S0-AXX-929

American Odyssey

The United States in the 20th Century

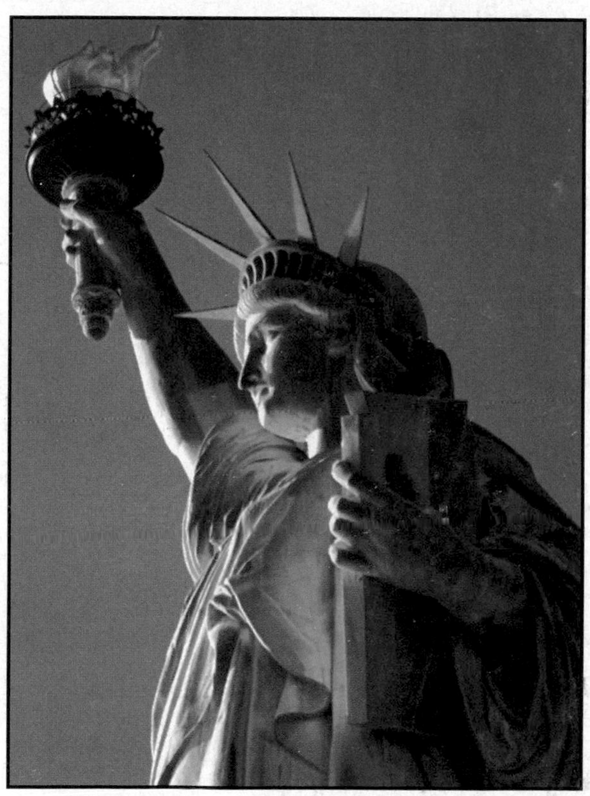

Gary B. Nash

Professor of History
University of California at Los Angeles

New York, New York   Columbus, Ohio   Woodland Hills, California   Peoria, Illinois

Author

Gary B. Nash is Professor of History at the University of California at Los Angeles and Director of the National Center for History in the Schools. He is author of *Red, White, and Black: The Peoples of Early North America,* Fourth Edition (Prentice-Hall, 2000) and *Forging Freedom: The Formation of Philadelphia's Black Community, 1720–1840* (Harvard University Press, 1988), among other publications. Nash served as president of the Organization of American Historians in 1994–1995 and is an elected member of the National Academy of Arts and Sciences.

Consultants

Program Consultants

Geography Consultant
Christopher L. Salter
Professor and Chair
Department of Geography
University of Missouri
Columbia, Missouri

Educational Consultant
Allan H. Scholl
Former Secondary Social Science Specialist
Office of Instruction
Los Angeles Unified School District
Los Angeles, California

Contributing Consultants

Multicultural Education
Gloria Contreras
Professor of Secondary Education
University of North Texas
Denton, Texas

American West Frontiers
Albert L. Hurtado
Associate Professor of History
Arizona State University
Tempe, Arizona

Reading and Bilingual Education
Eileen Mortensen
Assistant Professor of Education
National Louis University
Evanston, Illinois

Women's Studies and African American History
Cheryl Johnson Odim
Assistant Professor of History
Loyola University
Chicago, Illinois

Asian Studies
Gary Okihiro
Associate Professor of History
Cornell University
Ithaca, New York

African American History
Julius S. Scott
Assistant Professor of History
Duke University
Durham, North Carolina

Mexican American Women's History
Vicki L. Ruiz
Professor of Women's Studies
Arizona State University
Tempe, Arizona

Native American History
John Waukechan, M.A.
Member, American Indian Resource and Education Coalition
Austin, Texas

Glencoe/McGraw-Hill
A Division of The **McGraw-Hill** *Companies*

Printed in the United States of America.

Send all inquiries to:
Glencoe/McGraw-Hill
8787 Orion Place
Columbus, Ohio 43240-4027

ISBN 0-07-824482-X (student text)
ISBN 0-07-824483-8 (teacher's wraparound edition)

3 4 5 6 7 8 9 10 071/043 05 04 03 02

Cover: 1953 Buick Skylark convertible

Reviewers

Content Reviewers

David Anderson
Department of History and Political Science
University of Indianapolis
Indianapolis, Indiana

Assad Nimer Busool
Professor of Arabic and Islamic Studies
American Islamic College
Chicago, Illinois

D'Ann Campbell
Department of History
U.S. Military Academy
West Point, New York

Lynn Dumenil
History Department
Claremont-McKenna College
Claremont, California

Paula Fass
Department of History
University of California
Berkeley, California

Otis Graham
Department of History
University of California
Santa Barbara, California

James R. Grossman
Director, Family and Community History Center
Newberry Library
Chicago, Illinois

Warren F. Kimball
Department of History
Rutgers University
Newark, New Jersey

John Martz
Department of Political Science
Pennsylvania State University
University Park, Pennsylvania

Allen J. Matusow
School of Humanities
Rice University
Houston, Texas

David Oshinsky
Department of History
Rutgers University
New Brunswick, New Jersey

Herbert Parmet
Department of History
Queensborough Community College
Bayside, New York

Richard Polenberg
Department of History
Cornell University
Ithaca, New York

Bernard Reich
Professor of Political Science and International Affairs
George Washington University
Washington, D.C.

Athan Theoharis
Department of History
Marquette University
Milwaukee, Wisconsin

Educational Reviewers

David Bardow
Carmel High School
Carmel, Indiana

Edward Brickner
Woodbury High School
Woodbury, Minnesota

Carolyn Conner
Westbury High School
Houston Independent School District
Houston, Texas

Bruce Eddy
Evanston Township High School
Evanston, Illinois

Brook A. Goddard
Miami Norland Senior High School
Dade County Public Schools
Miami, Florida

Ronnie Granade
Arkadelphia High School
Arkadelphia, Arkansas

Robert Griesing
Toms River Regional School District
Toms River, New Jersey

Sonya Heckman
Greencastle-Antrim Middle School
Greencastle, Pennsylvania

Merle Knight
Lewis S. Mills High School
Burlington, Connecticut

Tom Laiches
Crossroads School
Santa Monica, California

Doris B. Meyers
Huntington High School
Huntington, West Virginia

Sheldon Obelsky
Arlington High School
Arlington, Massachusetts

Dennis Schillings
Homewood-Flossmoor High School
Flossmoor, Illinois

Jacob R. Seitz
Morgantown High School
Morgantown, West Virginia

Gloria Sesso
Half Hollow Hills School District
Dix Hills, New York

Louise Stricklin
Redondo Union High School
Redondo Beach, California

Larry Sutton
Madison High School
San Diego Unified School District
San Diego, California

Darla Weissenberg
Lincoln Park High School
Chicago, Illinois

CONTENTS

UNIT 1

A Nation of Nations, 40,000 B.C.–A.D. 1800

Chapter 1: A Geographic Perspective on History 4
1 The Five Themes of Geography 6
2 The Themes as Guides to History 11

Chapter 2: Encounters and Colonies 20
1 The Earliest Americans 22
2 Three Worlds Meet 30
3 Building Colonial America 36
4 Conflict and Growth in the Colonies 46

Chapter 3: The American Revolution 54
1 Toward Revolution 56
Declaration of Independence 61
2 War for Independence 66
3 Creating a New America 72

Chapter 4: A New Nation 78
1 From Federation to Constitution 80
2 Debate and Ratification 88
Constitution 91
3 Launching the New Government 112

UNIT 2

Rift and Reunion, 1800–1900

Chapter 5: The Expanding Nation 128
1 Territorial Expansion 130
2 The Economy Grows 140
3 A Changing People 150

Chapter 6: Civil War and Reconstruction 162
1 Slavery and Politics 164
2 The Civil War 172
3 Reconstruction 184

Chapter 7: New Frontiers 194
1 Moving West 196
2 Rise of Industrialism 204
3 Populism and Protest 212
4 Reaching for Empire 218

BROWN BROTHERS

UNIT 3

The Roots of a Modern Nation, 1880–1920

Chapter 8: Progressive Reforms 232
1 Facing a New Order 234
2 A Generation of Reformers 242
3 Progressive Agendas 250

Chapter 9: Progressivism Takes Hold 264
1 Theodore Roosevelt and the Modern Presidency 266
2 Woodrow Wilson and the New Freedom 274
3 Limits to Progressivism 281

Chapter 10: Expansionism and World War I 292
1 Becoming a World Power 294
2 Watching Europe's War 304
3 World War I: There and Here 314
4 Reshaping the World 321

UNIT 4

The New Era of the Twenties, 1920–1929

Chapter 11: Getting on With Business 336
1 Postwar Turmoil 338
2 The Republican Influence 346
3 Prosperity and American Business 353
4 The Changing Nature of Work 362

Chapter 12: A Prospering Society 374
1 Growth of the Middle Class 376
2 The Jazz Age 386
3 Cultural Conflicts 396

UNIT 5

Economic Crisis and the New Deal, 1929–1939

Chapter 13: The Great Depression 416
1 The Crash and Its Aftermath 418
2 The Dream on Hold 430
3 Life During the Depression 440

Chapter 14: The New Deal 450
1 FDR and the First New Deal 452
2 Criticism and Reformulation 464
3 The Impact of the New Deal 476

CONTENTS

UNIT 6

The United States Transformed, 1933–1945

Chapter 15: World War II **490**
1 The Road to War 492
2 The War Begins 500
3 The United States at War 508

Chapter 16: The Home Front **522**
1 Mobilizing the Home Front 524
2 The War and Social Change 534
3 The War and Civil Rights 542

UNIT 7

The Postwar World, 1945–1963

Chapter 17: The Uneasy Peace **560**
1 The Cold War Begins 562
2 The Cold War Deepens 569
3 Cold War in the Atomic Age 576
4 A New Battleground 587

Chapter 18: The Postwar Era **596**
1 Postwar Economy Booms 598
2 Suburban Lifestyles 606
3 Poverty and Plenty 618

Chapter 19: Cold War Politics **628**
1 Retreat From the New Deal 630
2 The Cold War at Home 640
3 The Eisenhower Years 652

UNIT 8

Toward Equality and Social Reform, 1954–1976

Chapter 20: The Civil Rights Struggle **666**
1 Challenging Segregation 668
2 Freedom Now 674
3 Government Response 680
4 Disappointed Hopes 690

Chapter 21: The Kennedy and Johnson Years **698**
1 New Frontier and Great Society 700
2 The Supreme Court and Civil Liberties 713

Chapter 22: Voices of Protest **722**
1 The Revival of Feminism 724
2 Hispanic Americans Organize 733
3 Land Claims of Native Americans 742
4 The Counterculture 748

UNIT 9

The Troubled Years, 1964–1980

Chapter 23: The Vietnam War **766**
1 War in Southeast Asia 768
2 1968: A Year of Crises 776
3 The War at Home 786
4 Ending the War 796

Chapter 24: From Nixon to Carter **806**
1 A New Majority 808
2 Nixon Foreign Policy 816
3 The Watergate Crisis 824
4 Ford and Carter 836

UNIT 10

New Challenges, 1980–Present

Chapter 25: The Reagan and Bush Years **854**
1 The Reagan Revolution 856
2 The Collapse of Communism 865
3 The Bush Presidency 876

Chapter 26: A Changing Nation in a Changing World **890**
1 The Clinton Agenda 892
2 In Search of Balance 906
3 Into a New Century 914

APPENDIX

Atlas **930**
United States Databank **944**
United States Presidents **950**
Primary Sources Library **958**
Glossary **970**
Spanish Glossary **977**
Index **986**
Credits **1010**

WHITE HOUSE HISTORICAL ASSOCIATION

Features

Primary Sources Library

This feature presents different types of primary sources and provides additional study material.

Working with Primary Sources 958
Unit 1: A Nation of Nations, 40,000 B.C.–A.D. 1800 960
Unit 2: Rift and Reunion, 1800–1900 960
Unit 3: The Roots of a Modern Nation, 1880–1920 962
Unit 4: The New Era of the Twenties, 1920–1929 962
Unit 5: Economic Crisis and the New Deal, 1929–1939 964
Unit 6: The United States Transformed, 1933–1945 964
Unit 7: The Postwar World, 1945–1963 966
Unit 8: Toward Equality and Social Reform, 1954–1976 966
Unit 9: The Troubled Years, 1960–1980 968
Unit 10: New Challenges, 1980–Present 968

TURNING POINTS

By examining pivotal decisions made by leaders and ordinary people, the cases provide insight into the decision-making process and highlight the significance of these historic events.

The Trial of Anne Hutchinson 42
Cherokee Expulsion 136
Woman Suffrage (Seneca Falls Convention) 258
The National Origins Act 404
Art and Politics at Rockefeller Center 472
Dropping the Bomb 516
The Hollywood Ten 648
The United Farm Workers and the Grape Boycott 738
The Attempted Impeachment of Nixon 832
Affirmative Action 922

Literature

A variety of literature selections at the beginning of each unit communicate the thoughts, feelings, and life experiences of people, past and present.

Castaways 2
Roots 126
Sister Carrie 230
The Great Gatsby 334
The Grapes of Wrath 414
Dispatches From the Front 488
The Book of Daniel 558
Voices of Change 664
Born on the Fourth of July 764
"Double Face" From The Joy Luck Club 852

One Day in History

Reminiscent of a daily newspaper, these "front pages" recall the dramatic—and the ordinary—events of ten special days in history.

The Shot Heard Around the World, April 19, 1775 64
Surrender at Appomattox, April 9, 1865 182
Edison's New Lamp, January 1, 1880 240
Lindbergh Crosses the Atlantic, May 21, 1927 394
Stock Market Crash, October 29, 1929 428
Attack on Pearl Harbor, December 7, 1941 506
Soviet "Moon" Circles Earth—Sputnik, October 4, 1957 584
JFK Assassination, November 22, 1963 718
Moon Landing, July 20, 1969 802
Fall of Berlin Wall, November 9, 1989 874

Visual and verbal displays appearing once per unit capture the popular culture of the time.

The Colonial Period 110
An Age of Ingenuity 202
Ragtime 288
The Roaring Twenties 370
Hard Times 446
The Big Band Era 532
Rock 'n' Roll Arrives 616
The Beat of the Sixties 756
An Era of Consciousness 784
The Rap on the Eighties 886

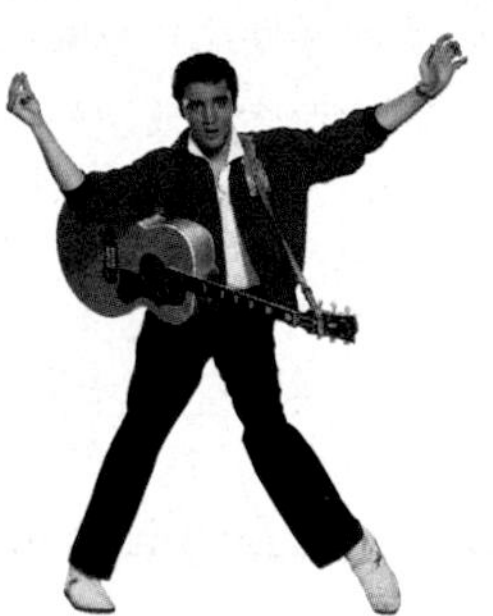

PHOTOPLAY ARCHIVES/LGI

Then and Now...

With photos and fun facts each feature examines in detail an artifact or phenomenon from each unit's time period and the influence of that item on what exists now.

Conestoga Wagon 122
Levi's Riveted Waist Overalls 226
Coca-Cola 330
Old Movie Houses 410
The DC-3 Passenger Plane 484

Women's Baseball 554
The 1955 Corvette 660
The First McDonald's 760
The Stereo 848
The Nintendo Entertainment System 928

Science, TECHNOLOGY, and Society

Through text, visuals, and a time line, this feature focuses on a technological advance and its short and long term impact on society.

Communication Media 86
The Steam Engine 158
The Radio 312
The Automobile 360
The Telephone 462
Medical Breakthroughs 550
Plastics 638
Television 710
Outer Space to the Kitchen 844
Personal Computers 862

Geography: Impact on History

The five geographic themes are explored through pivotal developments in United States history.

Native American Housing 28
The Rise of American Cities 148
The Panama Canal 302
Route 66 384
The Dust Bowl 438
A War Boomtown 540
Richmond, California: New American Landscape: Suburbia 604
Native American Urban Settlement 746
The Rise of the Sunbelt 814
America's Landfills 904

Skills

Skills features provide learning, practice, and technical literacy in the context of historical and geographical topics.

Social Studies Skills

Reading a Map 10
Combining Information From Maps 181
Reading Statistical Tables 211
Using Reference Materials 320
Interpreting Images 461
Reading Economic Graphs 549
Conducting Interviews 732
Understanding Public Opinion Polls 795
Interpreting Political Cartoons 823
Analyzing News Media 913

Study and Writing Skills

Interpreting a Primary Source 71
Analyzing Secondary Sources 586
Presenting Statistical Data 673

Critical Thinking Skills

Analyzing Information 119
Determining Cause and Effect 249
Making Comparisons 280
Synthesizing Information 393
Recognizing Ideologies 499
Distinguishing Fact From Opinion 657

Technology Skills

Using a Computerized Card Catalog 51
Using a Word Processor 157
Developing a Multimedia Presentation 369
Using E-Mail 437
Using the Internet 625
Building a Database 712
Using an Electronic Spreadsheet 864

DIAGRAPHICS

Through diagrams, maps, statistical information, and annotated visuals, complex concepts are clearly and accurately depicted.

Factors Influencing Vegetation 15
The Iroquois Longhouse 27
Supplying the Continental Army 69
The Three Branches of the United States Government 85
The First Modern Factories 142
The Cotton Gin 165
Horizontal and Vertical Integration 209
Forms of Municipal Government in the U.S. 251
The Anatomy of a Monopoly 270
Operating the Locks of the Panama Canal 296
The Effects of Henry Ford's Assembly Line 363
Creating a System for Roadways 379
A Depressed Economy 421
General Motors Sit-Down Strike of 1936–1937 466
The Nation Prepares for War 503
Distributing Rationed Goods 529

DIAGRAPHICS (continued)

The Cuban Missile Crisis: July–October, 1962 592
Hard Times in Appalachia 621
Television and Senator McCarthy 645
The Freedom Ride, Montgomery, Alabama, May 20, 1961 683
The Great Society 707
The Woodstock Festival, August 15–18, 1969 753
Vietnam Tour of Duty 790
The Watergate Scandal 827
The Origin of the Deficit 859
The Rising Cost of Health Care 895

MAPS

The Regions of the United States, 1995 10
Physical Map of the United States 12
Exploration by Early Settlers 19
Migration to North America 23
Eastern Native American Groups, 1500s 26
Native American Cultural Areas, 1500s–1800s 28
Major European Exploration, 1492–1550 31
European Land Claims, 1763 48
Population Growth in the Colonies 53
Eastern North America, 1763 57
Revolutionary War Battles, 1775–1781 67
Early Revolutionary War Battles, 1775–1776 77
The United States, 1812 121
The Settlement of the United States, 1783–1900 131
Native American Removal 135
Transportation Routes, 1800–1860 148

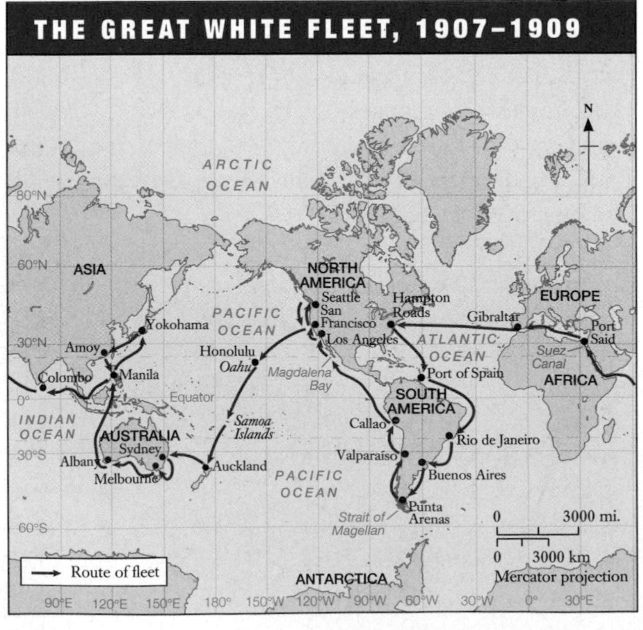

United States Territory, 1776–1803 161
Compromises On Slavery, 1820–1854 170
The Union and the Confederacy 173
Major Battles of the Civil War 175
Abolition of Slavery, 1777–1865 179
Agriculture and Industry, 1860 181
Mid-Atlantic Civil War Battles 193
The Election of 1892 214
The Philippines, 1898 223
The Caribbean, 1898 223
Second Native American Expulsion 225
Urban Growth in the United States, 1870–1920 235
Manufacturing Employment, 1899 263
Presidential Election, 1912 277
Labor's Struggle for Justice, 1880–1920 286
United States Parklands, 1909 291
The Caribbean, 1898–1917 297
Foreign Expansion in Eastern Asia 299
The Great White Fleet, 1907–1909 301
The Isthmus of Panama 302
Europe During World War I, 1914–1918 307
Europe After World War I, 1920–1922 326
United States in World War I 329
Woman Suffrage Before the Nineteenth Amendment 344
Steps Leading to the Dawes Plan 351
U.S. City Population, 1930 373
The Path of U.S. Route 66, 1926 384
Ku Klux Klan Distribution by Region, 1924 400
Prohibition Enforcement, 1929 409
Migrations of the Okies 431
Precipitation and Temperature, 1932–1939 437
The Shelterbelt, 1940 439
West Coast Crops, 1936 449
The Tennessee Valley Authority, 1930s 458
FDR Election Results, 1932-1940 483
The Expansion of European Totalitarianism, 1900–1939 494
The Expansion of the Japanese Empire, 1931–1942 505
World War II in Europe, 1939–1945 511
The Allied Advance in the Pacific, 1942–1945 514
D-Day Invasion, June 6, 1944 521
Population Shifts in the United States, 1940–1950 535
Richmond, California, 1943 540
African American Population, 1940–1950 553
Europe at the End of World War II 565
Divided Europe, 1955 571
Korean War, 1950–1953 574
CIA Actions in the World, 1950–1962 589
NATO Military Bases, 1950s 595
The Three Levittowns, 1950s 604
Los Angeles 607

Travel Routes of Migrant Workers 627
Interstate Highways, 1950s to Present 655
Truman's Whistle-Stop Tour, 1948 659
Segregation in United States Schools, 1950 669
Civil Rights Riots, Summer 1965, 1966, 1967 697
Distribution of Hispanic Americans, 1970 734
Land Recovery, 1950s–1970s 744
Native American U.S. Distribution, 1910 746
Native American U.S. Distribution, 1990 747
Equal Rights Amendment Ratification, 1972–1982 759
Vietnam, 1954–1967 769
Vietnam War, 1968–1973 777
Presidential Election Results, 1968 783
Physical Map of Southeast Asia 805
Emergence of the Sunbelt 814
The Middle East, 1973 837
Phoenix, Arizona, 1950-1994 847
Europe, 1995 870
Central America and the Caribbean, 1980s 872
Persian Gulf War, 1991 889
Presidential Election, 1992 893
The Former Yugoslavia, 1995 897
Health Insurance for Children 903
Election Night: Nov. 7, 2000 912

CHARTS AND GRAPHS

Grassland 15
Desert 15
Forest 15
The Ratification Debate 89
Abolitionism and William Lloyd Garrison: A Telescoping Time Line, 1619–1840 157
Confederacy/Union Resource Comparisons, 1861 177
Expansion of United States Railroads, 1840–1900 206
Labor Force and Employment, 1800–1960 211
Production and Price of Wheat, 1860–1900 213
Urban Growth in the United States, 1870–1920 235
Changing Sources of Immigrants 236
Lynchings in the United States 247
Length of School Year, 1880–1920 256
Mergers, 1895–1920 269
Heating Fuel Sources, 1902 271
Bank Failures, 1880–1915 279
Comparison Chart 280
Religious Membership in the United States 284
Exports of the United States, 1860–1920 295
World War I Casualties 316
Urban African American Population 341
Workers in Manufacturing, 1899–1925 365
Organizational Text Patterns 369
Average Annual Employee Income 377
Immigration, 1910–1930 401
Selected Stock Prices, 1927–1929 419
Labor Union Membership, 1929–1941 467
New Deal Legislation and Agencies, 1933–1938 481
World War II Deaths 515
Military Plane Production, 1941–1945 526
African American Jobs: 1940, 1944 544
Business Cycles in the United States, 1920–1945 549
Nuclear Fallout from Bravo H-Bomb Test, 1954 580
Nuclear Arms, 1945–1965 581
Farming Becomes Big Business 602
School Enrollment, 1910–1970, Grades K-8 610
Women in the Workplace, 1940–1960 615
Married Women Who Work, 1940–1960 615
Rising Food Prices, 1946 632
United States Freight Shipment, 1940–1988 654
Segregated Professional Schools, 1945 673
African American Voting Power, 1970–1976 689
Population Changes, 1950–1970 696
Highlights of the Kennedy Presidency 704
Business Behaviors 712
Warren Court Decisions on Key Issues of the 1960s 715
Georgia Reapportionment, 1964 721
Women in the Workforce 726
Women in Politics 726
Women in Education 726
Land Saga, 1794–1980 744
Making of an Activist Generation, 1946–1974 787
The Draft in the Vietnam Era 789
Public Opinion Poll, March 1969 795
United States Troop Commitment and Public Opposition to the War, 1965–1973 799
Presidential Election, 1972 822
Gallup Poll of Nixon's Popularity 830
The United States Economy, 1972–1980 839
Patterns of Immigration in the Twentieth Century 915
African Americans in the Middle Class, 1970–1997 916
Women in the Labor Force 917
Fastest-Growing Occupations, 1996–2006 920

African American Voting Power, 1970–1976

African American Elected Officials in Mississippi

Year	Officials
1970	81
1972	129
1974	191
1976	210

UNIT 1 A Nation of Nations

40,000 B.C.–A.D. 1800

HISTORY & YOU

The Americas had long been the home to a rich variety of Native American cultures. Hundreds of years ago, however, other peoples—Europeans and enslaved Africans—set foot in what was to them a new world. Together they created the United States of America—a nation founded on the promise of liberty and equality for all the diverse people who have contributed to its success.

Historic America Electronic Field Trips

Independence Hall, also known as the Old State House in Philadelphia, was the birthplace of the Declaration of Independence and the United States Constitution—the two documents that enshrine the rights and freedoms enjoyed by all Americans. To learn more about the unique role of Independence Hall in United States history, view videodisc Chapter 7: *Independence Hall* in **Historic America Electronic Field Trips.**

PRIMARY SOURCES
Library

See pages 960–961 for primary source readings that accompany Unit 1.

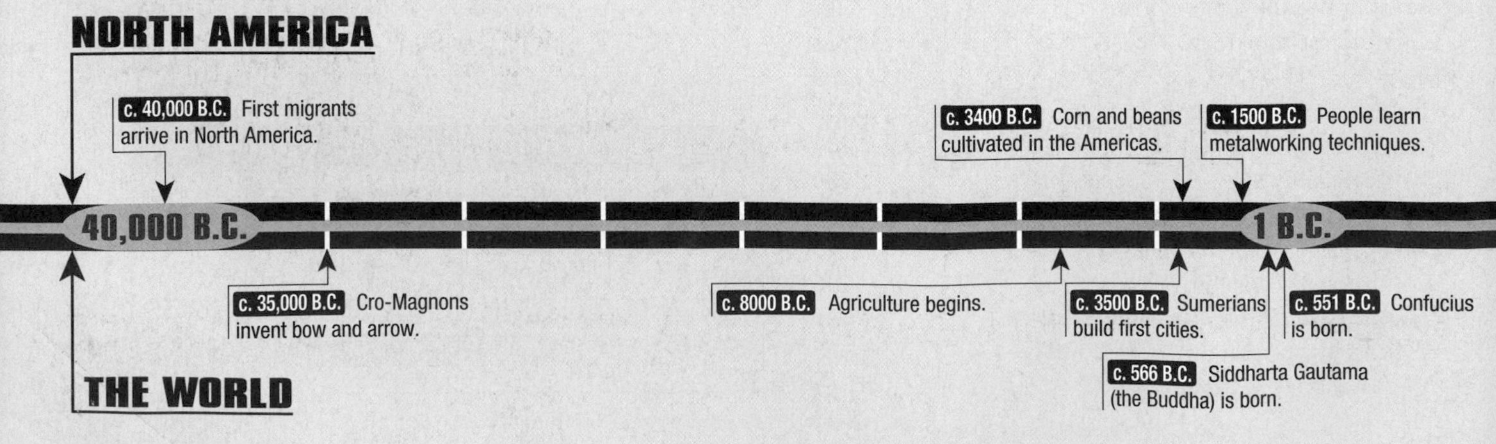

NORTH AMERICA
c. 40,000 B.C. First migrants arrive in North America.
c. 3400 B.C. Corn and beans cultivated in the Americas.
c. 1500 B.C. People learn metalworking techniques.
40,000 B.C.
1 B.C.
c. 35,000 B.C. Cro-Magnons invent bow and arrow.
c. 8000 B.C. Agriculture begins.
c. 3500 B.C. Sumerians build first cities.
c. 551 B.C. Confucius is born.
c. 566 B.C. Siddharta Gautama (the Buddha) is born.
THE WORLD

LAURIE PLATT WINFREY INC.

Native American art, such as this intricate Inca knife handle, shows the complexity of the cultures that first inhabited the Americas.

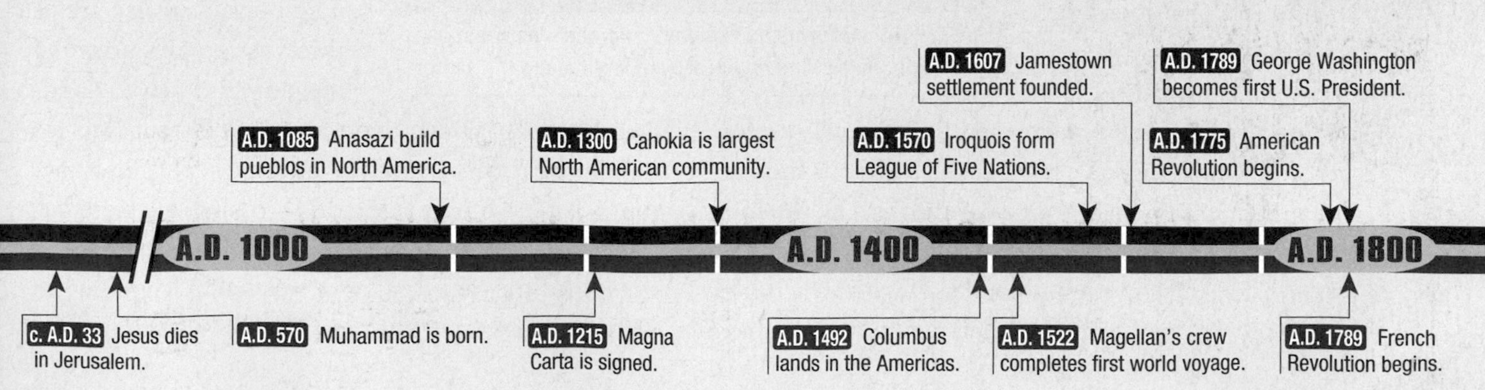
A.D. 1000
A.D. 1400
A.D. 1800
c. A.D. 33 Jesus dies in Jerusalem.
A.D. 570 Muhammad is born.
A.D. 1085 Anasazi build pueblos in North America.
A.D. 1215 Magna Carta is signed.
A.D. 1300 Cahokia is largest North American community.
A.D. 1492 Columbus lands in the Americas.
A.D. 1522 Magellan's crew completes first world voyage.
A.D. 1570 Iroquois form League of Five Nations.
A.D. 1607 Jamestown settlement founded.
A.D. 1775 American Revolution begins.
A.D. 1789 George Washington becomes first U.S. President.
A.D. 1789 French Revolution begins.

Castaways

BY ALVAR NÚÑEZ CABEZA DE VACA

Alvar Núñez Cabeza de Vaca landed in present-day Florida in 1528, part of an expedition that was to explore and claim territory for Spain. After losing contact with their ships, the Spaniards found themselves stranded in a harsh land with no supplies, among often hostile local peoples. Cabeza de Vaca and 3 others reached Spanish territory (in present-day Mexico) after an 8-year odyssey; the 4 were the only survivors from a group of 300. This excerpt from Cabeza de Vaca's account of the expedition concerns an attack on the Spaniards as they were crossing one of many lakes in Florida.

In view of this [the Indians' aggression] the governor ordered the horsemen to dismount and attack them on foot. The auditor dismounted with them, and they attacked the Indians and they all fought together in the lake, and so we forced our way through. In this affray some of our men were wounded, and the good weapons they carried were of no use; and there were men that day who swore they had seen two oak trees, each as thick as the lower part of a man's leg, shot clear through by the Indians' arrows. And this is not so much to be wondered at considering the strength and skill with which they shoot them, for I myself saw an arrow at the foot of a poplar tree that had penetrated into it two handbreadths. All the Indians that we saw, from Florida to here, use arrows; and they are so tall . . . they look like giants when seen from a distance. They are wonderfully handsome folk, very lean and extremely strong and agile. The bows they use are as thick as a man's arm and eleven or twelve handbreadths long, which they shoot at a distance of two hundred paces, so surely that they never miss anything. After we had made this crossing, a league farther on we came to another that was very like it, except for the fact that, as it was half a league wide, it was much worse; this one we crossed without hin-

Exploration European explorers approach the coast of Florida. Native Americans are gathered along the shore.

SUPERSTOCK/NEW YORK PUBLIC LIBRARY

drance and without attacks by Indians, for as they had used up all their supplies of arrows in the first encounter, they had nothing left with which they dared to confront us. On the following day, as we made another similar crossing, I found traces of people who had gone ahead of us and warned the governor of it, for he was in the rear guard; and so, although the Indians attacked us, they were unable to harm us because we were forewarned, and when we emerged on level ground they continued to follow us. We attacked them on two sides and killed two Indians, and they wounded me and two or three other Spaniards, and because they took shelter in the woods we were unable to do them any more harm or damage. We marched like this for eight days, and after the crossing I have described no more Indians attacked us until a league farther on, which is the place that, as I have said, we were going.

WE ATTACKED THEM ON TWO SIDES AND KILLED TWO INDIANS, AND THEY WOUNDED ME AND TWO OR THREE OTHER SPANIARDS . . .

As we were going our way, Indians came out of the woods without our hearing them and attacked the rear guard, and among them was a hidalgo [a man of the lower nobility in Spain] named Avellaneda who turned around on hearing the cries of a lad who was a servant of his and went to his aid, and the Indians hit him with an arrow at the edge of his cuirass [breastplate], and the wound was so severe that almost all the arrow went into his neck and he died on the spot, and we carried him to Aute [community near present-day Tallahassee, Florida]. We arrived after nine days of journeying from Apalachee [village near present-day Tallahassee], and when we reached there we found all the people fled, and the houses burned, and a great quantity of maize and pumpkins and beans, all ready to be harvested. We rested there for two days, and after that the governor asked me to go and find the sea, for the Indians said it was very close by: during this journey we thought we had discovered it because of a very large river that we found, which we named the Magdalena. In view of this, on the next day I set off to find it, along with the commissary and Captain Castillo and Andrés Dorantes and seven other mounted men and fifty on foot, and we marched until the hour of vespers, when we reached an inlet or arm of the sea where we found many oysters, which the men enjoyed greatly, and we gave great thanks to God for having brought us there.

Next morning I sent twenty men to explore the coast and find out what it was like; they returned on the following night saying that those inlets and bays were very large and entered so deeply into the land that they made it extremely difficult to find out what we wished to know, and that the coast was very far away. Once we had learned this, and considering the fact that we were ill prepared and ill equipped to explore the coast, I returned to the governor. When we arrived we found him and many others sick, and the previous night the Indians had come upon them and placed them in great peril owing to the illness they had suffered; also, one of the horses had died. I reported to him what I had done, and the unfavorable lie of the land. That day we stayed there.

Responding to Literature

1. **What difficulties did Cabeza de Vaca encounter while trying to explore Florida?**
2. **Do you find Cabeza de Vaca to be a careful observer? Support your answer with examples from the selection.**

A Geographic Perspective on History

LATE 1400s: EAGER EXPLORERS PORE OVER TRAVEL JOURNALS AND MAPS

"Just as we roof our houses or churches with lead, so this palace is roofed with fine gold. And the value of it is almost beyond computation."

Thus did Marco Polo describe Japan, a country he had never visited. Polo, a trader from Venice, lived in China for about 20 years in the late 1200s. While there, he heard stories about a mysterious country now called Japan. After returning home, Polo was commanding a Venetian ship in a war against Genoa when he was captured and held prisoner. During his imprisonment, he recorded the story of his travels.

During the 1200s, people copied books by hand, so books were scarce. About 1440, however, Johannes Gutenberg invented the printing press. Soon printing presses were common, and Europeans were exchanging ideas at an unprecedented rate. Polo's journal was now available to explorers. In 1492, the Genoese Christopher Columbus set sail to find the riches of Japan and China, he took along Polo's book as a guide. ■

HISTORY JOURNAL

As you read this chapter, write a description of the ways that the geography of your locale has affected the events that have occurred there in the past and in the present.

Chapter Overview

Visit the *American Odyssey* Web site at americanodyssey.glencoe.com and click on ***Chapter 1—Chapter Overview*** to preview the chapter.

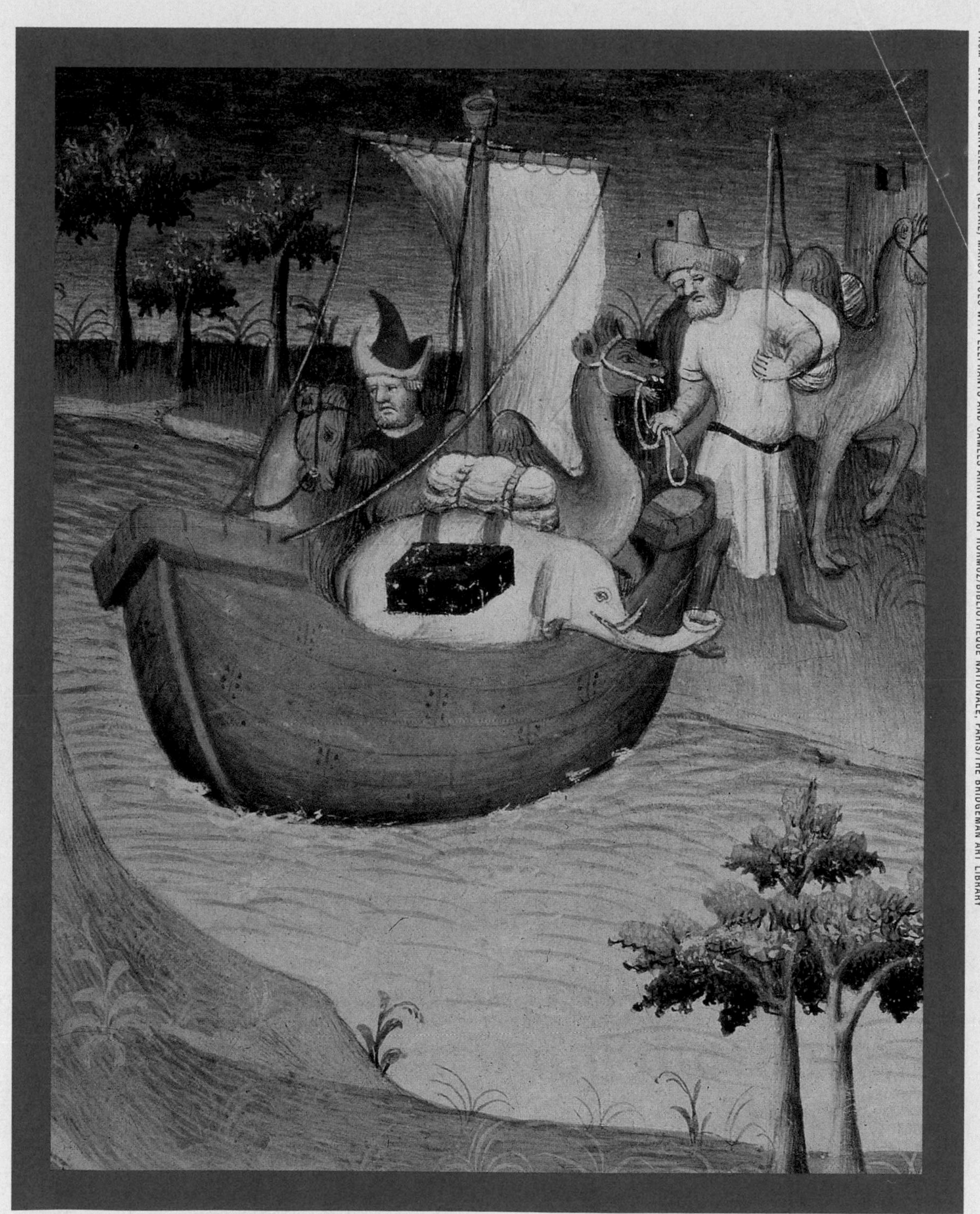

FROM "LIVRE DES MERVEILLES" (DETAIL) MARCO POLO WITH ELEPHANTS AND CAMELS ARRIVING AT HORMUZ/BIBLIOTHEQUE NATIONALE, PARIS/THE BRIDGEMAN ART LIBRARY

By sharing his discoveries about the geography of Asia, Marco Polo influenced the history of the world.

The Five Themes of Geography

1542: EXPLORER PUBLISHES SENSATIONAL TRAVEL JOURNAL

© SUPERSTOCK

A Land of Great Variety
Newcomers to the Americas saw animals and plants that they had never seen before.

It was a gripping story of survival that Alvar Núñez Cabeza de Vaca had to tell. This Spanish noble had been a member of an expedition sent to claim new lands in America for the Spanish king. The explorers experienced terrible misfortunes, including shipwreck and disease. In presenting his journal to King Charles V, Cabeza de Vaca admitted that the expedition had failed to achieve its goals. He was convinced, however, that his journal was a worthwhile offering to the king.

The value of his report, Cabeza de Vaca wrote, was its information about the new lands, including descriptions of native peoples, the environment, the kinds of food people ate, and the location of places and the distances between them.

In describing these discoveries to the king, Cabeza de Vaca was writing about **geography,** the study of people, places, and environments. Geography looks at space on the earth and how specific spaces are alike or different. It is a rich subject filled with intriguing, even astonishing information. To help organize such a huge body of information, today's geographers cluster their subject matter around five themes: location, place, movement, human/environment interaction, and region.

Guide to Reading

Main Idea

Geographers use five themes to study and describe spaces on the earth.

Vocabulary

- geography
- location
- place
- movement
- human/environment interaction
- region

Read to Find Out . . .

- what geography is and what it reveals about people, places, and environments.
- how the five themes of geography help organize geographical information.

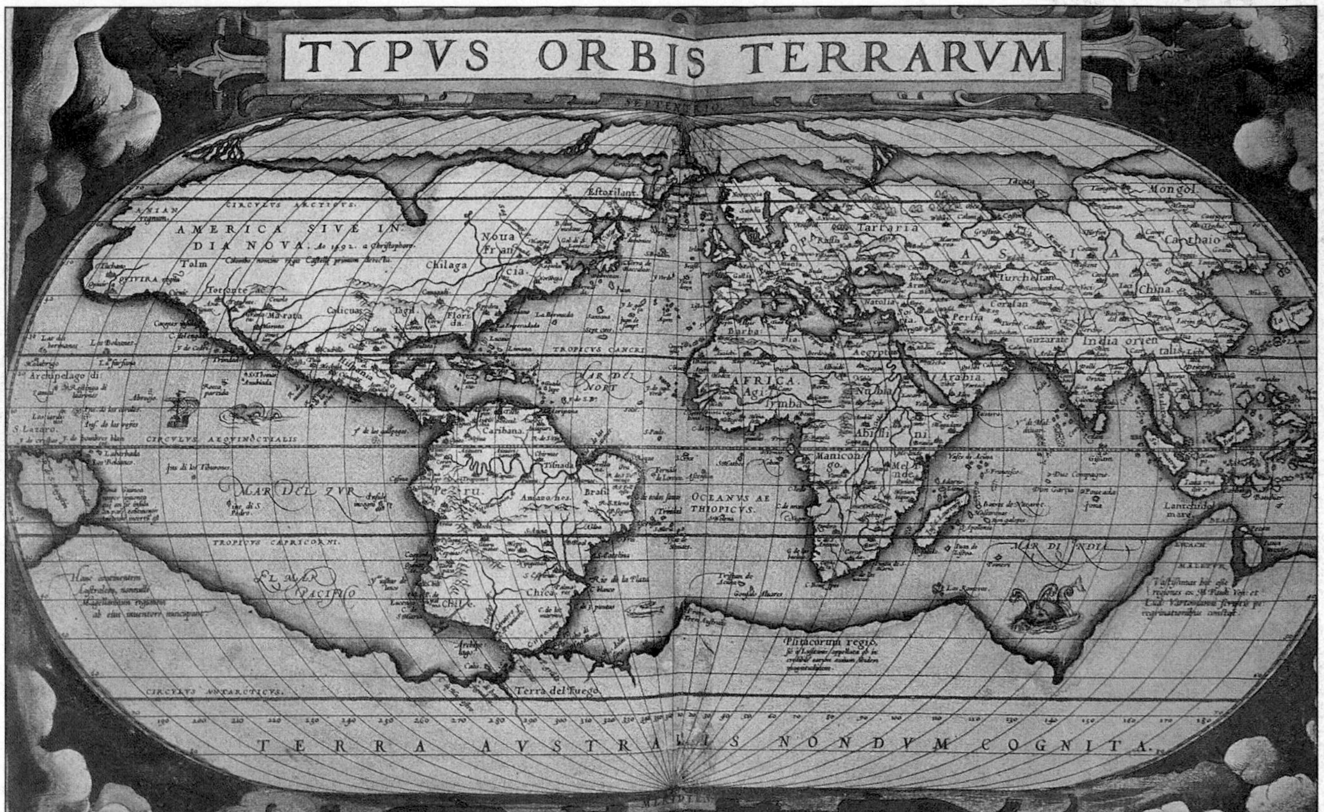

A World Map From 1570 This map shows many misunderstandings about the size and shape of North America, South America, Australia, and Antarctica. *Which parts of this map look like maps of today?*

Location

Finding Places Anywhere on Earth

The theme of **location** focuses on a specific place and considers the question of its position on the earth's surface. People may talk about the location of a place just out of curiosity, or they may actually want to visit it.

Absolute Location

In 25 B.C. a young man named Strabo visited Alexandria, then the Roman capital of Egypt. In a library built by Egyptian royalty, Strabo pored over an enormous collection of scholarly writings on geography and mapmaking. He later published his conclusions in an 18-volume book on geography. Two of Strabo's central conclusions were that the earth had the shape of a sphere and that the best map of the earth would employ a grid of intersecting lines, a plan that is still in use today.

One set of grid lines consists of the lines of latitude, which circle the earth parallel to each other and to the Equator, an imaginary line around the center of the earth. The Equator is measured at 0°, and the poles are measured at 90° N (north) or S (south). The other set of lines comprises longitude lines, which run from pole to pole and measure distance east or west of a starting line called the Prime Meridian. For a long time, individual mapmakers chose where to locate the Prime Meridian—usually putting it where they lived. Finally, in 1884, the United States held the First International Meridian Conference where delegates decided to locate the Prime Meridian at an observatory in Greenwich, England. The other meridians are measured east or west of the Prime Meridian up to 180°. This grid system enables people to give the exact, or absolute, location for any place on the earth.

Relative Location

People usually think of a place's location in relation to other known places, a concept called relative location. Even before there was a written language, people indicated relative location by drawing simple maps in sand or by saying, for example, that Europe is north of Africa. People still use directions based on relative location to get to their destinations.

Student Web Activity 1

Visit the *American Odyssey* Web site at americanodyssey.glencoe.com and click on ***Chapter 1—Student Web Activities*** for an activity relating to location.

Place

Describing a Location

Every **place,** or specific location, on the earth has a set of characteristics that distinguish it from other places. When geographers focus on place, they look at the physical features of a location as well as its human features.

A place's physical features include the nature of the land and water as well as the weather, soil, plants, and animals. The human features include the number and kinds of people who live in a place, the activities that occur there, and the cultures, languages, and religions represented. The combination of all these different characteristics gives each place its own distinctive flavor.

In 1596 explorer William Barents and his crew experienced the extremes of a place in the Arctic when their ship was frozen in the ice at 76° N latitude. Gerrit de Veer, one of the crew, recorded their experiences in a detailed account accompanied by illustrations.

Movement

Monitoring a Continuing Flow

From the beginning of human history, people have moved from one location to another, sometimes migrating great distances. They may have moved out of necessity, because of catastrophic natural events such as droughts or because of conflicts with other people. They may also have moved out of curiosity or from a desire to seek a better life. Such movements may be temporary, such as the travels of explorers or traders, or permanent, when people move to a new location and settle there. Geographers are also interested in the transfer of goods from place to place and the spread of information and ideas. All these activities are examples of the theme of **movement.**

Moving Into the Unknown Determining location at sea or in a new land presented explorers with a challenge. They used an astrolabe like the one shown (upper left) to determine latitude. *Which geography themes does this painting illustrate?*

Human/ Environment Interaction

A Story of a Close Relationship

The theme of **human/ environment interaction** explores the interdependence of people and their surroundings. People depend on the environment for fresh water, food, and shelter, their three most basic needs. For much of human history, people have settled near rivers, lakes, or other sources of fresh water.

The simplest and earliest way that people obtained food was as hunter-gatherers. They hunted, fished, or collected vegetables and fruits found where they lived. Of all the ways that people have lived, the hunter-gatherer way of life produces the fewest environmental changes.

About 10,000 B.C., some hunter-gatherer societies began to experiment with the domestication of plants and animals, leading to the development of agriculture. Agriculture revolutionized the way people interacted with their surroundings. It also changed the environment far more extensively than had their former way of life, a pattern that continues today.

Picturing New Discoveries Explorers returned to their European homelands with tales of new regions such as the Arctic (above). Books illustrated new kinds of plants (right). *What does the image above tell you about the explorer's life in the Arctic?*

Region

A Versatile Organizing Concept

The theme of region is the most flexible of the five themes. A **region** is an area that is defined according to one or more characteristics. Those characteristics may be physical features, or they may be based on other types of human concepts such as political divisions, kinds of languages, or types of industry.

Geographers often need to consider the physical features of an area, even when they are focusing on another type of region concept. The physical features of a region, such as the type of land, the bodies of water, the climate, and the vegetation, often influence whether or not the region will be heavily populated and what types of industries will flourish there.

Section Assessment

Main Idea

1. Use a diagram like this one to summarize how the five themes help geographers to study spaces on the earth.

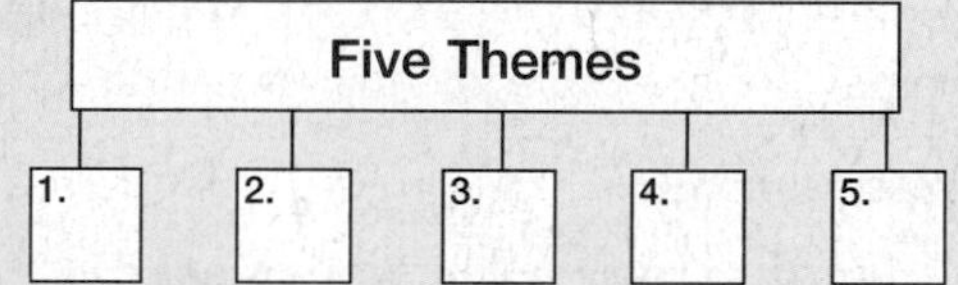

Vocabulary

2. Define: geography, location, place, movement, human/environment interaction, region.

Checking Facts

3. What is the difference between absolute and relative location?

4. What is the simplest method people have used to obtain food?

Critical Thinking

5. **Evaluating Information** Do you agree that region is the most flexible of the five geographic themes? Why or why not?

Social Studies Skill

READING A MAP

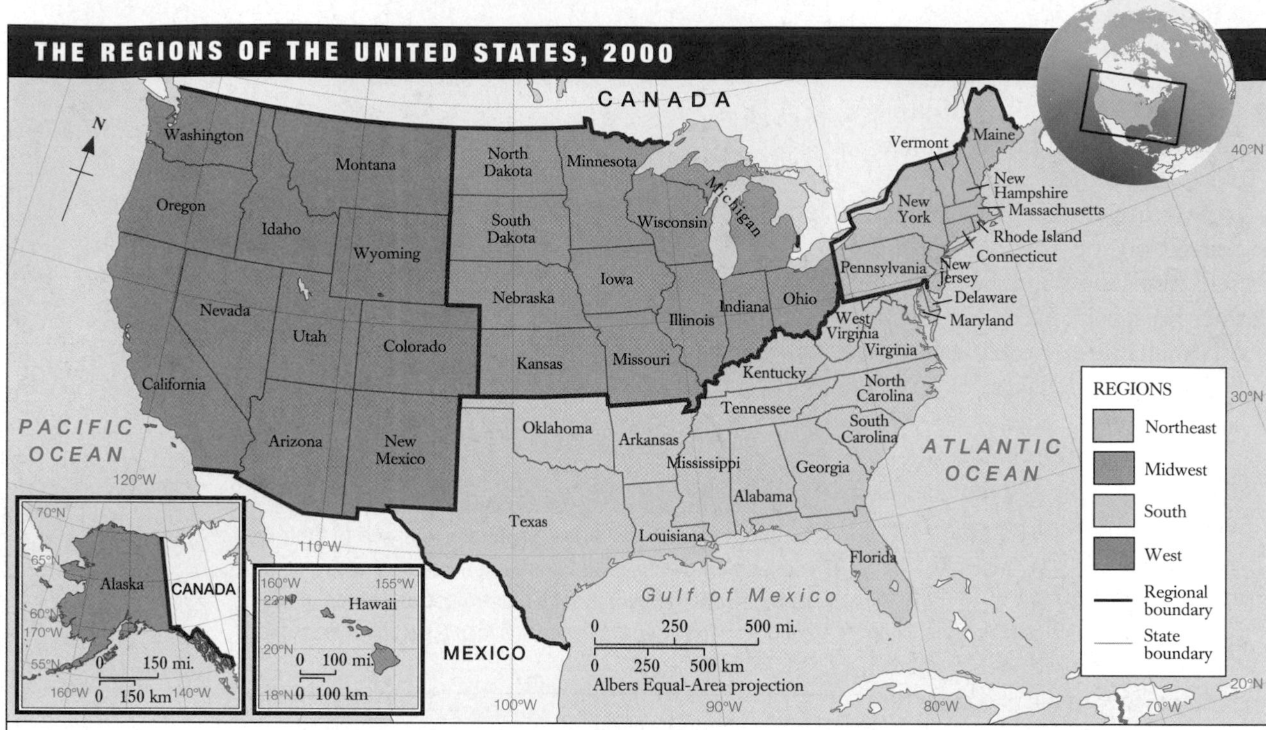

The four regions shown here are based partly on geographical location and partly on history and other factors such as climate. *In which region do you live? Which regions border your region?*

Learning the Skill

Maps are visual tools that show to scale the relative size, location, or even environmental aspects of specific geographic areas. Maps contain symbols and other elements that enable you to interpret them accurately.

Reading a Map

To read a map, follow these steps:

a. Examine the title to determine the map's content.

b. Examine the map's scale, which indicates the ratio between the map's size and the actual area being represented. A scale also shows the ratio between distance on the map and real distance on the earth.

c. Look for a compass rose or directional arrow to find the map's directions.

d. Examine the lines of latitude and longitude to find the absolute location of specific places. Express the latitude and longitude in degrees and direction. For example, the tip of Florida is about 80° W and 25° N.

e. Read the legend, or key, to interpret any boundary lines, shapes, or other symbols.

Practicing the Skill

Study the map above and answer the following questions.

1. Which region has no coastline?

2. Which region has the greatest number of states? Which has the fewest?

3. Which state is closest to the Equator?

4. Which state has a place with a location of 120° W and 45° N?

5. Approximately how long is the western border of the state of Idaho?

Applying the Skill

Use the map on page 15 to write two statements about your geographic area.

The **Glencoe Skillbuilder Interactive Workbook, Level 2** CD-ROM provides more practice in key social studies skills.

The Themes as Guides to History

EARLY 1500s: TRANSFER OF MAP A CRIMINAL ACT

(DETAIL) CHATEAU DE VERSAILLES/LAUROS-GIRAUDON/BRIDGEMAN ART LIBRARY, LONDON

Sailors Gossip
In the busy ports of Europe, sailors often spread news of new discoveries that rulers tried to keep secret.

"It is impossible to get a chart of the voyage because the king has decreed the death penalty for anyone sending one abroad." The king was Manuel I of Portugal, and the chart was a map of Vasco da Gama's travel route from Lisbon around Africa to India. The person making the complaint was a visitor to Portugal frantically trying to discover exactly how da Gama had accomplished his historic voyage.

Today, when many kinds of maps are freely available, people may find it hard to imagine that maps were once kept strictly secret. In the past, possession of a map could mean great power, in this case, control of the lucrative spice trade.

Spices were valuable because Europeans lacked the fodder to keep domesticated flocks alive through the winter. Each fall people butchered many of their animals and then salted the meat to keep it from spoiling. If the meat spoiled, people masked the taste of decay with spices.

Before da Gama's voyage, the merchants of Venice had monopolized trade in the spices that came westward by the traditional route from Asia. Now the Venetians saw their wealth disappearing, and they were desperate to counter Portugal's threat. This series of events was only one of countless occasions when knowledge about geography has had a major impact on historical events.

Guide to Reading

Main Idea

A knowledge of geographic concepts such as the five themes can illuminate the study of past events that have shaped the development of the United States.

Vocabulary

- history
- climate
- vegetation

Read to Find Out . . .

- how an understanding of geography helps people understand history.
- the ways in which the five themes of geography relate to United States history.

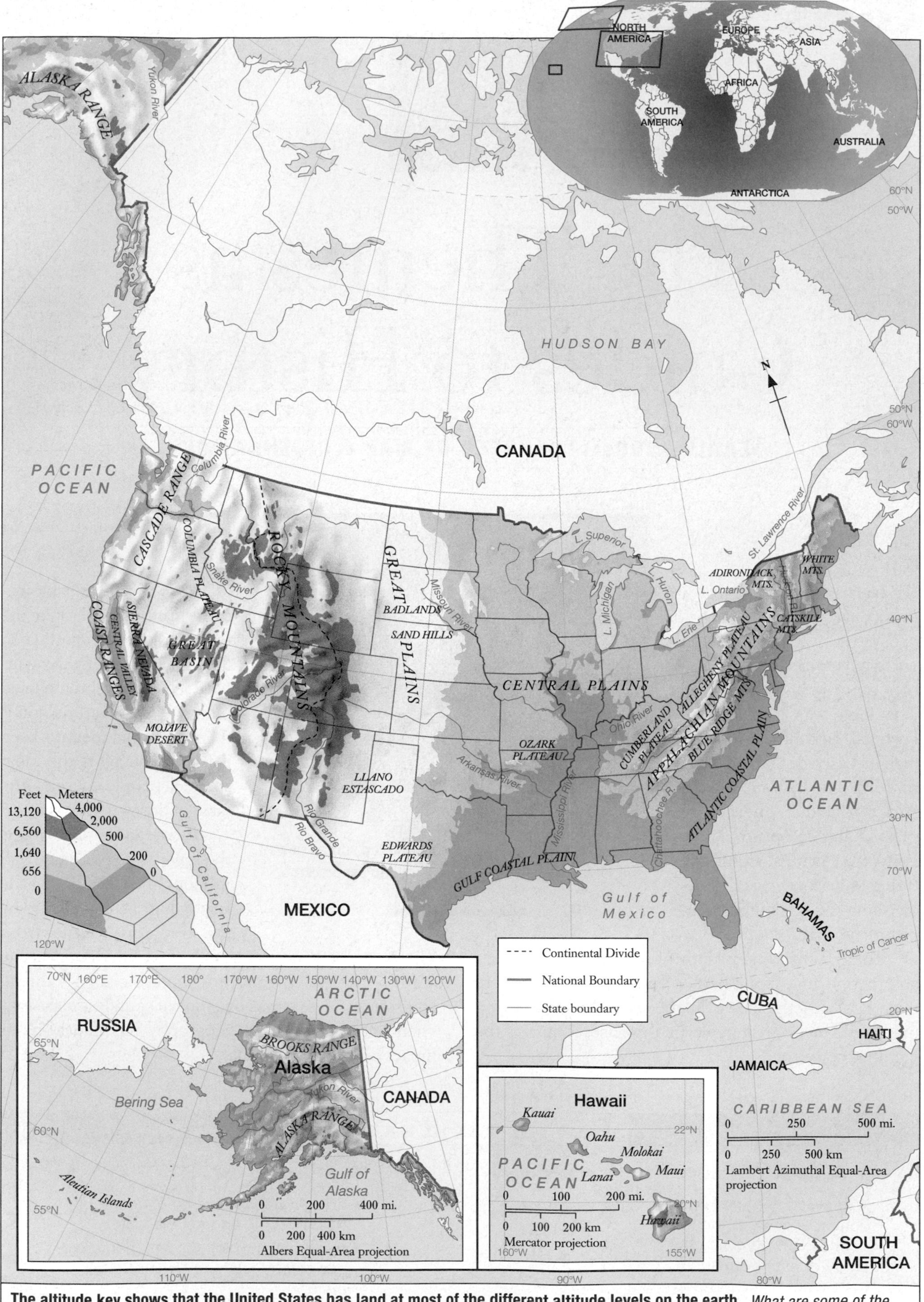

The altitude key shows that the United States has land at most of the different altitude levels on the earth. *What are some of the ways that the presence of these different landforms might influence people and events?*

© G. BRAD LEWIS/TONY STONE IMAGES © DAVID MUENCH © JON ORTNER/TONY STONE IMAGES © GEORGE SCHWARTZ/FPG INTERNATIONAL CORP.

A Country Characterized by Diversity These four locations—Oregon, Hawaii, New York, and Alaska (moving from left to right)—look very different from each other. *What are some of those differences?*

History is the study of people and events over time. Geography looks at people and events not over time but in space. Focusing on geographic concepts such as the five themes can illuminate the study of the past as well as make it easier to understand the present and the future.

The Location of the United States

Forty-eight Plus Two

The United States is located in the Northern Hemisphere west of the Prime Meridian. The United States currently includes 48 states that are contiguous, that is, that share borders, and 2 other states. The state of Alaska shares a border with Canada. The state of Hawaii is a group of islands located in the central Pacific Ocean.

A consideration of such a location can raise many questions about the history of the United States. How and when did the 48 states come together as a single political body? How and when did Alaska and Hawaii join the contiguous states? How has the location of the United States affected its relations with other nations in different parts of the world? The location of the United States has influenced many events in its history, including events that are occurring today.

Places in the United States

Richness and Variety

When a person pictures the physical characteristics of all the places in the United States, an extraordinary variety of environments becomes apparent. When the influences of all the different cultural heritages are added, the picture becomes even more amazingly diverse.

The concept of "place" can illuminate the study of history by showing how different people at different times came to this land and chose where to live. The earliest Americans settled in many diverse environments and developed ways of life that harmonized with those diverse places. Later settlers from Europe looked for harbors or farmland or opportunities for fur trapping. At each new stage of United States history, people have come seeking a place where they could live and prosper.

Regions of the United States

Natural Versus Human Divisions

The map on page 10 shows various political regions—areas defined by governments acting individually or jointly. The regions that nature has created are equally interesting and important.

Landforms

When someone looks at a physical map of the United States, like the one on page 12, the region that seems most prominent may be that of the mountain ranges that run down the west side of the continent. These westernmost mountains make up the Coast Ranges, with the Rocky Mountains slightly to the east. These impressive mountains arose millions of years ago when tectonic plates (the huge pieces of the earth's outer crust) collided.

To the east of the western mountains lies a series of Plains areas. The Plains are generally flat and lack significant changes in landforms, though the elevation drops gradually from west to east.

Between the Plains and the Atlantic Ocean lie the Appalachian Mountains, less impressive in height than their counterparts to the west. East and south of these mountains are the coastal lowlands.

For someone studying history, these landforms can suggest many questions. Where could people settle most easily? Which landforms are the easiest for people to traverse? When the early European settlers tried to migrate, for example, the Appalachian Mountains prevented easy access to western territories. For those hardy people who faced the challenge, moving uphill and through forests often meant carrying possessions on their backs and sometimes canoes as well. Most migrants chose to move along the coastal plain and up low-lying rivers instead, where the geography made movement easier.

Water Systems

Throughout history, people have settled near a supply of fresh water. In North America fresh water in lakes and river systems is abundant. Several lakes are so large that they are easily visible on the map on page 12.

Many lakes were formed as a result of the Ice Age that took place from about 2 million years ago to about 10,000 B.C., when sheets of ice moved down from the north as far as the valleys of the Missouri and Ohio Rivers. The ice blocked the water of some rivers and formed lakes, such as Great Bear Lake in northern Canada. The ice also dug out hollows as it moved over rocks, and water later filled these hollows creating, among other bodies of water, the Great Lakes, which lie between Canada and the United States.

The United States also contains several major river systems, which consist of brooks and streams that flow into small rivers that, in turn, flow into larger ones. The Mississippi River system is the largest in the United States both in the size of its drainage area and in its volume of water.

Throughout history, rivers have been important in the exploration, trade, and control of an area because rivers offer a natural route of transportation. For example, when settlers from the British colonies tried to migrate westward, they found their progress impeded by the French, who had built a network of settlements and forts that helped them control large parts of the Mississippi River system.

Climate Regions

The term **climate** refers to the set of meteorological conditions, including sunlight, temperature, precipitation, and wind, that characterize an area. An area having the same meteorological conditions is called a climate region. The United States has a wide variety of climate regions from the subarctic areas of Alaska to the tropical regions of Hawaii.

The climate of a region is like a meteorological boundary that sets limits for all aspects of life, including the extent to which humans can survive. In particular, climate determines the kinds of plants that can grow in an area and the kinds of animals that can thrive there.

Vegetation Regions

The term **vegetation** refers to the collection of plants that grow in an area. When people travel from one area to another that is very different, it is usually the vegetation that first draws their notice.

Given the variety of climate areas and landforms that characterize the United States, it is not surprising that the vegetation regions of the country are equally diverse. There are several kinds of forests, each with its own distinct family of trees. There are desert areas and flat grassland regions. Each type of vegetation supports a specific type of human lifestyle and activities.

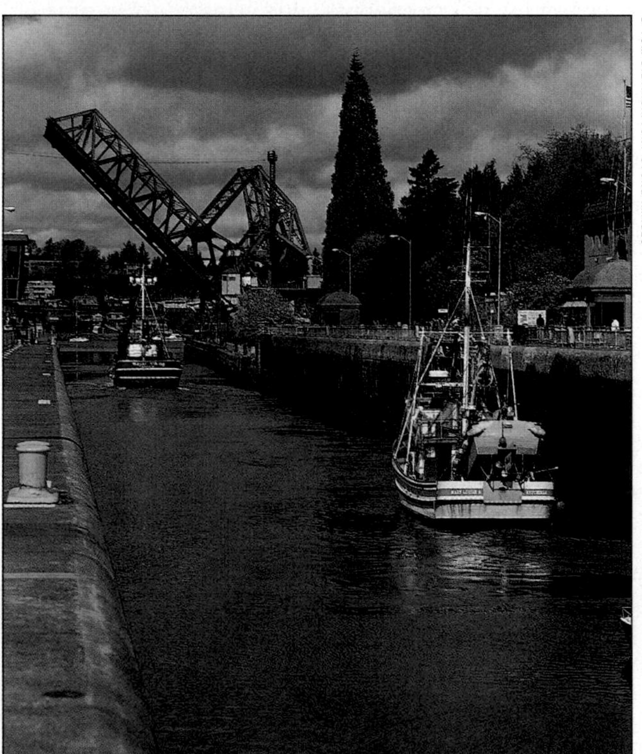

Moving Through the Locks Locks are sections of a waterway that can be closed off with gates so that the water level can be raised or lowered. *How can locks make it easier to travel on waterways that have variations in water level?*

FACTORS INFLUENCING VEGETATION

Climatic factors—such as the amount and intensity of sunlight, annual temperature patterns, and the annual rate of precipitation—limit the kinds of plants that grow naturally in a region. The type of soil and the local landforms also affect a region's vegetation.

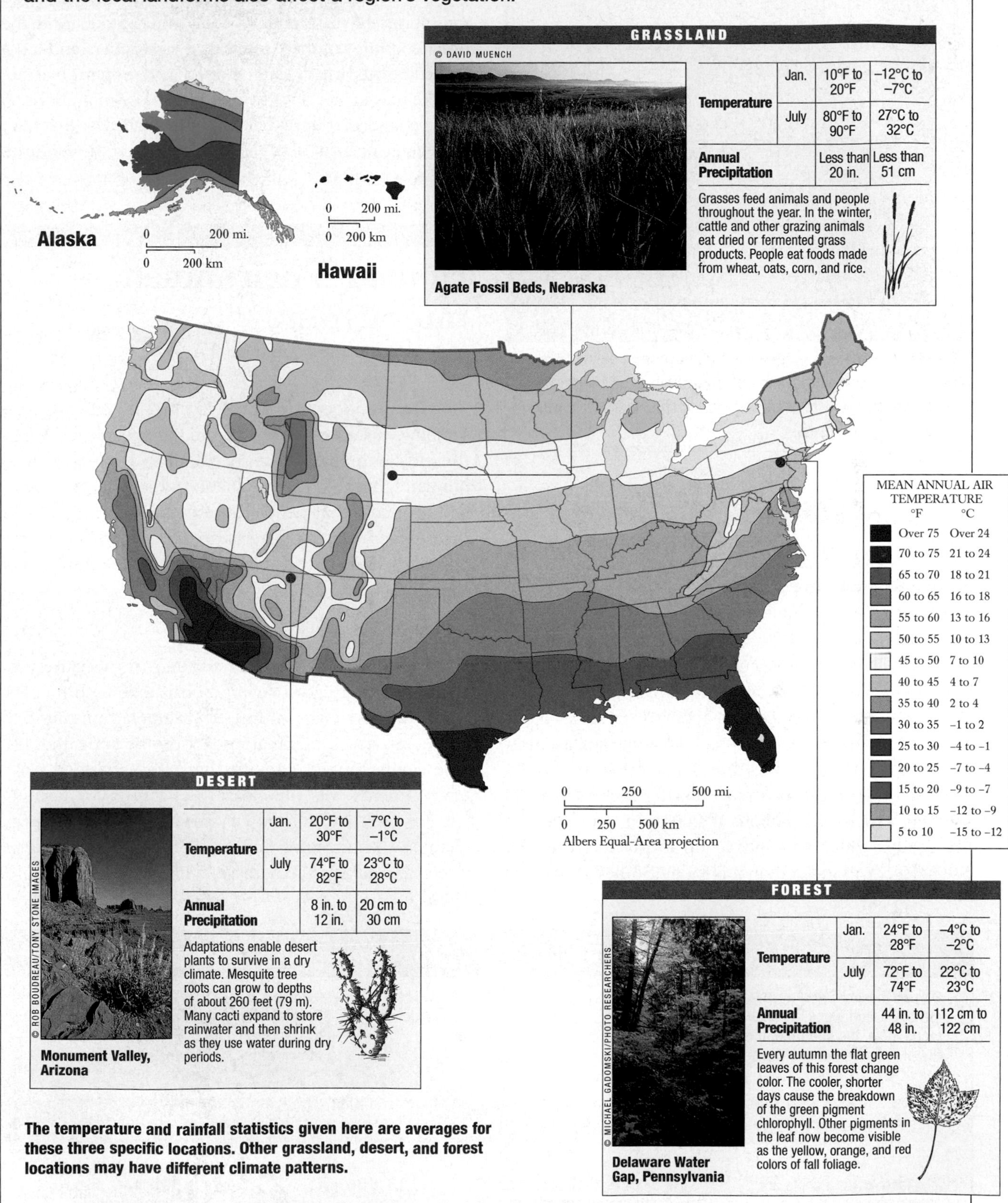

GRASSLAND

Agate Fossil Beds, Nebraska

Temperature	Jan.	10°F to 20°F	–12°C to –7°C
	July	80°F to 90°F	27°C to 32°C
Annual Precipitation		Less than 20 in.	Less than 51 cm

Grasses feed animals and people throughout the year. In the winter, cattle and other grazing animals eat dried or fermented grass products. People eat foods made from wheat, oats, corn, and rice.

DESERT

Monument Valley, Arizona

Temperature	Jan.	20°F to 30°F	–7°C to –1°C
	July	74°F to 82°F	23°C to 28°C
Annual Precipitation		8 in. to 12 in.	20 cm to 30 cm

Adaptations enable desert plants to survive in a dry climate. Mesquite tree roots can grow to depths of about 260 feet (79 m). Many cacti expand to store rainwater and then shrink as they use water during dry periods.

FOREST

Delaware Water Gap, Pennsylvania

Temperature	Jan.	24°F to 28°F	–4°C to –2°C
	July	72°F to 74°F	22°C to 23°C
Annual Precipitation		44 in. to 48 in.	112 cm to 122 cm

Every autumn the flat green leaves of this forest change color. The cooler, shorter days cause the breakdown of the green pigment chlorophyll. Other pigments in the leaf now become visible as the yellow, orange, and red colors of fall foliage.

The temperature and rainfall statistics given here are averages for these three specific locations. Other grassland, desert, and forest locations may have different climate patterns.

Climate and vegetation are interrelated. *How important is a region's vegetation to the people who live there?*

© TONY STONE WORLDWIDE

Facilitating Movement Modern highways include many features to improve safety, such as controlled traffic patterns at intersections. *How might a well-planned network of highways influence people's lives?*

Movement

People Come to the Two Continents

Fifty thousand years ago, North and South America were filled with a fascinating array of animals, but there were no people there at all. Anthropologists infer that the first human ancestors appeared in Africa a few million years ago. Their descendants migrated into Europe and Asia slightly less than 1 million years ago.

That migration took place during the most recent Ice Age, which ended about 10,000 years ago. Much of the earth's water was locked up in glaciers, and the ocean level was lower than it is today. Sometime toward the end of that Ice Age, while the ocean floor between Alaska and Asia was exposed and could serve as a "land bridge," the first humans migrated into North America from Asia.

From that moment until the present, a series of migrations have populated the United States and the other countries of the Americas. A rich understanding of United States history can be developed, in part, by tracing the reasons for and the effects of those migrations. A consideration of the goods, information, and ideas that have flowed into and out of the United States over the centuries can further enhance one's knowledge of history.

Human/Environment Interaction

An Inevitable Interdependence

Groups of people have always interacted with their surroundings in ways that affected the people as well as the environment. These interactions have produced human culture—the combination of institutions, ideas, and products that people have created and passed on from generation to generation. The time line below describes some of the milestones in the development of human culture.

The Early Centuries

The earliest Americans adapted to the variety of environments they discovered on the new continents. Some of their ways of life, for example, hunting and gathering, had a minimal impact on the surroundings. The single human activity that most changed early environments was the clearing of forests for farming and for fuel. Cutting down forests begins a series of changes that includes the loss of topsoil, the silting of rivers, and an overall increase in an area's temperature.

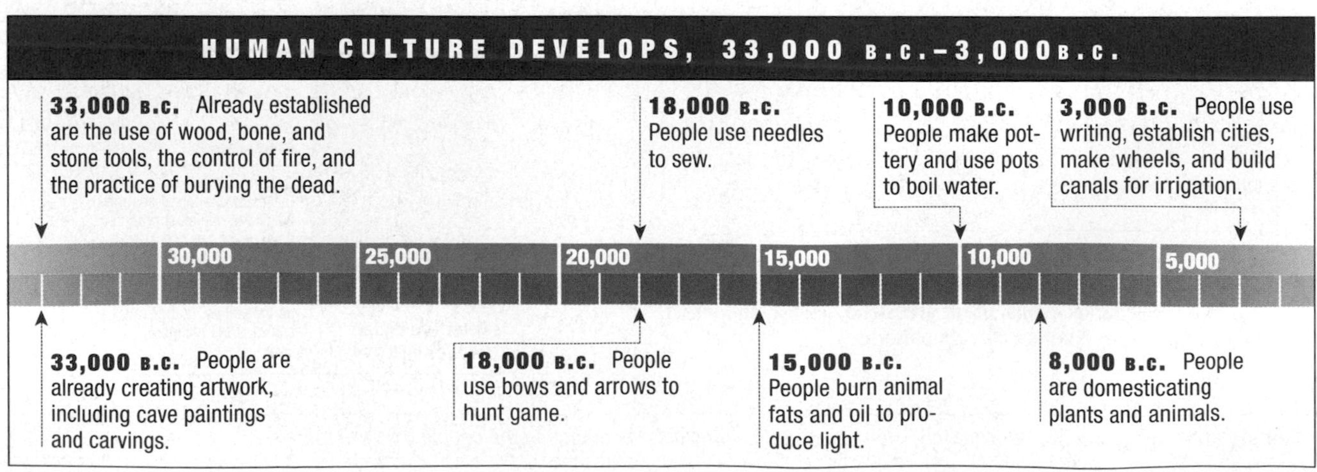

HUMAN CULTURE DEVELOPS, 33,000 B.C.–3,000 B.C.
33,000 B.C. Already established are the use of wood, bone, and stone tools, the control of fire, and the practice of burying the dead.
18,000 B.C. People use needles to sew.
10,000 B.C. People make pottery and use pots to boil water.
3,000 B.C. People use writing, establish cities, make wheels, and build canals for irrigation.
30,000
25,000
20,000
15,000
10,000
5,000
33,000 B.C. People are already creating artwork, including cave paintings and carvings.
18,000 B.C. People use bows and arrows to hunt game.
15,000 B.C. People burn animal fats and oil to produce light.
8,000 B.C. People are domesticating plants and animals.

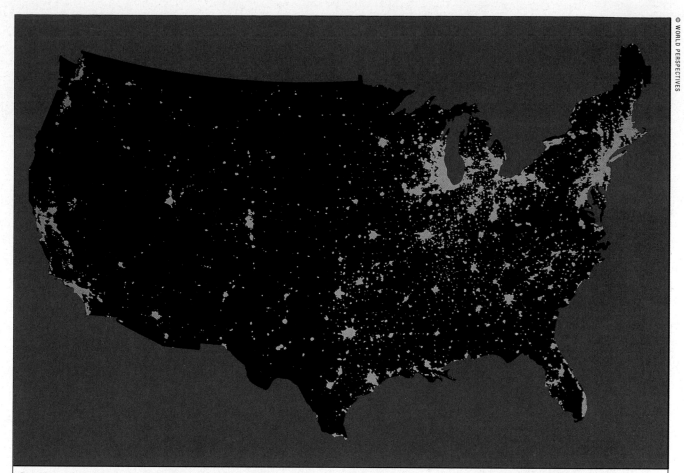

People's Night Lights This computerized composite image shows the light sensed by a satellite during the night. *In which two areas is the light the most concentrated?*

As the centuries have passed, the magnitude of the environmental changes caused by human activity has increased in a drastic way.

Monitoring Today's Conditions

In the late decades of this century, people have developed an amazing range of tools for looking at the environment. These tools can show the impact of natural events, such as volcanic eruptions, as well as human activities, such as burning fuel. The knowledge obtained from these tools will enable citizens and governments to make intelligent choices about the way people relate to their surroundings.

People can now use a modern understanding of the theme of human/environment interaction along with the other geography themes to illuminate the study of past events. The value of integrating the study of history and geography has been recognized for centuries. As one early historian noted:

> As Geography without History seems as carcass without motion, so History without Geography wanders as vagrant without a certain habitation.
>
> —John Smith, *The General History of Virginia, New-England, and the Summer Isles,* 1624

Section Assessment

Main Idea

1. Use a diagram like this one to show, using the five themes, how geography has influenced the development of the United States.

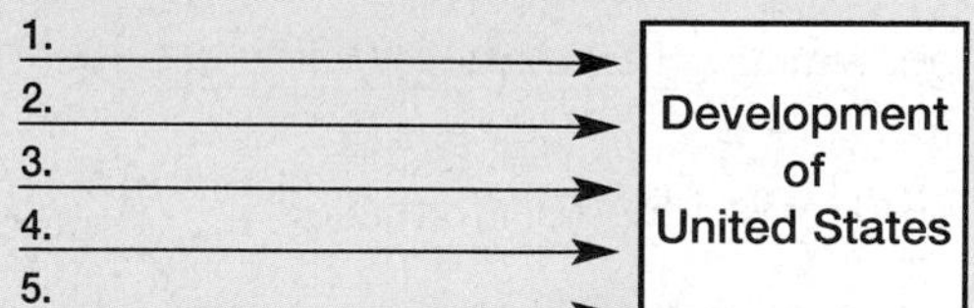

Vocabulary

2. Define: history, climate, vegetation.

Checking Facts

3. Give an example of a history question related to the location of the United States.
4. Why did the Mississippi River deter the westward migration of British colonists?

Critical Thinking

5. **Making Inferences** What historical changes might irrigation—the supplying of water to an area by ditches or pipes—bring to a dry region?

Chapter  Assessment

Self-Check Quiz

Visit the *American Odyssey* Web site at americanodyssey.glencoe.com and click on ***Chapter 1—Self-Check Quiz*** to prepare for the Chapter Test.

Reviewing Key Terms

Choose the vocabulary term that best matches each description below. Write your answers on a separate sheet of paper.

human/environment interaction
geography **location**
movement **place**
region

1. Theme that focuses on the distinctive characteristics of a specific location

2. An area that is defined according to one or more characteristics

3. Theme that explores the interdependence of people and their surroundings

4. The study of people, places, and environments

5. Theme that focuses on the relocation of people as well as the transfer of goods and information

Recalling Facts

1. Why do geographers often refer to the five themes of geography?

2. What does the theme of location emphasize?

3. How is absolute location described?

4. What is relative location?

5. What types of features describe a specific place?

6. What are some reasons why people migrate?

7. What three basic human needs does the environment satisfy?

8. What revolutionary event took place about 10,000 B.C.?

9. What three examples of region are based on human concepts?

10. What four examples of region are based on physical features?

11. Why did King Manuel I of Portugal want to keep a particular map a secret?

12. What is history?

13. Where is the United States located relative to the Prime Meridian?

14. How are the 50 states of the United States distributed?

15. What are political regions?

16. What are some of the landforms in the United States?

17. What is climate?

18. What does the term *vegetation* mean?

19. How were the first people able to migrate from Asia to North America?

20. What single human activity most changed the environment during the early centuries of life in North America?

Critical Thinking

1. Determining Relevance How does a knowledge of geography make it easier to understand history? Give examples to support your answer.

2. Analyzing Information Recall a region of the United States you have visited or read about. Describe the region using one of the five themes of geography.

3. Demonstrating Reasoned Judgment Use a diagram like this one to identify the distinctive features of the place where you live.

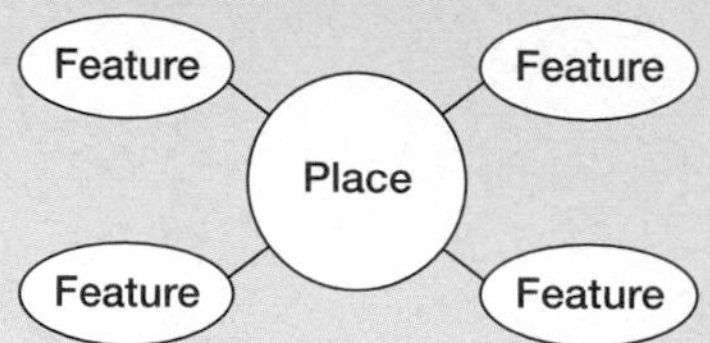

Portfolio Project

PORTFOLIO PROJECT

The geographer Harm de Blij has written, "If a picture is worth a thousand words, then a map is worth a million." Respond in writing to this statement, either agreeing or disagreeing with Harm de Blij. Explain the reasons for your opinion. Revise your work before placing it in your portfolio.

Cooperative Learning

In small groups, examine maps and use brainstorming to list the ways that all types of spatial boundaries can be established—from national borders to the property lines of private land. Then each member of the group should investigate one boundary that has changed at least once during its history. Find out what the boundary used to look like, what it looks like now, and why it changed. Report your findings to your group, and then choose one of the group's stories to share with the whole class.

Reinforcing Skills

Reading a Map Examine the map on page 19. Write a set of directions that would help someone read the map accurately.

GEOGRAPHY AND HISTORY

Exploration by Early Settlers

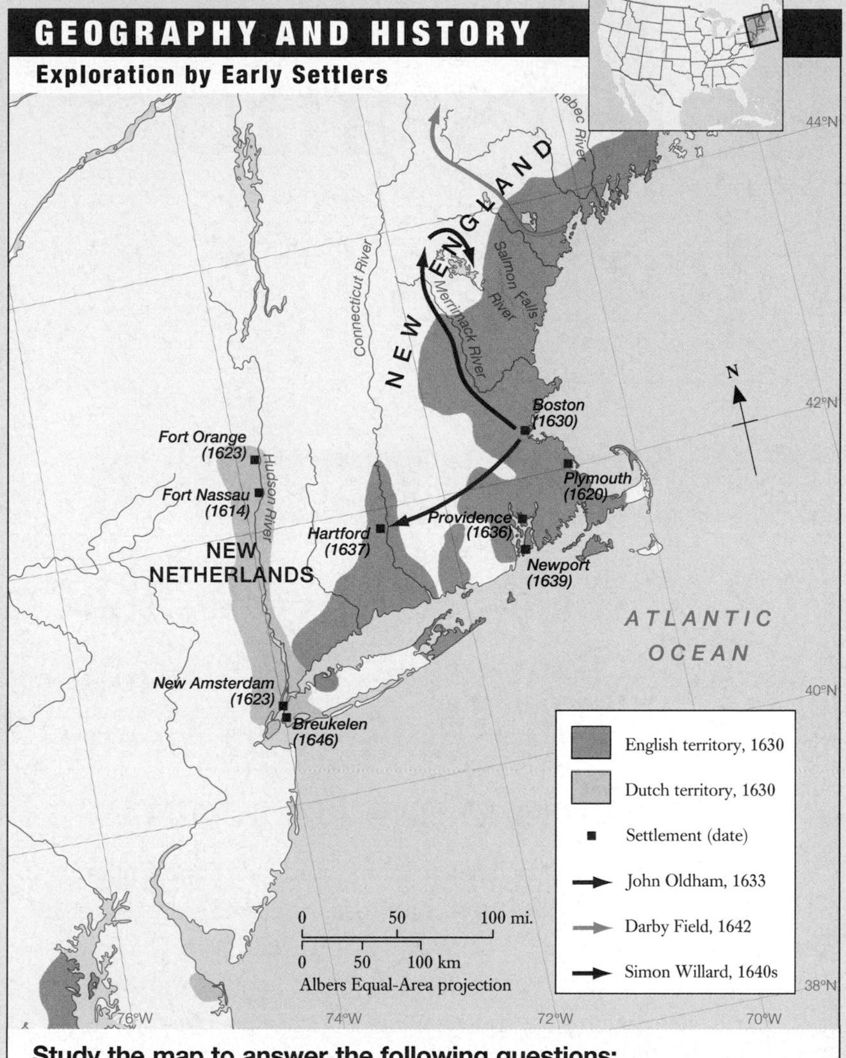

Study the map to answer the following questions:

1. Where were the Dutch settlements located?
2. How does the size of New Netherlands compare to the size of New England?
3. Describe John Oldham's explorations of 1633.
4. How does this map prove that rivers can affect history?

Technology Activity

Using the Internet Search the Internet for a Web site that has a political map of the world that you can print. Using this map as a focal point, create a bulletin board showing global interdependence. Include pictures and illustrations as examples.

Standardized Test Practice

1. Which of the following geographic themes would best help a historian to evaluate the significance of the invention of agriculture?

A region
B human/environment interaction
C movement
D place

Test-Taking Tip: The word *agriculture* means cultivating the land, growing crops, and raising animals. Eliminate any themes that do not directly focus on these activities.

2. All of the following are examples of the theme of movement EXCEPT

A publication of the journals of Marco Polo.
B the European spice trade.
C clearing forests for fuel and farmland.
D the travels of explorers.

Test-Taking Tip: Be careful—overlooking the word EXCEPT in a question is a common error. Read through all the answer choices and select the one that does NOT relate to the movement of people or the spread of ideas or goods.

Encounters and Colonies

APRIL 5, 1614: A WEDDING IS CELEBRATED IN JAMESTOWN

The bride was a Native American princess, the favorite daughter of King Powhatan. The groom, an English settler named John Rolfe, had been obliged to plead for the right to marry Pocahontas.

Rolfe received permission from Virginia's Governor Thomas Dale to wed for "the good of this plantation." The wedding brought a temporary if uneasy truce between the Powhatans and the English settlers of Jamestown, who would have starved if not for the Powhatans' gifts of corn.

Six years earlier, at the age of 12, Pocahontas had saved the life of Jamestown's leader, John Smith, by interposing herself between Smith and his Powhatan combatants. This intervention, which ended in Smith's being adopted into King Powhatan's family, allowed for the Powhatans to demonstrate their strength by establishing trade relations with the English settlers. When Smith returned to England, the settlers held Pocahontas hostage in exchange for the release of English prisoners and food. In captivity, she became an English-speaking Christian and met Rolfe.

When the Rolfes traveled to England with their infant son, the beautiful Pocahontas became an instant celebrity. She posed for a portrait, charmed the English king, and established a mythical presence that continues even today. Ironically, Pocahontas's celebrity also aroused the interest of potential English settlers who would soon flood the new colony and wage bloody warfare with her Powhatan relatives. ■

Write your reactions to the treatment of Pocahontas and the Powhatans by the English.

Chapter Overview

Visit the *American Odyssey* Web site at americanodyssey.glencoe.com and click on ***Chapter 2—Chapter Overview*** to preview the chapter.

(DETAIL) NATIONAL PORTRAIT GALLERY, SMITHSONIAN INSTITUTION/ART RESOURCE, NY

ALTHOUGH POCAHONTAS DIED BEFORE SHE WAS 22 YEARS OLD, SHE LEFT A LASTING MARK ON COLONIAL HISTORY.

The Earliest Americans

38,000 B.C.–10,000 B.C.: PEOPLE CROSS LAND BRIDGE TO NORTH AMERICA

SUPERSTOCK

Land of Plenty
As people moved south into the Americas, they found abundant herds of bison and other grazing animals such as mammoths.

ARCHAEOLOGICAL EVIDENCE INDICATES THAT ACROSS THE WIDE, GRASSY LAND BRIDGE THAT ONCE CONNECTED ASIA AND NORTH AMERICA TREKKED THE FIRST PEOPLE TO SETTLE IN NORTH AMERICA. With spears poised they may have pursued a mammoth, the huge game animal that once strode the earth. Today Beringia, the land bridge that allowed passage from Asia to Alaska, lies underwater. At several periods during the Ice Age, the glaciers that covered most of North America lowered sea levels by as much as 300 feet (91.44 m)—sufficient to expose a 1,000-mile (1609-km) wide passageway between continents.

The first settlers stalked big game such as mammoths and bison. Some settlers may have traveled by boat along the Pacific coast. Gradually, over thousands of years, the press of a growing population prompted the southward and eastward migration of smaller groups. Seeking new hunting grounds, the migrants followed their animal prey through the narrow pass between towering glaciers. When they reached the plains of North America, the earliest people beheld a paradise of plenty: animals from the antelope to the saber-toothed tiger; and berries, nuts, and grasses for the picking.

Over the centuries, groups continued breaking off and migrating farther southward and eastward. About 8,000 B.C. melting glaciers again boosted the sea level, burying Beringia underwater and drowning the land bridge back to Asia.

Scientists disagree on when and how people first came to the Americas and on how many waves of settlement they rode. Beringia, the land bridge, surfaced during 3 separate periods: between 70,000 and 30,000 years ago; between 25,000 and 15,000 years ago; and between 14,000 and 10,000 years ago. Some archaeologists speculate that people arrived from Asia as early as 40,000 years ago. Others suggest a much later date or a series of arrivals. Nevertheless, on several facts

GUIDE TO READING

Main Idea

Descendants of the early peoples who first settled North America adapted to the continent's diverse landscape and developed distinctive cultures.

Vocabulary

- nomadic
- sedentary
- egalitarian

Read to Find Out . . .

- how people first arrived in North America.
- the origins and ways of life of some Native American groups.
- how the League of the Iroquois formed.

scientists do agree: by 10,000 B.C. people had spread 15,000 miles (24,135 km) south to Tierra del Fuego, the southern tip of South America, and 6,000 miles (9,654 km) east to the East Coast of North America.

After generations of adapting to diverse climates and terrains, Native Americans practiced a staggering variety of lifeways and spoke several thousand languages. They became most populous in Mexico and Central America (Mesoamerica), but Native Americans also developed distinctive cultures throughout North America. There—in the deserts of the Southwest, along the fertile banks of the Mississippi, and in the woodlands of the East Coast—three contrasting cultures arose.

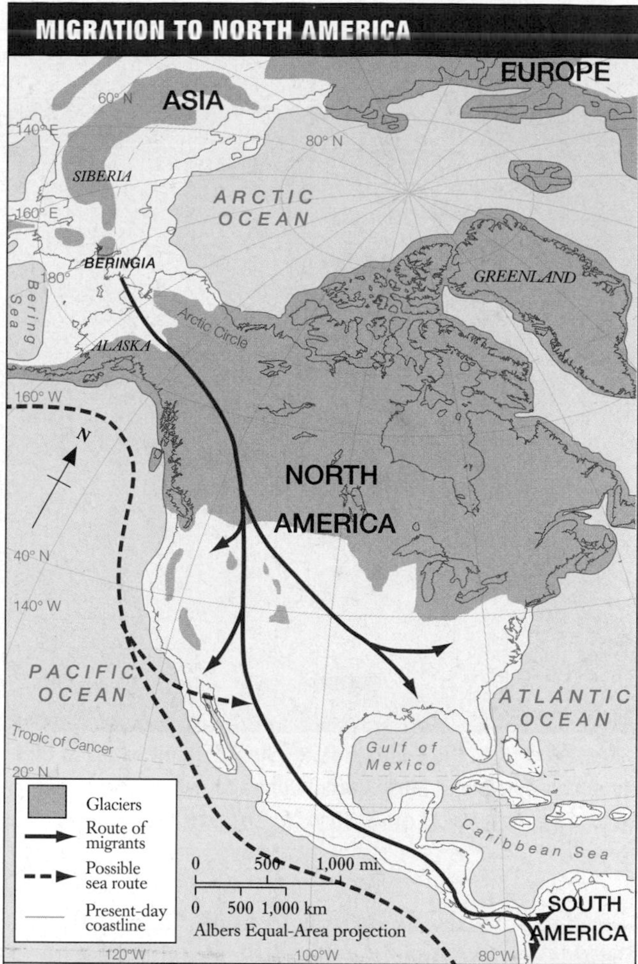

By 10,000 B.C. people occupied North America from present-day Alaska to the tip of what is now Chile. *In which areas did Native Americans become most populous?*

Cliff Dwellers of the Southwest

From Nomads to Farmers

During the Ice Age, descendants of the nomadic people who had followed their prey to North America hunted huge game animals such as mastodons in the southwestern part of what is now the United States. In time the weather warmed and the glaciers melted. As the climate grew drier, the larger game disappeared. The challenge of human survival in a newly arid environment launched a desert culture that depended on fishing, hunting small birds and animals, and on collecting edible foods that grew in the wild. This Southwestern desert culture survived for thousands of years.

Development of Agriculture

Between about 8,000 B.C. and 5,000 B.C., agriculture began to develop independently in Europe, Asia, Africa, and the Americas. As in other parts of the world, the cultivation of crops in the Southwest ushered in dramatic social changes. These changes included giving up a **nomadic,** or wandering, lifestyle for a more **sedentary,** or settled, one. A more dependable food supply stimulated population growth and reduced the amount of time people had to work to obtain food. Less time spent foraging afforded people more time for developing socially, politically, and religiously. In most places the growth of agriculture also decreed the division of labor. Now men hunted game and cleared the land that women then planted and cultivated.

Like their modern Pueblo descendants, but unlike most other highly developed early peoples, the Anasazi fostered an **egalitarian** culture in which people functioned as equals. Without kings, chiefs, or other official authority figures to compel cooperation, members of Anasazi farming villages built dams, reservoirs, and irrigation systems that harnessed the region's precious moisture to water corn and other crops. Beginning around A.D. 900, the Anasazi also constructed 400 miles (643.6 km) of roads and broad avenues leading to Chaco Canyon in northwest New Mexico, which became the heart of a thriving turquoise trade.

Anasazi Architecture

The leisure that accompanied the farming culture's prosperity allowed the Anasazi to turn out beautiful baskets and pottery, but their greatest creativity flowered in architecture. Generation after generation of Anasazi had lived in underground houses whose stonework walls and strong roofs provided shelter from the harshness of the seasons. Now, adapting their aboveground food storage houses for living quarters, the Anasazi transformed their underground pit houses into spiritual centers, or kivas. Some kivas in the populous valley held as many as 500 people. Constructing these kivas without horses (which were not brought to the Americas until the 1500s) required people to transport tons of timber to reinforce kiva roofs.

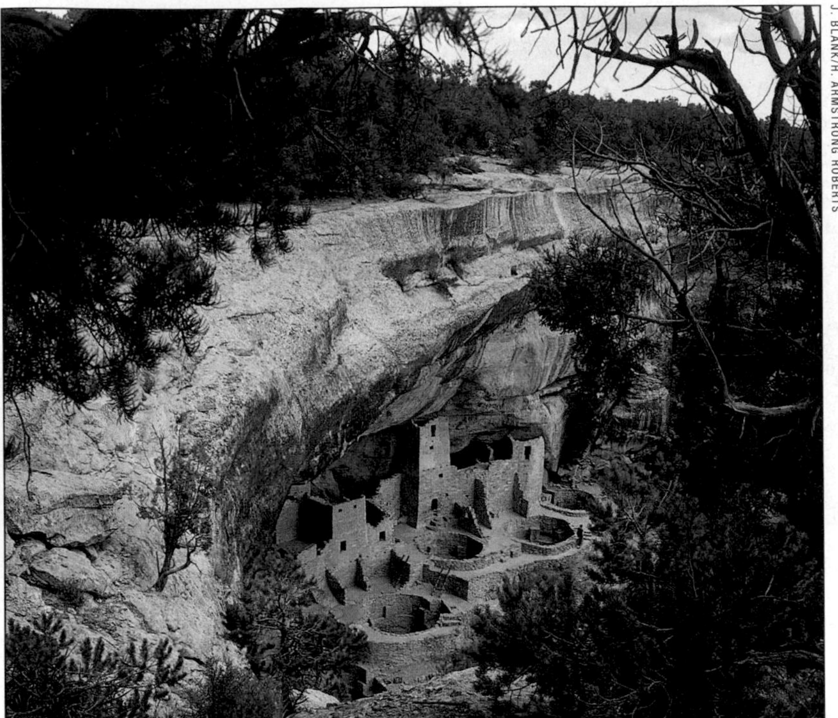
J. BLANK/H. ARMSTRONG ROBERTS

Ancient City **In the Southwest, the Anasazi built cities of cliff-side dwellings, such as this one at Mesa Verde, Colorado, which was constructed around 1100.**
What are the possible explanations for why the Anasazi abandoned Mesa Verde?

The Anasazi also began to build huge apartment complexes. At one dwelling site, Pueblo Bonito in Chaco Canyon, more than 1,000 residents lived in a free-standing 600-room structure. From the plaza amphitheater, some apartment sections towered 5 stories above the canyon floor. Until a larger apartment building went up in New York City in 1882, the size of this Anasazi building of the tenth century remained unsurpassed in the world.

When drought or a devaluation of turquoise prompted the Anasazis to abandon Chaco Canyon, about 3,000 Anasazi built stunning multifamily apartments within the protected cliff walls of Mesa Verde in Southwest Colorado. From their rooms in the cliff walls, the farmers used toeholds to clamber to the mesa top, where they cultivated corn, beans, and squash. The largest structure in Mesa Verde, later named the Cliff Palace, boasted 220 rooms that may have housed as many as 350 people.

By 1300, perhaps driven by drought or enemies, the Anasazi abandoned their homes in Mesa Verde. Among their descendants are today's Zuni, Hopi, and Taos Pueblo. The Taos Pueblo people of New Mexico repeat this myth about their beginnings, a story that may well have been told in this part of the world for more than 1,000 years: "The boy cried and cried. The blood came out, and finally he died. With his tears our lakes became. With his blood the red clay became. With his body our mountains became, and that was how Earth became."

Moundbuilders' Rich Culture

Metropolis on the Mississippi

About 1,000 years before the Anasazis began to farm mesa tops and construct apartment buildings in the dry Southwest, a friendlier eastern landscape had given rise to a very different culture. In the lushly watered country near the Ohio River, Native Americans farmed, hunted, and foraged for food. They also built gigantic earth mounds by the tens of thousands.

The First Moundbuilders

Used primarily as burial and ceremonial sites, the earth mounds rose as high as 70 feet (21.3 m). Their grandeur baffled the colonial settlers, who came upon the mounds after crossing the Appalachian Mountains in the late 1700s. Because the settlers had stereotyped eastern Native Americans as primitive forest dwellers, they invented myths to explain the imposing structures. Perhaps, they thought, survivors of the legendary sunken island of Atlantis or descendants of the ancient Egyptians had constructed the huge mounds.

Instead the mounds had been built by Native American people during the first century A.D. The building of such gigantic structures suggests a high degree of cooperation that required powerful leaders. These leaders were adorned at death and buried in special locations. Many excavations have shown individuals of high rank in the center of a group of people of secondary importance who had died earlier. One archaeologist described a Moundbuilder grave of a high-ranking female:

> At the head, neck, hips and knees of the female and completely encircling the skeleton were thousands of pearl beads and buttons of wood and stone covered with copper; extending the full length of the grave along one side was a row of copper ear ornaments; at the wrists of the female were copper bracelets . . . [she wore a necklace] of grizzly bear canines and [a] copper breastplate on the chest.
>
> —quoted in Joy Hakim's *The First Americans,* 1993

The contents of the burial mounds revealed the Moundbuilders as brilliant metalworkers and sculptors. The materials they worked with depended on a far-flung trading network, most likely based on a relay system.

The tentacles of the Moundbuilders' trading network reached west to Yellowstone (present-day northwest Wyoming) for obsidian, a natural glass used to make ceremonial blades; north to the Great Lakes for copper nuggets to beat out breastplates; east to the Appalachians for mica to fashion into decorated combs; and south to the Gulf of Mexico for turtle shells and alligator teeth to beautify ornaments.

The population of the Moundbuilders, ancestors of today's Creek, Choctaw, and Natchez, began to decline by about A.D. 500, perhaps due to the enmity of rivals or to a lingering cold spell that made farming and foraging less productive. West along the Mississippi River, however, another Moundbuilding culture arose. Centered at what is now East St. Louis, Illinois, on the Missouri border, this Mississippian culture encompassed thousands of villages from Wisconsin to Louisiana and from Oklahoma to Tennessee.

Cahokia

Like the Moundbuilders of the Ohio River valley, the Mississippians had strong leaders who directed the raising of huge mounds for burial and ceremonial purposes. The largest mound, built between A.D. 900 and 1100 rises 100 feet (30.5 m) from a rectangular base covering nearly 15 acres (6.1 ha) and containing 22 million cubic feet (616,000 cubic m) of earth. Its size surpasses that of the base of the Great Pyramid of Egypt.

This gigantic earthwork faces the site of a palisaded city that contains 100 smaller burial mounds and the remains of a busy urban settlement that archaeologists call Cahokia. Deemed "America's first metropolis" by one archaeologist, Cahokia once housed as many as 35,000 people. The city's residents worked at a variety of tasks, from jewelry making and weaving to hide dressing and salt making.

Mysteriously, the metropolis on the Mississippi lay abandoned centuries before the Europeans arrived on the Atlantic Coast. Before they disappeared, however, both the Mississippians and the Ohio River Moundbuilders passed on key agricultural skills to their trading partners in the Eastern Woodlands.

Eastern Woodland Native Americans

From Varied Lifeways, an Alliance

Like the Mississippians, the Native Americans who lived along the Eastern seaboard ate the fish they caught and the animals they hunted. Occasionally the men would don a deer head with antlers as a hunting ruse. Fertilizing the young plants with fish heads, the women cultivated corn, beans, and squash—which were called "the three sisters"—in the same plots. The sister plants supported each other as they grew, bean vines curling themselves around a supporting cornstalk. In addition, the nitrogen that beans brought to the soil benefited the other plants.

Like the Mississippians, the Eastern Woodland Native Americans also cleared their chosen planting grounds by girdling the trees. First they slashed the bark all the way around the trunk, leaving the tree to die.

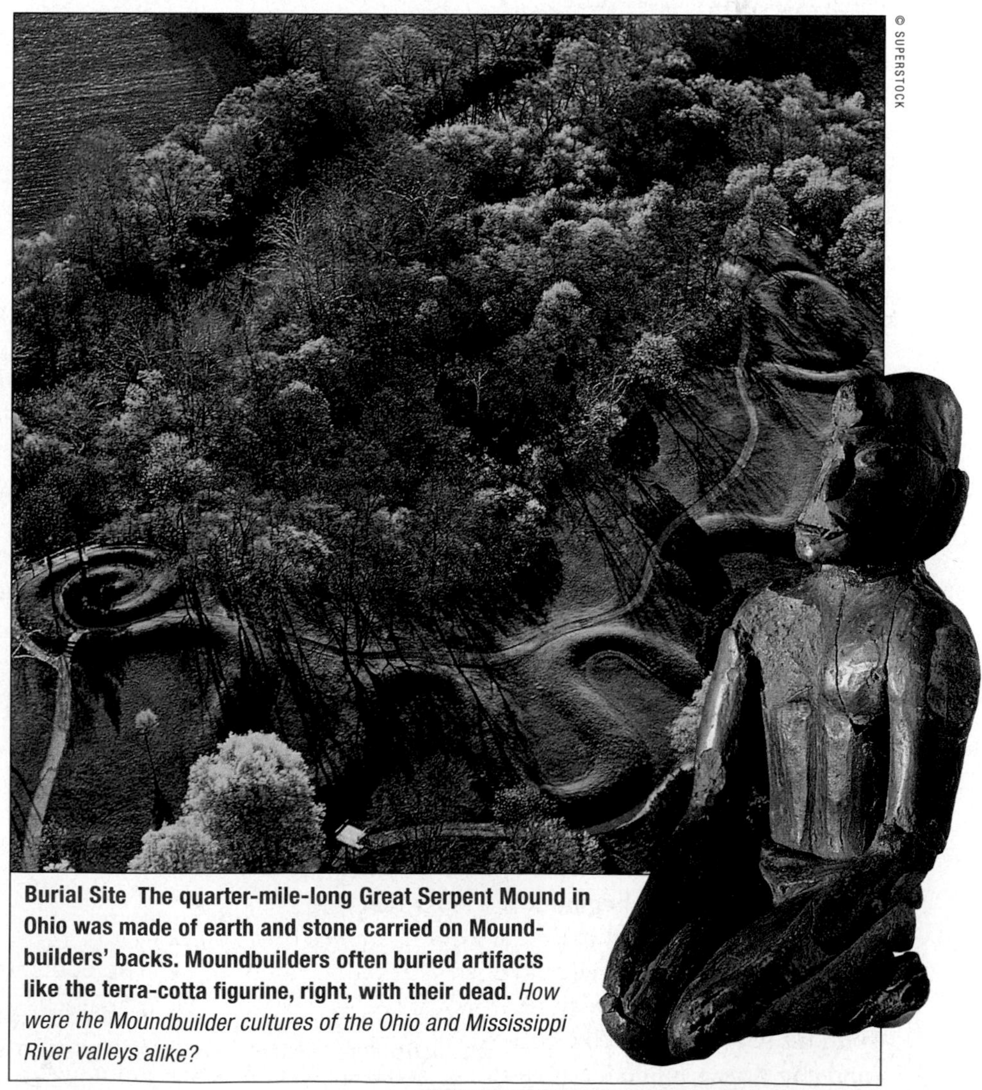

Burial Site The quarter-mile-long Great Serpent Mound in Ohio was made of earth and stone carried on Moundbuilders' backs. Moundbuilders often buried artifacts like the terra-cotta figurine, right, with their dead. *How were the Moundbuilder cultures of the Ohio and Mississippi River valleys alike?*

After burning the branches and leaves, they hoed the rich ash into the ground as a fertilizer.

The Mississippians passed on another influence, too. With their clusters of domed wigwams, occasionally surrounded by a palisade, the villages of many Eastern Woodland groups resembled the villages most Mississippians had called home. No Eastern Woodland village ever competed in size or sophistication with Cahokia. Still, excavation of one Huron town in the Great Lakes region revealed that it had housed about 5,000 people in more than 100 large structures. Its size exceeded that of the average European village of the 1500s.

The Iroquois Alliance

Eventually, the Iroquois became the most populous and powerful of all the groups that lived along the eastern seaboard. The group controlled territory from the Adirondack Mountains to the Great Lakes and from Pennsylvania to northern New York.

The power of the Iroquois derived from a longstanding alliance of 5 Native American groups—the Mohawk, Oneida, Onondaga, Cayuga, and Seneca. Europeans later called the Iroquois alliance the League of the Iroquois. The Iroquois themselves called their alliance *Ganonsyoni,* or The Lodge Extended Lengthwise, after the lodges, or longhouses, that as many as 20 families shared.

In an Iroquois longhouse, a woman and her female relatives ruled. The women owned the house and all its belongings. Women also controlled the fields where they planted their crops. When a son married, he left his mother's longhouse to move in with his wife's family. Iroquois women held power in the outside world as well. They chose the chiefs, or sachems, and could also depose them. Though only men could speak in the community councils, women exerted behind-the-scenes influence—determining, for example, the fate of captive warriors from enemies.

At one time, the 5 groups that formed the Iroquois League had themselves been enemies. By the late 1400s the constant feuding that had rendered the Iroquois people powerless in the face of their mutual enemy, the powerful Algonquian people, spurred them to form the league for mutual protection.

In Iroquois legend the league began when a Mohawk sachem named Hiawatha had a vision. In Hiawatha's vision a spirit named Dekanawidah dictated how the five groups should affiliate with one another. According to the legend, Dekanawidah spoke these words:

> We bind ourselves together by taking hold of each other's hands so firmly and forming a circle so strong that if a tree should fall upon it, it could not shake nor break it, so that our people and

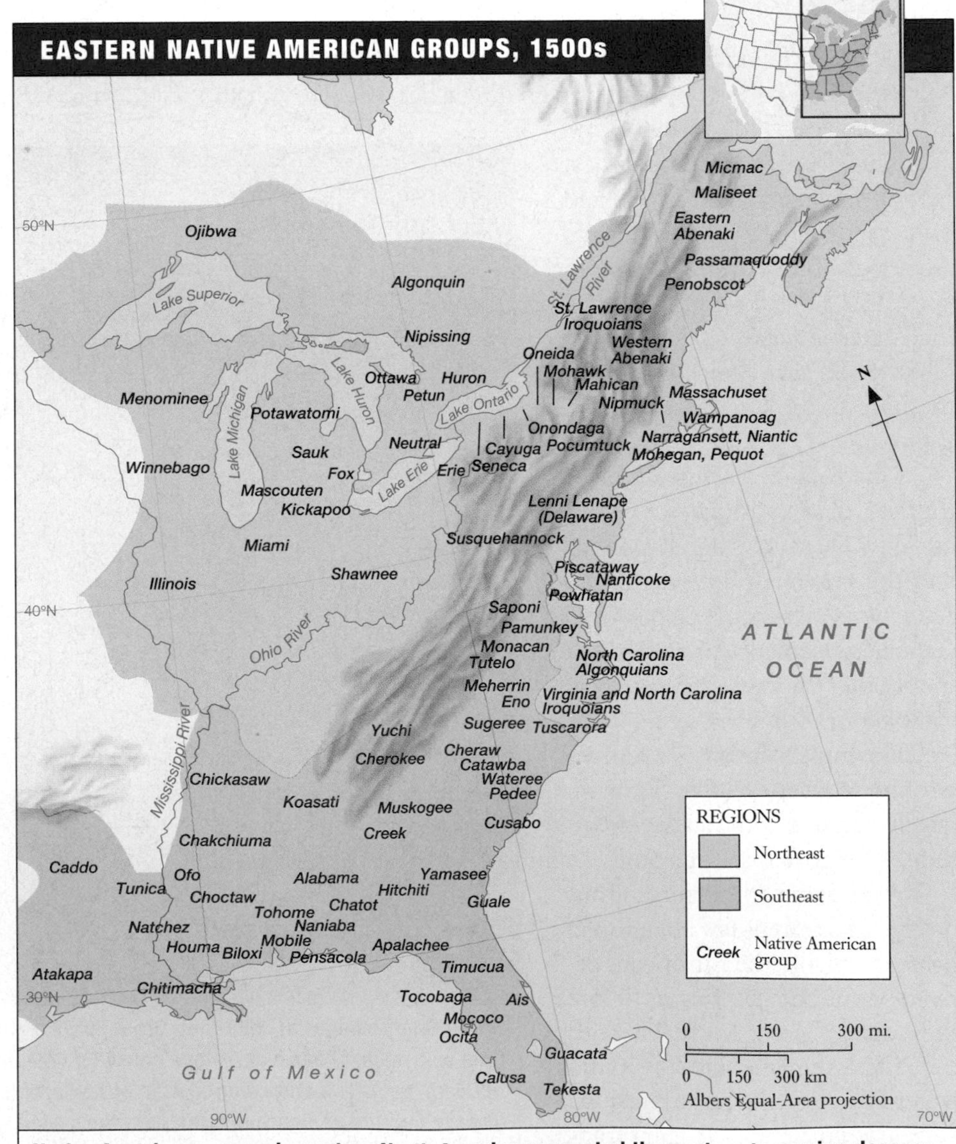

Native American groups in eastern North America supported themselves to varying degrees with agriculture. *In what areas are most groups of Native Americans concentrated?*

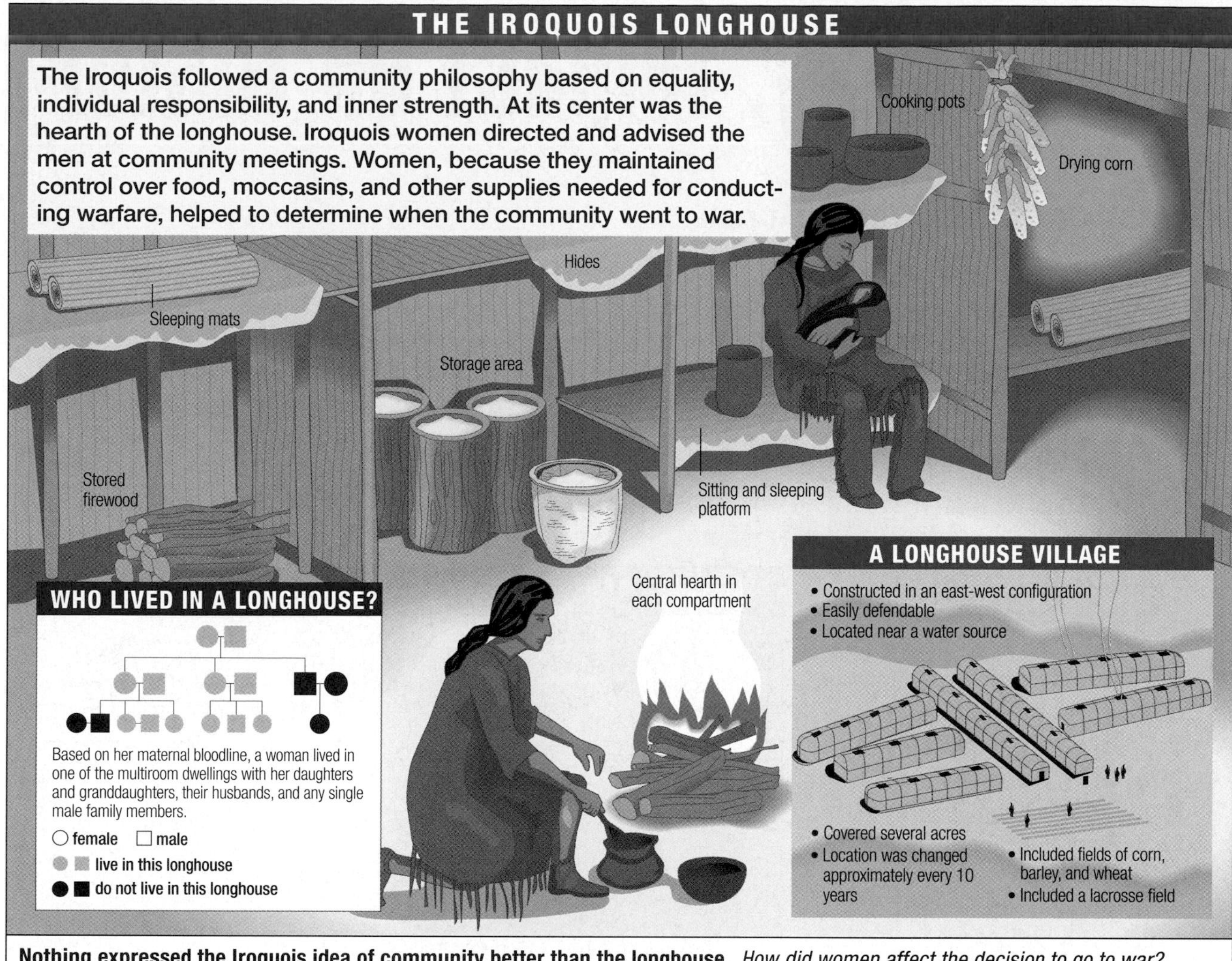

THE IROQUOIS LONGHOUSE
The Iroquois followed a community philosophy based on equality, individual responsibility, and inner strength. At its center was the hearth of the longhouse. Iroquois women directed and advised the men at community meetings. Women, because they maintained control over food, moccasins, and other supplies needed for conducting warfare, helped to determine when the community went to war.
Cooking pots
Drying corn
Hides
Sleeping mats
Storage area
Stored firewood
Sitting and sleeping platform
Central hearth in each compartment
WHO LIVED IN A LONGHOUSE?
Based on her maternal bloodline, a woman lived in one of the multiroom dwellings with her daughters and granddaughters, their husbands, and any single male family members.
female
male
live in this longhouse
do not live in this longhouse
A LONGHOUSE VILLAGE
• Constructed in an east-west configuration
• Easily defendable
• Located near a water source
• Covered several acres
• Location was changed approximately every 10 years
• Included fields of corn, barley, and wheat
• Included a lacrosse field

Nothing expressed the Iroquois idea of community better than the longhouse. *How did women affect the decision to go to war?*

grandchildren shall remain in the circle in security, peace, and happiness.

—quoted in Gary Nash's *Red, White, and Black: The Peoples of Early America,* 1982

European Attitudes

The Europeans who colonized the eastern seaboard wrongly considered the Native Americans to be ignorant savages. Nevertheless, they praised the organization of the Iroquois League. Benjamin Franklin wrote, "It would be a very strange Thing, if six Nations of ignorant Savages should be capable of forming a Scheme for such a Union . . . and yet that a like Union should be impracticable for ten or a Dozen English Colonies, to whom it is more necessary." For the European colonists, the Iroquois League offered a model for achieving unity among disparate states. For the Native Americans, the Iroquois League proved a powerful tool that enabled them to deal shrewdly with the European newcomers.

SECTION ASSESSMENT

Main Idea

1. Use a chart like this one to contrast the environment and cultures of the three groups shown on the chart.

Cliff Dwellers	Mound-builders	Eastern Woodland Groups

Vocabulary

2. Define: nomadic, sedentary, egalitarian.

Checking Facts

3. Why did people first cross into the Americas?
4. What spurred the Iroquois to form an alliance?

Critical Thinking

5. **Evaluating Information** Evaluate the accuracy of this statement: "Anasazi creativity flowered in architecture."

Geography: Impact on History

HUMAN/ENVIRONMENT INTERACTION

Native American Housing

Long before European settlers arrived, Native Americans had adapted to a broad range of environments, finding food and building homes using locally available resources. From the upper reaches of the Arctic to the Great Plains, the natural environment shaped Native American cultures.

Living on the Plains

On the Great Plains, Native American hunters and their families followed herds of millions of buffalo across the rolling grasslands. The Dakota, the Blackfeet, the Crow, and other Native American groups used the buffalo as a source of food, clothing, and shelter. They adapted their lifestyles to enable them to follow the buffalo, living nomadically in portable homes called tepees.

The Native Americans of the Plains built conical tepees by stretching buffalo hides across a frame of pine or cedar timbers. The tepees could be assembled and taken apart quickly. Because timber was scarce in the grasslands, the tepee poles were bundled together with the hides and transported from camp to camp. The hides formed a platform for carrying goods and even people across the Plains.

Northwest Coast Villages

In the rainy, mountainous forests of the Northwest Coast of North America, people lived in an environment of abundance. Rivers, streams, and the ocean teemed with fish, and the forest provided wild plants, berries, and a variety of game. Because a reliable supply of food was locally available, the

NATIVE AMERICAN CULTURAL AREAS, 1500s–1800s

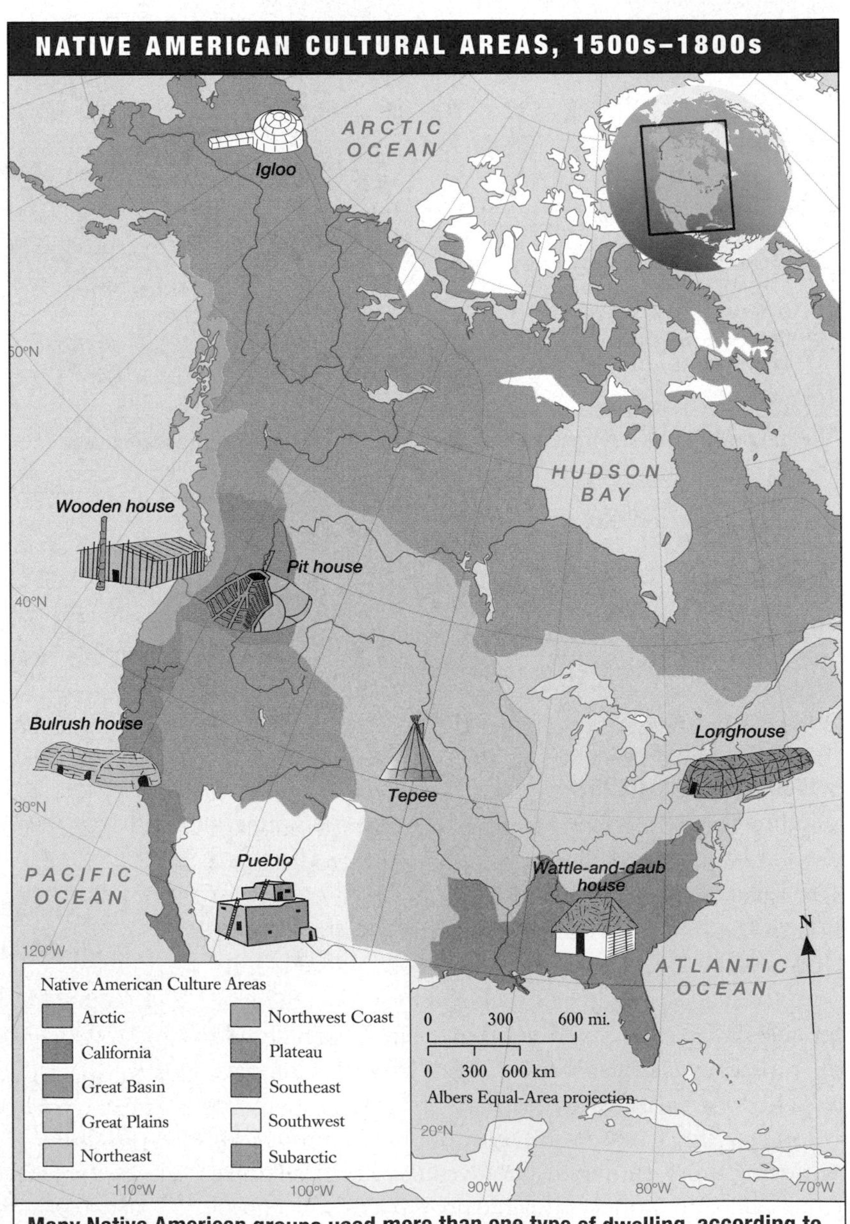

Many Native American groups used more than one type of dwelling, according to the season. *Why did Native American housing types vary by region?*

people of the Northwest developed a sedentary culture and lived in permanent homes and villages.

Using timbers hewn from the immense trees that blanketed the coastal mountains, the Native Americans of the Northwest built sturdy multi-family dwellings. Huge beams composed the frameworks of the houses. Planks made from split logs covered the frames. Pitched roofs shed the frequent rains. Craftspeople also made seaworthy canoes from hollowed-out logs. Water travel was a common form of transportation.

Native American villages nestled along narrow beaches or river shores. In only a few months' work each spring, villagers gathered enough food to last for the remainder of the year. Fishers caught large quantities of salmon, halibut, cod, and trout. The fish were dried on racks in the rafters of the houses and used as needed until the following spring.

STANLEY J. MORROW, COURTESY W.H. OVER STATE MUSEUM

Scraping Hides Cheyenne women scrape and stretch hides for use in tepee covers. *Why was the buffalo critical to the livelihood of the Native Americans of the Plains?*

Abodes of the Arctic

In the icy reaches of the Arctic, the Inuit used a variety of strategies to survive in an often harsh environment. Arctic peoples hunted and fished, moving in a rhythm that followed the seasons and the habits of their prey. Although they sometimes traveled great distances when hunting, the Inuit often built permanent homes and villages to which they returned between expeditions.

The Aleuts lived in small communities beside the sea. They built semisubterranean houses framed with whale bones and driftwood and covered with dirt, stone, and layers of sod. After a time, grass and other plants created a living roof that insulated against the cold. Most of their sustenance came from the sea, where they caught fish, hunted whales, seals, and other marine mammals, and gathered mussels and seaweed.

During the cold season, Inuit whalers moved north onto the Arctic ice to hunt seals. They traveled by dogsled and on foot, carrying few possessions. Lacking timber and other building materials, the whalers built ingenious dwellings called igloos from blocks of snow. The igloo's walls insulated occupants from the cold and wind. A small oil lamp or fire heated the igloo. Occupants carefully controlled the heat to prevent the igloo from melting.

Making the Geographic Connection

1. For each of the different types of Native American dwellings described, what was the main resource used?
2. What were some advantages of the materials selected for each type of dwelling?
3. **Human/Environment Interaction** How did the Native American groups discussed adapt their dwellings to their specific environments? List at least three examples for each environment.

Three Worlds Meet

OCTOBER 28, 1492: COLUMBUS EXPLORES CARIBBEAN

After 70 days at sea—weeks after he calculated he would reach Japan and days after his fearful crew had threatened mutiny—a sailor and his crew of 90 men finally made landfall on a tiny island in the Bahamas. At first the sailor delighted in everything he saw. The friendly people, whom the sailor called *los indios,* offered gifts of parrots and cotton thread in exchange for little glass beads.

Sixteen days after arriving in the Caribbean on October 12, Christopher Columbus wrote these words:

In Search of Asia
Columbus named the island where he first landed San Salvador—the present-day Bahamas.

> The houses of these Indians are the most beautiful I have ever seen, and I swear that the closer I get to the mainland, the better they become. They're like grand pavilions, like royal tents in an encampment without streets. One here, another there. They are well swept and quite clean inside, and the furnishings are arranged in good order. All are built of very beautiful palm branches. . . . The island is so beautiful, I could go on praising it forever.
>
> —Journal of Christopher Columbus

The skillful Genoese sailor had reckoned to reach the rich lands of India, China, and Japan by sailing west. Columbus, however, had stumbled upon the populous islands of Hispaniola (now Haiti and the Dominican Republic) and Cuba, which he assumed was the Asian mainland. Convinced that his quest had been successful, Columbus proudly returned to his Spanish royal sponsors. He brought cinnamon, coconuts, and a small amount of gold.

Columbus also carried human cargo: several kidnapped Arawaks. "There cannot be better or more gentle people than these anywhere in the world," Columbus wrote. Indifferent to the fate of the Arawaks and greedy for riches, Columbus's grateful patrons gave him more money and bigger ships to make three more expeditions.

Guide to Reading

Main Idea

Columbus's voyages brought together the peoples of Europe, the Americas, and Africa, producing the unique blend of culture that came to characterize the Americas.

Vocabulary

- western passage
- conquistador
- indigenous

Read to Find Out . . .

- the motives of European explorers in coming to the Americas.
- how Europeans and Native Americans interacted.
- why Africans were brought to North America and how they lived.

Columbus died convinced that he had found the **western passage**, or direct western route, to Asia. Instead the sailor had unwittingly accomplished something even more revolutionary. Columbus's voyages across the Atlantic forever connected the old world of Europe to the old world of the Americas and eventually to the old world of Africa. These links would blend the people and cultures of the old worlds. For good and ill a new world was born.

Europeans Cross the Atlantic

Cultures Collide

The first European to reach the shores of America preceded Columbus by almost 500 years. About A.D. 1000 a Viking sailor named Leif Eriksson landed in present-day Newfoundland. Eriksson named the spot Vinland because of its wild vines. The Vikings had sought new fishing grounds; for unknown reasons, their American settlements proved to be short-lived. In contrast the European hunger for gold and spices that fueled the voyages of Columbus forever married three worlds.

As the 1400s ended, Spain vied with its rival, Portugal, to discover western ocean routes offering direct access to the riches of Asia and Africa. Both powers sought to bypass the Middle Eastern merchants who controlled trade along eastern land routes to Asia. Bypassing these merchants would mean sharply higher profits for the Europeans.

Early Portuguese Dominance

Portugal forged an early lead in the race. Under the guidance of Prince Henry the Navigator, Portuguese sailors rounded West Africa, capturing a direct trade in gold and enslaved persons. Eventually, the Portuguese sailed all the way around Africa and onward to India and Asia.

The Portuguese had studied the works of Ptolemy, an astronomer of ancient Egypt. From their studies they knew that the earth was round, that distances on its surface could be measured in degrees, and that they could measure the position of the stars to determine their location on a map.

Two new inventions propelled Portuguese navigation in the second half of the 1400s. The quadrant, invented in 1450, notably improved the precision with which sailors could measure a star's altitude. By using a quadrant, sailors could determine their latitude much more accurately than was possible with a chart and compass.

A Moorish ship design inspired the second invention: the lateen-rigged caravel. A great improvement over European square-rigged vessels, the caravel with its triangular sails permitted Portuguese sailors to sail against the wind down the west coast of Africa.

The European powers vied for ocean routes to Asia and land claims in the Americas. Portugal's invention of the caravel (at left) enabled it to forge a lead in the exploration race. *Who were the French explorers who sailed to North America in 1524 and 1535?*

BIBLIOTECA NACIONAL, MADRID/BRIDGEMAN ART LIBRARY.

Conquest **The Aztec's defense was thwarted by the superior weapons of the Spanish.** *What other advantages did the Spaniards have over the Aztec?*

While the Portuguese made their way east around the cape of Africa, claiming the lucrative Asian spice trade, Columbus's voyages west staked Spain's title to the Americas. Within decades after Columbus's death in 1506, Spanish **conquistadors,** or conquerors, had cruelly subdued the **indigenous** peoples who inhabited the Americas.

The Conquest of Mexico and Peru

Two wealthy and ancient civilizations—the Aztec and the Inca—fell before the bloody onslaught of the Spanish conquerors. Mexico's Aztec civilization, weakened by internal strife, yielded in 1521 to the horses and firearms of Hernando Cortés's army. Like Mexico's Aztec, the Inca of Peru lived in populous cities under a well-organized social system. Before the Spanish conquest, domestic conflict had also undermined the Inca. Just 12 years after Cortés's bloody victory over the Aztec, the Spanish conquistador Francisco Pizarro led an army of 168 men to subdue the Incan capital of Cuzco. Pizarro's troops then used Cuzco as a base of operations from which to steal gold and silver from the other wealthy cities of the defeated Inca.

By the 1540s Catholic Spain laid exclusive claim to Central America, the southern parts of North America, and all of South America except Brazil, a Portuguese conquest. Spain now controlled an empire larger than the Western world had seen since the fall of Rome. The world would soon feel the effects of the Spanish conquest.

Profiting from the labor of enslaved Native Americans, the Spaniards plundered South American silver mines of millions of pounds of silver. As Spain grew wealthy, millions of Native Americans perished, mostly from disease. Bartolomé de Las Casas, a Dominican friar whose father and uncle had accompanied Columbus on his second voyage, condemned his fellow Spaniards' treatment of indigenous peoples:

> [The Spaniards] deal with them in any way they wish . . . without regard to sex, age, status, or dignity.
>
> —Bartolomé de Las Casas

Though Las Casas spent his life trying to stop Spanish exploitation of the Native Americans, his carefully documented efforts gained few supporters.

An Uneven Exchange

Livestock, Crops, and Disease

When Columbus first opened the Americas to European settlement, previously separate worlds became forever wed. The exchange favored the Europeans, but both sides contributed to the mix.

The Spaniards had come to the Americas, as one Spanish soldier explained, "to serve God and the king, and also to get rich." To serve God, priests attempted and sometimes succeeded in converting Native Americans to Catholicism. Because the Spanish men who served the king often traveled without women, they frequently took Indian wives, beginning a mixed-race culture that still permeates the Americas. In addition, as Bartolomé de Las Casas's passionate writings revealed, Spaniards forced Native Americans to mine gold and silver under unspeakable conditions.

Under two Spanish policies, known as the *encomienda* and *repartimiento,* Native Americans toiled to enrich Spanish colonists. The *encomienda* policy assigned to the Spanish a group of Native Americans who provided labor in return for protection and religious instruction. In practice this system meant virtual slavery for the Native Americans. As the Native American population fell, *repartimiento* replaced the *encomienda.* Like the *encomienda, repartimiento*—in which adult male Native Americans rotated their labor in Spanish factories, mines, farms, and ranches—also functioned as a slave labor system.

Native Americans did not succumb without a struggle. The European encroachment onto Native American lands engendered lethal warfare that continued for centuries. Disease, however, proved an even bigger killer.

The Scourge of Smallpox

Before 1492 Native Americans on the 2 continents numbered perhaps 50 million. Lacking immunities to smallpox and other European diseases, Native Americans saw their populations diminished by as much as 90 percent within a few generations. Many Native Americans who had never even seen a European perished from the diseases Europeans carried.

LAURIE PLATT WINFREY, INC.

A Conquistador on Horseback Without horses, the Spanish conquistadors might have failed in their conquests. *Why did Native Americans have to fight on foot?*

Smallpox, for example, a common scourge in the densely populated cities of Europe, had been unknown in the Americas before 1518. The smallpox epidemic that raged through Hispaniola decimated the indigenous people, who had barely survived warfare and enslavement. Las Casas wrote that the population of Hispaniola fell to no more than 1,000 "of that immensity of people that was on this island and which we have seen with our own eyes."

The horror of illness suggested to some Native Americans that their own gods had deserted them, and left many survivors susceptible to the belief that the Christian god had superior power. When the English pirate Sir Francis Drake raided Spanish Florida in the 1580s, he wrote that the Florida natives "died verie fast and said amongest themselves, it was the Inglisshe God that made them die so faste."

The scourge of disease and the promise of a powerful god were not the Europeans' only allies. Numerous European chroniclers of the invasion of the Americas expressed the sentiment that "after God, we owe the victory to the horses." Horses had died out on the American continent 10,000 years earlier. The return of the horse to the Americas on Spanish ships in the 1500s provided mounted Spanish conquistadors an easy victory over Native American foot soldiers. Eventually the horse would achieve near-sacred status among the buffalo-hunting Native Americans, whose life the horse revolutionized.

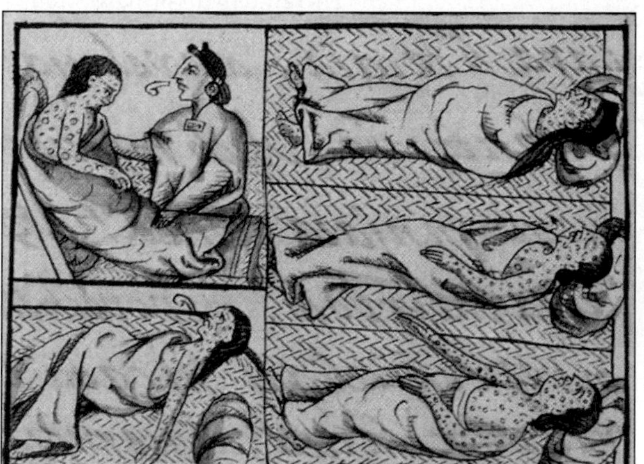

BIBLIOTECA MEDICEA LAURENZIANA, PHOTO ALBERTO SCARDIGLI

Epidemic This woodcut from the 1500s shows the devastating effects of smallpox on Native Americans. *Why did smallpox cause some Native Americans to turn to Christianity?*

Cultural Exchange

The Europeans also brought cows, chickens, and pigs to the Americas, and exchanged fruits and vegetables with the Native Americans. The exchange went both ways. From Europe Columbus brought oranges and sugarcane to the West Indies. To Europe went corn, beans, and potatoes—staple crops that would prove to be an even greater treasure than gold or silver.

Under optimal growing conditions, potatoes yielded far more calories per acre than the grain crops on which Europeans had traditionally relied. Potatoes carried another advantage. Grains such as rice, rye, or barley needed to be harvested and stored, making them an easy target for rent collectors or pillaging soldiers. Potatoes, however, could be left in the ground to be dug up one at a time, providing insurance against starvation. The potato's superior nutrient value prompted a population surge in Europe that laid the groundwork for the spread of industrialization in the 1700s.

The sugarcane that traveled from Europe to the Americas on Columbus's second voyage in 1493 opened the door to Africa's unwilling entrance into the Americas. The process of refining sugar from cane required backbreaking labor that Spaniards refused to do. The Native American populations that had provided forced labor lay decimated or had fled to the interiors of the North and South American continents. As a result the Spaniards looked to Africa. Enslaved Africans were first brought to the Caribbean as field-workers in 1505. Eventually 1 out of 4 of the 10 to 12 million Africans who were transported across the Atlantic as slaves would toil on Caribbean sugar plantations.

Africans in the Americas

A Forced Migration

The earliest Africans came to the Americas not only as slaves, but also as explorers. An African named Pedro Alonso Niño served on Columbus's crew. When the conquistador Hernando Cortés sailed to Mexico, Africans accompanied him; one African planted and harvested the first crop of wheat in North America. An African explorer named Estevanico opened up New Mexico and Arizona for the Spaniards, who followed cautiously when they discovered that hostile Native Americans had murdered the unlucky Estevanico.

The enslavement of millions of Africans followed rapidly upon the Europeans' arrival on American shores. The labor-intensive sugar, coffee, and tobacco plantations Spain established in the West Indies and in South America fueled African slavery. In time slavery expanded to North America as well.

A New Type of Slavery

Slavery itself was nothing new. During centuries of religious wars, Christians and Muslims had enslaved one another as infidels or unbelievers. Africans, too, had been involved for centuries in trading small numbers of slaves from West Africa across the Sahara to work as soldiers, servants, and artisans in Roman Europe and the Middle East. Before the American slave trade, however, slavery had never been permanent and irrevocable—nor had enslaved persons ever before been treated as subhuman, denied the rights of education, marriage, and parenthood, or forced to pass on their slave status to their descendants.

The European myth of African inferiority arose only after Europeans needed a rationalization for the profitable business of trading in human flesh. Far different from the European stereotype, West Africa had been the home of several advanced empires. For example, between the sixth and tenth centuries, the kingdom of Ghana ruled the territory between the Sahara and the Gulf of Guinea and from the Niger River to the Atlantic Ocean. In time the kingdom of Ghana fell, succeeded by the empire of Mali. At the center of the empire of Mali, the city of Timbuktu boasted great wealth and a distinguished Islamic university. Even the lesser kingdoms of Kongo and Benin boasted towns whose size rivaled that of European cities.

Life Enslaved

Before his capture from Benin in 1756, 11-year-old Olaudah Equiano "had never heard of white men or Europeans, nor of the sea." Equiano was enslaved in Barbados in the West Indies, and onboard a ship, he became the servant of a British naval officer. After buying his freedom and settling in Britain, Equiano published a 2-volume autobiography that powerfully indicted the slave trade.

Equiano's experience was atypical. Perhaps one of every six enslaved Africans died on the transatlantic journey. Survivors rarely had the opportunity to learn to read or write. Even fewer won their freedom. Still, Equiano's story reveals the harrowing experiences that transplanted Africans faced.

Captured and thrust onto a slave ship, Equiano described the wretched journey:

> I was soon put down under the decks, and there I received such a salutation in my nostrils as I had never experienced in my life: so that with the loathsomeness of the stench and crying together, I became so sick and low that I was not able to eat . . . but soon, to my grief, two of the white men offered me eatables, and on my refusing to eat, one of them held me fast . . . and laid me across I think the windlass, and tied my feet while the other flogged me severely . . . One day, when we had a smooth sea and a moderate wind, two of my wearied countrymen who were chained together . . . preferring death to such a life of misery, somehow made through the nettings and

CHRISTIE'S, LONDON/BRIDGEMAN ART LIBRARY, LONDON

Elaborate Art This bronze mask from Benin in Africa shows highly developed skills in metalworking and aesthetic expression. *Why did many Europeans believe that Africans were culturally inferior to them?*

THE L BRARY COMPANY OF PHILADELPHIA

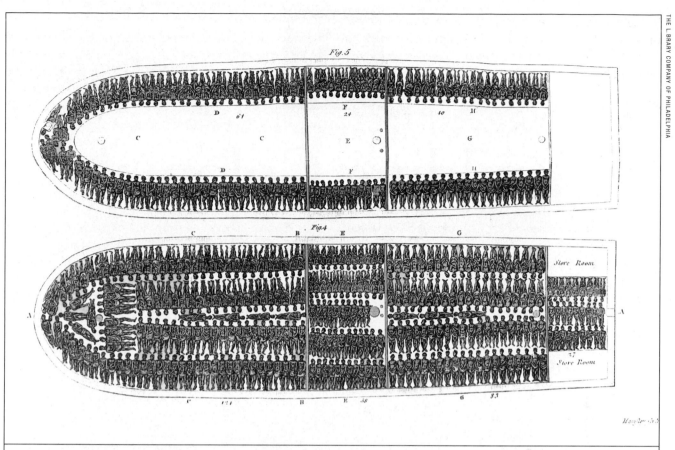

The Middle Passage Illustrations such as this one, which appeared in the early 1700s, showed slave traders how to pack their holds as efficiently as possible. *How many Africans died on slave ships during their journey to the Americas?*

> jumped into the sea, immediately another quite dejected fellow . . . also followed; and I believe many more would very soon have done the same if they had not been prevented by the ship's crew.
>
> —Autobiography of Olaudah Equiano

At least 10 million enslaved Africans made the same journey, unwillingly transported to the Americas in the largest forced migration the world has ever seen. By the mid-1700s, enslaved Africans represented about 40 percent of the population in America's Southern Colonies. In South Carolina after 1710, enslaved Africans outnumbered white colonists.

This migration not only enriched the European nations who traded in human flesh, it profoundly changed the character of the Americas. During the nearly 300 years between Columbus's journey and the American Revolution, 6 out of 7 persons who crossed the Atlantic came to the Americas against their will. These Africans soon learned European ways. With their complex religious and musical heritage as well as their agricultural knowledge, they also began to Africanize America's European culture.

Section Assessment

Main Idea

1. Use a before-and-after chart like this one to show the changes that Columbus's voyages brought to the Americas.

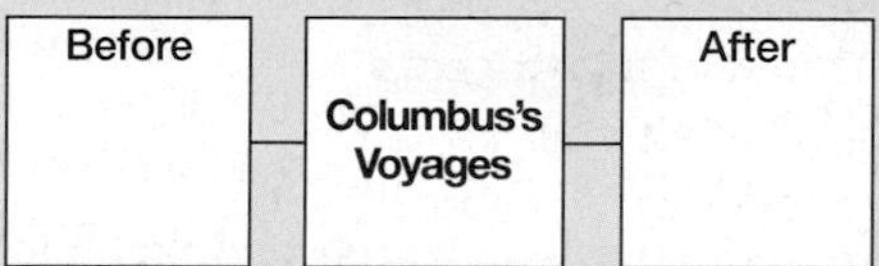

Vocabulary

2. Define: western passage, conquistador, indigenous.

Checking Facts

3. Where did Columbus think he had landed?
4. What accounted for most Native American deaths after contact with Europeans?

Critical Thinking

5. **Predicting Consequences** How would the early history of the Americas have been different if there had been no slave trade?

Building Colonial America

SPRING 1630: PURITANS ESTABLISH MASSACHUSETTS BAY COLONY

© NORTH WIND PICTURE ARCHIVES

Arrival of the Puritans
This etching depicts Winthrop's fleet of ships arriving in New England.

In the spring of 1630 the ship *Arbella* headed a fleet of 11 ships sailing for Massachusetts. Along with cows, horses, goats, pigs, and chickens, the ships carried 1,000 Puritans. In England these Puritans had failed to purify the Protestant Church of England of rituals they deplored as traces of Catholicism. The Puritans hoped Massachusetts would provide a more hospitable home for their strict religious practices.

Aboard the *Arbella,* John Winthrop, newly elected governor of the Massachusetts Bay Colony, summoned his fellow Puritans for a sermon. Although in England the Puritans had spurned church and state authority, Winthrop urged them to submerge their individuality in favor of a community that would adhere strictly to Christian ideals. Only if the Puritans could "rejoyce together, mourne together, labour and suffer together," Winthrop preached, could their settlement serve as an example to others:

> . . . for wee must Consider that wee shall be as a Citty upon a Hill, the eies [eyes] of all people are uppon us; so that if wee shall deale falsely with our god in this worke . . . wee shall be made a story and a by-word through the world, wee shall open the mouthes of enemies to speake evill of the wayes of god. . . .
>
> —John Winthrop, "A Model of Christian Charity," 1630

Guide to Reading

Main Idea

Spain, France, and England established colonies in North America, where settlers developed distinct ways of life and increased the cultural diversity of North America.

Vocabulary

- mission
- presidio
- selectman
- pacifism
- indentured servant

Read to Find Out . . .

- where Spanish, French, and English settlers established claims.
- how the European settlers adapted to the land and made their livings.
- the differences in the resources and economies of the New England, Middle, and Southern Colonies.

The Puritans were not the first English people to settle in North America. In 1607 English colonists established a settlement at Jamestown, Virginia. English Pilgrims, even stricter than the Puritans, had landed at Plymouth in 1620. English settlers in New England created communities, experimented with self-government, and struggled to create a "city upon a hill."

The English, however, were latecomers to the colonizing of North America. Well before the English settlements in Jamestown and Plymouth, the Spanish had carved out a much larger empire. Because the French also had made earlier claims, they would control far more territory than did England in the 1600s.

Spain and France in North America

Claiming the Land and Its Resources

Spain assumed a commanding lead in the settlement of the Americas. Within decades after Christopher Columbus died in 1506, Spanish conquistadors explored, conquered, and claimed most of South and Central America, as well as the southern portion of North America from Florida to California. In 1565 Spain built a fort at St. Augustine in what is now Florida, establishing the oldest continuously inhabited town in the continental United States. In the Southwest, as in Florida, the Spanish established **missions** to try to convert Native Americans to Christianity. They also constructed **presidios**, or garrisons, that served a dual purpose: to defend Spanish holdings and to serve as trading centers.

Because of the valuable silver Native American slave labor wrested from mines, Mexico and Peru dominated the Spanish Empire. Next in importance were Spain's Caribbean territories with their lucrative sugar plantations. Because they yielded no obvious riches, the Spanish territories that later became Florida, the Gulf states, Texas, New Mexico, Arizona, and California represented Spain's least important settlements in the Americas. Though Spain claimed huge territorial holdings in what would become the continental United States, Spanish colonists never settled there in large numbers. As late as 1700, fewer than 4,000 Spaniards dwelled in the northern border lands of Spain's territories.

Like the Spanish, the French staked an early claim to North America. In 1524 Giovanni da Verrazano sailed up the Atlantic coast for France, searching for the fabled passage to India. Though that search proved fruitless, Verrazano charted the Atlantic coastline between Florida and Newfoundland and established important trade contacts with Native American trappers. When he sailed up the St. Lawrence River in 1534, Jacques Cartier made further friendly contacts with Native Americans.

After the Portuguese and Spanish defeated French attempts to colonize Brazil and Florida, France chose to concentrate its settlements on the area around the St. Lawrence River. French fishing boats plied the cold waters of the North Atlantic for cod and salmon, but trading in furs soon proved even more profitable.

The fur trade required few settlers. The French simply brought manufactured goods such as iron and woolens across the Atlantic, anchored their ships in St. Lawrence's sheltered bay, and waited for Native Americans to bring their beaver pelts to barter at French trading posts. As late as 1643 fewer than 400 French people lived in Nova Gallia, or New France.

METROPOLITAN MUSEUM OF ART, NEW YORK/THE BRIDGEMAN ART LIBRARY, LONDON

Fur Traders **This painting by George Caleb Bingham depicts fur traders on the Missouri River.** *Which European nation established fur trading around the St. Lawrence River?*

Most of these settlers were traders or Jesuit priests. According to the royal government of France, the French in America had two concerns: the conversion of beaver and the conversion of souls. Thus, missions were often conveniently located at river junctions where the fur trade took place.

By the early 1600s the French government realized that they needed more settlers to protect understaffed French trading posts from their English and Dutch rivals. In the mid-1600s French explorers canoed down America's inland waterways. By 1660 New France's population was 2,000, and by 1690 France controlled the interior of North America. On the burgeoning coast, however, late-starting England reigned supreme.

Re-creating England in the Colonies

Thousands Settle the Atlantic Seaboard

From the beginning, England's settlements differed from those of Spain and France. Unlike the Spanish and French, whose settlements involved few colonists, the English came in large numbers, founding 13 colonies by 1732. In addition, while the royal governments of Spain and France sponsored and coordinated their settlers' activities, partnerships of merchants, who stood to win or lose large sums of money on the success of the colonies, privately financed the English ventures. As the 1600s drew to a close, moneyed investors became increasingly willing to speculate on the growing agricultural colonies on America's Atlantic seaboard.

Aside from needing money, English agricultural settlements on the Atlantic required a large body of willing migrants. During the 1600s thousands of English migrants streamed westward across the Atlantic, lured by an array of economic, religious, and political factors.

The glut of Spanish silver from the Americas had caused prices to rise on the European continent. When the rise in prices combined with population growth and the dispossession of small landowners, crime and poverty surged. John Winthrop, who would later lead the Puritans in Massachusetts, complained of England, "This land grows weary of her inhabitants, so as a man, which is the most precious of all creatures, is near more vile among us than a horse or a sheep."

In Europe religious wars between Catholics and Protestants made it harder to sell English woolen cloth and devastated once-thriving textile regions. Finally, the bloody political struggles between Catholics and Protestants within England itself made thousands of English settlers willing to brave everything to face an uncertain destiny. Between 1600 and 1640, 80,000 colonists fled England. By 1660 another 80,000 had followed.

Many of these English settlers stayed in the West Indies, but between 1630 and 1640, 20,000 Puritans headed for New England, moving from Hingham in Norfolk County, England, to Hingham, Massachusetts, or from Sudbury in Suffolk County, England, to Sudbury, Massachusetts. More than those who immigrated to the Middle or Southern colonies, English immigrants in New England sought to re-create English life and ways.

New England Colonies

A Puritan Stronghold

Because Puritan intolerance discouraged European immigrants of other countries from settling in the New England Colonies, most of the settlers in the northernmost colonies came from England. The Puritans sought to mold communities of pure Christians who would swear a covenant with God to achieve his ends on earth. As John Winthrop put it, if "the Lord shall please to . . . bring us in peace to the place wee desire, then hath hee

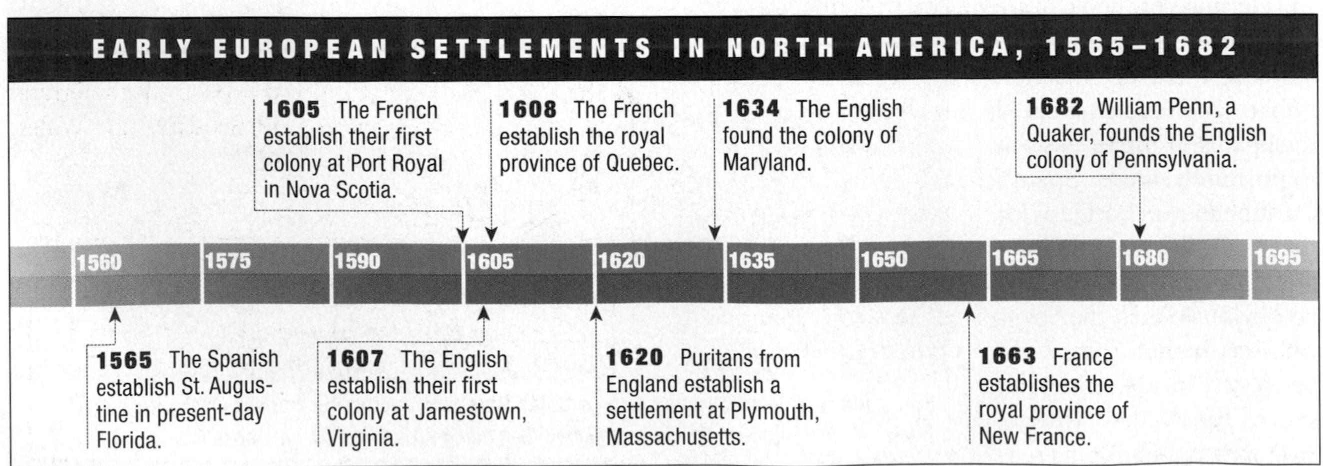

EARLY EUROPEAN SETTLEMENTS IN NORTH AMERICA, 1565–1682
1605 The French establish their first colony at Port Royal in Nova Scotia.
1608 The French establish the royal province of Quebec.
1634 The English found the colony of Maryland.
1682 William Penn, a Quaker, founds the English colony of Pennsylvania.
1560
1575
1590
1605
1620
1635
1650
1665
1680
1695
1565 The Spanish establish St. Augustine in present-day Florida.
1607 The English establish their first colony at Jamestown, Virginia.
1620 Puritans from England establish a settlement at Plymouth, Massachusetts.
1663 France establishes the royal province of New France.

ratified this Covenant and . . . will expect a strickt performance of the Articles contained in it." Puritan leaders such as Winthrop brooked no differences of opinion, even among their own members. When the pious Puritans Roger Williams and Anne Hutchinson threatened church authority, first Williams, then Hutchinson, were forced to flee to Rhode Island, where other dissidents soon settled.

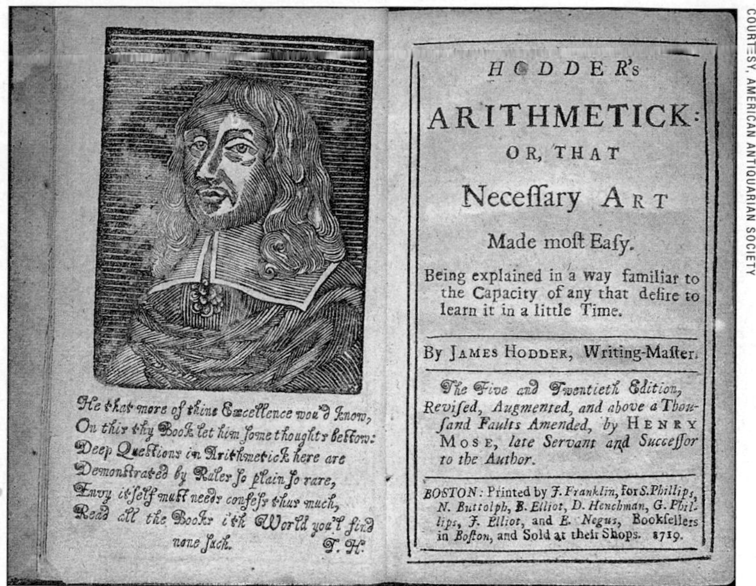
He that more of thine Excellence wou'd know,
On this thy Book let him some thoughts bestow:
Deep Questions in Arithmetick here are
Demonstrated by Rules so plain so rare,
Envy it self must needs confess thus much,
Read all the Books i'th World you'l find none such.
T. H.

HODDER'S
ARITHMETICK:
OR, THAT
Neceſſary ART
Made moſt Eaſy.
Being explained in a way familiar to the Capacity of any that deſire to learn it in a little Time.

By JAMES HODDER, Writing-Maſter.

The Five and Twentieth Edition, Reviſed, Augmented, and above a Thouſand Faults Amended, by HENRY MOSE, *late Servant and Succeſſor to the Author.*

BOSTON: Printed by *J. Franklin*, for *S. Phillips*, *N. Buttolph*, *B. Elliot*, *D. Henchman*, *G. Phillips*, *J. Elliot*, and *E. Negus*, Bookſellers in *Boſton*, and Sold at their Shops. 1719.

Teaching With the Primer Primers often combined teaching arithmetic or reading with teaching morals. *Why did the Puritans believe it was important that everyone be able to read?*

Establishing Communities

The single-mindedness that drove their religious ideals gave Puritans an economic edge. These New Englanders soon constructed a thriving economy based on agriculture, fishing, lumbering, shipbuilding, wool production, and trading for beaver furs with Native Americans.

Most Puritans emigrated with their families, or sent for them later. From New England John Winthrop wrote his wife, "Remember to come well furnished with linen, woollen, some more bedding, . . . and many other necessaries which I can't now think of, as candles, soap, and store of beef suet. . . ."

Striving to do God's work and avoid temptation, Puritan leaders dictated that single men and women not live on their own. Instead Puritan families clustered together in small towns that centered on the village meetinghouse, or "Lord's barn." There, even in New England's frigid winters, townspeople gathered to pray midweek as well as twice on Sundays.

Government and Education

Though the minister headed the community hierarchy, Puritans shared authority and developed a form of self-government. Voters, who were required to be male church members, elected **selectmen.** The selectmen dispensed land, determined taxes, and settled arguments. In addition all townsmen gathered yearly for a town meeting at which they chose town officers for the coming year and determined matters of community importance, such as teachers' salaries.

The Puritans' stress on literacy grew out of their belief that everyone should be able to read the Bible and psalmbooks. To train ministers, Puritans founded Harvard College in 1636, a mere 6 years after they had arrived. To ensure a healthy supply of students, the Massachusetts Bay Colony passed a law in 1642 dictating that parents must teach their children to read. A law that followed in 1647 mandated publicly funded education in towns of more than 50 residents.

In the healthy atmosphere of New England, the colonists' population doubled every generation. Between 1620 and 1700, the original immigrant population of 25,000 had burgeoned to 100,000 second- and third-generation Americans.

Middle Colonies

Northern Europeans Inhabit Farmlands

The lush farmland of the Middle Colonies attracted immigrants from most of northern Europe. As one settler wrote in 1681, "For the Soyl [soil] it is Good, and capable to produce any thing that England doth: (and) the Yearly Increase is far greater. The Air Temperate and Healthy." The Dutch established New Amsterdam (which later became New York City) in 1626, after purchasing Manhattan Island from Native Americans with goods worth about $24. Swedish settlers established a settlement called New Sweden along the banks of the Delaware River. New Jersey welcomed immigrants from the Netherlands, Sweden, England, France, and Finland. In addition to these groups, Pennsylvania also boasted immigrants from Denmark, Germany, Ireland, Scotland, and Wales.

HISTORY *Online*

Student Web Activity 2

Visit the *American Odyssey* Web site at americanodyssey.glencoe.com and click on ***Chapter 2—Student Web Activities*** for an activity relating to life in the Middle Colonies.

In the late 1600s England moved to expand its North American claims. In 1660 King of Great Britain Charles II granted New Amsterdam and the surrounding land to his brother, the Duke of York. The Duke kept the area he called New York for himself and granted New Jersey to a group of friends.

In 1681 Charles II made an even more generous grant. To repay a debt he had owed William Penn's father, the king offered young Penn a huge expanse of land. The land, including part of what is now the state of Delaware, became Pennsylvania, a holy experiment for its owner.

A Quaker, Penn had faced persecution in England for practicing his religious beliefs in human equality and **pacifism,** opposition to the use of force. Penn offered religious freedom to all Pennsylvanians and optimistically provided a governmental framework: "Let men be good and the government cannot be bad; if it be ill they will cure it." In contrast to New England Puritans, who seized Native American farming and hunting lands, Penn advocated maintaining good relations with the Native Americans. In a treaty in 1682, Penn wrote, "No advantage is to be taken on either side, but all is to be openness, brotherhood, and love."

Penn's enthusiastic advertisements attracted settlers from all over northern Europe. Pennsylvania soon became home to a mosaic of religious groups, including Quakers, Mennonites, Lutherans, the Dutch Reformed Church, Baptists, Anglicans, Presbyterians, Catholics, and Jews.

Lured to emigrate by the lush farmland, farmers in the Middle Colonies raised enough wheat, rye, beef, and pork to export to the other colonies and the West Indies. Prosperity from this agricultural trade turned cities such as Philadelphia, Lancaster, and New York into bustling commercial centers.

Farmers and business owners who needed additional workers often sent to Europe for **indentured servants,** people who would work for a number of years to repay the cost of their passage. An eyewitness account suggests both the harshness of the voyage and the devastating discovery many immigrants made at their destination:

> How sad and miserable is the fate of so many thousand German families who lost all the money they ever owned in the course of the long and difficult voyage, many of whom perished wretchedly and had to be buried at sea and who, once they have arrived in the new country, saw their old and young separated and sold away into places far removed one from the other.
>
> —Gottfried Mittelberger, *Journey to Pennsylvania,* 1756

Few indentured servants ever achieved their dream of owning land in America, but their labor boosted the prosperity of the Middle Colonies. In the Southern Colonies, the harshness of indentured servitude quickly gave way to the crueler institution of slavery.

Southern Colonies

Tobacco and Plantation Slavery

While the Middle and New England Colonies attracted people seeking religious freedom and farmland, the Southern Colonies drew fortune hunters. At Jamestown, the first English settlement in Virginia, however, most of the men who came seeking gold found death instead. Of the more than 900 settlers who arrived between 1607 and 1609, only 60 survived dysentery, malaria, and malnutrition.

The settlers who survived, and the land-hungry people who followed, soon discovered that the South's climate and soil were particularly well suited to growing tobacco. In London where tobacco brought high prices, people joked that Virginia had been built on smoke.

GIRAUDON/ART RESOURCE, NY

A Treaty With Native Americans **This painting shows how one artist imagined treaty negotiations between Native Americans and agents for William Penn.**
What relations did Penn seek to have with Native Americans?

The Plantation Economy

By the mid-1600s, a plantation economy had taken root in Maryland, Virginia, and parts of the Carolinas. The labor-intensive cultivation of tobacco demanded attention at many stages, from planting up through curing and packing. Other Southern cash crops, such as the rice and indigo that brought wealth to the Carolinas and Georgia, were similarly labor-intensive.

At first Southern planters relied on unskilled indentured servants to supply backbreaking labor in exchange for the hope of freedom and land. Most indentured servants came from the lowest rungs of society in England and Ireland. Probably no more than 1 in 20 indentured servants ever became free landholders. Instead the servants who survived the ocean journey and the unhealthy climate faced years of brutal treatment and an uncertain future.

Beginning in the early 1600s, Spanish and Dutch trading ships began to bring a few Africans to the Southern Colonies. The first Africans worked alongside whites as indentured servants, trading their work for the hope of freedom. By the late 1600s, however, the flow of enslaved Africans increased while the supply of white servants began to diminish. By the early 1700s, there were more enslaved Africans in the tobacco and rice fields than there were white indentured servants.

The institution of slavery quickly became a racial caste system in which even free Africans found their political and human rights obliterated. Laws controlling their rights and activities forbade enslaved persons to testify in court, engage in commerce or politics, travel independently, hold property, congregate in public, or marry. The holders of the enslaved Africans who toiled on Southern plantations viewed and treated African people as their private property.

Slavery Pervades the Colonies

Though the North never adopted plantation slavery, many enslaved Africans worked in Northern cities as artisans or domestic servants or on Northern farms as agricultural laborers. Still, every American colony dirtied its hands in the slave trade, from the wealthy Rhode Island shipbuilders whose fleets carried human cargo, to Pennsylvania wheat farmers whose crops fed the enslaved Africans of the West Indies.

In contrast to white settlers in New England and the Middle Colonies, white settlers in the South remained dispersed and isolated on small farms or plantations, where the gap between rich and poor loomed large. Power remained in the hands of a few wealthy plantation owners who could afford to educate their children privately or send them to Europe to study.

By 1682 English colonies lined the Atlantic seaboard from Massachusetts to South Carolina. In the late 1600s, both New England and Virginia fought major wars against Native Americans who resisted English settlement.

GUNSTON HALL PLANTATION LIBRARY & ARCHIVES

YALE UNIVERSITY ART GALLERY, MABEL BRADY GARVAN COLLECTION

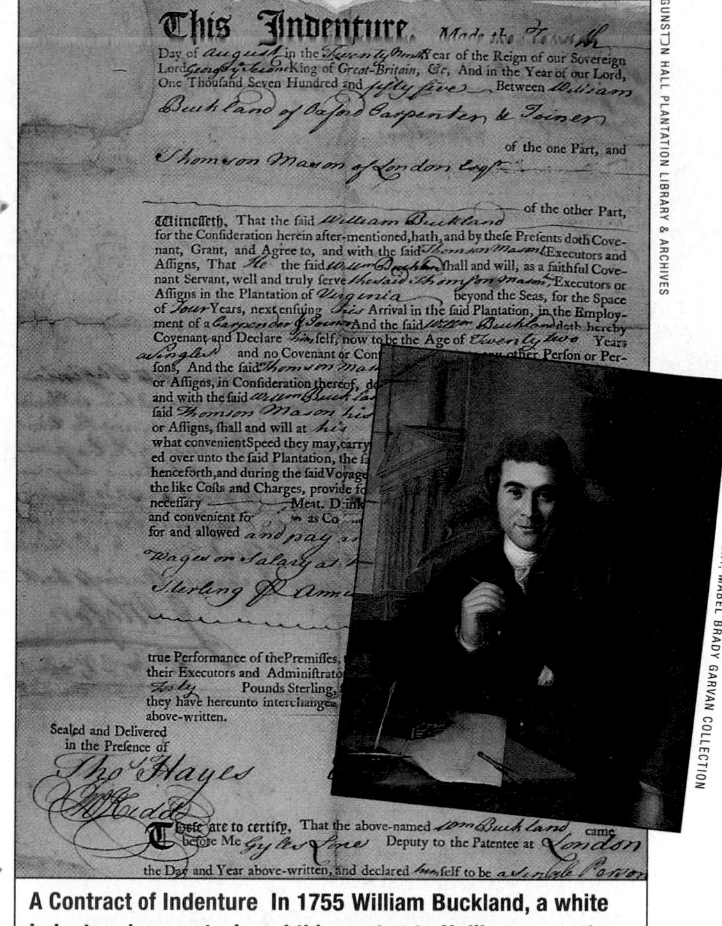
This Indenture, Made the Fourth Day of August in the Twenty Ninth Year of the Reign of our Sovereign Lord George the Second King of Great-Britain, &c. And in the Year of our Lord, One Thousand Seven Hundred and fifty five Between William Buckland of Oxford Carpenter & Joiner of the one Part, and Thomson Mason of London Esq. of the other Part,

Witnesseth, That the said William Buckland for the Consideration herein after-mentioned, hath, and by these Presents doth Covenant, Grant, and Agree to, and with the said Thomson Mason his Executors and Assigns, That He the said William Buckland shall and will, as a faithful Covenant Servant, well and truly serve the said Thomson Mason his Executors or Assigns in the Plantation of Virginia beyond the Seas, for the Space of Four Years, next ensuing his Arrival in the said Plantation, in the Employment of a Carpenter & Joiner. And the said William Buckland doth hereby Covenant and Declare himself, now to be the Age of Twenty two Years a Single Person and no Covenant or Con[...]

Sealed and Delivered in the Presence of

These are to certify, That the above-named William Buckland came before Me Gyles Lone Deputy to the Patentee at London the Day and Year above-written, and declared himself to be a Single Person

A Contract of Indenture In 1755 William Buckland, a white indentured servant, signed this contract. Unlike many other indentured servants, he was paid for his years of work.
Why did people sign such contracts?

SECTION ASSESSMENT

Main Idea

1. Use a chart like this one to compare Spanish, French, and English colonies in North America.

Colonies	Characteristics
Spanish	
French	
English	

Vocabulary

2. Define: mission, presidio, selectman, pacifism, indentured servant.

Checking Facts

3. Where did France concentrate its settlements?
4. What was the main occupation of English colonists along the Atlantic seaboard?

Critical Thinking

5. **Recognizing Ideologies** How did William Penn's ideology compare with that of the Puritans?

Turning Point

The Trial of Anne Hutchinson

NOVEMBER, 1637

TRANSCRIPT

From the Church Trial Against Anne Hutchinson

I look at her as a dangerous instrument of the Devil, raised up by Satan among us. . . . Whereas there was much love and union and sweet agreement amongst us before she came, yet since, all union and love have been broken and there have been censurings and judgings and condemnings one of another. . . . The misgovernment of this woman's tongue has been a great cause of this disorder. . . . Therefore, we should sin against God if we should not put away from us so evil a woman, guilty of such evils.

Reverend John Wilson,
Pastor, Church of Boston
March 1638

The Case

The General Court of the Massachusetts Bay Colony tried Anne Hutchinson in November 1637 for sedition, or working against the government. The Church of Boston tried Hutchinson for heresy in March 1638. By modern standards, Hutchinson committed no crimes. She had held meetings at her home to discuss the Sunday sermons given by Boston area ministers. At these meetings, she sometimes subtly criticized the teachings of some of the ministers. Challenging the authority of ministers and disputing their teachings was dangerous—especially for women, who were expected to bow to the authority of men at all times. Opposing the authority of church law was equal to speaking against the state.

The Background

Anne Hutchinson, a Puritan, left England and came to Boston with her family in 1634. They followed the minister John Cotton, who had been silenced in England and fled to the colonies. Anne's husband, William, held a considerable inheritance. He soon became a leading merchant in Boston. Anne worked as a midwife and healer and had contact with many Boston families.

Not long after the Hutchinsons landed in Boston, Anne invited a small group of women to her home to discuss religious doctrine. Anne was smart, eloquent, and well-versed in the Bible; she was also sensitive, supportive, and optimistic about life in the colonies. The gatherings quickly grew; as many as 80 people squeezed into her living room at once. Soon Anne was holding meetings twice a week to accommodate the crowds.

Through these meetings many Bostonians became familiar with Hutchinson's unorthodox views. She believed that a person's inner connection to God was more important than the person's appearance of following church laws. She thought that people could receive revelations—direct signs from God—without the help of a minister.

At that time in the Bay Colony many people considered it inappropriate for women to participate in public discourse. Hutchinson challenged this convention, as well as the authority of Boston's leaders, most of whom were men.

The Players

Within about a year of Anne Hutchinson's arrival, Massachusetts Bay Colony was divided into those who supported her and those who did not. Because of her neighborliness, her compelling egalitarian ideas, and her strength as a speaker and a leader, Hutchinson held wide popular support. Many businesspeople supported Hutchinson because religious leaders had placed severe restrictions on business. Some of the colony's most important political and religious figures opposed Hutchinson. John Winthrop, the colony's founder, lived across the street from Hutchinson. Winthrop knew about the popularity of Hutchinson's meetings. He also knew that his most powerful political rivals regularly attended. John Wilson, pastor of the Church of Boston, disliked Hutchinson because she had spoken against his teachings and walked out on his sermons. She had also tried to replace Wilson with Reverend John Wheelwright, her brother-in-law and one of her ardent supporters. John Cotton, Hutchinson's mentor, tried to remain neutral.

The Trial

By the fall of 1637, the balance of power had shifted in favor of the Bay Colony's founders. John Winthrop had recaptured the governorship; former governor Henry Vane, a Hutchinson supporter, had returned to England. Governor Winthrop and Reverend Wilson quickly acted against Hutchinson. First, they called a meeting of the ministers to evaluate her theologies. Not surprisingly, the ministers condemned Hutchinson's views, especially those on revelations. Ministers who preached these views

". . . you have maintained a meeting and an assembly in your house that hath been condemned by the general assembly as a thing not tolerable nor comely in the sight of God nor fitting for your sex. . . ."

Governor John Winthrop

"You have rather been a Husband than a Wife and a preacher than a Hearer; a Magistrate than a Subject."

Reverend Hugh Peter of Salem

CULVER PICTURES

"I'll bring you to a woman that preaches better than any of your black-coats . . . and for my part, sayeth he, I had rather hear such a one that speaks from the mere motion of the spirit without any study at all, than any of your learned scholars. . . ."

Chronicler Edward Johnson, quoting a male follower of Hutchinson's

"Here is no law of God that she hath broken nor any law of the country that she hath broke, and therefore she deserves no censure."

William Coddington, merchant and civic leader of Boston

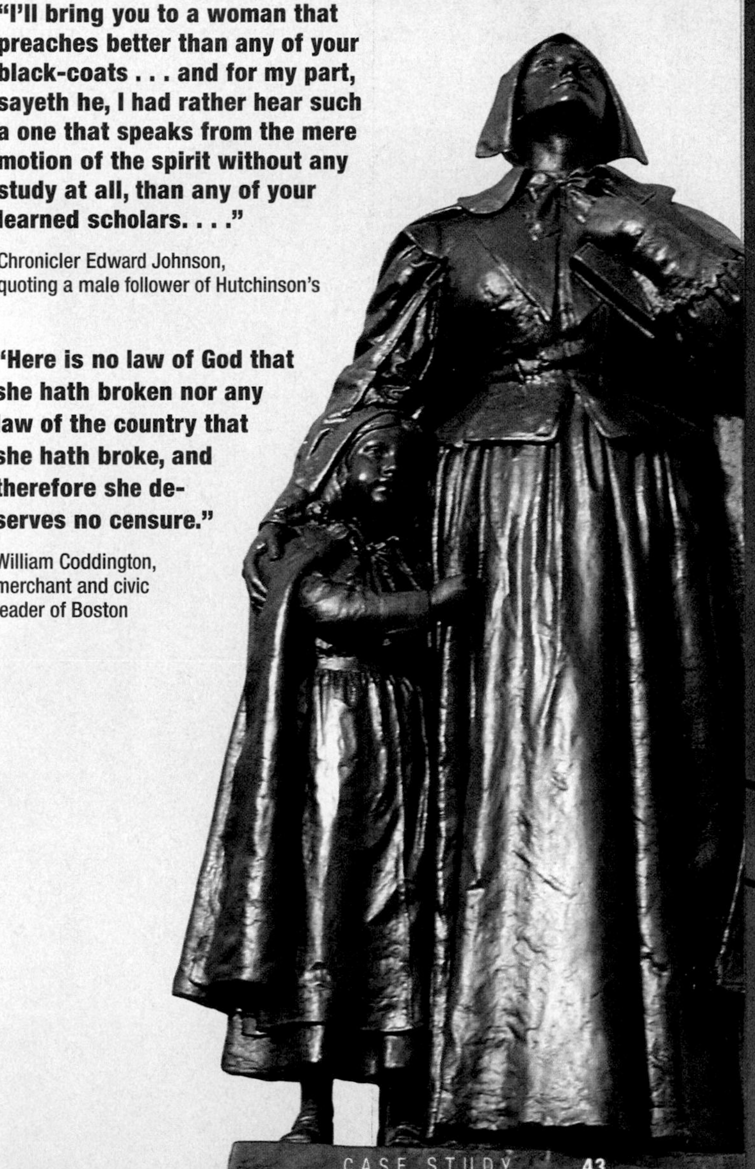

PHOTO BY JOHN JENKINS

Turning Point

were called to recant. Reverend Wheelwright refused and was banished from the colony, along with some of his supporters. Many other supporters were stripped of their citizenship.

The court called Anne Hutchinson to trial. Governor Winthrop sat as both judge and chief prosecutor. Anne Hutchinson addressed the court alone, without the benefit of a jury, lawyer, or witnesses.

The Opinions

The quotations on the previous page show divided opinions about Anne Hutchinson. Many in Boston were inspired by her, but they realized it was dangerous to speak against those in power. William Coddington, one of Boston's most successful business leaders, rallied to Hutchinson's defense.

Hutchinson spoke calmly, clearly, and eloquently in her own defense during the two-day trial. Although the governor and the ministers had little evidence against Hutchinson, they spoke strongly. Their strident judgments rang throughout the trial.

The Outcome

The verdict—banishment—surprised neither Hutchinson's supporters nor her detractors. Because winter was near, the court voted to allow Hutchinson to remain in the area under house arrest until spring.

The Bay Colony leaders still felt threatened by Hutchinson, who refused to alter her views. In March, they held a church trial. At the end of the trial, Hutchinson recanted her views in one breath and insulted the ministers in the next. They responded by excommunicating her.

The banishment was carried out a few days later. Hutchinson left with her family for the settlement of Aquidneck in present-day Portsmouth, Rhode Island. This region had become a haven for religious dissenters, including Roger Williams, who had been banished from the Bay Colony in 1635. Harassment by the Bay Colony continued. Ministers came to try to convince Hutchinson to reform; the colony also threatened to take over the Hutchinsons' land.

With the death of her husband in the summer of 1642, Anne Hutchinson decided to try to escape ever-present threats of the Bay Colony. The family eventually moved to the shores of Long Island, near Pelham Bay. Anne Hutchinson was killed there during a Native American attack in 1643.

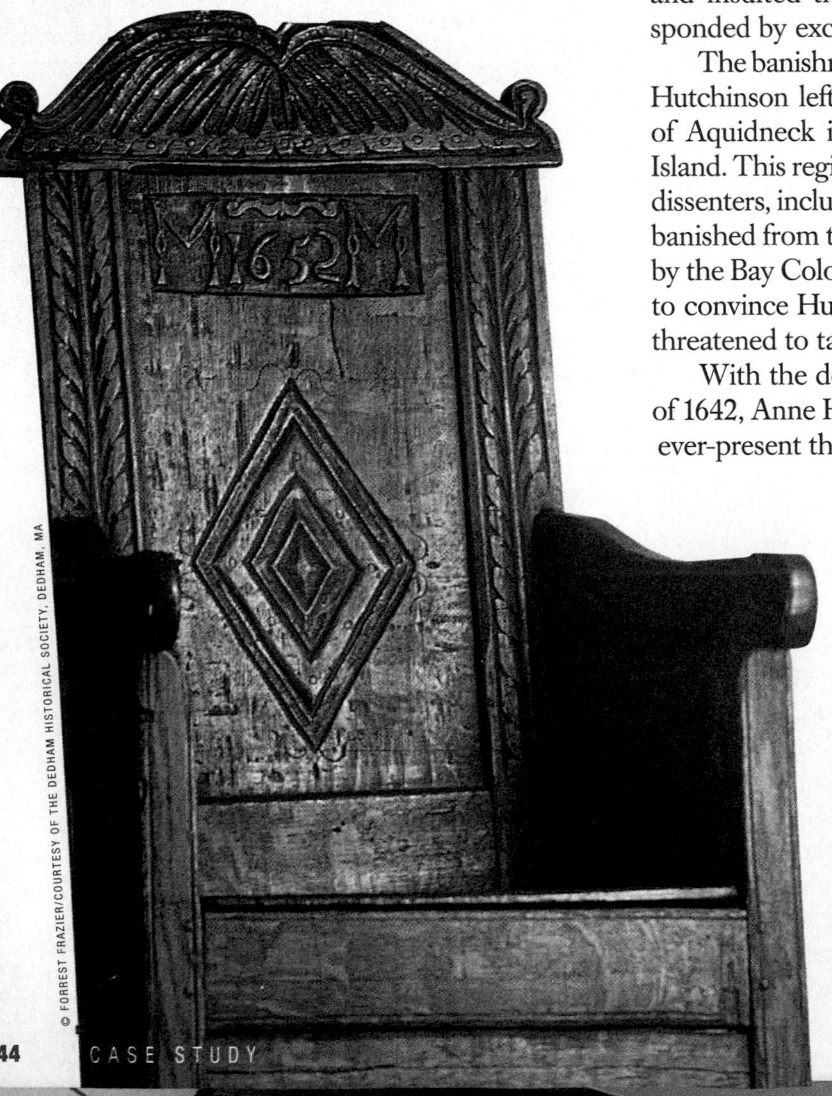

Most Puritan households contained only one chair, which was usually reserved for the man of the house. Anne Hutchinson sat in a chair when she held her meetings, thus violating this convention. One Hutchinson critic, Reverend Thomas Weld, sarcastically remarked that "the custom was for her scholars to propound questions and she (gravely sitting in the chair) did make answers thereunto."

Sir Henry Vane (left), a supporter of Hutchinson's, was governor of the colony from 1636–1637. When John Winthrop (right) succeeded Vane, he used the power of the governor's office against her.

COURTESY, AMERICAN ANTIQUARIAN SOCIETY

COURTESY, AMERICAN ANTIQUARIAN SOCIETY

The Significance

The religious controversy Anne Hutchinson sparked ravaged the Bay Colony. More than two dozen families left. Some followed Reverend Wheelwright to the settlement he founded at Exeter, now in New Hampshire. Most settled with the Hutchinsons in Aquidneck. As John Winthrop later noted, the colony's finest citizens were among the ranks of those who followed Hutchinson.

Winthrop himself eventually became disheartened about Hutchinson's banishment. In 1649 he refused to sign an order banishing another religious dissenter, saying, "No, of that work I have done too much already."

In the years between Hutchinson's banishment and Winthrop's expression of remorse, the Massachusetts Bay Colony slowly and subtly began a transformation. The power of traditional government authority, which had been intimately tied to the church, was curtailed. For instance, the personal power of the colony's main leaders was limited in 1641 when a written code of law was drawn up. The colony's laws were no longer based on the leaders' interpretations of the Bible but on the body of English common law.

The establishment of a two-house legislature in 1644 further cut into the power of the Bay Colony's traditional leadership. In 1646 business leaders who gained power in the lower house of the legislature pushed to suspend laws that discriminated against people who held unpopular religious views. With these acts, the intertwining of the church and the state gradually began to be disentangled. This separation of church and state became an important principle in the Massachusetts colonial government and a cornerstone of the United States Constitution.

RESPONDING TO THE CASE

1. In what ways was Anne Hutchinson a threat to the Massachusetts Bay Colony?

2. What do you think would have happened in Boston if Hutchinson's supporter Henry Vane had been reelected governor in 1637 and for several subsequent years?

3. Before Hutchinson was called to trial, the leaders of the colony had warned her to tone down her teachings. Do you think Hutchinson could have championed her views better if she had heeded their warnings, thereby avoiding banishment? Do you think she would have gained more influence if she had remained a citizen of Boston? Explain.

4. Many Puritans left England for New England so that they would be able to worship according to their own consciences. As you read in the chapter, however, they tolerated no dissent from their own religious views once they had their own colony. Based on what you know of this contradictory attitude, are you surprised, or do you think it was inevitable that religious toleration would become an issue for Puritans in America? Explain your views either way.

PORTFOLIO PROJECT

Using what you have learned about Anne Hutchinson, write a speech she might have given to the people who came with her to Aquidneck, thanking them for their support. In the speech, look to the future and describe the dreams you have for the settlement.

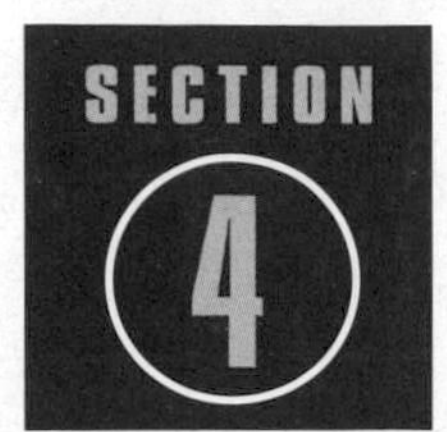

SECTION 4

Conflict and Growth in the Colonies

1744: VIRGINIANS OFFER EDUCATION TO NATIVE AMERICANS

BENJAMIN FRANKLIN WAS BORN IN BOSTON IN 1706, THE FIFTEENTH CHILD AND YOUNGEST SON OF A POOR CANDLE MAKER. Fleeing a hateful apprenticeship to his older brother, Franklin crafted a successful life as a printer in the bustling port of Philadelphia. In his pamphlet "Information to Those Who Would Remove to America," Franklin contrasted the world views held by white colonists and Native Americans, saying, "The learning on which we value ourselves, they regard as frivolous and useless." Franklin illustrated his point with the following story.

In 1744 the commissioners of Virginia had invited the chiefs of 6 Native American nations to send 6 of their sons to college in Williamsburg, Virginia. The chiefs declined with thanks and this explanation:

NATIONAL GALLERY OF CANADA/THE BRIDGEMAN ART LIBRARY

A Mohawk Leader
Joseph Brant, who once served as a missionary among his people, translated part of the New Testament into Mohawk.

> Several of our young people were formerly brought up at the colleges of the Northern Provinces; they were instructed in all your sciences; but when they came back to us, they were bad runners, ignorant of every means of living in the woods, unable to bear either cold or hunger; knew neither how to build a cabin, take a deer, or kill an enemy; spoke our language imperfectly; were therefore neither fit for hunters, warriors, or counsellors; they

GUIDE TO READING

Main Idea

Although Native Americans resisted European encroachment onto their homelands, British victory in the Seven Years' War opened the way to westward expansion by a booming and independent-minded colonial population along the Atlantic seaboard.

Vocabulary

- kachina
- legislature
- revivalism

Read to Find Out . . .

- why Native Americans rebelled against the colonists.
- how England became the dominant power in the colonies.
- how conditions in the colonies after the Seven Years' War fostered new ideas that foreshadowed independence.

were totally good for nothing. . . . if the Gentlemen of Virginia will send us a dozen of their sons, we will take great care of their education, instruct them in all we know, and make *men* of them.

—Zall, P.M., *Ben Franklin Laughing: Anecdotes from Original Sources by and about Benjamin Franklin,* 1980

In the 1600s and 1700s, conflicts erupted between colonists and Native Americans over such differences in values, but more importantly, over the colonists' persistent encroachment onto Native American territories.

Native American Wars

Colonists Conflict With Native Americans

In the Spanish Southwest, Native Americans succeeded for a time in ridding themselves of a hateful colonial presence. On the Eastern seaboard, however, coastal peoples soon succumbed to the English colonists' superior strength. The more powerful interior peoples would hold onto their own power only as long as France and England vied for supremacy on the continent.

Popé's Rebellion

In the 1600s Spain built missions in New Mexico. Nearby, Spanish soldiers occupied forts called presidios. With the aid of guns and horses, a few Spaniards subdued numerous Native Americans, converted them to Christianity, and forced them to toil for the Spaniards.

To destroy the Native American religion that competed with Christianity, the Spanish priests banned Native American dances, imprisoned and beat Taos Pueblo holy men, and burned sacred **kachina** dolls. In 1676 Spanish priests in New Mexico proudly reported the destruction of 1,600 Native American priestly masks.

Four years later, a Native American religious leader named Popé united Taos Pueblo people who spoke seven different languages into a formidable fighting force. Popé and his fighters leveled all but two Spanish villages in New Mexico and drove the hated priests back to Mexico, where they remained for more than a decade.

Victories such as Popé's did not occur in the East, where Native Americans came into conflict with American colonists who coveted their land. On the East Coast, two major defeats finally overpowered the Native American societies of the Atlantic seaboard.

King Philip's War

Massasoit, the Wampanoag chief, had befriended the earliest English colonists in Massachusetts, even bestowing the English names of Alexander and Philip on his sons, Wamsutta and Metacom. Eventually, Metacom (Philip) became chief. He detested the colonists, who had greedily overrun Wampanoag hunting and fishing lands. Unwilling to lose any more land or to be pushed westward, Metacom enlisted the aid of other seaboard peoples to fight the English. From 1675 to 1676, about 600 colonists and 3,000 Native Americans lost their lives in the bloody war.

COURTESY, AMERICAN ANTIQUARIAN SOCIETY

King Philip Almost 100 years after King Philip's War, Paul Revere created this engraved portrait of him. *How many Native Americans died in the war?*

Bacon's Rebellion

While New England colonists were fighting King Philip's War, settlers in Virginia were complaining that Virginia's royal governor, Sir William Berkeley, had reserved too much frontier land for Native Americans. Though his conciliatory policies pleased Native Americans and wealthy plantation owners, Berkeley's rulings infuriated new settlers and former indentured servants who coveted Native American lands.

In 1676 a planter named Nathaniel Bacon rallied troops of angry Virginians. First they declared war on all Native Americans, including those who were friendly, and then they battled the governor and his troops.

EUROPEAN LAND CLAIMS, 1763

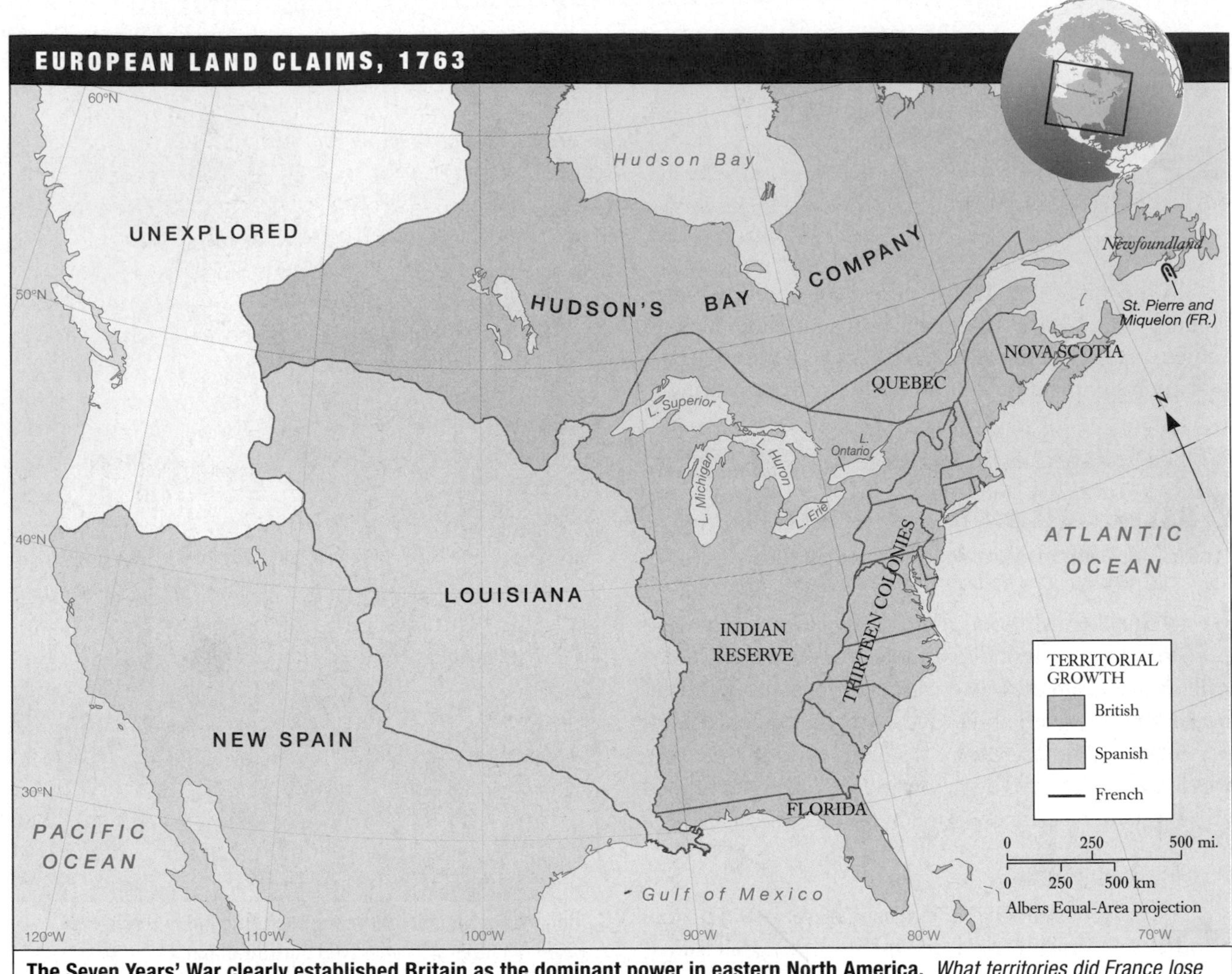

The Seven Years' War clearly established Britain as the dominant power in eastern North America. *What territories did France lose to Britain as a result of the war?*

Hundreds of settlers and Native Americans died in what became known as Bacon's Rebellion. Bacon was killed, but his followers later gained seats in the Virginia **legislature,** or lawmaking body, where they immediately voted to legalize Native American slavery. When English investigators arrived in 1677, they condemned the "inconsiderate sort of men who so rashly and causelessly cry up a war and seem to wish and aim at an utter extirpation [elimination] of the Indians."

France and Britain Struggle for Control

Britain Emerges Victorious

The Iroquois, Cherokee, Creek, and Choctaw of North America's interior wielded far greater power than did the smaller coastal peoples who submitted to the colonists in the 1600s. At first the interior Native Americans shrewdly protected their interests and maintained power by refusing to side with either France or England. As the growing white population of the English colonies pushed up against French-held territory, long-standing religious and commercial hostilities between the European rivals expanded into a deadly territorial struggle.

In 4 wars between 1689 and 1763, Protestant England sought to expel its Catholic French rival from the Americas. Foiled by weather, disease, and the hardship of transporting supplies, France and England each soon discovered that their best chance for success lay in recruiting colonial soldiers and in paying Native American allies to fight for them.

The fourth war, called the Seven Years' War in Europe and the French and Indian War in the colonies, proved climactic. By 1759, after the tide of victory turned indisputably toward Britain, the powerful Iroquois calculated that their interests would be best served by supporting the eventual victors. By the end of the Seven Years' War in 1763, France had lost Canada and all territory east of the Mississippi River except New Orleans; Britain held sway in the eastern part of North America; and thirteen separate colonies congratulated themselves on uniting against a common enemy. The Native Americans of North America's interior, however, had forever lost the power they had previously enjoyed from playing off one colonial power against another.

A People Emerges

New Ideas Foreshadow Independence

The Seven Years' War extracted a high price from the colonies. During the course of the long war, most working-class Boston men fought, and many died. In 1764 census takers in Boston counted 3,612 women but only 2,941 men. In addition the peace that put an end to the bloodshed precipitated an economic depression as 40,000 British troops suddenly departed.

Despite its heavy costs, the Seven Years' War left the colonists heady with victory and seeking westward expansion. Territory that had been newly wrested from French control grew even more attractive to colonists who wished to escape the crowded Eastern seaboard.

The Population Explosion

The population of the colonies had increased at an extraordinary rate between 1680 and 1770, rising more than tenfold from 150,000 to 1,700,000. A mere one-fourth of this increase stemmed from the willing immigration of indentured servants from Germany and Ireland, and the forced immigration of Africans. Fully three-quarters of the population explosion stemmed from a high birthrate accompanied by a low death rate. For European colonists and their descendants, North America's pure drinking water, healthful climate, and spacious territory made life both longer and healthier. Enslaved Africans who formed families also began to have children by the 1720s, producing as many children as whites and soon outnumbering enslaved persons who had been born in Africa.

THE BETTMANN ARCHIVE

George Whitefield **Drawn by his riveting style as a performer, more than 20,000 people attended Whitefield's farewell sermon in Boston.** *What did revivalism emphasize?*

Africans had brought to North America not only the agricultural know-how that enriched Southern farmers, but also the medical expertise that saved many white colonists from smallpox, a dreaded killer. The Boston minister Cotton Mather learned from a "Guramantee" servant—probably a West African man shipped from the Gold Coast fort at Kormantin—about a method of inoculation common in West Africa. In this method, "juice of small-pox" inserted into a cut produced a weakened form of illness, thereby conferring lifelong immunity. In July 1721 Mather wrote in his diary, "I have instructed our Physicians in the new Method used by the Africans . . . to prevent and abate the Dangers of the Small-Pox, and infallibly to save the Lives of those that have it wisely managed upon them." After inoculation took hold in colonial cities, smallpox virtually disappeared as a major killer.

A Great Awakening

At the same time that the population in the colonies was skyrocketing, many Americans came under the sway of **revivalism**—a movement that emphasized individual religious experience instead of church doctrine. A series of Christian revivals called the Great Awakening swept different regions between 1720 and 1760, arousing a widespread hunger for spiritual renewal. The timing and character of the Great Awakening differed from region to region. Still, regardless of region, revivalism posed a serious challenge to accepted sources of authority and introduced patterns of activity that helped fuel the revolutionary movement of the next generation. George Whitefield, a tiny 24-year-old Anglican priest with a magnificent voice, began by exciting audiences in his native Britain. In 1739 and 1740 Whitefield ignited the American Great Awakening on the first of 7 open-air preaching tours along the Atlantic Coast.

Awakeners like Whitefield preached that established congregations were dead because "dead men preach to them." The Awakeners shocked established clergy by encouraging individuals to participate by "lay exhorting." A lay exhorter could be any converted person—man or woman, young or old, African or white—who wished to preach "the Lord's truth."

Enslaved Africans were especially drawn to the revivalists of the 1740s and 1750s. Unlike professional Protestant clergy, whose sermons were typically dry and uninvolving, the revivalists preached personal rebirth in a freewheeling participatory style that gave Christianity mass appeal. Not surprisingly Africans' conversion experiences prompted many new African Christians to question the basis for their enslavement. On May 25, 1774, a group of Africans in Massachusetts addressed the following appeal to Thomas Gage, the royal governor: "There is a great number of us sincear . . . members of the Church of Christ(;) how can the master and the slave be said to fulfil that command Live in love. . . ."

All Americans, not just enslaved Africans, began to question received authority as a result of the Great Awakening. The ideas spread during this period led people to create new churches and to take responsibility in other matters, such as communal betterment and self-government.

NATIONAL PORTRAIT GALLERY, SMITHSONIAN INSTITUTION/ART RESOURCE, NY

Ben Franklin **Franklin's many accomplishments included founding the first city hospital and the University of Pennsylvania.** *What virtues did Franklin promote?*

Benjamin Franklin, Yankee Paragon

Though he shunned formal religion, the genial Benjamin Franklin offered George Whitefield accommodations on the preacher's 1745 visit to Philadelphia. Even if Franklin did not worship at any particular church, he nevertheless lived the maxim that "a good example is the best sermon." The sermon the self-educated Franklin preached promoted the Puritan virtues of thrift, hard work, education, and community responsibility. In his *Poor Richard's Almanack,* a collection of weather predictions and other practical information, Franklin coined many popular sayings. Two of these familiar sayings are "A stitch in time saves nine" and "Lost time is never found again." After the Bible, Franklin's annual almanac was the most popular book in the colonies.

Over a career that spanned decades, Franklin became the most famous colonial American. In the second half of the 1700s, thanks to his experiments with electricity and his lightning rod, Franklin's name crossed the Atlantic and became a household word in France. There the wealthy and famous man who had begun life as a poor boy seemed the embodiment of a freshly minted American spirit.

Colonial Self-Government

The American spirit Franklin celebrated expressed itself in the way the colonies governed themselves. Though each colony's government differed slightly, all the governments shared an important inheritance from the British system of government: an elected legislature. In most colonies, these legislatures consisted of two chambers that approximated the English House of Lords and House of Commons. Members of the council were wealthy appointees of the royal governor; members of the assembly were elected by white male property holders.

The legislatures provided a check on the power of the appointed royal or proprietary governors, many of whom proved to be corrupt at worst or mediocre at best. In the 1700s, the colonies' legislatures won the right to initiate bills, to settle contested elections, and to determine taxes.

Following the Seven Years' War, a French diplomat looked at the colonies' well-run governments and warned an unbelieving Britain that the colonies no longer needed its protection. He predicted, "You will call on them to contribute towards supporting the burden which they have helped to bring on you; they will answer you by shaking off all dependence."

SECTION ASSESSMENT

Main Idea

1. Use a chart like this one to show the central issue as seen by Native Americans in each of the following conflicts: Popé's Rebellion, King Philip's War, Bacon's Rebellion, Seven Years' War.

Conflict	Central Issue

Vocabulary

2. Define: kachina, legislature, revivalism.

Checking Facts

3. What prompted King Philip's War?

4. How did England win territory from France?

Critical Thinking

5. **Recognizing Ideologies** How did the practice of enslavement conflict with the practice of revivalism?

Technology Skill

USING A COMPUTERIZED CARD CATALOG

Learning the Skill

SUPERSTOCK

The Pilgrims, a radical Puritan group during the American Colonial period

If you want to write a paper on a topic related to the American colonial period, you will need to use a variety of reference materials for research. Familiarity with a computerized card catalog that you find in your school or local library will help you easily and quickly find the information you need. A computerized card catalog can help you find a specific book or a variety of resources about your chosen topic. Usually, you begin by submitting a specific kind of search, by title, by author's name, or by general subject. Once you have located an item you want, you can check its call number, availability, or other information such as the date of publication of the source.

Using a Computerized Card Catalog

Go to the computerized card catalog in your school or local library. Type in the name of an author; the title of a book, videotape, audiocassette, or CD; or a subject heading. This will access the computerized card catalog that lists all of the library's resources for that topic. The computer will list on screen the titles, authors, or subjects you requested.

The "card" that appears on screen also lists other important information, such as the year the work was published, who published it, what media type it is, and the language in which it is written or recorded. Use the information to determine if the material meets your needs. Then check to see if the material is available. Find the classification and call number under which it is shelved.

Additional Practice

For additional practice, see Reinforcing Skills on page 53.

Practicing the Skill

Your teacher has assigned a research report dealing with the Puritans. Follow the steps below to collect materials on this subject to aid you in the writing of this report.

1. Go to the computerized card catalog in your school or local library and conduct a subject search on the Puritans. What did you type in to start your subject search? Did you have to broaden or narrow your search?

2. A list of subjects should appear on the computer screen. Follow the instructions on the computer screen to display all the titles under your subject. List four titles of works that contain information on the Puritans.

3. Select one work on your subject that you want to learn more about. How do you find out more details on this work?

4. How many copies of this work are available in the library? Where can you find this work in the library?

Applying the Skill

Use the computerized card catalog in your school or local library to design a brochure that includes step-by-step directions on how to find material on the Massachusetts Bay Colony. Your brochure should include directions on how to begin a search, how to move from screen to screen, and how to find a specific work in the library. You may add illustrations to your brochure to help clarify your directions.

Chapter  Assessment

Self-Check Quiz

Visit the *American Odyssey* Web site at americanodyssey.glencoe.com and click on ***Chapter 2—Self-Check Quiz*** to prepare for the Chapter Test.

Reviewing Key Terms

Choose the vocabulary term that best completes each sentence below. Write your answers on a separate sheet of paper.

conquistador	**egalitarian**
indigenous	**pacifism**
indentured servant	**revivalism**

1. A colonist might hire an _________ to work for several years in exchange for passage to America.

2. The Anasazi functioned as equals and had no leaders because theirs was an _________ society.

3. Cortés was a Spanish _________ who conquered the Aztec.

4. As a Quaker, William Penn believed in _________, or an opposition to the use of force.

5. The Great Awakening, which swept colonial America between the 1720s and 1760s, was based on the movement called _________.

Recalling Facts

1. Who were the Moundbuilders?

2. What were "the three sisters," and how did they support each other?

3. What five Native American nations combined to form the Iroquois League?

4. What was Columbus seeking when he sailed west from Europe?

5. What two major inventions helped to advance Portuguese navigation in the second half of the 1400s?

6. Why did the enslavement of Africans occur soon after the Europeans explored and began colonizing in the Americas?

7. Why did the Puritans move to Massachusetts?

8. What physical and social factors lured people to the Middle Colonies, especially Pennsylvania?

9. How did Native Americans help establish Great Britain, rather than France, as the dominant power in North America?

10. What conditions in the thirteen colonies after the Seven Years' War fostered a spirit of independence?

Critical Thinking

1. Drawing Conclusions The Iroquois alliance was organized to end battles among Iroquois nations. A council of chiefs, delegated by the participating nations, governed the alliance and had the power to make decisions for all the Iroquois villages. Under the alliance, the Iroquois were more united and stronger than before. What does the success of the alliance, organized before Columbus arrived in North America, indicate about the Iroquois?

2. Identifying Assumptions What erroneous assumptions did Europeans make about the Native Americans living along the Eastern seaboard of North America?

The Princeton Review — Standardized Test Practice

1. Which of the following was NOT true of the system of slavery endured by Africans brought to the Americas?

A Enslavement was permanent and irrevocable.
B Enslaved Africans were treated as subhumans.
C Parents were forced to pass their slave status to their children.
D Enslaved Africans had little impact on European culture in the Americas.

Test-Taking Tip: Whenever you see the word NOT, find the answer that does NOT fit. For example, you may remember that an African taught colonists how to stem the spread of smallpox—an important clue to figuring out the correct answer.

2. The main occupation of English settlers living along the Eastern seaboard was

A manufacturing.
B fur-trading.
C farming.
D fishing.

Test-Taking Tip: Begin by eliminating the answers you know are incorrect. For example, English settlers cut down most of the forests along the coast, so answer B can be eliminated.

3. Making Comparisons Use a chart like this one to compare the advantages and disadvantages of life in each of the three colonial regions.

Colonies	Advantages	Disad-vantages
New England		
Middle		
Southern		

4. Demonstrating Reasoned Judgment The Puritans followed the European theory that unsettled land was open to claim by "civilized" people. In this way, they justified seizing lands where Native Americans "roamed." Do you think this distinction was just? Why or why not?

Portfolio Project

Imagine that you could ask Benjamin Franklin five questions about what life was like in colonial America after the Seven Years' War. Write these questions, and use them to do more research about this historic period. Put the results of your research into your portfolio.

Cooperative Learning

Working in small groups, research factors (other than epidemics) that contributed to the decline in the population of Native Americans and factors that contributed to the increase in the population of Africans in North America by 1750.

Reinforcing Skills

Using a Computerized Card Catalog
Use the computerized card catalog in your school or local library to identify four sources—books, videotapes, CDs, or audiocassettes—you can use to write a report on the founding of Boston, Massachusetts.

GEOGRAPHY AND HISTORY

Population Growth in the Colonies

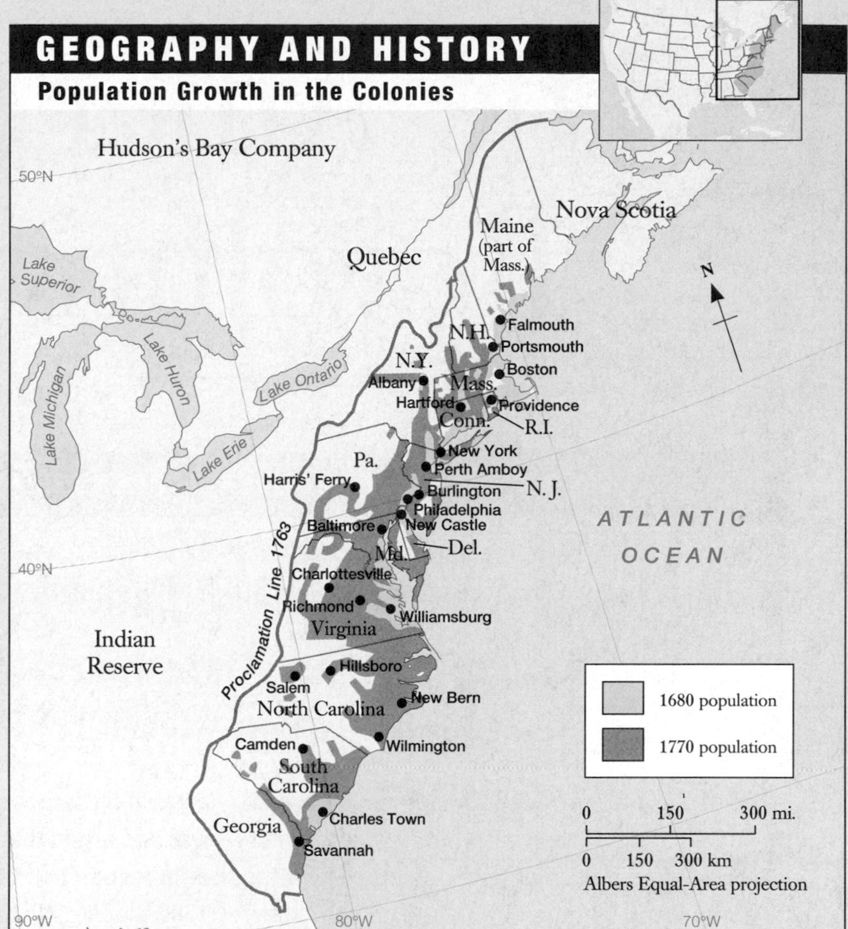

Study the map to answer the following questions:

1. Which colonies had no significant population in 1680?
2. Which colonies experienced the most growth from 1680 to 1770?
3. Locate the Proclamation Line established in 1763 after the Seven Years' War. Colonial governors were ordered to reserve all lands west of this line for Native Americans. Which colonies had people living closest to that line in 1770?
4. Which colonies—Northern, Middle, or Southern—were more likely to expand westward over the Proclamation Line first? Why?

Technology Activity

Building a Database Search the Internet or your library resources for information on Native Americans. Build a database, collecting information about as many different Native American cultures from North America as you can find. Include headings such as Name of People, Geographic Region, Language, Population, and Major Beliefs.

The American Revolution

OCTOBER 19, 1781: BRITISH SURRENDER AT YORKTOWN

An enslaved African named James gained permission from his owner, William Armistead, to join the Continental Army stationed nearby. It was March 1781.

The general commanding these American troops was Marie Joseph Lafayette, a young French aristocrat, who had volunteered to serve with the American army. That spring Lafayette sent many spies to the nearby British camp, but no one was as important as James. The secret information James gathered helped Lafayette and the Americans corner the British at Yorktown, Virginia. In October 1781 the British surrendered there, ending the fight for independence. At the end of the war, however, Lafayette went home a hero, and James went home an enslaved person.

Yet, with Lafayette's help, James was to be given his freedom. The Frenchman wrote a letter describing James's "essential services" during the war and urged that James be released by his owner in recognition of the value of those services. In 1786 the Virginia legislature finally freed James in thanks for his military efforts during the American Revolution.

James Armistead's story was exceptional, but the lives of many Americans—African and white, male and female, famous and unknown—changed during the Revolutionary era. Americans tasted new freedoms as they faced new challenges after the Revolutionary War. People of all backgrounds struggled together to forge their new nation. ■

HISTORY JOURNAL

Before reading the chapter, write about your understanding of the Revolutionary War and how you think the war may have changed people's lives.

Chapter Overview

Visit the *American Odyssey* Web site at americanodyssey.glencoe.com and click on ***Chapter 3—Chapter Overview*** to preview the chapter.

VIRGINIA HISTORICAL SOCIETY

JAMES ARMISTEAD BEGAN CALLING HIMSELF "JAMES LAFAYETTE," IN HONOR OF THE MAN WHO HELPED FREE HIM.

Toward Revolution

AUGUST 14, 1765: BOSTON CROWD PROTESTS NEW TAX

THE SOUND OF SCUFFLING FEET AND SHOUTING VOICES SHATTERED THE QUIET SUMMER EVENING. Hundreds of people, led by a poor, 28-year-old shoemaker named Ebenezer MacIntosh, stormed up the street. Men walking at the head of the crowd carried an effigy—a rag-stuffed dummy.

The effigy represented Andrew Oliver, a wealthy Boston merchant. Oliver had recently been made stamp officer for Massachusetts to help collect from the colonies a British tax authorized by the Stamp Act. Many Bostonians hated the tax; MacIntosh was leading a group to protest it.

THE METROPOLITAN MUSEUM OF ART, BEQUEST OF CHARLES ALLEN MUNN, 1924. (24.90.1566A)

Tax Protest
Mobs of colonists vented their anger on stamp officers, who were appointed by the British to see that taxes were collected.

The crowd carried the effigy through the streets of Boston. Then, after burning Oliver's effigy on a nearby hill, they attacked Oliver's luxurious house.

Oliver heard the crash of glass, the splintering of wood, and hoarse shouts. When the noise died down, Oliver found his "garden torn in pieces, his house broken open, his furniture destroyed." Standing before MacIntosh and his mob, Oliver "came to a sudden resolution to resign his office" as stamp agent. The common people had scored a victory.

On that hot August night, Ebenezer MacIntosh, the poor Boston shoemaker, found himself at the forefront of a movement that strained the bonds between Great Britain and its thirteen colonies. Yet MacIntosh did not always oppose the British. Only a few years before, he had proudly fought for Britain's colonies in the French and Indian War (also known as the Seven Years' War). As recently as 1763, he had joined with other colonists in celebrating Britain's victory over France in that war. In the intervening years, Britain's treatment of her subjects ignited the ire of MacIntosh and many other colonists.

GUIDE TO READING

Main Idea

British attempts to force the colonies to share in the costs of empire led colonists to defend their right to self-government—and ultimately to war.

Vocabulary

- external tax
- internal tax
- treason

Read to Find Out . . .

- what life was like in the thirteen English colonies in the 1760s.
- the changing relationship between Great Britain and the colonies in America at the dawn of the Revolution.
- the origins of the Revolution.

Paying for Security

Parliament Taxes the Colonies

Britain's leaders celebrated the end of the war in Europe and North America as heartily as did the colonists. The British victory ended more than 70 years of fighting with France in North America. As a result of a treaty signed in February 1763, King George III took possession of all French territory east of the Mississippi River, including lands in Canada. Yet the decades of fighting had left the British government struggling with a large national debt. British politicians also faced the expense of paying for an army in North America to secure the new borders and defend the enlarged territory.

This 1763 map of North America reflects many national interests. *Who would settlers come in conflict with as they moved westward and claimed lands between the Appalachian Mountains and the Mississippi River?*

The Proclamation of 1763

After the British victory, settlers began moving into the newly acquired lands west of the Appalachians. New settlers claimed the Native American hunting grounds that the French had protected. In May 1763, Native American resentment erupted in a bloody uprising led by Pontiac, an Ottawa chief. Within a few months, Native Americans captured or destroyed British forts on the frontier and killed many settlers.

To prevent another war, which Britain could not afford, King George III issued the Proclamation of 1763. The document proclaimed that all lands west of the Appalachians were reserved for Native Americans and closed to colonial settlement. For the British, the proclamation preserved peace with the Native Americans and prevented colonists from moving westward, farther from Britain's control.

Some colonists, however, felt that Britain had slammed shut a door of opportunity. They deeply resented being forbidden to settle on lands they had helped win from France. The colonists' resentment grew when Parliament demanded that they help pay for the army that Britain maintained to defend the frontier.

The Sugar Act

Beginning in 1764 Parliament tried to collect a series of taxes from the colonies to ease the war debt and strengthen the British Empire. The colonists' reaction was strong; it was most violent in Boston. The Sugar Act hurt Boston especially, because that city depended heavily on shipping and trade. Payment of all duties, or taxes, on molasses and sugar imported to North America from places outside the British Empire would now be strictly enforced. The act also placed new or higher duties on other foreign imports such as textiles, coffee, and wine.

These new duties caused the price of goods in the colonies to skyrocket, hurting businesses and customers alike. Just as important, the act also restricted smugglers by toughening the enforcement of customs laws. Smuggling formed a sizable part of colonial trade, in part because customs duties were high. The act had the overall effect of widening the division between Britain and the colonies. Americans resented having no representatives in Parliament to determine how the British rulers would spend their tax money.

Boston merchants protested the Sugar Act with orderly petitions. "If these taxes are laid upon us, in any shape," one petition read, "without our having a legal representation where they are laid, are we not reduced . . . to the miserable status of tributary slaves?" Yet these petitions had little impact on Parliament, and the Sugar Act remained law.

The Stamp Act

In 1765 Parliament passed a tax on all official documents and publications in the colonies. To be official, marriage licenses, mortgages, diplomas, bills of sale, and newspapers had to bear an official stamp, or seal, showing that a duty had been paid. The tax money was to pay for keeping British troops in North America.

The Stamp Act affected almost everyone, and most colonists hated it. Landowners and business owners despised it because the tax money raised went directly to the colonial governor. Colonists themselves had no say in how it was spent. Poorer people hated the tax because they had to pay extra for everyday items such as newspapers and playing cards.

Opposition to the stamp tax focused not just on the cost of the stamps but also on the method of taxation. Colonists agreed that Parliament had the right to levy an **external tax,** one to regulate trade in goods that came into the colonies. The Stamp Act, however, was an **internal tax,** one levied on goods made within the colonies, and designed only to raise revenue. Colonists argued that only their elected representatives should have the right to levy internal taxes. Because colonists could not elect representatives to Parliament, they believed that the right to levy an internal tax should belong to their elected colonial assemblies.

Protests over the Stamp Act united the colonists. Daniel Dulany, an attorney from Maryland, wrote a pamphlet rejecting Britain's right to impose internal taxes on Americans. John Dickinson of Pennsylvania published a pamphlet that denied the authority of Parliament to tax the colonists in any form. It was James Otis, a Massachusetts lawyer, who gave the colonists their rallying cry with his statement, "Taxation without representation is tyranny!"

COURTESY OF THE JOHN CARTER BROWN LIBRARY AT BROWN UNIVERSITY

COLONIAL WILLIAMSBURG FOUNDATION

No Stamp Act

Tea Protests Here colonists have tarred and feathered a tax collector and are forcing him to drink scalding hot tea. *How did the Stamp Act unite both wealthy colonists and common people in protest against Britain?*

The Coming of the Revolution

Tensions Explode in the Colonies

The taxation crisis of the 1760s heated the debate between Britain and its colonies. Colonists argued that Parliament violated their cherished right as British subjects to consent to all taxes levied on them. Feelings of resentment grew. People had been asking, Who has the power to tax us? Now the question became, Who has the power to govern? A movement toward self-government began to take shape. Protests against British authority intensified and, in some cases, became violent.

Sons of Liberty

Men like Samuel Adams of Boston felt that speeches and petitions against unjust British laws were not enough. A genial yet cagey politician, Samuel Adams came from a respected family and had attended Harvard College. He ran his own business, but after 20 years he was deep in debt. By the 1760s Adams was very involved in local politics and sought support for his ideas from the people of Boston.

Throughout 1765 Adams and leaders in other colonies formed a network of local groups called the Sons of Liberty to organize opposition to the Stamp Act. Often led by men of high position, these groups did not hesitate to resort to violence. They destroyed the homes of British officials and forced stamp agents to resign. To enforce a boycott of British goods, the Sons of Liberty threatened merchants. Anyone who imported or sold British goods risked being smeared with hot tar and covered with feathers.

In October 1765 delegates from nine colonies met in New York City and drafted a petition demanding repeal of the Stamp Act. This protest was effective, but the economic impact of the boycott was much stronger. The combination forced Parliament to repeal the Stamp Act in 1766. In its place Parliament passed the Declaratory Act. This law flatly declared Parliament's right to make laws concerning the colonists without their consent.

The Boston Massacre

Conflict over taxation prompted Britain to send troops to Boston to enforce laws and maintain order. The presence of British soldiers only raised tensions. Clashes between citizens and soldiers became common in Boston. On the evening of March 5, 1770, the tensions exploded into violence in an event that came to be called the Boston Massacre.

Accounts of the incident vary, but most agree that it began when a mob of townspeople taunted a British sentry on duty. Other British soldiers, led by Captain Thomas Preston, came to the sentry's aid. Tempers flared. The crowd threw snowballs and rocks at the soldiers. In the confusion, shots rang out. Some reports say that one soldier's musket went off by mistake, and then other soldiers began to fire. Others say an unidentified person commanded the soldiers to fire. Three colonists, including Crispus Attucks, a sailor of African and Native American ancestry, lay dead. Two more colonists later died from their wounds. Captain Preston was put on trial and acquitted. Two of his men were convicted of manslaughter and were branded on the hand.

A period of uneasy calm followed the Boston Massacre. Samuel Adams continued to use the incident to stir up anti-British feelings, but no violent protests resulted.

New trouble began in 1773. Parliament passed the Tea Act to save the East India Company, a British trading company, from bankruptcy. According to this law, only the East India Company could sell tea to the colonies. Though the tea would sell for a lower price than Americans were used to paying, they would still have to pay the import tax on it. Most of all, colonists resented the East India Company's monopoly on selling tea. To protest the tea tax, Boston's Sons of Liberty disguised themselves as Mohawks and went to the pier one night. There they tossed 342 chests of tea into the harbor.

As punishment for the so-called Boston Tea Party, Parliament closed Boston Harbor to all shipping until the tea was paid for. General Thomas George Gage, commander of British troops in North America, took over as governor of the colony to restore order to the rebellious city.

COURTESY, AMERICAN ANTIQUARIAN SOCIETY

Violence Erupts This engraving is called *The Bloody Massacre Perpetrated in King Street.* *Why would the colonists want to refer to the Boston shootings as a massacre?*

Committees of Correspondence

While Bostonians fought for their rights, people in other colonies also struggled against British control. Their struggle took different forms as tensions mounted. As early as the Stamp Act crisis in 1765, Virginia's assembly opposed Parliament with decrees worded so strongly that some colonists called them **treason,** or a betrayal of Britain. In 1768 merchants up and down the coast boycotted British goods to protest the Townshend Acts of 1767. Five years later, patriots from New

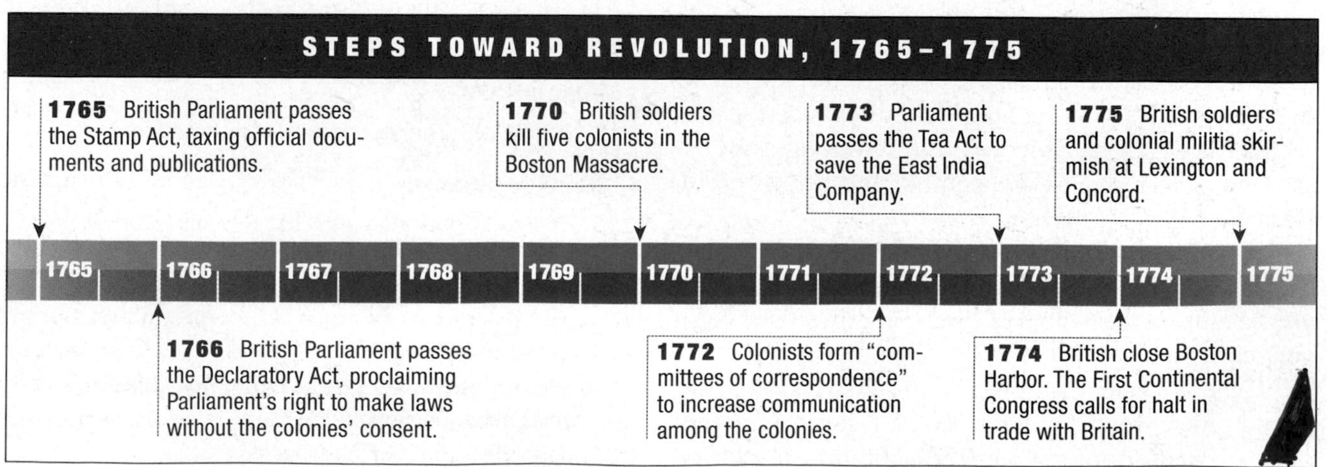

STEPS TOWARD REVOLUTION, 1765–1775
1765 British Parliament passes the Stamp Act, taxing official documents and publications.
1770 British soldiers kill five colonists in the Boston Massacre.
1773 Parliament passes the Tea Act to save the East India Company.
1775 British soldiers and colonial militia skirmish at Lexington and Concord.
1765 1766 1767 1768 1769 1770 1771 1772 1773 1774 1775
1766 British Parliament passes the Declaratory Act, proclaiming Parliament's right to make laws without the colonies' consent.
1772 Colonists form "committees of correspondence" to increase communication among the colonies.
1774 British close Boston Harbor. The First Continental Congress calls for halt in trade with Britain.

Hampshire to Virginia dumped or boycotted tea to protest the Tea Act. The Boston Tea Party was only the best known of these protests.

Most colonists, however, viewed the crisis with Britain as a local matter. A Philadelphia lawyer, a New England fisher, and a Carolina planter might all oppose a tax on tea, but they felt little in common with each other beyond that. Many colonists thought that Bostonians had brought trouble on themselves.

A group in Boston tried to change that attitude in 1772 by forming a "committee of correspondence." The committee would "state the rights of the colonists . . . and communicate and publish the same to the several towns and to the world." Soon dozens of towns in Massachusetts and assemblies from nearly every colony had created similar letter-writing committees.

The letters carried along the muddy roads leading from colony to colony did much to bring North and South, town and country, closer together in the struggle for self-government. Farmers had been slow to join the protests against Britain, but now they too argued against unfair taxes. Many farmers organized against the British as city people had done earlier.

News in 1774 that the British had closed Boston Harbor circulated through the committees of correspondence and outraged Americans everywhere. This news especially distressed merchants and planters, for if Britain closed the main ports of their colonies, they would be ruined. So when Bostonians called for a meeting to discuss the crisis, twelve of the thirteen colonies sent representatives.

Continental Congress

Fifty-six men from twelve colonies traveled to Philadelphia late in the summer of 1774 for the First Continental Congress. Most of them had served in colonial assemblies, but few knew any of the other representatives. John Adams of Massachusetts wrote, "We have numberless prejudices to remove here." Nobody knew what to expect of this unprecedented—and perhaps treasonous—meeting.

The First Continental Congress called for a halt in trade with Great Britain and resolved to meet again in the spring of 1775. In the process of discussing the crisis, the delegates had succeeded in removing some of their prejudices against one another and helped make Boston's crisis an American crisis.

By 1775 the machinery of the British Empire—governors, councils, courts—had broken down. In its place grew a ramshackle system of local committees and congresses of men who ignored British authority.

General Gage, the governor of Massachusetts, received orders from London to arrest just such a group of men. On an April night in 1775, 700 British soldiers marched toward Concord, about 15 miles from Boston. At Lexington, they encountered 70 American militia. A brief skirmish left 8 Americans dead on the village green, while the British marched on to Concord.

At Concord, fighting again broke out. As the British began the return march to Boston, colonists hid behind rocks, trees, and fences all along the road and picked off scores of British troops. By the time the British forces reached Boston, they had suffered 273 casualties, and 88 Americans had fallen. The struggle to defend the colonists' rights had become a war.

Old North Bridge At this site in Concord, Massachusetts, militia skirmished with British soldiers sent to destroy rebel supply stores. *Why was the exchange of gunfire at Lexington later referred to as "the shot heard round the world"?*

SECTION ASSESSMENT

Main Idea

1. Use a diagram like this one to show causes of the outbreak of fighting at Lexington and Concord.

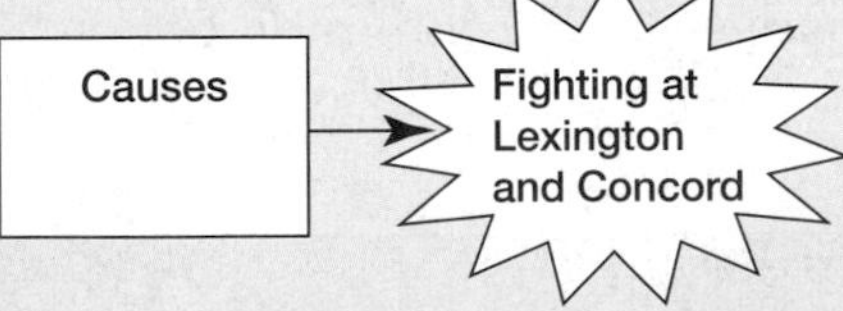

Vocabulary

2. Define: external tax, internal tax, treason.

Checking Facts

3. How did the British view the Proclamation of 1763?
4. What were the consequences of the Sugar Act?

Critical Thinking

5. **Making Inferences** How might the British have prevented the Revolution?

The Declaration *of* Independence

In Congress, July 4, 1776. The unanimous Declaration of the thirteen united States of America,

The printed text of the document shows the spelling and punctuation of the parchment original. To aid in comprehension, selected words and their definitions appear in the side margin, along with other explanatory notes.

Preamble

When in the Course of human events, it becomes necessary for one people to dissolve the political bands which have connected them with another, and to assume among the powers of the earth, the separate and equal station to which the Laws of Nature and Nature's God entitle them, a decent respect to the opinions of mankind requires that they should declare the causes which impel them to the separation.—

impel *force*

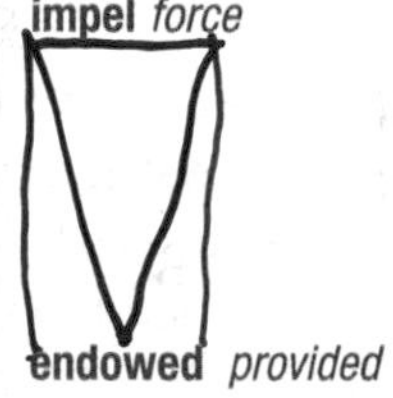

endowed *provided*

Declaration of Natural Rights

We hold these truths to be self-evident, that all men are created equal, that they are endowed by their Creator with certain unalienable Rights, that among these are Life, Liberty, and the pursuit of Happiness.—

That to secure these rights, Governments are instituted among Men, deriving their just powers from the consent of the governed,—

People create governments to ensure that their natural rights are protected.

That whenever any Form of Government becomes destructive of these ends, it is the Right of the People to alter or to abolish it, and to institute new Government, laying its foundation on such principles and organizing its powers in such form, as to them shall seem most likely to effect their Safety and Happiness. Prudence, indeed, will dictate that Governments long established should not be changed for light and transient causes; and accordingly all experience hath shewn, that mankind are more disposed to suffer, while evils are sufferable, than to right themselves by abolishing the forms to which they are accustomed. But when a long train of abuses and usurpations, pursuing invariably the same Object evinces a design to reduce them under absolute Despotism, it is their right, it is their duty, to throw off such Government, and to provide new Guards for their future security.—

If a government does not serve its purpose, the people have a right to abolish it. Then the people have the right and duty to create a new government that will safeguard their security.

Despotism *unlimited power*

List of Grievances

Such has been the patient sufferance of these Colonies; and such is now the necessity which constrains them to alter their former Systems of Government. The history of the present King of Great Britain is a history of repeated injuries and usurpations, all having in direct object the establishment of an absolute Tyranny over these States. To prove this, let Facts be submitted to a candid world.—

usurpations *unjust uses of power*

Each paragraph lists alleged injustices of George III.

He has refused his Assent to Laws, the most wholesome and necessary for the public good.—

He has forbidden his Governors to pass Laws of immediate and pressing importance, unless suspended in their operation till his Assent should be obtained; and when so suspended, he has utterly neglected to attend to them.—

relinquish *give up*

inestimable *priceless*

Annihilation *destruction*

convulsions *violent disturbances*

Naturalization of Foreigners *process by which foreign-born persons become citizens*

tenure *term*

Refers to the British troops sent to the colonies after the French and Indian War.

Refers to the 1766 Declaratory Act.

quartering *lodging*

Refers to the 1774 Quebec Act.

render *make*

abdicated *given up*

perfidy *violation of trust*

He has refused to pass other Laws for the accommodation of large districts of people, unless those people would relinquish the right of Representation in the Legislature, a right inestimable to them and formidable to tyrants only.—

He has called together legislative bodies at places unusual, uncomfortable, and distant from the depository of their public Records, for the sole purpose of fatiguing them into compliance with his measures.—

He has dissolved Representative Houses repeatedly, for opposing with manly firmness his invasions on the rights of the people.—

He has refused for a long time, after such dissolutions, to cause others to be elected; whereby the Legislative powers, incapable of Annihilation, have returned to the People at large for their exercise; the State remaining in the meantime exposed to all the dangers of invasion from without, and convulsions within.—

He has endeavoured to prevent the population of these States; for that purpose obstructing the Laws for Naturalization of Foreigners; refusing to pass others to encourage their migrations hither, and raising the conditions of new Appropriations of Lands.—

He has obstructed the Administration of Justice, by refusing his Assent to Laws for establishing Judiciary powers.—

He has made Judges dependent on his Will alone, for the tenure of their offices, and the amount and payment of their salaries.—

He has erected a multitude of New Offices, and sent hither swarms of Officers to harass our people, and eat out their substance.—

He has kept among us, in times of peace, Standing Armies without the Consent of our legislatures.—

He has affected to render the Military independent of and superior to the Civil power.—

He has combined with others to subject us to a jurisdiction foreign to our constitution, and unacknowledged by our laws; giving his Assent to their Acts of pretended Legislation:—

For quartering large bodies of troops among us:—

For protecting them, by a mock Trial, from punishment for any Murders which they should commit on the Inhabitants of these States:—

For cutting off our Trade with all parts of the world:—

For imposing Taxes on us without our Consent:—

For depriving us in many cases, of the benefits of Trial by Jury:—

For transporting us beyond Seas to be tried for pretended offences:—

For abolishing the free System of English Laws in a neighbouring Province, establishing therein an Arbitrary government, and enlarging its Boundaries so as to render it at once an example and fit instrument for introducing the same absolute rule into these Colonies:—

For taking away our Charters, abolishing our most valuable Laws, and altering fundamentally the Forms of our Governments:—

For suspending our own Legislatures, and declaring themselves invested with power to legislate for us in all cases whatsoever.—

He has abdicated Government here, by declaring us out of his Protection and waging War against us.—

He has plundered our seas, ravaged our Coasts, burnt our towns, and destroyed the Lives of our people.—

He is at this time transporting large Armies of foreign Mercenaries to compleat the works of death, desolation and tyranny, already begun with circumstances of Cruelty & perfidy scarcely paralleled in the most barbarous ages, and totally unworthy the Head of a civilized nation.—

He has constrained our fellow Citizens taken Captive on the high Seas to bear Arms against their Country, to become the executioners of their friends and Brethren, or to fall themselves by their Hands.—

He has excited domestic insurrections amongst us, and has endeavoured to bring on the inhabitants of our frontiers, the merciless Indian Savages, whose known rule of warfare, is an undistinguished destruction of all ages, sexes and conditions.

In every stage of these Oppressions We have Petitioned for Redress in the most humble terms: Our repeated Petitions have been answered only by repeated injury. A Prince, whose character is thus marked by every act which may define a Tyrant, is unfit to be the ruler of a free people.

Nor have We been wanting in attentions to our British brethren. We have warned them from time to time of attempts by their legislature to extend an unwarrantable jurisdiction over us. We have reminded them of the circumstances of our emigration and settlement here. We have appealed to their native justice and magnanimity, and we have conjured them by the ties of our common kindred to disavow these usurpations, which would inevitably interrupt our connections and correspondence. They too have been deaf to the voice of justice and of consanguinity. We must, therefore, acquiesce in the necessity, which denounces our Separation, and hold them, as we hold the rest of mankind, Enemies in War, in Peace Friends.—

insurrections *rebellions*

Petitioned for Redress *asked formally for a correction of wrongs*

unwarrantable jurisdiction *unjustified authority*

consanguinity *originating from the same ancestor*

Resolution of Independence by the United States

We, therefore, the Representatives of the united States of America, in General Congress, Assembled, appealing to the Supreme Judge of the world for the rectitude of our intentions, do, in the Name, and by Authority of the good People of these Colonies, solemnly publish and declare, That these United Colonies are, and of Right ought to be Free and Independent States; that they are Absolved from all Allegiance to the British Crown, and that all political connection between them and the State of Great Britain, is and ought to be totally dissolved; and that as Free and Independent States, they have full Power to levy War, conclude Peace, contract Alliances, establish Commerce, and to do all other Acts and Things which Independent States may of right do.—

And for the support of this Declaration, with a firm reliance on the protection of divine Providence, we mutually pledge to each other our Lives, our Fortunes and our sacred Honour.

rectitude *rightness*

The signers, as representatives of the American people, declared the colonies independent from Great Britain. Most members signed the document on August 2, 1776.

John Hancock
President from Massachusetts

GEORGIA
Button Gwinnett
Lyman Hall
George Walton

NORTH CAROLINA
William Hooper
Joseph Hewes
John Penn

SOUTH CAROLINA
Edward Rutledge
Thomas Heyward, Jr.
Thomas Lynch, Jr.
Arthur Middleton

MARYLAND
Samuel Chase
William Paca
Thomas Stone
Charles Carroll of Carrollton

VIRGINIA
George Wythe
Richard Henry Lee
Thomas Jefferson
Benjamin Harrison
Thomas Nelson, Jr.
Francis Lightfoot Lee
Carter Braxton

PENNSYLVANIA
Robert Morris
Benjamin Rush
Benjamin Franklin
John Morton
George Clymer
James Smith
George Taylor
James Wilson
George Ross

DELAWARE
Caesar Rodney
George Read
Thomas McKean

NEW YORK
William Floyd
Philip Livingston
Francis Lewis
Lewis Morris

NEW JERSEY
Richard Stockton
John Witherspoon
Francis Hopkinson
John Hart
Abraham Clark

NEW HAMPSHIRE
Josiah Bartlett
William Whipple
Matthew Thornton

MASSACHUSETTS
Samuel Adams
John Adams
Robert Treat Paine
Elbridge Gerry

RHODE ISLAND
Stephen Hopkins
William Ellery

CONNECTICUT
Samuel Huntington
William Williams
Oliver Wolcott
Roger Sherman

SPORTS: Sons of Liberty restrict extravagance of public sport as war with British approaches.

One Day in History

Wednesday, April 19, 1775

MARKET BASKET

Here is where money will go:

Ferry prices for taking cargo across the Susquehanna River at Wright's Ferry in Continental currency

A six-horse wagon...... $90
A horse and rider....... $12

THE BETTMANN ARCHIVES

Prices at the Ellery Tavern in Gloucester, Massachusetts: s.=shilling; d.=pence

Lodging for two......... 6d.
Bread and cheese....... 7d.
One dinner............. 9d.
One mug cider........ 1.5d.
Breakfast............ 9.5d.
15 lbs. (6.81 kg) tobacco........... 7s. 6d.

PRINT COLLECTION, MIRIAM AND IRA D. WALLACH DIVISION OF ART, PRINTS AND PHOTOGRAPHS THE NEW YORK PUBLIC LIBRARY

British Assault on Minutemen British troops led by Lieutenant Francis Smith vastly outnumbered the armed minutemen they fired upon in Lexington.

The Shot Heard Around the World

Patriot minutemen and British redcoats clash at Lexington and Concord

LEXINGTON, MA—Fighting broke out today in Lexington and Concord between British troops and volunteer minutemen. An unconfirmed number of deaths and casualties occurred.

Boston patriots learned last night of a plan for a British attack on the colonial arms depot at Concord. Paul Revere and William Dawes rode to warn the people of Lexington and Concord that the British were on the march.

In Lexington about 70 armed minutemen confronted some 700 British troops. Although no one knows who fired the first shot, 8 patriots lay dead when the smoke cleared. One group of redcoats then clashed with minutemen at the North Bridge in Concord, causing more casualties. The British then retreated to Boston, beset by residents who fired at them from behind stone walls and trees. It appears that a war for our freedom has begun.

NATION: The Continental Congress creates its own postal system and names Benjamin Franklin postmaster general.

Daniel Boone Cuts New Road

FORT BOONE, KY—With about 30 woodchoppers, Daniel Boone completed the Wilderness Road, which is 250 miles (402.25 km) long and runs through the Allegheny Mountains from North Carolina to Otter Creek near the Kentucky River. Settlers from Virginia and North Carolina plan to follow this road to found a fourteenth colony.

Daniel Boone

Treaty With Cherokee

KENTUCKY—By the terms of a treaty with the Cherokee, the Transylvania Land Company acquired all land south of the Ohio River, north of the Cumberland River, and west of the Appalachians in exchange for goods worth $10.

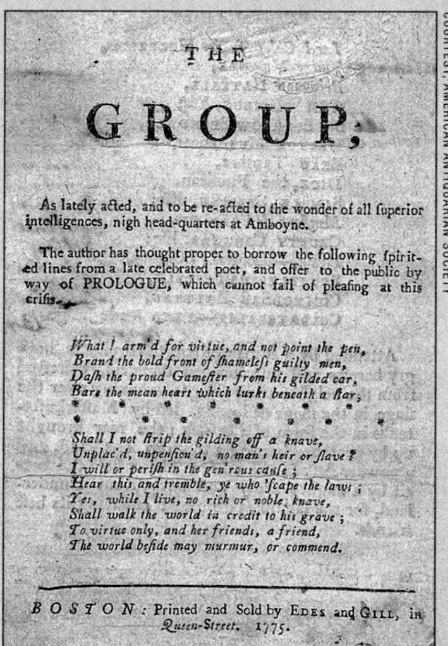

THE

GROUP;

As lately acted, and to be re-acted to the wonder of all ſuperior intelligences, nigh head-quarters at Amboyne.

The author has thought proper to borrow the following ſpirited lines from a late celebrated poet, and offer to the public by way of PROLOGUE, which cannot fail of pleaſing at this criſis.

What! arm'd for virtue, and not point the pen,
Brand the bold front of ſhameleſs guilty men,
Daſh the proud Gameſter from his gilded car,
Bare the mean heart which lurks beneath a ſtar;
* * * * * * *
* * * * * * *
Shall I not ſtrip the gilding off a knave,
Unplac'd, unpenſion'd, no man's heir or ſlave?
I will or periſh in the gen'rous cauſe;
Hear this and tremble, ye who 'ſcape the laws;
Yes, while I live, no rich or noble knave,
Shall walk the world in credit to his grave;
To virtue only, and her friends, a friend,
The world beſide may murmur, or commend.

BOSTON: Printed and Sold by EDES and GILL, in *Queen-Street*. 1775.

The Group, **a play about Puritan leaders written by Mercy Warren, draws enthusiastic audiences.**

IN PRINT

Women's Rights Written by Thomas Paine, the first article to expound women's rights in North America appears in *Pennsylvania Magazine.*

Nathaniel Law's *Astronomical Diary,* or *Almanack,* is published for 1775.

MUSIC

- **Popular song:** "Yankee Doodle"
- **First pianoforte:** John Behrent of Philadelphia makes North America's first pianoforte.

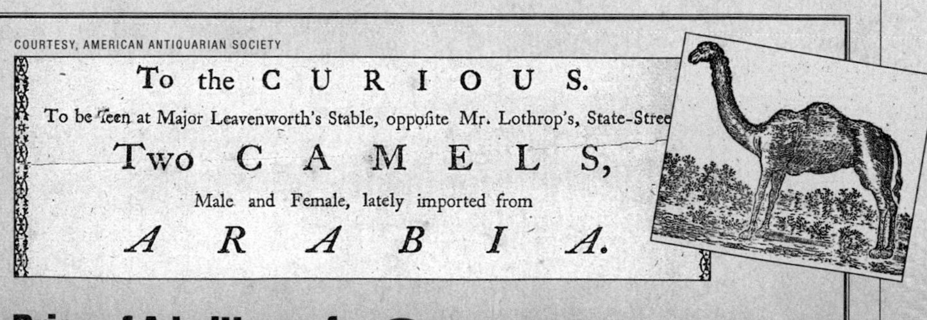

To the CURIOUS.

To be ſeen at Major Leavenworth's Stable, oppoſite Mr. Lothrop's, State-Stree

Two CAMELS,

Male and Female, lately imported from

ARABIA.

Price of Admittance for a Gentleman or Lady **9 pence**

War for Independence

MAY 1775: SECOND CONTINENTAL CONGRESS MEETS

ON MAY 10, 1775, THREE WEEKS AFTER THE BRITISH SPILLED COLONISTS' BLOOD AT THE BATTLES OF LEXINGTON AND CONCORD, THE DELEGATES OF THE SECOND CONTINENTAL CONGRESS ASSEMBLED IN PHILADELPHIA. They faced the challenge of leading thirteen colonies against the greatest empire and strongest army on earth. The Congress attempted to deal with that awesome task in two ways. First, the delegates called for the formation of a Continental Army of 20,000 men. Second, the delegates attempted to resolve the crisis with Britain. They sent King George III a petition blaming Parliament for the current problems and asking for the King's help in solving them. In December 1775, King George rejected the petition, declared the colonies in rebellion, and sent about 20,000 more British soldiers to America.

CHICAGO HISTORICAL SOCIETY

A Rallying Cry for Independence
Paine's *Common Sense* was the most widely circulated pamphlet in America in 1776.

One month later, in January 1776, colonists began reading a pamphlet that helped motivate and prepare them for independence. *Common Sense* appeared first in Philadelphia where its author, Thomas Paine, lived. Paine grew up in England and for a time worked as a tax collector. After meeting Benjamin Franklin, then the most famous American alive, Paine decided to move to Philadelphia in 1774 and soon became involved in the colonists' fight for independence.

Unlike other revolutionary writers, Paine wrote in the direct, colorful language of America's farmers and city workers. Paine called King George "the Royal Brute of Britain," and asserted that "a government of our own is our own national right." In 3 months, people purchased about 120,000 copies of *Common Sense*. Paine's arguments persuaded many Americans to join the cause.

GUIDE TO READING

Main Idea

After delegates to the Second Continental Congress approved the Declaration of Independence, Americans from all levels of society contributed to the cause of independence.

Vocabulary

- revolution
- suffrage

Read to Find Out . . .

- how the Second Continental Congress prepared for war with Britain.
- how the strategies used by George Washington helped win the war.
- the ways that the Revolutionary War affected the lives of the colonists on the battlefield and at home.

Declaring Independence

Planning the Revolution

Congress felt this popular push for independence. When it met in Philadelphia in June 1776, the Congress formed a committee to draft a declaration of the colonies' independence. The committee convinced 33-year-old Thomas Jefferson, a lawyer from Virginia, to write it.

The tall Jefferson owned a large plantation and also pursued a variety of interests: law, architecture, music, science, and politics. The document he created consisted of 3 parts. The first part contained a statement of what a government should do. "All men are created equal," Jefferson wrote, ". . . they are endowed by their Creator with certain unalienable Rights; . . . among these are Life, Liberty, and the pursuit of Happiness." Governments existed to "secure these rights." The second part contained 27 "reasons for separation" from Britain, while the third part officially declared independence.

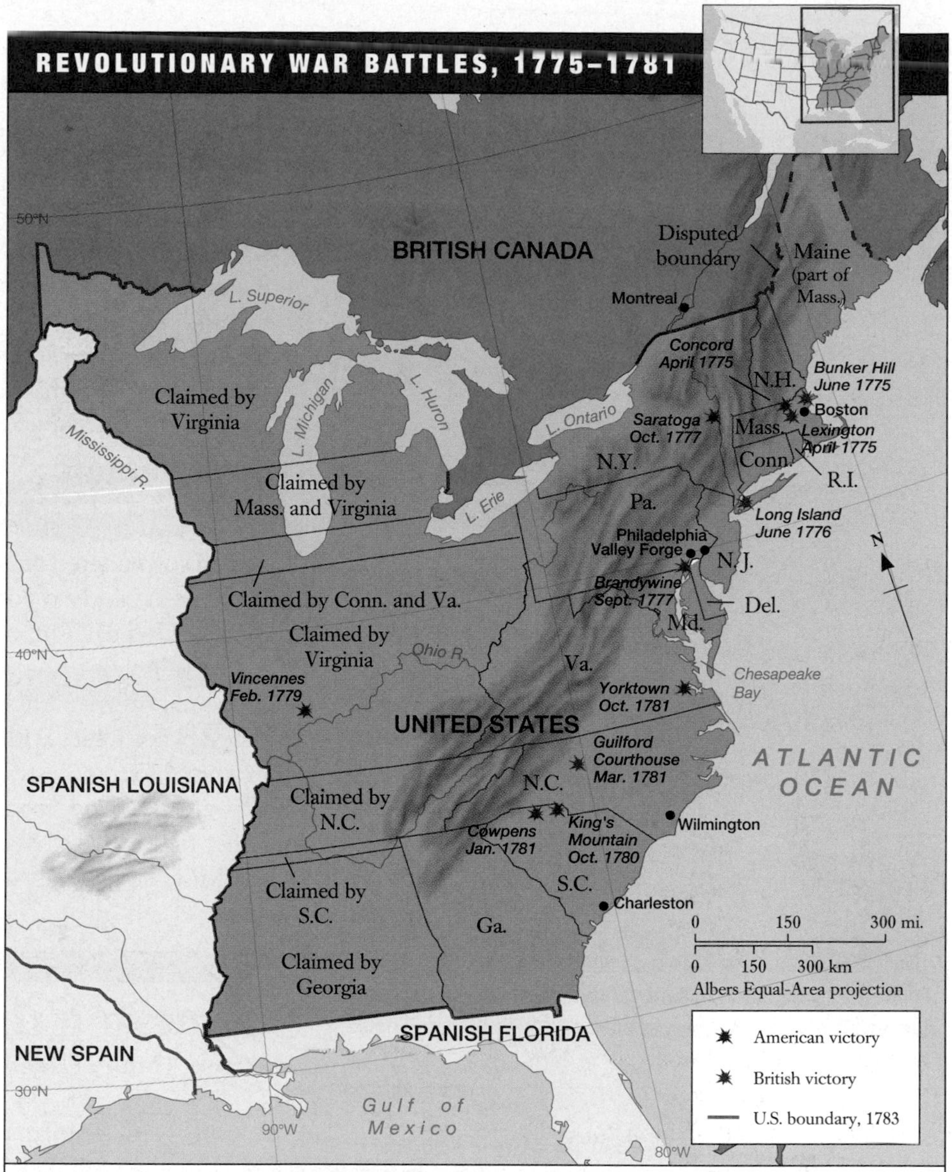

REVOLUTIONARY WAR BATTLES, 1775–1781

Compare the number of British and American victories between 1775 and 1781. *Prior to 1777 in what region of the country did most battles occur?*

Congress discussed the declaration for several days before voting unanimously for independence on July 2, 1776. On July 4 the delegates adopted the Declaration of Independence. Congress now turned to steering the new nation, the United States of America, through a **revolution,** a violent struggle to overthrow a government.

Winning the War

Congress had made its most important decision about the war a year earlier when it called for a commander for the Continental Army. John Adams worried that the war would remain New England's war unless a Southerner took command and brought the whole nation into the war together.

Adams had in mind a Virginian named George Washington. Washington had fought in the French and Indian War, where he had been an able soldier and leader. Delegates to the Congress approved of the aloof 43-year-old as the commander. Washington had the qualities they admired in themselves and others: rank, wealth, and integrity. He also had the discipline needed to turn a mass of poorly equipped, poorly trained men into an army that could survive the predicted long years of fighting.

Student Web Activity 3

Visit the *American Odyssey* Web site at americanodyssey.glencoe.com and click on ***Chapter 3—Student Web Activities*** for an activity relating to the American Revolution.

YALE UNIVERSITY ART GALLERY, GIVEN BY THE ASSOCIATES IN FINE ARTS AND MRS. HENRY B. LOOMIS IN MEMORY OF HENRY BRADFORD LOOMIS.

Portrait of a General This oil painting, *George Washington at the Battle of Princeton,* was done by Charles Willson Peale. *Why did the British finally surrender in 1781?*

During the six years of the war, Washington received little support from the Congress or the states, which bickered throughout. Still, he managed to maintain order through defeat, freezing winters, and starvation.

In the first years of the war, the British aimed to divide the rebellious colonies, cutting New England off from the rest of the nation. Only a surprise American victory at Saratoga, New York, in 1777 foiled their plan. The victory boosted the Americans' spirits and persuaded the French to enter the war to fight against their British rivals. After Saratoga, the British focused their energies in the South, where they hoped the region's many Loyalists, those who supported the British, might help them.

Washington learned valuable lessons during the first years of the war. The Americans, he knew, must avoid major battles with the better-trained British troops. They had to learn to use surprise tactics and familiar terrain to their advantage. If the Americans could not defeat the British in open combat, at least they could drag the war on until the British no longer cared to fight. This strategy paid off when Washington, supported by French troops and the French navy, trapped a large British force at Chesapeake Bay in Yorktown, Virginia, in 1781. The British surrendered at Yorktown; it became clear that after six years and no conclusive victories, the British no longer cared to fight, nor could they afford to.

The war finally ended in 1783, when Congress sent John Adams, Benjamin Franklin, and John Jay to negotiate a peace treaty with Britain. In the treaty, the British promised to remove their troops from America "with all convenient speed," to recognize officially the independence of the United States of America, and to agree that the Mississippi River was the nation's western border.

Surviving the War

Victory Through Sacrifice

More than 250,000 American soldiers fought for 6 years to break the back of British rule. During that time 1 out of every 10 Americans who fought died; the British captured and occupied most major cities, including Boston, New York, and Philadelphia; and many American lives were reshaped by the American Revolution.

When America mobilized for war in 1775 and 1776, all levels of society became involved. Elite politicians

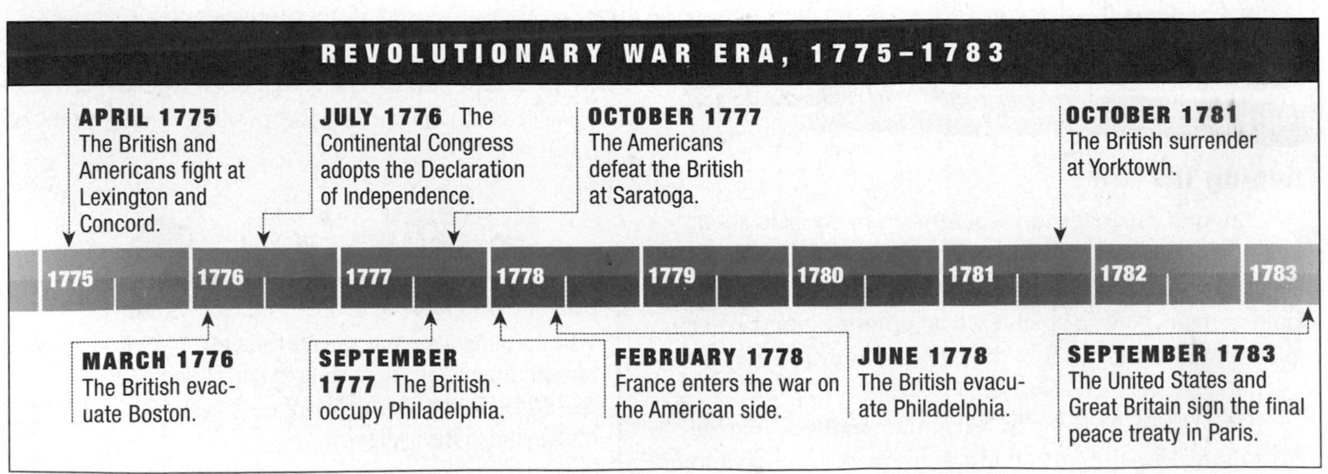
REVOLUTIONARY WAR ERA, 1775–1783
APRIL 1775 The British and Americans fight at Lexington and Concord.
JULY 1776 The Continental Congress adopts the Declaration of Independence.
OCTOBER 1777 The Americans defeat the British at Saratoga.
OCTOBER 1781 The British surrender at Yorktown.
1775
1776
1777
1778
1779
1780
1781
1782
1783
MARCH 1776 The British evacuate Boston.
SEPTEMBER 1777 The British occupy Philadelphia.
FEBRUARY 1778 France enters the war on the American side.
JUNE 1778 The British evacuate Philadelphia.
SEPTEMBER 1783 The United States and Great Britain sign the final peace treaty in Paris.

designed state and national governments. Men with military experience volunteered for army positions. Some merchants loaned money to the army and to the Congress; others made fortunes from wartime government contracts. Farmers tried to provide food for armies.

On the Battlefield

These many groups contributed to the war effort, but the poorest Americans did most of the actual fighting. Young city laborers, farm boys, indentured servants, and sometimes enslaved persons all fought bravely. A lack of money, food, and supplies made the usual wartime experiences—boredom, disease, bloodshed—worse for the soldiers in the Continental Army. In 1778 one young American gave this nightmarish description of a soldier's life: "Poor food, hard lodging, cold weather, fatigue, nasty clothes, nasty cookery."

Only the horror of battle relieved boredom. Ranks of soldiers standing in open fields fired their muskets once, reloaded, and fired again. Orderly troop movements soon broke down into hand-to-hand combat; soldiers inflicted many wounds with bayonets and knives. Mud, smoke, blood, curses, and cannon shot flew about the battlefield. Medical treatment barely existed on or off the battlefield, and most wounds were fatal.

African Americans also stood and fell on the battlefields of the Revolutionary War. One enslaved laborer named Jehu Grant escaped from his master and joined the colonists when he "saw liberty poles and people all engaged for the purpose of freedom." Yet only about 5,000 of the 500,000 African Americans living in the colonies served in the Continental Army during the war. Many more sided with the British, who promised them freedom if they fought. As many as 20,000 enslaved persons in the Carolinas and Georgia joined the British.

Many Native Americans also sided with the British. The British represented a last hope for keeping land-hungry Americans out of Native American territories. During the war, colonists fought Native Americans in bloody battles, creating long-lasting bitter feelings.

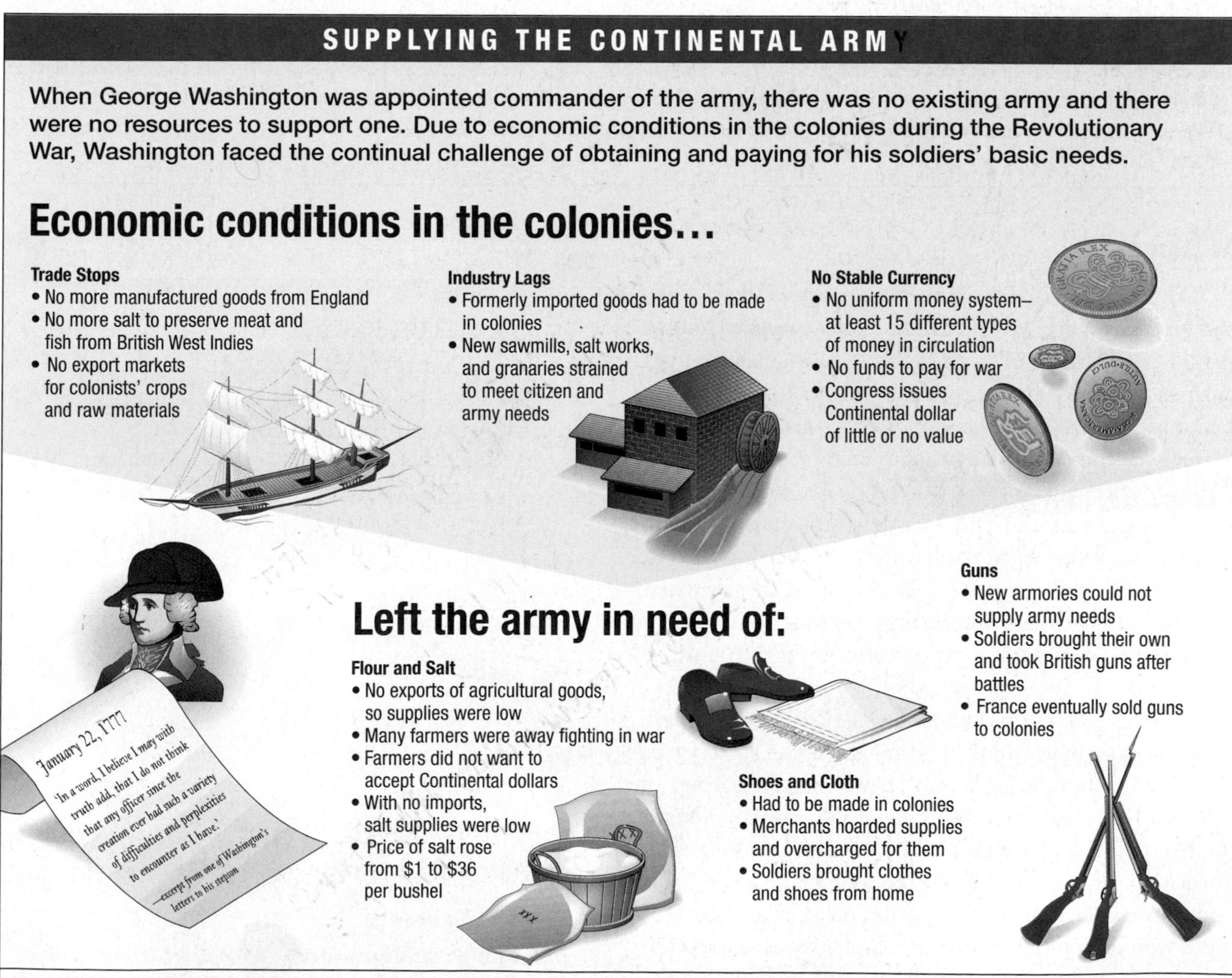
SUPPLYING THE CONTINENTAL ARMY
When George Washington was appointed commander of the army, there was no existing army and there were no resources to support one. Due to economic conditions in the colonies during the Revolutionary War, Washington faced the continual challenge of obtaining and paying for his soldiers' basic needs.
Economic conditions in the colonies...
Trade Stops
• No more manufactured goods from England
• No more salt to preserve meat and fish from British West Indies
• No export markets for colonists' crops and raw materials
Industry Lags
• Formerly imported goods had to be made in colonies
• New sawmills, salt works, and granaries strained to meet citizen and army needs
No Stable Currency
• No uniform money system—at least 15 different types of money in circulation
• No funds to pay for war
• Congress issues Continental dollar of little or no value
Left the army in need of:
Flour and Salt
• No exports of agricultural goods, so supplies were low
• Many farmers were away fighting in war
• Farmers did not want to accept Continental dollars
• With no imports, salt supplies were low
• Price of salt rose from $1 to $36 per bushel
Shoes and Cloth
• Had to be made in colonies
• Merchants hoarded supplies and overcharged for them
• Soldiers brought clothes and shoes from home
Guns
• New armories could not supply army needs
• Soldiers brought their own and took British guns after battles
• France eventually sold guns to colonies
January 22, 1777
'In a word, I believe I may with truth add, that I do not think that any officer since the creation ever had such a variety of difficulties and perplexities to encounter as I have.'
—excerpt from one of Washington's letters to his stepson

The lack of supplies left many soldiers in the Continental Army in tattered clothing, and some had to resort to eating their horses' food. *What were the three major economic problems in the colonies that caused these conditions?*

LOS ANGELES COUNTY MUSEUM OF ART, (DETAIL) BICENTENNIAL GIFT OF MR. AND MRS. J.M. SCHAAF, MR. AND MRS. WILLIAM D. WITHERSPOON, MR. AND MRS. CHARLES C. SHOEMAKER, MR. AND MRS. JULIAN GANZ, JR.

Home Front Tactics **Artist Emanuel Leutze portrayed the plight of many American colonists during the Revolutionary War in this 1852 painting, *Mrs. Schuyler Burning Her Wheat Fields on the Approach of the British.*** *In what other ways did the Revolutionary War change the lives of women?*

At Home

The war handed women new roles. Fathers, sons, and brothers marched off to fight—some never to return. While men shouldered guns, women managed farms and businesses. They also traveled with the army, working as cooks and nurses. These experiences gave satisfaction to many women who had never owned property nor had **suffrage,** the right to vote. Women began to express their thoughts more freely on such subjects as politics. As Philadelphia's Anne Emlen wrote to her husband in 1777, "How shall I impose a silence upon myself when the subject is so very interesting, so much engrossing conversation—and what every member of the community is more or less concerned in?"

Women openly participating in politics was a new phenomenon. In less than 20 years American society had changed in unpredictable and lasting ways. A group of colonies had challenged their governing country, fought the best army in the world, and won the right to be self-governing states. As the war ended, many Americans openly wondered how their experiment in self-government would eventually turn out. "The answer to the question," said Thomas Paine, "can America be happy under a government of her own, is short and simple—as happy as she pleases; she hath a blank sheet to write upon."

SECTION ASSESSMENT

Main Idea

1. Use a chart like this one to show how groups from all levels of colonial society contributed to victory in the American Revolution.

Group	Contribution

Vocabulary

2. Define: revolution, suffrage.

Checking Facts

3. What did the Second Continental Congress do to prepare for war with Britain?
4. What tactics did Washington use to survive?

Critical Thinking

5. **Identifying Alternatives** What alternatives did the colonists have to fighting the British in the Revolutionary War?

Study and Writing Skill

INTERPRETING A PRIMARY SOURCE

Learning the Skill

A primary source is direct evidence of an event, idea, or development. It is obtained firsthand, such as oral or written accounts from actual participants. Examples of such primary sources are official documents, speeches, diaries, autobiographies, and letters. A primary source may also consist of physical objects, such as tools or weapons, or visual evidence such as paintings, photographs, maps, or videotapes.

In contrast with a primary source, a secondary source is a written, oral, or visual account created after an event, usually produced using information from primary sources. Textbooks and biographies are examples of secondary sources.

Interpreting primary sources is a skill you can practice. One primary source to examine is the Declaration of Independence on pages 61–63. As you continue to read *American Odyssey,* you will encounter other primary source documents and speeches. Primary sources help to present a reliable and accurate picture of history. The ability to interpret a primary source allows you to make your own judgment about a historical event, one not based on secondhand interpretations.

I long to hear that you have declared independence. And by the way, in the new code of laws that I suppose you will make, I wish you would remember the ladies and be more generous and favorable to them than your ancestors. Do not put such unlimited power in the hands of husbands. Remember, all men would be tyrants if they could. If particular care and attention is not paid to the ladies, we are determined to stir up a rebellion and will not regard ourselves as bound by any laws in which we have had no voice or representation.

A Wife's Request This excerpt is from a letter Abigail Adams wrote to her husband when the Second Continental Congress was considering the Declaration of Independence. *What do her words suggest about her character?*

Interpreting a Primary Source

To interpret a primary source, use the following steps:

a. Examine the origins of the document or material to determine if it is a primary source.

b. Read the document and summarize the main ideas in your own words.

c. Read through it again, this time looking for details that support the main ideas.

d. Give an interpretation of the material in your own words.

To round out your interpretation, try putting the document or material within the context of what you know about history. It may be necessary to look at the person or people who created the source, to examine why it was created, or to explore the motive behind it. Sometimes, just looking at the title can give you insights.

Practicing the Skill

Read the passage from the Declaration of Independence and answer the questions that follow.

We hold these truths to be self-evident: that all men are created equal, that they are endowed by their Creator with certain unalienable rights; that among these are life, liberty, and the pursuit of happiness.

1. Why is this passage a primary source?

2. What is the main idea of the passage?

3. What are the supporting details?

4. What do you know about the writers of the Declaration of Independence?

5. Interpret the passage in your own words.

Applying the Skill

Read the passage from the letter above, and give your interpretation of it as a primary source.

The **Glencoe Skillbuilder Interactive Workbook, Level 2** CD-ROM provides more practice in key social studies skills.

Creating a New America

MAY 10, 1776: CONGRESS RECOMMENDS FORMING STATE GOVERNMENTS

On April 22, 1776, John Adams wrote to his friend, James Warren, about the Revolution that had just begun. Adams wrote that South Carolina had already adopted a constitution:

> The news from South Carolina has aroused and animated all the continent. It has spread a visible joy, and if North Carolina and Virginia should follow the example, it will spread through the rest of the colonies like electric fire.
>
> —John Adams, from a letter to James Warren

NATIONAL PORTRAIT GALLERY, SMITHSONIAN INSTITUTION/ART RESOURCE, NY

A Leader of the Revolutionary Era
John Adams served as the second President of the United States from 1797 to 1801.

At Adams's urging, the Congress officially recommended that each colony "adopt such a government as shall, in the opinion of the representatives of the people, best conduce to the happiness and safety of their constituents in particular, and America in general."

For the colonies, forming new governments was anything but a luxury. In colony after colony, royal colonial governments had collapsed at the onset of the war. After dissolving the colonial assemblies that had so boldly challenged royal authority, the British governors had escaped as best they could. Wartime responsibilities dictated the need for governmental authority to muster troops, collect money, and protect the public safety. Now the colonies hastily embarked on the daunting task of creating their own governments.

The idea that ordinary citizens could plan their own governments, draft written constitutions, and vote their approval of self-government represented something new in history, and Americans knew it. Crafting individual state constitutions also provided a rehearsal for the process of creating the national constitution during the decade that followed.

Guide to Reading

Main Idea

The constitutions written by state governments during the Revolution introduced new ideas in self-government and served as models for the later national constitution.

Vocabulary

- constitution
- abolition
- status quo
- coverture

Read to Find Out . . .

- how the state constitutions differed from colonial charters.
- how the lives of women and enslaved African Americans changed in the Revolutionary War era.

State Constitutions

A Variety of Democratic Documents

The British system on which colonists based their ideas of government did not reside in a **constitution,** one written document of a plan of government, but rather in a miscellaneous collection of laws and court cases that had developed over centuries. In contrast, American colonial leaders planned that state constitutions, and eventually the national constitution, would be documents written clearly, concisely, and specifically so that anyone who read a copy could understand the law.

Thomas Jefferson realized that the colonies could win the war for independence but lose the Revolution if they failed at these experiments in self-government: "In truth," he said, "self-government is the whole object of the present controversy." During the tumultuous war for independence, each state drafted a constitution that established self-government.

Virtually every state limited voting and government service to white male property holders. Still, most of the new constitutions established state governments that were more democratic than the colonial regimes they replaced. In place of governors appointed by a king, state executives now had to face elections. Furthermore, elected governors would wield less power than had their appointed predecessors, giving greater power to popularly elected assemblies. These assemblies in turn grew larger as farmers and artisans clamored to be represented.

Connecticut and Rhode Island merely adopted their colonial charters, carefully deleting all references to the British Crown. The other 11 states, awed by the opportunity before them, began afresh. In 1776 alone, 8 states crafted new constitutions. By 1780, all 13 states had adopted written constitutions.

Virginia's Conservative Constitution

In several states, conservatives drew up plans for governments that closely resembled the colonial regimes they replaced. For example, the Virginia constitution of 1776, drafted by Thomas Jefferson, preserved intact almost all of the institutions of the colonial era, including slavery. Though Jefferson had inserted a section in the constitution's first draft proposing **abolition,** an end to the practice of slavery, his attempt failed to win approval. Virginia's governor, now elected annually by the legislature and denied the power of the veto, held a somewhat weaker position than before the Revolution. On the other hand, Virginia's new House of Delegates looked nearly identical to its old House of Burgesses. The continuation of prewar property qualifications for voters as well as for officeholders ensured that wealthy landowners would still represent Virginians. Members of many of the same families who had served before the war continued to hold elected office after the war.

If its constitution maintained the **status quo,** or existing conditions, Virginia's Bill of Rights established a bold new tradition. This document, written by George Mason, enumerated rights, such as a jury trial and freedom of the press, that free citizens could expect from their representative governments. The Virginia Bill of Rights prompted other states to include similar documents in their constitutions. It also provided a model for the Bill of Rights that eventually crowned the national Constitution of 1787.

A Radical Document for Pennsylvania

Compared to the conservative Virginians, the liberals who wrote constitutions in other states sought to redistribute power more equitably. Georgia and Pennsylvania—a state that bordered Virginia—crafted the most liberal documents of all.

Pennsylvania, for example, cast off the British model of a balanced government consisting of two legislative houses and an executive, the governor. In the vacuum created by the departure of colonial leaders, the radical politicians who wrote Pennsylvania's constitution established a single legislative house. Its members would be elected each year and its debates would be open to the public. Going even further, the document also abolished the requirement that persons holding public

CULVER PICTURES

The Artisan Spirit Many hardworking blacksmiths and other artisans looked forward to better representation in state government after the Revolution. *How could they participate?*

office be property owners and opened the vote to any white male adult who paid taxes. The preamble that began the constitution clearly predicted the end of African slavery with its suggestion that government should "provide for future improvements, without partiality for or prejudice against any particular class, sect, or denomination of men whatever."

Even in liberal Pennsylvania, however, the long list of residents denied the vote included servants, dependent sons, the poor, Native Americans, and women. In only one state, for a brief period, did women get the vote. New Jersey's 1776 constitution granted suffrage to "all free inhabitants" who met property and residency requirements. Property-owning New Jersey women took advantage of their voting rights until their state reversed that ruling in 1807.

Constitutional Convention in Massachusetts

Like Virginia's conservative constitution and unlike Pennsylvania's liberal one, the Massachusetts document divided political power between a governor and two legislative houses. One house, the assembly, would represent the common people. Because the other house, the senate, would look after propertied interests, its members were required to own three times as much property as assemblymen. Constitutional architect John Adams defended this balance of power, saying, "power must be opposed to power, force to force . . . interest to interest . . . and passion to passion."

However conservative its constitution, Massachusetts took a radical new path to writing the document. Opposed to letting the existing legislature write the constitution, as most states had done, a Concord town meeting in October 1776 resolved that "a Constitution alterable by the Supreme Legislation is no security at all." To prevent the abuses that might follow if the legislature drafted the constitution by which it would rule, Concord suggested the novel idea of electing a special convention to do the job and requiring voters to approve the constitution. In 1780 the eligible voters of Massachusetts voted their approval of the document.

The preamble to Massachusetts's constitution read, "All men are born free and equal." Enslaved African men and women as well as white women began to wonder for how long these lofty words would exclude them.

COURTESY MASSACHUSETTS HISTORICAL SOCIETY

Abigail Adams During the war her letters provided her husband with information about the British in Boston. *What else did her letters to her husband reveal?*

Focus on Reforms

Expanding the Ideas of Liberty

The Revolutionary era fostered a climate of unprecedented political interest; the number of voters casting ballots doubled. A profusion of pamphlets and broadsides offered ordinary citizens instant access to Revolutionary affairs as well as exhortations about domestic matters. In his pamphlet *Common Sense,* Thomas Paine said, "We have it in our power to begin the world over again. The birthday of a new world is at hand." With a sense of unprecedented hopefulness, Americans began to write on the "blank sheet" Thomas Paine had set forth.

Republican Women

White women in Revolutionary America claimed few personal or political rights. For example, under an article of British law called **coverture,** any property a woman inherited passed into her husband's control when she married. Not until the 1900s would most American women regain the vote they so fleetingly enjoyed in New Jersey between 1776 and 1807.

Despite their inferior status compared to that of white men, white women aided the Revolution as nurses, innkeepers, suppliers of food and clothing, fund-raisers, farmers, and even as spies. Nevertheless, only the mediation of their fathers, husbands, brothers, or sons allowed those women who longed to do so to participate in the political ferment of the time.

Abigail Adams's letters to her husband John reveal a keen interest in women's rights. She marveled at the persistence of women's patriotism despite their forced exclusion from the political process: "Deprived of a voice in Legislation, obliged to submit to those Laws which are imposed upon us, is it not sufficient to make us indifferent to the publick Welfare? Yet all History and every age exhibit Instances of patriotic virtue in the female Sex; which considering our situation equals the most Heroick." After assisting at the polls in 1780, she consoled herself that her participation counted for something: "If I cannot be a voter upon this occasion, I will be a writer of votes. I can do some thing in that way."

Like Abigail Adams, Esther De Berdt Reed felt keenly that women should contribute to the Revolution. In a 1780 broadside, she wrote, "If opinion and manners did not forbid us to march to glory on the same paths as the Men, we should at least equal, and sometimes surpass them in our love for the public good." Reed helped organize the women of Philadelphia to collect funds for Washington's troops. The women refused Washington's request to deposit their $300,000 contribution into the Bank of the United States to be united "with the gentlemen." Instead, they used the money to buy linen shirts so the soldiers would recognize that women had sent the gifts.

COURTESY, THE HENRY FRANCIS DU PONT WINTERTHUR MUSEUM

Dr. Benjamin Rush This influential physician was a member of the Continental Congress and signed the Declaration of Independence. *What did he do to fight slavery?*

During the Revolution, the idea also took hold that mothers could help educate their sons toward a lifetime of civic participation. This notion of the "Republican mother" expanded the limited domain of women and gave them a rationale for increasing their political participation. Many Republican mothers began to insist on a better education for themselves and their daughters.

Trying to End Slavery

As white Americans fought for liberty from Britain, some enslaved Africans fought for liberty from slavery. In 1775, Lord Dunmore issued a proclamation in Virginia that offered freedom to any enslaved person or servant "able and willing to bear arms." The offer attracted more than 500 eager African Americans. The first volunteers formed a regiment of African American soldiers wearing chest sashes that proclaimed, "Liberty to Slaves!" As many as 20 percent of African Americans may have crossed behind British lines to struggle for their own freedom. Only a few thousand African Americans fought on the American side because the Americans did not promise them release from slavery.

If the Revolution did not end slavery, it did deal the institution a powerful blow. For one thing, the importation of enslaved persons almost stopped during the war. Though importation resumed briefly afterwards, 11 of the 13 states had outlawed it by 1790.

In addition, the Revolution brought the very institution of slavery under increased attack. In the South, the legislatures of Virginia and Maryland made it easier for slaveholders to free enslaved persons. A rapid increase in the population of freed African Americans fed expanding free African American communities in cities such as Richmond and Baltimore.

In the North, where enslaved persons made up a much smaller percentage of the population, the Revolution prompted states either to abolish slavery outright or to weaken it. In 1773, Dr. Benjamin Rush, the Pennsylvania leader who helped found America's first antislavery society, said, "The plant of liberty is of so tender a Nature, that it cannot thrive long in the neighborhood of slavery." In 1779 Pennsylvania legislated that all children born to enslaved women should be freed at age 21 if female and age 28 if male. Even such cautious steps showed an understanding that human slavery could never be reconciled with the ideal of liberty.

Section Assessment

Main Idea

1. Use a chart like this one to compare ways the new state constitutions advanced democracy and ways they limited it.

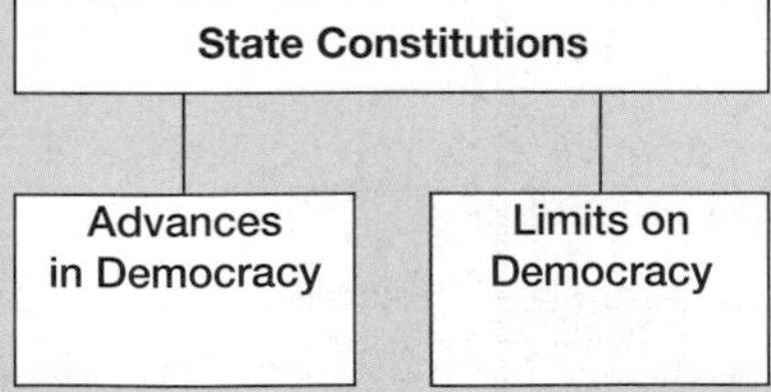

Vocabulary

2. Define: constitution, abolition, status quo, coverture.

Checking Facts

3. How did colonial leaders hope state constitutions would differ from British colonial charters?
4. In what ways were state governments more democratic than British colonial regimes?

Critical Thinking

5. **Making Comparisons** How did the state constitutions of Virginia, Massachusetts, and Pennsylvania differ?

Chapter  Assessment

Self-Check Quiz

Visit the *American Odyssey* Web site at americanodyssey.glencoe.com and click on ***Chapter 3—Self-Check Quiz*** to prepare for the Chapter Test.

Reviewing Key Terms

Choose the vocabulary word that best completes the sentences below. Write your answers on a separate sheet of paper.

internal tax	**revolution**
preamble	**external tax**
treason	**constitution**

1. Any goods that came into the colonies could be subject to an _________.

2. Many colonists believed strongly in the idea of a _________ or written plan of government.

3. The Continental Congress heeded the push for independence and began the _________.

4. Colonists meeting to defy the British government could be considered to be committing _________.

5. To raise revenue, Parliament levied an _________ on goods made within the colonies.

Recalling Facts

1. Identify 2 major taxation acts imposed upon the colonies in the 1760s. How did these acts move some colonists to look more favorably upon the idea of self-government?

2. What were committees of correspondence? How did colonists use them to gain sympathy for the revolutionary cause?

3. What action was taken by the First Continental Congress?

4. Who was Thomas Paine and what did he write? How did his publications influence colonial attitudes toward seeking independence?

5. What was the purpose of the Declaration of Independence? Who wrote it?

6. What was the British strategy at the beginning of the war? How did that plan change in 1777?

7. In which region of the colonies were most of the early battles of the Revolution fought? Why might war have broken out there first?

8. Why did each colony create its own constitution? Which people were allowed to vote and participate in government service?

9. Which colony initiated the idea that the Constitution should be ratified by voters? Why was this voter ratification an important development?

10. In what colony were women allowed to vote between 1776 and 1807? What requirements did these women voters have to meet?

Critical Thinking

1. Making Comparisons Compare external taxes and internal taxes. Were the colonists justified in protesting that Parliament had no right to levy internal taxes on them? Explain.

2. Making Generalizations Why do you think that the poorest Americans did most of the actual fighting in the Revolutionary War?

3. Making Inferences How did the ideals of freedom and independence that many colonists held during the Revolution help to change people's attitudes about slavery?

4. Drawing Conclusions Use a diagram like this one to show the causes and effects of the American Revolution.

Portfolio Project

What do you think a good citizen is? Is it someone who follows the law? Or might it be someone who breaks the law in order to stand up for an ideal? Do you think that people like the Sons of Liberty acted as good citizens? Are there groups like the Sons of Liberty today? Do you think they are good citizens? Write a persuasive paper explaining your views.

Cooperative Learning

Work with a group of classmates to evaluate the positive and negative effects of the Revolutionary War. Who benefited from the war? Whose lives remained the same? Who experienced negative consequences? Consider European American men and women, African Americans, and Native Americans. Discuss these issues and make a list of positive and negative consequences for each group. Share your group lists with your classmates.

Reinforcing Skills

Interpreting a Primary Source
Read the quotation by Anne Emlen on page 70. How do you know that this is a primary source? In your own words, explain what Anne Emlen means in her statement. Include any background information necessary.

GEOGRAPHY AND HISTORY

Early Revolutionary War Battles, 1775–1776

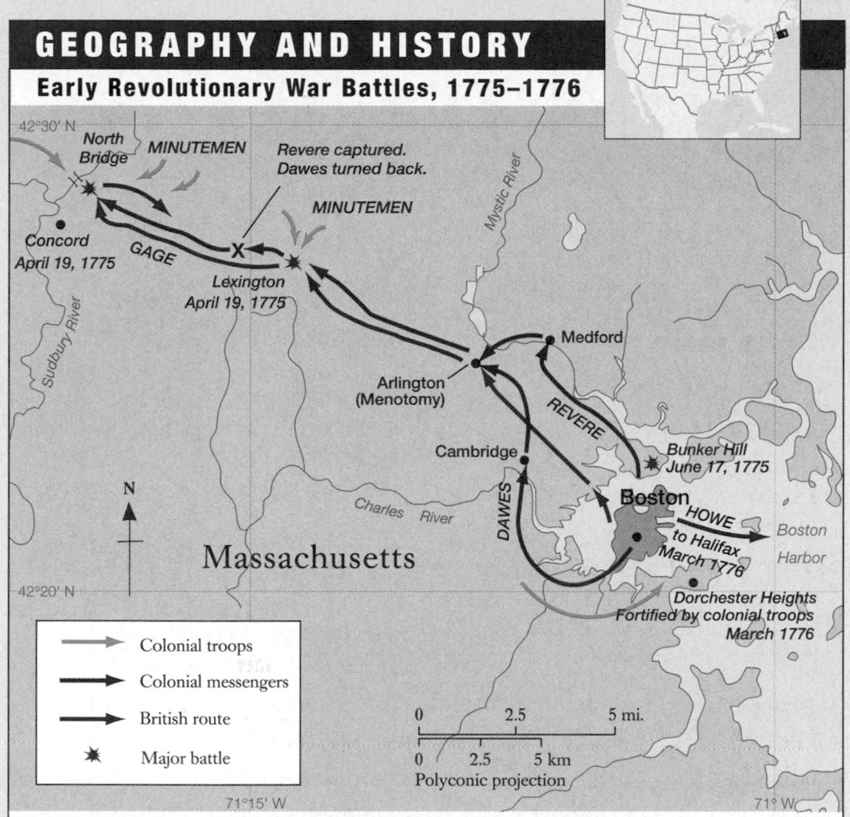

Study the map to answer the following questions:

1. How many major battles did the colonists and the British fight between April 1775 and the time when the British evacuated Boston?
2. Approximately how many miles did the British soldiers march from Lexington to Concord on April 19, 1775?
3. Describe the route taken by William Dawes when he rode to warn the colonists that the British were on the march.
4. What town marks the western limit of British troop movements on April 19, 1775?
5. For how many months after the start of the war were the British able to keep possession of Boston?

Technology Activity

Developing a Multimedia Presentation Use your library resources or the Internet to find additional information about the American Revolution. Create a multimedia presentation about the causes and effects of the American Revolution.

Standardized Test Practice

1. The American colonists complained about having to pay British taxes while not being allowed to vote for members of the British Parliament. Which of the following quotations best expresses this complaint?

A "Give me liberty or give me death."
B "No taxation without representation."
C "Government, even in its best state, is but a necessary evil."
D "Don't tread on me."

Test-Taking Tip: The important words in this question are *taxes* and *vote.* Which quotation *best* matches this information?

2. The main purpose of the Declaration of Independence was to

A outline colonists' reasons for separating from Great Britain.
B set forth the rights and duties of Congress.
C grant religious freedom to all citizens.
D question the practice of slavery.

Test-Taking Tip: Think about the meaning of the phrase *Declaration of Independence.* Eliminate any answers that don't relate to an announcement of freedom. Also, recall the mindset of colonists. Would they be likely to approve a document questioning slavery?

A New Nation

JULY 4, 1826: THE PASSING OF JEFFERSON AND ADAMS

It was the fiftieth anniversary of the signing of the Declaration of Independence. Thomas Jefferson, the nation's third President and principal author of the Declaration, lay gravely ill at Monticello, his home in Virginia.

Jefferson said to his grandson, "I am like an old watch, with a pinion worn out here, and a wheel there, until it can go no longer." He passed away shortly after noon.

John Adams died later that same day in Massachusetts, on his lips the words, "Thomas Jefferson survives!" He did not know that his old friend and rival was already gone.

Adams's words reflected his hope that at least one Founder would remain to watch over the young nation. While their relationship was strained at times by tensions in the country that pitted Democratic-Republicans against Federalists, Jefferson and Adams were bound together by the experiences they shared in the heady days of the Revolution.

Jefferson spent his vice presidency and two terms as President working to return the country to the Republican ideals of the Declaration of Independence and the Revolutionary era. He believed his predecessors, especially John Adams, had gone too far in strengthening the powers of the federal government. "I am not for transferring all the powers of the States to the general government, and all those of that government to the Executive branch," Jefferson wrote in a letter shortly before his election to the presidency. "I am for a government rigorously frugal and simple. . . ."

Confident in the strength of the American character, Jefferson never lost sight of his belief that the people's experiment in self-government was destined to set an example for the world. ■

What do you think is the meaning of Liberty feeding the American eagle in the painting on the right? Write your ideas in your journal.

Chapter Overview

Visit the *American Odyssey* Web site at americanodyssey.glencoe.com and click on ***Chapter 4—Chapter Overview*** to preview the chapter.

HENRY FORD MUSEUM & GREENFIELD VILLAGE

"Liberty" feeding the American eagle, circa 1800–1810

From Federation to Constitution

JUNE 17, 1788: VIRGINIANS DEBATE PROPOSED CONSTITUTION

NATIONAL PORTRAIT GALLERY, SMITHSONIAN INSTITUTION/ART RESOURCE, NY

Anti-Federalist
Patrick Henry led the opposition to the Constitution at Virginia's ratifying convention in 1788.

THE WINDOWS OF THE STATEHOUSE IN RICHMOND, VIRGINIA, STOOD OPEN ON THE HOT SUMMER AFTERNOON. Impassioned voices boomed from the building's main hall. There, 168 Virginia representatives heard arguments for and against a plan for a new government of the United States.

Patrick Henry stood before his fellow Virginians; they knew him as a former governor of their state and as a great public speaker. Henry explained his opposition to the proposed Constitution. It stripped powers away from the states, he said. It increased the powers of federal government, and it had been written by men with no authority to do so. He twisted the first words of the document into an attack on those men. "What right had they to say *We, the People?*" he asked. "Who authorized them to speak the language of *We, the People,* instead of *We, the States?*"

One of the men who helped design the new plan was at the convention. Edmund Randolph was as well known as Patrick Henry; he, too, had served as governor of the state and came from an old Virginia family. Randolph asked Virginia to accept the Constitution and unite the nation. Raising his right arm, Randolph exclaimed, "I will assent to the lopping of this limb before I assent to the dissolution of the Union."

The men debated the merits and faults of the Constitution through the rest of that warm June of 1788.

GUIDE TO READING

Main Idea

Experiences with government under the Articles of Confederation convinced delegates to the Constitutional Convention to draft a new plan of government and to compromise on issues that threatened their success.

Vocabulary

- ratify
- hard money
- checks and balances
- representation

Read to Find Out . . .

- the successes and failures of government under the Articles of Confederation.
- the difficulties in creating the Constitution.
- how the Constitution increased the power of the federal government and lessened the power of the state legislatures.

Patrick Henry and his supporters argued for the rights of the states. Randolph and others urged unity under a strong federal government that the new Constitution offered. The differences between the 2 men summed up tensions that pulled at the fabric of life in the United States in the 1780s.

A Firm League of Friendship

The Articles of Confederation

Hopes for unity under a strong central government stemmed from experiences with the Articles of Confederation, an earlier attempt at a federal constitution. A federal constitution had become necessary because state governments, established in the late 1770s, issued their own money, taxed their own citizens, and competed with other states in trade and for land beyond the Appalachians. By the 1780s states acted more like 13 small independent nations—each with its own government, economy, and interests—than like parts of a larger nation.

The Plan of the Articles

Around the same time that the former colonies were creating their state governments, the Second Continental Congress appointed a committee to draw up a plan for a national government. Congress, preparing for war, wanted its powers to be officially defined and recognized. Other Americans, too, realized that the states could not do everything on their own.

The Articles of Confederation created a national government in the form of a one-house legislature, similar to the Continental Congress. Each state, regardless of its size, had one vote in the Confederation Congress. This body was given only those powers that individual states could not fulfill alone: declaring war, conducting foreign policy, and establishing a postal system were examples. The Articles denied Congress the power to collect taxes, even for the support of an army or to enforce its own laws and treaties. One rule firmly established the power of the states over Congress: only a unanimous vote of the states could change the Articles of Confederation. Many Americans believed that this new system avoided the evils of a strong government—such as Britain's government—but allowed the states to work together for their common good and protection.

Ratification Difficulties

While all the newly formed states wanted a national government, it took almost four years to **ratify,** or officially accept, the Articles of Confederation (which could only be adopted if every state consented). The primary stumbling block to ratification was the question of control of the land between the Appalachian Mountains and the Mississippi River. Larger states such as Virginia claimed these Western lands in their colonial charters and were reluctant to give up control. Small states feared that control of this territory would make large states too powerful. Moreover, if the national government took control of the Western lands, their resources could benefit all the states in the union instead of just a few. States with no claims to Western lands pointed out that it was only fair that these lands be common property because they were being "wrested from the common enemy [the British] by the blood and treasure of the thirteen states." Small states hoped to see the Western lands opened for settlement and farming, so their poorer residents might make a new start.

Eventually most smaller states agreed to ratify the Articles despite their misgivings about control of Western lands. Maryland, however, refused to ratify until New York transferred its Western land claims to Congress in 1780, and Virginia followed suit in 1781. With all states' Western land claims ceded, or formally surrendered, Maryland announced its ratification of the Articles on March 1, 1781.

NATIONAL MUSEUM OF AMERICAN ART, WASHINGTON, DC/ART RESOURCE, NY

Unspoiled Lands The land that became the state of Tennessee (seen here in a later painting) was ceded by North Carolina in 1790. *Why did small states want the federal government to control Western lands?*

The 13 states would now be joined in a "firm league of friendship."

When the states worked together, the Confederation Congress succeeded in passing laws of lasting value. The Northwest Ordinance of 1787, for example, established rules for organizing the lush region west of the Appalachian Mountains. It reached a compromise on slavery, allowing it in territory south of the Ohio River and prohibiting the importation of slaves north of the river. The ordinance also provided rules for electing assemblies in the Western territories and for admitting territories "on an equal footing with the original states."

Although effective in passing the Northwest Ordinance, Congress faced a variety of difficult problems after the war that states refused to help solve. The worst of these problems involved paying off war debts and stabilizing the American economy.

In Debt

Congress had borrowed nearly $60 million from American investors and European governments during the war. After the war Congress lacked cash to pay its old debts. Because Congress was not allowed to tax the states, the only way it could pay its debts was to print massive amounts of paper money.

Continental paper currency was nothing more than a promise that Congress would pay the holder of the bill in **hard money**—gold or silver—at some time in the future. By the end of the war, the United States had a severe shortage of hard money. The more paper money Congress printed, therefore, the less it was worth. By the mid-1780s, Continental currency was worth only one-fortieth of its face value. Since Congress had no hard money to back up the millions of dollars printed during the war, people's confidence in paper money fell. Many merchants refused to accept Continental currency, and few Americans had any hard money to spend.

Desperately in need of a new way to raise taxes, leaders in Congress tried unsuccessfully to convince the states that it should have the power to tax imports. Meanwhile, the money problems began to have dire effects on the lives of common Americans.

NATIONAL PORTRAIT GALLERY, SMITHSONIAN INSTITUTION/ART RESOURCE, NY

In the Backcountry The Massachusetts Supreme Court sentenced Shays to death for his part in the uprising, then pardoned him in 1788. He is shown here with Jacob Shattuck, another leader in the farmers' rebellion. *What conditions in the country led to Shays's Rebellion?*

Shays's Rebellion

One of those Americans was Daniel Shays. Shays served as a captain in the Continental Army during the Revolution. When the war was over, he returned to his small farm in western Massachusetts. In the best of times, Shays had little extra money. After the war, he had none. In a time before banks, Shays and other farmers sometimes borrowed money from wealthy neighbors to buy food and supplies, or bought goods on credit from a store in town. When the wealthy neighbor or store owner asked the farmers to pay their debts—in hard money, of course—many could not pay.

For people who could not pay their debts, there were two alternatives. If they had property, a local court seized it and sold it to pay off the debt. If they had no property, they were sent to debtors' prison. In 1786 Shays and other farmers begged the Massachusetts legislature for extra time to pay their debts. The legislature ignored the requests, and the county courts continued to seize farms.

Daniel Shays recalled the early days of the crisis with Britain when legal attempts to solve disputes with government failed. He knew what to do in the face of an arrogant legislature. In August and September 1786, disgruntled farmers marched on courthouses in Northampton and Worcester. Muskets in hand, they closed the courthouses and prevented the courts from seizing any more farms or imprisoning any more farmers.

After those successes, Shays's group gathered near Springfield, where the state's supreme court was in session and where the state arsenal also happened to be located. When wealthy New Englanders learned that angry farmers were massing near the arsenal, they feared open rebellion and attacks on their property. They called the farmers traitors and provided the money that induced 4,400 militia from eastern Massachusetts to march against the gathering farmers.

In January 1787, Shays and 1,200 farmers marched on the arsenal. When Shays's men advanced, the militia opened fire. Four farmers died and the rest scattered. The revolt broke up soon afterward.

While Shays and the other farmers believed they were patriotic, other Americans were horrified. Men of wealth and power saw the rebellion as proof of social dis-

DEPOSITED BY THE CITY OF BOSTON, COURTESY, MUSEUM OF FINE ARTS, BOSTON

© NORTH WIND PICTURE ARCHIVES

THE THOMAS GILCREASE INSTITUTE OF AMERICAN HISTORY AND ART, TULSA, OKLAHOMA

Constitutional Convention at the Pennsylvania Statehouse James Madison (right) was among the most influential figures at the convention, where delegates shaped the new government and wrote the Constitution. Samuel Adams (above) refused to attend as a protest against the formation of a stronger federal government. *Why was the Confederation congress so anxious to replace the Articles of Confederation?*

order. Congress sent a veteran of Washington's army, General Henry Knox, to investigate. Knox reported that the farmers' uprising had "alarmed men of principle and property." He declared, "What is to afford our security against the violence of lawless men? Our government must be braced, changed, or altered to secure our lives and property."

A More Perfect Union

Reinventing Government

By 1787 the flaws in the Articles of Confederation were obvious to many Americans, including most members of the Confederation congress. A group of these men worried that the nation was headed for disaster unless the Articles were altered. They called on the states to send delegates to a convention where they might correct "such defects as may be discovered to exist" in the present government.

Meeting in Philadelphia

The group that gathered in Philadelphia in May 1787 contained some of the most distinguished men in America. Adoring crowds mobbed stern, proper George Washington, a delegate from Virginia. Americans still hailed him as the hero of the American Revolution. Another Virginia delegate, the short and frail James Madison, had spent much of the previous year reading about governments in past history to prepare for the convention. Benjamin Franklin was the elder statesman of the convention. At age 81, Franklin tired easily and had other Pennsylvania delegates read his speeches for him, but he enjoyed hosting the state delegates in his home city.

The other 52 delegates had experience drafting state constitutions and serving in state governments or the Confederation congress. The delegates' average age was 45, just past the prime of life in the 1700s. Many of them had attended college. All were white, male, and wealthy.

By May 25, delegates from 7 states had arrived and the meeting began. Delegates from 3 more states arrived late; delegates from Rhode Island never showed up.

Student Web Activity 4

Visit the *American Odyssey* Web site at americanodyssey.glencoe.com and click on ***Chapter 4—Student Web Activities*** for an activity relating to the Constitution.

Sworn to secrecy, and meeting behind closed doors, the delegates began their work at green felt-covered tables in the Pennsylvania statehouse. The delegates quickly agreed that the Articles were beyond repair. The Virginia delegation, headed by Edmund Randolph, proposed an entirely new system of government, based on James Madison's studies. This new government would be larger and more powerful than the Confederation congress.

That plan was the basis for discussion among the delegates throughout the long, hot summer of 1787. Working in a closed hall, the delegates suffered through sweltering heat. Six days a week, from May to September, they proposed and debated idea after idea. Angry delegates threatened to walk out of the convention and some did. Slowly, a plan for a new government emerged.

Reshaping the Government

Unlike the Confederation congress, the new government was to consist of three equal but separate branches: an executive branch, a legislative branch, and a judicial branch, or system of federal courts. The job of the executive branch, headed by a President, was to enforce federal laws. The responsibility of the legislative branch, or Congress, was to make laws. The judicial branch would rule on cases of federal laws. The responsibilities of these branches would overlap and interlock, creating **checks and balances** that would prevent one branch from being too powerful.

The new plan of government departed from the Articles in two major ways. First, it provided for a President with far-reaching powers. The President could veto acts of Congress, appoint judges, and put down rebellions. He also served as commander in chief of the army. These powers might not have been so great, said one delegate, "had not many of the members cast their eyes toward General Washington." Second, the new Constitution curbed the power of state legislatures. It banned them from issuing paper money and from allowing debts to be paid in farm produce instead of hard money. It also forbade states from "impairing the obligations of contracts"—meaning interfering with the settlement of contracts, which included debts owed by farmers.

The greatest difficulty the convention faced centered on Congress. The delegates agreed that Congress should consist of two houses, but they fiercely debated the question of **representation,** or how many votes each state should have. Delegates from small states insisted that each state have an equal vote in Congress. Those from larger states felt that representation should be decided by population.

Learning to Compromise

After seven weeks of deadlock on this issue, the two sides agreed to what historians call the Great Compromise. Both small and large states got part of what they wanted, but neither group got all they had hoped for. In the upper house, or Senate, each state would have two votes, regardless of its size. Representation in the lower house, called the House of Representatives, would be based on population.

Another conflict erupted over the way to figure the number of representatives a state could have. Southern delegates insisted that enslaved persons be counted in a state's population. Northern delegates objected. Some believed slavery was wrong; others realized that the proposal would increase Southern votes in the House. To complicate matters, some Northern delegates threatened to ban the slave trade.

YALE UNIVERSITY ART GALLERY, GIFT OF ROGER SHERMAN WHITE, B.A. 1899, LL.B. 1902

Federalist Leader Roger Sherman of Connecticut was one of the architects of the Great Compromise. *How did the delegates decide to compromise on slavery?*

THE THREE BRANCHES OF THE UNITED STATES GOVERNMENT

The United States Constitution separates and distributes the powers of the federal government among its three branches: the executive branch, the legislative branch, and the judicial branch.

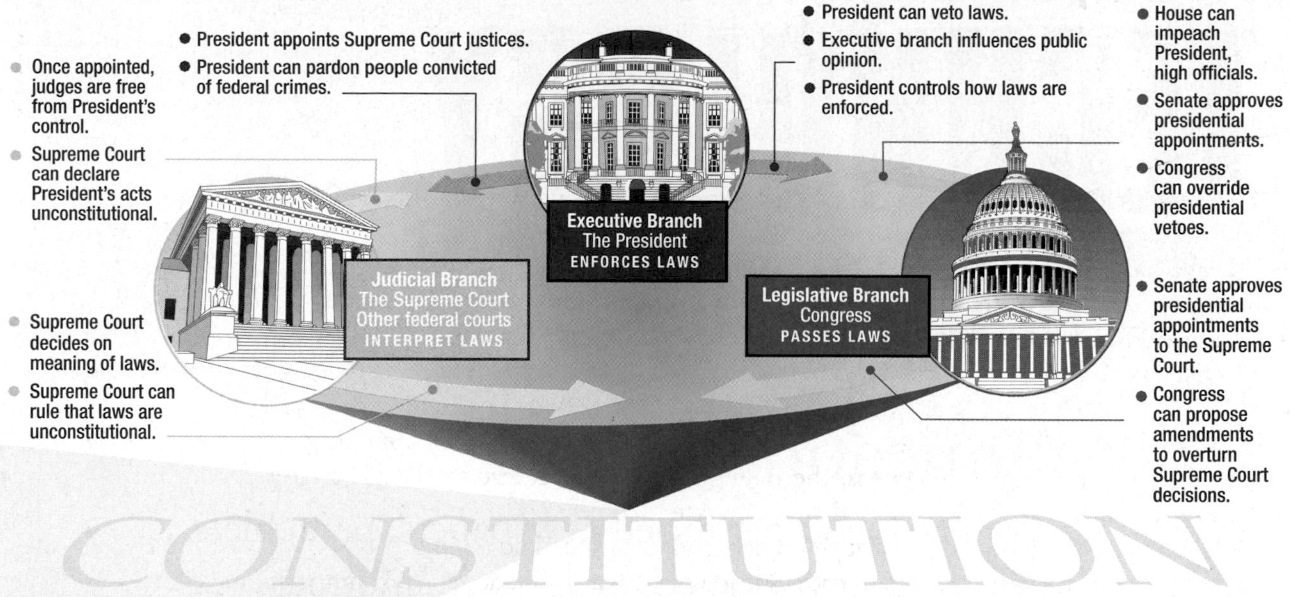

- Once appointed, judges are free from President's control.
- Supreme Court can declare President's acts unconstitutional.
- Supreme Court decides on meaning of laws.
- Supreme Court can rule that laws are unconstitutional.

- President appoints Supreme Court justices.
- President can pardon people convicted of federal crimes.

- President can veto laws.
- Executive branch influences public opinion.
- President controls how laws are enforced.

- House can impeach President, high officials.
- Senate approves presidential appointments.
- Congress can override presidential vetoes.
- Senate approves presidential appointments to the Supreme Court.
- Congress can propose amendments to overturn Supreme Court decisions.

Judicial Branch
The Supreme Court
Other federal courts
INTERPRET LAWS

Executive Branch
The President
ENFORCES LAWS

Legislative Branch
Congress
PASSES LAWS

CONSTITUTION

The Constitution prevents any one group from having total power by making the three branches of government depend on one another for their authority. *Using the graphic above, name two examples of the overlapping responsibilities of the branches.*

The two sides finally compromised. Representation in the House would be based on all the free inhabitants of a state, plus three-fifths of all enslaved people, even though they could not vote. The same formula would be used to figure the federal taxes owed by each state. Delegates also agreed that Congress could not ban the slave trade before 1808.

Many delegates feared that state governments would reject their new plan, which strengthened the central government. So they decided that the Constitution should be ratified in specially elected conventions of the people, rather than by the state legislatures. They also agreed that only 9 of the 13 states had to ratify the Constitution before it went into effect.

When the delegates saw the final document, many felt disappointed. They had compromised on issues of great importance to their states. "I confess there are several parts of this constitution which I do not at present approve," said Benjamin Franklin. He also said, however, that the new plan was better than their current government and encouraged the remaining delegates to sign it. All but 3 of them did so on September 17, 1787. (See pages 91–109 to read the Constitution.)

The next day, Major William Jackson, secretary of the convention, left Philadelphia by stagecoach, carrying a copy of the Constitution to the Confederation congress in New York. He also carried a letter from the convention explaining "the necessity of a different organization."

SECTION ASSESSMENT

Main Idea

1. Use a chart like this one to summarize the central question and final decision or compromise on each of the issues listed on the chart.

Issue	Central Question	Decision/Compromise
Articles of Confederation		
Representation		
Slavery		

Vocabulary

2. Define: ratify, hard money, checks and balances, representation.

Checking Facts

3. Why did smaller states want larger states to give up Western land claims?
4. What was the Great Compromise, and how did it satisfy all 13 states?

Critical Thinking

5. **Analyzing Information** Why did the delegates at the Constitutional Convention decide to compromise with each other?

Science, TECHNOLOGY, and Society

Communication Media

The colonial printer-publisher issued newspapers, pamphlets, and broadsides, or posters, that communicated information and opinions concerning the debate over British rule.

(DETAIL) PHOTO COURTESY PEABODY ESSEX MUSEUM, SALEM, MASS., ORIGINAL IN THE COLLECTION OF THE MARBLEHEAD HISTORICAL SOCIETY, MARBLEHEAD, MA

KEEPING IN TOUCH

Before the availability of printing presses in the Americas, colonists used letters and journals, such as the one at left, to keep records and disseminate information. These handwritten accounts had the obvious disadvantage of not being reproducible without great effort.

FILE PHOTO BY DOUG MINDELL

Pre-1650	1650	1700	1750

FIRST COLONIAL PRINTING PRESS is set up by Stephen Daye of Massachusetts in 1639.

The ***BOSTON NEWS-LETTER,*** the first successful newspaper in the colonies, is first published in 1704.

BALTIMORE PRINTER Mary Katherine Goddard prints and distributes the Declaration of Independence in 1777.

FREEDOM PRESS

Boston printer Isaiah Thomas learned his trade on this printing press in 1755, when he was 6 years old. At the start of the Revolution, Thomas removed his press to a town outside Boston to keep it out of British hands. There he printed the first accounts of the skirmishes at Lexington and Concord with the headline, "Americans!—Liberty or Death!—Join or Die!"

COLONIAL WILLIAMSBURG

COURTESY, AMERICAN ANTIQUARIAN SOCIETY

COURTESY, AMERICAN ANTIQUARIAN SOCIETY

REASONS WHY The *BRITISH* COLONIES, IN *AMERICA*, SHOULD NOT BE CHARGED WITH INTERNAL TAXES, BY AUTHORITY OF PARLIAMENT; HUMBLY OFFERED, For CONSIDERATION, In Behalf of the COLONY of *CONNECTICUT*.

NEW-HAVEN: Printed by B. MECOM. M,DCC,LXIV.

COURTESY, AMERICAN ANTIQUARIAN SOCIETY

PAPERS AND PAMPHLETS

The growth of small presses and improvements in the postal service made it much easier to find out what was going on. Connecticut Governor Thomas Fitch published a pamphlet (above, right) in 1740 that stated clearly and concisely his colony's objections to taxes. Between 1763 and 1775, the number of newspapers in the colonies doubled. The *Massachusetts Spy* (above, left) was founded in 1770.

COLONIAL WILLIAMSBURG

INTERNET NEWS

PORTFOLIO PROJECT

Comparisons have been made between colonial newspapers and today's electronic bulletin boards on the Internet. Do some research and write a brief report on how these media are alike and different.

1800 | 1850 | 1900 | 1950–2000s

THE TELEPHONE is invented by Alexander Graham Bell in 1876.

FIRST COMMERCIAL RADIO STATION, KDKA in Pittsburgh, goes on the air in 1920.

THE COMPUTER AGE begins when the first automatic digital computer is created in 1942.

THE INTERNET is born in 1969 out of a computer network built to study how the government could maintain communications in the event of nuclear war.

Debate and Ratification

SEPTEMBER 17, 1787: CONSTITUTIONAL CONVENTION ADJOURNS

As soon as the convention in Philadelphia ended, delegates rushed home to begin the campaign for ratification. That was a novel idea in itself. Never before had the nation's people at large been asked to ratify the laws under which they would live. The process of deciding for or against ratification produced perhaps the biggest, most informed political debate in American history.

News of the new Constitution spread rapidly through the states. Newspapers published the document and strongly worded arguments began to fill their pages. Those who favored the proposed Constitution called themselves Federalists. The Anti-Federalists opposed the new plan of government.

NATIONAL PORTRAIT GALLERY, SMITHSONIAN INSTITUTION/ART RESOURCE, NY

A Staunch Federalist
Alexander Hamilton was a major author of *The Federalist*, a series of 85 essays defending the Constitution.

The idea of a strong national government frightened some Americans. Many Anti-Federalists were small farmers who had learned to be self-sufficient and had found most of their contact with government unpleasant. The Anti-Federalist leaders, however, came from all classes and all regions. State politicians who dreaded losing power to the federal government were among the most active supporters of the Anti-Federalists.

The debate over the Constitution in newspapers, letters, and public discussions revealed divisions that remained in American society. One poor Anti-Federalist farmer mistrusted the people of "wealth and talent" who had framed the Constitution:

> These lawyers, and men of learning, and moneyed men, that talk so finely, and gloss over matters so smoothly, to make us, poor illiterate people swallow down the pill, expect to get into Congress themselves; they expect to be managers of this Constitution, and get all the power and all the money into their own hands, and then they will swallow up all us little folks, like the great Leviathan, Mr. President; yes, just like the whale swallowed up Jonah.
>
> —Amos Singletary, *Massachusetts Gazette*, January 25, 1788

Guide to Reading

Main Idea

The debate over the Constitution put Americans' faith in the new plan of government to the test and resulted in the addition of the Bill of Rights—one of the document's most important safeguards of individual liberties.

Vocabulary

- majority
- amendment

Read to Find Out . . .

- why opinions were divided about the proposed new Constitution.
- how the views of the Federalists differed from those of the Anti-Federalists.
- how the addition of the Bill of Rights enhanced the Constitution.

Toward Ratification

The Debate Over Basic Rights

NORTH WIND PICTURE ARCHIVES

The People Celebrate In this print New Yorkers are shown celebrating the ratification of the Constitution in 1788. *Why was New York a key state in the campaign for ratification?*

Many of the Anti-Federalists feared that a strong central government would not preserve the essential rights of the people. Even Britain guaranteed certain rights to its citizens, they argued. Why was there no bill of basic American rights?

The leading Federalists, including George Washington, Benjamin Franklin, and James Madison, did not believe a bill of rights was necessary. All basic rights, they argued, were protected by the Constitution or by state constitutions.

The Federalists found support in the area where America's elite had always dominated, the Atlantic Coast. Wealthy landowners in these areas wanted the protection a strong central government could provide. Merchants with overseas connections and artisans in large coastal cities also supported the proposed Constitution. These men had been hard hit by the inability of the Confederation congress to control the nation's economy; they saw a strong government that would pass import taxes on foreign goods as their best chance to succeed in business.

As the ratifying conventions began to convene, the Federalists knew they had clear **majorities,** or more than 50 percent of the votes, in some states. The vote was much closer in others, including large states such as Massachusetts, Virginia, and New York. If any one of those states did not ratify, the Federalists risked total failure.

The Ratification Debate

Anti-Federalist Objections to the Constitution	Federalist Defense of the Constitution
The Articles of Confederation were basically a good plan for government that could be amended.	The Articles of Confederation were weak and ineffective.
The Constitution made national government too strong.	National government needed to be strong in order to function.
Strong national government threatened the rights of the common people.	Strong national government was needed to quell rebellions by Native Americans and small farmers.
The Constitution favored wealthy men and preserved their power.	National government would protect the rights of the people.
The Constitution lacked a bill of rights.	Men of experience and talent should govern the nation.
	Constitutional and state governments protected individual freedoms without a bill of rights.

Both the Anti-Federalists and the Federalists held strong views regarding ratification of the new Constitution. *According to the Federalists, what safeguards would a strong national government provide for citizens?*

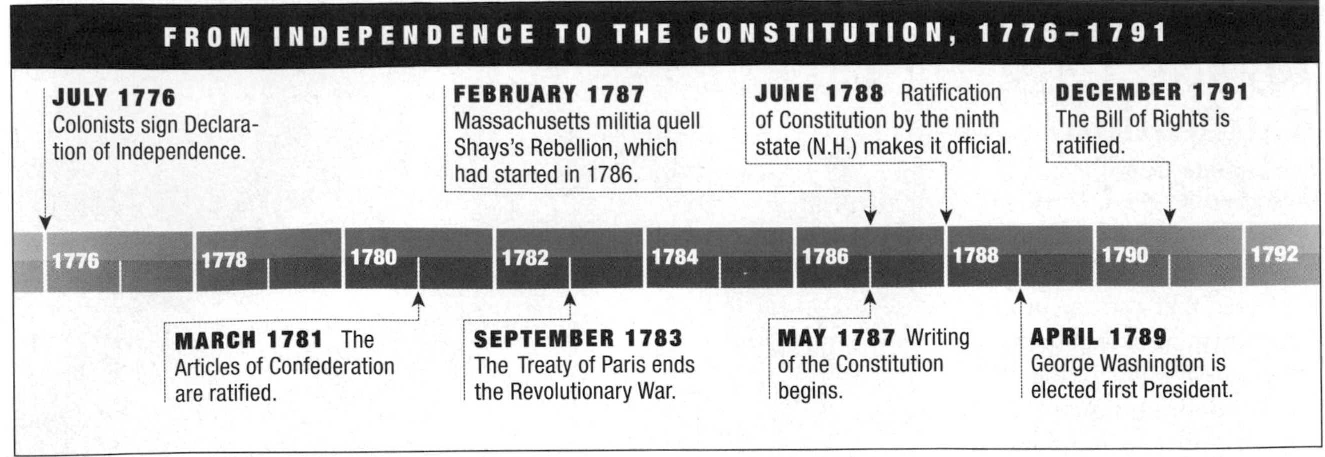

FROM INDEPENDENCE TO THE CONSTITUTION, 1776–1791
JULY 1776 Colonists sign Declaration of Independence.
FEBRUARY 1787 Massachusetts militia quell Shays's Rebellion, which had started in 1786.
JUNE 1788 Ratification of Constitution by the ninth state (N.H.) makes it official.
DECEMBER 1791 The Bill of Rights is ratified.
1776
1778
1780
1782
1784
1786
1788
1790
1792
MARCH 1781 The Articles of Confederation are ratified.
SEPTEMBER 1783 The Treaty of Paris ends the Revolutionary War.
MAY 1787 Writing of the Constitution begins.
APRIL 1789 George Washington is elected first President.

The People Vote

The first state conventions were held in December 1787 and January 1788. Delaware, New Jersey, Georgia, and Connecticut all ratified the Constitution.

The first real test occurred in Massachusetts. Opponents of the Constitution, including Samuel Adams, held a clear majority when the convention met in January 1788. The state's urban craftspeople—still the source of Samuel Adams's political power—sided with the Federalists, however, and persuaded Adams to vote for ratification. The Massachusetts convention agreed to the Constitution, but only if a bill of rights was added.

In June 1788, New Hampshire became the ninth state to ratify the Constitution. The Federalists had reached the minimum number required to make the new government legal. Virginia and New York, however, still had not yet ratified. Without these 2 large states the new government could hardly succeed.

George Washington and James Madison worked hard for ratification in Virginia, but Patrick Henry and other Anti-Federalists worked just as hard against it. Finally, at the urging of Thomas Jefferson, Madison compromised and agreed to add a bill of rights.

The contest was even closer in New York. Only a last-minute promise to add a bill of rights won ratification and secured the Federalists' victory.

Adding the Bill of Rights

Five states had ratified the Constitution with the understanding that Congress would add a bill of rights. They expected Federalist leaders to honor this promise. In September 1789, James Madison, who represented Virginia in Congress, presented 12 **amendments,** or written additions, to the Constitution.

Over the next 2 years, state legislatures ratified 10 of the 12 amendments. The Constitution now protected rights such as freedom of speech, religion, press, and assembly. In December 1791, these 10 amendments, or the Bill of Rights, were added to the Constitution.

The Preamble of the United States Constitution states that the Constitution is designed to "promote the general welfare, and secure the blessings of liberty" of "the people of the United States." It did not, however, address the rights of many Americans. The Constitution protected slavery, ignored women, and did not acknowledge Native Americans' rights. It left to future generations problems that it could neither foresee nor solve.

Yet through the process of ratification and with the addition of the Bill of Rights, the Constitution was shaped by more people than the flawed Articles of Confederation. As they headed into the 1790s, the American people watched—with hopes and fears—to see how this latest experiment would turn out.

Section Assessment

Main Idea

1. Use a diagram like this one to show pro and con arguments on the addition of a bill of rights to the Constitution.

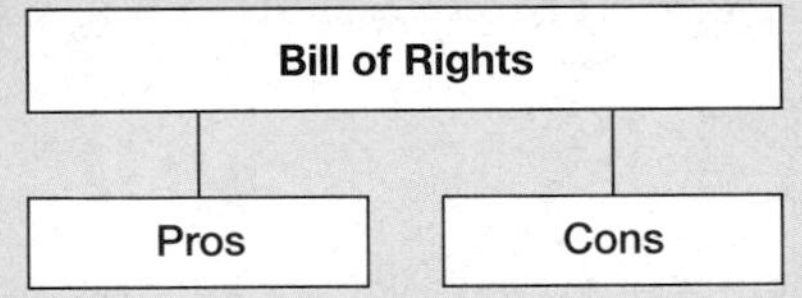

Vocabulary

2. Define: majority, amendment.

Checking Facts

3. Why did Anti-Federalists oppose the new Constitution?

4. Why did the Federalists favor the Constitution?

Critical Thinking

5. **Identifying Assumptions** What assumptions were many poorer Anti-Federalists making about the Federalists as a group?

The Constitution *of the* United States

For easier study of the Constitution, those passages that have been set aside or changed by the adoption of the amendments are printed in blue.

Preamble

We, the people of the United States, in Order to form a more perfect Union, establish Justice, insure domestic Tranquility, provide for the common defence, promote the general Welfare, and secure the Blessings of Liberty to ourselves and our Posterity, do ordain and establish this Constitution for the United States of America.

Article I

SECTION 1

All legislative Powers herein granted shall be vested in a Congress of the United States, which shall consist of a Senate and House of Representatives.

SECTION 2

1. The House of Representatives shall be composed of Members chosen every second Year by the People of the several States, and the Electors in each State shall have the Qualifications requisite for Electors of the most numerous Branch of the State Legislature.

2. No Person shall be a Representative who shall not have attained to the Age of twenty-five Years, and been seven Years a Citizen of the United States, and who shall not, when elected, be an Inhabitant of that State in which he shall be chosen.

3. Representatives and direct Taxes shall be apportioned among the several states which may be included within this Union, according to their respective Numbers, which shall be determined by adding to the whole Number of free Persons, including those bound to Service for a Term of Years, and excluding Indians not taxed, three-fifths of all other Persons. The actual Enumeration shall be made within three Years after the first Meeting of the Congress of the United States, and within every subsequent Term of ten Years, in such Manner as they shall by Law direct. The Number of Representatives shall not exceed one for every thirty Thousand, but each state shall have at Least one Representative; and until such enumeration shall be made, the State of New Hampshire shall be entitled to chuse three; Massachusetts eight, Rhode Island and Providence Plantations one, Connecticut five, New York six, New Jersey four, Pennsylvania eight, Delaware one, Maryland six, Virginia ten; North Carolina five, South Carolina five, and Georgia three.

Preamble

The Preamble introduces the Constitution and sets forth the general purposes for which the government was established. The preamble also declares that the power of the government comes from the people.

The printed text of the document shows the spelling and punctuation of the parchment original.

Article I. The Legislative Branch

Section 1. Congress

The power to make laws is given to a Congress made up of two chambers to represent different interests: the Senate to represent the states; the House to be more responsive to the people's will.

Section 2. House of Representatives

1. Elections and Term of Office

"Electors" means voters. Every two years the voters choose new Congress members to serve in the House of Representatives. The Constitution states that each state may specify who can vote. But the 15th, 19th, 24th, and 26th Amendments have established guidelines that all states must follow regarding the right to vote.

2. Qualifications

Representatives must be 25 years old, citizens of the United States for 7 years, and residents of the state they represent.

3. Division of Representatives Among the States

The number of representatives from each state is based on the size of the state's population. Each state is divided into congressional districts, with each district required to be equal in population. Each state is entitled to at least one representative. The number of representatives in the House was set at 435 in 1929. Since then, there has been a reapportionment of seats based on population shifts rather than on addition of seats.

Only three-fifths of a state's slave population was to be counted in determining the number of representatives elected by the state. Native Americans were not counted at all.

The "enumeration" referred to is the census, the population count taken every 10 years since 1790.

4. Vacancies
Vacancies in the House are filled through special elections called by the state's governor.

5. Officers
The speaker is the leader of the majority party in the House and is responsible for choosing the heads of various House committees. "Impeachment" means indictment, or bringing charges against an official.

Section 3. The Senate

1. Number of Members, Terms of Office, and Voting Procedure
Originally, senators were chosen by the state legislators of their own states. The 17th Amendment changed this, so that senators are now elected directly by the people. There are 100 senators, 2 from each state.

2. Staggered Elections; Vacancies
One-third of the Senate is elected every two years. The terms of the first Senate's membership was staggered: one group served two years, one four, and one six. All senators now serve a six-year term.

The 17th Amendment changed the method of filling vacancies in the Senate.

3. Qualifications
Qualifications for the Senate are more restrictive than those for the House. Senators must be at least 30 years old and they must have been citizens of the United States for at least 9 years. The Framers of the Constitution made the Senate a more elite body in order to produce a further check on the powers of the House of Representatives.

4. President of the Senate
The Vice President's only duty listed in the Constitution is to preside over the Senate. The only real power the Vice President has is to cast the deciding vote when there is a tie. However, modern Presidents have given their Vice Presidents new responsibilities.

5. Other Officers
The Senate selects its other officers, including a presiding officer (president pro tempore) who serves when the Vice President is absent or has become President of the United States.

6. Trial of Impeachments
When trying a case of impeachment brought by the House, the Senate convenes as a court. The Chief Justice of the Supreme Court acts as the presiding judge, and the Senate acts as the jury. A two-thirds vote of the members present is necessary to convict officials under impeachment charges.

7. Penalty for Conviction
If the Senate convicts an official, it may only remove the official from office and prevent that person from holding another federal position. However, the convicted official may still be tried for the same offense in a regular court of law.

4. When vacancies happen in the Representation from any State, the Executive Authority thereof shall issue Writs of Election to fill such Vacancies.

5. The House of Representatives shall chuse their Speaker and other Officers; and shall have the sole Power of Impeachment.

SECTION 3

1. The Senate of the United States shall be composed of two Senators from each State, chosen by the Legislature thereof; for six Years; and each Senator shall have one Vote.

2. Immediately after they shall be assembled in Consequence of the first Election, they shall be divided as equally as may be into three Classes. The Seats of the Senators of the first Class shall be vacated at the Expiration of the second Year, of the second Class at the Expiration of the fourth Year, and of the third Class at the Expiration of the sixth Year, so that one-third may be chosen every second Year; and if Vacancies happen by Resignations, or otherwise, during the Recess of the Legislature of any State, the Executive thereof may make temporary Appointments until the next Meeting of the Legislature, which shall then fill such Vacancies.

3. No person shall be a Senator who shall not have attained the Age of thirty Years, and been nine Years a Citizen of the United States, and who shall not, when elected, be an Inhabitant of that State in which he shall be chosen.

4. The Vice President of the United States shall be President of the Senate, but shall have no vote, unless they be equally divided.

5. The Senate shall chuse their Officers, and also a President pro tempore, in the absence of the Vice-President or when he shall exercise the Office of the President of the United States.

6. The Senate shall have the sole Power to try all impeachments. When sitting for that purpose they shall be on Oath or Affirmation. When the President of the United States is tried, the Chief Justice shall preside: And no person shall be convicted without the Concurrence of two-thirds of the Members present.

7. Judgment in Cases of Impeachment shall not extend further than to removal from Office, and disqualification to hold and enjoy any Office of Honor, Trust or Profit under the United States: but the Party convicted shall nevertheless be liable and subject to Indictment, Trial, Judgment and Punishment, according to Law.

SECTION 4

1. The Times, Places, and Manner of holding Elections for Senators and Representatives, shall be prescribed in each state by the Legislature thereof; but the Congress may at any time by Law make or alter such Regulations, except as to the Places of Chusing Senators.

2. The Congress shall assemble at least once in every Year, and such Meeting shall be on the first Monday in December, unless they shall by Law appoint a different Day.

SECTION 5

1. Each House shall be the Judge of the Elections, Returns and Qualifications of its own Members, and a Majority of each shall constitute a Quorum to do Business; but a smaller Number may adjourn from day to day, and may be authorized to compel the Attendance of absent Members, in such Manner, and under such Penalties as each House may provide.

2. Each House may determine the Rules of its Proceedings, punish its Members for disorderly Behaviour, and, with the Concurrence of two-thirds, expel a Member.

3. Each House shall keep a Journal of its Proceedings, and from time to time publish the same, excepting such Parts as may in their Judgment require Secrecy; and the Yeas and Nays of the Members of either House on any question shall, at the desire of one-fifth of those Present, be entered on the Journal.

4. Neither House during the Session of Congress, shall, without the Consent of the other, adjourn for more than three days, nor to any other Place than that in which the two Houses shall be sitting.

SECTION 6

1. The Senators and Representatives shall receive a Compensation for their Services, to be ascertained by Law, and paid out of the Treasury of the United States. They shall in all Cases, except Treason, Felony and Breach of the Peace be privileged from Arrest during their attendance at the Session of their respective Houses, and in going to and returning from the same; and for any Speech or Debate in either House, they shall not be questioned in any other place.

2. No Senator or Representative shall, during the Time for which he was elected, be appointed to any civil Office under the Authority of the United States, which shall have been created, or the Emoluments whereof shall have been encreased, during such time; and no Person holding any Office under the United States, shall be a Member of either House during his continuance in Office.

Section 4. Elections and Meetings

1. Holding Elections

In 1842 Congress required members of the House to be elected from districts in states having more than one Representative rather than at large. In 1845 it set the first Tuesday after the first Monday in November as the day for selecting presidential electors.

2. Meetings

The 20th Amendment, ratified in 1933, has changed the date of the opening of the regular session of Congress to January 3.

Section 5. Organization and Rules of Procedure

1. Organization

Until 1969 Congress acted as the sole judge of qualifications of its own members. In that year, the Supreme Court ruled that Congress could not legally exclude victorious candidates who met all the requirements listed in Article I.

A "quorum" is the minimum number of members that must be present for the House or Senate to conduct sessions. For a regular House session, a quorum consists of the majority of the House, or 218 of the 435 members.

2. Rules

Each house sets its own rules, can punish its members for disorderly behavior, and can expel a member by a two-thirds vote.

3. Journals

In addition to the journals, a complete official record of everything said on the floor, as well as the roll call votes on all bills or issues, is available in the *Congressional Record,* published daily by the Government Printing Office.

4. Adjournment

Neither house may adjourn for more than three days or move to another location without the approval of the other house.

Section 6. Privileges and Restrictions

1. Pay and Privileges

To strengthen the federal government, the Founders set congressional salaries to be paid by the United States Treasury rather than by members' respective states. Originally, members were paid $6 per day. Salaries for Senators and Representatives are $129,500.

The "immunity" privilege means members cannot be sued or be prosecuted for anything they say in Congress. They cannot be arrested while Congress is in session, except for treason, major crimes, or breaking the peace.

2. Restrictions

"Emoluments" means salaries. The purpose of this clause is to prevent members of Congress from passing laws that would benefit them personally. It also prevents the President from promising them jobs in other branches of the federal government.

SECTION 7

1. All Bills for raising Revenue shall originate in the House of Representatives; but the Senate may propose or concur with Amendments as on other bills.

2. Every Bill which shall have passed the House of Representatives and the Senate, shall, before it become a Law, be presented to the President of the United States; If he approve he shall sign it, but if not he shall return it, with his Objections, to that House in which it shall have originated, who shall enter the Objections at large on their Journal, and proceed to reconsider it. If after such Reconsideration two-thirds of that House shall agree to pass the bill, it shall be sent, together with the objections, to the other House, by which it shall likewise be reconsidered, and if approved by two-thirds of that House, it shall become a Law. But in all such Cases the Votes of both Houses shall be determined by Yeas and Nays, and the Names of the Persons voting for and against the Bill shall be entered on the Journal of each House respectively. If any Bill shall not be returned by the President within ten Days (Sundays excepted) after it shall have been presented to him, the Same shall be a Law, in like Manner as if he had signed it, unless the Congress by their Adjournment prevent its Return, in which Case it shall not be a Law.

3. Every Order, Resolution, or Vote to which the Concurrence of the Senate and House of Representatives may be necessary (except on a question of Adjournment) shall be presented to the President of the United States; and before the Same shall take Effect, shall be approved by him, or, being disapproved by him, shall be repassed by two-thirds of the Senate and House of Representatives, according to the Rules and Limitations prescribed in the case of a Bill.

SECTION 8

The Congress shall have the Power

1. To lay and collect Taxes, Duties, Imposts and Excises, to pay the Debts and provide for the common Defence and general Welfare of the United States; but all Duties, Imposts and Excises shall be uniform throughout the United States;

2. To borrow money on the credit of the United States;

3. To regulate Commerce with foreign Nations, and among the several States, and with the Indian Tribes;

4. To establish an uniform Rule of Naturalization, and uniform Laws on the subject of Bankruptcies throughout the United States;

5. To coin Money, regulate the Value thereof, and of foreign Coin, and fix the Standard of Weights and Measures;

6. To provide for the Punishment of counterfeiting the Securities and current Coin of the United States;

7. To establish Post Offices and post Roads;

Section 7. Passing Laws

1. Revenue Bills

"Revenue" is income raised by the government. The chief source of government revenue is taxes. All tax laws must originate in the House of Representatives. This insures that the branch of Congress which is elected by the people every two years has the major role in determining taxes. This clause does not prevent the Senate from amending tax bills.

2. How Bills Become Laws

A bill may become a law only by passing both houses of Congress and by being signed by the President. If the President disapproves, or vetoes, the bill, it is returned to the house where it originated, along with a written statement of the President's objections. If two-thirds of each house approves the bill after the President has vetoed it, it becomes law. In voting to override a President's veto, the votes of all members of Congress must be recorded in the journals or official records. If the President does not sign or veto a bill within 10 days (excluding Sundays), it becomes law. However, if Congress has adjourned during this 10-day period, the bill does not become law. This is known as a "pocket veto."

3. Presidential Approval or Veto

The Framers included this paragraph to prevent Congress from passing joint resolutions instead of bills to avoid the possibility of a presidential veto. A bill is a draft of a proposed law, whereas a resolution is the legislature's formal expression of opinion or intent on a matter.

Section 8. Powers Granted to Congress

1. Revenue

This clause gives Congress the power to raise and spend revenue. Taxes must be levied at the same rate throughout the nation.

2. Borrowing

The federal government borrows money by issuing bonds.

3. Commerce

The exact meaning of "commerce" has caused controversy. The trend has been to expand its meaning and, consequently, the extent of Congress's powers.

4. Naturalization and Bankruptcy

"Naturalization" refers to the procedure by which a citizen of a foreign nation becomes a citizen of the United States.

5. Currency

Control over money is an exclusive federal power; the states are forbidden to issue currency.

6. Counterfeiting

"Counterfeiting" means illegally imitating or forging.

7. Post Office

In 1970 the United States Postal Service replaced the Post Office Department.

8. To promote the Progress of Science and useful Arts, by securing for limited Times to Authors and Inventors the exclusive Right to their respective Writings and Discoveries;

9. To constitute Tribunals inferior to the Supreme Court;

10. To define and punish Piracies and Felonies committed on the high Seas, and Offenses against the Law of Nations;

11. To declare War, grant Letters of Marque and Reprisal, and make Rules concerning Captures on Land and Water;

12. To raise and support Armies, but no Appropriation of Money to that Use shall be for a longer Term than two Years;

13. To provide and maintain a Navy;

14. To make Rules for the Government and Regulation of the land and naval forces;

15. To provide for calling forth the Militia to execute the Laws of the Union, suppress Insurrections, and repel Invasions;

16. To provide for organizing, arming, and disciplining, the Militia, and for governing such Part of them as may be employed in the Service of the United States, reserving to the States respectively, the Appointment of the Officers, and the Authority of training the Militia according to the discipline prescribed by Congress;

17. To exercise exclusive Legislation in all Cases whatsoever, over such District (not exceeding ten Miles square) as may, by Cession of particular States, and the acceptance of Congress, become the Seat of Government of the United States, and to exercise like Authority over all Places purchased by the Consent of the Legislature of the State in which the Same shall be, for the Erection of Forts, Magazines, Arsenals, dock-Yards, and other needful Buildings; And

18. To make all Laws which shall be necessary and proper for carrying into Execution the foregoing Powers, and all other Powers vested by this Constitution in the Government of the United States, or in any Department or Officer thereof.

SECTION 9

1. The Migration or Importation of such Persons as any of the States now existing shall think proper to admit, shall not be prohibited by the Congress prior to the Year one thousand eight hundred and eight, but a tax or duty may be imposed on such importation, not exceeding ten dollars for each Person.

2. The privilege of the Writ of Habeas Corpus shall not be suspended, unless when in Cases of Rebellion or Invasion the public Safety may require it.

3. No Bill of Attainder or ex post facto Law shall be passed.

4. No capitation, or other direct, Tax shall be laid unless in Proportion to the Census or Enumeration herein before directed to be taken.

8. Copyrights and Patents
Under this provision, Congress has passed copyright and patent laws.

9. Courts
This provision allows Congress to establish a federal court system.

10. Piracy
Congress has the power to protect American ships on the high seas.

11. Declare War
While the Constitution gives Congress the right to declare war, the United States has sent troops into combat without a congressional declaration.

12. Army
This provision reveals the Framers' fears of a standing army.

13. Navy
This clause allows Congress to establish a navy.

14. Rules for Armed Forces
Congress may pass regulations that deal with military discipline.

15. Militia
The "militia" is now called the National Guard. It is organized by the states.

16. National Guard
Even though the National Guard is organized by the states, Congress has the authority to pass rules for governing its behavior.

17. Nation's Capital
This clause grants Congress the right to make laws for Washington, D.C.

18. Elastic Clause
This is the so-called "elastic clause" of the Constitution and one of its most important provisions. The "necessary and proper" laws must be related to one of the 17 enumerated powers.

Section 9. Powers Denied to the Federal Government.

1. Slave Trade
This paragraph contains the compromise the Framers reached regarding regulation of the slave trade in exchange for Congress's exclusive control over interstate commerce.

2. Habeas Corpus
Habeas corpus is a Latin term meaning "you may have the body." A writ of habeas corpus issued by a judge requires a law official to bring a prisoner to court and show cause for holding the prisoner. The writ may be suspended only during wartime.

3. Bills of Attainder
A "bill of attainder" is a bill that punishes a person without a jury trial. An "ex post facto" law is one that makes an act a crime after the act has been committed.

4. Direct Taxes
The 16th Amendment allowed Congress to pass an income tax.

5. Tax on Exports
Congress may not tax goods that move from one state to another.

6. Uniformity of Treatment
This prohibition prevents Congress from favoring one state or region over another in the regulation of trade.

7. Appropriation Law
This clause protects against the misuse of funds. All of the President's expenditures must be made with the permission of Congress.

8. Titles of Nobility
This clause prevents the development of a nobility in the United States.

Section 10. Powers Denied to the States
1. Limitations on Power
The states are prohibited from conducting foreign affairs, carrying on a war, or controlling interstate and foreign commerce. States are also not allowed to pass laws that the federal government is prohibited from passing, such as enacting ex post facto laws or bills of attainder. These restrictions on the states were designed, in part, to prevent an overlapping in functions and authority with the federal government that could create conflict and chaos.

2. Export and Import Taxes
This clause prevents states from levying duties on exports and imports. If states were permitted to tax imports and exports they could use their taxing power in a way that weakens or destroys Congress's power to control interstate and foreign commerce.

3. Duties, Armed Forces, War
This clause prohibits states from maintaining an army or navy and from going to war, except in cases where a state is directly attacked. It also forbids states from collecting fees from foreign vessels or from making treaties with other nations. All of these powers are reserved for the federal government.

Article II. The Executive Branch

Section 1. President and Vice President
1. Term of Office
The President is given power to enforce the laws passed by Congress. Both the President and the Vice President serve four-year terms. The 22nd Amendment limits the number of terms the President may serve to two.

5. No Tax or Duty shall be laid on Articles exported from any State.

6. No Preference shall be given by any Regulation of Commerce or Revenue to the Ports of one State over those of another: nor shall Vessels bound to, or from, one State, be obliged to enter, clear, or pay Duties in another.

7. No Money shall be drawn from the Treasury, but in Consequence of Appropriations made by Law; and a regular Statement and Account of the Receipts and Expenditures of all public Money shall be published from time to time.

8. No Title of Nobility shall be granted by the United States: And no Person holding any Office of Profit or Trust under them, shall, without the Consent of the Congress, accept of any present, Emolument, Office, or Title, of any kind whatever, from any King, Prince, or foreign State.

SECTION 10

1. No State shall enter into any Treaty, Alliance, or Confederation; grant Letters of Marque and Reprisal; coin Money; emit Bills of Credit; make any Thing but gold and silver Coin a Tender in Payment of Debts; pass any Bill of Attainder; ex post facto Law, or Law impairing the Obligation of Contracts, or grant any Title of Nobility.

2. No State shall, without the Consent of the Congress, lay any Imposts or Duties on Imports or Exports, except what may be absolutely necessary for executing its inspection Laws: and the net Produce of all Duties and Imposts, laid by any State on Imports and Exports, shall be for the Use of the Treasury of the United States; and all such Laws shall be subject to the Revision and Controul of the Congress.

3. No State shall, without the Consent of Congress, lay any duty on Tonnage, keep Troops, or Ships of War in time of Peace, enter into any Agreement or Compact with another State, or with a foreign Power, or engage in War, unless actually invaded, or in such imminent Danger as will not admit of delay.

Article II

SECTION 1

1. The executive Power shall be vested in a President of the United States of America. He shall hold his Office during the Term of four years, and together with the Vice-President chosen for the same Term, be elected, as follows:

2. Each State shall appoint, in such Manner as the Legislature thereof may direct, a Number of Electors, equal to the whole Number of Senators and Representatives to which the State may be entitled in the Congress: but no Senator or Representative, or Person holding an Office of Trust or Profit under the United States, shall be appointed an Elector.

3. The Electors shall meet in their respective States, and vote by Ballot for two Persons, of whom one at least shall not be an Inhabitant of the same State with themselves. And they shall make a List of all the Persons voted for and of the Number of Votes for each; which List they shall sign and certify, and transmit sealed to the Seat of the Government of the United States, directed to the President of the Senate. The President of the Senate shall, in the Presence of the Senate and House of Representatives, open all the Certificates, and the Votes shall then be counted. The Person having the greatest Number of Votes shall be the President, if such Number be a Majority of the whole Number of Electors appointed; and if there be more than one who have such Majority, and have an equal Number of Votes, then the House of Representatives shall immediately chuse by Ballot one of them for President; and if no Person have a Majority, then from the five highest on the List the said House shall in like Manner chuse the President. But in chusing the President, the Votes shall be taken by States, the Representation from each State having one Vote; a quorum for this Purpose shall consist of a Member or Members from two-thirds of the States, and a Majority of all the States shall be necessary to a Choice. In every Case, after the Choice of the President, the Person having the greatest Number of Votes of the Electors shall be the Vice-President. But if there should remain two or more who have equal votes, the Senate shall chuse from them by Ballot the Vice President.

4. The Congress may determine the Time of chusing the Electors, and the Day on which they shall give their Votes; which Day shall be the same throughout the United States.

5. No person except a natural born Citizen, or a Citizen of the United States, at the time of the Adoption of this Constitution, shall be eligible to the Office of President; neither shall any Person be eligible to that Office who shall not have attained to the Age of thirty-five years, and been fourteen Years a Resident within the United States.

6. In Case of the Removal of the President from Office, or of his Death, Resignation, or Inability to discharge the Powers and Duties of the said Office, the same shall devolve on the Vice-President, and the Congress may by Law provide for the Case of Removal, Death, Resignation or Inability, both of the President and Vice-President, declaring what Officer shall then act as President, and such Officer shall act accordingly, until the disability be removed, or a President shall be elected.

2. Election

The Philadelphia Convention had trouble deciding how the President was to be chosen. The system finally agreed upon was indirect election by "electors" chosen for that purpose. The President and Vice President are not directly elected. Instead, the President and Vice President are elected by presidential electors from each state who form the electoral college. Each state has the number of presidential electors equal to the total number of its senators and representatives. State legislatures determine how the electors are chosen. Originally, the state legislatures chose the electors, but today they are nominated by political parties and elected by the voters. No senator, representative, or any other federal officeholder can serve as an elector.

3. Former Method of Election

This clause describes the original method of electing the President and Vice President. According to this method, each elector voted for two candidates. The candidate with the most votes (as long as it was a majority) became President. The candidate with the second highest number of votes became Vice President. In the election of 1800, the two top candidates received the same number of votes, making it necessary for the House of Representatives to decide the election. To prevent such a situation from recurring, the 12th Amendment was added in 1804.

4. Date of Elections

Congress selects the date when the presidential electors are chosen and when they vote for President and Vice President. All electors must vote on the same day. The first Tuesday after the first Monday in November has been set as the date for presidential elections. Electors cast their votes on the Monday after the second Wednesday in December.

5. Qualifications

The President must be a citizen of the United States by birth, at least 35 years old, and a resident of the United States for 14 years. See Amendment 22.

6. Vacancies

If the President dies, resigns, is removed from office by impeachment, or is unable to carry out the duties of the office, the Vice President becomes President. (Amendment 25 deals with presidential disability.) If both the President and Vice President are unable to serve, Congress has the power to declare by law who acts as President. Congress set the line of succession in the Presidential Succession Act of 1947.

7. Salary

Originally, the President's salary was $25,000 per year. The President's current salary of $400,000 plus a $50,000 taxable expense account per year was enacted in 1999. The President also receives numerous fringe benefits including a $100,000 nontaxable allowance for travel and entertainment, and living accommodations in two residences—the White House and Camp David. However, the President cannot receive any other income from the United States government or state governments while in office.

8. Oath of Office

The oath of office is generally administered by the chief justice, but can be administered by any official authorized to administer oaths. All Presidents-elect except Washington have been sworn into office by the chief justice. Only Vice Presidents John Tyler, Calvin Coolidge, and Lyndon Johnson in succeeding to the office have been sworn in by someone else.

Section 2. Powers of the President

1. Military, Cabinet, Pardons

Mention of "the principal officer in each of the executive departments" is the only suggestion of the President's Cabinet to be found in the Constitution. The Cabinet is a purely advisory body, and its power depends on the President. Each Cabinet member is appointed by the President and must be confirmed by the Senate. This clause also makes the President, a civilian, the head of the armed services. This established the principle of civilian control of the military.

2. Treaties and Appointments

The President is the chief architect of American foreign policy. He or she is responsible for the conduct of foreign relations, or dealings with other countries. All treaties, however, require approval of two-thirds of the senators present. Most federal positions today are filled under the rules and regulations of the civil service system. Most presidential appointees serve at the pleasure of the President. Removal of an official by the President is not subject to congressional approval. But the power can be restricted by conditions set in creating the office.

3. Vacancies in Offices

The President can temporarily appoint officials to fill vacancies when the Senate is not in session.

7. The President shall, at stated Times, receive for his Services a Compensation, which shall neither be encreased nor diminished during the Period for which he shall have been elected, and he shall not receive within that Period any other Emolument from the United States, or any of them.

8. Before he enter on the execution of his office, he shall take the following Oath or Affirmation "I do solemnly swear (or affirm) that I will faithfully execute the Office of President of the United States, and will to the best of my Ability, preserve, protect and defend the Constitution of the United States."

SECTION 2

1. The President shall be Commander in Chief of the Army and Navy of the United States, and of the Militia of the several States, when called into the actual Service of the United States; he may require the Opinion, in writing, of the principal Officer in each of the executive Departments, upon any subject relating to the Duties of their respective Offices, and he shall have Power to Grant Reprieves and Pardons for Offences against the United States, except in Cases of Impeachment.

2. He shall have Power, by and with the Advice and Consent of the Senate, to make Treaties, provided two-thirds of the Senators present concur; and he shall nominate, and by and with the Advice and Consent of the Senate, shall appoint Ambassadors, other public Ministers and Consuls, Judges of the supreme Court, and all other Officers of the United States, whose Appointments are not herein otherwise provided for, and which shall be established by Law. But the Congress may by Law vest the Appointment of such inferior Officers, as they think proper, in the President alone, in the Courts of Law, or in the Heads of Departments.

3. The President shall have Power to fill up all Vacancies that may happen during the Recess of the Senate, by granting Commissions which shall expire at the End of their next Session.

SECTION 3

He shall from time to time give to Congress Information of the State of the Union, and recommend to their Consideration such Measures as he shall judge necessary and expedient; he may, on extraordinary occasions, convene both Houses, or either of them, and in Case of Disagreement between them, with respect to the Time of Adjournment, he may adjourn them to such Time as he shall think proper; he shall receive Ambassadors and other public Ministers; he shall take Care that the Laws be faithfully executed, and shall Commission all the Officers of the United States.

SECTION 4

The President, Vice-President and all civil Officers of the United States, shall be removed from Office on Impeachment for, and Conviction of, Treason, Bribery, or other high Crimes and Misdemeanors.

Section 3. Duties of the President

Under this provision the President delivers annual State-of-the-Union messages. On occasion, Presidents have called Congress into special session to consider particular problems.

The President's duty to receive foreign diplomats also includes the power to ask a foreign country to withdraw its diplomatic officials from this country. This is called "breaking diplomatic relations" and often carries with it the implied threat of more drastic action, even war. The President likewise has the power of deciding whether or not to recognize foreign governments.

Section 4. Impeachment

This section states the reasons for which the President and Vice President may be impeached and removed from office. (See annotations of Article I, Section 3, Clauses 6 and 7.)

Article III

SECTION 1

The Judicial Power of the United States, shall be vested in one supreme Court, and in such inferior Courts as the Congress may from time to time ordain and establish. The judges, both of the supreme and inferior Courts, shall hold their Offices during good Behaviour, and shall, at stated Times, receive for their Services, a Compensation, which shall not be diminished during their Continuance in Office.

SECTION 2

1. The judicial Power shall extend to all Cases, in Law and Equity, arising under this Constitution, the Laws of the United States, and treaties made, or which shall be made, under their Authority; to all Cases affecting ambassadors, other public ministers and consuls; to all cases of admiralty and maritime Jurisdiction; to Controversies to which the United States shall be a party; to Controversies between two or more states; between a State and Citizens of another State; between Citizens of different States; between Citizens of the same State claiming Lands under Grants of different States, and between a State, or the Citizens thereof, and foreign States, Citizens or Subjects.

2. In all Cases affecting Ambassadors, other public Ministers and Consuls, and those in which a State shall be Party, the supreme Court shall have original Jurisdiction. In all the other Cases before mentioned, the supreme Court shall have appellate Jurisdiction, both as to Law and Fact, with such Exceptions, and under such Regulations as the Congress shall make.

3. The trial of all Crimes, except in Cases of Impeachment, shall be by Jury; and such Trial shall be held in the State where the said Crimes shall have been committed; but when not committed within any State, the Trial shall be at such Place or Places as the Congress may by Law have directed.

Article III. The Judicial Branch

Section 1. Federal Courts

The term *judicial* refers to courts. The Constitution set up only the Supreme Court but provided for the establishment of other federal courts. There are presently nine justices on the Supreme Court. Congress has created a system of federal district courts and courts of appeals, which review certain district court cases. Judges of these courts serve during "good behavior," which means that they usually serve for life or until they choose to retire.

Section 2. Jurisdiction

1. General Jurisdiction

Use of the words *in law and equity* reflects the fact that American courts took over two kinds of traditional law from Great Britain. The basic law was the "common law," which was based on over five centuries of judicial decisions. "Equity" was a special branch of British law developed to handle cases where common law did not apply.

Federal courts deal mostly with "statute law," or laws passed by Congress, treaties, and cases involving the Constitution itself. "Admiralty and maritime jurisdiction" covers all sorts of cases involving ships and shipping on the high seas and on rivers, canals, and lakes.

2. The Supreme Court

When a court has "original jurisdiction" over certain kinds of cases, it means that the court has the authority to be the first court to hear a case. A court with "appellate jurisdiction" hears cases that have been appealed from lower courts. Most Supreme Court cases are heard on appeal from lower courts.

3. Jury Trials

Except in cases of impeachment, anyone accused of a crime has the right to a trial by jury. The trial must be held in the state where the crime was committed. Jury trial guarantees were strengthened in the 6th, 7th, 8th, and 9th Amendments.

Section 3. Treason

1. Definition

Knowing that the charge of treason often had been used by monarchs to get rid of people who opposed them, the Framers of the Constitution defined treason carefully, requiring that at least two witnesses be present to testify in court that a treasonable act was committed.

2. Punishment

Congress is given the power to determine the punishment for treason. The children of a person convicted of treason may not be punished nor may the convicted person's property be taken away from the children. Convictions for treason have been relatively rare in the nation's history.

Article IV. Relations Among the States

Section 1. Official Acts

This provision insures that each state recognizes the laws, court decisions, and records of all other states. For example, a marriage license or corporation charter issued by one state must be accepted in other states.

Section 2. Mutual Duties of States

1. Privileges

The "privileges and immunities," or rights of citizens, guarantee each state's citizens equal treatment in all states.

2. Extradition

"Extradition" means that a person convicted of a crime or a person accused of a crime must be returned to the state where the crime was committed. Thus, a person cannot flee to another state hoping to escape the law.

3. Fugitive-Slave Clause

Formerly this clause meant that slaves could not become free persons by escaping to free states.

Section 3. New States and Territories

1. New States

Congress has the power to admit new states. It also determines the basic guidelines for applying for statehood. One state, Maine, was created within the original boundaries of another state (Massachusetts) with the consent of Congress and the state.

2. Territories

Congress has power over federal land. But neither in this clause nor anywhere else in the Constitution is the federal government explicitly empowered to acquire new territory.

Section 4. Federal Protection for States

This section allows the federal government to send troops into a state to guarantee law and order. The President may send in troops even without the consent of the state government involved.

SECTION 3

1. Treason against the United States, shall consist only in levying War against them, or in adhering to their Enemies, giving them Aid and Comfort. No Person shall be convicted of Treason unless on the Testimony of two Witnesses to the same overt Act, or on Confession in open Court.

2. The Congress shall have power to declare the Punishment of Treason, but no Attainder of Treason shall work Corruption of Blood, or Forfeiture except during the Life of the Person attainted.

Article IV

SECTION 1

Full Faith and Credit shall be given in each State to the public Acts, Records, and judicial Proceedings of every other State. And the Congress may by general Laws prescribe the Manner in which such Acts, Records, and Proceedings shall be proved, and the Effect thereof.

SECTION 2

1. The Citizens of each State shall be entitled to all Privileges and Immunities of Citizens in the several States.

2. A Person charged in any State with Treason, Felony, or other Crime, who shall flee from Justice, and be found in another State, shall on demand of the executive Authority of the State from which he fled, be delivered up, to be removed to the State having Jurisdiction of the crime.

3. No Person held to Service of Labour in one State, under the Laws thereof, escaping into another, shall, in Consequence of any Law or Regulation therein, be discharged from such Service or Labour, but shall be delivered up on Claim of the Party to whom such Service or Labour may be due.

SECTION 3

1. New States may be admitted by the Congress into this Union; but no new State shall be formed or erected within the Jurisdiction of any other State; nor any State be formed by the Junction of two or more States, or parts of States, without the Consent of the Legislatures of the States concerned as well as of the Congress.

2. The Congress shall have Power to dispose of and make all needful Rules and Regulations respecting the Territory of other Property belonging to the United States; and nothing in this Constitution shall be so construed as to Prejudice any Claims of the United States, or of any particular State.

SECTION 4

The United States shall guarantee to every State in this Union a Republican Form of Government, and shall protect each of them against Invasion; and on Application of the Legislature, or of the Executive (when the Legislature cannot be convened) against domestic Violence.

Article V

The Congress, whenever two-thirds of both Houses shall deem it necessary, shall propose Amendments to this Constitution, or, on the Application of the Legislatures of two-thirds of the several States, shall call a Convention for proposing Amendments, which, in either Case, shall be valid to all Intents and Purposes, as part of this Constitution, when ratified by the Legislatures of three-fourths of the several States, or by Conventions in three-fourths thereof, as the one or the other Mode of Ratification may be proposed by the Congress; Provided that no Amendment which may be made prior to the Year One thousand eight hundred and eight shall in any Manner affect the first and fourth clauses in the Ninth Section of the first Article; and that no State, without its Consent, shall be deprived of its equal Suffrage in the Senate.

Article V. The Amending Process

There are now 27 Amendments to the Constitution. The Framers of the Constitution deliberately made it difficult to amend or change the Constitution. Two methods of proposing and ratifying amendments are provided for. A two-thirds majority is needed in Congress to propose an amendment, and at least three-fourths of the states (38 states) must accept the amendment before it can become law. No amendment has yet been proposed by a national convention called by the states, though in the 1980s a convention to propose an amendment requiring a balanced budget had been approved by 32 states.

Article VI

1. All Debts contracted and Engagements entered into, before the Adoption of this Constitution, shall be as valid against the United States under this Constitution as under the Confederation.

2. This Constitution, and the Laws of the United States which shall be made in Pursuance thereof; and all Treaties made, or which shall be made, under the Authority of the United States, shall be the supreme Law of the Land; and the Judges in every State shall be bound thereby, any Thing in the Constitution or Laws of any State to the Contrary notwithstanding.

3. The Senators and Representatives before mentioned, and the Members of the several State Legislatures, and all executive and judicial Officers, both of the United States and of the several States, shall be bound by Oath or Affirmation, to support this Constitution; but no religious Test shall ever be required as a Qualification to any Office or public Trust under the United States.

Article VI. National Supremacy

1. Public Debts and Treaties

This section promised that all debts the colonies had incurred during the Revolution and under the Articles of Confederation would be honored by the new United States government.

2. The Supreme Law

The "supremacy clause" recognized the Constitution and federal laws as supreme when in conflict with those of the states. It was largely based on this clause that Chief Justice John Marshall wrote his historic decision in *McCulloch* v. *Maryland.* The 14th Amendment reinforced the supremacy of federal law over state laws.

3. Oaths of Office

This clause also declares that no religious test shall be required as a qualification for holding public office. This principle is also asserted in the First Amendment, which forbids Congress to set up an established church or to interfere with the religious freedom of Americans.

Article VII

The Ratification of the Conventions of nine States shall be sufficient for the Establishment of this Constitution between the States so ratifying the same.

Done in Convention, by the Unanimous Consent of the States present, the Seventeenth Day of September, in the Year of our Lord one thousand seven hundred and Eighty-seven, and of the Independence of the United States of America the Twelfth. In Witness whereof We have hereunto subscribed our Names.

Article VII. Ratification of the Constitution

Unlike the Articles of Confederation, which required approval of all thirteen states for adoption, the Constitution required approval of only nine of thirteen states. Thirty-nine of the 55 delegates at the Constitutional Convention signed the Constitution. The Constitution went into effect in June 1788.

Signers
George Washington,
President and Deputy from Virginia

New Hampshire
John Langdon
Nicholas Gilman

Massachusetts
Nathaniel Gorham
Rufus King

Connecticut
William Samuel Johnson
Roger Sherman

New York
Alexander Hamilton

New Jersey
William Livingston
David Brearley
William Paterson
Jonathan Dayton

Pennsylvania
Benjamin Franklin
Thomas Mifflin
Robert Morris
George Clymer
Thomas FitzSimons
Jared Ingersoll
James Wilson
Gouverneur Morris

Delaware
George Read
Gunning Bedford, Jr.
John Dickinson
Richard Bassett
Jacob Broom

Maryland
James McHenry
Daniel of St. Thomas Jenifer
Daniel Carroll

Virginia
John Blair
James Madison, Jr.

North Carolina
William Blount
Richard Dobbs Spaight
Hugh Williamson

South Carolina
John Rutledge
Charles Cotesworth Pinckney
Charles Pinckney
Pierce Butler

Georgia
William Few
Abraham Baldwin

Attest:
William Jackson,
Secretary

Amendment 1. Freedom of Religion, Speech, Press, and Assembly (1791)
The 1st Amendment protects the civil liberties of individuals in the United States. The 1st Amendment freedoms are not absolute, however. They are limited by the rights of other individuals.

Amendment 2. Right to Bear Arms (1791)
The purpose of this amendment is to guarantee states the right to keep a militia.

Amendment 3. Quartering Troops (1791)
This amendment is based on the principle that people have a right to privacy in their own homes. It also reflects the colonists' grievances against the British government before the Revolution. Britain had angered Americans by quartering (housing) troops in private homes.

Amendment 4. Searches and Seizures (1791)
Like the 3rd Amendment, the 4th amendment reflects the colonists' desire to protect their privacy. Britain had used writs of assistance (general search warrants) to seek out smuggled goods. Americans wanted to make sure that such searches and seizures would be conducted only when a judge felt that there was "reasonable cause" to conduct them. The Supreme Court has ruled that evidence seized illegally without a search warrant may not be used in court.

Amendment I

Congress shall make no law respecting an establishment of religion, or prohibiting the free exercise thereof; or abridging the freedom of speech, or of the press; or the right of the people peaceably to assemble, and to petition the Government for a redress of grievances.

Amendment II

A well-regulated Militia, being necessary to the security of a free State, the right of the people to keep and bear Arms, shall not be infringed.

Amendment III

No soldier shall, in time of peace be quartered in any house, without the consent of the Owner, nor in time of war, but in a manner to be prescribed by law.

Amendment IV

The right of the people to be secure in their persons, houses, papers, and effects, against unreasonable searches and seizures, shall not be violated, and no Warrants shall issue, but upon probable cause, supported by Oath or affirmation, and particularly describing the place to be searched, and the persons or things to be seized.

Amendment V

No person shall be held to answer for a capital, or otherwise infamous crime, unless on a presentment or indictment of a Grand Jury, except in cases arising in the land or naval forces, or in the Militia, when in actual service in time of War or public danger; nor shall any person be subject for the same offence to be twice put in jeopardy of life or limb; nor shall be compelled in any criminal case to be a witness against himself, nor be deprived of life, liberty, or property, without due process of law; nor shall private property be taken for public use, without just compensation.

Amendment VI

In all criminal prosecutions, the accused shall enjoy the right to a speedy and public trial, by an impartial jury of the State and district wherein the crime shall have been committed, which district shall have been previously ascertained by law, and to be informed of the nature and cause of the accusation; to be confronted with the witnesses against him; to have compulsory process for obtaining witnesses in his favor, and to have the Assistance of Counsel for his defence.

Amendment VII

In suits at common law, where the value in controversy shall exceed twenty dollars, the right of trial by jury shall be preserved, and no fact tried by a jury, shall be otherwise reexamined in any Courts of the United States, than according to the rules of common law.

Amendment VIII

Excessive bail shall not be required, nor excessive fines imposed, nor cruel and unusual punishments inflicted.

Amendment IX

The enumeration in the Constitution, of certain rights, shall not be construed to deny or disparage others retained by the people.

Amendment X

The powers not delegated to the United States by the Constitution, nor prohibited by it to the States, are reserved to the States respectively, or to the people.

Amendment 5. Rights of Accused Persons (1791)

To bring a "presentment" or "indictment" means to formally charge a person with committing a crime. It is the function of a grand jury to see whether there is enough evidence to bring the accused person to trial. A person may not be tried more than once for the same crime (double jeopardy).

Members of the armed services are subject to military law. They may be tried in a court martial. In times of war or a natural disaster, civilians may also be put under martial law.

The 5th Amendment also guarantees that persons may not be forced in any criminal case to be a witness against themselves. That is, accused persons may refuse to answer questions on the ground that the answers might tend to incriminate them.

Amendment 6. Right to Speedy, Fair Trial (1791)

The requirement of a "speedy" trial insures that an accused person will not be held in jail for a lengthy period as a means of punishing the accused without a trial. A "fair" trial means that the trial must be open to the public and that a jury must hear witnesses and evidence on both sides before deciding the guilt or innocence of a person charged with a crime. This amendment also provides that legal counsel must be provided to a defendant. In 1963, the Supreme Court ruled, in *Gideon* v. *Wainwright,* that if a defendant cannot afford a lawyer, the government must provide one to defend the accused person.

Amendment 7. Civil Suits (1791)

"Common law" means the law established by previous court decisions. In civil cases where one person sues another for more than $20, a jury trial is provided for. But customarily, federal courts do not hear civil cases unless they involve a good deal more money.

Amendment 8. Bail and Punishment (1791)

"Bail" is money that an accused person provides to the court as a guarantee that he or she will be present for a trial. This amendment insures that neither bail nor punishment for a crime shall be unreasonably severe.

Amendment 9. Powers Reserved to the People (1791)

This amendment provides that the people's rights are not limited to those mentioned in the Constitution.

Amendment 10. Powers Reserved to the States (1791)

This amendment protects the states and the people from an all-powerful federal government. It provides that the states or the people retain all powers except those denied them or those specifically granted to the federal government. This "reserved powers" provision is a check on the "necessary and proper" power of the federal government provided in the "elastic clause" in Article I, Section 8, Clause 18.

Amendment 11. Suits Against States (1795)

This amendment provides that a lawsuit brought by a citizen of the United States or a foreign nation against a state must be tried in a state court, not in a federal court. This amendment was passed after the Supreme Court ruled that a federal court could try a lawsuit brought by citizens of South Carolina against a citizen of Georgia. This case, *Chisholm* v. *Georgia,* decided in 1793, was protested by many Americans, who insisted states would lose authority if they could be sued in federal courts.

Amendment 12. Election of President and Vice President (1804)

This amendment changes the procedure for electing the President and Vice President as outlined in Article II, Section 1, Clause 3.

To prevent the recurrence of the election of 1800 whereby a candidate running for Vice President (Aaron Burr) could tie a candidate running for President (Thomas Jefferson) and thus force the election into the House of Representatives, the Twelfth Amendment specifies that the electors are to cast separate ballots for each office. The votes for each office are counted and listed separately. The results are signed, sealed, and sent to the president of the senate. At a joint session of Congress, the votes are counted. The candidate who receives the most votes, providing it is a majority, is elected President. Other changes include: (1) a reduction from five to the three highest candidates receiving votes among whom the House is to choose if no candidate receives a majority of the electoral votes, and (2) provision for the Senate to choose the Vice President from the two highest candidates if neither has received a majority of the electoral votes.

The Twelfth Amendment does place one restriction on electors. It prohibits electors from voting for two candidates (President and Vice President) from their home state.

Amendment 13. Abolition of Slavery (1865)

This amendment was the final act in ending slavery in the United States. It also prohibits the binding of a person to perform a personal service due to debt. In addition to imprisonment for crime, the Supreme Court has held that the draft is not a violation of the amendment.

This amendment is the first adopted to be divided into sections. It is also the first to contain specifically a provision granting Congress power to enforce it by appropriate legislation.

Amendment XI

The Judicial power of the United States shall not be construed to extend to any suit in law or equity, commenced or prosecuted against one of the United States by Citizens of another State, or by Citizens or Subjects of any Foreign State.

Amendment XII

The Electors shall meet in their respective States and vote by ballot for President and Vice-President, one of whom, at least, shall not be an inhabitant of the same State with themselves; they shall name in their ballots the person voted for as President, and in distinct ballots the person voted for as Vice-President, and they shall make distinct lists of all persons voted for as President, and of all persons voted for as Vice-President, and of the number of votes for each, which lists they shall sign and certify, and transmit sealed to the seat of the government of the United States, directed to the President of the Senate; The President of the Senate shall, in the presence of the Senate and House of Representatives, open all the certificates and the votes shall then be counted; The person having the greatest number of votes for President, shall be the President, if such number be a majority of the whole number of Electors appointed; and if no person have such majority, then from the persons having the highest numbers not exceeding three on the list of those voted for as President, the House of Representatives shall choose immediately, by ballot, the President. But in choosing the President, the votes shall be taken by states, the representation from each state having one vote; a quorum for this purpose shall consist of a member or members from two-thirds of the states, and a majority of all the states shall be necessary to a choice. And if the House of Representatives shall not choose a President whenever the right of choice shall devolve upon them, before the fourth day of March next following, then the Vice-President shall act as President, as in the case of the death or other constitutional disability of the President. The person having the greatest number of votes as Vice-President, shall be the Vice-President, if such number be a majority of the whole number of Electors appointed, and if no person have a majority, then from the two highest numbers on the list, the Senate shall choose the Vice-President; a quorum for the purpose shall consist of two-thirds of the whole number of Senators, and a majority of the whole number shall be necessary to a choice. But no person constitutionally ineligible to the office of President shall be eligible to that of Vice-President of the United States.

Amendment XIII

SECTION 1

Neither slavery nor involuntary servitude, except as a punishment for crime whereof the party shall have been duly convicted, shall exist within the United States, or any place subject to their jurisdiction.

SECTION 2

Congress shall have power to enforce this article by appropriate legislation.

Amendment XIV

SECTION 1

All persons born or naturalized in the United States, and subject to the jurisdiction thereof, are citizens of the United States and of the State wherein they reside. No State shall make or enforce any law which shall abridge the privileges or immunities of citizens of the United States; nor shall any State deprive any person of life, liberty, or property, without due process of law, nor deny to any person within its jurisdiction the equal protection of the laws.

SECTION 2

Representatives shall be apportioned among the several States according to their respective numbers, counting the whole number of persons in each State, excluding Indians not taxed. But when the right to vote at any election for the choice of electors for President and Vice-President of the United States, Representatives in Congress, the Executive and Judicial officers of a State, or the members of the Legislature thereof, is denied to any of the male inhabitants of such State, being twenty-one years of age, and citizens of the United States, or in any way abridged, except for participation in rebellion, or other crime, the basis of representation therein shall be reduced in the proportion which the number of such male citizens shall bear to the whole number of male citizens twenty-one years of age in such State.

SECTION 3

No person shall be a Senator or Representative in Congress, or elector of President and Vice-President, or hold any office, civil or military, under the United States, or under any State, who, having previously taken an oath, as a member of Congress, or as an officer of the United States, or as a member of any State legislature, or as an executive or judicial officer of any State, to support the Constitution of the United States, shall have engaged in insurrection or rebellion against the same, or given aid or comfort to the enemies thereof. But Congress may by a vote of two-thirds of each House, remove such disability.

SECTION 4

The validity of the public debt of the United States incurred for payment of pensions and bounties for service, authorized by law, including debts in suppressing insurrections or rebellion, shall not be questioned. But neither the United States nor any State shall assume or pay any debt or obligation incurred in aid of insurrection or rebellion against the United States, or any claim for the loss or emancipation of any slave; but all such debts, obligations and claims shall be held illegal and void.

SECTION 5

The Congress shall have power to enforce, by appropriate legislation, the provisions of this article.

Amendment 14. Rights of Citizens (1868)

The clauses of this amendment were intended 1) to penalize southern states that refused to grant African Americans the vote, 2) to keep former Confederate leaders from serving in government, 3) to forbid payment of the Confederacy's debt by the federal government, and 4) to insure payment of the war debts owed the federal government.

Section 1. Citizenship Defined

By granting citizenship to all persons born in the United States, this amendment granted citizenship to former slaves. The amendment also guaranteed "due process of law." By the 1950s, Supreme Court rulings used the due process clause to protect civil liberties. The last part of Section 1 establishes the doctrine that all citizens are entitled to equal protection of the laws. In 1954 the Supreme Court ruled, in *Brown* v. *Board of Education of Topeka,* that segregation in public schools was unconstitutional because it denied equal protection.

Section 2. Representation in Congress

This section reduced the number of members a state had in the House of Representatives if it denied its citizens the right to vote. This section was not implemented, however. Later civil rights laws and the 24th Amendment guaranteed the vote to African Americans.

Section 3. Penalty for Engaging in Insurrection

The leaders of the Confederacy were barred from state or federal offices unless Congress agreed to revoke this ban. By the end of Reconstruction all but a few Confederate leaders were allowed to return to public life.

Section 4. Public Debt

The public debt incurred by the federal government during the Civil War was valid and could not be questioned by the South. However, the debts of the Confederacy were declared to be illegal. And former slave owners could not collect compensation for the loss of their slaves.

Section 5. Enforcement

Congress was empowered to pass civil rights bills to guarantee the provisions of the amendment.

Amendment 15. The Right to Vote (1870)
Section 1. Suffrage for African Americans

The 15th Amendment replaced Section 2 of the 14th Amendment in guaranteeing African Americans the right to vote, that is, the right of African Americans to vote was not to be left to the states. Yet, despite this prohibition, African Americans were denied the right to vote by many states by such means as poll taxes, literacy tests, and white primaries.

Section 2. Enforcement

Congress was given the power to enforce this amendment. During the 1950s and 1960s, it passed successively stronger laws to end racial discrimination in voting rights.

Amendment 16. Income Tax (1913)

The origins of this amendment went back to 1895, when the Supreme Court declared a federal income tax unconstitutional. To overcome this Supreme Court decision, this amendment authorized an income tax that was levied on a direct basis.

Amendment 17. Direct Election of Senators (1913)
Section 1. Method of Election

The right to elect senators was given directly to the people of each state. It replaced Article I, Section 3, Clause 1, which empowered state legislatures to elect senators. This amendment was designed not only to make the choice of senators more democratic but also to cut down on corruption and to improve state government.

Section 2. Vacancies

A state must order an election to fill a senate vacancy. A state may empower its governor to appoint a person to fill a Senate seat if a vacancy occurs until an election can be held.

Section 3. Time in Effect

This amendment was not to affect any Senate election or temporary appointment until it was in effect.

Amendment 18. Prohibition of Alcoholic Beverages (1919)

This amendment prohibited the production, sale, or transportation of alcoholic beverages in the United States. Prohibition proved to be difficult to enforce, especially in states with large urban populations. This amendment was later repealed by the 21st Amendment.

Amendment 19. Women's Suffrage (1920)

This amendment, extending the vote to all qualified women in federal and state elections, was a landmark victory for the woman suffrage movement, which had worked to achieve this goal for many years. The women's movement had earlier gained full voting rights for women in four western states in the late nineteenth century.

Amendment XV

SECTION 1

The right of citizens of the United States to vote shall not be denied or abridged by the United States or by any State on account of race, color, or previous condition of servitude.

SECTION 2

The Congress shall have power to enforce this article by appropriate legislation.

Amendment XVI

The Congress shall have power to lay and collect taxes on incomes, from whatever source derived, without apportionment among several States, and without regard to any census or enumeration.

Amendment XVII

SECTION 1

The Senate of the United States shall be composed of two Senators from each State, elected by the people thereof, for six years; and each Senator shall have one vote. The electors in each state shall have the qualifications requisite for electors of the most numerous branch of the state legislatures.

SECTION 2

When vacancies happen in the representation of any State in the Senate, the executive authority of such State shall issue writs of election to fill such vacancies: *Provided,* that the legislature of any State may empower the executive thereof to make temporary appointments until the people fill the vacancies by election as the legislature may direct.

SECTION 3

This amendment shall not be so construed as to affect the election or term of any Senator chosen before it becomes valid as part of the Constitution.

Amendment XVIII

SECTION 1

After one year from ratification of this article the manufacture, sale, or transportation of intoxicating liquors within, the importation thereof into, or the exportation thereof from the United States and all territory subject to the jurisdiction thereof for beverage purposes is hereby prohibited.

SECTION 2

The Congress and the several states shall have concurrent power to enforce this article by appropriate legislation.

SECTION 3

This article shall be inoperative unless it shall have been ratified as an amendment to the Constitution by the legislatures of the several States, as provided in the Constitution, within seven years from the date of the submission hereof to the states of the Congress.

Amendment XIX

SECTION 1

The right of citizens of the United States to vote shall not be denied or abridged by the United States or by any state on account of sex.

SECTION 2

Congress shall have power to enforce this article by appropriate legislation.

Amendment XX

SECTION 1

The terms of the President and Vice President shall end at noon on the 20th day of January, and the terms of the Senators and Representatives at noon on the 3rd day of January, of the years in which such terms would have ended if this article had not been ratified; and the terms of their successors shall then begin.

SECTION 2

The Congress shall assemble at least once in every year, and such meeting shall begin at noon on the 3rd day of January, unless they shall by law appoint a different day.

SECTION 3

If, at the time fixed for the beginning of the term of the President, the President elect shall have died, the Vice President elect shall become President. If a President shall not have been chosen before the time fixed for the beginning of his term, or if the President elect shall have failed to qualify, then the Vice President elect shall act as President until a President shall have qualified; and the Congress may by law provide for the case wherein neither a President elect nor a Vice President elect shall have qualified, declaring who shall then act as President, or the manner in which one who is to act shall be selected, and such person shall act accordingly until a President or Vice President shall have qualified.

SECTION 4

The Congress may by law provide for the case of the death of any of the persons from whom the House of Representatives may choose a President whenever the right of choice shall have devolved upon them, and for the case of the death of any of the persons from whom the Senate may choose a Vice President whenever the right of choice shall have devolved upon them.

SECTION 5

Sections 1 and 2 shall take effect on the 15th day of October following the ratification of this article.

SECTION 6

This article shall be inoperative unless it shall have been ratified as an amendment to the Constitution by the legislatures of three-fourths of the several States within seven years from the date of its submission.

Amendment XXI

SECTION 1

The eighteenth article of amendment to the Constitution of the United States is hereby repealed.

SECTION 2

The transportation or importation into any State, Territory, or possession of the United States for delivery or use therein of intoxicating liquors, in violation of the laws thereof, is hereby prohibited.

SECTION 3

This article shall be inoperative unless it shall have been ratified as an amendment to the Constitution by conventions in the several States, as provided in the Constitution, within seven years from the date of the submission hereof to the States by the Congress.

Amendment 20. "Lame-Duck" Amendment (1933)

Section 1. New Dates of Terms

This amendment had two major purposes: 1) to shorten the time between the President's and Vice President's election and inauguration, and 2) to end "lame-duck" sessions of Congress.

When the Constitution first went into effect, transportation and communication were slow and uncertain. It often took many months after the election in November for the President and Vice President to travel to Washington, D.C., and prepare for their inauguration on March 4. This amendment ended this long wait for a new administration by fixing January 20 as Inauguration Day.

Section 2. Meeting Time of Congress

"Lame-duck" sessions occurred every two years, after the November congressional election. That is, the Congress that held its session in December of an election year was not the newly elected Congress but the old Congress that had been elected two years earlier. This Congress continued to serve for several more months, usually until March of the next year. Often many of its members had failed to be reelected and were called "lame-ducks." The 20th Amendment abolished this "lame-duck" session, and provided that the new Congress hold its first session soon after the November election, on January 3.

Section 3. Succession of President and Vice President

This amendment provides that if the President-elect dies before taking office, the Vice President-elect becomes President. In the cases described, Congress will decide on a temporary President.

Section 4. Filling Presidential Vacancy

If a presidential candidate dies while an election is being decided in the House, Congress may pass legislation to deal with the situation. Congress has similar power if this occurs when the Senate is deciding a vice-presidential election.

Section 5. Beginning the New Dates

Sections 1 and 2 affected the Congress elected in 1934 and President Roosevelt, elected in 1936.

Section 6. Time Limit on Ratification

The period for ratification by the states was limited to seven years.

Amendment 21. Repeal of Prohibition Amendment (1933)

This amendment nullified the 18th Amendment. It is the only amendment ever passed to overturn an earlier amendment. It remained unlawful to transport alcoholic beverages into states that forbade their use. It is the only amendment ratified by special state conventions instead of state legislatures.

Amendment 22. Limit on Presidential Terms (1951)

This amendment wrote into the Constitution a custom started by Washington, Jefferson, and Madison, whereby Presidents limited themselves to two terms in office. Although both Ulysses S. Grant and Theodore Roosevelt sought third terms, the two-term precedent was not broken until Franklin D. Roosevelt was elected to a third term in 1940 and then a fourth term in 1944. The passage of the 22nd amendment insures that no President is to be considered indispensable. It also provides that anyone who succeeds to the presidency and serves for more than two years of the term may not be elected more than one more time.

Amendment 23. Presidential Electors for the District of Columbia (1961)

This amendment granted people living in the District of Columbia the right to vote in presidential elections. The District casts three electoral votes. The people of Washington, D.C., still are without representation in Congress.

Amendment 24. Abolition of the Poll Tax (1964)

A "poll tax" was a fee that persons were required to pay in order to vote in a number of Southern states. This amendment ended poll taxes as a requirement to vote in any presidential or congressional election. In 1966 the Supreme Court voided poll taxes in state elections as well.

Amendment 25. Presidential Disability and Succession (1967)

Section 1. Replacing the President

The Vice President becomes President if the President dies, resigns, or is removed from office.

Section 2. Replacing the Vice President

The President is to appoint a new Vice President in case of a vacancy in that office, with the approval of the Congress.

The 25th Amendment is unusually precise and explicit because it was intended to solve a serious constitutional problem. Sixteen times in American history, before passage of this amendment, the office of Vice President was vacant, but fortunately in none of these cases did the President die or resign.

This amendment was used in 1973, when Vice President Spiro Agnew resigned from office after being charged with accepting bribes. President Nixon then appointed Gerald R. Ford as Vice President in accordance with the provisions of the 25th Amendment. A year later, President Richard Nixon resigned during the Watergate scandal, and Ford became President. President Ford then had to fill the Vice Presidency, which he had left vacant upon assuming the Presidency. He named Nelson A. Rockefeller as Vice President. Thus both the presidency and vice-presidency were held by men who had not been elected to their offices.

Amendment XXII

SECTION 1

No person shall be elected to the office of the President more than twice, and no person who had held the office of President, or acted as President, for more than two years of a term to which some other person was elected President shall be elected to the office of the President more than once.

But this Article shall not apply to any person holding the office of President when this Article was proposed by the Congress, and shall not prevent any person who may be holding the office of President, or acting as President, during the term within which this Article becomes operative from holding the office of President or acting as President during the remainder of such term.

SECTION 2

This article shall be inoperative unless it shall have been ratified as an amendment to the Constitution by the legislatures of three-fourths of the several States within seven years from the date of its submission to the States by the Congress.

Amendment XXIII

SECTION 1

The District constituting the seat of Government of the United States shall appoint in such manner as the Congress may direct:

A number of electors of President and Vice President equal to the whole number of Senators and Representatives in Congress to which the District would be entitled if it were a State, but in no event more than the least populous State; they shall be in addition to those appointed by the States, but they shall be considered, for the purposes of the election of President and Vice President, to be electors appointed by a State; and they shall meet in the District and perform such duties as provided by the twelfth article of amendment.

SECTION 2

The Congress shall have power to enforce this article by appropriate legislation.

Amendment XXIV

SECTION 1

The right of citizens of the United States to vote in any primary or other election for President or Vice President, for electors for President or Vice President, or for Senator or Representative in Congress, shall not be denied or abridged by the United States or any State by reason of failure to pay any poll tax or other tax.

SECTION 2

The Congress shall have power to enforce this article by appropriate legislation.

Amendment XXV

SECTION 1

In case of the removal of the President from office or his death or resignation, the Vice President shall become President.

SECTION 2

Whenever there is a vacancy in the office of the Vice President, the President shall nominate a Vice President who shall take the office upon confirmation by a majority vote of both houses of Congress.

SECTION 3

Whenever the President transmits to the President pro tempore of the Senate and the Speaker of the House of Representatives his written declaration that he is unable to discharge the powers and duties of his office, and until he transmits to them a written declaration to the contrary, such powers and duties shall be discharged by the Vice President as Acting President.

SECTION 4

Whenever the Vice President and a majority of either the principal officers of the executive departments or of such other body as Congress may by law provide, transmit to the President pro tempore of the Senate and the Speaker of the House of Representatives their written declaration that the President is unable to discharge the powers and duties of his office, the Vice President shall immediately assume the power and duties of the office of Acting President.

Thereafter, when the President transmits to the President pro tempore of the Senate and the Speaker of the House of Representatives his written declaration that no inability exists, he shall resume the powers and duties of his office unless the Vice President and a majority of either the principal officers of the executive departments or of such other body as Congress may by law provide, transmit within four days to the President pro tempore of the Senate and the Speaker of the House of Representatives their written declaration that the President is unable to discharge the powers and duties of his office. Thereupon Congress shall decide the issue, assembling within forty-eight hours for that purpose if not in session. If the Congress within twenty-one days after receipt of the latter written declaration, or, if Congress is not in session, within twenty-one days after Congress is required to assemble, determines by two-thirds vote of both houses that the President is unable to discharge the powers and duties of his office, the Vice President shall continue to discharge the same as Acting President; otherwise, the President shall resume the power and duties of his office.

Amendment XXVI

SECTION 1

The right of citizens of the United States, who are eighteen years of age or older, to vote shall not be denied or abridged by the United States or by any State on account of age.

SECTION 2

The Congress shall have power to enforce this article by appropriate legislation.

Amendment XXVII

No law, varying the compensation for the services of Senators and Representatives, shall take effect, until an election of Representatives shall have intervened.

Section 3. Replacing the President With Consent

If the President informs Congress, in writing, that he or she cannot carry out the duties of the office of President, the Vice President becomes Acting President.

Section 4. Replacing the President Without Consent

If the President is unable to carry out the duties of the office but is unable or unwilling to so notify Congress, the Cabinet and the Vice President are to inform Congress of this fact. The Vice President then becomes Acting President. The procedure by which the President may regain the office if he or she recovers is also spelled out in this amendment.

Amendment 26. Eighteen-Year-Old Vote (1971)

This amendment made 18-year-olds eligible to vote in all federal, state, and local elections. Until then, the minimum age had been 21 in most states.

Amendment 27. Restraint on Congressional Salaries (1992)

Any increase in the salaries of members of Congress will take effect in the subsequent session of Congress.

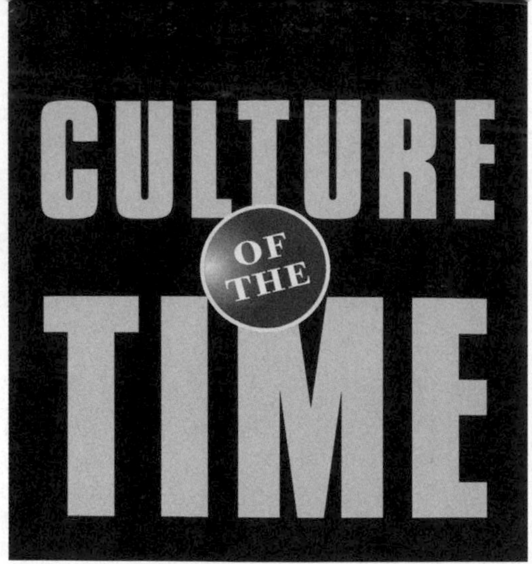

The Colonial Period

Immigrants brought European customs with them to the colonies. Familiar clothing styles, religious beliefs, amusements, and cookery helped settlers feel at home.

COURTESY, AMERICAN ANTIQUARIAN SOCIETY

KEEPING THE FAITH

Most newcomers to the colonies practiced Christianity. **Spiritual songs and writings** helped settlers keep their faith in spite of the challenges that faced them in this new land.

LUXURY GOODS

Throughout the period, wealthier colonists bought **imported European goods,** such as this elaborately dressed doll, and the fine items of clothing shown at bottom right.

COURTESY OF THE WENHAM MUSEUM, WENHAM, MA

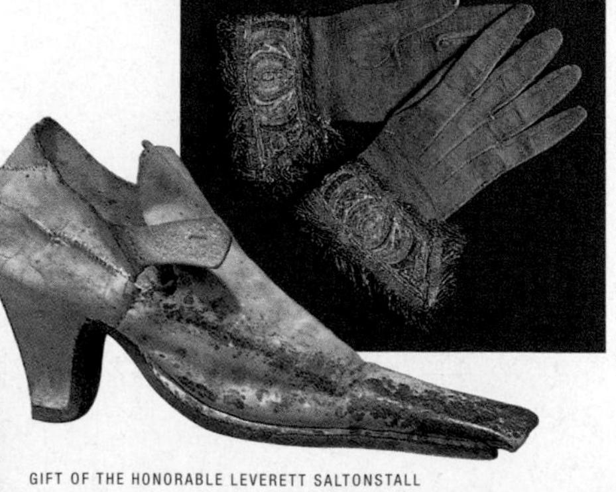

COURTESY PEABODY ESSEX MUSEUM, SALEM, MASS.

GIFT OF THE HONORABLE LEVERETT SALTONSTALL
COURTESY, MUSEUM OF FINE ARTS, BOSTON

COLONIAL CLOTHING

This colonial couple is dressed in clothing typical of the English middle class in the 1620s. Men's full baggy breeches were called **"slops."** Styles, of course, varied from region to region.

COURTESY OF PLIMOTH PLANTATION

GUILFORD COURTHOUSE NATIONAL MILITARY PARK

MAKING MUSIC

Craftspeople made instruments by hand, such as this painted **war drum.** Colonists played traditional European music and composed and played new music of their own.

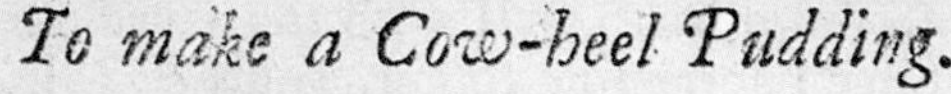

To make a Cow-heel Pudding.

TAKE a large Cow-heel, and cut off all the Meat but the black Toes; put them away, but mince the reſt very ſmall, and ſhred it over again, with three Quarters of a Pound of Beef-ſuet; put to it a Penny Loaf grated, Cloves, Mace, Nutmeg, Sugar, and a little Salt, ſome Sack, and Roſe-water; mix theſe well together with ſix raw Eggs well beaten; butter a Cloth and put it in, and boil it two Hours. For Sauce, melt Butter, Sack, and Sugar.
To

COURTESY, AMERICAN ANTIQUARIAN SOCIETY

HOME ECONOMICS

Colonial cooks adapted to scarcity when necessary. This recipe for **cow-heel pudding** shows one way colonists economized.

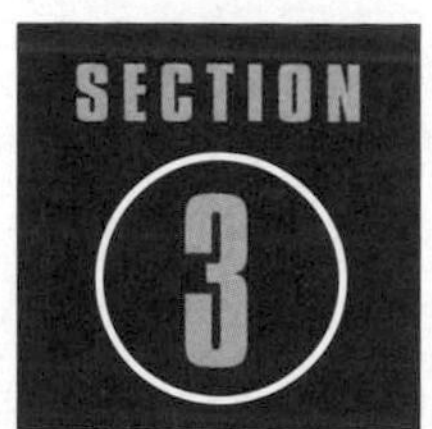

Launching the New Government

MARCH 4, 1801: A NEW PRESIDENT IN A NEW CAPITAL

JUST BEFORE NOON ON MARCH 4, 1801, THOMAS JEFFERSON LEFT HIS BOARDINGHOUSE AND WALKED THROUGH THE DUSTY STREETS OF WASHINGTON, D.C. As he stepped up the hill toward the unfinished Capitol building, one observer noted that his clothing was "usual, that of a plain citizen, without any distinctive badge of office." Yet that day Jefferson assumed the highest office in the nation: he became the third President of the United States.

Jefferson faced a number of firsts that day. He became the first President to be sworn into office in the nation's new capital city. He also became the first Chief Executive to succeed a political opponent in office. Jefferson had served as Vice President under President John Adams, but by the time of the election the two men headed conflicting political parties: Adams led the Federalists, and Jefferson led the Democratic-Republicans.

NATIONAL PORTRAIT GALLERY, SMITHSONIAN INSTITUTION/ART RESOURCE

A President for the Common Man
Thomas Jefferson believed strongly in the people's right to self-government and civil liberties.

When Jefferson won the presidential election, Americans feared that the transition from one political party to another might result in violence. Many Federalists worried that Jefferson would punish them as political enemies.

In his Inaugural Address, however, Jefferson asked all American people to "unite for the common good." "Every difference of opinion," he explained, "is not a difference of principle. We have called by different names brethren of the same principles. We are all Republicans—we are all Federalists."

GUIDE TO READING

Main Idea

The generation of leaders that launched the new government established new political precedents as it struggled to resolve challenges both at home and abroad.

Vocabulary

- cabinet
- national debt
- speculator
- neutral
- impressed
- embargo

Read to Find Out . . .

- how federal power was used in the 1790s.
- the conflicts between the Federalists and Democratic-Republican political parties.
- the role the Marshall court played in shaping the government.

After Jefferson's speech, many Americans breathed a sigh of relief. Yet their fears had been real. The struggles between the two parties threatened the stability of the nation. Even more disturbing, this political conflict had arisen in such a short time.

Washington and the Government

Stabilizing Economic Conditions

Just 12 years earlier, in 1789, George Washington took the same oath after being unanimously elected President. While bonfires and parties marked the people's excitement, Washington himself had grave concerns. "I walk on untrodden ground," he said. As the first President, Washington had no examples to follow. Every move he made set a precedent. He also knew the nation faced dire problems.

Congress created several departments to help the President run the country. The heads of those departments made up the President's **cabinet,** or official advisers. Among others in his cabinet, Washington appointed fellow Virginian Thomas Jefferson as secretary of state, in charge of relations with foreign countries. He named 34-year-old Alexander Hamilton of New York as secretary of the treasury.

The brilliant and handsome Hamilton had served as Washington's assistant during the Revolution, and the two men remained close friends after the war. Both served at the Constitutional Convention, and both fought for ratification. Hamilton felt, however, that the Constitution fell short of providing the type of government the United States needed.

As head of the Treasury Department, Hamilton hoped to increase the powers of the United States government. Under his guidance, he said, the government would work closely with "the rich, the well-born, and the good" to create wealth and stability in the young nation. Starting in 1790 he proposed a series of plans that helped to make this vision a reality.

Hamilton's Plans

The **national debt,** money owed from the American Revolution, remained the country's most serious economic problem. The United States government owed about $12 million to European countries and investors and about $40 million to American citizens. In addition the state governments had war debts of nearly $21 million. Most of these debts took the form of bonds that the government had sold to investors to pay for the costs of the war. Like Continental currency, bonds were worth a fraction of their face value in 1790 because people doubted that bondholders would ever be paid. Hamilton worried that if the United States could not make good on its own bonds, it would never establish credit—or credibility—with other nations or with its own citizens.

In 1790 Hamilton proposed to Congress that the government should pay off its bonds at full value and assume the debts of all the states as well. Congress agreed that foreign debts should be paid, but a storm of controversy arose over the rest of Hamilton's plan.

Some members of Congress argued that paying off domestic bonds at full value was unfair. The people who originally bought the bonds had given up hope of ever collecting on them. Many of them—mostly farmers and others who lacked cash—had sold their bonds at a discount to **speculators,** people who bought the bonds in the hopes that their value would go up again. Under the plan, wealthy speculators, not the common people who originally bought the bonds, would benefit. Hamilton believed that wealthy people were the key to the nation's economic development.

Other members of Congress complained about paying off the states' debts. Some Southern states had already paid their debts, while most New England states had not. Hamilton's plan favored the North, where most speculators lived. Southerners did not want to pay other states' debts after they had paid off their own.

ALL PHOTOS, COURTESY OF NATIONAL NUMISMATIC COLLECTION, SMITHSONIAN INSTITUTION

Money Problems "Not worth a Continental" became a popular saying after the war. *Why were Continental currency and bonds of little value to investors in 1790?*

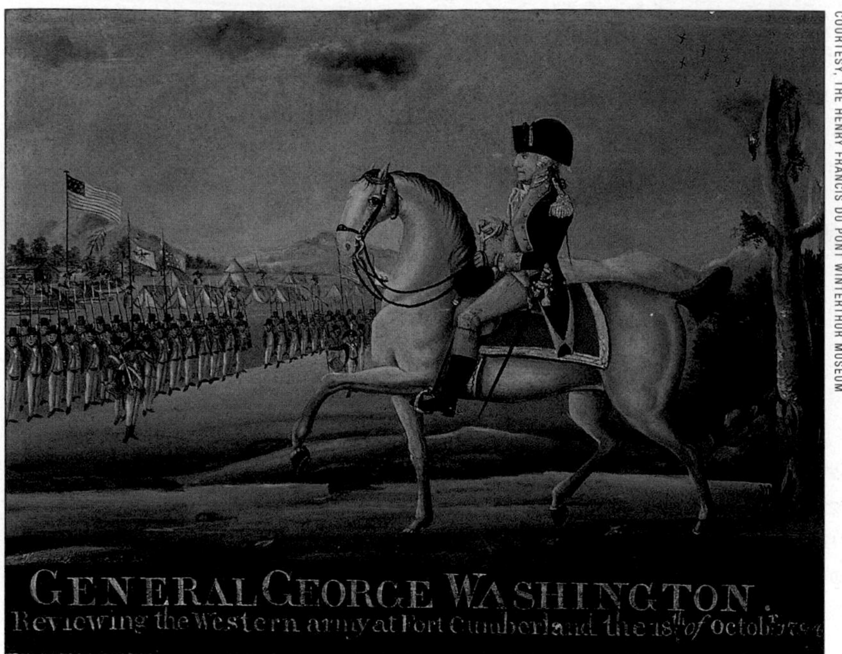

COURTESY, THE HENRY FRANCIS DU PONT WINTERTHUR MUSEUM

Quelling the Whiskey Rebellion In 1794 President Washington reviews federal troops at Fort Cumberland in Maryland. The Maryland militia was called in to help end the Whiskey Rebellion. *Why were the farmers so opposed to the tax on their whiskey?*

Hamilton brushed these criticisms aside. His intentions were to favor the commercial North over the agricultural South, and he hoped to ally the government with the wealthy men who had speculated in bonds. To get Congress to pass the plan, he struck a deal with Southern leaders. According to that deal, Southerners agreed to support Hamilton's debt plan, while Hamilton and other Northerners agreed to locate the proposed "federal city" near Virginia, away from Northern influence.

Hamilton then proposed the creation of a national bank. As a major stockholder, the government would have much influence on the operations of the Bank of the United States, as it would be called, but private citizens would own most of its stock. The bank would issue money, regulate the nation's financial affairs, and loan money to American citizens.

Before signing the bank bill into law, Washington asked the members of his cabinet to give him a written opinion of the plan. Jefferson argued that the plan was illegal; the Constitution said nothing about the government having the power to create a bank. Hamilton argued that, in addition to powers spelled out, the Constitution gave the government "implied" powers to do anything "necessary and proper" to carry out its responsibilities. The Bank, he said, was necessary for the government to regulate the economy. Washington carefully considered both Jefferson's strict reading of the Constitution and Hamilton's loose interpretation. Though not entirely convinced by Hamilton's argument, Washington sided with Hamilton and signed the bill in early 1791.

Whiskey and Taxes

Later that year Hamilton proposed a tax on distilled liquor. This tax would increase revenue and test the government's ability to tax—one of its most important powers, Hamilton thought.

The liquor tax aroused strong opposition from farmers in the hills of western Pennsylvania. Most backcountry farmers made whiskey to sell in the eastern part of the state. This had always been the best way to transport processed corn, and whiskey proved to be a reliable source of extra cash. Hamilton's tax threatened to make this practice unprofitable.

For these farmers the liquor tax brought back memories of the days before the American Revolution. At first the farmers simply refused to pay. Then they began to tar and feather tax collectors. Finally, in July 1794, 500 armed men surrounded the home of a local tax collector and demanded that he resign. When the farmers discovered soldiers in the house, they opened fire. In the violence that followed, several men were wounded, and the tax collector's house was destroyed.

When the farmers ignored several orders to obey the law and pay their taxes, Washington and Hamilton reacted vigorously. In the fall of 1794, Henry Lee, accompanied by Hamilton, led a federal army to put down the rebels and demonstrate the power of the federal government. Threatened with this force, the "whiskey boys" dispersed and the Whiskey Rebellion ended. Two of the farmers were later convicted of treason, but Washington pardoned them both.

Conflicts at Home and Abroad

Party Politics and Foreign Policy

The Whiskey Rebellion confirmed Hamilton's worst fears about the common people—"that great beast," as he called them collectively. "How can you trust people who own no property?" he asked. The army had been needed, Hamilton argued, to enforce the laws of the land and put down a dangerous rebellion.

Thomas Jefferson, however, believed that "such an armament against people at their ploughs" had shown unnecessary force. The differences between Hamilton and Jefferson went beyond the Whiskey Rebellion, however. The two men had very different ideas of what the United States should be.

Hamilton envisioned a nation with bustling cities, churning factories, big banks, and a powerful government. He found backers for his plans and ideas in large Northern cities and New England—places where trade and manufacturing thrived.

The freedom of the common people thrived in Thomas Jefferson's America. "I know of no safe depository," Jefferson wrote, "of the ultimate powers of the society but the people themselves." Democracy worked best, he believed, in a society of small farmers, living in quiet, rural areas. Jefferson found support on plantations in the South, farms in the Middle Atlantic states, and farms on the Western frontier.

The people that these men attracted formed America's first political parties, groups that promoted ideas and supported candidates. As Hamilton and his Federalists continued to appeal to people with commercial interests, support for Jefferson and the Democratic-Republicans grew among common people. The parties not only differed on domestic issues; their conflicts over foreign policy nearly split the nation in the 1790s.

EDWARD S. ELLIS, YOUTH'S HISTORY OF THE U.S., NY, 1887

Citizen Reaction Angry Americans burn an effigy of John Jay upon his return from treaty negotiations in Britain. *Why were Americans so upset by the terms of the Jay Treaty?*

France and Britain

In 1789 revolution erupted in France. What began as an effort to reform a corrupt monarchy turned into a violent, bloody battle that completely upset French society. Fearing the spread of revolt against monarchy and aristocracy, other nations, including Britain, declared war on France.

Jefferson, formerly the United States minister to France, supported the French. He and other Republicans believed the French Revolution continued the struggle for liberty that America had begun. They also remembered France's support during the American Revolution and argued that the alliance between the two countries remain intact. To Federalists like Hamilton and Vice President Adams, the French Revolution showed the destructiveness of the common people. They sided with the British, admired the stability of the British government, and believed that America's economic livelihood depended on close ties with Britain.

Despite mounting pressure to enter the war on one side or the other, Washington chose to keep the United States **neutral,** or not allied with any side. Washington's decision did nothing to calm tensions in the United States or on the Atlantic Ocean. Both French and British ships seized American merchant vessels bound for Europe, and American trade suffered. The British navy **impressed,** or forced into service, American sailors (and British deserters) and forced them to serve on British ships. In addition the British had not removed all of their troops from forts in the western United States after the American Revolution. In 1794 war between the United States and either France or Britain seemed likely.

Fearing Britain's military power, Washington sent John Jay, a Federalist, to London to negotiate a treaty. When Jay returned home in 1795, however, it became clear that the new treaty was not very successful. The British agreed to remove their troops from the western United States, but not until 1796. To get this, Jay gave up American rights to ship cotton and sugar to British colonies. In addition he resolved nothing about the impressment of American sailors. The treaty seemed to please no one but those Federalists who wanted to maintain good relations with Britain at all costs. Democratic-Republicans called the Jay Treaty "the death warrant of American liberty."

The Beginnings of Party Rivalries

The political harmony of Washington's early years in office had long since disappeared, and Washington decided to leave office in 1797. In his Farewell Address, he urged the new nation to avoid conflicts with foreign nations and warned about the dangers of political parties.

In 1797 President John Adams ignored Washington's plea and sent 3 Americans to secure a treaty with France. In Paris the French foreign minister demanded a bribe of $240,000 from the Americans and hinted that if they refused to pay it France would declare war on the United States. This threat allowed Adams to sway American public opinion away from the French and the Democratic-Republicans.

The Alien and Sedition Acts

Adams called for the formation of an army to defend against the expected French invasion in 1798; he also signed the Alien Act, giving him the power to expel any aliens, or foreign-born residents of the United States, who were "dangerous to the peace and safety of the United States."

Another law signed by Adams during the crisis—the Sedition Act—was aimed directly at the Democratic-Republicans themselves. This law made it a crime for anyone to "write, print, utter, or publish . . . any false, scandalous, and malicious writing" about the President or the government. As a result, about 10 Democratic-Republican editors, printers, and politicians were jailed.

The Alien and Sedition acts proved very unpopular, and public opinion turned against the President and the Federalists. When peaceful relations with France were restored in 1800, it appeared that the Federalists had manufactured the entire crisis. As a result, Adams and his party were in chaos as the presidential election of 1800 approached. Jefferson and his party were ready to challenge them.

ARCHIVE PHOTOS

Tie Vote The Twelfth Amendment, establishing separate balloting for President and Vice President, was ratified in 1804 in response to a tie between Jefferson and Aaron Burr (above) in the election of 1800. *Why were the Federalists in turmoil before the election?*

The Election of 1800

In 1800 the American people witnessed a hard-fought and noisy presidential campaign. Democratic-Republicans spread rumors that President Adams would soon name himself "King of America." New England Federalists whispered that Jefferson planned to burn every Bible in the nation. The final count of votes was close, but Jefferson won.

Jefferson chose to let the nation heal rather than churn up old political conflicts. He quietly stopped enforcing the Alien and Sedition acts and allowed them to expire. He reduced military spending. He even allowed the Bank of the United States to continue to exist.

John Marshall and Judicial Power

Strengthening the Supreme Court

After losing the election, John Adams sought ways to make Federalist ideas continue in a government dominated by Democratic-Republicans. He found his solution in the judiciary.

Packing the Courts

In the winter before their terms ran out, Adams and the Federalist Congress worked together to pass the Judiciary Act of 1801. This law added 21 positions to the roster of federal judges. Adams named Federalists to these positions. Adams also named John Marshall, a strong Federalist, chief justice of the United States.

Adams signed the appointments of the new Federalist judges the night before Jefferson's inauguration, leaving several of the appointments to be delivered by the new administration. Yet Jefferson's secretary of state, James Madison, refused to do this. When a Federalist named William Marbury did not receive his expected appointment, he appealed to the Supreme Court.

John Marshall found himself in a difficult position. As a Federalist, he would have liked to order Jefferson to make Marbury a federal judge. If he did, however, Jefferson and Madison would probably ignore the order, reducing the authority of the Supreme Court. Yet Marshall could not give in.

Marshall's Solution

Marshall's solution bypassed short-term gains for the Federalists, but it had long-term national effects. In 1803 he ruled that Marbury was entitled to his appointment and that Madison had violated the law in not delivering it. Marshall ruled, however, that the Court could not require delivery of the appointment because a part of the law giving the Court that right—the Judiciary Act of 1789—was unconstitutional, or violated the Constitution. Marshall had established the right of the Supreme Court to judge an act of Congress illegal. It is "the duty of the judicial department to say what the law is," he wrote. "A law repugnant to the Constitution is void."

What began as a petty political fight ended by strengthening the Supreme Court. John Marshall served as chief justice for 34 years, and during that time he consistently supported the Federalist program of a strong federal government. In this way, Marshall remained the chief adversary of Democratic-Republican Presidents for the next 16 years and helped Federalist policy endure long after the party ceased to exist.

Foreign Policy

The War of 1812: Another War With Britain

Along with the Federalist judiciary, conflicts with European nations troubled Thomas Jefferson's presidency. France and Britain continued to victimize the United States. Navies of the 2 nations seized nearly 1,500 American merchant ships. By 1807 the British had captured as many as 10,000 American sailors. The British fired on the American frigate *Chesapeake,* killing 3 Americans and wounding 18. Across the nation, Americans called for action against the British.

The Embargo Act

Jefferson did not believe that the United States could fight a war against Britain. He also remembered the trouble that foreign conflicts had caused during the 1790s, and he hoped to avoid such conflicts now.

Still, Jefferson knew that something had to be done. He believed that the European powers needed American food and materials. So in 1807 Jefferson signed the Embargo Act. The **embargo** stopped the export of all American goods and forbade American ships from sailing for foreign ports.

Jefferson thought that by depriving European countries of American products they would stop harassing the young nation. He was wrong. The Embargo Act had almost no effect on Britain and France. Instead, it proved to be a disaster for the United States, especially in the trading centers of New England. Depression and unemployment swept the country. Americans from South Carolina to New Hampshire openly defied the law.

Jefferson left office after 2 terms in 1809, but not before he convinced Congress to repeal the Embargo Act. James Madison won the presidency easily, but opposition to timid Democratic-Republican policies against the British grew. By 1811 a new breed of politician had swept into Congress.

The War Hawks

These politicians came from the West and were the first generation of politicians to come of age after the Revolution. They earned the name "war hawks" for their calls for action against the British.

The British had heaped one insult after another on the American people, the war hawks charged. They impressed American sailors, attacked American ships, and stirred up trouble between settlers and Native Americans. To Westerners accustomed to action, the economic warfare of Jefferson and Madison seemed pathetic. "Is the rod of British power to be forever suspended over our heads?" asked war hawk Henry Clay of Kentucky.

Madison recognized the growing power of these new politicians, and in 1812 he made a deal with them. If they supported him for reelection as President, he would ask for a declaration of war. The war hawks agreed, and by the summer of 1812 the United States and Britain were locked in combat.

COURTESY U.S. NAVAL ACADEMY MUSEUM

A British Defeat at Sea **This painting shows the frigate *USS Constitution,* nicknamed "Old Ironsides," defeating the British warship *Guerrière* in the War of 1812.**
What actions by the British led to war?

ANNE S.K. BROWN MILITARY COLLECTION, BROWN UNIVERSITY LIBRARY

Flames in Washington **This British cartoon shows President Madison fleeing the burning capital during the British attack on Washington in 1814.** *Why was the War of 1812 so significant for the United States?*

American goals in the war were unclear. The war hawks had boasted of conquering Canada and Florida, but these plans were squelched when the British invaded the United States. Each side scored victories in battles around the Great Lakes, near Washington, D.C., and on the Atlantic Ocean. By the end of 1814, British leaders, more concerned with European matters, offered to make peace. The treaty, ratified in 1815, resolved few of the problems. It simply ended the fighting and restored everything to what it had been before the war.

Although no one had won, the War of 1812 became an important event for the young nation. The war hawks hailed it as the "Second War for Independence." United States victories stimulated national pride and confidence. The war, which had been urged by Western politicians, also created a new Western hero: General Andrew Jackson of Tennessee, who scored a sensational victory near New Orleans. The War of 1812 also marked the end of United States involvement with European conflicts for more than a century.

After the war Americans looked eastward to Europe less and looked westward across their own continent more. At last the United States put its colonial past behind it and headed toward its future as a nation of lush prairies, growing cities, and a restless, changing people.

Section Assessment

Main Idea

1. Use a diagram like this one to show foreign and domestic challenges faced by leaders who put the Constitution into effect.

Vocabulary

2. Define: cabinet, national debt, speculator, neutral, impressed, embargo.

Checking Facts

3. How did Alexander Hamilton increase the powers of the federal government?

4. What were the main conflicts between the Federalists and the Democratic-Republicans?

Critical Thinking

5. **Demonstrating Reasoned Judgment** How did John Marshall's actions shape the role of the Supreme Court?

Critical Thinking Skill

ANALYZING INFORMATION

Learning the Skill

The newly independent Americans had to vote to ratify the laws under which they would live. They had to analyze information in order to decide how to vote. Analyzing information involves breaking it into meaningful parts so that it can be understood. Subsequently the reader or listener is able to form an opinion about it.

The ability to analyze information is important in deciding your position on a subject that could affect your life. You need to analyze a political document to determine if you should support it. You would analyze a candidate's position statements to determine if you should vote for him or her. You would analyze an article or editorial to arrive at your own opinion of it.

Analyzing Information

To analyze information, use the following steps:

a. Identify the topic that is being discussed.

b. Examine how the information is organized. What are the main points?

c. Summarize the information in your own words, and then make a statement of your own based on your understanding and what you already know.

Read the following passage from Article II, Section 1, of the Constitution of the United States.

No person except a natural-born citizen, or a citizen of the United States, at the time of the adoption of this Constitution, shall be eligible to the office of President; neither shall any person be eligible to that office who shall not have attained to the age of thirty-five years, and been fourteen years a resident within the United States.

The first step is to determine the general topic. This passage is about the qualifications for the President of the United States. Next, identify the three main points: the President must be a citizen of the United States by birth, must be at least thirty-five years old, and must have lived here for at least fourteen years. Then give a brief summary, such as: "People who want to become President must fulfill these three requirements." Finally, make a statement of your own, such as: "These requirements restrict the presidency to people who have a reasonable amount of life experience and keep from power people who were not born in the United States or who have not lived here very long."

ARTICLE II.—Sec. 1.—The power of this government shall be divided into three distinct departments; the Legislative, the Executive, and Judicial. . . .

ARTICLE III.—Sec. 1.—The Legislative power shall be vested in two distinct branches; a Committee and a Council, each to have a negative on the other, and both to be styled the General Council of the Cherokee Nation. . . .

ARTICLE IV.—Sec. 1.—The Supreme Executive Power of this Nation shall be vested in a Principal Chief, who shall be chosen by the General Council and shall hold his office four years. . . .

ARTICLE V.—Sec. 1.—The Judicial Powers shall be vested in a Supreme Court, and such Circuit and Inferior Courts as the General Council may from time to time ordain and establish. . . .

Constitution of the Cherokee Nation In 1827 elected delegates of the Cherokee Nation met to establish their own constitution. *How do these excerpts compare with related passages in the Constitution of the United States?*

Practicing the Skill

Read the excerpts above and practice analyzing information by answering these questions.

1. What is the subject of the document?

2. What are the most important points?

3. What do you notice about the organization of the document?

4. What does it mean that the Committee and the Council "each to have a negative on the other"? How is this similar to the "checks and balances" of the United States Constitution?

5. Summarize the passage in your own words, and make a statement of your own regarding it.

Applying the Skill

Find a short, informative piece, such as an editorial in a newspaper or an explanation of a new law. Analyze the information and make a statement of your own.

The **Glencoe Skillbuilder Interactive Workbook, Level 2** CD-ROM provides more practice in key social studies skills.

Chapter  Assessment

Self-Check Quiz

Visit the *American Odyssey* Web site at americanodyssey.glencoe.com and click on ***Chapter 4—Self-Check Quiz*** to prepare for the Chapter Test.

Reviewing Key Terms

Choose the vocabulary term that best completes the sentences below. Write your answers on a separate sheet of paper.

amendments	**embargo**
cabinet	**representation**
ratify	**impressed**

1. The smaller states demanded equal _________.

2. Ten _________, known as the Bill of Rights, were added to the Constitution.

3. American sailors were forcibly _________ into the British navy.

4. The President's _________ consists of department heads who serve as official advisers.

5. The state representatives urged the voters to _________ the Constitution.

Recalling Facts

1. What were the Articles of Confederation? Why were some states reluctant to accept them?

2. What limits on slavery were included in the Northwest Ordinance?

3. What was the difference between hard money and paper money? Which type of money did the Confederation Congress use? Why?

4. Why did the Constitution include a system of checks and balances for the new government?

5. What type of government did the Federalists support?

6. Why did the Anti-Federalists oppose the Constitution?

7. Identify at least five rights guaranteed by the Bill of Rights. What rights were not guaranteed by the Bill of Rights?

8. Why did Alexander Hamilton feel a national bank was necessary?

9. Who was John Marshall, and what effect did he have on the federal government?

Critical Thinking

1. Identifying Assumptions Were Daniel Shays and the farmers who followed him justified in going outside the law to address their grievances? Explain.

2. Drawing Conclusions Under the Alien and Sedition acts, was jailing people for publicly criticizing Federalist policies a violation of the First Amendment, or was it justified by the ongoing crises? Explain.

3. Making Comparisons Use a diagram like this one to compare the Articles of Confederation with the Constitution.

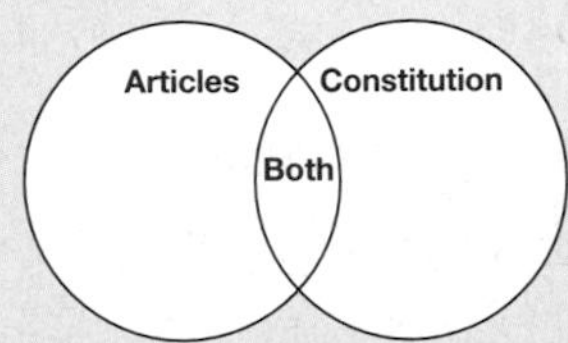

Standardized Test Practice

1. The Great Compromise was primarily a compromise between

A large states and small states.
B Federalists and Anti-Federalists.
C slave states and non-slave states.
D Northern states and Southern states.

Test-Taking Tip: Always read the question and all the answers carefully. Make sure you don't confuse the Great Compromise with the so-called "three-fifths compromise," which concerned the issue of slavery and the balance of power between Northern and Southern states.

2. Why did some revolutionary "patriots" such as Samuel Adams and Patrick Henry oppose the Constitution?

A They feared a strong central government.
B They did not favor the idea of a Bill of Rights.
C They felt the powers of the President were too weak.
D They believed the common people had too much say in government.

Test-Taking Tip: Look for key words in the question. The American Revolution was based on the concept of individual liberty. Therefore, it would be illogical for "patriots" to oppose the idea of a Bill of Rights (answer B). It would also be illogical to assume that "patriots" would trust a king-like President (answer C).

GEOGRAPHY AND HISTORY

The United States, 1812

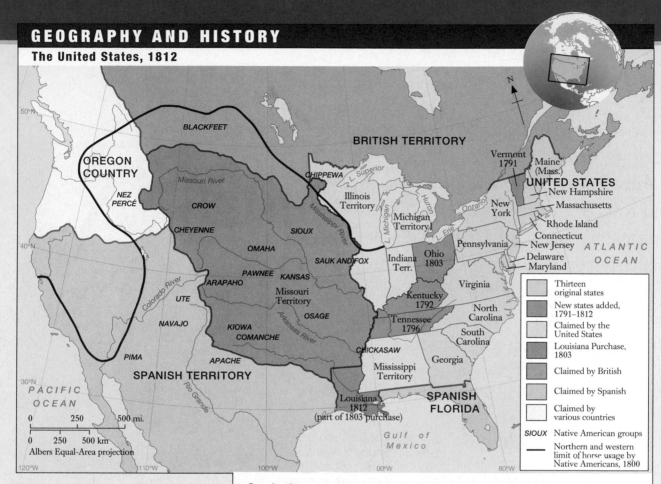

BRITISH TERRITORY
OREGON COUNTRY
SPANISH TERRITORY
SPANISH FLORIDA
UNITED STATES
PACIFIC OCEAN
ATLANTIC OCEAN
Gulf of Mexico
Missouri Territory
Illinois Territory
Michigan Territory
Indiana Terr.
Mississippi Territory
Ohio 1803
Kentucky 1792
Tennessee 1796
Vermont 1791
Louisiana 1812 (part of 1803 purchase)
Maine (Mass.)
New Hampshire
Massachusetts
Rhode Island
Connecticut
New York
New Jersey
Pennsylvania
Delaware
Maryland
Virginia
North Carolina
South Carolina
Georgia
BLACKFEET
NEZ PERCÉ
CROW
CHEYENNE
SIOUX
CHIPPEWA
OMAHA
PAWNEE
KANSAS
SAUK AND FOX
ARAPAHO
UTE
NAVAJO
KIOWA
COMANCHE
OSAGE
PIMA
APACHE
CHICKASAW
Missouri River
Mississippi River
Colorado River
Arkansas River
Rio Grande
L. Superior
L. Michigan
L. Huron
L. Erie
L. Ontario
0 250 500 mi.
0 250 500 km
Albers Equal-Area projection

- Thirteen original states
- New states added, 1791–1812
- Claimed by the United States
- Louisiana Purchase, 1803
- Claimed by British
- Claimed by Spanish
- Claimed by various countries
- SIOUX Native American groups
- Northern and western limit of horse usage by Native Americans, 1800

Study the map to answer the following questions:

1. In which direction does the United States seem to be expanding the most? Why do you think this was so?
2. United States territory expanded as a result of the Louisiana Purchase. Why do you think it was advantageous to have a state (Louisiana) in that region?
3. France and the United States negotiated the Louisiana Purchase without consulting the Native Americans who lived west of the Mississippi. How might this have contributed to future conflicts?
4. Consider the order in which the first 18 states were admitted to the union. Which areas are likely to have been next to gain statehood?

Portfolio Project

Prepare a chart that compares the American and French Revolutions. What were the causes of each? How long did each last? What were the results of each? In what ways were they similar? Different? When you are finished, put the chart in your portfolio.

Cooperative Learning

Working with a small group, read the Bill of Rights that was added to the Constitution (pages 91–109). Rewrite the amendments in your own words. Then compare the rewritten amendments with those done by your classmates. How do they differ from the original amendments?

Reinforcing Skills

Analyzing Information Find a copy of the Northwest Ordinance in an encyclopedia or history book. Read the slavery clause and analyze its importance to African Americans.

Technology Activity

Using a Word Processor On a word processor write an essay explaining how the Bill of Rights plays an important role in your life. Provide everyday examples from your community that show the freedoms guaranteed in the Bill of Rights in action.

Then...

Conestoga Wagon

By the mid-1700s, sturdy Conestoga wagons, called "Ships of the Inland Commerce," transported settlers and tons of their freight over the Appalachian Mountains. As people pushed even farther westward, the characteristic outline of the Conestoga was seen rolling across the plains toward Oregon and finally to California.

2 The boat-shaped wagon's high front and back kept goods from falling out on steep mountain trails.

1 Six to eight draft horses or a dozen oxen pulled the wagon. The driver rode or walked beside the animals.

NORTH WIND PICTURE ARCHIVES

Fun Facts

CRACKING THE WHIP

Wielding whips equipped with noisemaking "crackers" at the tips, drivers frequently had to snap them within inches of the ears of mules to keep the animals moving on the long treks over difficult terrain.

ALL PHOTOS, COURTESY THE LANDIS VALLEY MUSEUM, PHOTOS BY CARL SOCOLOW

3 **A high, white cloth cover stretched over hoops, or wagon bows, gave passengers protection from heat, rain, and snow.**

4 **A toolbox attached to the side of the wagon held spare parts for needed repairs.**

5 **Broad wheels helped keep the heavy wagon from being mired in the mud.**

Stats

WAGON NUMBERS

- Average wagon box: 21 feet long, 11 feet high, 4 feet in width and depth
- Average wagon weight: 1.5 to 2 tons (3,000 to 4,000 pounds)
- Wagon capacity: up to 6 tons (12,000 pounds) of cargo

COSTLY TRANSPORT

In the 1800s:

A team of horses: Approximately	$1,000
Construction of a wagon:	$250
Total:	**$1,250**

A TRANSPORTATION REPORT

PORTFOLIO PROJECT

Create a report about the length of Conestoga wagon journeys and how far they could typically travel in a day. Include a list of items that the settlers may have loaded for their trip. Then compare the modes of transportation available today, gathering statistics about how long a specific Conestoga trail would take by automobile or airplane.

THE "CONESTOGA STOGIE"

The wagons were named after the place where they were first built in the 1700s—the Conestoga Creek region of Lancaster, Pennsylvania. The word *stogie* derived from the cigars smoked by Conestoga wagon drivers.

Rift and Reunion

1800–1900

HISTORY & YOU

Westward expansion forced the nation to confront the divisive issues of states rights and the expansion of slavery. Compromise at first seemed to work in holding the nation together. However, the polarization of pro-slavery interests and abolitionists and the election of an anti-slavery President in 1860 catapulted the United States into a civil war. As the nation struggled to heal itself, it faced yet other upheavals in the form of rapid industrialization and increased global power.

Historic America Electronic Field Trips

Both before and after the Civil War, Frederick Douglass's outspoken views on the injustices suffered by African Americans made him one of America's greatest civil rights leaders. To learn more about Douglass's contributions to ending slavery and to keeping the issue of civil rights alive during America's new age of industry, view videodisc Chapter 9: *Frederick Douglass's Home* in **Historic America Electronic Field Trips.**

See pages 960–961 for primary source readings that accompany Unit 2.

UNITED STATES

- **1803** Senate approves the Louisiana Purchase.
- **1812** War with Great Britain begins.
- **1825** Erie Canal opens.
- **1836** Battle of the Alamo fought.
- **1838** Cherokee endure the "Trail of Tears."

1800 — 1825

THE WORLD

- **1815** Napoleon loses the Battle of Waterloo.
- **1821** Mexico declares independence from Spain.
- **1825** World's first public railroad opens in Great Britain.
- **1837** Victoria becomes Queen of Great Britain.
- **1848** Nationalist revolutions occur throughout Europe.

A Young Soldier **was painted by Winslow Homer during the Civil War.**

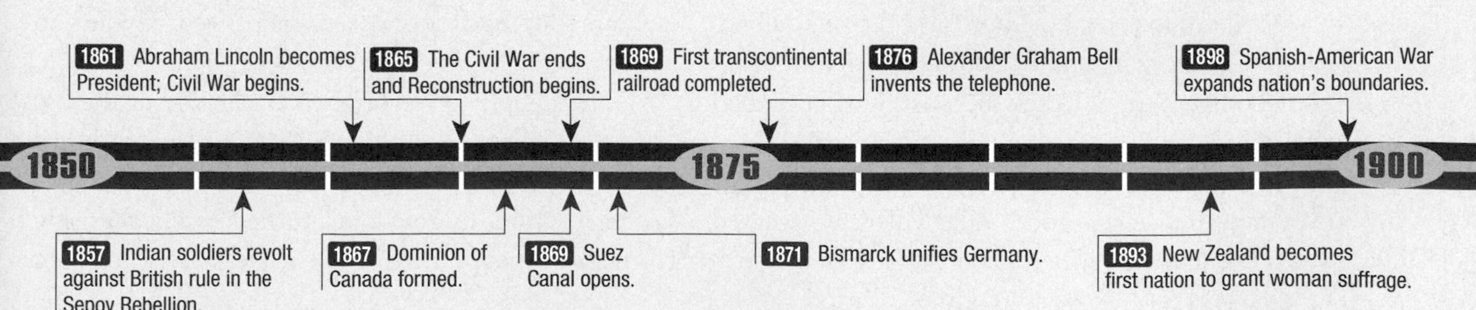
1850
1875
1900
1861 Abraham Lincoln becomes President; Civil War begins.
1865 The Civil War ends and Reconstruction begins.
1869 First transcontinental railroad completed.
1876 Alexander Graham Bell invents the telephone.
1898 Spanish-American War expands nation's boundaries.
1857 Indian soldiers revolt against British rule in the Sepoy Rebellion.
1867 Dominion of Canada formed.
1869 Suez Canal opens.
1871 Bismarck unifies Germany.
1893 New Zealand becomes first nation to grant woman suffrage.

Roots

BY ALEX HALEY

Oral history, folklore, and tradition connect us to the past. In this excerpt from the autobiographical novel Roots, *author Alex Haley learns his family history from a Mandinka griot, an elder who commits events of the past to memory and retells them to new generations.*

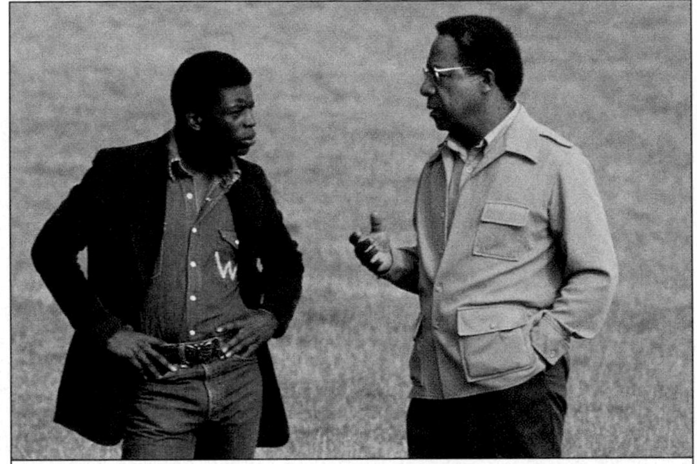

THE KOBAL COLLECTION

Recreating Roots LeVar Burton (left) played Kunta Kinte in the 1977 televised version of the family saga of Alex Haley (right). Nightly audiences of 80 million tuned in to the 8-part show, more than half of all American viewers.

There is an expression called "the peak experience"—that which emotionally, nothing in your life ever transcends. I've had mine, that first day in the back country of black West Africa.

When we got within sight of Juffure, the children who were playing outside gave the alert, and the people came flocking from their huts. It's a village of only about seventy people. Like most back-country villages, it was still very much as it was two hundred years ago, with its circular mud houses and their conical thatched roofs. Among the people as they gathered was a small man wearing an off-white robe, a pillbox hat over an aquiline-featured black face, and about him was an aura of "somebodiness" until I knew he was the man we had come to see and hear.

As the three interpreters left our party to converge upon him, the seventy-odd other villagers gathered closely around me, in a kind of horseshoe pattern, three or four deep all around; had I stuck out my arms, my fingers would have touched the nearest ones on either side. They were all staring at me. The eyes just raked me. . . .

One of my interpreters came up quickly and whispered in my ear, "They stare at you so much because they have never here seen a black American." When I grasped the significance, I believe that hit me harder than what had already happened. They hadn't been looking at me as an individual, but I represented in their eyes a symbol of the twenty-five millions of us black people whom they had never seen, who lived beyond an ocean.

The people were clustered thickly about the old man, all of them intermittently flicking glances toward me as they talked animatedly in their Mandinka tongue. After a while, the old man turned, walked briskly through the people, past my three interpreters, and right up to me. His eyes piercing into mine, seeming to feel I should understand his Mandinka, he expressed what they had all decided they *felt* concerning those unseen millions of us who lived in those places that had been slave ships' destinations—and the translation came: "We have been told by the forefathers that there are many of us from this place who are in exile in that place called America—and in other places."

The old man sat down, facing me, as the people hurriedly gathered behind him. Then he began to recite for me the ancestral history of the Kinte clan, as it had been passed along orally down across centuries from the forefathers' time. It was not merely conversational, but more as if a scroll were being read; for the still, silent villagers, it was clearly a formal occasion. The *griot* would speak, bending forward from the waist, his body rigid, his neck cords standing out, his words seeming almost physical objects. After a sentence or two, seeming to go limp, he would lean back, listening to an interpreter's translation. Spilling from the *griot's* head came an incredibly complex Kinte clan lineage that reached back across many generations. . . . To date things the *griot* linked them to events, such as "—in the year of the big water"—a flood—"he slew a water buffalo." To determine the calendar date, you'd have to find out when that particular flood occurred.

HE HAD JUST ECHOED WHAT I HAD HEARD ALL THROUGH MY BOYHOOD YEARS.

Simplifying to its essence the encyclopedic saga that I was told, the griot said that the Kinte clan had begun in the country called Old Mali. Then the Kinte men traditionally were blacksmiths, "who had conquered fire," and the women mostly were potters and weavers. In time, one branch of the clan moved into the country called Mauretania; and it was from Mauretania that one son of this clan, whose name was Kairaba Kunta Kinte—a *marabout,* or holy man of the Moslem faith—journeyed down into the country called The Gambia. He went first to a village called Pakali N'Ding, stayed there for a while, then went to a village called Jiffarong, and then to the village of Juffure. . . .

[His] youngest son, Omoro, stayed on in Juffure village until he had thirty rains—years—of age, then he took as his wife a Mandinka maiden named Binta Kebba. And by Binta Kebba, roughly between the years 1750 and 1760, Omoro Kinte begat four sons, whose names were, in the order of their birth, Kunta, Lamin, Suwadu, and Madi. . . .

Now after he had just named those four sons, again he appended a detail, and the interpreter translated—"About the time the King's soldiers came"—another of the *griot's* time-fixing references—"the oldest of these four sons, Kunta, went away from his village to chop wood . . . and he was never seen again. . . ." . . .

I sat as if I were carved of stone. My blood seemed to have congealed. This man whose lifetime had been in this back-country African village had no way in the world to know that he had just echoed what I had heard all through my boyhood years on my grandma's front porch in Henning, Tennessee . . . of an African who always had insisted that his name was "Kin-tay"; who had called a guitar a "*ko,*" and a river within the state of Virginia, "Kamby Bolongo"; and who had been kidnaped into slavery while not far from his village, chopping wood, to make himself a drum.

Responding to Literature

1. **Why does the author define listening to the griot as a "peak experience"? Describe a peak experience from your own life.**
2. **The griot relates a detailed history from several centuries ago. What devices does Haley use to recall and retell this history? Compare some of the techniques used in oral history and recorded history.**

The Expanding Nation

OCTOBER 26, 1825: ERIE CANAL OPENS

A large flatboat, the *Seneca Chief,* strung with flowers, led "a grand aquatic procession" through New York Harbor on November 4, 1825. The fleet sailed to a spot near Sandy Hook, New Jersey, where the other boats circled the *Seneca Chief.*

On deck stood DeWitt Clinton, governor of New York. He raised a small wooden keg, pulled the cork, and said: "May the God of the heavens and the earth smile on this work and render it subservient to the best interests of the human race." Then he emptied the keg, which contained water from Lake Erie, into the Atlantic Ocean.

The "Marriage of the Waters" concluded the official ceremonies marking the opening nine days earlier of the Erie Canal, the most important national waterway built in the United States. It stretched from the Hudson River to Lake Erie and connected New York City with the fertile regions to the West.

The building and subsequent success of the Erie Canal changed the way Americans traveled, conducted business, and practiced politics. This vital link between the East Coast and the Western frontier also changed the way many Americans thought about their country. The canal served as a symbol of pride and economic determination. ■

Write about some of the ways in which the United States might experience growth in the 1800s.

Chapter Overview

Visit the *American Odyssey* Web site at americanodyssey.glencoe.com and click on ***Chapter 5—Chapter Overview*** to preview the chapter.

NORTH WIND PICTURE ARCHIVES

New York Governor DeWitt Clinton leads the ceremonies opening the Erie Canal.

Territorial Expansion

NOVEMBER 7, 1805: EXPLORERS REACH THE PACIFIC OCEAN

A COLD RAIN FELL FROM THE GRAY SKY, DRENCHING THE EXPLORERS AS THEY PULLED THEIR CANOES ASHORE. Giant pines rose above them, green and full. Dense forest lined the sides of the river that emptied into the Pacific Ocean.

One man climbed a muddy hill to get a better look at the vast sea. For a year and a half he had traveled by boat and horseback, on foot and by canoe, to reach this spot. To mark the journey's end, he chose a tall yellow pine tree, pulled a knife from his belt, and began carving. "William Clark," he cut into the bark, dating his entry. "By land from the U. States in 1804 and 1805."

PHOTOGRAPH BY DAVID SCHULTZ, 1995. MISSOURI HISTORICAL SOCIETY, ST. LOUIS

The Expedition
In 1805 Lewis and Clark's tools included some that are still used in exploration today.

Clark and his friend Meriwether Lewis had set out from St. Louis in May 1804 on orders from President Thomas Jefferson. The United States had just purchased much of the territory west of the Mississippi River, and Jefferson wanted it explored.

Lewis and Clark traveled through the lands of many Native American nations—land unknown to all but a few fur-trading white Americans. When they reached the Pacific, they had pushed the American frontier all the way to the continent's western edge.

The Moving Frontier

Westward Advance

Only 40 years earlier, the **frontier**—the shifting zone where colonist-controlled lands met Native American-controlled lands—began at the Appalachian Mountains. Over the next decades, white settlers steadily displaced Native Americans as they pushed this frontier westward. One of these white men, Daniel Boone, played a major part in this movement.

GUIDE TO READING

Main Idea

Eager for land, white settlers pushed the frontier ever westward and displaced Native Americans from their ancestral homelands, often with the support of the federal government.

Vocabulary

- frontier
- flatboat

Read to Find Out . . .

- how westward movement was a central experience of American life in the early nineteenth century.
- the relationship between the federal government and the territories.
- federal policy toward Native Americans before 1860.

The Wilderness Road

Daniel Boone first learned about the land west of the Appalachians during the French and Indian War. He had heard a soldier describe a hunter's paradise, a land with buffalo so large that the earth sagged beneath them. The soldier told of a mountain pass, the Cumberland Gap, that led to this paradise.

After the war Boone searched for a route to the West. In 1769 he found a Native American trail across the mountains. Warriors' Path, as it was called, led Boone through the Cumberland Gap to the gentle hills of a land that came to be called Kentucky. For two years, he explored the region's dense forests and lush meadows.

In 1775 Boone rounded up 30 skilled foresters to build a path so that pioneer families could take it west. Boone's crew widened the Warriors' Path, cleared rocks from the Cumberland Gap, cut down trees in Kentucky, and marked the trail. The new Wilderness Road, as it became known, became the main Southern highway from the Eastern states to the West. More than 100,000 people traveled it between 1775 and 1790.

Meanwhile Boone continued his wandering. In 1799 he crossed the Mississippi River into present-day Missouri, then controlled by Spain. The Spanish governor awarded Boone a large piece of land. Boone, however, lost this land when this territory suddenly became the property of the United States in 1803.

The Louisiana Purchase

Boone's land was part of the Louisiana Territory, which included about half the land between the Mississippi River and the Pacific Ocean. Louisiana had once belonged to France, but it came under Spain's control after the French and Indian War. Then, in 1800, French Emperor Napoleon Bonaparte forced Spain to return ownership of Louisiana to France. Napoleon wanted Louisiana in order to expand France's American empire.

President Jefferson grew worried when he learned of this deal. He was anxious to ensure that New Orleans, a vital port, remain open to American trade. His fears turned out to be well founded, for the ruling official at New Orleans closed the port to American trade in 1802. Jefferson quickly planned his response.

Early in 1803 the President sent Virginian James Monroe to Paris with instructions to buy New Orleans. Congress had voted $2 million for the purchase, though Jefferson privately told Monroe to spend up to $10 million.

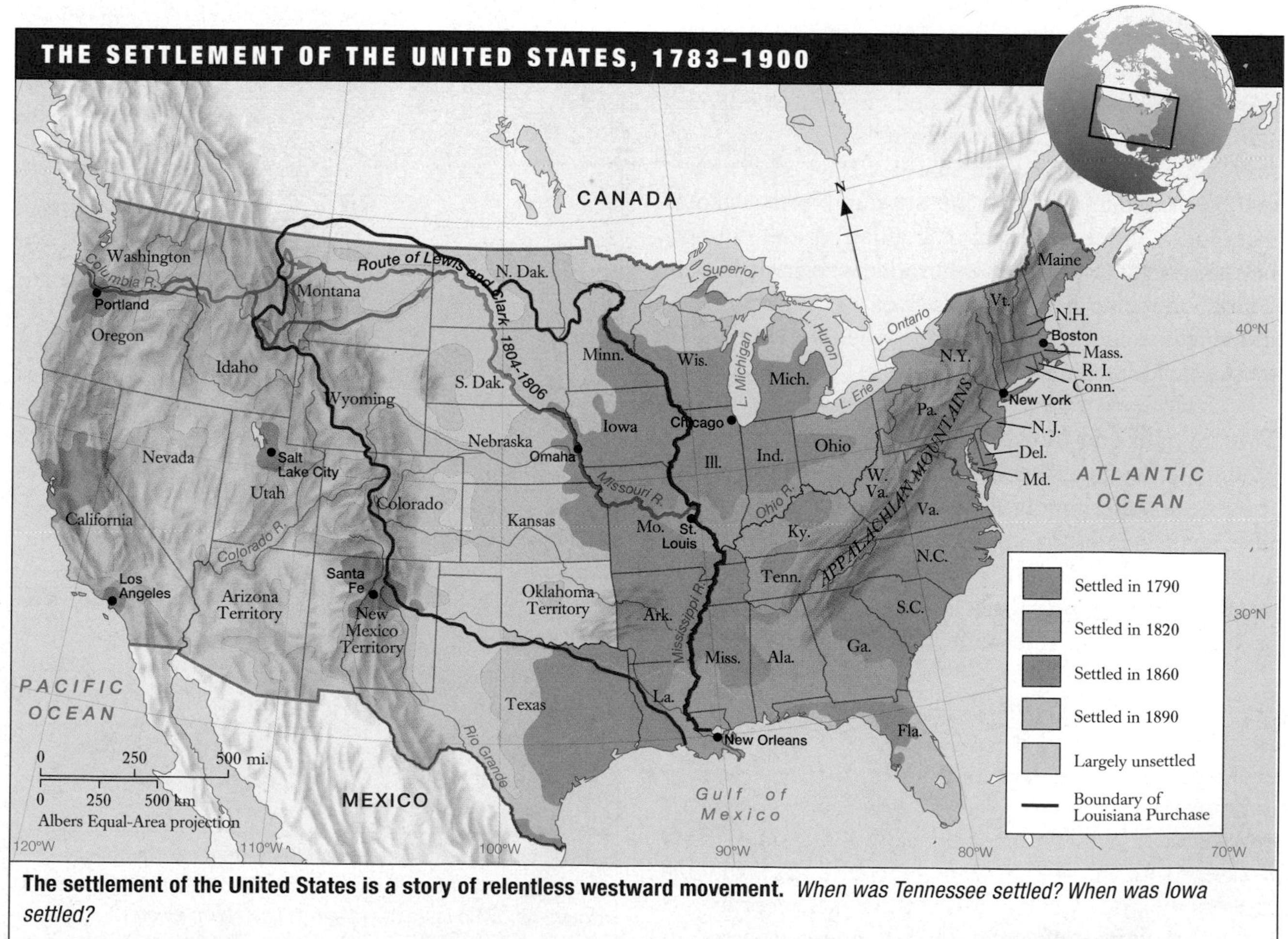

The settlement of the United States is a story of relentless westward movement. *When was Tennessee settled? When was Iowa settled?*

When Monroe reached Paris, Napoleon's situation had changed. A successful slave revolt in the French colony of Haiti had ended his hopes for an American empire. In addition war between France and Britain again seemed likely, and Napoleon needed money. The French offered Monroe all of the Louisiana Territory for $15 million. Monroe agreed.

When news of the purchase reached the United States, some people grumbled that the President had no right to buy land without Congress's approval. Ultimately, however, Congress approved the purchase. The United States thus gained nearly 830,000 square miles (2,149,700 sq. km) of land—doubling the size of the country.

Exploring the New Territory

President Jefferson knew that this region had to be explored. He selected Meriwether Lewis, his personal secretary, and army officer William Clark to lead the expedition. Jefferson instructed the explorers to establish friendly relations with Native Americans and to study their habits and languages. Jefferson wanted descriptions of wildlife they saw along the way. He also wanted detailed maps of the region.

Lewis and Clark chose about 45 men for the expedition, including 20 soldiers accustomed to living in the woods. Others were specialists in Native American sign language, gun repair, and carpentry. The group left St. Louis in the spring of 1804, navigating the Missouri River on **flatboats,** the square-ended, flat-bottomed craft used for transporting freight on inland waterways.

The explorers spent the winter of 1804–1805 near a friendly Mandan village in present-day North Dakota. There they met a French-Canadian trader named Toussaint Charbonneau, his Shoshone wife named Sacajawea, and their infant son. Sacajawea and Charbonneau joined up as guides and translators when the expedition set out again in the spring of 1805.

That summer Lewis and Clark crossed the Rocky Mountains. Using horses and supplies the Shoshone provided, they threaded their way through high mountain passes. After a month of climbing, the party reached the Pacific side of the range. From there they traveled quickly, arriving at the Pacific Ocean before the cold weather. The explorers built a fort and spent the winter at the ocean before returning to St. Louis in 1806.

Westward Migration

The reports and maps Lewis and Clark brought back sparked the interest of a nation that was already looking to its western frontier. Thousands of families crossed the Appalachians in the early 1800s. These new Western settlers were anxious to acquire the same political rights they had enjoyed in the East. According to the Northwest Ordinance, which Congress passed in 1787, each Western territory was permitted limited self-government. When its population reached 60,000, a territory could draft a constitution. If Congress approved the document, the territory became a state.

Western territories quickly lined up to join the union. Kentucky became a state in 1792, Tennessee in 1796, Ohio in 1803, and Illinois in 1818. Meanwhile, more settlers flocked to territories farther west. By 1820 more than 2 million Americans—about one-fourth of the population—lived west of the Appalachian Mountains.

Settling the West

Farming the New Frontier

In 1817 an English visitor to Ohio observed, "Old America seems to be breaking up and moving westward." The people who made this move were farmers, hunters,

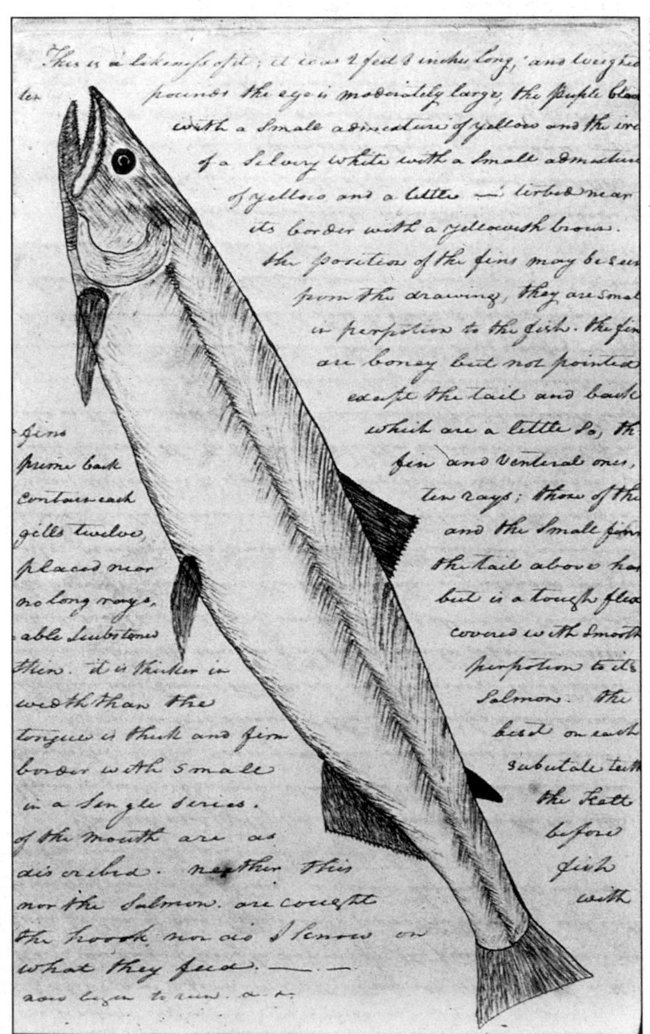

MISSOURI HISTORICAL SOCIETY, ST. LOUIS

A Salmon Observed Lewis and Clark kept excellent geographical and naturalistic records, often enhanced by Clark's drawings. *Who instructed them to keep such records?*

European immigrants, army veterans, artisans—a cross section of poor and middling people. The settlers brought their values and culture to their new homes in the West.

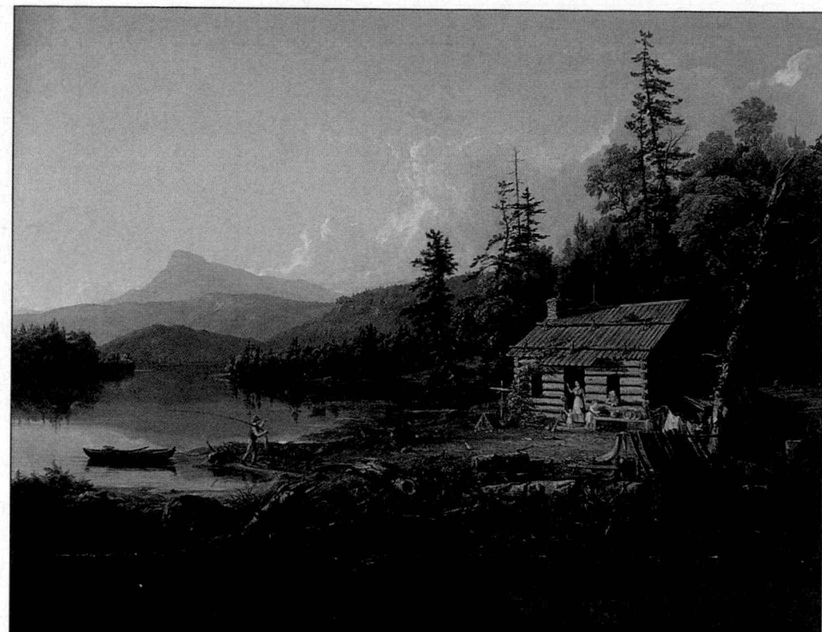

Cabin in the West This 1847 oil painting, ***Home in the Woods,*** is by Thomas Cole, a leader in the painting movement known as the Hudson River School. *In what ways did settlers on the frontier depend on one another?*

Paths to the New Land

Pioneers by the thousands gathered their belongings and loaded them into wooden wagons called Conestogas. These vehicles—20 feet (6.1 m) long and 4 feet (1.2 m) deep—were short on comfort but long on durability. They were also versatile. A Conestoga could serve as a wagon on roads, a sled in the mud, and a cozy camp at night.

Conestogas were a common sight along the rough roads of America. One traveler in New York counted 500 wagons a day rolling west in 1797.

Rivers provided another important route to the West. Some settlers traveled overland to Pittsburgh, Pennsylvania, where they climbed aboard flatboats and floated down the Ohio River. After reaching the desired spot in Ohio or Kentucky or the Indiana Territory, the pioneers unloaded their belongings and headed inland.

When settlers reached a spot they liked, they built a home, often a small log cabin, and began clearing land for farming. One observer in western New York noted in 1805 that "the woods are full of new settlers. Axes are resounding, and the trees literally falling about us as we passed."

Farms in the West

The new frontier farms generally resembled farms in the East. A few Southern settlers used enslaved Africans to plant and harvest cash crops like cotton. Most farmers on the Southern frontier, however, had no slaves, though many hoped to strike it rich and thus join the ranks of wealthy slaveholding planters. North of the Ohio River, where slavery was prohibited, farms were small and most produced only enough food to feed the families that worked them.

Northern and Southern farmers raised crops of corn and wheat and hunted to provide their families with food. "My old daddy," recalled one pioneer woman, "caught rabbits, 'coons, and possums. He would work all day and hunt at night." Women did almost everything else. One farm journal reported that women "spun their own yarn . . . made and mended their own chairs, braided their own baskets, wove their own carpets . . . picked their own geese, milked their own cows. . . ." They also cooked meals, raised children, and cared for the sick.

Frontier farmers felt close bonds with their neighbors. Community activities—churchgoing and barn raisings, weddings and funerals, barbecues and quilting bees—were necessary diversions from the rough life. Unlike the solitary explorers who first explored the frontiers, most settlers relied on the support of neighbors during good times and bad.

Bad times were an ever-present threat. In the lawless wilderness of the early 1800s, conflicts were often settled with fists and guns. Frigid winters and steamy summers brought disease and death. The land was lush, but a bad harvest could spell disaster for a farm family. The threat pioneers feared most, however, was an attack from Native Americans.

Native Americans and the Settlers

Promises Made and Broken

The greatest threat to Native Americans, in turn, was white settlers. For more than 150 years Native Americans had watched a tide of settlers stream west, threatening their ways of life. Usually, however, the conflicts between settlers and Native Americans arose over land.

In theory the United States government insisted on respect for Native American land claims. In 1787 the Northwest Ordinance declared:

The utmost good faith shall always be observed towards the Indians; their land and property shall never be taken from them without their consent; and, in their property, rights, and liberty, they shall never be invaded or disturbed.

—*The Northwest Ordinance,* 1787

This well-intentioned promise proved flimsy, however, in the face of land-hungry settlers.

Trouble in Ohio

During the 1700s several Native American nations—the Shawnee, the Miami, the Wyandot—shared the land that is today Ohio. They settled in villages and ate what they could hunt and grow. White settlers in this region pushed the Native Americans from their homes and hunting grounds. "Hear the lamentations of our women and children," cried one Shawnee leader. "Stop your people from killing our game."

When the United States government did nothing to stop this conflict, Native Americans in Ohio formed a confederation to halt white settlement. In 1790 and 1791 warriors repeatedly attacked settlers, killing more than 800 soldiers and handing the army several defeats.

In 1792 President Washington gave General Anthony Wayne command of an army in the Ohio country. After drilling some 3,000 soldiers for several months, Wayne led his army against the Ohio confederation. His troops fought about 2,000 warriors in the Battle of Fallen Timbers near Lake Erie in 1794. The Native Americans were soundly defeated. After the battle Wayne torched their homes and fields. Under the Treaty of Greenville that ended the war, Native Americans gave up much of their land.

THE FIELD MUSEUM

Tecumseh This oil portrait (artist unknown), painted not later than 1813, is from the collection of the Field Museum in Chicago. It is believed to portray the Shawnee military leader Tecumseh. *What was the name of the community Tecumseh and his brother established?*

CHICAGO HISTORICAL SOCIETY

After the Battle The Treaty of Greenville marked another loss of Native American lands. *Where did the Native Americans of the Ohio Valley go after the war ended?*

The Shawnee Solution

After the defeat many Native Americans of the Ohio Valley traveled west across the Mississippi, away from the settlers. Others tried to find new homes in Ohio.

One of those who remained in Ohio was a Shawnee named Tenskwatawa. Around 1805 Tenskwatawa began preaching a message of hope to the Shawnee. If the Shawnee returned to traditional ways, he said, he would lead them to "a rich, fertile country, abounding in game, fish, pleasant hunting grounds, and fine corn fields." Tenskwatawa told them to stop drinking the white man's whiskey, stop using his weapons, and stop eating "the food of the whites." Over time, Tenskwatawa's spiritual message turned into a political program, and his brother Tecumseh joined him as a leader of the Shawnee people.

The two brothers—the mystical prophet Tenskwatawa and the politically shrewd, militarily skillful Tecumseh—spoke of Native American pride, power, and unity. The brothers said they would reclaim lost land and draw a "boundary between Indians and white people." The magnetic presence and convincing speeches of the brothers attracted many impoverished Native Americans in Ohio and Indiana. In 1808 the two leaders established a community called Prophet's Town along Indiana's Tippecanoe River. William Henry Harrison, governor of the Indiana Territory, grew alarmed at the power of the Shawnee leaders. In 1811 he gathered a force of 1,000 soldiers and attacked and destroyed Prophet's Town. Though Tecumseh and Tenskwatawa survived to continue their resistance, Tecumseh was eventually killed in 1813 while fighting for the British in the War of 1812. With his death came the decline of effective Native American resistance in the North. Soon more Native Americans were moving across the Mississippi River, away from white settlers.

The Cherokee Solution

Not all Native Americans spurned new ways and resisted white trespassers. The Cherokee of the southeastern United States, for example, tried to live in peace with whites.

In many ways Cherokee villages resembled white settlements in the South. The Cherokee built roads and collected taxes. Some adopted the Christian religion most white settlers followed. One man named Sequoyah spent 12 years devising an alphabet for the Cherokee language. Using this alphabet the Cherokee printed a newspaper, the *Cherokee Phoenix*.

The Cherokee learned that many conflicts between white settlers and Native Americans were resolved using the written laws of the state governments. To protect their interests, the Cherokee adopted their own legal code in 1808, combining Cherokee and American laws. In 1827 the Cherokee nation adopted a written constitution based on that of the United States.

These efforts, however, did not protect the Cherokee from Southern whites who hungered to obtain Cherokee land to grow cotton. As the Case Study on pages 136–139 shows, the Cherokee were unable to stop the relentless westward advance of white people.

The Cherokee joined other Native Americans who had been expelled from the East and resettled in the "Great American Desert." Some Native Americans, however, remained in the East, the ancestors of today's Eastern Native Americans. Yet far more common was the experience of those who, in the words of one Native American, were "compelled to seek asylum [protection] from the craving desires of the white man, beyond the great river."

NATIVE AMERICAN REMOVAL

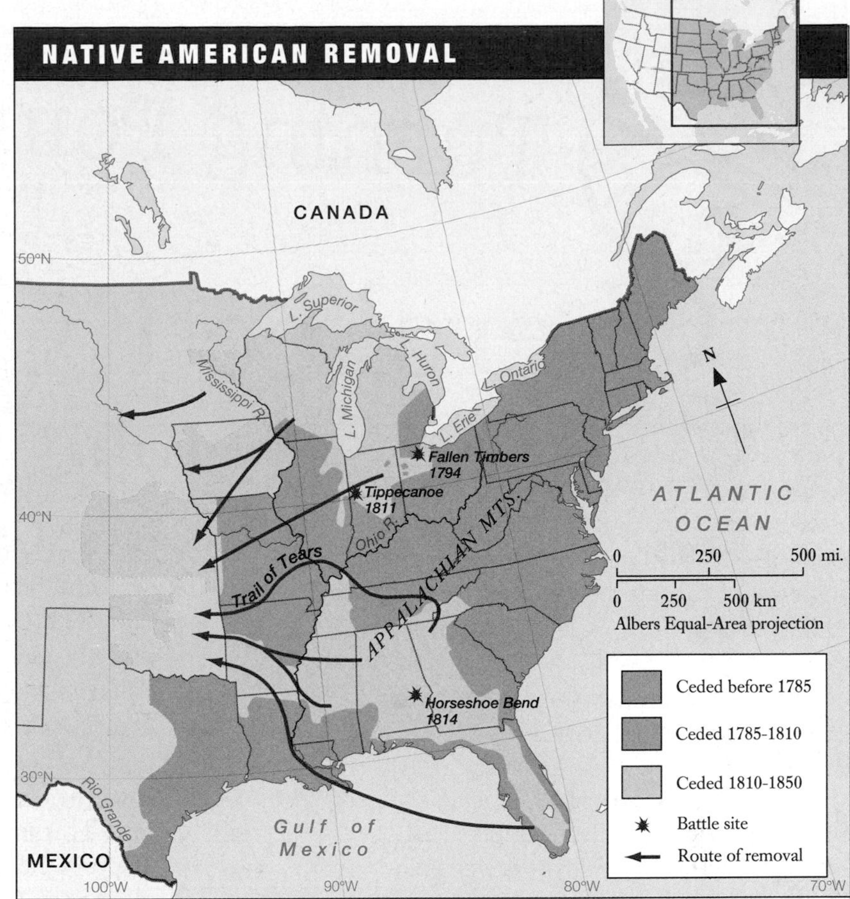

Frontier settlers often came into conflict with Native Americans; sooner or later the Native Americans lost their territories. *Identify the region where the Trail of Tears begins. How many states did the trail cross?*

SECTION ASSESSMENT

Main Idea

1. Use a diagram like this one to show the effects of westward expansion on Native Americans.

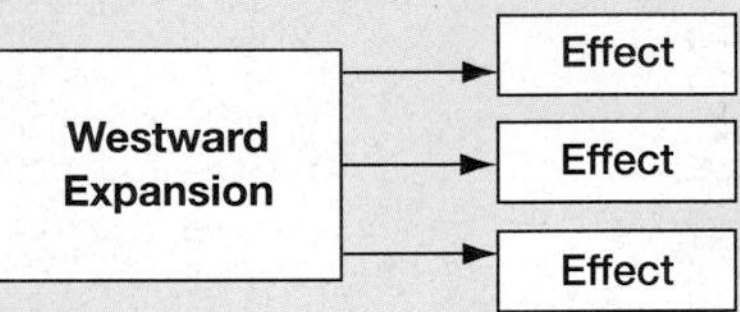

Vocabulary

2. Define: frontier, flatboat.

Checking Facts

3. How did a territory become a state?

4. What policy toward Native Americans did the federal government set forth in the Northwest Ordinance? What policy did it follow in its treatment of the Shawnee and Cherokee?

Critical Thinking

5. **Recognizing Ideologies** Did pioneer families who traveled west have any purposes other than to "strike it rich"? Explain your answer.

Turning Point

Cherokee Expulsion

WINTER 1838

DECISION

Chief Justice: John Marshall
Case: Worcester v. Georgia
Date: 1832

The Cherokee nation, then, is a distinct community, occupying its own territory, with boundaries accurately described, in which the laws of Georgia can have no force, and which the citizens of Georgia have no right to enter, but with the assent of the Cherokees themselves. . . .

It is the opinion of this court that the judgment of the superior court . . . of Georgia, condemning Samuel A. Worcester to hard labour, . . . was pronounced by that court under . . . a law which is void . . . and ought, therefore, to be reversed and nullified.

The Case

The Cherokee and their supporters were jubilant. The case of *Worcester* v. *Georgia* was decided, and the Supreme Court of the United States had ruled in favor of Samuel Worcester, reversing the state's earlier judgment against him.

Worcester, a missionary who had lived among the Cherokee for years, had broken a Georgia state law. This law stated that non-Cherokee people living on Cherokee lands could either sign an oath of allegiance to Georgia or leave the Cherokee land. Worcester refused to do either. Instead, he chose a prison sentence of four years and appealed his case to the United States Supreme Court.

The Supreme Court ruling promised far more than just freedom for Worcester. Chief Justice John Marshall's words implied that the Cherokee would be free to control their own fate, without interference from the state of Georgia. No one could enter the Cherokee Nation without the permission of the Cherokee, and the Cherokee could invite whomever they wanted to live on their land. The United States government would protect their lands.

The victory proved to be an empty one. President Andrew Jackson is said to have remarked, "John Marshall has made his decision; let him enforce it now if he can." It was true—the decision could not be enforced. Jackson did nothing to see that the ruling was obeyed, and Worcester stayed in prison.

The Background

The Cherokee had held their land long before European settlers arrived. Through treaties with the United States government, the Cherokee became a sovereign nation within Georgia.

By the early 1800s the Cherokee were principally an agricultural people, having adopted many of the customs and ways of life of neighboring white farmers. They had their own schools, their own newspaper, their own judicial system, and their own written constitution. Chief Sequoya's invention of a Cherokee alphabet enabled many of the Cherokee to read and write in their own language as well as in English. The Cherokee farmed some of Georgia's richest land, and in 1829 gold was discovered there. Settlers, miners, and land speculators were steadily encroaching on Cherokee territory in pursuit of its riches.

By the time of *Worcester* v. *Georgia* in 1832, federal and state laws had opened the door for Cherokee removal. In 1830 Congress had passed the Indian Removal Act, allowing Jackson to pursue his goal of relocating Eastern Native Americans to lands west of the Mississippi River.

That same year Georgia lawmakers had decreed that all Cherokee lands were under state jurisdiction, erasing Cherokee claims to sovereignty. Furthermore, the Cherokee could not testify against a white person or dig for the gold discovered in their own nation. Their laws were nullified. Finally, in December of 1830, Georgia restricted the presence of white settlers on Cherokee lands, a law that led to the *Worcester* case.

In 1832, when Jackson ignored the Supreme Court's ruling, the Cherokee realized their hopes for federal protection were in vain. Jackson recognized that the Cherokee had not been treated fairly. Nevertheless, he believed that the Eastern Native Americans would have to be relocated, because a separate nation could not continue to exist within an American state. Long before *Worcester* v. *Georgia,* Jackson had warned Congress against "encroachments upon the legitimate sphere of State sovereignty." It was no surprise that Jackson chose not to enforce the Supreme Court's ruling.

The Opinions

Read the opinions of some of the people involved in the Cherokee drama. President Jackson and Governor Lumpkin of Georgia favored removal, while Massachusetts Senator Everett sided with Cherokee Principal Chief Ross in upholding the sovereignty promised in earlier treaties and outlined in the Cherokee Constitution of 1827.

Among both United States and Cherokee officials, people's views on the issue of removal differed

LIBRARY OF CONGRESS

"My opinion remains the same, and I can see no alternative for them but that of their removal to the West or a quiet submission to the State laws."

President Andrew Jackson, 1831

LIBRARY OF CONGRESS

"Any attempt to infringe the evident right of a state to govern the entire population within its territorial limits . . . would be the usurpation of a power never granted by the states."

Wilson Lumpkin, governor of Georgia, 1832

MASSACHUSETTS HISTORICAL SOCIETY

"Whoever read of such a project? Ten or fifteen thousand families, to be rooted up. . . . There is not . . . such a thing in the annals of mankind. . . ."

Edward Everett, senator from Massachusetts, 1830

ARCHIVES AND MANUSCRIPTS DIVISION OF THE OKLAHOMA HISTORICAL SOCIETY

"The lands solemnly guaranteed and reserved forever to the Cherokee Nation by the Treaties concluded with the United States, . . . shall forever hereafter remain unalterably the same."

Constitution of the Cherokee Nation, formed by a convention of delegates led by Principal Chief John Ross, 1827

Turning Point

ROBERT LINDEUX, THE TRAIL OF TEARS. WOOLAROC MUSEUM, BARTLESVILLE, OK

Robert Lindeux's painting *The Trail of Tears* depicts the Cherokee on the forced march across the Appalachian Mountains from their homes in the Southeast. One soldier noted that he had seen 22 people die in a single night during the journey.

sharply. The government's removal policy would serve the interests of expansionists and miners, who wanted both rich soil and gold. On the other hand, most of the Cherokee wanted to remain on the land of their ancestors. Not only did they have a settled life on that land, they had also heard about the hardship and suffering of those who had already moved west.

The Assumptions

Quotations from the players involved reveal another basis for their opinions—underlying assumptions. For example, President Jackson professed to have "the kindest feelings" toward the Cherokee. Even so, his words and actions reveal a bias against them. On another occasion President Jackson had addressed the Cherokee, saying, "I tell you that you cannot remain where you now are. Circumstances that cannot be controlled, and which are beyond the reach of human laws, render it impossible that you can flourish in the midst of a civilized community." Notice the assumption that underlies Jackson's words in that last sentence.

Jackson based much of his argument for removal on his belief in state sovereignty. Governor Lumpkin had less sympathy for the Cherokee than Jackson and far less knowledge of them. Like Jackson, however, he based much of his argument against the Supreme Court's ruling on his belief that the powers of the state government took precedence over those of the federal government.

Everett's underlying assumptions caused him to speak passionately on behalf of the Cherokee. Unlike Jackson, Everett thought of them as "essentially a civilized people." This assumption led to his vehement expressions of indignation.

What about the Cherokee themselves? What were their assumptions? They at first assumed that the federal government would uphold the promises of previous administrations, such as those made during Thomas Jefferson's presidency. The Cherokee had worked hard, in the words of Cherokee orator John Ridge, ". . . to form a republican government, . . . cultivate the earth, and learn the mechanic arts." They made the basic assumption that the white senators would come to regard Native Americans as equals, with shared values and basic human rights.

The Outcome

For years John Ross, the principal chief of the Cherokee, was able to maintain unity among his people. He and other Cherokee leaders—such as Major Ridge and his son John Ridge—all opposed the Cherokee removal at first.

John Ridge When news of the *Worcester* v. *Georgia* decision reached John Ridge, he was exuberant. He believed that the Supreme Court, and therefore the Cherokee, would prevail over Georgia. Ridge then spoke to Jackson himself, however, and learned that the President had no intention of enforcing the decision. Jackson told him that the only hope for the Cherokee was in "abandoning their country and removing to the West."

By the mid-1830s John Ridge, his father, Major Ridge, and his cousin Elias Boudinot, the editor of the *Cherokee Phoenix,* had begun to believe that removal was inevitable. These Cherokee leaders and their supporters realized that the United States government would never protect the Cherokee lands in Georgia. They also believed the government was making the Cherokee a better offer in terms of land and assistance than ever before.

Two Factions The two factions that developed among the Cherokee were the Treaty party, which favored removal, and the National party, which continued to oppose it. John Ross and the National party viewed their opponents as traitors. They never came to accept removal. Major Ridge, knowing that many of the people he loved considered him an enemy, pleaded with them:

> I am one of the native sons of these wild woods. I have hunted the deer and turkey here more than fifty years. . . . The Georgians have shown a grasping spirit lately; they have extended their laws, to which we are unaccustomed, which harass our braves and make the children suffer and cry. . . . I know the Indians have an older title than theirs. We obtained the land from the living God above. . . . Yet they are strong and we are weak. We are few, they are many. We cannot remain here in safety and comfort. I know we love the graves of our fathers. . . . We can never forget these homes, I know, but an unbending, iron necessity tells us we must leave them.

Pressure to complete the Cherokee relocation intensified. The National party, representing about 16,000 Cherokee, adamantly resisted the move, yet the administration dealt only with the minority Treaty party. Its leaders signed a relocation treaty, ratified by Congress and the President in 1836.

Still, in 1838 after the deadline set for removal had passed, few Cherokee had moved voluntarily. Soldiers with rifles and bayonets forced more than 18,000 Cherokee from their homes and marched them approximately 1,000 miles to what is now Oklahoma. During the march nearly 4,000 Cherokee died from malnutrition, exposure to the cold, cholera, and physical hardship. Their grueling trek earned the name the Trail of Tears.

RESPONDING TO THE CASE

1. Jackson spoke of the Cherokee as hunters who had no right to "tracts of country on which they have neither dwelt nor made improvements, merely because they have seen them from the mountain or passed them in the chase." Why do you think Jackson made this statement? What was he purposely ignoring?

2. Senator Theodore Frelinghuysen, in a speech on the Indian Removal Act, asked: "Do the obligations of justice change with the color of the skin?" Which views presented on page 137 would Frelinghuysen probably agree with?

3. Before the Trail of Tears, the Ridges had decided that their people had no choice but to go west. Although at first they were opposed to relocation, what events changed their minds? Why?

4. In what respects was Major Ridge in sympathy with the Cherokee who continued to oppose removal? What were some of the values and assumptions he shared with them?

PORTFOLIO PROJECT

Imagine that you are a Cherokee leader faced with the threat of removal. Write a speech addressed to the Cherokee people urging the case of either the Treaty party or the National party. Keep the speech in your portfolio.

SECTION 2

The Economy Grows

APRIL 4, 1839: MILLWORKER DESCRIBES FACTORY LIFE

MUSEUM OF AMERICAN TEXTILE HISTORY, NORTH ANDOVER, MA

New Line of Work
The change from farm to factory meant a complete change in lifestyle for these young women.

AFTER 14 HOURS ON THE JOB, MALENDA EDWARDS WALKED TO HER BOARDINGHOUSE, WEARILY CLIMBED THE STAIRS, AND SAT AT THE DESK IN HER ROOM. Her ears still ringing from the din of the mill machinery, Malenda found a piece of paper and began a letter to her cousin Sabrina. "You have been informed, I suppose," she wrote, "that I am a factory girl." She continued:

> There are many young ladies at work in the factories that have given up millinery dressmaking and school keeping for to work in the mill. But I would not advise anyone to do it, for I was so sick of it at first I wished a factory had never been thought of. But the longer I stay the better I like it.
>
> —Malenda Edwards, from a letter to Sabrina Bennet, April 4, 1839

In 1839 Malenda Edwards had left her parents' quiet farm and moved to Nashua, New Hampshire, to work in a textile mill. She traded her days of milking cows, spinning thread, and raking hay for work in a 5-story, red-brick factory. Every day but Sunday, she started work at 5:00 A.M. and operated a power loom until 7:00 P.M., with only short breaks for meals. Most of the 250 workers in the factory were women.

Despite the long hours, Malenda was happy to work in the mill. For a 70-hour work week she earned $3.25—more than most women could make as teachers, seamstresses, or servants. In the years between 1839 and 1845, Malenda would work in the factory for part of the year, then return home to enjoy her earnings and take care of her aging parents.

GUIDE TO READING

Main Idea

The growth of factories and expansion of the nation's transportation system spurred domestic production and encouraged regional specialization.

Vocabulary

- textile
- wage
- turnpike
- tariff

Read to Find Out . . .

- how factories developed in the United States.
- how immigration contributed to the growth of American manufacturing.
- how roads, canals, and railroads united the country.

In 1845 Malenda Edwards got married, stopped working in the mills, and moved to a small town. She was just one of thousands of Americans who made the journey from farm to factory in the 1800s.

From Farms to Factories

Manufacturing Picks Up Speed

In 1800 most Americans worked on farms. Whether raising cotton in the South, planting in the meadow of a Western forest, or farming near an Eastern town, American farmers led a quiet, rural life. They prided themselves on being self-sufficient. Their farm supplied the family with food, and farm women made day-to-day necessities like soap, candles, and maple sugar.

Most other necessities could be found within a few miles of the farm. Items that could not be made at home were manufactured—by hand, one at a time—by local blacksmiths, shoemakers, and tailors in exchange for corn or wheat. In the more populous areas of the nation, small country stores provided farmers with hard-to-find goods, like gunpowder, coffee, and tea. **Textiles,** or cloth and fabric, from Europe were especially popular in American stores.

75 Young Women

From 15 to 35 Years of Age,

WANTED TO WORK IN THE

COTTON MILLS!

IN LOWELL AND CHICOPEE, MASS.

I am authorized by the Agents of said Mills to make the following proposition to persons suitable for their work, viz:—They will be paid $1.00 per week, and board, for the first month. It is presumed they will then be able to go to work at job prices. They will be considered as engaged for one year, cases of sickness excepted. I will pay the expenses of those who have not the means to pay for themselves, and the girls will pay it to the Company by their first labor. All that remain in the employ of the Company eighteen months will have the amount of their expenses to the Mills refunded to them. They will be properly cared for in sickness. It is hoped that none will go except those whose circumstances will admit of their staying at least one year. None but active and healthy girls will be engaged for this work as it would not be advisable for either the girls or the Company.

I shall be at the Howard Hotel, Burlington, on Monday, July 25th; at Farnham's, St Albans, Tuesday forenoon, 26th, at Keyse's, Swanton, in the afternoon; at the Massachusetts' House, Rouses Point, on Wednesday, the 27th, to engage girls,--such as would like a place in the Mills would do well to improve the present opportunity, as new hands will not be wanted late in the season. I shall start with my Company, for the Mills, on Friday morning, the 29th inst., from Rouses Point, at 6 o'clock. Such as do not have an opportunity to see me at the above places, can take the cars and go with me the same as though I had engaged them.

I will be responsible for the safety of all baggage that is marked in care of I. M. BOYNTON, and delivered to my charge.

I. M. BOYNTON,

[A]gent for Procuring Help for the Mills.

BAKER LIBRARY, HARVARD UNIVERSITY

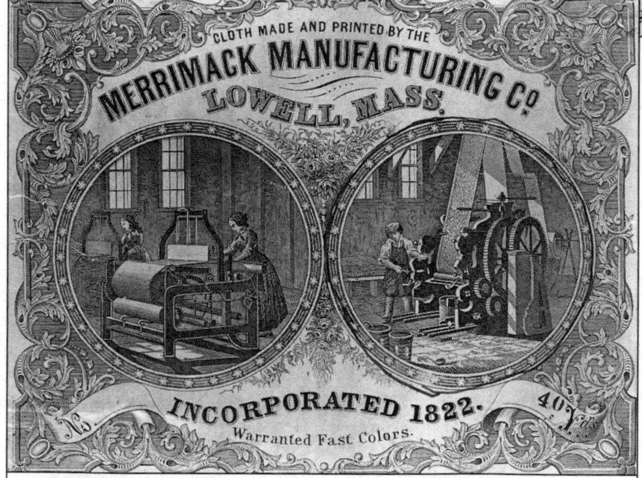

COURTESY AMERICAN ANTIQUARIAN SOCIETY

Millworkers The Merrimack label shows the weaving and printing of cloth under one roof. Mills recruited young women (poster, above) rather than young men because women were more easily spared from farmwork. *How did the Embargo Act spur the development of factories?*

By 1800 all but those farmers living on the most remote fringes of the frontier survived on a mix of homemade goods, handcrafted products of local artisans, and store-bought items imported from Europe. This way of living began to change in 1807.

A Changing Economy

Trade between the United States and Europe had increased steadily. In 1803, however, war broke out between Great Britain and France, resulting in harassment and capture of United States merchant ships. To avoid a war with Britain or France, President Jefferson signed the Embargo Act in 1807, stopping all trade between Europe and the United States. Trade remained choked until after the War of 1812. The resulting economic slowdown had several effects. First, the British wool, Irish linen, and Indian cotton that had flooded the American market no longer arrived. As a result, the home manufacture of textiles boomed. A second effect of this situation was that merchants who had traded with Europe now looked for other ways to make money.

One of those merchants, a Bostonian named Francis Cabot Lowell, recognized the demand for textiles in the United States. He had seen dozens of tiny spinning mills crop up across New England. Lowell took advantage of the postwar slowdown in trade with Britain and began a bold experiment. He started to organize an entirely new system of textile production that was bigger, more efficient, and more profitable than any in the United States.

Lowell's Experiment

In 1813 Lowell set about designing a new spinning and weaving machine. With help from employee Paul Moody, the machine was finally perfected. Lowell and his business partners built a three-story factory on the banks of the Charles River in Waltham, Massachusetts. The current of the river turned waterwheels, which were connected to gears and belts that ran the machinery in the factory.

Unlike the tiny spinning mills of New England, Lowell's plant contained all the stages of textile production under one roof: spinning, weaving, bleaching, dyeing, and printing. The fabric Lowell's factory turned out was rougher than the fine textiles of Europe, but it suited the needs of Americans who bought his cloth. Lowell's factory—larger and more ambitious than any other in the United States—launched the nation's Industrial Revolution, the change from manufacturing at home to manufacturing in factories.

New Workers

Where would Lowell find workers to operate his spinning and weaving machines? In the rural areas around Waltham, no farmer wanted to give up his property and independence to earn **wages,** or daily pay, in a textile factory. Lowell discovered, however, that the farmers' daughters were happy for an opportunity to earn money. Many parents were also happy to receive some of these earnings.

Lowell began recruiting young (mostly ages 15–29) farm women to live and work at his factory. He promised parents that their daughters would live under strict moral supervision in company dormitories, be required to attend church services, and be held to a nightly curfew. After persuading many parents to allow their daughters to move to Waltham, Lowell opened his factory in 1814.

Lowell's Waltham mill was an enormous success. It was so successful that following Lowell's death in 1817, his partners built a new, larger plant located on the Merrimack River in 1823. The town that grew up at that spot

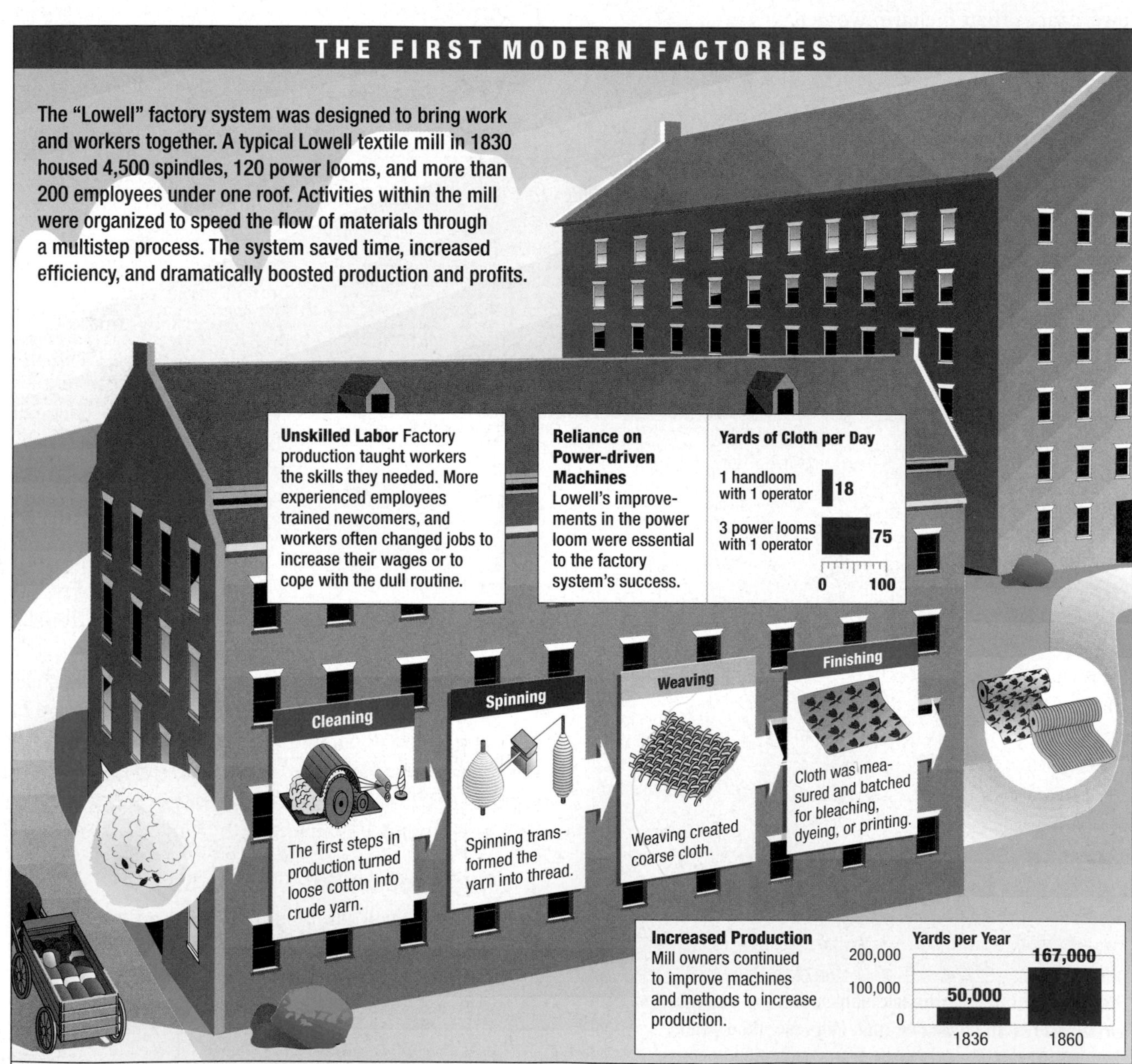

THE FIRST MODERN FACTORIES
The "Lowell" factory system was designed to bring work and workers together. A typical Lowell textile mill in 1830 housed 4,500 spindles, 120 power looms, and more than 200 employees under one roof. Activities within the mill were organized to speed the flow of materials through a multistep process. The system saved time, increased efficiency, and dramatically boosted production and profits.
Unskilled Labor Factory production taught workers the skills they needed. More experienced employees trained newcomers, and workers often changed jobs to increase their wages or to cope with the dull routine.
Reliance on Power-driven Machines Lowell's improvements in the power loom were essential to the factory system's success.
Yards of Cloth per Day
1 handloom with 1 operator
18
3 power looms with 1 operator
75
0
100
Cleaning
The first steps in production turned loose cotton into crude yarn.
Spinning
Spinning transformed the yarn into thread.
Weaving
Weaving created coarse cloth.
Finishing
Cloth was measured and batched for bleaching, dyeing, or printing.
Increased Production Mill owners continued to improve machines and methods to increase production.
Yards per Year
200,000
100,000
0
50,000
167,000
1836
1860

Technological innovation and economic opportunity combined to make the first textile mills possible. *How many more yards of cloth could an operator produce each day tending three power looms instead of one handloom?*

became known as Lowell, Massachusetts. Other textile mills that were located in Lowell also adopted the factory system. By 1840 textile mills employed 8,000 workers, almost 40 percent of Lowell's population.

Business leaders built textile mills all over New England and the mid-Atlantic states in the 1830s and 1840s. Most of the workers in these factories were women like Malenda Edwards. The rest of the labor force was made up of children from local farms and a growing number of men who sought factory work after failing at farming.

After 1840 another source of labor began arriving in the factories of the Northeast. Political turmoil and failed crops drove thousands of Germans and Irish from their European homes. Most of these immigrants arrived on American shores desperate for jobs. Many came to the textile mills of the Northeast and offered to work for lower wages than the farm women.

For factory owners this new, cheap source of labor came just in time. The success of the factory system had created intense competition between textile companies. Mill owners struggled to find ways to increase production and lower costs. Many cut wages and increased the workload of employees. Some women went out on strike to protest wage cuts. In response factory owners began to hire more and more immigrants. By 1860 European immigrants had replaced farm women as the largest group of workers in American factories. This influx of labor willing to work for low wages continued to make the factory system profitable in the United States.

A New Economy

The census of 1850 reported that in the past most "manufacturing was carried on in the shop and the household by the labor of the family." By 1850 it was done by "a system of factory labor, compensated by wages, and assisted by power." Factories producing textiles, shoes, furniture, carriages, and other goods appeared all across the Northeast. Many of these factories were built in growing cities that attracted immigrant workers.

The growth of factories meant that more Americans bought more goods in stores. After 1850 farmers did not get their shoes handmade from a cobbler two miles from home. Instead they bought factory-made shoes from a store that had ordered them from a merchant hundreds of miles away. The transportation revolution that also occurred after 1800 made more goods available to more people in more places than ever before.

The Transportation Revolution

Road, River, and Rail

By 1850 American manufactured goods and farm produce were being transported to most places where people wanted them, whether in Boston or Chicago. Moving goods and people from one place to another had not always been so simple, however.

Roads and Turnpikes

Before 1800 roads and rivers were the most important links between farms, villages, and cities. Yet travel over these roadways and waterways was impossible during some seasons and difficult during the best times. Dry seasons turned many rivers into trickling streams. Hot weather turned roads to dust and rain turned them into muddy troughs. Shipping goods from east to west was expensive: it cost more to haul a ton of goods 9 miles (14.5 km) inland from the ocean than it did to bring that same ton of goods from Europe.

An early solution to American transportation problems was the development of **turnpikes,** roads that required travelers to pay tolls. Private companies built the first turnpikes hoping to earn back the cost of the roads by charging tolls. Turnpike companies often built their roads of stone and gravel, making better traveling conditions. By 1832 the

WELLS FARGO BANK

Riding the Mail Coach Improving the transportation network helped industry and linked the people of different regions. *How might failure to improve transportation have affected the social development of the nation?*

United States had nearly 2,400 miles (3,861.6 km) of toll roads linking together most important cities.

Roads to the West were the most common projects during the turnpike era. The federal government funded construction of the most important route west, the National Road. Started in 1811, this stone road ran westward from Cumberland, Maryland. It measured 80 feet (24.3 m) wide and, by 1818, stretched about 130 miles (209.2 km) to Wheeling, in present-day West Virginia. By 1852 it spanned some 600 miles (965.4 km), ending in Vandalia, Illinois.

Rivers and Canals

Transportation by water was far less costly than by road. In the early 1800s, flatboats floated down the Ohio and Mississippi Rivers, carrying crops raised by Western farmers to export markets and to pioneers in other areas. Upstream travel was slow and expensive, but rivers remained a popular and cheap way to move people and goods.

The rise of steam power made the nation's rivers even more crowded. After 1810 steamboats began churning up and down the rivers, bringing trade in their wake. Between 1830 and 1860, riverboats on the Mississippi helped make Western farming profitable.

Student Web Activity 5
Visit the *American Odyssey* Web site at americanodyssey.glencoe.com and click on ***Chapter 5—Student Web Activities*** for an activity relating to the Erie Canal.

Of course, rivers had limited usefulness. For one thing, most run from north to south, so travel from east to west was often difficult. "Rivers are ungovernable things," Benjamin Franklin wrote. "Canals are quiet and always manageable." Franklin neglected to note that canals were also expensive and hard to build. Even so, the early 1800s witnessed a canal-building boom.

The biggest project was the Erie Canal linking the Hudson River to Lake Erie. At a time when the longest canal in the nation was less than 28 miles (45.1 km) long, the Erie Canal would extend some 363 miles (584.1 km). Starting in 1817, laborers dug by hand a canal 40 feet (12.2 m) wide and 4 feet (1.2 m) deep.

Completed in 1825, the Erie Canal was a phenomenal success. Thanks to the business the canal generated, by 1830 New York City replaced Baltimore as the

THE BETTMANN ARCHIVE

Big Dig The completion of the Erie Canal and other canals, together with the rise of steam power, solved many transportation problems. *What transportation problems could not be solved by the use of waterways?*

major Eastern port leading to the interior of the nation. Freight rates to western New York fell by 90 percent after the canal opened. The benefit of this modification to the nation's geography and transportation system was clear.

The Erie Canal's success spurred the construction of canals throughout the nation between 1830 and 1850. In the East, canals connected the backcountry to the ocean. Further inland canals linked Eastern cities with the growing settlements of the Ohio River valley. In the Midwest, canals connected the Great Lakes with the Mississippi River. By 1840 Americans had constructed more than 3,300 miles (5,309.7 km) of canals. In a land of mountains, forests, and plains, however, canals did not solve every transportation problem. Soon Americans were looking for another way to travel.

ENO COLLECTION, NEW YORK PUBLIC LIBRARY

Bird's-Eye View While transportation systems spawned new inland cities, they also built up older port cities such as New York, shown in this 1859 engraving. *What effect did the opening of the Erie Canal have on the commerce of New York City?*

Tracks and Steam Engines

The success of the Erie Canal took business away from Baltimore merchants who had profited from their location near the National Road. Some of them hatched a plan to restore Baltimore's importance as a seaport by building a railroad from Maryland to Ohio. In 1828 these merchants launched the Baltimore and Ohio, or B & O, Railroad.

Railroads had been invented in Britain. The idea, however, seemed tailor-made for the United States and its huge, varied landscape. Fast transportation that could cover virtually any terrain offered obvious advantages over canals. As a result, people eagerly invested large sums of money in infant railroad companies. During the 1830s more than 3,300 miles (5,309.7 km) of iron rails were built across the nation. A trip from New York to Cincinnati that had taken 2 months over roads took only 1 week by train in 1850.

WATER TRANSPORT DEVELOPMENTS, 1811–1850

1811 Robert Fulton's steamboat cruises down the Mississippi River. Previously, flatboats carried cargo along Western rivers.

1816 Capt. Shreve's steamboat, *The Washington,* travels upstream as well as down on the Ohio River.

1817 Construction on Erie Canal begins. First steamboat travels on the Great Lakes.

1825 Erie Canal is completed, connecting New York City to Great Lakes.

1833 Laborers, many of whom had worked on the Erie Canal, complete canal system in Ohio.

1840s Sharp decline in freight rates on canals and increase in allowed tonnage on lakes and rivers leads to heyday for water transport.

1848 Illinois and Michigan Canal connects the Great Lakes to the Mississippi.

1850s Private railroad companies break the transportation monopolies of state waterways. Toll rates decrease. Water and rail transport increase.

1810 | 1820 | 1830 | 1840 | 1850

By 1860 railroads carried goods and passengers at lower cost and in less time than roads, canals, or rivers. They made money for investors, merchants who shipped by rail, and people who settled in the towns and cities that sprouted along the track of the locomotive during the 1840s and 1850s. The need for railroads, like roads and canals before, came from industry and trade. The growth of railroads, in turn, created thousands of jobs and stimulated new industries, such as those for iron, steel, and railroad car manufacturing.

Politics and the Economy

National and Regional Interests Clash

"It is an extraordinary era in which we live," said Daniel Webster, a senator from Massachusetts, in 1847. "It is altogether new. The world has seen nothing like it." Revolutions in industry and transportation in the United States made this new world possible. While private investors had funded many of these developments, government also helped nurture America's economic growth in the 1800s.

PHOTO BY STEVE LASCHEVER/COURTESY OF MUSEUM OF AMERICAN POLITICAL LIFE, HARTFORD, CT

Henry Clay for President Clay began campaigning for President in 1824 and ran in three elections. Like other candidates of the period, his likeness appeared on practical and playful items, such as this bandanna. *What effect did Clay expect a new Bank of the United States to have on the national economy in 1816?*

One of the strongest supporters of government's role in the economy was Henry Clay. A member of Congress from Kentucky, Clay had gained prominence during the War of 1812 as a Western war hawk. At that time he opposed a strong national government and programs such as the Bank of the United States, which gave the federal government significant centralized economic power.

As America's economic power grew, however, Clay's views changed. He organized his new ideas into an economic plan called the American System.

The American System

Clay's American System was based on the idea that a stronger national government would benefit each of the different sections of the country. As part of this system Clay supported an 1816 bill to increase **tariffs,** or fees on imported goods. The tariffs were designed to protect American manufacturers—nearly all of whom were located in the East—from European competition. Clay believed that healthy Eastern industries would help the whole nation. This bill passed despite the objections of Southerners in Congress. The South, a region with little manufacturing, would gain nothing directly from the tariff. Consequently, the tariff would have the effect of higher prices for the South, because Southerners imported a great deal of foreign goods.

In 1816 Congress faced the decision of whether to charter a new Bank of the United States (the charter of the first Bank expired in 1811). Clay supported the Bank, arguing that it would stabilize the economy and encourage investments. The Bank bill passed.

Another part of Clay's American System met with less success than the first two. Clay wanted the government to supply money for improvements such as road and canal building. Other Westerners in Congress voted for these plans, which would greatly benefit the frontier regions they represented. Southerners in Congress generally favored Clay's plans because the South also stood to benefit from such improvements. Northerners, however, clashed with Clay over these improvements. For one thing, their roads and canals were already built and dug, so they would not

PHOTO BY STEVE LASCHEVER/COURTESY OF MUSEUM OF AMERICAN POLITICAL LIFE, HARTFORD, CT

Transportation Ticket This silk campaign ribbon shows the loyalty of a strong Clay contingent: the wagoneers, or cartmen. *What specific proposals did Clay put forward that could have won him the wagoneers' support?*

benefit directly from federal assistance. Also, many Northerners feared the growing power of the Westerners and did not want to help them grow stronger.

The greatest opposition to Clay's plans, however, came from the Executive Office of the President. Between 1817 and 1830, three of Clay's internal improvement bills were passed by Congress and then vetoed by three different Presidents. President James Madison, who argued that the Constitution did not give Congress the power to build roads, vetoed the first. On the same basic grounds, in 1822, President James Monroe vetoed a proposal to improve the National Road. Finally, in 1830 President Andrew Jackson vetoed the use of federal funds to improve Kentucky's Maysville Road.

Clay was disappointed that these Presidents paid so little attention to internal improvements, but the government did encourage the nation's growth in other ways. After 1816 Congress passed a series of tariffs that protected the nation's young industries. Between 1830 and 1860 New York, Pennsylvania, Ohio, and Virginia built many of their canals with state funds. Canal and railroad companies usually obtained land from federal and state governments at bargain prices. The combination of private investments and public policy reshaped American life after 1815.

A New Nation

Shortly after steamboats began to paddle down the nation's rivers, a newspaper editor exclaimed that steam power would "diminish the size of the globe." It would make Americans "one single people, one nation, one mind." In some ways, the nation did seem more unified after the transportation and industrial revolutions. After 1850 the farmer's solitary self-sufficiency no longer seemed practical. Cooperation between people with different interests and from different regions replaced it. New Englanders gave up most of their farming and devoted resources to manufacturing. Farmers from the western side of the Appalachians now produced most of the American grain. Southern planters devoted more land and slave labor to cash crops like cotton.

Regional specialization, however, could lead to conflicts. A law that helped Northern manufacturers, such as the tariff, might hurt Southern planters. Tensions between different sections of the nation and between different groups of people began to grow. The forces that changed America's economy in the 1800s also changed the politics and beliefs of its people.

Section Assessment

Main Idea

1. Use a diagram like this one to show the causes and effects of regional specialization.

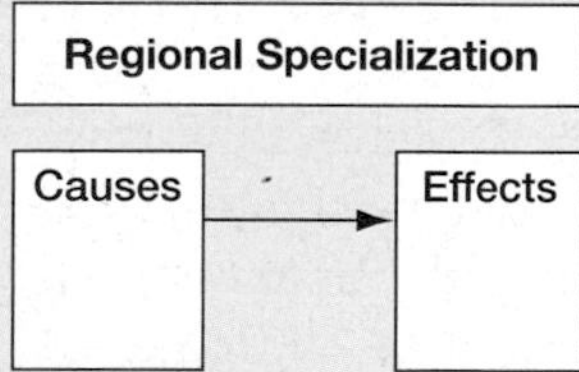

Vocabulary

2. Define: textile, wage, turnpike, tariff.

Checking Facts

3. What was the significance of Lowell's experiment?

4. Why did the Erie Canal and railroads succeed?

Critical Thinking

5. **Predicting Consequences** Why might factory owners have feared labor shortages in the 1830s? Who helped solve these problems?

Geography: Impact on History

MOVEMENT

The Rise of American Cities

Changes in trade and transportation set off a burst of urban growth from 1800 to 1860. All along trade and transportation routes, older cities grew larger and new ones were born. Topography, too, played a key role in this rise of American cities because terrain usually dictated locations of trade routes.

Early American Cities

Most American cities in the thirteen colonies grew up along the Atlantic coast. The ocean linked them with Britain and other countries. Ports and coastal cities such as New York, Charleston, and Boston are still important centers of transportation and industry today.

Inland cities tended to grow up along rivers that provided easy access to the coast and water power to run industries. As American technology overcame obstacles of distance and rugged terrain, the people moved steadily westward.

Steamboats bucked the currents in inland rivers to carry cargo; mules plodded along towpaths, pulling canal boats laden with everything from beeswax to lumber. Trains, spitting sparks and belching steam, hauled freight at the amazing speed of 15 miles per hour. With these 3 modes of transportation now in full swing west of the Appalachians, the pace of trade in the interior picked up. Soon river outposts, canal communities, and railroad whistle-stops developed into cities, while settlements off the beaten track stagnated, sometimes completely disappearing from the map.

Three cities exemplify how trade, transportation, and topography directed the course of urban growth in the United States.

Riverside City

A bonanza of waterways transformed the fur-trading center of St. Louis into a sizable city. Encircled by farmland, St. Louis is situated on the Mississippi just south of where that mighty river meets the Illinois and Missouri Rivers. By midcentury steamboats chugged into St. Louis from north and south, so many that sometimes they lined up for a mile along the docks. From St. Louis, both boats and barges traveled along the Illinois to the

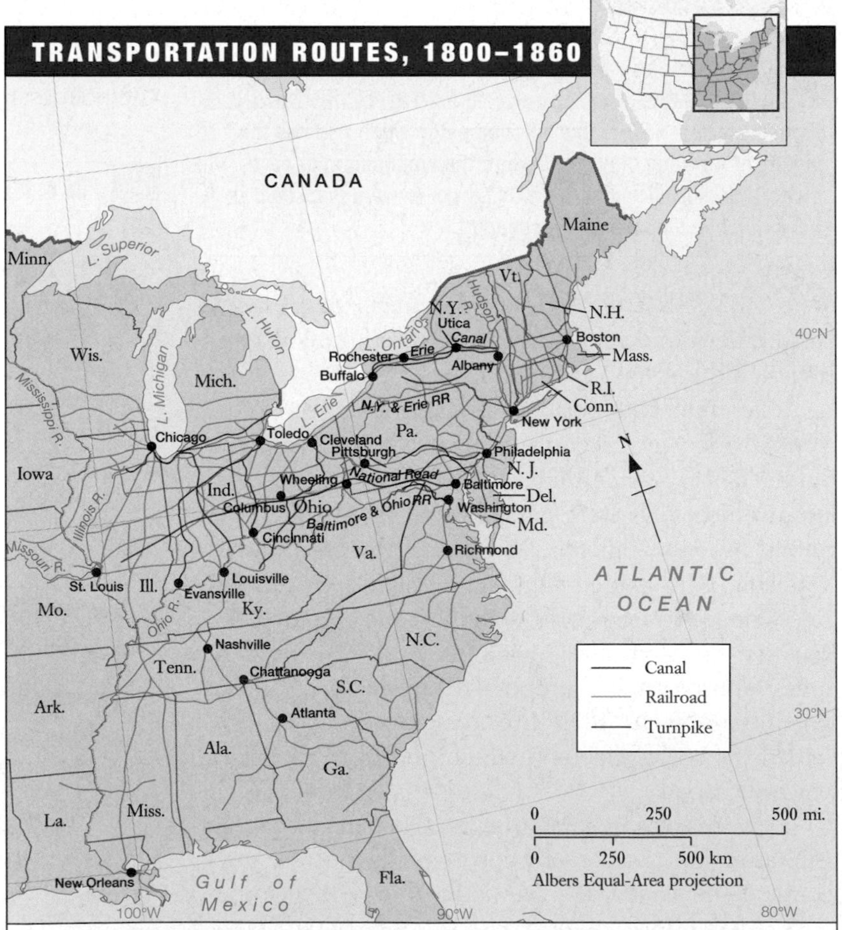

Three kinds of transportation routes linked American cities in the early 1800s.
How did geography help make Chicago a major transportation center?

NORTH WIND PICTURE ARCHIVES

A Busy Port **Between 1800 and 1860, major new cities like Chicago, St. Louis, and Buffalo developed along transportation routes. This print from the 1870s shows heavy traffic at the docks in St. Louis.** *What factors made St. Louis an ideal spot for urban growth?*

prairies, along the Missouri to the West, and down the Mississippi to New Orleans, gateway to the Gulf of Mexico. This intense activity helped boost the one-time fur-trade outpost to a city of 160,773 by 1860.

Along the Canal

In 1810, Buffalo, New York, was nothing but a settlement of 1,500 people at the east end of Lake Erie. When the Erie Canal opened in 1825, Buffalo's population grew to more than 2,400, and hundreds of new buildings were added. By 1860 the population had risen to 81,000.

The 363-mile (584-km) canal ran across New York State from Albany to Buffalo. At Albany, the Hudson River linked the canal with the coast, tying the Atlantic seaboard to the Great Lakes. Canal boats poked along at speeds of between 1 and 5 miles an hour, but rates were cheap. Shipping freight from New York City to Buffalo cost as little as $5 a ton. Transporting the same load by wagon cost $100 and took twice as long.

Although railroads soon outran canals, the Erie Canal remained in operation. Today it is part of the 524-mile (843-km) New York State Barge Canal System, and Buffalo remains a major transportation center.

The Hub of the Rails

As the railroad roared westward, Chicago changed its shape from swampy settlement to megacity. In 1840 the community numbered only about 4,500 people. Eight years later, as the first trains rumbled into town, grain, lumber, and livestock began opening up the city's growing market. Population rose to 109,260 by 1860.

Located on level land in the heart of the nation, with Lake Michigan at its front door, Chicago was perfectly placed for a rail center. Rail tycoons bypassed landlocked communities and charted their tracks to Chicago. By 1860 Chicago was the nation's top rail city, with 11 lines radiating from its hub.

Other industrial centers sprang up across Ohio and the Midwest; canal and rail networks gave them access to both raw materials and markets. Gradually these cities developed the political systems, educational facilities, and cultural institutions that were already flourishing in the older port cities.

MAKING THE GEOGRAPHIC CONNECTION

1. Identify the different kinds of transportation that linked American cities.
2. Trade and transportation often spur urban growth. What factors expand trade and transportation?
3. **Movement** In 1950 railroads carried 56 percent of American intercity freight. By 1988 they only carried 37 percent. What kinds of transportation are greatly affecting urban growth today?

A Changing People

AUGUST 1801: 20,000 WORSHIP AT KENTUCKY CAMP MEETING

THE NOISE RISING FROM THE CLEARING IN THE FOREST "WAS LIKE THE ROAR OF NIAGARA." The sound of singing, weeping, shouting, and moaning of thousands of people came from the meadow. "The vast sea of human beings," observed young James Finley, "seemed to be agitated as if by a storm." The power that stirred the people at Cane Ridge, Kentucky, on that warm August afternoon was religion.

COURTESY OF THE NEW YORK HISTORICAL SOCIETY, NEW YORK CITY

Open-Air Sermon
Camp-meeting preachers often held enormous audiences spellbound.

The Cane Ridge meeting began early one Friday and continued for 6 full days. More than 20,000 people flocked from the surrounding countryside to attend. For these people camp meetings were a rare chance for contact with others and for a religious service. At night they slept in a city of canvas tents; by day they heard sermons by traveling preachers.

"I counted seven ministers all preaching at once," reported Finley. Some stood on tree stumps, others in wagons. Using vivid images of Satan and fiery hell, the preachers evoked powerful feelings among the listeners. Their sermons offered straightforward choices: sin or salvation, evil or good, wrong or right. The decision was in each person's hands.

Like many others, James Finley was powerfully affected by what he heard at Cane Ridge. "A peculiar strange sensation came over me," he said. "My heart beat tumultuously, my knees trembled, my lips quivered, and I felt as though I must fall to the ground." Finley never forgot this experience; several years later he became a preacher himself.

To many people, religion was the solution to the problems facing the United States in the early 1800s. As the nation expanded, Americans became participants in disturbing conflicts—conflicts between rich and poor, Easterner and Westerner, Northerner and Southerner, African American and white. Some people tried to escape these tensions by joining religious communities.

GUIDE TO READING

Main Idea

A renewed interest in religion inspired the start of a broad-based reform movement that sought to perfect United States society by expanding democracy and ending evils such as slavery.

Vocabulary

- spoils system
- nullification
- secede
- temperance
- abolitionism

Read to Find Out . . .

- the changes in early nineteenth-century politics that brought Andrew Jackson to power.
- the connection between the Second Great Awakening and social reform.
- how participation in the abolition movement and other social movements gave women and African Americans a political voice.

Others tried to reform American society, while still others turned to politics as a way of bringing change to the nation.

A New Era in Politics

Courting the Common Man

New ideas about politics were sweeping the United States in the early 1800s. The most important of these ideas involved the question of who should be allowed to vote. Many Western states allowed all adult men to vote, regardless of how much land they owned. In the 1820s many Eastern states also eliminated property requirements for voters. During that decade, more white men than ever before gained the vote. Many of these new voters were Westerners, men who had left the East to seek wealth and opportunity on the frontier. These new voters wanted a new type of politician. They found one in Andrew Jackson.

Jackson and the Common Man

Thanks to his exploits in the War of 1812, Andrew Jackson became one of the nation's best-known heroes. Though he professed little interest in politics, friends persuaded him to run for President in 1824.

Jackson entered one of the wildest elections Americans had yet seen. After 23 years of solid control over the presidency, the Democratic-Republican party was split by factions battling along sectional lines. John Q. Adams, a Northerner and son of the second President, had the support of President James Monroe. Another veteran Democratic-Republican, Henry Clay, hoped to be elected by the Westerners he represented. A Southern candidate, William Crawford of Georgia, had won the support of many members of Congress.

Jackson was the fourth candidate. By far the least experienced politically, he nonetheless impressed people. His image as a no-nonsense frontiersman who had worked his way up the ladder of society, appealed to many voters. His political ideas were as direct as a frontier preacher's sermon: He favored a "Democracy of Numbers" over the "moneyed aristocracy."

Jackson's supporters in the West and South gave him the most electoral and popular votes in the contest, but no candidate had a clear majority. The contest—according to the Constitution's rule—was turned over to the House of Representatives. Henry Clay, who served as speaker of the House that year, threw his support to Adams. When the House vote was taken in February 1825, Adams won with the votes of 13 states to Jackson's 7 states. Jackson's supporters claimed that Clay and Adams had made a "corrupt bargain," a charge that seemed justified when Adams named Clay secretary of state.

The election of 1824 split the Democratic-Republican party once and for all. Supporters of Adams and Clay began to call themselves National Republicans. Jackson's supporters, calling themselves Democrats, began to make plans for the 1828 presidential election.

LABAN S. BEECHER/MUSEUM OF THE CITY OF NEW YORK

Andrew Jackson This figurehead representing Jackson was used on a ship in 1834. *Why do you think Jackson made enemies among traditional politicians?*

The Election of 1828

Both Adams and Jackson had observed the changing political climate, and both designed their campaigns with the "common man" in mind. The result was a mean-spirited but lively campaign that avoided most serious issues.

National Republicans called Jackson "a gambler, a cockfighter, a brawler, a drunkard, and a murderer." The Democrats attacked Adams as a "stingy, undemocratic" aristocrat. They asked Americans to choose between "John Quincy Adams, who can write, and Andrew Jackson, who can fight."

The political tide of democracy favored Jackson in 1828. Almost three times as many people voted as had in 1824, and these new voters helped deliver a resounding victory for Jackson.

After his Inaugural Address in March 1829, Jackson rode down Pennsylvania Avenue to the White House followed by thousands of his celebrating supporters. The crowd swarmed into the White House behind Jackson, grabbing the cakes, ice cream, and punch that had been set out for the inaugural reception. The people broke china, tore curtains, and knocked over furniture. Jackson had to escape the mob through a window. It was apparent to everyone in Washington that a new era in politics had begun.

"The people expect reform," Jackson said. "They shall not be disappointed." One of his first changes was to fire a number of allegedly "lazy" government workers, many of whom had supported Adams. Jackson replaced them with his own supporters.

This practice of rewarding government supporters with government jobs was known as the **spoils system.** Jackson claimed that replacing workers every so often made the government more democratic. The duties in most government jobs, he argued, were so "plain and simple" that anyone could do them. Dismantling the old bureaucracy, however, was a small matter compared with Jackson's war on the powerful Bank of the United States.

The Bank Crisis

The Bank of the United States was an important financial institution that exerted significant influence over Congress and the nation's economy. The United States owned 20 percent of the Bank's stock, and the government's money was deposited there. This money, along with private investments, was used to promote commerce and manufacturing. This had the effect of promoting the interests of Northeastern industries.

To Jackson, the Bank was undemocratic and unconstitutional. It represented the "moneyed aristocracy" that he so hated. He called the Bank a "monster" that threatened to "control the Government and change its character." Henry Clay and Daniel Webster knew how Jackson felt and planned to strengthen the Bank and embarrass the President at the same time. Clay and Webster drafted a bill rechartering the Bank, even though the Bank's original charter still had four years remaining. They reasoned that Jackson would not dare veto a bill—a rare occurrence in that era—in his reelection year. The bill passed Congress and reached the President's desk in July 1832.

Jackson saw this early bank bill as an attack. "The bank . . . is trying to kill me," he told an adviser, "but I will kill the bank." Jackson not only vetoed the Bank bill, he also made it the central issue in his campaign that fall. "When the laws," he said, "make the rich richer and the potent more powerful, the humble members of society—the farmers, mechanics, and laborers—. . . have a right to complain." Many people agreed, and in the 1832 election Jackson defeated his opponent Henry Clay.

People's Reception Andrew Jackson brought to Washington the spirit of the rugged frontier or a shocking lack of refinement, according to how one viewed him. *Do you think Jackson would have been as politically successful earlier in the history of the United States? Why or why not?*

During his second term, Jackson was determined to destroy the Bank. He closed the government's accounts at the Bank and moved federal funds to state banks. In 1836 the Bank's charter expired for good.

The Tariff Controversy

As Jackson battled the Bank, another crisis split his administration and threatened to divide the nation. Tariffs had been part of the country's economic policy since 1816. Tariffs were unpopular in the South, however. When Congress passed a high tariff on some European imports in 1828, many Southerners complained loudly. One of these angry Southerners was Jackson's Vice President, John Calhoun. Calhoun wrote an essay invoking states' rights and the theory of **nullification.** A state, wrote Calhoun, had the right to nullify, or reject, any law that the state felt violated the Constitution.

Jackson supported states' rights, but as President he could not accept nullification because it threatened the federal government's power and the states' unity. Still, some Southerners tried to win Jackson's support by inviting him to a large ceremonial dinner with Calhoun in 1830. When Jackson stood to make the toast before dinner, he let the nullifiers know exactly where he stood on the matter: "Our Federal Union: It must be preserved." Jackson's toast—which plainly put the power of the federal government above the power of the states—silenced the room. A stunned Calhoun rose with his own toast to defend states' rights: "The Union," he said, "next to our liberty, most dear."

In 1832 the controversy became a crisis when Congress passed yet another high tariff. This act enraged politicians in South Carolina. During the fall of 1832 the state legislature nullified the tariff. They also threatened to **secede,** or leave the Union, if the government tried to collect tariff duties in the state. John Calhoun resigned as Vice President and took over one of South Carolina's seats in the Senate.

In December, Jackson directed warships and troops to move toward South Carolina. Then Congress passed a Force Bill permitting the President to use military force to collect the state's tariff duties.

As tensions mounted, Henry Clay designed a compromise plan to reduce all tariffs for 10 years. South Carolina accepted this peace offering and withdrew its nullification of the tariff. Clay's compromise bill resolved the crisis, but states' rights would remain a burning issue for the next 30 years as Southern and Northern politicians battled over slavery.

The Whig Party

While Jackson remained a popular figure, he made many political enemies. By 1834 opposition to Jackson had unified as the Whig party. The new party included Republicans such as Henry Clay and Federalists such as Daniel Webster, plus supporters of the Bank of the United States, manufacturers who favored tariffs, and wealthy business leaders in large cities. The Democrats maintained their support among working people, immigrants, and the small farmers of the South and West.

The Democrats retained the White House in 1836 as Jackson's chosen successor, Martin Van Buren, won the election. In 1840, however, the Whigs retaliated. They portrayed Van Buren as an aristocrat who ate from gold plates. The Whig candidate was a military hero in the Jackson mold, William Henry Harrison. By ignoring the issues and portraying him as a common, cider-drinking man, the Whigs were able to capture the White House.

In the election of 1840, the Whigs made use of the Jacksonian idea that power and success were available to everyone, not just the elite. That idea was echoed in the sermons of preachers on the Western frontier.

An Awakening Interest in Religion

Revivalism Sweeps the Land

While voters were expressing displeasure toward the "moneyed aristocracy," many Americans were finding they had little in common with the traditional colonial Christian churches: the Anglican (Episcopal), the Congregationalist, and the Presbyterian. These churches often had an air of wealth and privilege. Services tended to be formal affairs that inspired little enthusiasm. As the nation expanded, Americans began seeking new forms of religion more in keeping with the spirit of a restless, growing young nation.

Western Revival

Beginning in the 1790s, a revival in religious interest known as the Second Great Awakening swept the Western frontier. The style of these growing churches—especially Methodist and Baptist—was less formal than the better established churches of the East. Circuit riders, or traveling ministers, rode about the frontier preaching to farmers. Rallies such as the camp meeting at Cane Ridge, Kentucky, attracted people from miles around.

The sermons delivered at these meetings and churches could be frightening—damnation awaited all sinners. The message behind them remained personal, emotional, practical, and even democratic. The idea that anything—even victory over sin—was possible with hard work and prayer appealed to many Americans.

Perfecting Society

As the powerful ideas of the Second Great Awakening spread through the country, the nature of its message changed. One preacher who took this message and developed it was Charles Grandison Finney. A tall man with thinning blond hair and blazing eyes, Finney began with the idea that sin was a failure of will. Those who could avoid the temptation of sin could make themselves perfect.

Finney went on to say that not only could Christians make themselves perfect, they could—indeed, must—make the world around them perfect. No Christian could fail to see a thousand evils that needed to be corrected, reformed, and eliminated. The ideas of Finney and other preachers unleashed enormous energy in Americans. The urge to perfect the nation grew stronger during the 1830s and thereafter.

Reforming American Society

Fighting Evils From Alcohol to Slavery

The Second Great Awakening inspired different responses from different groups. Some withdrew to create their own "perfect" communities. For example, the Shakers and the Mormons, two religious groups, attempted to build their own utopia, or ideal world, away from mainstream American life.

Others set about changing the mainstream itself. They saw a host of evils in the rapidly changing society of the 1800s. Churchgoers in the populous areas of the North were among the first to organize reform groups. These groups usually saw social problems in religious terms of "evil" and "sin."

In the Promised Land **These survivors of the 1847 Mormon trek across the plains and mountains to the Great Salt Lake were photographed 50 years later.** *What other religious society of the time set out to build its own utopia?*

In an era when women had limited opportunities for education or jobs, reform groups offered an outlet for their energy and skills. Women filled the ranks of many reform efforts during the mid-1800s, but others considered it "unfeminine" for women to play an active role in these movements. As a result of these tensions, women's rights became one of the dominant issues during the reform era.

While women's rights concerned some, other evils were more visible and easier to attack. Alcohol, for example, was blamed for crime, insanity, and the breakdown of the family. As a result, the **temperance,** or antidrinking, movement became one of the first organized reform movements in the United States.

Nine Steps to Destruction This illustration reflects the temperance movement's belief that alcohol drove people to ruin. *What other reform movements developed in the wake of the temperance movement?*

Demon Rum

Starting in the 1830s reformers targeted the evils of "demon rum." They flooded the nation with tracts and articles. One of the best-selling novels of the 1850s, *Ten Nights in a Bar Room and What I Saw There,* warned against the excesses of alcohol. Reformed alcoholics traveled to meetings in city after city, telling their stories. These efforts got results. Hard liquor sales fell by half during the 1830s alone.

Gradually the fight against drunkenness became a war on alcohol itself. More and more Americans chose to avoid all liquor and became "teetotalers." Reformers took their case to state legislatures. In 1838 Tennessee passed the first statewide regulation of liquor. Temperance reformers won another victory when Maine passed a tougher liquor law in 1851. While some citizens protested and bootleg liquor poured into the state from Canada, reformers counted the Maine law as a victory.

The success of the temperance movement inspired dozens of other reform efforts: the push for better prisons, mental health care, free public education, and aid for the blind and the deaf. Some reformers, however, perceived an evil much greater than all of these—an evil endorsed by politicians, protected by laws, and defended by an entire section of the nation. That evil was slavery.

Fighting Slavery

Slavery had troubled some Americans since before the Revolution. In 1787 the Northwest Ordinance forbade slavery in territories north of the Ohio River, and by 1804 every Northern state had provided for the end of slavery. Few white Americans, however, took an active stand on slavery between the passage of the Constitution and the 1820s.

At this time dozens of publications appeared spreading the ideas of **abolitionism,** the movement to end slavery. Most of these papers called for a gradual end to slavery, believing that the slow pace would bring liberation while it protected the businesses of Southern planters.

Other abolitionists had less patience. David Walker, a former slave living in Boston, called for an immediate end to slavery in 1829. He argued that enslaved individuals were entitled to use violence to obtain their freedom.

Two years later William Lloyd Garrison began publishing a newspaper called *The Liberator.* In his black suits and steel-rimmed glasses, Garrison looked more like a schoolmaster than a radical reformer. His pen, however, spouted fire as he called for the immediate emancipation of all enslaved persons. "I am in earnest," he wrote. "I will not retreat a single inch—AND I WILL BE HEARD!"

Freedom Fighters The abolition movement brought forth many notable historical figures. From left to right: top, Frederick Douglass and Sojourner Truth, both fugitives from slavery; bottom, William Lloyd Garrison, a member of the clergy, and Lucretia C. Mott, who was also a temperance leader. *What issues divided the abolition movement?*

Garrison was heard. In 1833 a group of his supporters met in Philadelphia and formed the American Anti-Slavery Society. The goals of the society were to end slavery in the United States by stirring up public sentiment and flooding the nation with abolitionist literature. The society grew throughout the 1830s. With success, however, came controversy. Southerners worried about the effect of Garrison's message on their enslaved laborers and mounted vicious verbal attacks on him. Northerners blasted his views on the Constitution, which he called a "compromise with tyranny" and "an agreement with hell" because it allowed slavery.

Tensions Within the Movement

White leaders of the abolitionist movement discovered that African Americans, especially those who had escaped from bondage, made the most convincing arguments against slavery. Soon, fugitives became the star attractions at meetings of the American Anti-Slavery Society. One of the best speakers was Frederick Douglass, a brilliant man who had made a dramatic escape from slavery in 1838 at age 21. Douglass was a spell-binding speaker. "I appear before this immense assembly," he addressed one crowd, "as a thief and robber. I stole this head, these limbs, this body from my master, and ran off with them."

Sojourner Truth, a tall, deep-voiced woman, had also become free after serving several masters for 30 years. In the 1840s she attracted large crowds throughout the North and West with her abolitionist speeches.

For all their talent, African American abolitionists found that white opponents of slavery were generally unwilling to accept them into their organizations. In addition, abolitionists often disagreed over how to attack slavery. Some abolitionists advocated the use of violence and urged enslaved persons to revolt. They felt that the speeches and tracts of the American Anti-Slavery Society were useless against a problem like slavery. Others, like Frederick Douglass, believed that change could only come from within the political system.

Women also chafed at their role as second-class citizens within the movement. Recognizing the important contributions of women, Garrison supported women's rights and encouraged their role in the movement. Other male leaders, however, refused to accept women as equals.

In 1840 all these tensions within the American Anti-Slavery Society splintered it. The split in the society, however, did not end abolitionism. In the 1840s and 1850s abolitionism was one of the issues—along with western expansion and the nation's changing economic identity—that widened the split between Northern and Southern states.

Section Assessment

Main Idea

1. Use a diagram like this one to show some of the major reform movements of the mid-1800s.

Reform Movements

Vocabulary

2. Define: spoils system, nullification, secede, temperance, abolitionism.

Checking Facts

3. How was William Henry Harrison's appeal to voters similar to Jackson's?
4. How did the Second Great Awakening relate to reform movements of the time?

Critical Thinking

5. **Making Comparisons** Compare differing abolitionist strategies for ending slavery.

Technology Skill

USING A WORD PROCESSOR

Learning the Skill

There are several ways to create a professional looking printed document. You may use a word processor or a computer word processing software program.

Using a Word Processor

When you open most word processors, you are initially presented with a blank document. To begin composition of a new document, simply begin typing. To begin composition of a new document, click the **New** button on the Standard toolbar. The following tips will help you format the document to make it look the way you want:

- Text attributes can be modified to make the text appear as *italicized,* **bold,** or <u>underlined</u>. These attributes can be set by first highlighting the text (drag the cursor over the text with the left mouse button depressed), then choosing the options mentioned above (the way you do this depends on the word processor you are using).
- The word processing program automatically "wraps" the text to the next line when the text reaches the right margin as you type. Do not press **Enter** at the end of each line of text; you should press **Enter** only when you wish to start a new paragraph.
- Text alignment can be modified to determine where the text appears on the page. Most word processors let you choose from left-justified, right-justified, or centered.
- Choices of text fonts and sizes also come standard with your word processor. Some common fonts are Times New Roman and `Courier`.
- To insert new text in a line, move the cursor to the point where you want the text to go, and type. The word processing program moves the existing text to the right to make room for the new text. If you wish to type over the existing text, switch to the "overtype" mode.
- To move several lines of text, select the copy using the drag method and click the **Cut** button on your toolbar. If you wish to move the text, click the **Copy** button on the toolbar. Then position your cursor in the location that you want to move the cut text and click **Paste.** The text reappears at your cursor. (If you accidentally drag or paste text to the wrong place, click the **Undo** or **Edit** button on the Standard toolbar.)
- Use a template, or a blueprint of a document, to easily create professional letters, memos, or reports.

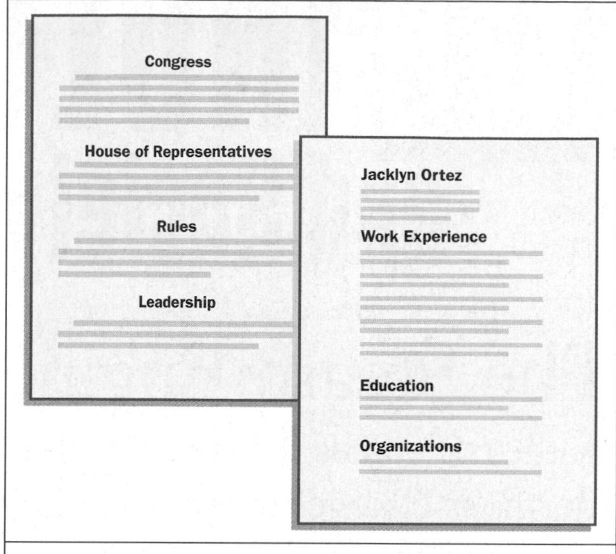

An example of a résumé template

- To learn about other word processing features, read your word processor user's manual or click the **Help** button on your Standard toolbar.

Practicing the Skill

Create a résumé using a template. Most word processing systems provide templates of commonly-used documents, including résumé. Choose **New** from the File menu. Then select **Template,** select the résumé option, and click **OK.** Replace the "boilerplate," or existing text, with your own information. You may choose your own font and style of print. Save your résumé.

Applying the Skill

Create a one- to two-page professional looking document using the subject of Andrew Jackson's election or presidency. For example, you might create a campaign brochure for Jackson or a newspaper clipping that details the Pendleton Act. You may use a template or create your own unique document with large and small heads. Be sure to title your document using a clear, yet attractive font.

Additional Practice

For additional practice, see Reinforcing Skills on page 16.

Science, TECHNOLOGY, and Society

© MICHAEL FREEMAN

The Steam Engine

By the mid-1800s the steam engine had wrought enormous changes in American society, especially in transportation. Steam engines were not only turning the wheels of steamboats and locomotives, but were powering manufacturing, mining, and agricultural machinery as well.

NATIONAL MUSEUM OF AMERICAN HISTORY, DIVISION OF ENGINEERING AND INDUSTRY, SMITHSONIAN INSTITUTE

TOWER OF POWER
A 40-foot-high (12.2-m) steam engine, built by George Corliss, supplied power to all 8,000 machines on display at the 1876 Centennial Exposition in Philadelphia.

HISTORY OF STEAM POWER

1760s | 1780s | 1800 | 1820s

STEAM ENGINE Building on earlier work, James Watt, a Scotsman, develops a true steam engine in 1769. He also devises a measure of output—*horsepower.*

HIGH-PRESSURE STEAM Oliver Evans in the U.S. and Richard Trevithick in England pioneer the high-pressure engine in 1801.

STEAMBOAT Robert Fulton's steamboat on the Hudson begins practical steam-powered travel in 1807.

LOCOMOTIVE The Liverpool & Manchester Line is the first public railroad to use steam power, 1830s.

NATIONAL MUSEUM OF AMERICAN ART, SMITHSONIAN INSTITUTION/ART RESOURCE, NY

GETTING UP STEAM

Steamboats, the floating palaces of their day, plied the Mississippi River from New Orleans to St. Paul. Steamboat captains and the public loved racing, despite its danger. In 1870 in a contest celebrated in story and song, the *Robert E. Lee* beat the *Natchez* in a race from New Orleans to St. Louis.

THE "IRON HORSE"

After the heyday of the steamboat, the steam locomotive took center stage. It sparked the railroad building boom that reached its climax with the completion of the transcontinental railroad in 1869.

RUNNING ON STEAM

PORTFOLIO PROJECT

Research and report on a machine mentioned on these pages—perhaps the steam locomotive or the steamboat—or another steam-driven machine such as the Stanley steamer car. Illustrate your report if you wish. Keep the report in your portfolio.

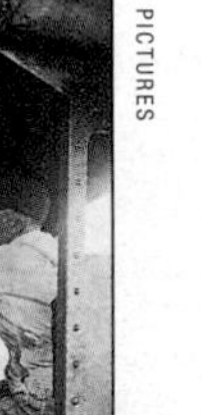

CULVER PICTURES

FULL SPEED AHEAD

The locomotive engineer was king, but no one worked harder than his understudy, the fireman, to keep the train "highballing"—going at top speed. In the early years the boiler was fueled by wood, but later by coal.

1840s | **1860s** | **1880s** | **1900s**

ON THE WATER The paddle wheeler dominates river transportation, but the young business is reaching its peak by the 1840s.

ON THE LAND By the 1860s the locomotive has transformed land transportation. Steam drives the Industrial Revolution in factories and mines, and on farms.

STEAM TURBINE In 1879 Irishman Charles Parsons invents a steam turbine to generate electricity to power ocean liners. Steam turbines are still used.

STEAM TAKES A BACKSEAT The steam engine gives way to electricity and to the internal combustion engine, though many uses for steam remain. Researchers are now developing steam-driven microchips; possible applications include microsurgery.

Chapter  Assessment

Self-Check Quiz

Visit the *American Odyssey* Web site at americanodyssey.glencoe.com and click on ***Chapter 5—Self-Check Quiz*** to prepare for the Chapter Test.

Reviewing Key Terms

Choose the vocabulary term that best completes each sentence below. Write your answers on a separate sheet of paper.

frontier	**turnpike**
tariffs	**spoils system**
nullification	**temperance**

1. Before they could travel on a ________, travelers were required to pay a toll.

2. One provision of Henry Clay's American System aimed to protect American manufacturers by raising the ________ on imported goods.

3. When Andrew Jackson was elected President, he rewarded his supporters with government jobs, a practice that became known as the ________.

4. Large numbers of new settlers began to take over Native American lands as they continued to push the ________ westward.

5. During the 1830s reformers in the ________ movement attacked the evils of alcohol, which was eventually banned by several states.

Recalling Facts

1. Identify three purposes of the Lewis and Clark expedition.

2. General Anthony Wayne defeated the Ohio confederation at the Battle of Fallen Timbers and then concluded the Treaty of Greenville. In what way did these events contradict the Northwest Ordinance?

3. Who were the brothers Tecumseh and Tenskwatawa? What was their message to the Shawnee about relations between Native Americans and white settlers?

4. Who was Sequoyah, and what was his contribution to Native American literacy?

5. Why were the early textile mills of New England built along rivers? What group formed much of the labor force of these mills?

6. What were some bodies of water linked by the canals built in the early 1800s? Why were the railroads able to take business away from the canals?

7. Describe the features of Henry Clay's American System. What parts of it were most successful? What part was less successful?

8. What changes in voting requirements gave rise to the era of the "common man"? How did President Jackson represent this era?

9. How was the question of women's rights related to the reform movement?

10. What were the goals of Sojourner Truth and Frederick Douglass?

Critical Thinking

1. Analyzing Information How did the Cherokee adapt to white settlement? What was the consequence of their adaptation?

2. Making Comparisons Compare the life of a young woman employed in a Lowell mill with the life of a young woman employed on the family farm.

3. Identifying Cause and Effect Use a diagram like this one to show the differences of opinion that caused the antislavery movement to split apart.

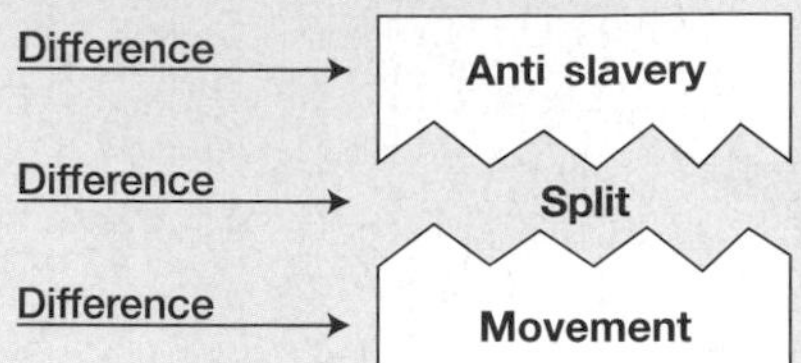

Portfolio Project

Choose one of the Native American peoples mentioned in the chapter—Mandan, Shoshone, Shawnee, Miami, Wyandot, or Cherokee—and research their history. Find out about their original way of life, their customs, and the regions they inhabited. Find out where and how they live today. Write a report and keep it in your portfolio.

Cooperative Learning

With a small group, construct a time line for the 1800s showing significant events in the history of industrial development. Beneath it, construct another time line showing the important developments in the history of women's rights. Add time lines for the antislavery movement, the addition of new states to the Union, and the growth of the railroads. What conclusions can you draw about the period based on these parallel timelines?

Reinforcing Skills

Using a Word Processor Use a word processor to create a time line for the years 1790 to 1840, showing major events discussed in this chapter. Focus on events during the presidencies of John Quincy Adams and Andrew Jackson, especially those related to political change and to development of national political parties.

GEOGRAPHY AND HISTORY

U.S. Territory, 1776–1803

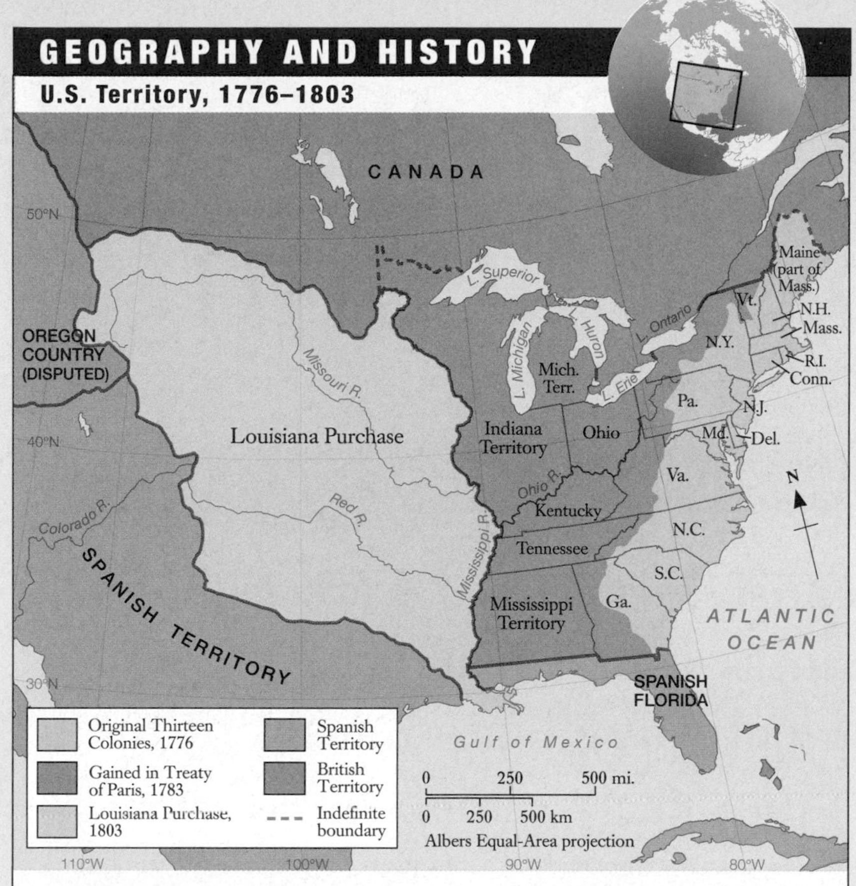

Study the map to answer the following questions:

1. What does the yellow area on the map indicate?
2. How did the United States acquire the territory that became the state of New York?
3. When did the Indiana Territory become a part of the United States?
4. Spain was distressed to learn that France had sold the Louisiana Territory to the United States. What inference can you make from the map about why the Spanish government might have been worried?
5. What was the northern boundary of the Louisiana Purchase? What geographical features marked the eastern boundary and part of the southern boundary?

Technology Activity

Using a Computerized Card Catalog Go to the computerized card catalog in your school or local library. Search for sources containing information about the Cherokee written language. Create a bulletin board about the Cherokee alphabet and its creator. Provide examples of the Cherokee written language and pictures to illustrate the meanings of words.

Standardized Test Practice

1. Which of the following issues was the *most* controversial in national politics during the years 1800 to 1850?

A exploration of the Louisiana Territory
B employment of women in textile mills
C white settlement of Native American lands
D increased tariffs to nurture American manufacturing

Test-Taking Tip: The key word in the question is *most.* Therefore, you can eliminate the answers that contain the *least* divisive issues. For example, reports by Lewis and Clark sparked American interest in the West, so you can eliminate answer A. How does this clue help you to eliminate answer C?

2. The Second Great Awakening helped fuel all of the following reform movements EXCEPT

A the temperance movement.
B the states' rights movement.
C the abolition movement.
D the women's rights movement.

Test-Taking Tip: This question tells you that the Second Great Awakening inspired a spirit of *reform*—a desire to change, improve, or perfect something for the better. Which answer choice seems *least* likely to achieve this goal?

Civil War and Reconstruction

MAY 1856: POTTAWATOMIE, KANSAS

Proslavery and antislavery forces were fighting for control of Kansas by 1855. Proslavery residents of Missouri had poured into Kansas by the hundreds to elect proslavery leaders to office.

The legislature that they elected then passed harsh laws to prohibit even the free expression of opinions against slavery. By the fall of 1855, however, more Kansas residents opposed slavery than supported it. These antislavery forces, determined to defy the proslavery laws, armed themselves, called for new elections, and then drafted a new state constitution.

In response, in the spring of 1856, a group of proslavery Missourians lugged five cannons to the outskirts of Lawrence, Kansas, the antislavery stronghold. The invaders ransacked and burned homes and businesses and killed several men. Outraged by this action, militant antislavery leader John Brown, with his four sons and two other men, kidnapped and brutally executed five proslavery settlers in Pottawatomie, Kansas.

In subsequent raids by the proslavery and antislavery forces, about 200 people were killed before federal troops could stop the violence. The confict in "Bleeding Kansas" foreshadowed the turmoil that later would engulf the nation. ■

HISTORY JOURNAL

Write in your journal about your reaction to the story of Pottawatomie and the picture on the opposite page. What kind of man do you think John Brown was?

Chapter Overview

Visit the *American Odyssey* Web site at americanodyssey.glencoe.com and click on ***Chapter 6—Chapter Overview*** to preview the chapter.

THE STATE HOUSE, TOPEKA, KANSAS/PHOTO COURTESY OF PHOTO ONE

In John Steuart Curry's mural, John Brown calls down the storm of civil war.

Slavery and Politics

MARCH 6, 1857: SUPREME COURT RULES ON *DRED SCOTT* CASE

FRANK LESLIE'S ILLUSTRATED NEWSPAPER

No. 82.—VOL. IV.] NEW YORK, SATURDAY, JUNE 27, 1857. [PRICE 6 CENTS.

Landmark Case
The Supreme Court handed Dred and Harriet Scott a grim decision. The Scotts' daughters, Eliza and Lizzie, are shown above them.

Dred Scott and his wife, Harriet Scott, anxiously awaited the Supreme Court decision. The Scotts were legally enslaved, but they were hoping the Supreme Court would set them free because they had resided with a former master in Illinois and in the Wisconsin Territory, where the Missouri Compromise prohibited slavery. The year was 1857, however, and people who were enslaved did not have any legal rights in the United States. Furthermore, the Scotts were again living in Missouri, a slave state.

At last Chief Justice Roger Taney read the majority opinion of the Court and crushed the Scotts' hopes for freedom. Enslaved African Americans were considered legal property, and no state could deprive citizens of their property without due process of law, Taney said. In addition the Court ruled the Missouri Compromise unconstitutional, declaring that Congress could not prohibit slavery in American territories.

Several weeks later the Scotts were again sold. Their new owner freed them, and they slipped quietly into obscurity. The decision from their lawsuit, however, did not travel quietly. The Court's ruling angered Northerners because it meant that new American territories could now become slave states. The ruling threatened to upset the balance of power between free and slave states, fueling a heated debate that in 1861 would erupt into a bloody war.

Guide to Reading

Main Idea

Economic and territorial expansion fueled sectional rivalries and made compromise over the issue of slavery increasingly difficult and more hostile.

Vocabulary

- sectionalism
- gospel tradition
- fugitive

Read to Find Out . . .

- methods of coping with bondage and various forms of resistance to slavery.
- the contrast between the Northern and Southern political agendas.
- the North's and the South's efforts at compromise and their effects.

The Roots of Conflict

Diverging Interests of North and South

In the late 1700s, many farmers in the upper South—Maryland, Virginia, and North Carolina—shifted from tobacco to grain crops because these crops required less labor. The result was that a once-booming slave trade declined in this region. In 1793, however, a single event abruptly stopped any possible downward trend in the enslaved labor trade. In that year Eli Whitney introduced the cotton gin, a machine that greatly reduced the amount of time and work required to remove the seeds from cotton.

Suddenly, large quantities of cotton could be profitably grown with the aid of the enslaved labor force. Almost overnight, vast numbers of landowners throughout the South converted their fields to cotton production and thousands of would-be cotton farmers poured into the South from other regions. These new cotton planters figured they could increase their profit margins if they used enslaved laborers to pick and clean their cotton.

With the profitability of cotton production ensured by Whitney's invention, slavery quickly gained a new economic foothold. It was a foothold white Southerners were determined to protect.

THE BETTMANN ARCHIVE

King Cotton A steamship in New Orleans carries a load of cotton bales. Most cotton bales weigh about 500 pounds or 227 kilograms. *How did increased cotton production affect the economies of the North and the South differently?*

By the mid-1800s, the Northern economy relied mostly on manufacturing and an ever-increasing immigrant workforce. Therefore, the Northern economy did not rely on enslaved laborers. Northern workers feared that if slavery were to extend northward, their own jobs

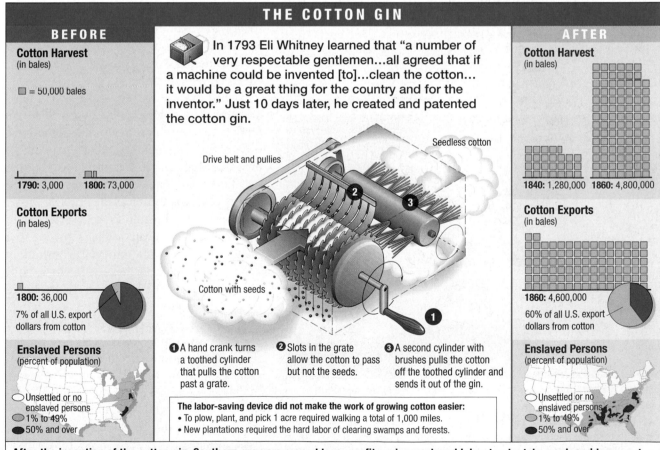

THE COTTON GIN

BEFORE

Cotton Harvest
(in bales)

■ = 50,000 bales

1790: 3,000 **1800:** 73,000

Cotton Exports
(in bales)

1800: 36,000

7% of all U.S. export dollars from cotton

Enslaved Persons
(percent of population)

Unsettled or no enslaved persons
1% to 49%
50% and over

In 1793 Eli Whitney learned that "a number of very respectable gentlemen...all agreed that if a machine could be invented [to]...clean the cotton... it would be a great thing for the country and for the inventor." Just 10 days later, he created and patented the cotton gin.

Seedless cotton

Drive belt and pullies

Cotton with seeds

1. A hand crank turns a toothed cylinder that pulls the cotton past a grate.
2. Slots in the grate allow the cotton to pass but not the seeds.
3. A second cylinder with brushes pulls the cotton off the toothed cylinder and sends it out of the gin.

The labor-saving device did not make the work of growing cotton easier:
- To plow, plant, and pick 1 acre required walking a total of 1,000 miles.
- New plantations required the hard labor of clearing swamps and forests.

AFTER

Cotton Harvest
(in bales)

1840: 1,280,000 **1860:** 4,800,000

Cotton Exports
(in bales)

1860: 4,600,000

60% of all U.S. export dollars from cotton

Enslaved Persons
(percent of population)

Unsettled or no enslaved persons
1% to 49%
50% and over

After the invention of the cotton gin, Southern growers reaped large profits using enslaved labor to plant, harvest, and transport cotton. *Approximately how closely did the increase in cotton production match the increase in enslaved labor?*

would be threatened. In addition Northern abolitionists opposed slavery on moral grounds. Abolitionists such as Frederick Douglass, Sojourner Truth, and William Lloyd Garrison had become adamant that slavery be abolished throughout the nation. As Garrison wrote in his antislavery newspaper, *The Liberator,* "I will be as harsh as truth and as uncompromising as justice. On this subject [slavery] I do not wish to think, or speak, or write, with moderation. No! No!"

By midcentury, North and South had developed two different political agendas based on their very different economies. The Northern agenda called for the extension of free labor into new states. The Southern agenda demanded the maintenance of slavery. The two regions drifted toward **sectionalism,** or an extreme allegiance to their own local interests.

This sectionalism developed because of Northern politicians' attempts to pass laws settling the slavery debate for the entire nation. White Southerners, angered over increasing federal intervention in their affairs, believed that they should be able to make more decisions—especially about slavery—at the state level of government. Meanwhile millions of African Americans wondered when their oppression would end.

Community Under Slavery

Inhuman Conditions and Human Response

From about 1800 to the Civil War, about half of all Southern African Americans lived on large plantations. On the plantation most enslaved laborers worked in the fields from sunup to sundown, six days a week. Although they were typically given Sundays off, many used that day to cultivate their own garden plots. Some worked as cooks, maids, and nursemaids in the Big House, where the plantation owner lived. There the enslaved servants might receive better food and clothing, but because they lived in Big House slave quarters (often in the basement), they saw their loved ones less often. On big plantations some enslaved African Americans also worked as shoemakers, seamstresses, and carpenters.

Most of the enslaved workers were periodically subject to physical abuse. Planters tended to use whips freely and sometimes even branded or maimed what they considered their human property to punish them.

The emotional torment slavery imposed was at least as common as the physical abuse. Planters would threaten to "sell a slave down the river," which meant selling someone to a distant plantation far removed from family and friends, usually farther south, where conditions were worse. Parents and children were frequently separated on the auction block. One way many families coped with these traumatic separations was by substituting "fictive kin" for blood ties, adopting new comrades as family.

A great number also turned to the Christian religion for comfort, adapting African religious beliefs and practices to suit their new circumstances. They took hope from biblical stories of slavery and liberation and transformed Protestant customs into their own African-

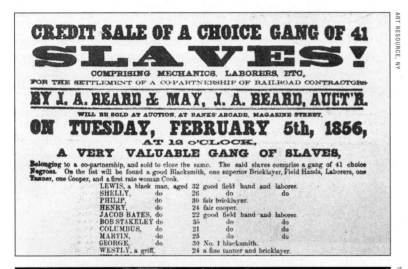

CREDIT SALE OF A CHOICE GANG OF 41
SLAVES!
COMPRISING MECHANICS, LABORERS, ETC.
FOR THE SETTLEMENT OF A CO-PARTNERSHIP OF RAILROAD CONTRACTORS
BY J. A. BEARD & MAY, J. A. BEARD, AUCT'R.
WILL BE SOLD AT AUCTION, AT BANKS' ARCADE, MAGAZINE STREET,
ON TUESDAY, FEBRUARY 5th, 1856,
AT 12 O'CLOCK,
A VERY VALUABLE GANG OF SLAVES,

Belonging to a co-partnership, and sold to close the same. The said slaves comprise a gang of 41 choice Negroes. On the list will be found a good Blacksmith, one superior Bricklayer, Field Hands, Laborers, one Tanner, one Cooper, and a first rate woman Cook.

LEWIS, a black man, aged 32 good field hand and laborer.
SHELLY, do 26 do do
PHILIP, do 30 fair bricklayer.
HENRY, do 24 fair cooper.
JACOB BATES, do 22 good field hand and laborer.
BOB STAKELEY do 35 do do
COLUMBUS, do 21 do do
MARTIN, do 25 do do
GEORGE, do 30 No. 1 blacksmith.
WESTLY, a griff, 24 a fine tanner and bricklayer.

ART RESOURCE, NY

THE BETTMANN ARCHIVES

Selling Humans The poster (above, top) advertises a slave auction in a matter-of-fact manner. Eyre Crowe's painting (above, bottom), *Slave Market in Richmond, Virginia,* clothes its subjects more finely than most who appeared on the auction block. A British observer, Crowe was one of few painters to dignify the subjects of slavery. *What were some psychological abuses of slavery?*

Christian blend. African dancing, drumming, music and chanting were incorporated into worship services. During the years of enslavement African Americans created a **gospel tradition,** a unique musical form that combines many African musical styles with the text of Protestant hymns. Characterized by passionate choral harmonizing and preaching through song, the spirituals were born from this tradition.

SOPHIA SMITH ARCHIVES, GARRISON COLLECTION

Underground Hero Harriet Tubman (far left) stands with a family she helped to freedom. Despite rewards of $40,000 for her capture, Tubman helped more than 300 people, including her parents, escape from slavery. *What did a conductor on the Underground Railroad do?*

In the Sea Islands of Georgia and South Carolina, African Americans known as the Gullah people were especially noted for infusing the Christian religion with African cultural practices. One observer described a worship service in 1867, noting, "Song and dance alike are extremely energetic, and often, when the shout lasts into the middle of the night, the monotonous thud, thud, thud of the feet prevents sleep within half a mile of the praisehouse. . . ."

Resistance to Slavery

Escape, Sabotage, and Revolt

Religious beliefs and practices could both offer comfort and inspire action. By the mid-1800s, hundreds were fleeing plantations each year to freedom in the North and in Mexico. Between 1830 and 1860, a network of abolitionists created the Underground Railroad that helped enslaved African Americans escape by conducting them to safe houses where they could hide on their way to free territories.

One of the most famous "conductors" along the Underground Railroad was Harriet Tubman, a woman who had herself escaped from slavery. Armed with a pistol she was not afraid to use, Tubman guided 19 expeditions of escape out of the South.

Jerry Loguen, another conductor, is said to have helped as many as 1,500 people escape from slavery. When Loguen's former owner, Sarah Logue, discovered his whereabouts, she wrote demanding that he return or pay her $1,000 to purchase his freedom and the horse he had stolen to escape. This was Loguen's reply:

Mrs. Sarah Logue . . . You say you have offers to buy me, and that you shall sell me if I do not send you $1000, and in the same breath and almost in the same sentence, you say, "You know we raised you as we did our own children." Woman, did you raise your own children for the market? Did you raise them for the whipping post? Did you raise them to be driven off, bound to a coffle in chains? . . . Shame on you!

But you say I am a thief, because I took the old mare along with me. Have you got to learn that I had a better right to the old mare, as you call her, than Manasseth Logue had to me? Is it a greater sin for me to steal his horse, than it was for him to rob my mother's cradle, and steal me? . . . Have you got to learn that human rights are mutual and reciprocal, and if you take my liberty and life, you forfeit your own liberty and life? Before God and high heaven, is there a law for one man which is not a law for every other man?

—J.W. Loguen, from a letter reprinted in *The Liberator* in the 1850s

Despite the threat of punishment, some enslaved laborers made annual forays off the plantations to visit family and friends. Others resisted their masters within the confines of the plantation grounds. They held secret meetings, staged work slowdowns, broke tools, feigned illnesses, and set fires.

Plantation owners feared open defiance from individuals but were even more afraid of a collective rebellion. A number of early slave revolts—such as Gabriel's Revolt in Richmond in 1800 and the Denmark Vesey Conspiracy in Charleston in 1822—aroused concern. This concern turned into panic in 1831 when, on August 22, an enslaved preacher named Nat Turner led 75 armed followers in a rebellion. During the 2 days before they were subdued, these rebels killed between 55 and 60 whites.

The hysteria that spread throughout the South after the Turner revolt prompted slaveholders to take elaborate precautions to protect themselves. They created a complicated system of permits for slave travel and patrols to enforce the system. Believing that literacy would lead to empowerment and revolt, masters tried to prevent enslaved workers from learning to read and write. Additionally, Southern legislatures passed laws that made it difficult for masters to free captive African Americans. They wanted to prevent the freed population from increasing because free African Americans could organize revolts much more easily than an enslaved group. While these tactics seemed to halt slave rebellion in the South, Northern opposition to the spread of slavery grew.

Conflict and Compromise

The Slavery Debate Gathers Fire

The majority of Northern politicians did not oppose slavery as a labor force or as a way of life. For purely political reasons, they opposed the extension of slavery into the new territories gained by the Louisiana Purchase. If these territories became slave states, the South would have greater representation in the Senate than the North. Greater representation would give Southern politicians a better chance of fulfilling their political agenda.

To protect slavery and their way of life, white Southerners insisted that the federal government keep out of all matters that the Constitution had not clearly defined. In addition, Southerners wanted tariff laws that encouraged Southern development.

As mentioned in Chapter 2, white Southerners opposed high tariff laws, which raised prices on many articles from overseas. Because the South bought large quantities of manufactured goods from Great Britain, which in turn bought the South's cotton for British cotton mills, the high tariffs threatened the South's prosperity. The Southerners argued that Congress did not have the right to make laws that caused one section of the country to suffer unfairly. They were determined to maintain the political balance.

The Missouri Compromise

Until 1818 there had been an equal number of slave and free states, and likewise an equal number of senators representing the interests of North and South. Then, in 1818 when Missouri petitioned to enter the Union as a slave state, this delicate balance of power was threatened. Northern legislators amended Missouri's petition by stipulating that Missouri could become a state only if it outlawed slavery. Southern politicians were outraged.

Lawmakers eventually resolved this conflict with a series of legislative compromises. The northern part of Massachusetts, which had petitioned for statehood soon after Missouri, would be admitted as the separate free state of Maine. Missouri would be admitted to the Union as a slave state. In addition, the region south of the 36°30′ latitude line in the Louisiana territory would be open to slavery, whereas all the land north of it, except Missouri, would be free. These agreements were collectively known as the Missouri Compromise.

SLAVE REVOLTS, 1600s–1831
1600s Rebellions frequently occur aboard ship during passage to the United States.
1700s Twice in New York enslaved and indentured servants join forces to attempt revolt. Harsh retaliation follows.
1800 Gabriel of Virginia answers "divine calling" to attack Richmond, but his plans fall short.
1600
1625
1650
1675
1700
1725
1750
1775
1800
1825
1850
1804 In the Caribbean Haiti gains independence from France when slaves revolt and claim the island.
1822 In South Carolina Denmark Vesey plans revolution based on Haiti's model, but he is betrayed.
1831 Nat Turner leads a revolt in which 60 whites are killed. Panic and retaliation follow.

White Southerners were unhappy with the compromise because it made more land available for settlement as free territory than as slave territory. Southerners were also concerned because the majority of immigrants pouring into the country were seeking jobs in Northern urban

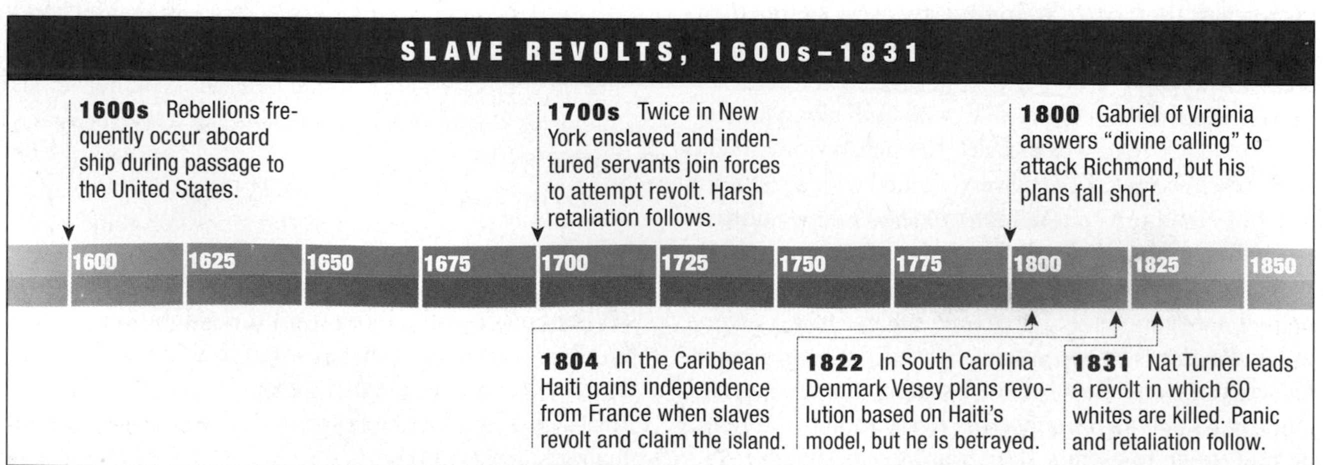

centers. This trend meant that the North's population would soon far exceed the South's. The North would then be entitled to far more seats in the House of Representatives and would be able to advance the goals of its free labor agenda. The North already had more seats, and this had helped them push the Missouri Compromise through.

A Treaty for Half of Mexico This nineteenth-century engraving shows General Zachary Taylor at Buena Vista, where he defeated General Santa Anna in 1847. Following Buena Vista it took five major battles to win the war. *What modern states are in the lands Mexico surrendered to the United States at the end of the war?*

NORTH WIND PICTURE ARCHIVES

War With Mexico

In 1836 when Texas declared its independence from Mexico, white Southerners hoped to acquire Texas as a new slave state. Northerners feared that the admission of Texas to the Union would not only increase the South's power in Congress but would also embroil the United States in a war with Mexico. Nevertheless by 1845 enough politicians were caught up in the fervor of westward expansion—believing that it was the destiny of the nation to reach from shore to shore—that white Southern politicians were able to prevail in getting Texas admitted to the Union as the twenty-eighth state. Mexico was outraged at this action. After a border skirmish between American troops and Mexican troops, the United States declared war on Mexico in May 1846.

On February 2, 1848, after almost two years of fighting, the nations ended the war by signing the Treaty of Guadalupe Hidalgo. This treaty gave the United States vast new regions that today include California, Arizona, New Mexico, Utah, Nevada, and parts of Colorado and Wyoming. The fear that these territories would organize into states intensified the sectional conflict between the North and the South. Many Northerners opposed the extension of slavery even into the newly acquired lands that lay south of the line established by the Missouri Compromise.

The Compromise of 1850

In 1850, 15 free states and 15 slave states made up the Union. California threatened this delicate balance of power by applying for admission to the Union as a free state. Congress once again faced the need to hammer out a legislative compromise. Senator Henry Clay of Kentucky introduced 4 compromise resolutions that became the basic proposals making up the Compromise of 1850: first, that California be admitted to the Union as a free state; second, that territorial governments in Utah and New Mexico let the people of the territories decide the slavery issue for themselves; third, that the slave trade—but not slavery—be prohibited in the District of Columbia; and fourth, that a new fugitive slave law require federal marshals to assist in recapturing **fugitives**—people who had escaped from slavery and were running from the law.

Clay's proposals touched off months of heated debate in Congress. Some of the greatest orators of the time lined up on opposite sides of the issue. John C. Calhoun of South Carolina bitterly opposed Clay's plan. Weak and near death, Calhoun sat silent while his final speech was read to the Senate. In it he warned that the Union could be saved only by giving the South equal rights in the acquired territory and by halting the agitation over slavery. Daniel Webster, who supported Clay's ideas, captivated the Senate with a sentence that has since become famous:

> I wish to speak today, not as a Massachusetts man, nor as a northern man, but as an American. . . . I speak today for the preservation of the Union. "Hear me for my cause."
>
> —Daniel Webster, March 7, 1850

Webster argued that there was no need to exclude slavery from the territories because it would not prosper there due to the soil and climate.

President Taylor opposed a compromise, but his untimely death in July 1850 brought Millard Fillmore to the presidency. With Fillmore's backing, Clay and his supporters succeeded in pushing the proposals through Congress. The package of four laws that became known as the Compromise of 1850 temporarily settled the question of slavery in the territories. The problems did not go away, however, because they were rooted in the issue of slavery itself.

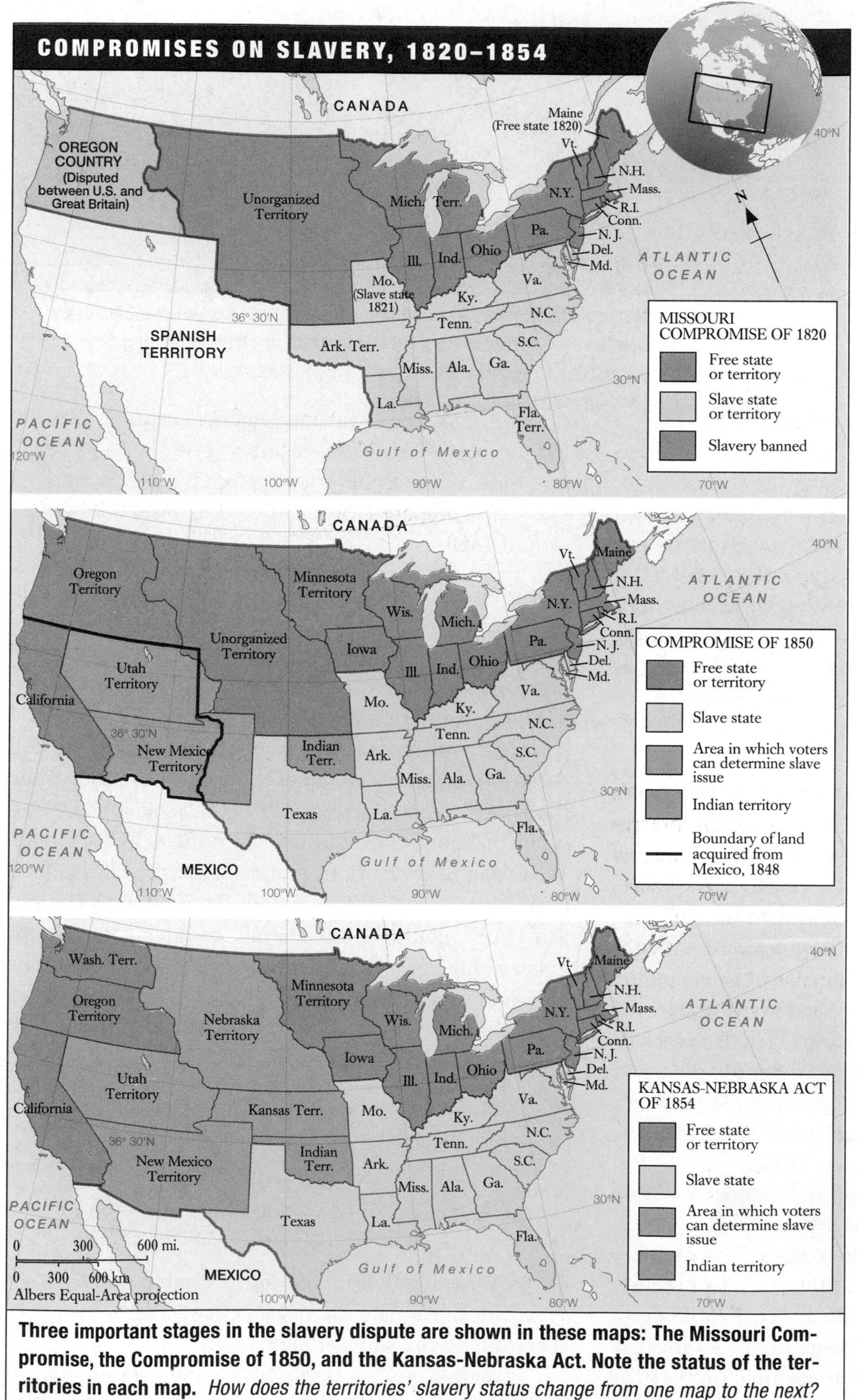

Three important stages in the slavery dispute are shown in these maps: The Missouri Compromise, the Compromise of 1850, and the Kansas-Nebraska Act. Note the status of the territories in each map. *How does the territories' slavery status change from one map to the next?*

The Kansas-Nebraska Act

Just four years later, in 1854, Illinois senator Stephen A. Douglas guided a highly controversial bill through Congress. This bill was the Kansas-Nebraska Act.

Douglas was serving as chairman of the Senate Committee on Territories. He wanted to see the unorganized territory west of Missouri and Iowa opened for settlement. This land lay north of the line established by the Missouri Compromise. Yet rather than letting the land become a free territory according to this legislation, Douglas proposed that the people in the territory decide for themselves whether or not they wanted slavery.

In 1854, after much negotiation, the Kansas-Nebraska Act was passed. It divided the Nebraska territory into two separate territories, Kansas and Nebraska; and it repealed the prohibition of slavery north of the Missouri Compromise line. The citizens of each territory would be able to determine by vote whether their state would be slave or free. In effect the act voided the Missouri Compromise, enabling slavery to expand northward.

Many of the antislavery politicians detested Douglas's bill as a violation of the "sacred pledge" of the Missouri Compromise: no slavery north of the 36°30′ line. These politicians broke from traditional party politics to form the Republican party in February 1854. The Republicans defended Northern sectional interests under the slogan Free soil, free labor, free speech, free men.

Kansas meanwhile became the battleground for sectional and party conflicts.

By 1856 Kansas had turned into a cauldron of violence between antislavery and proslavery groups.

Violence Reaches Washington, D.C.

"Bleeding Kansas" became the catchword for the escalating violence over slavery—and the blood spilled all the way to Capitol Hill. In May 1856 Congressman Preston Brooks of South Carolina entered the nearly empty Senate chamber and beat Massachusetts Senator Charles Sumner with a cane. Brooks felt that Sumner's "Crime Against Kansas" speech, which verbally attacked Brooks's kinsman, had warranted this retaliation.

Brawl on the Senate Floor Violence over slavery spread to Congress. *Who are the two men pictured in this famous cartoon and what prompted the attack?*

It was in the wake of these events that the Supreme Court handed down its decision in the *Dred Scott* case in March 1857. Free-Soil Republicans, who feared the spread of slavery into all territories, now gained popular support in the North, causing Southerners to defend slavery even more stubbornly.

An unsettled nation approached the 1858 elections. In this tense atmosphere, Abraham Lincoln, a little-known one-term congressman from Springfield, Illinois, opposed Senator Stephen A. Douglas in the race for the Senate and challenged him to a series of debates. The debates gave Lincoln the opportunity to make his political views, including his defense of Northern interests, nationally known. Lincoln lost the election, but the debates catapulted him into the national spotlight.

Hostilities Intensify

In October 1859 a violent clash captured the nation's attention when abolitionist John Brown led an interracial band of 21 men in an attack on the federal arsenal at Harpers Ferry, Virginia. Brown hoped to spark a slave rebellion that would "purge this land with blood."

Although Brown and his men were captured within 36 hours, the revolt prompted intense public reaction. White Southerners initially responded hysterically, fearing an outbreak of slave insurrections. The fear calmed as they realized that Brown had not, after all, managed to incite even one slave to join him in the Harpers Ferry revolt. Northern response was initially cool. Brown's eloquence during his trial, however, swayed public opinion. Some Northerners, including many African Americans, proclaimed Brown a hero.

By the time Brown was sentenced to hang, writer Ralph Waldo Emerson predicted that Brown would "make the gallows as glorious as the cross." The editor of a Kansas newspaper supported Emerson's prediction; he wrote, "The death of no man in America has ever produced so profound a sensation. A feeling of deep and sorrowful indignation seems to possess the masses." With Northerners gripped by indignation and most white Southerners gripped by fear or anger, the nation prepared for the upcoming presidential election of 1860.

Section Assessment

Main Idea

1. Use a chart like this one to show the central issue in each of the following crises over slavery: Missouri Compromise, Compromise of 1850, Kansas-Nebraska Act, *Dred Scott* case.

Crisis	Central Issue

Vocabulary

2. Define: sectionalism, gospel tradition, fugitive.

Checking Facts

3. What economic differences helped lead to the Civil War?

4. What were some ways that enslaved individuals coped with and fought the conditions of slavery?

Critical Thinking

5. Identifying Assumptions What did the Fugitive Slave Law assume about the North? Why did many Northerners oppose the law?

The Civil War

APRIL 2, 1865: THE FALL OF RICHMOND

PRIVATE COLLECTION/BRIDGEMAN ART LIBRARY, LONDON

Richmond in Ruins
Citizens flee the burning Confederate capital, shown in this Currier and Ives print.

On Sunday, April 2, 1865, Confederate president Jefferson Davis was praying in a Richmond, Virginia, church when a messenger rushed in. The Union army had broken through Confederate lines and was advancing on the city. In response General Lee had ordered his troops to pull out of Richmond. The city would have to be evacuated.

By midafternoon, troops, cavalry, and townspeople were clogging the roads in a frenzied attempt to escape the city. Then as the sun set, bands of devoted Confederates set fire to their own city of Richmond to destroy any remaining goods and shelter that might be of benefit to the Union soldiers.

On April 4, just 40 hours after Davis had left Richmond, President Lincoln entered the smoldering city. As Lincoln walked the streets of the fallen Confederate capital, freed slaves waved, shouted thanks and praise, and even reached out to touch him. One woman shouted, "I know I am free, for I have seen Father Abraham and felt him."

The Start of the War

"A Hornet's Nest"

In 1860 after a hard-fought campaign, Abraham Lincoln was elected President. Of the 4 candidates who had battled for the presidency, Lincoln had obtained an overwhelming majority of electoral votes—but only 40 percent of the popular vote.

Southerners, aware of Lincoln's pro-Northern political views, reacted by calling for **secession,** or formal withdrawal, from the nation. In December 1860, South Carolina became the first state to secede from the Union. The following year Mississippi, Florida, Alabama, Georgia, Louisiana, and Texas followed, declaring themselves a new nation, the Confederate States of America.

Guide to Reading

Main Idea

The Civil War established the authority of the federal government over the states and ended slavery but left a legacy of bitterness and unresolved questions about African American rights.

Vocabulary

- secession
- emancipation
- lynching
- scorched earth policy

Read to Find Out . . .

- what military and political consequences resulted from the decision of the Southern states to form their own government.
- the effects of the Emancipation Proclamation on African Americans in the Southern states.

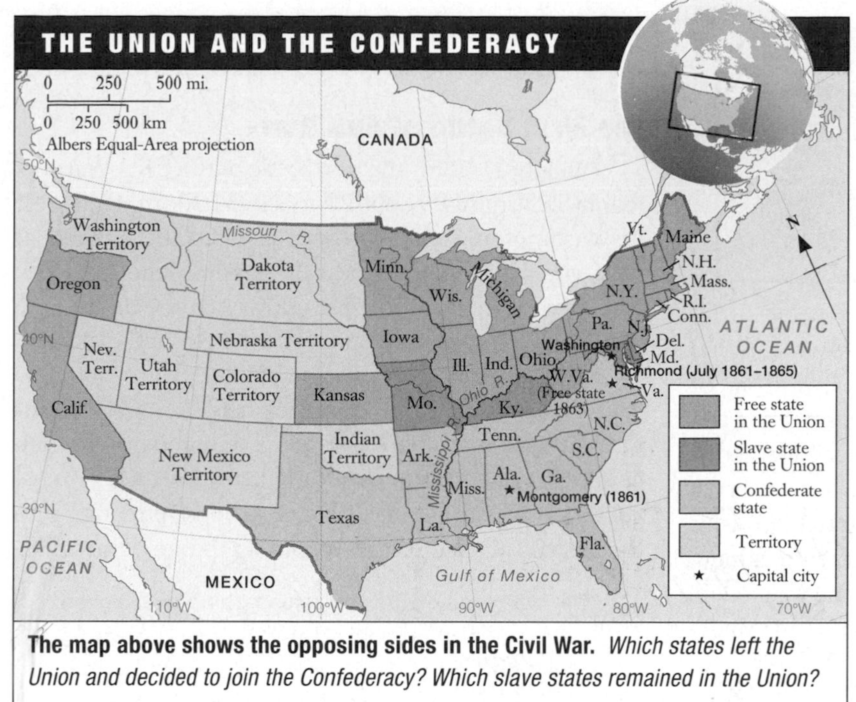

The map above shows the opposing sides in the Civil War. *Which states left the Union and decided to join the Confederacy? Which slave states remained in the Union?*

The Fall of Fort Sumter

The Confederacy's first military objective was to obtain control of Fort Sumter, a Union military installation in the harbor of Charleston, South Carolina. A prominent Southerner warned against firing on this army stronghold, "You will wantonly strike a hornet's nest. Legions now quiet will swarm out and sting us to death." Nevertheless, on April 12, 1861, the Confederate army began shelling Fort Sumter until its commander surrendered.

Proclaiming an insurrection in the South, Lincoln called for 75,000 volunteers to suppress the rebellion. In response, Virginia, Arkansas, North Carolina, and Tennessee joined the Confederacy. Headed by their newly elected president, Jefferson Davis, the Confederates prepared for a war of independence, likening their status to that of the American revolutionaries in 1776.

The Union and the Confederacy Compared

The Union could draw its fighting force from a population of 22 million that included foreign-born immigrants, free African Americans, and escaped slaves. With this size population, the North was able to raise a much larger army than the South. The 11 Confederate states had a population of only 9 million, nearly 3 million of whom the Confederacy refused to let fight because they were enslaved laborers.

What the South lacked in numbers, it made up for in military skill and experience. The Confederacy could draw from a talented pool of military minds that included many officers from West Point and veterans of the Mexican American War. It was a seasoned West Point general, Robert E. Lee of Virginia, who assumed command of the Confederate army. Also, many white Southerners were members of local militia units and were skilled marksmen.

Despite this superior military training, the South was at a disadvantage because almost all resources for waging war—steel mills and iron mines, important industries, transportation facilities and most naval facilities and ships—were located in the North. More than 70 percent of the nation's railroads ran through the North. By comparison the Confederacy possessed inferior natural resources, industry, and transportation. Furthermore the South lacked the financial resources to manufacture or acquire these necessities of war.

The South tried to make up for its disadvantages by fighting a defensive war. Southerners fortified their cities and waited for the Union to invade. Confederate strategists reasoned that Southerners then would be fighting on familiar terrain, amid supporters, and close to supplies.

African American Soldiers

Early in the war, Northern African Americans eagerly tried to enlist in the Union army in order to join the fight to end slavery, but they were not accepted. Outraged by the army's refusal, Frederick Douglass wrote: "Why does the Government reject the negro? Is he not a man? Can he not wield a sword, fire a gun, march and . . . obey orders like any other?"

African American Troops This print, showing troops training near Philadelphia, appeared on Union recruiting posters. *How did free and fugitive African Americans give the Union an advantage?*

HISTORY Online

Student Web Activity 6
Visit the *American Odyssey* Web site at americanodyssey.glencoe.com and click on ***Chapter 6—Student Web Activities*** for an activity relating to the Civil War.

In 1863, desperately needing more soldiers, Lincoln finally accepted African American troops. By the end of the war, about 180,000 African Americans served in the Union army, taking part in more than 500 engagements. During the Mississippi Valley campaign, one observer wrote: "The self-forgetfulness, the undaunted heroism, and the great endurance of the negro . . . created a new chapter in American history." In spite of the Confederate threat to shoot them on capture, 23 African American soldiers won the Medal of Honor.

Major Military Battles

The Bloodiest War

Neither the Union nor the Confederacy imagined that the war would last as long as it did, or that it would exact such a terrible toll. During four years of war, hundreds of thousands of Americans died in battle. Property damage was enormous.

The First Battle of Bull Run

On July 21, 1861, the first battle of the Civil War was fought in Virginia, about 20 miles (32.2 km) southwest of Washington, D.C. Northern civilians, believing that they would be able to witness the easy defeat of the Confederates, came out to picnic and watch the battle. The battle, however, did not end as the North had expected.

Even though Confederate soldiers were outnumbered more than two to one, they held their ground until reinforcements arrived. The Confederates then counterattacked, letting out bloodcurdling cries—"rebel yells"—that sent confused Union troops retreating into the crowds of spectators. According to one witness:

> Cruel, crazy, mad, hopeless panic possessed them, and communicated to everybody about in front and rear. The heat was awful, although now about six; the men were exhausted—their mouths gaped, their lips cracked and blackened with the powder of the cartridges they had bitten off in the battle, their eyes starting in frenzy; no mortal ever saw such a mass of ghastly wretches.
>
> —Congressman Albert Riddle

The defeat meant more than losing one battle. It was a psychological setback from which the Union did not quickly recover.

BOSTON ATHENAEUM

Images of War **Photographers as well as artists were pressed into service to document the horrors of war. The photo above, taken by Timothy O'Sullivan in 1863, is titled "Harvest of Death."** *How might documentary photos have affected Americans' view of the war in a way that paintings or engravings did not?*

Shiloh and Antietam

On April 6 and 7, 1862, the Union and Confederate armies clashed in the first of several massive battles at Shiloh, Tennessee. After the Battle of Shiloh, Americans realized that this conflict was not going to be a gentlemen's war; rather, it would be the wholesale slaughter of ill-fated men and boys. In just those 2 days of fighting at Shiloh, more than 20,000 Union and Confederate soldiers were killed or wounded—8,000 more than in several previous battles combined.

Another violent clash occurred at Antietam Creek on September 17, 1862, when General Lee marched his Confederate troops northward into Maryland. In the ensuing battle, which eventually stopped Lee's advance north, 30,000 soldiers died. The air, one army surgeon commented, was "vocal with the whistle of bullets and scream of shells." A Confederate officer said a nearby cornfield "looked as if it had been struck down by a storm of bloody hail." The Union's victory was of strategic importance because it made Britain reluctant to respond to the South's request for aid.

Using the map above, follow the war strategies of the Union and the Confederacy on land and on sea. *How does the location of most of the battles reflect the Confederates' plan to fight a defensive war? Where did the Union army attack along water routes? Why would the Union force want to gain control of the Mississippi River?*

Gettysburg

In 1863 Confederate general Lee tried once again to invade the North. Union troops met his advance, and during the first 3 days of July the 2 armies battled outside the town of Gettysburg, Pennsylvania. The Union suffered heavy losses on the first day of battle at Seminary Ridge. A gunner recalled "bullets hissing, humming and whistling everywhere; cannon roaring; all crash on crash and peal on peal."

On the third day, Lee ordered General George Pickett to lead 13,000 men in an assault on Union lines.

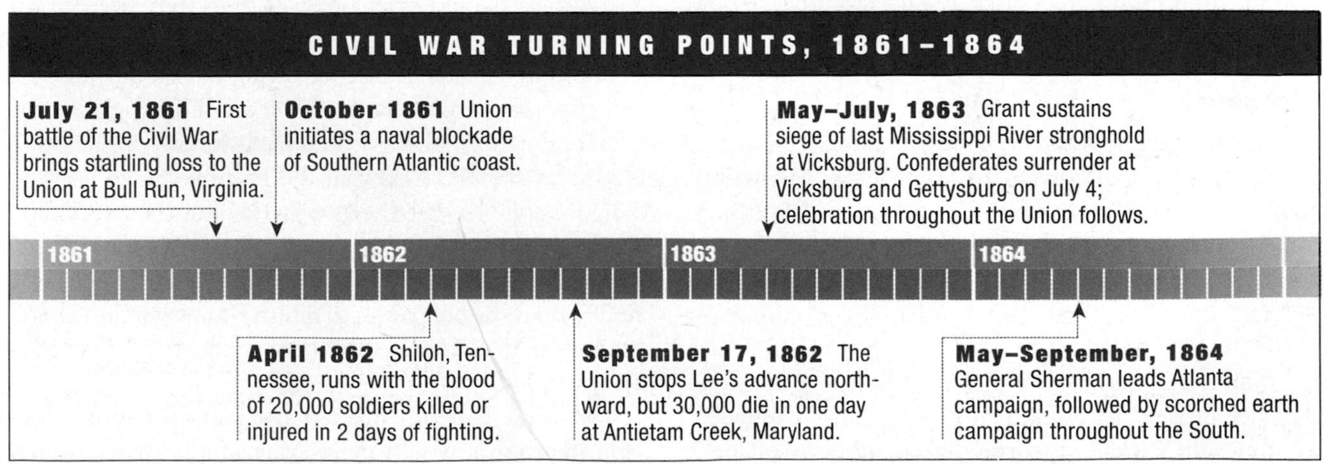

Nearly half the advancing Confederates were gunned down. By the time the Confederates retreated from Gettysburg, they had sustained 28,000 casualties; the Union had sustained 23,000. As wagons carried the Confederate wounded southward, a Quaker nurse wrote, "There are no words in the English language to express the suffering I witnessed today."

The Gettysburg Address

The Battle of Gettysburg cost both sides heavy casualties, but it was a crushing defeat for the South. The Confederacy would never recover from the losses it had suffered. On November 19, 1863, President Lincoln visited the battle site to dedicate a cemetery to honor the soldiers who had fallen there. In a short and eloquent address, the President stated:

> The world will little note nor long remember what we say here, but it can never forget what they [the fallen soldiers] did here. It is for us, the living, rather, to be dedicated here to the unfinished work which they who fought here have thus far so nobly advanced.
>
> It is rather for us to be here dedicated to the great task remaining before us—that from these honored dead we take increased devotion to that cause for which they gave the last full measure of devotion; that we here highly resolve that these dead shall not have died in vain; that this nation, under God, shall have a new birth of freedom; and that government of the people, by the people, and for the people, shall not perish from the earth.
>
> —Abraham Lincoln, November 19, 1863

Many people who were there that momentous day thought that Lincoln's remarks were too short and simple for such a serious occasion. The Address, however, is one of the significant developments in the history of individual rights in the United States. Here the President was telling a war-weary nation that *all Americans*—regardless of heritage—had a stake in the future of the nation. Along with that stake would eventually come equality.

Vicksburg

Yet the war was far from over in 1863. Union and Confederate forces battled to control the Mississippi River at the same time that troops fought at Gettysburg. Union troops occupied New Orleans, Baton Rouge, Natchez, and Memphis. Finally all that remained in Confederate hands was Vicksburg, located on bluffs high above the river. In mid-May 1863, Union general Ulysses S. Grant ordered a siege of the city. On July 4, the same day Lee began his retreat from Gettysburg, Confederate forces in Vicksburg surrendered. As news of the 2 strategic victories spread throughout the Union, there were, according to Carl Sandburg, "celebrations with torchlight processions, songs, jubilation, refreshments."

The War at Sea

While armies battled their way across the land, another aspect of the war took place in coastal waters and on inland rivers. At the outset of the war, Lincoln had ordered a blockade of all Southern ports. The Union navy's assorted ships patrolled the 3,500 miles (5,631.5 km) of Confederate coastline and eventually cut off Southern trade. The daring blockade runners that managed to escape capture could not carry enough goods to supply the South. The greatest blow to Confederate trade came in April 1862 when Commodore David Farragut sailed a fleet into the mouth of the Mississippi River. He steamed past the forts below New Orleans and went on to capture the South's largest city.

The Confederates almost succeeded in breaking the blockade at Chesapeake Bay. Southerners raised the frigate *Merrimack,* scuttled by Union forces when they abandoned the Norfolk navy yard, and converted it into an ironclad warship. In March 1862, the ship, renamed the *Virginia,* battled the Union's ironclad *Monitor.* Neither ship could sink the other, but the battle marked the beginning of a new era in naval warfare.

Social and Economic Battles

Controversy Over the War

The battles of 1863 turned the tide militarily for the Union, but Northerners still experienced difficulties on the home front. Social and economic difficulties plagued both sides.

Emancipation

Throughout the war, abolitionists pressured President Lincoln to free all enslaved African Americans. Abolitionists argued that Union soldiers were fighting not only to preserve the Union but also to end slavery. They also pointed out that freeing the slaves would create a new pool of recruits that could be drafted to fight for the North. Further, backers of **emancipation,** or liberation from slavery, reasoned that the Fugitive Slave Law no longer applied to Southerners, who after their secession from the Union could no longer claim to be protected by the Union's laws. By this reasoning, the North was finally rid of its obligation to return runaways, and Union troops could confiscate Southern property and slaves as spoils of war.

At first Lincoln evaded the issue of emancipation, fearing it would drive Maryland, Missouri, and

Kentucky out of the Union. On September 22, 1862, however, under extreme pressure from Republican senators to declare his position on slavery, Lincoln signed a preliminary version of the Emancipation Proclamation, which declared freedom for enslaved persons only in parts of the Confederacy not under the control of the Union army. The proclamation had no effect on enslaved African Americans in the border states that had not joined the Confederacy.

Although this proclamation freed some enslaved African Americans, it did not necessarily express Lincoln's personal views on the subject of slavery. Just a few months earlier, Lincoln had made his position known in a letter to the abolitionist Horace Greeley.

> My paramount object in this struggle is to save the Union, and is not either to save or destroy Slavery. If I could save the Union without freeing any slave, I would do it; and if I could save it by freeing all the slaves, I would do it; and if I could do it by freeing some and leaving others alone, I would also do that. What I do about Slavery and the colored race, I do because it helps to save this Union; and what I forbear, I forbear because I do not believe it would help to save the Union.
>
> —Abraham Lincoln, from a letter to Horace Greeley, 1862

CHICAGO HISTORICAL SOCIETY

Contributions to the War Effort Mary Rice Livermore worked throughout the Civil War in support of the Union cause. She organized women's aid societies such as the group pictured. The societies raised money and sent food and clothing to Union soldiers on the battlefield. *In what other ways did women's efforts make a difference during the Civil War?*

New Roles

As the war dragged on, Northern and Southern women had to assume many of the roles previously assigned to the men who had gone away to fight. The two armies needed food, clothing, and weapons. Women took responsibility for supplying many of these goods. In addition many women needed jobs to help support their families. So across the country, women managed their family farms, worked in factories, ran printing presses, shod horses, and also filled government positions. A handful of women even disguised themselves as men and fought in the war.

One of the many significant contributions women made to the war effort was caring for the wounded. Three thousand women served as nurses during the war. Nurses were in great demand to tend the wounded because twice as many soldiers died of infectious diseases as died of injuries sustained in combat. Doctors did not yet understand the importance of sanitation, sterile medical equipment, and a balanced diet. As a result deaths from dysentery, malaria, and typhoid were a by-product of war.

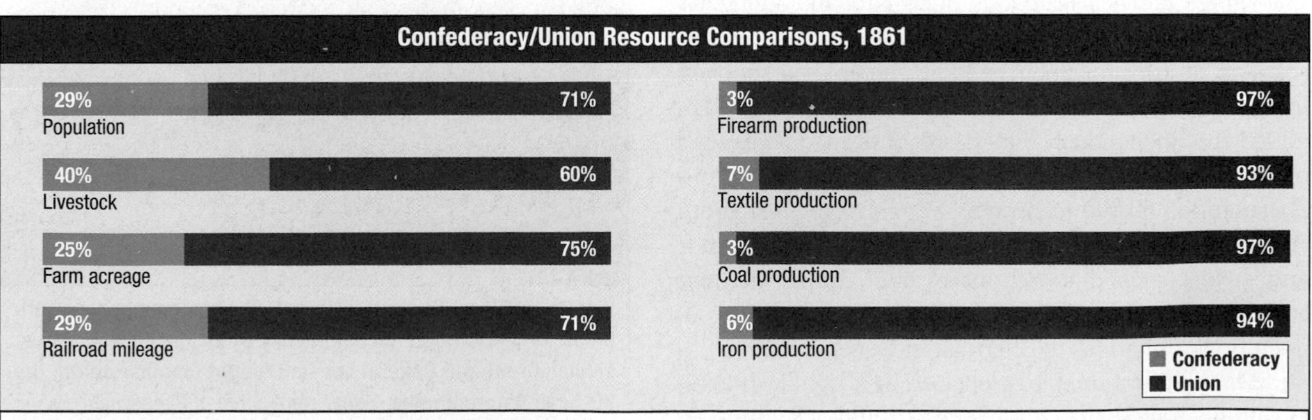

Compare the resources of the North and the South at the start of the Civil War. *In what two areas did the Union have the greatest advantage over the Confederacy? What, if any, advantages are shown for the South?*

Riots

As the bloody battles dragged on, both the North and the South experienced difficulties recruiting soldiers as well as raising money needed to keep up the fight. The Union draft law of March 1863 excused men from military service if they paid the government a $300 fee. Many Northerners who thought the law discriminated against the poor angrily took to the streets in protest.

The most violent draft riots erupted in New York City on July 13 in the wake of Union victories at Gettysburg and Vicksburg. There the draft riots had racial overtones as low-paid workers blamed African Americans for the war. Rioters set fire to an African American orphanage and began **lynching** African Americans, murdering them in ruthless mob attacks.

Resentment over the draft was also prevalent in the South. There, however, homelessness and hunger overshadowed the draft issue. Women, being the majority of those left at home to confront these issues, eventually took matters into their own hands. In 1863 riots broke out in which women looted stores, hijacked trains, and attacked Confederate supply depots to get bread and other food stored there.

The Road to Surrender

Smoldering Soil, Smoldering Resentment

Until 1864 Lincoln had been disappointed with the quality of his military commanders. Only General Ulysses S. Grant had performed close to Lincoln's expectations. In March the President appointed Grant commander of all Union forces.

One of Grant's first official actions was to order Generals William Tecumseh Sherman and Philip Henry Sheridan to pursue a **scorched earth policy** in the South. Following Grant's instructions, Sherman's and Sheridan's troops burned farmland, plantation homes, and cities in order to destroy the enemy's food, shelter, and supplies. In so doing they broke the South's will to fight. Sheridan raided the Shenandoah Valley, one of the Confederacy's main sources of food, to starve Lee's hungry troops. Sherman led 60,000 men on a "March to the Sea" from Atlanta to Savannah. On the way they burned homesteads and fields, sacked storehouses, and ripped up and twisted railroad tracks to render them useless. Consequently Savannah fell to Sherman in December 1864.

Meanwhile Grant battled Lee in Virginia, hoping eventually to take the Confederate capital of Richmond. Union and Confederate forces clashed in three major battles: in the Virginia wilderness and at Spotsylvania in May, and at Cold Harbor in early June. In three battles Grant lost almost as many Union soldiers as there were Confederates serving in Lee's army. Yet because of the Union's population advantage, Grant could replace his soldiers, while Lee could not. Grant then settled down to a long siege of Richmond.

By the fall of 1864, Lincoln called home as many Union troops as he could, hoping to generate support for his reelection. The Union victories in the South helped Lincoln win by an electoral college vote of 212 to 21 and a popular majority of more than 400,000 votes.

The War's End

Increasing desertions among Confederate troops prompted Jefferson Davis in November 1864 to allow enslaved African Americans to enlist. The Confederate Congress did not authorize the act, however, until it was too late to take effect. Still, Davis refused to surrender

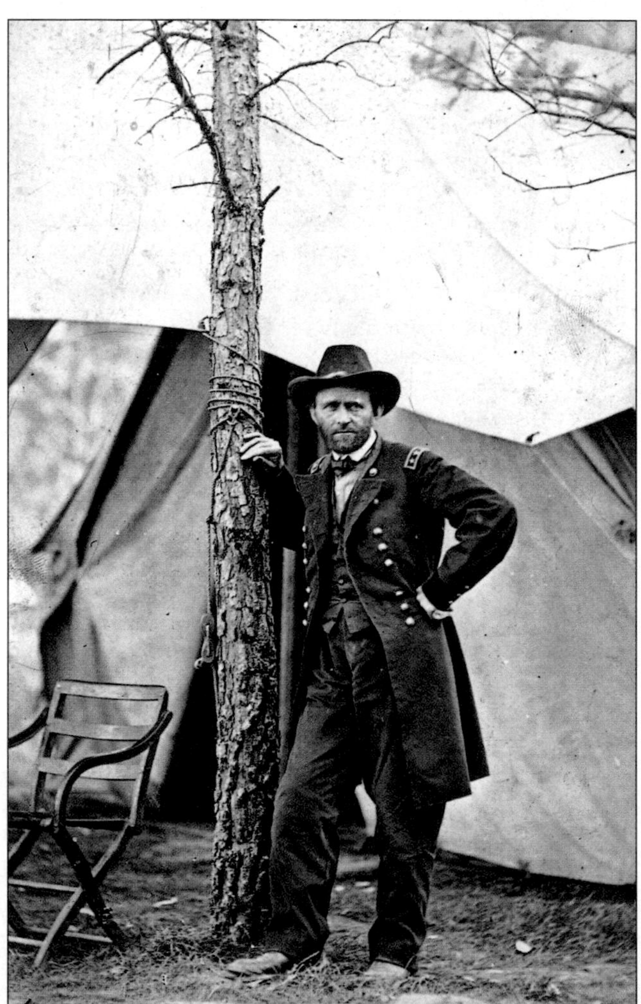

BROWN BROTHERS

Victory by Siege General Ulysses S. Grant, commander of all Union forces, exuded the confidence of a capable, aggressive soldier. Grant and General Lee had fought together during the Mexican American War. *What were some of the advantages Grant held over his former compatriot? How did Grant destroy Lee's remaining resources?*

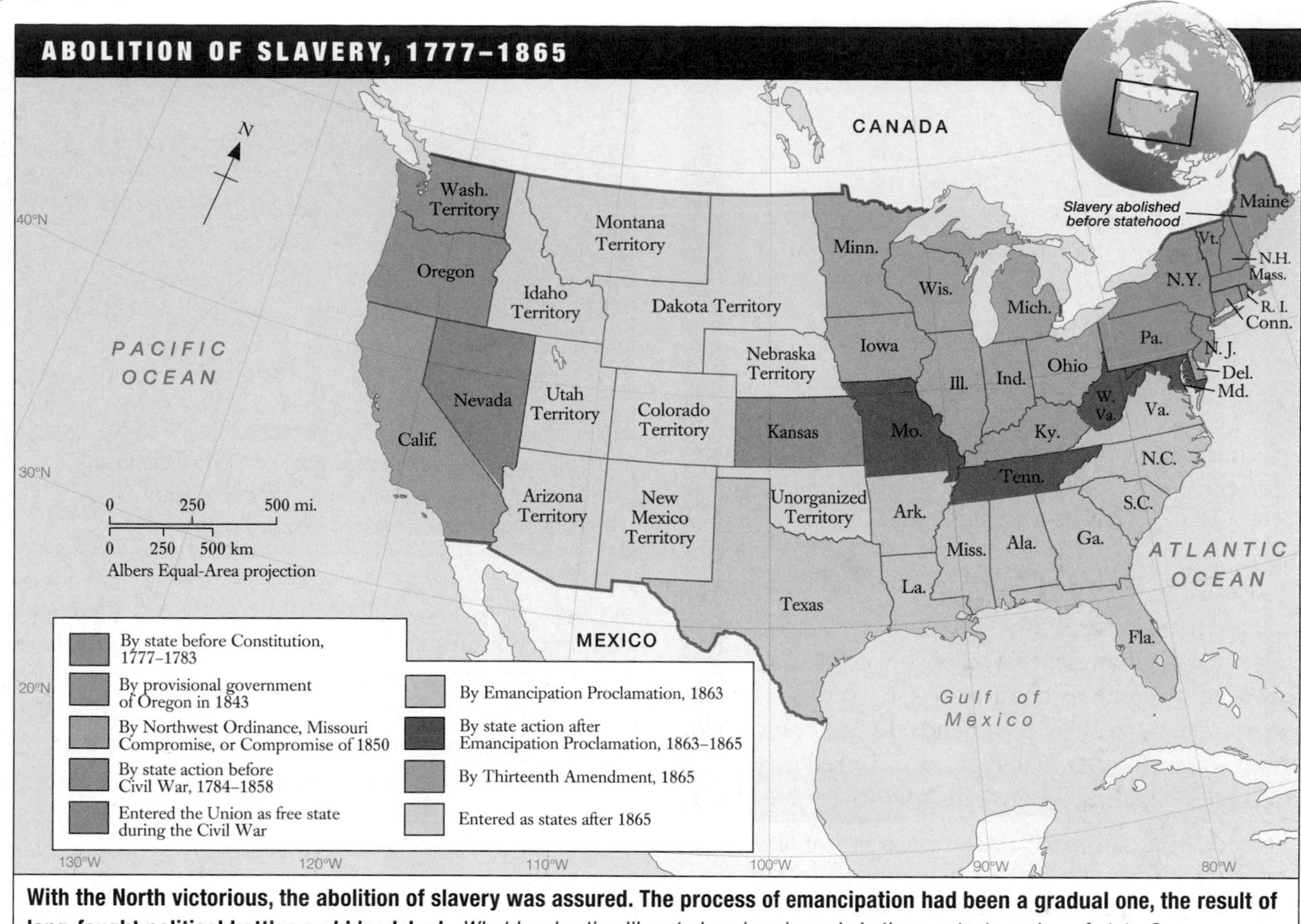

With the North victorious, the abolition of slavery was assured. The process of emancipation had been a gradual one, the result of long-fought political battles and bloodshed. *What legal action liberated enslaved people in the greatest number of states?*

unless Lincoln acknowledged the South as an independent nation.

Grant and Sheridan finally took Richmond on April 3, 1865, as the city smoldered from the fires set by retreating Confederates. Union troops pursued Lee and his exhausted army. The Confederates made feeble attempts to hold them off, but Lee's army had been reduced to about 30,000 hungry and demoralized men. On the morning of April 9, Lee led his troops into battle for the last time. Union forces had them almost surrounded and badly outnumbered. Facing an almost certain slaughter, Lee decided to surrender. That afternoon he met Grant at Appomattox Court House in Virginia. Grant's terms of surrender ensured that Confederate soldiers would not be prosecuted for treason and that artillery and cavalry soldiers would be permitted to keep their horses. Grant also arranged for 3 days' rations to be sent to the Confederate soldiers. Lee accepted.

When Union troops heard of the surrender, they began firing their guns to celebrate their victory. Grant put an end to the firing. "The war is over," he said, "the rebels are our countrymen again, and the best sign of rejoicing after the victory will be to abstain from all demonstrations."

Lee echoed these sentiments when he knew the Confederate army was defeated.

> The war being at an end, the southern states having laid down their arms, and the question at issue between them and the northern states having been decided, I believe it to be the duty of everyone to unite in the restoration of the country and the reestablishment of peace and harmony.
>
> —Robert E. Lee, April 1865

The human costs of the war were staggering. About 360,000 Union soldiers and 260,000 Confederates lay dead. Another 375,000 soldiers were wounded. Approximately 1 in 3 Confederate soldiers died in the war. These figures do not include deaths from imprisonment such as at Andersonville, a prison camp operated by Confederates in Georgia, where 13,000 out of 32,000 Union prisoners died.

Lincoln as Commander in Chief

Lincoln's main goal had been to preserve the Union. In his second Inaugural Address, he indicated that he would deal compassionately with the South after the war ended:

BROWN BROTHERS

"Peace Among Ourselves" Lincoln asked citizens to work for peace after the war. Matthew Brady's portrait of Lincoln (above) captures the peaceful spirit of the President. *How did Lincoln's agenda at the start of the war account for his post-war policy of leniency toward the South?*

> With malice toward none; with charity for all; with firmness in the right, as God gives us to see the right, let us strive on to finish the work we are in; to bind up the nation's wounds; to care for him who shall have borne the battle, and for his widow, and his orphan. . . .
>
> —Abraham Lincoln,
> *Second Inaugural Address,* March 1865

Unfortunately Lincoln never got to carry out his plan. On April 14, 1865, five days after the South surrendered, Confederate sympathizer John Wilkes Booth shot President Lincoln at a theater in Washington, D.C. Lincoln died the next morning. The nation, and indeed the world, mourned his death.

Even those who had sharply criticized Lincoln's policies acknowledged his leadership and accomplishments. The *New Orleans Tribune* stated: "Brethren, we are mourning for a benefactor of our race." An outpouring of sympathy came from Britain and others who had supported the Confederate cause. Admirers as well as critics agreed that replacing Lincoln would be difficult.

A funeral train carried Lincoln's body on a 1,700-mile (2,735.3-km) journey from Washington, D.C., to

ARCHIVE PHOTOS

Mourning Throngs of citizens flocked to view the President's open casket and mourn his untimely death. *What public memorials followed Lincoln's death?*

Springfield, Illinois. Millions of people lined the route. At night, bonfires and torches lit the way. By day, bells tolled and cannons fired.

Lincoln's second Inaugural Address, read at the cemetery, reminded Americans of his plan "to do all which may achieve and cherish a just, and a lasting peace, among ourselves, and with all nations." The future, however, now belonged to those who favored far harsher measures.

Section Assessment

Main Idea

1. Use a diagram like this one to show some of the social, economic, and political consequences of the Civil War.

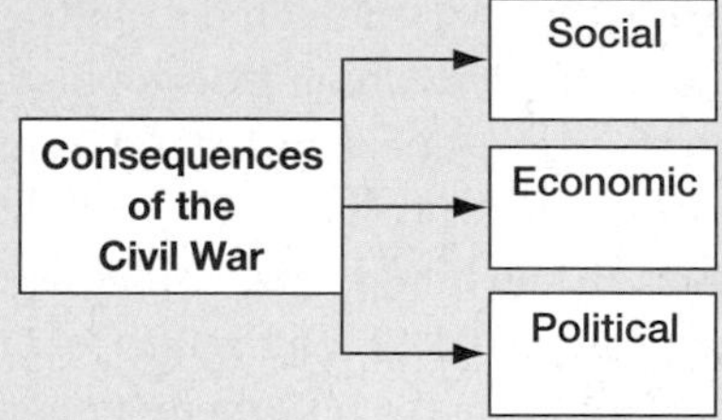

Vocabulary

2. Define: secession, emancipation, lynching, scorched earth policy.

Checking Facts

3. What advantages did the North have upon entering the war? The South?
4. What were the social and economic battles fought during the Civil War?

Critical Thinking

5. **Analyzing Information** Why do you think Lincoln initiated a postwar policy of leniency toward the South?

Social Studies Skill

COMBINING INFORMATION FROM MAPS

Learning the Skill

Thematic maps aid in the communication of information by presenting place-related data in a concise way. Sometimes two or more maps can convey information that cannot be presented easily on a single map.

Finding Connections

To find and combine geographic patterns:

a. First examine the map on this page to find information about industry and agriculture in 1860.

b. Note any significant patterns. For example, a quick look reveals that New England farmers mainly raised dairy cattle and hay, which are small farm enterprises.

c. Then examine the map on the abolition of slavery on page 179, which shows, for example, that the New England states prohibited slavery before the framing of the Constitution.

d. Try to visualize relationships between the two maps. In each, there are patterns differentiating the North and the South. Combining these maps suggests a state's decisions about slavery or abolition may have related to how the people in that state made a living.

Practicing the Skill

Study the map below and the map on page 179 and answer the following questions:

1. What relationship do you see between plantation crops and the abolition of slavery?

2. Compare industry in cotton-growing states and in other states. What pattern do you notice?

3. What connection can you make between a state's economy and its stand on slavery?

4. What was produced in the West and Midwest?

5. How might the economies of the West and Midwest have affected the slavery debate?

Applying the Skill

Using two other maps, draw five conclusions about the combined information they present.

The **Glencoe Skillbuilder Interactive Workbook, Level 2** CD-ROM provides more practice in key social studies skills.

AGRICULTURE AND INDUSTRY, 1860

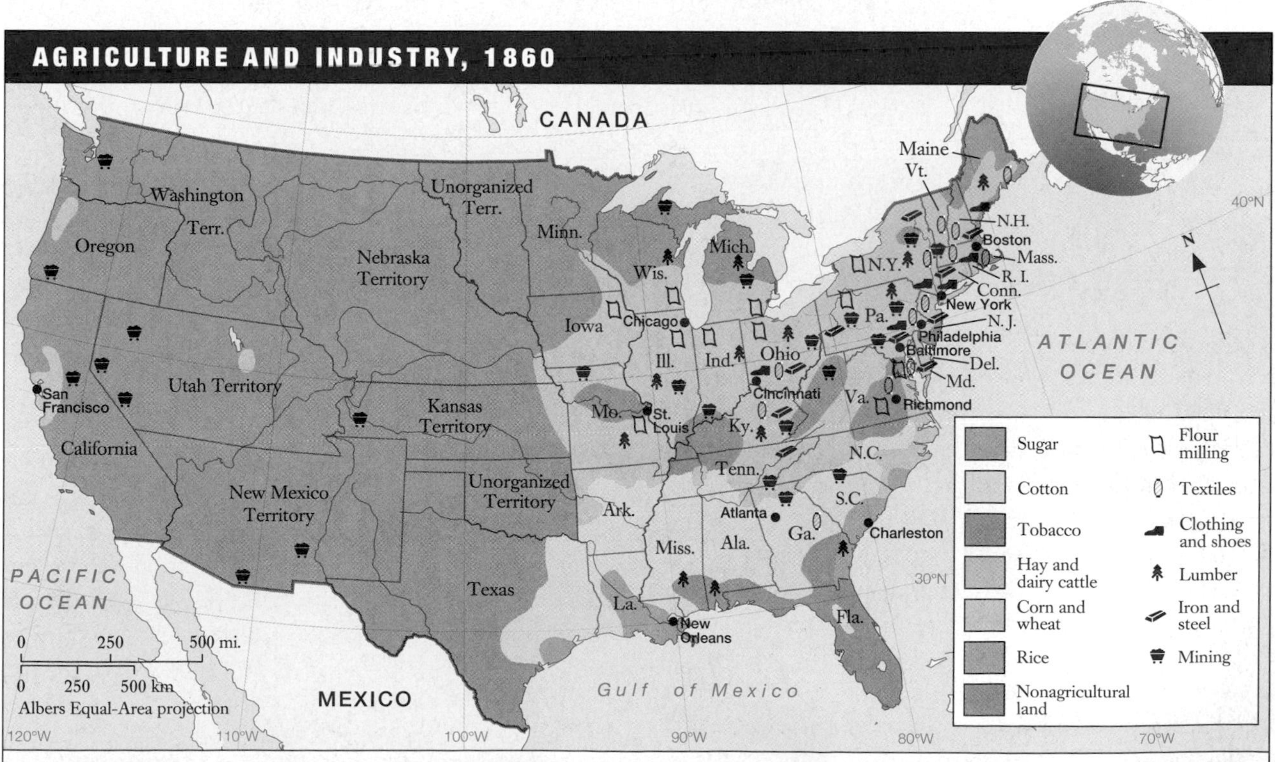

By 1860 textile and shoe factories fueled the economies of New York and New England, while plantation crops such as cotton and tobacco were the mainstay of the Southern economy. *What states depended on flour milling?*

SPORTS: "Fly rule" adopted: The baseball must be caught before it bounces to get the batter out.

One Day in History

Sunday, April 9, 1865

MARKET BASKET

Here is where a dollar will go:

Stereoscopic pictures $1.50/dozen
Barnum's American Museum ticket . . . . 15¢ child
. . . . 25¢ adult
Theater ticket . . . . . 25¢ child
. . . . 50¢ adult
Printing press $3,500

Collar $1.25/dozen
Coffee . . . . 7 to 25¢/lb.
Pocket watch $10
Artificial leg $75

HIGH IMPACT PHOTOGRAPHY, TIME-LIFE BOOKS

Daguerreotypes . . . . 25¢ to $1
Medical consultation fee . . $5
Harper's Weekly magazine . . . . 10¢
New York Times newspaper . . . . 3¢
Yarn . . . . 2¢/spool
Stove polish . . . . 10¢/cake
Sarsaparilla compound $1/bottle

LOVELL THOMAS © NATIONAL GEOGRAPHIC SOCIETY

Dignity in Defeat Rising to this sorrowful occasion, General Lee, in full dress uniform, agrees to peace terms with General Grant and signs the articles of surrender.

Confederates Surrender

Union Victory! Peace! General Lee Surrenders

APPOMATTOX COURT HOUSE, VIRGINIA—This afternoon General Robert E. Lee surrendered the Army of Northern Virginia to General Ulysses S. Grant, ending four years of bloody civil war and ensuring the survival of the American Union. Officers and men of the Confederate army will be allowed to return to their homes, and officers will retain their side arms and private property. All former Confederate fighters will be required to swear and sign an oath of loyalty to the Union.

The details of the treaty were negotiated at the home of a man named McLean, the same man who saw the first bombshell of the war fall on his front lawn. Colonel Ely S. Parker, a Seneca man and an aide to General Grant, recorded the proceedings.

One Day in History, Sunday, April 9, 1865

NATION: Maria Mitchell, discoverer of comet, is appointed to chair at Vassar; she becomes the first woman astronomy professor in the nation.

COURTESY OF SPECIAL COLLECTIONS, VASSAR COLLEGE LIBRARIES

Editorial

APRIL 1, 1865, from the *New Orleans Tribune,* an African American daily newspaper

Before 1863, the planters said that it was for the sake of the negroes that they kept them in slavery; it was from a feeling of humanity that they retained in bondage a race of men whom they proclaimed unfit to lie under any other status. . . . going so far as to have them whipped and put into the stocks—as a means of promoting their advancement. . . .

The planters defended slavery on the ground of sympathy for the negro. But it was all shame. They clung to slavery for the sake of making money. There is no disputing about it.

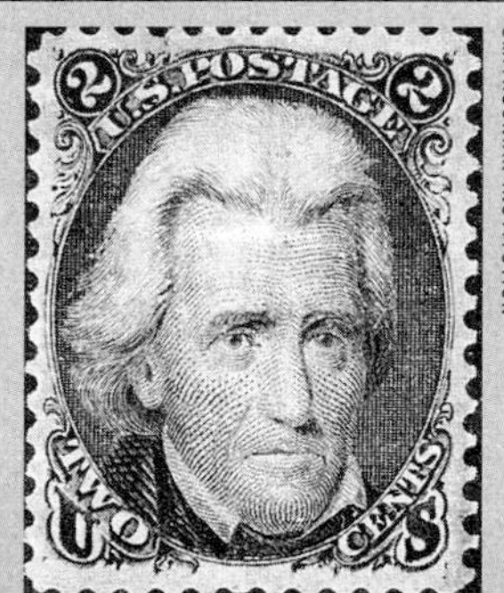

SMITHSONIAN INSTITUTION

Free Mail Delivery

WASHINGTON, D.C.—Mail will now be delivered free in all cities with populations of 50,000 or more. Recent improvements in rail and steamship transport make this free delivery possible.

THE BETTMANN ARCHIVE

Actor Edwin Booth, brother of John Wilkes Booth, appears in *Hamlet.*

MUSIC

"Battle Hymn of the Republic"
"When Johnny Comes Marching Home"
"Follow the Drinking Gourd"
"Many Thousand Gone"
"Oh, Susanna"
"Swanee River"
"My Old Kentucky Home"

COURTESY OF THE BARNUM MUSEUM, BRIDGEPORT, CT

Owner P.T. Barnum has improved his museum by hiring trapper Grizzly Adams to stock the menagerie.

AMUSEMENTS

At Barnum's American Museum:

The Great Dancing Giraffe
Punch and Judy
Bohemian Glass Blowers
Two Glass Steam Engines in Motion
Prof. Hutchins, lightning calculator
Poultry, pigeon, and rabbit show

Scovill's

Sarsaparilla Compound

For the cure of Liver Complaint, Dyspepsia, Scrofula, Dropsy, Neuralgia, Boils, Tumors, and Epilepsy

It's a sure cure! $1^{00}/bottle

BROWN BROTHERS

Reconstruction

FEBRUARY 24, 1879: BANKS OF THE MISSISSIPPI RIVER

Exodusters
This drawing from an 1880 *Harper's Weekly* contrasts the new exodus with the old (inset), as African Americans fled the South.

HUNDREDS OF AFRICAN AMERICANS, WITH THEIR BELONGINGS BUNDLED ON THEIR BACKS, WAITED ON THE SHORES OF THE MISSISSIPPI RIVER FOR THE STEAMER THAT WOULD CARRY THEM ACROSS TO ST. LOUIS. From there they would head by train to Kansas, where they hoped to begin new lives. These people were called the Exodusters, so named because they left their homes to make better lives in the dusty new land, just as the Israelites had done centuries earlier in their exodus from Egypt to Canaan.

During the exodus of 1879, more than 20,000 African Americans migrated to Kansas, their Canaan, or "promised land." A Louisiana preacher explained that they "were not emigrating because of inducements held out to them by parties in Kansas, but because they were terrorized, robbed, and murdered by the bulldozing desperadoes of Louisiana and Mississippi." The African Americans hoped that their journey to Kansas would take them far from the poverty and terrorism that they experienced in the South despite the many promises of the postwar government.

Presidential Reunion Plans

Attempts at Reconciliation

In 1863 before the war had ended, Lincoln made plans to reestablish state governments in the South that would be loyal to the Union after the war. According to Lincoln's plan, for a state to be recognized as legitimate, 10 percent of the men eligible to vote in 1860 had to have sworn allegiance to the Union.

Andrew Johnson, who assumed the presidency after Lincoln's assassination, had expressed harsh sentiments toward Confederate "traitors" during the war. He therefore surprised many Northerners when he began to promote policies that seemed to continue Lincoln's intentions of "malice toward none." Congress was not in session when Johnson took office, so he proceeded with

GUIDE TO READING

Main Idea

Conflicts sparked by harsh plans to reunite the Union exhausted a war-weary nation, causing many Northern politicians to leave the promise of full civil rights for African Americans unfulfilled.

Vocabulary

- amnesty
- black codes
- sharecropping
- carpetbagger
- gerrymandering

Read to Find Out . . .

- what possible approaches the North might have taken toward restoring the economic and social fabric of the defeated South.
- how Reconstruction brought both gains and hardships to African Americans.

his plans for Reconstruction—the process of restoring relations with the Confederate states.

In a Reconstruction proclamation issued in May of 1865, Johnson granted **amnesty,** or pardon, to Confederates who would sign an oath of loyalty to the Union. Political and military leaders and landowners whose property was worth more than $20,000 had to apply for special pardons. Johnson granted such pardons regularly. In addition Johnson appointed provisional governors and set forth minimal requirements for reorganizing Southern state governments. By December 1865 all former Confederate states except Texas had fulfilled the requirements and had elected representatives to Congress. Johnson announced that the Union had been restored.

HISTORICAL PICTURES/STOCK MONTAGE, INC.

Federal Troops Union soldiers roamed the streets of major Southern cities, protecting the rights of the recently freed. This cartoon shows how two Southern women might have looked upon such troops. *According to Sherman, what changes were impossible to accomplish with military presence?*

When Congress reconvened in December, it refused to seat the newly elected Southern representatives. Some members of Congress criticized Johnson's leniency toward the South. They pointed out that Johnson had done nothing to prevent new Southern state governments from passing **black codes,** laws that severely restricted the rights of newly freed African Americans. In Mississippi, for example, black codes prohibited free African Americans from receiving farmland and stipulated that freed African American orphans could be assigned to forced labor. Throughout 1866 and 1867, tensions increased as the President and Congress battled over Reconstruction.

Military Occupation

In 1867 Congress passed a series of Reconstruction Acts over Johnson's veto. These acts abolished the state governments formed under Johnson's plan. They also divided the South into five military districts, each under the command of a general. Federal troops were stationed in each district to carry out the process of readmitting states to the Union. The functions of the military forces, according to the acts, were "to protect all persons in their rights of person and property, to suppress insurrection, disorder, and violence, and to punish, or cause to be punished, all disturbers of the public peace and criminals."

The provision for military occupation of the Southern states changed the tone of Reconstruction. Leadership was in the hands of Congress, and the army administered Congress's plan. Many Northerners felt that the presence of federal troops was necessary to bring about political and social changes in the South. General Sherman, however, was more astute and expressed a different view: "No matter what change we may desire in the feelings and thoughts of people South, we cannot accomplish it by force. Nor can we afford to maintain there an army large enough to hold them in subjugation [control]."

The Supreme Court's Role

In the battle between the executive and legislative branches over Reconstruction, the Supreme Court at first seemed to support President Johnson's position. In *ex parte Milligan,* the Court ruled that civilians could not be tried in military courts when civil courts were functioning. Northerners defied this decision, however, and made military tribunals part of legislation. The Court further stated that the administration of military justice in the South was "mere lawless violence." In *ex parte Garland,* a case that involved a law requiring loyalty oaths from former Confederate teachers and others who wanted to resume their jobs, the Court handed down a split decision. The majority opinion ruled that such oaths were invalid. The dissenting opinion held that such requirements were valid qualifications for officeholders and voters.

The Court soon upheld Congress's authority to reconstruct the states. In 1867 Georgia and Mississippi sought an injunction preventing President Johnson from enforcing Congress's Reconstruction Acts. The Supreme Court refused on the grounds that executive functions were not subject to judicial restraint. Johnson, who had relied on the Court's record of sympathy toward the South, began to feel increasingly isolated.

Congressional Plans

The Push to Reform the South

The Radical Republican faction of Congress had been formulating plans for Reconstruction since the early 1860s. These Republicans earned the label "radical" because they were strongly antislavery and were not willing to forgive the Confederates. Lincoln's leniency had outraged them. They wanted sweeping political change in the South, which they believed would occur only with the strong presence of Union troops. As Thaddeus Stevens, a leading Radical Republican, said, any valid unifying plan "must revolutionize the southern institutions, habits, and manner . . . or all our blood and treasure have been spent in vain."

The Radical Republicans had responded to Lincoln's terms by passing the Wade-Davis Bill in 1864. This bill would have required a majority of a state's white male citizenry to swear both past and future loyalty to the Union; only then would the federal government recognize the state's government. Considering the bill too harsh, Lincoln had vetoed it.

Johnson further outraged the Radical Republicans by promoting Lincoln's lenient policies. In 1866 Northerners fought Johnson's policies by electing a Radical Republican majority to Congress. The Radical Republicans quickly enacted legislation designed to punish the former Confederate states, to increase Republican power in the South, and to create conditions that would promote economic development and racial equality in the South.

Much of the legislation passed during Reconstruction increased the rights and freedoms of African Americans. This benefited the Republicans in two ways: it made the Republicans popular with a large new pool of voters, and it diminished white Southerners' ability to dominate the South politically and economically. In 1866 Congress passed the Civil Rights Act, which granted citizenship to African Americans and prohibited states from diminishing the rights accompanying this citizenship. In addition ratification of the Fourteenth Amendment in 1868 prevented states from denying rights and privileges to any American citizen. The Fifteenth Amendment of 1870 guaranteed that no citizen could be denied the right to vote based on race, color, or former servitude. The Enforcement Act of 1870 empowered federal authorities to prosecute anyone who violated the Fourteenth or Fifteenth Amendments.

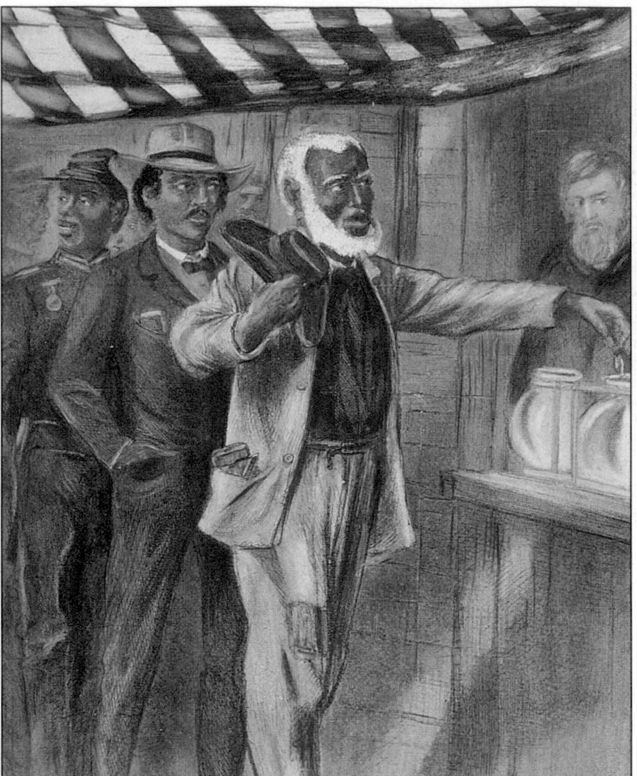

THE BETTMANN ARCHIVE

Influence at the Polls ***Harper's Weekly*** **celebrated full citizenship for African Americans with an illustration showing a soldier, a businessman, and an artisan casting their first ballots.** *What political faction promoted enfranchisement of African American citizens?*

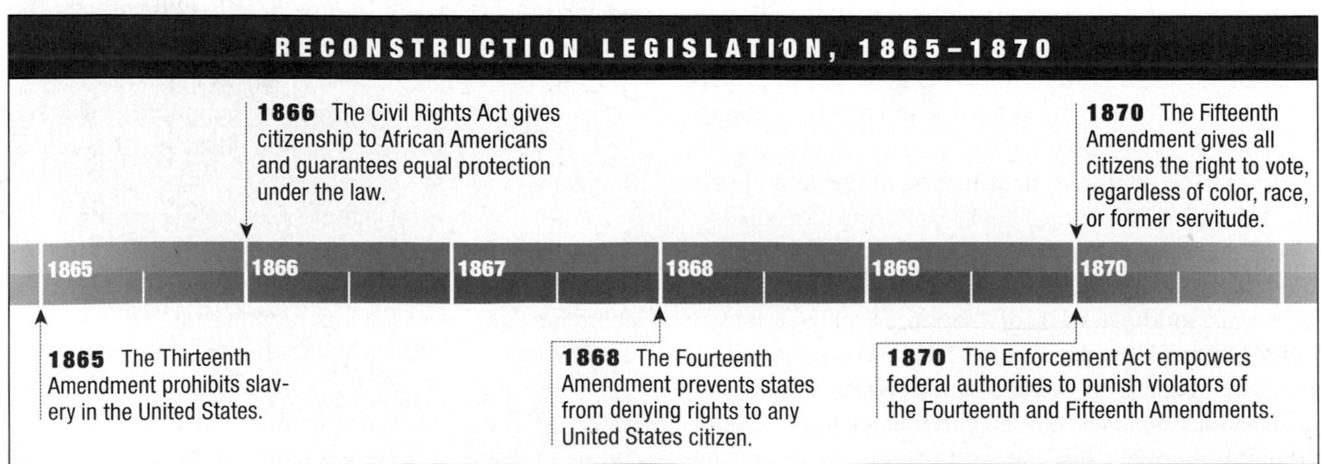

RECONSTRUCTION LEGISLATION, 1865–1870
1866 The Civil Rights Act gives citizenship to African Americans and guarantees equal protection under the law.
1870 The Fifteenth Amendment gives all citizens the right to vote, regardless of color, race, or former servitude.
1865
1866
1867
1868
1869
1870
1865 The Thirteenth Amendment prohibits slavery in the United States.
1868 The Fourteenth Amendment prevents states from denying rights to any United States citizen.
1870 The Enforcement Act empowers federal authorities to punish violators of the Fourteenth and Fifteenth Amendments.

HISTORICAL PICTURES/STOCK MONTAGE, INC.

Radical Republican **Thaddeus Stevens, a Radical Republican leader in Congress, wanted African Americans to receive full rights as citizens.** *Who was the chief opponent to Stevens's proposals?*

Radical Reconstruction

New state governments were established under the Reconstruction Acts. White Southerners who protested the acts refused to vote in the elections that set up these governments. Their protest had two results: Republicans, who had little support in the South before the Civil War, won control of every new state government; and African Americans began to exert influence at the polls. One white Southerner wrote in his diary:

> Bills have passed both houses of Congress which repudiate and destroy the present civil government of the lately seceded states and substitute in their place a military government. Most of the whites are disenfranchised [deprived of the right to vote] and ineligible for office, whilst the negroes are invested with the right of voting.
>
> —Henry William Ravenel, South Carolina, February 24, 1867

When African Americans were guaranteed their right to vote, they began to exert influence at the polls in states in which they were a majority of the population: Alabama, Florida, Louisiana, Mississippi, and South Carolina. African American representatives outnumbered white representatives in the South Carolina legislature.

Radical Republicans pushed their legislation through Congress in spite of President Johnson's vetoes. In 1866 Johnson vetoed the Civil Rights Act and a bill that would have enabled the Freedmen's Bureau, an organization that assisted formerly enslaved people, to continue. Congress overrode both vetoes.

The Invisible Empire

At about the same time that Johnson was undermining African Americans' efforts to obtain equality, white supremacist organizations such as the Ku Klux Klan began terrorizing them. These organizations used intimidation and violence to prevent African Americans from voting or holding positions of power. In this environment of violence and hatred, mobs of Southern whites periodically lashed out against the newly freed citizens among them. For example, in May 1866 in Memphis, Tennessee, a crowd of white supremacists killed 46 African Americans and 2 white sympathizers.

The Impeachment Effort

Johnson's attempts to undermine congressional legislation coupled with his inability or lack of desire to control terrorist organizations further angered Radical Republicans. Their anger peaked when the President defied the Tenure of Office Act, which required Senate approval for the removal of cabinet members. Johnson failed to obtain that approval before he fired Secretary of War Edwin Stanton in 1868.

The House responded by voting to impeach the President on 11 charges of misconduct. These included charges that Johnson had violated the Tenure of Office Act. The House appointed 7 representatives to present the charges to the Senate. Johnson was defended by a

THE BETTMANN ARCHIVE

The Invisible Empire of the South **Two African American attorneys are brutalized by the Ku Klux Klan in Pulaski, Tennessee, on Christmas Eve, 1865. The Klan began as an elite club for Confederate veterans but within months was terrorizing citizens with racist attacks.** *What did the Ku Klux Klan seek to prevent?*

team of lawyers. Chief Justice Salmon P. Chase presided over the trial. Johnson did not attend.

The trial dragged on for 8 weeks. Johnson's attackers accused him of everything from alcoholism to plotting Lincoln's murder. The President's lawyers presented a purely legal defense, arguing that the Tenure of Office Act was unconstitutional and did not apply to Stanton. Conviction required a two-thirds majority of the Senate. The final tally of 35 for conviction and 19 against acquitted Johnson by 1 vote.

Limits on Freedom

Freed but Not Free

At the end of the Civil War, most African Americans expected their lives to improve radically. A formerly enslaved woman recalled the excitement she and other freed men and women had felt when they learned of the Union victory and their new freedom:

> When the soldiers marched in to tell us that we were free . . . I remember one woman. She jumped on a barrel and she shouted. She jumped off and she shouted. She jumped back on again and shouted some more. She kept that up for a long time, just jumping on a barrel and back off again.
>
> —Anna Woods, a Federal Writers' Project interview, 1930s

After the initial happiness passed, however, African Americans realized that they would have to struggle to secure their rights as a freed people. At an 1865 convention in Alabama, African Americans demanded "exactly the same rights, privileges, and immunities as are enjoyed by white men—we ask nothing more and will be content with nothing less. . . ."

The Freedmen's Bureau, an office of the War Department, was established to provide freed African Americans with food, teachers, legal aid, and other assistance. The bureau also distributed horses, mules, and land that had been confiscated during the war. With the

THE BETTMANN ARCHIVE

Elected to Office **This lithograph shows the first African Americans who served in Congress. Top row, left to right: Representatives Robert C. De Large of South Carolina, Jefferson H. Long of Georgia. Bottom row, left to right: Senator H.R. Revels of Mississippi, Representatives Benjamin Turner of Alabama, Josiah T. Walls of Florida, and Joseph H. Rainy and R. Brown Elliot, both of South Carolina.** *What important civil rights did African Americans win during the 1860s?*

The Freedmen's Bureau **Education was the bureau's primary goal. A former Union commander, O.O. Howard (left), led the organization. The children here are students at one of many Freedmen's Bureau schools in the South.** *What role did the Freedmen's Bureau play in the fight for equality?*

bureau's help, about 40,000 African Americans were able to establish their own farms in Georgia and South Carolina. In the face of much opposition, African Americans obtained an education. At first, the Freedmen's Bureau and charitable organizations paid the cost of African American education. After 1871 the states began to take over the support of their own segregated schools. Many white Southerners resented African American schools, and teachers often faced intimidation or physical abuse. Progress was slow. Nevertheless, illiteracy among African Americans fell from more than 90 percent in 1860 to about 80 percent in 1870.

Voting Power

During Reconstruction African American voters exercised their political power for the first time. W.E.B. Du Bois, an important African American leader of the early 1900s, wrote: "With northern white leadership, the Negro voters . . . proved apt pupils in politics. They developed their own leadership. They gained clearer and clearer conceptions of how their political powers could be used for their own good."

African Americans were elected to office at the local, state, and national levels. Between 1869 and 1876, 2 African Americans served in the Senate and 14 served in the House of Representatives. Most of these men had been enslaved or were born of enslaved parents. Some critics claimed "they left no mark on the legislation of their time; none of them, in comparison with their white associates, attained the least distinction." Others observed: "The colored men who took seats in both Senate and House did not appear ignorant or helpless. They were as a rule studious, earnest, ambitious men, whose public conduct . . . would be honorable to any race."

Sharecropping

For many formerly enslaved African Americans, life changed little in the years after the Civil War. President Johnson returned confiscated estates to the previous Confederate owners. Freed people who had established farms on that land found themselves back on the plantations. Some worked under contract for meager wages. Others were forced into **sharecropping,** a system in which a wealthy patron would give seeds, supplies, and a small parcel of land to a farmer in exchange for a portion of the crop. If the patron required a large portion of the crop, the sharecropper might not be able to survive on what remained. If the crop failed, the sharecropper usually wound up hopelessly in debt to the patron.

"Freedom wasn't no difference I know of," complained one man. "I works for Marse John just the same." Many newly freed people did stay on the same plantations, where they worked under the same overseer. The wages or share of the crop they received hardly made up for the fact that freedom in no way meant equality.

Grant's Presidency

Corruption and Crisis

In 1868 the Republican Ulysses S. Grant won the presidency by a margin of 300,000 votes. The more than 500,000 African Americans who voted in the election certainly contributed to Grant's victory. Nevertheless, during Grant's two terms in office, from 1869 to 1877, the government began paying less and less attention to the problems of prejudice, discrimination, and racial harassment.

Government Scandal

Scandal and corruption plagued Grant's administration. A congressional investigation in the mid-1870s found that whiskey distillers and tax officials were stealing excise taxes from the government, and it linked a member of Grant's staff to the scandal. In addition, Grant's secretary of war, William W. Belknap, was accused of accepting bribes. Even Grant wrongly accepted personal gifts.

At the time successful politicians commonly rewarded their supporters by appointing them to government positions. These appointed individuals often lacked the skills and experience necessary to do their jobs. Quite often they were also greedy and dishonest. This was true of a number of the personal friends, relatives, and fellow army officers Grant appointed.

Such was also the case in the newly created Republican state governments in the South. Although these governments did implement legislation that helped to ease the South's social and economic difficulties, many of the Northerners involved in local Southern administrations were inexperienced and even corrupt. White Southerners called these Northern transplants **carpetbaggers,** mocking them for having arrived in the South with only the possessions they had been able to stuff inside their luggage. Most white Southerners believed the carpetbaggers wanted only to turn a profit or rise to power at the expense of the South. In addition, African Americans newly elected to political positions were often blamed for government wastefulness and dishonesty.

Democratic Success

As one after another of the carpetbag governments came under attack, Democrats began to regain control of Southern legislatures. They also used some underhanded tactics to neutralize the issues of equality that had begun to affect the election process.

One such technique, called **gerrymandering,** involved redividing voting districts to decrease African American representation in a particular area. Another tactic was to institute a poll tax, which the Democrats managed to do in several states. In these states voting became a privilege that required payment of a fee. Poll taxes excluded poor citizens of both races from the voting process. By 1875, aided by these strategies, Democrats had gained control of the House of Representatives for the first time since before the Civil War. By 1877 they had completely reestablished control over Southern state governments.

The Panic of 1873

Grant's administration faced economic as well as political problems. A financial crisis during his second term in office left the country in economic difficulty. The crisis was touched off in 1873 when financier Jay Cooke suddenly closed his Philadelphia bank. The bank closing prompted a panic during which 5,000 businesses closed, and thousands of people lost their jobs.

As the panic spread, concern for economic reform quickly replaced concern for social reform. In the North the demands of unemployed workers for economic relief supplanted demands for racial equality. By 1874 one-quarter of the population of New York City was out of work. In Chicago 20,000 unemployed people protested in the streets, demanding that government officials solve the problems of the economy.

In the South the sharecropping system cheated many African American farmers out of owning land or reaping profits from their labors. Meanwhile white farmers suffered devastating losses during these hard times and often accused African Americans of causing their economic troubles.

African Americans living in Northern states also faced economic and social problems. Although they had gained access to public education and transportation, they were usually trapped in low-paying, unskilled jobs; lived in poor housing; and had little voice in shaping government policies. Unlike the large freed population in the South, Northern African Americans comprised only 2 percent of the population. In both the North and the South, these newly enfranchised citizens had to struggle to claim the political and social rights that Reconstruction promised.

In the midst of the economic and social upheaval of Reconstruction, however, the United States celebrated its centennial in 1876. Ten million people paid 50 cents each to visit the Grand Exposition in Philadelphia. Displays of the nation's art, fashion, produce, appliances, and industrial development greeted the visitors. Many Americans were ready to push the problems of the Civil War into the past and forge on optimistically into the nation's second century.

The End of Reconstruction

Prejudice and Exodus

In the wake of social and economic crises, government scandals, and outbreaks of violence, the Radical Republicans lost their political power. So, too, the Radical Republican program of Reconstruction came to an end. No longer supported by the majority of voters, Republicans attempted to regain their foothold in the South by backing a moderate candidate for President—Rutherford B. Hayes, who appealed to both the North and South.

Hayes ran against Democratic candidate Samuel Tilden in what was possibly the closest presidential election battle in American history. A dispute arose over the election returns from four states. Three of these states were Southern states still under Reconstruction rule. The Democrats insisted that the majority of the people in these states favored Tilden but had been prevented from registering their votes. To settle the dispute, Congress appointed a special electoral commission.

To get Hayes elected, Republicans made many concessions to the Democrats, among which was the agreement to withdraw the Union troops that had been stationed in the South since the end of the war. These votes assured, Hayes won the election by one electoral vote. Shortly thereafter, the last Union troops withdrew from the South.

NATIONAL MUSEUM OF AMERICAN ART, WASHINGTON DC/ART RESOURCE, NY

Losing Ground By the turn of the century, conditions for African Americans in the South were in many ways indistinguishable from slavery, much like the scene in R.N. Brooke's painting, *Dog Swap*. *How were the civil rights gains during Reconstruction dismantled after 1870?*

Prejudice Persists

Without the presence of the Union army to combat terrorism, the rights of Southern African Americans were gravely jeopardized. Even before Hayes's election, the Supreme Court's 1876 ruling in *United States* v. *Cruikshank* overturned the Enforcement Act of 1870. The Court ruled that a state could not legally discriminate against African Americans, but nonstate institutions and individuals could. Specifically, the Court had overturned the convictions of three whites for their participation in a bloody massacre of African Americans on the grounds that the three individuals did not specify that their actions were racially motivated.

In subsequent administrations, the Supreme Court's support of African American rights diminished still further. For example, in 1883, during Chester A. Arthur's presidency, the Supreme Court nullified the Civil Rights Act of 1875.

Reconstruction Appraised

Although the period of Reconstruction had ended and Republicans and Democrats had temporarily united, African Americans felt as if their needs had been forgotten. Most of the legal decisions that had advanced African American rights during Reconstruction had been overturned. Furthermore the Radical Republican governments had failed to correct the problem of unequal land distribution in the South, a measure that might have provided the economic leverage that African Americans needed to protect their rights.

Discontented and afraid for their lives, African Americans left the South by the thousands. Many moved to Northern urban centers, such as Chicago and New York City. Some moved to Kansas, a state in which there was an abundance of fertile land and a strong Republican government that promised unbiased treatment under the law. There, many began to enjoy a decent existence.

Section Assessment

Main Idea

1. Use a diagram like this one to show reasons for the decline of Reconstruction.

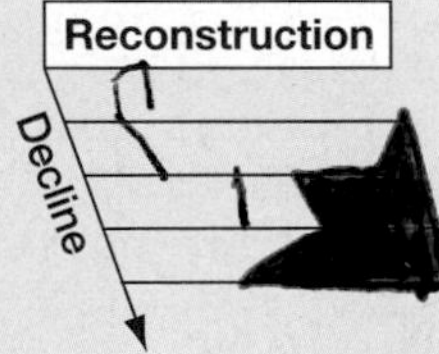

Vocabulary

2. Define: amnesty, black codes, sharecropping, carpetbagger, gerrymandering.

Checking Facts

3. What Reconstruction laws aided African Americans?
4. How did Congress react to Johnson's vetoes of Radical Republican bills in 1866?

Critical Thinking

5. **Determining Cause and Effect** Why did many Northern politicians lose interest in securing African Americans rights after 1868?

Chapter  Assessment

Self-Check Quiz

Visit the *American Odyssey* Web site at americanodyssey.glencoe.com and click on ***Chapter 6—Self-Check Quiz*** to prepare for the Chapter Test.

Reviewing Key Terms

Match each sentence below to the vocabulary term it defines or describes. Write your answers on a separate sheet of paper.

sectionalism	**black codes**
gospel tradition	**scorched earth policy**
emancipation	**gerrymandering**

1. Enslaved African Americans developed a unique musical form by combining African religious practices and beliefs with Christian practices and beliefs.

2. After the war President Johnson allowed Southern states to pass laws restricting the rights of newly freed African Americans.

3. In the years leading up to the war, the North and the South had developed entirely different political agendas based on their own regional economic interests.

4. Southern whites sometimes regained control of their state legislatures by the technique of redividing voting districts to dilute African American representation.

5. As commander of the Union forces, Grant ordered his generals to burn and destroy the South's crops, homes, and supplies.

Recalling Facts

1. Why was the *Dred Scott* decision significant?

2. Explain how Whitney's cotton gin helped increase sectionalism.

3. How did *(a)* the Missouri Compromise, *(b)* the Compromise of 1850, and *(c)* the Kansas-Nebraska Act reflect sectional interests?

4. Why were both Northerners and Southerners at first confident of victory in the Civil War?

5. What was the Emancipation Proclamation? Did it achieve all of the goals of the abolitionists? Explain.

6. What motivated the Radical Republicans to pass civil rights legislation on behalf of African Americans?

7. Despite laws passed during Reconstruction, African Americans in the South lost many of their civil rights until the 1950s and 1960s. Explain.

8. Did the Civil War and Reconstruction end sectionalism? Why or why not?

Critical Thinking

1. Recognizing Bias White Southerners tended to support policies that enlarged the powers of the states, while Northerners supported limiting the powers of the states in certain important ways. What caused this difference in outlook?

2. Making Inferences Explain what Jerry Loguen meant when he said, "Human rights are mutual and reciprocal." How has this idea been applied to other areas, for example, women's rights?

3. Making Comparisons Use a chart like this one to compare the strengths and weaknesses of the North and South at the start of the Civil War.

	North	South
Strengths		
Weaknesses		

4. Determining Cause and Effect President Lincoln believed that the South should be treated with compassion after the Civil War. Did Reconstruction fulfill this objective? Explain.

Portfolio Project

PORTFOLIO PROJECT

Civil war has torn apart many countries in the 1900s. Choose one country, such as China, Spain, Yugoslavia, or Mexico, and investigate its civil war period. Identify the causes and effects of its civil war. In what ways was the war similar to the American Civil War? In what ways was it different? Write a report and include it in your portfolio.

Cooperative Learning

The Civil War has inspired numerous books, plays, movies, and TV dramas. For example, Margaret Mitchell's novel *Gone With the Wind,* Stephen Crane's novel *The Red Badge of Courage,* and the 1989 movie *Glory* look at the war from different perspectives. With a group of your classmates, prepare a review of different works on the Civil War. Include in your review answers to the following questions: How historically accurate is the work in question? What evidence is there of character stereotyping? Has stereotyping changed over the years? Share the results of your review with your class.

Reinforcing Skills

Combining Information From Maps Compare the map of transportation routes on page 148 with the map of Civil War battles on page 175. What inference can you make about why Union victories in Tennessee and battles in New Orleans caused major hardships for the South?

GEOGRAPHY AND HISTORY

Mid-Atlantic Civil War Battles

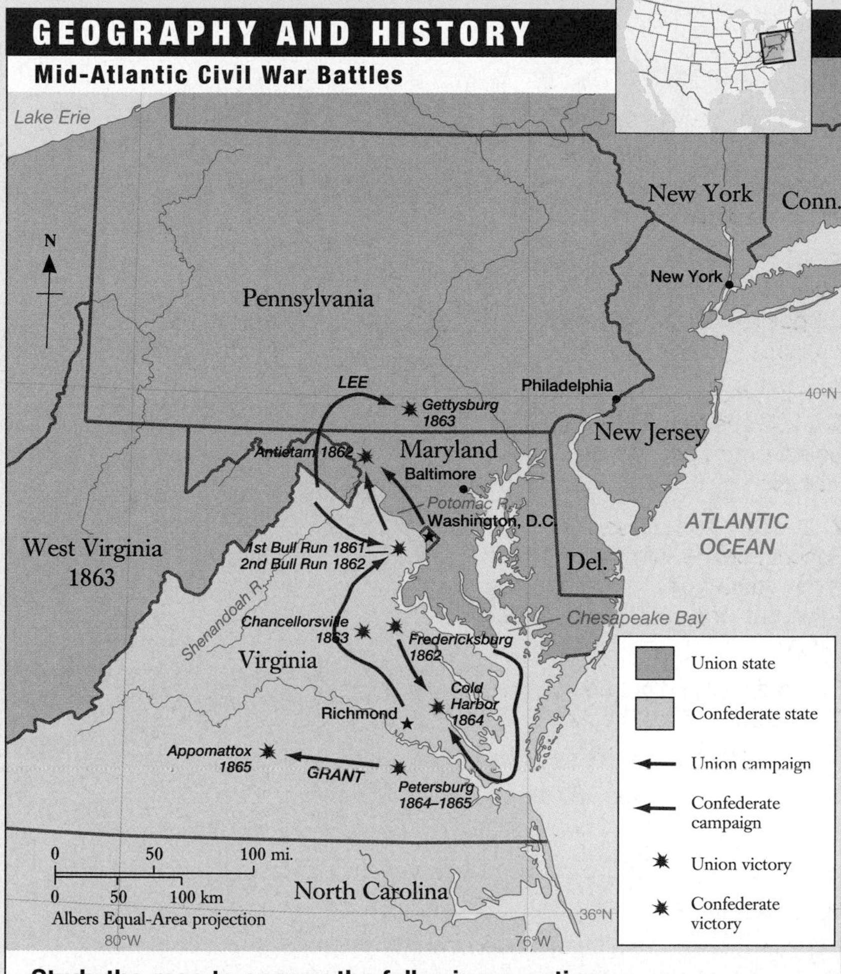

Study the map to answer the following questions:

1. In which mid-Atlantic state did the most battles take place? Which side won most of these battles?
2. Which of the battles shown on the map were victories for the Confederacy?
3. Which battles took place in Union states?
4. In which battles did the Confederate campaign appear to threaten Washington, D.C.?
5. What Confederate general was in command at Gettysburg?

Technology Activity

Using E-mail Search the Internet for the E-mail address of a Civil War historical organization. Compose a letter requesting additional information about a topic pertaining to the Civil War. Share your response with the class.

Standardized Test Practice

1. White Southerners feared the Underground Railroad because it

A strengthened the Fugitive Slave Law.

B provided an escape route for enslaved African Americans.

C benefited Northern manufacturing interests.

D increased the shipping rates on agricultural products.

Test-Taking Tip: Think about the meaning of the word *underground.* It either means, literally, "under the ground," or, metaphorically, "in secret." Since underground railroads, or subways, did not exist, you can eliminate any answers that relate to the literal meaning of the word.

2. Lincoln's primary goal at the start of the Civil War was to

A preserve the Union.

B break the power of the Democratic party.

C prevent expansion of the cotton kingdom.

D abolish slavery throughout the nation.

Test-Taking Tip: Do not confuse the *results* of the Civil War with the *primary,* or main, reason that Lincoln ordered Union troops into the South. Lincoln evaded the issue of slavery to prevent driving the border states out of the Union. Therefore, you can eliminate answer D.

New Frontiers

MAY 24, 1883: FANFARE MARKS BROOKLYN BRIDGE OPENING

Church bells rang out all over the city. Guns boomed from forts in New York harbor. After 14 years of construction, marred by worker injuries and deaths, New York City celebrated the opening of the Brooklyn Bridge.

President Chester A. Arthur and New York Governor Grover Cleveland joined thousands of New Yorkers in the opening ceremony. The steel bridge stretched over the East River, ready to open the way from the island of Manhattan to the borough of Brooklyn.

At the time it was opened, the bridge was the longest suspension bridge in the world. Costing nearly $15 million, the bridge was suspended by 4 cables. Each cable contained more than 5,000 small wires and could hold nearly 3,000 tons. More than 100,000 people would travel over it each day.

The Brooklyn Bridge reflected the tide of industrial progress sweeping the nation in the years following the Civil War. Factories and cities grew, while advancements in technology and communications transformed the way Americans lived. As the nation continued to push its boundaries outward, the United States emerged as one of the great powers of the 1900s. ■

HISTORY JOURNAL

Write in your journal about your reaction to the story and photograph of the Brooklyn Bridge. What makes a great bridge an appropriate symbol of industrial progress?

Chapter Overview

Visit the *American Odyssey* Web site at americanodyssey.glencoe.com and click on ***Chapter 7—Chapter Overview*** to preview the chapter.

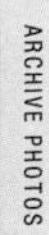

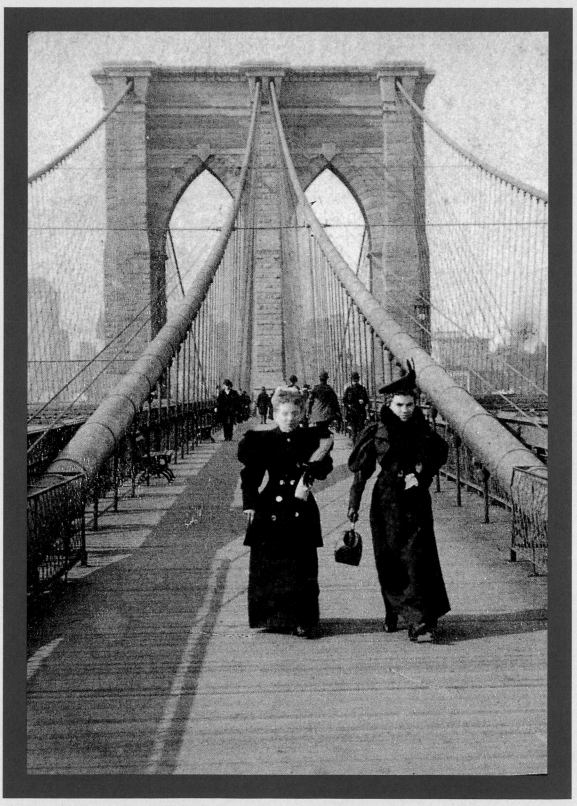

STROLLERS ENJOY THE BROAD PROMENADE ABOVE THE ROADWAY OF THE SOARING BROOKLYN BRIDGE.

SECTION 1

Moving West

APRIL 22, 1889: THOUSANDS GRAB LAND IN OKLAHOMA

THE CLOCK STRUCK NOON AND GUNSHOTS RANG OUT, BEGINNING ONE OF THE MOST REMARKABLE LAND GRABS IN AMERICAN HISTORY. Yancey Cravat, the hero in Edna Ferber's novel, *Cimarron,* describes the scene on April 22, 1889, when the federal government effectively gave away the almost 2 million acres (0.8 million ha) of land it had purchased from evicted Creek and Seminole.

> There we were, the girl on my left, the old plainsman on my right. Eleven forty-five. Along the border were the soldiers, their guns in one hand, their watches in the other. . . . Twelve o'clock. There went up a roar that drowned the crack of the soldiers' musketry as they fired in the air as the signal of noon and the start of the Run. You could see the puffs of smoke from their guns but you couldn't hear a sound. The thousands surged over the Line. It was like running water going over a broken dam. The rush had started, and it was devil take the hindmost. We swept across the prairie in a cloud of black and red dust that covered our faces and hands in a minute. . . .
>
> —Edna Ferber, *Cimarron,* 1930

ARCHIVES AND MANUSCRIPTS DIVISION OF THE OKLAHOMA HISTORICAL SOCIETY

Staking Claims
The rush into Oklahoma's Cherokee Outlet goes by in a blur of speed. Thousands of Americans claimed free land in the new territories. Claims often sparked violent disputes that took years to settle.

More than 50,000 men, women, and children participated in the rush. Although the land was free, the settlers would have to **homestead,** or settle on the land, for a number of years before they could own it. Some found their stakes too dry to farm, and disease-causing conditions drove others out; but a year later, the Oklahoma Territory boasted a population of about 259,000 people.

The success of the Oklahoma rush led the government to open more land in the West. The following year

GUIDE TO READING

Main Idea

A number of factors, including the construction of the transcontinental railroad, lured settlers ever westward, forcing Native Americans onto shrinking reservations.

Vocabulary

- homestead
- transcontinental railroad
- government boarding school

Read to Find Out . . .

- what influenced the development of American cowhand culture.
- what geographical factors led to settlement of the Plains and the West.
- how the transcontinental railroad was built.
- how federal policies adversely affected Native Americans.

federal authorities authorized settlement on millions of acres of Sioux land in South Dakota. The government could not hold back the tide of eager settlers, and after 1900 thousands descended on the former Native American reservation.

Expanding Frontiers

Farmers, Ranchers, and Miners Go West

As the nation's population boomed and Midwestern agricultural land filled up, farmers looked westward to the Great Plains. After completing the **transcontinental railroad** in 1869, the railroad companies encouraged eager farmers to buy some of their enormous land holdings. More encouragement came from the Homestead Act of 1862 that awarded 160 acres (64.8 ha) of public land free to any settler who would farm the land for at least 5 years. So enticed, many settlers, including thousands of immigrants from European countries, poured into the lands west of the Mississippi River.

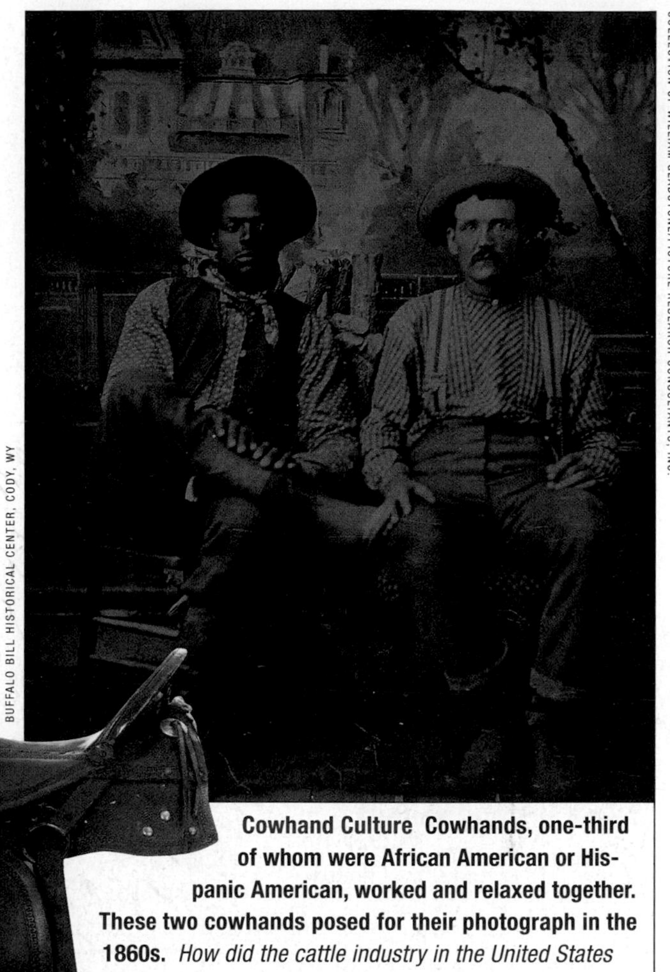

BUFFALO BILL HISTORICAL CENTER, CODY, WY

COLLECTION OF WILLIAM GLADSTONE/PICTURE RESEARCH CONSULTANTS, INC.

Cowhand Culture Cowhands, one-third of whom were African American or Hispanic American, worked and relaxed together. These two cowhands posed for their photograph in the 1860s. *How did the cattle industry in the United States begin?*

The Cattle Frontier

On the eastern high-grass prairie of the Great Plains, enough rain fell to cultivate grain crops. Settlers used the drier western lands for cattle grazing. Herds of longhorn and other cattle were fattened on the open range lands of Texas, Kansas, Nebraska, the Dakotas, Wyoming, and Montana. They were then driven to market, sold to packers, and sent east to feed beef-hungry city dwellers.

The profits from cattle ranching could be enormous. A Texas steer, purchased as a calf for \$5–\$6, could be set out to graze on public land and later sold for \$60–\$70. The "cattle kingdom" flourished for two decades after the Civil War until a drought and an oversupply of cattle in the late 1880s forced beef prices down.

Cowhands

The cattle industry in the United States developed from the livestock and horses that the Spanish introduced into the Americas. Similarly, the cowhand culture idealized in books and movies had a partly Spanish heritage. The unique way of life followed by cowhands evolved from that of the vaqueros, their Mexican counterparts. The chaps that protected a cowhand's legs from thorny brush came from the vaqueros' word *chaparajos*. The words *lariat* and *rodeo* also have Spanish origins.

The cowhands wore functional outfits. High-heeled boots kept their feet from slipping out of the stirrups. Broad-brimmed hats kept the sun, rain, and dust from their eyes. Because cowhands worked seasonally, few owned their own horses. Every cowhand, however, owned a saddle—a prized possession.

Ranchers hired cowhands for their skill at riding or roping. Cowhands branded cattle during the spring roundup and kept herds together during a trail drive, moving cattle as far as 1,000 miles (1,609 km) in 3 months. They worked hard for low wages—\$40–\$50 a month. As cattle rancher Joseph G. McCoy said of a cowhand in 1874: "He lives hard, works hard, has but few comforts and fewer necessities. He loves danger but abhors labor of the common kind, and never tires riding."

HISTORY Online

Student Web Activity 7

Visit the *American Odyssey* Web site at americanodyssey.glencoe.com and click on ***Chapter 7—Student Web Activities*** for an activity relating to the western frontier.

The profession was more integrated than most walks of American life. African American, Native American, Hispanic, and Anglo cowhands, as well as those of mixed ancestry, all met and worked together. Yet discrimination existed on the frontier as elsewhere. Vaqueros earned less than Anglos and seldom became foremen or trail bosses. Some saloons discriminated against Hispanics, segregated African Americans, and excluded Chinese altogether.

Few women worked as salaried cowhands. Ranchers' wives and daughters did help with many chores, such as tending animals and sewing leather britches. A widow sometimes took over her deceased husband's ranch.

During free time in the bunkhouse, cowhands entertained themselves with card games, tall tales, practical jokes, and songs. In town, after several months on the trail, many of them let off steam by drinking, gambling, and fighting in local saloons. Cow towns, where cattle were loaded on trains for shipment to market, had a reputation for lawlessness. Yet the "Wild West" gained its name not so much for gunfights as for the cowhands' rugged life.

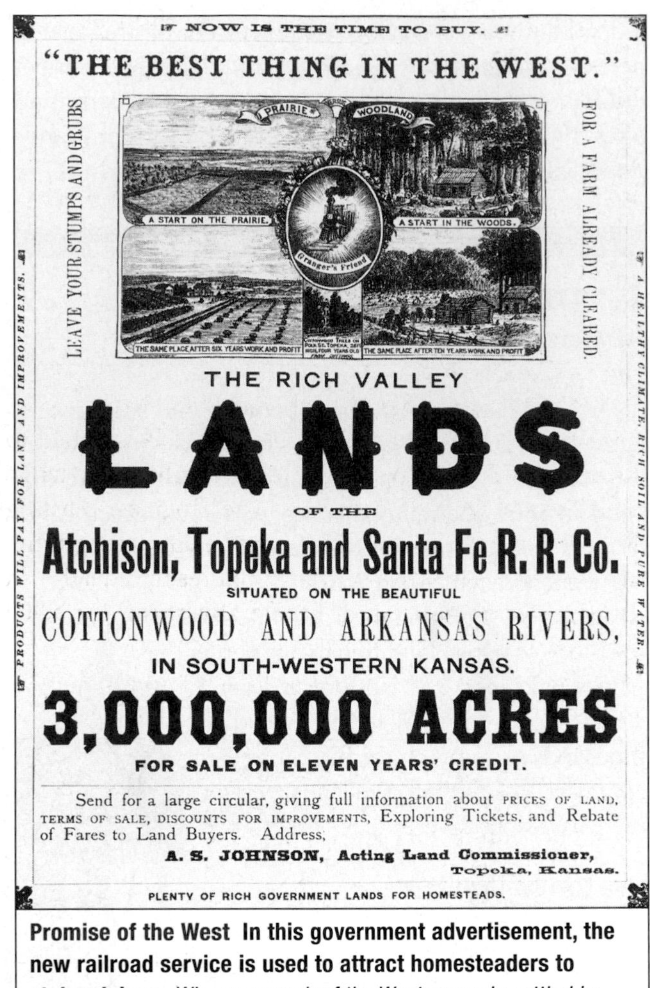

ASSOCIATION OF AMERICAN RAILROADS

Promise of the West In this government advertisement, the new railroad service is used to attract homesteaders to stake claims. *Why was much of the West sparsely settled before 1870?*

Mountains and Valleys

West of the Great Plains, people sought their fortune from the vast mineral and forest resources of the Rocky Mountain and Sierra Nevada regions. The timberlands of California and the Northwest yielded much of the wood necessary for thousands of miles of railroad ties, fence posts, and the building of hundreds of towns.

Gold and silver provided much of the capital for an industrializing country. The Comstock Lode, a rich vein of silver in Nevada, yielded more than $292 million between 1859 and 1882. Though Western tales celebrate the lone miner toiling with pick and shovel, huge companies did most of the mining of valuable metals. These companies, in pursuit of gold, silver, lead, copper, tin, and zinc, commanded great money and power. They could build railroad lines, bring in heavy machinery, and employ armies of miners.

In California the gold discovered under the ground proved less valuable than the ground itself. As one father told his son: "Plant your lands, these be your best gold fields." Farmland turned out to be California's most valuable asset. Eager miners, believing the California soil unsuitable for crops, willingly paid high prices for farm produce: "watermelon at from one to five dollars each, apples from Oregon at one and two dollars each, potatoes and onions at fifty cents to one dollar a pound . . . eggs at two dollars a dozen," according to one older resident. More often than not, provisioners in the West made money while miners did not. By 1862 California produced a surplus of some crops.

Like the cattle culture of the Great Plains, the agriculture of California had a partly Spanish heritage. Franciscan missionaries introduced grapes and citrus fruits to California's fertile soils in the late 1700s. With the end of the mission system in the mid-1800s, however, the vineyards and orchards fell into neglect. Enterprising settlers, once in search of gold, displaced Mexican ranchers and turned the rich California valleys into cornucopias of the Far West.

Building the Railroad

Across the Continent by Rail

California's population increased dramatically because of its gold rush and its agricultural successes. Other parts of the West remained sparsely settled, usually because they were far from transportation and markets. In the early 1860s, the federal government proposed that railroad lines should cross the entire United States.

The incredible engineering feat that provided transcontinental transportation began with the Pacific Railroad Act. Passed by Congress in 1862, the act authorized the Union Pacific Railroad to lay track westward from a point near Omaha, Nebraska, while the Central Pacific Railroad laid track eastward from Sacramento. The lines were to meet in Utah. In addition to government loans, the railroads received large land grants, 20 square miles (51.8 square km) of land for 1 mile (1.6 km) of track laid. The railroad barons made fortunes by selling this land to settlers.

Both railroads faced enormous challenges that required armies of laborers. The Central Pacific had to cross the Sierra Nevada in eastern California, while the Union Pacific had to cross the Rockies. Blasting and tunneling into rock and working through the winters, the crew suffered many injuries and deaths. In January 1865, the Central Pacific advertised for 5,000 more workers.

The quiet efficiency of Chinese laborers impressed the construction boss, and he began recruiting in China. Before the end of the year, about 7,000 Chinese laborers were at work on the line. The Union Pacific relied heavily on Irish immigrant labor, although one worker described the team as "a crowd of ex-Confederates and Federal soldiers, muleskinners, Mexicans, New York Irish, bushwackers, and ex-convicts," with a few African Americans as well.

By 1868 the work of laying track had become a race between the two railroads. The pace quickened as the lines approached each other. When the two sets of tracks met on May 10, 1869, at Promontory, Utah, special trains carrying railroad officials and their guests arrived for the completion ceremony. Leland Stanford, governor of California, drove in a gold spike, symbolically uniting the rail lines. A telegraph message informed the nation, "It is done!" By the end of the 1800s four more transcontinental rail lines crossed the United States. Passengers and freight began to crisscross the nation.

THE HARRY T. PETERS COLLECTION, MUSEUM OF THE CITY OF NEW YORK

A Dangerous Pass **This photo from 1877 shows the Secrettown Trestle, 62 miles (99.8 km) from Sacramento, California. The Chinese laborers shown used picks, chisels, hammers, wheelbarrows, and one-horse carts to build the timber structures and earthen embankments that bridged these chasms in the Sierra Nevada.** *When was the Pacific Railroad Act passed by Congress?*

LIBRARY OF CONGRESS

Forced Removal **This photograph shows federal agents preparing to relocate a group of Apache from Arizona to Oklahoma by train in the late 1800s. Geronimo, of the Chiricahua Apache, sat third from right in front.** *Why is this train bound for Oklahoma?*

The Second Great Removal

Native American Lands Taken

Not everyone benefited from the expansion of the railroads. In the summer of 1860, Lieutenant Henry Maynadier quoted one Sioux elder who warned about the expansion of the West, "We are glad to have the traders, but we don't want you soldiers and roadmakers; the country is ours and we intend to keep it."

The rapid settlement of the lands west of the Mississippi River after the Civil War led to a generation of violent conflict. Settlers fought the dozens of Native American nations that had inhabited these lands for generations.

In 1871 the federal government decreed that all Western Native American nations must agree to relocate to one of two reservation areas. The northern Plains nations were assigned to the western half of present-day South Dakota; the southern Plains nations were assigned to what is now Oklahoma. Once placed on the reservations, they would have to accept the federal government as their guardian.

Government policy, as well as military conflict with those who resisted, undermined Native American cultures. In 1871 the government ended the practice of treating each Native American nation separately. Under the new policy, Native Americans lost two rights. They could no longer negotiate treaties to protect their lands, and they could no longer vote on laws governing their fate. The Dawes Severalty Act of 1887 continued the attempt to break down Native American loyalty to their own nations. This act decreed that parcels of land be given not to nations but to individuals. Each family head was allowed 160 acres (64.8 ha). Reservation land left over was sold to white settlers.

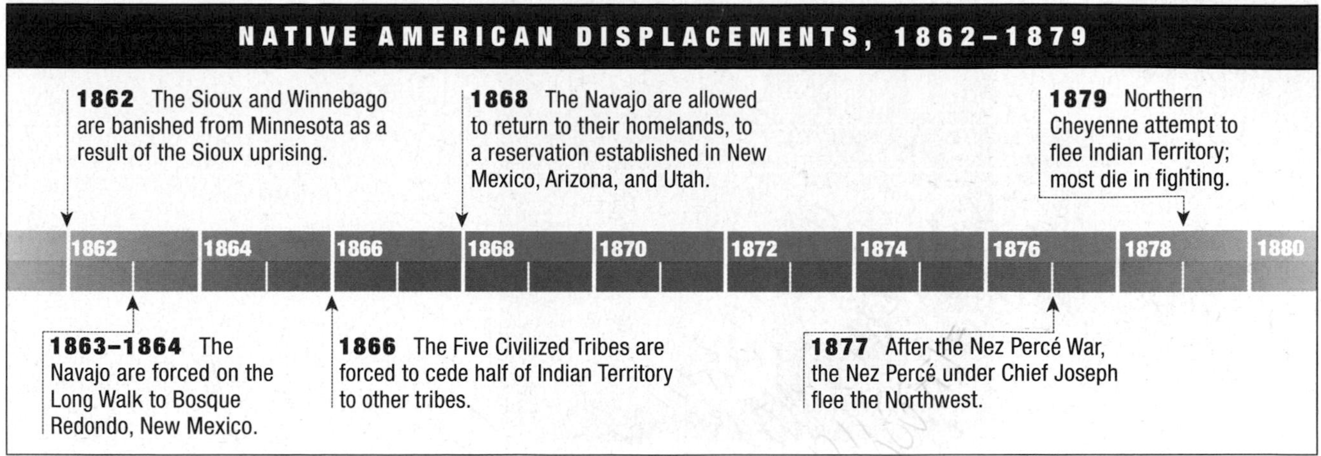

NATIVE AMERICAN DISPLACEMENTS, 1862–1879
1862 The Sioux and Winnebago are banished from Minnesota as a result of the Sioux uprising.
1868 The Navajo are allowed to return to their homelands, to a reservation established in New Mexico, Arizona, and Utah.
1879 Northern Cheyenne attempt to flee Indian Territory; most die in fighting.
1862
1864
1866
1868
1870
1872
1874
1876
1878
1880
1863–1864 The Navajo are forced on the Long Walk to Bosque Redondo, New Mexico.
1866 The Five Civilized Tribes are forced to cede half of Indian Territory to other tribes.
1877 After the Nez Percé War, the Nez Percé under Chief Joseph flee the Northwest.

Some reformers compared this act to the Emancipation Proclamation: just as enslaved people were set free, so Native Americans would gradually gain citizenship. Few reformers seemed to notice that sending Native American children to **government boarding schools,** where they were schooled in the white cultural tradition, was breaking down Native American culture.

Within 20 years after the Dawes Act, Native Americans retained control of only 20 percent of their original reservation lands. The southern Plains Native Americans in Oklahoma were severely hurt. By the time of Oklahoma statehood in 1907, most of their original acreage was in the hands of 500,000 white settlers. A newspaper editor in that year summed up the prevailing feeling among the settlers: "Sympathy and sentiment never stand in the way of the onward march of empire." The Oglala Sioux leader Red Cloud, who later represented Arapaho, Crow, and Cheyenne as well, expressed the corresponding Native American lament in 1870: "When we first had all this land we were strong; now we are all melting like snow on the hillside, while you are growing like spring grass."

S.J. MORROW COLLECTION/W.H. OVER MUSEUM

Red Cloud **A chief of the Oglala Sioux, Red Cloud led the opposition to the Bozeman Trail through Native American lands in Colorado and Montana. Under his leadership, representatives were able to negotiate removal of federal troops and forts from their lands.** *What was the impact of westward expansion on Red Cloud and his people?*

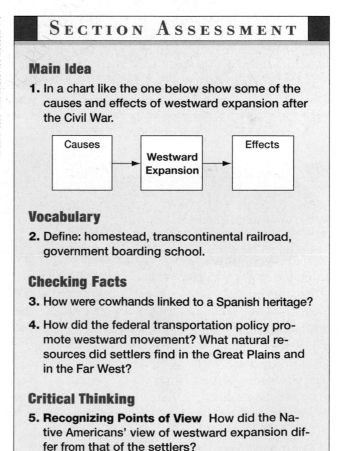

Section Assessment

Main Idea

1. In a chart like the one below show some of the causes and effects of westward expansion after the Civil War.

Causes	→	Westward Expansion	→	Effects

Vocabulary

2. Define: homestead, transcontinental railroad, government boarding school.

Checking Facts

3. How were cowhands linked to a Spanish heritage?
4. How did the federal transportation policy promote westward movement? What natural resources did settlers find in the Great Plains and in the Far West?

Critical Thinking

5. **Recognizing Points of View** How did the Native Americans' view of westward expansion differ from that of the settlers?

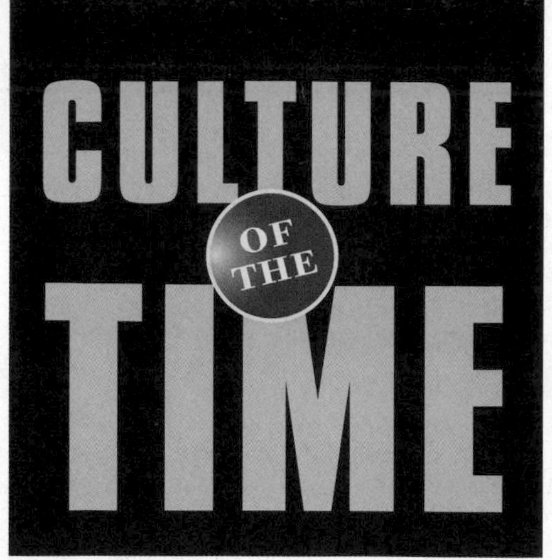

An Age of Ingenuity

After the Civil War, Americans yearned to shed painful memories. They channeled their creative energy into hopes for a brighter future. Inventors filed record numbers of patent applications for everything from the dentist's drill to the corn flake. They contrived new modes of travel and entertainment, and displayed their creations at exhibitions and fairs.

RON LABBE/STUDIO 3-D

SCHMITT COLLECTION, RJB

STEREO PHOTOGRAPHY

Stereoscopes filled the imaginations and parlors of Victorian viewers. In 1849 photographers began using a double-lensed camera to capture the perspectives of the left and right eyes. The resulting **stereographs** quickly became the most popular form of photography. Printed side by side, and seen through the little windows of the stereoscope, the two views on the stereograph merged into one and popped to life in 3-D.

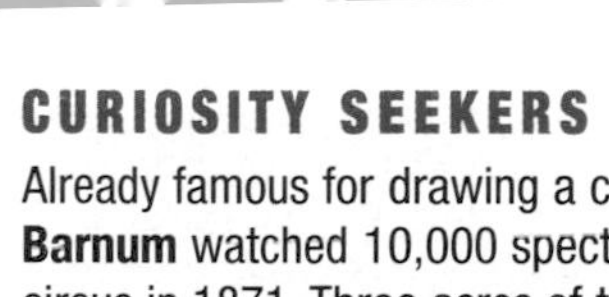

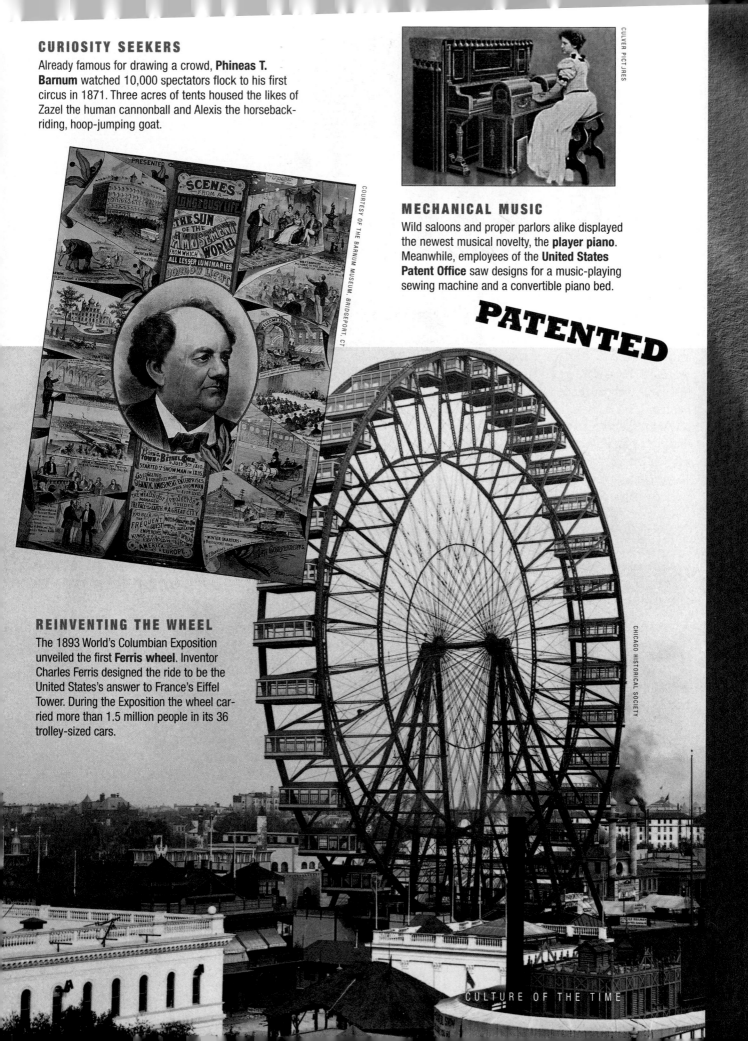

CURIOSITY SEEKERS

Already famous for drawing a crowd, **Phineas T. Barnum** watched 10,000 spectators flock to his first circus in 1871. Three acres of tents housed the likes of Zazel the human cannonball and Alexis the horseback-riding, hoop-jumping goat.

COURTESY OF THE BARNUM MUSEUM, BRIDGEPORT, CT

CULVER PICTURES

MECHANICAL MUSIC

Wild saloons and proper parlors alike displayed the newest musical novelty, the **player piano**. Meanwhile, employees of the **United States Patent Office** saw designs for a music-playing sewing machine and a convertible piano bed.

PATENTED

REINVENTING THE WHEEL

The 1893 World's Columbian Exposition unveiled the first **Ferris wheel**. Inventor Charles Ferris designed the ride to be the United States's answer to France's Eiffel Tower. During the Exposition the wheel carried more than 1.5 million people in its 36 trolley-sized cars.

CHICAGO HISTORICAL SOCIETY

Rise of Industrialism

LATE 1800s: CARNEGIE FORGES A STEEL EMPIRE

Innovator
Andrew Carnegie entered business when the use of steel was already widespread. He pioneered techniques to make steel processing more efficient and gradually took over the plants of his suppliers and distributors.

ANDREW CARNEGIE LEARNED ABOUT THE MEANING OF HARD WORK AS A YOUNG BOY. When his family fell on hard times in Scotland, he helped his mother sew shoes by threading her needles. In 1848 after the Carnegies left Scotland for the United States, 12-year-old Andrew worked with his father in a Pennsylvania cotton factory, earning $1.20 for a 72-hour week.

Little by little, Carnegie made himself a business success. At age 14 he started work in a telegraph office as a messenger and then quickly rose to the position of telegraph operator. The Pennsylvania Railroad hired Carnegie when he was 17, and his skills and hard work catapulted him in a few years to the job of assistant to the president. Through smart investments in a railroad car company and in oil wells, Carnegie made a small fortune by his early twenties and left the railroad to start his own business manufacturing iron bridges.

Carnegie was not only a shrewd investor but also a daring industrial innovator. In 1873 he began building a massive steel plant to produce railroad tracks in Pittsburgh, Pennsylvania. Carnegie introduced the revolutionary Bessemer converter and open-hearth steelmaking method, which converted iron ore into steel with much less labor than was previously required. Carnegie's mill also combined all stages of steel production—smelting, refining, and rolling—into one unified operation. As a result, the price of steel rails dropped from $107 per ton in 1870 to $32 per ton in 1890.

Innovation, ambition, and organizational skill made Carnegie hugely wealthy by the time he was 40 years old. Saying that hard work brought success, he also believed that those who acquired great

GUIDE TO READING

Main Idea

During the late 1800s, industrialization transformed the United States as manufacturing became the main source of economic growth.

Vocabulary

- industrialism
- national market
- merger
- horizontal integration
- vertical integration

Read to Find Out . . .

- the relationship between inventions and industrialism.
- how industrialism and the development of national markets affected business.
- how industrialists applied Social Darwinism to big business.

wealth had a responsibility to return a portion of their profits to society. "The man who dies rich, dies disgraced," the self-made Scottish immigrant avowed.

By the time of his death in 1919, Carnegie had donated more than $350 million to worthy causes, including thousands of libraries, and another $30 million was disbursed through his last will and testament. His generosity was legendary throughout the world.

Industrialism Triumphant

A New World of Manufacturing

The era during which Andrew Carnegie built his steel empire witnessed a dramatic economic transformation. Between the end of the Civil War in 1865 and the end of the 1800s, the United States became an industrial giant. Manufacturing replaced agriculture as the main source of economic growth; growing **industrialism** turned the United States into a land rich with machines, factories, mines, and railroads.

The Rise of Heavy Industry

Before the Civil War, manufacturing in the United States had been tied to the farming economy. Factories processed the products of the farm and forest into consumer goods—turning cotton and wool into cloth; hides into shoes and boots; and trees into ships, barrels, and furniture. After the Civil War, manufacturing branched out and concentrated increased funding and labor in heavy-industry consumer goods such as railroad tracks, steam engines, and farm tractors. Factories could now produce in huge quantities what craftspersons had painstakingly been making by hand.

Steelmaking was central to the new heavy industry. Hand in hand with steel production went the intensive development of the nation's mineral resources. Iron ore deposits in Michigan and Minnesota provided the raw substance for the steelmaking centers that sprang up in Illinois, Ohio, and Pennsylvania. Coal was equally important because it became the fuel that powered a nation of steam-run machines.

BROWN BROTHERS

Growing Employment **Cotton mills, such as this one in Greensboro, North Carolina, photographed in 1895, provided jobs for many Southerners who were forced out of farming by hard times. Whole families worked in the mills.** *How were factories linked to farming?*

The Technology Boom

In 1876 the most ingenious American inventor since Benjamin Franklin built a long wooden shed in a little town in New Jersey where he promised to produce "a minor invention every ten days and a big thing every six months or so." Thomas Alva Edison, a brash 29-year-old at the time, was nearly as good as his word.

Edison patented more than 1,000 inventions in his Menlo Park laboratory before his death in 1931. He lit up the nation through his stunning development of an incandescent lightbulb that provided a cheap and

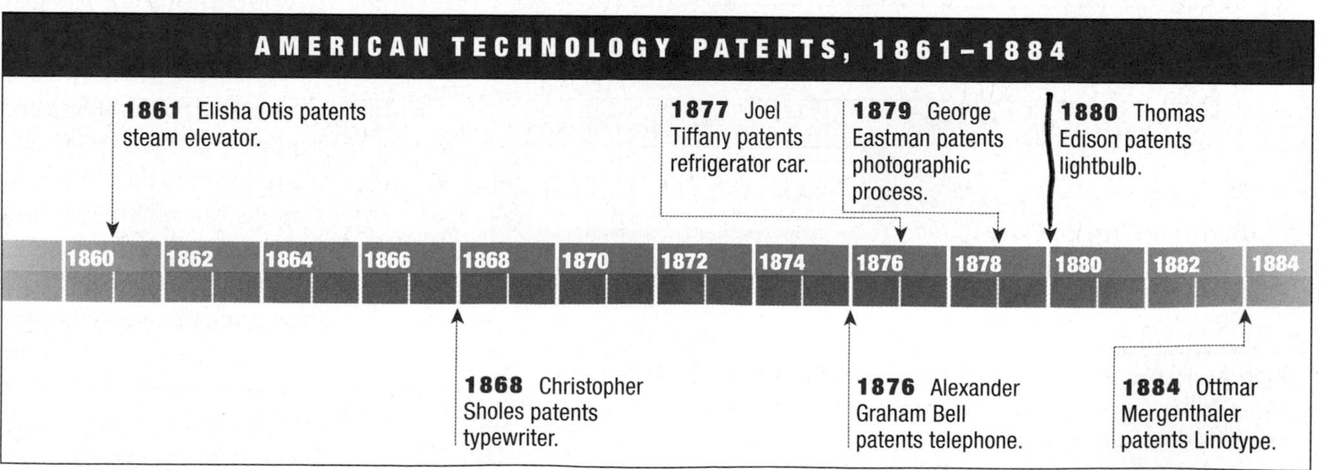

AMERICAN TECHNOLOGY PATENTS, 1861–1884
1861 Elisha Otis patents steam elevator.
1877 Joel Tiffany patents refrigerator car.
1879 George Eastman patents photographic process.
1880 Thomas Edison patents lightbulb.
1860
1862
1864
1866
1868
1870
1872
1874
1876
1878
1880
1882
1884
1868 Christopher Sholes patents typewriter.
1876 Alexander Graham Bell patents telephone.
1884 Ottmar Mergenthaler patents Linotype.

efficient replacement for candles and oil lamps. Of equal importance was his invention of the technology for producing and distributing electrical power.

Between 1860 and 1900, thousands of other inventors pushed forward the new age of machines and electrical energy. The United States Patent Office, which had issued a total of 36,000 patents in the 70 years before 1860, granted 676,000 between 1860 and 1900. Among the most important was Alexander Graham Bell's telephone. Patented in 1876, the telephone revolutionized communications.

By 1884 telephone service from Boston to New York City began the boom in rapid long-distance communication. By 1900 more than 1.3 million telephones were in operation nationwide.

Inventions and entrepreneurial skills combined to reshape the face of American manufacturing. New cotton machinery speeded up textile production. By 1886 a worker laboring for 10 hours could turn out 3 times as much as a worker in 1840 who toiled for 14 hours. Such developments made processed goods and consumer items cheaper and more readily available.

Everywhere in the United States the new technology could be seen in the form of mechanical reapers, blast furnaces, and telegraph offices; in the camera, typewriter, electric motor, and electric light; in the high-speed rotary printing press, iron and steel ships, pressed glass, wire rope, and petroleum. All of these products combined to create a new world of manufacturing, business, and consumerism.

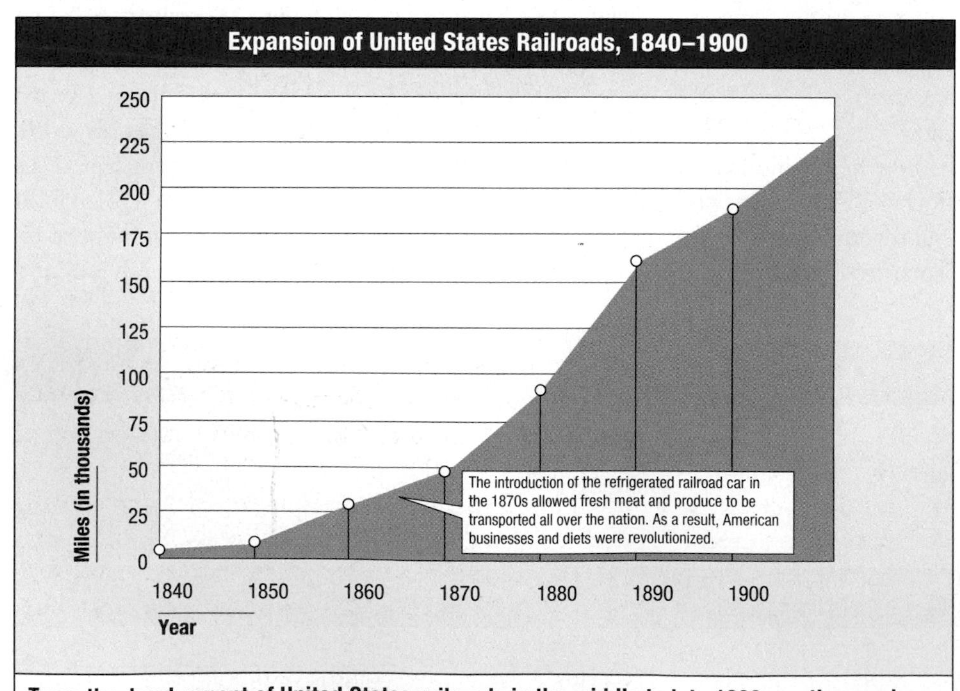

Trace the development of United States railroads in the middle to late 1800s on the graph. *When was the refrigerated railroad car introduced? What inference can you make about how it may have affected the growth of railroads?*

National Markets

Products Move Across the Nation by Rail

Closely linked to the maturing of the nation's industrial economy was the creation of a transportation network that turned the country into a huge, unified **national market.** Before the Civil War, canal and river boats had carried the bulky farm and forest products from one region to another. After the Civil War, the fledgling railroad system that began in the 1830s surged forward. Soon it became the most popular way of transporting people and goods.

Across these thousands of miles of railroad track, goods could move with such year-round, on-time efficiency that entire industries were revolutionized. One example was the meatpacking industry. Before the Civil War, Americans bought meat from their local butchers, who had purchased livestock from nearby farmers. The railroads, however, allowed for far more efficient cattle raising on the wide-open ranges of the Great Plains. This in turn lowered meat prices for the consumer. From the Great Plains, cattle were shipped in cattle cars to livestock markets—Chicago was the largest—and then were distributed by the railroads to be slaughtered in Eastern and Southern cities.

Refrigerated Railroad Cars

The invention of the refrigerated railroad car further revolutionized the business. Gustavus Swift, a clever Chicago cattle dealer, recognized that if slaughtering and preparing meat for market could be done in one place, money could be saved and meat sold more cheaply. What was needed was the ability to keep meat fresh during its journey to the local butcher shops. The refrigerated railroad car was the answer.

Using the newly invented refrigerated car, Swift created a gigantic national meatpacking network in the 1880s. His wagons carried chilled meat from regional packinghouses to local butcher shops. Four other meatpackers copied Swift's innovations, and by the 1890s these five companies completely dominated the nation's meat business.

ANDLER COLLECTION

New Consumer Markets **With the growth of a national market, merchandising took a leap from local department stores to national chain stores. Customers across the country could expect to find F.W. Woolworth stores that looked very similar to this one, which was in New Haven, Connecticut.** *What merchandising gimmick is advertised at this store?*

The refrigerated railroad car also created a national market for fruits and vegetables from the West Coast. By 1888 fresh apricots and cherries were able to survive the train ride from California to New York, and the nation's diet was transformed. Large parts of the country that only ate locally grown fruits and vegetables during the summer months could now have a Florida orange for breakfast, an Oregon apple for lunch, and a California lettuce salad for dinner at any time of the year.

Nationwide Businesses

Other businesses quickly followed the move to identify or create a national market. By the 1880s the McCormick Harvesting Machine Company had a national network of dealers who not only sold mechanized farm equipment that arrived by train but also provided credit and repair services. The Singer Sewing Machine Company dotted the land with retail stores and blanketed the country with door-to-door salespeople.

City dwellers also became connected to huge nationwide chain store systems. F.W. Woolworth's five-and-ten-cent stores sprouted in thousands of towns and cities. The Great Atlantic and Pacific Tea Company replaced "Ma and Pa" grocery stores all over the country because this large grocery chain could undersell the single retailer through mass purchasing. All of the products sold in chain stores moved across the nation by rail.

The Birth of Consumerism

The creation of a national marketplace changed the way people spent their money. In the cities people no longer purchased solely from pushcarts or small shops, but rushed to the new department stores. John Wanamaker of Philadelphia introduced fixed prices and window displays to entice customers in 1861. Macy's in New York, Marshall Field in Chicago, and Jordan Marsh in Boston soon joined him.

These lavish consumer palaces included leaded-glass skylights, polished marble staircases, expensive carpets, and chandeliers. Such stores introduced charge accounts and trained clerks to cater to the customer. They tried to convince buyers that shopping was a great pleasure to be enjoyed. Advertising played a significant role in this buying craze. Between 1870 and 1900 the amount of money spent on advertising increased dramatically, from $50 million to $542 million.

BROWN BROTHERS

Shopping at Home Montgomery Ward issued mail-order catalogs to rural families across the country. People could buy thousands of items, from barn nails to sunbonnets. *How did the mail-order business depend on railroads?*

The Growth of Big Business

Mergers Create Industrial Giants

The growth of heavy industry and the creation of vast nationwide markets brought about a fundamental change in business organization. Only large businesses gathering capital from many investors could afford to set up huge factories, install modern machinery, and employ hundreds of workers.

At the same time, the vast railroad system allowed national corporations to ship goods almost anywhere. While the typical railroad line in 1865 was only 100 miles long, by 1885 it had expanded to 1,000 miles (1,609 km) of track. Such a large enterprise, with enormous costs of construction, maintenance, and operation, demanded unprecedented amounts of capital and new methods of management.

The Managerial Revolution

In the early days of railroading, a superintendent could give his personal attention to every detail in running a 50- or 100-mile (80.45- or 160.9-km) operation. How, then, could one person oversee the operations of a business such as the Pennsylvania Railroad? By 1890 this railroad had 50,000 employees, properties spread over great distances, large amounts of capital invested, and hundreds of trains that had to be scheduled and coordinated with precision.

The answer was to separate the various functions of a business into departments and put each one under the direction of a separate manager. In a railroad, for example, one person would be in charge of people who maintained the tracks; another supervised cargo handling; another oversaw traffic. Managers reported to the central office through well-defined lines of communication.

The Merger Movement

Led by the railroads, the American industrial economy grew rapidly in the decades after the Civil War. The cutthroat competition of an uncontrolled marketplace, however, plagued businesses. Business owners feverishly overbuilt their operations in good times and cut back sharply when demand for their products slackened. In such a boom-or-bust marketplace, bankruptcy was common. In the depression of the 1870s, for example, 47,000 firms closed their doors, laying off hundreds of thousands of employees.

Some people felt that the solution to such business instability was a **merger,** or a combining of several competing firms under a single head. By merging companies in a particular industry, a junglelike market could become an orderly, predictable market. "I like a little competition now and then," exclaimed J.P. Morgan, a titan of mergers in the late 1800s, "but I like combination a lot better."

The pioneering figure in the late nineteenth-century merger movement was John D. Rockefeller. Rockefeller started out as a clerk in his boyhood town of Cleveland, Ohio. In the 1860s he founded a business that refined kerosene from petroleum and later became Standard Oil Company. Hundreds of oil refineries, mostly small and badly organized, competed fiercely in the Ohio and Pennsylvania regions.

Both wise and ruthless, Rockefeller purchased as many competing companies as possible, and by the late 1870s Standard Oil controlled almost all the oil refineries in Ohio. By 1882 Standard Oil had gobbled up most of the competition throughout the country. Rockefeller's 40 oil companies owned 90 percent of the nation's pipelines and refined 84 percent of the nation's oil. "The day of individual competition [in the oil business] is past and gone," Rockefeller pronounced.

Because he dominated the market, Rockefeller was able to demand rail shipping rates of ten cents a barrel as compared with his competitors' thirty-five cents. When Rockefeller turned the business over to his son in 1911, his fortune exceeded $1 billion.

The merger of competing companies in one area of business such as occurred to form Rockefeller's oil corporation was known as **horizontal integration.** It was often accompanied by **vertical integration** of industries, in which a firm would strive to control all aspects of production from acquisition of raw materials to final delivery of finished products. In this way a single business might gain total control over a national market, as the chart below shows. Note that when a business integrates horizontally, it merges all competing companies in one area of business. In vertical integration, one business controls all aspects of production.

In the merger movement, Swift and Armour dominated meatpacking, and the Duke family controlled tobacco. Andrew Carnegie, however, had the most success with vertical integration. Carnegie bought up coal mines and iron ore deposits for his steel mills, then bought railroads and ships to transport raw materials and send his products to market. By owning every aspect of steel production he could limit risk and guarantee profit.

When J.P. Morgan bought Carnegie's steel company in 1901, he consolidated it with several other firms to form the U.S. Steel Corporation, which controlled 60 percent of American steel production. It was the nation's first billion-dollar company. By 1913 J.P. Morgan controlled 314 directorships in 112 corporations, with an estimated collective worth of $22 billion.

The Spirit of the Gilded Age

Lavish Spending and Ruthless Competition

The wealth generated by industrial capitalism and big business led to the growth of a "nouveau riche" class with its own philosophy. Many of these self-made people proclaimed their importance with showy displays of wealth, leading humorist Mark Twain to call the late 1800s the Gilded Age.

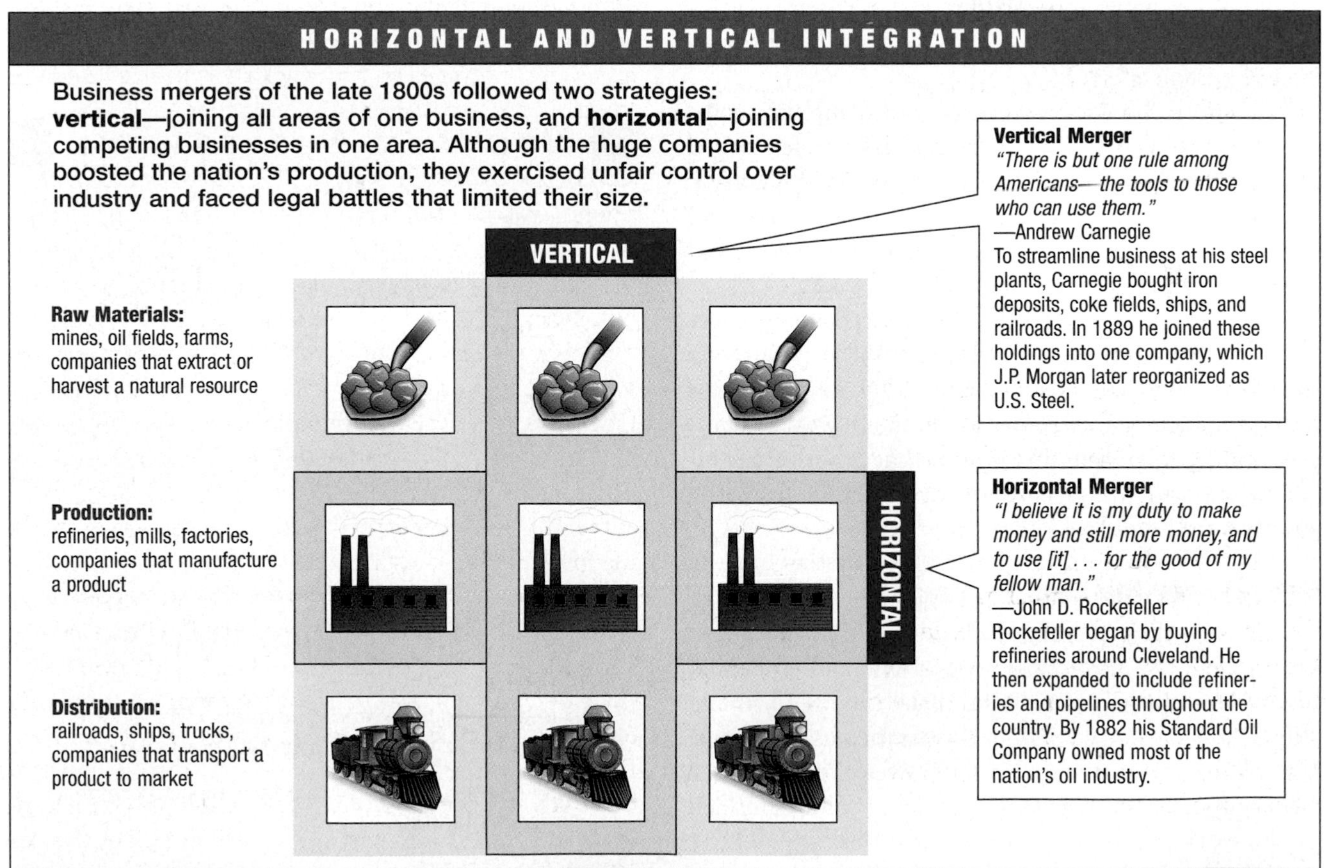

HORIZONTAL AND VERTICAL INTEGRATION
Business mergers of the late 1800s followed two strategies: **vertical**—joining all areas of one business, and **horizontal**—joining competing businesses in one area. Although the huge companies boosted the nation's production, they exercised unfair control over industry and faced legal battles that limited their size.
VERTICAL
HORIZONTAL
Raw Materials: mines, oil fields, farms, companies that extract or harvest a natural resource
Production: refineries, mills, factories, companies that manufacture a product
Distribution: railroads, ships, trucks, companies that transport a product to market
Vertical Merger
"There is but one rule among Americans—the tools to those who can use them." —Andrew Carnegie
To streamline business at his steel plants, Carnegie bought iron deposits, coke fields, ships, and railroads. In 1889 he joined these holdings into one company, which J.P. Morgan later reorganized as U.S. Steel.
Horizontal Merger
"I believe it is my duty to make money and still more money, and to use [it] . . . for the good of my fellow man." —John D. Rockefeller
Rockefeller began by buying refineries around Cleveland. He then expanded to include refineries and pipelines throughout the country. By 1882 his Standard Oil Company owned most of the nation's oil industry.

The chart above illustrates horizontal and vertical business integration. When a business integrates horizontally, it merges all competing companies in one area of business. In vertical integration, one business controls all aspects of production. *What kind of business integration does U.S. Steel represent in the chart? What did it own?*

Some of these people, known as robber barons, built lavish mansions in New York City complete with solid gold bathroom fixtures. For the summer months many built castlelike estates in Newport, Rhode Island, which they dubbed their "cottages." Railroad tycoon William Vanderbilt's summer home cost $11 million. Outrageous displays of wealth were popular. At one debutante ball in Philadelphia, a young woman's parents ordered thousands of live butterflies (many of which drowned in champagne glasses) as decorations at the $75,000 party.

Social Darwinism

In the heady, expensive atmosphere of the Gilded Age, the struggle for wealth became a way of life for the most ambitious Americans. How did business leaders, bent on killing off competition in order to increase their control of the marketplace and make as much money as possible, justify their activities to a public raised on the ideology of a fair and open society? A new theory of human behavior provided an answer. It rested on the scientific theories of Charles Darwin about the origin of species and the evolution of humankind. Darwin argued that the plant and animal world had reached its present state through a long process of "natural selection" in which only the fittest had survived. Herbert Spencer, an English philosopher, loosely adapted these ideas, in a theory known as Social Darwinism, to explain the evolution of human society.

Progress, Spencer argued, occurred through competition in which the weak fell and the strong forged ahead. His strongest American supporter, William G. Sumner, put it this way: "If we do not like the survival of the fittest, we have only one possible alternative, and that is the survival of the unfittest."

American business leaders flocked to honor Spencer when he visited the United States in 1882. Here was a man whose theories justified their aggressive business practices and their attempts to eliminate weaker competitors. They praised his notion that government interference with the separation of the weak from the strong would only hold back progress.

Concern for the Less Fortunate

Despite their seeming lack of regard for common people, many of the robber barons who had embraced Social Darwinism also believed that the more fortunate should give back to society to benefit the public at large. Carnegie was but one of a host of powerful, rich patrons who supported the arts, education, and culture; funded public works; and established foundations.

These individual efforts had their limitations, however. As Jane Addams, a reformer of this time, commented concerning her native city of Chicago, "Private beneficence [charity] is totally inadequate to deal with vast numbers of the city's disinherited." Americans would have to learn new ways to cope with and solve the enormous problems created by population growth and industrialization in the United States between the Civil War and the end of the nineteenth century.

CULVER PICTURES

Newport, Rhode Island While the wealthy lounged on the steps of summer "cottages," others worked in factories and mines. *Why were the late 1800s known as an age of excess?*

SECTION ASSESSMENT

Main Idea

1. Use a diagram like this one to show changes in the United States economy following the Civil War.

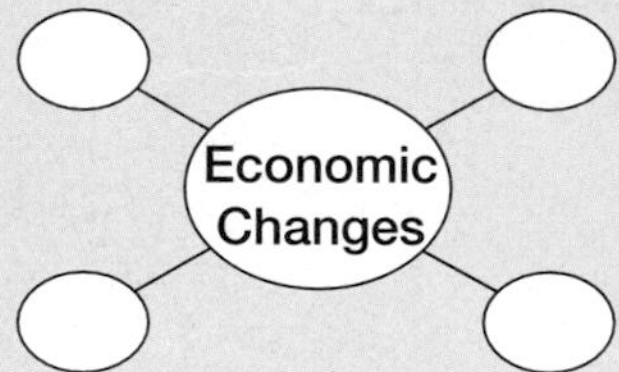

Vocabulary

2. Define: industrialism, national market, merger, horizontal integration, vertical integration.

Checking Facts

3. Name two technological advances that spurred industrial growth in the late 1800s.

4. How did the growth of railroads help to create national markets?

Critical Thinking

5. **Predicting Consequences** How might workers have reacted to the theory of Social Darwinism?

Social Studies Skill

READING STATISTICAL TABLES

Learning the Skill

Tables present statistical information by organizing it into categories. A statistical table can help you to identify patterns in employment in the United States.

Finding Information in a Table

To find the answers to statistical questions:

a. Read the title; then make sure that you understand the headings. There are three major headings: Total Labor Force, Labor Force, and Employment. Two of these heads are divided into smaller categories or heads; and of these, Manufacturing, Transport, and Service are subdivided again.

b. The lefthand column, the stub, lists another category of information, in this case, years. Find out which years the stub lists.

c. The columns of figures are the body of the table. They give data, by category, for each year.

d. Read down from one column heading and across from the corresponding year to find a measure of the labor force employed in a trade for that year.

Practicing the Skill

Study the table below, then answer the following questions:

1. In 1900 the Total Labor Force was 29,070,000. Why are there no figures in the next 2 columns?

2. What percentage worked in Trade in 1900?

3. Which category lost the most workers between 1800 and 1900?

4. By what percentage did employment in this field change?

5. Which categories gained the most workers?

Applying the Skill

Using another table, write 10 questions that can be answered from the table, and their answers.

The **Glencoe Skillbuilder Interactive Workbook, Level 2** CD-ROM provides more practice in key social studies skills.

Labor Force and Employment, 1800–1900

Year	TOTAL LABOR FORCE (IN THOUSANDS)	LABOR FORCE (PERCENT)		EMPLOYMENT (PERCENT)											
								Manufacturing				Transport		Service	
		Free	Slave	Agriculture	Fishing	Mining	Construction	Total	Cotton Textiles	Primary Iron and Steel	Trade	Ocean Vessels	Railways	Teachers	Domestics
1800	1,900	72	28	74	0.3	1.0	–	–	0.1	0.1	–	2.0	–	0.3	2
1810	2,330	68	32	84	0.3	0.5	–	3	0.4	0.2	–	3.0	–	1.0	3
1820	3,135	70	30	79	0.4	0.4	–	–	0.4	0.2	–	2.0	–	1.0	4
1830	4,200	72	28	71	0.4	1.0	–	–	1.0	0.5	–	2.0	–	1.0	4
1840	5,660	74	26	63	0.4	1.0	5	9	1.0	0.4	6	2.0	0.1	1.0	4
1850	8,250	76	24	55	0.4	1.0	5	15	1.0	0.4	6	2.0	0.2	1.0	4
1860	11,110	79	21	53	0.3	2.0	5	14	1.0	0.4	8	1.0	1.0	1.0	5
1870	12,930	–	–	53	0.2	1.0	6	19	1.0	1.0	10	1.0	1.0	1.0	8
1880	17,390	–	–	51	0.2	2.0	5	19	1.0	1.0	11	1.0	2.0	1.0	6
1890	23,320	–	–	43	0.3	2.0	6	19	1.0	1.0	13	1.0	3.0	2.0	7
1900	29,070	–	–	40	0.2	2.0	6	20	1.0	1.0	14	0.4	4.0	1.0	6

The United States Bureau of the Census compiled the statistical data for this table on labor and employment during the 1800s. *How many different fields of employment are represented? What are they?*

Populism and Protest

JULY 2, 1892: PEOPLE'S PARTY HOLDS FIRST CONVENTION

NORTH WIND PICTURE ARCHIVES

Stirring Words
Farmers and laborers listened to Ignatius Donnelly at the first Populist convention in 1892.

In July 1892, the delegates of a new political party met in Omaha to cement their alliance:

> We have witnessed for more than a quarter of a century the struggles of the two great political parties for power and plunder, while grievous wrongs have been inflicted upon the suffering people. . . . Assembled on the anniversary of the birthday of the nation . . . we seek to restore the government of the Republic to the hands of "the plain people."
>
> —Omaha Platform, July 1892

The delegates adopted the platform of the People's party, also called the Populist party, with great enthusiasm. The platform not only denounced the existing ills of society but also proposed a third-party remedy. The Populists represented a grand coalition of farmers, laborers, and reformers, which aimed to put government back into the hands of the people.

Populist leaders were as colorful and diverse as the causes they represented. Ignatius Donnelly of Minnesota, who had written the preamble to the party platform, was considered the greatest orator of Populism. Mary E. Lease, who forcefully represented farmers' interests, once advised Kansas farmers to "raise less corn and more hell." "Sockless Jerry" Simpson earned his nickname when he told a Kansas audience that he wore no silk socks like his "princely" Republican opponent. Georgia's Thomas E. Watson left the Democratic party to campaign for Populist ideals.

Guide to Reading

Main Idea

The economic imbalances caused by rapid industrialization and the power of big business led to the birth of the Populist movement among farmers and the rise of the labor movement among workers.

Vocabulary

- union
- strike
- injunction

Read to Find Out . . .

- the development of the Populist party.
- the problems facing farmers and their efforts to improve their situation.
- the development of labor unions in the late 1800s.

The Populists chose their candidates amid calls for restricted immigration and a shorter workday for industrial laborers. The party also aimed to convince the government to allow the free coinage of silver, a measure that would make silver, not just gold, legal tender. Many farmers thought this would cause inflation, thereby raising prices for farm goods, and would breathe new life into the faltering economy. The nomination for President in 1892 went to James B. Weaver, a seasoned campaigner from Iowa, who had been the candidate of the Greenback party in 1880. Second place on the ticket went to James G. Field, a former Confederate general from Virginia. As one historian observed, "Whether they knew it or not, the delegates were beginning the last phase of a long and perhaps losing struggle—the struggle to save agricultural America from the devouring jaws of industrial America."

Farmers Beleaguered

Falling Prices, Rising Debts

The rapid development of the agricultural West and the reorganization of Southern agriculture after the Civil War provided new opportunities for millions of American families. The changes also exposed these families to the financial hardships of rural life. The result was the first mass organization of farmers in American history.

Ironically the farmers' problem was rooted in their ability to produce so much. Immigrants as well as American-born farmers were tilling huge tracts of the Great Plains for the first time. Larger acreage, coupled with improved farming methods, meant bumper crops in most years. By the 1870s farmers produced more than the country—or the world—demanded. Prices dropped, as the graph shows. In addition two factors contributed to the farmers' financial problems: many farmers borrowed money to put more land under cultivation, and most of them had to pay high transportation costs to get crops to market.

Falling farm prices brought widespread rural suffering. On the Great Plains, many farmers had to borrow more money to keep afloat financially. In the South many lost their farms and became debt-ridden sharecroppers. When Eastern bankers began to foreclose on farm loans, thousands abandoned their homesteads.

Homesteaders in the late 1800s also faced nature's wrath. In 1874 a plague of grasshoppers devoured crops, clothes, and even plow handles. Droughts parched the earth in 1886. In January 1888, in the northern Plains the School Children's Storm killed more than 200 youngsters who were stranded at school or starting home.

Loneliness could be just as tormenting. One farm mother, who had not seen another woman for a year, walked across the prairie with her small children to see a woman who had come to live several miles away. The two strangers threw their arms around each other and wept.

Some families gave up and headed back East. They left behind bitter slogans: "In God we trusted, in Kansas we busted." The farmers who stayed began to seek political relief. The governor of Kansas received the following letter from a farm woman in 1894:

> I take my pen in hand to let you know we are starving. . . . My husband went away to find work and came home last night and told me that he would have to starve. He had been in 10 counties and did not get no work. . . . I haven't had nothing to eat today and it is 3 o'clock.

Farmers United

Farmers, like other beleaguered groups in society, realized that there is strength in numbers. As early as 1867 farmers banded together to form the Patrons of Husbandry, also known as the Grange. By 1875 there were about 1 million Grange members spread from New England to Texas, concentrated mainly in the South and the Great Plains. The Grangers wanted the government to

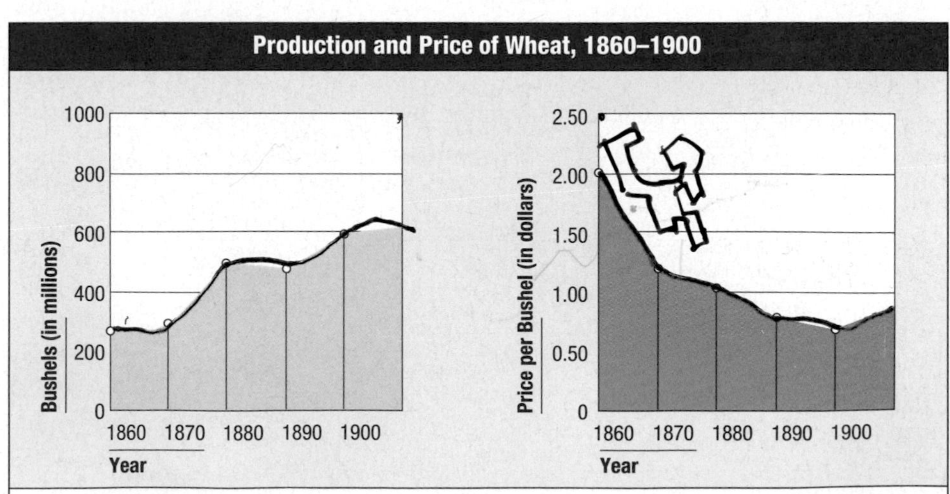

The graph on the left shows an increase in wheat production during the late 1800s. The graph on the right shows the price of wheat declining during this same period. *What conclusion can you draw from these two graphs?*

regulate railroad freight rates and to fund agricultural colleges. They also formed sales cooperatives, pooling their products and dividing profits.

In the 1880s farmers stepped up their political activism by forming groups known as Farmers' Alliances—one in the South, another on the Plains. The Alliances pooled the credit resources of their members to free themselves from the high interest rates banks charged. They formed marketing cooperatives to sell directly to large merchants and thus avoided paying extra costs to brokers. Such cooperatives could also buy bulk quantities of the supplies and machinery farmers needed.

The Populist Crusade

Despite action by the Farmers' Alliances and the Grangers, the plight of thousands of farmers worsened. By the 1890s they had become politically active as never before. The platform of the Populist party called for extensive reforms. Reformers believed that farmers and workers should be freed from the exploitative practices of banks, railroads, and merchants. Although James Weaver, the Populist candidate for President, soundly lost to Democrat Grover Cleveland in the election of 1892, his party made headway. The Populists gained 14 seats in Congress, won 2 governorships, and received the largest number of popular votes cast for any third party in the 1800s.

Shortly after the election of 1892, the nation plunged into the deepest depression the country had yet known. In 1893 more than 2.5 million Americans, about 20 percent of the labor force, were unemployed. By the following year, the ranks of the unemployed had swollen to 4 million.

President Cleveland's seeming indifference to the economic problems caused by the depression created a popular revolt. Jacob S. Coxey, a quiet Ohio business owner, led a march of about 500 people from Ohio to Washington, D.C., to dramatize the plight of the jobless. Leaders read their grievances on the steps of the Capitol and were arrested for unlawfully trying to enter the building.

By the time of the 1896 election, the Populist party itself had declined, but some of its ideas entered the mainstream. The continuing depression forced the Democratic party into a more radical position on one key issue—unlimited coinage of silver. This stance led many Populists to support the Democratic candidate, William Jennings Bryan of Nebraska. Bryan waged a campaign in favor of "free silver," and secured endorsement by the Populist party. He traveled extensively, logging 18,000 miles (28,962 km) on the campaign trail.

The Republican nominee, William McKinley, took a more relaxed approach. McKinley had the support of big business. Standard Oil's $250,000 donation to the Republicans nearly exceeded the total amount in the Democrats' treasury. McKinley merely warned voters of the dangers of radicalism.

McKinley won by a comfortable 600,000 votes, suggesting that Americans in towns and cities heeded his warning. The discovery of gold in Alaska in 1898 increased the nation's gold reserves and eased more money into circulation, stemming the money crisis for many farmers. Populism began to decline as a political force.

The South Withholds Support

One factor limited Populism's strength in the South. By 1890 more than 1 million farmers belonged to the Southern Alliance—the Southern branch of the two Farmers' Alliances. In December the Southern Alliance met with other farmers' groups at Ocala, Florida, and drew up a list of concerns. These included cheap currency, the abolition of national banks, and the restriction of land ownership to American citizens.

THE ELECTION OF 1892

VOTING FOR THE PEOPLE'S PARTY, 1892
Popular vote by state for the People's (Populist) party ticket of Weaver and Field

50% or more; 33% to 50%; 10% to 33%; 0% to 10%; Not yet a state in 1892

Nationally, the People's party received 8.54% of the popular vote

Albers Equal-Area projection

The Populist candidates for President and Vice President in 1892 received varying support from one state to the next. *In which states or regions did the Populists gain the most votes?*

Although this list resembled the Populist platform of 1892, the People's party failed to gain wide support in the South. The Southern Alliance advised its members to support major party candidates who favored agricultural interests.

The underlying reason for the failure of Populism in the South was the issue of white supremacy. The Southern Alliance feared that Populism might lead to gains for African Americans. Populist leader Thomas Watson tried to form an alliance of poor white and African American farmers. He argued that social class was more important than race. He urged citizens of both races to unite against the financial oppression that enslaved them.

Watson's career, however, mirrored the fate of Populism in the South. He was elected to Congress in 1890 but was defeated two years later as Democratic candidates who promised to exclude African Americans from political power gained support. Watson ran for President on the Populist ticket in 1904 and 1908. Embittered by his defeats, he turned against many who had supported him. He became racist, anti-Catholic, and anti-Semitic.

THE BETTMAN ARCHIVE

Mother Jones **Mary Harris Jones became known by company bosses as "the most dangerous woman in America."**
What obstacles did Mother Jones overcome in her early life before becoming a champion for poor workers?

Labor Organizes

Unions for Skilled Workers

As early as the 1810s, skilled workers such as carpenters, printers, and tailors had formed citywide organizations to try to get better pay. Construction workers in many Eastern cities succeeded in getting a 10-hour day in 1834. As the workplace changed, however, so did the labor movement. After the Civil War, factory production replaced skilled labor. Employers often cut the cost of wages by hiring women and children. Workers, like farmers, decided to organize to maintain control over their wages and working conditions.

The first nationwide labor organizations developed during the mid-1800s. In 1867 bootmakers and shoemakers, whose wares were being undersold by machine-made products, formed the Knights of St. Crispin to try to block competition from unskilled workers. By 1870 this **union,** an organization for mutual benefit, had nearly 50,000 members. Like most early unions, however, the Knights of St. Crispin could not survive the high unemployment of the 1870s.

In 1877 a national railroad **strike,** or work stoppage, was the first of many violent confrontations between labor and the large corporations in the post–Civil War era. Clashes between railroad workers and state militias or federal troops sent in to break the strikes recurred in the 1880s. Then in 1885 successful negotiations with railroad magnate Jay Gould helped workers in all fields by convincing millions that they needed stronger unions.

The Knights of Labor

The first national labor union to remain active for more than a few years was the Knights of Labor. Tailors in Philadelphia formed it as a secret society in 1869, and it grew to national proportions in the 1880s. The Knights of Labor differed from other labor unions by accepting all gainfully employed persons, including farmers, merchants, and unskilled workers. The union proposed new laws, including one to cut the workday to eight hours and one to authorize equal pay for men and women doing the same work. Both of these were radical propositions at the time.

Women workers played a role in this growing labor movement. When Irish immigrant Mary Harris Jones lost her husband and children to yellow fever in 1867, she moved to Chicago to work as a seamstress. After losing everything else in a fire, she turned to the Knights of Labor for help. Soon she was one of its strongest campaigners. She traveled on behalf of labor for nearly 50 years—later organizing for the United Mine Workers. Beloved by her followers, she became known as "Mother Jones." The bosses, however, feared her. A West Virginia lawyer working for the mining companies called her "the most dangerous woman in America."

The American Federation of Labor

In 1886 the Knights of Labor reached its peak with more than 700,000 members. A less reform-minded group, the American Federation of Labor (AFL), soon replaced it as the leading union. Led by Samuel Gompers, a cigar maker born in England, the AFL concentrated on organizing skilled workers. It advocated using strikes to improve wages and hours.

Gompers was willing to accept the new industrial system as it was, but only if labor got greater rewards. He also advocated boycotts—organized agreements to refuse to buy specific products—as one means of peaceful protest. This tactic had only limited success.

Protests and Violence

The Labor Movement Meets Resistance

Workers in the late 1800s customarily worked 10 hours a day, 6 days a week. A strike for an 8-hour workday at the huge McCormick Harvester factory in Chicago led to violent confrontation on May 3, 1886. After police killed 4 strikers in a scuffle outside the plant, about 1,000 workers turned out for a rally at Haymarket Square.

The Haymarket Riot

Someone in the crowd threw a bomb during the Haymarket protest, killing 7 police officers and injuring 67 bystanders. The police then fired into the crowd, killing 10 and wounding 50. Uproar over the Haymarket riot continued when 8 radical strike leaders were put on trial for murder. Although no direct evidence that any of them had thrown the bomb could be found, 7 of the 8 were sentenced to death, and 4 eventually were hanged. The public outcry against labor organizers helped employers defeat the 8-hour workday reform.

The Homestead Strike

In 1892 another violent dispute took place in Homestead, Pennsylvania. The steelworkers' union called a strike when the Carnegie Steel Company reduced wages. The company hired 300 guards from the Pinkerton Detective Agency to protect its factories. Several people were killed when violence broke out between the strikers and the guards. The Homestead strike failed when most workers quit the union and returned to work.

Coeur d'Alene

Labor unrest spread to the West as well. Disputes arose between miners and mine owners over pay and conditions. Disputes also flared between nonunion miners and members of the Western Federation of Miners. Strikes plagued the Coeur d'Alene mining region of Idaho during the 1890s. Twice the strikes were broken when the governor called in federal troops.

The Pullman Strike

The depression that lasted from 1893 to 1897 brought further setbacks for labor. In 1894 Eugene V. Debs, the founder of the new American Railway Union, led a labor action against the Pullman sleeping car works near Chicago.

George Pullman saw his company town as a model industrial village where workers were paid decently and were also disciplined. "We are born in a Pullman house," said one worker, "fed from the Pullman shop, taught in the Pullman school, catechized in the Pullman church, and when we die we shall be buried in the Pullman cemetery and go to the Pullman hell."

As the depression of 1893 worsened, Pullman cut wages by one-third and fired many workers. Prices in the company stores and rents for the company houses, however, stayed the same. Angry Pullman workers joined Debs's railroad union in droves and went on strike in the spring of 1894.

Debs then led a strike of all American Railway Union members across

CULVER PICTURES

Violent Clash **Angry strikers taunt security forces sent to break up the Pennsylvania Homestead strike in this 1892 print.** *Which company and which union were involved in the Homestead strike?*

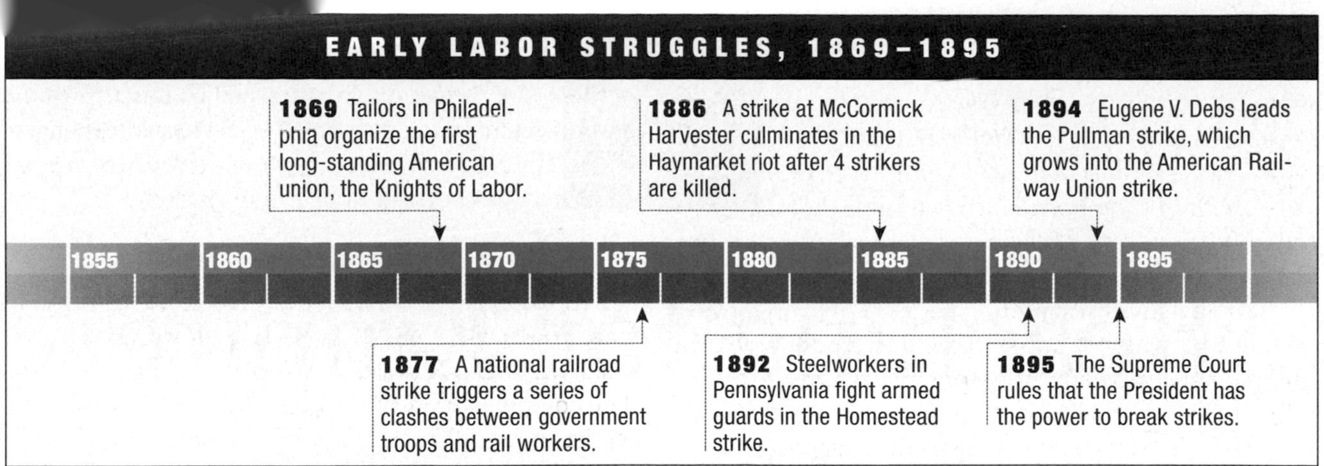

the country in sympathy with the Pullman workers. Debs promised to "use no violence" and to "stop no trains." Instead workers refused to handle trains with Pullman sleeping cars.

EARLY LABOR STRUGGLES, 1869–1895
1869 Tailors in Philadelphia organize the first long-standing American union, the Knights of Labor.
1886 A strike at McCormick Harvester culminates in the Haymarket riot after 4 strikers are killed.
1894 Eugene V. Debs leads the Pullman strike, which grows into the American Railway Union strike.
1855
1860
1865
1870
1875
1880
1885
1890
1895
1877 A national railroad strike triggers a series of clashes between government troops and rail workers.
1892 Steelworkers in Pennsylvania fight armed guards in the Homestead strike.
1895 The Supreme Court rules that the President has the power to break strikes.

Determined to break the growing union movement, 24 railroad owners persuaded President Cleveland to order United States Army troops to disperse the strikers. Violence once again centered in Chicago where strikers fought troops and railroad company guards. Strikers set boxcars on fire and brought rail traffic in the Midwest to a dead halt.

Labor did not stand united, however. Samuel Gompers refused to swing his powerful AFL behind the strike, causing it to collapse. The government arrested Debs and other union leaders and sentenced Debs to 6 months in prison. In 1895 the Supreme Court upheld the President's right to issue an **injunction,** an order to end a strike. Corporations thereby gained a powerful legal weapon that they used against unions for years.

Obstacles to Unity

Government intervention during major strikes repeatedly thwarted the nation's industrial unions. The unions, however, also tended to cripple themselves by largely excluding three important groups: women, members of minority groups, and unskilled workers. By 1900 only about 1 in every 33 American workers belonged to a union, and fewer than 100,000 of the 5.3 million working women belonged to unions.

In the South the great majority of African American workers could join only separate, segregated local unions. In the North and West white unionists feared the competition of African American workers, knowing that many bosses would pay them less.

The hostility of American-born workers toward immigrants also kept the unions weak. Suspicion often centered on German, British, or Russian immigrants, some of whom had more radical ideas about society and labor than Americans usually heard.

American-born workers strongly expressed their resentment of immigrants during the anti-Chinese movement in the West during the 1870s and 1880s. Angry mobs rampaged through Chinese areas in San Francisco, Tacoma, Seattle, and Denver in the 1870s. The Chinese Exclusion Act of 1882 reflected the widespread hostility against immigrant workers. The law halted immigration of Chinese workers and gained wide support from American labor unions.

By the turn of the century, big business had cast its shadow across most of the American economy, and in the turbulent labor struggles of the era, government took its place on the side of the employers against the workers.

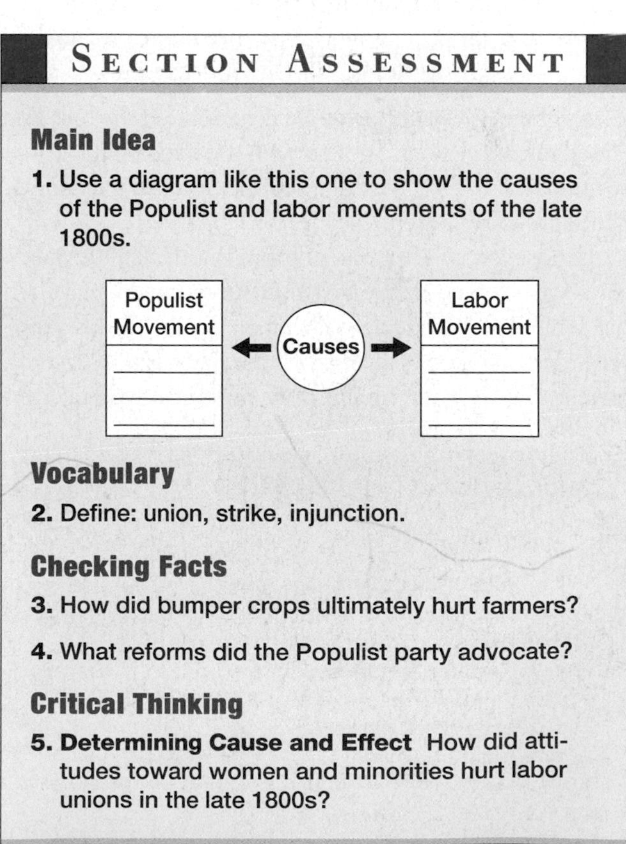

Section Assessment

Main Idea

1. Use a diagram like this one to show the causes of the Populist and labor movements of the late 1800s.

Vocabulary

2. Define: union, strike, injunction.

Checking Facts

3. How did bumper crops ultimately hurt farmers?
4. What reforms did the Populist party advocate?

Critical Thinking

5. **Determining Cause and Effect** How did attitudes toward women and minorities hurt labor unions in the late 1800s?

Reaching for Empire

JULY 1, 1898: ROUGH RIDERS STORM SAN JUAN HILL

SHOUTS OF "HURRAH!" WELCOMED TEDDY ROOSEVELT AND HIS BAND OF AMERICAN SOLDIERS AS THEY BATTLED THEIR WAY UP SAN JUAN HILL NEAR SANTIAGO, CUBA. Nonetheless Roosevelt barked at his troops: "Don't cheer, but fight. Now's the time to fight."

As the weary force struggled one last time to overpower the Spanish forces at the top of the hill, American wagons appeared, heaped with weapons. Grabbing rapid-fire rifles, American troops and the Cuban freedom fighters they supported finally captured the hill. The American and Cuban fighters won the battle, but the war continued. Finally, 16 days later, the Spanish garrison at Santiago surrendered.

THEODORE ROOSEVELT COLLECTION, HARVARD COLLEGE LIBRARY

The Rough Riders
Proud of his elite cavalry regiment, Roosevelt spent his own money to buy their rations.

Roosevelt was but one of more than 250,000 Americans who served in the Spanish-American War. When the United States declared war on Spain, Teddy Roosevelt was assistant secretary of the navy. Eager to fight, he resigned his government post, ordered a well-tailored uniform, and rushed to volunteer for military service. The secretary of the navy had mixed feelings about Roosevelt, saying, "He means to be thoroughly loyal, but the very devil seemed to possess him. . . . He has gone at things like a bull in a china shop."

Roosevelt proved to be a popular war figure. He organized the First Voluntary Cavalry Regiment, known as the Rough Riders. This odd collection of cowhands, college students, ranchers, and rich aristocrats fascinated the press. Roosevelt attracted a large following of wartime newspaper reporters with his colorful style and "bully" spirit. Reporters peppered their articles with Roosevelt's colorful quotes about the war.

The brief war with Spain was the climax of an era marked by the United States's growing involvement with foreign nations. In the late 1800s, the American people were in a mood for expansion as they pushed their boundaries westward, gained new lands, and created new businesses and markets in faraway places for American products.

GUIDE TO READING

Main Idea

In the late 1800s, an urge to expand gripped the American people as the nation gained new lands, created new business and markets in distant places, and waged a far-flung war against Spain.

Vocabulary

- expansionism
- missionary
- armistice

Read to Find Out . . .

- how the United States opened new avenues for trade.
- the reasons for acquiring Alaska, Hawaii, and the Philippines for the United States.
- how Manifest Destiny related to the expansion of the country's boundaries.

The Monroe Doctrine

A Legacy of Hemispheric Control

The United States had a long and complex relationship with its neighbors in the Western Hemisphere. President James Monroe's address to Congress in 1823 had a significant impact on this relationship. Monroe's message to the European powers was loud and clear: no more European colonies in the Western Hemisphere.

Any foreign military expeditions sent to the Western Hemisphere for whatever reason would be seen as a threat to the United States, Monroe warned. No European country should interfere in United States affairs, at home or abroad, he continued.

Spain's interest in regaining control over former colonies spurred the President into action. Yet Monroe did have some assurance as he made these bold statements. He knew that Britain was also determined to prevent Spain from gaining any new colonies in the Western Hemisphere.

The President, relying on this information, decided to seize the moment and chart American foreign policy with his strong words. This was a bold move, to volunteer to be the "police force" protecting emerging nations in the entire hemisphere.

At the time there was little discussion of Monroe's ground-breaking pronouncement. It was neither widely liked nor sharply contested. More than 20 years passed before President James K. Polk implemented this so-called Monroe Doctrine and laid a cornerstone for American foreign policy.

From Sea to Shining Sea

American settlers were flooding into territories throughout the country. Settlers in foreign-owned territories such as Oregon, Texas, and California wanted a government of their own, and they wanted to be part of the United States. Taking over these lands, however, would create conflicts with Britain, which owned part of Oregon, and with Mexico, which held Texas and California and much of today's southwestern United States.

James K. Polk was the settlers' champion. When Polk ran for President in 1844, he warmly supported **expansionism,** the process of increasing the territory of the United States. After his election, Polk set out to gain Oregon as well as the Southwest. Polk and many other Americans supported the concept of Manifest Destiny—the notion that the United States was a superior country and had a right to invade, conquer, and occupy the North American continent and beyond.

NATIONAL PORTRAIT GALLERY, SMITHSONIAN INSTITUTION/ART RESOURCE, NY

Manifest Destiny In 1845 Polk's campaigns to control more of the North American continent made him the settlers' champion. *What was Manifest Destiny?*

In 1845 Polk declared that no European colony could occupy the North American continent. When the British insisted that they would continue to share in the rich Northwest Territory, Polk decided to drive the British out.

In a compromise move in 1846, Britain claimed land above the forty-ninth parallel, and the United States retained what has today become the states of Oregon and Washington. War was avoided on the northern border as the United States prepared for battle with Mexico.

Mexico had broken diplomatic relations with the United States when Congress annexed Texas in 1845. In that same year Polk sent negotiators to Mexico in an attempt to buy other Mexican lands, such as California and the area known as New Mexico. Mexico refused the United States's $30 million offer. Shortly after, following a border dispute, war erupted. After 2 years of fighting, the 2 governments negotiated a peace, and the United States laid claim to nearly half of Mexico for the bargain price of $15 million, with an additional $3.25 million to compensate American citizens with claims against Mexico.

Policing the Hemisphere

The Civil War years, 1861 through 1865, considerably limited American dreams of expansion. The war so consumed American arms and energy that during the long conflict, European nations tried to gain control of weak nations south of the Mexican border.

In 1861, despite warnings by Secretary of State William Seward, Spain seized an opportunity to reclaim its former colony, the Dominican Republic, an island in the Caribbean.

At the same time that Spain sailed into the Caribbean, Britain and France sent troops to Mexico, pretending to collect war debts. The British soon retreated, but in 1864 the French leader Napoleon III installed Austrian Archduke Ferdinand Maximilian on the Mexican throne.

After the Union victory in the Civil War, however, American troops massed on the Mexican border, and Secretary of State Seward, citing the Monroe Doctrine, threatened war with France if its troops did not withdraw. By 1867 France complied, bringing new life to the Monroe Doctrine.

Worldwide Ambitions

Markets, Trade Routes, and Territories

Many factors contributed to the spread of expansionist fever in the United States after the Civil War. A patriotic fervor motivated many Americans. They felt that the acquisition of new lands would increase American glory and prestige throughout the world. Others saw the United States as a model country and felt a moral obligation to expand. They wanted to spread the American ideals of democracy and Protestant Christian values to people in other lands. **Missionaries,** or religious teachers, went to foreign lands to convert natives to Christianity. A new brand of American foreign policy maker supported these expansionist sentiments. These newly established foreign policy professionals wanted to make the United States a world power through trade, diplomacy, and conquest.

ARTHUR M. SACKLER GALLERY, SMITHSONIAN INSTITUTION

Amerikazin When trade with Japan began, Westerners exchanged culture as well as commodities. This 1861 woodblock print shows a family of American tourists. *What details of the figures and dress portray American style of the era?*

Perhaps the greatest motivation for expansion was the need for new economic markets. As settlers filled the Western frontier, farms and businesses produced more goods than Americans could buy. Henry Demarest Lloyd, a popular political writer at the time, wrote, "American production has outrun American consumption and we must seek markets for the surplus abroad."

Opening Closed Doors

The United States looked especially to Asia. American involvement in Asia actually began long before the Civil War. In 1844 the United States negotiated trade agreements with China and began to export cloth, iron, and fur to the Chinese in exchange for tea, silk, porcelain, and jade. Far Eastern trade became a boon to New England merchants and expanded naval production, especially after Commodore Matthew Perry "opened" Japan in 1854.

The Japanese had steadfastly refused contact with Western merchants and had closed their ports to European and American traders and missionaries for 250 years. Yet reports of Japan's great coal deposits had filtered out. Coal was an increasingly important resource for American steam-powered transportation and machinery. When Perry was sent to negotiate trade, it was important to the United States to be the first of the Western nations to access this resource. As he sailed into Tokyo's harbor under steam power, he so impressed the authorities that Japan began doing business with the United States.

By the 1880s the United States had made further inroads in the Far East by negotiating commercial treaties with Korea. The growth of these Asian markets stimulated the American economy and became a key factor in the United States's bid for world power.

Acquiring New Lands

Under the leadership of Secretary of State William Seward, foreign policy after the Civil War became more aggressive. Seward dreamed of an American empire that would include Canada, the Caribbean, Mexico, and Central America as well as Hawaii and other Pacific islands.

HAWAII STATE ARCHIVES

Hawaii for Hawaiians Queen Liliuokalani was determined to keep the United States from seizing Hawaii. *Why were the Hawaiian Islands so valuable to American interests in the Pacific?*

In 1867 Seward attempted to purchase Danish islands in the Caribbean for $7.5 million—a move that the Senate rejected. Congress also refused to approve Seward's plans for a United States naval base in the Dominican Republic.

He succeeded elsewhere, however. In 1867 the United States seized the Midway Islands in the Pacific Ocean, strategically located along the trade route to China and Japan. In the same year, Seward bought Alaska from Russia for $7.2 million.

Newspapers mocked Seward, and Alaska became known as "Seward's folly" and a worthless "polar bear garden." Seward, however, was wiser than his critics realized. Alaska paid for itself many times over with the gold that was discovered in the Yukon Valley, and its rich copper and oil resources, as well as seal and whale trade.

Moving into the Pacific

Expansionist ambitions continued in the Pacific in the last three decades of the 1800s. In 1878 the United States acquired rights to a naval station in Samoa, which was astride the trade route to Australia and New Zealand. Because Germany and England also had claims in Samoa, the three powers divided the islands in 1889.

The Hawaiian Islands were another Pacific prize. American planters and missionaries had thrived there after 1875 when the Senate allowed Hawaiian sugar to enter the United States duty-free. By 1881 the secretary of state declared the islands "essentially a part of the American system." In 1887, under strong pressure, King Kalakaua granted the United States rights to build a naval base at Pearl Harbor to protect American interests in the Pacific. Finally in 1893 American sugar planters in Hawaii staged a rebellion, determined to wrest control from Kalakaua's sister, Queen Liliuokalani. The queen had resisted American control with the slogan "Hawaii for the Hawaiians."

The United States Marines surrounded the palace, and the American minister cabled Washington: "The Hawaiian pear is now fully ripe, and this is the golden hour for the United States to pluck it." The palace coup succeeded, leaving American sugar planters and missionaries in political control of the islands. Congress moved toward official annexation, but this process would take another five years to complete.

War With Spain

Reports Become Real

The expansionist moves from the end of the Civil War through the early 1890s reached a peak in 1898 with the Spanish-American War. The war's outcome added significant new territory to the growing American overseas empire, and it demonstrated that the United States could turn its industrial muscle into formidable naval power in both of the oceans surrounding North America.

The origins of the Spanish-American War lay in the troubled island of Cuba, only 90 miles off the southern tip of Florida. The Cuban people had struggled since 1868 for independence from Spain.

Many Americans identified that struggle with their own revolution against Britain. Other Americans, beginning in the 1850s, had regarded Cuba as a natural part of the United States geographically and as an island of great economic potential because of its sugar-growing capability.

In 1895 Cuban rebels led by José Martí renewed their fight for independence, launching their first attacks from American soil. A ferocious war ensued. Spanish troops, commanded by Valeriano Weyler, forced some 300,000 Cubans into concentration camps, where tens of thousands died.

The war continued, and Americans elected William McKinley President in 1896. McKinley's campaign platform included claims to Hawaii and the Virgin Islands as well as support for Cuban independence. He had no desire for war with Spain, however, and in 1897 the President took encouragement from a new Spanish government that promised reforms in Cuba as well as some independence for Cubans.

Headline Wars

Dramatic events early in 1898 ruined McKinley's desire to avoid war. In February an explosion blew up the battleship *Maine*, killing 260 officers and men. Headlines screamed for revenge: "Remember the *Maine*! To Hell With Spain!" Two days later, a New York newspaper proclaimed: "Whole Country Thrills With the War Fever/Yet President Says 'It Was An Accident'." Most Americans believed the Spanish had blown up the *Maine*, and a naval board of investigation soon concluded that a Spanish mine had caused the explosions.

Against his conscience, President McKinley took action. On April 11, 1898, he sent a message to Congress that called for the use of troops to bring about "a national compromise between the contestants." Congress responded with a more warlike declaration that gave the President authority to use troops to end Spanish control of Cuba and declared the island independent. These acts amounted to a declaration of war against Spain. Spain responded with its own declaration of war on April 24, 1898.

Critics believed that journalists, with their sensational headlines and stories, pressed politicians into declaring war following the explosion of the *Maine*. Their views were justified 78 years later when Admiral Hyman Rickover conducted a study of the sinking of the *Maine*. Rickover concluded that an accident, probably a faulty boiler, caused the explosion—not a mine.

CHICAGO HISTORICAL SOCIETY

Media Hype Sensational stories and illustrations in newspapers misled the public and stirred Americans to war. *What may have been the real cause of the explosion of the* Maine?

From Havana to Manila

Although most American citizens focused on Cuba as the primary target for United States military might, others concentrated on the Philippines, a group of Pacific islands also under Spanish control. One reformer asked: "Why should Cuba with its 1.6 million people have a right to freedom and self-government and the 8 million people who dwell in the Philippine Islands be denied the same right?" Also, gaining a foothold in the Philippines would help the United States protect Asian business connections.

Shortly after the *Maine* explosion, Assistant Secretary of the Navy Teddy Roosevelt, anticipating war, instructed Commodore George Dewey to prepare to remove his squadron of six ships from the neutral port of Hong Kong and to attack the Spanish fleet in the Philippines.

Dewey confirmed this plan with President McKinley by cable and steamed across the China Sea to enemy waters more than 600 miles (965 km) away. The commodore sailed into Manila Bay on May 1, 1898, and demolished the old Spanish fleet protecting the city. Before noon every Spanish ship was sunk.

After Dewey's triumph, soldiers training in Florida felt eager to launch their attack in Cuba. The battle began on June 22 with great fanfare.

Within days most of the troops were under fire, wading through waist-deep swamps and dodging shrapnel day and night. American troops finally took San Juan Hill, near the city of Santiago, on July 1, but a strong Spanish naval force remained in the harbor.

On July 3, however, the United States Navy chased Spanish cruisers and defeated their fleet in a dramatic battle that left only 1 American sailor killed and another wounded. By contrast almost 500 Spanish were killed or wounded and 1,700 taken prisoner.

By July 17 the United States had secured Cuba, and only Puerto Rico remained under Spanish control. It fell to the United States in a few days. The United States stepped up the pace of the war in order to bring home the thousands of soldiers who were suffering from yellow fever and malaria. Occupation had proved more deadly than battle. By the end of 1898, the death toll exceeded 5,400 soldiers, fewer than 400 of whom had died in combat.

United States Victorious

On August 12, with two fleets and their colonial armies devastated, Spain signed an **armistice,** or ceasefire. Diplomats met in Paris in October to negotiate a permanent settlement. It took two months to iron out their differences. Spain granted independence to Cuba and ceded Guam, Puerto Rico, and the Philippines to the United States for $20 million.

Although the United States had claimed it was fighting to liberate the Philippines, the American gov-

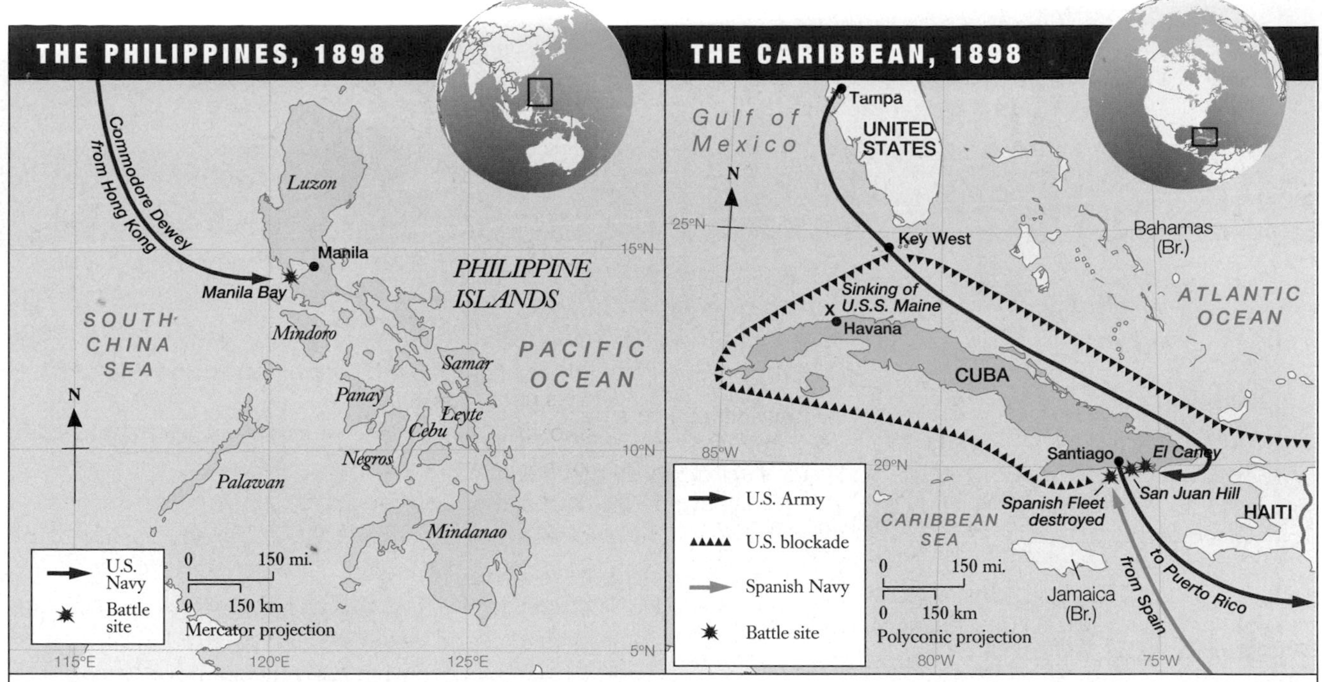

Fighting during the Spanish-American War took place in the Philippines and in the Caribbean. Note Dewey's successful strike in the Philippines and the United States's blockade of Cuba. *According to the two maps, in which area did more of the fighting take place?*

ernment refused to accept the pleas of Filipino nationalists for independence. The leader of the Filipino rebels against Spain, Emilio Aguinaldo, was deported from the islands when he refused to recognize American rule.

President McKinley felt it would be "cowardly and dishonorable" to return the islands to the Spanish and argued that the Filipinos were "unfit for self-government." To keep Europeans from taking over the Philippines, many Americans said that possession of the islands would uplift and Christianize the Philippines, overlooking the fact that the majority of Filipinos were already Catholic. Actually business interests outweighed all other considerations, as an editor at the *Chicago Times-Herald* wrote: "The commercial and industrial interests of Americans, learning that the islands lie in the gateway of the vast and undeveloped markets of the Orient, say 'Keep the Philippines. . . .'"

The war also gave the nation glory and many new heroes. Although Dewey's command to his subordinate, "You may fire when ready," was hardly stirring, the admiral became a cult figure. Eager for a hero, businesses capitalized on the naval commander's exploits: a song celebrated his bravery and a chewing gum was marketed as "Dewey's Chewies."

Teddy Roosevelt reveled in his image as a Rough Rider charging up San Juan Hill. He effectively used his military adventures during his political career, first as governor of New York and then as President. Roosevelt, like many Americans, believed the Spanish-American War had given the United States a new status. In 1898 he wrote, "the nation now stands as the peer of any of the Great Powers of the world."

By 1899 the United States had expanded its dominion to include Puerto Rico, Hawaii, and many Pacific islands, including the Philippines. The effects of global expansion would shape the course of United States's history well into the future.

Section Assessment

Main Idea

1. Use a diagram like this one to support the following generalization: "Expansionism formed a key theme in United States history during the 1800s."

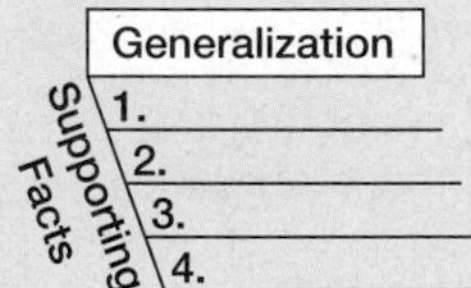

Vocabulary

2. Define: expansionism, missionary, armistice.

Checking Facts

3. How did the United States respond when Europeans tried to create new colonies in the Americas during the Civil War?
4. Why did Japan open its doors to United States trade?

Critical Thinking

5. **Drawing Conclusions** How did the small nations of the Pacific play a big role in United States plans for expansion?

Chapter  Assessment

Self-Check Quiz

Visit the *American Odyssey* Web site at americanodyssey.glencoe.com and click on ***Chapter 7—Self-Check Quiz*** to prepare for the Chapter Test.

Reviewing Key Terms

Choose the vocabulary term that best answers the questions below. Write your answers on a separate sheet of paper.

homestead	**union**
industrialism	**injunction**
merger	**expansionism**

1. If a corporation hoped to prohibit or end a strike, what kind of order might it ask a court to issue?

2. A settler who wanted to claim free land and who was willing to farm it for a number of years might do what?

3. What kind of foreign policy was the United States following when it set out to acquire new lands such as Puerto Rico, Hawaii, and Alaska?

4. What kind of economic and social system is marked by the large-scale industries centered in urban factories?

5. If a company's managers thought that market competition was too fierce in their industry, what solution might they choose?

Recalling Facts

1. How did cattle ranching and the work of cowhands promote the settlement of the Plains?

2. How did the early railroad lines influence where people settled on the Plains and in the Far West?

3. Which groups of people benefited from the settlement of the West? Which groups did not benefit? Why not?

4. Identify three important inventions from the era of 1865 to 1900. What effect did these and other inventions have on the productivity of workers?

5. John D. Rockefeller once said, "The day of individual competition is past and gone." How did Rockefeller's own business practices illustrate his statement?

6. Why was the term *robber barons* applied to people such as Andrew Carnegie and J.P. Morgan?

7. What were the main goals of the Populist party? Whose interests did the party represent?

8. How could labor unions have dramatically increased their size and power? What prevented them from doing so?

9. What was the Monroe Doctrine? Why was it important to the United States after the Civil War?

10. Why did the United States decide to keep control of the Philippines?

Critical Thinking

1. Making Inferences Wanamaker's, Macy's, and other department stores had marble staircases, expensive carpets, and chandeliers. Why do you think the owners spent so much money to decorate their stores? What values were they trying to appeal to in customers?

2. Making Comparisons Explain the difference between horizontal and vertical integration of industry. Why did Carnegie and other business leaders try to achieve both?

3. Supporting Generalizations Reread the material on the labor movements in Section 2. Then use a diagram like this one to record and support a generalization about efforts to organize laborers in the late 1800s.

Generalization

Supporting Facts

1. ______

2. ______

3. ______

4. Recognizing Bias President McKinley argued that the Filipinos were "unfit for self-government." What bias does this statement reveal? What might account for McKinley's bias?

Cooperative Learning

Form several groups to discuss the lives of Carnegie, Rockefeller, and other robber barons. Groups should consider the following questions: Do you admire that kind of success? What was its impact on ordinary citizens? How do the robber barons compare with today's wealthy industrialists? Choose a representative to present your group's conclusions to the rest of the class.

Reinforcing Skills

Reading Statistical Tables The *Statistical Abstract of the United States* publishes annual statistics from the Bureau of the Census and other governmental agencies. Look at the latest edition in the library for information on a topic discussed in this chapter—for example, labor union membership by state, mergers of corporations, or income levels of households. Pick one table and photocopy it. What information is given in the table's title and subtitle? According to the headings, in what categories and subcategories is the information grouped? Look at the column on the left side of the table to find out how items in the table are organized. Describe any changes or patterns shown by the statistics in the table.

GEOGRAPHY AND HISTORY

Second Native American Expulsion

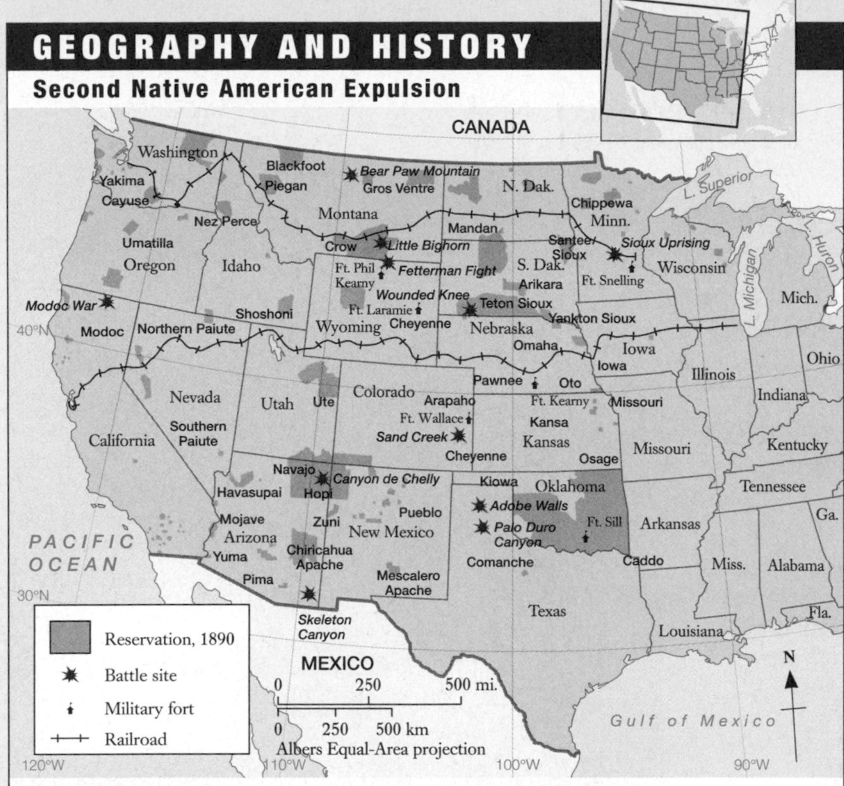

Study the map to answer the following questions:

1. What Native American lands lay along the two transcontinental railroads shown on the map?
2. What battle took place in South Dakota? What Native American nation was involved?
3. What Native American peoples inhabited the lands that are now Arizona and New Mexico?
4. Where did the Battle of the Little Bighorn—sometimes known as Custer's Last Stand—take place? What Native American nation fought there?

Portfolio Project

The history of United States expansionism in the 1800s includes efforts to acquire or at least to influence Cuba, Hawaii, Alaska, Puerto Rico, and the Philippines. Choose one of these places and investigate the history of United States involvement there, carrying your research up to the present. Use your research notes to build a time line showing the major events in that involvement. Keep your time line in your portfolio.

Technology Activity

Using a Spreadsheet Use library resources or the Internet to locate information about federal policies that affected Native Americans from 1860 to 1910. Create a spreadsheet to organize your information. Include headings such as Name of Policy, Year, Native Americans Affected, and Summary of Events.

Standardized Test Practice

1. Which of the following was NOT a result of the westward expansion of the railroad?

A improved living conditions for Native Americans

B increased immigration from Ireland and China

C settlement of lands along the railroad lines

D increased movement of freight across the country

Test-Taking Tip: Pay attention to the words NOT or EXCEPT in a question. These words tell you to look for an answer that does NOT fit. For example, you may recall that railroad owners recruited Irish and Chinese immigrants as workers. You can use this information to eliminate answer B.

2. "I like a little competition every now and then, but I like combination a lot better." When J.P. Morgan made this remark, he was talking about

A labor unions.

B business mergers.

C transcontinental railroads.

D Farmers' Alliances.

Test-Taking Tip: Make sure your answer strongly matches the main idea in the quote *and* reflects the thinking of J.P. Morgan. Only one answer is the kind of "combination" that Morgan liked.

Then...

Levi's Riveted Waist Overalls

One day businessman Levi Strauss received a letter from a customer, Jacob Davis, describing a new way to make pants. Davis, a tailor, could not afford to patent the process. Instead, he persuaded Strauss to become his partner. In 1873 the two men received a joint patent for riveted clothing.

1 **The word *denim* comes from the French "de Nimes," or "of Nimes," but the denim used by Strauss came from New Hampshire.**

2 **The pants all had button closings. The zipper was invented in 1891, but the Levi Strauss company did not use zippers in jeans until 1954.**

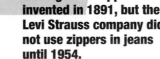

COURTESY LEVI STRAUSS & CO. SAN FRANSCISCO

FILE PHOTO BY DOUG MINDELL

SELLING STRENGTH

A leather patch was added to the design in 1886 depicting two workhorses attempting unsuccessfully to pull apart a pair of Levi pants. The company never tried the stunt, but rather used the patch as a symbol of strength.

3 Copper rivets reinforced pocket corners and the base of the fly. The fly rivet, however, fell by the wayside during World War II when the government ordered conservation of precious metals.

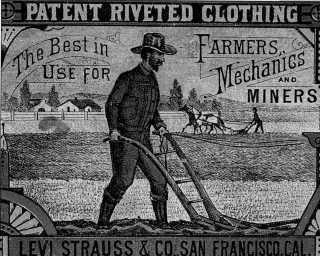

PATENT RIVETED CLOTHING

The Best in Use for Farmers, Mechanics and Miners!

LEVI STRAUSS & CO. SAN FRANCISCO, CAL.

COURTESY LEVI STRAUSS & CO. SAN FRANCISCO

COURTESY LEVI STRAUSS & CO. SAN FRANCISCO

Stats

PROFILE

In Buttenheim, Bavaria, Hirsch Strauss taught his peddler's business to his youngest son, Levi. Upon Hirsch's death in 1847, 18-year-old Levi immigrated to New York City.

Hoping prospectors' gold would end up in his cash register, Levi took his dry goods business to San Francisco, where he brought his four nephews on board as partners.

With the success of riveted clothing, Strauss became active in San Francisco's business and cultural community, serving on boards of both utility companies and orphanages. He belonged to San Francisco's first synagogue and helped to fund a gold medal for students of its Sabbath School.

PRICE

Levi Strauss & Co. sold riveted clothing to stores. In 1879, the catalog advertised:

Riveted XXExtra Heavy blue denim pants........$17.50 /doz

4 Originally the most popular blue dyes for fabrics like denim came from the indigo plant, first grown in the United States on plantations in South Carolina. In the 1880s a chemical version, *indigotin,* became available.

...Now

LEVI'S COMPARISON CHART

PORTFOLIO PROJECT

Consult the *Readers' Guide to Periodical Literature* to obtain information about Levi's clothing of today. Then draw or paste a picture of a pair of jeans in the center of a sheet of paper. Beside the left leg list the similarities between the Levi's jeans of 1873 and today's jeans. List differences beside the right leg. Include information on manufacturing, profitability, business, fashion, or culture.

JANE GRUSHOW/GRANT HEILMAN PHOTOGRAPHY, INC.

WHAT'S IN A NAME?

The patented pants were called waist overalls in the Old West. The term *jeans* was not used until the 1900s, and the name "Levi's" meaning riveted denim pants did not emerge in advertising until the 1960s.

UNIT
3

The Roots of a Modern Nation

1880–1920

HISTORY & YOU

As the United States headed into a new century, progressive-minded reformers sought to end a host of social ills while promoting a more democratic government through expanded suffrage and greater accountability of elected officials. The spirit of activism touched on foreign policy as the United States became more entangled in global affairs. These entanglements would lead the nation into World War I and a period of post-war disillusionment.

Historic America Electronic Field Trips

Feminists in the late 1800s and early 1900s kept alive the goals of the Seneca Falls Convention by agitating for passage of an amendment giving women the right to vote. To learn how possession of the vote has changed women's lives, view videodisc Chapter 6: *Seneca Falls* in **Historic America Electronic Field Trips.**

PRIMARY SOURCES
Library

See pages 962–963 for primary source readings that accompany Unit 3.

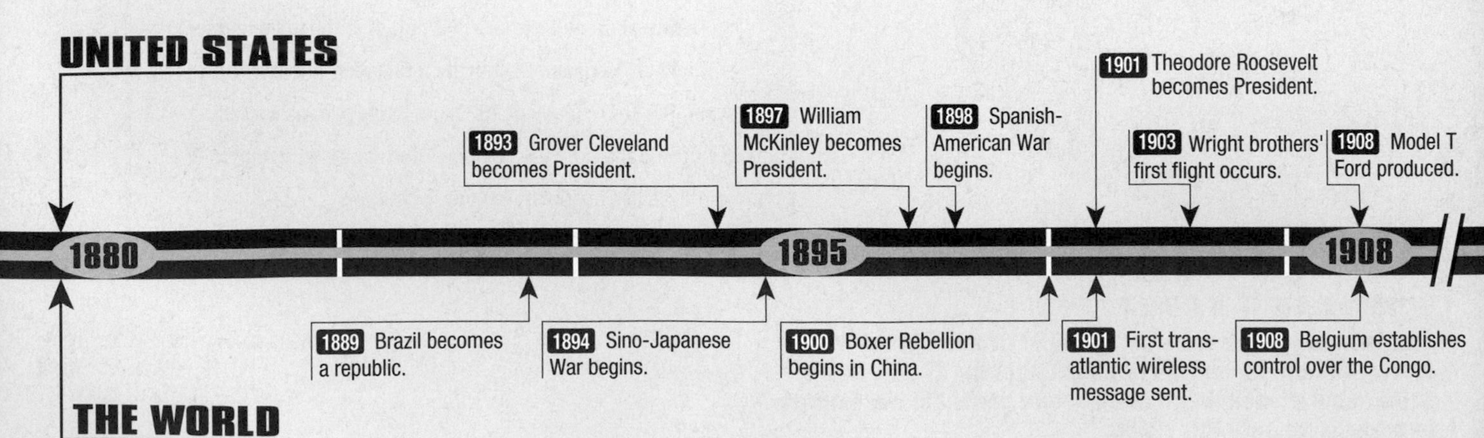
UNITED STATES
1893 Grover Cleveland becomes President.
1897 William McKinley becomes President.
1898 Spanish-American War begins.
1901 Theodore Roosevelt becomes President.
1903 Wright brothers' first flight occurs.
1908 Model T Ford produced.
1880
1895
1908
1889 Brazil becomes a republic.
1894 Sino-Japanese War begins.
1900 Boxer Rebellion begins in China.
1901 First trans-atlantic wireless message sent.
1908 Belgium establishes control over the Congo.
THE WORLD

LIBRARY OF CONGRESS

The World's Railroad Scene, rendered by Swaim and Lewis in 1882, symbolized a widely held American belief in growth and progress.

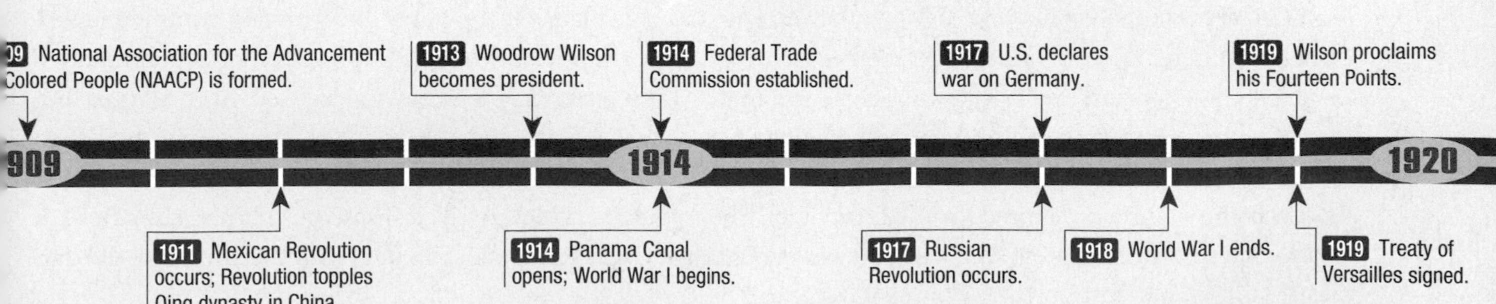

09 National Association for the Advancement
Colored People (NAACP) is formed.
1913 Woodrow Wilson becomes president.
1914 Federal Trade Commission established.
1917 U.S. declares war on Germany.
1919 Wilson proclaims his Fourteen Points.
909
1914
1920
1911 Mexican Revolution occurs; Revolution topples Qing dynasty in China.
1914 Panama Canal opens; World War I begins.
1917 Russian Revolution occurs.
1918 World War I ends.
1919 Treaty of Versailles signed.

Sister Carrie

BY THEODORE DREISER

In his novel Sister Carrie, *Theodore Dreiser captured the allure of rapidly expanding cities such as Chicago and New York for ambitious men and women in the late 1800s. Because he paid such careful attention to detail, Dreiser's portrait of city life at the time is as accurate as it is vivid.*

When she awoke at eight the next morning, Hanson had gone. Her sister was busy in the dining-room, which was also the sitting-room, sewing. She worked, after dressing, to arrange a little breakfast for herself, and then advised with Minnie as to which way to look. The latter had changed considerably since Carrie had seen her. She was now a thin, though rugged, woman of twenty-seven, with ideas of life coloured by her husband's, and fast hardening into narrower conceptions of pleasure and duty than had ever been hers in a thoroughly circumscribed youth. She had invited Carrie, not because she longed for her presence, but because the latter was dissatisfied at home, and could probably get work and pay her board here. She was pleased to see her in a way but reflected her husband's point of view in the matter of work. Anything was good enough so long as it paid—say, five dollars a week to begin with. A shop girl was the destiny prefigured for the newcomer. She would get in one of the great shops and do well enough until—well, until something happened. Neither of them knew exactly what. They did not figure on promotion. They did not exactly count on marriage. Things would go on, though, in a dim kind of way until the better thing would eventuate, and Carrie would be rewarded for coming and toiling in the city. It was under such auspicious circumstances that she started out this morning to look for work.

The Frenetic Movement of the City **The abstract geometric shapes of Max Weber's *Rush Hour, New York* (1915) convey the hustle and bustle of the burgeoning cities of the early part of the century.**

Before following her in her round of seeking, let us look at the sphere in which her future was to lie. In 1889 Chicago had the peculiar qualifications of growth which made such adventuresome pilgrimages even on the part of young girls plausible. Its many and growing commercial opportunities gave it widespread fame, which made of it a giant magnet, drawing to itself, from all quarters, the hopeful and the hopeless—those who had their fortune yet to make and those whose fortunes and affairs had reached a disastrous climax elsewhere. It was a city of over 500,000, with the ambition, the daring, the activity of a metropolis of a million. Its streets and houses were already scattered over an area of seventy-five square miles. Its population was not so much thriving upon established commerce as upon the industries which prepared for the arrival of others. The sound of the hammer engaged upon the erection of new structures was everywhere heard. Great industries were moving in. The huge railroad corporations which had long before recognised the prospects of the place had seized upon vast tracts of land for transfer and shipping purposes. Street-car lines had been extended far out into the open country in anticipation of rapid growth. The city had laid miles and miles of streets and sewers through regions where, perhaps, one solitary house stood out alone —a pioneer of the populous ways to be. There were regions open to the sweeping winds and rain, which were yet lighted throughout the night with long, blinking lines of gas-lamps, fluttering in the wind. Narrow board walks extended out, passing here a house, and there a store, at far intervals, eventually ending on the open prairie.

In the central portion was the vast wholesale and shopping district, to which the uninformed seeker for work usually drifted. It was a characteristic of Chicago then, and one not generally shared by other cities, that individual firms of any pretension occupied individual buildings. The presence of ample ground made this possible. It gave an imposing appearance to most of the wholesale houses, whose offices were upon the ground floor and in plain view of the street. The large plates of window glass, now so common, were then rapidly coming into use, and gave to the ground floor offices a distinguished and prosperous look. The casual wanderer could see as he passed a polished array of office fixtures, much frosted glass, clerks hard at work, and genteel business men in "nobby" suits and clean linen lounging about or sitting in groups. Polished brass or nickel signs at the square stone entrances announced the firm and the nature of the business in rather neat and reserved terms. The entire metropolitan center possessed a high and mighty air calculated to overawe and abash the common applicant, and to make the gulf between poverty and success seem both wide and deep.

Into this important commercial region the timid Carrie went. She walked east along Van Buren Street through a region of lessening importance, until it deteriorated into a mass of shanties and coal-yards, and finally verged upon the river. She walked bravely forward, led by an honest desire to find employment and delayed at every step by the interest of the unfolding scene, and a sense of helplessness amid so much evidence of power and force which she did not understand. These vast buildings, what were they? These strange energies and huge interests, for what purposes were they there? She could have understood the meaning of a little stone-cutter's yard at Columbia City, carving little pieces of marble for individual use, but when the yards of some huge stone corporation came into view, filled with spur tracks and flat cars, transpierced by docks from the river and traversed overhead by immense trundling cranes of wood and steel, it lost all significance in her little world.

ANYTHING WAS GOOD ENOUGH SO LONG AS IT PAID—SAY, FIVE DOLLARS A WEEK TO BEGIN WITH.

Responding to Literature

1. **Would you have wanted to live in a city at the turn of the century? Why or why not?**
2. **In *Sister Carrie* the main character believes the city will provide her with new opportunities and a new life. Explain why cities would or would not represent to you such a gateway to opportunity today.**

Progressive Reforms

JULY 7, 1903: WORKING CHILDREN MARCH TOWARD PRESIDENT'S MANSION

President Theodore Roosevelt faced a difficult decision. Should he meet with a handful of children who were marching 125 miles from Kensington, Pennsylvania, toward Oyster Bay, New York, to confront him at his home?

These marchers represented the thousands of children who worked in factories, mills, and mines. They were seeking the President's support for a law prohibiting child labor.

Though Roosevelt sympathized with the children, he feared supporting any demand voiced by their leader, radical organizer Mary Harris Jones, known as Mother Jones. President Roosevelt advocated reform, not revolution.

Finally, on July 27, after 20 days of marching, the children arrived. Through a representative, Roosevelt sent his reply: "No!" His fear outweighed his sympathy. Despite Roosevelt's refusal to meet with Jones and the children, the child labor debate did not go away.

The child labor debate was just one issue that Americans confronted between 1880 and 1920. Political corruption, labor unrest, and urban decay also plagued the United States during this period of rapid industrial and urban growth. By responding to these issues while avoiding radical upheaval, the American people fueled one of the greatest periods of reform in American history, the Progressive era. ■

HISTORY JOURNAL

Write your reaction to the working conditions for children as depicted in the photograph on page 233. What reforms would you initiate to change this situation?

Chapter Overview

Visit the *American Odyssey* Web site at americanodyssey.glencoe.com and click on ***Chapter 8—Chapter Overview*** to preview the chapter.

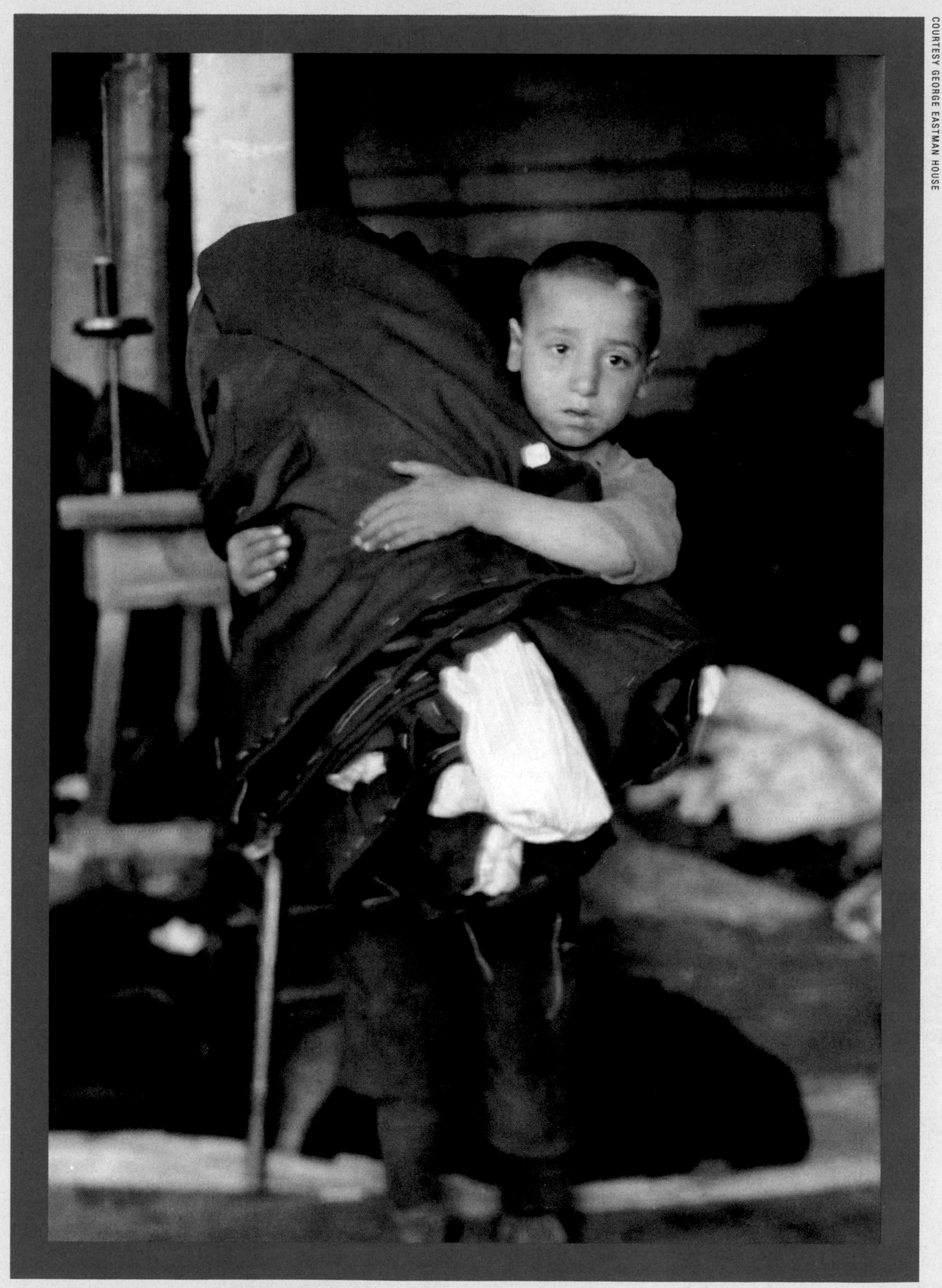

COURTESY GEORGE EASTMAN HOUSE

THIS YOUNG BOY IS CARRYING A BUNDLE OF WORK HOME AFTER FINISHING HIS DAY IN A NEW YORK CITY FACTORY.

Facing a New Order

1890: LIFE AND DEATH IN A NEW YORK CITY APARTMENT

PHOTOGRAPHER AND JOURNALIST JACOB RIIS HAD BREATHED ENOUGH STAGNANT AIR, SMELLED ENOUGH ROTTING FOOD, AND SEEN ENOUGH SICKLY CHILDREN TO KNOW HOW THE POOR OF NEW YORK CITY LIVED. In one of his writings he offered to take readers on a guided tour of an overcrowded apartment building:

THE JACOB A RIIS COLLECTION, MUSEUM OF THE CITY OF NEW YORK

Baxter Street Court
Jacob Riis photographed this tenement alley in New York City in 1888.

> Be a little careful, please! The hall is dark and you might stumble over the children pitching pennies back there. Not that it would hurt them; kicks and cuffs are their daily diet. They have little else.
>
> Here where the hall turns and dives into utter darkness is a step, and another, another. A flight of stairs. You can feel your way, if you cannot see it. Close? Yes! What would you have? All the fresh air that ever enters these stairs comes from the hall-door that is forever slamming, and from the windows of dark bedrooms. . . .
>
> Here is a door. Listen! That short hacking cough, that tiny, helpless wail—what do they mean? They mean that the soiled bow of white you saw on the door downstairs will have another story to tell—oh! a sadly familiar story—before the day is at an end. The child is dying with measles. With half a chance it might have lived; but it had none. The dark bedroom killed it.
>
> —Jacob Riis, *How the Other Half Lives,* 1890

Between 1880 and 1920 people flocked to the cities from the countryside and abroad. While they often found opportunity, many also suffered from low wages, diseases, and wretched housing. How concerned citizens responded to these problems reshaped American government in the Progressive era.

GUIDE TO READING

Main Idea

The rapid growth of cities in the late 1800s and early 1900s transformed the United States from a rural nation to an urban nation and created new challenges for the American people to solve.

Vocabulary

- tenement
- suburb
- urbanization
- immigrant
- political machine
- trust

Read to Find Out . . .

- reasons for the growth of cities in the United States.
- the impact of rapid urbanization on American life in the late 1800s.
- the experiences of immigrants in the United States.
- the reaction of middle-class people to industrialization, urbanization, and immigration.

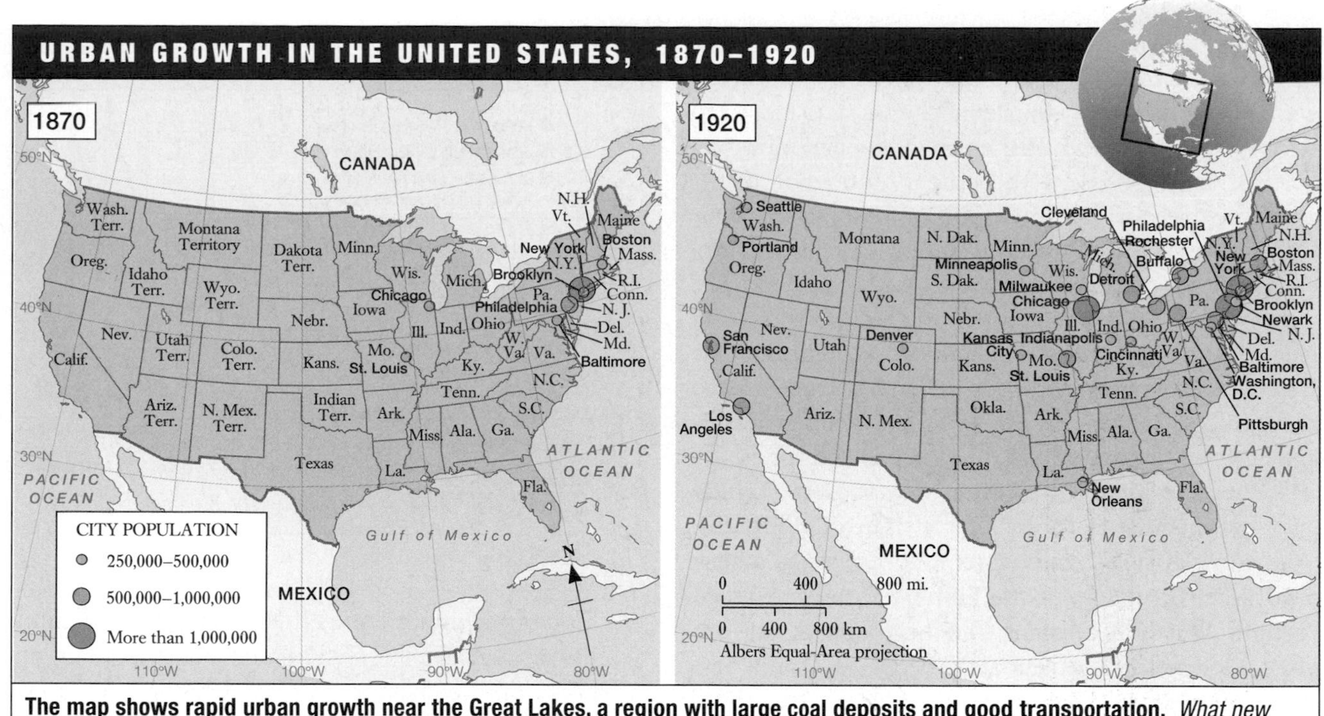

The map shows rapid urban growth near the Great Lakes, a region with large coal deposits and good transportation. *What new cities with populations of 500,000–100,000 appeared in 1920?*

Shame of the Cities

Urban Growth Brings Problems

The substandard conditions that Riis described in the New York apartment building, or **tenement,** could be found in many cities around the nation. As these cities grew, so did their problems.

Urban Growth

Cities in the United States expanded rapidly in the late 1800s. In 1860 only 20 percent of the people in the United States lived in towns or cities with populations greater than 2,500. By 1900 this percentage had doubled.

As American cities grew and became overcrowded, people who could afford to moved to **suburbs.** These communities blossomed at the edges of big cities. New forms of mass transportation developed; that enabled suburban residents to commute more easily to their jobs in the center of the city. In addition, these improvements helped everyone move around the city more efficiently. In 1873 San Francisco began construction of cable-car lines. A large cable powered by a motor at one end of the rail line moved passenger cars along. In 1888 Richmond, Virginia, pioneered the use of the trolley car, a motorized train that was powered by electricity supplied through overhead cables. In 1897 Boston opened the nation's first subway, or underground railway.

Changes in transportation were just one advancement in technology that fostered **urbanization,** the growth of cities. Before the mid-1800s water power ran machinery; therefore, factories had to be near rivers. With the application of steam power in the mid-1800s, though, factories could be established anywhere that fuel, usually coal, was available. Factory owners sought locations where they had dependable access to coal for fueling their steam-driven machinery and to minerals, sand, or other materials they needed to run their factories. They prized sites where rail lines linked with water routes, such as New York, Chicago, and St. Louis.

The opening of a factory in a city was a magnet that pulled in new residents looking for jobs. Many of these people came from rural areas where they could find no work. New machines—reapers, threshers, binding machines, combines—were rapidly replacing manual labor

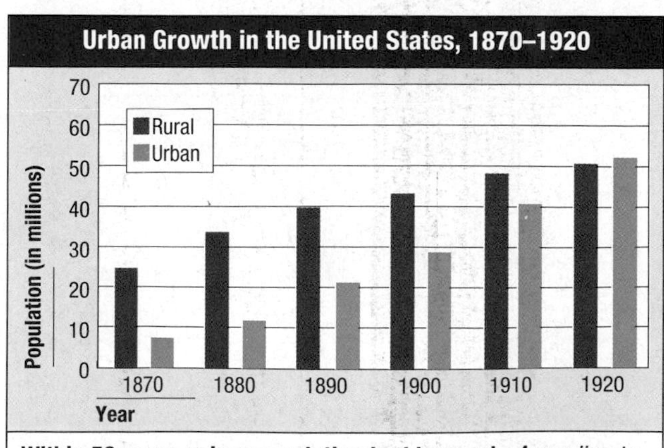

Within 50 years, urban population had boomed. *According to the chart, by how much did the rural population change between 1870 and 1920?*

on farms. One commentator noted in 1898 that "four men with improved agricultural implements now do the work formerly done by fourteen." Those who moved to cities often found work in the expanding factories.

Although jobs were the primary attraction of the cities, people also headed to cities for other reasons. Cities offered pleasures considered luxuries in rural areas—plays, concerts, and stores with fancy clothes. City dwellers got new technology, such as electricity and indoor plumbing, long before rural residents did. (See One Day in History, pages 240–241.) Finally, cities offered anonymity. In large urban areas people could easily disappear from the scrutiny of their friends and families.

The movement to the cities included both whites and African Americans. In 1865 at the end of the Civil War, most African Americans lived on farms and in small towns throughout the South. By the late 1800s, though, African Americans were beginning to move to cities. More than 40 percent of the people in Atlanta were African Americans. In most Northern cities, the African American population was increasing but did not exceed 3 percent in any given city in 1915.

Immigration

Like rural citizens of the United States, Europeans poured into American cities in the late 1800s and early 1900s. The United States had always been a land of **immigrants,** attracting people from other countries to live there. Beginning around 1880, however, the immigrant stream became a flood. Between 1880 and 1920 about 25 million immigrants entered the United States. That was half as many people as lived in the entire country in 1880.

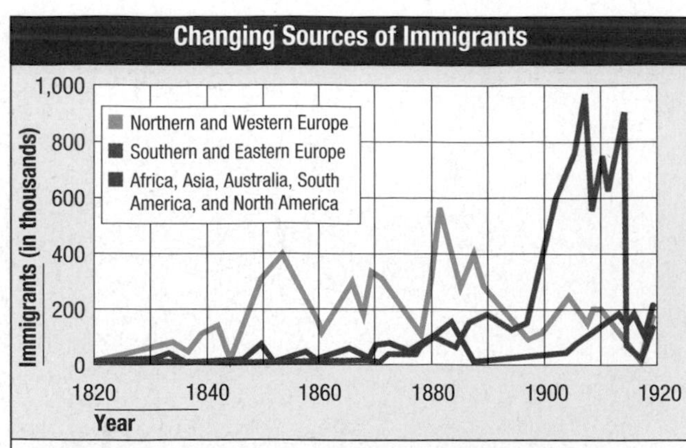

The numbers of immigrants from southern and eastern Europe increased dramatically in the early 1900s. *According to the chart, what range of years shows the greatest increase?*

Equally as important as the swelling tide of immigrants was the dramatic shift in their countries of origin, as shown on the chart on this page. Before 1890 most immigrants came from northern and western Europe—Great Britain, Ireland, Germany, and the Scandinavian countries. Many of these people spoke English, and most were Protestants. Between 1890 and 1920, though, about 80 percent of all immigrants came from southern and eastern Europe, from countries such as Italy, Greece, Poland, and Russia. They usually practiced the Roman Catholic, Eastern Orthodox, or Jewish faith. Most were poor, uneducated, and illiterate. The first sight of the United States for many of these newcomers was the Statue of Liberty and Ellis Island in New York Harbor. When Ellis Island opened in 1892, it marked the passage of processing immigrants from state to federal control.

Most immigrants arriving after 1880 settled in cities, because that was where jobs could be found. By 1920 nearly half of all urban dwellers were immigrants or the children of immigrants. The ethnic diversity of American cities impressed Danish immigrant Jacob Riis. Speaking of New York, he said, "A map of the city, colored to designate nationalities, would show more stripes than on the skin of a zebra, and more colors than any rainbow." One Polish immigrant found the large number of immigrants frustrating:

> I am polish man. I want be American citizen. . . . But my friends are polish people—I must live with them—I work in the shoeshop with polish people—I stay all the time with them—at home—in the shop—anywhere. . . . when

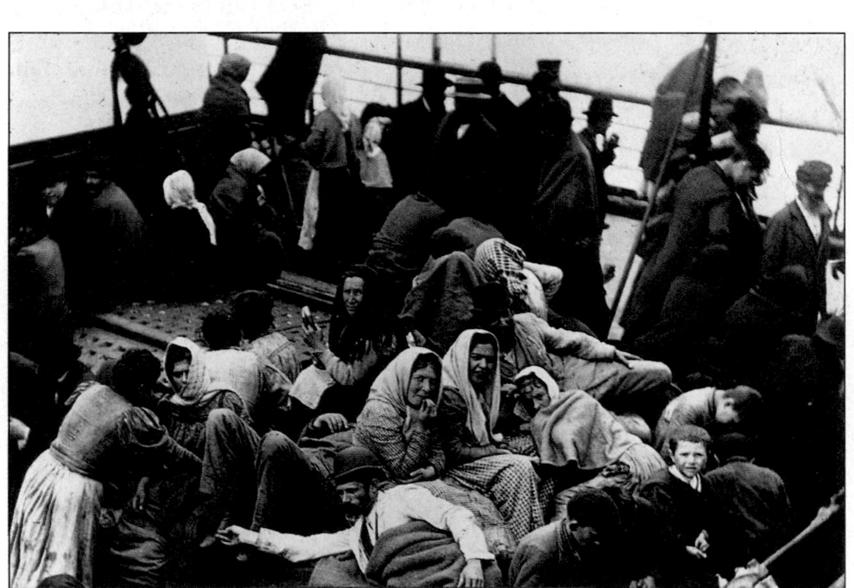

BROWN BROTHERS

Steerage Passengers Immigrants, such as those shown above arriving in New York in the early 1900s, often sailed on dangerously crowded ships. *Why did most immigrants to the United States settle in cities?*

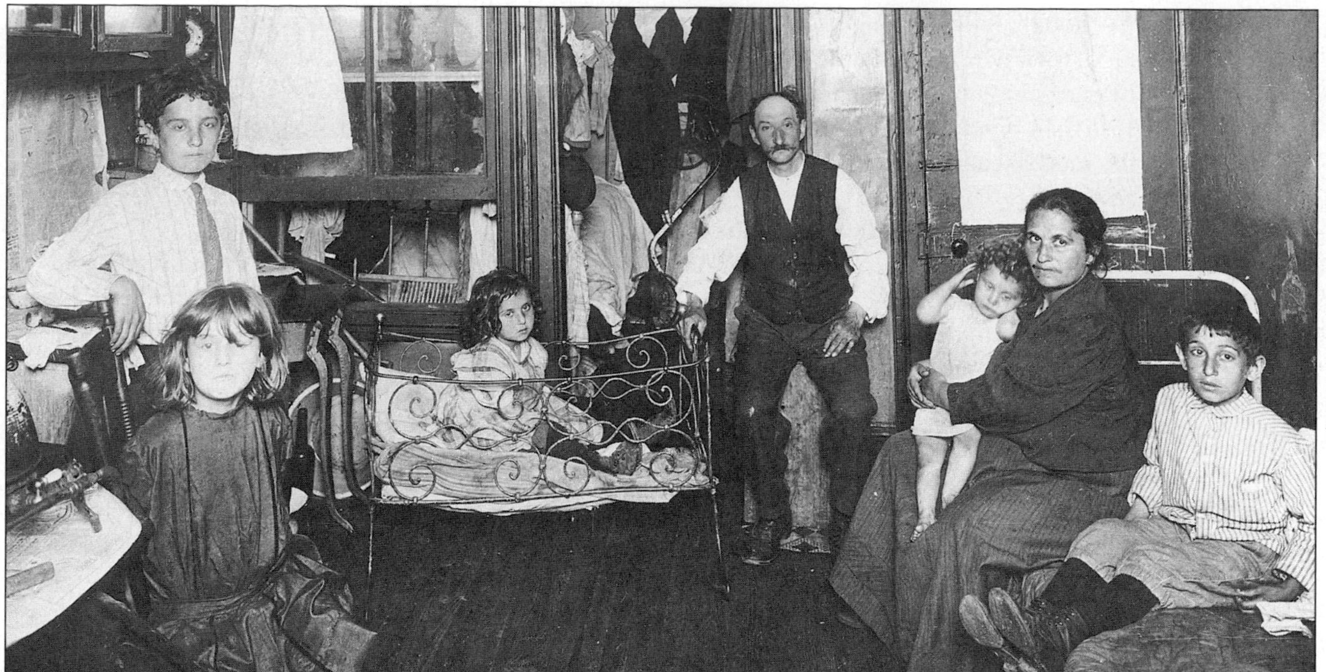
THE JACOB A RIIS COLLECTION, MUSEUM OF THE CITY OF NEW YORK

An Immigrant Apartment **Jessie Tarbox Beals took this photo, "Room in a Tenement Flat," in New York City in 1910. In poor areas of New York, where political machines were strong, apartments housed an average of 1.9 people per room.** *What other problems did city overcrowding create?*

I come home—I must speak polish and in the shop also. In this way I can live in your country many years—like my friends—and never speak—write well English—and never be good American citizen.

—Polish immigrant, Commission on the Problem of Immigration, 1914

Social Problems

Others found the growth of cities frustrating as well. Many Americans agreed with Congregationalist minister Josiah Strong that cities were wicked places and indeed posed threats to the very core of their civilization:

The city has become a serious menace to our civilization. . . . Here [in the city] is heaped the social dynamite; here roughs, gamblers, thieves, robbers, lawless and desperate men of all sorts, congregate; men who are ready on any pretext to raise riots for the purpose of destruction and plunder; here gather foreigners and wage-workers; here skepticism and irreligion abound.

—Josiah Strong, *Our Country,* 1885

Strong's attack on cities reflected his own dislike of immigrants. His views, however, also reflected the existence of real problems in cities. Many jobs paid so poorly that workers had to find other ways, sometimes illegal, to add to their income. Gambling, robbery, and extortion were widespread. In 1906 Chicago had an estimated 10,000 prostitutes, many of whom were under the age of 19. The city also had about 7,000 cocaine addicts. As cities grew, so did violence. The murder rate increased from 1.2 per 100,000 people in 1900 to 6.8 per 100,000 in 1920. Gang fights between rival political groups often marred election days.

Cities were not equipped to respond to their growing problems. Without enough police officers, crime was rampant. Without enough firefighters, fires quickly raged out of control. Without adequate sanitation systems, garbage and sewage piled up in the streets and polluted the drinking water. Two of the most severe urban problems were poor housing and political corruption.

Many of the people pouring into the cities could not afford their own apartments—and not enough places existed even if they could—so frequently they doubled up. Landlords divided small apartments into two or more even smaller units. Property owners converted horse stables, garages, and storage shacks into apartments. They added new buildings in the backyards of existing ones.

As buildings were carved up or constructed ever closer together, many apartments had no source of fresh air. Architects tried to combat this problem by designing dumbbell apartments. These structures were narrower in the middle than on the ends, like the letter I. With this design vertical spaces called air shafts could be left between buildings to allow light and air into each apartment.

The air shafts, though, became dangerous. Tenants threw garbage out of their windows into the shafts. The smell on a hot summer day could be so nauseating that tenants had to close their windows. Worse than the putrid smell were the rats, insects, and disease germs that thrived in the garbage.

Living conditions were bad for most newcomers to the city, but they were worse for African Americans. As a result of the racial prejudice of many whites, African Americans were restricted to living in only small parts of cities. As their population increased, the African American neighborhoods became even more overcrowded than the areas where immigrants lived.

Political Corruption

Politicians controlled the valuable contracts for building the new transportation lines, bridges, and firehouses that a growing city needed. Many showed more concern for filling their own pockets, however, than for solving the problems that Riis and others identified. A mayor could become wealthy overnight by accepting a bribe from a company trying to win a construction contract with the city. Businesses, then, usually added the cost of the bribe onto the contract with the city. Well-connected businesses prospered, and so did the politicians. Taxpayers paid the bill.

In order to keep the wealth flowing to themselves and their allies, politicians had to remain in office. They won the necessary votes by doing favors for people. The poor people of a city, especially immigrants and African Americans, often needed help—a job, a bag of coal, legal advice—that a wealthy politician could provide. All that the politician asked in return was a vote on Election Day. Some politicians developed and ran sophisticated organizations, known as **political machines,** to win votes. In each ward, or political district within a city, a machine representative controlled jobs, contracts, and favors. This person was the ward boss.

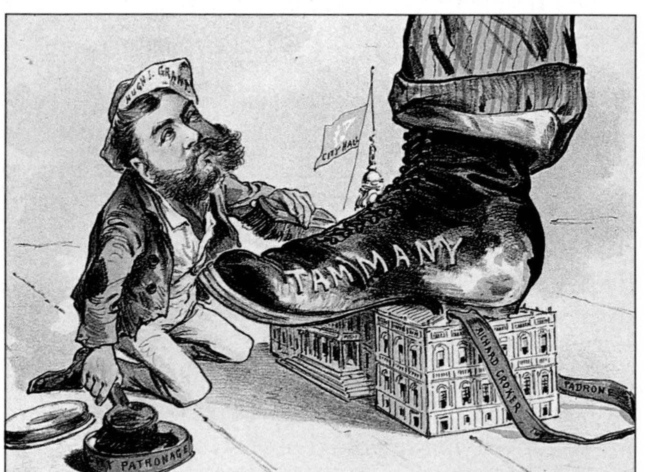

Controlling City Hall This lithograph by Joseph Keppler shows the power of Tammany Hall. *In what ways were political machines corrupt?*

The most famous political machine in the country controlled life in New York City and was headquartered in Tammany Hall. George Washington Plunkitt, a member of the New York State Assembly, was a minor boss in the Tammany Hall machine.

By observing Plunkitt in action and reading his diaries, a newspaper reporter pieced together a typical workday for Plunkitt. At 6:00 A.M., Plunkitt followed a fire truck to the scene of a fire and provided food, clothes, and temporary shelter for tenants who had just been burned out. "Fires," the reporter noted, "are considered great vote-getters." Later that morning, Plunkitt "paid the rent of a poor family" about to be evicted and "gave them a dollar for food." Then he found jobs for four men who had just been fired.

In the afternoon Plunkitt attended two funerals, one Italian and one Jewish. At each, he sat in the very front so everyone would see him. After dinner Plunkitt went to a church fair, where he bought tickets at every single fund-raising booth, and bought ice cream for all the children, "kissed the little ones, flattered their mothers, and took their fathers out for something down at the corner." At 9:00 P.M., he returned to his office, where he pledged to donate money to help a church buy a new bell. Later that night he attended a wedding reception and gave a "handsome wedding present to the bride." Finally, at midnight, after 18 hours of making friends and winning votes, Plunkitt went to bed.

Plunkitt's long hours paid off handsomely. His Tammany Hall associates rewarded him for his ability to deliver a large number of votes to party candidates each Election Day. For example, when the park board was planning a new park, they slipped word to Plunkitt of the location long before any plans had been made public. Then, from the unsuspecting owners, Plunkitt bought the land where the park would be established. Weeks later, when the board announced its decision to construct a new park, Plunkitt resold the land to the park board at a much higher price than he paid for it. By the time of his death, Plunkitt was a millionaire.

Industrial Disorder

Squeezing Small Businesses and Workers

Plunkitt was not the only person to prosper while others struggled just to survive. By 1910 the income of the wealthiest 2 percent of Americans accounted for almost 20 percent of the total income of all workers, double what it had accounted for in 1896.

LIBRARY OF CONGRESS

The Oil Industry This cartoon entitled *NEXT!* published in the magazine *Puck* depicts the control of Standard Oil over government and suppliers. *How did a large company also provide benefits to consumers?*

One reason for this growing concentration of wealth was the rash of business mergers and buyouts in the 1890s. Such consolidations usually resulted in the formation of **trusts,** a combination of companies dominating an industry, created for the purpose of reducing competition in that industry. Often a small handful of people, or even a single individual, ruled a trust.

The size of these large companies provided some benefits to consumers. Large firms could afford to develop and use expensive new machinery that, in turn, lowered the cost of producing goods. Even small cost-cutting measures could save enormous amounts of money for huge companies. For example, by reducing the cost of each oil storage can by only 15 cents, Standard Oil saved more than $5 million a year. Such production efficiency could lead to cheaper retail prices. Items that were once luxuries, such as glass bottles, were now widely available and inexpensive. "Never in human history was the creation of material wealth so easy and so marvelously abundant," pointed out one United States senator.

The senator cautioned, however, "Here are dangers it will behoove us to gravely contemplate." The new, efficient companies exacted a heavy cost in human suffering. Though wages increased slowly between 1890 and 1910, most workers lived just outside the reach of financial ruin. Everyday expenses such as rent, food, and clothes absorbed virtually all of the income of typical workers.

In between the wealthy owners and the poorly paid laborers was a growing middle class. This group consisted of managers, clerks, small-business owners, college professors, members of the clergy, lawyers, and other professionals. The middle class, which was able to afford the mass-produced goods, praised the technological triumphs that led to greater production efficiency. They felt threatened, however, by both the rich and the poor and blamed the growing problems of society on these groups:

> Nearly all problems which vex society have their sources above or below the middle-class man. From above come the problems of predatory wealth. . . . From below come the problems of poverty and of pigheaded and brutish criminality.
>
> —*California Weekly,* December 18, 1908

To many educated, honest, middle-class Americans, the traditional values that they prized were under assault. Trusts, though efficient, threatened to squeeze out small businesses. Workers, plagued by crime and poverty, seemed vulnerable to revolutionary calls for radical change. Middle-class Americans and their allies responded by working for a return to traditional values—economic opportunity, religious morality, political honesty, and social stability. This effort to reform the United States and preserve its democratic values became known as the Progressive movement.

Section Assessment

Main Idea

1. Use a diagram like this one to show the causes and effects of rapid urbanization.

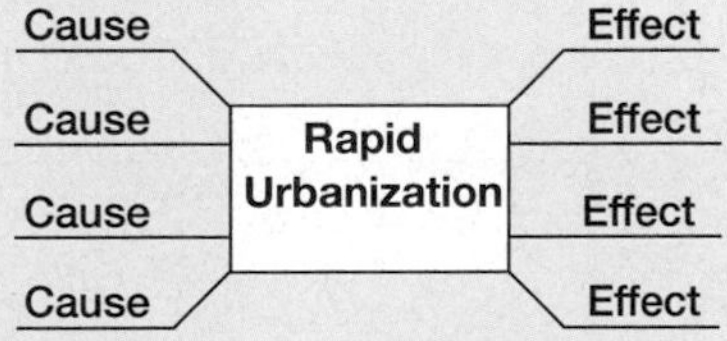

Vocabulary

2. Define: tenement, suburb, urbanization, immigrant, political machine, trust.

Checking Facts

3. Why did rural Americans as well as immigrants move to cities in the United States?

4. What effect did urban and industrial growth have on life in American cities?

Critical Thinking

5. Determining Cause and Effect How do you think the continuous flow of new workers into the cities affected the wages of all workers?

SPORTS: New baseball rule allows a batter to walk to first base after receiving nine balls.

One Day in History

Thursday, January 1, 1880

MARKET BASKET

Here is where a dollar will go:

Parasol .... 50¢
Perfumed kid gloves
Two-button $1
Four-button $1.50
Hat, trimmed $2.50

COURTESY THE OAKLAND MUSEUM HISTORY DEPARTMENT, OAKLAND, CA

Imitation-gold pocket watch $12
Corset $3
Muslin shirt $1
Neckwear—ties, bows, scarves .... 25¢
Baseball, by mail $1.50
Dental fee: vitalized or gas .... 25¢
Boys' short pantaloons .... 50¢
Walking skirt with ruffle .... 50¢
Black Elysian overcoat $4.50
Waterproof cape $8.25
Admission to New York circus ... 25¢, 50¢
Reserved .... 25¢ extra

UPI/BETTMANN

The Edison Lamp Inventor Thomas A. Edison stands in his laboratory holding the first incandescent vacuum light tube, which uses carbonized cotton thread as a filament.

Edison's New Lamp

An invention of great promise; Menlo Park illuminated

MENLO PARK—On New Year's Eve, the little hamlet of Menlo Park, New Jersey, was illuminated by 40 streetlamps lighted with electricity. Tonight the display will be repeated. In addition to the streetlamps, there were 100 electric burners in operation in machine buildings, private buildings, and Professor Edison's laboratory. The number of lights will be increased daily until there are 800. One of the lamps now in use has been lighted, day and night, for 17 days. The others have been used for 2 weeks. The Pennsylvania Railroad Company carried passengers to and from the park at a reduced fare, and as many as 3,000 people took the opportunity to witness the illumination.

NATION: By an act of Congress, women have won the right to practice law and to argue cases before the United States Supreme Court.

CULVER PICTURES

Latimer Joins Hiram Maxim

BOSTON—After illustrating the workings of the telephone's components for Alexander Graham Bell's 1876 patent, Lewis Howard Latimer has become interested in the incandescent lightbulb invented by Thomas Edison. Latimer has agreed to join Hiram Maxim's United States Electric Lighting Company as a patent draftsman. He will work on patenting methods for manufacturing superior carbon filaments used in the new electric lamps, hoping to make the lamps last longer and cost less.

PHOTOGRAPHS AND PRINTS DIVISION, SCHOMBURG CENTER FOR RESEARCH IN BLACK CULTURE, NEW YORK PUBLIC LIBRARY, ASTOR, LENOX AND TILDEN FOUNDATIONS.

Master Draftsman Lewis Latimer earns recognition for creating technical drawings that illustrate patents.

THE PIERPONT MORGAN LIBRARY, NEW YORK. THE GILBERT AND SULLIVAN COLLECTION.

Gilbert and Sullivan's New Opera Opens The *Pirates of Penzance,* direct from London, debuted last evening at the Fifth Avenue Theatre in New York City.

MUSIC

THIS YEAR'S HIT SONGS

"Oh! Dem Golden Slippers"

"In the Evening by the Moonlight"

"A Policeman's Lot Is Not a Happy One"

BOOKS

NEW AND SOON TO BE RELEASED

Ben-Hur by Lew Wallace

Daisy Miller by Henry James

Five Little Peppers and How They Grew by Margaret Sidney

The Brothers Karamazov by Fyodor Dostoyevsky

Dance the Night Away

Use Johnson's Powdered Wax for Dancing Floors

Sprinkle lightly over the surface of the floor and the feet of the dancer will do the rest.

A steal for less than 20¢

FILE PHOTO BY DOUG MINDELL

A Generation of Reformers

EARLY 1890s: "SAINT JANE" OPENS NURSERY FOR THE POOR

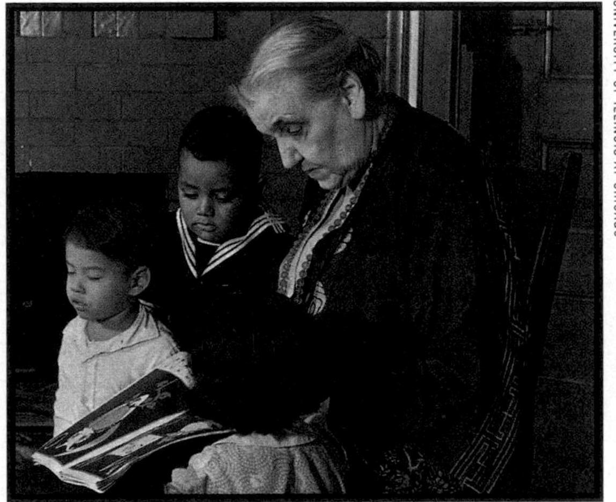
UNIVERSITY OF ILLINOIS AT CHICAGO

Children's Advocate
Jane Addams, founder of Hull House, reads a picture book to the young children in her nursery.

WITHIN A YEAR AFTER MOVING TO CHICAGO IN 1889, YOUNG, IDEALISTIC JANE ADDAMS MET THREE CHILDREN WHOM SHE NEVER FORGOT. "One had fallen out of a third-story window, another had been burned, and the third had a curved spine due to the fact that for three years he had been tied all day long to the leg of the kitchen table." The children had each been left alone, day after day, while their parents worked. Their parents earned so little money that they could not hire anyone to watch their children.

Addams, a quiet, dignified woman from a well-to-do family in a small Illinois town, had moved to Chicago because she wanted to help the poor. She and a friend had purchased a large, but run-down, old home known as Hull House in the midst of a densely populated immigrant neighborhood. They repaired the house and made it into a community center where neighborhood residents could learn to speak English, discuss political events, and hold celebrations. In addition, because of those three injured children, Addams opened a day nursery. Working parents no longer had to leave their young children unsupervised during the day. For her work, neighbors referred to her as Saint Jane.

Addams realized that the machines that had brought such great prosperity were also the engines of great

Guide to Reading

Main Idea

Many Americans at the turn of the 20th century advocated reforms to confront the problems caused by urbanization and industrialization.

Vocabulary

- progressive
- muckraker
- social gospel movement
- settlement house

Read to Find Out . . .

- the different types of people who became progressives.
- the aspects of American society that were criticized by the progressives.
- the different ways progressives tried to address problems associated with urbanization and industrialization.

misery. Jane Addams was just one of many Americans who, at the turn of the century, advocated reforms to confront the problems caused by industrialization and urbanization. The efforts of these reformers, the **progressives,** dominated the political landscape of the early 1900s.

Progressive Ideals

Protecting the Public Interest

During Jane Addams's youth the United States consisted mostly of small towns, small businesses, and small-scale problems. As Addams grew up, though, she watched larger cities, larger businesses, and larger problems develop. Small-town politicians never practiced corruption on the scale of George Washington Plunkitt and his Tammany Hall cronies. Rural poor people did not live in concentrations of garbage and stagnant air as did city tenement dwellers. A village blacksmith could never control a town the way a large steel company could dominate the people of a city.

Like the populists of the 1880s and 1890s, progressives feared the concentration of power in the hands of the wealthy few. While hardworking immigrants could not afford to provide for their hungry and ill children, financiers like J.P. Morgan became millionaires by manipulating ownership of the companies for which these immigrants toiled. Through campaign contributions and bribes, corporate trusts bought influence with lawmakers. Progressives wanted reforms to protect the public interest.

Unlike the populists, who usually lived in rural areas, the progressives generally lived in cities. By the 1890s cities faced crippling problems: housing shortages, political corruption, and spiraling crime rates. In the chaotic cities, progressives wanted to reestablish order and stability.

Progressives were also unlike populists in their greater faith in experts. While populists emphasized the wisdom of average people, progressives focused on the ability of knowledgeable experts to analyze and solve problems. Just as Thomas Edison had conquered technological problems in developing the lightbulb, progressives believed that trained experts could analyze and conquer crime, alcoholism, and political corruption. Many progressives praised business owners for their expertise in solving the problems of producing and distributing goods and in running a store or a factory smoothly. Though fearing the power of big businesses, progressives often respected the efficient methods they used.

Progressive Analysts

Analyzing and Publicizing Society's Problems

Progressives looked to government to solve problems. Virtually all progressives shared the hope that a well-run government could protect the public interest and restore order to society. Beyond this hope, though, progressives differed widely in their beliefs, goals, and actions.

New Intellectuals

Changes in higher education influenced many progressives. Between 1870 and 1920 college enrollment increased more than tenfold, and many schools established separate social science departments, such as economics, political science, and sociology. These departments attempted to analyze human society with the same objectivity that scientists used to study nature. Their establishment reflected a growing faith in the ability of people to analyze society and solve human problems. Many social science professors and the students they influenced became progressives. For example, Columbia University historian Charles Beard applied his knowledge of American history to reforming corrupt city governments. Not all the new intellectuals, however, worked for universities. Mary Ritter Beard, wife of Charles, wrote extensively about how scholars had ignored the contributions of women in history.

One of the influential members of the new social science fraternity was Lester Ward. Much of Ward's childhood was spent "roaming over those boundless

THE BETTMANN ARCHIVE

Lester Ward Brown University appointed Lester Ward professor of sociology in 1906 at the age of 65. *What did the new college social science departments attempt to analyze and why?*

prairies" of Illinois and Iowa in the mid-1800s "and admiring nature." After surviving three wounds as a Union army soldier in the Civil War, he got a job as a minor clerk in the United States Treasury Department. For the next 40 years, he held a variety of federal government jobs. For most of this period, he worked for the United States Geological Survey, studying rocks, plants, and animals in the lightly settled territories of the West.

In his free time, Ward taught himself Greek, Latin, French, and German, and participated in various book clubs, debating the latest ideas on science, history, and philosophy. In 1869 he began outlining his first book, *Dynamic Sociology,* which he completed in 1883. In this book and five others, Ward analyzed social concerns just as scientifically as he studied natural phenomena. He challenged the widely held belief that it was natural for the strong, such as the owners of large corporations, to prosper while the weak, the workers, suffered. What was natural, Ward argued, was for people to control and change their social environment—the laws, customs, and relationships among people—for their own benefit. "The day has come for society to take its affairs into its own hands and shape its own destinies."

Government's Job

The shaping of a society's destiny, according to Ward, was the job of the government. For example, if tenements were inadequate, then government should pass laws, spend money, or take other steps to improve housing. Ward believed that a larger role by government would improve the social environment and expand the options of individuals. "The true function of government," Ward proclaimed, "is not to fetter, but to liberate the forces of society, not to diminish but to increase their effectiveness."

In 1906 at age 65, Ward finally took his first full-time academic position. He became professor of sociology at Brown University. Social scientists such as Ward claimed that scientific study of human problems would provide better ways to run the cities. These new intellectuals often depended upon others, however, to motivate the public and to attack specific problems with specific solutions.

Angry Writers

Among those who motivated the public were many writers known as **muckrakers.** That label came from a character in a seventeenth-century book, *Pilgrim's Progress,* who spent all of his time raking up the dirt and filth, or muck, on the ground. The muckrakers combined careful research, vivid writing, and intense moral outrage. Most of these crusaders wrote long, investigative articles for popular magazines such as *McClure's, Collier's, Cosmopolitan,* and *American Magazine.* Writers attacked wealthy corporations that exploited child labor, corrupt police departments that protected prostitution rings, and prestigious churches that owned disease-ridden tenements. Ida Tarbell, a "conventional-minded lady, sweet and gracious," was one of the most famous of the muckrakers. She wrote a series of widely read articles detailing the rise of the Standard Oil Company. Tarbell exposed the ruthless methods used by its owner, John D. Rockefeller, to crush his competition—including Tarbell's father.

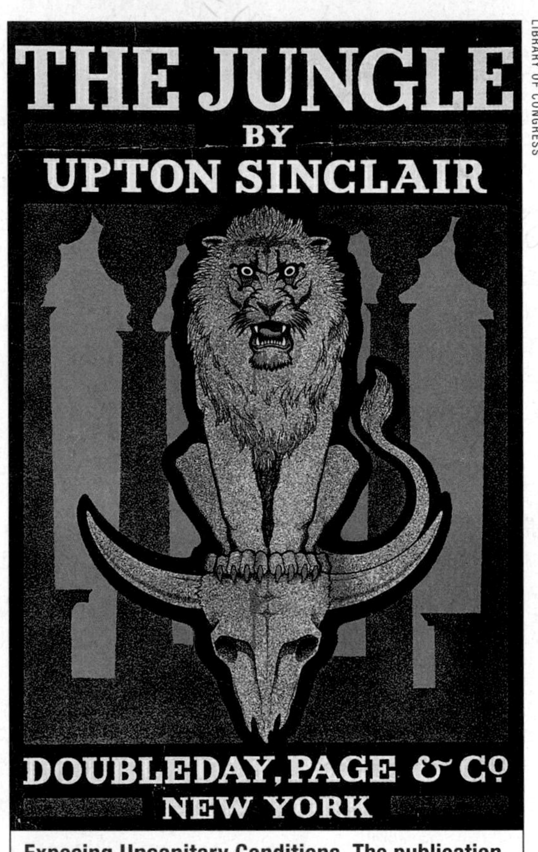

Exposing Unsanitary Conditions **The publication of *The Jungle* led to the passage of the first federal food-inspection laws.** *How did Sinclair prepare himself to write about exploited workers?*

In addition to articles, some muckrakers, such as Upton Sinclair, wrote novels. Sinclair grew up in near-poverty in Baltimore. His father, a salesperson, suffered from alcoholism and was never very successful. By 1904 the 26-year-old Sinclair was a gentle, innocent-looking young writer. He had already completed four novels, each featuring a courageous individual who fought against social injustice. In that year a radical newspaper, *Appeal to Reason,* hired Sinclair to write a novel about the exploitation of workers in the United States.

To prepare for the contracted novel, Sinclair lived among the stockyard workers of Chicago for seven weeks. He later recalled how he sat "in their homes at night, and talked with them and then in the daytime they would lay off their work, and take me around, and show me whatever I wished to see. I studied every detail of their lives."

Based on his close observations of how workers lived, Sinclair wrote *The Jungle,* a novel about a Lithuanian immigrant who worked in the meatpacking

BROWN BROTHERS

Preparing Meat for Consumers Complaints about unsafe meat preparation began in 1899, after United States soldiers got ill from eating spoiled canned meat. *How would photos like this one of the Chicago stockyards around 1900 support the charges made by Upton Sinclair?*

industry. In focusing on one worker's life, Sinclair intended to arouse public sympathy for the common laborer. His graphic descriptions of the unsanitary conditions in the packing plant, however, sparked a reaction to the meat industry itself. As Sinclair noted somewhat sadly, "I aimed at the public's heart, and by accident I hit it in the stomach." His book made consumers ill—and angry:

> There would come all the way back from Europe old sausage that had been rejected, and that was moldy and white—it would be dosed with borax and glycerine, and dumped into the hoppers, and made over again for home consumption. There would be meat that had tumbled out on the floor, in the dirt and sawdust, where the workers had tramped and spit uncounted billions of consumption germs. There would be meat stored in great piles in rooms; and the water from leaky roofs would drip over it, and thousands of rats would race about on it.
>
> —Upton Sinclair, *The Jungle,* 1906

Sinclair, like other muckrakers, had a vision of a just and orderly society: workers would receive adequate wages and consumers would purchase healthful food. The muckrakers' aim was to awaken people to the growing social, economic, and political evils and inequities in the nation.

Religious Reformers

Another group of progressives also appealed to the conscience of Americans. The **social gospel movement** included Christians who felt the church should improve life on the earth rather than just getting people into heaven.

One leader of the social gospel movement was Walter Rauschenbusch. Described by one journalist as "a tall, spare man, with a twinkle in his eyes," Rauschenbusch was a sixth-generation minister. After studying theology in Rochester, New York, and in Germany, he became pastor of the Second German Baptist Church in New York City.

Rauschenbusch's church bordered a region named Hell's Kitchen. Unemployment, alcoholism, and despair plagued residents of this poverty-stricken neighborhood.

Rauschenbusch turned to the Bible and his faith for a proper response to an industrial system that made "the margin of life narrow in order to make the margin of profit wide." He blamed fierce competition for many social ills. Owners and managers, many of whom practiced Christianity, believed they had to be ruthless or risk going out of business:

> Competitive commerce . . . makes men who are the gentlest and kindliest friends and neighbors, relentless taskmasters in their shops and stores, who will drain the strength of their men and pay their female employees wages on which no girl can live without supplementing them in some way.
>
> —Walter Rauschenbusch, *Christianity and the Social Crisis,* 1907

Rauschenbusch and other advocates of the social gospel believed that environmental conditions such as poverty, and not individual depravity, caused the ills in society. Hence, they believed, every Christian should strive to better economic and political conditions.

Student Web Activity 8

Visit the *American Odyssey* Web site at americanodyssey.glencoe.com and click on ***Chapter 8—Student Web Activities*** for an activity relating to progressive reformers.

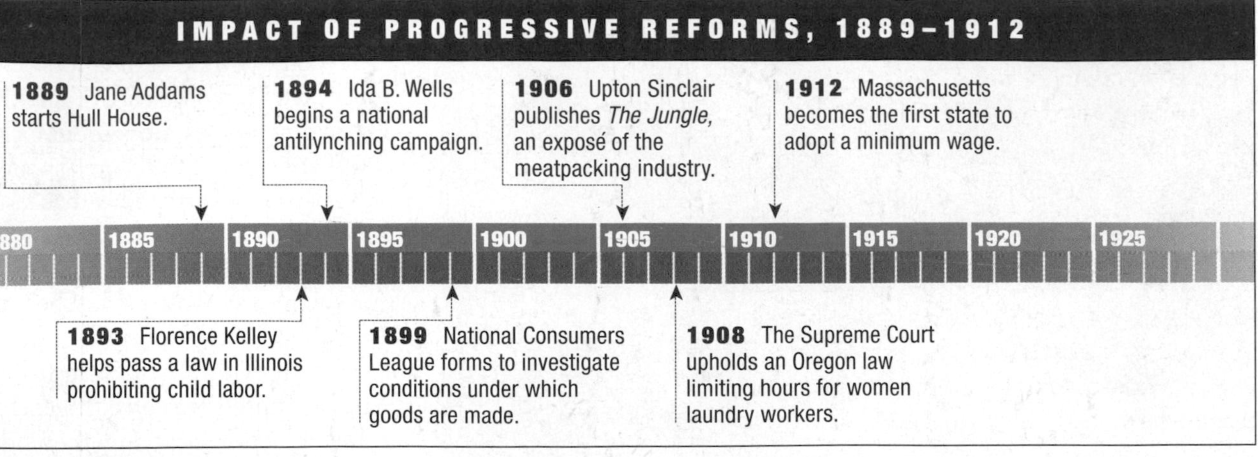
IMPACT OF PROGRESSIVE REFORMS, 1889–1912
1889 Jane Addams starts Hull House.
1894 Ida B. Wells begins a national antilynching campaign.
1906 Upton Sinclair publishes The Jungle, an exposé of the meatpacking industry.
1912 Massachusetts becomes the first state to adopt a minimum wage.
1880
1885
1890
1895
1900
1905
1910
1915
1920
1925
1893 Florence Kelley helps pass a law in Illinois prohibiting child labor.
1899 National Consumers League forms to investigate conditions under which goods are made.
1908 The Supreme Court upholds an Oregon law limiting hours for women laundry workers.

Progressive Activists

Solving Society's Problems

Most progressives who analyzed problems took action to solve them as well. Sinclair ran for Congress three times and for governor of California once. Rauschenbusch skillfully helped his parish members cope with unemployment, alcoholism, and other social ills. Sinclair and Rauschenbusch, like Ward, however, were more influential as analysts who identified and publicized problems than as activists who solved them.

Other progressives were more influential as activists who successfully won reforms on specific issues rather than as analysts. Progressives usually focused their efforts on the problems they saw firsthand or felt personally. For example, Sinclair wrote about the meatpacking workers he lived with. Rauschenbusch confronted the problems of the urban poor. Similarly, many women who were progressives emphasized the problems faced by women and children. Many African American progressives stressed issues affecting African Americans.

Concerned Women

In most families, whether urban or rural, women had more responsibility for raising the children than did men. Consequently, women were particularly outraged about the problems of children who labored in factories.

One of the leaders in the battle against child labor was Florence Kelley. Her father, a member of the United States House of Representatives, opposed slavery and supported women's right to vote. He taught Florence to read at a young age and to value education. She graduated from Cornell University in New York and attended graduate school in Switzerland.

In 1891 she went to live and work at Jane Addams's Hull House. During her seven years there, she investigated and reported on the use of child labor. "In the stores on the West Side," Kelley reported in 1895, "large numbers of young girls are employed thirteen hours a day throughout the week, and fifteen hours on Saturday."

Kelley was, in the words of a friend, "explosive, hot-tempered, determined . . . a smoking volcano that at any moment would burst into flames." What she unearthed in her investigations, though, outraged even many mild-mannered people. Kelley charged that "children are found in greatest number where the conditions of labor are most dangerous to life and health." Children working in the tobacco industry suffered from nicotine poisoning. Children in paint factories suffered

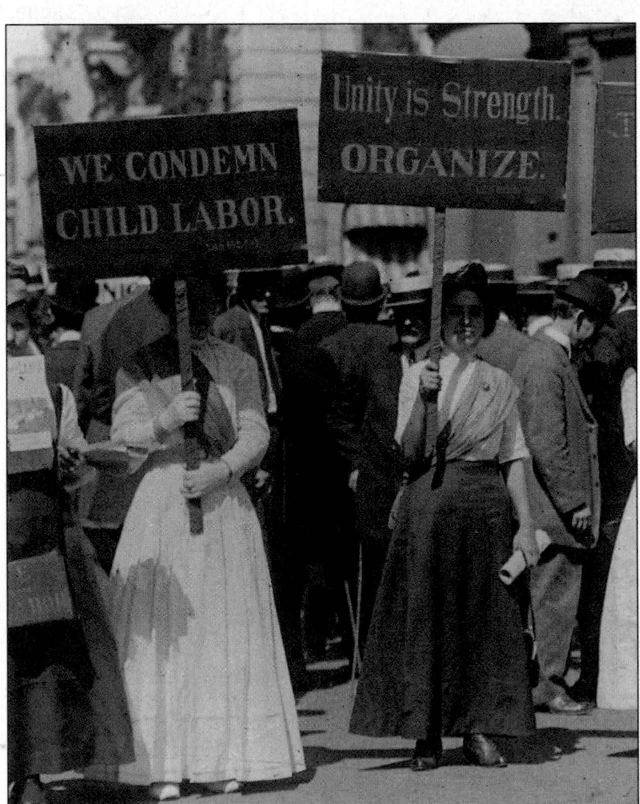
WE CONDEMN
CHILD LABOR.
Unity is Strength.
ORGANIZE.

BROWN BROTHERS

Child Labor Activists This photograph shows one of the many child labor protest marches held in the early 1900s.
Why are the women particularly upset about child labor?

from breathing in toxic arsenic fumes. Children in clothing factories suffered spinal curvature from hunching over sewing machines 48 hours each week.

Kelley pressed the federal government to outlaw the use of child labor. "Why," she thundered, "are seals, bears, reindeer, fish, wild game in the national parks, buffalo, [and] migratory birds all found suitable for federal protection, but not children?"

Kelley continued her battle against child labor after she left Hull House. As general secretary of the National Consumers League (NCL), she helped organize consumer boycotts of goods manufactured by children or by workers toiling in unsanitary or dangerous conditions.

The National Consumers League

Most members of the NCL were, like Kelley, middle-class or upper-class women concerned about problems such as exploitation of children in factories. Many NCL members also supported the work of **settlement houses,** institutions that provided educational and social services to poor people. Hull House was the best known of the 400 settlement houses established between 1886 and 1910. In addition to their work in settlement houses, women were very active in clubs that promoted the arts, education, and community health. By the early 1920s, almost 1 million women had joined such clubs. The NCL, the settlement houses, and the women's clubs indicate that women were taking a more active role in confronting political and economic problems than they had in the past.

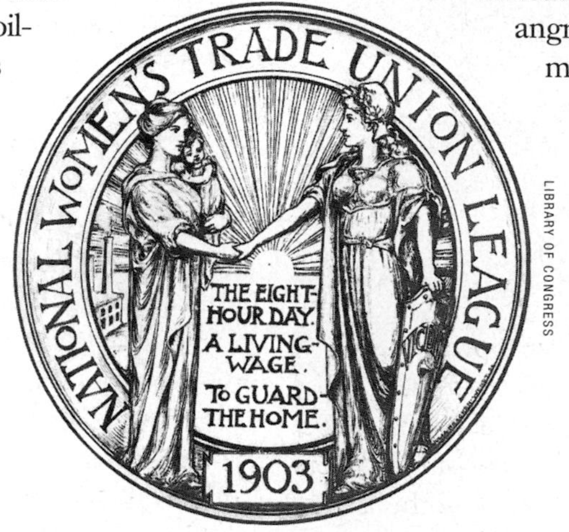

LIBRARY OF CONGRESS

NWTUL of Chicago The National Women's Trade Union League, like the National Consumers League, united workers and middle-class reformers. *How do its slogans reflect this?*

Some of the reforms advocated by Kelley and other women were not supported by many of the men who were progressives. For example, Walter Rauschenbusch opposed granting women the vote, even though this was a vital issue to Kelley and many female reformers.

African American Activists

For the urban African American family, racism intensified such problems as high unemployment and inadequate housing. Many white factory owners refused to hire African Americans—except as strikebreakers. In most cities African Americans could live only in well-defined areas, which quickly became overcrowded as cities grew. Furthermore, racism remained firmly entrenched in the minds of most whites, including most progressives. Many whites viewed African Americans as lazier, less intelligent, and more immoral than whites. In no other period of American history did state governments pass so many laws designed to restrict African Americans to a secondary role in society. African Americans working for reform often felt outside the Progressive movement.

The most dangerous problem for African Americans was lynching, murder by a mob without a trial, often by hanging. In 1892 about 230 people were lynched in the United States. Most of these people were African Americans, killed by groups of angry whites. Leading the antilynching movement was Ida B. Wells.

Born to enslaved parents in Holly Springs, Mississippi, in 1862, Wells remembered how much her parents emphasized education. "Our job," Wells recalled, "was to learn all we could."

When Wells was 14 her parents died in a yellow fever epidemic. Ida, the oldest of the 6 living children, refused to let her family be broken up. She lied about her age in order to get a job teaching school so that she could support her family.

In 1884 she got a better teaching job in Memphis and began writing for a local newspaper. Soon after arriving in Memphis, Wells became a controversial advocate of equality for African Americans because of an incident on a train. Upon taking a seat, she was told by the conductor that she was in a car reserved for whites and that she would have to move. Wells refused.

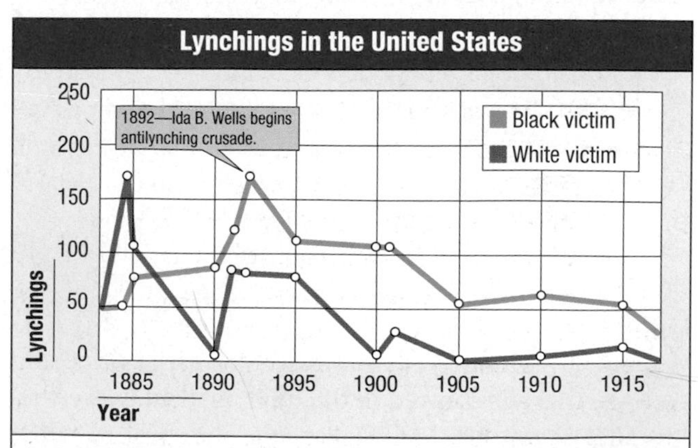

Before 1886 most lynchings were done by whites to whites. After that date the victims of lynchings, most of which occurred in the South, were usually African American. *According to the chart, when did lynchings of African Americans peak?*

Lynching Protest **Opponents of lynching (above) appealed to national pride as one reason to end the murder of African Americans. Ida B. Wells (above right) led a national battle against lynchings.** *How did Wells alert the public about the racism that motivated these mob murders?*

Though only about four and a half feet tall, Wells put up a fierce struggle:

> He tried to drag me out of the seat, but the moment he caught hold of my arm I fastened my teeth in the back of his hand. . . . He went forward and got the baggage-man and another man to help him and of course they succeeded in dragging me out. They were encouraged to do this by the attitude of the white ladies and gentlemen in the car. . . . I said I would get off the train rather than go in [to a segregated car]—which I did.
>
> —Ida B. Wells, *Crusade for Justice*

In her writing Wells expressed the same pride and courage that she showed in the train incident. Nevertheless, after writing articles criticizing the poor education that African Americans received in Memphis schools, she was fired from her teaching position. She became a full-time journalist, writing articles for several African American–owned newspapers.

The night of March 9, 1892, changed Ida Wells's life. That night a mob of angry whites lynched three African American men in Memphis. Wells wrote a scathing newspaper editorial attacking the lawless treatment of African Americans in Memphis. Moving to Chicago in 1894, Wells launched a national campaign to end lynching. From Chicago she wrote articles, gave speeches, and carried out investigations to expose the racism that motivated mob murderers. Within three years the number of lynchings went down by one-quarter.

Wells was not alone in fighting back. Racial oppression, in all its forms, triggered the founding of the National Association for the Advancement of Colored People (NAACP) in 1909 and the National Urban League in 1910. Both organizations worked to help African Americans improve their living conditions.

As Wells and the progressives awakened the public to social ills and organized campaigns to remedy these ills, the number of people pressuring the government to respond increased. Progressives set out their agenda to reform the political structure, to modify the economic system, and to improve the moral climate of communities across the nation.

Section Assessment

Main Idea

1. Use a diagram like this one to show some of the progressive reformers and the causes they supported. Add answer circles as needed.

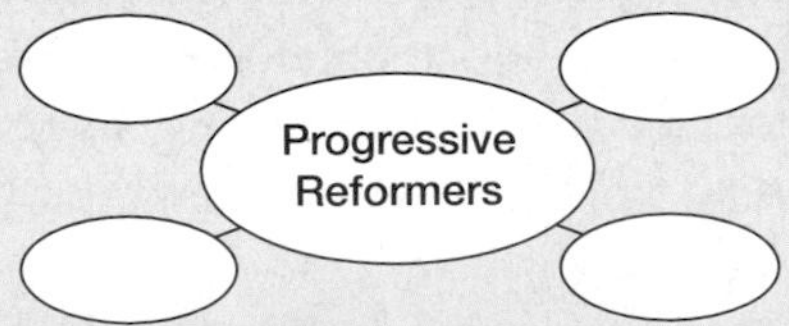

Vocabulary

2. Define: progressive, muckraker, social gospel movement, settlement house.

Checking Facts

3. Describe some of the different methods progressives used to combat injustice.
4. How did the methods of the activists differ from those of the analysts? How were they similar?

Critical Thinking

5. **Making Comparisons** Which of the progressive methods for reform were most effective? Give examples to support your opinion.

Critical Thinking Skill

DETERMINING CAUSE AND EFFECT

Learning the Skill

When reading and studying historical information, it is important to determine cause-and-effect relationships in order to comprehend the significance of various events.

The skill of determining cause and effect requires considering why an event occurred. A *cause* is the action or situation that produces an event. An *effect* is the result or consequence of an action or a situation.

How to Determine Cause and Effect

Follow these steps to determine cause and effect:

a. Ask questions about why events occur.

b. Identify two or more events.

c. Look for vocabulary clues to help decide whether one event caused the other. Words or phrases such as *because*, *as a result of*, *for this reason*, *therefore*, *thus*, *as a consequence*, *as an outgrowth*, and *if . . . then* indicate cause-and-effect relationships.

d. Identify the outcomes of the events.

e. Look for relationships between the events. Check for other, more complex, connections beyond the immediate cause and effect.

For example, read the passage below:

> **When Florence Kelley went to live and work at Hull House, she became an activist for outlawing child labor. Children's long working hours, detrimental health conditions, and poor factory environment were the causes of her activism. She helped organize consumer boycotts of goods manufactured by children and supported the work of settlement houses.**

When studying the reform movement mentioned in the passage above, a graphic organizer such as the one below aids in understanding multiple causes and effects.

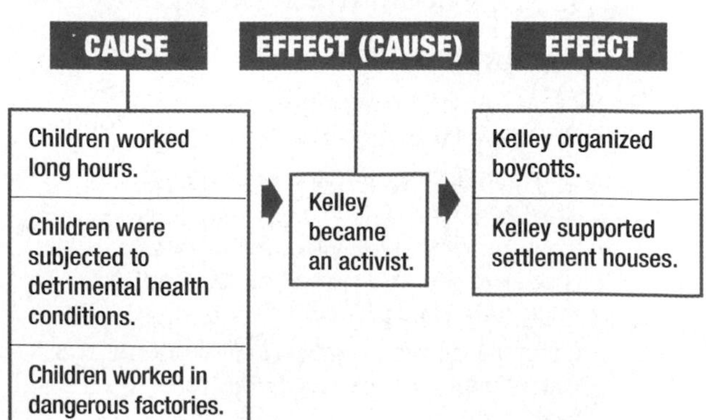

CAUSE
EFFECT (CAUSE)
EFFECT
Children worked long hours.
Children were subjected to detrimental health conditions.
Children worked in dangerous factories.
Kelley became an activist.
Kelley organized boycotts.
Kelley supported settlement houses.

Practicing the Skill

Use the model on this page to make a cause-and-effect diagram for each statement below by writing the cause on the left and the effect on the right. Then connect the two parts of the statement with an arrow.

1. Not all immigrants stayed in the United States. Some became homesick and returned to the land of their birth.

2. After meeting three neglected children, Jane Addams decided to open a day nursery to aid working parents.

3. To alert the public to social ills, the muckrakers wrote articles attacking wealthy corporations that exploited child labor, corrupt police departments that protected illegal activities, and churches that owned tenements.

4. As an outgrowth of Upton Sinclair's publication, *The Jungle*, public sympathizers began to consider providing adequate wages for workers and improving sanitary conditions in the meatpacking industry.

5. Ida B. Wells launched a national campaign to end lynching by writing articles, giving speeches, and carrying out investigations to expose the racism that motivated mob murders. For this reason, the number of lynchings went down by one-quarter within three years.

Applying the Skill

Choose a contemporary reform movement—such as changing affirmative action policies, providing universal health insurance, or ensuring Social Security benefits for retirees—or select your own area of interest. Write a paragraph detailing the causes and possible effects of the reforms you might institute. Then use the information in your paragraph to construct a cause-and-effect diagram.

The **Glencoe Skillbuilder Interactive Workbook, Level 2** CD-ROM provides more practice in key social studies skills.

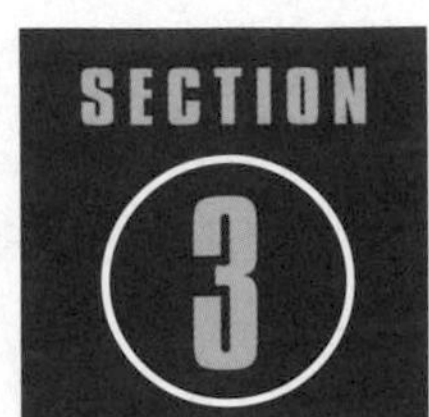

Progressive Agendas

SPRING 1901: WISCONSIN CHALLENGES THE RAILROADS

STOCK MONTAGE

Wisconsin Reforms
La Follette fought to loosen the railroad's control of state government.

THE YOUNG LEGISLATOR LOOKED TERRIFIED AS HE WALKED INTO THE OFFICE OF WISCONSIN GOVERNOR ROBERT LA FOLLETTE. The governor, hoping to protect the legislator's identity, referred to him by a letter. "E., what's the matter?" With that, E. burst into tears.

As a progressive, La Follette was fighting to break the tight grip of the railroad tycoons and political bosses on the state government. He needed E.'s support for his bill requiring the railroads to pay a fair share of taxes.

"Governor, I can't help it. I've got to vote against the railroad taxation bill," E. explained sorrowfully. He went on, "I haven't slept any for two or three nights. I have walked the floor. I have thought of resigning and going home."

"Tell me all about it," La Follette said.

"Well," E. replied, "you know that all I have in the world I have put into that factory of mine. I have told you about how proud I was of the thing. Now," he said, "this railroad lobby [people who try to influence the legislature] tells me that if I vote for that railroad taxation bill they will ruin me. . . . I can't beggar my family. I have a wife and babies." He knew that the railroads could put his factory out of business easily. They simply had to charge his competitors slightly lower rates for transporting their goods than they charged him. His goods would then cost more, and his sales would quickly vanish.

La Follette and E. talked for a long time about their duty as elected officials to protect the public interest. Then E. returned to the legislative chamber. Just before casting his vote, E. confessed to the legislator next to him, "It is a question between my honor and my bread and butter, and I propose to vote for my bread and butter." He voted against the bill.

GUIDE TO READING

Main Idea

Most progressives believed that political reform—making government more responsive to the people—paved the way to economic and social reform.

Vocabulary

- direct primary
- initiative
- referendum
- recall

Read to Find Out . . .

- the main elements of progressive reform at the state and local levels.
- the conflicting motives underlying progressive reforms.
- how progressives viewed the role of government and how they worked to eliminate corruption.
- reforms designed to help all workers, particularly women and children.

E.'s dilemma over how to vote demonstrated the clout of the railroads in 1901. The wealth and power of the railroads undermined the democratic process in Wisconsin and in many other states and cities. La Follette, however, did not give up. In 1903 he triumphed. The Wisconsin legislature passed the railroad tax hike. The choice between serving the public interest and giving in to powerful private interests, though, made life difficult for many progressives.

Political Reform

Making Government More Responsive to Citizens

Hoping to make it easier for dedicated officials like La Follette and E. to serve the public, progressives fought to end the stranglehold that the railroads and other powerful special interests had on government. Political machines, declared Kansas newspaper editor William Allen White, had to "be reduced to mere political scrap iron by the rise of the people." Most progressives agreed with White, but few agreed on how to destroy and supplant the machines and the corruption that made them powerful. Reforms in government were the first steps.

Galveston: Model of Efficiency

A hurricane helped initiate one alternative to machine politics on the city level. On September 8, 1900, driving rains and a tidal wave devastated Galveston, Texas. The storm killed 6,000 people. Almost the entire city was between 7 and 17 feet underwater.

Galveston's mayor and city council members were effective politicians but poor administrators. The task of rebuilding the city overwhelmed the weak city government. Reformers, including many Galveston business leaders, convinced the state legislature to set up a new local government to replace the large, slow-moving city council with a smaller, more centralized government. In March 1901, the legislature approved a new charter for Galveston that placed the power of the city government into the hands of five commissioners. Of the five, two were elected and three were appointed by the governor. With power centralized in just five people, the city could move quickly to clean up the damage from the storm.

Changing the type of people serving as government leaders was as important as changing the structure of city government. Four of the five commissioners were prominent local business leaders rather than Plunkitt-style politicians. They applied their experience in running businesses efficiently to the operation of Galveston's government. Under the guidance of its new

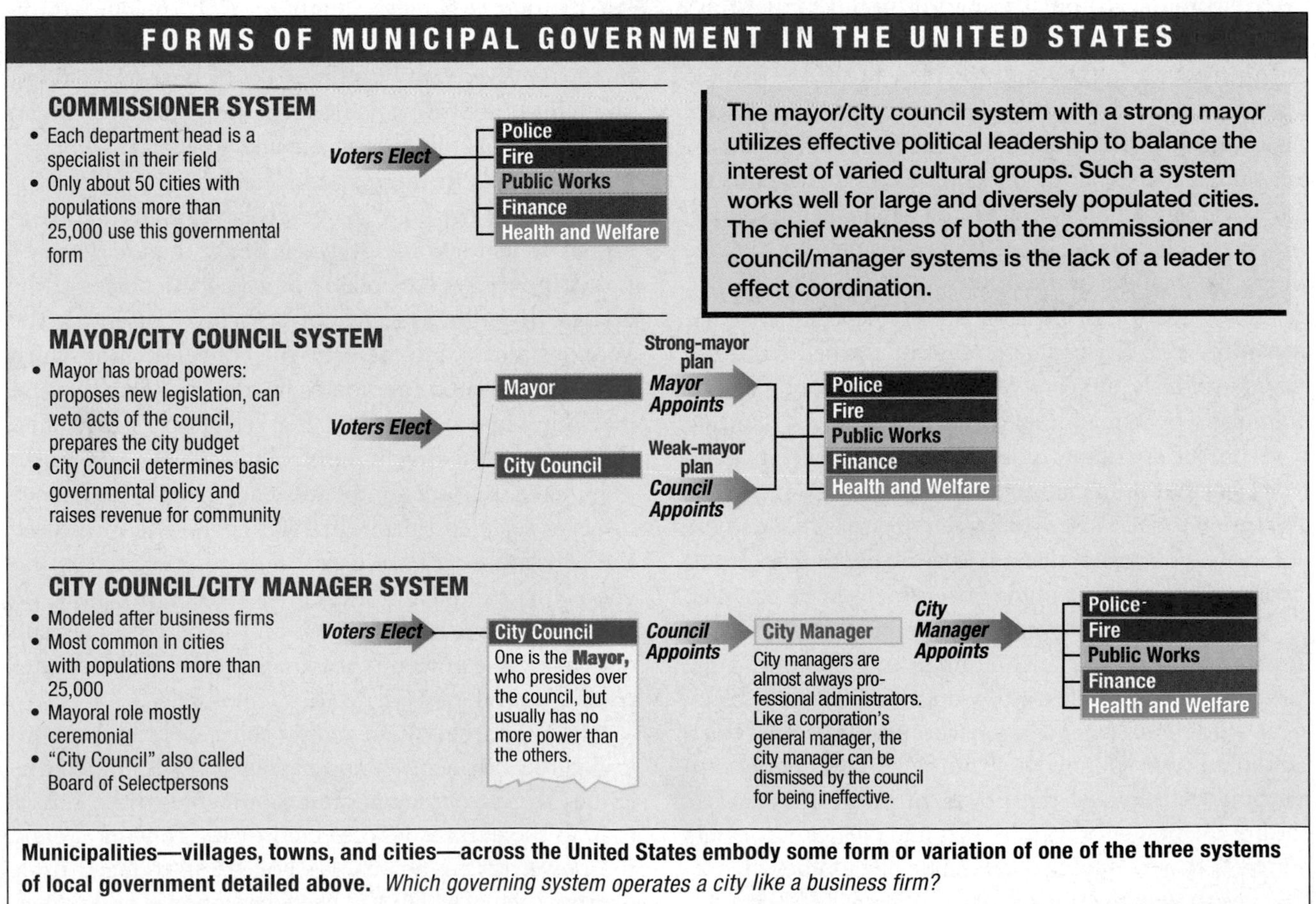

FORMS OF MUNICIPAL GOVERNMENT IN THE UNITED STATES
COMMISSIONER SYSTEM
• Each department head is a specialist in their field
• Only about 50 cities with populations more than 25,000 use this governmental form
Voters Elect
Police
Fire
Public Works
Finance
Health and Welfare
The mayor/city council system with a strong mayor utilizes effective political leadership to balance the interest of varied cultural groups. Such a system works well for large and diversely populated cities. The chief weakness of both the commissioner and council/manager systems is the lack of a leader to effect coordination.
MAYOR/CITY COUNCIL SYSTEM
• Mayor has broad powers: proposes new legislation, can veto acts of the council, prepares the city budget
• City Council determines basic governmental policy and raises revenue for community
Voters Elect
Mayor
City Council
Strong-mayor plan
Mayor Appoints
Weak-mayor plan
Council Appoints
Police
Fire
Public Works
Finance
Health and Welfare
CITY COUNCIL/CITY MANAGER SYSTEM
• Modeled after business firms
• Most common in cities with populations more than 25,000
• Mayoral role mostly ceremonial
• "City Council" also called Board of Selectpersons
Voters Elect
City Council
One is the Mayor, who presides over the council, but usually has no more power than the others.
Council Appoints
City Manager
City managers are almost always professional administrators. Like a corporation's general manager, the city manager can be dismissed by the council for being ineffective.
City Manager Appoints
Police
Fire
Public Works
Finance
Health and Welfare

Municipalities—villages, towns, and cities—across the United States embody some form or variation of one of the three systems of local government detailed above. *Which governing system operates a city like a business firm?*

STATE HISTORICAL SOCIETY OF WISCONSIN

"Fighting Bob" Robert La Follette was an eloquent spokesperson for the popular causes of his constituents. *How was La Follette able to attack the power of the political bosses?*

government, Galveston soon began to rebuild ruined buildings, to fix its destroyed streets, and to get its finances in order.

Reformers around the nation noted Galveston's quick recovery under its commissioner system. By centralizing power in the hands of a few business-oriented managers, Galveston had developed an efficient city government. Within 20 years more than 500 cities across the United States adopted a commissioner system. Another 158 cities had adopted a city-manager system in which the city council hired a professional to manage all the daily affairs of the city.

Even cities that did not adopt the commissioner system or the city-manager system learned from the example of Galveston and reduced the power of machine politicians by streamlining their government. Cutting government spending reduced the number of padded contracts that politicians could dole out to their friends. Trimming the bloated government payrolls reduced the number of jobs a politician had available to pass out as favors. These reforms made government more efficient.

In addition many cities changed their election procedures. Electing city council members at large, rather than from each ward, reduced the power of each local ward boss. Holding nonpartisan elections, in which candidates ran as individuals rather than as party representatives, reduced the power of parties. By undercutting the power of ward bosses and parties, reformers hoped that well-qualified candidates would have better chances to win elections.

Some progressives, hoping to make government more efficient, advocated reforms to undercut the machines. Others, though, supported reforms because they feared the power of immigrants and the poor. These progressives wanted to reduce the influence of immigrants and other poor people whom they blamed for causing the crime, prostitution, and disorder in the cities.

Wisconsin: Laboratory of Democracy

Many progressives believed that the solution to political corruption lay in making government more responsive to citizens. Governor Robert La Follette made Wisconsin the premier example of a state in which citizens directed and controlled their government.

La Follette was born in a two-room log cabin on a Wisconsin farm in 1855. By the time he was a student at the University of Wisconsin, he already displayed the traits that would lead him to political success. One classmate called him "the chairman of the undergraduate greeters" because of his friendly, outgoing manner. La Follette opposed with righteous indignation, however, any system by which a minority received special privileges. He felt an "overmastering sense of anger and wrong and injustice" at the gap between poor students like himself and the wealthy fraternity members.

La Follette's anger propelled him into politics. He served six years in Congress before he ran for governor. After losing two races, "Fighting Bob" finally won in 1900. Shortly after La Follette took office, one political boss swaggered into his office to cut a deal and to boast about his power over members of the legislature. "I own them," he told the newly elected governor. "They're mine!" La Follette, fiery and moralistic, refused to compromise with the boss. As he declared in his autobiography, "In legislation, *no bread* is better than *half a loaf*."

As governor, La Follette attacked the power of the bosses through a series of reforms known as the Wisconsin Idea. He opposed the conventions at which parties nominated candidates to run for office. Because machine bosses controlled the selection of delegates, the bosses effectively controlled whom the party nominated. Reform candidates had virtually no chance of being selected to run. In 1903 La Follette pressured the legislature to pass a law requiring each party to choose its candidates through a **direct primary,** an election open to all voters within the party. As a result of that law, the power to nominate and select candidates passed from the bosses to the electorate.

In Wisconsin, as in many states, bosses also controlled the introduction and passage of bills in the legislature. Legislators felt more accountable to the bosses than to the citizens who elected them. To work around the power of the bosses, La Follette introduced three reforms, each of which had been developed in other states.

ARCHIVE PHOTOS

The Bosses of the Senate **Locate the two doorways in this 1889 political cartoon by Joseph Keppler.** *How does the difference between the doors show Keppler's view of the Senate?*

The **initiative** allowed citizens to introduce a bill into the legislature and required members to take a vote on it. The **referendum** established a procedure by which voters cast ballots for or against proposed laws. The **recall** gave citizens a chance to remove an elected official from office before the person's term ended. Wisconsin adopted all three of these proposals, thereby giving citizens power to bypass or to punish machine-controlled legislators. Other states under progressive leadership followed the example of Wisconsin and instituted similar reforms.

Attacking Corruption in the Senate

Another reform La Follette and progressives favored affected the federal government: the direct election of senators. According to the United States Constitution, each state legislature elected the two senators from that state. When a powerful political machine or large trust gained control of a state legislature, it also captured two Senate seats. Then senators repaid the machine or trust with federal contracts and jobs. By the early 1900s, muckraker Charles Edward Russell charged, the Senate had become "only a chamber of butlers for industrialists and financiers."

To counter Senate corruption, progressives called for direct election of senators by the voters of each state. In 1912 Congress proposed a direct-election amendment to the Constitution. In 1913 the states ratified the Seventeenth Amendment.

Expanding Voting Rights

Some progressives tried to increase not only the influence but also the number of citizens participating in government. After an 1848 women's rights conference in Seneca Falls, New York, women began organizing to win suffrage, the right to vote. By 1890 women had won at least partial suffrage in 19 states. In most of these states, women could vote in local or state elections, but they could not vote in presidential elections. Only Wyoming and Utah gave women full voting rights.

The suffrage movement gathered momentum in the 1890s. The National American Woman Suffrage Association grew from 13,000 members in 1893 to 75,000 members in 1910. By 1912, 9 states, all west of the Mississippi River, allowed women to vote in all elections. Suffrage advocates continued to push for a constitutional amendment to grant women full voting rights in all states. They would not achieve that goal, however, until the passage of the Nineteenth Amendment in 1920.

While women fought to win the vote, African Americans struggled to regain it. Beginning in Mississippi in 1890, state after state in the South revised its constitution and laws to prevent African Americans from voting. In Louisiana, for example, more than 130,000 African Americans voted in 1896. In 1900, after changes in the constitution and the laws, the number of African Americans registered to vote there plunged to 5,320.

PHOTOGRAPHIC ARCHIVE, UNIVERSITY OF KENTUCKY LIBRARIES

Woman Suffrage Supporters In 1916 these activists from Kentucky traveled to St. Louis to urge delegates at the Democratic National Convention to support equal rights for women. *What other Americans were denied the right to vote?*

The drive to win voting rights for African Americans made little progress before 1915. African American progressives won little support from white progressives for their cause.

Economic Reform

Using Government to Protect Citizens

Progressives hoped that political reform would pave the way for economic reform. Once the political system was rescued from controlling private interests, citizens could use government to protect the public interest.

Regulating Big Business

Government regulation proved to be one means of taming powerful special interests. In Wisconsin La Follette established a state railroad commission. This group of experts, many from the University of Wisconsin, oversaw the operation of all railroads in Wisconsin. They held the power to revise, overturn, and thereby regulate rates charged by the railroads. Thus the commission prevented the railroads from unfairly overcharging small farmers whose livelihoods depended on the railroads for shipping their grain to market. Under regulation, factories could no longer bribe the railroads into giving them an unfair rate advantage over other factories in the state. La Follette declared that his goal "was not to 'smash' corporations, but to drive them out of politics, and then to treat them exactly the same as other people are treated."

Other states followed Wisconsin's lead, establishing commissions to regulate railroads, electric power companies, and gas companies. Some cities went beyond mere regulation, setting up and running utilities as part of city government.

Caring for Injured Workers

Owners and workers clashed repeatedly over issues such as how companies should treat injured workers. Factories, coal mines, and railroads were particularly dangerous places to work. In 1914 about 35,000 people died on the job; another 700,000 were injured. Companies often fired seriously injured workers because they could no longer do their jobs. In a fiercely competitive business climate, no company could afford the expense of caring for its injured workers unless all of its competitors did the same.

Articles by muckrakers and protests by unions slowly roused public anger at the irresponsibility of big business. In 1902 Maryland passed the first state law requiring employers to buy insurance that would compensate workers injured on the job. By 1916, the year that Congress passed the Workmen's Compensation Law, about two-thirds of the states required companies to have some type of workers' compensation program.

Limiting the Workday

In 1900 about one-fifth of all people working outside their homes were women. Most progressives believed that women were naturally weaker than men and thus

THE BETTMANN ARCHIVE

A Factory Tragedy **On March 25, 1911, a fire at the Triangle Shirtwaist Factory killed 146 female workers. Because the company locked the doors from the outside to prevent workers from taking breaks, many had no chance to escape. Outrage at the deaths caused New York City to pass a strict building code.** *What other laws were passed in the early 1900s to protect workers?*

more deserving of protection. Even a Tammany Hall boss, Big Tim Sullivan, worried about the ravages of work on young women: "I had seen me sister go out to work when she was only fourteen and I know we ought to help these gals by giving 'em a law which will prevent 'em from being broken down while they're still young."

In 1903 Oregon passed a law that prohibited employing women in a factory or a laundry for more than 10 hours a day. Portland laundry owner Curt Muller, fined $10 for breaking the law, challenged it. Muller, like other business owners, argued that the government had no right to interfere in a private contract between an owner and a worker. The Oregon Supreme Court disagreed with Muller and upheld the fine. Muller then appealed to the United States Supreme Court, which agreed to hear the case.

Progressives, including Florence Kelley and Josephine Goldmark of the National Consumers League, closely followed the *Muller* v. *Oregon* case. They had seen both state and federal courts strike down laws like the one passed by Oregon. If the Supreme Court upheld the Oregon law, though, similar laws in other states would also be valid.

Goldmark recruited her brother-in-law, Louis Brandeis, to defend the Oregon law. Brandeis, whose father was a Jewish immigrant from Bohemia, was a prominent Boston lawyer. Tall and wiry, with a shock of unruly hair, Brandeis earned his nickname of the "People's Lawyer" by donating his expertise to defending unions and attacking corrupt politicians.

In January 1908, Brandeis presented his brief, the statement of a client's case, to the Supreme Court. The brief included 95 pages of statistics, quotations, and other evidence collected by Goldmark showing that long hours damaged the health of women and, in effect, threatened the public interest. "The overwork of future mothers," Brandeis wrote, "thus directly attacks the welfare of the nation."

Goldmark's evidence proved persuasive. In a unanimous decision, the Supreme Court upheld the Oregon law. They agreed that a state government, to protect the public interest, had a right to regulate the work of women. After the *Muller* decision, Illinois, Virginia, Michigan, Louisiana, and other states quickly passed similar laws.

BROWN BROTHERS

A Crusading Lawyer **Louis Brandeis served as an associate justice of the United States Supreme Court from 1916 to 1939.** *What nickname did Brandeis earn and why?*

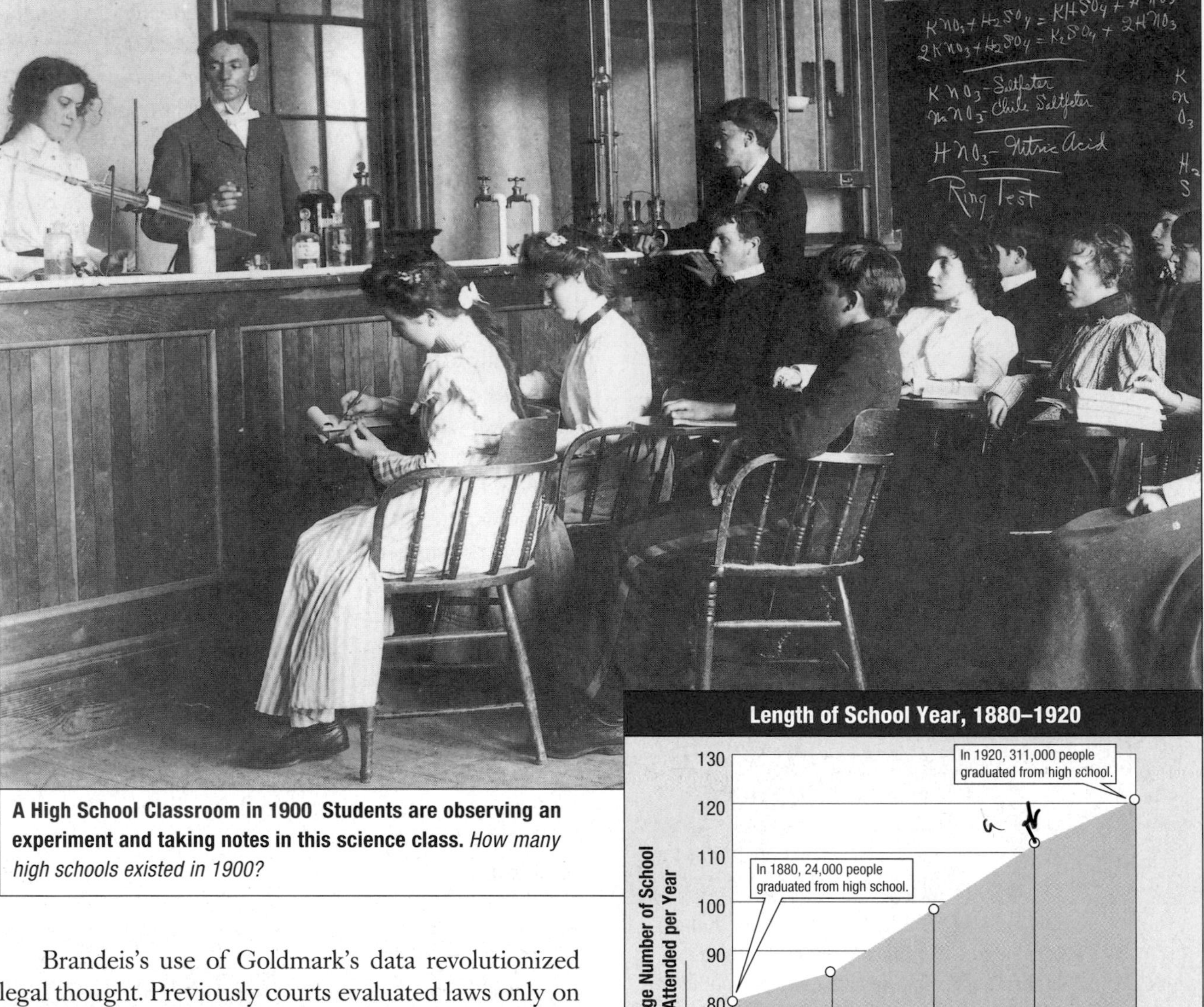

A High School Classroom in 1900 Students are observing an experiment and taking notes in this science class. *How many high schools existed in 1900?*

Progressives supported laws requiring attendance at school. *How many more days on average did students attend school in 1920 than in 1880?*

Brandeis's use of Goldmark's data revolutionized legal thought. Previously courts evaluated laws only on narrow legal grounds. Beginning with the *Muller* decision, courts considered the law's impact on people's lives. Brandeis and Goldmark won a major victory in the progressives' battle to carve out a new role for government as protector of the public interest.

Social and Moral Reform

Convincing Government to Support Children and Women

The progressives' desire to protect the public interest included a broad range of social reforms. Many reforms were designed to help children. For example, progressives supported establishing separate courts that would be sensitive to the needs and problems of juveniles. They also backed laws providing financial assistance to children in homes with no father present. One of the key progressive reforms for children was the expansion of public education.

Educating Children

During the late 1800s, state after state passed laws requiring young people to go to school. The number of schools jumped sharply. Before the Civil War, only a few hundred high schools existed across the nation. By 1900 there were 6,000 high schools; by 1920, there were 14,000. The expansion of public education then led to a sharp decline in illiteracy. In 1870 approximately 20 percent of the people in the United States were illiterate. By 1920 only 6 percent could not read.

In addition to growing, public education was changing. Philosopher John Dewey criticized schools for overemphasizing memorization of knowledge. Instead,

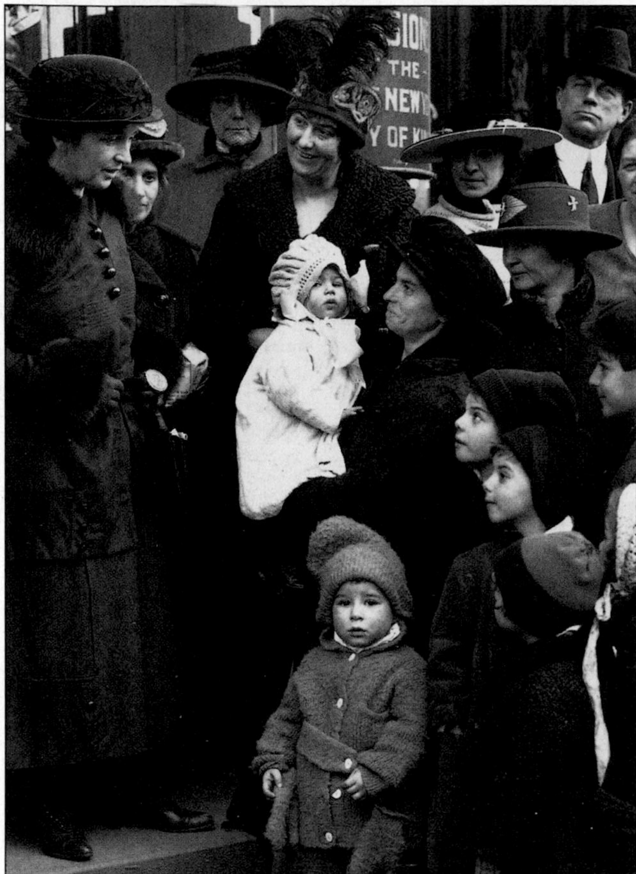

UPI/BETTMANN

Margaret Sanger **As Mrs. Margaret Sanger (left) and her sister Mrs. Ethel Byrne leave the Court of Special Sessions in Brooklyn, New York, on January 8, 1917, they are greeted by an immigrant family.** *What kind of crusade did Sanger undertake and what law did she break in the process?*

Dewey argued, schools should relate learning to the concerns of students. He felt the "true center" of a child's education was "not science, nor literature, nor history, nor geography, but the child's own social activities." Dewey wanted schools to teach students to be good citizens. "Education," he said, "is the fundamental method of social progress and reform." Most progressives agreed.

Protecting Women

Just as some progressives emphasized reforms to protect children, others focused on reforms that primarily affected women. The most controversial of these reforms was the birth control movement. A New York nurse, Margaret Sanger, had seen many women die from poorly performed abortions. In 1914 she launched a drive to inform women about ways they could prevent pregnancy. Under New York's Comstock Act of 1873, though, information describing birth control was considered obscene. Sanger was arrested almost immediately for violating the Comstock Act. Though the charges against her were dropped in 1916, Sanger faced constant opposition.

Another reform that aimed to protect women was the temperance movement, the drive to restrict or prohibit the use of alcohol. Intoxicated men sometimes beat their wives and children, and the temperance movement tried to stop the abusive behavior at the source—alcohol. By 1900, the Women's Christian Temperance Union (WCTU), founded in 1874, had almost 300,000 members. One-fourth of the United States population lived in areas with some restrictions on the sale or use of alcohol.

Frances Willard led the WCTU from 1879 until her death in 1898. She encouraged the organization to attack social ills other than the abuse of alcohol. The WCTU advocated voting rights for women, lobbied for prison reform, promoted world peace, and spoke out on various health issues. Willard's slogan was, Do everything.

The WCTU under Willard was typical of many progressive organizations. While it focused on one problem, it also supported several other reform causes. Although the problem it confronted was nationwide, the organization won its first victories on the city and state levels. In order to achieve a nationwide solution, the temperance movement, like other progressive reforms, would have to convince Congress and the President to take a more active role in social reform. The progressives needed to develop a new role for the federal government in the United States.

Section Assessment

Main Idea

1. Use a diagram like this one to show details that support the following main idea: The progressives tried to make government more responsive to citizens.

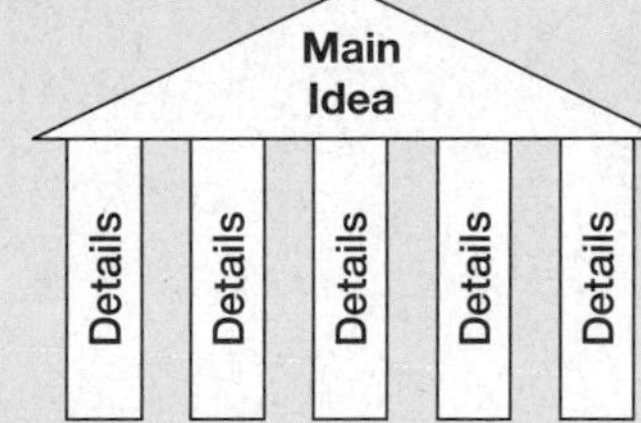

Vocabulary

2. Define: direct primary, initiative, referendum, recall.

Checking Facts

3. Explain the ruling in the case of *Muller* v. *Oregon.*
4. List reforms protecting women and children.

Critical Thinking

5. **Determining Cause and Effect** Why did the progressives think political reform had to come before economic reform?

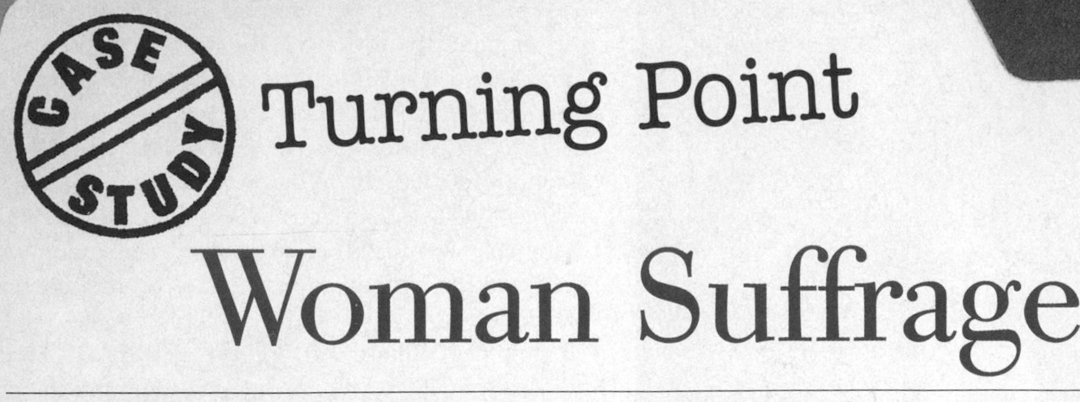

Turning Point

Woman Suffrage

SENECA FALLS WOMEN'S RIGHTS CONVENTION, JULY 19–20, 1848

MEMORANDUM

For: Concerned Women and Men

Subject: Women's Rights

A convention to discuss the social, civil and religious condition and rights of woman will be held in the Wesleyan Chapel of Seneca Falls, New York, on Wednesday and Thursday, 19th and 20th July current; commencing at 10 A.M. During the first day the meeting will be exclusively for women who are earnestly invited to attend. The public generally are invited to be present on the second day when Lucretia Mott of Philadelphia and other ladies and gentlemen will address the convention.

Advertisement
Seneca Court Courier
July 13, 1848

The Case

Elizabeth Cady Stanton and Lucretia Mott were amazed when about 300 people, including African American abolitionist Frederick Douglass among the 40 men, responded to their call to meet in a small chapel in Seneca Falls, New York, to discuss women's rights.

On the morning of Wednesday, July 19, organizers presented what one scholar calls "the single most important document of the nineteenth-century American woman's movement." By paraphrasing the Declaration of Independence of 1776, Mott, Stanton, Mary Ann McClintock, Jane Hunt, and Mott's sister Martha Wright produced a document they called a Declaration of Sentiments.

It stated:

> We hold these truths to be self-evident: that all men and women are created equal; that they are endowed by their Creator with certain inalienable rights; that among these are life, liberty, and the pursuit of happiness; that to secure these rights governments are instituted, deriving their just powers from the consent of the governed. Whenever any form of government becomes destructive of these ends, it is the right of those who suffer from it to refuse allegiance to it, and to insist upon the institution of a new government, laying its foundation on such principles, and organizing its powers in such form, as to them shall seem most likely to effect their safety and happiness.

Stanton had insisted on including in the declaration a resolution stating: "[I]t is the duty of the women of this country to secure to themselves their sacred right to the elective franchise"—a proposal considered unthinkable at the time. Even her husband, Henry Stanton, who was generally supportive of her views, was angry and embarrassed by her demand for entry into the white masculine domain of voting.

The Seneca Falls assembly unanimously adopted 11 resolutions, but Stanton's resolution on full voting rights for women—Resolution 9—met bitter resistance. Would it pass? More than that, what would happen when the convention was over?

"The family, and not th[...] been the political uni[...] family . . . has been th[...] tative of the rest. To give th[...] women would be to reject the pri[...] has thus far formed the basis of civiliz[...] government."

Historian Francis Parkman, "The Woman Question," *North American Review,* 1879

The Background

In 1776, shortly before the drafting of the Declaration of Independence, Abigail Adams wrote to her husband, John: "If particular care and attention is not paid to the ladies, we are determined to foment a rebellion, and will not hold ourselves bound by any laws in which we have no voice or representation." Her strong words went unanswered. Only New Jersey allowed women the vote in its state constitution, and the privilege was revoked in 1806. Adams's idea was not dead, but it lay dormant for some 42 years until woman suffrage was again seriously addressed—at Seneca Falls.

CULVER PICTURES

"Strange as it may seem to many, we now demand our right to vote according to the declaration of the government under which we live. . . . We have no objection to discuss the question of equality, for we feel that the weight of argument lies wholly with us, but we wish the question of equality kept distinct from the question of rights, for the proof of the one does not determine the truth of the other."

Elizabeth Cady Stanton, address delivered at Seneca Falls and Rochester, N.Y.

Seneca Falls leader Elizabeth Cady Stanton's position as a women's rights activist took shape at the 1840 World's Anti-Slavery Convention in London, England. There she began a lifelong friendship with Quaker abolitionist Lucretia Mott. When Stanton, Mott, and all other female delegates were banned from convention debate because of their sex and only allowed to listen from behind a screen, the famous abolitionist William Lloyd Garrison joined the evicted women as a nonparticipant. He declared, "After battling so many long years for the liberties of African slaves, I can take no part in a convention that strikes down the most sacred rights of all women."

As a result of their exclusion, Stanton and Mott spent much of their time together in London discussing the plight of women. They determined to organize a convention on women's rights, but, busied by other demands, they did not pursue the idea for another eight years.

Back in the United States, Stanton later joined Ernestine Rose and Paulina Wright Davis in a huge petition drive to demolish laws that forced married women to surrender everything they owned to their husbands. That campaign helped achieve passage of the Married Women's Property Act of New York

"All that distinguishes man as an intelligent and accountable being, is equally true of woman; and if that government only is just which governs by the free consent of the governed, there can be no reason in the world for denying to woman the exercise of the elective franchise, or a hand in making and administering the laws of the land."

Frederick Douglass, editorial, *North Star*, July 28, 1848

CULVER PICTURES

"The power of women is in her dependence, flowing from the consciousness of that weakness which God has given her for her protection, and which keeps her in those departments of life that form the character of individuals and of the nation."

Pastoral letter of the Congregational ministers of Massachusetts, 1837

Turning Point

in 1848, which states in part: "The real and personal property of any female who may hereafter marry, and which she shall own at the time of her marriage . . . shall not be subject to the disposal of her husband." Promotion of this act marked the first time that women had run a campaign directed specifically at furthering their own rights, and it set the stage for the Seneca Falls Convention.

U.S. POSTER COLLECTION 5084, HOOVER INSTITUTION ARCHIVES, STANFORD UNIVERSITY

Women's confidence about winning the vote increased with the victorious feeling that struck the nation at the end of World War I. This 1919 poster celebrates the passage of the Nineteenth Amendment. It was ratified by the states in 1920.

The Opinions

The opinions on the status of women excerpted on the previous page reflect the general spirit of the debate that emerged from Seneca Falls. The 1848 convention brought woman suffrage center stage. It remained a matter of fiercely divided opinion for the next 72 years.

The Outcome

The debate on suffrage divided the participants and the organizers of the Seneca Falls Convention. Stanton found support in Frederick Douglass, but many others opposed Resolution 9. Some feared that demanding suffrage at that point in time was too radical a step. Stanton's husband boycotted the convention (and even left town for the duration) because of Resolution 9. Even her dear friend Lucretia Mott told Stanton, "Thou will make us ridiculous. We must go slowly."

The convention broke temporarily and continued two weeks later in nearby Rochester, New York. There, with the influence of Stanton and Douglass, the resolution passed by a narrow margin. The demand for woman suffrage was officially added to the Declaration of Sentiments.

After the Convention As feared, the public and the press ridiculed the Seneca Falls Convention. Except for Douglass's *North Star* and Horace Greeley's *New York Tribune,* newspapers did not take the women or their meeting seriously.

The years following the convention, however, witnessed a growing number of women's meetings. These gatherings created widening public awareness of women's rights issues. For example, African American abolitionist leader Sojourner Truth attended the First National Woman's Rights Convention in Worcester, Massachusetts in 1850, and demanded the inclusion of African American women in the struggle for suffrage.

Civil War and Reconstruction When the Civil War erupted in 1861, women's rights activists put their own interests aside. Seneca Falls leaders and other women in the North worked long and hard for the Union cause. They consequently felt angry and betrayed when the Fourteenth Amendment, ratified in 1868, enfranchised African American men and omitted any reference to women. The abolitionist argument that African American male suffrage deserved precedence over women's issues resulted in a bitter rift between leaders of the woman suffrage movement and prominent abolitionists.

In the wake of the Fourteenth and Fifteenth Amendments, disagreements on how to proceed with the fight for suffrage plagued the women's rights movement. Some promoted a national amendment for woman suffrage; others promoted general reform, with suffrage in a list of demands. In 1890, however, Stanton and Susan B. Anthony merged their National Woman Suffrage Association with the rival (and more conservative) American Woman Suffrage Association, led by Lucy Stone and Julia Ward Howe. The resulting organization—the National American Woman Suffrage Association (NAWSA)—dampened the radical push for suffrage somewhat, but did restore unity to the movement.

The Twentieth Century The early years of the 1900s saw gradual advances in women's rights to education, employment, property ownership, and local election voting. Slowly the idea of women voting became slightly less terrifying or ludicrous to those in power.

Women continued to speak, march, hold meetings, and petition the government for suffrage. Finally, women's dramatic mobilization on the home front during World War I convinced many that it was wrong to withhold the vote from these citizens. One World War I era poster demanded: "We give our work, our men, our lives if need be. Will you give us the vote?"

In 1919 Congress at last voted to do just that. The states ratified the proposed amendment and it became the Nineteenth Amendment to the Constitution in 1920. That November the last surviving participant of the Seneca Falls Convention, Charlotte Woodward Pierce, voted for the President of the United States.

The Significance

The Seneca Falls Convention, though ridiculed at the time, now marks the birth of an organized women's movement for equality in the United States. The convention provided a precedent and model for women to speak publicly on their own behalf. The issues outlined in the Seneca Falls Declaration of Sentiments remained issues of concern for women well into the next century.

RESPONDING TO THE CASE

1. On passage of the 1848 Married Women's Property Act, Ernestine Rose said it was "not much . . . only for the favored few and not for the suffering many. But it was a beginning and an important step." How did the women's rights movement subsequently succeed in attracting less privileged people?

2. What impact did the Civil War years and postwar events have on the fight for woman suffrage?

3. Study the four opinions excerpted on page 259, and explain why they are said to "reflect the general spirit of the debate on woman suffrage."

4. Seneca Falls is often described as the birthplace of the woman suffrage movement. What was the turning point at that meeting?

5. Compare the original Declaration of Independence of 1776 to the adaptation for the Seneca Falls Declaration of Sentiments of 1848. Explain how language can generate enthusiasm for a cause.

PORTFOLIO PROJECT

Elizabeth Cady Stanton emerged as the leader at the Seneca Falls Convention, and she continued to be an activist for the rest of her life. Research one of the figures mentioned in this case study and write a brief biography of her or him to include in your portfolio.

Chapter  Assessment

Self-Check Quiz

Visit the *American Odyssey* Web site at americanodyssey.glencoe.com and click on ***Chapter 8—Self-Check Quiz*** to prepare for the Chapter Test.

Reviewing Key Terms

Imagine that you are a muckraker who is investigating the need for reform in your city. Use the following vocabulary words to write an article summarizing the corruption and stating your recommendations.

urbanization	**referendum**
recall	**political machine**
direct primary	**initiative**

Recalling Facts

1. Identify the major factors that contributed to the growth of cities in the late 1800s.

2. How did consumers benefit from the existence of large trusts?

3. Why did the average urban worker live on the edge of poverty?

4. How did men such as J.P. Morgan and John D. Rockefeller amass their huge fortunes?

5. How were the progressives different from the populists?

6. How did intellectuals such as Charles Beard, Mary Ritter Beard, and Lester Ward influence the thinking of the reformers?

7. Who were the muckrakers? How did the public react to Upton Sinclair's book *The Jungle*?

8. What were the principal features of the plan to rebuild Galveston?

9. What reforms did Robert La Follette bring about in Wisconsin?

10. How did progressive reforms benefit children?

Critical Thinking

1. Recognizing Ideologies Do you think progressives believed in democracy? In your answer clarify what you think democracy means. Then indicate whether the progressive view of democracy agrees with your view. Use examples from among the progressive reformers to support your answer.

2. Drawing Conclusions List and evaluate four changes caused by the growth of cities. Explain both the benefits and the costs of each change.

3. Making Generalizations Study the progressive reformers described in this chapter. Use this information to form a generalization, or true statement, about the personal background of most progressives.

4. Making Comparisons Use a diagram like this one to compare the women's suffrage movement with the African American struggle for equal rights.

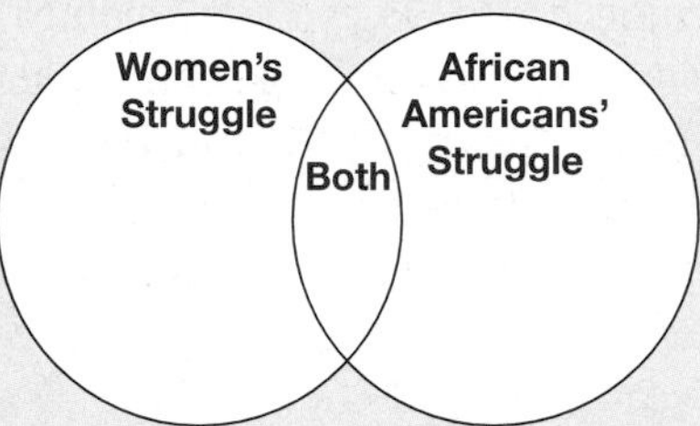

Standardized Test Practice

1. **"There would come all the way back from Europe old sausage that had been rejected, and that was moldy and white—it would be dosed with borax and glycerine, and dumped into the hoppers, and made over again for home consumption." The author of this passage is *most* likely**

   A a settlement worker.
   B a muckraker.
   C a suffragist.
   D a social scientist.

Test-Taking Tip: Identify the main problem addressed by this selection. Then recall the kind of problem that *most* concerned each of the reformers listed in the answers.

2. **All of the following were progressive reforms in the early 1900s EXCEPT**

   A passing child labor laws.
   B winning civil rights for African Americans.
   C regulating public utilities.
   D enacting workers' compensation laws.

Test-Taking Tip: This question asks you to develop a historical perspective. Think about the groups affected by the reforms—children, African Americans, consumers, workers. Which of these groups received the *least* support from progressives in the *early 1900s?*

GEOGRAPHY AND HISTORY

Manufacturing Employment, 1899

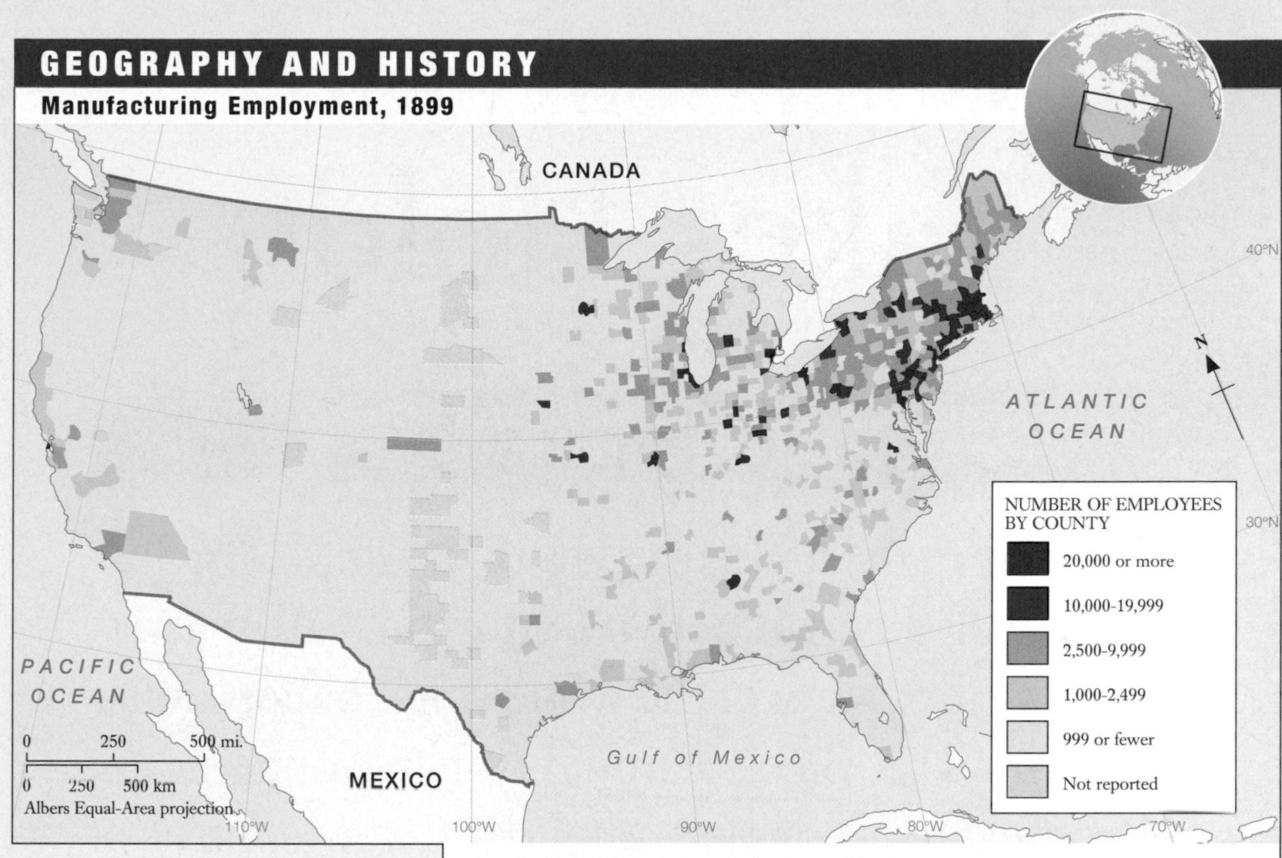

Study the map to answer the following questions:

1. Which region of the United States had the heaviest concentration of manufacturing employment?
2. In 1890 upstart Illinois passed venerable Massachusetts to take third place in the gross value of manufactured goods. It also passed Ohio to become the leader in agricultural machinery. In what direction was the center of industry shifting?
3. What areas in the West led manufacturing in 1899?
4. What correlation can you make between the growth of cities and the density of manufacturing employment?

Cooperative Learning

The progressives identified a set of problems that needed correction 100 years ago. What are the major problems facing your community today? Work with a few of your classmates to create a list for class discussion. Then, work in small groups to choose one problem and prepare to participate in a round-table discussion to explore ways of solving that problem.

Reinforcing Skills

Determining Cause and Effect

While progressive reformers worked to expose and solve social problems, politicians often showed more concern for filling their own pockets. How did politicians gain power in the cities during the Progressive Era? Why did this political power often lead to corruption?

Portfolio Project

What, in your opinion, is the major problem facing the United States today? Make a list of ways in which you could enlist people to work together to solve the problem. Choose a visual or graphic format to effectively display your ideas, and share them with your classmates. Then file your written list in your portfolio.

Technology Activity

Using E-mail Research the names of five modern organizations that have some of the same goals as the progressive reformers of the late 1800s and early 1900s. Choose one organization that interests you and make contact through E-mail to get more information about the group.

Progressivism Takes Hold

FEBRUARY 25, 1901: MORGAN CREATES THE FIRST BILLION DOLLAR CORPORATION

For J.P. Morgan, it was a day of triumph. In just 4 months of feverish activity, Morgan had masterminded the formation of the world's first billion dollar corporation, U.S. Steel. Through buying out leading steel companies, Morgan's steel trust won control of 60 percent of the nation's steel-making capacity.

For many people, though, Morgan's triumph was a frightening one. The 168,000 steelworkers, whose 12-hour days spent in dangerous mills made the steel industry so profitable, feared they would have no bargaining power with the giant new corporation. How low would Morgan drive wages? How high would he drive steel prices?

Only one institution seemed big enough to protect average citizens from Morgan: the federal government. Since the founding of the nation, however, the federal government had done far more to nurture corporations than to challenge them. In early 1901, with President McKinley in office, people had no reason to expect much change. Little did Americans realize that the role of the federal government in American life would soon change dramatically as progressives carried out their agenda. ■

HISTORY JOURNAL

After studying the cartoon on page 265, describe your impression of J.P. Morgan. How do you think the federal government could protect "average citizens" from him?

Chapter Overview

Visit the *American Odyssey* Web site at americanodyssey.glencoe.com and click on ***Chapter 9—Chapter Overview*** to preview the chapter.

CULVER PICTURES

THIS CARTOON SHOWS J.P. MORGAN ATTEMPTING TO FORM A TRUST WITH THE SUN AND PLANETS IN ORDER TO MONOPOLIZE THE LIGHT BUSINESS.

Theodore Roosevelt and the Modern Presidency

SEPTEMBER 6, 1901: PRESIDENT MCKINLEY ASSASSINATED

PRESIDENT MCKINLEY SHOOK HANDS WITH ADMIRERS AT THE PAN-AMERICAN EXHIBITION IN BUFFALO, NEW YORK, AS SECRET SERVICE DETECTIVE SAM IRELAND STOOD GUARD. Next in line to greet the President was a young man, anarchist Leon Czolgosz, who caught Ireland's eye:

> When Czolgosz came up I noticed that he was a boyish-looking fellow, with an innocent face, perfectly calm, and I also noticed that his right hand was wrapped in what appeared to be a bandage. I watched him closely, but was interrupted by the man in front of him, who held on to the President's hand an unusually long time . . . and it was necessary for me to push him along so that the others could reach the President. Just as he released the President's hand, and as the President was reaching for the hand of the assassin, there were two quick shots. Startled for a moment, I looked and saw the President draw his right hand up under his coat, straighten up, and, pressing his lips together, give Czolgosz the most scornful and contemptuous look possible to imagine.
>
> —Detective Sam Ireland, *In Our Times* by Mark Sullivan

CULVER PICTURES

McKinley's Assassin
Leon Czolgosz had a one-day trial and was executed a month later.

The doctors who came to the hospital emergency room where McKinley was taken thought the President might survive Czolgosz's attack. Despite surgery and

GUIDE TO READING

Main Idea

The activist policies of Theodore Roosevelt redefined the duties and powers of the presidency.

Vocabulary

- resource management
- holding company
- arbitration

Read to Find Out . . .

- how the background of Theodore Roosevelt shaped his actions as a politician.
- the similarities and differences in actions that Roosevelt and Taft took when each was President.

other efforts to save his life, President McKinley died 8 days later, on September 14. Czolgosz was later electrocuted, after admitting to a compulsion to kill a "great ruler."

Vice President Theodore Roosevelt was away on a hiking trip in the Adirondack Mountains at the time. He succeeded to the presidency shortly before his forty-third birthday. Upon taking the oath of office, Roosevelt became the nation's youngest President. This energetic young man soon changed the American people's idea of what the role of the President should be.

Early Political Career

Public Success, Personal Sorrow

Despite ridicule from his educated and respectable friends, Roosevelt entered politics immediately after graduating from Harvard College (and deciding against Columbia Law School) in 1880. Politics, his friends chided him, was for grasping, disreputable people, like the machine bosses whom they considered corrupt and uncultured. Roosevelt argued that "if this were so, it merely meant that the people I knew did not belong to the governing class, and that the other people did. . . . I intended to be one of the governing class." In 1881 Roosevelt showed the strength of his intention by winning election to the New York State Assembly.

He gained reelection twice before personal tragedy struck. On February 14, 1884, in a tragic coincidence, Roosevelt's young wife died in childbirth just hours after the death of his beloved mother. Emotionally shattered, Roosevelt left politics and fled New York for the Dakota Territory. There he ran a pair of cattle ranches in what he described as "a land of vast silent spaces, of lonely rivers, and of plains where the wild game stared at the passing horseman."

In 1886 after a disastrous winter demolished most of his cattle herd, Roosevelt returned to the East and to politics, his first love. For the next 12 years, he held various government positions, from civil service commissioner to assistant secretary of the navy. When the United States went to war against Spain in 1898, Roosevelt resigned and organized a group of volunteers called the Rough Riders. Their successful assault on San Juan Hill in Cuba made Roosevelt a national hero. He rode his new fame to victory in the 1898 race for governor of New York.

Roosevelt and McKinley

Balancing the Republican Ticket

When President McKinley prepared to run for reelection in 1900, he needed someone to replace Garret Hobart, his first Vice President, who had died in 1899. Roosevelt seemed a logical choice. After all, the governor of New York had earned public recognition as a war hero and was equally popular with ranchers in the West and reformers in the cities.

Basically a man of action, Roosevelt considered the vice presidency a do-nothing position leading to political oblivion. Political oblivion was exactly where New York's Republican party hoped to send the politician whose stubborn independence they found so irksome. The bosses schemed to kick Roosevelt out of New York to serve as McKinley's Vice President. After he and McKinley won the election, Roosevelt

★ ★ ★ Gallery of Presidents 

Theodore Roosevelt

1901–1909

"Our relations with the other powers of the world are important; but still more important are our relations among ourselves. Such growth in wealth, in population, and in power as this nation has seen . . . is inevitably accompanied by a like growth in the problems which are ever before every nation that rises to greatness."

Inaugural Address, March 4, 1905

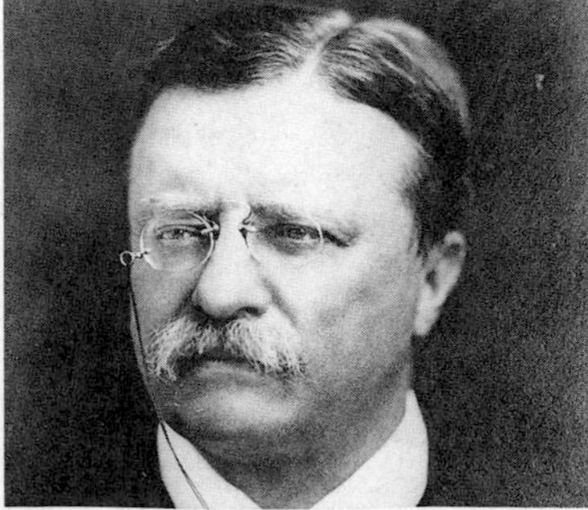

THE BETTMANN ARCHIVE

Background

- **Born 1858; Died 1919**
- **Republican, New York**
- **Elected Vice President 1900**
- **Assumed presidency 1901**
- **Elected President 1904**

Achievements in Office

- **Panama Canal begun**
- **Meat Inspection and Pure Food and Drug Acts (1906)**
- **United States Forest Service started (1905)**

HISTORY Online

Student Web Activity 9

Visit the *American Odyssey* Web site at americanodyssey.glencoe.com and click on ***Chapter 9—Student Web Activities*** for an activity relating to Teddy Roosevelt.

sadly wrote to a friend, "I do not expect to go any further in politics."

The reserved and serious McKinley provided a sharp contrast to his constantly moving Vice President. To one senator, Roosevelt resembled "a steam engine in trousers." Wherever Roosevelt went, he became the center of attention. "When Theodore attends a wedding he wants to be the bride," noted a relative, "and when he attends a funeral he wants to be the corpse."

Not all the Republican machine bosses had approved of Roosevelt. When Ohio Senator Mark Hanna heard of the Roosevelt nomination, he shouted at his allies, "Don't any of you realize that there's only one life between that madman and the Presidency?"

CULVER PICTURES

Roosevelt as Conservationist President Theodore Roosevelt and naturalist John Muir, right, survey Yosemite Valley. As a result of Muir's efforts, Yosemite became one of the nation's first national parks. *Why did Roosevelt start the Forest Service?*

Fifteen months later, that "one life" was gone. The "madman" was President. Though Roosevelt pledged to carry out McKinley's moderate policies, the new President's dramatic style transformed the presidency.

Thanks in part to his energetic speeches, Americans saw Roosevelt as a take-charge President. For his part, Roosevelt saw the presidency as a "bully pulpit" from which to preach his own ideas. The young President captivated audiences with his toothy grin, vigorous gestures, and somewhat squeaky voice.

Throughout his government career, Roosevelt supported progressive reform in strong language while in practice he pursued a more moderate course of action. In this way, Roosevelt persuaded the public that he was a reformer at the same time he reassured the business community of his basic conservatism. For example, as governor, Roosevelt had supported progressive labor legislation but repeatedly threatened to bring out armed troops to control strikers. "We Republicans," Roosevelt had written in 1896, "hold the just balance and set our faces as resolutely against the improper corporate influence on the one hand as against demagogy and mob rule on the other."

During the late 1800s, strong Congresses and relatively weak Presidents had predominated. Roosevelt reversed that tradition. As President, he employed the full powers of his office and his own personal magnetism to bypass congressional opposition. In doing so, Roosevelt became the first modern President.

Managing Natural Resources

New Ideas About the Environment

Roosevelt put his stamp on the presidency most clearly in the area of conservation. From his boyhood explorations, Roosevelt had viewed America's minerals, animals, and rugged terrain as priceless national resources. These treasures, thought Roosevelt, must be protected from greedy private developers. As President, Roosevelt eagerly assumed the role of protector. He argued that the government must distinguish "between the man who skins the land and the man who develops the country. I am going to work with, and only with, the man who develops the country."

Roosevelt quickly applied that philosophy in the dry Western states, where farmers and city dwellers competed for scarce water. To increase crop yields and to protect themselves from droughts, farmers demanded more water to expand their irrigation systems. Rapidly growing cities such as Los Angeles also thirsted for this precious resource. In 1902 Roosevelt

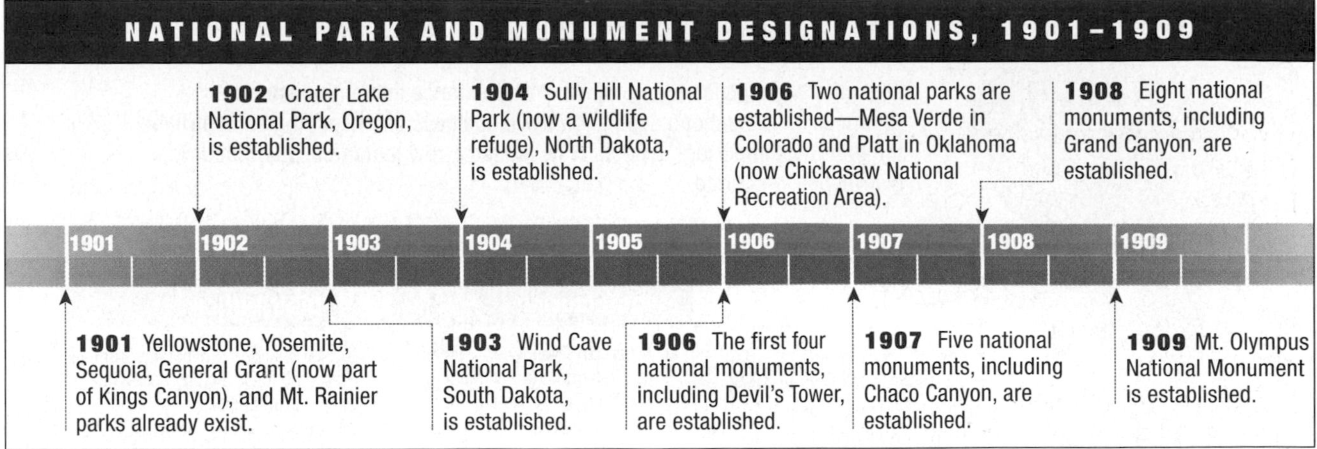

supported passage of the Newlands Reclamation Act, which authorized the use of federal funds from the sale of public lands to pay for irrigation and land development projects in the dry farms and cities of the West. Under the new law, Roosevelt supported the construction of 25 irrigation or reclamation projects.

NATIONAL PARK AND MONUMENT DESIGNATIONS, 1901–1909
1902 Crater Lake National Park, Oregon, is established.
1904 Sully Hill National Park (now a wildlife refuge), North Dakota, is established.
1906 Two national parks are established—Mesa Verde in Colorado and Platt in Oklahoma (now Chickasaw National Recreation Area).
1908 Eight national monuments, including Grand Canyon, are established.
1901
1902
1903
1904
1905
1906
1907
1908
1909
1901 Yellowstone, Yosemite, Sequoia, General Grant (now part of Kings Canyon), and Mt. Rainier parks already exist.
1903 Wind Cave National Park, South Dakota, is established.
1906 The first four national monuments, including Devil's Tower, are established.
1907 Five national monuments, including Chaco Canyon, are established.
1909 Mt. Olympus National Monument is established.

Roosevelt also backed efforts to save the nation's forests by preventing shortsighted lumbering companies from overcutting. He appointed his close friend Gifford Pinchot to head the United States Forest Service. Like Roosevelt, Pinchot was a firm believer in **resource management,** the rational scientific management of natural resources such as timber or mineral deposits.

With the President's support, Pinchot's department drew up regulations controlling lumbering on federal lands. This position satisfied neither business nor environmental interests. Business leaders, hoping to profit from unlimited cutting, criticized restrictions instituted by Pinchot as unwarranted government interference in the workings of private business. On the other hand, veteran environmental activists like John Muir of California criticized Pinchot for supporting any cutting in the few remaining unspoiled forests. They argued that forests should be kept in a completely unspoiled condition for people to enjoy.

In addition to supporting Pinchot's moderate actions in lumbering, Roosevelt took other steps to provide for the managed use of the nation's resources. He added 150 million acres to the national forests, quadrupling the amount of land they contained. Roosevelt also established 5 new national parks, created 51 federal bird reservations, and started 4 national game preserves. These solid conservation accomplishments hardly put an end to private exploitation of the country's natural treasures, but they did initiate government protection of such resources. At the very least, Roosevelt's constant championing of the causes of conservation and resource management served to place the issue on the national agenda.

Supervising Big Business

"Speak Softly and Carry a Big Stick" Does Not Apply

Other issues were already on the national agenda when Roosevelt took office. One involved the growth of large trusts—giant firms that controlled whole areas of industry by buying up all the companies with which they did business. This concentration of wealth and economic power under the control of large trusts had dramatically reshaped the American economy. Buyouts, takeovers, and mergers reached a feverish pitch between 1897 and 1903. By 1899 an elite group of 6 companies controlled about 95 percent of the railroads in the country.

Most Americans were suspicious of the trusts. By lowering prices trusts drove smaller companies out of business. They then established monopolies and were able to fix high prices without fear of competition. In 1890 Congress passed the Sherman Antitrust Act, which was designed to prohibit such monopolies, but it had proven

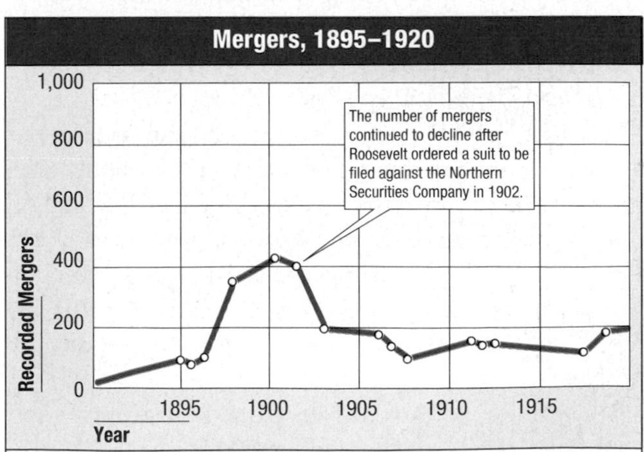

The Progressive era resembled the 1980s in terms of the large number of recorded mergers that occurred during that time. *According to the graph above, what effect did the Sherman Antitrust Act have on mergers?*

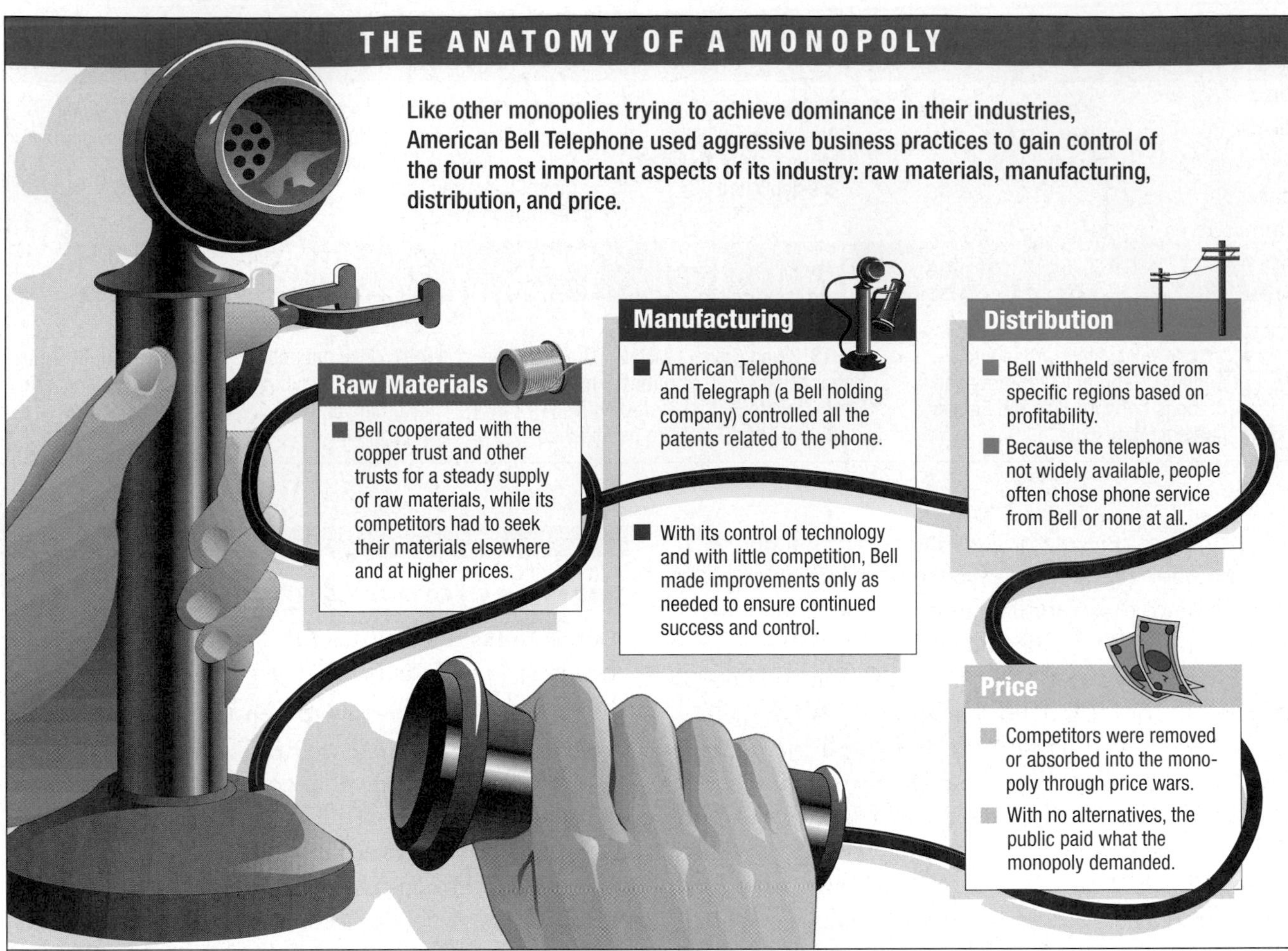

THE ANATOMY OF A MONOPOLY
Like other monopolies trying to achieve dominance in their industries, American Bell Telephone used aggressive business practices to gain control of the four most important aspects of its industry: raw materials, manufacturing, distribution, and price.
Raw Materials
Bell cooperated with the copper trust and other trusts for a steady supply of raw materials, while its competitors had to seek their materials elsewhere and at higher prices.
Manufacturing
American Telephone and Telegraph (a Bell holding company) controlled all the patents related to the phone.
With its control of technology and with little competition, Bell made improvements only as needed to ensure continued success and control.
Distribution
Bell withheld service from specific regions based on profitability.
Because the telephone was not widely available, people often chose phone service from Bell or none at all.
Price
Competitors were removed or absorbed into the monopoly through price wars.
With no alternatives, the public paid what the monopoly demanded.

American Bell Telephone was one of several large trusts and monopolies that existed at the turn of the century. Like others of his time, Alexander Graham Bell was a shrewd businessperson whose company rose to the top of a lucrative new industry. *What elements of the industry did Bell control?*

hard to enforce. Industrialists simply devised substitute methods of retaining control—for example, the **holding company.** Holding companies bought controlling interests in the stock of other companies instead of purchasing the companies outright. While the "held" companies remained separate businesses on paper, in reality the holding company controlled them.

In public Roosevelt capitalized on the widespread mistrust of the wealthy industrialists. He called them the "criminal rich," "malefactors of great wealth," and "a miracle of timid and short-sighted selfishness," yet Roosevelt avoided breaking up trusts whenever he could. "I have let up in every case," he said in describing his record of prosecuting trusts, "where I have had any possible excuse for so doing."

Cautious actions offset Roosevelt's outspoken comments. This behavior led one newspaper columnist, Finley Peter Dunne, writing in a thick Irish dialect, to summarize Roosevelt's trust policies as mixed: "On wan hand I wud stamp thim undher fut; on th' other hand not so fast."

Battling Monopolies

Roosevelt combined dramatic public relations with moderate action in 1902. J.P. Morgan, a powerful Wall Street banker, had joined with a handful of the nation's wealthiest men to finance the Northern Securities Company. This holding company combined the stock of the Union Pacific, Northern Pacific, and Burlington railroads to dominate rail service from Chicago to the Pacific Ocean. Roosevelt, deciding that the company was a monopoly in violation of the Sherman Antitrust Act, ordered his attorney general to file suit against the Northern Securities Company in 1902.

In 1904 the Supreme Court, in a 5–4 vote, sided with Roosevelt, ruling that the Northern Securities Company had indeed violated the Sherman Antitrust Act. Roosevelt declared victory, claiming it as "one of the great achievements of my administration. . . . The most powerful men in the country were held to accountability before the law."

Much of the public hailed Roosevelt as a trustbuster who challenged and defeated the most powerful financiers in the United States. The common, working people felt they had a fearless ally in the White House, one who would defend them from powerful corporations.

Despite the public praise, the Northern Securities case hardly changed the day-to-day operations of the railroads. The railroads west of Chicago continued to operate under the control of a few giant railroad firms, with little competition. None of the organizers of the trust went to jail or suffered significant financial loss for breaking the law. Instead they remained immensely powerful. Within a few months, Morgan would help Roosevelt further develop his image as a defender of the public interest.

Settling Strikes

In May 1902, the United Mine Workers (UMW) called a strike of the miners who dug the anthracite, or hard coal, that fired most of the furnaces in the United States. The UMW hoped to win a 20 percent pay increase and to reduce the miners' long workday to 8 hours, while at the same time securing the mine owners' recognition of the union. For their part, the mine owners firmly opposed a union that might force them to raise wages and improve mine safety conditions. They simply refused to negotiate with the striking workers.

The strike continued through the summer and into the fall. As the reality of a cold winter approached, the shivering public demanded a settlement. President Roosevelt stepped in and urged the union and the owners to accept **arbitration,** a settlement imposed by an outside party.

Although the UMW agreed, the owners did not. They intended to destroy the union, regardless of the public interest. One of the owners, George Baer, claimed that workers did not need a union, that they should trust the selfless, conscientious owners:

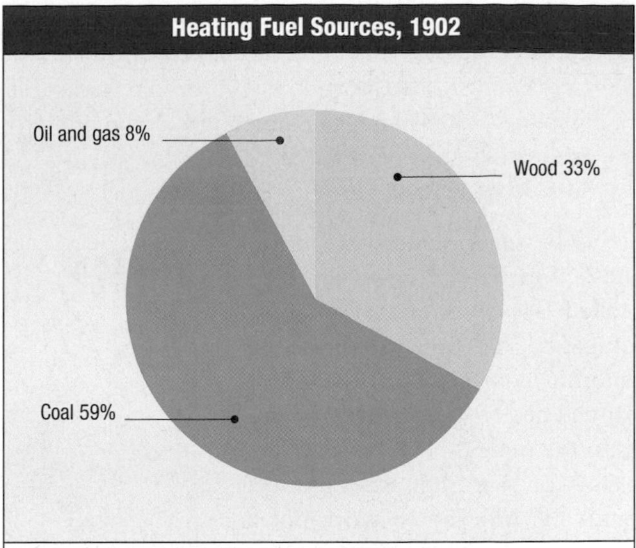

Many Americans used coal for cooking fuel as well as for heating. *How important a role did coal play as a heating resource?*

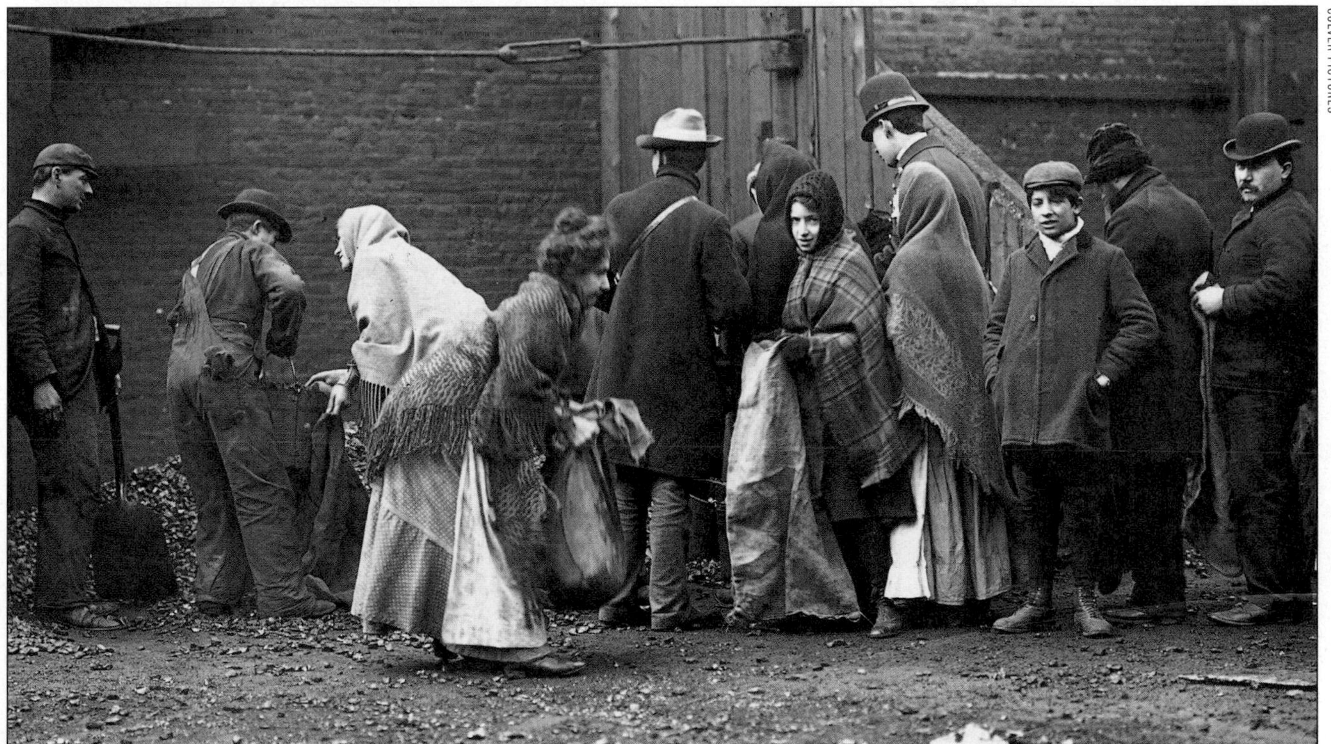

CULVER PICTURES

Coal Strike of 1902 As the coal supply dwindled during the coal strike of 1902, the lines of people fearful of facing a winter without coal grew longer. *Why did mine owners initially resist an arbitrated settlement?*

The rights and interests of the laboring man will be protected and cared for not by the labor agitators, but by the Christian men to whom God in His infinite wisdom has given the control of the property interests of the country.

—George F. Baer, *Letter to W.F. Clark*, July 17, 1902

The mine owners' stubbornness infuriated Roosevelt, who called Baer's comment "arrogant stupidity." If the owners refused to submit to arbitration, Roosevelt threatened to order federal troops into the mines. Then he sent Secretary of War Elihu Root to meet with J.P. Morgan to work out a settlement proposal. Fearing that Roosevelt would carry through on his threat and responding to the urging of the powerful Morgan, the mine owners finally accepted arbitration. The result was a compromise that gave each side part of what it had sought.

The miners won a 9-hour workday and a 10 percent pay increase, which was passed along to consumers in the form of higher coal prices. On the issue of union recognition, however, the owners won—they did not have to recognize the union.

In 1904, when Roosevelt ran for President in his own right, he coined a phrase that could have been used to describe his approach to the coal strike: "I shall see to it that every man has a square deal, no less and no more." Roosevelt saw himself standing above the battling classes, rendering to each a fair share of the spoils.

Despite the coal price hike, a relieved public felt it had been given a square deal. Americans hailed Roosevelt, whose powerful language shaped the public image of him as a fighter for their protection. Not since Abraham Lincoln had a President seemed to act so boldly on behalf of the public's interest.

THE GREAT HEALTH DRINK
Say! YOU OUGHT TO DRINK
Hires' Rootbeer
HIRES IMPROVED ROOT BEER

HIRES ROOT BEER: COURTESY OF THE PROCTER AND GAMBLE COMPANY

Buyer Beware Progressives were first to take action against false advertising claims by patent medicines and foods. *What legislation was passed to protect consumers?*

Protecting Consumers

Roosevelt also defended the public interest on consumer issues. He was President when Upton Sinclair published *The Jungle* in 1906, exposing the unsanitary practices of the meatpacking industry. *The Jungle* provoked a massive crusade. Roosevelt jumped to the head of the crusade and pushed the Meat Inspection Act through Congress.

The Meat Inspection Act of 1906 outlawed misleading labels and dangerous chemical preservatives. It also showed Roosevelt's willingness to compromise with the trusts. For example, Roosevelt agreed that the government, rather than the packers, should pay for the inspection. In addition, he dropped the requirement that meat be dated, which would have informed consumers about the meat's age.

★ ★ ★ Gallery of Presidents ★ ★ ★

William Howard Taft

1909–1913

"I have had the honor to be one of the advisers of my distinguished predecessor, and, as such, to hold up his hands in the reforms he has initiated. I should be untrue to myself, to my promises, and to the declarations of the party platform upon which I was elected to office, if I did not make the . . . enforcement of those reforms a most important feature of my administration."

Inaugural Address, March 4, 1909

THE BETTMANN ARCHIVE

Background

- **Born 1857; Died 1930**
- **Republican, Ohio**
- **Governor of the Philippines 1901–1904**
- **Secretary of War 1904–1908**
- **Chief Justice of the United States 1921–1930**

Achievements in Office

- **Postal Savings System (1910)**
- **Alaska given territorial government (1912)**

Though *The Jungle* focused specifically on meat, progressives worried about all of the foods and medicines that Americans consumed. Quack doctors sold concoctions of alcohol, cocaine, opium, and other drugs that claimed to heal everything from liver ailments to baldness. Many of these patent medicines, or nonprescription drugs, were worthless at best and addictive at worst. On the same day that Congress passed the Meat Inspection Act, it also passed the Pure Food and Drug Act. This act banned the manufacture, sale, or shipment of impure or falsely labeled food and drugs in interstate commerce. Later, in 1938, the Food and Drug Administration (FDA) was established. This agency broadly expanded the power of the federal government to protect consumers from fraudulent advertising claims by patent medicine dealers and from unsafe foods.

THE BETTMANN ARCHIVE

Taft's Style **"There is no use trying to be William Howard Taft with Roosevelt's ways," Taft said. He was happiest as a lawyer outside politics.** *What were Taft's strengths?*

Going Beyond Roosevelt

Taft Quietly Furthers Roosevelt's Work

No President had ever served more than two terms. In keeping with that tradition, Roosevelt decided not to run for reelection in 1908. Instead he chose William Howard Taft, an experienced diplomat and administrator, as his Republican successor. Taft, a large, slow-moving, but extremely intelligent man, ran a mild-mannered campaign. Thanks to Roosevelt's energetic efforts on his behalf, Taft won the election.

In office Taft repeated the pattern he had established on the campaign trail. Instead of dashing about, making fiery speeches and remaining in the public eye, Taft remained calm, quiet, and often almost unnoticeable.

Although he had none of Roosevelt's flair, Taft carried out—and went beyond—many of his predecessor's policies. In dealing with trusts, he rejected accommodation in favor of prosecution. In only four years as President, Taft prosecuted almost twice as many trusts as did Roosevelt in his nearly eight years, including two of the most powerful, Standard Oil and the American Tobacco Company.

In other areas, Taft was every bit a progressive. He expanded the number of acres of national forest. He supported laws requiring mine owners to improve safety. He established the Children's Bureau, a federal agency that protected the rights of children.

Despite all of these achievements, Taft never received the public acclaim Roosevelt did. Taft did not view the presidency as a bully pulpit. Rather, he considered it an administrative post, a job. He never had the eye for publicity that Roosevelt had. Nor did he have the ability to mobilize the nation with stirring speeches as Roosevelt had.

By 1912 Roosevelt had become upset over Taft's failure to exert strong public leadership. With a new presidential election on the horizon, Roosevelt wondered if Taft was enough of an activist to warrant his support.

Section Assessment

Main Idea

1. Use a diagram like this one to show actions taken by Roosevelt in regard to natural resources, trusts, labor, and consumers.

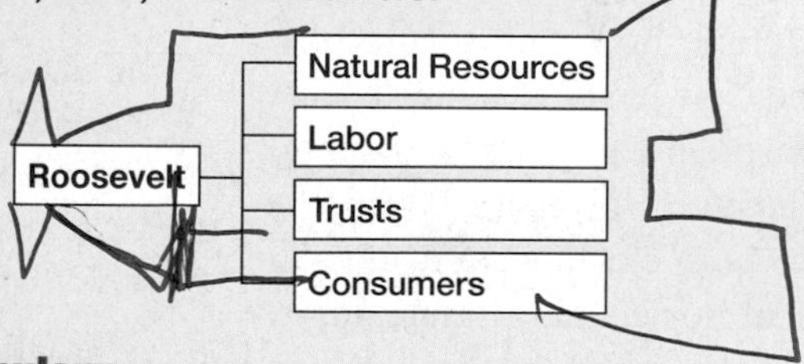

Vocabulary

2. Define: resource management, holding company, arbitration.

Checking Facts

3. Describe Roosevelt's resource-management plan. How did his background affect the plan?

4. How did Roosevelt's handling of the coal strike expand presidential power?

Critical Thinking

5. **Determining Cause and Effect** What effect did Roosevelt have on the attitude of the public toward the use of natural resources?

Woodrow Wilson and the New Freedom

SEPTEMBER 1910: BOSSES NOMINATE WILSON FOR GOVERNOR

"LOOK AT THAT MAN'S JAW!" EXCLAIMED A DELEGATE TO THE NEW JERSEY DEMOCRATIC CONVENTION UPON SEEING THE TALL, SHARPLY DRESSED WOODROW WILSON FOR THE FIRST TIME. That long, strong jaw of the just-nominated candidate for governor suggested an unbending moralist, one solidly in the progressive mold. Wilson, however, was not the candidate of New Jersey progressives; he was the handpicked choice of machine boss James Smith, Jr. The New Jersey machine backed Wilson, the popular president of Princeton University, because he was both electable and, as a political novice, nonthreatening to the entrenched machine. When Wilson rose to give his acceptance speech, however, he expressed views that neither the bosses nor the reformers expected from him:

WOODROW WILSON COLLECTION BOX 3 PRINCETON UNIVERSITY ARCHIVES. USED BY PERMISSION OF THE PRINCETON UNIVERSITY LIBRARIES

Thomas Woodrow Wilson
As an undergraduate, Wilson and his friends made a "compact" to become powerful and principled leaders.

> I shall enter upon the duties of the office of governor, if elected, with absolutely no pledge of any kind to prevent me from serving the people of the state with singleness of purpose.
>
> —Woodrow Wilson, Acceptance Speech, 1910

With these words, Wilson declared his independence from the machine. From a reformer in the delegation came the cry, "Thank God, at last, a leader has come!" "Go on, go on," other delegates shouted. Wilson went on to pledge his support for almost every progressive cause desired by New Jersey reformers, from direct election of senators

GUIDE TO READING

Main Idea

Democratic candidate Woodrow Wilson swept the presidency from the Republicans and brought his own brand of idealistic progressivism to the White House.

Vocabulary

- regulatory commission
- socialism
- capitalism

Read to Find Out . . .

- the similarities and differences among the presidential candidates in the 1912 election.
- examples of how Woodrow Wilson expanded the power of the presidency.

to the establishment of utility **regulatory commissions** to oversee the utilities' compliance with existing laws. At the end of his speech, the reformers, who had greeted him skeptically, applauded wildly. Some reformers ran up to the platform and tried to lift him to their shoulders, but Wilson would have none of that. His sponsors, figuring that the new politician was just playing to the crowd, assumed his backbone was not as strong as his jaw. They were wrong. Soon after election, Wilson began destroying the political machine that brought him to power.

Wilson's Rise to Power

From Professor to Progressive

Thomas Woodrow Wilson entered politics with a firm set of moral values that he had learned from his father, a Presbyterian minister, and his mother, the daughter of a Presbyterian minister. Wilson was born in Virginia in 1856 and grew up in Georgia and South Carolina. Although both of his parents were educated and avid readers, "Tommy" did not learn the alphabet until age 9 and could not read until age 11. Although he may have suffered from a learning disability, he persevered and became an excellent student. He attended law school, and eventually received a Ph.D. in political science from Johns Hopkins University in 1886. During his 16 years as a professor, he frequently won praise from students for his outstanding skills as a lecturer. In 1902 he was selected president of Princeton University, a post he held until he ran for governor.

When nominated, Wilson possessed no government experience. In dozens of articles and several books written during his academic career, however, he had expressed his political views. Wilson ridiculed Populists as "crude and ignorant" for their unquestioning trust in the wisdom of common citizens. He attacked Theodore Roosevelt and the Republicans for carrying political reforms to "radical lengths." The best model of government, he said, was the British system, which allowed for slow, orderly change under strong leadership from a well-educated elite. Because of his criticisms of most reformers and his praise for the British system, Wilson was generally branded a conservative rather than a progressive Democrat.

Once elected, however, Wilson proved that he was independent of the machine. Smith wanted to return to the seat he had once held in the United States Senate. Because the Seventeenth Amendment had not yet been ratified, the New Jersey legislature appointed the state's two senators. Smith, who had recruited Wilson to run for governor, expected Wilson's support in winning the

NEWARK EVENING NEWS

Boss Smith Wilson tried to dissuade Smith from running for senator and eventually backed Martine on principle. *How did Wilson's first actions as governor surprise people?*

votes of state legislators. In the Democratic primary, Smith had finished behind Thomas E. Martine. Wilson, calling machine bosses "warts upon the body politic," endorsed Martine. Without the governor's backing, an exasperated Smith and his machine lost. As one reporter put it, Wilson had "licked that gang to a frazzle."

From that battle onward, Wilson supported and won one progressive reform after another in New Jersey. He revamped election laws, established utility regulatory boards, and allowed cities to change to the commissioner form of government. To the embarrassment of the New Jersey machine, in less than two years as governor, Wilson transformed the state into a model of progressive reform.

The Election of 1912

Spoilers and Third Parties

Wilson's success in New Jersey attracted national attention. The Democratic party, which had elected only 1 President since the Civil War, needed a fresh new leader. The party met in Baltimore in June 1912, to choose its presidential nominee. The leading contenders were Wilson and Champ Clark, a Missouri representative and longtime reform activist. During a solid week of feverish politicking and 45 rounds of voting, the delegates could not reach agreement on a candidate. Finally the powerful Illinois machine threw its support to Wilson, and he won the nomination. In the 1912 election, as in 1910, Wilson owed his success to machine politicians.

BROWN BROTHERS

Socialist Candidate Debs **Eugene Debs (in the train window, wearing a bow tie) takes time out from his busy whistle-stop campaign to pose with his campaign workers.** *Why did some of Debs's supporters not vote for him?*

The Republicans

The Republicans were even more divided than the Democrats. Taft retained the support of most party officials, but few progressive Republicans stood by him. Widespread Democratic successes in the 1910 congressional elections convinced many Republicans that supporting Taft would cost them the White House in 1912. Progressive Republicans turned to the only person powerful enough to challenge an incumbent President: former President Roosevelt. Fearing that Taft was not progressive enough and that other leaders like Robert La Follette were too radical, Roosevelt entered the race. At the Republican Convention, though, Taft won the nomination.

The Bull Moose Party

Instead of quietly accepting defeat, Roosevelt bolted the Republican party. Declaring himself "fit as a bull moose," he created the Progressive party, often called the Bull Moose party. Social reformers, including Jane Addams, eagerly flocked to Roosevelt. "Roosevelt bit me and I went mad," confessed Kansas journalist William Allen White. The Progressive party platform included calls for many long-standing goals of the progressives: a minimum-wage law for women; prohibition of child labor; workers' compensation laws; a federal trade commission to regulate business and industry; woman suffrage; and initiative, referendum, and recall.

THE BETTMANN ARCHIVE

Bull Moose Paraphernalia **The Progressive party was loud, colorful, and often compared to a revival meeting.** *How did the Progressive party get its nickname?*

In addition to Wilson, Taft, and Roosevelt, Eugene Debs ran for President. Debs, leader of the American Railway Union during the Pullman strike in 1894, had run in 1908 and received about 420,000 votes. Debs believed in **socialism,** an economic theory advocating collective, or social, ownership of factories, mines, and other businesses. As a response to the problems caused by private ownership of big business, socialism gained considerable support in the United States in the early 1900s. Debs rejected the moral and economic basis of **capitalism,** in which private individuals own the means of production and profit by their ownership. If trusts did not serve the public interest, Debs passionately argued, then the government should take them over and run them. His faith in people and his energy won Debs many followers. One supporter commented, "That old man with the burning eyes actually believes that there can be such a thing as the brotherhood of man. And that's not the funniest part of it. As long as he's around I believe it myself."

Party Division The cartoon above was printed on September 4, 1912. Using political and mathematical symbols, the cartoonist reduced the election to its lowest common denominator. *Which party does each animal symbolize?*

Instead, government must be big enough and powerful enough to protect the public interest by controlling the excesses of big business. Just as La Follette in Wisconsin tamed the railroads by setting up a commission of experts to oversee their operation, so Roosevelt proposed establishing a federal regulatory commission to oversee trade practices of big businesses. He labeled that regulatory program the New Nationalism.

Wilson criticized Roosevelt's program as one that supported "regulated monopoly." If big businesses were destroying competition, Wilson argued, then government must break up big businesses. He urged that a strong federal government should dismantle—not regulate—the trusts so that small businesses could once again compete freely. Wilson referred to his program of restoring competition as the New Freedom. He

The Front-runners

Debs, despite his powerful oratory, and Taft, despite his influence as the incumbent, soon realized that they could not win. Taft recognized that many voters opposed him because they thought he lacked leadership on progressive causes. "I might as well give up," he lamented, "there are so many people in the country who don't like me." Debs attracted large crowds wherever he went, but he could not convince many of his supporters that he had a chance to win. They gave their vote instead to one of the two front-runners, Wilson or Roosevelt.

Wilson and Roosevelt agreed on many basic issues, such as the need for a stronger federal government to influence the economy, but to win votes the candidates highlighted their differences, particularly on the great question of the day—the trusts.

The Trust Issue

Roosevelt believed that trusts must be accepted and regulated. Though known as a trustbuster while President, in 1912 he maintained that breaking up the trusts was "futile madness." Big companies, Roosevelt decided, were as necessary to modern life as big factories, big stores, and big cities. He ridiculed efforts to promote competition in a trust-dominated economy as "preposterous."

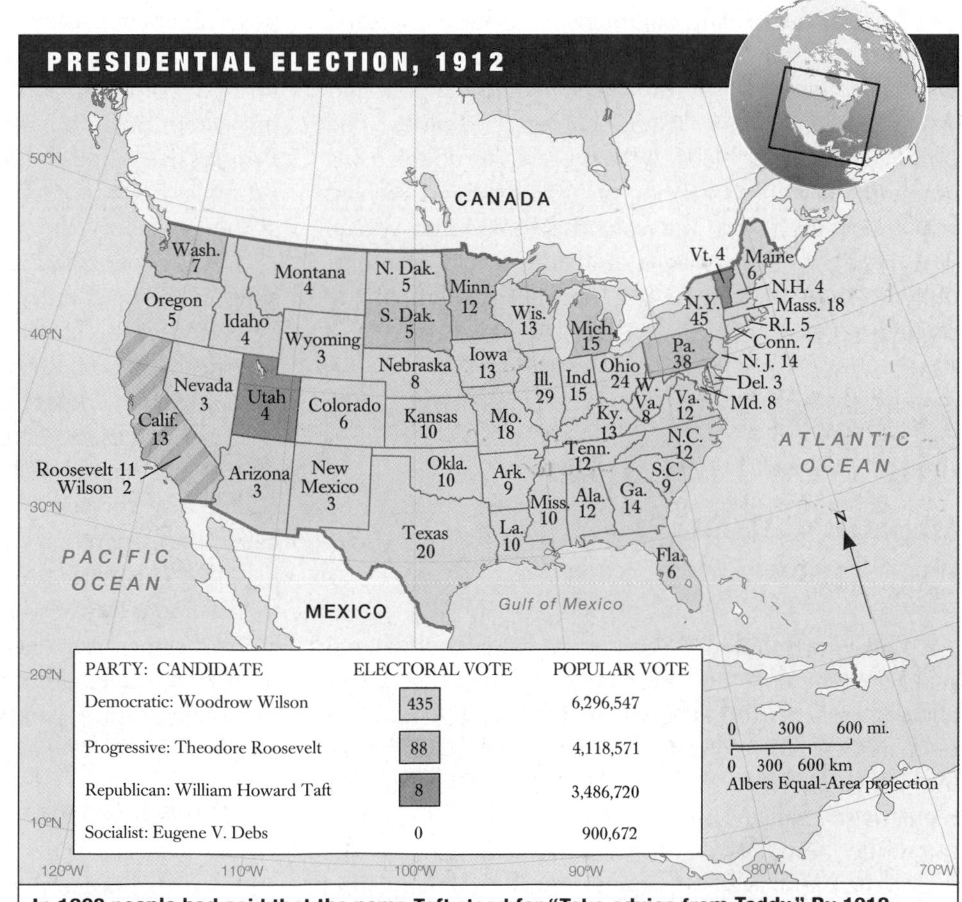

PARTY: CANDIDATE	ELECTORAL VOTE	POPULAR VOTE
Democratic: Woodrow Wilson	435	6,296,547
Progressive: Theodore Roosevelt	88	4,118,571
Republican: William Howard Taft	8	3,486,720
Socialist: Eugene V. Debs	0	900,672

In 1908 people had said that the name Taft stood for "Take advice from Teddy." By 1912, however, "Teddy" Roosevelt had abandoned the incumbent President Taft and formed a party to run against him. *Which states voted for President Taft?*

pledged to make the nation safe for aggressive young entrepreneurs once again: "What this country needs above everything else is a body of laws which will look after the men who are on the make rather than the men who are already made."

The Campaign Trail

Wilson, with a smooth, analytical speaking style honed during years of lecturing as a professor, and Roosevelt, with his energetic personality, captivated audiences wherever they spoke. Crowds of 10,000 people, straining to hear, stood and listened to hour-long speeches from each candidate. In Milwaukee on October 14, less than a month before the election, a would-be assassin shot Roosevelt as he prepared to give a speech. Slowed by his glasses case and the bulky speech still in his coat pocket, the bullet did not stop Roosevelt. "Friends," he began, "I shall have to ask you to be as quiet as possible. I do not know whether you fully understand that I have just been shot, but it takes more than that to kill a Bull Moose." He gave his speech, at times nearly fainting, before going to the hospital for treatment. Wilson, in a show of fair play, suspended his campaign until Roosevelt recovered.

The intensive campaigning and brilliant oratory, though, did not inspire the citizens. On Election Day, only 59 percent of the voters went to the polls and they seemed to follow traditional party loyalties. The only surprise was Debs, who more than doubled his vote total from 1908. Democrats united behind Wilson, while Roosevelt and Taft split the Republican voters. The result: Wilson won a landslide in the electoral college, even though he got only 42 percent of the popular vote.

The New Freedom in Operation

Wilson Increases Federal Power

Once inaugurated Wilson immediately took charge of the government. "The president is at liberty, both in law and conscience, to be as big a man as he can," Wilson had once written. "His capacity will set the limit." Two weeks into his term, Wilson became the first President to hold regularly scheduled press conferences. Allowing reporters to question him directly, Wilson knew, would make him a more powerful leader in shaping legislation. During his eight years as President, Wilson demonstrated his power as he crafted reforms affecting the tariffs, the banking system, the trusts, and the rights of workers.

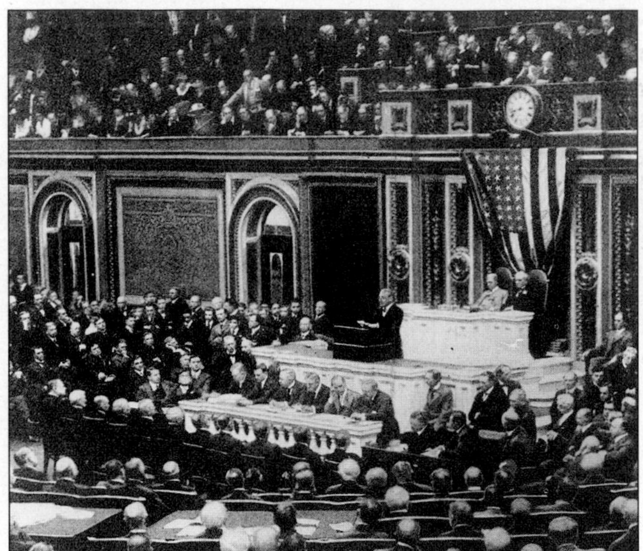

STOCK MONTAGE

Wilson in Action **Wilson broke a 113-year tradition by addressing Congress.** *What was Wilson's view of tariffs?*

Reducing Tariffs

Five weeks after taking office, Wilson appeared before Congress—something no President had done since John Adams in 1800—to present his bill to reduce tariffs. High tariffs symbolized the special treatment government accorded big business. Adding taxes to the price of imported goods protected businesses from foreign competition. The consumers paid for this protection of big business in the form of higher prices. Progressives had long attacked high tariffs as an example of how government served the special interests at the expense of the public interest.

Wilson personally lobbied members of Congress to support the tariff reduction bill. Rarely had a President, even Roosevelt, taken such an active role in promoting specific legislation. Representatives for the trusts flooded Washington to defeat the tariff reduction bill. Wilson took the offensive. Charging that the nation's capital was so full of lobbyists for big business that "a brick couldn't be thrown without hitting one of them," he called on Congress to defend "the interests of the public." In 1913, with the attention of the voting public focused on it by Wilson's charges, Congress passed and Wilson signed into law the Underwood Tariff, which reduced the average tariff on imported goods to about 30 percent of the value of the goods, or about half the tariff rate in the 1890s.

Reforming Banks

Wilson's second major legislative initiative attempted to bolster the banking industry. The United States had not had a central bank since the 1830s, when President Andrew Jackson destroyed the Second Bank of the United States. During the economic depressions

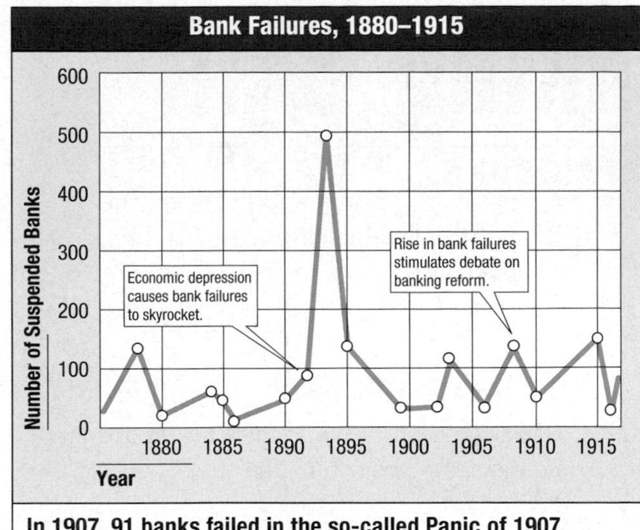

In 1907, 91 banks failed in the so-called Panic of 1907.
Which year shown on the graph saw the most bank failures?

that had hit the United States periodically over the decades that followed, hundreds of small banks went bankrupt, wiping out the life savings of many depositors. To restore public confidence in the banking system, Wilson proposed a Federal Reserve System. Banks would have to keep a portion of their deposits in a reserve bank, which would provide a financial cushion against unexpected economic downturns. Wilson reasoned fewer banks would go broke when depressions hit. A reserve system would also serve as a central bank for the entire economy, controlling interest rates and the amount of money in circulation.

Advocates of a reserve system disagreed about who should control the reserve banks. Wealthy bank presidents and industrialists argued that the big banks should control the system because they had the expertise. Many progressives favored a government regulatory agency directly controlled by the President and Congress and thereby responsive to the public. Wilson proposed a compromise system composed of 12 regional banks that a board appointed by the President would oversee. Congress approved Wilson's proposal at the end of 1913, creating the Federal Reserve System.

Regulating Trusts

As President, Wilson vowed to break up the trusts. In 1914 Congress passed the Clayton Antitrust Act, which broadened the Sherman Antitrust Act of 1890. For example, the Clayton Act prohibited interlocking directorates, which had allowed companies to work together to reduce competition. The Clayton Act also made corporate officers personally responsible for violations of antitrust laws.

Wilson also backed efforts to regulate trusts. In 1914 Congress established the Federal Trade Commission (FTC), which attempted to stop unfair trading and business practices. For example, the FTC could prevent companies from working together in order to keep prices high. Fair trade, Wilson hoped, would help small companies compete with larger companies.

Protecting Workers

As President, Wilson supported a variety of progressive federal labor laws. For example, in 1916, Wilson signed the first federal law regulating the use of children as workers in factories and mines. The Supreme Court struck down the law in 1918, however, claiming that whether or not children could work was a matter for the state courts.

Wilson also supported laws that required all federally contracted companies to provide their workers with compensation for injuries on the job. These laws greatly increased federal protection of workers.

During his presidency Wilson built upon Roosevelt's foundation. He expanded the role of the federal government and of the President. Like Roosevelt, Wilson saw himself as a crusader, using federal power to protect common citizens. In Wilson's view (and that of most progressives), however, the common citizens were white, native-born, and capitalists. Other Americans, such as African Americans, immigrants, and socialists, often suffered during the Progressive era.

Section Assessment

Main Idea

1. Use a diagram like this one to show the steps that led Woodrow Wilson to the White House. Modify the number of steps as necessary.

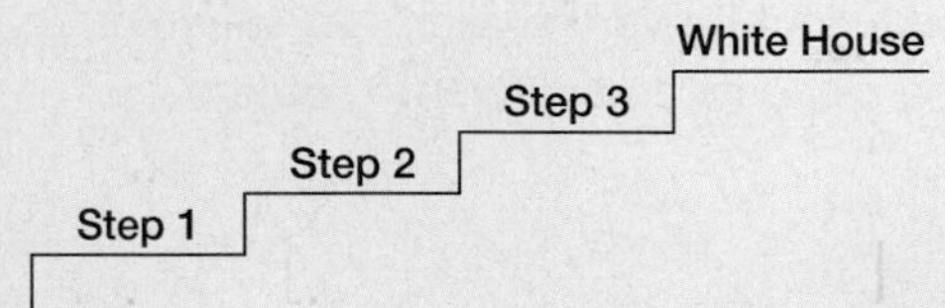

Vocabulary

2. Define: regulatory commission, socialism, capitalism.

Checking Facts

3. How did Wilson show his independence as governor? How did this independence shape his presidency?
4. How was the Clayton Antitrust Act an example of expanding presidential power?

Critical Thinking

5. **Making Generalizations** Based on the actions of Roosevelt, Taft, and Wilson, what statement can you make about the value of public relations to politicians?

Critical Thinking Skill

MAKING COMPARISONS

Learning the Skill

When you make comparisons, you determine similarities and differences between ideas, events, or objects. Knowing how to make comparisons helps you to understand the differing points of view voiced by the groups or individuals that shape history. For example, environmentalists may advocate the preservation of national parks as a necessary and beneficial government action; the logging industry may oppose the same preservation issue as government interference in the pursuit of their business. Comparing the positions can clarify an issue.

Making comparisons can help you organize information in your writing or thinking. It is also a citizenship skill that will help you choose between alternative candidates or policies.

The Process

Follow these steps to make comparisons:

a. Identify or decide what will be compared.

b. Determine a common area or areas in which comparisons can be drawn, such as positions on a certain issue, reactions to a certain event, goals of certain groups, and so on.

c. Look for similarities and differences within these areas. For example, two politicians' positions on labor rights might be very similar, very different, or similar in some respects and different in others.

d. If possible, find information that explains the similarities and differences.

Practicing the Skill

1. Using the chart below, identify the groups that share the same position on the strike.

2. Do those groups have the same reasons for their positions? Explain.

3. On what common grounds can you compare the various groups?

4. Which two groups' positions and reasons conflict the most?

5. Which point of view is probably most similar to that of the United Mine Workers?

Applying the Skill

Take an opinion poll among your classmates about a current issue in the news. Summarize the opinions and write a paragraph comparing the results. What reasons could explain any differences or similarities?

The **Glencoe Skillbuilder Interactive Workbook, Level 2** CD-ROM provides more practice in key social studies skills.

COMPARISON CHART

Who?	Position on the Coal Strike of 1902	Why?
United Mine Workers	Supports	They originated the strike, seeking an 8-hour workday and recognition of their union.
Mine owners	Oppose	They believe workers' demands are excessive and want to crush the union, keeping the industry free of regulation.
Coal-consuming public	Opposes	They suffer from the coal shortages and high prices that the strike engenders.
President Roosevelt	Officially neutral	He wants to halt the strike, but thinks owners are too selfish.
IWW	Supports	While not agreeing with the UMW on everything, the IWW promotes solidarity with all workers.

Limits to Progressivism

NOVEMBER 1914: AFRICAN AMERICAN ACTIVIST CHALLENGES WILSON

"TWO YEARS AGO YOU WERE THOUGHT TO BE A SECOND LINCOLN," WILLIAM MONROE TROTTER ANGRILY REMINDED PRESIDENT WILSON. Trotter, the outspoken editor of the Boston newspaper the *Guardian,* and four other African American leaders were meeting with Wilson to protest the segregation of African American and white workers in federal offices in Washington, D.C. These offices had been integrated for almost 50 years, since the end of the Civil War, and now thc President had tried to change that. Wilson agreed to meet with the African American delegation, but he had little sympathy for their complaints. After nearly an hour of tense discussion, an exasperated Trotter challenged President Wilson, "Have you a New Freedom for white Americans and a new slavery for 'your Afro-American fellow citizens'? God forbid!"

PHOTOGRAPHS AND PRINTS DIVISION, SCHOMBURG CENTER FOR RESEARCH IN BLACK CULTURE, NEW YORK PUBLIC LIBRARY, ASTOR, LENOX AND TILDEN FOUNDATIONS.

William Monroe Trotter
In 1901 Trotter founded the *Guardian,* which reached a circulation of 2,500 within 8 months.

Wilson resented anyone challenging his authority, particularly a defiant African American. "You have spoiled the whole cause for which you came!" barked Wilson, as he pointed to the door. The meeting was over, and the five men exited. Though unsuccessful in changing Wilson's policy, Trotter's final question did make his objective clear: he wanted progressives to address the needs of African Americans as well as white Americans.

Few white progressives thought to challenge the racism rampant in American society because they themselves had deeply negative attitudes toward all minority groups. As a result African Americans found themselves ignored by the mainstream of the Progressive movement. Two other groups—immigrants and radical workers—also found themselves battling progressives on many issues.

GUIDE TO READING

Main Idea

The progressive movement fell short of its lofty idealism when it came to the African Americans, immigrants, and radical workers who struggled for justice largely on their own.

Vocabulary

- accommodation
- melting pot
- nativism
- eugenics

Read to Find Out . . .

- the obstacles to and shortcomings of the Progressive movement.
- what areas of conflict existed between progressives and immigrants.
- the relationship between progressives and workers.

CULVER PICTURES

BROWN BROTHERS

Washington's Successes **Booker T. Washington (with Roosevelt, upper right) was the first African American invited to the White House for dinner. As founder and president of Tuskegee Institute (a vocational school, the print shop of which is shown above), Washington was the most admired African American leader in the beginning of the 1900s.** *What did Washington and his school promote?*

African Americans and Equality

"Jim Crow" Entrenched

For African Americans, continuing poverty and discrimination marked the Progressive era. About two-thirds of African Americans scratched out livings in the rural South. Most were sharecroppers, farmers who traded a share of their crop in return for land to plant and money to buy seeds and tools. Sharecroppers generally found that the tobacco or cotton they raised barely covered their rent and the money they had borrowed, so they were almost always in debt.

African Americans who could leave their farms joined the flood of rural people moving to cities in search of opportunity. Though most went to Southern cities, an increasing number headed north, hoping to escape racism. In Northern cities, though, African Americans found much of the same discrimination and segregation that they had experienced in the South. In addition, in the North, African Americans competed with immigrants for jobs. This competition created tension and sometimes violence between the two groups.

In both the North and the South, segregation was a matter of custom. Beginning in the 1880s, however, Southern states and cities started passing laws requiring racial segregation. Taking their name from a character in an old minstrel song, the Jim Crow laws required, for example, that trains have separate cars for African American and white passengers. They also mandated segregation in hotels, restaurants, parks, and every facility open to the public. Atlanta even required separate Bibles for African Americans and whites to swear upon when called as witnesses in court cases. In 1896, in *Plessy* v. *Ferguson,* the Supreme Court ruled that separate, segregated facilities were constitutional as long as they were equal. The only dissenter in the "separate but equal" decision was Justice John Harlan, a Southerner and former slaveholder. "Our Constitution is color-blind," protested Harlan fruitlessly.

Despite the requirements of the courts that separate facilities must be equal, they rarely if ever were. African American children received a second-class education compared to what white children received. For example, in 1900 in Adams County, Mississippi, the school system spent $22.25 per white student and only $2 per African American student.

Accommodating Racism

Leading one African American response to racism in the Progressive era was Booker T. Washington. The son of enslaved parents, Washington grew up in a log cabin with a dirt floor. He worked as a janitor to pay his way through Hampton Institute, a federally funded school in Virginia in 1868 established to educate African Americans freed from slavery. In 1881 the state of Alabama hired the mild-mannered but ambitious 25-year-old Washington to open a vocational school for African Americans in Tuskegee. Over the next 33 years, Washington molded Tuskegee Institute into a nationally prominent school where African American students could learn 38 trades and professions, including farming, forestry, plumbing, sewing, and nursing.

Washington believed that African Americans could achieve economic prosperity, independence, and the respect of whites through hard work as farmers, craft workers, and laborers. By succeeding at such jobs, African Americans would become valuable members of their communities without posing a threat to whites. Publicly Washington urged African Americans to bend to white racism by accepting without challenge Jim Crow laws, voting restrictions, and less desirable jobs. This policy, known as **accommodation,** emphasized economic success over racial equality.

Many African Americans, particularly poor farmers, agreed with Washington. Struggling to escape poverty, they believed that economic gains were more important than winning the vote, ending segregation, or directly challenging white domination.

ARCHIVE PHOTOS

William Edward Burghardt Du Bois Both Du Bois and Trotter opposed Washington's views. *What idea did Du Bois reject?*

Agitating for Equality

In spite of Washington's popularity, many African Americans opposed Washington's apparently meek acceptance of humiliating discrimination. The leading opponent of accommodation was W.E.B. Du Bois. Born in 1868 and raised in a free African American family in Massachusetts, Du Bois became the first African American to receive a Ph.D. from Harvard University. He taught history and social science at Atlanta University before helping found the National Association for the Advancement of Colored People (NAACP) in 1909. He served as that organization's director of publications for 24 years.

A proud and strong-willed man, Du Bois summoned African Americans to demand equality at once. "The way for a people to gain their reasonable rights," he pointed out, "is not by voluntarily throwing them away." Du Bois argued that the key to winning equality was not in developing vocational skills but in voting. With the vote African Americans would gain the political influence to end lynchings, to provide better schools for their children, and, in general, to challenge the white domination of society.

Reacting to African Americans

Most white people, including most progressives, ignored or actively opposed the efforts of Du Bois, Washington, and other African Americans to achieve equality. Many agreed with Theodore Roosevelt, who confided to a friend, "Now as to the Negroes! I entirely agree with you that as a race and in the mass [they] are : inferior to the whites."

Some progressives—usually women—d African American reformers. Jane Addams, fc criticized racial discrimination and helped o NAACP. The alliance between white female reformers and African Americans reached back to the 1830s. Many white women continued to identify with the cause for racial equality because, like themselves, African Americans were caught in a web of discrimination.

Among sympathetic whites, Washington's ideas were more acceptable than those of Du Bois because Washington did not directly challenge white social and political domination. These people might have been less supportive had they known that Washington privately supported many of the same goals as Du Bois. He quietly provided money to pay for court cases challenging Jim Crow laws, to win back voting rights for African Americans, and to support antilynching campaigns.

The activism of Washington, Du Bois, and other African Americans led to some advances in spite of the lack of support from progressives. For example, the African American illiteracy rate was cut in half between 1900 and 1910, and the number of African Americans owning land increased by 10 percent.

Immigrants and the Melting Pot

American Anxiety Comes to a Boil

Like African Americans, immigrants struggled to find their place in American society. After the flood of newcomers from eastern and southern Europe between 1890 and 1914, immigrants and their children constituted about one-third of the American population. The United States became even more of a **melting pot**—a society in which various racial, ethnic, and cultural groups were blended together—than it had been before 1890. Each immigrant went through the assimilation process of absorbing a new culture. For most the first steps in assimilating the culture of the United States, or

Americanization, were learning English and understanding the laws and system of government of the United States.

Americanizing the Newcomers

Few progressives valued the cultural diversity that immigrants brought to the United States. Most, like Theodore Roosevelt, considered the cultures of all immigrant groups inferior to the culture of the United States. Americanization, to Roosevelt, was a process of stripping away an immigrant's old habits and replacing them with new, American ones. With his usual confidence, Roosevelt had no doubt that the American melting pot could assimilate as many European immigrants as wished to come to the United States.

Not everyone shared Roosevelt's optimism about the melting pot. Among those who feared that the flood of immigrants was destroying American culture were some progressives, as well as advocates of **nativism,** a policy of favoring native-born individuals over foreign-born ones.

Many nativists were Protestants who opposed immigration because of the large number of Roman Catholics, Eastern Orthodox Christians, and Jews who arrived between 1890 and 1920. As the chart on this page shows, the Protestant domination of the United States was facing a challenge. Other nativists feared that radical immigrants, though few in number, would undermine the economic system and the government of the United States.

Opposition to immigration existed throughout society. Woodrow Wilson, while a professor at Princeton, complained that countries such as Hungary and Poland were "disburdening themselves of the more sordid and hapless elements of their population." A sign in a restaurant in California read: "John's Restaurant. Pure American. No Rats. No Greeks." Job advertisements often included a footnote, "No Irish Need Apply."

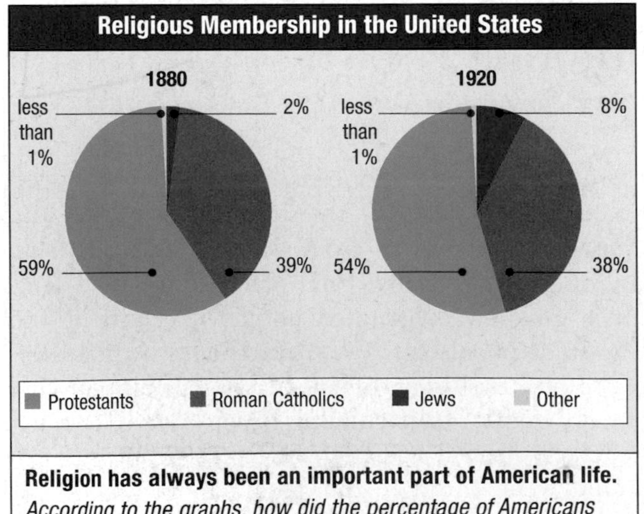

Religion has always been an important part of American life. *According to the graphs, how did the percentage of Americans who were Catholics and Jews change?*

Some opponents of immigration claimed to have scientific evidence proving that some racial or ethnic groups were superior to others. In particular they asserted that the Anglo-Saxon and Nordic peoples of northern and western Europe were smarter, stronger, and more moral than the Slavs and Mediterranean peoples of southern and eastern Europe. Jews, African Americans, and Asians, they claimed, were even more inferior. Based on these mistaken beliefs, some people advocated a **eugenics** movement, an effort to improve the human race by controlling breeding. The eugenics movement successfully convinced some state legislatures to allow forced sterilization of criminals and individuals who were diagnosed as having severe mental disabilities.

Imposing Restrictions

Nativists had begun calling for sweeping restrictions on immigration in the late 1840s. At that time about 150,000 Roman Catholics from Ireland were entering the United States each year because of a disastrous famine in their homeland.

As immigration swelled after 1880, reaching more than 1 million immigrants a year by 1905, the call for restriction became a loud chorus. The federal government began limiting Chinese immigration in 1882. In 1903 Congress prohibited individuals "dangerous to the public welfare," meaning political radicals, from immigrating. In 1907 Roosevelt worked out a "gentlemen's agreement" with Japan whereby the Japanese government limited the number of Japanese allowed to leave for the United States. All of these restrictions were targeted at specific groups. Still many Americans wanted much broader restrictions that would dramatically limit immigration from southern and eastern Europe.

In 1907, in response to the concerns of nativists, Congress established a commission to study how well immigrants were assimilating into American life. In its report issued in 1911, the Dillingham Commission concluded that the new immigrants from eastern and southern Europe were not assimilating as well as the older immigrants from western and northern Europe and that they never would. Hence, the commission recommended, Congress should restrict immigration, especially from eastern and southern Europe.

Some labor unions also called for immigration restrictions, hoping that a reduction in the number of people looking for work would help push wages upward. Ironically many labor union members were themselves recent immigrants.

Under these combined pressures, Congress adopted a wide-ranging restriction on immigration in 1917. This law refused entry to immigrants over the age of 16 who

BROWN BROTHERS

Closing the Door Behind Them Forgetting they were once immigrants themselves, many Americans demanded immigration restrictions. *What were some of the fears of those opposed to open immigration?*

could not pass a literacy test. Because schooling was limited in southern and eastern Europe, the literacy requirement affected immigration from these areas most sharply. More severe restrictions would come in the 1920s. (See Case Study, pages 404–407.)

Responding to Nativism

In a climate of restrictions and nativism, many immigrants relied upon one another for support. They formed mutual assistance societies, organizations that provided care for the sick and paid for funerals for members who died. Virtually every immigrant group had its own newspapers, its own athletic and social clubs, and its own theater groups. In many immigrant communities, churches and synagogues became centers of social as well as religious activity. There, new arrivals could meet people who spoke the same language and understood their customs.

Though old, ethnic hostilities frequently kept immigrant groups divided, they sometimes joined together for political battles, often in opposition to progressive reforms. For example, many immigrants supported the urban political machines that progressives tended to attack. Some poverty-stricken immigrant families who relied on the labor of their children to help them buy food and pay their rent opposed progressives who wanted to ban child labor. Immigrants from cultures in which drinking wine or beer was a traditional social behavior often resented progressives who advocated temperance. These conflicts over economic, social, and political issues increased tensions between immigrants and progressives.

Workers and Radicals

Progressives Uneasy as Unions Gain Strength

Progressives also had tense relationships with many labor unions and were deeply opposed to radical labor leaders and ideologies. On one hand progressives sympathized with workers in factories, mines, and mills who suffered from low wages, dangerous working conditions, and the constant threat of unemployment. Most progressives recognized that workers needed protection. On the other hand, progressives firmly supported capitalism and rejected all other economic systems. Most were horrified by socialists such as Eugene Debs, who argued that workers or the government should own the factories and operate them in the public interest.

Supporting Unions

Among progressives, the strongest advocates of unions were those who had the most contact with laboring people—the settlement house reformers. Jane Addams and others saw how unions won fairer wages, safer working conditions, and greater job stability for workers.

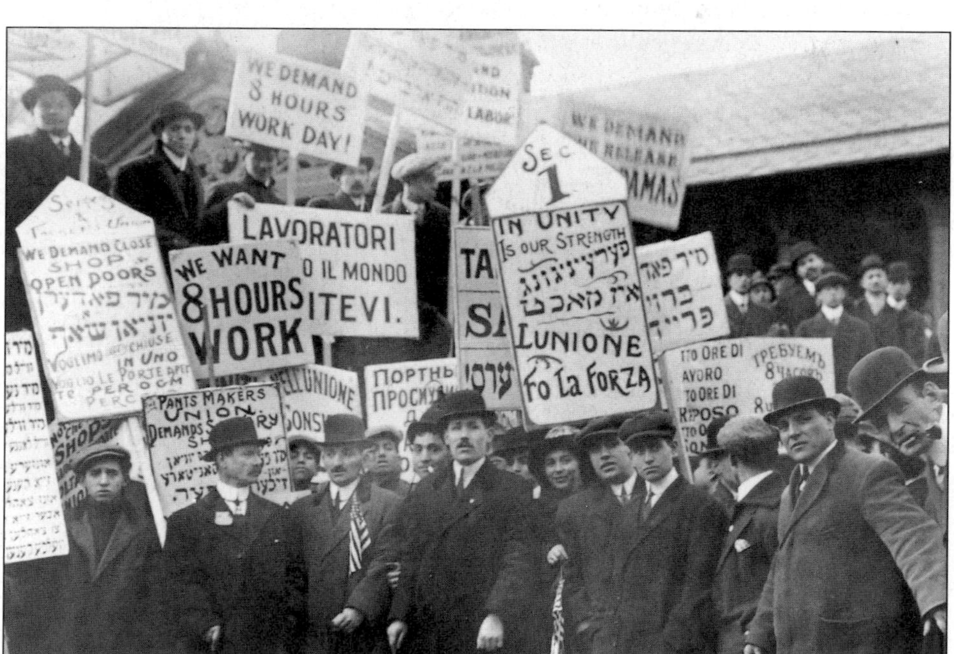

BROWN BROTHERS

United in Labor These picketers at a New York garment workers' strike carry signs in English, Greek, Yiddish, and Italian. *Why did some progressives dislike labor unions?*

In addition to backing unions, many progressives supported political reforms advocated by labor unions, such as limits on the length of the workday, a minimum wage for women, and an end to child labor. The largest labor organization was the American Federation of Labor (AFL), a coalition of unions that represented about 1.5 million workers by 1904. While the AFL called for these reforms, it trusted government less than did many progressives. The AFL realized that a government that could grant such reforms could also revoke them. The best protection for a worker, according to the AFL, was a strong union capable of negotiating with the owners.

AFL leaders also distrusted the government because they had frequently seen government side with owners to break strikes and crush unions. State governors or the President often sent in troops to reopen a plant shut down by striking workers. At other times courts ended strikes by declaring them illegal under the Sherman Antitrust Act, which banned all actions that restrained trade. Although this act was written to break up business monopolies, the courts used it to crack down on unions. Owners who knew that the courts or the troops would end a strike for them had almost no reason to negotiate with unions. Without that ability to strike, unions had little power.

Challenging Capitalism

Unions often included some socialists as members. While they envisioned radical changes in the long term, socialists often worked for short-term reforms that improved the lives of workers. They generally supported stronger unions that could fight for higher wages, shorter hours, and better working conditions. Socialists also called for public ownership of railroads, trolley lines, and utilities such as water and electricity. Most supported the right of women to vote.

Though the progressives shared many of the short-term goals of the socialists, the two groups analyzed problems differently and came up with different solutions. For example, when progressives saw a problem, such as the high number of workers killed on the job, they blamed insensitive owners and supported a factory safety law to solve the problem. Socialists seeing the same problem blamed the capitalist system of competition that forced owners to require workers to risk their lives so that the company could remain in business. Even if a law improved workplace safety, argued the socialists, the problems of workers would not go away until the competitive system that caused them was eliminated.

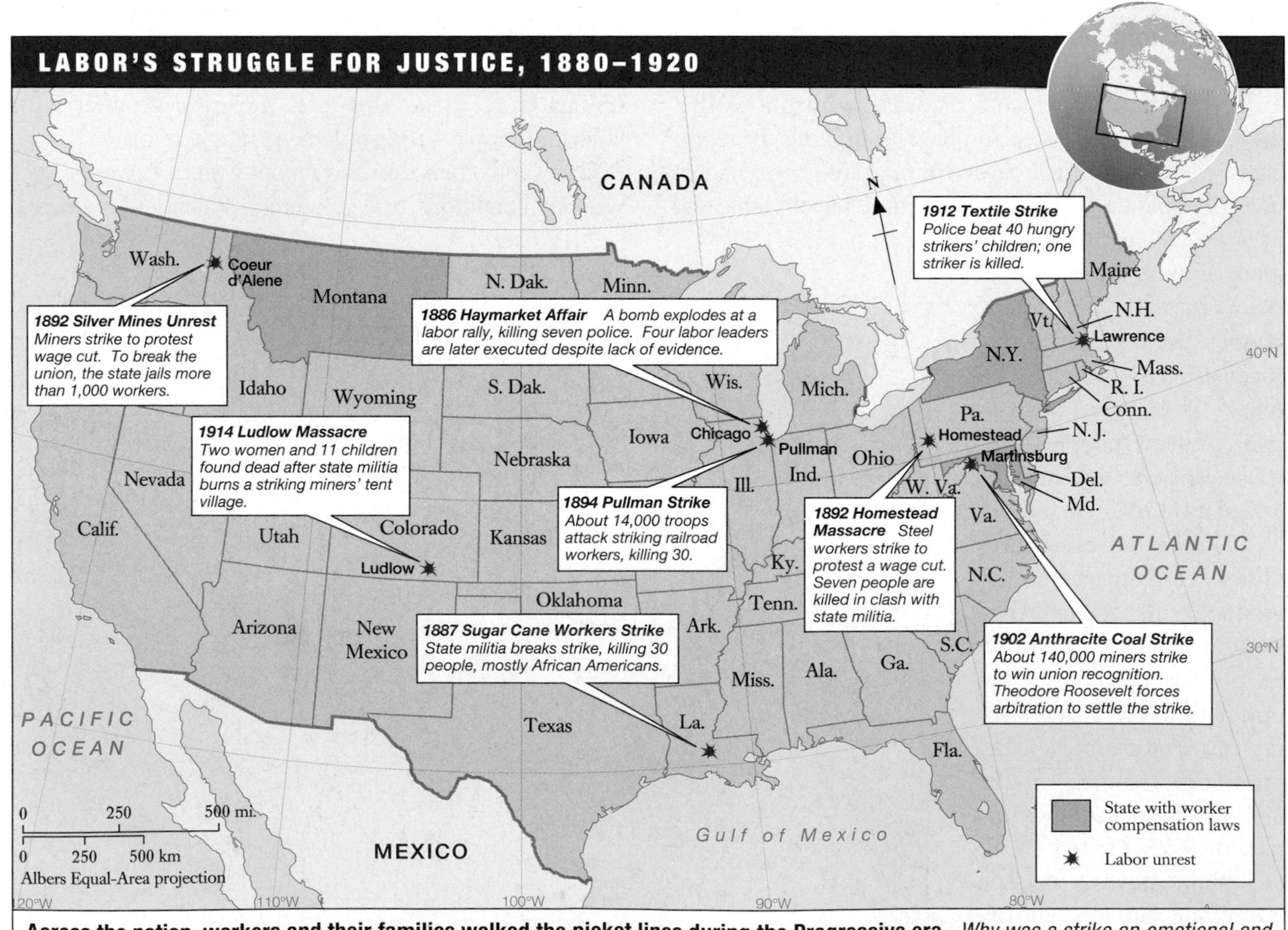
LABOR'S STRUGGLE FOR JUSTICE, 1880–1920
CANADA
N
1912 Textile Strike Police beat 40 hungry strikers' children; one striker is killed.
1892 Silver Mines Unrest Miners strike to protest wage cut. To break the union, the state jails more than 1,000 workers.
1886 Haymarket Affair A bomb explodes at a labor rally, killing seven police. Four labor leaders are later executed despite lack of evidence.
1914 Ludlow Massacre Two women and 11 children found dead after state militia burns a striking miners' tent village.
1894 Pullman Strike About 14,000 troops attack striking railroad workers, killing 30.
1892 Homestead Massacre Steel workers strike to protest a wage cut. Seven people are killed in clash with state militia.
1887 Sugar Cane Workers Strike State militia breaks strike, killing 30 people, mostly African Americans.
1902 Anthracite Coal Strike About 140,000 miners strike to win union recognition. Theodore Roosevelt forces arbitration to settle the strike.
Wash.
Coeur d'Alene
Montana
N. Dak.
Minn.
Maine
N.H.
Lawrence
Vt.
N.Y.
Mass.
R. I.
Conn.
Idaho
Wyoming
S. Dak.
Wis.
Mich.
Pa.
Homestead
N. J.
Iowa
Chicago
Pullman
Ohio
Martinsburg
Nebraska
Ind.
Del.
Md.
Nevada
Ill.
W. Va.
Calif.
Utah
Colorado
Kansas
Va.
Ludlow
Ky.
N.C.
Oklahoma
Tenn.
Arizona
New Mexico
Ark.
S.C.
Miss.
Ala.
Ga.
Texas
La.
Fla.
ATLANTIC OCEAN
PACIFIC OCEAN
Gulf of Mexico
MEXICO
40°N
30°N
120°W
110°W
100°W
90°W
80°W
0 250 500 mi.
0 250 500 km
Albers Equal-Area projection
State with worker compensation laws
Labor unrest

Across the nation, workers and their families walked the picket lines during the Progressive era. *Why was a strike an emotional and often frightening experience for the men, women, and children involved?*

Some radical labor organizations not only rejected capitalism, but they also rejected the willingness of socialists to run candidates for political office and to work with progressives. One such group was the Industrial Workers of the World (IWW), formed in Chicago in 1905. Wobblies, as IWW members were known, wanted a single union for all workers. They believed that workers should confront owners directly. "Shall I tell you what direct action means?" one IWW pamphlet asked. "The worker on the job shall tell the boss when and where he shall work, how long and for what wages and under what conditions." Under William D. ("Big Bill") Haywood, the IWW successfully organized unskilled workers that the AFL often ignored, such as miners, lumberjacks, and migrant farm laborers. In the most popular union song, sung to the tune of "Battle Hymn of the Republic," an IWW songwriter expressed the union's belief that workers needed to join together for their own protection:

IWW FILES

IWW Action Soldiers faced IWW workers at the so-called Bread and Roses Strike in Lawrence, Massachusetts, in 1912. One striker was killed; others went to prison. A union leader said, "Bayonets cannot weave cloth." *What did he mean?*

> When the union's inspiration through
> the workers' blood shall run,
> There can be no power greater anywhere
> beneath the sun.
> Yet what force on earth is weaker than the
> feeble strength of one?
> But the union makes us strong.
>
> Solidarity forever!
> Solidarity forever!
> Solidarity forever!
> For the union makes us strong.
>
> They have taken untold millions
> that they never toiled to earn,
> But without our brain and muscle
> not a single wheel could turn.
> We can break their haughty power,
> gain our freedom when we learn
> That the union makes us strong.
>
> —Ralph Chaplin, "Solidarity Forever," 1915

The members of the IWW, in addition to socialists, African Americans, and immigrants, often worked at cross-purposes to most progressives. Ironically these groups were the ones that suffered the most from the social ills that motivated progressives. Despite this irony, the progressives managed to expand government power to meet many of the problems caused by urbanization and industrialization. That expansion would have a significant and lasting effect on American life.

Section Assessment

Main Idea

1. Use a diagram like this one to show the limits of progressivism as it applied to African Americans, immigrants, and radical workers.

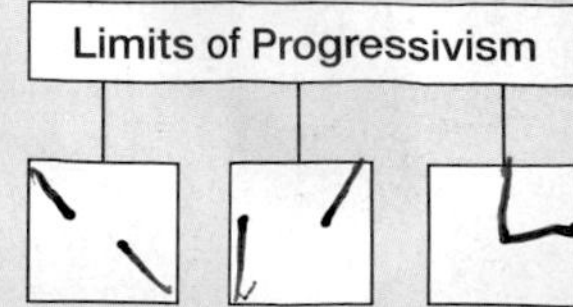

Vocabulary

2. Define: accommodation, melting pot, nativism, eugenics.

Checking Facts

3. What led to the immigration law of 1917? How did it differ from laws passed in 1882 and 1907?
4. How was the Sherman Antitrust Act of 1890 used against unions?

Critical Thinking

5. **Making Comparisons** How were progressives and Wobblies similar? How were they different?

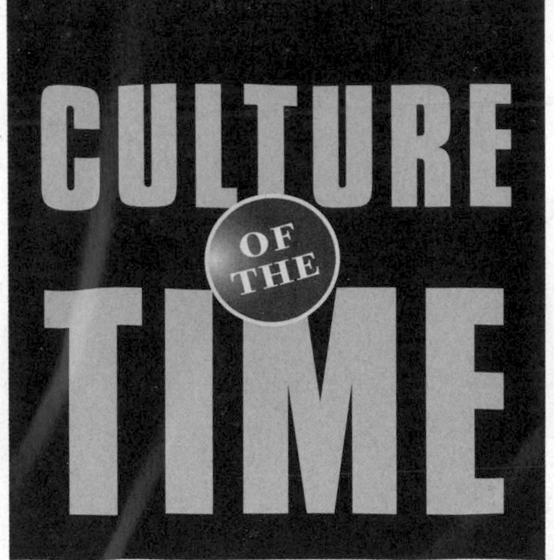

Ragtime

The ragtime years, named for the sprightly music of African American composer Scott Joplin, were an extraordinary time in the nation's history. Industrialization and innovation transformed the way Americans worked and played. Newly discovered "free time" presented the challenge of what to do with it. The invention of the camera made it possible to record many scenes of people eager to meet this new challenge.

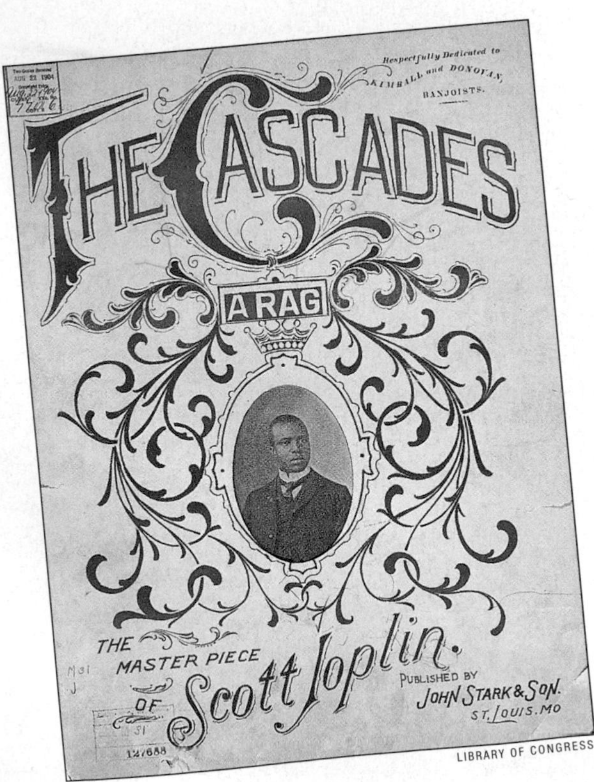

LIBRARY OF CONGRESS

THE BETTMANN ARCHIVE

WORLD TRAVELER

Ingenuity, determination, and achievement were some of the "American" virtues embodied by journalist **Nellie Bly.** Traveling around the world in 72 days (with one dress) in 1890, she outdid the record set in Jules Verne's popular novel *Around the World in 80 Days.*

POPULAR MUSIC

Sales of sheet music flourished when Scott Joplin began entertaining audiences with **ragtime piano music**—syncopated, high-stepping dance music born on the Mississippi Delta.

THE BETTMANN ARCHIVE

CULVER PICTURES

THE BETTMANN ARCHIVE

LIVE THEATER

The **vaudeville act,** unique to American theater, gave many actors and comedians who later became stars their start, often as children. The curtain behind the performers displayed the first commercial messages. Vaudeville, minstrel, and variety troupes toured the country, influencing community groups who then created their own shows.

EXCITING RIDES

Amusement parks, such as Luna Park on New York's **Coney Island,** provided a **"bully"** time for everyone. They offered exciting rides and elaborate slides for the young and daring.

SIDEWALK ENTERTAINERS

Traveling **organ grinders** in urban areas provided entertainment and amusement for city dwellers. Often they sold peanuts or popcorn and had trained animals (usually monkeys) who performed for the audience. People who lived during this time period had a chance to laugh and take a break from their tough daily routine of trying to make ends meet.

Chapter  Assessment

Self-Check Quiz

Visit the *American Odyssey* Web site at americanodyssey.glencoe.com and click on ***Chapter 9—Self-Check Quiz*** to prepare for the Chapter Test.

Reviewing Key Terms

Complete the sentences below with one of the vocabulary terms listed:

arbitration	**eugenics**
socialism	**accommodation**
capitalism	**nativism**
melting pot	**holding company**

1. _________ and _________ are two different economic systems.

2. Theodore Roosevelt helped resolve the coal miners' strike of 1902 when he imposed _________ by a third-party commission.

3. W.E.B. Du Bois opposed _________—Booker T. Washington's approach to racism.

4. One movement opposed to immigration was _________; another was the so-called science of _________.

5. A _________ can skirt antitrust laws by retaining controlling interests in companies or industries without owning them.

Recalling Facts

1. How did Theodore Roosevelt become President?

2. Why was the Sherman Antitrust Act difficult to enforce?

3. Identify three progressive reforms President Taft supported.

4. Why did Eugene Debs reject capitalism?

5. How did President Wilson restore public confidence in the banking system?

6. What effect did the Supreme Court decision in *Plessy* v. *Ferguson* have on the Jim Crow laws?

7. How did the views of Booker T. Washington differ from those of W.E.B. Du Bois?

8. Why did the concept of socialism frighten the progressives?

Critical Thinking

1. Recognizing Bias Reread the section entitled "Americanizing the Newcomers" on page 284. Find examples of bias in the attitudes of the progressives toward the immigrants and compare them to those of the nativists.

2. Formulating Questions Assume the role of an arbitrator in the United Mine Workers strike of 1902. Write at least three questions you would ask each side to understand their demands and identify opposing sets of values. Explain what you hope to learn from these questions.

3. Determining Cause and Effect Use a diagram like this one to show ways that Theodore Roosevelt and Woodrow Wilson increased the power of the presidency.

Standardized Test Practice

The Princeton Review

1. Which statement about the progressive Presidents is a FACT?

A Taft and Wilson did more to break up trusts than Roosevelt.

B The progressive Presidents upset the system of checks and balances.

C Taft was the most effective of the progressive Presidents.

D Roosevelt would have benefited the nation by seeking a third term.

Test-Taking Tip: The question asks you to distinguish between *fact* and *opinion.* A fact can be proved true, while an *opinion* expresses a personal view or judgment. Eliminate any obvious opinions such as answer D, which cannot be proved.

2. In contrast to Booker T. Washington, W.E.B. Du Bois argued that to achieve equality African Americans primarily needed to

A learn vocational skills.

B gain the right to vote.

C achieve economic prosperity.

D avoid direct challenges to white racism.

Test-Taking Tip: Eliminate answers that you know are wrong. Booker T. Washington argued that economic success would eventually win white respect. Eliminate answers that reflect this belief. Then look for an idea that is in *contrast* to this approach to winning equality.

GEOGRAPHY AND HISTORY

United States Parklands, 1909

National park
National monument

0 250 500 mi.
0 250 500 km
Albers Equal-Area projection

Study the map to answer the following questions:

1. Given that there were 5 national parks and no national monuments when Roosevelt took office in 1901, what does this map show about his contributions to the preservation of the country's wilderness?
2. In 1909 which part of the country contained the most national parks?
3. Which were the largest parks and monuments in 1909?
4. Were there more national parks or national monuments in 1909?

Portfolio Project

Traditionally, third parties have organized around a particular candidate, such as Theodore Roosevelt in 1912, or around an issue, such as prohibition. Identify a recent or current "third party" and research its platform. What was or is its goal? What role did or does it have in nationwide events? Write a short paper examining this party and include it in your portfolio.

Cooperative Learning

Work in 5 groups to research the 5 tariffs that were passed between 1890 and 1913. Then regroup into teams containing a representative from each of the original 5 groups. Each new group should choose its own means of presenting its findings.

Reinforcing Skills

Making Comparisons Politicians who support contrasting solutions often share similar beliefs. For example, Roosevelt, an ardent capitalist, agreed with most Socialists in blaming competition as the source of employees' overwork and inadequate pay. What other beliefs did Roosevelt and Socialists share?

Technology Activity

Using a Word Processor
Create a chart using a word processor to compare the views of activists Booker T. Washington and W.E.B. DuBois. Include headings such as Biographical Information, Major Contributions, and Personal Philosophy.

Expansionism and World War I

MARCH 1901: GEORGE WASHINGTON OF THE PHILIPPINES CAPTURED

Senator George F. Hoar once called Emilio Aguinaldo the "George Washington of the Philippines" when Aguinaldo sought to liberate his country from foreign rule. When that rule was Spanish, Hoar and others had encouraged the Philippine liberation struggle.

Aguinaldo had responded in kind, shouting *"Viva los Americanos!"* This enthusiasm, however, did not last long. The United States had promised its support of Philippine independence if Aguinaldo joined the United States in its fight against Spain. After the war, that promise was not kept. President McKinley wanted to "civilize" the Filipinos before granting independence.

When the United States refused to accept Aguinaldo as the legitimate head of government, a struggle ensued. American officials no longer praised him as a founder of his country. Instead, they plotted his capture. Aguinaldo marked the United States as an enemy and led a guerrilla war to rid his country of American forces.

Aguinaldo's capture in 1901 did not end the Filipino struggle. The war lasted for another year.

How the United States became the enemy of Aguinaldo is only part of the larger story of American foreign policy under the progressives—a policy guided by an uneasy mixture of idealism and self-interest. ■

HISTORY JOURNAL

Study the illustration of the famous piece of sheet music on page 293, and write your reaction to the mood it creates. Do you think American soldiers were always welcome in foreign countries? Why or why not?

Chapter Overview

Visit the *American Odyssey* Web site at americanodyssey.glencoe.com and click on ***Chapter 10—Chapter Overview*** to preview the chapter.

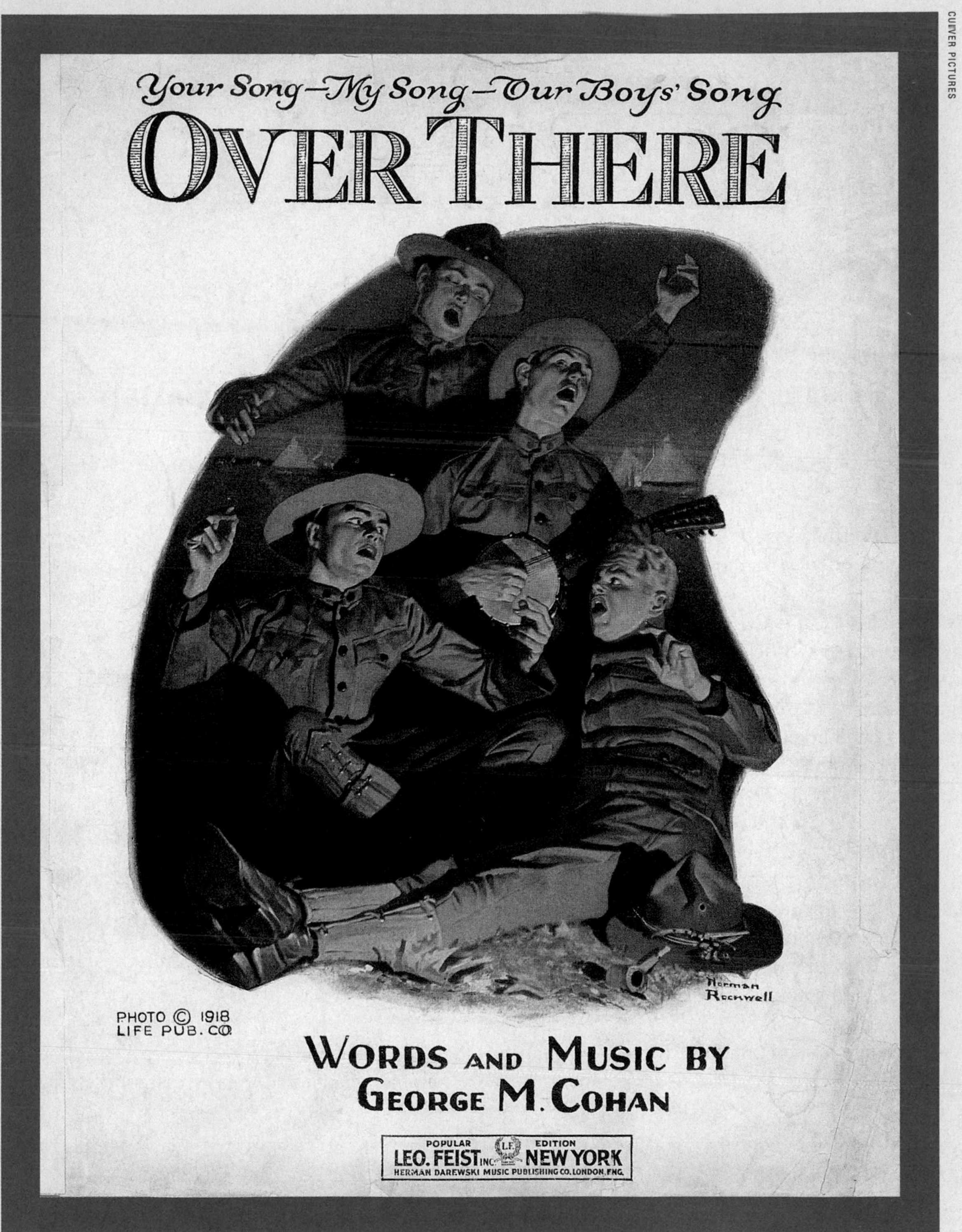

CULVER PICTURES

THIS SPIRITED PATRIOTIC SONG GLORIFIED THE ROLE OF THE UNITED STATES IN WORLD WAR I.

Becoming a World Power

JANUARY 9, 1900: BEVERIDGE DEFENDS IMPERIALISM

ALBERT J. BEVERIDGE, SENATOR FROM INDIANA, STOOD UP BEFORE THE UNITED STATES SENATE AND SPOKE WITH CANDOR. "Most future wars will be conflicts for commerce," he declared. He argued that the United States must secure new markets. As the United States acquired new markets in the countries of Asia and of Latin America, it should be willing to send troops, if needed, to protect those markets. It should even be willing to **annex,** or put under the dominion of the United States, new territories, so that only the United States could control the markets.

THE BETTMANN ARCHIVE

Coasting
The original caption states, "The old horse [Monroe Doctrine] was too slow for Uncle Sam."

As Beveridge argued his ideas, he recalled that the nation's Founders were not afraid to acquire the territories of Louisiana and Florida and other continental territories farther west. "The founders of the nation were not provincial," he noted. "Theirs was the geography of the world. They were soldiers as well as landsmen, and they knew that where our ships should go our flag might follow."

A Special Destiny

Upholding Freedom Overseas

Progressives responded to the possibility of gaining foreign commercial markets and annexing new territories in vastly different ways. Some

GUIDE TO READING

Main Idea

Foreign policies initiated during the progressive era led the United States to become increasingly tied to global markets and to the affairs of other nations.

Vocabulary

- annex
- imperialism
- corollary
- diplomacy
- territorial integrity

Read to Find Out . . .

- the purpose of Roosevelt's Big Stick foreign policy and Taft's Dollar Diplomacy.
- the importance of the Open Door policy for United States trade.
- the growth of United States political and economic involvement abroad.

of them wanted to forge ahead; others did not. They all kept in mind, however, that the United States was different from the many countries of Europe. For decades the United States had a special destiny to uphold liberty and freedom. Some progressives agreed with Senator Beveridge that the people of the United States had a duty to spread the American way of life to lands recently acquired during the Spanish-American War of 1898.

To some extent the idea of exporting American capitalism and democracy to foreign lands overseas gained strength from the Progressive movement itself. The progressives had shown that Americans had the ability to organize and mobilize for social, political, economic, and even moral reform within the United States. The progressives reasoned that they could export their knowledge and products to less developed countries overseas.

Deeply ingrained racial attitudes added support to the American impulse to become involved in the affairs of other countries. Some Americans believed that the people of the Philippines, as well as the people of most of the Caribbean islands, were racially inferior and that they should succumb to the leadership of the United States.

Overseas Markets

Not only progressive ideas but also economic realities helped to spur the debate about the United States's engaging in commercial expansion around the world. Senator Beveridge touched upon the economic realities affecting industries and the workforce:

> Today we are making more than we can use. Today our industrial society is congested; there are more workers than there is work; there is more capital than there is investment. We do not need more money—we need more circulation, more employment. Therefore we must find new markets for our produce, new occupation for our capital, new work for our labor.
>
> —Albert J. Beveridge, in *The American Spirit*

Beveridge's cry for new markets struck a responsive chord in American farmers, manufacturers, and investors. As shown by the graph on this page, exports of American products rose dramatically in the early 1900s. Investors, as well as farmers and manufacturers, favored new markets.

Railroads offered a good example of an American industry that was seeking new opportunities for investment. By the turn of the century railroads already crisscrossed North America. Entrepreneurs eagerly looked overseas to lands where railroads had yet to be built. One railroad entrepreneur at the World's Fair Railway Conference spoke eloquently on his desire for commercial expansion:

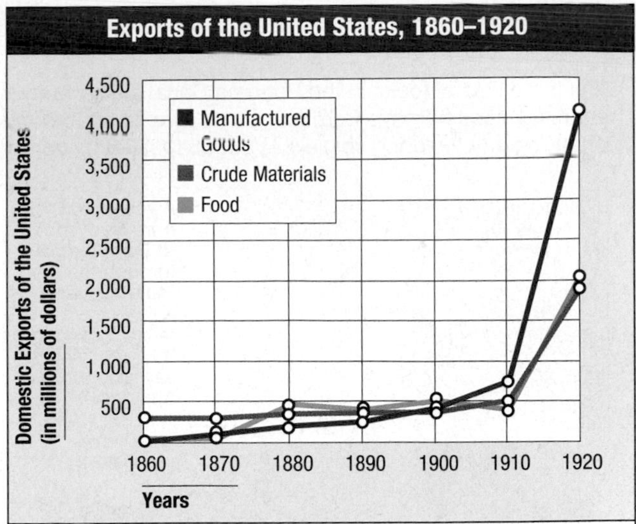

The rise of exports from the United States led to even more demands for commercial overseas markets by American farmers, manufacturers, and investors. *What types of products yielded the greatest number of export dollars in 1910?*

> We blow the whistle that's heard round the world, and all peoples stop to heed and welcome it. Its resonance is the diplomacy of peace. The locomotive bell is the true Liberty bell, proclaiming commercial freedom. Its boilers and the reservoirs are the forces of civilization. Its wheels are the wheels of progress, and its headlight is the illumination of dark countries.
>
> —Railway Conference Proceedings, in *Spreading the American Dream*

An Anti-imperialist Plea

Not all Americans favored expansion overseas. In 1902 the *Nation* magazine declared, "We made war on Spain four years ago for doing the very things of which we are now guilty ourselves." In this editorial the *Nation* pointed out that many Americans had previously opposed Spanish exploitation of local peoples, but now the government of the United States engaged in similar exploitation. Some Americans, like the author of the editorial, disapproved of **imperialism,** the policy of establishing economic, political, and military dominance over weaker nations, on humanitarian and moral grounds.

Other anti-imperialists prided themselves as Americans for being different from the Europeans, who were caught up in colonialism and militarism. They shared the sentiments of diplomat Carl Schurz, who lamented that extensive trading overseas would mean "wars and rumors of wars, and the time will be forever past when we could look down with condescending pity on the nations of the old world groaning under militarism and its burdens."

OPERATING THE LOCKS OF THE PANAMA CANAL

The three sets of locks in the Panama Canal are rectangular chambers, the largest concrete structures on earth, enabling ships to move from one water level to another by varying the amount of water in the locks. They are capable of raising and lowering vessels about 85 feet (26m), comparable to the height of a seven story building.

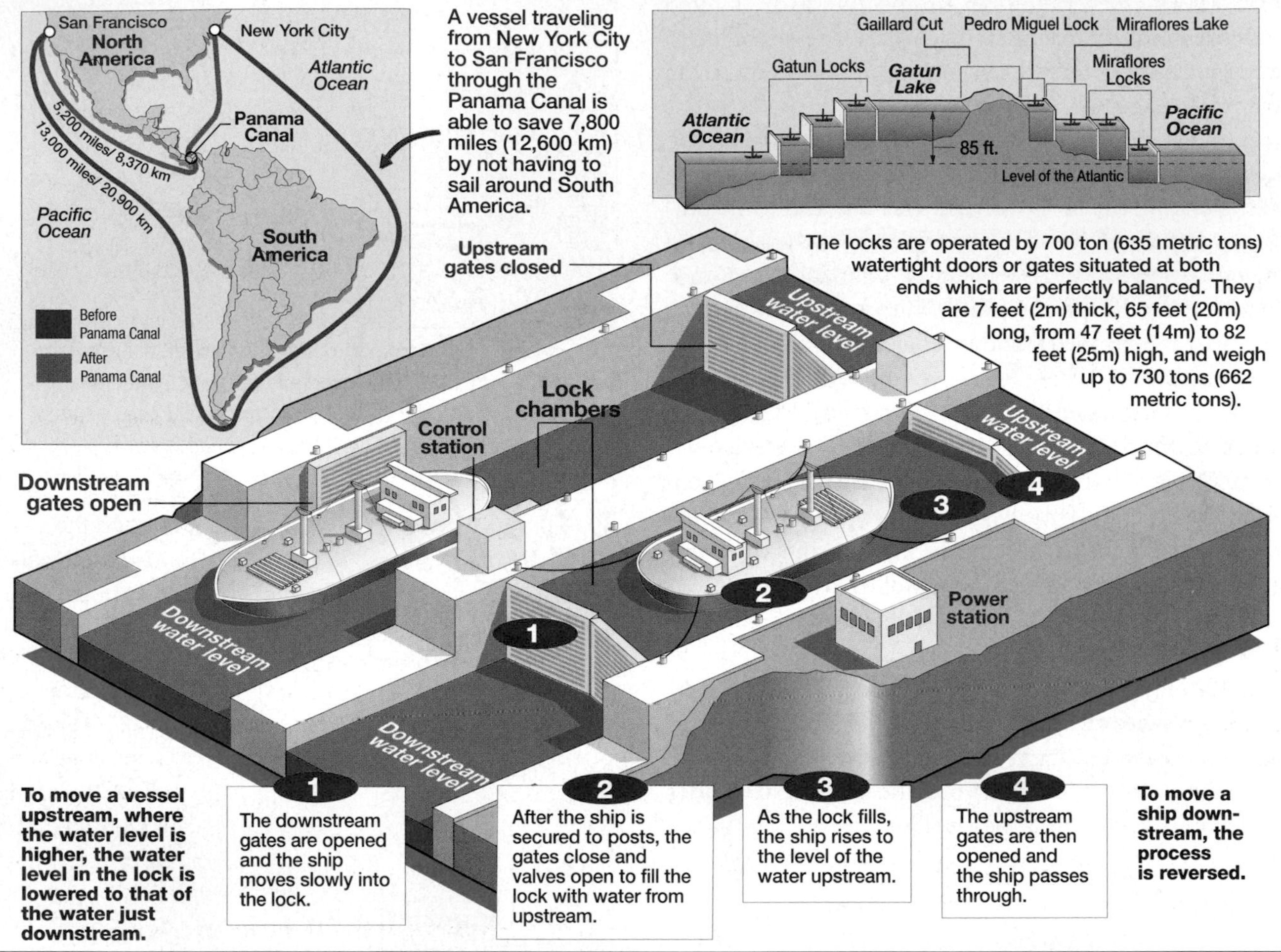

To move a vessel upstream, where the water level is higher, the water level in the lock is lowered to that of the water just downstream.

1. The downstream gates are opened and the ship moves slowly into the lock.
2. After the ship is secured to posts, the gates close and valves open to fill the lock with water from upstream.
3. As the lock fills, the ship rises to the level of the water upstream.
4. The upstream gates are then opened and the ship passes through.

To move a ship downstream, the process is reversed.

The opening of the Panama Canal reduced the average traveling time of early twentieth-century ships by 60 days. Today about 12,000 ships use its locks every year. *About how many feet can the locks raise or lower ships for passage through the canal?*

Policies in the Caribbean

Consolidating American Power

In spite of anti-imperialist arguments, the political and economic climate at the turn of the century favored commercial expansion, even if commercial expansion meant sending troops to keep order and defend markets. Such commercial and military endeavors suited the temperament of Theodore Roosevelt, who became President in 1901. "I have always been fond," Roosevelt explained, "of the West African proverb, Speak softly and carry a big stick; you will go far." Roosevelt preferred not to brag about American power, but rather to be so strong that other countries would bow to the United States. This philosophy came to be known as the Big Stick. Roosevelt's Big Stick policies in the Caribbean included the building of a canal in Panama and the extension of the Monroe Doctrine.

The Big Ditch

A canal across Central America linking the Pacific and Atlantic Oceans had been the dream of people of many different nationalities for years. The inset map above reveals the commercial and military advantages of such a canal. The reduction in travel time would save commercial fleets millions of dollars and increase the efficiency of naval fleets. The inefficiency of naval fleets during the Spanish-American War had underscored the need for a canal. When the war broke out in 1898, the battleship *Oregon* was sent from Seattle to Cuba. Because a canal did not exist at that time, the ship did not arrive until the war was nearly over.

The United States went on to negotiate the Hay-Herrán Treaty with Colombia in 1903, offering $10 million outright and $250,000 annually for a canal zone 6 miles wide in Panama, which at the time belonged to Colombia. When the Colombian legislature held out for more money, Roosevelt responded angrily and plotted to support a revolution that would make Panama an independent country—one the United States could more easily control.

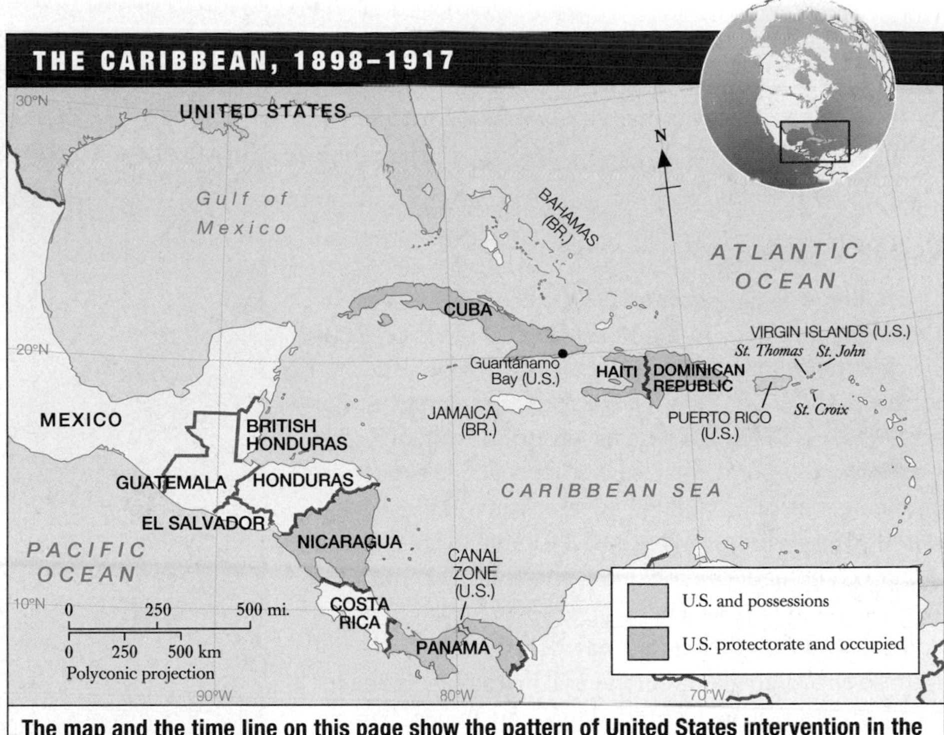

The map and the time line on this page show the pattern of United States intervention in the Caribbean from 1898 to 1917. *What islands became possessions of the United States?*

When the *Nashville,* a gunboat from the United States, arrived on November 2, 1903, the Panamanians began their rebellion. On November 4, 1903, the victorious rebels read a formal declaration of independence, and 2 days later the United States recognized the Republic of Panama. The new government had little choice but to accept the United States's terms for the building of a canal. The cutting of the canal began in 1904 and was completed 10 years later. Roosevelt took pride in having skillfully secured the canal, forging ahead in spite of reservations from Congress and legal advisers. He noted, "I took the Canal and let Congress debate."

Expansion of the Monroe Doctrine

Roosevelt had supported the revolution in Panama against Colombia to secure a canal for American interests. In general, though, he did not look kindly upon revolutions or any kind of disorder in the Caribbean. Striving to keep the region stable for American investment, he put down disorders in various Caribbean countries.

In 1904 and 1905 several European powers threatened the Dominican Republic. They wanted to collect money owed by Dominican customs, but could not do so peacefully because various factions in the Dominican Republic fought for control of customs revenues. Before Germany could send troops to collect the funds owed it, American troops seized Dominican customhouses and supervised the collection of customs fees and the repayment of debts. Roosevelt justified this action by issuing a **corollary,** or proposition, extending the Monroe Doctrine. His corollary asserted that "chronic wrongdoing" or "impotence" gave the United States the right to exercise "international police powers" in the Western Hemisphere. This changed the original intention of the Monroe Doctrine, which was to ward off European colonization. The United States now committed itself to

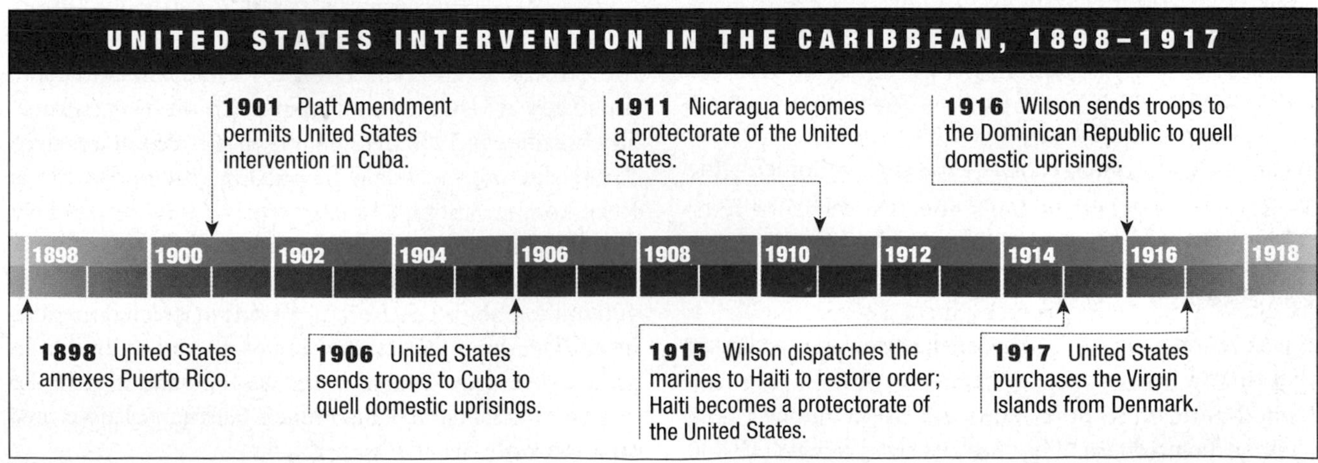

maintaining stability in the Western Hemisphere. The commitment would cause Roosevelt, Taft, and Wilson to send troops to a number of Caribbean countries—including Cuba, Nicaragua, and Haiti—during their respective terms of office.

Dollar Diplomacy

When William Howard Taft succeeded Roosevelt as President in 1909, he agreed with the spirit of Roosevelt's Big Stick policies, but not his tactics. Taft preferred a different form of conducting international relations, or **diplomacy.** His program, called Dollar Diplomacy—a somewhat milder approach to expansion and to interference in foreign governments—was one that substituted dollars for bullets. Hoping to gain more American influence in the hemisphere, Taft encouraged American bankers to lend money to Central American countries so that they could pay debts owed to Britain. He also encouraged entrepreneurial investment in the region. Investment in Central American mines, banana and coffee plantations, and railroads increased by $72 million from 1897 to 1914. Loans and investments had the effect of further impoverishing the fragile economies of Central American countries because most of their resources had to be used to pay back money, rather than to provide goods and services to their citizens. Throughout the 1900s, the United States State Department would use its power and influence in Latin America to protect American investors from loan defaults and unfriendly governments.

Missionary Influences In 1903 United States missionary Grace Roberts taught the Bible to Chinese women at a Manchurian outpost. *In what other ways did the missionaries try to spread American values, traditions, and the American way of life to the Chinese people?*

Policies in Eastern Asia

Establishing an American Presence

At the same time the United States consolidated its power in Latin America, it also turned to Asia to look for additional markets and to spread American values. Some Americans regarded Asia as a mysterious and alluring place. Others feared the growing Asian population, especially if it meant large numbers of Asians immigrating to the United States. The stereotypes that emerged in the 1800s lingered into the 1900s and characterized Asians as heathen and exotic—"the lawless hordes," "the yellow peril." Both prejudice against and fascination with Asia influenced foreign policy during the Progressive era.

The Chinese Market

While Americans at the turn of the century feared and discriminated against Chinese immigrants in the United States, the great numbers of people in China itself attracted them. The lure of souls, more than 400 million of them, to convert to Christianity inspired missionaries. The Student Volunteer Movement for Foreign Missions sprang up on college campuses all over the United States. During the 1890s the number of American missions in China doubled to more than 500.

Missionaries not only attempted to convert Chinese people to Christianity, but also built schools and hospitals and encouraged their converts to buy American products. As missionaries became more and more involved in China, they increasingly looked toward the American government for protection and help, especially when they confronted Chinese resentment and hostility. In 1900 missionaries asked for and received American military help in putting down the Boxer Rebellion, an attempt by a group of Chinese rebels to expel foreign influence from China.

Saving 400 million souls inspired missionaries, but 400 million bodies consuming goods inspired American businesspeople. The United States was not alone in its attraction to the Chinese market. China and its promise of wealth attracted Britain, France, Germany, Russia, and Japan as well.

By the latter half of the 1800s, these powers competed for influence in a China weakened by a decaying government, the Manchu dynasty. Each power vied for a chance to expand its interests in China. The United States wanted to share in these opportunities as well. Some Americans saw the possibility of building railroads, controlling ports, and selling manufactured products. At least two factors, however, put the United States at a distinct disadvantage: its geographical location, distant from China compared with Russia or Japan; and its navy, inferior to those of Japan, Germany, and Britain.

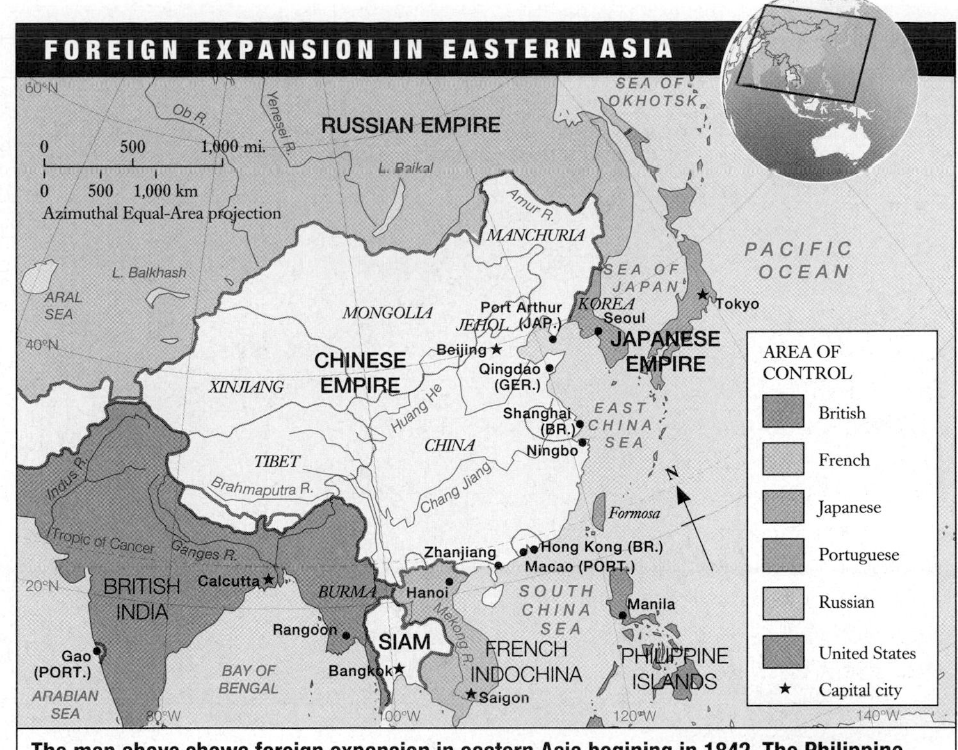

The map above shows foreign expansion in eastern Asia begining in 1842. The Philippine Islands provided a strategic location for the United States to establish commerce in eastern Asia. *How did the Open Door policy help the United States gain a foothold in eastern Asia?*

In 1899 and 1900 Secretary of State John Hay promoted a plan that would strengthen the American position in the scramble to gain control over specific regions of China. He sent notes to Japan and the key European powers asking them to accept the **territorial integrity** of China. In other words, Hay asked them not to control a specific part of China, but to leave the door open to trade for all nations in all parts of China. Because Russia, Japan, Britain, and France were jealous of one another's influence in China, they temporarily agreed with Hay's Open Door plan. The Open Door policy became a key concept in American foreign policy during the first decades of the 1900s. The hope of getting a share of the Chinese market continued to be the driving force in American policies in Asia and played a role in the American decision to annex the Philippines.

A War in the Philippines

As the United States celebrated its victory of 1898 against Spain, many wondered if the United States would allow the Philippines its independence. Before the Spanish-American War, the Filipinos had been waging a guerrilla war for independence from their colonial ruler, Spain. Filipino revolutionaries initially welcomed American forces into their country as liberators. The United States promised to support Philippine independence if the Filipino revolutionaries fought with the Americans against Spain. Moreover, the United States had drafted the Teller Amendment promising Cuba complete and unconditional freedom at the end of the war, and the Philippines expected similar treatment.

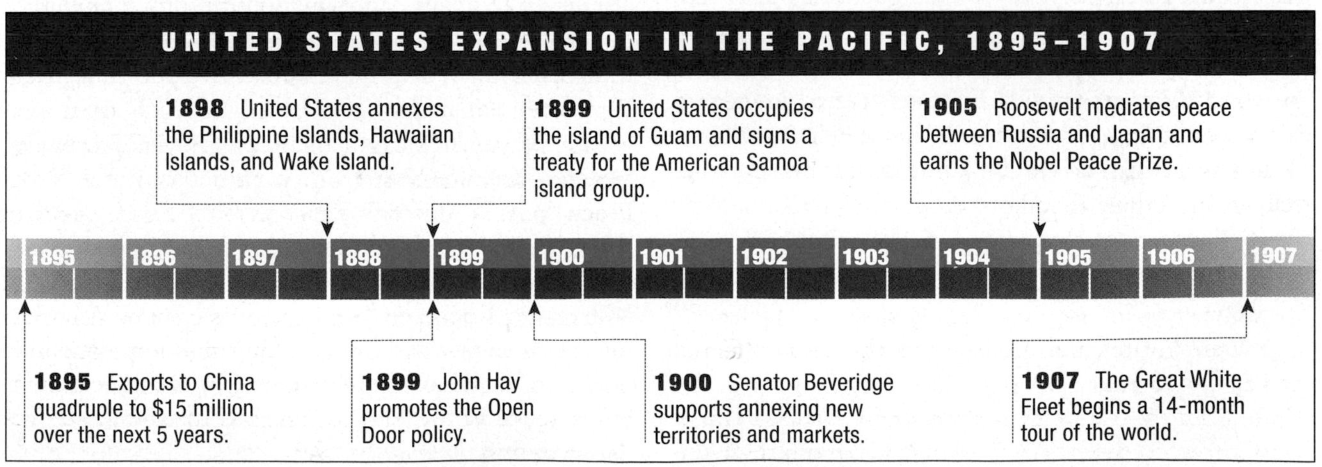

THE BETTMANN ARCHIVE

The Great White Fleet **Destroyers and battleships of the United States Navy were painted a dazzling white, giving the fleet its name.** *What would be the advantage to the United States of having a port in Manila?*

To justify annexation of the Philippines, expansionists used the arguments first put forth by President McKinley, who feared "anarchy" and vowed to "educate," "uplift," and "civilize" the population. Not far behind these lofty intentions, other considerations lurked: the Philippines could provide a rich variety of natural resources, as well as a foothold in Asia—a naval stop on the way to China. McKinley decided to hoist the American flag and take control of the country.

Filipino revolutionaries, led by Emilio Aguinaldo, did not accept the American decision to annex the Philippines without a fight. They waged guerrilla war at full force in the Philippines until 1902 and at reduced levels until 1906. In total, 120,000 American troops fought in the war, 4,200 of whom died. Filipinos suffered far greater casualties: at least 15,000 rebels and 200,000 civilians died. The novelist Mark Twain depicted the supreme irony of the situation:

> There must be two Americas: one that sets the captive free, and one that takes a once-captive's new freedom away from him, and picks a quarrel with him with nothing to found it on; then kills him to get his land.
>
> —Mark Twain, "To the Person Sitting in Darkness," 1901

Balancing Russia and Japan

The port of Manila would be a stop on the way to the tempting Chinese market, and this in part explained the willingness of the United States to fight for the Philippines. As Albert Beveridge put it: "[J]ust beyond the Philippines are China's illimitable markets." This dream also shaped American policies with Japan. When Theodore Roosevelt assumed the presidency in 1901, Russia posed the greatest danger to the Open Door policy in China because it controlled the large Chinese province of Manchuria. Like Hay before him, Roosevelt attempted to change the situation through diplomacy.

In 1904 Japan launched an attack against Russia, destroying much of its fleet. Roosevelt opportunistically supported Japan because he regarded Russia as a greater enemy. In 1905 he mediated a peace agreement between the two rivals, which earned him the Nobel Peace Prize. Roosevelt's mediation of the Russo-Japanese War pleased Japan. It gained control over Korea, as well as key ports in China and the railroad in southern Manchuria. Roosevelt, however, made a point of checking Japanese power by negotiating rights for Russia in northern Manchuria and by having Japan agree to noninterference in the Philippines. His main interest was in seeing that no single power reigned supreme in Asia.

THE GREAT WHITE FLEET, 1907–1909

The 14-month world tour of the Great White Fleet from 1907 to 1909 covered 46,000 miles (74,014 km). *What major canal was the fleet able to use to save mileage and time?*

Racial Politics

In addition to shifting the balance of power in China, the settlement of the Russo-Japanese War also had worldwide implications for racial politics. That an Asian people, the Japanese, had humiliated a white people, the Russians, kindled new national and racial pride in both the Chinese and the Japanese.

Japan reacted by protesting the 1906 segregation of Japanese children in San Francisco schools. A respected Japanese journal urged Japan to use its navy, if necessary, to end such humiliation:

> The whole world knows that the poorly equipped army and navy of the United States are no match for our efficient army and navy. It will be an easy work to awake the United States from her dream of obstinacy when one of our great admirals appears on the other side of the Pacific.
>
> —*Mainichi Shimbun*, 1906

Roosevelt soothed Japanese humiliation with "A Gentleman's Agreement" in 1907 that ended school segregation in San Francisco—while at the same time controlling Japanese immigration to California. As the controversy raged, Roosevelt began to calculate. Perhaps the delicate balance of power was shifting. Perhaps it was time for the United States to flex its muscles for the Japanese to see. Roosevelt had been building a stronger and more modern navy, and now he resolved to send the entire American fleet of 16 battleships around the world in a show of might. The Great White Fleet made a special stop in Japan in 1908.

Entanglement With Europe

Mediating Disputes

As the United States experimented in colonial and militaristic adventures overseas, its attitude toward Europe changed. For almost all of the 1800s, the United States had shunned entanglement with Europe. The democratic institutions of the United States set it apart from the colonial and militaristic ways of Europe—or so popular opinion believed. Nevertheless, when Hay shaped his Open Door policy and when Roosevelt mediated the Russo-Japanese War, they both participated in diplomacy that affected politics in Europe. They also showed that the United States could effectively resolve conflicts of interest in other parts of the world.

In the early 1900s the United States was often called upon to mediate disputes. In 1906 Roosevelt defused a crisis between Germany and France over Morocco. In 1911 Taft arbitrated a dispute between France and Great Britain over Liberia. In part, a desire for trading privileges in Africa motivated the efforts of Roosevelt and Taft in these cases. Far more than keeping an open door for American trade, the two Presidents hoped to keep peace in Europe. By 1900 the economy of the United States depended on markets all over the world. If tensions in Europe were to explode into war, American trade might suffer disastrously.

SECTION ASSESSMENT

Main Idea

1. Use a diagram like this one to compare arguments over United States foreign expansion.

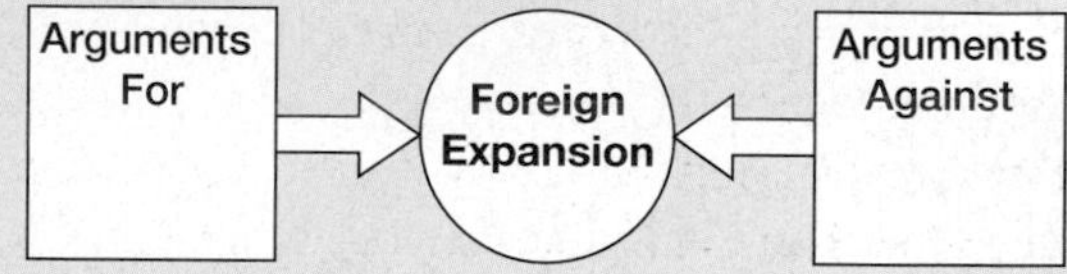

Vocabulary

2. Define: annex, imperialism, corollary, diplomacy, territorial integrity.

Checking Facts

3. How did feelings of superiority shape United States foreign expansion?

4. Why did Roosevelt mediate in the Russo-Japanese War?

Critical Thinking

5. **Making Comparisons** Compare how missionaries and investors viewed American involvement in China.

Geography: Impact on History

LOCATION

The Panama Canal

Still considered one of the greatest engineering feats in the world, the Panama Canal cuts more than 50 miles (80.5 km) through the Isthmus of Panama. The story of how the only link between the Atlantic and Pacific Oceans came to be built on this site reads like a novel—full of suspense and intrigue.

A Race for the First Canal

When California entered the Union in 1850, the United States saw that a canal joining its 2 oceans would be a great military and commercial boon. Between 1870 and 1875, the United States Navy made official surveys of desirable locations. In 1881 a United States commission decided that a canal through Nicaragua would be the cheapest to build. It would need locks, but it would involve the least digging. Convinced that a transoceanic canal was in the best interests of the United States, the government bought a concession for a canal from Nicaragua.

About the same time, France obtained a grant to build a canal across the Isthmus of Panama. In a race with the Americans, French government officials persuaded Ferdinand de Lesseps, builder of the Suez Canal, to build it. Although he was 75, de Lesseps could not resist the offer. He formed a private company to raise money and drew up plans for a sea-level canal.

During the 6 years that de Lesseps worked on the canal, 2 out of 3 workers died of yellow fever or malaria. In 1898 de Lesseps had to admit that his plan for a sea-level canal would not work. Cutting through the continental divide was

THE ISTHMUS OF PANAMA

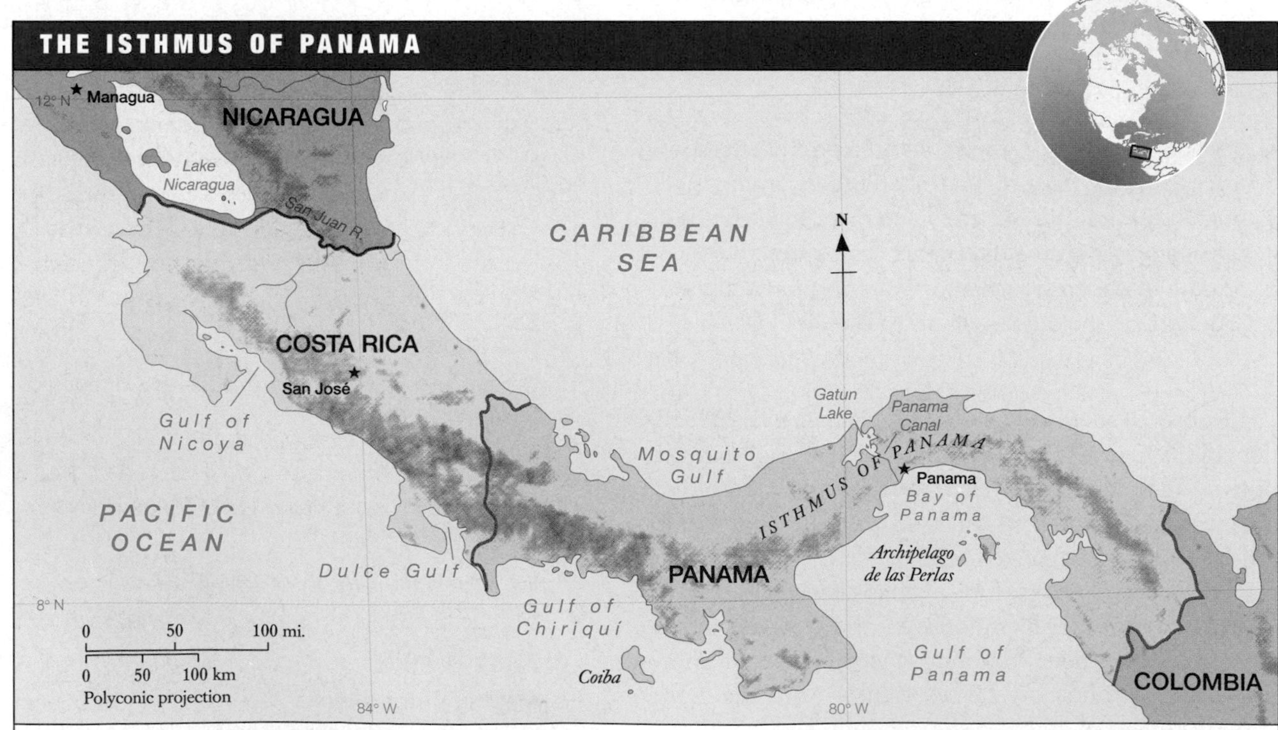

Panama is shaped in a long, thin curve, with a roughly east-west orientation. Ships traveling the canal from the Atlantic to the Pacific travel from northwest to southeast. *Why was Panama a good place for a transoceanic canal?*

not only extraordinarily expensive but almost impossible with the equipment he had. By then he had spent $320 million, at least 20,000 workers had died, and his company had gone bankrupt.

Panama or Nicaragua?

After the Spanish-American War, the United States renewed its interest in an American canal. Congress voted to build a canal in Nicaragua. Shortly afterward, the New Panama Canal Company (a French company that owned what was left of de Lesseps's canal in Panama) offered to sell the United States all of its canal rights and holdings for $40 million.

The United States would probably have stuck to its plan for a Nicaraguan canal, but a few days before Congress was to vote again on the canal's location, a volcano erupted in the French West Indies, killing 40,000 people. Philippe Bunau-Varilla, a representative of the French, seized the opportunity to remind Congress that potentially active volcanoes existed near the lake in Nicaragua where the approved canal was to be built. When Congress finally voted in 1902, Panama was in and Nicaragua was out as the site of the canal—by a margin of only 8 votes.

In the 1880s Nicaragua probably was the better choice for a canal, by the 1900s, Panama was a better site. The larger ships being built at that time would have had great difficulty negotiating the winding canal in Nicaragua. In hindsight, a Nicaraguan canal would have been a costly mistake because it soon would have become obsolete.

CULVER PICTURES

Miraflores Locks From the Pacific, the locks lift ships to Miraflores Lake and the next set of locks. *How long did it take to build the Panama Canal?*

Meanwhile, the intrigue continued. The Panama site depended upon the assent of Colombia, which controlled the isthmus. Colombia balked. Dissidents in Panama had long wanted to break with Colombia. Roosevelt spoke in favor of the rebels, who in turn favored an American canal. After Panama's successful revolt, it signed a treaty guaranteeing the United States the exclusive use and control of a canal zone 10 miles (16 km) wide across the isthmus, "in perpetuity."

Work Begins

In May 1904, a United States commission assumed the French property, and work began again on the Panama Canal. Colonel William C. Gorgas, an American physician who had wiped out yellow fever in Havana, Cuba, spent the first 2 years of construction clearing brush, draining swamps, and cutting out large areas of grass where mosquitoes carrying malaria and yellow fever lived. At the height of the project, more than 40,000 workers were employed. In 1914 the cost for the completed project came to more than $380 million.

The Panama Canal Today

The Panama Canal remains a crucial commercial and military waterway. Its importance diminished somewhat with the advent of supertankers and large aircraft carriers too large to go through the canal. The high speeds and low operating costs of these ships have undercut the time-saving advantage of the canal. After World War II, the canal's military importance changed, too. The United States Navy decided to maintain fleets in both the Atlantic and Pacific Oceans. Still, an average of 34 oceangoing vessels travel through the Panama Canal each day—for a total of about 12,500 ships every year.

Making the Geographic Connection

1. What was one of the main problems preventing the French from completing the canal?
2. Was the decision to locate the canal in Panama a simple one? Explain.
3. **Location** Where is Panama, and why was a canal there important to an expanding United States?

Watching Europe's War

MAY 7, 1915: GERMANY SINKS *LUSITANIA*

> Notice! Travellers intending to embark on the Atlantic voyage are reminded that a state of war exists between Germany and her allies and Great Britain and her allies; . . . and that travellers sailing in the war zone on ships of Great Britain or her allies do so at their own risk.
>
> —*New York World*, May 1, 1915

The passengers who sailed from New York on the British ship *Lusitania* that day seemingly ignored the warning that appeared in the newspaper. Bound for England, they enjoyed six days of dining and dancing on the luxury liner.

Early in the afternoon of May 7, in calm waters off the coast of Ireland, a German torpedo ripped into the side of the *Lusitania.* The huge ship sank within 18 minutes, taking with it the lives of nearly 1,200 men, women, and children, including 128 Americans.

"All the News That's Fit to Print."

The New York Times.

EXTRA 5:30 A.M.

LUSITANIA SUNK BY A SUBMARINE, PROBABLY 1,260 DEAD; TWICE TORPEDOED OFF IRISH COAST; SINKS IN 15 MINUTES; CAPT. TURNER SAVED, FROHMAN AND VANDERBILT MISSING; WASHINGTON BELIEVES THAT A GRAVE CRISIS IS AT HAND

STOCK MONTAGE

Headlines Influence Public Opinion
After reading this news report about the sinking of the *Lusitania* and the loss of life that resulted, Americans began to unify against Germany.

Germany defended its action on the grounds that the *Lusitania* carried a shipment of arms. It also pointed out that passengers had been warned not to sail in the war zone. Americans, however, were outraged. Some demanded a declaration of war, although most wanted to keep the United States out of the conflict. President Wilson chose to apply diplomatic pressure on Germany and try to hold it accountable for its actions. During the next few months Wilson sent increasingly severe protests to Germany. He insisted that it abandon unrestricted submarine warfare. Americans could no longer merely watch Europe's war.

GUIDE TO READING

Main Idea

World War I forced Americans to reexamine long-standing beliefs about noninvolvement in European wars.

Vocabulary

- self-determination
- coup
- alliance
- neutrality
- dogfight
- emigrate

Read to Find Out . . .

- reasons for the conflict between Wilson's belief in self-determination and his interventionist actions in Mexico and the Caribbean.
- the events that caused World War I.
- efforts taken by the United States to remain neutral during World War I.

MUSEO NACIONAL DE HISTORIA, MEXICO

Mexican Citizens Revolt This is just a portion of a mural found in Chapultepec Castle near Mexico City. It was created by David Alfaro Siqueiros. *How does this mural depict the period of the Mexican Revolution?*

Wilson's Foreign Policy

Intervention in Mexico

President Wilson brought to foreign policy an element of idealism that contrasted with the pragmatism of Roosevelt and Taft. He strongly believed that all peoples of the world had a right to **self-determination,** the right to choose the form of government they live under and to control their internal affairs. Yet President Wilson intervened in the affairs of other countries more than any previous President.

Revolution in Mexico

President Wilson, like Roosevelt, upheld the principles of the corollary to the Monroe Doctrine. Wilson maintained stability in the Western Hemisphere for American investment by sending American troops to quell domestic uprisings in Haiti in 1915, in the Dominican Republic in 1916, and in Cuba in 1917. He also continued Taft's Dollar Diplomacy policies by encouraging investors to buy out British enterprises in Central America. Dealing with Mexico and Europe, however, proved problematic for Wilson.

For 30 years the powerful Porfirio Díaz ruled Mexico. The stability of his rule encouraged American, British, and German investors, so much so that they controlled 90 percent of Mexico's mines, railroads, and industry. In 1911, however, Díaz fell from power, toppled by angry peasants whose land had been taken and middle-class Mexicans who had been deprived of their civil and voting rights.

Foreign investors feared that Francisco Madero, who replaced Díaz, would confiscate their property. Foreign diplomats—including the ambassador of the United States—and businesspeople plotted with discontented elements of the Mexican army to overthrow Madero. They wanted to replace him with Victoriano Huerta.

By the time President Wilson took office on March 4, 1913, Huerta had seized power, overthrowing the government and killing Madero in a bloody **coup.** Wilson thought the violence repulsive. He refused to recognize Huerta's government, vowing not to interfere directly.

> We shall have no right at any time to intervene in Mexico to determine the way in which the Mexicans are to settle their own affairs. . . . Things may happen of which we do not approve and which could not happen in the United States, but I say very solemnly that that is no affair of ours.
>
> —Woodrow Wilson, letter, 1914

American Intervention

A few months after expressing these beliefs, Wilson changed his mind, declaring that he had to teach Mexico to elect good officials. A minor incident concerning American honor was one reason for his shift. In April 1914, Mexican officials arrested several sailors from an American naval vessel in the port of Tampico. Local Mexican officials, as well as Huerta, quickly apologized for the incident. The American admiral in charge demanded a 21-gun salute to the American flag. Huerta demanded the same salute to the Mexican flag. This infuriated Wilson, who used the Tampico incident as a pretext for sending marines to the port city of Veracruz.

Another cause for Wilson's change of mind was a rumor that a German ship bound for Veracruz carried guns for Huerta's army. In spite of Mexico's ongoing revolution, the occupation of Veracruz outraged most Mexicans. Anti-American riots broke out in Mexico and throughout Latin America. The European press condemned the American military intervention, and so did many Americans. Shocked, Wilson backed off, and agreed to allow the ABC powers—Argentina, Brazil, and Chile—to mediate.

In 1915 Venustiano Carranza followed Huerta as president of Mexico. When Wilson backed Carranza, the rebel leader Pancho Villa struck back by killing 18 American mining engineers in Mexico. Villa's band then crossed the border and killed 17 Americans in the town of Columbus, New Mexico.

Wilson sent an expedition of 15,000 troops into Mexico under the command of John J. Pershing to find and capture Villa. Though they never found Villa, both Mexican and American lives were lost in battle.

Despite this military involvement, the United States failed to control events in Mexico. By late January 1917, Wilson decided to withdraw forces from Mexico. Another, much larger, war raged in Europe.

HULTON DEUTSCH COLLECTIONS LIMITED

Archduke Franz Ferdinand of Austria The Archduke poses with his wife, Sophie, and their family. *Why were Franz Ferdinand and his wife assassinated?*

Origins of World War I

Assassination and Alliances

What set off World War I in Europe? The bullet that killed the heir to the throne of the Austro-Hungarian Empire, Archduke Franz Ferdinand, started World War I. Austria-Hungary ruled over a large part of the Balkans, a mountainous area of southeastern Europe where many ethnic groups struggled for their independence. When a Serbian who supported Balkan independence assassinated Franz Ferdinand and his wife, all of Europe held its breath.

Entangling Alliances

By June 1914, almost any troublesome event could have sparked a war in Europe. Russia vied with Austria-Hungary and the Ottoman Empire for control over the Balkans. France, Russia, Britain, and Germany wrangled with one another to control ports and colonies overseas. The new naval force of Germany challenged Britain's long-established naval supremacy. Similarly, Germany's disciplined army struck fear into the hearts of neighboring Russia and France.

To gain security, many European countries organized themselves into a number of formal **alliances,** or unions. Each country that was part of a particular alliance vowed to help the allied countries in case of war. The members of the Triple Entente—which came to be called the Allies—were Britain, France, and Russia. Opposing the Allied Powers were the Central Powers, which consisted of Germany, Austria-Hungary, and the Ottoman Empire.

Because of the alliances, leaders in Europe knew that the assassination of Archduke Franz Ferdinand might mean world war. Russia reacted first by coming to the defense of the Serbian nationalists, in hopes of gaining influence in the Balkans. Russia's move brought the countries of the Triple Entente into the dispute, but Austria-Hungary and Germany needed to protect their interests too. Soon all of Europe erupted into war.

Early Years of the War

Austria-Hungary declared war on Serbia on July 28, 1914, and Germany declared war on Russia and France in the next few days. To avoid the strong defenses on the Franco-German border, German troops stormed through neutral Belgium. As a result, Great Britain, which was committed to the **neutrality,** or impartiality, of Belgium, declared war on Germany on August 4, 1914. A year later France, Russia, and Great Britain lured Italy into World War I on their side by promising Italy territory from the Austro-Hungarian Empire after the war was over. The map of Europe on page 307

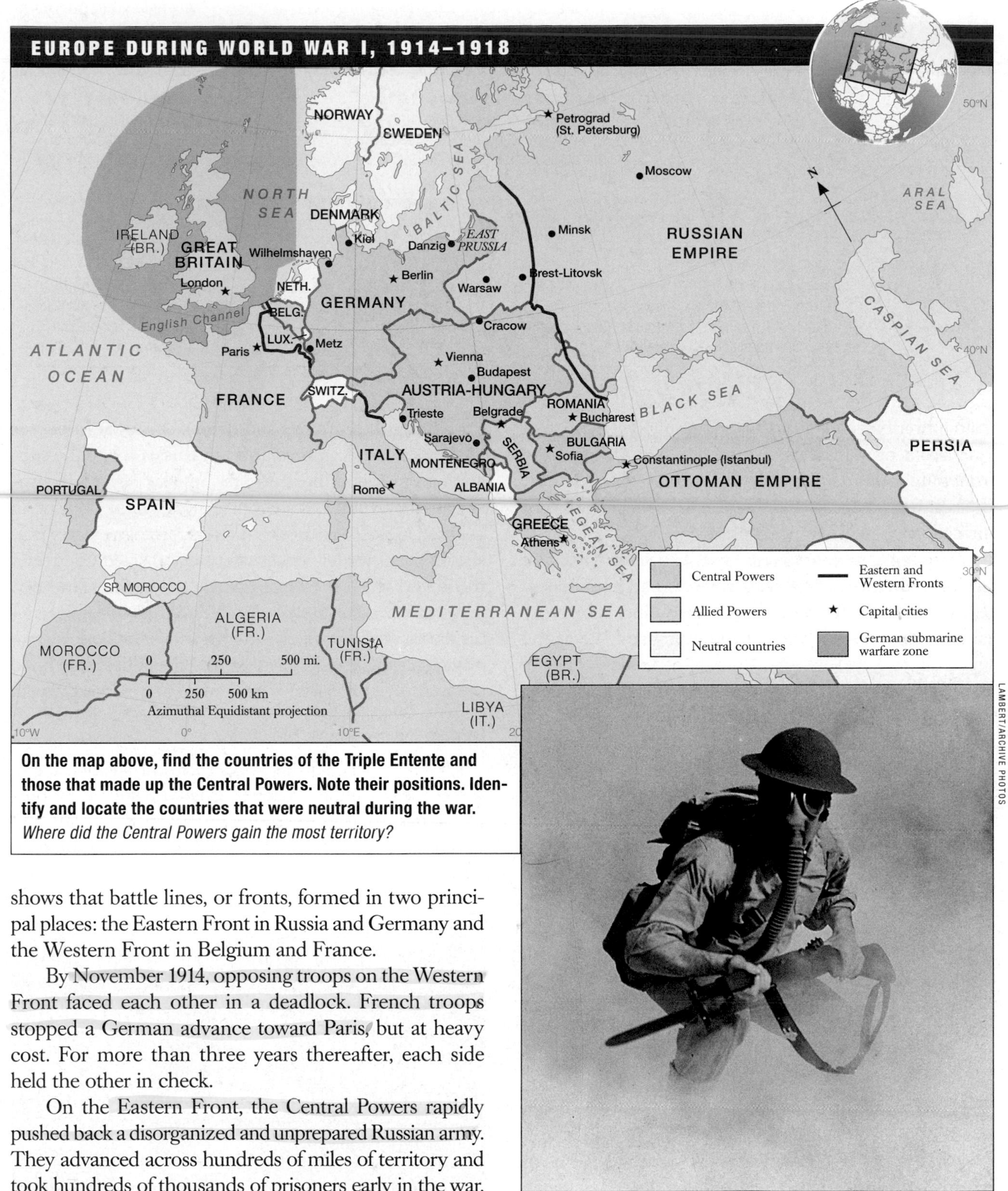

On the map above, find the countries of the Triple Entente and those that made up the Central Powers. Note their positions. Identify and locate the countries that were neutral during the war. *Where did the Central Powers gain the most territory?*

Preparing for a Gas Attack During the war many soldiers and civilians were killed by new weapons never before used—submarines, machine guns, poisonous gases, and tanks. *How did the loss of life and property in World War I compare with losses in previous wars?*

shows that battle lines, or fronts, formed in two principal places: the Eastern Front in Russia and Germany and the Western Front in Belgium and France.

By November 1914, opposing troops on the Western Front faced each other in a deadlock. French troops stopped a German advance toward Paris, but at heavy cost. For more than three years thereafter, each side held the other in check.

On the Eastern Front, the Central Powers rapidly pushed back a disorganized and unprepared Russian army. They advanced across hundreds of miles of territory and took hundreds of thousands of prisoners early in the war. Later Russian successes were less decisive. Hardship among the Russian people, coupled with plummeting confidence in the czar's leadership, threatened Russia's ability to fight at all. Talk of mutiny sped through the troops.

The Fields of Death

World War I resulted in greater loss of life and property than in any previous war. In the Battle of Verdun (February to July 1916), for example, French casualties numbered about 315,000 and German casualties about 280,000. In the Battle of the Somme, Britain suffered 60,000 casualties in one day of fighting. That battle raged

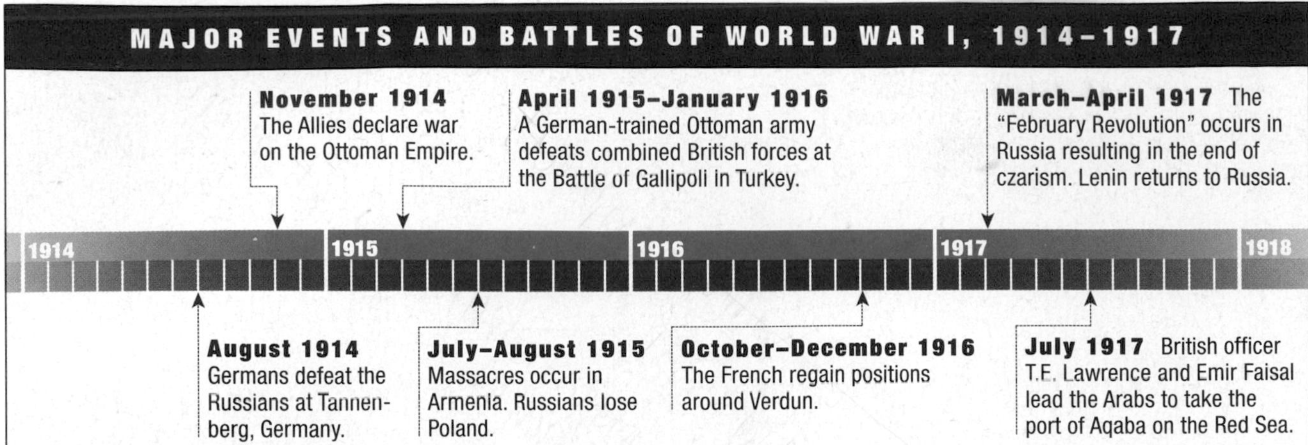

from July to November of 1916 and resulted in more than 1 million deaths. In the end, the Allies had advanced the front only about 7 miles. A battle at Tannenberg, in East Prussia, was so disastrous that the Russian general shot himself in despair over the defeat.

MAJOR EVENTS AND BATTLES OF WORLD WAR I, 1914–1917
November 1914 The Allies declare war on the Ottoman Empire.
April 1915–January 1916 A German-trained Ottoman army defeats combined British forces at the Battle of Gallipoli in Turkey.
March–April 1917 The "February Revolution" occurs in Russia resulting in the end of czarism. Lenin returns to Russia.
1914
1915
1916
1917
1918
August 1914 Germans defeat the Russians at Tannenberg, Germany.
July–August 1915 Massacres occur in Armenia. Russians lose Poland.
October–December 1916 The French regain positions around Verdun.
July 1917 British officer T.E. Lawrence and Emir Faisal lead the Arabs to take the port of Aqaba on the Red Sea.

The terrible destruction of World War I resulted from a combination of old-fashioned strategies and new technology. Military commanders continued to order massive infantry offensives. The command "Over the top!" sent soldiers scrambling out of the trenches to dash across a field with fixed bayonets, hurling grenades into enemy trenches. The attackers, however, were no match for automatic machine guns that could fire hundreds of rounds in rapid succession. Defensive artillery kept each side pinned in the trenches.

Both sides developed new weapons designed to break the deadlock. In April 1915, the Germans first used poison gas in the Second Battle of Ypres. The fumes caused vomiting and suffocation. When the Allies also began using poison gas as a weapon, gas masks became a necessary part of a soldier's equipment. Flamethrowers that shot out streams of burning fuel and tanks that could roll over barbed wire and trenches added to the destruction.

The fields of battle in World War I extended to the seas and to the skies. Germany challenged Britain's sea power with its submarine blockade. The two navies squared off in a major encounter on May 31 and June 1, 1916, in the Battle of Jutland, off the west coast of Denmark. Both sides claimed victory, but Britain retained control of the seas.

Great advances in aviation came about during World War I. At first planes were used mainly to observe enemy activities. Then Germany developed a machine gun timed to fire between an airplane's propeller blades. This invention led to the use of airplanes for combat. **Dogfights,** the name given to clashes between enemy aircraft, proved deadly for pilots but had little effect on the ground war.

During 1917 France and Britain saw their hopes for victory diminish. A revolution in Russia made the situation seem even more hopeless. In March 1917 (February in old Russian calendar), an uprising in Russia resulted in the overthrow of the czar. In November, Bolshevik party leader Vladimir I. Lenin seized control of the government and began peace talks with Germany. Thus, the Russian Revolution led to the end of fighting on the Eastern Front, freeing Germany to concentrate all its forces on the Western Front. The Allies' only hope seemed to be the entry of the United States into the war.

In the Trenches

The soldiers on the Western Front spent most of their time in muddy trenches. Enemy troops were protected from one another only by dirt, barbed wire, and a stretch of land—called no-man's-land—no more than 30 yards wide in some places.

ARCHIVE PHOTOS

Life in the Trenches British troops in a 1917 frontline trench near St. Quentin, France, rest before the next military assault. *What stretched between the trenches of enemy troops?*

PRIVATE COLLECTION

Pacifists in World War I Early in 1915 several feminist leaders formed the Woman's Peace party to advocate peace. After the *Lusitania* disaster, they staged a protest parade to urge the President to work for peace despite German actions. *What was the myth of neutrality?*

When not shooting at the enemy, soldiers in trenches fought lice, rats, and the dampness and cold, as well as such diseases as dysentery, gangrene, and trench mouth. All understood the suffering they faced daily, if not the politics that created the trenches. By the end of World War I roughly 10 million soldiers and about 20 million civilians had died. Exact numbers were impossible to collect.

Many soldiers took the war as a personal challenge. Others became disillusioned. One German novelist portrayed a young German soldier crying out in protest:

> While they [government officials] continued to write and talk, we saw the wounded and dying. While they taught that duty to one's country is the greatest thing, we already knew that death-throes are stronger. . . . We loved our country as much as they; we went courageously into every action; but also we distinguished the false from true.
>
> —Erich Maria Remarque, *All Quiet on the Western Front,* 1929

Struggle for Neutrality

Evolving Events Lead to War

Woodrow Wilson longed to keep the United States out of World War I. In August 1914, he asked for neutrality, urging the American people not to take sides. He said, "We must be impartial in thought as well as in action." Neither side deserved America's support, thought the righteous Wilson. The American people, however, many of whom had recently **emigrated** from Europe, leaving one country to settle in another, had their favorite sides. Millions had been born in Germany, England, Austria-Hungary, Russia, Ireland, or Italy; yet, for the most part, they too preferred to distance themselves from the bloodbath overseas.

Myth of Neutrality

While Wilson publicly proclaimed neutrality of the United States, American interests leaned toward the Allies. Although United States businesses traded with both sides in the European conflict, ties with the Allies were much stronger. A representative from the House of Morgan, the mighty New York financial institution, explained:

> Those were the days when American citizens were being urged to remain neutral in action, in word, and even in thought. But our firm had never for one moment been neutral: we didn't know how to be. From the very start we did everything that we could to contribute to the cause of the Allies.
>
> —Thomas W. Lamont, *Manchester Guardian,* January 27, 1920

American political and business sympathy pleased the Allies. They tried to sway popular support to their side too. One of the first things Britain did when war broke out was to cut the transatlantic cable to the United States, so all news had to come through Britain. The reports that arrived vilified the Germans. Soon many ordinary Americans favored the Allies in World War I.

Bryan and the Submarines

Although public sentiment was turning toward the Allies, Secretary of State William Jennings Bryan still favored neutrality—even after German submarines attacked ships on which American citizens traveled. The

HULTON DEUTSCH COLLECTION LIMITED

A German Submarine **This camouflaged German submarine, or U-boat, was typical of those that operated from 1914 to 1918.**
What strategy did the Germans employ to break the British blockade of Germany?

Germans had developed this new weapon, the submarine, and they used it to surprise enemy merchant ships in the war zone Germany monitored around the British Isles. That strategy was in response to a British blockade of Germany that had effectively begun to starve the German people. Bryan could see that both sides had military reasons for acting as they did. He encouraged Wilson to forbid Americans from traveling in the submarine zones as a way of avoiding trouble with Germany. Wilson argued, however, that free and safe travel was a right of citizens of a neutral country.

The issue reached a crisis on May 7, 1915, when German submarines attacked the *Lusitania,* a British passenger ship. More than 1,000 passengers died, including 128 Americans, as the torpedoed ship quickly sank. Germany knew that the *Lusitania* secretly carried arms and had warned ahead of time that it might be a target for attack. Nevertheless, Americans were outraged. "Damnable! Damnable! Absolutely hellish!" cried Billy Sunday, a fiery evangelist of the time. In spite of the tragedy, Wilson continued to believe that Americans should not be restricted from traveling the seas. In protest, Bryan resigned.

Reelection

The American people reelected Woodrow Wilson to the presidency in 1916 in a close race against Charles Evans Hughes. American voters responded to the Democratic campaign slogan: He kept us out of war! That slogan, however, made Wilson nervous. In spite of his neutrality efforts, he knew that the nation was edging closer to entering World War I.

The pressure on Wilson to enter the war came partly from his own moral commitment to the Allies; but it came also from American business leaders and

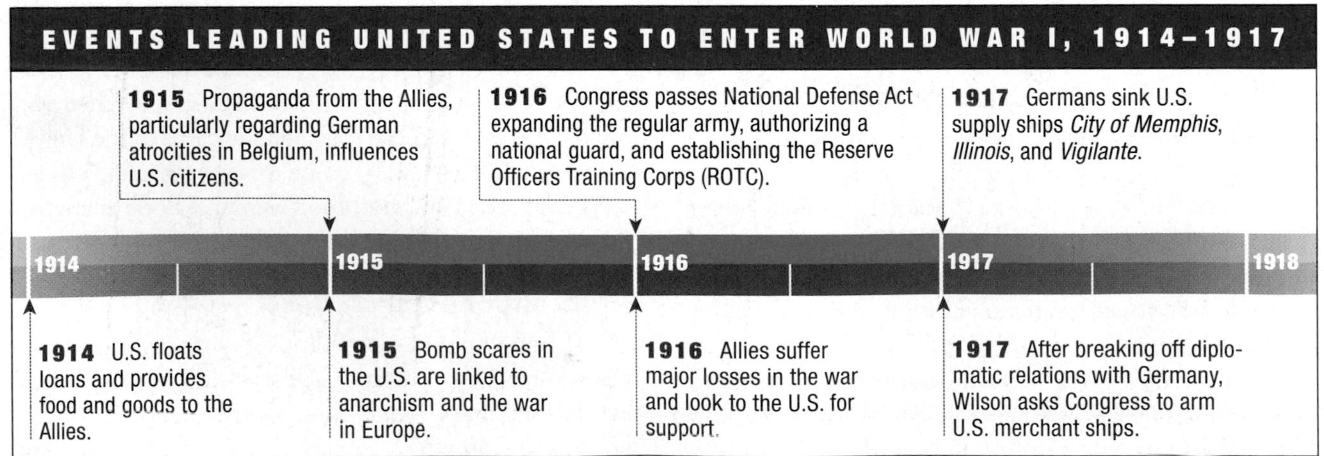

EVENTS LEADING UNITED STATES TO ENTER WORLD WAR I, 1914–1917
1915 Propaganda from the Allies, particularly regarding German atrocities in Belgium, influences U.S. citizens.
1916 Congress passes National Defense Act expanding the regular army, authorizing a national guard, and establishing the Reserve Officers Training Corps (ROTC).
1917 Germans sink U.S. supply ships *City of Memphis, Illinois,* and *Vigilante.*
1914
1915
1916
1917
1918
1914 U.S. floats loans and provides food and goods to the Allies.
1915 Bomb scares in the U.S. are linked to anarchism and the war in Europe.
1916 Allies suffer major losses in the war and look to the U.S. for support.
1917 After breaking off diplomatic relations with Germany, Wilson asks Congress to arm U.S. merchant ships.

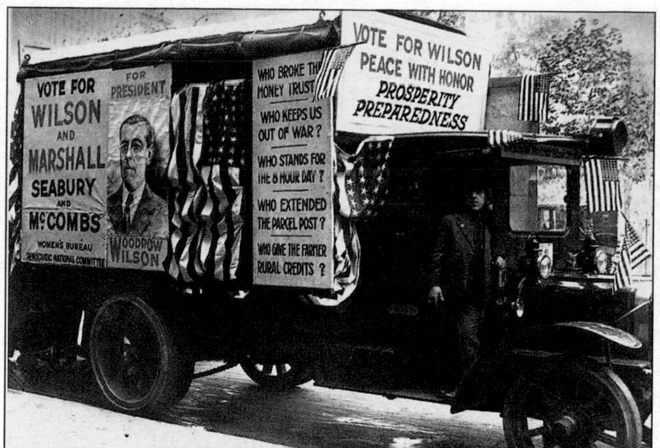

UPI/BETTMANN NEWSPHOTOS

Campaigning for Reelection This campaign van was used by supporters of President Wilson in 1916. *Why did President Wilson want to have a say in the peace settlement after World War I?*

investors. American companies had invested deeply in an Allied victory. By 1917 American loans to the Allies totaled $2.25 billion. If Wilson helped the Allies win, the money would be paid back. Even more important, his commitment to the Allies would ensure a place for American investment in postwar Europe.

In addition to these pragmatic motives, the idealistic Wilson truly wanted to have a say in a peace settlement. He longed to make sure that after World War I, no other war would ever threaten the world again. He felt that no one would listen seriously to his ideas unless the United States had actually proved itself in battle. Ironically, Wilson's desire for a peaceful world led him closer to war.

Closer to War

Several events led the United States to finally enter the war. In January 1917, a German official named Arthur Zimmermann cabled the German ambassador in Mexico instructing him to make an offer to the Mexican government. Zimmermann proposed that Mexico ally itself with Germany. In return, Germany would make sure that after the war Mexico would receive some of the region that it lost to the United States in 1848. A British official intercepted Zimmermann's telegram and spread the news to the United States. This incident occurred shortly after Wilson withdrew from the Pancho Villa chase, so the Zimmermann note made many Americans eager to humiliate both Mexico and Germany.

Another declaration from Germany led the United States even closer to war. On January 31, 1917, Germany announced an unrestricted submarine campaign. German people were starving, and the country was desperate to end the war. Because the United States was not truly neutral, the Germans felt they had nothing to lose by an onslaught. The Germans sank one ship after another, including the American supply ship *Illinois* on March 18, 1917.

By April 1, President Wilson was brooding and pacing the floor. "Once I lead these people into war," he confided to editor Frank Cobb, "they'll forget there was ever such a thing as tolerance. To fight you must be brutal and ruthless, and the spirit of ruthless brutality will enter into the very fabric of our national life." Despite his anguish, on April 2, 1917, the President stood before the United States Congress and asked its members to declare war on Germany.

> It is a fearful thing to lead this great peaceful people into war, into the most terrible and disastrous of all wars, civilization itself seeming to be in the balance. But the right is more precious than peace, and we shall fight for the things which we have always carried nearest our hearts,—for democracy, for the right of those who submit to authority to have a voice in their own Governments, for the rights and liberties of small nations. . . . [W]e dedicate our lives and our fortunes, everything that we are and everything that we have, . . . America is privileged to spend her blood and her might for the principles that gave her birth and happiness and the peace which she has treasured.
>
> —Woodrow Wilson,
> War Message, April 1917

Section Assessment

Main Idea

1. Use a diagram like this one to show events leading to United States entry into World War I.

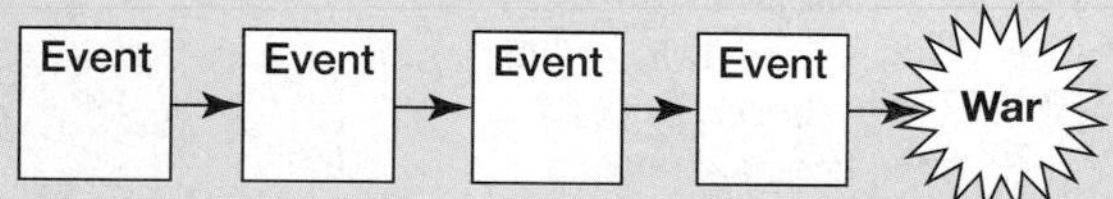

Vocabulary

2. Define: self-determination, coup, alliance, neutrality, dogfight, emigrate.

Checking Facts

3. How did Wilson continue the policies of Roosevelt and Taft?

4. What single act set off World War I? Why?

Critical Thinking

5. **Drawing Conclusions** Why was the British government so eager to inform the United States of Germany's offer to Mexico? What did it hope to gain? How did this information affect Wilson's thinking on the war?

Science, TECHNOLOGY, and Society

The Radio

With the invention of the radio, communication improved worldwide. The radio connected governments, as well as average citizens, providing information about international events and ending isolation across the globe. As a form of entertainment, the radio also impacted everyone's leisure time.

THE MARCONI COMPANY

GENERATING POWER

The use of wireless telegraphy during World War I affected the development of offensive and defensive fronts. This soldier is pedaling a stationary bike to generate the power needed to make radio contact between troops. The primary concern was communicating information between a fixed and a moving point.

IMPERIAL WAR MUSEUM

KDKA RADIO PHOTO, PITTSBURG, PA

THE "MUSIC BOX"

Frank Conrad, an engineer for Westinghouse, began broadcasting music from his garage after World War I. As interest in the broadcasts grew, Harry P. Davis, a Westinghouse vice president, launched the sale of the first commercial radio receiver in 1920 called the "music box" (above).

THE EVOLUTION OF RADIO BROADCASTING

Pre-1900s | 1900s | 1910s | 1920s

ELECTROMAGNETIC WAVES, the precursor to radio, radar, and television, are demonstrated by James Maxwell in 1864.

ELECTROMAGNETIC WAVES first transmit sounds in a 1900 experiment by R.A. Fessenden.

TRIODE VACUUM TUBE, which allows for amplification of weak signals, is developed by Lee De Forest in 1906.

BROADCASTING INDUSTRY, including hundreds of radio stations and millions of receivers, is envisioned by David Sarnoff in 1916.

WESTINGHOUSE

TRANSMITTING SIGNALS

On November 2, 1920, KDKA of Pittsburgh conducted the world's first scheduled broadcast. By the mid-1920s, KDKA personnel were testing an experimental antenna, carried aloft by a big balloon (left). This was a far cry from the first mobile radio in 1901 (below), with its cylindrical aerial that allowed telegraphic transmissions around the country and to sailing vessels. Guglielmo Marconi, standing at the extreme right, is credited with the invention of wireless telegraphy.

THE MARCONI COMPANY

ENTERTAINMENT

Singing into an early microphone, Dame Nellie Melba's clear soprano soared across European and Atlantic airwaves on June 15, 1920, from the Marconi wireless factory in Chelmsford, England. This was the first advertised program of entertainment on the radio—until then the radio had been used mostly as a news service. Civilians were prohibited from using the wireless during the war.

THE CHANGING SHAPE OF RADIO

PORTFOLIO PROJECT

How has the radio changed since its inception in 1920? What impact has this form of communication had on other sectors of life? Make a collage labeling the different forms of radio technology available today.

1930s	1940s	1950s–1970s	1980s–2000s

FM RADIO becomes available in 1929.

TRANSISTOR RADIOS become commercially available in 1952. Stereophonic radio broadcasting begins in the 1960s. Sony introduces the first personal stereo, the Walkman, in 1979.

INTERNET RADIO comes into existence with the birth of the World Wide Web in 1991. Within less than a decade, radio stations around the world broadcast radio programs via the Internet.

World War I: There and Here

FALL 1918: INFLUENZA AND BONDS SWEEP NATION

In her novella *Pale Horse, Pale Rider,* Katherine Anne Porter describes life on the home front through the experiences of a woman named Miranda. During 1918 Miranda's problems, like those of other young working women, were intimately linked to the war. One morning, she awakened with a headache and a queasy feeling in her stomach—symtoms of influenza. This disease had infected the people of Denver, where Miranda worked, and other cities across the nation. Thousands died. The deadly epidemic struck other countries too. It proved fatal to more American soldiers than did the war itself. About 57,000 American soldiers died from influenza while the United States was at war; about 53,500 died in battle.

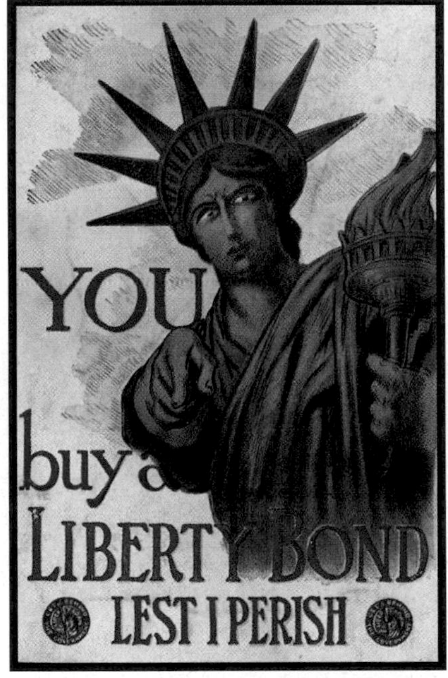

CULVER PICTURES

Patriotic Sales
Emotional appeals and celebrity endorsements characterized the sale of Liberty Bonds during World War I.

Miranda tried to ignore her headache and the funeral processions that wound down the city's streets. She needed to concentrate on two other problems. She had fallen in love with a young man, Adam, who had to leave for the front in a few days. She also was being hounded to buy liberty bonds—loan certificates the government issued to help pay for the war. Bonds were sold at rallies throughout the country. Miranda could not afford a bond, but she was afraid she would lose her job if she refused to buy one.

That evening Miranda met Adam. The couple strolled to the theater. They could not, however, escape the hawking of the war. When the curtain rose for the third act, the audience beheld not the actors, but an American flag draped

Guide to Reading

Main Idea

Involvement in World War I tested the resolve of Americans to work together as a nation and to confront questions of liberty and freedom at home.

Vocabulary

- mobilization
- conscription
- doughboys
- propaganda

Read to Find Out . . .

- what efforts the United States made in mobilizing for World War I.
- the nature of American military participation in World War I.
- the negative effect the war had on civil liberties.

across a backdrop. In front of the flag, a middle-aged man began to sell Liberty Bonds. All of the words Miranda had ever heard about the war ran together in her mind:

> WAR to end WAR, war for Democracy, for humanity, a safe world forever and ever—and to prove our faith in Democracy to each other, and to the world, let everybody get together and buy Liberty Bonds and do without sugar and wool socks.
>
> —Katherine Anne Porter, *Pale Horse, Pale Rider,* 1939

Mobilization

Military Draft and Civilian Pressure

The pressures Miranda felt to back the war effort were typical for her generation. When President Wilson asked Congress to declare war, he knew that he needed the support of all Americans. War, he said, would involve **mobilization,** or preparation, by citizens and business enterprises. Wilson warned that any disloyalty would be met "with a firm hand." Support in Congress for the war resolution was very strong. To fund the war, Wilson raised income taxes and organized a vigorous Liberty Bond campaign. Secretary of the Treasury William Gibbs McAdoo also pressed the public for financing. "A man who can't lend his government $1.25 per week at the rate of 4 percent interest," he said, "is not entitled to be an American citizen."

Drafting an Army

In addition to raising money, the President initiated **conscription,** or compulsory enrollment in military service. The United States had not enforced a draft since the Civil War, and some Americans spoke out against it. "I feel it is my sacred duty to keep the stalwart young men of today out of a barbarous war 3,500 miles away," said Congressman Isaac Sherwood. Jeannette Rankin of Montana, the first woman elected to Congress, also opposed both conscription and the war declaration.

Many progressives, however, supported the war and the draft. They argued that the draft might prove to be a great equalizer. Young men from upper and lower classes and from many ethnic origins would serve side by side, learning to live together as brothers. This equality might then translate into reforms at home.

Secretary of War Newton D. Baker called June 5, 1917, the official day of registration for the draft, "a festival and patriotic occasion." Draft registration proceeded in the midst of local fairs and picnics. Men aged 21 to 30 (later the draft age was extended from 18 to 45) registered by the millions. A lottery decided those to be actually inducted into the military. About 11,000 women also volunteered as nurses, clerical workers, and telephone operators.

Segregating African Americans

The military was not an equalizer for African Americans, who were strictly segregated. The National Association for the Advancement of Colored People (NAACP) demanded that African Americans be allowed to become officers. Its persistence paid off, when more than 600 African Americans graduated from an officer-training program at Fort Des Moines. The military, however, did not give high rank to any of these officers. White officers commanded the African American Ninety-Second Division. Some African American troops were integrated with white French troops once they arrived in Europe. This tolerance abroad added to African Americans' discontent with prejudice back home.

UPI/BETTMANN NEWSPHOTOS

Segregated Military The Fifteenth Negro Regiment shown above was made up of New Yorkers and nicknamed "the Buffalos." *How did the experience of African Americans in the war spur the desire for equal rights at home?*

Fighting Over There

American "Pep" and Strength in Numbers

Under the command of General John J. Pershing, the United States infantry—nicknamed **doughboys** after a cake traditionally baked for sailors—began coming ashore in France in late June 1917. The Allies desperately needed "men, men, men," as one French officer put it. Although most Americans fought separately from the European units, the Allies welcomed the relief the American Expeditionary Force (A.E.F.) offered.

The doughboys arrived in France singing "Pack Up Your Troubles in an Old Kit Bag" and "It's a Grand Old Flag." Aside from their confident air, the doughboys were unprepared for war. Pershing, known for his unbending will and a personality embittered by the death of his wife and children in a fire, described the problem: "A large percentage of them [American troops] were ignorant of practically everything pertaining to the business of the soldier in war." By late 1917, about 200,000 had arrived. Though they lacked training, American soldiers gained a reputation for courage and "pep."

The Eastern Front

The A.E.F. filled a breach left by heavy Allied losses on the Western Front and Russia's pullout from the war. Russia had suffered huge losses on the Eastern Front. Its new revolutionary government wanted no part of what they considered to be the czar's imperialistic—and now unwinnable—war. Russia signed a peace treaty with Germany on March 3, 1918, and gave up large amounts of territory, including Finland, Poland, Ukraine, and the Baltic states.

Yet Germany's strength was waning. American troops and military hardware added punch to the Allied attack in the west, and the military position of all of the Central Powers deteriorated rapidly in the fall of 1918. Bulgaria surrendered on September 29. British forces caused the surrender of the Ottoman Empire on October 30. Italy, with the help of France and Britain, brought about the surrender of Austria-Hungary in November.

World War I Casualties*

	Country	Killed	Wounded
Allied Powers	Russia	1,700,000	4,950,0000
	France	1,358,000	4,266,000
	British Empire	908,400	2,090,000
	Italy	650,000	947,000
	Romania	335,700	120,000
	United States	116,500	234,400
Central Powers	Germany	1,773,000	4,216,000
	Austria-Hungary	1,200,000	3,620,000
	Turkey	325,000	400,000
	Bulgaria	87,500	152,400

*Figures are approximate. Not all countries are listed.

World War I devastated many countries. *Which four countries suffered most of the casualties?*

The Expeditionary Force's Role

More than 2 million American soldiers went to France during the war, the peak arriving in July 1918. Of these troops, nearly 1.4 million took part in active combat. Most were in the army or marines, but 50,000 United States naval forces, under the command of William S. Sims, were indispensable too. They convoyed troop transports and helped the British fleet chase submarines and keep German ships out of the North Sea.

Beginning in March 1918, the Germans launched a last desperate series of offensives on the Western Front. In June United States troops helped the French forces block a German advance at Château-Thierry. American troops then captured the town of Cantigny. The turning point of the war was at the Second Battle of the Marne in July. About 85,000 American troops helped end the German offensive. After that, the Allies advanced steadily.

Britain and France attacked the Germans near Amiens, and General Pershing led United States troops to a major victory at St.-Mihiel. The last major offensive of the war took place between the Meuse River and the Argonne Forest, beginning in September 1918. More than 1 million

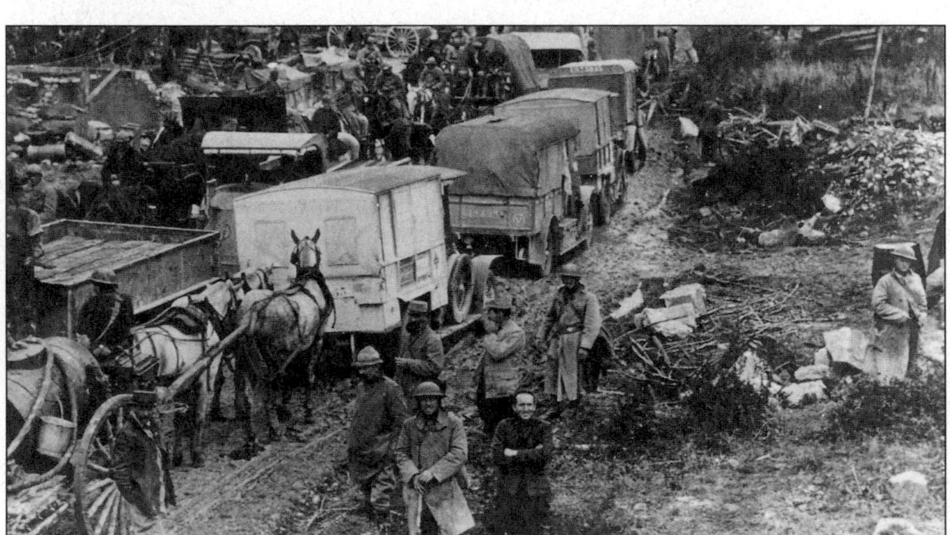

THE BETTMANN ARCHIVE

Preparing for Battle **At the end of the St.-Mihiel offensive, about 600,000 American troops moved northeast to the Meuse-Argonne region. Bad roads and tired horses slowed movement of supplies to 2 miles (3.22 km) an hour.** *On which front were American troops concentrated?*

American troops took part in a campaign that finally convinced the Germans they could not overcome the superior strength of the Allies. Germany signed the armistice on November 11, 1918, and World War I came to an end.

Americans had fought in Europe for just over a year. They felt neither the despair nor the suffering of their European counterparts. Many doughboys, never away from home before, regarded the "Great War" as a dashing adventure, a romantic scene from movies they had seen in boot camp.

Not all soldiers, however, could romanticize the war. They had witnessed sobering scenes such as this one described in the diary of an American draftee:

> Many dead Germans along the road. One heap on a manure pile. . . . Devastation everywhere. Our barrage has rooted up the entire territory like a ploughed field. Dead horses galore, many of them have a hind quarter cut off—the Huns need food. Dead men here and there.
>
> —Battlefield diary, November 3, 1918, in *The American Spirit*

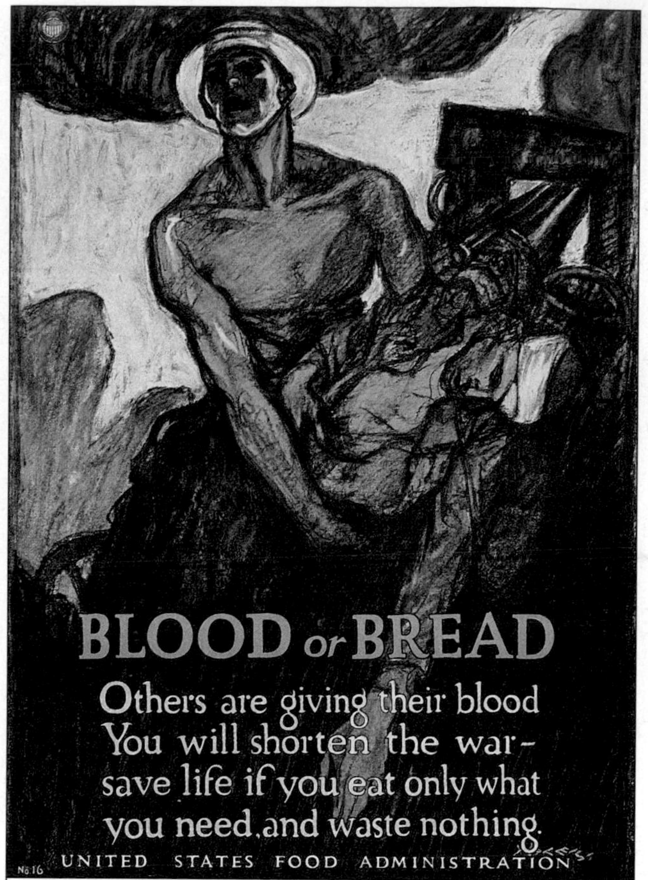

BLOOD or BREAD
Others are giving their blood
You will shorten the war-
save life if you eat only what
you need and waste nothing.
UNITED STATES FOOD ADMINISTRATION

Propaganda This poster by Henry Raleigh influenced public opinion in the United States during 1917 and 1918. *What message did this poster attempt to send to the American public?*

The War Effort at Home

Adversaries United—or Arrested

Unity, cooperation, conformity—these words described the war effort at home. **Propaganda,** a form of public information used to mold public opinion, became the tool by which American opinion would be molded to fight and win the war. Secretary of the Treasury McAdoo relentlessly pitched patriotism in his Liberty Bond campaigns. Herbert Hoover, food administrator, used slogans to urge housewives to conserve: Food will win the war, Use all leftovers, and Serve just enough. George Creel, who headed Wilson's Committee on Public Information, also relied on emotion and peer pressure to mold public opinion. Some regarded his numerous flyers, movies, conferences, speeches, posters, news bulletins, headlines, and exhibits as heavy-handed. Creel, however, defended his mission, calling it "the world's greatest adventure in advertising."

Response From the Heartland

The patriotism campaigns of McAdoo, Hoover, and Creel reached every corner of the United States. In Geneva, Illinois, for example, women formed the Women's Council of Defense to conserve food for the war effort. Because the Allies desperately needed food, many crops were shipped overseas and Americans at home were asked to conserve. Besides conserving food, women, along with adolescent girls and boys, pitched in to plow fields and plant and harvest corn. The corn crops of the Midwest fed the whole nation.

Women and teenagers in Geneva also worked at the Burgess-Norton Company, a factory booming with war business. In 1916 the government awarded the factory a contract to produce ammunition. Burgess-Norton later received contracts to produce fuses for navy shells, as well as meat cleavers, saws, and brush axes for the army.

Cooperation of Business

The Burgess-Norton Company, like thousands of other small companies, willingly cooperated with the government. By helping the war effort, they seized an opportunity to grow and increase profits. For large corporations, the war promised even bigger rewards.

In the name of unity (and expecting abundant profit), big businesses joined with the government in forming cooperative committees. They supervised the purchasing of war supplies and the granting of contracts. Progressives who lauded efficiency and cooperation smiled upon this centralized regulation, forgetting, in the heat of the moment, their former distrust of big business. Corporate profits tripled between 1914 and 1919.

Student Web Activity 10

Visit the *American Odyssey* Web site at americanodyssey.glencoe.com and click on ***Chapter 10—Student Web Activities*** for an activity relating to World War I.

Cooperation of Labor

Would labor cooperate with government and big business to win the war? In 1917 that question did not have a ready answer. Antiwar sentiment among ordinary workers had soared since 1914, and labor leadership was sharply divided. The American Federation of Labor and the Women's Trade Union League supported the war, while Socialists (members of the American Socialist party and the Industrial Workers of the World) opposed it as an imperialist ploy to protect the profits of big business. Likewise, some women suffragists in the labor movement opposed the war, questioning Wilson's commitment to democracy. After all, women still could not vote in most states.

Samuel Gompers, who headed the American Federation of Labor, became a key figure in labor's support of the war. He shed his earlier pacifist ideals as he calculated the opportunities war might bring to the labor movement. If he cooperated with government, Gompers believed he could gain concessions from company leaders: higher pay and better working conditions; the right to organize and bargain collectively.

Even before the country entered the war, Gompers had pledged support to Wilson. In return, the government's Committee of Public Information secretly channeled money to Gompers's American Alliance for Labor and Democracy, a group organized to discredit Socialists in the labor movement.

The American Federation of Labor did attract thousands of workers to its ranks during the war years. By 1918, with its membership swelled to nearly 3 million, labor had won important concessions such as an 8-hour workday in many industries previously opposed to it.

These gains came at a price. For example, during the war workers labored under no-strike contracts. Later, women of all races and African American and Hispanic men quickly lost their jobs when soldiers returned home to claim them. The labor movement itself lost some of its diversity as Gompers, in cooperation with the government, muzzled Socialist opponents. Thus weakened, the labor movement was unable to effectively face the backlash that would come after the war.

War and Civil Liberties

The lack of diversity in the labor movement reflected a similar pattern in society as a whole as the government passed legislation to unify everyone behind the war effort. The Espionage Act of 1917 and the Sedition Amendment of 1918 made any obstruction of the war effort illegal and curbed the civil liberties, or democratic rights, of those who spoke against the war. Government agencies broadly interpreted the new laws. Loyalty Leagues, organized by George Creel, encouraged Americans to spy and report on those who might be "disloyal." The Post Office withdrew circulation privileges from Socialist and antiwar newspapers such as the *Masses* and the *Milwaukee Leader,* and it even hired college professors to translate foreign periodicals to find out if they contained antiwar messages. Wilson's fears of April 1, 1917, seemed prophetic. Just before he declared war, Wilson had expressed concern that the war would result in widespread intolerance.

During the war, freedom of speech took a severe beating. Socialist Rose Pastor Stokes was punished for a letter she sent to the *Kansas City Star* stating that

THE BETTMANN ARCHIVE

War Protesters Those against the war risked official punishment and often the ridicule of their fellow citizens. *Which groups tended to oppose American involvement in the war?*

EUGENE V. DEBS FOUNDATION

Courage of Convictions **Before his arrest and 10-year sentence, Eugene Debs proclaimed to a crowd, "The master class has always declared the wars. The subject class has always fought the battles."** *What law curtailed free speech?*

"no government which is for the profiteers can also be for the people, and I am for the people, while the Government is for the profiteers." For her words, a local court sentenced her to 10 years in prison. That decision was later reversed through a higher court. Socialist leader Eugene Debs served time in prison for telling his followers to "resist militarism, wherever found."

This atmosphere of legal repression, or official restriction of dissent, soon led to mindless crowd reaction. One night in Tulsa, Oklahoma, "gowned and masked gunmen" terrorized members of the Industrial Workers of the World. One member remembered the ordeal: "After each one [of us] was whipped another man applied the tar with a large brush, from the head to the seat. Then a brute smeared feathers over and rubbed them in."

Americans of German descent, like Socialists, suffered wartime harassment. All things German became suspect. Advertisers began to call sauerkraut "liberty cabbage" and hamburgers "liberty sausage" because they wanted to avoid German names. Many schools dropped German language classes from their curricula. In some small towns, anti-German feeling turned into violence. A mob numbering 500 in Collinsville, Illinois, lynched a young German-born man whom they suspected of disloyalty. When a jury found the mob leaders innocent, they shouted, "Nobody can say we aren't loyal now!"

Defending Free Speech

Not all Americans were caught up in the wartime frenzy. Some spoke out against the espionage and sedition laws and what they considered to be violations of free speech. Senator Robert La Follette and Professor Zechariah Chafee, Jr., of the Harvard Law School openly defended Americans' rights to exercise freedom of speech with regard to war. Groups formed to protect the rights of antiwar protesters. The Civil Liberties Union assisted pacifists and conscientious objectors who had been subjected to ridicule and abuse. Most Americans, however, gave little thought to restrictions of speech and supported the war without questioning the rights they were giving up.

After the war Supreme Court Justice Oliver Wendell Holmes, Jr., ruled that a citizen's freedom of speech should only be curbed when the words uttered constitute a "clear and present danger." He used yelling a false alarm of "Fire!" in a crowded theater as an example of a situation in which freedom of speech would be superseded by others' right to safety. The question remained whether critics of the war constituted a "clear and present danger" to the nation.

Section Assessment

Main Idea

1. Use a chart like this one to show examples of cooperation and opposition to mobilization.

Response to Mobilization	
Cooperation	Opposition

Vocabulary

2. Define: mobilization, conscription, doughboys, propaganda.

Checking Facts

3. How did United States troops help win the war?
4. What were the espionage and sedition laws?

Critical Thinking

5. **Recognizing Bias** Look at the posters on pages 314 and 317. Explain how language and images can stir up enthusiasm for war.

Social Studies Skill

USING REFERENCE MATERIALS

Learning the Skill

If you want to write a paper on a topic related to World War I, you will need to use a variety of reference resources. Familiarity with such materials sharpens your research skills and helps you decide where to look for information. Try to locate the following resources in a library's reference department:

Encyclopedias

Encyclopedia articles give an overview of a topic. Most offer suggestions for further research at the end of an article, including a bibliography, list of related articles in the encyclopedia, or additional sources of information.

Indexes of Periodicals

Periodicals from the past reflect the culture, events, and concerns of their time; current periodicals provide the most recent research on a given topic. Several indexes can help you find information in periodicals. The *Readers' Guide to Periodical Literature* is a popular set of reference books that lists magazine articles by topic.

Historical Atlases

These contain maps with information about people and events of the past, and may also have articles and time lines. National Geographic's *Historical Atlas of the United States* is one source for United States history.

Statistical Sources

For information about the United States, the *Statistical Abstract of the United States* is a good place to start. Compiled by the Bureau of the Census, it contains data on more than 30 topics. The information dates back to 1790, the year the first census was taken.

Biographical Dictionaries

These tell about the life or achievements of noteworthy people. Webster's *American Biographies* and the *Dictionary of American Biography* are good sources.

Practicing the Skill

Study the chart below and answer the following questions.

1. For each source, make up your own research question based on material in Chapter 10.

2. Find answers to the questions you wrote in question 1 in the appropriate reference materials.

3. Write a short report about a key figure in this chapter. Tell what sources you used.

4. Where would you look to find out more about World War I battlefields?

5. Look up the Philippines in two sources, and list two facts from each source.

Applying the Skill

Check today's newspaper for a story that interests you; where would you look for more information on the subject?

The **Glencoe Skillbuilder Interactive Workbook, Level 2** CD-ROM provides more practice in key social studies skills.

ORGANIZATIONAL PATTERNS		
Source of Information	**Uses**	**Sample Research Questions**
Encyclopedias	Provide topic overviews; suggest further research	What were the main provisions of the Versailles Treaty
Periodicals	Reflect the past; supply current research on a topic	How did journalists react to the November Revolution?
Historical Atlases	Provide geographic context for historical information	Locate the Eastern and Western fronts during World War I.
Statistical Sources	Convey statistical information	What was the estimated total cost of World War I to the United States?
Biographical Dictionaries	Describe the backgounds and achievements of historical figures	Who were Emilio Aguinaldo, V.I. Lenin, and Georges Clemenceau?

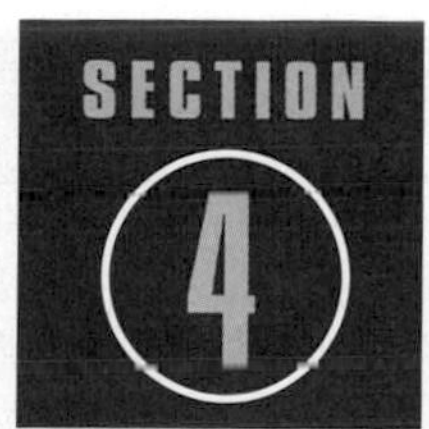

Reshaping the World

DECEMBER 1918: EUROPEANS CHEER WILSON

"WE WANT WILSON," THE WAR-WEARY CROWD ROARED. "Long live Dr. Wilson!" "Honor to Wilson the just!" British students with American flags smiled, tossing flowers in the President's path. Everywhere in Europe the Wilsons visited—Paris, Rome, Milan—the reception was jubilant. An Italian laborer spoke for millions when he said of Wilson:

> They say he thinks of us—the poor people; that he wants us all to have a fair chance; that he is going to do something when he gets here that will make it impossible for our government to send us to war again. If he had only come sooner! I have already lost my two sons. Do you believe he is strong enough to stop all wars?
>
> —Overheard conversation, 1918, *My Diplomatic Education*

NATIONAL ARCHIVES

Celebrating Wilson and Peace
Jubilant crowds greet President Wilson and British officials on Wilson's arrival in London.

Europeans had lost about 10 million soldiers in the war and twice as many civilians. Soldiers still suffered from wounds in crowded hospitals. French towns had been obliterated from the map. Ordinary Europeans had sacrificed, scrimping on food, often going cold and hungry. No wonder they looked for a savior—someone to end such brutality forever. They hailed Wilson hopefully because of his plan for a just and lasting peace. The President had outlined the plan in a 14-point document; his ideas came to be known simply as the Fourteen Points.

European leaders, however, regarded Wilson with skepticism. French Premier Georges Clemenceau observed, "God has given man Ten Commandments. He broke every one. President Wilson has his Fourteen Points. We shall see."

GUIDE TO READING

Main Idea

The destruction of World War I and the rise of radical bolshevism in Russia produced stiff resistance to Wilson's Fourteen Points both in Europe and the United States.

Vocabulary

- bolshevism
- irreconcilables
- reservationist

Read to Find Out . . .

- the terms of Wilson's Fourteen Points and international reaction to them.
- how events in Russia affected other nations.
- the 1919 Paris Peace Conference negotiations and the Treaty of Versailles.
- why the Senate rejected the Treaty of Versailles.

Points for Peace

Fear and Hope for the Postwar World

Wilson's Fourteen Points for peace had been a brilliant propaganda ploy as well as an earnest effort to steer a middle course between a radical peace settlement and a conservative, opportunistic peace settlement. Wilson gave his Fourteen Points speech to Congress on January 8, 1918, 10 months before the end of World War I. George Creel chose the most lyrical phrases from the speech to print in leaflets—about 60 million of them. He eagerly distributed them around the world, even dropping them from the air above Central Power countries.

Why had Wilson outlined his terms for peace so long before the war was over? The answer lay in the momentous events of the war years. Wilson believed that if he did not act quickly, he might lose the initiative to the Bolsheviks in Russia, who had powerful ideas of their own about reshaping the world.

Impact of Bolshevism

Russia had dealt a hard blow to the Allied cause when it withdrew from the war in early 1918. On March 3, 1918, Vladimir Ilyich Lenin, the new leader in Russia, signed the Treaty of Brest-Litovsk with Germany, formally ending Russian-German conflict. Lenin gave up large areas of land to the Germans because he needed peace to concentrate on domestic reform and on internal opposition by czarist forces, called the Whites. Events in Russia during the war help explain why **bolshevism,** a radical socialist ideology, posed such a threat to President Wilson.

COURTESY STEPHEN WHITE

Early Soviet Art The translated title of this El Lissitsky poster is *Beat the Whites With the Red Wedge.* It was created in 1920 to dramatize abstractly the social revolution in Russia. *How does this piece illustrate the conflict?*

When World War I began, an autocratic czar ruled Russia. Wilson's initial hesitation to enter the war stemmed, in part, from his distaste for associating with the absolute monarchy of the czarist rulers. By July 1917, the czar had already surrendered his power, and the Russian parliament had set up a provisional government led by moderate Socialist Aleksandr Kerensky. His liberal policies and commitment to keep Russia in the war made Kerensky very popular with the Allies.

At home, however, domestic problems overwhelmed Kerensky. Chief among them was the war's unpopularity and the disintegration of the Russian army. In the midst of chaotic discontent, the Bolsheviks, led by Lenin, seized power from Kerensky in November 1917

★ ★ ★ Gallery of Presidents ★ ★ ★

Woodrow Wilson

1913–1921

"The world must be made safe for democracy. Its peace must be planted upon the tested foundations of political liberty. We have no selfish ends to serve. We desire no conquest, no dominion. We seek no indemnities for ourselves, no material compensation for the sacrifices we shall freely make. We are but one of the champions of the rights of mankind."

War Message, April 2, 1917

BROWN BROTHERS

Background

- **Born 1856; Died 1924**
- **Democrat, New Jersey**
- **President of Princeton University 1902–1910**
- **Governor of New Jersey 1911–1913**

Achievements in Office

- **Underwood Tariff Act (1913)**
- **Federal Reserve Act (1913)**
- **Clayton Antitrust Act (1914)**
- **Child Labor Act (1916)**

(October in old Russian calendar). All of Europe, as well as the rest of the world, watched the tumultuous events in Russia. American journalist John Reed described the "October Revolution" in *Ten Days That Shook the World.*

This revolution frightened world leaders. They knew that bolshevism could potentially attract millions of discontented, war-weary workers to its ranks. Lenin's beliefs were rooted in the Communist ideology of philosopher Karl Marx, who called for class war between workers and capitalists rather than world war between capitalist governments. Lenin blamed the war on capitalism and named workers of all nationalities as its hapless victims.

Wilson and other world leaders feared the Bolsheviks' radical message. They were embarrassed when Lenin published copies of secret pacts made between allied European powers early in the war. The pacts revealed that the Allies were not simply fighting for democracy but also hoped to divide the world among themselves. The publication of the pacts put Wilson in a difficult position. He did not want to be associated with them, nor did he want to support the Bolsheviks. His answer to this dilemma emerged as the Fourteen Points. Wilson hoped that his plan for lasting peace would attract the attention of common people, distracting them from bolshevism.

Wilson's Fourteen Points

The Fourteen Points promised that all countries signing the peace treaty would enjoy equality of trade and "removal, as far as possible, of all economic barriers" in the postwar world. This provision reassured Germany, who feared harsh reprisals. The points stressed the importance of territorial integrity and self-determination for countries invaded during the war, including Russia, Belgium, France, and Italy. They outlined specific recommendations for adjusting borders after the war, so that the Austro-Hungarian Empire would be divided into several new states based on nationality.

The Fourteen Points also suggested new forms of international conduct: freedom of ocean travel and trade, open agreements instead of secret pacts, and arms reductions. One point called for "impartial adjustment" of colonial claims, with a voice for both the colonial populations and the foreign governments claiming dominion over them.

Wilson believed the most important point to be the establishment of a League of Nations, an international mediating body "affording mutual guarantees of political independence and territorial integrity to great and small states alike." He thought that such a league could bond all nations of the world together. If the League provided for the security of each individual state, then the ancient dream of peace among nations might succeed.

Reaction to the Fourteen Points

While the European masses greeted the Fourteen Points with great enthusiasm, British and French leaders were more restrained. They did not have time to sit down with Wilson and discuss his grand ideas. The war needed their attention. Nonetheless, David Lloyd George, the pragmatic prime minister of Great Britain, knew that he could never agree to freedom of the seas, thus giving up British naval dominance. Likewise, Georges Clemenceau knew that France would never concede to ignoring the damage inflicted by Germany. From the outset the Fourteen Points were no match for the fierce determination of France to punish Germany.

One of the Fourteen Points was ignored seven months after the points were announced—the right of Russia to have "institutions of her own choosing." Yielding to pressure from the Allies, Wilson sent American battalions to the Russian ports of Vladivostok and Murmansk. He did so under the pretense of helping Czech troops stranded there after Russia pulled out of the war. In reality the intervention gave aid to the White Army that was engaged in a civil war against the Bolsheviks.

CULVER PICTURES

Program for the Peace of the World

By *PRESIDENT WILSON* January 8, 1918

I. Open covenants of peace, openly arrived at, after which there shall be no private international understandings of any kind, but diplomacy shall proceed always frankly and in the public view.

II. Absolute freedom of navigation upon the seas, outside territorial waters, alike in peace and in war, except as the seas may be closed in whole or in part by international action for the enforcement of international covenants.

III. The removal, so far as possible, of all economic barriers and the establishment of an equality of trade conditions among all the nations consenting to the peace and associating themselves for its maintenance.

IV. Adequate guarantees given and taken that national armaments will reduce to the lowest point consistent with domestic safety.

V. Free, open-minded, and absolutely impartial adjustment of all colonial claims, based upon a strict observance of the principle that in determining all such questions of sovereignty the interests of the population concerned must have equal weight with the equitable claims of the government whose title is to be determined.

VI. The evacuation of all Russian territory and such a settlement of all questions affecting Russia as will secure the best and freest coöperation of the other nations of the world in obtaining for her an unhampered and unembarrassed opportunity for the independent determination of her own political development and national policy, and assure her of a sincere welcome into the society of free nations under institutions of her own choosing; and, more than a welcome, assistance also of every kind that she may need and may herself desire. The treatment accorded Russia by her sister nations in the months to come will be the acid test of their good-will, of their comprehension of her needs as distinguished from their own interests, and of their intelligent and unselfish sympathy.

VII. Belgium, the whole world will agree, must be evacuated and restored, without any attempt to limit the sovereignty which she enjoys in common with all other free nations. No other single act will serve as this will serve to restore confidence among the nations in the law which they have themselves set and determined for the government of their relations with one another. Without this healing act the whole structure and validity of international law is forever impaired.

VIII. All French territory should be freed and the invaded portions restored, and the wrong done to France by Prussia in 1871 in the matter of Alsace-Lorraine, which has unsettled the peace of the world for nearly fifty years, should be righted, in order that peace may once more be made secure in the interest of all.

IX. A readjustment of the frontiers of Italy should be effected along clearly recognizable lines of nationality.

X. The people of Austria-Hungary, whose place among the nations we wish to see safeguarded and assured, should be accorded the freest opportunity of autonomous development.

XI. Rumania, Serbia and Montenegro should be evacuated; occupied territories restored; Serbia accorded free and secure access to the sea; and the relations of the several Balkan States to one another determined by friendly counsel along historically established lines of allegiance and nationality; and international guarantees of the political and economic independence and territorial integrity of the several Balkan States should be entered into.

XII. The Turkish portions of the present Ottoman Empire should be assured a secure sovereignty, but the other nationalities which are now under Turkish rule should be assured an undoubted security of life and an absolutely unmolested opportunity of autonomous development, and the Dardanelles should be permanently opened as a free passage to the ships and commerce of all nations under international guarantees.

XIII. An independent Polish State should be erected which should include the territories inhabited by indisputably Polish populations, which should be assured a free and secure access to the sea, and whose political and economic independence and territorial integrity should be guaranteed by international covenant.

XIV. A general association of nations must be formed under specific covenants for the purpose of affording mutual guarantees of political independence and territorial integrity to great and small States alike.

Wilson's Hope The Fourteen Points were brief but influential, condensing Wilson's plan for peace to one page. *How did other world leaders react to Wilson's plan?*

Wilson also unwittingly endangered his Fourteen Points with a political move at home. As the midterm congressional elections of 1918 drew near, Wilson issued an appeal urging Americans to vote Democratic. This appeal enraged Republicans, who took it as an affront to their patriotism. When voters later elected Republican majorities to Congress, Wilson lost credibility at the negotiating table with European leaders.

A Troubling Treaty

Vision and Vengeance Clash

Woodrow Wilson walked into the Paris Peace Conference at the Palace of Versailles in January 1919 with the cheers of the European crowds still ringing in his ears, but he was in a very weak bargaining position. As the conference dragged on for five long months, he would give up more and more of his Fourteen Points as well as his own good spirits and health. By April he appeared thinner, grayer, grimmer, and more nervous. His face twitched as he spoke, and he expressed greater moral rigidity than ever before. This irritated the European leaders around him. "I never knew anyone to talk more like Jesus Christ," said Clemenceau in exasperation.

An Atmosphere of Exclusion

One of the Fourteen Points promised that international negotiations and agreements would be made in the open, eliminating secret pacts. From early on, however, this principle was ignored. The press was kept away from the negotiations. The Allied Powers also pared down the number of countries actually shaping the final outcome to the "Big Four"—the United States, Great Britain, France, and Italy. Germany and Russia—two countries whose futures hinged on the outcome of the treaty—were completely shut out of negotiations.

Great Britain, Italy, and France insisted on the exclusion of a German representative. France even refused Germany the right to have observers at the proceedings. Wilson had argued for peace among equals, but now he deferred to the wishes of his three wartime allies. Before the conference concluded, France obtained concessions to occupy an industrial region of Germany for 15 years, won back its northeastern territories of Lorraine and Alsace, and established a reparations commission to assess money Germany would pay for French losses.

The exclusion of Russia at the conference stemmed from confusion and fear. In 1919 Europe seemed on the brink of revolution. Bolshevik forces had not fallen to the White Russian opposition, in spite of American and Japanese intervention. In Germany radical groups threatened to overthrow the newly established Social Democratic government. Communists gained power in Hungary. Leaders of the Western democracies at Versailles were worried about the revolutionary movements sweeping Europe.

The Big Four vacillated and disagreed. Should they include Russia to try to soften its impact, or should they use direct military action to subdue the Bolsheviks? Neither extreme won the day. Instead, they simply excluded Russia from the conference, but as a contemporary observer noted, "the black cloud" of Russia remained, "threatening to overwhelm and swallow up the world."

An Atmosphere of Self-Interest

The Fourteen Points dwindled to even fewer as the Big Four debated what to do about German and Turkish colonies in Asia and Africa. In Wilson's original plan, all colonies would have a say in their own destiny. Colonies of Allied Powers hoped this principle would include them. To victorious France and Great Britain, however, the self-determination of their colonies was completely unacceptable. Rather than losing their own colonies, they were eager to enjoy the spoils of war by absorbing the colonies of their defeated enemies.

The final compromise did little to honor Wilson's call for "impartial adjustment of all colonial claims." Allied Powers would retain their own colonies and the League of Nations would give them control over Central

THE BETTMANN ARCHIVE

Germany Impoverished **Germany's huge postwar debt helped bankrupt its economy and made it fertile ground for the rise of fascism. Some poorer citizens turned to rummaging through refuse heaps in hopes of finding everyday necessities.** *How was Germany treated at the Paris Peace Conference?*

NEGOTIATION OF THE TREATY OF VERSAILLES

Japanese Delegates Like the Big Four, Japan sent 5 delegates to Versailles; 22 other nations had 1 to 3 delegates each. *What did Japan request at the peace conference?*

Power colonies. These mandated colonies, however, would be ruled in the name of the League.

Italy presented another challenge to the Fourteen Points. It, too, wanted some of the spoils of war—parts of the Austro-Hungarian Empire including the ports of Fiume and Trieste. Wilson resisted Italy's expansion because his plan advocated forming Balkan states from the land of Austria-Hungary. Much of what Italy wanted would go to the newly created state of Yugoslavia (shown on the map on page 326). Soon Italians would turn to Benito Mussolini, who vowed to avenge their humiliation.

Japan, the mighty force of the Pacific, also came to Versailles to make its demands as the world shifted and realigned. Japan wanted full recognition of its rights in the Shandong Province of China, which Germany had controlled before the war. During the heat of the war, world powers had little time to protect their stake in China, leaving Japan to consolidate its interests there. Japan's demand to control the province directly opposed the self-determination provisions of the Fourteen Points.

Nonetheless, Japan devised a scheme to secure its control of Shandong. Japanese delegates asked that an article formally declaring the equality of all races be attached to the peace agreement. This request exposed the limitations of Wilson's progressive approach. Much of progressive foreign policy, especially in the Caribbean, had been based on the assumption that white people knew best. While the Fourteen Points provided for a degree of self-determination, Wilson was not ready to change the power structure of the world so radically. The Japanese proposal directly challenged not only Wilson, but all of the colonial powers at the conference who held dominion over people of color in Asia and Africa. Rather than deal with this troubling situation, the conference let Japan expand its influence in China, provided it drop its racial equality proposal. Thus, by cleverly manipulating the issue of race, Japan gained power in China. The Japanese victory enraged student radicals in China, who rioted in protest through the streets of Beijing.

By June 28, 1919, when the Treaty of Versailles was signed, a beleaguered and ill Woodrow Wilson had only one consolation left: the provision for the League of Nations had not been rejected, even though most of his original Fourteen Points had vanished. He returned to the United States driven by the idea that the League of Nations must not fail. Only an international league could deal with the injustices built into the Treaty of Versailles.

Rejection at Home

Political and Personal Obstacles

Woodrow Wilson's long stay in Europe took its toll on his health. Moreover, his rivals in Congress had united against him. Approval for the League of Nations now hinged on ratification of the Treaty of Versailles by the United States Senate.

Opposition in Congress

Opposition to the League was consolidated in two camps in Congress. One camp, the **irreconcilables,** was mostly progressive Republicans, many of whom had been in elected office since the turn of the century. They included Robert La Follette, William Borah, Hiram Johnson, and a handful of others. They called themselves irreconcilables because under no circumstances would they be reconciled to voting for the League of Nations.

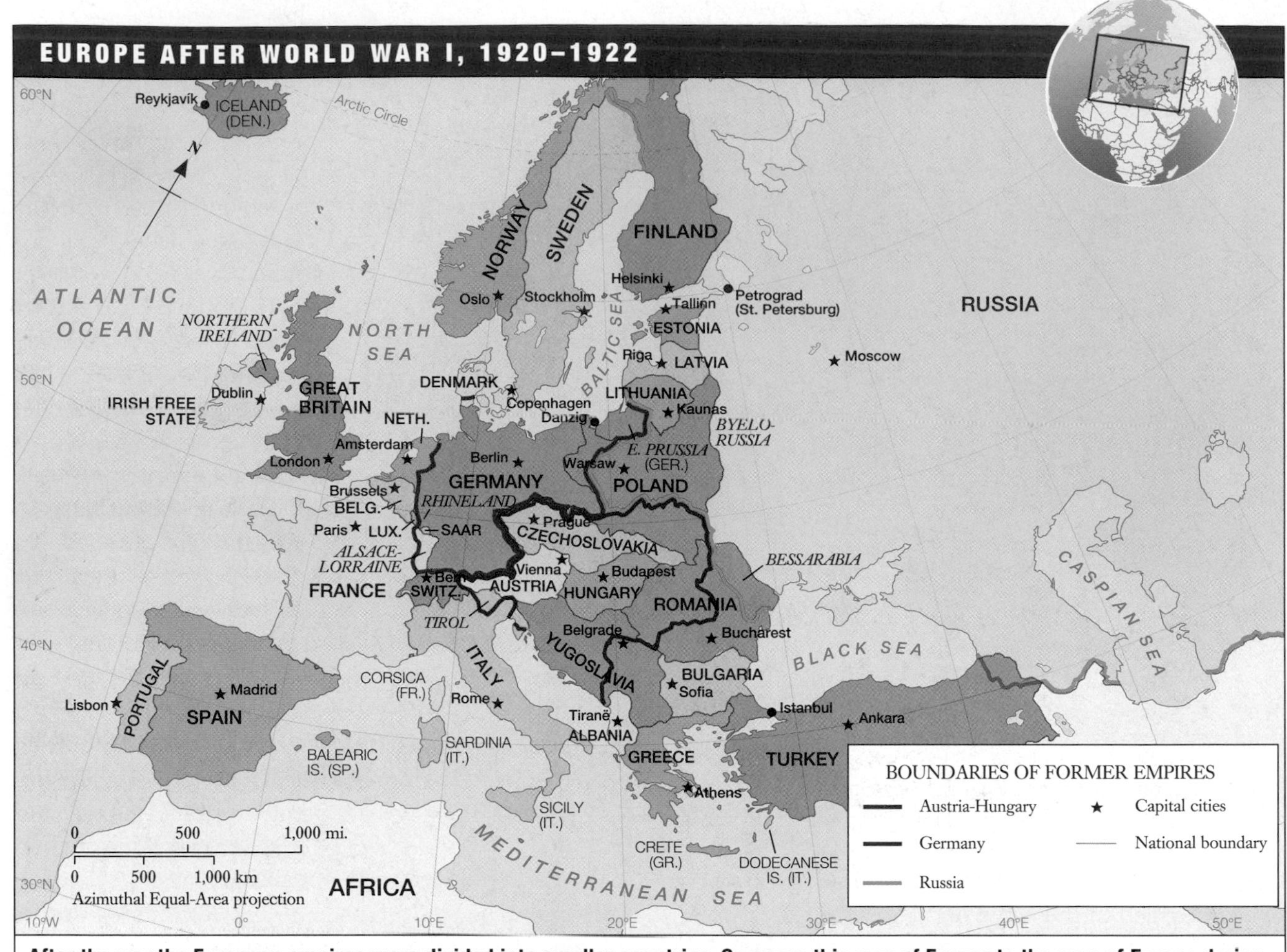

After the war the European empires were divided into smaller countries. Compare this map of Europe to the map of Europe during World War I on page 307. *Which new countries make up what were once Austria-Hungary and the German and Russian Empires?*

Irreconcilables clung to the old argument that the United States was better off steering clear of the corrupting influence of Europe. They were mainly anti-imperialists and feared that if the United States joined the League of Nations, it would be put in the immoral position of defending the colonial activities of European powers. They preferred to focus attention on reform at home rather than on politics abroad. Nevertheless, they did not completely favor isolationism—a policy that supported indifference in affairs outside the United States.

The **reservationists,** on the other hand, approved of the idea of the League of Nations but wished to modify Wilson's particular proposal. They disliked the article specifying that the League preserve "the territorial integrity and existing political independence of all Members of the League." Vague wording described how such an obligation would be fulfilled. Both reservationists and irreconcilables feared that this article —Article 10—could involve the United States in armed conflict. It also seemed to suggest that the League itself would have the authority to decide if and when the United States, or any League members, would enter a conflict in defense of a member nation's independence. If this were so, the power of the League superseded the power of Congress to declare war.

By late summer 1919, anti–League of Nations sentiment spread from Washington throughout the country. An advertisement in the *Boston Herald* on July 8, 1919, for an anti-League meeting warned: "AMERICANS, AWAKE! Shall We Bind Ourselves to the War Breeding Covenant? It Impairs American Sovereignty! Surrenders the Monroe Doctrine! . . . Entangles us in European and Asiatic Intrigues!"

Besides the reservationists' concern about Article 10, they also objected to the League for other reasons. Led by Senator Henry Cabot Lodge, they hoped to embarrass the President. Lodge, like Wilson, had formerly been a scholar. Though Lodge often acted in an aristocratic manner, he resented the same behavior in Wilson. He seethed with anger at the thought of Wilson getting full credit for the League when he himself had often suggested an international peacekeeping body. Motivated by anger as well as genuine misgivings, Lodge fought to attach his amendments to the original proposal for the League. Wilson refused to consider a compromise.

WILLIAM TELL, REVERSED.
—Harding in the Brooklyn *Eagle*.

Wilson Shot Down This cartoon shows partisan opposition to the League. *How can personal opinions about an individual affect decisions to support that individual's policies?*

Speaking to the People

Growing impatient with senators and critics, President Wilson decided to take his case to the American people. If he had their overwhelming support, the Senate would not dare defy him. In September 1919, Wilson organized a grueling 9,000-mile (14,481-km) cross-country speaking tour by train: 26 different stops in 27 days.

As in Europe, cheering crowds greeted Wilson. Despite failing health, he often spoke eloquently:

> For the first time in the history of a civilized society, a great international convention, made up of the leading statesmen of the world, has proposed a settlement which is for the benefit of the weak and not the benefit of the strong.
>
> —Woodrow Wilson, speech in Los Angeles, September 1919

Crowds gathered and cheered. The President waved and rallied. His dream, though, was not to be. On September 25, 1919, as he spoke in Pueblo, Colorado, he fell violently ill and was rushed back to Washington, D.C. A few days later, he suffered a paralytic stroke. For weeks Wilson could not function as President. When finally he was able to make decisions, he refused to modify any of his ideas. As both Lodge and Wilson remained entrenched in their positions, the Senate voted to reject the Treaty of Versailles with its League of Nations.

Wilson refused to give up. He looked forward to the presidential election of 1920. The Democratic party did not seriously consider renominating President Wilson because of his illness. Wilson, however, pinned his hopes on the party's nominee, Governor James M. Cox from Ohio. Woodrow Wilson saw the election of 1920 as a "solemn referendum" on the League of Nations.

Most of the country, however, was not listening. Other concerns captured their attention. The Red Scare—a fear of bolshevism—spread throughout the United States. Wilson himself had contributed to this hysteria during the war by supporting the Espionage Act of 1917 and the 1918 Sedition Amendment that had led to the arrest of several Socialist labor leaders.

In the election of 1920, the country responded to this fear by isolating itself, turning away from Europe and the world's troubling revolutions. Repudiating the League of Nations and the idea of internationalism, the American people opted for a promise of "normalcy" by electing the Republican Warren G. Harding to the presidency. Woodrow Wilson lived for three years after leaving office, but he never regained his health. He died on February 3, 1924, shortly after telling some of his friends that he was "tired of swimming upstream."

Section Assessment

Main Idea

1. Use a chart like this one to show causes of European opposition to Wilson's Fourteen Points and American opposition to the Treaty of Versailles.

Opposition to Wilson's Peace Plans	
Fourteen Points	Treaty of Versailles

Vocabulary

2. Define: bolshevism, irreconcilables, reservationist.

Checking Facts

3. How did Russia's withdrawal from World War I and its separate peace with Germany affect other nations?

4. Why was the League of Nations so important to Wilson? Why did the Senate oppose it?

Critical Thinking

5. **Drawing Conclusions** Why did leaders at the Versailles Conference agree to Japan's request to expand its influence into China?

Chapter  Assessment

Self-Check Quiz

Visit the *American Odyssey* Web site at americanodyssey.glencoe.com and click on ***Chapter 10—Self-Check Quiz*** to prepare for the Chapter Test.

Reviewing Key Terms

Imagine that you have kept a diary of events covering the outbreak of World War I and the United States involvement in the war. Write headlines for 10 diary entries, using each of the following terms.

alliance	**doughboys**
neutrality	**propaganda**
dogfight	**bolshevism**
mobilization	**irreconcilable**
conscription	**reservationist**

Recalling Facts

1. Why did overseas markets appeal to many Americans? Why did some oppose commercial expansion overseas?

2. What policies did Roosevelt and Taft implement in the Caribbean?

3. What is self-determination? What actions did Wilson take that were not consistent with his belief in self-determination?

4. Describe the United States's involvement in Mexico during the first 2 decades of the 1900s.

5. Why did Wilson claim neutrality before World War I?

6. Give examples of print media that historians might use to study public opinion during World War I.

7. Describe the racial bias that existed in the United States military during World War I.

8. What actions were taken to support the war on the home front?

9. How did George Creel help spread Wilson's ideas about peace?

10. Why did bolshevism frighten President Wilson and other world leaders?

Critical Thinking

1. Recognizing Bias When Roosevelt negotiated peace between Russia and Japan, he claimed neutrality. What evidence suggests that he actually favored one side? Why would it be to his advantage to pretend he was unbiased?

2. Predicting Consequences Think about the convictions of Eugene Debs and Rose Pastor Stokes and the terrorization of IWW members in Oklahoma. In what ways might the abridgement of civil liberties lead to mob rule?

3. Determining Cause and Effect President Woodrow Wilson did not want to involve the United States in World War I. Instead he wished to remain neutral, supporting neither Germany nor Russia. The President wanted the people of the United States to be "impartial in thought as well as in action." On April 2, 1917, however, the President asked the members of Congress to declare war on Germany. What factors or international incidents involving the United States caused President Wilson to reverse his position?

4. Determining Cause and Effect Use a diagram like this one to summarize the causes and effects of World War I. Add answer lines as needed.

World War I	
Causes	Effects
1. 2. 3.	1. 2. 3.

Portfolio Project

PORTFOLIO PROJECT

Select a country in Europe that was involved in World War I. Research what life was like for the citizens of that country during the war. Try to locate and review primary sources to supplement textbook and other secondary source materials. Primary sources might include letters, diaries, personal memoirs, and legal documents such as wills and titles. Prepare a written report about "life during World War I." You may want to support your report with appropriate visuals—pictures from newspapers and magazines, photographs, paintings, and drawings. Share your report orally with your classmates before filing your written account in your portfolio.

Cooperative Learning

With a small group, stage the debate over the selective exclusion that occurred during the 1919 Paris Peace Conference. Use information from Section 4, as well as additional research, to represent the Big Four countries. Try to identify the reasons the Big Four finally excluded Germany and Russia from the peace negotiations.

Reinforcing Skills

Using Reference Materials
Imagine that you are a reporter who was assigned a feature story commemorating Theodore Roosevelt. Think about the various reference materials that could be sources of information about his family, his accomplishments, and his career. Refer to the Tools of Reference chart on page 320 as you list the various reference materials you could use. Explain the type of information that you expect to learn from each source.

GEOGRAPHY AND HISTORY

United States in World War I

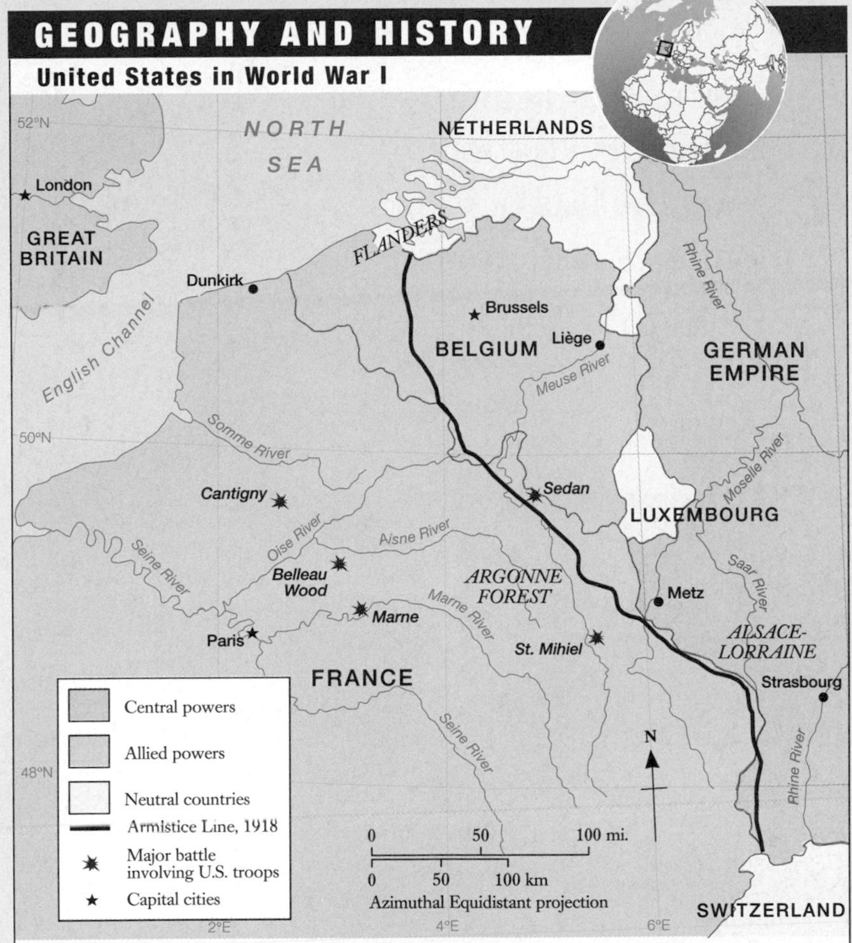

Study the map to answer the following questions:

1. Name two important World War I battles involving United States troops. In what country did the fighting occur?
2. Which French city was an important naval landing site for British and Allied replacement troops? Why?
3. Which capital city of western Europe was most threatened by nearby warfare? How did this affect the way the war was fought?
4. Through what countries did the Armistice Line extend? Were these countries primarily Allied Powers or Central Powers?

Technology Activity

Using the Internet Search the Internet to find out more details about the "Great War"—World War I. Use the information you find to create a chart titled "World War I —A Closer Look." Focus on causes of the war for various countries. Include the number of casualties and costs of rebuilding.

Standardized Test Practice

1. The United States did not enter World War I until 1917. Which of the following was the *most* important factor in convincing the American public to support the war?

- **A** German submarine attacks on American ships
- **B** the threat of a German invasion
- **C** failure of British and French troops to defeat Germany
- **D** use of poison gas by the Central Powers

Test-Taking Tip: Use reasoned judgment to eliminate weak answers. For example, since the majority of Americans favored an isolationist policy, answers C and D were probably not strong enough reasons to change public opinion.

2. One of the effects of World War I on the American economy was

- **A** a sharp rise in unemployment.
- **B** more favorable contracts for labor unions.
- **C** a huge increase in business profits.
- **D** increased progressive efforts to regulate big business.

Test-Taking Tip: This question asks you to identify a cause-and-effect relationship. Look for an answer that can be *directly related* to the needs of a wartime economy. For example, mobilization requires increased production, which means that answer A would be unlikely.

Then...

Coca-Cola: Symbol of America

In the heyday of American cure-all medicines and soda fountains, Dr. John S. Pemberton decided to create a "medicine" tasty enough to top the lists of soda fountain flavors. In 1886, after months of taste-testing, he produced his famous "nerve tonic"—actually 99 percent sugar water—and Coca-Cola was born.

PRINTS SUPPLIED BY THE COCA COLA COMPANY

PRINTS SUPPLIED BY THE COCA COLA COMPANY

1 Pemberton's partner Frank Robinson created the product's name and its flowing script. His adjectives "delicious and refreshing" became almost synonymous with the drink. Bottles, advertising, and recipes changed, but the Coca-Cola script remained the same.

PRINTS SUPPLIED BY THE COCA COLA COMPANY

Fun Facts

FOR LOVE OF TRADITION

When the Coca-Cola Company tried altering its recipe in 1985, the popular uproar forced a reintroduction of "Coke Classic" within 3 months.

ADVERTISING AT ITS BEST

Some say that "Coca-Cola" is the second most recognized term on the earth, after "OK."

2 **Pemberton spent $150 in advertising during the first year—at a time when a streetcar sign cost a penny and 1,000 free-sample coupons could be printed for a dollar. Soon the Coca-Cola name was visible on all kinds of items, such as the 1910 baseball scorecard, below.**

PRINTS SUPPLIED BY THE COCA COLA COMPANY

PRINTS SUPPLIED BY THE COCA COLA COMPANY

Stats

PRODUCT DEVELOPMENT

	Originated	Patent Registered
Coca-Cola name	1886	1893
Coke name	1941	1945
Contoured bottle	1916	1960

ORIGINAL RECIPE

Water, sugar, lime juice, coco, citric acid, vanilla, caffeine, orange, lemon, nutmeg, cinnamon, coriander, neroli, alcohol

THE COMPETITION

- Before Pepsi Cola became a threatening competitor, Coca-Cola refused two offers to buy out the nearly bankrupt company.
- Hire's Root Beer and Dr. Pepper were already on many soda fountain menus by the time Coca-Cola arrived.
- Dr. Pemberton originally called his concoction "my temperance drink," in response to the growing temperance movement of the day.

3 **At soda fountains, Coca-Cola syrup was often stored in urns like this one. It was mixed with carbonated water at soda fountains and served in a glass for 5 cents. Many soda fountains were inside drugstores, emphasizing the belief (popular since Roman times) that carbonated water had healing properties.**

...Now

ANALYZING ADVERTISING

PORTFOLIO PROJECT

Coca-Cola is one of the best advertised products in the country. From the start, the product name has appeared on matchbooks, blotters, clocks, calendars, lamps, serving trays, and playing cards, among other things. In what ways do you see Coca-Cola advertised today? How are today's approaches similar to and different from those of the past? What do you consider to be the most effective forms of advertisement today? Why? Compile examples and explanations for your portfolio.

PRINTS SUPPLIED BY THE COCA COLA COMPANY

EVOLUTION OF DISTRIBUTION

Bottles of ready-to-drink Coca-Cola were not widely distributed until the turn of the century when the crimped-crown bottle cap became the industry standard.

The New Era of the Twenties

1920–1929

HISTORY & YOU

World War I sapped the nation's energy for sacrifice and reform. During the 1920s, many Americans turned inward, enjoying the economic boom triggered by the growth of big business. An expanding middle class took advantage of its new-found buying power to purchase new consumer goods and to escape in pastimes such as movies or baseball. However, there was no escaping the explosive issues that still troubled American society—cultural conflicts over religion, immigration, the rights of African Americans, and more.

See pages 962–963 for primary source readings that accompany Unit 4.

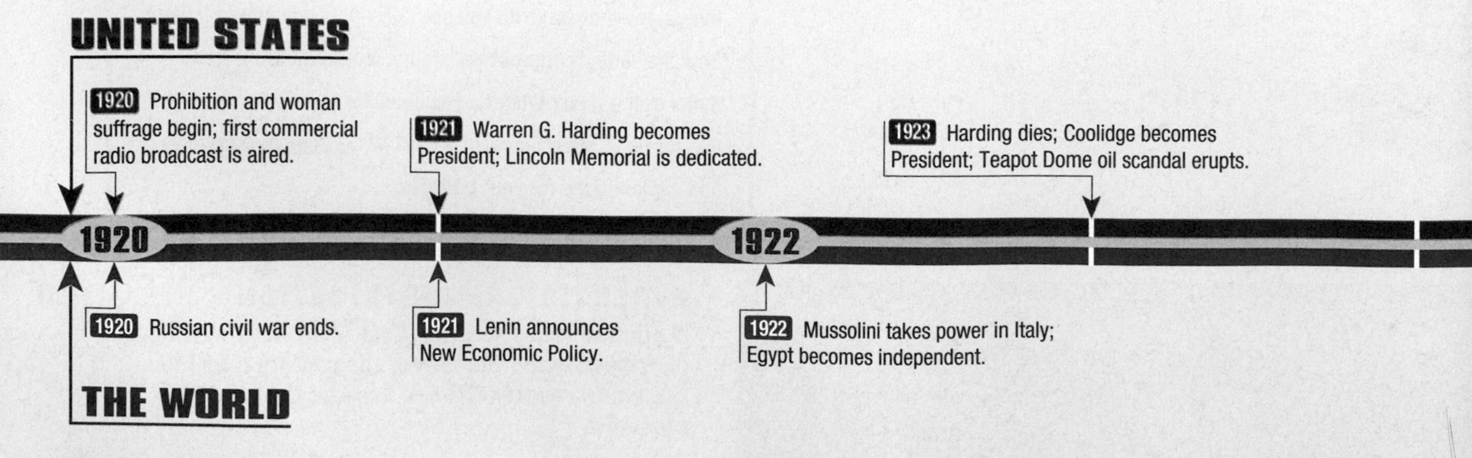

UNITED STATES
1920 Prohibition and woman suffrage begin; first commercial radio broadcast is aired.
1921 Warren G. Harding becomes President; Lincoln Memorial is dedicated.
1923 Harding dies; Coolidge becomes President; Teapot Dome oil scandal erupts.
1920
1922
1920 Russian civil war ends.
1921 Lenin announces New Economic Policy.
1922 Mussolini takes power in Italy; Egypt becomes independent.
THE WORLD

PHOTOGRAPH COURTESY NIAGARA MOHAWK POWER COMPANY

Created by an unknown artist, this example of an Art Deco panel entitled *Illumination* captures the urban sophistication that characterized the 1920s.

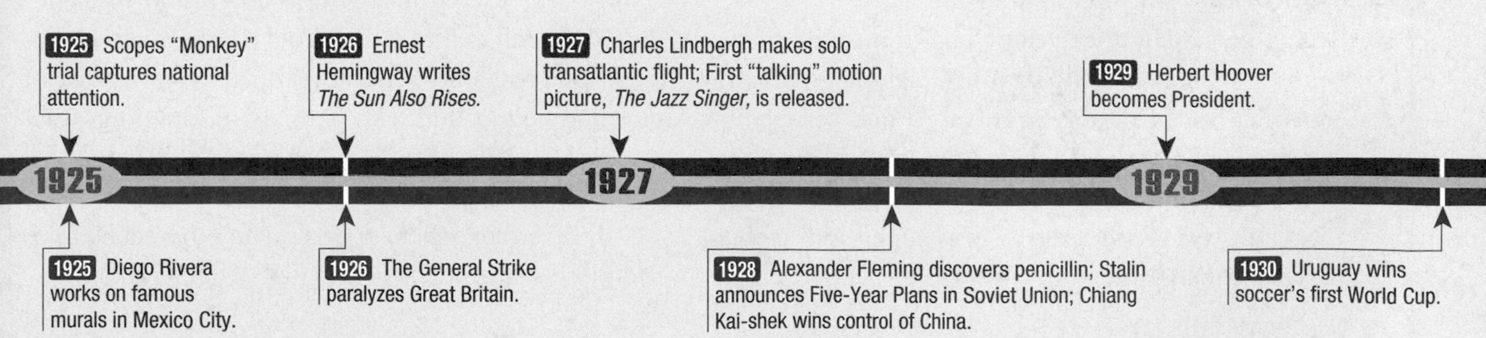

1925 Scopes "Monkey" trial captures national attention.
1926 Ernest Hemingway writes *The Sun Also Rises.*
1927 Charles Lindbergh makes solo transatlantic flight; First "talking" motion picture, *The Jazz Singer,* is released.
1929 Herbert Hoover becomes President.
1925
1927
1929
1925 Diego Rivera works on famous murals in Mexico City.
1926 The General Strike paralyzes Great Britain.
1928 Alexander Fleming discovers penicillin; Stalin announces Five-Year Plans in Soviet Union; Chiang Kai-shek wins control of China.
1930 Uruguay wins soccer's first World Cup.

The Great Gatsby

BY F. SCOTT FITZGERALD

In this excerpt from F. Scott Fitzgerald's novel The Great Gatsby, *the narrator describes a party at a mansion on Long Island. Music, dancing, and carefree parties—with a hint of emptiness—typified the Jazz Age of the 1920s.*

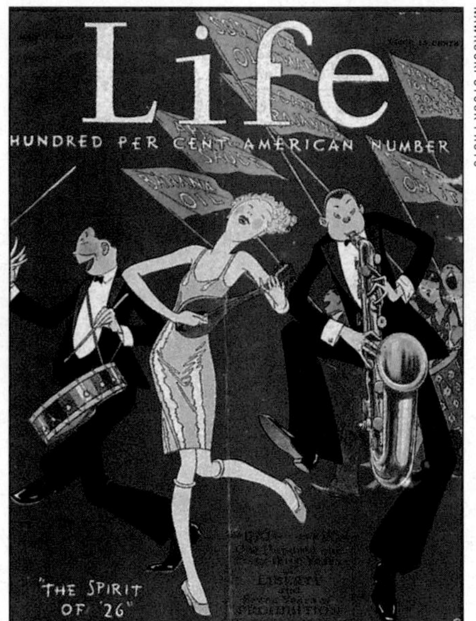

NAWROCKI STOCK PHOTO

The Spirit of '26 **Illustrator John Held, Jr., captured the jazzy verve of the 1920s in this 1926 *Life* magazine cover.**

There was music from my neighbor's house through the summer nights. In his blue gardens men and girls came and went like moths among the whisperings and the champagne and the stars. At high tide in the afternoon I watched his guests diving from the tower of his raft, or taking the sun on the hot sand of his beach while his two motor-boats slit the waters of the Sound, drawing aquaplanes over cataracts of foam. On weekends his Rolls-Royce became an omnibus, bearing parties to and from the city between nine in the morning and long past midnight, while his station wagon scampered like a brisk yellow bug to meet all trains. And on Mondays eight servants, including an extra gardener, toiled all day with mops and scrubbing-brushes and hammers and garden-shears, repairing the ravages of the night before.

Every Friday five crates of oranges and lemons arrived from a fruiterer in New York—every Monday these same oranges and lemons left his back door in a pyramid of pulpless halves. There was a machine in the kitchen which could extract the juice of two hundred oranges in half an hour if a little button was pressed two hundred times by a butler's thumb.

At least once a fortnight a corps of caterers came down with several hundred feet of canvas and enough colored lights to make a Christmas tree of Gatsby's enormous garden. On buffet tables, garnished with glistening hors-d'oeuvre, spiced baked hams crowded against salads of harlequin designs and pastry pigs and turkeys bewitched to a dark gold. In the main hall a bar with a real brass rail was set up, and stocked with gins and liquors and with cordials so long forgotten that most of his female guests were too young to know one from another.

By seven o'clock the orchestra has arrived, no thin five-piece affair, but a whole pit full of oboes and trombones and saxophones and viols and cornets and piccolos, and low and high drums. The last swimmers have come in from the beach now and are dressing upstairs; the cars from New York are parked five deep in the drive, and already the halls and salons and verandas are gaudy with primary colors, and hair shorn in strange new ways, and shawls beyond the dreams of Castile. The bar is in full swing, and floating rounds of cocktails permeate the garden outside, until the air is alive with chatter and laughter, and casual innuendo and introductions forgotten on the spot, and enthusiastic meetings between women who never knew each other's names.

The lights grow brighter as the earth lurches away from the sun, and now the orchestra is playing yellow cocktail music, and the opera of voices pitches a key higher. Laughter is easier minute by minute, spilled with prodigality, tipped out at a cheerful word. The groups change more swiftly, swell with new arrivals, dissolve and form in the same breath; already there are wanderers, confident girls who weave here and there among the stouter and more stable, become for a sharp, joyous moment the center of a group, and then, excited with triumph, glide on through the sea-change of faces and voices and color under the constantly changing light.

Suddenly one of these gypsies, in trembling opal, seizes a cocktail out of the air, dumps it down for courage and, moving her hands like Frisco, dances out alone on the canvas platform. A momentary hush; the orchestra leader varies his rhythm obligingly for her, and there is a burst of chatter as the erroneous news goes around that she is Gilda Gray's understudy from the *Follies.* The party has begun.

THERE IS A BURST OF CHATTER AS THE ERRONEOUS NEWS GOES AROUND THAT SHE IS GILDA GRAY'S UNDERSTUDY.

I believe that on the first night I went to Gatsby's house I was one of the few guests who had actually been invited. People were not invited—they went there. They got into automobiles which bore them out to Long Island, and somehow they ended up at Gatsby's door. Once there they were introduced by somebody who knew Gatsby, and after that they conducted themselves according to the rules of behavior associated with amusement parks. Sometimes they came and went without having met Gatsby at all, came for the party with a simplicity of heart that was its own ticket of admission. . . .

Dressed up in white flannels I went over to his lawn a little after seven, and wandered around rather ill at ease among swirls and eddies of people I didn't know —though here and there was a face I had noticed on the commuting train. I was immediately struck by the number of young Englishmen dotted about; all well dressed, all looking a little hungry, and all talking in low, earnest voices to solid and prosperous Americans. I was sure that they were selling something: bonds or insurance or automobiles. They were at least agonizingly aware of the easy money in the vicinity and convinced that it was theirs for a few words in the right key.

As soon as I arrived I made an attempt to find my host, but the two or three people of whom I asked his whereabouts stared at me in such an amazed way, and denied so vehemently any knowledge of his movements, that I slunk off in the direction of the cocktail table—the only place in the garden where a single man could linger without looking purposeless and alone.

Responding to Literature

1. **Fitzgerald has been called the "chronicler of the Jazz Age." Based on this excerpt, how would you define the era?**
2. **What is the narrator's attitude toward the lifestyle and values of the wealthy? Explain.**

Getting on With Business

OCTOBER 28, 1925: MISSING EPISODE OF *ANNIE* PUBLISHED

From the moment the orphan with the frizzy curls appeared in American homes on August 5, 1924, she found her way into the hearts of all.

On October 27, 1925, the *Chicago Tribune* accidentally left *Little Orphan Annie* out of the newspaper. Reader response was so strong that an apology, along with 2 *Annie* comic strips, was seen in the next day's paper.

How could a comic strip capture so much attention? In part, Annie's innocent strength seemed to reflect the self-image of the United States in the era following World War I. Annie's creator, Harold Gray, had left her without relatives or entanglements. This gave Annie the freedom to do what she wanted and go where she pleased.

Annie's foster father, Daddy Warbucks, was a weapons tycoon who showered Annie with kindness, gifts, and love. His character sent a resounding message that businesspeople could be honest and decent. In the big business era of the 1920s, millions of people seemed to agree. ■

How does the image on the opposite page illustrate the bustle of business that characterized the 1920s? Identify details from the photograph to support your answer.

Chapter Overview

Visit the *American Odyssey* Web site at americanodyssey.glencoe.com and click on ***Chapter 11—Chapter Overview*** to preview the chapter.

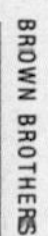

THIS 1922 PHOTO OF NEW YORK CITY'S TIMES SQUARE CAPTURES THE HIGH ENERGY THAT FILLED THE COUNTRY AFTER WORLD WAR I.

Postwar Turmoil

AUGUST 23, 1927: SACCO AND VANZETTI EXECUTED; WORLDWIDE RIOTS

IN 1921 NICOLA SACCO AND BARTOLOMEO VANZETTI HAD BEEN CONVICTED OF MURDERING A PAYMASTER AND A SHOE FACTORY GUARD DURING A ROBBERY IN SOUTH BRAINTREE, MASSACHUSETTS. Many people believed that the men had been found guilty only because they were immigrants and **radicals,** advocating political and social revolution. By 1927 Sacco and Vanzetti had exhausted every legal appeal. Now they were about to be executed.

In his final defiant words to Judge Thayer, Vanzetti declared that he was innocent of the murders but unshakable in his unpopular beliefs:

> I am suffering because I am a radical and indeed I am a radical; I have suffered because I was an Italian, and indeed I am an Italian; I have suffered more for my family and for my beloved than for myself; but I am so convinced to be right that if you could execute me two times, and if I could be reborn two other times, I would live again to do what I have done already.
>
> —Bartolomeo Vanzetti, speech to Judge Thayer, 1927

UPI/BETTMANN

Vanzetti (left) and Sacco (right)
The pair arrive for trial at the Dedham Courthouse in Massachusetts.

The years of the trial of Sacco and Vanzetti showed the United States desperately struggling to defend itself against the dangers following World War I. Many Americans feared immigrants whose ways appeared different and threatening. For a time, many Americans also believed that the radical politics of the 1917 Russian Revolution might overtake this country. Sacco and Vanzetti seemed to represent all the fears of the United States during the turbulent postwar years.

GUIDE TO READING

Main Idea

Social unrest gripped the nation during the postwar era as Americans reacted to the rise of communism, the Great Migration of African Americans to the North, and ongoing progressive demands for reform.

Vocabulary

- radical
- anarchism
- prohibition

Read to Find Out . . .

- the factors that led to the Red Scare.
- the causes and effects of the Great Migration.
- ways in which the Progressive movement continued during the 1920s.
- the reasons that progressivism declined during the 1920s.

Sacco and Vanzetti

A Miscarriage of Justice

Some criminal evidence linked Sacco, a shoemaker, and Vanzetti, a fish peddler, to the murders. Neither man had ever been accused of a crime before his arrest, and none of the money from the robbery was ever traced to the men.

Their trial, too, was marked by serious breaches of fairness. The judge, Webster Thayer, had repeatedly denounced Sacco and Vanzetti for their immigrant backgrounds and for their belief in a radical political theory called **anarchism.** Anarchists believe that the restraint of one person by another is evil, and they do not recognize the authority of any government.

During the six years the men stayed in jail, Judge Thayer refused repeated motions for a new trial. Finally, the Massachusetts governor appointed a special committee to review the case one more time. The committee included Abbott Lawrence Lowell, president of Harvard, and Dr. Samuel W. Stratton, president of the Massachusetts Institute of Technology.

One witness told the committee that, even before the trial, the foreman of the jury had declared, "They ought to hang anyway." The committee agreed that the judge had not behaved properly when he had referred to Sacco and Vanzetti as "dagos" and worse. The committee, however, still backed Judge Thayer's decision to execute the prisoners.

Prominent Americans, including future justice of the Supreme Court Felix Frankfurter, protested the scheduled executions. Sacco and Vanzetti, Frankfurter argued, were being punished for their "alien blood and abhorrent philosophy," rather than for murder.

Americans were not the only protesters. During the six years of appeals, the Sacco and Vanzetti case had become world famous. When Sacco and Vanzetti were executed, riots broke out from Japan to Warsaw, from Paris to Buenos Aires. Crowds menaced the United States Embassy in Rome, and workers went on strike in France, Italy, and the United States.

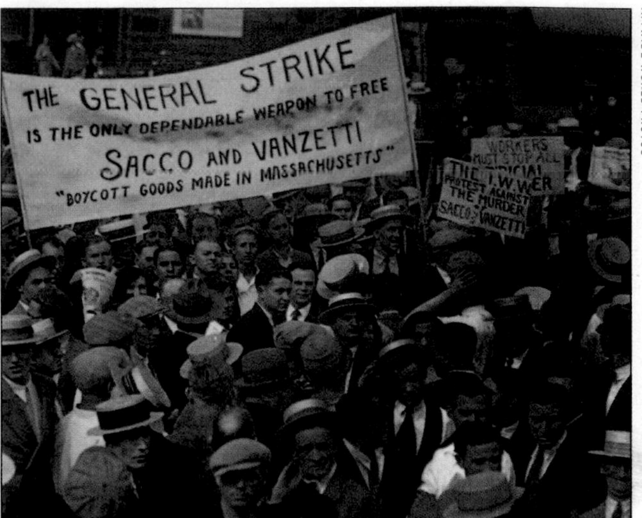

AP/WIDE WORLD PHOTOS

Sympathizers Protest Supporters of organized labor protest the Sacco and Vanzetti guilty verdict. *How widespread was support for Sacco and Vanzetti?*

Sacco's last words were "Long live anarchy!" Before he died, Vanzetti gave an interview to a reporter. In broken but eloquent English, he said:

> If it had not been for these thing, I might have live out my life, talking at street corners to scorning men. I might have die, unmarked, unknown, a failure. Now we are not a failure. This is our career and our triumph. Never in our full life can we hope to do such work for tolerance, for joostice [justice], for man's onderstanding [understanding] of man, as now we do by an accident.
>
> —Bartolomeo Vanzetti, *New York World,* May 13, 1927

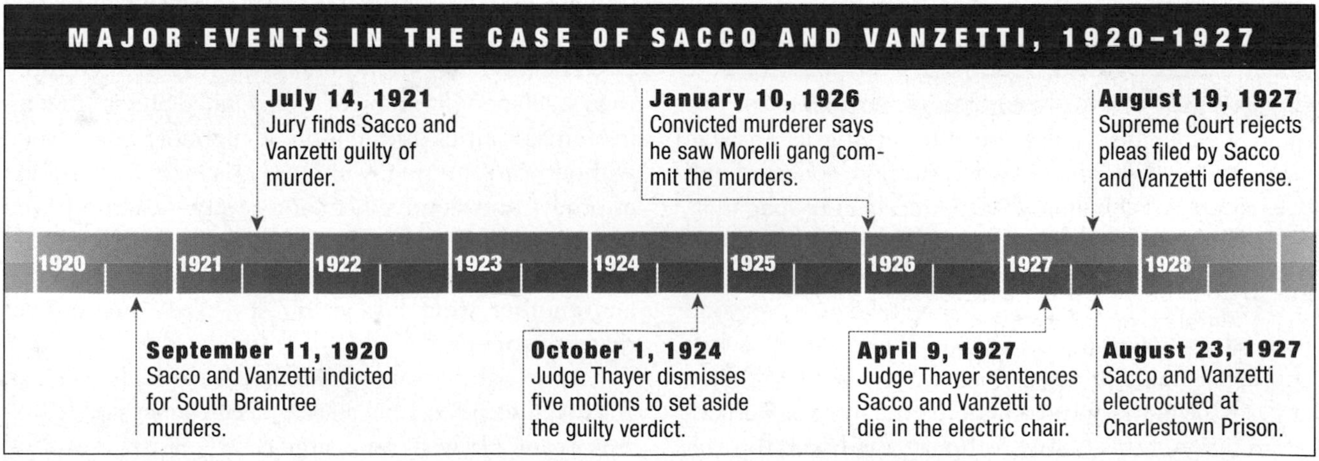

MAJOR EVENTS IN THE CASE OF SACCO AND VANZETTI, 1920–1927
July 14, 1921
Jury finds Sacco and Vanzetti guilty of murder.
January 10, 1926
Convicted murderer says he saw Morelli gang commit the murders.
August 19, 1927
Supreme Court rejects pleas filed by Sacco and Vanzetti defense.
1920
1921
1922
1923
1924
1925
1926
1927
1928
September 11, 1920
Sacco and Vanzetti indicted for South Braintree murders.
October 1, 1924
Judge Thayer dismisses five motions to set aside the guilty verdict.
April 9, 1927
Judge Thayer sentences Sacco and Vanzetti to die in the electric chair.
August 23, 1927
Sacco and Vanzetti electrocuted at Charlestown Prison.

Fifty years to the day of their execution, August 23, 1977, Massachusetts governor Michael Dukakis cleared the names of Sacco and Vanzetti. Their trial, Dukakis said, had been "permeated with prejudice."

The Red Scare

Anti-Communist Panic

Judge Felix Frankfurter described the atmosphere in Boston during the Sacco and Vanzetti trial. He said that outside the courtroom "the Red hysteria was rampant; it was allowed to dominate within."

Indeed, Boston had become one of the centers for the Red Scare, a violent wave of anti-Communist panic that swept through the United States in 1919 and 1920. In November 1917, the Bolshevik Revolution had installed a Communist government in Russia. Communist uprisings in Hungary and Bavaria made it seem as though communism were spreading rapidly.

Two small Communist parties had formed in the United States in 1919. Their total membership never exceeded 70,000, just one-tenth of 1 percent of the adult population. Even so, many people began to fear that a Communist revolution like the one in Russia was brewing in this country.

During World War I, George Creel's Committee on Public Information had whipped up public hatred of Germans. After the war many Americans transferred this hatred to anyone who had been born in another country. Foreigners were especially vulnerable to attack when, like Sacco and Vanzetti, they favored radical politics.

Public officials, business leaders, and the press all contributed to the Red Scare. More than any other person, President Wilson's attorney general, A. Mitchell Palmer, directed the Red Scare.

A Climate of Fear

A progressive lawyer and politician from Pennsylvania, Palmer had no doubt that Communists were about to take over his country's government. For one thing, Palmer had spent the war serving as an alien property custodian. In this job he had collected and been shocked by reams of anti-American propaganda. As a pacifist Quaker, Palmer despised the Bolshevik theory that promoted violent revolution.

To Palmer the Bolshevik plan to take over the world seemed to become a reality on June 2, 1919, when bombs exploded in eight cities throughout the United States. One of the bombs shattered the front of Palmer's Washington, D.C., home. Although the bomb thrower was killed in the blast, evidence suggested he was an Italian immigrant and anarchist.

"Put Them Out and Keep Them Out" **The title of this political cartoon expressed the sentiments of those who were influenced by the Red Scare.** *What was the Red Scare?*

After the bombings, Palmer asked for and got an appropriation of $500,000 from Congress to launch a campaign to "tear out the radical seeds that have entangled American ideas in their poisonous theories." Within the Justice Department's Bureau of Investigation, Palmer established the General Intelligence—or antiradical—division. Under the direction of J. Edgar Hoover, this division began to gather information about domestic radical activities.

The Palmer Raids

In November 1919, Palmer's men staged raids on the Union of Russian Workers in 12 cities. In December, 249 aliens were deported to Russia on a ship the popular press nicknamed "The Soviet Ark." Most of the deportees had never participated in any terrorist or criminal activity but merely favored nonviolent radical causes.

The following month Palmer's men arrested more than 4,000 people, many of them United States citizens, in 33 major cities during a single night of raids. Seized without warrants, many of these prisoners were denied attorneys and deprived of food, water, heat, and even bathroom facilities. In Boston one detainee leaped 5 stories to his death, 2 prisoners died of pneumonia, and another went insane. In New York guards beat many prisoners.

Some critics challenged Palmer's methods. William Allen White, newspaper editor, called Palmer's raids "un-American." He went on to argue:

> And if a man desires to preach any doctrine under the shining sun, and to advocate the realization of his vision by lawful, orderly, constitutional means—let him alone. If he is Socialist, anarchist, or Mormon, and merely preaches his creed and does not preach violence, he can do no harm. For the folly of his doctrine will be its answer. The deportation business is going to make martyrs of a lot of idiots whose cause is not worth it.
>
> —William Allen White, *Emporia* (Kansas) *Gazette,* January 8, 1920

The public, however, generally applauded Palmer's January raids. Even though most of the prisoners eventually were released because they had nothing to do with radical politics, the *Washington Post* proclaimed that this was "no time to waste on hairsplitting over infringement of liberty." Six hundred radicals were expelled from the country before the Department of Labor, in charge of aliens, halted the deportations.

By midsummer the height of the Red Scare seemed to be over. The raids and deportations had demoralized American radicals. Businesses had broken a rash of strikes. Bolshevism had failed to spread beyond Russia.

In September 1920, a bomb exploded at the corner of Broad and Wall Streets, the center of New York City's financial district, killing more than 30 people and injuring hundreds more. If the bombing had occurred the year before, Americans might have interpreted it as part of a plot to overthrow the government. Now the United States seemed to be determined not to give way to panic. One newspaper reported:

> The public is merely shocked, not terrorized, much less converted to the merits of anarchism. Business and life as usual. Society, government, industry functioning precisely as if nothing had happened.
>
> —*Cleveland Plain Dealer,* September 18, 1920

Labor Unrest

In the middle of the Red Scare, an outbreak of strikes brought the threat of revolution uncomfortably close to home. The cost of living had more than doubled from prewar levels. When their wages lagged far behind, angry workers went on strike.

Of the 3,600 strikes during 1919, the Seattle general strike, the police strike in Boston, the steel strike, and the coal strike proved the most disruptive. Each major strike further inflamed an already fearful public. During the Boston police strike, all the Boston newspapers called the strike "Bolshevistic." When labor leader Samuel Gompers asked Massachusetts governor Calvin Coolidge to help settle the strike, Coolidge wired back the refusal that launched his national political career: "There is no right to strike against the public safety by anybody, anywhere, anytime."

The 350,000 steelworkers who went on strike in September 1919 worked a 12-hour day, 7 days a week. Each time they changed between the day and the night shift, they had to work 24 hours straight, risking injury and death. Elbert Gary, the head of United States Steel, denied their simple demand—one day's rest out of the week. At first the public sympathized with the strikers. Supported by the press, however, the steel companies portrayed the strike as a radical outbreak and dangerous uprising. As public opinion began to turn against them, the strikers had little chance.

The steel owners provoked riots, broke up union meetings, and employed police and soldiers to end the strike. African Americans recruited from the impoverished South to replace the striking workers also helped break the strikes. In the end, 18 strikers were killed, and the steelworkers' union won none of its demands.

The coal strike lasted for a month in the late fall of 1919 and threatened to paralyze a country that depended on coal to heat its homes and run its factories. When the 394,000 striking miners finally obeyed a presidential order to go back to work, they went back to the same working conditions.

All the major strikes of 1919 were portrayed in the press as anti-American actions that threatened the United States government. The issues of long hours and poor working conditions got lost in the shuffle.

The Great Migration

Opportunities in the North

Between 1916 and 1920, half a million African Americans left the South for new jobs in the North. Many of these migrants were World War I veterans. These

Urban African American Population

City	1920	1930	Increase
Atlanta	62,831	90,119	43%
Birmingham	70,256	99,127	41%
Chicago	109,458	233,903	114%
Cleveland	34,815	73,339	111%
Detroit	40,838	120,066	194%
Los Angeles	15,579	38,894	150%
New York	152,467	327,706	115%
Philadelphia	134,229	219,599	64%
Washington, D.C.	110,701	132,955	20%

African American populations increased in urban areas across the United States from 1920 to 1930. *What two cities had the largest increases?*

INDIANA STATE LIBRARY

Firefighter Recruits **Service workers such as these firefighter recruits were part of growing African American communities in the North.** *What other salaried jobs did African Americans perform in Northern communities?*

soldiers bitterly resented the discrimination they had experienced in the war. No longer satisfied to struggle on Southern farms, African Americans began to seek better opportunities in the North.

Many African Americans corresponded with a newspaper, the *Chicago Defender,* a key source of information about jobs and conditions in the North. One man wrote to the *Defender* to explain why so many African Americans were migrating north. In the South, he wrote, the wages of a grown man were 50 to 75 cents a day for all labor. "He is compelled to go where there is better wages and sociable conditions, . . . many places here in this state the only thing that the black man gets is a peck of meal and from three to four lbs. of bacon per week, and he is treated as a slave."

African Americans Find Better Pay

In the North, African Americans took jobs as meatpackers, metalworkers, and autoworkers, all for more pay than they could have made in the South. A migrant to Chicago who had found employment in the sausage department of a meatpacking plant wrote: "We get $1.50 a day and we pack so many sausages we don't have much time to play but it is a matter of a dollar with me. . . ."

Only 50 African Americans worked for the Ford Motor Company in 1916. By 1920 Ford had 2,500 African American employees. Six years later their numbers had quadrupled to 10,000.

Between 1910 and 1930, the Great Migration swelled Chicago's African American population from 44,000 to almost 234,000. Cleveland, the home of 8,500 African Americans in 1910, sheltered 68,000 by the end of the 1920s.

Northern whites, however, were no more eager than Southern whites had been to share power and opportunity with African Americans. Many Northern whites reacted violently to this Northern migration.

Racial Unrest

In 1917 race riots erupted in 26 Northern cities. Racial conflicts escalated even further after the war. Riots broke out in many cities, including the nation's capital, during the hot summer of 1919.

Southern African Americans who had migrated to Washington, D.C., during the war had been competing for jobs in an atmosphere of mounting racial tension. Newspaper reports of rumored African American violence against whites contributed to the tension.

Following one such newspaper story, 200 sailors and marines marched into the city, beating African American men and women. A group of whites also tried to break through military barriers to attack African Americans in their homes. Determined to fight back, a group of African Americans boarded a streetcar and attacked the motorman and the conductors. African Americans also exchanged gunfire with whites who drove or walked through their neighborhoods.

President Wilson had to call in federal troops to control the crowds, which finally dispersed in a driving rain. When the Washington riot ended, 4 days after it began, 4 men had been killed, 11 had suffered serious wounds, and dozens more had been injured. Three hundred people were arrested for rioting or for carrying weapons.

Few cities escaped racial violence during the early 1920s. Knoxville, Omaha, and Tulsa all experienced deadly attacks on African American neighborhoods. Several radical African American groups sprang out of this ferment. Marcus Garvey's "Back to Africa" movement became the most famous.

The Garvey Movement

A black man from Jamaica, Marcus Garvey had grown up at the very bottom of Jamaican society. Black Jamaicans had no economic or political voice in this white-controlled British colony.

Educated as a journalist and filled with ambition, Garvey arrived in New York City at the age of 28. There he found an enthusiastic audience for his particular version of Booker T. Washington's African American self-help doctrine.

Where Washington advocated separate development in the United States, Garvey encouraged African Americans to return to Africa "to establish a country and a government absolutely on their own." To this end, Garvey founded the Universal Negro Improvement Association, which peaked at a membership of 250,000. With its program of African American pride and power, Garvey's "Back to Africa" movement foreshadowed the Black Muslim movement of the 1960s.

Garvey's message encouraged poor African Americans, who were his most fervent supporters. A member of the NAACP's board of directors said:

> The sweeper in the subway, the elevator boy eternally carrying fat office men and perky girls up and down a shaft, knew that when night came he might march with the African army and bear a wonderful banner to be raised some day in a distant, beautiful land.
>
> —Mary White Ovington, *Portraits in Color,* 1927

Thousands invested in Garvey's Black Star Line of ships that would take back African Americans to their "home" in Africa. The Black Star Line collapsed, however, partly because unscrupulous white business dealers sold Garvey leaky ships and faulty equipment. Arrested and charged with mail fraud, Garvey was deported as an undesirable alien.

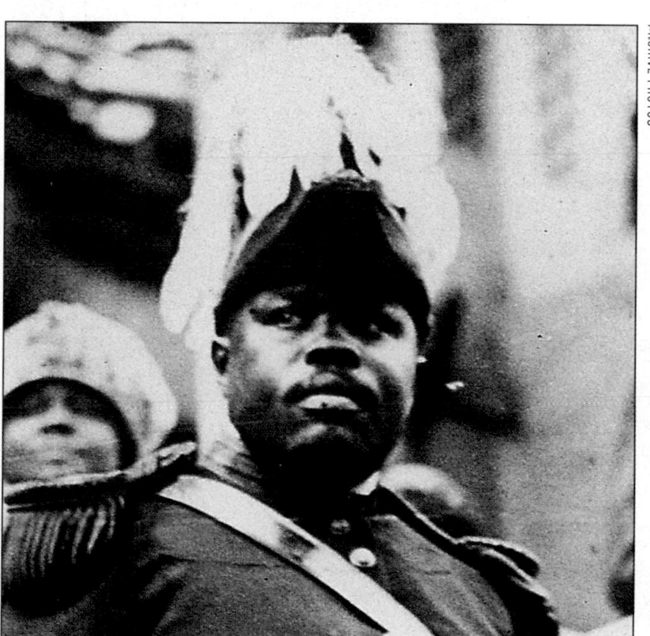

ARCHIVE PHOTOS

A Master Showman Marcus Garvey dressed in a hat with a white plume and a fancy colorful uniform, declaring himself president of the African empire. *What did Marcus Garvey advocate?*

Whites called Garvey the "Moses of the Negroes," but some African American leaders, particularly W.E.B. Du Bois, criticized his unconventional methods and personal flamboyance. Marcus Garvey, however, gave African Americans pride and hope for the future.

Progressivism Endures

New Social Reforms Enacted

Even during this period of labor unrest and social tension, the reform impulse endured. For example, Senator George Norris of Nebraska successfully resisted efforts to turn over the government power plant at Muscle Shoals to business interests. The Women's Joint Congressional Committee lobbied for social reforms throughout the 1920s. On the state level, reformers also succeeded in instituting such programs as old-age pensions, workers' compensation, and city planning.

The postwar decade began with two important reforms whose roots were firmly planted in the Progressive Era. The Eighteenth Amendment established national Prohibition in 1919, and the Nineteenth Amendment gave women the right to vote in 1920.

Prohibition

Between 1906 and 1919, 26 states had passed laws limiting the sale of liquor. Progressives supported **prohibition,** or a ban on alcohol. They championed national Prohibition, a law that would forbid the manufacturing, transporting, and selling of liquor, arguing that an outright ban on drinking would be a great boon to society. In the House of Representatives debate on the Prohibition amendment, Congressman Richard Austin from Tennessee predicted that "a [prohibition] law which has emptied the jails in Tennessee and virtually wiped out the criminal side of the dockets of the courts will do the same in every State."

During the war, antisaloon advocates successfully linked Prohibition with patriotism. Conserving the grain that would have gone into liquor became part of the war effort. The antisaloon league also stirred up the country's anti-German hysteria, blaming German brewers for making American soldiers unfit.

By 1918, three-quarters of the population lived in "dry" states or counties. The cities, with their large immigrant populations, however, remained "wet" until the national amendment was ratified in 1919. This amendment was enforced by the Volstead Act, a law passed in 1919 declaring beverages containing one-half of 1 percent of alcohol intoxicating. When the Volstead Act took effect in January 1920, many Americans had high hopes that the new law would reduce poverty and wipe out

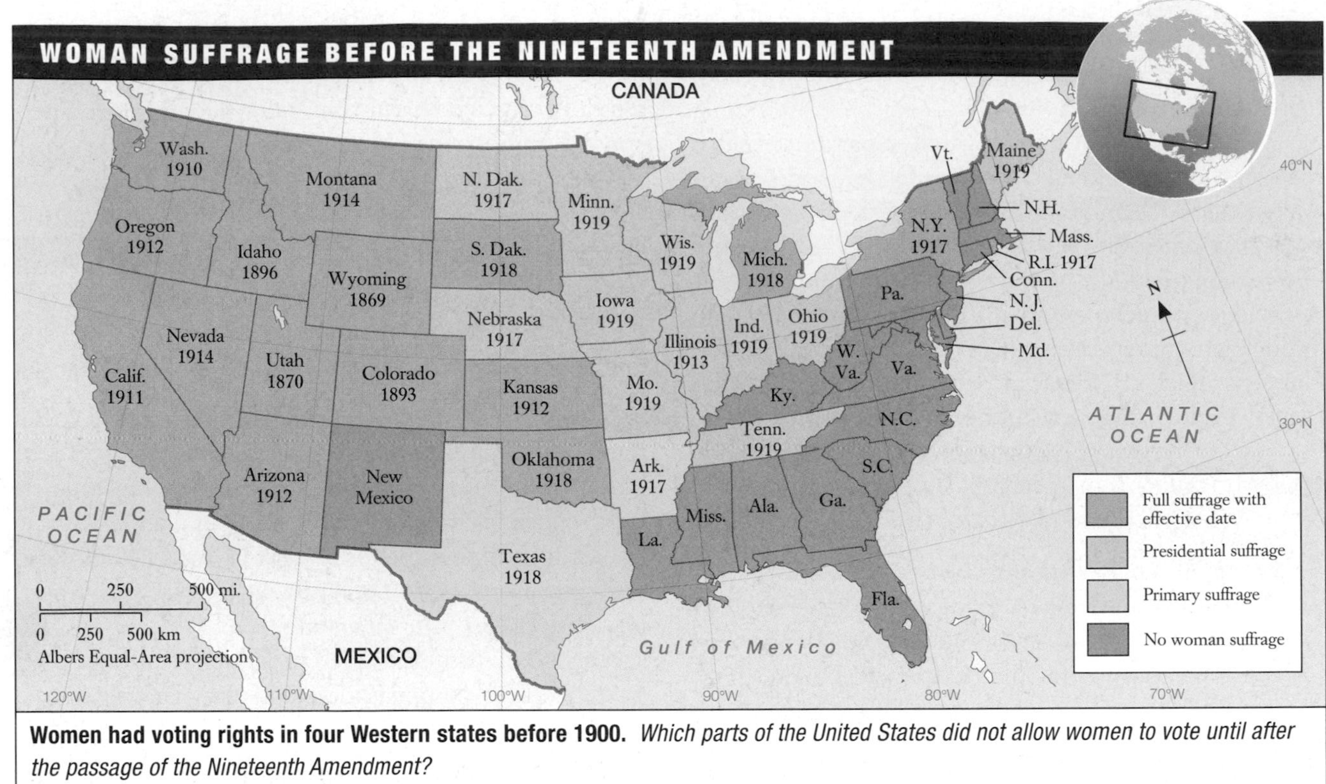

Women had voting rights in four Western states before 1900. *Which parts of the United States did not allow women to vote until after the passage of the Nineteenth Amendment?*

prostitution and crime. John Kramer, the first Prohibition Commissioner of the United States, enthusiastically proclaimed: "We shall see that it [liquor] is not manufactured. Nor sold, nor given away, nor hauled in anything on the surface of the earth or under the earth or in the air."

Suffrage

Like the fight for Prohibition, women's struggle for voting rights got its final push from the war experience. Women had begun pursuing the right to vote in 1848, but the fight died down in the decades before the Progressive Era.

Progressives supported suffrage because they believed women's votes could help pass a variety of reforms, especially those that protected women and children. A new period of activism, beginning around 1910, won rewards when several states—mostly in the West—approved suffrage.

Agnes Geelan, who later became mayor of her town and state senator from North Dakota, remembered: "We were allowed to vote in state elections . . . but there were restrictions. Women could only vote for women candidates. Men could vote for either men or women, and I didn't like that discrimination."

The campaign for national suffrage gathered steam in 1916, thanks to Carrie Chapman Catt's National American Woman Suffrage Association (NAWSA) and Alice Paul's Congressional Union, later the National Woman's party. The two groups argued intensely over tactics. The Woman's party favored radical actions, such as picketing the White House and going on hunger strikes when arrested. In a somewhat less radical way, NAWSA

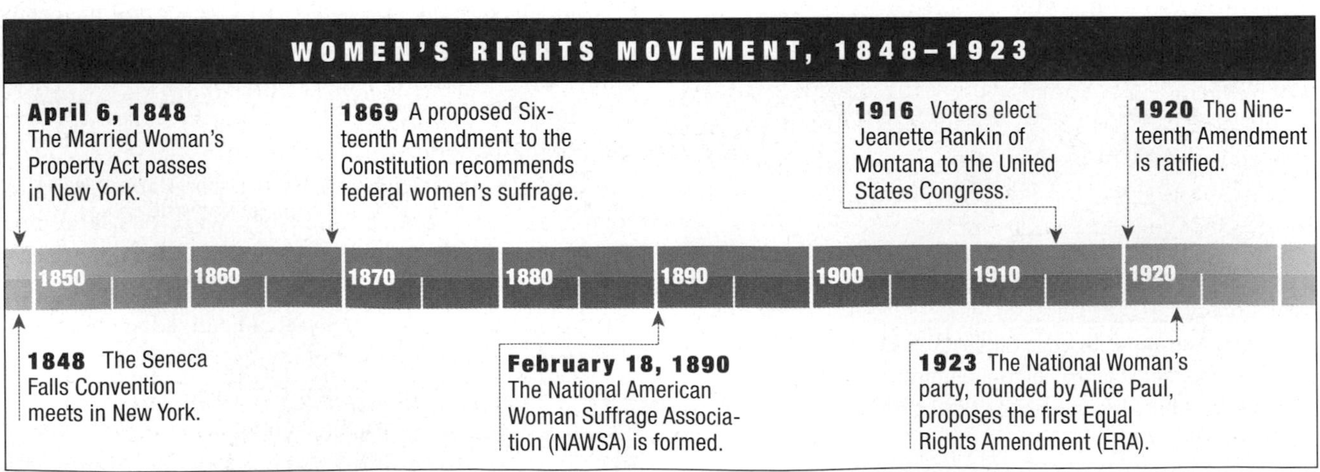

CULVER PICTURES

Carrie Chapman Catt Catt waves to supporters in New York City in 1920. *What group did Catt lead and what suffrage tactics did she support?*

publicized women's contributions to the war effort, an argument President Wilson used in urging Congress to approve suffrage. Ratification of the national suffrage amendment finally came on August 26, 1920.

The right to vote did not grant women full equality. In many states, a woman still could not serve on juries, hold office, enter business, or sign contracts without her husband's permission. Despite the years of hard work that went into gaining the right to vote, two out of three women who had the vote failed to use it in the 1920 election.

After winning the vote, women united to support one important piece of legislation, the Sheppard-Towner Maternity Act of 1921. Stimulated by high rates of maternal and infant mortality, the act provided funds for states to employ public health nurses, hold child-care conferences, and educate new mothers. The Sheppard-Towner Act was the first allocation of federal funds for welfare purposes. It had faced opposition from the American Medical Association. Other opponents argued that the bill was "inspired by foreign experiments in communism." Even so, Congress passed the Sheppard-Towner Act almost unanimously. It stayed in effect until 1929 when Congress failed to renew it.

Decline of Progressivism

Despite the passage of Sheppard-Towner, the 1920s hardly proved friendly for reform. Progressive legislation that survived Congress or state legislatures frequently fell victim to a hostile Supreme Court.

For example, in 1916 Congress had passed a Child Labor Act, controlling the employment of children. Two years later the Court declared the act unconstitutional on the grounds that Congress could not use its commerce power to regulate labor conditions. To make it uneconomical for businesses to hire children, Congress passed a new law establishing a prohibitive tax on child-manufactured products. The Court found the new law unconstitutional as well.

Laws to benefit working women fared little better. In 1923 the Court struck down a Washington, D.C., law enacting a minimum wage for women.

Progressivism declined for other reasons besides a hostile Supreme Court. After the brutality of World War I, many reformers had lost faith in finding political solutions to social problems. The turmoil of the postwar years also helped to weaken the Progressive movement. Many progressives were middle-class property owners. Shocked by violent strikes and fearful of radical political ideas, many progressives began to sympathize more firmly with big business.

SECTION ASSESSMENT

Main Idea

1. Use a diagram like this one to show causes of social tensions during the postwar era.

Cause	Postwar Social Tensions
Cause	
Cause	
Cause	

Vocabulary

2. Define: radical, anarchism, prohibition.

Checking Facts

3. How did Sacco and Vanzetti symbolize the fears of many Americans in the postwar era?

4. Identify progressive reforms that continued in the 1920s.

Critical Thinking

5. **Determining Cause and Effect** List the factors that led many African Americans to seek better employment opportunities in the North.

The Republican Influence

NOVEMBER 2, 1920: HARDING DEFEATS COX

Richard Strout began reporting for the *Christian Science Monitor* in 1922 and continued for 62 years. The first three Presidents he covered—Warren Harding, Calvin Coolidge, and Herbert Hoover—could not have been more different.

Richard Strout said that Warren Gamaliel Harding, a fun-loving man who was elected in a landslide in 1920, did not have the answers. "He was furthermore aware of his inadequacies, and he was pathetic. . . . He said, 'Gentlemen, gentlemen, go easy on me. I just want to go out on the golf course today and shoot a round.'"

Calvin Coolidge, Harding's stern Vice President, succeeded to the presidency when Harding died. Coolidge then handily won the 1924 election. In an interview concerning the thirtieth United States President, Strout said:

FILE PHOTO BY RALPH J. BRUNKE

Campaign Buttons
Republicans held the White House through the 1920s.

> Calvin Coolidge only answered written questions from the press, and so, one time, we all got together and wrote down the same question. We wanted to know if he was going to run for re-election in 1928. So Coolidge looked at the first question and put it aside. Then he looked at the second and did the same thing. He went through all the slips of papers, I think there were a total of twelve, and on the last one he paused, read it to himself, and went on dryly: "I have a question about the condition of the children in Poland." We all smiled. He may have smiled too. And that concluded the press conference.
>
> —As told to Tom Tiede, *American Tapestry*, 1988

Guide to Reading

Main Idea

Rejecting the social reforms of the Progressive Era, the three Republican Presidents of the 1920s—Harding, Hoover, and Coolidge—put their faith in big business, both at home and abroad.

Vocabulary

- internationalism
- disarmament

Read to Find Out . . .

- how the policies of Harding, Coolidge, and Hoover supported big business.
- how Republican foreign policy moved away from military and political involvement in Europe.
- the reasons for United States involvement in Latin America.

Herbert Hoover, the engineer who had performed brilliantly as secretary of commerce under Harding and Coolidge, easily won the presidency in 1928 after Coolidge declined to run. In the same interview, Strout said:

> Herbert Hoover was the first great man in my life. I thought he was going to be the greatest president we ever had. . . . He had each of us ask our questions, and then he would remember all of the questions and answer them one by one. It was remarkable. "As for your question, Mr. Strout, blah, blah, blah." He did it perfectly. I always thought he had a great mind, and he did.
>
> —As told to Tom Tiede, *American Tapestry,* 1988

Although their personalities were strikingly different, the three Republican Presidents pursued similar policies in the 1920s. Rejecting the social reforms of the Progressive Era, the Republican Presidents—Harding, Coolidge, and Hoover—put their faith in big business, both at home and abroad. If government allowed business to prosper, all Americans would reap the rewards.

Harding and the Teapot Dome

Scandals Strike the Administration

In 1920 Warren G. Harding trounced Democrat James M. Cox in the general election. Many observers saw this as a rejection of Woodrow Wilson's brand of **internationalism**, his policy of cooperation and involvement with other countries. As a senator, Harding had fought against joining Wilson's League of Nations. Now he promised, "We do not mean to be entangled."

THE BETTMAN ARCHIVE

Harding's Style **Harding (third from left) enjoys an outing in 1922 with Henry Ford and Thomas Edison.** *Who was Harding's opponent in the 1920 presidential election?*

Harding owed his success to Americans' exhaustion with the war years, with progressivism, and with the turbulence of 1919. Tired of reformers' attacks and President Wilson's demands for self-sacrifice, the country longed for a rest.

Return to Normalcy

Harding reassured the American people. In a campaign speech in 1920 he said, "America's present need is not heroics, but healing; not nostrums, but normalcy; not revolution, but restoration; not agitation, but adjustment; not surgery, but serenity."

★ ★ ★ **Gallery of Presidents** ★ ★ ★

Warren G. Harding

1921–1923

"Our supreme task is the resumption of our onward normal way. Reconstruction, readjustment, restoration—all these must follow. If it will lighten the spirit and add to the resolution with which we take up the task, let me repeat for our nation we shall give no people just cause to make war upon us. We hold no national prejudice; we entertain no spirit of revenge."

Inaugural Address, March 4, 1921

CULVER PICTURES

Background

- **Born 1865; Died 1923**
- **Republican, Ohio**
- **Elected lieutenant governor of Ohio 1903**
- **Elected to the Senate 1914**
- **Elected President 1920**

Achievements in Office

- **Washington Disarmament Conference (1921)**
- **Signing of peace treaties with Austria and Germany (1921)**

Teapot Dome Affair This 1923 cartoon depicts the fall of public officials as the oil scandal was revealed. *Why did people not blame Harding when scandals during his administration came to light?*

People were not always sure exactly what the word *normalcy* meant—it was not even in the dictionary. Harding sounded presidential, however, and he most certainly looked presidential—tall, handsome, and stately.

Harding's first two years in office began well. He called a presidential conference to consider the problem of unemployment. Well aware of his own limitations, Harding named some bright and able officers to his cabinet: Secretary of State Charles Evans Hughes, Secretary of the Treasury Andrew Mellon, and Secretary of Commerce Herbert Hoover.

Harding also surrounded himself with his old friends from Ohio. People called these friends "The Poker Cabinet" or "The Ohio Gang." Alice Roosevelt Longworth described the White House atmosphere under Harding: "the air heavy with tobacco smoke, . . . cards and poker chips at hand—a general atmosphere of waistcoat unbuttoned, feet on desk, and spittoons alongside."

Some of Harding's poker buddies used their positions to line their pockets with money. The head of the Veterans Bureau was fined and sent to jail for selling off veterans hospital supplies for a personal profit. Eventually, another adviser resigned in disgrace and another narrowly avoided going to prison. Two of Harding's other advisers committed suicide rather than face public humiliation.

Teapot Dome Affair

Of the many scandalous situations that occurred during Harding's administration, the Teapot Dome Affair became the most famous. Harding's secretary of the interior, Albert Fall, leased government oil fields—one at Teapot Dome, Wyoming—to wealthy friends in exchange for hundreds of thousands of dollars in bribes. Eventually, Fall made history by being the first cabinet officer to go to prison, but the wealthy businesspeople who bribed him were never punished. A popular joke at the time quipped, "In America, everyone is assumed guilty until proved rich."

Upon hearing the news of a Senate investigation of oil leases, Harding grew depressed and distraught over his friends' betrayal. He became ill in Seattle, contracted pneumonia, and died in San Francisco on August 2, 1923, before the press began to reveal news of his administration's corruption. Americans mourned Harding, whom they had loved. Indeed the public seemed less angry at the corrupt government officials than they did at the exposers of the scandals. Senators Thomas J. Walsh and Burton K. Wheeler, who attempted to bring the crimes to light, were labeled "the Montana scandalmongers" by the *New York Tribune* and "assassins of character" by the *New York Times.* After decades of exposure, the American public had tired of muckraking and truly wanted a return to "normalcy." They got it when Harding's Vice President, Calvin Coolidge, succeeded to the presidency.

Silent Cal and Big Business

Business Prospers Under Republicans

Coolidge had a dry personality that symbolized the old-fashioned virtues of the New England in which he had been raised. The journalist William Allen White once remarked that Coolidge had the expression of one "looking down his nose to locate that evil smell which seemed forever to affront him." Alice Roosevelt Longworth said he looked as if he had been "weaned on a pickle."

Yankee Background

Born on a Vermont farm that his family had worked for five generations, Coolidge attended a one-room schoolhouse. After Harding's death, Coolidge's father, a justice of the peace, administered the presidential oath to his son by the light of a kerosene lamp. With his upright Yankee background and unquestioned reputation for complete honesty, Coolidge soon erased any damage the Harding scandals had caused the Republican administration.

Although he lacked Harding's personal warmth, Coolidge carried out Harding's programs. Both administrations rejected government programs to help ordinary citizens. When the victims of a Mississippi River flood appealed to the government for help, for example, President Coolidge replied, "The government is not an insurer of its citizens against the hazards of the elements." (See One Day in History, pages 394–395 for more on the 1927 flood.)

Policies Toward Business

Big business was another matter. The *Wall Street Journal* could justly brag that "Never before, here or anywhere else, has a government been so completely fused with business." The Harding and Coolidge administrations gave big business a boost in three ways. They appointed businesspeople to commissions that were supposed to regulate business. They selected Supreme Court justices who ruled against progressive legislation. Finally, they named conservatives to powerful cabinet positions.

Harding and Coolidge appointed to regulatory commissions people who opposed regulation. The Interstate Commerce Commission, the Federal Trade Commission, and the Bureau of Corporations soon began to overlook business's violations of antitrust laws.

Harding and Coolidge made 5 conservative appointments to the Supreme Court. From its origin in 1789 until 1925, the Supreme Court had struck down only 53 acts of Congress. During the 1920s the Supreme Court found 12 progressive laws unconstitutional, including the child labor law and the Washington, D.C., minimum wage law for women.

Cabinet positions in the Republican administrations went to wealthy business leaders who used their positions to protect big business interests. Andrew Mellon—secretary of the treasury under Harding, Coolidge, and Hoover—showed where the heart of 1920s politics lay. The third wealthiest person in the United States, Mellon immediately set out to cut government spending and reduce taxes on corporations and on people with high incomes.

Andrew Mellon's Influence

Mellon feared that if high taxes deprived a business person of too much earnings, "he will no longer exert himself and the country will be deprived of the energy on which its continued greatness depends." The multimillionaire with the straggly bow tie almost completely overturned the progressive tax policies of the Wilson years. Thanks to Mellon's efforts, a person making a million dollars a year in 1926 paid less than one-third of the taxes a millionaire had paid in 1921.

Coolidge agreed with Mellon; government should interfere with big business as little as possible. "Four-fifths of all our troubles in this life would disappear if we would only sit down and keep still," said Silent Cal. When Coolidge chose not to run in 1928, America's beloved humorist, Will Rogers, commented that Coolidge retired a hero "not only because he hadent [sic] done anything, but because he had done it better than anyone."

Herbert Hoover, The Wonder Boy

From Engineer to President

As secretary of commerce under both Harding and Coolidge, Herbert Hoover was a key architect of the Republican era. An intelligent and dedicated President, Hoover inherited the blame when the Republican prosperity later came crashing down.

★ ★ ★ **GALLERY OF PRESIDENTS** ★ ★ ★

Calvin Coolidge

1923–1929

"I favor the policy of economy, not because I wish to save money, but because I wish to save people. The men and women of this country who toil are the ones who bear the cost of the Government. Every dollar that we carelessly waste means that their life will be so much the more meager. Every dollar that we prudently save means that their life will be so much the more abundant."

Inaugural Address, March 4, 1925

AP/WIDE WORLD PHOTOS

BACKGROUND

- **Born 1872; Died 1933**
- **Republican, Massachusetts**
- **Elected governor of Massachusetts 1918**
- **Elected Vice President in 1920**
- **Assumed presidency 1923**
- **Elected President 1924**

ACHIEVEMENTS IN OFFICE

- **Kellogg-Briand Pact (1928)**
- **Improved relations with Mexico**
- **Support of American business**

Hoover, a successful mining engineer (once chief engineer for the Chinese Imperial Bureau of Mines), had brilliantly managed the United States Food Administration during World War I. As director of the Belgian Relief Committee, which provided food to starving Europeans, Hoover's name was a household word in the United States years before he became President.

Secretary of Commerce

Coolidge, who prided himself on restraint, sneered at Hoover's optimistic energy and called his secretary of commerce the "Wonder Boy." Indeed, during the 1920s, it seemed there was nothing the "Wonder Boy" could not do.

Hoover expanded the Commerce Department to control and regulate airlines, radio, and other new industries. He helped organize trade associations—groups of firms in the same line of business—to minimize price competition, which Hoover thought inefficient. Hoover also pushed the Bureau of Standards to standardize everything manufactured in the nation from nuts and bolts to tires, mattresses, and electrical fixtures.

Hoover supported zoning regulations, eight-hour workdays in major industries, improved nutrition for children, and conservation of natural resources. He even pushed through the Pollution Act of 1924, the first effort to control coastline oil pollution.

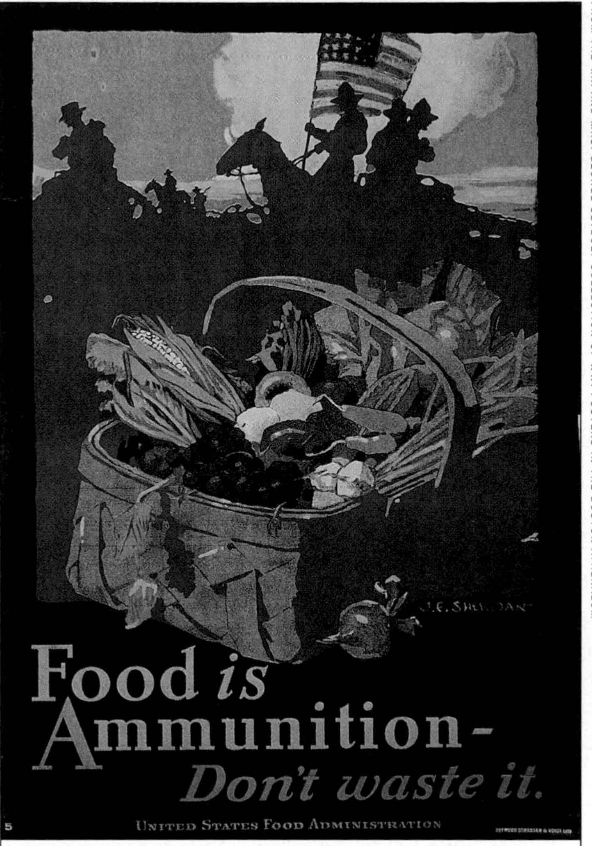

FROM THE MR. AND MRS. GEORGE SEYBOLT COLLECTION OF WWI POSTERS IN THE BOSTON ATHENAEUM

Hoover's Achievements Herbert Hoover gained a reputation for competence during World War I. *How did Hoover's view of big business differ from his predecessors'?*

Attitudes Toward Business

Hoover believed above all in volunteer effort and free enterprise. As secretary of commerce, Hoover had argued that American business was entering a new era. With the growth of trade associations, Hoover hoped businesses would show a new spirit of public service.

In 1928 many Americans agreed with Will Rogers, who said, "I always did want to see [Hoover] elected. I wanted to see how far a competent man could go in politics. It has never been tried before."

Republican Foreign Policy

Business Ties Replace Political Ties

After World War I, the United States shied away from political involvement in Europe. Nevertheless, all three Republican administrations increased the country's economic ties to Europe and the rest of the world. During the 1920s military assistance gave way to economic expansion and control. Herbert Feis, who was an influential historian of United States policy, wrote, "The soldiers and sailors had done their part, [and now] the dollar was counted on to carry on their work. It was regarded as a kind of universal balm."

In the 1920s the government encouraged United States firms to dramatically expand their international business. During this decade, American businesses came to dominate world markets in cars, tractors, electrical equipment, and farm machinery. "World peace through world trade" was how business leaders like Thomas J. Watson of International Business Machines (IBM) put it.

The Dawes Plan

Although the United States government did not direct this worldwide economic expansion, its policies fostered the international expansion of big business. The Dawes Plan showed how the United States influenced European economics without direct government intervention.

After World War I, the Allies owed $10 billion in war debts to the United States. Americans insisted on repayment, but the Allies could not pay unless they got the $33 billion Germany owed them in war reparations.

When Germany defaulted on its payments in December 1922 and January 1923, French soldiers marched into Germany's Ruhr Valley. To avert another war, the United States stepped in. The United States sent a business leader instead of an army. Charles G. Dawes, a wealthy Chicago banker, negotiated loans from

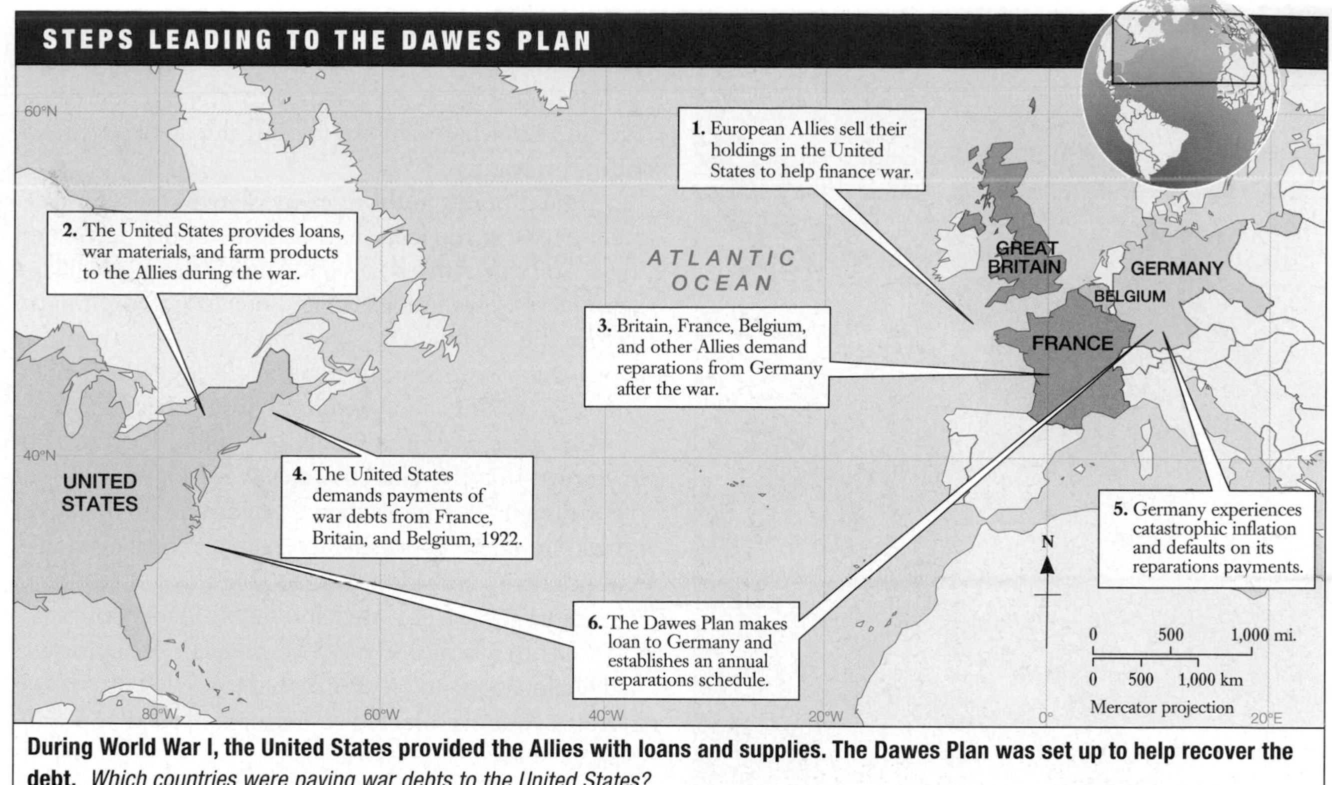

STEPS LEADING TO THE DAWES PLAN
60°N
40°N
1. European Allies sell their holdings in the United States to help finance war.
2. The United States provides loans, war materials, and farm products to the Allies during the war.
ATLANTIC OCEAN
GREAT BRITAIN
GERMANY
BELGIUM
FRANCE
3. Britain, France, Belgium, and other Allies demand reparations from Germany after the war.
UNITED STATES
4. The United States demands payments of war debts from France, Britain, and Belgium, 1922.
5. Germany experiences catastrophic inflation and defaults on its reparations payments.
N
6. The Dawes Plan makes loan to Germany and establishes an annual reparations schedule.
0 500 1,000 mi.
0 500 1,000 km
Mercator projection
80°W
60°W
40°W
20°W
0°
20°E

During World War I, the United States provided the Allies with loans and supplies. The Dawes Plan was set up to help recover the debt. *Which countries were paying war debts to the United States?*

private American banks to Germany and set up a new payment schedule.

These negotiations took shape as the Dawes Plan, a way for Germany to meet its financial obligations and avoid war. United States banks loaned Germany $2.5 billion so that Germany could make war reparations to the Allies. In turn, the Allies repaid this money to the United States government. Even though this money represented only a fraction of what the Allies and the United States were actually owed, the Dawes Plan restored payments that otherwise would not have been made. As a result, the potential for war on that score was reduced.

The most powerful nation in the world during the 1920s, the United States proved to be a reluctant giant. To stay clear of Europe's power struggles, the United States embarked on a twofold policy. The United States attempted to destroy the weapons of war through the Washington Conference. The United States also signed the Kellogg-Briand Pact to outlaw armed struggle.

The Washington Conference

In November 1921, Charles E. Hughes addressed the nine nations meeting at the Washington Naval Conference to discuss **disarmament**, the limitation or reduction of weapons. The delegates knew they were to discuss specifically the limitation of naval arms. Hughes, United States secretary of state, shocked his fellow world leaders when he asked them to destroy their battleships. Eventually, three major treaties emerged—making this the first successful disarmament conference in modern history.

After much controversy, the United States, Great Britain, Japan, France, and Italy pledged to limit the number of their largest ships and to stop constructing new ships. Great Britain and the United States got to keep 500,000 tons of ships each; Japan, 300,000 tons; and France and Italy, 167,000 tons each. The Japanese ambassador complained that the ratio of 5:5:3 sounded like "Rolls-Royce, Rolls-Royce, Ford." Japan agreed only after winning concessions that prohibited new American, British, and Japanese naval bases on the western Pacific islands.

For its part, Japan promised to respect China's sovereignty and independence. Despite this pledge, which kept the China market open to American business, the United States was concerned about Japanese power and ambitions in the Pacific.

The Kellogg-Briand Pact

The United States's second attempt to free itself from involvement in Europe, the Kellogg-Briand Pact, began as a two-nation pact initiated by France's foreign minister, Aristide Briand, to outlaw war and ensure France's security. Secretary of State Frank Kellogg, however, wanted a world treaty to outlaw war.

Fourteen nations initially signed the Kellogg-Briand Pact of 1928. Although the treaty declared war illegal, it failed to include punishments for future attackers.

LIBRARY OF CONGRESS

César Augusto Sandino Sandino opposed the United States Marines and was a hero in his country. *Why were United States troops in Nicaragua?*

Many people scorned it as a "parchment peace," but the pact demonstrated Americans' high hopes for an end to military entanglements with Europe.

Relations with Latin America

Although the United States wanted to avoid political involvement in Europe, it chose to protect its interests in Latin America. During the 1920s, American business firms continued their long-standing expansion to the south, searching for markets and raw materials. By 1924 the United States controlled the financial policies of 14 out of 20 Latin American countries.

United States control of Latin America represented more than an extension of business-government cooperation. The United States felt it had the right and the duty to extend its civilization south of the border.

Though the United States government had begun to reduce its military presence in Latin America after World War I, it still did not hesitate to use soldiers to protect its business interests. From 1909 to 1933, United States Marines were present almost continuously in Nicaragua, where American bankers and policymakers essentially controlled the economy. Coolidge withdrew troops from Nicaragua briefly in 1925, but sent them back in 1926 when factional fighting threatened to destabilize the country.

United States authorities mediated a peace agreement between the factions, but some of the players on the liberal side refused to sign. Among them was liberal nationalist César Augusto Sandino. At first fighting to restore the Nicaraguan constitutional government, he kept his grassroots army together to fight the United States forces until they withdrew from the country.

Congress criticized Coolidge's military action, but he argued that the United States was "not making war on Nicaragua any more than a policeman on the street is making war on passersby." Yet congressional resistance and popular opposition to Coolidge's use of troops in Nicaragua hinted at a shift in United States policy toward Latin America. By 1929 American policymakers had finally begun to recognize that United States troops in Latin America created resentment abroad and criticism at home.

Domestically and internationally the Harding, Coolidge, and Hoover administrations showed a firm commitment to promoting the country's business interests. Most Americans shared the firm belief that United States business could spread peace and prosperity to the nation and to the world at large.

SECTION ASSESSMENT

Main Idea

1. Use a diagram like this one to show Republican policies that promoted the growth of big business, both at home and abroad.

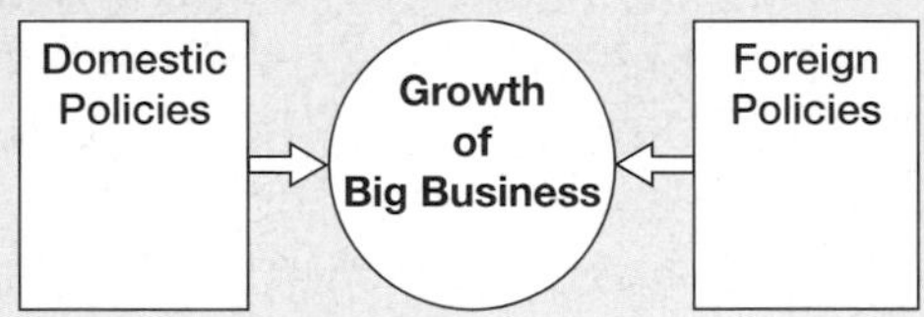

Vocabulary

2. Define: internationalism, disarmament.

Checking Facts

3. What did the Dawes Plan show about Republican attitudes toward business and government?
4. What were American businesses looking for in Latin America?

Critical Thinking

5. **Making Comparisons** Briefly compare and contrast Harding, Coolidge, and Hoover.

Prosperity and American Business

1925: *THE MAN NOBODY KNOWS* IS BEST-SELLER

BRUCE BARTON'S SUBJECT—BIG BUSINESS—AND HIS HERO—JESUS—SEEMED AN UNLIKELY COMBINATION FOR A BOOK. Surprisingly, Barton's *The Man Nobody Knows* became America's best-seller during 1925 and 1926. A one-time journalist and the founder of a large advertising agency, Barton told Americans that Jesus had been the first modern business leader. After all, he wrote, Jesus "picked up twelve men from the bottom ranks of business and forged them into an organization that conquered the world."

Barton explained that when Jesus said he must be about his father's business, he had meant more than simply religion. Barton wrote:

THE BETTMANN ARCHIVE

Best-selling Author Bruce Barton
Barton stressed the human life of Jesus with perky prose and chapter titles such as "The Sociable Man" and "His Advertisements."

Ask any ten people what Jesus meant by his "Father's business," and nine of them will answer "preaching." To interpret the words in this narrow sense is to lose the real significance of his life. It was not to preach that he came into the world; nor to teach; nor to heal. These are all departments of his Father's business, but the business itself is far larger, more inclusive. For if human life has any significance it is this—that God has set going here an experiment to which all His resources are committed. He seeks to develop perfect human beings, superior to circumstance, victorious over Fate. No single kind of human talent or effort can be spared if the experiment is to succeed. The race must be fed and clothed and

GUIDE TO READING

Main Idea

Increased production, new management methods, and a booming economy elevated the public image of big business in the minds of many Americans in the 1920s.

Vocabulary

- industrial productivity
- capital
- corporation
- oligopoly
- welfare capitalism

Read to Find Out . . .

- the causes of the prosperity of the 1920s.
- the changes that occurred in the structure and management of American businesses during the 1920s.
- how corporate policies of the 1920s reduced the appeal of the unions.

housed and transported, as well as preached to, and taught and healed. Thus all business is his Father's business. All work is worship; all useful service prayer.

—Bruce Barton, *The Man Nobody Knows,* 1925

The Glorification of Business

Business Grows in Power and Prestige

The America that made Bruce Barton's book a best-seller changed business almost into a religion and elevated the successful businessperson to the status of a religious hero. In 1921, after touring and examining 12 of the country's biggest businesses, writer Edward Earl Purinton published an article idolizing big business. He praised the business manager of Gary, Indiana, the world's largest one-industry city, saying that successful business leaders were naturally suited to be powerful religious leaders:

He is called upon by the pastors and priests of churches of a dozen different faiths and nationalities, whose members are employees of the U.S. Steel Corporation, to address the congregations in some helpful, appropriate way. Because he is a fine business man, with power, skill and money back of him, the men of the city want to hear what he has to say. And because he is a gentleman, kind, thoughtful, and sympathetic, the women of the church listen gladly to his lay sermons.

—Edward Earl Purinton, "Big Ideas from Big Business," *The Independent,* April 16, 1921

Not only wealthy Americans revered business. After all, President Coolidge had said, "The man who builds a factory builds a temple—the man who works there worships there." As profits, salaries, dividends, and industrial wages rose during this decade, the gospel of big business became a national creed. Popular magazines printed articles praising corporate leaders, such as Walter Chrysler, *Time* magazine's Man of the Year in 1929.

A list of 59 people who "ruled" the United States appeared in newspapers in the 1920s. The list omitted all elected officials but included John D. Rockefeller, J.P. Morgan, a number of Du Ponts, and Treasury Secretary Andrew Mellon. The person who had compiled the list explained, "These men rule by virtue of their ability." Too busy to hold public office themselves, "they determine who shall hold such office."

Even universities, traditionally hostile to business matters, joined in the admiration for business leaders. In 1925 the Princeton University newspaper asked:

What class of men is it that keeps governments, businesses, families, solidly on their feet? What class of men is it that endows universities, hospitals, Foundations? . . . What class of men are the fathers of most of us—fathers who provide decently for their families, who educate their children, who believe in order and justice, who pay taxes to support jails, insane asylums and poor houses, which neither they nor theirs are likely to occupy?

—*Daily Princetonian*, January 7, 1925

Predictably, the one answer to all the questions was *business*men.

A Booming Economy

Industry on the Go

Americans thanked big business for the prosperity they enjoyed during the 1920s. The nation had emerged from World War I in a splendid economic position. At

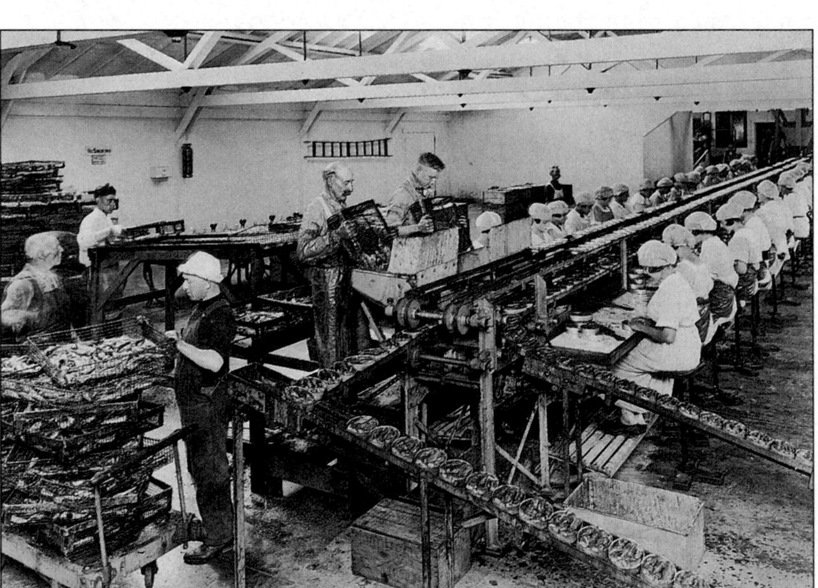

BROWN BROTHERS

Increased Productivity The development of assembly lines and the use of electric generators boosted industrial productivity. *How did new technology contribute to the expanding economy?*

the beginning of the war, the United States had owed other countries money. Now the United States was a creditor nation, collecting debts from war-torn Europe.

Unlike other major powers whose farms and factories had been devastated by the war, America's productive capacity had expanded. Following a short period of postwar social and economic unrest, the United States bounded into several years of record-breaking prosperity.

Between 1922 and 1928, **industrial productivity**—the amount of goods each hour of labor produced—rose by 70 percent. Corporate investors reaped the largest rewards, but many ordinary workers also earned higher wages than at any other time in United States history.

America's productivity soared as new technology and techniques increased manufacturing efficiency. Electrical motors powered 70 percent of machines in 1929, compared with only 30 percent in 1914. The assembly line that revolutionized the auto industry in 1914 soon moved into other industries as well.

When American business boomed, companies needed bigger and better offices. A growing urban population required new apartment buildings, and a spreading suburban population demanded new roads and houses. As a result, building and road construction took off during the decade.

New Industry

New industries also added to the decade's rapid growth. Production of light metals, such as aluminum; a brand-new synthetics industry; motion picture production; and radio manufacturing all provided new jobs and products for the American public.

Automobile manufacturing ranked as the most important of all the new industries. Henry Ford was one of several automobile makers, but it was his name that became a synonym for the booming new industry. In 1923 a public opinion poll declared Henry Ford would be a more popular candidate for President than President Harding. In another contest, college students voted Ford the third greatest figure of all time. Only Napoleon and Jesus got more votes.

In 1907 Ford had declared:

> I will build a motor car for the great multitude. It will be large enough for the family but small enough for the individual to run and care for. It will be constructed of the best materials, by the best men to be hired, after the simplest designs that modern engineering can devise. But it will be so low in price that no man making a good salary will be unable to own one—and enjoy with his family the blessing of hours of pleasure in God's great open spaces.
>
> —Henry Ford, quoted in *American Civilization in the First Machine Age: 1890–1940,* 1970

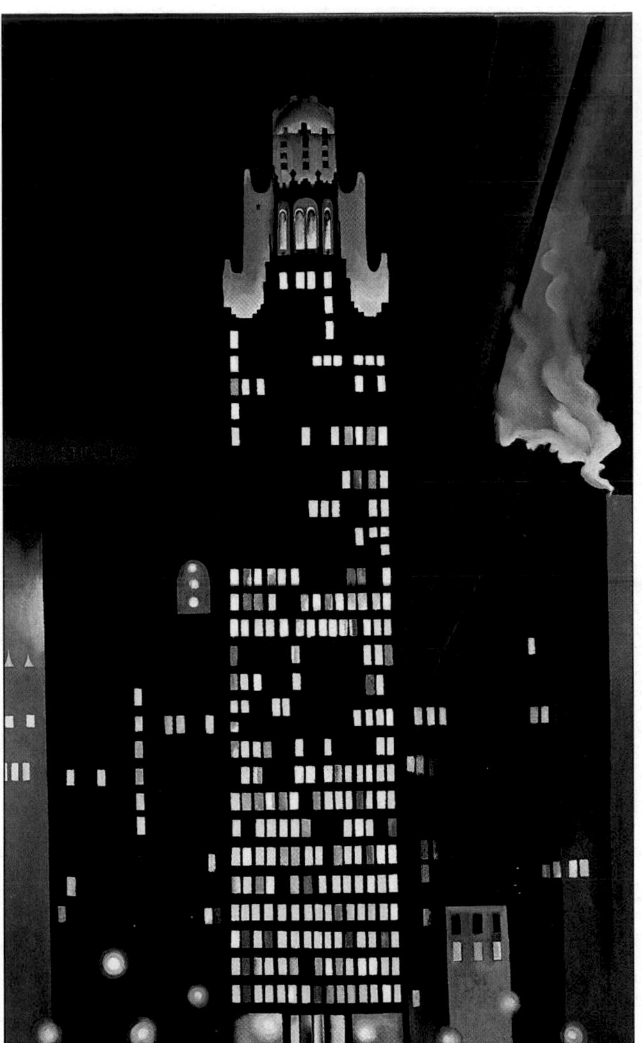

ALFRED STIEGLITZ COLLECTION, FISK UNIVERSITY, NASHVILLE

The Radiator Building, Night, New York The skyscraper, represented in this 1927 painting by Georgia O'Keeffe, symbolized the new age of business. *Why were skyscrapers built?*

During 1913 and 1914, Ford introduced the moving production line, an innovation that made it possible to assemble his car in 93 minutes instead of the 14 hours it had taken a year before. By 1925 a completed auto rolled off the Ford assembly lines every 10 seconds. The auto industry's dramatic expansion in the 1920s gave birth to a host of related industries: steel, rubber, petroleum, machine tools, and road building.

The New Commercial Downtowns

As roads and automobiles remade the horizontal landscape of the United States, skyscrapers began to revolutionize the country's vertical landscape. During the war, construction had been abruptly halted. Now it seemed Americans were reaching for the sky as they made up for lost time.

In 1910 travelers to New York City had been surprised by 20-story skyscrapers. On May 1, 1931, the new Empire State Building dwarfed even the Bank of Manhattan's 71 stories and the Chrysler Building's

Student Web Activity 11
Visit the *American Odyssey* Web site at americanodyssey.glencoe.com and click on ***Chapter 11—Student Web Activities*** for an activity relating to the era of big business.

77 stories. At 102 stories, with a slender mast, the Empire State Building had become the tallest building in the world.

If New York had its skyscrapers, the rest of the United States would have theirs, too. Houston had its Petroleum Building, Chicago its Tribune Tower, and Cleveland its Terminal Tower. Even prairie towns raised the giant buildings. Tulsa and Oklahoma City had not even existed when the first skyscraper was completed in 1885. By the end of the 1920s, these cities, too, celebrated their own new skylines.

The Corporate Revolution

New Ideas in Business Management

The 1920s witnessed the culmination of the corporate revolution that had begun in the late 1800s. Many family-run firms could no longer raise enough **capital**–an accumulation of money—to invest in research and development. Unable to purchase the new technology or to afford national advertising, small companies could not compete. American business became big business, as thousands of small firms went out of business or were absorbed into larger companies or **corporations**—businesses owned by multiple stockholders, whose personal rights and responsibilities are legally separate from the organization's.

The Urge to Merge

Between 1920 and 1928, more than 5,000 such mergers joined firms together in larger and increasingly powerful entities that could then buy out smaller companies. Thus the total number of firms dropped by hundreds. The Federal Trade Commission (FTC) had been created to protect small businesses against such takeovers. The person President Coolidge appointed to the chairmanship of the FTC, however, scorned the commission as a "publicity bureau to spread socialistic propaganda" and "an instrument of oppression and disturbance and injury instead of help to business." Under William E. Humphrey, the FTC soon began to encourage instead of to prosecute trade associations and business mergers.

Some of the most obvious examples of business mergers were seen among utility companies. Many local electric companies were absorbed into huge regional systems and utility empires. From 1919 to 1927, 3,700 local power companies turned their lights off for good. By 1930, 10 holding companies supplied 72 percent of the nation's power.

Four meatpackers, 3 major baked goods companies, and 4 tobacco producers dominated their industries during the 1920s. Such a situation, in which a few major producers influence an entire industry, is called an **oligopoly**. Oligopoly prevailed in banking,

THE NATIONAL DOLLAR STORES, LTD.

Growth of Chain Stores Chinese American Joe Shoong founded National Dollar Stores, Inc., with one small store in 1903. It had grown into a chain of stores by the 1920s. *How might management of a group of chain stores differ from that of a single store?*

Growth of Business Associations Booker T. Washington (seated, second from left) founded The National Negro Business League. The League encouraged African American enterprises in the 1920s. *How do you think such associations could help prevent small businesses from takeovers?*

too, as large banks swallowed smaller ones. By 1929, 1 percent of the banks controlled more than 46 percent of the country's banking resources.

A smaller and smaller number of American businesses began to wield unmatched economic power. By 1929 half of America's corporate wealth belonged to its 200 largest corporations.

As small firms went out of business, chain stores and other large companies thrived. The Great Atlantic and Pacific Tea Company (A & P) expanded from 400 stores in 1912 to 15,500 stores by 1932. A single strong leader could no longer run big businesses like the A & P. The new companies demanded a new type of leadership.

The Managerial Revolution

Everyone knew who Henry Ford was, but during the 1920s, the average American could no longer identify the chairperson of the board of directors of any other large corporation. Anonymous, replaceable managers rather than the strong personalities of the past now directed big firms.

Colleges stepped in to train the new leaders for the large corporations. Indeed, during the 1920s, almost every leading university established its own business school. In 1924 the Harvard Graduate School of Business Administration dedicated 23 elegant new buildings on a site across the Charles River from the university. The president of the First National Bank of New York had given $6 million toward the building of Harvard's business school.

During the 1927–1928 school year, Northwestern University offered more than 30 courses on business, from "Bank Practice and Policy" to "Psychology of Business Relations." New York University students could even take a course in "Restaurant, Tea Room, and Cafeteria Organization."

Smaller businesses that had grown more complicated also required a more specialized kind of managerial know-how. New college-trained business managers soon began to replace the company-trained general managers of an earlier generation.

By 1924 in Muncie, Indiana, for example, the old job of general manager of the glass factory had been divided into five new jobs: production manager, sales manager, advertising manager, personnel manager, and office manager. Companies grew by adding laborers. To supervise these larger workforces, however, they now seemed to need more layers of management.

Another plant in the same city had employed 200 workers in 1890 and supervised them with a small staff: a president, a vice president who was also general manager, a secretary, treasurer, and two foremen. By 1924 the same plant had 6 times as many workers, but now required 15 times as many foremen, as well as the addition of 2 superintendents, an auditor, and assistants to the secretary and treasurer.

Industry's Labor Policies

Suppressing Union Organization

Big corporations with specialized managerial staffs had almost complete control over the workforce during the 1920s. Immediately after the war, the Red Scare had struck a crushing blow to labor by associating unions with Communists. For the rest of the decade, corporations kept labor submissive with an effective combination of punishment and reward. The American Plan was the punishment, and welfare capitalism was the reward.

The American Plan

The American Plan was made up of a variety of activities companies used after the war to demoralize and destroy unions. Corporations called it the "American Plan" to give it the ring of patriotism. One of the plan measures, open-shop associations, allowed employers to stick together in blacklisting union members.

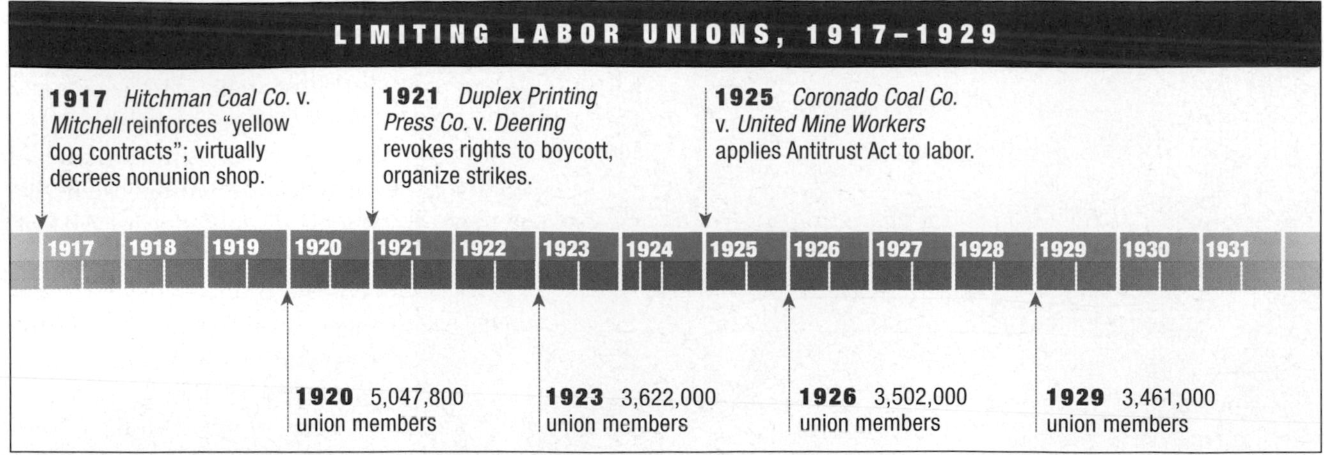
LIMITING LABOR UNIONS, 1917–1929
1917 Hitchman Coal Co. v. Mitchell reinforces "yellow dog contracts"; virtually decrees nonunion shop.
1921 Duplex Printing Press Co. v. Deering revokes rights to boycott, organize strikes.
1925 Coronado Coal Co. v. United Mine Workers applies Antitrust Act to labor.
1917 1918 1919 1920 1921 1922 1923 1924 1925 1926 1927 1928 1929 1930 1931
1920 5,047,800 union members
1923 3,622,000 union members
1926 3,502,000 union members
1929 3,461,000 union members

Companies also employed spies who joined unions and then informed employers about labor discontent and identified labor organizers.

As part of the American Plan, many companies offered their workers only "yellow-dog" contracts. With a yellow-dog contract as a condition of employment, an employee agreed not to become a member of a union or to organize fellow employees.

Big business, of course, tried to make it sound as though the American Plan was in the worker's best interest. Elbert H. Gary, head of U.S. Steel, wrote:

> The principle of the "open shop" is vital to the greatest industrial progress and prosperity. It is of equal benefit to employer and employee. It means that every man may engage in any line of employment that he selects and under such terms as he and the employer may agree upon; that he may arrange for the kind and character of work which he believes will bring to him the largest compensation and the most satisfactory conditions, depending upon his own merit and disposition.
>
> —Elbert H. Gary, *New York Times*, September 18, 1919

The Supreme Court favored management over labor with several key rulings. In 1915 the Court had upheld the yellow-dog contract. In 1921 it declared a union boycott illegal and drastically limited workers' rights to picket. In the 1925 *Coronado* case, the same Court that so carefully guarded the rights of big businesses ruled that unions could be sued for damages under antitrust rules.

Between 1921 and 1929, union membership dropped from about 5 million to about 3.5 million. Phil Bart, a lifelong union organizer, recalled how difficult it was to organize strikes in the auto industry in 1928:

> There were no laws to protect strikers then, and there wasn't much public sympathy either. We had to struggle against the place and time. The authorities were intolerant, and when we set up a line the police might come right in and knock hell out of us. The strikers could try to protect themselves by putting up a fight or something, but you could not go to the courts, you could not go to the government; they didn't care. . . . We never forced management to bargain, but working conditions did get better.
>
> —Phil Bart, quoted in *American Tapestry,* 1988

Welfare Capitalism

Working conditions got better partly because employers sought to reduce the appeal of independent unions. The combination of programs employers adopted in order to convince workers they did not need unions became known as **welfare capitalism**.

During the 1920s most employers improved plant conditions, hired company doctors and nurses, and provided a variety of activities from glee clubs to sports teams. For example, the Hammermill Paper Company sold its workers cheap gasoline, while Bausch and Lomb established dental and eye care clinics for its employees.

In 1922 the president of General Electric Company, Gerard Swope, had told a group of foremen in Schenectady, New York, "You are constantly being hounded to increase your output. One of the ways of getting it is to have your men cooperate with you." American business leaders heeded this message and began practicing welfare capitalism in their own companies.

During the 1920s most United States companies offered safety programs and group insurance. A few of the largest corporations instituted stock purchase opportunities and pension plans. In the 1920s U.S. Steel alone paid out more than $10 million a year in worker benefits. Even Elbert Gary, the head of U.S. Steel, had come to believe that such generosity to workers actually profited his company. In 1923 he told his stockholders, "It pays to treat men in that way."

LIBRARY OF CONGRESS

Keeping the Workforce Content **A company-sponsored basketball team was a benefit these employees received under welfare capitalism.** *What other benefits did welfare capitalism offer, and why?*

Many companies also began programs in which workers could elect representatives to speak to management. Employers called this "industrial democracy" and boasted that it would erase the differences between workers and bosses. Edward Purinton wrote that by providing employee representation on the board of directors, "owners of a business now give the manual workers a chance to think and feel in unison with [the bosses]. All enmity is between strangers. Those who really know each other cannot fight."

Employers may have believed that the interests of worker and employer were identical and that company unions were a form of democracy. The workers knew that the company unions had no real power and called them "Kiss Me Clubs." Welfare capitalism maintained the power inequalities that gave management full authority over labor. Indeed, Charles M. Schwab, the head of Bethlehem Steel Corporation, made the owners' position very clear: "I will not permit myself to be in a position of having labor dictate to management."

Welfare capitalism may not have ended the vast inequities between employer and employed, but by the 1920s, worker-led unions were in sharp decline. By 1929 only about 1 in 12 workers belonged to a union.

While the United States was prosperous, welfare capitalism seemed to keep the workforce content. In January 1929, the head of the Chicago and Alton Railroad boasted, "In our shops since the strike of 1922, the shop employees have been very quiet. The employee is much happier. . . . He is a peaceful worker and a peaceful citizen."

As employee well-being increased efficiency and profits, welfare capitalism paid off for big business. Corporations also used welfare capitalism to restore their public image after the muckraking scandals of the Progressive Era.

During the 1920s, professional public relations experts promoted the idea of humane businesses that not only looked to the welfare of their employees but also acted in the service of society. The Western Electric Company, for example, offered to send literature teaching household management to women.

> The science of managing a home indicates the use of electrical appliances, but the company wants to teach the science whether it sells the goods or not. This is "good business" because [it is] genuine service.
>
> —Edward Earl Purinton, "Big Ideas from Big Business," *The Independent*, April 16, 1921

The idea of public service became an ideal for big business during the 1920s. Business leaders joined service groups such as the Rotary Club, whose motto became "He profits most who serves best." According to the Rotarians, "the businessman was no longer a profit-maker or even a bread-winner, he was a public servant."

Section Assessment

Main Idea

1. Use a diagram like this one to show how big businesses improved their public image in the 1920s.

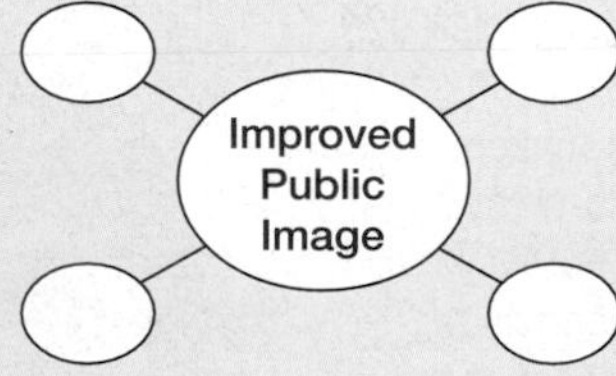

Vocabulary

2. Define: industrial productivity, capital, corporation, oligopoly, welfare capitalism.

Checking Facts

3. List three examples showing the respect Americans had for big business.

4. What two methods did corporations use to manage labor in the 1920s?

Critical Thinking

5. Recognizing Ideologies Why would Coolidge appoint someone opposed to the activities of the FTC to be its chairperson?

Science, TECHNOLOGY, and Society

The Automobile

By the 1920s Ford, General Motors, and Chrysler dominated auto manufacturing, and gasoline-burning internal combustion replaced the once wide array of power sources. Gasoline and automobile industries and related businesses drastically changed the look, pace, and values of the country.

BROWN BROTHERS

AUTOMOTIVE STATUS

Even as more people could afford automobiles, cars remained symbols of status and glamour, such as this 1929 Packard Roadster. Many independent auto makers did not survive the de-pression of 1920–1921, but Packard survived to become the leading luxury car of the decade. Sales of luxury cars peaked in 1928 and 1929.

PHOTOGRAPH: BENJAMIN MAGRO.COURTESY OF THE SEAL COVE AUTO MUSEUM

AUTOMOBILE DEVELOPMENTS

1920s	1930s	1940s	1950s
POST–WORLD WAR I The industry adopts wartime technology with superchargers for greater speed and shock absorbers for a better ride.	**NEW FEATURES** By 1930 balloon tires are widely used for a smoother ride; electric lights become standard.	**POST–WORLD WAR II** Wartime gas rationing ends and pleasure driving returns, with bigger, more powerful cars.	**STYLE** Decorative tail fins inspired by Lockheed P-38 fighter planes dominate styling.

PUBLIC SERVICES

Motorization of public services gave increased speed and efficiency to police and fire departments, the post office, even library bookmobiles. The United States Postal Service's rural free delivery (RFD) reduced rural people's isolation, and door-to-door package delivery boosted mail-order sales of companies such as Sears, Roebuck and Montgomery Ward.

THE BETTMANN ARCHIVE

PHOTO BY DECIO GRASSI

THE WORLD THAT CARS MADE

PORTFOLIO PROJECT

How have cars affected your environment? Look around your neighborhood and identify and describe features that are there only because of cars. How would it look if electricity were the primary car fuel?

ROADSIDE SIGNS

Mass auto travel prompted businesses to advertise in big, loud signs that would catch the eye of passing motorists. In the 1920s, Elizabeth Boyd Lawton led a movement to reform what she saw as a threat to outdoor beauty. She formed the Committee for the Restriction of Outdoor Advertising in 1923. One Lawton supporter lamented, "Where highways run, where the motor car goes [one sees an] eruption of filling stations, hot-dog stands, Tumble Inns, garages, vegetable booths, scarifying field and forest for rods around."

GASOLINE

Originally a little-used waste product of kerosene production, gasoline was an essential commodity by the 1920s. It was sold on city street corners and on country roads. The "pump" evolved from a hand-operated tank with a measurement container to a self-measuring, price-calculating machine.

1960s

IMPORTS American small cars first compete with imports.

1970s

OIL The Volkswagen Beetle surpasses the Model T as the best-selling car ever. After the 1973 oil crisis, government mandates high mileage standards.

1980s

NEW METHODS Computer-aided design, computer-aided engineering, and factory robots replace traditional design and manufacturing processes.

1990s

OLD IDEAS Environmental concerns and limited oil resources renew interest in electric cars and alternative power sources.

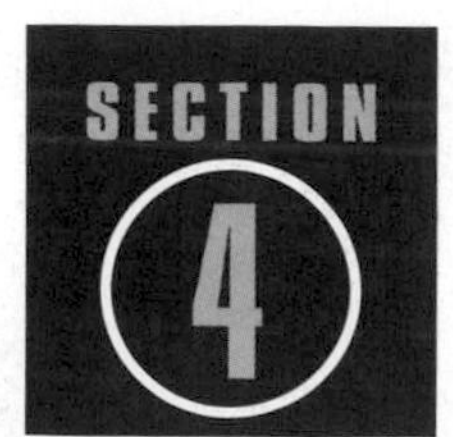

The Changing Nature of Work

1924: ASSEMBLY LINE BOOSTS SALES AND EARNINGS

IN 1924 THE TYPICAL FACTORY WORKER WORKED ON AN ASSEMBLY LINE, REPEATING ONE SMALL TASK. Sociologists Robert and Helen Lynd wrote of one such worker: "The worker is drilling metal joint rings for the front of a well-known automobile. He stands all day in front of his multiple drill-press, undrilled rings being brought constantly to his elbow and his product carted away."

The man described above drilled a pair of joint rings 3 times each minute, over and over again. In a 9-hour day, he performed his job 1,620 times.

BROWN BROTHERS

Early Ford Assembly Line
Workers place tires and steering wheels on the Model T.

Although a worker's contribution to making an automobile usually involved tedious work, many factory laborers could still hop into their own cars and drive home at the end of the workday. In that sense, Henry Ford's dream of 1907 had come true. The assembly line sped up car manufacturing and reduced the cost of producing automobiles. Ford passed that savings on to his customers by slashing the prices of his cars.

Henry Ford

Workers' Lives Change

Henry Ford was one of the first **industrialists,** people who dealt with the commercial production and sale of goods and services, to act

GUIDE TO READING

Main Idea

Automation of manufacturing helped create new jobs and dramatically changed the work environment in both factories and offices.

Vocabulary

- industrialist
- scientific management
- white-collar worker

Read to Find Out . . .

- how scientific management changed the workplace.
- the reasons for the growth of white-collar work.
- the kinds of white-collar jobs most women held.
- what office work was like in the 1920s.

on the realization that each worker is also a consumer. If workers had more money, Ford reasoned, they could purchase more of his cars. So in 1914 Ford took the revolutionary action of doubling the wages of the workers at his plant in Highland Park, Michigan.

Working for Henry Ford

In an era when $2 a day was considered a generous wage, Ford offered $5 a day to workers of "thrifty habits." Workers who refused to learn English, rejected the company detective's advice, gambled, drank, or pursued "any malicious practice derogatory to . . . moral behavior" did not get the raise. In 2 years, three-quarters of Ford's workers made $5 a day.

Other industrialists called Ford a "traitor to his class" because his actions defied the conventional wisdom of keeping wages low and prices high. Ford, however, reasoned that well-paid workers would be less likely to seek other jobs and more likely to do their boring jobs willingly. In 1926 Ford again delighted the workers and shocked the business world by reducing the workweek at his plant from a 48-hour, 6-day week to a 40-hour, 5-day week.

Ford could easily afford to cut back his workers' hours and increase their pay beyond the standards of the time. The assembly line methods that permitted mass production made tremendous profits for Ford, whose company earned an estimated $264,000 per day in 1922.

In addition to their increased wages, Ford's workers gained some other benefits from the new assembly line work. Because the jobs required no skills and little training, laborers could master their work quickly. Almost anyone who wanted to work could do the new jobs.

Henry Ford employed ex-convicts, as well as the physically and mentally challenged. He believed a worker to be "equally acceptable whether he has been

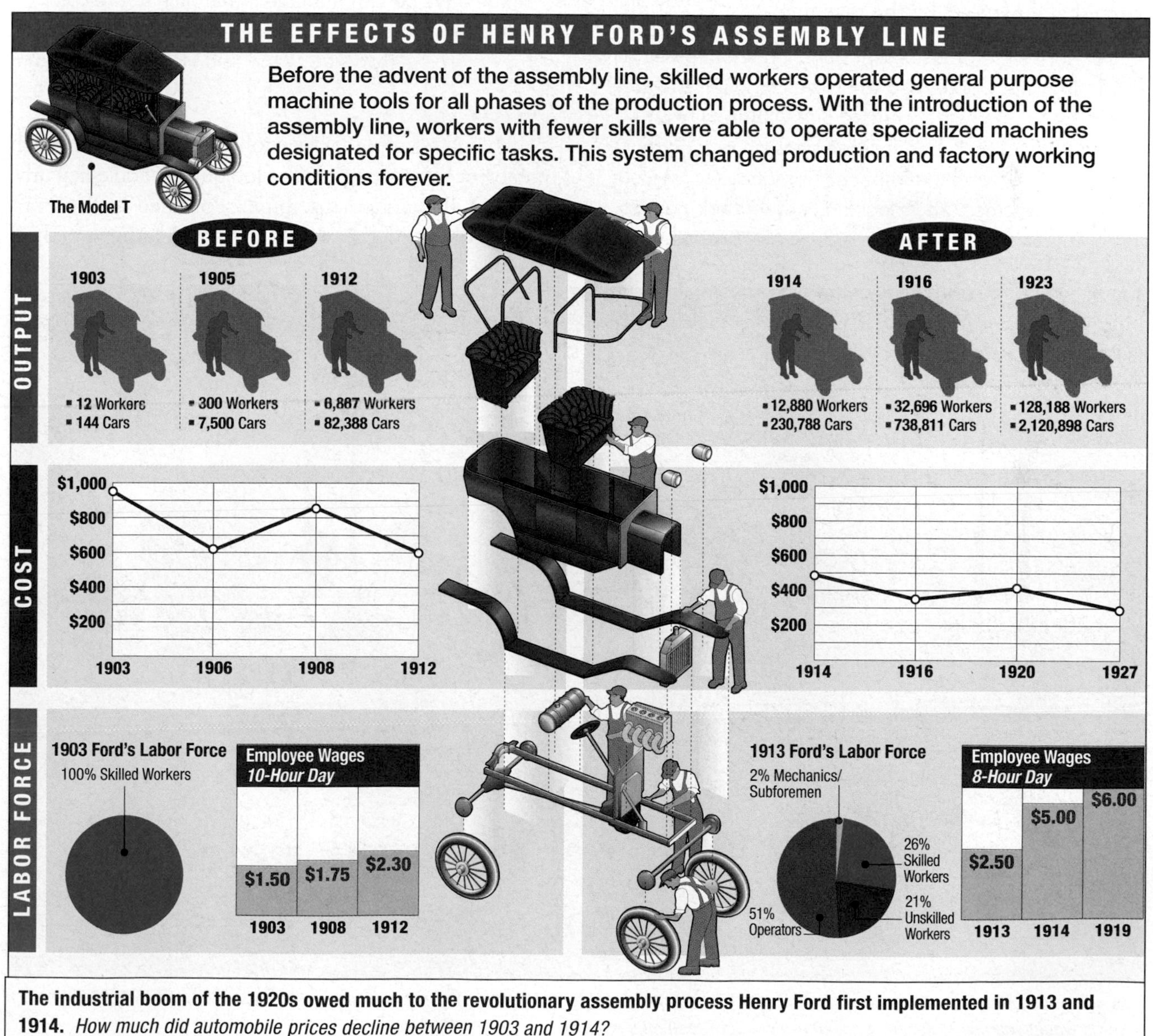

The industrial boom of the 1920s owed much to the revolutionary assembly process Henry Ford first implemented in 1913 and 1914. *How much did automobile prices decline between 1903 and 1914?*

in Sing Sing or at Harvard and we do not even inquire from which place he has graduated. All that he needs is the desire to work." Henry Ford prided himself on hiring thousands of immigrants and members of minority groups who might not otherwise have had good job opportunities.

Man or Machine?

The Czech immigrants who worked for Henry Ford and in other factories brought a new word to the United States during the 1920s. The word *robot* came to mean a machine that acts like a person or a person who acts like a machine. In the new factories, it began to be difficult to tell where the worker ended and the machine began.

Typically, a mechanized assembly line delivered the material to workers at waist level, so they did not have to waste valuable time walking, stooping, reaching, or bending. Each worker, doing a tiny part of the total job, worked at a pace set by the machine:

> There were presses that punched sheet steel. All that the worker had to do was to insert the steel before the press descended and withdraw his hands quickly. But some men became fatigued, or surrendered to the numbness or monotony, or were simply careless. The machines cut off their hands.
>
> —Geoffrey Perrett, *America in the Twenties,* 1982

The steel company prevented these accidents by chaining the workers' hands to their machines. All day, the men's hands jerked back and forth, even when they were out of material. As one visitor to a model steel plant wrote, "There they work, chained to their machines, as galley slaves were chained to their oars."

Mass production meant skilled jobs got broken down into their most basic operations, to be repeated without pause almost all day long. Many workers, not just those who worked in Ford plants, held these repetitive jobs on assembly lines. Skills that had taken a lifetime to master soon became unnecessary. In 1924 a steelworker lamented:

> You had to know how to use the old carbon steel to keep it from gettin' hot and spoilin' the edge. But this "high speed steel" and this new "stelite" don't absorb the heat and are harder than carbon steel. You can take a boy fresh from the farm and in three days he can manage a machine as well as I can, and I've been at it twenty-seven years.
>
> —Robert S. Lynd and Helen Merrell Lynd, *Middletown*, 1929

The new simple factory jobs did not require much training or thought. To do the job quickly and efficiently, however, demanded discipline. Foremen at the Ford plant prohibited the workers from leaning on their

MOVIE STILL ARCHIVES

Downtrodden Workers The owner exploits factory workers in this image from the classic movie *Metropolis* filmed in 1925. *What words would you use to describe how these workers seem like robots?*

machines, sitting, squatting, singing, talking, whistling, smoking, or smiling on the job. Laborers had to talk like ventriloquists, not moving their lips, in what they called the "Ford whisper." They set their faces in frozen grimaces that became known as "Fordization of the face." Describing the atmosphere in his auto plant, Ford explained, "There is not much personal contact. The men do their work and go home."

Breaking down skilled work into tiny jobs increased production and profits, raised the wages of laborers, and provided jobs for thousands of people in need of work. It also, however, threatened to turn the workers into machines. Although Henry Ford was the first to use the assembly line for large-scale mass production, the blessings and the curses of the new mass production stemmed from the theories of Frederick Taylor.

Scientific Management

Efficiency Equals Profits

Born into an upper-class family in Pennsylvania, Frederick Taylor joined the Midvale Steel Works in Philadelphia as a laborer in 1878 at the age of 22. Within 6 years, the young man had become chief engineer and a careful observer of his coworkers.

For himself, Taylor appreciated the virtue of hard work, calling it "the real monotonous grind which trains character." The wealthy young man concluded, however, that most of his fellow factory workers were lazy and sloppy in performing their jobs. Taylor argued that developing more efficient working methods would heighten the workers' productivity, raise their wages, and profit the company.

Taylor's theory, which came to be known as **scientific management**, suggested that efficiency, or time-study, experts analyze each work operation and find ways to minimize the time necessary to do a job. Breaking each job into its simplest operations, time-study experts would train workers to carry out their simplified tasks and then time them to see if they could meet the new standards. Taylor advised management to offer cash incentives to workers who produced more than the standard quantities that had been established for their jobs.

Taylor successfully tested scientific management at Midvale Steel. At first both management and labor criticized Taylor's ideas. The bosses at Midvale opposed scientific management because it disrupted their long-established routines. For their part, the workers remained unimpressed by the money incentives. They suspected scientific management of being simply the "scientific sweating of labor."

One new industry, however, had no traditional routines to be upset by Taylor's revolutionary new methods. The auto industry adapted Taylor's ideas from the very beginning.

In 1911 Taylor published his major work, *The Principles of Scientific Management*. That same year, the Taylor Society was founded to spread Taylor's ideas. Four years later, Taylor's book had been translated into eight European languages and Japanese.

By the 1920s many established industries had gotten the message that saving time meant greater profits. Scientific management truly came into its own during the antiunion era that followed the post-World War I strikes. In the 1920s the Taylor Society boasted new members from some of the country's biggest corporations: General Electric, Du Pont, and American Telephone and Telegraph Company (AT&T).

Workers in Manufacturing, 1899–1925

Year	Blue-Collar Workers	White-Collar Workers	Ratio of Blue: White
1899	4,496,000	349,000	11.4 : 1
1904	5,173,000	546,000	9.5 : 1
1909	6,256,000	750,000	8.3 : 1
1914	6,592,000	911,000	7.2 : 1
1919	8,482,000	1,384,000	6.1 : 1
1921	6,487,000	1,087,000	5.8 : 1
1925	7,873,000	1,270,000	6.2 : 1

The ratio of blue-collar wage earners to salaried white-collar workers decreased from 1899 to 1925. *What was the ratio of blue-collar to white-collar workers in 1925?*

The New White-Collar Workers

Business Occupations Surge

Frederick Taylor's ideas about the organization of the workplace influenced these new workers. During the 1920s even the physical layout of offices began to resemble factories with their assembly lines. Papers passed from worker to worker along a moving belt. A writer described one such firm in 1929:

> Orders are passed along by means of a belt and lights from a chief clerk to a series of checkers and typists, each of whom does one operation. The girl at the head of the line interprets the order, puts down the number and indicates the trade discount;

the second girl prices the order, takes off the discount, adds carriage charges and totals; the third girl gives the order and number and makes a daily record; the fourth girl puts this information on an alphabetical index; the fifth girl time-stamps it: it next goes along the belt to one of several typists, who makes a copy in sextuplicate and puts on address labels; the seventh girl checks it and sends it to the storeroom.

—C. Wright Mills, *White Collar*, 1951

During the 1920s more new workers than ever before were going to work each day dressed in business clothes. Although women were among their ranks, these workers—professionals, wholesale and retail salespeople, and clerks—became known as **white-collar workers** because of the white shirts and ties uniformly worn by the men.

As corporations grew larger and more complex, the industrial transformation of the early twentieth century gave rise to a host of new occupations—from typist, clerk, and stenographer to junior manager. Thriving insurance and banking industries added to the growing need for still more white-collar jobs.

Scientific Management Creates New Jobs

Moreover, between 1920 and 1930, the ranks of white-collar workers swelled by 36 percent, from 10.5 million people to 14.3 million people. During the same decade, the number of manual workers increased only 13 percent, from 16.9 million to 19.2 million.

White-collar work got another boost from thriving United States factories. By 1929, led by the supercharged automobile industry, 9 of the 20 biggest United States corporations were turning out consumer goods. Exploding with new products, businesses now needed to persuade consumers to buy these new goods. Two growing white-collar professions—sales and advertising—proved indispensable to big business.

CAUFIELD & SHOOK COLLECTION, PHOTOGRAPHIC ARCHIVES, UNIVERSITY OF LOUISVILLE

Lining Up the Salesforce As electricity became available to all, salespeople like these found a ready market for their wares. *What kind of tactics might these salespeople use to be successful?*

The Lure of Sales

Popular magazines in the 1920s advertised, "Don't envy successful salesmen—be one!" Descriptions of salespeople making $5,000 to $30,000 a year, at a time when even autoworkers were earning less than $2,000 a year, lured thousands of young people into the profession.

If they showed brashness and drive, salespeople could make a lot of money. The pressure to succeed, however, could be devastating. Many companies used the quota system in which, to keep the job, each salesperson had to sell 20 percent or 25 percent more every year.

To make a quota, a salesperson needed to learn and apply sales psychology taught in a variety of books. According to a 1925 essay by famed lawyer Clarence Darrow, a leading sales textbook of the time even compared selling to hunting for prey: "The expert fisherman tries out the fish—if one kind of bait doesn't get the strike, he changes . . . He carefully lays his snares, places his bait and then the unsuspecting Prospect falls into the trap."

Sometimes a salesperson simply could not wait for a prospect to fall into the trap. A more aggressive approach was in order. *Selling News,* a magazine for salespeople, awarded a cash prize for this winning entry to a "sales ideas" contest. An electric cleaner salesperson who had seen a woman shaking a rug out of a second-story window told the following story. Because the door to her upstairs rooms was open, the salesperson walked right in, pretending to have an appointment to clean the woman's house. In the words of the salesperson, the woman was "very much surprised, assuring me that I had the wrong number. But during my very courteous apologies I had managed to get my cleaner connected and in action. The result was that I walked out minus the cleaner, plus her contract and check."

The salespeople who could succeed, using whatever methods, won the biggest rewards. One company gave a yearly banquet at which the best salesperson feasted on oysters, roast turkey, and ice-cream dessert. The runner-up was served the same feast, but without the oysters. So it went, down to the one with the worst sales record. This poor person's humiliation was served up before the group on a small plate of boiled beans and crackers.

The Advertising Worker

If the salesperson sold Americans what they needed and wanted, it was the advertising worker who persuaded Americans to need and want what was being sold. By 1925, United States corporations spent more than $1 billion a year on advertising. In the 1920s advertiser and author Bruce Barton argued, "Advertising is the spark plug on the cylinder of mass production . . . and sustains a system that has made us leaders of the free world." The advertising company Barton began started with a $10,000 loan in 1919 and eventually became a multimillion-dollar business.

THE BETTMANN ARCHIVE

Skilled Labor in the 1920s Office **In the 1920s many young women spent their working hours in large typing "pools" like this one.** *What skills did a typist need to possess?*

Who worked for a typical large advertising company? Most advertising workers were young, white college graduates or former newspaper writers. Advertising companies hired women for the special knowledge they could provide about the products women used and wanted. In the largest ad agencies, however, male employees outnumbered females by 10 to 1. As in many other businesses, men in advertising occupied almost all the executive positions. Even the best-paid women copywriters earned far less than men who performed the same jobs.

Advertising workers produced at a hectic pace. One ad copywriter later recalled, "If you have never wrapped a cold towel around your head at three o'clock in the morning in an effort to get a piece of copy ready for delivery before nine, you have never given it your all." The job turnover was high: More than 1 out of 3 advertising workers switched employers each year. Yet, if an advertising worker could stand the exhausting pace, he or she could earn over $5,000 a year—more than 3 times what an automobile worker earned. Advertisers prided themselves on knowing what Americans wanted. Indeed, they liked to consider themselves not advertising workers but "consumption engineers." Great business leaders, a 1920s advertising magazine boasted, might someday "learn almost as much about what the people of the United States really know about and are interested in as does the junior copywriter of a fourth rate advertising agency."

Women in the Workforce

From Factories to Offices

At the turn of the century, less than 1 in 5 women workers held clerical, managerial, sales, and professional positions. When women began to flood the workforce during the 1920s, however, many left their houses dressed in black skirts and starched white blouses. These women workers were heading for offices and stores, not factories. By 1930, 44 percent of employed women worked at white-collar jobs.

Typecasting Women

It all started with the typewriter. E. Remington and Sons sold the first typewriting machines in 1874. Almost all the new typists were middle class, high-school educated, and female. Why? To do the job, a worker needed to be a good speller and possess a knowledge of grammar, capitalization, and punctuation. Most lower-class men and women lacked these skills; a middle-class man with a high-school diploma could find a much better-paying job.

For female high-school graduates, however, the story was different. Before the typewriter an educated working woman had few choices: she could become a teacher or a nurse or take a factory job for which she was overqualified. Even if typing paid no better than operating a machine in a factory, the new office work allowed an educated young woman to work in a clean, attractive environment.

ARCHIVE PHOTOS

Operating the Switchboards **Ever-growing communications systems provided employment opportunities for women of the 1920s.** *Why did women choose this kind of work?*

Previously, one man or a small group of male clerks, who could expect eventual promotion to managerial positions, had done the clerical work in a typical office. Women, who did not command high wages or look forward to advancement, could operate all the new office technology—typewriters, dictaphones, telephones.

Because any of the new jobs could be performed as easily at one firm as another, the stenographer or typist found herself in a large "pool" of similarly skilled workers. In a book called *The Job,* Sinclair Lewis described such a pool in which an "unrecognized horde of girls . . . merely copied or took the bright young men's dictation." He added, "They were expected to keep clean and be quick-moving; beyond that they were as unimportant to the larger phases of office politics as frogs to a summer hotel."

Shop Clerks and Telephone Operators

In the same way that secretarial work provided an alternative to nursing or teaching for female high-school graduates, telephone companies and the new department stores offered women without a high-school diploma a pleasant alternative to factory work or domestic service. By 1930, 736,000 women had gone to work as shop clerks, cash girls, wrappers, stock clerks, cashiers, or switchboard operators.

Women employees eagerly accepted the challenges of their new positions. Shop work involved less manual labor than factory work, and the environment was cleaner. The pay equaled or exceeded what women workers could earn with unskilled labor. The jobs were important, too. It was up to the salesclerk, for example, to see that people's new needs and wants were satisfied.

Men and Women in the Office

By the 1920s offices and stores had two distinct cultures, neatly divided by sex. Women dominated in the clerical, unskilled occupations. There neatness, orderliness, and courtesy played a big role, but job responsibility involved simple, repetitive routines. Women's jobs provided little chance for advancement except to the positions of cashier or executive secretary, or perhaps to marriage. Secretarial work taught a woman endurance, modesty, and obedience, so many people considered it perfect preparation for marriage.

Men, on the other hand, found jobs as managers, senior cashiers, chief clerks, head bookkeepers, floorwalkers, salespeople, or advertising workers. In these jobs energy, initiative, and creativity paid off and could lead to a better position in the company.

Though the new work environment of the 1920s clearly defined the separate jobs of each gender, it also provided for the first time an opportunity for educated men and women to meet and share the workplace. These new coworkers would soon become consumers of a host of new products thriving United States factories produced.

SECTION ASSESSMENT

Main Idea

1. Use a diagram like this one to show the effects of automation on both factory and office work.

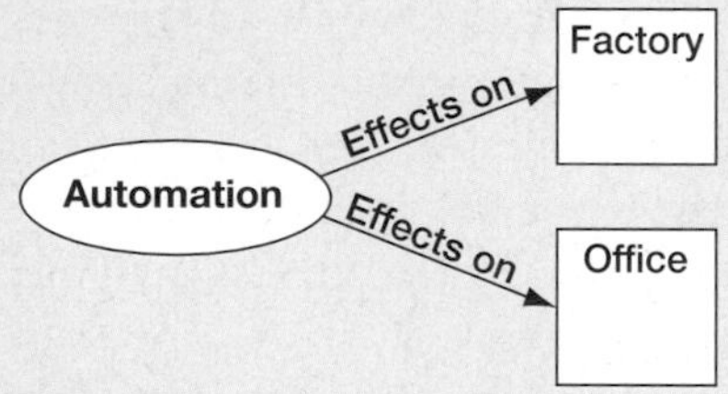

Vocabulary

2. Define: industrialist, scientific management, white-collar worker.

Checking Facts

3. Why did management and labor at Midvale Steel oppose scientific management at first? Why did the auto industry adopt the new methods from the beginning?

4. List three white-collar jobs men held in the 1920s. Compare these with white-collar jobs women held, in terms of qualifications, salary, and opportunity for advancement.

Critical Thinking

5. **Determining Cause and Effect** Why were there suddenly so many new white-collar workers during the 1920s?

Technology Skill

DEVELOPING A MULTIMEDIA PRESENTATION

Learning the Skill

Your history teacher has assigned a presentation on the Prohibition era. You want to develop an interesting presentation that really holds your classmates' attention. How do you do this? Most presentations are more dynamic and easier to follow if they include diagrams, photographs, videos, or sound recordings. Equipment you may have at home, plus classroom or library equipment and resources, can help you develop interesting multimedia presentations.

Developing a Multimedia Presentation

A multimedia presentation involves using several types of media. To discuss the history of Prohibition, for example, you might create and show timelines of significant events during the period of Prohibition. You could also play recordings of speeches for and against Prohibition made in Congress or present a video about the history of Prohibition.

Another way to develop a multimedia presentation is with computer programs. Multimedia as it relates to computer technology is the combination of text, video, audio, and animation in an interactive computer program. In order to create multimedia productions or presentations on a computer, though, you need to have certain tools. These may include traditional computer graphic tools and draw programs, animation programs that make still images move, and authoring systems that tie everything together. Your computer manual will tell you which tools your computer can support.

AARON HAUPT

Various types of media that can be used in multimedia presentations

Practicing the Skill

Plan a multimedia presentation on a topic found in the chapter, such as women's struggle for voting rights. List three or four major ideas you would like to cover. Then think about how multimedia resources could enhance your presentation. Use your school or local library to do a preliminary survey of materials that may be available and list them. Use your imagination when planning your presentation. Answer the following questions:

1. Which forms of media do I want to include? Video? Sound? Animation? Photographs? Graphics? Other?

2. Which forms of media on my chosen topic are available at my school or local library?

3. Which of these media forms does my computer support?

4. What types of media can I create myself to enhance my presentation?

5. Is there a "do-it-all" program I can use to develop the kind of presentation I want?

Applying the Skill

Make the presentation you planned a reality. Create a multimedia presentation about some topic in the chapter. Use as many multimedia materials as possible, including those that you create, such as photographs, drawings, charts, graphs, posters, music recordings, or videotapes. Share your multimedia presentation with the class.

Additional Practice

For additional practice, see Reinforcing Skills on page 373.

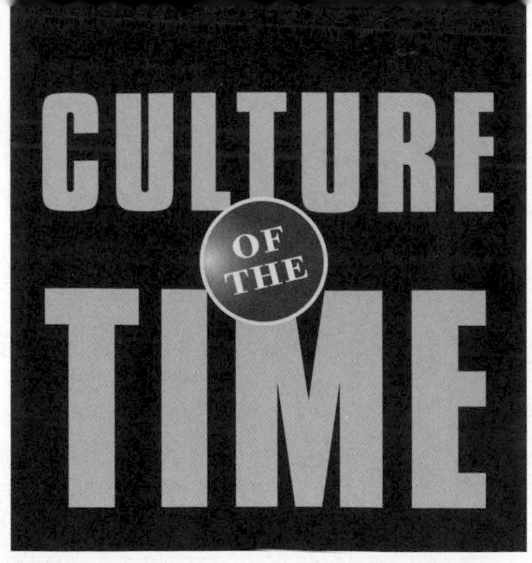

The Roaring Twenties

During the 1920s—the golden age of jazz—Americans danced to the decade's joyous music at a frantic and ever accelerating pace. Inspired by jazz, Americans began to improvise leisure time activities that had no purpose other than having fun. People roared through the decade intent on enjoying every exciting moment of it, as though everyone shared an unspoken premonition that it could not last.

COMIC HERO

Charlie Chaplin's comic film character, "the Tramp," captured the country's imagination. His mustache, derby hat, bamboo cane, and outsize shoes were recognized around the world—and often imitated, as these young fans attest.

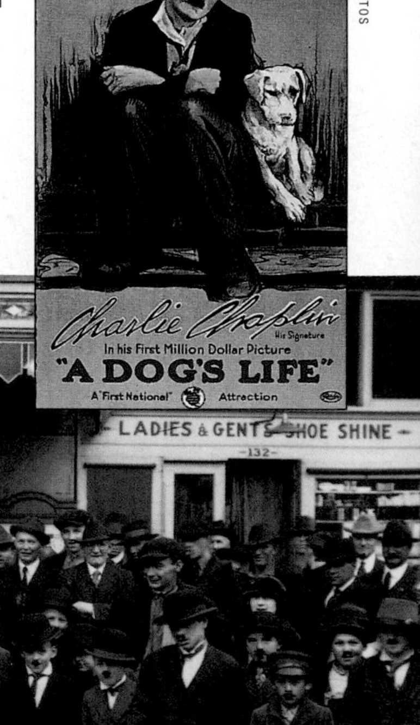

ARCHIVE PHOTOS

#203, J. WILBUR SANDISON COLLECTION, WHATCOM MUSEUM OF HISTORY AND ART, BELLINGHAM, WA

UPI/BETTMANN

DAREDEVILS IN THE AIR

A passion for flying possessed the nation, and novelty-crazed audiences were not satisfied by planes simply flying in straight lines. At almost any open field, **stunt flyers** looped, spiraled, and even played airborne tennis for thrilled spectators.

LIBRARY OF CONGRESS

FAD FEVER

Of the fads that roared in and out of the 1920s, **flagpole-sitting** may have been the oddest. Started as a publicity stunt by "Shipwreck" Kelly in 1924, the idea took off. In Baltimore, Maryland, flagpole fervor reached epic proportions after Avon Foreman set an endurance record there. One week in 1929, as many as 20 people perched on poles at various points around the city.

UPI/BETTMANN NEWSPHOTOS

SINGING THE BLUES

In the flourishing world of African American music, arts, and letters in the Jazz Age, singer **Bessie Smith** reigned as "Empress of the Blues." Guitarist Danny Barker said, "She could bring about mass hypnotism."

UPI/BETTMANN

DANCE CRAZES

The **Charleston** and the **tango** were the hot dances of the decade. The dance-until-you-drop marathons inspired other wacky dance endeavors, such as this couple's tango from Santa Monica to downtown Los Angeles.

Chapter  Assessment

Self-Check Quiz

Visit the *American Odyssey* Web site at americanodyssey.glencoe.com and click on ***Chapter 11—Self-Check Quiz*** to prepare for the Chapter Test.

Reviewing Key Terms

On a separate sheet of paper, identify the person, people, or group from the following list that was associated with each concept in the numbered list below.

- Frederick Taylor and Henry Ford
- large employers
- César Augusto Sandino
- Woodrow Wilson
- industry-dominating businesses
- Sacco and Vanzetti

1. anarchism
2. internationalism
3. oligopoly
4. welfare capitalism
5. scientific management

Recalling Facts

1. Name at least three contributing causes of the Red Scare.

2. Why did so many African Americans migrate from the South to the North from 1916 to 1920?

3. List three factors that contributed to the decline of progressivism in the 1920s.

4. What do you think Harding meant by *normalcy*?

5. Why did Andrew Mellon believe millionaires should not pay taxes?

6. How did technology affect productivity in the 1920s?

7. Name two factors that contributed to the development of oligopolies in the 1920s.

8. List three types of welfare capitalism programs.

9. Give three reasons why Henry Ford doubled his workers' wages in 1914.

10. How did Henry Ford apply the theory of scientific management?

Critical Thinking

1. Drawing Conclusions Women and men had been organizing, marching, and asking for the vote for 72 years. Using information in the text, why do you think women were able to win the vote in 1920?

2. Synthesizing Information The Republican Presidents of the 1920s supported big business and rejected programs for the public welfare. How did the government's support of big business affect ordinary citizens both positively and negatively?

3. Making Comparisons Compare the careers of women and men in white-collar professions in the 1920's.

4. Making Comparisons Use a diagram like this one to compare the careers of women and men in the white-collared professions in the 1920s.

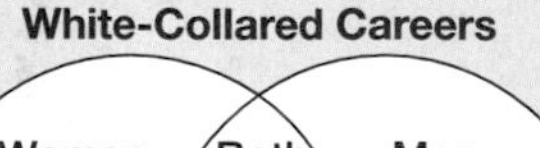

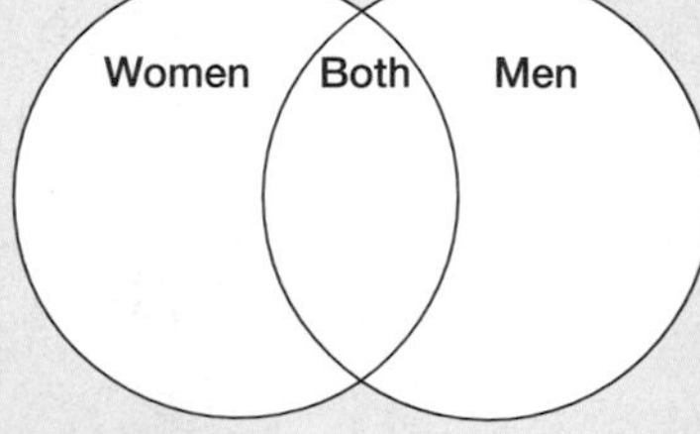

5. Determining Cause and Effect The idolization of business and business leaders created a national climate that benefited big business. What do you think might have been some negative effects of the glorification of business?

Portfolio Project

PORTFOLIO PROJECT

Research the requirements for setting up a small business in your community. Investigate areas such as government regulations, financing, and the costs of leasing space and buying equipment. The local chamber of commerce might direct you in your research. Write a report on your findings, and include your final report in your portfolio.

Cooperative Learning

Work in small groups to research and report on one of the following industries between 1919 and 1929: textiles, railroads, shipping, farming, aviation, or chemistry. As part of your research, find out whether the industry did well or had problems, and describe the causes of the success or struggle. As a group, choose a medium for presenting your findings, such as a newspaper article, skit, or collage, and share your project with the rest of the class.

Reinforcing Skills

Developing a Multimedia Presentation Study the list of topics below and select one. Write a brief summary describing the 3 types of media you would use in a presentation to teach the topic most effectively to your class.

- The Red Scare
- The Garvey Movement
- Prohibition

GEOGRAPHY AND HISTORY

U.S. City Population, 1930

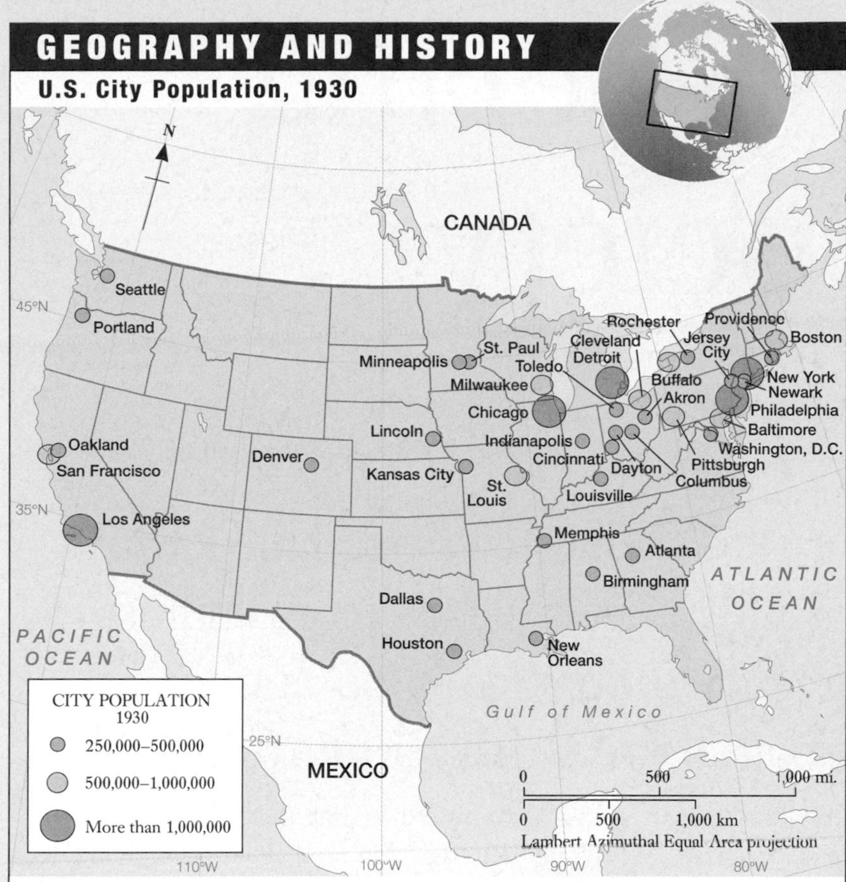

Study the map to answer the following questions:

1. Which cities had more than 1 million residents in 1930?
2. Which regions of the country had the densest urban population? Which had the sparsest? What might explain this population distribution?
3. How does this population map from 1930 reflect the Great Migration of African Americans from the South?
4. How does the location of the nation's five largest cities show the importance of geography in determining where large population centers are located?
5. Note that few states in the West had large population centers in 1930. How do you account for this?

Technology Activity

Developing a Multimedia Presentation Search the Internet or your local library to find additional information about the 1920s. Create a multimedia presentation about the 1920s comparing the social climate of great innovations and conservatism. Identify who did well and who struggled during this period.

Standardized Test Practice

11 The term that *best* describes the business policies promoted by Presidents Harding, Coolidge, and Hoover is

A socialism.
B free enterprise.
C bolshevism.
D anarchism.

Test-Taking Tip: Eliminate any answers that do not make sense. For example, the Communist revolution in Russia made Americans fear all radical political theories, which eliminates answers C and D.

2. "The Afro-American population of the large cities of the North and West is being constantly fed by a steady stream of new people from the Southern States." –*The New York Age*, 1907

These words describe an early 1900s African American exodus from the South known as the

A Garvey Movement.
B American Plan.
C Great Migration.
D Great Awakening.

Test-Taking Tip: This question asks you to remember facts about movements of people during the early 1900s. The dates rule out the the Great Awakening (answer D), a religious revival movement that took shape in the mid-1700s.

A Prospering Society

OCTOBER 6, 1926: THE BABE SETS WORLD SERIES RECORD!

In St. Louis, Missouri, 40,000 fans witnessed the fourth game of baseball's World Series. Millions more enthusiastic fans were listening to popular radio announcer Graham McNamee as Babe Ruth came to bat.

McNamee reported, "The Babe is waving that wand of his over the plate. Bell is loosening up his arm. The Babe hits it clear into the center-field bleachers for a home run! For a home run! Did you hear what I said? Oh, what a shot! . . . Oh, boy! Wow! That is a World Series record, three home runs in one series game, and what a home run!"

No one better symbolized the period of the 1920s than home run hitter Babe Ruth. He was a contradictory man with an amazing athletic talent, a gigantic appetite for pleasure, and a casual disregard for rules.

Like its baseball hero, the United States also exhibited some basic contradictions during the 1920s. At the same time most of the country was plunging breathlessly into the new era, many Americans sought to return to a simpler past. Deep conflicts in the United States over religion and immigration added turmoil to the excitement of this decade, which was rapidly becoming full of radios, newspapers, movies, and advertising.

Babe Ruth was a perfect hero for a country undergoing vast change in a bold, hungry, and lawless era. ■

HISTORY JOURNAL

Before you read the rest of this chapter, write any other information you know about the history of baseball. Then write what societal changes you think took place in the 1920s.

Chapter Overview

Visit the *American Odyssey* Web site at americanodyssey.glencoe.com and click on ***Chapter 12—Chapter Overview*** to preview the chapter.

NATIONAL BASEBALL LIBRARY, COOPERSTOWN, N.Y.

THE EMERGENCE OF MASS COMMUNICATION IN THE 1920S MADE SPORTS STARS LIKE BABE RUTH FAMOUS WORLDWIDE.

Growth of the Middle Class

1922: SINCLAIR LEWIS PUBLISHES *BABBITT*

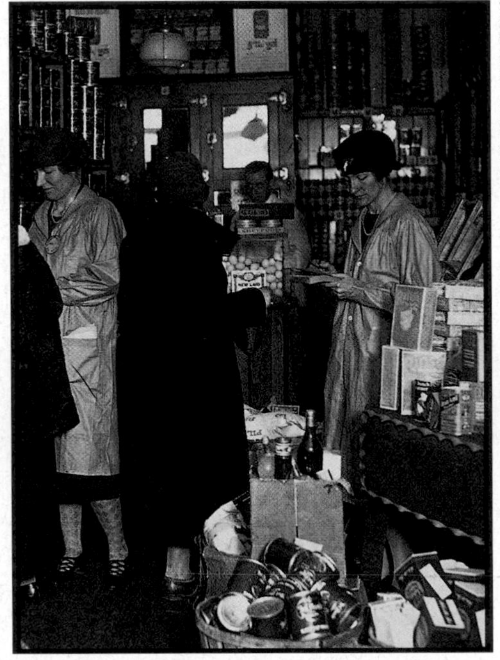

UPI/BETTMANN NEWSPHOTOS

A New Era of Consumer Goods
Self-service was an innovation in retail shopping.

WRITER SINCLAIR LEWIS INVENTED THE BOOMING TOWN OF ZENITH IN 1922 FOR HIS NOVEL *BABBITT*. It could have been any one of many American cities in the 1920s. The novel's main character, George Babbitt, declared:

> Zenith manufactures more condensed milk and evaporated cream, more paper boxes, and more lighting-fixtures, than any other city in the United States, if not in the world. But it is not so universally known that we also stand second in the manufacture of package-butter, sixth in the giant realm of motors and automobiles, and somewhere about third in cheese, leather bindings, tar roofing, breakfast food, and overalls!
>
> . . . When I add that we have an unparalleled number of miles of paved streets, bathrooms, vacuum cleaners, and all the other signs of civilization; that our library and art museum are well supported and housed in convenient and roomy buildings; that our park-system is more than up to par, with its handsome driveways adorned with grass, shrubs, and statuary, then I give but a hint of the all-round unlimited greatness of Zenith!
>
> —Sinclair Lewis, *Babbitt,* 1922

GUIDE TO READING

Main Idea

The availability of affordable consumer goods, coupled with new methods for purchasing them, convinced many American workers that they were part of a growing middle class.

Vocabulary

- standard of living
- credit
- mass media
- flapper

Read to Find Out . . .

- how and why the standard of living of many, though not all, Americans rose during the 1920s.
- the effects of the automobile on the economy and culture of the 1920s.
- how advertising and mass media affected American buying habits and fashions in the 1920s.

Americans as Consumers

Buying Power Increases for Most

The industrialization of the late 1800s was finally beginning to offer real rewards to residents of towns like Zenith. Between 1923 and 1929, American workers saw their real income rise 11 percent. With more than just enough money to live on, many American workers could buy more of the goods they produced. They began to feel that they were part of a growing middle class.

In the 1920s many middle-class American consumers improved their **standard of living.** That is, necessities and luxuries were more available—and affordable. Compared to people overseas, Americans like George Babbitt could afford to buy more goods and, compared to people overseas, Americans like George Babbitt had a higher standard of living.

New Consumer Products

Thanks to refrigeration, Americans ate fresh fruits and vegetables, that were available in stores year-round. Thanks to improved packaging, they bought a wider variety of packaged food, including that great invention, sliced bread. They now purchased ready-made clothes, which replaced home-sewn or tailored garments.

Some regional differences between Americans began to blur as clothing and other mass-produced goods became cheaper and more popular. In most parts of the country, people bought identical vacuum cleaners, electric irons, toasters, washing machines, and refrigerators.

These marvelous machines reduced the time it took to do housework. In their newfound leisure time, Americans could now listen to radios and phonographs or talk to each other on the telephone.

Without electricity, all these machines would have stayed on their inventors' drawing boards. During the 1920s electrical current needed to run machines became more widely available, not just in the houses of the wealthy but also in the homes of many average Americans.

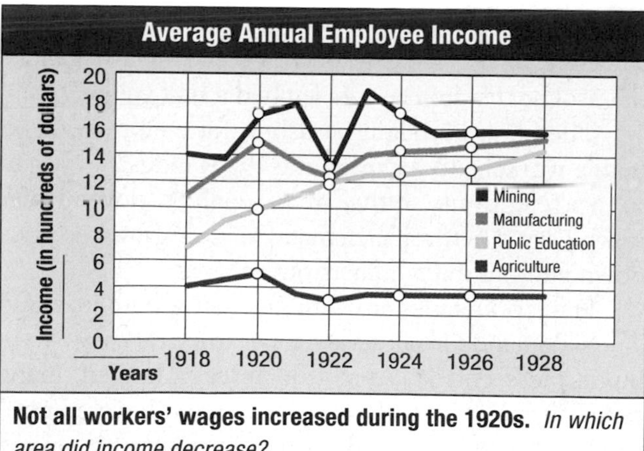

Not all workers' wages increased during the 1920s. *In which area did income decrease?*

Not all American homes had electricity. Many parts of rural America, especially in the South, were not electrified for many years. Even without electricity, some working-class homes showed an improvement in their standard of living during this decade. Many poor people traded wood fuel for coal, walked on linoleum floors instead of wooden ones, and retired their water buckets when fresh water began to gush from indoor faucets.

Poverty in the Midst of Plenty

Not all Americans were able to improve their standard of living during this period. Low wages and unemployment combined to drive many American families into poverty. Farmers and other workers suffered when the goods they produced dropped in price.

For example, thousands of farmers had replaced their workhorses with Ford's Fordson tractors. With this efficient machine farmers produced more wheat and corn than the country could consume. In a market economy, when supply exceeds demand, prices tend to drop.

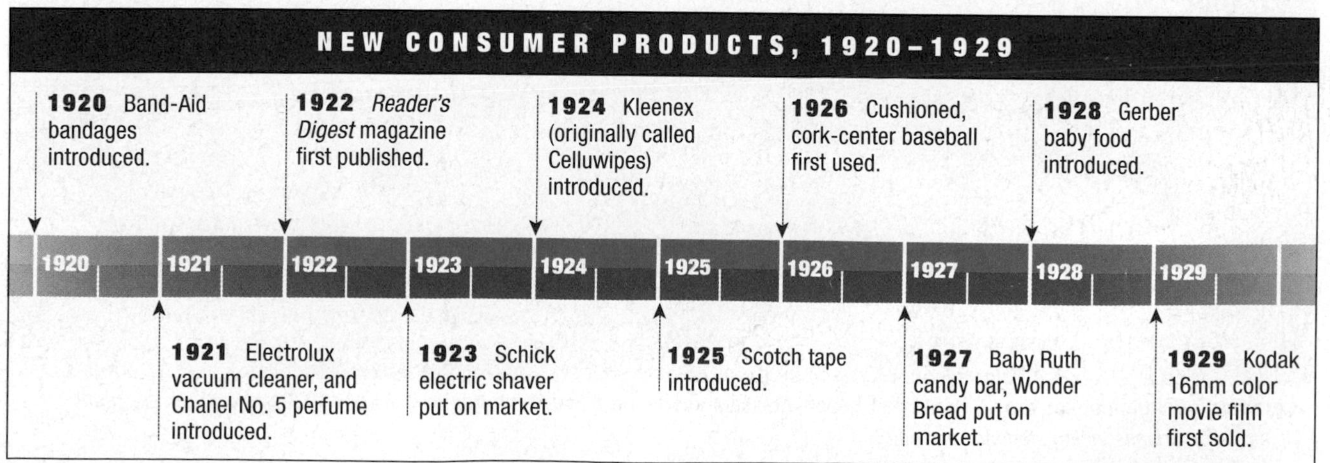

NEW CONSUMER PRODUCTS, 1920–1929
1920 Band-Aid bandages introduced.
1922 *Reader's Digest* magazine first published.
1924 Kleenex (originally called Celluwipes) introduced.
1926 Cushioned, cork-center baseball first used.
1928 Gerber baby food introduced.
1920
1921
1922
1923
1924
1925
1926
1927
1928
1929
1921 Electrolux vacuum cleaner, and Chanel No. 5 perfume introduced.
1923 Schick electric shaver put on market.
1925 Scotch tape introduced.
1927 Baby Ruth candy bar, Wonder Bread put on market.
1929 Kodak 16mm color movie film first sold.

During the 1920s a glut of produce sent farm prices into a decline. In 1919 a bushel of corn could buy five gallons of gasoline. By 1921 it only fetched a half gallon.

The period brought hardships for coal miners and textile workers, too. During the 1920s industries began to use electricity rather than coal to power their machinery. This drop in demand for coal drove the price down and put many miners out of work.

Due to changes in fashion—rising hemlines and a new demand for silk stockings—Americans now were buying less cotton. As cotton prices plunged, many textile factories in the Northeast and South were forced to shut down. For the first time in a century, overall factory employment decreased.

By some estimates, a third of American families lived below minimum levels for a decent life. Their inability to buy what the United States produced would contribute to the unraveling of the booming economy by the end of the decade. Despite the plight of farmers and workers in depressed industries, however, most Americans in the 1920s shared George Babbitt's satisfaction. The automobile was beginning to give even ordinary Americans a share in the United States's plenty.

America Hits the Road

Automobiles Redefine the Country

More than any other single consumer item, the automobile defined the United States of the 1920s. In 1927 Americans owned 4 out of 5 of the world's cars, averaging 1 motor vehicle for every 5.3 persons. The Model T car Henry Ford introduced in 1908 transformed the automobile from a high-priced item to one many moderate-income families could afford. On May 27, 1927, when the last of 15 million Model Ts rolled off the line, the average American family made $2,000 a year and could buy a new car for less than $300.

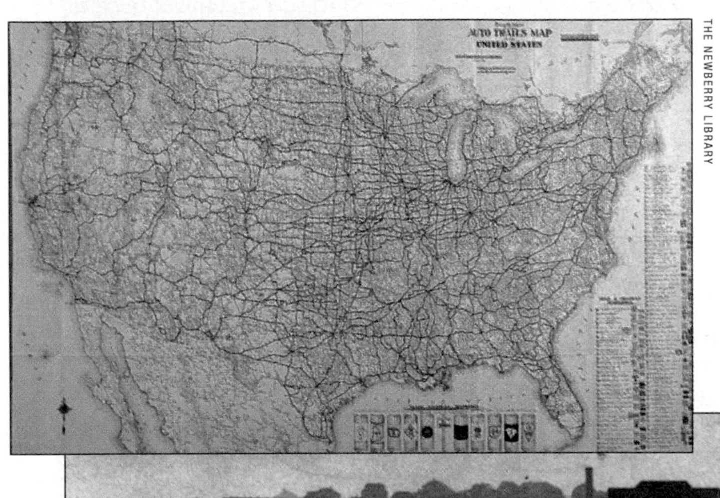

THE NEWBERRY LIBRARY

HIRZ/ARCHIVE PHOTOS

Cars for Fun Automobiles crowd Nantasket Beach, Massachusetts, on a Fourth of July in the early 1920s. *How does this photo illustrate Americans' rising standard of living?*

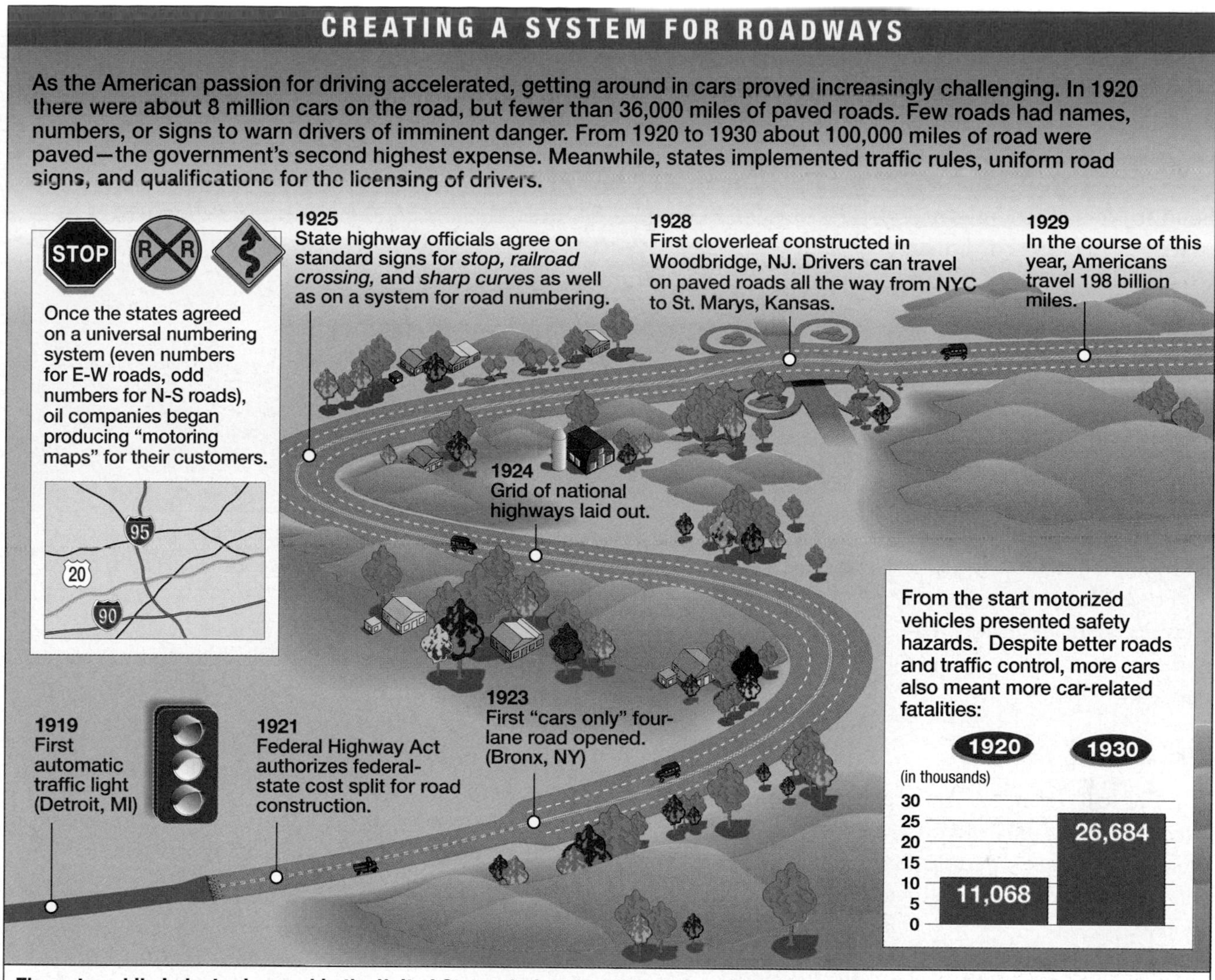

CREATING A SYSTEM FOR ROADWAYS
As the American passion for driving accelerated, getting around in cars proved increasingly challenging. In 1920 there were about 8 million cars on the road, but fewer than 36,000 miles of paved roads. Few roads had names, numbers, or signs to warn drivers of imminent danger. From 1920 to 1930 about 100,000 miles of road were paved—the government's second highest expense. Meanwhile, states implemented traffic rules, uniform road signs, and qualifications for the licensing of drivers.
STOP
R R
Once the states agreed on a universal numbering system (even numbers for E-W roads, odd numbers for N-S roads), oil companies began producing "motoring maps" for their customers.
95
20
90
1925 State highway officials agree on standard signs for stop, railroad crossing, and sharp curves as well as on a system for road numbering.
1928 First cloverleaf constructed in Woodbridge, NJ. Drivers can travel on paved roads all the way from NYC to St. Marys, Kansas.
1929 In the course of this year, Americans travel 198 billion miles.
1924 Grid of national highways laid out.
1923 First "cars only" four-lane road opened. (Bronx, NY)
1919 First automatic traffic light (Detroit, MI)
1921 Federal Highway Act authorizes federal-state cost split for road construction.
From the start motorized vehicles presented safety hazards. Despite better roads and traffic control, more cars also meant more car-related fatalities:
1920
1930
(in thousands)
30
25
20
15
10
5
0
11,068
26,684

The automobile industry boomed in the United States during the 1920s. *How many more traffic fatalities were there in the United States in 1930 than in 1920? What steps did state and federal agencies take to bring order to crowded roadways?*

Sharing so visibly in the wealth of society, more and more Americans came to feel that the booming Coolidge economy was working for them. They enthusiastically entered a new era, the age of the automobile. In turn, the age of the automobile would revolutionize American life for decades to come.

Shifting the Economy

Automobile manufacturing became America's biggest industry during the 1920s and soon boosted the entire economy. Cars required vast quantities of steel, lead, nickel, and gasoline. Workers in all these industries thrived. Another 5 million Americans worked to produce glass and rubber that automobile making demanded.

Businesses flourished to serve the needs of a newly mobile nation. Garages, filling stations, hot dog stands, restaurants, tearooms, tourists' roadside camps—all sprang into existence only after the automobile drove onto the American scene.

Besides boosting industry, the automobile radically changed the face of the country. Villages along the new automobile routes thrived, while villages along the railroad lines began to disappear.

At the end of World War I, the United States had just 7,000 miles (11,263 km) of concrete roads. By 1927 a network of 50,000 miles (80,450 km) was growing at the rate of 10,000 miles (16,090 km) each year. Even-numbered highways like Route 66 ran east-west; odd-numbered highways ran north-south. Few Americans minded that states paid for these roads by taxing gasoline. (See Geography, pages 384–385.)

The Romance of the Automobile

The automobile was more than just a convenient way to get from one place to another. It soon became an integral part of the American dream. Henry Ford boasted that his customers could have a Model T in any color "so long as it is black." By the middle 1920s though, Americans wanted their cars to make a fashion statement. With the invention of lacquer finishes, automobiles of 1925 and 1926 delighted buyers with bold new shades from Arabian Sand to Versailles Violet.

Even Henry Ford had to give in. At the end of May 1927 he shut down the plant that had produced the Model T—America's first real car. Ford's announcement of the brand-new Model A was a major event of 1927. Beginning at 3:00 A.M. on December 2, almost 1 million people lined up in front of Ford Motor Company's New York headquarters, eagerly trying to catch the first glimpse of Ford's colorful new cars.

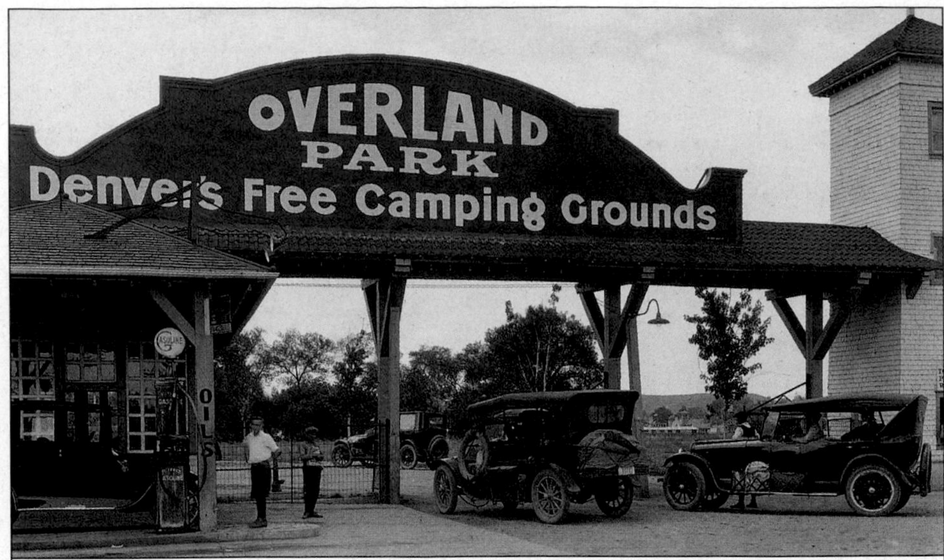

Automotive Leisure Autocamping became a favorite vacation; car owners could buy special tents to attach to their cars. *Did people have mixed feelings about cars? What were they?*

The Driving Culture

The car changed American culture in countless ways. Dating habits of young people, Sunday outings of families, places people lived and vacationed, and ways people shopped—all were affected by the automobile.

By 1927, 4 out of 5 cars had closed tops, compared with only 1 in 10 in 1919. The new, closed car was a room on wheels. Now protected from the weather, teenagers especially enjoyed the privacy of closed cars.

On Sundays many families hopped into their cars for short day trips. With "auto-mobility," many city workers moved to houses in the new suburbs. Car owners now traveled easily to once distant places.

One such traveler described his stay at a roadside camp in North Carolina. The tourists had come from as far away as Washington state:

> There were fourteen cars in the camp, ranging all the way from dusty Fords to big and glittering limousines with balloon tires and tremendous horsepower. . . . And for the first time in history, the common, ordinary "fo'kes" of the North and South are meeting one another on a really large scale, mostly by means of the National chariot—the Ford car.
>
> —C.P. Russell, "The Pneumatic Hegira," *The Outlook,* December 9, 1925

In addition to bringing far-flung Americans together for the first time, the automobile also saddled many people with their first debt. Eager to own a car, a person could now put a deposit down, drive a new car away, and pay off the balance, plus interest, in installments. By 1927, two out of three cars were purchased on the installment, or time-payment, plan.

A banker who loaned money to prospective car buyers bemoaned the change in American habits of thrift, including his own, in an essay written in 1925:

> The ease with which a car can be purchased on the time-payment plan is all too easy a road to ruin. The habit of thrift can never be acquired through so wasteful a medium as an automobile. Instead, the habit of spending must be acquired, for with the constant demand for fuel, oil, and repairs, together with the heavy depreciation, the automobile stands unique as the most extravagant piece of machinery ever devised for the pleasure of man. But—I still drive one myself. I must keep up with the procession.
>
> —William Ashdown, "Confessions of an Automobilist," *Atlantic Monthly*, June 1925

Selling America

New Ways to Buy

Even thrifty Americans such as William Ashdown felt pressured to buy cars on the installment plan. One reason was the brash salesmanship the dealers practiced.

A Ford dealer speaking with reporter Jesse Rainsford Sprague said his boss had instructed him to sell 20 cars a month in a depressed rural area. In speaking of one customer, the dealer said:

The man was a poor devil of a renter seven or eight miles out of town who never had enough cash ahead to buy a wheelbarrow, but Burke insisted that one of my salesmen go out there with him to try and land a sale. When they got there a couple of the children were down with whooping cough and a hailstorm had laid out his bean crop, but Burke came back and told me he would expect me to put over a Ford on the fellow before he came on his next trip.

—Jesse Rainsford Sprague, "Confessions of a Ford Dealer," *Harper's Monthly Magazine*, June 1927

Buying on Time

Automobiles were not the only product Americans were buying on **credit**—putting money down and paying the balance in installments. In 1928, 85 percent of furniture, 80 percent of phonographs, 75 percent of washing machines and radios, and 70 percent of refrigerators were also bought on credit.

Buying on time could add as much as 40 percent to the price consumers eventually paid; but for the first time, buyers could have an item without saving the money to pay for it. That $43.50 phonograph became irresistible when the price read, "$5 down and $5 a month."

Most Americans no longer looked at debt as shameful. They began to regard installment buying as an easy way to raise their standard of living.

Chain Stores

If Americans were buying more and buying on the installment plan, they were also shopping in a different type of store. In the 1920s Americans flocked to the new chain stores that began to spring up all over the country—grocery stores such as A&P, Safeway, and Piggly Wiggly and department stores such as J.C. Penney and Sears, Roebuck. In 1918 there were 29,000 such stores. By 1929 there were 160,000.

Now that customers could hop into their cars and drive to a chain store, the owners of the traditional corner stores lost their main advantage—convenience. Besides being convenient, the chain stores also offered lower prices, greater reliability, better service, and wider choice. At F.W. Woolworth, for example, a shopper with 10 cents or less could buy anything from Rosh Hashanah cards to Venetian Night incense, from an ice cream sundae to a packet of gumdrops or foreign stamps.

Advertising

Americans' buying habits changed most of all because of the sudden growth of advertising. Advertising itself was not new, of course. Since colonial times, American retailers had used newspapers to inform the public about products and prices. What revolutionized advertising in the 1920s was the idea of using it to create consumer demand.

Even tight-lipped and thrifty Calvin Coolidge acknowledged the power of advertising to make "new thoughts, new desires and new actions" seem attractive to an impressionable public. He added, "It is the most potent influence in adopting, and changing the habits and modes of life, affecting what we eat, what we wear, and the work and play of the whole nation."

Advertising suddenly sprang into prominence because Americans' purchases could barely keep pace with the factories' explosion of new goods. Advertisers helped sell their clients' products.

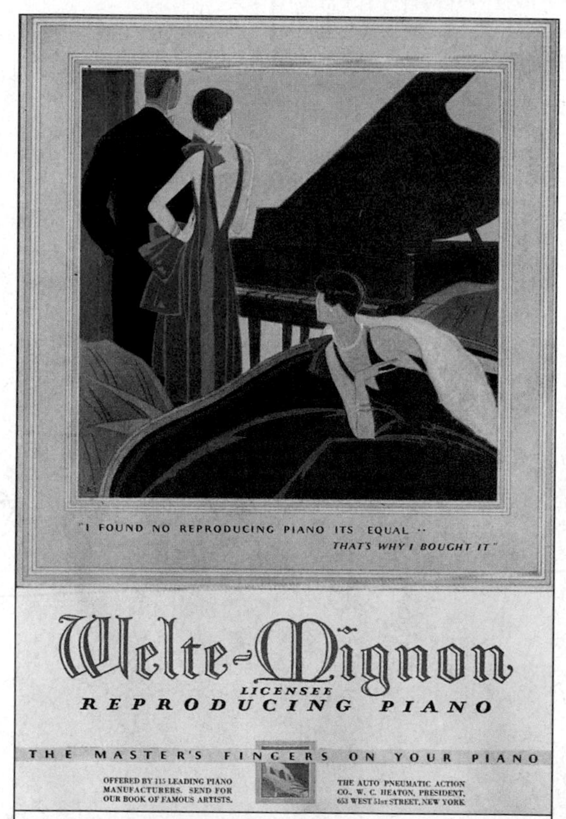

"I FOUND NO REPRODUCING PIANO ITS EQUAL ··
THAT'S WHY I BOUGHT IT"
Welte-Mignon
LICENSEE
REPRODUCING PIANO
THE MASTER'S FINGERS ON YOUR PIANO
OFFERED BY 115 LEADING PIANO MANUFACTURERS. SEND FOR OUR BOOK OF FAMOUS ARTISTS.
THE AUTO PNEUMATIC ACTION CO., W. C. HEATON, PRESIDENT, 653 WEST 51st STREET, NEW YORK

The Advertising Industry **Glamorous-looking advertisements such as this one enticed Americans to buy all kinds of products, from the grand to the mundane. The ads often featured well-known artists' work, and tended toward flowery language.**
How did advertisements create consumer demand?

The new **mass media** (a term first used in 1923 to refer to modes of communication that reached large numbers of people) gave advertisers a huge audience of potential consumers. Newspapers, radio stations, billboards, and national magazines all bombarded consumers with one message: Buy, buy, buy!

Advertising became big business in the 1920s. Critics complained that for every dollar spent to educate consumers in what to buy, a mere 70 cents went to pay for schools.

Youth Sets the Scene

Creating the "Roaring Twenties"

During this decade advertisers took advantage of the nation's growing fascination with youth to sell products that promised youthful vitality or style. Never before had American culture idolized the young as it did in the 1920s. The loss of so many young men in World War I seemed to place a special premium on youth. Now, instead of young people modeling themselves on their elders, adults tried to act like children.

Fashions and Fads

As youth came to mean stylishness, young people became the models for fashion, dress, music, and language. Styles that began on college campuses spread quickly to the public, thanks to cheap mass production and advertising in the national mass media. Women everywhere wore yellow rain slickers and multicolored bandanas at the waist. Men sported raccoon coats and golf stockings.

Other fads spread equally quick. The 1920s could be called the age of the fad—a sudden explosion of interest in some product or activity. In Baltimore, for example, 15-year-old Avon Foreman sat on a flagpole for 10 days, 10 hours, 10 minutes, and 10 seconds in 1929. For months Americans everywhere tried to do the same. Then they turned their attention elsewhere. Like the automobile, mass-produced items, and national advertising, the fads of the 1920s helped establish a common culture.

New Ideals of Beauty

The Gibson Girl, an ideal of feminine beauty before World War I, had long, flowing hair. Her dress emphasized her womanly figure, highlighted her tiny waist, and covered her legs.

The 1920s girl—at least the one promoted in advertising and movies—turned this modest image upside down and inside out and emerged as a **flapper.**

BROWN BROTHERS

The Influential Young **Revealing bathing suits, as seen on this beach in the late 1920s, were part of the daring attire of both men and women.** *In what way was the obsession with youth a reaction to World War I?*

THE BETTMANN ARCHIVE

Flappers Flaunt Tradition **Dashing flappers were sometimes called shebas; their male counterparts sheiks.** *How did the flapper differ from the Gibson Girl?*

Named for the open galoshes she flapped around in, the flapper bound her chest to flatten it, loosened her blouse and dropped its waist, lifted her hemline, and rolled down her stockings. She bobbed her hair short and crowned the shorn locks with a close-fitting hat.

In 1928 the *Journal of Commerce* estimated that in the previous 15 years the average woman had stripped away 12 ¼ yards (11.2 m) of material from her outfit, leaving only a scant 7 yards (6.4 m) of cloth in addition to her rolled-down stockings. These were now silk or the new rayon, no longer the practical cotton or wool ones of the past.

The flapper may have looked like a little girl or even a little boy, but she applied makeup with a bold hand. So did her mother.

Women's New Freedoms

Before World War I, women had been arrested for smoking or using profanity in public. Appearing at the beach without stockings or going without a corset was considered indecent exposure, even in cities as large and sophisticated as Chicago. Ten years later, flappers smoked, drank, left corsets in the cloakroom at the dance, and went joyriding in automobiles. Society, far from curbing women's new behavior, seemed to encourage it.

For one thing, the women's movement and new laws gave women a greater measure of economic and intellectual independence than they had been allowed before the war. In addition, the automobile gave the young a new and exciting independence from their families.

School Days

If American teenagers were taking to the road in the evening, they were spending more time at school during the day. Many Americans now kept their children in school longer because they no longer depended upon the children's wages. By 1930, 51 percent of all high-school-age youths were in school, compared with less than 6 percent in 1890.

The schools Americans built for their children looked nothing like the little red schoolhouses of the past. In the 1920s the new high school building, with its huge gym and gleaming laboratory, was the pride of the neighborhood.

Only one out of eight young people went to college in 1930, but that was three times the number who had attended college at the turn of the century. Both high school and college students were eager consumers who helped set trends for fashion and amusement. The mass media helped to make youth the best-selling image of the 1920s.

Section Assessment

Main Idea

1. Use a diagram like this one to show new ways of selling and buying consumer goods in the 1920s.

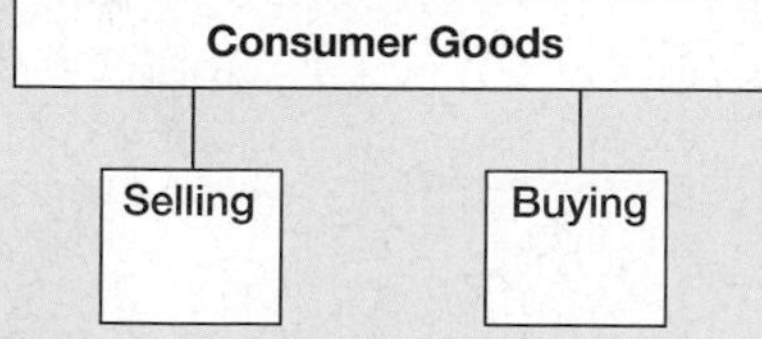

Vocabulary

2. Define: standard of living, credit, mass media, flapper.

Checking Facts

3. How did the automobile change living patterns?
4. What was the link between increasing school attendance and American prosperity?

Critical Thinking

5. **Determining Cause and Effect** How did changes in women's fashion affect the cotton industry?

Geography: Impact on History

MOVEMENT

Route 66

The construction of U.S. Route 66 provided Americans with a main artery for travel that linked the Midwest with the Far West. The ensuing movement of people and goods had dramatic effects on the nation's culture and economy.

Building a Spirit of Travel

Pulitzer Prize–winning author James Agee described the American story as having five main characters: the continent, the people, the automobile, the road, and the roadside. According to Agee, these five characters met because of the restless nature of Americans:

> **The twenties made him [the American] rich and more restive still and he found the automobile not merely good but better and better. It was good because continually it satisfied and at the same time greatly sharpened his hunger for movement.**
>
> —James Agee, *Fortune,* September 1934

Cars alone could not satisfy the American hunger for movement. Only the construction of a vast network of highways would finally enable Americans to travel freely. This increased movement of people and goods contributed to the reduction of regional differences.

One famous highway, U.S. Route 66, allowed Americans to fulfill their desire to take to the road. How did the United States highway system, including roads such as Route 66, develop?

Building the Roadway

Americans enjoyed driving their cars and soon wanted better roads. People were interested in what Americans in other parts of the country were doing and how they lived.

Car owners and manufacturers were not the only ones demanding new roads. Since the early 1900s, farmers in the Midwest and the Southwest had cried out for roads on which to transport their products

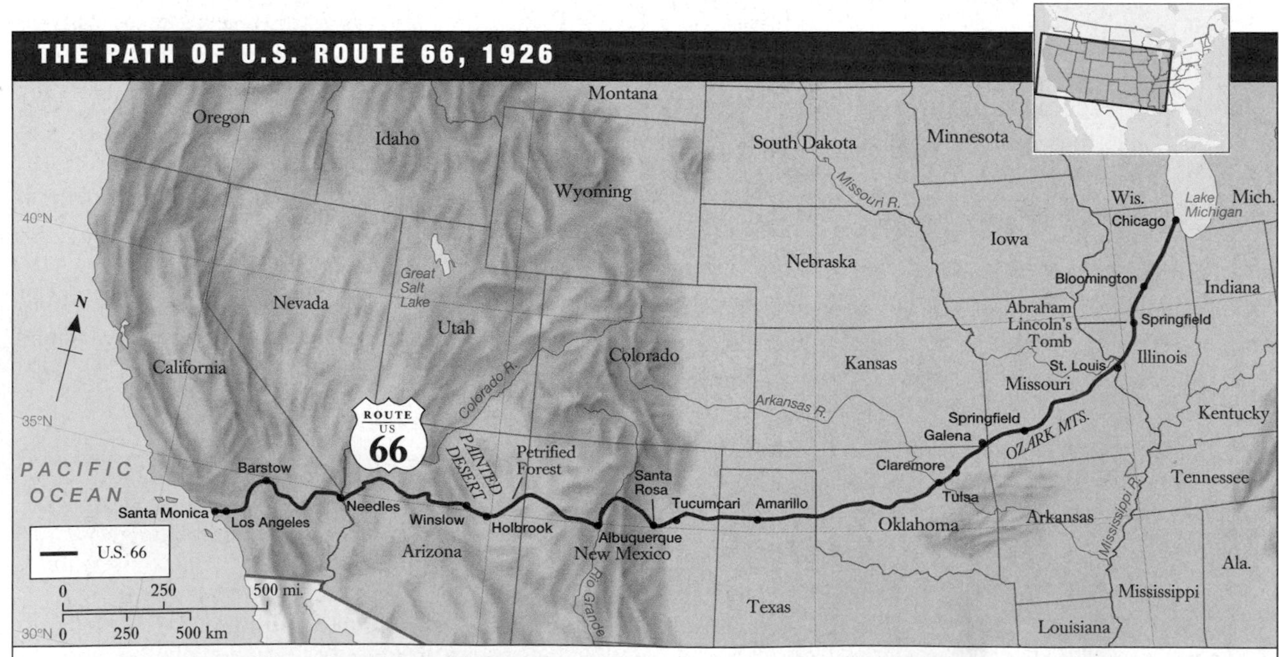

The path of U.S. Route 66 was the subject of intense negotiating as many small towns petitioned to have the road run through their community. *What other points of interest besides towns were located on Route 66?*

to market. Farmers had been dependent on trains to freight their produce at whatever rate the railroad monopoly set.

Local political-action groups pressed Congress to legislate highway building and to break the railroad's stranglehold over transportation. In 1916 the Federal Aid Road Act responded to the pleas of these groups. The Road Act provided federal aid for half of the construction costs of any rural highway intended to carry mail. The new state highway departments were to plan the routes of the new roads. A second federal provision in 1921 granted money to states that would connect their roads to the roads of other states, forming a main thoroughfare. These acts set the basis for a national highway system.

When U.S. Route 66 officially opened on November 11, 1926, it became one of the main arteries of the national highway system. This "great diagonal highway" between Chicago and Los Angeles cut through the Middle West, straddled the Great Plains, crossed the deserts of the Southwest, and reached to the very edge of the Pacific Ocean. Route 66 spanned 8 states and ran through 200 towns, covering 2,400 miles (38,616 km). In the late 1920s, Route 66 was an autotourist's vacationland.

During the Depression of the 1930s, Route 66 became famous as the road that migrants in search of jobs in California followed. John Steinbeck once wrote, "66 is the mother road, the road of flight."

BROWN BROTHERS

A Roadside Autocamp **Americans enjoyed the fresh air and fellowship found at roadside autocamps.** *What goods and services did these autotourists require?*

Building the Roadside

The car and the highways provided Americans with a new form of recreation and business in the 1920s: autocamping. Millions of Americans packed tents and headed for the countryside. Car dealers even advertised autotourism as a way to strengthen the family. They pictured the prosperous middle-class family traveling down Route 66 exploring the United States.

Much of the land Route 66 crossed had not experienced the same prosperity as the rest of the nation in the 1920s. The same technology that brought cars and highways also revolutionized farming with new machinery. When the overproduction of grains glutted the market, however, prices fell. Many farmers went bust, losing their farms as well as their jobs.

The unemployed farmers and other people who lived in rural areas throughout the western states were not quite sure what the new highways were, nor what businesses the highways could bring to their communities. When Route 66 opened, though, they soon found out.

Many unemployed farmers enthusiastically joined the retail petroleum business selling gasoline, oil, and other services to passing tourists. After these new entrepreneurs opened gas stations, they went on to build tourist courts and cafes where tourists could rest and try local foods. Billboards began advertising such roadside attractions as man-eating pythons. In those days any promise became fair in the battle to get the tourist to stop and spend money.

Making the Geographic Connection

1. What did Americans want to learn as they drove to other parts of the United States?
2. What events led to the establishment of a national highway system?
3. **Movement** As Americans traveled along roads such as Route 66, what impact did they have on the economy of local cities and towns?

SECTION 2

The Jazz Age

OCTOBER 6, 1927: FIRST TALKING MOTION PICTURE RELEASED

MOVIE STILL ARCHIVES

The Jazz Singer **Opens in New York**
Crowds gather at Warners' Theatre to view the first film using the Vitaphone sound system.

TEENAGERS ENTERED THE HUSHED THEATER AS THOUGH IT WERE THE PALACE IT LOOKED LIKE. Furniture, statues, and rugs from all over the world filled the lobby. One couple stopped in surprise as they caught sight of themselves in the huge mirrors that covered every wall. For just a moment, they thought they had become their favorite movie stars. Like guests at a grand ball, the girl and her date got ready to ascend the marble staircase. Inside the huge auditorium with its painted ceiling, the couple rested back in their plush seats. Fans blowing over ice cooled the summer air. The movie started!

More than any other entertainment, movies defined and helped create American culture in the 1920s. Glamorous settings like the movie house described above showed that many Americans in the 1920s had new-found leisure as well as the wealth to enjoy it. By the millions, Americans were now discovering the pleasures of movies, sports, live music, dancing, radio, and an abundance of newspapers, magazines, and books. (See Then and Now, pages 410–411.)

At the Movies

Connecting Americans

In the 1920s Americans went to the movies about once a week. Sociologists Robert S. Lynd and Helen Merrell Lynd profiled an average American city—Muncie, Indiana—in their 1929 book *Middletown.* In the 1920s Muncie boasted 9 motion picture theaters for a town of 35,000. The movies at these theaters operated from 1:00 P.M. to 11:00 P.M. every day of the year.

GUIDE TO READING

Main Idea

Americans in the 1920s had new-found wealth and more leisure time to support expanding forms of mass entertainment and to read an outpouring of literature, which was often critical of these changes to American society.

Vocabulary

- syndicate
- tabloid
- materialism

Read to Find Out . . .

- how people used their leisure time during the Jazz Age.
- the musical and literary contributions of the 1920s.
- how the writers of the Lost Generation and Harlem Renaissance reacted to American society, particularly the materialism, of the 1920s.

COURTESY OF THE ACADEMY OF MOTION PICTURE ARTS AND SCIENCES

Silent Film Stars Rudolph Valentino, a famous silent film actor, and Agnes Ayres starred in *The Sheik* (1921). *What kind of role made Rudolph Valentino so popular with women?*

Escaping Together

At the movies, Americans escaped to a different world, both on and off the screen. The movies—silent until *The Jazz Singer* in 1927—spoke powerfully to their audiences. A *Saturday Evening Post* ad encouraged Americans to "Go to a movie . . . and let yourself go." Each week, Americans of all ages, but especially high school and college students, paid as little as 10 cents for a few hours of fantasy.

Because every seat in the movie palace cost exactly the same admission price, going to the movies helped level the differences among Americans. A team of white-gloved ushers treated modest workers with the same courtesy they showed to rich businesspeople.

Even more important, because many of the major movie studios had chains of outlets, people in Muncie were now watching exactly the same stories people watched in California. The movies quickly became more popular than regional forms of entertainment.

Some people worried that the movies promoted immoral behavior. The ads for a movie called *Flaming Youth,* for example, promised "neckers, petters, white kisses, red kisses, pleasure-mad daughters, sensation-craving mothers, . . . the truth—bold, naked, sensational." In 1922 the Motion Picture Producers and Distributors Association tacked a moral message onto the end of each movie. Yet the movies themselves stayed as suggestive as ever.

Wishing on Stars

Seated in the dark, audiences could easily imagine themselves on the screen. Americans also relished reading about the stars' private lives in gossip columns by Louella Parsons and Hedda Hopper. The major movie studios hired publicity departments to make up and publicize stories that kept fans attached to "their" stars' loves, marriages, and divorces. When the romantic leading man Rudolph Valentino died at age 31 in 1926, nearly 30,000 tearful women thronged his funeral.

Through the fans' identification with stars, movies transformed Americans' tastes and behaviors. When stars like Mary Pickford or Gloria Swanson appeared in a new dress style or hairstyle, millions of women suddenly began to demand the same look.

New American Heroes

Sports and Individual Triumphs

Now that so many Americans had the time, the energy, and the money to play, they took to sports almost as avidly as they had embraced the movies. Before this decade, 300 private clubs and a handful of public courts easily served the few people who played tennis. By the late 1920s, the United States boasted nearly 1,000 tennis clubs and enough municipal courts to accommodate more than 1 million players, who swatted at 300,000 new tennis balls each month.

Golf, too, became widely popular during the 1920s. Before the war, golf had been a game for the wealthy. By 1927, 2 million players were putting away on 5,000 courses, many of them open to working-class people. Cities also constructed swimming pools, baseball diamonds, summer camps, playgrounds, and recreation centers.

Sports Stars

Hard-playing Americans also provided huge audiences for professional sports. The era's popular sports heroes—baseball's Babe Ruth and Oscar Charleston, boxing's Jack Dempsey, tennis's Helen Wills, football's Red Grange, golf's Bobby Jones—became as newsworthy off the field as movie stars. Explaining America's fascination with sports heroes, the historian George Mowry wrote:

AP/WIDE WORLD PHOTOS

Jack Dempsey Heavyweight boxing champion Jack Dempsey was a hero to millions of Americans. *What other professional sports provided heroes for Americans?*

On the battlefield, in the factory production line, at home in a city apartment, and increasingly even in the business world the individual was becoming lost in a welter of the hive. The sporting field was one of the few remaining areas of pure individual expression where success or failure depended precisely upon individual physical and intellectual prowess. And if the masses themselves could not or would not participate directly they could at least, by a process of identification, salute the old virtues.

—George E. Mowry, *The Twenties: Fords, Flappers, & Fanatics,* 1963

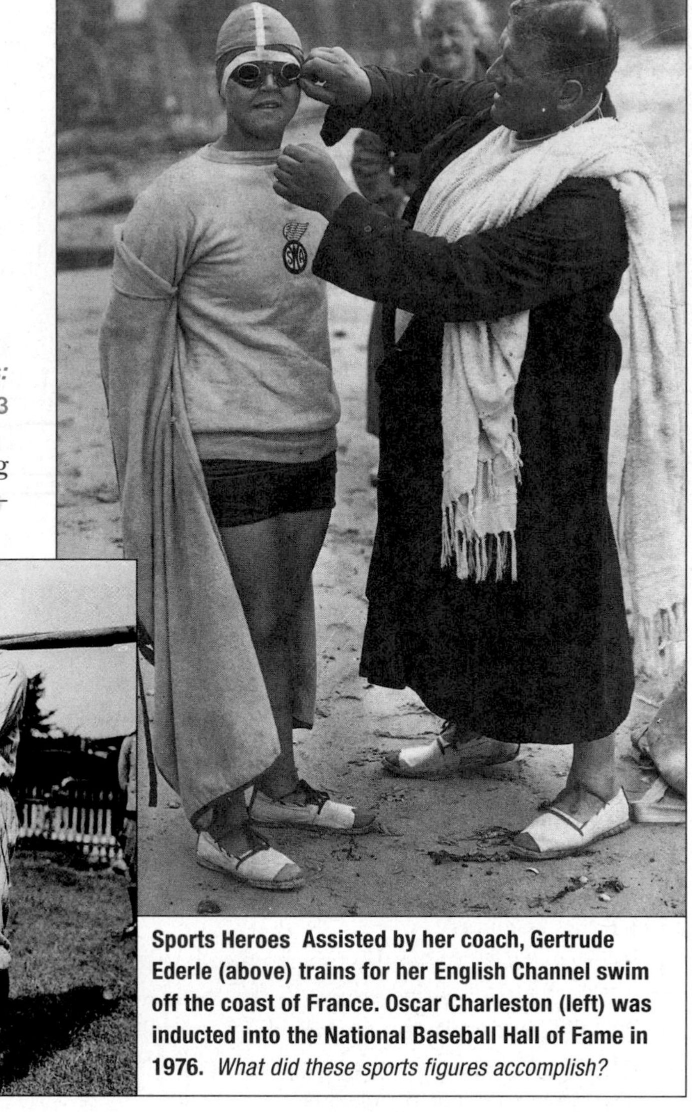

FPG INTERNATIONAL CORP.

NATIONAL BASEBALL LIBRARY & ARCHIVE, COOPERSTOWN, NEW YORK

Sports Heroes **Assisted by her coach, Gertrude Ederle (above) trains for her English Channel swim off the coast of France. Oscar Charleston (left) was inducted into the National Baseball Hall of Fame in 1976.** *What did these sports figures accomplish?*

Americans learned about their heroes by watching them perform. They also devoured newspaper and magazine articles about them. In 1926 Jack Dempsey, the "Manassa Mauler," lost his heavyweight boxing title to Gene Tunney. Sports fans all over the country chuckled at the aging fighter's answer when his wife asked him what had happened. "Honey," Dempsey answered, "I forgot to duck."

In 1926 a 19-year-old girl named Gertrude Ederle, popularly known as "Our Trudy," became the first woman to swim the English Channel, beating the fastest man's record by a full two hours. Before her swim, W. O. McGeehan wrote in the *New York Herald Tribune,* "If there is one woman who can make the swim, it is this girl, with the shoulders and back of Jack Dempsey and the frankest and bravest pair of eyes that ever looked into a face." After swimming the English Channel, Gertrude Ederle said simply, "I just knew if it could be done it had to be done, and I did it." A huge ticker tape parade greeted her return to New York City.

One of the greats in baseball's Negro League, Oscar Charleston led the league in home runs six times between 1921 and 1933. Regarded as one of the greatest players of all time, Charleston was never allowed to play in the major leagues because of the color of his skin.

The Lone Eagle

No American hero of the 1920s equaled Charles Lindbergh, whose solo flight across the Atlantic in 1927 excited more enthusiasm than any single event before, or perhaps since. The modest young man in his flying machine served to join America's pioneer past with an optimistic view of the country's technological future.

Lindbergh's flight and the public response to it never could have taken place without modern machinery and the combined efforts of thousands of people. Still, many Americans preferred to regard their hero as a traditional pioneer, "the lone eagle." To them, Lindbergh's accomplishment seemed to demonstrate the triumph of individual American heroism in a bewildering new age of machines. Amelia Earhart, who became the first woman to fly across the Atlantic Ocean, matched his feat in 1928.

New Rhythms in the Air

Blues, Jazz, and the Charleston

During the 1920s Americans entertained themselves at movies and sports events. They also began to listen to two exciting new types of music: soulful blues and frantic jazz that would give its name to the entire era.

King Oliver's Creole Jazz Band **Louis Armstrong played the cornet, and his wife, Lil Hardin, played the piano in this Chicago band later known as King Oliver's Dixieland Jazz Band.** *How did jazz make its way to Northern cities?*

Imitating African American jazz bands, white bands, such as those of Paul White man and Bix Beiderbecke, performed widely at dances for young people. Supper clubs and country clubs provided settings for the slow dancing and the Charleston that young people so enjoyed and that older people declared immoral, shocking, and scandalous.

The Charleston was by no means the only dance of the 1920s, an era that has been called "The Dance Age" as well as "The Jazz Age." With its flying beads, knocking knees, and crossing hands, however, the Charleston will forever represent the 1920s. The Charleston first appeared in an African American revue called "Runnin' Wild" in 1924. Although initially considered too difficult for amateurs to master, within a year this whirlwind had swept the country.

The blues grew out of work songs and field chants of enslaved African Americans. In the 1920s African American singers, such as Bessie Smith and Gertrude "Ma" Rainey, sang their sad songs to huge audiences in clubs on Chicago's South Side and recorded them on African American labels for major record companies.

Jazz began in New Orleans and moved north when African Americans migrated there during World War I. Not a single note was written down, but the musicians all seemed to know what to play.

Singing of joy in the face of oppression, jazz contains strands of music from many European countries. Nevertheless, jazz is above all an African American creation, and it could have developed only in a city in the United States. In 1925 J.A. Rogers wrote, "With its cowbells, auto horns, calliopes, rattles, dinner gongs, kitchen utensils, cymbals, screams, crashes, clankings and monotonous rhythm [jazz] bears all the marks of a nerve-strung, strident, mechanized civilization."

When it moved to Chicago in 1920, Joseph "King" Oliver's Creole Jazz Band found a ready audience of urban African Americans. In 1922 King Oliver invited his talented former cornet student to join the band. When the student, Louis Armstrong, later switched to the trumpet, he became perhaps the most famous jazz musician of all time.

While live music defined the 1920s, recorded music became part of the mainstream only after electricity made the phonograph and radio possible. Commercial radio had a modest start when stations in Detroit and Pittsburgh broadcast the 1920 presidential election returns. By the middle of the decade, few people found themselves out of earshot of a radio speaker. In the late 1920s, the roof of practically every tenement house on the Lower East Side of New York City looked like a forest of radio antennae. Radio brought entertainment and advertising to a mass market and helped spur the explosive growth of the mass-market economy.

Time to Read

The Rise of Print Media

With time on their hands and with more education than any previous generation, more Americans in the 1920s read. During the 1920s scores of new magazines came into existence. At least 20 magazines boasted circulations of a million readers. *Reader's Digest* debuted in 1922, *Time* in 1923, and *The New Yorker* in 1925.

More people were reading newspapers as well, although the number of newspapers dropped as papers gathered into **syndicates**—chains of newspapers under centralized direction. The contents of the newspapers began to look more similar as the syndicates provided editorials, sports, gossip, and Sunday features for a national audience.

With their small pages and large type, **tabloid** newspapers made ideal reading for crowded, rocking subway cars. Tabloids swept the country in the 1920s. New York alone had 3, with a combined circulation of 1.6 million readers. The tabloids battled each other, attempting to sell papers by publicizing scandals or fads, such as dance marathons in which young people danced until they dropped.

Most of the fads reported in the tabloids grew old very quickly. One fad though thrived long enough to launch a publishing empire. Two young men, Richard Simon and Lincoln Schuster, began their publishing company by bringing out a crossword puzzle book that eventually sold two million copies.

Americans were hungry for books and the 1920s saw the birth of several major publishing houses, including Simon and Schuster, Morrow, Viking, and Harcourt, Brace. The Book-of-the-Month Club and the Literary Guild began mass distribution of books within months of each other in 1926.

A Painting of Gertrude Stein **The Spanish artist Pablo Picasso painted Gertrude Stein in 1906. Stein encouraged experimental painters such as Picasso and Henri Matisse.** *What phrase did Stein create that described the 1920s literary era?*

The Lost Generation

Attacking Materialism

While ordinary Americans happily pursued new leisure activities—movies, radio, music, dance, and reading—some writers began to attack America's **materialism.** They questioned a society that placed more importance on money and material goods than it did on intellectual, spiritual, and artistic concerns.

Leaving the United States Behind

During the 1920s some prominent American writers and artists moved to Europe, partly because they felt the United States was "the enemy of the artist, of the man who cannot produce something tangible when the five o'clock whistle blows." The expatriates also felt that it was cheaper to live in Europe than it was to stay at home.

The dollar was especially strong in Paris where writers Gertrude Stein, Ernest Hemingway, and F. Scott Fitzgerald took up residence in the 1920s. Gertrude Stein made bold experiments with language in her plays, operas, and books. She also gave the literary era its name when she told her friend Hemingway, "You are all a lost generation."

Ernest Hemingway set most of his novels in Europe and portrayed the ruined innocence of his postwar generation. His masterpiece *The Sun Also Rises,* published in 1926, quoted Gertrude Stein's comment on its title page. The book tells of Jake, an expatriate American who bears physical and psychological wounds from the war. It ends on a note of quiet despair.

F. Scott Fitzgerald's earliest novels and stories were set in the United States where he wrote about daring college students. *The Great Gatsby,* published in 1925 and considered Fitzgerald's greatest work, explored the empty lives of Americans with too much money. Daisy, the main female character, feels purposeless and lost.

Criticizing the United States From Within

Many of the most significant writers of the 1920s never left the United States or left for only brief periods. Like the expatriates, American writers who stayed home took up their pens to expose what they considered the shallow and money-centered culture of their nation.

In his trilogy, *U.S.A.,* John Dos Passos suggested the United States had become two nations, one rich and one poor. Experimenting with free-form writing and leaving punctuation behind, Dos Passos wrote,

"... on the streets you see only the downcast faces of the beaten the streets belong to the beaten nation . . . we stand defeated America."

Sinclair Lewis attacked the materialism of small-town America in satiric novels such as *Main Street,* which was a best-seller in 1920, and *Babbitt,* which was equally popular two years later. The term *Babbitt* is still used to refer to the ordinary 1920s American—a narrow-minded, obsessed businessperson whose deepest desires are determined by advertising.

Ironically, just as intellectuals were ridiculing the lack of serious art, American writers were publishing some of the country's best literature ever.

The targets of H.L. Mencken, one of the wittiest critics at the time, often richly deserved his nasty insults. Yet, when Mencken labeled the South the "Sahara of the Bozard," or wasteland of fine arts, he could not have been more mistaken. In Oxford, Mississippi, William Faulkner was crafting the brilliant works destined to win him the Nobel Prize.

DENVER CENTER THEATRE COMPANY

Emperor Jones **The plays of Eugene O'Neill such as *Emperor Jones* (1920) brought serious themes to Broadway in the 1920s.** *What issues did writers of the 1920s address?*

The Harlem Renaissance

A Literary and Artistic Movement

While the Lost Generation of white writers questioned materialistic American culture, African American writers began to express their own identity and a rising anger at Northern racism. Harlem, a section of New York City bustling with nightclubs and alive with blues and jazz, lured African American and white intellectuals. The African American literary and artistic movement that resulted became known as the Harlem Renaissance.

Alain Locke was a professor of literature at Howard University, a graduate of Harvard, and the first African American Rhodes scholar. Locke urged his fellow African Americans to create a new literature. In *The New Negro,* Locke wrote that the younger generation of African Americans is "vibrant with a new psychology . . . the new spirit is awake in the masses."

ENTERTAINMENT, 1920–1929
1920 National Football League is organized.
1923 Bessie Smith records first blues song.
1925 Satchel Paige begins his baseball career in the Negro League.
1929 First Academy Awards are presented.
1920
1921
1922
1923
1924
1925
1926
1927
1928
1929
1930
1920 Edith Wharton's *The Age of Innocence* is published.
1921 Opera singer Enrico Caruso dies.
1924 George Gershwin writes "Rhapsody in Blue."
1927 Harlem Globetrotters begin playing basketball.
1928 First Mickey Mouse movie with sound, *Steamboat Willie,* is released.

Inspired by Locke, writers like Langston Hughes and Claude McKay spoke out in the strongest voices of the Harlem Renaissance. Hughes, a gifted poet, was one of the first African American writers to use jazz and blues themes and rhythms in his poetry. In a 1926 essay called "The Negro Artist and the Racial Mountain," Hughes argued that what was truly worth expressing would be found in the culture of the poorest African American people: "If white people are pleased we are glad. If they

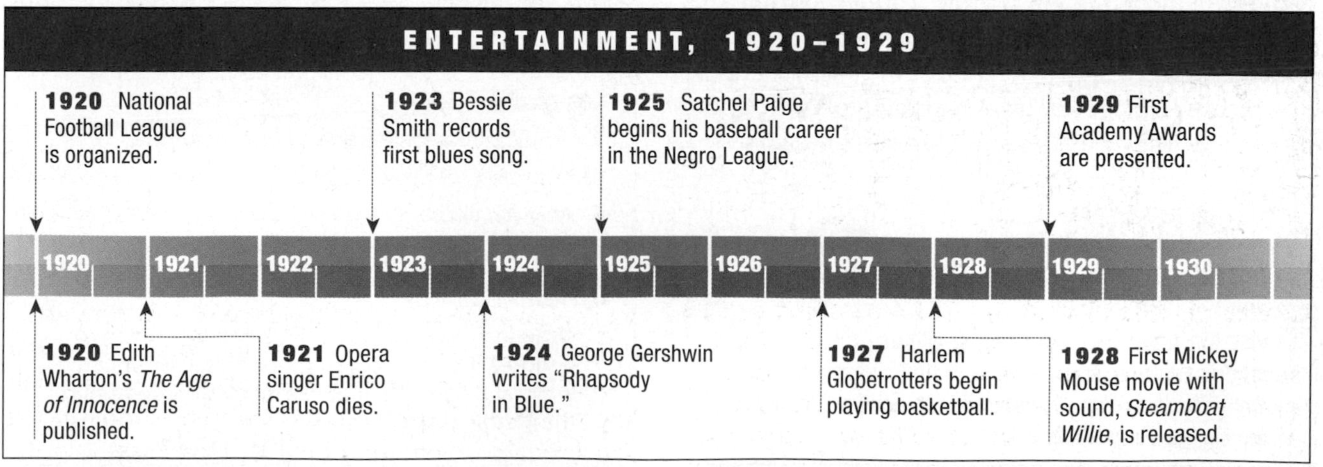

PHOTOGRAPHS AND PRINTS DIVISION, SCHOMBURG CENTER FOR RESEARCH IN BLACK CULTURE, NEW YORK PUBLIC LIBRARY, ASTOR, LENOX AND TILDEN FOUNDATIONS. MORGAN AND MARVIN SMITH PORTFOLIO.

Langston Hughes A pioneer of modern African American literature, Hughes was descended from a prominent family of abolitionists. *What themes did Hughes use in his poetry?*

are not, it doesn't matter. We know we are beautiful. And ugly too. The tom tom cries and the tom tom laughs."

Claude McKay migrated from his native Jamaica to Harlem. There he wrote poems such as "If We Must Die" that challenged African Americans to fight for their rights. McKay's autobiographical novel, *Home to Harlem,* published in 1928, expressed his fascination with all the shades of people who could be called black: "Brown girls rouged and painted like dark pansies. Brown flesh draped in soft colorful clothes . . . The cabaret singer, a shiny coffee-colored girl in a green frock . . . chocolate, chestnut, coffee, ebony, cream, yellow. . . ."

Many other talented African American men and women launched their writing careers during this exciting period. For example, Arna Bontemps, a poet and a friend of Langston Hughes, wrote the following poem in which the images of planting grain pointed out the inequalities between African Americans and whites:

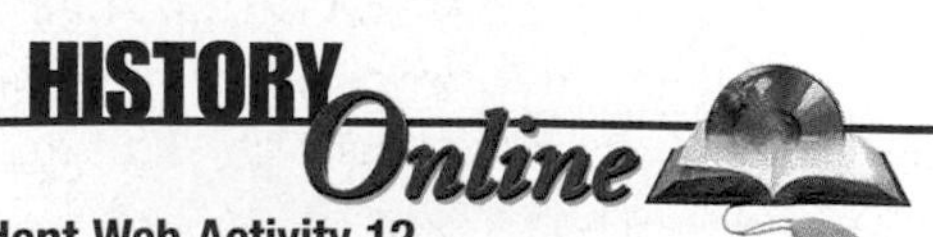

Student Web Activity 12

Visit the *American Odyssey* Web site at americanodyssey.glencoe.com and click on ***Chapter 12—Student Web Activities*** for an activity relating to the Harlem Renaissance.

I have sown beside all waters in my day.
I planted deep, within my heart the fear
That wind or fowl would take the grain away.
I planted safe against this stark, lean year.

I scattered seed enough to plant the land
In rows from Canada to Mexico
But for my reaping only what the hand
Can hold at once is all that I can show.

Yet what I sowed and what the orchard yields
My brother's sons are gathering stalk and root,
Small wonder then my children glean in fields
They have not sown, and feed on bitter fruit.

—Arna Bontemps, "A Black Man Talks of Reaping," 1927

Of the many gifted African American women writers, a young anthropologist named Zora Neale Hurston became the best known. Hurston's plays, short stories, and articles began to appear in the 1920s, and featured the African American folklore she had listened to as a child. Her 1937 masterpiece, *Their Eyes Were Watching God,* portrayed the first heroic African American woman in American literature.

In the 1920s African Americans expressed their own unique voices in exciting new literature. Harlem Renaissance members proclaimed that African Americans would not accept second-class citizenship in any area of life.

Section Assessment

Main Idea

1. Use a diagram like this one to show forms of popular entertainment during the 1920s.

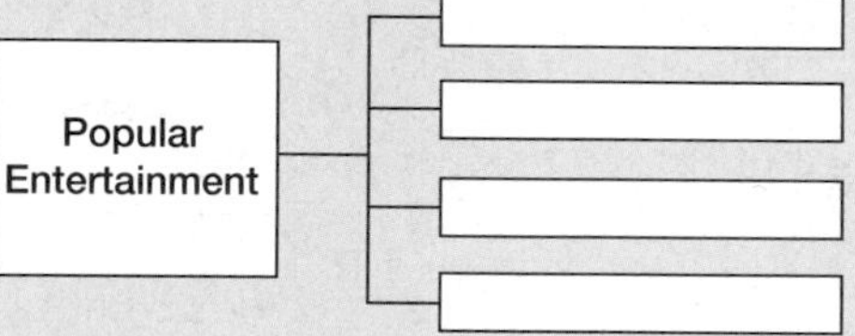

Vocabulary

2. Define: syndicate, tabloid, materialism.

Checking Facts

3. How did movies and radio increase the similarities among Americans?
4. Why did so many American writers criticize American values during the postwar period?

Critical Thinking

5. **Drawing Conclusions** Give two examples to support the conclusion that African American writers developed a powerful new voice during the Harlem Renaissance.

Critical Thinking Skill

SYNTHESIZING INFORMATION

Learning the Skill

The author of this book gathered information from many sources to present a story of how Americans lived in the 1900s. To integrate all the evidence into a cohesive story, the author used a process called synthesis.

The skill of synthesizing involves combining and analyzing information obtained from separate sources or at different times to make logical connections.

Follow these three basic steps to synthesize data:

a. Select relevant information.

b. Analyze information and build connections.

c. Reinforce or modify connections as you acquire new information.

Being able to synthesize can be a useful skill for you as a student. Suppose you needed to write a research paper on the status of women in the 1920s. You would need to synthesize what you learn to inform others.

Organizing Existing Ideas and Adding New Data

Begin by detailing the ideas you already have about the status of women in the 1920s. A graphic organizer such as the one below aids in categorizing facts.

SYNTHESIZING	
Women's Status in the 1920s	
Economic	Many women worked in factories and offices at low-level, low-paying jobs.
Political	Women gained the right to vote in 1920.
Social	Women had new social freedoms—smoking, drinking, freer clothing styles.
Educational	Many women had a high school education.

Then select an article about women in the 1920s such as the following:

In 1923 the National Woman's party first proposed an equal rights amendment to the Constitution. This amendment stated that "men and women shall have equal rights throughout the United States and every place subject to its jurisdiction." The National Woman's party pointed out that legislation discriminating against women existed in every state. For example, in some states, the law gave husbands control over the earnings of their wives and prevented women from sitting on juries. Women could not attend some of the best schools, and they were delegated to the lower levels of professions.

Some progressive women reformers, however, opposed the goals of the National Woman's party. They favored protective legislation, which had brought shorter hours and better working conditions for many women. These progressives succeeded in defeating the amendment.

Practicing the Skill

1. On a sheet of paper, revise the graphic organizer to incorporate relevant information in the article by verifying and modifying the original ideas.

2. Using only your existing knowledge, write a paragraph about how the automobile affected Americans in the 1920s. Next, review Section 1 of this chapter to rewrite your paragraph, integrating ideas from the text and illustrations.

3. Create a visual display that includes relevant information about baseball today. Support your design with text that will help viewers synthesize the message you are presenting.

4. In Section 2 of this chapter, Gertrude Stein described the literary era of the 1920s in her statement, "You are all a lost generation." Write a response to this assertion.

5. Find three different newspaper or magazine reviews of the same movie and synthesize the information in a single critique.

Applying the Skill

Discuss and list with a partner ideals of the 1920s, synthesizing information from Chapter 11 and Sections 1 and 2 of Chapter 12. Highlight those ideals that exist today and discuss which ones have changed. Then make a list of present-day ideals, incorporating those from the 1920s that still exist and adding any new ones.

The **Glencoe Skillbuilder Interactive Workbook, Level 2** CD-ROM provides more practice in key social studies skills.

SPORTS: Princeton crew beats Yale in rowing regatta; Yale's first loss in 5 years

One Day in History

Saturday, May 21, 1927

MARKET BASKET

Here is where a dollar will go:

Mobil oil . . . . 30¢/quart
Memorial wreath for Memorial Day. . . . . 89¢
Men's cotton broadcloth pajamas. $1.69
Gallon-size Auto Vacuum jug (keeps hot drinks hot in the car) $1.89

Wrigley's chewing gum . . . 5¢
Cotton fabric . . . . . . 39¢/yard
Silk and rayon hose. . 50¢/pair
Hatbox $2.69
6-volt battery for all small cars $5.99
2-car garage, built $350
Electric waffle iron. $5
Hy-Dyve swimsuit . . . . $4–$5
Balloon-cord car tire. . . $7.98
Apartment: 5 rooms, gas, set tubs, stove. $28/mo
White Mountain icebox . . . . $27.50 . . . . . . ($5 down, $1 weekly)
Kelvinator refrigerator (installment plan available) $210

Lindbergh Crosses the Atlantic

"Lone Eagle" Lands—World Sighs in Relief

PARIS—Just 33 hours and 29 minutes after he took off from New York, Captain Charles E. Lindbergh landed at Le Bourget airfield in Paris. The 25-year-old "Lone Eagle" became the first person to survive a nonstop flight across the Atlantic. "No man before me had commanded such freedom of movement over the earth," said Lindbergh. "For me the *Spirit of St. Louis* was a lens focused on the future, a forerunner of mechanisms that would conquer time and space."

The *New York Times* reported from Paris:

> *Lindbergh did it. Twenty minutes after 10 o'clock tonight suddenly and softly there slipped out of the darkness a gray-white airplane as 25,000 pairs of eyes strained toward it. At 10:24 the* Spirit of St. Louis *landed and lines of soldiers, ranks of policemen and stout steel fences went down before a mad rush as irresistible as the tides in the ocean.*

UPI/BETTMANN

"The Lone Eagle," Charles Lindbergh, becomes the first to fly across the Atlantic from New York (not Newfoundland) to Paris, and the first to do it alone.

One Day in History, May 21, 1927

WORLD: Yesterday Great Britain recognized Saudia Arabian independence and sovereignty in the Treaty of Jeddah.

INFORMATION OFFICE, ROYAL EMBASSY OF SAUDI ARABIA

BROWN BROTHERS

Deluge Devastates Louisiana

NEW ORLEANS—The Associated Press reports, "The restless gurgle of muddy water echoed from the northern boundary of Louisiana tonight to within 50 miles (80.5 km) of the Gulf of Mexico." About 100,000 people have taken refuge in LaFayette; more are still fleeing the water. The flood has cut a path 150 miles (241 km) long and 50 miles (80.5 km) wide across the state.

Secretary of Commerce Herbert Hoover says, "There has never been a calamity such as this flood."

The flood threatened weak points along the Atchafalaya River 140 miles (225 km) north of New Orleans. The current was tearing the embankment to pieces in McCrea, where more than 200 workers fought in the mud and rain to keep the flood off the sugar plantations of 5 parishes.

THE CARSON COLLECTION

Clara Bow, "the 'It' Girl" of the 1920s, is a huge box office draw.

MUSIC

Popular Songs of 1927:

"Ol' Man River"

"Let a Smile Be Your Umbrella"

"My Blue Heaven"

BOOKS

This Week's Best-Sellers:

Twilight Sleep by Edith Wharton

Revolt in the Desert by T.E. Lawrence

MOVIES

- ***Rough House Rosie,*** with Clara Bow
- ***Mr. Wu,*** starring Lon Chaney
- ***Slide, Kelly, Slide,*** starring William Haines, a Metro-Goldwyn Mayer picture
- Cecil B. DeMille's ***King of Kings,*** which premiered last Thursday at the grand opening of Graumann's Chinese Theater in Hollywood, California

Cultural Conflicts

JULY 10, 1925: SCOPES TRIAL BEGINS, DAYTON, TENNESSEE

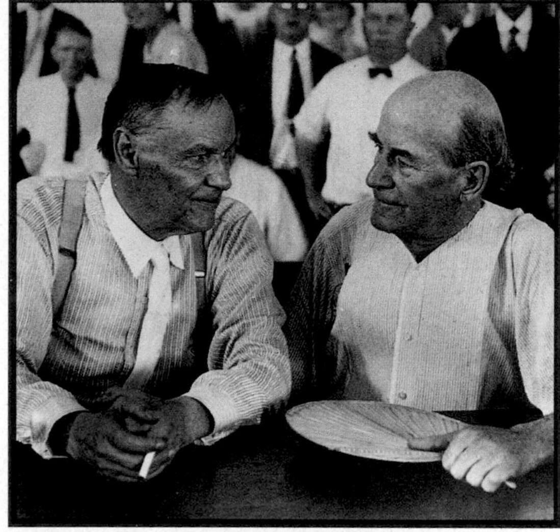

AP/WIDE WORLD PHOTOS

Celebrities in the Scopes Trial
Clarence Darrow (left) and William Jennings Bryan (right) were said to have respected each other, in spite of their differences.

DURING A SIZZLING HOT JULY IN 1925, A SIMPLE TRIAL IN THE SMALL TOWN OF DAYTON, TENNESSEE, TURNED INTO A SHOWDOWN BETWEEN RELIGION AND SCIENCE. A local science teacher, John Scopes, was on trial for teaching evolution. Scopes and all the other teachers who used the state-approved textbook had broken the Butler Act, a new state law against teaching "any theory that denies the story of the Divine Creation of man as taught in the Bible."

When the Butler Act was passed in 1925, Tennessee's governor had signed it reluctantly, commenting, "Nobody believes that it is going to be an active statute." He was wrong. When a small item about the law appeared in the *New York Times*, the American Civil Liberties Union (ACLU) raised money to test the law in court. All it needed was a Tennessee teacher to volunteer to be arrested for breaking the Butler Act.

In 1925 John Scopes agreed to go on trial to test the legality of the Butler Act. Clarence Darrow, an urban liberal, volunteered as defense lawyer for Scopes. William Jennings Bryan, three times a candidate for President and a hero to rural America, joined the prosecution to testify as an expert on the Bible.

Broadcast over the radio and reported in hundreds of newspapers, the Scopes trial symbolized many of the bitter conflicts that rocked the United States during the 1920s. In this decade, struggles between Americans erupted over religion, over drinking, and even over who was considered an American.

GUIDE TO READING

Main Idea

Bitter conflicts rocked the United States during the 1920s, as Americans found themselves thrust, sometimes unwillingly, into a modern and urban world.

Vocabulary

- fundamentalism
- evangelist
- speakeasy
- bootlegger
- quota

Read to Find Out . . .

- how the social changes of the 1920s caused conflicts among various groups of people in the United States.
- possible reasons for and effects of the widespread disregard of Prohibition.
- the reasons for a resurgence of the Ku Klux Klan in the 1920s.

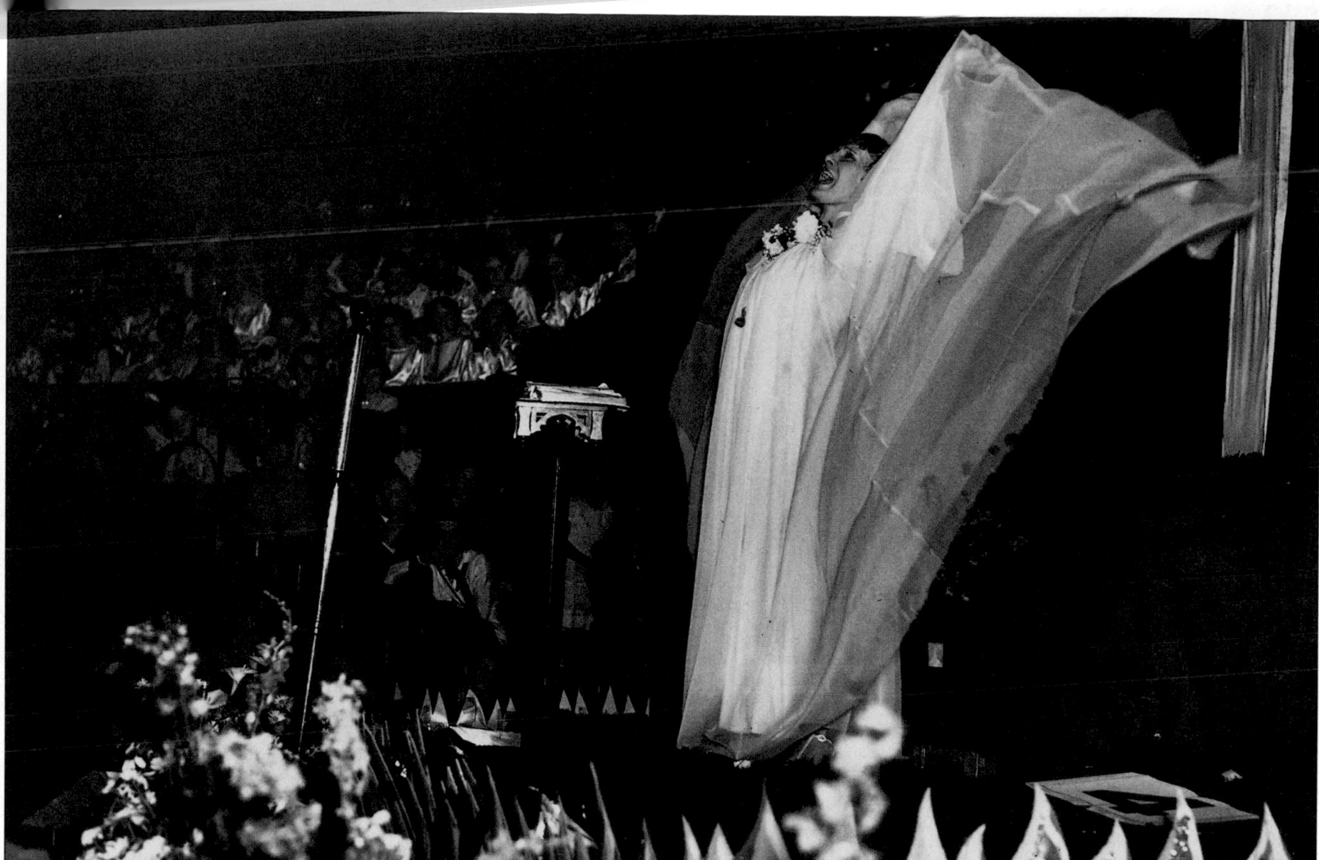
AP/WIDE WORLD PHOTOS

Charismatic Preacher Aimee Semple McPherson **Some 1920s evangelists mixed religion and show business. Here Aimee Semple McPherson dramatically pleads with her Los Angeles congregation for contributions.** *In which regions of the country was fundamentalism strongest?*

The Power of Religion

Something Familiar In Changing Times

The turning point of the Scopes trial came on the last day, when Darrow put Bryan on the stand and questioned him at length about the Bible's account of creation, which Bryan claimed to believe literally. Darrow, who saw the case as an important constitutional issue, asked Bryan if he thought the earth had been made in 6 days, and Bryan had to admit, "Not 6 days of 24 hours." The judge finally halted the questioning when the 2 adversaries ended up shaking their fists at each other.

When the trial was over, both sides claimed victory: the jury had taken less than 10 minutes to find John Scopes guilty and fine him $100, but the Tennessee Supreme Court later acquitted him on a technicality. Although some biology teachers continued to teach evolution, the Butler Act remained the law in Tennessee (until 1967, when it was repealed). To many it seemed that **fundamentalism**—a movement that affirmed the literal truth of the Bible—had won.

Nonetheless, Darrow's piercing questions disturbed Bryan, who had been forced to admit that a "day" in the Bible might be a million years or more. Because Bryan had based his position on the idea that the Bible must be read literally and not interpreted, he was aware of contradicting himself. The elderly statesman died less than a week later and was mourned by millions.

The Scopes case may have dealt fundamentalism a blow, but the movement continued to thrive in the United States. Rural people, especially in the South and Midwest, remained faithful to their churches. When large numbers of farmers migrated to cities during the 1920s, they brought fundamentalism with them. The familiar religion helped them make sense of their new lives.

At the same time, however, the traditional religions began to take on some modern aspects. In Southern California several fundamentalist preachers, or **evangelists,** used radio to reach many people.

Aimee Semple McPherson used show business techniques to attract a radio following to her "Foursquare Gospel." McPherson barnstormed the country in 1921 and 1922, raising $1.5 million for the construction of her Angelus Temple. After the temple was completed in 1923, McPherson kept it filled every night.

The Failure of Prohibition

Gangsters and Citizens Ignore the Law

Like the battle over whether fundamentalism belonged in schools, the struggle to enforce Prohibition, enacted by an amendment in 1919, pitted small-town residents and farmers against a newer, more urban America. Most fundamentalists stood firmly in favor of Prohibition, claiming that strict laws could and should control people's behavior. Opponents of Prohibition, on the other hand, preferred more tolerance.

Prohibition succeeded in eradicating the saloon. The demise of the saloon decreased alcohol consumption among people who could not afford to go to the new **speakeasies,** clubs where liquor was sold in violation of the law. Most middle-class people, however, simply refused to obey the Volstead Act, which was passed to enforce Prohibition. This widespread refusal gave the 1920s its well-deserved reputation as a lawless decade.

Enforcement Problems

Prohibition was hard to enforce for many reasons. For one thing the United States had more than 10,000 miles (16,090 km) of coastlines and land borders where smugglers were all too happy to sneak in the alcohol that many Americans refused to give up. People who made, sold, or transported illegal liquor were known as **bootleggers.** A former bootlegger from Barre, Vermont, later recalled, "We ran mostly ale. We got it in Canada for five bucks a case and sold it here for fifteen or twenty. You could load a lot of ale into those big crates we had. We kept five or six cars on the road at the time."

In 1924 the Department of Commerce estimated the value of liquor smuggled into the country at $40 million. In addition, hundreds of ships that anchored in international waters dispensed legal liquor to anyone who came out by boat.

Thousands of druggists sold alcohol quite legally on doctors' prescriptions. During the 1920s some doctors began to prescribe alcohol for a variety of real and imagined complaints. Women who had not been able to drink in saloons went to the new speakeasies, where both men and women eagerly gulped down Prohibition's new drink, the cocktail.

Illegal distilling could and did take place anywhere. An industrious bootlegger could make his own home brew with a portable still that sold for six or seven dollars. Between 1919 and 1929, the production of corn sugar increased sixfold, and most of it ended up in illegal liquor.

Prohibition had other ill effects. Americans came to have a casual attitude about disobeying the law. A tiny

THE BETTMANN ARCHIVE

Ordinary Criminals During Prohibition, many Americans devised creative ways to carry illegal alcohol, such as these strap-on containers. *What were other ways people avoided the Prohibition laws?*

force of Prohibition agents received very little pay for the thankless job of enforcing a law many Americans hated. In 1923 one Prohibition agent toured several American cities to see how difficult it would be to purchase an illegal drink. It took him only 3 minutes in Detroit; in New Orleans, a drink could be had in a mere 35 seconds.

Many people simply refused to take the law seriously. One San Francisco jury in a Prohibition case drank up liquor that had been used in court as evidence!

Big City Crime

As federal courts choked on too many liquor cases, many government officials took part in the bribery and corruption that accompanied the unenforceable law. Fiorello La Guardia, a member of Congress from New York who would later become a reform-minded mayor of New York City, estimated it would take a police force of 250,000 to enforce Prohibition in New York, and another 200,000 agents to police the police.

Perhaps the worst effect of Prohibition was its contribution to the explosive growth of big-city crime. Gangsters had been around before Prohibition, but when they took over bootlegging, crime soared to new heights.

The gangs bought out hundreds of breweries and transported illegal beer in armored trucks. They stationed "soldiers" to hijack other gangs' shipments, and killed their rivals in a series of gruesome slayings. Al Capone, the head of a gang of Chicago bootleggers, became a multimillionaire driving through the streets in an armored car with bulletproof windows.

THE BETTMAN ARCHIVE

Organized Intolerance Ku Klux Klan members share their values with the next generation. *Did the Klan generally support or oppose Prohibition?*

UPI/BETTMANN NEWSPHOTOS

Celebrity Criminals Chicago gangster Al Capone broke laws flagrantly but was eventually convicted of income tax evasion. *How did Prohibition contribute to a soaring crime rate in the 1920s?*

Crosses in the Night

Klan Terrorism Surges and Subsides

The forces favoring Prohibition centered in rural areas and small towns where fundamentalist preachers warned their congregations against the sinful ways of the big city. The Ku Klux Klan, which suddenly blazed back onto the American scene in the 1920s, also flourished in small towns, and it fought some of its fiercest battles with the liquor interests. The rebirth of the Klan pointed up many of the conflicts that divided American society during this period.

Like the hooded secret order of Reconstruction days, the new Klan began in the South under a burning cross, sparking some Southern whites' hatred for African Americans. When the Klan spread from Georgia in the 1920s, however, it added new enemies to its list. In Texas

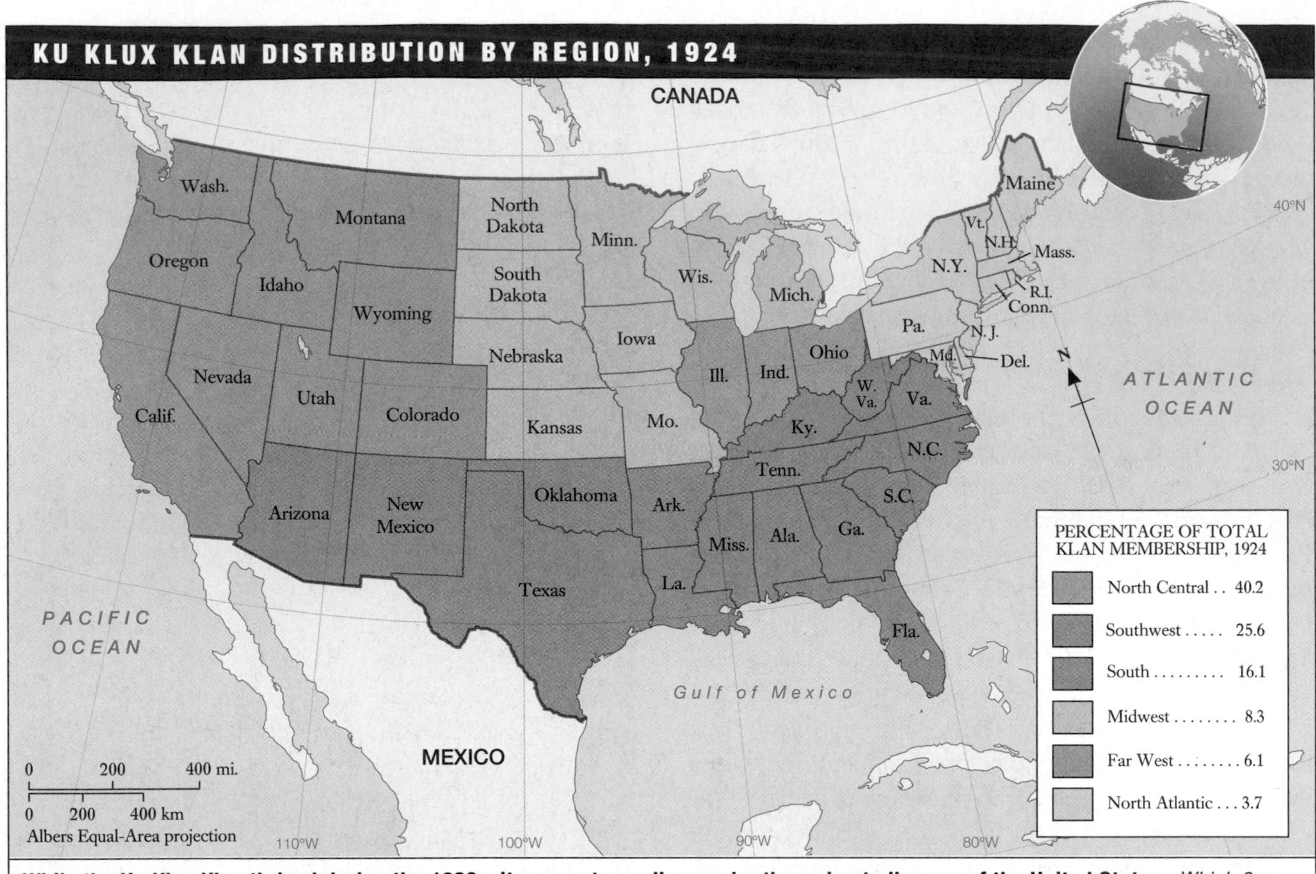

While the Ku Klux Klan thrived during the 1920s, it was not equally popular throughout all areas of the United States. *Which 3 regions of the country accounted for more than 80 percent of Klan membership?*

the Klan attacked Mexican Americans; in California it fought Japanese immigrants; in New York the Klan's targets were Jews and European immigrants; and in New England, it stirred up hatred of French Canadians.

All over the country, Klan members participated in violent activities—tarring and feathering, flogging, and lynching. The Southwest saw some of the worst terror. In a single year, Oklahoma's Klan was responsible for no less than 2,500 floggings.

With its secret initiation rites, hooded robes, and burning crosses, the Klan mainly provided a fellowship of prejudice for ill-educated men whose lives offered few other satisfactions. It soon became strong in Northern cities such as Detroit, Pittsburgh, and Indianapolis, where many African Americans had recently migrated.

The Ku Klux Klan claimed its greatest strength in Indiana where almost half a million men had joined. David Stephenson, state head of the Klan in Indiana, bragged with some truth, "I am the law in Indiana." On parade night in Kokomo, the police disappeared and white-sheeted figures directed traffic.

The new Klan even gained a foothold in the industrial Northeast and in California. In 1923, 10,000 New Jersey Klan members burned a cross in New Brunswick, New Jersey, almost in sight of Manhattan. Similar scenes took place in Anaheim, California.

Klan members believed that as "pure" Americans, they should be the guardians of society's behavior and morals. In America's cities, Klan members enjoyed a feeling of superiority in their common hatred for whichever group they thought was beneath them.

Under Hiram Wesley Evans, a Texas dentist and the Klan's Imperial Wizard and Emperor, the secret society's rolls swelled to almost 5 million members. Evans believed the Klan represented "the great mass of Americans of the old pioneer stock." By this, he meant "a blend of various peoples of the so-called Nordic race, the race which, with all its faults, has given the world almost the whole of modern civilization."

Evans and his followers felt modern America had forced them to become strangers in their own land:

> One by one all our traditional moral standards went by the boards, or were so disregarded that they ceased to be binding. The sacredness of our Sabbath, of our homes, of chastity, and finally even of our right to teach our own children in our own schools fundamental facts and truths were torn away from us.
>
> —Hiram Wesley Evans,
> "The Klan's Fight for Americanism,"
> *The North American Review,* March–May, 1926

Evans expected to win "a return of power into the hands of the everyday, not highly cultured, not overly intellectualized, but entirely unspoiled and not de-Americanized, average citizen of the old stock."

The Klan prided itself on its pure-blooded Americanism, but it shared many similarities with German and Italian movements of this period. Like the European groups, the Klan stressed nationalism and racial purity, attacked alien minority groups, disapproved of the urban culture, and called for a return to the past.

The Ku Klux Klan began to sink back into obscurity in 1925 when David Stephenson, who had insisted he was the law in Indiana, went to jail for the second-degree murder of a woman he had kidnapped and brutally abused. Klan members who had believed in its stated ideals of chastity and morality deserted the organization in large numbers.

In 1928 the Klan could not prevent the nomination of Al Smith, a Catholic, for President of the United States. Although Smith could see crosses burning in the fields as his campaign train crossed Oklahoma, the Klan itself was almost burned out.

Closing the Doors

Popular Pressure Against Immigration

The Ku Klux Klan's drive for "pure Americanism," if not their methods, found a sympathetic echo in mainstream America. Many Americans associated immigrants with radicalism and disloyalty. These fears had fueled the Red Scare, the Palmer raids, and the case against Sacco and Vanzetti. Rural Americans in particular believed that immigrants had somehow caused erosion of old-fashioned American values.

An immigration act in 1921 attached the force of law to bigotry when it reversed the century-long tradition of open immigration from Europe. The law limited the number of immigrants by applying a **quota** system, in which the number of immigrants from any country in a year could not exceed 3 percent of the number of people in the United States from that country according to the 1910 census. That favored immigrants from northern and western Europe because most of the immigrants from these areas had arrived by this time.

In 1924 the National Origins Act reduced the number of immigrants and excluded Asians altogether. It also decreased the quota percentage to 2 percent of the number of any given nationality residing in the United States in 1890. By using the 1890 census instead of the 1910 census, the law slashed the number of immigrants allowed in from eastern and southern Europe—nationalities that arrived largely after 1890.

In the debate on the bill, members of Congress vented their hatred of immigrants, especially immigrants who lived in New York. One representative from Kansas contrasted the "beer, bolshevism, unassimilating settlements and perhaps many flags" to his idealized view of the United States: "constitutional government; one flag, stars and stripes."

The law attempted to maintain the ethnic mixture that the United States had in 1890 in order to ensure that the country would stay "American." The authors of the law assumed that Asians, Italians, and Poles were less American than were Irish and Germans who had come in large numbers in the 1800s and therefore had a larger quota in the law.

The National Origins Act made it exceptionally difficult for people from countries with low quotas to immigrate to the United States. In the 1930s immigration to the United States dwindled to a trickle. (See the Case Study on pages 404–407.)

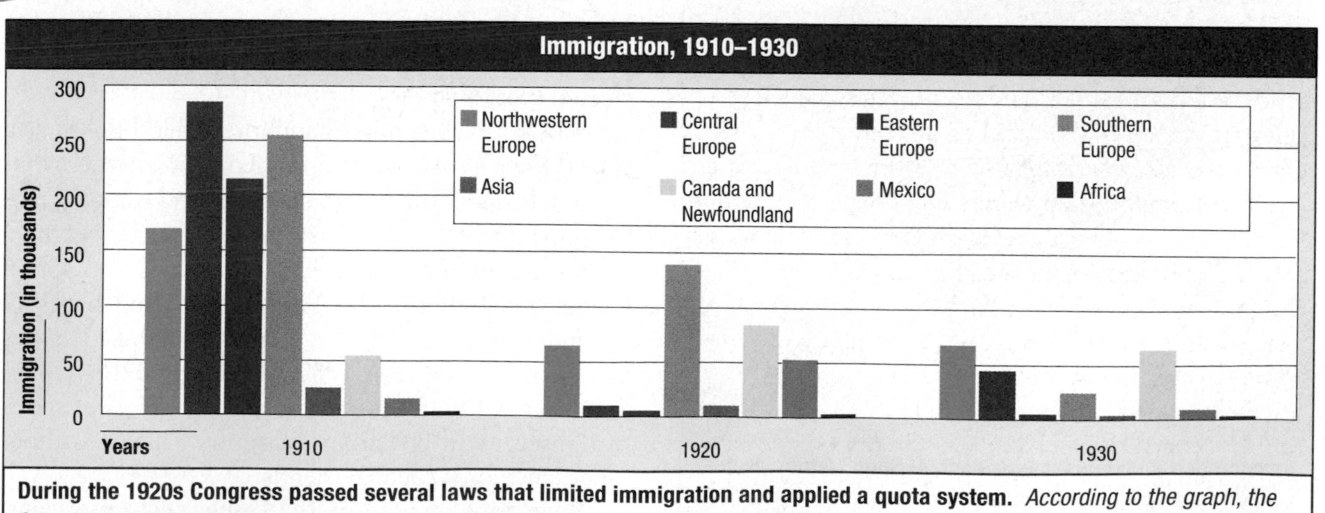

During the 1920s Congress passed several laws that limited immigration and applied a quota system. *According to the graph, the fewest immigrants came from which four areas in the 1920s?*

The Challenge of Change

Conflict Personified in the 1928 Election

During the 1920s Americans found themselves suddenly thrust, sometimes unwillingly, into a modern, urban world. In 1910 more than half of all Americans lived in villages of less than 2,500 people. During the 1920s, 6 million people left the farm for the city, and by 1930 only 44 percent of Americans still lived in rural areas.

Hostility and Fear

The battles fought in the 1920s over religion, over drinking, and over who could be considered an American shared a common thread of fear and hostility to everything an urban society seemed to represent. At best, the laws passed to try to stop change merely postponed it.

LIBRARY OF CONGRESS

Democratic Candidate for President, Al Smith Smith inspired supporters and frightened others. *How might radio have hurt his presidential campaign?*

For example, Tennessee's law to prevent the teaching of evolution received world attention in the Scopes trial. The Eighteenth Amendment to curb Americans' thirst for liquor was often ignored before its repeal in 1933. After the late 1920s, the Ku Klux Klan and the values it represented had all but disappeared, except in the South. While the National Origins Act stemmed the tide of eastern European immigration, it did not stop immigrants from the Western Hemisphere. After the 1920s Mexicans, French Canadians, and Puerto Ricans became the new American immigrants.

FILE PHOTO BY RALPH J. BRUNKE

City Versus Country

Tensions between the city and the country erupted into national election politics for the first time in 1928 when New York Governor Al Smith made his bid for national power. Probably no Democrat could have defeated Republican Herbert Hoover in the middle of this prosperous decade. Smith, furthermore, seemed to stand for everything small-town Americans feared most: the big city with sinful and foreign ways.

For example, the governor had been born in a tenement house near the East River in New York City. Fearful voters saw Smith as a voice for immigrants. He openly opposed Prohibition, which small-town Americans supported.

Rural voters and city voters who held traditional values gaped at Smith's brown derby hat, his expensive tailor-made suits, and his ever-present cigar. Even the accent with which Smith pronounced "radio" as "raddio" or said "foist" for "first" made the candidate seem un-American. Most important of all, many Americans wondered whether the devout Catholic governor could remain independent of the pope if he were to be elected President.

Hoover, on the other hand, presented himself as a typical Iowa farm boy, who recalled diving in the swimming hole under the willow branches and trapping rabbits in the woods. Of course, he had since become a millionaire mining engineer. Hoover had also spearheaded relief efforts after World War I and had successfully served under two Republican Presidents as secretary of commerce. When he accepted the Republican nomination for President, however, Hoover spoke of himself as "a boy from a country village, without inheritance or influential friends."

The popular vote of 1928 reflected Americans' intense interest in the election. Only half the eligible

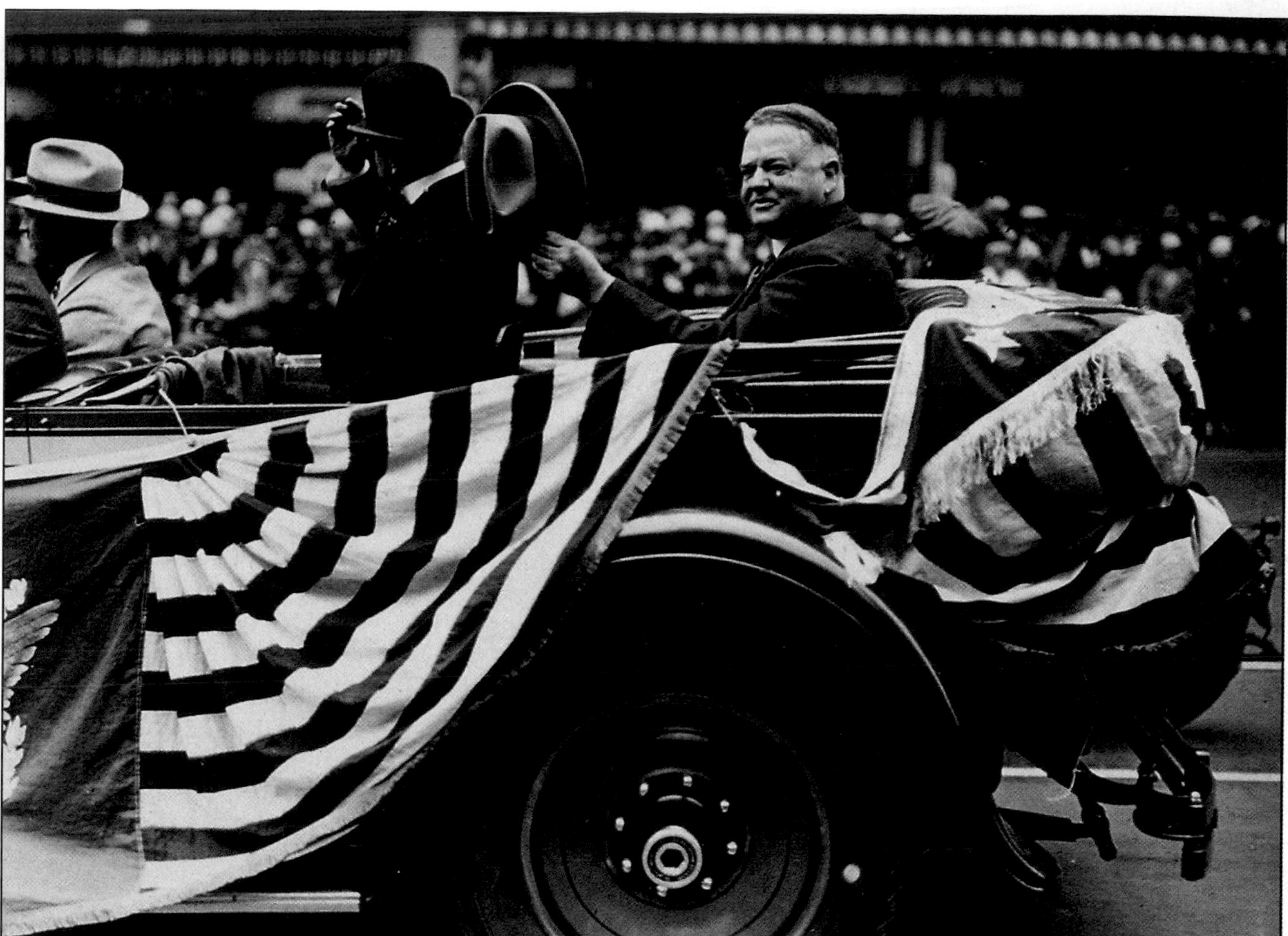
ARCHIVE PHOTOS

Hoover Triumphant **Herbert Hoover won the 1928 race for President with a pro-business platform.** *How did he present himself to Americans in his campaign?*

voters had cast ballots in the 1924 contest. In 1928 more than two-thirds of the eligible voters turned out. Many of the new voters in 1928 were Catholic women, casting ballots for the first time.

To no one's surprise, Hoover won in a landslide. Lost in the excitement of Hoover's victory was the fact that for the first time in a decade of Republican prosperity, a President had failed to win the 12 largest cities in the United States. In 1924 the Republicans had carried these big cities by 1.3 million votes. Political change was clearly in the wind.

The 1920s, a time of rapid social change in the United States, was an exciting and troubling decade. The promise of an easier, more bountiful and modern life existed side by side with old suspicions, fears, and hatreds. The change that thrilled some people threatened others who tried unsuccessfully to cling to older ways. The people in power—white, Protestant, and male—still gave lip service to the small-town virtues of the past, but in the 1920s the United States was changing rapidly into a modern, urban society. It would change even more with the Great Crash in 1929.

Section Assessment

Main Idea

1. Use a chart like this one to summarize the central issues in some of the major conflicts of the 1920s.

Conflicts	Central Issues

Vocabulary

2. Define: fundamentalism, evangelist, speakeasy, bootlegger, quota.

Checking Facts

3. Explain the resurgence of the Ku Klux Klan. Why did the Klan's popularity decline?

4. Why was the presidential election of 1928 seen as a contest between rural and urban values?

Critical Thinking

5. **Making Inferences** Why do you think Prohibition failed?

Turning Point

The National Origins Act

MAY 26, 1924

MEMORANDUM

"American institutions rest solely on good citizenship. They were created by people who had a background of self-government. New arrivals should be limited to our capacity to absorb them into the ranks of good citizenship. America must be kept American. For this purpose, it is necessary to continue a policy of restricted immigration. . . . I am convinced that our present economic and social conditions warrant a limitation of those to be admitted. . . . Those who do not want to be partakers of the American spirit ought not to settle in America."

President Calvin Coolidge,
State of the Union Address,
December 6, 1923

The Case

A few months after Coolidge's speech, Congress took him at his word. Led by Representative Albert Johnson of Washington and Senators Henry Cabot Lodge of Massachusetts and Hiram Johnson of California, Congress passed the Immigration Act of 1924, also called the National Origins Act.

The act strictly limited immigration from every country outside the Western Hemisphere by imposing quotas. Until 1929, quotas would be based on the national origins of the United States population using the 1890 census. After that, quotas would be set using the 1920 census. The bill limited total immigration to about 150,000 people per year starting in 1929, a drastic reduction from the almost 1 million that arrived each year from 1900 to 1914.

For a nation founded by immigrants, the National Origins Act seemed a complete reversal of its traditional policy. For a nation worried about its future, the act seemed a promise to keep America for Americans. What did it mean to be an American? Who was able, or qualified, to become one? Should the country continue its relatively open policy, or were tighter restrictions needed? These questions were central to the debate over the National Origins Act.

Despite certain objections, President Coolidge signed the bill into law on May 26, 1924.

The Background

Before the Civil War, most Americans agreed that an open immigration policy was essential to the country's growth. Immigration provided settlers for the territories and workers for expanding industry. Most immigrants of the time—like most Americans—had roots in northern and western Europe. That did not mean all new arrivals were equally welcomed: early Irish and German immigrants, for example, often faced a hostile reception. Nonetheless, because most early immigrants and Americans shared similar roots, few saw immigration as a threat to the country's values, and most viewed it as an integral part of the national character and tradition. While the United States had a surplus of land and a shortage of labor, an open policy seemed to serve its needs.

Changing Views This view had changed dramatically by the late 1800s. Regional and national economies experienced a frightening series of depressions. The Western frontier was disappearing; the South was in transition. Urban problems of overcrowding, disease, and labor unrest worried many Americans. Newcomers were blamed for these problems—especially the "new" immigrants who came from Asia and southern and eastern Europe.

Prejudice and anti-immigrant feelings grew in the late 1800s, as did calls to limit immigration. In California, Chinese immigrants were unfairly blamed for many social and economic ills. Riding the wave of anti-Chinese feelings, Congress passed the Chinese Exclusion Act of 1882, preventing Chinese immigrants from becoming United States citizens. For the first time, the United States had restricted immigration based solely on national origin. Prior restrictions were based on keeping criminals or those with contagious diseases out of the country.

Eugenics In arguing for the exclusion of new immigrants, restrictionists promoted eugenics, the idea that heredity, or genetics, determined who was "fit" or "unfit," and thus superior or inferior. Eugenics suggested that persons from northern or western European stock could be true Americans because they were "fit"—intelligent, strong, and self-reliant. People from southern and eastern Europe, Asians, Africans, and Jews were deemed "unfit" and therefore unable to become Americans.

Evidence for eugenics came from biased studies, but Americans increasingly believed in it. Senator William Dillingham's 1911 commission published a report stating that the new immigrants were a threat to the nation and that certain ethnic groups should be considered undesirable. Madison Grant's widely read book, *The Passing of the Great Race* (1916),

"Unless the U.S. adopts this biologic principle [of racial differences] they will be flooded over by people of inferior stock because of their greater fecundity [birth rate]."

Dr. Harry H. Laughlin, speaking for the United States secretary of labor in support of the National Origins Act

"I felt confident that the President would sign the Immigration bill, for I know he sympathizes with the general purposes of the legislation and realizes fully its great importance. It is a very great measure, one of the most important if not the most important, that Congress has ever passed. It reaches far into the future."

Senator Henry Cabot Lodge (right)

AP/WIDE WORLD PHOTOS

AP/WIDE WORLD PHOTOS

"Immigrants have contributed greatly to the industrial development of this country; contributed not alone by their numbers but also by their age, sex and training."

Constantine Panunzio (left) in his 1927 book, *Immigration Crossroads,* in defense of open immigration

"This association protests against the enactment of said measures as . . . intolerant in purpose and effect, unfounded upon any fair, useful or logical test for fitness for American citizenship, and unjust to race stocks which have proved pre-eminently loyal in peace time and in war, law abiding and productive. . . ."

Emily S. Bernheim, Executive Secretary of the United Neighborhood Houses of New York, in a letter to President Coolidge opposing the act

supported this view. Grant claimed that heredity was the key factor in all human progress. These works seemed to "prove" that the new immigrants were inferior and an "alien menace."

World War I convinced many that the open immigration tradition had failed, since foreign ties had involved the country in a horrible war. The 1917 revolution of the Bolsheviks in Russia linked fears of communism with foreigners in American minds. Labor unrest and domestic terrorism inspired dread that the United States might collapse from internal strife.

Congress passed the first widely restrictive immigration law in 1921, with a limit of 357,000 people per year based on a national quota system. Many felt the 1921 law did not do enough. It failed to decrease southern and eastern European immigration. Representative Albert Johnson and Senators Lodge and Hiram Johnson pressed for an even stronger law. With the National Origins Act of 1924, restrictionists won the debate over immigration. This law would govern immigration until 1965.

The Opinions

Since the nation's founding, opinions have been split between open and restrictive immigration policy. Restrictionists were dominating the debate by the early 1900s, but many Americans held firm to the belief that immigration was one of the country's greatest strengths. They championed a more open policy. The quotes on the preceding page reveal the conflict in opinions on immigration and the National Origins Act.

The Outcome

The Response Many foreign governments reacted angrily to the new immigration policy. Japanese Lieutenant General Bunjiro Horinouchi stated, "We must be determined to undergo whatever hardships are necessary in avenging the insult which America has done our country." Another Japanese leader said, "If history teaches anything, an eventual collision between Japan and America on the Pacific is inevitable." Some Americans felt the act would harm all foreign relations.

Public opinion and newspaper editorials in the United States, though, reflected widespread support for the National Origins Act. The *Cleveland Plain Dealer* stated in an editorial, "Immigration is a domestic problem. The Japanese are neither as unsophisticated nor so domineering as to try to override the clearly expressed will of friendly America."

Congress soon moved to strengthen immigration restrictions even more. It created a border patrol to prevent illegal immigration—not by Mexicans or Canadians, but by Europeans trying to get around quota restrictions. It also gave immigration officers more power to arrest suspected illegal residents.

Border Patrol **In 1926 these Border Patrol officers in Laredo, Texas, show off their equipment and personnel for a photo portrait by Eugene Goldbeck. They hoped to prevent Europeans from evading quotas by coming in through Mexico.**

Immediate Effects The act had immediate effects on immigration. For the most part, it ended legal Chinese and Japanese immigration. The goal of encouraging more immigrants from northern and western Europe and restricting the number from other areas was achieved. The Quota Board set up by the act raised the British quota from 34,007 under the 1921 law to 65,721, while setting the Italian quota at 5,802, Poland's at 6,524, and Greece's at 307.

The National Origins Act was the main catalyst for changes in the character of United States immigration. First, total immigration fell sharply. From 1906 to 1915, 9.4 million people had immigrated to the United States. Less than 2 million immigrated to the United States from 1925 to 1948.

More notably, the national origins of immigrants changed dramatically, just as restrictionists had desired. From 1900 to 1910, northern and western Europe had sent 21.7 percent of all United States immigrants; southern and eastern Europe, 70.8 percent; Canada and Mexico, 2.6 percent; and all other countries, 4.9 percent. From 1924 to 1946, northern and western Europe sent 43.1 percent of immigrants; southern and eastern Europe, 18.9 percent; Canada and Mexico, 33 percent; and all others, 5 percent.

People scrambled to get the required visas before their country's annual quota was filled. Irma Busch from Germany recalled, "I went to Hamburg in 1924, and it was one year before I finally got my quota number. . . . At the consulate, they said to me, that if I had been born a little bit further down in Silesia, in the Polish sector, I couldn't have come here, because that would have been under a different quota. There were always more people applied from that part than there was a quota for."

Later Effects Even before and during World War II, the quotas held fast. Thousands desperate to flee the terror of fascism were shut out, including many Jews. Boats of hopeful immigrants were turned away. In 1938, as anti-Jewish violence erupted in Germany, Congress rejected a proposal to admit about 20,000 German children, most of them Jews. Congress claimed that it might draw the nation into war—and would violate the quota system. Yet in 1940 Congress admitted 15,000 English children to the United States.

As a result of the National Origins Act, the United States suffered a labor shortage, especially agricultural workers, during World War II. The United States asked Mexico to help ease the shortage. The resulting bracero program allowed Mexicans to enter the United States as short-term farmworkers. More than 4 million Mexicans served as braceros in the United States until Congress ended the program in 1964.

The Significance

For more than 40 years, the National Origins Act remained in force. Americans continued to support it, but as the early 1960s civil rights movement grew, President Kennedy and others questioned whether the act truly reflected American values. In 1965 Congress passed a new immigration law, ending the National Origins Act. The 1965 law seemed to return the United States to its former, more open status. While limiting open immigration to 200,000, it allowed in any number of relatives of United States citizens. It gave each country the same quota, 20,000, but did not end the quota system.

The main results of the National Origins Act —limits on total immigration and the use of a quota system—remained unaffected. More than 70 years after the act, its restrictive principles continue to dominate United States immigration policy.

RESPONDING TO THE CASE

1. Why did the restrictionists support a quota system for immigration? What did they hope such a system would accomplish?

2. One of the effects of the National Origins Act was that immigration from Canada and Mexico increased greatly. Would supporters of the act have welcomed these immigrants? Explain.

3. Did the National Origins Act achieve the goals of its supporters? Explain.

PORTFOLIO PROJECT

Suppose you are an opponent of the National Origins Act in the 1920s. You have the opportunity to address Congress before they decide on the bill. What would you say to them to convince them of your argument? Write a brief address you could give to the House of Representatives and the Senate explaining your views.

Chapter  Assessment

Self-Check Quiz

Visit the *American Odyssey* Web site at americanodyssey.glencoe.com and click on ***Chapter 12—Self-Check Quiz*** to prepare for the Chapter Test.

Reviewing Key Terms

In each of the following lines, the two terms are related in some way. On a separate piece of paper, write a sentence for each pair that clearly explains the relationship between the two terms.

credit	**standard of living**
tabloid	**syndicate**
evangelist	**fundamentalism**
speakeasy	**bootlegger**
mass media	**materialism**

Recalling Facts

1. How much did the real income of American workers increase between 1923 and 1929? How did this increase affect their standard of living?

2. Give examples of some occupations left out of the prosperity of the 1920s.

3. How did advertising reflect the materialism of the 1920s?

4. Identify three sports heroes of the 1920s. What ideals of the age did these people represent?

5. How did Charles Lindbergh's accomplishment link the values of the nation's past and future?

6. Who inspired the Harlem Renaissance? Identify three writers of this literary movement and a work of each.

7. How was David Stephenson responsible in part for the decline of the Ku Klux Klan?

8. Why did many Americans seek to restrict immigration during the 1920s? How did the National Origins Act of 1924 affect Asian immigration to the United States?

9. How did the Scopes trial test fundamentalism?

Critical Thinking

1. Drawing Conclusions How did the Model T and chain stores such as F.W. Woolworth and J.C. Penney diminish the differences between city and country life? What other 1920s innovations had a similar influence?

2. Making Generalizations This chapter discusses the work of writers such as Sinclair Lewis, Alain Locke, Langston Hughes, Gertrude Stein, and Zora Neale Hurston. What generalization can you make about the topics these writers selected?

3. Recognizing Points of View Use a diagram like this one to identify the groups that supported and opposed Prohibition and the Volstead Act and their reasons for doing so.

Standardized Test Practice

1. Which of the following did NOT occur during the 1920s?

A Secondary education became available to many more Americans.
B A large number of people migrated from cities to farms.
C Motion pictures became an extremely popular form of entertainment.
D A new generation of African American artists arose in Harlem.

Test-Taking Tip: Look for the exception—the answer that does NOT fit the question. Since the availability of secondary education, the rise of motion pictures, and the Harlem Renaissance all *did* occur during the 1920s, answers A, C, and D can be ruled out.

2. Which of the following represented a clash between religious beliefs and science in the 1920s?

A the Scopes trial
B the passage of Prohibition
C the Palmer raids
D the Sacco-Vanzetti case

Test-Taking Tip: This question asks you to identify the central issue in key *clashes,* or conflicts, in the 1920s. Eliminate any answers that do NOT center on conflicts between *religion* and *science.* For example, the issue in the Palmer raids (answer A) and the Sacco-Vanzetti case (answer C) was a fear of radicalism.

GEOGRAPHY AND HISTORY

Prohibition Enforcement, 1929

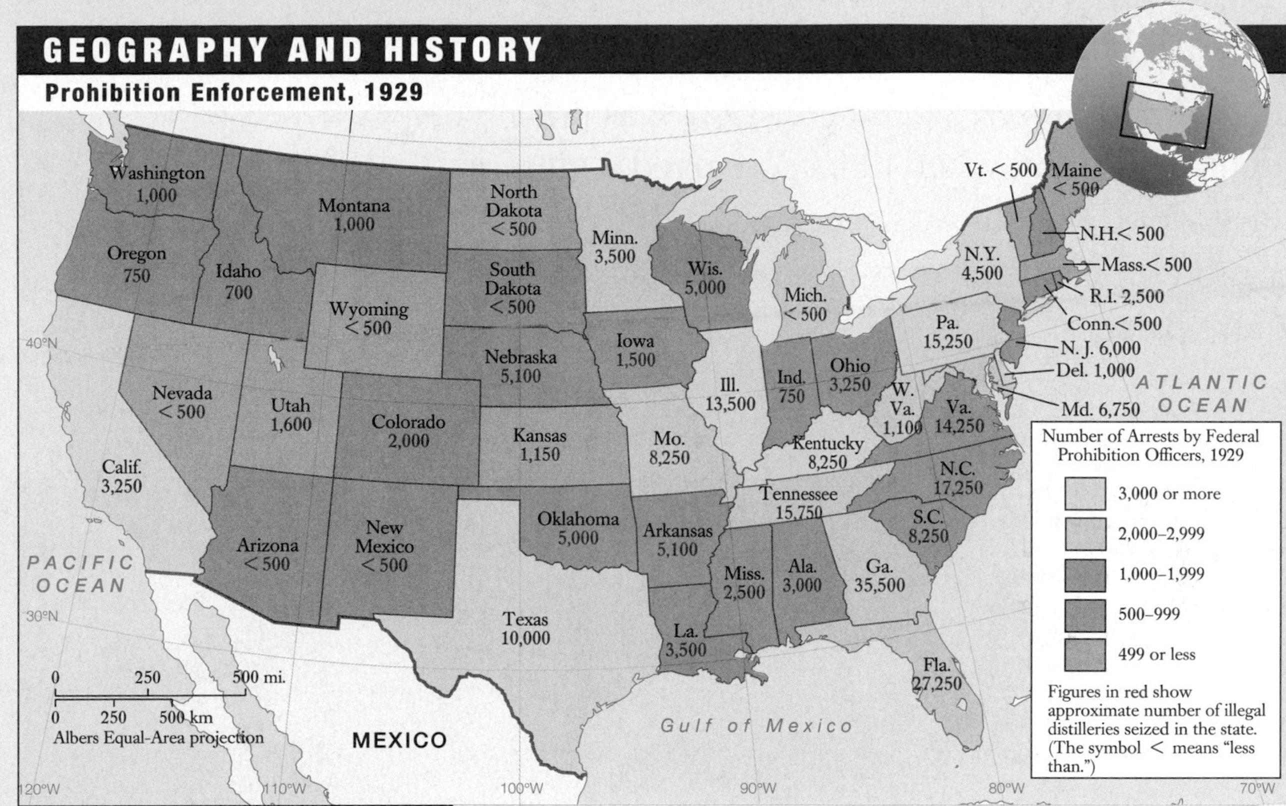

Study the map to answer the following questions:

1. The 1920s have sometimes been called "the lawless decade." How does this map's information reinforce that nickname and connect to the geographic theme of movement?
2. In which states did federal Prohibition officers make the most arrests?
3. Name the two states where the most illegal distilleries and equipment were seized.
4. What region or regions had the fewest arrests? Why might this be so?

Portfolio Project

PORTFOLIO PROJECT

Research the lives of people who were teenagers during the 1920s. Your local history museum or back issues of newspapers may be helpful. Try to learn about some of the following topics: education, styles of clothing, forms of recreation, and music. You may wish to explore family albums. Look for pictures that record styles of clothing, hairdos, and social events of that period. Report your findings orally to the class. You may also want to share a display of any supporting visuals. Then file a written summary of the activity in your portfolio.

Cooperative Learning

In small groups discuss how organizations such as the Ku Klux Klan often violate the civil rights of other citizens. To what extent are such organizations protected by the Constitution? What laws protect citizens from the threats and intimidation practiced by such groups?

Reinforcing Skills

Synthesizing Information Imagine that you are living in the 1920s. Decide whether you are a city or a farm dweller. Select material from each section of Chapter 12, and synthesize the material into a written account of a day in your life.

Technology Activity

Using a Word Processor The 1920s was a time of fads. Look through current store catalogs and magazines for fads of today. Choose one that you think is particularly interesting. On your word processor, write a two-paragraph explanation of why or how you think this fad developed.

Then...

Old Movie Houses

The *Alabama Theatre* opening of 1927 was part of the golden age of film, when films portrayed a glittering fantasy world. To show these films, architects designed ever more opulent theaters that people nicknamed "picture palaces."

1 A local newspaper proclaimed, "Birmingham Gets a $1,500,000 Christmas Gift" when the *Alabama Theatre* opened in 1927. This movie palace has 2,500 seats spread over the three-tiered interior. Above a giant proscenium arch is an oval dome that caps the room.

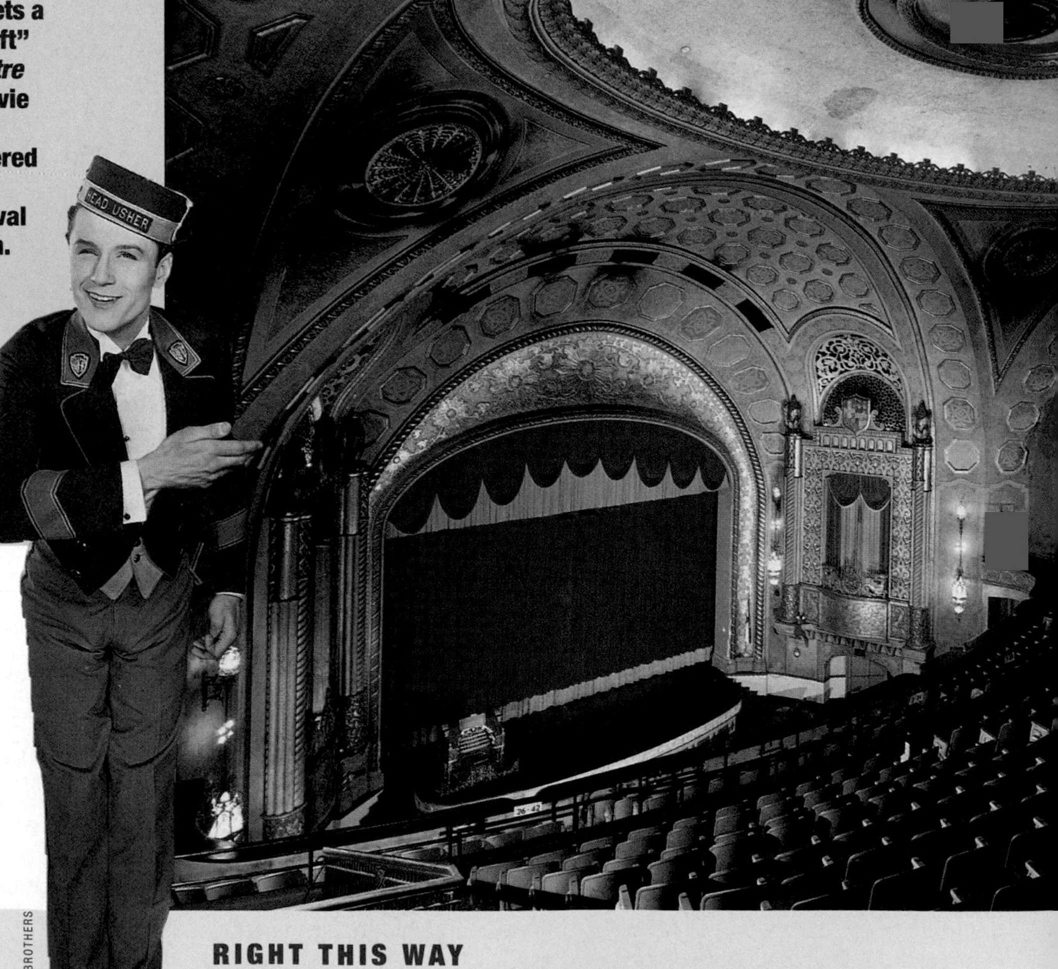

BROWN BROTHERS

Fun Facts

RIGHT THIS WAY

Being an usher often required the talents of a police officer, diplomat, and valet. During a formalized training program, ushers were drilled in the proper and polite treatment of the public, including learning a variety of hand signals.

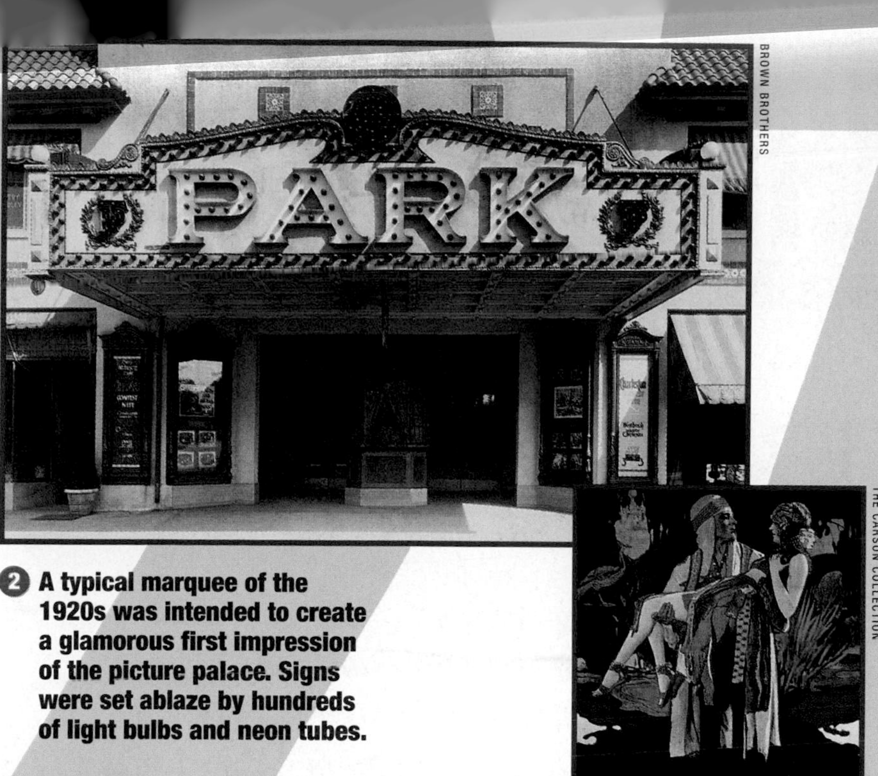

BROWN BROTHERS

2 A typical marquee of the 1920s was intended to create a glamorous first impression of the picture palace. Signs were set ablaze by hundreds of light bulbs and neon tubes.

THE CARSON COLLECTION

3 Most people learned about new films through word of mouth, newspapers, and posters. The finest posters, such as this one advertising the posthumous release of Rudolph Valentino's last feature in 1926, were as powerful as the films they promoted.

M. LEWIS KENNEDY, KENNEDY STUDIOS

Stats

ATTENDANCE

By 1922 average weekly theater admissions totaled 40 million. By 1929 theater admissions totaled 80 million. In May 1924, there were reported to be 578 cinemas in New York City alone, with seating for 428,926.

TICKET PRICES

Ticket prices were never less than 10 cents, and at first-run theaters they were often more than 75 cents.

STAR SALARIES

In June 1927, Louis B. Mayer renewed Greta Garbo's MGM contract at a salary of $5,000 per week.

SOUND PRICES

- According to a 1929 article in *Variety,* equipping cinemas with sound systems would cost close to $3 million.
- *Broadway* (1929) was one of the first sound films to use a movie camera mounted on a special crane that was built for Universal Studios at a cost of $75,000.

...Now

M. LEWIS KENNEDY, KENNEDY STUDIOS

MOVIE HOUSE COMPARISON

PORTFOLIO PROJECT

How do the cinemas of today compare with the 1920s movie houses? Select one contemporary theater and create a booklet for your portfolio that includes pertinent information and visuals. Be sure to include any data you can think of that would help someone make a Then and Now kind of comparison in the future.

THE MIGHTY WURLITZER

To the average moviegoer, any pipe organ that accompanied a silent movie was a "Wurlitzer." The organ often rose high above the stage floor on a lift, sometimes reaching balcony level. On several occasions, organists had to be rescued when the lift became stuck in the highest position.

Economic Crisis and the New Deal

1929–1939

HISTORY & YOU

The "Roaring Twenties" came to a roaring halt with the stock market crash of 1929. Grossly inflated stock prices—coupled with a prolonged agricultural slump, industrial overproduction, and high tariffs—contributed to the worst economic depression in the nation's history. Belief in the American dream had all but vanished until Franklin and Eleanor Roosevelt restored hope with their buoyant pledge to hand Americans a "new deal." The impact of the New Deal, particularly the expanded role of government, can be felt to this day.

See pages 964–965 for primary source readings that accompany Unit 5.

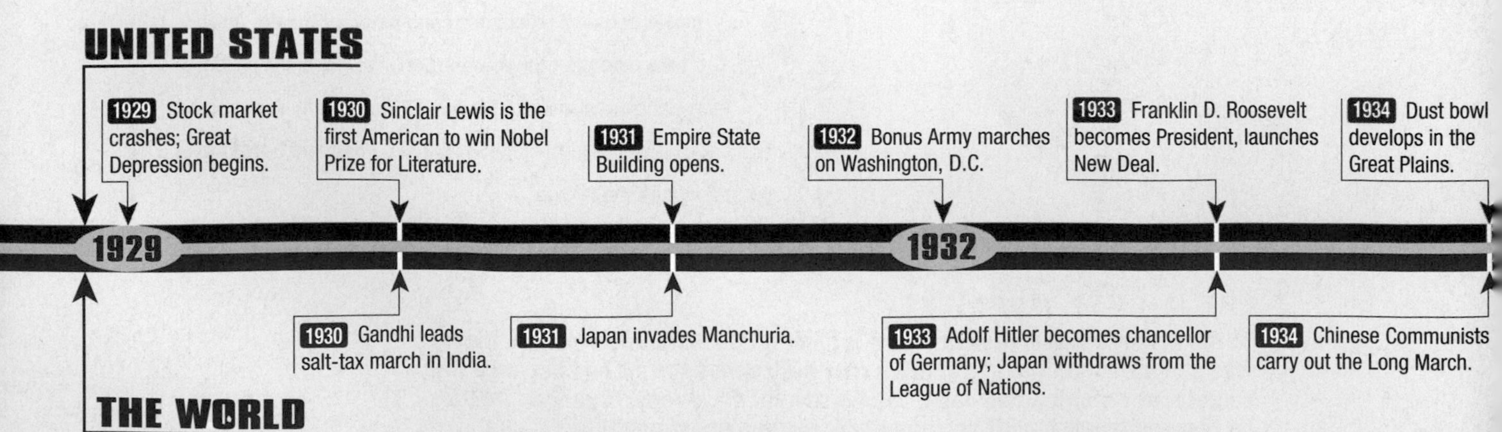

UNITED STATES
1929 Stock market crashes; Great Depression begins.
1930 Sinclair Lewis is the first American to win Nobel Prize for Literature.
1931 Empire State Building opens.
1932 Bonus Army marches on Washington, D.C.
1933 Franklin D. Roosevelt becomes President, launches New Deal.
1934 Dust bowl develops in the Great Plains.
1929
1932
1930 Gandhi leads salt-tax march in India.
1931 Japan invades Manchuria.
1933 Adolf Hitler becomes chancellor of Germany; Japan withdraws from the League of Nations.
1934 Chinese Communists carry out the Long March.
THE WORLD

PHOTO BY DOROTHEA LANGE/LIBRARY OF CONGRESS

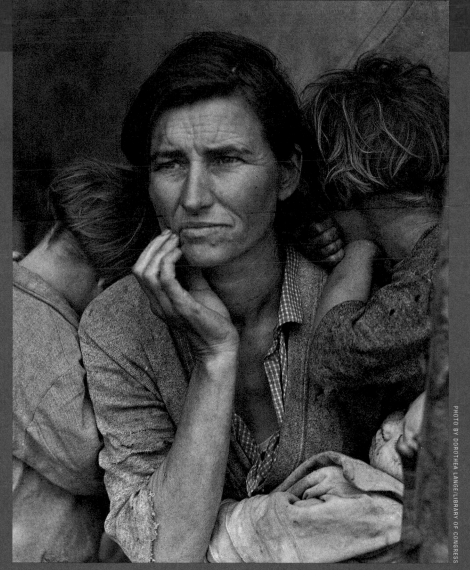

Migrant Mother, **by Dorothea Lange, 1936, shows the hopelessness many people felt during the Great Depression.**

1935 Social Security Act is passed.
1936 Roosevelt is reelected.
1937 *Gone With the Wind* wins Pulitzer Prize.
1939 John Steinbeck publishes *Grapes of Wrath*.
1935
1937
1939
1936 Spanish Civil War begins; Keynes publishes his economic theories.
1937 Picasso paints *Guernica*.
1938 Mexico nationalizes oil wells; Venezuela becomes third-largest oil-producing nation in the world.
1939 Germany invades Poland; World War II begins.

The Grapes of Wrath

BY JOHN STEINBECK

At the height of the Depression, drought gripped the Great Plains. In this excerpt from The Grapes of Wrath, *novelist John Steinbeck conveys the Oklahoma farmers' frustration at the prospect of losing their farms.*

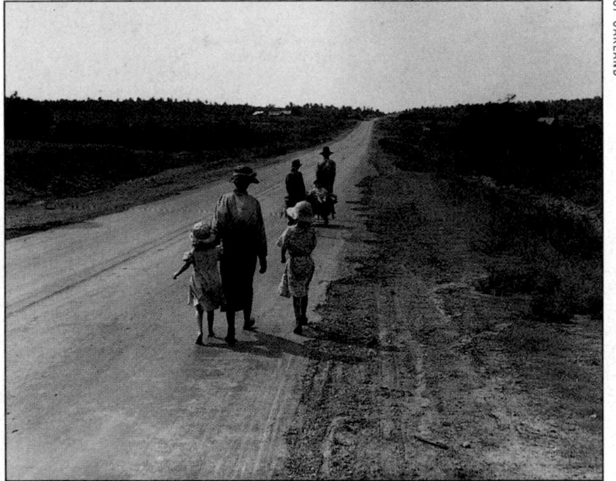

On the Road Dorothea Lange's portrait, "Homeless Family," tells a Depression story of uprooting.

Some of the owner men were kind because they hated what they had to do, and some of them were angry because they hated to be cruel, and some of them were cold because they had long ago found that one could not be an owner unless one were cold. And all of them were caught in something larger than themselves. Some of them hated the mathematics that drove them, and some were afraid, and some worshiped the mathematics because it provided a refuge from thought and from feeling. If a bank or a finance company owned the land, the owner man said, the Bank—or the Company—needs—wants—insists—must have—as though the Bank or the Company were a monster, with thought and feeling, which had ensnared them. These last would take no responsibility for the banks or the companies because they were men and slaves, while the banks were machines and masters all at the same time. Some of the owner men were a little proud to be slaves to such cold and powerful masters. The owner men sat in the cars and explained. You know the land is poor. You've scrabbled at it long enough, God knows.

The squatting tenant men nodded and wondered and drew figures in the dust, and yes, they knew, God knows. If the dust only wouldn't fly. If the top would only stay on the soil, it might not be so bad.

The owner men went on leading to their point: You know the land's getting poorer. You know what cotton does to the land; robs it, sucks all the blood out of it.

The squatters nodded—they knew, God knew. If they could only rotate the crops they might pump blood back into the land.

Well, it's too late. And the owner men explained the workings and the thinkings of the monster that was stronger than they were. A man can hold land if he can just eat and pay taxes; he can do that.

Yes, he can do that until his crops fail one day and he has to borrow money from the bank.

But—you see, a bank or a company can't do that, because those creatures don't breathe air, don't eat side-meat. They breathe profits; they eat the interest on money. If they don't get it, they die the way you die without air, without side-meat. It is a sad thing, but it is so. It is just so. . . .

The squatting men looked down again. What do you want us to do? We can't take less share of the crop—we're half starved now. The kids are hungry all the time. We got no clothes, torn an' ragged. If all the neighbors weren't the same, we'd be ashamed to go to meeting.

And at last the owner men came to the point. The tenant system won't work any more. One man on a tractor can take the place of twelve or fourteen families. Pay him a wage and take all the crop. We have to do it. We don't like to do it. But the monster's sick. Something's happened to the monster.

But you'll kill the land with cotton.

We know. We've got to take cotton quick before the land dies. Then we'll sell the land. Lots of families in the East would like to own a piece of land.

The tenant men looked up alarmed. But what'll happen to us? How'll we eat?

You'll have to get off the land. The plows'll go through the dooryard.

And now the squatting men stood up angrily. Grampa took up the land, and he had to kill the Indians and drive them away. And Pa was born here, and he killed weeds and snakes. Then a bad year came and he had to borrow a little money. An' we was born here. There in the door—our children born here. And Pa had to borrow money. The bank owned the land then, but we stayed and we got a little bit of what we raised.

We know that—all that. It's not us, it's the bank. A bank isn't like a man. Or an owner with fifty thousand acres, he isn't like a man either. That's the monster.

Sure, cried the tenant men, but it's our land. We measured it and broke it up. We were born on it, and we got killed on it, died on it. Even if it's no good, it's still ours. That's what makes it ours—being born on it, working it, dying on it. That makes ownership, not a paper with numbers on it.

We're sorry. It's not us. It's the monster. The bank isn't like a man.

Yes, but the bank is only made of men.

No, you're wrong there—quite wrong there. The bank is something else than men. It happens that every man in a bank hates what the bank does, and yet the bank does it. The bank is something more than men, I tell you. It's the monster. Men made it, but they can't control it.

The tenants cried, Grampa killed Indians, Pa killed snakes for the land. Maybe we can kill banks—they're worse than Indians and snakes. Maybe we got to fight to keep our land, like Pa and Grampa did.

And now the owner men grew angry. You'll have to go.

But it's ours, the tenant men cried. We——

No. The bank, the monster owns it. You'll have to go. . . . And the owner men started their cars and rolled away.

IT'S NOT US. IT'S THE MONSTER. THE BANK ISN'T LIKE A MAN.

Responding to Literature

1. The tenants say about the land, "That's what makes it ours—being born on it, working it, dying on it." Do you agree or disagree? Explain.
2. Who do you think Steinbeck believes is ultimately responsible for the tenants' loss of their land? Explain.

The Great Depression

DECEMBER 1932: NEW YORK RESPONDS TO ITS NEEDIEST CASES

Daily stories in the *New York Times* in 1932 described the city's neediest families and asked readers to contribute to a fund to help them. One story described an unemployed plasterer, Mr. C., who had starved himself so that his 2-year-old could have enough food.

One morning Mr. C. "fell to the floor and could not rise. A doctor said he had injured himself so seriously by voluntarily starving himself that an operation was imperative. Help is asked to keep the family in food and shelter until Mr. C. is able to work."

Mr. C. was only one of millions of people who had enjoyed prosperity during the 1920s but whose fortunes fell in the early 1930s. Between 1929 and 1932 millions of hardworking men and women lost their jobs. Most of these people were proud and used to providing for their own families. They felt ashamed to take charity.

The 1930s witnessed one of the longest, deepest, and most devastating economic depressions ever experienced by the United States. After a decade of high living, the abrupt financial breakdown came as a severe shock. The affluence enjoyed by many Americans during the Roaring Twenties began to evaporate in the fall of 1929. ■

Based on the picture on page 417, write what you think the Great Depression was like and what the chapter will be about.

Chapter Overview

Visit the *American Odyssey* Web site at americanodyssey.glencoe.com and click on ***Chapter 13—Chapter Overview*** to preview the chapter.

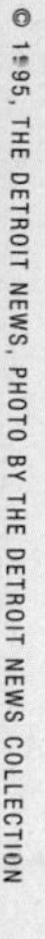

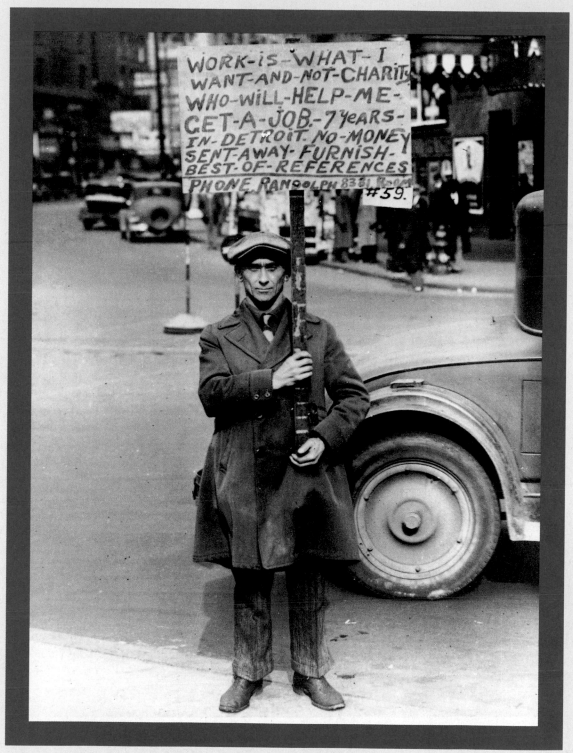

AN UNEMPLOYED WORKER
GETS HIS MESSAGE ACROSS.

The Crash and Its Aftermath

OCTOBER 24, 1929: NEW YORK STOCK EXCHANGE CRASHES

Gloomy Investors
Crowds of stockholders gather on Wall Street as they prepare to sell at a loss.

THURSDAY MORNING AT 10:00, WALL STREET WAS JAMMED. A crowd of thousands gathered outside the New York Stock Exchange, waiting for news. The rumble of loud voices hinted to spectators of the bedlam inside. Traders shouted out their orders to sell, sell, sell. Few were willing to buy the **stocks,** shares in business ownership whose price and value constantly fluctuate, so prices plunged steeply in the stampede.

At noon, five of the nation's leading bankers met in the building across the street from the stock exchange. In an effort to stabilize the plummeting market, these men pledged to pump undisclosed millions into the stock market. By buying stocks, they hoped to make prices rise. Rumors of the meeting had a calming effect on the stock market. Selling slowed and the panic began to subside. When the bankers' representative, Richard Whitney, strode across the floor later that afternoon to deliver his orders for large blocks of stock above asking prices, the stock market had already begun to rally. At closing time stock prices started to rebound from the morning's slump.

The stock market's recovery was short-lived. The following Monday the stock exchange opened with a rush of sales that wiped out all the gains of the preceding week. The bankers met again and decided they could do nothing

GUIDE TO READING

Main Idea

The stock market crash of 1929 ended dreams of permanent prosperity and unleashed a chain of events leading to the Great Depression.

Vocabulary

- stock
- speculation
- margin
- depression
- unemployment

Read to Find Out . . .

- the causes of the stock market crash.
- other factors that contributed to the country's economic decline.
- the nature and effectiveness of President Hoover's response to the Depression.

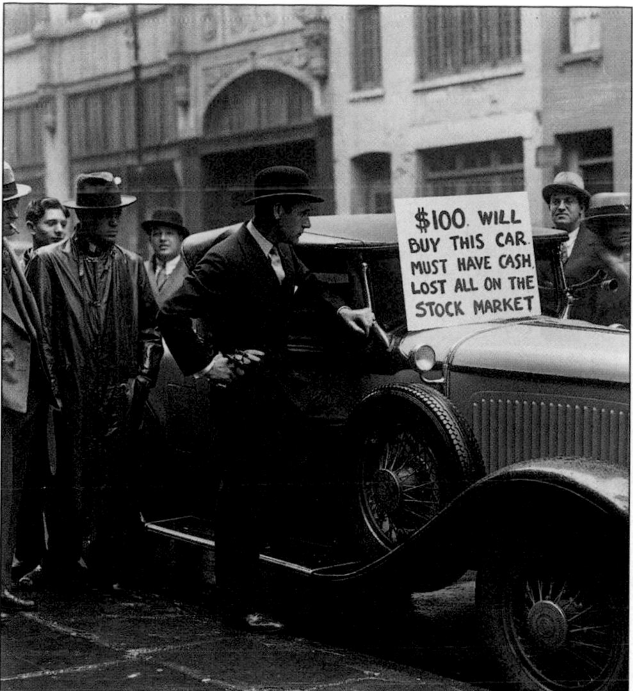

THE BETTMANN ARCHIVE

Driven to Ruin Forced to pay off debts for stocks that were suddenly worthless, people such as this man made drastic adjustments. *Why had so many people invested so heavily in the stock market?*

to check the decline. On Tuesday, October 29, the flood of sales continued. Historians have called this "the most devastating day in the history of markets." A gloomy quiet pervaded the trading floor. The week before, traders ran across the floor in panic, trying to submit their orders before prices dropped further. That day, however, the stock exchange was as dour as a funeral parlor. A reporter from the *New York Times* described the somber scene: "Orderly crowds lined up before each [selling] post, talking in subdued tones, without any pushing." In that last week in October 1929, the stock market began a momentous decline that came to be known as the great crash. During that time $30 billion in stock value—about the same amount of money the United States had spent in World War I—evaporated completely along with people's dreams of achieving permanent prosperity.

Why Did the Crash Occur?

Margin Buying Fuels Speculation

According to economists and politicians of the late 1920s, the United States had entered a new era in which everyone could be rich. Many people agreed with the words of a leading politician:

> If a man saves $15 a week, and invests in good common stocks, and allows the dividends and rights to accumulate, at the end of twenty years he will have at least $80,000 and an income from investments of around $400 a month. He will be rich.
>
> —John J. Raskob, Democratic National Committee chairman, 1929

Stock Market Speculation

Such advice inspired thousands of people to pour their savings into stocks. Many investors, however, wanted to make their fortunes immediately. Hoping that heavy financial risks would pay off quickly, people in the late 1920s speculated in the stock market. **Speculation** was a way of gambling with short-term investments. Speculators would buy stocks they thought would quickly rise in price. After the price of their stocks went up, they would sell the stocks for a profit.

Stocks made large gains between 1927 and 1929. A speculator who bought stock in Hershey Chocolate in August 1928, for example, and sold it in September 1929, made more than 100 percent profit on the investment. Banks at the time commonly paid an annual rate of under 7 percent on savings accounts. The

Selected Stock Prices, 1927–1929

Stock	Aug. 31, 1927	Aug. 31, 1928	Sept. 3, 1929	Oct. 29, 1929	Nov. 15, 1929
American and Foreign Power	$23.86	$38.00	$167.75	$73.00	$67.86
American Telephone and Telegraph (AT&T)	$169.00	$182.00	$304.00	$230.00	$222.00
Detroit Edison Co.	$151.00	$205.00	$350.00	not listed	$195.00
General Electric Co.	$142.00	$168.13	$396.25	$210.00	$201.00
Hershey Chocolate	not listed	$53.25	$128.00	$108.00	$68.00
International Business Machines (IBM)	$93.00	$130.86	$241.75	not listed	$129.86
People's Gas Chicago	$147.13	$182.86	$374.75	not listed	$230.00

Stock values peaked just before the crash, and then tumbled sharply. *If you had bought 10 shares of AT&T in August 1927 and sold them in September 1929, how much would you have profited? If you had bought them in September 1929 and sold them in November 1929, how much would you have lost?*

NATIONAL MUSEUM OF AMERICAN ART, SMITHSONIAN INSTITUTION, MUSEUM PURCHASE

Black Tuesday The Latin words *Dies Irae* literally mean "Day of Wrath," but colloquially the expression means "Judgment Day." *What do you see in the picture that shows how the artist feels about the date October 29?*

dramatic difference between the return on a savings account and the return on stock speculation made the stock market an attractive gamble for thousands of Americans.

The common practice of buying on **margin** involved paying only a fraction of a stock's dollar value. In such a transaction, an investor put down as little as 5 percent of the stock price and borrowed the rest of the money from a stockbroker. The stock itself was collateral for the loan. In other words, if the investor could not repay the loan, the broker gained ownership of the stock. Investors buying on margin could buy more stock with their money than investors who did not borrow from brokers. For example, an investor with $500 could buy 5 shares of a stock costing $100 per share. Buying on margin, however, the investor could use the $500 to buy 100 shares, in effect buying $10,000 worth of stock. As long as the price of the stock continued to rise, the buyer could sell later, pay back what had been borrowed, and realize a tidy profit.

In the boom years of the late 1920s, savvy margin buyers made fortunes. Buying stocks at low prices, they watched gleefully as stock values soared. When they thought a stock had reached its peak price, they sold it, paying off the stockbroker with the money they made from the sale.

As long as stock prices kept going up, brokers were happy to lend money to speculators. After all, they received up to 20 percent interest on their loans. As soon as prices began to slide, brokers had to protect their loans. Because the stocks were their only collateral, when stock prices began to decline, brokers called in their margins. In other words, they asked investors who had borrowed money from them to put down more cash. If the customer could not pay, the broker sold the stock, keeping the proceeds as repayment for the loan.

The Beginning of the End

By the summer of 1929, brokers had lent out more than $6 billion in margin loans to their customers. Realizing that the huge number of people investing in the stock market meant the market was saturated, a few investors began to sell, and stock prices slowly declined in the autumn of 1929. Brokers began calling in their margins. Many investors did not have cash to pay for their stocks, so brokers were forced to sell. Enforced selling pushed prices down further. Noticing the downturn, other investors began selling their stock in panic. Amid the flood of unmet margin calls and the deluge of panic selling, the crash gained speed and force.

By the last week in October, the bottom fell out of the stock market. Stocks tumbled even further in November. In a few months the prices of major stocks fell 75 percent. People who had been millionaires suddenly were deep in debt.

Stock market investors, however, were not the only people brought down by the crash. Many banks had lent their cash reserves to stockbrokers. The brokers lost the money when their customers could not respond to the margin calls and failed to repay their loans. Because savings deposits were not federally insured, people who had prudently tucked their money in banks found their savings had vanished. Thus, the stock market crash caught millions of innocent bystanders in the financial crunch.

The Onset of the Depression

In the first few months after the crash, business leaders and economists spoke confidently, predicting a quick recovery. In December 1929, Secretary of the Treasury Andrew Mellon announced, "I see nothing in the present situation that is either menacing or warrants pessimism." As the new decade dawned, however, the United States fell into a deep business depression that spread to almost all nations.

A period of severely reduced economic activity, known as a **depression,** is characterized by a sharp rise in **unemployment** as people lose their jobs and are unable to find new ones. The depression that began in October 1929 was the most devastating economic downturn in the nation's history. Raging through most of the 1930s, this sickening decline became known as the Great Depression.

The Causes of the Great Depression

Weaknesses in the Economy

After the crash, the economy began to unravel. Economists then saw flaws few had noticed during the get-rich-quick era of the mid-1920s. Each weakness in the economy contributed to the Depression.

Depressed Farms and Industries

The shiny glow of prosperity had not rubbed off on all Americans in the 1920s. Farmers' incomes fell throughout the decade. The textile, lumber, mining, and railroad industries also declined. In the months preceding the crash, the automobile and construction industries

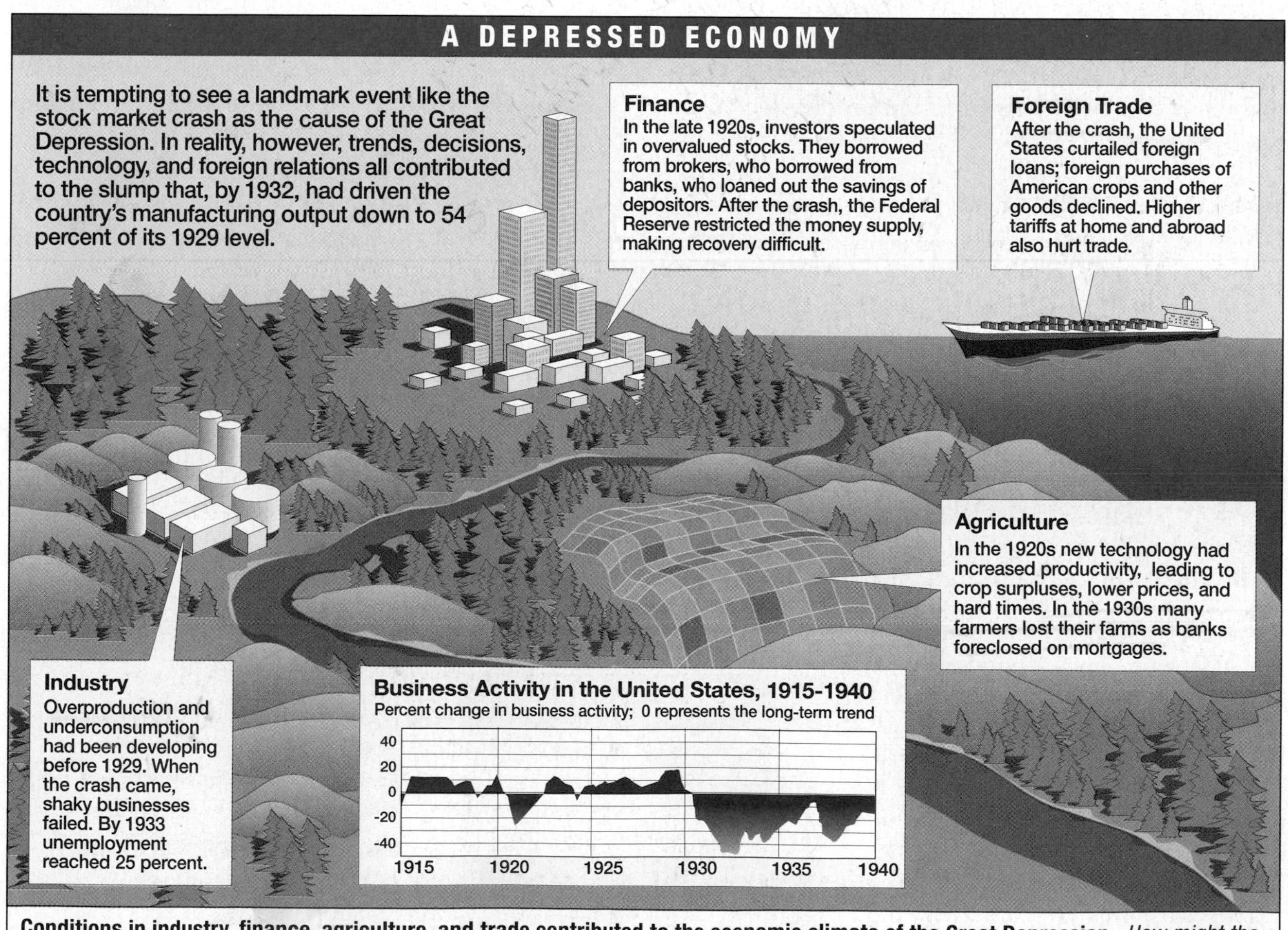

A DEPRESSED ECONOMY
It is tempting to see a landmark event like the stock market crash as the cause of the Great Depression. In reality, however, trends, decisions, technology, and foreign relations all contributed to the slump that, by 1932, had driven the country's manufacturing output down to 54 percent of its 1929 level.
Finance
In the late 1920s, investors speculated in overvalued stocks. They borrowed from brokers, who borrowed from banks, who loaned out the savings of depositors. After the crash, the Federal Reserve restricted the money supply, making recovery difficult.
Foreign Trade
After the crash, the United States curtailed foreign loans; foreign purchases of American crops and other goods declined. Higher tariffs at home and abroad also hurt trade.
Agriculture
In the 1920s new technology had increased productivity, leading to crop surpluses, lower prices, and hard times. In the 1930s many farmers lost their farms as banks foreclosed on mortgages.
Industry
Overproduction and underconsumption had been developing before 1929. When the crash came, shaky businesses failed. By 1933 unemployment reached 25 percent.
Business Activity in the United States, 1915-1940
Percent change in business activity; 0 represents the long-term trend
40
20
0
-20
-40
1915
1920
1925
1930
1935
1940

Conditions in industry, finance, agriculture, and trade contributed to the economic climate of the Great Depression. *How might the decline in industrial production have affected the agricultural surplus? How might the decline in the amount of money in circulation have affected industrial production?*

suffered from a decrease in orders. As a result, wages dropped and employers laid off workers. With their incomes cut, many farmers and workers could not afford the manufactured goods that the nation's industries had been churning out in the 1920s. This underconsumption became a weakness in the economy.

Wealth Distribution

Another factor contributing to the underconsumption that fueled the Depression was the growing gap in wealth between rich people and Americans of more ordinary means. Although business profits in many industries rose throughout the 1920s, not all workers received much of these profits. This reduced consumer buying power. By the late 1920s, radios, telephones, refrigerators, washing machines, and other goods were piling up in warehouses across the country.

Monetary Policy

Inept monetary policy also contributed to the crash—and then to the Depression's severity and length. After the crash the Federal Reserve System, charged with regulating the amount of money in circulation, followed a restrictive policy that dried up credit. This policy left the country with a supply of money in circulation that was not large enough to allow the economy to bounce back after the stock market bubble burst.

Decline in Foreign Trade

Weaknesses in the American economy also sapped the strength of foreign economies, some of which were already unstable. Throughout the 1920s the United States served as a bank for other nations, lending money to aid foreign industries and speed recovery from the Great War. During the late 1920s, however, as Americans began pouring borrowed money into the stock market, bank funds for loans to other nations dried up. International trade slowed down because, without American loans, other nations had less money to spend on our nation's goods. High tariffs—taxes on imported products—further blocked international trade. This decline fed into the cycle of underconsumption, weakening the American economy even more.

After the stock market crash, all these problems with the economy began to take their toll. The economic slowdown frightened everyone, from East Coast executives to Midwestern store owners, from Utah miners to the President of the United States.

Hoover's Response

Voluntary and Local Action Fail

Herbert C. Hoover occupied the White House when the Depression began. Nicknamed the Great Engineer, Hoover was elected President by a wide margin in 1928. Orphaned at age 8, he left his Iowa home to move in with relatives in Oregon. Although his early childhood was sad, in young adulthood Hoover buried unhappiness with driving ambition. He graduated from Stanford University in 1895 with an engineering degree. For the next 18 years he worked on engineering projects all over the world, building an unshakable reputation for solving technical problems and amassing a personal fortune.

Hoover's Quaker upbringing gave him a strong desire to serve humanity. After the outbreak of World War I, he coordinated war relief efforts in Europe and

★ ★ ★ Gallery of Presidents ★ ★ ★

Herbert C. Hoover

1929–1933

"Ours is a land rich in resources; stimulating in its glorious beauty; filled with millions of happy homes; blessed with comfort and opportunity. . . . No country is more loved by its people. I have an abiding faith in their capacity, integrity, and high purpose. I have no fears for the future of our country. It is bright with hope."

Inaugural Address, March 4, 1929

HERBERT HOOVER PRESIDENTIAL LIBRARY-MUSEUM

Background

- **Born 1874; Died 1964**
- **Republican, Iowa**
- **Headed the Commission for Relief in Belgium 1914–1917**
- **Secretary of Commerce 1921–1928**

Achievements in Office

- **Federal Farm Board (1929)**
- **Smoot-Hawley Tariff Act (1930)**
- **Reconstruction Finance Corporation (1932)**

food production in the United States. Efficient and successful, Hoover inspired confidence. He quickly rose as an important political figure. President Harding appointed him secretary of commerce in 1921.

From this influential post, Hoover tried to put into practice his vision for the United States. He encouraged voluntary associations of business leaders to eliminate inefficiency in industry. He suggested that federal, state, and local governments coordinate efforts to dampen harmful swings in the business cycle. With these and other measures, Hoover was sure that the United States in 1928 was "nearer to the final triumph over poverty than ever before in the history of any land." His optimism and confidence matched the mood of the country and won him the presidency.

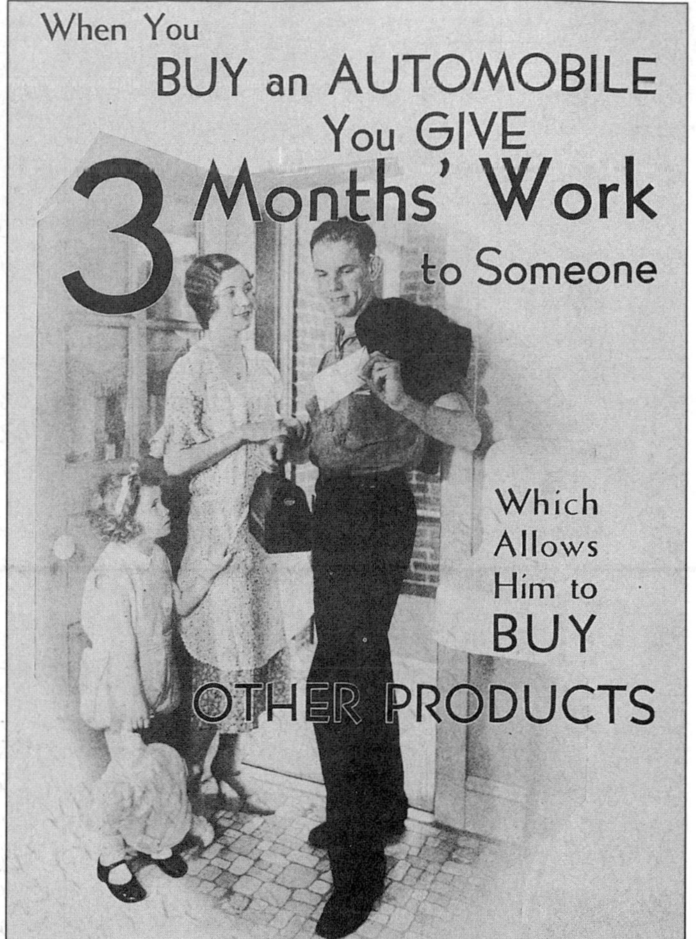

PHOTO COURTESY OF HALBERT F. SPEER

Wishful Thinking **Auto companies urged Americans to help the economy by spending money—money that most Americans did not have.** *In what ways did Hoover's efforts to end the Depression fall short?*

Initial Reaction to the Depression

Only months after Hoover made that prediction, the stock market crashed. Realizing that people's plummeting faith in the economy hindered chances of recovery, Hoover tried to bolster confidence. "We have now passed the worst," he told Americans in May 1930, "and . . . shall rapidly recover."

Even with his optimistic pronouncements, the President took immediate action to try to arrest the economic downturn. Following his own faith in voluntary action, he called a meeting of business leaders and asked them to pledge not to cut wages or production of goods. He suggested that city and state governments stimulate their local economies by funding building projects to provide new jobs.

Hoover also funneled aid to farmers through the Agricultural Marketing Act, which Congress had passed even before the economy began to weaken in the aftermath of the crash. Through this legislation, the federal government established the Farm Board, which lent money to farmers to help them set up cooperative marketing associations. Farmers who joined these associations agreed to sell their crops as a group. If they could not get the prices they wanted at the time of the harvest, they would store their crops until prices rose.

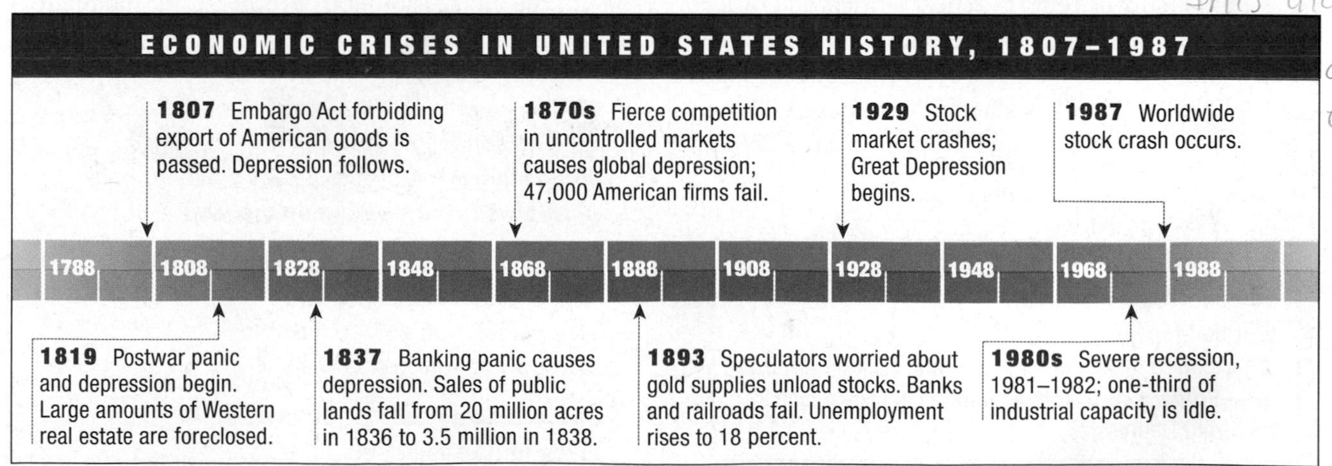

ECONOMIC CRISES IN UNITED STATES HISTORY, 1807–1987
1807 Embargo Act forbidding export of American goods is passed. Depression follows.
1870s Fierce competition in uncontrolled markets causes global depression; 47,000 American firms fail.
1929 Stock market crashes; Great Depression begins.
1987 Worldwide stock crash occurs.
1788 1808 1828 1848 1868 1888 1908 1928 1948 1968 1988
1819 Postwar panic and depression begin. Large amounts of Western real estate are foreclosed.
1837 Banking panic causes depression. Sales of public lands fall from 20 million acres in 1836 to 3.5 million in 1838.
1893 Speculators worried about gold supplies unload stocks. Banks and railroads fail. Unemployment rises to 18 percent.
1980s Severe recession, 1981–1982; one-third of industrial capacity is idle.

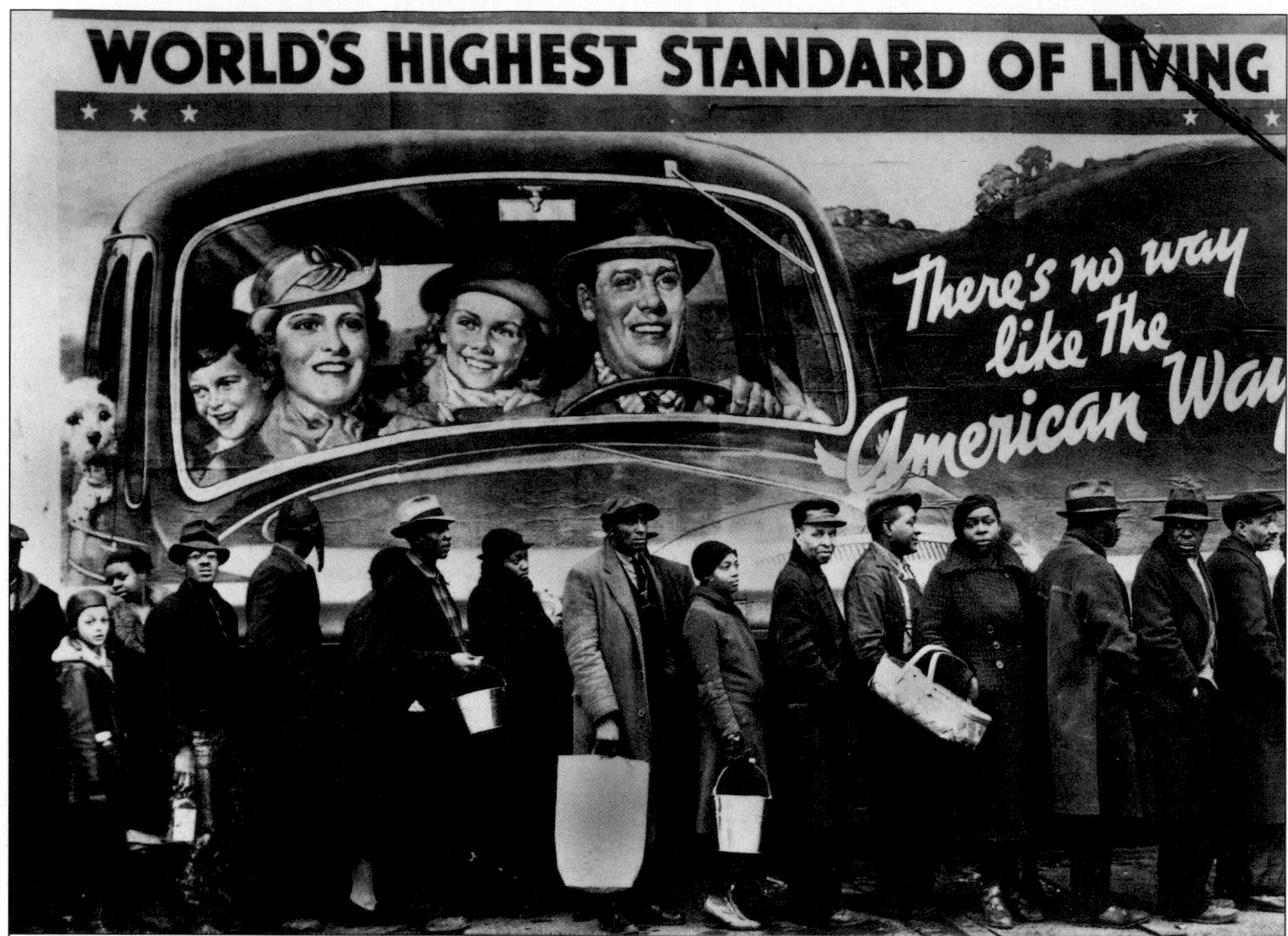

WORLD'S HIGHEST STANDARD OF LIVING
There's no way like the American Way

MARGARET BOURKE-WHITE/LIFE MAGAZINE, ©1937 TIME INC.

Natural Disaster **Margaret Bourke-White, one of the four original staff photographers for *Life* magazine, took this photograph at a flood relief station in Louisville, Kentucky, in 1937.** *What examples of irony do you see in this photo?*

Voluntary marketing associations might, in time, have raised crop prices. Many farmers, however, needed immediate help paying the mortgages on their land. The Farm Board was not authorized to lend money to individual farmers, so thousands of families went bankrupt in the early 1930s, losing their jobs and their homes.

The Depression Deepens

Despite Hoover's efforts to help farmers and others, business conditions in the United States worsened in the 2 years after the crash. About 23,000 businesses failed in 1929. In 1932, 32,000 businesses went under. The average family's annual income dropped from $2,300 in 1929 to $1,600 in 1935. Unemployment rose from about 5 percent in 1929 to almost 25 percent in 1932.

The early 1930s saw mounting poverty and destitution. In major cities bread lines stretched for blocks, as people waited for one scant meal a day.

E.Y. (Yip) Harburg, a song lyricist, captured the prevailing mood of desperation and shock at the time. Harburg wrote the words to the most famous song of the Depression era, "Brother, Can You Spare a Dime?"

HISTORY Online

Student Web Activity 13

Visit the *American Odyssey* Web site at americanodyssey.glencoe.com and click on ***Chapter 13—Student Web Activities*** for an activity relating to the Great Depression.

They used to tell me I was building a dream,
And so I followed the mob—
When there was earth to plow or guns to bear
I was always there—right on the job.

They used to tell me I was building a dream
With peace and glory ahead—
Why should I be standing on line
Just waiting for bread?

Once I built a railroad, made it run,
Made it run against time.

Once I built a railroad,
Now it's done—
Brother, can you spare a dime?

Once I built a tower, to the sun.
Brick and rivet and lime,
Once I built a tower,
Now it's done—
Brother, can you spare a dime?

Once in khaki suits,
Gee we looked swell,
Full of that Yankee Doodle-de-dum
Half a million boots went sloggin' through Hell,
I was the kid with the drum.

Say don't you remember, they called me Al—
It was Al all of the time.
Say don't you remember I'm your pal—
Buddy, can you spare a dime?

—E.Y. Harburg,
"Brother, Can You Spare a Dime?"

Bands played this song in 1930 and 1931. During the 1932 presidential campaign, the Republicans tried to discourage the radio networks from broadcasting it, but the song had already impressed voters.

Ironically, Harburg also wrote one of the decade's optimistic songs, "Somewhere Over the Rainbow." He himself saw the Depression as a release from the business world. With the downward economic trend came a change of ideals that he deemed positive:

With the Crash, I realized that the greatest fantasy of all was business. The only realistic way of making a living was versifying. Living off your imagination.

We thought American business was the Rock of Gibraltar. We were the prosperous nation, and nothing could stop us now. A brownstone house was forever. You gave it to your kids and they put marble fronts on it. There was a feeling of continuity. If you made it, it was there forever. Suddenly the big dream exploded. The impact was unbelievable.

—E.Y. Harburg, in *Hard Times* by Studs Terkel

With the number of unemployed growing every month, charity funds soon proved inadequate. Toledo, Ohio, could afford to spend only 2 cents per relief meal per day. New York City gave only $2.39 per week to each family on relief. Thousands of people were turned away. The Federal Reserve compounded the problem by squandering chances to rescue the collapsing banking system.

With poverty pressing down on them, some people wrote President Hoover in anger and frustration:

Why should we hafto . . . have foodless days . . . and our children have Schoolless days and Shoclcss days and the land full of plenty and Banks bursting with money? Why does Every Thing have Exceptional Value Except the Human being? Why are we reduced to poverty and starving and anxiety and Sorrow So quickly under your administration?

—Robert S. .McElvaine,
Down & Out in the Great Depression

Too Little Too Late

Discontent Continues to Rise

Facing such harsh criticism, Hoover reluctantly introduced new government programs to deal with the economic crisis. He still insisted that voluntary action and local programs were the best ways to relieve the Depression. By early 1932, however, he had to admit that these measures had failed.

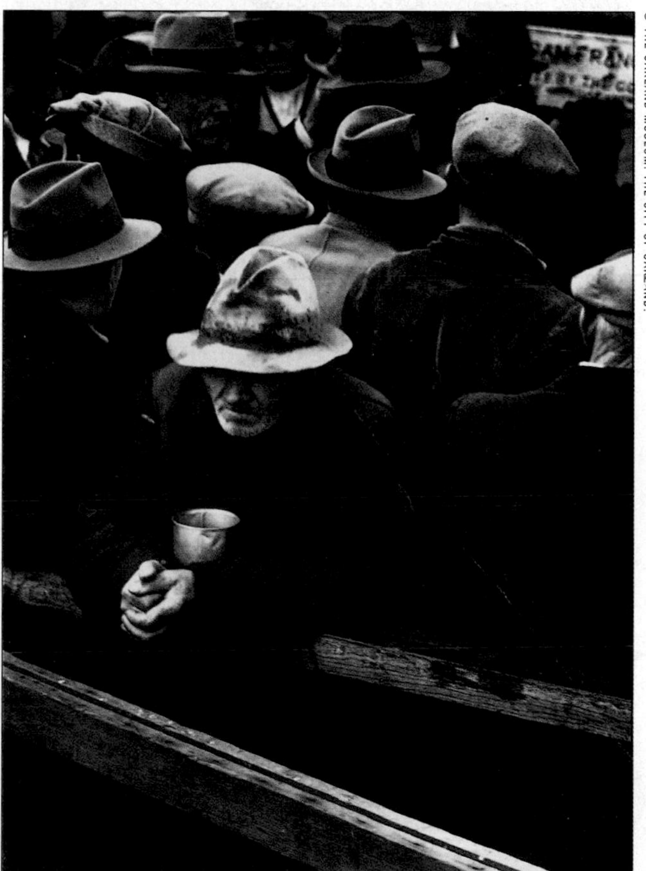

"Why should I be standing on line?" Dorothea Lange described "White Angel Bread Line" as her most famous photograph and added that life for people in 1932 had begun to crumble on the edges. *According to Yip Harburg's lyrics, what might some of these men have done before the Depression?*

Trying to respond to the deepening economic crisis, Hoover obtained congressional approval for a federal relief agency called the Reconstruction Finance Corporation (RFC) in February 1932. The RFC was the largest federal program of economic aid that any President had ever proposed. The agency was authorized to dispense $2 billion in loans to faltering banks, insurance companies, and railroads. Hoover hoped that the RFC would inspire confidence in business. The theory was that funding such institutions would stimulate industry and eventually create more jobs.

The trickle-down measure, however, could not relieve the immediate suffering of the unemployed. The Emergency Relief Act, passed in July 1932, enabled the RFC to distribute an additional $300 million in loans to state governments for unemployment relief. These governments did not qualify for RFC loans, however, unless they were on the verge of bankruptcy. By the end of the year, the RFC had distributed only half of its available money.

Mounting Protests

With wages dropping, unemployment growing, and so little money trickling into relief measures, resentment grew among people beaten down by the Depression. One group, veterans of the Great War, organized a massive lobbying effort to get aid for themselves and their families. The government had promised these veterans a bonus for serving in the war, payable in 1945. Organizing themselves into disciplined companies, a group of jobless veterans from Portland, Oregon, traveled to Washington, D.C., in May 1932 to try to persuade Congress to grant them their bonus 13 years early. The bonus army, as this group was called, enforced strict rules to keep the movement united and respectable. Among these rules were "no panhandling, no drinking, and no radicalism."

The group from Portland started with 1,000 veterans. By the time Congress was to vote on the bonus in June, the ranks of the bonus army had swelled to 17,000. Setting up camp in abandoned buildings in Washington, D.C., and on the marshy flats along the shores of the Anacostia River, the veterans remained orderly. Many veterans had brought their families with them. Wives set up housekeeping while the children made new friends from all over the country.

On June 17, the day the Senate was slated to vote on the bonus bill, the veterans marched to the Capitol steps to await the outcome. Late in the afternoon, Senator Elmer Thomas of Oklahoma appeared on the Capitol steps and told the leader of the group, Walter W. Waters, that the bill had been defeated. As the men began to hiss and boo, Waters took charge: "Let us show them that we can take it on the chin. Let us show them that we are patriotic Americans. I call on you to sing 'America.'" Thousands of the men joined in singing and then formed ranks and marched back to their camps.

With the bonus bill dead, several thousand veterans left Washington. About 2,000 remained throughout the month, however, hoping that the bill would be revived before the congressional session ended in July. After Congress again refused to approve the bonus bill, the veterans slowly began to disperse. They did not leave quickly enough for Hoover, however, who saw the bonus army as a hostile force. On July 28, Hoover dispatched Army Chief of Staff Douglas MacArthur and his aide

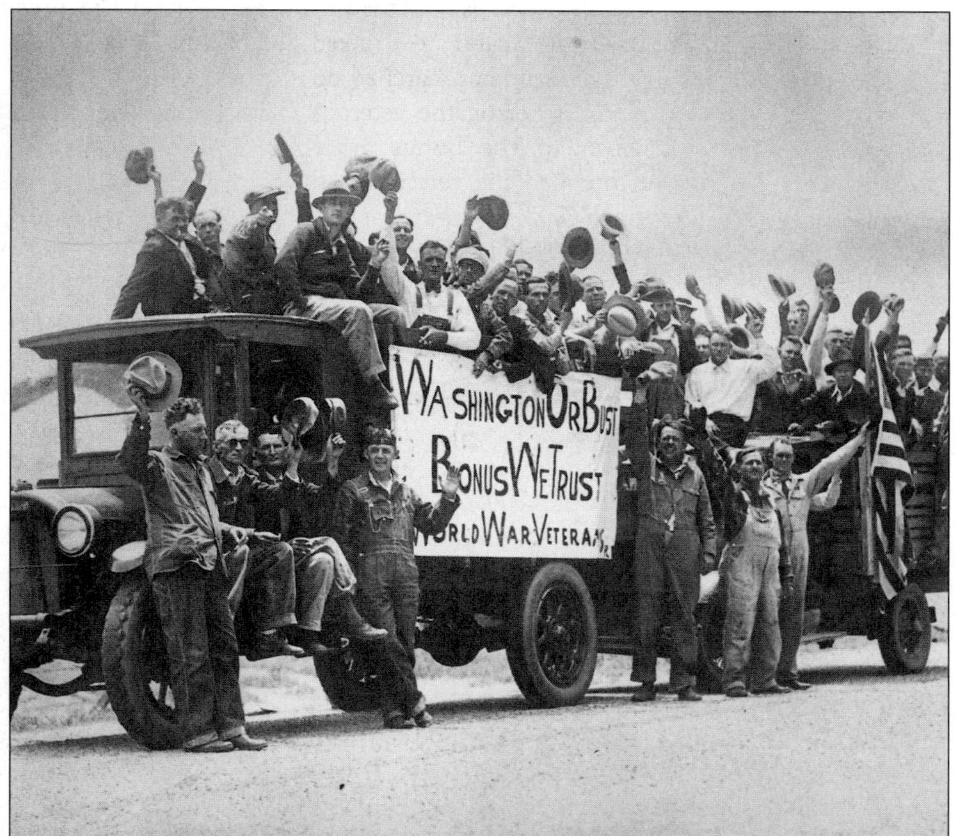

AP/WIDE WORLD PHOTOS

The Bonus Army **Led by Walter W. Waters, veterans of World War I marched peacefully from Portland, Oregon, to Washington, D.C., to lobby for early payment of their promised benefits.** *How was the military training of these men reflected in their protest?*

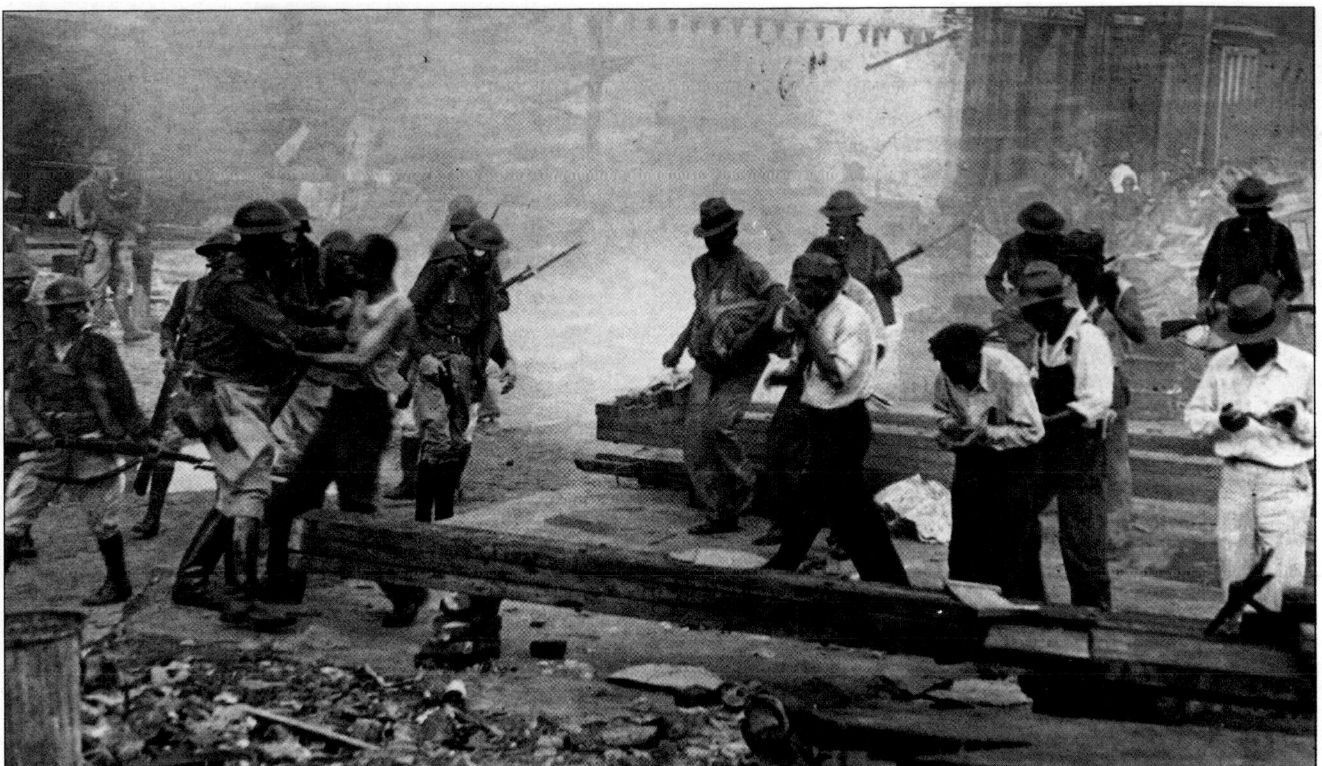

WIDE WORLD

Hostile Reception **Bonus-seeking veterans were attacked by soldiers near the veterans' makeshift shacks in the Anacostia Flats, approximately three miles from the White House.** *How did Hoover respond to the bonus army?*

Dwight D. Eisenhower to clear the veterans from the federal buildings. Cavalry units, tanks, infantry with fixed bayonets, and a machine-gun detachment marched on the unarmed veterans. Fleeing in terror, the veterans crossed the Anacostia River to the bonus army encampments. MacArthur pursued the veterans and torched the camp. More than 100 people were injured and a baby died, asphyxiated by tear gas. The press, appalled at the brutal attack, commented: "What a pitiful spectacle is that of the great American Government, mightiest in the world, chasing unarmed men, women, and children with Army tanks."

The Election of 1932

The routing of the bonus army was the last nail in Hoover's political coffin. The public, which already considered the President cold and unfeeling because he refused to pay for unemployment relief, now saw him also as a vicious bully. On hearing about the attack on the veterans at Anacostia by MacArthur's troops, Democratic presidential candidate Franklin D. Roosevelt turned to his friend Felix Frankfurter and said, "Well, Felix, this will elect me."

Roosevelt's prediction proved correct. Hoover stayed in Washington through most of the campaign. When he did make public appearances, he was often booed into retreat. On Election Day, on his way to vote, people hurling stink bombs attacked his car. Roosevelt won the presidency by a landslide. Herbert Hoover, for all of his early optimism and organizational skills, was defeated by the Depression and its crushing economic problems.

Section Assessment

Main Idea

1. Use a diagram like this one to show the immediate and underlying causes of the stock market crash of 1929.

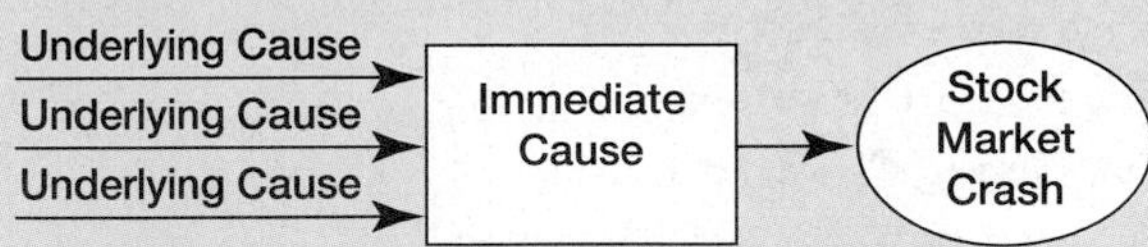

Vocabulary

2. Define: stock, speculation, margin, depression, unemployment.

Checking Facts

3. Describe Hoover's approach to the Depression.

4. What was the Bonus Army?

Critical Thinking

5. Determining Cause and Effect Discuss the major causes of the Depression.

SPORTS: Babe Ruth of the New York Yankees hits 500th home run.

One Day in History

Tuesday, October 29, 1929

MARKET BASKET

Here is where a dollar will go:

Average cost to produce a Hollywood film . . . $360,000
One-year subscription to a survey of best stocks . . $65
Double room at the Lexington Hotel, N.Y.C. . . $5
Dinner at a Hollywood restaurant $1.50

W.L. HAMILTON/SUPERSTOCK

Studebaker automobile . . . . $1,185–$2,350
Boston to New York one way via rail or boat $4
Movie ticket . . . . 25¢–75¢
Phonograph record . . . . . 50¢
Bottle of Moxie . . . . . 9¢ small . . . . 15¢ large
Daily local newspaper . . . . 2¢

ARCHIVE PHOTOS

Pair of shoes . . . . $2–$5
One dozen oranges . . . . . . 39¢
Loaf of bread . . . . 9¢
One pound of ham . . . . . . 50¢

ARCHIVE PHOTOS

Panic Looms Large: Today's stock market activity caused so much chaos and confusion that analysts are already calling the day "Black Tuesday."

Stocks Hit the Skids

Market sees biggest losses yet

NEW YORK—Trading in record numbers today on the New York Stock Exchange, investors rushed to sell. Despite last week's optimism and the efforts of bankers to pump money into the market, today's activity brought the panic that everyone had feared since Thursday's crash. On the brink of ruin, investors collectively unloaded 16,338,000 shares. By the end of the day, prices had plummeted $14 billion.

One man on the street was overheard muttering to himself, "Don't tell me it's going up. It's down and it's going down. It will never go up again." A New York drugstore owner reports leaving his store because of "hysterical demands for sleeping potions, sedatives, and other nerve potions." On Broadway, a young marketeer was seen unsuccessfully hawking his $12,000 Duesenberg automobile for $1,500 in cash.

Meanwhile, rumors say that John D. Rockefeller, Jr., has been quietly liquidating his stocks for weeks.

NATION: Madame Curie visits White House to receive America's gift of $50,000. The money will buy a gram of radium for cancer research.

AP/WIDE WORLD PHOTOS

Byrd Explores the South Pole

LITTLE AMERICA, Antarctica—Commander Richard E. Byrd has built an air base at his Little America camp on the Ross Ice Shelf. From here he plans to fly over the South Pole, matching his feat of being the first to fly over the North Pole. His party is currently exploring by snowmobile, and fighting frostbite.

AP/WIDE WORLD PHOTOS

Commander Richard E. Byrd

THE CARSON COLLECTION

MUSIC

Popular Songs of 1929:

"Stardust" by Hoagy Carmichael, Mitchell Parish

"St. James Infirmary" by Joe Primrose

"Honeysuckle Rose" by Fats Waller, Andy Razaf

"Ain't Misbehavin'" by Fats Waller

RADIO

Premieres:

- ***The Back Home Hour***
- ***The Fleischmann Hour* (with Rudy Vallee)**
- ***The Rise of the Goldbergs***
- ***The Hour of Charm* (with Phil Spitalny and his all-girl orchestra)**

Wisecracking, roughhousing Marx Brothers complete their first film, *The Cocoanuts.* Filming takes place between performances of their current Broadway hit, *Animal Crackers.*

Happy Days?

HOLLYWOOD—By bizarre coincidence, the Casa Loma Orchestra recorded a new tune today heralding cheerful times. The song, "Happy Days Are Here Again," couldn't have come at a more needed time, but the lyrics just don't ring true on this unhappy day. Milton Ager and Jack Yellen wrote the tune for the film *Chasing Rainbows.*

$5 Down! 52 Weeks to Pay!

Trade in your old radio or Victrola for $20–$75 toward a *NEW* Jackson-Bell radio!

"Peter Pan" model: $85.00

© 1995 CLASSIC PIO PARTNERS

The Dream on Hold

APRIL 14, 1935: DUST STORM SOCKS MEADE COUNTY, KANSAS

UPI/BETTMANN NEWSPHOTOS

Black Blizzard
Lifting topsoil from a farmer's wheat fields, this dust storm obscures the sun's light.

One person thought that life itself was coming to an end. Another was sure that Judgment Day had arrived. A third simply brought her rocking chair to the center of her living room and waited out the storm. She was content because the tape over her window frames was blocking out almost every particle of dust. She boasted that under such conditions "almost any housewife could have died happily."

On Sunday, April 14, 1935, one of the biggest dust storms of this century swept over the Great Plains of the United States. Huge black clouds of dust, more than 1,000 feet (304.8 m) high, formed a wall miles wide. Birds flew frantically trying to escape suffocation in the roiling storm. Motorists were stranded for hours along the highway, totally blinded by the impenetrable cloud. The rain sent mud balls splattering to the ground. Dust from the "black blizzard" piled up on railroad lines, and it took snowplows several days to clear off the tracks.

Dust storms like these plagued the Great Plains during the drought years of 1932 to 1939. Especially hard hit were the Dakotas, Nebraska, Kansas, Oklahoma, eastern Colorado and New Mexico, and the Texas Panhandle. Burying crops and killing livestock, the natural disasters of dust storms and drought worked in tandem with the economic disaster of the Depression to bring thousands of farmers to financial ruin. Although Dust Bowl farmers were among the hardest hit, farmers throughout the country suffered severe hardship during the Depression.

Guide to Reading

Main Idea

The worsening Depression affected all Americans, but farmers and unemployed urban workers were among the hardest hit, both economically and psychologically.

Vocabulary

- foreclosure
- penny auction
- repatriation

Read to Find Out . . .

- how the Depression affected people differently in rural and urban areas.
- the ways communities responded to the sudden arrival of hard times.
- how men, women, and families were each affected differently by the economy.

On the Farms

From Foreclosures to Migration

Heading into their second decade of economic depression, farmers received severely low prices for their crops. Falling incomes made it impossible for many to pay their mortgages. A bank that held an unpaid farm loan would have a **foreclosure,** whereby it would take back ownership of the property without letting the farmer pay off the rest of the mortgage. In the early years of the Depression, thousands of farmers lost their land. As the Depression deepened, however, some of the farmers thought of their own inventive ways to get around their financial problems. One Iowan recalled how farmers connived to resist the foreclosures by the banks, saying, "[The] mortgaging of farms was getting home to us. . . . [The bankers would] put up a farmer's property and have a sale." He continued:

> All the neighbors'd come in, and they got the idea of spending twenty-five cents for a horse. They was paying ten cents for a plow. And when it was all over, they'd all give it [the property] back to him [the farmer being foreclosed upon]. It was legal and anybody that bid against that thing, that was trying to get that man's land, they would be dealt with seriously, as it were.
>
> —Harry Terrell, in *Hard Times*

Penny auctions—staged sales of property for pennies to friends, who simply returned it later—helped some farmers stay on their land. Borrowing money from relatives saved the farms of others. On the drought-ridden plains, however, where for seven successive years crops were pulverized, thousands of farmers had no choice but to abandon their fields. The Okies, as these Great Plains farmers were called, headed west in search of a better life for themselves and their families.

Migration of the Okies

The plight of the Okies dramatized that of the desperately unemployed throughout the United States. They exhausted any savings they had. They sacrificed everything they owned except what they could carry with them. Uprooted, the Okies drifted anywhere they thought they might have a chance to find work. California, with its huge farms, lured many. Leaflets advertising jobs for seasonal work drew them onward, across the highways. A writer late in the 1930s described it this way:

> They came along U.S. Highway 30 through the Idaho hills, along Highway 66 across New Mexico and Arizona, along the Old Spanish Trail through El Paso, along all the other westward trails. They came in decrepit, square-shouldered 1925 Dodges and 1927 La Salles; in battered 1923 Model-T Fords that looked like relics of some antique culture; in trucks piled high with mattresses and cooking utensils and children, with suitcases, jugs, and sacks strapped to the running boards.
>
> —Frederick Lewis Allen, *Since Yesterday*

When they reached California, the Okies were in for even more hard times. Although a few jobs were

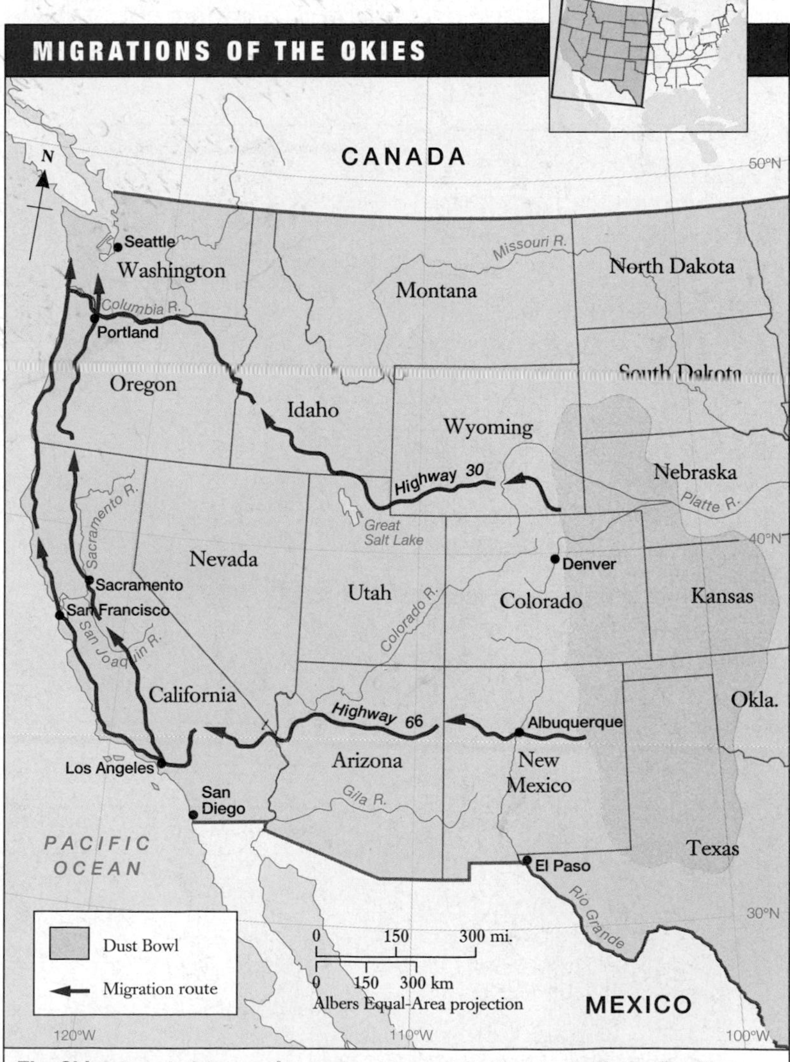

The Okies traveled two major routes to reach California. Both the Rockies and the Sierra Nevadas lay between the Dust Bowl and the West Coast. *At what points did these routes diverge or connect?*

available, competition for those jobs was fierce. With Okies entering the state by the hundreds daily, the number of unemployed in the labor market quickly skyrocketed. Yet, bouncing down rutted roads, driven by hope and false rumor, the Okies still kept coming. For the California farm owners, the migration of the Okies was a boon. The owners could lower wages nearly to starvation levels and still find takers for the most wretched of jobs. Huddled on the outskirts of farm towns, luckless Okies without employment set up temporary camps. People living within the towns often saw these unemployed as dirty, ignorant outsiders and sent the police to dislodge them. Bitter and dispirited, the Okies continued their migration, wandering up and down the West Coast, searching for a lucky break.

Tenant Farmers

The farm crisis of the 1930s also hit tenant farmers, most of whom lived in the South. Tenant farmers did not own the land that they farmed. Therefore they were extremely vulnerable to changes in the farm economy during the thirties.

As the Depression dragged on, the government began to pay landowners to let some of their land lie fallow, or go unplanted. This reduced surplus crops, causing prices for those remaining crops to rise. Most landowners decided to take out of production the land their tenant farmers used rather than the land they used. Tenant farmers lost their jobs and were also thrown off the land where some had worked and lived for many years. Also, as landowners used their government checks to buy farm equipment such as tractors and cultivators, they no longer needed year-round farmhands. Instead, they would hire a few day laborers on a temporary basis for the essential seasonal work.

The following letter, from a Georgia farmer to a government relief official, highlights the tenant farmers' situation:

> I have Bin farming all my life. But the man I live with Has Turned me loose taking my mule [and] all my feed. . . . I have 7 in my family. I ploud up cotton last yeare. I can rent 9 acres and plant. . . . But I haven't got a mule [or] no feed.
>
> —From a letter to Harry Hopkins

UPI/BETTMANN

Sharecroppers These former farmers of Caruthersville, Missouri, have been evicted and are forced to move on. *What made a tenant farmer so vulnerable?*

Evicted from the farms, with little hope of finding work with other landowners, tenant farmers and their families took to the roads to look for work, often leaving behind many possessions of a lifetime. Since most of the African Americans living in the South had been tenant farmers, they suffered disproportionately from the upheaval in agriculture. However, white tenant farmers suffered severe hardship as well.

Mexican American Workers

The tenant farmers were not the only group who faced discrimination during the Depression. Mexican Americans, many of whose families had been in this country for several generations, found themselves branded illegal aliens, foreigners who had no right to live and work in the United States.

Although farm owners in California welcomed a surplus of Mexican and Mexican American migrant workers to help keep wages low during the harvest season, city officials wanted to send all people of Mexican descent back to Mexico. For example, between 1931 and 1934, Los Angeles officials rounded up more than 12,000 people of Mexican descent and forced them to return to Mexico. A number were United States citizens. Nevertheless, they were denied their legal rights and threatened with deportation if they refused to leave on their own. With no choice in the matter, many Mexican Americans gathered their belongings and boarded the government-sponsored trains that dumped them across the border.

Mexicans and Mexican Americans living in the Southwest and Texas also faced increased discrimination and threats of deportation during the Depression years. Many were agricultural workers caught in the crunch of the depressed farm economy of the United States. Out of work, they fled to the cities to apply for relief. Here, they were easy prey for immigration officials, who denied them fair hearings and summarily deported them. Seeing the hopelessness of the situation, many Mexican Americans decided to seek **repatriation,** or return to a former homeland, and they applied to the Mexican consulate for permission to return. In Austin, Texas, for example, 60 percent of all people of Mexican descent had returned to Mexico by January 1931.

In the City

Jobless, Homeless, and Penniless

The prospect for people without jobs was just as bleak in the cities as on the farms. By 1933 one of every four people was out of work. In some cities, however, the jobless rate soared above the national level. Unemployment ran 30 percent in Buffalo, 50 percent in Chicago and Cleveland, and 80 percent in Toledo.

Evidence of the economic crisis was clearly visible in most cities. "For Rent" notices festooned closed-down shop windows. Apple sellers hawked their wares on street corners. These unemployed men and women had bought

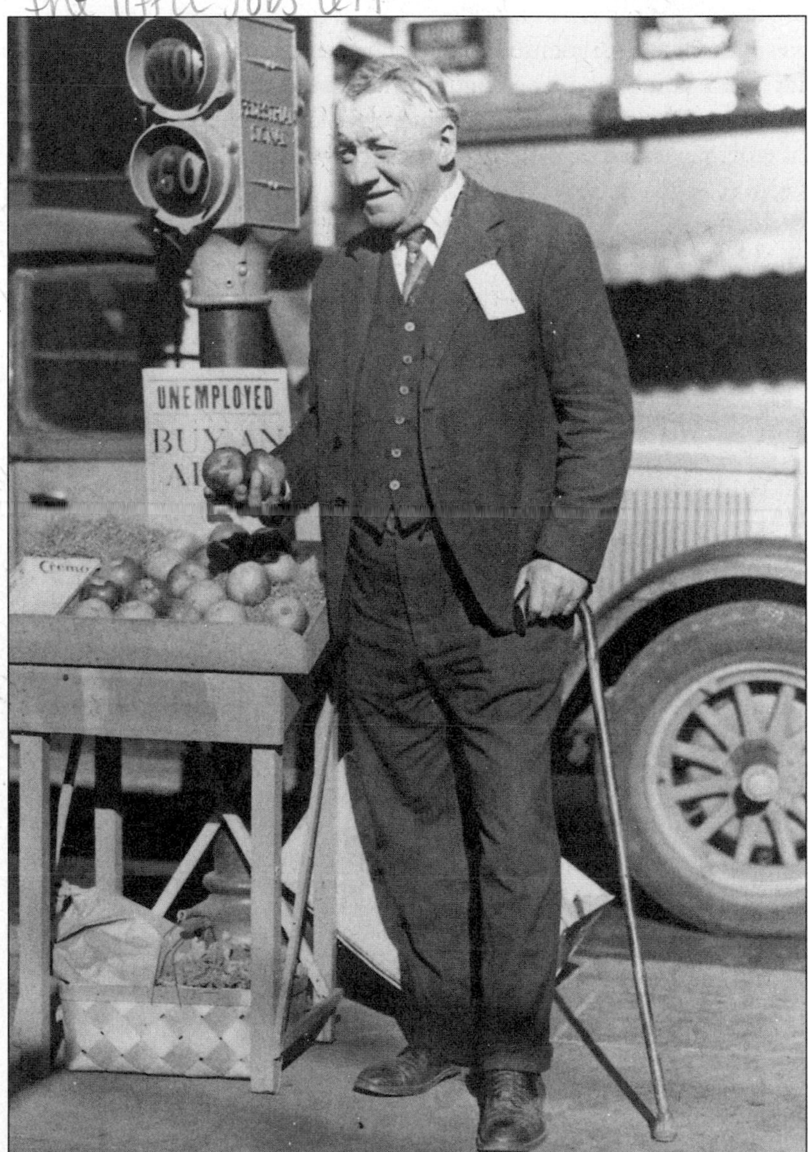

AP/WIDE WORLD PHOTOS

On Every Corner Fred Bell, known as "Champagne Fred" in San Francisco, had inherited a fortune in the 1920s, but in 1931 he joined the ranks selling apples on the street. *How did many people who had no money acquire bushels of produce to sell?*

surplus apples on credit from Pacific Coast apple growers and hoped to sell the fruit to passersby at a small profit. Those with less of an entrepreneurial spirit turned to panhandling. Beggars roved the sidewalks in most cities, accosting better-off citizens for spare change.

The most telling sign of the Depression, however, was the absence of activity. In the most depressed areas, factory smokestacks spewed no smoke. Loading docks received no deliveries. Construction sites were eerily silent, the skeletons of half-finished buildings rusting in the rain. Pedestrians slowed their pace. Time seemed to dawdle during the Depression years. This was especially true for the unemployed who had little but time on their hands.

Unemployed Workers

Despite promises to President Hoover to keep factories running full tilt, many factory owners began to lay off workers after a year or two of economic decline. The layoffs followed a pattern. African Americans and members of other minorities were usually the first to lose their jobs. Next, full-time employees were asked to share their jobs with others. Then, even these scaled-down jobs were cut. With wage reductions many working people were no better off than people who qualified for relief. In many cities the jobless and those with jobs became economic equals.

To reduce living expenses, people moved in with relatives. As many as 15 people would crowd into an apartment built for a couple or a family of 3. Evictions of renters who could not make their monthly payments were so common in some neighborhoods that children invented a new game based on their own experience:

> They would pile all the doll furniture up first in one corner and then in another. "We ain't got no money for the rent, so we's moved into a new house," a tot explained to the teacher. "Then we got the constable on us, so we's moving again."
>
> —Caroline Bird, *The Invisible Scar*

Just as these children adapted to their transient situation by making a game out of it, people from all levels of society had to adapt to immense changes and learn how to do without. People lost their jobs, their homes, most of their possessions, but still they survived. Among the saddest and most touching testaments to hu-

ARCHIVE PHOTOS

Living in Hoovervilles People called shantytown slums Hoovervilles, newspapers became Hoover blankets, and empty pockets turned inside out were Hoover flags. *What other makeshift plans did people devise when they faced losing their homes?*

man adaptability and survival were the makeshift cities that sprang up on the fringes of metropolitan areas. People sarcastically nicknamed these communities Hoovervilles.

Hoovervilles and the Homeless

During the early years of the Depression, the number of homeless people in the United States skyrocketed. Although no one ever took an official census, it was estimated that by 1932 about 2 million people were on the road, job seekers and their families looking for work and a place to settle. At least that many had constructed temporary or not-so-temporary shelters in Hoovervilles. One woman described her amazement when she first saw the sprawling Hooverville in Oklahoma City:

> Here were all these people living in old, rusted-out car bodies. I mean that was their home. There were people living in shacks made of orange crates. One family with a whole lot of kids were living in a piano box. This wasn't just a little section, this was maybe ten-miles wide and ten-miles long. People living in what ever they could junk together.
>
> —Peggy Terry, in *Hard Times*

For some, life on the Hooverville streets was squalid beyond belief. Garbage scraps were all these poor people could scrounge for food. For other people life was simple and pleasant. They kept their homes, however humble, sparkling clean and shared food with neighbors.

Helping others became a way of life, even among people who had not previously known each other. Those who did know each other often developed a trust that transcended the hard times. A young girl, orphaned during the Depression, remembered her friendship with the owners of a local grocery store.

> Louise was a Bohemian girl. Her mother had a grocery store that they lived behind. Louise used to do the books, and there was always owing. You never said to the people: "Do you have the money to pay me?" They would say, "Write it in the book." And you wrote it in the book, because this was their family food, and they had to have it. It wasn't that you were giving it away. Eventually, you'd be paid.
>
> —Dorothe Bernstein, in *Hard Times*

The Better-Off

Even relatively well-to-do people sometimes had to depend on the aid and charity of their neighbors during the Depression. For example, people who owned rental property did not qualify for food supplements in most city relief programs. Unable to collect rents, some landlords let their unemployed tenants stay on for free, and the tenants shared their food with the landlord.

Nevertheless, people who were wealthy before the Depression had much greater chances of weathering the economic storm and coming out with minimal financial damage. Such people might have had to sell a summer home or give up a vacation trip. They might have had to postpone buying a new car or forgo the latest fashions. Most were able to make ends meet, however, and live a comfortable, if less luxurious, life.

A handful of people took advantage of the rock-bottom prices brought on by the Depression to increase their wealth. For example, J. Paul Getty eventually became one of the richest men in the world by buying up oil companies at bargain prices during the 1930s. Such people were the exception.

For most Americans the loss of money and material possessions was not nearly as damaging as the sense of lost hope and pride brought on by years of unemployment or underemployment. These losses, along with changing roles and expectations, were most apparent within families.

In the Family

Making Do With Less

In many families the father—the traditional provider—lost status and self-esteem during the Depression. With loss of income, many men were no longer able to support their families or maintain their former lifestyles. Some hid out at home, discouraged, listless, and cranky. Others hit the pavement every day, hoping against hope to land a new job. Still others set themselves daily tasks to keep busy. One person remembered:

> My father spent two years painting his father's house. He painted it twice. It gave him something to do. It prevented him from losing all his—well, I wouldn't say self-respect, because there were many, many people who were also out of work. He wasn't alone.
>
> —Bob Leary, in *Hard Times*

The Woman's World

Women, traditionally taking the role of homemakers, suffered less upheaval throughout the Depression years. Their families came to depend on them even more during those lean years, because their efforts at economizing kept many families from starvation. Many

ARCHIVE PHOTOS

Women on the Job **In spite of rising unemployment, the number of women in the workforce increased.** *How did unemployment for men and women contribute to domestic upheaval?*

women revived traditional home crafts, such as canning vegetables, drying food, and sewing clothes. They started home industries, such as taking in laundry, selling baked goods, or renting out rooms to boarders. In many families not only did women run the household, but they also held a job outside the home.

Although women faced increasing discrimination in professional fields, jobs that traditionally went to women, such as clerical work and retail sales, did not decline as extensively as the professional and manufacturing jobs that traditionally went to men. Therefore, many job opportunities remained open to women, and the number of working women grew in the 1930s.

Growing Up in the Thirties

Domestic upheaval—unemployed fathers and mothers working long hours for low wages—took its toll on families. Many of the hoboes who hitchhiked across the country on freight trains were unemployed men who had at first set out in search of work in other parts of the country. Unsuccessful and ashamed to return home, they deserted their families and lived together in hobo camps along the side of the railroad tracks.

With other families hard times actually brought family members closer. Hope Moat's family, from Cincinnati, Ohio, lost everything during the Depression, and they had to split up. Hope's mother and brother went to live with her grandparents on their farm. Her father traveled in search of work, and Hope herself worked in town in exchange for board.

On weekends and holidays, I'd go traipsin' up to grandma's and we'd all be together, the whole family; and everybody played an instrument and we sang. We just got closer as a family during that time.

—Hope Moat, in *Making Do: How Women Survived the '30s* by Jeane Westin

Although some people came away from the Depression with an increased sense of inner strength or with stronger bonds to their family, for most the Depression was aptly named. It was a time of psychological and spiritual as well as economic depression. People stayed home and avoided socializing, ashamed of their worn clothes or their decline in fortune. Young people put off getting married, and married couples avoided having children. Undernourishment in children was common throughout the country. Milk consumption dropped in state after state. Economic factors shaped these choices, but so did a deep lack of hope and faith in the future. Everywhere, health officials reported that at the city and state levels child welfare and public nursing were usually the first services to be cut. During the 1930s deep despair entered the grain of American life. Some have called the Depression an invisible scar, one that, though unseen, would take many years to heal.

SECTION ASSESSMENT

Main Idea

1. Use a diagram like this one to compare the conditions faced by farmers and unemployed urban workers in the early 1930s.

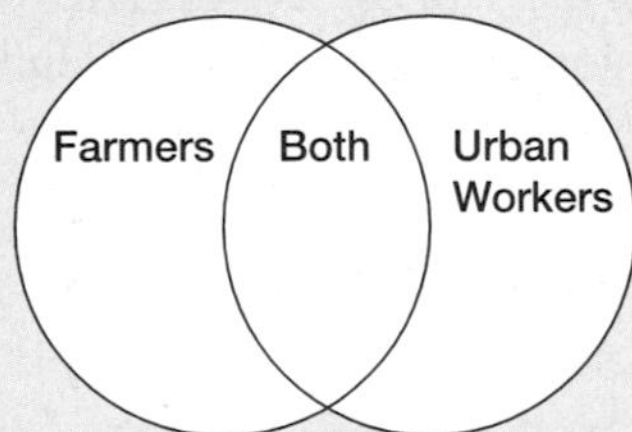

Vocabulary

2. Define: foreclosure, penny auction, repatriation.

Checking Facts

3. Why were the Hoovervilles established?
4. Discuss three ways the Depression affected women's roles in the family.

Critical Thinking

5. **Predicting Consequences** Discuss both the economic and the psychological effects of the Depression on a typical American family.

Technology Skill

USING E-MAIL

Learning the Skill

World leaders and ordinary citizens communicate over great distances all the time. *Telecommunications* refers to communication through the use of such equipment as a telephone, video, or computer. A computer is ready for telecommunications after two items are added to it. The first piece of equipment is a *modem.* A modem is a device that enables computers to communicate with each other through telephone lines. The second item is *communications software,* which lets your computer prepare and send information to the modem. This software also allows your computer to receive and understand the information it receives from the modem.

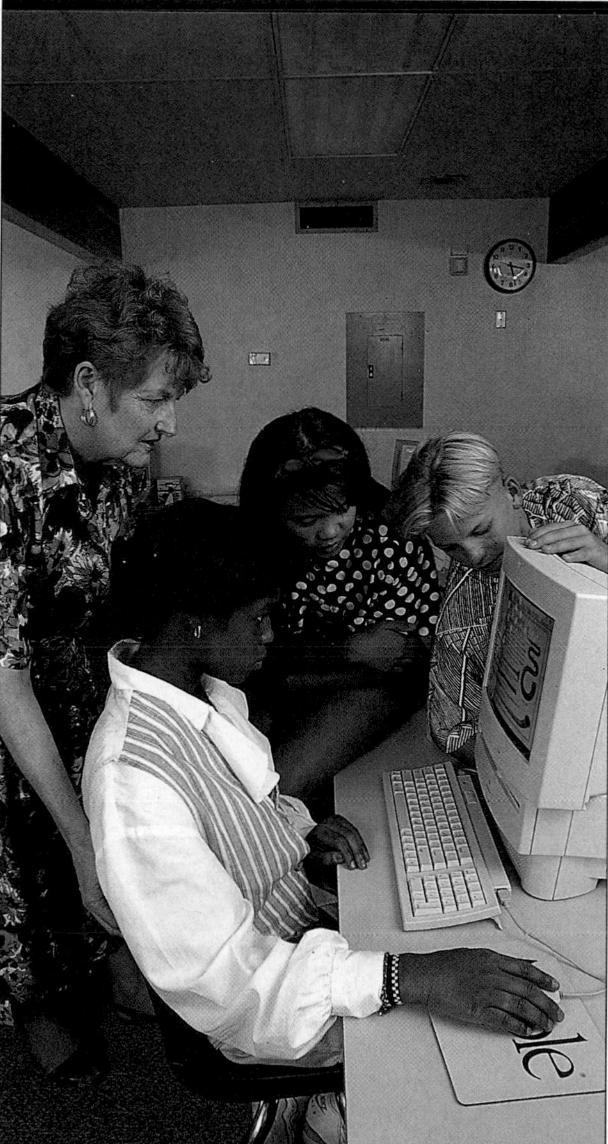
MARK BURNETT

Students using E-mail

Using E-Mail

Electronic mail, or E-mail, enables users to send and receive messages and data worldwide, to and from anyone connected to the Internet. By simply clicking a send button, a user immediately sends a message. The computer (called a server because it serves several other computers) for the *Internet Service Provider (ISP)* receives the message and stores it in an electronic "mailbox"; the message is available whenever the recipient chooses to retrieve it. If you are on an E-mail network, you have a specific address. This address identifies the location of your electronic "mailbox"—the place where you receive your E-mail. To send E-mail, you must include the address of the recipient.

Practicing the Skill

To send an E-mail message, complete the following steps:

1. Select the "message" function from your communications software.

2. Type in your message—and proofread it for errors.

3. When the message is ready, select the "send" button.

The E-mail system places the message in the receiver's mailbox. He or she may read the message at any time, and send you a return message.

Applying the Skill

Prepare a "Did You Know?" fact sheet about the Great Depression. E-mail your fact sheet to a student in another class. Have that student E-mail you back with additional information about the Great Depression. Share your response with the rest of the class.

Additional Practice

For additional practice, see Reinforcing Skills on page 449.

Geography: Impact on History

REGION

The Dust Bowl

With Manifest Destiny achieved, Americans thought that they had conquered the continent. The Dust Bowl of the 1930s proved them wrong. The devastation of the Dust Bowl taught people that nature cannot simply be conquered—it must be adapted to and protected.

The Prairie Ecosystem and the Prairie Farms

The Great Plains is a semidesert region lying in the "rain shadow" of the Rocky Mountains. The rain shadow is the lee side of a mountain barrier, which receives much less precipitation than the windward side. Weather systems moving up from the Gulf of Mexico and down from the Arctic collide over the prairie, causing storms with high winds and massive updrafts.

The native grasses of the Great Plains grew deep roots, which enabled them to survive fires and to hold moisture in the soil. These grasses formed a thick, dense sod that sheltered the soil from wind and rain erosion. Thus the soil and the grasses protected each other.

After the Louisiana Purchase (1803), Americans began to settle west of the Mississippi. The Homestead Act (1862) spurred the growing movement to "conquer" the prairie. The "sodbusters" plowed up the sod and planted wheat to sell for a profit. In the early part of the twentieth century, especially during World War I, world demand for wheat grew sharply. Tens of thousands of square miles of prairie were converted to wheat fields. The plowing continued after the war, as falling prices put pressure on farmers to produce more, and huge tractors increased productivity.

Portrait of a Dust Storm

The problems in the Great Plains remained hidden until below-average rains fell from 1930 to 1933. After the severe drought of 1934, the prairie grasses were so frail and withered that even the remaining grasslands were in danger. Where the grasses had been plowed, however, the land did not stand a chance.

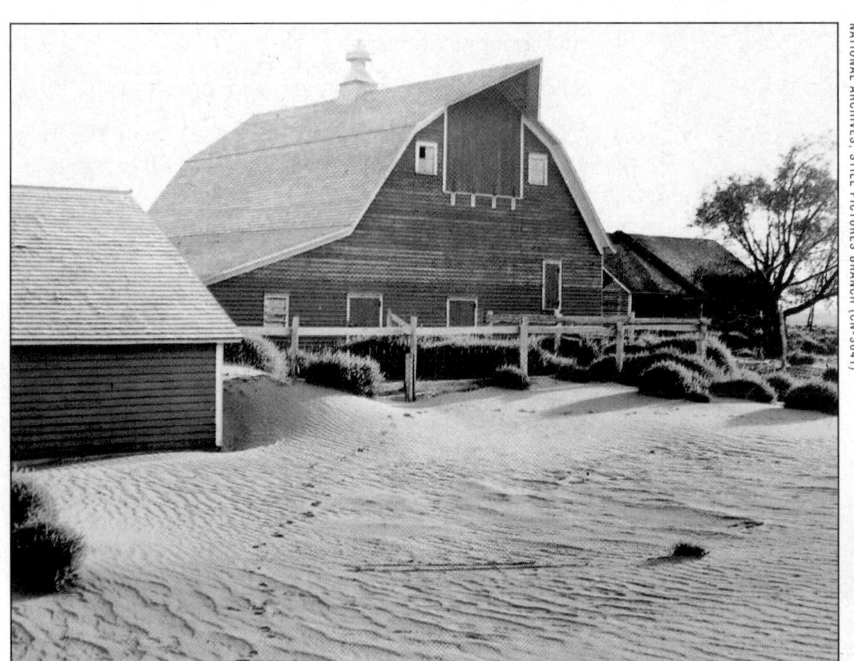

NATIONAL ARCHIVES, STILL PICTURES BRANCH (CN-3641)

NATIONAL ARCHIVES, STILL PICTURES BRANCH (CN-3640)

Before and After **At this ruined farm, emergency plantings of sugar cane, shown at right, reduced wind erosion and added organic matter to the soil.** *Which causes of Dust Bowl conditions are not subject to human control?*

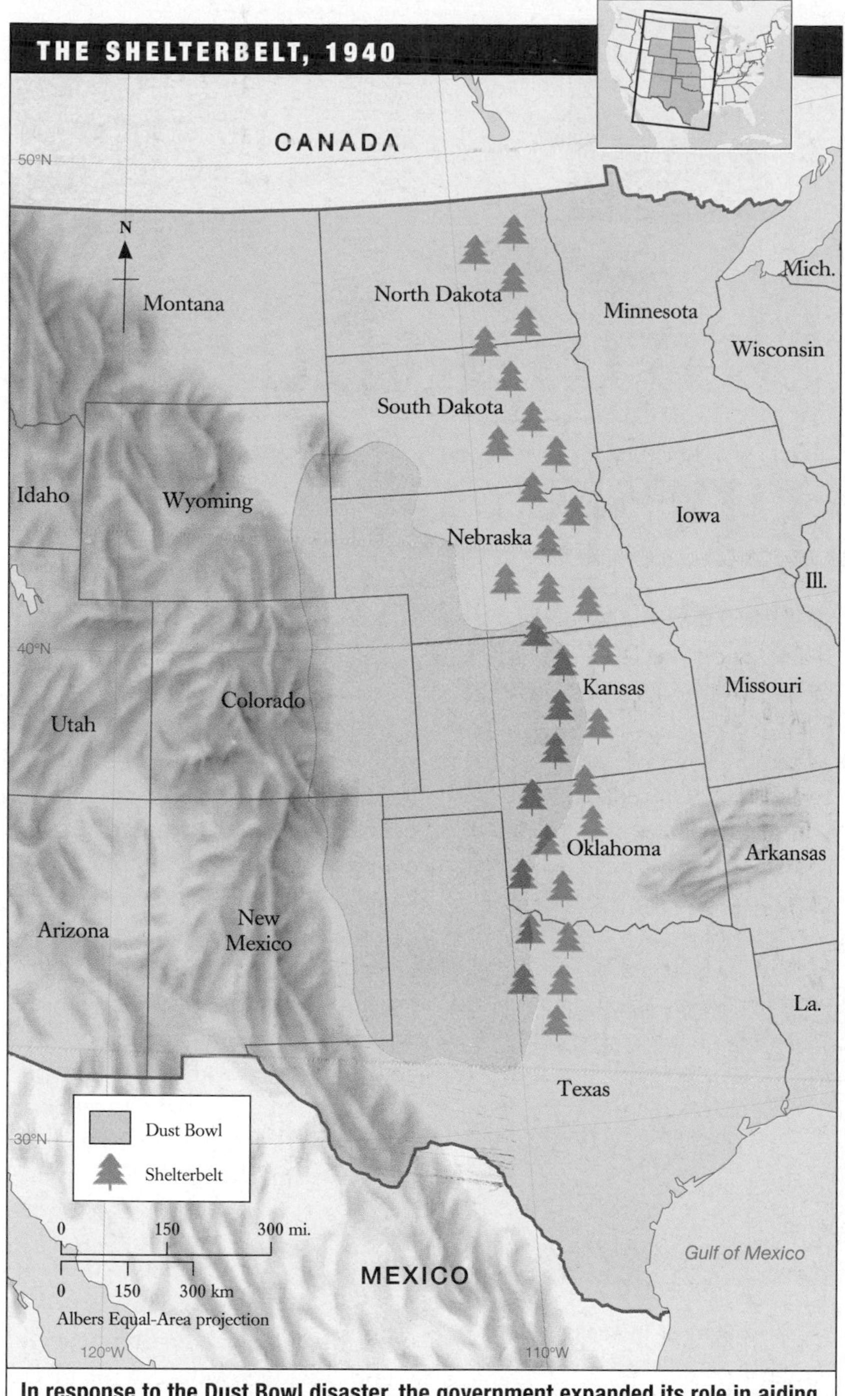

In response to the Dust Bowl disaster, the government expanded its role in aiding agriculture. Government workers planted trees in shelterbelts to fight the effects of windstorms. By 1940 more than 40 million trees had been planted. *What agricultural practices contributed to Dust Bowl conditions?*

When the winds came in the spring of 1934, the dust rose in great black clouds, forming swirling masses that darkened the sky. Folksinger Woody Guthrie reported, "The storm was as black as tar and as big as an ocean. It looked like we was done for." Once the strong winds subsided, the topsoil—reduced to dust—was blown in drifts that made farms, homes, and businesses literally worthless. People left the region in droves to find work and food and to escape the ravaged land.

Protecting the Heartland

Nothing could bring back six feet of lost topsoil, but Dust Bowl farmers welcomed New Deal efforts to rehabilitate the land and to protect it from drought, wind erosion, and water erosion.

The Soil Conservation Service, created in 1935, encouraged farmers to use contour plowing and terracing, practices that reduce runoff, water loss, and soil erosion. The service taught farmers not to plow fields under after a harvest, but to leave the stubble to protect the soil, and it taught them about crops that offered better soil protection.

The Forest Service planted strips of trees to make shelterbelts, or windscreens (see map). It also provided saplings to individual farmers.

These measures were successful in returning the land to production. Once the worst was over, though, many farmers returned to their old practices. The climate and landforms of the Great Plains, however, have not changed, and soil erosion remains a great danger.

Making the Geographic Connection

1. What geologic and climatic features define the Great Plains region? How did each of these features contribute to the dust storms of 1934?
2. What change did the farmers of the Great Plains make to their environment? How did this change contribute to the dust storms?
3. **Region** What changes did the government introduce to rehabilitate and protect the land?

Life During the Depression

JUNE 30, 1936: *GONE WITH THE WIND* SMASHES SALES RECORDS

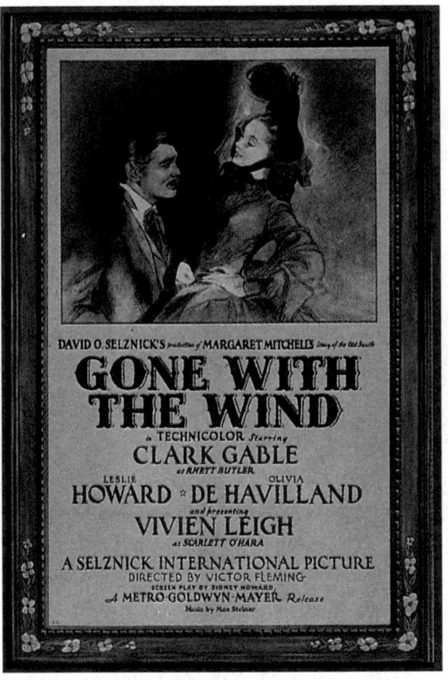

COURTESY OF THE ACADEMY OF MOTION PICTURE ARTS AND SCIENCES

A Story of Triumph
Margaret Mitchell's novel went on to break box office records as a film in 1939.

Penned by an unknown journalist who had never written a full book before, Margaret Mitchell's novel, *Gone With the Wind,* became an instant success during the Depression. Through its pages readers stepped back in time to the world of Scarlett O'Hara and Rhett Butler in plantation Georgia, during and after the Civil War. Vivid with description, the book told of plantation life in a land only recently tamed:

> It was a savagely red land, blood-colored after rains, brick dust in droughts, the best cotton land in the world. It was a pleasant land of white houses, peaceful plowed fields and sluggish yellow rivers, but a land of contrasts, of brightest sun glare and densest shade. The plantation clearings and miles of cotton fields smiled up to a warm sun, placid, complacent. At their edges rose the virgin forests, dark and cool even in the hottest noons, mysterious, a little sinister, the soughing pines seeming to wait with an age-old patience, to threaten with soft sighs: "Be careful! Be careful! We had you once. We can take you back again."
>
> —Margaret Mitchell, *Gone With the Wind,* 1936

The outbreak of the Civil War brought upheaval to this peaceful world. Readers were caught in the flames of Atlanta burning and dragged through the decimated

Guide to Reading

Main Idea

Americans coped with the Depression in a variety of ways, from seeking temporary escape to capturing the grim reality in literature and art.

Vocabulary

- status symbol
- mass media

Read to Find Out . . .

- how people lived, coped, and even escaped during the Depression era.
- the forms of escape that people sought or created in the 1930s.
- the themes that predominated in art, literature, and entertainment during the Depression.

fields of the O'Hara family's plantation, Tara. Lost in this broken world of postwar Reconstruction, millions of readers momentarily escaped from their own troubled time. They put aside their worries as they experienced the epic drama, defeat, and triumphs of Margaret Mitchell's memorable cast of characters.

Gone With the Wind won the 1937 Pulitzer Prize for fiction and in 1939 was made into one of the most popular movies of all time. During the Depression fans had the fun of reading the book and anticipating the casting of the movie before finally seeing the characters come to life on the big screen. Other works of historical fiction also enjoyed immense popularity, transporting readers to another era and allowing them to forget the ordeals of the Depression.

The Car Craze Continues

The United States Hits the Highway

Just as reading books provided an emotional escape from the dire circumstances of the Depression, owning an automobile gave people the sense that they could physically escape their problems. America's romance with cars, which began in the prosperous years of the 1920s, continued through the poverty-ridden 1930s. Auto shows drew tens of thousands. Then, as now, a new car was a **status symbol,** a sign of wealth or great prestige.

Cars for Show

The Depression highlighted the status value of the automobile. Even people who could not afford the fuel to drive considered their cars among their most prized possessions. One person recalled his grandfather's car:

> My grandfather owned a car [during the Depression] but it never left the garage. He had it jacked up for two years. Gasoline was just too expensive. He told how he polished the car once a week. How he took good care of it, but he never drove it. Couldn't afford it.
>
> —Ben, in *Hard Times*

Whether they could afford their cars or not, many Americans kept the autos and continued to drive them despite the expense. A restless spirit lured thousands to the highways during the Depression.

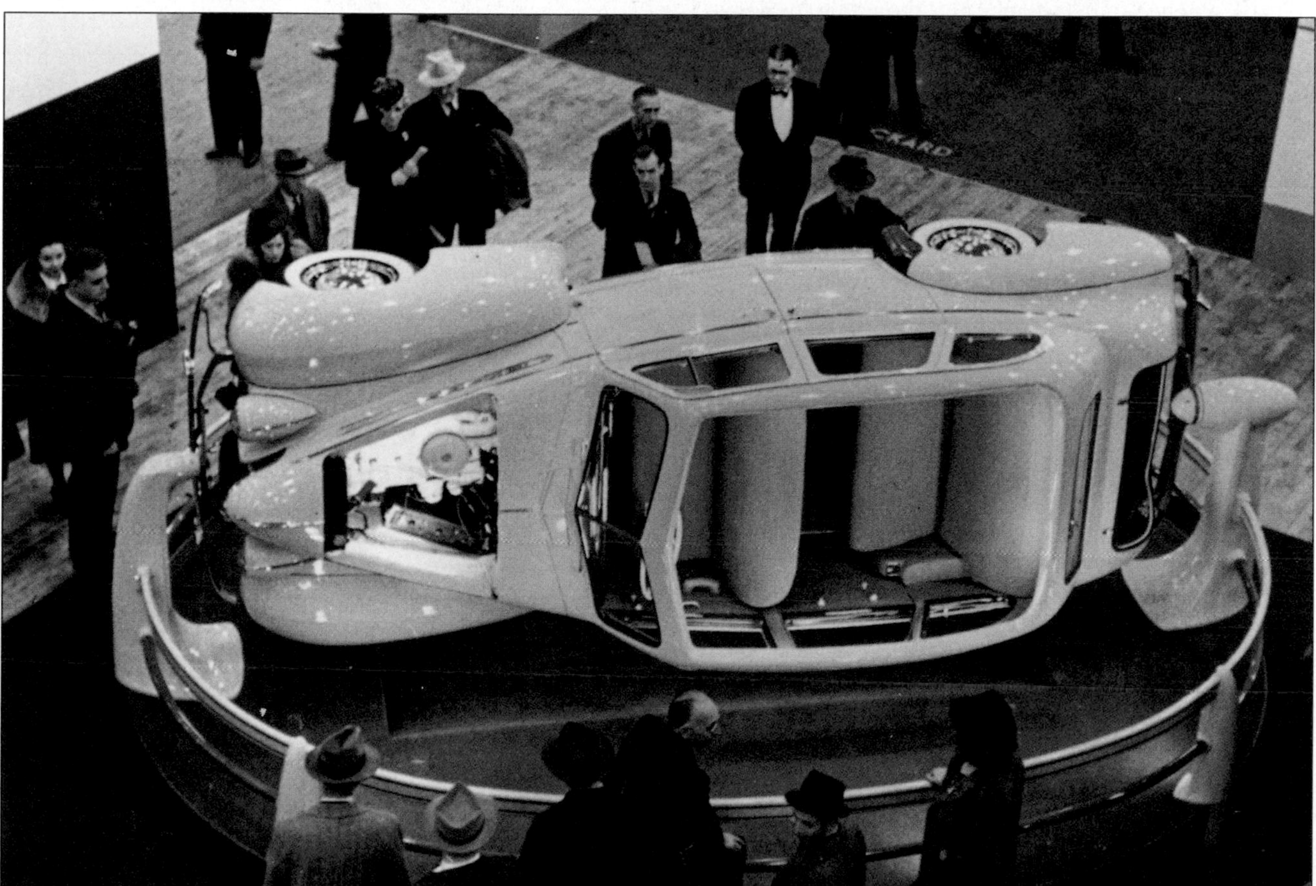

THE BETTMANN ARCHIVE

Year of the Auto The year 1935 was a banner year for the American automobile. Auto show attendance zoomed, and car sales dramatically increased. *What did automobiles symbolize to their owners in the 1930s?*

On the Move

By the mid-1930s a maze of two-lane roads crisscrossed the United States. Heading down these bumpy byways, people took off for parts unknown. Some were searching for work. Others were seeking adventure. Many were pioneering what would soon become an American institution: the driving trip as a family vacation.

During the 1930s tourism grew to be the third largest industry in the United States. Thirty-five million vacationers took to the roads in 1935 alone. One woman recalled a yearlong journey she took with her husband and son in the middle of the decade:

> The roads in those days were not the way they are now, and there weren't many motels, although in the East they had what they called auto courts; sometimes these were little better than primitive log cabins. We camped beside the road when we couldn't find a tourist home or a hotel. . . .
>
> This country was so different for families traveling in the thirties. You stayed with local people and ate the food the region was famous for. For instance, in the South there were antebellum houses that were turned into tourist homes, and I think it only cost about $1.50 a night—for the three of us—with an absolutely gigantic dinner and breakfast thrown in.
>
> —Marion Conrad, in *Making Do: How Women Survived the '30s*

FILE PHOTO BY RALPH J. BRUNKE/COURTESY DOW CHEMICALS

Light Work Electrical appliances manufactured in the 1930s were making housework lighter and easier. *What messages about housework are shown in this ad?*

Trailers—mobile homes that could be hitched to the back of a car—became popular in the 1930s. Ideal for vacations in isolated areas or for rent-free accommodations in a city, trailers tapped into the American dream, promoting freedom and opportunity. The trailer fad peaked in the summer of 1937, when a Florida observer reported that an average of 25 trailers entered his state each hour.

The automobile industry itself just kept growing. The number of registered automobiles in the United States jumped from 24 million in 1933 to 32 million in 1940. Even in the early 1930s, more than half of the families in the United States owned a car.

Escape From Household Drudgery

Electricity Transforms the Home

The car was the ultimate escape machine for the Depression decade. It was not the only machine prized for its powers. The appliance revolution that began in the 1920s continued into the 1930s. As more and more houses were wired with electricity, the market for remarkable new household appliances grew. In the late 1930s, government programs helped bring electricity to many isolated regions of the country, such as the mountains of Arkansas.

The refrigerator was, by far, the most sought after of the new appliances. Even during the worst years of the Depression, refrigerator sales continued to climb. Replacing the clunky old icebox, the refrigerator promised a cleaner, safer way to store food. Gone was the incessant drip-drop of melting ice and the creeping puddle of water that always seemed to spill over the edge of the icebox's collecting pan. With the hum of the refrigerator's whirring motor, families could rest assured that their food would stay fresh.The spread of electrification also eased burdensome household chores such as washing and ironing clothes. Doing laundry had traditionally involved a whole day of bending over tubs full of scalding water and another full day of heating and reheating a heavy iron for pressing. Simple washing machines and the electric iron transformed this work from a weekly ritual of torture. With modern appliances, doing laundry became a set of relatively painless tasks to be squeezed in between other household chores.

For some people electrical power seemed no less than a miracle. An Arkansas congressman remembered the day it miraculously appeared:

> I wanted to be at my parents' house when electricity came. It was in 1940. We'd all go around flipping the switch to make sure it hadn't come on yet. We didn't want to miss it. When they finally came on, the lights just barely glowed. I remember my mother smiling. When they came on full, tears started to run down her cheeks.
>
> —Clyde T. Ellis, in *Hard Times*

People in these regions welcomed the escape from drudgery that new appliances afforded them.

Escape Through Entertainment

Song, Spectacle, and Fantasy

For a child in the 1930s, a dime would buy a round-trip fare on a streetcar, two apples from a corner vendor, a malt at the drugstore fountain, or an afternoon at the movies. Faced with these choices, many adults as well as children did without afternoon snacks and saved their pennies in order to claim a seat in the local theater for a Saturday double-feature matinee.

MOVIE STILL ARCHIVES

Dynamic Duo Ginger Rogers and Fred Astaire set the standard for lighter-than-air dance steps with nine Hollywood hits. *Why were dance numbers especially popular in the 1930s?*

The Silver Screen

Movies changed dramatically as "talkies"—movies with sound—became more common in the early 1930s. At first, all sound was taped live in the studio at the same time the movie was being filmed. Any editing of the movie threw the sound track out of sync with the picture. As a result the actors looked as if they were mouthing their lines, but the words did not match up. Immobile microphones also stunted acting and directing styles. When speaking, the actors and actresses had to stand in place in front of the microphones. They could not change positions or even turn their heads for fear of spoiling the sound. For these reasons, early talkies had a stiffness to them that contrasted with the smooth pace of the old silent movies.

Continued improvement of sound technology ushered in the era of musicals. Watching such gems as *Flying Down to Rio* and *42nd Street,* audiences swooned at the sensuous steps of Fred Astaire and Ginger Rogers. They thrilled at the spectacle of rows of high-stepping dancers. So far removed from the dreariness of the Depression, these sumptuous pageants transported people to a world of glitz and glamour.

Color-film technology added another appealing dimension to 1930s movies. Over the decade more and more movie theaters bought the equipment to project the full-color films the studios began making. The release of the movie version of *Gone With the Wind* in 1939 converted any diehards who preferred black and white. The searing scenes of Atlanta under Union General William Sherman's torch had some viewers shielding their eyes from the imagined heat of dancing flames.

Gone With the Wind was the epitome of a Depression era film. It drew viewers into a romantic, faraway world. It engaged them with a twisting, dramatic plot.

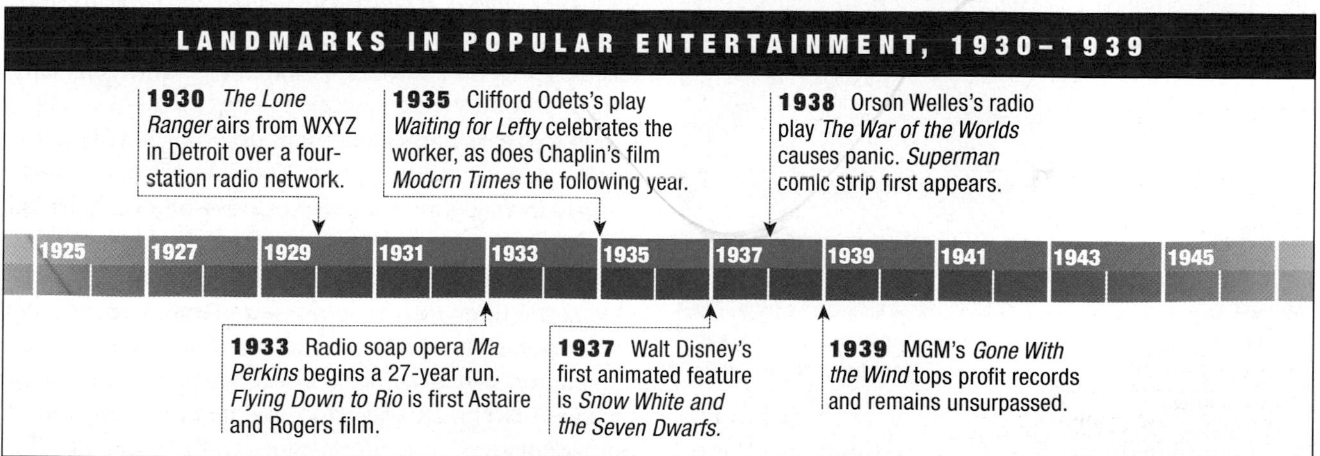

LANDMARKS IN POPULAR ENTERTAINMENT, 1930–1939
1930 The Lone Ranger airs from WXYZ in Detroit over a four-station radio network.
1935 Clifford Odets's play Waiting for Lefty celebrates the worker, as does Chaplin's film Modern Times the following year.
1938 Orson Welles's radio play The War of the Worlds causes panic. Superman comic strip first appears.
1925
1927
1929
1931
1933
1935
1937
1939
1941
1943
1945
1933 Radio soap opera Ma Perkins begins a 27-year run. Flying Down to Rio is first Astaire and Rogers film.
1937 Walt Disney's first animated feature is Snow White and the Seven Dwarfs.
1939 MGM's Gone With the Wind tops profit records and remains unsurpassed.

It tugged at all the emotions—love, anger, fear, pity, and hope. Best of all, it lasted for nearly four hours, not including an intermission for a meal. A more satisfying afternoon of entertainment could not be had for the price of just one thin dime.

During an average week in the mid-1930s, between 60 million and 90 million people flocked to the movies. For their daily entertainment, however, most people turned on the radio.

The Golden Age of Radio

Unlike today's compact radio that can be carried in the palm of the hand, the radio of the 1930s was a substantial piece of furniture. Granted an honored place in the living room, the radio, with its rich wood cabinet, often served as a visual focus, the mantel for family photographs and mementos. It also served as a social focus, the gathering place for hours of spirit-lifting amusement.

More than 10 million households owned radios in 1929. A decade later that number had almost tripled. Like television today, radio served many purposes. It was the family's communication link to the outside world. It was the housewife's companion as she did her daily chores. It gave the unemployed the comfort of company. It occupied young children when they returned home from school. Radio enlivened long winter evenings with engrossing family entertainment.

Radio programming in the 1930s set a pattern that television would follow for years. Daytime radio included soap operas, panel discussions, and quiz shows designed to appeal to women working at home. During the late afternoon, children's programs came on. Adventure stories, such as *The Lone Ranger* and *Superman,* originated in the 1930s and captured young audiences well into the 1950s. The evening was reserved for news programs, variety shows, comedy hours, dramatic presentations of plays, and live musical performances.

Sponsored by big-name corporations, radio programs tended to avoid controversial issues. Audiences of the **mass media**—movies, radio, and other large networks of communication—were most often seeking a means of escape. A few used it as a forum to discuss difficult questions or controversial views.

UPI/BETTMANN

Entertainment Center **The radio was a piece of furniture that became the entertainment center and focal point of the living room in many homes.** *What sorts of shows were broadcast in the mornings, afternoons, and evenings?*

Voices That Would Not Be Stilled

Bleak Visions of Reality

Despite many Americans' obsession with escape, quite a few people took an interest in defining the nation's problems and exploring solutions. Angry at injustices, they spoke out candidly. Many were artists—writers, painters, photographers, playwrights—whose works still inspire social awareness and empathy today.

The Mirror of Literature

During the 1930s many serious writers shifted their focus from the anxiety of the individual to the mass struggles of people caught in a system that robbed them of their vitality. John Steinbeck and John Dos Passos, two writers acclaimed during this turbulent decade, stressed the struggles of individuals in society. In addition, both writers evaluated the effectiveness of society in upholding the rights of people of different classes. They intended that their writing serve as a mirror in which society could see itself. These writers wanted their readers to take a long, hard look at the evils and injustices of society. They wanted to inspire their readers to fight for social change.

The Grapes of Wrath by Steinbeck was one of the most famous and influential novels of the 1930s. This American classic focused on an Okie family driven from their land:

> Pa borrowed money from the bank, and now the bank wants the land—wants tractors, not families on the land. Is a tractor bad? Is the power that turns the long furrows wrong? If this tractor were ours it would be good—not mine, but ours. If our tractor turned the long furrows of our land, it would be good. Not my land, but ours. We could love that tractor then as we have loved this land when it was ours. But this tractor does two things—it turns the land and turns us off the land. There is little differ-

THE BETTMANN ARCHIVE

CEDAR RAPIDS MUSEUM OF ART ARCHIVES, GIFT OF JOHN B. TURNER IN MEMORY OF HAPPY YOUNG

Regionalism The models for Grant Wood's *American Gothic* were the artist's sister Nan and his dentist, Dr. McKeeby, shown in the photo. *What sentiments does this painting convey?*

ence between this tractor and a tank. The people are driven, intimidated, hurt by both. We must think about this.

—John Steinbeck, *The Grapes of Wrath,* 1939

Statements in the Arts

No less insistent than the 1930s writers were the artists of the time who clamored for social change. They sought to show the United States in all its Depression era bleakness. Thomas Hart Benton, Edward Hopper, and Grant Wood each focused on a particular region of the country and tried to convey the flavor of life there as they saw it. Through these works of art, viewers perceived the trials of poor farmers, unemployed workers, and others struggling to hold on to their ideals during years of hardship.

Playwrights and theater directors also used their works to make statements about society. Emphasizing the struggle of labor against exploitative factory owners, the play *Waiting for Lefty* by Clifford Odets glorified the Depression era worker. This and other plays promoted the visions of playwrights for a just world.

In contrast, documentary photography showed the United States of the Depression era stripped of hopes and dreams. Staring into the faces of destitute migrant workers from Alabama, the evicted wheat farmers from the Dust Bowl, and the hungry children in Hoovervilles, few viewers could avoid sensing these people's anger, shame, and misery. The photographs immediately convey the scope of the Depression, which shattered the lives of so many Americans.

Section Assessment

Main Idea

1. Use a diagram like this one to show how people coped with the Depression, either through escape or through artistic social statements.

Vocabulary

2. Define: status symbol, mass media.

Checking Facts

3. Why did America's romance with cars continue into the poverty-ridden 1930s?

4. What household machines changed people's lives?

Critical Thinking

5. Drawing Conclusions Unemployment remained high during the 1930s, but movie attendance and sales of cars rose. Do you feel the 1930s were a depressing time to be a teenager? Explain.

Hard Times

The harsh reality of the Great Depression was something that Americans faced every day. Most people could hope for only a few hours a week of escape into a fantasy world where life was beautiful and problems could be easily solved. Movies, radio, comics, and new novelty games provided that escape.

"THE GREAT ZIEGFELD", 1936. MGM/MOTION PICTURE & TELEVISION PHOTO ARCHIVE

MUSICAL SPECTACLE

In sharp contrast to daily life during the Depression, musicals such as **The Great Ziegfeld** sparkled with lavish sets and cascades of smiling dancers. This tribute to theatrical producer Florenz Ziegfeld won Academy Awards for best picture and best director in 1936.

© PARKER BROTHERS/NATIONAL GEOGRAPHIC S

FANTASY TYCOONS

Players of **Monopoly** could pretend to own railroads and luxury hotels. Even though the game had many rules, it became an instant success in 1935, sending its unemployed inventor, Charles Darrow, into six-figure wealth.

FILE PHOTO BY DOUG MINDELL/ PERMISSION COURTESY OF PARKER BROTHERS

REPRINTED BY PERMISSION: TRIBUNE MEDIA SERVICES, INC., 2-13-38.

THRILLS AND CHILLS

Monsters in films such as *Dracula, Frankenstein,* and ***King Kong*** could make people forget about ordinary troubles. In 1933 Kong's battle atop the **Empire State Building** also gave moviegoers the chance to see "the world's tallest building," built just two years earlier.

THE CARSON COLLECTION

SUPERHEROES

As real gangsters ran wild, Chester Gould's **Dick Tracy** upheld law and order in the daily comics. Flash Gordon, Tarzan, Buck Rogers, and Superman kept the universe safe from other cartoon villains.

"TUNE IN TOMORROW . . ."

Heard but not seen, these **actors at NBC** played realistic murder victims. Soap operas and serials such as *Ma Perkins, One Man's Family,* and *Our Gal Sunday* kept listeners riveted to the radio.

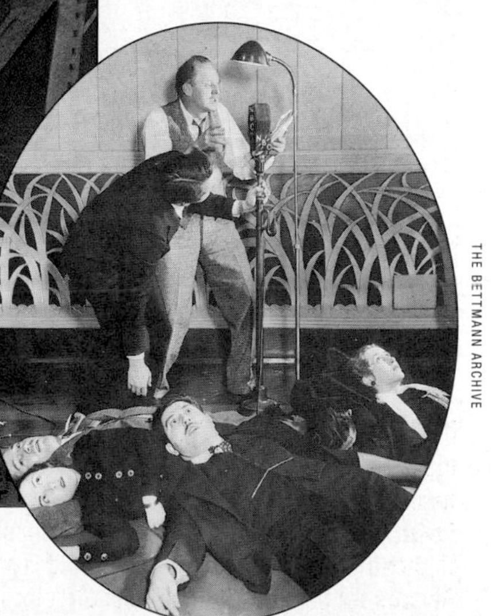

THE BETTMANN ARCHIVE

Chapter  Assessment

Self-Check Quiz

Visit the *American Odyssey* Web site at americanodyssey.glencoe.com and click on ***Chapter 13—Self-Check Quiz*** to prepare for the Chapter Test.

Reviewing Key Terms

Choose the vocabulary term that best completes the sentences below. Write your answers on a separate sheet of paper.

speculation	**repatriation**
margin	**status symbol**
foreclosure	**mass media**

1. Because of the depressed farm economy in the Southwest and Texas, many Mexican American workers were deported or sought _________ to Mexico.

2. Even during the Depression people took pride in automobile ownership. Their automobile, whether they could afford to drive it or not, was a _________ that established their position in the community.

3. One cause of the stock market crash of 1929 was reckless short-term investment _________ in overvalued stocks.

4. As farmers fell behind in making their farm mortgage payments, they feared a _________ by the bank that held the mortgage.

5. Often investors paid only part of a stock's value and borrowed the rest; such buying on _________ hastened the crash.

Recalling Facts

1. State two steps President Hoover took to end the Depression. Why were these steps unsuccessful?

2. Why did the Republican party try to discourage radio stations from playing "Brother, Can You Spare a Dime?"

3. State three reasons why many farmers were out of work during the Depression.

4. What farming practices contributed to Dust Bowl conditions?

5. During the Depression why was so much of the entertainment extravagant and unrealistic?

6. Give examples of realistic art and literature that highlighted social problems in the Depression.

Critical Thinking

1. Recognizing Cause and Effect Use a diagram such as this one to summarize the economic, political, and social effects of the Depression.

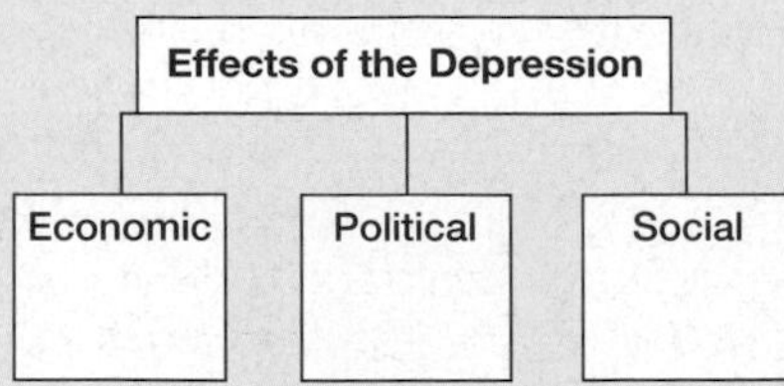

2. Making Comparisons Compare the ways that people in cities and rural areas helped one another during the Depression.

3. Drawing Conclusions Mexican Americans and African Americans were among the first to lose their jobs during the Depression. Why did this occur?

Standardized Test Practice

1. A major reason for the collapse of the United States economy after 1929 was

A an increased money supply.
B decreased farm production.
C low tariffs at home and abroad.
D overproduction of consumer goods.

Test-Taking Tip: If you are not sure of the answer to a question, use the process of elimination. For example, farmers had been left out of the general prosperity of the 1920s because of their ability to produce larger crops, which in turn forced down agricultural prices. Therefore, answer B is incorrect.

2. "Highway 66 is the path of a people in flight, refugees from the dust and shrinking land, . . . from the twisting winds that howl out of Texas. . . ."

Who was John Steinbeck describing when he wrote this description in *The Grapes of Wrath?*

A the Bonus Army
B Southern tenant farmers
C the Okies
D residents of the Hoovervilles

Test-Taking Tip: The question provides two clues to the answer. Both the geographic description and Steinbeck's book are about the Dust Bowl. Which of the groups listed in the answers were *refugees* from the Dust Bowl?

Portfolio Project

The Depression of the 1930s was a worldwide event. Investigate and write a report on how another country handled the hard times and unemployment of the Depression. You might choose Great Britain or Germany or any country in which you have a special interest. Keep your report in your portfolio.

Cooperative Learning

Form a film-review group and divide up the responsibility for analyzing videotapes of some of the film classics of the 1930s, such as *King Kong, Gone With the Wind*, or one of the films starring Fred Astaire and Ginger Rogers. Present a panel discussion on these films, evaluating them and comparing them with some of the popular films of the 1990s.

Reinforcing Skills

Using E-mail Using the Internet, locate the E-mail address of a historical organization that maintains information on the Great Depression. Compose an E-mail letter asking the organization for information about a specific aspect or topic of that era which you want to research. If you need additional information, write to other organizations. Share the responses to your E-mails with the class.

Technology Activity

Using a Computerized Card Catalog Go to your school or local library's computerized card catalog. Locate sources that provide information and tips on how to create an oral history. Prepare a list of ten questions you will use to interview a person who lived during the Great Depression.

GEOGRAPHY AND HISTORY

West Coast Crops, 1936

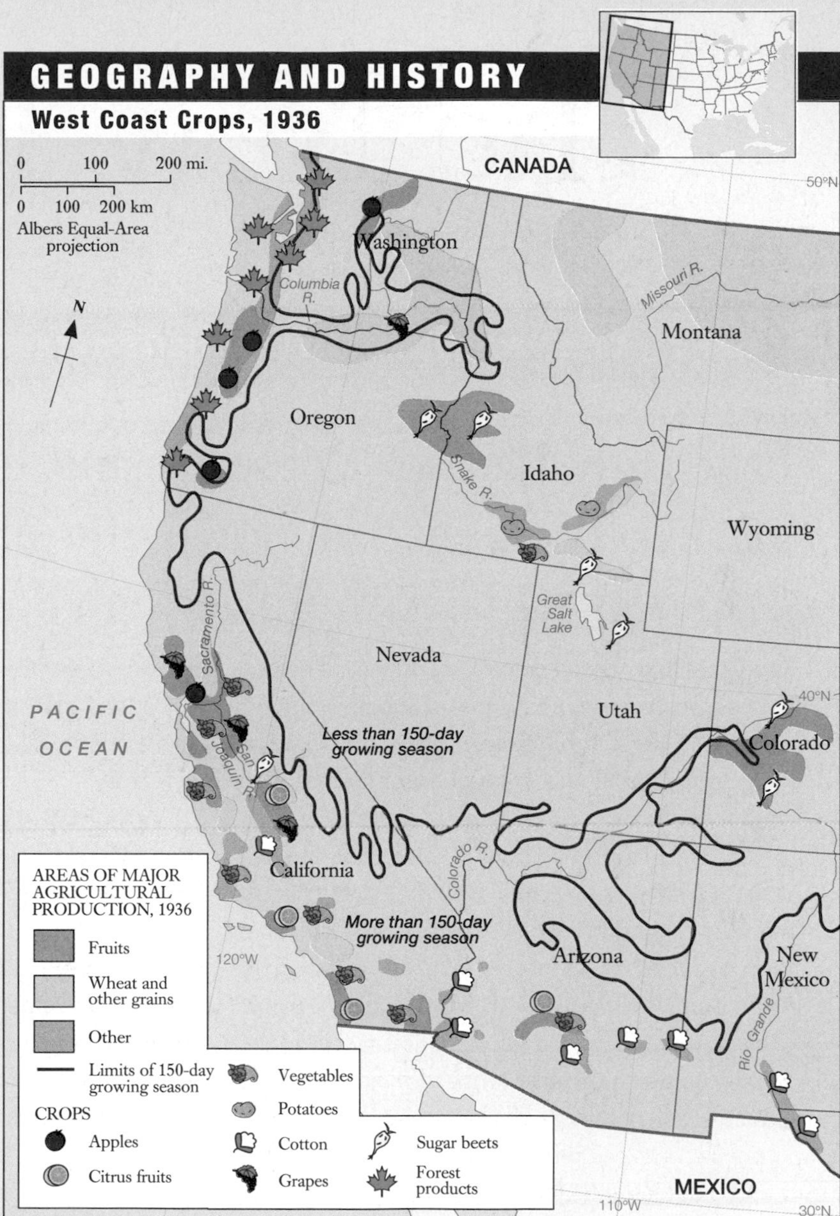

Study the map to answer the following questions:

1. What does the red line on the map mean? Would Dust Bowl farmers be more likely to settle in areas west and south of the red line or in areas east and north of it? Why?
2. What special opportunities for farming would California's growing season offer?
3. If migrant wheat farmers from Dust Bowl states hoped to grow wheat again, in which West Coast states would they settle?
4. In which states were forest products a major crop? What other crops were grown in those states?

The New Deal

MAY 27, 1938: ELEANOR ROOSEVELT VISITS ARTHURDALE, WEST VIRGINIA

First Lady Eleanor Roosevelt and her square dance partner promenaded down the aisle of clapping onlookers in the Arthurdale High School auditorium.

Five years had passed since Mrs. Roosevelt helped to establish the resettlement community of Arthurdale, West Virginia, and she wanted to be on hand to celebrate the graduation of its first high school senior class.

In 1933 in the midst of the Depression, the federal government persuaded a number of families to move from Morgantown, West Virginia, where most farm families could barely eke out a living, to Arthurdale. Residents there would ideally be able to remain employed and self-sufficient during the year by combining subsistence farming with small industry. To encourage people to make the move to Arthurdale, the federal government promised that each family would have a house with plumbing and electricity, a plot of land, and a job in a nearby factory.

Arthurdale was the first of the government-sponsored communities established by the Resettlement Administration, one of President Roosevelt's New Deal programs. These communities gave hope to people mired in the Depression. Under the President's leadership, the United States government assumed a new responsibility for the welfare of the American people and for the future of the nation's economy. ■

HISTORY JOURNAL

Consider the problems people were facing as the Hoover administration ended. What does the picture on 451 show about how people might have reacted to the idea of a "new deal"? Write your ideas in your journal.

Chapter Overview

Visit the *American Odyssey* Web site at americanodyssey.glencoe.com and click on ***Chapter 14—Chapter Overview*** to preview the chapter.

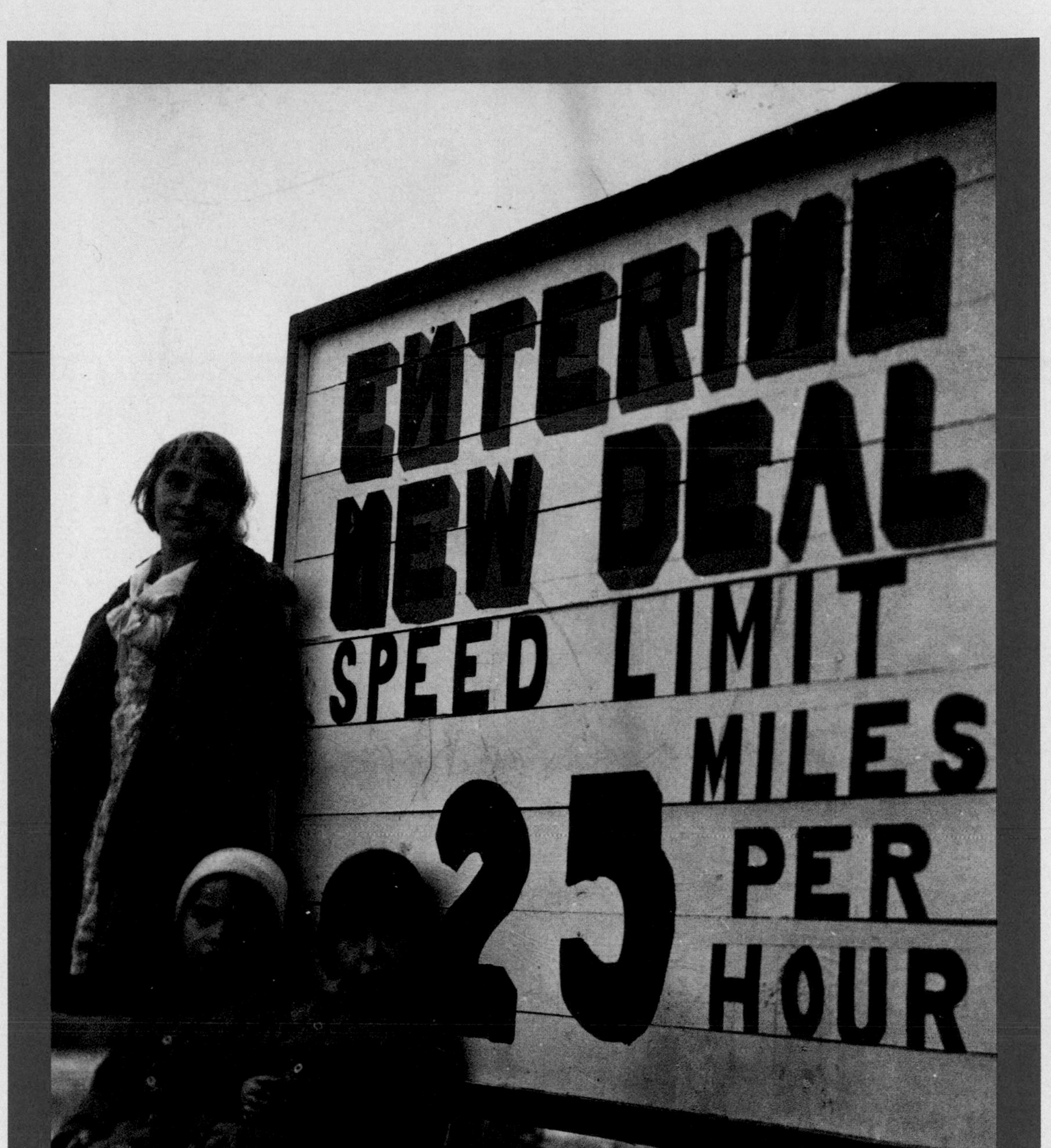

THIS WESTERN TOWN TOOK ITS NAME FROM ROOSEVELT'S PROMISE TO GIVE AMERICANS A NEW DEAL.

FDR and the First New Deal

MARCH 4, 1933: FRANKLIN D. ROOSEVELT TAKES PRESIDENTIAL OATH

DULL, GRAY SKIES HUNG OVER WASHINGTON. An icy wind gusted down the city's broad boulevards, chilling the crowd that packed the walk in front of the Capitol steps. Suddenly the high, clear notes of a bugle sounded out a fanfare. Franklin Delano Roosevelt, partially paralyzed from polio, leaning on the arm of his son, mounted the inaugural platform. As he walked up the steps to the podium, the band began playing "Hail to the Chief."

After Roosevelt took the oath of the office of the President, he turned to face the crowd. He had planned his first words as President carefully, because he knew that the nation would be listening closely to find out just what kind of President he would be.

FRANKLIN D. ROOSEVELT LIBRARY

New Leader
Roosevelt's inauguration was the result of a landslide win.

Three and a half years of economic depression had left millions unemployed, hungry, and homeless. Thousands of banks had closed. Assembly lines had ground to a halt while breadlines stretched for blocks down city streets. Farmland lay fallow, abandoned by angry farmers unable to recover even the costs of planting. Americans had lost faith in their country. Roosevelt considered his first major task was to restore that faith.

His voice echoing over the public-address system, Roosevelt declared the following:

GUIDE TO READING

Main Idea

Franklin Roosevelt tried to fulfill promises of a new deal for the American people through a period of intense legislative activity known as the Hundred Days.

Vocabulary

- moratorium
- dole
- subsidy

Read to Find Out . . .

- the issues and events that persuaded voters to elect FDR.
- the legislation of the Hundred Days.
- FDR's relationship with the public during the Hundred Days.

This great Nation will endure as it has endured, will revive and will prosper. So, first of all, let me assert my firm belief that the only thing we have to fear is fear itself—nameless, unreasoning, unjustified terror which paralyzes needed efforts to convert retreat into advance.

—Inaugural Address, March 4, 1933

Cheers and roaring applause burst from the crowd at the end of the President's address. For the first time that day, Roosevelt grinned. Then he descended the steps, determined to lead this country out of its prolonged economic depression.

FDR Takes the Helm

Personal and Political Victories

Franklin Delano Roosevelt was born on January 30, 1882, into a wealthy, well-connected family. As a child Roosevelt was popular with his classmates and received good grades in school. Nevertheless, the future President showed no signs of distinction.

A classmate described Roosevelt as "nice but colorless." Several decades later, when Roosevelt was running for office, a political analyst would confirm the classmate's opinion:

Franklin Roosevelt is no crusader. He is no tribune of the people. He is no enemy of entrenched privilege. He is a pleasant man who, without any important qualifications for the office, would very much like to be President.

—Walter Lippmann, 1932

Marriage to Eleanor Roosevelt

Franklin's distant cousin Eleanor introduced him to a world he had not seen in his sheltered youth. At the age of 20, Eleanor had volunteered at a settlement house in the slums of New York City. Franklin, accompanying Eleanor to the home of one of her students, exclaimed, "I didn't know people lived like that!"

On March 17, 1905, Franklin and Eleanor were joined in marriage. Republican President Theodore Roosevelt, Franklin's distant cousin and Eleanor's uncle, led Eleanor down the aisle. A few years later, Franklin followed in Theodore Roosevelt's footsteps, launching a political career.

An Emerging Politician

In 1910 FDR, as Franklin Roosevelt came to be known, was elected as a Democrat to the New York state legislature. In 1913 President Wilson appointed him assistant secretary of the navy. He served in this post for 7 years until 1920, when, at the age of 38, he gained the Democratic nomination for Vice President. Roosevelt did not become Vice President, however, because the Democratic presidential candidate lost the election.

In 1921, while vacationing at his family's summer home, FDR suffered an attack of poliomyelitis that left his legs completely paralyzed. Nevertheless, Roosevelt was determined to return to an active political life.

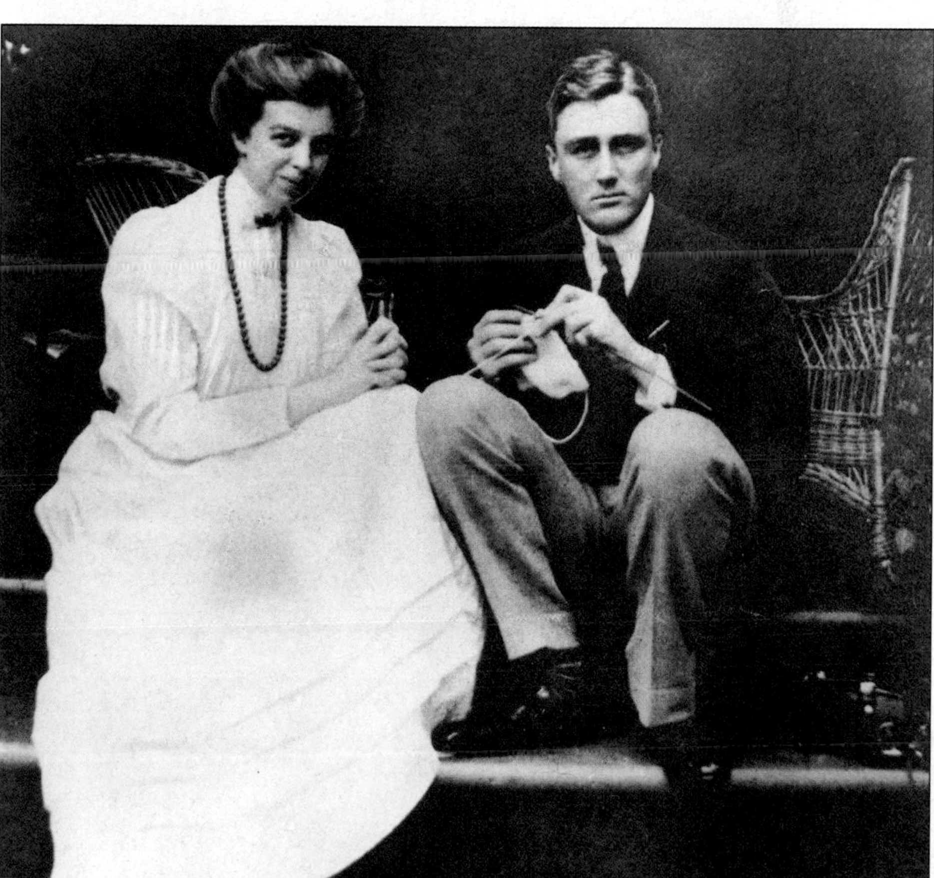

FRANKLIN D. ROOSEVELT LIBRARY

Two Visions Joined **In this 1905 photograph, newlyweds Eleanor and Franklin Roosevelt pose on the steps of their Hyde Park home. Eleanor's volunteer activities helped expand Franklin's awareness of social issues.** *What qualities of Franklin and Eleanor Roosevelt prepared them for leadership?*

Years of treatment never did restore the use of his legs, but the experience increased his ability to empathize with others and strengthened his spirit. As he remarked, "If you have spent two years in bed trying to wiggle your big toe, everything else seems easy."

At the Democratic convention in 1924, Roosevelt made his first public political appearance since having been stricken with polio. From that appearance on, Roosevelt's political career skyrocketed. Twice he won the governorship of New York—in 1928 by a slim margin and in 1930 by a landslide. His innovative relief measures, including a statewide relief program, won him national praise. Then in 1932 he accepted the Democratic nomination for President.

The Roosevelt Victory

Both Roosevelt and Hoover promoted conservative measures to end the Depression. President Hoover, however, was reluctant to institute direct relief measures, and he projected a grim attitude. Both of these things made him widely unpopular. Roosevelt, on the other hand, possessed a buoyant spirit and a warm smile and promised direct action. These were enough to sweep him into office and to get a wide Democratic majority elected to both houses of Congress.

An experimenter at heart, Roosevelt was open to all ideas. He employed Republicans as well as Democrats, conservatives as well as liberals, university intellectuals as well as experienced politicians.

The day Roosevelt took office a flurry of activity began that did not let up for more than three months. This time of intensive legislation and policy setting came to be called the Hundred Days.

The Hundred Days

Drastic Reform Measures

Months before Roosevelt's inauguration, thousands of panicky Michigan residents had begun flocking to their local banks to withdraw cash from savings accounts. This activity depleted bank funds to such an extent that many banks actually closed. In mid-February 1933, the governor of Michigan declared a banking **moratorium,** a temporary shutdown of operations, in effect closing all state banks. He hoped that this would give the banks enough time to replenish their supplies of ready cash and, thus, restore depositors' confidence. The moratorium, however, actually had the opposite effect: It caused the panic to spread and intensify. Overnight, people throughout the nation began to panic. By Inauguration Day, 38 states had closed their banks, and the remaining 10 states had sharply restricted banking operations. The majority of Americans, having lost faith in their financial institutions, were hoarding money, hiding cash under mattresses, and storing gold in pillowcases.

Stemming the Bank Crisis

Even before the inauguration, Roosevelt had directed his future secretary of the treasury, William Woodin, to develop a plan for dealing with the bank crisis. Woodin proposed that Roosevelt call a special session of Congress and declare a partial bank holiday for all financial institutions until after Congress met on March 9. The President announced the plan on the afternoon of March 5, directing the banks to accept all deposits and make emergency loans for food and animal

★ ★ ★ GALLERY OF PRESIDENTS ★ ★ ★

Franklin Delano Roosevelt

1933–1945

"There is a mysterious cycle in human events. To some generations much is given. Of other generations much is expected. This generation of Americans has a rendezvous with destiny."

Nomination acceptance speech, Democratic National Convention, 1936

FRANKLIN D. ROOSEVELT LIBRARY

BACKGROUND

- **Born 1882; Died 1945**
- **Assistant secretary of the navy 1913–1920**
- **New York governor 1929–1932**
- **Elected President in 1932, 1936, 1940, and 1944**

ACHIEVEMENTS IN OFFICE

- **Agricultural Adjustment Act**
- **National Industrial Recovery Act**
- **The Social Security Act of 1935**
- **Yalta Conference (1945)**

feed over the course of the next four days but to refrain from conducting any other business.

From March 5 to noon on March 9, Secretary Woodin and his advisers worked around the clock to hammer out legislation that would end the banking crisis. When Congress met on the afternoon of March 9, the President's representative read the bill aloud. It stated that banks in sound financial shape would be reopened immediately. Those lacking assets would remain closed until the government could develop a way to open them safely. Congress promptly passed the bill, and Roosevelt signed it that evening.

FDR reassured people that their money would be safer in the newly reopened banks than hidden in their homes. Within a few days, deposits exceeded withdrawals. The banking crisis was over.

A New Deal

When Roosevelt accepted the Democratic nomination for President, he had pledged "a new deal for the American people." Now that he had taken office, it was time to fulfill that promise and put the rest of his legislative program, the New Deal, into effect.

The overwhelming approval that the Democrat-controlled Congress gave his banking bill persuaded Roosevelt to extend the special session to work on other New Deal legislation. The bills Roosevelt introduced—some of which actually had been first proposed by the Hoover administration—addressed the three R's: relief for the unemployed, recovery measures to stimulate the economy, and reform laws to help lessen the threat of another economic disaster.

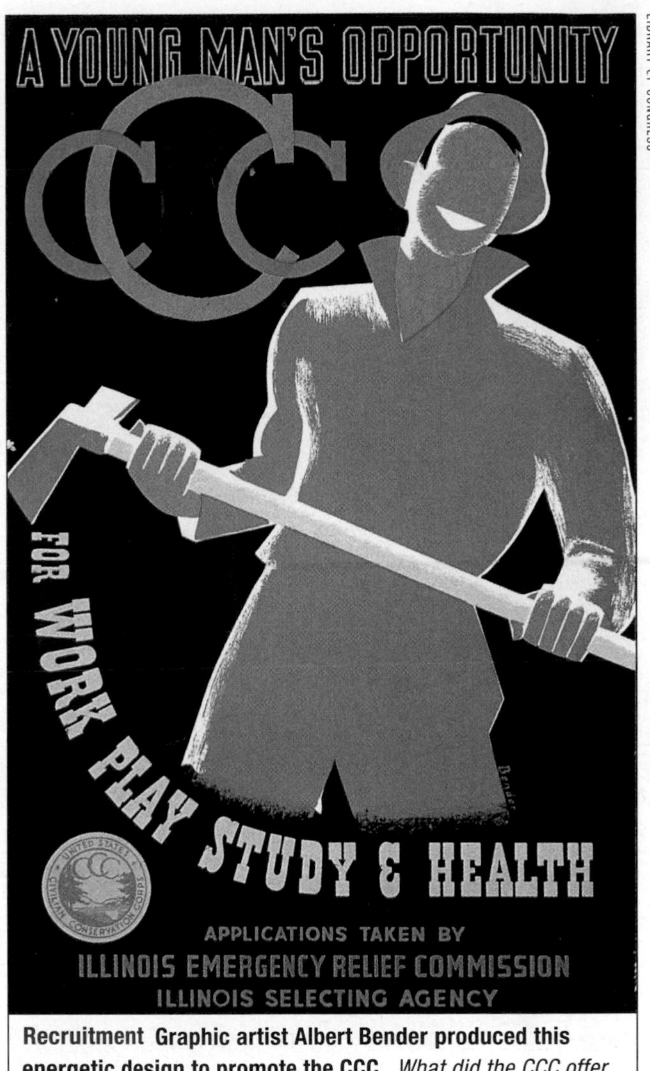

Recruitment Graphic artist Albert Bender produced this energetic design to promote the CCC. *What did the CCC offer to its recruits that the dole did not?*

Emergency Relief

By 1933 many of the millions of people who had been unemployed for more than three years had no choice left to them but to apply for public aid. Local relief agencies, however, could not meet the growing demand for aid. In response, FDR asked Congress to appropriate $500 million that a new agency, the Federal Emergency Relief Administration (FERA), would distribute to state and local relief agencies. The bill passed on May 12.

Eight days later the FERA swung into action. Headed by experienced administrator and social worker Harry Hopkins, the agency distributed $5 million in its first 2 hours of operation. One government official, worried about this fast pace of spending, suggested that a slower, more conservative distribution of funds might work out better in the long run. Hopkins responded, "People don't eat in the long run—they [have to] eat every day."

Although Hopkins disbursed the millions allotted to FERA quite freely, he disliked the **dole,** which is what government charity was called. He, along with Roosevelt, felt that giving money to people broke down their self-respect and their will to work. To combat this weakening of morale, Roosevelt proposed relief programs that would put people back to work.

Civilian Conservation Corps

One of these programs was the Civilian Conservation Corps (CCC). The CCC put hundreds of thousands of unemployed men to work each season on environmental projects. The CCC constructed many of the facilities in the state and national parks.

Roosevelt hoped the CCC would create "a mass exodus of unemployed to the forests." Instead of going on relief, unmarried men between the ages of 18 and 25 would work in the corps to preserve the environment. According to Roosevelt's plan, the Labor Department would recruit the workers, the War Department would run the camps, and the Interior Department would supervise the work projects.

NATIONAL MUSEUM OF AMERICAN ART, WASHINGTON, DC/ART RESOURCE, NY

Work and Happiness **William Gropper painted the mural *Construction of the Dam* in 1939. In it Gropper depicts the energy and productivity New Deal programs engendered. He also conveys a sense of harmony among the construction workers.** *How does Gropper achieve this effect?*

CCC members lived in barracks, ate together in mess halls, and followed a strict schedule. Room and board and a salary of $30 a month were provided to each man in exchange for his labor. The workers sent most of their salaries back to their families.

All told, by 1942 when the CCC was disbanded, 2,650 camps had been built and a total of 2.5 million men had served in them. The CCC excluded women and limited the numbers of African Americans, Hispanic Americans, and Native Americans it accepted into its ranks. Furthermore, the minorities who were permitted to join the corps were segregated from the white workers. So, although the CCC helped many people, it still discriminated against minorities and women—some of the people hardest hit by the Depression.

Among the first recruits to the CCC were several thousand members of the bonus army. This army had returned to Washington, D.C., in the spring of 1933 to lobby again for early payment on the bonus certificates they had received as veterans of World War I. Roosevelt, like Hoover, was reluctant to grant them the money. Instead of sending in troops to run the veterans out of Washington as Hoover had done, however, Roosevelt had coffee served to the veterans and then arranged for them to meet with his aides. These aides first gave the veterans the idea of seeking employment in the CCC.

Public Works Administration

The Public Works Administration (PWA) was another New Deal program that helped provide jobs for the unemployed. With a grant of $3.3 billion to carry out public projects, the PWA put people back to work building schools and dams, refurbishing government buildings, planning sewage systems, improving highways, and generally modernizing the nation. The PWA's massive spending on wages, materials, and supplies for projects nationwide was intended to stimulate industry and spur economic recovery.

National Recovery Administration

Another of Roosevelt's goals was to increase the productivity of industry. Between 1929 and 1933, America's factories had decreased their production levels by about 40 percent. To help factories recover, Roosevelt sponsored the National Industrial Recovery Act (NIRA). After its passage on June 16, 1933, the NIRA established the National Recovery Administration (NRA) to carry out the new law.

The NIRA relaxed the antitrust laws of the early 1900s and called for business leaders to confer and establish codes to set quality standards, production levels, prices, maximum work hours, and minimum wages. The NIRA also declared that workers should be allowed to

NRA
MEMBER
U.S.

CULVER PICTURES

Working Eagle Hired by the Works Progress Administration, Charles Coiner created the best-known symbol of the New Deal. *What was the function of a blue-eagle poster?*

organize labor unions and to bargain collectively. Shortening individual workers' hours forced businesses to hire more people, which, in turn, created 2 million additional jobs.

The NRA could not effectively penalize business leaders who decided not to adhere to the industry-set standards. So to encourage business leaders to comply voluntarily with the codes, the NRA launched a huge publicity campaign. It adopted as its symbol a dark blue eagle and asked businesses that followed the codes to prominently display a blue-eagle poster. Then the NRA asked people to buy their goods only from businesses displaying the blue eagle.

The public rallied in support of businesses displaying the eagle. Despite the public's enthusiasm, the NRA's policies had controversial results. Owners of large companies established codes that put small businesses at such a disadvantage that many small-business owners felt that they were being forced into bankruptcy, and for this they blamed the NRA.

Agricultural Adjustment Administration

The Agricultural Adjustment Administration (AAA) was equally controversial. This agency was established to help farmers who had been hard hit by the Depression. The AAA paid farmers a **subsidy,** or financial assistance, to reduce the production of crops and the number of animals they raised. Such cutbacks would help bring the supply of agricultural products more in line with the demand for them, causing prices to rise.

Although the plan was sound in theory, problems developed as it was put into practice. For example, by the time the AAA was established in the spring of 1933, farmers had already planted their fields and farm animals had already produced many young. Therefore, in order to meet the AAA's guidelines, farmers had to plow under portions of their crops and kill the newborn animals. At a time when thousands of people were suffering from malnutrition, this action struck many as immoral and wasteful.

In response, Roosevelt authorized the FERA to buy some of the crops and livestock before they were destroyed and to distribute them to the needy. Yet not all the farm products could be redistributed. For example, most of the animals that were slaughtered were too young to be used as food. To explain the apparent waste, Secretary of Agriculture Henry A. Wallace stated, "Agriculture cannot survive in a capitalistic society as a philanthropic enterprise." His explanation did little to appease the people who were distressed by the AAA's policies.

Tennessee Valley Authority

Another New Deal recovery program was the Tennessee Valley Authority (TVA). The TVA built dams in the Tennessee River to turn the river's water

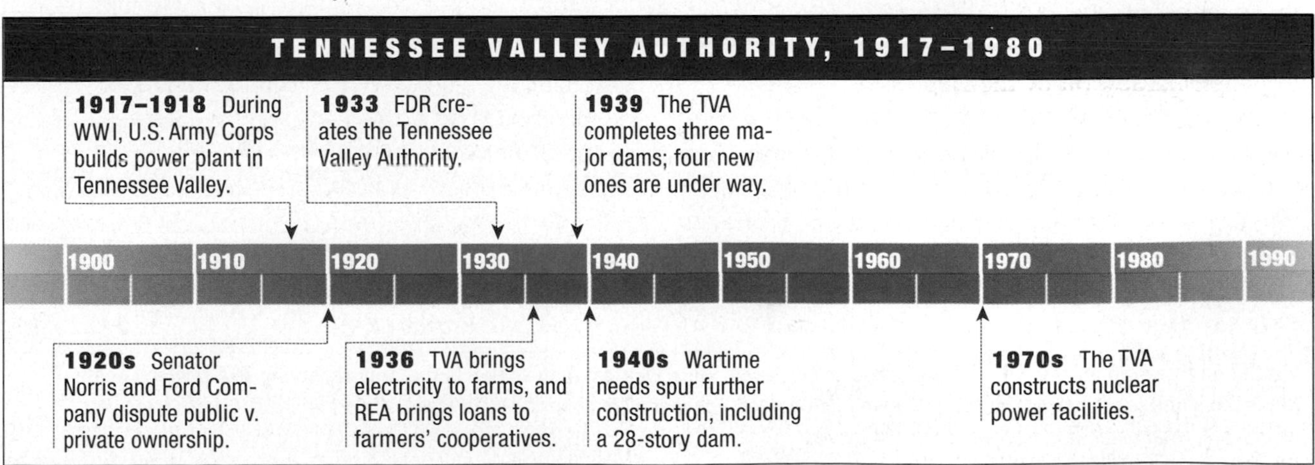
TENNESSEE VALLEY AUTHORITY, 1917–1980
1917–1918 During WWI, U.S. Army Corps builds power plant in Tennessee Valley.
1933 FDR creates the Tennessee Valley Authority.
1939 The TVA completes three major dams; four new ones are under way.
1900
1910
1920
1930
1940
1950
1960
1970
1980
1990
1920s Senator Norris and Ford Company dispute public v. private ownership.
1936 TVA brings electricity to farms, and REA brings loans to farmers' cooperatives.
1940s Wartime needs spur further construction, including a 28-story dam.
1970s The TVA constructs nuclear power facilities.

power into electricity. A reporter outlined the TVA's plan as follows:

> First, says the TVA, you fill up your gullies, terrace your land, strip-plow your slopes, and let the water flow down as slowly as possible. You collect the water behind dams and produce power. You use part of this power to make phosphate fertilizer, and with the fertilizer you grow legumes which enrich and hold your soil. You use some of the rest of the power on the farm itself.
>
> —"A Dream Takes Form in TVA's Domain," *New York Times Magazine,* April 19, 1936

The TVA aimed to do much more than just generate electricity. It was also intended to enrich the land, to create fish-filled lakes that would, in turn, increase tourism, and to provide jobs for the residents of the Tennessee Valley. Although the TVA achieved some of these goals, it was not well received by everyone. Farmers whose lands were permanently flooded by backwaters the dams created were certainly not pleased by the project. Also, some business leaders considered the government-sponsored agency an unfair competitor, resenting the rock-bottom rates the TVA charged. They lobbied to prevent similar programs from being approved for other regions of the country.

Reform Laws

In addition to providing relief and stimulating recovery, the New Deal legislation enacted reform measures. Among the most important reform measures were the Truth-in-Securities Act and the Glass-Steagall Banking Act.

The Truth-in-Securities Act was designed to eliminate fraud in the stock market. Under this law, a company that deliberately deceived investors about its financial status could be sued. The Glass-Steagall Banking Act prohibited banks from investing savings deposits in the stock market, which was too unpredictable to assure the safety of these funds. It also established the Federal Deposit Insurance Corporation (FDIC) to insure bank deposits in all member banks. With this insurance people regained confidence that their money would be safe in FDIC banks.

THE TENNESSEE VALLEY AUTHORITY, 1930s

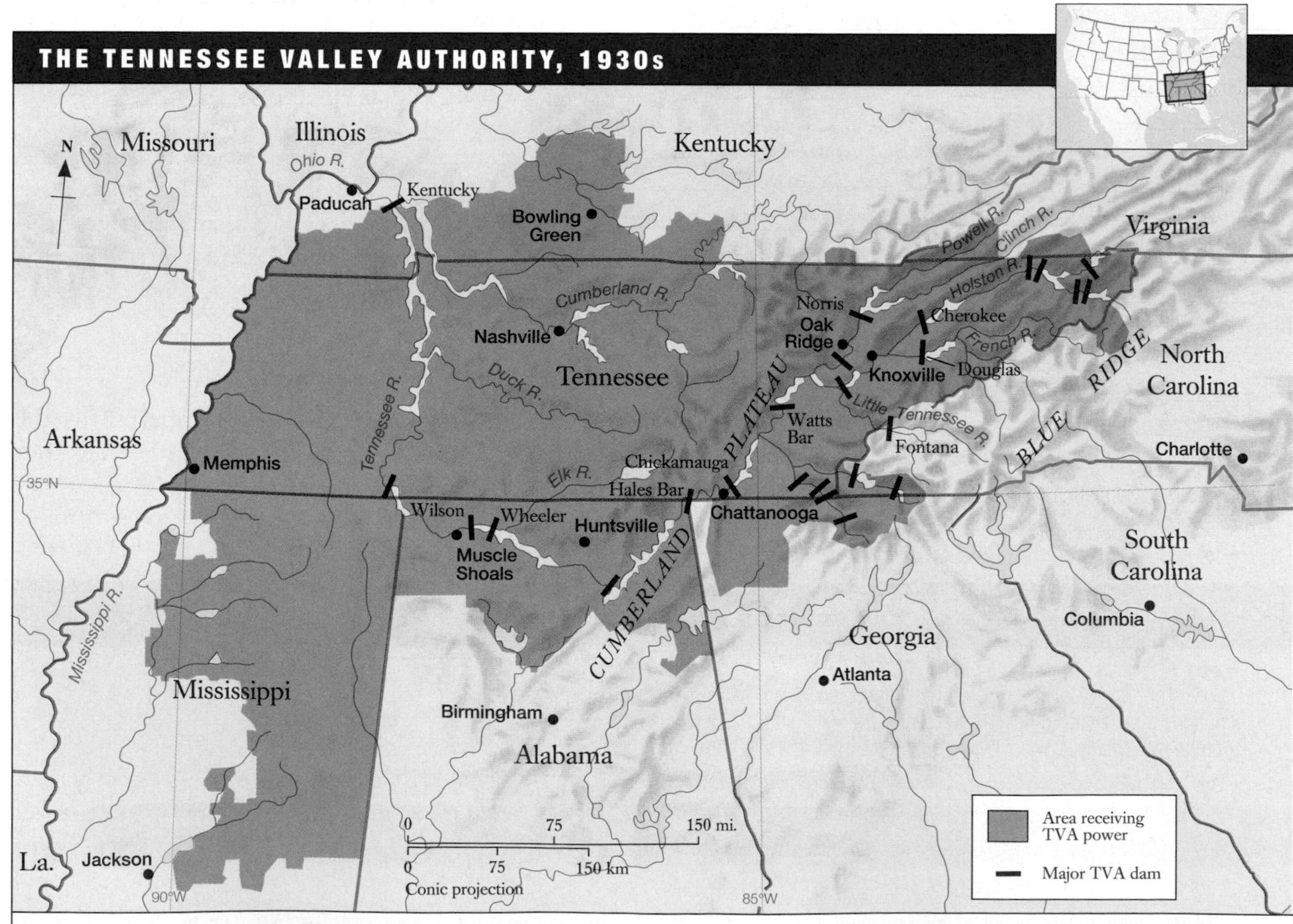

Plotted on this map are the sites at which major TVA dams were located. Also shown is the area receiving TVA power. Locate these sites and identify the area that receives TVA power. *In what other states besides Tennessee are there TVA dams? Besides Tennessee, what other states benefit from TVA power?*

COURTESY TENNESSEE VALLEY AUTHORITY

Electricity for Farms Under the Rural Electrification Act, low-interest, 20-year loans were granted to farmers' cooperatives to help connect rural homes to cheap power sources such as the TVA. *Why were some business leaders opposed to the TVA? Why did some farmers oppose it?*

During the Hundred Days between March 9 and June 16, President Roosevelt proposed 15 bills. These came to be known collectively as the First New Deal. Congress, with only minor changes, passed all 15 of his proposals. For a President to be able to collaborate so successfully with a Congress was a major victory. FDR, however, was a Democrat at a time when Democrats controlled Congress, a fact that greatly facilitated the passage of FDR's legislative programs.

The President and the People

Access to the White House

President Roosevelt's positive, vigorous style was reflected not only in his legislative programs but also in life at the White House, where glumness had reigned during the last few months of the Hoover administration. On Inauguration Day the head of the secret service, Colonel Edmund Starling, drove the brooding former President and his wife to the train station. When Starling returned, he reported that the White House was "transformed during my absence into a gay place, full of people who oozed confidence." The friendly informality of the White House made many Americans feel personally connected to the President.

Fireside Chats

FDR promoted this feeling by informally addressing the American public in frequent radio broadcasts known as fireside chats. In these chats, Roosevelt explained the legislation of the New Deal in simple, straightforward terms. Humorist Will Rogers quipped that in Roosevelt's first fireside chat, on March 12, 1933, the President explained the complex subject of banking in terms that even bankers could understand. His steady, relaxed voice reassured people across the nation that their problems would be solved and, more importantly, that they could participate in solving them. In his broadcast about the NRA, Roosevelt said the following:

> The essence of the plan is a universal limitation of hours of work per week for any individual by common consent, and a universal payment of wages above a minimum, also by common consent. I cannot guarantee the success of this nation-wide plan, but the people of this country can guarantee its success. . . . [I] do have faith, and retain faith, in the strength of common purpose, and in the strength of unified action taken by the American people.
>
> —Franklin D. Roosevelt, Fireside Chat, July 24, 1933

FDR's skillful handling of the press matched his masterful management of radio publicity. Hoover had met infrequently with reporters and only answered questions that had been written out beforehand. Roosevelt, on the other hand, held weekly press conferences in which he was willing to answer all questions. This made him very popular with reporters—a relationship that often worked to his advantage.

AP/WIDE WORLD PHOTOS

Woman of Action **While touring Puerto Rico in 1934, Mrs. Roosevelt listens to a young girl read from her schoolbook. In addition to speaking English, the First Lady spoke Spanish, French, and German.** *In what ways did Eleanor Roosevelt affect the presidency?*

Eleanor's Influence

Eleanor Roosevelt first became involved in politics during her husband's battle with polio. Hoping to keep FDR's name before the public, Eleanor became active in the Democratic party. She soon took up other causes, joining the Women's Trade Union League and the League of Women Voters. When FDR returned to politics, Eleanor did not give up her own political activities. Instead, she lobbied for laws to end child labor, worked for better conditions in state hospitals, discussed with her husband the appalling plight of people stranded by the Depression, and used her influence to help relieve their suffering.

Eleanor gave people the sense that they had access to the President. She received hundreds of thousands of letters each year, seeking help or offering solutions to problems.

> This letter comes to you from the . . . lead and zinc field of southeastern Kansas. Thirty-eight percent of the entire world supply of lead and zinc ore is produced in this district. We have here health hazards known as "lead poisoning" in the smelters and silicosis, the most dreaded industrial disease known to medical science. . . . These health hazards can be eliminated if the mining trusts will install air cleaning devices. This, of course, costs money and the greedy, grasping employers apparently haven't any extra. . . . Why [doesn't] the labor department make a health and hygiene survey of this district? Will you add your voice to ours in requesting this be done[?]
>
> —Letter from the Cherokee County Central Labor Body, Columbus, Kansas, 1938

Eleanor saw to it that all the letters that she received were answered. Those letters that were of special concern to her, like the one reprinted above, she showed to the President, often persuading him to take action.

She held her own press conferences regularly and traveled across the country giving lectures on a variety of topics that were of great concern to her and the American people. According to her friend Adlai Stevenson, "What rendered this unforgettable woman so extraordinary was not merely her response to suffering; it was her comprehension of the complexity of the human condition." Showing concern for everyone she met, the First Lady symbolized the energy, empathy, and responsiveness of the Roosevelt administration.

The Roosevelts' warm public images aligned the majority of Americans behind President Roosevelt and his New Deal. Throughout 1934, however, the country remained mired in economic depression. Critics quickly arose to attack Roosevelt and the New Deal.

Section Assessment

Main Idea

1. Use a chart like this one to organize New Deal legislation according to the three R's: relief, recovery, and reform.

New Deal Legislation		
Relief	Recovery	Reform

Vocabulary

2. Define: moratorium, dole, subsidy.

Checking Facts

3. What are some of the reasons why Roosevelt won the election of 1932?

4. How did the CCC and the PWA differ?

Critical Thinking

5. **Predicting Consequences** What might have happened if Roosevelt's legislation had failed to address any one of the three R's?

Social Studies Skill

INTERPRETING IMAGES

Learning the Skill

Many painters and photographers have documented American life. You can learn about a period from their works; you can get an idea of how people dressed, what technology they used, and where they lived and worked. Paintings and photographs are artists' impressions, however, and not objective records of the subjects they portray. To interpret an image, therefore, you must understand how it reflects the views of the person who created it. Both painter and photographer make choices about what to include and how to show it. These choices affect the impressions their works give.

Interpreting a Painting or Photograph

When you look at an image, ask yourself the following questions:

a. What has the painter or photographer chosen to portray? The artist might have represented only a small segment of society or symbolized the subject rather than documenting it precisely. What has been left out?

b. What is the central impression created by the image? Through the use of form and color, the artist might have idealized the subject, for example, or made it frightening.

c. How is the impression communicated? Photographers can control what the lens "sees" just as painters can control what appears on a canvas. Photographers can pose people and can exclude elements that do not support the impression they want to convey.

Practicing the Skill

1. Look below at the section of Thomas Hart Benton's mural *America Today*. How has Benton idealized the steelworkers and the industry?

2. Study the photograph below. What impression does it convey about the steelworkers' relationship to the city? How has the photographer communicated this impression?

3. Examine the mural on page 456. What can you learn about the New Deal from this image?

4. Review the two photographs of Eleanor Roosevelt on pages 453 and 460. How does each photograph give a different impression of her?

5. Look at the poster on page 455. How does the artist use the drawing to support the text on the poster?

Applying the Skill

Find a painting or photograph that interests you in a book or magazine. Apply what you have learned about interpreting images.

The **Glencoe Skillbuilder Interactive Workbook, Level 2** CD-ROM provides more practice in key social studies skills.

© THE EQUITABLE LIFE ASSURANCE SOCIETY OF THE UNITED STATES

America Today **Thomas Hart Benton depicts steelworkers in this section from a large mural.** *How does Benton convey the atmosphere of a steel mill?*

CULVER PICTURES

High Above New York This 1912 photograph shows men at work on the Woolworth Building, then the world's tallest building. *How does the photographer capture the danger?*

Science, TECHNOLOGY, and Society

The Telephone

Although the telephone industry shared in the hard times of the 1930s, technical development went forward. Replacement of operator-assisted calling with dial telephones continued; one operator at the switchboard could now do the work of six. By the end of 1935, 48 percent of telephones were dial operated.

FRANKLIN D. ROOSEVELT LIBRARY

HELLO GIRL

FDR had a special switchboard installed in the White House with Louise Hachmeister ("Hacky") as operator. He called her the phone detective and the hello girl. Eleanor Roosevelt said, "I doubt that there is a more consistently courteous group in America than telephone operators."

A TELEPHONE HISTORY

1870s | 1880s | 1890s | 1900s | 1910s | 1920s | 1930s

ALEXANDER GRAHAM BELL patents the first operational telephone in 1876; this patent was probably the most valuable patent ever issued.

FIRST COAST-TO-COAST CALL connects Bell and his assistant, Watson, in 1915. Dial phones are in use by 1919, and the work of the operator grows more mechanical.

SHORTWAVE RADIO helps make the first transatlantic telephone transmission possible in 1927. A handheld unit containing both earpiece and mouthpiece comes into use in the 1930s.

THE LAST WORD

The 1930s model, at left, was one of the earliest to combine the receiver and transmitter in a handheld, dial-operated instrument. This model and its later variations were standard for decades.

PHONE LOG

PORTFOLIO PROJECT

Keep a personal record for one week of your incoming and outgoing calls, both local and long-distance. Classify the calls as family, school-related, or social. Then assess the impact of the telephone on your life. How might you have sent or received each message without using a telephone?

THE
HECHT & MacARTHUR'S
FRONT PAGE
LINCOLN CENTER THEATER at the VIVIAN BEAUMONT

JAMES McMULLAN INC.

GET THAT STORY

By the 1930s the telephone was as essential to the reporter as the notepad and pencil—as vital to newspapering as it was to almost every other kind of business.

BROOKLYN MUSEUM

THE PAY PHONE

During the Depression years, the pay phone was a blessing to those who had to defer their dream of a household telephone. This telephone booth, called the Yin-Yang, was designed for the 1939 New York World's Fair.

1940s	1950s	1960s	1970s	1980s	1990s

DIRECT DIAL connects domestic long-distance calls by 1951. An undersea cable with long-life amplifiers and polyethylene insulation improves transatlantic calls in 1956.

SATELLITE TRANSMISSION and Touch-Tone phones help handle high volumes of calls by the early 1960s. International direct dialing begins in 1970.

MOBILE TELEPHONES make use of cellular radio technology in 1982. The Department of Justice ends the Bell monopoly in 1984. The 1990s introduce widespread use of conference calls, fiber optics, faxes, voice mail, and videoconferences.

Criticism and Reformulation

SEPTEMBER 1933: DOCTOR LAUNCHES CRUSADE TO AID THE ELDERLY

UPI/BETTMANN NEWSPHOTOS

Rage for Reform
The popularity of Townsend's pension program influenced the passage of the 1935 Social Security Act, even though economists considered his plan to be unworkable.

ONE DAY IN 1933, DR. FRANCIS E. TOWNSEND, A 66-YEAR-OLD RETIRED PHYSICIAN, WITNESSED SOMETHING THAT CHANGED HIS LIFE. While standing at his bathroom window shaving, he saw "three very haggard old women, stooped with great age, bending over the [trash] barrels, clawing into the contents." That these elderly people should be reduced to such poverty and degradation infuriated him.

Townsend channeled his fury into formulating a plan to aid America's aged and, at the same time, to stimulate the economy. According to his plan, every person over age 60 would be asked to retire, freeing up jobs for younger people. Each retired person would receive a pension of $200 per month on the condition that the person spend the entire sum in 30 days. Townsend claimed that the pension would rescue the elderly from poverty, and the enforced spending would act as a transfusion of cash into the economy. Furthermore, it would create a demand for products, which, in turn, would result in a demand for more workers to produce them. Townsend believed that his social security program would bring about an immediate end to the Depression.

In the southern California community where Townsend lived, the idea gained widespread appeal. To publicize the plan, Townsend began circulating petitions, speaking at meetings, and organizing

GUIDE TO READING

Main Idea

Roosevelt faced opposition not only from people who demanded the government do more to help the needy, but also from people who demanded it do less.

Vocabulary

- unionization
- demagogue

Read to Find Out . . .

- the objections of tenant farmers, labor unions, radicals, conservatives, and the Supreme Court to the New Deal.
- the legislation of the Second New Deal.
- the impact of Roosevelt's proposed change in the Supreme Court on the momentum of the Second New Deal.

clubs. Within a few years, Townsend clubs had sprung up throughout the nation.

The success of Dr. Townsend's movement indicated the level of discontent many elderly people felt during Roosevelt's first term. Older people, however, were not the only ones to find fault with Roosevelt. By the end of 1934, people from all walks of life were attacking Roosevelt's policies.

New Deal: Big Deal!

Discontent With the Pace of Recovery

Under Roosevelt's New Deal, the economy had begun to recover. Between 1933 and 1934, the national income rose 25 percent. By 1934 hundreds of factories that had closed in the early 1930s were again producing goods. Many farmers had refinanced their mortgages with government assistance. Millions of people who had been unemployed were receiving relief or holding federally funded jobs.

Nevertheless, the recovery was incomplete. Although by 1934 incomes had risen substantially, they were still far below precrash levels. On average, workers in the cities made 13 percent less than they had made in 1929. Farm prices lagged 28 percent behind 1929 prices. More than 20 percent of the working population were still unemployed. For many farmers, factory workers, and unemployed citizens, the New Deal had taken too long to accomplish too little.

Protests of Tenant Farmers

The New Deal's agricultural program, the AAA, actually did some farmers more harm than good. To reduce the amount of crops that would be produced, the AAA paid landowners to let some of their land lie unused. Technically, the landowners were supposed to divide their AAA checks with their tenant farmers. In reality, however, few landowners complied with this

AP/WIDE WORLD PHOTOS

Common Cause Although African Americans and whites were segregated in most work and social situations, in the Southern Tenant Farmers' Union (STFU), African American and white tenant farmers joined forces to fight the landowners who had unjustly evicted them. *What did the AAA require of landowners?*

GENERAL MOTORS SIT-DOWN STRIKE OF 1936–1937

Union organizing efforts in the mid-1930s focused on the auto industry, where the United Automobile Workers (UAW) pioneered the sit-down, a work stoppage in which workers refuse to leave their place of employment until their demands are met.

LIBRARY OF CONGRESS

Inside the Plant: Most of the strikers are orderly and disciplined. They organize an orchestra and chorus, games, sports, and classes in labor history and other subjects.

UPI/BETTMANN NEWSPHOTOS

June 1936 UAW tries to organize autoworkers. Spies hired by General Motors (GM) infiltrate meetings. Union activists are fired. GM refuses to recognize the union.

January 11 GM cuts off heat to the plant and blocks delivery of food. Police attack with tear gas; strikers fight back with firehoses and improvised projectiles; 13 strikers are wounded by gunfire.

1 Day | 10 Days | 20 Days | 30 Days | 40 Days

December 30 Workers at GM's Fisher Body #1 plant in Flint, Michigan, begin a sit-down strike.

January 6 An injunction against the strike is voided when the judge is found to own GM stock. Strikers ignore a later injunction.

Strike spreads: Soon 18 other GM plants in 10 cities are closed. Public opinion turns against GM.

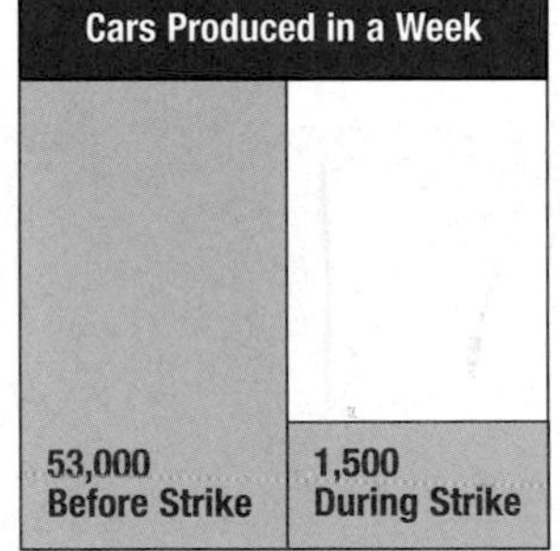

Support: John L. Lewis, head of the CIO, and Governor Frank Murphy of Michigan, support the strikers. A local restaurant offers its facilities; a Women's Emergency Brigade prepares food and marches in picket lines.

A watershed in labor history was the push by the Congress of Industrial Organizations (CIO) to organize workers on an industry-wide basis rather than on a craft basis, as in the older American Federation of Labor (AFL). *Judging from the membership graph, when did industrial unions begin to take hold?*

requirement. Instead, they tended to reduce the number of acres planted by evicting their tenant farmers and did not even share with them the AAA subsidy. Poverty-stricken before the New Deal, tenant farmers were then also homeless and jobless.

A group of Southern tenant farmers who were outraged by this situation organized the interracial Southern Tenant Farmers' Union (STFU). They went on strike to obtain raises for working tenant farmers and day laborers. They petitioned the Department of Agriculture to give them a guarantee that tenant farmers would get their fair share of AAA payments. They also promoted nonviolent protest and showed that African Americans and whites could work together effectively.

The STFU met with strong opposition. Landowners worked with law enforcement agents to harass STFU leaders, threaten union members, and break up STFU meetings. Desperate for help, the STFU appealed to Roosevelt for aid. Roosevelt responded with promises but no action. Bitterly disappointed, one STFU leader wrote, "Too often he [Roosevelt] has talked like a cropper [tenant farmer] and acted like a planter [landowner]."

Voices of Labor

The National Industrial Recovery Act (NIRA) of 1933 had permitted all workers to join unions of their choice, bargain collectively for wage increases and other work benefits, and go on strike to try to force employers to meet their demands. The NIRA thus renewed most workers' hopes for change. In just the first 2 years following its passage, unions added about 1 million new workers to their ranks.

Although unions organized workers' efforts and provided them with leaders who could negotiate with owners and managers, some workers believed that unions were not as effective as worker-organized strikes and protests. Unions tended to dissipate revolutionary energy by focusing on contracts and negotiations rather than on rebellion.

"When Mr. Knudsen put his name to a piece of paper and says that General Motors recognizes the UAW-CIO—until that moment, we were non-people, we didn't even exist. [Laughs] That was the big one. [His eyes are moist.]"

Bob Stinson, a striker
quoted in *Hard Times* by Studs Terkel

The End [February 11] GM agrees to negotiate. The union wins recognition and a six-month contract. Workers are no longer afraid to join the union.

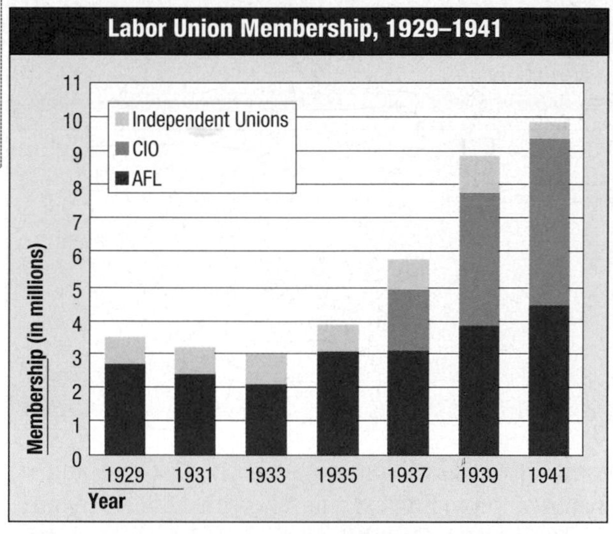

Unionization, or the formation of unions, did not generally ease the conflict between workers and management, however. The number and intensity of such conflicts increased after passage of the NIRA. An especially heated conflict occurred in 1934 when Minneapolis truck drivers tried to get local business representatives to negotiate with their union. Business leaders responded by banding together to break the strike. Then, on July 16, the police opened fire on unarmed picketers, shooting 67 people and killing 2. One hundred thousand Minneapolis citizens marched in the funeral procession for the slain workers. Confronted by such strong union sympathy, business leaders agreed to negotiate with unions.

During 1934 similarly bitter strikes took place throughout the nation. Textile workers from Georgia to Massachusetts staged a massive strike, while San Francisco workers from various unions struck together. That year more than 1.5 million workers staged 1,800 strikes.

Because unionization tended to increase the number of strikes and protests, business leaders and factory owners generally tried to prevent workers from unionizing. Although it was illegal, many employers fired or intimidated workers who tried to start unions. Even Roosevelt, who had supported the NIRA, worried more about labor's power to halt economic recovery with strikes than he did about protecting the rights the bill supposedly ensured.

Reactionary and Radical Voices

Frustrated with the slowness and the limited scope of Roosevelt's New Deal, many Americans turned to leaders who promised simple and sometimes radical solutions to the nation's pressing problems. These leaders gained huge followings during the mid-1930s.

Dr. Townsend, who organized more than 5 million supporters for his pension plan, was one such leader. Townsend focused on getting Congress to approve his plan. In 1935, however, Townsend's plan was soundly defeated in Congress.

Another popular leader was Father Charles E. Coughlin, a Roman Catholic priest with his own weekly radio show. Coughlin was a **demagogue,** a leader who gains power by appealing to people's prejudices and fears rather than by appealing to reason.

In 1933 and 1934, Coughlin supported Roosevelt because he thought the President agreed with his ideas, such as nationalizing the banks and running them as a federal business like the post office. By 1935, Coughlin realized that Roosevelt had no intention of changing the nation's financial system. At that point he began calling the President a "great betrayer and a liar."

FDR was not the only person Coughlin attacked. He also spoke out against powerful bankers and later extended his hatred of particular bankers who happened to be Jewish to hatred of all Jews. Although the Jewish people were clearly not responsible for the economic plight of the nation, Coughlin's anti-Semitism gave his

AP/WIDE WORLD PHOTOS

Police and Strikers Clash **During the 1934 strike, truckers fought with police in an attempt to prevent loaded vehicles from leaving a warehouse.** *How did Minneapolis citizens react to the violence?*

AP/WIDE WORLD PHOTOS

FROM THE COLLECTION OF THE LOUISIANA STATE MUSEUM

Two of a Kind Father Charles Coughlin, above, claimed approximately 9 million supporters before the church ordered him to step out of the public spotlight. Huey P. Long, right, also had an enormous following. *How did Long maintain control of Louisiana while he was a member of the United States Senate?*

followers a group of people to blame for their troubles. Coughlin also preached that the wealth of the few should be redistributed among the many, an idea that appealed to many in the working class.

Coughlin's impassioned speeches increased his following. In the mid-1930s he commanded a radio audience of 30 million. Superiors in the church, however, embarrassed by Coughlin's behavior, finally imposed silence upon the priest in 1942.

A contemporary of Coughlin, Senator Huey P. Long of Louisiana was equally popular and just as opposed to FDR's programs. Long had achieved almost instant popularity when, as governor of Louisiana, he had pushed through new taxes to raise funds for schools and hospitals that would serve the poor. Long had seen to it that roads were improved and bridges were built in previously neglected areas of the state.

While still governor, Long was elected to the United States Senate in 1930. Just before he left the office of governor to take his seat in the Senate, he replaced the lieutenant governor with two successors who would follow his commands while he was in Washington, D.C. Then, as senator, he abolished local Louisiana governments, putting himself in control of all appointments to government offices such as those of the police and fire departments.

As senator he also launched his Share Our Wealth campaign with the slogan: Every man a king, but no one wears a crown. According to Long's proposal, all incomes above $5 million would be confiscated and redistributed, providing each family with a $5,000 income. Long's plan, like Coughlin's, appealed to many in the working class, helping him to gain widespread support.

Having taken complete control of the Louisiana government, Long then set his sights on controlling the United States government. In September 1935, however, Long was assassinated, putting an end to his plans.

New Deal: No Deal!

Conservatives and Courts Oppose FDR

Roosevelt not only faced opposition from people who demanded that the government do more for the needy, but also from people who demanded it do less. Among his greatest enemies were bankers and politicians with whom he had worked so successfully when he first took office.

Attack From the Conservatives

Many business leaders charged that Roosevelt was interfering too much with private businesses and spending an excessive amount of money on relief. They attacked the President's top advisers for lacking the political and business experience necessary to address adequately the needs of businesses. Most claimed that

Roosevelt had created an unmanageable bureaucracy and was leading the nation toward socialism.

In 1934 a number of unhappy politicians and busi nesspeople formed the American Liberty League, an organization dedicated to "upholding the Constitution." This stated goal masked the league's real purpose: to destroy the New Deal. By waging a propaganda war, league members hoped to force Roosevelt supporters out of office. The Liberty League, described by one reporter as "the largest collection of millionaires ever assembled under the same roof," never gained much support.

Attack From the Courts

The courts were more successful in attacking the New Deal than were the millionaires. In the mid-1930s the Supreme Court overturned two key pieces of New Deal legislation, the NIRA and the AAA, on the grounds that they were both unconstitutional. It objected to the multitude of NIRA codes the executive branch had helped design and found that the NIRA's regulation of all industries—from dog food to shoulder pads—gave the executive branch too much power over small local businesses. In addition, the Court faulted NIRA codes that regulated intrastate as well as interstate business, arguing that the Constitution gave the federal government power only to regulate commerce between states—not within states. The Court also objected to the means by which the AAA funded its agricultural subsidies: by levying a processing tax on businesses that bought the agricultural products. The Court deemed taxation was an improper method of regulating agricultural production.

Faced with attacks by radicals, liberals, and conservatives and hampered by the Supreme Court, Roosevelt revamped his recovery and reform policies. In 1935 he launched his new program—the Second New Deal.

The Second New Deal

Extending Relief and Reform

Like the First New Deal, the Second New Deal included sweeping legislation in many different areas. The new laws expanded relief programs, aided farmers and workers, and provided economic reforms.

Expanding Relief

Despite the success of the First New Deal, 10 million people remained unemployed in 1934. To put more people back to work, Roosevelt proposed a $4.8 billion relief program, the Works Progress Administration (WPA), in his Second New Deal.

Congress approved the proposed WPA in April 1935. Headed by Harry Hopkins, the administrator who had so forcefully taken charge of the FERA, the WPA then began processing the applications it received for projects nationwide. Building projects, including construction of hospitals, schools, airports, and playgrounds, were the mainstay of the program. The WPA also put unemployed teachers, artists, writers, and actors back to work. Teachers taught people to read. Painters designed murals for public buildings. Writers wrote guidebooks describing America's historical and cultural heritage. Actors traveled the country, bringing live theater to people who had never seen a play before.

A single WPA project might benefit a community in a variety of ways. For example, in San Antonio, Texas, in 1939

NATIONAL MUSEUM OF AMERICAN ART, WASHINGTON, DC/ART RESOURCE, NY

Jobs for Artists This 1935 Moses Soyer painting, *Artists on WPA*, depicts painters preparing works to be hung in public buildings. *How does Soyer convey the effect that WPA projects had on the morale of artists?*

the WPA sponsored a $300,000 project that included building a scenic walkway along the San Antonio River, deepening the river channel to permit small-craft navigation, landscaping the riverfront, and building an outdoor theater. This project stimulated the local economy and beautified the city.

Both directly and indirectly, the WPA improved the quality of life in communities across the nation. In all, during its 5 years of operation, the WPA gave jobs to more than 8 million people.

In August 1935 another program, the Social Security Act, was passed. With its passage, the government accepted direct responsibility for meeting the basic needs of its citizens. This program instituted pension and survivors' benefits for the elderly and the orphaned and aid to individuals injured in industrial accidents. Monthly Social Security payments ranged from $12 to $85. Millions of people, however, did not even qualify for the program. Many of those who did not qualify were members of minority groups.

Aiding Recovery

Roosevelt further aided recovery by restoring to workers and farmers the rights and privileges that the Supreme Court had revoked. When the Supreme Court declared the NIRA unconstitutional in May 1935, workers lost their right to join unions of their choice and to bargain collectively. The July 1935 Wagner Act, however, restored those rights. It also set up a federal agency, the National Labor Relations Board (NLRB), to ensure that employers followed the new law.

After the Supreme Court struck down the AAA, Roosevelt proposed the Soil Conservation Act of 1936, which required farmers to reduce the acreage of the same crops the AAA had previously paid them not to plant. Under this act, the money for farm subsidies would not come from a processing tax—as it had under the AAA—but from the treasury.

The Rural Electrification Act (REA) of 1935 lent money to groups of farmers who organized to build power plants. For years utility companies had refused to extend service to isolated rural areas, arguing that it was not profitable. As a result, before the REA, fewer than 1 in 10 American farms had electricity. By the late 1940s, however, electricity had been extended to 90 percent of all farms.

Pushing for New Reforms

The REA indirectly attacked utility companies by enabling people to obtain electricity without them. Roosevelt also attacked these huge conglomerates directly with the Public Utility Holding Company Act, passed in June 1935. This act, which pared down the holding companies, helped eliminate corruption and inefficiency in the utility industries and reduced consumers' costs.

The legislation regulating the utility companies enraged many business leaders who believed that the

CULVER PICTURES

A Powerful Project In this 1938 photograph, a skilled WPA employee works on intricate wiring. *In what ways did the WPA improve the quality of life during the Second New Deal?*

government was assuming too much power over businesses. These people became even angrier when the President proposed increased taxes on the incomes of wealthy corporations and individuals. This revenue bill passed Congress in 1935.

The Revenue Act of 1935 as well as other Second New Deal legislation convinced millions of Americans that the President was on their side. Roosevelt's popularity soared as the 1936 election season began.

Reelection and Redirection

Victory Won and Momentum Lost

Roosevelt geared his campaign toward the lower and middle classes, who had been hardest hit by the Depression. He promised voters legislation that was not only charitable but that helped people to help themselves. The Republican candidate, Kansas's Governor Alfred Landon, supported most of Roosevelt's New Deal programs but said that he would run them more efficiently. Nevertheless, Landon gave people little reason to switch to him. In the most lopsided election since 1820, FDR won the majority of votes in every state but Maine and Vermont. Backed by 60 percent of the voters, Roosevelt believed the American people had endorsed his New Deal.

Conflict Over the Judicial Branch

Forging ahead, in February 1937 Roosevelt introduced a bill to increase the number of justices on the Supreme Court. Having been distressed by the Court's rulings against New Deal legislation, FDR wanted to appoint additional judges sympathetic to his programs. Publicly, however, Roosevelt insisted that he was merely trying to ease the workload of the aging justices. People reacted negatively to his tampering with the delicately balanced judicial system. Republican critics accused Roosevelt of wanting to become a dictator.

Although even some Democrats eventually criticized him, Roosevelt stuck to his proposal. Then, in the middle of the fight, the Supreme Court upheld several key New Deal programs. At this point, FDR backed down. To save face, he eventually signed a watered-down bill enacting measures to speed up judicial processes.

Fair Labor Standards Act

Opposition to Roosevelt's proposed judicial system changes and an economic recession that began in 1937 slowed down his political momentum. In 1937 and 1938, Roosevelt proposed numerous other programs. He only secured passage of one New Deal law in 1938, the Fair Labor Standards Act, which regulated wages and working hours. Then, as tensions in Europe and Asia grew, the President began to concentrate on international issues and the New Deal slowly ground to a halt.

BROWN BROTHERS

An Unpopular Proposal **When FDR proposed adding seats to the Supreme Court, most people thought he meant to "pack the court" with justices who would sustain his New Deal legislation.** *How did this controversy end?*

SECTION ASSESSMENT

Main Idea

1. Use a diagram like this one to show people who challenged Roosevelt and their reasons for doing so. Add more answer boxes as needed.

Roosevelt's Challengers	
Group / Person	Reason

Vocabulary

2. Define: unionization, demagogue.

Checking Facts

3. How did the Second New Deal meet some of the criticisms of the First New Deal?

4. Why did the New Deal slow down in 1937 and 1938?

Critical Thinking

5. **Recognizing Bias** Why might tenant farmers and landowners differ on the issue of AAA reimbursement?

Turning Point

Art and Politics at Rockefeller Center

SPRING 1933

May 4, 1933

Dear Mr. Rivera,

While I was in the No. 1 building at Rockefeller Center yesterday viewing the progress of your thrilling mural, I noticed that in the most recent portion of the painting you had included a portrait of Lenin. This piece is beautifully painted but it seems to me that his portrait, appearing in this mural, might very easily seriously offend a great many people. . . . As much as I dislike to do so I am afraid we must ask you to substitute the face of some unknown man where Lenin's face now appears. . . .

With best wishes, I remain sincerely,
Nelson A. Rockefeller

The Case

Nelson Rockefeller, grandson of oil magnate John D. Rockefeller, Sr., commissioned Mexican muralist Diego Rivera to paint a fresco mural into the fresh plaster of the RCA Building's grand hall in Rockefeller Center. The mural's middle panel was nearly 41 feet by 19 feet (12.5 m by 5.8 m). The mural's proposed title was *Man at the Crossroads Looking with Hope and High Vision to the Choosing of a New and Better Future.* The Rockefeller family approved a preliminary sketch by Rivera that showed man standing between the bad times of the past and the good times of the future. A faceless leader united the people and brought order out of chaos.

Rivera began painting the mural in March 1933. On May Day (May 1), an international day in honor of workers, Rivera painted a portrait of the late Russian Communist ruler V.I. Lenin in place of the faceless leader. Rivera described his mural:

> **On the left . . . I showed a night club scene of the debauched rich, a battlefield with men in the holocaust of war, and unemployed workers in a demonstration being clubbed by the police. On the right, I painted corresponding scenes of life in a socialist country: a May Day demonstration of marching, singing workers; an athletic stadium filled with girls exercising their bodies; and a figure of Lenin, symbolically clasping the hands of a black American and a white Russian soldier and worker, as allies of the future.**

When Rockefeller asked Rivera to alter the design by eliminating the image of Lenin, Rivera responded:

> **I am sure that that class of person who is capable of being offended by the portrait of a deceased great man, would feel offended, given such a men-**

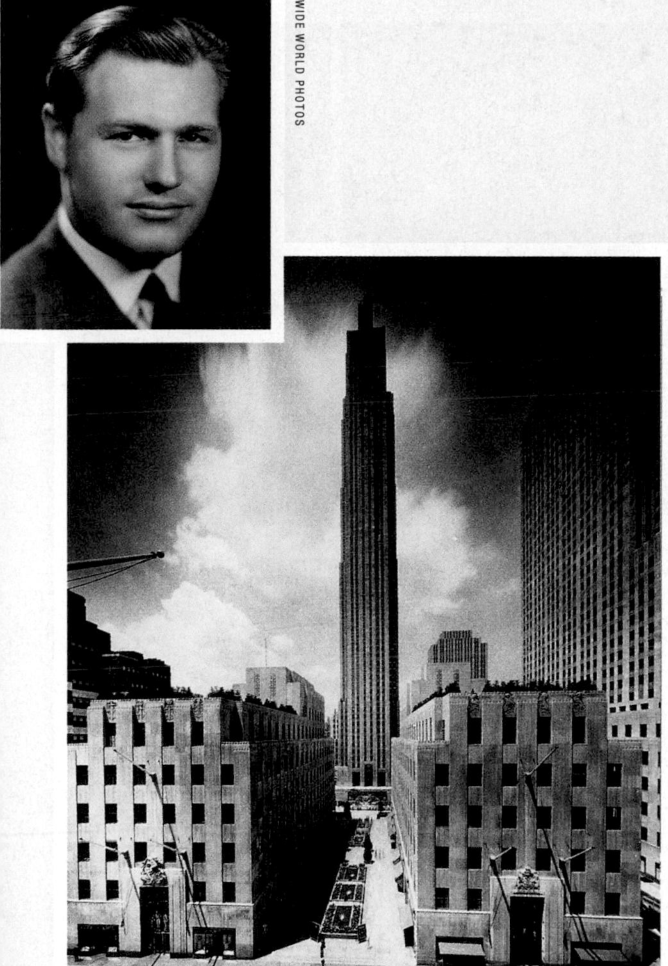

AP/WIDE WORLD PHOTOS

SOPHIA SMITH COLLECTION, SMITH COLLEGE, NORTHAMPTON, MA, AND MRS. AUBREY NIEL MORGAN

Diego Rivera, above, painted a controversial mural in Rockefeller Center, New York, left. Nelson Rockefeller is shown at upper left.

tality, by the entire conception of my painting. Therefore, rather than mutilate the conception, I should prefer the physical destruction of the conception in its entirety, but conserving, at least, its integrity. . . . I could change the sector which shows society people playing bridge and dancing, and put in its place, in perfect balance with the Lenin portion, a figure of some great American historical leader, such as Lincoln, who symbolizes the unification of the country and the abolition of slavery.

The next move was up to Rockefeller. If he insisted that Rivera change the portrait of Lenin to an unknown man, would that constitute censorship? Who owns a work of art—the artist who creates it, the person who buys it, or the public?

The Background

The Rockefeller family developed Rockefeller Center between 1929 and 1939. When 64 percent of the workers in the building trades were unemployed, 75,000 men were employed in constructing Rockefeller Center. John D. Rockefeller, Jr., was the epitome of the successful American capitalist. While all around him workers were losing faith in an economy that could not employ them, Rockefeller provided meaningful, profitable work.

Mrs. John D. Rockefeller, Jr., was a founder of the Museum of Modern Art in New York City. In 1931 she brought Rivera to the United States, where he gave a show the next year. Some of the images in that show had realistically depicted starving workers and idle mills in the United States. She was also aware that in his Mexico City murals Rivera had painted a mocking caricature of John D. Rockefeller, Sr., the founder of the family's fortune.

Rivera regarded Lenin as the father of a unified and successful working class. Lenin provided the rallying point for what Rivera thought

Turning Point

MUSEO DEL PALACIO DE BELLAS, MEXICO CITY

When Diego Rivera could not complete his mural for Rockefeller Center, he asked the Mexican government for a duplicate space and was given a wall on the third floor of the Palacio de Bellas Artes (Palace of Fine Arts) in Mexico City.

was an impending world revolution. Rivera explained the use of Lenin in the mural in this way:

> If the United States wished to preserve its democratic forms, it would ally itself with Russia against [Nazi] fascism. Since Lenin was the preeminent founder of the Soviet Union and also the first and most altruistic theorist of modern communism, I used him as the center of the inevitable alliance between the Russian and the American [against fascism].

The Opinions

To Rivera this dispute was between individual ownership as championed by capitalism and collective ownership as advocated by communism. He stated:

> There are only two real points of view from which to choose: the point of view of capitalist economy and morality . . . the right of individual property . . . and the point of view of socialist economy and morality . . . the rights of the human collectivity.
>
> —quoted in Bertram Wolfe, *Diego Rivera: His Life and Times,* 1939

Many artists saw the issue of censorship at the heart of the dispute, claiming that the Rockefellers were attempting to suppress Rivera's free speech.

To refute this view, a newspaper editorial expressed the opinion that it was not censorship that was at issue but rather logic. It was illogical to have a communistic mural in a capitalist building:

> The issue between Rivera and Rockefeller Center would thus have nothing to do with the right of the artist to represent the world as he sees it. The mural painter is not concerned with visions and intuitions but with telling a story and inculcating a lesson. His message must therefore make sense. There is no sense in making a monumental wall-painting cry "Liar" to the wall on which it is spread.
>
> —*New York Times,* May 11, 1933

The Decision

On May 9 Rockefeller ordered Rivera to stop work on the mural, and the carpenters covered it with large frames of stretched canvas. After the guards drove Rivera from his scaffold, the building manager paid off the artist's $21,000 contract and gave him a letter of dismissal.

Nearly 100 admirers of Rivera's art paraded in front of the RCA Building, carrying signs that read Save Rivera's Art and We Want Rivera. There was a great uproar; committees of artists agitated for and against the mural.

Rockefeller was eager to avoid controversy and said in a letter to his father, "We are hoping that the disagreeable public criticism which has been leveled at us this past week will be turned to sympathetic understanding of our position." On May 12, 1933, the *World-Telegram* reported Rockefeller's assurance that the "uncompleted fresco of Diego Rivera will not be destroyed or in any way mutilated, but . . . will be covered, to remain hidden for an indefinite time."

The Rockefellers allowed the mural to remain covered until February 9, 1934. At midnight, just as the weekend was beginning, workers rolled wheelbarrows into the building and crumbled the fresco into powder, which was wheeled away.

The lawyers of Rockefeller Center completely deflated the protests that were planned by the artistic community. They made public the year-old letter in which Rivera told the Rockefellers that he would prefer to see the whole mural destroyed rather than change Lenin's portrait.

The Significance

When Rivera learned that his painting had been smashed, he made his goal clear: "My object was attained when the painting was destroyed. I thank the Rockefellers for its destruction because the act will advance the cause of the labor revolution."

In Mexico City, Rivera applied to the Mexican government for a wall at the Palace of Fine Arts where he could let people see what kind of painting it was that these "patrons of the arts" had chosen to destroy. He introduced into the new mural's nightclub scene a portrait of John D. Rockefeller, Jr., drinking champagne. Rockefeller actually did not drink alcohol.

To Rivera the significance of the dispute lay in the distinction between the individual's rights (as represented by capitalism) and the rights of the group (as represented by communism):

> Let us take, as an example, an American millionaire who buys the Sistine Chapel, which contains the work of Michelangelo. . . . Would that millionaire have the right to destroy the Sistine Chapel?. . . In human creation there is something which belongs to humanity at large, and . . . no individual owner has the right to destroy it or keep it solely for his own enjoyment.
>
> —Diego Rivera

RESPONDING TO THE CASE

1. Make two columns on a sheet of paper. On one side list the arguments made by Rivera and on the other side list the arguments made by Nelson Rockefeller on behalf of his family. Explain which side appears to have the stronger position.

2. Discuss whether a person who owns a work of art but does not let it be seen is guilty of censorship. For example, could a newspaper publisher/owner who stopped an objectionable story from being printed be considered guilty of censorship?

3. Which, if any, of Rockefeller's responses constituted censorship: his request that Lenin's portrait be changed, his covering the mural with canvas for nine months, or his chiseling it off the wall? Defend your answer.

4. Discuss whether a painting is owned by the painter who created it, the person who bought it, or the general public.

PORTFOLIO PROJECT

Write a letter to the editor of the *New York Times* either defending or opposing Rivera's position, Rockefeller's position, or the *Times*'s position. In your letter, begin by stating fairly the view you are discussing, and then present your best arguments either for or against it. Conclude with a clear statement summarizing your own position.

The Impact of the New Deal

EASTER 1939: MARIAN ANDERSON DAZZLES CROWD AT LINCOLN MEMORIAL

THE WHITE MARBLE OF THE LINCOLN MEMORIAL GLEAMED IN THE SUNSHINE. A crowd of 75,000 people gathered in front of it on the grassy hill and beside the reflecting pool. At the dedication ceremony 10 years earlier, African Americans had been assigned seats in a separate, roped-off section across the road. This Sunday, however, African Americans and whites sat together, awaiting the appearance of the famous opera singer Marian Anderson.

The crowd hushed as Anderson appeared at the foot of the monument and turned to face the crowd. She began singing, "My country 'tis of thee, sweet land of liberty." She sang slowly as if singing a solemn hymn.

UPI/BETTMANN

Open-Air Concert
Contralto Marian Anderson, celebrated in the concert halls of Europe, sings on the steps of the Lincoln Memorial.

It was an inspiring moment because plans for the concert had almost had to be abandoned. There was no concert hall in the capital large enough to seat the enormous crowd expected to attend her performance other than Constitution Hall. The Daughters of the American Revolution (DAR), which owned the hall, had refused Anderson the right to sing there, however, simply because she was an African American. Dismayed, Anderson had turned to the Roosevelts for help.

When Eleanor Roosevelt heard about the DAR's refusal to

GUIDE TO READING

Main Idea

The New Deal had an enormous impact on the United States, greatly increasing the role of the federal government in the lives of ordinary citizens.

Vocabulary

- discrimination
- federal regulation

Read to Find Out . . .

- the impact that New Deal legislation had on women, African Americans, and Native Americans.
- the new responsibility the government began to take for the welfare of its citizens.

host the famous singer, she not only resigned from the organization but also encouraged Anderson to apply for permission to give a free concert on the steps of the Lincoln Memorial. Almost immediately Anderson's request was approved. Thus, with help from the White House, Anderson's thousands of fans were not disappointed, and the concert was a majestic success.

Although the Roosevelt administration's record on gender and race was mixed, to the nation's women and minority groups it was the most accessible and sympathetic administration in the nation's history. The Roosevelt administration passed legislation, created programs, and made other significant changes that benefited African Americans, Native Americans, and women. Such changes were among the most important legacies of FDR's New Deal.

Women Gain Political Recognition

New Deal Furthers Women's Rights

On March 6, 1933, 2 days after President Roosevelt's inauguration, approximately 35 reporters gathered in the Red Room of the White House to wait for the First Lady. The scene looked like any other press conference—reporters quietly talking and reviewing their lists of questions—except that all of the reporters were women. This was the first of what Eleanor Roosevelt promised would be weekly press conferences.

In addition to what the First Lady had to say to the press, the mere fact that she had decided to hold weekly press conferences made news in Washington. Mrs. Hoover had met with reporters just once in her four-year tenure as First Lady—and then only reluctantly. Eleanor Roosevelt had been politically active even before she came to the White House, and, as First Lady, she increased her political activities. One of her causes was helping women gain economic and political power. She restricted her press conferences to women reporters to help them keep their jobs. During the Depression many newspapers cut back their staffs, and women were often the first to be let go. Eleanor Roosevelt felt that if she would only meet with women reporters, at least these women would be retained by their employers.

Partly because of Eleanor's influence, women gained political recognition. Women, she felt, were in the best position to promote child welfare, education, fair labor standards, and even world peace. To this end, in addition to publicizing these causes, the First Lady worked to get women appointed to political posts. Women's roles in government expanded substantially during the Roosevelt years.

HISTORICAL PICTURES SERVICE, CHICAGO

Meet the Press The candid and informal way the Roosevelts addressed reporters won the press over completely. Here Eleanor Roosevelt (center) is holding one of her regular press conferences. *Why did the First Lady restrict her press conferences to women reporters?*

Women in Power

In his first term as President, Roosevelt appointed the first woman in United States history to a cabinet post: Frances Perkins, a former social worker, who had served as industrial commissioner for New York State. As secretary of labor, Perkins pushed hard to obtain a social security program and a minimum-wage law that would boost the pay of thousands of poorly paid women in the workforce.

Roosevelt also appointed the first woman to the federal appeals court, the first women ambassadors, and a woman as director of the mint. Women were asked to serve as advisers in many New Deal agencies. In all, more than 100 women held senior positions in the federal government during FDR's administration. This was still only a fraction of the number of such positions held by men.

Facing Discrimination

Although many women entered public life during Roosevelt's administration, in general they still faced **discrimination,** or prejudicial treatment. For example, Roosevelt supported women's rights, but he still tended to appoint women to government posts where they would be least likely to conflict with men. Thus the women in his administration had more limited influence than it might seem.

Therefore, women in government usually could not prevent women in the workforce from experiencing unfair treatment. NRA codes often granted women lower pay than men, even for the same jobs. Many businesses refused to hire married women, and married women whose husbands worked were often forced to resign.

The reasons for these severe practices were twofold. First, most people believed that unless a woman's wages were essential for family survival, the woman should stay at home. Second, the majority of Americans thought that because jobs were so scarce, working wives should give up their jobs so that men could take their places. People believed in these arguments despite logical contradictions. For example, many men would not have taken the jobs vacated by women anyway because they were jobs thought to be inappropriate for men.

FRANKLIN D. ROOSEVELT LIBRARY

African American Concerns Seen here with actress Hattie McDaniel, Mary McLeod Bethune (right), led meetings of the black cabinet. *How did the black cabinet reflect Roosevelt's progressive yet cautious civil rights policies?*

African Americans Gain a Voice

Change Comes Slowly

The year 1934 was a dramatic one in United States political history. In the congressional elections, most African Americans switched their allegiance from the Republican party to the Democratic party. Although they had voted overwhelmingly for Republicans since Reconstruction, they changed allegiance mainly to support Roosevelt and the New Deal.

Student Web Activity 14

Visit the *American Odyssey* Web site at americanodyssey.glencoe.com and click on ***Chapter 14—Student Web Activities*** for an activity relating to the impact of the New Deal.

At the urging of Eleanor Roosevelt and other key political advisers, FDR kept himself informed about issues important to African Americans. Much of his information came from a group of about 50 African American appointees who served in various branches of his administration. This group came to be known as the black cabinet.

The Black Cabinet

Although most African Americans in the Roosevelt administration were appointed to secondary posts, they nevertheless exerted influence collectively as the black cabinet. Mary McLeod Bethune, head of the Negro Affairs Division of the National Youth Administration, was the most influential member of the black cabinet. A personal friend of Eleanor Roosevelt's, Bethune often shared the black cabinet's ideas with her. The First Lady then discussed them with FDR.

Harold Ickes, secretary of the interior, also worked closely with African Americans to improve race relations, and he passed along their concerns to FDR. He integrated his department, appointing several prominent African Americans to key positions. Under Ickes, the PWA allocated funds for the construction of African American hospitals, universities, and housing projects. PWA building contracts also contained a clause requiring that the number of African Americans hired be at least equal in proportion to their number in the local population. This practice would become a basis for civil rights legislation in the 1960s and the 1970s.

Other New Deal agencies also greatly aided civil rights during the Depression. The WPA gave jobs to hundreds of thousands of African Americans. The FERA and other relief agencies granted aid to 30 percent of all African American families.

Failure to Stand for Justice

The Roosevelt administration exceeded all previous administrations in the number of African Americans that it appointed to government positions and in the amount of federal aid that it provided African Americans. The President, however, failed to take a strong stand on civil rights issues.

Roosevelt did little to eliminate unfair hiring practices and discriminatory job conditions. Some government agencies, such as the TVA, often refused to hire African American workers. Most of the government agencies that did hire African Americans, including the CCC and the armed forces, segregated African Americans and whites. In addition, African American workers often received lower wages and were prevented from obtaining many jobs by stiff hiring restrictions.

Roosevelt also failed to push for a federal antilynching law. Acts of mob violence, such as lynching, increased during the early years of the Depression. Unlike Hoover, Roosevelt publicly condemned what he called "that vile form of collective murder." Roosevelt, however, hesitated to support antilynching legislation because he was afraid that he would alienate the Southern white leaders who strongly opposed such laws.

Roosevelt's desire to maintain the support of Southern whites also kept him from abolishing the poll tax. Election officials levied this tax to prevent poor African Americans and whites from voting in elections.

Roosevelt expressed the views of many liberal Americans at the time about race relations. He advocated only slow, cautious change, a stand that exasperated racial and ethnic minorities. Nevertheless, the President recognized the vital importance of working toward social equality. During a meeting with black cabinet member Mary McLeod Bethune, FDR said the following:

> People like you and me are fighting and must continue to fight for the day when a man will be regarded as a man regardless of his race or faith or country. That day will come, but we must pass through perilous times before we realize it.
>
> —Franklin D. Roosevelt

Native Americans Gain an Ally

Preserving Tribal Ownership

Native Americans, like African Americans, had long been subject to discrimination, deprivation, and degrading policies. Earning an average annual income of $48, Native American families were the poorest in the nation. New Deal agencies and policies provided many Native Americans with jobs and aid.

The most significant New Deal program to aid Native Americans was the Indian Reorganization Act of 1934, authored by John Collier, the commissioner of Indian affairs. Collier had been involved in Native

AP/WIDE WORLD PHOTOS

Navajo Meet With Collier **Showing one of the woolen products by which they make their living, Navajo protest a government limit on the number of sheep they may raise. Left to right: Dan Phillipe, interpreter; John Collier, commissioner; Johnnie Chief and Slim Salt, Navajo representatives.** *What was the average annual income of Native American families at the start of the New Deal?*

***Harvest* by Joe Jones In this work, painted about 1935, and in similar works, Jones wanted "the working people, the people producing useful things with their hands" to enjoy seeing themselves portrayed with understanding.** *What aspects of the painting depict skills needed for farmwork?*

American politics since 1923, when he had founded the American Indian Defense Association. In this and the Indian Reorganization Act of 1934, Collier built upon the ideas and initiatives of Winnebago teacher Henry Roe Cloud and Sioux writer Gertrude Bonnin. The goals of both the association and the Reorganization Act were to promote Native American cultures and to preserve tribal ownership of reservation lands.

Collier's Indian Reorganization Act furthered these goals by preventing the government from seizing unclaimed reservation land and selling it to people who were not Native American. Government seizure of reservation territory, which had been going on since the late 1800s, had deprived Native Americans of their most valuable lands and reduced the reservations to one-third of their original sizes. With the Indian Reorganization Act, Native Americans gained control of their reservations and could decide how their lands would be used and managed.

The Indian Reorganization Act also encouraged Native Americans to establish their own governments on reservations. Once these governments had been established, the Indian Bureau was authorized to provide the funds needed to build schools and hospitals, to establish businesses, and to start arts and crafts cooperatives.

An Expanded Government Role

The Government Takes on New Tasks

By including the excluded—women, African Americans, Native Americans, farmers, common laborers, the poor—the New Deal brought government closer to all

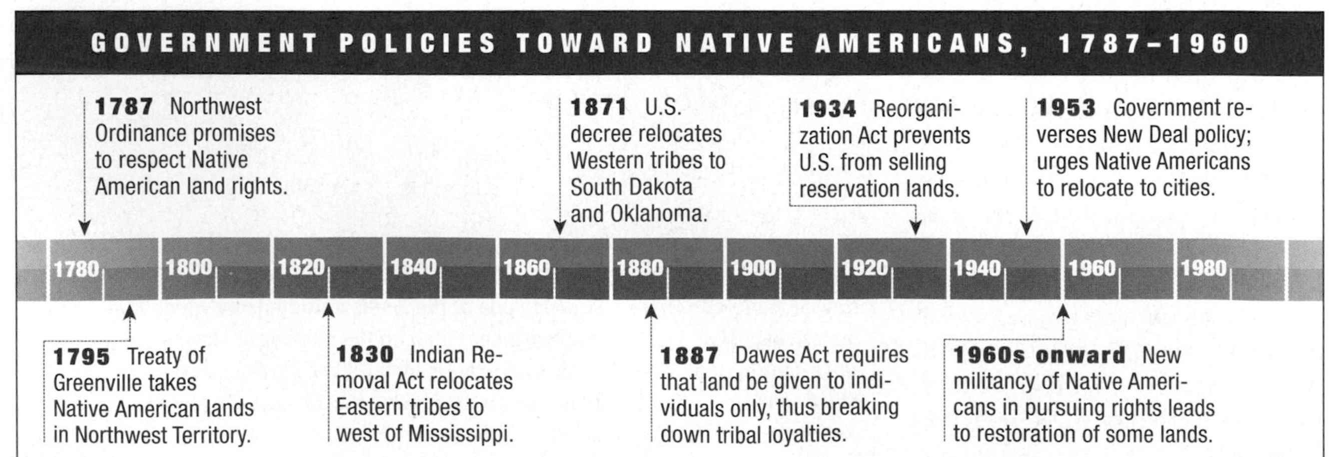

GOVERNMENT POLICIES TOWARD NATIVE AMERICANS, 1787–1960
1787 Northwest Ordinance promises to respect Native American land rights.
1871 U.S. decree relocates Western tribes to South Dakota and Oklahoma.
1934 Reorganization Act prevents U.S. from selling reservation lands.
1953 Government reverses New Deal policy; urges Native Americans to relocate to cities.
1780
1800
1820
1840
1860
1880
1900
1920
1940
1960
1980
1795 Treaty of Greenville takes Native American lands in Northwest Territory.
1830 Indian Removal Act relocates Eastern tribes to west of Mississippi.
1887 Dawes Act requires that land be given to individuals only, thus breaking down tribal loyalties.
1960s onward New militancy of Native Americans in pursuing rights leads to restoration of some lands.

New Deal Legislation and Agencies, 1933–1938

Year	Name and Purpose	Year	Name and Purpose
1933	**Emergency Banking Act:** Reopened banks under government supervision	1935	**Resettlement Administration (RA):** Helped resettle destitute farmers on better land and unemployed workers in planned communities
	Civilian Conservation Corps (CCC): Employed young men in environmental projects		**Works Progress Administration (WPA):** Employed people for construction, maintenance, education, and creative projects
	Federal Emergency Relief Act: Provided funds for local and state relief organizations		**Social Security Act:** Instituted pension and survivors' benefits for the elderly and the orphaned and provided aid to people injured in industrial accidents
	Agricultural Adjustment Act (AAA): Subsidized farmers to reduce crop and livestock production		**National Labor Relations Board (NLRB):** Guaranteed workers the right to join labor unions of their choice, bargain collectively, and call strikes
	Emergency Farm Mortgage Act: Provided funds for the refinancing of farm mortgages		**Rural Electrification Act (REA):** Lent money to rural cooperatives for the building of power plants
	Tennessee Valley Authority (TVA): Provided funds for the development and electrification of the Tennessee River Authority		**Public Utility Holding Company Act:** Allowed a maximum of only two holding companies to control any one utility company
	Truth-in-Securities Act: Required full disclosure of information about stocks and bonds	1936	**Soil Conservation Act:** Subsidized farmers to reduce soil-depleting crops and to employ soil conservation measures
	Home Owners' Loan Act: Provided funds for the refinancing of home mortgages	1937	**National Housing Act:** Authorized low-rent public housing projects
	National Industrial Recovery Act (NIRA): Created work codes and industry standards		**Farm Security Administration (FSA):** Lent money to sharecroppers and tenant farmers to help them buy their own farms; established camps for migrant workers
	Public Works Administration (PWA): Funded projects to revive industry and fight unemployment	1938	**Fair Labor Standards Act:** Established minimum wages and maximum hours for all employees of businesses engaged in interstate commerce
	Glass-Steagall Banking Act: Guaranteed bank deposits with the Federal Deposit Insurance Corporation (FDIC)		
1934	**Federal Housing Administration (FHA):** Insured bank loans for the construction and rehabilitation of homes		
	Indian Reorganization Act: Restored tribal ownership of reservation land to Native Americans		

Examine the legislation of Roosevelt's New Deal shown on the chart. List each piece of legislation under one or more of the following heads, as appropriate: housing, agriculture, labor, civil rights, relief, unemployment, banking, industry, utilities. *Judging from your list, what issues concerned FDR most? What issues concerned him least?*

the people. During the Roosevelt administration, 14 percent of all families obtained aid or relief from the federal government. Millions were able to stay off of relief because of government jobs with the CCC, the PWA, and the WPA. Other New Deal agencies helped people hold on to their farms, keep their homes, stay in business, and bargain with employers for better pay.

Federal regulation, or the expansion of the federal government into almost all aspects of people's lives, was a direct legacy of the New Deal. Under President Roosevelt, for the first time, the federal government assumed responsibility for the economic welfare of individuals as well as for the health of the nation's economy at large. In taking on such obligations, FDR's New Deal proved to be a turning point in the country's history.

The New Deal increased many people's confidence in the nation's political and economic systems. The government programs of the New Deal, however, neither eliminated individual poverty nor ended the Depression. The economy did not completely recover from the Depression until World War II was well under way.

Section Assessment

Main Idea

1. Use a diagram like this one to show social and political legacies of the New Deal.

Vocabulary

2. Define: discrimination, federal regulation.

Checking Facts

3. What was the Black Cabinet?
4. What duties did the government assume under FDR?

Critical Thinking

5. **Identifying Assumptions** List the goals of the Indian Reorganization Act. What assumptions about Native American cultures underlie these goals?

Chapter  Assessment

Self-Check Quiz

Visit the *American Odyssey* Web site at americanodyssey.glencoe.com and click on ***Chapter 14—Self-Check Quiz*** to prepare for the Chapter Test.

Reviewing Key Terms

Match the sentences below to the vocabulary term they define or describe. Write your answers on a separate sheet of paper.

moratorium	**unionization**
dole	**demagogue**
subsidy	**discrimination**

1. A certain kind of leader gains power by appealing to the public's fears and prejudices rather than to their reason.

2. Although women and minority groups made some advances during the New Deal, they still faced many barriers based on prejudice.

3. When he first came to office, Roosevelt declared a temporary shutdown of most banking operations.

4. In order to bring supply in line with demand, the Agricultural Adjustment Administration gave farmers financial assistance in return for voluntary crop reductions.

5. Workers joined together and chose their own leaders to negotiate wages and working conditions with factory owners and managers.

Recalling Facts

1. What major problems did Roosevelt face as he began his first term of office in 1933?

2. What were the Hundred Days?

3. Describe the life of a member of the Civilian Conservation Corps.

4. Why was the National Recovery Administration (NRA) controversial?

5. What New Deal legislation created problems for farmers? What were those problems?

6. What opposition did Roosevelt meet from business leaders? From the Supreme Court?

7. Why was the Rockefeller family so concerned about Diego Rivera's painting of Lenin during this time of economic depression?

8. How did Eleanor Roosevelt help to advance the cause of women in politics?

9. What did the Roosevelt administration do to improve conditions for African Americans? What did it do for Native Americans?

10. What legislation benefited organized labor during the 1930s?

Critical Thinking

1. Making Comparisons Use a diagram like this one to show how Roosevelt's solutions to the Depression differed from those of Hoover.

Solutions to Depression

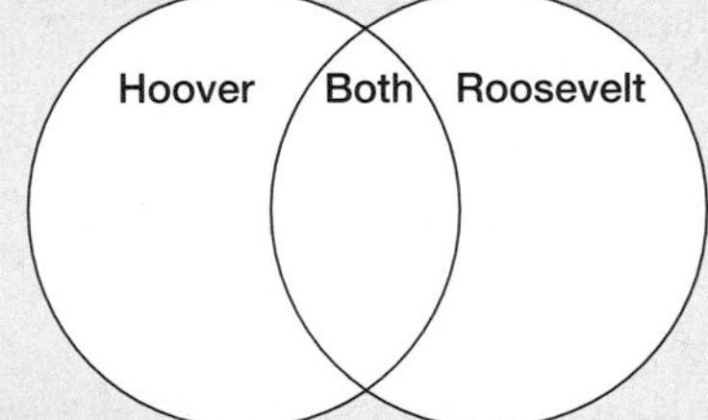

2. Determining Cause and Effect How might the circumstances of FDR's earlier years have contributed to making him the kind of President he became?

3. Demonstrating Reasoned Judgment What conditions of the times made some Americans willing to listen to the messages of demagogues such as Father Coughlin and Huey Long?

4. Drawing Conclusions What kinds of political recognition did women and minority groups achieve during the New Deal administrations? What barriers still remained?

Portfolio Project

Interview a friend or relative who is a senior citizen. Ask for that person's opinions about the present Social Security program. Also consider possible changes currently discussed in Congress. Report your findings in a letter to an imaginary newspaper editor. In your letter urge people to support legislation that will either leave Social Security as it is, modify it, or abolish it. Be sure to include the reasons for your opinion. Keep the letter in your portfolio.

Cooperative Learning

Work with two or three other students to research the life of one person prominent during the Roosevelt years. For example, you could look up Frances Perkins, the first woman to serve in a President's cabinet, or John Collier, the innovative commissioner of Indian affairs. Each group member might find out about a different aspect of the person's life, such as his or her childhood, education, or early career. Then, as a group, prepare a presentation of your material for the rest of the class.

Reinforcing Skills

Interpreting Images Turn to page 471. Examine the cartoon and read the caption. How does the artist convey the unpopularity of FDR's proposal to add several justices to the Supreme Court? What detail in the cartoon shows that the President's own party disliked his proposal? What seems to be FDR's reaction to the criticism?

GEOGRAPHY AND HISTORY

FDR Election Results, 1932–1940

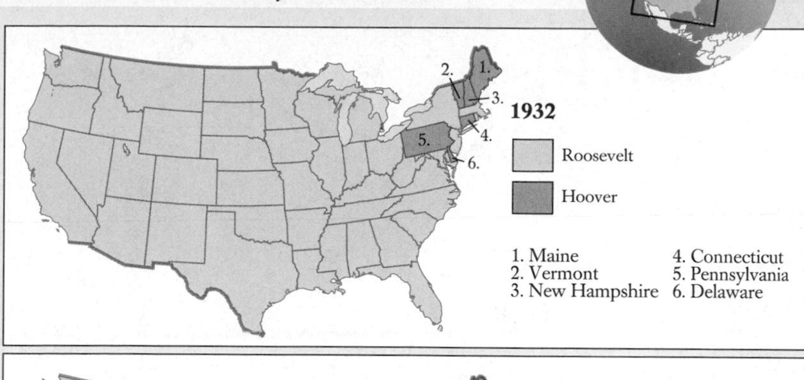

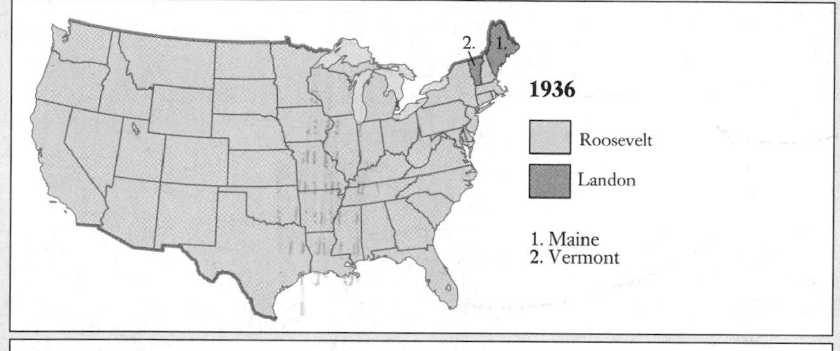

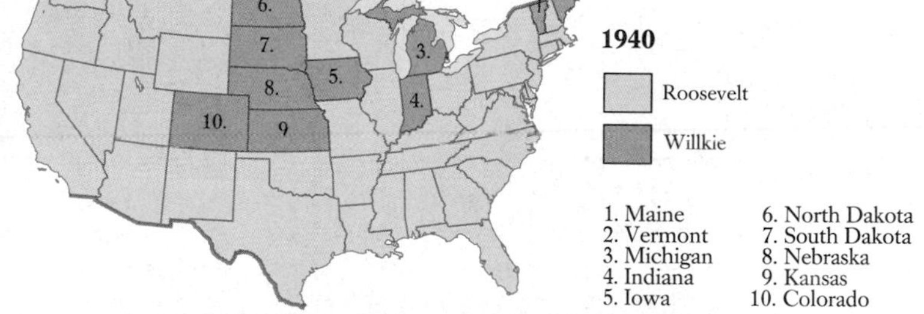

Study the maps to answer the following questions:

1. Which states voted Republican in all three of the elections shown? In what part of the country are they located? Where did the Republicans make gains in 1940?
2. Compare the 1932 and 1936 maps. What does the comparison show you about the popular appeal of Roosevelt's policies during the First New Deal?
3. Compare the 1936 and 1940 maps. How many more states did Roosevelt lose in the election of 1940?

Technology Activity

Building a Database Use the Internet to locate information about federal programs from the time of the New Deal to the present that directly aid Americans. Build a database of key information on each program. Include headings such as Program, Year of Creation, and Purpose.

Standardized Test Practice

1. The Public Works Administration, the Tennessee Valley Authority, and the Civilian Conservation Corps were all examples of

A programs to create new jobs.
B laws to stabilize banks.
C reforms to ensure the stability of the stock market.
D programs intended to increase military size and readiness.

> ***Test-Taking Tip:*** The important word in this question is *all.* Think about what *all* three programs had in common. The names of programs provide some clues. For instance, does *public works* have anything to do with the stock market or banks? If not, you can probably eliminate answers B and C.

2. Which of the following was NOT one of the "three R's" of the New Deal?

A *relief* for the unemployed.
B *recovery* measures to stimulate the economy.
C *restriction* of labor unions.
D *reform* to lessen the threat of another economic disaster.

> ***Test-Taking Tip:*** Remember, the word *NOT* means an *exception.* You are looking for an answer that is *false.* For example, you probably remember that the "three R's" were intended to combat the effects of the Great Depression, so answer A is *true,* and therefore, definitely not the correct answer.

Then...

The DC-3 Passenger Plane

In the early 1930s, TWA adviser Charles Lindbergh asked that the new Douglas passenger plane be able to cross the Rockies with only one engine running. By 1935 the DC-3 not only passed this test, but, according to American Airlines president C.R. Smith, was the first plane to "make money just by hauling passengers."

1 The all-metal body was easy to maintain and clean. Cowl flaps and engine mounts made service speedy.

PHOTO BY BOB SHANE

2 The multicellular wings survived pressure tests with lead weights and even a steamroller.

UNITED AIRLINES/PHOTO COURTESY OF ED DAVIES

3 The soundproof cabin could accommodate 21 seats or 14 sleeping berths.

UNITED AIRLINES/PHOTO COURTESY OF ED DAVIES

Fun Facts

ATTENDANTS OF THE AIR

A nurse from Iowa, Ellen Church, proposed adding attendants to passenger flights and became the first American stewardess in 1930. The nursing background of early flight attendants reassured passengers.

Stats

PERFORMANCE

- Maximum speed:
  230 miles per hour (370 kmph)
  Average speed:
  180 miles per hour (257.4 kmph)
- Average range:
  1,500 miles (2,413.5 km)

SIZE

- Weight: 25,200 pounds (11,440.8 kg)
- Height: 16 feet 11 inches (5.2 m)
- Length: 64 feet 6 inches (19.7 m)

PROFITS

- The DC-3 was the first American passenger plane to turn a profit; it earned the Douglas Aircraft Company more than $1 billion.
- With space for 21 passengers, the DC-3 provided 50 percent more space than its predecessors, and only increased operating costs by 3 percent.
- Sample fares: $18.95, one way, Los Angeles to San Francisco; $288, round trip, New York to the West Coast

4 **Automatic pilot and dual controls provided safety, and meant that pilots no longer had to reach across each other while flying the plane.**

...Now

5 **Strong retractable landing gear made use of a new "pork chop" joint.**

FLYING MAGAZINE ARCHIVES

MODERN AIR TRAVEL

PORTFOLIO PROJECT

Find pictures and information about a modern passenger plane in books or brochures. What features of this new plane represent improvements over its forerunners? Using a photo or your own drawing of the plane, create a diagram with call-out lines highlighting some of the plane's features. Include service, performance, and profitability as well as physical characteristics.

IN-FLIGHT SERVICE

Amenities included lavatories with running water, electric razors, heating and cooling systems, and meals served on tables with linens, silverware, and china.

UNIT
6

The United States Transformed

1933–1945

HISTORY & YOU

While the Great Depression threatened the nation's economic system, the Axis powers of Germany, Italy, and Japan threatened the future of global democracy. American resistance to intervening in a second world war melted with the bombing of Pearl Harbor, Hawaii, on December 7, 1941. The American people committed themselves to the Allied victory, waging a two-front war in Europe and Asia. Mobilization ended the Depression and established the United States as the leading world power.

Historic America Electronic Field Trips

The entire crew of the U.S.S. *Arizona* lost their lives when a 1,760 pound Japanese bomb slammed through the ship's deck and ignited onboard ammunition. To honor those who died in the attack on Pearl Harbor, the United States government approved construction in 1958 of a memorial over the *Arizona's* sunken hull. To learn more about the emotional impact of Pearl Harbor on American public opinion, view videodisc Chapter 8: *The U.S.S. Arizona Memorial* in **Historic America Electronic Field Trips.**

Primary Sources
Library

See pages 964–965 for primary source readings that accompany Unit 6.

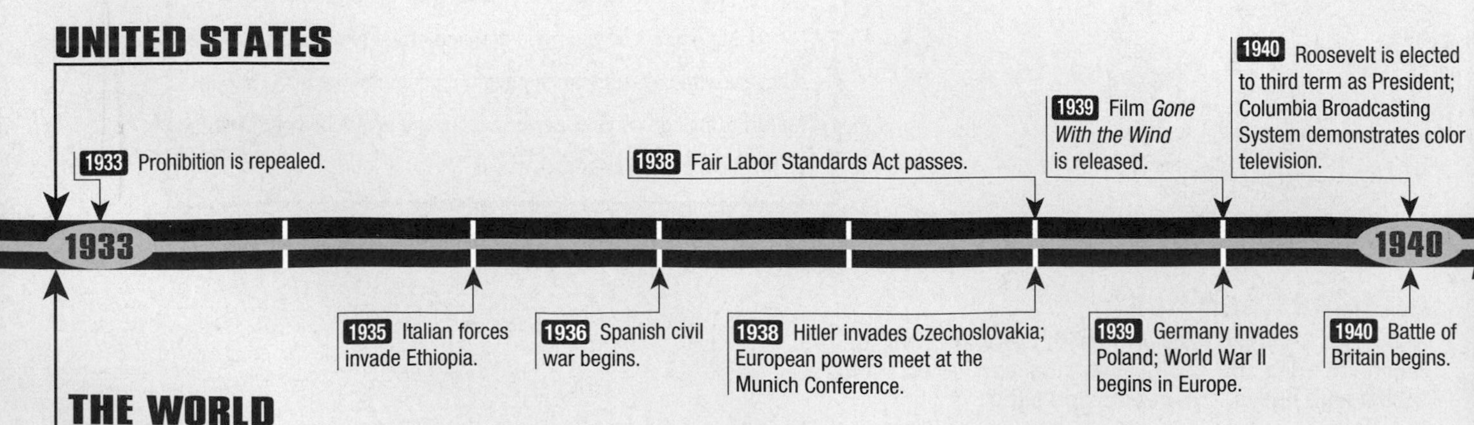
UNITED STATES
1933 Prohibition is repealed.
1938 Fair Labor Standards Act passes.
1939 Film *Gone With the Wind* is released.
1940 Roosevelt is elected to third term as President; Columbia Broadcasting System demonstrates color television.
1933
1940
1935 Italian forces invade Ethiopia.
1936 Spanish civil war begins.
1938 Hitler invades Czechoslovakia; European powers meet at the Munich Conference.
1939 Germany invades Poland; World War II begins in Europe.
1940 Battle of Britain begins.
THE WORLD

Two United States planes that proved effective against the Japanese Zero fighters were the Wildcat (above foreground) and the Hellcat (above rear).

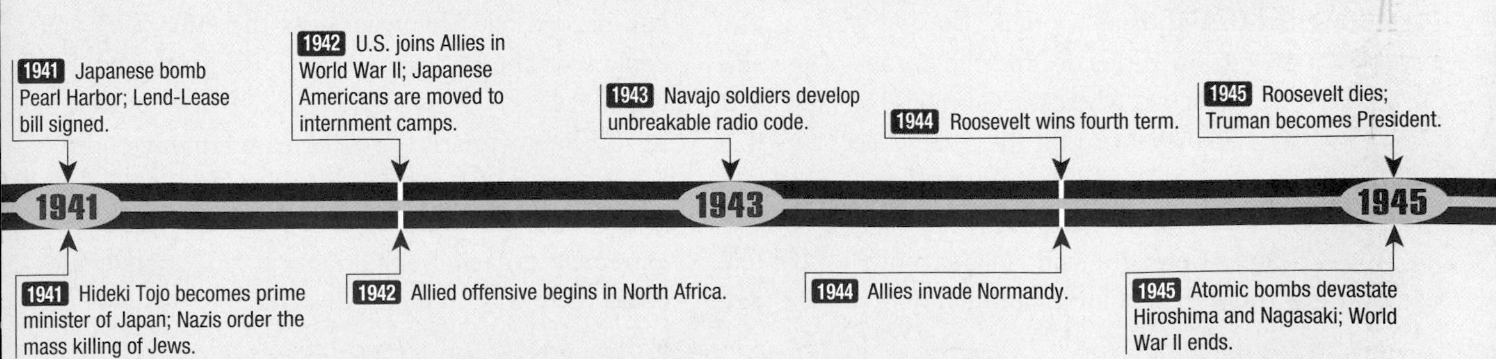

1941 Japanese bomb Pearl Harbor; Lend-Lease bill signed.
1942 U.S. joins Allies in World War II; Japanese Americans are moved to internment camps.
1943 Navajo soldiers develop unbreakable radio code.
1944 Roosevelt wins fourth term.
1945 Roosevelt dies; Truman becomes President.
1941
1943
1945
1941 Hideki Tojo becomes prime minister of Japan; Nazis order the mass killing of Jews.
1942 Allied offensive begins in North Africa.
1944 Allies invade Normandy.
1945 Atomic bombs devastate Hiroshima and Nagasaki; World War II ends.

Dispatches From the Front

Personalizing the War

BY ERNIE PYLE

Popular World War II correspondent Ernie Pyle brought the war home by writing about the experiences, thoughts, and feelings of army soldiers at the front lines of combat. The following excerpt from one of Pyle's columns recounts the Ninth Infantry Division's fight to recapture a French town from the Germans.

In Normandy, July 17, 1944—Tank Commander Martin Kennelly wanted to show me just where his tank had been hit. As a matter of fact he hadn't seen it for himself yet, for he came running up the street the moment he jumped out of the tank.

So when the firing died down a little we sneaked up the street until we were almost even with the disabled tank. But we were careful not to get our heads around the corner of the side street, for that was where the Germans had fired from.

The first shell had hit the heavy steel brace that the tread runs on, and then plunged on through the side of the tank, very low.

"Say!" Kennelly said in amazement. "It went right through our lower ammunition storage box! I don't know what kept the ammunition from going off. We'd have been a mess if it had. Boy, it sure would have got hot in there in a hurry!"

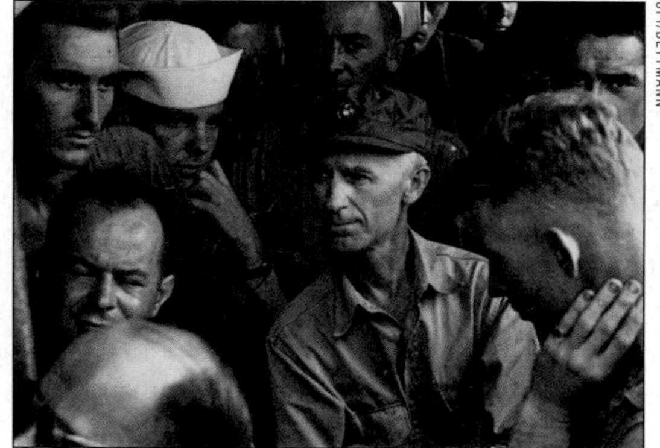

UPI/BETTMANN

At the Front Ernie Pyle accompanied Allied forces in the invasions of North Africa, Italy, and Okinawa, in addition to Normandy.

The street was still empty. Beyond the tank about two blocks was a German truck, sitting all alone in the middle of the street. It had been blown up, and its tires had burned off. This truck was the only thing you could see. There wasn't a human being in sight anywhere.

Then an American soldier came running up the street shouting for somebody to send up a medic. He said a man was badly wounded just ahead. He was extremely excited, yelling, and getting madder because there was no medic in sight.

Word was passed down the line, and pretty soon a medic came out of a doorway and started up the street. The excited soldier yelled at him and began cussing, and the medic broke into a run. They ran past the tanks together, and up the street a way they ducked into a doorway.

On the corner just across the street from where we were standing was a smashed pillbox. It was in a cut-away corner like the entrances to some of our corner drugstores at home, except that instead of there being a door there was a pillbox of reinforced concrete, with gun slits.

The tank boys had shot it to extinction and then moved their tank up even with it to get the range of the next pillbox. That one was about a block ahead, set in a niche in the wall of a building. That's what the boys had been shooting at when their tank was hit. They knocked it out, however, before being knocked out themselves.

NOW AND THEN BLASTS FROM A 20-MM GUN WOULD SPLATTER THE BUILDINGS AROUND US.

For an hour there was a lull in the fighting. Nobody did anything about a third pillbox, around the corner. Our second tank pulled back a little and just waited. Infantrymen worked their way up to second-story windows and fired their rifles up the side street without actually seeing anything to shoot at.

Now and then blasts from a 20-mm gun would splatter the buildings around us. Then our second tank would blast back in that general direction, over the low roofs, with its machine gun. There was a lot of dangerous-sounding noise, but I don't think anybody on either side got hit.

Then we saw coming up the street, past the wrecked German truck I spoke of, a group of German soldiers. An officer walked in front, carrying a Red Cross flag on a stick. Bob Capa, the photographer, braved the dangerous funnel at the end of the side street where the damaged tank stood, leapfrogging past it and on down the street to meet the Germans.

First he snapped some pictures of them. Then, since he speaks German, he led them on back to our side of the invisible fence of battle. Eight of them were carrying two litters bearing two wounded German soldiers. The others walked behind with their hands up. They went on past us to the hospital. We assumed they were from the second knocked-out pillbox.

I didn't stay to see how the remaining pillbox was knocked out. But I suppose our second tank eventually pulled up to the corner, turned, and let the pillbox have it. After that the area would be clear of everything but snipers.

The infantry, who up till then had been forced to keep in doorways, would now continue up the street and poke into the side streets into the houses until everything was clear.

That's how a strong point in a city is taken. At least that's how ours was taken. You don't always have tanks to help, and you don't always do it with so little shedding of blood.

But the city was already crumbling when we started in on this strong point, which was one of the last, and they didn't hold on too bitterly. But we didn't know that when we started.

I hope this has given you a faint idea of what street fighting is like. If you got out of it much more than a headful of confusion, then you've got out of it exactly the same thing as the soldiers who do it.

Responding to Literature

1. **If you had been a teenager during World War II, how might Ernie Pyle's dispatches from the front have influenced you?**
2. **Does Pyle's writing make you feel as if you are an eyewitness to the war? Explain.**

World War II

SEPTEMBER 1, 1939: GERMANY INVADES POLAND

President Franklin Roosevelt was awakened by a telephone call at 2:30 A.M. on September 1, 1939. Bill Bullitt, United States ambassador to France, reported an urgent call from Tony Biddle in Warsaw.

"Several German divisions are deep in Polish territory, and fighting is heavy. Tony said there were reports of bombers over the city. Then he was cut off."

"Well, Bill," Roosevelt said, "it's come at last. God help us all."

"It" was war in Europe. Only 21 years after the end of World War I, war had begun again. In response to Germany's invasion of Poland, Great Britain began mobilizing troops. Two days later Great Britain and France declared war on Germany.

Bringing the United States out of the Great Depression was Roosevelt's most pressing concern, but growing political unrest in Europe and Asia also demanded his attention. The invasion of Poland was only the latest international crisis of the 1930s.

Looking back, Roosevelt could see the roots of the crisis in Europe in the rise to power of Benito Mussolini and Adolf Hitler. He had also watched as Japan flexed its military might. It was clear to him that these events could hurl the United States into global conflict. He could not know that the war to come would be the most devastating in history, or that it would make the United States the richest and most powerful nation in the world. ■

HISTORY JOURNAL

Using the picture on page 491 and your own knowledge of history, write down all that you know about World War II. Speculate on major topics in this chapter.

Chapter Overview

Visit the *American Odyssey* Web site at americanodyssey.glencoe.com and click on ***Chapter 15—Chapter Overview*** to preview the chapter.

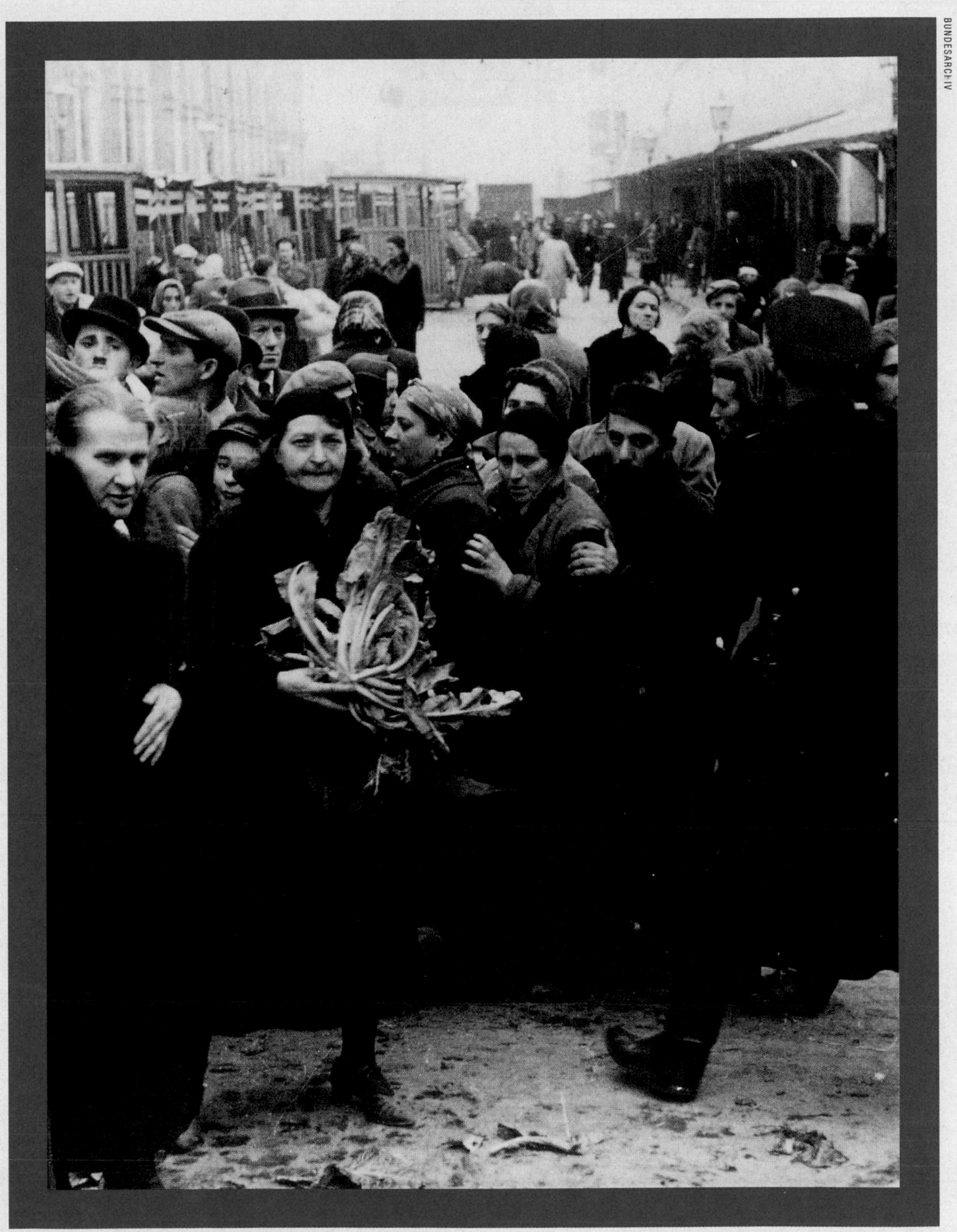

BUNDESARCHIV

THE DAY AFTER GERMANY DEFEATED POLAND, MEMBERS OF HITLER'S SS BEGAN ROUNDING UP GROUPS OF POLISH JEWS IN KRAKÓW.

The Road to War

JULY 13, 1934: HITLER ADDRESSES THE REICHSTAG

ADOLF HITLER RECOGNIZED AND MADE USE OF THE POWER OF THE SPOKEN WORD. "Every great movement on this globe owes its rise to the great speakers," he had said. As he stood before the Reichstag, the German house of representatives, on July 13, 1934, Hitler sensed that the moment for a powerful speech was at hand. Two weeks before, he had ruthlessly eliminated those members of his own political party who stood in the way of his rise to absolute power. In a night of blood and terror, Hitler's storm troopers had shot or stabbed hundreds of Hitler's political enemies.

THE BETTMANN ARCHIVE

Hitler
Speaking with power and emotion, Hitler tried to sway the minds of his people.

Though he began speaking in a hoarse whisper, Hitler's voice soon rose to a screech. Stabbing the air with his hands, he spat out words such as *traitor, poison,* and *blood.* As Reichstag members sat in stunned silence, Hitler took full responsibility for the murders. He had killed, he declared, from the highest of motives—his love for the German people and the German state:

> I gave the order to shoot those who were the ringleaders in this treason, and I further gave the order to burn out down to the raw flesh the ulcers of this poisoning of the wells in our domestic life and of the poisoning of the outside world. And I further ordered that if any of the mutineers should attempt to resist arrest, they were immediately to be struck down with armed force. . . . I am ready to undertake the responsibility at the bar of history for the twenty-four hours in which the bitterest decisions of my life were made . . . to hold fast to the dearest thing that has been given us in this world—the German people and the German Reich!
>
> —Adolf Hitler, 1934

GUIDE TO READING

Main Idea

Although memories of World War I and the suffering of the Great Depression led most Americans to support a policy of neutrality, they found it increasingly impossible to ignore aggression overseas.

Vocabulary

- fascist
- totalitarian
- appeasement
- blitzkrieg

Read to Find Out . . .

- reasons behind the rise of totalitarianism in Europe and the rise of militarism in Asia.
- how acts of aggression threatened world peace and why the United States at first adopted a policy of neutrality.

Hitler's bold justification of the murders swept millions of Germans off their feet and united them behind his government. It also frightened into silence those Germans who still opposed his rule. Hitler's speech warned the rest of the world that this new German Reich was a force not to be ignored.

The Rise of Dictators

Mussolini and Hitler on the Move

Before 1934 Americans had been too preoccupied with their own problems to take Hitler's emotional speeches seriously. The suffering the Great Depression caused convinced most people in the United States that their first priority lay at home, not overseas. The enormous cost of victory in World War I—both in money and in lives—convinced many that the nation should stay out of Europe's troubles.

Keeping with public sentiment, President Roosevelt's foreign policy concentrated at first on making the United States a "good neighbor" to the countries in this hemisphere. At his inauguration in 1933, he announced the Good Neighbor policy. This policy supported the idea of nonintervention among nations. Roosevelt pledged that the United States would not interfere in the internal affairs of its Latin American neighbors. Events in Italy and Germany, however, would soon make it impossible for the United States to avoid intervention in Europe.

AP/WIDE WORLD PHOTOS

Il Duce on Horseback Mussolini, shown here in 1933 reviewing troops in Rome, ruled Italy for almost 21 years. *How did economic conditions in Italy after World War I make his rise to power easier?*

Mussolini's Rise in Italy

The events that brought Italy to the center of the world stage began after World War I. Although Italy had fought on the victorious Allied side, the war had left the country in economic chaos. Thousands of soldiers returning to civilian life could not find jobs.

THE SPREAD OF DICTATORSHIP, 1929–1939
1929 Hitler denounces Treaty of Versailles.
1933 Hitler becomes chancellor of the Nazi party. Hitler empowered to make laws.
1936 Mussolini and Hitler both send troops to Spain to fight for General Franco.
1938 Hitler occupies Austria and the Sudetenland in Czechoslovakia.
1929
1930
1931
1932
1933
1934
1935
1936
1937
1938
1939
1932 Nazi party becomes most powerful in Germany.
1934 Hitler abolishes office of president, declares himself the führer.
1935 Mussolini's troops invade Ethiopia.
1939 Germany and Soviet Union sign nonagression pact. Hitler invades Poland.

A wounded veteran himself, Benito Mussolini burst onto the Italian political scene with a threat and a promise of change. Painting himself as a modernizer and as a champion of order and efficiency, *Il Duce* (the leader), as he called himself, challenged Italians to join with him in rebuilding their shattered economy and in restoring Italy's power in the Mediterranean region. Mussolini gained a following of political demonstrators

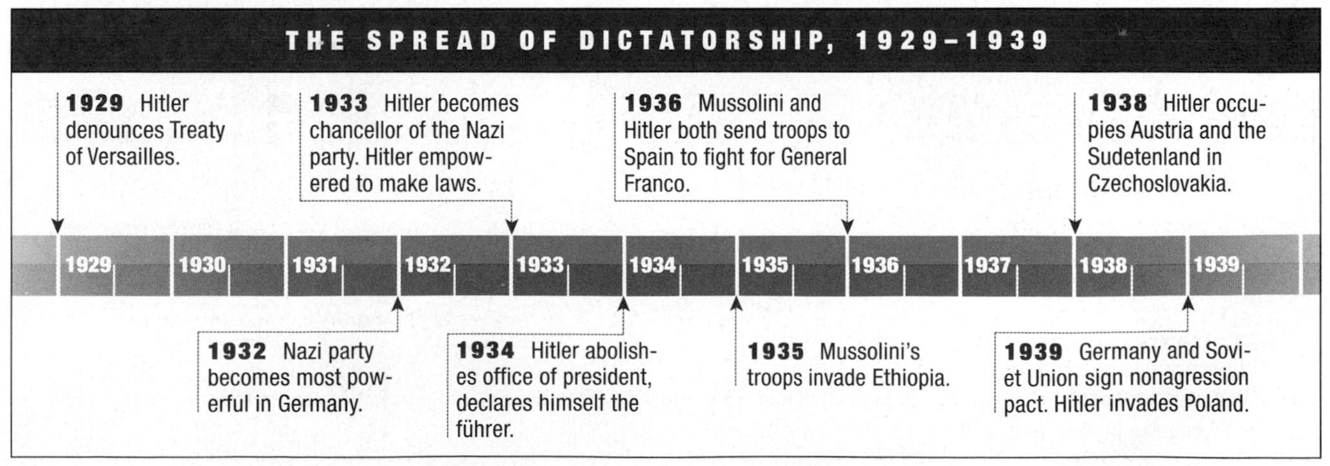

who became known as **fascists,** followers of a political philosophy that preached that the nation and the race were more important than the individual. Fascists won elections by frightening people into supporting them. Black-shirted gangs roamed the streets smashing the offices of opposing political parties and breaking up their meetings. As the leader of the Fascist party, Mussolini became a **totalitarian** dictator, completely controlling all aspects of Italian life.

In spite of these ruthless tactics, many Italians, and even some Americans, saw Mussolini as a model of strength and determination. Once in power, he succeeded in bringing energy and discipline to Italian society with a flood of new government economic and social programs. Under Mussolini, for example, Italian trains ran on time, and engineers built 400 new bridges and 4,000 miles (6,436 km) of roads.

Mussolini also kept his promise to restore Italy's power in the Mediterranean. In October 1935, his armies invaded the African nation of Ethiopia. Ethiopian soldiers on horseback, armed with outdated guns and spears, were no match for the bombers and machine guns of the modern Italian army. By May 1936, Mussolini controlled Ethiopia.

Hitler Founds the Nazi Party

As Mussolini did, Adolf Hitler rose to power in Germany during the troubled times after World War I. Wounded and gassed during the war, Hitler nursed his bitterness by transforming a tiny workers' party into the mighty National Socialist German Workers' party, which became known as the Nazi party. In a series of speeches during the 1920s, Hitler spelled out the Nazi program. The German people, he said, had been divided into warring social classes for too long. By eliminating the differences between rich and poor, the Nazis would make the German people strong and united. Moreover, Hitler said, Jews and others who were not blond, blue-eyed members of what he called the "Aryan" or Germanic race had betrayed Germany in World War I. The Jews, Hitler said, were to blame for Germany's economic problems.

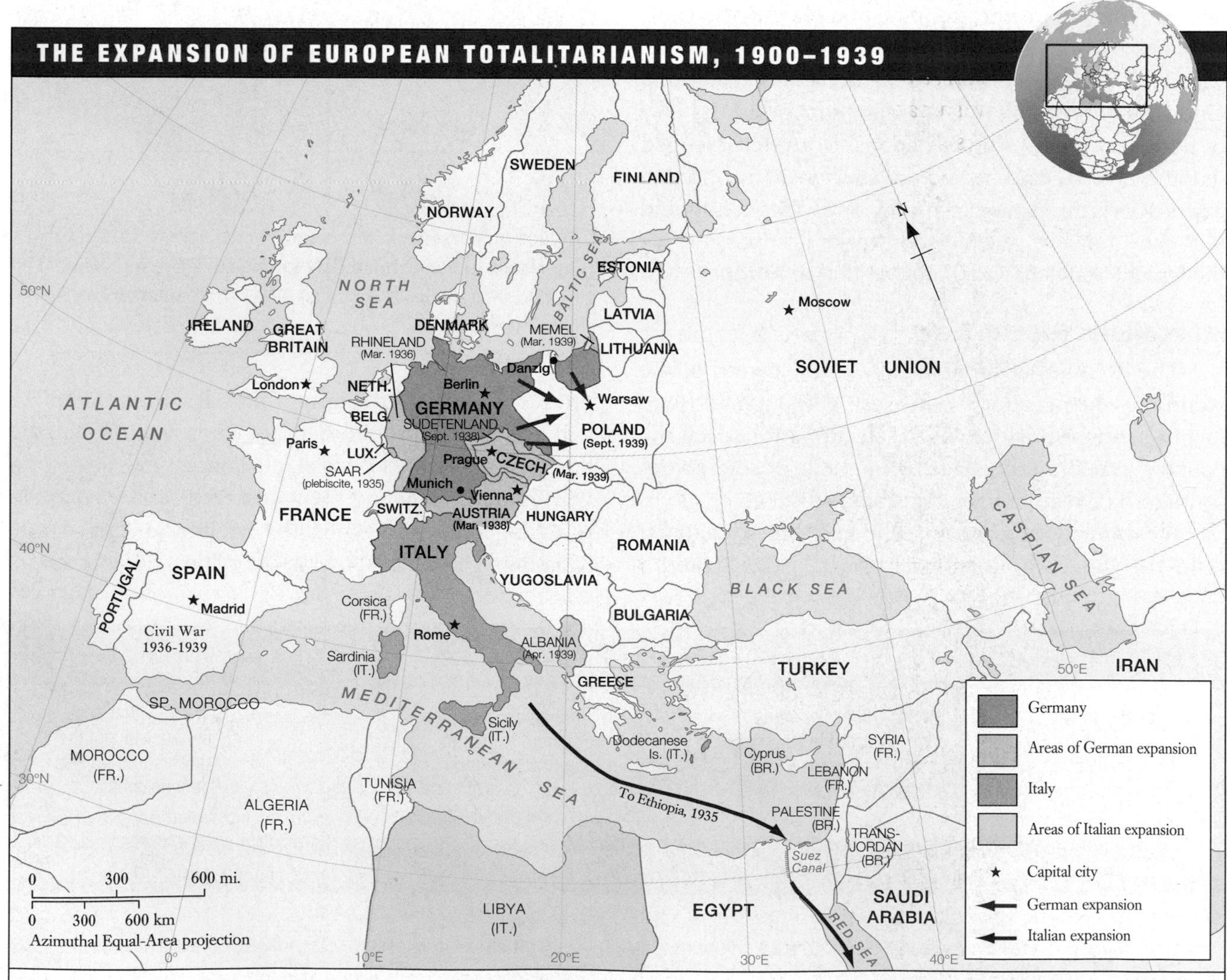

Once in power, the totalitarian regimes of Mussolini and Hitler moved across Europe and parts of Africa, conquering every small and weak country in their paths. *When did Germany take over Austria?*

Protest Through Art **Pablo Picasso's famous painting *Guernica* is a masterpiece of protest against the bombing of the town of Guernica during the Spanish civil war.** *How does his unconventional portrayal of this event contribute to its overall effect as a protest statement against war?*

Building the Third Reich

When the Depression struck Germany in 1929, the German government was unable to find jobs for 6 million unemployed workers. Hitler took advantage of the discontent to appeal to the German people to rebuild their economy and to revive their honor by bringing him to power. He denounced the Treaty of Versailles, which dismantled the German military and required Germany to pay huge sums of money to the Allies. In an election held in July 1932, the Nazi party became the most powerful in Germany, though it failed to win a clear majority. Nevertheless, Hitler held out for full powers as chancellor, which he got in January 1933.

Once in power Hitler moved to eliminate opposition. In February 1933, he persuaded German president Paul von Hindenburg to suspend most German civil rights. A month later, by false promises and threats of violence, Hitler convinced the Reichstag to give him the power to make laws without its consent. In June 1934, Hitler demanded that members of the military swear personal allegiance to him. After Hindenburg's death in August 1934, Hitler abolished the office of president and declared himself the führer, or supreme leader of the Third Reich, the German Empire. Thus, Hitler also became a totalitarian dictator.

With all power concentrated in his hands, Hitler defied the Treaty of Versailles by rebuilding the German military. In 1936 he took his defiance a step further and sent troops into Germany's Rhineland. This put German soldiers on the eastern border of France. When Great Britain and France did not resist the action, Hitler's plans grew even more ambitious.

The Axis Tests Its Strength

Mussolini and Hitler Join Forces

Hitler and Mussolini were two powerful leaders who had dreams of expanding their borders, and both were building armies mighty enough to seize new lands at will. When these two dictators formed an alliance in 1936, dubbed the Axis Powers, fear struck the hearts of many Europeans, including the Soviets whose communism clashed with fascism.

Fighting the Spanish Civil War

The outbreak of a bitter and bloody civil war in Spain complicated the situation in Europe. In 1931 a parliamentary government under a democratic constitution replaced the Spanish monarchy. Led by Spanish army General Francisco Franco, conservative and pro-monarchy rebel troops attempted to overthrow the Spanish government in 1936. The war quickly grew into an international struggle. Because Franco, like Mussolini, strongly opposed communism, Mussolini felt compelled to aid Franco's cause. He sent airplanes and thousands of soldiers from the Italian army. Hitler also sent Franco bombers and troops.

On the other side, the Soviet Union supported the Republicans who fought for their elected government. Though the governments of Great Britain, France, and the United States were officially neutral, many citizens in these countries backed the Republicans. Some 3,000 Americans who opposed Franco's facism formed the Abraham Lincoln Brigade and fought in Spain for the Republican cause. Many belonged to the American Communist Party. Other volunteers were socialists, liberals, trade-unionists, and even zionists. All were united by a hatred of facism and a belief that if Germany and Italy could help overturn a democracy in Spain, nothing would stop them from moving on to France. "And after France?" many asked. In the end, Franco's fascist forces prevailed.

Appeasing Hitler in Munich

Intervening in the Spanish civil war did not satisfy Hitler's drive for power. In March 1938, he proclaimed that Austria was part of Germany and sent German tanks into the Austrian capital Vienna to seal the deal. Six months later Hitler's armies occupied the Sudetenland region of Czechoslovakia, an area with a large ethnic German population. To justify his aggression, Hitler explained that he had taken the Sudetenland to satisfy the wish of Germans living there to become part of Germany. His only goal, he said, was to defend the German-speaking people of Czechoslovakia against political oppression by the Czechs.

Eager to avoid another war, the leaders of Great Britain and France adopted a policy of **appeasement** toward Hitler, in which they gave in to his demands in an attempt to keep the peace. At a conference in Munich in September 1938, British Prime Minister Neville Chamberlain and French Premier Edouard Daladier agreed not to oppose Hitler's move against the Sudetenland. Hitler in turn promised to respect the rest of Czechoslovakia and to make no new territorial demands in Europe. A joyful Chamberlain, supported by President Roosevelt, told a jittery world that the Munich Pact ensured "peace for our time." Not all British politicians agreed. Winston Churchill, who would soon replace Chamberlain as prime minister, remarked, "Britain and France had to choose between war and dishonor. They chose dishonor. They will have war."

Invading Poland Leads to War

When Hitler seized the rest of Czechoslovakia just five and a half months later, Churchill's words proved prophetic. Any remaining hope that Hitler could be stopped short of waging all-out war was shattered on August 23, 1939, when Germany signed a nonaggression pact with the Soviet Union. The agreement pledged that neither country would attack the other. By securing his eastern border against Soviet attack, Hitler freed himself to direct his forces against the rest of Europe.

The suspense concerning where Hitler would strike next was short-lived. Poland, a country historically beset by its stronger neighbors, was once again the fuse igniting the powder keg. In a secret section of their nonaggression treaty, Germany and the Soviet Union had already agreed to divide Poland between them. With Soviet approval, Hitler's tanks rumbled across the border into Poland at dawn on September 1, 1939, while his *Luftwaffe* (air force) bombarded Polish cities. This swift, all-out style of attack, known as **blitzkrieg** (lightning war), was devastatingly effective. Two days later, Great Britain and France, who had pledged to defend Poland against outside aggression, declared war on Germany. World War II had begun.

ARCHIVE PHOTOS

Returning to London On September 30, 1938, Prime Minister Neville Chamberlain, home from the Munich Conference, speaks to a crowd. *What did he believe he had accomplished?*

The Rise of Militarism

Japan Flexes Its Muscles

Japan was as aggressive a nation in Asia as Hitler's Germany was in Europe. During the 1930s ambitious Japanese military leaders began a policy of territorial expansion. Confined to a chain of small islands and Korea, Japan's growing population strained its resources. Though rich in industrial know-how, Japan was poor in land for agriculture and in raw materials for its industries. It depended on imports from the United States and other countries for such essential commodities as wheat, petroleum, rubber, coal, iron, and timber. Japanese military leaders resented this dependence on foreign suppliers, which made them vulnerable to economic and military pressure from abroad. To make Japan secure and self-sufficient, these leaders pushed to expand Japan's borders beyond its home islands onto the Asian mainland.

Military leaders occupied a special place in Japanese society. The chiefs of the Imperial Army and Navy were independent of the civilian government and answered only to the emperor in matters of national defense. These leaders regarded foreign conquest as a badge of personal honor. They had already savored the sweetness of victory when Japan won the large and potentially productive island of Taiwan in a war with China in 1895. Ten years later, they tasted conquest again when Japan won footholds in Manchuria and Korea on the Asian mainland by defeating Russia in the Russo-Japanese War in 1904 and 1905. Now they looked to the rest of Manchuria and East Asia for new lands to add to their empire.

Japan Invades Manchuria

The most tempting target for Japanese expansion was Manchuria, in northern China. This vast region was poorly defended, and it had abundant resources. Japanese military leaders hoped that Manchuria would provide living space for Japan's surplus population and enough raw materials, food, and manufactured goods to make Japan self-sufficient. In September 1931, Japan launched an attack on Manchuria. Within a few months, the Japanese army had overpowered the province. In September 1932, Japan installed a Japanese-controlled puppet government and renamed the region "Manchukuo."

UPI/BETTMANN NEWSPHOTOS

Symbol of Power Emperor Hirohito, shown above right in 1934, was emperor of Japan from 1926 until he died in 1989.
Why was the Japanese military so powerful?

The League of Nations, of which Japan was a key member, condemned Japan for its aggression. In contempt, Japan merely withdrew from the League. Meanwhile, Japan argued that its military actions in Manchuria were essential to its long-term security. The world remained unconvinced.

Shutting the Open Door

The United States protested Japan's expansion into China but did little more. Roosevelt refused to recognize Japan's puppet government in Manchuria. Later, when Japan used its base in Manchuria to launch a full-scale assault on China, Roosevelt authorized small loans to the government of China to help them buy military supplies. He also urged Americans to boycott Japanese silk.

Perhaps the strongest critics of Japanese aggression against China were the American people. Many Americans felt a special sympathy and kinship with the Chinese. Fiction such as *The Good Earth* by Pearl Buck painted a picture of Chinese peasants as noble and long-suffering. Chiang Kai-shek (Jiang Jieshi), the leader of China, and Soong Meiling, his American-educated wife, were popular figures in the United States, even appearing on the cover of *Time* magazine. American missionaries had long been active in China, and many Americans saw themselves as China's protectors. Some Americans even believed that, in time, China would come to resemble the United States.

The most important reason for Americans' alarm at the invasion of China, however, was economic. The American business community saw China as a boundless market for American goods. To protect this market, the United States had long asserted its Open Door policy, assuring all countries equal access to China's markets. If Japan succeeded in conquering China and in closing that open door, the United States stood to lose close to $100 million in annual cotton sales. As Japan grew stronger and gained control of more natural resources, its industries would be better able to compete with American businesses for world sales. For these reasons, many feared Japan's continued aggression in China.

The "China Incident"

By 1937 Japanese forces moved south from Manchuria against Shanghai and Nanjing, major Chinese cities. Japanese soldiers killed tens of thousands of Chinese civilians. Leaders in Tokyo tried to play down the military actions in China, referring to them as the "China Incident." In reality the "China Incident" was a full-scale war.

The Japanese attacks on Shanghai and Nanjing alarmed already anxious Americans. Even such a strong opponent of American involvement in foreign conflicts as Senator George Norris condemned the Japanese actions as "disgraceful" and "barbarous." The United States, however, leveled nothing stronger than words at the Japanese.

Assault on Nanjing **Japanese invaders march behind one of their tanks in 1937 during the violent assault on the Chinese capital that claimed the lives of about 200,000 citizens.** *What was the American sentiment toward the Chinese?*

Nonneutral Neutrality

Resistance to Another War

With hostilities spreading in Europe and Asia, Congress tried to block American involvement. After Italy's invasion of Ethiopia in 1935, and again after the outbreak of the Spanish civil war in 1936, Congress passed the so-called Neutrality Acts. These laws prohibited the sale of weapons to nations at war and tried to keep American citizens from traveling on ships belonging to warring countries. The laws also required that countries at war pay cash for nonmilitary trade goods like cotton or wheat.

Roosevelt reluctantly signed the Neutrality Acts. In doing so he bowed to a strong anti-war sentiment. A 1937 Gallup poll found that nearly two-thirds of Americans thought that the nation's participation in World War I had been a mistake. Although Roosevelt regarded both Germany and Japan as serious threats to the nation's security, he faced an uphill battle in preparing the United States for the possibility of another war.

Roosevelt knew that to fight a war, the United States would need tanks, planes, guns, and other supplies. To this end, he asked Congress in 1938 for $300 million in additional spending. By 1939 Roosevelt was asking Congress for a $1.3 billion military budget. He had decided that Hitler and Mussolini were "two madmen," who "respect force and force alone." History would prove Roosevelt correct.

Section Assessment

Main Idea

1. Use a diagram like this one to summarize causes of United States neutrality and the foreign threats that made that policy hard to follow.

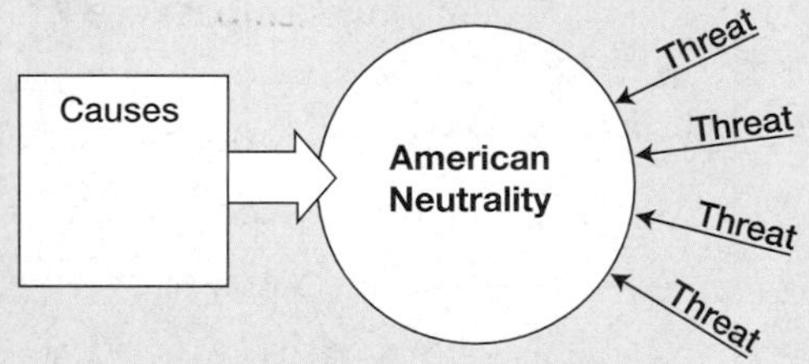

Vocabulary

2. Define: fascist, totalitarian, appeasement, blitzkrieg.

Checking Facts

3. What similarities existed between the rise of totalitarianism in Italy under Mussolini and in Germany under Hitler?
4. Why were Americans alarmed by Japan's aggressiveness in China?

Critical Thinking

5. **Recognizing Ideologies** Many Americans condemned the "China Incident," which in reality was a full-scale war. Why did the United States respond with only words?

Critical Thinking Skill

RECOGNIZING IDEOLOGIES

Learning the Skill

Ideology is a basic set of beliefs about freedom and equality, life, culture, and the desired role of the state and government. Recognizing ideology in a speech or statement can help you to identify a person's political beliefs.

The lists below show the ideologies characteristic of a totalitarian dictatorship and of a democracy.

Totalitarian Dictatorship

- The leader has total and absolute power.
- People have no power to limit their leaders.
- Government is not accountable for its actions.
- Power is gained by military force.

Democracy

- People hold the power to rule.
- People have individual liberty and equal opportunity.
- Majority rule combines with respect for minority rights.
- People choose their leaders.

HULTON DEUTSCH COLLECTION

Political Rally Hitler staged spectacular political shows to highlight his speeches, such as at this rally at Bückeberg in 1934. *How does this scene reflect the ideology behind Hitler's rise to power as a dictator?*

How to Recognize Ideologies

To recognize ideologies in written passages, follow these steps:

a. Read the passage and state it in your own words.

b. Identify the important or key words in the passage.

c. Identify unstated beliefs, ideas, facts, or opinions.

d. Compare this to what you know about the characteristics of specific ideologies.

Read this sentence once spoken by John F. Kennedy:

Ask not what your country can do for you; ask what you can do for your country.

The first step is to restate the sentence in your own words; for example, "People should help their country instead of expecting the country to do things for them."

Next, identify key words such as "what you can do." Then look for any unstated ideas, such as, "people have a responsibility to make changes in their country."

Finally, use what you know about political ideologies to make a statement about the author's political beliefs; for example, "In this statement, the author wants people to take action, so the passage reflects a democratic ideology."

Practicing the Skill

Read the following passage by Adolf Hitler and use what you have learned about recognizing ideologies to answer the questions.

There must be no decisions by majority, but only responsible persons, and the word *council* is once more reduced to its original meaning. At every man's side there stand councilors, indeed, but one man decides.

1. What does "no decisions by majority" mean?

2. State the main idea of the passage in your own words.

3. Note the key words and important ideas in the passage.

4. What do you think are the unstated ideas or beliefs in this passage?

5. In your opinion, what political ideology does this passage reflect? Explain your answer.

Applying the Skill

Find a passage from a political statement or speech. Analyze the passage and write what it tells you about the author's political ideology.

The **Glencoe Skillbuilder Interactive Workbook, Level 2** CD-ROM provides more practice in key social studies skills.

The War Begins

JUNE 14, 1940: GERMAN TROOPS OCCUPY PARIS

© BLACK STAR

Surrender of Paris
The French surrender Paris to the Germans.

PARIS WAS SILENT AND OMINOUSLY DESERTED AS DAWN BROKE ON FRIDAY, JUNE 14, 1940. The shutters over house and shop windows were closed and barred. The Metro was not running. No cars, trucks, or bicycles moved down the magnificent boulevards or along the narrow, twisting streets. Three million of the nearly 5 million people who lived in Paris and its surrounding neighborhoods had already fled. The rest stayed indoors and waited.

The night before, under a flag of truce, French officers had met with German officials near Paris. The French knew Paris would fall under a German assault. Rather than see their beautiful city destroyed, they handed it over to the Germans.

By 5 A.M. on Friday morning, columns of German infantry were marching three abreast toward railroad stations and other key points inside Paris. Roger Langeron, chief of the Paris police, watched as German soldiers entered the city. Writing in his diary for that fateful Friday, Langeron described the "terrible thing" that had befallen France. He mourned the "interminable defile of motorized troops" that made its way through Paris from Saint-Denis toward Montrouge. He recorded in his diary the dark parade of leather-clad motorcyclists and armored tanks that moved down empty streets before "shuttered" houses.

In the midafternoon, Langeron was summoned to meet the new German military governor at the Crillon Hotel. By then swastika flags were already flying over the public buildings of Paris.

GUIDE TO READING

Main Idea

As Europe once again plunged into war, Americans debated United States intervention, while President Roosevelt cautiously took steps to aid the Allies.

Vocabulary

- interventionism
- isolationism

Read to Find Out . . .

- the events that led to the outbreak of war in Europe and the response of Americans to the idea of United States intervention.
- the link between United States embargoes against Japan and the attack on Pearl Harbor.

Hitler Crushes Europe

The Continent Gives Up

The unopposed German occupation of Paris was a triumph for Hitler's forces, which in two months had conquered most of Western Europe. On April 9, 1940, more than seven months after invading Poland, Hitler unleashed an air and sea assault against Denmark and Norway. A few weeks later, German tanks and bombers drove the Netherlands, Belgium, and Luxembourg to their knees. "The small countries are smashed up, one by one, like matchwood," England's new prime minister, Winston Churchill, complained.

UPI/BETTMANN

AP/WIDE WORLD

Britain in the War In the photo above, British destroyers loaded with troops that had been stranded at Dunkirk arrive safely at a British port. The photo at the left shows civilians huddled in a cramped subway tunnel during the London blitz. *Why did Germany begin to strike Great Britain after dark?*

France Surrenders

Despite Germany's victories, the French had prepared to make a stand. About a million French soldiers held positions along the Maginot Line, a system of heavily armed steel and concrete bunkers built after World War I and stretching hundreds of miles along the German border, from Belgium to Switzerland. In addition, England had sent troops and supplies to aid in the defense of France.

In early May 1940, German tanks stormed across the French border from Belgium, swept around the north end of the Maginot Line, and attacked French positions from the rear. Fixed firmly in concrete and pointing toward Germany, the heavy artillery pieces of the Maginot Line were never fired.

France had placed its faith in the strength of the Maginot Line, and its failure demoralized the French. Within a few short weeks, France's fate was sealed. The pulverizing attacks of the German tank corps, supported by massive air power, sent the French and British armies reeling backward. By the end of May, French soldiers were throwing down their weapons in the face of the German advance, and the British forces had retreated to the French seacoast town of Dunkirk on the English Channel. A fleet of military and private vessels saved the British army from destruction by evacuating 338,000 French and British troops from Dunkirk between May 28 and June 4, 1940. French forces were left to face the German invaders alone.

French resistance lasted only a few weeks more. On June 3, German bombers had attacked Paris airports. A week later Italy declared war on France, and Mussolini's forces attacked from the south. On June 14, German troops marched into Paris. Finally, in a railway car on June 22, a jubilant Hitler personally accepted the French surrender.

The Battle of Britain

With France secure, Hitler began an all-out attack on Great Britain in the summer of 1940. Great Britain, however, was not as easily conquered. Although badly outnumbered, Britain's Royal Air Force had excellent fighter planes and highly dedicated pilots. So many German planes were shot down by British fighter pilots that Germany had to abandon daylight attacks. A proud Prime Minister Churchill declared that "never in the field of human conflict was so much owed by so many to so few."

Hoping to avoid further defeat, Hitler sought the cover of darkness. From September 1940 to May 1941, German aircraft dropped tons of bombs on London almost every night. The blitz, as the British called the bombing raids, killed more than 20,000 Londoners alone. The entire city of Coventry and large parts of London were reduced to smoking rubble. In the face of this assault, Churchill pleaded for more American aid. The future course of the United States at this point, however, was far from clear.

The Americans Respond

A Conflict of Attitudes

The rapid fall of France stunned people in the United States, but Americans still disagreed about what should be done. Some who supported **interventionism** believed the United States should give all possible support to Britain short of declaring war on Germany. Others who supported **isolationism** thought the United States should stay out of the war.

One influential interventionist was William Allen White, a Kansas City journalist. He formed the Committee to Defend America by Aiding the Allies. With more than 600 local branches, the group promoted vigorous American support of Britain, short of active participation in the war.

Isolationists banded together to form the Committee to Defend America First. Its members thought the United States should keep out of Europe's business. America First drew support from a broad range of Americans, including pacifists and socialists, Democrats and Republicans. Former President Herbert Hoover, union activist John L. Lewis, and architect Frank Lloyd Wright belonged, as did representatives from German and Italian ethnic groups. Robert E. Wood, the chairman of Sears, Roebuck and Co., headed the governing committee. The most famous speaker for the group was aviator Charles Lindbergh. He argued that the United States was strong enough to stand alone, despite Hitler's victories. Within a few months of its founding, America First had about 60,000 members.

Selective Service

Aware of the split in public opinion and mindful of the upcoming presidential election, Roosevelt cautiously aided the Allies while refraining from a strong public attack on facism. In September 1940, he arranged the transfer of 50 overage American destroyers to Britain. In return, the United States won the right to establish naval and air bases on British territory in Newfoundland, Bermuda, and British Guiana (now Guyana). The same month the President signed the Selective Training and Service Act, establishing the nation's first peace-time draft. The law applied to all men between 21 and 35. More than 1 million men were to serve in the military for 1 year, but only within the Western Hemisphere. The Selective Service Act laid the groundwork for a United States military capable of fighting a global war.

To Help or Not to Help Many Americans were indecisive about involvement in World War II. *Does this cartoon support interventionism or isolationism?*

On the surface, these moves brought the United States closer to involvement. Yet Roosevelt explained them as strengthening United States defenses and keeping the nation out of the war. Roosevelt took a similar stance during the 1940 election campaign: "Your President says this country is not going to war!" Approving voters returned him to the presidency for a third term.

Lend-Lease

With the election won, Roosevelt moved to support the Allies openly. In January 1941, he proposed the Lend-Lease bill. This bill gave the President the right to sell, lend, or lease military supplies to any nation deemed "vital to the defense of the United States." Roosevelt defended this plan by explaining that Britain did not have the money to purchase arms. If a neighbor's house were on fire, Roosevelt argued, you would loan that person your garden hose without worrying about the price. The United States, the President declared, must become the "great arsenal of democracy."

Polls indicated that most Americans agreed with Roosevelt. Nearly 80 percent of those questioned in one poll favored the Lend-Lease plan. Given these results,

Congress approved the Lend-Lease Act in March 1941, providing an initial budget of $7 billion. Before Lend-Lease ended, more than $50 billion in weapons, vehicles, and other supplies would go to support the Allied war effort. Shipments to Britain began at once. Economically, at least, the United States was at war with Germany.

Lend-Lease heated up the United States's involvement in the war in another way. During the spring and summer of 1941, German submarines patrolling in "wolf packs" sent tens of thousands of tons of British and American supply ships to the bottom of the Atlantic every week. To make sure that Lend-Lease supplies arrived safely in Britain, in April Roosevelt ordered the United States Navy to help the British track German U-boats. By summer the navy had orders to guard British ships as they traveled across the Atlantic and to destroy enemy submarines that threatened their passage.

The undeclared war between German and American ships worsened in the fall of 1941. In September a German submarine fired on the *Greer,* an American destroyer. Calling the Germans "the rattlesnakes of the Atlantic," Roosevelt ordered the navy to shoot Axis vessels on sight. In October German U-boats torpedoed the destroyer *Kearny* and sank the destroyer *Reuben James,* killing about 100 Americans. Congress revised the Neutrality Acts to allow armed American merchant ships to carry munitions directly to England.

Though Lend-Lease aid to the Allied Powers seemed to be pulling the United States into the war, most citizens supported it in principle. When Germany suddenly attacked the Soviet Union in June 1941, however, the United States extended Lend-Lease aid to the USSR. Some people in the United States were outraged at the idea of sending Lend-Lease aid to a Communist country. Isolationist Charles Lindbergh said he would prefer an alliance with Nazi Germany, with all its faults, to an alliance with "the godlessness and barbarism that exist in the Soviet Union."

Churchill, who had criticized the Communists for years, however, cheered the United States aid to the Soviets. "I have only one purpose," Churchill remarked, "the destruction of Hitler. . . . If Hitler invaded Hell I would at least make a favorable reference to the Devil in the House of Commons." Churchill was aware that Germany's opening of an eastern front would take some pressure off Britain. Battles against the Soviets in the east tied up 200 German divisions that might otherwise have been used in an invasion of Britain.

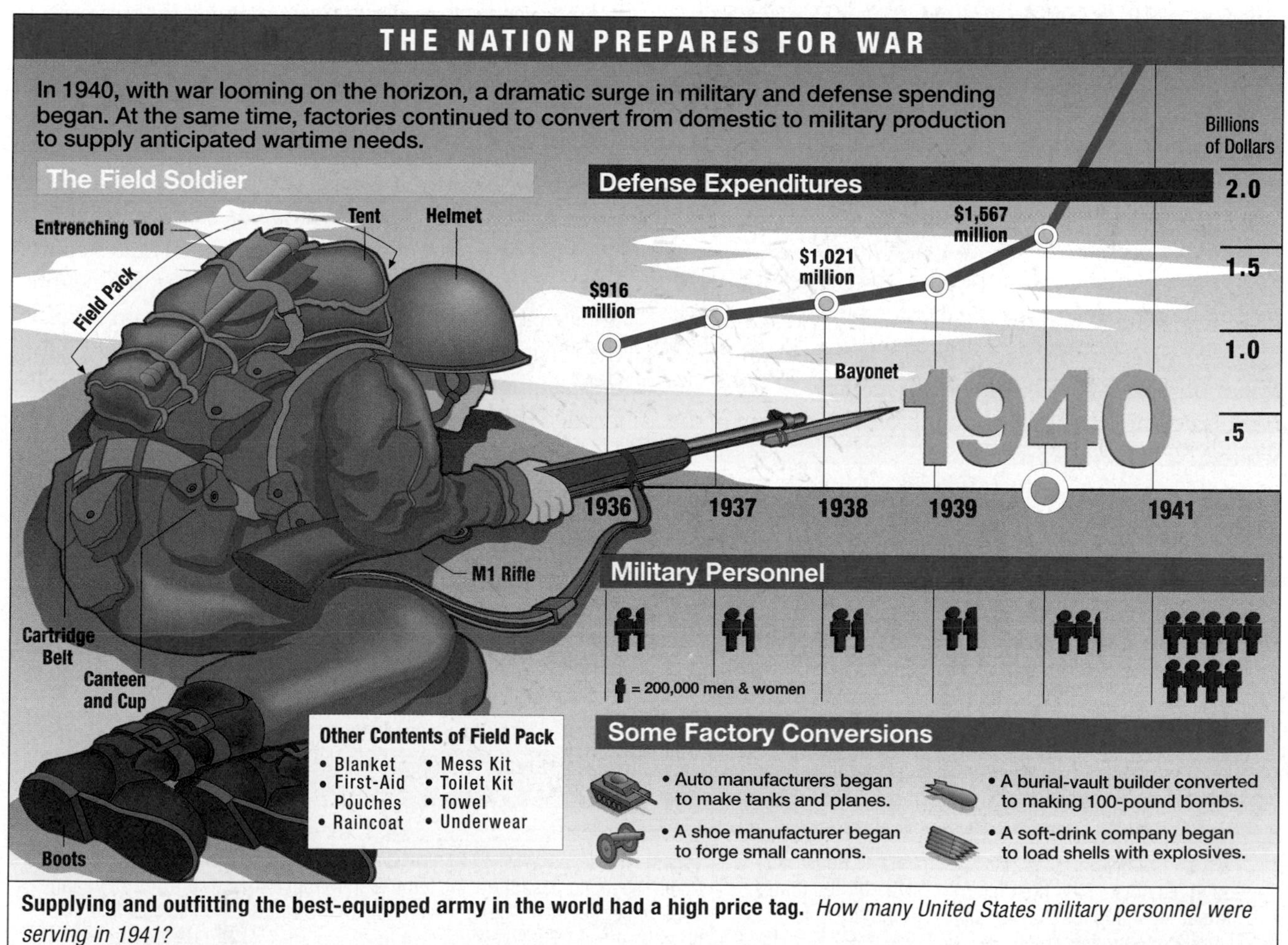

Supplying and outfitting the best-equipped army in the world had a high price tag. *How many United States military personnel were serving in 1941?*

LIBRARY OF CONGRESS

Roosevelt and Cordell Hull Cordell Hull, above right, served as secretary of state from 1933 to 1944. He was a leader in the drive to create the United Nations. *What goal prompted the formation of the United Nations?*

The Atlantic Charter

Stopping Hitler was not the only goal Roosevelt and Churchill shared. In August 1941, the two met for four days on a warship off the coast of Newfoundland. In addition to discussing military strategy, Roosevelt and Churchill agreed on a set of common principles establishing their goals for a postwar world. Their joint public statement was known as the Atlantic Charter. Recalling Wilson's Fourteen Points, the Charter affirmed each nation's right to choose its own government, free from fear of aggression. To protect this right, the United States, Britain, and the 15 others who had signed the charter by September 24 resolved to create an international organization to protect the security of all countries. Later, this dream took shape in the founding of the United Nations (UN).

The Japanese Threat Increases

Rome–Berlin–Tokyo Axis Formed

In the Pacific, Japan's continued aggression clearly violated the principles that Roosevelt and Churchill supported in the Atlantic Charter. In July 1940, Japan announced a plan for the future of Asia called the Greater East Asia Co-Prosperity Sphere. The sphere was in reality a Japanese empire, to include much of China, Southeast Asia, and the western Pacific. On September 27, Japan made an alliance with Germany and Italy, the Rome-Berlin-Tokyo Axis, which promised that each would defend the other if they were attacked by the United States.

The United States Responds

The United States responded to Japan's aggressive stance by applying economic pressure. Roosevelt's goal was to limit Japanese expansion by cutting off supplies, without provoking Japan to war. He placed an embargo on the sale of scrap metal to Japan. In September 1940, when Japan occupied French colonial possessions in northern Indochina, Roosevelt extended the embargo to include aviation fuel, all metals, chemicals, machine parts, and other products with military uses to Japan. This game of check and countercheck continued into 1941. When, in July of that year, Japan seized control of the rest of Indochina, Roosevelt retaliated by freezing all Japanese assets in the United States and ending all trade with Japan.

Despite mounting tensions, the United States continued to negotiate with the Japanese. In part, the negotiations were an attempt to buy time for the nation to fortify the Philippines and to build the "two-ocean navy" Congress authorized in 1940. Roosevelt's secretary of state, Cordell Hull, however, did not budge from his principles. He refused to meet with General Hideki Tojo in October

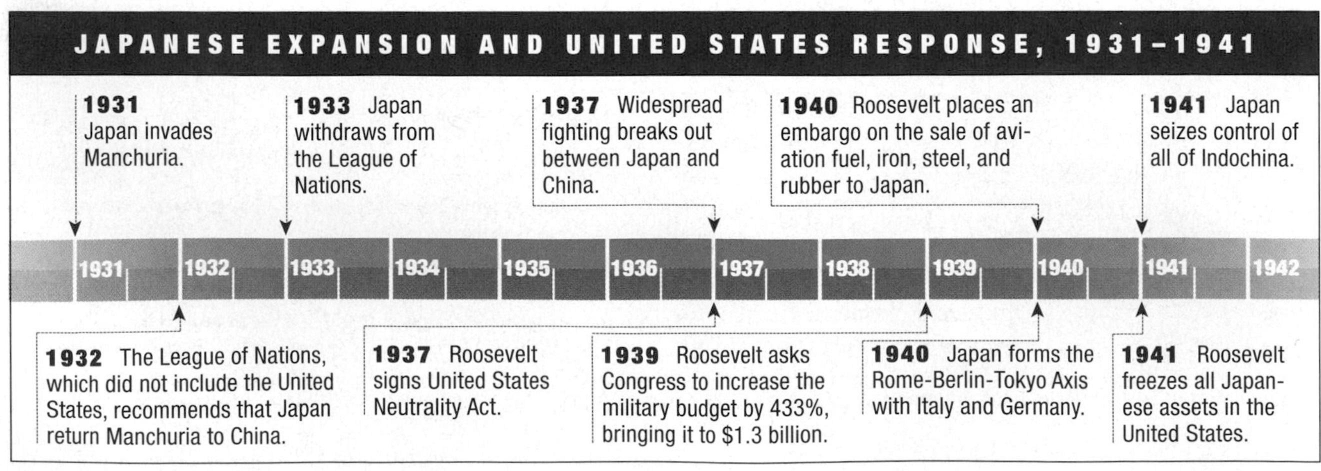

JAPANESE EXPANSION AND UNITED STATES RESPONSE, 1931–1941
1931 Japan invades Manchuria.
1933 Japan withdraws from the League of Nations.
1937 Widespread fighting breaks out between Japan and China.
1940 Roosevelt places an embargo on the sale of aviation fuel, iron, steel, and rubber to Japan.
1941 Japan seizes control of all of Indochina.
1931 1932 1933 1934 1935 1936 1937 1938 1939 1940 1941 1942
1932 The League of Nations, which did not include the United States, recommends that Japan return Manchuria to China.
1937 Roosevelt signs United States Neutrality Act.
1939 Roosevelt asks Congress to increase the military budget by 433%, bringing it to $1.3 billion.
1940 Japan forms the Rome-Berlin-Tokyo Axis with Italy and Germany.
1941 Roosevelt freezes all Japanese assets in the United States.

THE EXPANSION OF THE JAPANESE EMPIRE, 1931–1942

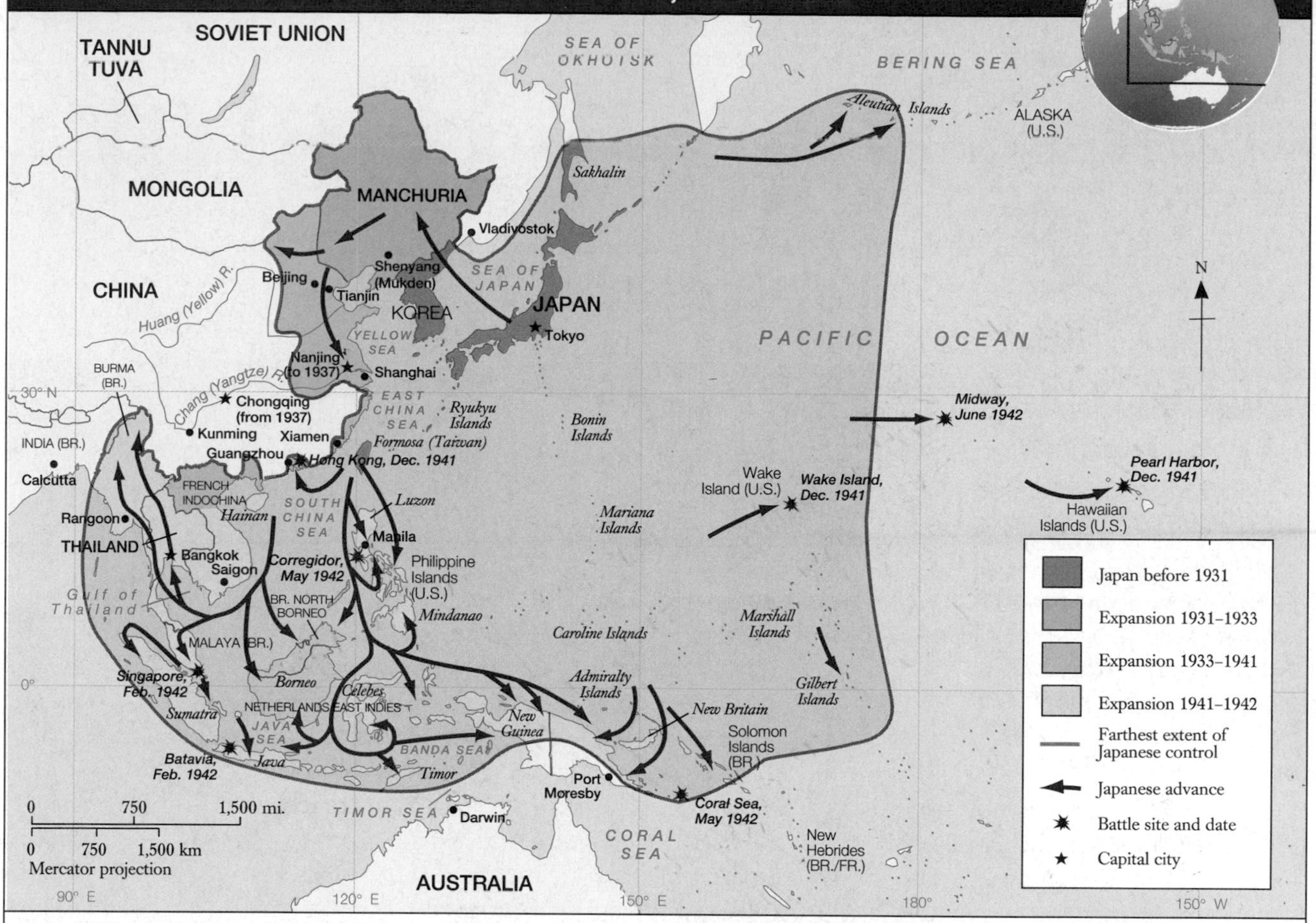

From 1931 to 1941 Japan's expansionism led to its control of most of East Asia. When Japan decided to attack the United States, Pearl Harbor was the chosen target. *Geographically, what might have influenced this decision?*

1941 and insisted that Japan honor the Open Door policy with China and that it stop its expansionism. The United States would resume trade with Japan, Hull said, only if Japan withdrew from China and Indochina.

Yamamoto's Plan

By November 1941, the United States government knew that war with Japan would come. With negotiations deadlocked and its oil supplies dwindling, the Japanese decided to take the offensive. Some Americans suspected an attack on Malaya or the Philippines. The Japanese, however, had accepted the plan of Admiral Isoroku Yamamoto, who advised striking the United States closer to home. An attack on the American naval base at Pearl Harbor offered Japan the possibility of delivering a knockout blow to the American fleet. Yamamoto, however, was far from optimistic about Japan's long-range prospects. "In the first six months to a year of war with the United States and England I will run wild," Yamamoto told his government prophetically. "I will show you an uninterrupted succession of victories, but if the war is prolonged for two or three years I have no confidence in the ultimate victory."

SECTION ASSESSMENT

Main Idea

1. Use a diagram like this one to show the steps Roosevelt took to aid the Allied cause.

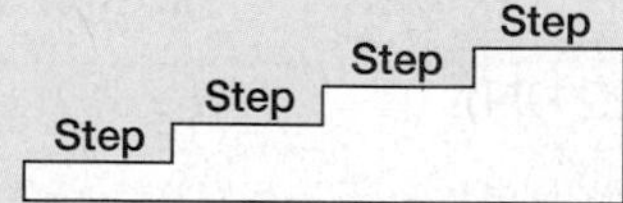

Vocabulary

2. Define: interventionism, isolationism.

Checking Facts

3. What led to the French surrender to Hitler?
4. Why did Roosevelt place embargoes on Japan?

Critical Thinking

5. **Making Inferences** After war broke out, Roosevelt said, "This nation will remain a neutral nation, but I cannot ask that every American remain neutral in thought as well." What can you infer from these words?

SPORTS: Ted Williams bats .406 for the season and also has 37 home runs.

One Day in History

Sunday, December 7, 1941

MARKET BASKET

Here is where a dollar will go:

Movie ticket . . . . 40¢
Eastman Brownie camera $2.56
Chevrolet Aerosedan $880.00
Wool sports jacket . . . $15.00
Boy's haircut. . . . . 50¢
Flashlight battery . . . . 4¢

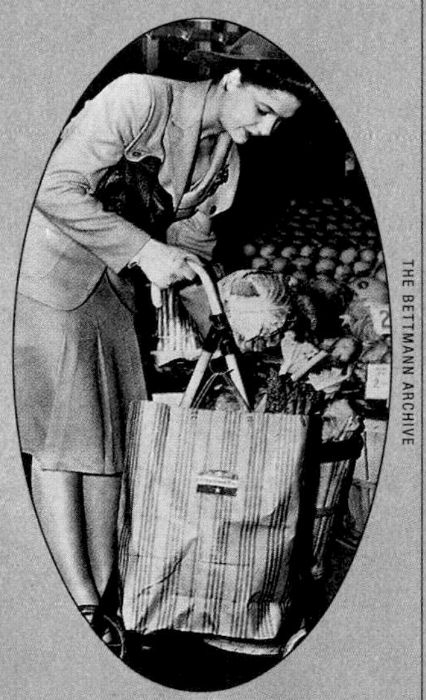

THE BETTMANN ARCHIVE

Coffee (1 lb.) . . . . 24¢
Chicken (1 lb.). . . . . 23¢
Frozen shrimp (1 lb.) . . . . 15¢
Salad dressing (1 qt.). . . . 33¢
Coca-Cola (6-pack) . . . . . 25¢
Milk (1 qt.). . . . . 14¢

NATIONAL ARCHIVES

Unprovoked Attack: Set aflame by Japanese bombs, United States battleships burn in their moorings at Pearl Harbor. The first attack occurred at 7:55 in the morning, local time, and most of the damage to the fleet occurred during the first 30 minutes of the sneak attack.

Japan Attacks Fleet

Japanese forces attack the United States Pacific Fleet in Pearl Harbor, Hawaii

NEW YORK—Sudden and unexpected attacks by the Japanese air force and navy on Pearl Harbor, Honolulu, and other United States possessions in the Pacific have plunged the nation into World War II.

The initial attack on the United States Pacific Fleet at Pearl Harbor, Hawaii, apparently launched by Japanese submarines and bombers carrying torpedoes, caused widespread damage and death. United States military casualties totaled more than 3,400. Of these, more than 2,300 were killed. The major targets of the Pearl Harbor attack were the 8 United States battleships moored there. The battleship *Arizona* was completely destroyed. The *California, Nevada,* and *West Virginia* sank, and the *Oklahoma* capsized. More than 180 United States aircraft were also destroyed.

Although radar indicated a large number of incoming planes, military personnel thought they were United States B-17s that were due to arrive.

NATION: Yale, Harvard, and Princeton Universities cut their programs from four to three years by staying in session all year.

War Fashions

NEW YORK—Reflecting the military influence of the day, a "Sentry Duty" cape is modeled at a benefit for the British-American Ambulance Corps held at the Rainbow Room. The show also previewed air-raid fashion.

UPI/BETTMANN

"Sentry Duty" Cape

First Lady at Radcliffe

CAMBRIDGE, MA—On December 12, Eleanor Roosevelt will be initiated into the Radcliffe College chapter of Phi Beta Kappa at its annual dinner. Her speaking topic will be "Women—Nazi, Fascist, and Democratic."

THE CARSON COLLECTION

***The Maltese Falcon* premieres, starring Humphrey Bogart.**

THE BETTMANN ARCHIVE

Martha Graham's New York City dance company performs *Letter to the World*.

MOVIES

- ***How Green Was My Valley,*** starring Walter Pidgeon and Maureen O'Hara
- ***Citizen Kane,*** starring Orson Welles
- ***Dr. Jekyll and Mr. Hyde,*** starring Spencer Tracy and Ingrid Bergman

MUSIC

Hit songs: "Deep in the Heart of Texas," "I'll Remember April," "The Anniversary Waltz"

Top records: "Chattanooga Choo Choo" by Glenn Miller, "Buckle Down, Winsocki" by Benny Goodman

REPRINTED COURTESY EAST.

REPRINTED COURTESY EASTMAN KODAK COMPANY

The United States at War

DECEMBER 7, 1941: JAPANESE ATTACK PEARL HARBOR

WITHOUT WARNING, JAPANESE DIVE BOMBERS AND TORPEDO PLANES SWOOPED OUT OF THE CLEAR, BLUE HAWAIIAN SKY AND RAINED DEATH AND DEVASTATION ON AMERICAN SHIPS ANCHORED IN THE HARBOR AND ON AMERICAN PLANES AT NEARBY AIR BASES. John Garcia, like others who witnessed the attack on Pearl Harbor, never forgot it:

> I was sixteen years old, employed as a pipe fitter apprentice at Pearl Harbor Navy Yard. On December 7, 1941, oh, around 8:00 a.m., my grandmother woke me. She informed me that the Japanese were bombing Pearl Harbor. I said, "They're just practicing." She said, no, it was real and the announcer is requesting that all Pearl Harbor workers report to work. I went out on the porch and I could see the anti-aircraft fire up in the sky. . . . I was asked . . . to go into the water and get sailors out that had been blown off the ships. Some were unconscious, some were dead. So I spent the rest of the day swimming inside the harbor, along with some other Hawaiians. . . . We worked all day at that.
>
> —As told to Studs Terkel, *"The Good War,"* 1984

AP/WIDE WORLD PHOTOS

Declaring War
On December 8, 1941, President Franklin Roosevelt asked for and received a declaration of war on Japan from a joint session of Congress.

In less than 3 hours, the Japanese destroyed 19 ships, including 5 battleships, and 188 planes. More than 2,400 Americans were killed. It was the worst defeat by a foreign power in United States military history. Yet Pearl Harbor aroused and united Americans as nothing else could have done. It hurled the nation into war, bent on revenge and committed to victory.

GUIDE TO READING

Main Idea

After mobilizing, the United States fought a two-front war, first giving priority to the defeat of Germany while staving off Japan, whose defeat was completed with the use of the atomic bomb.

Vocabulary

- unconditional surrender
- sonar technology

Read to Find Out . . .

- the roles of women and minorities in the war.
- the strategies that the Allies used to win the war and how the war changed the world.

Mobilizing at Home

Organizing the Fighting Forces

On December 8, President Roosevelt asked Congress to declare war on Japan to avenge what he called a "date which will live in infamy." Because the United States had not attacked first, the pact between the Axis Powers did not require Hitler and Mussolini to follow Japan into war against the United States. Nevertheless, Germany and Italy declared war a few days later. Now the United States had to prepare quickly for global war on two fronts.

Boosting the Number of Troops

The Selective Service Act had been in force for more than a year, but United States armed forces had only 1.8 million men when war was declared. Increased draft calls soon began to fill the ranks.

Reasons for signing up varied. Patriotism, anger toward the Axis, a desire for adventure, and joblessness all played parts in the decision to enlist. By 1942 nearly 3.9 million Americans were in uniform. The number more than doubled by 1943 and more than tripled by 1945. When the war ended, more than 15 million men and nearly 216,000 women had served.

Minorities in Uniform

The armed forces included about 1 million African Americans. Like much of the rest of United States society, the military was officially segregated. When African Americans enlisted, they were assigned to all African American units, usually commanded by white officers. African Americans were often given jobs as cooks or laborers. Many white commanders would not send African American units into combat.

Those African American units that did fight, however, performed with distinction. In late 1944 General Dwight D. Eisenhower called for African Americans to volunteer for combat in integrated units. Eisenhower became convinced that racially integrated combat units were more successful than segregated units.

Other minority groups also enlisted. Nearly 350,000 Hispanic Americans served, and they suffered many of the same kinds of discrimination as African Americans. Hispanics were the most decorated of American ethnic groups, while the Japanese American 442nd Regiment was the most decorated unit. Japanese American soldiers fought loyally during the war in spite of the severe discrimination suffered by their families back home. Many Native Americans also joined the war effort. Navajos in the Marine Signal Corps outwitted the Japanese by sending messages in a code based on the Navajo language.

THE BETTMANN ARCHIVE

Combat Skills African American troops in France during 1944 proved their skill in field artillery units. *By serving in combat, how did African American soldiers begin to alter the United States military's attitude toward minorities?*

The European Front

The Struggle to Defeat Germany

Shortly after Pearl Harbor, Allied political leaders met to determine their war strategy. Roosevelt and Churchill decided that defeat of Germany would be their top priority. Later, in 1943 at the Casablanca Conference in Morocco, at which Stalin was absent, the Allied leaders agreed to wage war until the Axis Powers accepted an **unconditional surrender**—a surrender without any concessions. The United States would fight a defensive war against Japan in the Pacific while the Allies concentrated their joint efforts on defeating the Nazis.

Invasion of the Soviet Union

Although the Soviets and the Nazis had signed a nonaggression pact in 1939, Soviet leader Joseph Stalin distrusted Hitler. The German invasion of the Soviet Union on June 22, 1941, however, shocked the Soviets.

HISTORY Online

Student Web Activity 15

Visit the *American Odyssey* Web site at americanodyssey.glencoe.com and click on ***Chapter 15—Student Web Activities*** for an activity relating to World War II.

SOVFOTO

After the Battle The Soviet defense of Stalingrad gave the Allies an advantage in Europe. *Why was Stalin angry with the Allies after the battle of Stalingrad?*

Using blitzkrieg tactics on a vast scale now, German troops surged north toward Leningrad and south toward the Crimean peninsula. By November they had begun to encircle Moscow. An unusually severe winter and the determination of Soviet troops and civilians drove back the attackers. In the north, German troops surrounded Leningrad for almost 900 days, starving to death more than half a million residents.

In the spring of 1942, the Germans launched a new attack on the Soviet oil fields in southwestern Russia. By September, 300,000 Nazi troops had begun a major assault on the city of Stalingrad. The battle continued for five months amid the ruins and rubble of the city, until the Germans surrendered in February 1943. As many as 250,000 German troops, and many more Soviets, were killed or they froze to death. The Battle of Stalingrad halted Germany's eastward advance, but Stalin never forgave the Allies for failing to help defend the Soviets. His country had suffered more casualties at Stalingrad than the United States did during the entire war. After the war, United States General George C. Marshall called the refusal of the British and Soviet people to accept defeat "the great factor in the salvage of our civilization."

Allied Offensives

Rather than face a winter deep within Russia, the Allies decided on a less risky assault. In November 1942, American and British troops landed in North Africa, advancing into Morocco and Algeria against a German tank division led by General Erwin Rommel, dubbed "the Desert Fox." The British gained an important victory in Egypt at El Alamein. This battle, like Stalingrad, marked a turning point in the war. Although 5,000 Americans died in a German counterattack in Tunisia, the Allies were victorious in North Africa by May 1943.

The Allies used bases in North Africa to launch an invasion of southern Europe, landing in Sicily in July 1943. They battled German troops for more than a month before driving them out of Sicily. Meanwhile, Mussolini's Fascist government fell from power. British forces invaded Italy from Sicily. On September 8, Italy announced its unconditional surrender to the Allies.

Germany, however, was determined to fight the Allies for control of Italy. Some of the most bitter fighting of the war occurred at Anzio beach and at Cassino Pass in central Italy. It was this kind of fighting—months of bombing, destruction, and death—that led cartoonist Bill Mauldin to write one of his darker captions: "Look at an infantryman's eyes and you can tell how much war he has seen." The Allies finally broke through German defenses in May, and Rome was liberated on June 4, 1944.

D-Day

The spotlight on the victory in Italy quickly shifted west. On June 6, 1944, General Eisenhower directed the largest combined land-sea-air invasion in history. The code name for the offensive was Operation Overlord, but most Americans remember the assault as D-Day. The D-Day invasion was, according to Churchill, "the most difficult and complicated that has ever taken place." Some 175,000 Allied soldiers began to come ashore before dawn along a 60-mile (96.5-km) stretch of the coast of Normandy in France. Once they had established a beachhead, at a cost of 2,245 killed and 1,670 wounded, the Allied forces had a base from which they would try to sweep the Germans out of France.

The success of D-Day also hinged on American industry. For months before the invasion, United States and British planes had dropped thousands of tons of bombs on German railroad lines, factories, and cities. Moreover, the huge Allied invasion force had been carried by American transports of all kinds. Without the industrial workers who had made this equipment, the Allied forces could not have landed in or retaken France.

The Beginning of the End

As the war progressed, the Allies gradually proved their dominance in the skies. Both experienced and new pilots flew fighters, bombers, and spy planes. That done, ground troops could advance cautiously eastward toward Germany. On August 25, 1944, American and French forces liberated Paris to great rejoicing by most inhabi-

WORLD WAR II IN EUROPE, 1939–1945

The European phase of World War II lasted five years, eight months, and seven days. Civilians suffered heavy losses in life and property from bombings, forced evacuations, and starvation. *What countries shown on the map were not directly affected by World War II? Why?*

tants. In the meantime, Allied forces had launched an invasion of France's Rhône Valley from the south. By summer's end France, Belgium, and Luxembourg were in Allied hands. Soviet troops advanced on Germany from the east.

Sea power was also crucial to Allied planning. Before the United States had entered the war, German U-boats had preyed on North Atlantic shipping, even briefly threatening cities on the east coast of the United States. While at sea sailors faced the triple peril of attack from above, from the surface, and from below—from planes, battleships, and U-boats. By late 1943 advances in **sonar technology**—technology allowing detection of submerged objects by means of sound waves—had given the Allies an edge in locating and sinking U-boats. More and more Allied naval convoys were safely crossing the Atlantic, keeping the Allies' enormous armies well provisioned. This lifeline made possible an offensive, not just a defensive, strategy.

While the Allies prepared for an invasion of Germany itself, Hitler launched a last desperate strike. In December Germany mounted a counteroffensive in the Ardennes Forest of Belgium. Hitler's tanks drove a bulge of troops and artillery 80 miles (128.7 km) long and 50 miles (80.5 km) deep into the Allied lines. After weeks of heavy fighting, during which 76,000 Allied soldiers were killed or wounded, the Germans were pushed back. The so-called Battle of the Bulge was the final German offensive of the war. The road into Germany, blocked for 6 weeks, was now open. As the Allied armies advanced, however, they had to confront the horrors committed by Hitler's government.

The Holocaust

When Allied soldiers entered Germany in 1945, they found the terrible consequences of Hitler's fanatical hatred of Jews and other peoples. In early 1942 Hitler had put into action what he called "the final solution" to his "Jewish problem." Nazi soldiers rounded up Jews from all over Europe and shipped them to concentration camps. In these camps Jews were used for slave labor, subjected to medical experiments and other atrocities,

THE BETTMANN ARCHIVE

AP/WIDE WORLD PHOTOS

Nazi Atrocities **The horror of Nazi persecution is evident in the photo above of emaciated survivors of one of the concentration camps at Evensee, Austria. In the photo at the left, Nazi troops take Jewish people in Warsaw, Poland, from their homes.** *What other civilian groups in Europe did the Nazis persecute and kill?*

starved, beaten, shot, and put to death in gas chambers. Their bodies were buried in mass graves or incinerated in fiendishly efficient crematoriums.

Reports about these horrors were circulating as early as 1942. Only when the Allies liberated the death camps in 1945, however, did the world learn for certain the ghastly extent of Hitler's plan to wipe out the Jews of Europe. Walter Rosenblum, an American soldier, helped liberate Dachau, a concentration camp in southern Germany. He recalled:

> The first thing I saw as I went down this road to Dachau were about forty boxcars on a railroad siding. . . . I looked into these boxcars and they were full of emaciated bodies, loaded all the way to the top. Forty boxcars full of dead people.
>
> —As told to Studs Terkel, *"The Good War,"* 1984

Hitler's henchmen, along with thousands of Nazi collaborators, massacred about 6 million Jewish men, women, and children. More than two-thirds of the total Jewish population in Europe was destroyed. They also killed some 6 million Slavs, Gypsies, Communists, homosexuals, and others, most of them civilians. This mass extermination lives in infamy as the Holocaust, which has come to mean the "great destruction."

Some critics have charged that Roosevelt could have lessened the extent of this tragedy, pointing out that only 21,000 Jewish refugees were admitted to the United States in the early 1940s. This was a small fraction of the number permitted under existing immigration quotas. Moreover, some people thought Roosevelt was indifferent to the mass suffering of European Jews. In 1944 the United States War Department resisted proposals to bomb the gas chambers at the Auschwitz concentration camp. Roosevelt countered that his policy was to defeat Germany quickly and thus save all Hitler's victims from further persecution.

Victory in Europe

After turning back the Nazi onslaught on their homeland, Soviet troops moved west. They ousted Nazi governments or aided anti-German forces throughout eastern and central Europe in 1944 and 1945. They encircled Vienna and Prague, prize capitals of central Europe, and warned off the western Allies from challenging their control. Residents of the formerly Nazi-occupied countries, fearing new foreign armies, were not always sure which army to surrender to. Already it was clear to the world that the Soviet Union and the United States were replacing Germany as superpowers in Europe.

Allied forces began their final assault on Germany early in 1945. Soviet troops crossed Poland, as British and American troops swept into northern Germany from the Netherlands. Crossing rivers was among the gravest dangers, as retreating Nazis often tried to mine the bridges. By the end of March, American forces had crossed the Rhine River and were advancing steadily toward Berlin, Germany's capital.

In the midst of Allied successes in Europe a tragedy occurred in the United States. On April 12, Franklin Roosevelt died, after 12 years in office. Vice President Harry S Truman took the oath of office and assumed leadership of the country. Roosevelt's death did not halt the Allied advance. By late April Soviet troops had surrounded the city of Berlin. On April 30, Hitler committed suicide.

Berlin fell on May 2, and Germany surrendered unconditionally on May 7. War-weary Allied soldiers could look forward to being sent home. Sergeant Harold Murphy of Decatur, Illinois, expressed the feelings of thousands of other fathers in a postcard mailed to his baby daughter that day: "The War ended today, honey, and I hope to see you soon." The Allies declared May 8, 1945, V-E Day, or Victory in Europe Day.

The Pacific Front

To Japan Through the Islands

The war in Europe was over, but the United States continued to fight a very different kind of war in the Pacific. After its brutal attack on Pearl Harbor, the Japanese army swept to victory after victory. In early 1942 Japanese forces captured the Dutch East Indies, which were rich in oil and other natural resources. Then they took Burma, Wake Island, and Guam and forced the surrender of 12,000 American soldiers in the Philippines.

By May 1942, United States forces in the Pacific began to reverse the tide that had been flowing against them. In the battle of the Coral Sea, American carrier-based planes bombarded the Japanese fleet, stopping the Japanese advance toward Australia. A month later at the Battle of Midway, American planes sank 4 Japanese aircraft carriers and destroyed more than 300 planes. This was the first major Japanese defeat, and it greatly reduced the threat to Hawaii.

Despite these setbacks, Japan still held many fortified Pacific islands. To counter this advantage, American military planners adopted an "island hopping" strategy. Hoping to surround Japanese strongholds and cut them off from supplies, United States Marines captured key islands, building bases from which to attack the Philippines and eventually Japan itself.

Guadalcanal

A typical United States offensive in the Pacific was the attack on Guadalcanal in the Solomon Islands. During the summer of 1942, the Japanese began building an airfield on the island, preparing for an invasion of Australia. To keep the Japanese from finishing the airfield, 10,000 marines waded ashore to seize the island on August 7, 1942.

Once on land, the marines battled both the enemy and the steaming jungle environment. Scorching heat, relentless humidity, rotting gear, poisonous insects, and tropical fevers, such as malaria and dysentery, were the everyday conditions of jungle warfare.

The battle for Guadalcanal continued over six grueling months, as Japanese soldiers were ordered to fight to the death to hold the island. Even after the United States Navy destroyed Japanese ships in the area, isolating the enemy remaining on the island, it took three months to drive off the Japanese.

Guadalcanal was the first territory Japan lost in the war. In their unsuccessful attempt to hold the island, the Japanese lost 25,000 men. Americans learned that every Pacific battle would be bloody and hard fought and that the Japanese could be beaten.

Battles for islands like Guadalcanal cost thousands of American lives from 1942 to 1945. In a 6-week battle for Iwo Jima in early 1945, for example, the marines

UPI/BETTMANN NEWSPHOTOS

Mobile Rocket Unit A barrage of explosives are launched from a United States Marine rocket unit during a 1945 assault on the Japanese on an island in the Pacific. *What advantage would a unit on wheels provide?*

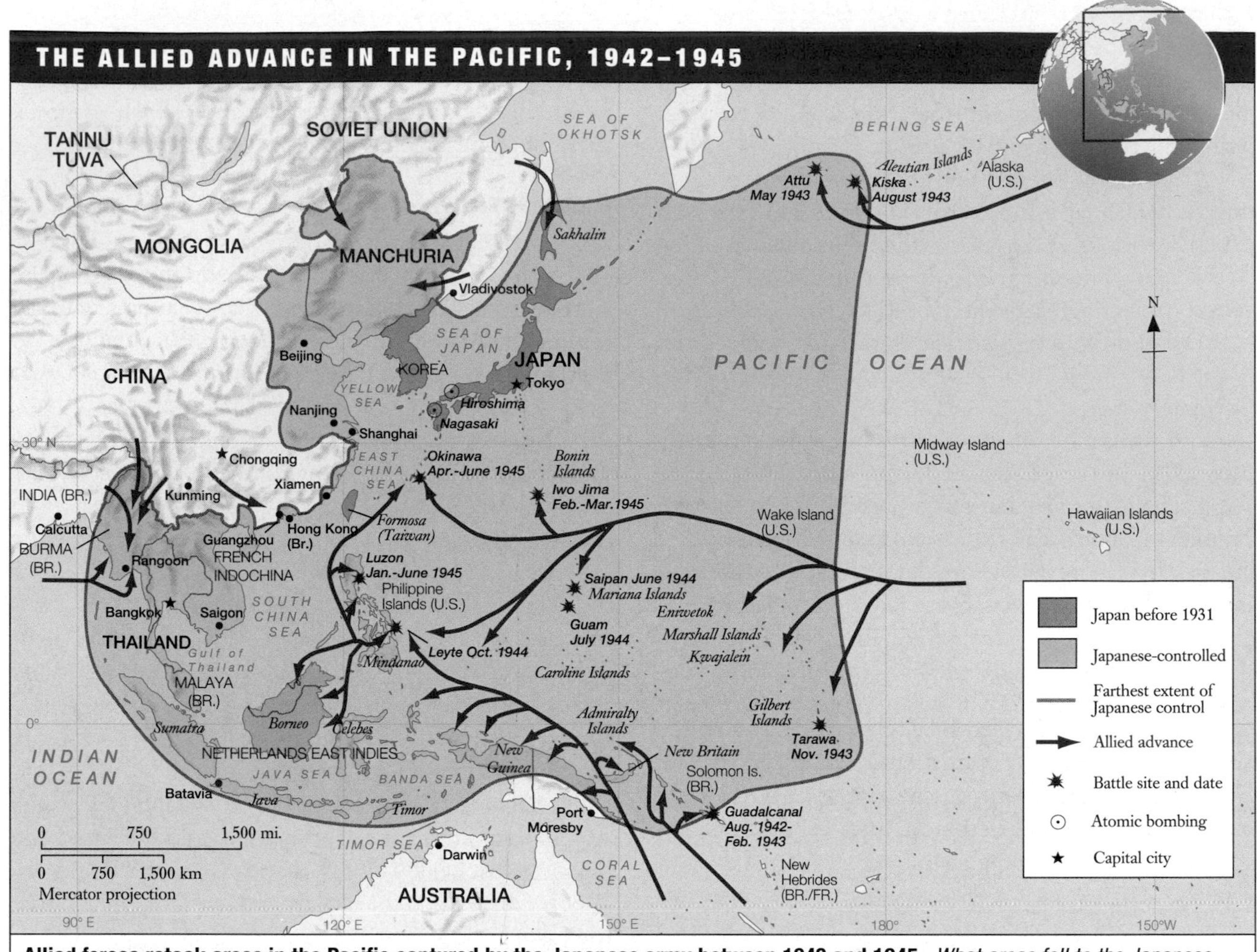

Allied forces retook areas in the Pacific captured by the Japanese army between 1942 and 1945. *What areas fell to the Japanese during these years? What major battles occurred during their recapture?*

suffered about 20,000 casualties to secure this tiny island 700 miles (1,126.3 km) from Japan. At about the same time, the United States achieved another objective when General Douglas MacArthur directed the American recapture of the Philippines. The strategy of inching island by island toward an eventual invasion of Japan was working. The United States and its allies agreed, however, that it might take years and up to a million deaths to conquer the Japanese home islands.

To step up the pressure on Japan, American long-range B-29 bombers began sustained strikes on the Japanese mainland in June 1944. By November they were bombing Tokyo itself. In one raid on Tokyo in March 1945, napalm bombs caused a firestorm in the city, incinerating 83,000 Japanese citizens. Despite casualties like these and the near total destruction of Japanese sea and air power, Japanese military leaders refused to accept the unconditional surrender that the United States demanded.

The Atomic Bomb

With little hope of forcing a Japanese surrender, President Truman scheduled an invasion of Japan for late 1945 and early 1946. Then on July 16, 1945, American scientists, led by physicist J. Robert Oppenheimer, gave Truman another choice when they successfully detonated the first atomic bomb in the desert near Alamogordo, New Mexico. Truman chose to use the bomb on Japan with the hope of ending the war without an invasion. (See page 516.) On August 6, 1945, the *Enola Gay,* an American B-29, dropped a single atomic bomb code-named Little Boy on the Japanese city of Hiroshima. A Japanese journalist described the bomb's devastating effects:

> Suddenly a glaring whitish pinkish light appeared in the sky accompanied by an unnatural tremor. . . . Within a few seconds the thousands of people in the streets . . . and in the gardens in the center of town were scorched by a wave of searing heat. . . .
>
> By the evening the fire began to burn down and then it went out. There was nothing left to burn. Hiroshima had ceased to exist.
>
> —Barrington Boardman, *From Harding to Hiroshima,* 1987

World War II Deaths*		
Country	**Military Deaths**	**Civilian Deaths**
United States	405,000	2,000
Great Britain	271,000	60,600
Germany	2,850,000	2,300,000
France	210,700	173,300
USSR	14,500,000	7,000,000
Poland	850,000	5,778,000
Italy	279,800	93,000
China	1,324,000	10,000,000
Japan	1,506,000	300,000
Spain	12,000	10,000

*approximate

The United States suffered approximately 2,000 civilian deaths during World War II. *What factors account for this comparatively low estimate?*

The atomic blast killed 100,000 people instantly, and another 100,000 men, women, and children died later from burns, radiation, or other wounds caused by the blast. The bomb destroyed more than 4 square miles of the city. On August 8, the Soviet Union entered the war against Japan as it had promised. When the Japanese still did not surrender, the United States dropped a second atomic bomb on the city of Nagasaki on August 9. The bomb killed 40,000 more Japanese citizens. Five days later, on August 14, the Japanese government surrendered. After 6 years of fighting, World War II was over.

The Impact of War

A Changed World

World War II was the most devastating war in history and the first to bring mass civilian deaths. Grigori Baklanov, who served in the Soviet army, expressed the tragedy: "Of my generation, out of one hundred who went to fight, three came back. Three percent." Baklanov noted with despair, "I was the only one from our class of all the boys who went to the front who remained alive after the war. What else is there to say?"

The war devastated thousands of cities and villages throughout Europe and Asia, leaving national capitals in ruins. Everywhere, transportation systems were mangled, factories were destroyed, and economies were left in shambles.

As the chart on this page indicates, the United States suffered fewer deaths than many other nations, and it had less destruction of property. Fewer than 1 percent of United States citizens were killed or wounded in the war. By contrast, the Soviet Union lost more than 8 percent of its population. Also, the demand for war supplies pulled the American economy out of the Great Depression and made it more productive and prosperous.

The war changed the lives of the men and women who served in it. Many left their homes for the first time to travel across the country and around the world. They were exposed to new ideas and opinions. Anne Bosanko Green described life in the WACs (Women's Army Corps):

> We suddenly left our humdrum lives, our jobs, and schools and were moved all around the vast United States or across the Atlantic and Pacific oceans to lands we had never thought we would see. We did not have to worry about our families and homelands being destroyed while we were off seeing the world. We were learning new skills, [and] meeting new people. . . .
>
> —Anne Bosanko Green, *One Woman's War,* 1989

In addition to its effects on returning servicemen and servicewomen, the war transformed the lives of millions of Americans on the home front. In all areas of United States society—business, agriculture, labor, and government—the war brought varied and lasting changes.

Section Assessment

Main Idea

1. Use a diagram like this one to show key battles or military actions that were critical in achieving victory in Europe and in the Pacific.

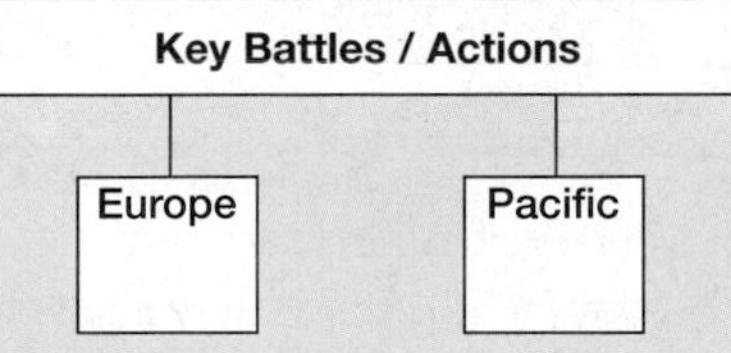

Vocabulary

2. Define: unconditional surrender, sonar technology.

Checking Facts

3. What was the overall Allied war strategy?
4. What was the social impact on the people and the countries involved in World War II?

Critical Thinking

5. **Determining Cause and Effect** How did the use of advanced technology make World War II the most devastating war in history?

Turning Point

Dropping the Bomb

AUGUST 6, 1945

MEMORANDUM

For: The President

Subject: Dropping the Bomb

I think it is very important that I should have a talk with you as soon as possible on a highly secret matter.

I mentioned it to you shortly after you took office, but have not urged it since on account of the pressure you have been under. It, however, has such a bearing on our present foreign relations and has such an important effect upon all my thinking in this field that I think you ought to know about it without much further delay.

Secretary of War Henry L. Stimson
April 24, 1945

The Case

When Truman received Stimson's note on April 24, 1945, he had been President for only 12 days. Stimson wanted to talk with Truman about the atomic bomb. The war in Europe was drawing to a close, and the President was turning his attention to ending the war with Japan and to the negotiations that would shape the postwar world. Truman met with Stimson the next day, and the information Stimson shared would significantly influence Truman's strategy for ending the war.

Truman faced a critical question: Now that the atomic bomb was almost ready, would the United States use this fearsome new weapon against Japan? Truman later insisted that he "regarded the bomb as a military weapon and never had any doubt that it should be used." Some others did have doubts, but the evidence available today indicates that Truman and other leading policy makers did not. The decisions they made about when and how to use the weapon, however, had major military, political, and ethical consequences for the postwar world.

The Background

Truman's meeting with Stimson gave him his first knowledge of the atomic bomb; Stimson informed him that the bomb would probably be ready within four months. Although Stimson supported using the bomb to end the war, he also pointed out serious problems that the bomb would pose for the world after the war. Chief among these were a possible atomic arms race and the danger of an atomic war. To address these challenges, Stimson proposed that Truman appoint a committee to advise him on policy regarding atomic weapons. The President took Stimson's advice, and the Interim Committee, as it was called, met in Washington on May 31.

The goal of Truman and the Interim Committee appears to have been to find the most effective way to use the bomb to shock Japan into surrendering. Even though the Russians had promised to enter the war against Japan by August 8, many American military leaders assumed that an amphibious landing on the Japanese mainland would be necessary to end the war. The cost in American lives would be high, and many believed that using the bomb could end the war without an invasion.

The Opinions

The quotes on this page represent the range of opinions about using the atomic bomb that were expressed during the summer of 1945. Stimson's statement expresses the majority opinion—that the bomb had to be used to end the war quickly and to save American lives. The other statements question the use of this new weapon.

The Options

The opinions you have read indicate that Truman had these options to consider:

1. Drop the bomb on Japanese cities to force an immediate end to the war.
2. Carry out a demonstration of the weapon to persuade Japan to surrender.
3. Launch an invasion of Japan.
4. Rely on Japan's deteriorating military situation and the entry of the Soviet Union into the war to force Japanese surrender.
5. Negotiate surrender terms acceptable to Japan and the United States.

The Decision

The Interim Committee made its decision and gave it to Truman on June 1:

> The present view of the Committee was that the bomb should be used against Japan as soon as possible; that it be used on a war plant surrounded by workers' homes; and that it be used without prior warning.
>
> —Recording Secretary R. Gordon Arneson, from minutes taken on May 31

"In the light of the alternatives which, on a fair estimate, were open to us I believe that no man, in our position and subject to our responsibilities, holding in his hands a weapon of such possibilities for accomplishing this purpose and saving those lives, could have failed to use it and afterwards looked his countrymen in the face."

Henry L. Stimson
Secretary of War

AP/WIDE WORLD PHOTOS

"I told him [Stimson] I was against it on two counts. First, the Japanese were ready to surrender and it wasn't necessary to hit them with that awful thing. Second, I hated to see our country be the first to use such a weapon."

General Dwight D. Eisenhower
Supreme Allied Commander

AP/WIDE WORLD PHOTOS

AP/WIDE WORLD PHOTOS

"I have had a feeling that before the bomb is actually used against Japan that Japan should have some preliminary warning of say two or three days in advance. . . . The position of the United States as a great humanitarian nation and the fair play attitude of our people generally is responsible in the main for this feeling."

Ralph A. Bard
Undersecretary of the Navy

BROWN BROTHERS

"If the United States were to be the first to release this new means of indiscriminate destruction upon mankind, she would sacrifice public support throughout the world, precipitate the race for armaments, and prejudice the possibility of reaching an international agreement on the future control of such weapons."

James Franck
University of Chicago

Turning Point

AP/WIDE WORLD PHOTOS

HULTON DEUTSCH COLLECTION

Above, a column of smoke billows 20,000 feet over Hiroshima, Japan, after the first atomic bomb strike. The aftermath is shown on the left.

Secretary of State Byrnes informed the President of the Interim Committee's decision. Later, he said that "with reluctance [Truman] had to agree that he could think of no alternative and found himself in accord with what I told him the Committee was going to recommend." Why did Truman choose Option 1?

Apparently Truman rejected Option 2, a demonstration, for reasons offered by the Interim Committee and its scientific panel. A demonstration would not help to end the war. The committee did not offer evidence to support this judgment. They knew, however, that a successful test would not necessarily cause the Japanese to surrender unconditionally. An unsuccessful test, they believed, would be worse than none.

Truman placed the highest value on ending the war with the loss of as few American lives as possible. Both Options 3 and 4 would cost countless American lives and bring an indefinite extension of the war with no certain outcome. The Japanese might never surrender. They seemed prepared to fight to the end, whatever that would mean, even the loss of many Japanese lives. Option 4 had an added disadvantage. If the Soviets entered the fighting, they would gain an advantage in postwar negotiations about new governments in Eastern Europe. Truman and other United States leaders preferred not to be indebted to the Soviets for any help in ending the war with Japan.

Truman probably never viewed Option 5 as a real possibility. The only surrender acceptable to American leaders would be unconditional. The only surrender acceptable to the Japanese would include at least one condition: that they be allowed to keep their emperor. Truman saw the bomb as just another weapon—legitimate in wartime, when the goal was to win.

The Outcome

The bomb was successfully tested on July 16, 1945, at a remote desert site near Alamogordo, New Mexico. On August 6, 1945, the United States dropped an atomic bomb carrying more power than 20,000 tons of TNT on Hiroshima, Japan, an important military center. The next day President Truman gave a statement that included the following: "Let there be no mistake: we shall completely destroy Japan's power to make war. Only a Japanese surrender will stop us."

Most Americans and their allies breathed a sigh of relief, knowing that the war would soon end. Yet they also recognized that, as the *London Daily Express* put it, "The world has changed overnight."

The Interpretations

More than half a century has passed since that summer in 1945. The years have brought knowledge and perspectives unavailable to Truman and other decision makers of that time. During these years three main interpretations have emerged.

One is that Truman and Stimson were correct in their idea that the bombings were necessary to end the war and save lives. According to this view, these were the only significant motives of those who ordered the bombing of Hiroshima and, three days later, Nagasaki.

Another interpretation is that dropping the bomb was unnecessary, even immoral. People holding this view argued that while Truman and the others were honest, they were also naive; they failed to take into account the long-term effects of dropping the bomb, such as the arms race and the cold war.

A third group also saw the bombings as unnecessary and unwise. In addition, they said that Truman and the other policy makers had ulterior motives, that they engaged in "atomic diplomacy." They used the bombings to try to intimidate the Soviets. As a result, said this group, they failed to consider seriously alternatives to dropping the bomb.

Today controversy over the decision to drop the atomic bomb continues. As time passes new evidence becomes available. For example, the first viewpoint found support in later evidence from Japan that seemed to show that without the bombings the war might have continued for many months. Such findings support the often repeated but much challenged idea that the bombings saved as many as 1 million American lives.

Another source of new evidence has been medical reports about those who survived the bombings at Hiroshima and Nagasaki. Many sickened and died soon afterward. Over the years more evidence has emerged about long-term effects of atomic radiation. Today, for example, survivors of the bombings have a higher than average incidence of leukemia and thyroid cancer. Thus medical reports about survivors add to the evidence used by those who raise ethical questions about the bomb.

UPI/BETTMANN

A Japanese prisoner of war weeps at the news of Japan's surrender.

RESPONDING TO THE CASE

1. Look again at the opinions of Henry L. Stimson and James Franck and contrast their predictions of the consequences of using the bomb. Why do you think they differed so much?

2. Which consequences of using the bomb did Truman predict correctly? Which were different from what he might have expected?

3. Some scientists were more likely than political leaders to oppose the use of the atomic bomb. What could account for these differences?

4. What conflicts in values did you discover as you read the quotations on page 517? Have our values as Americans changed over time, giving new meanings to the events of the 1940s?

PORTFOLIO PROJECT

Even today, more than 50 years after the bombing of Hiroshima, many people still debate whether the bombing should have taken place. Write down your opinion and your reasoning, and place your work in your portfolio.

Chapter  Assessment

Self-Check Quiz

Visit the *American Odyssey* Web site at americanodyssey.glencoe.com and click on ***Chapter 15—Self-Check Quiz*** to prepare for the Chapter Test.

Reviewing Key Terms

Match the vocabulary term from the list below to the sentence that describes it. Write your answers on a separate sheet of paper.

blitzkrieg **interventionism**
totalitarian **isolationism**
unconditional surrender **appeasement**

1. The United States insisted upon _________ in negotiations with the Japanese.

2. Early in the war, the policy of _________ enabled Hitler to occupy the Sudetenland region of Czechoslovakia without any official opposition from Great Britain or France.

3. A _________ type of government demands complete control over the lives of its citizens.

4. Those people who supported a policy of _________ thought the United States should not become involved in the war.

5. _________ was a rapid and devastating style of attack that helped Hitler to gain control of Poland quickly.

Recalling Facts

1. In his speech before the Reichstag, how did Hitler justify his orders to murder those who stood in his way to political power? What effect did his words have on the German people?

2. Germany and Italy formed an alliance in 1936 known as the Axis Powers. How did this alliance affect the outcome of the Spanish civil war?

3. Why did Japan wish to expand its territory during the 1930s and 1940s?

4. What was the function of the Neutrality Acts?

5. Why was the Battle of Britain an initial failure for Germany? What strategy did Hitler try in his "blitz" of London to ward off further failure?

6. Describe the Lend-Lease Act. How did its passage signify a deeper American commitment to the war?

7. Why did the Battle of Stalingrad cause Stalin to resent Great Britain and the United States?

8. What famous battle led to the liberation of France? How was liberation accomplished?

9. Why is the name Holocaust used to describe Hitler's atrocities against Jews in Europe during World War II?

10. What was the effect of the war on the cities of Asia and Europe?

Critical Thinking

1. Identifying Assumptions Many people in the United States supported the Republican cause in Spain. Some even volunteered to fight in the Spanish civil war. What assumptions might they have made about the expansion of totalitarian governments in Europe that led them to become involved in what could have been seen as strictly Spain's problem?

2. Determining Cause and Effect Admiral Isoroku Yamamoto promised Japan a series of victories for the first year of a war with the United States and Great Britain if Japan took his advice to strike the United States close to home. He also said, however, that unless Japan won the war quickly victory would be impossible. Considering what you now know about Japan during this time period, identify the cause-and-effect relationship that caused Yamamoto to hold this view.

3. Formulating Questions Use a diagram like this one to write questions that you would like to ask a man or woman who volunteered for duty in World War II. Each of the questions should begin with one of the six questions words—*who? what? where? when? why? how?*—commonly used by reporters.

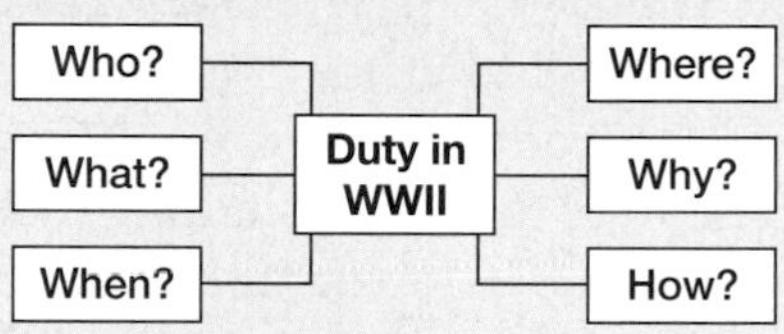

4. Determining Relevance World War II was the most destructive war ever waged in terms of lives lost and property destroyed. What can people of today learn from this period in history?

Cooperative Learning

Working in small groups, analyze the various types of propaganda used during World War II by the Axis Powers and by the Allies. Assign group members specific tasks of gathering information, writing descriptions and summaries of what you find, analyzing the propaganda, and then making a class presentation. Try to include some visuals in the presentation.

Reinforcing Skills

Recognizing Ideologies Research a political slogan or choose one that you already know. Write out the slogan and explain what it reveals about the ideology of the person or group who has adopted the slogan.

GEOGRAPHY AND HISTORY

D-Day Invasion, June 6, 1944

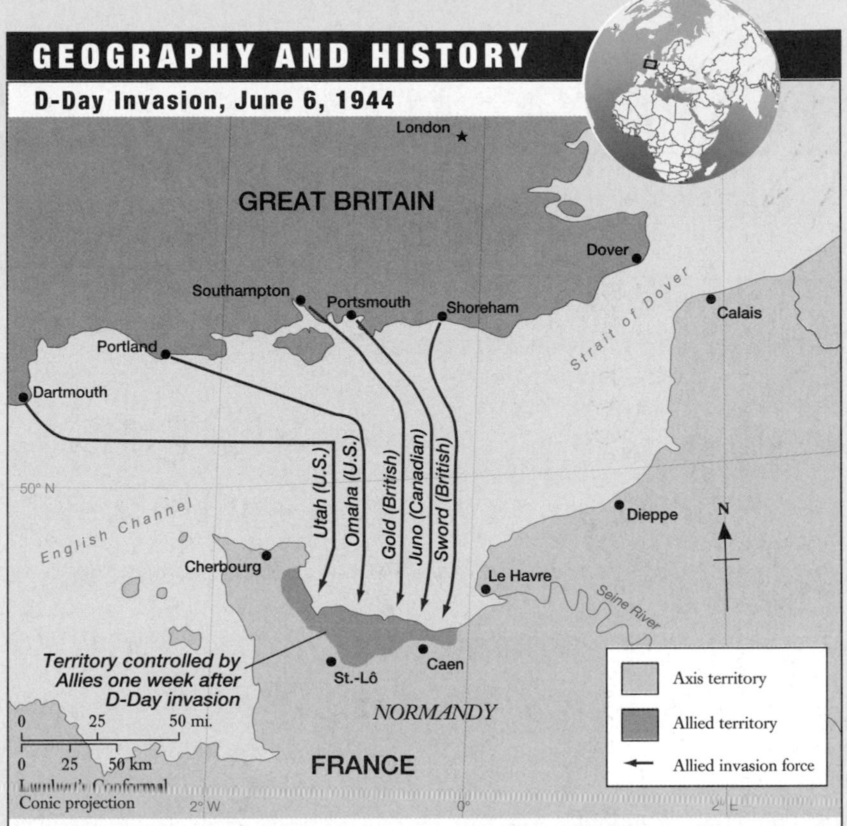

Study the map to answer the following questions:

1. The map shows the Allied invasion routes from Great Britain to Normandy beginning June 6, 1944. Utah, Omaha, Gold, Juno, and Sword were code names for the Normandy beaches. Write an explanation of the Allied attack.
2. Why do you think the invasion was launched from five sites rather than from one?
3. The Nazis were fooled into thinking the D-Day invasion would come near Calais. Why do you think the Allies chose to land on the Normandy peninsula instead?

Portfolio Project

PORTFOLIO PROJECT

Isolationists and interventionists had different opinions about United States involvement in World War II. Write a summary of the basic views, priorities, and values of each group. Explain your own position on this issue and give reasons for taking that position. Place your finished work in your portfolio.

Technology Activity

Using the Internet Search the Internet for a World War II Web site that includes memoirs or excerpts from survivors of the Holocaust. Copy or print parts of the memoirs. Create a bulletin board by posting the excerpts under the heading "Voices of the Holocaust."

Standardized Test Practice

1. When Roosevelt signed the Lend-Lease Act in 1941, he said that the United States must become the "great arsenal of democracy" in order to

A end the Depression.
B help the Axis powers.
C remain neutral.
D help Great Britain and France.

> ***Test-Taking Tip:*** Think about the meaning of the word *arsenal:* a stockpile or storehouse of weapons. Eliminate any answer that does not strongly relate to using the United States *arsenal* to protect democracy. Because the Axis powers were totalitarian states, you can rule out answer B.

2. The Allies agreed in early 1942 that their first military goal would be the

A defeat of Japan.
B invasion of the Soviet Union.
C development of the atomic bomb.
D defeat of Germany.

> ***Test-Taking Tip:*** This question involves a sequence of events and a knowledge of the nations that comprised the Allies. For example, by 1942, the Soviet Union had joined with the Allies. Therefore, you can rule out answer B.

The Home Front

1942: AMERICANS PULL TOGETHER

World War II jolted the American people—who were still troubled by a depressed economy—with an electric sense of purpose. After a decade of severe job shortages, thousands of American men and women willingly served in the armed forces.

Others worked on farms and in factories to produce the food and weapons needed to win the war. During the war years, the United States became a country on the move. Many of the new recruits had never before left their hometowns.

The war disrupted the homes, families, and lives of all Americans. Many women followed their husbands to military bases. Both men and women went in search of high-paying jobs in the defense industry. Many African Americans traveled north and west hoping to escape poverty and discrimination.

This mingling of people from different backgrounds altered the way Americans looked at themselves. The American people began to recognize some of the political, social, and economic consequences of living in such a diverse society. The prosperity that Americans experienced from a full-employment economy during the war years enabled them to live better after the war. ■

HISTORY JOURNAL

Starting with your reactions to the above description and the picture on page 523, write down what you think life was like for Americans on the home front.

Chapter Overview

Visit the *American Odyssey* Web site at americanodyssey.glencoe.com and click on ***Chapter 16—Chapter Overview*** to preview the chapter.

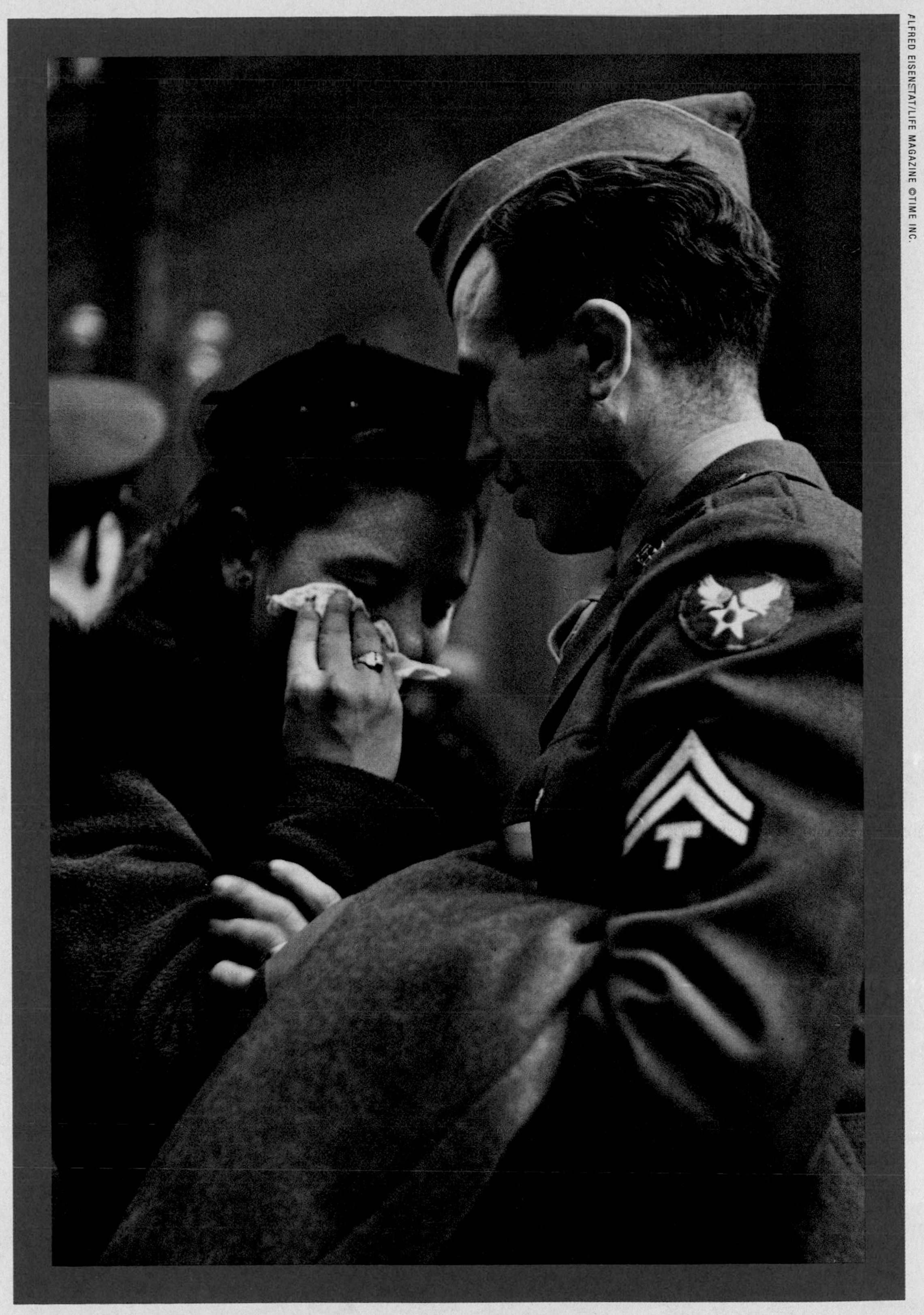

THE WAR BROUGHT SADNESS AND ANGUISH TO SEPARATED FAMILIES AND FRIENDS.

Mobilizing the Home Front

DECEMBER 7, 1941: JAPANESE BOMB PEARL HARBOR

AT THE BEGINNING OF DECEMBER 1941, THE UNITED STATES WAS AT PEACE, AND MOST AMERICANS WERE PREPARING FOR THE HOLIDAYS. The Japanese attack on Pearl Harbor on December 7 stunned Americans and permanently changed their lives. Everyone had a story to tell about how he or she first heard the startling news. Maxine Andrews, one of the famous Andrews Sisters singing trio, remembers that day:

> But oh, I remember the day war was declared. We were in Cincinnati. It looked like we were gonna break the house record in the theater. It didn't matter how cold it was or how high the snow, people were lined up for blocks. . . . This Sunday morning, I walked over and there were no lines. I thought, "Now, this is funny." I walked onto the stage, which was very dark. The doorman and the stagehands were sitting around the radio. They had just one light on. They were talking about Pearl Harbor being bombed. I asked the doorman, "Where is Pearl Harbor?"
>
> —As told to Studs Terkel, *"The Good War,"* 1984

CULVER PICTURES

Gearing Up
Posters like this one encouraged Americans to increase their wartime efforts at home.

The Andrews Sisters, like other stars and celebrities, bolstered the morale of Americans both at home and abroad. In small towns and big cities, on army posts and navy ships, entertainers lifted spirits and helped unify the country.

GUIDE TO READING

Main Idea

After Pearl Harbor, Americans from all backgrounds committed themselves to mobilizing for war and to the defense of what President Roosevelt called the Four Freedoms.

Vocabulary

- gross national product
- inflation
- consumer price index
- bond

Read to Find Out . . .

- the problems the U.S. government faced in maintaining morale and directing a wartime economy.
- how the war affected labor and the employment opportunities for women.
- the purpose of rationing.

Building National Morale

Motivating Citizen Efforts

Japan's surprise attack on Pearl Harbor ended the bitter argument between isolationists and those who favored intervention in the war. Shocked and angered by the attack, Americans rallied to support their government. Most believed they were fighting for what President Roosevelt called the Four Freedoms: freedom of speech and expression, freedom of worship, freedom from want, and freedom from fear.

Salvage for Victory **Stores posted signs such as the one above to show they were supporting the war effort. Neighborhood children such as these in New York City, who are members of a recycling group called the Tin Can Club Number One, cut, washed, and flattened cans for war use.** *How did salvaging scrap materials help the war effort?*

Calling All Volunteers

To raise and maintain the country's morale, the government created the Office of Civilian Defense (OCD). Citizens were asked to contribute "an hour a day for the U.S.A." They could choose from a number of civil defense projects. For example, volunteer air-raid wardens enforced blackouts while spotters scanned the skies for enemy planes.

Many other Americans helped the war effort by growing their own vegetables. In 1941 the secretary of agriculture suggested that because farmers were busy feeding the army, people who wanted fresh vegetables should plant "victory gardens." A few months later, backyards, vacant lots, and such unlikely places as zoos, racetracks, and jails sprouted colorful arrays of vegetables planted by conscientious citizens. Victory gardens eventually produced 40 percent of all the vegetables grown in the country during the war.

Volunteers also collected materials for the war effort. Newspapers, rubber, scrap metal, aluminum pots, tin cans, box springs—anything that could be turned into armaments—were deposited on designated street corners. Students brought these materials to collection centers. By June 1942, the Boy Scouts had salvaged so much wastepaper that paper collection was temporarily called off. Eventually these efforts supplied much of the steel, half of the tin, and half of the paper that was needed to fight the war.

The Media Go to War

To keep Americans informed about the war, the government established the Office of War Information. Its function was to coordinate war news from various federal agencies. The office also encouraged newspapers, radio stations, and the movie industry to help Americans understand the progress of the war and the government's policies.

The entertainment industry, however, needed no encouragement from the government. Hollywood rushed to copyright titles such as *Bombing of Honolulu, Yellow Peril, My Four Years in Japan,* and *V for Victory.* A month after Pearl Harbor, filmmakers were hard at work on their versions of the war. The heroes were gallant Americans played by actors such as John Wayne. The villains—all stereotypes—were sadistic Germans, bumbling Italians, and sneaky Japanese.

Comic strip characters also went to war. Terry of *Terry and the Pirates* fought the Japanese instead of pirates. Little Orphan Annie called on readers to collect scrap metal, and her father, Daddy Warbucks, served as a general. Superman promoted the Red Cross and war bonds. New comic strips with titles such as *G.I. Joe, War,* and *Don Winslow of the Navy* appeared.

Songwriters, too, joined in. A popular song told how the war changed one musician's life:

> He was a famous trumpet man from
> out Chicago way,
> He had a boogie sound that no one else could play,
> He was top man at his craft.
> But then his number came up and he
> was called in the draft.
> He's in the army now ablowin' reveille.
> He's the boogie woogie bugle boy of Company B.
>
> —Hughie Price and Don Raye, "The Boogie Woogie Bugle Boy of Company B," 1941

Patriotic songs such as "This Is the Army Mister Jones," and "American Patrol" were popular at the beginning of the war. After 1942, though, patriotism gave way to more sentimental songs such as "I Left My Heart at the Stage Door Canteen" and "You'd Be So Nice to Come Home To."

Advertisements in magazines and newspapers and on billboards and radio shows also stimulated national unity. Advertisers reversed their usual emphasis on selling goods and instead urged Americans to use less rather than buy more. The popular slogan was "Use it up, wear it out, make it do or do without." The materials and energy that ordinarily went into producing consumer goods would now be needed to make the instruments of war.

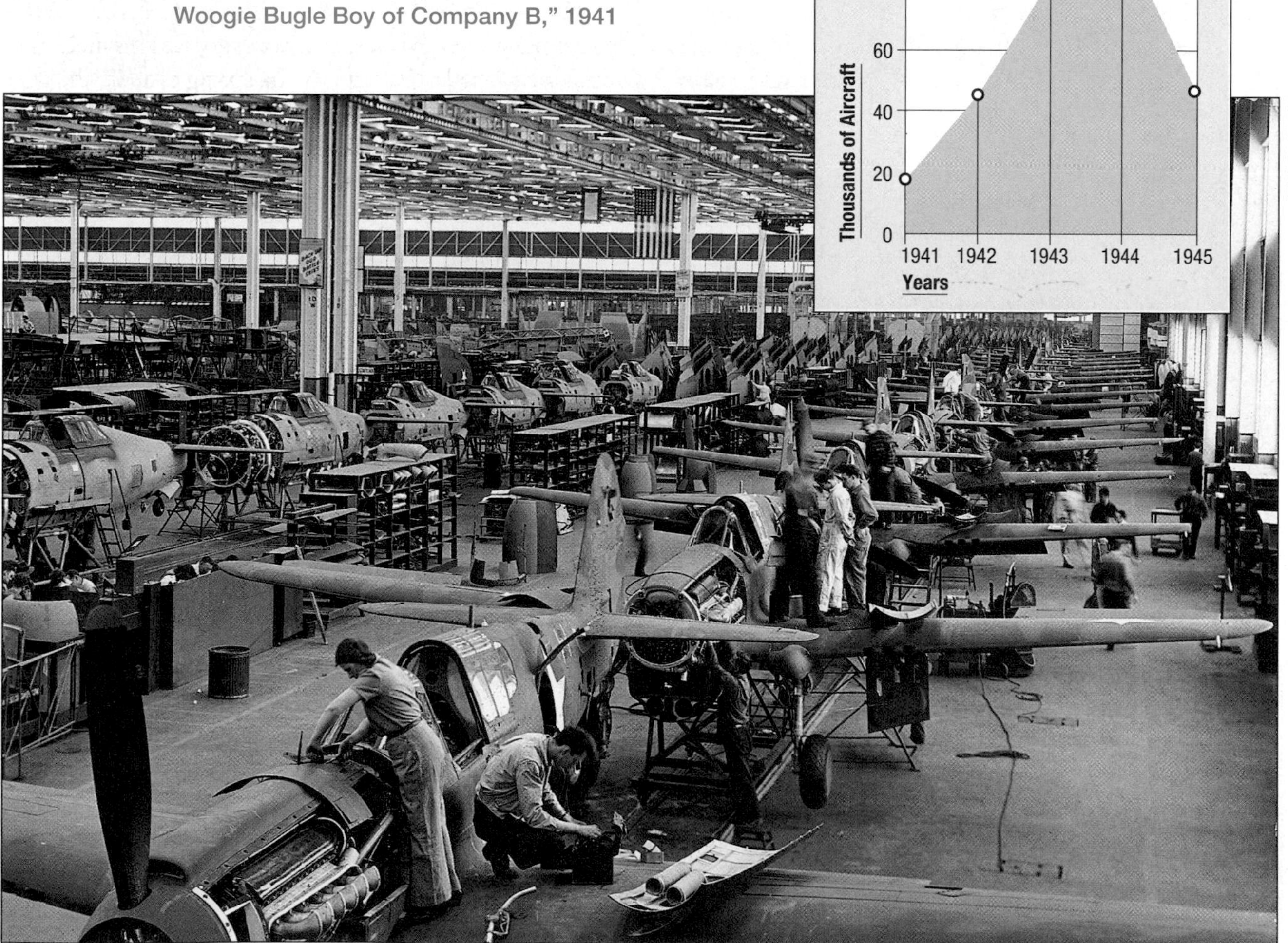

The Plane Production Push At defense plants and converted factories throughout the nation, mechanized assembly lines doubled the daily output and reduced production hours. As the graph on the right shows, production had not yet reached peak capacity by 1943. *At the peak in 1944, approximately how many planes were produced?*

Staging a Production Miracle

Manufacturing War Machines

Although the Roosevelt administration had taken steps to prepare the country for war before Pearl Harbor, much remained to be done. In 1941 only 15 percent of industrial production was going to military needs. To help United States industry convert to war production, President Roosevelt created the War Production Board (WPB) in January 1942. The WPB's job was to "exercise general responsibility" over the nation's economy.

First came the task of getting industrialists to convert their factories from civilian to military production. To accomplish this the WPB issued orders limiting the production of materials not essential to the war effort. Manufacturers switched from making consumer goods such as shirts, toys, and cars to making uniforms, bombs, tanks, and aircraft.

Next came the job of convincing businesses to build new plants to increase production. The government often paid for the new plants and equipment and also agreed to grant relief from antitrust laws to war-related industries. To eliminate the risk for businesses, military contractors were reimbursed for their costs and guaranteed a fixed and generous profit. "If you . . . go to war . . . in a capitalist country, you have to let business make money out of the process or business won't work," said Secretary of War Henry Stimson.

The WPB's plan succeeded, and industrial production nearly doubled. This was accomplished with the help of people like Henry Kaiser, the genius of ship construction. His Richmond, California, shipyard cut the time needed to build merchant ships from 105 days to 46, then to 29, then to 14 days from start to finish! By 1944 the United States had created such a surplus of armaments that the government ordered some defense plants to stop hiring and to cut back on items like antitank guns and trainer planes.

At a meeting between Roosevelt, Churchill, and Stalin in Tehran, late in 1943, the Soviet leader offered a toast: "To American production, without which this war would have been lost."

Directing a Wartime Economy

Controls, Rationing, and Taxes

The United States economy grew at a staggering rate during the war. The **gross national product (GNP),** the dollar value of all goods and services produced annually, increased in the United States from $90.5 billion in 1939 to $211.9 billion in 1945.

The war created 17 million new jobs, and many workers put in long hours of overtime. Farmers shared in the prosperity as crop prices doubled between 1940 and 1945. As people made more money, they sought more of the consumer goods that were in short supply. This increased demand pushed prices up. By the spring of 1942, the cost of living had risen 15 percent above 1939 levels.

Roosevelt worried about the effects of this **inflation,** or general rise in wages and prices. The first step he took to control inflation was to freeze wages. Trade unions, however, opposed a wage freeze. Because they were enthusiastic political supporters of FDR, the administration moved slowly and cautiously.

Controlling Wages and Prices

The administration set up the National War Labor Board (NWLB) to control wages and monitor inflation. In July 1942, the NWLB adopted a wage formula that allowed wage increases up to 15 percent over January 1,

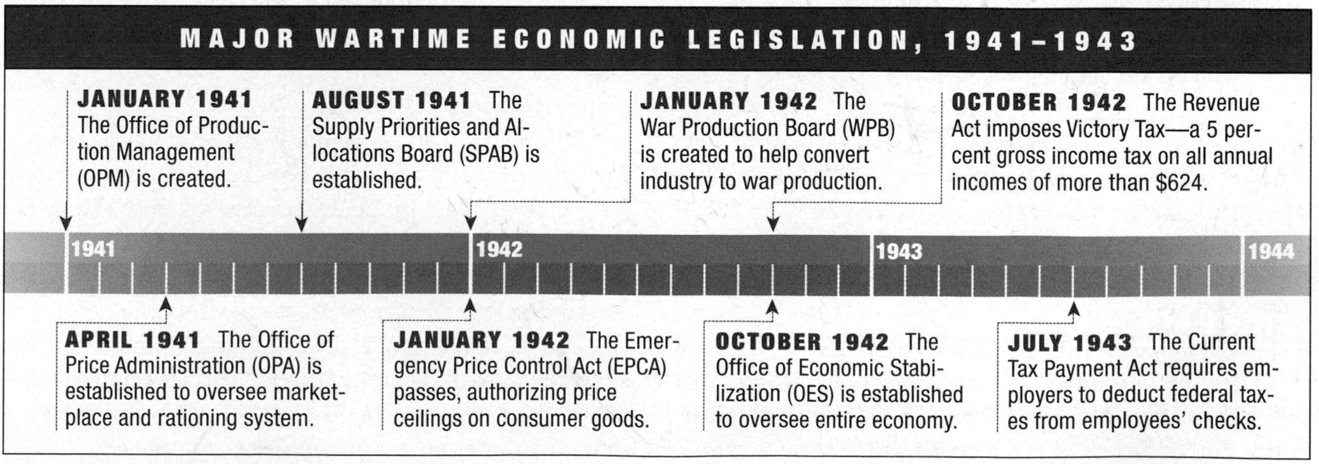

MAJOR WARTIME ECONOMIC LEGISLATION, 1941–1943
JANUARY 1941 The Office of Production Management (OPM) is created.
AUGUST 1941 The Supply Priorities and Allocations Board (SPAB) is established.
JANUARY 1942 The War Production Board (WPB) is created to help convert industry to war production.
OCTOBER 1942 The Revenue Act imposes Victory Tax—a 5 percent gross income tax on all annual incomes of more than $624.
1941
1942
1943
1944
APRIL 1941 The Office of Price Administration (OPA) is established to oversee marketplace and rationing system.
JANUARY 1942 The Emergency Price Control Act (EPCA) passes, authorizing price ceilings on consumer goods.
OCTOBER 1942 The Office of Economic Stabilization (OES) is established to oversee entire economy.
JULY 1943 The Current Tax Payment Act requires employers to deduct federal taxes from employees' checks.

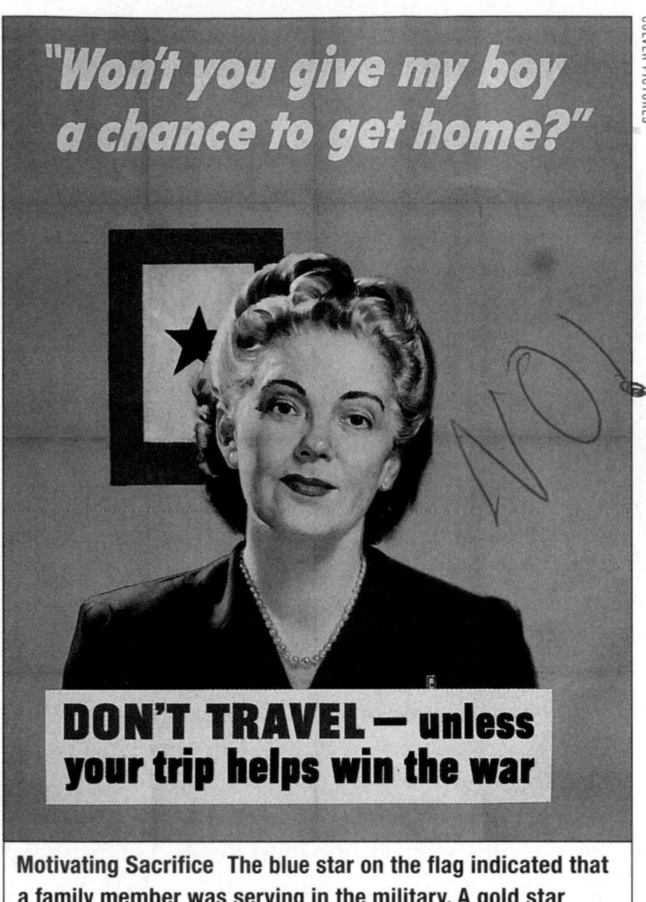

CULVER PICTURES
"Won't you give my boy a chance to get home?"
DON'T TRAVEL – unless your trip helps win the war

Motivating Sacrifice **The blue star on the flag indicated that a family member was serving in the military. A gold star would indicate that an individual had been killed.** *How does this flag strengthen the poster's image?*

1941, levels—the amount the NWLB had estimated living costs had risen.

In April 1943, faced with continued inflation, the government issued a "hold the line" order. Restrictions, however, applied to hourly wages, not to weekly earnings. By working overtime, workers could still earn a good deal more money. Consequently, while wage rates rose by a relatively modest 24 percent during the war, weekly earnings rose by a tremendous 70 percent.

If wages were to be limited, workers wanted prices controlled as well. Early in 1942 Congress let the Office of Price Administration (OPA) fix maximum prices. The OPA soon set a ceiling on all prices.

Overall, however, a reasonable balance existed between wages and prices throughout the war. The **consumer price index (CPI),** a statistic showing the price change of selected goods and services, rose about the same percentage as wages between 1939 and 1945.

Reducing Demand Through Rationing

One method the OPA used in hopes of keeping prices down was rationing, a way of distributing limited goods fairly. Rationing reduced demand because ration coupons were needed to purchase many goods, such as meat and butter. The OPA set up local rationing boards that set quotas for each family's coupons. Families received ration coupons based on the number of people in a household and their needs. They presented coupons when buying rationed items. Merchants, in turn, gave these coupons to suppliers in order to restock their shelves. In this way the government controlled demand and kept prices from rising.

Rationing was one of the most controversial elements of the war effort. Although Americans were earning more, government restrictions limited their spending. They could afford automobiles and gasoline, but Detroit was producing tanks, not cars, and gasoline was limited. Because they found gasoline rationing so irritating, some Americans learned to bend the rules.

> I was a certified ski instructor and was with the National Ski Patrol, so the army hired me to certify skiers and mountaineers for the mountain troops that were trained in Leadville, Colorado. They gave me a 'C' card for an unlimited amount of gasoline to go skiing on the weekends. . . .
>
> But you'd better believe I had a long waiting list of people to ride up to the mountains with me every weekend. One of the guys who went with me owned a small butcher shop and had a contract to supply a hotel, and he seemed to be able to get unlimited quantities of meat. So every month I turned my meat stamps over to him and was able to get meat anytime I wanted it. You had to work the angles—good old American ingenuity I guess—and it didn't hurt anything.
>
> —As quoted by Archie Satterfield, *The Home Front,* 1981

Paying for a Costly War

World War II cost the United States 10 times more than World War I did. From 1941 to 1945, the government's operating budget was $321 billion, nearly twice as much as its total spending in the preceding 150 years. Taxes met about 40 percent of the war costs; the government borrowed the rest.

Before the war began, many Americans did not pay any federal income tax. Only about 26 million tax returns were filed in 1941. In 1942 Congress passed a Revenue Act that FDR called "the greatest tax bill in American history." This legislation increased corporate taxes and required nearly all Americans to pay income taxes.

In 1943 Congress approved a system for withholding taxes through monthly payroll deductions. Now the modern tax structure, begun in 1913 when Congress instituted a direct tax on income, was completed.

While taxes provided for 40 percent of the cost of the war, borrowing, mostly from Americans, paid for the remaining 60 percent. To borrow money, the government sold **bonds,** certificates that promised that the government would pay the holder the amount borrowed plus interest. The bonds also controlled inflation by reducing the money consumers had to spend and they helped sell the war to the American public.

The Treasury Department recruited both Madison Avenue advertisers and Hollywood stars to help sell bonds. Creative public relations stunts boosted sales. The publishers of *Batman* comic books devoted a cover to a picture of their hero urging the purchase of war bonds. Hollywood stars traveled across the country to perform at rallies and auctioned their personal possessions. In the first big war bond sale in 1942, some 337 actors and actresses participated, working 18 hours a day.

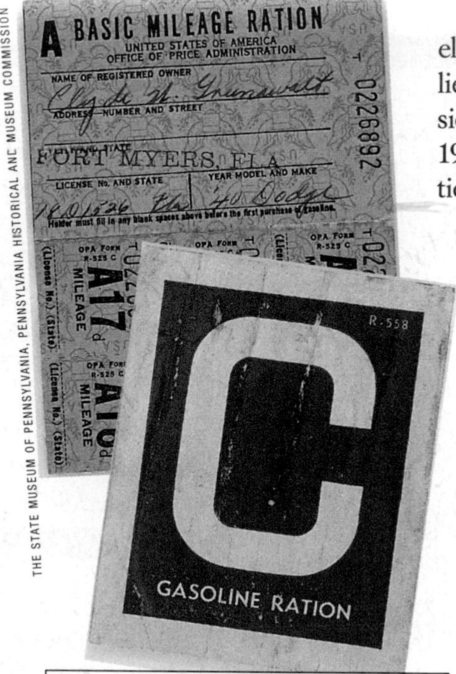

THE STATE MUSEUM OF PENNSYLVANIA, PENNSYLVANIA HISTORICAL AND MUSEUM COMMISSION

Rationing Every World War II family in the United States was familiar with ration coupons like these. *Do you agree with the principle of rationing? Why or why not?*

Even children helped pay for the war. At the post office, they bought war stamps that they pasted into albums. When their stamps totaled $18.75, they received a war bond redeemable for $25 10 years later. Adult Americans bought bonds to help family members in the armed services, to invest their money safely, to preserve "the American way of life," to combat inflation, and to save for postwar purchases. When the war ended, Americans had saved $129 billion that they could spend on homes, appliances, and goods they were unable to buy during the war.

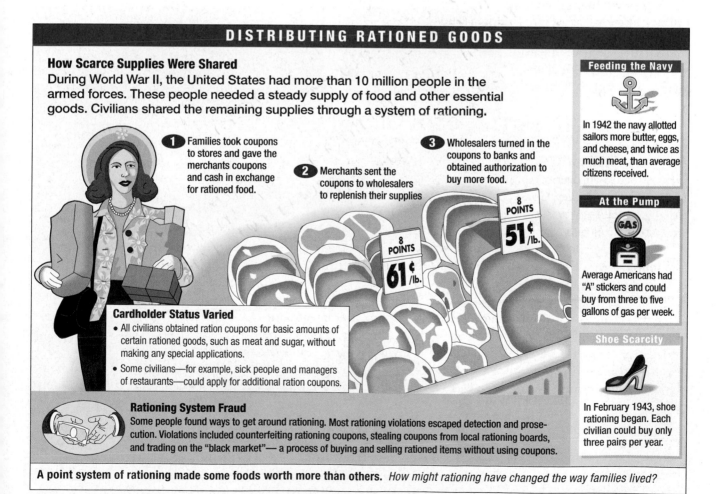

DISTRIBUTING RATIONED GOODS

How Scarce Supplies Were Shared

During World War II, the United States had more than 10 million people in the armed forces. These people needed a steady supply of food and other essential goods. Civilians shared the remaining supplies through a system of rationing.

1. Families took coupons to stores and gave the merchants coupons and cash in exchange for rationed food.
2. Merchants sent the coupons to wholesalers to replenish their supplies
3. Wholesalers turned in the coupons to banks and obtained authorization to buy more food.

8 POINTS 61¢/lb.

8 POINTS 51¢/lb.

Cardholder Status Varied

- All civilians obtained ration coupons for basic amounts of certain rationed goods, such as meat and sugar, without making any special applications.
- Some civilians—for example, sick people and managers of restaurants—could apply for additional ration coupons.

Rationing System Fraud

Some people found ways to get around rationing. Most rationing violations escaped detection and prosecution. Violations included counterfeiting rationing coupons, stealing coupons from local rationing boards, and trading on the "black market"— a process of buying and selling rationed items without using coupons.

Feeding the Navy

In 1942 the navy allotted sailors more butter, eggs, and cheese, and twice as much meat, than average citizens received.

At the Pump

GAS

Average Americans had "A" stickers and could buy from three to five gallons of gas per week.

Shoe Scarcity

In February 1943, shoe rationing began. Each civilian could buy only three pairs per year.

A point system of rationing made some foods worth more than others. *How might rationing have changed the way families lived?*

Trying to Uphold a No-Strike Pledge

Labor's Wartime Efforts

While the wages of many Americans increased dramatically during the war, not everyone shared in this prosperity. The major labor unions, however, had issued a pledge that, as long as the war continued, their workers would not strike for higher salaries and better working conditions.

In return, the NWLB enforced settlements between companies and their workers on hours, wages, and working conditions. It also had authority to seize plants whose owners refused to cooperate. The no-strike pledge, however, was not legally binding, and more than 3 million workers went on strike in 1943.

The most serious strikes occurred in the coalfields. Wages had been frozen in 1942, but prices and profits had continued to rise, and miners thought they were entitled to a raise. United Mine Workers president John L. Lewis, a miner himself, led nearly 450,000 coal miners out on strike in 1943 when the NWLB denied them a raise. At congressional hearings, when Lewis was reminded that the government was trying to hold down wages to control inflation, he replied, "Do you mind first inflating the stomachs of my members?"

After his pleas to miners to return to work failed, President Roosevelt took over the mines. When FDR was urged to put striking miners in jail, however, one adviser cautioned: "There are not enough jails in the country to hold these men, and, if there were, I must point out that a jailed miner produces no more coal than a striking miner." Eventually Lewis, the mine operators, and the administration agreed on a raise.

Workers in the coal, steel, and railroad industries went out on strike during the war. Despite these strikes, labor largely lived up to the no-strike pledge.

Recruiting New Workers

Women Fill the Gap

More than 15 million Americans left work to serve in the armed forces during the war. Many of the remaining adults, as well as adolescents, assumed those positions. As new war-related plants were built, the need for civilian workers increased dramatically.

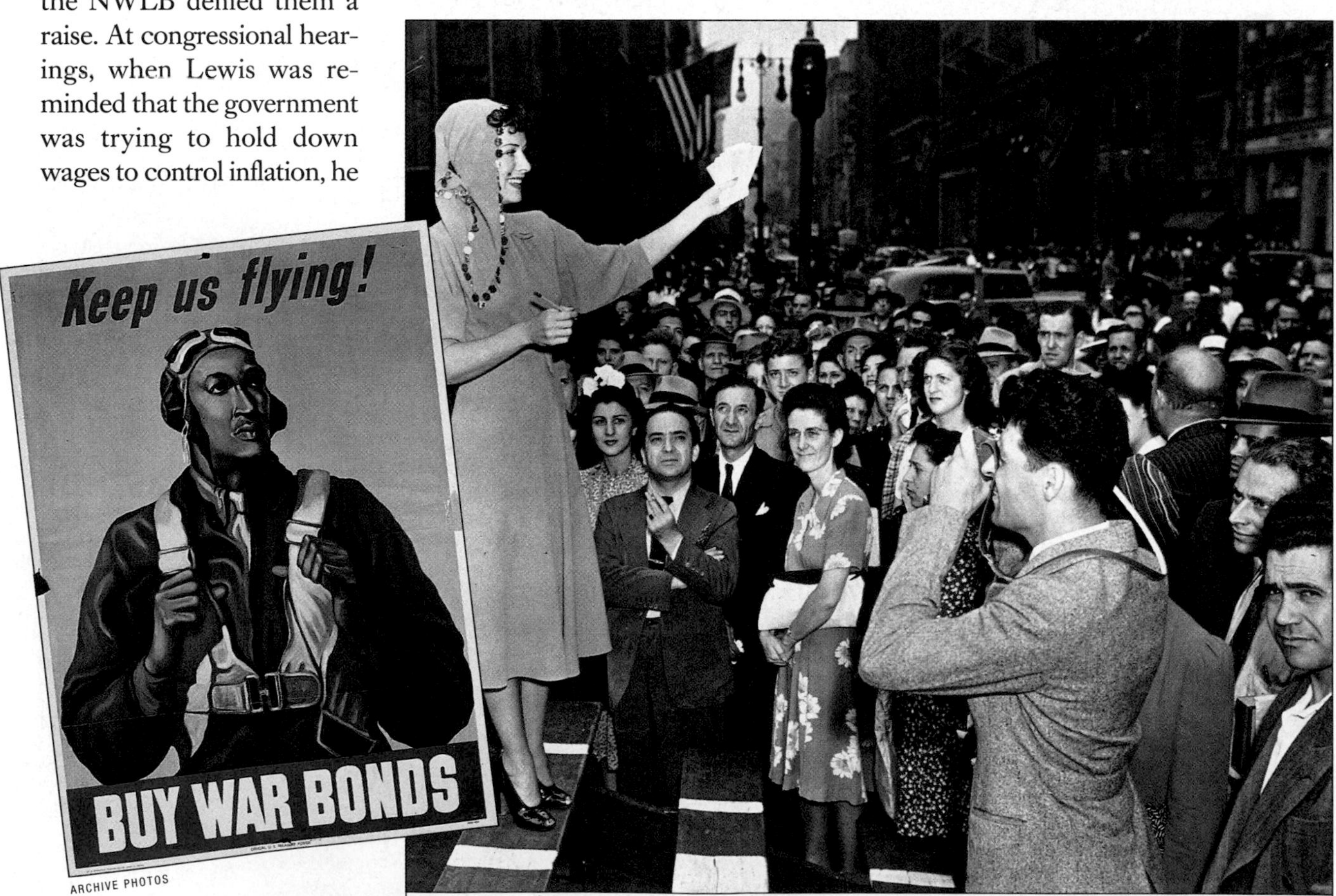
Keep us flying!
BUY WAR BONDS

ARCHIVE PHOTOS

UPI/BETTMANN NEWSPHOTOS

Movie Star Promotes War Bonds Actress Paulette Goddard campaigned for the war effort. *How much do you think celebrity appearances influence people's decisions?*

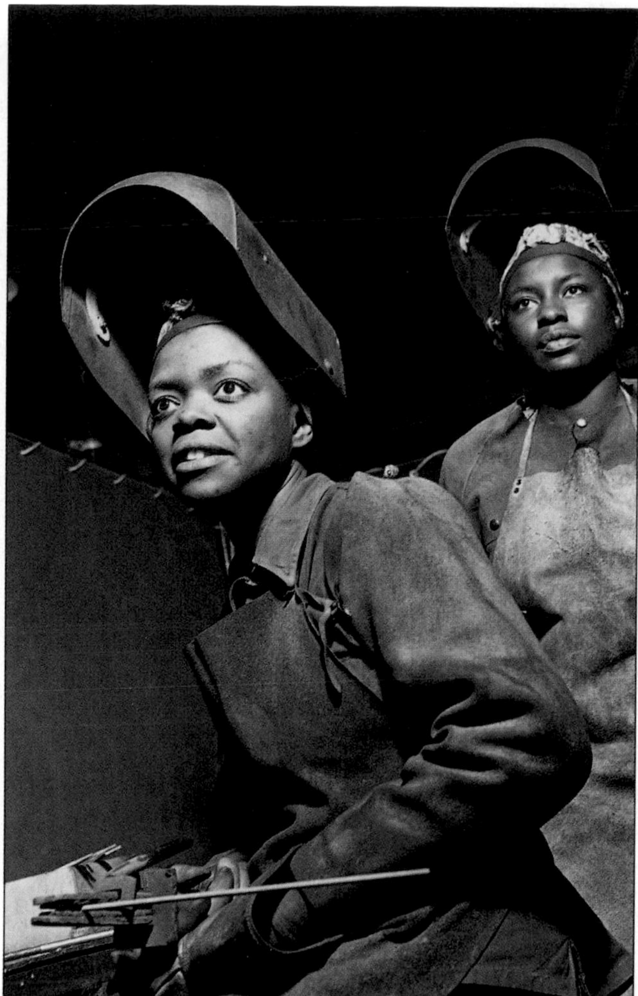

LIBRARY OF CONGRESS

A New Workforce **Women already working in domestic service or in textile-related jobs were among the first to be hired for wartime defense jobs. As the need grew, recent high school graduates were also recruited.** *How did these workers help to change society's opinion of women's capabilities?*

At first, jobs were easily filled by the unemployed. Wartime labor demands wiped out the unemployment of the Depression years and created other opportunities. Between 1940 and 1945, about 6 million women joined the civilian labor force. The proportion of women who worked rose from 27 percent to 37 percent as women replaced the men who were at war.

The labor shortage opened up doors for women in many occupations. The most startling increase in numbers of working women occurred in defense industries, such as airplane manufacturing and shipbuilding, where female employment jumped by 460 percent. In plants and shipyards, women worked on assembly lines as welders, riveters, and mechanics. Although "Rosie the Riveter" transformed the nature of the labor force, women generally had a hard time gaining acceptance by male workers. Helen Studer, a riveter at Douglas Aircraft in Los Angeles during the war, told her story:

> The men really resented the women very much, and in the beginning it was a little bit rough. . . . The men that you worked with, after a while, they realized that it was essential that the women worked there, 'cause there wasn't enough men and the women were doing a pretty good job. So the resentment eased. However, I always felt that they thought it wasn't your place to be there.
>
> —As reported by Sherna B. Gluck, *Rosie the Riveter Revisited,* 1987

Women suffered two disadvantages. They received 60 percent less pay than men, and they had little job security. The NWLB called for equal pay for equal work, but women were often given lower job classifications, so the income gap between men and women actually increased.

In spite of income gaps, women workers, like most other laborers, performed production miracles. Nearly three of every four new women workers were married, and most wanted to help loved ones serving overseas.

Yet fighting the war on the home front created new problems. For one, most employment opportunities for women were temporary. Between 1944 and 1946, as the war drew to a close, about 4 million women either lost their jobs or left the workforce. The war also strained the American family and society in new ways.

Section Assessment

Main Idea

1. Use a diagram like this one to show the Four Freedoms that most Americans believed were at stake in the war.

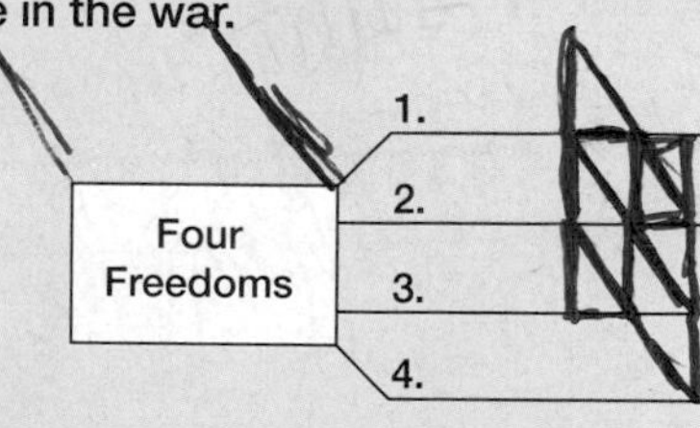

Vocabulary

2. Define: gross national product, inflation, consumer price index, bond.

Checking Facts

3. How did the government raise morale at home?
4. What two major tasks faced the nation as it converted to wartime production?

Critical Thinking

5. **Expressing Problems Clearly** What problem was rationing designed to solve?

The Big Band Era

Thousands of families bid tearful farewells as loved ones left for war. Newspaper headlines screamed of battles and bombings. Paychecks hit an all-time high, but goods were few because everything from silk to steel was needed to fuel the war. No wonder people turned to entertainment for escape.

HERB GEHR/LIFE MAGAZINE. © 1943 TIME, INC.

THE CROONER

The idol of millions of fans, singer **Frank Sinatra** put some members of his adoring audiences into a swoon, or faint, as he sang his romantic lyrics. Although during wartime many of his fans were teenagers, his tunes were popular with all generations.

UPI/BETTMANN

3-D MANIA

After the seriousness of war, fads in the later 1940s reflected the need for pure fun. These boys, members of New York's Madison Square Boys' Club, wear special glasses to read their **3-D comics.**

UPI/BETTMANN

SOOTHING SOUNDS

Big-name bands like Duke Ellington's played the music of the day on stage and even in the movies. **The Duke** and his band are shown here in a scene from the movie *Reveille With Beverly*.

FRANK DRIGGS COLLECTION

FRANK DRIGGS COLLECTION

A DANCING CRAZE

Jitterbuggers went wild in the war years with routines that demanded rhythm and stamina. Couples jived to both live bands and jukebox recordings.

BOB LANDRY/LIFE MAGAZINE, ©1947 TIME, INC.

A GI SIGNATURE

The name and image of the whimsical character **Kilroy** was scribbled on walls, bunkers, and in other locations. Kilroy left the message that GI Joe had been there.

UPI/BETTMANN

PATRIOTIC LEGWEAR

When silk and nylon were needed to make parachutes, women improvised by painting their legs with makeup to create **simulated stockings.** They even used devices to draw seams—with some difficulty, of course.

The War and Social Change

1941–1945: AMERICANS MIGRATE

BETWEEN 1941 AND 1945, ONE IN EVERY FIVE AMERICANS MOVED FROM ONE AREA OF THE COUNTRY TO ANOTHER. Among them were more than 700,000 African Americans. Since the end of Reconstruction, African Americans had faced grueling hardships. As the economy boomed during the war, many African Americans sought opportunities outside the South. Most hoped to escape grueling working hours, poverty, and demeaning segregation. Sybil Lewis was one of these Americans. This is what she said about leaving Oklahoma and heading west:

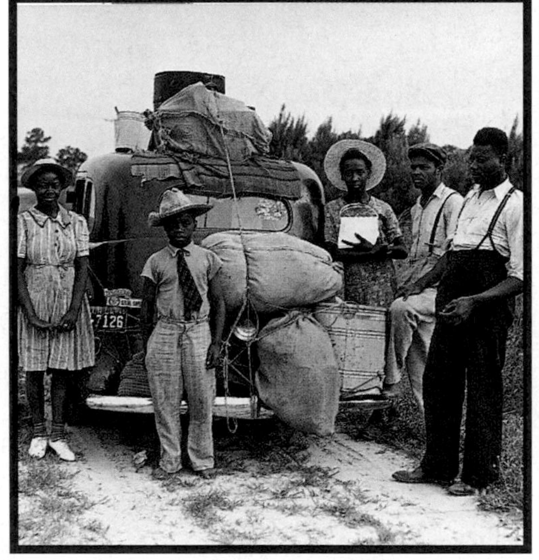
LIBRARY OF CONGRESS

Moving
Many families moved to cities for freedom from prejudice and for economic opportunity.

I had always been told that California was a liberal state and there was no segregation there. "Go west," that was the theme. "Everything is great in California, all doors are open, no prejudice, good jobs, plenty of money." . . . When I arrived, though, I found it wasn't quite the way I had imagined. . . .

In many ways California was no different from Oklahoma or the South, because people brought their feelings with them.

—As told to Mark Jonathan Harris, Franklin D. Mitchell, and Steven J. Schechter, *The Homefront*, 1984

GUIDE TO READING

Main Idea

New wartime jobs offered opportunity for millions of Americans, but their rapid migration to war production sites created severe social stresses and strained family relationships.

Vocabulary

- migration
- deficit spending

Read to Find Out . . .

- the population shifts in the United States during World War II, and the relationship between mobility, overcrowding, and social stress.
- the status of New Deal social programs during the war.

Americans on the Move

A Population Reshuffled

When more than 15 million Americans left civilian jobs to join the military, African Americans and whites who remained at home sought jobs that opened up in shipyards, aircraft plants, munitions factories, and military bases. This reshuffling made up the greatest short-term **migration,** or movement, of people in American history.

In general, Americans migrated from rural areas to urban areas, from the East to the West, and from the North to the South. The largest gains were in the Far West, which included California, Washington, and Oregon. Much of the wartime shipbuilding and airplane manufacturing took place there. More than 1.4 million Americans migrated to California alone. Next in population gain were Texas and the three South Atlantic states of Maryland, Florida, and Virginia.

Other areas of the country also grew. Big war contracts went to the auto manufacturers of Detroit and the arms manufacturers of New England. New arsenals, new steel and other metal plants, and new military bases sprang up in both rural and urban areas.

The movement of Americans from farms to cities reflected both the wartime demand for workers and the changes in American agriculture. Between 1940 and 1945, the number of farm workers fell by 11 percent while farm output increased by more than 15 percent. By using more fertilizer and more machinery and by consolidating small farms into larger ones, fewer farmers were able to grow more crops.

It seemed that almost everyone in the United States was moving. Migrants drove their cars until the tires were worn smooth. Others stood on crowded trains and buses. Young wives with babies joined their husbands at defense jobs or in army camps. Old men and young boys went west and south for jobs.

African Americans made up a large part of this migrating stream. In areas where the most wartime

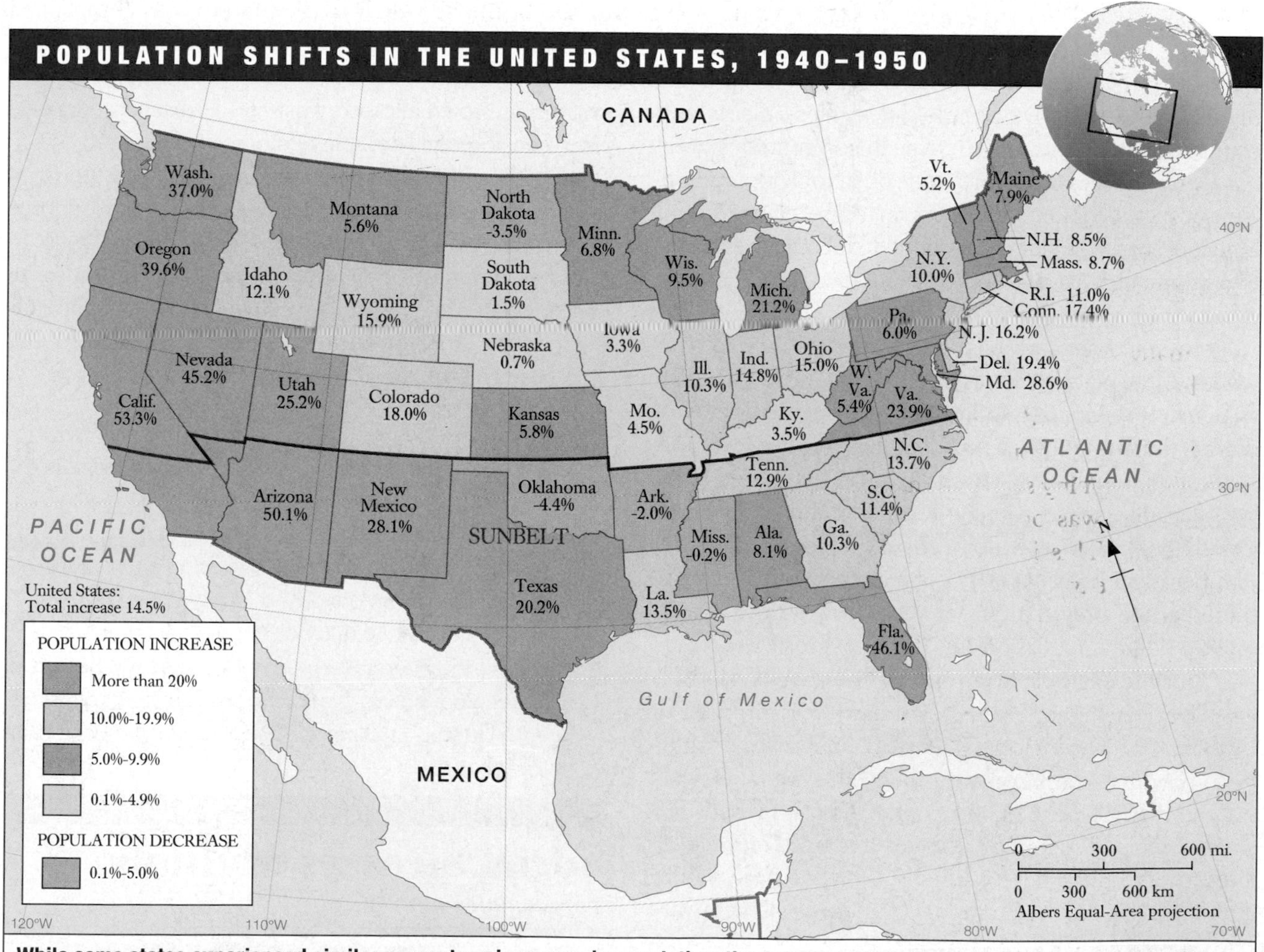

While some states experienced similar percentage increases in population, the actual number of people gained was quite different. For example, Nevada and Florida had similar percentage gains, but Nevada actually gained 50,000 people while Florida gained 874,000 people. *Which states experienced actual population losses?*

production took place, the African American population almost doubled. In contrast to other groups who stayed only temporarily, African Americans tended to remain in their new homes.

One of the most congested areas was Mobile, Alabama. From 1940 to 1943, Mobile's population climbed by 61 percent. The novelist John Dos Passos described the impact of this massive population growth on Mobile:

> Sidewalks are crowded. Gutters are stacked with litter that drifts back and forth in the brisk spring wind. . . . Cues [lines] wait outside of movies and lunchrooms. The trailer army has filled all the open lots with its regular ranks. In cluttered backyards people camp out in tents and chickenhouses and shelters tacked together out of packingcases.
>
> —John Dos Passos, *State of the Nation,* 1944

UPI/BETTMANN NEWSPHOTOS

Race Riots An explosion showers burning gasoline on a passenger-packed trolley car during the Detroit race riots of June 21, 1943. *What conditions contributed to the race riots of 1943?*

Boomtowns Emerge

Coping with Overcrowding

Many migrants headed for large industrial cities. Others went to the small towns that grew into boomtowns in the shadows of smoking defense plants and shipyards. The rapid growth of such communities overburdened services that Americans often took for granted. New arrivals looking for work in these places found housing scarce, medical facilities inadequate, sanitary conditions terrible, schools overcrowded, and day-care centers almost nonexistent.

Housing was a problem for almost all migrant war workers. The National Housing Agency figured that it had to house 9 million migrating workers and their families during the war years. Thus, lodgings for new workers were often temporary—barracks, trailers, and even tents.

Schools lacked money, teachers, and equipment. One high school in Mobile accommodated twice the number of students for which it was designed. Teachers there earned only $1,150 per year while a typist could make $1,440 and a laborer in the shipyards $2,600.

A prime example of a troubled boomtown was Willow Run, Michigan, located 27 miles (43.4 km) west of Detroit. The Ford Motor Company built a huge factory to produce bomber planes there, and the factory attracted more than 32,000 people. They crowded into small trailers, drank impure water, and lived in dread of a fire or an epidemic. Eventually, the government built about 10,000 units of temporary housing, which only partially solved the overcrowding.

Other boomtowns experienced similar problems, though on a smaller scale. Pascagoula, Mississippi, a small town with a fine shipyard, nearly quadrupled its population during the war. Older residents often refused to accept the new arrivals. Recent arrivals complained that they were made to feel inferior because they lived in trailers instead of houses. Lacking an adequate sewage system, the town allowed waste to be discharged into a river, causing considerable ecological damage.

San Diego, California, was once a quiet waterfront town, but an aircraft factory there grew from a workforce of 6 in the 1930s to more than 50,000 in the 1940s. In addition, San Diego was the home of the largest naval base on the West Coast as well as a thriving shipbuilding center. One longtime resident remembered the changes brought about by this population increase:

> We used to go to bed by ten, or anyway, by eleven. Now some theaters and cafes never close! I remember it was like that in the Klondike. Now when boatloads of sailors hurry ashore, and all those soldiers from Fort Rosecrans and Camp Callan swarm in on payday, this town goes crazy. In one day they eat 50,000 hot dogs! Even shoe shine boys get the jitters. Sherman's Cafe has ten bars, and a dance floor so big that 5,000 can dance at once.
>
> —Quoted in *National Geographic,* January 1942

Social Stresses Multiply

Communities in Crisis

The rapid movement of migrants into new regions and cities created severe social stresses. Native residents of cities such as Los Angeles, San Diego, and Detroit often resented the newcomers. Midwesterners labeled the migrants from Arkansas, Oklahoma, Tennessee, and Kentucky "hillbillies" and stereotyped them as poor and lazy. Workers in the shipyards and factories discriminated against African Americans who came in search of jobs. The situation was especially tense in Detroit.

Racial Tensions Explode

By 1943 Detroit was home to about half a million migrants, including many Southern whites and 60,000 African Americans. As a result, housing, transportation, and recreational facilities were overcrowded. Most African Americans, both the newly arrived and the native Detroiters, were wedged into an area called Paradise Valley. There, according to the Detroit Housing Commission, more than half the dwellings were substandard. Bottled-up racial tensions finally erupted in violence on a hot summer night in June 1943. Picnickers, most of them African Americans, were returning home from a Sunday outing when a fight broke out. Nobody remembered why. Apparently some African American teenagers had bumped a white sailor and his girlfriend. Sailors from the navy arsenal nearby joined the fray. As rumors spread of sexual assaults and murders, rioters smashed windows and stoned cars. African American crowds attacked white workers returning from the night shift. The overworked police force, shorthanded because many experienced officers had joined the military, could not control the violence.

The next day, Bloody Monday, large crowds of whites roamed up and down Detroit's main street in search of African Americans to beat or kill. Whites dragged African Americans off trolley cars and beat them; police shot looters and battled with rooftop snipers. After a day of violence, the governor of Michigan requested federal assistance. Six thousand soldiers moved into Detroit to control the crowds and restore order. In the 36 hours of rioting, 25 African Americans and 9 whites lost their lives, and nearly 700 people were injured. Also, $2 million worth of property was destroyed.

UPI/BETTMANN

Zoot Suits **Some people objected to the roomy zoot suits because the amount of wool cloth used in men's suits was supposed to be rationed after March 1942.**
Why did some men wear zoot suits and defy the rule on rationing?

Discrimination led to other race riots in 1943. African American soldiers, who resented unfair treatment, inferior housing, and the brutality of military police, were involved in riots at 9 army training camps, mostly in the South. In August 1943, Harlem exploded when rumors circulated that a white New York City police officer had killed an African American soldier. Unlike the Detroit riot, the Harlem riot did not see pitched battles; however, 5 African Americans were killed and 410 people were injured before the police restored order.

The Zoot Suit Riots

African Americans were not the only minority group involved in violent clashes in the summer of 1943. Opportunities for farmworkers in the Southwest brought thousands of Mexicans illegally to the United States. At the same time, many Americans of Mexican descent shifted from agricultural work to industrial and manufacturing jobs. They worked at factories in and around Los Angeles. There, as elsewhere, they suffered discrimination and prejudice. They were segregated from other Americans, insulted by police, and given only the lowest-paying jobs.

In Los Angeles this prejudice turned into hatred of Hispanic American teenagers, many of whom wore zoot suits. A zoot suit included a long jacket that reached to the fingertips and had heavily padded shoulders and pleated trousers tightly tapered at the cuffs.

Mexican Americans did not have a monopoly on zoot suits, however. On the whole, zoot-suiters were young people seeking escape from the burdens of life in the slums. The zoot suit set them apart from the rest of society and served as a badge of independence. In Los Angeles, many of the zoot-suiters were underemployed teenagers, many of whom were caught between two cultures.

For several months, zoot-suiters and white sailors had clashed in Los Angeles. Sailors stationed at the nearby Chavez Ravine Naval Base blamed zoot-suiters for stabbing and robbing military personnel. In June they cruised the Mexican American sections of Los Angeles in cars, beating up people they found wearing zoot suits. Even though the sailors had started the trouble, the police arrested only the zoot-suiters. To end the violence, the city had to be declared off-limits to naval personnel. When the city council outlawed zoot suits, the situation cooled.

The violence in Los Angeles and other cities prompted Philip Murray, president of the Congress of Industrial Organizations (CIO), to write President Roosevelt. He urged the administration to prepare an educational campaign "to eradicate the misconceptions and prejudices" that had contributed to the riots. The President replied in a short note that read in part, "I join you and all true Americans in condemning mob violence, whatever form it takes and whoever its victims."

One idealistic African American student had expected that Roosevelt would stand behind the demands of minorities for fair treatment. After Roosevelt's reply to Murray, she expressed her feelings of hopelessness in this poem entitled "Mr. Roosevelt Regrets."

> What'd you get, black boy,
> When they knocked you down in the gutter,
> And they kicked your teeth out,
> And they broke your skull with clubs,
> And they bashed your stomach in?
> What'd you get when the police
> shot you in the back,
> And they chained you to the beds
> While they wiped the blood off?
> What'd you get when you cried
> out to the Top Man?
> When you called the man next to God,
> as you thought,
> And you asked him to speak out to save you?
> What'd the Top Man say, black boy?
> Mr. Roosevelt regrets. . . .
>
> —Pauli Murray, as printed in *The Crisis,* August 1943

Wartime Family Stresses

Children on Their Own

Other stresses caused by the war itself fell on both whites and African Americans. As families migrated, children and adolescents were moved from familiar neighborhoods to strange surroundings. Men and women worked long hours of overtime at their defense jobs, sometimes leaving children unattended. Single-parent families became common as men went into the armed forces, leaving their wives and children behind.

As more mothers of young children took jobs, newspapers and magazines complained about "latchkey children" and "eight-hour orphans." Agnes Meyer, the wife of the publisher of the *Washington Post,* traveled around the country investigating social conditions in boomtowns. She wrote:

> In the San Fernando Valley, in the city limits of Los Angeles, where several war plants are located, a social worker counted 45 infants locked in cars of a single parking space [lot]. In Vallejo, the children sit in the movies, seeing the same film over and over again until mother comes off the swing shift and picks them up. Some children of working parents are locked in their homes, others locked out.
>
> —Agnes E. Meyer, *Journey Through Chaos,* 1943

Teenagers were often left to care for themselves. Unlike younger children, they could get jobs. From 1940 to 1944, the number of teenage workers nearly tripled to 2.9 million. More than 1 million teenagers dropped out of school. Although child labor laws governed the kind of work they did and the number of hours they could work, these laws were often ignored. Because of the widespread disregard for these laws, 19 states extended the number of hours teenagers could work.

With teenagers left to fend for themselves in society, it was not surprising that juvenile delinquency increased. During the war years, a widely viewed documentary film, *Youth in Crisis,* aroused public concern. The film described how adolescents, abandoned by their parents and subjected to wartime stress, picked up a "spirit of recklessness and violence." To help curb rising juvenile delinquency, some communities enforced curfews.

Teens at Work This 16-year-old worked on a transport plane's fuselage on an assembly line at a West Coast aircraft plant. *What advantages and disadvantages might working teens have experienced?*

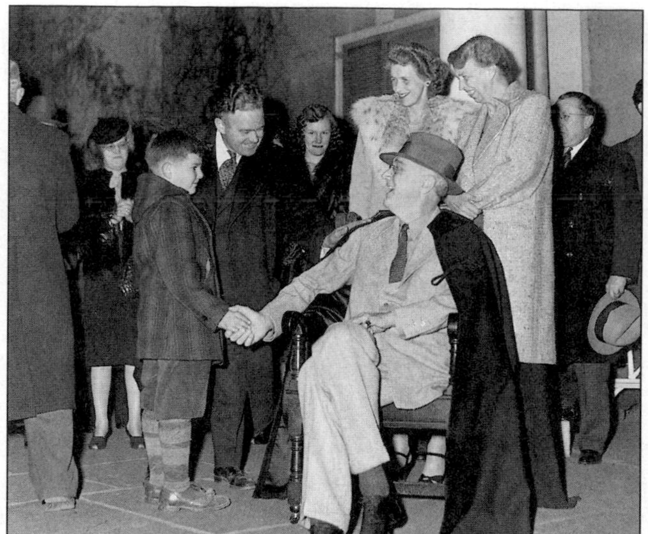
UPI/BETTMANN

A Fourth Win **Citizens visit Roosevelt after his reelection.**
Why do you think Roosevelt was reelected?

Even though the war caused new problems for American children, many later remembered this period as the most exciting time of their lives. Memories include collecting scrap, watching war movies in which the "good guys" always won, and being intensely interested in news of the war.

The End of the New Deal

Military Objectives Take Over

In December 1943, President Roosevelt announced that "Dr. New Deal" had outlived his usefulness and would have to make way for "Dr. Win-the-War." In other words, military objectives took priority over social reform. Many of the New Deal programs, such as Social Security, unemployment compensation, old-age benefits, and the Tennessee Valley Authority (TVA), however, had become a permanent part of American life. Even the Republican party had, by 1944, accepted most New Deal programs.

Both liberals and conservatives agreed that the nation should shelve any reforms that could interfere with war production. The government delayed electrifying rural areas because copper wire was needed for the war. The workweek was increased from 40 to 48 hours in order to boost industrial output. Many antitrust cases were suspended to avoid interfering with well-run businesses. Child labor laws were changed to permit teenagers to join the labor force. "Progressives should understand that programs which do not forward the war must be given up or drastically curtailed," wrote David Lilienthal, head of the TVA.

The war made it possible to phase out a number of New Deal agencies. These included the Civilian Conservation Corps, the Works Progress Administration, and the National Youth Administration. Congress had created these agencies to ease unemployment. With full employment during the war, they were no longer needed.

World War II, however, extended the New Deal in some respects by continuing the role of government in economic planning. Wartime economic growth convinced many people that government spending could ensure full employment and prosperity. In the future the government would resort to **deficit spending,** using borrowed money, to counteract economic downturns.

The war also made possible the election of Franklin D. Roosevelt to an unprecedented fourth term as President in 1944. His margin of victory over Republican Thomas E. Dewey, however, was the narrowest in all of his four campaigns.

Americans on the home front suffered from housing shortages, overcrowding, a breakdown of law and order, and juvenile delinquency during the war years. At the same time, most people reaped the financial rewards of a wartime, full-employment economy. Although minority groups did not yet enjoy many benefits, the war did provide new opportunities in employment and enabled them to make some headway in their struggle for civil rights. Some of the New Deal reform measures had to be set aside during the war but were not forgotten. They would be taken up again when the war ended.

Section Assessment

Main Idea

1. Use a diagram like this one to show problems created by wartime migrations.

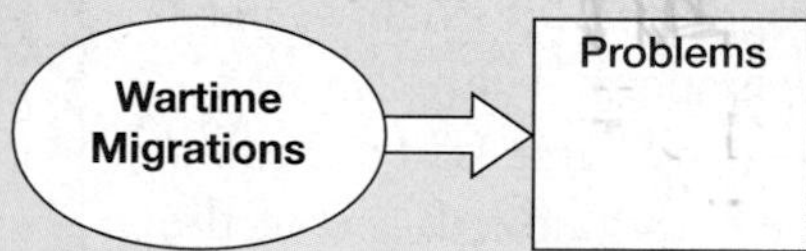

Vocabulary

2. Define: migration, deficit spending.

Checking Facts

3. How did the war change the lives of teenagers?
4. What effect did the war have on New Deal agencies and reforms?

Critical Thinking

5. **Synthesizing Information** How did wartime migrations affect industrial cities in the short and long run?

Geography: Impact on History

PLACE

Richmond, California: A War Boomtown

Located in California on San Francisco Bay, Richmond was transformed almost overnight during World War II. Between 1940 and 1943, Richmond's population grew nearly 400 percent, from 23,642 to 93,738. Like other suburban towns in California, Richmond had large tracts of undeveloped land, a major rail line, and a deepwater harbor—a perfect mixture for shipbuilding.

Kaiser's Role in Richmond

After being awarded major contracts to build Liberty ships, huge merchant ships used to supply troops with jeeps, tanks, and rations, industrialist Henry J. Kaiser located four of his shipyards in Richmond. Resolved to beat his deadlines and to lower his costs, he applied mass-production methods to his shipbuilding operations. Like other industrialists, however, Kaiser soon faced a severe shortage of workers.

To attract and keep good workers, Kaiser raised his wages to some of the highest in the country, instituted a company health plan, and—prompted by First Lady Eleanor Roosevelt—organized one of the first day-care centers for children of working women.

Kaiser's efforts paid off. At their peak, his Richmond shipyards employed more than 90,000 workers, including significant numbers of whites and African Americans from the South, Chinese Americans, Native Americans, women, and teenagers. Although only 240 African Americans called Richmond home in 1940, more than 10,000 worked at Kaiser's shipyards there during the war. Kaiser's employees succeeded in transforming the nation's entire shipbuilding industry, and their accomplishments earned Kaiser the nickname "Sir Launchalot."

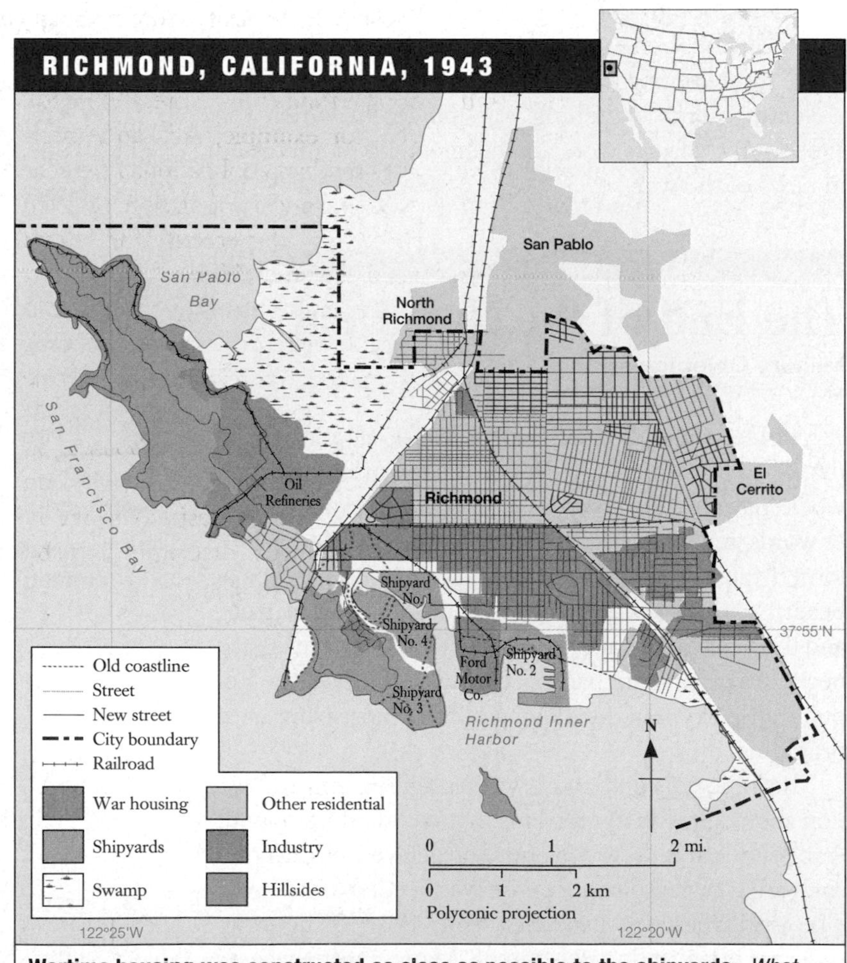

Wartime housing was constructed as close as possible to the shipyards. *What industries other than shipbuilding are indicated on the map?*

Social Strains

Richmond's rapid growth strained social relations. The first migrants, or "newcomers," often arrived to find public housing in short supply. Racial quotas limited any available public housing slots, forcing most African Americans to live in overcrowded rooming houses in the segregated part of Richmond.

Longtime residents, or "oldtimers," resented the presence of the newcomers, many of whom lived in tents, cars, and homemade shanties because of the lack of housing. In the workplace, union leaders, most of whom were oldtimers, pressured the newcomers to join their unions. Unions then restricted these new members from skilled-job classes, thus preserving the best-paying jobs for the oldtimers. African Americans and women faced extra burdens in the workplace. Often employers tried to keep them in menial, low-paying jobs, and coworkers regularly harassed them. At first many unions also tried to exclude them from their ranks. As the war neared its end, African Americans, women, and other newcomers were usually the first ones to be laid off.

Richmond Shipyard No. 2 Celebrates Hundreds of Kaiser workers gather for the launch of the Liberty ship *Robert E. Peary*—built in a record-breaking 4 days, 15 hours, and 29 minutes. *Where did many of these workers live?*

COURTESY OF THE BANCROFT LIBRARY, KAISER PICTORIAL COLLECTION

The Boomtown Legacy

The wartime boom permanently changed Richmond. After the war many migrant workers remained and settled there. By 1950 Richmond's population had stabilized at about 100,000 people—compared to about 24,000 in 1940. It now housed a greater diversity of people than ever before. Before the war, for example, African Americans made up only about 1 percent of Richmond's population. By 1950 more than 13 percent of the city's residents were African American.

As urban areas like Richmond became more diverse, outer suburbs expanded, largely due to "white flight." Developers quickly built subdivisions and tract housing in response. Although many African Americans also desired to live in these suburbs, discrimination by real estate brokers and others limited their opportunities.

Boomtowns also contributed to a lasting shift in the relationships of work, community, and home in the United States. More and more Americans now lived in one place, worked in another, and maintained family roots in yet another part of the country. Changing jobs and homes became more common as people tried to advance in corporate positions.

Ultimately, millions of workers who remained on the home front during World War II, including many African Americans, gained valuable skills and made economic gains. Steady work in boomtowns like Richmond enabled them to support their families, pay off debt incurred during the Great Depression, and save money for new cars and homes. In turn, their new economic wealth and political power would help fuel the vast economic growth and social change of the 1950s and 1960s.

Making the Geographic Connection

1. What geographical features of Richmond made it suitable for shipbuilding?
2. What were some of the social tensions that occurred in Richmond? Describe their causes.
3. **Place** How did the large increase in Richmond's population during World War II have a lasting effect on life there? How did the growing population of Richmond affect the surrounding landscape?

The War and Civil Rights

1941: RACIST HIRING PRACTICES MEET WITH RESISTANCE

ALTHOUGH AFRICAN AMERICANS FOUGHT AND DIED FOR THE UNITED STATES IN BOTH WORLD WARS, THEY FACED DISCRIMINATION AS THEY SEARCHED FOR JOBS AT HOME. The hiring policy of North American Aviation, one of the nation's largest aircraft manufacturers, was typical of the discrimination many companies practiced. The president of North American Aviation publicly stated its policy in 1941:

> While we are in complete sympathy with the Negro, it is against company policy to employ them as aircraft workers or mechanics . . . regardless of their training, but there will be some jobs as janitors for Negroes.
>
> —As quoted by Daniel S. Davis, *Mr. Black Labor,* 1972

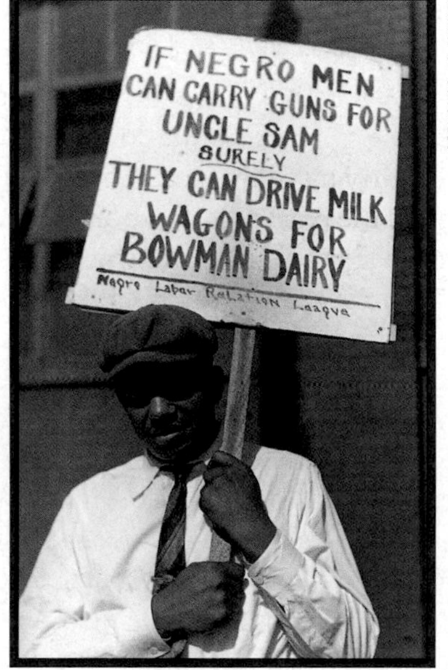

LIBRARY OF CONGRESS

Protesting for Fair Employment This sign reflects one form of racial injustice that occurred during the war.

Other executives shared this view. As one steel company head said in 1941, "We haven't had a Negro worker in twenty-five years and do not plan to start now."

Civil Rights Movement Grows

Fighting Racism

During World War II, the demands of African Americans for equal treatment grew louder. Many whites as well as African Americans came to recognize the uncomfortable similarity between racial tensions in the United States and Hitler's belief in a superior race. A leading African

GUIDE TO READING

Main Idea

Nazi theories of racial superiority heightened awareness of racism within the United States, particularly the unequal treatment of African Americans and the unjust internment of Japanese Americans.

Vocabulary

- racism
- civil liberties

Read to Find Out . . .

- how African Americans fought racism during World War II.
- the effect of the March on Washington Movement.
- why internment violated the civil liberties of Japanese Americans.

American newspaper, the *Amsterdam News,* deplored the "race discrimination and segregation, mob brutality—the entire Nazi pattern of U.S. racial conditions."

Racism is the belief that race determines human capacities and that some races are superior to others. Racism was the basis for the system of segregation and discrimination that existed in law and in fact throughout most of the United States. For many years anthropologists had been challenging the once popular idea that certain races were superior. By the 1940s scholars considered doctrines of racial supremacy to be unscientific and false. The differences that mattered, they said, were not between races but between individuals. Racial traits or characteristics were really a product of environmental influences, they concluded. White Americans who continued to justify segregation felt increasingly uncomfortable with comparisons of discrimination in the United States and Hitler's theories of racial superiority. One Southern politician conceded in 1944 that the Nazis "have wrecked the theories of the master race with which we were so contented so long."

African Americans responded to this heightened awareness of racism with a new militancy. As they moved from the South, where they could not vote, to the North and the West, African Americans began to flex their political muscles. They became more vocal, insisting on opportunities that they had long been denied. Some picketed factories with signs such as: Hitler Must Own This Plant, Negroes Can't Work Here. If We Must Fight, Why Can't We Work?

The African American press pushed a "Double V" campaign—victory at home as well as abroad. They insisted that fighting the war should not diminish the struggle for equality; on the contrary, progress toward equality should help win the war.

Civil Rights Gains

The March on Washington Movement

In the South, African Americans were legally segregated from whites in all public facilities. In much of the rest of the country, trains, buses, restaurants, and movie theaters were segregated, too. Throughout the nation, poverty kept most African Americans confined to slums and ghettos, and those who could afford better housing faced exclusion by homeowners and real estate salespeople in middle-class neighborhoods.

The war led civil rights groups to develop new forms of protest against these injustices. In the summer of 1941, A. Philip Randolph led the movement for African American equality. The son of a minister, he had grown up in the South where the Ku Klux Klan terrorized African Americans to keep them in line. After arriving in New York in 1906 at the age of 17, Randolph attended college at night and worked at various jobs during the day.

Quiet but determined, Randolph became a respected leader of African Americans. By following his goal of "creating unrest among the Negroes," Randolph

AP/WIDE WORLD PHOTOS

Testifying for Civil Rights A. Philip Randolph, on the right, is shown before the Senate Armed Services Committee testifying that millions of African Americans would refuse to register for or to be drafted into the military unless racial segregation and discrimination ended. *How did the war serve to attract attention to the unjust treatment of minority groups?*

eventually became known as the Father of the Civil Rights Movement.

Randolph's leadership qualities first surfaced in 1925 when he led a movement to organize the porters who worked on the sleeping cars of the nation's trains. The Brotherhood of Sleeping Car Porters, which Randolph organized, worked to obtain higher wages and better working conditions for its members. New Deal reforms before the war, such as the Wagner Act, helped the organization win its fight to bargain as a union.

By May 1941, Randolph had turned his energies to battles in the national political arena. He was appalled by discrimination in the armed forces, in which African Americans had already fought for their country during World War I. The exclusion of African Americans from well-paying jobs in war industries to which billions of federal dollars were flowing also angered him. To help right these wrongs, Randolph organized a March on Washington Movement (MOWM). Supporters rallied behind the slogan: We loyal American citizens demand the right to work and fight for our country.

Randolph's approach differed from the mainstream civil rights organization of the time, the National Association for the Advancement of Colored People (NAACP). The NAACP, the largest organization fighting for equal treatment for African Americans, urged African Americans to "persuade, embarrass, compel and shame our government and our nation" to end discrimination. In contrast to the NAACP, Randolph called for direct action, a "thundering march" on Washington rather than the use of cumbersome political and legal processes. In addition, Randolph demanded changes that would benefit Northern urban African Americans as well as those living in the South. Finally, he excluded white people from the MOWM because he maintained that the victims of discrimination must assume responsibility for abolishing it. "No one will fight as hard to remove and relieve pain as he who suffers from it," Randolph counseled.

African American Jobs: 1940, 1944

Occupation	Percentage of Workforce	
	1940	1944
Agriculture	32.1%	21%
Business, repair, and recreation	1.5%	1.2%
Construction	2.5%	1.9%
Domestic services	36.5%	29.3%
Government	1.2%	3.5%
Manufacturing	9.5%	18.3%
Mining	0.9%	2.1%
Professional services	4.3%	5.3%
Trade and finance	8.1%	11.9%
Transportation and utilities	3.4%	5.5%

African Americans experienced both gains and losses in nonagricultural jobs during World War II. *Despite the gains, what field continued to account for the highest percentage of African American workers?*

Roosevelt and Randolph Compromise

As preparations for the March on Washington moved ahead, government officials began to worry. Roosevelt wanted to prevent the march, which would embarrass the government. He was also afraid that a march that brought 50,000 to 100,000 people to Washington might end in violence. The President sent his wife, Eleanor, as well as government officials, to persuade Randolph to call off the march. To show his sympathy, Roosevelt publicly condemned job discrimination and ordered his defense chiefs to do something about it.

When Randolph refused to call off the march, Roosevelt finally met with him. Randolph demanded three key changes in government policy, all of which an executive order of the President could bring about. First, he wanted defense contracts denied to employers who practiced discrimination. Next, he asked that job segregation in federal agencies be abolished. Finally, he asked for the desegregation of the armed forces.

Randolph did not get all he demanded, but his threat of a mass demonstration in the nation's capital marked a real breakthrough in equal treatment and opportunities for African Americans. Roosevelt's Executive Order 8802, issued on June 25, 1941, stipulated that government agencies, job training programs, and defense contractors put an end to discrimination. It also created the Fair Employment Practices Committee (FEPC) to investigate violations of the order. The President, however, did not agree to integrate the armed forces.

As Randolph canceled the march, African American leaders hailed the executive order as a major step forward. The MOWM, however, did not disband. Randolph continued to urge mass marches and protest rallies to focus attention on discrimination. He also encouraged boycotts of segregated facilities and acts of civil disobedience to show nonviolent opposition to government laws or policies. African American protesters willingly accepted punishment for such illegal actions.

Other Victories

Encouraged by Randolph's success in protesting discrimination, other African American civil rights leaders organized the Congress of Racial Equality (CORE) in 1942. CORE continued the strategy of mobilizing mass resistance to discrimination and employed acts of

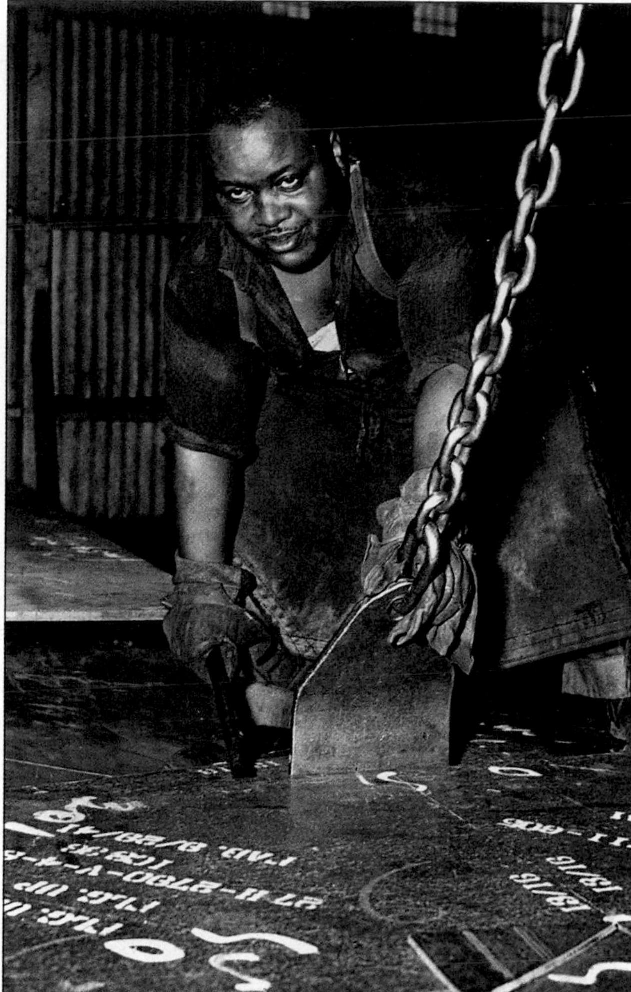
UPI/BETTMANN

Skilled Labor Some African Americans held skilled-labor jobs during the war, while others were excluded. *How did African Americans work to lessen discriminatory labor practices?*

nonviolent civil disobedience such as sit-ins at movie theaters and restaurants. Through the use of such tactics, shunned by more conservative organizations, CORE helped end segregation in public accommodations in several Northern cities.

Meanwhile, the membership of the NAACP grew. By 1946 it had risen to 450,000, almost 10 times the membership in 1940. The NAACP continued to rely on traditional, noncontroversial means of protesting, such as education, political pressure, and legal action. The organization won an important victory in 1944 when the Supreme Court ruled that it was unconstitutional to bar African Americans from voting in Democratic primaries in eight Southern states. In *Smith* v. *Allwright,* the Court held that political parties were agents of the state and they could not nullify the right to vote by practicing racial discrimination.

The FEPC Fights Discrimination

Obstacles to Success

Through the efforts of the NAACP, CORE, and MOWM, but mainly due to the critical labor shortage during the war, the share of jobs African Americans held in war industries grew. In addition, the FEPC helped open up some jobs in the federal government for African Americans and Hispanic Americans.

The FEPC faced major obstacles, however, in battling racial discrimination. The committee could act only on formal complaints about hiring practices or discrimination on the job, but many people were afraid to file complaints. Moreover, the committee's authority was severely limited. The FEPC was given no power to enforce its orders but had to rely on support from other federal agencies. For example, the only action the FEPC could take against defense contractors who discriminated against minorities was to recommend that their government contracts be canceled. Because canceling defense contracts would jeopardize military production, however, the cancellation was unlikely to occur.

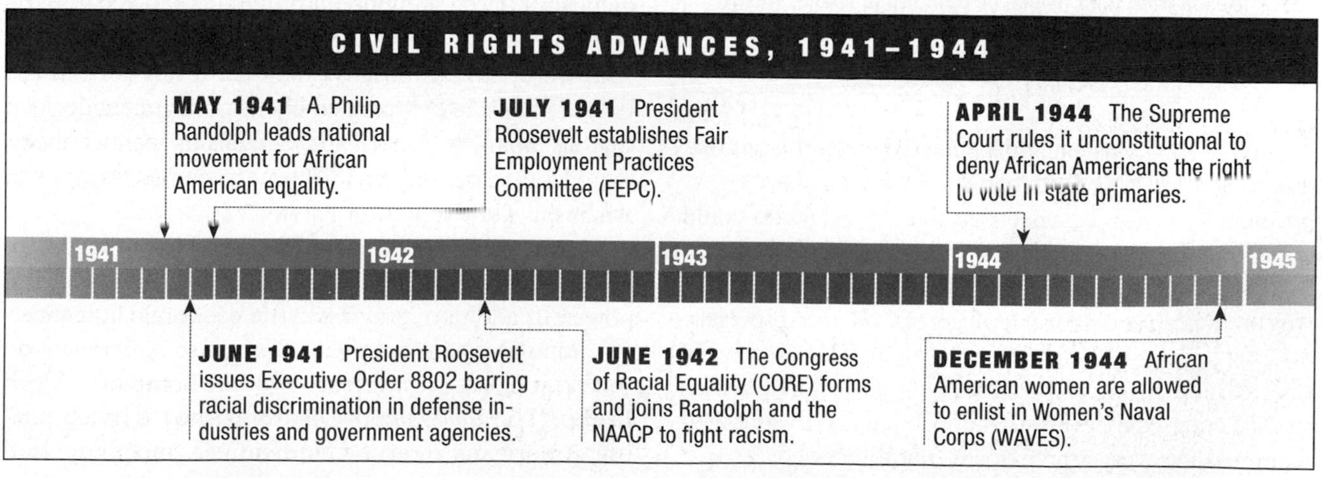

CIVIL RIGHTS ADVANCES, 1941–1944
MAY 1941 A. Philip Randolph leads national movement for African American equality.
JULY 1941 President Roosevelt establishes Fair Employment Practices Committee (FEPC).
APRIL 1944 The Supreme Court rules it unconstitutional to deny African Americans the right to vote in state primaries.
1941
1942
1943
1944
1945
JUNE 1941 President Roosevelt issues Executive Order 8802 barring racial discrimination in defense industries and government agencies.
JUNE 1942 The Congress of Racial Equality (CORE) forms and joins Randolph and the NAACP to fight racism.
DECEMBER 1944 African American women are allowed to enlist in Women's Naval Corps (WAVES).

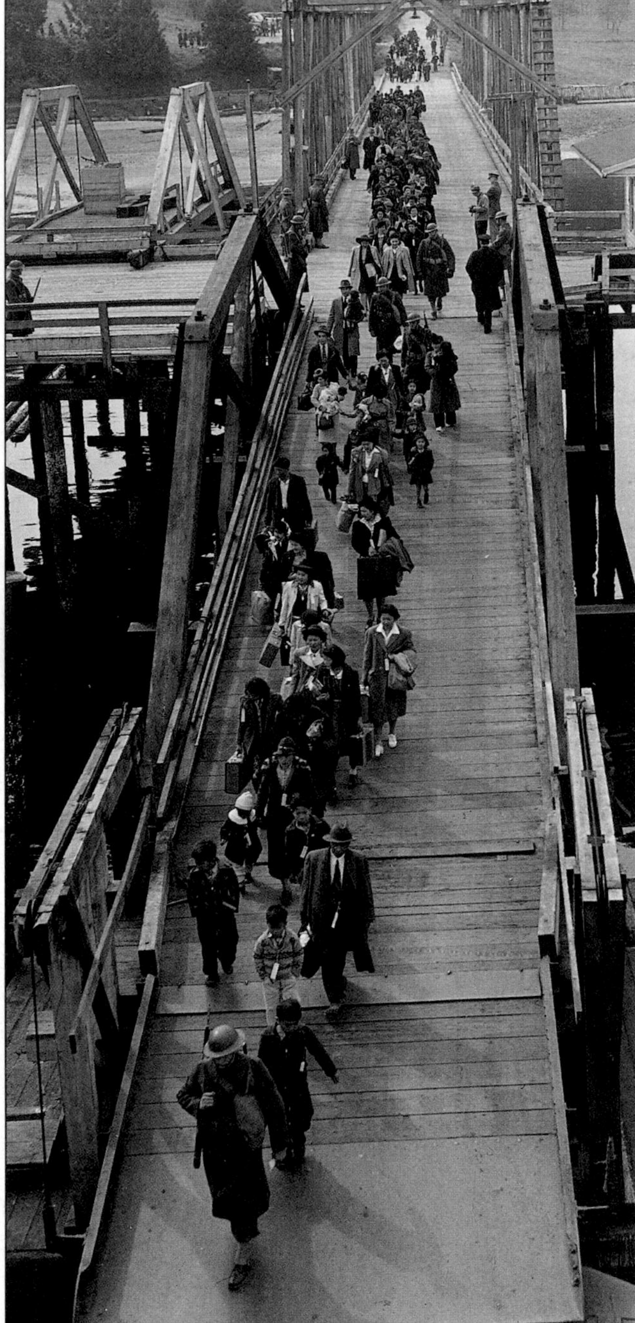
MUSEUM OF HISTORY AND INDUSTRY, SEATTLE WA

Internment On March 30, 1942, Japanese American evacuees are led from their homes on Bainbridge Island, Washington. *What does the armed escort suggest about the nature of the relocation?*

The FEPC was equally ineffective when the railroad unions ignored its order to end discrimination. Other government agencies reasoned that the United States could not afford a nationwide transportation walkout in wartime.

The committee also fought public opinion, which was prejudiced against it. Members of Congress, especially Southern Democrats, claimed the agency fostered racial discord and promoted communism. The FEPC withstood a congressional investigation, but it had to fight with Congress for every scarce dollar that it received.

Ironically, the FEPC was led by moderates who moved cautiously. The FEPC did not consider segregation, as opposed to discrimination, a cause for action. In several cases, the FEPC approved the creation of separate facilities for African American and white workers.

In all, the FEPC received 8,000 complaints, only one-third of which were resolved successfully. More often than not, employers defied its directives. In 1945, just before the war ended, Congress cut the FEPC's budget in half and shortly thereafter dissolved the agency.

Internment of Japanese Americans

Fear Leads to Relocation

Generally, World War II brought about few restrictions on **civil liberties,** or rights guaranteed to all citizens. Almost no one vocally opposed the war after Pearl Harbor, and little danger existed of an attack on the United States. As a result, there was not a repetition of the hysteria and pressure to conform that had occurred during World War I. Most Americans showed tolerance toward persons of foreign ancestry. The treatment of Japanese Americans was the exception.

Relocation

Spring 1942 brought events that are burned into the memories of Japanese Americans. Even though they showed no evidence of disloyalty, more than 120,000 Japanese Americans were moved from their homes to relocation camps. One evacuee, Helen Murao, explained why. "We looked like them [the enemy]. That was our sin."

Of the 120,000 Japanese Americans who lived on the West Coast and in Hawaii, about one-third were Issei—foreign-born Japanese who had entered the United States before the National Origins Act of 1924 had dramatically cut the number of immigrants allowed into the country. Two-thirds were Nisei—mainly children of Issei who were citizens because they had been born in the United States. In February 1942, the government decided that all Japanese Americans, citizens as well as aliens, would be relocated to internment camps located in Arkansas and the Western states.

Japanese Americans were vulnerable because they could easily be singled out and they lacked political power. In addition, they had little economic influence.

Popular sentiment against Japanese Americans on the West Coast grew intense after the bombing of Pearl Harbor. The *San Francisco Chronicle* pushed to have Japanese Americans interned. Individuals, including Earl

Warren, attorney general of California, (later chief justice of the United States), and several members of Congress, supported relocating Japanese Americans. Finally, on February 19, 1942, President Roosevelt signed Executive Order 9066 authorizing the removal of Japanese Americans from the West Coast.

Economic Hardship

The executive order subjected Japanese Americans to extreme economic hardship. Because they were permitted to take only a few belongings with them to the camps, they were forced to sell most of their possessions. Signs began to appear reading Evacuation Sale—Furniture Must All Be Sold. In the end most Japanese American families received about 5 cents for every dollar's worth of their possessions. Property not immediately sold was either stored or left with friends. Much of this was stolen, vandalized, or sold through legal loopholes. Even more devastating was the loss of farms, houses, and places of business. Estimates of this loss hover around $500 million.

Over the course of several months, the Japanese Americans were ordered to report to relocation centers. The military justified this action on the basis that Japanese Americans would commit sabotage to aid Japan in an attack on the West Coast. General John DeWitt, head of the Western Defense Command argued: "The very fact that no sabotage to aid Japan has taken place to date is a disturbing and confirming indication that such action will be taken."

Other motives played a role, too. Farmers and business associations thought they would profit by eliminating Japanese American competitors. Politicians believed they would win popular support by favoring relocation. General DeWitt expressed the commonly held view, "the Japanese race is an enemy race."

Life in the Camps

From the relocation centers, Japanese Americans were moved to 1 of 10 armed and guarded internment camps located in sparsely settled areas. For example, Topaz, a camp in Utah, was 4,600 feet (1,402.08 m) above sea level. Here inmates endured temperatures ranging from 106° F (41.1° C) in summer to –30° F (–34.5° C) in winter. They also lived in a constant whirlwind of dust.

The other camps were similarly barren. Japanese Americans taken to Heart Mountain, Wyoming, also suffered from winter temperatures as low as –30° F (–34.5° C). For those from the mild California valleys, the camps were tolerable at best. One camp resident wrote a poem in the camp newspaper, the *Sentinel.*

> Snow upon the rooftop
> Snow upon the coal;
> Winter in Wyoming—
> Winter in my soul.

One evacuee, Peter Ota, recalled the camp where he was interned:

> It's a desolate, flat, barren area. The barracks was all there was. There were no trees, no kind of

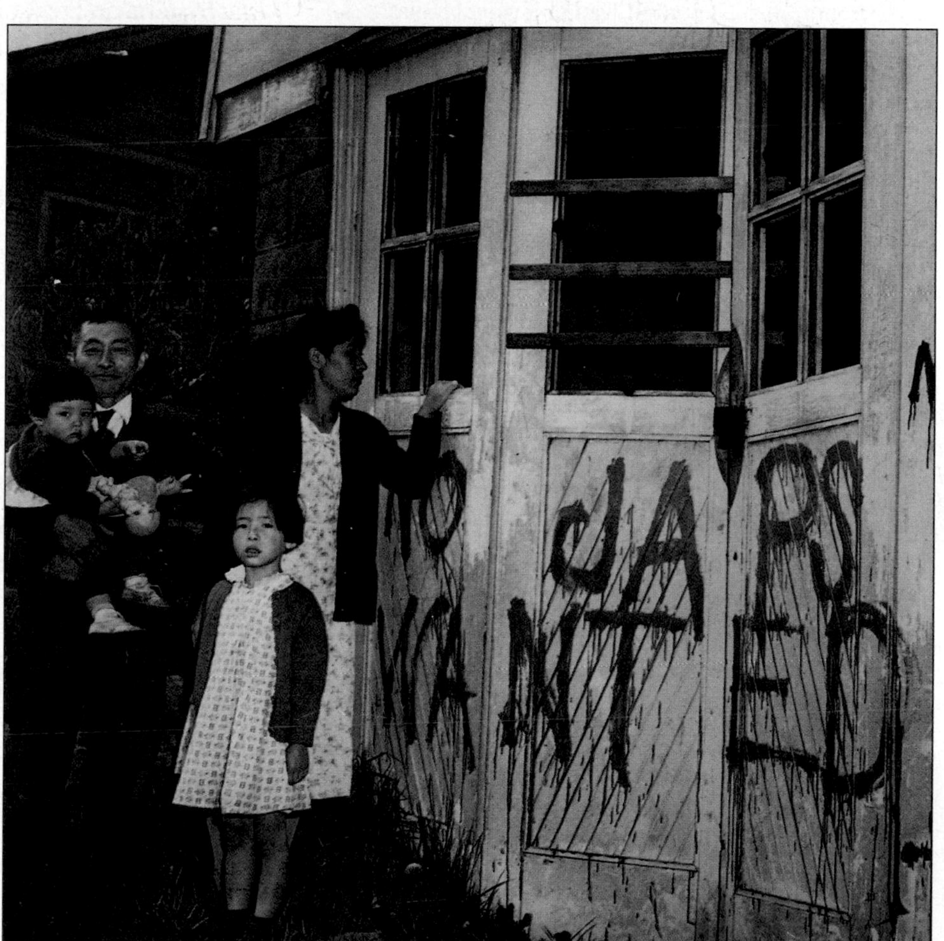

AP/WIDE WORLD PHOTOS

Internees Return Shigeo Nagaishi and his Nisei family find broken windows in their home and garage when they return to Seattle, Washington, from the relocation center in Hunt, Idaho, on May 10, 1945. *Why was this treatment of Japanese Americans unfair?*

AP/WIDE WORLD PHOTOS

Compensation for Internees **On August 10, 1988, President Ronald Reagan signed Public Law 100-383. Among other things, this law makes apologies and restitution to individuals of Japanese ancestry who were interned during World War II. Each eligible person received $20,000 in tax-free payments over a 10-year period.** *Do you think that this compensation was adequate? Why or why not?*

> landscaping. It was like a prison camp. Coming from our environment, it was just devastating.
>
> —As told to Studs Terkel, *"The Good War,"* 1984

This was no exaggeration. Entire families lived in a single room in the barracks, sparsely furnished with cots, makeshift dressers, and bare lightbulbs.

Despite the stark surroundings, the evacuees created a number of alternative communities to serve their cultural needs. The Japanese Americans published newspapers; started schools, churches, bands, Boy Scout groups, and softball leagues; built tennis courts; landscaped flower and vegetable gardens; and gave trumpet and tap dancing lessons. They were determined to replenish their lives with the dignity and the resources that they and their children would need when the war ended.

Some of the evacuees were released to work at jobs in the interior of the United States before the end of the war. They were allowed to resettle in the East or the Midwest. Most, however, remained in the camps for the duration of the war.

HISTORY Online

Student Web Activity 16

Visit the *American Odyssey* Web site at americanodyssey.glencoe.com and click on ***Chapter 16—Student Web Activities*** for an activity relating to internment of Japanese Americans.

Judicial Rulings Support Relocation

The Supreme Court upheld the wartime policies toward Japanese Americans. In 1943, in *Hirabayashi* v. *United States,* the Court unanimously ruled that a curfew order affecting only Japanese Americans did not violate their civil rights. Chief Justice Harlan Fiske Stone wrote: "In time of war residents having ethnic affiliations with an invading enemy may be a greater source of danger than those of a different ancestry."

In December 1944, in *Korematsu* v. *United States,* the Court upheld the order providing for internment. It based its ruling largely on the grounds that the judiciary could not second-guess military decisions. One of the dissenting justices, however, termed the decision a "legalization of racism." Although the Court ruled that citizens could not be held in relocation centers once their loyalty was proven, the camps were being closed down by then. In 1998, Fred Korematsu, who had refused to report for transport to an internment camp, won the Presidential Medal of Freedom.

During the war, the nation saw both gains and losses in civil rights and liberties. While African Americans fought hard to win small victories, Japanese Americans were treated as enemies of the United States. As the war ended, Americans could only hope for a more just, prosperous, and peaceful postwar world.

SECTION ASSESSMENT

Main Idea

1. Use a diagram like this one to show gains and losses in civil rights and liberties during World War II.

Civil Rights and Liberties	
Gains	Losses

Vocabulary

2. Define: racism, civil liberties.

Checking Facts

3. How did A. Philip Randolph's approach to protest compare to that of the NAACP?
4. Describe the Japanese American internment camps.

Critical Thinking

5. **Recognizing Bias** What obstacles hindered the work of the FEPC?

Social Studies Skill

READING ECONOMIC GRAPHS

Learning the Skill

During the 1940s dramatic economic changes affected many Americans. In the early 1940s, government spending on war materials boosted production. To meet rising production, manufacturers hired more workers, who then had more money to spend, further increasing demand and production. Then in 1942 thousands of American men left their jobs to serve in the armed forces. Production dropped. Soon other Americans filled the open positions, stopping the decline in production. Patterns of this kind—in prices, interest rates, or wages—form what is called a business cycle. Business cycle graphs can help you visualize the direction and extent of economic change.

Line graphs illustrate change over time. A business cycle graph, such as the one below, is a type of line graph that shows changes in economic activity, as measured by the value of goods and services produced. In the graph below, the horizontal line in the center represents the trend line of economic activity over the period. The data points show how the value of goods and services produced at a given time varies above (+) or below (–) the trend line.

Patterns of Economic Activity

To interpret this type of graph, follow these steps:

a. First compare each data point to the trend line. It tells you how much economic production increased or decreased in a given year.

b. Next determine if the line connecting a group of data points has a downward or upward slope. A downward slope shows falling production and an upward slope shows rising production.

c. Identify the business cycle of which a given year is a part. Look for a pattern of rising production, peak, declining production, and bottom. A given year may belong to a business cycle that began in an earlier year; for example, the business cycle that includes 1923 begins with rising production in 1922.

Practicing the Skill

Use the graph to answer these questions.

1. How much did production decline during the period 1930–1931?

2. Find the business cycle that began with rising production during 1942. When did this cycle end?

3. The 1920s and the 1940s were both periods of economic prosperity, yet their business cycles appear quite different. How do you explain this?

4. During which Depression years might Americans have felt most hopeful? Explain.

Applying the Skill

Find a graph in a newspaper or newsmagazine that shows a trend in economic activity. Write a paragraph identifying the trend and explaining how you recognized it.

The **Glencoe Skillbuilder Interactive Workbook, Level 2** CD-ROM provides more practice in key social studies skills.

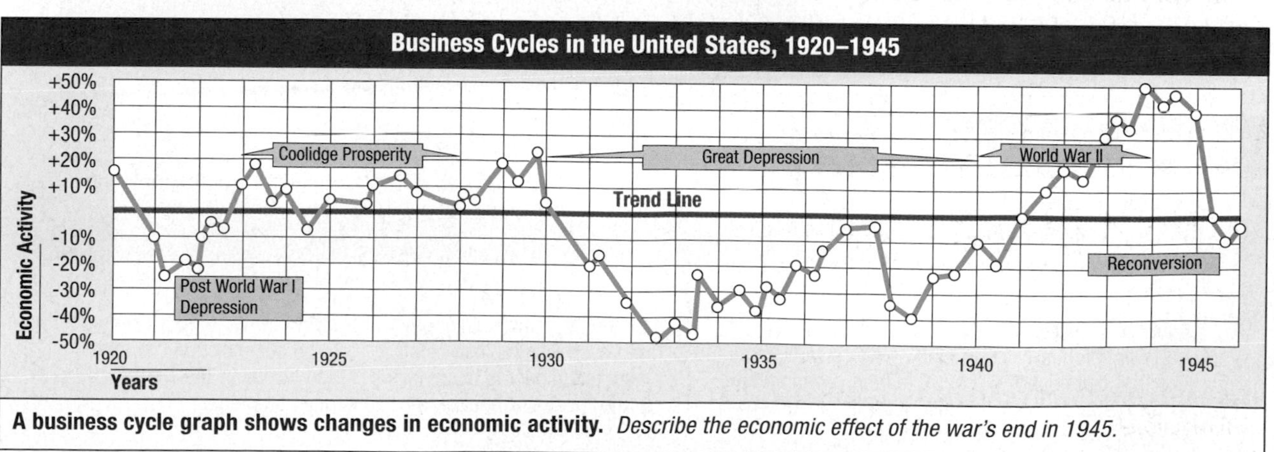

A business cycle graph shows changes in economic activity. *Describe the economic effect of the war's end in 1945.*

Science, TECHNOLOGY, and Society

Medical Breakthroughs

Medical advances reduced the overall mortality rate of the wounded in World War II to 3 percent, down from 6 percent in World War I. The innovations of wartime surgeons and researchers, aided by government funding, greatly enriched civilian medicine after the war.

HELP FOR INJURED VETERANS

Vast numbers of soldiers lost limbs in World War II, encouraging the development of lighter, better-functioning prostheses and increasing social acceptance of their use. This veteran is wearing an artificial arm developed at the United States Army Prosthetic Research Laboratory after the war. The wearer's muscle contractions activate electrodes that generate the electric currents that control the limb.

UPI/BETTMANN

MEDICAL BREAKTHROUGHS

Pre-1938 | 1940 | 1942

SULFA DRUGS, early antibiotics, are first developed in the 1930s.

BLOOD PLASMA is found by U.S. scientists in 1939 to be a useful substitute for whole blood in transfusions.

ALBUMIN, a protein separated from whole blood using a new technique, is found in 1940 to be a useful alternative to plasma.

PENICILLIN is first used on a large scale in 1943 to treat Allied troops in the North Africa campaign.

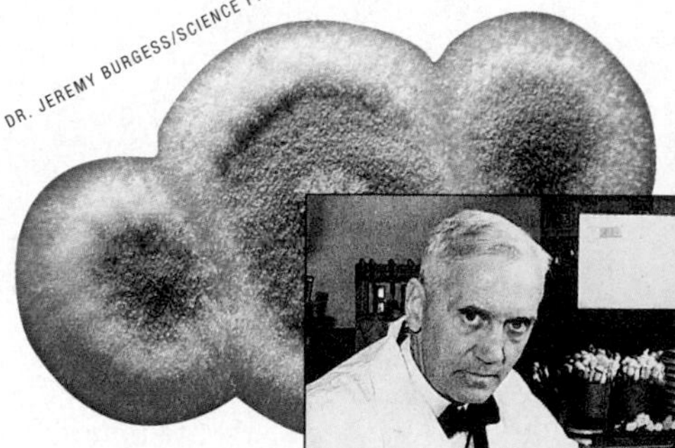

DR. JEREMY BURGESS/SCIENCE PHOTO LIBRARY

BROWN BROTHERS

PLASMA, THE LIFE GIVER

One of the most important medical breakthroughs was the use of blood plasma to prevent shock, a life-threatening condition resulting from blood loss that caused arteries to collapse, cutting off circulation to vital organs. Plasma, the liquid part of the blood, was easier to preserve than whole blood and caused far fewer allergic reactions. When transfused, plasma kept arteries open and helped the wounded live long enough to be evacuated and to undergo surgery. Plasma, General George Patton said, "saves more lives than you could believe."

MIRACLE DRUG

Penicillin replaced sulfa drugs as the antibiotic of choice because it actually killed bacteria instead of just stopping their growth and it had fewer side effects. The strange story of the discovery of penicillin dates back to 1928, when British physician Alexander Fleming, above, accidentally grew a new variety of mold that killed all nearby bacteria. The significance of Fleming's discovery was not recognized until the early 1940s.

© FPG INTERNATIONAL CORP.

HOW ARE DISCOVERIES MADE?

PORTFOLIO PROJECT

What factors account for the large number of medical advances made during World War II? Which factor do you think was most important? Explain your reasoning in a paragraph.

1944 | 1946 | 1948 to 2000s

ALEXANDER FLEMING, Howard Florey, and Ernst Chain receive the Nobel Prize in 1945 for the discovery of penicillin.

U.S. ARMY SURGICAL RESEARCH UNIT is founded in 1945, the forerunner of the specialized burn treatment centers of today.

GENES responsible for hereditary breast, colon, and kidney cancers are isolated in the early 1990s; giving hope for new tests and treatments in the 2000s.

Chapter  Assessment

Self-Check Quiz

Visit the *American Odyssey* Web site at americanodyssey.glencoe.com and click on ***Chapter 16—Self-Check Quiz*** to prepare for the Chapter Test.

Reviewing Key Terms

Match each of the following sentences with the vocabulary term that best defines or describes it. Write your answers on a separate sheet of paper.

inflation	**deficit spending**
migration	**racism**
gross national product	**civil liberties**

1. By 1942 the annual cost of living had rapidly increased by 15 percent.

2. In relocating and interning Japanese Americans, the United States denied them these rights.

3. This total value of all goods and services produced annually in the United States more than doubled during the war years.

4. This pattern of discrimination has disadvantaged African Americans.

5. During the wartime economic growth, the government used borrowed money to ensure full employment and prosperity.

Recalling Facts

1. How did civilians contribute to the war effort?

2. Explain why inflation occurred during the war and how the government tried to fight it.

3. How did rationing help the war effort?

4. How did the government raise the money to finance World War II?

5. Who was John L. Lewis?

6. What kind of work did women do during the war?

7. Describe migration patterns in the United States during World War II.

8. What happened to the cities when large numbers of migrant war workers arrived?

9. How did the native residents of the boomtowns feel about the newcomers?

10. What are some of the advantages and disadvantages that society experienced as a result of having women enter the workforce during World War II?

11. What aspects of the New Deal became a permanent part of United States political policy?

12. Who was A. Philip Randolph? What did he accomplish? Explain the March on Washington Movement, and tell what this movement accomplished.

13. What is civil disobedience?

14. Give examples of how the war furthered the cause of racial equality.

15. Describe what life was like for those held in the Japanese internment camps.

Critical Thinking

1. Recognizing Bias Navy personnel roamed the streets of Los Angeles in 1943 beating zoot-suiters, but only the zoot-suiters were arrested. What can you infer about the attitudes of the arresting police officers?

2. Identifying Assumptions How did the military justify the relocation of Japanese Americans? On what assumptions was the justification based?

3. Making Comparisons Use a diagram like this one to compare A. Philip Randolph's methods for bringing about social change with those of the NAACP. Record which methods you think were most effective.

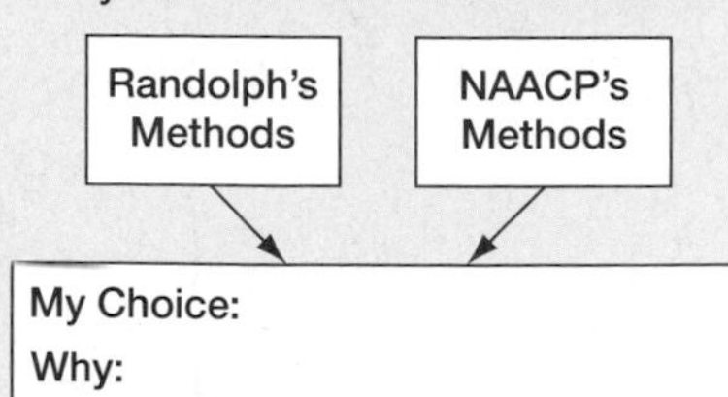

Portfolio Project

Write an essay that discusses ways in which an individual can cope with and ease racial tensions today. You might relate incidents or comments that you may have witnessed. Conclude by making recommendations that you can apply to everyday social situations. (An example might be speaking out among peers when racial comments or jokes are made.)

Cooperative Learning

In small groups plan an oral history project. Interview family members or older neighbors who lived at home during World War II. Find out about their memories of social changes and the importance of entertainment. Write down their stories. You might bring to class examples of some of the time's popular music.

Reinforcing Skills

Reading Economic Graphs Use what you know about economic graphs to answer these questions.

1. What kinds of information might be represented on a business cycle graph?

2. What kinds of events or activities might have an effect on the business cycle?

3. Why is it helpful to include a long-term average on an economic graph?

GEOGRAPHY AND HISTORY

African American Population, 1940–1950

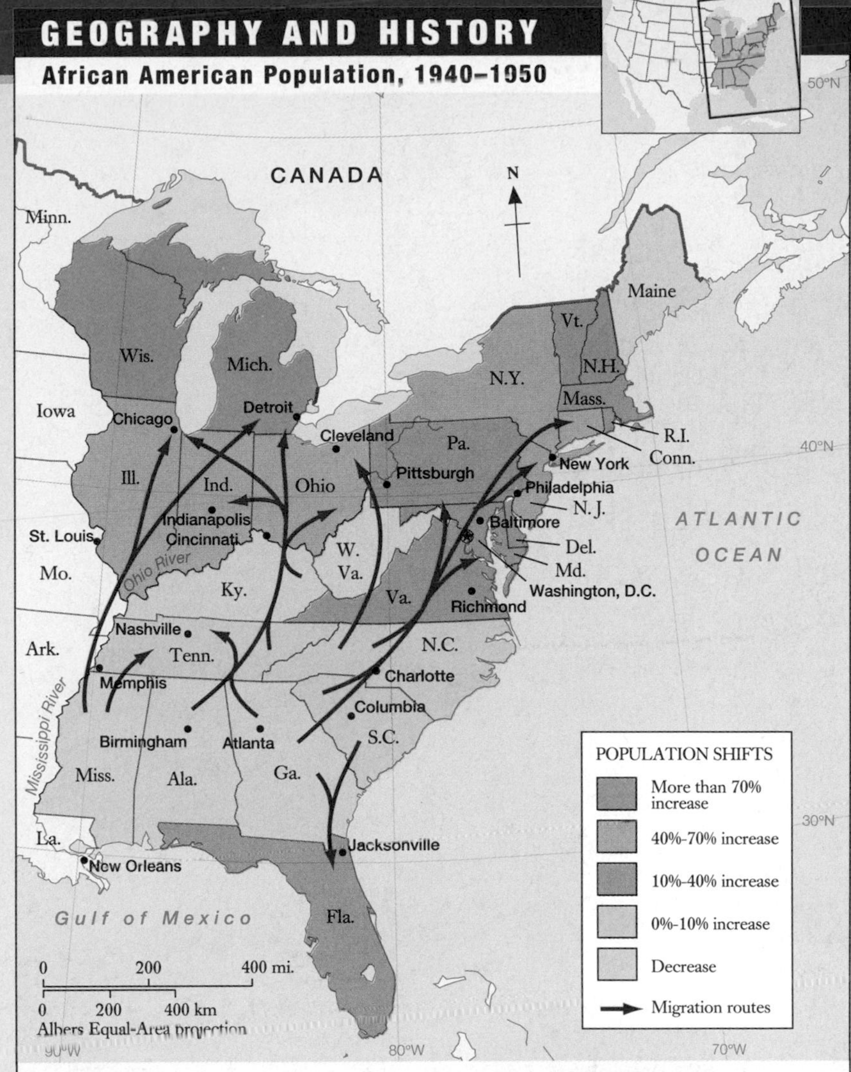

Study the map to answer the following questions:

1. Which states experienced a decrease in their African American populations?
2. Which states experienced the greatest increase in their African American populations?
3. Which states experienced the smallest increase in their African American populations?
4. Use the map to summarize the migration routes of African Americans east of the Mississippi River from 1940 to 1950.

Technology Activity

Using a Spreadsheet The population in the United States has increased rapidly since 1940. Create a spreadsheet showing actual population statistics on how the United States population has increased each decade from 1940 to the present. Based on population indicators, predict the population growth for the next five decades.

Standardized Test Practice

1. An economic policy begun in World War II that is still in effect today is federal

A wage-and-price controls.
B withholding taxes on income.
C rationing of consumer goods.
D war-bond drives.

Test-Taking Tip: This question requires you to link past with present. All four of these economic policies were implemented in World War II, but only *one* has remained in practice. Which of these policies would be important today?

2. World War II brought about all the following long-term changes in the United States EXCEPT

A population gains for states in the West and South.
B the end of the Great Depression.
C a growing civil rights movement.
D permanent new employment opportunities for women.

Test-Taking Tip: The key word in this question is *long-term.* Three of the changes lasted; one did NOT. For instance, the full-employment economy and forced savings of the war years made possible a post-war economic boom. Therefore, you can eliminate answer C.

Then...

Women's Baseball

In 1943, when half of the male professional baseball players were serving in World War II, Philip Wrigley, owner of the Chicago Cubs, organized the All-American Girls Baseball League. The league's athletes thrilled and entertained thousands of war-weary fans with their skill and left a lasting mark on the history of baseball.

1 The Muskegon Lassies played from 1946 through 1950, managed by Ralph "Buzz" Boyle. All league managers were men.

GREATER MUSKEGON GIRLS PROFESSIONAL BALL CLUB
MUSKEGON LASSIES
21503
OFFICIAL
10¢
SCORE CARD
A-A GBBL
"Watch the girls play ball"
All American Girls
PROFESSIONAL BALL
MARSH FIELD

NATIONAL BASEBALL LIBRARY HALL OF FAME, COOPERSTOWN, NEW YORK

2 The league's skirted uniforms left legs unprotected. Scrapes, or "strawberries," were continually created as skin met the ground when players slid into bases.

Fun Facts

KEEPING UP APPEARANCES

In the early years of the league, players were required to attend "charm school," where they learned how to apply makeup and act in social situations. They were also fined $50 if they appeared "unkempt" in public.

Stats

NATIONAL BASEBALL LIBRARY HALL OF FAME, COOPERSTOWN, NEW YORK

PLAY-OFF CHAMPIONS, 1943–1945

- 1943, Racine Belles
- 1944, Milwaukee Chicks
- 1945, Rockford Peaches

STARTING SALARY

- $55 per week

LEAGUE BATTING CHAMPS, 1943–1945

- 1943, Gladys Davis
- 1944, Betsy Jochum
- 1945, Mary Crews

4 Dorothy "Kammie" Kamenshek of the Rockford Peaches, the league batting champion in 1946 and 1947, was offered a contract by a men's professional baseball team.

NATIONAL BASEBALL LIBRARY HALL OF FAME, COOPERSTOWN, NEW YORK

3 The 1945 Rockford Peaches, above, won the team's first league pennant. Between 1943 and 1954, when the league's last teams disbanded, more than 550 women played on a total of 15 teams.

...Now

NATIONAL BASEBALL LIBRARY HALL OF FAME, COOPERSTOWN, NEW YORK

A SPORTS REPORT

PORTFOLIO PROJECT

Create a report about any sport that women participated in 50 years ago and continue to participate in today. Collect facts about past and current individual female athletes, including records they have set, and money they have earned. In your report describe if and how the status of women in the sport has changed.

FAN HOSPITALITY

Fans housed the teams as they traveled, raised money to pay injured players' medical expenses, and hosted celebrations. One family in Racine, Wisconsin, gave the Racine Belles a yearly picnic, serving each player's favorite food.

UNIT
7

Economic Crisis and the New Deal

1945–1963

HISTORY & YOU

Within months after the end of World War II, the United States and the Soviet Union entered into a period of intense confrontation known as the cold war. Rivalries extended from the arms race to the space race. American leaders tried to maintain workable links with the Soviets while containing the spread of communism abroad. The often chaotic world situation created an intense desire among Americans for stability at home and the chance to lavish the benefits of a pumped-up economy on their children.

PRIMARY SOURCES
Library

See pages 966–967 for primary source readings that accompany Unit 7.

UNITED STATES
1946 United Nations headquarters established in New York.
1947 Truman Doctrine is announced; Jackie Robinson becomes first African American major-league baseball player.
1953 Dwight D. Eisenhower becomes President; McCarthyism stirs the nation.
1954 Brown v. Board of Education declares segregation in schools unconstitutional.
1945
1950
1945 Yalta Conference held.
1946 Winston Churchill makes "iron curtain" speech.
1948 Berlin Airlift takes place.
1949 Mao Zedong's Communist forces take China; NATO created.
1950 Korean War begins.
THE WORLD

PHOTO COURTESY OF THE NORMAN ROCKWELL MUSEUM AT STOCKBRIDGE

New Television Antenna, **by Norman Rockwell, 1949, demonstrates the post-war prosperity and innovation that shaped life in the 1950s.**

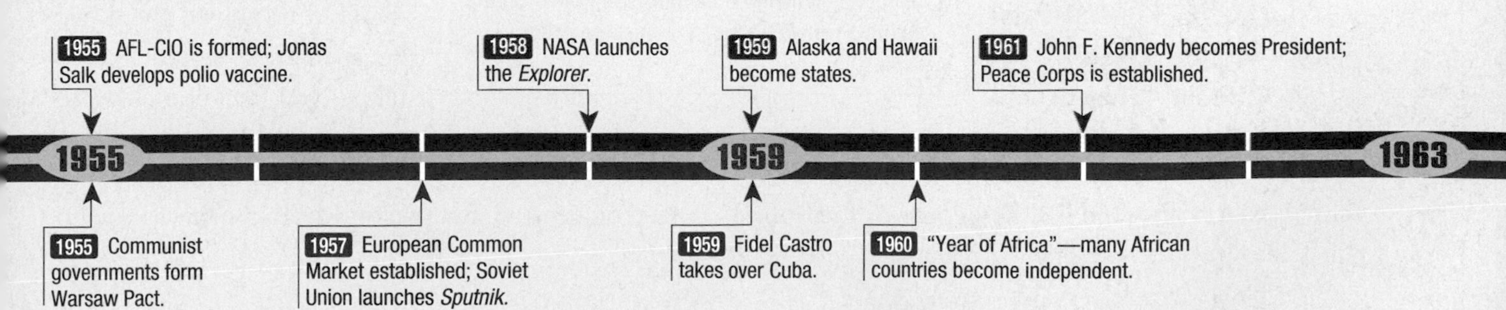

1955 AFL-CIO is formed; Jonas Salk develops polio vaccine.
1958 NASA launches the *Explorer*.
1959 Alaska and Hawaii become states.
1961 John F. Kennedy becomes President; Peace Corps is established.
1955
1959
1963
1955 Communist governments form Warsaw Pact.
1957 European Common Market established; Soviet Union launches *Sputnik*.
1959 Fidel Castro takes over Cuba.
1960 "Year of Africa"—many African countries become independent.

The Book of Daniel

BY E.L. DOCTOROW

E.L. Doctorow captures anti-Communist paranoia in this excerpt from the novel The Book of Daniel. *The FBI, who suspects Daniel's parents of Communist espionage, visits Daniel's home.*

Early the next morning, as I was leaving for school, the doorbell rang and I opened the door and two men were standing on the porch. They were dressed neatly, and did not appear to be of the neighborhood. They had thin, neat faces and small noses, and crew-cut hair. They held their hats in their hands and wore nice overcoats. I thought maybe they were from one of those Christian religions that sent people from door to door to sell their religious magazines.

"Sonny," said one, "is your mother or father home?"

"Yes," I said. "They're both home."

NATIONAL MUSEUM OF AMERICAN ART, WASHINGTON DC/ART RESOURCE, NY

The Postwar Era **After reading the literature selection, consider how this 1959 Franz Kline painting reflects a mood of menace or foreboding.**

My mother did not allow me to delay going to school just because the FBI had come to the door. I don't know what happened on that first visit. The men went inside and, going down the splintery front steps, I turned and caught a glimpse of Paul coming out of the kitchen to meet them just as the door closed. My mother was holding the door and my father was coming forward in his ribbed undershirt, looking much skinnier than the two men who rang the bell.

When the FBI knocks on your door and wants only to ask a few questions, you do not have to consent to be asked questions. You are not required to talk to them just because they would like to talk to you. You don't have to go with them to their office. You don't have to do anything if you are not subpoenaed or arrested. But you only learn the law as you go along.

"They don't know what they want," Paul says to Rochelle. "It's routine. If you don't talk to them, they have nothing to pin their lies on. They are clumsy, obvious people."

"I'm frightened," my mother says. "*Polizei* don't have to be smart."

"Don't worry," Paul says. "Mindish won't suffer from anything we said." He is walking back and forth in the kitchen and he is pounding his fist into his palm. "We have done nothing wrong. There is nothing to be afraid of."

It develops that all of Mindish's friends are being questioned. Nobody knows what he is being held for. There has been no announcement on the radio, there has been no story in the newspaper. Sadie Mindish is in a state of hysterical collapse. Her apartment has been searched. Her daughter has stayed home from school. Nobody knows if they even have a lawyer.

The next day the same two FBI men come back again, this time in the early evening. They sit on the stuffed, sprung couch in the living room parlor with their knees together and their hats in their hands. They are very soft-spoken and friendly. Their strange names are Tom Davis and John Bradley. They smile at me while my mother goes to the phone to call my father.

"What grade are you in, young fellow?"

I don't answer. I have never seen a real FBI man this close before. I peer at them, looking for superhuman powers, but there is no evidence that they have any. They look neither as handsome as in the movies nor as ugly as my parents' revulsion makes them. I search their faces for a clue to their real nature. But their faces do not give clues.

When Paul comes home, he is very nervous.

"My lawyer has advised me that I don't have to talk to you if I don't want to," my father said. "That particular fact you neglected yesterday to mention."

"Well, yes sir, Mr. Isaacson, but we were hoping you would be cooperative. We're only looking for information. It's nothing mysterious. We thought you were a friend of Doctor Mindish. As his friend, you may be in a position to help him."

"I will be glad to answer any questions in a court of law."

"Do you deny now that you know him?"

"I will answer any questions in a court of law."

The two men leave after a few minutes, and then they sit in their car, double-parked in front of the house, for ten or fifteen minutes more. They appear to be writing on clipboards or on pads, I can't tell exactly. It is dark and they have turned on the interior car light. I am reminded of a patrol man writing a parking ticket. But the sense is of serious and irrevocable paperwork, and I find it frightening. There is some small, grey light in the dark sky over the schoolyard. The wind is making whistling noises at the edges of the window.

"Danny!" Rochelle says sharply. "Get away from there."

My father takes my place at the curtains. "That is outrageous," he says. "Don't you see, it is part of the treatment. They are trying to shake us up. But we're too smart for them. We're onto them. They can sit out there all night for all I care."

WHEN THE FBI KNOCKS ON YOUR DOOR AND WANTS ONLY TO ASK A FEW QUESTIONS, YOU DO NOT HAVE TO CONSENT.

Responding to Literature

1. **What kind of view of the postwar United States does this passage suggest?**
2. **Daniel later likens the FBI investigation to a searchlight in a Nazi concentration camp. Why is this ironic in the 1950s?**

The Uneasy Peace

OCTOBER 22, 1962: THE WHITE HOUSE

President John F. Kennedy walked into the Oval Office at 6:59 P.M., stepping over TV cables on the way to his desk. He was about to deliver some frightening news to the American people—news of a mounting Soviet threat in Cuba.

In a controlled, almost dull tone, Kennedy explained what the United States would do in response to the threat caused by the Russians installing missiles in Cuba. It would ask for a United Nations meeting. It would blockade Cuban shipping lanes with American destroyers to keep more weapons from reaching the island, and it would put the United States military on full alert. If even one missile were fired from Cuba toward any nation in the Western Hemisphere, the United States would launch a nuclear attack on the Soviet Union. Suddenly the world teetered on the brink of disaster.

What had happened? Just 17 years before, people of the United States and the Soviet Union embraced and toasted their stunning World War II victory. Franklin Roosevelt's warmth and diplomacy in dealing with the Soviets near the end of the war had raised hopes of cooperation between the two powers. Now, however, the wartime alliance had soured into a bitter and dangerous rivalry—a cold war—affecting the entire world. ■

HISTORY JOURNAL

Think about what you have heard or know about the Cuban missile crisis or early cold war. Now look at the picture of President John F. Kennedy on page 561. Write down what it might have been like to be President during these tense times.

Chapter Overview

Visit the *American Odyssey* Web site at americanodyssey.glencoe.com and click on ***Chapter 17—Chapter Overview*** to preview the chapter.

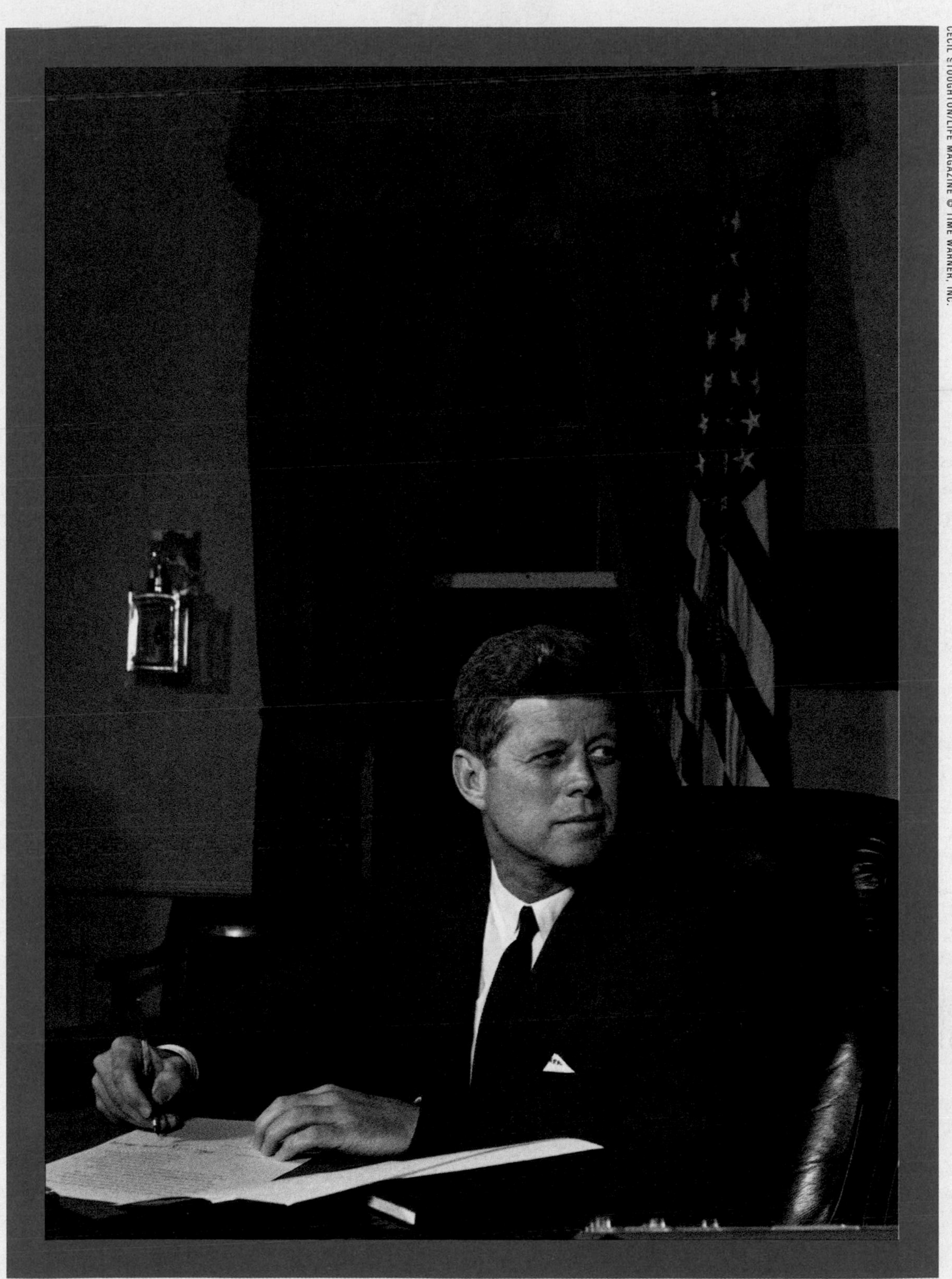

President John F. Kennedy pauses to reflect during the Cuban missile crisis.

The Cold War Begins

APRIL 25, 1945: GIs MEET SOVIET TROOPS

LILACS BLOOMED AND THE SUN SHONE ON APRIL 25, 1945, AS AMERICAN SOLDIERS BATTLING THE GERMANS FROM THE WEST APPROACHED THEIR SOVIET ALLIES FIGHTING FROM THE EAST. Victory was in the air, and as the armies neared the Elbe River south of Berlin, small patrols of Americans drove out in jeeps to meet their Soviet comrades-in-arms. Throughout the day Soviet and American soldiers embraced for the first time. Andy Rooney, staff writer for the armed forces newspaper, *Stars & Stripes,* caught the moment:

AP/WIDE WORLD PHOTOS

War's End
American and Soviet soldiers congratulate each other on the fall of Nazi Germany.

> There was a mad scene of jubilation on the east and west banks of the Elbe at Torgau as infantrymen of Lieutenant General Courtney H. Hodges . . . swapped K rations for a vodka with soldiers of Marshal Kornian's Ukrainian Army, congratulating each other . . . on the linkup.
>
> Men of the 69th Division sat on the banks of the Elbe in warm sunshine today with no enemy in front of them or behind them and . . . watched their new Russian friends and listened to them as they played accordions and sang Russian songs.
>
> The Russian soldiers are the most carefree bunch . . . that ever came together in an army. They would best be described as exactly like Americans, only twice as much. . . . You get the feeling of exuberance, a great new world opening up.
>
> —Andy Rooney, "Good Soldiers Meet," *Stars & Stripes,* April 28, 1945

GUIDE TO READING

Main Idea

The United States and the Soviet Union emerged from World War II deeply distrustful of each other and with conflicting visions for the future.

Vocabulary

- containment
- cold war

Read to Find Out . . .

- the events that led to Soviet domination in Eastern Europe, the Truman Doctrine, and the Marshall Plan.
- how ideological differences between the Soviet Union and the United States fueled the cold war.

An Iron Curtain Falls

Soviets Break With Allied Nations

The possibility of the opening of that "great new world" evaporated quickly. The war left the United States and the Soviet Union as the world's dominant powers. Cautious allies during the struggle, the two nations emerged from the war with misgivings about one another. Each viewed the other with deep mistrust. Each had special interests to protect. Each carried the weight of its own history to the moment.

An Uneasy Alliance

During the war, Britain, the Soviet Union, the United States, and 23 other nations had joined forces as the Allied Powers. Having pooled their military might, the 26 set out to crush the Axis Powers in Europe and Asia.

The organization was a strong, but uneasy, alliance. Among its members were nations with old hatreds and misunderstandings of one another, bound together by a common enemy. At the heart of the alliance stood the United States and the Soviet Union.

While the Soviets praised the courage of American soldiers and the leadership of President Roosevelt, old hostilities simmered beneath the surface. The Soviets resented that American troops, along with British and French forces, had tried to undo their revolution of 1917. When that attempt failed, the United States still refused to recognize the Soviet government until 1933. Furthermore, Soviet propaganda stirred up popular fears of American capitalism with its divisions between rich and poor and its swings between prosperity and depression.

The Allies' delay in launching a second front also made Stalin suspicious. He had counted on an invasion of France in 1942 to divert German forces from his country. The United States and Britain delayed the attack for two years, making Stalin think that the Americans secretly wanted a weakened Soviet Union.

Americans also harbored fears of the Soviet Union. Communism, with its emphasis on world revolution, had always frightened Americans. Furthermore, past Soviet agreements with Germany rankled Americans. In 1918 the Soviets struck a separate peace with Germany, forcing the West to fight Germany without Soviet help. In 1939 Stalin signed a short-lived nonaggression pact with Hitler. Adding to American fears were memories of Stalin's bloody attacks on his internal enemies in the 1930s.

During the war Roosevelt struggled to keep the Allies focused on military issues—the common problem—and off the areas of disagreement. As the war came to an end, the United States and the Soviet Union faced their greatest challenge.

EASTFOTO

Victory in Europe After World War II, victory celebrations took place in both American and Soviet cities. *What effects of the war are evident in this picture?*

Two Views of the World

At the end of the war, the western Soviet Union was a scene of awful destruction. More than 20 million Soviets had died in the struggle. Ground fighting and air bombing had destroyed more than 4.7 million homes, nearly 2,000 towns, and 70,000 villages. Through the ruins wandered the hungry and homeless—25 million of them—seeking a place to settle.

Nothing was more important to Soviet leaders than protecting themselves from a rearmed Germany and rebuilding their shattered economy. One key to their security, they believed, was a permanently weakened Germany. Another was a ring of pro-Soviet nations protecting their western border. From Napoleon's attack on Moscow in 1812 through the German invasions of World Wars I and II, enemy armies had always swept in from the west.

Unlike the Soviets, the Americans emerged from the war more powerful than when they entered it. American deaths of 405,000 were tragic, but the number was small compared with the millions of Soviet dead. A booming American economy controlled nearly 50 percent of the world's wealth, and most Americans felt proud of their successful fight for democracy.

American leaders envisioned a future of international peace and prosperity. They imagined a world patterned after the United States—democratic, open to business expansion and free trade. In this world free nations would solve their differences by talking, not by fighting. Like the Puritans and the believers in Manifest Destiny before them, many Americans felt they had a mission: to build a free world with the United States leading the way.

Turning Point at Yalta

Soviets Take Power in Eastern Europe

In February 1945, near the end of the war, the Big Three—Roosevelt, Churchill, and Stalin—met in the Soviet city of Yalta to work out control of the postwar world. The three men and their advisers arrived at a moment when victorious Soviet armies were sweeping across Eastern Europe.

Each leader brought his own concerns to the table. Churchill hoped to save the British Empire; Stalin intended to protect his borders and rebuild his country. Unlike Churchill and Stalin, who believed in great powers controlling spheres of influence, Roosevelt sought the worldwide spread of democracy and free trade. The American President, however, also needed Soviet aid in the war against Japan. All agreed, ultimately, that working out these interests together was the only path to peace.

Every day for a week, the Big Three met in the ballroom of the former czar's palace along the Black Sea. They talked, debated, and compromised.

The meeting at Yalta marked a high point of cooperation among the Big Three. It also became a turning point in the relationship between the major powers, and in many ways it determined the form the postwar world would take.

Big Three Agreements

Many key agreements came out of the Yalta talks. Much to Roosevelt's relief, Stalin agreed to join the fight against Japan "two or three" months after Germany surrendered. In return, Stalin would receive territories in Asia. Stalin also pledged Soviet support for the United Nations (UN), an international body that would be formed to help keep world peace.

Agreement broke down over Germany and Eastern Europe. Even though all three leaders feared a rearmed Germany, they disagreed on how to keep Germany under control. Stalin wanted to punish Germany by demanding $20 billion in war payments. Half of the money would go to the Soviet Union to help rebuild its shattered economy. Roosevelt and Churchill knew that Germany could not afford the payments without their help; they feared having to support Germany so it could pay Stalin.

Rather than debate the issue, the three agreed that each nation would control the part of Germany its troops held at the end of the war. Later a commission would solve the problem of war payments.

NATIONAL ARCHIVES

The Big Three Meet **At Yalta, Churchill, Roosevelt, and Stalin reached a number of historic agreements.** *Which of these agreements affected the future of Germany?*

Control in Eastern Europe

Eastern Europe and Poland were even touchier issues. Stalin demanded recognition of Soviet power in Poland, Romania, Bulgaria, Austria, Hungary, and Czechoslovakia to protect his western border. Soviet forces already occupied much of Eastern Europe, and Stalin had installed a government in Poland. Roosevelt and Churchill protested strongly. Britain went to war "so that Poland should be free," Churchill exclaimed.

In the end, however, Roosevelt and Churchill had little choice but to give in. With the Pacific war still raging, they had no means of forcing Stalin to back down. Reluctantly they agreed to Soviet influence in Eastern Europe but insisted that Stalin hold "free and unfettered elections" at an "early date."

In the weeks after the conference at Yalta, Roosevelt worried as the Soviets installed Communist governments in country after country. Still, he had faith in his ability to win Stalin's trust of the West. Newly elected to a fourth term, Roosevelt believed he could persuade Stalin that the Soviets had nothing to fear and could relax their iron grip on Eastern Europe. Any such hopes were dashed, however, when Roosevelt died suddenly on April 12, 1945.

Truman Comes to Power

Truman Gets Tough With Stalin

"I don't know whether you fellows ever had a load of hay or a bull fall on you, but last night the moon, stars, and all the planets fell on me." Harry S Truman could well feel overwhelmed on his first day as President—April 13, 1945. Nations were still battling, and the world had reached a turning point in its history: The old system of

At the close of World War II, the political map of Europe underwent massive changes. *Which European nations fell under the control of the Soviet Union at the end of the war?*

power was crumbling and a new, unknown system remained to be built.

Truman stepped into the presidency unprepared. Raised in a small Missouri town with little chance for an education, the gritty, intelligent Truman worked his way up from the farm to business and finally to the United States Senate. Nominated as Roosevelt's running mate in 1944, he spent only 12 weeks as Vice President before Roosevelt's death.

During those 83 days, Truman got little information from Roosevelt. The President shared no details of key military or foreign policies with him, and Truman received only two short foreign relations briefings. According to Roosevelt's key adviser, Harry Hopkins, Truman himself knew "absolutely nothing of world affairs." Yet only 10 days after Truman assumed the presidency, international events took center stage.

Formation of the United Nations

At Yalta, the Big Three had agreed in principle to an international peacekeeping organization. On April 25, 1945, 50 countries met in San Francisco to draft the charter for the United Nations. United States support was voiced in Truman's address to the conference: "We must build a new world, a far better world—one in which the eternal dignity of man is respected."

The first article of the charter stated that the purpose of the United Nations was to maintain international peace and security. By October 1945, a majority of the participating nations had ratified the charter, and the United Nations officially came into existence.

The United States hoped that the United Nations would help to bring about a world in which every country would be free to run its own government. The Soviet Union—and to a lesser extent Great Britain—believed, however, that self-determination applied only to those countries that did not have strategic value to Soviet, or British, interests. In particular, the Soviets were determined to control Eastern Europe as a protection against future aggression from the West.

Truman's advisers urged him to get tough with the Soviets, and Truman exhibited his hard-line approach during the visit of Soviet ambassador V.M. Molotov. Truman sharply criticized Molotov for failing to support the Yalta agreements. Specifically, Truman demanded to know why the Soviets had not held free elections in Poland.

Accustomed to Roosevelt's friendly, patient style, Molotov was shaken. "I have never been talked to like that in my life," he reportedly said to Truman.

"Carry out your agreements and you won't get talked to like that," Truman snapped.

Meetings at Potsdam

In this mood of growing hostility, Truman, Stalin, and Churchill met in Potsdam, a suburb of Berlin, in July 1945. Germany had surrendered in May, but the fight with Japan wore on. At this final wartime meeting, the three leaders tried to tie up some loose ends from Yalta, especially the future of Germany.

Truman and Stalin were meeting for the first time, and Truman was determined to be hard-nosed. A few days into the sessions, the already determined Truman learned that American scientists had successfully exploded the atomic bomb. He kept the news to himself, but it was soon clear that something had happened. Churchill recalled, "When he [Truman] got to the meeting after having read the report he was a changed man. He told the Russians just where they got off and generally bossed the whole meeting."

In spite of Truman's attitude, the three leaders reached agreement on Germany. The country would be completely disarmed and its war industries dismantled. Each occupying nation would be allowed to take war payments from its zone.

With this decision the three leaders began moving down the path to a divided Germany. The western half of Germany would remain under British, French, and United States control. The eastern half would stay in Soviet hands. The capital city of Berlin, 110 miles (177 km) deep in the Soviet zone, would also be carved up among the four nations.

All too quickly the world was dividing into two camps. The United States dominated one. The Soviet Union dominated the other.

The Idea of Containment

Over the next seven months, Truman's and Stalin's mistrust of one another grew. Stalin continued to oppress most of Eastern Europe, forcing loyalty to the Soviet Union through phony trials and executions. In the Middle East, Stalin kept his troops in Iran long after United States and British troops had pulled out. Iran complained before the United Nations, and Truman protested as well. In early 1946 the United States gave Britain a $3.5 billion loan but ignored a Soviet request for help.

On February 9, 1946, Stalin added to the growing tension with an important speech in which he declared that capitalism was a danger to world peace. Capitalism and communism, he said, would eventually clash. Because of that danger, he would protect Soviet security by stopping trade with the West and developing modern weaponry no matter how high the cost. In the United States, Supreme Court Justice William Douglas said the speech sounded like "a declaration of World War III."

Truman then received a momentous 16-page telegram from George Kennan, a brilliant young diplomat at the American embassy in Moscow. An expert in Soviet history and culture, Kennan advised Truman that the United States needed to pursue "long-term, patient, but firm and vigilant containment of Russian expansive tendencies." **Containment**—the restriction of communism to its current borders—was the only way to secure the peace.

A few weeks later, in March 1946, Winston Churchill supported this view in a famous speech at Westminster College in Fulton, Missouri. Somberly he warned that "from Stettin in the Baltic to Trieste in the Adriatic, an

★ ★ ★ Gallery of Presidents ★ ★ ★

Harry S Truman

1945–1953

"The American people desire, and are determined to work for, a world in which all nations and all peoples are free to govern themselves as they see fit. . . . Democracy alone can supply the vitalizing force to stir the peoples of the world into triumphant action, not only against their human oppressors, but also against their ancient enemies—hunger, misery, and despair."

Inaugural Address, January 20, 1949

THE HARRY S TRUMAN LIBRARY

Background

- **Born 1884; Died 1972**
- **Democrat, Missouri**
- **Served in the Senate 1935–1944**
- **Elected Vice President 1944**
- **Assumed presidency 1945**
- **Elected to full term 1948**

Achievements in Office

- **United Nations founded (1945)**
- **Marshall Plan (1947)**
- **North Atlantic Treaty Organization (1949)**

iron curtain has descended across the continent." Furthermore, Churchill warned, English-speaking people should join forces against the Soviet threat. "There is nothing the Communists admire so much as strength and nothing for which they have less respect than for military weakness."

Cold War Is Declared

Foreign Aid Blocks Communism

Churchill's speech gave the world a clear picture of the future: The West, led by the United States, would resist any Soviet attempts to expand its influence in the world. The **cold war** had begun—a United States–Soviet conflict in which the two powers would avoid fighting each other directly but would block each other's goals around the world.

The Truman Doctrine

In February 1947, the British gave the United States a chance to put containment to work. Nearly bankrupt at the end of the war, the British asked the United States government to take over support of the Greek and Turkish governments. The Soviet Union was trying to force the Turks to share control of a key shipping channel between the Black Sea and the Mediterranean. In Greece the government was fighting Communist rebels, although the Soviet Union was not directly involved.

Truman talked to his advisers, who convinced him that the United States had to act. Otherwise, they believed, the Communists might succeed, and that would "open three continents to Soviet penetration."

Truman agreed but knew he had to convince a Congress that wanted to reduce taxes—not raise them. He would have to "scare the American people" and Congress into supporting the plan.

UPI/BETTMANN

Iron Curtain Speech Winston Churchill speaks at Westminster College. *What was Churchill's famous speech about?*

On March 12, 1947, Truman called a joint session of Congress. In his speech he grimly pictured a threatening world:

> At the present moment, nearly every nation must choose between alternative ways of life. The choice is too often not a free one.
>
> One way of life is based upon the will of the majority and is distinguished by free institutions, representative government, free elections, guarantees of individual liberty, freedom of speech and religion, and freedom from political oppression.
>
> The second way of life is based upon the will of a minority forcibly imposed upon the majority. It relies

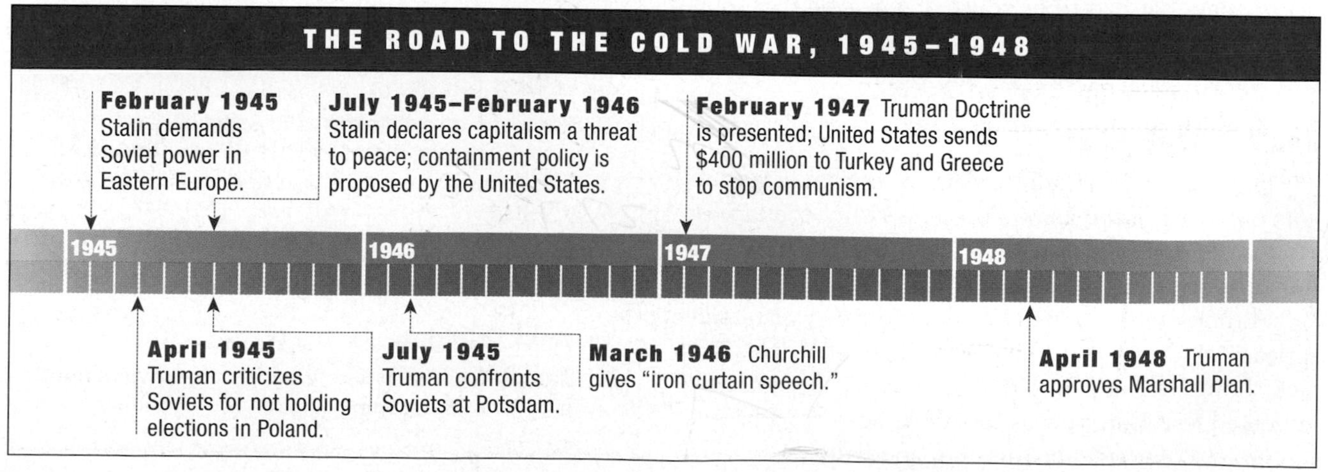

THE ROAD TO THE COLD WAR, 1945–1948
February 1945 Stalin demands Soviet power in Eastern Europe.
July 1945–February 1946 Stalin declares capitalism a threat to peace; containment policy is proposed by the United States.
February 1947 Truman Doctrine is presented; United States sends $400 million to Turkey and Greece to stop communism.
1945
1946
1947
1948
April 1945 Truman criticizes Soviets for not holding elections in Poland.
July 1945 Truman confronts Soviets at Potsdam.
March 1946 Churchill gives "iron curtain speech."
April 1948 Truman approves Marshall Plan.

sève nouvelle
vie meilleure
coopération inter-européenne
GEORGE C. MARSHALL FOUNDATION

Marshall Plan **A poster urges European cooperation with the Marshall Plan, which is seen as an opportunity for new growth and new life.** *How did nations qualify for Marshall Plan aid?*

upon terror and oppression, a controlled press and radio, fixed elections, and the suppression of personal freedoms.

—Harry S Truman, Speech to Joint Session of Congress, March 12, 1947

Truman went on to state that the United States must help all free people who were "resisting attempted subjugation by armed minorities or outside pressures." Then he asked for $400 million in military and economic aid to support the Greek and Turkish governments. Although many observers felt that Truman painted too harsh a picture, his dramatic appeal worked. Congress approved the request about one month later.

The so-called Truman Doctrine defined United States foreign policy for the next 20 years. Most Americans now saw communism as a worldwide threat to democracy that had to be resisted. The cold war soon became not just a struggle for territory but a fight between two opposing views of the world.

The Marshall Plan

Truman and his advisers knew that military aid was only part of the answer. In June 1947, Secretary of State George Marshall suggested another way to bolster freedom—a plan for helping Europe rebuild.

Although the war had been over for two years, Europeans still struggled to survive. Millions of people were sick, homeless, and hungry. In May 1947, Churchill lamented that Europe was "a rubble heap . . . a breeding ground of pestilence [disease] and hate."

Conditions like these were not only heartbreaking but also dangerous. Such terrible suffering provided ideal conditions for communism to grow, and already Communist parties were gathering strength in France and Italy. A ruined, starving Europe would drain the American economy—and American businesses desperately depended on European markets.

Marshall's plan involved spending billions of dollars to help put Europe, including the USSR, back on its feet. To qualify for the aid, nations had to agree to spend the dollars on American goods. At first many conservatives in Congress disagreed with the plan, but events in Eastern Europe soon changed their minds. The Soviets rejected the plan, criticizing it as the United States's way of taking over Europe. In February 1948, the Communist party seized control of Czechoslovakia, completing the Soviet domination of Eastern Europe.

Two months later Truman approved Congress's bill for $17 billion in aid to Europe over 5 years. Sixteen nations participated in the plan, and by 1952 it was more successful than anyone had dreamed. The Communist party in Western Europe was severely weakened. Western European industries had increased their output by 64 percent, and the prosperity of the United States was ensured. At the same time, however, tensions with the Soviet Union continued to grow.

Section Assessment

Main Idea

1. Use a diagram like this one to show how differing world views paved the way for a cold war between the United States and Soviet Union.

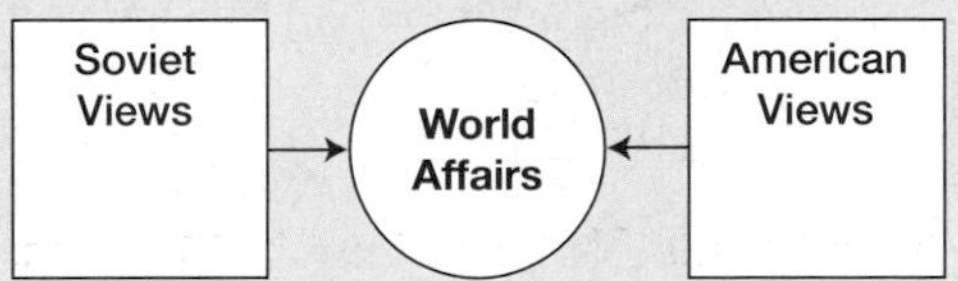

Vocabulary

2. Define: containment, cold war.

Checking Facts

3. What was the toll taken in Russian life and property during World War II? Which six Eastern European nations did Stalin demand control over at Yalta?

4. Describe the commitment of the United States to rebuild Europe as part of the Marshall Plan.

Critical Thinking

5. **Making Comparisons** Why did the Soviets prefer Roosevelt's style of diplomacy to Truman's?

The Cold War Deepens

JUNE 1948: UNITED STATES AIR FORCE HEADS FOR BERLIN

ON A LAZY SATURDAY MORNING IN 1948, LIEUTENANT COLONEL GUY B. DUNN, JR., HEADED FOR A GOLF GAME NEAR BROOKLEY AIR FORCE BASE IN ALABAMA. Before he could get to the course, though, Colonel George S. Cassidy told him they had to get to work—fast. They had to organize 12 aircraft, 3 crews per aircraft, and 62 maintenance people to start a squadron of planes. Their destination—Berlin.

UPI/BETTMAN

Berlin Airlift
Young Berliners are glad to see cargo planes arrive with much-needed supplies.

Dunn and his group got under way quickly. Once airborne and droning over the Atlantic, Dunn's colleague Lieutenant Colonel Jim Haun got on the radio. From the air he organized the rest of the squadron, calling on crews from Travis Air Force Base in California and Great Falls Air Force Base in Montana.

The 12 planes heading to Berlin were cargo planes on a mission of mercy—not bombers. Just two weeks later, though, Truman ordered 60 B-29 bombers—the "atomic bombers"—to bases in Great Britain. There they would be within easy striking range of Moscow.

Berlin Crisis

Soviets in Germany

Not since the cold war began had the United States and the Soviet Union inched so close to war. Threatening speeches and hostile policies had deepened the two countries' fear of each other. Now they had a powder keg on their hands—Berlin.

Since the end of the war, Soviet and American plans for Germany had put the two nations on a collision course. The United States wanted a strong Germany to promote the recovery of Western Europe and to help contain communism. The Soviets demanded a powerless Germany that could never attack the Soviet Union again.

GUIDE TO READING

Main Idea

Both the Soviets and Chinese Communists tested the United States policy of containment, triggering a dangerous arms race and the Korean War.

Vocabulary

- land reform
- arms race
- limited war

Read to Find Out . . .

- the causes of the Berlin blockade and the Communist takeover of China and the effect of each event on United States foreign policy.
- how the Korean War strengthened the powers of the presidency and the United States military.

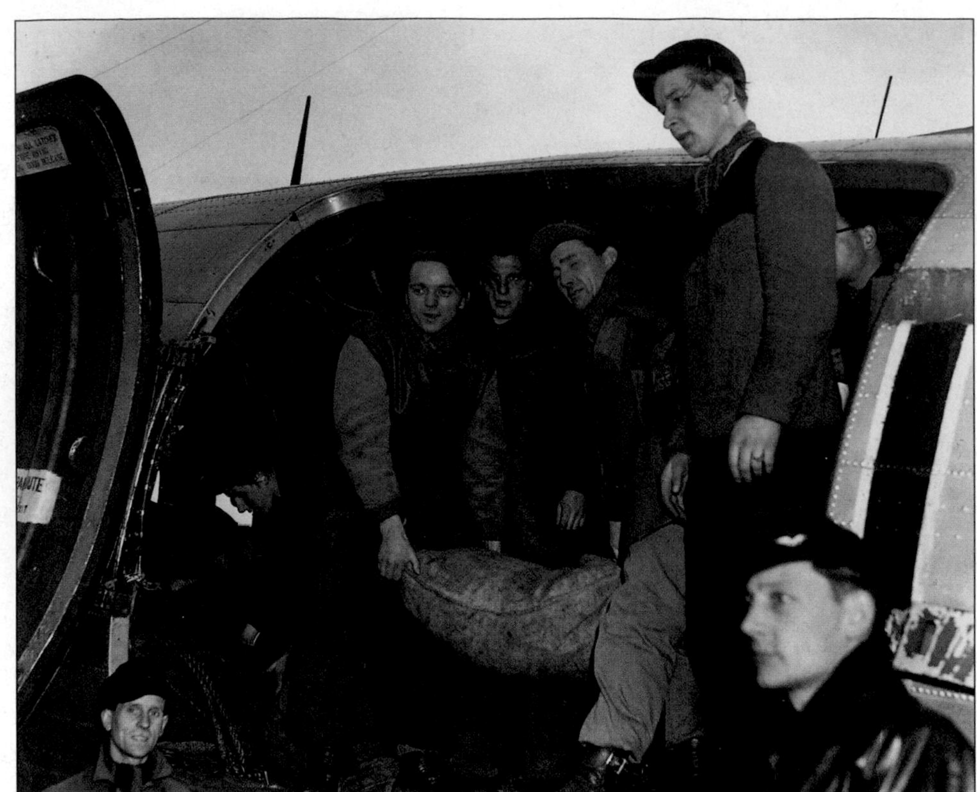

UPI/BETTMANN NEWSPHOTOS

Help Arrives This plane carries the first shipment of coal to Berlin. *Why did Truman choose an airlift rather than troops to open the roads to Berlin?*

Unable to find a common solution, the two powers pursued their own aims in the zones of Germany and Berlin that they controlled. The United States, Britain, and France hammered out plans to rebuild the three western zones, tie their economies to the rest of Europe, and lay the groundwork for a free West German state. The Soviets viewed these plans with growing anger and alarm.

On June 18, 1948, tensions reached a breaking point when the United States, Britain, and France announced a new currency for the three western zones and West Berlin. Outraged, the Soviet government angrily reminded the Western powers that at Potsdam they had agreed to treat Germany as one country. The Soviets warned them to scrap their currency plan or accept a Soviet currency system for the eastern zone and *all* of Berlin.

Over the next three days, tempers flared. Western leaders reminded the Soviets they had no authority in West Berlin. The Soviets insisted that Berlin was part of their territory. At meetings on June 22, the powers searched for a compromise but gave up at 10:00 P.M.

Showdown in Berlin

The next morning, Soviet leaders declared that their currency would start circulating the following day. It would be the official currency in the Soviet zone and all four zones of Berlin. Soviet troops then blockaded the highways and railroads crossing the eastern zone to West Berlin and shut off electric power in West Berlin.

Suddenly 2 million West Berliners found themselves sealed off from the outside world, with no way to import food and fuel. By isolating West Berlin, Stalin hoped to force the Allies into giving up their plans for West Germany or surrendering Berlin to the Communists.

Truman seemed to have two choices—order American troops to open Berlin and risk World War III, or surrender Berlin to Stalin. His advisers, however, had another idea. After Truman heard it, he declared, "We are going to stay—period."

Taking advantage of a 1945 agreement to keep three air corridors open to Berlin, Truman launched an airlift. He ordered more than 50 C-54 and 80 C-47 cargo planes, all war-weary and in need of repair, to fly everything from milk, potatoes, blankets, and coal to clothing and vitamins into West Berlin's Tempelhof and Gatow airports.

Student Web Activity 17

Visit the *American Odyssey* Web site at americanodyssey.glencoe.com and click on ***Chapter 17—Student Web Activities*** for an activity relating to the cold war.

Airlift Saves Berlin

For 11 months American and British pilots worked to exhaustion. At first they landed every 3 minutes, carrying in 2,400 pounds (1,089.6 kg) of supplies a day. At the peak of the airlift, the planes set down on makeshift runways every 45 seconds, day and night. Feverishly, crews unloaded some 13,000 tons (11,791 t) of supplies a day. The effort—some 277,000 flights delivering 2 million tons (1.8 million t) of supplies—melted wartime hatred between the Americans and Germans.

Before long West Berliners by the hundreds were traveling out to Tempelhof to thank the pilots. They brought whatever gifts they had—flowers, hand-knitted sweaters, treasured family heirlooms. "An old man, so thin you could see through him, showed up with a watch that would have fed him for months on the black market," recalled the American public affairs officer. "He insisted on giving it to an American. He called it 'a little token from an old and grateful heart.' "

The blockade was a complete disaster for Stalin. World opinion turned against the Soviet Union and its tactic of starving innocent people to achieve its ends. The United States, however, emerged a resourceful hero, and Berlin quickly became a symbol of America's fight against communism.

In May 1949, Stalin lifted the blockade, but the strong West Germany he had tried to prevent now became a reality. Late in May the United States, Britain, and France agreed to form the Federal Republic of Germany, sealing tight the once loose border between the eastern and western zones. In October 1949, Stalin countered by declaring the German Democratic Republic of Eastern Germany. With those decisions Europe lay divided in half, and the Allied Powers saw that a new alliance was needed.

Allies Form NATO

The Berlin blockade convinced the Allies that Western Europe needed military as well as economic support to remain free. In April 1949, a month before Stalin lifted the blockade, the United States, Canada, and 10 European nations formed the North Atlantic Treaty Organization (NATO). Not since the Revolutionary War had the United States joined a military alliance with Europe.

In Truman's mind, NATO would work like a "tripwire." If the Soviet Union dared to invade Western Europe, it would "trip the wire" and set off an American military response. Said Truman, "An armed attack against one or more [nations] in Europe or North America shall be considered an attack against them all." NATO knit Western Europe together as a force and discouraged individual countries from staying uncommitted to the rest.

Truman also persuaded Congress to spend $1.5 billion for military aid to NATO countries, beginning a military buildup in the United States. A few years later, in 1955, the Soviet Union matched NATO with the Warsaw Pact, a Soviet–Eastern Europe alliance planted squarely across the iron curtain.

The Cold War in Asia

Changes Rock the Far East

While the cold war unfolded in Europe, massive changes rocked the Far East. Throughout Asia, British, French, and Dutch colonies began demanding their

In 1955 NATO and the Warsaw Pact divided Europe into two sections as shown. *What correlation existed between NATO members and participants in the Marshall Plan?*

EASTFOTO

Mao Inspects the Red Army **Mao Zedong reviews his troops as they prepare to march behind enemy lines.** *Why did Chinese Communist and Nationalist forces unite during World War II?*

freedom. Stretched thin by the job of rebuilding at home, the European powers had little choice but to give in. In 1947 Britain granted freedom to India and to Pakistan—which later split into Pakistan and Bangladesh—and in 1949 the Dutch gave up control of Indonesia.

Civil War in China

At the end of World War II, revolution was also raging in China, one of the key allies of the United States. There, Jiang Jieshi (Chiang Kai-shek), leader of the Nationalist government, was fighting a civil war with Mao Zedong (Mao Tse-tung), leader of the Communist forces.

To most Americans, Jiang's success seemed essential to world peace. They believed a strong anti-Communist government in China, the most populous country in the world, would block Soviet expansion and give the United States an important trading partner. Mao's success, many feared, could open Asia to Soviet control.

Yet this view of China was too simple. For one thing, Americans did not understand the Soviets' mistrust of Mao. A brilliant leader, Mao described himself as part tiger and part monkey—part ruthless and part clever. Stalin did not trust Mao or his brand of communism, saying once that "the Chinese Communists are not really Communists. They are 'margarine' Communists." A weak China, like a weak Germany, would have pleased Stalin more. Likewise, Americans failed to understand a major cause of the Chinese civil war—the oppression by a landlord class of millions of peasant farmers.

In the early 1910s, the Nationalist party swept into power, promising to rid China of foreign powers and to institute **land reform**—redistribution of property to the land-hungry peasants. Once in power, however, the Nationalists ignored the needs of the peasants and put up with corruption at all levels of government. Furthermore, Jiang forced the Communists who helped put him in power out of the government. By the late 1920s, the Communists and the Nationalists were locked in battle.

When the Japanese invaded China in 1937, the Nationalists and the Communists joined forces to defeat the Japanese. As the fighting wore on, however, the fortunes of the Nationalists and the Communists changed dramatically.

Within a year Japanese forces crushed the Nationalist armies and conquered China's coast and river valleys—the industrial and farming heart of the country. With this defeat, the Nationalists lost much of their military strength and their power base.

By contrast, the Communists took advantage of the war to expand their control in the countryside. Stepping in where the Japanese had destroyed normal life, the Communists set up governments and small police forces. They gave peasants their own plots of land. In time, more and more people felt Mao's Communists protected and took care of them.

By the end of World War II, Communist forces had grown from about 100,000 in 1937 to more than 900,000. As their shoestring army attracted more followers, they began to fight Jiang. Soon they welcomed deserters from Jiang's poorly fed, sickly army into their own ranks.

Truman Steps In

Late in 1945 Truman sent George Marshall to meet with Jiang and Mao and find a way for the two leaders to share control. The idea, however good, was doomed. Both Mao and Jiang wanted to control China alone.

At this point, Truman had to choose a side, and he chose Jiang's. To fuel the Nationalist cause, the United States sent more than $3 billion to help solve China's problems. In return Truman told Jiang to stop his friends from helping themselves to the treasury, to take care of his tattered army, and to answer the cry for land reforms by dividing the land more fairly among the people.

Jiang continued to ignore these problems, while Mao's forces began winning battles. By January 1949, Jiang's forces abandoned Beijing. In May Mao seized Shanghai; in October he took Guangzhou and declared the People's Republic of China. Jiang fled to the offshore island of Taiwan in December, and in the American view, 500 million Chinese were "lost" to communism.

The Response of the United States

To many Americans, Mao's victory represented a frightening failure of containment. The most populous nation on the earth had fallen into the enemy camp. "Who lost China?" many demanded to know.

Republican leaders blamed Truman and the State Department. They believed more military support would have stopped Mao.

Truman responded that China was not America's to lose. Jiang, Truman said, lost because he refused to solve his nation's problems. The United States already had expensive programs to pay for in Europe. A full-scale war in China would have been too costly.

Still, the failure of containment was disturbing. To anchor freedom in Asia, the National Security Council urged the President to support the remaining friendly nations in Asia. Jiang's government was one. Another was Bao Dai's regime in Vietnam.

The Arms Race Begins

As hard as the Truman administration tried to keep people calm, events in Berlin and China unnerved everybody—including Truman himself. In January 1950, he ordered a high-level study of the defenses of the United States. The outcome of that study—the top secret National Security Council Report NSC-68—suggested beginning a massive buildup of weapons to stay ahead of the Soviets. The subsequent competition between the United States and the Soviet Union for greater military strength became known as the **arms race.**

According to NSC-68, the Soviet Union should be considered an enemy with a "design for world domination." As the leader of the "free world," only the United States could be expected to lead the fight against Soviet expansion. That job, however, required a huge army and navy and the best weapons that money could buy. To pay for such a massive defense system would require more than three times the $13 billion defense budget.

Truman and his advisers agreed with the report, but they worried about persuading Congress and the public to support a huge increase in taxes. "We were sweating over it," said a State Department aide, "and then, thank God, Korea came along."

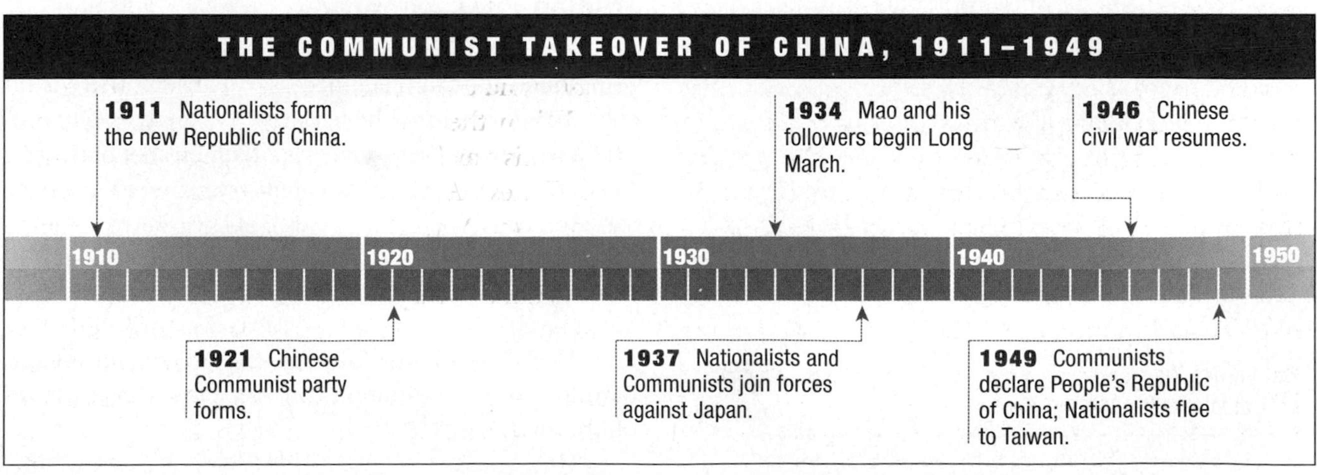

THE COMMUNIST TAKEOVER OF CHINA, 1911–1949
1911 Nationalists form the new Republic of China.
1934 Mao and his followers begin Long March.
1946 Chinese civil war resumes.
1910
1920
1930
1940
1950
1921 Chinese Communist party forms.
1937 Nationalists and Communists join forces against Japan.
1949 Communists declare People's Republic of China; Nationalists flee to Taiwan.

Hot War Flares in Korea

North Korean Communists Invade South

Korea, which had been brutally ruled by Japan since 1910, suffered a fate much like Germany's. At the end of World War II, the victors divided Korea at the 38th parallel, leaving a Communist government in the north and a pro-Western government in the south. Each government wanted to reunite Korea; however, it wanted to do so on its own terms. North Korea struck first.

On June 25, 1950, some 90,000 North Korean troops following Soviet-made tanks poured across the 38th parallel. In a matter of days, they overran the South Korean capital of Seoul. They "struck like a cobra," recalled General Douglas MacArthur.

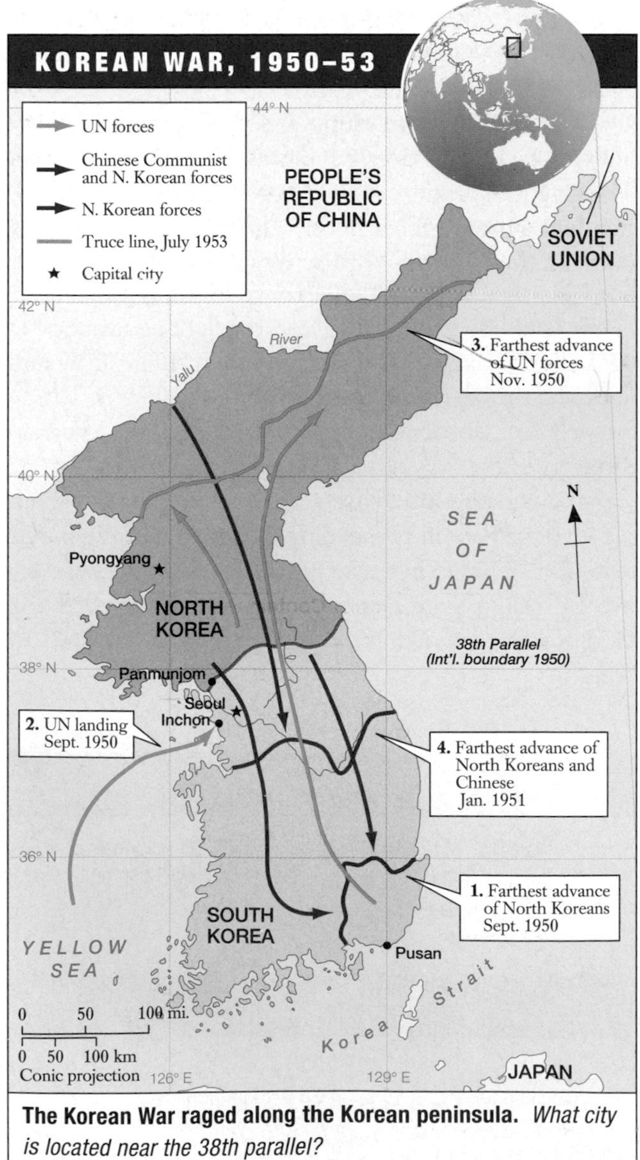

The Korean War raged along the Korean peninsula. *What city is located near the 38th parallel?*

Truman Responds

Truman saw the assault as a test of containment. On June 27, without seeking approval from Congress, he ordered air and naval forces to Korea. He then sought the help of the United Nations.

The Soviet delegate to the UN Security Council was not present to block Truman's request. He had walked out in protest of the council's refusal to seat a representative from Mao's China. The rest of the council condemned the Korean invasion and voted money to help South Korean, American, and supporting UN forces repel the attack.

By the summer the well-trained North Korean army had cornered poorly trained UN troops in the southeast around Pusan. UN air forces, led by American pilots, inflicted heavy damage on North Korean ground troops in a "scorched earth" campaign that destroyed thousands of villages and exacted a huge civilian toll. On September 15, MacArthur landed UN forces behind enemy lines at Inchon, a port city near Seoul. With some 18,000 marines and tanks, he freed Seoul and then drove the North Koreans back to the 38th parallel.

MacArthur smelled victory and persuaded Truman to let him attempt to unify Korea under Western control. By November MacArthur had pinned North Korean troops against the Chinese border at the Yalu River. Stubborn and overconfident, he ignored warnings from Mao to back off, bombed bridges crossing into China, and launched yet another attack to the north.

In late November, Mao sent Chinese soldiers streaming across the Yalu, taking MacArthur by surprise. Through the bitterly cold winter, Chinese forces drove UN troops back across the 38th parallel, recaptured Seoul, and inflicted terrible losses on UN units. The war slowed to a brutal stalemate, with soldiers on both sides fighting and dying over small, snow-covered hills.

Truman Fires MacArthur

MacArthur demanded permission to attack China, using nuclear weapons if necessary. "In war there is no substitute for victory," he insisted. "We are trying to prevent a world war—not start one," Truman shot back. The President made clear his intentions to seek a peace settlement.

MacArthur publicly criticized Truman's policy of **limited war**—containing the conflict to one area and avoiding the use of nuclear weapons. In April 1951, Truman fired MacArthur for insubordination and for undermining the Constitution's provision for civilian control of the military.

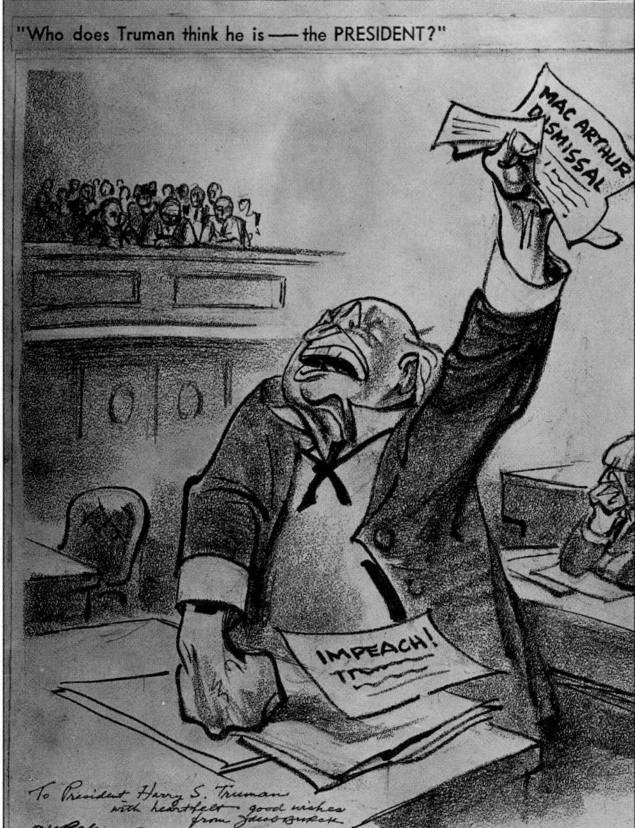

HARRY S TRUMAN LIBRARY

MacArthur Fired Truman's firing of General Douglas MacArthur was the beginning of a decline in the President's popularity. *Why was Truman criticized throughout his second term?*

President Truman's action ignited a storm of public fury. After all, Americans had just won a world war. Why not let MacArthur, a warrior and a hero, rid Asia of communism? Truman's popularity took a nosedive; only 31 percent of the public agreed with him, even though the Joint Chiefs of Staff had unanimously recommended MacArthur's dismissal. Returning home for the first time since World War II, MacArthur initially received widespread public support.

Many government officials supported Harry Truman, however. They knew that the United States could not afford to provoke the Soviet Union into open warfare. Nor could the United States expend all of its resources in Asia, leaving the continent of Europe unprotected. After a much-publicized United States Senate investigation of MacArthur's dismissal, popular support for his position declined sharply.

In July 1951, shortly after General MacArthur's firing, United Nations representatives and North Koreans met to begin peace talks. The fighting and the talks dragged on for two more years in a bloody stalemate. The peace talks were finally settled by the next President of the United States, Dwight D. Eisenhower.

The Korean War's Impact

Support Grows for a Stronger Military

The Korean War settled little. When the fighting ended in 1953, the official border was set at the cease-fire line, not far from where the fighting began. Korea continued to have a Communist regime in the north and a pro-Western government in the south. Still, the conflict had far-reaching effects.

First, the Korean War claimed more than 2 million civilian lives and left a legacy of bitterness lasting into the 2000s. Second, it convinced Americans to support a huge military buildup. Moving faster than NSC-68 suggested, Congress increased defense spending from $22.3 billion in 1951 to $50.4 billion in 1953. The United States emerged from the Korean War with an army of 3.5 million, overseas military bases, and powerful new weapons like the long-range B-52 bomber. Plus, the country now had a stockpile of 750 nuclear warheads, an increase of 600 in 2 years.

The public also supported Truman's decisive actions in Korea, overlooking the fact that he never sought a declaration of war from Congress. His independent action enhanced the power of the presidency and laid the basis for later undeclared wars.

Section Assessment

Main Idea

1. Use a chart like this one to show Communist challenges to containment and the United States response.

Policy of Containment	
Soviet Challenges	United States Response

Vocabulary

2. Define: land reform, arms race, limited war.

Checking Facts

3. What does the acronym NATO stand for? What was the name of NATO's Soviet counterpart?
4. Why did Truman fire General MacArthur?

Critical Thinking

5. **Drawing Conclusions** How might a Nationalist victory in the Chinese civil war have affected the outcome of the Korean conflict?

Cold War in the Atomic Age

AUGUST 1949: THE SOVIET UNION JOINS THE NUCLEAR CLUB

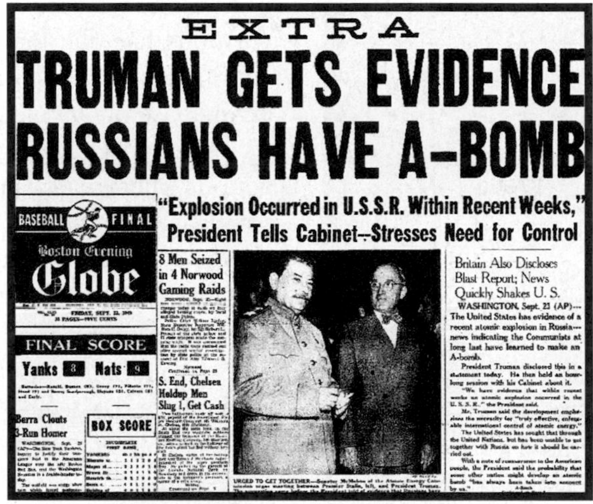

EXTRA

TRUMAN GETS EVIDENCE RUSSIANS HAVE A-BOMB

"Explosion Occurred in U.S.S.R. Within Recent Weeks," President Tells Cabinet—Stresses Need for Control

BASEBALL FINAL

Boston Evening Globe

FINAL SCORE

Yanks 8 Nats 9

Berra Clouts 3-Run Homer

BOX SCORE

8 Men Seized in 4 Norwood Gaming Raids

S. End, Chelsea Holdup Men Slug 1, Get Cash

Britain Also Discloses Blast Report; News Quickly Shakes U. S.

WASHINGTON, Sept. 23 (AP)—The United States has evidence of a recent atomic explosion in Russia—news indicating the Communists at long last have learned to make an A-bomb.

President Truman disclosed this in a statement today. He then held an hour-long session with his Cabinet about it.

"We have evidence that within recent weeks an atomic explosion occurred in the U. S. S. R.," the President said.

Mr. Truman said the development emphasizes the necessity for "truly effective, enforceable international control of atomic energy."

The United States has sought that through the United Nations, but has been unable to get together with Russia on how it should be carried out.

URGED TO GET TOGETHER—

THE BOSTON GLOBE

Atomic Scare

The world became a more frightening place for many Americans when they learned that the USSR had exploded an atomic bomb.

Thunder boomed ominously, and hail clattered down on the White House roof the morning of September 23, 1949. Just after 10:30 A.M., White House reporters finished a routine meeting with Charles Ross, President Harry S Truman's press secretary. On their way out, however, Ross's secretary, Myrtle Bergheim, told the reporters to stick around. She called them out of the nearby pressroom and back into Ross's office just seconds before 11:00 A.M. None of them knew what was coming, and none of them realized how perfectly the storm outside would fit the news.

As the last reporter filed in, Ross said, "Close the door. Nobody is leaving until everybody has this statement."

Ross handed each reporter a short statement by Truman. The first reporter to scan the copy gasped; in seconds the whole group tore out of Ross's office and down the hall for the pressroom phones. In the mad rush, somebody crashed into a stuffed deer head and broke off its nose.

When the presidential statement hit the papers, it stunned the nation. "We have evidence," Truman announced, "that within recent weeks an atomic explosion occurred in the USSR."

Guide to Reading

Main Idea

Soviet nuclear tests and the launching of a Soviet satellite made the arms race more deadly—and peace more imperative—than at any time in history.

Vocabulary

- massive retaliation
- brinksmanship
- military-industrial complex

Read to Find Out . . .

- how the Soviet atomic bomb affected United States society and the arms race.
- reasons for the policy of massive retaliation and how it helped spur the growth of a disarmament movement.
- how *Sputnik* brought far-reaching changes to the United States.

Living With Fear

Two Nuclear Powers

With this chilling announcement, the United States's sense of security went up in a cloud of smoke—a dark, fearsome mushroom-shaped cloud. The world now had two nuclear powers, and what happened to Hiroshima and Nagasaki could just as easily happen to New York or Chicago or Los Angeles.

Public Worry

When the atomic age burst into history at Hiroshima in 1945, Americans were shocked, confused, and terrified. Like children whistling in the dark, they also joked about the bomb. Stores had atomic sales, bars sold atomic cocktails, musicians wrote ballads and polkas about the bomb, but under the surface laughter ran a deep current of fear. Months passed before Americans got used to the idea of life with the bomb.

With Truman's announcement America's fears surged back to the surface. The media jumped on the story, both soothing the panic with helpful advice and intensifying fears with hair-raising descriptions. One radio show broadcast the following account of a make-believe nuclear attack on Chicago:

> Most of those in the center of the city were violently killed by the blast or by the following vacuum, which explosively burst their stomachs. . . . Those few who escaped the blast, but not the gamma rays, died slowly after they had left the ruined city. No attempt at identification of the bodies or burial ever took place. Chicago was simply closed.
>
> —NBC radio program, August 1949

To help calm the public's jangled nerves, Truman organized the Federal Civil Defense Administration (FCDA). Within months the agency flooded the country with posters and booklets telling people they *could* survive a nuclear war—if they were prepared.

How should Americans prepare? Best of all, they could build some kind of underground bomb shelter. A simple one could be a trench covered with dirt. They could also take shelter in the family car or a well-stocked basement protected with piles of dirt around the outside walls.

If a shelter was not handy when an attack came, people learned to "jump in any . . . ditch or gutter" and "bury their faces in their arms." Grade schools instructed children in these procedures. To keep from panicking during an attack, people were encouraged to use "little tricks to help steady their nerves—reciting jingles or the multiplication tables."

Once again, all of America seemed preoccupied with nuclear war. Real estate agents offered houses in "safe locations." Doctors and ministers took courses on coping with radiation injuries and panic. Entrepreneurs tried to sell every product they could dream up—burn medicine, ready-made bomb shelters, dog tags, even radiation-proof clothing for dad, mom, kids, and the dog.

The Game Gets Deadlier

Scary as nuclear bombs were, most Americans thought the best way to prevent nuclear war was to have more and better bombs than the Soviets. Truman agreed. In January 1950, after a heated debate with his advisers, the President ordered scientists to develop a deadly hydrogen bomb, a superbomb. By late 1952, the scientists were ready to test the first H-bomb–nicknamed Mike—on a coral island in the South Pacific.

No one who saw the explosion after the bomb was dropped ever forgot it. Out of a blast of white heat, 5

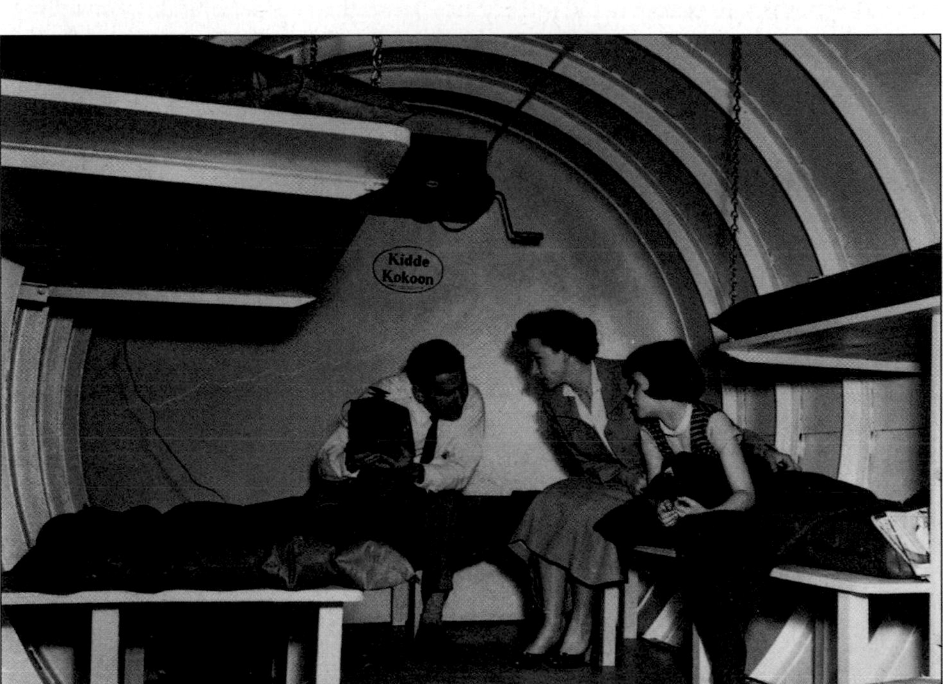

UPI/BETTMANN NEWSPHOTOS

Bomb Shelter Public fear of nuclear attack resulted in the building of backyard bomb shelters and numerous publications from the Federal Civil Defense Administration. *What caused Americans to become so fearful during the 1950s?*

times hotter than the center of the sun, billowed a monstrous mushroom-shaped cloud. Purple, gray, and yellow and nearly 100 miles (160.9 km) wide, it climbed 25 miles (40.2 km) into the sky. The blast carved a mile-long (1.6 km) crater in the bottom of the ocean and spilled radioactive dust over thousands of square miles. Nuclear scientists had let a terrible genie out of the bottle, and now there was no way to put it back.

Eisenhower Elected

A War Hero in the White House

Three days after the H-bomb Mike blew a coral island to smithereens, Republican Dwight D. Eisenhower won the 1952 presidential election. The World War II hero stepped into the White House at the height of the cold war. China had fallen. United States troops were bogged down in Korea. Growing stockpiles of atomic bombs had Americans on edge. In the midst of mounting danger, Ike seemed like the perfect leader.

Raised on the Kansas frontier and honed into a tough army officer by West Point and World War II, Eisenhower was both a seasoned soldier and a grandfather figure. He had an instinct for people, and his homespun charm won hearts instantly. Said one of Eisenhower's World War II compatriots: "He has the power of drawing the hearts of men towards him as a magnet attracts bits of metal. He merely has to smile at you, and you trust him at once." People, as the campaign buttons said, liked Ike.

Eisenhower in Korea

Americans found President Eisenhower's upbeat outlook and his practicality comforting in dangerous times. They also liked his determination to settle the Korean War.

Before the election in 1952, Eisenhower had accused the Democrats of "mishandling the war," and vowed that his first job as President would be "to bring the Korean war to an early and honorable end. If that job requires a personal trip to Korea," Eisenhower had declared, "I shall make that trip."

True to his word, three weeks after the election, Eisenhower toured the Korean front and confirmed his hunch that peace talks offered the only way out. "Small attacks on small hills would not end this war." Still, Eisenhower took time to review other ways of ending the war, including full-scale war against China and nuclear attacks on Korea. Finally, though, he decided to demand peace talks backed up by a veiled threat to use nuclear weapons.

AP/WIDE WORLD PHOTOS

The First Family **Mamie and Ike's eight years in the White House was the longest they had lived in one place.** *What qualities did Eisenhower project to Americans?*

The death of Joseph Stalin in March 1953 aided Eisenhower's search for peace. Communist leaders in China and North Korea could no longer be sure of Soviet help; nor could they be sure whether Eisenhower was bluffing or telling the truth about a nuclear attack. With little choice but to settle the fight, United Nations and Communist delegates finally signed an agreement in July 1953 dividing Korea into two parts at the truce line.

Eisenhower and Dulles

With the Korean War behind him, Eisenhower could focus on the cold war and the arms race. Like Truman, Eisenhower was a passionate anti-Communist. Unlike Truman, however, Eisenhower stepped into office with a solid grasp of world affairs. He had lived in Latin America, Europe, and Asia. As a World War II general and, later, the commander of NATO, he had mingled with heads of state. Even so, Eisenhower wanted a secretary of state who would hold the line on communism and advise him on areas like the Middle East and Asia.

John Foster Dulles fit the bill. A polished international attorney, Dulles had spent more than 40 years in foreign relations. The son of a Presbyterian minister, white-haired Dulles was also deeply religious and fiercely anti-Communist. Many Americans found Dulles humorless and argumentative. Churchill once said that Dulles was the only "bull he knew who carried his own china shop with him." Premier Nikita Khrushchev of the Soviet Union would later say of Dulles that he "knew how far he could push us and he never pushed us too far."

UPI/BETTMANN

John Foster Dulles Dulles speaks before the United Nations. *What policy did Eisenhower and Dulles propose to fight communism?*

A New Strategy

Cold War Questions

Together, Eisenhower and Dulles took a fresh look at the cold war game board. Problems and unknowns were everywhere. Who would replace Stalin in the Soviet Union? How long could the United States afford to build bigger armies and navies and bombs? Was containment the best defense against communism? How did nuclear weapons figure into all of this?

In May 1953, Eisenhower assigned three top-level groups to study the situation, while he worked with defense officials to cut military costs. Out of these studies emerged a new containment policy.

Massive Retaliation

Instead of depending on costly armies and navies to fight limited wars as Truman did, Eisenhower decided to rely on cheaper air power and nuclear weapons. This program, called the New Look, would retire 500,000 soldiers and 100,000 sailors but would increase the air force by 30,000 men. The new defense plan would save about $4 billion a year, thereby providing "a bigger bang for the buck."

Smaller armies and navies required a different way to fight communism, so Eisenhower and Dulles proposed a new policy. If the Soviet Union attacked any nation, the United States would launch **massive retaliation**—an instant nuclear attack "by means and at places of our own choosing." Such a vague threat, Eisenhower believed, would force the Communists to think twice before attacking because they could not be sure where the United States might strike.

Critics called this tough stance **brinkmanship**—the art of never backing down from a crisis, even if it meant pushing the nation to the brink of war. By keeping the Communists from testing every weak spot along their borders, the United States could stay out of small, limited wars that cost huge amounts of money.

To back up this tough stance, Eisenhower and Dulles also circled the Soviet Union and China with more American military bases and allies. By the end of the decade, Dulles had worked out mutual defense treaties with 43 countries around the globe.

★ ★ ★ **GALLERY OF PRESIDENTS** ★ ★ ★

Dwight David Eisenhower

1953–1961

"We must be ready to dare all for our country. For history does not long entrust the care of freedom to the weak or the timid. We must acquire proficiency in defense and display stamina in purpose. We must be willing, individually and as a Nation, to accept whatever sacrifices may be required of us. A people that values its privileges above its principles soon loses both."

Inaugural Address, January 20, 1953

THE BETTMAN ARCHIVE

BACKGROUND

- **Born 1890; Died 1969**
- **Republican, Kansas**
- **Graduated West Point 1915**
- **Commanding general of United States forces in Europe 1942**
- **Supreme commander of the Allied Expeditionary Force in Europe 1943**

ACHIEVEMENTS IN OFFICE

- **Southeast Asia Treaty Organization formed (1954)**
- **NASA formed (1958)**

Policy Dangers

The policy of massive retaliation had two dangerous results. First, it gave the United States only two extreme ways of responding to a Communist attack: either fight a nuclear battle or do nothing. The middle ground, using armies to fight small wars, virtually disappeared. The United States had to gamble on threats and Soviet insecurity to keep the peace.

Second, the Soviets did not sit idly by and let the United States sprint ahead in the arms race. Heavy spending by the United States for nuclear weapons spurred the Soviets to step up their own research, and in July 1953, they exploded an H-bomb in Siberia. "The U.S. and Soviet Union are like two scorpions in a bottle, each capable of killing the other but only at the risk of his own life," observed J. Robert Oppenheimer, father of the atomic bomb. The world had reached, in Churchill's words, a new "balance of terror."

UPI/BETTMANN

H-bomb Test A mushroom-shaped cloud from a nuclear test looms over the Marshall Islands in the fall of 1952. *What was the name of the biggest H-bomb the United States tested?*

Eisenhower Wages Peace

A Plan for Nuclear Disarmament

Eisenhower was a realist. He knew he had to be tough with the Soviets, so he kept the war machine working. Like Oppenheimer, he understood that nuclear war was pointless. From the early days of his presidency, Eisenhower searched for ways to disarm atomic weapons.

A few weeks after Stalin's death, Eisenhower made his famous "Chance for Peace" speech before a group of newspaper editors. "An era ended with the death of Joseph Stalin," Eisenhower said, inviting friendlier relations with the Soviet Union. He went on to spell out the high costs of cold war. "Every gun that is made, every warship launched, every rocket fired signifies . . . a theft from those who hunger and are not fed, those who are cold and not clothed." Eisenhower closed with an appeal for nuclear disarmament.

In December 1953, Eisenhower carried his appeal to the United Nations. There he proposed an "atoms for peace" plan in which Soviets and Americans would contribute radioactive materials to a stockpile for peaceful uses.

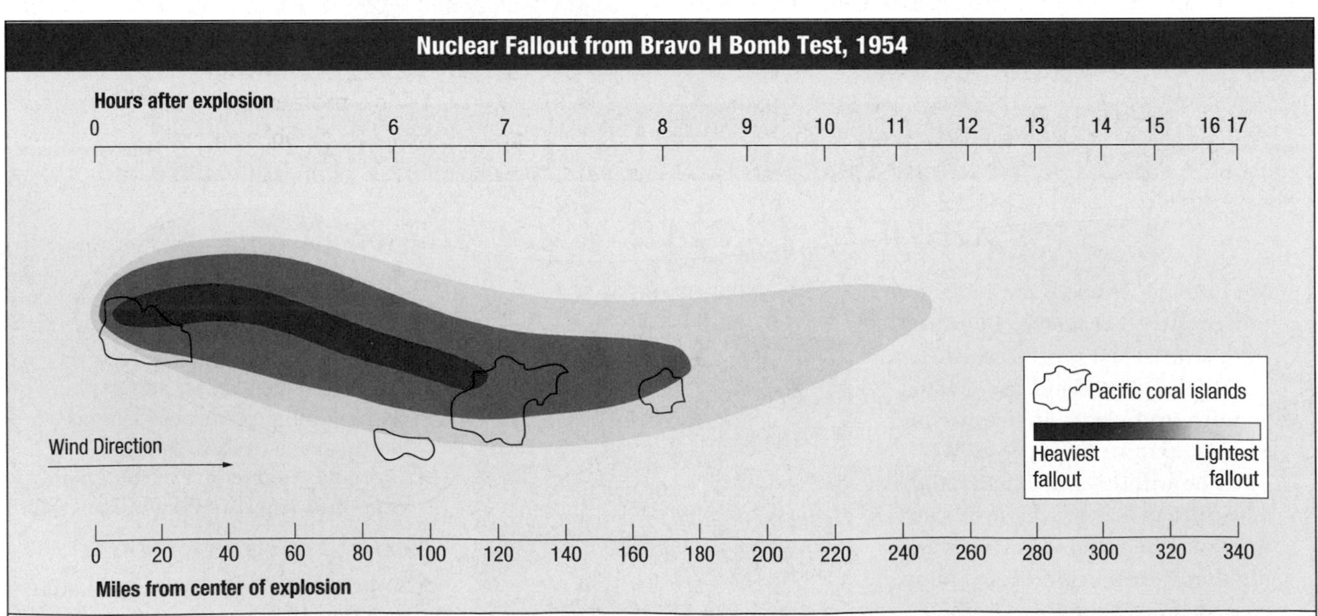

The radioactive fallout from Bravo affected 239 of the inhabitants of the Marshall Islands and 28 American service personnel. *How far did the heaviest fallout travel? The lightest fallout?*

Fallout Fears

As Eisenhower worked for peace, arms research continued. On March 1, 1954, the United States set off the biggest H-bomb it had ever tested—the equivalent of 15 million tons (13.6 million metric tons) of TNT, nicknamed Bravo.

The massive explosion in the South Pacific created a radioactive cloud that rained deadly silver ash on 7,000 square miles (18,130 sq km) of ocean waters and islands. Worst of all, radioactive ash fell on 23 Japanese fishers aboard the *Lucky Dragon,* some 80 miles (128.7 km) from the blast. By the time the fishers got back to Japan, all 23 were sick with radiation poisoning. A few months later, Aikichi Kuboyama, the radioman, died.

Suddenly people had something new to worry about—radioactive fallout. It was possible to live hundreds of miles from a nuclear blast and still be killed. Around the world, concern grew about nuclear tests and the effects of their deadly radioactive clouds.

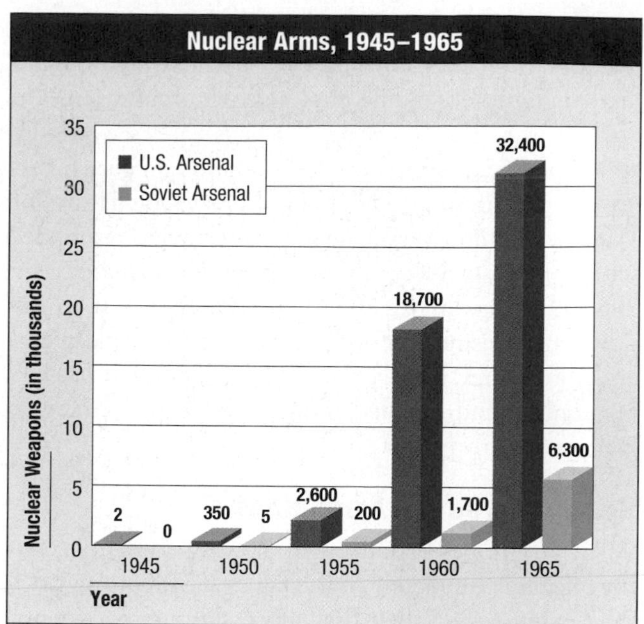

Nuclear Arms, 1945–1965
U.S. Arsenal
Soviet Arsenal
Nuclear Weapons (in thousands)
35
30
25
20
15
10
5
0
2
0
350
5
2,600
200
18,700
1,700
32,400
6,300
1945
1950
1955
1960
1965
Year

The arms race led to a dramatic rise in the number of nuclear warheads. *How does the number of Soviet warheads in 1960 compare with the number of American warheads that year?*

Talks in Geneva

By the autumn of 1954, international voices were clamoring for a halt to the arms race. Late that year Soviet and Western leaders finally agreed to meet the following summer—their first face-to-face talk since 1945.

Eisenhower flew to the meeting in Geneva, Switzerland, with high hopes of improving relations between the United States and the Soviet Union. The first few days of meetings went poorly, however. The Soviet leaders—Nikolay Bulganin and Nikita Khrushchev, the real power—"drank little and smiled much," Eisenhower commented. Their actions seemed unnatural, rehearsed.

After several days, Eisenhower decided to loosen things up. Speaking earnestly to the Soviet leaders, he proposed the "open skies" idea in which the two nations would inspect each other's military sites from the air. Bulganin agreed to think about the idea, but Khrushchev dismissed the plan as an obvious spying ploy. Ten years of bitter mistrust stood in the way of the idea, and in the end the Soviets let it die. Even so, the Geneva conference did end on an upbeat note—the powers had begun to talk again.

The Deep Freeze Returns

Soviet Power in Hungary

Through the rest of 1955 and into 1956, the cold war seemed to be thawing. The talks in Geneva had broken the ice, and back home Khrushchev made some astounding statements. In a momentous speech before the Party Congress in February 1956, he openly condemned Stalin's crimes against the Soviet people. Moreover, he

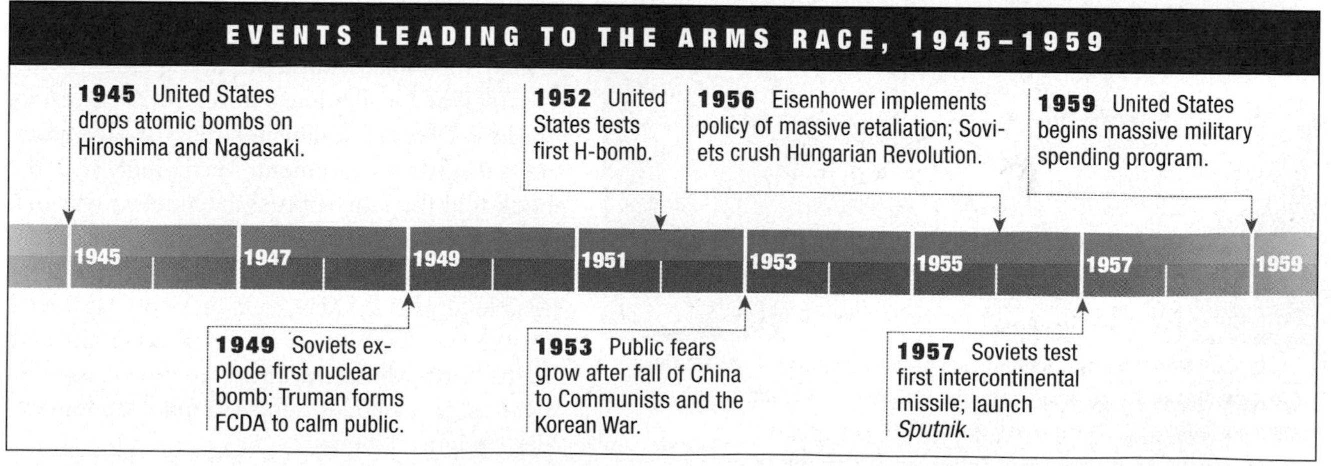

EVENTS LEADING TO THE ARMS RACE, 1945–1959
1945 United States drops atomic bombs on Hiroshima and Nagasaki.
1952 United States tests first H-bomb.
1956 Eisenhower implements policy of massive retaliation; Soviets crush Hungarian Revolution.
1959 United States begins massive military spending program.
1945
1947
1949
1951
1953
1955
1957
1959
1949 Soviets explode first nuclear bomb; Truman forms FCDA to calm public.
1953 Public fears grow after fall of China to Communists and the Korean War.
1957 Soviets test first intercontinental missile; launch *Sputnik*.

stated that Communists and capitalists might be able to live together peacefully and even declared that the Soviets might tolerate different kinds of communism.

All over Eastern Europe, Khrushchev's words inspired people to seek more freedom. In Hungary a new government announced that the country would leave the Warsaw Pact and remain neutral. The Soviets responded with force. On November 4, 1956, Khrushchev sent 200,000 troops and 2,500 tanks into Budapest to put down an uprising of poorly armed students and workers. Khrushchev, the "bare-knuckle slugger" who was taking control, had revealed another side. Clearly, the cold war was far from over.

Sputnik Fires the Arms Race

If any hopes remained of slowing the arms race, they fizzled completely in the fall of 1957. On August 1, the Soviets tested their first successful intercontinental missile, a long-range missile carrying a nuclear warhead. On October 4, the Soviets jolted Americans when they launched *Sputnik,* a 184-pound (83.5 kg) satellite, into orbit around the earth.

People read the news with awe and fear: the United States was running second in the survival race. Critics accused Eisenhower of "permitting a technological Pearl Harbor." A missile gap had developed, they cried, and now the United States was threatened by satellites they feared were capable of carrying weapons!

Sputnik shifted the arms race into high gear. Almost immediately Eisenhower increased the funding for missile development from $4.3 billion in 1958 to $5.3 billion in 1959. He launched the National Aeronautics and Space Administration (NASA), which worked feverishly to close the missile gap. With large new congressional appropriations, the Defense Department expanded the B-52 bomber fleet, built submarines outfitted with nuclear missiles, and installed a ring of short-range missiles in Europe.

To make sure the United States would not be caught short again, the government poured money into education to train scientists and engineers. Billions of dollars also went to universities; nearly one-third of all university scientists and engineers directed their energies to full-time weapons research. A powerful military-educational-industrial combination was taking shape.

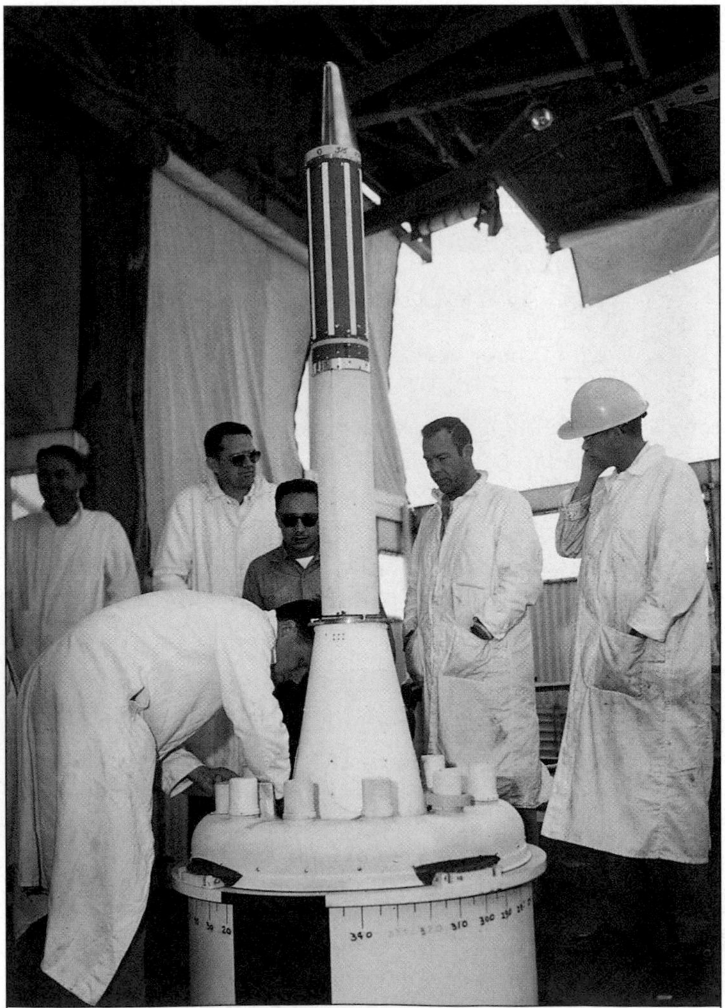

NASA

The Space Race Begins Technicians prepare *Explorer I*, the United States's first artificial earth satellite, for launch. *Why did Eisenhower increase funding for missile development?*

Protests Slow Testing

In spite of the Soviets' military achievements and the United States's headlong race to keep up, strong pressure was still building for arms control. The nuclear fallout scare of 1954 continued into 1955 when radioactive rain fell in Chicago. Scientists and doctors began to warn of fallout dangers like bone cancer and leukemia.

In 1957, the same year that *Sputnik* roared into orbit, a group of business, scientific, and publishing leaders established SANE, the Committee for a Sane Nuclear Policy. Within a year its membership grew to 25,000, and SANE began pressuring for change with powerful newspaper ads: "We must stop the contamination of the air, the milk children drink, the food we eat."

In 1957 Nevil Shute's novel *On the Beach* hit the best-seller list, adding its strength to the growing antinuclear movement. Terrifyingly real, the book told the story of massive nuclear war that destroyed the Northern Hemisphere and sent clouds of radioactive dust swirling into the Southern Hemisphere. There, millions of people talked, planned, worried, cried—and waited for the end. In the book, Moira Davidson, a young Australian woman, rages at her friend, submarine commander Dwight Towers:

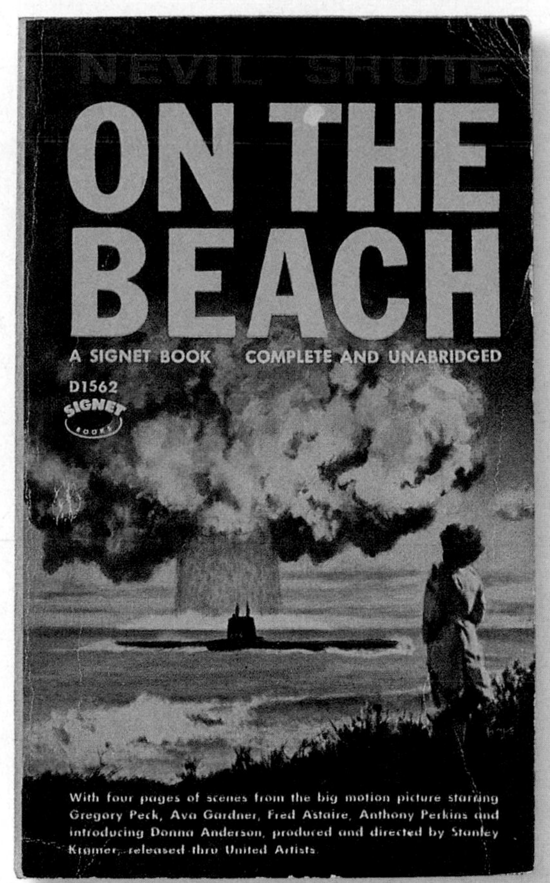

COURTESY, SIGNET BOOKS/PHOTO BY DOUG MINDELL

People Fear Nuclear Fallout **Nevil Shute's novel helped galvanize public opinion against nuclear testing.** *What percentage of Americans in 1957 wanted the United States to stop H-bomb testing?*

It's not fair. No one in the Southern Hemisphere ever dropped a bomb. . . . We had nothing to do with it. Why should we have to die because other countries nine or ten thousand miles away from us wanted to have a war? . . ."

There was a pause, and then she said angrily, "It's not that I'm afraid of dying, Dwight. We've all got to do that sometime. It's all the things I'm going to have to miss. . . . All my life I've wanted to see the Rue de Rivoli. I suppose it's the romantic name. It's silly, because I suppose it's just a street like any other street. But that's what I've wanted, and I'm never going to see it. Because there isn't any Paris now, or London, or New York."

—Nevil Shute, *On the Beach,* 1957

Forty newspapers serialized *On the Beach,* and eventually the book was made into a movie. The book contributed its weight to shifting public opinion. In 1957 a Gallup Poll found that 63 percent of Americans wanted the government to halt H-bomb tests.

The United States and the Soviet Union bowed to a growing world outcry and agreed to limit nuclear testing. In 1963 the two nuclear powers signed a test-ban treaty that banned nuclear tests in the atmosphere but permitted them underground and in outer space.

The Military-Industrial Threat

Changes in nuclear testing solved one problem, but the United States and the Soviet Union continued to invent and stockpile new doomsday weapons. In the process, a new threat was born in the United States—the vast, interwoven military establishment and arms industry. At the end of his presidency, Eisenhower alerted the nation to the danger of this **military-industrial complex.**

In the councils of government we must guard against the acquisition of unwarranted influence . . . by the military-industrial complex. The potential for the disastrous rise of misplaced power exists and will persist.

We must never let the weight of this combination endanger our liberties or democratic processes.

—President Dwight Eisenhower, Farewell Speech, 1961

Section Assessment

Main Idea

1. Use a diagram like this one to show ways in which the arms race became more deadly during the 1950s.

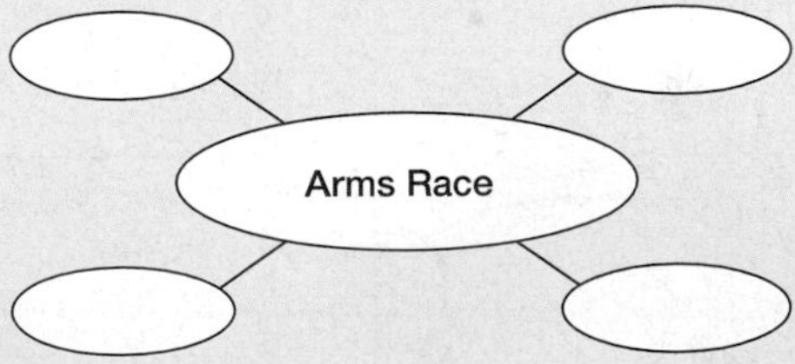

Vocabulary

2. Define: massive retaliation, brinkmanship, military-industrial complex.

Checking Facts

3. Why did Eisenhower appoint Dulles as his secretary of state?
4. What steps did the United States take to close the missile gap after the launching of *Sputnik*?

Critical Thinking

5. **Predicting Consequences** In 1961, Eisenhower predicted the rise of a military-industrial complex. What are some possible consequences of an alliance between industry and the military?

SPORTS: Brooklyn mourns loss of the team they love to hate: The Dodgers ("dem bums") head to L.A.

One Day in History

Friday, October 4, 1957

MARKET BASKET

Here is where a dollar will go:

8-oz. bottle of Coca-Cola . . 5¢
Loaf of bread. . . . . 19¢
Roll of film. . . . . 42¢
Hotel room, per night $5
Men's leather shoes . . $19.95

COURTESY THE OAKLAND MUSEUM HISTORY DEPARTMENT, OAKLAND, CA

Bicycle $64.95
Record $9.98
Steak, per pound $1
Phonograph $28.50

FILE PHOTO BY DOUG MINDELL

Magazine . . . . 25¢
Movie projector $89.95
Television set $550
Ford sedan. $2,272
4-bedroom house . . . $19,500

© SOVFOTO/EASTFOTO

Sputnik I Soviet students look at a model of the Soviet Union's artificial satellite. The name *Sputnik* means "fellow traveler," a reference to its companion satellite, Earth.

Soviet "Moon" Circles Earth

Reds Win Race Into Outer Space

MOSCOW, OCTOBER 4—The Soviet Union today launched the first manufactured "moon." Named *Sputnik*, the Soviet satellite is now spinning around Earth at a speed of five miles a second.

Weighing 185 pounds and measuring 23 inches in diameter, the artificial moon was launched by an intercontinental ballistic missile, which gave the satellite the necessary spin to circle the world in 1 hour and 35 minutes.

THE CAT IN THE HAT introduces Thing One and Thing Two in Dr. Seuss's new series of Beginner Books. *Cat* nets $8 million.

Hoffa to Head Teamsters

WASHINGTON—James R. Hoffa was elected president of the giant Teamsters Union last night in open defiance of the AFL-CIO order that the union clean its house of corrupt elements like Hoffa. His election is certain to spur support for federal legislation to crack down on labor racketeering. The AFL-CIO has warned the Teamsters that it faces expulsion if it doesn't rid itself of corruption and those responsible for it.

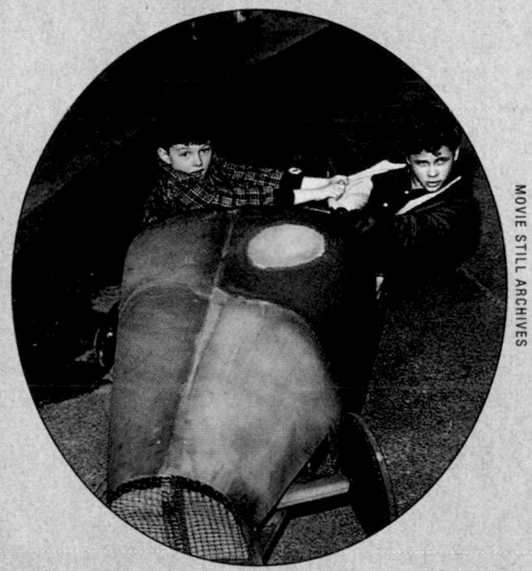

MOVIE STILL ARCHIVES

Beaver and Wally Cleaver

Leave It to Beaver Debuts

NEW YORK—The Cleaver family, with Beaver and big brother Wally, makes its first television appearance. In the first episode, Beaver tried to avoid being "spelled from school."

UPI/BETTMAN

Althea Gibson (right) and Darlene Hard

New Champion Honored

NEW YORK—A ticker-tape parade welcomed home tennis champion Althea Gibson after her dual victory at Wimbledon. Gibson first won the women's singles title and then won the women's doubles.

THE CARSON COLLECTION

***West Side Story*, based on *Romeo and Juliet*, with music by Leonard Bernstein, opens on Broadway.**

MUSIC

DETROIT—Entrepreneur Berry Gordy, Jr., invests $700 to start Motown, a new record company that promotes African American rock musicians such as Stevie Wonder and Diana Ross and the Supremes.

For the best in TV dining!

Swanson's TV dinners

Meals like Mom's
in only 25 minutes!
No thawing!
No dishes!

for only 98¢

COURTESY CAMPBELL SOUP COMPANY

Study and Writing Skill

ANALYZING SECONDARY SOURCES

Learning the Skill

A source created at or near the time of the events it reports is a primary source. Historians often use primary sources such as letters, original documents, speeches, and photographs as the basis for their descriptions or analyses of events. Books or other materials that draw from primary sources to explain a topic are secondary sources. Most history books are secondary sources.

The book *War and Peace in the Nuclear Age,* by John Newhouse, is a secondary source that analyzes the cold war events described in this chapter. The value and accuracy of a secondary source depend on how its author uses primary sources.

To determine whether an author uses primary sources effectively, ask these questions:

a. Are there references to primary sources in the acknowledgments, footnotes, or text?

b. Who are the authors of the primary sources? What insights or biases might these people have?

c. Is the information from the primary sources interwoven effectively to support or describe an event?

d. Are different kinds of primary sources considered? Do they represent varied testimony?

e. Is the interpretation of the primary sources sound?

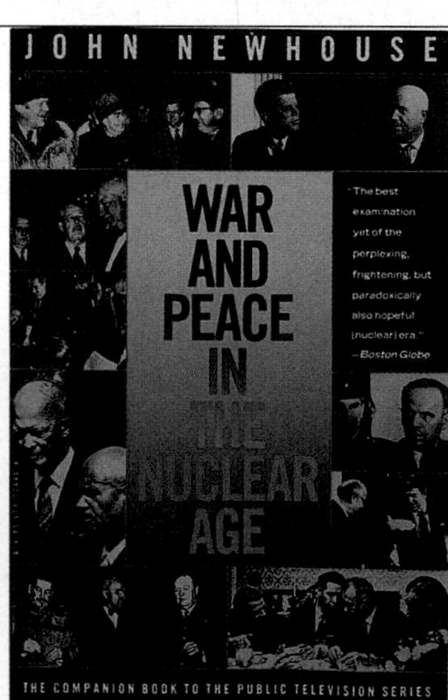

Secondary Sources Good secondary sources synthesize information from primary sources to give a full picture of events. *Judging from the information on the book's cover, what do you think are some of the sources it analyzes?*

Practicing the Skill

Read this excerpt from *War and Peace in the Nuclear Age*. Identify the primary source Newhouse uses. Then answer the questions below.

Eisenhower was very taken with the Open Skies idea. . . . Eisenhower described in his memoirs the . . . [reaction] of Soviet Prime Minister Bulganin, who said it had real merit and would be studied sympathetically. "The tone of his talk seemed as encouraging as his words," wrote Eisenhower. A few minutes later, walking toward the bar with Khrushchev, he was disabused but enlightened. " 'I don't agree with the Chairman,' Khrushchev said, smiling—but there was no smile in his voice. I saw clearly then . . . the identity of the real boss of the Soviet delegation." "From then on," said Eisenhower, "I . . . devoted myself exclusively to an attempt to persuade Mr. Khrushchev of the merits of the Open Skies plan."

1. What primary source does Newhouse quote?

2. Why is Eisenhower an excellent primary source to explore the topic?

3. How well has Newhouse used the excerpt to convey Eisenhower's feelings? To create a sense of immediacy?

4. Is the information from the primary source interwoven effectively into the text?

5. What other primary sources could you use to explore the cold war years?

Applying the Skill

Find and read an in-depth article in a newspaper or magazine today. Then analyze how reliable you think the primary sources are. List the primary sources the writer used. How effectively does the author interweave information from the primary sources?

The **Glencoe Skillbuilder Interactive Workbook, Level 2** CD-ROM provides more practice in key social studies skills.

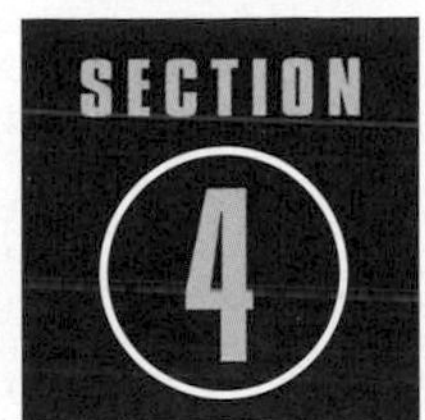

A New Battleground

MIDNIGHT, AUGUST 2, 1953: CIA PLOTS THE TAKEOVER OF IRAN

THE BETTMANN ARCHIVE

Kermit Roosevelt
This dapper-looking man was actually a spy for the United States.

LATE IN THE SUMMER OF 1953, TROUBLE WAS BREWING IN IRAN, AND EISENHOWER WAS WORRIED. This Middle Eastern country was important to the United States for two reasons: Iran bordered the Soviet Union, and it had some of the richest reserves of oil in the world.

Eisenhower worried about Iran's troubled economy and its increasing reliance on the Soviet Union. If the Communists seized Iran's government, yet another country—and one with a huge supply of valuable oil—would join the Soviet bloc. Something had to be done quickly. That something began this way:

A large, ornate garden in Teheran [Iran's capital]. A medium-sized, medium-height, rather nondescript American wearing a dark turtleneck shirt, Oxford gray slacks, and Persian sandals, opens the gate to the garden, slips out, glances up and down the street, and silently climbs into the back seat of an ordinary-looking black sedan. Without a backward glance, the driver pulls away slowly, smoothly and heads toward the royal palace. In the back seat, the American huddles down on the floor and pulls a blanket over him.

At the palace gate, the sentry flashes a light in the driver's face, grunts, and waves the car through. Halfway between the gate and the palace steps, the driver parks, gets out, and walks away. A slim, nervous man walks down the drive, glancing left and right as he approaches. The American pulls the blanket out of the way and sits up as the man enters the car. . . .

GUIDE TO READING

Main Idea

Cold war rivalries led the United States and the Soviet Union to spy on each other and to interfere in the affairs of developing countries in Asia, Africa, and Latin America.

Vocabulary

- emerging nation
- covert operation
- nationalization

Read to Find Out . . .

- how the United States and Soviet Union competed for the loyalty of emerging nations.
- reasons for United States interest in the Middle East and the policies adopted to protect American influence in the region.
- causes and effects of the Cuban missile crisis.

They look at each other. Then His Imperial Majesty, Mohammed Reza Shah Pahlavi, Shahanshah of Iran, Light of the Aryans, allows himself to relax and even smile.

—Kermit Roosevelt, *Countercoup: The Struggle for Control of Iran,* 1979

The American hiding under the blanket in the backseat that night was Kermit (Kim) Roosevelt, the grandson of President Theodore Roosevelt and a cousin of Franklin Delano Roosevelt. A top United States spy, Roosevelt had entered Iran under a phony name to meet secretly with Iran's 34-year-old Shah, or ruler.

Why were Roosevelt and the Shah sneaking around in the middle of the night? What was going on?

New Worlds to Conquer

Movements for National Independence

Iran, like many developing countries, found itself in turmoil after World War II. These **emerging nations**—developing countries in Asia, Latin America, and Africa—were shaking off colonial rule and taking charge of their futures. So widespread and powerful were these movements for national independence that between 1946 and 1960 alone 37 new countries emerged. Loyal to neither the United States and its democratic allies nor the Soviet Union and the Communist bloc, these newly independent nations became a new cold war battleground.

United States Interests

Winning the loyalty of emerging nations was crucial to Eisenhower. The United States depended on rich stores of rubber, oil, and other natural resources from developing countries and on their vast markets for American products. Just as important, emerging nations that were allied with the United States could help defend against Communist expansion.

Eisenhower and Dulles believed they needed to act decisively. They assumed that struggles for self-determination in the developing world were really revolutions directed by the Soviet Union. Left unopposed, these revolutions could result in neutral states or, worse, Communist ones throughout the Southern Hemisphere. If the Soviets managed to increase their influence in these regions, said Dulles, the scales would tip decisively against the Western democracies.

The Views of Emerging Nations

Drawing emerging nations into the American camp was difficult, however. Many newly independent countries, such as India and Egypt, wanted no part of outside control—United States or Soviet. Having just gotten rid of one foreign ruler, they had no desire for another.

Even establishing friendships with emerging nations proved difficult. For the millions of poor people in developing nations, life was a grim daily struggle to stay alive. They resented the United States's wealth, which they glimpsed in the luxurious lifestyles of American tourists and diplomats. Likewise, Soviet propagandists pointed to America's troubled race relations and asked nonwhite people in these nations: If the United States does not treat its fellow citizens equally, how will it treat you? Finally, in the struggles of emerging nations, the United States often sided with the wealthy, not the common, people. Even though America itself was born of revolution, the United States now worried about protecting its overseas investments and military bases. To people struggling for freedom, the United States seemed like just another threat.

Facing resistance from emerging nations, the United States used many methods to win friends and wage cold war. Massive amounts of foreign aid—the primary method—helped improve farming, schools, and medical care in developing countries. When Eisenhower became President, he relied increasingly on the Central Intelligence Agency, the CIA, to promote the allegiance of newly independent nations. The CIA spied and conducted **covert operations,** or undercover missions, of all kinds.

The CIA Joins the Fight

Agents Spy on the Soviet Union

The CIA was not Eisenhower's idea but rather a government agency President Truman created. After World War II, Truman decided that peacetime America no

COURTESY, THE CENTRAL INTELLIGENCE AGENCY

The CIA President Truman approved the seal of the CIA on February 17, 1950. *What actions did the CIA take during Truman's administration?*

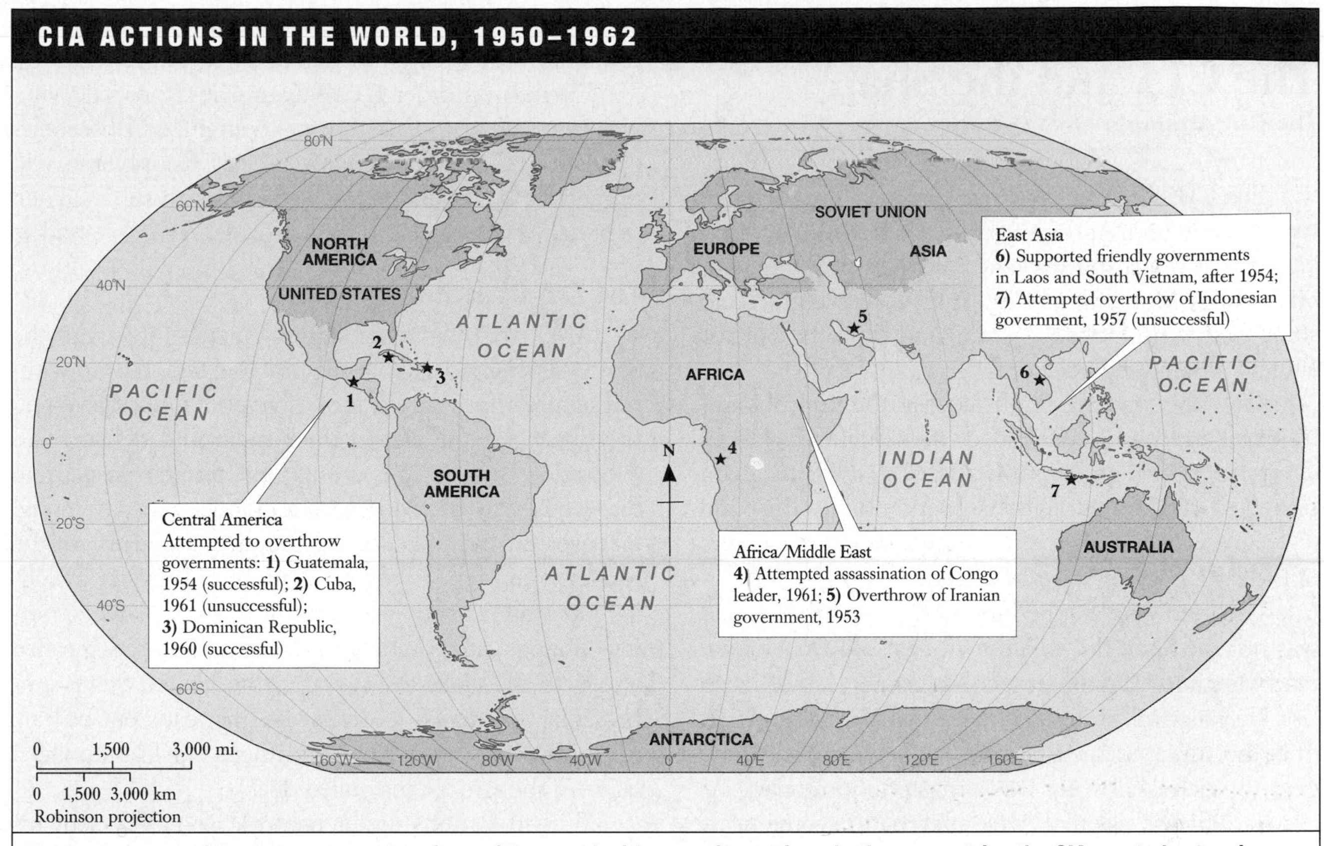

The green areas of the map represent regions of the world with emerging nations. In these countries the CIA exerted extensive covert powers. *How did the United States justify the interference of the CIA in foreign governments?*

longer needed a network of spies. By 1946, however, Truman changed his mind as United States–Soviet relations soured and intelligence gathering began to seem necessary again.

CIA Powers

In 1947 Congress passed the historic National Security Act, which streamlined the defense system and created the CIA and the National Security Council (NSC). The newly created NSC and CIA reported directly to the President.

The act also gave the CIA sweeping powers with this loose definition of its job: The CIA shall perform "functions and duties related to intelligence affecting national security as the National Security Council will direct." This language left the CIA free to spy and to carry on covert operations. Used with care, the CIA enabled the President to take quick, controversial action in foreign trouble spots without waiting for congressional or public approval. This resource gave the White House virtual control of foreign policy.

In its early years, the CIA carried out few covert operations. Its main job was to spy on the Soviet military and prop up European democracies by secretly funding democratic political parties, labor unions, and other pro-Western groups.

The CIA was so successful that in 1949 Congress gave that agency the right to spend unlimited amounts of money without telling anyone except the director where the money went and what it was used for. This authority gave the President and the CIA a free hand. In time they would bribe overseas politicians, hire secret armies, and plot the assassinations of troublesome leaders.

The CIA Grows Powerful

With its increase in power and funding, the CIA mushroomed. In 1949 the agency had about 300 employees and spent $4.7 million. Just 3 years later, the CIA had grown to 20 times its original size. It employed nearly 6,000 people all over the world and spent nearly $82 million.

As the CIA grew, more Americans saw it as "the good way to fight communism." Exciting, glamorous, and challenging, the agency attracted talented young graduates from Harvard, Yale, and other top universities. Eventually the CIA would have an important role, instead of just a hand, in shaping events all over the world. As the map above shows, CIA agents worked behind the scenes worldwide to overthrow neutral or pro-Soviet governments and to prop up pro-Western ones.

The CIA and the Shah

The CIA Attempts an Overthrow

The CIA's first attempt to overthrow a government took place in Iran. At the end of World War II, a monarch and a two-house parliament ruled oil-rich Iran. The Shah (king), Mohammad Reza Pahlavi, was a dark, handsome man who looked dashing and powerful but was actually young and insecure.

After the war the Shah faced a tough problem—Iranian hatred of the British-owned Anglo-Persian Oil Company. Through Anglo-Persian Oil, the British controlled most of Iran's oil industry and drained the country of great wealth. Angry Iranians wanted to take control of their oil, but they needed a leader.

The man who stepped forward to lead the Iranians was not the Shah but wealthy 70-year-old Dr. Mohammad Mossadeg. On the surface Mossadeg seemed harmless. He was small, thin, and often emotional. He appeared to be no threat to the Shah. Beneath the surface, however, the rich landowner was a masterful politician.

In 1951 the popular Mossadeg had become prime minister and pushed through the legislature a bill authorizing **nationalization** of the oil fields—that is, declaring them the property of Iran. Outraged, the British refused to accept the payment Mossadeg offered. Instead, the British shut down their refineries, stopped buying Iranian oil, and convinced other countries to do the same. As Iran's oil market dried up, its economy slipped toward bankruptcy.

Eisenhower Steps In

By the time Eisenhower took office, Iran was in serious trouble. In Eisenhower's mind the situation was a perfect breeding ground for communism. The best way to protect Iran's oil supply for the West, Eisenhower thought, was to keep the Shah and get rid of Mossadeg.

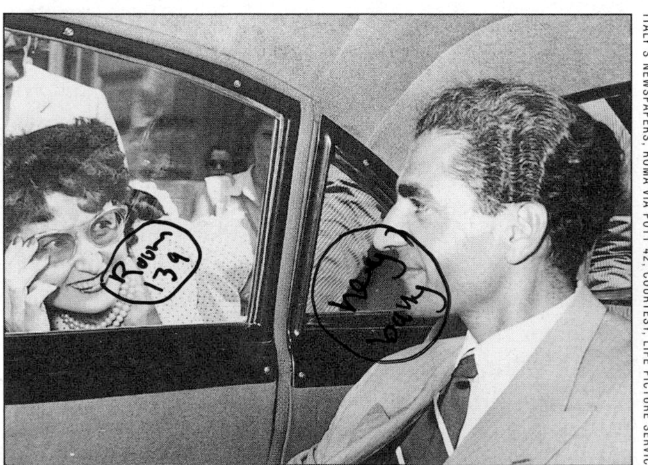

ITALY'S NEWSPAPERS, ROMA VIA POTT 42, COURTESY, LIFE PICTURE SERVICE

The Shah Flees Tehran A woman in Rome peers into the Shah's Buick. *Why did the Shah flee Tehran?*

Eisenhower ordered CIA agent Kim Roosevelt, who was in a "safe house" in Tehran, to engineer Mossadeg's overthrow. In a plan nicknamed AJAX, Roosevelt would organize military and public support for the Shah. Then the Shah would sign a royal decree deposing Mossadeg.

The CIA Operation

AJAX got off to a bad start in August 1953 when the Shah grew nervous about the plot and fled Tehran without signing the decree. It took Roosevelt four days to find the Shah, get the signed document, and deliver it to Mossadeg. By that time, though, the prime minister had discovered the plot. Mossadeg announced the attempted takeover on the radio and demanded the arrest of the Shah's supporters. In response, mobs of Iranians, including Communist supporters, ran wild in the streets, rioting, looting, and searching for enemies. Mossadeg called a stop to the violence only after the United States ambassador threatened to order all Americans out of Iran. Mossadeg knew that his government would look like a failure if the Americans pulled out.

With the mobs under control, Roosevelt sent his Iranian agents into action. On August 19, 200 Zirkaneh giants—huge, frightening-looking weight lifters—marched through Tehran's bazaars chanting, "Long live the Shah!" Other agents ran alongside, passing out money and gathering a crowd of artisans, students, police, and professionals. As the crowd headed for Mossadeg's house, Roosevelt rounded up the Shah's military supporters, who set off with tanks and guns.

The CIA agents and the Shah's men met and clashed with Mossadeg's supporters near Mossadeg's house. The battle lasted several hours and left 400 dead or injured. When Mossadeg's forces ran out of ammunition, the resistance ran out of steam. On the following day Mossadeg surrendered, and the Shah's supporters begged the Shah to return.

The Shah returned victorious. Soon after, Mossadeg was jailed. With the Shah in power, a group of Western oil companies was able to sign an agreement to buy and sell Iranian oil and share the profits with the Shah. AJAX had ensured the CIA's future. It had also planted the seeds of Iranian hatred of the United States.

War in Egypt

A Suez Canal Crisis

Three years later another hot spot ignited in the Middle East. This time the CIA was not involved, but the event showed Eisenhower that the developing coun-

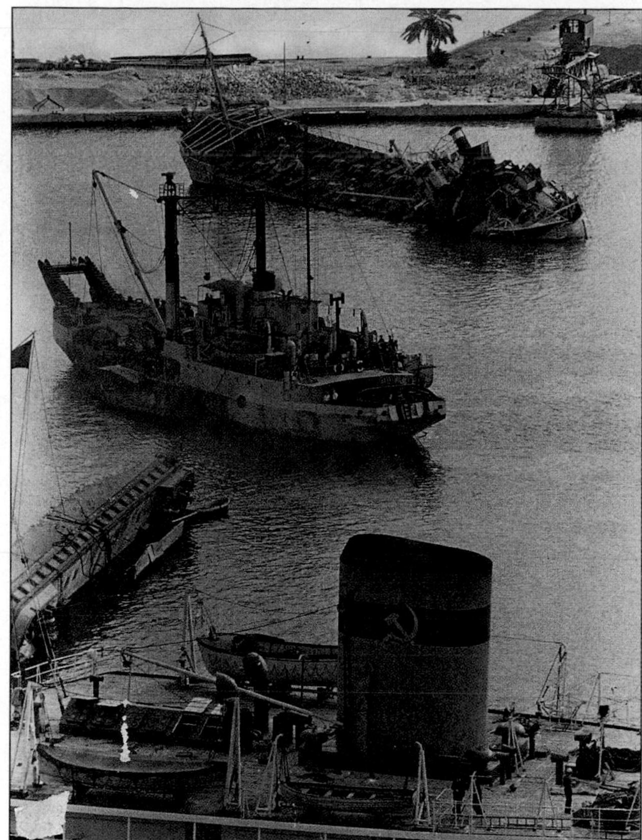
© BLACK STAR

Suez Canal Sunken ships obstruct the canal in Port Said.
Who sank the ships and why?

tries of the world presented difficult and dangerous problems.

In 1953 Egypt declared itself an independent republic, and in 1954 the passionate Arab nationalist General Gamal Abdel Nasser demanded that Britain give up control of the Suez Canal, which cut through his country. More than 75 percent of Western Europe's oil imports were shipped through the Suez Canal, a key link between the Persian Gulf and the Mediterranean Sea. Nasser wanted to collect the $25 million in annual profits from tolls. As part of his plan for modernizing Egypt, Nasser also wanted to build a dam on the Nile River to provide electric power and irrigation water for farms.

To help draw Egypt into the United States camp, Dulles had offered to help Nasser build his dam. Soon afterward, though, the independent Nasser made an arms deal with the Soviets, and Dulles angrily canceled the loan. In July 1956, Nasser fought back by seizing the Suez Canal. With the millions in tolls from the canal, Egypt would finance the Nile River dam itself.

In October 1956, before Eisenhower could work out a solution to the crisis, Israel, Britain, and France invaded Egypt to seize the canal. Eisenhower and Dulles were appalled, fearing the action would drive the Middle East into the Soviet camp and threaten vital oil resources. Eisenhower called for a UN resolution condemning the actions of the three American allies. Without United States support, they pulled out, and the canal was returned to Egypt—full of sunken ships.

While Eisenhower managed to head off a full-scale war, the incident had serious consequences. It opened the Middle East to the Soviets, who appeared to side with Egyptian nationalists and eventually built Nasser's dam. The conflict also revealed weaknesses in the Western camp and pulled the United States deeper into Middle Eastern affairs. Afraid of growing Soviet influence in the oil-rich Middle East, Eisenhower promised aid, both economic and military, to pro-Western governments in the region. This policy, known as the Eisenhower Doctrine, would soon involve fighting communism and the Arab governments that did not join the Western camp.

Latin America

The Cold War Arrives

The spirit of nationalism fired up people in Central and South America during this period, too. For decades the United States had invested in the region's economies, and by the mid-1950s, United States companies controlled more than $7 billion of oil, mineral, and agricultural resources in Latin America. These firms enjoyed rich profits from their investments in the region, but little wealth trickled down to the masses of people who lived in poverty. Nationalistic leaders knew they had to loosen the grip of the United States firms on their economies. Revolution was simmering.

Revolution in Cuba

By the early 1950s, United States corporations virtually controlled the island nation of Cuba. Nearly 90 percent of Cuba's mines, ranches, and oil, half of its sugar crop, and 3 million acres of its land belonged to Americans. Only a few high-level Cubans lived well. Most suffered in grinding poverty.

In 1952 Fulgencio Batista overthrew the government and installed himself as dictator, friendly to the United States. He did little to improve life for the Cuban people, however, and in 1958 a young lawyer named Fidel Castro led a group of peasants and middle-class Cubans in a successful revolt against Batista.

Once in power, Castro moved quickly to solve Cuba's problems by demanding control of American properties. When the United States refused to discuss the matter, Castro turned to the Soviets for economic help. Soon after, Eisenhower ordered the CIA to train a secret force of anti-Castro Cubans called La Brigada, which could be used to overthrow Castro. Before

Eisenhower left office in 1961, Castro had seized all American businesses and signed a trade agreement with Moscow. The United States and Cuba had broken diplomatic relations.

Kennedy and Cuba

In 1961 John F. Kennedy became President and faced, in his words, the problem of a "Communist satellite on our very doorstep." With Castro's success in Cuba and growing crises in Africa and Southeast Asia, Kennedy feared a Soviet upper hand in the cold war. Before leaving office Eisenhower had urged Kennedy to step up the training of La Brigada. Now in office, Kennedy took the advice of CIA operatives and ordered La Brigada to land secretly in Cuba, inspire a popular uprising, and sweep Castro out of power.

The invasion on April 17, 1961, failed miserably. When the 1,500 commandos tried to land at the Bay of Pigs on Cuba's southern coast, they met disaster at every turn. Their boats ran aground on coral reefs, Kennedy canceled their air support to keep United States involvement secret, and the promised uprising of the Cuban people never happened. Within 2 days Castro's forces killed several hundred members of La Brigada and captured nearly all the rest.

The Bay of Pigs was a dark moment for Kennedy. The action exposed an American plot to overthrow a neighbor's government, and the clumsy affair made the United States look weak, like a paper tiger.

To the Brink of War

To assert the United States's strength, Kennedy searched for other ways to unseat Castro. Using the CIA in a plan called Operation Mongoose, he interrupted Cuban trade, ordered more raids by exiles, and even plotted Castro's assassination.

For Castro and Khrushchev, these activities were outrageous. Khrushchev did not want to lose his foothold in the Western Hemisphere, and Castro did not want to lose his freedom from United States influence. "We had

THE CUBAN MISSILE CRISIS: JULY – OCTOBER, 1962

Citing Fidel Castro's fear of an American invasion of Cuba, the Soviet Union transformed the island into an enormous military base during the summer of 1962. It was a stunning move that put the Soviet threat less than 100 miles from American shores. The standoff that ensued between the two cold war leaders placed the world close to its first nuclear war.

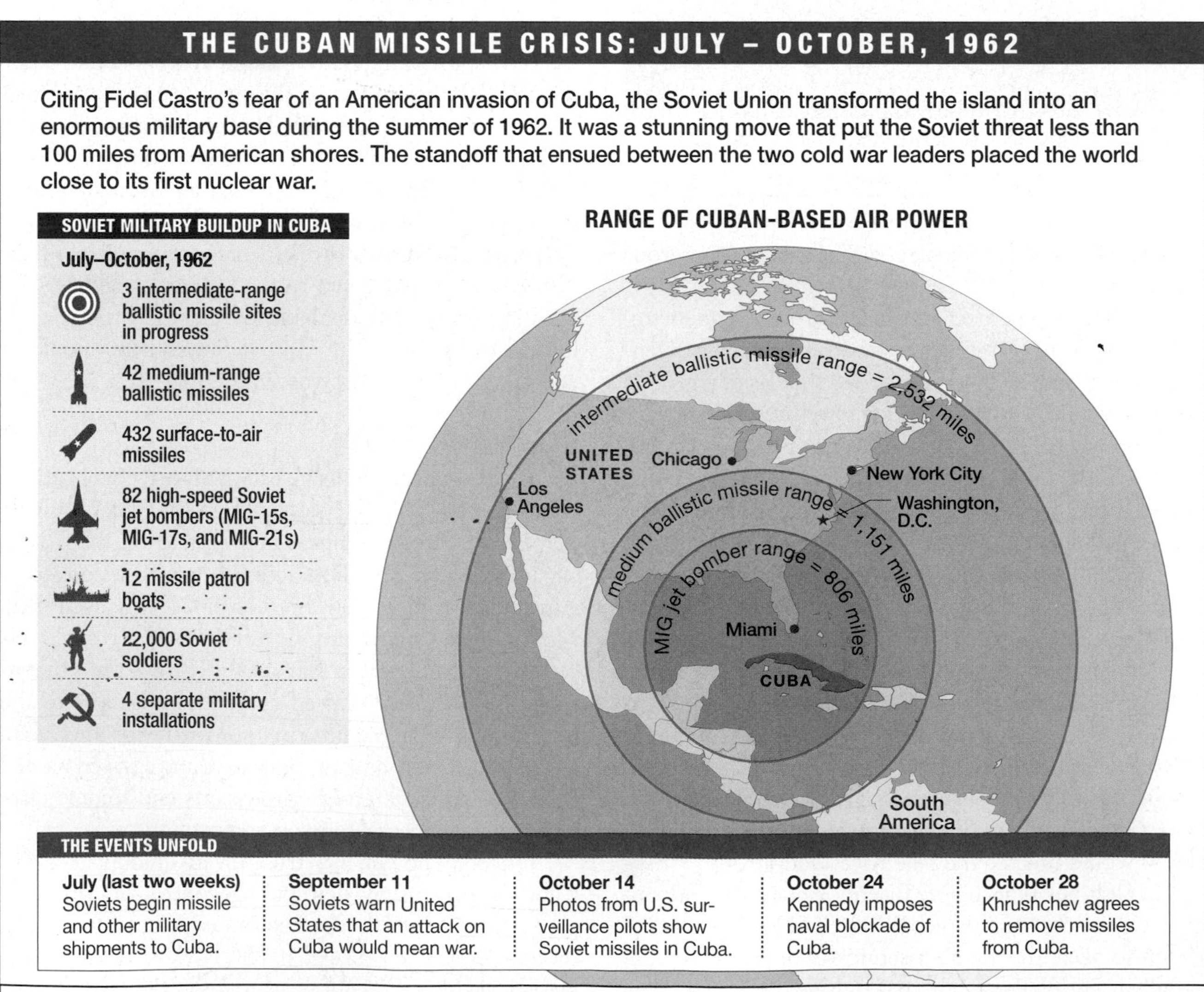

SOVIET MILITARY BUILDUP IN CUBA
July–October, 1962
3 intermediate-range ballistic missile sites in progress
42 medium-range ballistic missiles
432 surface-to-air missiles
82 high-speed Soviet jet bombers (MIG-15s, MIG-17s, and MIG-21s)
12 missile patrol boats
22,000 Soviet soldiers
4 separate military installations
RANGE OF CUBAN-BASED AIR POWER
intermediate ballistic missile range = 2,532 miles
medium ballistic missile range = 1,151 miles
MIG jet bomber range = 806 miles
UNITED STATES
Chicago
New York City
Washington, D.C.
Los Angeles
Miami
CUBA
South America
THE EVENTS UNFOLD
July (last two weeks)
Soviets begin missile and other military shipments to Cuba.
September 11
Soviets warn United States that an attack on Cuba would mean war.
October 14
Photos from U.S. surveillance pilots show Soviet missiles in Cuba.
October 24
Kennedy imposes naval blockade of Cuba.
October 28
Khrushchev agrees to remove missiles from Cuba.

Enemy nuclear warheads positioned close to the United States posed an immediate danger to the country and raised the specter of all-out nuclear war between the United States and the Soviet Union. *Which United States cities are not in range of Cuban missiles?*

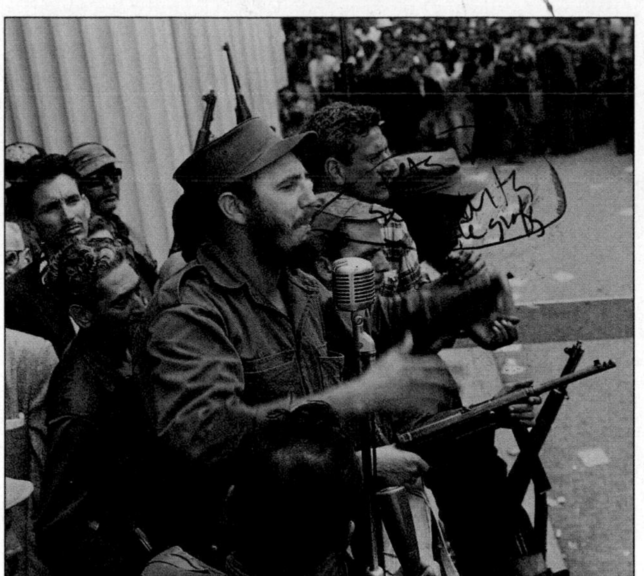

UPI/BETTMANN

The March to Havana Fidel Castro addresses a crowd of Cuban people. *How did Castro ascend to power?*

to think of some way of confronting America with more than words," Khrushchev recalled. Their solution was to install Soviet nuclear missiles and bombers near Havana, Cuba's capital, as a warning to the United States.

On October 14, 1962, a United States spy plane flying over Cuba got clear photos of crews installing Soviet missiles. Kennedy called a meeting of his closest advisers to decide what to do.

For a solid, nerve-racking week, the group thrashed out every possible response. Negotiations were ruled out at once; the group feared that drawn-out talks would give the Soviets time to install the missiles. Bombing the missile sites and invading Cuba were both proposed, but Kennedy feared that either could ignite a nuclear war. He finally agreed to block Cuban shipping lanes, while pushing Khrushchev to remove the missiles.

On the evening of October 22, Kennedy announced this decision on national television. Within 2 days 180 warships were sailing to Cuba, B-52 bombers loaded with nuclear weapons were in the air, and military forces worldwide were on full alert—more than 200,000 in Florida alone. For the next 2 days, Soviet ships steamed toward Cuba, and the world held its breath. It was a time when "the smell of burning hung in the air," Khrushchev remembered later. The United States and the Soviet Union had edged to the brink of nuclear war.

On October 26, Khrushchev agreed to remove the missiles if the United States vowed never to attack Cuba. The next day he demanded the removal of United States missiles from Turkey. Kennedy agreed to the first demand but ignored the second. He told Khrushchev to get the missiles out of Cuba—or the United States would do it. On October 28, Khrushchev backed down.

After the Crisis

As the missiles left Cuba, the world stepped back from the brink and breathed a huge sigh of relief. War had been averted.

The standoff also changed the character of the cold war. At last the United States and the Soviet Union accepted each other's power and admitted the importance of negotiation. In this spirit, American and Soviet leaders installed a hot line, a Teletype link for communication when future crises arose.

The brush with nuclear war did nothing to slow the arms race, however. For the Soviet Union, the missile crisis had ended in public humiliation. The Soviets vowed, in the words of one official, "never [to] be caught like this again." Back home they launched a huge military buildup.

The United States's victory in the missile crisis renewed the nation's pride and its belief in containment. Through the rest of Kennedy's administration, the United States continued to stockpile nuclear weapons and serve as the world's police force. Before long, though, America's beliefs would be put to the test in the small Asian country of Vietnam.

Section Assessment

Main Idea

1. Use a diagram like this one to show why and how the United States became involved in the affairs of emerging nations.

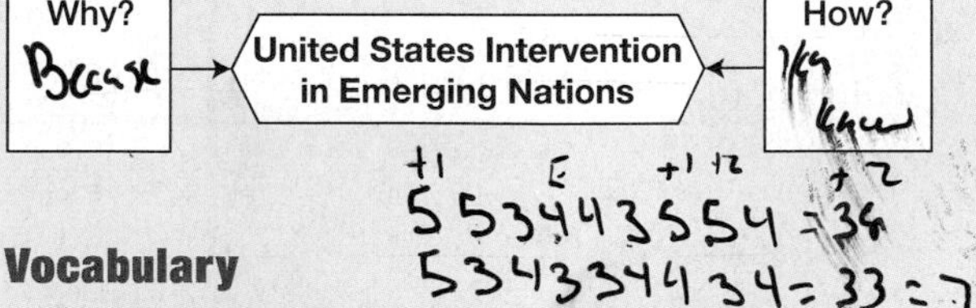

Vocabulary

2. Define: emerging nation, covert operation, nationalization.

Checking Facts

3. What sparked the controversy between Iran and Great Britain in 1951?

4. Why did Castro's revolution threaten United States interests?

Critical Thinking

5. **Predicting Consequences** How would the United States benefit if Castro's revolution failed?

Chapter  Assessment

Self-Check Quiz

Visit the *American Odyssey* Web site at americanodyssey.glencoe.com and click on ***Chapter 17—Self-Check Quiz*** to prepare for the Chapter Test.

Reviewing Key Terms

Match each vocabulary word to its definition below. Write your answers on a separate sheet of paper.

containment **cold war**
limited war **land reform**
brinksmanship
massive retaliation

1. confining war to one area rather than letting it grow into a global confrontation

2. securing peace by restricting communism to its current borders

3. a policy in which the United States would launch a nuclear strike against the Soviet Union if it attacked any ally

4. attempt to keep peace by stating one will never back down

5. redistribution of property to land-poor peasants

Recalling Facts

1. How did the United States's position at the end of World War II compare with the Soviet Union's position?

2. Describe the events that prompted the United States to adopt the containment policy of keeping communism confined within its current borders.

3. How did the Marshall Plan help the United States implement its foreign policy following World War II?

4. Why did most Americans hope for a Nationalist victory in China?

5. How did Mao and the Communists win the support of the Chinese people?

6. What were some advantages and some dangers of a policy of massive retaliation?

7. Why did Nikita Khrushchev refuse to agree to Dwight Eisenhower's proposal to inspect each other's military sites?

8. What methods did the United States use to gain the friendship of emerging nations? How was the CIA involved?

9. What conditions in Cuba helped prepare the way for Fidel Castro's takeover?

Critical Thinking

1. Recognizing Points of View Use a diagram like this one to show the concerns of Roosevelt, Churchill, and Stalin when they met at Yalta.

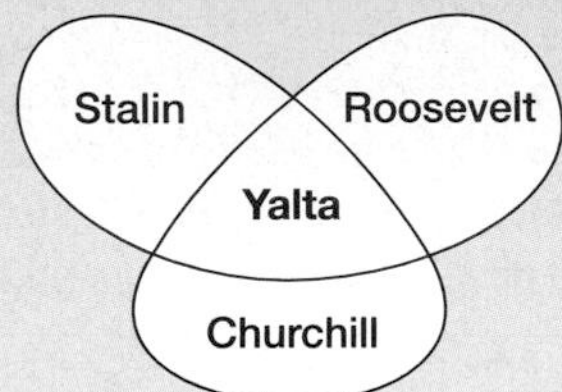

2. Identifying Assumptions In 1956 Nikita Khrushchev spoke of tolerating different kinds of communism. What did Eastern European nations assume this statement meant? How were these assumptions proven false in Hungary?

Standardized Test Practice

1. The United States's policy during the cold war can best be described as

A maintaining isolation and neutrality.
B destroying communism through expansionism.
C preventing the spread of communism through containment.
D providing aid for communist nations to rebuild their economies.

Test-Taking Tip: The *cold war* was a time of tension between the Soviet Union and the United States. Therefore, the United States had little reason to provide economic aid to the communist block. Answer D can be ruled out.

2. "The U.S. and Soviet Union are like two scorpions in a bottle, each capable of killing the other but only at the risk of his own life." This quote by J. Robert Oppenheimer best reflects a major shortcoming in the policy of

A containment.
B nationalization.
C limited war.
D massive retaliation.

Test-Taking Tip: Think of the meaning of the word *shortcoming:* a defect or failure. Despite their power, what *shortcoming* does each of the two "scorpions" have if it strikes? Which of the listed policies has a similar defect?

GEOGRAPHY AND HISTORY

NATO Military Bases, 1950s

■ U.S. military bases or ports

NATO members

Warsaw Pact members

0 500 1,000 mi.

0 500 1,000 km

Polar Stereographic projection

Study the map to answer the following questions:

1. How many military bases are on the map?
2. Near what part of the Soviet Union do you see the most bases?
3. Where are the Soviet Union and the United States closest together?
4. Which NATO bases may have been the most serious threat to the Soviets?

3. Determining Cause and Effect What caused the mistrust between Harry S Truman and Joseph Stalin? How did this mistrust affect the way in which each nation handled its foreign affairs?

Portfolio Project

Interview someone who lived through the Cuban missile crisis. Ask the person to describe what it was like. Write a summary and keep it in your portfolio.

Cooperative Learning

Create a newspaper about a topic from this chapter. Include editorials, political cartoons, and feature articles.

Reinforcing Skills

Analyzing Secondary Sources The photo on page 577 is a primary source that catches a glimpse of childhood during the cold war. Write a paragraph for a secondary source explaining what it was like to grow up at the height of cold war tensions.

Technology Activity

Using the Internet Search the Internet for information on how the United Nations is organized. Design a flowchart that shows the names of each of the main bodies of the UN and how they relate to each other.

The Postwar Era

1955: MIDDLE-CLASS SUBURBANITES BLIND TO URBAN POVERTY

The sun glinted off the tail fins and chrome bumpers of the new Buick in the driveway as the Wilsons piled into the car for their weekly ritual—the Sunday afternoon drive. After a brief struggle over who would get the window seats, Sally, Tom, and Susan settled themselves in the backseat.

The car turned onto one of Chicago's newly completed expressways, and shortly the Wilsons were driving north on Michigan Avenue with its exclusive shops and fine restaurants. They parked to window-shop a bit, and when the children clamored for ice cream, the family stopped at an ice-cream parlor. Then they headed home to the tree-lined streets of their comfortable suburb of Morton Grove.

The Wilsons were a lucky family. Exactly 10 years ago, John Wilson was one of thousands of exhausted GIs marching on the road to Berlin. Now John and Julie had 3 great kids with a fourth on the way and a beautiful home in the suburbs. Thanks to the GI Bill, John had a college degree (something his parents had never achieved) and a promising future with a large company.

On their drive the Wilsons never saw the not-so-lucky Americans who lived on Chicago's West Side: women talking on the steps of decaying buildings; men slumped in doorways; children playing ball on a sidewalk strewn with broken glass. ■

Based on your own knowledge of the 1950s and the picture on page 597, write down what you think this chapter will be about.

Chapter Overview

Visit the *American Odyssey* Web site at americanodyssey.glencoe.com and click on ***Chapter 18—Chapter Overview*** to preview the chapter.

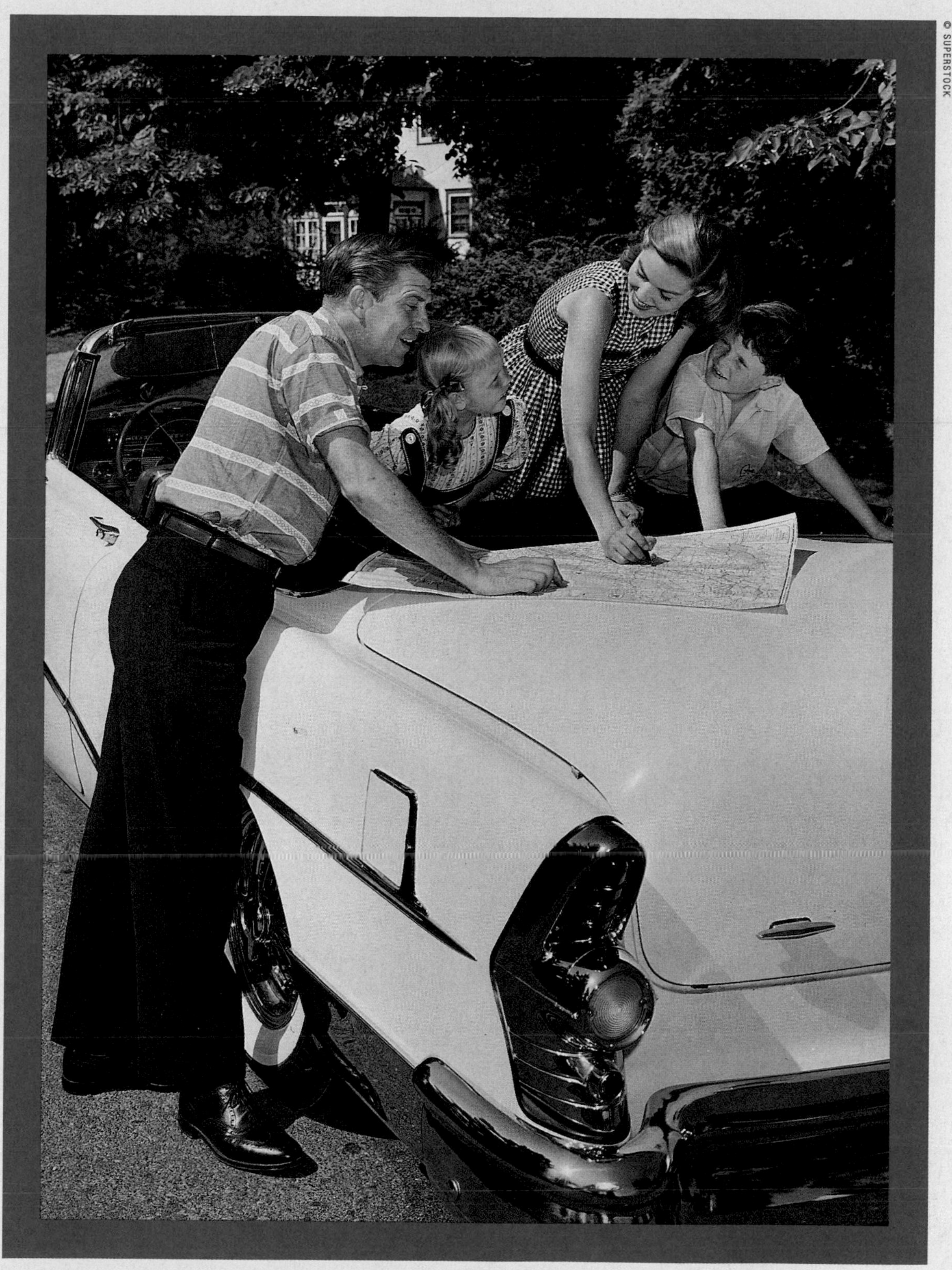

© SUPERSTOCK

THE SUBURBAN VALUES OF THE 1950S STRESSED TOGETHERNESS, FAMILY, AND THE "GOOD LIFE."

Postwar Economy Booms

FALL 1947: VETS ENROLL IN COLLEGE ON GI BILL

WORLD WAR II VETERAN KENNETH BAKER, HIS WIFE, LAURA, AND THEIR BABY DAUGHTER ARRIVED ON THE CAMPUS OF THE UNIVERSITY OF MINNESOTA ON A COOL SEPTEMBER MORNING IN 1947. Ken was one of 6,000 married "vets" on campus ready to begin the fall semester. His family was assigned to one of the 674 housing units in Veterans' Village, a university community for ex-GIs, where rents were based on each vet's ability to pay. Veterans who had the most seniority were assigned to the best units—converted steel barracks with gas heat and indoor bathrooms. As newcomers, Kenneth and Laura would be living in a trailer with no plumbing. That meant that they would have to use the public bathhouse and the public laundry.

UNIVERSITY OF MINNESOTA

GI Housing
Veterans flooded college campuses after the war. Some ex-GIs and their families at the University of Minnesota lived in quonset units.

Nevertheless, the Bakers considered themselves lucky. As Ken observed, "Even a hovel in Veterans' Village is heaven compared to the way I lived in the service." Living in Veterans' Village meant that Ken and Laura could get by on their monthly government allowance of $90.

Life in Veterans' Village fostered a spirit of cooperation. With more than 900 babies among the village population, every adult became a guardian to every child. The Bakers shopped in the village grocery store, which the veterans' campus community owned and operated. Ken and several of his buddies joined the veterans'

GUIDE TO READING

Main Idea

A postwar economic boom and benefits extended to veterans under the GI Bill contributed to a general prosperity and a higher standard of living for most Americans.

Vocabulary

- demobilization
- real income
- discretionary income
- conglomerate

Read to Find Out . . .

- reasons for continued prosperity during the postwar era and how the growth of a consumer culture helped fuel that prosperity.
- the programs that helped returning GIs reenter society.

bowling league. Laura took special classes in sewing, cooking, and child care. On Friday nights, Laura and Ken joined other residents of Veterans' Village in the recreation center to dance to the recorded music of popular big bands of the day.

Similar veterans' communities could be found on most large college campuses in the postwar United States, thanks to the GI Bill of Rights. The GI Bill was designed to ease the transition from military to civilian life by providing veterans with financial aid for education and housing and to begin small businesses. Nearly 8 million veterans took advantage of educational assistance. Armed with college degrees or technical training, the vets contributed their energy and talent to what would become the nation's longest unbroken period of prosperity.

From War to Peace

Returning GIs Spur Economy

More than 16 million Americans had served in the armed forces during World War II. **Demobilization,** the dismantling of the huge United States war machine, was a daunting task, somewhat like trying to reverse the direction of a river's flow. After peace was achieved in 1945, war-weary soldiers stationed around the world waited eagerly to come home. After thousands of citizens appealed to their congressional representatives to speed up the process, the number of soldiers on active duty dropped from 12 million in 1945 to 1.6 million by mid-1947. This rapid demobilization provided much-needed workers for United States industry, which was in the process of converting from wartime to peacetime production.

Economic Growth

After years of "going without" during the Great Depression and the war, Americans hungered for new cars, electronics, appliances, and gadgets. Industry set out to fill the growing demand for consumer goods. The automobile industry produced 2 million cars in 1946 and nearly 2 times that many by 1955. Americans bought 975,000 television sets in 1948, and 2 years later they bought 7.5 million sets. By 1960 about 75 percent of all American families owned at least 1 automobile, and 87 percent owned at least 1 television set. Consumers also purchased more refrigerators, washing machines, vacuum cleaners, and cameras than ever before. Electric can openers, electric garage door openers, and electric pencil sharpeners appeared on the market and quickly became part of the new American way of life.

The GNP, or gross national product (the total value of a country's goods and services), rose rapidly—

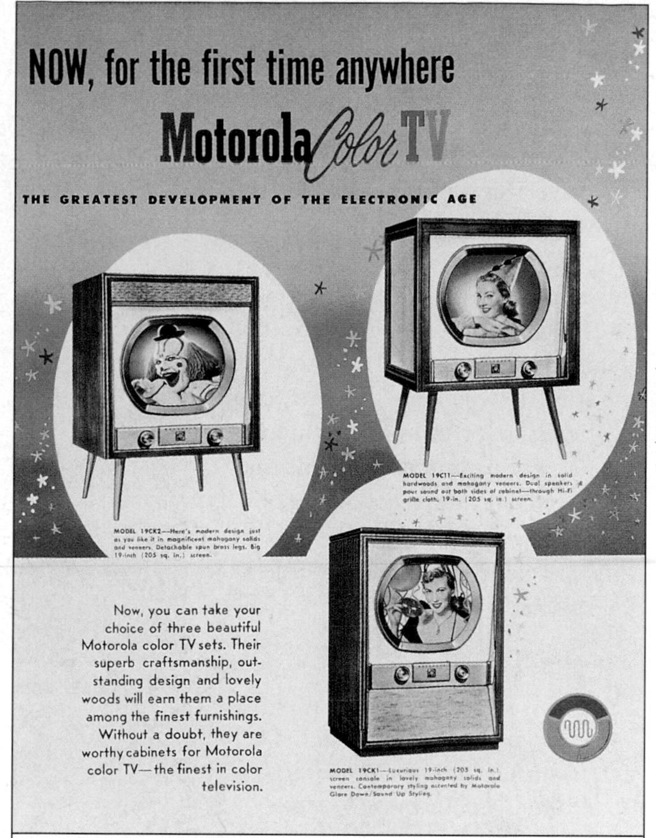

NOW, for the first time anywhere
Motorola Color TV
THE GREATEST DEVELOPMENT OF THE ELECTRONIC AGE
Now, you can take your choice of three beautiful Motorola color TV sets. Their superb craftsmanship, outstanding design and lovely woods will earn them a place among the finest furnishings. Without a doubt, they are worthy cabinets for Motorola color TV—the finest in color television.

A 1950s Spending Spree During the 1950s, electricity consumption more than doubled, due in large part to the purchases of electrical appliances and televisions. *Why did Americans have so much money to spend?*

from just more than $100 billion in 1940 to about $300 billion in 1950 and then to $500 billion by 1960. This increase in goods and services that characterized the postwar period gave Americans the highest standard of living the world had ever known. People lived more comfortably than ever before. The United States, home to just 6 percent of the world's population, produced and consumed nearly half the world's goods.

Wage and Price Issues

The reconversion to a peacetime economy brought problems, too. During the war, civilian paychecks included plenty of overtime pay. In addition, government policies had kept a lid on prices. When postwar wages failed to keep up with now-rising prices, blue-collar workers launched a wave of strikes and work stoppages, refusing to work until their demands were met.

Despite rising prices, most American workers continued to prosper. Average annual earnings for factory workers rose from $3,302 in 1950 to $5,352 in 1960. **Real income,** the amount of income earned taking into account an increase in prices, increased more than 20 percent during the same period. Working-class Americans began to accumulate **discretionary income**—money to buy what they wanted as well as what they needed. This increased purchasing power further fueled the rapid economic growth.

Persuading the Consumer

Advertising became the fastest growing industry in the postwar United States. Manufacturers employed new marketing techniques. These techniques were carefully planned to whet the consumer's appetite. It was also the purpose of these advertisers to influence choices among brands of goods that were essentially the same. In his 1957 best-seller, *The Hidden Persuaders,* Vance Packard described the role of advertisers:

TV Commercials Advertisers discovered that television was a good way to reach consumers. Advertising was the fastest growing industry in the postwar United States. *What techniques did advertisers use?*

> These motivational analysts . . . are adding depth to the selling of ideas and products. They are learning, for example, to offer us considerably more than the actual item involved. A Milwaukee advertising executive commented to colleagues in print on the fact that women will pay two dollars and a half for skin cream but no more than twenty-five cents for a cake of soap. Why? Soap, he explained, only promises to make them clean. The cream promises to make them beautiful.
>
> —Vance Packard, *The Hidden Persuaders,* 1957

According to these hidden messages, a freezer became a promise of plenty, a second car became a symbol of status, and a mouthwash became the key to immediate social success.

The increased popularity of television played a major role in the development of the advertising industry and the gospel of consumerism. Television networks depended on advertising revenues to pay for the programs they produced. At the same time, advertisers found television a perfect medium for reaching consumers. Television, after all, was still a novelty for most people in the United States during the early 1950s, and they watched the television commercials just as avidly as the television programs.

Television ads became something of an art form in themselves. They not only sold products, they also entertained the viewers with showy dramatizations and catchy jingles. As the decade progressed, the presence and influence of television advertising became pervasive, and acquiring material goods like those shown on TV became a goal of the growing, status-conscious middle class.

Impact of the GI Bill

A Boom for Colleges and Housing

More than any other factor, the GI Bill of Rights, Congress passed in 1944, shaped American society in the postwar period. One veteran concurred:

> The GI Bill of Rights, of course, had more to do with thrusting us into a new era than anything else. Millions of people whose parents or grandparents had never dreamed of going to college saw that they could go. . . . Essentially I think it made us a far more democratic people.
>
> —Nelson Poynter, in *Americans Remember the Home Front*

As a result of the GI Bill, the greatest wave of college building in the nation's history took place during the postwar years. Many states vastly increased their support of higher education. For example, during the postwar period California State University opened campuses at Sacramento, Los Angeles, Long Beach, Fullerton, Hayward, Northridge, and San Bernardino.

In addition to educational benefits, the GI Bill offered low-interest mortgages to veterans who wanted to purchase homes. This spurred a huge demand for housing after the war, creating a construction boom and fostering a trend toward mass production. Using mass production methods, the housing industry built 13 million new homes during the 1950s. Home ownership had always been a part of the American dream. The rate of home ownership increased between 1940 and 1960 from 44 to 62 percent of American households. The GI Bill allowed millions of Americans to achieve a standard of living that was generally better than that of their parents.

The New World of Business

Corporate Values Stress Conformity

During the postwar years, the motto of major corporations became "bigger is better." Business mergers, the combining of several companies, created **conglomerates**—firms that had holdings in a variety of unrelated industries. Many of the nation's biggest corporations grew even bigger during the postwar years. The net sales of IBM jumped from $119.4 million in 1946 to $1.7 billion in 1961. General Motors doubled its net assets during the 1950s from $1.5 billion in 1951 to $2.8 billion in 1960.

Up the Corporate Ladder

Rapid corporate growth during the 1950s gave rise to new employment opportunities and a new lifestyle for the nation's white-collar workers (clerical and professional workers) who viewed the corporate life as a secure career. Major corporations provided their employees with everything from company neckties to memberships in exclusive country clubs. Training programs encouraged employees to adopt the company point of view. Companies such as IBM sent their managers to schools to learn not only management techniques, but company beliefs as well.

Critics charged corporations with destroying individuality by expecting employees to conform to company standards of thinking, dressing, and behaving. As sociologist C. Wright Mills commented, "When white-collar people get jobs, they sell not only their time and energy but their personalities as well."

Major corporations greatly influenced American life and values in the 1950s. To those climbing the corporate ladder—that is, being promoted to higher and higher levels of responsibility—wages were but one concern. Equally important were benefits such as a pension plan, medical insurance, a performance bonus, an expense account, a paid vacation, and a company car. For employees who dedicated themselves to the corporate lifestyle and successfully met the expectations of their superiors, the rewards of corporate life were further proof that the United States was a land of opportunity—at least for some Americans.

During the 1950s positions of power and authority within the corporate world belonged mostly to white males. Minority representation was very rare. Women were expected to fill different roles in the postwar American workforce. The widely read *Life* magazine explained women's roles one way:

> Household skills take her into the garment trades; neat and personable, she becomes office worker and saleslady; patient and dexterous, she does well on repetitive, detailed factory work; compassionate, she becomes teacher and nurse.
>
> —*Life,* 1956

IBM

Corporate Image **Large corporations encouraged conformity and offered training programs that helped develop the "corporate image." At some companies, holding the proper beliefs was just as important as wearing the proper necktie.**
What might be the benefits and disadvantages of working for a large corporation?

The Service Sector

The nation's public and private service industries enjoyed tremendous expansion during the postwar years. Government jobs at the national, state, city, and county levels included social workers, teachers, and civil servants. In private business, there was a big growth in the number of secretarial and clerical workers, bank tellers, and telephone operators, as well as service workers in the insurance, transportation, and retail sales areas. Hospitality and recreation industries needed more service workers with the increased number of bowling alleys, skating rinks, movie theaters, hotels, and restaurants. The unprecedented number of cars, appliances, radios, and television sets purchased by consumers created a need for skilled mechanics and repairpeople. For the first time in United States history, workers who performed services began to outnumber those who manufactured products.

Farms Become Big Business

Small Farmers Leave for the City

The postwar years also saw a transformation in agriculture from family business to corporate enterprise. Two studies conducted of Plainville, a pseudonym for a small rural community in southeast Missouri, told a large story. The first study, conducted in 1939, revealed a community of small farms. Here, farmers grew a variety of small crops, raised a few chickens, and bred a few cows. Fifteen years later, Plainville had been transformed. Farming had become big business. As incomes doubled, or even tripled, residents joined the consumer society. Nearly every home had a television set. The way of life in rural Plainville was almost indistinguishable from that in suburban areas.

Plainville was typical of the changing nature of farming throughout the postwar United States. The size of farms increased. Farmers learned that large-scale farming lowered the cost of production. For example, in 1960 the average cost of corn production was $61 per acre when grown on 160 acres (64.8 ha); the cost dropped to $54 per acre on 640 acres (259.2 ha). As the size of farms grew, the value of fertile farmland rose rapidly.

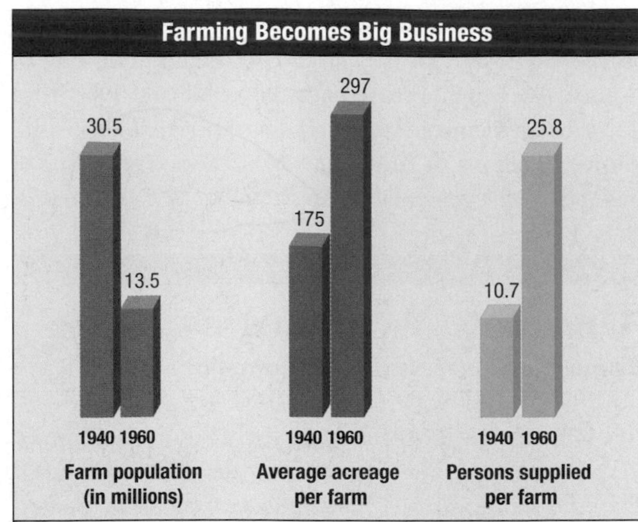

As farms grew larger, the number of people needed to work on them dropped. *What happened to the number of people supplied per farm?*

While a few farmers benefited from these changes, others suffered. Because small farms could not compete with large farms, many small-farm families sold their land and migrated to urban areas. As farm size doubled, the total number of farms dropped from more than 6 million in 1940 to fewer than 4 million in 1960, and the farm population fell from about 30 million to about 13 million. By 1960 only 8 percent of the population lived on farms.

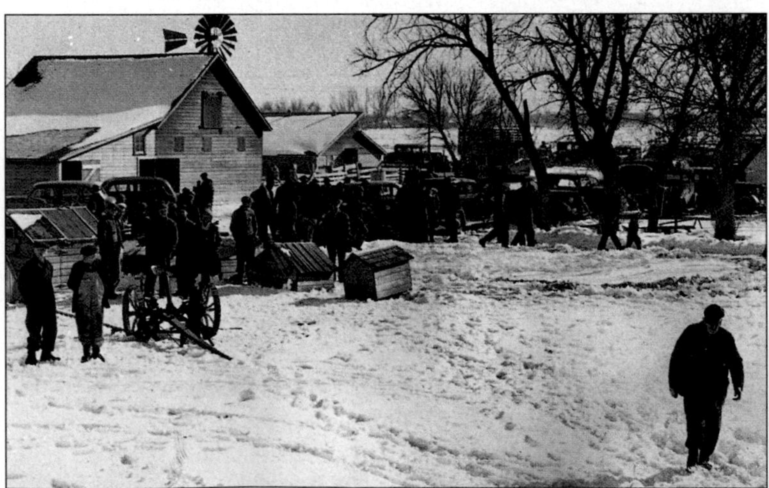
UPI/BETTMANN NEWSPHOTOS

Farm Auction A farmer, defeated by weather and economic conditions, must auction off his Nebraska farm. *Why were small farms unable to compete with large farms?*

An Automobile Culture

The 1950s' Fascination With Cars

The migration of farm families to the city was characteristic of the population as a whole. Americans were on the move, and the automobile became indispensable to their way of life. Auto dealers sold a record 58 million cars during the 1950s. Car manufacturers kept the public buying by changing body styles and adding more options, which made the previous year's models obsolete, at least in style. Turning out large, high-powered, steel-and-chrome fantasies in every color of the rainbow, the automakers provided sparkling steel chariots for every taste and income level.

Curb Service and Drive-ins

Americans practically lived in their automobiles. "Come as you are, eat in your car" became a popular slogan of fast-food drive-ins that provided curb service. Traveling on roller skates, waitresses and waiters, called carhops,

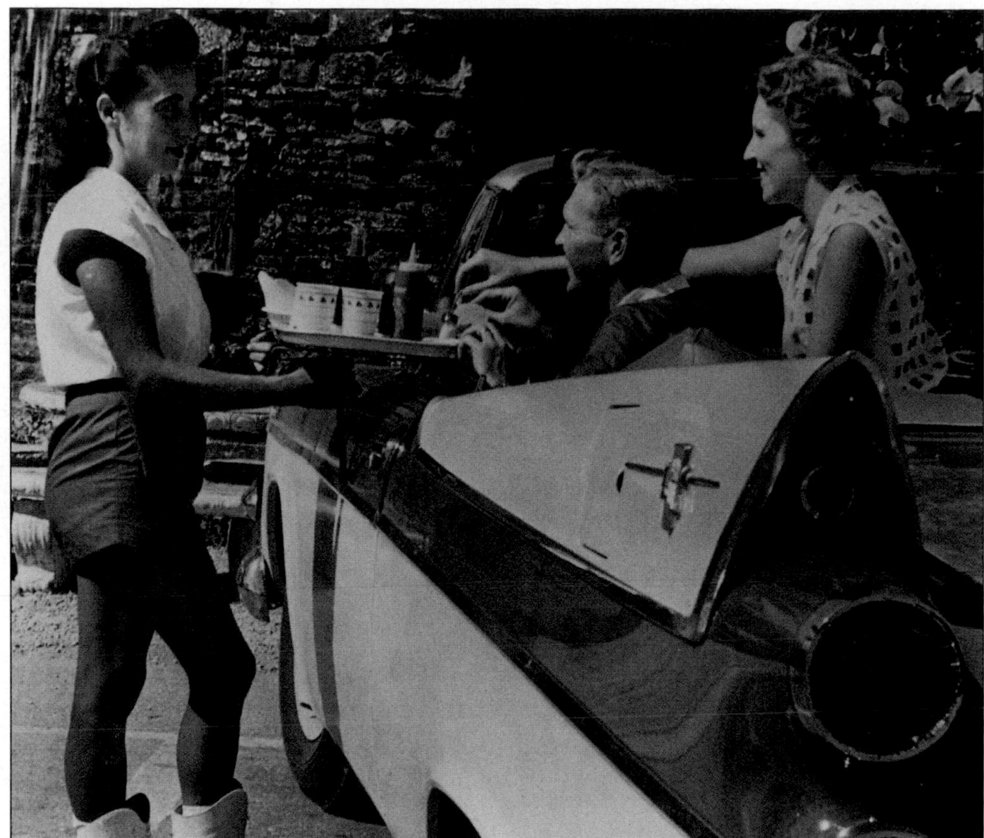

UPI/BETTMANN

Drive-in Restaurant Hamburgers, french fries, and Cokes were drive-in favorites during the 1950s. *What encouraged automobile travel?*

took orders and delivered food to the customer's car window. Drive-in theaters showed movies on outdoor screens as audiences watched from inside their cars.

Ribbons of Highway

The development of an extensive interstate highway system encouraged automobile travel. The Highway Act of 1956 authorized $32 billion for the construction of more than 40,000 miles of federal highways. President Eisenhower proudly described his administration's commitment to the interstate highway system:

> The amount of concrete poured to form these roadways would build . . . six sidewalks to the moon. . . . More than any single action by the government since the end of the war, this one would change the face of America.
>
> —President Dwight D. Eisenhower

Migration to the Suburbs

The moving van became the new symbol of American mobility. During each year of the 1950s, nearly one-fifth of the population changed residences. Attracted by warm climates and plentiful jobs, Americans began to head to the West and the Southwest. Cities such as Houston, Dallas, Phoenix, and Albuquerque boomed. The greatest population surge took place in California. By 1963 it had surpassed New York as the nation's most populous state.

By far the most significant population shift was the migration of white Americans from cities to suburbs. The greater availability of automobiles, the expansion of the highway system, and the affordability of mass-produced housing spurred suburbinization. By the end of the 1950s, more than one-fifth of all Americans lived in the suburbs, changing the landscape of the nation and the lifestyle of middle-class America.

Section Assessment

Main Idea

1. Use a diagram like this one to show the causes and effects of the postwar prosperity enjoyed by most Americans.

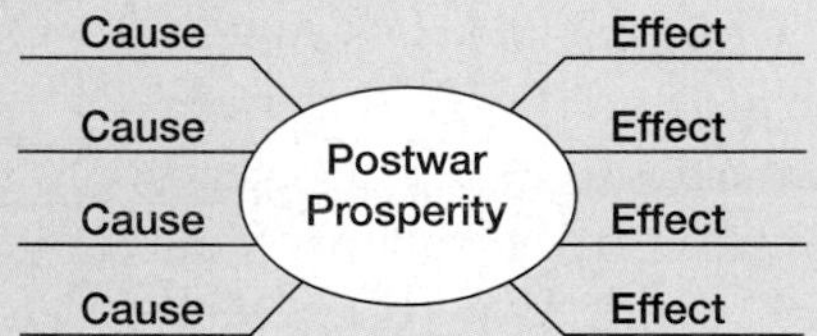

Vocabulary

2. Define: demobilization, real income, discretionary income, conglomerate.

Checking Facts

3. What benefits did the GI Bill of Rights offer?
4. What caused the heavy demand for consumer goods after the war?

Critical Thinking

5. **Analyzing Information** How did the return of the GIs change the job market for women? Were any of the changes positive? Explain.

Geography: Impact on History

MOVEMENT

New American Landscape: Suburbia

By 1945 a severe housing shortage had developed in the United States. During the war new housing starts had slowed to a standstill. Then hundreds of thousands of GIs came home, got married, and began looking for homes. The nation needed 5 million new housing units—the sooner, the better.

The Suburbs

The construction industry in the United States had to meet quite a challenge. Cities were too crowded for new construction to occur, and relocating millions of people to remote, sparsely populated areas of the country would be expensive and impractical. The builders' solution was to create a new addition to the country's landscape—planned communities on the outskirts of cities. This decision would transform not only the landscape of the country but also the lifestyles of the mostly white, middle-class Americans who began migrating from crowded cities to the open, quieter environment of the suburbs. Following World War II, several planned communities were constructed just outside many of the nation's big cities.

Levittown, U.S.A.

The first and most famous postwar planned community was begun in 1946 on Long Island, New York, about 30 miles (48.2 km) from midtown Manhattan. The community, called Levittown, was named for the company that built it, Levitt & Sons, and was constructed on 1,200 acres (486 ha) of potato farmland.

Levittown's design included single-family homes, parks, playgrounds, shopping centers, swimming pools, baseball diamonds, handball courts, and clubhouses for fraternal and veterans organizations. Each home was exactly the same and sold for the same price: $7,990.

The homes at Levittown were mass-produced. Specialized construction crews hurried from one home site to the next, digging foundations, pouring concrete, erecting walls and roofs, and installing plumbing and electrical fixtures. During the height of the construction at Levittown, workers finished a new home every 15 minutes.

Levittown was an immediate success. Just 3 years after construction began, 10,600 houses had been built, and Levittown's population

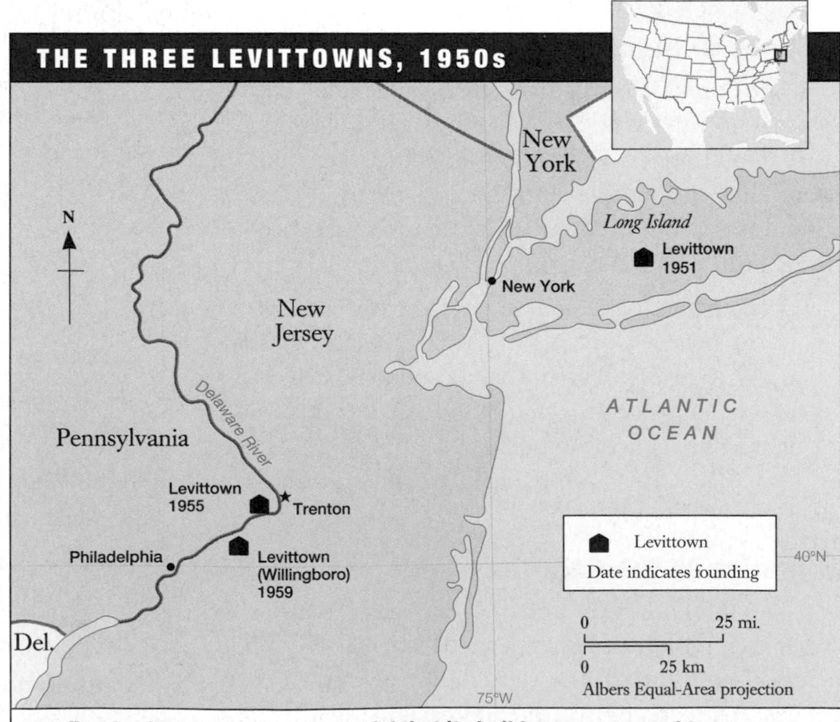

The first Levittown was so successful that its builders constructed two more—one in Pennsylvania and one in New Jersey. *What cities were they near?*

had swelled to more than 40,000. The residents loved their new community. One former GI who had moved to Levittown with his wife and another relative from a 1-bedroom apartment in Brooklyn said, "That was so awful I'd rather not talk about it. Getting into this house was like being emancipated."

A New Landscape

The construction of planned communities such as the three Levittowns accounted for several important changes in the landscape. First, these types of planned communities, or subdivisions, had never existed before. They combined elements of city life with features of rural living, blurring the distinctions that had once existed between these two ways of life.

Second, the new communities were an attractive alternative to the increasingly crowded, dirty cities in which most Americans lived. People who could afford to move did so, resulting in a migration of white middle-class Americans from the cities to surrounding suburbs.

Finally, the suburbs created a new way of life for many Americans. Long daily commutes to and from jobs in the cities became more and more common. New local governments were created to administer the affairs of these fledgling communities and new school systems were needed to educate the children of the suburbs. In short, the postwar housing shortage led to a transformation in the way the nation looked and in the way many Americans lived.

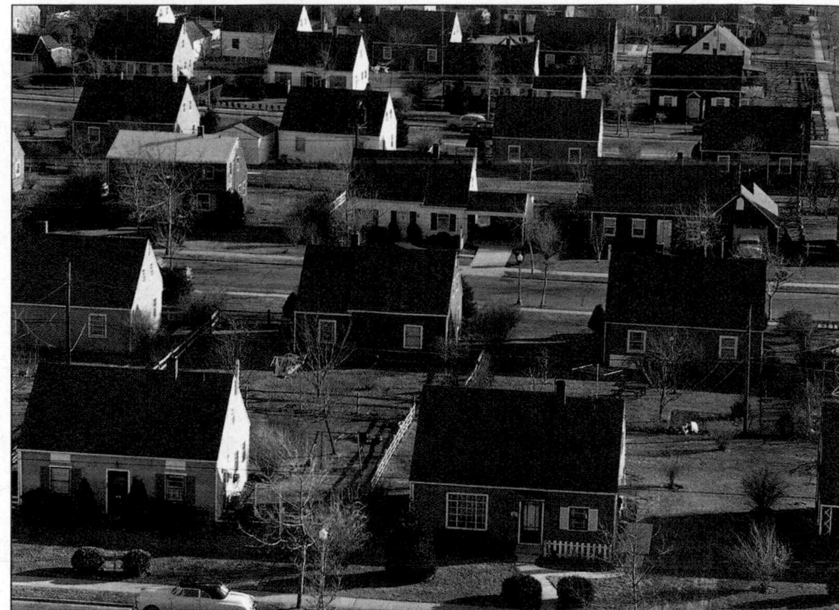

Suburban Living **All the streets in Levittown curved at exactly the same angle, and trees were planted along them, 1 every 28 feet (8.5 m). Despite such rigid conformity, residents from the city loved the openness and country feel of this new suburb.** *How many homes were constructed in the first Levittown?*

Modern Conveniences **Homes in Levittown had a living room with a fireplace, two bedrooms, and a large attic that could be converted into two additional bedrooms. They also had the latest conveniences: radiant heat, an electric kitchen, an automatic washing machine, and a built-in television.** *How much did these homes cost when they were first built?*

Making the Geographic Connection

1. Where was the first Levittown built, and what major city was it near? Where do you think many of the Levittown residents had lived before they moved to Levittown?
2. How were the homes in Levittown mass-produced? During the height of construction at the Levittown on Long Island, how often was a new home completed?
3. **Movement** After a decade of middle-class migration to the suburbs, the quality of life in most big cities began to decline. What were possible reasons for this decline?

Suburban Lifestyles

1950s: AMERICANS MIGRATE TO SUBURBS

JILL JOHNSON PARKED THE GREEN AND WHITE STATION WAGON NEXT TO A NUMBER OF OTHER SIMILAR VEHICLES AT THE TRAIN STATION. As Bob Johnson joined the crowd waiting for the 8:22 A.M. commuter into the city, the Johnson children waved and blew kisses to their dad. Jill Johnson's next stop was Eisenhower Elementary School where Bill, a fourth grader, and Susan, a second grader, spent their day. Mary Ann, age four, and baby Jimmy then accompanied their mom to the shopping center.

© SUPERSTOCK

Family Values
Following World War II, many families moved to the suburbs in search of the good life.

The Village Market Mall provided ample parking for its 30 or more stores and offices. Shoppers had access to a large department store, a bank, a beauty salon and a barber shop, a drugstore, a dry cleaner, and a supermarket. Physicians, dentists, and attorneys occupied offices on the second floors of the two-story buildings in the shopping center.

Jill dropped off Bob's suits at the dry cleaner and then stopped at the supermarket to pick up cookies for the Cub Scout meeting and steaks to barbecue on Sunday. She also picked out frozen TV dinners so that the family could eat while they watched *The Adventures of Ozzie and Harriet* on Friday night.

With the morning errands completed, Jill Johnson and her children headed for home, a neat one-story frame house with a picture window and an attached garage, located on a street with many similar houses. The neighborhood's well-kept lawns and newly planted flowers and trees reflected pride of ownership. The Johnsons, along with 60 million other white Americans, were enjoying the comfortable lifestyle of the suburbs.

GUIDE TO READING

Main Idea

For some people, the child-centered suburban culture fulfilled the American dream; for others, it represented a dream unfulfilled and the shortcomings of postwar society.

Vocabulary

- suburbia
- baby boom

Read to Find Out . . .

- the major population patterns that helped reshape American society in the 1950s.
- the suburban values of the 1950s.
- that status of women and children during the 1950s.

Growth of Suburbia

Cities Lag Behind as Suburbs Grow

During the 1950s, 85 percent of new home construction took place in **suburbia**—residential areas outside the city. The number of suburban dwellers doubled, while the population of central cities rose only 10 percent. Reasons for the rapid growth of suburbia varied. Some whites wanted to escape the crime and the congestion of city neighborhoods. Others fled because of their prejudices against African Americans and Hispanic Americans who were moving to cities in growing numbers. Generally, middle-class white Americans considered migration to the suburbs a move upward to a better life for themselves and their children.

In contrast to city life, suburbia offered a retreat to the picturesque countryside. As developers in earlier periods had done, the developers of the 1950s attracted home buyers with promises of fresh air, green lawns, and trees. Many suburbs had "park," "forest," "woods," "grove," or "hill" as part of their names.

The new suburbs were usually located on the fringes of major cities. Farmland or vacant wooded areas became sites for new subdivisions. In southern California, development of the San Fernando Valley, formerly sprinkled with orange groves, helped make Los Angeles the fastest growing area in the postwar period.

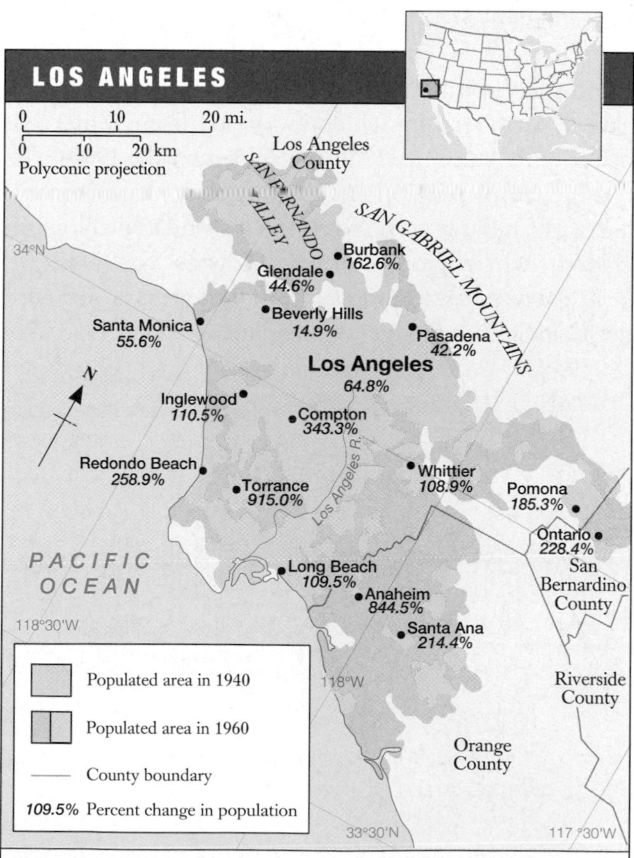

The Los Angeles area was one of the most rapidly growing parts of California between 1940 and 1960. *Which counties experienced the most growth between 1940 and 1960?*

African American Suburbs In Richmond, California, a group of African American community leaders developed a planned community, named Parchester Village, for middle-class African Americans. *Why was suburban life denied to many Americans in the 1950s?*

Suburbs had low population densities compared with cities. Single-family homes on large plots of land, wide streets, and open spaces gave suburbs the "country" feeling that new middle-class homeowners craved. They could enjoy this openness because residents owned automobiles, which allowed them to travel to jobs, schools, and shopping facilities.

Affordability became a key factor in attracting home buyers to the suburbs. Because the GI Bill offered low-interest loans, new housing was more affordable during the postwar period than at any other time in American history. Equally attractive was the government's offer of income tax deductions for home mortgage interest payments and property taxes.

Though affordable, the suburbs did not offer opportunities for homeownership to everyone. Many American cities had small but growing populations of middle-class minorities, particularly African Americans and Hispanic Americans, who also longed to escape the noise, the dirt, and the crime of the cities. By and large, however, the developers of the nation's postwar suburbs refused to sell homes to minorities. By 1960, for example, Levittown, Long Island, had a population of more than 65,000, but it had not a single African American resident. Despite having achieved a measure of financial success, America's middle-class minorities were still denied full access to the American dream.

LAMBERT/ARCHIVE PHOTOS

Suburban Ideal Togetherness was an important value during the 1950s. *What criticisms were leveled at the suburban dream?*

Such criticism would not have rung true with most suburbanites. Emerging from an era of depression and a world war, the residents of suburbia during the 1950s saw themselves creating thousands of new communities built on a common desire for a decent existence. They prized the informality and togetherness of suburban life. The Welcome Wagon, a community organization that provided information and offered gifts and coupons from local stores, greeted new families. Most newcomers moved easily into the social life of their new neighborhood by joining a bowling league, a bridge club, or a church group. One suburban resident observed: "Before we came here, we used to live pretty much to ourselves. . . . Now we stop around and visit with people or they visit with us. I really think [suburban living] has broadened us."

Cooperation and group participation helped forge community spirit in the suburbs. This spirit extended to church membership, which increased from 48 percent of the population in 1940 to 63 percent in 1960. The resurgence of religion became evident in all areas of life, from movies to politics. Hollywood's hit films included such religious extravaganzas as *The Robe, The Ten Commandments,* and *Ben Hur.* Congress added "under God" to the Pledge of Allegiance and "In God We

The American Dream

Community Spirit in the Suburbs

Low-income and minority groups were largely excluded from suburban society. Millions of white, middle-class Americans, however, shared a lifestyle that represented to them the American dream. They owned their own homes, sent their children to good schools, lived in safe communities, and were economically secure. Such were the dreams of the immigrants who had sailed into New York Harbor half a century before, and now those dreams finally had been realized by many of their children and grandchildren.

Nevertheless, some Americans found fault with the "dream." Social critics of the 1950s deplored the conformity of suburban life. They mocked what they regarded as the sameness of the "cookie-cutter" houses, the lack of privacy, and the decline of individuality. Folksinger Malvina Reynolds satirized the middle-class suburbanites in a popular song titled "Little Boxes":

And they all play on the golf course
And drink their martinis dry,
And they all have pretty children
And the children go to school,
And the children go to summer camp
And then to the university,
Where they are put in boxes
And they come out all the same.

—Malvina Reynolds,
"Little Boxes"

"Cookie-cutter" Houses A cartoonist pokes fun at the sameness of suburban life. *Why did many people like the suburbs?*

Billy Graham **An ordained Southern Baptist minister, Graham first gained recognition through his radio broadcasts, tent revivals, and appearances at "Youth for Christ" rallies. During the 1950s, many considered him fundamentalism's chief voice.** *How did religion help shape values during the 1950s?*

Trust" to all United States currency. President Eisenhower told Americans, "Everybody should have a religious faith, and I don't care what it is."

Religious leaders helped spread religious commitment with the aid of modern media. They had their own radio and television programs, best-selling books, and newspaper columns. Billy Graham, a popular Protestant minister, attracted thousands of people throughout the United States and in other parts of the world with his huge evangelical campaigns. Fulton J. Sheen, a Roman Catholic bishop, became a television personality through his weekly program optimistically titled *Life Is Worth Living*. Protestant minister Norman Vincent Peale attracted followers with his message of "positive thinking."

Critics claimed that churches downplayed faith and emphasized comfort and security. Instead of searching for God, the critics said, most Americans turned to religion for peace of mind and a sense of belonging. For whatever reasons, American families flocked to their churches and synagogues throughout the 1950s. Billboards and television commercials proclaimed: "Bring the whole family to church" and "The family that prays together stays together." Messages like these clearly indicated that postwar society was focused on the family.

Baby Boom

A Child-centered Culture

Like the economy, the family enjoyed unprecedented growth in the postwar years. The nation's population increased by 19 million in the 1940s and by almost 30 million in the 1950s. The fertility rate—the number of births per thousand women—peaked at 123 in 1957, up about 20 percent from the Depression years of the 1930s. That meant that a baby was born in the United States every 7 seconds! This phenomenal population growth, known as the **baby boom,** continued until the mid-1960s.

HISTORY Online

Student Web Activity 18

Visit the *American Odyssey* Web site at americanodyssey.glencoe.com and click on ***Chapter 18—Student Web Activities*** for an activity relating to society and culture in the 1950s.

Like the resurgence of religion in the 1950s, the emphasis on family reflected a desire for close social and emotional ties. A *McCall's* magazine article in 1954 coined the term "togetherness" to describe young married couples whose lives centered on raising large families. Americans in the 1950s married at an earlier age and had more babies than their parents. Between 1940 and 1960, the birthrate for third and fourth children in a family more than doubled.

The baby boom further fueled the economy and helped sustain prosperity. Growing families needed larger houses, so the construction industry prospered. As the baby boomers progressed from diapers to school classrooms to college diplomas, industries and institutions grew to satisfy their needs. During the 1950s, school enrollments increased by 13 million. School districts struggled to erect new buildings and temporary classrooms to accommodate the nation's children. In California a new school was completed every 7 days throughout the 1950s, and still the state faced a shortage of classrooms.

Catering to the Kids

Many baby-boom kids enjoyed a lifestyle of unprecedented privilege. Schools became not only institutions of learning but also centers of social activity. After-school programs included an endless variety of lessons and sports events. Parents, who wanted to give their children all the advantages their new prosperity allowed, enthusiastically supported these activities. Music lessons in the schools drove up the sale of musical instruments from $86 million in 1950 to $149 million in 1960. The number of Girl Scouts and Brownies doubled, and the number of Little Leagues grew from about 800 to nearly 6,000 during the 1950s.

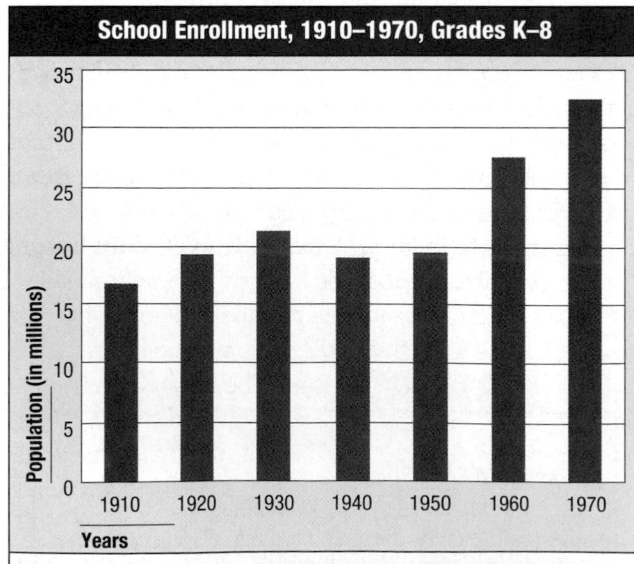

School enrollments skyrocketed in the 1950s. *How many students were enrolled in schools in 1910? In 1970?*

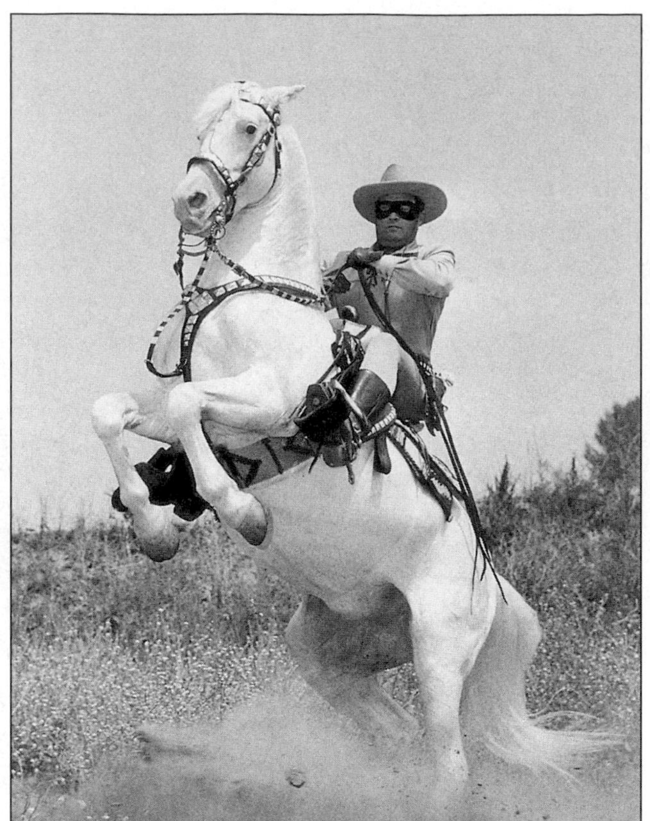

The Lone Ranger In this very popular television western, the Lone Ranger and his Native American friend, Tonto, set out to bring law and order to the West. *Who were some of the other television heroes of the 1950s?*

Baby boomers were the nation's first generation raised on television from their earliest years. Programming for children included everything from puppet shows to tales of the Old West. Young viewers gathered around the television to watch Buffalo Bob and his freckle-faced marionette, and when the youngsters heard the familiar opening line, "Say kids, what time is it?" they responded in unison, "It's Howdy Doody time!" At its height the popular *Kukla, Fran, and Ollie* puppet show attracted an audience of 10 million viewers. Kukla (a clown), Ollie (a snaggle-toothed dragon), and several other Kuklapolitan puppets visited with Fran Allison in an unrehearsed weekly program that charmed adults as well as children.

Television heroes included the Lone Ranger, Hopalong Cassidy, and Captain Video (Guardian of the Universe). Also popular were shows featuring heroic dogs and horses—*Lassie, Rin-Tin-Tin,* and *My Friend Flicka.* On *Ding Dong School,* kindly Miss Frances led her television audience in constructive preschool activities and songs. Millions of viewers joined Annette, Cubby, Karen, and the other Mouseketeers on *The Mickey Mouse Club.* Captain Kangaroo, Mr. Green Jeans, and a collection of puppet friends entertained more than one generation of youngsters.

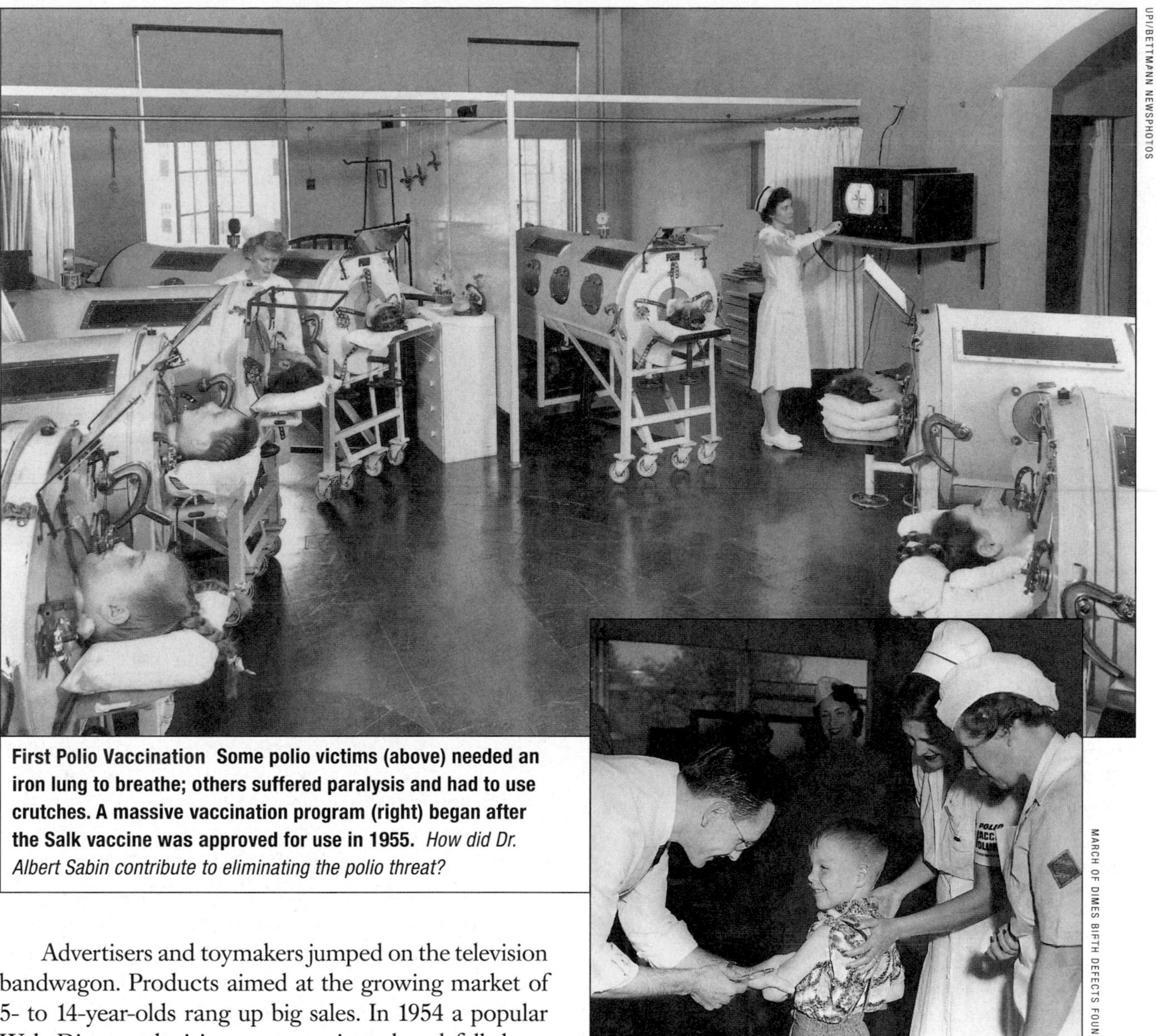
UPI/BETTMANN NEWSPHOTOS

MARCH OF DIMES BIRTH DEFECTS FOUNDATION

First Polio Vaccination **Some polio victims (above) needed an iron lung to breathe; others suffered paralysis and had to use crutches. A massive vaccination program (right) began after the Salk vaccine was approved for use in 1955.** *How did Dr. Albert Sabin contribute to eliminating the polio threat?*

Advertisers and toymakers jumped on the television bandwagon. Products aimed at the growing market of 5- to 14-year-olds rang up big sales. In 1954 a popular Walt Disney television program introduced folk hero Davy Crockett, portrayed by Fess Parker. The resulting Davy Crockett "cult" created a $100 million market for coonskin caps and dozens of other items with Davy's picture on them. The show's theme song, "The Ballad of Davy Crockett," sold 4 million records.

Critics argued that television produced passive children. Children's programming, they claimed, was boring, mindless, and often violent. Still, some programs carried positive messages. Good triumphed over evil. Gentleness, kindness, and truthfulness prevailed. The joy and wonder of childhood were encouraged and celebrated.

Healthier, Happier Children

By the 1950s medical science had made great strides toward combating childhood diseases. Antibiotics and vaccines helped control diseases such as diphtheria, influenza, and typhoid fever. Polio, however, continued to baffle the medical profession. In 1952 a record number of 58,000 cases of polio was reported in the United States. Those who survived were often permanently paralyzed. The most severe cases were confined to iron lungs—large metal tanks with pumps that helped patients breathe. Polio became the most feared disease of the postwar period.

Dr. Jonas Salk finally developed an effective vaccine against polio and in doing so became the medical hero of the 1950s. Salk first tested the vaccine on himself, his wife, and their three sons. In 1954, 2 million schoolchildren took part in a mass testing program. The test, which was the largest effort of its kind in history, utilized the services of thousands of physicians and millions of volunteers. On April 12, 1955, the Salk vaccine was declared a safe and effective weapon against polio. Through the work of Dr. Salk, who became a hero to people throughout the world, and Dr. Albert Sabin, who developed an oral version of the vaccine, the threat of polio was virtually eliminated.

AP/WIDE WORLD PHOTOS

Dr. Benjamin Spock The famous doctor visits the Anderson quintuplets. *How did his books influence the rearing of children?*

Dr. Salk's fame was paralleled by that of another medical person, Dr. Benjamin Spock. During the 1950s only the Bible sold more copies than Spock's book *Baby and Child Care.* Spock popularized the theory that early childhood experiences influence an individual's entire life. He urged mothers to spare the rod and to devote themselves to creating an atmosphere of warmth and trust for their children so that they would grow into happy, well-adjusted adults. "You can think of it this way: useful, well-adjusted citizens are the most valuable possessions a country has, and good mother care during early childhood is the surest way to produce them." Dr. Spock suggested that the government should pay mothers so that they would not have to seek outside employment. This idea failed to gain popular support, and opponents even suggested that it smacked of socialism.

A Woman's Place

Back Into the Labor Force

Spock's theories helped reinforce the concept of motherhood as a profession in itself and strengthened the old idea that a woman's place was in the home. "No job is more exacting, more necessary, or more rewarding than that of housewife and mother," stated an article in the *Atlantic* in 1950. Statistics indicated that American women agreed. The median age of marriage for women fell from 21.5 in 1940 to 20.1 in 1956. By 1950 nearly 60 percent of all women between the ages of 18 and 24 were married.

Mother and Homemaker

In the 1950s women were discouraged from attending college. A high-school textbook on family living counseled young women that "Men are not interested in college degrees, but in the warmth and humanness of the girls they marry." Many women who did graduate from college concentrated their studies in such fields as home economics or child development. A survey found that most college women believed "it is natural for a woman to be satisfied with her husband's success and not crave personal achievement."

The suburban lifestyle strengthened the distinctions between male and female roles. Fathers often left home early in the morning to commute to jobs in the city. When they returned home in the evening, the children had been fed, bathed, and dressed for bed. Most mothers assumed responsibility for the daily routine of child rearing in addition to cooking, cleaning, shopping, washing clothes, and participating in school and community activities. John Cheever, who set many of his novels and short stories in the suburbs of New York, described one such woman:

> She gets up at seven and turns the radio on. After she is dressed, she rouses the children and cooks the breakfast. Our son has to be walked to the school bus at eight o'clock. When Ethel returns from this trip, Carol's hair has to be braided. I leave the house at eight-thirty, but I know that every move that Ethel makes for the rest of the day will be determined by the housework, the cooking, the shopping, and the demands of the children. I know that on Tuesdays and Thursdays she will be at the A & P between eleven and noon, that on every clear afternoon she will be on a certain bench in a playground from three until five, that she cleans the house on Mondays, Wednesdays, and Fridays, and polishes the silver when it rains. When I return at six, she is usually cleaning the vegetables or making some other preparation for dinner. Then when the children have been fed and bathed, when the dinner is ready, when the table in the living room is set with food and china, she stands in the middle of the room as if she has lost or forgotten something, and this moment of reflection is so deep that she will not hear me if I speak to her, or the children if they call. Then it is over. She lights the four white candles in their silver sticks, and we sit down to a supper of corned-beef hash or some other modest fare.
>
> —John Cheever, "The Season of Divorce" from *The Stories of John Cheever*

Popular culture reinforced the image of women as cute and perky rather than intelligent or career-minded. Actresses such as Doris Day, Debbie Reynolds, and Sandra Dee became role models for white women of the 1950s. Each portrayed the sweet, funny, innocent, wholesome, blond girl-next-door in popular box-office hits of the decade. Television situation comedies (sitcoms) emphasized the role of woman as wife and mother. In such shows as *Father Knows Best* and *Leave It to Beaver,* Dad dispensed wisdom and advice while apron-clad Mom tended to domestic matters. In programs such as *Our Miss Brooks* and *Private Secretary,* the main character was an unmarried career woman whose goal in life was simply to find a husband.

The educational system often encouraged schoolgirls of the 1950s to follow in their mothers' footsteps. While boys studied woodworking, auto mechanics, or courses preparing them for college, girls learned typing, cooking, and etiquette. However, a Gallup Poll in 1962 showed that 90 percent of the mothers surveyed hoped that their daughters would not lead the same lives as they had.

LAMBERT/ARCHIVE PHOTOS

Housework In the 1950s, hanging the laundry outside to dry was common.
What did Dr. Spock think was the most rewarding profession?

Women Question Their Role in Society

Despite the apparent happiness of the middle-class American woman, something was amiss. Many of these women did not feel the complete fulfillment that devotion to their homes and families was supposed to provide. Yet many considered women who were dissatisfied with this role to be either mentally disordered, unfeminine, or both. For example, psychiatrist Helene Deutsch declared that truly feminine women related to the outside world only through identification with their husbands and children.

In 1957 Smith College graduates of the class of 1942 answered an alumnae questionnaire prepared by Betty Friedan that raised the issue of a woman's role in society. Years of such research and interviews with women led to Friedan's landmark book, *The Feminine Mystique,* published in 1963. Friedan described the situation:

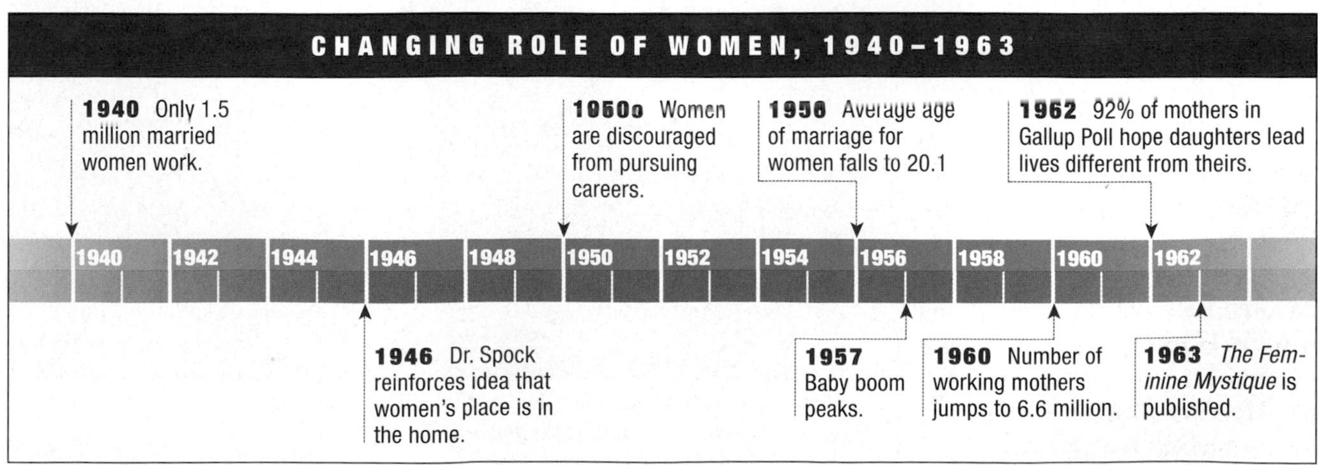

CHANGING ROLE OF WOMEN, 1940–1963
1940 Only 1.5 million married women work.
1950s Women are discouraged from pursuing careers.
1956 Average age of marriage for women falls to 20.1
1962 92% of mothers in Gallup Poll hope daughters lead lives different from theirs.
1940
1942
1944
1946
1948
1950
1952
1954
1956
1958
1960
1962
1946 Dr. Spock reinforces idea that women's place is in the home.
1957 Baby boom peaks.
1960 Number of working mothers jumps to 6.6 million.
1963 The Feminine Mystique is published.

The problem lay buried, unspoken, for many years in the minds of American women. It was a strange stirring, a sense of dissatisfaction, a yearning that women suffered in the middle of the twentieth century in the United States. Each suburban wife struggled with it alone. As she made the beds, shopped for groceries, matched slipcover material, ate peanut butter sandwiches with her children, chauffeured Cub Scouts and Brownies . . . she was afraid to ask even of herself the silent question—"Is this all?"

—Betty Friedan, *The Feminine Mystique,* 1963

UPI/BETTMANN NEWSPHOTOS

Betty Friedan After the publication of *The Feminine Mystique,* Friedan organized the National Organization for Women. *What was Friedan's book about?*

Friedan had finally identified the "problem that had no name." While many American women were happy with their roles as housewives and mothers, many others felt social pressures had relegated them to roles as lifelong domestics.

Women in the Workforce

At the end of World War II, the government and industries urged women to "go back home" and "give your job to a vet." Women, who were largely excluded from important jobs in the corporate world, were also squeezed out of the manufacturing jobs they had held during the war.

Whether by pressure or by choice, many women who had taken on nontraditional jobs during the war returned to the familiar roles of full-time homemakers and mothers. For women in the lower economic ranks, however, staying at home was not an option. Millions of such women continued to enter the job market while still maintaining their roles as housewives and mothers. During the 1950s the rate of female employment increased 4 times faster than that of males. The number of working wives nearly doubled from 17 percent in 1940 to 32 percent in 1960. The number of working mothers leaped from 1.5 million to 6.6 million. By 1960 nearly 40 percent of women with children between the ages of 6 and 17 had jobs outside the home.

Married women over 35 represented the greatest increase in female employment in the 1950s. Many of these women had worked outside the home before having a family. They then had stayed home to raise their children, who were now either married or off to school. These women filled the millions of clerical and secretarial positions created in the postwar period that the relatively small number of young single women who were entering the job market could not fill.

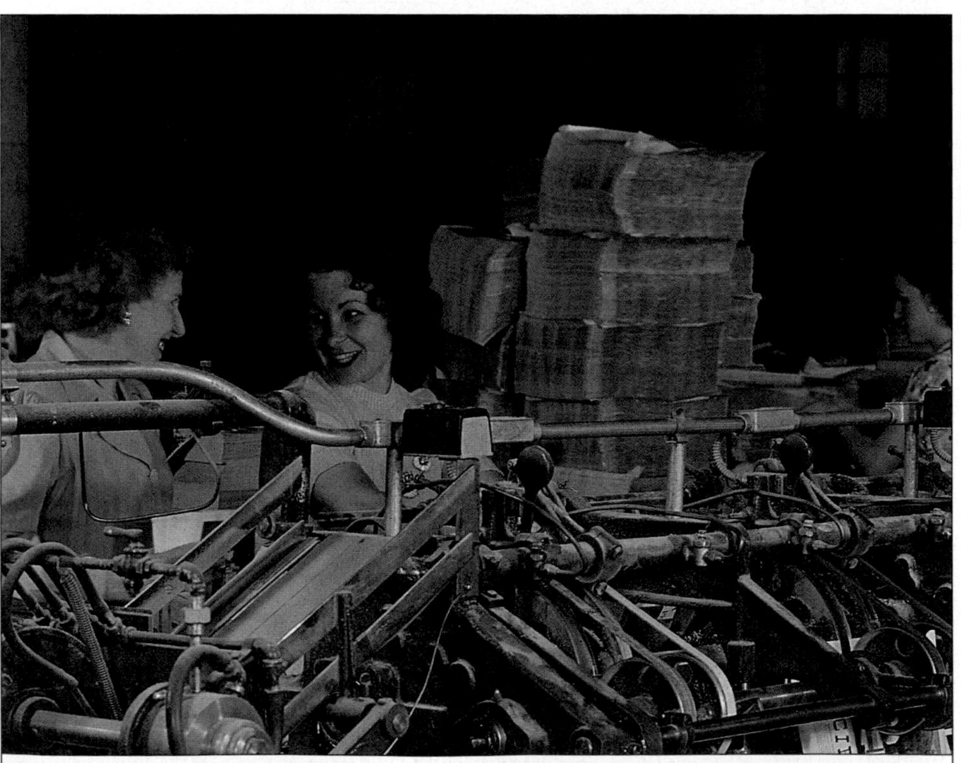

© ARTHUR D'ARAZIEN/SUPERSTOCK

Women at Work Women run folding machines at this plant in Chicago. *How much faster did the rate of female employment increase than that of males in the 1950s?*

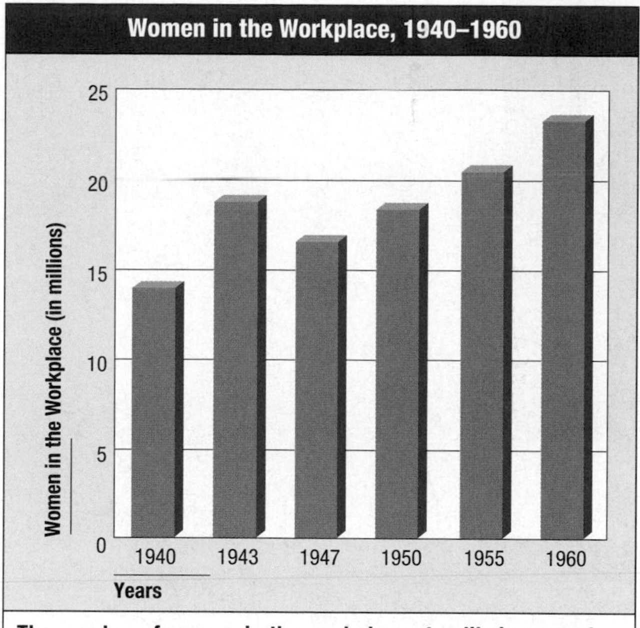

The number of women in the workplace steadily increased from 1940 to 1960. *How many women worked in 1940? In 1960?*

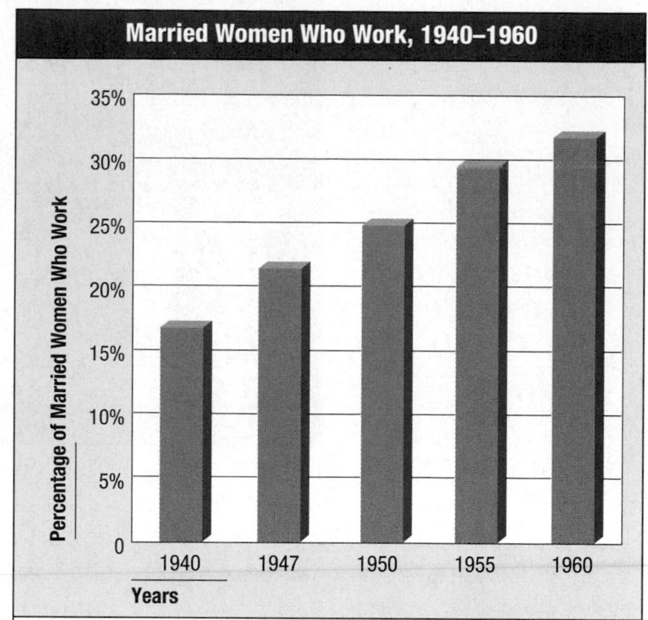

The percentage of married women who work also steadily increased. *What percentage of married women worked in 1940? In 1960?*

When surveyed about why they worked, married women no longer talked about professional advancement. Many women said they wanted to help pay for the children's education or the mortgage or a second car or a vacation—in other words, to get a piece of the American dream. In households where the husband earned between $7,000 and $10,000 a year, the rate of women's employment increased from 7 percent in 1950 to 25 percent in 1960. The 1960 United States census indicated that the number of households earning $15,000 or more would be cut in half if women's earnings were excluded. Women thus faced a dilemma. Economic pressures to maintain a comfortable lifestyle forced them into the workplace, while social pressures led them to believe their proper place was at home.

Most women's jobs, however, were low-paying and were either temporary, part-time, or held no opportunity for advancement. In areas such as insurance and banking, for example, women made up 50 percent or more of the workforce, but they held 20 percent or less of higher-level managerial positions. Many women in these industries worked as bank tellers or secretaries. High-level positions were reserved for men.

Stereotyped images of women's roles erected barriers to equal treatment. After World War II, the salary gap between full-time male and full-time female wage earners widened. In 1955 women earned 64 percent of average male wages; in 1963 they earned only 60 percent as much as men. A 1959 study concluded that women could not expect a professional career. Men simply would not take their professional goals seriously.

Women were not alone in their plight. Despite the prosperity of postwar society, many Americans—victims of racial prejudice and discrimination, neglect, and cultural differences—were denied full participation in the American dream.

Section Assessment

Main Idea

1. Use a diagram like this one to show the pros and cons of suburban life.

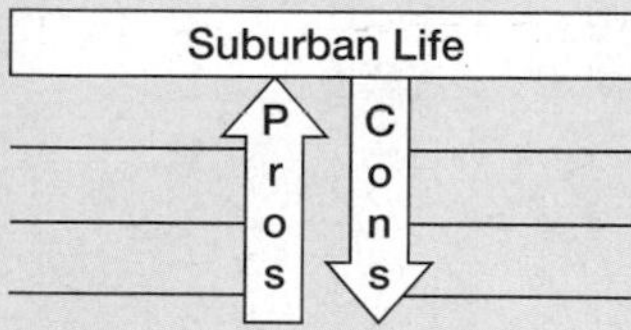

Vocabulary

2. Define: suburbia, baby boom.

Checking Facts

3. How and why did baby-boom kids enjoy privileges not available to their parents?

4. What role did religion play in the 1950s?

Critical Thinking

5. **Recognizing Bias** In 1955 women earned only 64 percent of the average wages men earned. What bias does this statistic reflect?

Rock 'n' Roll Arrives

After the upheaval of World War II, Americans sought security in an uncertain world. Many women left wartime jobs to become full-time housewives. Veterans returned to a pumped-up economy full of opportunity. Parents who had experienced the Depression lavished their newly acquired affluence on their children.

MOVIE STILL ARCHIVES

UNIVERSAL APPEAL

Little Richard (Richard Wayne Penniman) started his career as a gospel singer. In the mid-1950s, however, his single "Tutti Frutti" became a hit. Pat Boone's rendition of the song made it popular among white teenagers and introduced them to the rock music already popular among African Americans. Until the record company Motown began releasing the records of African American artists, most of these musicians were relatively unknown to white audiences.

© SID AVERY, 1956/MOTION PICTURE & TELEVISION PHOTO ARCHIVE

POPULAR ICON

With the popularity of the Mouseketeers on the ***Mickey Mouse Club*** television show and the opening of Disneyland in Southern California, Walt Disney became one of the most well-known and beloved figures in the United States.

FILE PHOTO BY RALPH BRUNKE

ROCK 'N' ROLL IS HERE TO STAY

On ***American Bandstand,*** hosted by the youthful-looking Dick Clark, teen fans danced in front of the TV camera to the live music of hit singers. From its studio in Philadelphia, *Bandstand* helped spread the urban rock scene throughout the country and tapped into a growing market for records.

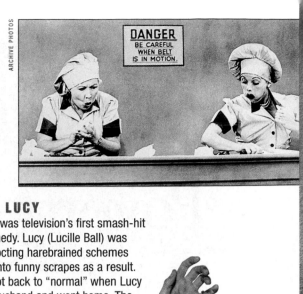

PAUL SCHUTZER/LIFE MAGAZINE, © TIME, INC.

DANGER
BE CAREFUL
WHEN BELT
IS IN MOTION.

ARCHIVE PHOTOS

LOVABLE LUCY

I Love Lucy was television's first smash-hit situation comedy. Lucy (Lucille Ball) was always concocting harebrained schemes and getting into funny scrapes as a result. Everything got back to "normal" when Lucy obeyed her husband and went home. The show mirrored and reinforced the prevailing attitudes about male and female roles.

PHOTOPLAY ARCHIVES/LGI

"THE KING"

In 1956 **Elvis Presley** skyrocketed to rock 'n' roll stardom—despite the objections of parents all over the country, who deplored his suggestive onstage antics. Nicknamed "Elvis the Pelvis," the country singer from Tennessee was the most popular rock star in history.

C O O L

DANCE WITH ME, BABY

Dancing became extremely popular among teenagers in the 1950s. Teenagers continued to dance the jitterbug that their parents had originated, in addition to their own creations—**line dances, the twist, the bop, the Watusi, the stroll, the slide, the pony, and the monkey.**

© SID AVERY, 1956/MOTION PICTURE & TELEVISION PHOTO ARCHIVE

Poverty and Plenty

1955: FAMILIES STRUGGLE IN EL BARRIO

PEDRO AND MARIA LOPEZ AND THEIR FIVE CHILDREN LIVED IN AN UNFURNISHED APARTMENT IN EAST HARLEM. El Barrio, as this section of New York City was called, had become one of the most densely populated places in the world, with nearly 300,000 people per square mile.

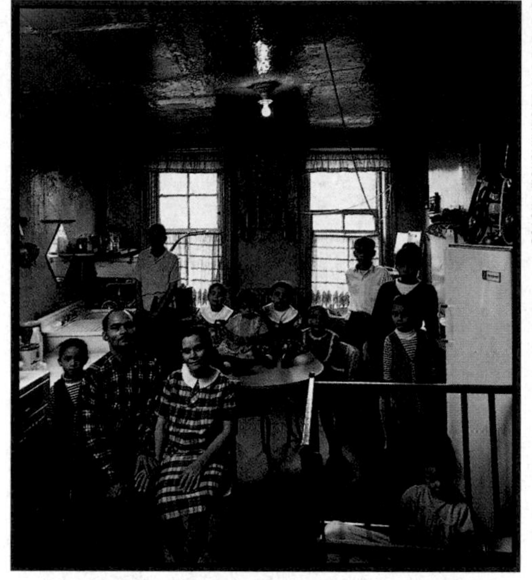

© BRUCE DAVIDSON/MAGNUM PHOTOS

El Barrio
Families like the Lopezes worked hard but struggled to make ends meet. The urban poor, who flooded cities after World War II, had little or no political representation.

The Lopez family paid $40 a week in rent for their fourth-floor walk-up, which consisted of a living room, a bathroom, a kitchen, and one bedroom. Despite Maria's scrupulous housekeeping, the apartment was infested with rats and roaches.

Six days a week, Pedro got up at 4:30 A.M. to commute to his job as a die cutter, for which he earned $75 weekly. Maria earned another $60 weekly by working part-time and weekends in a supermarket, which was a 45-minute trip from home.

When Pedro had to miss work because of a stomach ulcer, Maria applied for temporary aid from the Department of Social Services. The application was denied because her son Anthony had been suspended from school for truancy.

Because of additional medical expenses, Pedro and Maria came up $5 short that month when the rent was due. Their landlord promptly issued an eviction notice. In desperation, Pedro ignored his doctor's orders and returned to his job and even took a second job evenings and Sundays. Ten-year-old Manuel dropped out of school and found a job to help pay his family's bills.

Like many American families in the 1950s, the Lopezes were dedicated to the values of thrift, hard work, and a good education. The American dream, however, seemed always beyond

GUIDE TO READING

Main Idea

Overshadowed by the general affluence of the 1950s was a culture of poverty made up of the groups barred from the mainstream of American life by prejudice and discrimination.

Vocabulary

- culture of poverty
- termination policy

Read to Find Out . . .

- how groups of people—young and old, rural and urban—got caught in the cycle of poverty and why the poor often felt invisible.
- the hardships of poverty during an age of general affluence.

their grasp. Pedro, Maria, and their children belonged to a class of Americans whose dreams rarely came true and whose problems went largely unnoticed by the rest of society. The Lopezes were unfortunate members of the nation's **culture of poverty,** the poor—largely invisible—members of a generally affluent American society.

The Invisible Poor

The Causes of Poverty

Picture postcards of New York City in the 1950s reflected the glory of the postwar United States. Skyscrapers soared heavenward; the waters swarmed with commercial traffic; sleek passenger jets cruised a cloudless sky; and in the harbor, Madame Liberty beckoned with promises of freedom, equality, and opportunity.

Hidden Poverty

Hidden behind the tall buildings, away from the bustling harbor, was a very different United States. It was a nation of crumbling streets and tenements, of hungry and sometimes homeless people; a nation not of freedom and equality but of prejudice and discrimination; a nation not of plenty but of desperate need.

The "invisible poor" were so well hidden that many Americans believed that poverty in the United States had been nearly eliminated. In 1956 historian Arthur Schlesinger stated that "the central problems of our times are no longer problems of want and privation." Four years later *Fortune* magazine declared that there were fewer than 1 million poor people left in the United States and predicted that by 1970 there would be none at all.

Reasons for Invisibility

Social and political factors combined to make the poor invisible. Prosperous Americans, for example, simply closed their eyes to the poverty around them because the postwar popular culture glorified the "good life."

As the middle class moved to the suburbs after World War II, they left the poor behind. The inner cities became isolated islands of poverty—out of sight and out of mind. The population of midtown Manhattan dropped from 1.5 million during the day to 2,000 at night. Writer John Brooks noted that midtown Manhattan was "tidally swamped with bustling humanity every weekday morning . . . and abandoned again at nightfall when the wave sucked back." Working in midtown Manhattan, the suburbanites rarely saw the hundreds of thousands of poor families who lived in the Bronx, Brooklyn, and Queens.

AP/WIDE WORLD PHOTOS

Michael Harrington When Harrington published *The Other America,* many denied that poverty was a problem in the United States. *What was Harrington's definition of poverty?*

The lack of any effective political voice also kept the poor invisible. In the past the urban poor had included large numbers of European immigrants who were aided by big-city political bosses, most of whom had European backgrounds themselves. With such aid the immigrants and their children often struggled out of poverty and fled the noisy, dirty cities for the calm and quiet of the suburbs. Progressive urban reforms of the 1900s and the increase in federal programs in the 1930s, however, helped undermine the political-boss system's monopoly on social services. The urban poor of the 1950s, who flooded the cities during and after World War II, included displaced white people from Appalachia, African Americans, Hispanic Americans, and Native Americans.

In 1962 author Michael Harrington shocked prosperous Americans by revealing the extent of poverty in their midst. In his book, *The Other America,* Harrington wrote that 50 million Americans lived in poverty. He explained that poverty was defined not only by a lack of money but also by the absence of hope:

> The poor live in a culture of poverty . . . [and] for reasons beyond their control, cannot help themselves. . . . The poor get sick more than anyone else in the society. . . . When they become sick, they are sick longer than any other group in the society. Because they are sick more often and longer than anyone else, they lose wages and work, and find it difficult to hold a steady job. And because of this, they cannot pay for good housing, for a nutritious diet, for doctors . . . [and] their prospect is to move to an even lower level . . . toward even more suffering.
>
> —Michael Harrington, *The Other America,* 1962

The Culture of Poverty

The Downside of Government Programs

Harrington and others pointed out that the poverty of the 1950s was a "new" poverty. The poverty of the Depression era was a general condition that affected large parts of society. Nationally organized, large-scale social welfare programs and labor organizations had responded with work programs and relief payments. When the economy began to recover, so too did the people. In contrast, the poor in the postwar era had no such massive social welfare programs to enable them to break out of poverty.

Additional studies supported Harrington's findings. One study concluded that 40 percent of the American people were ill-housed, ill-clothed, and ill-fed. Another study found that 34.5 million Americans lived on less than $2.10 a day. Americans could no longer deny that poverty was a major social problem.

The reasons for poverty in the United States were varied. Some of the poor, particularly African Americans and Hispanic Americans, faced long-standing racial and ethnic prejudice and discrimination. The poor also included jobless Appalachian whites, who moved to the cities because of the lack of opportunity in the hills, and Native Americans, who lived both in the cities and on reservations. Finally, there were the growing numbers of elderly Americans who were not covered by Social Security and had never received pensions from their employers. Whatever the reasons for the existence of poverty, the problem was not limited by age, race, or ethnic heritage.

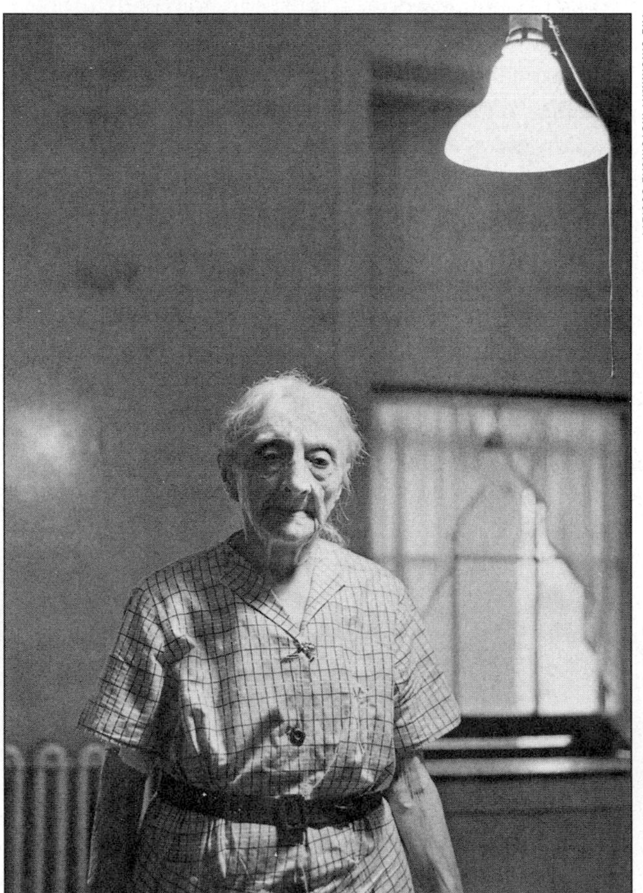

THE CINCINNATI HISTORICAL SOCIETY

The Elderly Harrington estimated that there were more than 8 million elderly poor in the United States. *What contributed to the poverty of elderly people?*

The Young and the Old

Almost half of the poor were children under the age of 18. By the early 1960s, many of the nation's poor children were the third generation in their families to have been raised on welfare. A depressing cycle of poverty was born—generation after generation totally dependent on government aid for their sustenance, knowing no other way of life.

While many children were born into poverty, many elderly Americans simply grew into it. Approximately 8 million Americans over the age of 65 had incomes of less than $1,000 a year. The following testimony details the problems afflicting the elderly during the 1950s and 1960s:

> Louise W_____, age 73, lives by herself in a single furnished room on the third floor of a rooming house located in a substandard section of the city. In this one room, she cooks, eats, and sleeps. . . . Widowed at 64, she has few friends remaining from her younger years. Those who do remain do not live near her, and it is difficult for her to see them. . . . And so she stays confined to her one room and the bathroom shared by nine other people. When the weather is warm enough, she ventures down the long flight of stairs about once a week for a walk to the corner and back.
>
> —Testimony at the 1960 Senate hearing on the aged

The plight of the nation's elderly citizens was, ironically, partly the result of scientific and technological progress. Modern medicine prolonged their lives, while modern technology often left them unemployed. Mechanization wiped out the farm chores and factory jobs formerly available to older workers. Thus, many elderly Americans spent their final years without work and without dignity.

Rural and Urban Poverty

At least a third of the poor worked on farms or lived in depressed rural areas. Changes in modern farming created deep pockets of rural poverty. As corporate farms and large-farm owners came to dominate production, many small independent farmers found it difficult to

HARD TIMES IN APPALACHIA

Mining companies in Appalachia determined and controlled every aspect of a miner's life. Companies provided "cradle to grave" benefits: housing, utilities, meals, transportation, hospital care, and even funerals. As shown in the deductions column on the pay slip below, miners paid exorbitantly high fees for "mandatory benefits." Consequently, a work-related dispute meant a miner lost not only his job, but housing and food for his family as well.

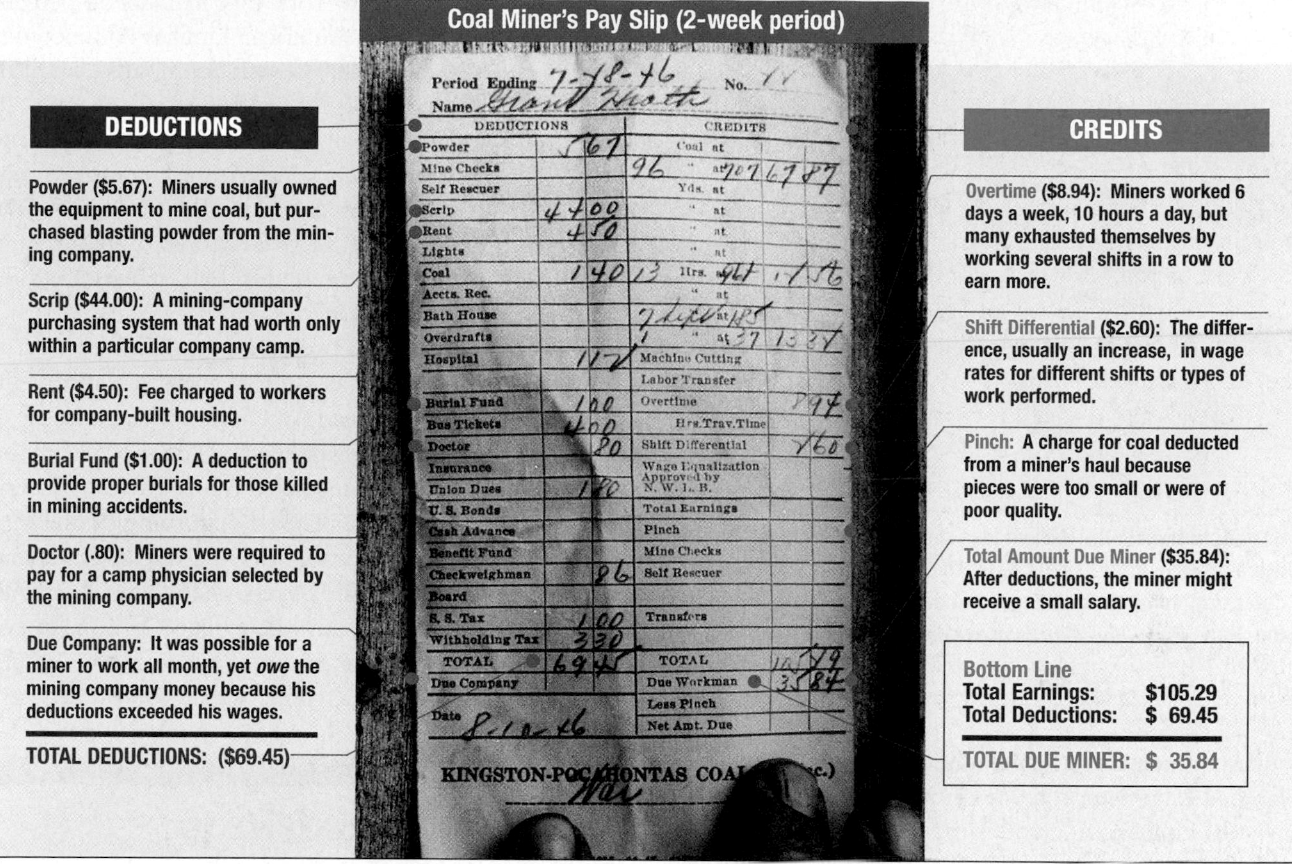

Coal Miner's Pay Slip (2-week period)
DEDUCTIONS
Powder ($5.67): Miners usually owned the equipment to mine coal, but purchased blasting powder from the mining company.
Scrip ($44.00): A mining-company purchasing system that had worth only within a particular company camp.
Rent ($4.50): Fee charged to workers for company-built housing.
Burial Fund ($1.00): A deduction to provide proper burials for those killed in mining accidents.
Doctor (.80): Miners were required to pay for a camp physician selected by the mining company.
Due Company: It was possible for a miner to work all month, yet *owe* the mining company money because his deductions exceeded his wages.
TOTAL DEDUCTIONS: ($69.45)
CREDITS
Overtime ($8.94): Miners worked 6 days a week, 10 hours a day, but many exhausted themselves by working several shifts in a row to earn more.
Shift Differential ($2.60): The difference, usually an increase, in wage rates for different shifts or types of work performed.
Pinch: A charge for coal deducted from a miner's haul because pieces were too small or were of poor quality.
Total Amount Due Miner ($35.84): After deductions, the miner might receive a small salary.
Bottom Line
Total Earnings: $105.29
Total Deductions: $ 69.45
TOTAL DUE MINER: $ 35.84
Period Ending
Name
DEDUCTIONS
CREDITS
Powder
Mine Checks
Self Rescuer
Scrip
Rent
Lights
Coal
Accts. Rec.
Bath House
Overdrafts
Hospital
Burial Fund
Bus Tickets
Doctor
Insurance
Union Dues
U. S. Bonds
Cash Advance
Benefit Fund
Checkweighman
Board
S. S. Tax
Withholding Tax
TOTAL
Due Company
Date
Coal at
Yds. at
Hrs.
Machine Cutting
Labor Transfer
Overtime
Hrs.Trav.Time
Shift Differential
Wage Equalization Approved by N. W. L. B.
Total Earnings
Pinch
Mine Checks
Self Rescuer
Transfers
TOTAL
Due Workman
Less Pinch
Net Amt. Due
KINGSTON-POCAHONTAS COA

Few workers were able to save enough money to enable them to leave a mining company; so it was not unusual to see three generations of a single family working the same mine, side by side. It was difficult, if not impossible, to rise above the cycle of debt created in a mining camp. *What put 70 percent of Appalachia's coal miners out of work by 1960?*

compete and slipped into poverty. Across the Southern United States, thousands of small-farm families lacked adequate diets in the midst of the world's most productive agricultural system.

Residents of Appalachia, a region covering 80,000 square miles (207,200 sq. km) and parts of 9 states, suffered severely. In 1960 about three-fourths of Appalachia's 8 million people had a median family income of about $2,000 a year. A drop in the demand for coal coupled with the increased use of machinery put almost 70 percent of the region's coal miners out of work.

Rural poverty drove thousands of people to the cities, straining already inadequate housing, school systems, and transportation facilities. Governmental efforts to provide low-cost housing often did more harm than good. Slum clearance merely shoved the poor from one part of the city to another. The projects—low-rent public housing complexes—imposed harsh restrictions on tenants. Large families with low incomes had priority. A family could be evicted if the marriage broke up or the family income exceeded the limits set by the housing authority. Housing projects often actually contributed to the cycle of poverty.

The African American Experience

Overcoming Racial Roadblocks

The poverty of African Americans had a unique quality that other groups did not share. African Americans, unlike many of the other poor, had to contend with deep-seated racial prejudice. While Southern African American farmers suffered the same poverty as their

Harlem in the 1950s Harlem was the home of a great African American literary circle in the 1920s. After the Depression, however, overcrowding, the deterioration of old buildings, and high unemployment had their effect on the area. *How did James Baldwin describe the problems facing the people of Harlem?*

white counterparts, the rural South harbored that force of racial terrorism, the Ku Klux Klan. The Klan used physical violence, including many instances of torture and lynchings, to intimidate African Americans and keep them "in their place."

African Americans carried this fear of white terrorism with them when they migrated to Northern cities. By the mid-1950s, nearly half of the African American population lived in cities. Atlanta, Los Angeles, Detroit, Chicago, New York—each had its ghetto. James Baldwin, African American novelist, essayist, and activist, described Harlem in the postwar period:

> Harlem, physically at least, has changed very little in my parents' lifetime or in mine. Now as then the buildings are old and in desperate need of repair, the streets are crowded and dirty, there are too many human beings per square block. Rents are 10 to 58 percent higher than anywhere else in the city; food, expensive everywhere, is more expensive here and of an inferior quality; and now that the war is over and money is dwindling, clothes are carefully shopped for and seldom bought. Negroes, traditionally the last to be hired and the first to be fired, are finding jobs harder to get, and, while prices are rising implacably, wages are going down. All over Harlem now there is felt the same bitter expectancy with which, in my childhood, we awaited winter: it is coming and it will be hard; there is nothing anyone can do about it.
>
> —James Baldwin, *Notes of a Native Son,* 1955

In New York City in 1955, 50 percent of African American families had incomes under $4,000 a year (compared with 20 percent of the white families), and 40 percent of all New York's welfare recipients were African American. Unemployment among African American workers was double that of white workers, and average wages were about half of what white workers earned.

Racial prejudice formed a barrier to economic as well as social advancement. Many African American workers, because of their color, were denied access to all but the lowest-paying jobs. Many African American students lacked opportunities in a segregated school system. African American doctors and lawyers often found it difficult to practice anywhere but in African American neighborhoods where they would never earn as much as their white colleagues.

Hispanic Hardships

The Search for Migrant Farmwork

Spanish-speaking Americans made up the nation's second largest minority group. Puerto Ricans, like Pedro and Maria Lopez, who were described earlier, flocked to the United States in the 1950s, drawn by stories of abundance and a desire to escape the poverty of their island homeland. During the decade, the Puerto Rican population of the United States grew from 300,000 to nearly 1 million. Many of these immigrants crowded into the slum neighborhoods of New York City.

Puerto Rican immigrants faced other difficulties in addition to their poverty. The language barrier slowed their assimilation into United States society. Native culture and strong family traditions were slowly lost as young Puerto Ricans adopted American ways. Women found jobs more easily than men did, which strained the traditional husband–wife relationship.

Mexican Americans suffered from the same discriminations that Puerto Ricans faced, with an added burden—they rarely felt politically secure. Because Puerto Rico is a commonwealth of the United States, Puerto Ricans are United States citizens, free to travel, work, and live within the country. Mexico, however, is a sovereign foreign state, and Mexican immigrants are legally defined as aliens. Officers of the Immigration and Naturalization Service were charged with tracking down immigrants who were in this country illegally. In the process, they could stop any Mexican American on the street and demand proof of citizenship.

WAYNE STATE UNIVERSITY

Living Conditions A 1960 television documentary titled *Harvest of Shame* revealed the shocking living conditions of the nation's 2 million migrant workers. *What was the* bracero *program?*

Agricultural Workers

Many Mexican American families had been citizens of the United States for generations. Many lived in urban centers, especially in California, Texas, and the Midwest. They were less noticed than the migrant farmworkers, however. While Mexican Americans made up the largest group of migrant farmworkers, African Americans, Puerto Ricans, and poor whites lived and worked under the same oppressive conditions. Migrant workers followed the crops from state to state for 7 or 8 months a year, from harvesting spring vegetables in Texas to picking fall apples in Washington. They slept in shacks or in labor camps and worked 10 or 12 hours a day in the fields. Some migrant workers worked for piece rates; others received an hourly wage of 50 cents. Migrant workers toiled outside the protection of labor laws. Children worked the fields with their parents, often on ladders or using hazardous machinery. Injured farmworkers received no workers' compensation.

LIBRARY OF CONGRESS

Field Work Agriculture depended heavily on migrant workers to do the stoop labor associated with harvesting crops such as tomatoes and beans. *What is the work and travel cycle of a typical migrant family?*

Some Mexicans illegally entered the United States to work in the fields. Others entered this country legally, under the *bracero* program—an agreement forged with the Mexican government during World War II to permit seasonal immigration of farmworkers. State employment officials recruited Mexican braceros, or temporary workers, to harvest crops. Braceros were expected to return to Mexico after the harvest, but many stayed on illegally.

In 1953 the government launched a deportation program that became known as Operation Wetback. Illegal Mexican aliens were called wetbacks—a derogatory term—because thousands of them entered the United States by swimming across the Rio Grande. In 3 years, Operation Wetback deported more than 3 million people.

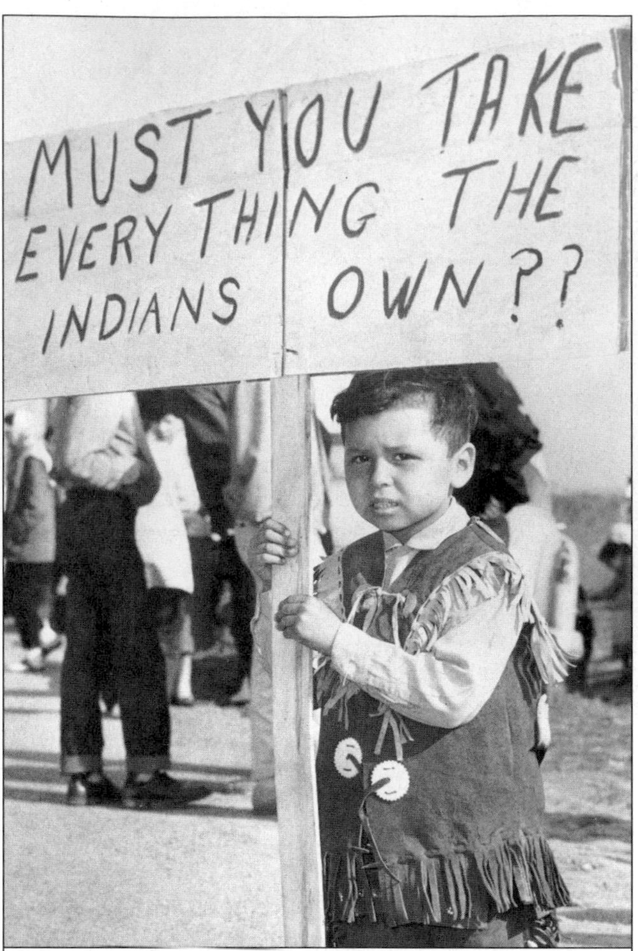

WIDE WORLD PHOTOS

Relocation Under the Voluntary Relocation Program, more than 60,000 Native Americans moved to cities. Nearly one-third later returned home. *Why did the government urge Native Americans to leave their reservations?*

Displaced Native Americans

The Government's Termination Policy

Native Americans were one of America's smallest, poorest, and most ignored minority groups. By 1960 almost two-thirds of some 600,000 Native Americans lived on reservations. Unemployment rates were staggering—more than 70 percent among the Blackfeet of Montana and the Hopi of Arizona; 86 percent among the Choctaw of Mississippi. Native Americans who migrated to the cities faced much of the same discrimination and poverty as African Americans and Hispanic Americans.

In 1953, the federal government adopted the **termination policy.** While the Indian Reorganization Act of 1934 had attempted to restore lands to Native American ownership, the new policy tried to end the reservation system and related federal services. The policy resulted in the loss of thousands of acres of Native American lands to agricultural, lumber, and mining interests.

As an incentive to leave the reservations, the government helped Native Americans relocate to cities through the Voluntary Relocation Program. Relocation offices provided moving expenses, help in finding housing and jobs, and temporary living expenses. Relocating to the cities, however, proved to be culturally wrenching for thousands of Native Americans who left their Native American groups. A Seminole petition to President Eisenhower spoke for all Native American groups who struggled for identity in the 1950s:

> We do not say that we are superior or inferior to the White Man and we do not say that the White Man is superior or inferior to us. We do say that we are not White Men . . . do not wish to become White Men but wish to . . . have an outlook on all things different from the outlook of the White Man.
>
> —Seminole Petition to President Eisenhower

The termination policy of the 1950s, like nearly every Native American policy before it, ended up victimizing Native Americans. Individual Native American nations and organizations of Native Americans officially protested termination. Lacking political representation, their protests went unanswered, and Native Americans remained the most "invisible" of all minority groups.

Section Assessment

Main Idea

1. Use a diagram such as this one to describe features of the culture of poverty.

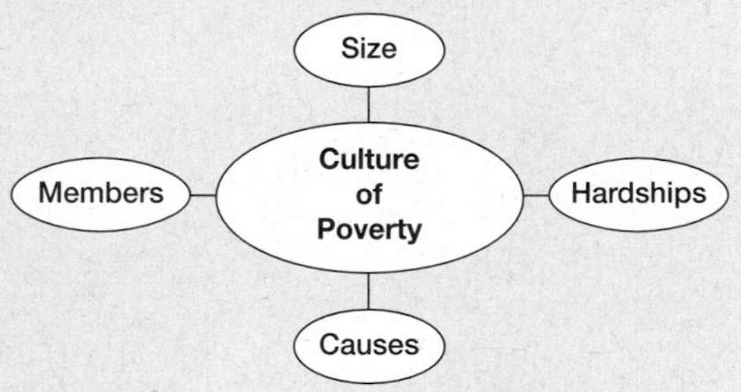

Vocabulary

2. Define: culture of poverty, termination policy.

Checking Facts

3. How did the poverty of the 1950s differ from the poverty of the Great Depression?
4. Why did Mexican Americans rarely feel politically secure in the United States?

Critical Thinking

5. **Identifying Assumptions** Keeping in mind that during the 1950s the poor were "invisible," what do you think many middle-class Americans of the 1950s assumed about the poor?

Technology Skill

USING THE INTERNET

Learning the Skill

To learn more about almost anything, use the Internet. The Internet, often referred to as the "Net," is a global network of computers. The Internet provides a medium in which you can research information, share information, and collaborate with others on a variety of subjects. The Internet offers many features, such as E-mail, online discussion groups, and even shopping services. To get on the Internet, you will need three things:

- A personal computer
- A modem—a device that connects your computer to a telephone line
- An account with an Internet service provider, such as AOL or a local Internet Service Provider (ISP). An Internet Service Provider is a company that enables you to log on to the Internet (usually for a fee).

Using the Internet

Once you are connected, the easiest way to access Web sites and information is to use a "Web browser." A Web browser is a program that lets you view and explore information on the World Wide Web. The World Wide Web consists of documents called Web pages. Each page on the Web is referred to as a site. Each Web page has it own address, or URL. Many URLs start with a prefix of *http://*

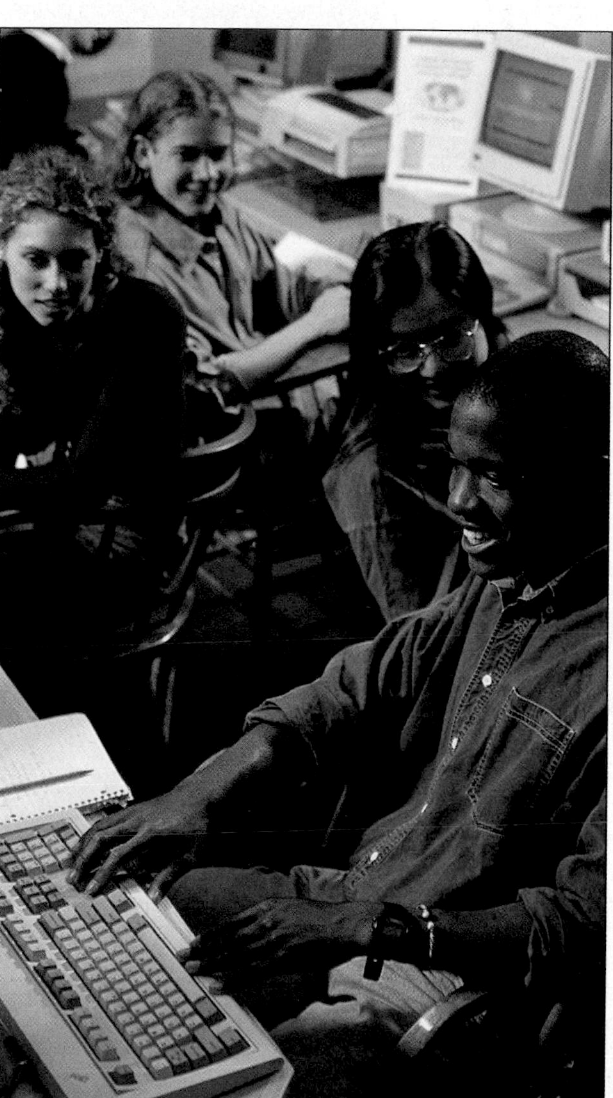
T. ROSENTHAL/SUPERSTOCK

Students using the Internet.

Practicing the Skill

This chapter focuses on the postwar period of World War II. Follow these steps to learn more about life in American society during the 1950s.

1. Log on to the Internet and access a World Wide Web search engine, such as Yahoo, Lycos, or WebCrawler.

2. Search by selecting one of the listed categories or by typing in the subject you want to find, such as *american society during the fifties.*

3. Continue your search by scrolling down the list that appears on your screen. When you select an entry, click on it to access the information. Sometimes the information you first access will not be exactly what you need. If so, continue searching until you find the information that you want. Use your findings to create a short report on different aspects of American society during the 1950s.

Applying the Skill

Go through the steps described to search the Internet for information about popular music trends during the 1950s. Based on your information, create a bulletin board comparing popular music trends of today with trends of the 1950s.

Additional Practice

For additional practice, see Reinforcing Skills on page 627.

Chapter  Assessment

Self-Check Quiz

Visit the *American Odyssey* Web site at americanodyssey.glencoe.com and click on ***Chapter 18—Self-Check Quiz*** to prepare for the Chapter Test.

Reviewing Key Terms

Choose the vocabulary term that best completes the sentences below. Write your answers on a separate sheet of paper.

demobilization	**conglomerates**
suburbia	**baby boom**
culture of poverty	**termination policy**

1. The rapid population growth after World War II is referred to as a _________ .

2. This population increase fueled the growth of _________ , communities on the outskirts of cities.

3. Shifting people and business back to peacetime pursuits was called _________ .

4. The "bigger is better" philosophy of the postwar years led to the formation of huge _________.

5. The _________ resulted in the loss of hundreds of thousands of acres of Native American lands to agricultural, mining, and lumber interests.

Recalling Facts

1. Describe a Veterans' Village. How many veterans took advantage of the educational assistance offered by the GI Bill?

2. What happened to the economy as working-class Americans accumulated discretionary income?

3. How did advertising affect the demand for consumer goods?

4. Where were most new homes built in the 1950s?

5. What kind of people lived in suburbia? Describe their lifestyle.

6. As their parents' discretionary income increased, teenagers had more money to spend as well. How did this affluence affect the culture of the 1950s?

7. What was the problem Betty Friedan identified in *The Feminine Mystique*?

8. How did poor people's lack of an effective political voice contribute to the cycle of poverty?

9. How was the poverty of the 1950s different from the poverty of the Depression era?

10. Describe some of the hardships in the lives of most migrant farmworkers.

Critical Thinking

1. Synthesizing Information What were some of the advantages and disadvantages inherent in corporate life in the 1950s?

2. Analyzing Information Look at the information about Appalachia on page 621. Why did this region suffer so much during the 1950s?

3. Determining Cause and Effect Use a diagram like this one to summarize the causes and effects of the growth of suburbia.

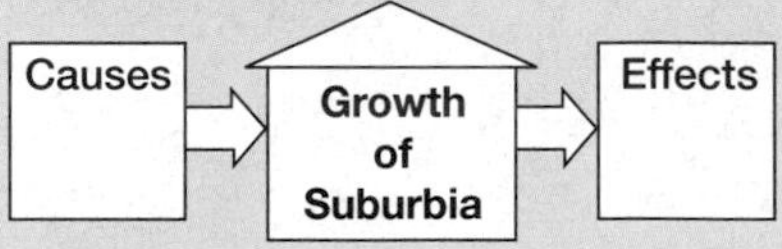

The Princeton Review — Standardized Test Practice

1. The postwar baby boom of the 1950s had all the following effects EXCEPT

A child-oriented television programming.
B sustained economic prosperity.
C marriages at later ages than previous generations.
D increased school enrollments.

Test-Taking Tips: Think about the meaning of the term *baby boom:* a surge in the population due to high birth rates. Predict some of the consequences of such a boom. For example, school enrollments would probably rise along with the number of children. So you can rule out answer D.

2. As a result of an agreement reached with Mexico in World War II, many Mexicans were allowed to enter the United States legally as seasonal workers through

A Operation Wetback.
B the Voluntary Relocation Program.
C the *bracero* program.
D the termination policy.

Test-Taking Tip: Eliminate answers that do not make sense. For example, the *termination policy* refers to government efforts to end federal services to Native Americans. Therefore, answer D is obviously incorrect. Do any of the other listed programs refer to groups other than Mexicans?

GEOGRAPHY AND HISTORY

Travel Routes of Migrant Workers, 2000s

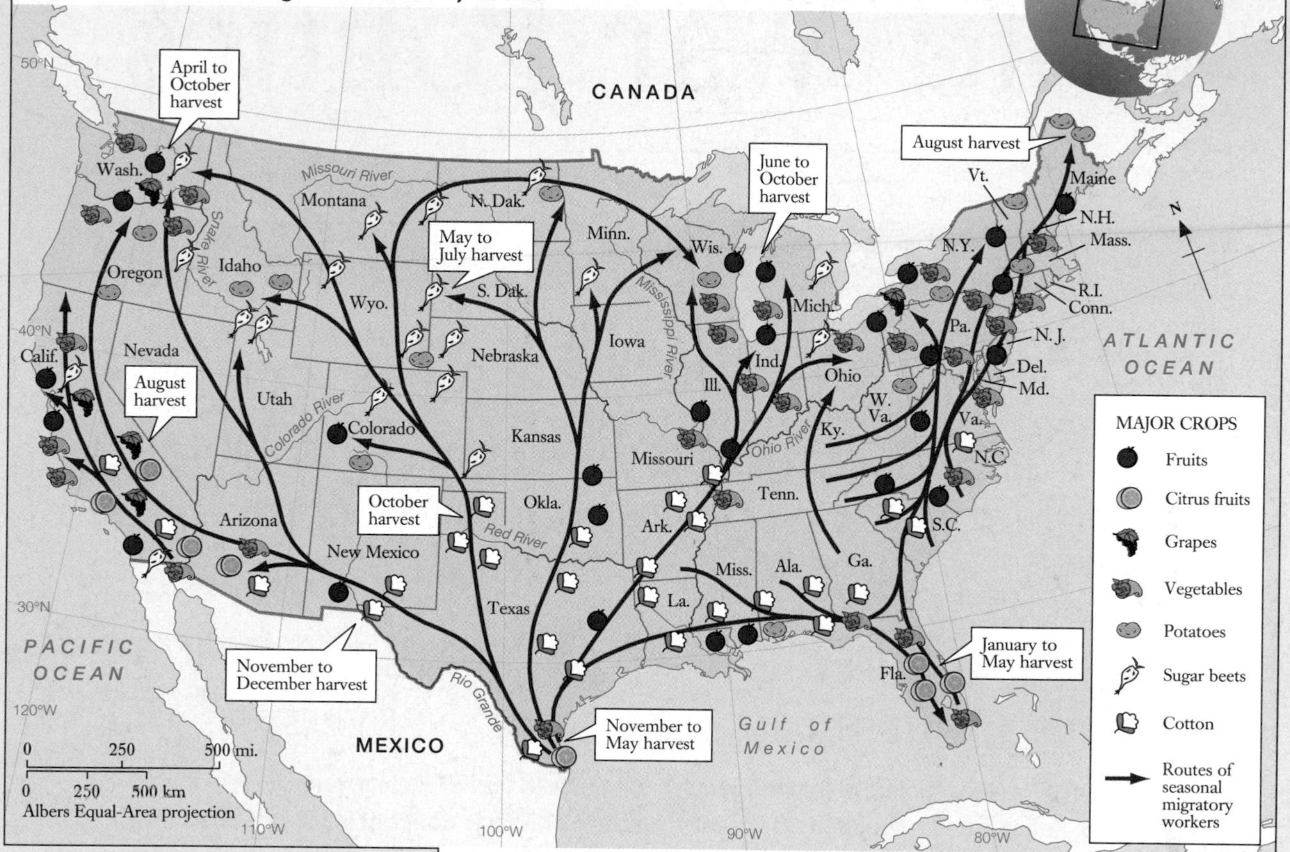

MAJOR CROPS: Fruits; Citrus fruits; Grapes; Vegetables; Potatoes; Sugar beets; Cotton; Routes of seasonal migratory workers

April to October harvest; August harvest; May to July harvest; June to October harvest; August harvest; October harvest; November to December harvest; November to May harvest; January to May harvest

Albers Equal-Area projection

Study the map to answer the following questions:

1. To which states do migrant workers travel to harvest citrus fruits?
2. To which parts of the country do migrant workers go in winter?
3. In how many states do migrant workers pick cotton?
4. Which areas of the country have the longest harvests?

Portfolio Project

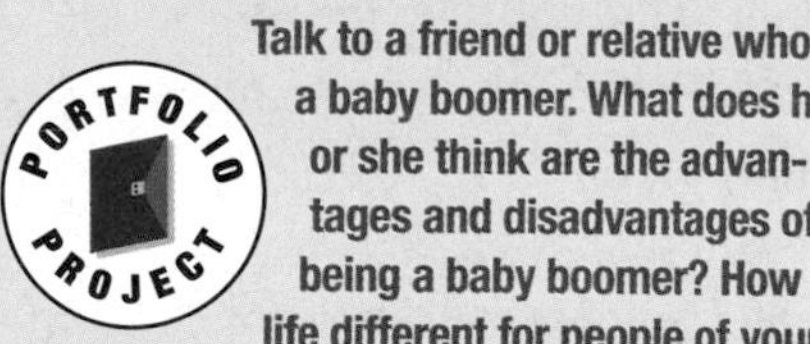

Talk to a friend or relative who is a baby boomer. What does he or she think are the advantages and disadvantages of being a baby boomer? How is life different for people of your generation? What do you think baby boomers' effect on society will be when they retire? Write a report that focuses on these questions. Place it in your portfolio.

Cooperative Learning

Form groups to research the special hardships placed on one of the following groups: displaced Native Americans, Hispanics (one group can discuss Mexicans and another Puerto Ricans), and Southern African Americans. Share your findings.

Reinforcing Skills

Using the Internet Go through the steps described on page 625 to search the Internet for information about fads of the 1950s such as telephone booth stuffing or the hula hoop. Use a search engine to help focus your search by using phrases such as *1950s fads* or *beatniks.* Use your findings to create a bulletin board illustrating all the different fads.

Technology Activity

Using E-mail One by-product of the computer revolution is the hundreds of new computer-related words we have added to our language, such as *modem* and *surfing*. Using E-mail, send a message to a friend requesting a list of words that probably did not exist before computers were invented.

Cold War Politics

JUNE 9, 1954: McCARTHY VERSUS THE ARMY

Joseph Welch was one of many people caught up in the controversy surrounding congressional hearings on Communists. Dozens of people, under questioning, had helplessly watched their careers and their reputations slip away. They left the hearings branded "Communists," "spies," or "subversives."

Welch faced his questioner, Senator Joseph McCarthy, the nation's self-appointed Communist hunter of the early 1950s. He was a dreaded man who was determined to prove that Communists were lurking in every office and department of the United States government.

McCarthy rarely offered any evidence against people he accused, but in the cold war atmosphere of the 1950s, proof did not matter. Fear, rather than reason, ruled.

The McCarthy hearings were an example of the extreme conservatism that dominated the politics of the time. His campaign of intimidation went unchecked for nearly four years. Few people were willing or able to confront McCarthy effectively.

Welch, a Boston attorney, appeared before McCarthy to defend the United States Army against allegations that it was harboring Communists. Under the glare of hot lights and with the nation closely watching on TV, Welch, weary of McCarthy's slander, replied calmly and firmly. His famous rebuttal challenged the senator. "I think I never really gauged your cruelty or your recklessness, . . ." Welch said. "Have you no sense of decency, sir, at long last? Have you left no sense of decency?" ■

HISTORY JOURNAL

Look at the picture on page 629. Then recall what you know about communism and the Red Scare. Write down what you think happened to people accused of being Communists by Joseph McCarthy.

Chapter Overview

Visit the *American Odyssey* Web site at americanodyssey.glencoe.com and click on ***Chapter 19—Chapter Overview*** to preview the chapter.

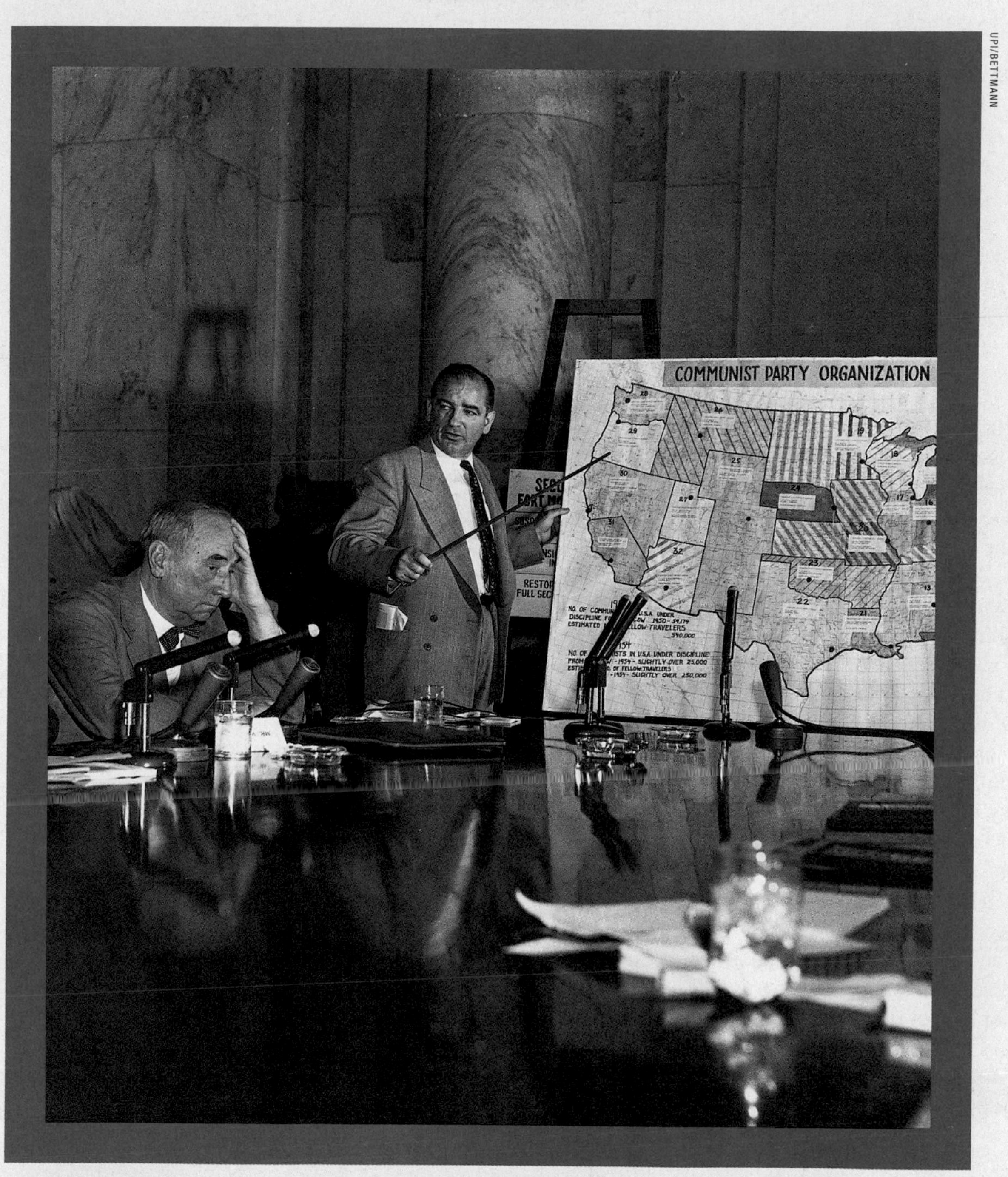

UPI/BETTMANN

SENATOR JOSEPH McCARTHY TESTIFIES ON COMMUNIST PARTY ORGANIZATION IN THE UNITED STATES AS A WEARY JOSEPH WELCH LISTENS.

Retreat From the New Deal

1946: VETERANS RETURN TO A CHANGING COUNTRY AFTER WORLD WAR II

THE NEWSREELS SHOWED THOUSANDS OF CHEERING SAILORS, SOLDIERS, AND AIRMEN CROWDING INTO TIMES SQUARE OR POURING OFF TROOP SHIPS. Their families and girlfriends and wives leaped into their arms, shedding tears of joy. They flung caps into the air. They kissed the ground. When the homecomings were over, however, World War II veterans faced the task of rebuilding their lives and careers in a very uncertain time.

Many men were able to pick up their jobs more or less where they had left off before the war. Others, however, had put education and career decisions on hold to serve in the military. There was at first a great deal of turmoil in the job market, as the economy adjusted to peacetime production and to the flood of returning workers.

UPI/BETTMANN

A Changing Country
After the war, thousands of veterans returned to a country in flux. Americans now wanted to put the war behind them and enjoy the freedoms for which they had sacrificed and fought.

The 1946 movie *The Best Years of Our Lives* dramatized the difficulties of veterans during the first weeks of their return. In the following scene, a drugstore manager, Mr. Thorpe, is talking to Fred Derry, a much-decorated bombardier:

> Thorpe: I can see that you had a splendid war record, Derry.
>
> Derry: Just average, Mr. Thorpe.
>
> Thorpe: But you'll understand that since this business changed hands we're

GUIDE TO READING

Main Idea

As Americans searched for a sense of security in an increasingly turbulent world, many turned to conservative politicians who opposed programs or movements that threatened to bring even greater changes to the United States.

Vocabulary

- closed shop
- right-to-work law
- union shop
- whistle-stop tour

Read to Find Out . . .

- causes of the postwar backlash against New Deal policies.
- the struggle that President Harry S Truman faced in implementing his Fair Deal.

under no legal obligation to give you your old job back.

Derry: I wasn't thinking of getting my old job back, Mr. Thorpe. I'm looking for a better one.

Thorpe: What are your qualifications, your experience?

Derry: Two years behind a soda fountain, and three years behind a Norden bomb sight. . . . I was only responsible for getting the bombs on the target. I didn't command anybody.

Thorpe: I see; I'm sure that work required great skill. But unfortunately, we've no opportunities for that with Midway Drugs.

—RKO Pictures, *The Best Years of Our Lives,* 1946

Not everybody faced what Fred Derry did, going back to the drugstore where he once worked. One of Derry's compatriots resumed his prestigious work as a bank manager. The nation as a whole was looking in a new direction. People wanted to put wartime sacrifices behind them, put veterans back to work, and enjoy the prosperity and freedom for which they had fought.

ARCHIVE PHOTOS

Nixon The congressman speaks on the campaign trail. *Why did many voters turn against the Democrats in 1946?*

A Conservative Turn

Shortages Create Demand for Change

Richard M. Nixon carried a law degree and a modest war record with him when he came home. Like thousands of other veterans, he was looking for a job. Within two years he would begin to work the levers of power in Washington.

Nixon's quick political climb began when a group of California business leaders backed him as a candidate for Congress in 1946. Nixon was part of the conservative backlash, or opposition, to the New Deal. He was also an outspoken anti-Communist who would soon become a prominent figure in the cold war politics of the 1950s.

The Twelfth Congressional District in southern California in many ways mirrored the political makeup of the nation. There were slightly more Democrats than Republicans registered in the voting rolls, but that advantage was vanishing because of a growing resentment among voters over postwar shortages in jobs, goods, and housing. Business leaders, farmers, and bankers were generally hopeful but nervous about the nation's economic outlook.

Often in times of uncertainty, voters look with suspicion at the policies of the party in power. In 1946 many voters turned against the Democrats and the New Deal.

There were "two definite opinions on the American system," Nixon told a group of prominent people in his congressional district. "One advocated by the New Deal is government control regulating our lives. The other calls for individual freedom and all that initiative can produce." He was talking to a handful of California Republicans, but he might as well have been addressing disaffected voters in many states who would soon sweep Republicans into Congress.

In congressional districts throughout the country, growing fears about communism resulted in particularly nasty campaign battles. Candidates whipped up anti-Communist rhetoric, publicly and subtly accusing their opponents of being "Red," the slang term for Communists and Communist sympathizers. The accusations, even if unfounded, were often hard to erase from the minds of voters.

When the Eightieth Congress convened in January 1947, many incumbents had been replaced. The conservative shift brought a new group of Republicans to Washington and gave the Republican party control of Congress. They came ready to correct what they saw as a threat to the nation's peacetime economy: the New Deal. That meant taking on the man who now embodied the spirit of the New Deal—President Harry Truman.

Fears About the Economy

Rising Costs Blamed on Unions

While Nixon and the other 1946 congressional hopefuls were campaigning, the nation's economy had been following a precarious path. Business leaders and conservatives were pressuring Truman to lift the government's wartime limits on prices. Finally he gave in and prices for basic goods immediately shot up.

The President called on businesses to keep prices down voluntarily as a patriotic measure to help stabilize the economy. Nevertheless, the inflation rate climbed to about 25 percent in mid-1946. The price hikes did little to dampen the spending desires of more prosperous Americans, who eagerly snatched up items, such as refrigerators, that were now beginning to return to stores after wartime shortages. Many workers watched the purchasing power of their wages shrink. They began to protest. Labor union membership had been growing during the war, but the unions generally had neither asked for nor received wage increases. After the war unions grew restless and began to make more and more demands on employers.

Rising Food Prices, 1946

Month	A Loaf of Bread	A Pound of Butter	A Dozen Eggs
March	$0.09	$0.55	$0.48
June	$0.11	$0.61	$0.51
September	$0.12	$0.83	$0.67
December	$0.12	$0.92	$0.70

Rising Food Prices The price of basic goods skyrocketed after price controls were lifted. *For which of the three types of food shown on the chart did the price rise the most?*

Americans started their days with a full breakfast of news about strikes in their morning papers. Unions were stopping production in industries across the nation. There were more strikes, measured in lost work hours, than at any other time in American history.

In 1946 and 1947 many people were getting fed up with rising prices and with lingering shortages in basics such as beef and gasoline. Many targeted their frustrations at the unions. They felt that the unions had become greedy in their demands, forcing up the cost of goods. Critics accused the Truman administration of not having the courage, or the alertness, to confront the economic problems.

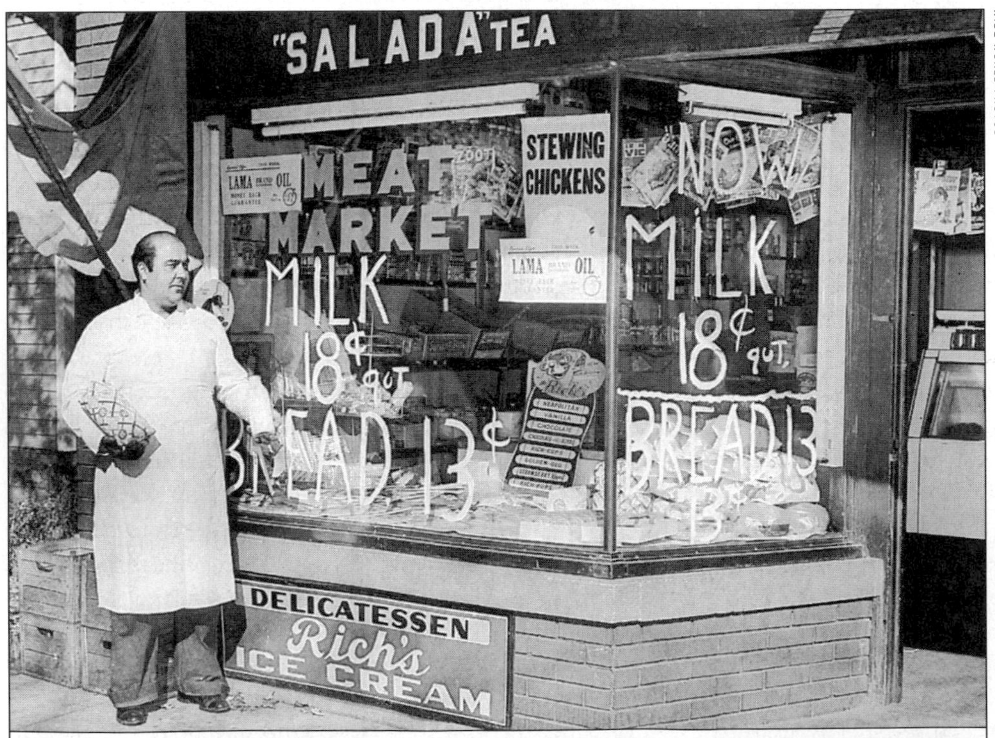

A Typical Grocery Store Tedaldo Guido stands in front of his grocery store in North Tonawanda, New York, in 1947. *Why did some people blame the unions for the rising cost of goods?*

Backlash Against the New Deal

The Republicans in the Eightieth Congress had been elected, by and large, on the promise to "clean up the mess in Washington." Senator Robert Taft of Ohio observed that their task was "the restoration of freedom and the elimination or reduction of constantly increasing interference with family life and with business" by the government. His comment was reflected in two of the Republicans' goals: to cut back New Deal spending and to rein in labor. The

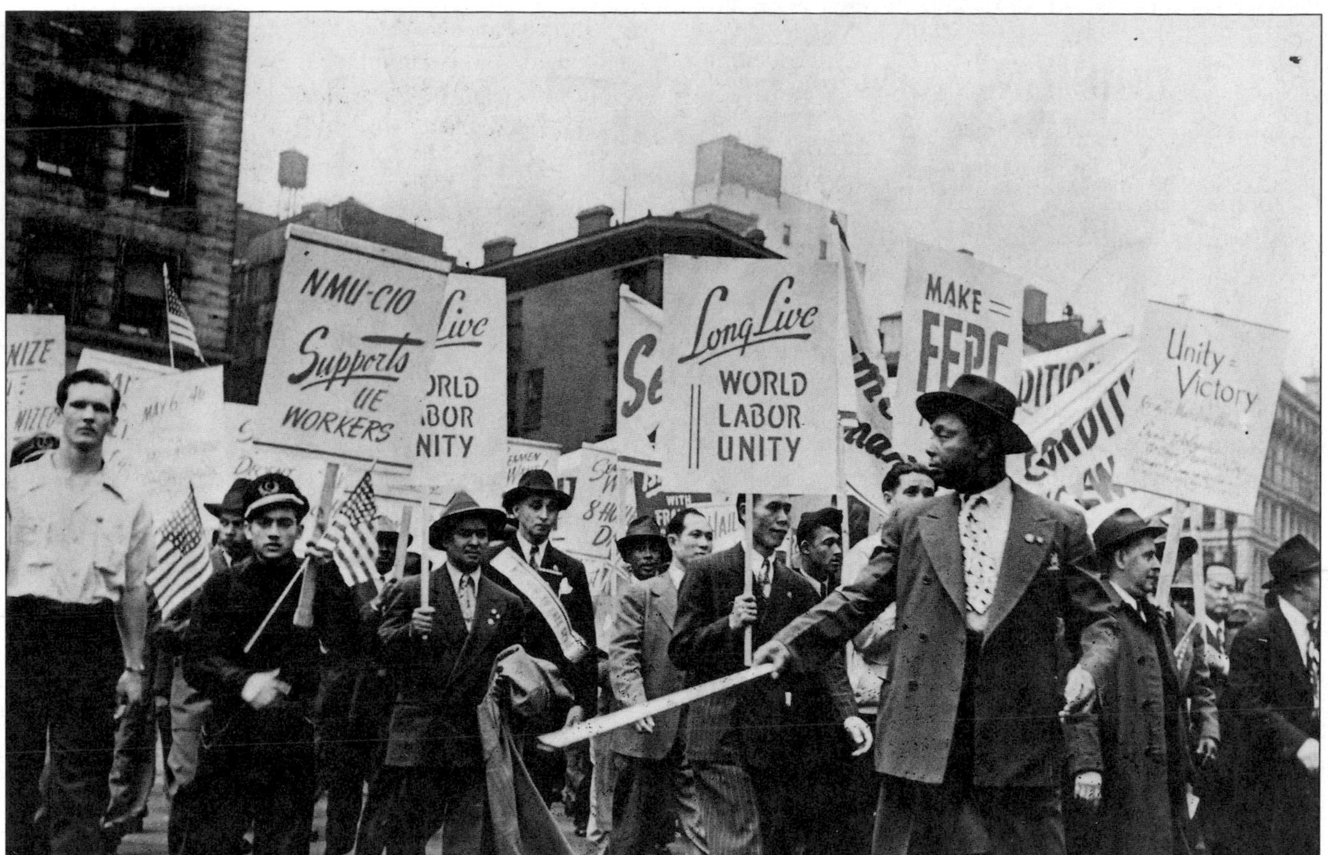

Labor Strikes Begin Workers march through New York City in a 1946 labor parade. Truman's sour relations with labor turned sweeter after his veto of the Taft-Hartley bill. *Why was labor unhappy with Truman? What did Truman do that improved his relationship with organized labor?*

controversy over labor quickly became focused on a single issue: the Taft-Hartley bill.

The 1935 National Labor Relations Act, a major New Deal protection for workers, had recognized the unions' right to bargain collectively. Employers complained that the act had given unions too much power. Companies cited crippling strikes and agreements broken by unions and complained that they had lost the ability to manage their employees. Conservative members of Congress thought the time had come to strengthen the management position.

The Taft-Hartley bill sought to ban the **closed shop,** a workplace where only union members could be hired. The bill also allowed states to pass **right-to-work laws,** which outlawed **union shops** (shops in which new workers were required to join the union).

The bill tipped the balance of power in other ways as well. It allowed employers to sue if the unions did not live up to their contracts. It provided for "cooling off" periods during which labor and management would resume bargaining. The bill also enabled the President to intervene in strikes that endangered national health and safety by ordering workers back to their jobs for 80 days.

Truman Fights the Taft-Hartley Bill

Truman and the Congress went to war over the Taft-Hartley bill, which the President called "a slave labor bill." The President shared the public concern about union power. He had on some occasions locked horns with union leaders and forced them to back down in their demands, but he felt that the new bill threatened important worker protections. Congress passed the bill, Truman vetoed it, and Congress voted to override the veto.

The bill proved to be less of a threat to labor than was feared, but it had an important side effect. Truman's strong opposition to the measure gave him a new political ally—labor. After months of souring relations with the unions, Truman had in a single stroke become a friend of the worker. "I don't give a hang what the unions say about me, or do to me politically: that isn't my job," Truman had growled to his aides after tangling with striking mine and railroad workers. "But when they run a balance sheet on Harry Truman, they'll realize they got a fine fair shake."

Truman's balance sheet got plenty of credit from his veto of the Taft-Hartley bill. It gave Truman labor support—a formidable weapon he would carry into the 1948 presidential election. He would need all the help he could get in this election.

The Uphill Race in '48

Truman Defends Civil Rights Program

Harry Truman never wanted to be President. Over and over again, he wished out loud that someone else would take the dubious honor of toiling away in the big drafty house he and his family referred to as the "Great White Jail."

Yet a strange paradox resided in this outwardly simple man. He knew he lacked the understanding of foreign policy and the passion for domestic reform of his predecessor, but he had one quality in himself that he trusted supremely: the determination to do the right thing. In the end Harry Truman trusted his ability to do the right thing more than he trusted anybody else he saw looming on the presidential horizon. The man who as senator had called himself "just a country jake who works at the job" liked being Just Plain Harry and thought a "country jake" could run the country just fine.

Daunting Prospects

Political experts and members of Truman's own Democratic party thought he should let someone else run for President in 1948. Only 36 percent of the voters approved of his administration. His public image floundered. Many saw him as soft on labor and on communism.

Prices had doubled since 1939, and Truman was blamed. In many opinion columns, news stories, and cartoons, he was portrayed as weak and incompetent. A popular quip of the time was, "To err is Truman." One of his campaign jingles, "We're just wild about Harry," was mockingly rendered as "We're just mild about Harry."

Before confronting the Republicans, Truman first had to face attacks from his own party that promised to rob him of votes from conservative and liberal Democrats. Henry Wallace, a former member of Truman's cabinet, split from the Democratic party to form the Progressive party and took many liberals with him. Wallace advocated stronger civil rights legislation, more federal spending for social programs, and a less confrontational stance toward the Soviet Union. The latter position gained him the support of the Communist party, which he did not reject. Wallace's refusal to take an anti-Communist stand proved disastrous to his candidacy. For a time, however, the Progressive party appeared to be a serious political contender that could spoil Truman's chances for reelection.

Civil Rights

The other threat to Truman's campaign came over the issue of civil rights. The President was a longtime supporter of equal rights for African Americans. He had begun the desegregation of the armed forces and had urged the Justice Department to prosecute cases in which African Americans were deprived of their civil rights. Before the 1948 Democratic convention he had unveiled a civil rights plan that included an antilynching bill and a ban on poll taxes, which had previously blocked poor people from voting.

UPI/BETTMANN

Civil Rights Legislation **Truman received the Robert S. Abbott Award for making the most significant contribution to democracy in 1948. Truman's civil rights plans earned him the respect of many African Americans.** *How did the Southern congressional delegation react to Truman's civil rights program?*

Civil rights issues shattered the Democratic national convention. Liberals managed to insert into the Democratic platform a mildly worded plank affirming the party's commitment to eliminate "racial, religious, and economic discrimination." It also commended Truman's "courageous stand" on civil rights.

A group of conservative Southern Democrats, the so-called Dixiecrats, broke from the party to form a States' Rights Democratic party. It nominated South Carolina governor Strom Thurmond as its candidate. The party attracted some conservatives who wanted a repeal of New Deal measures, but the Dixiecrats' main issue was their own support of racial segregation and

UPI/BETTMANN

Running on the Rails **Truman won the support of thousands of Americans as he crossed the country on his whistle-stop campaign tour.** *What did Truman claim about the Republicans?*

their opposition to federal government action on civil rights—action they insisted violated the authority of states. Asked why Southern members of Congress revolted against Truman's civil rights proposals when Roosevelt had advocated virtually the same measures, Dixiecrat Strom Thurmond replied, "Yeah, but he means it."

During the campaign friends warned Truman to soften his stand so as not to offend Southern conservative Democrats. To one such friend Truman wrote:

> I am not asking for social equality, because no such thing exists, but I am asking for equality of opportunity for all human beings and, as long as I stay here, I am going to continue that fight. When the mob gangs can take four people out and shoot them in the back, and everybody in the country is acquainted with who did the shooting and nothing is done about it, that country is in a pretty bad fix from a law enforcement standpoint. . . . I am going to try to remedy it and if that ends up in my failure to be reelected, that failure will be in a good cause.
>
> —Harry S Truman, August 18, 1948

Truman indeed faced failure. With the Democrats in disarray and their candidate weakened, the Republicans believed that anyone they nominated could crush Truman in November.

The Republican nomination went to the man FDR had trounced in 1944, New York governor Thomas E. Dewey. He presented a sharp contrast to Truman's feisty, freewheeling style: Dewey was reserved and meticulous. He was known as an intelligent and efficient administrator.

Although dapper and confident, Dewey was not going to sweep the nation off its feet with charisma. The Republicans, however, were not worried. In his speeches, Dewey never even referred to Truman; he campaigned like a man who had already won the election. It seemed that the race was Dewey's to win.

Running on the Rails

Although Truman's campaign staff was pessimistic about his chances, the President remained confident. In a particularly shrewd move, Truman waited until the end of the Republican national convention and then called a special session of Congress. He challenged Republicans to make good on their platform promises. He handed Congress a string of his own proposals, including his civil rights legislation. When Congress failed to pass a single bill, Truman was able to claim that the Republicans were not serious about solving the nation's problems.

Truman could now point to a whole menu of New Deal–style measures that the Eightieth Congress rejected: aid to farmers, a minimum-wage hike from 40 to 75 cents, a housing bill, increased Social Security coverage, and new price controls. This gave him the

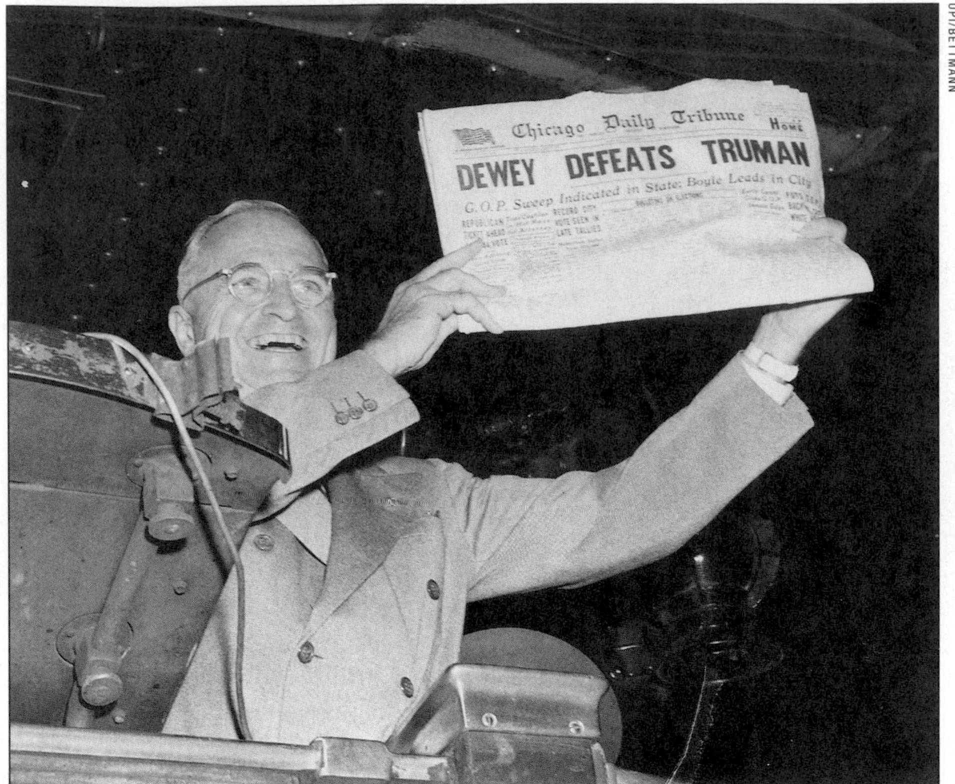

UPI/BETTMANN

Election Results **In one of the most famous photos in United States history, Truman holds up the *Chicago Daily Tribune* with its headline erroneously announcing the 1948 election results.** *Why did people think Dewey was sure to win the presidential election?*

ammunition he needed against the Republicans in an unprecedented national campaign tour.

Many past Presidents had stayed put in the White House during their campaigns—to do otherwise was thought undignified. Truman, however, wanted to take his case to the people, so he took the White House on the road. From Labor Day to Election Day, Truman conducted his famous train trip, or **whistle-stop tour,** of the country in the Ferdinand Magellan, an ornately appointed suite of railroad cars that once belonged to FDR. More than 20 staff members and dozens of reporters accompanied the President on his 32,000-mile (51,488km) trip.

Stopping in town after town, he spoke to enthusiastic crowds from the rear platform of the train. To people who had only seen pictures of the President and heard him speak on the radio, the impression was strong. Truman told his listeners about the troubles in Washington. He ticked off the failures of "that do-nothing Eightieth Congress." After that he asked the crowd if they wanted to meet his family. They did, of course. His wife, Bess, and daughter, Margaret, joined him on the platform. The crowds ate it up.

Still, few people believed Truman could win. In the last weeks before the election, polls showed him trailing by up to 10 percentage points. *Newsweek* polled 50 experts from across the country; not one gave Truman a chance. When one of his aides handed the magazine to Truman, he looked at it, grinned, and said, "Forget it, they're always wrong."

On Election Day, Truman went home to Independence, Missouri, where he voted, took a Turkish bath, and confidently awaited the results. He went to bed early and was awakened at midnight and again at 4:00 A.M. by aides telling him he was winning. Radio commentators kept predicting that Dewey would come on strong as new precincts reported in. The *Chicago Daily Tribune* went to press with the historic and later embarrassing banner headline, "Dewey Defeats Truman." Nothing of the sort happened. Truman won big.

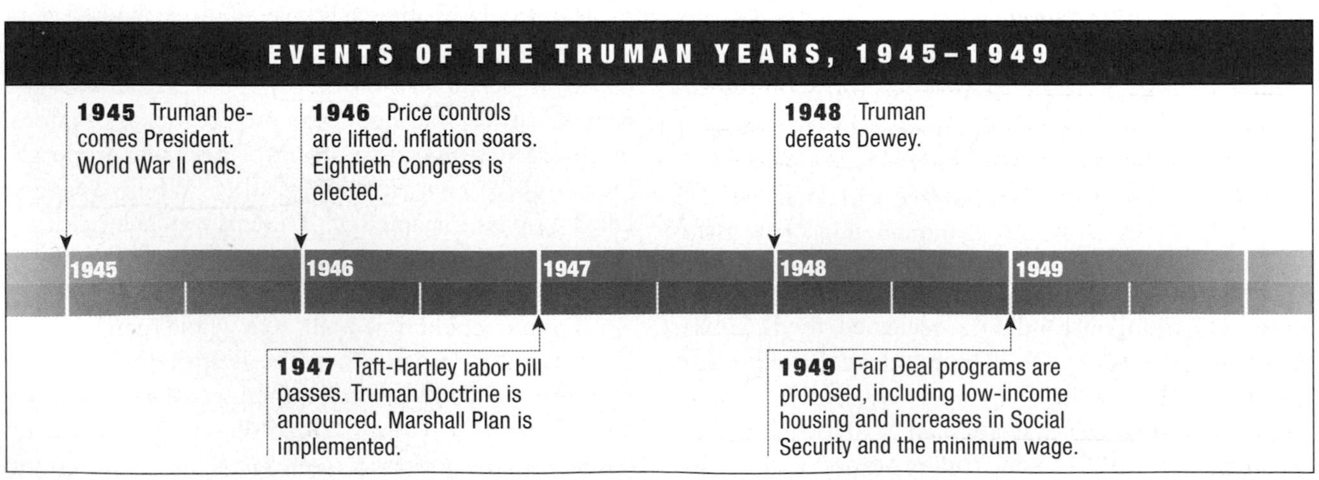

EVENTS OF THE TRUMAN YEARS, 1945–1949
1945 Truman becomes President. World War II ends.
1946 Price controls are lifted. Inflation soars. Eightieth Congress is elected.
1948 Truman defeats Dewey.
1945
1946
1947
1948
1949
1947 Taft-Hartley labor bill passes. Truman Doctrine is announced. Marshall Plan is implemented.
1949 Fair Deal programs are proposed, including low-income housing and increases in Social Security and the minimum wage.

The Fair Deal

Roosevelt's New Deal Revisited

The romantic view of the 1948 election is that of the underdog overcoming the odds through grit and determination. In recent times, historians have noted that President Truman's reelection victory was really due to the resilience of FDR's Democratic party, which was sufficient to overcome even Truman's unpopularity. The vote to reelect Truman was, in effect, a vote for Franklin Roosevelt's fifth term. The strength of the party was also evident because the Democrats regained the majority in both houses of Congress in the 1948 election.

For nearly four years, the Republican-controlled Congress had thwarted President Truman's hopes of continuing and expanding the New Deal. Now, fresh from his victory, Truman marched into the Democrat-controlled Congress with a State of the Union message that unveiled the Fair Deal, his new lease on life for the New Deal. It called for legislation favoring such causes as national medical insurance, extension of Social Security, new public power projects, public housing, and repeal of the Taft-Hartley Act. It was bold, ambitious, and liberal.

The Fair Deal registered its successes. The Social Security system was broadened to cover 10 million more people than it had before. The minimum wage rose from 40 to 75 cents per hour. The Housing Act of 1949 authorized the construction of about 800,000 low-income units.

In many ways the Fair Deal was doomed. Republicans and conservative Dixiecrats often voted as a bloc to defeat many of Truman's legislative proposals, especially in the area of civil rights. Events in the country, and in the world, also helped to undermine the Fair Deal. The fresh wave of support Truman gained in the election gradually faded as charges of corruption riddled his administration.

In addition, President Truman was blamed for not taking stronger action to prevent the Communist takeover of China. The United States became bogged down in a costly and stalemated war in Korea. As military spending again soared, Congress had little interest in funding social programs.

Truman's presidency fell victim to these changes. By the end of his term, when he decided not to run for reelection, his popularity had sunk to a new low. Events inside and outside of Washington contributed to Truman's fall. Another factor was the nation's fear of communism—a fear that Truman himself had helped to create.

The Fair Deal Truman's struggle with the Dixiecrats is captured by this cartoon. *How did this struggle help to defeat Truman's Fair Deal?*

Section Assessment

Main Idea

1. Use a diagram like this one to show causes and effects of the conservative backlash of the 1950s.

Vocabulary

2. Define: closed shop, right-to-work law, union shop, whistle-stop tour.

Checking Facts

3. What issue did Republican candidates raise in the 1946 election? How successful or unsuccessful were they? Why?

4. How successful was Truman's Fair Deal? Explain.

Critical Thinking

5. **Recognizing Ideologies** How did President Truman's values both help and hurt him?

Science, TECHNOLOGY, and Society

FILE PHOTO BY DOUG MINDEL

Plastics

Plastics are human-made materials that can be shaped into many forms. They can be as hard as steel or as soft as a pillow. A shortage of raw materials during World War II led to both the development of new plastics and the use of old plastics in new ways. Mass production helped plastics come into common use in American homes and businesses.

NEW PLASTICS

New types of plastics invented during World War II led to new ways of using them in medicine, including this plastic heart valve.

© DAN MCCOY/RAINBOW

POPPERFOTO

NEW USES FOR OLD MATERIALS

Nylon, once used mostly for women's hosiery, is used to make parachutes for the war effort, May 1944.

THE HISTORY OF PLASTICS

1930s

LUCITE AND PLEXIGLAS are used in airplane windows; nylon for hosiery; vinyl for garden hoses and raincoats; polystyrene for food containers, tiles, and electrical equipment.

1940s

POLYESTER is used in car bodies, luggage, and magnetic tape. Polyethylene, silicone, and epoxy are developed but are not in widespread use.

1950s

POLYETHYLENE is inexpensive to produce and is used for plastic bags, plates, and cups. Silicones are used for lubricants and heart valves. Epoxy is a strong adhesive.

1960s

HIGH-TEMPERATURE plastics are developed and used for electronics and missiles.

HULTON DEUTSCH COLLECTION LIMITED

AIRCRAFT WINDOWS

Plexiglas, a light, transparent, weather-resistant thermoplastic, was used for windows in World War II planes.

PLASTICS EVERYWHERE

PORTFOLIO PROJECT

To better understand the effect plastics have had on people's lives, keep a list for one day of everything you use that is made of plastic. Are the lenses of your glasses made of plastic? What about your sneakers? How pervasive are plastics? Write down the results of your inquiry and keep a copy in your portfolio.

FILE PHOTO BY DOUG MINDEL

© GREG ANTHONY LIGHT SOURCES

JUKEBOXES

After the war, plastics found their way into products used for entertainment (such as this jukebox), products used in nuclear and space research and architecture, as well as toys, automobiles, and household items.

1970s

PLASTIC microwave cookware, computer housing, and CDs are developed. Biodegradable plastics are introduced.

1980s

HEAT-RESISTANT plastic foam covers space-shuttle fuel tanks. Photodegradable plastics are introduced.

1990s

PLASTICS that carry an electric current are developed for batteries, wiring, and static-resistant fabrics.

2000s

ALL-PLASTIC CARS with lightweight body structures that reduce fuel emissions and pollution are introduced.

The Cold War at Home

MAY 1, 1950: WISCONSIN TOWN FALLS TO THE "COMMUNISTS"

The Red Star

Official Soviet Proclamation!

Instructions To Citizens Released

Legion Now Is Entirely Dead

Proclamation

Confiscation of Autos Ordered

History of Stalin, Our Valiant Leader

COURTESY MOSINEE TIMES

The Spread of Anticommunism
Mosinee, Wisconsin, like many American towns, thought the threat of communism a serious problem. This newspaper depicts what life would be like under Communist rule.

Mosinee, Wisconsin, was a typical quiet American town—until the day the "Communists" took over. On May 1, 1950, armed soldiers stormed into Mosinee, seizing Mayor Ralph Kronenwetter. The mayor and Police Chief Carl Gewiss were arrested and taken to city hall, where the Soviet hammer-and-sickle flag was raised high. When Gewiss refused to cooperate with the invaders, he was "liquidated."

The Communist forces circled the town and set up roadblocks to prevent escape. Red guards took over the Mosinee power plant; they arrested the local newspaper editor and began converting his printing presses to publish the new propaganda paper, *The Red Star*.

Soldiers then raided the public library and private homes to "purge" them of anti-Communist literature. Members of the clergy and business leaders were rounded up and put in concentration camps.

Meanwhile, at the high school, Communist party workers organized a parade to celebrate the new regime. They marched down Main Street and gathered for a rally in the center of town—newly dubbed "Red Square."

Then, at 7:00 P.M., the soldiers put down their weapons, the prisoners were freed, and Mosinee residents held a good old-fashioned picnic to celebrate the joys of freedom and democracy. They raised the American flag as the high school band played "The Star-Spangled Banner." An American Legion commander addressed the crowd about the virtues of the American way of life.

The takeover was a hoax, of course. The armed subversives were actually patriotic United States sol-

Guide to Reading

Main Idea

Widespread fear of a Communist takeover of the United States, enflamed by many politicians and commentators, gave rise to a wave of anticommunism and a climate of accusation in the McCarthy era.

Vocabulary

- vigilante
- blacklisting

Read to Find Out . . .

- the causes and effects of the anti-Communist sentiments of the McCarthy era.
- how blacklisting affected aspects of American life.

diers; the leader of the "coup" was an ex-Communist. Project organizers, including the American Legion, chose May Day as their date because in the Soviet Union it was a major holiday celebrating communism. The Mosinee event received nationwide news coverage.

Although the takeover seems rather humorous now, it reflected a pervasive fear. Mayor Kronenwetter died the next day of a heart attack; a clergyman died days later. Town historians said the deaths were associated with stress. The Mosinee story is an extreme example of a wave of anticommunism that swept the country during the late 1940s and early 1950s. Watching the spread of communism around the world, and listening to the rhetoric of politicians and commentators, millions of Americans feared that seemingly friendly citizens—the local PTA president, a bank secretary, the railroad worker next door—were working for a Communist takeover of the United States.

The menace of Communist traitors seemed very real to many people. Some of them felt their fellow citizens were not taking the threat seriously enough.

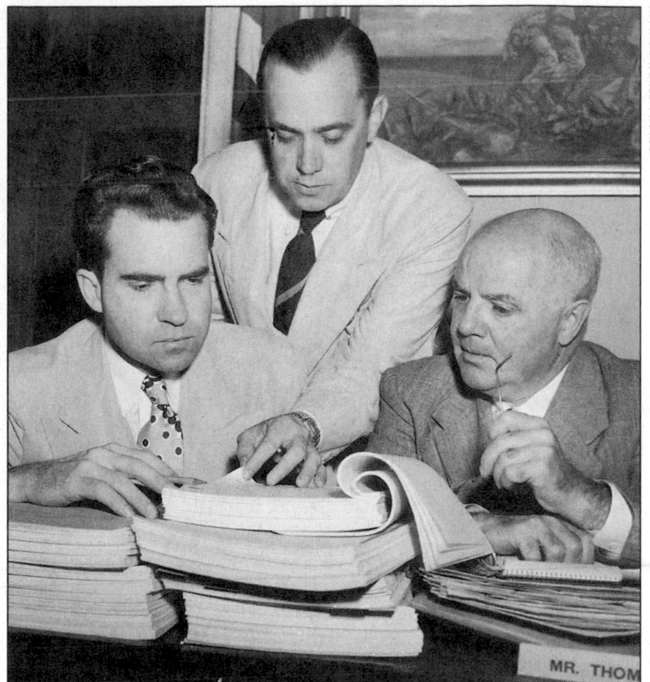

AP/WIDE WORLD PHOTOS

The House Un-American Activities Committee Richard Nixon looks over testimony in the trial of Alger Hiss. *Why was Nixon considered the voice of reason during the hearings?*

The Hunt for Communists

Fear Tactics and Intimidation

The fear of communism did not start with the cold war. It grew, explosively, in the climate produced by the development of the Soviet atomic bomb, the spread of communism in the world, and the efforts of some unscrupulous Americans to use fear as a way to defeat their enemies and to grab political power.

Long after the Red Scare of 1919 and well before the heyday of anticommunism in the 1950s, conservatives in Congress had looked for a way to discredit President Roosevelt and his New Deal administration. The House Un-American Activities Committee, or HUAC, held hearings that explored the issue of Communist influence in the New Deal. Little came of the hearings, largely because of World War II. Concern about communism was put aside as Stalin's Soviet government became a temporary ally.

When the war ended, however, Stalin turned more openly belligerent toward the United States. Winston Churchill delivered his famous "iron curtain" speech. The cold war was launched, and the HUAC resumed hearings. For months the committee publicly probed for Communists in the Truman administration but failed to find any. Then in 1947 the HUAC got a new cast of characters, most notably a young congressman with an ability to skewer a reluctant witness during cross-examination. The postwar history of the HUAC quickly became the story of Richard Nixon and Alger Hiss. It was a case that made one man and broke another.

The American Communist Party

Surrounded by men who were at times emotional, vindictive, and racist, Congressman Nixon became the voice of reason on the HUAC. Some committee members resorted to demagoguery—stirring people up by appealing to their emotions—and to character assassination. Nixon, by contrast, spoke quietly, usually from a brief of carefully gathered facts.

To be sure, there were Communists and Communist sympathizers to be found, but there were far more former Communists. The American Communist party was in its heyday during the Depression, when much of the nation was suffering and out of work. Marxist and Leninist writings and the speeches of Stalin—touting the rights of the working class and criticizing the failures of capitalism—appealed to many liberals in the United States. The party drew workers, intellectuals, artists, and college students to its ranks. In a time of extensive poverty, racial injustice, and the abuse of workers by powerful corporations, communism seemed to promise

Student Web Activity 19

Visit the *American Odyssey* Web site at americanodyssey.glencoe.com and click on ***Chapter 19—Student Web Activities*** for an activity relating to the Red hunt.

relief. The ideology had not yet acquired an association with evil and repression.

This association came in the late 1930s, when Stalin stepped up his campaign of terror against his enemies and tightened internal security in the Soviet Union. His strong-arm tactics caused many sympathizers in the United States to become disillusioned with communism. By World War II, public interest in communism in the United States had virtually died.

The rise of the cold war, however, caused changes that brought the HUAC's activities into the spotlight once again. The cold war resulted in increased espionage activity by Stalin against the United States. That legitimized fears that the Soviet Union was trying to undermine the United States government.

The Case of Alger Hiss

Politicians and voters wanted to see a strong case brought against the spies they thought had infiltrated the government. That case came along in 1948 when Nixon met Whittaker Chambers, a senior editor at *Time* magazine. Like many intellectuals, Chambers had been attracted to the Communist party in the 1930s, but unlike most intellectuals, he had become deeply involved in Communist espionage activities. He later joined the ranks of those disillusioned with the party and became as staunch an anti-Communist as he had been a fervent Communist.

Chambers told Nixon and the HUAC that during his Communist days he had become closely involved with a man named Alger Hiss. Hiss was the spy suspect Red hunters dreamed of catching. He had served in influential positions in government and society. If it could be proved that Hiss was a Communist, it would support the allegations that the HUAC had been making for years.

AP/WIDE WORLD PHOTOS

Alger Hiss Hiss listens to a question during his trial. *What made Hiss a perfect villain for Communist-hunting politicians?*

Alger Hiss was a graduate of Harvard Law School who had gained a coveted spot as clerk for Supreme Court Justice Oliver Wendell Holmes. He had served as a New Dealer under Roosevelt and had even gone to Yalta as a member of FDR's staff.

Many conservative Republicans believed that Roosevelt had sold out to the Soviet Union at Yalta, and the Hiss connection made that argument even more plausible. At the time of his arrest, Hiss was president of the Carnegie Endowment for International Peace. Peace organizations in general were highly suspect as instruments for "softening" the United States, so the Soviets could take over the nation by surprise. Hiss was the perfect target for the HUAC.

The Role of Whittaker Chambers

Chambers had been seeking an audience for his accusations against Hiss for almost a decade by the time he was introduced to Nixon. The FBI had investigated the case and had been unable to make much of the charges by Chambers. FDR heard about the allegations and dismissed them. A New York grand jury failed to bring an indictment against Alger Hiss.

Now Chambers told Nixon that Hiss had been, and probably still was, a high-ranking Communist party operative. In highly publicized hearings, Nixon staked his personal career on the guilt of Hiss and the integrity of Chambers. Showing talents honed as a high school and college debater and as an experienced lawyer, Nixon bore down on Hiss and discredited him with a style of questioning that observers called both brilliant and ruthless. At first Hiss denied ever knowing Chambers. Then, confronted with Chambers in person, Hiss lost his composure and admitted having known Chambers under another name.

Although the FBI continued its investigation of Hiss, the attorney general's office did not yet have sufficient evidence from Chambers to press its case against Hiss in the hearings. The story seemed to end there, with Hiss's reputation smeared but with nothing proven.

Proof in a Pumpkin Patch?

It was at this point that the case took its most bizarre turn. Late in 1948 two investigators visited Chambers's farm in Maryland, and Chambers, who had not

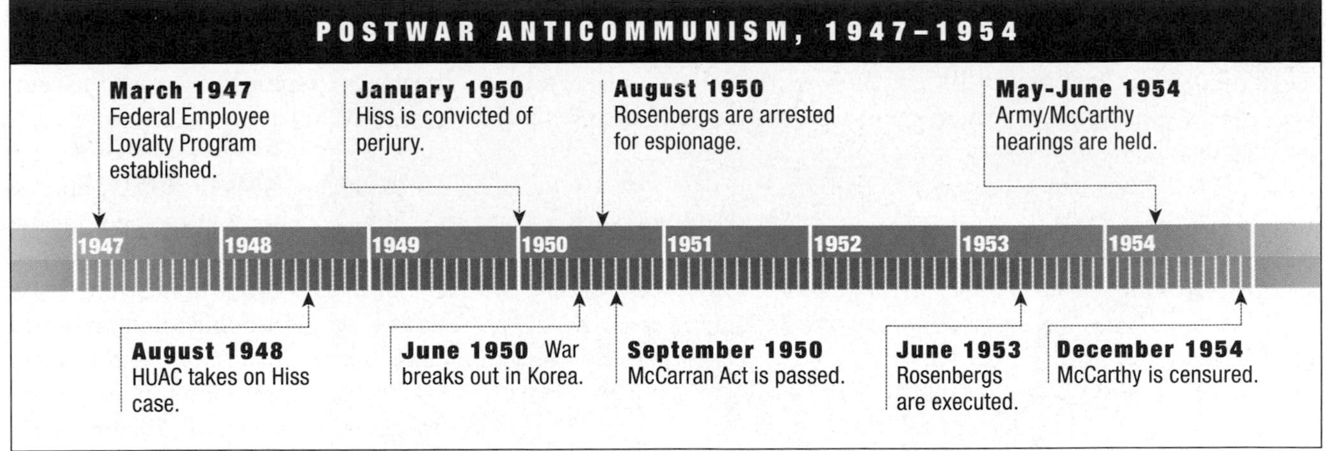

POSTWAR ANTICOMMUNISM, 1947–1954
March 1947 Federal Employee Loyalty Program established.
January 1950 Hiss is convicted of perjury.
August 1950 Rosenbergs are arrested for espionage.
May-June 1954 Army/McCarthy hearings are held.
1947
1948
1949
1950
1951
1952
1953
1954
August 1948 HUAC takes on Hiss case.
June 1950 War breaks out in Korea.
September 1950 McCarran Act is passed.
June 1953 Rosenbergs are executed.
December 1954 McCarthy is censured.

previously accused Hiss of engaging in espionage, suddenly said: "I think I have what you're looking for." Taking the investigators out to a pumpkin patch, he rummaged through the pumpkins, finally finding the one for which he was looking. As his guests watched in amazement, Chambers dramatically pulled off the top, reached into the pumpkin, and pulled out a roll of microfilm.

The microfilm showed copies of secret State Department documents that became known in national headlines as the Pumpkin Papers. Some documents had been copied on a typewriter that was eventually traced to Alger Hiss.

This was the bombshell Nixon and the HUAC had been looking for. The committee hearings led the courts to take up the case against Alger Hiss again. He could no longer be tried for espionage, since the alleged spying had taken place so long before. Hiss was convicted in 1950 on two counts of perjury and sentenced to five years in prison.

Many books have been written debating Hiss's guilt or innocence. In many he is portrayed as a man who destroyed himself, partly with statements like: "Until the day I die, I shall wonder how Whittaker Chambers got into my house to use my typewriter." When he made the statement in court, laughter erupted in the room. Alger Hiss was a ruined man.

Richard Nixon emerged the real victor in the case. The press, which initially supported Hiss, wound up running dramatic pictures of Nixon scrutinizing the microfilm and making tough public statements about the case. He became identified as a relentless pursuer of Communist subversion. In his memoirs Nixon explains, regarding his later decision to run for the Senate, "I recognized the worth of the nationwide publicity that the Hiss case had given me—publicity on a scale that most congressmen only dream of achieving."

Truman Joins the Red Hunt

Compared with FDR, Harry Truman had a far greater suspicion and dislike of Communists. His own rhetoric about "the enemy within" contributed to the fears of subversion, but he was forced into taking an even stronger, highly public stand on the subject to defend himself against the accusations of headline-hunting congressmen.

Responding to the label of being "soft," Truman in 1947 instituted the Federal Employee Loyalty Program,

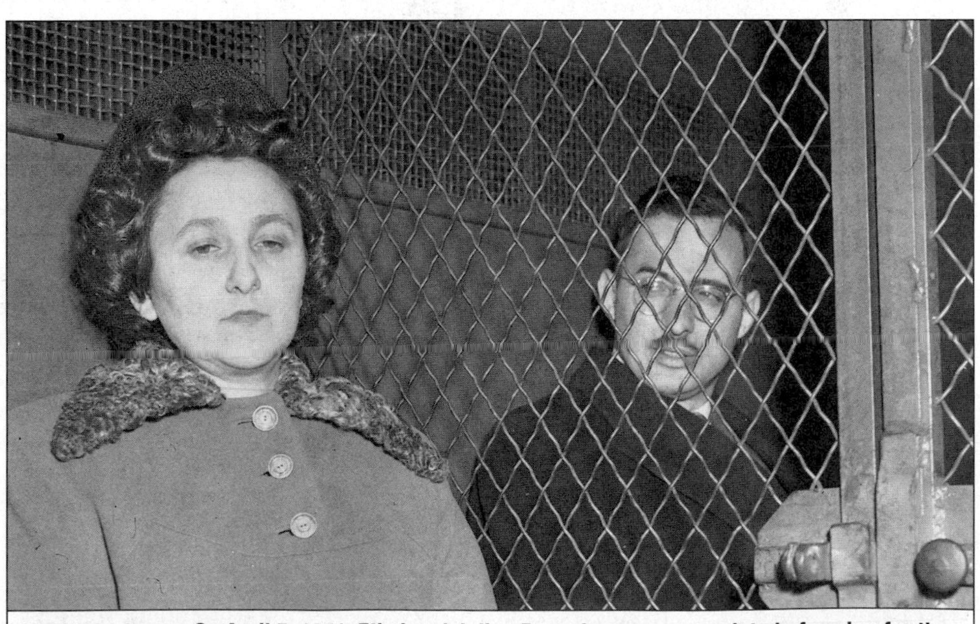

UPI/BETTMANN

The Rosenbergs On April 5, 1951, Ethel and Julius Rosenberg were convicted of spying for the Soviet Union. *Why did Truman join the Red hunt?*

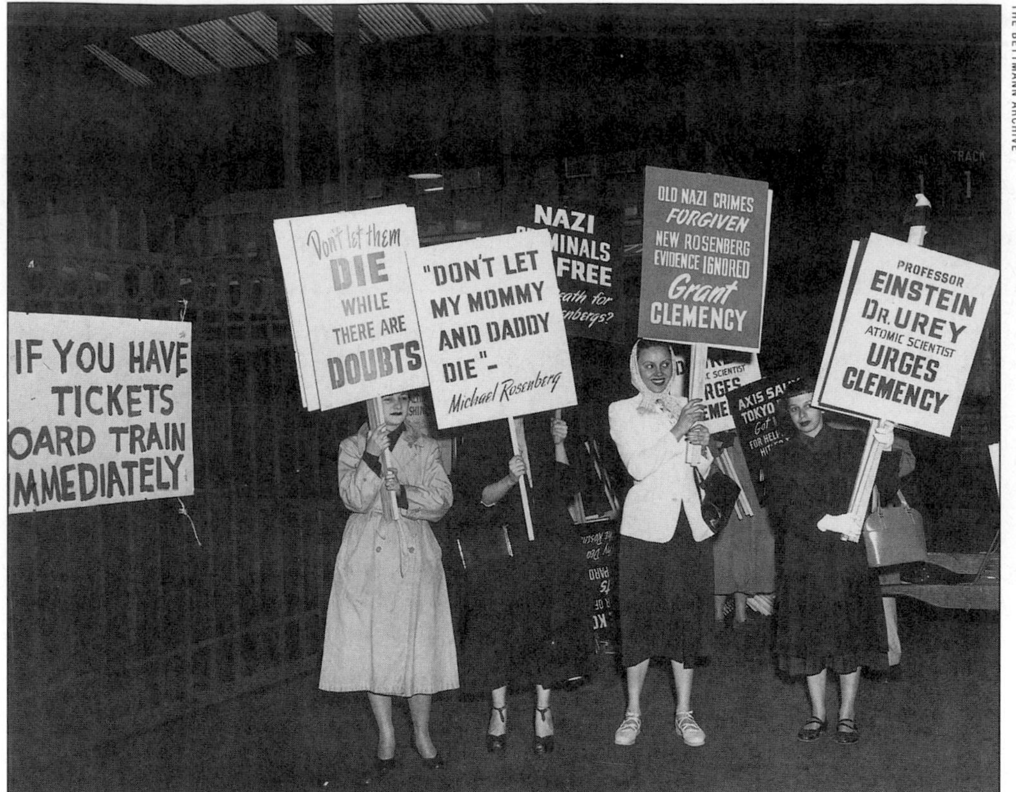

THE BETTMANN ARCHIVE

The Red Scare Women demonstrate against the conviction of Ethel and Julius Rosenberg. *What message do these demonstrators want to send?*

designed to evaluate the loyalty of government employees. Although the program had checks meant to protect individuals' rights, it was often abused by ambitious officials.

Under the program, even the slightest suspicion of disloyalty or the slimmest connection to a Communist party member was enough to put a government worker out of a job. Employees were suspect for openly criticizing American foreign policy, advocating equal rights for women, owning books on socialism, and attending foreign films. Others lost jobs because of associations or former associations with radicals, or because they belonged to a group classified as dangerous. From 1947 to 1951 a "loyalty board" investigated more than 3 million government employees; nearly 3,000 were forced to resign, and 212 were fired. Yet the probes uncovered no positive proof of subversion or espionage.

To many in Congress, Truman's anti-Communist measures were not enough. So in 1950 Congress passed its own tough law, the McCarran Act. This act did not directly outlaw the Communist party but made it illegal for Americans to engage in activities that would create a Communist government. It required Communist organizations to register with the federal government. Communists were not allowed to work in defense plants or to obtain United States passports.

Truman vetoed the McCarran Act, declaring, "In a free country, we punish men for crimes they commit, but never for the opinions they hold." Congress easily overrode the veto.

Seeking United States Secrets

On the heels of the Hiss conviction, a new case broke into the headlines and served to heighten people's fears of Communist espionage. In 1950 a young British scientist, Klaus Fuchs, admitted he had handed over to the Soviets American government specifications for the manufacture of the atomic bomb. A bizarre series of circumstances led investigators to Ethel and Julius Rosenberg, a New York City couple who had likely been members of the Communist party.

The government charged the Rosenbergs with conspiracy in a plot that prosecutors said was intended to transmit top secret bomb specifications to the Soviets. Ethel's brother, a soldier stationed at the Manhattan Project in New Mexico, accused the Rosenbergs of recruiting him to collect the information. The couple were convicted and sentenced to death.

On June 19, 1953, at 8:06 P.M., Julius Rosenberg walked calmly into the electric chair chamber at Sing Sing prison in New York State. Moments later, his wife Ethel followed him. A reporter who witnessed the executions said of Ethel afterward that she had "gone to meet her maker, and would have a lot of explaining to do."

Ethel and Julius Rosenberg died protesting their innocence. Appeals and worldwide protests failed to save them. Ethel's brother served 10 years of a 15-year sentence.

The Rosenbergs had frequently been offered a deal: Testify against others and avoid the death penalty. "Since we are guilty of no crime, we will not be party to the nefarious plot to bear false witness against other innocent progressives to heighten hysteria in our land," Julius wrote.

Ever since, in books, movies, and magazine and newspaper articles, people have been trying to uncover the truth about the Rosenbergs. Arguments abound on both sides, but recently released Soviet documents seem to confirm the Rosenbergs' guilt.

The McCarthy Era

Unfounded Accusations Ruin Many

Even before Ethel and Julius Rosenberg had been arrested and charged with spying for the Soviet Union in July 1950, Senator Joseph McCarthy took up the anti-Communist cause. McCarthy had impressed few people in his first three years in Congress, which began in 1947. The congressional press corps sized him up as a small-time politician. He drank too much and could get offensive and even violent at times. He was not well liked; but he learned how to be feared.

On February 9, 1950, McCarthy stood up at a Republican women's club meeting in Wheeling, West Virginia, waved some papers in the air, and announced he had a list of 205 Communists working in the State Department. In follow-up investigations of McCarthy's claim, he wavered on the exact number—from 205 to 81 to 57 to "a lot." His basic theme, however, remained the same: Communists thrived in Truman's administration. They had to be rooted out. Joe McCarthy was the one to do it.

McCarthy never produced a shred of credible evidence; however, in hearings and public statements, he attacked and ruined official after official of the United States government. Almost nobody was safe from his accusations. The accused either resigned under a cloud of suspicion or were fired as security risks.

These accusatory, anti-Communist times were named after the Wisconsin senator. They became known as "the McCarthy era." He gave a new word, *McCarthyism,* to the language. It referred to the use of intimidation and often unfounded accusations in the name of fighting communism.

Despite his tactics, McCarthy won considerable public support, at least at first. Millions of Americans believed that he was fighting a lonely battle—that he was a patriot challenging traitors and subversives. He was making the country safe for democracy.

TELEVISION AND SENATOR McCARTHY

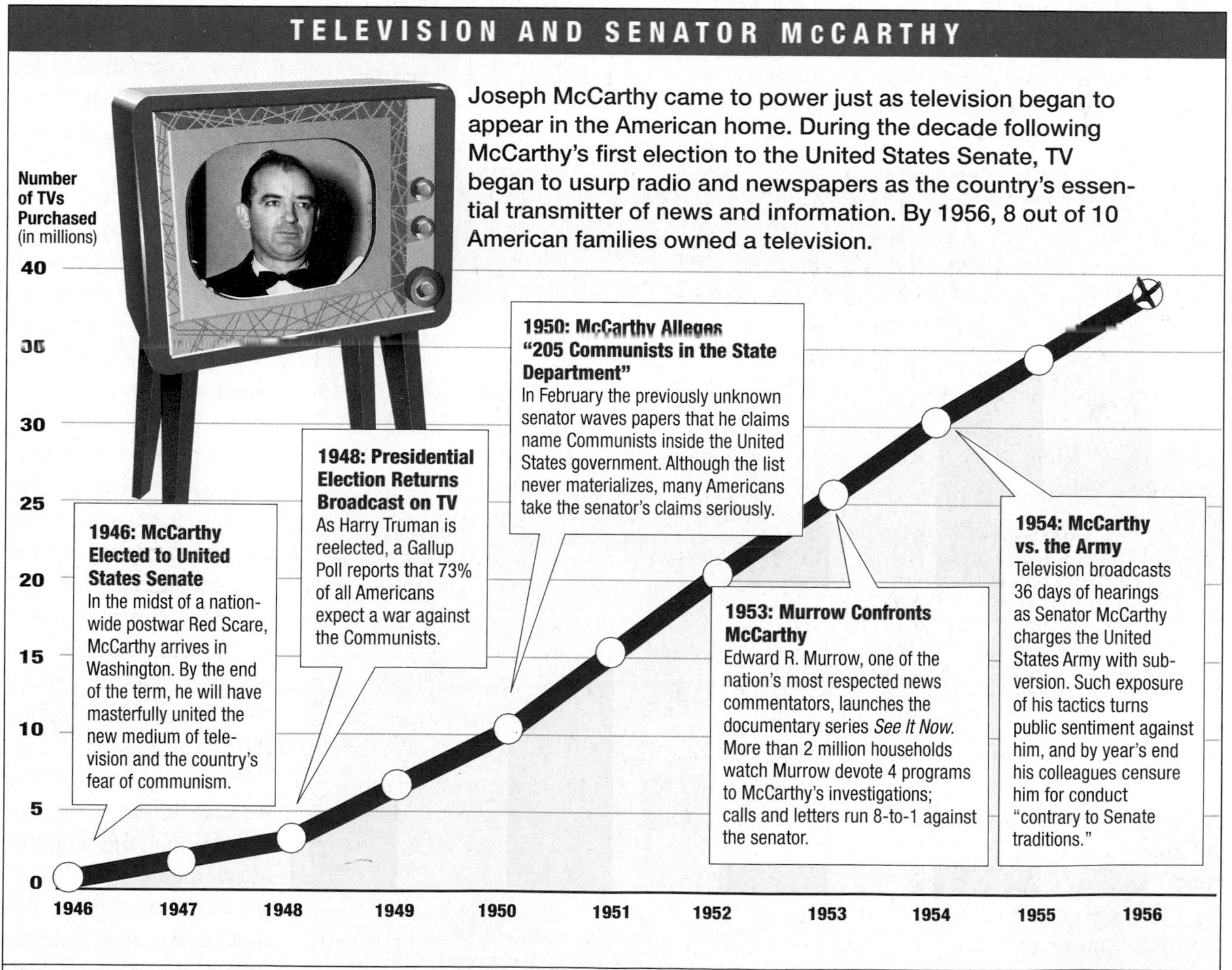

Joseph McCarthy came to power just as television began to appear in the American home. During the decade following McCarthy's first election to the United States Senate, TV began to usurp radio and newspapers as the country's essential transmitter of news and information. By 1956, 8 out of 10 American families owned a television.
Number of TVs Purchased (in millions)
40
35
30
25
20
15
10
5
0
1946
1947
1948
1949
1950
1951
1952
1953
1954
1955
1956
1946: McCarthy Elected to United States Senate
In the midst of a nationwide postwar Red Scare, McCarthy arrives in Washington. By the end of the term, he will have masterfully united the new medium of television and the country's fear of communism.
1948: Presidential Election Returns Broadcast on TV
As Harry Truman is reelected, a Gallup Poll reports that 73% of all Americans expect a war against the Communists.
1950: McCarthy Alleges "205 Communists in the State Department"
In February the previously unknown senator waves papers that he claims name Communists inside the United States government. Although the list never materializes, many Americans take the senator's claims seriously.
1953: Murrow Confronts McCarthy
Edward R. Murrow, one of the nation's most respected news commentators, launches the documentary series See It Now. More than 2 million households watch Murrow devote 4 programs to McCarthy's investigations; calls and letters run 8-to-1 against the senator.
1954: McCarthy vs. the Army
Television broadcasts 36 days of hearings as Senator McCarthy charges the United States Army with subversion. Such exposure of his tactics turns public sentiment against him, and by year's end his colleagues censure him for conduct "contrary to Senate traditions."

McCarthy's media savvy helped him take advantage of the new medium of television. *How many televisions did Americans purchase in 1954?*

The Senate subcommittee on investigations, of which McCarthy became chairman in 1953, provided him with an official forum from which to launch public attacks on government employees. His was not the only show in town. Numerous other congressmen conducted their own hearings and investigations, and the HUAC's activities continued as well.

For Republicans, McCarthy was a loose cannon, and his conservative colleagues often distanced themselves from him, except when it suited their own purposes. Although few people liked him, some took advantage of his talent for keeping himself and his issue in the spotlight.

In his highly public role, the senator accumulated enormous power. At the height of his power, he could make politicians, bank presidents, network executives, and average citizens quake. For a long time, few people dared challenge him. Harry Truman, in his retirement, acknowledged the extent of McCarthy's hold on the nation's affairs:

> McCarthyism . . . the meaning of the word is the corruption of truth, the abandonment of our historical devotion to fair play. It is the abandonment of 'due process' of law. It is the use of the big lie and the unfounded accusation against any citizen in the name of Americanism and security. . . .
>
> This horrible cancer is eating at the vitals of America and it can destroy the great edifice of freedom.
>
> —Harry S Truman, radio and TV address, November 17, 1953

McCarthy's rise to power was swift and heady. The senator eventually grew reckless with it, throwing accusations around fearlessly—but also, many noted, with a growing sense that if he ever ran out of names to smear, his bubble would burst.

McCarthy Goes Too Far

That is just what happened. McCarthy went too far. When President Eisenhower took office in 1953, he decided to ignore the senator as much as possible, hoping McCarthy would do himself in. In addition, Eisenhower did not want to offend conservatives in his own party by engaging in a risky battle with one of their own.

Hunting for ever more sensational targets, McCarthy hurled his next accusations against the United States Army in 1954; and the army was ready. Meeting the senator's unsupported allegations with a quiet presentation of the facts, army attorney Joseph Welch calmly shredded McCarthy's charges of a Communist conspiracy in the United States Army. To a nation watching the subcommittee hearings on TV, Welch presented an intelligent contrast to McCarthy's sensational theatrics. McCarthy sealed his own fate.

A political cartoon of the time showed McCarthy trapped in a spider's web, crying, "I can't do this to me!" He did, though, along with a growing number of opponents who broke their silence to take a public stand against him. In 1954 the Senate voted to condemn McCarthy.

When the senator died in 1957, sickened from alcohol and exhaustion, few people mourned. Many hoped an era had died with him—but it had not.

AP/WIDE WOLRD PHOTOS

McCarthyism Joseph McCarthy acknowledges the cheers of a flag-waving crowd at New York's Carnegie Hall. *Who did McCarthy accuse in 1954?*

The Red Hunt Goes On

Spying on Neighbors Encouraged

Just as Red hunting did not begin with McCarthy, it did not end with him, either. Government films and brochures urged citizens to expose anyone they suspected of having Communist leanings—neighbors, friends, teachers, even clergy.

The McCarthy era spawned hundreds of watchdog groups run by private citizens. The motives and methods of these **vigilantes**—self-appointed doers of justice—could be vicious and illegal. John Henry Faulk found this out in 1957, the year McCarthy died.

A Texan with a quick mind and a fondness for radical ideas, Faulk had a radio show in New York City in which he dispensed his own brand of humor. In the mid-1950s Faulk was elected vice president of a local chapter of the American Federation of Television and Radio Actors. He won partly because of his stand against **blacklisting,** the effort to brand people as Communists and prevent them from holding jobs. One such group, called AWARE, had ruined many, and Faulk and others sought to stem its influence. AWARE responded by trying to link Faulk with communism. It pressured the advertisers on Faulk's radio show to cancel their ads. Faced with negative publicity and the loss of advertising dollars, CBS fired Faulk.

Faulk countered with a lawsuit against AWARE that took 6 years to settle. In 1963 a jury awarded him $3.5 million in damages, although the award was reduced to $550,000 on appeal. In the meantime, Faulk's career had been ruined. Ironically, CBS later made a highly successful television movie sympathetic to Faulk.

By 1963, when Faulk's name was cleared, the legacy of the Red hunters had faded—but was not forgotten. There remained the living memory of the thousands of people who had been smeared, blacklisted, and ostracized. As late as 1960, for instance, city and state employees all over the country were forced to swear to and sign a loyalty oath. In Massachusetts, teachers had to make the following promise:

> I do solemnly swear or affirm that I will uphold and defend the Constitution of the United States of America and the Commonwealth of Massachusetts and that I will oppose the overthrow of the government of the United States of America or of the Commonwealth by force or violence or any illegal or unconstitutional method: I am not a member of the Communist party.
>
> Subscribed by me under penalty of perjury, this ___ day of ___________, 1960.

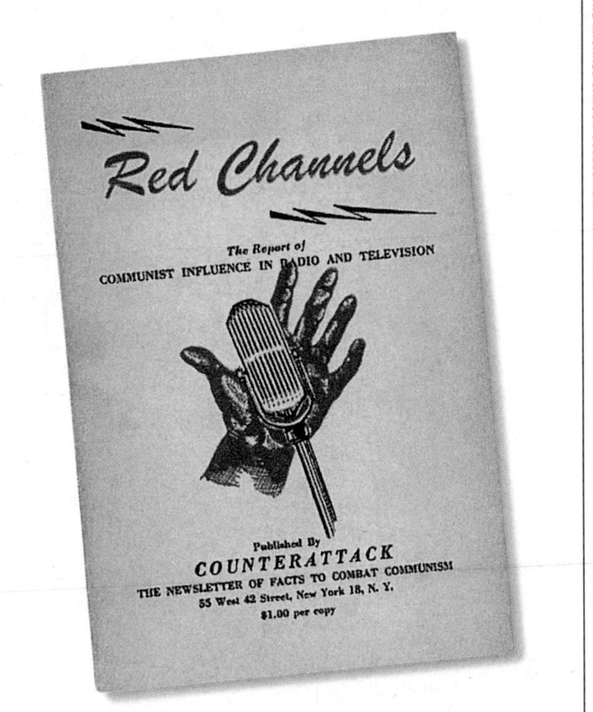

THE MICHAEL BARSON COLLECTION/PAST PERFECT

The Red Hunt Vigilante groups published brochures such as this to expose suspected Communists. *Why was John Henry Faulk accused of being a Communist?*

SECTION ASSESSMENT

Main Idea

1. Use this diagram to write six questions about the McCarthy era using the question words commonly asked by reporters: who? what? when? where? why? and how? Record your answers to each question.

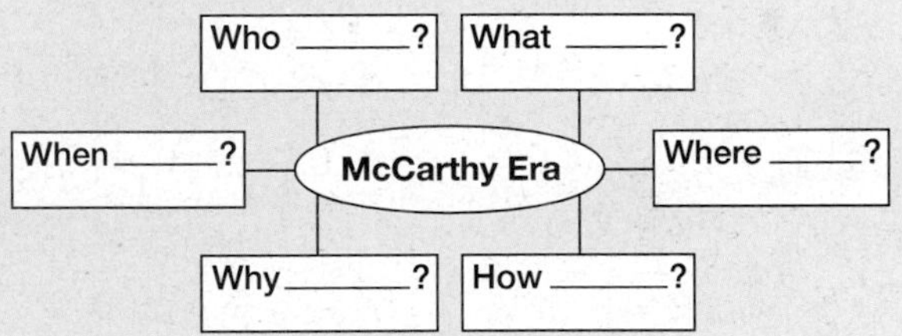

Vocabulary

2. Define: vigilante, blacklisting.

Checking Facts

3. Give two examples of the government's response to growing fears of communism.
4. How did Red hunting continue after McCarthy?

Critical Thinking

5. **Identifying Bias** Given the nation's preoccupation with communism, what can you conclude about the stereotype of Communists at the time?

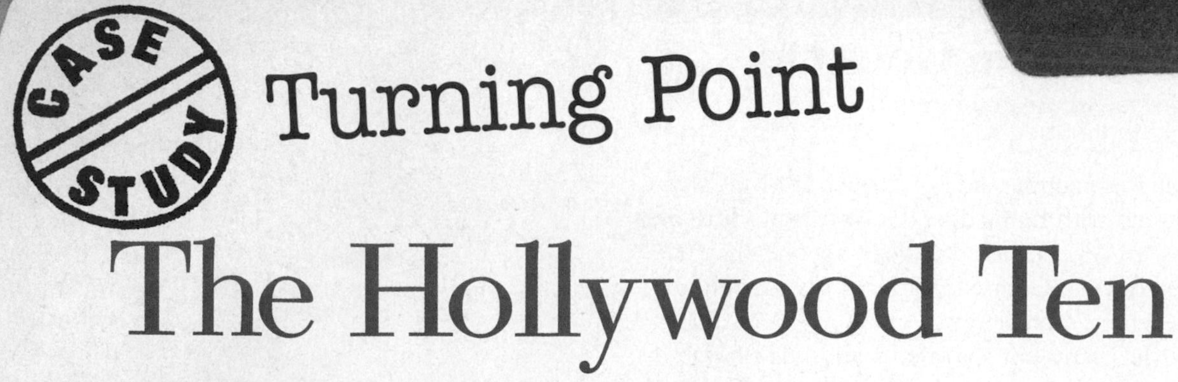

Turning Point

The Hollywood Ten

OCTOBER, 1947

TRANSCRIPT

Robert Stripling [Chief Investigator]: Mr. Lawson, are you now or have you ever been a member of the Communist party of the United States?

John Howard Lawson [Screenwriter #1]: The question of Communism is in no way related to this inquiry, which is an attempt to get control of the screen and to invade the basic rights of American citizens in all fields.

Ring Lardner, Jr. [Screenwriter #2]: I could answer that question, but I'd hate myself in the morning.

J. Parnell Thomas [Committee Chairman]: Any real American would be proud to answer that question.

The Case

Congress formed the House Un-American Activities Committee (HUAC) in the late 1930s to combat extremist movements. Following World War II, the committee became concerned about Communists in Hollywood. In 1947 the committee obtained membership files of the Communist party in Hollywood and subpoenaed prominent writers and directors on the list to ask them what the committee already knew—whether they had ever been members of the Communist party. During the committee hearings, the following witnesses became known in the press as the Hollywood Ten:

Alvah Bessie, screenwriter

Herbert Biberman, screenwriter and director

Lester Cole, screenwriter

Edward Dmytryk, director

Ring Lardner, Jr., screenwriter

John Howard Lawson, screenwriter

Albert Maltz, screenwriter

Samuel Ornitz, screenwriter

Adrian Scott, screenwriter and producer

Dalton Trumbo, screenwriter

The committee had no legal power to prosecute, and it was not illegal to belong to the Communist party. In the words of Chairman J. Parnell Thomas, the committee's goal was to "uncover the truth and let Hollywood and the American public do the rest."

The Background

From the mid-1930s to the mid-1950s, about 300 film directors, actors, writers, and designers, along with many people in other walks of life, joined the Communist party. Interest in Communist philosophy grew among people who had doubts about capitalism and felt that it led to the exploitation of workers. Communism seemed to promise improved conditions for workers and equity for people of all races. Joining the party was popular in the 1930s, when being a Communist often meant being concerned about workers' rights and about racism. By the late 1930s, many craft unions in the film industry were formed, and the Communist party was involved in a struggle for workers' benefits. During World War II, the Communists in the Soviet Union were allies of the United States against Nazi Germany. Before and during World War II, the federal government encouraged Hollywood movie moguls to make upbeat movies about the Soviet Union so that Americans would support the fight against the Nazis.

With the defeat of Germany and the end of World War II, however, attitudes toward the Soviet Union began to shift. Americans became increasingly fearful of Soviet leader Joseph Stalin and his interest in the spread of communism worldwide. As the cold war heightened, tolerance of communism dissolved. Stalin's repressive tactics against his people caused many party members to quit. Although membership in the Communist party was never illegal, the party lost popularity.

People became worried that Communists were influencing many aspects of American society. They suspected that Communists in Hollywood were not just working to secure the rights of workers, but also to control the content of films. The federal government now encouraged movies showing Communists in a bad light and depicting the Soviet Union as an enemy. In this atmosphere, the House Un-American Activities Committee decided to turn a spotlight on Hollywood and investigate Communists in the movie business. The probe was a way to influence the movie industry and gain publicity for the HUAC.

The Opinions

People in Hollywood were divided on whether to cooperate with the HUAC. Some Hollywood witnesses who appeared before the committee were people who saw evidence of Communist activity around them. The committee responded favorably to these "friendly witnesses." Those less willing to cooperate with the committee received less cordial treatment. These people were termed "unfriendly witnesses."

AP/WIDE WORLD PHOTOS

There has been a small group within the Screen Actors Guild which has consistently opposed the policy of the Guild board and officers of the Guild. . . . That small clique . . . has been suspected of more or less following the tactics that we associate with the Communist Party.

Ronald Reagan,
president of the
Screen Actors Guild

THE GRANGER COLLECTION

I am convinced that these Hollywood Commies are agents of a foreign country. If I have any doubt that they are [Communists], then I haven't any mind.

Sam Wood,
producer and director

CULVER PICTURES, INC.

Today J. Parnell Thomas is engaged in a personally conducted smear campaign of the motion picture industry. . . . Silence the artist and you have silenced the most articulate voice the people have.

Katharine Hepburn,
movie star

AP/WIDE WORLD PHOTOS

You [the committee] are using the old technique . . . to create a scare . . . in order that you can smear the motion picture industry . . . . The Bill of Rights was established . . . to prevent the operation of any committee which could invade the basic rights of Americans.

John Howard Lawson,
screenwriter

CASE STUDY Turning Point

The press reported on the witnesses and committee members alike and publicized the time the HUAC Chairman Thomas smashed a gavel to splinters while calling for order. On the editorial page of the *New York Times*, the hearings themselves were deplored:

> **Finally, an investigation of this kind, once begun, has no ready stopping-place. One of the Government's witnesses has already declared that Broadway is worse than Hollywood in the matter of Communist penetration, and that the reading departments of the publishing houses are "very, very heavily infiltrated with Communists." Are we now to go on from Hollywood to Broadway, and then from Broadway to the publishing houses, searching for suspects all along the line, and after that carry the hunt into the radio and then into the . . . press?**
>
> —*New York Times*

HISTORICAL PICTURES SERVICE, CHICAGO

Nine of the Hollywood Ten await fingerprinting after their surrender.

The Options

Witnesses who appeared before the HUAC were asked, "Are you now or have you ever been a member of the Communist party?" When responding, the witnesses had several options.

1. Refuse to answer on the grounds that Congress has no authority to investigate behavior protected by the First Amendment, the right to freedom of speech and thought. The witnesses' lawyers warned that this response might bring a charge of contempt of Congress because the Supreme Court had established Congress's right to inquire. The Hollywood Ten maintained that Congress could not legislate away the First Amendment of the Bill of Rights and, therefore, had no right to investigate where they could not legislate.
2. Refuse to answer, pleading the Fifth Amendment, which gives people the right not to testify against themselves. Using this tactic was assumed by many to be an admission of Communist party membership.
3. Answer yes and place themselves at the mercy of the committee. This tactic would make them subject to more questions, such as requests for the names of other people in the Communist party.
4. Answer no and risk being charged with perjury if the committee proved they were not telling the truth. Perjury carried a greater penalty than contempt of Congress.

The Outcome

In October 1947 the Hollywood Ten agreed among themselves to plead the First Amendment and remain silent as a protest against questions they believed the HUAC had no right to ask.

The Ten were held in contempt of Congress for refusing to testify. In December 1947 a grand jury indicted them and found them guilty of contempt. The appeals process ran until 1950, when the Supreme Court refused to hear the case and let the verdict stand. The Ten served jail terms of about one year.

In one of the ironies of history, some of the Hollywood Ten and Chairman Thomas would meet again. A newspaper columnist discovered that Thomas had raised the salaries of his staff members in return for payments, or kickbacks, from the grateful employees. Thomas was indicted for fraud and pleaded no contest. He was fined $10,000 and served a 9-month sentence in the same prison in which some of the Hollywood Ten were confined.

HISTORICAL PICTURES SERVICE, CHICAGO

Hollywood celebrities protest the tactics of the HUAC's investigation into alleged Hollywood communism.

In December 1947, one week after the Hollywood Ten were cited for contempt, the film industry fired them. The industry, facing a serious economic crisis, desperately needed favorable publicity. Industry officials hoped that firing the Ten would boost Hollywood's image.

Fifty top film executives met at the Waldorf-Astoria Hotel in New York City. After two days of conferences, they fired the Hollywood Ten and released a statement saying, "We will not knowingly employ a Communist."

In addition to the jail sentences and firings, the Hollywood Ten were blacklisted. Many were unable to find any work in the film industry for the next 10 years. Others, like Ring Lardner, Jr., could work only under pseudonyms. The Hollywood Ten were not the only ones to be penalized, however.

Some of the Ten's colleagues stood up for them. Famous actors, such as Gene Kelly, Judy Garland, and Humphrey Bogart, took part in benefits and speeches on behalf of the Ten. Because of their support, these actors' reputations were also tainted. MGM Studios received so many letters criticizing Katharine Hepburn that they told the famous actress they could not use her in films again until public opinion of her improved.

The Significance

The HUAC hearings on communism in Hollywood ended a few days after the Ten refused to testify. Four years later in 1951, the HUAC again investigated communism in the film industry. This time witnesses pleaded the Fifth Amendment to avoid contempt charges. The committee sent no one to jail, but the industry again responded by denying work to 250 actors, writers, and directors.

Following the HUAC hearings, there was a noticeable increase in the number of movies with an anti-Communist point of view. By some estimates, between 1947 and 1954 more than 50 films were released preaching the view that Communists were the enemies of the United States.

The Hollywood Ten decided to go to prison rather than submit to questioning from the HUAC. They believed that the United States Constitution protected them from having to answer to the committee. Screenwriter Dalton Trumbo expressed his feelings about the experience in this poem, which he wrote to his family from prison:

Say then but this of me:
Preferring not to crawl on his knees
In freedom to a bowl of buttered slops
Set out for him by some contemptuous clown,
He walked to jail on his feet.

RESPONDING TO THE CASE

1. List reasons the House Un-American Activities Committee felt it needed to investigate communism in the Hollywood film industry. List the arguments of the Hollywood Ten for not answering the committee's questions. Explain which side appears to have the stronger position.

2. How might the Hollywood Ten have responded to the committee's questions without showing contempt but at the same time remain true to their beliefs in the freedom of thought guaranteed in the Bill of Rights?

3. What might have happened if the Hollywood Ten had testified at the HUAC hearings?

PORTFOLIO PROJECT

The First Amendment of the Bill of Rights guarantees a person's freedom of speech and thought. Do you think the Hollywood Ten's First Amendment rights were violated by the HUAC? Explain your reasoning. What dangers or benefits do you see in clamping down on unpopular opinions?

The Eisenhower Years

APRIL 5, 1954: PRESIDENT EISENHOWER ADDRESSES THE NATION

We Like Ike
These campaigners in San Francisco show their support for Dwight David Eisenhower, who won the confidence of the nation in the 1950s.

HIS WAS A VOICE OF REASON IN AN UNREASONABLE AGE. He had the inner assurance and five-star strength of a man who had met the enemy and won. When he spoke, people felt that things might come out all right, if they would all pull together, as they had on the battlefields of Europe during World War II.

Dwight David Eisenhower won the confidence of the American people. Maybe it had something to do with the innocent smile he wore when he held up a big fish he had just caught; or the commanding presence one saw in his eyes; or his baldish dome, which made him appear taller than he was. Maybe it was his halting speech, which seemed to hold six decades of experience and caution in each pause.

Dwight Eisenhower was not a fist-pounding speech maker. He did not have the flair for dropping verbal bombs on an audience the way General Douglas MacArthur and General George Patton did. Eisenhower counseled calmly, like the family doctor. He spoke to a generation of Americans who were uneasily watching communism advance on the world's continents, who built bomb shelters in their backyards and bought lead-lined suits in the naive hope of surviving a nuclear holocaust. Both his words and his tone had a soothing effect:

> No one can say to you that there are no dangers. Of course there are risks, if we are not vigilant. But we do not have to be hysterical. . . . We can stand up and hold up our heads and say, "America is the greatest force that God has ever allowed to exist on his footstool." As such it is up to us to lead this world to a peaceful and secure existence.
>
> —President Eisenhower, radio and TV address, April 5, 1954

GUIDE TO READING

Main Idea

Although the presidency of Dwight Eisenhower gave the nation a sense of security and prosperity at home, ongoing cold war tensions created an opportunity in 1960 for John F. Kennedy to seize back the White House for the Democrats.

Vocabulary

- consensus decision making
- electronic media

Read to Find Out . . .

- how the process of consensus decision making worked under Eisenhower.
- the growing political role of the electronic media during the 1950s.
- how Kennedy defeated Nixon for the presidency in 1960.

Warrior in the White House

An Efficient Campaigner and President

The United States's favorite patriot, the supreme allied commander in Europe, had never voted in his life when the Republicans began urging him to run for the presidency in 1952. Living in Paris, General Eisenhower began reading United States history books and studying economics, but he was not quick to commit himself to a run for the White House. In fact, he even refused an offer of $40,000 from *McCall's* magazine just to say whether he was a Republican. Ike was not a man of haste. In 1952, however, he answered the call of duty to his country.

AP/WIDE WORLD PHOTOS, COURTESY UNIVERSITY OF SOUTHERN CALIFORNIA LIBRARY

Richard and Pat Nixon In his "Checkers" speech, Nixon introduced his wife, Pat, to the viewers and emphasized his family values. *How did Nixon portray his critics in his Checkers speech?*

A New Kind of Campaign

Given Eisenhower's popularity and lack of involvement in political controversy, the outcome of the election was never much in doubt. The Democratic candidate, Governor Adlai E. Stevenson of Illinois, conducted a respectable, even admirable, race. The governor was a witty, eloquent speaker who appealed to liberal intellectuals, but the country as a whole was not in a liberal frame of mind in 1952.

For every voter who found Stevenson sophisticated, there were two who dubbed him and his followers eggheads. He was articulate and sophisticated, not a man who could win the average voter with a folksy style. Stevenson's greatest obstacle, however, was that he belonged to the same party as Harry Truman.

Although new to politics, Eisenhower did not lack political instincts, as shown by his choice of Senator Nixon as his running mate. By adding an experienced politician and champion of anticommunism to his ticket, Ike clinched the conservative vote and eased the fears of those who wondered about his grasp of domestic issues.

At first, however, the choice of Nixon threatened to blow up in Ike's face. Early in the campaign, a newspaper revealed the existence of a "secret fund" of contributions from citizens, which it said was used to support Nixon in an extravagant lifestyle. Some party members called for Nixon to quit the ticket.

Nixon, the prosecutor, went on the offensive. At Ike's suggestion, he took his case to the voters in a live TV broadcast on September 23, 1952. In quiet tones Nixon gave a lengthy and thorough accounting of all his financial holdings, which were quite modest. The fund, he said, was used for travel from his Washington home to California, and it was neither illegal nor immoral.

In this politically shrewd talk, he clearly implied that those who attacked him were those who opposed his efforts to fight communism. Nixon did admit to one contribution for his personal use. An admirer had sent his family a dog. His young daughters loved that dog, which they named Checkers, and he was not going to give it back.

The emotional appeal from Nixon won him a wave of support from viewers. The broadcast became known as the Checkers speech. As in the Hiss case, Nixon came out on top. Calling him "my boy," Ike embraced Nixon, and the campaign rolled on.

Ike's election campaign resembled his military campaigns: It was organized, efficient, and determined. His speeches offered little in the way of specifics—he promised to "clean up the mess in Washington." Adlai Stevenson warned that the Republican platform was "as slippery as a bunch of eels—you can't stand on it." It did not matter. The Republicans hammered away at the themes of Truman-era weakness and incompetence—with Nixon slamming the "scandal-a-day administration," and Ike promising to go to Korea himself to put an end to the war. This was what voters wanted to hear. "We like Ike" echoed in the auditoriums of the country, and the Republicans marched on to victory. The 1952 election was not so much a win for the Republican party as it was a measure of the personal popularity of the smiling hero of World War II.

A New Command

A seasoned soldier knows that in battle lives depend not only on good generals but also on the cooperative efforts of every fighter. It is no surprise, then, that

President Eisenhower used **consensus decision making,** a management style based on group efforts, to solve problems. "No one has a monopoly on the truth," he declared.

Eisenhower had a clear vision of what he thought was right, and he was comfortable in an administrative role. He focused on major issues only, delegating other matters to his advisers. Everything moved through proper channels in the new administration.

The President had great respect for successful business leaders, and he was convinced that the country would function best on proven business principles. In fact, he named corporate executives to most key posts in his administration. To the government's regulatory agencies, he appointed business leaders friendly to the industries they were supposed to regulate.

One of President Eisenhower's major initiatives during his first term in office was to encourage private development of hydroelectric and nuclear power plants. He unsuccessfully urged Congress to turn over to private companies the operation of one New Deal program, the Tennessee Valley Authority. He did, however, approve the Atomic Energy Act of 1954, which allowed private companies to operate nuclear power plants. The first nuclear-powered generator to produce electricity for public use began operation in Arco, Idaho, in 1955.

Ike unwaveringly followed "middle of the road" policies. Political observers increasingly criticized his emphasis on consensus decision making as cumbersome and ineffective. As a columnist noted in 1959, however, "The public loves Ike. The less he does, the more they love him. That, probably, is the secret. Here is a man who doesn't rock the boat."

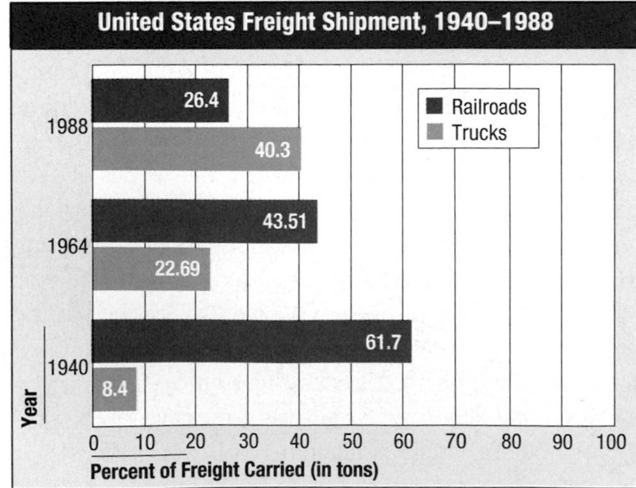

From 1940 to 1988, the amount of freight that trucks carried rose. The amount that trains carried decreased. Trains, however, remained an important means of transporting freight.
How much freight was carried by trains in 1940 and in 1988?

A Second Term

Ike Builds Interstate System as Cold War Deepens

This "secret" was the strategy that successfully carried him through a second presidential race in 1956. The race was practically a rerun of 1952. Once again Eisenhower squared off against Adlai Stevenson and won.

Although the outcome of the two campaigns was the same, the tone was different. Eisenhower had suffered a heart attack in 1955 and was running a less energetic campaign on his record of "peace, progress, and prosperity." The nation still liked Ike but was lukewarm to his party. Democrats retained control of Congress in 1956.

Eisenhower's second term was notable for decisions both made and postponed. As in his first term, domestic problems took a backseat to foreign policy. Trouble threatened when Castro came to power in Cuba. Although the President had ended the Korean War, the cold war grew icier. In 1957 the Soviets shocked the United States by sending up *Sputnik I,* the first space satellite.

The United States hurried to catch up in the space race, although Eisenhower was not eager to spend too much money to do it. *Explorer I,* the country's answer to *Sputnik I,* went up less than four months later, on January 31, 1958. Later that year, Congress created the National Aeronautics and Space Administration (NASA).

Paving America

Ike was less concerned with blazing a path into space than he was with paving new roads across the nation. The second Eisenhower term witnessed the most ambitious and expensive public works program in American history: construction of the federal interstate highway system.

Eisenhower's pet program, launched in 1956, was a departure from his generally conservative approach to spending. The President believed the country needed a network of highways to increase road safety, promote commerce, and preserve the nation's unity.

Besides Ike's personal support, the program had the backing of a powerful coalition that included oil companies, automobile and rubber manufacturers, letter carriers, bakers, truckers, and other groups. All stood to benefit from the road building.

Congress appropriated $32 billion to build 41,000 miles (65,969 km) of highways. Ten years later, cars and trucks crisscrossed the nation along the world's finest highway system. The final cost was more than $80 billion.

Ike's Legacy

Ike described himself as "conservative when it comes to money and liberal when it comes to human beings." During his terms, Congress extended Social Security to cover another 7 million people and unemployment compensation to cover another 4 million people. The minimum wage increased from 75 cents per hour to $1, and federally financed housing for low-income families increased. The President also approved building the St. Lawrence Seaway, connecting the Great Lakes to the Atlantic Ocean.

By 1960 the Eisenhower administration was stalled. Lack of progress in easing the cold war was crushing to Ike. The President's health, mirroring the prestige of the nation, sank. It was an opportunity tailor-made for a young political hopeful from Massachusetts, John F. Kennedy.

In With the New

Television Gives Kennedy a Victory Over Nixon

The 1960 presidential contest between Richard Nixon, son of a California shopkeeper, and John F. Kennedy, son of a Massachusetts millionaire, pitted against each other two men and two political philosophies that seemed to offer the country a real choice.

On the surface, Kennedy versus Nixon meant Catholic versus Protestant, a member of the Harvard elite facing a self-styled middle American. It was Kennedy the spender against Nixon the fiscal conservative, the Kennedy style and wit versus the proven Nixon experience.

In reality many of these much-celebrated differences mattered little. The two men had similar opinions on foreign and domestic issues. When Nixon ran for the Senate in 1950 against Helen Gahagan Douglas, Kennedy showed up at his office with a $1,000 contribution from his father for Nixon's campaign. The Kennedys thought Douglas just as dangerously left-leaning as Nixon did.

When Kennedy advocated an armed invasion of Cuba during the campaign, he was taking just the position Nixon had privately urged under Eisenhower. Ironically, Nixon had to disagree publicly with Kennedy because he had to support his administration's view. In 1960 Kennedy was not a vigorous advocate of civil rights, and Nixon had long been a moderate on the issue.

INTERSTATE HIGHWAYS, 1950s TO PRESENT

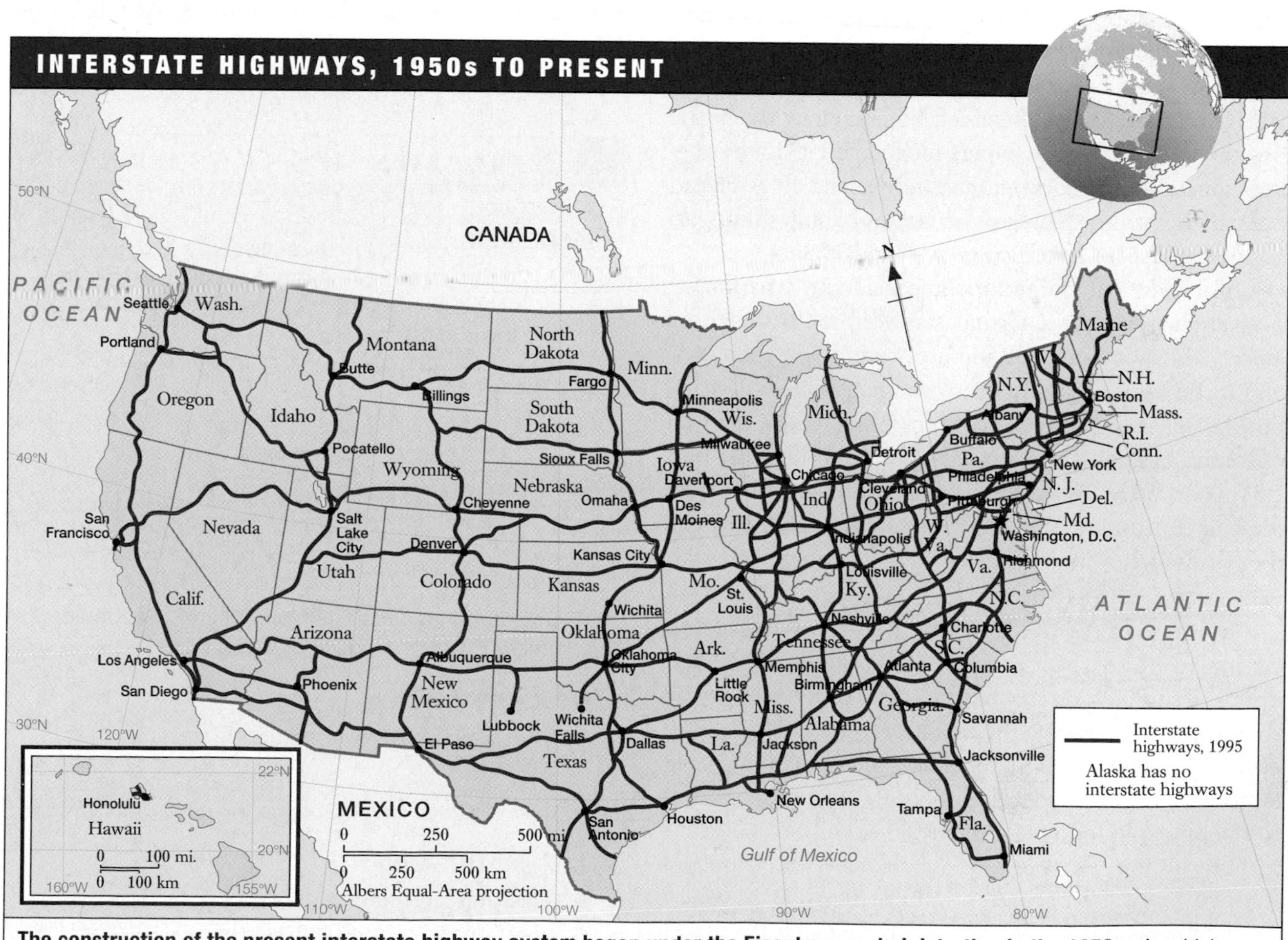

The construction of the present interstate highway system began under the Eisenhower administration in the 1950s. *In which regions of the United States were the most interstate highways built?*

AP/WIDE WORLD PHOTOS

The Nixon-Kennedy Debates **During the 1960 televised debates between Nixon and Kennedy, the public was influenced by Kennedy's wit and youthful appearance.** *How did Nixon's whistle-stop campaign strategy hurt him in his run for the presidency?*

Campaign Issues

Actually, the 1960 campaign provided something much more interesting than the stereotypes of the two men. It was a political battle waged over issues of national and international importance. Cuba, just off the tip of Florida, was fast becoming a perceived Communist threat. The United States had been left behind again when the Soviets sent a dog—the papers nicknamed it "mutnik"—into space. Violent Communist movements in Asia had not ended with the Korean War but were only shifting to Southeast Asia in a little country called Vietnam.

The 1960 campaign for the presidency was fought over such issues to a virtual standoff, indicating how closely the two young candidates resembled each other. Of the two, Kennedy was younger by several years, but that did not seem to cost him many votes. He was a Roman Catholic, and surveys indicated that cost him 1.5 million votes. Nixon had far more foreign experience: He had confronted anti-American crowds in Venezuela, met Khrushchev in a debate in Moscow, and talked with leaders around the world.

It was Nixon's decision to adopt the whistle-stop campaign strategy of Harry Truman that proved his undoing. Truman's recipe for victory turned out to be Richard Nixon's recipe for defeat. For the first time, the **electronic media**—TV and radio—were becoming a big factor in a presidential campaign, something that Kennedy exploited with his boyish good looks and infectious humor. The televised debate between Nixon and Kennedy in 1960 became a contest between a weary campaigner who was being squeezed dry by his grueling campaign schedule and a candidate whose aides knew how to help him work smarter, not harder.

The candidates met in a tide-turning televised debate on September 26, 1960. Viewers saw in Nixon a man stretched to his limits. Early in the whistle-stop campaign, Nixon had injured his knee. For weeks it continued to jolt him with pain, but he had carried on, racking up mile after mile to keep a promise to campaign in every state. He lost weight and looked haggard and drawn.

Kennedy, meanwhile, arrived for the debate tan and fit from a rest in Florida. It did not matter that radio listeners scored the debate for Nixon on the strength of his arguments. Television conveyed Kennedy's warmth and ease to 70 million viewers.

The Election

The election returns were one of the closest in history. Kennedy took 49.7 percent of the popular vote to 49.5 percent for Nixon, although the difference in electoral votes (303 to 219, respectively) proved far greater. Many Republicans and some independent observers, claimed election fraud in Texas and Illinois, where a single county might have wiped out Kennedy's victory of just over 100,000 votes out of the 69 million that were cast. A *New York Herald Tribune* writer, Earl Mazo, who had long been friendly to Nixon, started a journalistic investigation of vote fraud. Nixon, however, called him off. "Earl," he said, "no one steals the presidency of the United States."

Section Assessment

Main Idea

1. Use a diagram like this one to evaluate reasons for Eisenhower's public appeal and the legacy of his presidency.

Public Appeal		Legacy
	Eisenhower	

Vocabulary

2. Define: consensus decision making, electronic media.

Checking Facts

3. What was Eisenhower's attitude toward business?

4. How did television influence the election of 1960?

Critical Thinking

5. **Recognizing Ideologies** What does Eisenhower's emphasis on consensus decision making tell you about his values?

Critical Thinking Skill

DISTINGUISHING FACT FROM OPINION

Learning the Skill

Distinguishing fact from opinion is often not easy. Senator Joseph McCarthy convinced many Americans that Communists thrived in Truman's administration. Yet he never produced credible evidence.

Learning to distinguish fact from opinion can help you make reasonable judgments about what others say. A fact is a statement that can be proven by evidence such as records, documents, government statistics, or historical sources. An opinion is a statement that may contain some truth but also contains a personal view or judgment.

The following steps will help you to sift facts from opinions and to judge the reliability of what you read or hear.

a. Identify the facts. Ask yourself the following: Can these statements be proved? Where can I find information to verify them?

b. Check the sources for the facts. Reliable sources include almanacs, encyclopedias, the *Congressional Record,* and so on. Often statistics sound impressive but they come from an unreliable source such as an interest group trying to gain support for its programs.

c. Identify the opinions. Sometimes opinions contain phrases such as *in my view, I believe, it is my conviction, I think.*

d. Identify the purpose. What does the speaker or author want you to believe or do?

UPI/BETTMANN

Recognizing Opinion Senator McCarthy waves a report that he says proves presidential candidate Adlai Stevenson's associations with groups promoting "the suicidal Kremlin-based policies" of the Soviet Union. *What do you think was McCarthy's purpose in making such allegations?*

Practicing the Skill

The following is from John F. Kennedy's opening remarks in the September 26, 1960, debate with Richard M. Nixon.

This is a great country, but I think it could be a greater country; and this is a powerful country, but I think it could be a more powerful country. I'm not satisfied to have 50 percent of our steel mill capacity unused. I'm not satisfied when the United States had last year the lowest rate of economic growth of any major industrialized society in the world, because economic growth means strength and vitality; it means we're able to sustain our defenses; it means we're able to meet our commitments abroad.

1. Identify the facts. Is there a way to prove that 50 percent of the steel mill capacity was unused or that economic growth was slow? What could you do to check these facts?

2. Identify the opinions. What phrases does Kennedy sometimes use to signal his opinions? Which of his opinions do not use signal words?

3. What is the purpose of Kennedy's statement? What does Kennedy want listeners to do?

4. How does knowing this purpose help you listen more objectively?

Applying the Skill

Record or take notes on a television interview. List three facts and three opinions that were stated. Then answer the following questions.

Do the facts seem reliable? Why or why not? How could you verify the facts? What opinions were stated? Were signal words used? If so, what were they? Was the person being interviewed trying to convince viewers of some position? Explain that position. Does knowing the position help you to listen more effectively? How?

The **Glencoe Skillbuilder Interactive Workbook, Level 2** CD-ROM provides more practice in key social studies skills.

Chapter  Assessment

Self-Check Quiz

Visit the *American Odyssey* Web site at americanodyssey.glencoe.com and click on ***Chapter 19—Self-Check Quiz*** to prepare for the Chapter Test.

Reviewing Key Terms

Choose the vocabulary word that best completes the sentences below. Write your answers on a separate sheet of paper.

closed shop **blacklisting**
vigilante **electronic media**
consensus decision making **whistle-stop tour**

1. During the Nixon-Kennedy presidential campaign, TV and radio, also known as the _________, became an important factor.

2. Truman took his campaign to the people by conducting his famous 32,000-mile (51,500-km) _________.

3. A workplace at which only union members can be hired is called a _________.

4. Efforts to brand people as Communists and prevent them from working by placing them on a list of suspected Communists is called _________.

5. Dwight Eisenhower practiced a management style based on group agreement called _________.

Recalling Facts

1. Why were consumers eager to purchase new cars and appliances following the war?

2. Who were the Dixiecrats, and how did they influence politics?

3. Name 3 international events that contributed to cold war fears at home in the 1940s; then name 3 events from the 1950s.

4. How did television affect the outcome of the Army-McCarthy hearings?

5. Explain the impact of *Sputnik I* on the mood of the United States.

Critical Thinking

1. Recognizing Ideologies Identify ways in which the methods of Joseph McCarthy ran counter to American political ideals and constitutional protections.

2. Evaluating Information The McCarthy hearings were broadcast, showing the senator attacking the witnesses. How might McCarthy's performance have affected public perception of him?

3. Making Generalizations Use a diagram like this one to identify the achievements and limitations of Truman's Fair Deal and to record a generalization about the program's overall success.

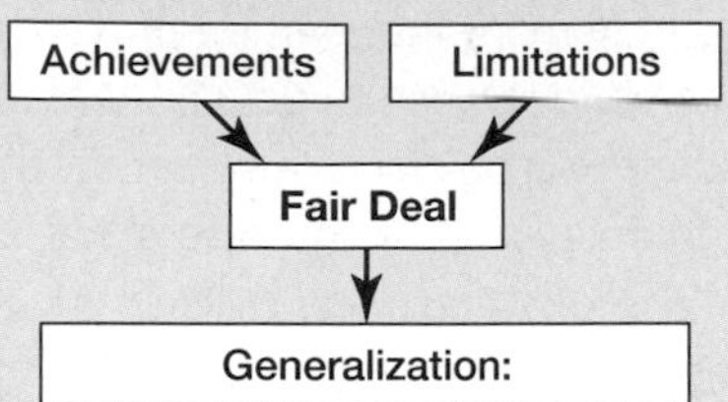

4. Analyzing Information Identify a trend regarding the role of government during the cold war.

The Princeton Review — Standardized Test Practice

1. One historical lesson learned from the McCarthy Era was the realization that

A loyalty oaths prevent spying by government employees.
B communism gains influence in times of economic prosperity.
C Communist agents had infiltrated all levels of U.S. government.
D public fear of traitors can weaken constitutional liberties.

Test-Taking Tip: Think about what the term *McCarthyism* has come to mean: the practice of using unsubstantiated accusations or unfair methods of investigation to discredit people. Which of the answers relates most strongly to this definition?

2. Which of the following was NOT an accomplishment of the Eisenhower administration?

A construction of the interstate highway system
B creation of the National Aeronautics and Space Administration (NASA)
C expansion of social security benefits and unemployment compensation
D passage of the Taft-Hartley Act

Test-Taking Tip: Remember, whenever you see the word NOT, the question asks you to find an *exception.* First think about the time period when Eisenhower was in office. Then eliminate the event that could not have taken place during this time.

GEOGRAPHY AND HISTORY

Truman's Whistle-Stop Tour, 1948

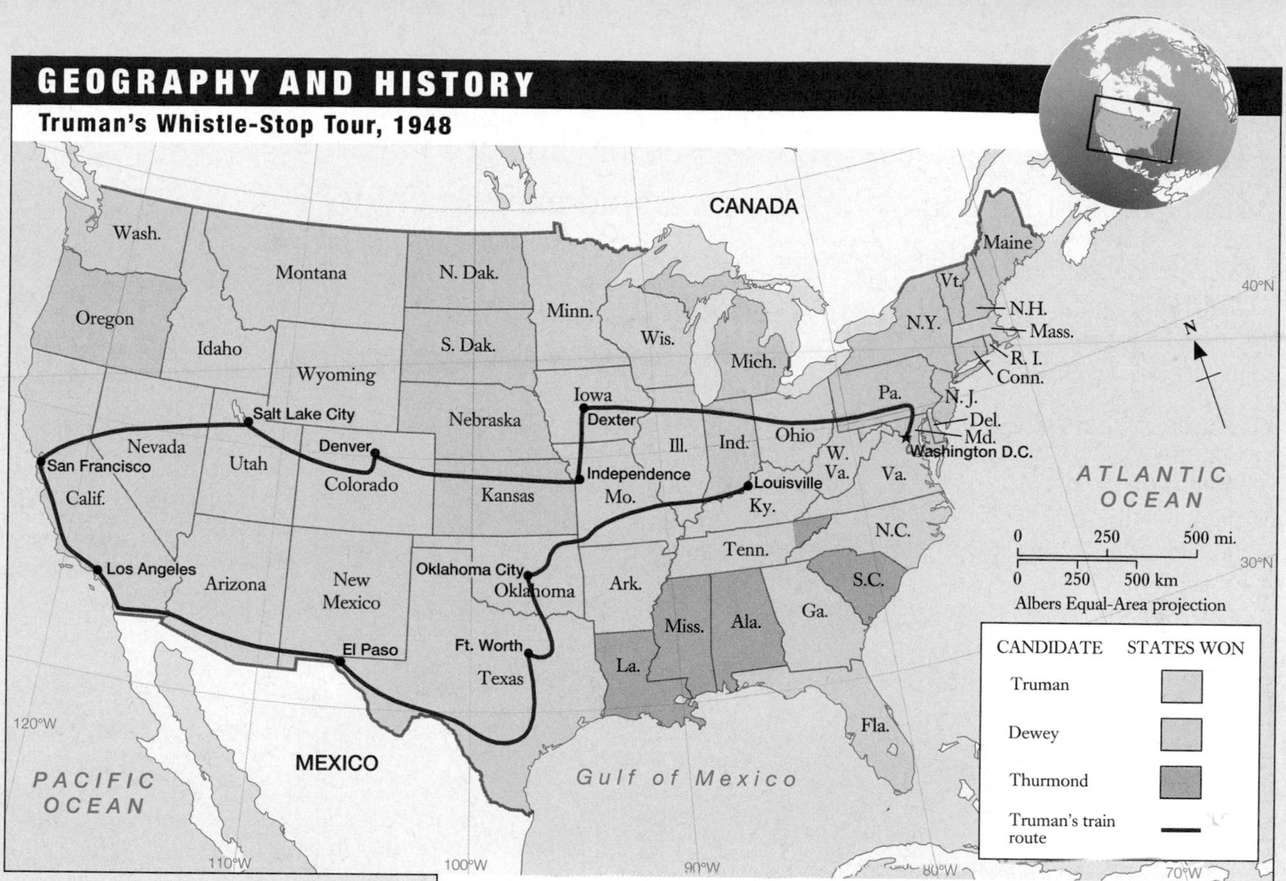

Albers Equal-Area projection

CANDIDATE	STATES WON
Truman	
Dewey	
Thurmond	
Truman's train route	

Study the map to answer the following questions:

1. According to the map, through how many states did Truman travel on his whistle-stop campaign?
2. Notice the states that Truman visited. Which way did most of these states vote?
3. Conservative Southern Democrats nominated Strom Thurmond as their presidential candidate. According to the map, where was Dixiecrat support strongest?
4. In which regions of the country was support for Dewey strongest?
5. Of the states Truman visited on his tour, how many voted for Dewey?

Portfolio Project

Identify a current labor dispute, local or national, and summarize in a report the points at issue between labor and management. How would you decide this particular case? Does the Taft-Hartley Act apply? Keep your report in your portfolio.

Cooperative Learning

Form two groups. One group should portray supporters of Senator McCarthy. The other group should portray his critics. Select spokespersons to conduct a debate on the following topic: Senator McCarthy's attacks on Communists were justified, although he went too far. Some innocent people had to suffer to protect the nation.

Reinforcing Skills

Distinguishing Fact From Opinion Read the excerpt on page 646 from Truman's 1953 speech on McCarthyism. Which statements are opinions, and which are facts? How can you tell? Are there facts in the lesson text on pages 644–645 that support or dispute the opinions? If so, list them.

Technology Activity

Using a Computerized Card Catalog Search your school or local library's computerized card catalog to locate sources on the 1950s' Red Scare and McCarthyism. Write a report analyzing how the phenomenon of McCarthyism affected American society.

Then...

The 1955 Corvette

The first Corvette rolled off the assembly line in Flint, Michigan, on June 30, 1953. It was a bold experiment for General Motors officials, who wanted to compete with sleek European sports cars. GM produced only 300 of the 1953 Corvettes—in white only. In 1955 GM introduced 2 new colors—Gypsy red and Corvette copper.

1 The revolutionary fiberglass body is still a Corvette trademark.

2 Imitation knock-on hubcaps looked like race car hubcaps.

Fun Facts

© RON KIMBALL

THE FIRST CORVETTES

Most of the 300 Corvettes made in 1953 went to GM employees. Of these 300 Corvettes, 225 can be accounted for today. A 1953 Corvette in good condition could be worth as much as $500,000 today.

© RON KIMBALL

© NICKY WRIGHT

© RON KIMBALL

© RON KIMBALL

3 The Corvette's logo was two crossed flags that looked like those used at racetracks.

4 Wire mesh guarded the headlights from bouncing rocks.

Stats

PRODUCTION

The 1955 Corvette came with either a 6-cylinder (V-6) or a V-8 engine. The V-8 also had an enlarged gold "V" in the word *Chevrolet* on the front fenders. The overwhelming majority of 1955 Corvettes were V-8 powered. Like other Corvettes, the 1955s had a fiberglass body, a chrome-framed grille, no side windows or outside door handles, and a wraparound windshield.

PERFORMANCE

- 0 to 60 mph in 8.7 seconds
- Top speed of 106 mph
- V-8 (12-volt electrical system)

Standard equipment: Powerglide automatic transmission with floor shift, whitewall tires, clock, cigarette lighter, driver's side mirror

PRICE

Base Price:	$2,934.00
Heater:	$91.40
AM Radio:	$145.15
V-8	$135.00
Total:	**$3,305.55**

...Now

CORVETTE COMPARISON

PORTFOLIO PROJECT

How does the 1955 Corvette compare with Corvettes today? Research newspapers and magazines for advertisements and articles about Corvettes. If possible, interview a Chevrolet dealer and get a price list. What do today's options say about how people use their cars? Create a brochure from the information you gather.

GLASS WITH CLASS

The "Vette" was the first mass-produced car to have a "fiberglass skin," body panels made up of compressed fibers of glass. Its most popular new rival in 1955, the Thunderbird, used steel.

FAIR-WEATHER FRIEND

The number one owner complaint was rain leaking in. As one owner put it, "Strictly a dry-weather car. Floor can hold 4 gallons of water."

Toward Equality and Social Reform

1954–1976

HISTORY & YOU

Not everyone accepted the conformity of the 1950s. African Americans, in an organized movement, rejected their second-class citizenship and the practice of forced segregation. Inspired by the African American example, other groups—feminists, Hispanic Americans, Native Americans, and young people—also raised their voices in protest of unfair practices or their assigned roles in society. The social turbulence led the federal government to revive the activism of the New Deal in an effort to remove barriers to equal opportunity.

See pages 966–967 for primary source readings that accompany Unit 8.

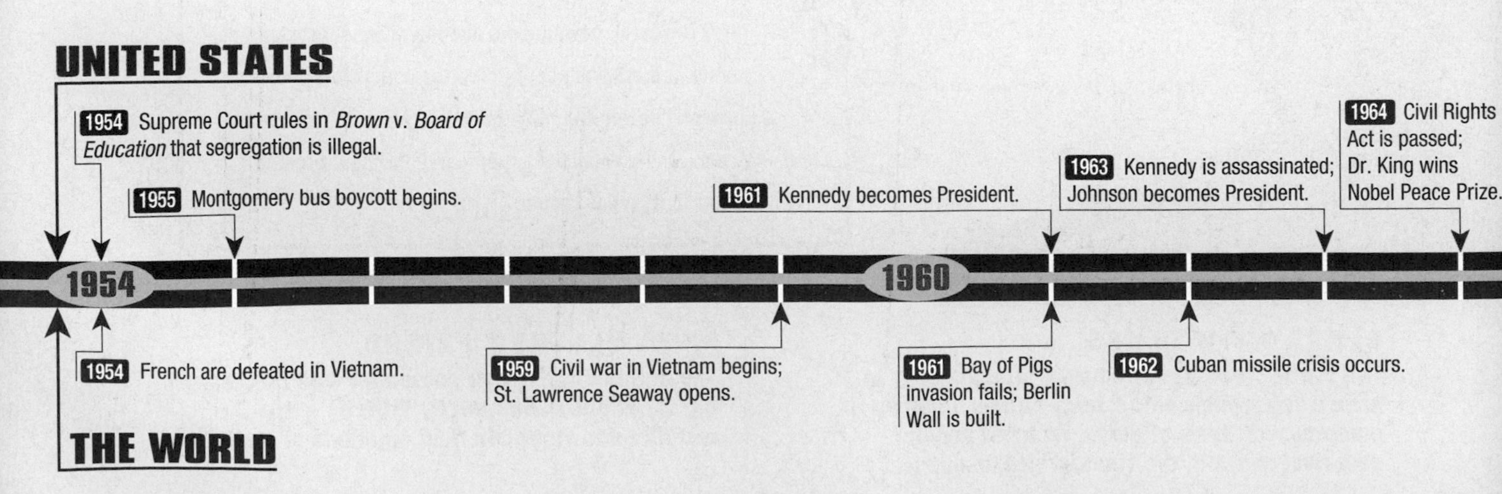

UNITED STATES
1954 Supreme Court rules in *Brown* v. *Board of Education* that segregation is illegal.
1955 Montgomery bus boycott begins.
1961 Kennedy becomes President.
1963 Kennedy is assassinated; Johnson becomes President.
1964 Civil Rights Act is passed; Dr. King wins Nobel Peace Prize.
1954
1960
1954 French are defeated in Vietnam.
1959 Civil war in Vietnam begins; St. Lawrence Seaway opens.
1961 Bay of Pigs invasion fails; Berlin Wall is built.
1962 Cuban missile crisis occurs.
THE WORLD

FRANCIS MILLER/LIFE MAGAZINE © TIME INC.

Dr. Martin Luther King, Jr., speaks at the march on Washington, August 28, 1963.

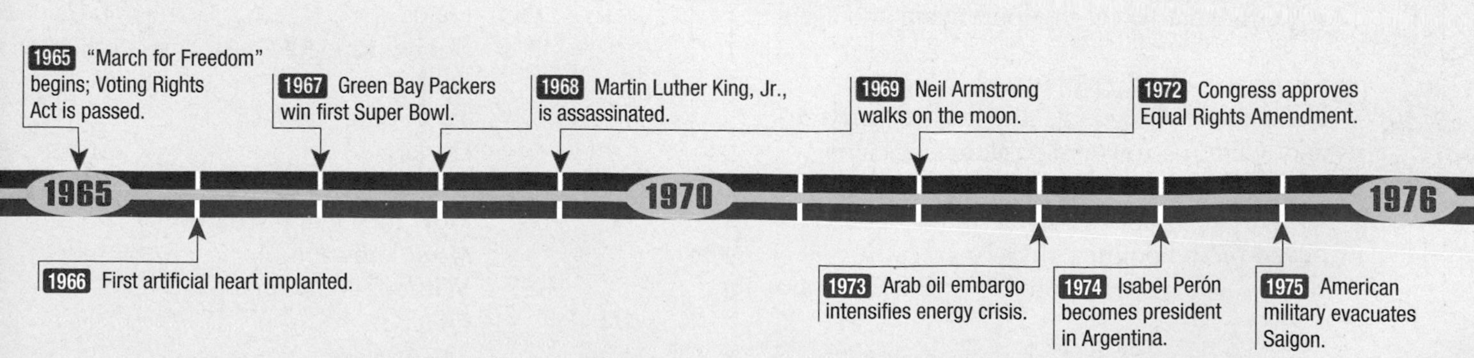

1965 "March for Freedom" begins; Voting Rights Act is passed.
1967 Green Bay Packers win first Super Bowl.
1968 Martin Luther King, Jr., is assassinated.
1969 Neil Armstrong walks on the moon.
1972 Congress approves Equal Rights Amendment.
1965
1970
1976
1966 First artificial heart implanted.
1973 Arab oil embargo intensifies energy crisis.
1974 Isabel Perón becomes president in Argentina.
1975 American military evacuates Saigon.

Voices of Change

During the 1960s and 1970s, women and people of color began to challenge predominant ethnic, racial, and gender stereotypes and worked to overturn laws that restricted their rights and freedoms. The authors of the following poems assert their identities by linking personal experiences to a broader understanding of culture, gender, tradition, and family. They represent the diversity of American culture during this period.

To Be of Use

by Marge Piercy

The people I love the best
jump into work head first
without dallying in the shallows
and swim off with sure strokes almost out of sight.
They seem to become natives of that element.
the black sleek heads of seals
bouncing like half-submerged balls.

I love people who harness themselves, an ox to a heavy cart.
who pull like the water buffalo, with massive patience,
who strain in the mud and the muck to move things forward,
who do what has to be done, again and again.

I want to be with people who submerge
in the task, who go into the fields to harvest
and work in a row and pass the bags along,
who stand in the line and haul in their places,
who are not parlor generals and field deserters
but move in common rhythm
when the food must come in or the fire be put out.

Women

by Alice Walker

They were women then
My mama's generation
Husky of voice—Stout of
Step
With fists as well as
Hands
How they battered down
Doors
And ironed
Starched white
Shirts
How they led
Armies
Headragged Generals
Across mined
Fields
Booby-trapped
Ditches
To discover books
Desks
A place for us
How they knew what we
Must know
Without knowing a page
Of it
Themselves.

Dinner Quilt **Faith Ringgold's "soft" quilt art tells of growing up as an African American in Harlem. *Dinner Quilt* tells about Christmas dinners with Aunt Connie, who would embroider place mats with names of famous African American women, such as Fannie Lou Hamer.**

The Immigrant Experience

by Richard Olivias

I'm sitting in my history class,
The instructor commences rapping,
I'm in my U.S. History class,
And I'm on the verge of napping.

The Mayflower landed on Plymouth Rock.
Tell me more! Tell me more!
Thirteen colonies were settled.
I've heard it all before.

What did he say?
Dare I ask him to reiterate?
Oh, why bother,
It sounded like he said,
George Washington's my father.

I'm reluctant to believe it,
I suddenly raise my *mano*.
If George Washington's my father,
Why wasn't he Chicano?

Responding to Literature

1. **Why does Alice Walker admire the women of her mother's generation? What does she mean by "Headragged Generals"?**
2. **In what ways do you think Richard Olivas would change the way American history is taught in high school?**

The Civil Rights Struggle

SEPTEMBER 4, 1957: SCHOOL OPENS AT LITTLE ROCK CENTRAL HIGH

Elizabeth Ann Eckford and her mother made a crisp black and white dress for Elizabeth to wear her first day in the new school. The eight other African American students arranged to go to school together, but Elizabeth never got the message.

She went instead by bus to Little Rock Central High School. As she headed for the front door, she found the way blocked by an angry crowd of white townspeople and hundreds of armed soldiers, Arkansas National Guard members sent by the governor.

Elizabeth tried to follow a white student through the door but was stopped by a soldier. "When I tried to squeeze past him," she recalled later, "he raised his bayonet, and then the other guards moved in and raised their bayonets. . . . Somebody started yelling, 'Lynch her! Lynch her!'"

Elizabeth and the 8 other students never made it into Central High that day. It took 3 more weeks, intervention by the President, 1,000 paratroopers, and 10,000 members of the Arkansas National Guard to integrate the school.

It was a pattern repeated often in the years to come. Legislation, court orders, grassroots efforts, and nonviolent demonstrations alone were not enough. It took all of these efforts together to bring the Constitution's promise of equality for all closer to reality. ■

HISTORY JOURNAL

Based on what you know and the picture on page 667, write your understanding of some of the problems faced by African Americans in their struggle for full civil rights.

Chapter Overview

Visit the *American Odyssey* Web site at americanodyssey.glencoe.com and click on ***Chapter 20—Chapter Overview*** to preview the chapter.

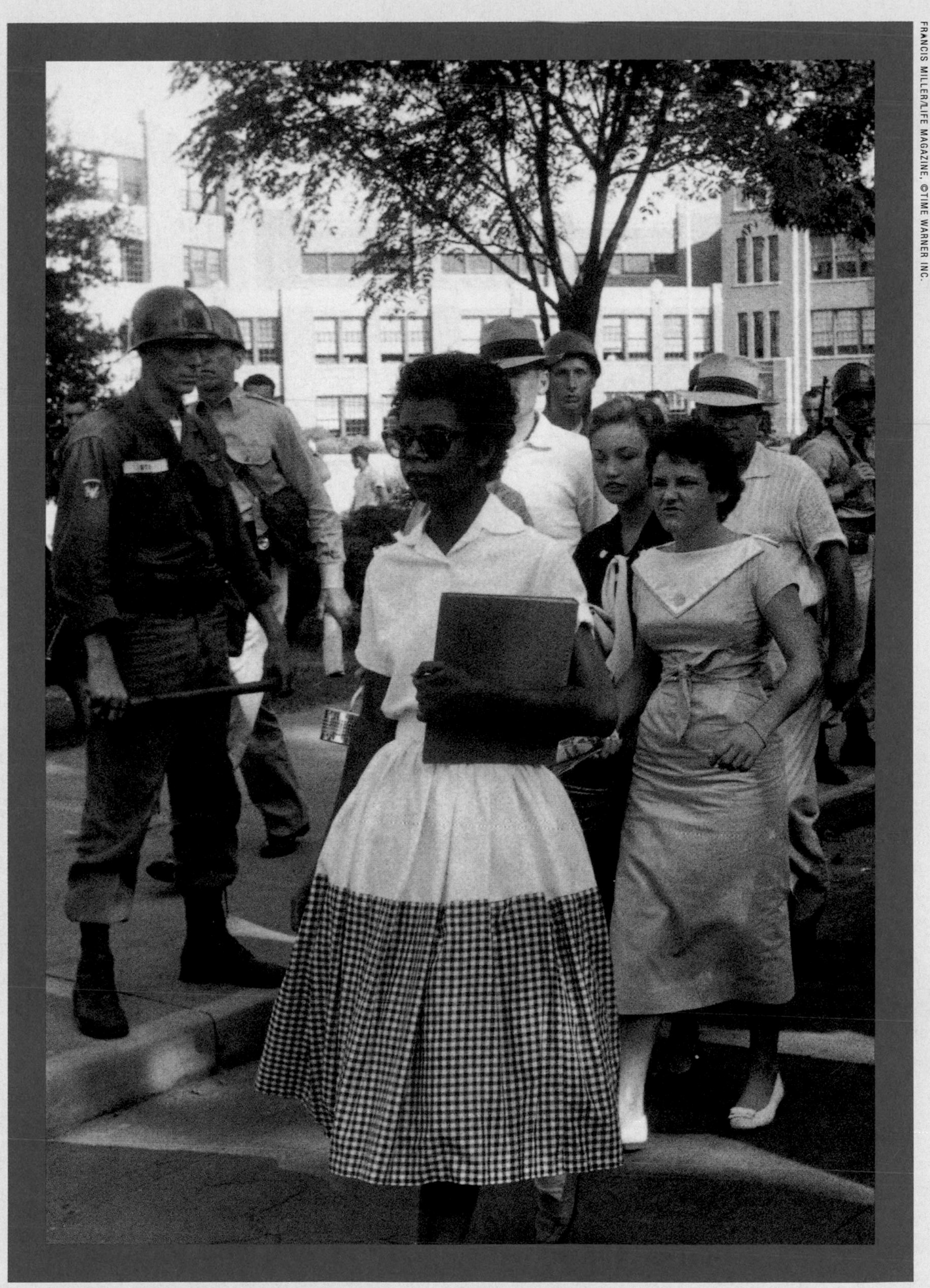

FRANCIS MILLER/LIFE MAGAZINE, ©TIME WARNER INC.

STATE TROOPS HAD DEFENDED SEGREGATION; LATER FEDERALIZED TROOPS ENABLED INTEGRATION.

Challenging Segregation

EARLY 1950s: THE UNITED STATES

AFRICAN AMERICANS MADE GAINS DURING WORLD WAR II. Yet they did not share in the promise and prosperity that followed, and most white Americans seemed unaware of this. Novelist Ralph Ellison wrote:

> I am an invisible man. . . . I am invisible, understand, simply because people refuse to see me. . . . When they approach me they see only my surroundings, themselves, or figments of their imagination—indeed everything and anything except me.
>
> —Ralph Ellison, *Invisible Man,* 1952

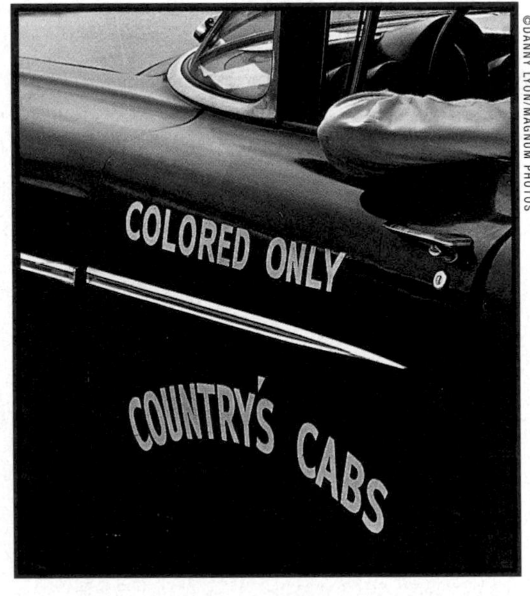

Two Americas
African Americans were not allowed to ride in the same cabs as white patrons.

In the South, laws that ensured **segregation** enforced this invisibility. Indeed, separation of blacks and whites formed a fundamental part of southern culture. All across the region, African Americans had to enter public buses by the back door, sit in separate waiting rooms at train stations, eat in separate restaurants, and attend separate schools. The power to vote was regularly withheld.

In the North, the pattern of urban life often resulted in *de facto* segregation—segregation in fact though not by law. As African Americans migrated to Northern cities, white people moved out to the suburbs.

GUIDE TO READING

Main Idea

African Americans in the post–World War II era stepped up efforts to end the system of segregation that divided the United States into two separate and unequal societies, one black and one white.

Vocabulary

- segregation
- civil rights

Read to Find Out . . .

- the importance of *Brown* v. *Board of Education* to the civil rights movement.
- the ways whites in the South resisted the *Brown* decision and the chain of events that led a reluctant Eisenhower to enforce school desegregation.

Other, more subtle, means of separating whites and African Americans emerged. For example, school districts were carefully drawn so that they included only black neighborhoods or only white ones.

The country had two societies, one white and one black. The invisible world of the African Americans, however, was about to make its presence known. This happened dramatically when Jackie Robinson, a star athlete at UCLA, broke the color line in 1947 to become an infielder for the Brooklyn Dodgers. Facing hostile teammates and opponents, Robinson held his temper and won over the fans with his spirited play. African Americans, formerly confined to segregated leagues, soon began moving into professional sports.

The Segregation System

The North Eases, the South Intensifies

If integrated major league baseball worked, asked many African Americans, why should segregation prevail elsewhere? In the country they had bravely helped to defend, why should they not be entitled to fair housing and fair employment protections?

However, the issue that most inflamed both segregationists and integrationists was public education. Because public schools placed children in daily social situations of playing and learning, attitudes learned in the classroom could be expected to influence students for the rest of their lives.

In the early 1950s, 17 states and the District of Columbia prohibited African American and white children from attending school together. Only 16 states required their public schools to be integrated, and individual school districts often violated these requirements.

Then in 1950 three Supreme Court decisions handed down on a single day gave a new direction to those who were fighting for **civil rights,** the rights of all citizens. First, railroad dining cars operating in the South now had to provide equal service to all travelers, regardless of race. Second, African American students could not be segregated within a school also attended by whites. Third, "intangible factors," not just buildings or books, had to be considered when comparing the education provided for African Americans and whites.

The Challenge of the Courts

Supreme Court Rules Against Segregation

For more than 50 years, *Plessy* v. *Ferguson* had stood as the legal precedent for the "separate but equal" doctrine. This 1896 Supreme Court opinion held that if separate accommodations provided in railroad cars were

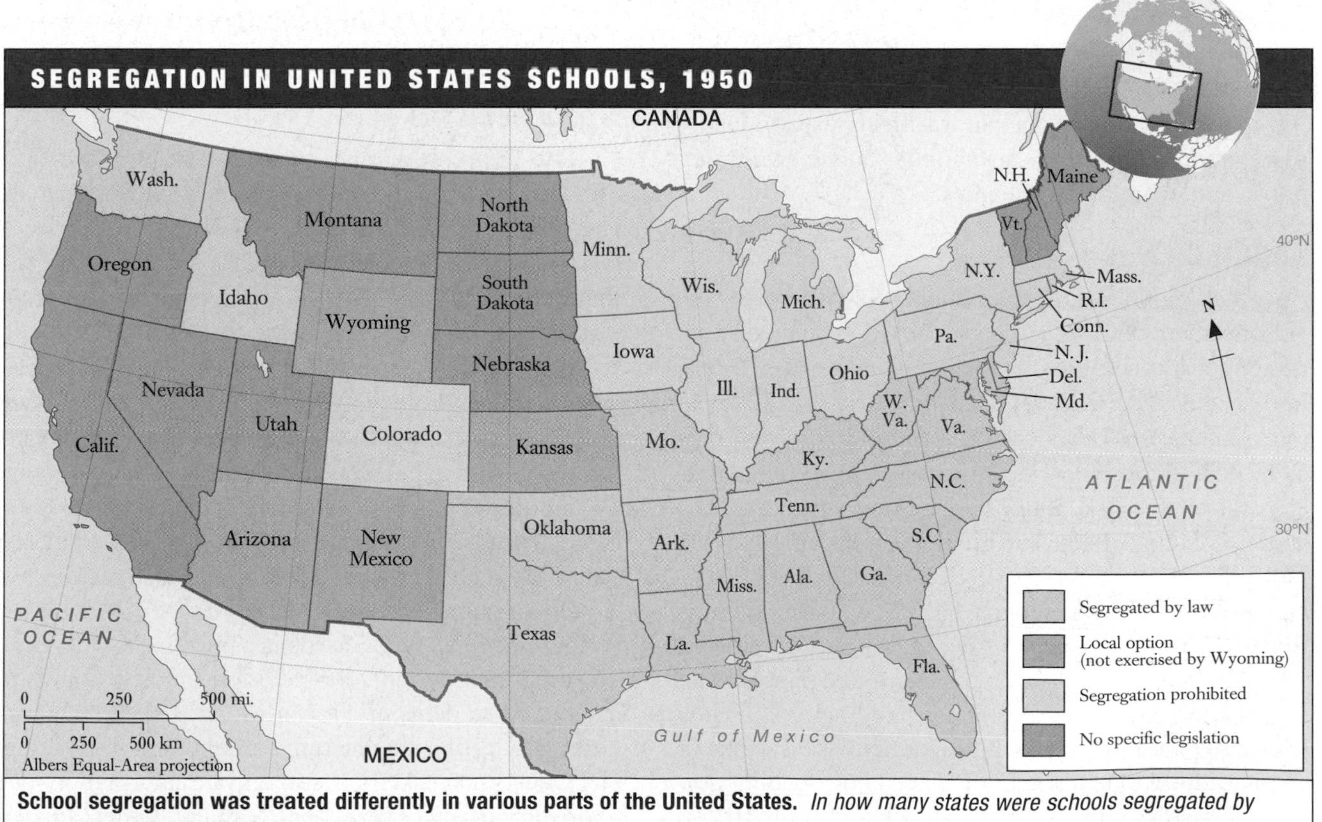

School segregation was treated differently in various parts of the United States. *In how many states were schools segregated by law? In what region was segregation predominant?*

©UPI/BETTMANN

Fighting Segregation Through the System Thurgood Marshall and Mrs. L.C. Bates, president of the Arkansas NAACP, talk with Arkansas students outside the Supreme Court. *In what way was the* Brown *case different from previous segregation cases?*

equal for African American and white passengers, then the resulting segregation was constitutional. Soon the "separate but equal" principle was being used to justify segregation in housing, restaurants, public swimming pools, and other public facilities.

NAACP Strategy

After World War II, the National Association for the Advancement of Colored People (NAACP) initiated a series of court cases that chipped away at the *Plessy* ruling. In case after case, the Supreme Court held that the separate facilities provided for African Americans were not, in fact, equal to those provided for white people. This strategy was engineered largely by Charles Houston, a Harvard Law School graduate who later taught at the all-black Howard University. As chief legal counsel for the NAACP, he was assisted by Thurgood Marshall, who later became the first African American justice on the Supreme Court.

The NAACP's strategy concentrated first on desegregating graduate and specialized schools. They hoped to prove that the facilities for nonwhites were not equal to those of whites. Then, instead of building new school buildings for use by only a handful of African American students, states would be forced to integrate. After succeeding on this level, the NAACP planned to attack segregation in elementary and high schools. In 1950 the NAACP made a bold decision. Rather than trying to prove case by case that the "separate but equal" doctrine was unworkable, they agreed to fight segregation head-on. They would challenge the courts that segregation itself was illegal.

When Houston died in 1950, Thurgood Marshall continued the effort for the NAACP. Marshall was popular among most African Americans. As one supporter explained, Marshall was "of the people. He knew how to get through to them. Out in Texas or Oklahoma or down the street here in Washington at the Baptist Church, he would make these rousing speeches that would have them all jumping out of their seats."

Then the NAACP decided which segregated school district to bring before the Supreme Court. A suitable case required parents courageous enough to sign a court petition despite pressure from local officials. It also required patience. The NAACP expected to lose when the suits were first tried, allowing for an appeal to the Supreme Court.

Brown Decision

The Supreme Court case that helped overturn school segregation did not originate in the South at all. The case was called *Brown* v. *the Board of Education of Topeka, Kansas.* By selecting a case from outside the South, the Court hoped to emphasize that the question of school segregation was a national one.

The "separate but equal" school facilities in Topeka were of comparable quality. Seven-year-old Linda Brown, however, had to cross through a railroad switching yard to catch the bus to her all-black elementary school, which was miles away. Why, her father insisted, couldn't she attend the all-white school just a few blocks from her home instead of riding a bus to a school located miles away?

Oral arguments before the Supreme Court were set for December 9, 1952. As usual, the NAACP lawyers rehearsed their presentation before the mostly nonwhite faculty and students of Howard Law School in Washington, D.C. After the hearing came months of waiting. The Court then asked for some more information, but before arguments were heard again, Chief Justice Fred M. Vinson died suddenly. President Eisenhower appointed in Vinson's place the former governor of California, Earl Warren.

Warren felt that such a sensitive decision required a unanimous decision. Such a decision would send a clear message to all parts of the country. Again, weeks of negotiations went on before the Court announced its decision. That historic moment came on May 17, 1954. Chief Justice Warren, in delivering the opinion, said:

> Does segregation of children in public schools solely on the basis of race, even though the physical facilities and other tangible factors may be equal, deprive children of the minority group of equal educational opportunities? We believe it does. . . . To separate them from others of similar age and qualifications solely because of their race generates a feeling of inferiority as to their status in the community that may affect their hearts and minds in a way very unlikely ever to be undone.
>
> We conclude that in the field of public education the doctrine of 'separate but equal' has no place. Separate educational facilities are inherently unequal.
>
> —*Brown* v. *Board of Education,* 1954

Resistance to *Brown*

The South Resists Integration

When the Supreme Court declared in 1954 that school segregation was illegal, they said nothing about how integration was to be carried out. That announcement came a year later. The rather vague ruling of the Court, pronounced in May 1955, was that integration should take place "with all deliberate speed" and "at the earliest possible date." The reluctance to give definite guidelines for ending segregation may have been the price that Chief Justice Warren had to pay for his justices' unanimous decision. After all, the integration decision was not a popular one among many groups. Polls showed that 80 percent of Southern whites opposed the *Brown* decision.

Some of the nation's school districts took steps to comply with the ruling. Other districts, particularly in the South, devised plans to resist the decision.

Massive Resistance

In Southern districts where resistance was strong, white students, encouraged by parents, refused to attend integrated schools. The Ku Klux Klan reemerged, while other white Southerners joined the less militant White Citizens' Councils.

Resistance often received encouragement from those in high offices. Virginia's governor, Thomas Stanley, declared, "I shall use every legal means at my command to continue segregated schools in Virginia." Southern state legislatures passed more than 450 laws and resolutions aimed at preventing enforcement of the *Brown* decision. In 1956 the Virginia state legislature passed a massive resistance measure that cut off state aid to all desegregated schools.

In the same year, 100 Southern members of Congress signed what came to be called the Southern Manifesto, praising "the motives of those states which have declared their intention to resist forced integration by any lawful means." One of the three Southern representatives who refused to sign was Lyndon B. Johnson of Texas, future President of the United States.

Eisenhower and *Brown*

When elected President in 1952, Dwight Eisenhower carried 4 of the 11 states of the old Confederacy, only the second time the Republicans had made inroads in the solidly Democratic South since Reconstruction. Out of personal conviction, and out of loyalty to his Southern constituents, Eisenhower attempted to be neutral toward desegregation. He neither endorsed nor refuted the Supreme Court decision, saying instead, "I don't believe you can change the hearts of men with laws or decisions." Privately, he called his appointment of Earl Warren to the Supreme Court his biggest mistake.

In 1956 the African American student Autherine Lucy was suspended and then expelled from the University of Alabama after whites rioted to prevent her from remaining. Eisenhower said, "I would certainly hope that we could avoid any interference with anybody as long as that state, from its governor down, will do its best to straighten it out." The university continued to exclude African Americans for the next seven years.

Crisis at Little Rock

Desegregation Meets Violent Resistance

Little Rock, Arkansas, seemed an unlikely place for a showdown on school segregation. Just 5 days after the *Brown* decision, the Little Rock school board announced its willingness to obey the new law. The school district superintendent worked out a careful plan that consisted in its first stage of placing 9 African American students in Central High School, a school with approximately 2,000 white students. Then on September 2, 1957—the night before the first day of school—Arkansas governor, Orval Faubus, appeared on statewide television. He

UPI/BETTMANN NEWSPHOTOS

State and Federal Authorities Struggle Opposition to school desegregation by white citizens of Arkansas was so strong that armed soldiers had to protect African American students. *What were the results of this military intervention?*

announced that soldiers from the state's National Guard would surround Central High School the next morning. The move was necessary, Faubus claimed, because of "evidence of disorder and threats of disorder."

The nine new students stayed away from school the next day, as school plans to delay and federal court orders to desegregate followed one another in quick succession. Many saw the issue as a fight between federal and state authority, but President Eisenhower was reluctant to intervene. Finally Governor Faubus met with Eisenhower. Faubus asked for but was denied a one-year delay in implementing desegregation. The meeting ended with the President thinking he had persuaded Faubus to allow integration of the school.

Chaos Erupts

Then, in a surprising show of defiance, Faubus removed the National Guard and left Little Rock. As an angry crowd of nearly 1,000 white people gathered at the school the next day, the so-called "Little Rock Nine" were forced to leave class at midday under police protection.

Reluctantly Eisenhower ordered federal troops into Little Rock and nationalized the Arkansas National Guard. For the first time since Reconstruction, a President had sent federal troops into the South to enforce the Constitution. On September 25, the day after the President's action, paratroopers lined the route to the high school. The nine students arrived in a military convoy, escorted by armed federal soldiers.

The paratroopers left at the end of the month, but the federalized National Guard remained for the rest of the school year. The next year, Little Rock public schools closed entirely.

White students attended private schools, schools outside the city, or none at all. Most African American students had no school to attend. Finally, in August 1959, following another Supreme Court ruling, the Little Rock school board reopened and integrated its public schools.

Section Assessment

Main Idea

1. Use a diagram like this one to show the steps in the NAACP strategy to end segregation in public education.

Step 1 → Step 2 → Step 3 → Integrated Schools

Vocabulary

2. Define: segregation, civil rights.

Checking Facts

3. What did *Brown* v. *Board of Education* say about the "separate but equal" doctrine?
4. How did many white Southerners react to the *Brown* decision? What were some results of this reaction?

Critical Thinking

5. **Making Inferences** Why did President Eisenhower say that appointing Earl Warren to be chief justice of the Supreme Court was his worst mistake?

Study and Writing Skill

PRESENTING STATISTICAL DATA

Learning the Skill

Effectively presented statistical data can strengthen and clarify oral and written material. NAACP lawyers, for example, used statistical data to present each of the cases brought against segregated school systems.

Understanding how to show statistical data in graph or chart form allows you to present information clearly and effectively, often focusing on a specific aspect of a broad topic. Data thus presented can be used to answer specific questions or to draw conclusions.

Below is a list of four visual-presentation formats and the main features of each.

Statistical Data Presentation Formats

Format	Characteristics
Bar graphs	Compare data using colored bars
Charts	Show various aspects of data, using columns and rows
Circle graphs	Show percentages of a whole using a segmented circle
Line graphs	Show changes or trends over time using lines on a grid

To present statistical data, follow these steps:

a. Define the topic you want to cover.

b. Collect data about the topic (you can ask a reference librarian for assistance).

c. Decide which aspect(s) of the data to highlight.

d. Organize and present the data, highlighting the aspects you selected.

Practicing the Skill

Analyze the presentation of the data in the bar graph, the chart, and the circle graph below.

1. The bar graph uses labeled, colored bars to present information. What does the bar graph show? What do the divided bars indicate?

2. The chart presents data in labeled rows and columns. What does the chart show? Does it present more or less data than the bar graph?

3. The circle graph uses a circle to represent the total number of schools (74). What percentage accepted only white students?

4. Which seems most effective to you—the bar graph, the chart, or the circle graph? Why?

5. You could also use a line graph to show a trend such as the number of law schools open to African American students over a specified period of time. What is another trend you could show with a line graph, using the data on this page?

Applying the Skill

Choose a chart or graph in a current newspaper or magazine. Analyze the information it presents. How else might this data be visually presented? Would it be more or less effective? Why?

The **Glencoe Skillbuilder Interactive Workbook, Level 2** CD-ROM provides more practice in key social studies skills.

Segregated Professional Schools, 1945

Bar Graph

Profession	White	African American
Dentistry	4	
Law	16	4
Medicine	15	
Pharmacy	14	
Social Work	9	
Library Science	11	1

Number of Schools: 0 2 4 6 8 10 12 14 16 18 20 22

■ White ■ African American

Chart

Profession	Total	White	African American
Dentistry	4	4	0
Law	20	16	4
Medicine	15	15	0
Pharmacy	14	14	0
Social Work	9	9	0
Library Science	12	11	1

Circle Graph

93% White Students

7% African American Students

Freedom Now

DECEMBER 1, 1955: MONTGOMERY, ALABAMA—BUS BOYCOTT BEGINS

ROSA PARKS WAS TIRED. It was the Christmas shopping season, and the 43-year-old bespectacled woman worked hard as a tailor's assistant in a Montgomery, Alabama, store.

When Parks boarded the Cleveland Avenue bus, she was pleased to find a seat in the middle section. In Montgomery, African American riders could occupy the middle section seats unless the front seats reserved for whites were fully occupied. Then, in order to provide more seats for white riders, African American passengers had to move to seats farther back in the bus or stand.

By the third stop, the seats reserved for whites had filled up, and one white man was standing. The other African American passengers in Parks's row of seats got up and stood in the back, but she did not move.

The bus driver, James Blake, called out, "If you don't stand up, I'm going to have to call the police and have you arrested." "You may do that," Rosa Parks replied.

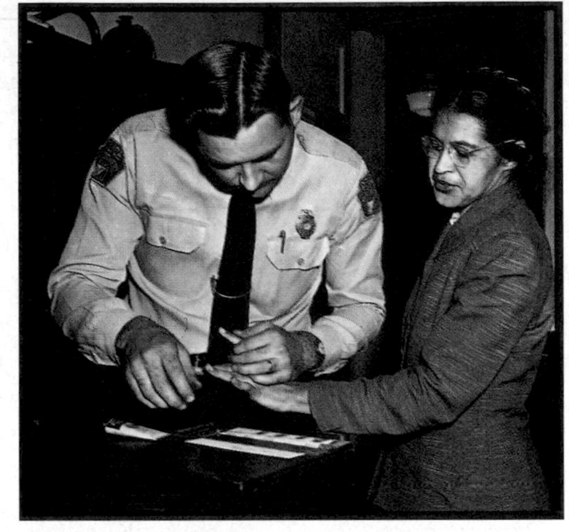

AP/WIDE WORLD PHOTOS

Simple Refusal Stirs Boycott
Rosa Parks was prepared to fight for her civil rights.

The Bus Boycott

Economic Means to Attain Goals

Rosa Parks's simple decision not to give up her seat set in motion a series of events with far-reaching consequences for the whole country. Later, many people came to regard her action as the true beginning of the civil rights movement of the 1950s and the 1960s. Out of Montgomery emerged the courage, leadership, and strategies for an entire movement.

The news of Parks's arrest soon spread through Montgomery's African American community. Protests like Parks's were not new, but hers was the kind of case community leaders had been waiting for. Parks was dignified, soft-spoken, well liked. She was a former secretary of the local NAACP chapter and was active in her church. The previous summer she had attended an interracial workshop at the Highlander Folk School in Tennessee. Now, local civil rights leaders asked if she would

GUIDE TO READING

Main Idea

A civil rights movement began to take shape in the South as African Americans, working initially through the NAACP and churches, used a variety of nonviolent tactics to protest segregation.

Vocabulary

- boycott
- nonviolent resistance
- civil disobedience

Read to Find Out . . .

- how the Southern Christian Leadership Conference countered segregation in the South.
- the role that the Student Nonviolent Coordinating Committee played in the civil rights movement.

be willing to fight her case for as long as it took to win. Despite her mother's and husband's fears, she said yes.

DAN WEINER, COURTESY SANDRA WEINER

Supporting the Movement **Dr. Martin Luther King, Jr., was a powerful communicator.** *How did King use his communication abilities to promote civil rights?*

The Boycott Begins

Immediately the call went out for a **boycott** of the Montgomery bus system. By refusing to use the services of the bus company, African Americans would exert economic pressure on the company. Jo Ann Robinson, an English professor at Alabama State College, worked through the night writing and mimeographing 35,000 leaflets that instructed, "Don't ride the buses to work, to town, to school, or anywhere on Monday."

Meanwhile, ministers and community leaders met and pledged their support of the one-day boycott. They agreed to a second meeting at Holt Street Baptist Church on Monday evening to decide whether to continue the boycott.

Dr. Martin Luther King, Jr., the new minister of the Dexter Avenue Baptist Church, announced the boycott during his Sunday morning services, asking for the congregation's support. So did other ministers, including the white minister of the Trinity Lutheran Church.

A Successful Strategy

On Monday, nearly empty buses rolled through Montgomery. Although Rosa Parks was found guilty and fined $10 plus $4 in court charges, the boycott was a success. Of the 52,000 passengers who normally rode the bus every day, 40,000 were African American, and they had stayed away in droves. That afternoon the ministers and community leaders met again. They named themselves the Montgomery Improvement Association and selected a president—Dr. King.

That evening some 5,000 people packed into the Holt Street Baptist Church. Loudspeakers were set up for thousands of people outside. King declared:

> There comes a time when people get tired. We are here this evening to say to those who have mistreated us so long that we are tired—tired of being segregated and humiliated, tired of being kicked about by the brutal feet of oppression . . .
>
> If you will protest courageously and yet with dignity and Christian love, in the history books that are written in future generations, historians will have to pause and say "there lived a great people—a black people—who injected a new meaning and dignity into the veins of civilization." This is our challenge and our overwhelming responsibility.
>
> —Dr. Martin Luther King, Jr., 1955

The Montgomery bus boycott lasted nearly 400 days. At first the city's 18 African American–owned cab companies filled in by agreeing to accept African American passengers for 10 cents, the price of bus fare. Then the city threatened to fine the taxi companies for not charging the full 45-cent taxi fare.

Next, boycott leaders worked out an elaborate plan of car pooling. Station wagons picked up riders at 42 separate locations. Funds to buy and operate the station wagons—called "rolling churches" because they were painted with the names of churches—came from white and African American supporters in Montgomery and throughout the nation. When city officials tried to prevent the "rolling churches" from getting the necessary insurance, King arranged coverage with Lloyd's of London, known for insuring almost any risk.

City officials had not expected such strong resistance. As the bus company continued to lose money day after day, the segregationists in power became increasingly frustrated. The mayor, the city commissioners, the police commissioner, and the city council all publicly joined the White Citizens' Council. King's house was bombed. King and 88 other African American leaders were arrested and fined for conspiring to boycott.

Student Web Activity 20

Visit the *American Odyssey* Web site at americanodyssey.glencoe.com and click on ***Chapter 20—Student Web Activities*** for an activity relating to the civil rights movement.

DAN WEINER, COURTESY SANDRA WEINER

Impact of Boycott Felt Although African Americans enjoyed few rights in the South, their numbers gave them economic power. *What finally ended the Montgomery bus boycott?*

The end of the boycott finally came when the United States Supreme Court ruled that segregation on Montgomery buses was unconstitutional. City officials challenged this ruling on the grounds that it violated states' rights. When the Court's written order was received on December 20, 1956, however, the segregationists gave up. All riders sat where they pleased on buses that rolled through Montgomery.

> Ain't gonna ride them buses no more,
> Ain't gonna ride no more.
> Why don't all the white folk know
> That I ain't gonna ride no more.
>
> —Sung by Montgomery boycotters, 1955–1956

Martin Luther King, Jr.

An African American Leader Emerges

After the Montgomery boycott, Dr. Martin Luther King, Jr., emerged as the unchallenged leader of the African American protest movement. Short in stature and gentle in manner, King was at that time only 27 years old. What had propelled him into this demanding role in history?

The son of a Baptist minister, King, like his father, was named after Martin Luther, the founder of the Protestant branch of Christianity. The younger King grew up in a comfortable, middle-class home in Atlanta. He attended Morehouse College there and when he was 18 years old decided on a career in the ministry. He already showed a gift for the eloquent, emotion-arousing art of speaking popular in Southern churches. After a trial sermon in his father's Ebenezer Baptist Church, he was ordained a Baptist minister.

King then went north for more schooling—to Crozer Theological Seminary in Pennsylvania and then to Boston University for a Ph.D. in religion. By the time he first arrived in Montgomery in September 1954 as pastor of the Dexter Avenue Baptist Church, he had also met and married Coretta Scott.

The Creation of SCLC

Following the success of the Montgomery bus boycott, King faced the issue of how to extend the lessons learned there to other cities and other civil rights arenas. In January 1957, King called a meeting in Atlanta of 60 Southern ministers to discuss nonviolent integration.

The news that the home and the church of King's friend and fellow minister Ralph Abernathy had been bombed marred the beginning of the conference. After a hurried trip back to Montgomery to survey the damage, King returned to Atlanta to assume the presidency of the newly formed Southern Christian Leadership Conference (SCLC).

Nonviolence

From the beginning of the Montgomery boycott, King encouraged his followers to use **nonviolent resistance.** This meant that those who carried out the demonstrations should not fight with authorities, even if provoked to do so.

The SCLC and the Fellowship of Reconciliation (FOR), the latter an interracial organization founded in 1914, conducted workshops in nonviolent methods of resistance for civil rights activists. Those attending learned how to sit quietly while others jeered at them, called them names, and even spat on them. Workshop participants also learned how to guard themselves against blows and how to protect one another by forming a circle of bodies around someone under attack.

King's use of nonviolent tactics has often been compared to those Mohandas Gandhi used in India's struggle for independence from Great Britain. In both cases the final victory depended on using moral arguments to change the minds of the oppressors. King linked nonviolence to the Christian theme of loving one's enemy. He was certainly familiar with Gandhi's teachings, however, and in 1959 traveled to India to talk with some of Gandhi's followers.

The Gandhian strategy of nonviolence involved four steps: investigation, negotiation, publicity, and demonstration. Applied to civil rights actions, this meant that the activists ought first to look into a situation and gather the facts. Next, the activists should attempt to negotiate with the party responsible for the segregation. Failing that, others should be made aware of the situation and what the activists intended to do. Only then should action, such as a march or a demonstration, be carried out.

Soon after the victory in Montgomery, nonviolent methods began to be applied in a startlingly fresh way. Students in universities and colleges all over the country were tired of waiting for change. They vowed to integrate the nation's segregated lunch counters, hotels, and entertainment facilities by a simple new strategy of nonviolent resistence—sitting.

A Season of Sit-ins

Students Sit to Protest

The first sit-in was not elaborately planned. The four African American freshmen from North Carolina Agricultural and Technical College had never attended a workshop on nonviolence, but late one night they began to talk about what they could do to fight segregation. Earlier in the day Joseph McNeil, one of the four, had tried to get something to eat at the local bus station but had been turned down. He was hurt and resentful.

"We should just sit at the counter and refuse to go until they serve us," one suggested.

"You really mean it?" his friend asked.

"Sure I mean it," the first replied.

The next day, February 1, 1960, the four walked into a local store. Nervous, they first tested the waters to see if their business was welcome. One bought a tube of toothpaste, another some school supplies. Then the four sat down at the whites-only lunch counter and asked for coffee and doughnuts.

"I'm sorry but we don't serve colored here," the waitress said.

STATE HISTORICAL SOCIETY OF WISCONSIN

Sit-ins: A Powerful Instrument of Integration Employing nonviolent tactics brought abuse not only from authorities but also from people who disagreed with the protesters. *Who started the sit-ins?*

"I beg your pardon," Franklin McCain said. "You just served me at a counter two feet away. Why is it that you serve me at one counter and [not] at another?"

The 4 continued to sit at the counter until it closed about half an hour later. The next day they came back, accompanied by 27 other students. The third day, 63 students sat down at the lunch counter. They were not served, so they just sat. On the fourth day, 3 white students from the Women's College of the University of North Carolina joined them. By Friday, the fifth day, the number of demonstrators had grown to about 300. They sat in shifts. If some students had to leave to attend class, other students who stood waiting behind them took their place at the lunch counter.

On Saturday evening 1,600 students attended a victory rally, exhilarated by the announcement that the company was ready to negotiate. They soon discovered that the celebration was premature, however, for the company was willing to make only token changes in its segregation policy.

Two months later students resumed their lunch-counter sit-ins. Adopting a new hard line, the city arrested 45 students and charged them with trespassing. This in turn so enraged the students and their supporters that they launched a massive boycott of stores with segregated lunch counters. As sales dropped by a third, the merchants reluctantly gave in. Six months after the 4 freshmen had first sat down and asked for coffee, they were finally served.

The Sit-ins Spread

Meanwhile, the spontaneous grassroots movement started a reaction that spread like a brushfire throughout the border states and the upper South. By April 1960, college and high school students in 78 communities had staged sit-ins, and 2,000 protesters had been arrested. A year later those numbers had nearly doubled. By September 1961, 70,000 African American and white students were sitting in for social change.

The targets of many sit-ins were Southern stores that were part of national chains. In some Northern cities, however, students picketed stores of the same chains, carrying signs that read We Walk So They May Sit. As more lunch counters integrated under the pressure of sit-ins, variations of the technique emerged. Students held "kneel-ins" to integrate churches, "read-ins" in libraries, "wade-ins" at beaches, and "sleep-ins" in motel lobbies.

A Student Movement

The driving center of the civil rights movement had spread from the legal committees of the NAACP and African American churches to college campuses. The students were impatient. As schoolchildren in 1954 when the Supreme Court ruled on the *Brown* decision, they had expected immediate results, but progress had been slow. In 1957 African Americans had shared in the excitement of Ghana's independence from Great Britain. During 1960 alone, 11 African countries threw off the shackles of colonialism. "All of Africa will be free before we can get a lousy cup of coffee," writer James Baldwin complained.

The nonviolence of the students provoked increasingly hostile reactions from those who opposed them. In Nashville, after four students had successfully desegregated a bus terminal, they were badly beaten. In other cities white teenagers poked students in the ribs, ground cigarettes out on their backs, or threw ketchup on them as they ate.

The Creation of SNCC

Ella J. Baker, executive secretary of King's SCLC, was impressed with the students' commitment and courage, but she was concerned about their lack of coordination and leadership. She invited 100 student leaders of the sit-ins to a conference at Shaw University in Raleigh, North Carolina, over Easter weekend in April 1960. To her surprise, some 300 students showed up,

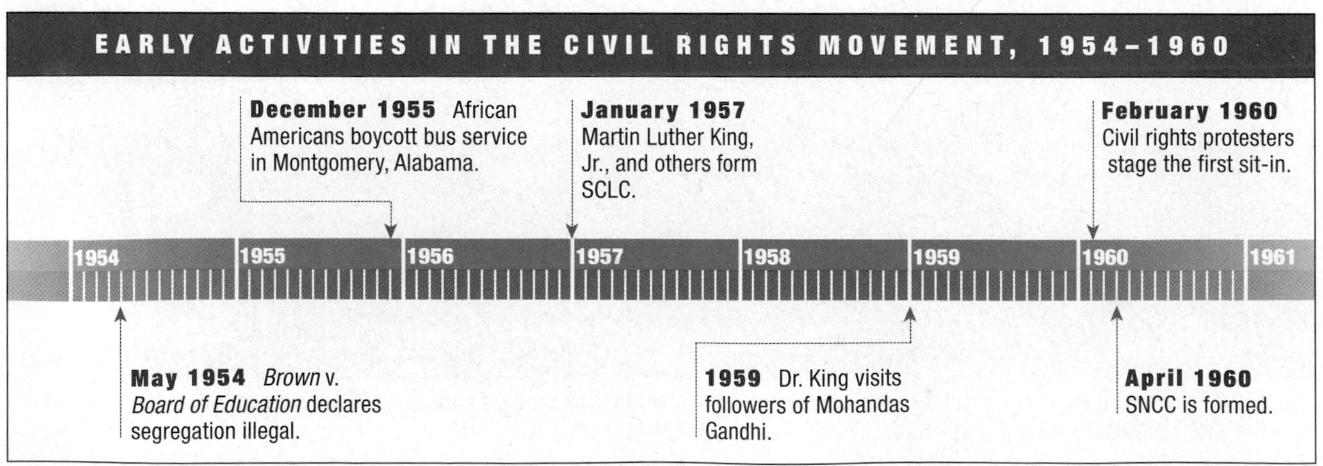

EARLY ACTIVITIES IN THE CIVIL RIGHTS MOVEMENT, 1954–1960
December 1955 African Americans boycott bus service in Montgomery, Alabama.
January 1957 Martin Luther King, Jr., and others form SCLC.
February 1960 Civil rights protesters stage the first sit-in.
1954
1955
1956
1957
1958
1959
1960
1961
May 1954 *Brown* v. *Board of Education* declares segregation illegal.
1959 Dr. King visits followers of Mohandas Gandhi.
April 1960 SNCC is formed.

most from Southern African American communities, but a few also from Northern colleges. Out of that meeting came a new civil rights organization, the Student Nonviolent Coordinating Committee (SNCC, pronounced *snihk*).

King addressed the students that weekend. He stressed the moral power of nonviolence, saying, "The tactics of nonviolence without the spirit of nonviolence may become a new kind of violence."

One of the slogans students warmly applauded at the conference was "jail not bail." The decision to refuse bail and to remain in jail came about for practical as well as philosophical reasons. Supporters of the sit-ins throughout the country had been contributing bail money so that students who were arrested could be quickly released on bail. As the number of arrests grew, the bail money became a heavy drain on the treasuries of civil rights organizations. Philosophically, opting for jail placed the burden of supporting the arrested protesters onto the police and local officials. Also, through press coverage, jail service kept the eyes of the nation focused on the protesters and their conflicts with the authorities.

In adopting "jail not bail," SNCC followed an American tradition of **civil disobedience,** or nonviolent resistance of unfair laws. Henry David Thoreau, for example, had spent a night in jail in 1846 for refusing to pay his poll tax as a protest against slavery and the Mexican War. He later wrote:

> How does it become a man to behave toward this American government today? I answer, that he cannot without disgrace be associated with it. I cannot for an instant recognize that political organization as my government which is the slave's government also.
>
> —Henry David Thoreau, "Civil Disobedience," 1849

Within a year SNCC evolved from an activity that students engaged in between classes to a full-time commitment. The most active students postponed their studies, dropping out of college to work for the movement. In the fall of 1961, SNCC sent 16 "field secretaries" to areas most resistant to integration. By early 1964 that number had grown to 150.

A field secretary could count on only about $10 a week from SNCC, so most roomed and boarded with local African American residents. This arrangement could mean considerable hardship to many Southern African Americans who lived constantly on the edge of poverty. SNCC workers and their hosts were also subject to physical harassment, even danger.

Yet, more than federal court decisions and civil disobedience would be required before the segregation system of 100 years would finally break down. The active commitment of the nation's President and the force of the executive branch also would be needed. The year that the sit-ins erupted and SNCC was formed, John F. Kennedy became the presidential nominee of the Democratic party.

come let us build a new world together
STUDENT NONVIOLENT COORDINATING COMMITTEE

Student Activism Grows **Student activism powered SNCC, an organization that helped bring the civil rights movement out of the courtroom and into the segregated communities of the South.** *How did the policy of "jail not bail" focus public attention on civil rights issues?*

SECTION ASSESSMENT

Main Idea

1. Use a diagram like this one to show some of the nonviolent tactics used to protest segregation.

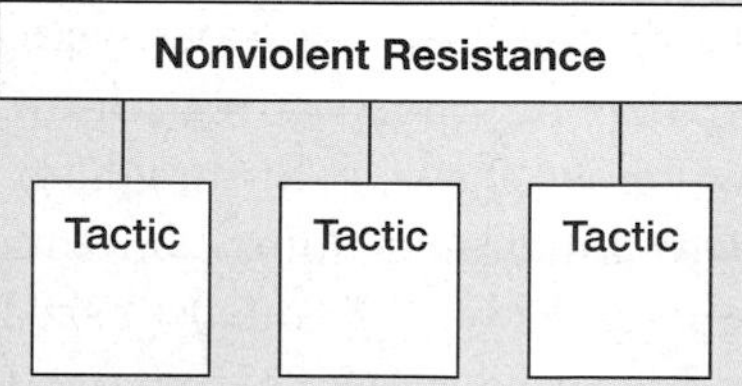

Vocabulary

2. Define: boycott, nonviolent resistance, civil disobedience.

Checking Facts

3. What was the major goal and the primary tactic of SCLC?
4. Why did SNCC adopt the slogan "jail not bail"?

Critical Thinking

5. **Determining Cause and Effect** What effect did the student sit-ins have on the integration of public facilities in the South?

Government Response

MAY 21, 1961: FREEDOM RIDERS MOBBED IN MONTGOMERY, ALABAMA

THE PASSENGERS WERE EXPECTING TROUBLE. On the way to Birmingham, Alabama, from Atlanta, Georgia, one of their buses had been firebombed, burned to an iron skeleton. An angry, violent mob had met the second bus as it limped into the Birmingham terminal. After that the bus drivers, all white, refused to go on. For two days the "Freedom Riders," as the passengers were called, waited for the bus company to find other drivers. Others of their group recuperated in hospital beds. Finally, frustrated, they left the city by plane.

Some thought the Freedom Rides were over then. However, a group of students fresh from sit-ins in Nashville, Tennessee, flew to Birmingham intent on continuing the integrated journey. United States Attorney General Robert Kennedy asked for, and thought he had received, a pledge from the governor of Alabama to protect the bus and its passengers.

Freedom Riders Face Violence
Soldiers guard a bus carrying Freedom Riders.

The ride was calm during the first leg of the journey to Montgomery, Alabama. Alabama state patrol cars were seen at intervals. When the bus pulled into the Montgomery terminal, however, an angry mob of about 1,000 white people quickly surrounded the bus. No police were present.

John Doar, a Justice Department lawyer on the scene, placed a call to the attorney general's office as the bus rolled into the station. "Now the passengers are coming off," Doar reported. "They're standing on a corner of the platform. Oh, there are fists, punching. A bunch of men led by a guy with a bleeding face are beating them," Doar continued. "There are no cops. It's terrible. It's terrible. There's not a cop in sight. People are yelling, 'Get 'em, get 'em.' It's awful."

The mob violence and the city's indifference became front-page news throughout the world. Deeply disturbed and faced with international embarrassment,

GUIDE TO READING

Main Idea

Media coverage of violent attacks on nonviolent civil rights activists forced President Kennedy to chose sides in the segregation struggle, paving the way for the civil rights legislation of the Johnson administration.

Vocabulary

- enfranchisement
- militant
- filibuster

Read to Find Out . . .

- how politics shaped Kennedy's civil rights policy.
- why Kennedy sided with Dr. Martin Luther King, Jr.
- successes of the civil rights movement during the Johnson presidency.

President Kennedy and his brother Robert sent federal marshals to keep order in Alabama. The segregationists would never forgive them for that move.

The next night Robert Kennedy called Governor John Patterson and pleaded with him to reinforce the marshals protecting Martin Luther King, Jr., and a group of his followers who were trapped inside a church by a crowd of several thousand whites. At the last minute, Patterson did send in Alabama National Guard troops to assist the marshals, but not until after the following exchange:

"You are destroying us politically," Patterson told Kennedy.

Kennedy replied, "It's more important that the people in the church survive physically than for us to survive politically."

Politics and Civil Rights **The Kennedys were politicians who understood the political significance of the civil rights issue.** *What was John Kennedy's position on civil rights during the presidential campaign?*

JFK and Civil Rights

Kennedy Supports Civil Rights

John F. Kennedy had not demonstrated a strong commitment to civil rights when he had become a candidate for the presidency in 1960. Like many other politicians on the state and national scene, his views on the civil rights issue reflected mainly its political importance to him. The question to him was how his stand would help him defeat his Republican opponent, Richard Nixon.

On the Campaign Trail

The dilemma Kennedy faced was this: To win, he needed both the segregationists' vote in the South and the African Americans' vote in the North. Kennedy relied upon his vice-presidential running mate, Texas Senator Lyndon Johnson, to bring the Southern white vote. Republican Eisenhower had attracted significant African American support in the 1956 election, and Kennedy expected that Nixon would make a bid for that support by endorsing civil rights.

Kennedy decided to make an all-out effort for the African Americans' vote. He endorsed the sit-ins and promised to sponsor a civil rights bill during the next congressional session. He also pledged—"with a stroke of the presidential pen," he said—to end racial discrimination in federally supported public housing.

In the closing days of the campaign, King's arrest during a sit-in at an Atlanta department store put both presidential candidates to the test. The other protesters were quickly released, but not King. The judge had ruled that King's sit-in arrest was a violation of his probation, which King had received as a result of an earlier conviction for driving without a valid driver's license. King was sentenced to four months of hard labor on a Georgia road gang. He was led off in handcuffs and shackles to a rural state prison.

Coretta King and other King supporters feared that King might not come out of that prison alive. There followed a flurry of phone calls to whomever the civil rights leaders thought might be able to help.

Nixon did nothing. John Kennedy, however, telephoned Coretta King and expressed to her his concern, and Robert Kennedy phoned the judge on King's behalf. When King was released a day later, the Kennedys were given much of the credit. "It's time for all of us to take off our Nixon button," Martin Luther King, Sr., exclaimed gratefully.

John Kennedy won the election by the narrowest margin of popular votes in any presidential election in the twentieth century. His ability to carry 7 of the 11 states of the old Confederacy and 70 percent of the African American vote was a major factor in his political success at that time.

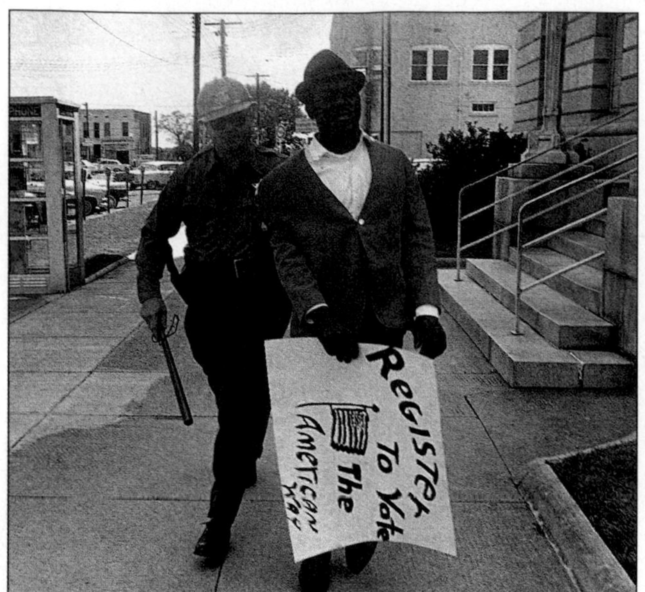

The Push for Voter Participation In Selma, an African American man carrying a voter registration sign is arrested by an Alabama State Trooper. *Why was the initial attempt at enfranchisement unsuccessful?*

Kennedy's Civil Rights Strategy

Despite his campaign promises, Kennedy made no mention of civil rights in his Inaugural Address. Instead, during his first two years in office he tried to avoid losing either Southern white or African American support. He failed to back the promised civil rights bill, which would have required Southern school districts to submit desegregation plans by 1963. When he finally did issue an executive order on housing discrimination in late 1962, it was so weak that it had little effect.

Rather than attacking segregation, Kennedy sought to keep black support by promising African Americans jobs and votes. To find more jobs, Kennedy created a presidential committee, headed by Vice President Johnson. The committee was charged with ending job discrimination in federal government departments and businesses that contracted with the federal government. Johnson chose to rely on voluntary efforts instead of using strict measures such as canceling contracts. The result was that during Kennedy's term the committee accomplished little.

Kennedy was not any more successful in helping African Americans obtain voting rights. In 100 counties of the Deep South, only 5 percent of voting-age African Americans were registered to vote. The civil rights acts passed in 1957 and in 1960 gave the attorney general power to sue in federal courts on behalf of African Americans denied the right to vote because of their race. Accordingly, Robert Kennedy had sent a group of lawyers to the South, to sue when necessary. In 3 years the Justice Department had filed 50 voting-rights cases.

The results of this effort at **enfranchisement,** or obtaining the rights of citizenship, for African Americans through the courts was, however, largely unsuccessful. This was so in part because President Kennedy himself had appointed a number of federal judges who were unsympathetic to civil rights.

Although President Kennedy could produce neither the jobs nor the votes he promised, he did appoint a number of African Americans to his administration. He invited prominent African Americans to social events at the White House and made other symbolic gestures that the African American community applauded. At the same time, many politicians appreciated his reluctance to address segregation issues head-on. His efforts to appeal to both sides of the civil rights issue might have continued if **militants**—activists who would not tolerate any compromise—on both sides had not forced his hand.

Kennedy and the Militants

Kennedy Sides With Civil Rights Protesters

Civil rights demonstrators demanded "Freedom now!" and white segregationists cried "Segregation forever!" If violent whites attacked nonviolent demonstrators, Kennedy would have to make a choice. Either he would have to stay aloof, losing the support of those aligned with the civil rights movement, or he would have to intervene, alienating segregationists. This presented Kennedy with a difficult political dilemma.

The Freedom Riders

The first crisis occurred with the arrival on the scene of the Freedom Riders. James Farmer, executive director of the Congress of Racial Equality (CORE), organized these carefully selected interracial groups of bus passengers. In December 1960, the Supreme Court had ruled that all bus stations and terminals serving interstate travelers should be integrated. The purpose of the Freedom Rides was to test the execution of that decision.

On May 4, 1961, the first busload of 13 CORE volunteers rolled out of the Washington, D.C., bus terminal, bound for New Orleans. On the bus, whites sat in the back, and African American volunteers sat in the front. At each stop, African American volunteers got off the bus and entered the whites-only waiting rooms to test whether the facilities were integrated.

The first leg of the journey went well. Violence, however, soon caught up with the Freedom Riders at Anniston, Alabama, where one of the buses was firebombed. When Robert Kennedy finally intervened in Montgomery, he appealed to the Freedom Riders to wait for the situation to calm down before continuing. They insisted, however, on moving on to Jackson, Mississippi, and potentially more danger. Each of the 26 African Americans and 2 whites aboard the bus wrote out the names and addresses of persons to be notified in case they were killed. "Everyone on the bus was prepared to die," one Freedom Rider recalled.

Kennedy made a deal with Mississippi Senator James O. Eastland. Kennedy would not interfere by sending in federal marshals if Eastland would guarantee there would be no mob violence.

There were no mobs waiting for the Freedom Riders in Jackson; however, police, state troopers, and Mississippi National Guard soldiers were everywhere. As the Riders stepped off the bus and tried to enter the whites-only waiting room, they were quickly arrested for trespassing and taken to jail.

Despite the violence and the jail sentences, more Freedom Riders kept coming all summer. More than 300 were jailed in Jackson alone. Finally, the attorney general petitioned the Interstate Commerce Commission to issue a ruling against segregation of interstate facilities. The ICC made such an announcement on September 22; CORE's victory was secured.

The Voter Education Project

In an effort to steer the civil rights organizations away from violent confrontations with Southern segregationists, Robert Kennedy began to stress the importance of African American voter registration. He reasoned that if more

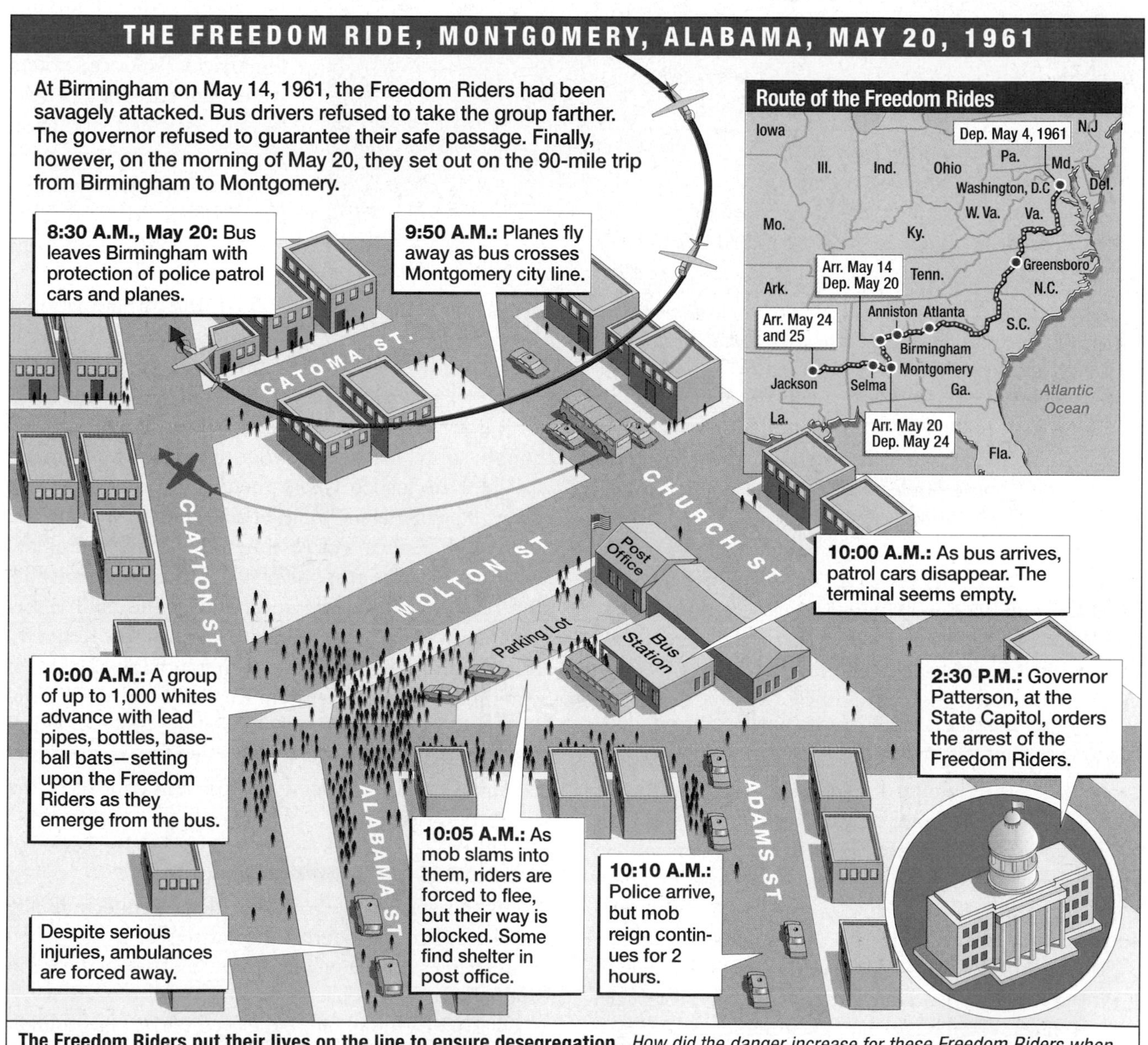
THE FREEDOM RIDE, MONTGOMERY, ALABAMA, MAY 20, 1961
At Birmingham on May 14, 1961, the Freedom Riders had been savagely attacked. Bus drivers refused to take the group farther. The governor refused to guarantee their safe passage. Finally, however, on the morning of May 20, they set out on the 90-mile trip from Birmingham to Montgomery.
8:30 A.M., May 20: Bus leaves Birmingham with protection of police patrol cars and planes.
9:50 A.M.: Planes fly away as bus crosses Montgomery city line.
10:00 A.M.: As bus arrives, patrol cars disappear. The terminal seems empty.
10:00 A.M.: A group of up to 1,000 whites advance with lead pipes, bottles, baseball bats—setting upon the Freedom Riders as they emerge from the bus.
10:05 A.M.: As mob slams into them, riders are forced to flee, but their way is blocked. Some find shelter in post office.
10:10 A.M.: Police arrive, but mob reign continues for 2 hours.
2:30 P.M.: Governor Patterson, at the State Capitol, orders the arrest of the Freedom Riders.
Despite serious injuries, ambulances are forced away.
CATOMA ST.
CLAYTON ST
MOLTON ST
CHURCH ST
ALABAMA ST
ADAMS ST
Post Office
Bus Station
Parking Lot
Route of the Freedom Rides
Dep. May 4, 1961
Arr. May 14
Dep. May 20
Arr. May 24
and 25
Arr. May 20
Dep. May 24
Iowa
Ill.
Ind.
Ohio
Pa.
N.J
Md.
Del.
Washington, D.C
W. Va.
Va.
Mo.
Ky.
Greensboro
N.C.
Ark.
Tenn.
Anniston
Atlanta
S.C.
Birmingham
Montgomery
Jackson
Selma
Ga.
La.
Fla.
Atlantic
Ocean

The Freedom Riders put their lives on the line to ensure desegregation. *How did the danger increase for these Freedom Riders when they crossed the line from Montgomery to Birmingham?*

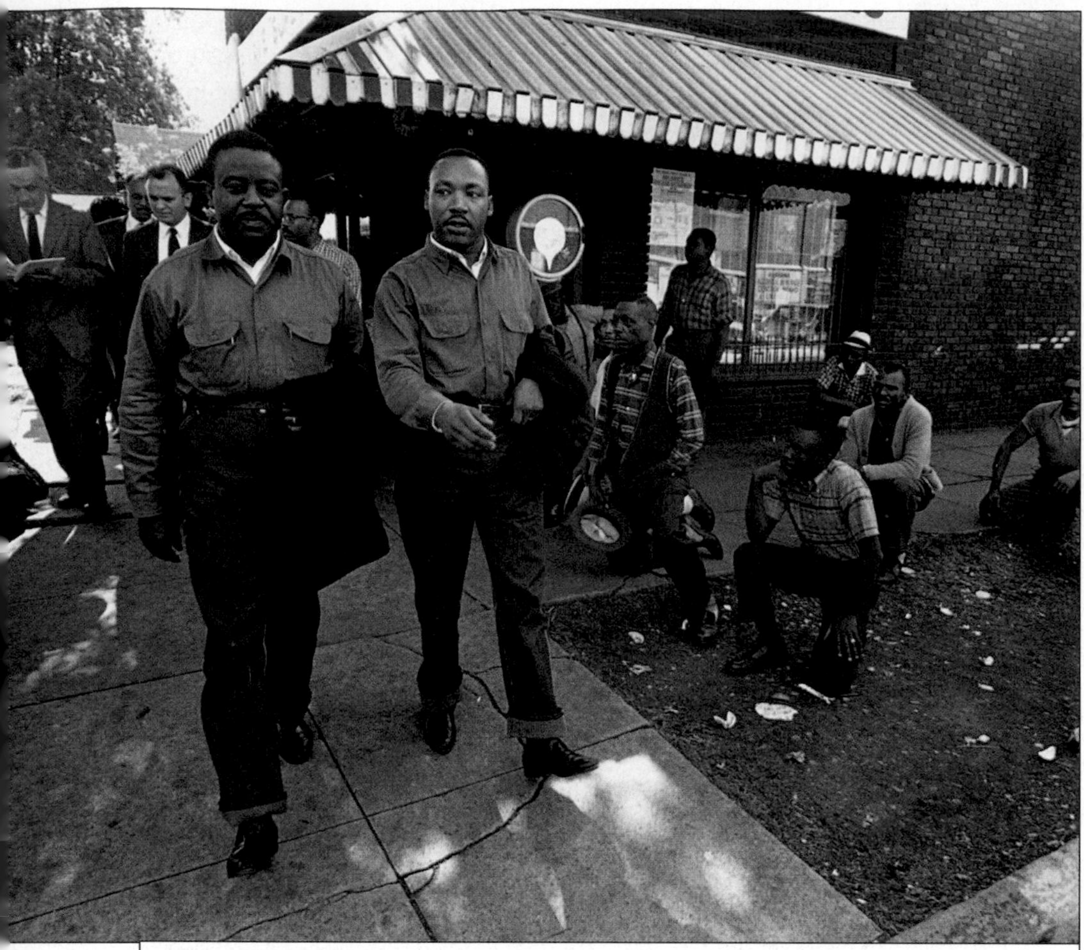

©CHARLES MOORE/BLACK STAR

Protest Leaders March for Equality Ralph Abernathy and Martin Luther King, Jr., lead a group of demonstrators in Birmingham, Alabama. *What were civil rights demonstrators protesting in Birmingham?*

African Americans voted in elections, they would be able to wield some power on important issues, such as housing and education.

Of course, the idea of encouraging voter registration of African Americans was not a new idea. Groups such as SNCC had been working to increase African American registration for some time. To encourage collaboration on voter registration, Kennedy called for a meeting in June 1961 of representatives of SCLC, SNCC, CORE, and NAACP. The result was the Voter Education Project, staffed mainly by SNCC workers. An umbrella group called the Council of Federated Organizations, or COFO, carried out voter registration in Mississippi.

To increase the number of African Americans on voting rolls, SNCC workers held workshops. They explained the sometimes lengthy application forms and accompanied eligible voters to the registration offices.

Few of the eligible voters were able to get their names on the rolls. They were turned away because the registration dates were changed, or they made spelling mistakes, or they failed outrageously difficult tests on the state constitutions. "Sometimes out of 20 or 25 Negroes who went to register, only one or two would pass the test," SNCC worker Anne Moody recalled. "Some of them were flunked because they used a title (Mr. or Mrs.) on the application blank; others because they didn't."

The presence of so many SNCC workers and their effectiveness in organizing local African American communities brought terrorist responses from some white segregationists. In Georgia four churches that had been used to register African American voters were bombed. Workers were beaten, assaulted, and shot. African Americans who dared to vote were evicted from their land, fired from their jobs, and cut off from their credit.

At the organizational meeting, Robert Kennedy's representatives had seemed to pledge money and protection for the workers. Although some private foundation funds were made available, the Justice Department failed to protect the civil rights volunteers it had encouraged to work in the South. The department reasoned that maintaining law and order was the responsibility of local governments. The result was that the militants in the civil rights movement became as alienated from the Kennedy administration as the white segregationists. Then, on September 30, 1962, President Kennedy had to send the United States Army to enforce a court order to enroll James Meredith in the University of Mississippi. It had become clear that Kennedy was losing control of the segregation issue.

Decision at Birmingham

In the spring of 1963, President Kennedy finally chose sides in the segregation struggle. It happened during King's campaign of massive civil disobedience in Birmingham, Alabama.

In 1962 Birmingham had closed parks, playgrounds, swimming pools, and golf courses to avoid desegregating them. "We believed that while a campaign in Birmingham would surely be the toughest fight of our civil rights careers," King wrote later, "it could, if successful, break the back of segregation all over the nation."

The Demonstrations

Civil rights leaders planned the demonstrations to gradually increase in frequency and size. The effect was to keep the attention of newspaper and television reporters focused on the streets of Birmingham.

The conflict was dramatic. Representing one side was the police commissioner, Eugene "Bull" Connor. Thickset and heavily jowled, Connor took pride in the toughness with which he handled integrationists. People around the world watched in horror as he set snarling police dogs on demonstrators or washed small children across streets with the powerful impact of fire hoses.

Representing the opposition was King, who timed the demonstrations to include his arrest on Good Friday, the Christian holy day marking the death of Jesus. During King's two weeks in jail, he wrote the eloquent "Letter from Birmingham Jail." King began the letter on the margins of a full-page newspaper ad that a group of white ministers had taken out. The ad called for an end to the demonstrations. King's letter from jail attempted to explain his use of civil disobedience:

> We know through painful experience that freedom is never voluntarily given by the oppressor; it must be demanded by the oppressed. Frankly, I have yet to engage in a direct-action campaign that was "well-timed" in the view of those who have not suffered unduly from the disease of segregation. For years now I have heard the word "Wait!" It rings in the ear of every Negro with piercing familiarity. This "Wait" has almost always meant "Never." We must come to see, with one of our distinguished jurists, that "justice too long delayed is justice denied."
>
> —Martin Luther King, Jr.
> "Letter From Birmingham Jail," 1963

After his release from jail, King began a new tactic of using African American schoolchildren in the demonstrations. To those who protested that the children, who ranged in age from 6 to 18, were too young, King replied, "Children face the stinging darts of segregation as well as adults."

On the first day, about 1,000 singing children marched out from the church headquarters and in small groups headed toward the city's downtown. They were quickly arrested. The next day the police cast aside all restraint and set upon the child marchers with dogs, clubs, and fire hoses. At one point more than 2,000 children and adults were in jail.

The police tactics swung public opinion squarely around in favor of the protesters. Adult demonstrators came out into the streets in record numbers. King described the scene on May 27, 1963, when white business leaders were meeting privately to work out a settlement:

> On that day several thousand Negroes had marched on the town, the jails were so full that police could only arrest a handful. There were Negroes on the sidewalks, in the streets, standing, sitting in the aisles of downtown stores. There were square blocks of Negroes, a veritable sea of black faces. They were committing no violence; they were just present and singing. Downtown Birmingham echoed to the strains of freedom songs.
>
> —Martin Luther King, Jr., *Why We Can't Wait,* 1964

Local business leaders gave in and agreed to desegregate the big department stores. King called off the demonstrations; but shortly after, on May 11, 1963, bombs exploded at King's motel and at his brother's home, and rioting erupted. Alarmed that the protest might turn violent, President Kennedy decided to cast his lot with Martin Luther King, Jr.

Power Through Song Civil rights workers often sang together in nonviolent protest. *What was the result of police violence against nonviolent protesters in Birmingham?*

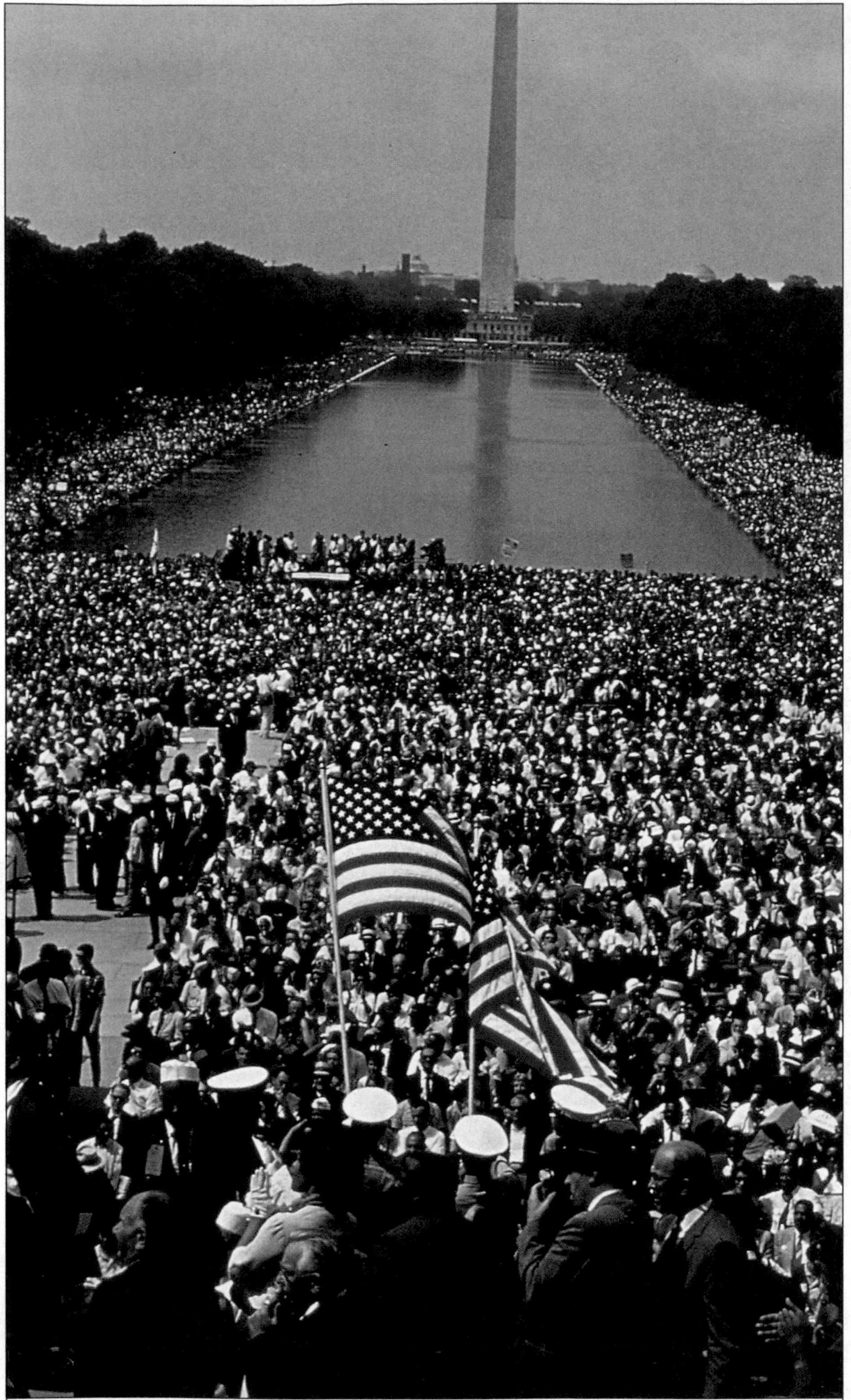

The People March **More than 200,000 gathered at the Lincoln Memorial to call for civil rights reforms.** *Who were the organizers of the march?*

June 11, 1963, was a historic day for the civil rights movement. In the afternoon President Kennedy federalized the Alabama National Guard to enforce a court order requiring the admission of two African American students to the University of Alabama. That evening the President appeared on national television. "We are confronted primarily with a moral issue," he said. "It is as old as the Scriptures and is as clear as the American Constitution." He then announced that he would send Congress a civil rights bill, which, it turned out, would deliver crushing blows to segregation.

Later that night in Jackson, Mississippi, a white sniper killed Medgar Evers, head of the state NAACP. By the time President Kennedy was assassinated in November 1963, his civil rights bill was moving toward passage in the House.

The March on Washington

The massive protest march on the nation's capital on August 28, 1963, began as a cry for jobs. As planning went on, however, the goals of the march grew to embrace the entire civil rights movement. A key demand was support for passage of Kennedy's civil rights bill. The march's organizers were a coalition of labor leaders, clergy, liberals, and grassroots workers.

Trains and buses brought in thousands of demonstrators from all over the country. It was the largest crowd ever to attend a civil rights demonstration. There were two highlights, most agreed, in a day of memorable songs, speeches, and appearances: Mahalia Jackson's singing of the spiritual "I Been 'Buked and I Been Scorned" and King's delivery of a speech, in which he cried, "I have a dream that one day this nation will rise up and live out the true meaning of its creed: 'We hold these truths to be self-evident, that all men are created equal.' "

The Triumph of Civil Rights

Johnson Signs Civil Rights Act

Following President Kennedy's assassination on November 22, 1963, presidential leadership of civil rights efforts fell on Lyndon B. Johnson. Born and raised in the South, Johnson had removed himself from the segregationist ranks in 1956 when he refused to sign the Southern Manifesto. In addition, Johnson had overseen the passage of a limited civil rights act in 1957.

LBJ Carries On

Johnson was determined to overcome liberal doubts about his presidency by achieving passage of Kennedy's civil rights bill without compromising any of its most important elements. The bill passed the House in February 1964 but faced an uncertain future in the Senate.

The Southerners in the Senate intended to prevent a vote by launching a **filibuster**—that is, they would debate the bill nonstop to keep it from coming to a vote. According to Senate rules, a motion to end debate could carry only if it had the support of two-thirds of those present and voting. With Southern Democrats solidly behind the filibuster, 26 of the 33 Republicans in the Senate would have to vote with Northern Democrats in order to end it.

The one man who could deliver these votes was the Senate minority leader, Everett McKinley Dirksen. A conservative Republican from Illinois, he was not known as a friend of civil rights. Yet Dirksen ended months of suspense by lining up the Republican votes to end debate and to pass the bill. Dirksen explained his decision with a quote from Victor Hugo: "No army can withstand the strength of an idea whose time has come."

On July 2, 1964, President Johnson signed into law the most comprehensive civil rights legislation enacted up to that time. It met the demands of the civil rights activists in several key ways. For example, the civil rights movement had protested the forced exclusion or separation of African Americans and whites in public places. Title II of the 1964 Civil Rights Act forbade segregation in hotels, motels, restaurants, lunch counters, theaters, and sporting arenas that did business in interstate commerce. As a result, most businesses in Southern cities and large towns desegregated immediately after passage of the Civil Rights Act. The act also relieved individuals of the responsibility for bringing discrimination complaints to court. The act made bringing discrimination cases the job of the federal government.

Protest in Selma

The passage of the Civil Rights Act did not mean that the work of the civil rights movement was over. Legislation still did not exist to enforce the Fifteenth Amendment, which forbids any state from depriving citizens of the right to vote because of race. King decided to force this issue by mounting another campaign of nonviolent resistance, this time in Selma, Alabama. At the start of King's campaign there, only 383 African American citizens out of a possible 15,000 were registered.

Selma was an excellent choice for another reason as well. After Birmingham, King had begun to rely increasingly on the power of television and newspapers to reach the conscience of America. Selma had in the person of its sheriff, Jim Clark, a civil rights antagonist who rivaled Birmingham's Bull Connor for ruthlessness.

After 2 months of beatings, arrests, and 1 murder, civil rights leaders in Selma announced a climactic protest march from Selma to the state capital in Montgomery, 54 miles (87 km) away. Though Governor George Wallace banned the march, Hosea Williams, who was King's chief aide in Selma, and John Lewis, a SNCC leader, decided to defy Wallace and march anyway.

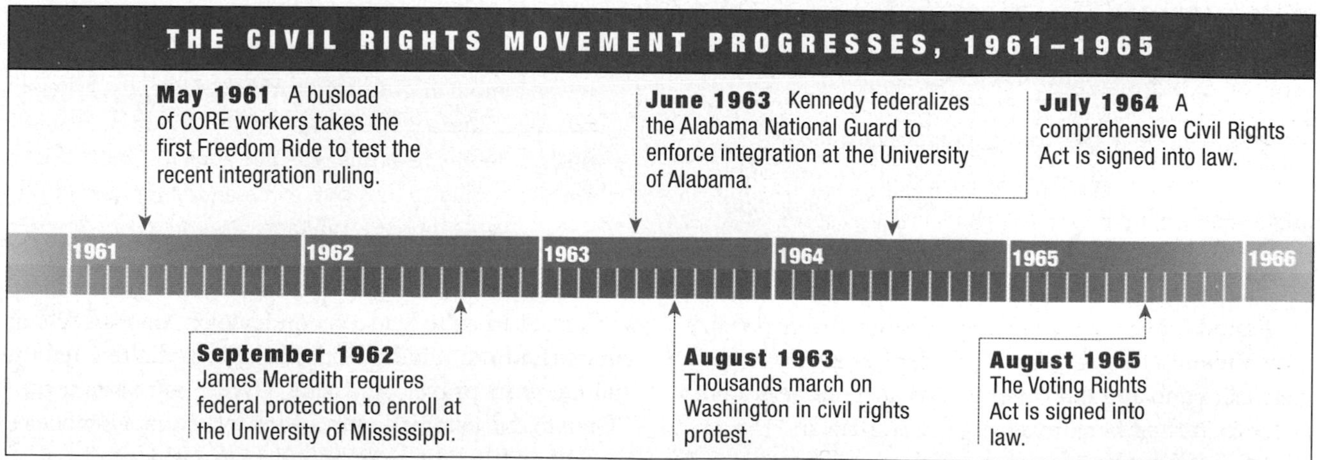

THE CIVIL RIGHTS MOVEMENT PROGRESSES, 1961–1965
May 1961 A busload of CORE workers takes the first Freedom Ride to test the recent integration ruling.
June 1963 Kennedy federalizes the Alabama National Guard to enforce integration at the University of Alabama.
July 1964 A comprehensive Civil Rights Act is signed into law.
1961
1962
1963
1964
1965
1966
September 1962 James Meredith requires federal protection to enroll at the University of Mississippi.
August 1963 Thousands march on Washington in civil rights protest.
August 1965 The Voting Rights Act is signed into law.

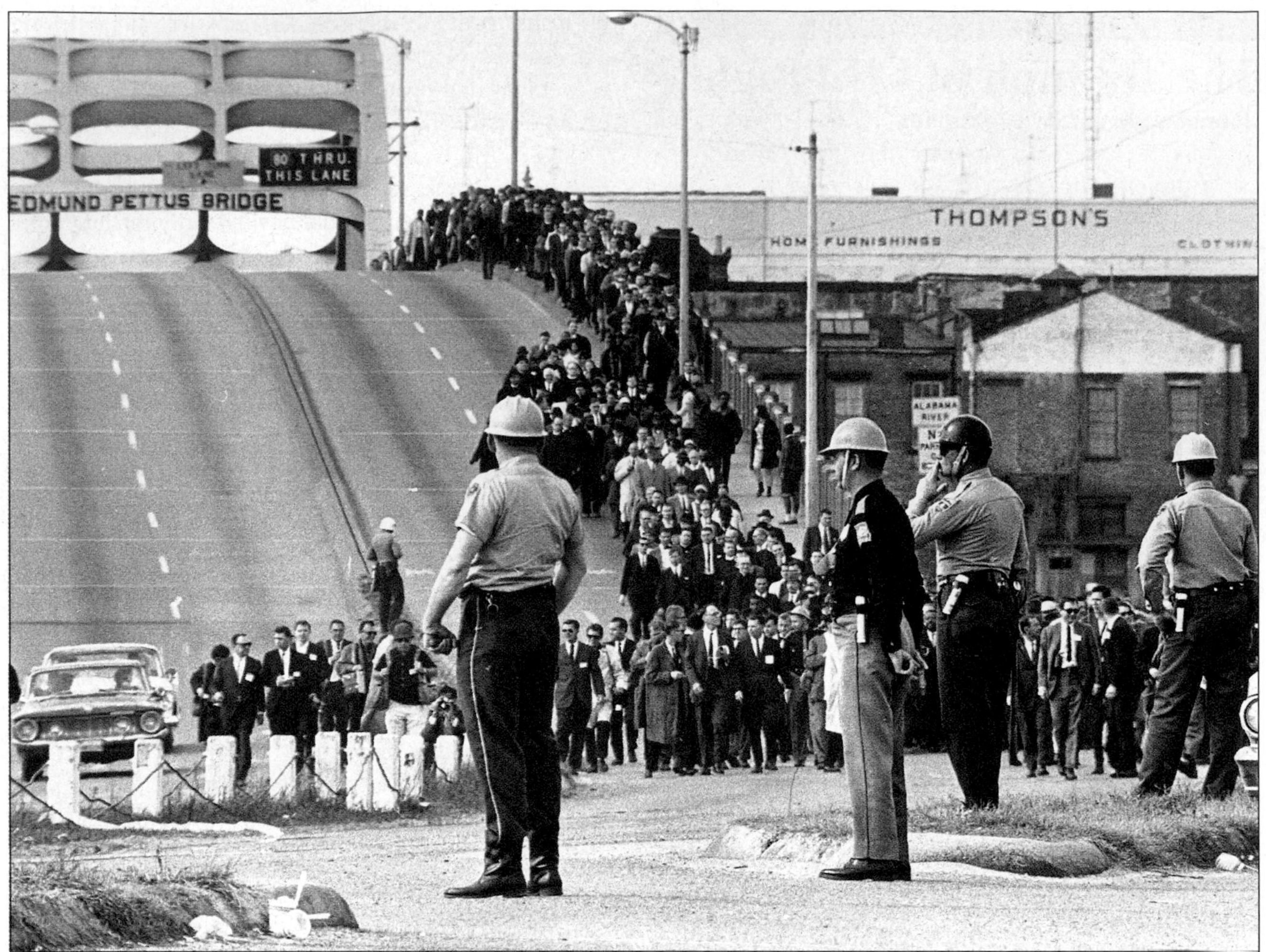

UPI/BETTMANN

Push for Enforcement of the Fifteenth Amendment At Edmund Pettus Bridge civil rights activists in Alabama met violence—and won sympathy for their cause. *How did the troopers drive the marchers back?*

On March 7, 1965, Williams and Lewis led 600 demonstrators onto the Edmund Pettus Bridge outside Selma on the way to Mongtomery. Sheriff Clark's deputies lined both sides of the bridge, and 100 state troopers blocked the opposite end.

The leader of the troopers gave the marchers two minutes to disperse, then set upon them with tear gas and clubs, driving them back to Selma and into the reach of Sheriff Clark's men.

Sheyann Webb remembered her experience as an eight-year-old marcher:

> I saw those horsemen coming toward me and they had those awful masks on; they rode right through the cloud of tear gas. Some of them had clubs, others had ropes or whips, which they swung about them like they were driving cattle. . . .
>
> I began running and not seeing where I was going. I remember being scared that I might fall over the railing and into the water. . . . I heard more horses and I turned back and saw two of them and the riders were leaning over to one side. It was like a nightmare seeing it through the tears. I just knew then that I was going to die. . . .
>
> —Sheyann Webb, from *Selma, Lord, Selma: Girlhood Memories of the Civil Rights Days,* by Sheyann Webb and Rachel West Nelson, as told to Frank Sikora

Governor George Wallace had different memories:

> As Major Cloud tells the story, he gave no orders to attack, and because of the noise of the melee it was almost impossible to hear commands. When it was over, there were mercifully no serious injuries—and no deaths. But this was not at all the way I had wanted things to turn out. I was saddened and angry.
>
> —George C. Wallace, *Stand Up for America*

King, who had been out of town for the Sunday march, returned to lead a second one on March 9. When he reached the middle of the bridge, he halted, led the marchers in prayer, and sang "We Shall Overcome." Then, to the astonishment of his followers, he wheeled around and led the marchers back to Selma.

No one knew that King had reluctantly agreed, at the request of the Johnson administration, not to complete the march. King needed the support of the President. In addition, he felt that the first bloody march had accomplished its purpose.

Once again public opinion in the North rallied to King's cause, and once again a President moved to join him. On March 15, 1965, in an emotional televised speech to Congress, Johnson promised to send a bill to Congress that would guarantee African Americans the most basic right of citizenship—the right to vote. Finally on March 21, the march from Selma to Montgomery, already twice turned back, proceeded peacefully under the protection of the federalized Alabama National Guard.

The Voting Rights Act of 1965

At Selma the civil rights movement protested laws designed to prevent African Americans from voting. Of special concern were literacy tests, which were used to deny African Americans the right to vote in Alabama, Mississippi, Louisiana, South Carolina, Georgia, Virginia, and 39 counties of North Carolina.

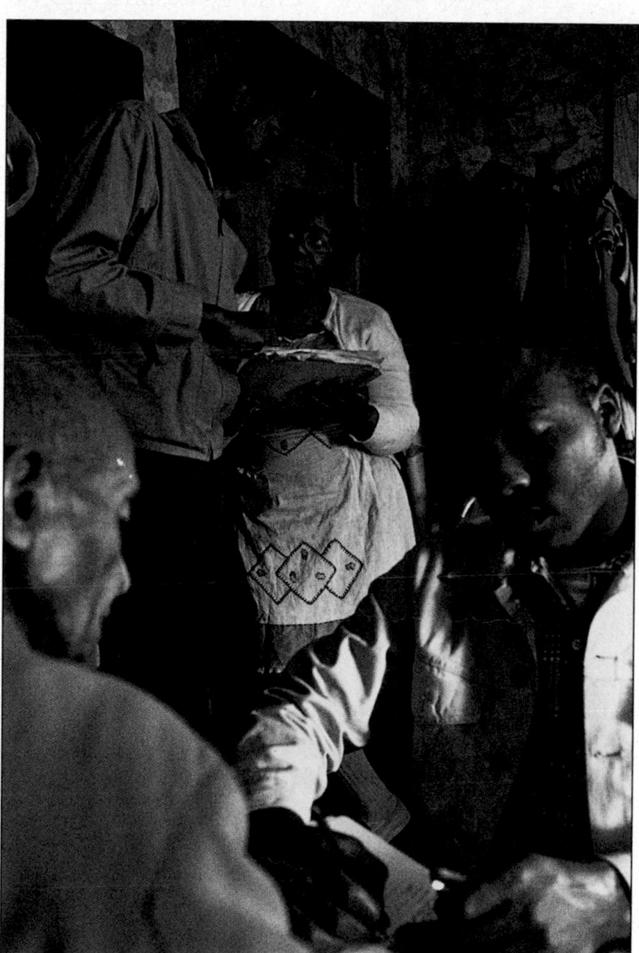

©CHARLES MOORE/BLACK STAR

Voter Registration These Mississippi residents get help registering to vote. *How did African Americans use their new political power?*

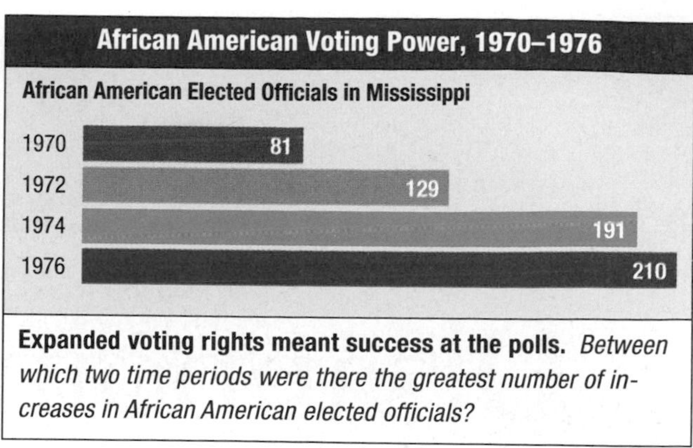

Expanded voting rights meant success at the polls. *Between which two time periods were there the greatest number of increases in African American elected officials?*

The 1965 Voting Rights Act provided that if literacy or other similar tests were used, and if less than 50 percent of the voting-age citizens were registered, then racial discrimination could be presumed. In such cases literacy tests were automatically suspended, and eligible African American citizens were allowed to enroll whether or not they could read. The act further provided that if local registrars would not enroll African Americans, the President could send federal examiners who would.

As a result of the act, 740,000 African American voters registered to vote in 3 years. They used their new political power to help win elections for hundreds of African American officials. African Americans also used their power to help defeat Selma Sheriff Jim Clark, who lost his reelection campaign to a racial moderate.

Section Assessment

Main Idea

1. Use a chart like this one to show key civil rights confrontations during the years 1961 to 1965 and the presidential response to each confrontation.

Civil Rights Confrontation	Presidential Response

Vocabulary

2. Define: enfranchisement, militant, filibuster.

Checking Facts

3. How did politics and actions by militants help shape Kennedy's civil rights policies?
4. How did Johnson exert leadership in the civil rights struggle after Kennedy's death?

Critical Thinking

5. **Determining Cause and Effect** How do you think the media affected Kennedy's views on segregation?

Disappointed Hopes

JUNE 1966: KING AND SNCC MARCH TOGETHER ONE LAST TIME

WHAT BEGAN IN JUNE 1966 AS A SOLO MARCH THROUGH MISSISSIPPI IN DEMONSTRATION OF AFRICAN AMERICANS' RIGHT TO VOTE TURNED INTO ONE LAST MARCH IN UNITY. After that the civil rights movement disintegrated into separate factions with radically different goals, ideals, and strategies.

©BOB FITCH/BLACK STAR

Split Emerges
Stokely Carmichael speaks out.

James Meredith, who in 1962 became the first African American to attend the University of Mississippi, undertook the 220-mile (354-km) walk to demonstrate African Americans' right to vote and their right to move without fear through the state. When he fell wounded on the roadside, his back full of buckshot, civil rights workers rushed to Mississippi to complete his march.

During the day they trudged down U.S. Highway 51 arm in arm: Martin Luther King, Jr., of SCLC; Floyd McKissick, of CORE; and Stokely Carmichael, of SNCC. As they stopped to speak in courthouse squares, King and Carmichael preached two separate gospels.

King, despite the increasing numbers of killings and assaults, continued to call on his followers to answer violence with nonviolence. The SNCC and CORE marchers, however, had given up on nonviolence and sang a new tune. When King and his supporters began their theme song, "We Shall Overcome," they were often drowned out by the militants' new version, "We Shall Overrun."

The climactic moment came in Greenwood. Carmichael, just released from a few hours in jail for erecting a tent against a state trooper's orders, leaped onto a flatbed truck and raised his hand in a clenched-fist salute. "This is the twenty-seventh time I have been arrested—and I ain't going to jail no more," he shouted.

GUIDE TO READING

Main Idea

Disappointed by the slow pace of change, some African Americans adopted different strategies for gaining equality, causing splits within the civil rights movement.

Vocabulary

- martyr
- black separatism
- black pride
- black power

Read to Find Out . . .

- how splits developed in the civil rights movement and why some African Americans turned to radical protests.
- the causes of rioting in northern cities during the mid-1960s.

"We been saying freedom for six years and we ain't got nothin'. What we gonna start saying now is Black Power!" King tried to calm the crowd, but the new cry of "Black Power" drowned out his call of "Freedom *Now!*" By the time the march reached Jackson, Mississippi, the new call had replaced the old one.

New Directions in Civil Rights

African Americans Turn to Radical Protest

The change in direction in SNCC had been in the making for a long time. In the early 1960s the students shared in the ideal of a new, better American society. After the 1964 and 1965 civil rights acts, when the new laws were not immediately enforced, SNCC volunteers became disillusioned. Indeed, the progress that did occur seemed to come at enormous cost. One **martyr,** or person who dies in the name of an important cause, followed another: the four young girls killed when their church was bombed in Birmingham in 1963; the three civil rights workers shot in Mississippi in 1964; and on and on. As time went on, SNCC leaders began to discuss three key issues: the role that white volunteers should play within the organization; a growing movement among some African Americans toward **black separatism,** or the separation of the races in America; and the continued use of nonviolence as a strategy for change.

Seeking Political Support Fannie Lou Hamer (center) and two other MFDP candidates visit the Capitol. *What was the result of their efforts?*

SNCC's efforts to work within the political system also left members disillusioned. In 1964 the Mississippi Freedom Democratic Party (MFDP), a grassroots group that SNCC supported, asked to be recognized at the national Democratic party convention as the legitimate Democratic party in the state. They challenged the regular Democratic party principally on the grounds that fewer than 5 percent of the African American population in the state was allowed to vote.

President Johnson, however, was not sympathetic to the MFDP. He did not want the convention distracted from its main job of enthusiastically supporting his policies. Also, he did not want to risk sending white Southern Democrats in flight to the Republican party. Johnson assigned Minnesota senator Hubert Humphrey the job of sidetracking the MFDP challenge, suggesting that at stake might be the vice-presidential nomination that Humphrey was hoping for.

The compromise Humphrey pushed through gave the MFDP only 2 of the 40 Mississippi seats. SNCC and MFDP members, who had risked their lives by openly challenging the local regular Democrats, felt the white liberals at the convention had let them down. Fannie Lou Hamer, sharecropper and member of the MFDP, summed it up by exclaiming, "We didn't come all this way for no two votes."

Black Pride

The success of the civil rights movements in the early 1960s gave rise to **black pride,** a pride in being African American. Ralph Bunche, famous for his skills as a diplomat, wrote in 1961, "I am confident that I reflect accurately the views of virtually all Negro Americans when I say that I am proud of my ancestry, just as I am proud of my nationality." Other African American leaders also recognized the importance of black pride, as well as the harm done by the feelings of inferiority that had long afflicted African Americans. Malcolm X, a strong African American leader, bitterly recalled his youthful efforts at straightening his hair in order to look more like a white person:

> This was my first big step toward self-degradation: when I endured all of that pain, literally burning my flesh to have it look like a white man's hair. I had joined that multitude of Negro men and women in America who are brainwashed into believing that the black people are "inferior"—and white people "superior."
>
> —Malcolm X, *Autobiography of Malcolm X,* 1965

©UPI/BETTMANN

Differences Deepen The growing movement for black separatism and militancy, led by people such as Malcolm X, unsettled many white people. *What did black separatists propose as the best way of achieving their goal of black separatism?*

As the 1960s progressed, younger and more race-conscious African Americans adopted natural "Afro" haircuts and put on African-inspired dashikis in place of shirts and ties. The new pride was reflected also in language, music, lifestyle, and many other aspects of African American culture. Even the words that African Americans used to describe themselves changed. The term *Negro,* used for years by many prominent leaders, was abandoned because of its evocation of the slave trade. The word *colored* was rejected as not being sufficiently precise. The new preferred term was the simple adjective *black,* turned into a noun.

Sometimes the powerful desire of African Americans to proclaim their own self-worth was expressed in anti-white feelings. This was part of the reason that some SNCC workers raised in their planning group the troublesome question of the role of white volunteers.

Some within SNCC argued that white college-trained workers thoughtlessly took over the jobs that African Americans with little schooling were just learning to do. Moreover, some accused white volunteers of being insensitive to the local conditions under which African Americans lived. "Let the whites go fight racism in their own communities," they said. Others, however, pointed out the sacrifices and efforts that white SNCC workers made. Some activists protested that by excluding whites, SNCC itself could be accused of racism. Ultimately, the new view won, and the white workers were asked to give up leadership positions in SNCC.

Malcolm X and Black Separatism

Emerging African American pride was one factor in the move toward black separatism. According to the promoters of black separatism, this could best be achieved by African Americans returning to Africa or by their occupying an exclusive area within the United States on land that the federal government supplied to them.

Black separatism was the antithesis of the civil rights movement's goal of racial integration. It was a view promoted by, among others, the Nation of Islam, a subgroup of the Islamic religion commonly known as the Black Muslims.

The most vocal Black Muslim was Malcolm X. A brilliant and bold orator, Malcolm X preached a message that included religious justification for black separatism. He was ousted from the Nation of Islam in a fight over leadership and went on a pilgrimage to the Islamic holy city of Makkah. There he was exposed to more traditional Islamic religious teachings, which do not include racial separatism. On his return to the United States, he softened his views on the separation of blacks and whites. On February 21, 1965, three members of the Nation of Islam assassinated Malcolm X as he spoke in Harlem.

Though Malcolm X's views on separatism gradually softened toward the end of his life, he never supported King's nonviolent methods. Instead, he advocated the use of weapons for self-defense, believing that African American nonviolence simply emboldened violent white racists. Shortly before his death, Malcolm X pointed out in a speech at Selma, "The white people should thank Dr. King for holding black people in check."

SNCC's New Leadership

The rhetoric of Malcolm X lived on long after his death and influenced SNCC members and other young militants. The final turnaround in SNCC's orientation came in 1966 with the election of Stokely Carmichael as chairman.

Carmichael was arrested many times during Freedom Rides, sit-ins, and marches. Jailers were happy to see him go because he was never reluctant to argue with them over the condition of mattresses and other jail comforts. Once, when six other Riders were put in solitary confinement, he banged on his cell door asking for equal treatment, which he finally received.

One of Carmichael's projects during his leadership of SNCC was the formation of an African American political party in Lowndes County in Alabama. The party failed to put any of its candidates into office in the

1966 election. It was, however, a bold attempt to seize political power, or **black power** as it was called. The symbol used for the Lowndes County Freedom Organization was a black panther about to spring.

The Long, Hot Summers

Riots Erupt in Northern Cities

Although civil rights activists fought their major campaigns in the South, the pattern of segregation was not confined to states that belonged to the former Confederacy. It was a growing frustration among African Americans over conditions in the North that led to some of the most dramatic and tragic confrontations of the 1960s.

The migration to Northern cities that began in the early 1900s had by 1965 resulted in the relocation of some 3 million Southern African Americans. More than two-thirds of the total African American population were now urban dwellers. Of these, more than half were concentrated in just 12 cities.

Perhaps more than in the South, life in Northern cities bred frustration among many African Americans. Problems of poverty, unemployment, and racial discrimination followed the migrants as they fled the South. The empty promise of racial equality in the North ignited a smoldering fire of rage in many African American communities. The following poem by Langston Hughes, written in 1951, captures the emotions of many city-dwelling African Americans of the mid-1960s:

> What happens to a dream deferred?
> Does it dry up
> like a raisin in the sun?
> Or fester like a sore—
> And then run?
> Does it stink like rotten meat?
> Or crust and sugar over—
> like a syrupy sweet?
>
> Maybe it just sags
> like a heavy load.
>
> *Or does it explode?*
>
> —Langston Hughes, "Harlem," 1951

Watts, First of a Series

The arrest for a traffic violation of the young African American in the Los Angeles ghetto should have been routine. Perhaps it was the warm, humid August weather that drew people onto the streets. Or perhaps it was the time, 7:00 P.M., still early enough in the evening to attract a restless crowd.

For whatever reason, that simple arrest in Watts on August 11, 1965, exploded into a major riot that lasted 6 days. Before it was over, 34 people were dead, 1,072 were injured, and 4,000 had been arrested. Close to 1,000 buildings were damaged or destroyed, with a property loss that totaled nearly $40 million.

The Watts riot was the first, but not the most destructive, of a series of racial disorders that hit cities throughout the United States in the summers of 1965, 1966, and 1967. Like some kind of seasonal plague, a fever of rage, looting, and arson seemed to erupt in one crowded city after another.

Many of the riots began in similar ways, with an arrest or a police raid that was followed by rumors of resistance and police brutality. The numbers of men, women, and children involved were immense: there were 30,000 rioters in Watts, while another 60,000 milled about in the streets; in the 1967 Detroit, Michigan, riot, 7,000 people were arrested.

Typically, looters headed for white-owned businesses, stripping them clean of merchandise, then setting fire to the buildings. Some stores escaped destruction by putting up signs that read Negro Owned or Blood (meaning African American). Nevertheless, African American–owned businesses were often destroyed. As the fires burned, snipers prevented firefighters from

© DECLAN HAUN, BLACK STAR

Violence Erupts The riots in the Watts section of Los Angeles in 1965 were the first of many to break out in cities in the United States. *What sparked the riots in Watts?*

©JOFFRE T. CLARKE/BLACK STAR

The Panthers Members of the Black Panther party attend the funeral of one of their members in Seattle, Washington. *In what way did the Black Panthers differ from other groups of African Americans at the time?*

doing their work. As a result, whole blocks were left to burn. In Watts in 1965, and again in Detroit in 1967, National Guard troops were sent in to help local police. While the riots were raging, a new African American political group appeared. In 1966 the Black Panther party was formed in Oakland, California. Its goals included protecting African American communities from police harassment and assuming neighborhood control of police, schools, and other services. The Black Panthers differed significantly from other African American groups in that they supported the use of weapons for self-defense and retaliation.

Reasons Why

During the first 9 months of 1967, more than 150 cities in the United States reported incidents of racial disorders. In Newark, New Jersey, and in Detroit, Michigan, the incidents erupted into full-scale riots.

To identify and address the causes of the riots, President Johnson appointed a National Advisory Commission on Civil Disorders, headed by Governor Otto Kerner of Illinois. The Kerner Report, as the commission's findings came to be known, was released in March 1968. As a basic cause of the rioting, the Kerner Report pointed to the "racial attitude and behavior of white Americans toward black Americans." This could be visible, the report said, in patterns of racial discrimination and prejudice, in African American migration to the cities followed by white flight to the suburbs, and in the existence of African American ghettos. The report cited three triggers for the racial violence: frustrated hopes of African Americans; the approval and encouragement of violence, both by white terrorists and by some African American protest groups; and the sense many African Americans had of being powerless in a society dominated by whites.

The Kerner Report concluded that "the nation is rapidly moving toward two increasingly separate Americas." To divert that move, the report recommended the elimination of all racial barriers in jobs, education, and housing; greater public response to problems of racial minorities; and increased communication across racial lines.

One More Assassination

The Death of King

The Kerner Report did not end race riots in the United States. One more outburst of rage swept through nearly 130 ghettos following the April 4, 1968, death of Dr. Martin Luther King, Jr., at the hands of a white assassin. The 39-year-old minister was shot while standing on a balcony with friends in Memphis, Tennessee.

The acceptance of violence as a means of social protest continued to concern King up until his death. Protesters against the war in Vietnam had long been pressing him to come out with an antiwar statement. The issue was not only the war itself but also its financial cost, which was at the expense, many thought, of the war against poverty at home.

King was reluctant to oppose Johnson, a stand he knew would be unpopular among many of his supporters. The logic of his commitment to nonviolence, however, demanded it. Finally, in 1967 he began to make speeches denouncing the war. He declared that "the promises of the Great Society," the name given Johnson's social program, "have been shot down on the battlefield of Vietnam."

VERNON MERRITT/©BLACK STAR

Leadership Void **Coretta Scott King mourns the death of her husband.** *How did King's death affect the civil rights movement?*

King did lose many supporters because of his antiwar statements. Partly in an effort to rebuild his political strength, he turned toward organizing an interracial coalition of the poor. His final trip to Memphis was to rally support for the mostly African American garbage collectors who were attempting to unionize.

The night before his death King spoke at a church rally. He might have had a premonition when he said, "We've got some difficult days ahead. But it doesn't matter with me now. Because I've been to the mountaintop." King went on to say, "I may not get there with you, but I want you to know tonight . . . that we as a people will get to the promised land!"

The Movement Appraised

Civil Rights Gains

Without strong leadership in the years following King's death, the civil rights movement floundered. Middle-class Americans, both African American and white, tired of the violence and the struggle. The war in Vietnam and crime in the streets at home became the new issues at the forefront of the nation's consciousness.

In retrospect, the 14 years between the Supreme Court's momentous *Brown* decision and King's death were years of great progress in civil rights. Not since the passage of the Thirteenth, Fourteenth, and Fifteenth Amendments during Reconstruction had so many gains been made. For this reason, these years are sometimes called the Second Reconstruction. Some civil rights leaders today fear that, as in the original Reconstruction, hard-won victories will gradually slip away. To guard against this, civil rights groups remain vigilant in their quest for progress.

Because of the combined efforts of state and federal legislatures, the courts, and the people themselves, some measure of political power was given to African Americans. The next gains would have to come through the political process. Meanwhile, other minorities who also thought of themselves as disenfranchised looked to the civil rights movement of the 1950s and the 1960s as a model for their own efforts.

SECTION ASSESSMENT

Main Idea

1. Use a diagram like this one to show the factors that helped cause discontent within the civil rights movement.

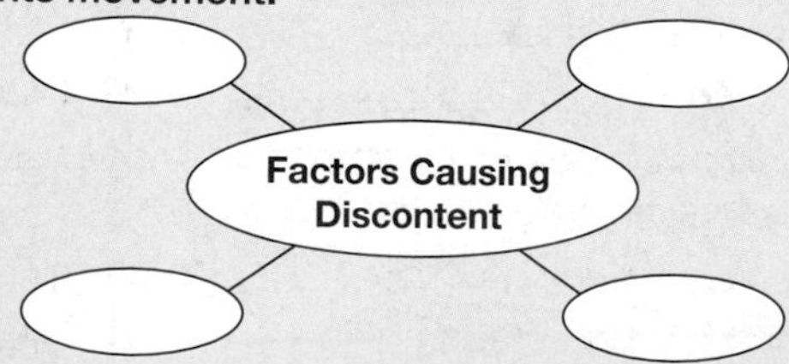

Vocabulary

2. Define: martyr, black separatism, black pride, black power.

Checking Facts

3. In what ways did the militant civil rights groups disagree with the strategies and attitudes of Martin Luther King, Jr.?
4. Describe the racial unrest that spread to major cities in the North during the mid-1960s.

Critical Thinking

5. **Predicting Consequences** What do you think would have happened in the civil rights movement had King not been assassinated?

Chapter  Assessment

Self-Check Quiz

Visit the *American Odyssey* Web site at americanodyssey.glencoe.com and click on ***Chapter 20—Self-Check Quiz*** to prepare for the Chapter Test.

Reviewing Key Terms

On a separate sheet of paper, write the number of each phrase and the term it describes.

segregation	**civil rights**
boycott	**militant**
sit-in	**enfranchisement**

1. the attainment of the rights of citizenship, especially the right to vote

2. the political, economic, and social rights of a citizen

3. the enforced separation of racial groups in schools, housing, and public areas

4. one who aggressively pursues or defends a cause

5. an organized agreement not to use certain goods or services in order to exert pressure for change

Recalling Facts

1. What was the major issue at the start of the civil rights movement?

2. What principle was overturned in *Brown* v. *Board of Education*?

3. What do the acronyms NAACP, SNCC, CORE, and SCLC stand for? What kinds of groups were these?

4. What techniques were used to keep African American citizens from registering to vote?

5. What did John Kennedy say about civil rights during his campaign for the presidency? What did he say at his inauguration? Why did he change his mind?

6. Who were the Freedom Riders, and what was the purpose of the Freedom Rides?

7. How did Lyndon Johnson show support of civil rights issues both before and during his presidency?

8. What was the Kerner Report? What did it identify as the causes of urban violence? What recommendations did it make?

Critical Thinking

1. Determining Cause and Effect In the mid-1960s, most people in the United States watched the evening news on television. Why was this custom significant to the civil rights movement?

2. Predicting Consequences If the Supreme Court had given definite guidelines for carrying out school desegregation early on and if President Eisenhower had taken an early stand for desegregation, how do you think desegregation might have progressed? Explain.

3. Recognizing Points of View Use a diagram like this one to describe how Malcolm X and Dr. Martin Luther King, Jr., differed in their views on how to combat racism.

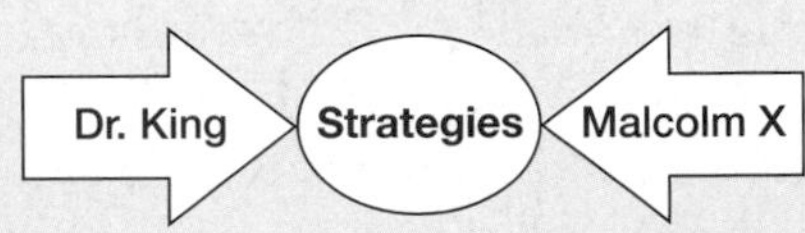

Standardized Test Practice

1. Which of the following was the result of the other three?

A In some places, state and local laws upheld racial segregation.

B Congress passed a new civil rights act and a new voting rights act.

C Several civil rights groups were organized.

D Some state and local governments barred African Americans from voting.

Test-Taking Tip: This question asks you to identify a cause-and-effect relationship. *One* event was caused by the other three. Remember that racial segregation and restrictions on voting were two major causes of the civil rights movement, so you can rule out answers A and D.

2. "We have never initiated violence against anyone, but we do believe that when violence is practiced against us we should be able to defend ourselves. We don't believe in turning the other cheek."

This quote best reflects the ideas of

A Dr. Martin Luther King, Jr.

B Rosa Parks.

C Malcolm X.

D Ella J. Baker.

Test-Taking Tip: Remember the methods that each of these speakers used to challenge racial injustice. For example, Dr. King supported nonviolent resistance, or refusing to fight, even if provoked. So you can eliminate answer A.

GEOGRAPHY AND HISTORY

Civil Rights Riots, Summer 1965, 1966, 1967

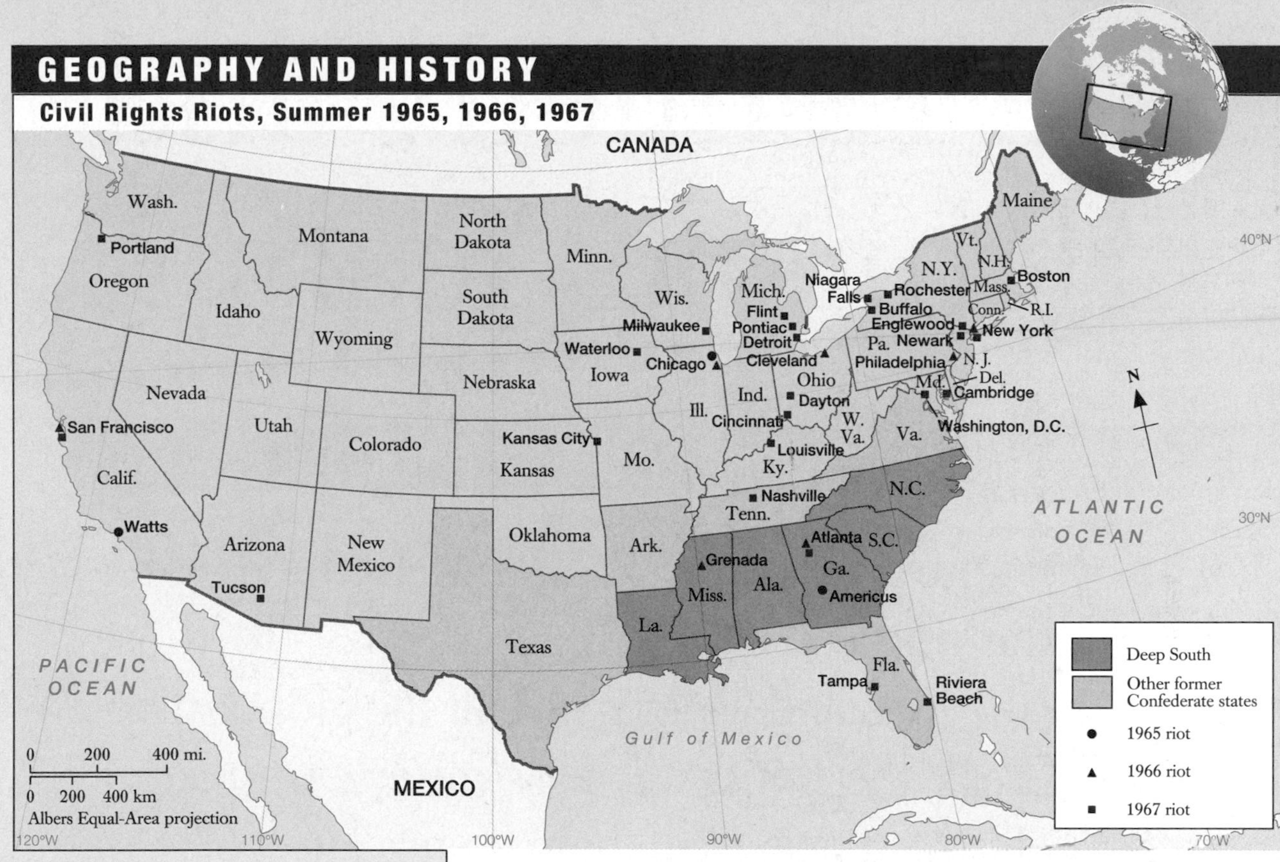

Study the map to answer the following questions:

1. Which cities had civil rights riots in 1965? In what regions of the country are these cities located?
2. In what 2 regions of the country did most of the 1966 and 1967 riots take place?
3. Which cities had more than one riot? Why might this have happened?
4. Which areas of the country experienced few or no riots? What might be a reason for this?

Portfolio Project

Choose a civil rights figure such as Martin Luther King, Jr., Rosa Parks, Fannie Lou Hamer, Mahalia Jackson, Malcolm X, or Stokely Carmichael. Research this person, and write a personal profile. Include copies of photographs, speeches, and so on, as appropriate.

Cooperative Learning

In *Brown* v. *Board of Education,* the Supreme Court handed down a unanimous decision. In some recent civil rights cases, however, the Court has been divided. With a few other students, consult newspapers and periodicals to identify some of these cases. Choose one, research it, and create a chart that lists the arguments on both sides. Share your findings with other groups in the class.

Reinforcing Skills

Presenting Statistical Data

Study the map on page 669. Then turn its data into a statistical table. Use each category in the map key as a column head. Present totals at the end of each column. What generalization can you form about segregation in 1950 based on this table?

Technology Activity

Using the Internet The National Association for the Advancement of Colored People (NAACP) is very active today. Search the Internet for information about this organization and create a brochure that explains its goals.

The Kennedy and Johnson Years

1961: THE BIRTH OF THE PEACE CORPS

In his Inaugural Address, President Kennedy proclaimed the purpose of the Peace Corps: "To those people in the huts and villages of half the globe struggling to break the bonds of mass misery, we pledge our best efforts to help them help themselves. . . ."

Kennedy and his vision deeply inspired many Americans, as Roger Landrum, volunteer to Nigeria from 1961 to 1963, remembers:

". . . when he [Kennedy] announced the Peace Corps idea, I wrote him a letter saying, 'If you will do it, I will volunteer.'"

"I grew up in rural Michigan and I'd never been overseas before. I was at my mother's house when the telegram came inviting me to train for Nigeria. I remember my hands were shaking as I opened it. I had never heard of Nigeria but I definitely felt I was participating in history. This was a new era of American participation in the world. Peace Corps volunteers were the front-line people making fresh contact with a whole bunch of newly independent nations. There was a sense of exhilaration about maybe carrying forth democracy and establishing new relations with Asia, Africa, and South America."

Landrum and thousands of other volunteers went on to make Kennedy's dream a reality, symbolizing the best of the "New Frontier." ■

HISTORY JOURNAL

Based on what you already know and the picture on page 699, write down your first impressions of the Kennedy and Johnson years and what you think this chapter may be about.

Chapter Overview

Visit the *American Odyssey* Web site at americanodyssey.glencoe.com and click on ***Chapter 21—Chapter Overview*** to preview the chapter.

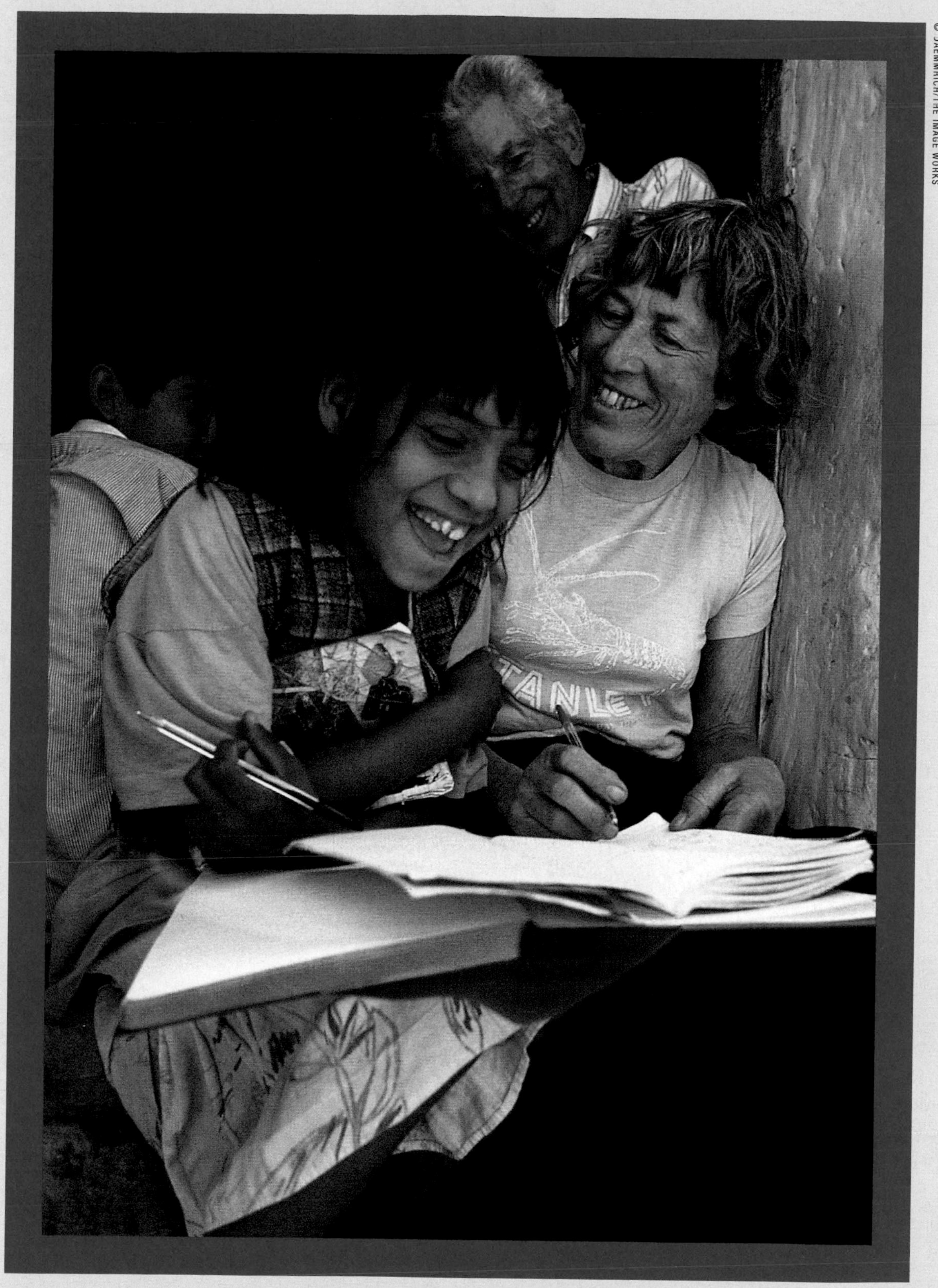

PEACE CORPS VOLUNTEERS
IN HONDURAS

New Frontier and Great Society

JANUARY 20, 1961: JOHN F. KENNEDY SWORN IN AS PRESIDENT

THEY STOOD TOGETHER ON THE INAUGURAL PLATFORM: THE 43-YEAR-OLD JOHN F. KENNEDY, TANNED, VIGOROUS, AND COATLESS DESPITE THE SUBFREEZING WEATHER, AND 70-YEAR-OLD DWIGHT D. EISENHOWER, WEARING A MUFFLER, LOOKING LIKE A TIRED GENERAL. The appearances of the two men, a generation apart in age, symbolized the change of leadership. Kennedy, many voters believed, would get the United States moving again.

Behind Kennedy on the platform were other members of his glamorous family: his beautiful wife, Jackie; his younger brother Robert, soon to be attorney general of the United States; and his parents, Rose and Joseph P. Kennedy, founders of a political dynasty. As Kennedy began his Inaugural Address, his hands chopped at the air in the style that was familiar to those who had seen his campaign appearances on television. His speech promised so much:

UPI/BETTMANN

Camelot Begins
President Kennedy inspired a spirit of optimism.

> Let the word go forth . . . that the torch has been passed to a new generation of Americans—born in this century, tempered by war, disciplined by a hard and bitter peace. . . .
>
> Let every nation know, whether it wishes us well or ill, that we shall pay any price, bear any burden, meet any hardship, support any friend, oppose any foe to assure the survival

GUIDE TO READING

Main Idea

The optimistic message of John F. Kennedy helped propel the nation into a new political era of social reform, both under Kennedy and his successor Lyndon B. Johnson.

Vocabulary

- mandate
- coalition
- pragmatist

Read to Find Out . . .

- how the goals and accomplishments of Kennedy and Johnson compared.
- some of the major reform programs of the 1960s.

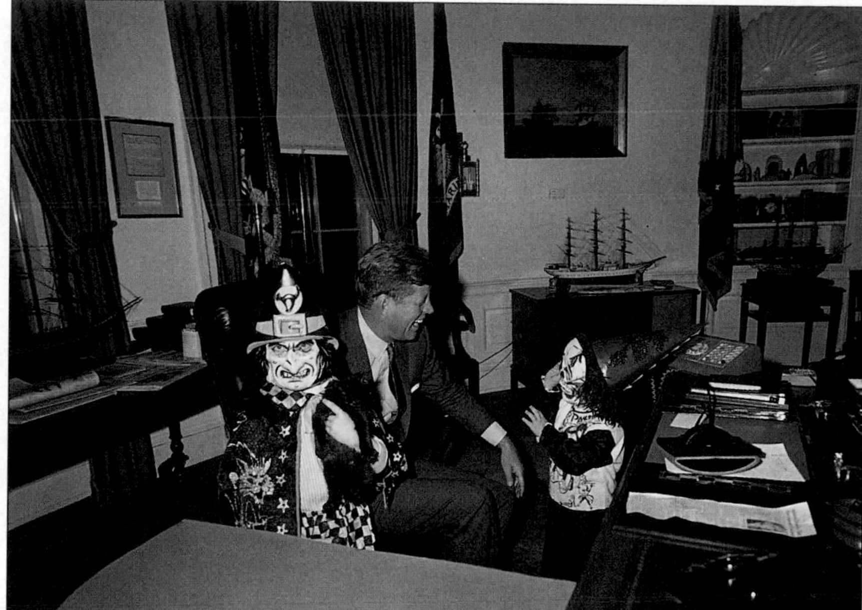

JOHN F. KENNEDY LIBRARY, BOSTON

The President and Helpers President Kennedy's two children, Caroline and John, Jr., were frequent visitors to the oval office. *What did Kennedy ask of his fellow Americans in his Inaugural Address?*

and the success of liberty. . . . All this will not be finished in the first 100 days. Nor will it be finished in the first 1,000 days. . . . But let us begin. . . . And so, my fellow Americans—ask not what your country can do for you—ask what you can do for your country.

—John F. Kennedy, Inaugural Address, 1961

The promise John Fitzgerald Kennedy gave the United States was never realized. JFK had scarcely more than 1,000 days himself—1,036 to be exact—before an assassin's bullet cut him down. Looking back at his brief presidency, from the buoyant, wintry inaugural in January 1961 to the funeral procession through the grief-soaked streets of Washington, D.C., in 1963, what survives is a strong impression of the Kennedy spirit. It was a force that propelled the nation into a new political era.

The Kennedy Years

Kennedy Pursues a New Frontier

In the eyes of most historians, the scattered accomplishments of Kennedy's abruptly ended term hardly amounted to a finished political record. Compared to the hard-driving presidencies of FDR and Lyndon Johnson, whose first years were packed with new initiatives, Kennedy's young administration moved slowly. He came into office with the narrowest margin of victory of any modern President—not enough to claim a **mandate** (a clear endorsement of his ideas) from the American public. In Congress, Kennedy faced a powerful conservative **coalition,** or temporary alliance with a common purpose. He, therefore, pursued his course with more caution than boldness.

He grew into the job. His days were long, hard, and fast-paced. As his term progressed, his initiatives became bolder, and his handling of Congress became more aggressive and assured.

★ ★ ★ Gallery of Presidents ★ ★ ★

John Fitzgerald Kennedy

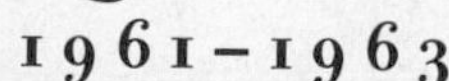

"Now the trumpet summons us again—not as a call to bear arms, though arms we need—not as a call to battle, though embattled we are—but a call to bear the burden of a long twilight struggle . . . against the common enemies of man: tyranny, poverty, disease, and war itself."

Inaugural Address, January 20, 1961

UPI/BETTMANN

Background

- **Born 1917; Died 1963**
- **Democrat, Massachusetts**
- **Served in the navy 1941–1945**
- **Elected to the House of Representatives 1946**
- **Elected to the Senate 1952**
- **Assassinated, November 1963**

Achievements in Office

- **United States Peace Corps (1961)**
- **Trade Expansion Act (1961)**
- **Nuclear Test Ban Treaty (1963)**

The New Frontier

Kennedy may not be remembered as a President who accomplished sweeping domestic legislation. He may stand, however, as one who instilled Americans with renewed idealism.

> We stand today on the edge of a new frontier—the frontier of the 1960s, a frontier of unknown opportunities and paths, a frontier of unfulfilled hopes and threats. . . . The new frontier of which I speak is not a set of promises—it is a set of challenges.
>
> —John F. Kennedy, Presidential nomination acceptance speech, 1960

The New Frontier became the label for Kennedy's vision of progress at home. It was not an organized set of legislative initiatives for economic change, like Roosevelt's New Deal or Johnson's Great Society, which was yet to come. Kennedy often reacted to events—such as civil rights disturbances and the Cuban missile crisis—instead of blazing new trails. The New Frontier, then, was more a personal vision of Kennedy's, a progressive ideology but by no means a radical one.

As Kennedy began the campaign that had ushered him into office, many liberals had become complacent. Although in 1960 the economy was sluggish, the country still enjoyed the post-war prosperity. Issues that had consumed the liberals of the New Deal era—economic inequalities and the overhaul of large corporations—no longer seemed so critical. As economist John Kenneth Galbraith said in a 1958 study, "[Capitalism] works, and in the years since World War II, quite brilliantly."

Liberals in the 1960s reasoned that if the country maintained its current progress, those at the bottom of the economic heap would in time better themselves. The two major issues still to be resolved were civil rights and civil liberties. Other problems, such as inadequate education and poverty, could be solved by fine tuning.

The Kennedy Aura

The Kennedy image captivated the media. "Since the thirty-fifth president and his wife are about the most physically attractive people to have lived in the White House, the urge of the publicists, magazines, networks, and photographers to fuse two American dreams and reveal the White House as the ultimate movie set is irresistible," Alistair Cooke wrote in 1963. "To put it mildly, the president has yielded to this urge and has manipulated it."

Many considered JFK a hero. Others distrusted him. Their reasons ranged from dislike of his wealthy father and the threat of a family dynasty to anti-Catholic and anti-Eastern biases. "All that Mozart string music and ballet dancing down there, and all that fox hunting and London clothes," one congressman said. "He's too elegant for me."

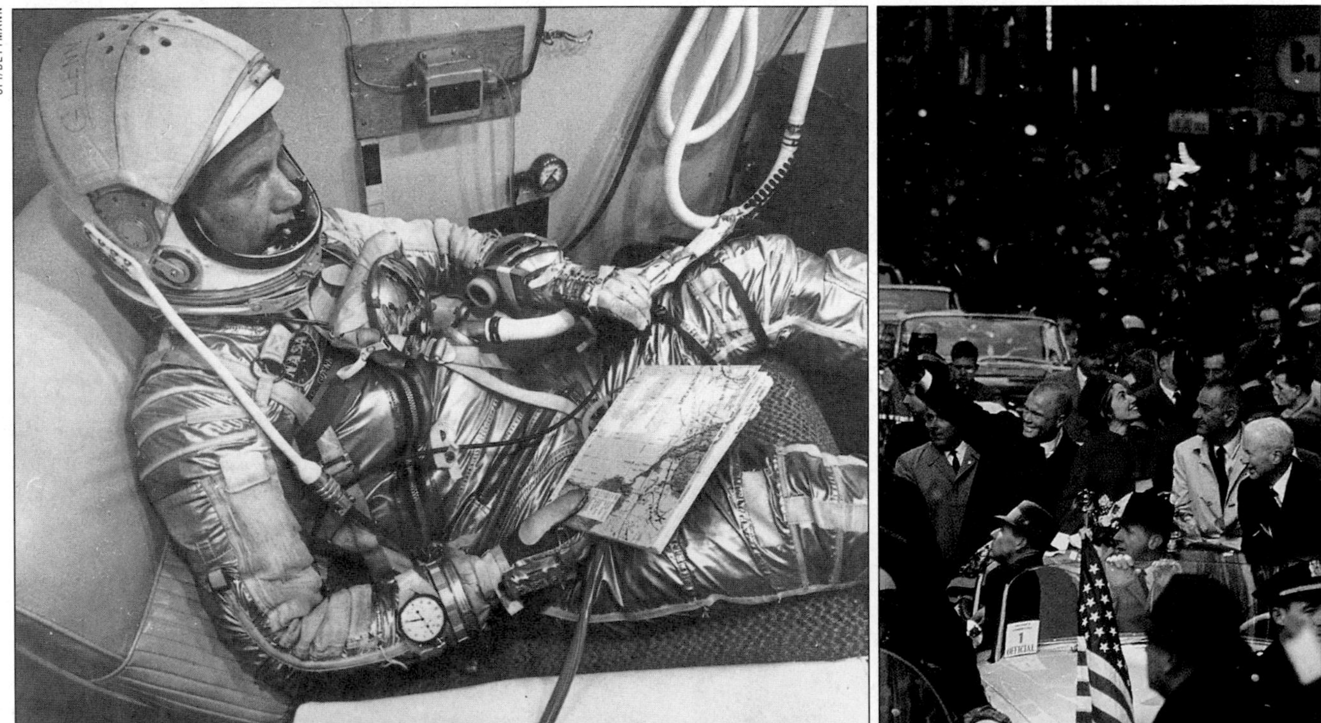
UPI/BETTMANN

RALPH MORSE, © TIME, INC.

Success in Space **In the spacecraft *Friendship*, John Glenn became the first American to orbit the earth—and the country celebrated!** *Space was part of the New Frontier; how did Kennedy define the New Frontier in his acceptance speech?*

JOHN F. KENNEDY LIBRARY, BOSTON

A Warm Send-off **JFK greets early Peace Corps volunteers and wishes them well.**
What was the main function of Peace Corps volunteers?

Kennedy's Working Style

The team that Kennedy gathered around him in his administration were, as one journalist noted, "the best and the brightest" of the President's generation. Most were educated at top Eastern schools, and many were recruited from the executive rooms of big business.

Kennedy and his team were content, on the domestic front, to nudge along economic growth and to strengthen public programs. This is what he meant by "getting the country moving again" and restoring United States prestige abroad. The President's interests were centered on foreign policy—the cold war and the containment of communism.

In August 1961, Communists built a wall between East Berlin and West Berlin to prevent East Germans from fleeing to the West. Kennedy reaffirmed his support for West Berliners in a speech delivered near the Berlin Wall in 1963. He said, "All free men, wherever they may live, are citizens of Berlin, and, therefore, as a free man, I take pride in the words, 'Ich bin ein Berliner.'"

Kennedy saw himself more as a **pragmatist,** someone interested in practical solutions to problems, than as a liberal. Most of the nation's problems "are technical . . . administrative problems," he explained. "They [involve] sophisticated judgments which do not lend themselves to the great sort of 'passionate movements' which have stirred this country so often in the past."

The Space Race

During the early 1960s, a nation's accomplishments in space became a test of leadership in technology and defense. The Soviet Union gained an edge in the so-called space race when cosmonaut Yuri Gagarin orbited the earth in April 1961. The following month, in a message to Congress, President Kennedy asked for a commitment to the goal of "landing a man on the moon and returning him safely to earth" before 1970.

The challenge fueled public imagination and ensured the dedication of American astronauts. The space agency, National Aeronautics and Space Administration (NASA), developed a three-stage program to put Americans in space. The first stage, Project Mercury, consisted of a series of test flights between 1961 and 1963. John H. Glenn, Jr., became the first American to orbit the earth during a Mercury flight in February 1962. During 1965 and 1966 Project Gemini launched a second series of flights in which two-man teams practiced maneuvering and docking spacecraft while orbiting the earth. The Apollo program, which would accomplish the goal of a moon landing, began in 1968.

Programs at Home and Abroad

Kennedy's efforts to perk up the economy largely succeeded. Increased spending for defense and for the space program poured billions of dollars into government contracts, which in turn increased employment. The Area Redevelopment Act channeled funds into needy regions. Congress raised the minimum wage from $1 to $1.25 an hour. These measures contributed to an economic upswing that lasted until the early 1970s.

During his administration Kennedy initiated several programs for international development. The Alliance for Progress was a series of aid projects undertaken cooperatively with Latin American countries that agreed to democratic reform. The Peace Corps sent volunteers to developing countries, where they lived among the local people and assisted in education and rural development projects. In its first 34 years, the Peace Corps sent 140,000 volunteers to 100 countries. The popular program continues today.

Student Web Activity 21

Visit the *American Odyssey* Web site at americanodyssey.glencoe.com and click on ***Chapter 21—Student Web Activities*** for an activity relating to the Kennedy presidency.

Highlights of the Kennedy Presidency		
1961	**1962**	**1963**
January • John F. Kennedy is inaugurated on January 20. *March* • Peace Corps is assembled. • Committee on Equal Employment Opportunity is established. • Twenty-third Amendment grants the right to vote to District of Columbia. *May* • Alan Shepard, Jr., is the first United States astronaut in space. • Minimum wage is raised from $1.00 to $1.25. *August* • Alliance for Progress is initiated. • Communist East Germany builds the Berlin Wall.	*February* • John Glenn, Jr., is the first United States astronaut to orbit the earth. *May* • United States naval forces and ground troops are sent to Laos. *June* • Supreme Court declares school prayer unconstitutional. *September* • Race riots erupt at University of Mississippi. *October* • JFK "quarantines" Cuba; Soviets remove missiles. *November* • JFK lifts quarantine of Cuba.	*May* • Telstar II communications satellite is launched. *June* • National Guard assists with integration of University of Alabama. • President's Advisory Council on the Arts is created. • JFK recommends strong civil rights legislation. *August* • "Hot line" is established between United States and USSR. • Civil rights protesters march on Washington. *September* • United States treaty is ratified banning nuclear testing in the atmosphere, outer space, and under water.

The Kennedy administration was a time of new frontiers—at home, around the world, and in space. *When did the first American orbit the earth?*

Kennedy's efforts to pass an education aid bill showed the obstacles he faced in Congress. The coalition of Republicans and Southern Democrats feared that increased federal support for education might mean less state control. The issue of aid to parochial schools was a further complication. Kennedy felt that supporting such aid would expose him to the accusation that as a Catholic he favored parochial schools. As negotiations wore on, both Protestants and Catholics became displeased with him. Kennedy was unable to push the education bill through Congress, something that Lyndon Johnson, a Protestant, later managed to do.

Hopes Cut Off

Assassin Kills Kennedy

Many people expected more than they were getting from Kennedy on issues such as civil rights. "I was furious with the administration's civil rights posture," recalled Roger Wilkins, a lawyer with the Agency for International Development. "I thought it was slow, lethargic, and unresponsive."

Arthur Schlesinger, Jr., who served as special assistant to Kennedy, however, notes that the President "was soon educated by events. . . ." Later in his term, Kennedy seemed to be seizing control of events. He called for a thawing of the cold war with the Soviet Union. Two months later the two nations signed a treaty limiting nuclear testing. As one of his last efforts, Kennedy requested his economic advisers to prepare a plan directed at poverty in the United States. He also promised action on civil rights.

Kennedy's hope was to achieve a greater mandate for his programs in the 1964 election. With this in mind, in late November 1963 he took a trip to Dallas, Texas, to smooth over party differences and gather electoral support.

Tragedy in Dallas

CBS television news anchor Walter Cronkite cried as he gave the nation the news: President Kennedy had been fatally shot in Dallas while riding in a motorcade. For four days people across the United States sat hunched in front of their television sets, as images of violence and of mourning were etched forever into their minds. They pored over newspaper accounts of the grisly shooting, trying to understand why or how the tragedy could have happened.

They saw the pictures of Kennedy waving to cheering crowds as his open limousine wove through the streets of Dallas shortly before noon on November 22. As the motorcade approached an expressway, shots rang out and Kennedy slumped forward in his seat. Jackie Kennedy cradled her dying husband's head in her lap as the limousine raced to nearby Parkland Hospital. Kennedy was pronounced dead at 1:00 P.M. Vice President Lyndon Johnson was sworn in almost immediately as President.

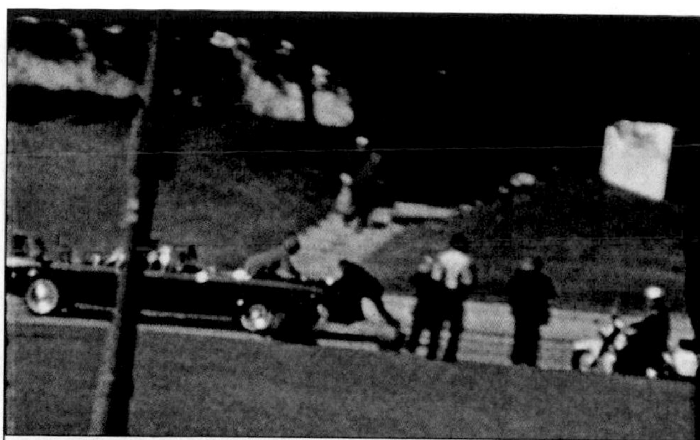

Tragedy Strikes **A bystander, using home movie equipment, recorded scenes from the unexpected and tragic assassination of the President.** *Whom did police charge with the murder?*

Police determined that the shots had been fired from a warehouse that overlooked the route of the motorcade. They arrested Lee Harvey Oswald, a 24-year-old warehouse worker, and charged him with the murder. Two days later Oswald was transferred from the city jail to the county jail. Television cameras covered the event live. As viewers across the country watched in disbelief, a Dallas nightclub owner, Jack Ruby, pushed through a circle of police officers and journalists and shot and killed Oswald at point-blank range.

The death of Oswald hampered investigations of the assassination. The Warren Commission, headed by Chief Justice Earl Warren, however, concluded in 1964 that Oswald had acted alone and not in a conspiracy of any kind. Critics of the Warren Commission maintain that the investigations were hastily concluded and that some group whose identity is as yet unknown most likely aided Oswald.

The Nation Mourns

The answer to the question, "Where were you when Kennedy was shot?" became frozen in people's memories. "I was in social studies class at Woodlands High School," said Bonnie Steinboch of White Plains, New York. "In the corridor, I saw Mr. Courtney, the art teacher, sobbing against the wall, and I was astonished that a grown-up, a teacher, would be so openly upset. Kennedy was the most important person in my life to die. . . . Months after he died, I realized one night in bed that I would never hear his voice again, and I sobbed for a long time."

Americans cried as they saw three-year-old John F. Kennedy, Jr., salute his father's funeral procession, and they stared at the riderless horse in the procession, a symbol of the fallen hero. The nation grieved as much for the President that John F. Kennedy might have become had he lived, as for the leader he had been. Commentator

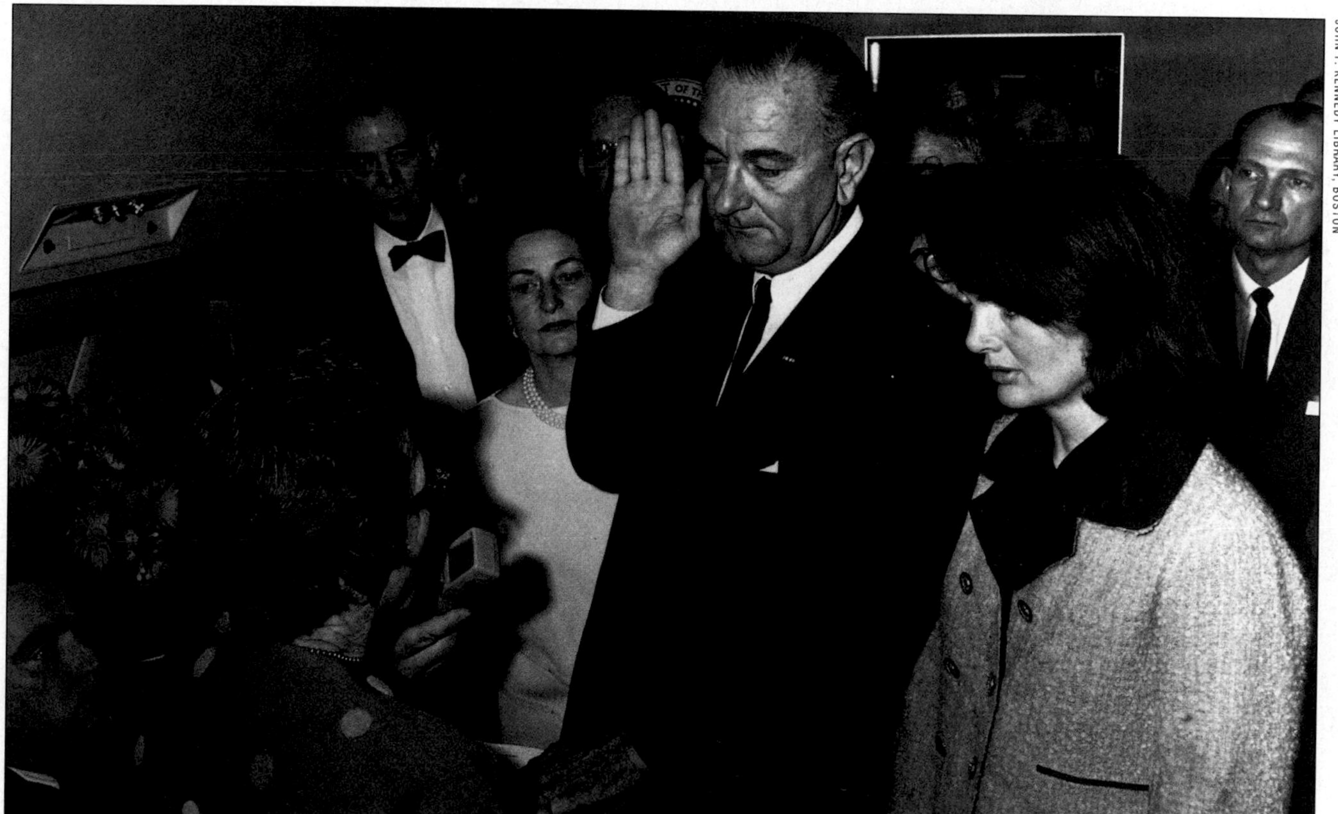

JOHN F. KENNEDY LIBRARY, BOSTON

A Change of Leaders **Vice President Lyndon Johnson takes the oath of office aboard *Air Force One* almost immediately after the assassination of President Kennedy.** *What part did Jack Ruby play in the events surrounding the Kennedy assassination?*

Richard Neustadt wrote, "He left a broken promise, that 'the torch has been passed to a new generation,' and the youngsters who identified with him felt cheated as the promise, like the glamour, disappeared."

His widow compared the Kennedy years in the White House to Camelot, the site of the legendary King Arthur's court, about which a popular musical was written in the 1960s. The romantic hero and heroine, the battle between good and evil, a time of great happiness forever lost—all these images were more commonly applied to ballads and to myths than to political figures.

Johnson's Great Society

Johnson Pushes Social Reform

Johnson's administration began in the tragedy of Kennedy's assassination and ended in the tragedy of the disastrous war in Vietnam. In between Johnson carried forward Kennedy's dream of a New Frontier, then went beyond Kennedy's domestic programs to launch his own vision of the Great Society.

In the days following Kennedy's assassination, Johnson took several steps to reassure the world that he would carry on in the same tradition as Kennedy. In his first speech following his succession to office, he said, "All I have, I would have given gladly not to be standing here today," and asked for the nation's prayers and support. Looking back on those days, Johnson told his biographer, Doris Kearns Goodwin:

> We were all spinning around and around, trying to come to grips with what had happened, but the more we tried to understand it, the more confused we got. We were like a bunch of cattle caught in the swamp, unable to move in either direction, simply circling 'round and 'round. I understood that; I knew what had to be done. There is but one way to get the cattle out of the swamp. And that is for the man on the horse to take the lead, to assume command, to provide direction. In the period of confusion after the assassination, I was that man.
>
> —Doris Kearns Goodwin, *Lyndon Johnson and the American Dream,* 1976

COURTESY BENNY ANDREWS

Federal Support for the Arts In 1965 Congress established a funding program for artists and arts organizations. This 1969 painting uses strong images to comment on African Americans' fight for civil rights in the United States. *What do you think the symbols represent?*

The differences between the two men, Kennedy and Johnson, were striking. Whereas Kennedy was handsome, sophisticated, and well-educated, Johnson could be crude and intimidating. Politeness and polish were not

★ ★ ★ GALLERY OF PRESIDENTS ★ ★ ★

Lyndon Baines Johnson

1963–1969

"Let us now join reason to faith and action to experience, to transform our unity of interest into a unity of purpose. For the hour and the day and the time are here to achieve progress without strife, to achieve change without hatred—not without difference of opinion, but without the deep and abiding divisions which scar the union for generations."

Inaugural Address, January 20, 1965

LYNDON BAYNES JOHNSON LIBRARY

BACKGROUND

- **Born 1908; Died 1973**
- **Democrat, Texas**
- **Representative, 1937–1948**
- **Served in the Senate 1949–1960**
- **Assumed the presidency 1963; elected to full term 1964**

ACHIEVEMENTS IN OFFICE

- **Civil Rights Act (1964)**
- **Voting Rights Act (1965)**
- **Medicare (1965)**

among Johnson's attributes; but he was, as he said, the man for the job. He had been an apt student of politics. A member of the House in 1937 at age 29, he advanced to the Senate in 1949 and rose quickly to the powerful position of Senate majority leader in 1955.

Johnson was a genius at building coalitions. "Let us reason together," he would say, with a touch of understatement. He then used what those who received it called "the Treatment."

Johnson's method was to find out everything he could about the person he was talking to—family, friends, strengths, weaknesses, special interests. Then Johnson would proceed to flatter, cajole, promise, threaten, all the while suggesting that the other person's decision was going to make the difference between success or failure. "Lyndon got me by the lapels and put his face on top of mine and he talked and talked," a colleague said. "I figured [the choice] was getting drowned or joining."

Fashioning a Legacy

President Johnson had boundless confidence in himself, and he knew what he wanted to do. He promised to realize the Kennedy vision, and he did—perhaps better than Kennedy ever could have.

In 1963 Kennedy's program for social change was only an emerging vision. His liberalism was cautious and uncertain. Johnson had no such uncertainties. He was a man determined to do great things, and now he had the power to change the country. What then needed changing?

The answer depended on where you looked. In the suburban shopping malls that were springing up around

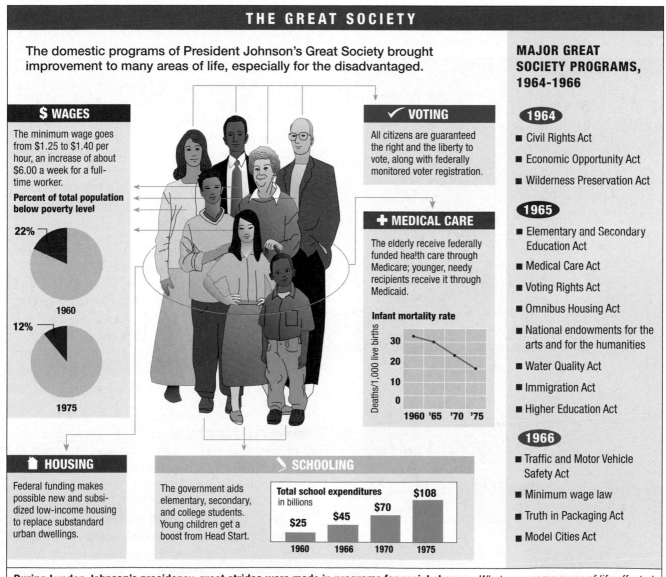

THE GREAT SOCIETY

The domestic programs of President Johnson's Great Society brought improvement to many areas of life, especially for the disadvantaged.

$ WAGES

The minimum wage goes from $1.25 to $1.40 per hour, an increase of about $6.00 a week for a full-time worker.

Percent of total population below poverty level

✓ VOTING

All citizens are guaranteed the right and the liberty to vote, along with federally monitored voter registration.

✚ MEDICAL CARE

The elderly receive federally funded health care through Medicare; younger, needy recipients receive it through Medicaid.

Infant mortality rate

HOUSING

Federal funding makes possible new and subsidized low-income housing to replace substandard urban dwellings.

SCHOOLING

The government aids elementary, secondary, and college students. Young children get a boost from Head Start.

Total school expenditures in billions

1960	1966	1970	1975
$25	$45	$70	$108

MAJOR GREAT SOCIETY PROGRAMS, 1964-1966

1964
- Civil Rights Act
- Economic Opportunity Act
- Wilderness Preservation Act

1965
- Elementary and Secondary Education Act
- Medical Care Act
- Voting Rights Act
- Omnibus Housing Act
- National endowments for the arts and for the humanities
- Water Quality Act
- Immigration Act
- Higher Education Act

1966
- Traffic and Motor Vehicle Safety Act
- Minimum wage law
- Truth in Packaging Act
- Model Cities Act

During Lyndon Johnson's presidency, great strides were made in programs for social change. *What were some areas of life affected by Great Society programs? What age groups were affected?*

the country, the United States looked robust. Measured in auto sales and economic indicators, the country hummed with prosperity. This was the nation that television viewers watched on *The Lucy Show* and other situation comedies, where everyday problems were solvable within a 22-minute show.

There was, of course, another America, as Michael Harrington revealed in his book, *The Other America.* He described a country within a country, where people were hungry when they went to bed, if in fact they had a bed. Chronic joblessness, unbudged by the New Deal or the postwar economic boom, was set like cement in rural towns and big-city slums. During the 1960s a vision of this other America slowly revealed itself to public consciousness. Strangely enough, it was Lyndon Baines Johnson (LBJ), the wheeling-dealing politician and friend of the rich, who understood the problem.

Johnson's homespun tales of his rag-poor past may have stretched the truth a bit, but he certainly knew hard times as a child growing up in central Texas. Later, as a teacher of the rural poor in his home state, he felt a great empathy for people living in grinding, persistent poverty.

© E. CREWS/THE IMAGE WORKS

A Head Start **This 3-year-old Hispanic girl is "reading" in a Head Start program.** *What was the purpose of these programs?*

LBJ cared about the poor, and he cared about his place in history. He felt he could become the first President to create a just society that all but eliminated chronic poverty and hardship in the United States.

Johnson told Congress on March 16, 1964, that "in the past we have often been called upon to wage war against foreign enemies which threaten our freedom today. Now, we are asked to declare a war on a domestic enemy which threatens the strength of our nation and the welfare of our people."

That enemy, of course, was poverty. LBJ's ambitious war on poverty would be the cornerstone of his Great Society.

The Great Society

Johnson moved quickly to push Kennedy initiatives, including the Civil Rights Act, through Congress. He launched his war on poverty with the Economic Opportunity Act, the most ambitious attempt to aid the poor in the nation's history. It established Volunteers in Service to America (VISTA), a kind of domestic peace corps of citizens working in poor neighborhoods. The act also funded Project Head Start, to give preschoolers from disadvantaged families a leg up on elementary education.

The mood of the country, still affected by the shock of Kennedy's assassination, worked in Johnson's favor during the 1964 presidential election. Johnson overwhelmingly defeated Arizona senator Barry Goldwater and seized the mandate to introduce his own program of reform.

> The Great Society rests on abundance and liberty for all. It demands an end to poverty and racial injustice . . . [It] is a place where every child can find knowledge to enrich his mind . . . where the city of man serves not only the needs of the body and the demands for commerce, but the desire for beauty and the hunger for community.
>
> —Lyndon B. Johnson, University of Michigan commencement address, 1964

The President knew that what he called the "honeymoon" of his election would not last for long. "You've got to give it all you can that first year," he said. The result was the most comprehensive reform package to pass through Congress since the New Deal reforms of 1935.

Among the most significant pieces of legislation were Medicare, federally funded health care for the elderly, and Medicaid, its companion program for the needy who were too young to qualify for Medicare. These programs were the first to make health care available to those who could not afford it. The Voting Rights

Transformed Living Spaces Improved urban housing was one of the many benefits of the Great Society programs. *What new housing department was created as part of Johnson's Great Society?*

Act of 1965 put teeth into the Fifteenth Amendment by providing for federal supervision of voter registration. Cities benefited from the Model Cities Act, which encouraged slum rehabilitation. A new department of Housing and Urban Development was created; its secretary, Robert Weaver, became the first African American to serve in a presidential cabinet.

Immigration legislation did away with a quota system that had existed for more than 50 years. As a result, people from a variety of cultures entered the United States, creating considerable variety in the ethnic mix of the population.

Successes and Limitations

Johnson's Great Society program of social and political reform is often compared with FDR's New Deal. The goals of the two were somewhat different. The New Deal sought social reforms in some areas—the creation of the Social Security system is an example. Its main goals, however, were to provide relief for the unemployed and the poor and to stimulate economic recovery.

The Great Society was more successful in creating legislative programs than in implementing them. It was underfunded, partly because the financing of the Vietnam War claimed a greater and greater proportion of the tax dollar. Still, the percentage of impoverished Americans, as measured by government standards, dropped from 22 percent in 1959 to 12 percent in 1969. The civil rights acts of 1964 and 1965 were landmark achievements of the Johnson presidency. Perhaps the greatest weakness in the Great Society program was that it promised so much that, despite its successes, critics could always point to problems yet unresolved.

Section Assessment

Main Idea

1. Use a chart like this one to show how Johnson fulfilled—and in many cases went beyond—Kennedy's idealistic vision for America.

Fulfilling a Vision	
Kennedy's Vision	Johnson Programs

Vocabulary

2. Define: mandate, coalition, pragmatist.

Checking Facts

3. How was Kennedy's pragmatism reflected in his approach to legislative reforms?
4. How did the Great Society differ from the New Deal?

Critical Thinking

5. **Making Comparisons** Compare the political styles of Kennedy and Johnson.

Science, TECHNOLOGY, and Society

Television

For decades people in the United States had learned about the world through newspapers, radio, or newsreels. That changed, however, when television came on the scene—bringing comedy, education, social issues, politics, and violence right into viewers' living rooms. By 1960 more than 45 million households had TV sets.

COMEDY

The 1962–63 top-rated comedy, *The Beverly Hillbillies,* featured a mountain family that struck oil and moved to Beverly Hills, yet remained unaffected by the posh surroundings.

TELEVISION HIGHLIGHTS

1920s

PHILO FARNSWORTH invents the first electronic television system.

1940s

COLOR TELEVISION is demonstrated in the United States for the first time in 1940. Today 90 percent of households have a color set.

1950s

REMOTE CONTROL is invented by Robert Adler and introduced by Zenith in 1955. Today at least 66 million households have remote-control devices.

UPI/BETTMANN

VIOLENCE AND MOURNING

Across the nation viewers watched in profound sadness and near-disbelief as John F. Kennedy, Jr., saluted the casket carrying his assassinated father, President John F. Kennedy.

TELEVISION PROGRESS

PORTFOLIO PROJECT

Research one of the developments in television listed on the time line. Describe the innovation and explain its effect on society. Include photographs and other graphic aids. Share your findings with your classmates, and place your written report in your portfolio.

AP/WIDE WORLD PHOTOS

RACIAL UNREST

The often violent treatment of nonviolent civil rights protesters in the 1960s was brought to the public eye. Coverage such as this of a protester taking part in a 1963 sit-in in Greensboro, North Carolina, swung public sympathy to the side of the civil rights movement.

© SWERSEY/GAMMA LIAISON

EDUCATIONAL INROADS

Since its debut in 1969, *Sesame Street* has demonstrated the power of television as an educational tool—with characters such as Big Bird helping with the lessons.

1960s

TELSTAR, a communications satellite, launches international television broadcasting in 1962 by linking the United States and Europe for up to 20 minutes.

1980s

CABLE SYSTEMS are connected to 30 percent of homes in the United States. By 1987, half of United States households have cable.

1990s

PORTABLE VIDEO CAMERAS and videotapes let families record their own activities to play back on television. *America's Funniest Home Videos* is a hit.

Technology Skill

BUILDING A DATABASE

Learning the Skill

A computerized database program can help you organize and manage a large amount of information. Once you enter data in a database table, you can quickly locate information according to key criteria. For example, if you start your own business collecting newspaper, plastic, and glass from businesses to recycle, you could have the program list all of your clients that live in a particular area. You could also identify all clients that need you to collect their recyclables on Saturdays.

Building a Database

An electronic database is a collection of facts that are stored in a file on the computer. The information is organized into different *fields.* For example, one field may be the names of your clients. Another field may be the street addresses of your clients.

A database can be organized and reorganized in any way that is useful to you. You give commands to the computer telling it what to do with the information, and it follows your commands. When you want to retrieve information, the computer searches through the records, finds the information, and displays it on the screen. By using a database management system (DBMS)—special software developed for record keeping—you can easily add, delete, change, or update information.

© BRAD MARKEL/GAMMA LIAISON

The United States Supreme Court

Practicing the Skill

This chapter mentions many landmark Supreme Court cases. Follow these steps to build a database on landmark Supreme Court cases and their significance.

1. Determine what facts you want to include in your database and research to collect that information. For example, besides the case titles, what information is important in summarizing the cases? Should you include the year, the name of the chief justice at the time, and the topic of each case? Should you list the outcome and its significance in a special field?

2. Follow the instructions in the DBMS that you are using to set up fields. Then enter each item of data in its assigned field. Take as much time as you need to complete this step. Inaccurately placed data is difficult to retrieve.

3. Determine how you want to organize the facts in the database—chronologically by the date of the case, or alphabetically by the title of the case.

4. Follow the instructions in your computer program to sort the information into order of importance.

5. Check that all the information in your database is correct. If necessary, add, delete, or change information or fields.

Applying the Skill

Research and build a database that organizes information on some other aspect of the Supreme Court. For example, you may wish to examine Supreme Court cases that have to do with the Bill of Rights or cases dealing directly with presidential powers. Build your database and explain to a partner why the database is organized the way it is and how it might be used in this class.

Additional Practice

For additional practice, see Reinforcing Skills on page 721.

The Supreme Court and Civil Liberties

JANUARY 8, 1962: GIDEON PETITIONS THE SUPREME COURT

CLARENCE EARL GIDEON WAS A MAN BEATEN DOWN BY LIFE'S CIRCUMSTANCES AND BY HIS OWN FOOLISH MISTAKES. In 1962 he was an inmate of the Florida state prison, serving time for breaking into a poolroom and stealing money. He was a frail man, 51 years old, though he looked 10 years older. His face was gray and wrinkled and his lower lip continually trembled.

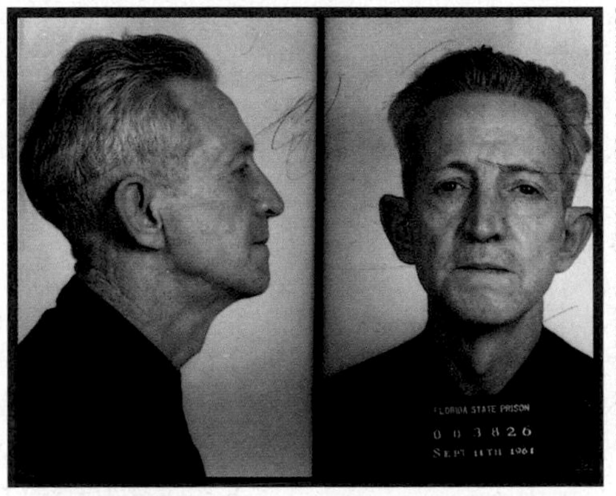
DEPARTMENT OF CORRECTIONS OF THE STATE OF FLORIDA

Civil Liberties Strengthened
The Clarence Earl Gideon case was one of many landmark decisions made by the Warren Court.

Prison life was not new to Gideon. He had served 4 previous jail terms. Poverty was also no stranger, since he had been a runaway at age 14; but now he wanted out. He worried about his family; his wife had started drinking, and his children were in foster homes. He insisted he was convicted in an unfair trial for a crime he did not commit.

So Gideon wrote the Supreme Court a letter. In pencil, on lined prison paper, he petitioned the Court to release him on the grounds that the state had denied him his rights. At the time of his trial, with no money for a lawyer, he had asked the lower court to provide him with one, but the court had refused. Gideon had conducted his own defense.

Fourteen months after Gideon mailed off his plea to the Supreme Court, his conviction was overturned. The *Gideon* v. *Wainwright* ruling reversed an earlier

GUIDE TO READING

Main Idea

Between 1954 and 1969, the Supreme Court handed down a series of decisions that brought far-reaching changes to the meaning and protection of civil liberties in the United States.

Vocabulary

- reapportionment
- due process

Read to Find Out . . .

- how reapportionment related to equal representation.
- important rulings by the Warren Court and how these rulings expanded the power of the Supreme Court.

UPI/BETTMANN

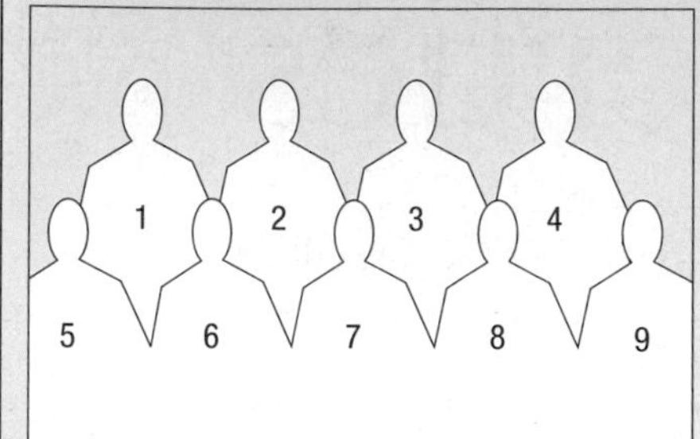

1. Byron R. White, 1962–1993
2. William J. Brennan, Jr., 1956–1990
3. Potter Stewart, 1958–1981
4. Abe Fortas, 1965–1969
5. Tom C. Clark, 1949–1967
6. Hugo C. Black, 1937–1971
7. Earl Warren, 1953–1969
8. William O. Douglas, 1939–1975
9. John M. Harlan, 1955–1971

The Warren Court, 1965 These Supreme Court justices were instrumental in one of the most extensive periods of social reform the country had ever known. *What did critics say about this reform-minded Court?*

decision and declared that, according to the Sixth Amendment, if a defendant cannot afford a lawyer, the court must supply one. The appeal to the Supreme Court by Gideon, a poor man with few resources, made legal history.

The Court's Authority

The Supreme Court Expands Its Boundaries

The Supreme Court, the branch of government that Alexander Hamilton called "the weakest of the three departments of power," has become mighty throughout its history. In its earliest days, the Court simply ruled on whether laws had been broken. In 1803 the Court expanded its powers by taking on the role of judging the validity, or constitutionality, of laws. That step sent shock waves through the young government. Presidents from Jefferson to Lincoln bridled at the expansion of judicial power that followed—but there was much more to come.

A further question remained, and it was one that would touch the lives of politicians, families, minorities, and children in modern times: Should the Court have a hand in making the country a better, safer, fairer place? That is, when legislatures are failing to bring about reform in social, economic, and political systems, should the Court step in? At issue was whether Court rulings should merely take into account precedents and laws, or consider the needs of the country.

Dwight Eisenhower did not realize it, but when he appointed Earl Warren as chief justice of the United States, he was answering these questions for some time to come. No Supreme Court in United States history went further in making reform its business than the Warren Court of the 1950s and the 1960s.

The Warren Court

The Warren Court Supports Social Reform

When Earl Warren came to Washington, D.C., in 1953, most Americans saw their country as a place of prosperity, liberty, and justice. The Warren Court, however, saw a place where equal justice under the law was elusive if you happened to be an African American, a poor person, an accused criminal, an immigrant, or a city dweller. When Warren finished his historic 16-year term as chief justice in 1969, the Court had taken direct, far-reaching action to correct what it saw as the nation's social ills. In doing so, the reform-minded Court wielded more power and made a bigger impact on the country than had many Presidents.

President Eisenhower appointed Warren to head the nation's highest court, following Warren's years as a crime-fighting district attorney and then as governor of California. Despite his conservative image, Warren's beliefs grew more liberal over the years. The chief justice's written opinions were sometimes a reversal of positions he had taken as a governor.

The Warren Court era of liberal activism was launched with the 1954 *Brown* v. *Board of Education* decision on school desegregation. Critics from Joseph McCarthy to more moderate thinkers said the Court was stepping far beyond its limits—infringing on the rights of state and local governments, intruding on family life, and threatening the moral fabric of the United States.

Calls for the chief justice's impeachment were heard periodically throughout his tenure. "Impeach Earl Warren" billboards and pamphlets appeared throughout the South and even at Earl Warren High School in Downey, California. The movement, to which Warren gave little heed, heated up when the Court entered its most active period of reform in the early 1960s.

In 1962 changes in the makeup of the Supreme Court gave Warren a clear majority of judges who were likely to side with him on most issues. In the 1960s the Court handed down a series of historic decisions affecting the nation's political process, the civil liberties of individuals, and the operation of the criminal justice system. The chart on this page highlights some of those decisions.

One Person, One Vote

Warren called *Baker* v. *Carr* "the most important case of my tenure on the Court." He was referring to one of a series of cases from 1962 to 1964 that redistributed political power in the United States.

The old methods by which states carved up voting districts were devised when this was a nation of country dwellers. When twentieth-century industrialization drew more and more people to cities, however, the size and shape of districts did not change to reflect the shifts in population.

For example, 6 million people lived in Los Angeles County in 1960. Yet, 1 state legislator, whose vote carried the same weight as the legislator from a rural district of 14,000 people, represented the city.

This, in effect, made the vote of each citizen in Los Angeles County worth less than the vote of a resident of that rural district. Farm groups and others who wished to preserve their voting power opposed a **reapportionment** proposal—a plan changing the number of legislative seats assigned to each district. The plan was defeated with the help of the governor of California at the time, Earl Warren.

In 1962, however, Chief Justice Earl Warren had a new constituency—the nation. In many places legislative districts were drawn in ways that favored a particular political party, a practice known as gerrymandering. Throughout the nation, there was a need for a redrawing of political districts according to a "one person, one vote" principle of equal representation.

In Florida, for example, one-fifth of the population lived in Dade County, where Miami is located, but Dade County residents elected only 4 of Florida's 133 state legislators. Traditionally, the Supreme Court had left such political matters as apportionment up to the state legislatures. Some citizens, however, frustrated when the legislatures did not take action, brought suits against state officials. In time, these suits came before the Supreme Court on appeal.

In the *Baker* v. *Carr* suit, the residents of Memphis, Tennessee, complained that their votes were worth less than the votes of rural residents. The Supreme Court ruled that the federal courts, which had originally declined to hear the case, should decide it. The Court's 1962 decision opened the door for the lower courts to involve themselves with reapportionment. "Never in American history has a single judicial decision opened the gates for such a massive change in the nation's political structure," printed the *Washington Post*.

Subsequent cases went further in forcing states to reorganize their voting systems. In 1964 the Court

Warren Court Decisions on Key Issues of the 1960s

Reapportionment

***Gomillion* v. *Lightfoot*, 1960**
Outlawed racial gerrymandering in case involving the city limits of Tuskegee, Alabama

***Baker* v. *Carr*, 1962**
Established federal authority to oversee that state voting districts ensure equal representation for all citizens; the ruling opened the door to Supreme Court involvement in what previously had been seen as a "political" issue outside the Court's jurisdiction

***Wesberry* v. *Sanders*, 1964**
Required that states redraw their voting districts for the United States Congress according to population; each district had to have roughly the same number of people, so every citizen's vote carried the same weight, according to the "one person, one vote" principle

***Reynolds* v. *Sims*, 1964**
Applied the "one person, one vote" standard to their state legislatures, requiring state elective districts to be reapportioned; the ruling also demanded the apportionment by population of both houses of a bicameral state legislature

School Prayer

***Engel* v. *Vitale*, 1962**
Ruled unconstitutional a nondenominational prayer drafted by the State of New York and read voluntarily in school classrooms; the decision banned prayer in public schools

***Abington* v. *Schempp*, 1963**
Banned Bible reading and other religious exercises in public schools, saying this constituted the government establishment of religion

Rights of the Accused

***Gideon* v. *Wainwright*, 1963**
Established that people accused of a crime have the right to a lawyer, even if they cannot afford one

***Escobedo* v. *Illinois*, 1964**
Ruled that people have the right to a lawyer from the time of arrest or when they become the subject of a criminal investigation

***Miranda* v. *Arizona*, 1966**
Required that accused people be informed of their right to a lawyer and their right not to testify against themselves

The Warren Court extended the reach of the Supreme Court. *What were some areas the Warren Court dealt with in its historic decisions of the 1960s?*

demanded that states redraw their voting districts—for representation to state legislatures as well as to Congress—to make them roughly equal in population. The Court also directed that in state legislatures with two houses, both should be apportioned according to population. Warren wrote the majority opinion:

> Legislators represent people, not trees or acres. Legislators are elected by voters, not farms or cities or economic interests. As long as ours is a representative form of government, and our legislatures are those instruments of government elected directly by and directly representative of the people, the right to elect legislators in a free and unimpaired fashion is a bedrock of our political system.
>
> —*Reynolds* v. *Sims,* 1964

The 1964 reapportionment rulings and the cases grouped with them affected one-third of the nation's states. In time all 50 states reshaped their legislatures.

Prayer in Schools

People knew Earl Warren to be a very religious man who read the Bible regularly. Justice Hugo Black had been a Sunday school teacher for 20 years. Yet in 1962 these two justices led the Court in banning prayer in public schools, a decision that was shocking to many Americans.

At issue in *Engel* v. *Vitale* was a 22-word nondenominational prayer drafted by the state of New York and recommended to be recited daily by public school children. The prayer read: "Almighty God, we acknowledge our dependence upon Thee, and we beg Thy blessings upon us, our parents, our teachers, and our country."

Parents of 10 students in Hyde Park, New York, objected to the voluntary readings. The Court agreed with them, saying that even voluntary prayer subjected religious minorities or nonbelievers to "indirect coercive pressure." Citing the First Amendment provision that "Congress shall make no law respecting an establishment of religion," Justice Black wrote in the majority opinion that this "must at least mean that in this country it is no part of the business of government to compose official prayers for any group of the American people to recite as a part of a religious program carried on by government."

In later decisions, the Court also prohibited Bible reading and other religious exercises in the classroom. The rulings disturbed some parents and clergy. Others, including some teachers, atheists, and religious people, were relieved. Legislators tried, and failed, to pass a constitutional amendment permitting school prayer.

The Rights of the Accused

When police arrested Ernesto Miranda at his home on charges of kidnapping and rape, he had no idea that his name would become a shorthand term for the rights of accused criminals and that his case would be a required course of study for every police recruit and law student. In *Miranda* and other key cases, however, the Warren Court handed down decisions that revolutionized how criminal justice is exercised in this country.

Warren, a former prosecutor, personally showed a great deal of concern for the rights of accused criminals and the conduct of police during the arrest and interrogation of suspects. The Court's rulings reinforced the right of accused citizens to **due process,** or the established legal rules and procedures.

The last major criminal justice ruling had come in 1936, when police were barred from torturing suspects in order to obtain confessions from them. The new wave of reform rulings began in 1963 when Clarence Earl Gideon won his appeal to the Supreme Court. The ruling upheld the right of an accused to have an attorney, even when the accused could not afford one. The decision resulted in a new trial for Gideon, in which he was represented by a local attorney and was acquitted.

In the 1964 case of *Escobedo* v. *Illinois,* the Court ruled that the right to legal counsel begins at the moment of arrest or as soon as someone becomes the subject of police suspicion. Warren felt, however, that the Court needed to take stronger action to protect accused criminals. This led to one of the most controversial rulings in the Supreme Court's history.

The case was *Miranda* v. *Arizona,* which came before the Court in 1966. Police had ar-

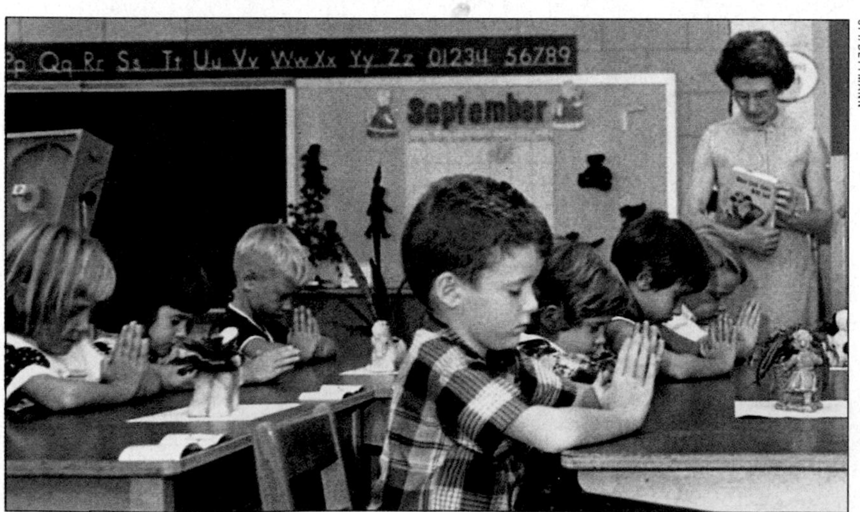

UPI/BETTMANN

Prayer in the Classroom ***Engel*** **v.** ***Vitale*** **raised the issue of prayer in public schools.** *According to Justice Black's written opinion, what part should government play in issues relating to religion?*

UPI/BETTMANN

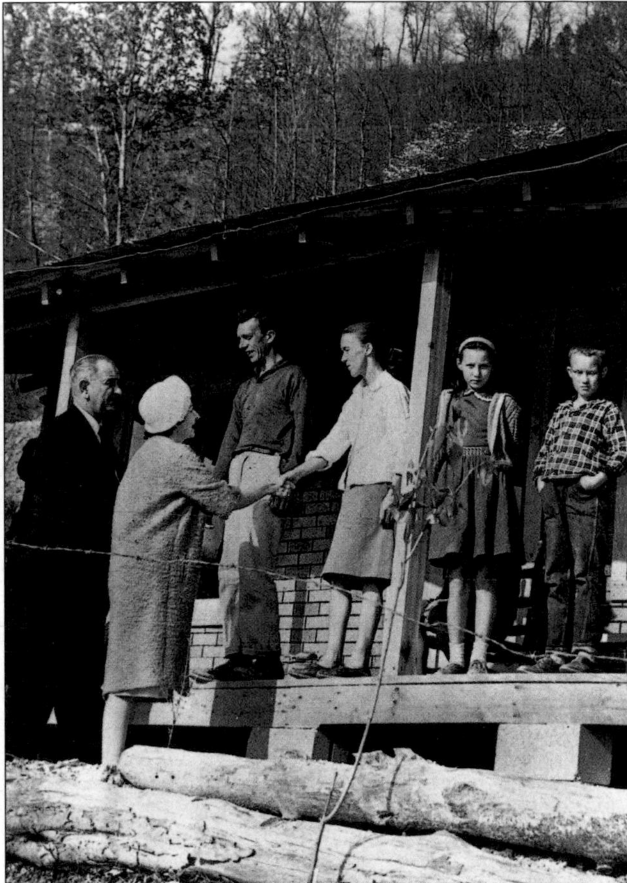

Extending a Helping Hand President and Mrs. Johnson visit with the Fletcher family in Inez, Kentucky. *What three groups benefited greatly from LBJ's reform programs?*

rested Ernesto Miranda for kidnapping and rape. After the police interrogated him for 2 hours, Miranda signed a confession. In a divided 5–4 ruling, the Court set aside his conviction.

Chief Justice Warren gave specific instructions that would sound familiar to anyone who has watched police shows on television: "Prior to any questioning, the person must be warned that he has a right to remain silent, that any statement he does make may be used as evidence against him, and that he has a right to the presence of an attorney, either retained or appointed."

The "Miranda card" that police departments use today lists instructions to read to suspects at the time of their arrest. Arresting officers must prove that a defendant has waived the right to legal counsel.

Police departments were disturbed by the *Miranda* ruling, saying it restricted them in performing their duties. Richard Nixon used the ruling to boost the "crime in the streets" issue during the 1968 presidential race. On the other hand, a supporter of the ruling quoted Winston Churchill: "The quality of a nation's civilization can be largely measured by the methods it uses in the enforcement of its criminal law."

The Reform Achievements

Far-reaching Reforms Require Follow-up

The Supreme Court, Congress, and the President did not always agree on social reform. Controversies marked the reform period from 1954 to 1969. Decisions made during this time are still being argued about today, and Congress faces tough decisions about how to pay for the aid programs launched more than 30 years ago.

Nevertheless, the efforts of the 3 branches of government combined to bring about the greatest package of reform measures since FDR's New Deal. One measure of the change is to recall how, in 1948, civil rights proposals by President Truman splintered the Democratic party. Some 20 years later, a Democratic President, Lyndon Johnson, worked with Congress in providing for minorities, the poor, and the elderly. The Supreme Court upheld much of this legislation and extended individual liberties.

Yet some groups still remained in the shadows in regard to reform. One group was women, who were not a minority in terms of their numbers, but who frequently played a secondary role to men. Women watched the changes of the Kennedy–Johnson era with interest and planned their own strategies for reform.

Section Assessment

Main Idea

1. Use a diagram like this one to write and support a generalization about the effect of the Warren Court on individual civil liberties in the United States.

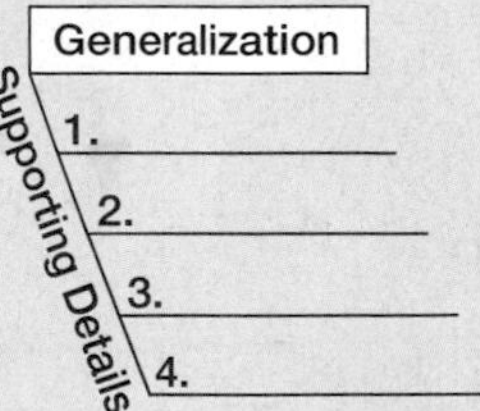

Vocabulary

2. Define: reapportionment, due process.

Checking Facts

3. Why did the Supreme Court rule that prayer in the public schools was unconstitutional?
4. What were the main Supreme Court decisions protecting the rights of the accused?

Critical Thinking

5. **Determining Cause and Effect** Why did Chief Justice Warren consider the reapportionment decisions the most significant ones made by the Court during his tenure?

SPORTS: The Harvard/Yale football game is canceled

One Day in History

Friday, November 22, 1963

IN MEMORIAM

- **Broadway theaters closed and musical events were canceled.**
- **Memorial programs preempted regular shows on television networks.**
- **Holiday lighting was turned off.**
- **The lights in Times Square were turned off.**
- **Wall Street stopped business early.**
- **The conductor of the Boston Symphony Orchestra led the orchestra in the funeral march from Beethoven's third symphony. More than 2,600 people stood solemnly with bowed heads.**

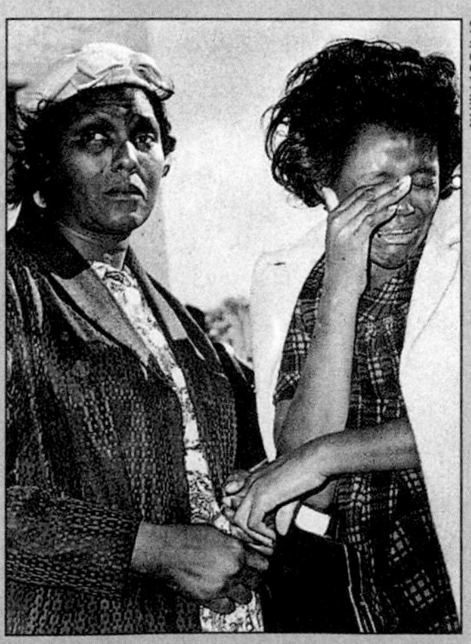

Two women outside Parkland Hospital react to news of Kennedy's death. Much came to a standstill as a result of this tragic event.

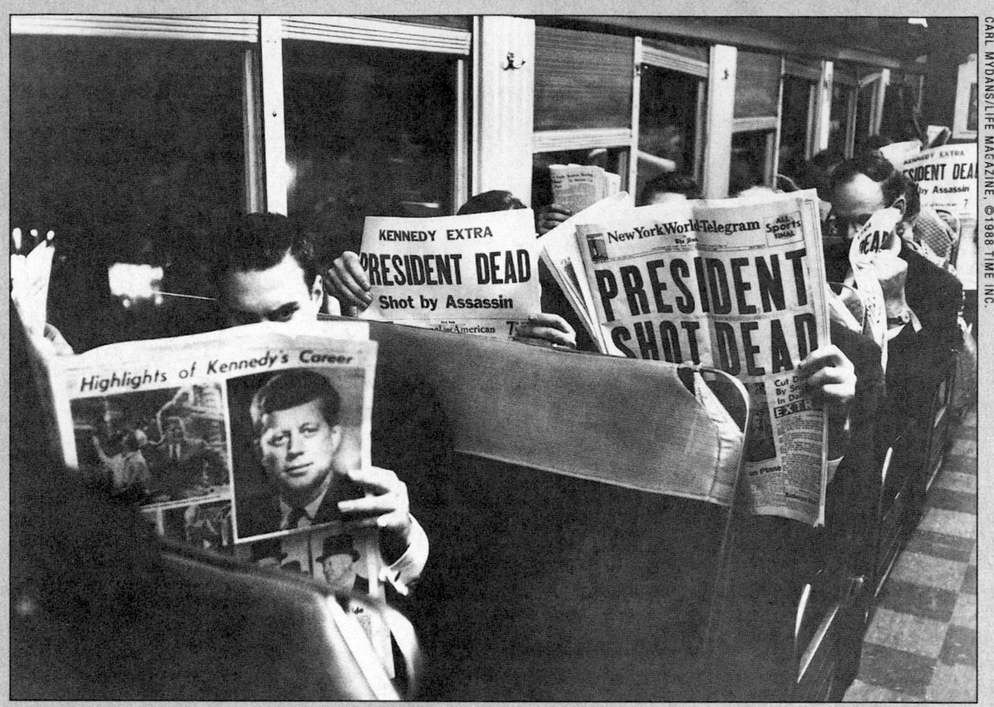

Heads Bowed These commuters, like most people across the nation, are solemnly focused on details of the Kennedy assassination.

Kennedy Assassinated

The President is shot and killed as he rides in a motorcade in downtown Dallas

DALLAS—President John F. Kennedy was shot and killed shortly after 12:30 P.M. today as he rode in an open Lincoln Continental in a motorcade through downtown Dallas. Kennedy was rushed to Parkland Memorial Hospital. He did not regain consciousness and was declared dead 30 minutes later. Mrs. Kennedy was near her husband at the hospital when he died.

With Kennedy in the limousine were his wife, Jacqueline, and Texas governor and Mrs. John Connally. The governor sustained serious injuries.

Ninety-nine minutes after Kennedy was declared dead, District Judge Sarah T. Hughes, on board *Air Force One* at Love Field, swore in Vice President Lyndon B. Johnson as the thirty-sixth President of the United States.

One Day in History, Friday, November 22, 1963

NATION: Lee Harvey Oswald, a worker in the Texas School Book Depository, has been charged with the murder of President Kennedy.

AP/WIDE WORLD PHOTOS

Top TV Shows

1. *The Beverly Hillbillies*
2. *Bonanza*
3. *The Dick Van Dyke Show*
4. *Petticoat Junction*
5. *The Andy Griffith Show*
6. *The Lucy Show*
7. *Candid Camera*
8. *The Ed Sullivan Show*
9. *The Danny Thomas Show*
10. *My Favorite Martian*

ARCHIVE PHOTOS

POPULAR FILMS

- ***Lilies of the Field***
- ***Hud***
- ***The V.I.P.s***
- ***Tom Jones***

DANCE

The Limbo Rock This acrobatic dance became popular in 1963, introduced by Chubby Checker, father of the original twist.

© MICHAEL OCHS ARCHIVES

MUSIC

Beach Boys This clean-cut group from Southern California, with their melodic songs about hot rods and surfing, had 5 hit songs in 1963.

MARKET BASKET

Here is where a dollar will go:

First-class stamp . . . . 5¢

FILE PHOTO BY DOUG MINDELL

Eggs, one dozen . . . . 55¢
Bacon, one pound . . . . 69¢
Bread, one loaf . . . . 19¢
Coffee, one pound . . . . 38¢
Kodak Brownie camera $22

FILE PHOTO BY DOUG MINDELL

Royalite portable typewriter $49.95
Woman's cardigan sweater $7.99
Man's chambray shirt $1.47
Movie ticket . . . . 75¢
Flashlight battery . . . . 32¢
Schoolbag $3
New York subway token . . . . 15¢
Bicycle $47.95
Ford Fastback Coupe $3,095

Chapter  Assessment

Self-Check Quiz

Visit the *American Odyssey* Web site at americanodyssey.glencoe.com and click on ***Chapter 21—Self-Check Quiz*** to prepare for the Chapter Test.

Reviewing Key Terms

On a separate sheet of paper, write the vocabulary term that best completes each sentence below.

mandate	**reapportionment**
coalition	**due process**
pragmatist	**liberalism**

1. A ________ comes up with practical solutions to individual situations.

2. Through ________ the rights of the accused are protected.

3. People united by a common purpose form a strong ________.

4. Voting power was put in proportion to population by ________.

5. Winning an election by a large margin would indicate a clear ________ from the people.

Recalling Facts

1. Why did John Kennedy call himself a pragmatist, not a liberal? Cite an example of his pragmatism.

2. What ideals of the Kennedy years does the establishment of the Peace Corps reflect?

3. What kinds of reforms had Kennedy begun to take action on when he was assassinated?

4. What was the conclusion of the Warren Commission related to the assassination of Kennedy? What have critics said about the commission's findings?

5. What is a mandate? How were Kennedy's and Johnson's abilities to carry out their programs affected by their respective electoral mandates?

6. Explain how the New Frontier differed from the Great Society. Which was more effective? Why?

7. What was the limitation to many Great Society programs?

8. How did gerrymandering affect voters' rights? How did the Supreme Court address this in the 1960s?

9. What was the Supreme Court's reasoning for banning prayer and religious exercises in public schools?

10. How were the rights of accused people expanded during the 1960s?

Critical Thinking

1. Making Generalizations Identify a common theme in the various laws and Supreme Court decisions described in this chapter.

2. Making Comparisons Use a chart like this one to compare the public image, political style, and political experience of Presidents Kennedy and Johnson.

	Kennedy	Johnson
Public Image		
Political Style		
Political Experience		

3. Demonstrating Reasoned Judgment Some have argued that expanding the rights of the accused has made it more difficult to prosecute criminals and has been responsible for an increase in crime. Write an essay giving your opinion.

4. Evaluating Information When Johnson became President, he initially kept all of Kennedy's cabinet appointees—even though there were political differences, and Johnson knew that Kennedy's appointees might resent him. Why do you think Johnson retained these officials?

Portfolio Project

PORTFOLIO PROJECT

In *Baker* v. *Carr* and subsequent rulings, the Supreme Court made decisions that led to the reapportionment of state electoral districts. Do library research (books, newspaper stories, magazine articles) to find out how reapportionment, including recent Supreme Court rulings, has affected your state. Write a summary, and place it in your portfolio.

Cooperative Learning

With a small group, research one of the Kennedy or Johnson reform programs—the Peace Corps, the Alliance for Progress, Project Head Start, or the Job Corps, for example. In addition to using library reference sources, you may also find listings of local program offices in the government listings of your telephone directory. Use your research to answer questions such as these: Did the program achieve its goals? Is it still in existence? Has it expanded or contracted? What problems has it faced or is it facing? Share what you learn with your class. Display visual aids if appropriate.

Reinforcing Skills

Building a Database Prepare a database of Supreme Court rulings in the last six months. Use the resources at your local library to find information on the majority opinions, dissenting opinions, and subjects of the rulings. You may add any other information to your database that you consider appropriate.

GEOGRAPHY AND HISTORY

Georgia Reapportionment, 1964

In 1964 Georgia had 10 congressional districts; if split up equally, the average population of each was 394,312.

- ■ Within 15% above or below average district population
- ■ More than 15% below
- ■ More than 15% above

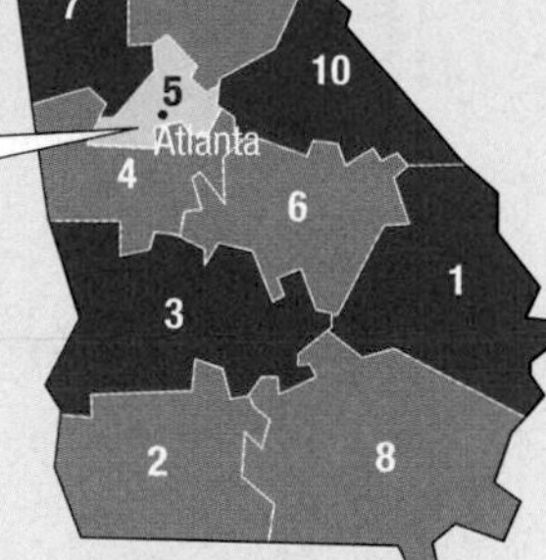

Population of heavily urban Fifth District: 823,680—108% above average district population

Before Reapportionment

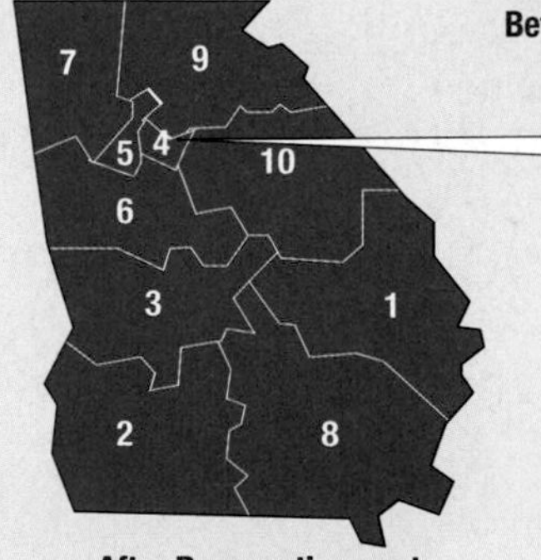

Old Fifth District split into two; other more rural districts shrink

After Reapportionment

Study the maps to answer the following questions:

1. How many congressional districts did Georgia have before reapportionment in 1964? After reapportionment?
2. Before reapportionment, how many state legislative districts were more than 15 percent below average in population? How far above average was the Fifth District?
3. Legislative seats were tied to districts, regardless of the population of the districts. What, therefore, was the political significance of the population differences among districts before reapportionment?
4. What happened to the old Fifth District after reapportionment?
5. After reapportionment, how many districts fell above or below the average in population?

Technology Activity

Using a Word Processor Use library resources or the Internet to locate information about the assassinations of John F. Kennedy, Martin Luther King, Jr., and Robert Kennedy. Use the information you find and your word processor to compose a ballad-type song honoring their memory. Experiment with different fonts, graphics, and borders to create an attractive song sheet.

Standardized Test Practice

1. The New Deal and the Great Society were *most* alike in that they both

A emphasized expanded civil rights for African Americans.

B had as their main goals relief for the unemployed and economic recovery.

C increased the role of the federal government in people's lives.

D went into effect despite strong presidential opposition.

Test-Taking Tip: Eliminate answers that do not make sense. For example, both programs came about largely through the efforts of Presidents Roosevelt and Johnson. Therefore, you can rule out answer D.

2. All of the following were effects of rulings by the Warren Court EXCEPT

A involvement of federal courts in the reapportionment of state election districts.

B extended rights for people accused of crimes.

C protection of religious minorities through greater separation of church and state.

D increased state authority at the expense of federal authority.

Test-Taking Tip: This question calls for an answer that does NOT fit the question. The Warren Court expanded individual civil liberties and the power of the judicial branch. Eliminate answers that had either of those *effects.*

Voices of Protest

1966: GRAPE GROWERS AND WORKERS MEET

Picking grapes in the California fields was hot, dirty, difficult work. When thirsty, workers had to go for their own water, costing them valuable picking time. To remedy such conditions, a new union, the United Farm Workers (UFW), headed by César Chávez, sent its best negotiator to talk with the ranch owner.

Cofounder of the UFW with César Chávez, Dolores Huerta was a tough negotiator. She demanded protective clothing for the workers and a pollution-reduction device for the tractors. She insisted that each crew receive a can of drinking water. She demanded better wages for the grape pickers.

"Sister, it sounds to me like you're asking for the moon for these people," said one of the rancher's lawyers.

"Brother, I'm not asking for the moon for the farmworkers. All we want is just a little ray of sunshine for them," Huerta replied.

Huerta and her fellow Mexican Americans, like members of other minority groups, followed the civil rights movement with great interest. They hoped the time was right for them to achieve progress in their own struggle for equality.

Meanwhile, the nation itself faced social turbulence that turned into a social revolution. White, middle-class women began questioning their traditional role in society. Many young people began to reject the values of their parents. Some attempted to establish their own culture, a counterculture to the one they had known before. ■

HISTORY JOURNAL

Based on what you already know, write down why you think Hispanic Americans, Native Americans, women, youth, and other groups may have organized protest movements in the post–World War II era.

Chapter Overview

Visit the *American Odyssey* Web site at americanodyssey.glencoe.com and click on ***Chapter 22—Chapter Overview*** to preview the chapter.

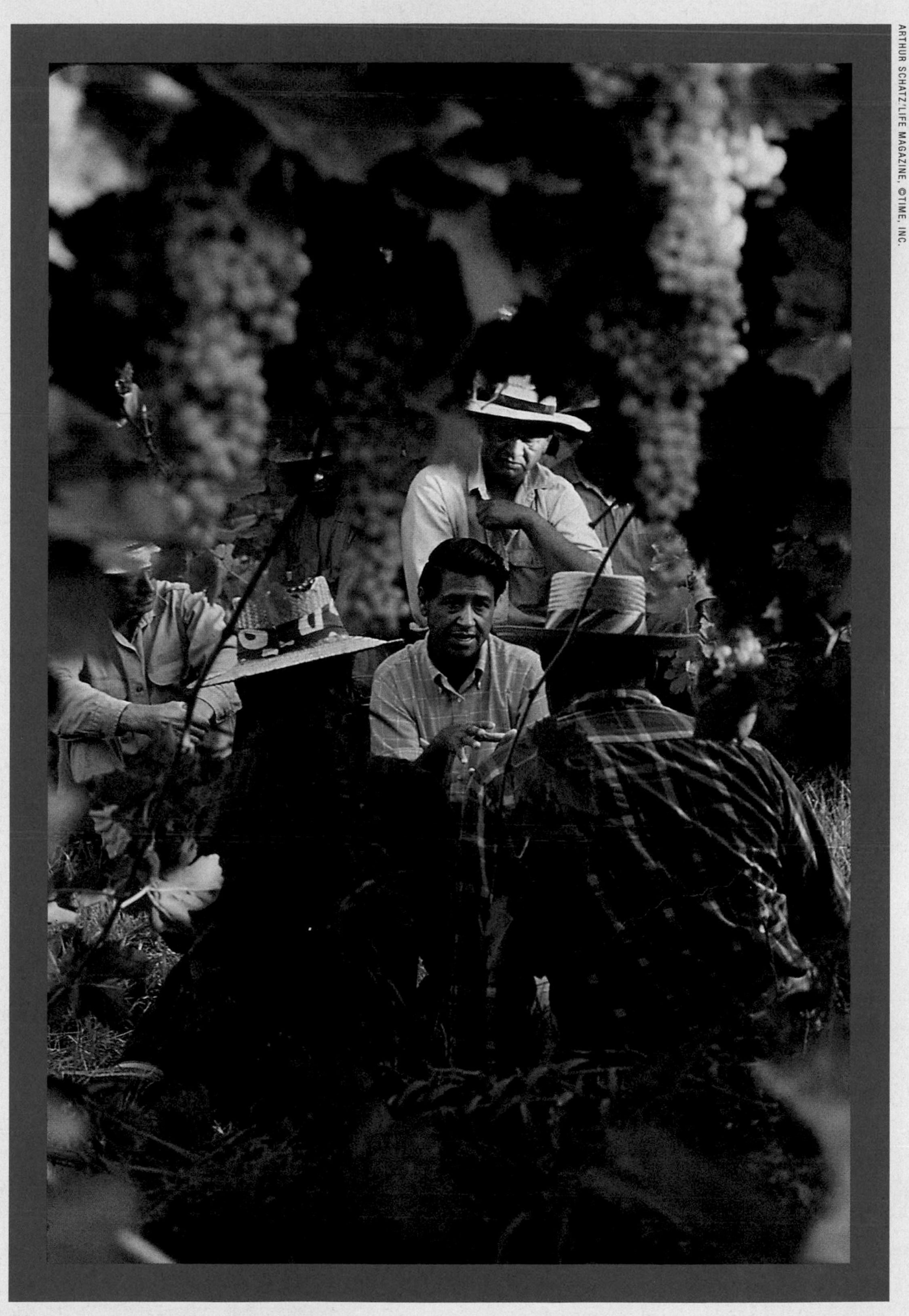

ARTHUR SCHATZ/LIFE MAGAZINE, ©TIME, INC.

LEADERS SUCH AS CÉSAR CHÁVEZ HELPED MINORITY GROUPS FIGHT FOR CIVIL RIGHTS.

The Revival of Feminism

NOVEMBER 1964: WOMEN SPEAK OUT AGAINST OPPRESSION

AP/WIDE WORLD PHOTOS

Second-Class Citizens
Casey Hayden checks students' credentials.

DURING THE SUMMER OF 1964, CASEY HAYDEN AND MARY KING SHARED WITH OTHER STUDENT NONVIOLENT COORDINATING COMMITTEE (SNCC) MEMBERS THE DANGERS OF WORKING FOR CIVIL RIGHTS IN THE SOUTH. Tear gas, water from fire hoses, snarling dogs, and police clubs did not distinguish between women or men, but hit both with equal force. Hayden and King, both white women, learned about bravery by seeing their African American "sisters" beaten so badly they could only whisper the word *freedom.* They learned about commitment from Fannie Lou Hamer, who was evicted from her home when she tried to register to vote, but who never gave up.

Hayden and King also gained insight from working for SNCC that summer. They concluded that as white, middle-class women, they too were second-class citizens.

In the early 1960s nearly half the students sitting in at the lunch counters and riding the freedom buses were women. Yet few women had leadership roles within SNCC itself. Ironically, "women's work" was to type memos, make sandwiches, take minutes at meetings, and perform other menial tasks, but not to make decisions. Finally, Hayden and King wrote an unsigned memo protesting the men's attitude:

> Assumptions of male superiority [among SNCC men] are as widespread and deep-rooted and every much as crippling to the woman as the assumptions of white supremacy are to the Negro. . . . [We need to] stop the discrimination and start the slow process of changing values and ideas so that all of us gradually come to understand that this is no more a man's world than it is a white world.
>
> —SNCC Position Paper, 1964

GUIDE TO READING

Main Idea

The women's movement that took shape in the 1960s sought to redefine the role of women at home, in school, at work, and in professional and personal relationships.

Vocabulary

- women's liberation
- feminist

Read to Find Out . . .

- the issues and goals of the women's movement in the 1960s.
- how actions by Congress and the Courts advanced women's rights and why some people opposed these actions.

The response to the memo was laughter and scorn. The next fall the two women tried again, this time in a signed memo addressed to other SNCC women. "Perhaps we can start to talk with each other more openly than in the past," they wrote, "and create a community of support for each other." The time was not right for such an appeal, though. Then, a few months later, the pressures of black separatism pushed whites of both sexes out of SNCC.

Hayden and King concluded that the fight for **women's liberation**—freedom from the limits of traditionally female roles—was a separate fight. The women's experience in the civil rights movement provided them with some strategies, but equality for women would require its own organization and its own movement.

Origins of the Women's Movement

Women Express Growing Discontent

The women's movement that sprang up in the 1960s had multiple origins, which perhaps accounts for how quickly it swept the country. One wing of the women's movement, founded on the experiences of women like Hayden and King, grew out of the civil rights struggle. Another got its start with Betty Friedan, who first identified the "problem that had no name." In addition, President Kennedy in 1961 appointed a Presidential Commission on the Status of Women, chaired at first by Eleanor Roosevelt and later by Esther Peterson.

Although the movement began primarily among white, middle-class women, by the 1970s it had spread across all racial, social, and economic lines. The movement did not achieve all its legislative goals. Nevertheless, it accomplished major changes in the status of women at home, in school, at work, and in professional and personal relationships.

The Early History

In the 1800s the struggle for women's rights was a parallel movement to the antislavery crusade and involved many of the same people. Susan B. Anthony and Elizabeth Cady Stanton, for example, were reformers who were active in both struggles. For a time, achieving both objectives seemed possible. An 1838 issue of the abolitionist newspaper *The Liberator* stated, "As our object is universal emancipation, to redeem women as well as men from a servile to an equal condition—we shall go for the rights of women to their utmost extent." The women, however, eventually split with the abolitionist men, who worried that the issue of women's equality might weaken support for the fight against slavery.

Women gained the right to vote only after a long struggle. As late as 1910 only Wyoming, Colorado, Utah, and Idaho had given women full voting rights. Then in 1919 Congress finally passed the Nineteenth Amendment, guaranteeing these rights to all women. The amendment was ratified the following year. After the voting rights victory, little happened in the women's movement. Although more and more women joined the labor force, most of them were steered into low-paying categories of so-called women's work, such as clerical, teaching, and factory jobs.

Such was the situation when Betty Friedan published her landmark book *The Feminine Mystique* in 1963. The book ridiculed the notions that women were only suited for low-paying jobs and that achievement for women could be measured only by their success as wives and mothers. Her ideas struck a chord with many women across the country, and they began to consider alternatives to marriage, childbearing, and homemaking. Yet at the same time, the book inspired strong opposition among many women who rejected Friedan's ideas as an attack on traditional roles.

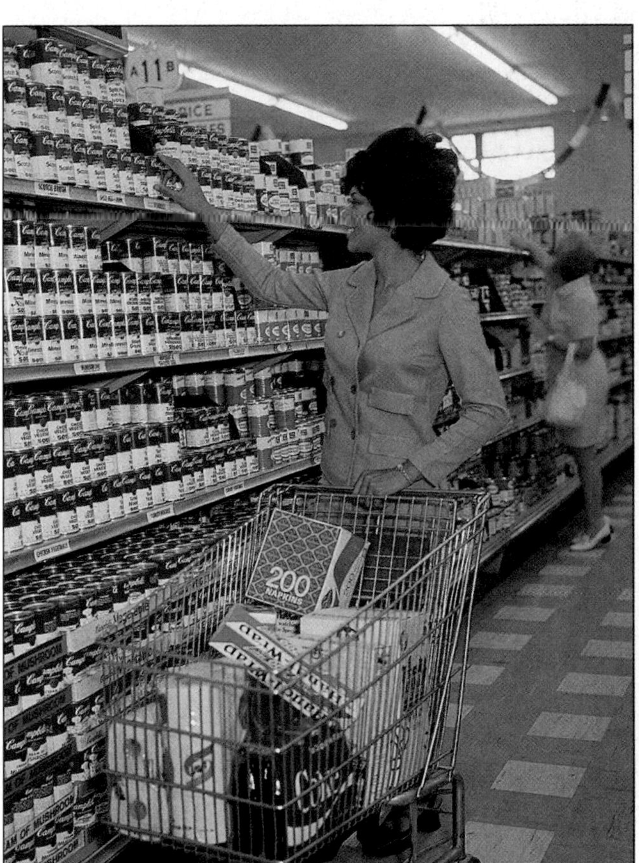

© LAMBERT/ARCHIVE PHOTOS

Women's Roles Until the women's movement of the 1960s, it was believed that women's fulfillment came only through the roles of wife and mother. *What person challenged that belief?*

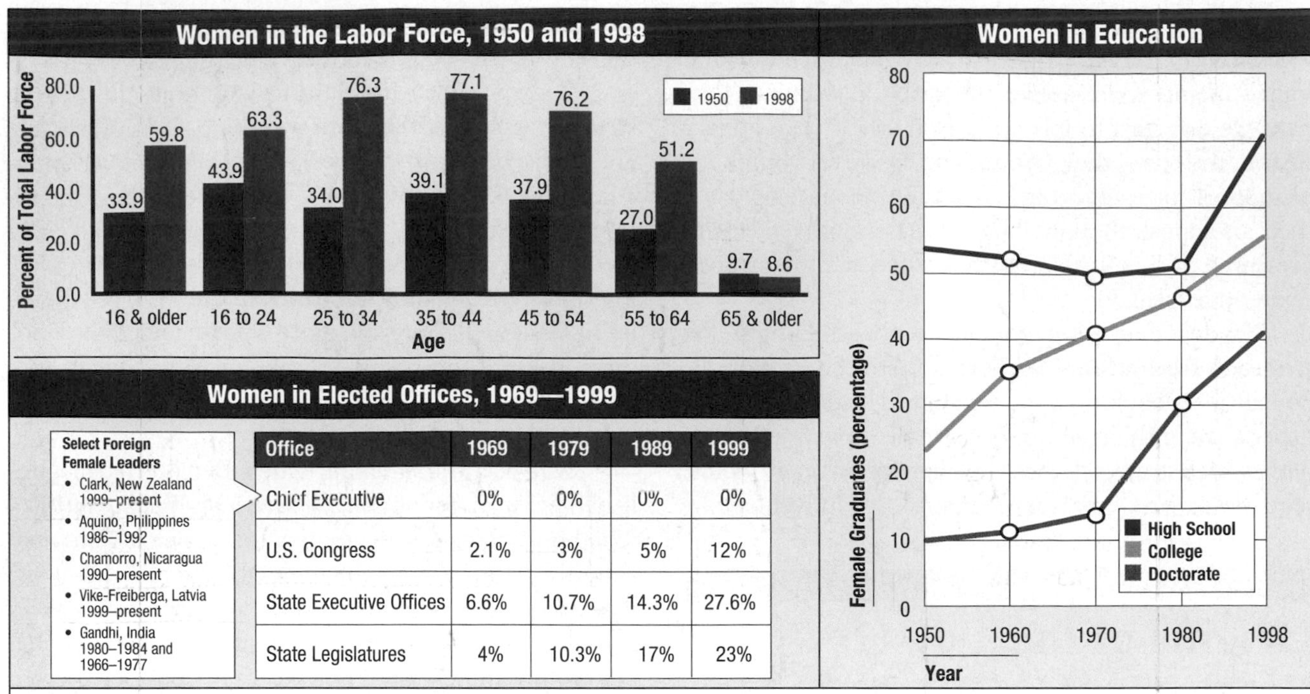

Office	1969	1979	1989	1999
Chief Executive	0%	0%	0%	0%
U.S. Congress	2.1%	3%	5%	12%
State Executive Offices	6.6%	10.7%	14.3%	27.6%
State Legislatures	4%	10.3%	17%	23%

Statistics reveal that women have made strides in the areas of work, schooling, and politics—although obstacles to equal opportunity still exist. *What story do the graphs and charts above tell you about the progress of women in the last half of this century?*

For an online update of this graph, visit americanodyssey.glencoe.com and click on ***Textbook Updates—Chapter 22.***

The Woman's Dilemma

Minority women faced a special problem in that they encountered both sexual and racial discrimination. They experienced sexual discrimination by white and African American men and racial discrimination by whites, men, and other women. In describing that period, author Toni Morrison says African American women "look at white women and see the enemy, for they know that racism is not confined to white men and that there are more white women than men in this country."

Many African American, Hispanic American, Native American, and Asian American women chose to delay their fight for equality in one sphere while they struggled for recognition in the other. Many women chose to seek full civil liberties for their ethnic group as their first objective. Equality between men and women would have to come later.

Women's Issues in the 1960s

Women Demand Equal Rights

When the President's Commission on the Status of Women issued its report in October 1963, relatively few people noticed. The civil rights struggle at home and the Vietnam War abroad claimed much more public attention. As a follow-up to the commission, however, a permanent Citizens' Advisory Council on the Status of Women was formed, and 32 states set up their own commissions. These actions produced a strong network for the future of **feminists,** or activists for women's equal rights. The commission's report identified many of the issues that would occupy feminists over the next decades. It presented statistics on how women fared in employment, in education, and in government.

Economic Rights

In 1960 women made up one-third of the nation's workforce. Most of their jobs, however, offered less pay and prestige than the positions held by men. For example, women made up only 5 percent of the nation's managers and administrators and 12 percent of all professional and technical workers.

On average, for every dollar that a man earned on a job in the 1960s, a woman with the same job earned only 59 cents. The Equal Pay Act of 1963 required employers to pay women the same as men for the same work. This act did not, however, address the discrimination women faced in actually getting jobs.

More important gains came through the inclusion of women in Title VII of the Civil Rights Act of 1964, which prohibited discrimination in employment on the basis of sex as well as of race.

Still, women would need to receive equal education and training, or laws alone would never be able to ensure them equal job opportunities. In 1960 women made up only 37 percent of the nation's undergraduate college students and received just 10 percent of the doctoral degrees conferred.

Political Rights

By the early 1960s women had been voting for 40 years, but they had achieved little success in obtaining political office, either elected or appointed. In 1963, for example, 351 women served in state legislatures, holding only 5 percent of the total legislative seats. Thirteen women held seats in Congress, down from a record number of 19 in 1961. The chart on page 726 gives information about the number of women holding high office in the United States and in other nations.

Reproductive Rights

At the same time that women were growing more aware of the limits on their economic and political freedoms, many also began demanding more personal freedoms. The right to control their own sexuality and reproductivity became a rallying cry of many feminists.

In 1960 the Food and Drug Administration approved the sale of the birth control pill, ushering in a period of new sexual freedom. Married and unmarried women became more knowledgeable about their own health and their bodies. Many women felt that the pill gave them the freedom to be sexually active without the risk of pregnancy. The pill gave these women more opportunity to make their own decisions about their bodies.

Meanwhile, many women had been making these decisions another way—through abortion. Because abortions were illegal, finding a qualified physician who was willing to perform the procedure was difficult and costly. Many who could not afford to have a safe abortion resorted to procedures performed by unqualified people. Many women suffered injury, sterility, or death because of unsafe abortions.

Some women took this risk because they did not want to be mothers; others chose abortion because they felt they were too poor or otherwise unfit to care for a baby. Still others were terrified of being pregnant and unmarried, a condition that carried a heavy social stigma at the time.

The push for reform of existing abortion laws came first from some doctors and lawyers, who were acutely aware of the dangers of illegal abortions. Many feminists soon joined them. Many other people, however, believed that abortions should not be allowed. By the time of the 1972 Democratic party convention, abortion had become an explosive political issue. Although feminists were not successful in including a plank on abortion in the 1972 Democratic platform, the issue has refused to fade and is still bitterly contested today.

Social and Gender Relationships

As women reexamined their roles in society, old ways of relating to family members, husbands, friends, bosses, and fellow workers all came under question. Women postponed marriages as they prepared themselves for careers, and the divorce rate climbed as more and more women chose to exercise their options rather than remain in unsatisfactory marriages.

Many men willingly examined and adjusted their attitudes in response to the evolving consciousness of women. For other men, understanding their changing roles proved frustrating; many found it difficult to get beyond the most trivial issues. "It's getting so you don't know what to do when you come to a door," one man complained. "Open it and a women's libber comes through, you get a dirty look. Don't open it and you feel like an unmannered slob who just kicked his grandmother in the shins."

Women's Responses to the Issues

Feminists and Antifeminists Organize

Two types of women's rights organizations had sprung up in the United States by the mid-1960s, and both were made up primarily of white, middle-class, college-educated women. The organizations differed in the age groups they represented and in their organizational structures. Both groups, however, frequently worked together on legislative and political issues, exchanging ideas and strategies.

The Founding of NOW

It started as a statement scribbled on Betty Friedan's luncheon napkin. It became a large and powerful national organization that has helped elect politicians, that has helped correct inequality in women's employment, and that wields considerable lobbying power today in the halls of government in Washington, D.C.

Hot Buttons NOW quickly became a leader in the fight for women's rights. *What kinds of issues does NOW deal with?*

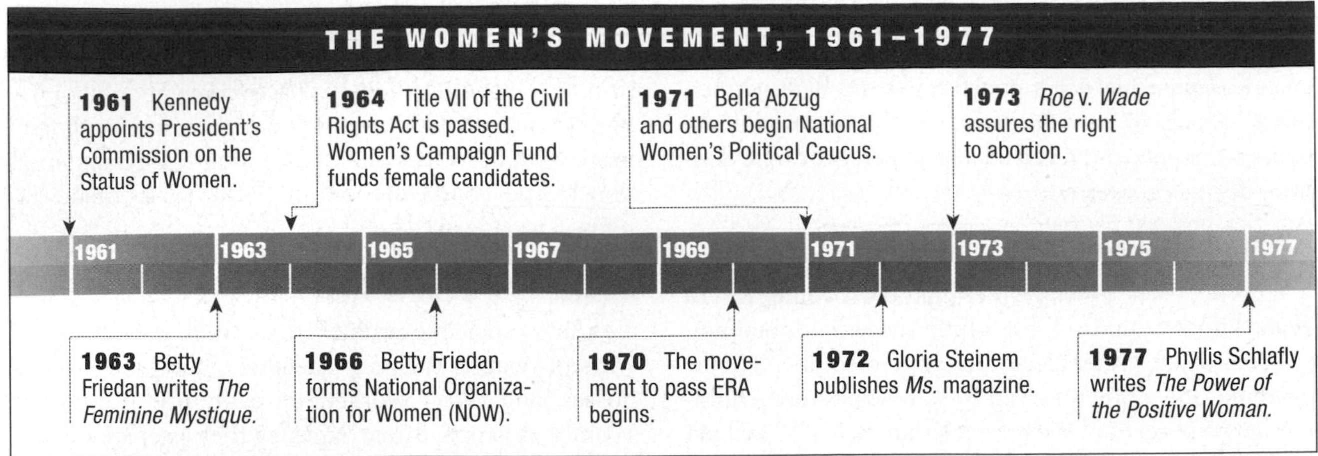

THE WOMEN'S MOVEMENT, 1961–1977
1961 Kennedy appoints President's Commission on the Status of Women.
1964 Title VII of the Civil Rights Act is passed. Women's Campaign Fund funds female candidates.
1971 Bella Abzug and others begin National Women's Political Caucus.
1973 Roe v. Wade assures the right to abortion.
1961
1963
1965
1967
1969
1971
1973
1975
1977
1963 Betty Friedan writes The Feminine Mystique.
1966 Betty Friedan forms National Organization for Women (NOW).
1970 The movement to pass ERA begins.
1972 Gloria Steinem publishes Ms. magazine.
1977 Phyllis Schlafly writes The Power of the Positive Woman.

The National Organization for Women (NOW) began in 1966 at a conference on the status of women. The women were concerned that complaints of sex discrimination before the Equal Employment Opportunity Commission (EEOC) were not being given serious consideration. Whereas cases of racial discrimination were filed by organizations or government agencies, cases of sex discrimination were filed by individuals and, therefore, received less attention. Conference participants, therefore, decided to form a civil rights organization for women.

During lunch the following day, 28 women and men each contributed $5 for expenses, and Friedan scribbled on a paper napkin the name of the new organization and its purpose. The statement of purpose was accepted virtually unchanged 4 months later at the first formal meeting of the organization, which named Friedan president. The statement of purpose read:

© ADAM SCULL/GLOBE PHOTOS

Momentum Grows Bella Abzug, left, represented New York in Congress and helped found the National Women's Political Caucus. Gloria Steinem, right, helped Abzug establish the caucus; she also founded *Ms.* magazine. *How did NWPC help the women's movement make progress?*

> To take action to bring women into full participation in the mainstream of American society now, assuming all the privileges and responsibilities thereof in truly equal partnership with men.
>
> —NOW, Statement of Purpose, 1966

Eight years later NOW's membership had soared to 40,000 people in 1,000 chapters. By 1995 its membership had reached 250,000, and the organization had an approximate annual budget of $7 million. At its first national conference, NOW outlined its goals: passage of a constitutional amendment guaranteeing equal rights for all, enforcement of Title VII of the Civil Rights Act, maternity leave benefits, better child care, equal and unsegregated education, equal job training opportunities, and abortion rights.

NOW's success has helped inspire the creation of several other women's organizations. The National Women's Political Caucus (NWPC), founded in 1971, worked to put women in public office and also supported political candidates of both sexes who were sympathetic to feminist issues. In 1974 the Women's Campaign Fund began to raise money for female candidates. Two women achieved important political breakthroughs that year. Ella Grasso was elected governor of Connecticut, the first woman to head a state in her own right, not as a successor to her husband. Voters in San Jose, California, elected Janet Gray Hayes as mayor, the first woman to head a large city.

Minority women also formed separate organizations. These included the North American Indian Women's Association in 1970, a conference of Mexican American women in 1971, the Conference of Puerto Rican Women in 1972, and the National Black Feminist Organization in 1972.

The growing momentum of the women's movement was evident by July 1972, when *Ms.*, a feminist magazine, published its first issue. A preview edition of 300,000 copies completely sold out in eight days. The magazine took up issues that up until then had never found their way into the pages of more traditional women's magazines such as *Good Housekeeping* and *Cosmopolitan. Ms.* also helped popularize the title "Ms." as an alternative to "Miss" or "Mrs." when a woman's marital status was unknown or irrelevant. Women's studies courses appeared at universities, and several men's colleges began opening their doors to women. By 1980 women made up 51 percent of all college undergraduates and received 30 percent of all doctorates.

Radical Feminism

Because to many women in the United States equality of the sexes was a revolutionary idea, NOW was by definition a radical organization. To some women, however, it was not radical enough. These more radical women were mostly white and well educated but generally younger than their counterparts in NOW. Many of them had learned about social reform through their civil rights and student protest activities.

The younger feminists lacked the national network of NOW but excelled in grassroots organization. The women practiced participatory democracy—every woman had a voice in discussions and a chance to develop her own skills and talents.

Small, informal discussion groups met regularly at participants' homes for "consciousness-raising" sessions. Women talked openly about their experiences in childhood, school, families, marriages, and careers. They analyzed issues of common concern to all women and tried to identify those for which political changes seemed most attainable.

The radical feminists tended to favor more dramatic protests than their NOW sisters. They ridiculed the 1968 Miss America contest by crowning a sheep as the winner. In one widely reported episode, they threw girdles, bras, hair curlers, false eyelashes, and other symbols of what they called feminine enslavement into a "freedom trash can." Such events resulted in a great deal of media attention and often produced negative reaction from the public.

The Opposition

Not all women embraced the new ideas of women's liberation with equal enthusiasm. A great many women accepted certain feminist ideas but rejected others. Some disagreed with the radical feminists' methods. Some were adamantly opposed to the movement's general support of a woman's right to abortion. Still other women viewed feminism as an attack on traditional values, which included the subordination of women to men and the importance of a full-time commitment to family.

Among the most prominent of the antifeminists was author and attorney Phyllis Schlafly. Schlafly had long

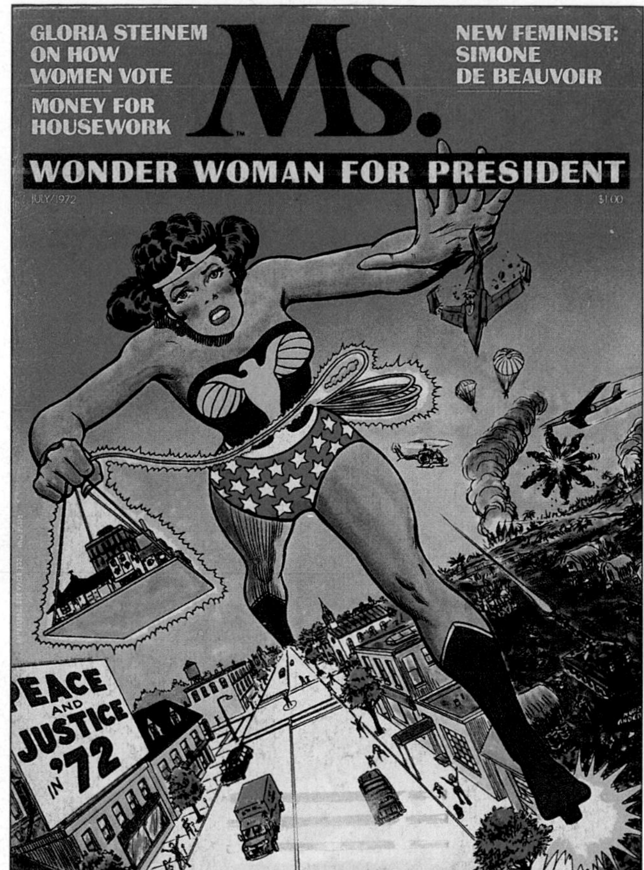

Women's Issues *Ms.* magazine articles addressed issues important to feminists. *What were some traditional women's magazines in 1972?*

been active in Illinois and national politics where she was a strong voice for conservative causes. As the feminist movement gained strength, Schlafly directed her energies against it. In her 1977 book, *The Power of the Positive Woman,* she argued that a woman's most important and satisfying role was in the home and that the primary duty of women was to uphold the traditional values of the church, family, and country. Schlafly asserted that feminist organizations did not represent the views of all women. Her leadership offered a powerful choice for many women.

Responses of Congress and the Courts

Strides and Conflicts

Despite the opposition of the antifeminists, the accumulated effect of the women's movement began to be visible in the responses of Congress and the courts. In 1970 the Labor Department issued an order calling for all federal contracts to require the employment of a certain percentage of women. In 1972 the Education Amendments Act outlawed sex discrimination in education. On the local level, that meant that school boards had to rewrite policies that limited cooking classes to girls and shop classes to boys. It also obliged schools to increase their support of girls' athletics. The United States armed forces relaxed some restrictions against women in 1973 and in 1976 opened up the military academies of Annapolis and West Point to women.

In the 1970s, however, two legislative and court issues divided American society into opposing camps. These were the proposed Equal Rights Amendment (ERA) and the Supreme Court's decision on abortion. These two issues galvanized the opposition—which until that time had been somewhat dispersed—and gave it a new focus and sense of purpose.

The Fight for ERA

The idea of a constitutional amendment specifically addressing the issue of women's equality was not a new one. The National Woman's party had first proposed an Equal Rights Amendment in 1923 and reintroduced it in every subsequent session of Congress.

As late as 1962, the President's Commission on the Status of Women did not favor the passage of the amendment. This view was shared by many women's groups, including the League of Women Voters, who were concerned that passage of the ERA would cancel legal protections women already enjoyed. In the late 1960s, however, the courts began to strike down these protective laws because they were in conflict with Title VII of the Civil Rights Act of 1964. As a result, the League withdrew its objection to the amendment.

The proposed amendment was a simple one. It read: "Equality of rights under the law shall not be denied or abridged by the United States or by any State on account of sex." Two other brief clauses provided Congress with enforcement power and established that the amendment would go into effect two years after ratification.

The proponents of the amendment felt that in 1970 the time was right for its passage. That year the amendment flew through the House of Representatives on a voice vote of 350 to 15. Two years later, it carried the Senate by a vote of 84 to 8. To become law, however, the amendment needed to be ratified, or approved, by three-fourths of the state legislatures within the next seven years.

Opposing Sides Pro-ERA activists and anti-ERA activists such as Phyllis Schlafly, with loudspeaker above, felt strongly about their positions. *What did the ERA propose?*

Thirty states quickly approved the amendment by 1973; then the drive for ratification stalled. NOW, which had assumed leadership of the drive for ratification, was taken by surprise.

The feminists had underestimated the opposition to the amendment and the ability of conservative women's groups to organize grass-roots opposition. Although opinion polls showed that the majority of Americans favored the concept of equality between men and women, the same polls also indicated that an even larger percentage of the population did not wish to change men's and women's social and family roles. For these concerned people, the ERA seemed too radical a change. They vowed to kill the amendment.

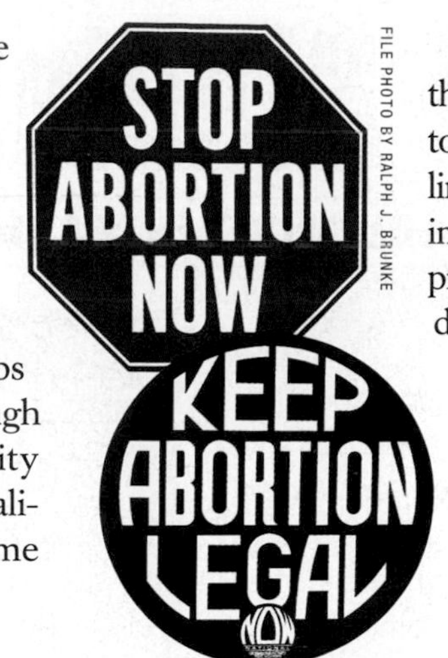

FILE PHOTO BY RALPH J. BRUNKE

An Issue Divided **Much of today's women's rights debate focuses on the issue of abortion.** *Why do some people oppose abortion?*

The Defeat of ERA

Schlafly and her supporters charged that passage of the ERA would lead directly to women in combat in wartime, the breakdown of the family, government funding of abortion, and elimination of separate public bathrooms for men and women. The "Stop ERA" forces dramatized their concerns in California by presenting state senators with live mice and asking, "Do you want to be a man or a mouse?" In Illinois they handed out apple pies in the state legislature as symbols of traditional homemaking values, and they brought in baby girls bearing signs that read Don't Draft Me.

As the original ratification period ran out, supporters of ERA managed to obtain a 3-year extension from Congress. They failed, however, to add a single state during that period, and by the 1982 deadline, they were still 3 short of the 38 state approvals required. The amendment was never added to the Constitution.

Roe v. *Wade*

In 1973 the Supreme Court announced its decision in *Roe* v. *Wade*, which established a woman's right to have an abortion. Even before the Court's historic pronouncement, several states had modified their laws to permit abortion under specific conditions. Many feminists, however, wanted all abortion limits repealed on the grounds that women should have absolute control over their own bodies. Many other people, however, including some feminists, were against abortion. These people believed that life begins at conception and that abortion at any time during pregnancy constitutes murder. Therefore, they opposed abortion on moral grounds.

The Supreme Court's decision set forth the manner in which states could limit the right to abortion. The decision established that no limitations could be imposed by the states during the first trimester, or first three months, of pregnancy. State law could legalize abortions during the second trimester in situations that were potentially dangerous to a woman's health. The state could choose to restrict abortion during the third trimester to protect the life of an unborn child capable of sustaining life outside the womb.

A Shift in Focus

In the process of moving through the Supreme Court, the abortion issue shifted in focus from the rights of the mother to the rights of the unborn child. Rather than settling the issue of abortion, however, the Supreme Court decision intensified controversy.

The political and moral battle between the "pro-choice" supporters (those favoring the individual's right to abortion) and the "pro-life" forces (those opposed to abortion) dominated many political contests. The debate has continued no less passionately in the 2000s.

Section Assessment

Main Idea

1. Use a diagram like this one to show some of the economic, political, and social inequities that helped spark the women's movement of the 1960s.

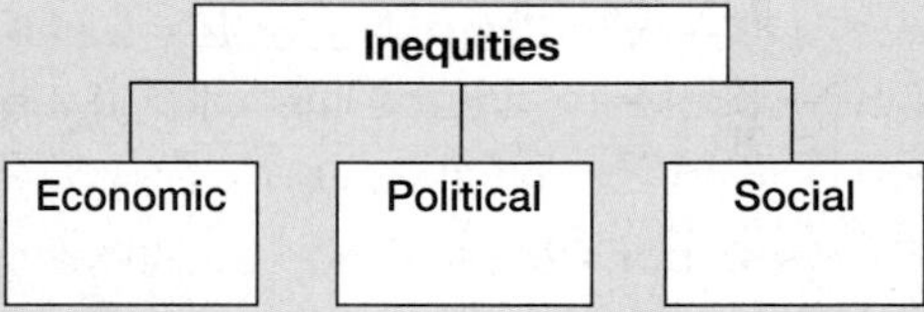

Vocabulary

2. Define: women's liberation, feminist.

Checking Facts

3. What were some major issues facing women in the 1960s?
4. Why did the ERA provoke such controversy?

Critical Thinking

5. **Expressing Problems Clearly** How did the decision in *Roe* v. *Wade* clarify the focus of the women's movement?

Social Studies Skill

CONDUCTING INTERVIEWS

Learning the Skill

Interviews allow you to gather information about interesting people such as Betty Friedan, the founder and first president of the National Organization for Women (NOW). Friedan (pictured right) became a leader in the struggle for women's rights. In 1970 Friedan made the following assessment of the barriers facing women.

We are beginning to know that no woman can achieve a real breakthrough alone, as long as sex discrimination exists in employment, under the law, in education, in mores, and in denigration of the image of women.

Even those of us who have managed to achieve a precarious success in a given field still walk as freaks in a "man's world" since every profession—politics, the church, teaching—is still structured as a man's world.
—Betty Friedan, *Voices of the New Feminism,* 1970

To interview Betty Friedan or anyone else, you would want to follow these steps.

a. Make an appointment. Contact the person, and explain why you want the interview, what kinds of things you hope to learn, and how you will use the information. Discuss where and when you will conduct the interview, and ask if you may use a tape recorder.

b. Gather background information. Find out about the early life, education, career, and other accomplishments of the person you will interview. Familiarize yourself with books or articles the interviewee has published. Then do research on the topics you will discuss.

c. Prepare questions. Group questions into subject categories, beginning each category with general questions and moving toward more specific questions. Formulate each question carefully, phrasing it in a way that encourages a well-developed answer. If the answer could be simply yes or no, rephrase the question.

d. Conduct the interview. Introduce yourself and restate the purpose of the interview. Ask questions and record responses accurately. Ask follow-up questions to fill gaps in information.

e. Transcribe the interview. Convert your written or tape-recorded notes into a transcript, a written record of the interview presented in a question-and-answer format.

A Powerful Leader **Betty Friedan, founder of NOW, has been very influential in the women's liberation movement.**

Practicing the Skill

If you were to interview Betty Friedan, you might consider the following:

1. What kind of background information might you gather?

2. What are some broad categories of questions you might ask based on the quotation to the left?

3. What are some specific questions you might ask, based on the quotation?

4. What would you do if you ran out of prepared questions and there was a lull in the interview?

5. What might you do with information gathered in an interview with Friedan?

Applying the Skill

The women's movement probably included some women you know—your mother, aunts, grandmothers, neighbors. Interview one or more women of three different generations. Ask about their experiences as women in the United States. Ask about their attitudes toward feminist issues, past and present. As you transcribe the interviews, be aware of any common themes or surprising differences. You may want to summarize your findings or create a comparison chart.

The **Glencoe Skillbuilder Interactive Workbook, Level 2** CD-ROM provides more practice in key social studies skills.

Hispanic Americans Organize

1966: SUPPORT GROWS NATIONWIDE FOR UFW GRAPE BOYCOTT

DURING THE LATE 1960S IT WAS A SCENE REPEATED IN MANY SUPERMARKETS AND NEIGHBORHOOD GROCERY STORES THROUGHOUT THE UNITED STATES. Grapes were on sale—green and purple, luscious, full of juice, appealing to the sight and to the taste. If you were doing the family shopping, you might be tempted to reach for a bunch—until you remembered what you had seen on TV or read in the newspapers about the California grape industry. The industry's problems were reaching consumers. Some grocers even posted this sign above the fruit as a reminder:

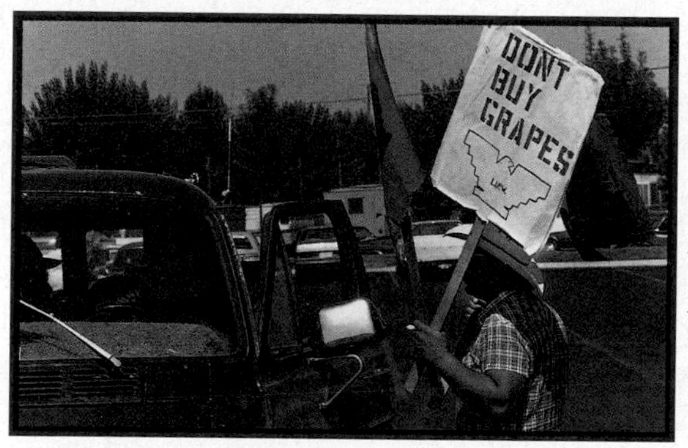

ARTHUR SCHATZ/LIFE MAGAZINE, ©TIME, INC.

Powerful New Strategy
Consumers make decisions.

> Notice: California Grape Boycott United Farm Workers led by César Chávez are calling for a boycott of California table grapes. . . . It is this grocer's current policy to inform consumers of the boycott request so that each consumer can make his or her own purchase decision. It's your decision—to boycott or not.
>
> —Table grape boycott notice, 1966

Shoppers did decide, and many put the grapes back into the bin. By appealing to the nation's consumers, César Chávez, founder of the United Farm Workers (UFW) of America, gained the support he needed to win recognition of his union among California farm owners. The union used the new strategy of a nationwide boycott alongside the more familiar tactics of strikes, pickets, and demonstrations. Chávez would use it successfully again, when bargaining with the owners of vineyards and lettuce fields.

GUIDE TO READING

Main Idea

In an effort to make their growing numbers felt, Hispanic Americans began to organize in the 1960s and 1970s, demanding representation and opportunities equal to those of other groups in the United States.

Vocabulary

- extended family
- undocumented immigrant
- representation
- bilingualism
- assimilation

Read to Find Out . . .

- the five major Hispanic American groups.
- the issues facing Hispanic Americans in the 1960s and 1970s and how they addressed these issues.

Recent Hispanic American History

Diverse Yet Similar

Look at a map of the United States. Read out the names of places in the Southwest and Southeast: San Francisco, Los Angeles, Santa Fe, San Antonio, Rio Grande, Ponce de Leon Bay. These names all suggest the long history of Hispanic culture in North America. From the first explorers in the 1500s to the most recent immigrants, Hispanic Americans have added a distinctive element to the language and culture of the United States.

The term *Hispanic American* refers to those Americans who have come, or are descended from others who came, from Spanish-speaking lands such as Mexico, Puerto Rico, and Cuba. Hispanic Americans are the fastest-growing minority in the country. From 3 million in 1960, the Hispanic population rose to 15 million in 1980 and approximately 30.3 million in 1998. As many feminists began to demand their rights in the 1960s and 1970s, many Hispanic Americans did as well. Both groups were characterized by diversity: their members came from many different places and had varying interests.

Similarities and Differences

Regardless of their country of origin, Hispanic Americans shared a Spanish ancestry that included, among other things, practice of the Catholic religion and strong ties with the **extended family**—an individual's grandparents, parents, aunts, uncles, cousins, and brothers and sisters. Economic and social pressures also forced many urban Hispanic Americans to live in mostly Spanish-speaking neighborhoods, or barrios.

In other ways, Hispanic Americans were and are a diverse group, coming to the United States for differing reasons and at differing times. As a result, their goals and concerns have historically varied.

Five Major Groups

Hispanic Americans may be divided into five major subgroups: Mexican Americans, Puerto Ricans, Cuban Americans, those from Central America, and those from South America. Each group has its own history and settlement pattern.

Many Mexican Americans were grandchildren or great grandchildren of the 1 million people who fled Mexico in the 20 years following Mexico's 1910 revolution. Others traced their origins to families who lived in Mexican territories that were incorporated into the United

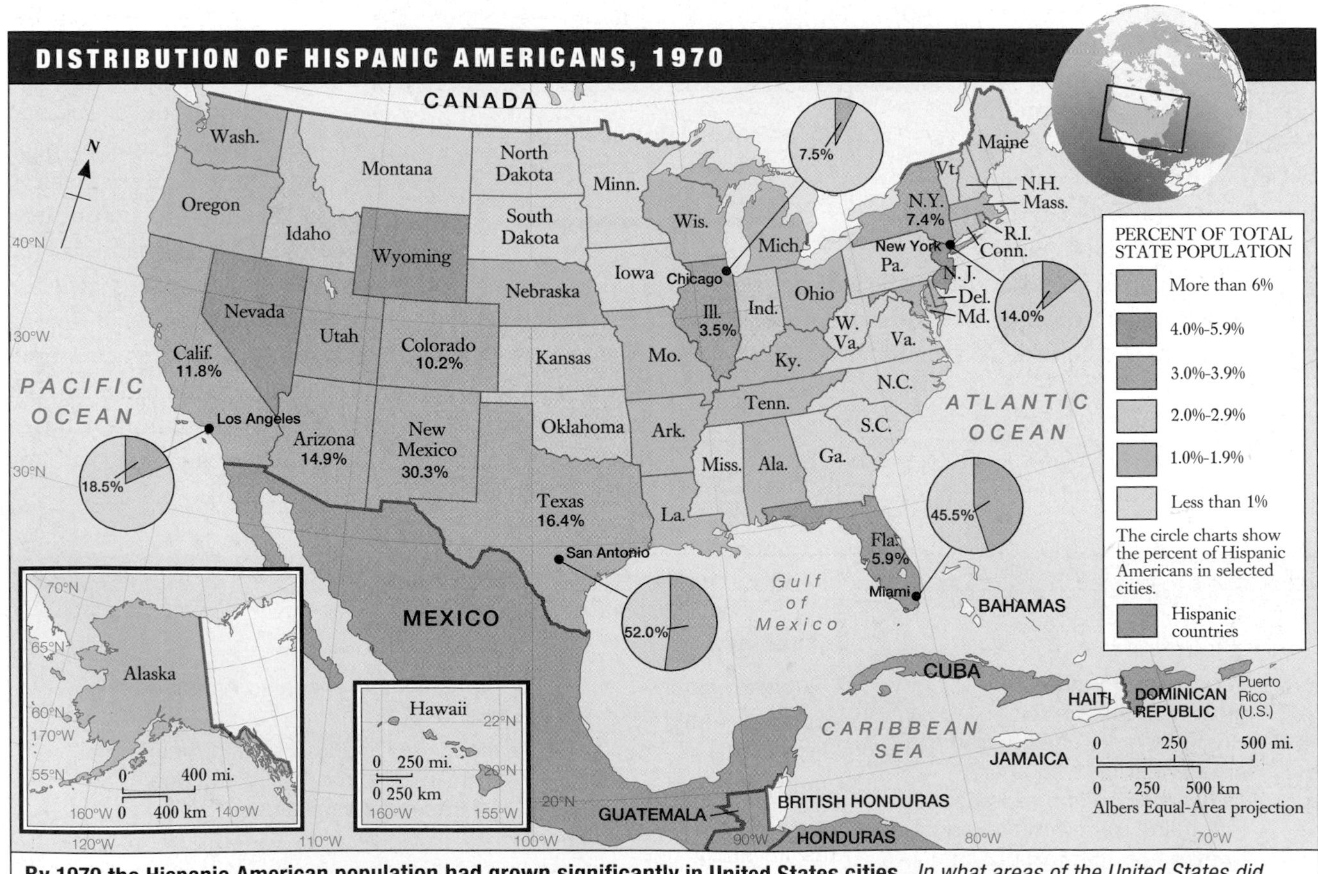

By 1970 the Hispanic American population had grown significantly in United States cities. *In what areas of the United States did Hispanic Americans tend to settle?*

© ERICH HARTMANN/MAGNUM PHOTOS

Enrichment Celebrations such as this Puerto Rican Day parade add to the nation's diversity. *Why did many Puerto Ricans come to the United States?*

States after the Mexican War. Others first came to this country as *braceros,* farmworkers who were issued temporary work permits by the United States government during World War II and after. Still others were **undocumented immigrants**—people who lacked legal papers for residing in the United States. Many Mexican Americans maintained ties with relatives and friends in Mexico through frequent visits or moves back and forth.

Because Puerto Rico is a possession of the United States, Puerto Ricans may enter this country as citizens. After World War II, 1 out of every 6 Puerto Ricans came to the mainland in search of economic opportunity. In the 1960s, of the 1 million Puerto Ricans in the United States, 600,000 lived in New York City, often working at low-paying jobs.

Cubans began arriving in this country in large numbers after Fidel Castro took over Cuba in 1959. One great migration began after the Cuban missile crisis of 1962, when 3,000 people a week arrived for several months. A second migration took place between 1965 and 1970, when 368,000 Cubans immigrated to the United States. In 1980, 130,000 Cubans left their homes for this country in what is known as the Mariel Boatlift. Although most Cuban Americans settled in and around Miami, large Cuban communities also grew up in New York City and in New Jersey. Many of these immigrants left Cuba for political, not economic, reasons and had little difficulty reestablishing themselves.

Two other groups of Hispanic Americans are those with roots in Central America and South America. Civil war caused tens of thousands of Salvadorans, Guatemalans, and Nicaraguans to seek asylum here. Economic changes and chronic poverty led many of South Americans to enter this country. The largest number of these are from Colombia. More than 100,000 Colombians immigrated between 1966 and 1979. Most settled in New York City, Miami, and Los Angeles.

Hispanic Americans Respond

Hispanic Americans Organize

While the numbers of Hispanic Americans increased dramatically during the 1960s and 1970s, their development as a political force occurred more slowly. Because of the Hispanic Americans' diversity, it was difficult for any one leader to unite all the segments into a single force.

Political Issues

For Hispanic Americans, as for other minorities, a major political issue was **representation,** which would result from electing to public office people to represent their views. In some border towns such as El Paso, Texas, Hispanic American voters outnumbered other voters two to one, but few Hispanic American candidates were nominated or elected to office. Gerrymandering in other cities, such as Los Angeles, helped to keep Hispanic Americans from massing their votes. Gradually, with changes such as reapportionment, a few Hispanic American candidates were elected. For example, in 1961 voters in San Antonio, Texas, elected Democrat Henry B. González to the House of Representatives. In 1964 Texans elected E. "Kika" de la Garza to represent the Lower Rio Grande Valley in the House.

Gradually, Hispanic Americans began to organize politically. La Raza Unida, which translates roughly as "the people united," resulted from an effort to organize a national political party that would unite the sometimes divided Hispanic American elements. José Angel Gutiérrez, a 25-year-old Texan, formed the party early in 1970 to give Mexican Americans political control over some 20 southern Texas counties in which they made up the majority of the population. In September of that year, Rodolfo "Corky" González, an activist and poet from Colorado, formed the Colorado La Raza Unida. Two years later a national convention drew 3,000 Chicanos, the ethnic label adopted by many Mexican Americans.

Another pressing political issue concerned the *bracero* program. In periods of labor shortage such as occurred during World War II, American growers pressed the

Student Web Activity 22

Visit the *American Odyssey* Web site at americanodyssey.glencoe.com and click on ***Chapter 22—Student Web Activities*** for an activity relating to Mexican Americans.

Hard Work Hispanic Americans often toiled in grape and lettuce fields like these. *What problems did Hispanic Americans face?*

United States government to allow farm laborers to enter on temporary, restricted permits. Although Mexico disliked the program, fearing that the workers would face ethnic discrimination, it reluctantly consented to accept it. The program was scrapped in 1965 when Mexican Americans complained about the poor working conditions that the workers suffered.

The plight of the undocumented immigrant and the related problem of controlling the United States–Mexico border were other troublesome issues. Poverty in Mexico was the source of much illegal immigration. No one really could be sure how many people had crossed over the 2,000-mile (3,218-km) border without proper documents.

The journey to the United States was a difficult and dangerous one for these undocumented immigrants. They were vulnerable to exploitation by "coyotes," the often unscrupulous guides who charged huge sums of money for transporting the immigrants across the border. Coyotes frequently robbed the immigrants and sometimes abandoned them in the wilderness. Immigrants who reached the United States then faced exploitation by employers. Because they were here illegally, they had no place to turn for protection and often worked under poor conditions for little pay.

Other challenges awaited undocumented immigrants once they reached this country. Communities generally provided education and emergency health care to anyone who needed it, but undocumented immigrants were often denied other social services, such as unemployment insurance and food stamps, even though most of them paid taxes. In addition, families in need often would not apply for aid for fear of being deported—that is, sent back to their native land.

Undocumented immigrants were not the only ones who suffered. Many Hispanic Americans who were in this country legally faced discrimination from employers as the federal government's Immigration and Naturalization Service (INS) pressured businesses not to hire undocumented immigrants. Many employers, in order to avoid attracting the attention of the INS, simply stopped hiring people of color or those with Hispanic-sounding names, regardless of the workers' legal status.

Economic Issues

Among minorities, economic subjects such as wages and working conditions were not easily distinguished from broader political and social issues. César Chávez believed that they all must be treated as a single issue.

Partly as a result of Chávez's leadership, farmworkers became unionized for the first time. Chávez, a soft-spoken, patient man, has been called a "quiet explosion." Much of his work centered on the grape-growing area around Delano, in California's San Joaquin Valley. There he faced bitter opposition from the growers as well as from the Teamsters Union, which had received permission from the growers to represent the workers even though the workers had not been consulted.

In his union work, Chávez followed the nonviolent philosophy of India's Mohandas K. Gandhi and our own country's Martin Luther King, Jr. Chávez explains:

If someone commits violence against us, it is much better—if we can—not to react against the violence, but to react in such a way as to get closer to our goal. People don't like to see a nonviolent movement subjected to violence. . . . That's the key point we have going for us. . . . By some strange chemistry, every time the opposition commits an unjust act against our hopes and aspirations, we get tenfold paid back in benefits.

—César Chávez, *Labor Leaders in America,* 1987

Realizing the limits of his resources in Delano, Chávez hit upon the idea of organizing national and international boycotts of farm products. He first used the boycott tactic when negotiating with the growers of table grapes. He then later called successfully for boycotts of wine grapes and of lettuce.

Social and Cultural Issues

All Hispanic Americans share some social and cultural problems. As people of color, most have been subject to some degree to the pervasive racial and ethnic prejudices in United States society.

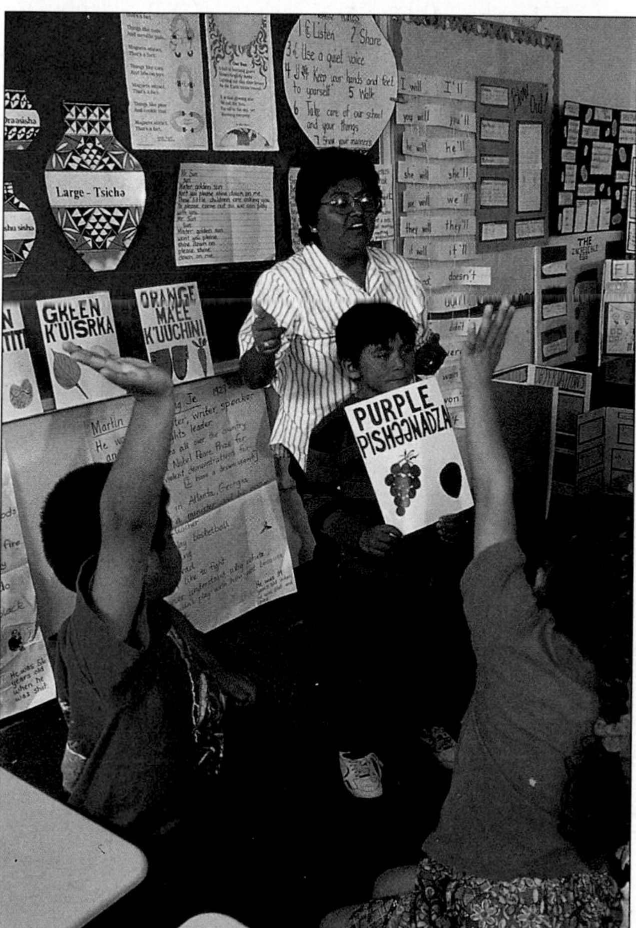

©DAEMMRICH/THE IMAGE WORKS

Bilingual Education These first graders of Acoma Pueblo in New Mexico enjoy the benefits of a bilingual classroom.
What were the arguments against bilingual education?

Social reforms brought about through the civil rights movement did not immediately benefit Hispanic Americans. Hispanic Americans were regarded as white, and therefore they did not receive many of the legal protections granted other minorities. Not until 1970 did a federal district court rule that Mexican Americans constituted an "identifiable ethnic minority with a pattern of discrimination."

In the 1970s **bilingualism,** the use of two languages, became a center of stormy controversy. The proponents of bilingualism claimed that educating children in their native tongue as well as in English was the only way to ensure that minority students would receive an education equal to that of English-speaking classmates. Those who objected to bilingualism felt it delayed the successful **assimilation,** or incorporation, of minorities into the mainstream of society. Some opponents argued that the United States would become a bilingual country.

In 1968 the Bilingual Education Act had provided federal assistance to school districts for developing bilingual education programs. In 1974 the legal issues were decided in favor of bilingual education, when the Supreme Court ruled that schools had to meet the needs of those children who had a limited knowledge of English. Nevertheless, the issues of bilingualism and assimilation remain contentious ones in communities across the nation.

Section Assessment

Main Idea

1. Use a diagram like this one to show some of the goals that Hispanic Americans shared as they began to organize.

Shared Goals

Vocabulary

2. Define: extended family, undocumented immigrant, representation, bilingualism, assimilation.

Checking Facts

3. What are the five major Hispanic American subgroups, and what similarities do they share?
4. What were some major problems facing Hispanic Americans in the 1960s and 1970s?

Critical Thinking

5. **Making Comparisons** Compare what César Chávez said about the gains made through nonviolent resistance to the actual experiences of civil rights protesters.

Turning Point

The United Farm Workers and the Grape Boycott

JANUARY, 1968

MEMORANDUM

Mr. President, in September the United Farm Workers Organizing Committee, AFL-CIO—UFWOC—began the third year of their strike and boycott against California growers of fresh table grapes. They are solemnly dedicated to non-violent, direct action as a tactic to obtain human dignity, and to guarantee by contract improved living and working conditions through collective bargaining with their employers.

Senator Harrison Williams, D-N.J.
Chair, Subcommittee on Migratory Labor
Congressional Record, October 11, 1968

The Case

In January 1968, labor organizer Dolores Huerta and 60 other members of the United Farm Workers Organizing Committee (UFWOC) set off from California on a cross-country bus trip. They were headed for New York City, the biggest market for West Coast grapes, to kick off UFWOC's latest campaign in its struggle for farmworkers' rights—a boycott of California table grapes. As they crossed the United States, the farmworkers set up boycott committees in dozens of communities. At each stop, they spoke in churches, schools, and homes, urging people to support their efforts to unionize farmworkers by not buying grapes.

The grape boycott grew out of earlier efforts to force grape growers to let their workers join the union. When those pickets, strikes, and negotiations failed, UFWOC turned to the boycott.

The growers insisted that the boycott was illegal and that most farmworkers did not want a union. In the months and years that followed, the growers and the farmworkers would each try to win consumers to their side. The boycott would be won or lost in supermarket aisles across the country.

The Background

California's farmworkers—mainly Mexican Americans, but also whites, African Americans, Filipino Americans, and others—were among the poorest of the poor. Many were migrants, following the harvest up and down California's Central Valley, picking grapes, lettuce, and other crops. Even though the entire family, including the children, worked long hours in the fields, the average yearly income for a migrant farmworker's family was well below the poverty level of $3,000. Exposed to pesticides in the fields and with little access to health care, the average migrant worker could expect to live only 49 years compared with 70 years for the average United States citizen.

Farmworkers had never been able to organize an effective union. They had been excluded from the National Labor Relations Act (NLRA), passed in 1935, which guaranteed other workers the right to join unions and to bargain collectively with their employers.

Organizing Workers In the 1960s, however, farmworkers in California were beginning to build a union. One of the leaders of this new movement was César Chávez. Chávez, a Mexican American, grew up in a migrant farmworker family in California. Like many other farmworker children, Chávez left school at 14 to work full-time in the fields. In the 1950s Chávez began working with a group that was helping Mexican American communities in California organize to fight discrimination.

In 1962 Chávez set off on his own to organize agricultural workers in Delano, California, the heart of California's grape-growing empire. He called his organization the Farm Workers Association (FWA). Within 3 years the FWA had more than 1,000 members and had begun to use traditional labor tactics, including strikes, to win wage increases. In 1966 the FWA joined with the Agricultural Workers Organizing Committee (AWOC), another farmworker organization, to form the United Farm Workers Organizing Committee (UFWOC). The new organization was headed by Chávez and other FWA leaders along with Larry Itliong and Philip Vera Cruz, Filipino American labor organizers from AWOC.

Building Support UFWOC members went from vineyard to vineyard talking to workers about the union and pressing growers to allow elections so that workers could choose a union to represent them. Once workers had a union, UFWOC argued, they could use collective bargaining to win contracts that would guarantee higher wages, better working conditions, and benefits.

"Gandhi taught that the boycott is the most nearly perfect instrument of nonviolent change, allowing masses of people to participate actively in a cause. . . . Even if people cannot picket with us or contribute money or food, they can take part in our struggle by not buying certain products."

César Chávez

"Employer importation and use of strikebreakers, presence of Mexican alien greencarders, and court injunctions severely limiting the union's right to picket, left no recourse for the workers but to seek public support through a consumer boycott of grapes."

Senator Harrison Williams

"If we, as farmers and employers, accept the union as bargaining agent, we are taking away the individual laborer's right of choice—his right to freedom of work. This is a struggle for the right of a farmer to deal directly with his employees—a stand for free enterprise."

Louis Rozzoni, president, California Farm Bureau

"When we tried to fight back in the past, we found the grower was too strong, too rich, and we had to give up. César Chávez has shown us we can fight back."

Farmworker

© PAULFUSCO/MAGNUM PHOTOS

Farmworker

UPI/BETTMANN

César Chávez

© PAUL FUSCO/MAGNUM PHOTOS

Boycotters

Turning Point

© PAUL FUSCO/MAGNUM PHOTOS

César Chávez leads marches for farmworkers' rights.

In 1967 UFWOC targeted the Giumarra Vineyard Corporation, the largest table-grape grower in California. Giumarra, however, refused to allow union elections, and the vineyard's workers voted to strike. Giumarra then brought in other workers in an attempt to break the strike. To force Giumarra to negotiate, UFWOC called on consumers to boycott Giumarra grapes. To evade the boycott, Giumarra began shipping its grapes under other companies' labels. UFWOC decided that the only way to make the boycott work was to expand it to all table grapes. Chávez later explained, "It was the only way we could do it. We had to take on the whole industry. The grape itself had to become a label."

The Opinions

The growers insisted that most farmworkers did not want a union. They claimed that California farmworkers were the highest paid of any American farmworkers and that they were already adequately protected by labor laws. The growers argued that they could not afford to pay higher wages and warned that increased farmworker wages would mean higher prices for consumers. The growers also maintained that the boycott was illegal—prohibited by the NLRA.

Many conservative politicians, including California Governor Ronald Reagan and President Richard Nixon, supported the growers. Nixon said the boycott should be condemned "with the same firmness we condemn . . . any other form of lawbreaking."

Many supermarkets also supported the growers, claiming to do so under the banner of consumer rights. They argued that they should continue to stock grapes so that consumers could choose for themselves whether or not to support the boycott.

Chávez and UFWOC argued that the growers should at least allow the workers themselves to decide whether or not they wanted a union by letting them hold elections. UFWOC pointed out that they had always offered growers the option of holding elections before calling for strikes or boycotts. At the few vineyards where elections were held, workers overwhelmingly voted to join UFWOC.

UFWOC maintained that farmworkers' wages were unfairly low. Raising these wages would mean only a slight increase in the price of grapes at the supermarket, they said, since United States Department of Labor records showed that only 2 cents to 5 cents of every dollar invested in grape production went to the workers. Furthermore, UFWOC claimed the consumer boycott was legal because the provisions of the NLRA that restricted the use of boycotts did not cover farmworkers.

People across the United States and Canada supported the boycott. They set up more than 400 boycott committees and raised more than $20,000 a month for UFWOC. Boycott supporters picketed supermarkets, calling on store managers to stop selling grapes and shoppers to stop buying them. Students demanded that school cafeterias stop serving grapes. In Boston, one group dumped grapes into the harbor in a protest reminiscent of the Boston Tea Party. Religious leaders, including California's Catholic bishops, defended the farmworkers' right to unionize. Politicians, too, began to stand up for the farmworkers. All the major Democratic presidential candidates and the mayors of three dozen cities, including New York, declared their support for the boycott.

The Players

César Chávez Director of UFWOC. Chávez was a firm believer in nonviolence as a means of bringing about social change. To make this point and to draw public attention to the boycott, Chávez fasted for 25 days. He said, "Social justice for the dignity of man cannot be won at the price of human life."

FILE PHOTO BY RALPH J. BRUNKE

Boycott Button

Growers Just 30 growers grew 85 percent of California table grapes. Giumarra alone had 10 percent of the market. Many growers were suspicious of Chávez's motives. Some even called him a Communist.

Consumers The farmworkers called on shoppers to stop buying grapes, and many did. *New York* magazine reported that many Americans "would rather eat a cyanide pellet than a California grape these days."

The Outcome

The grape boycott turned out to be one of the most successful consumer boycotts in United States history. In New York City, sales of grapes declined by 90 percent during the summer of 1968. National grape sales fell by 12 percent. Prices for grapes dropped too. One grower admitted, "It is costing us more to produce and sell our grapes than we are getting paid for them. . . ."

Finally, in the summer of 1970, most growers gave in and signed agreements with UFWOC. The new contracts called for pay increases, employer contributions to worker health and welfare funds, union control over hiring, and joint worker-grower committees to regulate pesticide use.

The Significance

Most historians consider the grape boycott to be a landmark in twentieth-century American labor history. For the first time, United States farmworkers gained the right to unionize. The contracts negotiated by the union led to increased pay and better working conditions for many farmworkers.

The grape boycott also demonstrated the power of grassroots organizing and of the boycott as a tool for social change. Other groups would later adopt these same tactics to bring about change in other areas, such as the environment.

Perhaps most importantly, the grape boycott heralded the emerging political power of Hispanic Americans and others who took part in the struggle. In the years that followed, Hispanic Americans would join together in the National Council of La Raza to lobby Washington on behalf of Hispanic Americans. They would use their newfound political muscle to oppose discrimination, to fight for bilingual education and changes in immigration law, and to elect Hispanics to government posts.

RESPONDING TO THE CASE

1. Make a chart in which you list the growers arguments against the boycott and UFWOC's responses. Which arguments do you find most convincing?

2. In your opinion, why was the boycott successful?

3. What are some of the advantages and disadvantages of a boycott as a strategy for bringing about change? Should groups involve consumers in disputes through boycotts?

PORTFOLIO PROJECT

Imagine you are in charge of a public relations campaign for the grape growers. Write a newspaper ad in which you try to persuade shoppers not to boycott grapes. Then take the position of a supporter of the grape boycott, picketing a grocery store. How would you convince a shopper not to buy grapes? Write a script of a conversation you might have with a shopper. Also, design a poster to carry while picketing. Place the ad, the script, and the poster design in your portfolio.

Land Claims of Native Americans

DECEMBER 15,1970: TAOS PUEBLO PEOPLE REGAIN SACRED BLUE LAKE

BLUE LAKE HAS ALWAYS BEEN SACRED TO THE TAOS PUEBLO PEOPLE. Physically, Blue Lake is a small body of water in the Sangre de Christo range of the Rocky Mountains in northern New Mexico. In 1966 Pueblo governor John C. Reyna tried to explain the deeper importance of the lake to the Taos people. "The lake," he said,

> Is as blue as turquoise. It is surrounded by evergreens. In the summer there are millions of wildflowers. Springs are all around. We have no buildings there, no steeples. There is nothing the human hand has made. The lake is our church. . . . We pray to the water, the sun, the clouds, the sky, the deer. Without them we could not exist."
>
> —John C. Reyna

© DAVID MUENCH/DAVID MUENCH PHOTOGRAPHY

Sacred Lands
The Taos Pueblo people fight for their sacred lands.

Reyna was speaking for the Taos Pueblo people, who were working to regain control of Blue Lake and the surrounding land. Control had been stripped from them in 1906 when the United States government made the area part of the Carson National Forest. The Taos Pueblo had used the land for centuries, yet the United States government never gave them title or **compensation,** money or something else in return for a loss.

What ultimately turned the tide for the Taos Pueblo was the fact that President Nixon looked favorably on their cause. The Native Americans' desire to avoid integration dovetailed neatly with Nixon's belief that peoples should not be forced together if they wanted to remain independent. Nixon's administration had been

GUIDE TO READING

Main Idea

In the 1960s and 1970s, Native Americans organized to resist government programs that limited their self-determination and threatened their cultural identities.

Vocabulary

- compensation
- liberate

Read to Find Out . . .

- the relationship between Native Americans and the federal government.
- the concerns of Native Americans in the 1960s and 1970s and how they responded to these concerns.

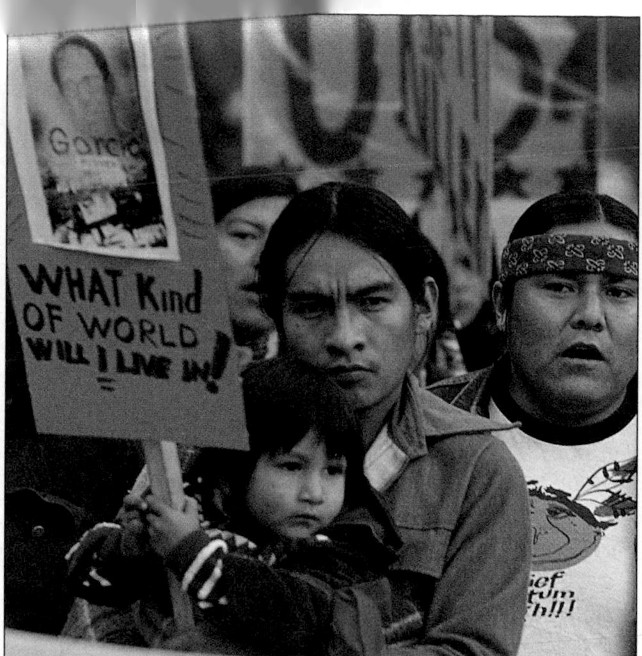

© PAUL FUSCO/MAGNUM PHOTOS

Demonstrations Native Americans in New Mexico take part in a civil rights protest. *What are some other methods Native Americans have used to regain control of thier lives?*

seeking a way to gain credibility in the eyes of the Native American nations in order to help them move toward desired independence. Furthermore, it was evident that the Taos Pueblo had been seriously wronged when control of Blue Lake had been taken from them. Their victory, decades in coming, was realized on December 15, 1970, when President Nixon signed into law legislation to return the sacred site of Blue Lake to the Taos Pueblo.

Recent History of Native Americans

United States Controls Native Americans

As with Hispanic Americans, assimilation was an issue among Native Americans and a factor in government decisions for several decades. Unlike other minorities, Native Americans had never been immigrants, for they were already here when Europeans first colonized the country. Nevertheless, starting in the late 1880s, Native Americans became virtual wards of the state—powerless, with little voice in their own affairs. FDR's administration returned a limited amount of control to Native Americans living on reservations. Eisenhower's administration, however, reversed Roosevelt's New Deal policy on Native Americans.

In spite of the changing federal policy between the 1930s and the 1950s, the cultural identity of the Native American was still threatened as the 1960s began. From 1960 to 1970, their population soared from 551,500 to 792,730, a rate of increase four times the national average. About two-thirds of all Native Americans lived off the reservations. Most were in large cities such as Los Angeles and Chicago. The federal government's Bureau of Indian Affairs managed the 285 reservations, mostly west of the Mississippi River, with little input from the Native Americans themselves.

During this time, on and off the reservations, Native Americans were the most disadvantaged of this nation's racial and ethnic minorities. More than 38 percent lived below the poverty line, as compared to 33 percent of African Americans and only 12 percent of the United States as a whole. Unemployment was widespread, frequently as high as 50 percent. With a school dropout rate of 50 percent, many Native Americans were unprepared to compete. Life expectancy was lower than the national average. The rates of tuberculosis and alcoholism were the highest in the nation, while the suicide rate among Native Americans was double that of the rest of the country.

Native American Responses

A Fight to Regain Control

During the 1960s and 1970s, Native Americans began to organize in order to combat these problems. They met on and off their reservations, on college campuses, in tribal powwows, and in conferences. They negotiated with museums and universities to regain sacred objects that had been removed from Native American lands. They sued to reclaim land, water, and other rights lost when treaties were broken. Some of the younger activists formed militant groups, such as the American Indian Movement (AIM), and tried to achieve social reform by force.

Many Native Americans did not want to blend their traditional cultures with the American mainstream. They wanted self-determination, the opportunity to participate themselves in the political and economic decisions that affected their lives.

Radical Movements

Frustrated by what they saw as their failure to achieve justice through legal channels, a group of Oglala Sioux decided to take matters into their own hands. On the evening of February 27, 1973, a caravan of 54 cars rolled into a small, quiet town just after dusk. Many of the cars' occupants were armed. First they shot out streetlights; then they seized ammunition and rifles from a trading post. All the town's white people were herded into one house. Roadblocks were set up on all the roads leading into the town, which the Sioux then declared **liberated,** or freed from outside control.

The liberated town was Wounded Knee, little more than a fork in the road on the Pine Ridge reservation in southwestern South Dakota. To its liberators Wounded Knee was significant as the site of a massacre more than 80 years earlier where United States troops had killed almost 300 Sioux men, women, and children. Responding to the present-day Sioux militancy, United States marshals began a 71-day siege of the town to starve out the captors. Members of AIM and other sympathetic Native Americans from across the nation soon joined the captors at Wounded Knee.

When the siege lifted, two Native Americans had been killed and one marshal wounded. The issues cited—alleged corruption in the white-sponsored government on the reservation, broken treaties, and lack of self-determination—were not resolved.

What the demonstration did achieve was to focus the nation's attention on the deplorable living conditions of Native Americans. Like earlier dramatic occupations of United States property—at Alcatraz Island in 1969 and the Bureau of Indian Affairs building in Washington, D.C., in 1972—the occupation of Wounded Knee brought into the open a problem that had been ignored for almost a century.

Land Saga, 1794–1980

1794 Passamaquoddy and other local Native American groups sign treaty with the state of Massachusetts.

1820 The territory that is now Maine breaks away from Massachusetts. Native American lands are now part of Maine.

1957 Passamaquoddy leader John Stevens discovers a copy of the 1794 treaty. Stevens tries to get compensation for lands lost to white settlers over the years.

1975 Eastern Native American groups win protection under the 1790 Trade and Non-Intercourse Act, which had required congressional approval of all treaties.

1977 Carter administration steps in to help negotiate an out-of-court settlement.

1980 Maine Indian Claims Settlement Act provides more than $80 million for Native Americans to buy back land lost under the treaty. Native Americans begin to buy back huge tracts of tribal land.

The Passamaquoddy and Penobscot people used the courts to fight for lands they had lost to white settlers. *What group took over the work of the ICC after it was dissolved in 1978?*

Challenges Through the Courts

In spite of their frustrations, Native Americans did have some success in the courts. In 1946 President Truman created the Indian Claims Commission (ICC) to hear and settle all outstanding land claims that Native Americans brought against the government. When the commission was dissolved in 1978, the United States Court of Claims continued its work. During its lifetime the ICC heard 670 cases and awarded about $775 to each claimant. Most of the claims stemmed from broken treaties and seizures of Native American land without agreement or compensation. Many Native Americans were not satisfied with the results of the settlements. They would have preferred to have had their lands restored to them instead of receiving cash payments. The act setting up the ICC, however, had provided that compensation could be made only with money.

As time went on, though, some land restorations were made in addition to cash settlements. The claims of Native American peoples in Alaska, who include Aleut and Inuit, had not been dealt with since the purchase of the Alaskan territory from Russia in 1867. The Alaska Native Land Claims Settlement Act of 1971 gave more than 40 million acres (16,200,000 ha) to native peoples and paid out $962.5 million in cash. The act established 12 regional corporations to manage these resources. This action helped fulfill the Alaskan natives' desire for self-determination but created many difficulties. Few Alaskan natives were experienced in managing large corporations. Also, the regional division tended to weaken the traditional pattern of organization important in Native American societies.

In 1980 the Sioux were awarded $106 million for lands in South Dakota that had been taken from them illegally. In 1988 the Puyallup people of Washington received $162 million in settlement of claims from a treaty signed in the 1850s.

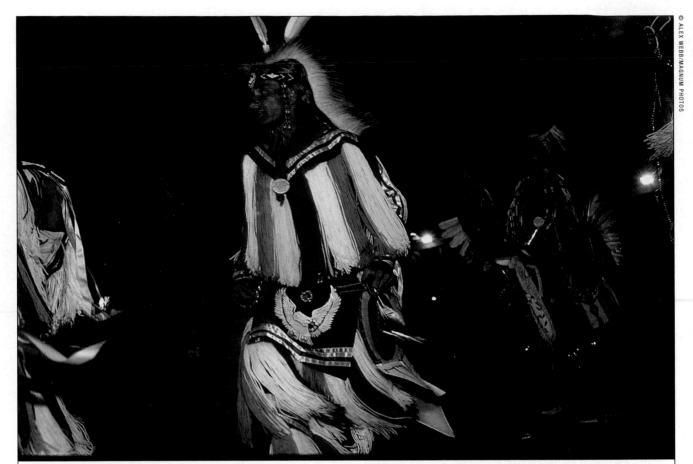

Cultural Pride **Native Americans have taken part in powwows such as this one to keep in touch with their cultural traditions.**
What Native American issues have United States courts dealt with?

Sacred Lands

Congress also addressed the issue of lands sacred to Native Americans. The Taos Pueblo people of New Mexico, for example, struggled for decades to regain possession of their sacred Blue Lake. After the ICC finally acknowledged the Taos title to the land, Congress passed an act in 1970 approving a return of a portion of the national forest and the lake area to the Taos people. In exchange, the Taos gave up their claims to the Taos township.

The courts of the United States have also helped resolve long-standing disputes among Native American nations. For example, disagreements between the Hopi and the Navajo stemmed from the government's establishment of reservation borders in 1882. The Hopi claimed that these borders favored the Navajo. The courts' 1962 ruling restored some of the disputed land to the Hopi and provided joint use of a larger area. The ruling, however, required the relocation of some 13,000 Navajo. Also at issue were water and timber rights, oil and mineral rights, and hunting and fishing rights. Many of these cases were not completely resolved by the ICC and continue to be fought in the United States courts.

Section Assessment

Main Idea

1. Use a diagram like this one to show some of the causes and effects of the Native American rights movement.

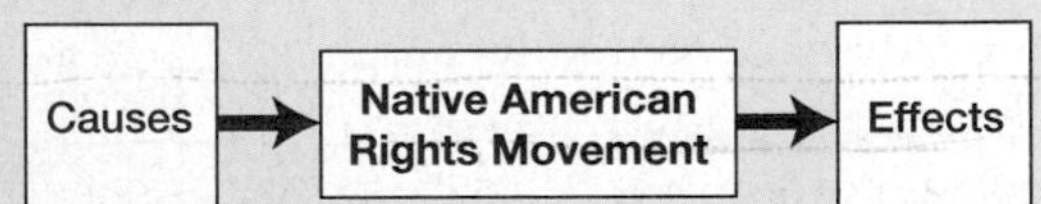

Vocabulary

2. Define: compensation, liberate.

Checking Facts

3. What major problems faced Native Americans during the 1960s and 1970s?

4. How did Native Americans try to address the problems?

Critical Thinking

5. Making Inferences Native Americans have expressed a preference for regaining control of their traditional homelands rather than receiving cash settlements. What does this tell you about their values?

Geography: Impact on History

MOVEMENT

Native American Urban Settlement

Beginning in the 1950s, large numbers of Native Americans left the reservations and moved to cities. This urban migration brought many changes to Native American individuals and communities.

Living on Reservations

In the nineteenth century, the United States government implemented the reservation policy, primarily during two major removal periods. This policy forced Native Americans to move from traditional lands to prescribed reservation areas, which were ultimately broken down further into individual parcels of land. Deprived of large expanses of land on which to hunt and gather and unable to support themselves by farming or ranching, Native Americans faced lives of poverty.

Moving to the Cities

Before the 1950s most Native Americans lived rural lives—on reservations or on traditional lands. During the 1950s, however, the federal government began to push for the assimilation of Native Americans into mainstream culture. Toward this goal the government sought to move Native Americans off reservations and into cities, where it seemed jobs were plentiful and assimilation would be rapid.

To hasten the process even more, the government adopted a policy known as termination. Under this policy the federal government began to cut off aid to Native American nations. Without this aid many nations could not survive on the reservations. Federal officials hoped this policy would eventually allow the government to abolish the reservations altogether.

To further encourage Native Americans to move to cities, the Bureau of Indian Affairs (BIA) set up the Voluntary Relocation Program. BIA offices provided money and services to help Native American families relocate. Many Native Americans took advantage of the program and moved to cities such as Minneapolis, Chicago, Denver, Oklahoma City, Seattle, San Francisco, and Los Angeles.

Such government policies and programs brought many Native Americans to cities. Other Native Americans, however, moved on their own. Opportunities for edu-

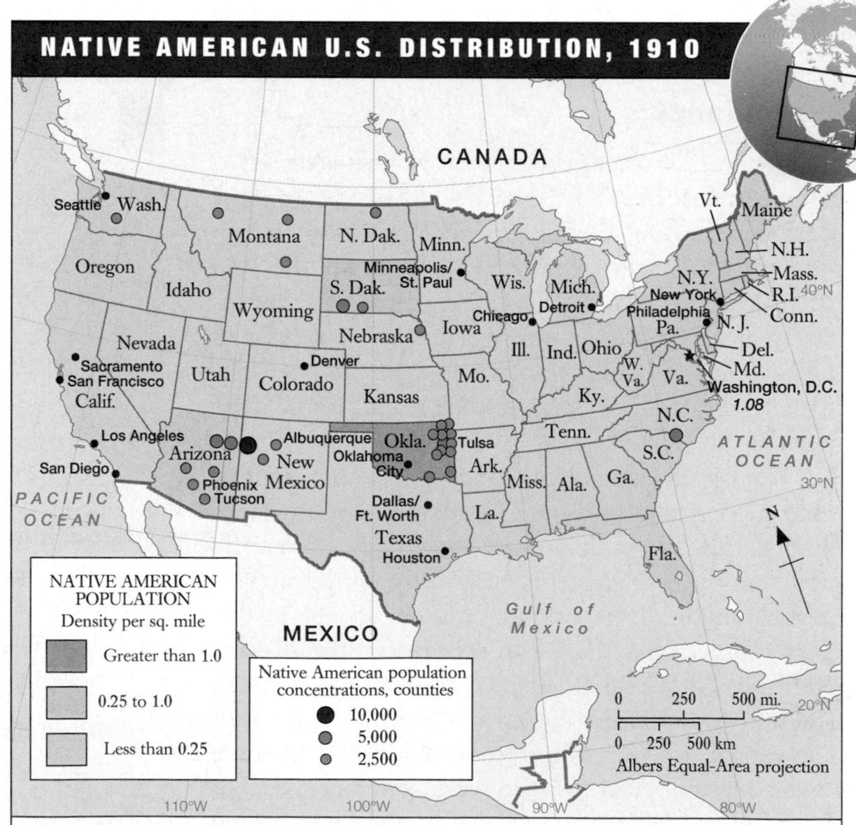

Before World War II, most Native Americans lived on reservations or in areas that had once been tribal lands. *In what areas of the country was most of the Native American population located?*

cation and employment were limited on most reservations, and many Native Americans came to cities in search of better schools and jobs. Still others came to join family members and friends.

The urban migration that began in the 1950s brought tens of thousands of the Native American population to United States cities. In 1930 less than 10 percent of the Native American population lived in urban areas. By 1970 that figure had climbed to 45 percent, and still the migration continued. By 1990 nearly 67 percent of Native Americans lived in cities.

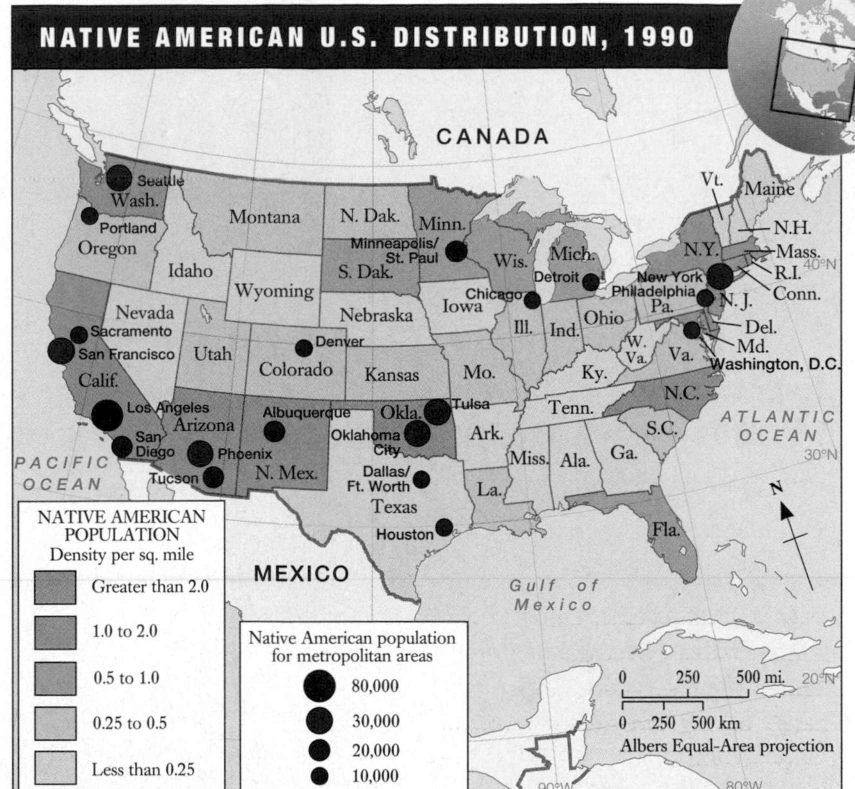

By 1990 more Native Americans lived in cities than in rural areas. *What states included cities with more than 30,000 Native American residents?*

Urban Life

Despite the help offered by relocation programs, Native Americans who moved to cities faced many problems. Moving from rural to urban environments, surrounded by non-Native American culture and discrimination, many Native Americans wrestled with painful questions about their cultural identities. How could they live in two worlds at once?

One young Native American man who had grown up in a city said, "What is an Indian? I don't know. Perhaps that is because I have been raised in white society. My mother was raised on the reservation so perhaps I should know what an Indian is. People say, 'It doesn't matter how much Indian you are if you feel Indian.' I don't 'feel' Indian. . . . Perhaps this feeling of Indian is feeling kinship for people with Indian blood. . . . I search for something to validate myself as an Indian. I know Indians are sharing and giving people, they lack materialism—but that's a hard way to live in the city. . . ."

Some urban Native Americans built successful careers in law, medicine, and education. For many Native Americans, however, city life proved to be a life of poverty. At the time of the 1980 census, one-quarter of all urban Native Americans were living below the federal poverty level. Often these urban newcomers lacked education and thus found it hard to get jobs that paid well. Without a decent income, they could not afford adequate housing, food, or health care.

Urban Native Americans also had to deal with unaccustomed necessities such as rent, transportation, and child care. On the reservations these services had been unnecessary or had been provided by the federal government.

Faced with the challenges of urban life, some Native Americans found strength in their traditional values. They began to establish cultural centers to keep their traditions alive. They set up community programs and clinics to meet their own needs for social services and health care. Many urban Native Americans also maintained close ties to the reservations (those that had not been destroyed by termination), trying to maintain a balance between a rural life that no longer sustained them and an urban life that was not yet comfortable.

Making the Geographic Connection

1. What did the United States government do to get Native Americans to leave the reservations? Why?
2. What were some problems Native Americans faced when they moved to cities?
3. **Movement** Why did Native Americans begin moving to cities during the 1950s?

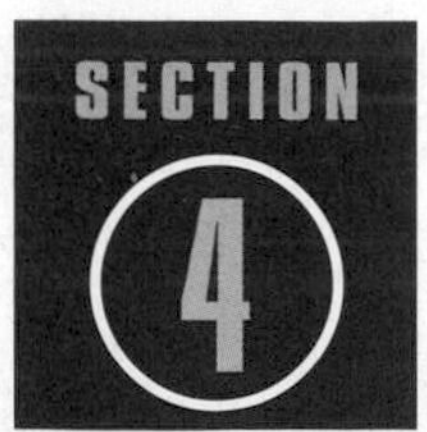

The Counterculture

1965: ROCK MUSIC PROVIDES A VOICE FOR THE COUNTERCULTURE

THE YOUNG PEOPLE WHO STRUGGLED FOR SOCIAL REFORM IN THE 1960S HAILED BOB DYLAN AS THEIR GUERRILLA MINSTREL. He fought for social justice with a guitar and a song. More than any other musician of the time, Dylan gave popular music a social consciousness. Many agreed that he was the spokesperson for his generation. In a 1962 song, Dylan asked one question after another about racism, war, pollution, apathy—the major issues of the day:

> How many roads must a man walk down
> Before you call him a man? yes, 'n'
> How many seas must a white dove sail
> Before she sleeps in the sand? yes 'n'
> How many times must the cannon balls fly
> Before they're forever banned?
> The answer, my friend, is blowin' in the wind,
> The answer is blowin' in the wind.
>
> —Bob Dylan, "Blowing in the Wind," 1962

© JOHN LAUNOIS/BLACK STAR

Music Icon
Bob Dylan's music caught the mind, heart, and beat of a generation.

Then in 1965 Dylan changed his tune. In albums such as *Bringing It All Back Home* and in an appearance at the Newport Folk Festival he signaled that change by playing half his music on an acoustic guitar and half on an electric guitar backed up by a rock group. The reaction was electrifying. Where had the old Dylan gone? Who was this new hard-driving musician with tousled hair who sounded so sarcastic, so sneering, so accusing:

> How does it feel,
> To be without a home,
> Like a complete unknown,
> Like a rolling stone?
>
> —Bob Dylan, "Like a Rolling Stone," 1965

Once again Bob Dylan had caught the heartbeat of American youth, even before they felt the beat themselves. His unbridled energy, explosive anger, and rejection of what had gone before were signs of the arrival of

GUIDE TO READING

Main Idea

Many young people in the 1960s challenged the values and beliefs of mainstream America and adopted ways of life that, in varying degrees, left their mark on United States society.

Vocabulary

- counterculture
- generation gap
- hippie
- commune
- cultural diffusion
- entrepreneur

Read to Find Out . . .

- the beliefs and values of the counterculture and how some aspects of the counterculture were adopted by mainstream America.
- how communes prior to the 1960s compared to the communes set up by the counterculture.

the **counterculture,** a culture of young people with values that ran counter to those of the established culture.

Profile of a Generation

Youth Reacts to Tradition

The 1950s had been a turbulent time politically. The majority of American youth, however, did not seriously challenge the social order of the time. Of course, that age had its social critics, writers such as Jack Kerouac and Allen Ginsberg, who turned their backs on the social and cultural values of their time. These critics, however, were few in number and did not gain many followers.

In the 1960s the first of the baby boomers became teenagers. Having grown up during the cold war, many of these young people felt they were living on the edge of disaster. The threat of nuclear war was ever present as was the possibility of fighting in a faraway jungle war. Many blamed their elders, who included not only their parents but everyone over the age of 30, for creating the world in which they lived. The differences in attitudes between people of different age groups, or the **generation gap,** became a divisive force in society.

Music was perhaps the main instrument of communication within the young generation. Listening to and discussing the new music—rock and roll—was the way these young people identified one another as members of the same group. The affluence that carried over from the 1950s and the availability of small, cheap, portable radios and of record players meant that teenagers could listen to their own music while parents were tuned in to something completely different.

Beliefs and Values

Not all the young people of the 1960s hopped on the counterculture bandwagon. For that matter, a few of those who did could no longer be considered young. There was no such thing as a typical member of the movement, and different counterculture groups had different goals. What the members of the counterculture did have in common was a rejection of the prevailing middle-class values, the attitudes and beliefs of what they called the "Establishment"—people and institutions that represented power, authority, and the status quo.

In the counterculture's way of thinking, the older generation was inhibited, so the young placed a premium on "doing your own thing." The Establishment was materialistic, so the youth culture attempted to break from habits of regular employment and consumerism. Better, so the thinking went, to make what you need, share what you have with others, and not want what you do not have. Science, technology, and the emphasis on reason were blamed for bringing the world to the brink of nuclear disaster, so the counterculture stressed intuition and inner feelings over intellect.

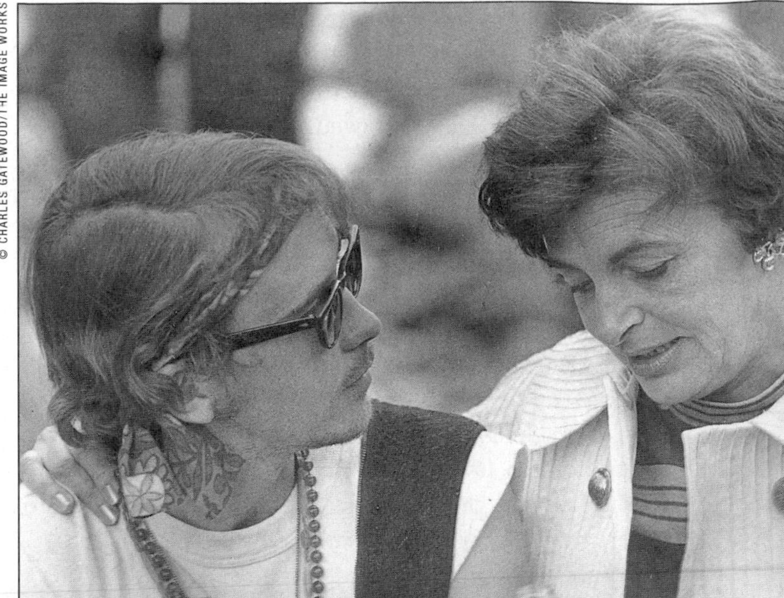

Questioning Authority The generation gap was not unique to the 1960s. Conflict between young and old is a common theme in history. *Why did young people in the 1960s feel they were living in danger?*

New Views

Hippies, as members of the counterculture came to be called, searched for peak moments, or emotional highs, in sex and drugs. Their rejection of more conservative morals against premarital sex, plus the availability of the birth control pill, opened the door to a new era of sexual freedom. These new views attempted to separate sex from love. Some of the flaunting of the new sexuality, such as explicit song lyrics or public nudity, were self-indulgences meant to shock the older generation; however, there was a price to be paid. For example, venereal disease climbed at an alarming rate among young people during the 1960s.

The self-appointed guru, or spiritual leader, of many drug users was Timothy Leary, an academic dropout who experimented with the mind-altering drug lysergic acid diethylamide (LSD). He was fired by Harvard University for violating a pledge not to involve undergraduates in his experiments. Leary then became an advocate of drug use and coined the slogan: Turn on, tune in, drop out.

The use of LSD declined when word got around about its unpleasant side effects, "bad trips," and possible genetic effects. Meanwhile, the smoking of marijuana, also known as grass or pot, increased. In the absence of today's scientific evidence of marijuana's dangers, its proponents favorably compared the use of the drug to the older generation's use of alcohol and tobacco. Some marijuana users moved on later to more powerful and more harmful drugs.

New Religious Movements

In their rejection of materialism, many members of the counterculture embraced spirituality. This included a broad range of beliefs, from astrology and magic to Eastern religions and new forms of Christianity. Many of the religious groups centered around charismatic leaders, individuals who possessed remarkable personal appeal. Some of the religious groups had strict rules against drug use and premarital sex. Their centers, therefore, were frequently refuges to young people searching to recapture their lives from drug abuse.

Although not all religious groups were authoritarian in structure, some were. In these groups, the leader dominated others and controlled their lives, sometimes to the point of arranging marriages between members. Religion became the central experience in the believer's life. The authoritarian figure was a sort of parent figure, and believers formed an extended family that took the place of the family into which a member had been born. Some followers seemed to reject many aspects of their previous lives when they entered these groups. This could lead to painful conflicts. Parents accused religious sects of using mind-control methods; some attempted to recapture and deprogram their children. Also at issue was the right to choose one's own religion, even when that religion was at odds with widely held beliefs about individual free will.

Age of Aquarius Counterculture youth often went beyond the boundaries of customary behavior. The use of drugs was one development that troubled older people. *What did many members of the counterculture use to replace materialism?*

Two examples of authoritarian, mind-controlling religious groups that attracted considerable attention beginning in the 1960s were the Unification Church and the Hare Krishna movement. Both were the offspring of established religions, and both were imports from abroad. Members of the Unification Church were popularly known as "Moonies," after their Korean-born founder, the Reverend Sun Myung Moon. He claimed to have had a vision in which Jesus told him that he, Moon, was the next messiah and was charged with restoring the Kingdom of God on Earth. The Hare Krishnas traced their spiritual lineage through Swami Bhaktivedanta, founder of the American sect, to a Hindu sect that began in fifteenth-century India and that worshiped the god Krishna. In dress, diet, worship, and general style of living they tried to emulate Hindu practitioners of another time and place.

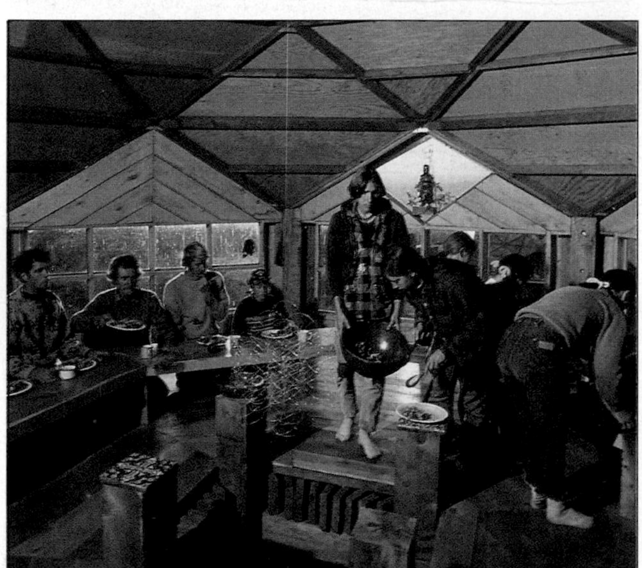

Sharing In this New Mexico commune, as in others, members shared food and eating space. *About how many communes existed in 1970?*

Living Arrangements

Young People Live in Groups

Looking at American society in 1967, author Joan Didion wrote:

> Adolescents drifted from city to torn city sloughing off both the past and the future as snakes shed their skins, children who were never taught and would never now learn the games that had held the society together.
>
> —Joan Didion, *Slouching Towards Bethlehem,* 1967

In San Francisco such adolescents gravitated to Haight-Ashbury, a district near Golden Gate Park. In New York City they concentrated in the East Village.

City Hangouts

A common practice was for individuals to organize into groups that shared living quarters, without regard to sex or marital status. Many coffeehouses had a "pad"—a room with a few mattresses on the floor or horizontal space sufficient at least to roll out a sleeping bag—where anyone who wished could "crash" for a night. The Diggers, a loosely formed group in San Francisco, operated a "free store" of used clothing. Something was always happening in the street—a performance by a free theater or an unplanned concert. Drugs were readily available.

Thousands of young people converged on the cities during the summer; some of them were disturbed runaways. City hangouts became crowded. In the fall of 1967 some particularly violent murders shook up everyone. Small groups began retreating to the country, where they formed **communes,** communities that shared property in common.

Rural Communes

The practice of people with similar religious, political, or cultural ideals retreating into the countryside to create their own utopian community has a long tradition in American society. Two highly successful examples were the Shakers, a religious order founded in the 1700s, and the Harmony Society, which lasted from 1804 to 1906.

At the height of the modern commune movement in 1970, the *New York Times* estimated the number of rural communes at more than 2,000, though few of them had more than 30 members. Some held meetings, wrote out bylaws, and discussed the ideal community. Communes such as Twin Oaks near Louisa, Virginia, for example, responded to the new women's liberation movement by eliminating distinctions between women's work and men's work. Any member was as likely to work in the kitchen as in the fields.

Other communes, as one observer noted, searched for "Eden rather than Utopia." They sought out secluded spots of natural beauty where commune members could act as they wished without disturbing their neighbors. They also praised spontaneity and resisted making decisions, imposing order, or doing anything else that resembled planning or organization.

Community relationships were prized. One member of a Vermont commune described her experience:

> The things that make up community are terribly subtle; it's the little things . . . someone getting his hair cut on the porch, the children around sweeping up the hair, each taking a turn snipping . . . making dinner with a crew once a week, remembering who's a vegetarian and needs a special meal. Expanded consciousness of others . . . nothing big and spectacular. The scenes that move me are the little things about our life together.
>
> —Rosabeth Moss Kanter, *Commitment and Community,* 1971

The problems that arose on the Edenlike communes often stemmed from lack of organization. Without rules regarding visitors and new members, the communes were often overrun by the curious or the "weekend hipster." Privacy was in short supply. So was money, and without an economic base such as a home industry, some residents were forced to work outside the commune to raise cash. Despite the counterculture rhetoric of equality, women were often assigned traditional cooking and child-rearing roles. Nearly all of the communes were short-lived, or changed members frequently.

Marching to a New Beat Drama, color, and public display were important elements of the counterculture. *What kinds of entertainment took place on city streets?*

Counterculture and the Mainstream

Counterculture Affects the Mainstream

Those whom the counterculture influenced responded in various ways. The radicals rejected mainstream American culture and dropped out for a few years or permanently. The moderates enjoyed aspects of the counterculture such as the music, yet managed to hold down demanding jobs. In cities across the nation some young professionals in the 1960s lived together in familylike urban communes. During the day they practiced law or accounting, and in the evening returned to the house or apartment they shared with like-minded professionals who sought an alternative lifestyle.

While many, if not most, members of the counterculture generation eventually returned to more conventional lifestyles, the main stream adopted some aspects of the counterculture in a process called **cultural diffusion.** Examples of cultural diffusion can be seen in aspects of the mainstream's diet, fashion, music, and art.

Psychedelic **This colorful poster advertises The Yardbirds, The Doors, and others.** *What effect did counterculture musicians hope their music would have?*

Diet

The rapid growth of health food stores and of vegetarian restaurants across the nation, along with the availability of many new food products, can be credited partly to the counterculture's interest in diet and food production. The back-to-the-land movement made consumers aware of the advantages of stone-ground cereals and organically grown produce. New items in the American diet, such as yogurt and ranch-fed chicken, became available in supermarkets. Environmental concerns prompted people to analyze the economics of feeding a nation on beef as opposed to fish, poultry, or vegetables. Some adopted an exclusively vegetarian diet.

Fashion

The counterculture generation, as one observer of the 1960s noted, dressed in costumes rather than in occupational or class uniforms. The colorful, beaded, braided, patched, and fringed garments that both men and women wore turned the fashion industry upside down. The international world of high fashion took its cues from young men and women on the street. Men's clothing became more colorful and women's clothing became more comfortable.

Protest often expressed itself in clothing. The counterculture adopted military surplus attire not only because it was inexpensive, but also because it expressed rejection of materialist values and blurred the lines of social class. For the same reasons, clothing of another age was recycled, and worn-out clothing repaired with patches. A mark of high distinction was to wear a patch that had been patched.

Ethnic clothing was popular for similar reasons. Beads and fringes imitated Native American costumes; tie-dyed shirts borrowed techniques from India and Africa. Ideally, each person created his or her own costume, but specialists became **entrepreneurs**—small-business owners—and sold their products at street fairs and rock concerts.

Perhaps the most potent symbol of the era was hair; a popular 1967 musical about the period was titled, fittingly, *Hair*. Long hair on a young man was the ultimate symbol of defiance. Slogans appeared, such as, Make America beautiful—give a hippie a haircut. School officials debated the acceptable length of a student's hair—could it curl over the collar or not? Once the initial shock wore off, longer hair on men and more individual clothes for both men and women became generally accepted. What was once anti-Establishment clothing was soon mainstream.

Music and Dance

Counterculture musicians hoped that their music—rock and roll—would be the means of toppling the Establishment and reforming society. It did not succeed because rock stars and their music were absorbed into the mainstream where the music brought material success worth billions of dollars to performers, promoters, and record companies.

Rock and roll was an international phenomenon that combined African American music with elements of popular white music. In the early 1950s only African American musicians played rhythm and blues (R & B), a high-energy music that emphasized the beat over the lyrics. When a few African American singers such as

Chuck Berry and Little Richard began to add lyrics that spoke to the trials and tribulations of adolescents, they created a whole new audience.

Sam Phillips, a Memphis recording engineer, said in 1951, "If I could find a white man who had the Negro sound and the Negro feel, I could make a billion dollars." A few years later he found that man in Elvis Presley. Not only did Presley have the sound and the feel, he also put on an electrifying show, dancing wildly while singing and playing his guitar. Other white performers such as Buddy Holly soon joined Presley in stardom.

Meanwhile, in England, four young men from Liverpool with working-class backgrounds began learning popular music by listening to the recordings of African American musicians. Calling themselves the Beatles, they took England by storm in 1963 and a year later made their American debut on the Ed Sullivan TV show. "Beatlemania" soon swept the country, inspiring many rock and roll imitators.

The final ingredient in the rock and roll mix was the addition of lyrics that spoke to the fears and hopes of the new generation and to the widening rift between the young and their parents. Bob Dylan provided these lyrics, as did the Beatles and many other musicians; while spirited performers like Janis Joplin made songs seem to come alive.

The use of electrically amplified instruments also drastically changed the sound and feel of the new music. One master of this new guitar sound was Jimi Hendrix, a musician from Seattle who lived overseas and achieved stardom only after returning to the United States with the influx of musicians from Great Britain.

At rock festivals such as Woodstock, in August 1969, and Altamont, in December of that same year, hundreds

THE WOODSTOCK FESTIVAL, AUGUST 15–18, 1969

On one hot weekend in 1969, 400,000 of the nation's youth gathered for the "Woodstock Music and Art Fair, An Aquarian Exposition." The event made headlines around the country, shocking adults and raising young people's hopes for a peaceful, alternative culture.

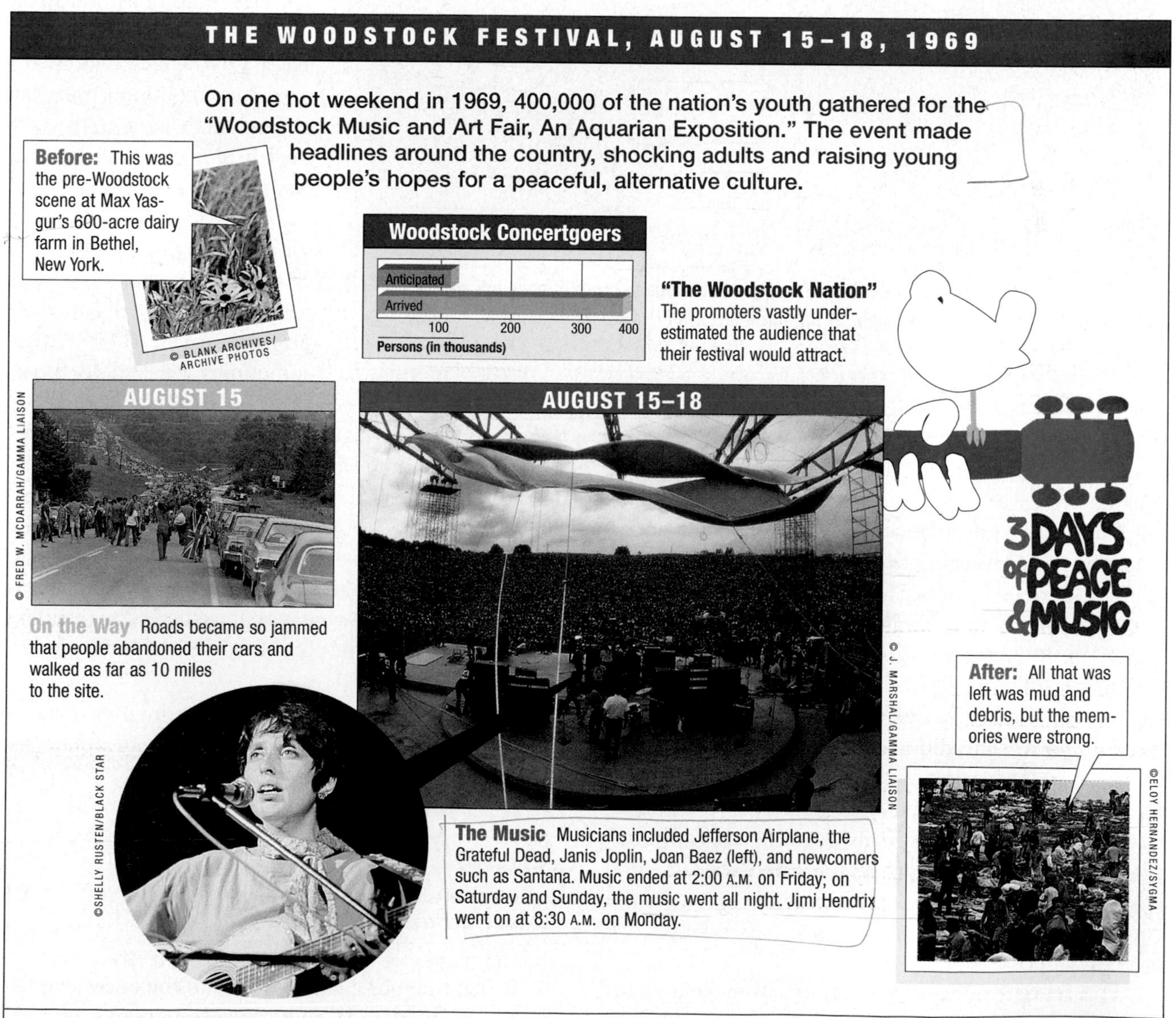

Before: This was the pre-Woodstock scene at Max Yasgur's 600-acre dairy farm in Bethel, New York.

© BLANK ARCHIVES/ARCHIVE PHOTOS

"The Woodstock Nation" The promoters vastly underestimated the audience that their festival would attract.

© FRED W. MCDARRAH/GAMMA LIAISON

On the Way Roads became so jammed that people abandoned their cars and walked as far as 10 miles to the site.

© J. MARSHAL/GAMMA LIAISON

After: All that was left was mud and debris, but the memories were strong.

©ELOY HERNANDEZ/SYGMA

©SHELLY RUSTEN/BLACK STAR

The Music Musicians included Jefferson Airplane, the Grateful Dead, Janis Joplin, Joan Baez (left), and newcomers such as Santana. Music ended at 2:00 A.M. on Friday; on Saturday and Sunday, the music went all night. Jimi Hendrix went on at 8:30 A.M. on Monday.

Despite rain and crowded conditions, the mood at Woodstock was one of fun and friendship. *What was the "schedule" of music, and who were some of the performers?*

COLLECTION OF JOHN JENKINS III

Pop Art **Andy Warhol's reproductions of images of famous personalities, such as this one of Elizabeth Taylor, made icons out of the familiar.** *What role did many pop artists want observers to take?*

of thousands of people got together to celebrate the new music. Though the fast-paced, energetic beat of rock and roll was made for dancing, the style of dancing had changed dramatically. Each individual danced without a partner, surrounded by others who also danced alone—a perfect metaphor for the counterculture, which stressed individuality within the group.

Art

During the 1960s, one art critic observed, the distinctions between traditional art and popular art, or pop art, dissolved. The primary purpose of pop art seemed to be to entertain. The entertainment, however, had a bite to it—a bite that for many gave the art enormous significance. In poking fun at the established culture, pop artists selected many of the same targets as did the counterculture—for example, a consumer society's love of material possessions.

Pop art derived its subject matter from elements of the popular culture, such as photographs, comics, advertisements, and brand-name products. Artist Andy Warhol, for example, used images of famous people, such as Marilyn Monroe and Elizabeth Taylor, and repeated them over and over. Warhol also reproduced items such as boxes of household cleaning products, making the pictures as realistic as possible. Roy Lichtenstein used as his inspiration frames from comic strips. He employed the bold primary colors of red, yellow, and black, and in comic book fashion put words like *blam* and *pow* into his paintings.

Robert Rauschenberg incorporated actual objects into his art to break down the distinction between art and reality. A 1955 composition titled "Bed" included a real quilt and pillow. Claes Oldenburg reproduced common, everyday objects such as a three-way electric plug or a toilet bowl in giant scale.

Pop artists expected these symbols of popular culture to carry, as art, some of the same meaning as they did in their original form. The artists sometimes referred to themselves as only the "agents" of the art and said it was up to the observer to give meaning to the work and thus become part of it.

An outgrowth of this philosophy was a new kind of theater staged by pop artists in the 1960s, called a "happening." An artist would set a scene, which differed at each performance, and allow each observer to express his or her reaction to what was presented. The response of the audience became part of the drama, and each performance was unique.

The Counterculture Appraised

Counterculture Expands Consciousness but Takes a Toll

When the music faded away and the crowds at the corner of Haight and Ashbury packed up and returned home, what remained? The young people of the 1960s had forced people all across the country to take a look

© SHELLY RUSTEN/BLACK STAR

Feeling the Music Janis Joplin and others used music as a form of self-expression. *In what ways was the counterculture an expression of inner adventure?*

inside themselves for a brief moment and to question some fundamental values about the individual and society. Musical sounds were never the same again; colors were forever brighter.

Dangers and Divisions

On the other hand, casual sex and the use of drugs took a great toll. Many plans for social change were never achieved. People learned the hard way that ideals, such as love not war and sharing versus possessing, are not effective unless there is a plan to put them into action. Planning required organization and careful thought, which many rejected as characteristic of the Establishment.

The complications and contradictions in the movement were also apparent in the diversity of its members. Although there were those who were sincerely dedicated to specific goals of social justice for African Americans, women, Native Americans, and Hispanic Americans, even within these groups there were differences in thought and strategy that often undermined their efforts at social change.

An Inner Adventure

In the last analysis, was the counterculture a real movement? Not in the sense of the other modern efforts at social reform. These other efforts generally worked within the established social system and advocated organized political, legislative, and economic measures to accomplish concrete goals.

Although there were many in the counterculture who chose to effect change by working within the existing social system, there were also those who completely rejected this strategy. Commune members, for example, hoped that their success in establishing new ways for people to live together would encourage others to do the same. Some people were mainly interested in economic reforms, such as better wages and working conditions for the poor. Still others were dissatisfied with their lives and found in the symbols of the counterculture—long hair, peace signs, unconventional dress—the security and status of belonging to a group. Many members of the counterculture were more concerned about their own inner adventures than social reform.

There was one issue, however, that had the power to draw together different elements from the counterculture and beyond—war in Vietnam. The war itself, in turn, became the dominant issue on the social and political landscape of the United States, an issue that would reshape the nation's self-image in the decades to come.

Section Assessment

Main Idea

1. Use a diagram to compare what the United States was like before and after the counterculture movement.

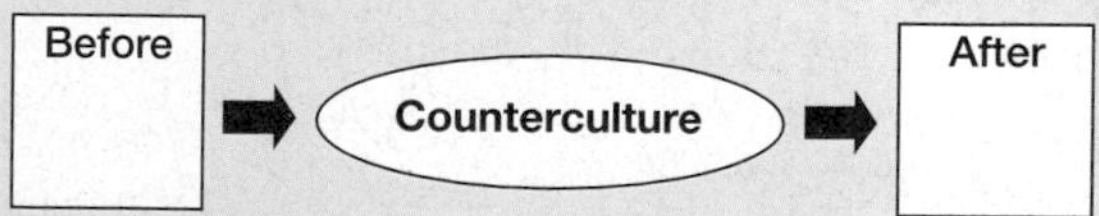

Vocabulary

2. Define: counterculture, generation gap, hippie, commune, cultural diffusion, entrepreneur.

Checking Facts

3. What were the major beliefs and values of the counterculture?

4. Why did urban and rural communal living fail in the counterculture?

Critical Thinking

5. **Synthesizing Information** In what ways did the counterculture become an "establishment"?

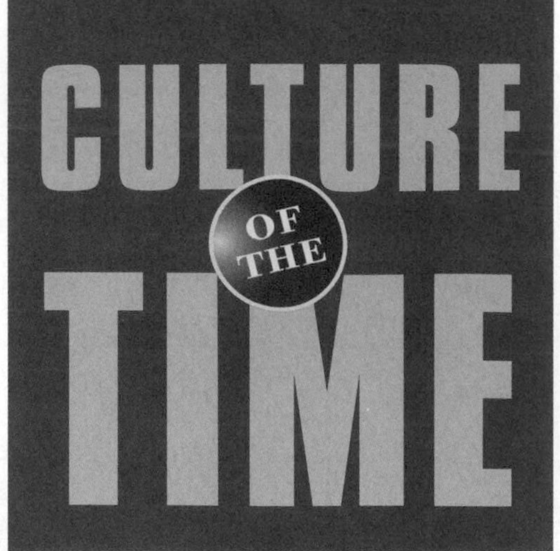

The Beat of the Sixties

The youth of the 1960s marched to a new beat. The Beatles, Jimi Hendrix, Janis Joplin, the Doors, and others revolutionized music. A nonconformist, optimistic attitude prevailed. Bright colors, flamboyant designs, and long hair decorated the scene. Fast-paced comedy with a political bite sharpened entertainment.

© 1967 BOB WILLOUGHBY/MOTION PICTURE & TV PHOTO ARCHIVE

THE GRADUATE

This topical movie comedy reflected both the vulnerability of youth and the **anything-goes attitude** that was prevalent in the 1960s.

FILE PHOTO BY DOUG MINDELL

© JOHN LAUNOIS/BLACK STAR

THE BEATLES

In the mid-1960s, 4 British rock singers took the United States by storm. Their melodies were complex and their lyrics socially relevant. Millions of youth listened to their music and imitated their optimistic, flamboyant style—**Beatlemania** was born.

LAUGH-IN

This **innovative, fast-paced TV comedy** combined sketches, one-liners, and celebrity cameo appearances with sight gags and catch phrases ("Sock it to me," "You bet your bippy") in a loosely structured frenetic whole that was highly appealing to viewers in the late 1960s.

JIMI HENDRIX

The electric guitar revolutionized music, and Jimi Hendrix revolutionized the electric guitar. His hyper-amplified, magnetic performances of **heavy rock** and **psychedelic blues** were embellished by his flashy outfits and outrageous stage antics—such as smashing or burning his guitar. Hendrix was a gifted rock musician—one of the most innovative of the 1960s.

Chapter  Assessment

Self-Check Quiz

Visit the *American Odyssey* Web site at americanodyssey.glencoe.com and click on ***Chapter 22—Self-Check Quiz*** to prepare for the Chapter Test.

Reviewing Key Terms

On a separate sheet of paper, write the vocabulary term that best completes each sentence.

generation gap	**amendment**
compensation	**feminist**
undocumented immigrant	**cultural diffusion**

1. Each ______ in the women's liberation movement was striving for equal rights with men.

2. An ______ comes to the United States without paper documents.

3. Native Americans wanted ______ for lands they had lost to the United States government.

4. Differences in opinion between youth and their elders resulted in a ______.

5. Through ______, many aspects of the counterculture became incorporated into the mainstream.

Recalling Facts

1. What were 3 origins of the women's movement of the 1960s?

2. How does each of the following relate to the women's movement: Phyllis Schlafly, *The Feminine Mystique, Roe* v. *Wade*, the ERA?

3. For what reasons did Hispanic Americans come to the United States?

4. Hispanic Americans are not a single group. How has this diversity affected their attaining civil rights?

5. In what ways were Native American issues similar to and different from the issues of other groups seeking civil rights?

6. What general and specific aspects of traditional culture did the counterculture reject?

7. What were people seeking in rural communal living in the 1960s and 1970s? What did they find?

Critical Thinking

1. Stating Problems Clearly How did the issue of undocumented immigrants affect Hispanic Americans legally in the United States, either as citizens or on special visas?

2. Making Comparisons Use a diagram like this one to compare the methods used by women, Hispanic Americans, and Native Americans to achieve equality. Place a check mark by the methods you think have been most effective for each group.

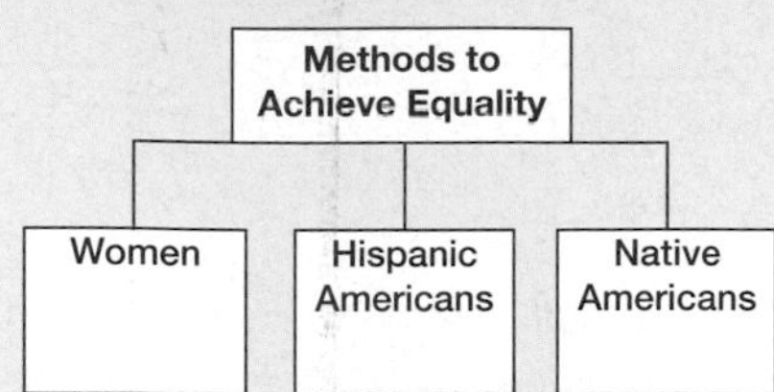

3. Making Generalizations How does bilingualism for Hispanic Americans relate to self-determination for Native Americans?

The Princeton Review — Standardized Test Practice

1. One of the major issues that concerned Native Americans in the 1960s and 1970s was

A self-determination.
B undocumented immigration.
C bilingualism.
D cultural diffusion.

Test-Taking Tip: Eliminate obviously incorrect answers. For example, Native Americans had never been immigrants, for they were already here when Europeans first colonized the Americas. Therefore, answer B would not be a leading issue and can be ruled out.

2. All of the following helped shape the counterculture of the 1960s EXCEPT

A the threat of nuclear war.
B a rejection of the consumerism of the 1950s.
C the popularity of rock and roll.
D an acceptance of prevailing middle-class values.

Test-Taking Tip: The question asks for an *exception,* or an answer that would NOT have caused or been associated with the counterculture. Remember that the counterculture was made up of mostly young people whose values ran *counter,* or opposite, to those of the established culture.

GEOGRAPHY AND HISTORY

Equal Rights Amendment Ratification, 1972–1982

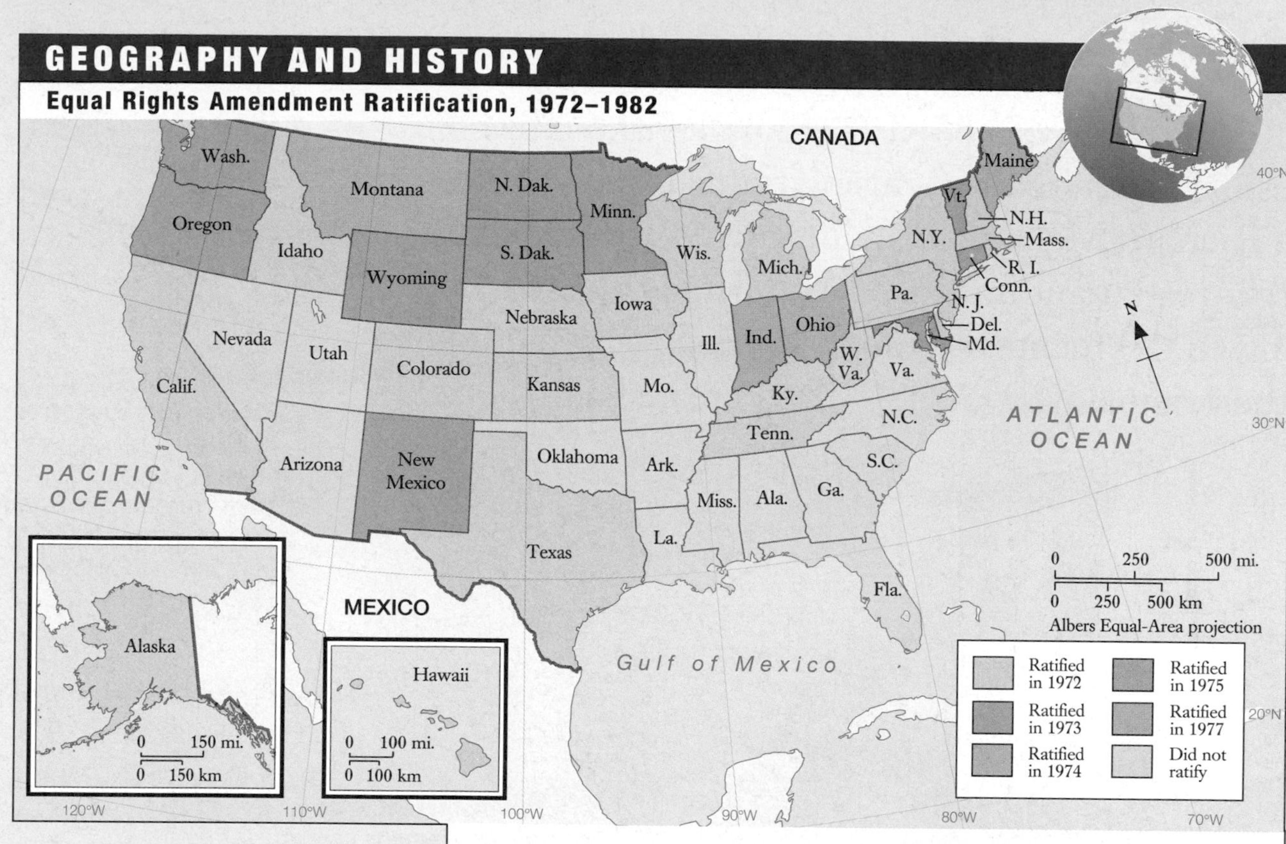

Study the map to answer the following questions:

1. How many states ratified the ERA early, in 1972? In 1973?
2. How many states ratified the ERA from 1974 to 1977?
3. How many states never ratified the ERA?
4. Did your home state ratify the ERA? If so, when?
5. What regional trends do you notice in terms of ratification?

Portfolio Project

Choose and research one of the reform groups covered in this chapter. What have been the group's successes and failures over the years? Is the group still active today? If so, what are the group's current makeup and concerns? Does its membership still reflect the same type of people (age, social and economic status, and so on)? Write a report based on your findings, including copies of photographs, articles, or graphics, if possible. Place the results in your portfolio.

Cooperative Learning

With three or four other students, choose and research one controversial issue mentioned in this chapter—feminism, ERA, bilingualism, restoration of land and sacred sites, for example. Look at both sides of the issue, and conduct an informal debate within your group, with two or more students representing each point of view.

Reinforcing Skills

Conducting Interviews Review the steps used to prepare for an interview with Betty Friedan on page 732. Then repeat these same steps to prepare for an interview with Phyllis Schlafly. How would your background information and questions differ for the two women?

Technology Activity

Building a Database Use the Bureau of Indian Affairs Web site to locate information about Native American land claims against the United States government, starting with the Indian Claims Commission (1946). Build a database with the information you've collected. Headings to include are Claimant, Date, Summary of Case, and Result of Settlement.

Then...

The First McDonald's

In 1955 Ray Kroc, a 53-year-old milkshake-mixer salesman, acquired franchising rights from Maurice and Richard McDonald, owners of a successful hamburger restaurant franchise. The detail-oriented Kroc followed the menu and the food-processing method of the original McDonald's—and created an empire.

2 McDonald's employees follow set procedures for food preparation and presentation, established by the McDonald brothers and refined over the years.

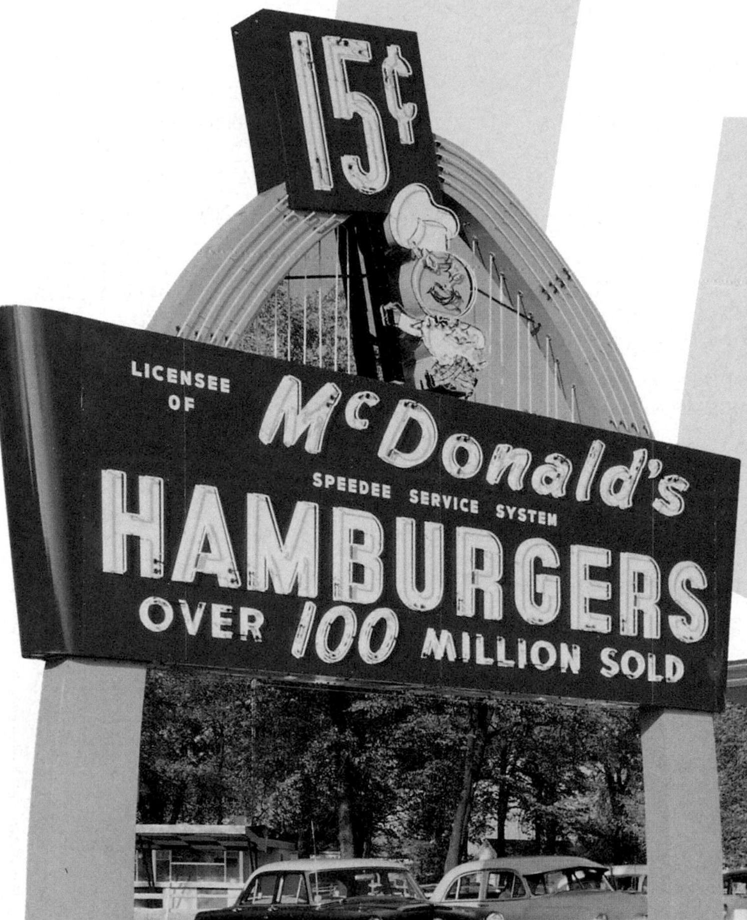

15¢
LICENSEE OF
McDonald's
SPEEDEE SERVICE SYSTEM
HAMBURGERS
OVER 100 MILLION SOLD
McDonald's

1 This restaurant, with the now-famous golden arches, was typical of McDonald's in the 1950s.

Fun Facts

© MCDONALD'S CORPORATION

RONALD McDONALD

Ronald McDonald made his first public appearance in 1963 in Washington, D.C. Ronald was played by Willard Scott, who later became the weatherperson on NBC's *Today Show*.

3 McDonald's Original Menu Items and Prices

Hamburger	15¢
Cheeseburger	19¢
French Fries	10¢
Milk	10¢
Milk Shake	10¢
Root Beer	10¢
Orangeade	10¢
Coca-Cola	10¢
Coffee	10¢

Try McDonald's ALL-AMERICAN
McDonald's
FRENCH FRIES · HAMBURGER ·

McFacts

1955 Ray Kroc acquires franchising rights to McDonald's

1955 "Speedee" becomes company symbol

1961 Ray Kroc buys McDonald's name for $2.7 million

1963 Ronald McDonald makes his debut

1967 First McDonald's restaurants outside U.S. open, in Canada and Puerto Rico

1968 Big Mac is introduced

1972 McDonald's becomes a billion-dollar corporation

1973 McDonald's makes the cover of *Time* magazine

1975 First drive-through opens, in Oklahoma City, Oklahoma

1986 Complete food product ingredient listing is introduced

1990 Foam packaging is phased out

1993 McDonald's is in 69 countries; 95 billion+ hamburgers sold

1995 McDonald's opens franchises in Estonia, Romania, Malta, Colombia, Jamaica, and Slovakia

4 This cheerful, winking fellow is Speedee, an early McDonald's symbol.

...Now

IMPACT OF FAST FOOD

PORTFOLIO PROJECT

Write a one-page magazine article on how fast-food restaurants such as McDonald's affect what and how teenagers eat today. Gather information from library resources, from your own experiences, and from talking with others. You may want to include suggestions for future fast-food establishments. Place the article in your portfolio.

RONALD'S FRIENDS

Ronald has many friends in McDonaldland, all of whom like and respect him. Some of Ronald's friends are Hamburglar, Grimace, Birdie the Early Bird, The Fry Kids, The Happy Meal Guys, CosMc, McNugget Buddies, Mayor McCheese, The Professor, The Captain, and Uncle O'Grimacy.

UNIT
9

The Troubled Years

1960–1980

HISTORY & YOU

The Vietnam War ushered in an era of conflict among the American people. Disagreement over the war in Southeast Asia created seemingly insurmountable rifts. The Watergate crisis during the waning years of the war weakened the nation's trust in its elected leaders. The two events deeply shook the nation's self-confidence and imposed a new sense of limits on the actions undertaken by the federal government both overseas and at home.

Historic America Electronic Field Trips

On November 13, 1982, a monument was dedicated in Washington, D.C., to honor Americans who served in the Vietnam War. It also helped to heal the deep wounds caused by debate and protest over the war. To learn more about the history of United States involvement in Vietnam and the effect of protest on the troops who served there, view videodisc Chapter 10: *The Vietnam Veterans Memorial* in **Historic America Electronic Field Trips.**

Primary Sources
Library

See pages 968–969 for primary source readings that accompany Unit 9.

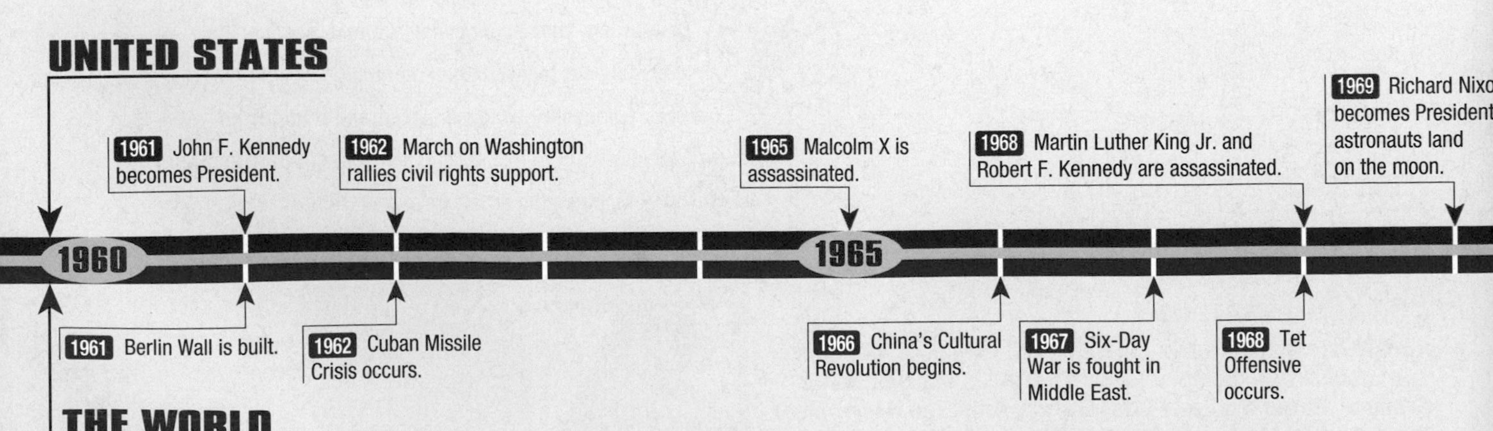
UNITED STATES
1961 John F. Kennedy becomes President.
1962 March on Washington rallies civil rights support.
1965 Malcolm X is assassinated.
1968 Martin Luther King Jr. and Robert F. Kennedy are assassinated.
1969 Richard Nixo becomes President astronauts land on the moon.
1960
1965
1961 Berlin Wall is built.
1962 Cuban Missile Crisis occurs.
1966 China's Cultural Revolution begins.
1967 Six-Day War is fought in Middle East.
1968 Tet Offensive occurs.
THE WORLD

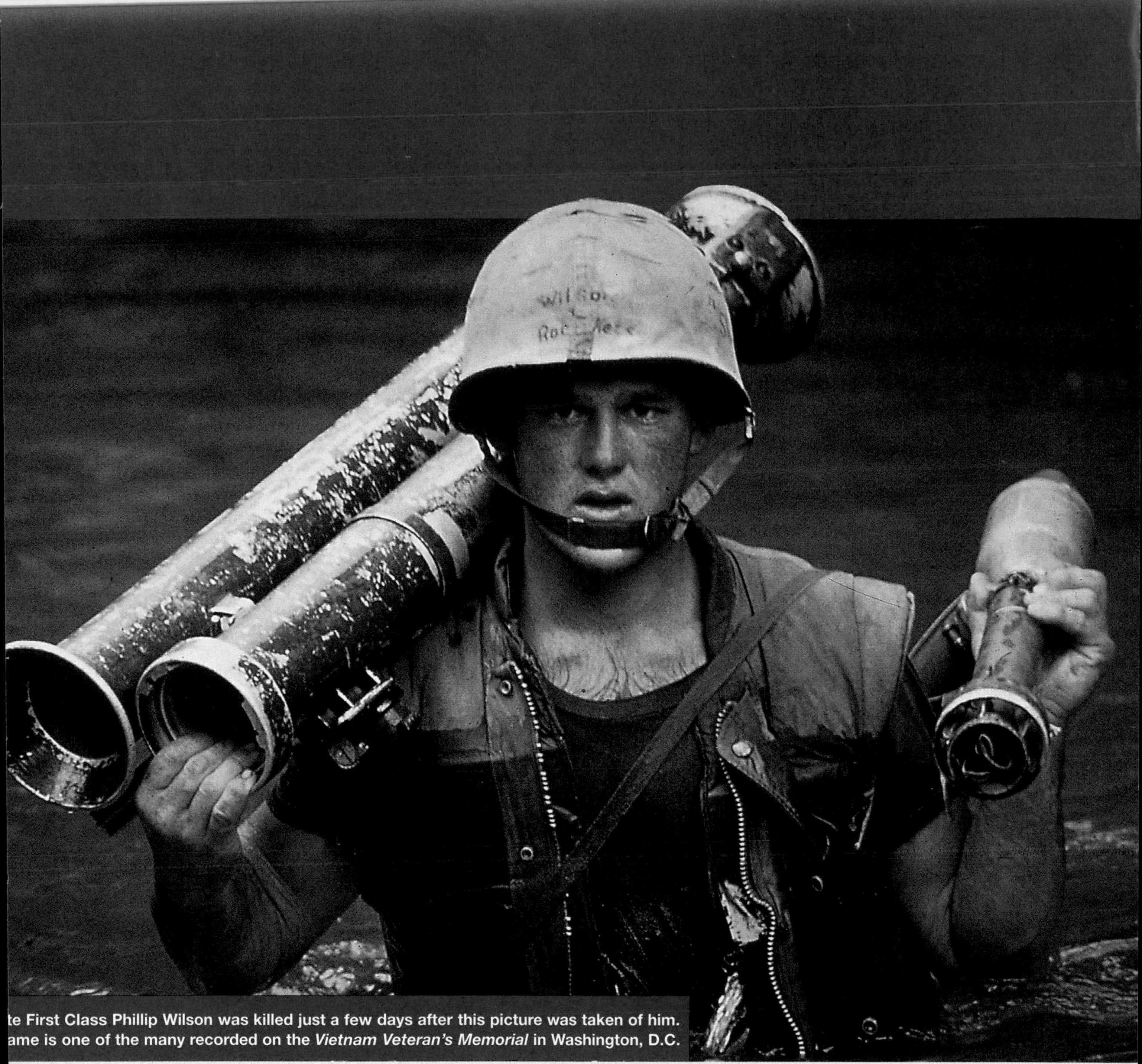

te First Class Phillip Wilson was killed just a few days after this picture was taken of him. ame is one of the many recorded on the *Vietnam Veteran's Memorial* in Washington, D.C.

LARRY BURROWS/© TIME, INC.

- **1970** National Guard troops shoot students at Kent State and Jackson State.
- **1970** Henry Kissinger's trip to China begins détente.
- **1972** SALT arms limitation agreement is signed.
- **1973** Oil embargo begins.
- **1973** U.S. troops leave Vietnam; Yom Kippur War is fought in Middle East.
- **1974** Nixon resigns; Gerald Ford becomes President.
- **1977** Jimmy Carter becomes President.
- **1979** Nuclear accident occurs at Three Mile Island.
- **1979** Camp David Agreement is signed.

1970 — 1975 — 1980

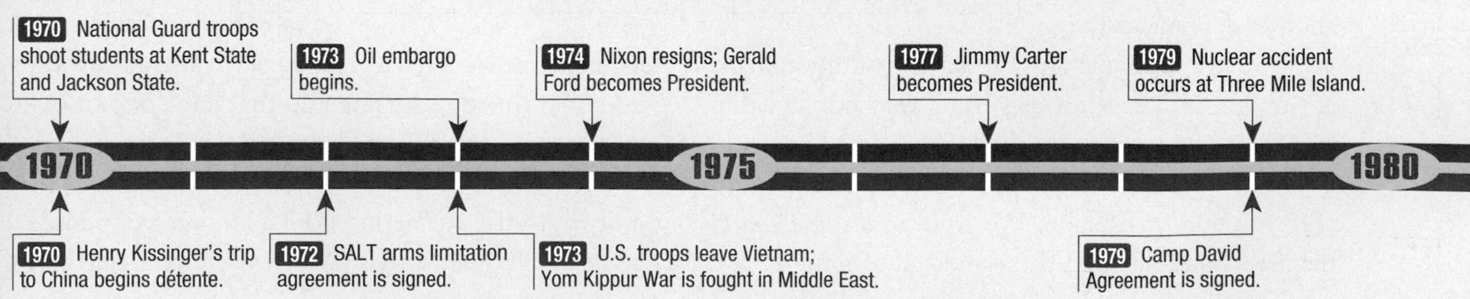

Born on the Fourth of July

BY RON KOVIC

Some Americans tried to end the Vietnam War by protesting at home. Others went to fight in Vietnam. After being shot and permanently paralyzed in Vietnam, Ron Kovic began to question the war effort. This excerpt from his personal narrative shows how Kovic's experience at a peace rally in Washington, D.C., helped him decide to join the antiwar movement.

A young girl sat down next to me and handed me a canteen of cool water. "Here," she said, "have a drink." I drank it down and passed it to Skip who passed it to someone else. That was the feeling that day. We all seemed to be sharing everything.

We listened as the speakers one after another denounced the invasion of Cambodia and the slaying of the students at Kent State. The sun was getting very hot and Skip and I decided to move around. We wanted to get to the White House where Nixon was holed up, probably watching television. We were in a great sea of people, thousands and thousands all around us. We finally made it to Lafayette Park. On the other side of the avenue the government had lined up thirty or forty buses, making a huge wall between the people and the White House. I remember wondering back then why they had to put all those buses in front of the president. Was the government so afraid of its own people that it needed such a gigantic barricade? I'll always remember those buses lined up that day and not being able to see the White House from my wheelchair.

COLLECTION OF WHITNEY MUSEUM OF AMERICAN ART, NY. PHOTOGRAPHY BY GEOFFREY CLEMENTS, NY

Three Flags **Jasper Johns and other pop artists incorporated everyday objects into their paintings and sculptures. Johns's *Three Flags* (1958) invites viewers to question their feelings about the American flag.**

We went back to the rally for a while, then went on down to the Reflecting Pool. Hundreds of people had taken off their clothes. They were jumping up and down to the beat of bongo drums and metal cans. A man in his fifties had stripped completely naked. Wearing only a crazy-looking hat and a pair of enormous black glasses, he was dancing on a platform in the middle of hundreds of naked people. The crowd was clapping wildly. Skip hesitated for a moment, then stripped all his clothes off, jumping into the pool and joining the rest of the people. I didn't know what all of this had to do with the invasion of Cambodia or the students slain at Kent State, but it was total freedom. As I sat there in my wheelchair at the edge of the Reflecting Pool with everyone running naked all around me and the clapping and the drums resounding in my ears, I wanted to join them. I wanted to take off my clothes like Skip and the rest of them and wade into the pool and rub my body with all those others. Everything seemed to be hitting me all at once. One part of me was upset that people were swimming naked in the national monument and the other part of me completely understood that now it was their pool, and what good is a pool if you can't swim in it.

I remember how the police came later that day, very suddenly, when we were watching the sun go down—a blue legion of police in cars and on motorcycles and others with angry faces on big horses. A tall cop walked into the crowd near the Reflecting Pool and read something into a bullhorn no one could make out. The drums stopped and a few of the naked people began to put their clothes back on. It was almost evening and with most of the invading army's forces heading back along the Jersey Turnpike, the blue legion had decided to attack. And they did—wading their horses into the pool, flailing their clubs, smashing skulls. People were running everywhere as gas canisters began to pop. I couldn't understand why this was happening, why the police would attack the people, running them into the grass with their horses and beating them with their clubs. Two or three horses charged into the crowd at full gallop, driving the invading army into retreat toward the Lincoln Memorial. A girl was crying and screaming, trying to help her bleeding friend. She was yelling something about the pigs and kept stepping backward away from the horses and the flying clubs. For the first time that day I felt anger surge up inside me. I was no longer an observer, sitting in my car at the edge of a demonstration. I was right in the middle of it and it was ugly. Skip started pushing the chair as fast as he could up the path toward the Lincoln Memorial. I kept turning, looking back. I wanted to shout back at the charging police, tell them I was a veteran. When we got to the memorial, I remember looking at Lincoln's face and reading the words carved on the walls in back of him. I felt certain that if he were alive he would be there with us.

I WANTED TO SHOUT BACK AT THE CHARGING POLICE, TELL THEM I WAS A VETERAN.

I told Skip that I was never going to be the same. The demonstration had stirred something in my mind that would be there from now on. It was so very different from boot camp and fighting in the war. There was a togetherness, just as there had been in Vietnam, but it was a togetherness of a different kind of people and for a much different reason. In the war we were killing and maiming people. In Washington on that Saturday afternoon in May we were trying to heal them and set them free.

Responding to Literature

1. **What do you think contributed most to changing Ron Kovic's attitude about the Vietnam War?**
2. **If you had been a teenager during the Vietnam War, what do you think your attitudes toward the war and war protesters might have been? Why?**

The Vietnam War

JANUARY 30, 1968: COMMUNIST GUERRILLAS ATTACK UNITED STATES EMBASSY

It was nearly 3 A.M. on the first night of Tet, the Vietnamese New Year. A small truck and a taxicab filled with Vietcong guerrillas rolled through the quiet city streets. As they turned onto Thong Nhut Boulevard, a broad, tree-lined avenue that ran past the American embassy, the guerrillas opened fire.

Two United States soldiers inside the embassy grounds returned the fire. One soldier, 23-year-old Charles Daniel, shouted: "They're coming in! They're coming in! Help me! Help me!" Moments later Daniel and his companion, 20-year-old William Sebast, lay dead.

Thus began a bloody 6-hour assault on the United States embassy in Saigon, the capital of South Vietnam. When the fighting was over, 19 guerrillas and 5 American soldiers had lost their lives. According to one reporter, the embassy grounds looked like "a butcher shop in Eden."

By 1968 United States troops had been fighting for 3 years. Policy makers saw Vietnam as a battle to prevent the spread of communism in Southeast Asia. In pursuing this policy of containment, the United States had become entangled in a tragic war thousands of miles from its shore.

This would be the nation's longest war, claiming the lives of more than 58,000 United States soldiers and more than 2 million Vietnamese. It would leave Southeast Asia in ruins and divide American society as had no other issue since the Civil War. ■

HISTORY JOURNAL

Before you read the rest of this chapter, write briefly what you know about the domestic turmoil caused by the war in Vietnam and what you think this chapter will be about.

Chapter Overview

Visit the *American Odyssey* Web site at americanodyssey.glencoe.com and click on ***Chapter 23—Chapter Overview*** to preview the chapter.

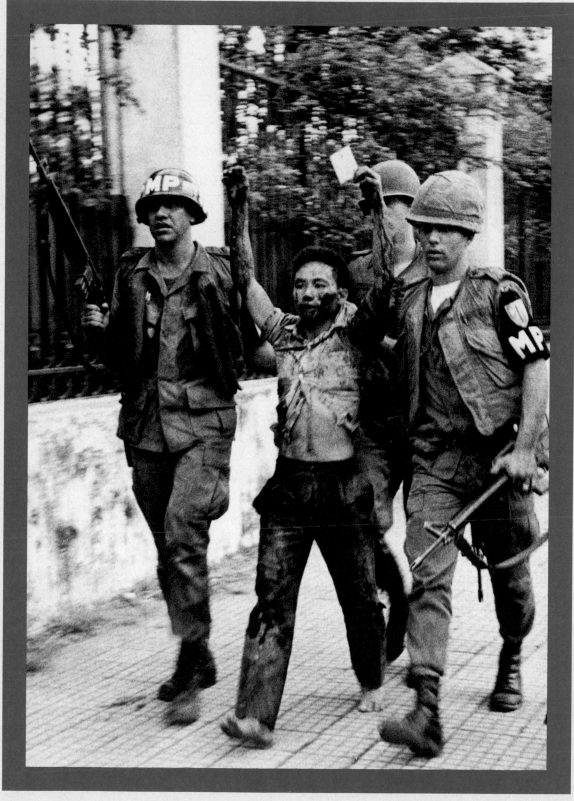

A SURVIVING MEMBER OF THE GUERRILLA TEAM THAT ATTACKED THE UNITED STATES EMBASSY IN SAIGON IS LED AWAY.

War in Southeast Asia

SEPTEMBER 2, 1945: VIETNAM DECLARES ITS INDEPENDENCE

UPI/BETTMANN

Independence
Ho Chi Minh makes an appeal to the United States for support.

HALF A MILLION VIETNAMESE FILLED BA DINH SQUARE IN CENTRAL HANOI. Peasants in straw hats, many of whom had come on foot from distant villages, mingled with Hanoi residents on the grassy square. At noon a frail figure with piercing black eyes and a wispy black beard climbed onto a wooden platform set up at one end of the square. He was Ho Chi Minh, the 55-year-old leader of the Vietnamese nationalist force known as the Vietminh. The crowd began chanting, "Doc-Lap, Doc-Lap" ("independence, independence"). For several minutes Ho stood there smiling, buoyed by the crowd's enthusiasm. Finally he raised his hands, and the crowd grew still.

"We hold these truths to be self-evident, that all men are created equal, that they are endowed by their creator with certain unalienable rights, among them life, liberty, and the pursuit of happiness." With those words borrowed from the American Declaration of Independence, Ho proclaimed the independence of Vietnam from French colonial rule. The crowd roared its approval.

Later in the day, United States Army officers joined Vietnamese leaders to celebrate Vietnam's liberation. During World War II Japan had occupied Vietnam. The Americans and the Vietminh had fought side by side to drive out the Japanese. When the Japanese surrendered in August 1945, the Vietminh took over the capital of Hanoi and declared Vietnam independent.

Yet the warm friendship of that September day soon chilled, as Vietnam became a battleground in the cold war that followed World War II. In just 20 years, Vietnamese nationalists and the United States would become bitter enemies, embroiled in war.

GUIDE TO READING

Main Idea

After the French withdrew from Indochina, U.S. Presidents tried to stop the spread of communism in the region through increasing involvement in a civil war waged between Communists and non-Communists in Vietnam.

Vocabulary

- national liberation
- containment
- domino theory
- guerrilla warfare
- pacification program

Read to Find Out . . .

- why most Vietnamese wanted a communist form of government.
- what the United States feared would happen if Communists took control of Vietnam.
- the experiences of U.S. troops and military nurses sent to Vietnam.

The French War in Indochina

Ho Chi Minh Leads Vietminh Against the French

Although the Vietnamese had declared their independence, the French were unwilling to give up the empire they had ruled for more than 60 years. The colonies in Indochina—the present-day nations of Cambodia, Laos, and Vietnam—were among the richest of France's overseas colonies, supplying such valuable resources as rice, rubber, and tin.

The French, however, faced a powerful foe in Ho Chi Minh. Ho was a staunch, and at times ruthless, revolutionary committed to the struggle for Vietnamese independence. Ho founded the Vietminh in 1941 to drive the French from Vietnam. Like Ho, most Vietminh leaders were committed Communists. Their primary goals were extensive land reform and the creation of an independent unified Vietnam. They were waging a war of **national liberation** to free their country from foreign control.

By 1945 the Vietminh army numbered 5,000 and had a firm base of support in northern Vietnam. The French, meanwhile, tried to regain control of southern Vietnam as the Japanese withdrew. Tensions mounted, and fighting broke out between the French and the Vietminh. In November 1946, a French ship shelled the city of Haiphong, setting off a full-scale war.

The French entered the war confident of victory. Ho, however, predicted a different outcome. "If ever the tiger [the Vietminh] pauses," he said, "the elephant [France] will impale him on his mighty tusks. But the tiger will not pause, and the elephant will die of exhaustion and loss of blood."

The French soon controlled the major cities and towns, while the Vietminh retreated into the countryside. There they waged a relentless war—avoiding major battles, ambushing French troops, and staging hit-and-run raids on French outposts—while building support among the peasants.

United States Support for the French

In 1950 the French, unable to crush the Vietminh, appealed to Washington, D.C., for aid. President Truman was not eager to support France's colonial ambitions. Yet the cold war had increased tensions in Europe. Truman was afraid to lose France as an ally against the Soviets, who in August 1949 had exploded their first atomic bomb.

Also Indochina had assumed a new importance. The Communist victory in China in 1949 fed American fears of Communist takeovers elsewhere in Asia.

If the United States failed to stop communism in Indochina, Truman believed, it would sweep across the rest of Asia. The United States policy of **containment**—opposing communism wherever it appeared in an effort to "contain" its spread—would pull the United States closer to war in Southeast Asia.

In 1950, just before the outbreak of the Korean War, Truman agreed to send $20 million in direct military aid to the French. Over the next 4 years, the United States paid for most of the French war effort, pumping more than $2.6 billion into the French attempt to "save" Vietnam from communism.

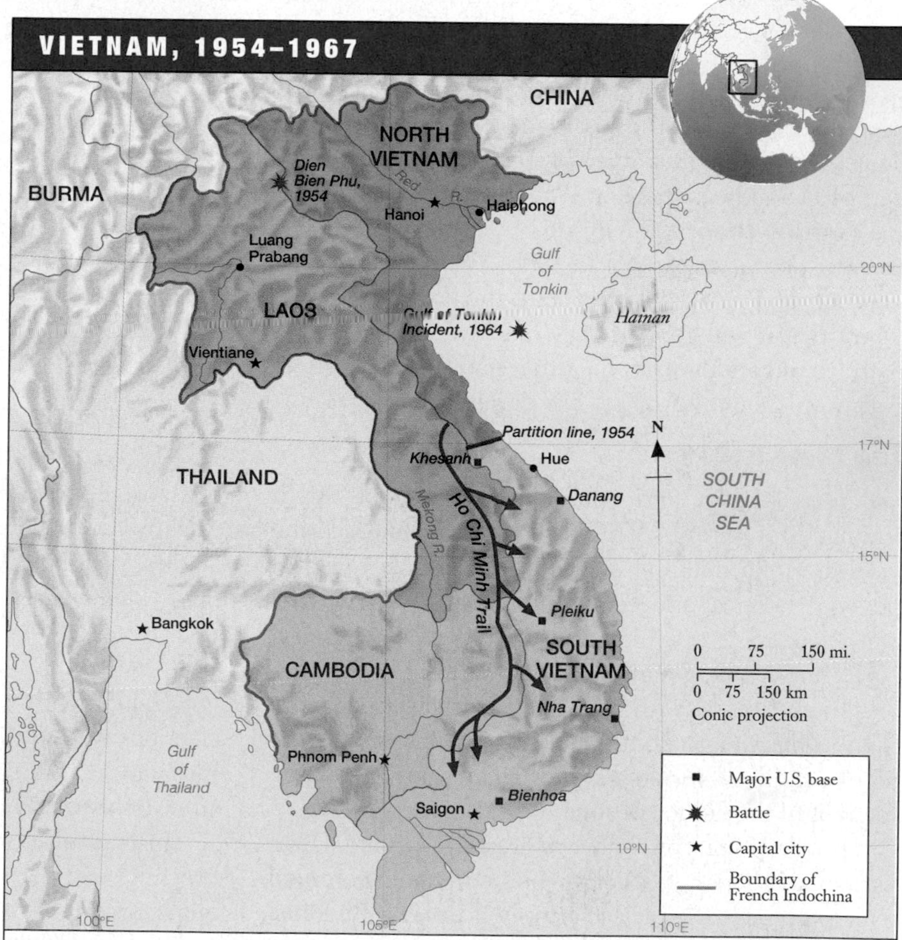

The division of Vietnam left the North without its main source of rice in the South. Emergency imports from Burma prevented a famine. *What United States military base is located near the partition line between North and South Vietnam?*

The End of French Rule

Despite American aid, France was losing the war. When in May 1954 the Vietminh overran Dien Bien Phu, a French outpost in northwestern Vietnam, it signaled the end of French control of Vietnam.

The day after the French surrendered at Dien Bien Phu, representatives of the United States, Great Britain, France, the Soviet Union, China, Laos, Cambodia, and the Vietminh met in Geneva to hammer out a peace agreement. According to its terms, Vietnam would be temporarily divided along the 17th parallel. The Vietminh would withdraw north of that line, and the French would withdraw to the south. Vietnam would be reunified in 1956 after national elections. The Vietminh agreed, confident that they would win the promised elections.

The United States Enters the War

Fear of the Spread of Communism Spurs Action

Fearful of just such a Communist victory, the United States refused to sign the agreement. President Eisenhower believed that the loss of South Vietnam would deny the United States access to the resources and markets of all Southeast Asia. In 1954 Eisenhower explained the **domino theory** to a group of reporters. "You have a row of dominoes set up," he said. "You knock over the first one, and what will happen to the last one is a certainty that it will go over very quickly." If South Vietnam fell to communism, the other nations of Southeast Asia would fall in turn, just like dominoes.

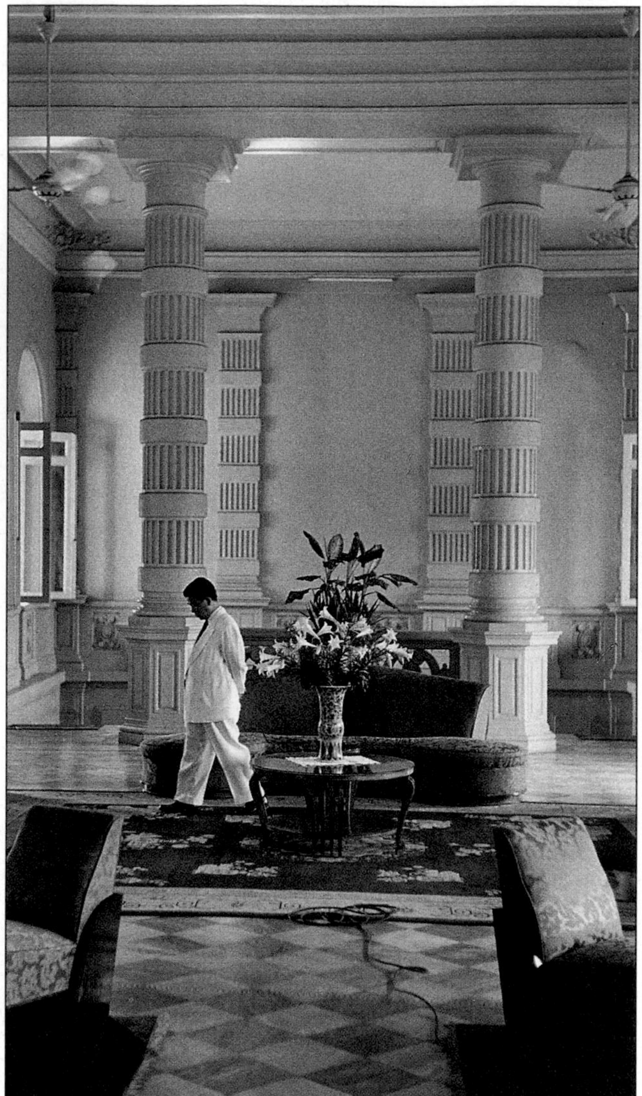

HOWARD SOCHUREK/LIFE MAGAZINE, ©TIME, INC.

An Isolated Leader Diem did not understand the concerns and needs of his people. *Why did the United States support Diem?*

The Diem Regime

Years of war and colonial rule had left South Vietnam in disarray. A tiny ruling class controlled the wealth, while millions of landless peasants toiled in poverty. Political and economic reforms were desperately needed. The United States pinned its hopes on Ngo Dinh Diem, a nationalist and fierce anti-Communist. From 1954 to 1961, the United States pumped more than $1 billion into South Vietnam, but $4 out of every $5 of the aid was spent on the military, leaving only a fraction of the aid for economic development.

An aloof man who always dressed in white, Diem was an aristocratic Catholic who had little in common with the people he ruled, most of whom were Buddhist peasants. He ran the country as if it were a personal empire. Half his cabinet members were relatives, and he imprisoned anyone who dared to speak out against his autocratic rule.

United States advisers urged Diem to try to win peasant support by breaking up the huge estates of wealthy landowners and handing out farming plots to the landless peasants. Diem, however, rejected any reforms that would weaken the ruling class.

Civil War

In 1957, with American support, Diem canceled the elections promised by the Geneva Accords. As even Eisenhower admitted, if the elections had been held, Ho Chi Minh would have won.

Instead of elections Diem held a "referendum" to prove he had the support of the people in South Vietnam. American advisers assured Diem that they would be satisfied if he had 60 percent approval, but he rigged the vote so that he won by a whopping 98 percent. In Saigon, for example, he claimed 605,000 votes even though the city had only 405,000 registered voters.

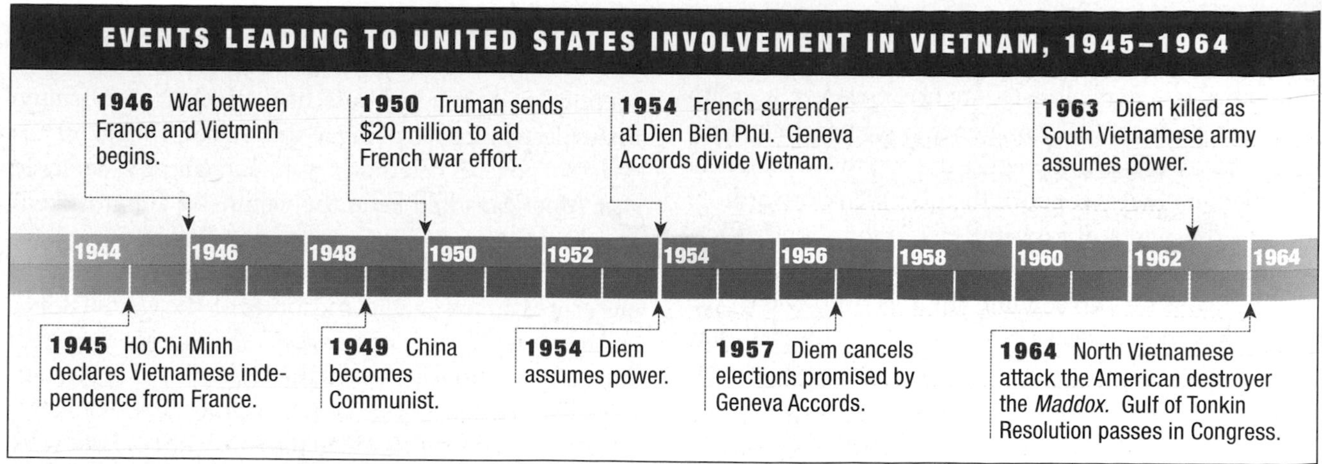

EVENTS LEADING TO UNITED STATES INVOLVEMENT IN VIETNAM, 1945–1964
1946 War between France and Vietminh begins.
1950 Truman sends $20 million to aid French war effort.
1954 French surrender at Dien Bien Phu. Geneva Accords divide Vietnam.
1963 Diem killed as South Vietnamese army assumes power.
1944
1946
1948
1950
1952
1954
1956
1958
1960
1962
1964
1945 Ho Chi Minh declares Vietnamese independence from France.
1949 China becomes Communist.
1954 Diem assumes power.
1957 Diem cancels elections promised by Geneva Accords.
1964 North Vietnamese attack the American destroyer the *Maddox*. Gulf of Tonkin Resolution passes in Congress.

Diem's brutal policies and his refusal to hold elections angered many Vietnamese. Their discontent proved fertile ground for the Vietminh. As one Vietminh soldier later said, the peasants were "like a mound of straw ready to be ignited."

In late 1960 the Vietminh and other groups opposed to Diem united in South Vietnam to form the National Liberation Front (NLF). Like the Vietminh, most of the NLF leaders were Communists. They promised economic reform, reunification with the North, and genuine independence. They also waged a campaign of terror, assassinating 2,000 government officials in 1960. The NLF, also known as the Vietcong, had close ties to the government of Ho Chi Minh. Over the years the NLF would get increasing support from North Vietnam and, indirectly, from China and the Soviet Union as well. The new President of the United States, John F. Kennedy, faced a difficult choice: abandon Diem or deepen American involvement in Vietnam.

The Kennedy Years

Like Truman and Eisenhower, President Kennedy saw Vietnam as part of the global struggle in the fight against communism. "Vietnam represents the cornerstone of the Free World in Southeast Asia," he declared. Despite some misgivings, Kennedy greatly expanded the United States's role in Vietnam. Kennedy's plan was twofold. The first part was to strengthen the South Vietnamese army with United States technology and military advisers to help them win the war against the Vietcong. The second was to pressure Diem to make political and economic reforms to eliminate the conditions that had allowed communism to take root in the first place. By 1963 Kennedy had tripled the amount of aid and increased the number of United States military advisers to 16,000.

Once again, however, Diem refused to go along. Instead of paying for new schools, health clinics, or land reform, American funds often ended up in the pockets of corrupt Saigon officials. Despite United States aid, the ineffective South Vietnamese army failed to score major victories against the Vietcong.

The Overthrow of Diem

The crisis in Vietnam deepened in the spring of 1963. As a crowd of Buddhists gathered in the city of Hue on May 8 to protest a government ruling forbidding the display of Buddhist flags, government troops fired on them. The attack stirred new and powerful protests.

A month after the attack at Hue, a Buddhist monk set himself on fire as a protest against the Diem regime. Other monks soon followed his example. A horrifying photograph of a monk engulfed in flames appeared in newspapers and on television screens around the world. Almost overnight, world opinion turned against Diem.

AP/WIDE WORLD PHOTOS

Ultimate Protest The Buddhist monk Thich Quang Duc sacrificed himself to protest the government persecution of Buddhists. Other monks lay in front of nearby fire trucks to prevent their moving to assist Duc. *What caused the crisis in Vietnam to deepen?*

By early August the Diem regime teetered on the brink of collapse; yet Kennedy feared he had no alternative to Diem. In late August, however, a group of South Vietnamese army generals met secretly with United States officials to propose the overthrow of Diem. With United States support, the plan went forward.

On the night of November 1, 1963, South Vietnamese army officers seized control of the government. In the confusion surrounding the takeover, Diem was killed. Just three weeks later, Kennedy himself was assassinated, and the war in Vietnam now troubled his successor, President Lyndon B. Johnson.

Johnson's War

Involvement Expands in 1964

Like his predecessors, President Johnson believed that Vietnam was a key battle in the cold war. He rejected any settlement of the war that did not guarantee a non-Communist government in South Vietnam.

Also like Truman, Johnson was haunted by the loss of China. "I am not going to be the president who saw Southeast Asia go the way China went," he vowed. Johnson also believed he had to take a strong anti-Communist stand to fend off the 1964 election challenge by conservative Republican Barry Goldwater.

Also like Truman, Johnson took over the presidency with little experience in international affairs. He surrounded himself with the same team that had guided Kennedy's foreign policies—Secretary of State Dean Rusk, Secretary of Defense Robert McNamara, and National Security Adviser McGeorge Bundy—the architects of the United States war in Vietnam. Johnson, like Kennedy, hoped to keep the Vietcong from overrunning South Vietnam. By 1964, however, Diem's successors had proved just as unsuccessful in waging the war and just as unpopular with the South Vietnamese. Only massive economic and military aid from the United States would keep the regime from toppling.

Johnson did not want to lose Vietnam, but he did not want to be seen as recklessly plunging the nation deeper into war. He needed the support of Congress and of the American public to expand United States involvement. He got it in August 1964.

The Gulf of Tonkin Resolution

In early August Johnson announced that North Vietnamese torpedo boats had attacked two United States destroyers patrolling in the Gulf of Tonkin off the coast of North Vietnam. Johnson angrily declared that Americans had been the victims of "unprovoked" attacks. He urged Congress to pass a resolution giving him authority to "take all necessary measures to repel any armed attack against the forces of the United States and to prevent further aggression." An alarmed Congress almost unanimously passed the Gulf of Tonkin Resolution. The resolution was not a declaration of war, but it authorized Johnson to widen the war. The resolution, he said, "was like grandma's nightshirt—it covered everything."

Few Americans questioned the President's account of the incident. Years later, however, it was revealed that Johnson had withheld the truth from the public and Congress. The American warships had been helping South Vietnamese commandos raid two North Vietnamese islands the night of the attacks.

Operation Rolling Thunder

Six months later a second incident provided another excuse for deeper involvement. In February 1965 Vietcong forces attacked a United States military base at Pleiku, South Vietnam, and killed eight Americans. Johnson retaliated by ordering the first American bombing of North Vietnam. Code-named Operation Rolling Thunder, the bombing would continue almost nonstop for three years.

In addition to bases, roads, and railways in North Vietnam, the air attacks targeted the so-called Ho Chi Minh

The Pain of War The sheer horror of the fighting is captured in this photo taken during Operation Prairie. *How did President Johnson respond to the attack on Pleiku?*

Trail, a tangled network of dirt roads and muddy trails along which soldiers and supplies flowed from North Vietnam through Laos and Cambodia into South Vietnam. Yet the raids failed to cut off North Vietnamese aid to the NLF. The South Vietnamese army continued to suffer heavy losses at the hands of the Vietcong.

Meanwhile in 1967 a new regime had taken power in South Vietnam under General Nguyen Van Thieu. Like Diem, Thieu lacked popular support. As a result, the NLF continued to grow, soon controlling the majority of villages in the countryside. Johnson believed that the Saigon government would fall without direct American support. In March of 1965, he made a fateful decision.

United States Troops in Vietnam

One month after the attack on Pleiku, two battalions of American Marines waded ashore at Da Nang, South Vietnam. General William Westmoreland, the commander of United States forces in Vietnam, had asked Johnson to send the troops to guard the United States air base at Da Nang. Johnson agreed, assuring Americans that peace was on the horizon.

The trickle of United States troops soon swelled to a torrent. By the end of 1965, more than 180,000 American troops were fighting in South Vietnam. By the end of 1966, that number had doubled; and by the end of 1967, nearly 500,000 soldiers had been sent to Vietnam—more than all the United States troops in Korea at the height of that conflict.

Vital Supply Line The North Vietnamese kept the Vietcong in the South resupplied by sending men, equipment, and ammunition down the Ho Chi Minh Trail. *Why did the United States bomb this trail?*

Fighting the War

Early Optimism Turns to Frustration

The first United States troops to land in Vietnam shared the optimism of policy makers at home. As Marine Lieutenant Philip Caputo wrote, "When we marched into the rice paddies on that damp March afternoon, we carried, along with our packs and rifles, the . . . conviction that the Vietcong would be quickly beaten." Within just two years, however, that optimism had turned to bitter frustration.

Through relentless bombing and combat, the United States hoped to destroy the Vietcong's will to fight in order to force them to the bargaining table. The measure of the United States's success in the war was not territory gained but body counts—a tally of the number of enemy killed. Optimistic reports of body counts from the field led many at home to believe the United States was winning the war.

American officials, however, underestimated the Vietcong and their North Vietnamese allies. As Ho Chi Minh had warned the French, "You can kill ten of my men for every one I kill of yours, but even at those odds, you will lose and I will win." Although United States forces claimed to have killed 220,000 Communists by the end of 1967, the war raged on.

The Air War

Because bombing cost fewer American lives than ground combat, the United States relied more and more on air power. Once Johnson unleashed Operation Rolling Thunder, the air war over Vietnam escalated dramatically—from 25,000 bombing raids in 1965 to more than 108,000 in 1967.

At first the attacks were limited to military targets and supply routes in North Vietnam, but soon the B-52s hammered roads, railways, factories, and homes in South

Vietnam and neighboring Laos and Cambodia. By 1967 the United States had dropped more bombs on Vietnam than the Allies dropped during all of World War II. The air raids leveled dozens of cities, killed thousands of civilians, and turned the once lush rice fields and forests into a moonscape pitted with craters.

Yet the immense firepower of the United States Air Force failed to rout the Vietcong. To evade the bombers, the Vietcong used and expanded a vast network of underground tunnels dug during the conflict with the French in the 1940s. Soldiers and supplies continued to flow south from North Vietnam through more than 30,000 miles of tunnels.

The Ground War

While United States bombers rained terror on Vietnam from above, United States ground forces attempted to wipe out the Vietcong through "search-and-destroy" missions. To the inexperienced United States troops, the first challenge was simply finding the enemy in these unfamiliar jungles. Flying into Vietnam for the first time, Philip Caputo described the terrain:

> An unbroken mass of green stretched westward, one ridgeline and mountain range after another, some more than a mile high and covered with forests that looked solid enough to walk on. It had no end. It just went on to the horizon.
>
> I could see neither villages, nor fields, roads, or anything but endless rain forests the color of old moss. . . . "Out there" they called that humid wilderness where the Bengal tiger stalked and the cobra coiled beneath its rock and the Viet Cong lurked in ambush.
>
> —Philip Caputo, *A Rumor of War,* 1977

AP/WIDE WORLD PHOTOS

AP/WIDE WORLD PHOTOS

Routing Out the Enemy A chemical defoliant, Agent Orange, was used to eliminate Vietcong staging areas. The top photo shows a forest before spraying in 1965; the lower photo shows the same area in 1970. *What happened to the vegetation?*

Once on the ground, the troops slogged through the countryside on endless patrols—plagued by suffocating heat, clouds of mosquitoes, razor-sharp jungle grasses, and hungry leeches. Soaked in sweat and weighed down by 50 to 70 pounds of equipment, United States soldiers waded knee-deep along muddy trails and through flooded rice fields. Cautiously they inched along. Each rock, each clump of weeds, might hide a mine that would cripple or kill in an instant. American soldiers called one especially lethal booby trap a "Bouncing Betty." It leaped out of the ground just before it exploded.

All South Vietnam became a war zone, as United States troops searched the fields, forests, and villages for Vietcong. Yet how could they be sure whether a peasant was friend or enemy? They were all Vietnamese. As one soldier explained, "The Vietcong would be the farmer you waved to from your jeep in the day who would be the guy with the gun out looking for you at night." The enemy was everywhere and nowhere.

Guerilla Tactics

The Vietcong employed **guerrilla warfare** tactics, using small bands of fighters to harass United States troops. Unlike conventional forces, guerrilla fighters avoid open battles. Instead they try to wear down the enemy—with ambushes, hit-and-run raids, and sabotage—and force them to withdraw. As one observer noted, "The guerrilla wins if he does not lose; the conventional army loses if it does not win." By that definition, the United States was losing the war.

The Vietcong guerrillas had two advantages over the United States forces. First, they knew the terrain and could move unseen through the mountains and jungles. Second, through a combination of terrorism and the genuine appeal of their nationalist struggle, they had the support of many peasants who supplied food and shelter and kept them informed of American troop movements.

To deprive the Vietcong of their peasant support, United States troops undertook a **pacification program,** uprooting entire villages and forcing the people to move to cities or refugee camps. The soldiers then burned the fields and empty villages.

The program, however, failed to stop the Vietcong, who simply moved elsewhere. Moreover, the pacification program alienated the peasants who were forced to leave the beloved land of their ancestors. "I have to stay behind to look after this piece of garden," one grandfather pleaded with Americans evacuating his village. "Of all the property handed down to me by my ancestors, only this garden now remains. . . . If I leave, the graves of my ancestors, too, will become forests. How can I have the heart to leave?"

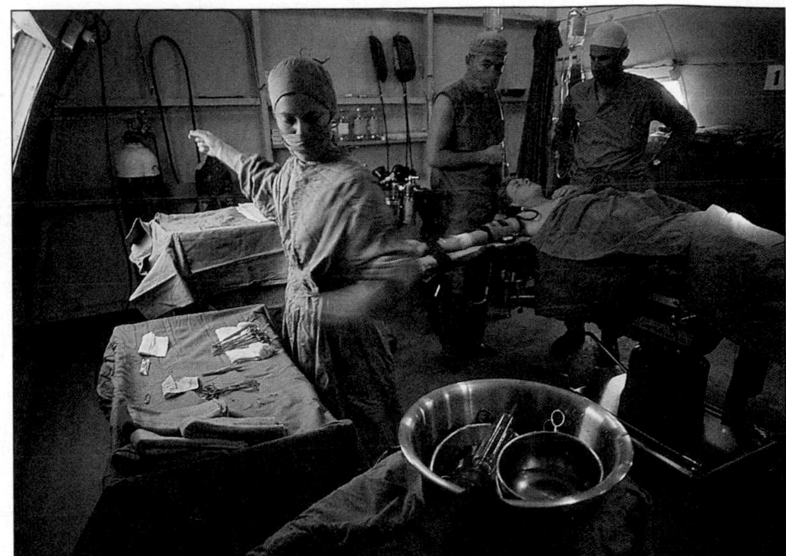

© RAY CRANBOURNE, EMPIRE/BLACK STAR

Nurses Battle **More than 7,500 nurses served during the war in Vietnam.**
What is a MASH unit?

The United States tried to offset these policies through development projects in which teams of volunteers visited villages offering medical care and farming advice. United States bombs and bullets, however, undercut any efforts to win Vietnamese "hearts and minds."

Meanwhile American losses in Vietnam continued to mount. By 1967 more than 14,000 United States soldiers had been killed. Yet United States military power still failed to crush the Vietcong. As one reporter observed, every powerful blow from the American war machine "was like a sledgehammer on a floating cork. . . . Somehow the cork refused to stay down."

The Endless War

For Americans fighting a seemingly unwinnable war, Vietnam was a frustrating and terrifying nightmare. Nurses working in mobile army surgical hospital (MASH) units near the front and on hospital ships off the coast probably had a better feeling for the Vietnam tragedy than anyone. They saw the wounded every day, day after day. Ruth Sidisin of the Air Force Nurse Corps said: "Vietnam was not John Wayne. In Vietnam, every day was disaster day." Most of the United States troops were young and inexperienced; the average soldier was just 19 years old, 7 years younger than the average soldier in World War II. These young people were miles from home in a steamy jungle filled with daily horrors—mud, heat, booby traps, and an invisible enemy. They fought bravely, but the war seemed endless. Some turned to drugs to escape. Some snapped under pressure, no longer able to tell friend from foe. David Ross, a 19-year-old army medic, had volunteered to fight in Vietnam, but 2 years of war had shaken his faith in his country's goals.

I volunteered, you know. Ever since the American Revolution my family had people in all the different wars, and that was always the thing—when your country needs you, you go. You don't ask a lot of questions, because the country's always right. This time it didn't turn out that way.

—David Ross, in *Everything We Had,* 1981

Section Assessment

Main Idea

1. Use a diagram like this one to show the steps leading to United States military involvement in the war in Vietnam.

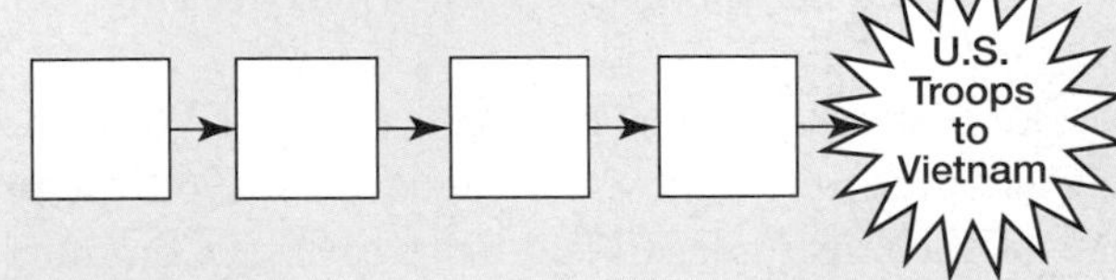

Vocabulary

2. Define: national liberation, containment, domino theory, guerrilla warfare, pacification program.

Checking Facts

3. Why did the United States support the French war effort in Vietnam?
4. How did the war escalate under Johnson?

Critical Thinking

5. **Recognizing Biases** In what ways did the United States military planners fail to understand the Vietnamese culture? How did this affect pacification programs in South Vietnam?

1968: A Year of Crises

NOVEMBER 21, 1967: GENERAL WESTMORELAND REPORTS END IS NEAR

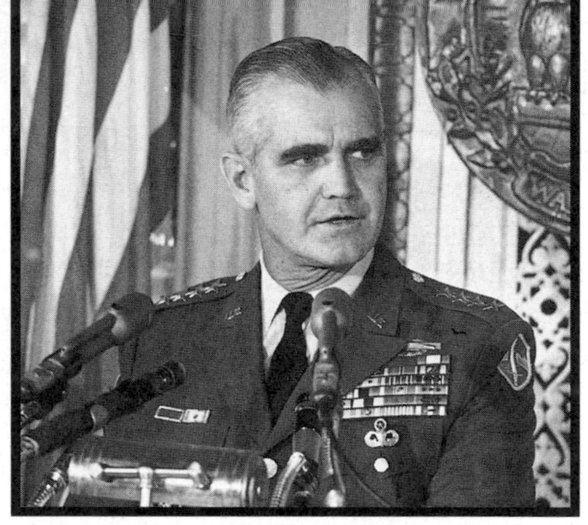
AP/WIDE WORLD PHOTOS

The War's General
General William Westmoreland was an architect of United States military action in Vietnam from 1964 to 1968.

FACED WITH GROWING OPPOSITION TO THE WAR AT HOME, PRESIDENT JOHNSON BROUGHT GENERAL WILLIAM WESTMORELAND BACK FROM SAIGON TO REASSURE THE AMERICAN PUBLIC ABOUT THE WAR. On November 21, 1967, in an address to the National Press Club in Washington, D.C., Westmoreland delivered an upbeat report: "I am absolutely certain that whereas in 1965 the enemy was winning, today he is certainly losing," he said. "There are indications that the Vietcong and even Hanoi know this. . . . We have reached an important point when the end begins to come into view."

Just 10 weeks later, however, General Westmoreland's words rang hollow. On January 30, 1968, the first day of the Vietnamese New Year, or Tet, Communist forces launched a massive attack, striking without warning at civilian and military targets throughout South Vietnam. Within 24 hours about 84,000 Communist soldiers had stormed more than 100 South Vietnamese cities and towns, a dozen United States military bases, and even the United States embassy in Saigon.

Tet Offensive: A Turning Point

Losses High on Both Sides

Though United States and South Vietnamese forces retook most of the targets within hours or days, a bitter battle over the ancient city of Hue raged for nearly three weeks. To recapture the city, United States forces hammered its streets with bombs and artillery fire. The fighting left the beautiful city of old temples and palaces a "shattered, stinking hulk, its streets choked with rubble and rotting bodies."

GUIDE TO READING

Main Idea

The ongoing war in Vietnam and political turmoil within the United States made the year 1968 a turning point in American history.

Vocabulary

- conservative era
- liberal era

Read to Find Out . . .

- how the Tet offensive and the 1968 presidential campaign altered the political direction of the United States.
- how the assassinations of Dr. Martin Luther King, Jr., and Robert F. Kennedy affected the civil rights and antiwar movements.

United States forces routed the Vietcong, killing an estimated 33,000 enemy troops in the first 2 weeks of the month-long Tet offensive. The cost was high, however. More than 1,100 American soldiers, 2,300 South Vietnamese troops, and 12,500 Vietnamese civilians were killed. More than 1 million Vietnamese became refugees. Dozens of towns and villages lay in ruins. As one American army officer said of the battle for the village of Ben Tre, "We had to destroy the town to save it."

General William Westmoreland quickly claimed Tet as a victory for the United States and boasted that "the enemy is on the ropes." Even the Communists admitted that Tet had not achieved their major goal, "to spur uprisings throughout the South." Tet also marked a turning point in the war. It showed that no place in South Vietnam—not even the American embassy—was safe from attack. It shattered American confidence and raised grave doubts about Johnson's policies in Vietnam.

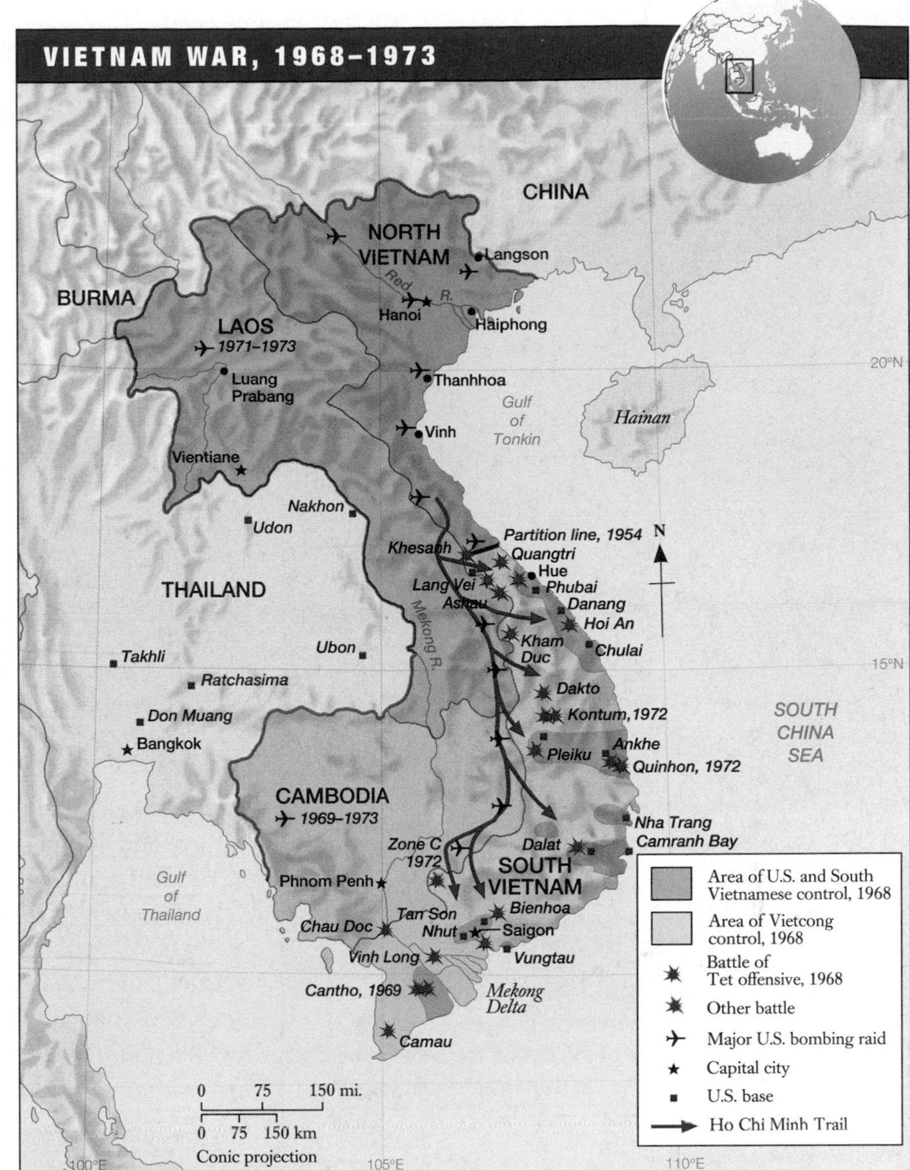

The United States depended heavily on the use of air power in the war in Vietnam because it cost fewer American lives. *Why did the United States stage so many bombing raids in Laos and Cambodia, just west of Vietnam?*

Critics of United States Policy

"What the hell is going on?" asked Walter Cronkite, the respected CBS newscaster. "I thought we were winning the war!" After returning from a trip to Saigon after the Tet offensive, Cronkite reported that "it seems now more certain than ever that the bloody experience in Vietnam is to end in a stale-mate . . . [and] that the only rational way out . . . will be to negotiate."

"If I've lost Walter," lamented President Johnson, "then it's over. I've lost Mr. Average Citizen." Editorials in *Newsweek, Time,* and the *Wall Street Journal* also called for a negotiated settlement of the war and a prompt withdrawal of American troops.

Televised reports challenged official statements and brought home the brutality and hopelessness of the war. The desperate struggle to regain the United States embassy and the destruction of Hue stunned Americans. The brutality of the United States's ally shocked millions as they watched a South Vietnamese police chief draw his revolver, place it against the head of a young Vietcong prisoner, and pull the trigger. Such images prompted Americans to question United States policy: Was the United States really defending democracy in Vietnam? If so, at what cost?

The horrifying images of Tet contradicted the rosy picture of the war Westmoreland had painted the previous fall. Public opinion polls showed that in the 6 weeks after the Tet offensive, the percentage of Americans who approved of Johnson's handling of the war plunged from 40 to 26; Johnson's overall approval ratings dropped from 48 to 36 percent. The massive antiwar protests of the previous year grew even larger. Crowds of angry demonstrators chanted, "Hey, hey, LBJ. How many kids did you kill today?"

© DONALD McCULLIN, MAGNUM PHOTOS

The Horror of War **Three marines in flak jackets drag a sniper victim out of the line of fire during the battle of Hue.**
What effect did Tet have on the 1968 presidential campaign?

Democratic Challengers

As President Johnson's popularity took a nosedive, he faced another crisis. The liberal Minnesota Senator Eugene McCarthy had entered the New Hampshire Democratic primary. Running on an antiwar platform, McCarthy challenged Johnson for the presidential nomination.

Since the summer of 1967, antiwar Democrats had been searching for a candidate to replace President Johnson. They first tried to recruit New York Senator Robert Kennedy, a vocal critic of the war and the brother of slain President John Kennedy. Reluctant to challenge the President and split the party, Kennedy at first refused. The antiwar Democrats then turned to McCarthy.

At the beginning of January, with support from just 17 percent of the Democratic party, McCarthy had seemed to pose little threat to Johnson's reelection bid. Then came Tet.

McCarthy's antiwar stand attracted thousands of college students. With the motto Be clean for Gene, the students trimmed their hair, dressed in suits and ties, and swarmed across New Hampshire, knocking on doors and urging residents to vote for McCarthy. On March 12 McCarthy surprised everyone by winning nearly half the popular vote as well as 20 out of 24 state delegates to the national nominating convention.

Not all of those who voted for McCarthy favored United States withdrawal from Vietnam; many favored stepping up the United States effort to win the war. Whatever their politics, New Hampshire voters agreed that Johnson's policies had failed.

On March 16 another antiwar candidate entered the race—Robert Kennedy. His challenge, however, embittered many of McCarthy's supporters, who feared that McCarthy and Kennedy would split the antiwar vote. With a promise to carry on the goals of his brother's New Frontier, Kennedy attracted widespread support from minorities, the poor, and the working class, as well as wealthier mainstream Democrats. As the Vietnam War drained more and more money from social reform at home, the ranks of Kennedy's supporters swelled.

Johnson's Decision

Shaken by Tet, McCarthy's success in New Hampshire, and Kennedy's entry into the presidential race, President Johnson faced a further dilemma. Following the Tet offensive, General Westmoreland and the Joint Chiefs of Staff had requested an additional 206,000 American troops—a 40 percent increase. Westmoreland claimed that Tet losses had weakened the Vietcong. With additional troops, he argued, the United States

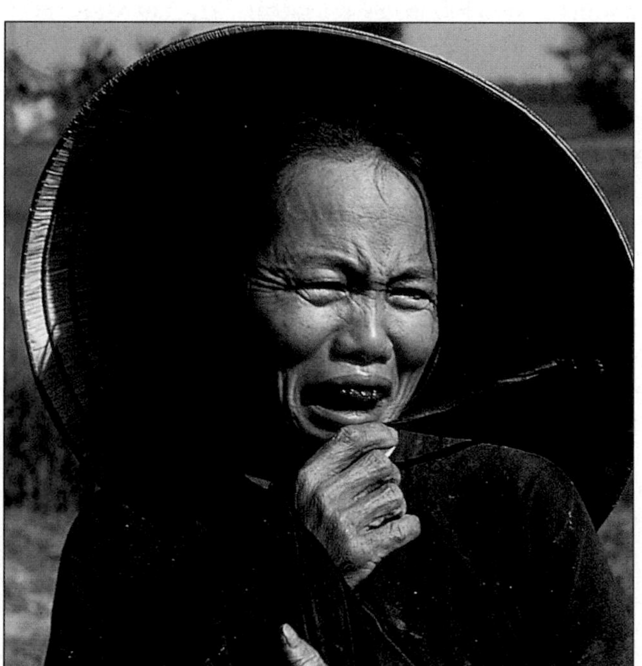
© JAMES PICKERELL/BLACK STAR

The War Touches Both Sides **The Tet offensive brought widespread destruction and affected thousands of civilians.**
What did Westmoreland want to do to follow up the Tet offensive?

could take advantage of their weakness and score a military victory. Uneasy about the request for additional troops, Johnson asked his new secretary of defense, Clark Clifford, to make a recommendation.

After questioning the Joint Chiefs of Staff, Clifford became convinced that "the military course we were pursuing was not only endless but hopeless." The top military commanders could give him no reason to believe the Communists could be beaten by "an additional 200,000 American troops, or double or triple that quantity."

As a result Clifford recommended that the President reject Westmoreland's request and instead encourage the South Vietnamese to do more of the fighting. Bitterly Johnson accepted Clifford's recommendation—he would send only a few thousand additional troops to Vietnam. For the first time in three years of war, Johnson refused to support Westmoreland.

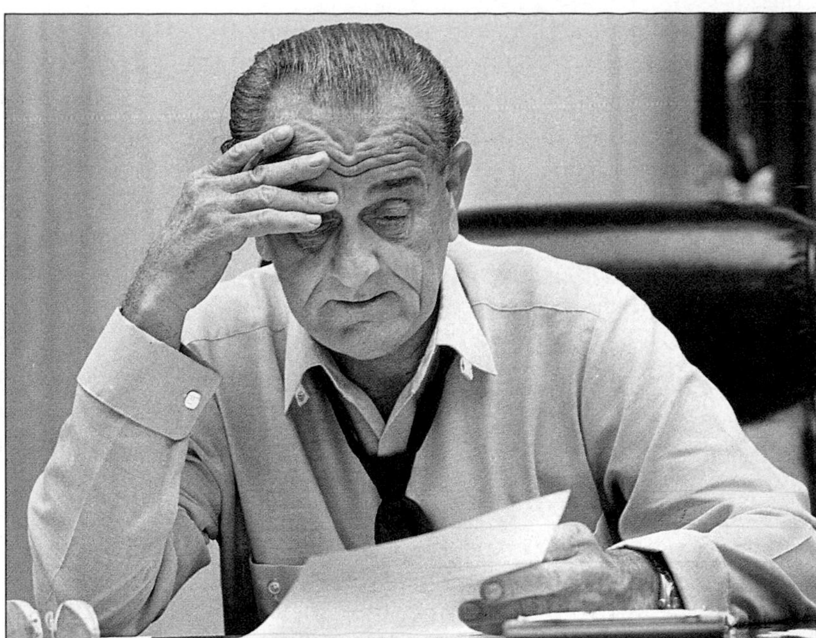

UPI/BETTMANN

A Surprise Announcement **The day before Johnson withdrew from the presidential race, his eldest daughter, Lynda, sent her husband, Charles Robb, off to Vietnam.** *Why did Johnson decide not to run for reelection?*

On March 31, three years after the first American troops landed in Vietnam, Johnson made a televised speech. He announced that the United States would limit the bombing of North Vietnam, and he appealed to Ho Chi Minh for a negotiated settlement to the war. Then Johnson dropped his own bombshell: "I have decided that I shall not seek and I will not accept the nomination of my party for another term as your president."

Unable to build a Great Society at home and wage a war at the same time, Johnson got out of the race. He later confided to his biographer Doris Kearns Goodwin the reasons why:

> On one side, the American people were stampeding me to do something about Vietnam. On the other side, the inflationary economy was booming out of control. Up ahead were dozens of dangerous signs pointing to another summer of riots in the cities. . . . And then the final straw. The thing I feared from the first day of my presidency was actually coming true. Robert Kennedy had openly announced his intention to reclaim the throne in the memory of his brother. . . . The whole situation was unbearable to me.
>
> —Doris Kearns Goodwin, *Lyndon Johnson and the American Dream,* 1976

Two days later, McCarthy swept the Wisconsin Democratic primary.

Tragedy and Turmoil

Bloodshed and Political Upheaval Dominate 1968

According to Vietnamese tradition, the first guest through the door during the Tet holiday serves as a sign of the year to come. The Vietcong commandos who burst into the United States embassy in the early morning hours of Tet ushered in a troubled year for Americans, a year of turmoil, frustrated hopes, and shattered dreams.

Tensions over the war in Vietnam and the civil rights struggle at home had been building for years. Now they exploded. The troubling events of 1968 would lead many Americans to reject the liberalism of the 1960s and embrace a new conservatism in hopes of bringing an end to the war and restoring peace at home.

King's Assassination

A nation still reeling from the shock of Tet and Johnson's refusal to run for reelection suffered another blow in April—the assassination of civil rights leader Martin Luther King, Jr. One of the earliest critics of United States involvement in Vietnam, King had linked the struggle for racial equality and economic justice to the struggle for peace. "The black revolution is much more than a struggle for the rights of Negroes," he declared. "It is forcing America to face all its interrelated flaws—racism, poverty, militarism, and materialism."

The news of King's murder stunned the nation. Thousands of his admirers took part in peaceful marches and memorial services, but the shock and grief soon turned to rage. Within hours many African Americans stormed through the streets of cities around the country. Their anger and frustration exploded in rioting, looting, and burning. In Chicago fires raged through a 20-block area of the city's heavily African American West Side. In Washington, D.C., soldiers armed with rifles and machine guns stood guard outside the White House and the Capitol as African Americans looted and burned.

The Democratic Primaries

While the nation agonized over unrest at home and war abroad, the presidential race picked up speed. Three candidates now scrambled for the Democratic nomination: Eugene McCarthy, Robert Kennedy, and Vice President Hubert Humphrey.

Although Humphrey championed civil rights and social reform, his ties to Johnson's Vietnam policies repelled the antiwar liberals. To line up convention support, Humphrey avoided the primaries and courted the Democratic party bosses, who in some states chose the delegates.

McCarthy waged a spirited crusade against the war and social injustice, but his low-key, intellectual style appealed mainly to educated middle-class liberals. "He has wit, charm, and grace," columnist I.F. Stone observed, "but he seems to lack heart and guts."

Robert Kennedy, on the other hand, made passionate appeals on behalf of the have-nots of American society. Campaigning against poverty, racism, and the war, Kennedy reached out to African Americans, Native Americans, Hispanic Americans, and young protesters. With Johnson out of the race, Kennedy quickly became the front-runner.

Kennedy won early primary victories in Indiana and Nebraska, but McCarthy rebounded and scored a victory in the Oregon primary. California, the nation's most populous state, was next. Both candidates campaigned energetically, but when the polls closed on June 4, Kennedy had won 46 percent of the popular vote and McCarthy just 41 percent. California was a winner-take-all state, so Kennedy claimed all the convention delegates.

Kennedy's Assassination

That evening, moments after the victorious Kennedy spoke to cheering supporters at a Los Angeles hotel, he lay dying, the victim of an assassin's bullet. The nation reeled in shock. Within two months two liberal leaders—both critics of the war and advocates of civil rights—had been killed. The deaths of King and

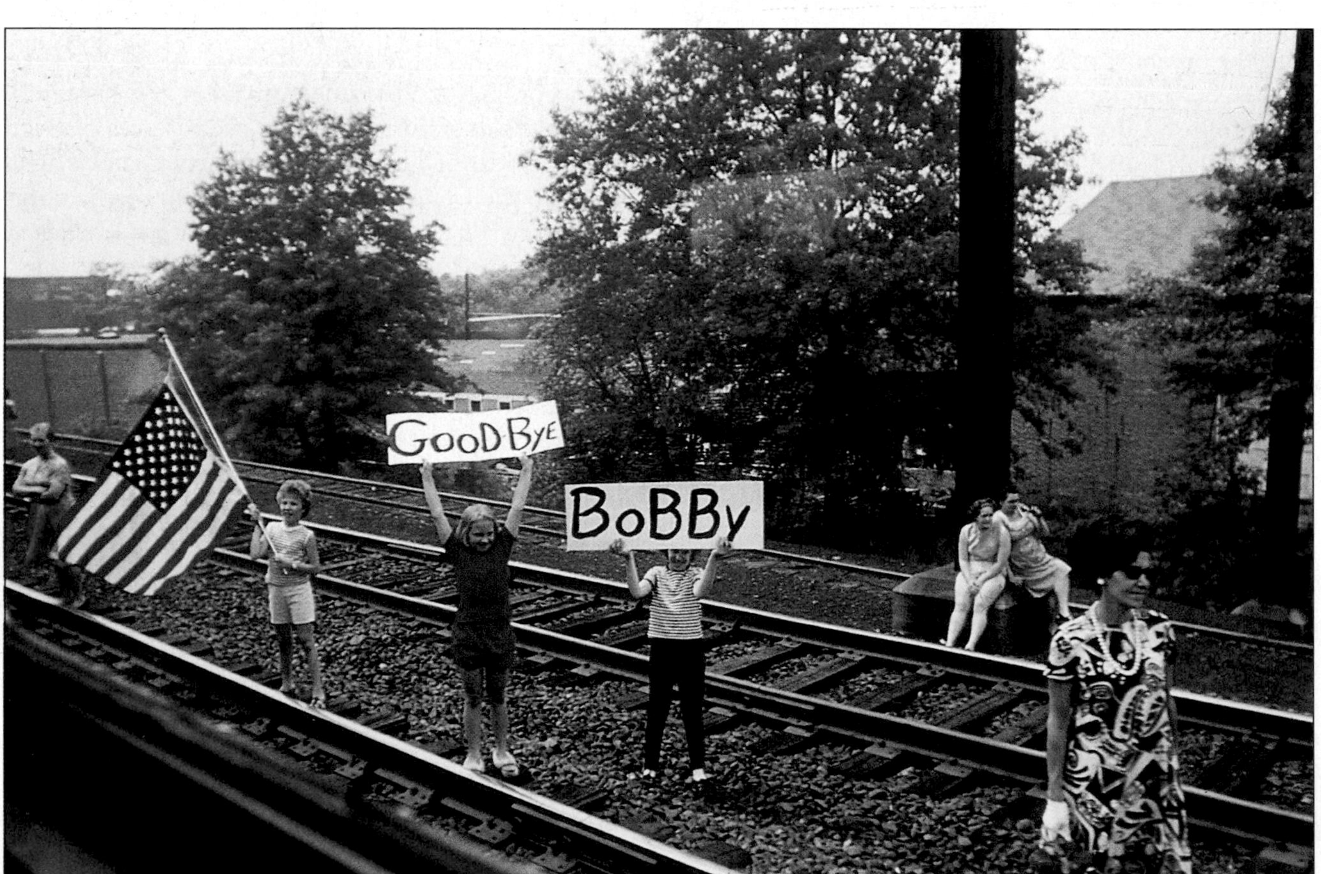

The Last Farewell **Mourners lined the route as a special funeral train carrying the body of Robert F. Kennedy traveled from New York City to Washington, D.C., for burial in Arlington National Cemetery.** *To what groups did the Kennedy campaign appeal?*

Kennedy shattered the hopes of antiwar and civil rights activists who had sought to work within the political system. Many despaired that politics would ever be an effective way to enact change. "I won't vote," one young African American from New York declared. "Every good man we get they kill."

The Election of 1968

National Politics Become More Conservative

The simmering anger and frustration many Americans felt over the deaths of King and Kennedy would boil over in the August heat, as Democrats met in Chicago to nominate a candidate for President. The resulting convention turmoil would shock the nation and splinter the Democratic party. In the process, it would help pave the way for a new **conservative era** in presidential politics in which the role of government would be limited and individuals would depend less on the government for assistance.

The Democratic Convention

With Kennedy dead and McCarthy unable to rally more than a few convention delegates, Hubert Humphrey looked like a sure winner of the Democratic nomination. Humphrey's support for Johnson's Vietnam policies, however, angered many antiwar activists. Nearly 10,000 of them flocked to Chicago to protest, if they could not prevent, Humphrey's nomination.

Most of the demonstrators had come to pressure delegates to adopt an antiwar platform. Some, however, hoped to provoke violence that would discredit the Democrats. With memories of the riots after King's death still fresh, Chicago Mayor Richard Daley mobilized 12,000 Chicago police officers and put 5,000 members of the National Guard on call. "As long as I am mayor," he vowed, "there will be law and order."

Daley's forces ringed the convention hall with barbed wire. On August 28, as convention delegates cast their ballots for Hubert Humphrey, helmeted police savagely clubbed demonstrators and bystanders in downtown Chicago. The protesters chanted, "The whole world is watching." As television cameras broadcast the brutal scene to homes across the nation, the image of the Democrats as the party of disorder was etched in the minds of millions of Americans.

Nixon and the Republicans

The Republicans presented themselves as the party of stability. According to writer Norman Mailer, the Republican convention in Miami was a "convention

© DENNIS BRACK/BLACK STAR

The Whole World Watched **Democratic delegates, reporters, and ordinary citizens, as well as demonstrators, were attacked by police and members of the National Guard.** *What effect did the violence in Chicago have on Humphrey's chances in the coming presidential election?*

of the clean, the brisk, the orderly, the efficient"—a marked contrast to the Democratic convention. Republican delegates quickly picked Richard Nixon, the former Vice President, to once again be their candidate for President.

Just six years earlier, Nixon's political career seemed dead. In 1962 after losing the race for governor of California, Nixon had announced that he was retiring from politics, telling reporters, "You won't have Nixon to kick around anymore." Richard Nixon was a fighter, not a quitter. Now he was making a comeback.

A shrewd politician, Richard Nixon saw that the disorder and violence of the 1960s frightened many Americans. They were impatient with urban violence and campus unrest, and they resented the counterculture's challenge to traditional values. Nixon would try to appeal to those who, as one reporter put it, yearned for "a kind of Eisenhowerian calm, after the pains and shocks and tragedies of the Democratic years."

In his acceptance speech at the Republican convention, Nixon echoed that deep yearning:

> As we look at America, we see cities enveloped in smoke and flame. We hear sirens in the night. We see Americans hating each other; killing each other at home. And as we see and hear these things millions of Americans cry out in anger: Did we come all this way for this?
>
> —Richard M. Nixon, Republican convention, 1968

Nixon promised to end the turmoil and to protect the "first civil right of every American . . . to be free from domestic violence." He attacked Johnson's Great Society, declaring that it was "time to quit pouring billions of dollars into programs that have failed." To Americans weary of the Vietnam War, he promised "peace with honor."

© CHARLES BONNAY/BLACK STAR

Nixon's the One Sensing victory as Election Day drew near, Nixon supporters were jubilant as their candidate arrived to speak at a campaign rally. *What did Nixon pledge to do if he was elected?*

The Wallace Campaign

The only threat to Nixon's presidential campaign came from further right. The conservative governor of Alabama, George Wallace, was running as the candidate of the American Independent party. In his campaign for the presidency, Wallace was attempting to capture the same conservative voters that Nixon sought—those who feared school integration, resented the Great Society's antipoverty programs, and despised antiwar protesters.

As governor of Alabama, Wallace had once pledged to enforce "segregation now . . . segregation tomorrow . . . segregation forever." As a presidential candidate, he tried to appeal to the fears and prejudices of blue-collar workers around the country by lashing out at the "brief-case-totin' bureaucrats, ivory-tower guideline writers, bearded anarchists, smart-aleck editorial writers, and pointy-headed professors looking down their noses at us."

Wallace called for victory in Vietnam, and he denounced the antiwar protesters. "If any demonstrator ever lays down in front of my car," he pledged to his supporters, "it will be the last car he will ever lay down in front of."

Wallace's popularity climbed as his attacks grew more shrill. By mid-September, polls showed that he had won the support of 21 percent of the voters. His campaign suffered a setback, however, when he picked Curtis LeMay, a retired air force general, as his running mate. LeMay frightened even devoted Wallace supporters when he argued that the United States should "drop nukes on Vietnam."

The Election

By the end of September, polls showed Humphrey trailing Nixon by 15 percentage points and leading Wallace by only 7 points. Crippled by his loyalty to Johnson's Vietnam policy, Humphrey was falling further and further behind. In mid-October he tried to salvage his campaign by calling for a halt to the bombing of North Vietnam. Johnson tried to help by ordering a complete halt to the bombing on October 31.

Humphrey managed to close in on Nixon, but it was too late. On Election Day Nixon won 43.4 percent of the popular vote, edging out Humphrey by less than 1 percent. Nearly 14 percent of the voters rejected both the Republican and Democratic parties and cast their votes for Wallace.

The 57 percent of voters who supported Nixon or Wallace signaled the rise of a new conservative major-

PRESIDENTIAL ELECTION RESULTS, 1968

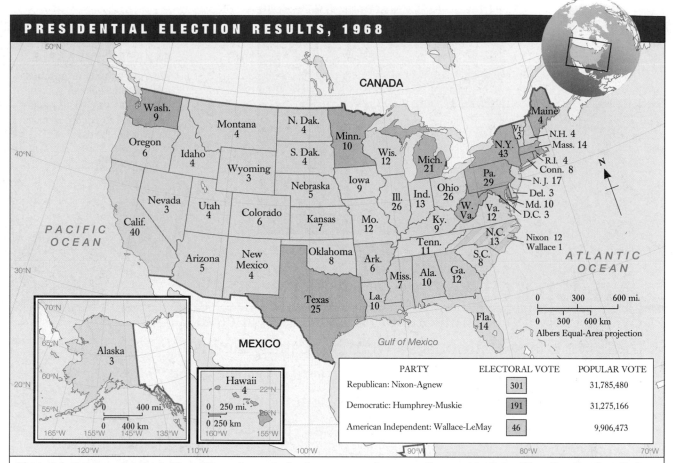

PARTY	ELECTORAL VOTE	POPULAR VOTE
Republican: Nixon-Agnew	301	31,785,480
Democratic: Humphrey-Muskie	191	31,275,166
American Independent: Wallace-LeMay	46	9,906,473

Nixon defeated Humphrey by half a million votes, ushering in a new era of conservative presidential politics. "In city after city," one observer noted, "racial conflicts had destroyed the old alliance. The New Deal had unraveled block by block." *Where did Nixon obtain most of his support? Where was Wallace particularly strong?*

ity. Since the election of 1964, the Democrats had lost nearly 12 million voters, including many in the once solidly Democratic South. The New Deal **coalition**, or alliance, of liberals, African Americans, and Southern whites was finally shattered over two divisive issues—civil rights and the war in Vietnam. Many of those who abandoned the Democrats felt that the party's social reforms—particularly the push for civil rights—had gone too far and that the Democrats had failed in Vietnam.

Some observers interpreted the election as a sign that the American political system was still alive and healthy. One British journalist noted, "The enormous power of the presidency passed peacefully from one man to another [despite] the fear that the country was coming apart."

The outcome of the 1968 election, however, disheartened others. For them, Nixon's election signaled more than just the end of a **liberal era,** a time when government power was used to promote social progress. It marked a defeat for those who had tried to work within the American political system to bring about racial equality, economic justice, and an end to the war in Southeast Asia.

SECTION ASSESSMENT

Main Idea

1. Use a diagram like this one to show some of the events in 1968 that made the year a turning point in American history.

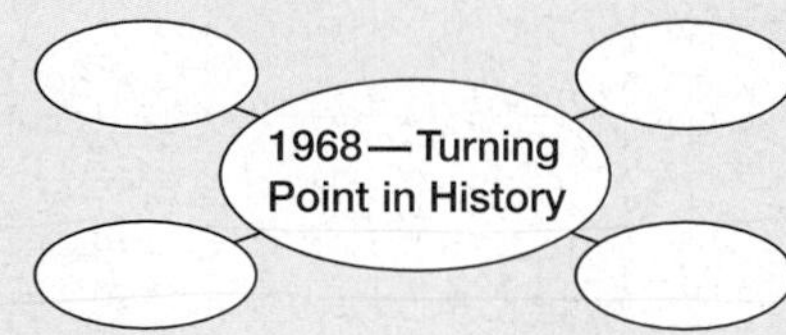

Vocabulary

2. Define: conservative era, liberal era.

Checking Facts

3. What was the Tet offensive?

4. What were some of the effects of the 1968 assassinations of King and Kennedy?

Critical Thinking

5. Synthesizing Information Why did Johnson deny the request by General Westmoreland for an additional 206,000 troops?

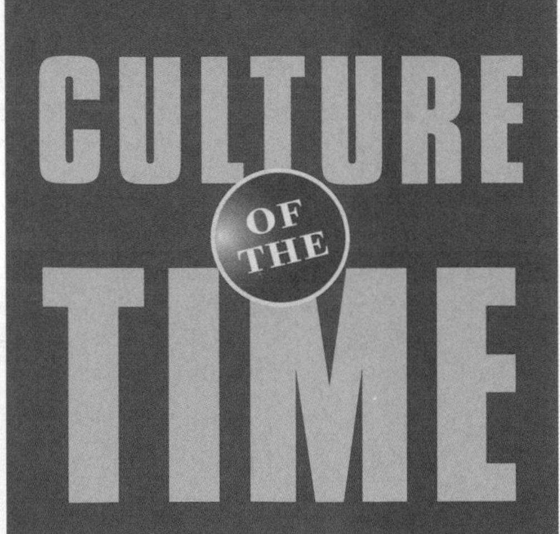

EXPRESS YOURSELF

Wearing buttons or patches and attaching bumper stickers to one's car were popular and visual ways to express opinions on issues of the day.

FILE PHOTO BY JEFF WILLS

FILE PHOTO BY DOUG MINDELL

An Era of Consciousness

By the early 1970s, millions of Americans—especially those on college campuses—were protesting the ills of society. Attitudes concerning authority, politics, the environment, and many traditional American values shifted dramatically during this period. The entire society, it seemed, was under siege.

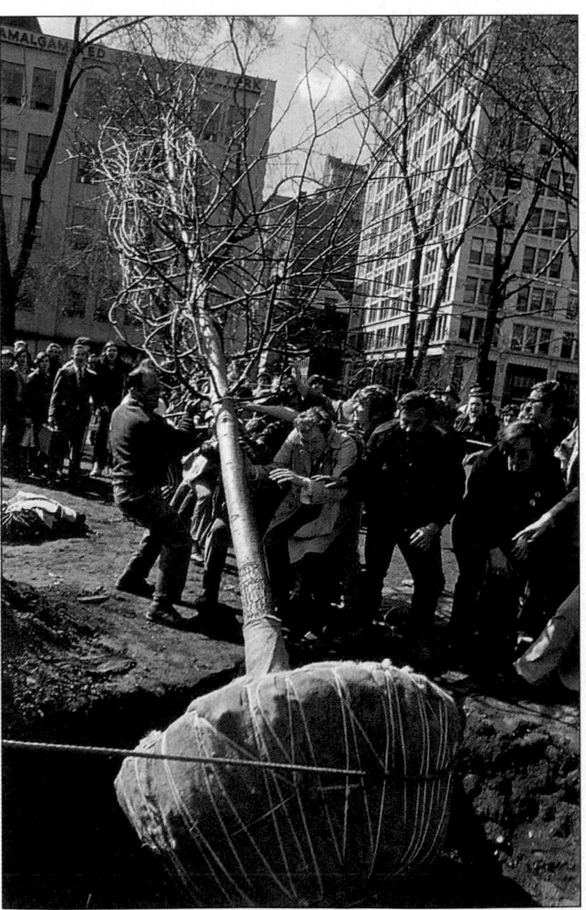

© BERNARD GOTFRYD/WOODFIN CAMP

© BILL PIERCE/SYGMA

MUSIC AND POLITICS

The lyrics of many songs revealed strong antiwar and antiestablishment sentiments. "I-Feel-Like-I'm-Fixin'-To-Die Rag," sung by **Country Joe and the Fish,** described the threat of the draft and service in Vietnam.

EARTH DAY

A new **awareness of the environment** and the limits of our natural resources was emerging. The first Earth Day on April 20, 1970, celebrated this new national consciousness and brought environmental concerns into the political mainstream.

PROM NIGHT

While thousands of students protested on campuses and in the streets, many other young men and women were more concerned about **less political issues** such as going to school, getting a job, and finding a date for the prom.

THE SMALL SCREEN

In 1971 a brash new series, ***All in the Family,*** debuted. Many of the period's conflicts were highlighted by the show's characters: outspoken, bigoted Archie Bunker, the husband; conservative, peacemaking Edith, his wife; and their daughter, Gloria, and liberal son-in-law, Michael.

MOVIE STILL ARCHIVES

The War at Home

FALL 1964: BERKELEY STUDENTS DEMAND RIGHT TO FREE SPEECH

MARIO SAVIO, A 21-YEAR-OLD STUDENT AT THE BERKELEY CAMPUS OF THE UNIVERSITY OF CALIFORNIA, SENT A LETTER TO A FRIEND IN AUGUST OF 1964. "I'm tired of reading about history," he wrote. "I want to make it." Savio got his chance that fall when he returned to Berkeley. Uneasy about student activism, university officials had banned on-campus recruitment for off-campus political activities. Led by Savio, a group of students founded the Berkeley Free Speech Movement (FSM) to protest the ban.

AP/WIDE WORLD PHOTOS

Student Movement Launched
Mario Savio was suspended from school for organizing student protests.

On December 2, nearly 6,000 students rallied on the steps of Sproul Hall, the administration building of the university. Folksinger Joan Baez joined the throng, singing the civil rights anthem, "We Shall Overcome." Savio stirred the students to action with a fiery speech. Universities, he claimed, had become vast knowledge factories serving only the interests of United States corporations. Students were treated not as human beings but as products rolling off an assembly line, diploma in hand. He called on his fellow students to resist:

> There is a time when the operation of the machine becomes so odious, makes you so sick to heart, that . . . you've got to put your bodies upon the gears and upon the wheels . . . and you've got to make it stop.
>
> —Mario Savio, December 2, 1964

Inspired by Savio's speech, more than 1,000 students marched into Sproul Hall and staged a sit-in. This was the first, but by no means the last, time students would use civil disobedience to press their demands on campus. Just after 3:00 A.M., police began clearing the building, arresting nearly 800 demonstrators.

GUIDE TO READING

Main Idea

Student protests and uncensored media coverage brought the war in Vietnam home to the United States as internal dissent and government crackdowns rocked the nation.

Vocabulary

- draft
- deferment
- conscientious objector
- hawk
- dove

Read to Find Out . . .

- the causes and goals of the student movement.
- reasons the antiwar movement became more diverse.
- how the media shaped public opinion on the war.

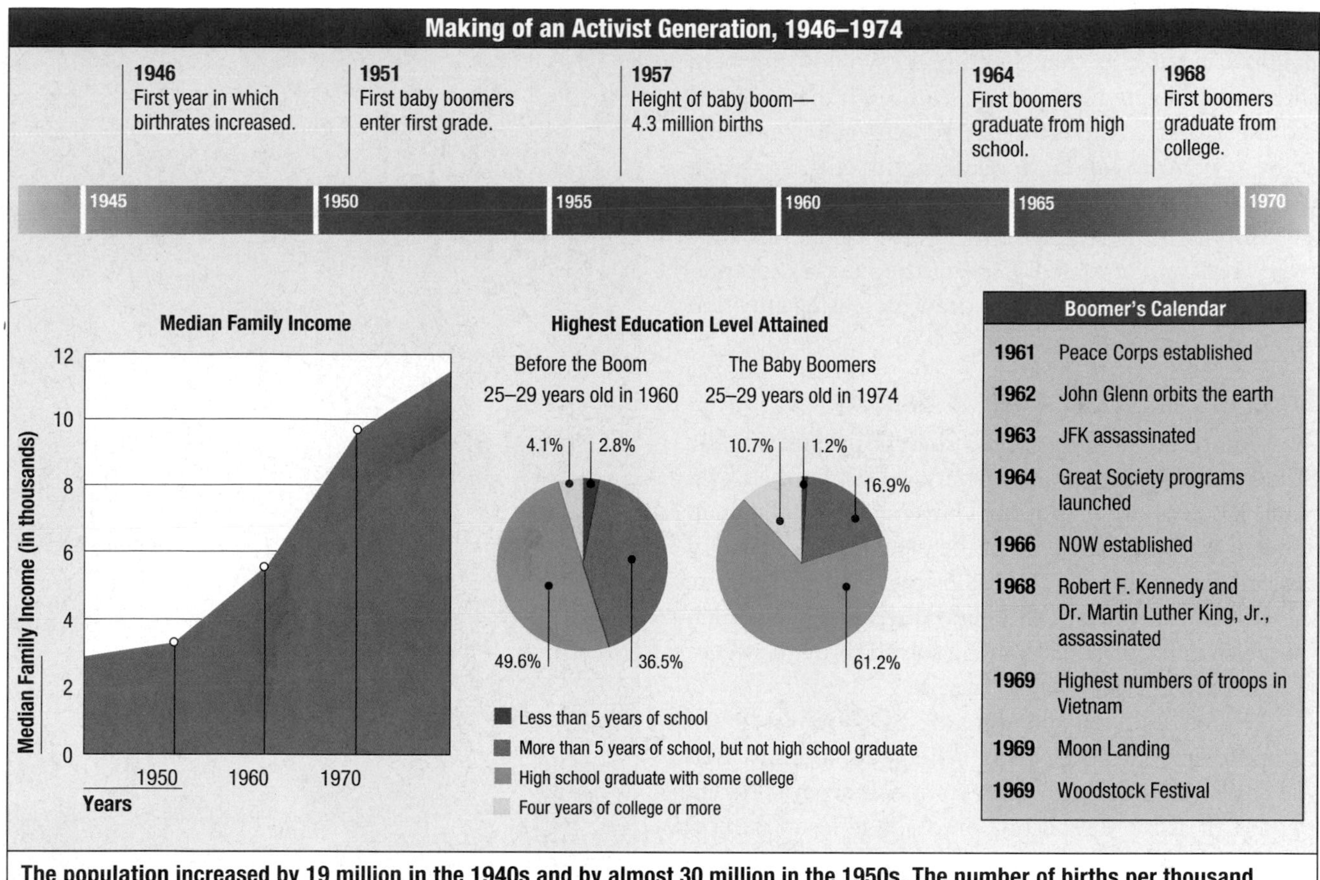

The population increased by 19 million in the 1940s and by almost 30 million in the 1950s. The number of births per thousand women peaked in 1957. *How many babies were born in 1957?*

In the days following the arrests, nearly 70 percent of Berkeley students protested. They picketed administration buildings brandishing signs that read Shut This Factory Down and I Am a U.C. Student: Do Not Fold, Bend, or Mutilate.

University officials eventually backed down. In early 1965 they lifted the ban on campus political activity. By 1965, however, student protests had spread like wildfire across the nation's campuses. Unlike the "silent generation" of the 1950s, the rebellious students of the 1960s became outspoken critics of American society. At first, their protests focused on students' rights. Soon a new issue would arise to fuel student passions—the war in Vietnam.

The Student Movement

Student Activism Emerges in the Early 1960s

The students who protested at Berkeley were children of the post–World War II baby boom. Having grown up in the 1950s, they were now attending college in unprecedented numbers. In 1950 only 1 million young Americans attended college. By 1960 that number had jumped to 4 million. By the end of the decade, nearly 8 million students flooded the nation's campuses.

Raised in the prosperity of the postwar years, the college students of the 1960s had grown up in economic security, free of the worries that had troubled their Depression-era parents. Seventy-five percent of them came from families with incomes above the national average. Mostly white and middle class, student activists could afford to be idealistic and rebellious.

A youthful President Kennedy, who appealed to young Americans in 1961 to "ask not what your country can do for you—ask what you can do for your country," stirred their idealism. Thousands responded, joining the Peace Corps and VISTA, its domestic counterpart.

Others, like Mario Savio, joined the civil rights movement. Inspired by African Americans who risked their lives in the struggle for racial equality, nearly 1,000 Northern white students volunteered for SNCC's Mississippi Freedom Summer Project in 1964. As the white volunteers journeyed south, they got a firsthand look at racism and poverty in the United States. They returned to their Northern campuses that fall schooled in the techniques of nonviolent civil disobedience and determined to fight injustice.

Only a minority of American college students joined the protest movement. At the height of campus unrest in 1970, only 12 percent identified themselves as part of the radical New Left. The majority of students joined fraternities and sororities, cheered at football games, and majored in subjects that they hoped would help them earn a good living after college. Although they rejected radical politics, many of these students still shared the activists' concerns about students' rights, civil rights, and the war in Vietnam.

Although the student rebels were a minority, they were vocal and attended some of the nation's top universities. Their protests would draw increasing attention as the decade progressed.

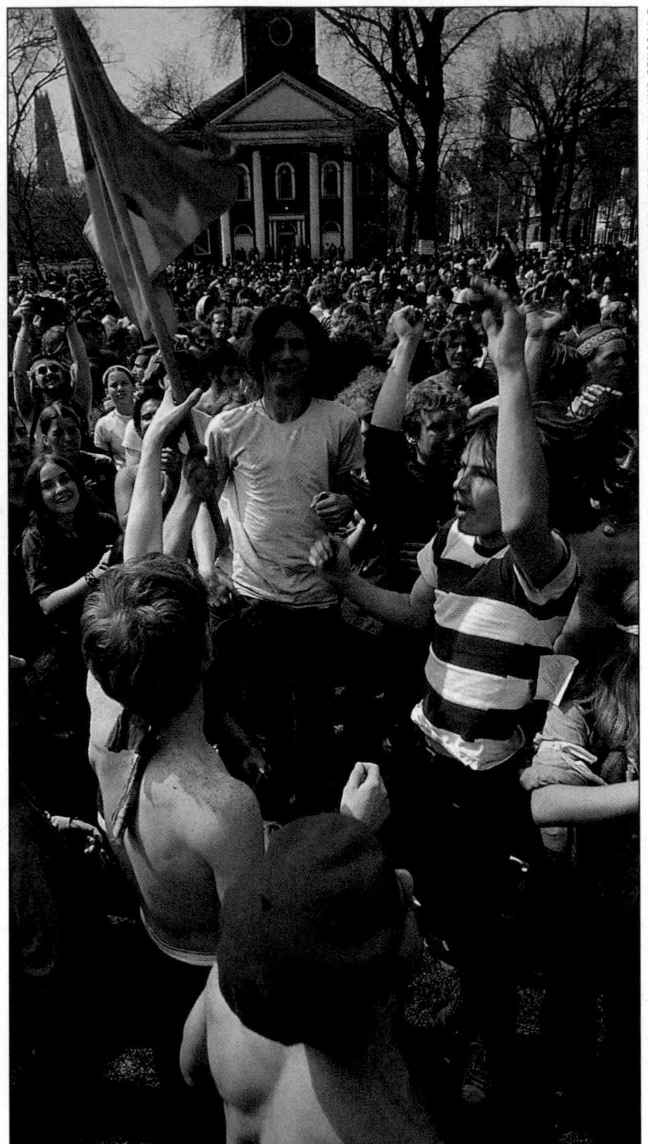

A National Organization SDS members at Yale University mobilized antiwar activities on campus. *How many members did SDS have in 1965?*

Students for a Democratic Society

One of the earliest radical student groups was the Students for a Democratic Society (SDS). Formed by a small group of students at the University of Michigan in 1960, SDS formed the core of the New Left, a rebirth of radical American politics. Disillusioned with liberalism, members of the New Left believed that problems such as racism and war could only be solved through sweeping changes in American society.

In June 1962, 60 members of SDS from a dozen campuses met at Port Huron, Michigan, to draft what they called an agenda for a generation. It began: "We are people of this generation, bred in at least modest comfort, housed now in universities, looking uncomfortably to the world we inherit."

Written for the most part by Tom Hayden, a 22-year-old student from the University of Michigan, the document went on to spell out the ills afflicting the United States. The United States, Hayden argued, was controlled by massive government, corporate, and educational bureaucracies that left individuals powerless. As a cure SDS envisioned a radical movement to bring about "participatory democracy," in which citizens would seize control over decisions affecting their lives.

The Port Huron Statement signaled the political awakening of a generation of students and the beginning of an era of student activism. As SDS member Sharon Jeffrey recalled, "It was exalting. We felt that we were different, and that we were going to do things differently. . . . It felt like the dawn of a new age."

Protesting the War

At first SDS tackled domestic issues. In the summer of 1964, SDS volunteers moved into poor urban neighborhoods and organized residents to fight for jobs, better housing, schools, and community services.

By the fall of 1964, SDS had organized chapters on nearly 50 campuses around the country. Then a new issue loomed—the war in Vietnam. At its December 1964 national convention, SDS members voted to protest the war by organizing a march on Washington for the following April. Because United States involvement in Vietnam was still limited to military advisers and aid, opposition to the war remained muted. No one expected more than a few thousand marchers. Then President Johnson began to escalate the United States commitment to South Vietnam.

When Johnson ordered the large-scale bombing of North Vietnam in 1965 and sent in the first combat troops, the antiwar movement mushroomed. Some Americans felt betrayed by Johnson, whom they had considered a peace candidate in 1964. SDS now led a crusade to end the war in Vietnam. Within a single year, the ranks of SDS had swollen to more than 150 chapters with 10,000 members.

On April 17, more than 20,000 people crowded around the Washington Monument for the SDS antiwar march—the first of increasingly massive, and eventually more militant, protests. Folksinger Judy Collins sang

"The Times They Are A-Changin'." The words seemed prophetic:

> Come senators, congressmen
> Please heed the call
> Don't stand in the doorway
> Don't block up the hall.
> For he that gets hurt
> Will be he who has stalled.
> There's a battle
> Outside and it's ragin'
> It'll soon shake your windows
> And rattle your walls
> For the times they are a-changin'.
>
> —Bob Dylan,
> "The Times They Are A-Changin'," 1963

That spring SDS also helped organize several university teach-ins. The first teach-ins took place at the University of Michigan at Ann Arbor. On March 24, 1965, shortly after the first United States ground combat troops landed in South Vietnam, more than 3,500 students and professors jammed into 4 lecture halls. They sang folk songs, analyzed United States foreign policy, and debated the war until dawn. In the following weeks, similar teach-ins sprang up at campuses across the nation.

Resisting the Draft

Opposition to the war led some students to resist the **draft,** a system of selecting individuals for military service. Since the early 1950s, all 18-year-old men had been required to register for the draft. In theory all those who registered were eligible to serve in the armed forces if needed. Individuals could be given **deferments,** or postponements of military service, however, due to their health or occupation. College students were among those who received deferments in large numbers during the Vietnam War.

Critics of the draft pointed out that, partly because of college deferments, the burden of the war fell unfairly on the poor, the working class, and minorities. Poor and working-class men were twice as likely to be drafted and, if drafted, twice as likely to fight as men from the middle class. African Americans made up 18 percent of those drafted to fight in Vietnam, although they were only 10 percent of the nation's population.

During the Vietnam War, thousands of defiant young men challenged the idea that citizens have a military obligation to their country. "The war in Vietnam is criminal and we must act together, at great individual risk, to stop it," the resisters declared. They argued that without a draft, the government could not continue to wage the war.

Some became **conscientious objectors,** claiming that their moral or religious beliefs prevented them from fighting in the war. Others, in defiance of federal law, refused to register for the draft or burned their draft cards. Protesters harassed campus recruiters for the military and disrupted campus Reserve Officers' Training Corps (ROTC) classes. Some went to jail for refusing to be drafted. Thousands more fled the country.

As the number of young men called up by the draft increased from 5,000 per month in 1965 to 50,000 per month in 1967, the ranks of draft resisters swelled. By the fall of 1966, more than 3 dozen draft resistance groups had sprung up on college campuses around the country.

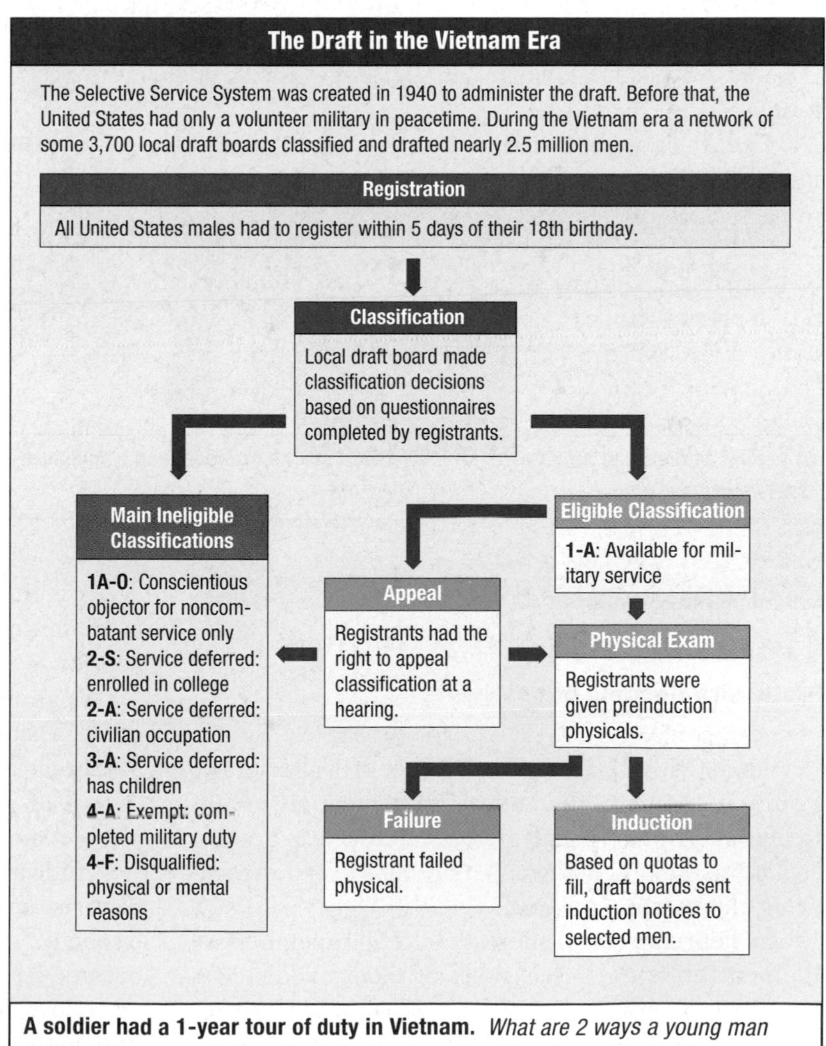

The Draft in the Vietnam Era
The Selective Service System was created in 1940 to administer the draft. Before that, the United States had only a volunteer military in peacetime. During the Vietnam era a network of some 3,700 local draft boards classified and drafted nearly 2.5 million men.
Registration
All United States males had to register within 5 days of their 18th birthday.
Classification
Local draft board made classification decisions based on questionnaires completed by registrants.
Main Ineligible Classifications
1A-O: Conscientious objector for noncombatant service only
2-S: Service deferred: enrolled in college
2-A: Service deferred: civilian occupation
3-A: Service deferred: has children
4-A: Exempt: completed military duty
4-F: Disqualified: physical or mental reasons
Eligible Classification
1-A: Available for military service
Appeal
Registrants had the right to appeal classification at a hearing.
Physical Exam
Registrants were given preinduction physicals.
Failure
Registrant failed physical.
Induction
Based on quotas to fill, draft boards sent induction notices to selected men.

A soldier had a 1-year tour of duty in Vietnam. *What are 2 ways a young man could avoid serving in the military?*

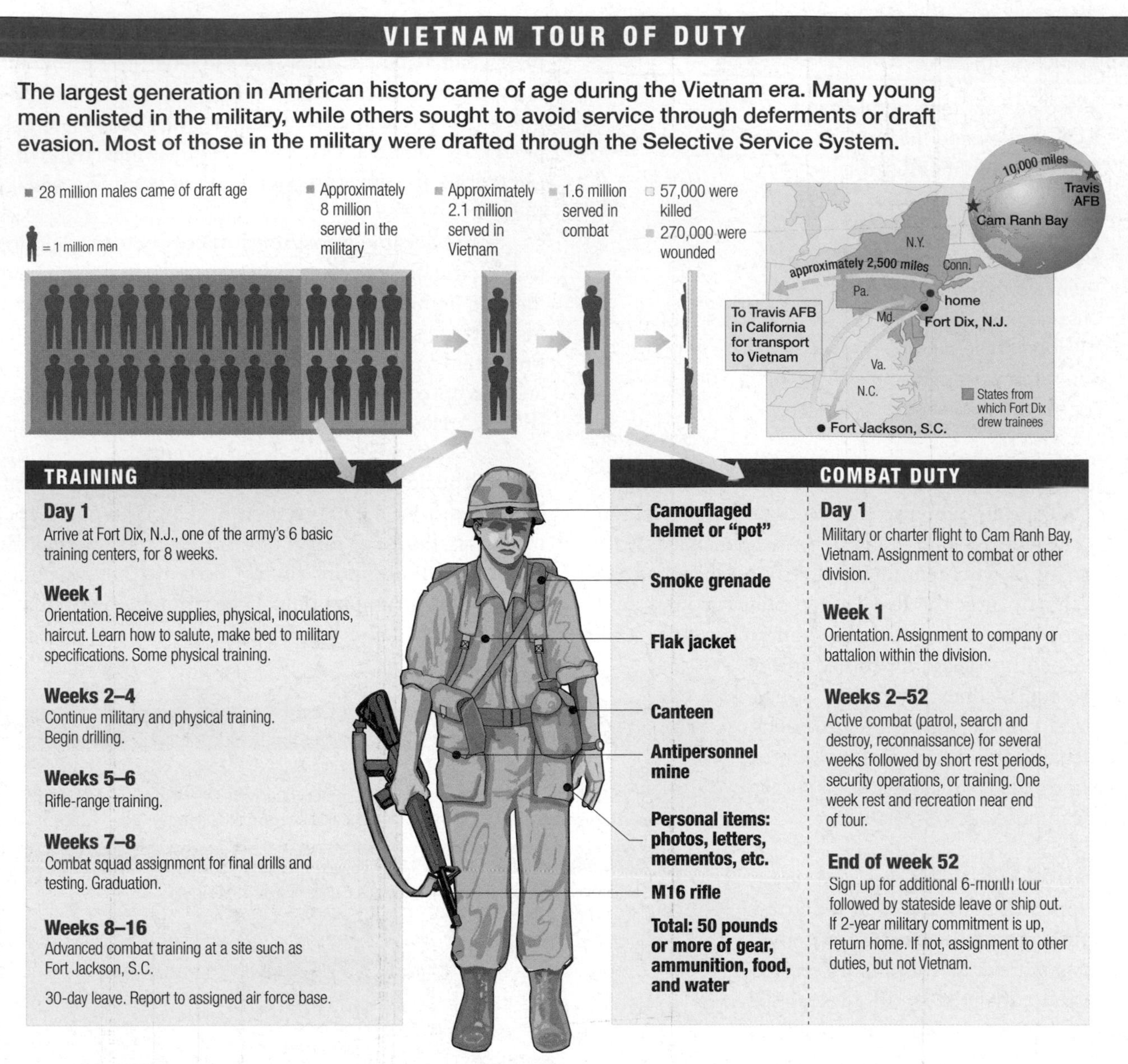

VIETNAM TOUR OF DUTY
The largest generation in American history came of age during the Vietnam era. Many young men enlisted in the military, while others sought to avoid service through deferments or draft evasion. Most of those in the military were drafted through the Selective Service System.
28 million males came of draft age
= 1 million men
Approximately 8 million served in the military
Approximately 2.1 million served in Vietnam
1.6 million served in combat
57,000 were killed
270,000 were wounded
10,000 miles
Travis AFB
Cam Ranh Bay
N.Y.
approximately 2,500 miles
Conn.
Pa.
home
Md.
Fort Dix, N.J.
To Travis AFB in California for transport to Vietnam
Va.
N.C.
States from which Fort Dix drew trainees
Fort Jackson, S.C.
TRAINING
Day 1
Arrive at Fort Dix, N.J., one of the army's 6 basic training centers, for 8 weeks.
Week 1
Orientation. Receive supplies, physical, inoculations, haircut. Learn how to salute, make bed to military specifications. Some physical training.
Weeks 2–4
Continue military and physical training. Begin drilling.
Weeks 5–6
Rifle-range training.
Weeks 7–8
Combat squad assignment for final drills and testing. Graduation.
Weeks 8–16
Advanced combat training at a site such as Fort Jackson, S.C.
30-day leave. Report to assigned air force base.
Camouflaged helmet or "pot"
Smoke grenade
Flak jacket
Canteen
Antipersonnel mine
Personal items: photos, letters, mementos, etc.
M16 rifle
Total: 50 pounds or more of gear, ammunition, food, and water
COMBAT DUTY
Day 1
Military or charter flight to Cam Ranh Bay, Vietnam. Assignment to combat or other division.
Week 1
Orientation. Assignment to company or battalion within the division.
Weeks 2–52
Active combat (patrol, search and destroy, reconnaissance) for several weeks followed by short rest periods, security operations, or training. One week rest and recreation near end of tour.
End of week 52
Sign up for additional 6-month tour followed by stateside leave or ship out. If 2-year military commitment is up, return home. If not, assignment to other duties, but not Vietnam.

A typical soldier was armed with an M16 rifle, a smoke grenade, and a claymore—an antipersonnel mine. *How many men were sent to Vietnam?*

Opposition to the War

Protesters Become More Diverse

Along with the increasing number of United States troops in Vietnam, the antiwar movement also grew. Religious groups, peace groups, antinuclear groups, civil rights groups, and women's groups joined the students in protesting the war.

In February 1967, more than 2,500 members of Women Strike for Peace, most of them middle-class homemakers, stormed the Pentagon demanding to see "the generals who send our sons to Vietnam." When refused entrance, the women began pounding on the doors with their shoes. Secretary of Defense Robert McNamara eventually ordered that the women be allowed to enter and present their petition to an aide.

Huge antiwar rallies in the spring of 1967 drew hundreds of thousands of protesters to New York City and San Francisco. Marching alongside the students were Americans from all walks of life: priests, businesspeople, and mothers pushing children in strollers.

Antiwar protests grew as more and more Americans demonstrated a willingness to risk arrest in acts of civil disobedience protesting the war. The SDS rallying cry became "From Protest to Resistance." Thousands responded in what organizers called a dramatic confrontation between the "people" and the "warmakers," the March on the Pentagon. On October 21, 1967, more than 50,000 protesters crowded onto the Pentagon steps where armed troops awaited. Scores of young men burned their draft cards as supporters chanted, "Burn cards, not people!" Some protesters, pleading with the troops to join them, placed flowers in the barrels of the rifles. Hundreds of protesters were arrested, and many were beaten.

FILE PHOTO BY RALPH J. BRUNKE

A Soldier's Voice Opinions on the war were visible at home and on the battlefield. *What message was this soldier trying to convey with his helmet sticker?*

Key leaders, too, began to criticize the war in 1967. Senator William Fulbright, once a supporter of the war, held a series of televised hearings in which critics of the war analyzed United States policy. Martin Luther King, Jr., pointed out that each dollar spent in Vietnam was one dollar less for social reform at home. By early 1966 the federal government was pouring nearly $2 billion a month into Vietnam—more than the Johnson administration ever spent in a single year on the war on poverty.

War Divides the Nation

By 1967 the United States was deeply divided over the war. **Hawks,** those who supported the war, urged stepping up the war effort to win a military victory. **Doves,** those who supported the withdrawal of United States troops and a negotiated end to the war, questioned both the cost and the morality of the war.

Many Americans were neither hawks nor doves but were disturbed both by the war and the protests against it. A December 1967 poll showed that 70 percent of Americans believed the protests were "acts of disloyalty" to the soldiers fighting the war. As the war raged on, however, many became convinced that the United States was hopelessly bogged down in an unwinnable war. That frustration could be heard in the words of one Iowa homemaker: "I want to get out, but I don't want to give up."

Bringing the War Home

In the aftermath of the Tet offensive, public opinion on the war shifted dramatically. In early January 1968, hawks outnumbered doves by 62 to 22 percent. By March the number of hawks had fallen to 41 percent, while the number of doves had climbed to 42 percent.

Antiwar protests increased in size and number on the nation's campuses. From January to June 1968, nearly 40,000 students at more than 100 colleges staged protests. Though most protests were peaceful, violence occasionally erupted.

The most violent uprising took place that spring at Columbia University in New York City and reflected the growing militancy of SDS. The protest at Columbia linked two potent issues—civil rights and the Vietnam War. At noon on Tuesday, April 23, more than 600 students rallied to protest university ties to military research. They also objected to a university plan to build a gym on public parkland in a nearby Harlem neighborhood.

When university officials refused to listen to student demands, the protest escalated. Led by the SDS and the students' Afro-American Society, the protesters took over five university buildings, including the office of the university president. "We are fighting to recapture a school from business and war," wrote student James Kunen, "and rededicate it to learning and life." A week later New York City police officers stormed the buildings to arrest the students and drag them off to waiting police vans.

The Media and the War

Coverage Sways Public Opinion

The antiwar protesters gained a powerful ally as the war continued on—the mass media. Television, especially, played an important role in molding public opinion. Satellite technology meant that the war could be broadcast at home almost as it happened. The scenes of brutal fighting, desperate refugees, and dying United States soldiers shocked the more than 60 million Americans who tuned in to the nightly news.

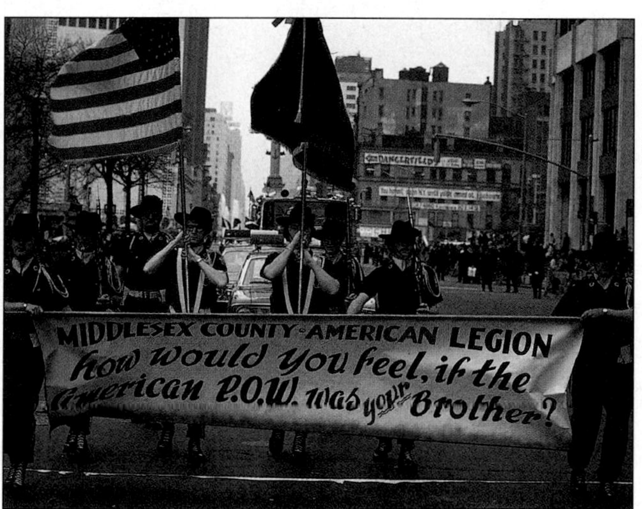

© BURT GLINN/MAGNUM PHOTOS

Support for the War The message on the banner in this photo captures the sentiment that war protests were "acts of disloyalty" to the fighting soldier. *How do you think you would feel about antiwar protesters if you knew someone who was a POW?*

In contrast with earlier wars, the military did not censor the press in Vietnam. Reporters and photographers easily got press passes and tramped through the muddy jungle, side by side with American patrols. In 1968, at the height of United States involvement, 800 reporters covered the Vietnam War.

Early Reporting on the War

During the early years of the war, most reporters agreed that the United States was fighting the spread of communism and that South Vietnam deserved and needed American support. They applauded South Vietnamese leader Diem. In June 1960, *Newsweek* called him "one of Asia's ablest leaders."

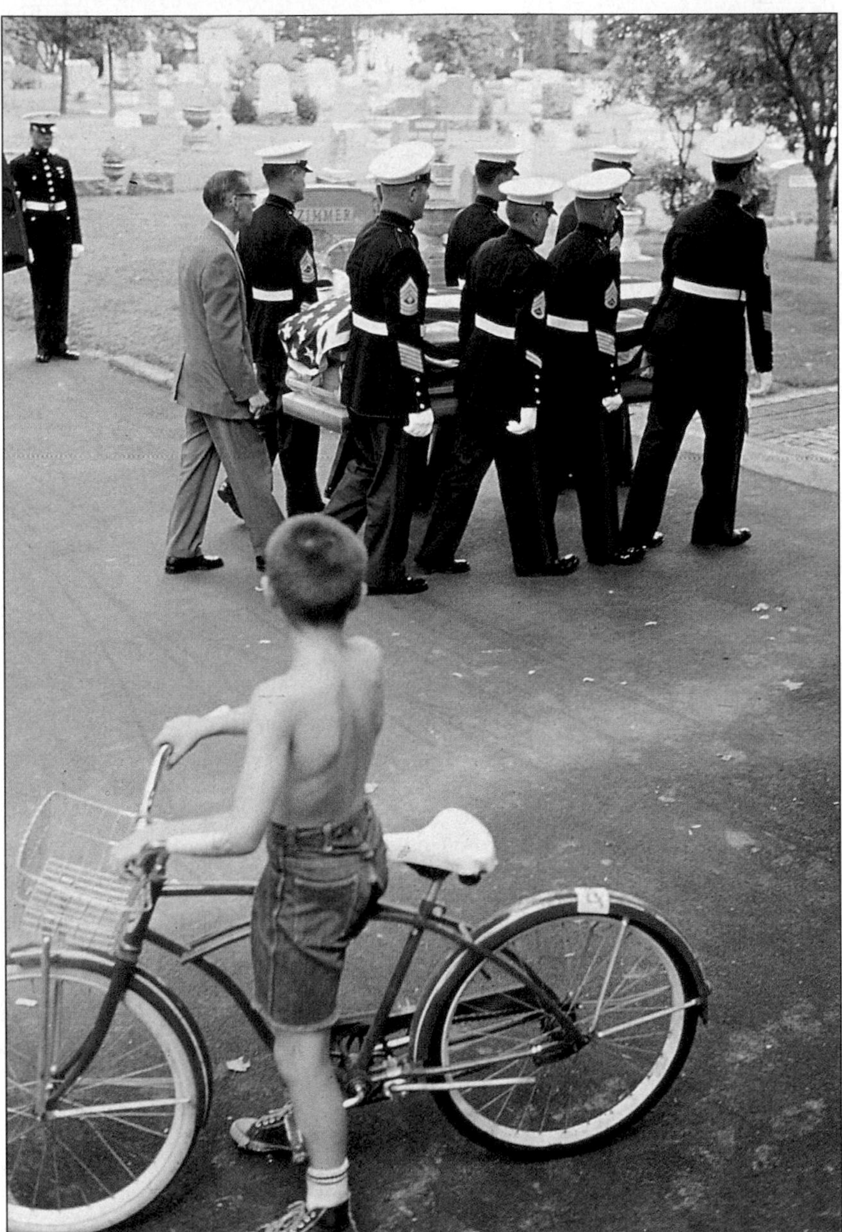

BILL RAY/LIFE MAGAZINE, ©TIME, INC.

The War Touches Home **A boy stops to watch the funeral of Private First Class Robert Damian Wuertz, Jr., the first casualty of war from Massillon, Ohio.** *Give an example of how the media brought home the personal cost of the war.*

A More Critical Press

After the Tet offensive in early 1968, however, respected reporters such as Walter Cronkite began to raise serious questions about the war. After a trip to Saigon in 1968, Cronkite told viewers, "To say we are closer to victory today is to believe, in the face of the evidence, the optimists who have been wrong in the past." Such reports undercut official optimism and eroded public support for the war.

Reporters not only questioned official reports that the war could be won but also raised more fundamental questions: Should the United States be in Vietnam? Was Vietnam worth the cost? In the wake of Tet, James Reston, a columnist for the *New York Times,* asked: "What is the end that justified this slaughter? How will we save Vietnam if we destroy it in the battle?"

The media also brought home the immense tragedy of the war—its cost in human lives. In June 1969, *Life* magazine published the photos of 242 Americans who had been killed in 1 week in Vietnam. Their young faces served as a reminder that the nightly casualty figures represented real people—the sons, brothers, husbands, and fathers of those at home.

The My Lai Massacre

One of the most shocking incidents of the war surfaced in November 1969. Journalist Seymour Hersh discovered that, in March 1968, United States forces under the command of Lieutenant William L. Calley, Jr., had massacred nearly 350 Vietnamese civilians in the village of My Lai. Americans read the account of 22-year-old Private Paul Meadlo: "We huddled them up. We made them squat down. . . . I poured about four clips into the group. . . . The mothers was hugging their children. . . . Well, we kept right on firing."

Lieutenant Calley was court-martialed and sentenced to life imprisonment. Though the actions of the United States forces shocked Americans everywhere, some felt a certain amount of sympathy for Calley, who claimed he was "following a direct order." The military eventually reduced Calley's sentence.

Nixon and the Antiwar Movement

Nixon Seeks to Silence Protesters

Public pressure had made the Vietnam War a key issue during the 1968 election. President Johnson had been forced out of the race for his failed Vietnam policies. Richard Nixon had been elected President in part because he promised an end to the unpopular war.

In June 1969, President Nixon announced that he would start bringing United States troops home as part of his plan to "Vietnamize" the war. The fighting continued, however, and so did the protests. On October 1, nearly 2 million Americans across the nation demonstrated for peace in Vietnam. One month later more than 300,000 protesters flooded Washington, D.C., taking their plea for peace to the White House. By the end of the year, doves outnumbered hawks on college campuses by 3 to 1.

To rally support for his policies, President Nixon appealed to what he called the silent majority. In a November 3 speech, he declared that a minority now threatened the nation's security "by mounting demonstrations in the streets." "North Vietnam cannot defeat or humiliate the United States," Nixon insisted. "Only Americans can do that." To fend off this "enemy" at home, Nixon appealed "to you, the great silent majority of my fellow Americans—I ask for your support."

Conflict over the war would come to a head the following spring. A new wave of demonstrations and violence would rock the country and cause many on both sides of the issue to fear for the nation's future.

The War Comes Home

On April 30, 1970, President Nixon announced that he had ordered United States troops to invade Vietnam's neutral neighbor, Cambodia, to clean out Communist bases there. His expansion of the war soon led to massive protests across the country.

The Cambodian invasion outraged students at Ohio's Kent State University. Two days after the President's announcement, they surrounded the campus ROTC building, pelting it with firecrackers and rocks. Then they burned it to the ground. In response Ohio Governor James Rhodes called members of the National Guard to Kent State on May 3.

The next day at noon, about 600 students held a peaceful protest on the Kent State campus commons. A campus police officer bellowed through a bullhorn: "This assembly is unlawful! This is an order—disperse immediately!"

A Different Kind of Violence A shocked young woman kneels beside the body of a Kent State student killed by a National Guard member's bullet. *What prompted the student protest at Kent State?*

The students refused to leave. Some lobbed stones and sticks at the soldiers, shouting, "Pigs off campus!" In reply the troops hurled tear gas at the students. Then their commander ordered, "Prepare to move out and disperse this mob."

The members of the National Guard, many as young and nervous as the students they confronted, pointed their bayonets at the demonstrators and marched toward them. Choking and weeping from the tear gas, dozens of students fled. A group of soldiers retreated to the top of a nearby hill. Suddenly they turned, raised their rifles, and fired into the crowd.

"My God," a girl screamed, "they're killing us!" Seconds later, nine students had been wounded, and four students were dead. None of them were radical activists. One was an ROTC student, and two had simply been crossing the campus on their way to lunch.

The soldiers claimed they had fired in self-defense. A later investigation found otherwise, declaring the action of the National Guard "unwarranted and inexcusable."

Public reaction following the shootings revealed just how deeply divided the country was during the 1960s. Some Americans blamed the students for the violence at Kent State. They resented the college students for

HISTORY Online

Student Web Activity 23

Visit the *American Odyssey* Web site at americanodyssey.glencoe.com and click on ***Chapter 23—Student Web Activities*** for an activity relating to the Vietnam War era.

their privileges, their countercultural values, and their rebelliousness. Other people condemned the government. The grief-stricken father of Allison Krause, one of the slain students, asked, "Is this dissent a crime? Is this a reason for killing her?"

Jackson State

Violence flared again a week later at the nearly all-African American college of Jackson State in Mississippi. An outbreak of vandalism in downtown Jackson prompted local officials to call in 500 National Guard troops to back up 80 state highway patrol officers and 125 city police officers.

On the evening of May 14, rocks and bottles began to fly in downtown Jackson, and a city truck was set on fire. At 10:30 P.M., police, highway patrol officers, and National Guard troops approached the nearby campus where students had gathered. Suddenly a bottle crashed near an officer. Without warning, police and highway patrol officers opened fire. The hail of bullets lasted nearly 30 seconds; 12 students were wounded, and 2 were killed, both innocent bystanders.

The End of a Decade

The protests after the Cambodian invasion marked the climax of a decade of student protest. Although some protests would continue until the war ended in 1973, the massive demonstrations of the 1960s were over. Their failure to end the war frustrated many students. One of the pioneers of the student movement, SDS, splintered into smaller extremist groups such as the militant Weathermen. Other students gave up political action altogether.

Government harassment of the New Left also took a toll. Although prohibited by law from spying on American citizens, the Central Intelligence Agency collected files on 7,200 Americans. Federal Bureau of Investigation agents secretly joined leftist groups and triggered feuds between members or instigated violent encounters with the police. Racked by internal dissent and weakened by government crackdowns, the New Left fell apart as the war in Vietnam wound down and United States troops returned home.

Although the student movement failed in its goal of radically transforming United States society, it did succeed in effecting change. The antiwar protests helped to force a shift in United States policy. The campus demonstrations brought about reforms in how universities were governed and enlarged students' role in campus life.

The radicalism of students during the 1960s alarmed many Americans and fueled growing conservatism. Along with inner-city riots, assassinations, and the Vietnam War, widespread campus unrest seemed to be a sign that something was deeply wrong with the country.

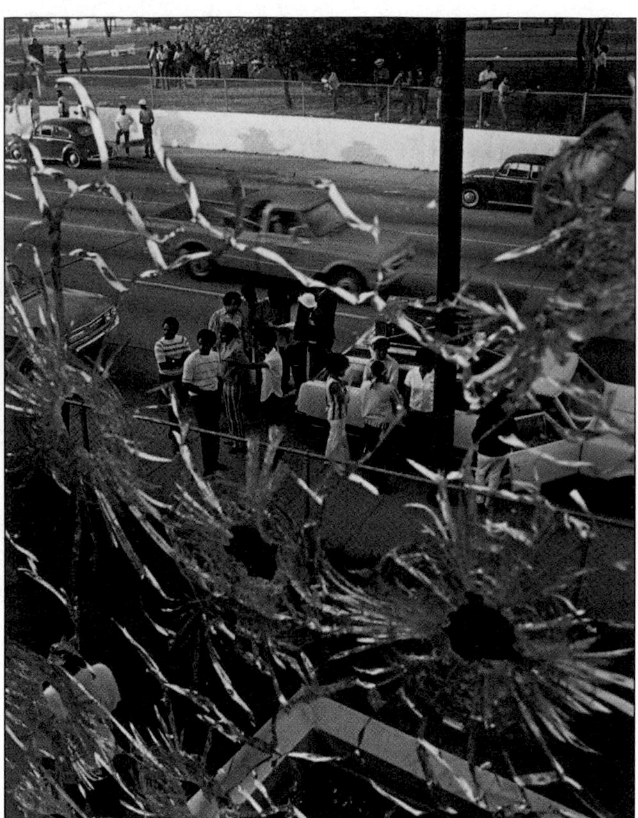

AP/WIDE WORLD PHOTOS

Jackson State A total of 230 bullet holes riddled Alexander Hall, a women's dormitory at Jackson State. *Why do you think the authorities reacted so violently to student unrest?*

SECTION ASSESSMENT

Main Idea

1. Use a diagram like this one to write and support a generalization on how student protests and media coverage affected public opinion of the war.

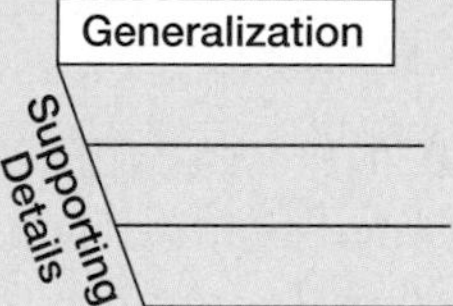

Vocabulary

2. Define: draft, deferment, conscientious objector, hawk, dove.

Checking Facts

3. Why did many students shift their attention from domestic issues to antiwar activities?

4. Why was the Vietnam War a "living room war"?

Critical Thinking

5. Determining Relevance How did the lyrics of "The Times They Are A-Changin' " reflect the goals of many New Left groups?

Social Studies Skill

UNDERSTANDING PUBLIC OPINION POLLS

Learning the Skill

Public opinion polls have become a major factor in political life. For example, eroding public support for the war in Vietnam was a key factor in President Johnson's decision not to seek reelection in 1968. Polls, however, can only offer a snapshot of public opinion at one point in time, and only about the specific questions asked.

A public opinion poll should collect information in an objective and scientific way. Pollsters often use "random sampling," a method that employs the mathematical rules of probability, to obtain a representative segment of the population for questioning—called a "sample."

Sampling allows pollsters to infer something about a whole group by looking closely at a small part of it. Before pollsters can make inferences from their data, however, they must account for a "margin of error" in their sampling.

Questions must be written so the pollsters will find out what they want to know without influencing the results. Questions should be phrased to be as neutral as possible.

Knowing how to read and understand data from a public opinion poll will help you judge what other citizens are thinking and feeling about people, issues, and events of the day.

Use these steps to analyze a public opinion poll:

a. Look at the date and title for the overall context of the poll.

b. Look to see who was questioned. How large was the sample?

c. Read the questions carefully and decide whether they were phrased in an unbiased way.

d. State the numerical results in sentence form.

Public Opinion Poll, March 1969

What do you think the United States should do next in regard to the Vietnam War situation?	
Margin of error: 3–4 percentage points	Sample size: 1,500*
Escalate war (go all-out)	32%
Pull out (let South Vietnamese take over)	26%
Continue present policy (work for cease-fire at Paris, stay in Vietnam as long as necessary)	19%
End the war as soon as possible	19%
Other	4%

*Twenty-one percent expressed no opinion.

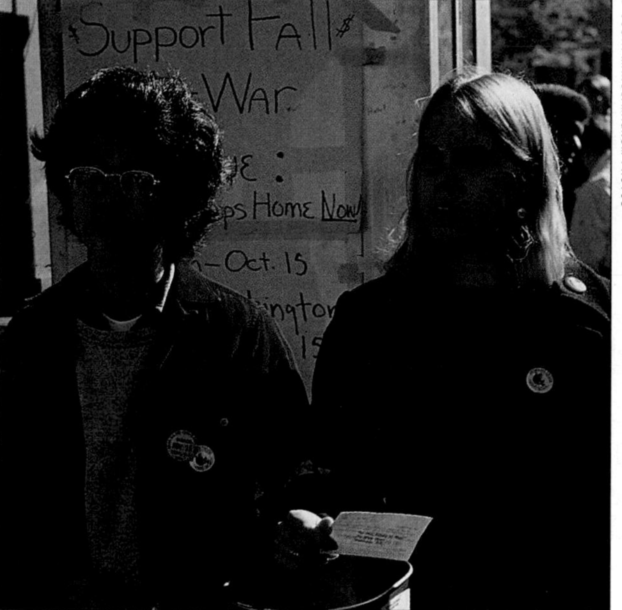

Rallying Support Opinions about the war varied among students. *What is the opinion of these students about the war?*

Practicing the Skill

Look carefully at the poll results shown on this page and answer the following questions:

1. What is this poll about?

2. Is the question phrased objectively?

3. What is the sample size?

4. What is the margin of error?

5. State the numerical results in sentence form.

Find a public opinion poll in a newspaper or magazine, and use the questions above to analyze the results.

Applying the Skill

Pick an issue that concerns students in your school. Develop a nonbiased question to poll opinion on this issue. Then randomly select a sample population, conduct the poll, and tally results in a chart. State the results in sentence form.

The **Glencoe Skillbuilder Interactive Workbook, Level 2** CD-ROM provides more practice in key social studies skills.

Ending the War

NOVEMBER 13–15, 1969: PROTESTERS DEMAND AN END TO WAR

© BONNIE FREER

A Solemn Moment
Each soldier killed in Vietnam is honored.

During the evening of Thursday, November 13, thousands of people assembled outside the gates of Virginia's Arlington National Cemetery. Across the Potomac River lay Washington, D.C. The lights of the capital twinkled in the distance as the group stood in the darkness and biting cold.

In single file the protesters set off to walk the four miles (6.4 km) across the river to the White House. Each marcher carried a lighted candle and a placard bearing the name of a United States soldier killed in Vietnam or of a Vietnamese village destroyed by the war. Six drummers beating out a funeral march led the way. Just outside the gates of the White House, each marcher paused for a moment and spoke aloud the name on the placard.

The first marcher was Judy Droz, a 23-year-old widow and the mother of a 10-month-old child. Softly she spoke the name of her husband, Lieutenant Donald G. Droz, who had been killed in Vietnam the previous April. Behind her, in turn, another woman angrily shouted out her dead brother's name. Hour by hour, 1 by 1, they came. Forty-five thousand marchers, 45,000 names—through 2 nights and days, the March Against Death continued.

On Saturday, November 15, 2 hours after the last marcher filed past the White House, nearly 300,000 Americans swarmed around the Washington Monument. They had journeyed to Washington, D.C., from all over the nation to protest United States involvement in the Vietnam War. This November mobilization, which was the largest demonstration in the nation's history, reflected the mushrooming opposition to the war. The protesters were no longer just long-haired student radicals but ordinary Americans like Judy Droz.

Guide to Reading

Main Idea

Faced with increasing pressure to end the war, President Nixon negotiated a settlement that, in the end, brought neither peace to Vietnam nor honor to the United States.

Vocabulary

- negotiate
- nationalist movement

Read to Find Out . . .

- the steps Nixon took to end the war in Vietnam.
- the terms of the peace accords negotiated by the United States.
- the costs of the Vietnam War.

Working Toward Peace

Four Years of Struggle

By the end of the 1960s, Vietnam had become, in the words of one Nixon aide, "a bone in the nation's throat." By 1969, about 15 years after United States advisers were first sent to Vietnam, more than 36,000 Americans had come home in flag-draped coffins.

Nixon knew he had to end this unpopular war. During the 1968 campaign, he had claimed to have a secret plan for ending the war quickly and achieving peace with honor in Vietnam. The war would drag on, however, for four more years. In the end the settlement would bring neither peace to Vietnam nor honor to the United States.

Vietnamization

Despite pressure to end the war quickly, Nixon was determined to keep an independent pro–United States government in South Vietnam and to preserve the prestige of the United States as the leader of the free world.

Even the most optimistic military advisers estimated that it would take eight more years for the United States to win the war in Vietnam. The President realized that the American people would never accept eight more years of war. Public pressure was increasing to bring American troops home—now.

In May 1969, Nixon unveiled his secret plan: South Vietnamese soldiers would be trained and equipped to take the place of American troops, a process that came to be known as Vietnamization. As the South Vietnamese took over more of the fighting, United States troops would start coming home.

Vietnamization was part of a larger shift in foreign policy, known as the Nixon Doctrine. On an Asian tour in 1969, Nixon redefined the United States's role in Southeast Asia and the rest of the developing nations. The United States would no longer step in militarily to protect its Asian allies from Communist threats. Although the United States would continue to provide weapons and financial aid to Asian nations, in the future they would have to fight their own wars.

In November 1969, Nixon announced the withdrawal of 60,000 troops from Vietnam. Over the next 3 years, the number of American troops in Vietnam dropped from more than 500,000 to less than 25,000. The troop withdrawals, Nixon believed, would help silence antiwar protesters and buy him time to pursue a more favorable settlement on the battlefield and in the Paris peace talks.

The Paris Peace Talks

Peace talks had begun in Paris in 1968 but had yielded few results. Around the table sat representatives of the United States; its ally, the Thieu government of South Vietnam; North Vietnam; and its ally, the South Vietnamese Communists, known as the Vietcong. Each side had interests to protect; neither the Communists nor the anti-Communists were willing to compromise.

The United States and South Vietnam insisted that all North Vietnamese forces withdraw from South Vietnam and that the Thieu regime remain in power. The North Vietnamese and the Vietcong demanded that United States troops withdraw from South Vietnam and that a coalition government that included the Vietcong would replace the Thieu regime.

Nixon sought to continue the peace talks by sending his national security adviser, Henry Kissinger, to

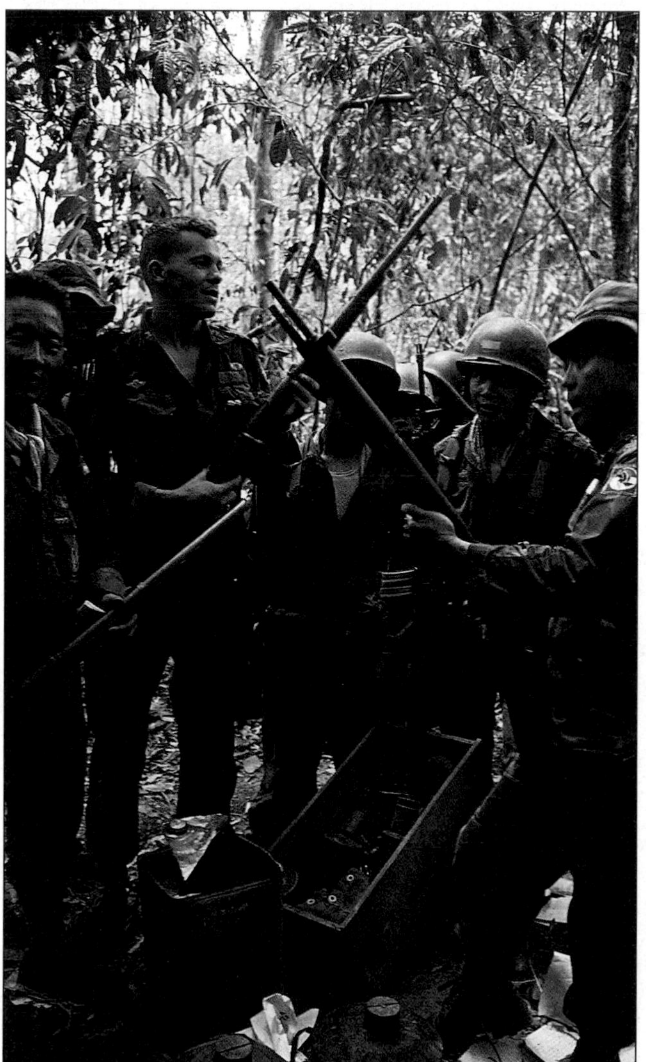

Vietnamization United States military officers train South Vietnamese soldiers to take over more of the fighting in the war. *Why did the concept of Vietnamization become politically necessary for President Nixon?*

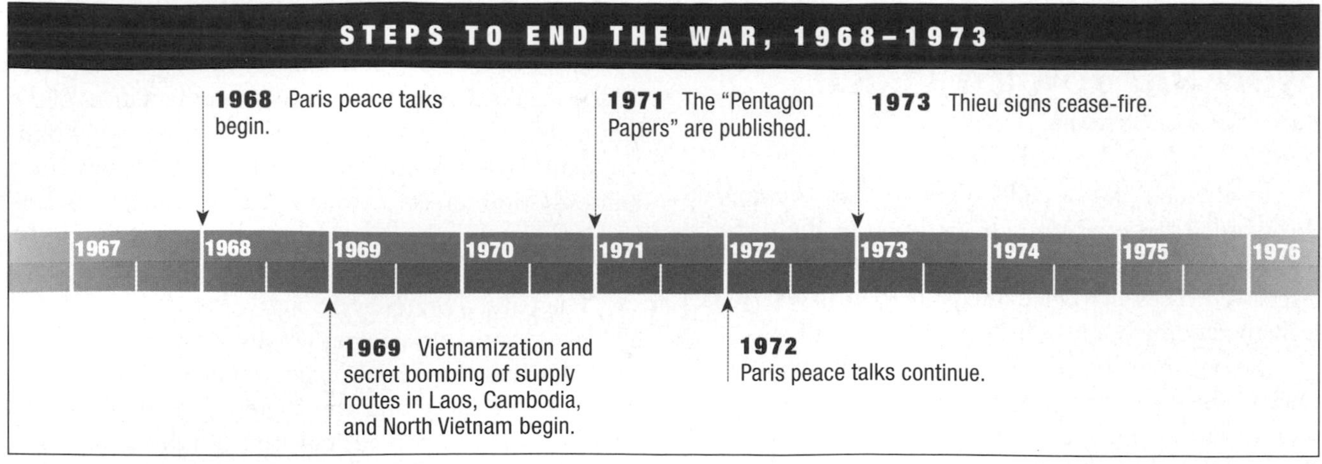
STEPS TO END THE WAR, 1968–1973
1968 Paris peace talks begin.
1971 The "Pentagon Papers" are published.
1973 Thieu signs cease-fire.
1967
1968
1969
1970
1971
1972
1973
1974
1975
1976
1969 Vietnamization and secret bombing of supply routes in Laos, Cambodia, and North Vietnam begin.
1972 Paris peace talks continue.

negotiate secretly with North Vietnam's foreign minister, Le Duc Tho. Kissinger, a Jewish refugee who had escaped Nazi Germany, was a respected professor of international relations at Harvard University when Nixon tapped him for government service. Kissinger, a skilled negotiator, was also ambitious. "What interests me," he once said in an interview, "is what you can do with power."

Nixon shared that interest. Over the years he relied more and more on Kissinger alone to help him carry out foreign policy, eventually appointing him secretary of state. Convinced that debate would weaken their ability to negotiate, Kissinger and Nixon kept their foreign policy moves hidden from the American press, the public, and even from Nixon's own cabinet.

The Secret War

One such hidden policy lay at the core of Nixon's strategy for winning the war in Vietnam. To force the North Vietnamese to negotiate as American forces withdrew, Nixon ordered the secret bombing of enemy supply routes and bases in Cambodia, Laos, and North Vietnam in March 1969. As Nixon confided to aide H. R. Haldeman:

> I call it the madman theory, Bob. I want the North Vietnamese to believe I've reached the point where I might do anything to stop the war. We'll just slip the word to them that "for God's sake, you know Nixon is obsessed about communism. We can't restrain him when he's angry—and he has his hand on the nuclear button"—and Ho Chi Minh himself will be in Paris in two days begging for peace.
>
> —H. R. Haldeman, *The Ends of Power,* 1978

The bombing raids failed to cut completely the supply lines or bring the North Vietnamese to the bargaining table. Instead the attacks spread the war to Cambodia and Laos. Despite the failure of the air attacks, Nixon and Kissinger believed that eventually their strategy would work. For the next four years the United States would pursue the same carrot-and-stick policy—tempting North Vietnam with the carrot of negotiations, and then threatening them with the stick of escalating war.

United States Fire Power Bombing brought death and destruction to the neutral countries of Laos and Cambodia. *Why did Nixon begin the secret bombing of Laos and Cambodia?*

A Bigger Stick

More than 3,600 secret bombing missions and 110,000 tons of bombs had failed to wipe out Communist bases in Cambodia. Nixon decided he needed a bigger stick. On April 30, 1970, he went on television to announce that he was sending United States troops across the border into Cambodia to attack North Vietnamese bases.

Secretary of Defense Melvin Laird and Secretary of State William Rogers opposed Nixon's decision. Both men feared the reaction of the American public. Nixon insisted, convinced that his bold move would stun the North Vietnamese and force them to negotiate.

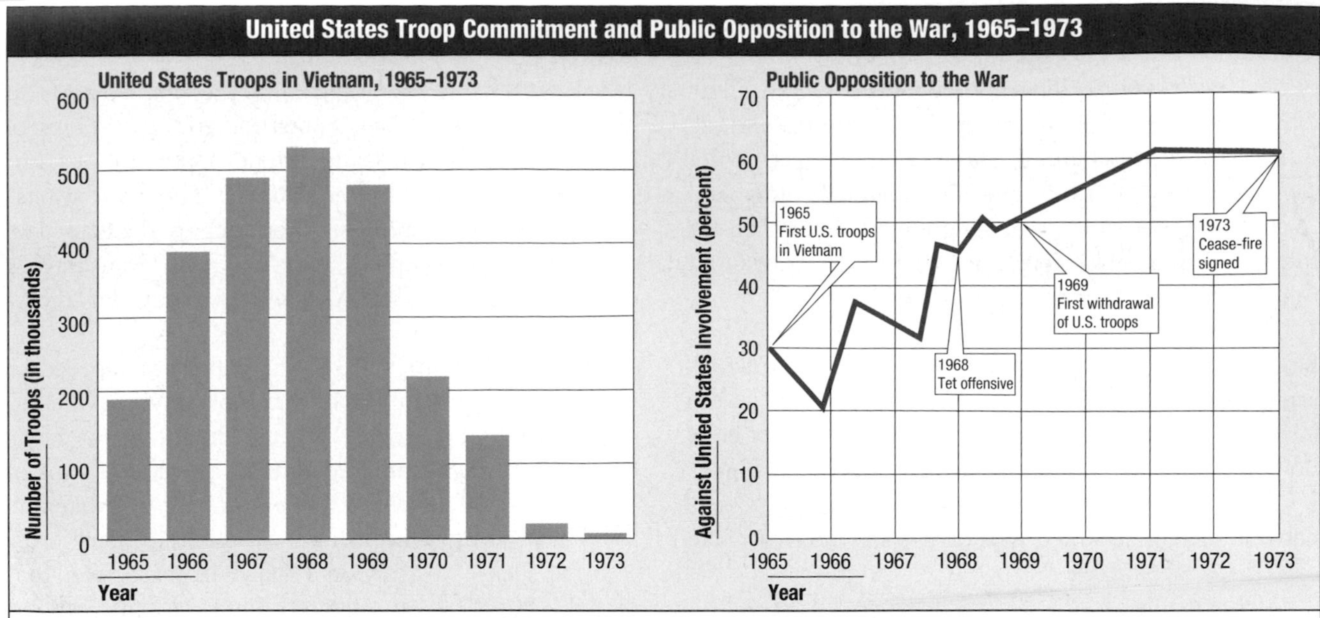

The Vietnam War never had complete public support, but as the war dragged on, opposition increased. *In what year did opposition peak?*

The Home Front

Growing Opposition

Nixon hoped to rally support for his policy by making it public. Instead the news provoked widespread protests. College campuses exploded in demonstrations and violence as the National Guard fired on and killed antiwar protesters at Kent State. Local police did the same at Jackson State.

Despite the public outcry, Nixon and Kissinger insisted that their strategy would bring the war to an honorable end. Others disagreed. An editorial in a respected Midwest newspaper argued:

> In asking the American people to support the expansion of the Vietnam war to Cambodia, as he has already expanded it to Laos, [Nixon] asks them to believe the same false promises which have repeatedly betrayed them against their will into ever deeper involvement on the mainland of Asia.
>
> They are asked to seek peace by making war; to seek withdrawal of our troops by enlarging the arena of combat; to diminish American casualties by sending more young men to their death.
>
> —*St. Louis Post-Dispatch,* May 3, 1970

Further damage to the government's credibility came in June 1971, when the *New York Times* published the "Pentagon Papers," a secret Defense Department study of United States involvement in Vietnam prepared during the Johnson administration. Leaked to the press by a former Defense Department analyst, Daniel Ellsberg, the report offered evidence that in the past the government had lied to the public about the war. Publicly, American Presidents had insisted that the United States was fighting to keep South Vietnam free from communism. According to the "Pentagon Papers," the real reason for pouring troops into Vietnam was to "avoid a humiliating defeat." Although there was nothing in the work damaging to the Nixon administration, the White House tried to block publication of the report. The Supreme Court upheld the right of the *New York Times* to print the "Pentagon Papers."

The Final Years of War

The Agony Continues

Despite United States training and billions of dollars in military aid, the South Vietnamese troops proved unable to defeat the Communist forces. In a disastrous test of Vietnamization in February 1971, South Vietnamese troops invaded neighboring Laos to cut off the flow of supplies from North Vietnam to South Vietnam. Alerted to South Vietnamese battle plans by Vietcong agents, the North Vietnamese troops crushed the South Vietnamese forces in just 6 weeks.

Renewed Peace Talks

Finally, in October 1972, talks reopened in Paris. For the first time in nearly 10 years of war, peace seemed within reach. The North Vietnamese agreed to drop their demand that a coalition government replace South Vietnam's President Thieu. Kissinger, too, offered critical concessions. The United States would allow North Vietnamese troops to remain in South Vietnam. Furthermore the United States would agree to let the Vietcong play a role in a final political settlement. A cease-fire agreement was negotiated that called for the withdrawal of all remaining American troops and the return of all American prisoners of war.

With the 1972 election approaching, the White House was eager to reach a firm agreement of peace. A settlement of the festering war in Vietnam would assure Nixon's reelection. Just days before the November election, a beaming Kissinger announced, "Peace is at hand."

The settlement fell apart, however, when South Vietnamese President Thieu refused to sign the treaty. He knew he was doomed if North Vietnamese troops were allowed to remain in the South.

Again Nixon used the military to force Hanoi to negotiate. On December 18, he ordered the bombing of North Vietnam's major cities, Hanoi and Haiphong. For 12 days bombers hammered away. The "Christmas" bombings—the most massive bombings of the war—laid waste to homes, hospitals, and factories. Thousands of civilians were killed. The *New York Times* called it "diplomacy through terror."

In January 1973, the North Vietnamese agreed to return to the bargaining table. It took just one week to **negotiate,** that is, to reach an agreement, nearly identical to the one hammered out the previous October. What broke the stalemate? The bombing had taken its toll, but even more important was United States pressure on Thieu. Nixon promised that the United States would "respond with full force should the settlement be violated by North Vietnam" and sent $1 billion in military equipment to the South Vietnamese. Reassured, Thieu signed the cease-fire.

UPI/BETTMANN

Fleeing to Safety In the 19 hours before the collapse of the capital, United States helicopters evacuated more than 7,000 American personnel and selected South Vietnamese citizens. *Why did President Thieu eventually agree to the cease-fire?*

Although Nixon claimed he had achieved peace with honor, many Americans believed that the agreement brought neither. These critics pointed out that the same peace agreement could have been reached 4 years earlier. In those 4 years approximately 107,000 South Vietnamese, 500,000 North Vietnamese, and 21,000 more American troops had been killed.

The Fall of Saigon

The peace accords failed to bring peace to Vietnam. Issues unresolved by the treaty would be settled by soldiers on the battlefield, not politicians in Paris.

Shortly after the last American troops left in March 1973, the cease-fire collapsed. Fighting broke out not only in Vietnam but also in Laos and Cambodia. In March 1975, North Vietnam launched an offensive against the weakened forces of South Vietnam. Thieu turned to Washington for aid, and Congress refused to grant it.

In April 1975, Communist troops marched into Saigon. American television audiences watched

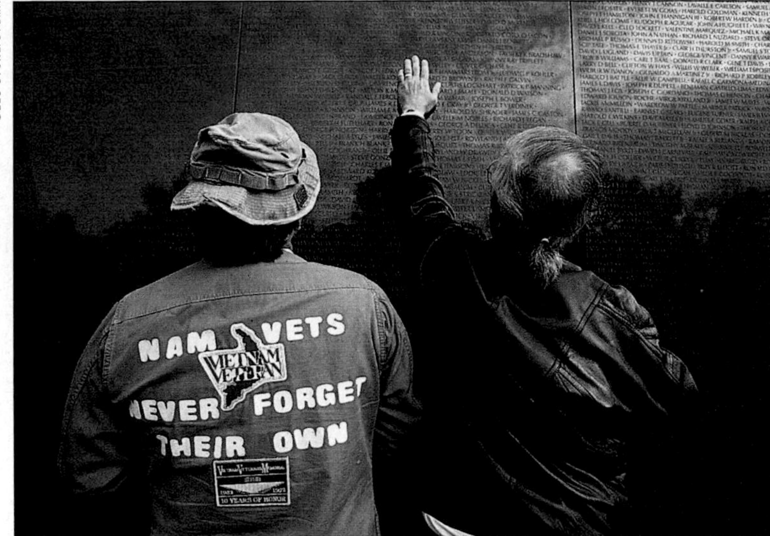

A Sacred Place **The Vietnam Veterans Memorial in Washington, D.C., is made of black granite panels that carry the names of 58,000 Americans who died in Vietnam. Visitors come and touch the names of those they knew and often make a rubbing of a soldier's name.** *Why do you think this memorial has had such an impact on those who have come to visit it?*

as desperate South Vietnamese, many of whom had supported the Americans, scrambled to escape. A United States Army medic described the turmoil on an aircraft carrier offshore:

> There were people coming out in boats, half-sinking boats. . . . There were all these choppers we had left there; they were using these to fly out, the Vietnamese. This flight deck was so full of choppers that we had to push them overboard because there was no room, we couldn't get our own choppers in. . . . It was total chaos.
>
> —Al Santoli, *Everything We Had*, 1981

In the dawn hours of April 30, 1975, Saigon fell to the Communists; soon after, South Vietnam surrendered to North Vietnam.

The Costs of the War

Thousands of Lives and Billions of Dollars

The nation paid a high price to end the war in Vietnam. More than 58,000 Americans were dead; 300,000 were wounded, many of them permanently disabled. More than $150 billion had been poured into the war, while social programs at home went underfunded.

For the first time in history, the United States had lost a war. The optimism and self-confidence inspired by World War II had been shattered. Despite its wealth and technology, the United States had been unable to defeat a **nationalist movement,** the desire of a group of people to be free of any foreign influence.

The people of Southeast Asia also paid a great price for the war in Vietnam. More than 8 million tons of bombs—the equivalent of 640 Hiroshimas—had been dropped on Southeast Asia. Two million Vietnamese and uncounted Cambodians and Laotians were dead. Their land lay in ruins; their villages—to the Vietnamese the heart of their ancient culture—had been destroyed.

Section Assessment

Main Idea

1. Use a diagram like this one to show the causes and effects of the peace accords ending United States military involvement in Vietnam.

Vocabulary

2. Define: negotiate, nationalist movement.

Checking Facts

3. Explain the steps Nixon took to end the war.

4. Describe the costs of the war in Vietnam for the United States and for the people of Southeast Asia.

Critical Thinking

5. **Predicting Consequences** What consequences might have made the Thieu government unwilling to sign a peace treaty that allowed North Vietnamese troops to remain in South Vietnam?

SPORTS: Baseball's centennial year is one of many changes.

One Day in History

Sunday, July 20, 1969

MARKET BASKET

Here is where a dollar will go:

Minimum wage per hour $1.60
Transistor radio $29.95
1 gallon regular gas . . . . . 33¢

© SUPERSTOCK

Body paint kit $6
Deodorant . . . . 69¢
Box of cereal . . . . 27¢
Concert ticket for Newport Jazz Festival $3.50
One-bedroom apartment at the Watergate, Washington, D.C. . . $28,000
Hairdryer $35

© MIA & KLAUS/SUPERSTOCK

NASA

Explorer Edwin Aldrin "Beautiful! Beautiful!" exclaimed the astronaut. About seven hours after landing, both *Apollo* astronauts began their exploration of the moon.

The *Eagle* Has Landed!

Man steps on the moon for the first time in history

HOUSTON—At 10:56 P.M. astronaut Neil Armstrong declared, "That's one small step for man, one giant leap for mankind," when he took his first cautious steps on the lunar surface. Television cameras mounted on the outside of the *Eagle* landing craft recorded Armstrong's movements live for the whole world to watch.

Edwin "Buzz" Aldrin joined Armstrong 15 minutes later for a 2-hour tour of the moon. They collected samples, took photographs, performed experiments, and radioed their feelings and findings back to the earth. They also spoke via telephone link with President Nixon.

Astronaut Michael Collins was in the *Apollo 11* mother ship in lunar orbit 70 miles (113 km) above the surface.

Landing on the moon was not easy. The astronauts had to manually fly their ship over the rocky surface to find a level site for their craft in the plain known as the Sea of Tranquility.

NATION: Charles Evers was sworn in as the first African American mayor of Fayette, Mississippi.

UPI/BETTMAN

Packaged Politics

NEW YORK—*The Selling of the President (1968),* written by 26-year-old reporter Joe McGinniss, is a shocking, often funny, insider's account of how Nixon's team of technicians, ghostwriters, and pollsters helped him capture the presidency from Hubert H. Humphrey.

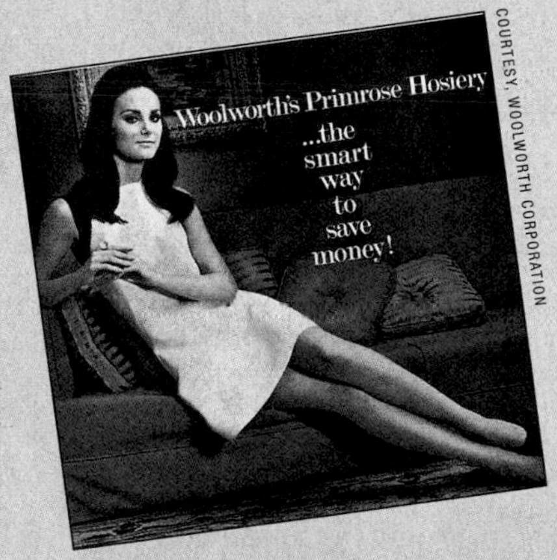

COURTESY, WOOLWORTH CORPORATION

Pantyhose find an eager market.

Hosiery Revolution

NEW YORK—More women are making the switch from nylon stockings to panty hose. Spurred by the popularity of the miniskirt, panty hose have found a place in fashion. Lively designs, colors, and better fit have also fueled phenomenal growth. Sales rose this year to 624 million pairs, up from 200 million last year.

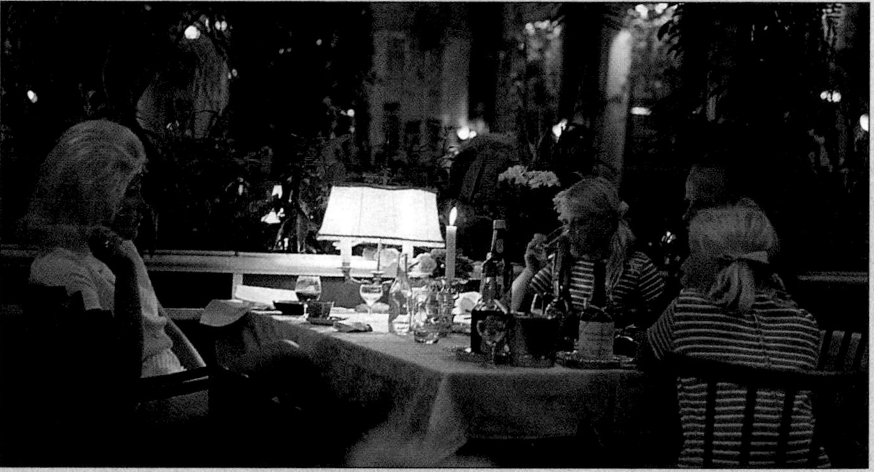

© 1968 ELLIOT ERWITT/MAGNUM PHOTOS

Spending is up as Americans engage in more leisure activities.

LIFESTYLE

Cash registers at restaurants, movie theaters, concert halls, and clothing stores are ringing across the United States. Per capita spending on clothing this year was $189.96. More surprising was the increase in entertainment expenditures—$198.86 per person, up $58.93 from 1965.

Americans Are Talking

More than one-half of the 225 million telephones in service all over the world are used in the United States.

© 1995 CLASSIC PIO PARTNERS

ENTERTAINMENT

Easy Rider, starring Peter Fonda and Dennis Hopper, is one of the most popular and controversial movies of the year. Some moviegoers think the film reflects the fears and concerns of today's youth about national problems; others feel the movie glorifies drug use and escapism. Many believe it will capture an academy award for Fonda, son of movie legend Henry Fonda.

© FOTOS INTERNATIONAL/ARCHIVE PHOTOS

The hip heroes of *Easy Rider* find violence and bigotry on their cross-country journey.

Chapter  Assessment

Self-Check Quiz

Visit the *American Odyssey* Web site at americanodyssey.glencoe.com and click on ***Chapter 23—Self-Check Quiz*** to prepare for the Chapter Test.

Reviewing Key Terms

Choose the vocabulary term that best completes each sentence below. Write your answers on a separate sheet of paper.

dove	**guerrilla warfare**
deferment	**domino theory**
hawk	**conservative era**

1. One way to avoid military service was to obtain a _________ .

2. The Vietnamese used _________ to their advantage in fighting the Americans.

3. Someone who supported the war and wanted a military victory was called a _________ .

4. By the late 1960s, the nation had entered the _________, in which many Americans favored limiting government.

5. The _________ was an accepted concept during the cold war.

Recalling Facts

1. Identify Ho Chi Minh, his goals, and his role in the Vietnam War.

2. What happened at Dien Bien Phu?

3. Why did the United States support Ngo Dinh Diem?

4. What was the Gulf of Tonkin Resolution?

5. List some of the guerrilla warfare tactics the Vietcong used.

6. Who was General William Westmoreland?

7. Explain why the Tet offensive was a turning point in the war.

8. How did Dr. Martin Luther King, Jr., link the civil rights movement to his opposition of United States policy in Vietnam?

9. What was Richard Nixon's strategy for winning the presidency in 1968?

10. Explain how the media influenced public opinion during the war.

11. What was public reaction to the shootings at Kent State? At Jackson State?

12. What impact did student and other antiwar protest groups have on government policies both domestically and in Vietnam?

13. What did the Pentagon Papers reveal about the government's motivation for fighting in Vietnam?

14. What concessions did the United States and the North Vietnamese make at the Paris peace talks that finally ended the war?

15. What happened in Vietnam after the last American troops left?

Critical Thinking

1. Demonstrating Reasoned Judgment President Johnson made the decision not to run for re-election in 1968. Determine whether you believe that President Johnson's decision was a good one or a bad one for him and the country. Write at least three reasons to support your decision.

2. Identifying Alternatives Imagine that you are a student during the Vietnam era and you are going to be drafted into the military. List several choices you could make in response to the draft. Explain the advantages and disadvantages of each possible decision.

3. Making Comparisons In a diagram like this one, compare the plans by Johnson and Nixon to fight and win the Vietnam War.

War Strategies

Johnson | Both | Nixon

Portfolio Project

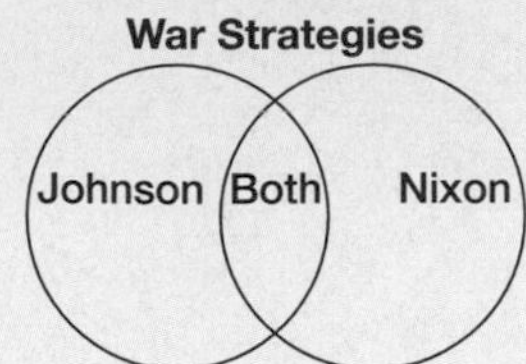

Use books, periodicals, and newspapers to learn about the plight of American POWs (prisoners of war) and MIAs (soldiers missing in action) in Vietnam. Make a time line to show what the government and private citizens have done on their behalf. Explain at least two courses of action that one might take to further the cause of verifying that prisoners are still in Vietnam and promoting their return.

Cooperative Learning

Work with your classmates to organize the class into two groups. One group should contact friends, relatives, or veterans groups to locate two Vietnam veterans and arrange to have the veterans visit the class. The other group should create a list of questions to ask the veterans. It will be useful to think about questions that will help you learn about how the veterans joined the military, their combat or other training, their experiences in Vietnam, and their adjustment to civilian life after their return.

Reinforcing Skills

Understanding Public Opinion Polls Write a brief explanation of how public opinion polls can affect government decisions or public policy. Include at least one example from either the period discussed in this chapter or the present.

GEOGRAPHY AND HISTORY

Physical Map of Southeast Asia

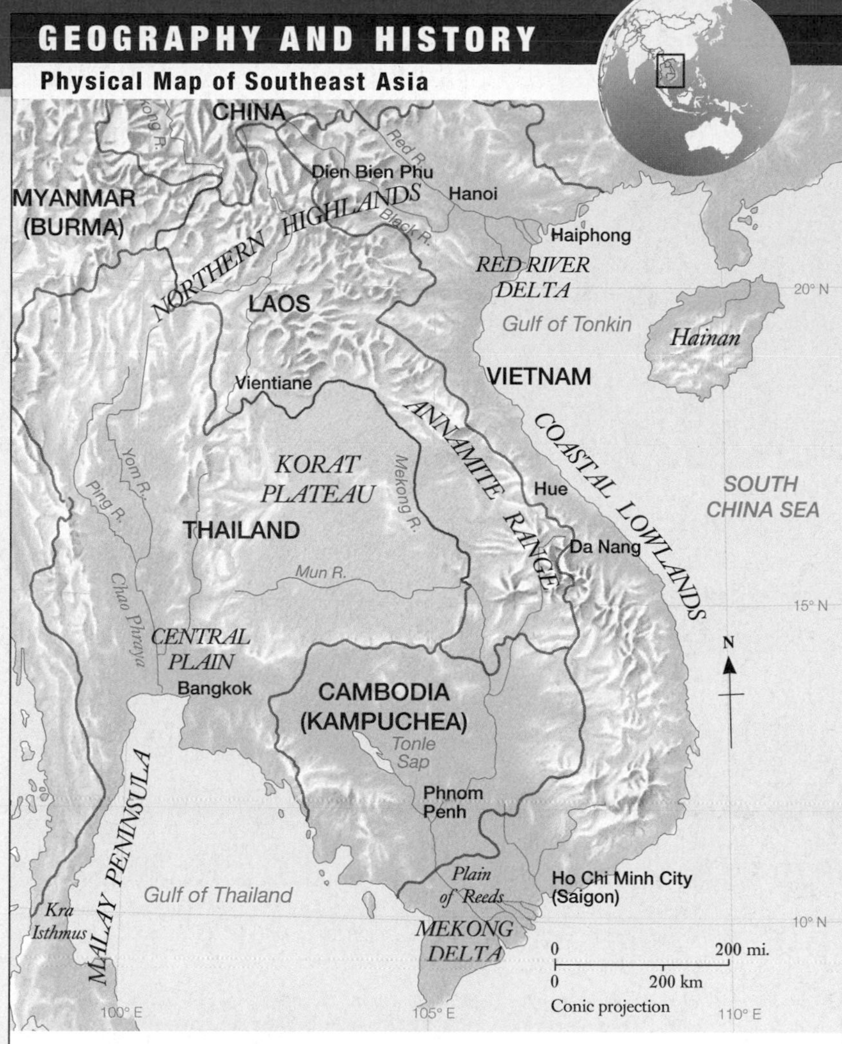

Study the map to answer the following questions:

1. Do the countries that border Vietnam share any of the same physical characteristics? Explain.
2. What are the two principal river deltas in Vietnam?
3. What countries share the Northern Highlands?
4. How did the topography of Vietnam affect the kind of battles that were fought during the war?
5. What clues does the latitude of Vietnam give you about its climate? How would the climate affect how the war was fought?

Technology Activity

Using a Computerized Card Catalog Use the computerized card catalog in your school or local library to locate information about American attitudes during the Vietnam War. Find quotes from the late 1960s and early 1970s that show America's feelings toward the war. Then use the quotes to create a bulletin board. Include photographs and other memorabilia.

Standardized Test Practice

1. When the United States entered the fighting in Vietnam, leaders were following the cold war policy of

A national liberation.
B containment.
C pacification.
D Vietnamization.

> ***Test-Taking Tip:*** The clue phrase in this question is *cold war policy.* Remember that the goal of U.S. foreign policy during the cold war was to stem the spread of communism. Identify the term that best reflects this goal.

2. The greatest escalation of United States troops in Vietnam took place during the administration of President

A Eisenhower.
B Kennedy.
C Johnson.
D Nixon.

> ***Test-Taking Tip:*** This question requires you to think chronologically about U.S. involvement in Vietnam. For example, the number of ground forces in Vietnam peaked in the late 1960s. Neither Eisenhower nor Kennedy served then, so you can rule out answers A and B.

From Nixon to Carter

AUGUST 8, 1974: THE PRESIDENT DECIDES

After a week of sleepless nights, an exhausted, pale President Nixon walked into the Oval Office of the White House and sat down behind his desk. He was alone except for a few television technicians and the White House photographer, Ollie Atkins. His voice cracked as he joked nervously with the crew.

At 9 P.M. the television crew signaled Nixon to begin. The President gazed into the camera: "Good evening. This is the thirty-seventh time I have spoken to you from this office in which so many decisions have been made that shape the history of this nation." Then came the moment that so many people had anticipated. For the first time in the nation's history, a President resigned from office.

Less than two years before, a beaming, triumphant President Nixon had addressed the nation, fresh from a landslide reelection victory. He had forged a new conservative coalition and was widely hailed for his bold foreign policy moves.

Yet he had overstepped the limits of the presidency and had broken the laws he had sworn to uphold. Richard Nixon had defied the American constitutional system, and now that system had taught him that no one is above the law, not even the President of the United States. ■

HISTORY JOURNAL

Before you read this chapter, use what you already know to write briefly about the political, economic, and environmental crises that faced the nation during the 1970s.

Chapter Overview

Visit the *American Odyssey* Web site at americanodyssey.glencoe.com and click on ***Chapter 24—Chapter Overview*** to preview the chapter.

UPI/BETTMANN

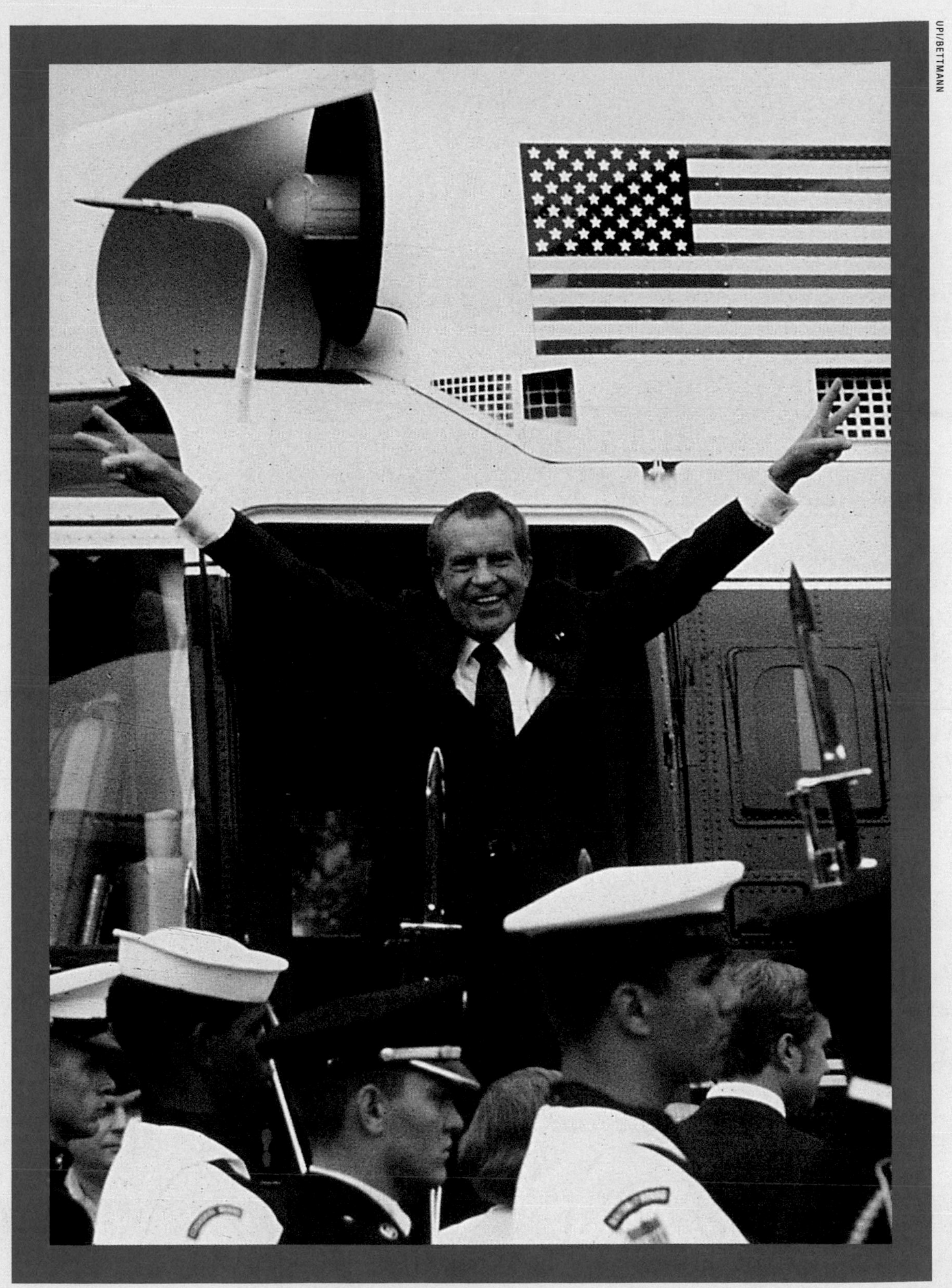

After resigning the presidency, Richard Nixon boarded a helicopter to begin his return to private life in California.

A New Majority

MAY 8, 1970: WORKERS BATTLE ANTIWAR PROTESTERS

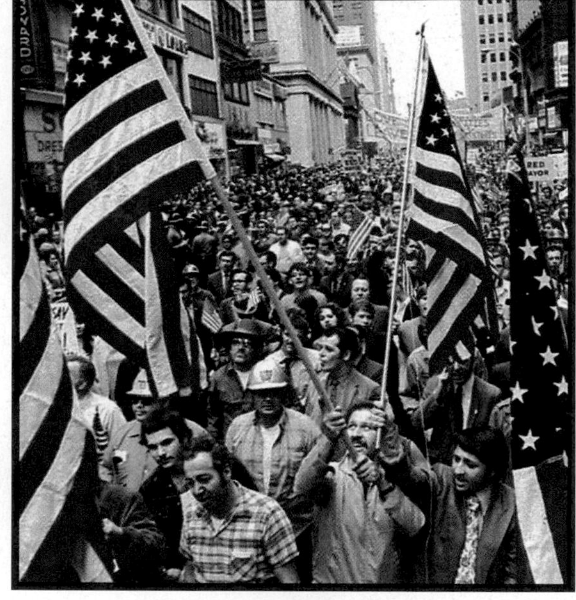
AP/WIDE WORLD PHOTOS

A Need to Be Heard
Working-class Americans take to the streets in support of President Nixon and his policies.

"When you were still up on Broadway you could hear the ruckus, the hollering. The peace demonstrators trying to outshout the construction workers. The construction workers hollering, 'U.S.A., all the way' and 'We're Number One.' And the peace demonstrators screaming up there that the war was unjust and everything else."

Thirty-one-year-old Joe Kelly, construction worker and family man, was one of several hundred workers who battled peace demonstrators in New York City that day. Wearing a yellow construction helmet bearing the message For God and Country, Kelly joined in, hurling insults and throwing punches.

The violent noon-hour rampage marked the beginning of two weeks of flag-waving marches in support of the Nixon administration and its Southeast Asia policies. The marchers were fed up with those they called flag-burning radicals who opposed the war.

Although other workers joined in, the construction workers led the way. Their hard hats soon became a symbol of traditional American values. Many, like Joe Kelly, were demonstrating for the first time in their lives.

Their message found a sympathetic ear at the White House. A few days after the Wall Street riots, President Nixon himself was awarded his own hard hat inscribed Commander in Chief.

Guide to Reading

Main Idea

Richard Nixon was carried into the White House by a conservative backlash that allowed him to reshape the political landscape of the United States.

Vocabulary

- backlash
- silent majority
- revenue sharing
- Southern strategy

Read to Find Out . . .

- why Nixon's conservatism appealed to so many Americans in the 1970s.
- the strategies that Nixon used to build support for a broad domestic policy known as New Federalism.

The War Within

Conflicts Set the Stage for Change

Like the workers and demonstrators who came to blows on Wall Street, American society at the end of the 1960s was divided into hostile camps. A decade of war and social change had ripped the nation apart. Not since the Civil War had the country seemed so divided—with conservatives pitted against liberals, workers against students, whites against African Americans, old against young.

As the 1960s drew to a close, the United States seemed to be at war with itself. Riots rocked 125 American cities following the assassination of Dr. Martin Luther King, Jr., in April 1968. In August of that year, police battled protesters at the Democratic National Convention in Chicago. Then, in October 1969, nearly 300 members of the Weather Underground, a militant wing of the Students for a Democratic Society (SDS), swept through the streets of Chicago smashing windows and shouting, "Long live the victory of the people's war!" Scenes of these so-called days of rage filled the television news, fueling the fears of millions of Americans.

The Conservative Backlash

Like construction worker Joe Kelly, a growing number of Americans became fed up with the social protests of the 1960s. The result was a conservative **backlash,** a sudden reaction against the liberalism of the 1960s. Mostly white working-class and middle-class Americans, these people saw the protests as an unprincipled attack on traditional values: hard work, family, religion, patriotism, and respect for law and order. They feared that unchecked violence and social disorder would destroy the country.

In part, they blamed the liberal policies of the Johnson years for the unrest of the decade. They resented the Warren Court for "meddling" in social issues and for "coddling" criminals. According to one poll, by 1968, 3 out of 5 Americans disagreed with the Warren Court's decisions.

They also resented paying taxes to support federal programs that they believed benefited only the poor and minorities. As one middle-class Chicagoan put it, "We are the forgotten men. We don't get one cent from the government." The cost of living rose steadily during the 1960s (by more than 7 percent in 1969), and income failed to keep pace. Many Americans saw the good life slipping away from them, and they resented it. They yearned for a return to traditional values and an end to the turmoil.

Nixon and the Silent Majority

In his 1968 campaign for President, Richard Nixon shrewdly tapped the deep well of discontent felt by these Americans, whom he called the **silent majority.** He promised to listen to "the great majority of Americans, the forgotten Americans, the non-shouters, the non-demonstrators."

Raised in a hard-working middle-class family, Nixon seemed to share the silent majority's values. He campaigned against the Great Society's "welfare mess" and pledged to "quit pouring billions of dollars into programs that have failed." He railed against Supreme Court decisions that he claimed had "tipped the balance against the peace forces in this country and strengthened the criminal forces." He promised to end the Vietnam War honorably and to restore law and order.

His appeal to what one writer called "the unblack, the unyoung, and the unpoor" paid off. In his victory speech after defeating Hubert Humphrey, Nixon promised to end the years of turmoil and unite the country: "We want to bridge the generation gap. We want to bridge the gap between the races. We want to bring America together."

Nixon at the Wheel Nixon is driving backwards—in effect driving to reverse 1960s civil rights gains. *What groups were divided against one another during the late 1960s?*

Despite his promises of unity, Nixon divided Americans even further. Intent on holding onto power, he took to heart the advice of one of his aides who claimed that the art of politics was the art of discovering who hated whom. Nixon played on the anger and fears of the silent majority as he set about building a new conservative coalition.

Nixon's New Conservatism

A Policy Born of Anger and Resentment

Once in office, Nixon sought to address the two major concerns of the silent majority—resentment of the federal government and fear of social disorder. A powerful civil rights movement, a broad antiwar coalition, and a Congress controlled by Democrats, however, would limit his attempts to advance conservative legislation. A practical man as well as a fighter, President Nixon compromised when necessary and pursued his conservative agenda whenever possible. Thus, in his first term, Nixon accepted many liberal programs and signed bills to boost Social Security benefits, expand the Job Corps, and build low-cost housing. He approved Democrat-sponsored legislation to lower the voting age to 18 and established the Environmental Protection Agency (EPA) and the Occupational Safety and Health Administration (OSHA).

Nixon's New Federalism

Even as he signed these liberal bills, Nixon began to steer a more conservative course. He introduced what he called the New Federalism—a series of programs that would "reverse the flow of power and resources from the states and communities to Washington and start power and resources flowing back . . . to the people."

To shift power back to the states, Nixon established a program of **revenue sharing** through which the federal government returned some of its tax money to local governments. He and his supporters hoped that more conservative state and local governments would use the money for law enforcement and civic projects instead of liberal programs to create jobs for the unemployed.

In one of his most controversial moves, Nixon sought to reduce the federal government's role in the nation's welfare system. In August 1969, the President introduced the Family Assistance Plan (FAP), an attempt to streamline the massive federal welfare bureaucracy and reduce welfare cheating. Instead of piecemeal handouts and a maze of federal agencies, regulations, and caseworkers, the FAP was a simple plan designed to give poor families a minimum annual income and then let them take responsibility for themselves. The FAP proposed a guaranteed minimum yearly income of $1,600 for a family of 4. To qualify for aid, heads of households had to sign up for job training.

The FAP quickly came under fire from both conservative and liberal camps. Conservative critics rejected the idea of a guaranteed annual income and insisted that the new program would only increase the number of people on the welfare rolls. Liberals denounced the plan, claiming that the payments were inadequate and that the job training program prepared trainees for low-paying jobs that held little chance for advancement. Although the plan passed in the House, it died in the Senate.

Despite his failure to overhaul the welfare system, Nixon successfully chipped away at the Great Society's base by cutting off federal grants for urban renewal, job

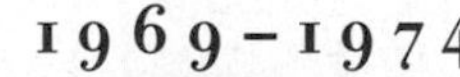

★ ★ ★ GALLERY OF PRESIDENTS ★ ★ ★

Richard Milhous Nixon

1969–1974

"The greatest honor history can bestow is the title of peacemaker. This honor now beckons America—the chance to help lead the world . . . onto that high ground of peace that man has dreamed of since the dawn of civilization. If we succeed, generations to come will say of us now living that we helped make the world safe for mankind."

Inaugural Address, January 20, 1969

BACKGROUND

- **Born 1913; Died 1994**
- **Republican, California**
- **Served in the navy 1942–1946**
- **Elected to the Senate 1950**
- **Resigned as President 1974**

ACHIEVEMENTS IN OFFICE

- **Environmental Protection Agency (1970)**
- **First United States President to visit China (1972)**

training, and education. In 1973 he abolished the Office of Economic Opportunity, a cornerstone of Johnson's antipoverty program.

When the Democratic majority in Congress opposed his bids to reduce funding for certain programs, Nixon defied them by impounding, or refusing to spend, the funds. By 1973 Nixon had impounded nearly $15 billion in funds, crippling more than 100 federal programs. Programs in the areas of health, housing, education, and the environment were the hardest hit.

UPI/BETTMANN

Under Arrest Black Panther leader Bobby Seale and police come face-to-face in this 1971 photo. *What kind of actions did FBI undercover agents promote in the Black Panthers?*

The courts eventually ruled that impoundment was illegal because it gave the President a veto power not granted in the Constitution. Only Congress, they ruled, had the authority to decide how federal funds should be spent.

Law and Order

To combat crime and social unrest, Nixon appointed his former law partner, John Mitchell, attorney general. A steely-eyed political veteran, Mitchell was an archconservative. He boasted, "This country is going so far right you won't recognize it."

As head of the Justice Department, Mitchell promoted measures to strengthen police powers—even at the cost of civil liberties. For example, he supported the use of wiretaps without a court order and the detention of criminal suspects without bail.

To silence antiwar and civil rights protesters and other critics, Nixon and Mitchell marshaled the forces of several federal agencies. The President used the Internal Revenue Service to harass enemies by auditing their tax returns. The Federal Bureau of Investigation (FBI) illegally tapped their phones and broke into their homes and offices, searching for information to embarrass and discredit them.

In addition undercover FBI agents joined the ranks of SDS and African American militant groups such as the Black Panthers. In some cases the agents deliberately set up violent clashes between these groups and the police. In 1969, for example, when the FBI targeted the Black Panther party, police killed an estimated 28 Panthers. Hundreds more were arrested.

Building a New Majority

Nixon Woos Disaffected Democrats

While shifting the national agenda toward more conservative programs, Nixon was also looking ahead to 1972 elections. He had been elected in 1968 by a slim plurality—less that 1 percent of the popular vote. Congress remained in Democratic hands. Nixon realized that to regain Republican control of Congress and to be reelected he would need to forge a new majority.

Shortly after the 1968 election, Nixon adopted a strategy that would guide his policies for the remainder of his presidency. In a report entitled "The Emergence of a Republican Majority," Kevin Phillips, a Nixon campaign aide, analyzed the results of the 1968 election. He claimed that conservative Democrats—primarily white ethnic voters, Southern whites, suburbanites, and blue-collar workers—were tired of the liberals who had come to control the Democratic party. He argued that these voters were ready to leave the Democrats and join the Republicans to form a new conservative majority under Nixon's leadership.

An Appeal to the South

According to Phillips's report, a growing number of conservative Americans lived in the Sunbelt—the Southern states, plus Texas, California, New Mexico, Oklahoma, and Arizona. Since the end of World War II, these states had more than doubled in population.

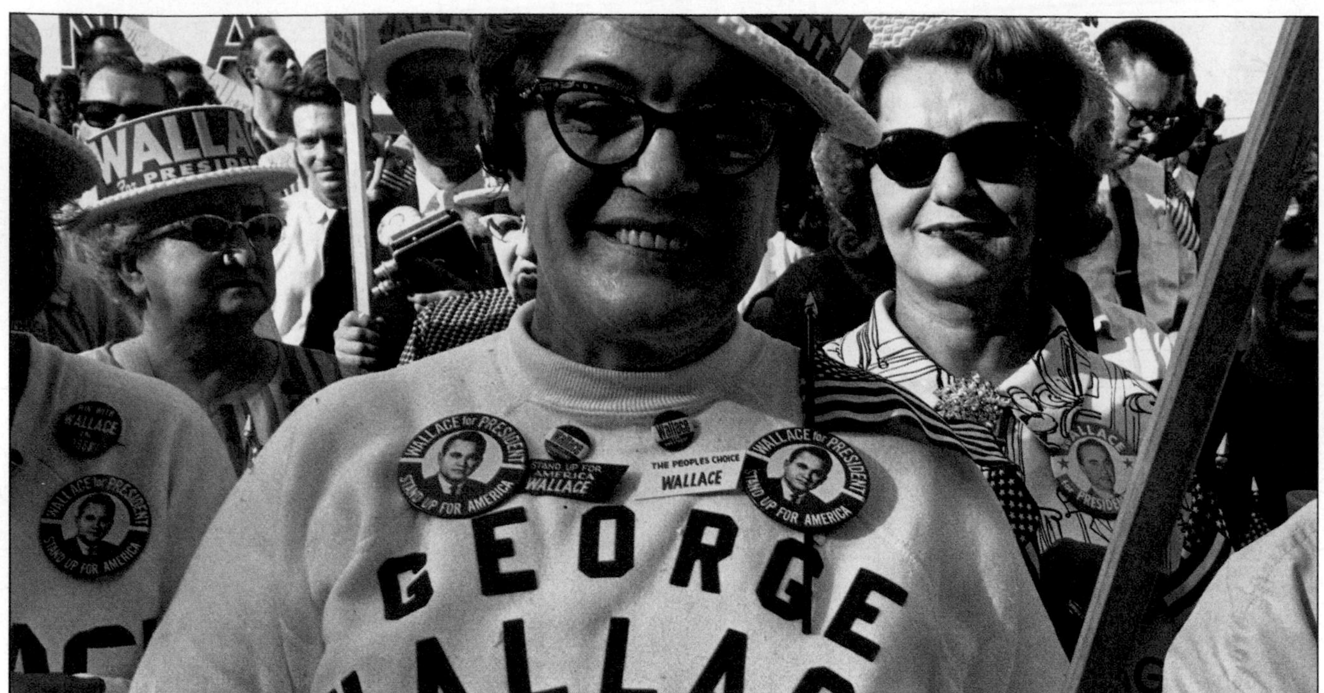

Wallace Supporters Nixon's Southern strategy was designed to lure voters like this one away from George Wallace. *What does the slogan on the woman's button tell you about Wallace's political platform?*

The South had long been a Democratic stronghold, but many white Southern Democrats believed that the party had become too liberal. As a result some of them had left the party and supported the conservative segregationist George Wallace in the 1968 presidential election. These conservative Democrats had helped Wallace—the former governor of Alabama—win 13.5 percent of the popular vote and carry 5 Southern states. Nixon planned to lure these voters away from Wallace with his conservative agenda. By adding the Wallace voters and other discontented Democrats to the 43.4 percent of Americans who had voted for Nixon in 1968, the Republicans hoped to build a powerful new majority that would help them recapture Congress and hold on to the White House.

Nixon adopted a **Southern strategy**—a plan designed to appeal directly to Southern white conservatives. To bring these voters into the Republican camp, the President appealed to their discontent with racial integration, a liberal Supreme Court, and Eastern liberals.

Student Web Activity 24

Visit the *American Odyssey* Web site at americanodyssey.glencoe.com and click on ***Chapter 24—Student Web Activities*** for an activity relating to President Richard M. Nixon.

Attacks on Civil Rights

In the 1968 election, Nixon won barely 13 percent of the African American vote, and he knew he was unlikely to attract more African American voters in 1972. To gain votes in the South, Nixon believed he could afford to alienate African Americans on civil rights issues. He made his position clear in a September 1968 press conference when he stated: "There are those who want instant integration and those who want segregation forever. I believe we need to have a middle course between those two extremes." In effect Nixon sided with those who wanted to delay desegregation and inferred that African Americans were extremists.

Once in office Nixon used the Department of Health, Education and Welfare (HEW) to carry out his strategy. In 1969 HEW stepped in to delay desegregation plans for school districts in South Carolina and Mississippi, despite a Supreme Court ruling that school desegregation begin at once. Shocked by the turnaround in federal policy, the NAACP responded, "For the first time since Woodrow Wilson we have a national administration that can be rightly characterized as anti-Negro."

Two years later the Supreme Court ruled that courts could order the desegregation of school systems by busing if necessary. Nixon publicly denounced the ruling and urged Congress to prohibit forced busing. Although Congress did not heed his call, Southern segregationists got the message—President Nixon was on their side. The message also reached Northerners—including many Democrats—who opposed busing.

Nixon further angered civil rights supporters by opposing the extension of the Voting Rights Act of 1965. This act had added 1 million African Americans to the voting rolls, greatly increasing African American political power. Despite the President's opposition, Congress voted to extend the act.

The Nixon Court

Many conservatives also resented the liberalism of the Warren Court. In their eyes recent Supreme Court rulings on questions such as integration and school prayer were an attack on traditional values.

To reverse the liberal decisions of the Warren Court, Nixon sought to fill vacancies on the Court with conservative judges. When Chief Justice Earl Warren resigned in 1969, Nixon nominated conservative federal judge Warren Burger to head the court. Later that year Nixon selected a conservative Southerner, South Carolina federal circuit judge Clement F. Haynsworth, Jr., to fill another opening. He hoped this appointment would help solidify his support among white Southerners.

Haynsworth, however, quickly came under fire for his record of antilabor and anti–civil rights rulings, and the Senate rejected his appointment. Furious at the defeat, Nixon chose another, less qualified conservative Southern judge—Florida federal appeals court judge G. Harrold Carswell. Civil rights groups were outraged. During a state election campaign in 1948, Carswell had affirmed his belief in white supremacy. Even more damaging was his poor record as a federal judge; higher courts had overturned many of his rulings. Even Carswell's promoters were half hearted in their support.

When the Senate rejected Carswell's nomination, Nixon claimed the votes against Haynsworth and Carswell reflected the Democratic Senate's prejudice against the South. He used the defeat to further align himself with Southern conservatives. "I understand the bitter feelings of millions of Americans who live in the South," Nixon declared.

Nixon's subsequent Supreme Court nominees—Harry A. Blackmun, Lewis F. Powell, Jr., and William H. Rehnquist—were all well qualified and conservative. The Senate confirmed the nominations with little debate.

Although Nixon appointed four conservative justices, the Supreme Court did not always rule conservatively. On issues such as abortion, desegregation, and the death penalty, it took a liberal stance. On other issues, such as civil liberties, police power, and censorship, however, the Court's rulings reflected a shift to the right.

Attacks on Liberals

In his bid to capture the Wallace vote, Nixon launched shrill attacks on his liberal opponents—the press, the liberal Democrats, and the student protesters. To carry out the broadsides, he enlisted the aid of his outspoken Vice President, Spiro Agnew. In speeches across the country, Agnew used his knack for colorful language to characterize the administration's opponents. He called liberal Democrats "sniveling hand-wringers." The television news media drew Agnew's scorn for what he saw as a liberal bias.

The Nixon administration also had a fear of what they saw as the Eastern establishment. As a result Agnew called media executives "curled-lip boys in eastern ivory towers." While Nixon insisted his goal was to bring Americans together, Agnew revealed a different strategy: "If in challenging, we polarize the American people, I say it is time . . . to rip away the rhetoric and to divide on authentic lines."

Nixon's Southern strategy failed to yield major Republican victories in the 1970 state and congressional elections. The Southern strategy did, however, lay the groundwork for Nixon's own reelection campaign in 1972. Coupled with the policy of New Federalism, the Southern strategy helped shift the national agenda to the right. While the policies of Johnson's Great Society had promised to protect the rights of the poor and minorities, Nixon's new conservatism promised to look out for the middle class. Yet even as Nixon was reshaping the political landscape at home, a far more pressing issue demanded his attention abroad—the Vietnam War.

SECTION ASSESSMENT

Main Idea

1. Use a diagram like this one to show features of Nixon's policy of New Federalism.

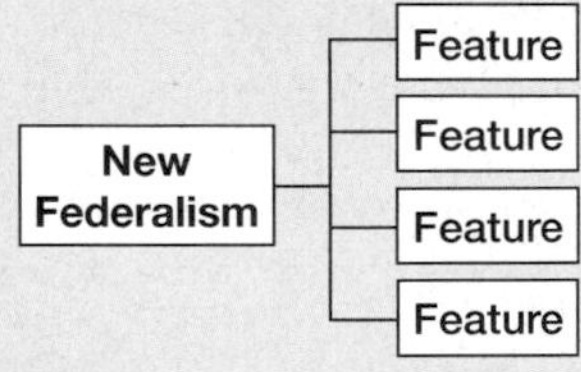

Vocabulary

2. Define: backlash, silent majority, revenue sharing, Southern strategy.

Checking Facts

3. What issues concerned the people that Nixon sought as supporters?
4. How did Nixon try to build a new coalition of voters?

Critical Thinking

5. **Evaluating Information** Evaluate the pros and cons of Nixon's law-and-order campaign.

Geography: Impact on History

REGION

The Rise of the Sunbelt

Regions can be defined by many different criteria—climate, vegetation, geographic features, or industrial characteristics, for example. Since the 1970s a new region has emerged with its own distinctive political and economic characteristics—the Sunbelt, the fastest growing area in the United States.

The Sunbelt

This region includes 15 states, each with a generally mild and sunny climate, and extends from Virginia on the East Coast to Southern California in the West. The states are Virginia, North Carolina, South Carolina, Tennessee, Georgia, Florida, Alabama, Mississippi, Arkansas, Texas, Louisiana, New Mexico, Arizona, and the southern part of California.

Why the Region Grew

During World War II, the United States military established scores of training bases in the South. Thousands of civilians followed military personnel south to take advantage of the business opportunities the bases provided. Cities such as San Diego, California; Mobile, Alabama; and Norfolk, Virginia, had huge increases in population. In

EMERGENCE OF THE SUNBELT

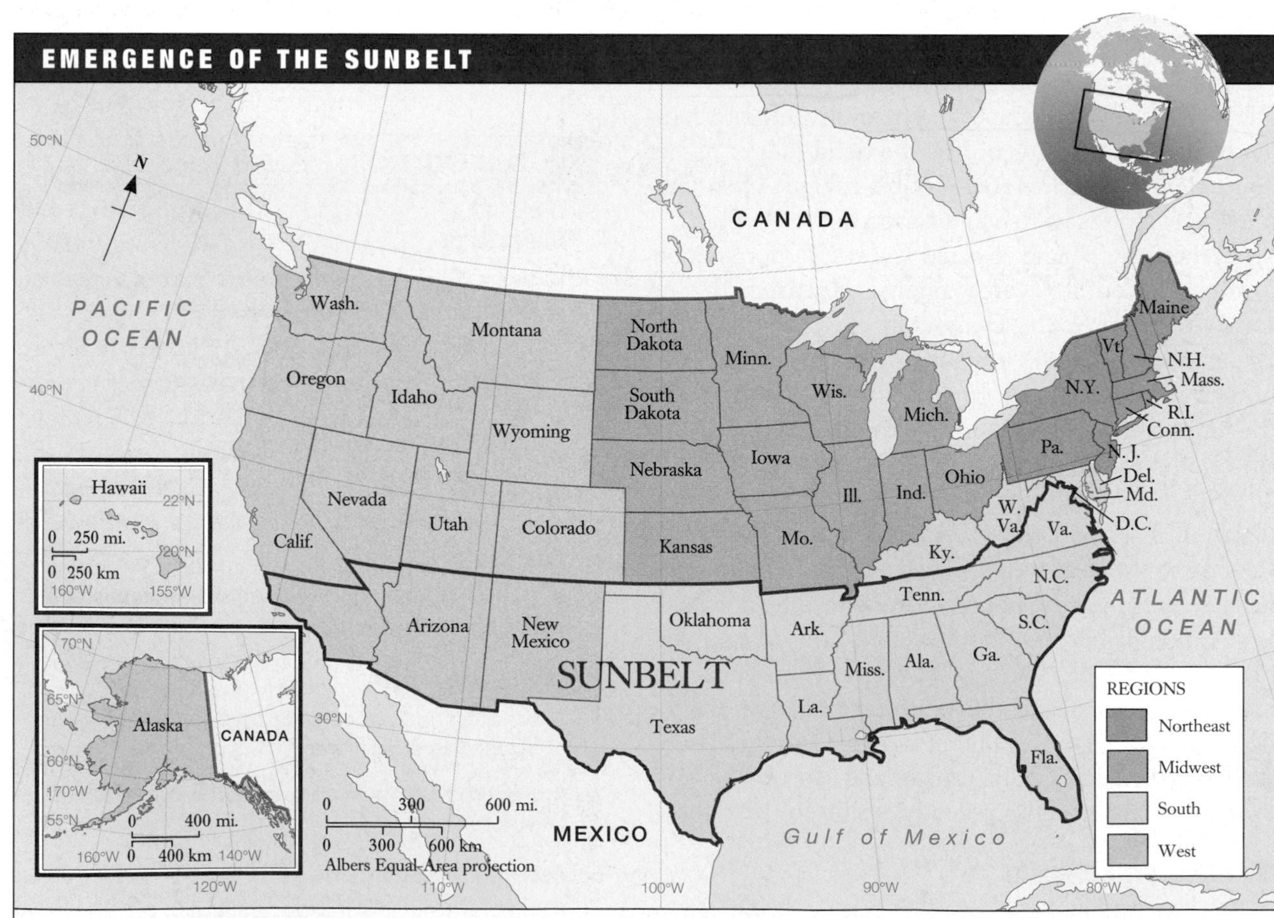

Since the end of World War II, the American population has been shifting from the Northeast and Midwest to the Sunbelt.
What is the southernmost state in the Sunbelt?

the 1950s the testing and development of rockets, missiles, space vehicles, and military aircraft often took place on or near military facilities and brought still more jobs and people to the area.

The economic climate of the late 1970s forced many changes on businesses and individuals. New government policies and a severe drought created a crisis for American farmers, for example. Between 1979 and 1988, nearly 1 million jobs on farms and in related businesses disappeared. As a result, many people from farming regions were forced to look for work elsewhere.

The recession of the late 1970s and early 1980s deeply affected the auto and steel industries of the Northeast and Midwest. Factory after factory in these states closed, leaving unemployed workers little choice but to leave the area.

States began to compete with each other to lure new business to their area. Offers of tax incentives and the lenient labor laws in the South and West drew companies to the region. Some industries that moved were new (such as the computer industry), but many others were not.

There were other attractions to the Sunbelt. Lower cost of living, lower taxes, available energy sources, and inexpensive land all prompted business growth. Several large dams provided sources of water and abundant, cheap electricity. New air and highway transportation networks also helped the Sunbelt to grow.

Finally, air conditioning—no longer a luxury affordable only to the rich—made working in the Sunbelt's stifling summer heat more bearable and the region more attractive to potential employers.

© F. FOURNIER/WOODFIN CAMP

Urban Growth Sun City businesses and neighborhoods spill into the Arizona desert. *Why have retirees moved to the Sunbelt?*

The Attraction of Prosperity

On the heels of corporate moves to the South and West came service, entertainment, and retail industries. As the population exploded, once quiet residential communities began to look more like cities, with malls, industrial parks, and large housing developments replacing open fields and wooded areas.

The warm climate and sandy beaches along the Gulf of Mexico and the southern Atlantic fueled growth in the tourist industry. Warm weather, planned retirement communities, and the lower cost of living also lured many retirees to the Sunbelt states. Sun City, Arizona, is an example of an area whose growth has been largely the result of the interregional migration of retirees.

Increased Political Power

As the population has shifted to the South and West, the political importance of the Sunbelt has also increased. According to 1990 census reports, some of the Sunbelt states have grown by as much as 20 percent since 1980. As a result, Sunbelt states have gained 11 seats (excluding California, which had a total state gain of 7 seats) in the House of Representatives. Northern and Midwestern states have lost 21 seats in the House during the same period. Current Census Bureau estimates indicate that this trend will continue into the 2000s.

Making the Geographic Connection

1. What have been some of the political consequences of the growth of the Sunbelt region?
2. What kinds of businesses and industries have moved to the Sunbelt?
3. **Region** What has made the Sunbelt so attractive to people and companies since the end of World War II?

Nixon Foreign Policy

JULY 1971: KISSINGER MAKES TOP-SECRET CHINA TRIP

In the early-morning darkness, United States Security Adviser Henry Kissinger boarded a Pakistani jet for a secret flight into mainland China. His mission, code-named Polo after Marco Polo, another trailblazing China traveler, was to arrange a presidential visit to the People's Republic of China. His cover was a "stomach indisposition" he had supposedly developed during a stopover in Pakistan. To help Kissinger's plane evade Soviet and Indian radar, Chinese navigators teamed with the Pakistani crew to guide the plane on a special route over the Himalayas. According to the plan, Kissinger would not contact the United States until he returned to Pakistan; if successful, he was simply to send the code word *Eureka.*

© DENNIS BRACK/BLACK STAR

A Step Toward Détente
The secrecy of Kissinger's trip was nearly revealed by a newspaper reporter.

Kissinger's trip to mainland China was in itself a major breakthrough; he was the first high-level United States official to visit that country in more than 20 years. Now, after months of careful diplomatic moves and secret messages relayed by third parties, Kissinger was meeting China's leaders face-to-face.

Back in the United States, Nixon and a few trusted aides waited anxiously for news from Kissinger. On July 11, Kissinger cabled his deputy at the White House, Alexander Haig, who then put a call through to Nixon's home in San Clemente, California.

"What's the message?" Nixon asked.

"Eureka," Haig replied.

Four days later, on network television, Nixon told the world of Kissinger's mission. The news amazed many in Nixon's audience because Republicans had adamantly opposed recognition of the People's Republic of China and had barred the country's admission to the United Nations.

Guide to Reading

Main Idea

Although Nixon angered many Latin Americans by intervening in their affairs, he won widespread praise for his efforts to reduce cold war tensions and to promote peace in the Middle East.

Vocabulary

- détente
- realpolitik
- balance of power
- liberation theology

Read to Find Out . . .

- how Nixon and Kissinger changed United States relationships with the Soviet Union and China.
- why Nixon continued a United States policy of intervention in Latin American affairs.
- why Nixon won the 1972 election.

Détente

A Shift in Foreign Policy

Although President Nixon's policy in Vietnam provoked fierce criticism, he was widely hailed for a series of bold moves in other parts of the world. Envisioning a new world order, Nixon abandoned the cold war policy of confrontation and initiated a policy of **détente,** an attempt to repair strained relations between the United States and the Communist powers. In a dramatic reversal of nearly 25 years of cold war politics, Nixon sought better relations with both China and the Soviet Union.

A New World View

The world in 1970 little resembled the world of the 1950s, when the cold war policy of containment was forged. Five economic superpowers—the United States, the Soviet Union, Japan, China, and the European Economic Community, a coalition of the nations of Western Europe—had replaced the 2 superpowers, the United States and the Soviet Union. President Nixon believed that economic power was the key to political power and that these 5 superpowers would determine the political future.

Nor was the Communist world united in 1970. Tensions between the Soviet Union and China had erupted in the 1960s, resulting in armed clashes between the two former allies in 1969. By playing one Communist power against the other, Nixon and Kissinger hoped to gain concessions from both.

Nixon and Kissinger shared a belief in **realpolitik,** practical politics. According to this view, a nation should pursue policies and make alliances based on its national interests rather than on any particular view of the world. Thus, if improved relations with China and the Soviet Union would benefit the United States, then the United States should set aside its bias against communism and pursue those relations.

UPI/BETTMANN

An Official Review Premier Zhou Enlai and President Nixon inspect troops during Nixon's 1972 visit to China. *Why did the United States initiate a policy of détente?*

Kissinger and Nixon promoted a foreign policy based on a **balance of power** among nations. "It will be a safer world and a better world," the President declared in 1971, "if we have a strong, healthy United States, Europe, Soviet Union, China, Japan—each balancing the other."

Nixon and Kissinger believed that détente was the key to this balance. Détente would limit Communist expansion and curb the nuclear arms race through negotiation rather than armed conflict.

Détente made sense economically, too. The United States was not eager to pour billions of dollars into another regional conflict like Vietnam. In addition trade with the Soviet Union and China would open up new markets for American products.

Nixon was able to undertake this bold shift in foreign policy in part because of his reputation as a cold warrior. Elected to Congress in 1946 on an anti-Communist platform, he gained fame in the 1940s as a member of the House Un-American Activities Committee. Certainly no one could question Nixon's genuine commitment to anticommunism.

Kissinger: The Master Player

Kissinger and Nixon's shared love of secrecy and personal power also contributed to Nixon's success in international relations. As national security adviser and later as secretary of state, Kissinger reported directly to Nixon, devised policy with him, and often conducted secret negotiations on his behalf. This working style frequently excluded other government officials and avoided public debate. In dealing with China, however, Nixon and Kissinger's system of secrecy helped them achieve a foreign policy breakthrough.

The People's Republic of China

Since the Communist takeover of China in 1949, the United States had refused to recognize the People's Republic of China, the most populous nation on the earth. Diplomatic relations between the 2 nations had been cut off. Instead the United States recognized the anti-Communist Chinese government in exile on the island of Taiwan.

The United States had treated the People's Republic as an outlaw nation; it had cut off trade and vetoed the country's admission to the United Nations. To the cold war policy makers, the People's Republic was a "red menace" threatening to gobble up its Asian neighbors.

By the time Nixon became President, however, each side had good reasons for wanting to heal the rift. After years of border disputes and the Soviet invasion of Czechoslovakia, China distrusted and feared the Soviet Union. The United States hoped that recognition of China would help end the war in Vietnam, drive a deeper wedge between the two Communist superpowers, and pressure the Soviet Union into making greater negotiating concessions on limiting nuclear arms.

The winds of change began to blow in the fall of 1970 when Nixon confided to a *Time* magazine reporter that he wanted to go to China. Then, in April 1971, a ping-pong ball made headline news when the Chinese hosted an American table tennis team in the first official contact between the 2 nations in more than 2 decades. Only 1 week later the United States announced the end of the trade embargo against China.

In July 1971, Nixon sent Kissinger on a secret mission to Beijing. Soon afterward Nixon stunned the world with the announcement that he would travel to China to normalize relations between the 2 countries. That fall, after the United States abandoned its opposition, China was admitted to the United Nations.

In February 1972, Nixon arrived in China for a week-long visit. Accompanied by reporters and television camera crews, the President visited the Great Wall and met with Chinese leaders Mao Zedong and Zhou Enlai. Friendly gestures abounded. Chinese musicians played "America the Beautiful," and Nixon quoted lines from Mao's poetry.

The United States and China agreed to allow greater scientific and cultural exchange and to resume trade. Although formal diplomatic relations were not established until 1979, Nixon's trip marked the first formal contact with China in more than 25 years.

© J.P. LAFFONT/SYGMA

Cold War Begins to Warm Soviet Premier Leonid Brezhnev and President Nixon share a lighter moment during Nixon's trip to Moscow in 1972. *Why was the Soviet Union anxious to meet with the United States?*

The Soviet Union

In a second dramatic foreign policy move, Nixon visited Moscow only three months after his trip to China. The Soviets eagerly welcomed the thaw in cold war politics. They wanted to prevent a Chinese-American alliance and to slow the costly arms race. They also hoped to gain access to United States technology and to buy badly needed American grain.

During his visit Nixon met with Soviet leader Leonid Brezhnev and signed agreements on trade and technological exchange. Even more important, Nixon signed a landmark arms agreement, the result of negotiations known as the Strategic Arms Limitation Talks (SALT). The economic and military pacts were linked: the United States promised to allow the Soviets to buy wheat and corn and other consumer goods if the Soviets agreed to make arms concessions.

The SALT Agreement

SALT made history with the openness of the negotiations and the limits it placed on specific nuclear missiles. It limited the number of missile defense systems in each country to one system for the capital city and one system for the main missile launching center. It allowed the addition of certain weapons only if others were dismantled. SALT had weaknesses: it did not limit long-range bombers or missiles loaded with multiple independently targeted warheads; it did not prohibit the development of new nuclear weapons systems. Even so, by restricting the number of some nuclear weapons, it eased tensions between the United States and the Soviet Union and put a brake on the expensive and perilous nuclear arms race. It also laid the groundwork for the more substantive SALT II negotiations.

Middle East

Kissinger and Shuttle Diplomacy

By 1973 Nixon foreign policy stood at a turning point. Nixon and Kissinger's major theories—realpolitik, maintenance of an equilibrium of power among nations, and détente—had worked well in relations with China and the Soviet Union. Their foreign policy approach was soon to be tested severely in the Middle East.

© ABBAS/MAGNUM PHOTOS

Occupied Golan Heights Israeli Defense Minister Moshe Dayan looks out from an observation post in Syria. *What prompted the Yom Kippur War?*

The Yom Kippur War

Armed and advised by the Soviet Union, Egypt and Syria attacked Israel on October 6, 1973, the Jewish holy day of Yom Kippur. They were attempting to regain territories lost to Israel in the 1967 Six-Day War. Almost immediately, Nixon and Kissinger saw this conflict as an opportunity for the United States to assume a peacemaking role in the Middle East and thus gain an edge over the Soviet Union in the region.

To make their plan work, Kissinger, now secretary of state, tried to determine the war's outcome by alternately withholding and granting supplies to Israel. The stakes rose when the Arab oil-producing countries stopped shipments to the United States to protest its aid to Israel. Fuel prices skyrocketed and so did United States inflation. Nixon and Kissinger now had an urgent economic need to establish better relations with Arab countries, even at the expense of Israel. When the Israelis violated a cease-fire, Kissinger forced them to back down by cutting off supplies. On October 26, a new cease-fire took effect.

Searching for Lasting Peace

During the next two years, Kissinger shuttled back and forth between Middle Eastern cities, trying to resolve the oil crisis and broker a lasting peace. Arab nations ended the oil embargo in March 1974, and in September 1975, Egypt and Israel signed a historic peace agreement: Egypt officially recognized Israel for the first time, and the Israelis gave up part of the Sinai Peninsula, their first-ever withdrawal from occupied lands. As part of the settlement, the United States promised massive military aid to both parties.

Pleased by Kissinger's negotiations and the United States's promises of aid, Egypt abandoned the Soviet Union in favor of the United States. With Kissinger's help, Arabs and Israelis met to talk about long-term peace for the first time. Kissinger also carefully staked out a more neutral territory for the United States in Arab-Israeli affairs, thus reducing the likelihood of future oil embargoes.

Nonetheless shuttle diplomacy had its costs. By shutting the Soviets and the Palestinians out of Middle East negotiations, Nixon and Kissinger endangered détente and encouraged the Soviet Union to arm radical Arab factions such as the Palestinian Liberation Organization (PLO). Kissinger's shuttle diplomacy also created suspicions among the negotiating parties that the United States was playing one country against another.

Latin America Since 1945

The Region Undergoes Many Changes

The years following World War II brought sweeping changes to Latin America. Economies grew rapidly, and democracy flourished. Yet by the 1970s, 2 shadows loomed over Latin America—deepening economic crises and the rise of military dictatorships.

Economic Growth

In the postwar prosperity of the 1950s, the rapidly growing economies of North America and Western Europe clamored for Latin American exports such as oil, minerals, coffee, bananas, and sugar. As the world economy grew, Latin America prospered.

Export income and loans helped fund Latin America's own industrial development. In 1950 Latin America produced just $11 billion worth of manufactured goods. By 1974 that total had climbed to $66 billion.

Foreign investment mounted too. By the mid-1960s, United States investment in Latin America reached $9 billion, and in 1980 it topped $35 billion.

The Growing Debt

As industrial production grew, Latin American nations began borrowing from banks in the United States and Western Europe to finance their economic growth. Bankers flocked to Latin America. Latin American countries sank even deeper in debt when oil prices rose in 1974 and 1979.

The ability of these borrowers to repay their loans, however, depended on an expanding international market for products from Latin America and stable interest rates. In the 1980s the demand for Latin American oil

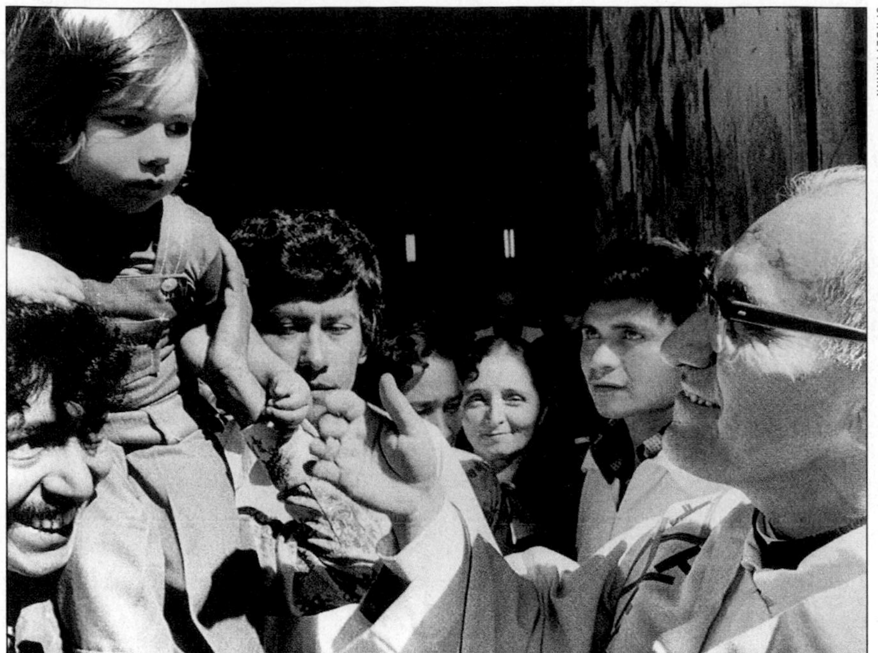
UPI/BETTMANN

Government Target Archbishop Romero greets his parishoners after a Sunday mass at the San Salvador Basilica. *Why were left-leaning clergy often targets of government repression?*

fell when Western industrial nations suffered a recession. As their export earnings declined, Latin American nations were also hit by rising interest rates. The results were disastrous. The debt consumed most of Latin America's export earnings. Once eager to make loans, bankers now closed their doors to the struggling debtors. One despairing manager of a Mexican oil company lamented in September 1982, "Six months ago, there were so many bankers in [my office] you couldn't walk across the room. Now they don't even answer my telephone calls."

The Rise of Democracy

The victory of democracy over dictatorship during World War II led many Latin Americans to demand democracy at home. A group of Brazilians opposed to the dictator ruling their country in the 1940s declared, "If we fight against fascism at the side of the United Nations so that liberty and democracy may be restored to all people, certainly we are not asking too much in demanding for ourselves such rights and guarantees."

In addition postwar prosperity was creating an emerging middle class that believed that its interests would be best served by democracy. By 1946 dictators had been forced out of Peru, Cuba, El Salvador, Guatemala, Colombia, Venezuela, and Brazil. New political parties sprouted, and women gained the right to vote. By 1959 only 4 military governments remained.

The new democracies faced serious challenges—poverty, illiteracy, and hunger. Often their attempts at economic change, such as land reform, disturbed the upper classes, who feared the loss of their wealth and power. The elite turned to their traditional allies, the military, to halt the reforms. From 1962 to 1964, democratic governments in 8 countries fell to military dictatorships.

An Era of Change

Governments Topple

The failure of Latin American democracies and the rise of repressive military governments led some Latin Americans to choose more radical means of bringing about change. During the 1960s, left-wing revolutionary guerrilla movements sprang up throughout Latin America. Revolutionaries were willing to postpone democratic reforms such as free elections and a free press until basic social reforms had been achieved.

The Catholic Church, which served 80 percent of the population, added its voice to those clamoring for reform in Latin America. The church had long been an ally of the rich and powerful. In the 1960s, however, thousands of young priests and nuns began to speak out, asserting that the church must side with the poor in the struggle for social justice. This doctrine, known as **liberation theology,** led many religious leaders to call for Socialist reforms. As Mexican Bishop Sergio Mendes declared in 1970, "Only socialism can give Latin America a true development. . . . I believe that a socialist system best conforms to Christian principles of true brotherhood, justice, and peace."

A Troubled Era

By 1970 the military ruled most of Latin America. Only Costa Rica, Uruguay, Chile, Mexico, Colombia, and Venezuela enjoyed democracies. Chile and Uruguay fell to dictators during the 1970s. Economic crises in the 1970s and massive opposition to repression, however, led to the fall of many military governments during the 1980s.

United States-Latin American Relations

After World War II, the United States wanted democratic governments and the free enterprise system to flourish in Latin America so that these nations would be good allies and trading partners. It also wanted to protect United States investments and to prevent the spread of communism. On occasion these foreign policy goals conflicted with each other and with the aims of the Latin American countries involved.

Mexico in particular had a love-hate relationship with the United States. It welcomed United States investments and wanted its northern neighbor to allow millions of Mexicans to cross the border to find work, yet it fought to stay clear of United States-sponsored trade agreements. Although the United States still offered many advantages that Mexico depended on—jobs for migrant workers, large oil markets, technology, and investments—Mexico, along with the rest of Latin America, was beginning to challenge the United States's domination of its economic development.

To break the American grip on their economies, many Latin American countries wanted to create their own industries rather than just supply raw materials and cheap labor for United States businesses. Some reform-minded politicians also wanted to break up large plantations and redistribute land to small farmers. Some wanted to nationalize certain industries—to take them from private owners and run them as national government businesses. The United States government joined major landowners and businesspeople in opposing such socialist reforms.

A Policy of Intervention

To protect United States business interests and to prevent leftist politicians from achieving successes in Latin America, the United States government often supported the region's right-wing dictators. Interventionism, government interference in the political or economic affairs of another country, had been practiced by the United States in Latin America for nearly 100 years. After World War II, intervention came to mean anything from providing weapons and training for Latin American armies to economic sanctions and invasions.

MICHAEL MAUNEY/LIFE MAGAZINE © TIME INC.

Physician Turned Politician Salvador Allende tried to build a socialist society within a parliamentary democracy. *Why did Nixon and Kissinger fear Allende's presidency?*

Allende Pushes for Change

In 1970 a Socialist named Salvador Allende ran for the presidency of Chile, promising land reform and nationalization of foreign industries. Although Nixon and Kissinger discounted the importance of most of South America, they saw Allende's candidacy as a major threat to the United States. Both Nixon and Kissinger feared that a Socialist Chile would ally with Cuba and the Soviet Union and perhaps start a Communist "domino effect" in South America. An undercover campaign to defeat Allende thus began. Nixon authorized the CIA to try to "fix" the election with bribes, propaganda, and other "dirty tricks." When Allende won, Nixon ordered the CIA to incite a military coup before Allende actually took office. CIA operatives even conspired with right-wing groups to assassinate Allende. Those tactics also failed, but Nixon and Kissinger did not give up.

By now, with the CIA's reputation on the line, the secret war against Allende intensified. While the United States cut off all aid to Chile, the CIA spent millions of dollars financing antigovernment media and military opposition. Finally in 1973 a military force headed by General Augusto Pinochet seized the government and killed Allende. Even though Pinochet's government abolished civil liberties, executed thousands, and ended economic reforms, the United States quickly resumed trade and economic relations with Chile.

Congress later investigated the involvement of the United States in the overthrow of Chile's elected government and condemned Nixon and Kissinger's maneuvers against Allende. This episode also weakened détente, because it was a clear violation of an earlier United States-Soviet pledge to use negotiations rather than force in dealing with regional crises.

The Election of 1972

A Republican Triumph

Nixon's trips to China and the Soviet Union boosted his popularity at home. In the summer of 1971, following the invasion of Laos, only 31 percent of the American public supported Nixon's policies. By the summer of 1972, however, after his well-publicized visits abroad, his approval rating soared to nearly 62 percent. As Election Day neared, a Republican victory seemed certain.

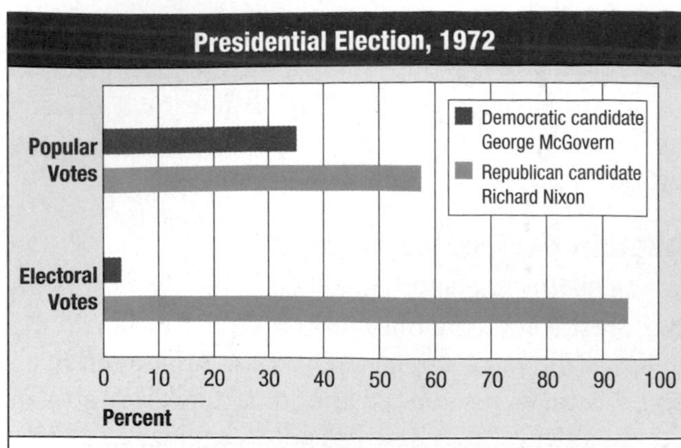

A Sweeping Victory Nixon captured approximately 47 million votes and McGovern nearly 30 million. *What percentage of the electoral vote did Nixon obtain?*

The Divided Democrats

The Democratic party was hopelessly split. Four major candidates competed for the presidential nomination: former Vice President Hubert Humphrey, Maine Senator Edmund Muskie, South Dakota Senator George McGovern, and former governor of Alabama George Wallace.

Humphrey, who had lost to Nixon in 1968, was unable to muster support for a rematch. The moderate Muskie started strong, but the liberal McGovern soon overtook him. McGovern's opposition to the Vietnam War gave voters a clear alternative to Nixon's war policies.

Wallace posed the greatest threat to Nixon. Wallace had galvanized many conservative voters with his attacks on busing, criminals, protesters, and "pointy-headed intellectuals." As a Democratic nominee or a third-party candidate, Wallace could pull these voters away from Nixon. Wallace won a string of Southern primaries and came in a close second in some Northern states. His campaign was cut short in May 1972 by the bullet of a would-be assassin. The attack left Wallace paralyzed for life and forced him to withdraw from the campaign.

An early opponent of the Vietnam War and a social reformer, McGovern won a number of key primaries. Recent reforms in Democratic party rules had increased the number of women, minority group members, and young persons among the delegates at the convention, assuring McGovern's nomination. McGovern was not a middle-of-the-road candidate. He called for a $30 billion cut in defense spending, immediate withdrawal from Vietnam, and pardons for Vietnam draft resisters.

Many traditional Democratic supporters were unhappy with the party's drift to the left. Denied a seat at the convention, AFL-CIO President George Meany ordered union members—traditionally staunch Democrats—to withhold support from McGovern.

The Republican Campaign

Nixon's campaign suffered no setbacks. His trips to China and the Soviet Union and his withdrawal of troops from Vietnam helped silence his foreign policy critics. An upturn in the economy further bolstered his popularity. He easily won over voters who had previously supported Wallace with promises to fight busing and end "the age of permissiveness."

Nixon also capitalized on the Democrats' disarray and their choice of the liberal McGovern. He called them the party of "hooligans, hippies, and radical liberals." Many conservative Democrats agreed and voted Republican on Election Day.

Nixon won the 1972 election by a landslide, carrying every state but Massachusetts. He won 60.8 percent of the popular vote and 520 of the 537 electoral votes. The Southern strategy had paid off.

Yet a shadow loomed over Nixon's victory. He had been accused of authorizing a "dirty tricks" campaign against the Democrats. Shortly before the election, burglars hired by the Committee to Re-Elect the President had been caught breaking into Democratic national headquarters in Washington. Nixon and his aides denied any involvement, and at first the public believed them. As Nixon began his second term, however, the tangled story behind the burglary began to unravel.

Section Assessment

Main Idea

1. Use a chart like this one to show what you consider to be triumphs and shortcomings of Nixon's foreign policy.

Nixon's Foreign Policy	
Triumphs	Shortcomings

Vocabulary

2. Define: détente, realpolitik, balance of power, liberation theology.

Checking Facts

3. Why were both the Soviet Union and China receptive to visits by President Nixon?

4. Why was Nixon so popular in 1972?

Critical Thinking

5. Analyzing Information Give several examples of how the relationship between the United States and Latin America has changed since 1945.

Social Studies Skill

INTERPRETING POLITICAL CARTOONS

I claim executive privilege

Learning the Skill

For more than 200 years, American newspapers and magazines have published political cartoons. Reading political cartoons from the past can help you appreciate how people of other times felt about important issues. Interpreting current political cartoons can increase your awareness of differing views on today's important issues.

A cartoon is meant to entertain, usually by using a play on words or by creating amusing images. A political cartoon also makes a comment on a current political issue by using caricatures, symbols, and analogies.

To help you interpret a political cartoon, study the use of each of the visual techniques described below. Then combine the individual messages to determine what impression the cartoonist wants to leave with the reader.

Caricature

A caricature is an exaggerated picture. By deliberately exaggerating unusual or distinctive features of a well-known subject, the cartoonist produces a comic image and also helps the reader to recognize the subject. The cartoon on this page, for example, exaggerates two of President Nixon's most recognizable facial features—the size of his nose and the dark circles around his eyes.

Symbol

A symbol is an idea, image, or object that stands for or suggests something else. Some symbols are widely used and need no explanation. For example, a dove as a symbol of peace is recognized almost anywhere. In the cartoon on this page, the person labeled Congress symbolizes the father figure in the story of George Washington and the cherry tree. The axe behind Nixon's back is a symbol of his guilt. The cartoonist in this case expects the reader to be familiar with the cherry tree story and to recognize these symbols.

Analogy

An analogy compares two related things or ideas by using one as a reference for illustrating the other. For example, an analogy might be drawn between the benefits of walking and the benefits of reading, as follows: reading is to the mind as walking is to the body.

In this cartoon, evidence of President Nixon's actions is compared to George Washington's axe. The analogy is that the evidence in the Watergate affair was to Congress what the axe was to George Washington's father—proof of his involvement. In this unfavorable comparison, Nixon does not admit his offense as young Washington did. Instead he uses his privilege as the nation's Chief Executive to try to hide the evidence of his actions.

Practicing the Skill

1. Look at the political cartoon on page 825 of your textbook. What does the crown in the cartoon represent?

2. What feature of John Ehrlichman is exaggerated in this cartoon?

3. Why do you think the cartoonist chose this setting for the drawing?

4. What is the message shown by having Nixon with his hand in the mouth of Arthur Burns?

5. What does it mean that Kissinger and Ehrlichman also have headwear?

Applying the Skill

Find a cartoon in a newspaper or magazine. Write a brief summary of the cartoon's message.

The **Glencoe Skillbuilder Interactive Workbook, Level 2** CD-ROM provides more practice in key social studies skills.

The Watergate Crisis

JUNE 17, 1972: BURGLARS BREAK INTO DEMOCRATIC PARTY HEADQUARTERS

SHORTLY AFTER MIDNIGHT ON JUNE 17, 1972, SECURITY GUARD FRANK WILLS WAS MAKING HIS ROUNDS OF THE WATERGATE BUILDING, A VAST OFFICE-APARTMENT COMPLEX IN WASHINGTON, D.C. As he checked the doors connecting the building to an underground parking garage, the 24-year-old Wills noticed something odd. The locks on the doors had been taped to keep them from locking. "I took the tape off, but I didn't think anything of it," he said later. "I thought maybe the building engineer had done it." Wills finished his rounds and then strolled across the street to a diner for a cheeseburger, french fries, and a shake.

An hour later Wills was back at work. Once again he checked the garage doors. They had been retaped! This time Wills called the police.

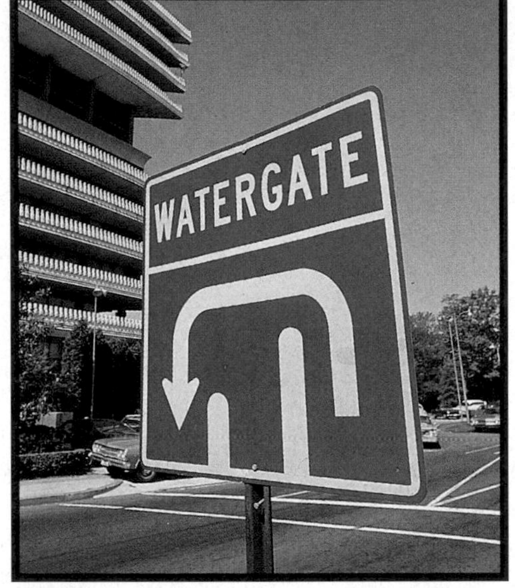

© DENNIS BRACK/BLACK STAR

A Turn in the Presidency
The Watergate burglary was one of several "dirty tricks" in a larger plan called Gemstone.

The police found more taped doors on the building's sixth floor, headquarters of the Democratic National Committee (DNC). They cautiously began to search the DNC offices one by one.

Suddenly, behind a glass and wood partition, one of the police officers spotted an arm. "Hold it!" he shouted. "Come out!" A moment later, not 2 but 10 hands shot up. Five men dressed in business suits emerged. On the floor lay lock picks, 40 rolls of film, 2 cameras, 2 "bugs"—tiny electronic devices for listening—and $1,754 in cash.

When police returned the next day, they found more electronic equipment, several suitcases, and $3,566.58 in cash. They also found a tiny black address book. In it, next to the name Howard Hunt, were a telephone number and the phrase: *W. House.*

GUIDE TO READING

Main Idea

The Watergate scandal challenged, and ultimately proved, the stability of the nation's constitutional government, particularly its system of checks and balances.

Vocabulary

- impeachment
- pardon

Read to Find Out . . .

- how President Nixon abused the powers of his office.
- how a free press and the system of checks and balances helped preserve the integrity of the federal government.

It would take 22 months and the combined efforts of Congress, the press, and the courts to bring the Watergate story to light. What emerged was not just the story of a burglary but a tale of crimes committed by the man sworn to uphold the Constitution and the nation's laws—the President of the United States.

The Nixon White House

An Imperial Presidency

When Richard Nixon first took office in 1969, the White House was already the seat of considerable power. Since the outbreak of World War II, United States Presidents had gradually assumed powers in foreign policy making that the Constitution seemed to reserve for Congress. During the war President Roosevelt had, in effect, made treaties with foreign nations without the advice or consent of the Senate. Both Truman and Johnson had sent troops into combat without a congressional declaration of war. When national security was at stake, they argued, the President had to be able to respond quickly—even if that meant Congress was not consulted.

Nixon, however, outdid his predecessors in ignoring constitutional checks on presidential powers. He impounded funds for federal programs he opposed, defying the constitutional mandate that Congress control spending. He ordered United States troops to invade Cambodia without seeking congressional approval. As the executive branch flexed its muscles, the legislative branch weakened, and the balance of powers set forth in the Constitution tipped in favor of a more powerful presidency. By the 1970s the constitutional presidency had become what some critics called the imperial presidency.

President Nixon

Richard Nixon reached the White House after nearly 25 years in politics. A skilled lawyer and a shrewd politician, Nixon loved public life and hoped to be remembered as a great statesman. He greatly admired former Presidents Woodrow Wilson and Teddy Roosevelt.

Yet Nixon had a darker side. At times mean-spirited and suspicious, he made his reputation in the late 1940s by hounding alleged Communists in the United States government. This was the Nixon who thrived on the power of the imperial presidency and whom his critics dubbed King Richard.

The Inner Circle

Nixon surrounded himself with a small group of trusted and loyal aides. At the head of what some critics called the palace guard stood Harry Robins "H. R." Haldeman, the President's chief of staff, and John Ehrlichman.

Haldeman was Nixon's closest aide. A former advertising executive, Haldeman first worked for Nixon in 1956 when Nixon was campaigning for Vice President. The uncomplaining Haldeman described his role: "I get done what he wants done, and I take the heat for it." Ehrlichman, a former Seattle lawyer, handled domestic policies. Together with Henry Kissinger, Haldeman and Ehrlichman formed an inner circle that wielded more power than the President's cabinet.

The Enemies List

By surrounding himself with aides who almost always agreed with him, Nixon created his own house of mirrors, where all opinions reflected his own. Protected from criticism, Nixon grew increasingly isolated.

All the President's Men **This cartoon shows how those who wanted to be heard by the President had to press hard to do so. His most powerful assistants are positioned closest to him.** *Whom does Nixon seem most willing to listen to here?*

One Nixon aide recalled: "You were either for us or against us, and if you were against us we were against you." In 1971 Nixon ordered his special counsel, Chuck Colson, to put together an enemies list. Colson, who described himself as a "flag-waving . . . anti-press, anti-liberal, Nixon fanatic," eagerly set about his task.

Colson drew up a list of more than 200 individuals and 18 organizations that the administration regarded as enemies. The list included many notable liberal Americans. Among them were politicians such as Senators Edward Kennedy and George McGovern, Representatives Bella Abzug and Shirley Chisholm, and the entire African American leadership of the House; college presidents, such as Kingman Brewster of Yale University; Hollywood stars, such as Steve McQueen, Paul Newman, and Jane Fonda; and 57 members of the media.

Once the list was complete, Nixon asked the FBI to spy on these individuals and try to discredit them. He also ordered the IRS to harass them with tax audits.

The Huston Plan

A concern that the antiwar movement might undo him as it had toppled Johnson in 1968 fed Nixon's fears. The massive public outcry following the announcement of the Cambodian invasion in April 1970 had shaken the President. He believed he had to silence his critics or face defeat at the polls in 1972.

In June 1970, White House aide Tom Huston submitted a plan for a secret police operation to combat the antiwar movement. The Huston plan would expand and unify the work of the FBI, the CIA, the National Security Agency, and the Defense Intelligence Agency. The entire operation would be run out of the White House. To defend what the White House considered to be national security, agents would infiltrate antiwar groups, open people's mail, and tap telephones. They would break into homes and offices in search of information that could be used to discredit or even blackmail Nixon's critics.

Although Huston admitted that much of the plan was illegal and would violate the rights of United States citizens, President Nixon approved it. FBI Director J. Edgar Hoover, however, feared that the plan would reduce the FBI's power and blocked it.

CREEP

As the 1972 presidential election neared, Nixon's worries mounted. The Republican party had failed to regain control of either the House or the Senate in the congressional elections of 1970. Past campaign losses, to John F. Kennedy for President in 1960 and to Pat Brown for governor of California in 1962, haunted Nixon. He wanted 4 more years in the White House.

In early 1971, Nixon looked like a loser. A poll in February showed Democratic presidential hopeful Edmund Muskie out in front of Nixon, 43 to 40 percent. By March Muskie was ahead 44 to 39 percent, and by May he led Nixon by a still greater margin at 47 to 39 percent.

Taking no chances with his reelection campaign, the President put his trusted friend John Mitchell in charge. In March 1971, Mitchell resigned as attorney general and set up the Committee to Re-Elect the President (CREEP). The burly, pipe-smoking Mitchell soon launched a massive illegal fund-raising campaign. Of the nearly $60 million collected, more than $350,000 was squirreled away in a special fund to pay for "dirty tricks" operations against Nixon's Democratic foes.

The Plumbers

Nixon feared that the press might expose his illegal campaign activities. Those fears deepened that summer when the *New York Times* published the "Pentagon Papers." Although the papers dealt with Vietnam policy before the Nixon administration, Nixon feared their publication would lead to leaks of classified documents damaging to his administration. To prevent such a disaster, CREEP created a special investigations unit, nicknamed "the plumbers," to stop security leaks.

The plumbers' first target was Daniel Ellsberg, the Defense Department analyst who had leaked the Pentagon Papers to the press. In an attempt to uncover embarrassing details about Ellsberg's personal life, the plumbers broke into the office of Ellsberg's psychiatrist. They found nothing they could use against Ellsberg.

Then, in January 1972, CREEP aide G. Gordon Liddy came up with a daring plan. A team of plumbers would break into Democratic National Committee headquarters, copy documents, and wiretap the phones. By doing so the White House could keep tabs on Democratic election strategies. The plan, okayed by John Mitchell, was set in motion on the morning of June 17, 1972, at the Democratic party offices in the Watergate complex.

Unraveling Watergate

The Press, the Courts, and Congress at Work

Later, on the morning of June 17, *Washington Post* reporters Bob Woodward and Carl Bernstein got a call about the Watergate break-in. Woodward, a 29-year-old Yale graduate, and Bernstein, a 28-year-old college dropout, were an unlikely team. Inexperienced but ambitious, the 2 young reporters worked tirelessly to uncover the entire story.

Their investigations soon revealed that two of the Watergate conspirators—G. Gordon Liddy and E. Howard Hunt—were employees of CREEP. They also learned that the burglars had been paid from a CREEP fund the White House staff controlled. The deeper the two reporters dug, the more evidence they found that the Watergate break-in was one of many illegal activities planned and paid for by the President's advisers.

Eager to put a lid on the investigation, Nixon held a press conference that August. He assured the public that White House counsel John Dean had conducted an investigation of the incident and found that "no one on the White House staff was involved in this very bizarre incident." At the same time Nixon secretly authorized the payment of more than $460,000 in CREEP funds to keep the Watergate burglars quiet about White House involvement.

Woodward and Bernstein kept digging. In a front-page story on October 10, the 2 reporters pulled together the evidence they had unearthed that summer.

> FBI agents have established that the Watergate bugging incident stemmed from a massive campaign of political spying and sabotage conducted on behalf of President Nixon's re-election and directed by officials of the White House and the Committee for the Re-election of the President.
>
> —Bob Woodward and Carl Bernstein, *Washington Post,* October 10, 1972

THE WATERGATE SCANDAL

As individuals one by one decided on a course of action, the truth concerning the Watergate scandal began to reveal itself. The national media followed and sustained the drama from the beginning of the scandal to its historical conclusion.

The media profiled the men in the Watergate spotlight.

THE JUDGE

© THE WASHINGTON POST

John J. Sirica
Chief Judge
U.S. District Court
He thrust Watergate into the midst of the Senate Select Committee proceedings by reading McCord's letter publicly.

THE SENATOR

© THE WASHINGTON POST

Mike Mansfield
Senate Majority Leader
In order to maintain public confidence in the political process, he urged the Senate to examine the recent campaign and how it was waged.

© THE WASHINGTON POST

The media investigated leads and verified leaks.

THE COUNSEL

© THE WASHINGTON POST

John Dean
White House Counsel
While still working at the White House, he created a legal safety net for himself before giving his Senate testimony.

THE PRESIDENT

President Nixon resisted all efforts to reveal information to Congress or the courts about his administration and his involvement in Watergate. Only upon the collapse of his political base did Nixon offer his resignation.

THE AIDE

© THE WASHINGTON POST

Alexander Butterfield
White House Aide
Only when threatened with arrest by the Senate sergeant-at-arms did he testify publicly about the existence of the White House taping system.

The media uncovered the link between the White House and the Watergate break-in.

THE SUPREME COURT

© THE WASHINGTON POST

Warren Burger
Chief Justice
The Supreme Court upheld the lower courts' rulings about the tapes and reaffirmed that the Court, not the executive branch, had the power to define the law.

THE PROSECUTOR

© THE WASHINGTON POST

Archibald Cox
Special Prosecutor
He rejected the White House offer of tape summaries and limited access to further evidence believing it would compromise his investigation.

The media kept the public informed about the proceedings.

The truth about Watergate emerged as a result of the investigatory activities of the courts, Congress, and the media. *Why did Senator Mansfield assemble a Senate committee to investigate the 1972 presidential election?*

It was sensational news. The White House fought back, calling the *Post's* story "a senseless pack of lies" put together by the liberal paper to discredit the administration. As the 1972 election neared, Nixon worked to bury the Watergate story.

For a time the President's strategy seemed to work. Few other journalists picked up the story. Just before the 1972 election, polls showed that only 48 percent of Americans had even heard of Watergate.

The Watergate Trial

The Watergate story might have remained just a bizarre incident, but early in 1973, shortly after Nixon began his second term, the Watergate burglars went on trial before federal judge John J. Sirica. Nicknamed Maximum John because of his reputation for handing out long prison terms, Sirica was a no-nonsense judge who warned the Watergate defendants, "Don't pull any punches—you give me straight answers." Angered by the Watergate scandal, Sirica was determined to use his courtroom to search for the real story behind the Watergate break-in.

Afraid of a lengthy prison sentence, one of the Watergate burglars, James W. McCord, agreed to cooperate. In a letter to Judge Sirica, McCord alleged that White House officials had lied about their involvement in the affair and had pressured the defendants "to plead guilty and remain silent." McCord's letter blew the lid off the case.

The Senate Hearings

While Judge Sirica pursued the case in a Washington courtroom, the Senate began its own investigation of Watergate. From May to November in 1973, the Senate Select Committee on Presidential Campaign Practices heard testimony from a parade of White House officials. Sam J. Ervin, the 76-year-old senator from North Carolina, chaired the committee. Ervin was a Harvard Law School graduate who had earned the respect of his colleagues during his 18-year Senate career.

Ervin was known to be a staunch defender of First Amendment rights. He called the Constitution "the finest thing to come out of the mind of man." Ervin steered the hearings with a commanding wit and down-to-earth common sense.

On April 30, 1973, Nixon made another attempt to shield the White House from the gathering storm by announcing the resignations of Dean, Haldeman, and Ehrlichman. All 3 men had been involved in Watergate. Speaking on television, the President denied any attempt at a cover-up and vowed: "There can be no whitewash at the White House." Polls, however, showed that half of those watching believed the President had taken part in a cover-up.

Under pressure from Congress and the public, Nixon ordered Attorney General Elliot Richardson to appoint a special prosecutor to investigate Watergate. Richardson chose Harvard law professor Archibald Cox and promised the Senate that Cox would have complete independence from the White House and broad powers of investigation.

Public interest in the case grew that summer as the Senate committee began televised hearings. Each day millions of Americans watched—fascinated—as the story unfolded.

The most damaging testimony came from John Dean, the White House counsel. Dean testified for nearly 30 hours. He claimed that there had been a cover-up and charged that the President himself had directed it.

Then, in July, another bombshell exploded. White House aide Alexander Butterfield told the Senate

The Washington Post
SUNDAY, APRIL 29, 1973
3 Top Nixon Aides Tied to Cover-Up
Dean Cites Haldeman, Ehrlichman
Kalmbach Hush Fund Link Probed
Senate Won't Cry Over 'Those Two'
D.C. Mayor Might Run In Future
New Army: Magnet for Poor
Volunteers View Service as Opportunity
Petersen Role in Probe Q

The Washington Post
FINAL
WEDNESDAY, MAY 1, 1974
President Hands Over Transcripts
Nixon Debated Paying Blackmail, Clemency
'Keep Cap on Bottle'
Dean Warned of Furor
Initial Reaction On Hill Divided Along Party Lines
Judiciary Committee Unsure How to Respond
Meeting Set For Tonight
White House Strategy Shifts
President in Private: Lonely, Cynical

The Washington Post
SUNDAY, JULY 28, 1974
Judiciary Committee Approves Article To Impeach President Nixon, 27 to 11
6 Republicans Join Democrats to Pass Obstruction Charge
Reinecke Convicted Of Perjury
Majority Switches, Gets to Specifics

COURTESY THE WASHINGTON POST

Headline News By the spring of 1973, Watergate was big news, and the byline of Woodward and Bernstein was familiar to readers following the story. *What event brought the Watergate burglary back into the news in 1973?*

© FRED WARD/BLACK STAR

UPI/BETTMANN

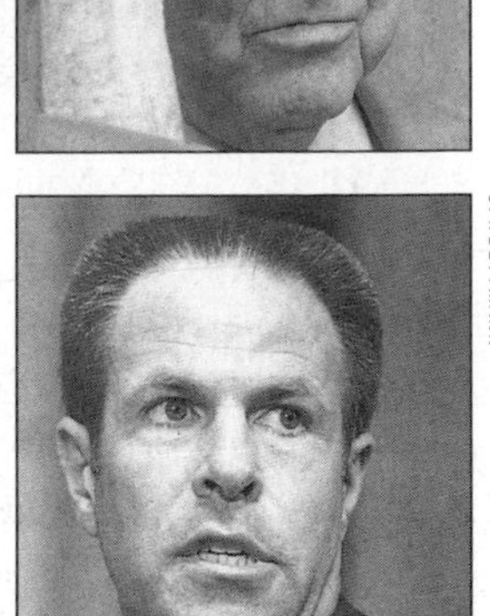

UPI/BETTMANN

UPI/BETTMANN

UPI/BETTMANN

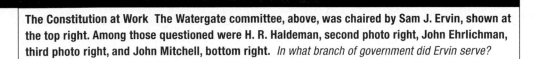

The Constitution at Work The Watergate committee, above, was chaired by Sam J. Ervin, shown at the top right. Among those questioned were H. R. Haldeman, second photo right, John Ehrlichman, third photo right, and John Mitchell, bottom right. *In what branch of government did Ervin serve?*

committee that early in 1971 Nixon had installed a tape recording system in the White House. The news that the President had bugged his own office was electrifying. Here was proof of Nixon's guilt or innocence.

By August the hearings were the top-rated daytime television show. Democrat Sam Ervin became a national hero as he grilled Mitchell, Haldeman, Ehrlichman, and other White House figures about Watergate. Republican Senator Howard Baker asked each witness the question to which all Americans wanted the answer: "What did the President know and when did he know it?"

The Tapes

Both the Senate committee and Special Prosecutor Cox called on Nixon to surrender tapes of conversations that might pertain to the Watergate break-in. Nixon refused and claimed executive privilege, insisting that the release of the tapes would endanger national security. Cox and Ervin persisted. Cox declared, "There is no exception for the president from the guiding principle that the public, in the pursuit of justice, has a right to every man's evidence." He sought a court order to force Nixon to hand over the tapes.

Nixon again tried to shift attention away from the scandal. On August 15 he urged Americans to put Watergate behind them. He felt that after 12 weeks and 2 million words of televised testimony, it was time to get on with the "urgent business of our nation." Few Americans agreed.

Finally Nixon ordered Attorney General Richardson to fire Cox. Richardson, remembering his promise to the Senate, refused and resigned. When Richardson resigned, Nixon ordered the deputy attorney general, William Ruckelshaus, to fire Cox. Ruckelshaus refused and was himself fired. Finally Solicitor General Robert Bork fired Cox. Public outcry over what came to be known as the Saturday Night Massacre forced Nixon to appoint another special prosecutor, attorney Leon Jaworski. Jaworski renewed the demand for the tapes. Nixon balked, and Jaworski took the case to court.

The crisis was deepening. Already nearly 50 Nixon administration officials, including Mitchell, Haldeman, and Ehrlichman, faced criminal charges.

That fall Nixon's troubles multiplied. In October 1973, Vice President Spiro Agnew pleaded no contest to charges of income tax evasion and accepting bribes while governor of Maryland and resigned. Nixon nominated Gerald R. Ford, a popular, conservative member

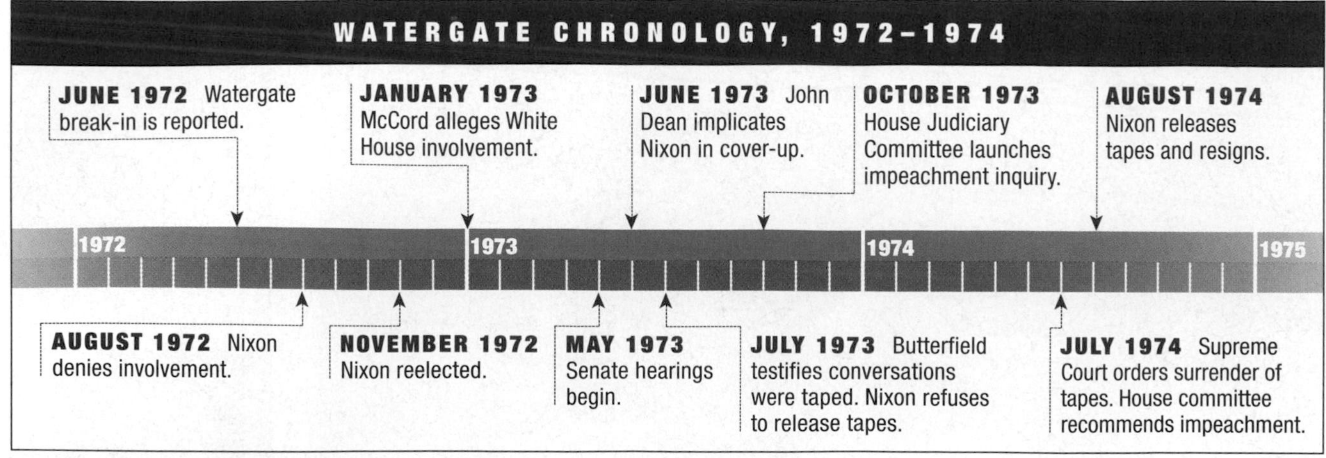
WATERGATE CHRONOLOGY, 1972–1974
JUNE 1972 Watergate break-in is reported.
JANUARY 1973 McCord alleges White House involvement.
JUNE 1973 John Dean implicates Nixon in cover-up.
OCTOBER 1973 House Judiciary Committee launches impeachment inquiry.
AUGUST 1974 Nixon releases tapes and resigns.
1972
1973
1974
1975
AUGUST 1972 Nixon denies involvement.
NOVEMBER 1972 Nixon reelected.
MAY 1973 Senate hearings begin.
JULY 1973 Butterfield testifies conversations were taped. Nixon refuses to release tapes.
JULY 1974 Supreme Court orders surrender of tapes. House committee recommends impeachment.

of Congress from Michigan, to fill the post. Congress quickly confirmed the nomination.

Then, in December, Nixon's own finances came under fire. Federal investigators reported that in 1970 and 1971 the President had paid only about $800 a year in federal taxes on an annual salary of $200,000. Since 1969 he had paid no state income tax even though he was still a legal resident of California.

Pressure for the tapes was also mounting. In April 1974, the President released edited transcripts of some of the tapes in question. Although his aides had cut the most incriminating comments, the profanity, pettiness, and ethnic insults that peppered the President's conversations shocked many people.

Even more revealing was what was missing from the tapes. Gaps in the tapes indicated the President was not telling the public the whole truth. When Nixon again refused to release the unedited tapes, Jaworski took the case to the Supreme Court. On July 24, in *United States* v. *Nixon,* the Supreme Court unanimously ruled that President Nixon had to release the tapes.

The Move for Impeachment

Also in July the House Judiciary Committee began to draft articles of **impeachment,** or charges of misconduct, against the President. The impeachment process allows Congress to check the power of officials in the executive and judicial branches. Impeachable offenses include criminal activity, but are not limited to acts that are illegal.

Under the Constitution the House of Representatives determines whether impeachment charges are justified. If so, the Senate then serves as the jury for the trial. Only one President, Andrew Johnson, had ever been impeached.

On July 30, following several days of televised debate, the House committee voted to recommend impeachment of President Nixon on 3 counts: obstructing justice by trying to cover up the role of the White House in the Watergate burglary; violating the rights of United States citizens by using the FBI, the CIA, and the IRS to harass critics; and defying congressional authority by refusing to turn over the tapes. The articles of impeachment would now go to the House of Representatives for a vote.

Nixon was trapped. On August 5, he handed over the tapes, confessing that they were "at variance with some of my earlier statements." The tapes revealed that just days after the Watergate break-in, the President had ordered the CIA to halt the FBI investigation of the case: "Don't go any further into this case, period." Impeachment charges seemed certain.

The Final Days

For three days Nixon paced, brooded, and conferred with his few remaining friends in Congress. No matter how he counted the votes in the House and Senate, they added up to certain impeachment and probable conviction in the Senate.

By Wednesday, August 7, key Republican leaders had joined the chorus demanding the President's resignation. Nixon made his decision.That evening Nixon met with

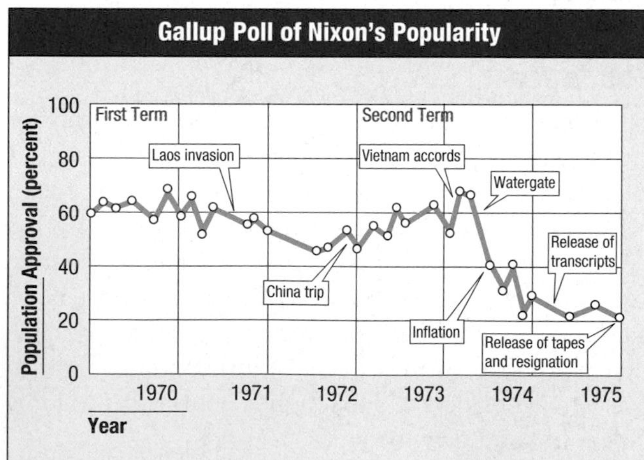
Gallup Poll of Nixon's Popularity
Population Approval (percent)
100
80
60
40
20
0
First Term
Second Term
Laos invasion
Vietnam accords
Watergate
Release of transcripts
China trip
Inflation
Release of tapes and resignation
1970
1971
1972
1973
1974
1975
Year

With changing events, Nixon's popularity rose and fell like a roller coaster. *What was Nixon's approval rating when he resigned?*

You Be the Judge In their work, cartoonists made use of the personalities, attitudes, and actions of those involved in the Watergate scandal. *What kind of attitude about cover-ups and lies is suggested by the White House dialogue in this cartoon?*

a group of 46 loyal congressional leaders. In a long, rambling speech, he thanked them for their years of support. Twenty minutes later he would address the nation—the first American President ever to resign from office.

The following day Nixon and his family flew back to California, and Gerald Ford was sworn in as President. President Ford declared, "Our long national nightmare is over." A President had fallen, but the American political system had survived.

The Aftermath

A Pardon, New Laws, and Continuing Doubts

A month later President Ford **pardoned,** or excused, Nixon for any crimes he had committed or might have committed while in the White House. Many Americans felt Nixon had escaped justice. Others, however, believed it was time to put Watergate to rest and to look to the future.

To counter the trend toward greater presidential power and curb future abuses, Congress enacted a series of laws. The War Powers Act of 1973 required the President to consult with Congress before sending American troops into prolonged action. In 1974 Congress passed the Congressional Budget and Impoundment Control Act, which prohibited the impounding of federal money by the President.

Also in 1974 Congress strengthened the Federal Election Campaign Act of 1972, setting limits on campaign contributions. Finally Congress extended the Freedom of Information Act by passing the Privacy Act, allowing citizens to have access to the files that the government may have gathered on them.

The Nixon White House had threatened the foundation of American democracy—constitutional law. Yet, as many pointed out, the system worked. The legislative and judicial branches used their powers to rein in the executive branch. Congress investigated the charges, and the independent judiciary forced the President to release evidence. Eventually 31 Nixon officials were convicted and went to prison for Watergate-related offenses.

At the same time, Watergate was deeply disquieting. The nation's leaders had committed serious crimes. Then the new President had pardoned the most important offender. Had a deal been made? How could Americans continue to trust their government? Coming on the heels of the war in Vietnam, Watergate further undermined the nation's self-confidence.

SECTION ASSESSMENT

Main Idea

1. Use a diagram like this one to show events leading to Nixon's resignation.

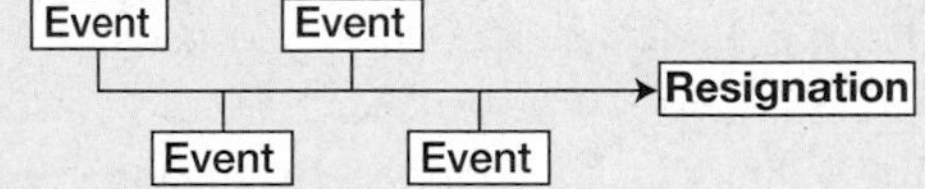

Vocabulary

2. Define: impeachment, pardon.

Checking Facts

3. Identify examples of Nixon's abuse of power.
4. What laws did Congress pass after Watergate to curb abuses of presidential power?

Critical Thinking

5. **Drawing Conclusions** What were some of the consequences of Ford's decision to pardon Nixon?

Turning Point

The Attempted Impeachment of Nixon

SUMMER 1974

MEMORANDUM

For: Judiciary Committee of the House of Representatives

Subject: Impeachment of Richard M. Nixon

Richard M. Nixon has acted in a manner contrary to his trust as President and subversive of constitutional government, to the great prejudice of the cause of law and justice, and to the manifest injury of the people of the United States.

Wherefore Richard M. Nixon, by such conduct, warrants impeachment and trial, and removal from office.

The articles of impeachment voted by the Judiciary Committee of the House of Representatives, July 27–30, 1974

The Case

The impeachment proceedings against President Richard Nixon in 1974 revolved around 4 words in the United States Constitution—"high Crimes and Misdemeanors." Article II, Section 4, grants Congress the power of impeachment:

> The President, Vice President and all civil Officers of the United States, shall be removed from Office on Impeachment for, and Conviction of, Treason, Bribery, or other high Crimes and Misdemeanors.

The Constitution, however, does not define "high Crimes and Misdemeanors." In the summer of 1974, the members of the Ninety-third Congress faced the difficult task of deciding for themselves what that definition was.

These four words served as the constitutional battleground for the impeachment case against Nixon. This battle would involve all three branches of government, as well as the "fourth estate"—the press. It would challenge the fundamental political will of the American people and their leaders—and put the Constitution to one of its greatest tests.

The Background

In late July 1974, more than 2 years after the Watergate break-in, the House Judiciary Committee voted for 3 articles of impeachment against President Richard Nixon based on his actions in the Watergate affair:

- Article I—that the President "prevented, obstructed, and impeded the administration of justice" (obstruction of justice)—passed 27 to 11.

- Article II—that the President "repeatedly engaged in conduct violating the constitutional rights of citizens. . . ." (abuse of presidential powers)—passed 28 to 10.
- Article III—that the President "failed without lawful cause or excuse to produce papers and things as directed by duly authorized subpoenas. . . ." (contempt of Congress)—passed 21 to 17.

The chairman of the House Judiciary Committee, Representative Peter W. Rodino, Jr., a Democrat from New Jersey, hoped to bring these articles before a full vote of the House, the next step in the impeachment process, on August 19. If the House voted for any one of these articles, Nixon would be brought to trial before the Senate sometime that fall. Lastly, if the Senate convicted Nixon, he would be removed from office.

Charting a New Course History provided little guidance for members of the Ninety-third Congress as they moved through the process. Before 1974 the House had voted to impeach only 13 officials, including 1 President, Andrew Johnson, in 1868. To many in Congress, however, the evidence against Nixon seemed overwhelming, and there was no need to consider historical precedent. In addition, the Senate Watergate Committee, Special Prosecutor Leon Jaworski and his staff, and the press all compiled their own evidence. Representative Jack Brooks of Texas, a Democratic member of the House Judiciary Committee, listed Nixon's offenses: "The cover-up of crimes, obstructing the prosecution of criminals, surreptitious entries, wiretapping for political purposes, suspension of civil liberties of every American, tax violations and personal enrichment at public expense, bribery and blackmail; flagrant misuse of the FBI, the CIA and the IRS."

Support for the President Still, the President's supporters in Congress—most of them fellow Republicans—remained convinced that the evidence failed to prove Nixon had committed an impeachable offense. Ten Republican members of the House Judiciary Committee, led by Charles Wiggins of California, stayed firm in their support of Nixon. Each had voted against all three articles of impeachment.

Nixon hoped that his congressional supporters could slow down or even stop the impeachment

"I have revered all Presidents and I have searched within my heart and my conscience and searched out the facts, and when I test the facts I find that the President of the United States . . . must be found wanting."

Peter Rodino, chairman of the House Judiciary Committee (HJC)

AP/WIDE WORLD PHOTOS

". . . My faith in the Constitution is whole, it is complete, it is total, and I am not going to sit here and be an idle spectator to the diminution of the Constitution. . . . The framers confided in the Constitution the power if need be to remove . . . a President swollen with power and grown tyrannical."

Barbara Jordan, Democrat from Texas, member of the HJC

UPI/BETTMAN

"For those who are looking for the smoking pistol, I am just afraid they are not going to find it, because the room is too full of smoke."

Hamilton Fish, Republican from New York, member of the HJC

© DENNIS BRACK/BLACK STAR

"It's a . . . weak circumstantial case. . . . The committee has avoided any kind of standard on what is an impeachable offense."

Charles Wiggins, Republican from California, member of the HJC

UPI/BETTMAN

Turning Point

UPI/BETTMAN

House Judiciary Committee members (left to right): Harold D. Donohue, D-Massachusetts, John Doar, chief counsel, Chairman Peter Rodino, D-New Jersey, Edward Hutchinson, R-Michigan, and Albert Jenner, minority counsel.

process. After the Judiciary Committee's vote in late July, however, hope waned that there would be enough votes to stop the momentum. Nixon's presidency depended on keeping the support of at least 34 senators. Nixon felt he could count on 36 senators—8 Democrats and 28 Republicans. To convict the President of impeachment took a two-thirds majority in the 100-member Senate. As long as Nixon could count on these 36 senators, he could complete his term.

The Opinions

Nixon's supporters viewed the House Judiciary Committee's vote and the continuing momentum for impeachment as a political act, not a constitutional one. Some Republicans even believed that the "liberal" Democrats hoped to overturn the national election results of 1972 that had swept Nixon into office. Like Nixon, his supporters held an intense dislike and distrust for members of the press, which they felt had prejudiced the country against the President. More importantly to them, no "smoking gun" that proved the President had directly committed a crime had yet been found—after more than 2 years of investigations. Without this evidence, his supporters believed no grounds for his impeachment existed.

Nixon's opponents, both Democrats and Republicans, also did not like the impeachment process, but for vastly different reasons. To them, evidence clearly showed that Nixon had abused the power of the presidency. If impeachment proceedings stopped, a serious injustice would be committed against the constitutional system of checks and balances.

The Decision

After the House Judiciary Committee's vote, members of Congress felt a grave sense of urgency. It was August of an election year. Could Congress avoid a prolonged impeachment battle with Nixon? Could it persuade him to resign and avoid a brutal fight?

Rodino, House Speaker Carl Albert, and House Majority Leader Thomas "Tip" O'Neill, resolved to move the impeachment process forward. They cleared the House's calendar and set a firm date of August 19 for impeachment proceedings. Wiggins and other Nixon supporters tried to delay the process with procedural matters. Although the President's supporters knew they might lack the votes to delay, they were determined to remain loyal to Nixon. Then, in the midst of all the activity, Wiggins learned of the existence of a "smoking gun"—and of his betrayal by the President.

The "Smoking Gun" On July 24, the Supreme Court had voted 8 to 0 that Nixon must turn over 64 unedited tape recordings to Special Prosecutor Jaworski. Although no President had ever disobeyed a Supreme Court decision, Nixon delayed handing over the tapes until early August. Nixon realized that if he did not comply with the Court's order, the House would consider that a high crime. In turning over the tapes, however, Nixon worried that he was giving evidence to both his supporters and opponents that would reveal that he had directed a cover-up attempt soon after the Watergate break-in and had lied about it—the tapes would become the "smoking gun."

Alarmed by Nixon's hesitation and his deteriorating health, the President's chief of staff, Alexander Haig, asked Wiggins to meet with him and James St. Clair, the special counsel to the President, on August 2. Having just learned the contents of the transcripts of the tapes, Haig and St. Clair let Wiggins read 5 or 6 key pages before the documents were made public. Once Wiggins read the transcript pages he felt betrayed and could no longer defend the President. On August 5, Wiggins made public his change of mind: ". . . I am prepared to conclude that the significant career of public service of Richard Nixon must be terminated involuntarily."

Nixon's White House staff continued to try to convince the President that efforts to fight were hopeless—that the country would be best served by his resignation. Nixon, however, still resolved to carry the fight, mistakenly believing he continued to have enough support in the Senate to block his conviction.

The Decision to Resign The country was approaching a crisis. Finally, in a face-to-face meeting with Senator Barry Goldwater and a few other supporters on August 7, Nixon realized he had only 2 choices: have the Senate remove him from office, or resign.

On August 9, Nixon turned in his resignation, by Constitutional requirement, to the Secretary of State: "I hereby resign the Office of President of the United States." This one-sentence letter made Nixon the first President in United States history to resign. His resignation ended the impeachment process, but ensured a smooth and peaceful transition of power from Nixon to Vice President Gerald R. Ford, who became the thirty-eighth President.

The Significance

Although Nixon resigned from office without seeming to admit his guilt, the constitutional system of checks and balances did its work. Some Americans believed that Nixon's resignation merely revealed that corruption existed at even the highest level of government, but most agreed that it proved that Article II, Section 4, of the United States Constitution worked as intended.

RESPONDING TO THE CASE

1. Why did some in Congress support the President in his fight against impeachment? Why did others want him removed from office?

2. In your opinion, did Nixon commit "high Crimes and Misdemeanors"? Defend your viewpoint.

3. Do you agree or disagree that Nixon's resignation proved that the constitutional system worked? Defend your viewpoint.

4. The Ninety-third Congress never defined "high Crimes and Misdemeanors" during the impeachment process. Should the Constitution be amended to define this term? Why or why not?

PORTFOLIO PROJECT

The media, both print and electronic, played an important role in keeping the public informed throughout the Watergate saga. President Nixon's resignation was the culmination of more than two years of investigation and litigation. Write a news story about Nixon's resignation and the immediate events that led up to it. Be sure to include this story in your portfolio.

Ford and Carter

WINTER 1973: OIL EMBARGO FUELS GAS PANIC

DURING THE WINTER OF 1973–1974, AN UNFAMILIAR DRAMA WAS ENACTED AT GAS STATIONS ALL ACROSS THE UNITED STATES. From dawn to dusk, cars queued up at the gas pumps, forming lines that often snaked down the street for blocks. Panicky motorists rushed to any gas station that had a supply, and they often had to wait for 2 hours or more. When they finally did reach the pump, they were often limited to buying only a few gallons of gas—and at a higher price! Even after the oil embargo was over, gas prices continued to rise. Another round of sharp increases occurred during the energy crisis of 1979. By 1980 the price of gasoline was more than $1 a gallon, more than twice the 1973 price.

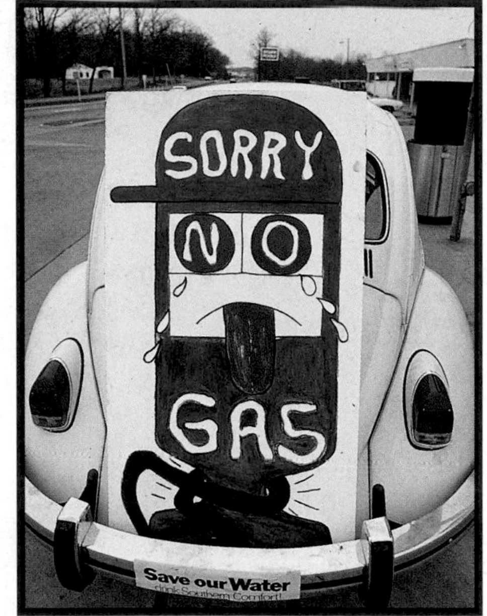

© DENNIS BRACK/BLACK STAR

A Scarce Commodity
Many Americans had to rearrange their lives around the availability of gasoline.

The competition for fuel frayed people's nerves and rattled their tempers. Drivers fought with one another, waved guns at harried service station employees, and sometimes even smashed gas pumps in rage and frustration. "These people are like animals foraging for food," said the owner of a station in Miami. "If you can't sell them gas, they'll threaten to beat you up, wreck your station, run over you with a car."

A feeling of powerlessness intensified the motorists' anger. Political and trade decisions made halfway around the globe hindered their freedom to drive to work or the shopping center. The forces at work at the gas pumps would continue to overshadow American life throughout most of the 1970s: religious fervor and political unrest in North Africa and Southwest Asia, the unstable politics that governed the international flow of oil, and a runaway United States economy.

GUIDE TO READING

Main Idea

Ford and Carter tried to rebuild the integrity of the presidency and to instill Americans with a new sense of confidence; however, a series of economic, foreign, and environmental challenges undermined their efforts.

Vocabulary

- inflation
- stagflation
- embargo
- recession
- human rights
- dissident

Read to Find Out . . .

- the causes and effects of the economic policies adopted by Ford.
- the foreign policy initiatives pursued by Carter.
- reasons Americans developed a new environmental awareness in the late 1970s.

Ford Follows Nixon

Ford Faces Many Challenges

When Richard Nixon resigned the presidency in disgrace, he left to his successor, Vice President Gerald R. Ford, a nation in crisis. A humiliating defeat in Vietnam had battered American prestige, and the Watergate scandal had left the American people deeply shaken.

Ford tried to pull the country together. On September 8, 1974, in an effort to consign the Watergate scandal to history, Gerald Ford pardoned Richard Nixon for any federal crimes he might have committed as part of the Watergate break-in and cover-up. The pardon outraged many Americans who strongly believed that all citizens, even the President, must be accountable to the Constitution and the laws of the land. Despite Ford's best intentions, the United States remained a troubled and divided nation.

The Stagflation Dilemma

Perhaps the greatest obstacle to President Ford's effort to restore public faith in government was his inability to control the economy. Since the end of World War II in 1945, most Americans had become used to a rising standard of living. Now, however, two economic conditions that rarely occur at the same time shattered American prosperity: slowing productivity and rising **inflation**—or the steady increase of prices.

Industry had begun stagnating, or slowing down. During the 1970s industrial productivity—the rate of goods produced per hour—had slowed, causing the cost of producing goods to rise. At the same time, foreign firms, especially those in Japan and West Germany, were able to manufacture high-quality goods quickly and inexpensively and to market them successfully in the United States. American consumers spent more on these high-quality, less expensive products, causing United States productivity to slow down even more.

The second cause of the American economic dilemma was rising inflation. As a result of inflation, the dollar fell in value against foreign currencies, and its purchasing power at home and abroad fell dramatically. A pair of gloves that once sold for $5 might now sell for $10. The annual inflation rate, which had been 3.3 percent in 1972, soared to 11 percent by 1974. Economists referred to this combination of stagnating growth and spiraling inflation as **stagflation.**

An Energy Crisis Is Born

The major cause of the United States's inflationary spiral was an international oil crisis with roots in the turbulent politics of North Africa and Southwest Asia. The United States economic machine demanded huge amounts of oil. Foreign oil suppliers—principally Arab nations—met nearly one-third of that demand.

Since 1960 many oil-rich nations in Africa, Southwest Asia, and South America had sold their oil as part of the Organization of Petroleum Exporting Countries (OPEC). OPEC countries set common prices and regulated production quotas and ceilings. These trade practices allowed them to control both the price and availability of oil throughout the world.

During the Yom Kippur War in 1973, in which Israel fought Syria and Egypt, Saudi Arabia imposed an **embargo,** or a restriction of trade, on oil shipped to Israel's allies, including the United States. At the same

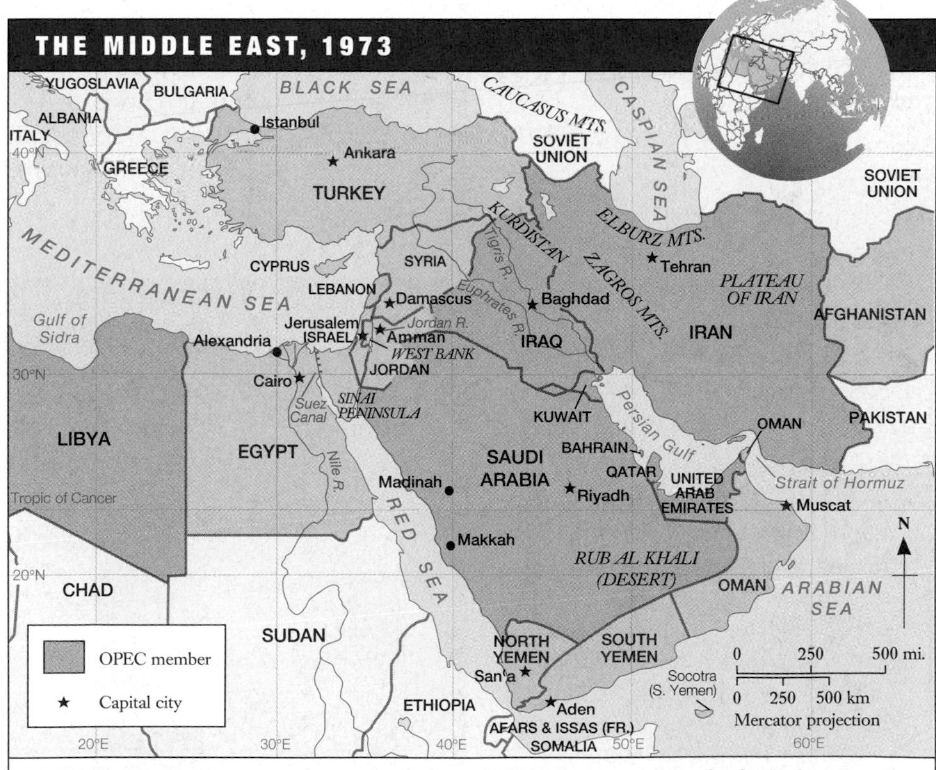

OPEC oil price increases sent a message to the United States and the Soviet Union: Developing countries would no longer cater to the needs of the superpowers. *What Southwest Asian nations belong to OPEC?*

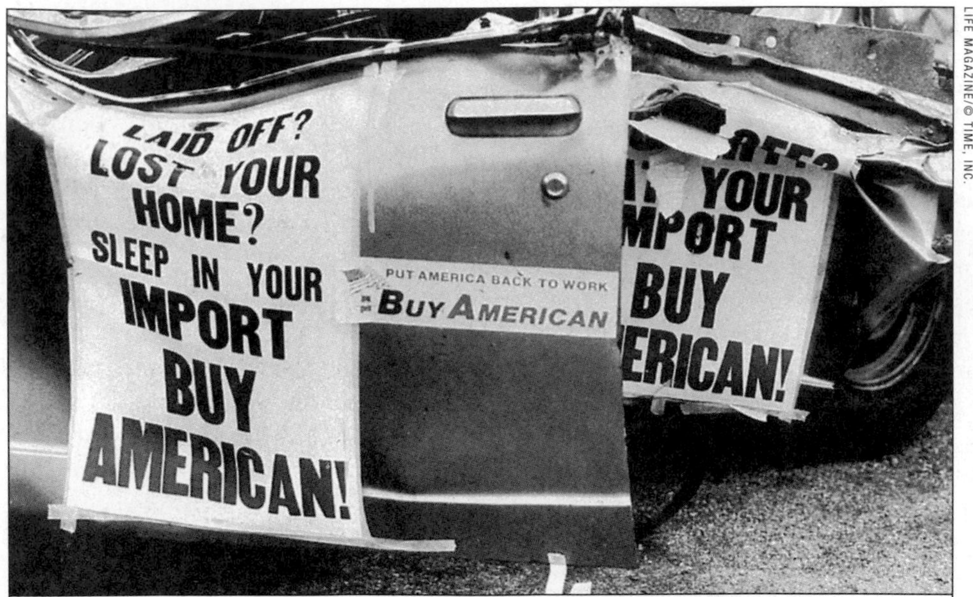

LIFE MAGAZINE/© TIME, INC.

Steel Industry in Decline **Angry at the rapidly rising numbers of imported cars, unemployed steelworkers in Fairfield, Alabama, vented their frustration by bashing this Toyota.** *Why were Americans buying so many Japanese cars during the 1970s?*

time, other OPEC countries nearly quadrupled their prices. Although the embargo was lifted in 1974, its economic effects continued through the end of the decade.

Wheels and Steel

The oil embargo had a profound effect on United States auto and steel industries. The big, gleaming cars produced in Detroit had long represented American know-how around the world. Now, more than any other product, they symbolized the United States's industrial decline.

When the Arab oil embargo and OPEC price increases hit the United States economy in 1973, most American car buyers wanted nothing to do with Detroit's oversized "gas-guzzlers." Many consumers switched to foreign cars, especially those manufactured in Japan. Imported autos, which held only a 17 percent share of the United States market in 1970, captured a whopping 37 percent by 1980. By that year, a dozen American auto plants had closed, and 300,000 autoworkers had lost their jobs.

The steel industry came close to a complete collapse. In 1946 the United States provided 60 percent of the world's steel. By 1980 that figure had fallen to 14 percent, and steel executives questioned whether their industry could survive.

Again foreign steel manufacturers presented stiff competition. Because of their computerized and automated production facilities, they were able to keep production costs down. United States steel companies, whose plants were old-fashioned by foreign standards, saw their costs rise 10 percent a year, forcing them to raise the price of American steel. As a result American manufacturers began buying nearly one-fifth of their steel from foreign producers. The steel industry appealed

★ ★ ★ Gallery of Presidents ★ ★ ★

Gerald R. Ford

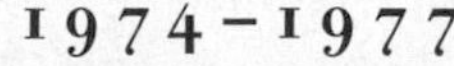
1974–1977

"I have not sought this enormous responsibility, but I will not shirk it. Those who nominated me and confirmed me as Vice President were my friends. . . . They were of both parties, elected by all the people and acting under the Constitution in their name. It is only fitting then that I should pledge to them and to you that I will be the President of all the people."

August 9, 1974

COURTESY GERALD FORD LIBRARY

Background

- **Born 1913**
- **Republican, Michigan**
- **Served in the navy 1942–1946**
- **Elected to House of Representatives 1948**
- **Succeeded to presidency 1974**

Achievements in Office

- **Amnesty program for Vietnam War draft dodgers**
- **Council on Wage and Price Stability (1974)**

to Congress to use stiff quotas, tariffs, and other international agreements to set limits on imports. Congress refused, fearing retaliation by foreign governments against American trade.

The President Responds

President Ford decided that the economy could best be revived by attacking inflation. At press conferences, he wore a red and white lapel button emblazoned with the letters WIN, the acronym for "Whip Inflation Now." In addition he supported high interest rates, which made money more expensive for everyone to borrow, including the government. By tightening credit Ford hoped to reduce spending, which would result in an oversupply of goods and thus lower prices. Ford also clamped down on government spending by vetoing new health, housing, and education legislation.

The measures Ford took helped to cool inflation, which fell to 6 percent by 1976. As a result of Ford's restrictions, however, industrial production plummeted and unemployment rose. Before long, almost 1 out of every 10 people was out of work. During 1974 and 1975, the country plunged into its worst **recession,** or economic slowdown, since the Great Depression.

Carter Takes Charge

Recession: An Election Issue

The struggling economy was the key issue as Americans went to the polls in 1976 to elect a President. Although Americans liked Gerald Ford well enough as a person, they rejected his leadership, especially his economic policies. James Earl Carter, a peanut farmer and former governor of Georgia, was elected the nation's thirty-ninth President.

Jimmy Carter knew that he had to cure the economic ills that were draining the nation's vitality. He tried to jolt the economy out of recession by increasing government spending and cutting taxes. Both measures were meant to stimulate economic growth. Unemployment came down, but inflation took off. For 2 years the annual inflation rate hovered above 10 percent.

Further fueling inflation was a dramatic OPEC price increase in 1979. The cost of a barrel of OPEC oil zoomed to $30, and another oil shortage ensued. Businesses, industries, and homeowners faced energy shortages, and once again motorists lined up at gas stations to buy expensive fuel.

Carter asked Americans to turn down their thermostats to 68 degrees in the winter, switch off unnecessary lights, and go "gasless" on Sundays. Businesses reduced their operating hours and schools extended vacations, all in an effort to conserve energy. As a result of these dramatic lifestyle changes, Carter's approval rating fell to 26 percent, almost as low as Nixon's had been at the darkest moments of his presidency. Americans were weary of want and sacrifice, and they directed their anger and frustration at Washington.

Human Rights and Foreign Policy

Fostering Peace and Respect for Sovereignty

Standing up for **human rights** at home and abroad was the cornerstone of Jimmy Carter's foreign policy. A devout man, Carter tried to apply the religious principles that governed his private life to the conduct of

The United States Economy, 1972–1980

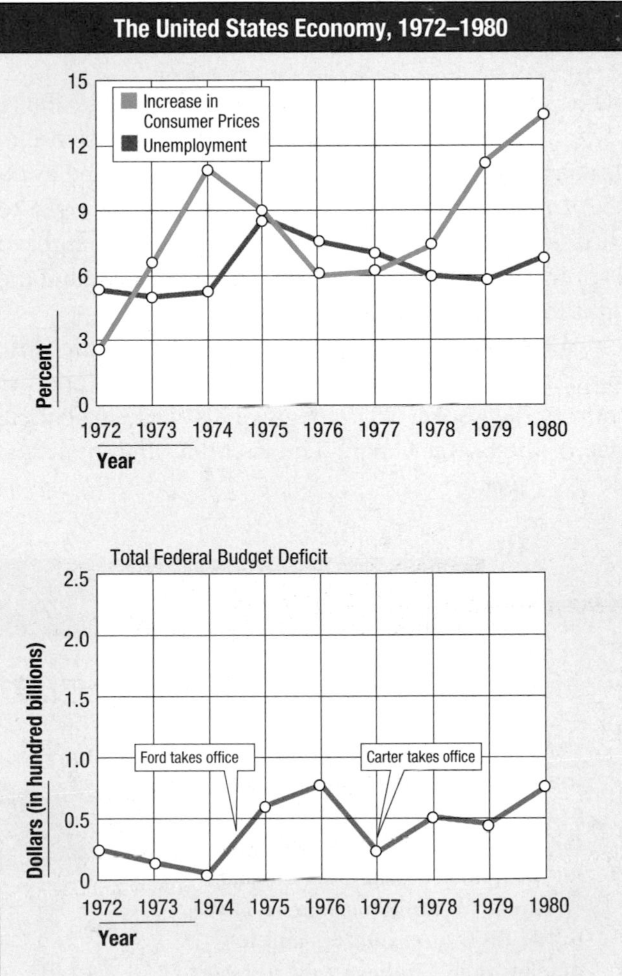

Economic stagflation began during the Nixon years. Presidents Ford and Carter tried short-term methods to cure the economy's woes. *According to the charts, what effect did these methods have on the United States economy?*

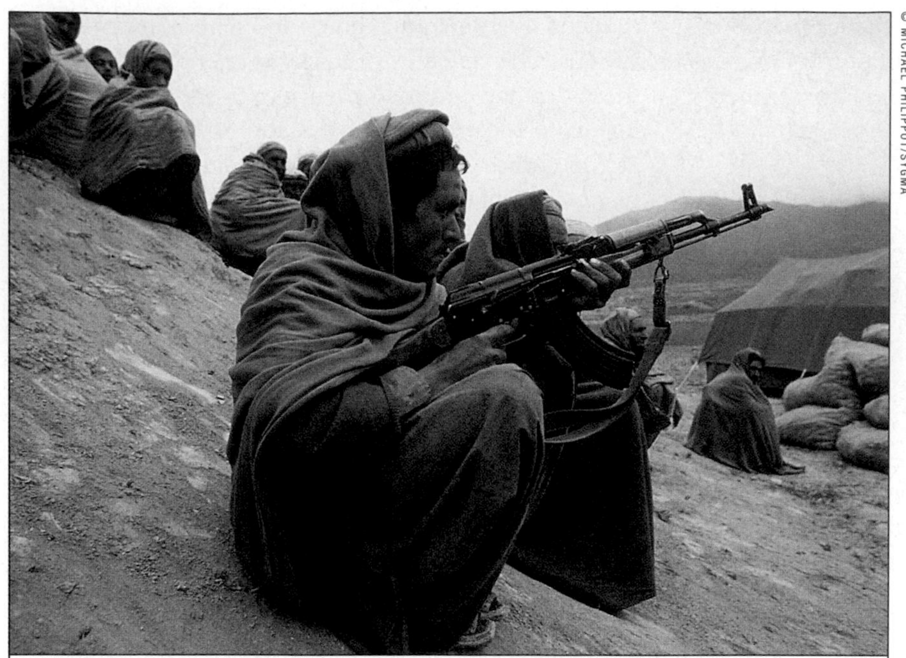

© MICHAEL PHILIPPOT/SYGMA

Resistance Fighters The Afghan rebels used guerrilla tactics to overcome the superior equipment of the Soviets. *What was Carter's response to the Soviet attack of Afghanistan?*

public affairs. Like Woodrow Wilson early in the 1900s, Carter crafted a foreign policy based on the defense of basic rights and freedoms he believed should be available to all people throughout the world: the right to choose leaders in fair and honest elections, the right to a fair trial, the right to worship and travel freely, and the right to free expression.

When Carter thought a nation had violated the human rights of its own citizens or citizens of another country, he spoke out strongly. This was particularly true of the Soviet Union. The Kremlin often punished **dissidents,** those who openly criticized Soviet policies. When Carter offered imprisoned or exiled dissidents his moral support, Soviet leaders accused him of meddling in their internal affairs.

In 1979 the Soviet Union invaded Afghanistan. Outraged at what he considered to be interference in the affairs of a sovereign nation, Carter ordered sanctions against the Soviet Union. The United States and other nations refused to participate in the 1980 Olympic Games in Moscow; in addition the United States government imposed a grain embargo on the Soviet Union.

Playing the Peacemaker

Carter's stand on human rights was reflected in other areas of his foreign policy. His primary goals were to foster peace and respect for other nations' sovereignty.

For example, Carter sought to slow down the arms race between the United States and the Soviet Union. American and Soviet negotiators worked hard to draft a treaty limiting the number of missiles, bombers, and nuclear warheads each side could stockpile. Finally, in June 1979, Carter and Soviet leader Leonid Brezhnev signed the second Strategic Arms Limitation Treaty (SALT II), expanding the first agreement negotiated during President Nixon's administration.

James Earl Carter, Jr.

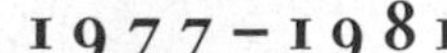

"Let us learn together and laugh together and work together and pray together, confident that in the end we will triumph together in the right. The American dream endures. We must once again have full faith in our country—and in one another. I believe America can be better. We can be even stronger than before."

Inaugural Address, January 20, 1977

COURTESY JIMMY CARTER LIBRARY

BACKGROUND

- **Born 1929**
- **Democrat, Georgia**
- **Graduated naval academy 1946**
- **Served in the navy 1946–1953**
- **Elected state senator 1962**
- **Elected governor 1970**

ACHIEVEMENTS IN OFFICE

- **Negotiated Israeli-Egyptian peace treaty (1978)**
- **Negotiated SALT II (1979)**

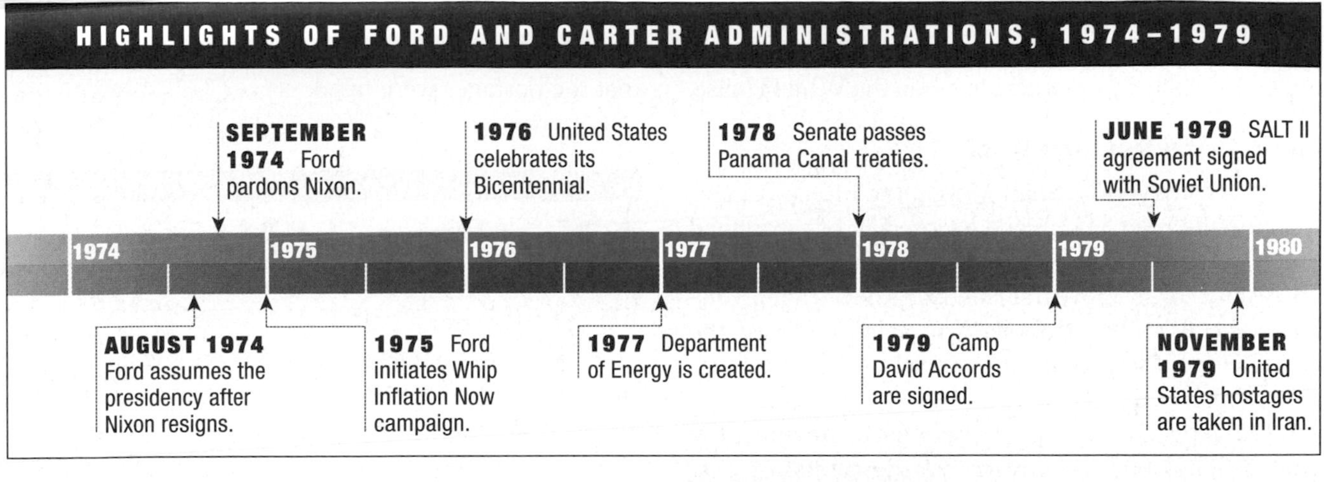
HIGHLIGHTS OF FORD AND CARTER ADMINISTRATIONS, 1974–1979
SEPTEMBER 1974 Ford pardons Nixon.
1976 United States celebrates its Bicentennial.
1978 Senate passes Panama Canal treaties.
JUNE 1979 SALT II agreement signed with Soviet Union.
1974
1975
1976
1977
1978
1979
1980
AUGUST 1974 Ford assumes the presidency after Nixon resigns.
1975 Ford initiates Whip Inflation Now campaign.
1977 Department of Energy is created.
1979 Camp David Accords are signed.
NOVEMBER 1979 United States hostages are taken in Iran.

Continuing Nixon's policy of détente, Carter hoped to reduce the "balance of terror" between the United States and the Soviet Union. Strong opposition to the SALT II agreement surfaced in the United States. Congress did not believe the limits set forth by the treaty could be verified. The treaty languished in the Senate. In response to the Soviet invasion of Afghanistan, Carter asked the Senate to delay consideration of the pact. In the end SALT II was never ratified.

Continuing President Nixon's efforts, Carter established normal diplomatic relations with the People's Republic of China. In doing so, he cleared the way for valuable technical and commercial exchanges between the two formerly hostile nations.

The Panama Canal

Carter also tried to encourage peace and sovereignty in Latin America and to develop a more favorable image of the United States in that region. His administration cut back military aid to South and Central American dictators and negotiated an agreement to give control of the Panama Canal to that nation by the year 2000. Despite strong conservative opposition, the United States Senate ratified this agreement in 1978, along with a second treaty that gave the United States the right to defend the neutrality of the canal.

© DIRCK HALSTEAD/GAMMA LIAISON

Former Enemies Begin (left) and Sadat (right) celebrate their efforts toward peace. *Why was Carter able to bring the two men together?*

The Camp David Accords

President Carter's most successful foreign policy initiative was to assist in forging a peace treaty between Israel and Egypt. These age-old enemies had fought four wars since the creation of Israel in 1948. When their most recent conflict ended in 1973, a tense, bitter diplomatic stand-off ensued between the victorious Israelis and the defeated Egyptians.

In 1978 President Anwar el-Sadat of Egypt told American news reporter Walter Cronkite that he would do whatever he could to make peace with Israel. Carter then seized what he knew was a unique opportunity. In September of that year, Carter invited Israeli Prime Minister Menachem Begin and President Sadat to Camp David. For two weeks, Carter, Secretary of State Cyrus Vance, and others patiently talked the 2 leaders through their differences and tried to reconcile them. Finally Carter was able to make the historic announcement that the two leaders had constructed a "framework for peace." In March 1979, Begin and Sadat flew to Washington to sign the formal agreement in the White House.

The Iranian Hostage Crisis

In February 1979, Shah Mohammad Reza Pahlavi, the absolute ruler of Iran and a close ally of the United States, was deposed in a revolution sparked by extreme liberal and conservative Iranians. Iran's new leader, Muslim cleric Ayatollah Ruholla Khomeini, despised the United States for its political, financial, and military support of the Shah.

On November 4, an armed mob stormed the United States embassy in Tehran, the capital of Iran, and seized diplomats and military personnel. Angry and frustrated, Americans stared helplessly at their television screens while an angry, chanting Iranian mob set up a giant poster that defiantly proclaimed in English: U. S. Can Not Do Anything.

For many months, it seemed that the message on the Iranian poster told the truth. Finally, in April 1980, President Carter authorized a daring commando raid to rescue the hostages. The raid was a disaster for the United States. Encountering a violent dust storm over southern Iran, several of the helicopters ferrying the commandos to Tehran suffered mechanical failures. The raiders landed to assess the situation and decided to scrub the mission. As the commandos beat a hasty retreat from the Iranian desert, a helicopter collided with a cargo plane, killing 8 men and wounding 5.

Months later Carter agreed to release $8 billion in Iranian assets he had ordered "frozen" in the United States at the start of the crisis. It was not until January 20, 1981, President Ronald Reagan's Inauguration Day, that the hostages were freed.

A New Sense of Limits

Foreign Affairs and Economy Questioned

The United States's troubled economy and apparent weakening of power and influence in foreign affairs left many Americans worried and pessimistic about the future. Throughout the 1970s, Americans faced change in nearly every facet of their lives. The nation that had sent men to the moon, the nation where everything had seemed attainable, was developing an unfamiliar sense of limits.

The Polluting of America

A newly urgent concern for the environment typified this sense. Environmentalists warned that two forces were abusing and destroying the United States's natural resources. The first was governmental reluctance to curb unrestricted industrial growth and commercial development. The second was the greed of businesses that some claimed placed profit before responsibility. Environmental horror stories became front-page news. Birds hatched chicks deformed by severe genetic abnormalities. Commercial fishing crews returned from the deep oceans with catches contaminated by mercury and a wide variety of industrial chemicals. Oil spills fouled stretches of coastline with heavy crude that destroyed scenic beauty and sometimes killed the local wildlife.

Then in 1978 the problem hit home. The soil and groundwater of Love Canal, New York, a community near Niagara Falls, was found to be so polluted by poisonous chemicals from nearby industries that the Environmental Protection Agency (EPA) declared the entire town unfit for human habitation. The residents of Love Canal were evacuated, their homes boarded up, and the community sealed off by a tall, chain-link fence. The United States had its first toxic-waste ghost town.

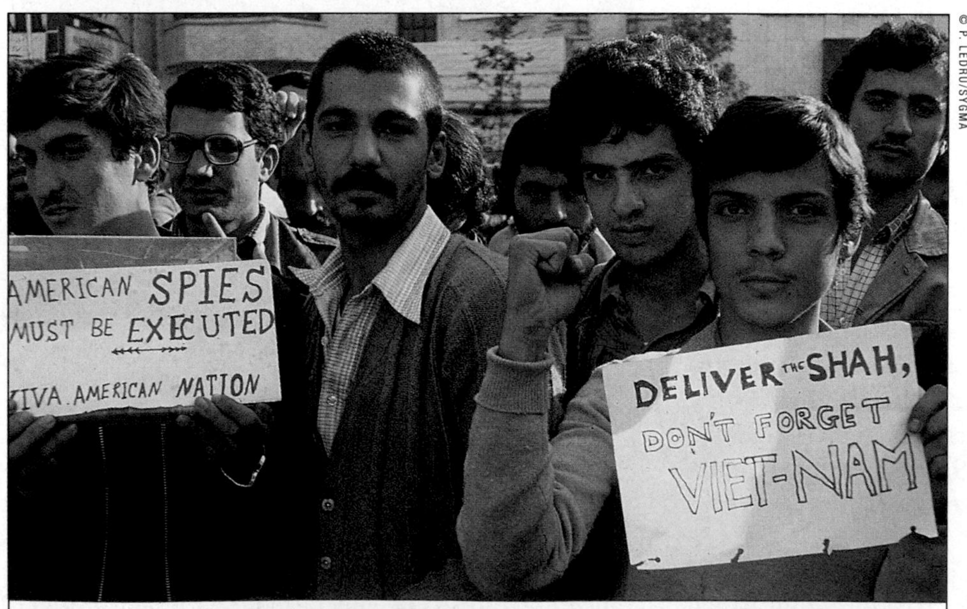

Anti-American Fervor **These young men wanted the Shah, who was in the United States seeking medical treatment, returned to Iran.** *Why was there anti-American feeling in Iran?*

© NEAL PALUMBO/GAMMA LIAISON

A Near Miss **The cooling towers of Three Mile Island loom large in this downtown scene of Goldsboro, Pennsylvania.**
What happened to the Unit 2 reactor during the nuclear accident?

Throughout the 1970s, legislation was proposed to protect the environment. Congress toughened air pollution standards and imposed strict regulations on the logging industry. In 1972 the government told business and industry that the release of toxic waste into United States waterways must stop by 1985. To further improve water quality, the EPA distributed $19 million to local governments for the construction of waste treatment plants. In 1978 Interior Secretary Cecil Andrus extended for 2 decades restrictions against development on 40 million acres of federal lands in Alaska. In addition President Carter placed more than 100 million acres of Alaskan land under the federal government's protection as national parks, national forests, and wildlife refuges.

The Nuclear Power Dilemma

Environmentalists also objected to the spread of nuclear power plants. Well-organized protesters appeared in every part of the country to condemn the construction and operation of the power plants. Although the protesters filed legal challenges, waged spirited public information campaigns, and sometimes resorted to civil disobedience, their concerns went largely unheeded—that is, until one fateful day in March 1979.

On that day a series of human and mechanical errors in the Unit 2 reactor of the Three Mile Island nuclear power station near Harrisburg, Pennsylvania, combined to produce the worst nuclear power accident in United States history. The reactor's core overheated, releasing radioactive water and steam. Fearing a massive release of radiation, officials evacuated 100,000 nearby residents. The disaster never came, but the Unit 2 reactor, littered with radioactive debris, was shut down.

The nuclear dilemma typified the difficult 1970s, a decade in which every advance harbored a setback and every promise included a threat. Looking back, some observers believe the decade forced a fundamental change in the American outlook, described by economist Robert Lekachman as "a shift from the easy politics of growth to the era of limits."

SECTION ASSESSMENT

Main Idea

1. Use a chart like this one to show the foreign and domestic challenges faced by Ford and Carter. Place a check mark next to any challenge that you think they resolved successfully.

Challenges	Ford	Carter
Domestic		
Foreign		

Vocabulary

2. Define: inflation, stagflation, embargo, recession, human rights, dissident.

Checking Facts

3. What happened during the OPEC oil embargo?
4. What happened to the economy during the Ford administration?

Critical Thinking

5. **Determining Cause and Effect** What caused Americans to see limits on the power and stature of the United States?

Science, TECHNOLOGY, and Society

Outer Space to the Kitchen

After the Soviet Union launched *Sputnik,* the first artificial satellite, politics drove the space race. As scientists overcame technological barriers, and political tensions between the United States and the Soviets eased, much of what was learned from space research began to make its way into our everyday lives. Scientists continue working to make outer space more habitable.

SPACE FOOD

The need for lightweight, nutritious food for astronauts led to the development of the freeze-drying process and to the improved packaging and processing methods for many of our foods today.

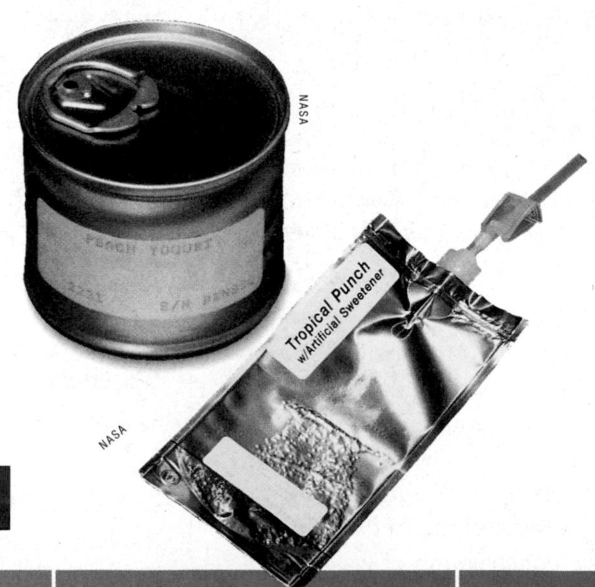

STEPS INTO SPACE

1950s	1960s	1970s
SPACE RACE BEGINS The Soviets launch *Sputnik* and put the first animal into orbit. National Aeronautics and Space Administration is established.	**MEN IN SPACE** Soviet Yuri Gagarin is first human in space; Alan Shepard is the first American in space; *Apollo 11* lands men on the moon.	**SPACE EXPLORATION** First U.S. space station, *Skylab,* launched. *Viking* space probes reach Mars. First U.S.-Soviet mission, *Apollo-Soyuz,* launched.

FIRST SPACE WALK

Edward H. White, the first American to walk in space, floats outside his *Gemini 4* spacecraft. He had to fire a maneuvering gun to move around in the zero gravity during this 1965 mission.

NASA

SYNTHETIC SOIL

Researchers are developing synthetic soil to use in growing plants as part of a recyclable life support system in a future spacecraft.

NASA

SPACE RACE SPINOFFS

Research other applications of space technology that have made their way into workplaces, homes, hospitals, or the entertainment industry. Try to include illustrations in the report. Be sure to place this work in your portfolio.

WRITING UNDER WATER

The pen used here was originally developed for NASA astronaut record keeping on Apollo missions. Its special cartridge allows ink to flow regardless of gravity or atmospheric pressure.

1980s

WORKSHOPS IN SPACE The first United States reusable spacecraft, the shuttle *Columbia,* orbits the earth for the first time. Sally Ride becomes the first American woman in space.

1990s

EXPANDING FRONTIERS Hubble Space Telescope, an orbiting observatory, is launched with a 15-year lifetime in space. Launch of the space probe *Cassini* to Saturn.

2000s

INTERNATIONAL SPACE STATION Permanent crew members move to the space station, built through the cooperation of 16 nations, to conduct scientific research.

Chapter  Assessment

Self-Check Quiz

Visit the *American Odyssey* Web site at americanodyssey.glencoe.com and click on ***Chapter 24—Self-Check Quiz*** to prepare for the Chapter Test.

Reviewing Key Terms

Match the key term below with the phrase that best defines its meaning. Write the word and the appropriate phrase on a separate sheet of paper.

détente	**realpolitik**
recession	**revenue sharing**
impeachment	**silent majority**

1. an accusation, a charge against

2. a plan where the federal government returns some tax money back to the states

3. "forgotten" Americans who did not protest the war

4. an attempt to repair relations with China and the Soviet Union

5. an economic slowdown

Recalling Facts

1. Identify some events and policies that helped bring about the conservative backlash of the late 1960s.

2. Name two Democratic-sponsored pieces of legislation that Nixon supported and signed into law.

3. Give two examples of conservative policies Nixon implemented.

4. Name the four Supreme Court justices President Nixon appointed.

5. Identify Henry Kissinger. Describe the various roles he held in the Nixon administration.

6. Explain why President Nixon was eager to implement a policy of détente with the People's Republic of China and the Soviet Union.

7. Briefly explain the United States policy of interventionism in Latin America. Give an example.

8. Give three examples of Nixon's unlawful exercise of the power of his office.

9. Describe what happened in the Saturday Night Massacre. Who was involved?

10. Briefly explain how the impeachment process works according to the Constitution.

11. What is OPEC? Describe how it contributed to the economic problems of the United States in the 1970s.

12. What were some of the basic beliefs that drove President Carter's foreign policy?

13. Why were the Camp David Accords so important?

14. How did the Iranian hostage crisis hurt the Carter administration?

15. Name two environmental crises that took place during the Carter administration.

Critical Thinking

1. Making Generalizations Use a diagram like this one to make and support a generalization about Nixon's view of the presidency and the power given to that office.

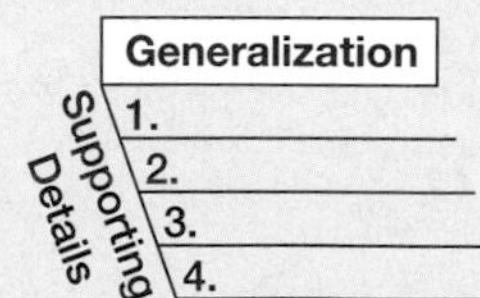

2. Making Comparisons Two segments of society with different values disagreed over the Vietnam War. Compare how the silent majority and social protesters felt about the issues of patriotism and law and order.

3. Analyzing Decisions How did Nixon's belief in realpolitik influence decisions he made about the Soviet Union and the People's Republic of China?

4. Determining Cause and Effect What actions of the Nixon administration caused Congress to enact the War Powers Act and the Congressional Budget and Impoundment Act?

Portfolio Project

List five qualities you think a President should possess. If you were able to vote tomorrow, what three domestic issues would concern you the most? What three global issues would concern you? Write an essay to explain how you would determine your choice if no candidate held your views on all issues.

Cooperative Learning

The Vietnam War polarized U.S. citizens. Work in small groups to identify a social or political issue today that deeply divides people. Each group should then report their issue to the class. Try not to duplicate any issues another group has worked on. The groups should also research each side of their selected topic and prepare a report to share with the class. As you prepare your reports, be sure to give each side of the issue equal conviction.

Reinforcing Skills

Interpreting Political Cartoons

Locate a political cartoon in your local newspaper or in a national news magazine. Identify the main issue addressed by the cartoon and the techniques used by the cartoonist to influence people's opinion of this issue. Share your findings with the rest of the class.

GEOGRAPHY AND HISTORY

Phoenix, Arizona, 1950–1994

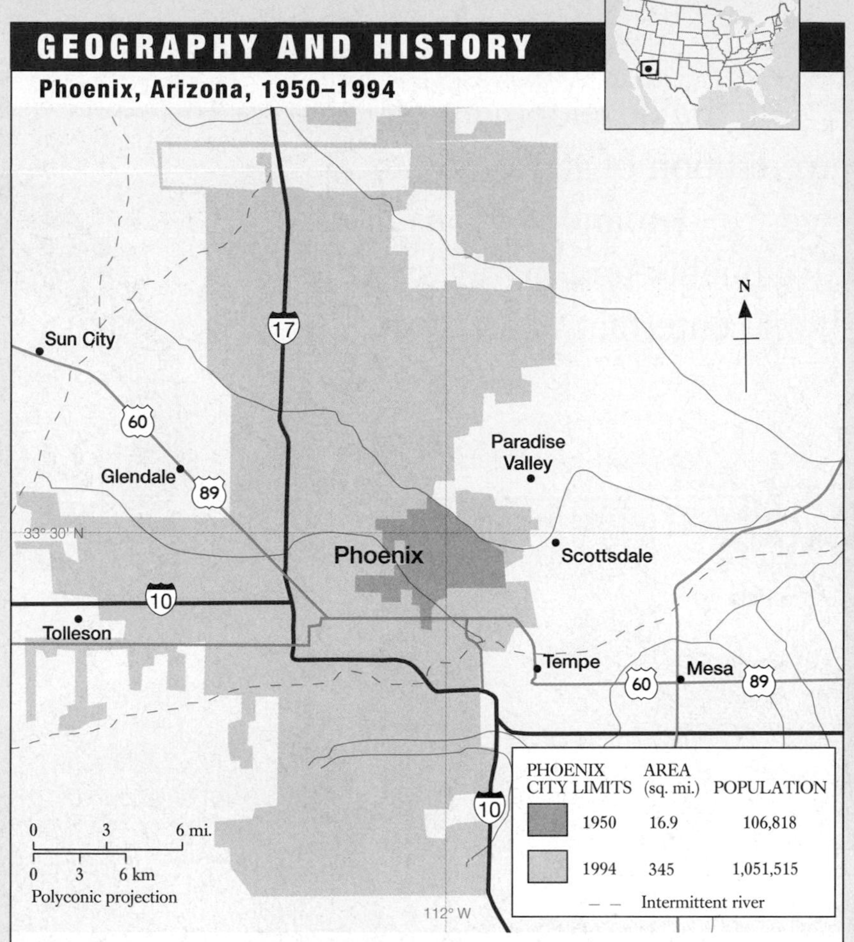

Study the map to answer the following questions.

1. How large was the growth in square miles in the Phoenix area between 1950 and 1994?
2. How much did the population of Phoenix increase from 1950 to 1994?
3. In which direction did the city undergo the largest area of growth?
4. Beyond the city limits of Phoenix, where do you think population will increase?

Technology Activity

Using a Word Processor The Freedom of Information Act of 1974 allowed public access to many government records. Before 1974 and prior to the abuses of the CIA and FBI in the 1970s, those records were kept secret. Research how to use the Freedom of Information Act to examine government records. Then, using your word processor, write a step-by-step guide explaining the procedure.

Standardized Test Practice

1. **The purpose of the War Powers Act, passed in 1973, was to ensure that the President would**

   A have greater authority over the military.
   B consult Congress before committing troops to extended conflicts.
   C have the authority to sign treaties without Senate approval.
   D have a freer hand in fighting the spread of communism.

> ***Test-Taking Tip:*** The War Powers Act was partly a reaction to the Vietnam War and to Watergate. Congress wanted to make sure the President was not becoming too powerful in relation to the other branches. Three of the answers actually do the *opposite*—they give the President *more* power. Which choice limits presidential power?

2. **As a political conservative, President Nixon wanted to**

   A increase federal welfare programs.
   B speed the desegregation process.
   C return power to state governments.
   D appoint reform-minded Supreme Court justices.

> ***Test-Taking Tip:*** Think of the meaning of *political conservative:* someone who generally believes the government role in society should be limited and that individuals should be responsible for their own well-being. Choose the answer that would *best* accomplish this goal.

Then...

The Stereo

The popularity of rock 'n' roll, the development of stereo records, and the introduction of stereo sound in radio broadcasting all fueled the demand for consumer products that could produce quality and higher volume sound. A new industry—home entertainment—was born during the 1960s.

1 A component stereo system in the 1960s had at least 6 separate units, which made it bulky, heavy, potentially confusing to assemble, and often visually unattractive.

© ROY DOTY, COURTESY POPULAR SCIENCE

Fun Facts

FILE PHOTO BY RALPH J. BRUNKE

MUSIC MAKES MONEY

By the 1980s the recording industry employed nearly 31,990 men and women and had total annual sales of nearly $4 billion.

2 **A 1960s turntable (shown right) was one unit of a component stereo system. Its parts were the drive system, the stylus, the cartridge, and the tone-arm. Other components of a stereo included an amplifier and speakers or headphones.**

FILE PHOTO BY DOUG MINDELL

DR. JEREMY BURGESS/SCIENCE PHOTO LIBRARY

3 **The waves in the grooves of a record make the stylus, or needle, vibrate. An enlarged image of this part is shown above. The vibrations then become electric signals that the speakers or headphones change into sound.**

Stats

RECORDS

A long-playing vinyl record (LP) is 12 inches in diameter.

An LP plays at $33\frac{1}{3}$ rpm (revolutions per minute) and has about 30 minutes of sound on each side.

There are about 250 grooves per inch on an LP.

COSTS

In 1968 a stereo LP cost $4.98; a monaural LP cost $3.98.

The average price for a stereo component system in 1969 was about $200.

SALES

Record sales for 1968 were $1.1 billion.

In 1975 there were 73 million phonographs in the United States.

...Now

MUSIC TO YOUR EARS

PORTFOLIO PROJECT

Write a brief report on the different ways music can be played in the home. Compare contemporary systems with those available during the years covered in this unit. Compare them in terms of cost, technology, quality, and portability. Be sure to include this report in your portfolio.

SUPERSTOCK

SOUND IN EVERY SHAPE AND SIZE

A console stereo system was available in a variety of shapes and designs—it could look like a fireplace, a cube, a grandfather clock, a tea cart, or a chest. Some were even shaped like hexagons!

ARCHIVE PHOTOS

UNIT
10

New Challenges

1980–Present

HISTORY & YOU

The United States witnessed sweeping changes as the 20th century drew to a close. The collapse of Soviet communism ended the cold war and ushered in a new world order. A series of regional crises challenged the nation to reexamine its role in world affairs, its commitment to human rights, and its willingness to adopt a global outlook. The leaders who guided the nation into the 21st century grappled with ways to protect the economic well-being of all Americans and to prevent the abuses of power that can infringe on freedom.

Primary Sources
Library

See pages 968–969 for primary source readings that accompany Unit 10.

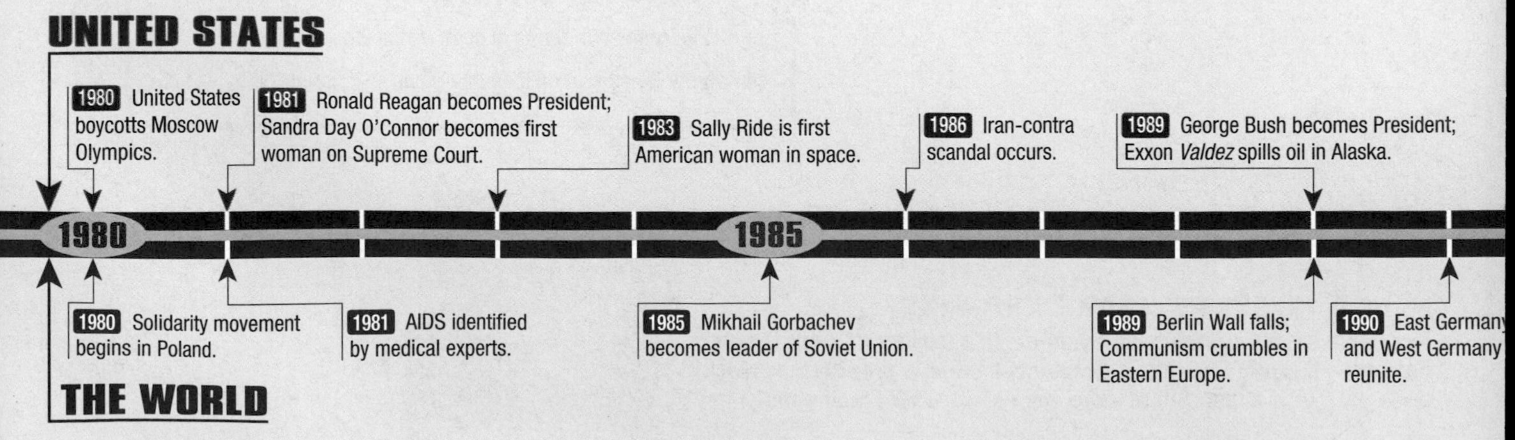
UNITED STATES
1980 United States boycotts Moscow Olympics.
1981 Ronald Reagan becomes President; Sandra Day O'Connor becomes first woman on Supreme Court.
1983 Sally Ride is first American woman in space.
1986 Iran-contra scandal occurs.
1989 George Bush becomes President; Exxon *Valdez* spills oil in Alaska.
1980
1985
1980 Solidarity movement begins in Poland.
1981 AIDS identified by medical experts.
1985 Mikhail Gorbachev becomes leader of Soviet Union.
1989 Berlin Wall falls; Communism crumbles in Eastern Europe.
1990 East Germany and West Germany reunite.
THE WORLD

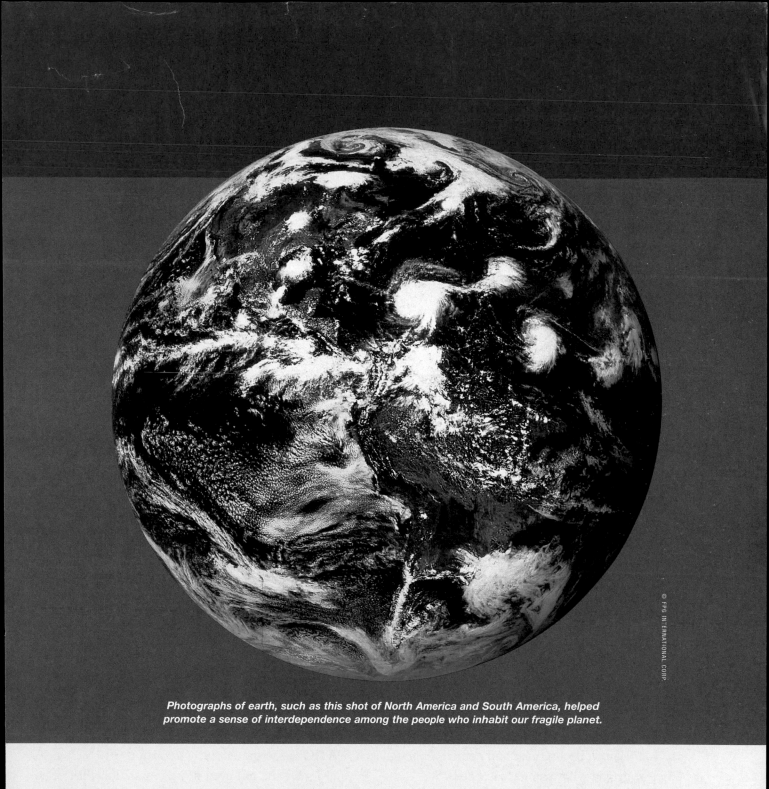

Photographs of earth, such as this shot of North America and South America, helped promote a sense of interdependence among the people who inhabit our fragile planet.

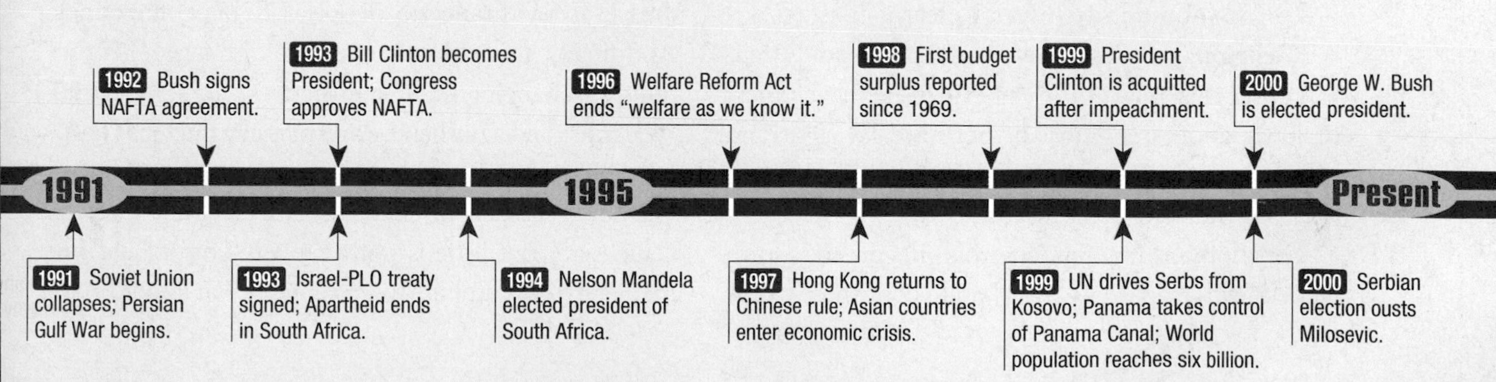

1992 Bush signs NAFTA agreement.
1993 Bill Clinton becomes President; Congress approves NAFTA.
1996 Welfare Reform Act ends "welfare as we know it."
1998 First budget surplus reported since 1969.
1999 President Clinton is acquitted after impeachment.
2000 George W. Bush is elected president.
1991
1995
Present
1991 Soviet Union collapses; Persian Gulf War begins.
1993 Israel-PLO treaty signed; Apartheid ends in South Africa.
1994 Nelson Mandela elected president of South Africa.
1997 Hong Kong returns to Chinese rule; Asian countries enter economic crisis.
1999 UN drives Serbs from Kosovo; Panama takes control of Panama Canal; World population reaches six billion.
2000 Serbian election ousts Milosevic.

"Double Face"

FROM *THE JOY LUCK CLUB* BY AMY TAN

The United States is a nation of immigrants who came in search of new opportunities. Throughout our history immigrants have faced the same dilemma: how to preserve their language and culture in the face of pressure to adapt to a new society. The narrator in the following selection explores differences between her Chinese culture and the culture of her new country.

THE KOBAL COLLECTION

Mothers and Daughters **These characters in the movie *The Joy Luck Club* face problems related to preserving their heritage and adapting to American ways.**

It's hard to keep your Chinese face in America. At the beginning, before I even arrived, I had to hide my true self. I paid an American-raised Chinese girl in Peking to show me how.

"In America," she said, "you cannot say you want to live there forever. If you are Chinese, you must say you admire their schools, their ways of thinking. You must say you want to be a scholar and come back to teach Chinese people what you have learned."

"What should I say I want to learn?" I asked. . . .

"Religion, you must say you want to study religion," said this smart girl. "Americans all have different ideas about religion, so there are no right and wrong answers. Say to them, I'm going for God's sake, and they will respect you."

For another sum of money, this girl gave me a form filled out with English words. I had to copy these words over and over again as if they were English words formed from my own head. Next to the word NAME, I wrote *Lindo Sun.* Next to the word BIRTHDATE, I wrote *May 11, 1918,* which this girl insisted was the same as three months after the Chinese lunar new year. Next to the word BIRTHPLACE, I put down *Taiyuan, China.* And next to the word OCCUPATION, I wrote *student of theology.*

I gave the girl even more money for a list of addresses in San Francisco, people with big connections. And finally, this girl gave me, free of charge, instructions for changing my circumstances. "First," she said, "you must find a husband. An American citizen is best."

She saw my surprise and quickly added, "Chinese! Of course, he must be Chinese. 'Citizen' does not mean Caucasian. But if he is not a citizen, you should immediately do number two. See here, you should have a baby. Boy or girl, it doesn't matter in the United States. Neither will take care of you in your old age, isn't that true?" And we both laughed.

"Be careful, though," she said. "The authorities there will ask you if you have children now or if you are thinking of having some. You must say no. You should look sincere and say you are not married, you are religious, you know it is wrong to have a baby."

I must have looked puzzled, because she explained further: "Look here now, how can an unborn baby know what it is not supposed to do? And once it has arrived, it is an American citizen and can do anything it wants. It can ask its mother to stay. Isn't that true?"

But that is not the reason I was puzzled. I wondered why she said I should look sincere. How could I look any other way when telling the truth?

See how truthful my face still looks. Why didn't I give this look to you? Why do you always tell your friends that I arrived in the United States on a slow boat from China? This is not true. I was not that poor. I took a plane. I had saved the money my first husband's family gave me when they sent me away. And I had saved money from my twelve years' work as a telephone operator. But it is true I did not take the fastest plane. The plane took three weeks. It stopped everywhere: Hong Kong, Vietnam, the Philippines, Hawaii. So by the time I arrived, I did not look sincerely glad to be here.

Why do you always tell people that I met your father in the Cathay House, that I broke open a fortune cookie and it said I would marry a dark, handsome stranger, and that when I looked up, there he was, the waiter, your father. Why do you make this joke? This is not sincere. This was not true! Your father was not a waiter, I never ate in that restaurant. The Cathay House had a sign that said "Chinese Food," so only Americans went there before it was torn down. Now it is a McDonald's restaurant with a big Chinese sign that says *mai dong lou*–"wheat," "east," "building." All nonsense. Why are you attracted only to Chinese nonsense? You must understand my real circumstances, how I arrived, how I married, how I lost my Chinese face, why you are the way you are.

When I arrived, nobody asked me questions. The authorities looked at my papers and stamped me in. I decided to go first to a San Francisco address given to me by this girl in Peking. The bus put me down on a wide street with cable cars. This was California Street. I walked up this hill and then I saw a tall building. This was Old St. Mary's. Under the church sign, in handwritten Chinese characters, someone had added: "A Chinese Ceremony to Save Ghosts from Spiritual Unrest 7 A.M. and 8:30 A.M." I memorized this information in case the authorities asked me where I worshipped my religion. And then I saw another sign across the street. It was painted on the outside of a short building: "Save Today for Tomorrow, at Bank of America." And I thought to myself, This is where American people worship. See, even then I was not so dumb! Today that church is the same size, but where that short bank used to be, now there is a tall building, fifty stories high, where you and your husband-to-be work and look down on everybody.

> **"SAVE TODAY FOR TOMORROW, AT BANK OF AMERICA." I THOUGHT TO MYSELF, THIS IS WHERE AMERICANS WORSHIP.**

My daughter laughed when I said this. Her mother can make a good joke.

Responding to Literature

1. **What did Lindo Sun do to prepare herself for her move to the United States? How well did it prepare her?**
2. **Explain why this passage from Amy Tan's book is called "Double Face."**

The Reagan and Bush Years

NOVEMBER 13, 1979: RONALD REAGAN DECLARES HIMSELF A CANDIDATE FOR PRESIDENT

The New York Hilton banquet hall glittered with diamonds at the $500-per-plate dinner that launched Ronald Reagan's third try for the presidency. Far from California where he had been an actor and governor, Reagan wanted to prove that he appealed to the entire nation.

Throughout his campaign, Reagan implied that life had been better in an earlier time. People were good. They believed in family and trusted in God. They stood on their own two feet. People might have been poor, as Reagan had been, but with hard work and a bit of luck, a person could still achieve the American dream.

Such a simple, sturdy United States was part myth, part reality. The future President's poignant picture of it, though oversimplified, tapped into a deep longing in Americans who were weary of the turmoil of the 1960s and 1970s and frightened by declining economic fortunes at home and reduced political and military influence abroad. ■

HISTORY JOURNAL

Why do you think many Americans found Ronald Reagan appealing? Write down your thoughts about whether his popularity would last throughout his presidency.

Chapter Overview

Visit the *American Odyssey* Web site at americanodyssey.glencoe.com and click on ***Chapter 25—Chapter Overview*** to preview the chapter.

UPI/BETTMANN

Ronald and Nancy Reagan waltz during the dinner at which Reagan declared himself a candidate for President.

The Reagan Revolution

JANUARY 20, 1981: AMERICAN HOSTAGES LEAVE TEHRAN

YOUNG ISLAMIC MILITANTS CALLED OUT INSULTS AS AMERICAN HOSTAGES, STILL BLINDFOLDED, WERE LED OUT ONTO THE TARMAC AT THE TEHRAN AIRPORT. The 52 captives climbed into an Algerian 727 that waited there to carry them on the first leg of a journey that would return them to the United States after 444 days in captivity.

After what seemed like endless delays, the plane rose into the blue desert sky above Iran. Bill Belk, one of the captives, remembers, "When the wheels lifted off the runway there was a great shout of rejoicing. 'We are off! We are free!' I think lifting off of that runway was the greatest thrill of my entire life. It was a moment of pure joy." The time was 12:25 P.M. Eastern Standard Time.

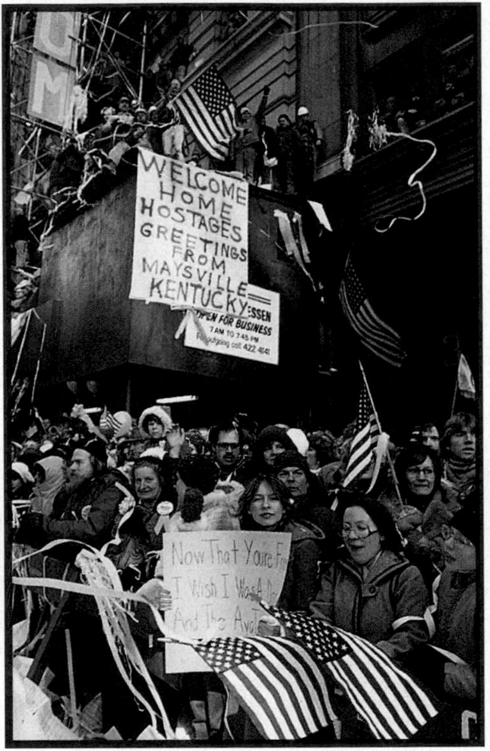

© DIEGO GOLDBERG/SYGMA

Released!
Jubilant crowds welcome the released hostages home.

The sequence of events could not have been better for Ronald Reagan. At the exact moment the plane became airborne, the newly elected President was concluding his Inaugural Address in Washington, D.C. One hour later, when he was sure the plane had cleared Iranian airspace, the new President announced the happy news that the nation had waited so long to hear.

The freeing of the hostages and the swearing in of the fortieth President marked an important shift for the nation. Many hoped the United States was leaving behind the self-doubt and indecisiveness of the post-Vietnam years and entering a new era. To them it looked as though it would be "morning in America" again as candidate Reagan had promised.

GUIDE TO READING

Main Idea

Reagan's personal appeal and his views on limited government won him the popular support to pursue a conservative vision for America.

Vocabulary

- mandate
- neoconservatism
- supply-side economics
- deregulate

Read to Find Out . . .

- the political and religious coalition that brought Reagan to the presidency.
- how Reaganomics affected the economy.
- the successes and shortcomings of the "Reagan revolution."

A Broad New Coalition

Neoconservatives, the Religious Right, and Reagan

Reagan's race for the presidency came at a time when the country's mood was changing. Many Americans were unsympathetic to the protest movements and boisterous freedoms of the 1960s and the expensive social programs of the 1970s. A powerful conservative groundswell had been building momentum for years.

The changing mood of the country found its voice in Reagan. He received support from nearly all segments of American society: Democrats and Republicans, the rich and the poor, insiders as well as outsiders. This broad-based support swept Reagan into office with a **mandate**—an order from the voters—to make changes in the way the nation was run. The people were eager for Reagan to deliver on his promise to "get the government off people's backs" and restore the old-fashioned virtues of the heartland.

A New Conservatism

As the 1980s began, many conservative Americans believed that government had grown too large in the 1960s and 1970s. They challenged the central beliefs of liberalism: that a fair and equal society can be achieved and that government ought to play a major role in guaranteeing and regulating it. These conservatives believed that the government had spent too much of the taxpayers' money; created bloated, inefficient bureaucracies; and kept the economy from flourishing on its own.

Reagan's appeal most attracted those Americans who were convinced that some problems just could not be solved by the government and must simply be accepted. Government, they believed, should withdraw from most areas of American life, and people should behave with more restraint. Businesses, in particular, should be freed from government restraint so they could become more profitable and thus strengthen the country. This was **neoconservatism,** a new type of conservatism. It signaled a return to the type of conservative thinking that was popular in the early years of the 1900s.

The Religious Right

Neoconservatism was not the only new doctrine to gain favor during the 1970s. When President Carter proclaimed himself "born-again," he spotlighted a major trend in American culture—the emergence of evangelical Christianity as a powerful religious and political force.

The most recent wave of evangelism began in the 1950s with the spiritual crusades of the Reverend Billy Graham. The movement grew rapidly in the 1960s and 1970s with the advent of television ministers—dubbed televangelists—who preached to huge home audiences via television. By the middle of the 1970s, as many as 70 million Americans identified themselves as born-again.

The Religious Right The Reverend Jerry Falwell, leader of the Moral Majority, becomes a force in national elections. *What beliefs did Falwell and other members of the Moral Majority favor that influenced the election of 1980?*

In contrast to Jimmy Carter, a moderate political liberal, many evangelicals saw their religious zeal reflected in political conservatism. Like conservatives, they were morally opposed to drugs, pornography, and abortion. They firmly rejected liberal social policies and strongly favored free enterprise and a foreign policy backed up by a strong military.

During the 1980 presidential campaign, a California-based group called Christian Voice flooded the Midwest and the South with political literature. Their candidate was Ronald Reagan. Through Reagan, the evangelicals believed, biblical principles could become law.

One of the most effective political organizations of the religious right was the Moral Majority, founded in 1979 by another televangelist, the Reverend Jerry Falwell. In a little over a year, the Moral Majority registered between 2 and 3 million new voters. Falwell and his associates enjoyed the confidence of President Reagan and exerted powerful political influence—that is, until the organization was disbanded in 1989. This followed a series of scandals and financial wrongdoings within other groups of the religious right that, in the minds of many Americans, had discredited the moral force of the entire movement.

Shifting Political Allegiance

Ronald Reagan's triumph over President Carter was much more than a victory for neoconservatism and the religious right. It also represented a reshuffling of many historic voting patterns in the United States.

Reagan captured 44 of the 50 states, giving him 489 electoral votes to Carter's 49. The Republicans also captured the Senate. This landslide was primarily due to the force of Reagan's personality. Many voters simply liked him as a person, and they had enormous confidence in Reagan's ability to cure the nation's ills.

Reagan ran strongly in the West and the Southwest, where Republicans usually do well. He also captured the industrial states around the Great Lakes and in the Northeast, which had become Democratic strongholds. In those states, his supporters were mostly blue-collar and ethnic voters who responded to his pledges to revive the economy, fight communism, and oppose abortion. The South was another Democratic stronghold. Yet Reagan, boosted by his support from the religious right, won every Southern state except Carter's home state of Georgia. Many older voters also viewed the 69-year-old Reagan as a politician who would be sensitive to their needs.

Reagan + Economics = Reaganomics

Balanced Budget Pledge Not Achieved

Ever since the 1930s, most American Presidents had subscribed to the ideas of British economist John Maynard Keynes. Keynes believed that the key to stimulating an economy was government spending, which often required higher taxes.

President Ronald Reagan and his economic advisers replaced this approach with what was called **supply-side economics.** According to this theory, the key to economic vitality was reducing taxes, especially those on wealthy individuals and large corporations. Lower taxes would encourage more saving and investment, which would lead to business expansion and more jobs. The result would be a larger supply of goods for consumers who, thanks to tax cuts, now had more money to spend.

Within months of taking office, Reagan got Congress to approve one of his biggest campaign promises: a major reduction of income taxes that favored, above all, the wealthiest Americans. That raised a tough question. Lower taxes meant less money flowing into the Treasury, but Reagan was also sharply increasing military spending. How was he going to balance the budget, as he had also promised voters?

His answer was to chip away at domestic programs. Welfare benefits were cut, and a million recipients of food stamps were removed from the government rolls. Fewer government programs were available to revitalize big cities and pay for children's meals in the nation's public schools. Medicare benefits were slashed, requiring the elderly to pay more for health care, and unemployment compensation was reduced.

Most of the scaled-down programs had grown out of the liberal social agenda that had dominated presidential and congressional politics for decades. Cutting them back fit Reagan's conservative view that the government should be less involved in the lives of its people, even those people who needed help.

★ ★ ★ **GALLERY OF PRESIDENTS** ★ ★ ★

Ronald Reagan

1981–1989

"We are a nation that has a government—not the other way around. And this makes us special among the nations of the Earth. Our government has no power except that granted it by the people. It is time to check and reverse the growth of government which shows signs of having grown beyond the consent of the governed."

Inaugural Address, January 20, 1981

AP/WIDE WORLD PHOTOS

BACKGROUND

- **Born 1911**
- **Republican, California**
- **Governor of California, 1967–1975**

ACHIEVEMENTS IN OFFICE

- **Economic Recovery Tax Act (1981)**
- **Proposal for SDI (1983)**
- **INF Treaty with the Soviet Union (1987)**
- **Three appointments to the Supreme Court**

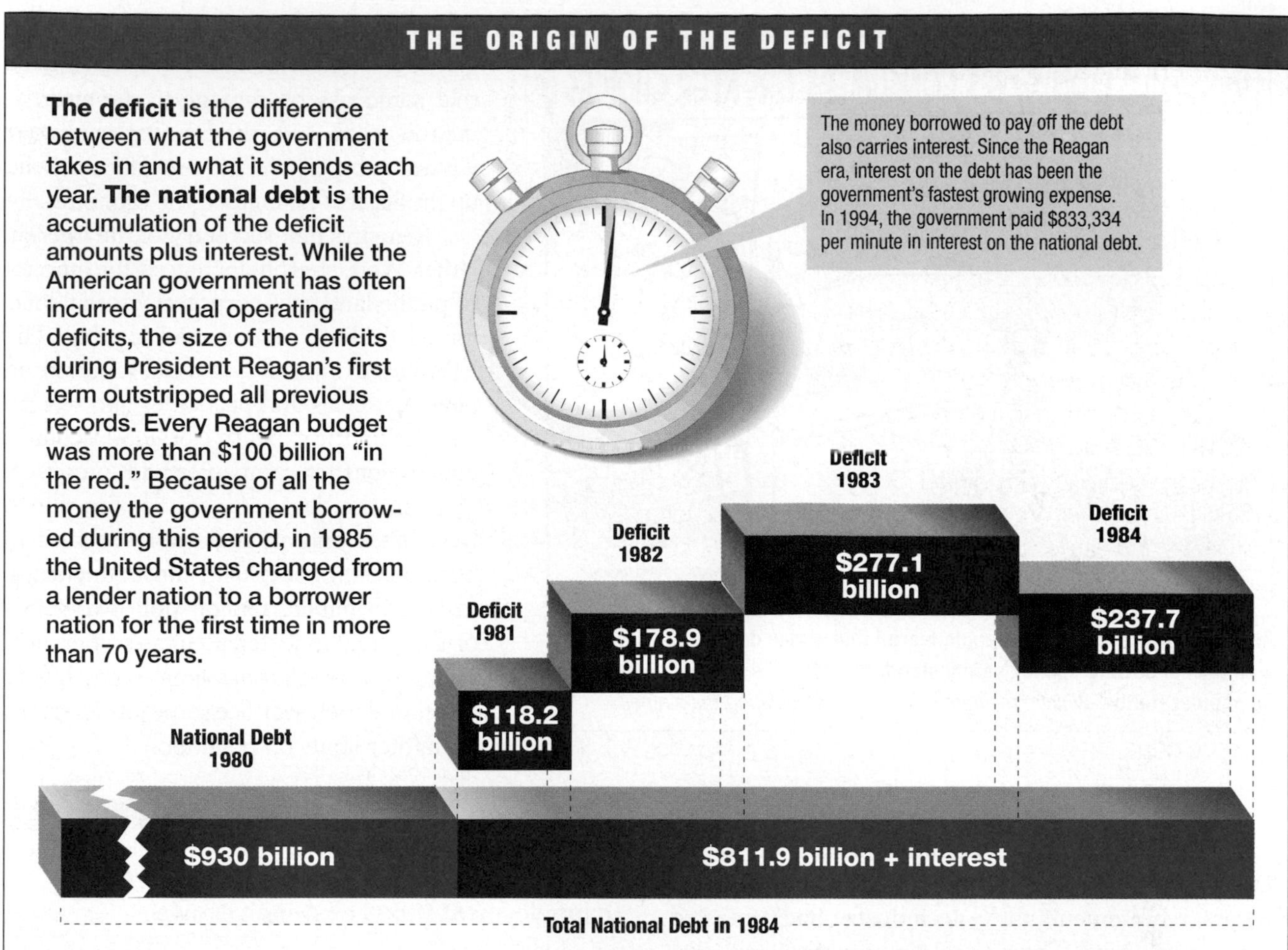

THE ORIGIN OF THE DEFICIT
The deficit is the difference between what the government takes in and what it spends each year. **The national debt** is the accumulation of the deficit amounts plus interest. While the American government has often incurred annual operating deficits, the size of the deficits during President Reagan's first term outstripped all previous records. Every Reagan budget was more than $100 billion "in the red." Because of all the money the government borrowed during this period, in 1985 the United States changed from a lender nation to a borrower nation for the first time in more than 70 years.
The money borrowed to pay off the debt also carries interest. Since the Reagan era, interest on the debt has been the government's fastest growing expense. In 1994, the government paid $833,334 per minute in interest on the national debt.
Deficit 1981
$118.2 billion
Deficit 1982
$178.9 billion
Deficit 1983
$277.1 billion
Deficit 1984
$237.7 billion
National Debt 1980
$930 billion
$811.9 billion + interest
Total National Debt in 1984

Reagan's economic policies halted runaway inflation and unemployment. At the same time, government spending (mostly on defense) outpaced revenues. The resulting deficit made people wonder if the prosperity of the Reagan years was built on borrowed money. *When did consumers see the benefits of Reaganomics?*

Recession and Recovery

Reagan's economic policies, dubbed Reaganomics, sparked a radical change in government fiscal policy. The policies succeeded in controlling the double-digit inflation of the Carter years. High interest rates, however, prevented many Americans from borrowing the money to make major purchases or expand businesses.

The nation slumped into another severe 2-year recession as productivity declined. A third of the nation's factories and mines stood idle. Detroit's auto sales plunged to their lowest levels in 2 decades. By late 1982, 10 percent of the labor force, or about 11 million people, were out of work—the greatest number since 1940.

Many farmers and businesspeople were caught in a bind. They had taken out loans at high interest rates during the 1970s, when prices were high. Now, with income down, they could not make their payments.

Many farmers lost their farms, and business bankruptcies skyrocketed. During a single week in August 1982, a record 572 businesses failed, the highest weekly total since the Great Depression.

By the end of 1982, the tide turned. Interest rates dropped to about half of the all-time high of 21.5 percent that they had hit in 1981. With interest rates falling, companies could afford to invest again. With inflation edging down, people could keep more of their tax cuts and buy houses, cars, and smaller consumer items.

Unemployment was still above 9 percent in 1983, but increased business activity did create more jobs. Productivity turned upward. A cycle of growth was restored. In 1984 the gross national product increased by more than 9 percent, the biggest 1-year gain since 1951.

The Drive to Deregulate

In Reagan's view government red tape hamstrung business and industry, kept companies less profitable, and ultimately weakened the American economy.

Reagan signaled that his administration would **deregulate,** giving companies more leeway to operate freely. He set up a task force to advise him on how to ease regulations and to find appropriate people to work in the federal agencies that watched over various industries.

DEREGULATION GIVES CONSUMERS GREATER CHOICES
... AND WOULD YOU FOLKS LIKE MAINTENANCE OR NO MAINTENANCE?
ROULETTE AIR
LET US TAKE YOU FOR A SPIN
WASSERMAN
©'87 THE BOSTON GLOBE
DIST. BY L.A. TIMES SYNDICATE

DAN WASSERMAN/COURTESY BOSTON GLOBE

Airline Deregulation Some people feared that airline deregulation would lead to cost cutting and lax safety standards; others welcomed lower prices on popular routes. *Which President first began deregulating the airlines?*

To the environmentalists' dismay, Reagan often sided with business. He suggested that some risk or damage to the environment was the price the country had to pay if it wanted companies to provide jobs, build up profits, and strengthen the economy.

Reagan's first secretary of the interior, James Watt, sharply increased the amount of public land that corporations could use for oil drilling, mining, and logging. The EPA eased the safety checks required on new chemicals and pesticides and relaxed its rules on the expensive pollution-control equipment that companies had to use.

On the issue of the environment, Reagan's economic philosophy seemed to put him out of step with most Americans. In a 1985 public opinion poll, two-thirds of the public rejected Reagan's approach, saying they would be willing to pay higher prices and even sacrifice some jobs in return for tighter limits on pollution.

Soon the new approach took effect. The National Highway Traffic Safety Administration slowed its demands for air bags and tighter fuel-efficiency standards for cars, requirements the auto industry had protested were too expensive. The Federal Communications Commission took a hands-off attitude toward cable television, allowing almost unrestricted growth in that new field.

At the direction of President Carter, Congress had begun to free the airline industry of regulations controlling its fares and routes. The Reagan administration encouraged the process. Passengers reaped a bonanza of additional flights and cheaper fares as the airlines cut into one another's territory and waged bruising price wars. Away from the big cities, however, the effect was that some small communities lost service altogether.

The Environmental Rearguard

The restrictions that Reagan lifted from American industry were not all just red tape. Many laws tried to curb pollution and regulate the disposal of dangerous wastes. Thus Reagan's deregulation policy ran counter to the environmental movement of the 1970s.

Student Web Activity 25

Visit the *American Odyssey* Web site at americanodyssey.glencoe.com and click on ***Chapter 25—Student Web Activities*** for an activity relating to the Reagan era.

The Reagan Legacy

Unemployment Drops as Deficit Grows

In many ways Reagan's leadership and popularity unified the nation. Many of his policies, however, increased long-standing divisions. Strains were showing between different economic and racial groups as well as between conservatives and liberals.

Successes of the Revolution

Although some people opposed President Reagan's proposals, he had personal qualities that helped to promote his positions: a great ability to communicate with his audience and a sense of humor. For many people he represented a restored faith in the American way of life.

As the economy recovered from the 1982 recession, the President's popularity soared. The inflation rate dropped just as the 25 percent cut in income taxes was putting more money into the hands of consumers. Feeling new confidence in the economy, Americans made purchases they had put off during the recession. Sales of every type of goods and service shot upward, and industries hired back workers who had been laid off. By the end of Reagan's second term in 1988, unemployment had dropped to 5.5 percent—the lowest in 14 years.

To celebrate, President Reagan went before Congress in 1984 saying, "America is back—standing tall, looking to the '80s with courage, confidence, and hope. . . . Send away the hand-wringers and doubting Thomases."

Shortcomings of the Revolution

The Reagan revolution, however, did not benefit all Americans equally. Although the tax cuts benefited everybody, they benefited the rich most of all. At the same time, the cuts in social programs drove some of those at the bottom of the economy deeper into poverty, creating what social scientists called a new urban underclass.

Reagan's pro-family philosophy had appealed to many women voters in the 1980 election. Increasingly, however, Reagan's seeming lack of concern for women's issues alienated many women. In 1983 the *New York Times* identified a "gender gap" in attitudes toward Reagan, as more women opposed him.

Reagan's supporters and opponents alike worried about one notable failure of Reaganomics: its inability to produce a balanced budget. During the 1980 campaign, Reagan had attacked the Carter administration for spending $73.8 billion more than it took in that year. By 1985, however, the deficit had zoomed to more than $212 billion. By the following year, the Reagan administration had run up a greater total deficit than all the administrations in American history combined.

The Supreme Court In 1981 Arizona judge Sandra Day O'Connor became the first woman to serve on the Supreme Court. Reagan nominated her in part because of her conservative views. *What Supreme Court decisions did Reagan oppose?*

A New Orientation on the Supreme Court

Reagan's conservative philosophy included passionate opposition to two major Supreme Court decisions—that prayer in public schools is unconstitutional and that women have a constitutional right to abortion. On both of these deeply emotional issues, Reagan sought constitutional amendments that would reverse the Court's decisions. Meanwhile, he waited for his chance to appoint justices who would leave policy making to the legislative and executive branches of government.

Reagan's first Supreme Court appointment was a historic one. In 1981 he named Sandra Day O'Connor the first woman justice in the Court's history. Later he appointed other conservative justices.

The Supreme Court began to hand down some conservative decisions that pleased the President. For example, the Court curtailed affirmative action and limited the rights of criminal suspects.

Nevertheless, the Court's direction proved to be a slow drift toward conservatism, not a sharp turn. At the conclusion of Reagan's presidency in 1989, the existing decisions about abortion and prayer in public schools were still the law of the land.

Section Assessment

Main Idea

1. Use a diagram like this one to show features of Reagan's conservative vision for America.

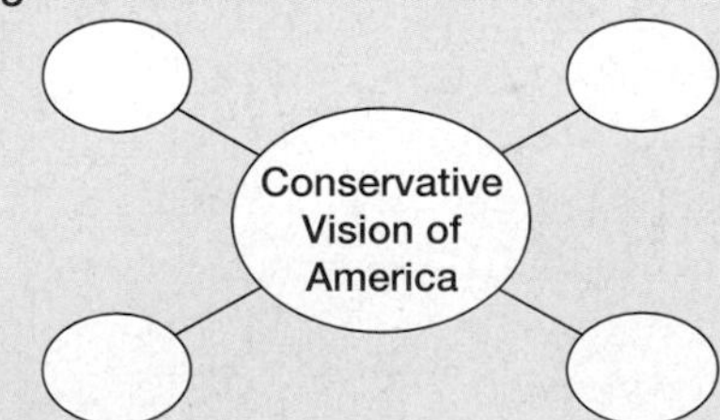

Vocabulary

2. Define: mandate, neoconservatism, supply-side economics, deregulate.

Checking Facts

3. How did Reagan's election reshuffle traditional American political patterns?
4. How did Reaganomics differ from Keynesian economics?

Critical Thinking

5. **Predicting Consequences** What might be some of the long-term consequences of a conservative Supreme Court?

Science, TECHNOLOGY, and Society

Personal Computers

Before their workings could fit on miniature chips, computers were huge machines in back rooms of offices. Hundreds of people could log on at work, but they had no access to computers at home or at school. Once personal computers (PCs) became easily available in the 1980s, their use soared. By the end of the 1980s, PCs sat on desks nationwide.

UPI/BETTMANN NEWSPHOTOS

ENIAC

The University of Pennsylvania's ENIAC computer cost $500,000. It could carry out operations at electronic speed, but it had no memory. Scientists had to rewire the computer for each new problem it tackled. Six full-time technicians scurried about replacing any of the 17,000 vacuum tubes that randomly blew out.

© DAN McCOY/RAINBOW

HISTORY OF PERSONAL COMPUTERS

1940s

In 1946 **ENIAC,** the first general-purpose electronic digital computer, fills a huge room. It weighs 30 tons.

1950s

In 1951 **UNIAC,** the first commercially available computer, accurately predicts Eisenhower's election 45 minutes after the polls closed. It is the first computer to use letters as well as numbers. First **TRANSISTORIZED COMPUTERS** introduced in 1958.

1960s

COMPUTER circuits are placed on chips. More than 10,000 computers are in use worldwide by 1961.

NOTEBOOK COMPUTERS

Some notebook computers today weigh less than 3 pounds. The first "portable" notebook computer weighed 30 pounds and needed an electrical outlet. It was not until 1985 that rechargeable batteries and LCD screens made computers truly portable.

© TOM McCARTHY/RAINBOW

FILE PHOTO BY DOUG MINDELL

SMALLER AND SMALLER

Transistors, such as the one on the left, replaced the much larger vacuum tubes. Today computers can contain thousands or millions of transistors and related circuitry on a chip smaller than a fingernail (above).

PCs DO EVERYTHING

Modern computers have made typewriters (still common in the 1980s) virtually obsolete. They can replace many other office items as well, including adding machines, erasers, and carbon paper. Computers can send letters, fax documents, and create artwork. They can analyze volumes of data or provide access to libraries of information around the world. A modern desktop computer has more computing power than the huge room-filling computers of the early 1960s.

COMPUTERS TODAY

PORTFOLIO PROJECT

Think about how computers affect you. Keep a list for one day or one week detailing every use you make of a computer. How would someone have performed these activities a decade ago? How pervasive are computers in your life? Keep your results in your portfolio.

1970s

Entire workings of computers can now be placed on **CHIPS.** More than 100,000 computers in use in 1971. **APPLE** personal computer introduced in 1977.

1980s

IBM personal computer is introduced in 1981. In 1984 Apple introduces the first Macintosh powerful enough to support a mouse, windows, and elaborate software.

1990s

BY 1997, more than one in three American households had computers and more than 70 percent of school-aged children used computers someplace, either at school or at home.

Technology Skill

USING AN ELECTRONIC SPREADSHEET

Learning the Skill

People use electronic spreadsheets to manage large groups of numbers quickly and easily. You can use an electronic spreadsheet to perform the mathematical functions with any data that involves numbers that can be arranged in columns and rows.

Using an Electronic Spreadsheet

A spreadsheet is an electronic worksheet. It is made up of numbered cells that form rows and columns. Each column (vertical) is assigned a letter or number. Each row (horizontal) is assigned a number. Each point where a column and row intersect is called a *cell*. A cell's position on the spreadsheet is labeled according to its corresponding column and row—Column A, Row 1 (A1); Column B, Row 2 (B2) and so on. See the diagram below.

A1	B1	C1	D1	E1
A2	B2	C2	D2	E2
A3	B3	C3	D3	E3
A4	B4	C4	D4	E4
A5	B5	C5	D5	E5

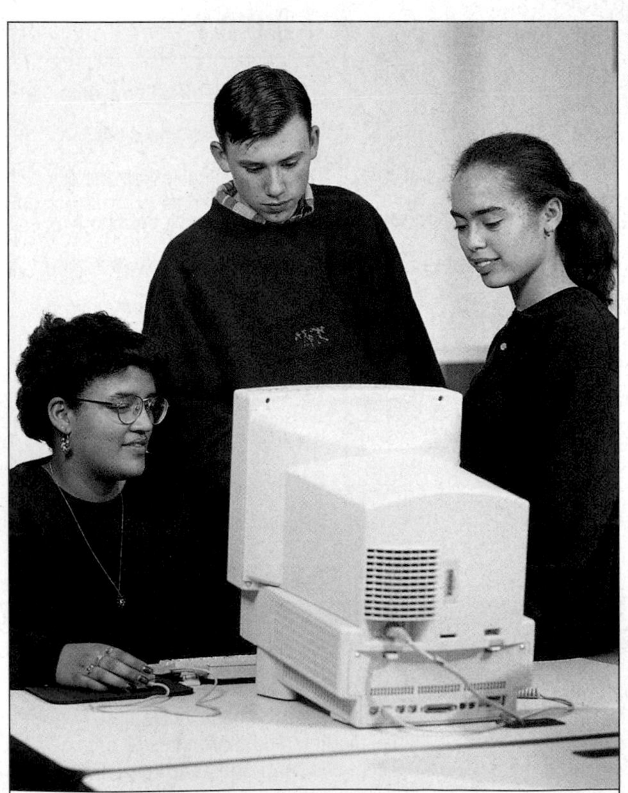

LIFE IMAGES

Students learning how to use electronic spreadsheets

Spreadsheets use *standard formulas* to calculate the numbers. By entering a simple equation into a specific cell, you command the computer to add, subtract, multiply, or divide the numbers in rows or columns.

To make changes in a spreadsheet, use a mouse or the cursor keys on the computer to move to the cell you choose. That cell will be highlighted or have a border around it. If you change a number in any cell, your equation will automatically change the totals to reflect the new number. The computer will even copy a formula from one cell to another.

Practicing the Skill

Suppose you wanted to chart the number of votes the Republican, Democratic, and third-party candidates received in the last five presidential elections. Use these steps to create a spreadsheet that will provide this information:

1. In cells B1, C1, and D1 respectively, type the name of the political party. In cell E1, type the term *total*.

2. In cells A2-A6, type the year of a presidential election. In cell A7, type the word *total*.

3. In row 2, enter the number of votes each party received in the year named in cell A2. Repeat this process in rows 3-6.

4. Create a formula to calculate the votes. The formula for the equation tells what cells (B2 + B3 + B4 + B5 + B6) to add together.

5. Copy the formula down in the cells for the other years.

6. Use the process in steps 4 and 5 to create and copy a formula to calculate the total number of votes each party received over the five-year period.

Applying the Skill

Use a spreadsheet to enter your test scores and your homework grades. At the end of the grading period, the spreadsheet will calculate your average grade.

Additional Practice

For additional practice, see Reinforcing Skills on page 889.

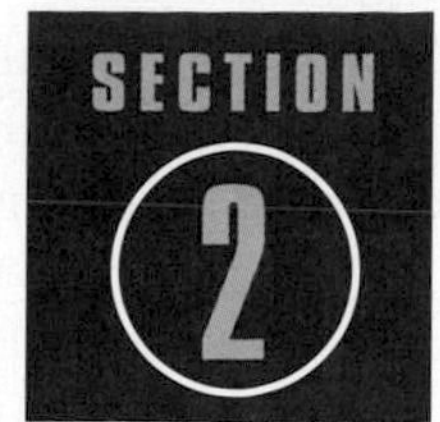

The Collapse of Communism

MAY 6, 1992: GORBACHEV COMES TO FULTON, MISSOURI

© DOUG MINER/SYGMA

Mikhail Gorbachev
Addressing the students of Westminster College, Gorbachev announces that the cold war has at last come to an end.

THE SPRING SUN SHONE DOWN ON THE CAMPUS OF WESTMINSTER COLLEGE IN FULTON, MISSOURI, WHERE MORE THAN 10,000 PEOPLE HAD GATHERED. They had come to hear a speech by Mikhail Gorbachev, the former president of the Soviet Union.

Carolyn O'Donley, a college student, basked in the thrill of seeing a major historical figure on her campus of just 750 students. "Gorbachev and his wife, Raisa, walked through the crowd shaking people's hands," she said. "Everyone was very excited—it was a very positive feeling to have them here." She added, "I think there were reporters from every country in the world, too."

The reporters were there to cover more than a speech, for Gorbachev was only the second major historical figure to visit the school. In 1946—before any of the students present on that day were born—Winston Churchill, prime minister of Great Britain during World War II, had spoken at Westminster. In a famous speech, Churchill warned of the onset of the cold war and of Soviet oppression in Europe. "From Stettin in the Baltic to Trieste in the Adriatic, an iron curtain has descended across the continent," Churchill had said.

Now Gorbachev—who did more than any other person to end the cold war and lift the iron curtain from Europe—looked out on the sea of

GUIDE TO READING

Main Idea

The collapse of Soviet communism brought profound changes to United States foreign policy, particularly toward nations in Eastern Europe, Central America, and the Caribbean.

Vocabulary

- mutual deterrence
- glasnost
- perestroika

Read to Find Out . . .

- why Soviet-American relations were transformed dramatically during Reagan's second term.
- the causes for the breakup of the Soviet Union in the late 1980s.
- how the cold war's end changed the foreign policy of the United States.

faces assembled. He picked up on Churchill's theme when he said that the world was no longer divided between East and West, but "between the rich and the poor countries, between the North and the South."

People in the crowd applauded enthusiastically, as they did throughout his speech, for this was an amazing moment. Many that day recalled that little more than 10 years earlier, President Reagan had called the Soviet Union an "evil empire." Now they were listening to a speech by the man in charge when that empire collapsed. It was remarkable evidence of the changes that had occurred in the world and in the United States since the beginning of the Reagan administration.

A Challenge to the Soviets

Strong Military Gives Reagan Negotiating Power

When Ronald Reagan was a young film actor in Hollywood, he played the part of a Wild West hero in such films as *Santa Fe Trail* (1940) and *Law and Order* (1953). When he arrived in Washington in 1981, he brought with him some of the swagger and steely resolve of the Western heroes he had portrayed on the screen.

Ever since his days as president of the Screen Actors Guild, from 1947 to 1952 and again in 1959, Reagan had been a fervent anti-Communist. During congressional investigations into Communist activity in the movie industry in the late 1940s and early 1950s, Reagan worked to expose suspected Communists.

In 1982 Reagan told an audience that the Soviet Union was the "focus of evil in the modern world." The President served notice on the Soviets that he intended to confront them whenever possible.

The Arms Buildup

Since the dawn of the nuclear age, the United States and the Soviet Union had maintained a nuclear balance called **mutual deterrence.** This theory held that as long as accurate missiles capable of complete destruction targeted both countries, neither nation would ever start a nuclear war. In their efforts to prevent each other from tipping that balance, both superpowers engaged in an ever-escalating arms race.

© FRANK FOURNIER/CONTACT PRESS IMAGES

East Meets West Soviet President Mikhail Gorbachev stands with President Ronald Reagan during White House ceremonies. *Explain the irony in this picture.*

Although Reagan preached economy in government and cut many domestic programs, he proposed the biggest arms buildup in American history. Reagan wanted to develop new weapons systems and enlarge the fleet. He urged Congress to vote funds for an untried system of orbiting satellites that could fire laser beams to shoot down any Soviet missiles launched toward the United States. Reagan called the system the Strategic Defense Initiative (SDI). The press quickly dubbed it "Star Wars," and critics assailed its feasibility.

The President said that military power would make the nation feel good again about itself and its place in the world. "America is back, standing tall," he said. The cost was a breathtaking $1.5 trillion over a 5-year period.

While Reagan pressed for more planes, missiles, and ships, Soviet foreign policy strengthened his hand. The Soviet war in Afghanistan raged on, and Soviet support for Communist guerrilla activity in Central America, Africa, and the Philippines remained active.

Two incidents in 1983 confirmed Reagan's worst fears about the Soviet Union. The first occurred in Poland, where the Soviets installed a new, repressive government and jailed members of a popular democratic revolution. Some analysts think that only the intervention of Pope John Paul II, himself a Pole, prevented Soviet military intervention.

In a second incident, the Soviets earned worldwide condemnation in 1983 for shooting down a Korean Airlines passenger jet that had accidentally entered Soviet airspace. The jet, attacked by a MIG fighter, plunged into the Pacific, killing all 269 passengers and crew.

Negotiation Through Strength

While building up American military strength, Reagan offered the Soviets numerous proposals for controlling or reducing nuclear and conventional arms. The President believed that by making the United States strong and taking a hard line, he could intimidate the Soviets into concessions at the bargaining table.

For example, Reagan made a blunt offer to the Soviets. If they would agree to destroy some of their missiles aimed at Western Europe, then the United States would call off the placement in Western

Europe of additional missiles targeted at the USSR. Talks on this question began in 1981. Dissatisfied with their progress, Reagan ordered the installation of more missiles in 1983. The talks collapsed, and it became clear to the Soviets that Reagan was a tough negotiator.

Reagan's refusal to consider any unilateral, or one-sided, reduction of the American nuclear stockpile prompted an intense debate throughout the country during 1982 and 1983. Politicians, scientists, and church leaders formed a nuclear freeze movement, calling for a halt to the production and placement of nuclear weapons. In June 1982, 1 million Americans marched in support of the movement. The march was the largest peacetime protest ever staged by Americans.

© MITSUHIRO WADA/GAMMA LIAISON

Gorbymania Fascinated by Gorbachev, Americans were eager to buy souvenirs—such as these Gorby dolls—of his visit. *Why did Gorbachev's proposals surprise Reagan?*

A Thaw in the Cold War

Superpowers Agree to Reduce Nuclear Arms

A remarkable transformation in Soviet-American relations began to take shape at the beginning of Ronald Reagan's second term as President. The impetus for change came in part from the two leaders of the superpowers. One was Mikhail Gorbachev, a dynamic leader committed to reforming his country's collapsing economy and establishing productive ties with the West. The other was Ronald Reagan, whose every action in foreign policy had, according to Donald Regan, his chief of staff, "been carried out with the idea of one day sitting down at the negotiating table with the leader of the USSR and banning weapons of mass destruction from the planet."

Ice Breaking

The setting for this transformation was a series of summit meetings between the two leaders. In 1985 at the first one in Geneva, Switzerland, the two leaders sized each other up. Their exchanges were direct. Gorbachev held to his view that outer space should be weapon free. Reagan stood firm, reserving the right of the United States to implement SDI as protection against Soviet missiles.

In October 1986, the two leaders met in Reykjavik, Iceland. At this meeting, Gorbachev unveiled a broad range of new arms control proposals covering topics such as long-range missiles and the Strategic Defense Initiative. The sweep of Gorbachev's proposals stunned President Reagan and his advisers. In an attempt to capture a historic opportunity, both sides worked long beyond the scheduled close of the meetings. Neither Reagan nor Gorbachev, however, would compromise on the issue of weapons in space. In the end, this second meeting produced no agreement.

Arms Cuts

Reagan and Gorbachev met twice more to discuss arms control. In December 1987, Gorbachev and his wife, Raisa, visited Washington, D. C. In the spring of 1988 the Soviets hosted the Reagans. At both meetings, style overshadowed substance. Americans caught "Gorbymania"; Soviets marveled at Ron and Nancy in Red Square.

In the midst of the social activities, the Intermediate-Range Nuclear Forces (INF) treaty went into effect in June 1988. The treaty was the first agreement of its kind; it aimed to reduce the number of nuclear missiles in each superpower's arsenal. Although covering only one type of missile, the treaty cleared the way for later arms pacts.

The INF treaty was perhaps the greatest foreign policy triumph of Reagan's presidency. After escalating the arms race and increasing tensions between the superpowers, Reagan ended his presidency on much friendlier terms with the Soviets. During the Reagan years, the United States had gone further than in any previous presidency to stabilize Soviet-American relations.

Further Arms Reduction

George Bush, Reagan's successor, continued to press the merits of democratic capitalism and to speak out vigorously against communism. Bush, too, believed in bargaining from a position of military strength.

By late 1989 the Reagan and Bush strategy produced results. Bush and Gorbachev met aboard a ship in the Mediterranean Sea to discuss ending the arms race. Less than a year later, the superpowers agreed to limit their troops and conventional weapons in Europe and Asia. Bush also ordered the Strategic Air Command to relax its 24-hour-a-day combat-ready status. Gorbachev called Bush's order a "great event." Then he ordered the

©PETER MARLOW/MAGNUM PHOTOS

Lech Walesa After seeing protesters shot down in a 1970 demonstration, Walesa became a leader in Poland's trade union movement. Despite arrest and harassment for his political activism, Walesa continued to fight for democracy. *What was the name of Walesa's labor union?*

destruction of all Soviet short-range nuclear missiles and halted nuclear testing for 1 year. In October 1991, NATO responded by cutting its nuclear forces in Europe by 80 percent. Such cutbacks offered relief to both sides after a decade of unprecedented arms buildup.

The Soviet Breakup

Eastern Bloc Countries Declare Independence

Relief from defense spending came too late, however, to save the faltering Soviet economy. When Gorbachev took office in March 1985, he spoke of **glasnost,** opening up Soviet society to new ideas. He hoped to improve everyday life for Soviet citizens and to get more consumer goods into stores by easing the government's near-total control over the economy. This restructuring of the way Soviets did business was called **perestroika.**

Perestroika and glasnost extended into the realm of politics as well. In 1989 Soviet citizens were allowed to vote for non-Communists for the first time, breaking down the USSR's one-party system.

Eastern Europe Changes

By 1989 no Communist leader in Eastern Europe could count on Soviet tanks to suppress his opponents. The first country to loosen communism's grip was Poland. Lech Walesa, a shipyard worker in the Baltic port of Gdansk, led the labor union Solidarity in the 1980s as it won concessions from the government. Even after Solidarity was banned, Walesa's character inspired the antigovernment movement. Pope John Paul II, a fellow Pole, also lent inspiration from afar to the forces of democracy. Under growing public protest, the Communist president was obliged to step aside. Walesa was elected president of Poland in a December 1990 landslide.

Czechoslovakia's relatively smooth passage to democracy resulted in the election in 1989 of playwright Vaclav Havel as president. Slovaks in the eastern portion of the country, however, wanted a separate nation, and Czechs in the western portion were obliged to concede. Havel, a Czech, lost office in 1992 in a democratic vote mainly because few Slovaks would vote for him. He reluctantly agreed to the nation's split into the Czech Republic and Slovakia in 1993.

Europe's worst violence since World War II began in June 1991 in Yugoslavia. Throughout the early 1990s, the world watched helplessly as ethnic groups that had lived side by side for generations turned on each other. Secretary-General Boutros Boutros-Ghali of the UN termed the bloodbath "tragic, dangerous, violent, and confused."

A New Germany

The USSR's declining influence in the late 1980s set off a political chain reaction. Unification of the two Germanies, divided since 1949, came swiftly on the heels of Gorbachev's sweeping reforms.

Months of protests in East Germany, for 40 years a Soviet ally, led to the ouster of Communist leader Erich Honecker in October 1989. All summer East Germans had been fleeing their country through Hungary, and now the trickle became a flood. On November 9, 1989, the government capitulated and said it would issue exit visas to anyone who asked. Hordes of citizens immediately began to break through the Berlin Wall, a symbol of Germany's division, built on Soviet orders in 1961.

Plans for unifying the 2 countries began immediately. On October 3, 1990, far sooner than anyone had predicted, the 2 nations joined as the Federal Republic of Germany. Overnight the 62 million West Germans and 16 million East Germans became

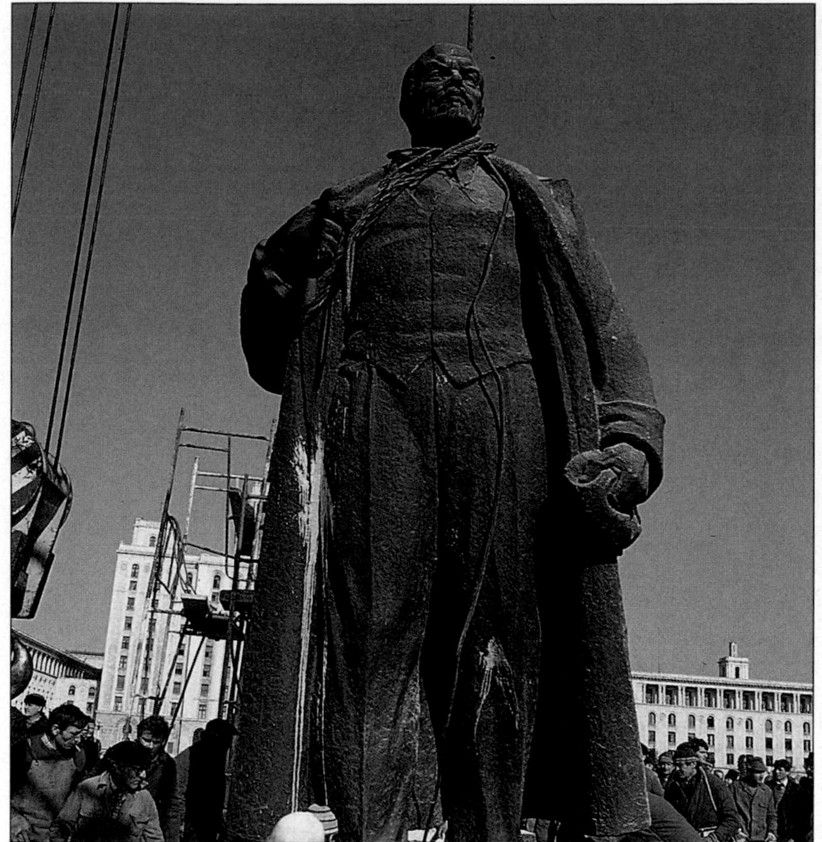
© BI/GAMMA LIAISON

A New Russia Soviet citizens dismantle a giant statue of Lenin to signify their dissatisfaction with the old regime. *In what other ways did people in the former Soviet Union indicate they wanted change?*

a European powerhouse with a combined economy worth $1 trillion a year.

The excitement of reunification soon faded, though, as Germans faced the difficult task of raising the living standard of the former East Germans. Adding to the instability of reunification was the arrival of thousands of refugees from other eastern European countries. Right-wing groups called neo-Nazis, disturbed by the changes, launched violent attacks on the foreigners. By the mid-1990s, however, the German economy was beginning to recover. Terrorist attacks abated, though they continued to cause grave concern among the majority of the nation's citizens. The international community remained firm in its opposition to such violence.

The Attempted Gorbachev Coup

In the Soviet Union, Gorbachev's policies of glasnost and perestroika led Communist party loyalists to fear for their jobs and privileges. It was this faction—the Soviet Union's political elite—that plotted a coup against Gorbachev in August 1991.

The coup attempt was met with condemnation from world leaders as well as Soviet citizens. Defiantly opposing the coup was Boris Yeltsin, president of the Russian Federation, the largest republic in the USSR. From his office in Moscow, Yeltsin rallied a fearful but growing crowd to oppose the coup, at times speaking from a balcony to thousands gathered in the streets. His effort succeeded, and the coup instigators ended their attempt to take over the government.

The Collapse of the Soviet Union

Mikhail Gorbachev resigned as Communist party leader and banned any party involvement in government affairs. With these moves, the party's 73-year monopoly on political power came to an end, and with the loss of centralized control, the Soviet Union began to break up.

THE FALL OF COMMUNISM, 1985–1993
1985 Mikhail Gorbachev comes to power in the Soviet Union.
1990 East and West Germany united. Lech Walesa elected president of Poland.
1992 Havel loses reelection in Czechoslovakia. Yugoslavia erupts into civil war.
1985
1986
1987
1988
1989
1990
1991
1992
1993
1989 Vaclav Havel is elected in Czechoslovakia. Berlin Wall falls. Bush and Gorbachev hold first arms talks. Soviet Union holds first free election.
1991 Slovenia and Croatia declare independence. Coup against Gorbachev fails; Soviet Union crumbles; Yeltsin becomes Russian leader.
1993 Czechoslovakia splits into two nations—the Czech Republic and Slovakia.

People living in many of the USSR's 15 republics agitated for autonomy. The first to break from the union were the peoples of Lithuania, Latvia, and Estonia. They had voted to secede in early 1991. Ukraine, breadbasket

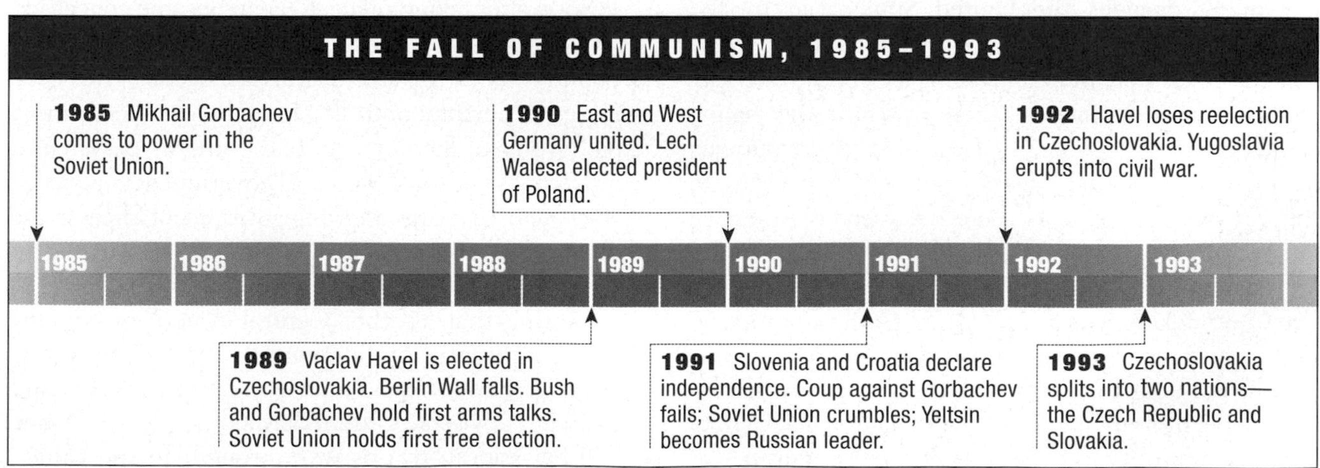

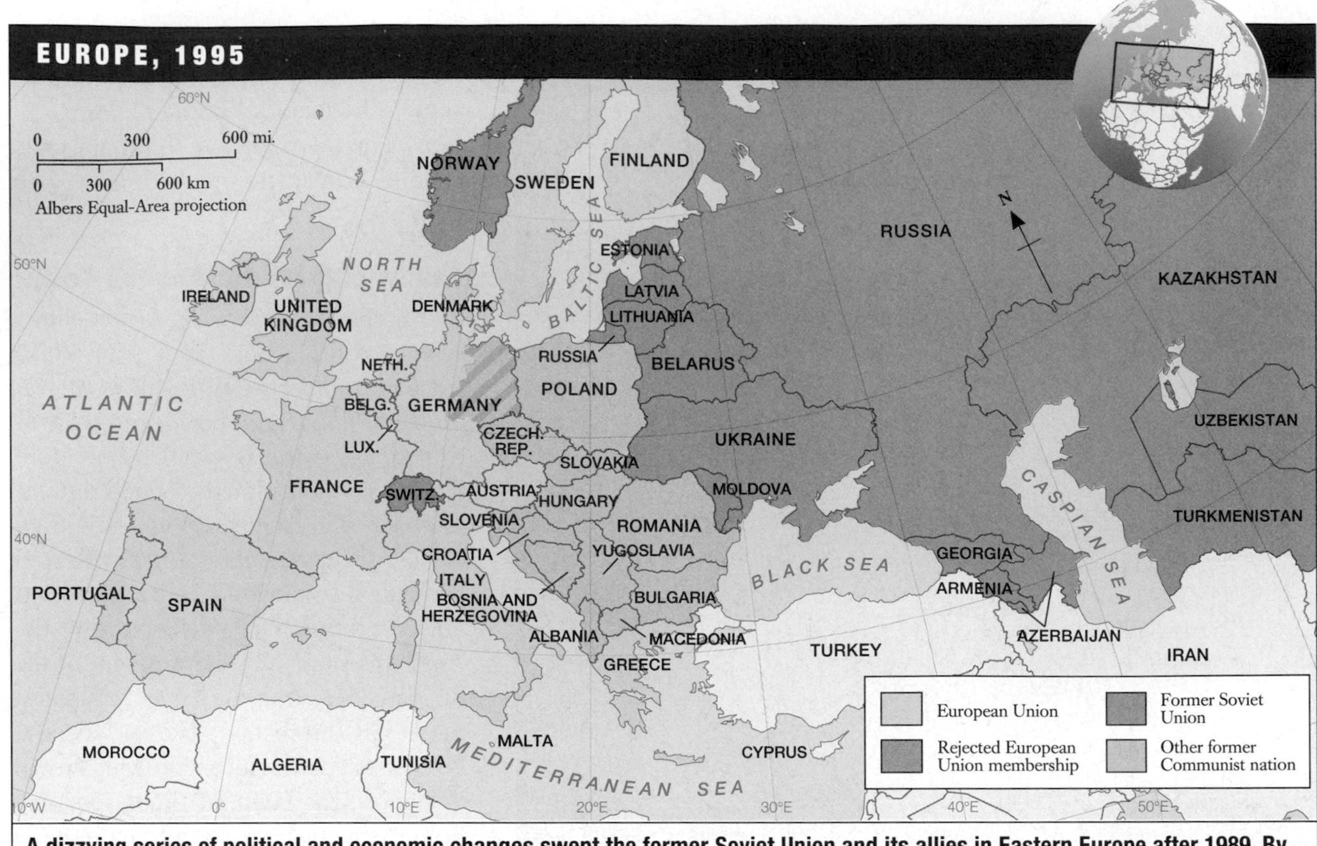

A dizzying series of political and economic changes swept the former Soviet Union and its allies in Eastern Europe after 1989. By 1995 the region had fragmented into many independent nations. *Which of the countries shown above used to be a part of the Soviet Union?*

of the Soviet Union, declared its independence just days after the August coup, as did 9 other republics. The USSR no longer existed.

Central America

United States Involvement Creates Controversy

The United States's strong military stance in the early 1980s and the subsequent end to the cold war had a profound effect on relations with Central America. For many decades the United States had treated the nations of that region with casual disdain. When the United States thought that invading a Central American country was in its interest, there was little that nation could do except protest. The United States encouraged democracy in Central America but was also willing to support corrupt dictators there who served American interests.

Partly in response to American support for repressive Central American governments, Communist movements and guerrilla resistance flourished throughout the region. Pointing to Soviet and Cuban involvement in these rebel movements, President Reagan made Central America a priority in his war against communism.

"The national security of all the Americas is at stake in Central America," Reagan told a joint session of Congress in 1983. "If we cannot defend ourselves there, we cannot expect to prevail elsewhere." During his first administration, Reagan demonstrated this point dramatically. In October 1983, leftists on the tiny Caribbean island of Grenada staged an uprising. Uneasy over reported Cuban and Soviet influence in the area, Reagan dispatched an invasion force to oust the leftists and install a prodemocracy government.

El Salvador

Soon after taking office, Reagan became concerned about the instability of the government in El Salvador, a country about the size of Massachusetts. The right-wing government, controlled by military officers and a small group of landowners, had come to power in a coup two years earlier. Now this government was shaky. Leftist guerrillas were attacking government forces in the countryside, where peasant people had struggled in poverty for decades.

Fearing that another Central American country would go the way of Communist Cuba, Reagan persuaded Congress to send military aid to El Salvador and American "advisers" to train Salvadoran soldiers. Some 1,600 Salvadoran troops were brought to the United

States for training. The United States had to act, the administration felt, because the Salvadoran guerrillas had the backing of Cuba and Nicaragua, and ultimately of the Soviet Union.

Opponents of Reagan's policy claimed that poverty and government oppression were the real causes of the rebellion. The Reagan administration pressed the government of El Salvador to speed up its land reform and to outlaw the military "death squads" that roamed the country killing anyone suspected of sympathizing with the guerrillas. In 1983 these right-wing squads killed as many as 200 people a week.

Throughout the rest of the 1980s, the civil war continued. By the end of 1988 the fighting had cost the lives of between 65,000 and 70,000 Salvadorans. The United States had contributed $3 billion to the government during that time.

It was not until the ending of the cold war that real progress toward a peaceful settlement was possible. In 1991 the United States and the Soviet Union urged UN Secretary-General Javier Pérez de Cuéllar to intervene in the peace negotiations between the government and the guerrillas. At a meeting between the 2 sides in New York, plans for a new peace initiative were announced. The next year, some 1,000 UN peacekeeping troops were dispatched to El Salvador, and within days a formal peace accord was ratified as the United States secretary of state, James Baker, looked on.

Nicaragua

In Nicaragua, as in El Salvador, the Reagan administration decided to fight communism with military aid. The Nicaraguan government was made up of Marxist revolutionaries who called themselves Sandinistas. In 1979 the Sandinistas, after years of guerrilla warfare, had overthrown the brutal Nicaraguan dictator Anastasio Somoza. The Somoza family had ruled the country with iron fists and American support since the 1930s.

Now the Sandinistas found themselves opposed by right-wing guerrillas, including some former officers of Somoza's despised paramilitary National Guard. Not unexpectedly, President Reagan backed the right-wing guerrillas, called *contras,* after the Spanish word *contra,* meaning "against." As part of a cover operation, the CIA trained and armed approximately 10,000 *contras,* at bases in Honduras and Costa Rica.

Reagan justified these actions by portraying Nicaragua as "a Soviet ally on the American mainland only two hours' flying time from our own borders." Cuban military advisers, medical experts, and teachers were aiding the Sandinistas. In addition, the Soviet Union

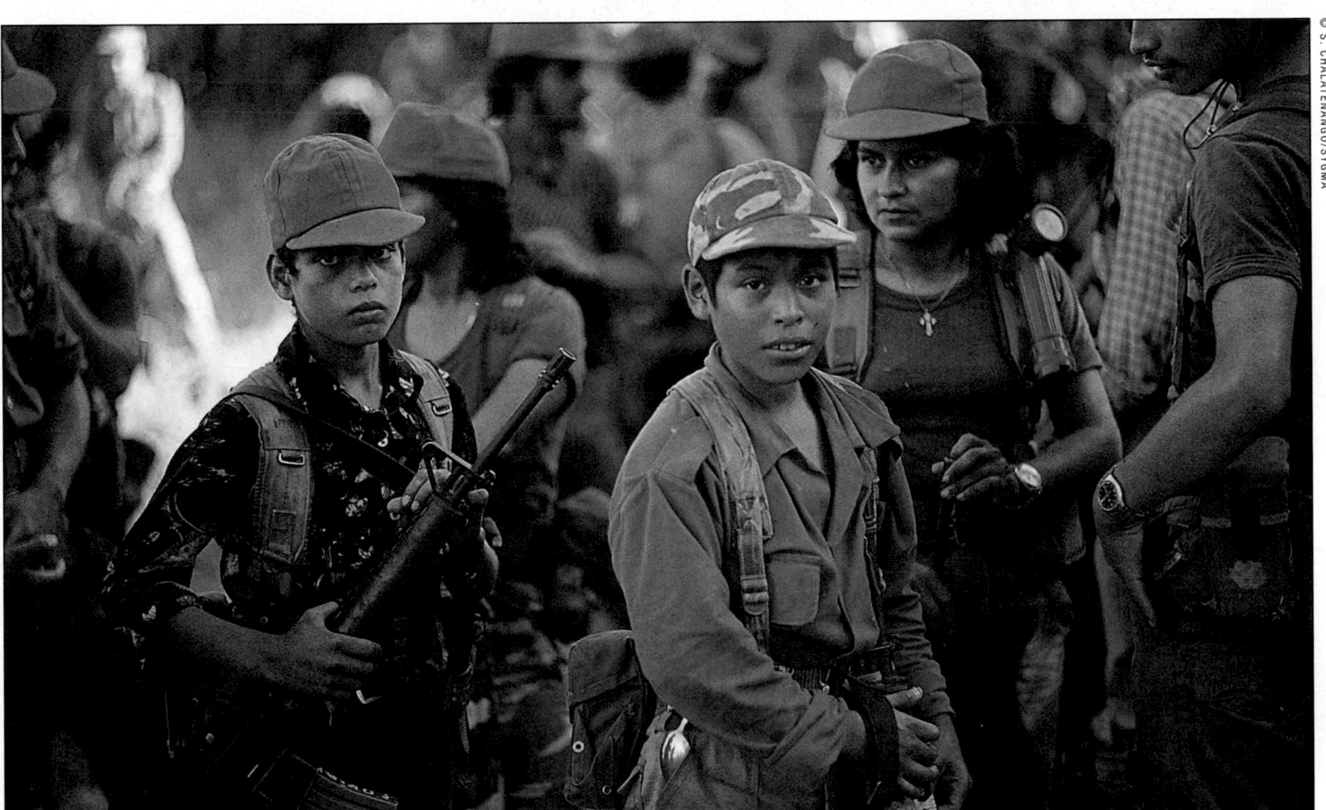

Guerrilla Warfare in El Salvador Young boys and girls joined the guerrillas to fight Salvadoran soldiers. *Why did the Reagan administration support the right-wing government of El Salvador?*

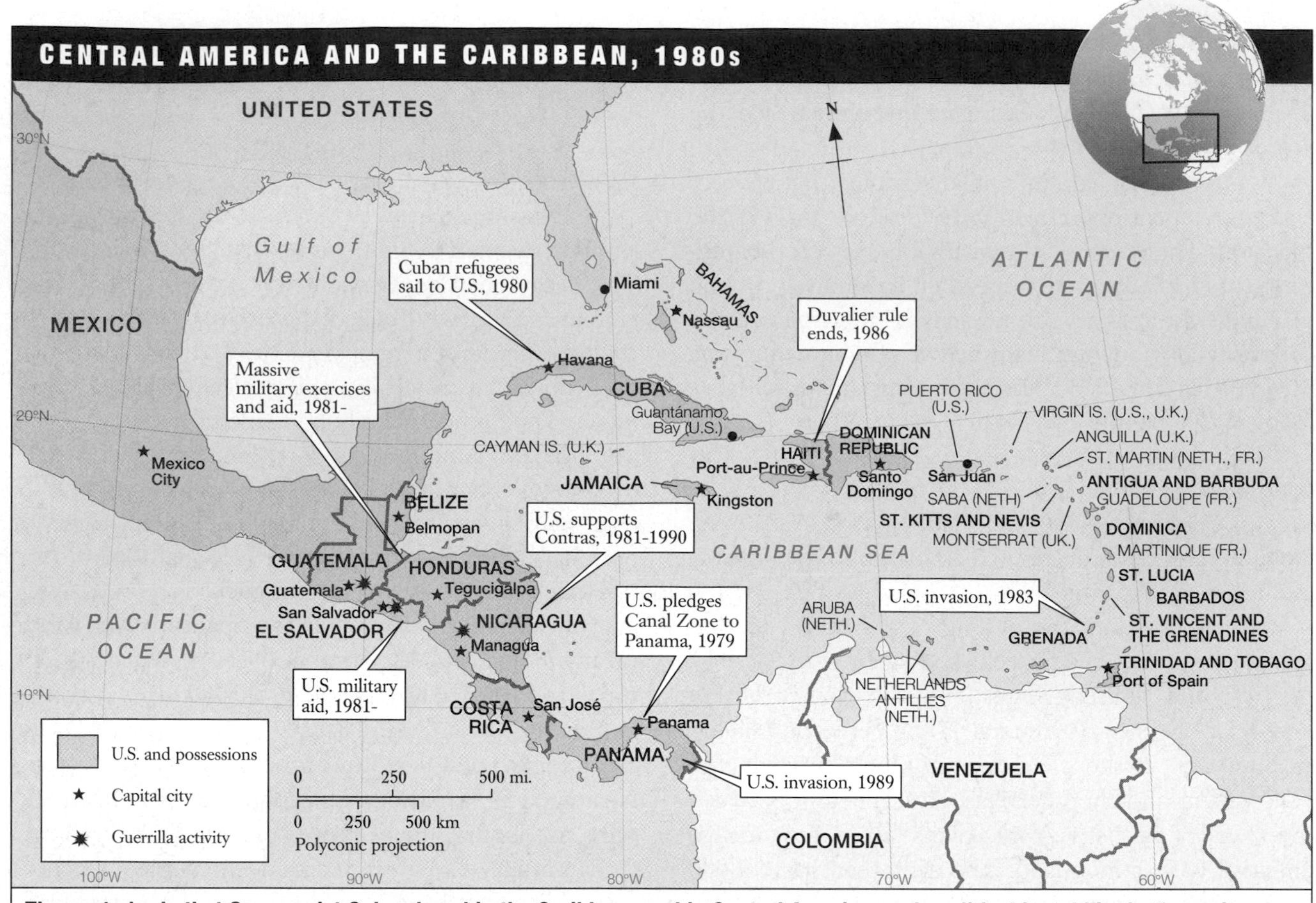

The central role that Communist Cuba played in the Caribbean and in Central America made political instability in the region a major concern of President Reagan. He feared the domino effect: one nation after another falling to communism. *Use this map to describe the role of the United States in the Caribbean and Central America.*

was also sending military aid, including fighter planes and attack helicopters. Intelligence reports also indicated that the Sandinistas were sending military aid to the leftist rebels in El Salvador.

As the CIA role in Nicaragua became more widely known, heated debate erupted in the United States. News emerged early in 1984 that the CIA had placed mines in the harbors of Nicaraguan ports and trained the *contras* to incite mob violence and to murder their political opponents. An angry Congress forbade any more military aid to Nicaragua. Congress relaxed its ban in 1986. By that time, however, allegations that Reagan and his aides had broken the law in their efforts to support the *contra* resistance were undermining the President's Nicaraguan policy.

The Iran-*contra* Scandal

Throughout the summer of 1987, millions of Americans sat riveted to their TV screens, following 1 of those rare congressional hearings that achieve major importance and high drama. The hearings reminded many of the Watergate hearings 14 years earlier.

Once again, as with Watergate, Congress was looking into wrongdoing by officials in the administration, including some close to the President. Once again, the abuses concerned officials taking the law into their own hands. Once again, the key questions were: Who authorized the illegal activities? Was the President involved?

According to Hawaii senator Daniel K. Inouye, cochairperson of the congressional committee, the Iran-*contra* scandal was "much more serious than Watergate, not because of who was (or was not) involved but because of what was involved: the formulation and conduct of American foreign policy."

The details of the Iran-*contra* scandal were complicated and murky. In essence, United States officials privately arranged arms sales to Iran, presumably with the hope that Iran would use its influence to free American hostages being held by pro-Iranian groups in Lebanon. This was at a time—the mid-1980s—when Washington was publicly condemning Iran as a terrorist nation and insisting that the United States would make no deals for the hostages' release. To make matters worse, profits from the arms sales were secretly funneled to the Nicaraguan *contras* to help finance their guerrilla war against the Sandinistas. Congress had specifically forbidden any military aid to the *contras.*

The President's National Security Council (NSC), which was supposed to be a research and advisory body, carried out these activities. An NSC aide, Colonel Oliver North of the Marine Corps, and his boss, Admiral John Poindexter, ran the secret operation.

The report of the congressional committees stopped short of accusing the President of wrongdoing, but it took a dim view of his hands-off management style. Reagan was portrayed as "fuzzy" on specific details and out of touch with important activities within his administration.

The scandal made the President look bad either way. If he did not know what Poindexter and North were doing in his name, then, his critics contended, he must be incompetent. If he did know, then he was guilty of breaking the law forbidding military aid to the *contras*—a law that he himself had signed.

North and Poindexter were tried and convicted of scandal-related offenses. North was sentenced to perform community service, but his sentence was set aside on appeal. Poindexter received a six-month jail term.

Overall, the scandal seemed to have little effect on the public's opinion of Reagan, leading some to dub him the "Teflon" President. He appeared to have a nonstick surface to which bad news would not adhere. At the end of Reagan's second term, polls showed that two-thirds of the public approved of his conduct.

The Caribbean

Moving Toward Democracy

Oppressive dictatorship had long been the norm in the island nation of Haiti. In 1957 Dr. François Duvalier was elected president. The popular leader soon established himself as a dictator, maintained in power by an intimidating private army called the *Tontons Macoutes*. On the eve of his death in 1971, Duvalier appointed his son, Jean-Claude Duvalier, as his successor. Repression, grinding poverty, and corruption continued.

It was not until late 1986 that Jean-Claude and his family were forced to flee the island. Euphoria over his overthrow was short-lived, however. Rioting and repeated coups d'état threatened the stability of the nation.

In 1990 voters in Haiti elected Father Jean-Bertrand Aristide, a left-wing Catholic priest, as president. Unfortunately, the Aristide government proved no more stable than its predecessors. Within eight months, a military junta overthrew the government in a violent coup. Aristide fled to exile in the United States.

Following the coup, thousands of Haitians attempted to flee the country in makeshift boats. Most headed for the United States, where instead of welcoming them, the Bush administration attempted to return them to Haiti.

During the campaign for the presidential election of 1992, candidate Bill Clinton promised to reverse this policy. Yet when he became President, fearing a mass exodus of Haitians seeking refuge, he ordered the repatriation continued. He promised the Haitian people that he would continue to work on their behalf to secure a democratic solution to their island's turmoil.

Perhaps no country in the Western Hemisphere was more profoundly affected by the changes in the Soviet Union than Cuba. Ever since Fidel Castro aligned himself with the Soviet bloc in the early 1960s, Cuba was perceived as a threat to the United States and to the security of the region.

In 1989 President Gorbachev visited Fidel Castro. Although the two leaders signed a treaty of friendship, serious rifts had developed in their relationship. The meeting signaled a reduction of Soviet financial aid that had long kept the Cuban economy afloat. To counter the effects of the cutbacks, Castro moved to reduce government spending by making deep cuts in the Cuban bureaucracy. He expanded rationing to include all consumer products. These measures, however, were not sufficient to revitalize the economy.

In 1992 President Bush stepped up pressure on Castro by ordering a ban that prevented any ship doing business with Cuba from entering American ports. By 1993 Castro had begun to allow some free enterprise in an effort to bolster Cuba's sinking economy.

Section Assessment

Main Idea

1. Use a diagram like this one to show some of the leading world issues facing United States policymakers before and after the collapse of Soviet communism.

Vocabulary

2. Define: mutual deterrence, glasnost, perestroika.

Checking Facts

3. List the ways in which Mikhail Gorbachev helped to bring about an end to the cold war.
4. Summarize United States policy toward El Salvador, Nicaragua, Haiti, and Cuba.

Critical Thinking

5. **Determining Cause and Effect** What factors contributed to the breakup of the Soviet Union?

SPORTS: Cincinnati Reds' Pete Rose is banned from baseball for life for betting on baseball.

One Day in History

November 9, 1989

MARKET BASKET

Here is where a dollar will go:

Loaf of bread. . . . . 65¢
Movie ticket $4
1-liter soft drink $1
Velour shirt $14.95
Theater ticket $20
CD player $229.95

FILE PHOTO BY DOUG MINDELL

Cellular phone. $995
Microwave oven $219.99
19-inch color TV. $209
Apple II computer. $795
Dodge Medallion $8,995

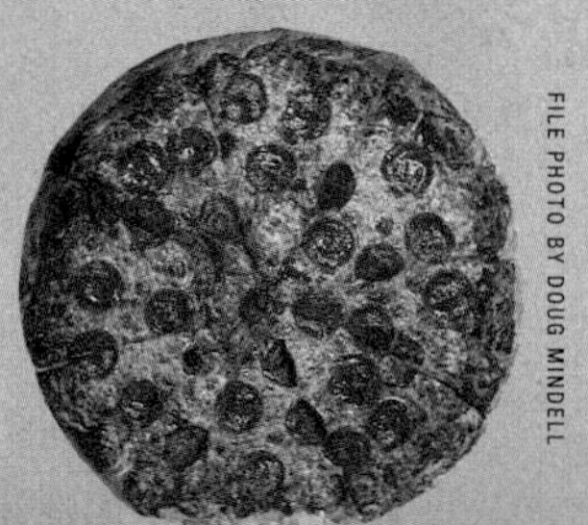

FILE PHOTO BY DOUG MINDELL

Pizza. $7.95
Camcorder $893
4-bedroom house . . . $73,900

© ANTHONY SUAU/GAMMA LIAISON

Jubilation: East and West Berliners celebrate atop the infamous Berlin Wall near the Brandenburg Gate after East Germany announces the opening of its borders.

Berlin Wall Falls

East Berliners rush through Berlin Wall—symbol of the cold war—as travel limits are lifted

WEST BERLIN—Today East Germany lifted its 28-year-old restrictions on travel to the West. Within hours, thousands of East Berliners swarmed across the infamous Berlin Wall for a boisterous celebration.

East Berliners walked, biked, or drove to crossing points (including the notorious Checkpoint Charlie) to enter the other half of their city, a place they could only gaze at just hours before. Cheers, champagne, flowers, and applause greeted their arrival. Border guards, who formerly had orders to fire on any escape attempts, smiled and took snapshots. "This is what we have dreamed of all these years," asserted an elderly East Berlin woman.

NATION: By a narrow margin, Douglas Wilder is the first African American elected governor.

© CYNTHIA JOHNSON/GAMMA LIAISON

The Big One?

SAN FRANCISCO—North America's most destructive earthquake since 1906 hits the Bay Area minutes before the beginning of the 3rd World Series game between the Oakland Athletics and the San Francisco Giants. Measuring 7.1 on the Richter scale, the 15-second tremor kills 90 people, buckles highways and the Bay Bridge, and causes $6 million in damages.

© JAMES A. SUGAR/BLACK STAR

Earthquake Damage

Market Plunges

NEW YORK—Wall Street's Dow Jones Industrial Average drops 190.58 points in 1 day as confidence weakens in "junk" bond financing of company mergers and acquisitions, marking the most drastic 1-day slide in the market since the stock market crash of 1929.

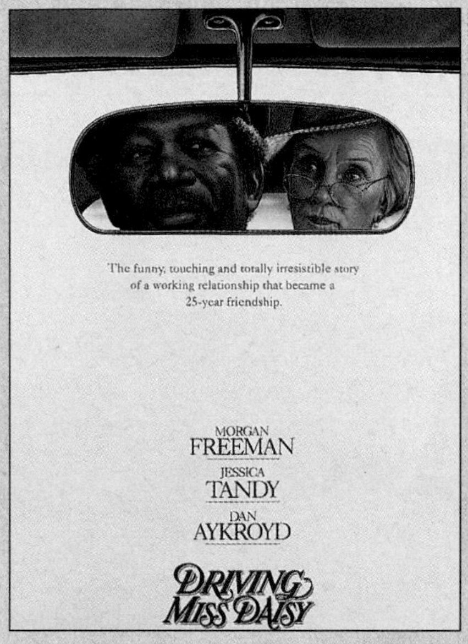

The funny, touching and totally irresistible story of a working relationship that became a 25-year friendship.
MORGAN FREEMAN
JESSICA TANDY
DAN AYKROYD
DRIVING MISS DAISY

RICHARD C. ALLEN

Morgan Freeman and Jessica Tandy (best actress) star in Oscar winner.

MOVIES

Popular Movies: *Field of Dreams ("If you build it, he will come"), When Harry Met Sally, Glory, Dead Poet's Society, Batman, The Little Mermaid, Indiana Jones and the Last Crusade, My Left Foot, Born on the Fourth of July, Do the Right Thing*

NBC PHOTO BY AL LEVINE

The new "typical American family": *The Cosby Show* garners an Emmy.

TELEVISION

- **Top Ten shows:** ***The Golden Girls, A Different World, The Cosby Show, Cheers, Roseanne, Dear John, 60 Minutes, The Wonder Years, L.A. Law, Empty Nest***
- **Specials:** ***Lonesome Dove, Billy Crystal, War and Remembrance***

LPs Become History

An era comes to an end when almost all music stores stop carrying records and begin selling CDs and audiocassettes exclusively. It's good that Thomas Edison is not around to see his invention replaced by the new technology.

FILE PHOTO BY DOUG MINDELL

SECTION 3

The Bush Presidency

JULY 18, 1988: JESSE JACKSON ADDRESSES THE DEMOCRATIC NATIONAL CONVENTION

THE REVEREND JESSE JACKSON STOOD BEFORE THE THOUSANDS OF NOISY DELEGATES WHO HAD COME TO ATLANTA, GEORGIA, TO NOMINATE THE DEMOCRATIC CANDIDATE FOR PRESIDENT. His mission that night, as it had been throughout the primary campaigns, was to give voice to those people who had been termed forgotten Americans. In a rich Southern accent he intoned, "They catch the early bus. . . . They raise other people's children. . . . They drive dangerous cabs. . . . They work in hospitals. . . . No job is beneath them and yet when they get sick they cannot lie in the bed they made up every day. America, that is not right. We are a better nation than that."

© DENNIS BROCK/BLACK STAR

The Democrats
During the 1988 primaries, Jesse Jackson and Michael Dukakis competed for the Democratic nomination.

Jackson was one of several candidates vying for the Democratic nomination that year. During the 1960s he had worked in the civil rights movement with Martin Luther King, Jr. With the support of many African Americans, Jackson attracted a "rainbow coalition" of supporters from various ethnic and racial groups. Jackson's supporters believed that he addressed problems that other major party candidates generally avoided, such as homelessness, unemployment, and inequality.

1988 Election
Bush Versus Dukakis

As Ronald Reagan's second term drew to a close, the election campaign for his successor heated up. The Republicans' clear choice to follow him was his Vice President, George Bush.

On the Democratic side, Jackson won several primaries, but he did not gain enough votes to win the

GUIDE TO READING

Main Idea

The end of the cold war forced the United States to redefine its role in world affairs and to weather the economic dislocations caused by new patterns of federal spending and global trade.

Vocabulary

- apartheid
- trade deficit
- global economy
- working poor

Read to Find Out . . .

- what the Persian Gulf War revealed about the roles of the United States and United Nations in the post–cold war world.
- how the arms build-down and the competitive global market affected the way Americans lived and worked.

nomination. Ultimately the Democrats nominated Michael Dukakis, governor of Massachusetts. Dukakis was credited with having brought his home state out of a deep recession with the so-called Massachusetts Miracle of the early 1980s.

AP/WIDE WORLD PHOTOS

Campaigning In the 1988 election, George Bush won the votes of most Reagan supporters. *What kind of policies did the voters want Bush to follow?*

Electronic Campaigning

In 1988 both Bush and Dukakis relied heavily on expert consultants to produce expensive, carefully scripted television commercials and promotional materials for their campaigns. The candidates were packaged and promoted as if they were consumer products like laundry detergent or breakfast cereal. Instead of concentrating on the issues, TV ads were often personal attacks on the opposing candidate. The ads themselves became the topic of news coverage.

When the votes were counted, Bush carried 40 states, giving him 426 electoral votes to 112 for Dukakis. Polling results showed that 85 percent of those who had supported Ronald Reagan voted for Bush. Voters seemed to be saying not only that they wanted Bush for President, but also that they wanted him to continue Reagan's policies.

Bush Faces New Problems

When George Bush took the oath of office, he looked out on a world far different from the one his predecessor faced. As Communist governments in Eastern Europe fell, the United States had to reevaluate its diplomatic and military goals. Now free of the burden of containing communism, the nation could commit a greater share of its resources to domestic matters: revitalizing the cities, restoring respect for public schools, and building a domestic economy that could compete internationally.

The public consensus that both the military force and the defense budget should be reduced touched off arguments about how much and how fast. In early 1992

★ ★ ★ Gallery of Presidents ★ ★ ★

George Bush

1989–1993

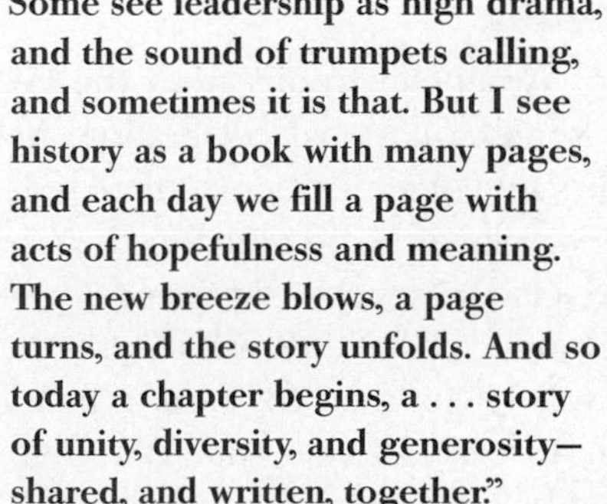

"Some see leadership as high drama, and the sound of trumpets calling, and sometimes it is that. But I see history as a book with many pages, and each day we fill a page with acts of hopefulness and meaning. The new breeze blows, a page turns, and the story unfolds. And so today a chapter begins, a . . . story of unity, diversity, and generosity—shared, and written, together."

Inaugural Address, January 20, 1989

AP/WIDE WORLD

Background

- Born 1924
- Republican, Texas
- Elected to the House of Representatives 1966
- Elected Vice President 1980, 1984

Achievements in Office

- Americans with Disabilities Act (1990)
- Clean Air Act (1990)
- START Treaty (1991)

© S. COMPOINT/SYGMA

The Persian Gulf **As they fled the country, Saddam Hussein's troops set fire to hundreds of Kuwaiti oil wells. The dense smoke polluted skies over many parts of Southwest Asia and Northeast Africa.** *Why did Hussein try to pull Israel into the war?*

the Pentagon ordered personnel cuts and other cuts that would save $103 billion over 5 years. Ironically, these cutbacks were announced just weeks after fighting men and women had proved their effectiveness by winning a war on a Southwest Asia battleground.

The Persian Gulf War

A Battle Over Oil

In early August 1990, news reached the White House that Iraqi forces had invaded neighboring Kuwait and taken over its capital. In the view of President Bush, Iraq's dangerous dictator, Saddam Hussein, had threatened half the world's oil supply and was thumbing his nose at the United States. The attack seemed to threaten the post–cold war order, and the President and his secretary of state, James Baker, were quick to respond.

The two men devoted themselves to putting together a coalition of countries to fight Iraq. Bush promised Saudi Arabia, an Iraqi neighbor, that he would commit American military forces to defend that country from Hussein's aggression. "I will see this through with you," he told the Saudi ambassador.

Twenty-eight nations joined the effort, including several Arab states. The most personnel came from the United States—half a million troops. Additional military support came from Saudi Arabia, Egypt, Great Britain, Syria, and France.

A Quick Victory

On January 17, 1991, a United States–led military force launched air strikes against Iraqi military targets in Baghdad, the capital, and other Iraqi cities. For 5 weeks Allied aircraft flew more than 40,000 sorties, demolishing Iraqi industrial and military sites and draining the fighting spirit of Iraqi troops. Many Iraqi civilians were killed also. The ground war began on February 24, 1991, when Allied tanks and personnel advanced against Iraqi troops in Kuwait.

Hussein had tried to draw Israel into the war in a desperate ploy to detach the Arab members from the coalition. Here too his efforts failed. Israel, although hit by numerous "Scud" missiles launched from Iraq, stayed out of the war at the urging of the American government.

The Allies pressed forward to a quick victory. When the 1,000-hour air battle and 100-hour ground blitz ended, about 100,000 Iraqi soldiers lay dead, and Kuwait was liberated. Fewer than 300 Allied troops died as a result of the war. When it ended, more than 90 percent of the American public approved of how President Bush had handled the war.

While fleeing Kuwait, Hussein's forces set fire to Kuwait's oil fields, filling the skies with thick black smoke and coating both sea and land with oily sludge. Scientists could not gauge the long-term effects of this environmental sabotage.

A New World Order

The return of American troops from the Persian Gulf War was a time of national celebration. Yellow ribbons, the nation's sign of remembrance, fluttered from tree trunks. After weeks of being glued to their televisions, people were glad to see the war over.

At the time few noticed that the celebration at the end of this small war was bigger than any held to honor the end of more than 40 years of cold war. The Gulf War probably could not have happened during the cold war. The United States would not have risked a confrontation with the Soviets. By 1991 that risk had disappeared.

The Gulf War seemed to help the United States regain the prestige it had lost in Vietnam. It also boosted American influence in the Arab world and set the stage for new peace talks in Southwest Asia. These held the most promise yet that Israel and its Arab neighbors would come to terms. The war also brought new respect to the United Nations (UN), which had unanimously condemned Iraqi aggression and sponsored the Allied military effort.

New Role for the United Nations

The Persian Gulf War signaled the UN's changing role in world affairs. Created in 1945 the UN was often ignored by the superpowers or their allies. Yet it contributed to world peace as UN negotiators arranged cease-fire agreements in dozens of conflicts. These conflicts ranged from the 1949 Arab-Israeli war to the 1988 end of hostilities between Morocco and the Polisario Front in a battle over the Western Sahara.

When Iraq invaded Kuwait, the United Nations took on new importance in battling aggression. For the first time, United States and Soviet leaders, cooperating with the UN, worked together to end a world crisis. In addition, between 1988 and 1992, UN forces, wearing blue helmets or berets, continued to police the world's hot spots and attempted to bring order to troubled lands. Altogether, it was engaged in 13 actions during that time—as many as it had undertaken in the previous 42 years of its existence. These actions took place all over the world.

In Cambodia the United Nations organized elections and provided materials for new homes for the country's 370,000 refugees. UN troops monitored the civil war in the former Yugoslavia and attempted to enforce sanctions against government forces. In Somalia UN peacekeepers tried to safeguard supply lines carrying food to the starving people of the nation. Many of the UN's efforts were thwarted, however, because sanctions failed to halt conflict, and rebels carried off food, clothing, and medicine intended for victims.

International Politics

New Nations, New Governments

With the end of the cold war came both new hope and new challenges to maintain a peaceful world. After Gorbachev's landmark steps to open Soviet society to democracy and a free-market economy, optimism blossomed worldwide. Cooperation extended even to Antarctica, as 25 leading nations signed an accord in October 1991 to protect that frozen continent's environment from exploitation.

China proved an exception in at least one important way. Although its aging leaders allowed some free enterprise to take root, they generally clamped down on political freedom. In June 1989, China's rulers ordered troops to crush a democracy movement in Beijing. Television carried pictures to the United States of Chinese tanks rolling into a peaceful crowd of some 5,000 student demonstrators in Tiananmen Square. Two images in particular were imprinted on the public mind. One was of a replica of the Statue of Liberty called the Goddess of Democracy, which the students erected as a symbol of their desire for freedom. The other was of a lone protester facing a row of oncoming tanks—an unarmed youth standing against the military might of a repressive regime.The Chinese government never released casualty figures for the massacre at Tiananmen Square, and estimates vary widely, from 700 to 5,000.

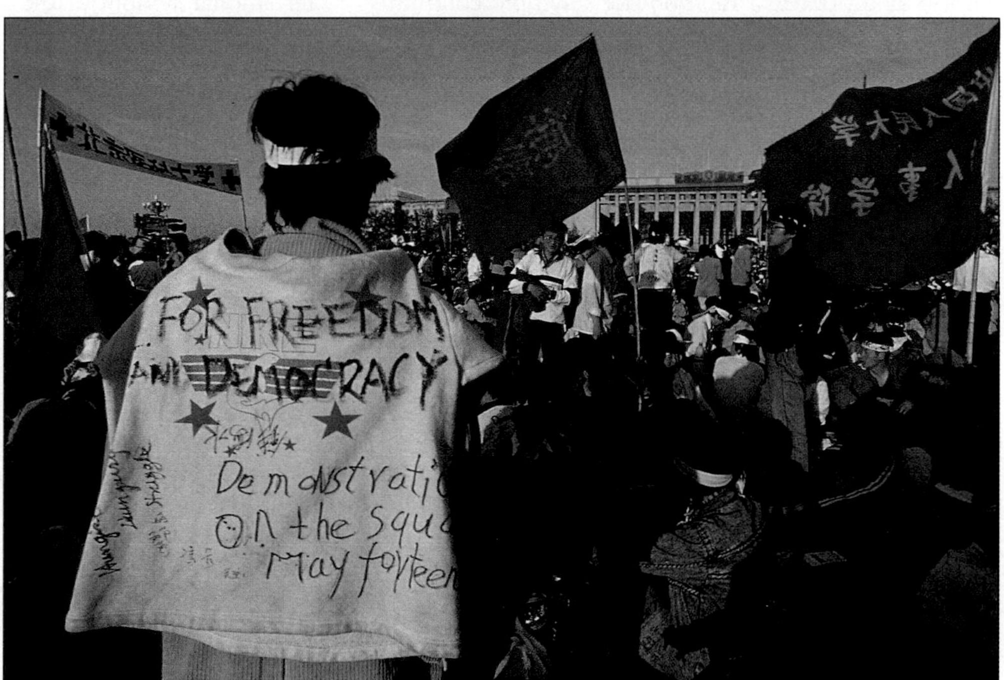

Tiananmen Square This demonstration by students in Tiananmen Square occurred on the day of Mikhail Gorbachev's arrival. *How did the world community react to China's crackdown on the pro-democracy activists?*

The power of the images set off a debate in the United States. President Bush, drawing on his diplomatic experience in China as the head of the United States Liaison Office in Beijing from 1974 to 1975, attempted to dampen the moral outrage many Americans felt because he feared a breakdown in Chinese-American relations. A majority in Congress, on the other hand, wanted to impose stiff sanctions on the Chinese. It was later revealed that Bush, ignoring the wishes of Congress, had sent a secret mission to China to discuss relations between the two countries. Despite concerns over human rights violations, the United States continued to pursue trade relations with China.

Mandela Freed! After Nelson Mandela was freed from a South African prison, anti-apartheid groups all over the world rejoiced. *What did the release of Mandela signify?*

Peaceful Revolution in South Africa

At the end of a century that had seen almost every African country throw off the yoke of colonial government, racism was still the law of the land in South Africa. Whites clung to the system of **apartheid,** a policy of racial segregation, which excluded black South Africans from meaningful participation in the government.

For decades the world community had treated the nation as an outcast. In 1968 the Olympic committee banned South African participation in the games. In 1977 the United Nations imposed an arms embargo. In 1986 the United States Congress, over President Reagan's veto, imposed economic sanctions. Most American companies stopped doing business with South Africa, and the nation began to slip into recession. Even white South Africans began to realize that apartheid was a dead-end street.

The 1990s saw an enormous transformation take place in South Africa. Credit for the change goes largely to two remarkable leaders: Nelson Mandela and F.W. de Klerk. Nelson Mandela was the leader of the African National Congress (ANC), the outlawed organization that struggled to win rights for blacks in South Africa. In 1964 the white government sentenced Mandela to life imprisonment for treason, yet he continued to be an international symbol of the struggle against apartheid in South Africa.

De Klerk was elected president of South Africa in 1989. Recognizing that his nation could no longer survive under apartheid, he announced that he was going to release Nelson Mandela from jail and to legalize the ANC. Following that dramatic moment, he began the tough negotiations with the ANC that resulted in the first-ever multiracial election in his country.

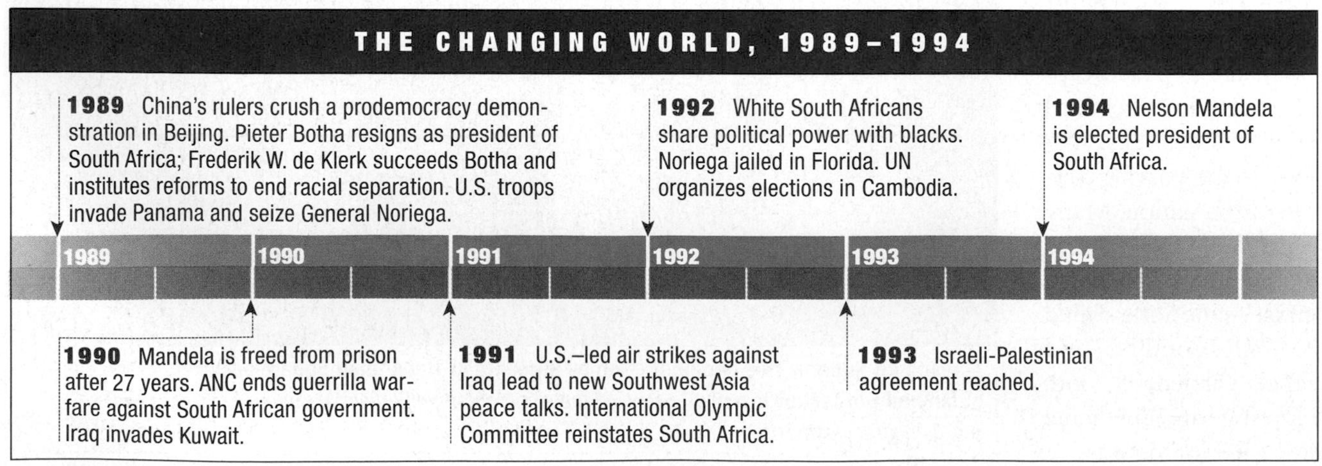

THE CHANGING WORLD, 1989–1994
1989 China's rulers crush a prodemocracy demonstration in Beijing. Pieter Botha resigns as president of South Africa; Frederik W. de Klerk succeeds Botha and institutes reforms to end racial separation. U.S. troops invade Panama and seize General Noriega.
1992 White South Africans share political power with blacks. Noriega jailed in Florida. UN organizes elections in Cambodia.
1994 Nelson Mandela is elected president of South Africa.
1989
1990
1991
1992
1993
1994
1990 Mandela is freed from prison after 27 years. ANC ends guerrilla warfare against South African government. Iraq invades Kuwait.
1991 U.S.–led air strikes against Iraq lead to new Southwest Asia peace talks. International Olympic Committee reinstates South Africa.
1993 Israeli-Palestinian agreement reached.

On April 27, 1994, lines of voters—black and white—stretched across the South African landscape. Many waited for hours in pouring rain. Observed white playwright, Athol Fugard, "White South Africans should consider themselves one of the luckiest groups of people on the face of the earth. In spite of our terrible history, we weren't torn apart by the violence disemboweling countries like Yugoslavia."

When the votes were counted, 75-year-old Nelson Mandela was president of South Africa, and F.W. de Klerk was deputy president. The nation entered the new era with hopes high.

American Troops in Panama

In the Western Hemisphere, the United States once more used military force to achieve its aims. In February 1988, a United States federal grand jury indicted Panamanian leader Manuel Antonio Noriega on drug-dealing charges. American troops stormed the Central American nation in December 1989 to overthrow Noriega and bring him to trial. The United States alleged that he had turned Panama into a depot to launder illicit money and channel drugs between Colombian drug cartels and American dealers. In April 1992, a jury in Florida convicted him of these crimes.

Middle East Peace Talks

The Persian Gulf War prodded many Arabs and Israelis to try again to bury their ancient hostilities and live in peace. Using diplomatic influence gained in the war, Secretary of State James Baker brought together negotiators from many countries and factions in late 1991.

The massive changes Gorbachev had unleashed also had a ripple effect in Israel. Almost 400,000 Soviet Jews were allowed to immigrate to Israel in the late 1980s and early 1990s. Israel asked for a $10 billion loan from the United States to help resettle the immigrants. In return, Israeli leaders agreed to come to the negotiating table in Washington, D.C. The talks held out the most promise in years for a resolution of the Arab-Israeli conflict. After months of intense negotiations, in 1993 Palestinians and Israelis signed an agreement for limited Palestinian self-rule in Gaza and in the West Bank.

The next year saw the United States play a pivotal role in another historic accord. In 1994 Israel and neighboring Jordan signed a declaration in the Rose Garden of the White House, ending a state of war that had existed for 46 years. Said Jordan's King Hussein, "Out of all the days of my life, I do not believe there is one such as this." It seemed clear that the two leaders hoped to leave a legacy of peace in the long-troubled region. The road to peace, however, was anything but smooth. In November 1995, an assassin's bullets killed Israeli Prime Minister Yitzhak Rabin. The attack cast a pall over the peace negotiations.

Battles for Markets

United States, Canada, and Mexico Open Trade Doors

Although the cold war had ended, competition and even conflict over trade continued. Through most of the 1980s, the United States led the world in exporting goods to other nations. Beginning in the late 1980s, however, Americans imported more than they exported each year, creating a costly **trade deficit.** The country was losing ground to its main competitors, including the European Union (EU)—formerly called the European Community—a 12-nation trade bloc, and the Asian nations of Japan, Taiwan, South Korea, and China.

One response to global economic competition was to form a United States–led trade bloc. In 1988 the United States signed an agreement with Canada to gradually remove tariffs and other obstacles to trade on everything from lumber to cassettes to cars. Then, in a momentous event, the two nations joined with Mexico to sign the North American Free Trade Agreement (NAFTA) in August 1992.

© SERGIO DORANTES/SYGMA

Homage to a Leader Jordan's King Hussein traveled to Israel to speak at Prime Minister Rabin's funeral. *Why was this speech such a historic event?*

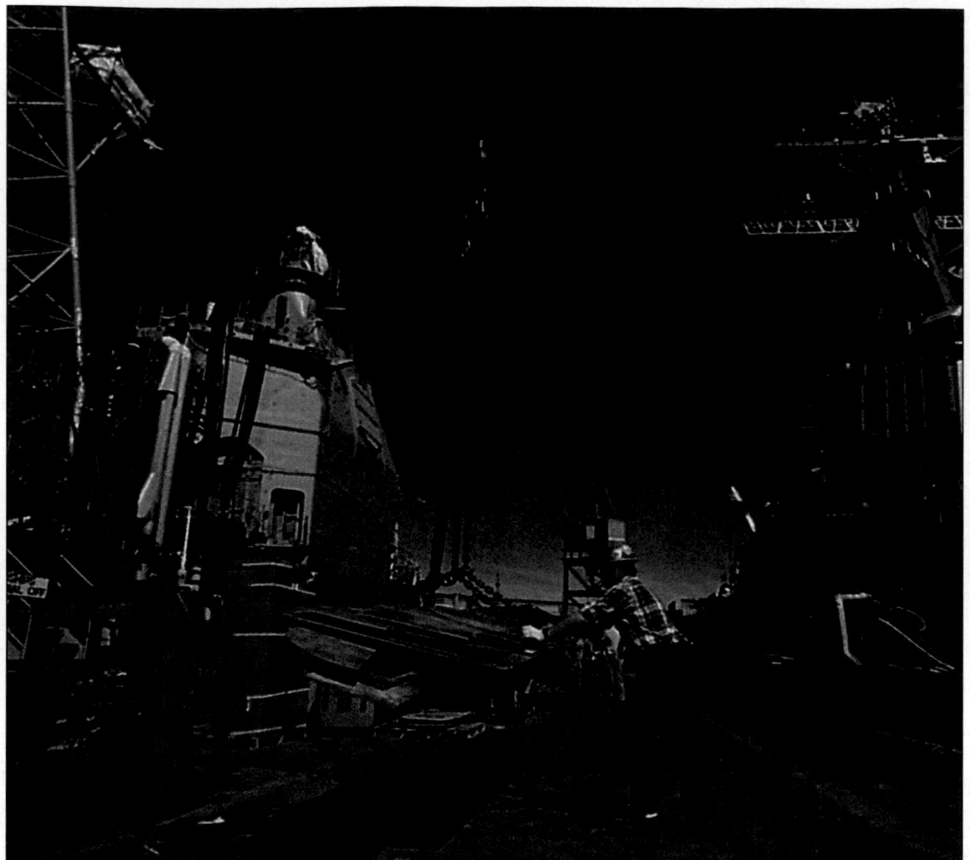

© RICHARD HOWARD

The Recession This defense-related shipyard in Bath, Maine, once employed thousands of people, but as defense spending was cut, so were jobs. As the 1990s began, Americans were buying more imported goods. *Who did defense cuts affect?*

The pact offered two main benefits. It would end most cross-border tariffs and quotas on goods and services by the year 2000, and it would give the NAFTA members greater leverage in negotiating with the EU and the Asian powers. With this leverage, businesses could nurture potential new markets while maintaining old ones. American and Canadian labor unions and some corporate leaders opposed NAFTA. Their main fear was that manufacturing jobs would move to lower-wage plants in Mexico and thus hurt American and Canadian workers. Environmentalists also worried about pollution controls.

Recession Adjustments

Defense and Automobile Industries Lose Markets

By early 1991 the American economy was fraught with problems: economic growth had halted; unemployment was rising; and the after-tax income for most workers was falling. Defense spending, still the single largest allocation of the federal budget, had been cut drastically. The economy and the nation needed to readjust.

The Arms Build-Down

Americans realized the economy was in serious trouble as the effects of military budget cuts spread across the country. The terms of treaties signed with the Soviet Union in the late 1980s called for major troop reductions. The Pentagon moved to eliminate 500,000 active duty military personnel by 1997. Army, navy, marine, and air force reserve units throughout the country also felt the budget cutters' axe. The 1990 cuts, affecting about one-fourth of the American military facilities in Europe, touched airfields, barracks, and even remote weather stations. These first cuts set the pace for those to follow. "General Motors is eliminating seventy-four thousand employees over three years," said General Colin Powell, chairman of the Joint Chiefs of Staff. "We're doing that many alone from January to September [of 1992]."

The defense cuts also affected American civilians. An estimated 1.35 million defense industry workers would lose their jobs by 1997. Demand was dropping for everything from soldiers' socks to billion-dollar B-2 bombers. Following the cancellation of the Seawolf nuclear submarine program, General Dynamics, Connecticut's second largest employer, planned to lay off nearly a quarter of its 17,000 workers. Smaller companies serving the defense industry were particularly hard hit. In Dallas-Fort Worth half the manufacturing jobs lost were defense related. In San Diego similar defense-related positions accounted for one-third of all lost jobs. Across the country, two-thirds of the 190,000 manufacturing jobs lost in 1990 were in military-related industries.

Military contracts from foreign governments saved some defense-related jobs. Workers at the McDonnell-Douglas complex in St. Louis, for example, prepared to supply Saudi Arabia with 72 new F-15 fighters. Nevertheless, cuts in defense spending cost defense contractors a major portion of their business. To make matters worse, the recession limited the industry's ability to retool factories and retrain employees to work in other high-tech fields, such as environmental protection or the construction of power plants or high-speed trains. Companies and workers began looking to the government to help pay for transforming the factories. "Priming the pump is the way to go," said John O'Brien, chairman of Grumman Corporation, a leading defense contractor.

Economic Woes The budget deficit caused George Bush problems during his presidency. *What weakened the nation's economy?*

the windows and doors of stores, restaurants, movie theaters, and offices.

Meanwhile, in Washington, D.C., the Bush administration and Congress struggled to find ways to jump-start the economy. Bush proposed a cut in the capital gains tax that he said would stimulate new investment. Calling the proposal a tax break for the rich, the Democrats in Congress defeated it. Faced with an ever-growing deficit, Bush broke his "no new taxes" campaign pledge. After a series of budget summits with congressional leaders, Bush agreed to a tax increase that fell mostly on those with low and average incomes. The Federal Reserve System carried out another recession-fighting strategy, cutting interest rates 18 times between 1989 and the end of 1992. Lower interest rates had spurred the economy out of every recession since 1948 by fueling consumer spending and increasing demand for manufactured goods. The recession of the early 1990s, however, proved unyielding. Interest rates on savings accounts went down as well, driving investors to the stock market, where they hoped for greater returns. For retirees who depended on the interest income from their savings accounts, lower interest rates often meant real hardships.

The recession persisted, and by late 1992 the United States economy stood trapped in the longest stagnant period since World War II. Sales at major corporations and neighborhood shops alike kept declining, forcing more layoffs—of white-collar workers as well as blue-collar. Government, businesses, and consumers found themselves with little cash to promote economic growth.

The Stubborn Recession

Defense was not the only industry caught in a changing world. Automobile makers, like many manufacturers, found themselves losing out to worldwide competition. In 1988 American automakers earned a record $11 billion in profits. Three years later they lost a record $7.5 billion. Falling revenue was only a symptom of their economic ills: the United States's share of worldwide automobile sales fell from 75 percent in 1950 to just 19 percent in 1991. American industry had come face-to-face with the realities of a **global economy.** This new system of worldwide trade was evident in the variety of inexpensive, foreign-made goods that American consumers found in local stores. The popularity of those foreign products upset the balance of trade between the United States and other countries. By the 1990s, each year the total value of goods the United States bought from other countries was about $100 billion more than the total value of goods it sold to other countries. This trade deficit weakened the nation's economy and hurt the ability of American companies to compete with foreign companies.

The nation's inability to compete hit home in the nation's industrial towns and cities. In the video documentary *Roger and Me,* filmmaker Michael Moore recorded what happened to his hometown of Flint, Michigan, as General Motors closed its facilities there. Once a thriving middle-class community, Flint began to resemble a ghost town. Unemployed autoworkers left town to seek jobs elsewhere, and local businesses quickly lost most of their customers. Deputies evicted people from their homes because they could not pay their rent or meet their mortgages. Along Flint's main street, boards covered

Ballooning Debt

Many economists believed that the recession's stubbornness was due in part to the nation's enormous debt. For years the federal government had operated with a budget deficit, spending more money each year than it collected in taxes and revenues. In 1992 the deficit reached $333 billion. Some economists estimated that the deficit could soar to $500 billion, 5 percent of the nation's income, by the year 2002. The government financed the deficit by selling billions of dollars worth of bonds each month, often to overseas investors. Paying the interest on those bonds reduced the government's resources for combatting the recession. In addition, interest payments diverted spending away from programs to improve education, end drug abuse, rebuild the nation's roads and railways, and fight urban decay. Government economists kept predicting that the economy would rebound by mid-1992, but high levels of personal and corporate debt worked against recovery. Like the government, individuals and corporations were paying interest on their own debts.

Wealth and Poverty

Stock and Banking Scandals Hurt Working Class

The recession and the economic policies that resulted from it touched people at all income levels. The effects on the wealthy, the middle class, and the poor were vastly different. In 1989 the richest 1 percent of American households owned 36 percent of the country's total private wealth. This represented a 5 percent increase in the wealthy elite's share since 1983. At the same time, the number of people living in poverty rose from about 11 percent of the population in the 1970s to about 15 percent in 1991.

The Income Gap

The rich got richer for a number of reasons. Top corporate executives commanded ever-higher salaries. Even during the layoffs and plant closings of the late 1980s and early 1990s, pay for top executives continued to rise, soaring to 160 times the pay of an average worker. Many well-off people also benefited from tax law changes. The Reagan administration argued that giving the wealthy more capital to invest would expand business. The effects would "trickle-down" to the middle and lower classes. In 1986 tax reform decreased taxes on the wealthy from 70 percent to 30 percent of their taxable income, but the "trickle down" effect did not occur for everyone.

Others became rich through elaborate and sometimes illegal business deals. In the 1980s a wave of corporate takeovers swept the country. One of the largest was Chevron's takeover of Gulf Oil at a cost of $13.4 billion. The 2 brokerage houses involved in the merger together received $45 million. Corporate mergers offered great profits to some merger specialists while extracting a high price from the nation's economy. Corporations that might be takeover targets often sacrificed long-term performance in favor of short-term profits. This practice weakened the economy.

The deregulation of the banking industry opened another avenue for enrichment. Officers in institutions such as Lincoln Savings and Loan in California made large loans to businesses that had little chance of succeeding. Often, the bankers knew or were related to the businesses' top executives. The borrowers paid themselves huge salaries; the banking executives pocketed fat commissions. When the businesses failed, the bank often failed as well. There was no money to repay the investors or to cover the deposits of the customers. Taxpayers got the bill for more than 1,000 bank or savings-and-loan failures, at an estimated cost of $500 billion.

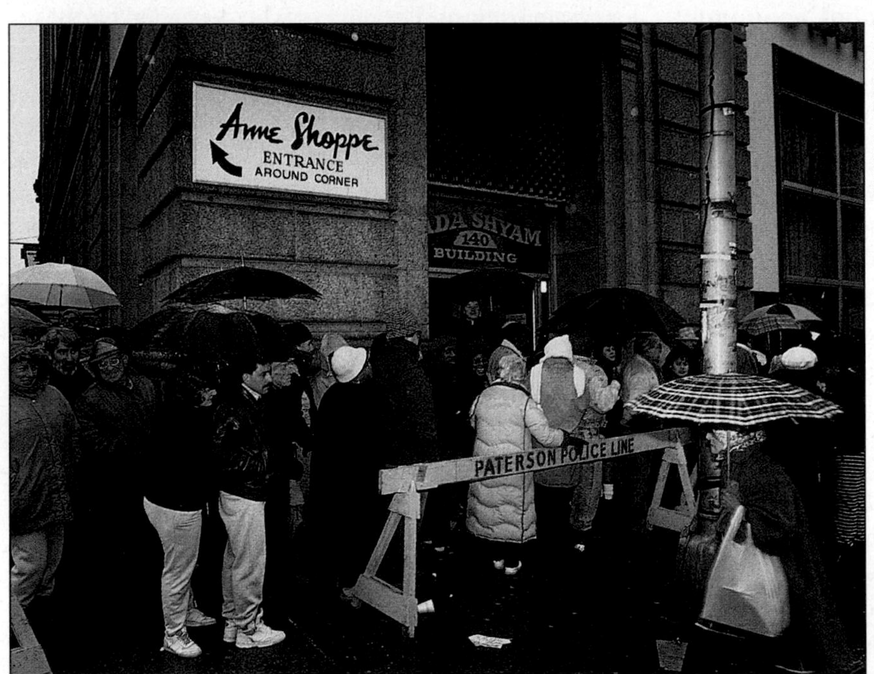

© PETER BYRON/BLACK STAR

Banks Close Many banks failed in the 1980s because of their irresponsible lending practices. *Who benefited most from these loans? Who ended up paying for the failed loans?*

Pressures on the Middle Class

American taxpayers shouldered the bulk of the tax burden for the failed savings-and-loan institutions. In the late 1980s and early 1990s, working people coped with stagnant incomes and a declining quality of life. More and more businesses were moving factories and jobs to cheaper, less regulated foreign labor markets; and changing technologies were making many blue-collar jobs obsolete. For Americans in the middle and the lower classes, affordable health care became increasingly difficult to find. Some retirees learned that their union pension plans had been mismanaged. Most of all, they watched their children's opportunities for a better future dwindle.

Unlike previous downturns, the recession of the early 1990s also barreled through the suburban United States. Forty percent of the jobs lost in the recession of the early 1990s were white-collar jobs. Hardworking members of the middle class, like Ben D'Cruz, saw the American dream evaporate before their eyes. In 1991 D'Cruz was laid off from a $48,000-a-year job at Norden Systems in New York. He looked in vain for a comparable position; he applied for jobs paying as little as $19,000 without success. After spending most of his retirement savings, D'Cruz relied on unemployment compensation and his wife's earnings to make ends meet. "It's very tough out there," he said. "Even if you go out of Long Island, it's happening all over." Many of the white-collar layoffs turned out to be permanent, as global competition forced companies to cut costs aggressively.

© MARK LUDAK/IMPACT VISUALS

Urban Poverty A young mother in a San Francisco homeless shelter feeds her son. *How many children lived in poverty in 1989?*

Otherwise encouraging economic developments failed to make a difference for hard-pressed middle-class Americans in the early 1990s. Home mortgage rates fell to their lowest levels in two decades, while prices dropped for numerous consumer goods. Nevertheless, consumer purchases did not increase because consumer incomes had not kept pace with rising costs. The increased taxes on the middle class had left them with less money to spend than they had had a decade earlier.

The Frayed Safety Net

As the recession deepened, the people with the least money to spend lost the most economic ground. Half the adults living in poverty, 14 million people, were classified as **working poor.** These adults earned less than $12,195 a year, too little to pull a family of 4 out of poverty. The nation's poorest people had been left out of the business boom of the 1980s. Like the middle class, the working poor lost jobs to foreign labor and automation. Workers fortunate enough to hold on to basic jobs watched their earning power plummet.

These circumstances affected some more than others. Between 1983 and 1989 the net worth of white families fell 8 percent. During the same period, the net worth of African American and Hispanic families fell 42 percent. Women and children were now the poorest of the poor; the number of poor single-parent families increased. By 1989, nearly 1 of every 5 children was living in poverty; 14 percent of these children were white, 35 percent were Hispanic, and 43 percent were African American.

The economic losses of African Americans and Hispanic Americans were mainly felt in cities. City revenues fell, and urban dwellers began to see crumbling streets, leaking sewers, and broken bridges. Some cities closed schools and eliminated educational programs due to decreased revenues for education. While city problems multiplied, cities found that their share of federal dollars fell. Federal aid to cities in 1992 was 64 percent less than it had been in 1980.

Section Assessment

Main Idea

1. Use a diagram like this one to show some of the post–cold war adjustments that the United States faced in terms of diplomatic goals, global trade, and federal spending.

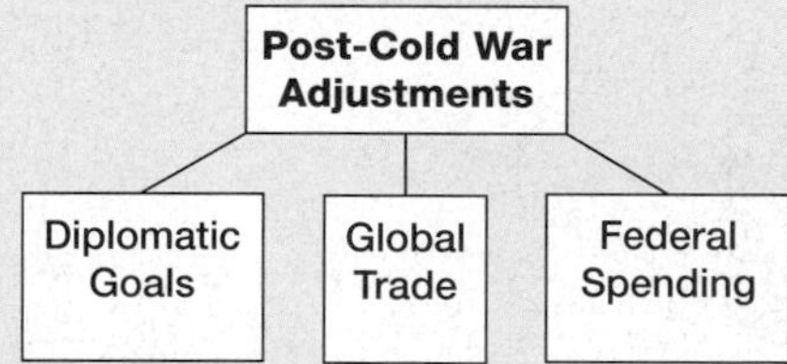

Vocabulary

2. Define: apartheid, trade deficit, global economy, working poor.

Checking Facts

3. What effects did cuts in defense spending have on civilians in the United States?
4. What triggered the Persian Gulf War, and what were the results of the war?

Critical Thinking

5. **Predicting Consequences** How is global economic competition changing relations between the United States and its neighbors Canada and Mexico?

© STEVE SCHAPIRO/SYGMA

The Rap on the Eighties

In the 1980s many Americans focused on comfort and appearance, trying to live well and look good. Technology changed, too. Compact discs (CDs), juice boxes, and cordless telephones appeared. A new movie rating, PG-13, was invented. New words, such as *couch potato* and *yuppie,* entered our language.

APPEARANCE COUNTS

Baby boomers placed low-fat, high-fiber foods, designer clothes, and health clubs high on their agendas. **Jane Fonda workout** books and videos sold well.

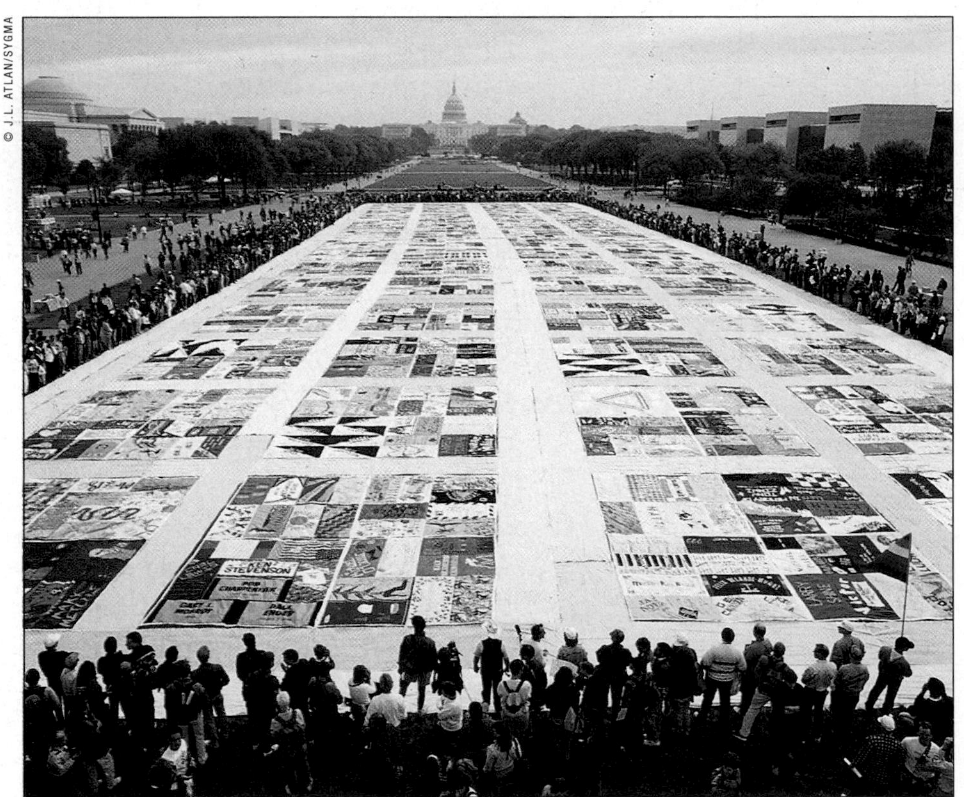
© J.L. ATLAN/SYGMA

A DEADLY DISEASE

In 1981 medical experts identified a mysterious disease that came to be called AIDS. Rock Hudson raised public awareness of the disease when he acknowledged in 1985 that he was battling AIDS. On October 11, 1987, thousands of people gathered in Washington, D.C., to display an **AIDS quilt.** Each square of the quilt represented someone who had died of the disease.

MTV: MUSIC TELEVISION LOGO USED BY PERMISSION. MTV NETWORKS, A DIVISION OF VIACOM

CABLE TV ARRIVES

MTV, which began the rock video business, was one of many new cable television stations that originated during the 1980s. Others included CNN, the Disney Channel, the Discovery Channel, A&E, and TNT. VCRs also became popular during this period, increasing 72 percent in sales from 1980 to 1981.

MUSICIANS COME TOGETHER

In 1985 musicians from around the world performed to raise money for drought-stricken Africa. The concert, called **Live Aid,** was staged in both Philadelphia and London, and almost 2 billion people watched it. It grossed $70 million. The "We Are the World" (the concert's theme song) record and video raised another $50 million.

© BENSON/GAMMA LIAISON

© TOM MIHALEK/SYGMA

PHOTO OF ALBUMS BY DOUG MINDELL

THE MATERIAL GIRL

One of many musicians to appear at Live Aid, **Madonna** had 5 best-selling albums in the 1980s. Her stage shows, along with clever promotion, helped ensure her success in the 1980s.

RAPPERS ROAR

Its syncopated, rhythmic beat and its chanted, rhyming lyrics made **rap music** a form of expression almost anyone could enjoy. The most popular rappers projected an image of power, independence, and arrogance that appealed to their fans.

Chapter  Assessment

Self-Check Quiz

Visit the *American Odyssey* Web site at americanodyssey.glencoe.com and click on ***Chapter 25—Self-Check Quiz*** to prepare for the Chapter Test.

Reviewing Key Terms

Choose the vocabulary term that best completes each sentence below. Write your answers on a separate sheet of paper.

trade deficit **glasnost**
global economy **perestroika**
apartheid

1. A _________ is created when a country imports more than it exports.

2. Gorbachev's policy of _________ encouraged Soviet citizens to look beyond communism to new ways of doing things.

3. South Africa used _________ to keep blacks separated from whites and out of the government.

4. Economic competition among nations is a feature of the ________ .

Recalling Facts

1. What forces combined to sweep Ronald Reagan into office in 1980?

2. How did Reaganomics differ from Keynesian economic theories?

3. How did Reagan and Bush tax policies affect wealthy Americans? Poor Americans?

4. How did Reagan's deregulation policies affect the environment?

5. What was Reagan's greatest achievement in foreign policy? Why was it so important?

6. What led to the collapse of communism in the Soviet Union? How was Gorbachev himself instrumental in bringing about the collapse?

7. How did the focus of United States foreign policy shift after the end of the cold war?

8. Who were the Sandinistas? What was the United States's role in the Nicaraguan civil war?

9. How did the Iran-*contra* scandal affect Ronald Reagan's presidency?

10. Why did President Bush and Secretary of State Baker seek to involve a large number of nations in the coalition against Iraq in the Persian Gulf War?

11. Explain the steps by which apartheid was abolished in South Africa.

12. What were the advantages of the NAFTA pact? Why were some people so opposed to it?

13. What prompted the military cutbacks in the United States in the early 1990s?

14. How did the trade deficit weaken the nation's economy?

15. In what ways did the recession of the early 1990s change both the suburban and urban United States?

Critical Thinking

1. Making Comparisons Compare the end of communism in East Germany to its end in Poland.

2. Identifying Assumptions Some critics of NAFTA argued that free trade would drive down Americans' wages to Mexican levels. What assumptions does this argument make?

3. Making Comparisons Use a diagram like this one to compare the Great Depression of the 1930s with the recession of the early 1990s.

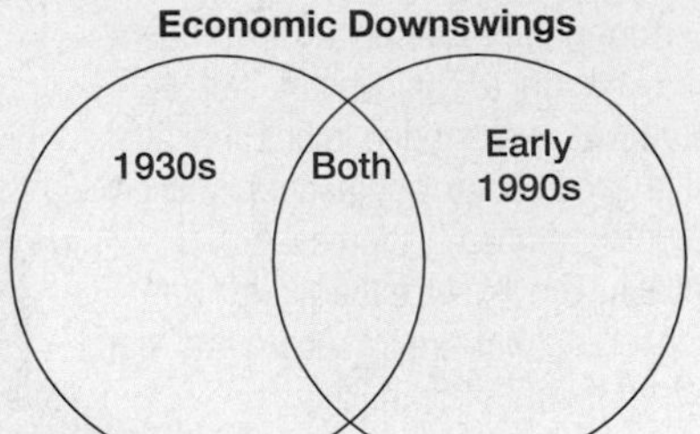

4. Determining Cause and Effect In the early 1990s, home mortgage rates were lower than they had been in 20 years, and yet sales of new homes rose slowly. What caused the slow sales?

Portfolio Project

PORTFOLIO PROJECT

Imagine that you are a resident of East Berlin the day the Wall goes down. Write down what you think your reactions to that event might be. What would you now be able to do that you could not do before November 9, 1989? If possible, read some newspapers or newsmagazines from that period to learn the actual reactions of Berliners. Keep the results of your research in your portfolio.

Cooperative Learning

Form small groups and take turns explaining the following economic terms and concepts and describing how they work: the deficit, the national debt, supply-side economics, balanced budget, global economy, recession, trade deficit, and trickle-down economics.

GEOGRAPHY AND HISTORY

Persian Gulf War, 1991

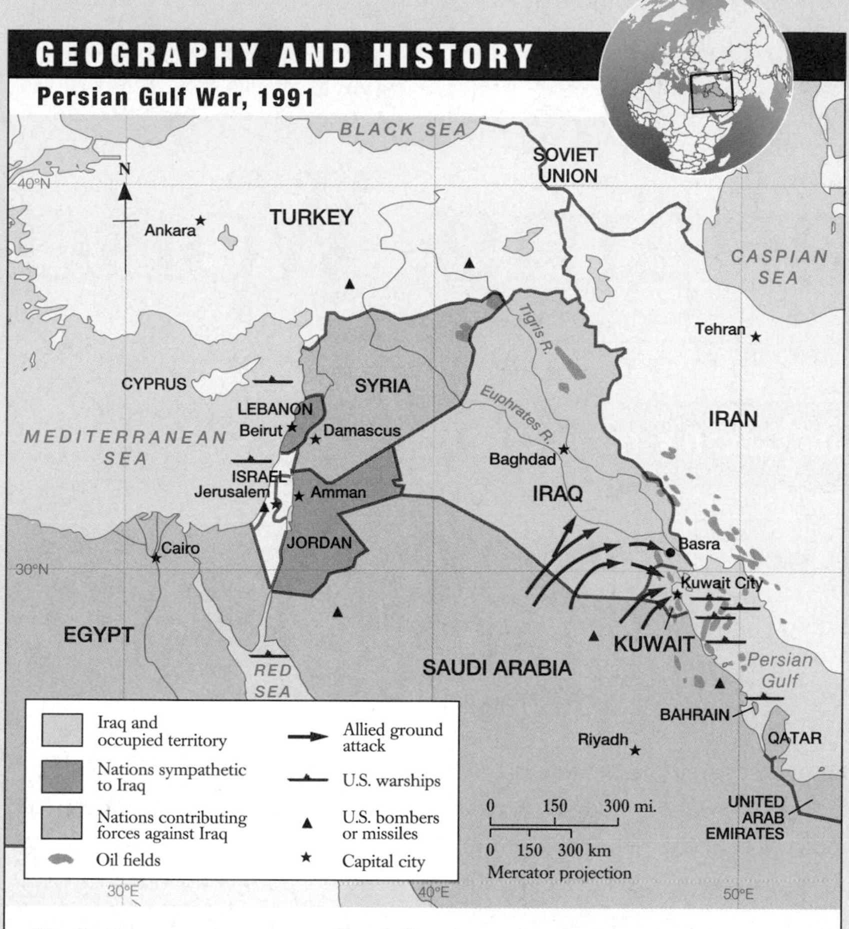

Study the map to answer the following questions:

1. In which countries were United States bombers located?

2. Which countries were sympathetic to Iraq?

3. Where did the Allied ground attack take place?

4. Locate the oil fields in Southwest Asia.

5. Which nations helped in the Allied invasion?

Reinforcing Skills

Using an Electronic Spreadsheet Over a 4-week period, note both the high and low temperatures for each day. Insert an equation to calculate the average temperature for the first day. Copy the equation to calculate the average temperature for each day. Using your spreadsheet software, create a line graph showing the daily high, the daily low, and the daily average temperatures and the daily average temperature for this 4-week period.

Technology Activity

Using the Internet Search the Internet for current information about Kuwait since the Persian Gulf War. Write a short description of what a traveler visiting this nation might expect to find today.

Standardized Test Practice

1. Reaganomics failed in that the program was unable to

A produce a balanced budget.
B reduce unemployment.
C lower inflation.
D scale back interest rates.

> ***Test-Taking Tip:*** Think of the meaning of *Reaganomics:* an economic policy that favored tax cuts, especially for wealthy individuals and large corporations. How might such a policy affect the spending of individuals, businesses, and government? Which would have *less* money to work with?

2. "It is time to check and reverse the growth of government which shows signs of having grown beyond the consent of the governed." This quote by President Reagan *best* reflects the idea of

A a new world order.
B neoconservatism.
C democratic capitalism.
D mutual deterrence.

> ***Test-Taking Tip:*** Eliminate answers that do not strongly relate to the quote. For example, the terms *new world order* and *mutual deterrence* reflect beliefs about foreign policy, rather than the role of government. Therefore, answers A and D can be ruled out.

A Changing Nation in a Changing World

NOVEMBER 7, 2000: ELECTION TURNS INTO A CLIFFHANGER.

Who would be the first President of the 21st century? Americans asked that question not only on Election Day, but in the days and weeks thereafter.

The confusion began on election night when paper-thin margins in the popular vote turned a close election into an election too close to call. As the night wore on, the lead in electoral votes seesawed between the Democratic candidate, Vice President Al Gore, and the Republican candidate, Texas Governor George W. Bush. By 1:30 A.M. Eastern time on November 8, each candidate had 242 electoral votes—28 short of the 270 votes required to win the presidency.

While a handful of states were too close to call, Florida with its 25 electoral votes held the key to the White House. Based on early results, TV networks projected Gore the winner of Florida. However, by 2:15 A.M., Bush led by 50,000 votes, and the media proclaimed him the winner. Gore telephoned Bush to concede the election. Then, about an hour later, new results posted on the Florida Board of Elections Web site melted Bush's lead to several hundred votes. Gore telephoned to retract his concession. In the closest national election since 1880, the razor-thin margin in Florida forced an automatic recount under state law.

The chaotic election, and the ensuing legal battles over thousands of undercounted ballots that would determine the nation's 43rd President, turned into a 37-day national civics lesson. With lawsuits flying, federal district courts, the Florida Supreme Court, and the U.S. Supreme Court all entered the fray. In the end, a narrowly divided U.S. Supreme Court brought the cliffhanger to a close. ■

Before you read the chapter, write down factors that you think influenced voter behavior as the nation headed into the 2000s.

Chapter Overview

Visit the *American Odyssey* Web site at americanodyssey.glencoe.com and click on ***Chapter 26—Chapter Overview*** to preview the chapter.

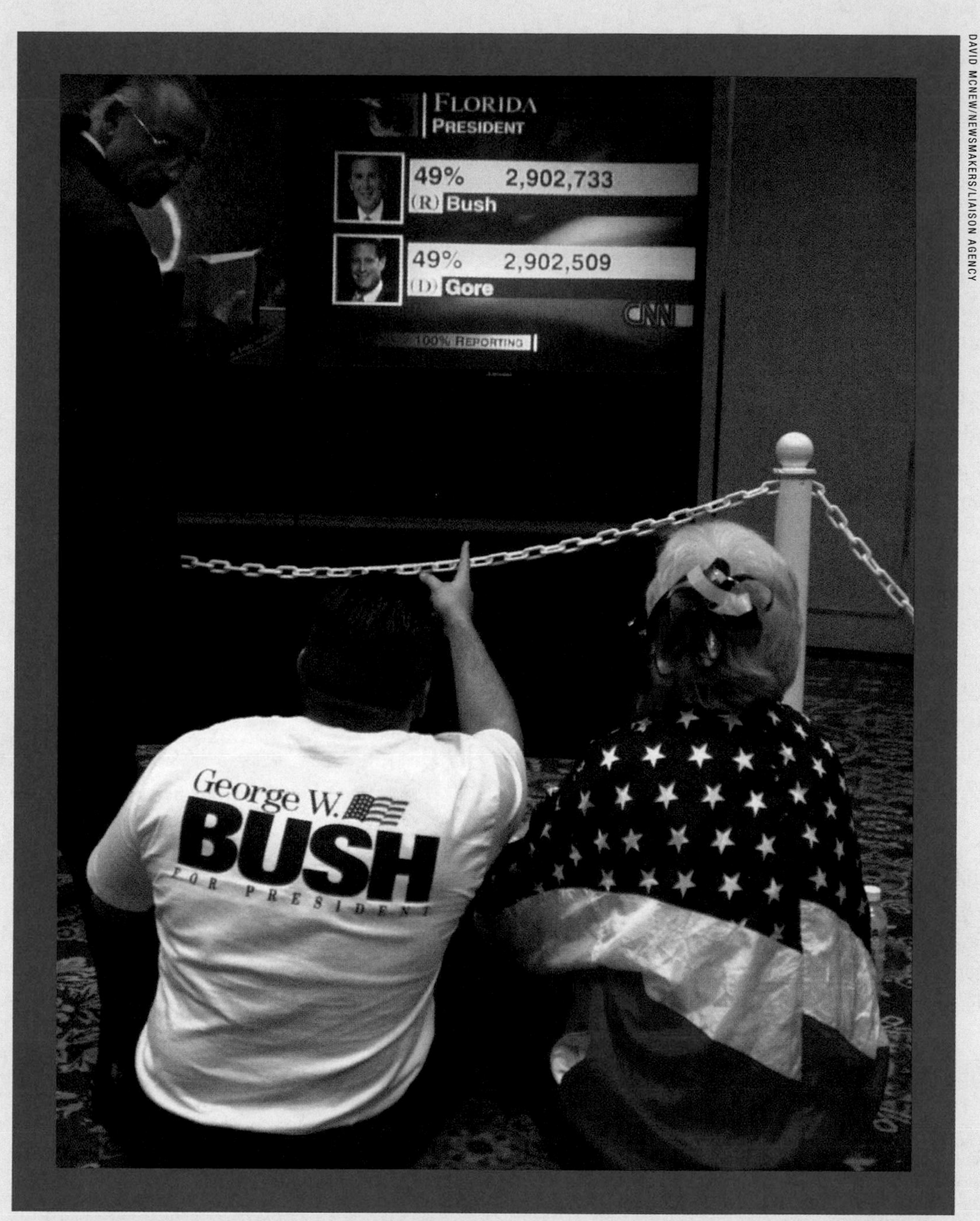

DAVID MCNEW/NEWSMAKERS/LIAISON AGENCY

TWO BUSH SUPPORTERS WATCH TELEVISION REPORTS OF ONE OF THE NATION'S CLOSEST AND MOST CHAOTIC PRESIDENTIAL ELECTIONS.

The Clinton Agenda

AUGUST 1992: CLINTON BUS TOUR ON THE ROAD

© BLACK STAR

The 1992 Clinton Campaign Presidential candidate Bill Clinton takes his bus tour to North Carolina.

The campaign bus rolled through farm country that lay along the banks of the Mississippi River. On board were Arkansas governor Bill Clinton, the Democratic presidential candidate, and his vice-presidential running mate, Senator Albert Gore, Jr., of Tennessee. Traveling with the candidates were their wives, Hillary Rodham Clinton and Tipper Gore. About 150 reporters trailed along as the bus made its way from St. Louis to Minneapolis. During the day, the candidates gave radio and television interviews, met with local politicians, and visited factories and coffee shops.

Working men and women, their jobs done for the day, appeared at the roadside. Women sat in lawn chairs, kids bounced on trampolines, and, in one place, a farmer sat atop his combine holding a homemade sign: Clinton-Gore in '92. Wherever 500 or more people gathered, the bus stopped for an impromptu rally. The candidates made speeches, but they listened, too. What they heard helped shape the Democratic strategy to recapture the White House from the Republican President George Bush and his running mate Vice President Dan Quayle.

1992 Election

The Economy

Hard hit by the recession, American voters approached the 1992 presidential election with one chief concern: the economy. The Democrats and Republicans interjected their fundamental economic differences

Guide to Reading

Main Idea

Efforts by President Clinton to fulfill his campaign promises met with mixed success, paving the way for a Republican takeover of Congress in the 1994 midterm elections.

Vocabulary

- universal coverage
- family leave
- crime bill
- bipartisan coalition
- unfunded mandate
- pork barrel legislation

Read to Find Out . . .

- how Clinton tried to reverse Reaganomics and to introduce policies aimed at balancing the budget.
- how the United States tried to work with other nations in resolving international crises.
- why the Republicans took control of Congress in 1994 and what their goals were once in power.

TIMOTHY HENDRIX/LIAISON AGENCY

Sluggish Economy The economy remained weak in the early 1990s. This family resorted to living in a national forest. *What were some of the solutions proposed to fix the economy?*

into the heart of the campaign. Republicans favored increased incentives to businesses, both big and small, to encourage economic expansion and the creation of more jobs. Democrats favored higher taxes on the wealthy, more funds for job retraining, and increased investment in the nation's educational system and in its transportation and communication networks.

The weak economy overshadowed the fact that, for the first time in more than 40 years, the nation was not threatened by a nuclear war with the Soviets. The chief concerns in this election were domestic: skyrocketing health-care costs, an increase in violent and drug-related crimes, a need for improved education—and the question of how to finance solutions to these problems.

Three-Way Race

Disgruntled voters turned a two-way race into a three-way race by supporting Texas businessman H. Ross Perot, the owner of a highly successful data-processing company. Perot capitalized on voter discontent by criticizing the legislative gridlock between a Republican President and a Democrat-controlled Congress. He outlined a program to cut the federal budget deficit in five years—a plan that asked all Americans to "share the pain" of fixing the problems.

To a large extent, the outcome of the race depended upon the ability of each of the three candidates—Bush, Clinton, and Perot—to convince voters that he was the one best able to lead the nation out of its economic decline. Bush painted Clinton as a "tax-and-spend" Democrat. Clinton attacked Bush's emphasis on foreign policy and his neglect of domestic concerns. The campaign grew complicated with Perot's witty participation in the televised presidential debates and his 30-minute campaign commercials.

In the end a frustrated electorate, concerned about the economy and a government that they saw as expensive and inefficient, voted for change, ousting Bush after one term. Clinton became the first Democrat elected to the White House since Jimmy Carter in 1976.

★ ★ ★ Gallery of Presidents 

William Jefferson Clinton

1993–2001

"America has called upon me to be our next president. But our forebears call on all of us at this moment to honor their efforts, their sacrifices, their ideals, and their lives, by working hard and working together to improve this good and great nation. . . . They call on us to take our dreams and our hopes, and make them real. Thank you, and God bless America."

Address to media, November 4, 1992

ROBERT TRIPPETT/SIPA PRESS

Background

- **Born 1946**
- **Elected attorney general of Arkansas 1976**
- **Elected governor of Arkansas 1978, 1982, 1984, 1986, 1990**

Achievements in Office

- **Family Leave Act (1993)**
- **Brady Act (1993)**
- **Crime Act (1993)**
- **NAFTA (1993)**
- **Welfare Reform (1996)**
- **Balanced Budget (1997)**

JEFFREY MARKOWITZ/CORBIS SYGMA

Women in Government Contributing to greater diversity, a record number of women won congressional seats in 1993—54 in all. *What African American woman was the first to be elected to the Senate?*

The Budget

Clinton entered office intending to reverse Reaganomics and redirect the nation's resources from consumption to investment in transportation, schools, and industry. He proposed a "stimulus package" aimed at revitalizing industry and creating jobs throughout the nation. To offset these spending increases, Clinton supported cutbacks in wasteful or unnecessary federal programs, a modest reduction in defense spending, and some higher taxes and fees, primarily on the most affluent 1 percent of taxpayers.

The President faced two major obstacles in implementing his plans. One was the deficit, which in the public's mind loomed as a major threat to the nation's economic well-being. The other was entitlement programs, such as Social Security, Medicare, and veterans' benefits. Although entitlements consumed almost half the budget and were rising in costs, Clinton's budget only made minor cuts in them.

Clinton pledged to reduce the federal deficit through fiscal 1998 by $496 billion. Even so, many people felt the budget was not bold enough. It made cuts in 150 programs, but eliminated only 6. One was a subsidy for beekeepers that Clinton often referred to in his speeches. As it turned out, even this program was spared.

After many amendments the final budget squeaked through Congress without a single vote of support from Republicans. The timid performance by Congress and the President only fueled voter frustrations, which would ignite during the 1994 midterm elections.

New Faces in Government

Voters' desire for change rippled through the nation. A record number of legislators either chose not to run again or were defeated. A record 164 women stepped forward to run for Congress, and another 8 women sought governorships.

Government, especially Congress, now reflected the ethnic diversity of the nation more than ever before. In California voters sent two women to the Senate and elected the first person of Korean ancestry—Jay C. Kim—to serve in Congress. In Colorado Ben Nighthorse Campbell became the first Native American in the Senate. In Illinois Carol Moseley Braun became the first African American woman to hold a Senate seat. Across the country 14 more African Americans, 9 more Hispanics, and 23 more women won seats in the Congress.

First-Term Domestic Issues

Ups and Downs

As Inauguration Day approached, Clinton held a nationally televised economic summit aimed at developing a consensus on the direction of economic policy for the next four years. Out of that meeting came his first budget plan and a surprising call for massive health-care reform. He would later propose other programs that centered on family leave, gun control, and crime. This ambitious agenda met with mixed legislative success.

Health-Care Issues

Shortly after Clinton's pre-inaugural economic summit, he delivered an impassioned, table-pounding speech on the issue of health care. In it, he asserted that the cost of caring for the nation's sick or injured was "going to bankrupt the country."

Few questioned the skyrocketing costs of health care. By 1993 nearly 14 percent of the gross domestic product—$2.7 billion a day—was spent on doctors, nurses, hospitals, medicines, and a vast array of high-tech equipment. At the same time people were becoming fed up with a system that looked at the bottom line rather than at the concerns of the sick.

Equally troubling was the huge number of people with no health insurance at all. Many claimed they

THE RISING COST OF HEALTH CARE

The total cost of health care has risen dramatically in the United States. In 1972 the average American's health-care costs were $387 a year. By 1994 that number had risen almost 10 times to $3,510. Contributing reasons for this rise include (1) an exploding bureaucracy of regulators and insurers and the subsequent expansion of hospital billing departments; (2) rising hospital costs and doctors' fees; and (3) new technology, drugs, and medical procedures.

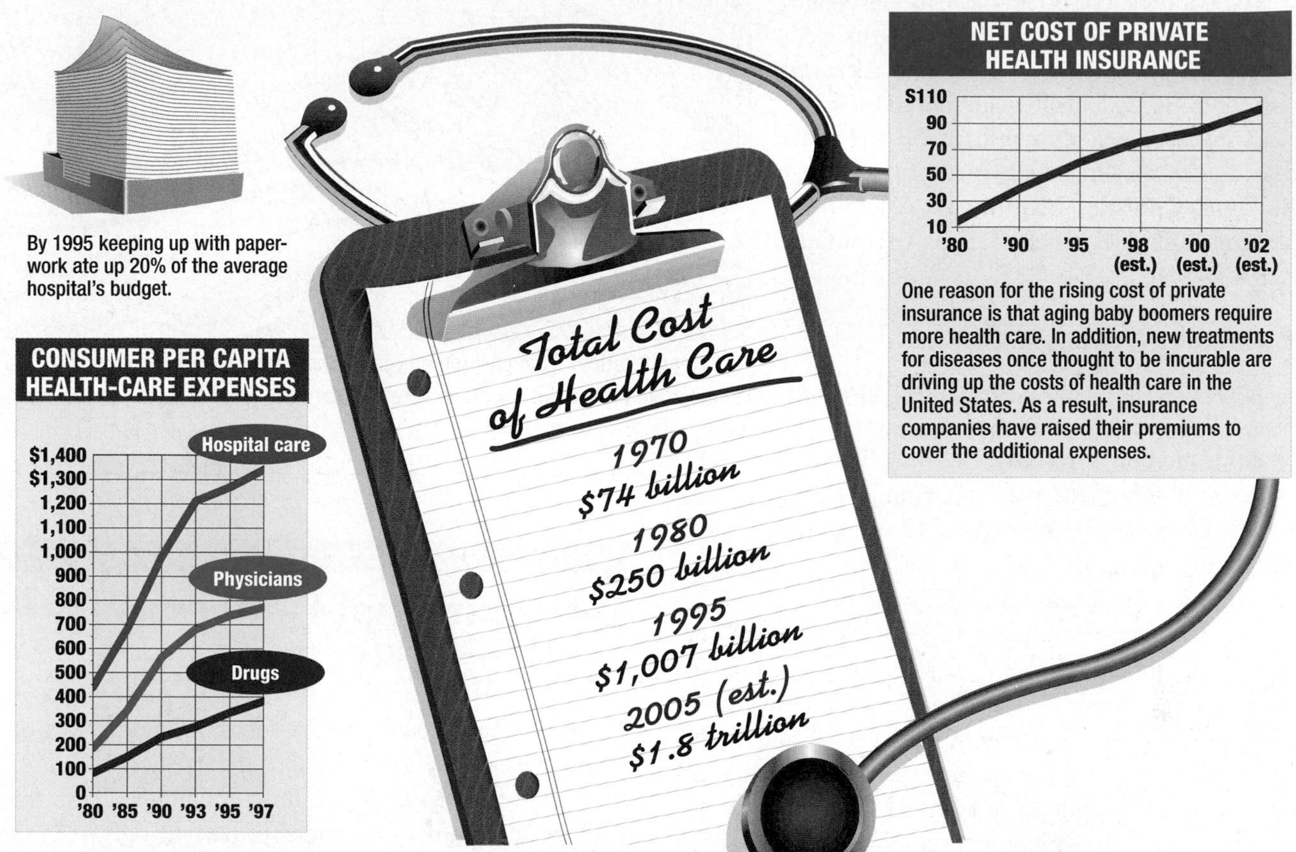

The skyrocketing costs of health care concern most Americans. *What do experts believe health care will cost in 2005?*

For an online update of this graph, visit americanodyssey.glencoe.com and click on ***Textbook Updates—Chapter 26.***

earned too much money to qualify for Medicaid and were too poor to afford private health insurance. Of the estimated 39 million uninsured people, 10 million were children who, without regular medical checkups, risked developing chronic illnesses. Added to these individuals were the millions of people who feared losing coverage if their jobs fell victim to the ongoing recession.

Health-Care Reform

Clinton thought people needed assurance that health care would be available whenever they needed it. Despite the looming federal deficit and the shaky economy, he decided to overhaul the nation's health care system. Within days of his inauguration, the new President established a 500-member health care task force chaired by Hillary Rodham Clinton.

The task force met in secret to hammer out proposals that would both reduce health-care costs and guarantee **universal coverage**, or health insurance for all. The administration wanted to build on the existing principle of employer-provided health insurance, making it mandatory instead of voluntary, and to put more discipline into health costs by cutting out waste and fraud. All of this was to be accomplished without new taxes, with a minimal increase to employers or people already insured, and without any reduction in medical services.

This was a tall order. When the Clinton administration finally submitted its reform bill to Congress in October 1993, the document totaled 1,342 pages. Few people understood the entire plan, and many groups, including the American Medical Association, pharmaceutical companies, insurers, and business associations, spent millions of dollars opposing it. Critics of the health-care bill claimed the program would increase medical costs and result in rationed care. The situation was further complicated by Democrats and Republicans who introduced other, more modest plans.

In August 1994, with the midterm elections fast approaching, the Senate recessed without bringing a health-care bill to the floor. Most involved felt that reform on the scale imagined by the President was not possible at the time. Clinton's inability to resolve the dilemma ranked as a major failure in the minds of many voters.

JOHN BRANCH/©1993 SAN ANTONIO EXPRESS-NEWS

Bowling Politics. This cartoon suggests the mixed nature of Clinton's legislative record during his first term in office. *What does the cartoonist suggest was Clinton's main failure?*

Legislative Successes

Despite the gridlock over health-care reform, Clinton still managed to steer several major domestic bills through Congress. The first bill to pass Congress was the Family Leave Act, which gives workers up to 12 weeks per year of unpaid **family leave** for the birth or adoption of a child or for the illness of a family member.

Another important piece of legislation passed during Clinton's first term was the Brady Act, signed in November 1993. Named after President Reagan's press secretary, who was permanently injured during a 1981 shooting attempt on Reagan's life, the law requires a waiting period for the purchase of hand guns to allow police time to check criminal records. Vigorously opposed by the National Rifle Association (NRA), the act still gained wide national support. In 1997 the Brady Act was weakened after the Supreme Court ruled against mandatory checks of handgun buyers' records.

Gun control also played a major role in the debate over a third piece of legislation, the **crime bill.** This bill provided for more police on the streets, the construction of prisons, new applications of the death penalty, and bans against 19 types of assault weapons. It also included money for crime prevention, such as creating midnight baseball leagues that would get people off the streets and into the stadiums.

The crime bill had many opponents. Conservative Republicans and Democrats, under pressure from the NRA and from many constituents who opposed gun control, opposed the weapons ban and argued that the bill spent too much money on crime prevention. The Black Caucus opposed increased use of the death penalty. Others challenged funds allocated to increase police and prisons. In the end, however, few wanted to disregard public concern with rising crime rates, and the bill passed.

International Concerns

Post-Cold War Policies

As Congress and the President struggled over domestic policies, events abroad forced the nation to confront the issue of the nation's role in international affairs, particularly in regard to violations of human rights. As the world's sole superpower, questions emerged over whether the nation should intervene in regional conflicts and, if so, whether it should act alone or in tandem with other international agencies. The nation also was forced to view its economic policies within the context of an increasingly interdependent world, particularly in terms of trade.

North American Free Trade Agreement

Trade was one of the first foreign policy issues to confront the Clinton administration. Under President Bush, the United States had signed the North America Free Trade Agreement (NAFTA), which called for gradual elimination of tariffs and trade barriers among Canada, Mexico, and the United States. The goal was to create a three-nation market of 370 million people producing and consuming goods and services. Hopefully, NAFTA would produce an entity able to compete with the European Union (formerly called the European Community).

In 1993 both Canada and Mexico ratified the treaty. In the United States, business groups praised the treaty, saying it would create jobs, lower the cost of goods, and make the United States more competitive. Labor unions, however, argued that the treaty would hurt workers because businesses would try to lower labor costs by moving jobs to Mexico, where wages were lower. Farmers also opposed NAFTA, fearing that low-priced Mexican produce would undercut American goods. Environmentalists joined the fray by contending that United States businesses would move to Mexico to escape antipollution laws at home.

In the end the treaty passed both houses of Congress with comfortable majorities, due largely to the lobbying efforts and compromises backed by President Clinton. At least 100,000 American jobs have migrated to Mexico since the signing of NAFTA, but the drop in unemployment to the lowest rate in nearly half a century has offset this loss.

Conflict in the former Yugoslavia triggered one of the most serious foreign crises during the Clinton administration. *What three major groups fought over the territory?*

Crisis in the Balkans

In the early post–cold war years, the Clinton administration faced a number of crises in trouble spots around the world, but one of the most difficult conflicts emerged in the Balkans, a peninsula in southeastern Europe. There the former Communist nation of Yugoslavia, made up of six republics, began to break apart when Slovenia, Croatia, and Macedonia declared their independence in 1991. Bosnia-Herzegovina followed suit in 1992. The remaining republics, Serbia and Montenegro, declared themselves to be the new Federation of Yugoslavia, but most countries did not recognize this declaration.

The breakup of Yugoslavia triggered long-standing rivalries among three major groups: Serbs, Croats, and Muslims. The announcement of independence led to fighting in Croatia, where minority Serbs, afraid of domination by the Croats and backed up by Yugoslavia's Serbs, seized control. Brutal fighting continued for six months before the United States, acting with its NATO allies, declared an embargo on arms shipments to all of the Balkan republics. The United Nations sent peacekeepers to the area to monitor a cease-fire. Although scattered fighting continued, Croatia generally remained quiet for several years.

Bosnia-Herzegovina

Civil war also broke out in Bosnia-Herzegovina as the Serb minority attacked the Muslim-dominated government. As in Croatia, Yugoslavia's arms supported Serb forces in Bosnia, and the outgunned Muslims called on the international community for help. The United Nations responded by imposing a trade and oil embargo on Yugoslavia and by sending food and medicine to help soldiers and civilians in the region.

Then came word that the Bosnian Serbs, under the leadership of Communist party head Slobodan Milosevic, were practicing *ethnic cleansing*—killing thousands of Bosnian Muslims, including civilians, in a manner that evoked memories of Adolf Hitler's World War II death camps. In 1993 the United Nations set up several safe areas to protect Muslim civilians.

Debate Over the American Role

In 1995 the UN-sponsored protected areas began to fall. The prospect of renewed gross violation of human rights set off intense debate over whether Congress should lift the general arms embargo and provide weapons so that the Muslims could fight back. Although deeply divided over the arms embargo, the President and Congress were of one mind in their reluctance to commit United States ground troops in the region.

As in Croatia, the United States decided to work from within the framework of NATO. NATO unleashed a fearful bombing campaign against the Bosnian Serbs—the first such action in its history. With heavy American involvement, NATO air strikes forced Bosnian Serbs to the UN-sponsored peace talks held in Dayton, Ohio. These talks, which where attended by the presidents of Bosnia, Serbia, and Croatia, led to the signing of the Dayton Peace Accord.

POOL/AP/WIDE WORLD PHOTOS

U.S. Foreign Policy As secretary of state, Madeleine Albright played an important role in negotiating peace in Bosnia-Herzegovina. *Where was the UN-sponsored treaty negotiated?*

The peace accord outlined a plan that would bring peace to Bosnia-Herzegovina. As part of that plan, Bosnia would remain a country but would be divided into two substates—one Muslim-Croat (controlling 51 percent of the region) and one Serb (controlling 49 percent). The accord also required people convicted of war crimes to be barred from holding military or political office. NATO troops, 65,000 strong, remained in the area through the late 1990s to prevent renewed fighting.

The peace attained in Bosnia-Herzegovina was fragile at best. Milosevic, the president of Yugoslavia, ignored the peace accord and continued to finance Bosnian Serb soldiers. Former Bosnian President Radovan Karadzic, who was forced from office in 1996, was twice charged with genocide, the deliberate killing of Bosnian Muslims, by the United Nations War Crimes Tribunal. Then the situation worsened in 1999.

Kosovo

In Kosovo, a southern Yugoslavian province, ancient hatreds of Serbian domination fueled a movement for Kosovar independence. Milosevic horrified the world with a ferocious campaign of ethnic cleansing, driving most of the Kosovars into Albania and Montenegro. Milosevic appealed to Serbian hard-line nationalism, arguing that he would restore Serbia to greatness by deporting Muslims, Catholics, and non-Serbs.

NATO again intervened with an air campaign, the largest allied operation in Europe since World War II. Air strikes drove the Yugoslav forces out of Kosovo, allowing most of the refugees to return.

In September 2000, Yugoslavian voters, weary of Milosevic's harsh regime, elected a new president, Vojislav Kostunica. Milosevic did not concede defeat until rural workers, previously his staunch supporters, stormed the government and state television facilities in Belgrade. In October he turned over the government.

However, the world had not seen the last of Milosevic. In late November 2000, he staged a defiant comeback, winning reelection as leader of Serbia's Socialist party. An unrepentant Milosevic gave no indication that he would easily retire from political life.

Invasion of Haiti

Closer to the United States, unrest in the Caribbean nation of Haiti also posed difficult challenges. In 1991, the Haitian military had overthrown the nation's first democratically elected president, Jean Bertrand Aristide, and instituted a policy of repression. The UN used economic sanctions, including an embargo on arms and trade, to topple the junta.

Faced with severe food shortages and a ruthless government, thousands of Haitians fled to the United States in makeshift boats. Fearing a huge influx of Haitian immigrants, Clinton at first refused to admit the refugees. But as political pressure mounted, he offered refugees a safe haven at the U.S. naval base in Guantanamo Bay, Cuba. The haven spurred the massive flight of Haitians—as many as 2,000-3,000 refugees a day! The only way to stop the migration, many felt, was for the United States military to reinstate President Aristide.

BRACA NADEZDIC/NEWSMAKERS/LIAISON AGENCY

LIAISON AGENCY

Revolution in October 2000. Yugoslavians forced Slobodan Milosevic to hand over the government to popularly elected Vajislav Kostunica. *What segment of the population led the mass protest?*

In fall 1994 the United Nations authorized a United States invasion of Haiti. American troops returned Aristide to power and kept the peace for almost two years, during which time Haitians elected René Préval to succeed Aristide. By the middle of 1996, all U.S. troops had left Haiti, although about 900 UN forces remained to help keep the peace.

Midterm Elections

A New Conservatism

As Clinton sought to guide the nation in a new foreign policy, ups and downs in his domestic policy produced growing discontent at home. With the midterm elections approaching, pollsters expected some Republican gains. But nobody was prepared for the stunning upset of November 8, 1994. Republicans had garnered the biggest midterm victory of the century, overthrowing 40 years of Democratic dominance in Congress.

Election Results

Before the election, Democrats had a 56 to 44 majority in the Senate; after the votes were counted, that majority had been reversed to favor the Republicans 52 to 48. In the House the election of 53 new Republicans, who now controlled that body by a margin of 230 to 178, shattered the old Democratic majority of 256 to 178.

Not one incumbent Republican senator, representative, or governor lost a race, but many leading Democrats, including House Speaker Tom Foley of Washington State, did. Foley's defeat was the first one for a sitting speaker since before the Civil War. The Republican sweep extended to the state level, where the GOP captured 11 new governorships and 9 new state legislatures. Many called the results a revolution.

Looking for Reasons

In the aftermath, journalists, academics, and media commentators searched for explanations. Much of the Republican success, of course, could be attributed to voter frustration at the inability of a Democratic administration to deliver on changes promised in 1992. As one former Democrat who voted Republican said, "We always vote for change and we never get it."

In looking closer some observers credited the win to the skillful use of new methods of communication by the Republicans. To keep congressional candidates informed of the issues and abreast of new ideas, an operation led by Representative Newt Gingrich of Georgia sent out 700,000 videotapes preceding the 1994 election. Conservative Republicans funded a cable TV network called National Empowerment Television that carried their message to millions of viewers. The boom in talk shows, hosted by conservatives such as Rush Limbaugh,

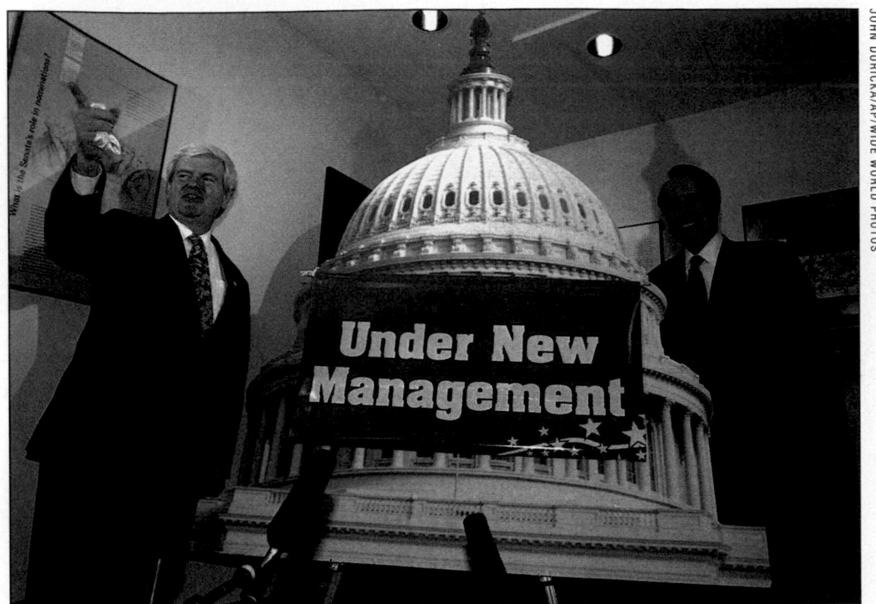

JOHN DURICKA/AP/WIDE WORLD PHOTOS

New Leaders in Congress **Newt Gingrich (left) and Bob Dole (right) celebrate Republican control of Congress in 1994.** *How long had the Democrats led Congress?*

allowed the public to listen to around-the-clock discussions of issues important to the right wing of the party. Computer networks, with more than 30 million subscribers, offered yet another channel of communication.

Other observers felt the Republican sweep may have been a white male backlash against Clinton's pledge to create a multicultural administration staffed by women and men who "looked like America." A profile of the average Republican voter showed him to be a white, male, high school or college graduate who listened to talk shows and owned a gun. He might also have contributed to United We Stand, the organization of presidential candidate Ross Perot, because a majority of Perot's supporters also voted Republican. The Congress elected by these voters was largely white and male, suburban or rural, and socially traditional. Many new members were baby boomers between the ages of 32 and 48. If 1992 was the year of the woman in American politics, 1994 might have been called the year of the young white man.

With the retirement of many moderate members of Congress in both parties, the coalition of New Deal Democrats and moderate Republicans that had held sway in American politics since the New Deal seemed to have collapsed. No one doubted that the Democratic party had been rebuffed. The nation now turned to a conservative legislature to see if they could deliver on their promises.

The Contract With America

The Republicans had based their campaign promises on their Contract With America, which proclaimed government had become "too big, too intrusive, and too easy with the public's money." It said that a new Republican majority would "be the beginning of a Congress that respects the values and shares the faith of the American family." In a carefully honed list, the contract called for tax cuts, reduced spending on everything but Social Security and defense, a balanced budget amendment, and term limits for members of Congress. Divisive issues, such as abortion rights and gun control, received no mention in the contract.

In the days following the election, jubilant Republicans paraded the Contract With America before television cameras and promised to enact its main provisions in the first 100 days of the 104th Congress. They even distributed a "citizen's scorecard" on which voters could keep track of their Republican legislator's performance. "Hold your elected officials accountable in the promises they've made!" they said.

Congressional Leadership

House and Senate

Republican domination of Congress meant new leadership at all levels. Newt Gingrich, a nine-term member of Congress who had devoted his political career to ousting the Democrats, became Speaker of the House. The position of House Majority Leader went to Richard Armey, a conservative representative from Texas and one of the main authors of the Contract With America. Robert Dole of Kansas, a long-time Minority Leader with a lengthy record of bringing Republicans and Democrats together in **bipartisan coalitions,** now became Senate Majority Leader. In addition, Republicans took over the chairs of every committee in both houses of Congress. To these leaders fell the task of fulfilling their promises.

The First 100 Days

The new Congress opened with a bustle of activity. As part of its promise to reduce the size of government, the House eliminated several committees and cut its staff by a third. By the end of their first 100 days in office, members of the Republican-controlled Congress passed all 34 of the bills in the Contract With America. Two of these bills—with substantial Democratic support—were then approved by the Senate and signed into law by the President.

The first of these two laws required that all laws that apply to the nation also apply to Congress. This brought the House and Senate into compliance with civil rights and equal employment regulations. The second law restricted the federal government's ability to pass **unfunded mandates**, or laws that states or businesses must comply with but for which Congress supplies no money. The Congressional Budget Office estimated that such regulations had cost state and local governments about $10 billion between 1983 and 1990.

At this point, however, the Contract With America collapsed. Five of the bills were passed by both the House and Senate but failed to get signed by the President. Twenty-eight other bills were passed by the House but not the Senate, where moderate Republicans and Democrats prevented their passage.

The problem of unfilled promises was compounded by a string of ethics complaints levied against Gingrich. He was accused of misusing tax-exempt donations to pay for televising a college course that promoted the Republican agenda. He was also questioned about a $4.5 million book deal with a publisher who would have been affected by legislation before the House. Gingrich at first proclaimed his innocence, but he was found guilty by the House and later apologized to the Congress, both for his actions and for lying to the investigating committees.

Wrestling With Tough Issues

Conflicting Agendas

Once again, legislation stalled as Republicans in Congress came face-to-face with the stubborn and politically astute Democratic President. Each side had an agenda to fulfill, and both actively pursued it. What voters saw was a government mired in debate over three critical issues—a balanced budget amendment, national health-care reform, and reform of the welfare system.

Balanced Budget Amendment

For years politicians of both parties had railed against a government that did not, in the words of the Contract With America, "live under the same budget constraints as families and businesses." Balancing the budget seemed prudent. However, the Republicans proposed a constitutional amendment, which complicated the issue.

Supporters of the amendment failed to note a number of factors. For example, they neglected to mention the deficit financing used by individuals and businesses that apply for mortgages, make purchases with credit cards, or apply for business loans. Also, while many states and cities have balanced-budget laws, the laws typically exempt bond issues, which invoke long-term debt to finance projects such as construction of schools or highways.

Another stumbling block in the way of balancing the budget was the issue of **pork barrel legislation**, or "pork," the laws or projects that bring jobs and money into a legislator's district. Once the Republicans won power, many of them proved to be as hungry for "pork" as the Democrats had been. In 1995 much of the pork was found in the defense budget. Congress appropriated $7 billion more than the Department of Defense requested for projects ranging from the construction of a physical fitness center at a naval shipyard to the construction of two B2 bombers at a cost of $1 billion each. The extravagance led some House members to set up a bipartisan coalition, nicknamed the "pork busters," to curb such excesses.

In the end, the balanced budget amendment passed the House but lost in the Senate by one vote. Following the fight over the amendment, both the Republicans in Congress and the President proposed plans that would lead to a balanced budget. For all the venting of the issue, it was the return of a flourishing economy that balanced the budget and in fact began to produce surpluses by late in Clinton's first term.

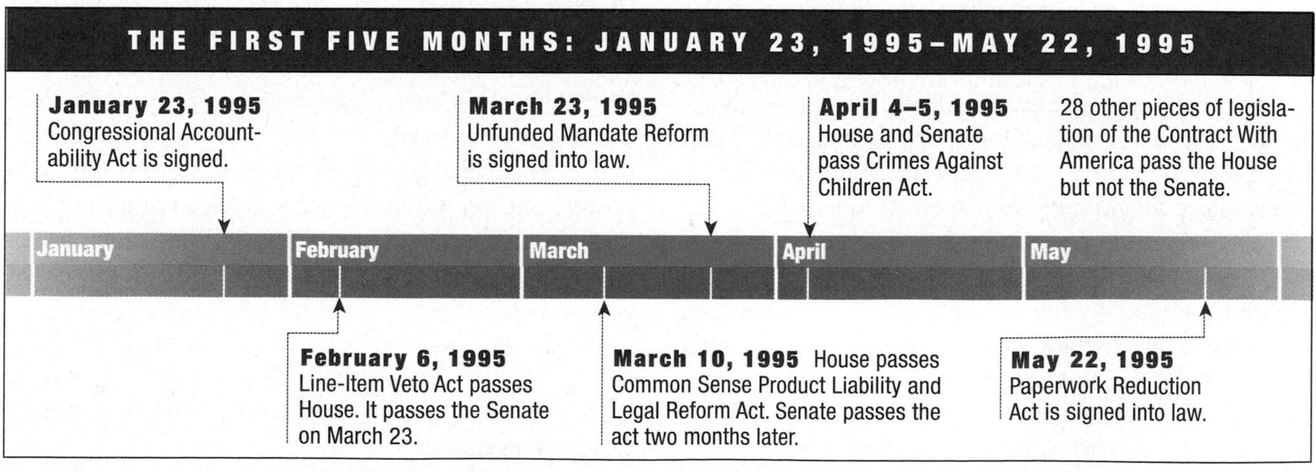

THE FIRST FIVE MONTHS: JANUARY 23, 1995–MAY 22, 1995
January 23, 1995 Congressional Accountability Act is signed.
March 23, 1995 Unfunded Mandate Reform is signed into law.
April 4–5, 1995 House and Senate pass Crimes Against Children Act.
28 other pieces of legislation of the Contract With America pass the House but not the Senate.
January
February
March
April
May
February 6, 1995 Line-Item Veto Act passes House. It passes the Senate on March 23.
March 10, 1995 House passes Common Sense Product Liability and Legal Reform Act. Senate passes the act two months later.
May 22, 1995 Paperwork Reduction Act is signed into law.

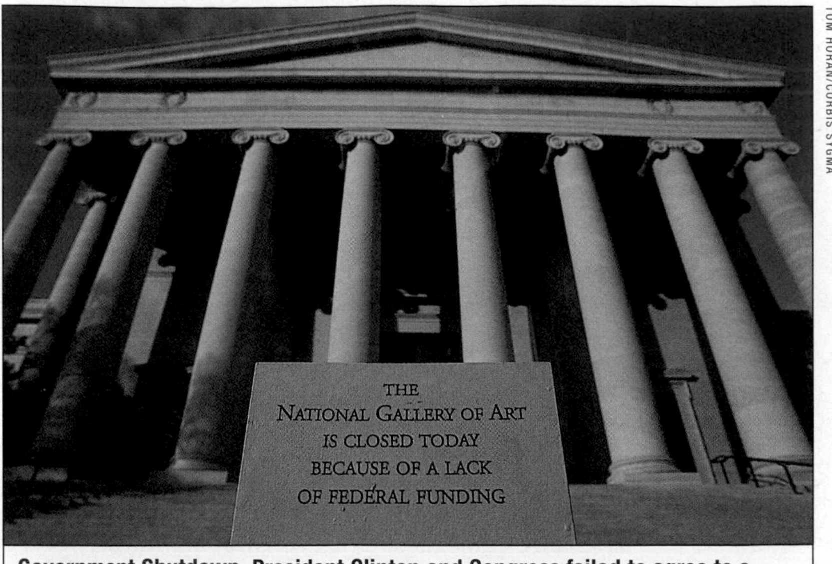

TOM HORAN/CORBIS SYGMA

Government Shutdown President Clinton and Congress failed to agree to a budget in late 1995. *Who was the speaker of the House?*

However, after the resounding defeat of his sweeping health-care reform, President Clinton realized he needed to take more moderate stands on some issues. Among these issues was welfare reform. Before his first term ended, President Clinton made good on his promise to "end welfare as we know it" by signing into law a welfare-reform measure that ended the federal government's Aid to Families with Dependent Children—a program established in 1935 as part of the Social Security Act. Under the Welfare Reform Act, the federal government no longer reimburses states for payments to poor families with children. Instead, states receive lump-sum payments from the federal government, and they must cut off payments after two consecutive years. In addition, lifetime benefits are limited to five years of assistance.

Health Care Reform—Again

Deciding how to change Medicare proved as difficult for the 104th Congress as for previous ones. President Clinton, discouraged after his health-care reform attempts failed in 1993, advocated only minor cutbacks. He maintained it would be impossible to overhaul Medicare without reforming the health-care system.

Republicans, anxious to deliver on their promises of a balanced budget and tax cuts, hinted at major changes in the way Medicare delivered services, changes that they argued would provide more options for senior citizens and simultaneously curtail spending. When the debate opened, the government was acting as the insurer, paying doctors and hospitals for services rendered. The Republican plan would have had the government provide a "defined contribution," a fixed amount of money, or voucher, that a person could use to purchase coverage from any number of health insurance plans. In the end, though, neither Republicans nor Democrats were willing to introduce the sweeping reform that experts said were necessary to deal with rising Medicare costs.

Welfare Reform

For many Americans, the idea of people receiving money without working for it was repugnant. They wanted, in the words of the Contract With America, to "discourage illegitimacy and teen pregnancy by prohibiting welfare to minor mothers and denying increased AFDC (Aid to Families with Dependent Children) for additional children while on welfare." As with so many measures in the contract, a bill aimed at fulfilling this goal passed the House and later stalled in the Senate, where members on both sides were concerned for children who would suffer from severe cutbacks.

Targets of Spending Cuts

The Arts, Humanities, and the Environment

In the mid-1990s, as the Republican-controlled Congress began to make budget cuts, few people remained unaffected. More than half the people in the United States received some kind of direct government assistance. While some Republican spending cuts resulted from efforts to balance the budget, others were symbolic of the Republicans' desire to reduce the reach of the federal government.

Funding the Arts and Humanities

Conservatives directed much of their criticism at the National Endowment for the Arts (NEA), the National Endowment for the Humanities (NEH), and similar agencies. They charged that such programs too often funded liberal or even obscene works. They also argued that funding for music, theater, museums, libraries, and public broadcasting was best left to philanthropists. Supporters of these programs were quick to point out that the United States funded the arts and humanities far less than any other industrialized nation and that these programs should therefore be kept intact.

In the end, neither side got what it wanted. The NEA and NEH were not abolished. However, the Republican-controlled Congress slashed funding of the agencies by nearly 40 percent.

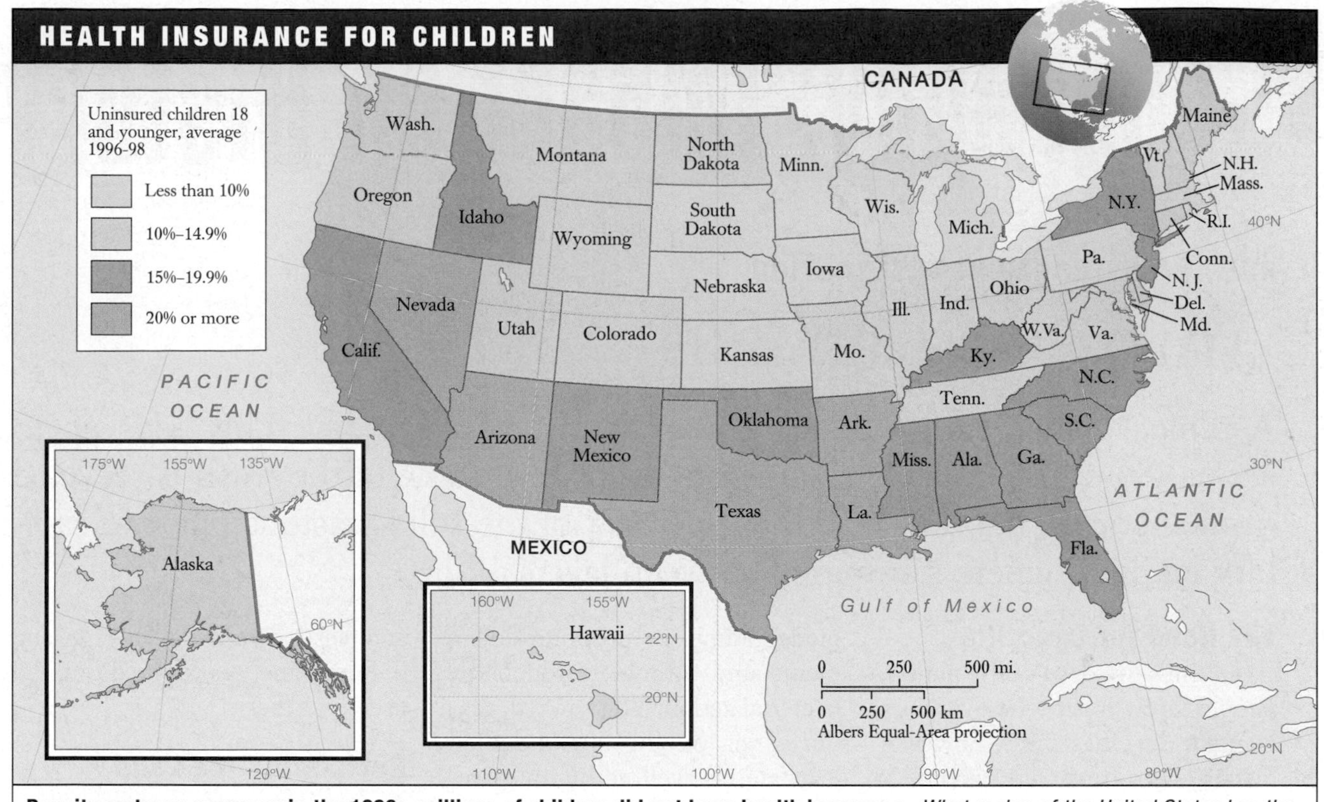

Despite a strong economy in the 1990s, millions of children did not have health insurance. *What region of the United States has the highest percentage of uninsured children?*

For an online update of this graph, visit americanodyssey.glencoe.com and click on ***Textbook Updates—Chapter 26.***

Environmental Protection

The Republican father of conservation was Theodore Roosevelt, the first President to make conservation a national goal. Other Republican Presidents added legislation to protect the environment. Richard Nixon supported creation of the Environmental Protection Agency (EPA) and signed a new Clean Air Act in 1970. George Bush strengthened the law's provisions by signing the Clean Air Act of 1990. Yet, once in power, Republicans in the 104th Congress curbed environmental protection.

The Republican plan aimed to cut the EPA budget by 34 percent and to lift environmental restrictions on ranchers, loggers, and miners who used federal lands. Even national parks were not exempt from cuts. A proposal before Congress would have set up a park closure commission modeled after the one that closed military bases. At risk would be 314 of 368 national parks and historic sites, including Mount Rushmore, the Statue of Liberty, and the Washington Monument. Supporters of the proposals argued that since the government did not have enough money to manage the lands properly, they would be better off in private hands, where they would be run as businesses.

Even some Republicans found such cutbacks too drastic. Concerned that these stands might backfire with voters at the polls, they joined Democrats in voting down the measures. Other Republican members of the 104th Congress would learn that the extreme positions they had taken on some issues, such as the environment, education, and health care, would cost them reelection.

Section Assessment

Main Idea

1. Use a diagram like this one to show successes and failures of Clinton's first-term administration.

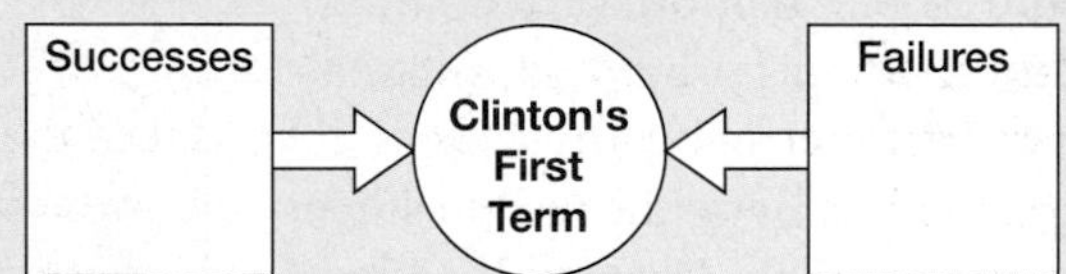

Vocabulary

2. **Define:** universal coverage, family leave, crime bill, bipartisan coalition, unfunded mandate, pork barrel legislation.

Checking Facts

3. What were the most important issues of the 1992 presidential campaign?

4. What were some of the possible reasons for the sweeping Republican victories in 1994?

Critical Thinking

5. **Evaluating Information** Some people described the 1994 midterm election as a "revolution." Do you agree? Why or why not?

Geography: Impact on History

HUMAN/ENVIRONMENT INTERACTION

America's Landfills

A typical American generates 4 pounds of garbage a day. This adds up to about 180 million tons of solid waste each year. Some of the trash is recycled or incinerated, but about 70 to 80 percent of the solid waste is put into sanitary landfills, where it is buried between layers of dirt.

The Need for Landfills

In the early days of the nation, people threw trash wherever they wanted. As cities grew, however, disposing of trash did become a problem. In 1930, New York City became one of the first cities to send its trash to sanitary landfills. Now many communities have municipal landfills to take care of their own waste. Densely populated areas such as New York State, however, have less space available for landfills. They have to ship their garbage out to other areas of the country.

Despite the fact that moving trash from one area of the country to another has created conflict, huge loads of garbage are still sent out daily by truck or by train. The problem came to a head during a 1992 rail strike. Trainloads of East Coast garbage were stranded in the Midwest and people got an eyeful (and noseful) of the trash. Then, as now, no one wants a landfill nearby, but the garbage must go somewhere.

Environmental Impact

Many people are worried that landfills will harm the environment because of problems with surface and groundwater pollution, dangerous gas emissions, and noxious fumes. Landfills work by biodegrading, or breaking down, plants and animal products by bacterial action. This process produces an oozing liquid called leachate, as well as highly flammable methane gas.

New landfills are being built to be more environmentally sound. The landfill site is lined with clay and plastic to prevent leakage, and the methane gas is piped out and used as a fuel.

Reclaiming the Land

When landfills are full, they are covered over with earth, and the land is "reclaimed." Newark and JFK International Airports were

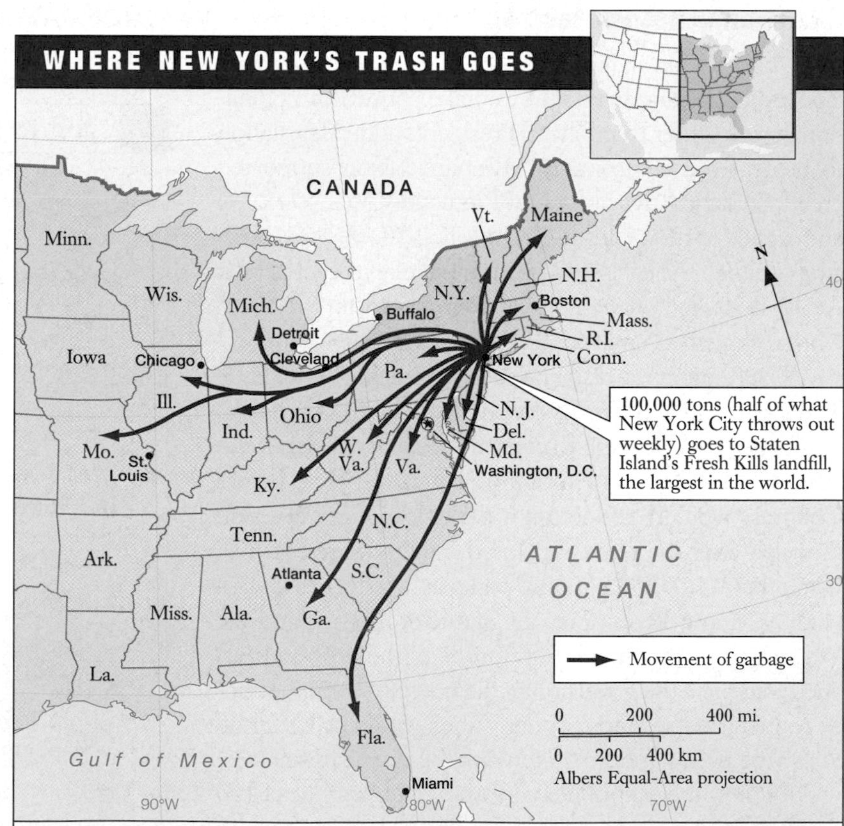

New York City ships 200,000 tons of garbage to landfills each week. *Where else does New York City ship its garbage? What is the most distant state to which New York City ships its garbage? The closest?*

Landfills This landfill in Massachusetts is a repository for trash from all over the state. The largest landfill in the world is Fresh Kills in New York. It receives 17,000 tons of garbage each day. The landfill covers 3,000 acres and takes up 2.4 billion cubic feet of space. Contents of the landfill include: paper (50%), miscellaneous (20%), organic (13%), metal (6%), glass (1%), and plastic (less than 1%). *When was Fresh Kills built? Where was it built?*

built on top of landfills. Hospitals, golf courses, and community parks have all been built on top of land that has been reclaimed.

Fresh Kills landfill in New York is the largest in the world. As parts of it become full, they are covered over with earth. Trees and wildflowers are then planted to help them revert back to their natural state. Fresh Kills landfill, however, was begun in 1948 on top of a salt marsh before people were environmentally conscious. Although it was eventually cleaned up, for many years it leaked more than a million gallons of leachate (waste percolated into a liquid state) into the water.

Long-range Plans

How will the United States deal with its waste problems? Other methods of disposal include incineration, waste-to-energy programs, and recycling. These methods account for a relatively small percentage of waste disposal, however. The use of sanitary landfills puts an ever-increasing burden on rural and less heavily populated areas, whose residents often resent their urban neighbors. The best answer may be to decrease the amount of solid waste being generated and by reusing and recycling goods.

Making the Geographic Connection

1. What are some of the problems that landfills create for the environment? How are these problems being solved today? How does land reclamation fit into these solutions?
2. What methods of waste disposal other than landfills are being used today? Which method is used most often? What are some solutions currently being considered to alleviate the problem?
3. **Human/Environment Interaction** What impact do you think the recycling of paper, plastic, metal, and glass could have on future landfills?

In Search of Balance

JULY 28, 1997: CLINTON BASKS IN BIPARTISAN BUDGET DEAL

IN A ROSE GARDEN PRESS CONFERENCE, REPUBLICAN AND DEMOCRATIC CONGRESSIONAL LEADERS APPLAUDED AS PRESIDENT CLINTON ANNOUNCED PASSAGE OF A LONG-PROMISED GIFT TO THE AMERICAN PEOPLE: A BALANCED BUDGET. The deal marked the end of the President's long march to the political center, a journey that almost none of the Democrats who stood behind him in the budget celebration had backed. Even staunch Clinton opponents, such as Republican Trent Lott, were jubilant: "Today we celebrate the beginning of a new era of freedom."

The deal had nearly broken down at several points, with the Clinton administration pushing for increased spending and the Republicans calling for deeper tax cuts. Compromises between the White House and Republican congressional leaders produced shouting matches within the ranks of both parties, as some members of Congress, both Democratic and Republican, threatened to vote against any deal.

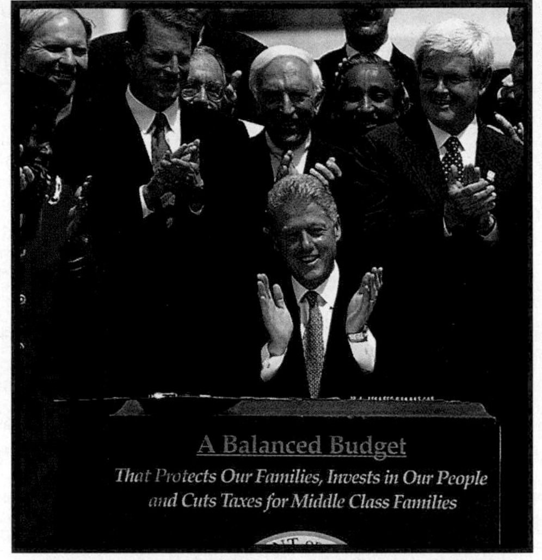

BRAD MARKEL/LIAISON AGENCY

Clinton/Gore announce balanced budget

In the end, several factors pulled the budget bill back from the edge of defeat, not the least of which was the President's willingness to moderate his views on the need for bold reforms. Burned by the battles over health-care reform, Clinton focused on fiscal responsibility, something that both parties had pledged and yet repeatedly failed to deliver. He then began to hammer out the compromises needed to achieve a political success that few people would dispute—a balanced budget.

A booming economy helped the brokers of the deal. By May 1997 the economy was growing at a rate of 6 percent, which put an additional $65 billion in tax dollars in the nation's coffers. With hundreds of billions more expected by 2002, there was suddenly money for everyone. Republicans won the largest tax cut in 16 years, while Democrats got more money to spend on education, children's health, cities, and welfare.

GUIDE TO READING

Main Idea

Investigations into alleged scandals overshadowed the accomplishments of President Clinton's second term and influenced the way voters looked at the election of his successor in 2000.

Vocabulary

- e-commerce
- soft money
- perjury

Read to Find Out . . .

- some of Clinton's second-term accomplishments.
- the outcome of Clinton's impeachment trial.
- how the disputed Election 2000 was resolved.

The Election of 1996

The Comeback Kid

The budget victory came on the heels of an even bigger personal victory for Clinton—triumph in the 1996 presidential election. Once again, he had lived up to his reputation as the Comeback Kid, a nickname he earned when he won back the Arkansas governorship in 1982 after being voted out of the office two years earlier.

When the presidential primary season first opened in January 1996, Clinton seemed likely to join the ranks of one-term Presidents. In the *Doonesbury* comic strip, he was characterized as a free-floating waffle, a leader without direction. Yet eleven months later, Clinton scored a stunning victory over his opponents, Republican Senate Majority Leader Bob Dole and Reform Party candidate Ross Perot. He took 49 percent of the popular vote to Dole's 41 percent and Perot's 8 percent. The electoral count was even more telling: 376 votes for Clinton, 159 for Dole, 0 for Perot. He became only the seventh Democratic President to be elected to a second term and the first since Franklin Delano Roosevelt.

The Vital Center

In his victory speech, Clinton stood before a hometown crowd in Little Rock, Arkansas, and told the nation, "Tonight we proclaim that the vital American center is alive and well. It is the common ground on which we have made our progress." The remark held one of the keys to Clinton's victory. In effect, he promised to cut a middle course between liberals and conservatives in both parties and avoid the "gridlock" between himself and Republicans in Congress that had stalled legislation in his first term.

The President now crafted positions that would anchor him in the political center. In his whistle-stop train campaign across the country, Clinton opposed Republican proposals to restrain the costs of Medicare, while embracing the GOP's demand for a balanced budget. He courted socially traditional voters by calling for teen curfews, V-chips to block violent television shows, and school uniforms.

Keying in on the public's concern over school violence, Clinton vowed in one speech, "If it means that teenagers will stop killing each other over designer jackets, then our public schools should be able to require their students to wear school uniforms." Later Bob Dole would criticize Clinton by saying, "You're for school uniforms and curfews, and you're opposed to truancy. Now that's not reform, Mr. President." In fact, Clinton had come close to the very same positions supported by Republicans like Dole.

DIRCK HALSTEAD/TIMEPIX

Defying Predictions Clinton's prospects looked dim at the beginning of the 1996 campaign, but he triumphed in the end, winning a second term as President. *What kind of policies were key to Clinton's victory?*

On July 31, 1996, in an action that firmly fixed Clinton to the political center, the President made good on his promise to "end welfare as we know it" by agreeing to support a Republican welfare reform bill. After vetoing two earlier bills, he signed into law a welfare-reform measure that ended the federal government's Aid to Families with Dependent Children—a program established in 1935 as part of the Social Security Act. Under the Welfare Reform Act, the federal government no longer reimburses states for payments to poor families with children. Instead, states receive lump-sum payments from the federal government, and they must cut off payments after two consecutive years. In addition, life-time benefits to recipients are limited to five years of assistance.

The Balance of Power

Although the voters handed Clinton a victory, they also returned Republicans to power in both houses of Congress. For the first time in 56 years, the Republicans had maintained their congressional majorities for two consecutive elections.

However, of the 70 first-term Republican representatives who had helped spearhead Gingrich's assault on Democratic power, 13 lost the reelection. All told, the Republicans lost nine seats in the House, leaving them with a 227 to 207 majority over the Democrats, with 1 independent. In the Senate, the Republicans picked up 2 seats, giving the GOP 55 senators and the Democrats 45.

In the end, however, the big news on November 5, 1996, was not the reelection of a Democratic President for the first time since 1936 or a Republican Congress for the first time since 1930. In 220 years no Democratic candidate had ever been elected to the White House while the opposing party controlled Congress. In a sense voters had delivered a message to politicians: Work together to deliver the moderate agenda that you have promised.

Economic Recovery

The Real Political Bottom Line

One of the most important deciding factors in Clinton's 1996 campaign for the White House was the economy, just as it had been in 1992. However, instead of focusing on an economic recession, Clinton focused on an economic boom.

In one telling moment in the first televised debate, moderator Jim Lehrer of the Public Broadcasting System asked Dole if he agreed with Clinton's claim that Americans were better off in 1996 than in 1992. "Well he's better off than he was four years ago," quipped Dole. That got a big laugh but did not change the fact that most Americans agreed with Clinton's claim.

Winning Numbers

The economic recovery, though modest, began early in Clinton's first term and grew stronger year by year. News commentators, aware of American interest in the economy, began reporting economic and financial statistics in a way more commonly associated with sports scores. As stocks prices rose, mortgage rates fell, and interest rates held steady or even dropped, the economy became major news. Despite fears of renewed inflation, prices edged up only slightly.

Throughout Clinton's first term, employment rates rose. By November 1996 employment in the United States was 2.6 million higher than in November 1995. During the same period, the number of unemployed declined by 200,000, bringing down the jobless rate to 5.3 percent as compared to 5.6 percent a year earlier.

Perhaps the best news, from a politician's viewpoint, was the decline in the budget deficit—an issue that captured the attention of liberals and conservatives alike. When Clinton won his first term in 1992, the budget deficit exceeded a record $290 billion. By July 1998, just one year after hammering out the balanced-budget deal, the nation enjoyed a $69 billion surplus—the first surplus in 29 years and by far the largest in the nation's history. As the economy churned along, the surplus kept mounting—$79 billion in fiscal 1999 and more than $167 billion in fiscal 2000.

The "Long Boom"

The economic recovery puzzled many economists. In December 1996 Alan Greenspan, the Federal Reserve chairman, remarked that Americans were "irrationally exuberant" about the recovery, pointing out that growth was only half that at equivalent stages of the nation's two longest economic expansions in the 1960s and 1980s. But the expansion continued, and in February 2000 the "long boom," as many economists called it, officially became the longest in the nation's history.

A number of factors contributed to the boom, though economists do not agree on which should get the most credit, nor do they fully understand the reason for its unprecedented length. The collapse of the Soviet Union caused the United States to shift resources from massive defense spending, which had rapidly increased the national debt, to other budget areas. Cutting the defense budget also reduced the budget deficit. At the same time, export markets expanded and foreigners invested heavily in the United States economy as it began to boom. Also, the Federal Reserve deftly manipulated interest rates to hold down inflation without putting the brakes on economic expansion.

Yet another factor in the "long boom" was the fantastic growth of **e-commerce**, the many companies on the Internet that sell everything from books to airline tickets to information services. From 1995 to 2000, the estimated number of online shoppers increased from 3 million to 33 million, generating shopping revenues that increased from about $.7 billion in 1996 to $17 billion in 2000. The advent of the "Net Economy" generated thousands of new jobs in the 1990s and encouraged a new entrepreneurial spirit, especially among young people who grew up with the Internet.

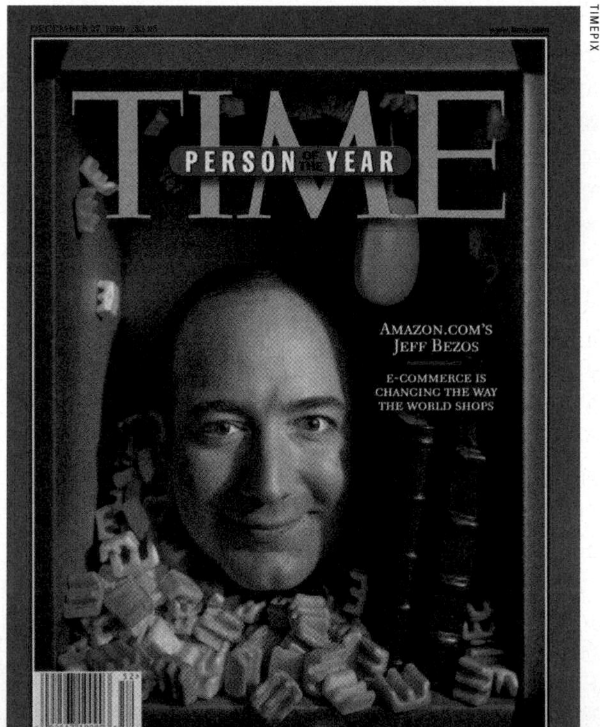

TIMEPIX

Internet Pioneer **Jeff Bezos fueled e-commerce growth when he founded Amazon.com. *TIME* magazine recognized e-commerce when it made him 1999 person of the year.**
What statistics show e-commerce growth in the 1990s?

Uneven Gains

The economic boom reached far and wide. Economic gains, however, were uneven. The poverty rate for Hispanic Americans reached an all-time high. The nation also had the highest child-poverty rate among the world's industrialized nations.

The situation was compounded by the difficult transition from welfare to self-sufficiency forced by the Welfare Reform Act of 1996. The booming economy helped. However, most of the jobs available for single mothers—the group that forms a large proportion of welfare recipients— turned out to be short-term or part-time low-paying jobs.

As Clinton began his second term of office, fewer people lived in poverty. However, the gap between the rich and poor had grown immensely, with a disproportionate number of the poor being children.

BOB DAEMMRICH/PICTOR

Day-care Shortages Despite a booming economy, many single-parent families were handicapped by a lack of good child care. *What impact did this problem have on the effort to move welfare recipients to greater economic independence?*

Clinton's Second Term

Defining a Legacy

Keenly aware of the problems facing the nation as well as his own place in history, William Jefferson Clinton celebrated his reelection by calling upon Americans to help build what his campaign slogan referred to as a "bridge to the 21st century." As 1997 opened, Americans wondered what kind of bridges Clinton would build. Would he hold to his new-found central course, or would he veer off in other political directions?

The Benefits of Prosperity

For Clinton the capstone of his administration was the return of economic well-being to the United States. During his second term, unemployment dropped, falling to 3.9 percent in late 2000, the lowest rate in more than 30 years. That same year Clinton announced that the Treasury Department had made the largest one-year debt payment in American history—$221 billion—and would pay off the entire national debt by 2013, if the budget stayed on track.

After passage of the Balanced Budget Act of 1997, the President outlined plans for using the newfound budget surpluses. He argued in favor of diverting some of the funds to protect Social Security and Medicaid rather than to cut taxes. He also set forward plans to relieve school crowding, reduce teenage smoking, improve child care, and protect the environment through the creation of nine new national monuments, such as Agua Fria, an area near Phoenix, Arizona, that includes many Native American ruins.

In his remaining years in office, the President took steps to ensure the success of the Welfare Reform Act of 1996. In 1997 he announced the Welfare to Work Partnership, which provided subsidies and tax incentives to businesses that agreed to create jobs for people still on welfare. He also committed the federal government and its contractors to hiring welfare recipients. By 2000 more than 20,000 businesses had joined the partnership, hiring an estimated 1.1 million welfare recipients.

Clinton also implemented a provision in the Welfare Reform Act that allowed the President to award bonuses to states that successfully moved people into jobs. He had fought hard for this provision and in December 1999 awarded the first $200 million in bonuses to 27 states. The following year the President put in place funds for future bonuses for states that moved families "from dependence to independence."

Although Clinton had been stung by health-care measures in the past, he did not turn his back on reform. Instead he focused on the millions of uninsured children of low-income working families—an issue on the agenda of both Democrats and Republicans. In 1997, with bipartisan support, the Clinton Administration created the State Children's Health Insurance Program. This program extends health care coverage to the uninsured children.

Promoting Peace

Clinton, one of the most widely traveled Presidents in history, set several major foreign policy goals, including the promotion of democracy in the developing world, encouragement of peace negotiations between warring factions or nations, and opposition to terrorism and the construction of weapons of mass destruction.

ZOOM 77/AP/WIDE WORLD PHOTOS

No Peace in Middle East In 2000 Palestinians clashed with Israeli soldiers over independence. *When was the Camp David summit?*

Impeachment

Clinton's Narrow Escape

More than a failed peace effort threatened to undermine the Clinton legacy. Rumors of scandal increasingly overshadowed the President's accomplishments.

Especially serious were questions raised in 1996 and 1997 about the fund-raising practices of the White House and the Democratic party. Republicans charged that the 1996 election had been funded, in part, by **soft money,** donations supposedly used only for party-building activities such as issue ads. Unlike hard money, or contributions used directly to elect candidates, soft-money funds are not subject to federal limits. Critics also charged that the Democrats had used loopholes in the law to violate the ban on foreign contributions, leading presidential candidate Bob Dole to comment in 1996, "We've finally got foreign aid coming to America and it's all going to the Democratic National Committee."

Starr Power

In late 1997, Kenneth W. Starr, appointed as an independent counsel by the attorney general, uncovered another scandal—an extra-marital affair. When Starr pursued inquiries into the affair, Clinton resisted the investigation, publicly denying the charges. However, evidence submitted to Congress by Starr left little doubt that the President had lied.

The Impeachment Question

The scandal did not stop with the grand jury hearings, however. In September 1998 Starr submitted a 445-page summary of his investigation, containing what he claimed was "substantial and credible information . . . that may constitute grounds for impeachment." The principal charges included **perjury,** or lying under oath, and obstruction of justice.

Nobody doubted that Clinton's conduct had soiled the dignity of the Oval Office. But were his actions in denying the affair impeachable offenses? Most Republicans in Washington thought so, while most Democrats believed the Constitution set a much higher bar for impeaching an elected President.

Public opinion polls confounded politicians by showing that Americans, although deploring the President's personal behavior, overwhelmingly approved Clinton's policies as chief executive. Nonetheless, Re-

During his second term, Clinton made a historic six-nation tour of Africa, becoming the first U.S. President to visit Ghana, Uganda, Rwanda, South Africa, Botswana, and Senegal while in office. He pledged to help Americans "see the new Africa with new eyes" and to provide aid for combating disease, improving education, and increasing food production. He also visited a number of other nations to encourage peace talks, ease old cold war tensions, and prevent renewed warfare among rival nations. To promote these goals, he helped broker a peace in Northern Ireland, became the first-ever President to visit Vietnam, and encouraged the leaders of India, Pakistan, and Bangladesh, to resolve long-standing differences peacefully.

Clinton also made clear United States opposition to the illegal manufacture and sale of weapons of mass destruction. In 1998 the United States and Great Britain led a bombing blitz, known as Operation Desert Fox, on Iraq to force Saddham Hussein to comply with terms ending the Persian Gulf War. That same year, the President visited U.S. troops near the Demilitarized Zone in Korea to show his concern over North Korea's weapons program. In 2000, in an effort to reduce tensions on the Korean Peninsula, Clinton approved a visit to North Korea by Secretary of State Madeline Albright, the first ever by a high-ranking government official.

Clinton hoped to be remembered as the President who brought peace to the Middle East. However, the outbreak of renewed violence between Palestinian Arabs and Israelis in 2000 undercut this dream. Despite a July summit at the Camp David presidential retreat, conflicts continued. As clashes persisted, the gains of the 1993 peace accord, brokered by Clinton, became threatened.

publicans continued to push for impeachment. They rejected a Democratic resolution to censure the President, officially disapproving of his actions. Instead, they voted to bring impeachment charges against him. On January 7, 1999, the case moved to the Senate for trial, where for the first time in 131 years a President faced possible removal from office.

On February 12, 1999, the U.S. Senate voted on two articles of impeachment. The final tallies—45-55 to convict on the charge of perjury, 50-50 on the count of obstruction of justice—fell far below the two-thirds majority required to convict a President. Two hours after the votes, a subdued Clinton delivered a brief speech. After more than a year of turmoil, he declared "how profoundly sorry I am for what I said and did to trigger these events and the great burden they have imposed on the Congress and the American people."

Clinton was now free to complete the remaining 708 days of his second term as President. Against the backdrop of impeachment hearings, both political parties jumpstarted the contest to succeed Clinton. In assessing the upcoming race, David Broder, a columnist for the *Washington Post,* predicted, "The Number 1 Democrat, Bill Clinton, has seeded the atmosphere with so many doubts about his presidential character that the hunger for a trustworthy successor could trump any issues on which the rival nominees choose to run."

Election 2000

And the Winner Is . . .?

After more than a year of politicking, the 2000 election campaign narrowed to three candidates: Republican nominee George W. Bush, Democratic nominee Al Gore, and Green Party nominee Ralph Nader, a longtime fighter for consumer safety and environmental protection. "The battle lines are clearly drawn," declared Bush. But in the end, the election could not have been much closer.

Although Gore was ahead in popular votes, no candidate had the required 270 electroal votes to win. Whoever won the too-close-to-call vote in Florida would become President. Both candidates battled with each other over the final count in Florida's popular vote. Lawyers replaced political consultants as the race entered the courts. Legal maneuvering centered first on suits that claimed a confusing ballot design had led people to mistakenly vote for the wrong candidate. Later other suits focused on the logistics of recounting votes to make sure machines had correctly read punch ballots. On these ballots, pieces of paper were punched by voters, tearing the pieces, or chads, off the ballot forms. Some ballots still had these chads partially attached, while others showed only indentations, or dimples.

When a 5 P.M. deadline for certifying the vote arrived on November 26, a painstaking recount by hand was still not complete. Nonetheless, Florida secretary of state Katherine Harris certified Bush the winner by 537 votes. "How can we teach our children that every vote counts if we are not willing to make a good-faith effort to count every vote?" asked Al Gore's running mate Joseph Lieberman. As Bush prepared a short victory speech, Gore prepared the next round of legal battles.

Suits filed by both candidates—to uphold or to reject the recounts—went to the Florida supreme court and to the U.S. Supreme Court, with each side pressing for decisions before the December 12 deadline for selecting the elector slates for each state. In the end, the Court ruled that the hand recounts violated the equal protection clause of the Fourteenth Amendment. This ruling effectively threw the election to Bush who became only the fourth presidential candidate in history to lose the popular vote and still win the election.

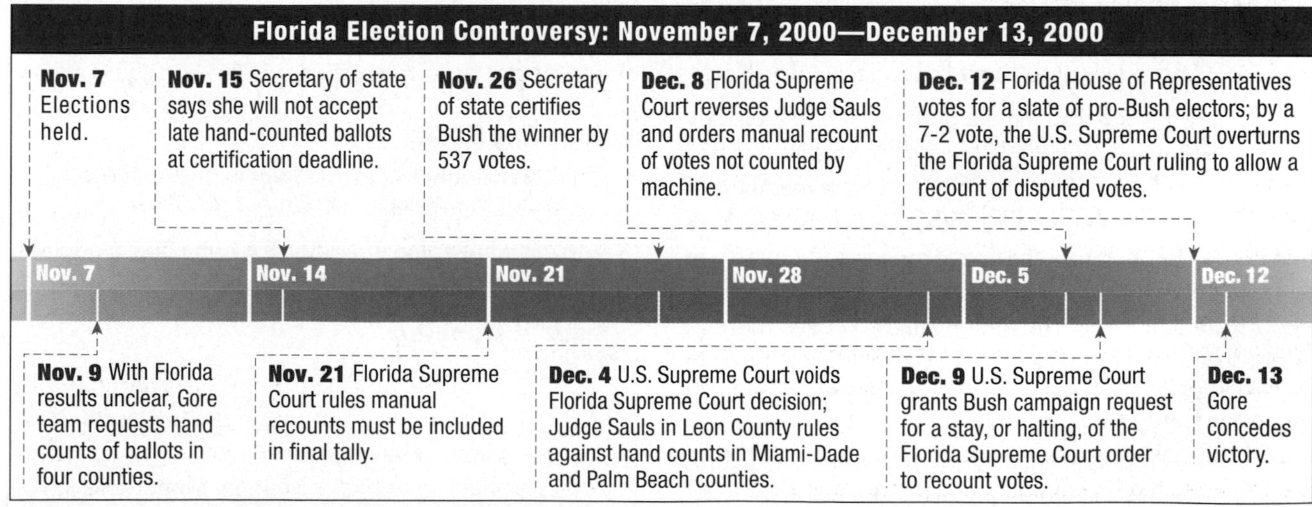

Florida Election Controversy: November 7, 2000—December 13, 2000
Nov. 7 Elections held.
Nov. 15 Secretary of state says she will not accept late hand-counted ballots at certification deadline.
Nov. 26 Secretary of state certifies Bush the winner by 537 votes.
Dec. 8 Florida Supreme Court reverses Judge Sauls and orders manual recount of votes not counted by machine.
Dec. 12 Florida House of Representatives votes for a slate of pro-Bush electors; by a 7-2 vote, the U.S. Supreme Court overturns the Florida Supreme Court ruling to allow a recount of disputed votes.
Nov. 7
Nov. 14
Nov. 21
Nov. 28
Dec. 5
Dec. 12
Nov. 9 With Florida results unclear, Gore team requests hand counts of ballots in four counties.
Nov. 21 Florida Supreme Court rules manual recounts must be included in final tally.
Dec. 4 U.S. Supreme Court voids Florida Supreme Court decision; Judge Sauls in Leon County rules against hand counts in Miami-Dade and Palm Beach counties.
Dec. 9 U.S. Supreme Court grants Bush campaign request for a stay, or halting, of the Florida Supreme Court order to recount votes.
Dec. 13 Gore concedes victory.

ELECTION NIGHT: NOVEMBER 7,2000

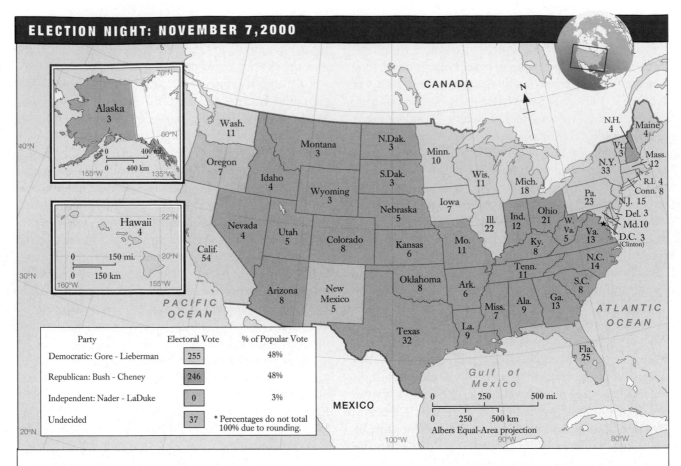

Party	Electoral Vote	% of Popular Vote
Democratic: Gore - Lieberman	255	48%
Republican: Bush - Cheney	246	48%
Independent: Nader - LaDuke	0	3%
Undecided	37	* Percentages do not total 100% due to rounding.

Election Day 2000 did not produce a clear presidential winner because several states were too close to call. *Which state became the focus of the post-election battle?*

The Job Ahead

Winning the election was just the beginning of the struggle for President Bush. Sidetracked by the ballot recounts, Bush faced the unsettling makeup of the 107th Congress, which in many ways reflected the outcome of the election itself. The elections awarded Democrats and Republicans a 50-50 split in the Senate. In the House the Republicans held 221 seats to the 212 for the Democrats and 2 independents. In commenting on the situation facing the President, New York Senator Chuck Schumer warned, "He has to make a decision—work the middle or get nothing done."

To compound matters, the President and Congress faced a slowing economy and a number of bills tabled by the 106th Congress, including spending measures shaped largely by President Clinton. One of the new members of Congress to determine the fate of these bills was New York Senator Hillary Clinton, the first former First Lady to win elected office. Even before Senator Clinton began work, people predicted that the nation might yet see more of her husband, the Comeback Kid. "We're going to be dealing with Bill Clinton for a long time to come," predicted Skip Rutherford, a longtime Arkansas friend. "He'll be the youngest ex-President since Teddy Roosevelt. He figures at age 54, there's a lot more history to be made."

SECTION ASSESSMENT

Main Idea

1. Use a diagram like this one to support your opinion of Clinton's second-term legacy to the nation.

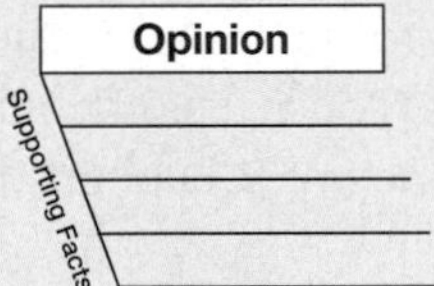

Vocabulary

2. Define: e-commerce, soft money, perjury.

Checking Facts

3. What actions did Clinton take to ensure the success of the Welfare Reform Act of 1996?
4. What were some of Clinton's foreign policy goals during his second term?

Critical Thinking

5. **Evaluating Information** Do you agree with the claim by Senator Chuck Schumer that President Bush must "work the middle—or get nothing done"? Why or why not?

Social Studies Skill

ANALYZING NEWS MEDIA

Learning the Skill

Every citizen needs to understand current events in order to make decisions about election issues, causes, and career choices. To stay informed, people use a variety of news sources, from broadcast media (television and radio) to print media (newspapers and newsmagazines).

How to Analyze the News

To get an accurate profile of current events, you must learn to think critically about the news you hear or read:

a. First, think about the source of the news story: reports that reveal sources are more reliable than those that don't because if you know the sources, you can evaluate them. Can all facts be verified?

b. Second, many news stories also analyze and interpret events. Such analyses may be more detailed than other reports, but they also reflect a reporter's biases. See if you can identify biases as you read or listen.

c. Finally, ask yourself whether the news is even-handed and thorough. Is it reported on the scene or secondhand? Does it fairly represent both sides of an issue? How many sources are used? The more sources cited for a fact, the more reliable it is.

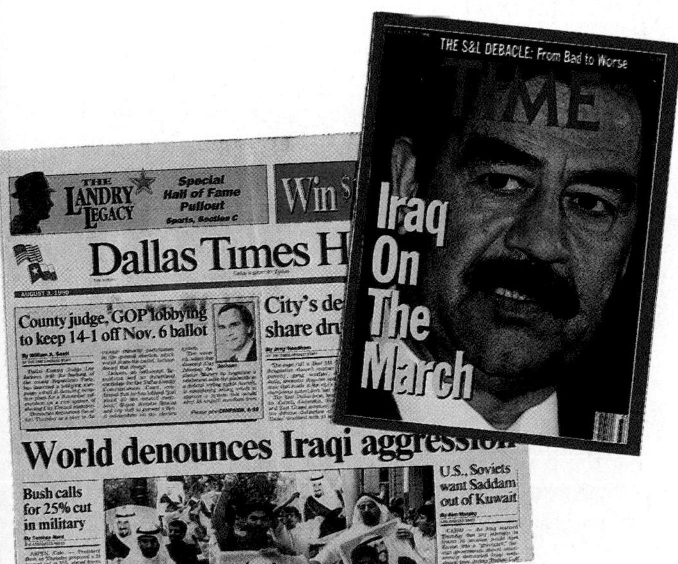

Media Representations Iraq's invasion of Kuwait in August 1990 immediately dominated news in the United States. *How do the headlines in the newspaper and the newsmagazine shown here emphasize different aspects of the event?*

Broadcast Media

Visual impact and immediacy are television's main strengths. Both television and radio replace a written account with an oral presentation. Both are up-to-the-minute. Stories can be edited and updated almost until airtime. Reporters can even interrupt their broadcasts to include new information.

Print Media

Print media carry a greater variety of news stories, as well as features and editorials, than broadcast media do. Reader comment and opinion sections offer interaction with subscribers. Print news is less immediate than broadcast news and becomes out-of-date more quickly.

Practicing the Skill

1. Find two articles, one in a current newspaper and the other in a newsmagazine, on a topic involving Latin America. Which article provided more in-depth coverage?

2. What points were the articles trying to make? Were the articles successful? Can the facts be verified?

3. Did either of the articles reflect bias? List any unsupported statements.

4. Was the news reported on the scene or secondhand? Do the articles seem to represent both sides fairly?

5. How many sources can you identify in the articles? List them.

Applying the Skill

Think of an issue in your community on which public opinion is divided. Read newspaper features and editorials about the issue and listen to television reports. Can you identify biases? Which reports most fairly represent the issue and the solutions? Why? Which reports are the most reliable? The least reliable? Why?

The **Glencoe Skillbuilder Interactive Workbook, Level 2** CD-ROM provides more practice in key social studies skills.

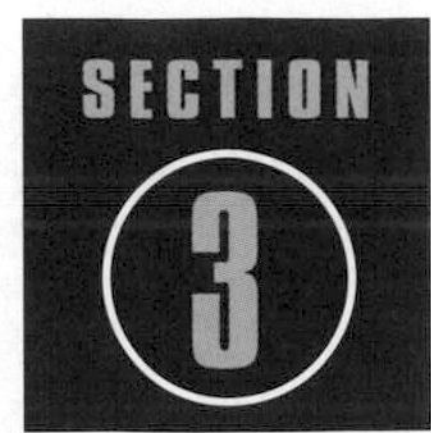

Into a New Century

JULY 4, 2000: AMERICANS CELEBRATE 224 YEARS OF FREEDOM

SHORTLY AFTER THE CONTINENTAL CONGRESS FORMALLY ADOPTED THE DECLARATION OF INDEPENDENCE ON JULY 4, 1776, JOHN ADAMS REPORTEDLY CALLED FOR A GRAND CELEBRATION. Said the leader who would follow George Washington into the presidency,

> It ought to be solemnized with pomp and parade, with shows, games, sports, guns, bells, bonfires, and illuminations, from one end of this continent to the other, from this time forward forevermore.
>
> —John Adams, July 1776

PICTOR

July 4, 2000
Fireworks light up the Washington Monument

And so Americans have done every year since 1776. However, the celebrations on July 4, 2000, held a special meaning for Americans as the nation headed into a new century.

Across the United States people set aside their differences to "solemnize with pomp and parade" the nation's 224th birthday. A fife-and-drum band performed at a reading of the Declaration in Washington, D.C. About 150 tall sailing ships from more than 50 nations plied the waters of New York's harbor. The city of Dallas hosted old-time games like sack races, horseshoe pitching, and a pie eating contest, while San Francisco set off one of the nation's biggest fireworks displays. The celebrations reached all the way into outer space, where astronauts aboard the U.S. space shuttle Columbia broadcast live, coast-to-coast television pictures to the nation.

To honor the diversity that is the United States of America, a group of 80 immigrants from 27 different countries—Cuba, China, Russia, Iran, the Dominican Republic, and more—took part in a naturalization ceremony at Monticello, the Virginia home of Thomas Jefferson, author of the Declaration.

GUIDE TO READING

Main Idea

New forces are shaping the United States in the 2000s, changing both the makeup of the American people and the way they live.

Vocabulary

- affirmative action
- community policing

Read to Find Out . . .

- how immigration patterns have changed in recent years.
- arguments for and against affirmative action.
- the issues that face the nation during the 21st century.

Immigration

And Still They Come

When the immigrants at Monticello took their oaths of citizenship, they joined about 375,000 immigrants who had already become citizens that year. They arrived at a time when the nation's foreign-born population—nearly 26 million people—was the largest in United States history. Their arrival made a diverse nation even more diverse.

© BLACK STAR

Newcomers New American citizens are sworn in under a tent in Washington, D.C. *What did the amendments to the Immigration and Nationality Act do?*

Easing Immigration Requirements

The large-scale arrival of immigrants helped shape the closing decades of the 20th century. Between 1970 and 1997, the nation's foreign-born population jumped by 168 percent. The rapid increase resulted in large part from passage of the Immigration Act of 1965, which reopened the doors to the United States after 40 years of restricted immigration. The act, wrote one observer, created "a stampede, almost an invasion" of people "who hungered to enter." It also ended the government bias against newcomers from Asia and Latin America.

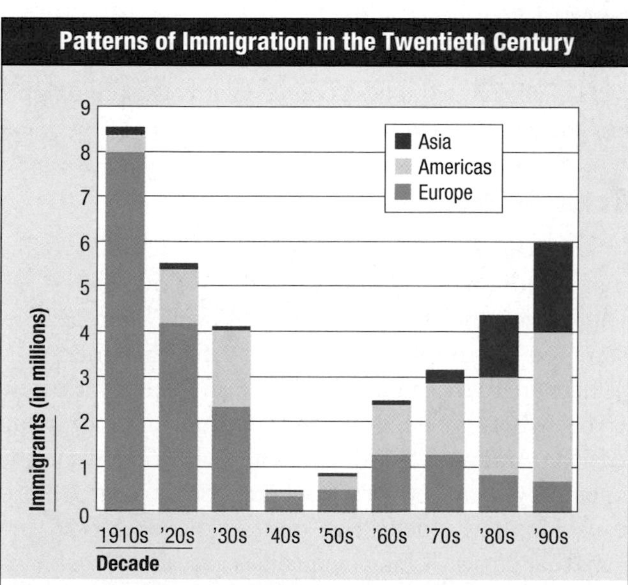

Immigration into the United States has grown steadily since 1940. *What legislative changes have affected the number of people legally entering the country?*

For an online update of this graph, visit americanodyssey.glencoe.com and click on ***Textbook Updates—Chapter 26.***

Changes in Immigration Law

Amendments to the Immigration and Nationality Act in 1990 increased the number of immigrants allowed into the United States. The annual ceiling was raised to 700,000 immigrants for the years 1992 to 1994 and to 675,000 beginning in 1995. The amendments placed no limit on the immigration of immediate family members of U.S. citizens and strengthened preferences for skilled workers. "America has revived one of its greatest traditions: that of being a nation of immigrants," remarked the director of the National Immigration Forum.

During the 1970s, 1980s, and 1990s, poverty and political conflicts in several parts of the world drew people to the United States. Devastating wars in Southeast Asia, for example, created waves of political refugees, 500,000 of whom entered the United States. By 1997, 10 percent of the population was foreign born, the highest percentage since 1930.

The opportunities for economic success and political freedom that attracted legal immigrants also attracted undocumented immigrants—people living in the United States without the proper visas. In 1986, Congress passed the Immigration Reform and Control Act. The law offered undocumented immigrants who had lived in the United States since 1981 a chance to become legal residents. More than a million immigrants took advantage of the law during its first year in effect.

Settlement Patterns

In the nation's greatest sustained era of immigration, from 1880 to 1914, immigrants spread out all over the United States, often becoming farmers, craftworkers, or small business owners in villages or rural areas. But in the era of immigration from 1970 to 2000, three quarters of all the new arrivals concentrated geographically in six states: California, Texas, New York, Illinois, New Jersey, and Florida. By 2000, for example, white Californians had become a "minority," with the state's Hispanic population standing at 30 percent, Asian Pacific Islanders at 12 percent, and African Americans at 8 percent. New Mexico and Hawaii also have a minority of white Americans, with Texas and Florida fast approaching the tipping point.

Even more striking, immigrants have chosen coastal ports of entry–San Francisco, Los Angeles, Houston, New Orleans, Boston, New York, Philadelphia, Washington, and Miami—as a place to find the American Dream. Chicago is the one city in the American heartland that stands out as a magnet for immigrants.

Equality for Minorities

Race and Gender Issues

The population changes added new twists in a long-standing debate over **affirmative action**—programs created through a series of executive orders and laws designed to aid racial minorities and women in their quest for equality. Many people argued that these programs unfairly discriminated against whites, who in several states like California were becoming a minority themselves.

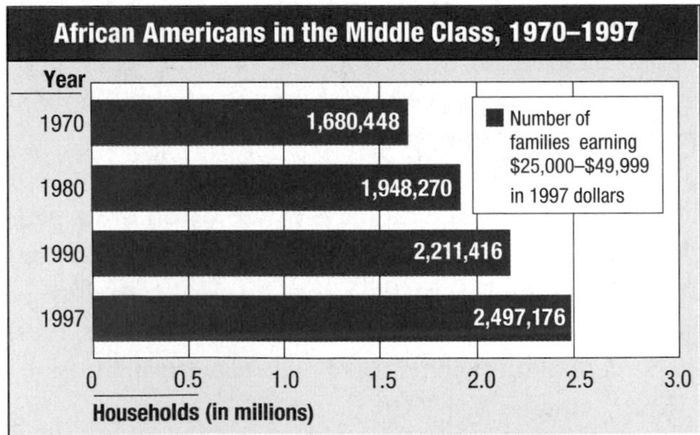

The size of the African American middle class has grown since the 1970s. *How many African American families were middle class in 1997?*

For an online update of this graph, visit americanodyssey.glencoe.com and click on ***Textbook Updates—Chapter 26.***

Origins of Affirmative Action

Affirmative action programs had their roots in the 1960s when President Kennedy encouraged government contractors to "take affirmative action" to treat all job applicants without discrimination based on their race, gender, ethnicity, or religion. After Kennedy's death, President Johnson issued an executive order that required employers to search aggressively for minority job applicants by such methods as placing ads in minority newspapers or advertising jobs in minority neighborhoods.

President Nixon built on this precedent by ordering craft unions to admit members of racial minorities so that they could receive training. In a groundbreaking action, he tightened hiring rules by requiring federal contractors to show evidence of "affirmative action" to meet the goal of increased minority employment. This plan, known as the Philadelphia Plan, set the stage for subsequent regulations and court rulings that expanded the scope of the original version to include not only racial minorities but women as well.

Affirmative action, as defined by these regulations and court cases, entailed creating outreach programs, preparing minority high school students for college admissions, and in some cases establishing quotas that defined how many female or minority openings were available in schools or companies. By the 1990s, the effects of affirmative action, coupled with other civil rights legislation, were beginning to be felt.

Gains in Equality

African Americans profited, but slowly, after affirmative action was implemented. In November 1999 Hugh Price, the president of the National Urban League, summed up the situation facing African Americans. "There are two headlines," said Price. "Things have never been better," he explained, pointing to a growing African American middle class and historic lows in the unemployment and poverty rates for African Americans. He then added, "But, on the downside, there are gaps that persist," citing inequalities in academic achievement, income, and financial assets.

Women also experienced progress. By 1999 women all but matched men in terms of educational attainment, with 23.1 percent of women completing 4 or more years of college compared to 27.5 percent for men. In the 1990s, women accounted for nearly 50 percent of the labor force, with expanded employment oppor-

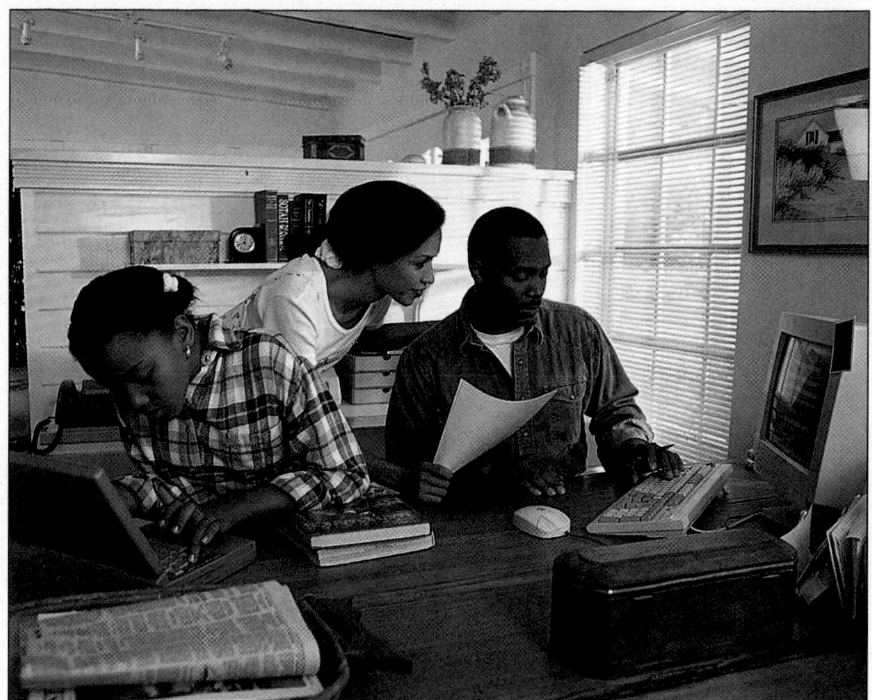

PAUL BARTON/THE STOCK MARKET

The Middle Class More African American families than ever before are part of the middle class. *How did affirmative action help African Americans leave inner city neighborhoods?*

tunities in occupations predominated by men, such as corporate management and the military. The number of women in high-paying managerial and professional jobs, such as law or medicine, rose from 11 million in 1985 to 16.5 million in 1995. Close to 6.5 million owned businesses, which collectively employed more people than all the Fortune 500 companies combined. Despite these gains, women's pay still lagged behind that of men, though the "income gap" narrowed somewhat in the 1990s.

The Future of Affirmative Action

As the United States entered the 2000s, many people questioned the success—and even the legality—of affirmative action. Proponents of affirmative action said that these policies broadened the pool for jobs and college admissions to include a wide range of qualified people. Opponents argued that affirmative action policies favored less-qualified women and minority applicants over better-qualified white males. Both proponents and opponents, however, seemed to be united on one point: They felt that establishing quotas was unfair.

The debate over affirmative action took place in individual states. In 1995 California's state university system voted to stop considering race and gender in student admissions. The following year Californians voted in favor of the California Civil Rights Initiative (CCRI), also known as Proposition 209, which ended affirmative action policies in all of the state's public agencies. Two years later, Washington followed California's example and passed Initiative 200. In February 2000, Florida Governor Jeb Bush and the state's independently elected cabinet voted to voluntarily ban affirmative action in both college admissions and state contracts.

The United States Supreme Court moved to narrow the scope of many affirmative action programs by declaring that they must "serve a compelling government interest . . . and be narrowly tailored to their goals." In 1996 the Supreme Court ruling in *Texas et al.* v. *Hopwood et al.* limited affirmative action when it agreed to let stand a lower-court decision that barred the University of Texas from considering race in its admission policies.

Violence in America

Americans React

As the new century dawned, one of the biggest issues on the minds of Americans, regardless of their

Women in the Labor Force

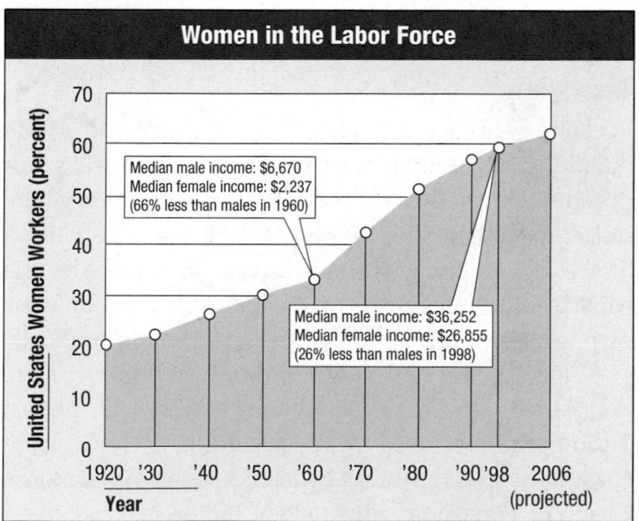

By 1998 more than 60% of women worked outside the home. *How did their median salary compare to that of men?*

For an online update of this graph, visit americanodyssey.glencoe.com and click on ***Textbook Updates—Chapter 26.***

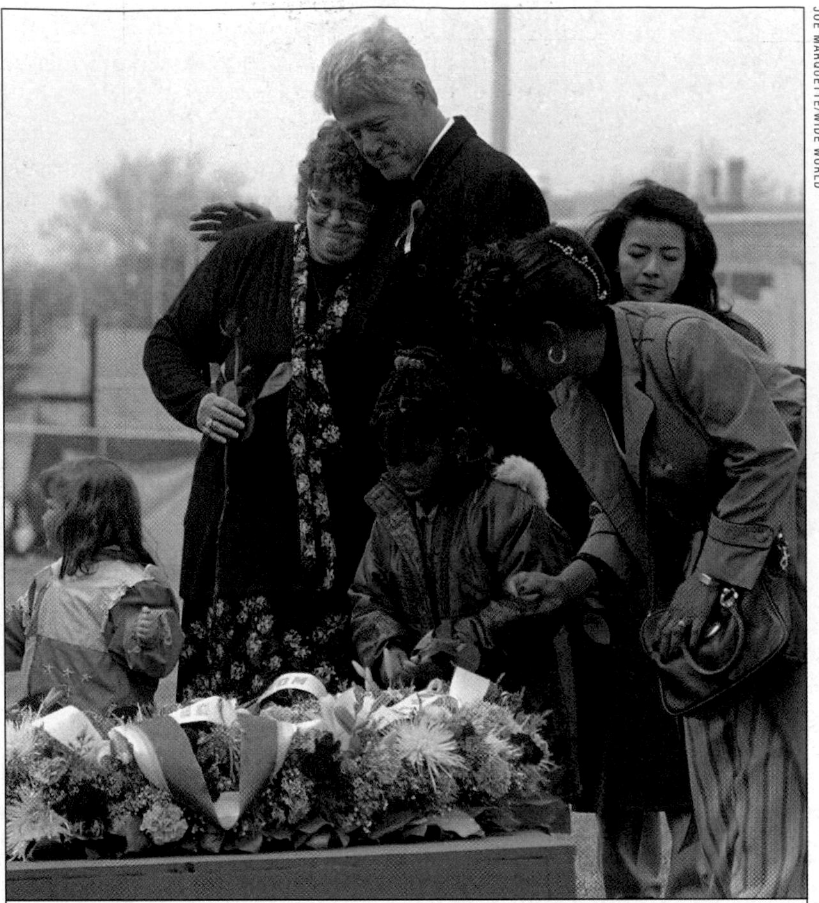
JOE MARQUETTE/WIDE WORLD

Domestic Terrorism President Clinton comforts family members of victims in the Oklahoma City bombing. *Who was convicted of the crime?*

ancestry, was the rise of violence. Although the nation might be free of war abroad, a war of another sort took place on American soil, as acts of terrorism and use of guns to commit violent crimes made many people fear for their personal safety and the safety of their children.

Terrorism

The February 1993 bombing of the World Trade buildings in New York City by foreign terrorists opposed to U.S. policies in the Middle East created a new sense of vulnerability among Americans. The United States, like other nations, was exposed to actions by terrorists, either individuals or groups, who acted on their own, usually without any formal government support.

Nor was the nation free of homegrown terrorism. A little after 9 A.M. on the morning of April 19, 1995, a 2-ton bomb produced from agricultural chemicals tore apart the Alfred P. Murrah Federal Building in Oklahoma City. The explosion, which killed 168 people, including 19 children, was the worst act of terrorism ever perpetrated in the United States. At first some people suspected foreign terrorists. In the end, both of the men convicted in the case—Timothy McVeigh and Terry Nichols—however, were Americans.

On July 27, 1996, terrorism struck again when a bomb exploded during the Olympic Games in Atlanta, Georgia, killing 1 and injuring 111. While a suspect was found very quickly, he was later released, after weeks of investigations proved him innocent. As a result of such bombings, governments took extra precautions to protect Americans during celebrations to mark the arrival of the 21st century. Contrary to fears, however, the ceremonies went peacefully.

Street Violence

Despite the intense emotional impact of terrorist acts, the incidence of street violence was far higher. The principal victims of the violence were young African American and Hispanic men living in cities. One out of every 20 African American and Hispanic men in the 1990s was killed before age 20. Their death rate exceeded the rate of soldiers killed in World War II, which was one out of every 40.

To curb street violence, Americans tried a variety of approaches. In Bridgeport, Connecticut, Police Chief Thomas J. Sweeney pioneered **community policing,** which involves sending more foot patrols into neighborhoods and establishing better relationships between the police and community. "You've got to redevelop a sense of neighborhoods," warned Sweeney, this is "not something you're going to change in a presidency or a two-year term of a mayor. You need long-term focus."

Meanwhile, a nervous public formed neighborhood watches to keep their communities safe. Although the homicide rate has begun to drop in many urban centers, including New York and Detroit, most Americans agree that the issue of street violence will not easily resolve itself.

School Violence

On April 20, 1999, Littleton, Colorado—and the entire nation—was devastated by the attack of two teenage boys on their classmates at Columbine High School. The boys used bombs and attack weapons to kill 15 schoolmates and wound 23 others before turning their guns on themselves. The Columbine shootings sounded the alarm to parents and students everywhere. As one expert on children and violence claimed,

> There is a growing recognition that the epidemic of youth violence has now reached a point

where virtually every school contains boys who are troubled, angry, and violent enough, who have access to weapons and violent scenarios and images, to become the next tragedy.

Challenges for the Future

Building a Better Nation

As the nation moved into the 2000s, Americans paused to look back at what the United States had accomplished during the 1900s—a time many historians referred to as the "American Century." They also cast their eyes to the future speculating on what accomplishments and challenges might lay ahead.

The Long Reach of Technology

By the 2000s the idea of humans strolling on Mars seemed possible. This dream was inspired by images transmitted back to Earth from cameras aboard the Mars probe *Pathfinder* and the arrival of astronauts aboard the world's first international space station in late 2000. "My imagination is taking me out there," declared astronaut Story Musgrave enthusiastically.

Technology not only carried humans into space, it was also reshaping life on Earth. The computerization of America brought sweeping changes to the nation. Computers, along with industrial robots, streamlined the manufacturing methods used by factories, which now required fewer—and better skilled—workers. By the late 1990s computers could be found on the desks of more than half of all American workers.

Computers and other technological advances also affected farming, turning many farms into "agribusinesses," large high-tech farms run much like a corporation. Technological advances—including genetically altered crops—produced higher yields, which in turn reduced the number of farming jobs and speeded the movement of people from rural areas into the suburbs and cities.

The trend toward automation forced many workers to undergo retraining or seek new jobs, either voluntarily or because of downsizing. The fastest-growing occupations were in the service industry. Service positions—jobs in retail stores, restaurants, hotels, computer software companies, insurance companies, stock brokerages, accounting firms, and other service business—accounted for 90 percent of the 42.6 million new jobs in the past three decades. This trend is expected to continue in the years ahead, with one of every five new jobs created by the year 2005 projected to be in the field of health-care services. Child-care will also account for many new jobs, as the number of dual wage-earner families increases.

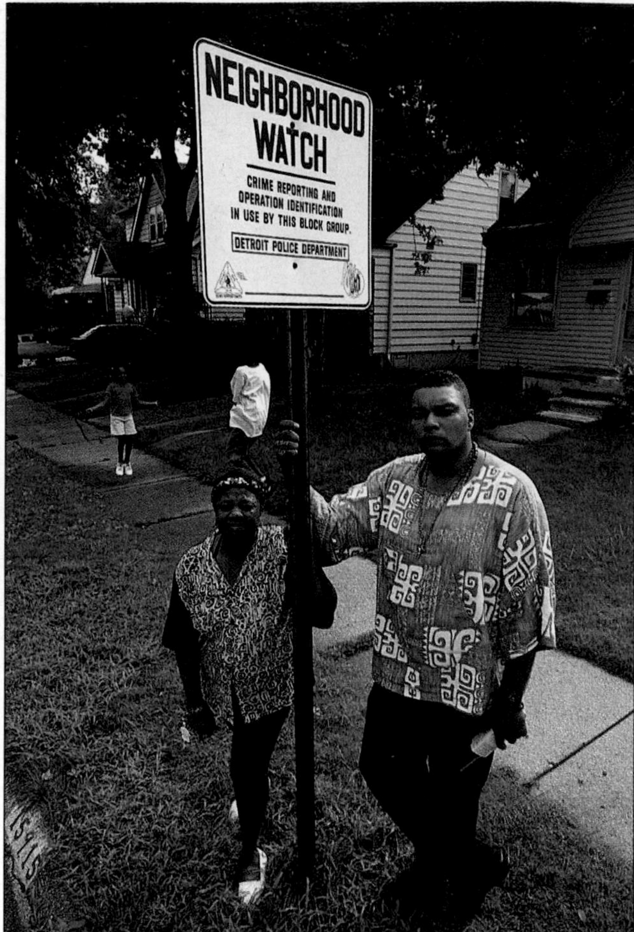

© PHIL PUGLIANO/GAMMA LIAISON

Communities Fight Back People in this Detroit neighborhood worked together to form a Neighborhood Watch group to keep their community safe. *What happened to the homicide rate in Detroit in the mid-1990s?*

Putting the World Online

The rise of the Internet, a worldwide linking of computer networks via communication satellites and telephone lines, increased "globalization" as people and businesses came in contact with each through a click of the mouse.

The Internet revolutionized communications and methods of doing business, but at the same time it threat-

Student Web Activity 26

Visit the *American Odyssey* Web site at americanodyssey.glencoe.com and click on ***Chapter 26—Student Web Activities*** to find out more about education in the United States.

AP/WIDE WORLD PHOTOS

Counting the People Census Director Kenneth Prewitt works to count Inuit residents for the 2000 census. *How is the ethnic makeup of America changing?*

ened users with "information overload." It also exposed them to invasions of privacy as people and companies posted all kinds of data on the Net—everything from telephone numbers to bank accounts.

Conquering Disease

One of the most stunning accomplishments of the 20th century was the improved medical care that increased life spans through new medicines such as penicillin and prevention of diseases such as polio. Americans in the 21st century looked forward to yet other medical advances, including cures or new methods of treatment for cancer and acquired deficiency syndrome (AIDS), a disease identified in 1981.

AIDS, which has reached epidemic proportions in some parts of the world, presents a special challenge to scientists. They know that it is caused by the HIV virus, but they have not yet been able to find a vaccine that prevents people from contracting the virus. Neither have they been able to produce less costly drugs that prevent the HIV virus from developing into AIDS once it invades the body.

Scientists are also focused on finding a cure for Alzheimer's disease, a gradual degeneration of the brain's processes commonly associated with aging. This disease presents a special problem to the United States, where the nation's aging baby boomers will push the number of people age 65 and over to more than 69.4 million people by 2030. To speed work on a vaccine to prevent Alzheimer's disease, the Clinton administration allocated $50 million in July 2000 to fund Alzheimer's research over a five-year period.

Meeting Educational Challenges

A 1983 presidential commission on education found that American students lagged behind students in other industrialized nations. An "education summit" held at the White House in 1989 established the goal of raising the academic level of students from near the bottom among industrialized nations to the top in math and science.

To address educational issues, President Clinton asked Congress to authorize the "America Reads" initiative—a program that would send work-study students, AmeriCorps students, and other groups into elementary schools to make sure students can read independently by the end of third grade. In addition, his 1997 budget included the single largest increase in aid to education in more than 30 years. Clinton also increased the overall investment in educational technology from $23 million in 1993 to $769 million in 2000, with the goal of connecting all public schools to the Internet.

At the same time, schools throughout the nation tried to improve their educational systems. Iowa, Arkansas, Utah, Ohio, and other states experimented with school-choice programs, such as charter schools, schools run by private individuals or organizations under district super-

Fastest-Growing Occupations, 1996–2006

Occupation	Employment (in thousands) 1996	2006	Percent Change
Database administrators, computer support specialists, and all other computer scientists	212	461	118%
Computer engineers	216	451	109%
Systems analysts	506	1,025	103%
Personal and home care aides	202	374	85%
Physical and corrective therapy assistants and aides	84	151	79%
Home health aides	495	873	76%
Medical assistants	225	391	74%
Desktop publishing specialists	30	53	74%
Physical therapists	115	196	71%
Occupational therapy assistants and aides	16	26	69%

Source: U.S. Department of Labor, Bureau of Labor Statistics, *Monthly Labor Review*, November 1997.

The United States government tracks the predictions for future job growth. *Which field will have the most growth?*

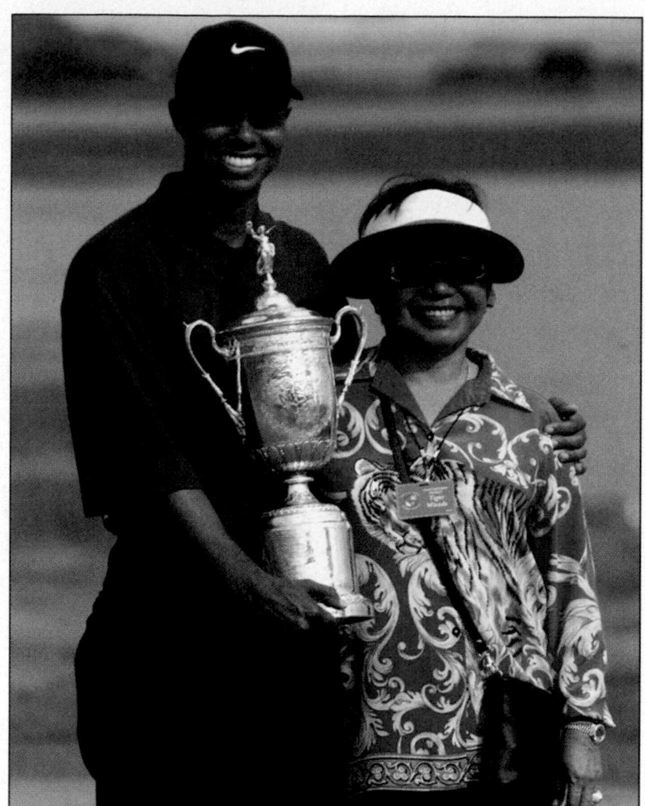
LIAISON AGENCY

Savoring Victory Tiger Woods has emerged as America's top golfer. *What is his ethnic background?*

vision. Milwaukee, Wisconsin, and Cleveland, Ohio, experimented with school vouchers, which could be used as tuition for any participating school.

Educators also pushed forward with the establishment of standards for core disciplines. Every state except Iowa—and most large school districts—approved written standards to guide teaching priorities and to provide the basis for state-wide proficiency tests.

Two other reforms also helped improve student performance. First, many school districts reduced class size, which had ballooned to more than 40 students in some areas, to a create better learning environment. Second, a growing number of districts raised teachers' salaries and provided cash incentives for teachers whose students made significant progress in mastering basic skills.

Finding Common Ground

Uniting All Americans

In his 2000 State of the Union Address, President Clinton told the nation:

> In a little more than 50 years, there will be no majority race in America. In a more interconnected world, this diversity will be our greatest strength. . . . Therefore, we should do more than just tolerate our diversity—we should honor and celebrate it.
>
> —William Jefferson Clinton, State of the Union, 2000

The President urged Americans to look beyond their individual differences and to see "our common humanity." In a silent but steady way, that process had already begun. In every part of the country, people who had been divided by race or ethnicity were beginning to cross the color line in friendship, love, and marriage.

Professional golfer Tiger Woods, the son of an African American father and a Thai mother, took a progressive view of race relations at the start of the 21st century. Said Woods in an interview,

> It's kind of neat to be able to be raised in two cultures and understand them both and fit in. In this country I'm a minority, but around the world I'm treated a little bit differently. We would be ignorant to say racism doesn't exist. But I think things are changing, and changing for the good.
>
> —Tiger Woods

If the changes continue, perhaps Americans can indeed meet on a common ground to celebrate the diversity that characterizes our nation.

SECTION ASSESSMENT

Main Idea

1. Use a diagram like this one to show some of the changes in the United States during the late 1990s and early 2000s.

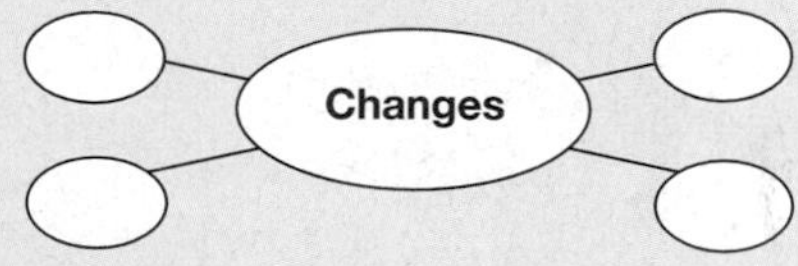

Vocabulary

2. Define: affirmative action, community policing.

Checking Facts

3. From what two regions do most recent immigrants come, and where do they tend to settle in the United States?
4. What are educators doing to improve the quality of education?

Critical Thinking

5. **Recognizing Points of View** Some educational reformers think that increased funding will solve most of the problems facing schools. What is your point of view on this issue?

Turning Point

Affirmative Action

SPRING 1995

MEMORANDUM

For: People of the Court

Subject: racial classifications

Any individual suffers an injury when he or she is disadvantaged by the government because of his or her race. . . . We hold today that all racial classifications, imposed by whatever federal, state, or local governmental actor, must be analyzed by a reviewing court under strict scrutiny. In other words, such classifications are constitutional only if they are narrowly tailored measures that further compelling governmental interests. . . .

Justice Sandra Day O'Connor
Supreme Court, June 12, 1995

The Case

In 1990 the state of Colorado was rebuilding a stretch of highway in the San Juan National Forest. The prime contractor on the job, Mountain Gravel and Construction, invited subcontractors to bid on the installation of guardrails along the 4.5-mile (7.24-km) road.

Randy Pech, the white owner of Adarand Constructors, was one of the bidders. Adarand's sole business was guardrail installation, and he had been in business for 14 years. Adarand did about $2.5 million of business per year.

Frank Gonzales, a Hispanic man who owned Gonzales Construction, was a second bidder. Gonzales Construction was a 10-year-old company engaged in environmental cleanup, demolition work, and road building as well as guardrail installation. Gonzales's company did about $3 million of business per year.

Both bids were in the $100,000 range. Of the two, however, Adarand's was lower. Adarand agreed to do the work for $1,700 less than Gonzales Construction.

Adarand, however, did not get the job. Instead the contract went to Gonzales. Mountain Gravel and Construction hired the company because it was minority-owned. Under a federal program, administered by the United States Department of Transportation, the prime contractor would receive a bonus of about 1.5 percent for hiring what was called a Disadvantaged Business Enterprise.

Randy Pech claimed that the policy discriminated against him because he was a white owner of a company. Of the five companies in Colorado that installed guardrails, three were minority-owned, and one was owned by a woman. Pech said his company was the only one adversely affected by the set-aside—the percentage of federal contracts set aside for minority firms.

Pech sued the Department of Transportation, which was headed by Federico Pena. Although two lower courts rejected Adarand's claims, Pech's lawyers persisted, arguing that race-based set-asides violate the equal protection component of the Fifth Amendment's due process clause. They took the case all the way to the Supreme Court, which in 1994 agreed to hear the case.

The Background

By the mid-1990s, the United States had spent more than 30 years implementing the Civil Rights Act of 1964. In this effort, hundreds of regulations and thousands of lawsuits had opened jobs to groups who for generations had suffered from discrimination and unequal treatment. These groups included women, African Americans, Hispanic Americans, Native Americans, Asians, and the disabled.

One powerful tool used to win job equality was a policy called "affirmative action." President Kennedy instituted the policy in 1961 to encourage government managers and contractors to "take affirmative action" to ensure that all workers and applicants were treated without discrimination on the basis of race, religion, sex, or ethnic background.

President Johnson continued to support the policy after Kennedy's death. In the beginning employers were required to seek out minority applicants, but when it came time to hire, they could hire without regard to race or sex. In 1969, however, President Nixon tightened the rules. Through the "Philadelphia Plan," he opened Philadelphia's construction unions to minority apprentices.

Companies now had to hire minorities in proportion to their numbers in the local workforce. This rule led to more widespread quotas, which forced companies to hire a certain percentage of women and minorities, due to set-asides. By 1995 the effect of 162 federal affirmative action regulations was felt in the nation's private businesses, universities, hospitals, and thousands of other public institutions across the nation.

The Debate

During the late 1980s and early 1990s, increasing numbers of people, mostly white males, began to chafe under affirmative action regulations, saying the regulations had gone too far. They contended

"Government cannot make us equal; it can only recognize, respect and protect us as equal before the law . . . As far as the Constitution is concerned, it is irrelevant whether a government's racial classifications are drawn by those who wish to oppress a race or by those who have a sincere desire to help those thought to be disadvantaged."

Clarence Thomas,
Supreme Court Justice

". . . Discrimination's lingering effects, . . . reflective of a system of racial caste only recently ended, are evident in our work places, markets and neighborhoods. Job applicants with identical resumes, qualifications and interview styles still experience different reception, depending on their race."

Ruth Bader Ginsburg,
Supreme Court Justice

"We should reaffirm the principle of affirmative action. . . . We should have a simple slogan: 'Mend it but don't end it.'"

William Clinton,
President of the United States

"The only time they get a break is when it's against me. When I'm the low bidder they get a break."

Randy Pech,
Owner, Adarand Constructors

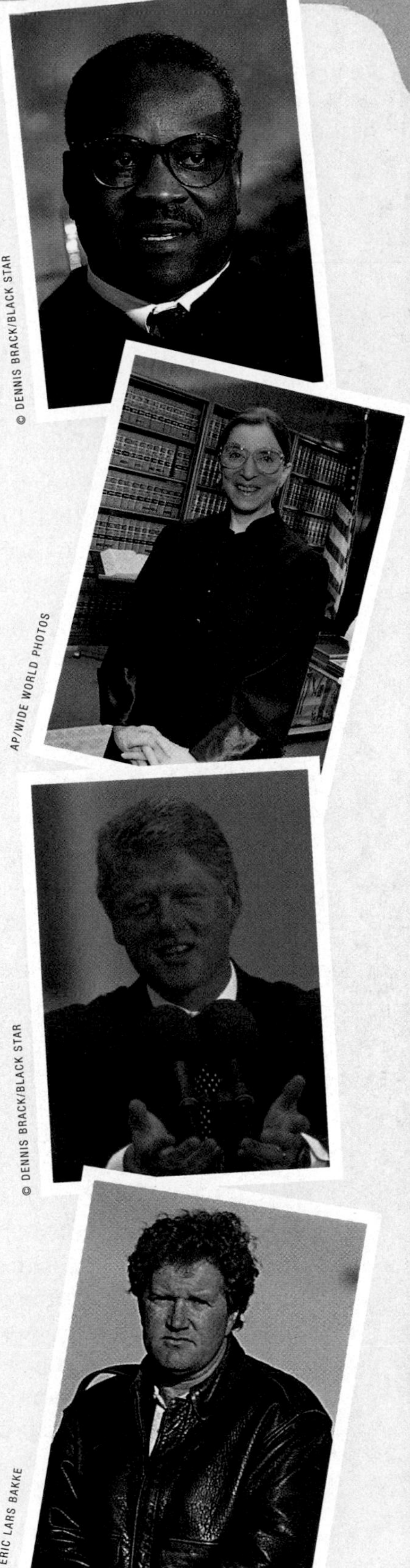
© DENNIS BRACK/BLACK STAR
AP/WIDE WORLD PHOTOS
© DENNIS BRACK/BLACK STAR
© ERIC LARS BAKKE

Turning Point

that jobs should not be awarded to anyone because of race or gender. After the Republicans won control of Congress in 1994, opponents of affirmative action gained a stronger voice in the debate. Supporters of affirmative action stood their ground. They insisted that few white males suffered any substantial losses, while women and minorities, long deprived, were given a chance to prosper. They pointed out, for example, that only 266,000 African American families belonged to the middle class in 1967, while more than 1 million African American families were middle class in 1989. They added that affirmative action programs were still needed to fight ongoing discrimination.

Critics of affirmative action called the policies undemocratic because they gave preferential treatment to women and minorities and discriminated against white males. These critics also claimed that affirmative action policies helped well-off minorities, but were useless weapons for fighting inner-city poverty.

The Precedents

In 1980 the Supreme Court upheld the public works set-aside program in a ruling on the *Fullilove* v. *Klutznick* case. By the end of the decade, however, a more conservative Supreme Court, with 3 Reagan-appointed justices and a new chief justice, weighed into the debate with a series of decisions that made substantial inroads into affirmative action regulations.

In one important 1989 case, *Richmond* v. *Croson*, the Court ruled that state and local governments had to prove that discrimination existed before they could set quotas for minority contractors. This proof was called "strict judicial scrutiny." Wrote Justice Sandra Day O'Connor, "An amorphous claim that there has been past discrimination in a particular industry cannot justify the use of an unyielding racial quota." Further, the Court ruled, affirmative action programs must be "narrowly tailored" to address specific cases of discrimination. Liberal justice Thurgood Marshall, writing in dissent, called the decision "a deliberate and giant step backward in this court's affirmative-action jurisprudence."

For a number of years after the *Richmond* decision, a two-tiered system remained in place. Local and state programs were subject to "strict scrutiny," while federal programs were held to a more relaxed standard, a standard that Randy Pech's attorneys argued against before the Supreme Court.

The Decision

The decision the Court rendered in *Adarand* v. *Pena* was in part a compromise between two extreme positions. Justices Antonin Scalia and Clarence Thomas, while concurring with the majority opinion, nevertheless issued separate opinions, which expressed their conclusion that all affirmative action programs were inherently unconstitutional. Wrote Scalia: "To pursue the concept of racial entitlement even for the most admirable and benign of purposes is to reinforce and preserve for future mischief the way of thinking that produced race slavery, race privilege, and race hatred."

On the other side, three of four justices, Ruth Bader Ginsberg, David A. Souter, and John Paul Stevens, filed dissenting opinions. They claimed that the Court should follow the precedent it set in *Fullilove* v. *Klutznick* and continue to allow federal set-asides for minorities. "There is no moral equivalence or constitutional equivalence between a policy that is designed to perpetuate a caste system and one that seeks to eradicate racial subordination," wrote Justice Stevens. "Remedial race-based preferences reflect . . . a desire to foster equality in society." In the minority's judgment, an interest in "consistency" did not justify treating differences as though they were similarities.

The Response

In the wake of the decision, both sides tried to put a positive spin on the news. Supporters of affirmative action claimed that the ruling was, in the words of Penda Hair, a senior attorney at the National Association for the Advancement of Colored People (NAACP), "a setback but not a disaster." She asserted that NAACP research showed "federal contracting programs would survive strict scrutiny be-

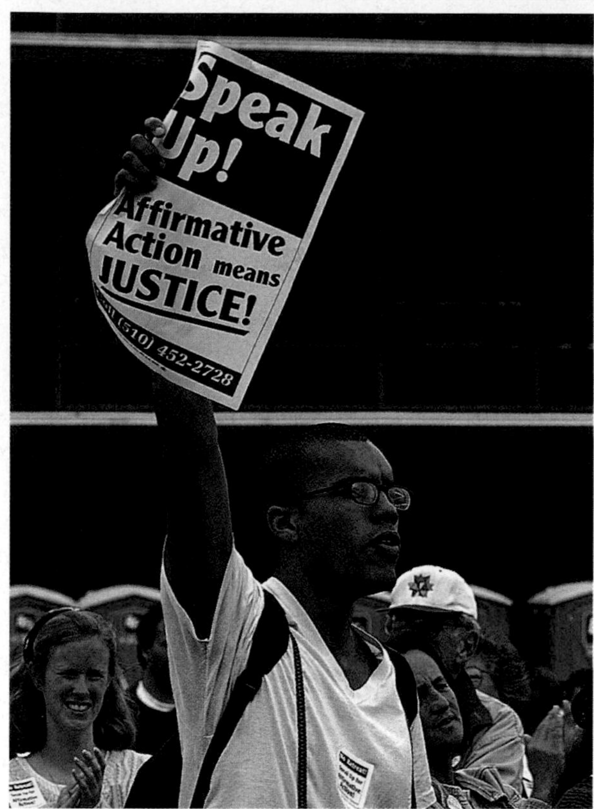

A man demonstrates at an affirmative action rally in San Francisco in July 1995.

cause there's a very compelling reason for them. Right now, women- and minority-owned businesses are getting less than 6 percent of all federal contracts."

Opponents of affirmative action also saw reason to be optimistic about the decision. Clint Bolick of the Institute for Justice was quoted as saying, "The era of racial preferences is finally coming to an end. The Court said it had erred in creating one standard for government, another for everyone else. It's really the Court saying, 'Enough is enough'."

President Clinton, whose administration had vowed to study the controversy, issued a response the next month. The President outlined a compromise position. Affirmative action, he said, has not always been perfect. He looked forward to a day when it would have succeeded to the point where it would no longer be necessary: "I am resolved that that day will come, but the evidence suggests, indeed screams, that that day has not come. The job of ending discrimination in this country is not over. That should not be surprising. We had slavery for centuries before the passage of the 13th, 14th, and 15th Amendments. We waited another 100 years for the civil rights legislation. Women have had the vote less than 100 years."

On June 13, 1995, Clinton remarked, "The court has approved affirmative action that is narrowly tailored to achieve a compelling interest. The constitutional test is now tougher than it was, but I am confident the test can be met in many cases."

Toward Resolution

Opinion polls taken after the *Adarand* decision have suggested a path toward resolution. They show that most Americans disapprove of preferential treatment, regardless of how any group was once treated. Most Americans, however, approve of compensatory actions, such as Head Start, college aid, job training, and other programs that help disadvantaged people catch up. Ideally these programs give everyone an equal opportunity to compete, but they do not guarantee who will win the race.

RESPONDING TO THE CASE

1. Why did Randy Pech decide to sue the United States Department of Transportation?

2. Why did supporters of affirmative action feel that the programs should be kept in place?

3. Sandra Day O'Connor's opinion in *Adarand* v. *Pena* was seen as a compromise by some on the Supreme Court. Who took more extreme positions, and what did they say?

4. Why do you think most Americans support compensatory actions rather than affirmative action policies that give preferential treatment to minorities and women?

PORTFOLIO PROJECT

Consider both sides of the affirmative action debate. Collect newspaper and magazine articles presenting both sides as well as solutions to the conflict. Prepare a paper describing what you believe is the best way to resolve the affirmative action debate. Support your position with strong factual arguments.

Chapter  Assessment

Self-Check Quiz

Visit the *American Odyssey* Web site at americanodyssey.glencoe.com and click on ***Chapter 26—Self-Check Quiz*** to prepare for the Chapter Test.

Reviewing Key Terms

Match each vocabulary word to its definition below. Write your answers on a separate sheet of paper.

bipartisan coalition	**unfunded mandate**
pork barrel legislation	**community policing**
universal coverage	**militia group**

1. laws that require states to take action without providing money to enable them to do so

2. sending more foot patrols into neighborhoods and establishing a better relationship between residents and police

3. a group of Republicans and Democrats working together

4. laws that usually involve spending money on projects of questionable necessity in order to bring money into a legislator's home district

5. health insurance that covers everyone regardless of ability to pay

Recalling Facts

1. What were some of the issues involved in the debate over the health care system in the 1990s? Why was it so difficult to pass reform?

2. What were some of the biggest foreign policy challenges faced by the United States in the 1990s?

3. What promises did Republicans make in their Contract with America? How successful were they in keeping them?

4. What were some of President Clinton's successes and failures?

5. What trends are reshaping the United States job market?

6. Why was the 2000 presidential election so unique?

7. How has immigration to the United States changed in recent decades? How have these changes affected American society?

8. What issues concerned educational reformers in the late 1990s and early 2000s?

Critical Thinking

1. Making Comparisons Explain why organized labor, farmers, and environmentalists feared NAFTA, while the Bush and Clinton administrations pushed for it.

2. Identifying Central Issues What were some of the central issues involved in the fighting that erupted in former Yugoslavia? What role did the United States play in resolving these conflicts?

3. Recognizing Points of View Use a diagram like this one to analyze arguments for and against continuing affirmative action policies in the 21st century and to record your prediction for its fate.

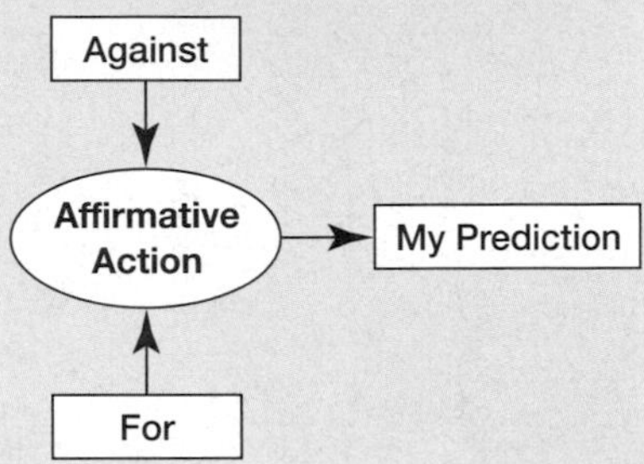

The Princeton Review — Standardized Test Practice

1. In the late 1990s, more than 30 years after Lyndon Johnson signed Medicare into law, the program was

A replaced by universal coverage.
B seen as adequately fulfilling the nation's health-care needs.
C slashed to achieve a balanced budget.
D threatened by the rising costs of medical care.

Test-Taking Tip: Eliminate answers that do not make sense. For example, as the 2000s opened, nearly 39 million people had no health insurance. Therefore, *universal coverage,* or health care for all, had not been put into effect, ruling out answer A.

2. The final victory in the 2000 presidential election—the closest election in United States history—was decided by the

A electoral college.
B Congress.
C Supreme Court.
D popular vote.

Test-Taking Tip: This question asks you to remember a fact about the election process. The Supreme Court played an important role in the 2000 election, but it did not actually pick the President. That rules out answer C.

GEOGRAPHY AND HISTORY

Recent Immigration to the United States, 1990–2000

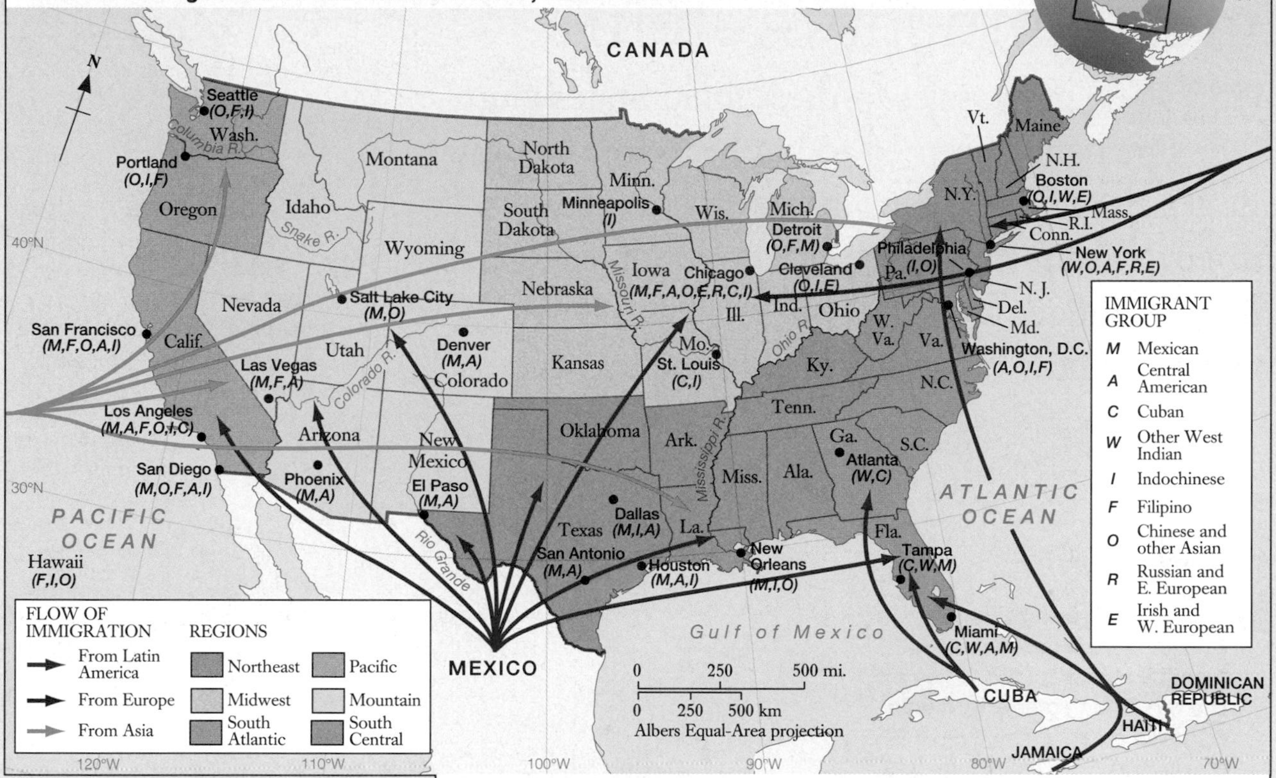

CANADA
Seattle (O,F,I)
Wash.
Portland (O,I,F)
Oregon
Idaho
Montana
North Dakota
South Dakota
Wyoming
Minn.
Minneapolis (I)
Wis.
Mich.
Detroit (O,F,M)
Iowa
Chicago (M,F,A,O,E,R,C,I)
Cleveland (O,I,E)
Ill.
Ind.
Ohio
Nebraska
Nevada
Salt Lake City (M,O)
Utah
San Francisco (M,F,O,A,I)
Calif.
Las Vegas (M,F,A)
Denver (M,A)
Colorado
Kansas
Mo.
St. Louis (C,I)
Ky.
W. Va.
Va.
N.C.
Tenn.
Los Angeles (M,A,F,O,I,C)
Arizona
New Mexico
Oklahoma
Ark.
Miss.
Ala.
Ga.
Atlanta (W,C)
S.C.
San Diego (M,O,F,A,I)
Phoenix (M,A)
El Paso (M,A)
Dallas (M,I,A)
Texas
La.
San Antonio (M,A)
Houston (M,A,I)
New Orleans (M,I,O)
Fla.
Tampa (C,W,M)
Miami (C,W,A,M)
Vt.
Maine
N.H.
N.Y.
Boston (O,I,W,E)
Mass.
R.I.
Conn.
Philadelphia (I,O)
Pa.
New York (W,O,A,F,R,E)
N.J.
Del.
Md.
Washington, D.C. (A,O,I,F)
Columbia R.
Snake R.
Colorado R.
Missouri R.
Ohio R.
Mississippi R.
Rio Grande
PACIFIC OCEAN
Hawaii (F,I,O)
ATLANTIC OCEAN
Gulf of Mexico
MEXICO
CUBA
JAMAICA
HAITI
DOMINICAN REPUBLIC
40°N
30°N
120°W 110°W 100°W 90°W 80°W 70°W
0 250 500 mi.
0 250 500 km
Albers Equal-Area projection

IMMIGRANT GROUP
M Mexican
A Central American
C Cuban
W Other West Indian
I Indochinese
F Filipino
O Chinese and other Asian
R Russian and E. European
E Irish and W. European

FLOW OF IMMIGRATION
From Latin America
From Europe
From Asia

REGIONS
Northeast
Midwest
South Atlantic
Pacific
Mountain
South Central

Study the map to answer the following questions:

1. In which regions of the United States do most immigrants from Asia settle?
2. Where do many immigrants from the Caribbean settle?
3. Which immigrant groups have settled in Los Angeles and Atlanta?
4. How does Chicago's location help explain why it gets immigrants from so many parts of the world?

Portfolio Project

PORTFOLIO PROJECT

Interview or read newspaper or newsmagazine accounts of someone who recently immigrated to this country. Write about his or her reasons for coming and the challenges and successes that they have had in a new country. Keep your report in your portfolio.

Cooperative Learning

In small groups, conduct research to find out more about the changing electorate or the changing demographics of this nation. Each group should analyze information to make some predictions about the future. Groups might want to compile their reports into a classroom book entitled *The Future of the United States*.

Reinforcing Skills

Analyzing News Media Choose one current issue and compare its coverage in two different media. Which medium supplies the most facts? Is the information accurate? What are the advantages and disadvantages of each medium?

Technology Activity

Using the Internet Search the Internet for information about the latest technological innovations that are influencing our global culture. Post the information you found on a bulletin board. Include illustrations of those innovations that you consider the most important to our lives.

Then...

The Nintendo Entertainment System®

In 1985 video game sales in the United States plummeted. The nation seemed to have reached its saturation point. Then Nintendo introduced its Nintendo Entertainment System (NES), which revolutionized video games. No longer found only in arcades, Nintendo games could now be played on a home television set.

NINTENDO OF AMERICA, INC.

2 In Super Mario Bros., Luigi and Mario® help the peaceful Mushroom People in their battle against the Koopa turtle tribe.

1 The Nintendo Entertainment System used a control pad or joystick to control the action on the television screen. Nintendo released a new game, Super Mario Bros.®, for play on its new system.

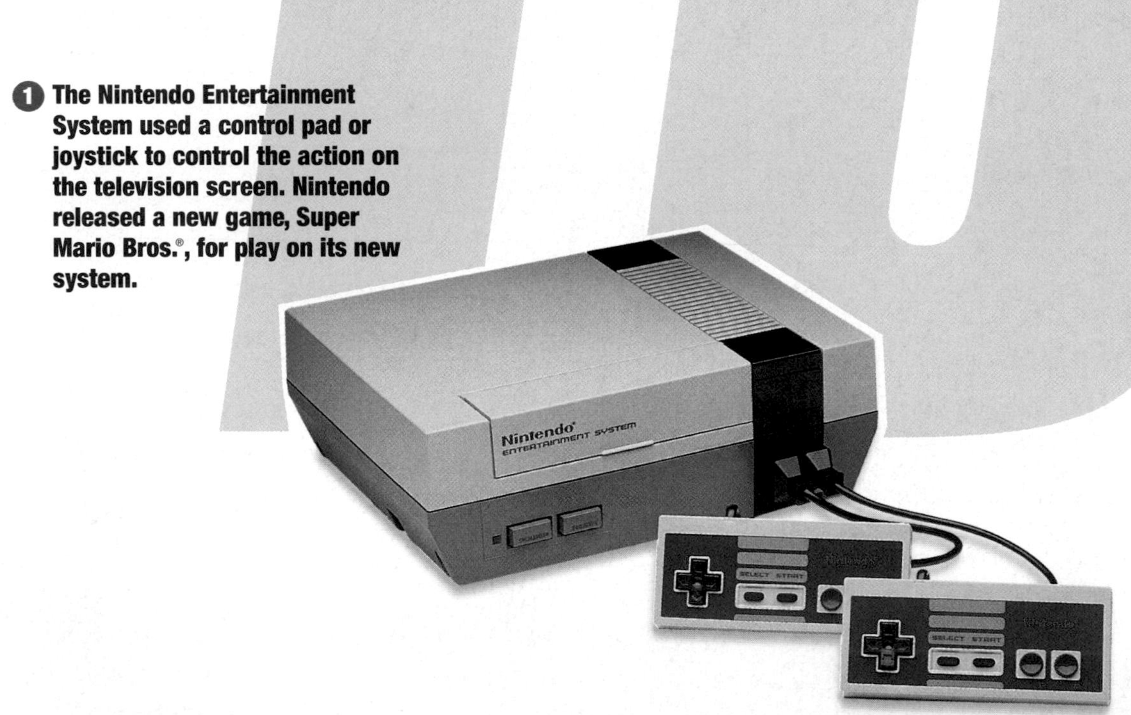

NINTENDO OF AMERICA, INC.

Fun Facts

IN THE BEGINNING WAS PONG

The first successful totally electronic video game in the United States was Pong, a video Ping-Pong game. The three young engineers who invented Pong formed a company called Atari in 1974 to distribute the game.

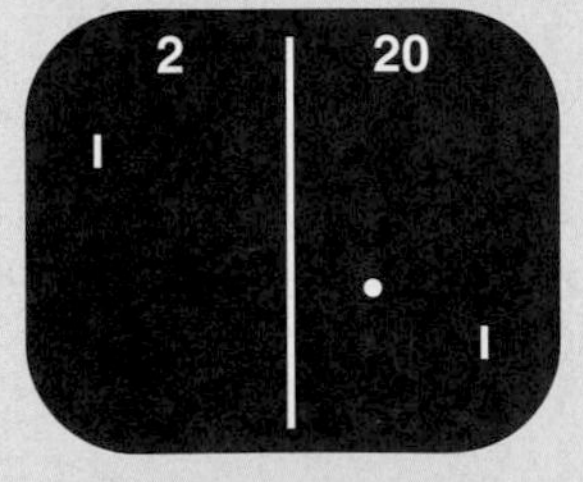

4 **Super Mario Bros. sold over 2.5 million copies in its first 4 months. It generated numerous sequels, television shows, magazines, fan clubs, and tie-ins.**

FILE PHOTO BY DOUG MINDELL

NINTENDO OF AMERICA, INC.

Stats

MARIO TRIVIA

- Mario first appeared in Donkey Kong® in 1981. Mario was named Jumpman in this game.
- Mario was named after Mario Segali, the landlord of Nintendo's first warehouse in the United States.

VIDEO GAME FACTS

- In the United States, consumers spend more on video games than on any other form of entertainment, including movies and CDs.
- If Nintendo were a country, it would be more prosperous than many nations of the world.
- If all the Nintendo game paks sold around the world were laid end to end, they would stretch for about 82,860 miles (133, 322 km) —three and one-half times around the earth's equator.

...Now

3 **Mario untiringly attempts to rescue Princess Toadstool from Bowser, the King of the Koopas.**

NINTENDO OF AMERICA, INC.

VIDEO GAMES

PORTFOLIO PROJECT

Some people think that eventually the video game boxes that sit near the TV will link to a worldwide network. You might compete with a player overseas, order a pizza, or transfer money. Compare the video games of today with the video games of 1985, and then make predictions about the games of the future. Keep your report in your portfolio.

MARIO'S FIRST APPEARANCE

Donkey Kong derived its name from *donkey*, a stubborn, wily creature, and the mighty ape *King Kong*. To American video game salespeople, who were used to names with words such as *destroy* and *annihilate*, the name made no sense. Donkey Kong, however, was a huge success despite its name.

NINTENDO OF AMERICA, INC.

Reference Atlas

World Physical	932
United States Political	934
United States Physical	936
Canada Physical/Political	938
Middle America Physical/Political	940
Pacific Rim Physical/Political	942

ATLAS KEY

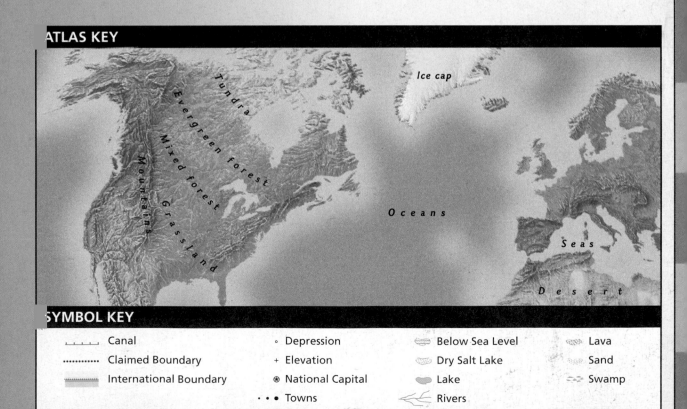

Ice cap
Tundra
Evergreen forest
Mixed forest
Mountains
Grassland
Oceans
Seas
Desert

SYMBOL KEY

Canal	Depression	Below Sea Level	Lava
Claimed Boundary	Elevation	Dry Salt Lake	Sand
International Boundary	National Capital	Lake	Swamp
	Towns	Rivers	

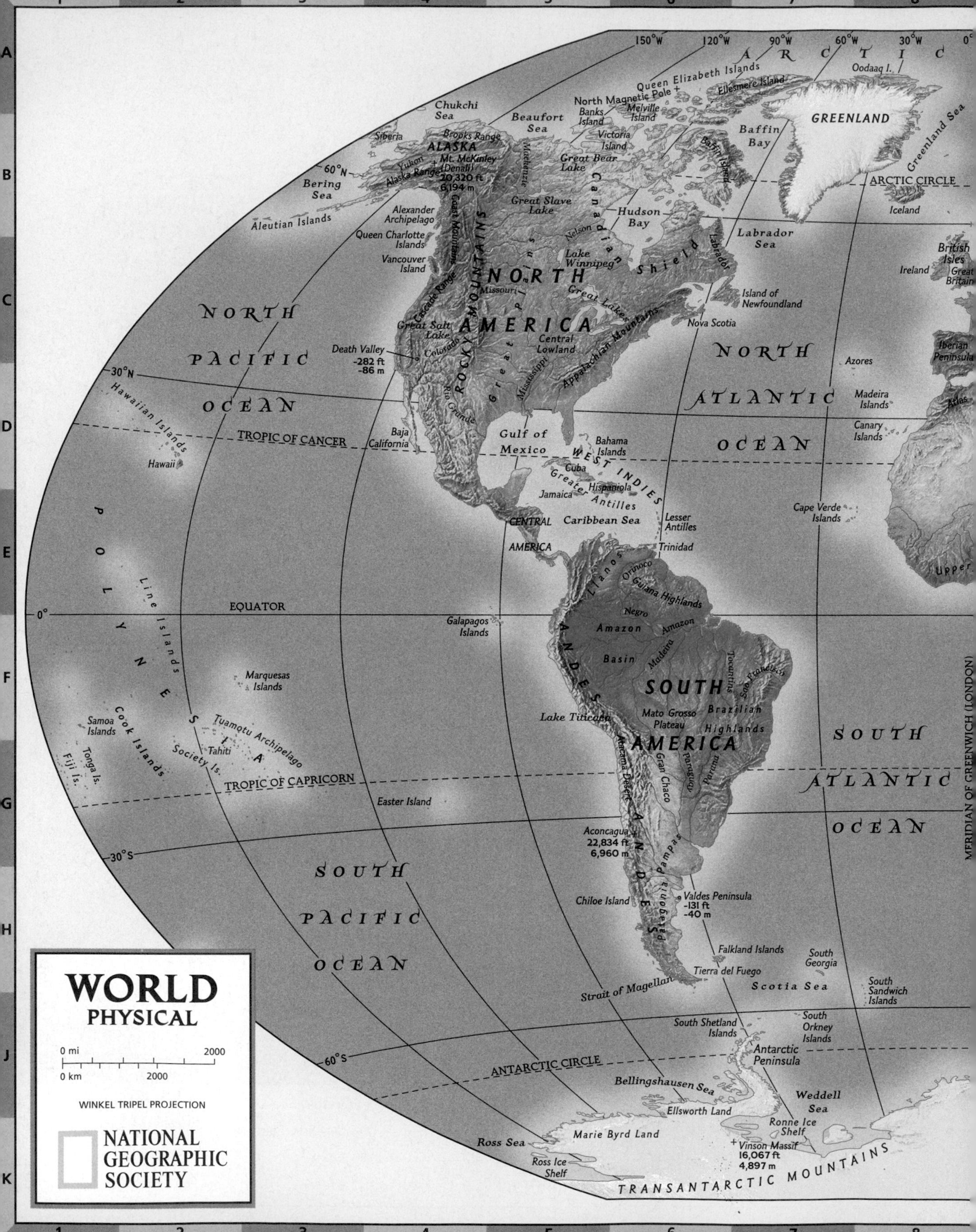
WORLD
PHYSICAL
0 mi
2000
0 km
2000
WINKEL TRIPEL PROJECTION
NATIONAL
GEOGRAPHIC
SOCIETY
1
2
3
4
5
6
7
8
A
B
C
D
E
F
G
H
J
K
150°W
120°W
90°W
60°W
30°W
0°
60°N
30°N
0°
30°S
60°S
ARCTIC
Oodaaq I.
Queen Elizabeth Islands
Ellesmere Island
North Magnetic Pole
Banks Island
Melville Island
Victoria Island
Chukchi Sea
Beaufort Sea
GREENLAND
Greenland Sea
Baffin Bay
Baffin Island
Siberia
Brooks Range
ALASKA
Yukon
Mt. McKinley (Denali)
20,320 ft
6,194 m
Alaska Range
Bering Sea
Aleutian Islands
Mackenzie
Great Bear Lake
Great Slave Lake
Canadian Shield
ARCTIC CIRCLE
Iceland
Hudson Bay
Labrador Sea
Labrador
Alexander Archipelago
Coast Mountains
Queen Charlotte Islands
Vancouver Island
Nelson
Lake Winnipeg
British Isles
Ireland
Great Britain
ROCKY MOUNTAINS
NORTH AMERICA
Cascade Range
Missouri
Great Lakes
Island of Newfoundland
Nova Scotia
NORTH PACIFIC OCEAN
Great Salt Lake
Colorado
Great Plains
Central Lowland
Appalachian Mountains
Death Valley
-282 ft
-86 m
Mississippi
NORTH ATLANTIC OCEAN
Iberian Peninsula
Azores
Hawaiian Islands
Rio Grande
Madeira Islands
Atlas
TROPIC OF CANCER
Baja California
Gulf of Mexico
Bahama Islands
Canary Islands
Hawaii
WEST INDIES
Cuba
Greater Antilles
Hispaniola
Jamaica
Cape Verde Islands
CENTRAL AMERICA
Caribbean Sea
Lesser Antilles
Trinidad
POLYNESIA
Line Islands
Llanos
Orinoco
Guiana Highlands
Upper
EQUATOR
Negro
Amazon
Amazon Basin
Galapagos Islands
ANDES
Madeira
Tocantins
São Francisco
Marquesas Islands
SOUTH AMERICA
Mato Grosso Plateau
Brazilian Highlands
Lake Titicaca
Samoa Islands
Cook Islands
Tuamotu Archipelago
Tahiti
Society Is.
Tonga Is.
Fiji Is.
Atacama Desert
Gran Chaco
Paraguay
Paraná
SOUTH ATLANTIC OCEAN
TROPIC OF CAPRICORN
Easter Island
MERIDIAN OF GREENWICH (LONDON)
Aconcagua
22,834 ft
6,960 m
Pampas
SOUTH PACIFIC OCEAN
Chiloe Island
Patagonia
Valdes Peninsula
-131 ft
-40 m
Falkland Islands
South Georgia
Tierra del Fuego
Scotia Sea
South Sandwich Islands
Strait of Magellan
South Shetland Islands
South Orkney Islands
Antarctic Peninsula
ANTARCTIC CIRCLE
Bellingshausen Sea
Weddell Sea
Ellsworth Land
Ronne Ice Shelf
Ross Sea
Marie Byrd Land
Vinson Massif
16,067 ft
4,897 m
Ross Ice Shelf
TRANSANTARCTIC MOUNTAINS

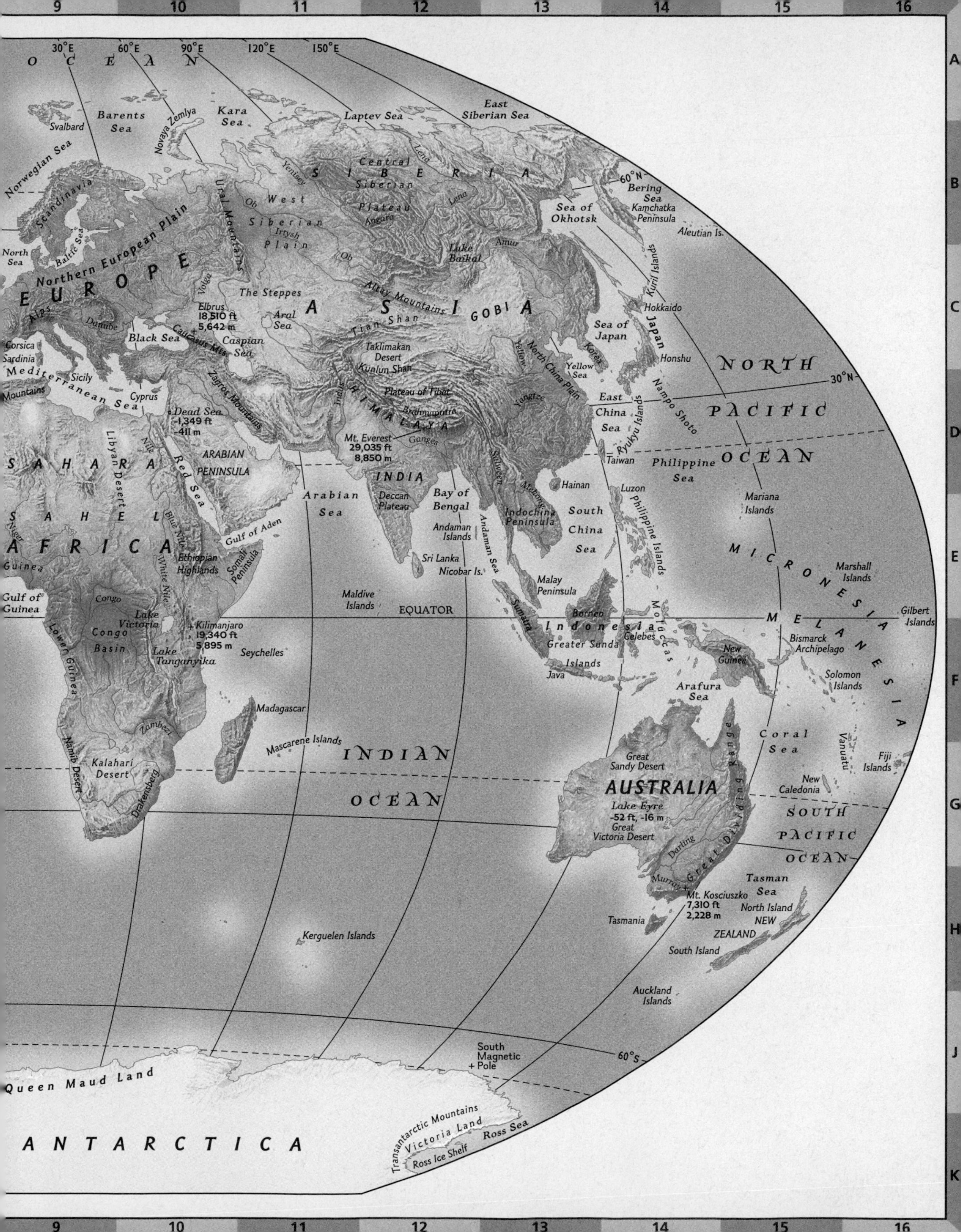
9
10
11
12
13
14
15
16
A
B
C
D
E
F
G
H
J
K
30°E
60°E
90°E
120°E
150°E
O C E A N
Svalbard
Barents Sea
Novaya Zemlya
Kara Sea
Laptev Sea
East Siberian Sea
Norwegian Sea
Scandinavia
Baltic Sea
North Sea
Northern European Plain
EUROPE
Alps
Danube
Corsica
Sardinia
Sicily
Mediterranean Sea
Mountains
Cyprus
Black Sea
Caucasus Mts.
Elbrus
18,510 ft
5,642 m
Caspian Sea
Volga
Ural Mountains
Ob
West Siberian Plain
Irtysh
The Steppes
Aral Sea
Yenisey
Central Siberian Plateau
SIBERIA
Angara
Lena
Lake Baikal
Amur
Altay Mountains
ASIA
GOBI
Tian Shan
Taklimakan Desert
Kunlun Shan
Plateau of Tibet
HIMALAYA
Brahmaputra
Indus
Ganges
Mt. Everest
29,035 ft
8,850 m
INDIA
Deccan Plateau
Yellow
North China Plain
Yangtze
Korea
Yellow Sea
Sea of Japan
Japan
Hokkaido
Honshu
Kuril Islands
Sea of Okhotsk
Kamchatka Peninsula
Bering Sea
60°N
Aleutian Is.
Ryukyu Islands
Nampo Shoto
East China Sea
Taiwan
NORTH PACIFIC OCEAN
30°N
Philippine Sea
Mariana Islands
Dead Sea
-1,349 ft
-411 m
Zagros Mountains
ARABIAN PENINSULA
Red Sea
Nile
Libyan Desert
SAHARA
SAHEL
Niger
AFRICA
Blue Nile
White Nile
Ethiopian Highlands
Somali Peninsula
Gulf of Aden
Arabian Sea
Bay of Bengal
Andaman Islands
Andaman Sea
Nicobar Is.
Sri Lanka
Salween
Mekong
Hainan
Indochina Peninsula
South China Sea
Luzon
Philippine Islands
MICRONESIA
Marshall Islands
Gilbert Islands
Guinea
Gulf of Guinea
Congo
Congo Basin
Lake Victoria
Kilimanjaro
19,340 ft
5,895 m
Lake Tanganyika
Lower Guinea
Seychelles
Maldive Islands
EQUATOR
Malay Peninsula
Sumatra
Borneo
Indonesia
Celebes
Moluccas
Greater Sunda Islands
Java
New Guinea
Bismarck Archipelago
MELANESIA
Solomon Islands
Arafura Sea
Zambezi
Madagascar
Mascarene Islands
Namib Desert
Kalahari Desert
Drakensberg
INDIAN OCEAN
Great Sandy Desert
AUSTRALIA
Lake Eyre
-52 ft, -16 m
Great Victoria Desert
Great Dividing Range
Darling
Murray
Mt. Kosciuszko
7,310 ft
2,228 m
Tasmania
Coral Sea
Vanuatu
Fiji Islands
New Caledonia
SOUTH PACIFIC OCEAN
Tasman Sea
North Island
NEW ZEALAND
South Island
Kerguelen Islands
Auckland Islands
60°S
South Magnetic Pole
Queen Maud Land
ANTARCTICA
Transantarctic Mountains
Victoria Land
Ross Ice Shelf
Ross Sea

RUSSIA
ARCTIC OCEAN
Point Barrow
Bering Strait
St. Lawrence Island
Seward Peninsula
Norton Sound
Brooks Range
Beaufort Sea
Yukon
Nunivak Island
ALASKA
Fairbanks
Aleutian Islands
Alaska Range
Bristol Bay
Anchorage
Alaska Peninsula
Kodiak I.
Gulf of Alaska
Juneau
Alexander Archipelago
PACIFIC OCEAN
Tacoma
Seattle
Olympia
WASH.
Spokane
Portland
Salem
Eugene
Cascade Range
OREGON
Snake
IDAHO
Boise
Butte
Great Salt Lake
Salt Lake City
UTAH
Reno
Carson City
NEVADA
Sacramento
San Francisco
CALIFORNIA
Sierra Nevada
Las Vegas
ARIZONA
Los Angeles
San Diego
Phoenix
Tucson
Honolulu
HAWAII
Hilo
TROPIC OF CANCER
170°E
180°
170°W
160°W
150°W
140°W
130°W
120°W
110°
70°N
60°N
50°N
40°N
30°N
20°N
10°N

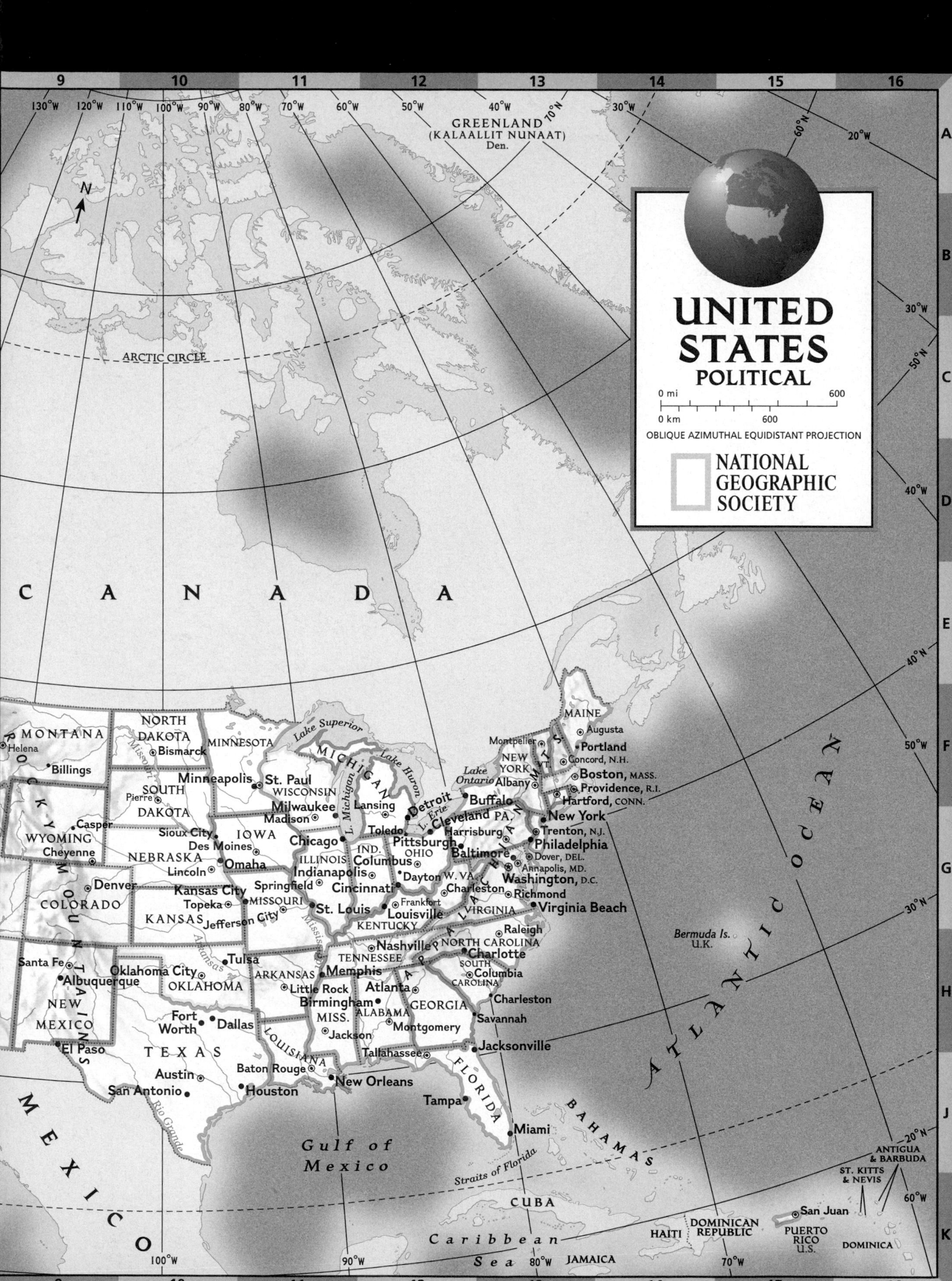
UNITED STATES
POLITICAL
0 mi 600
0 km 600
OBLIQUE AZIMUTHAL EQUIDISTANT PROJECTION
NATIONAL GEOGRAPHIC SOCIETY
GREENLAND (KALAALLIT NUNAAT) Den.
ARCTIC CIRCLE
CANADA
MONTANA
Helena
Billings
NORTH DAKOTA
Bismarck
MINNESOTA
SOUTH DAKOTA
Pierre
Minneapolis
St. Paul
WISCONSIN
Milwaukee
Madison
Lake Superior
MICHIGAN
Lake Huron
L. Michigan
Lansing
Detroit
L. Erie
Lake Ontario
Buffalo
Albany
Toledo
Cleveland
WYOMING
Casper
Cheyenne
NEBRASKA
Lincoln
Omaha
Sioux City
IOWA
Des Moines
Chicago
ILLINOIS
IND.
Indianapolis
OHIO
Columbus
Pittsburgh
PA.
Harrisburg
Baltimore
Dayton
Cincinnati
W. VA.
Charleston
Springfield
COLORADO
Denver
KANSAS
Topeka
Kansas City
MISSOURI
Jefferson City
St. Louis
Louisville
Frankfort
KENTUCKY
VIRGINIA
Richmond
Virginia Beach
Washington, D.C.
Annapolis, MD.
Dover, DEL.
Philadelphia
Trenton, N.J.
New York
MAINE
Augusta
Portland
Montpelier
NEW YORK
VT.
N.H.
Concord, N.H.
Boston, MASS.
Providence, R.I.
Hartford, CONN.
ROCKY MOUNTAINS
APPALACHIAN MTS.
Missouri
Mississippi
Arkansas
Raleigh
NORTH CAROLINA
Charlotte
Nashville
TENNESSEE
SOUTH CAROLINA
Columbia
Charleston
Memphis
ARKANSAS
Little Rock
Atlanta
GEORGIA
Birmingham
ALABAMA
MISS.
Jackson
Montgomery
Savannah
Jacksonville
Tallahassee
Santa Fe
Albuquerque
NEW MEXICO
Oklahoma City
OKLAHOMA
Tulsa
Fort Worth
Dallas
El Paso
TEXAS
Austin
San Antonio
Houston
Rio Grande
LOUISIANA
Baton Rouge
New Orleans
FLORIDA
Tampa
Miami
MEXICO
Gulf of Mexico
Straits of Florida
BAHAMAS
CUBA
Caribbean Sea
JAMAICA
HAITI
DOMINICAN REPUBLIC
PUERTO RICO U.S.
San Juan
ANTIGUA & BARBUDA
ST. KITTS & NEVIS
DOMINICA
Bermuda Is. U.K.
ATLANTIC OCEAN
N

PACIFIC OCEAN
CANADA
GREAT BASIN
ROCKY MOUNTAINS
GREAT PLAINS
COAST RANGES
CASCADE RANGE
SIERRA NEVADA
COLUMBIA PLATEAU
Cape Flattery
Mt. Olympus 7,966 ft 2,428 m
Seattle
Columbia
Blue Mts.
Clearwater Mts.
Bitterroot Range
Salmon River Mts.
Great Sandy Desert
Snake
Snake River Plain
Shoshone Falls
Absaroka Range
Bighorn Mts.
Wind River Range
Black Hills
Missouri
Laramie Mts.
N. Platte
Sand Hills
Platte
High Plains
Cape Mendocino
Great Salt Lake
Wasatch Range
Uinta Mts.
Lake Tahoe
Central Valley
San Francisco
Denver
Mt. Elbert 14,433 ft 4,399 m
Mt. Whitney 14,494 ft 4,418 m
Death Valley -282 ft, -86 m
Lake Powell
Lake Mead
Colorado
Arkansas
San Juan Mts.
Sangre de Cristo Mts.
Point Conception
Mojave Desert
Grand Canyon
Colorado Plateau
Los Angeles
Channel Islands
Salton Sea
San Diego
Phoenix
Sonoran Desert
Rio Grande
Sacramento Mts.
Llano Estacado
Red
Dallas
Brazos
Edwards Plateau
MEXICO
TROPIC OF CANCER
ARCTIC OCEAN
Point Barrow
Beaufort Sea
Chukchi Sea
RUSSIA
North Slope
Brooks Range
Bering Strait
ARCTIC CIRCLE
Seward Pen.
ALASKA
CANADA
St. Lawrence Island
Yukon
Tanana
Kuskokwim
Alaska Range
Mt. McKinley (Denali) 20,320 ft, 6,194 m
Anchorage
Nunivak Island
Bering Sea
Bristol Bay
Gulf of Alaska
Alexander Archipelago
Alaska Peninsula
Kodiak I.
PACIFIC OCEAN
0 mi 300
0 km 300

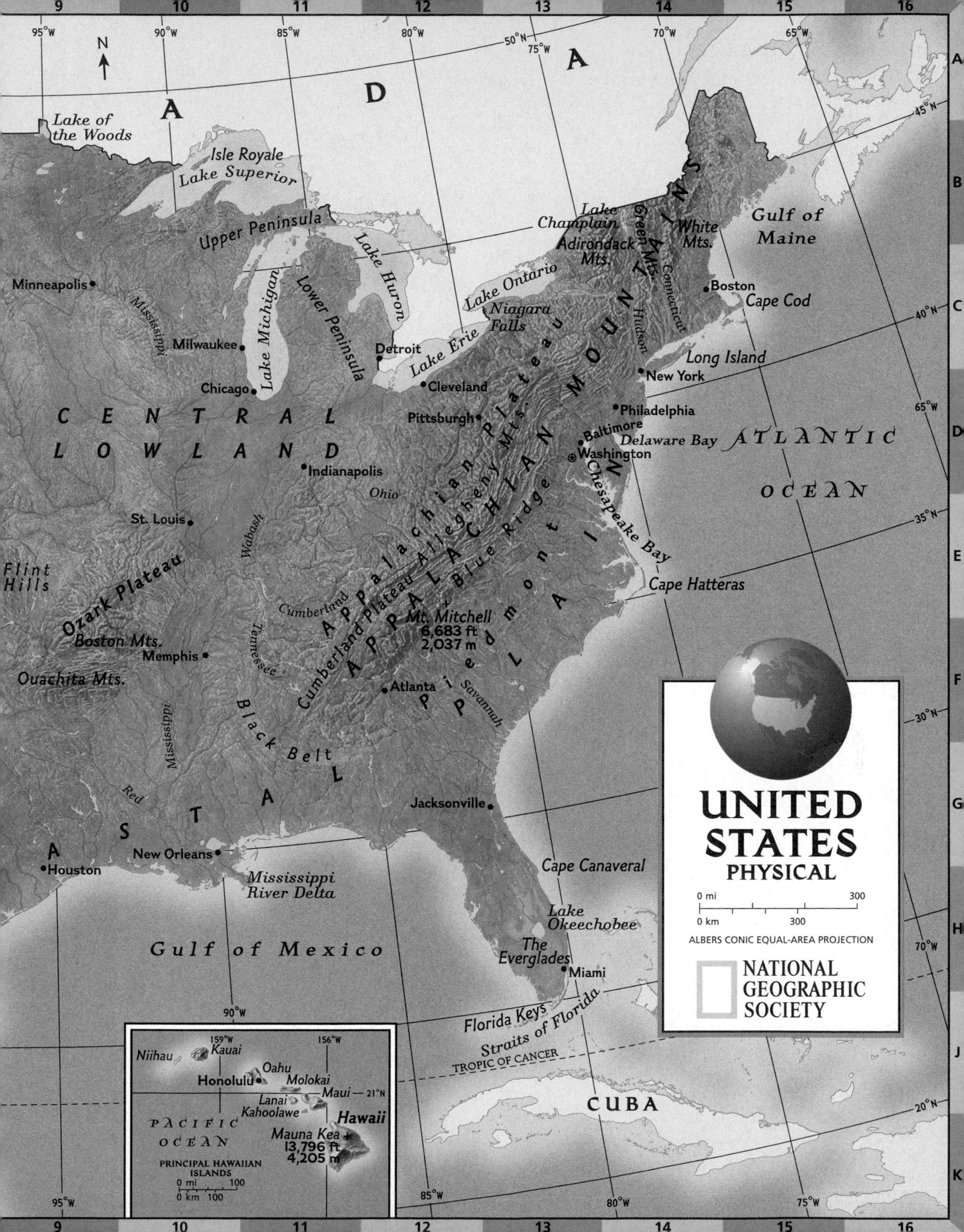
UNITED STATES
PHYSICAL
0 mi 300
0 km 300
ALBERS CONIC EQUAL-AREA PROJECTION
NATIONAL GEOGRAPHIC SOCIETY
CANADA
Lake of the Woods
Isle Royale
Lake Superior
Upper Peninsula
Lake Michigan
Lower Peninsula
Lake Huron
Lake Ontario
Lake Erie
Niagara Falls
Lake Champlain
Adirondack Mts.
Green Mts.
White Mts.
APPALACHIAN MOUNTAINS
Gulf of Maine
Boston
Cape Cod
Connecticut
Hudson
Long Island
New York
Philadelphia
Baltimore
Delaware Bay
Washington
Chesapeake Bay
ATLANTIC OCEAN
Cape Hatteras
Minneapolis
Mississippi
Milwaukee
Chicago
Detroit
Cleveland
Pittsburgh
CENTRAL LOWLAND
Indianapolis
Ohio
St. Louis
Wabash
Appalachian Plateau
Allegheny Mts.
Blue Ridge
Piedmont
Cumberland Plateau
Cumberland
Mt. Mitchell
6,683 ft
2,037 m
Flint Hills
Ozark Plateau
Boston Mts.
Memphis
Tennessee
Ouachita Mts.
Atlanta
Savannah
Black Belt
COASTAL PLAIN
Red
Jacksonville
New Orleans
Houston
Mississippi River Delta
Cape Canaveral
Lake Okeechobee
The Everglades
Miami
Gulf of Mexico
Florida Keys
Straits of Florida
TROPIC OF CANCER
CUBA
Niihau
Kauai
Oahu
Honolulu
Molokai
Maui
Lanai
Kahoolawe
Hawaii
Mauna Kea
13,796 ft
4,205 m
PACIFIC OCEAN
PRINCIPAL HAWAIIAN ISLANDS
0 mi 100
0 km 100

RUSSIA
ARCTIC OCEAN
Queen Elizabeth Islands
North Magnetic Pole
Prince Patrick I.
Melville Island
Bathurst Island
Banks Island
Somerset Island
Prince of Wales I.
Victoria Island
Boothia Peninsula
Beaufort Sea
ARCTIC CIRCLE
ALASKA
U.S.
Inuvik
YUKON TERRITORY
Mackenzie Mts.
Mackenzie
Mt. Logan
19,551 ft
5,959 m
Yukon Plateau
Whitehorse
Great Bear Lake
NORTHWEST TERRITORIES
NUNAVUT
Coast Mountains
Virginia Falls
Yellowknife
Great Slave Lake
ROCKY MOUNTAINS
Slave
Peace
Lake Athabasca
Queen Charlotte Islands
BRITISH COLUMBIA
ALBERTA
Churchill
Fraser Plateau
Prince George
Athabasca
GREAT PLAINS
Fraser
Columbia Mts.
Nelson
CANADIAN
PACIFIC OCEAN
Edmonton
SASKATCHEWAN
MANITOBA
Vancouver Island
Saskatchewan
Lake Winnipeg
Vancouver
Victoria
Calgary
Saskatoon
Lake Winnipegosis
Regina
Winnipeg
Lake of the Woods
UNITED STATES
60°N
70°N
80°N
50°N
40°N
170°W
160°W
150°W
140°W
130°W
120°W
110°W
100°W
1
2
3
4
5
6
7
8
A
B
C
D
E
F
G
H
J
K

CANADA
PHYSICAL/POLITICAL
0 mi 400
0 km 400
AZIMUTHAL EQUIDISTANT PROJECTION
NATIONAL GEOGRAPHIC SOCIETY
GREENLAND
(KALAALLIT NUNAAT)
Den.
ICELAND
Ellesmere Island
Devon Island
Baffin Bay
Baffin Island
Davis Strait
Labrador Sea
Melville Peninsula
Foxe Basin
Southampton Island
Iqaluit
Hudson Strait
Ungava Bay
Hudson Bay
Belcher Islands
James Bay
NEWFOUNDLAND
LABRADOR
Cartwright
Schefferville
Happy Valley-Goose Bay
Smallwood Reservoir
Churchill Falls
Island of Newfoundland
St. John's
Avalon Peninsula
QUEBEC
Manicouagan Reservoir
Sept-Iles
Anticosti I.
Gulf of St. Lawrence
St.-Pierre & Miquelon Fr.
Gaspe Pen.
PRINCE EDWARD ISLAND
Cape Breton I.
Charlottetown
NOVA SCOTIA
NEW BRUNSWICK
Fredericton
Saint John
Halifax
Bay of Fundy
ATLANTIC OCEAN
ONTARIO
SHIELD
Lake Nipigon
Thunder Bay
Lake Superior
Rouyn-Noranda
Chicoutimi
Quebec City
St. Lawrence
Montreal
Ottawa
Sudbury
Lake Huron
Lake Michigan
Toronto
L. Ontario
Niagara Falls
London
L. Erie

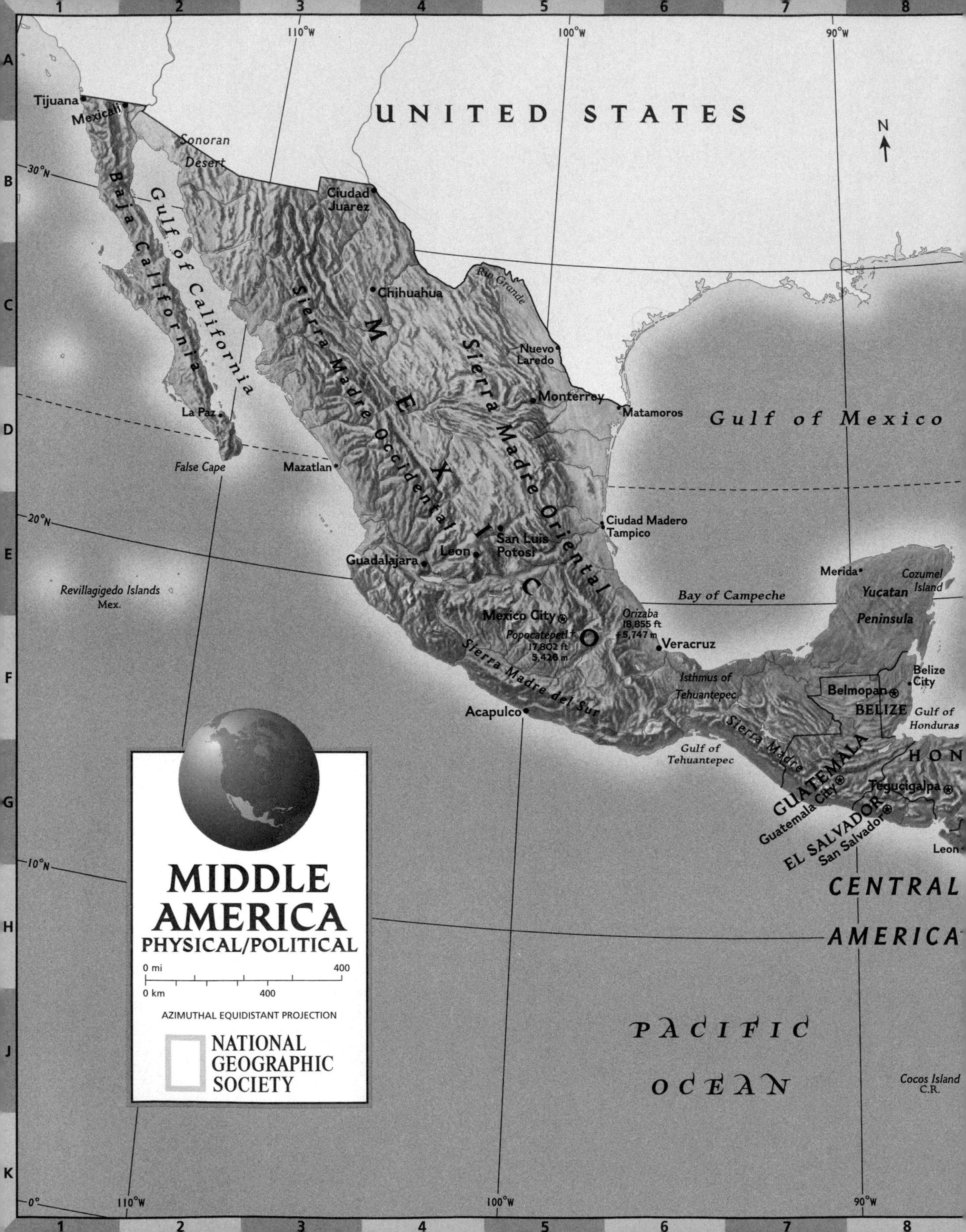

MIDDLE AMERICA
PHYSICAL/POLITICAL
0 mi
400
0 km
400
AZIMUTHAL EQUIDISTANT PROJECTION
NATIONAL GEOGRAPHIC SOCIETY
UNITED STATES
MEXICO
CENTRAL AMERICA
PACIFIC OCEAN
Gulf of Mexico
Bay of Campeche
Gulf of California
Baja California
Sonoran Desert
Sierra Madre Occidental
Sierra Madre Oriental
Sierra Madre del Sur
Sierra Madre
Rio Grande
Yucatan Peninsula
Cozumel Island
Isthmus of Tehuantepec
Gulf of Tehuantepec
Gulf of Honduras
Revillagigedo Islands Mex.
Cocos Island C.R.
False Cape
Orizaba 18,855 ft 5,747 m
Popocatepetl 17,802 ft 5,426 m
Tijuana
Mexicali
Ciudad Juarez
Chihuahua
Nuevo Laredo
Monterrey
Matamoros
La Paz
Mazatlan
Ciudad Madero
Tampico
San Luis Potosi
Leon
Guadalajara
Mexico City
Veracruz
Acapulco
Merida
Belmopan
Belize City
BELIZE
GUATEMALA
Guatemala City
EL SALVADOR
San Salvador
HON
Tegucigalpa
Leon
N
110°W
100°W
90°W
30°N
20°N
10°N
0°

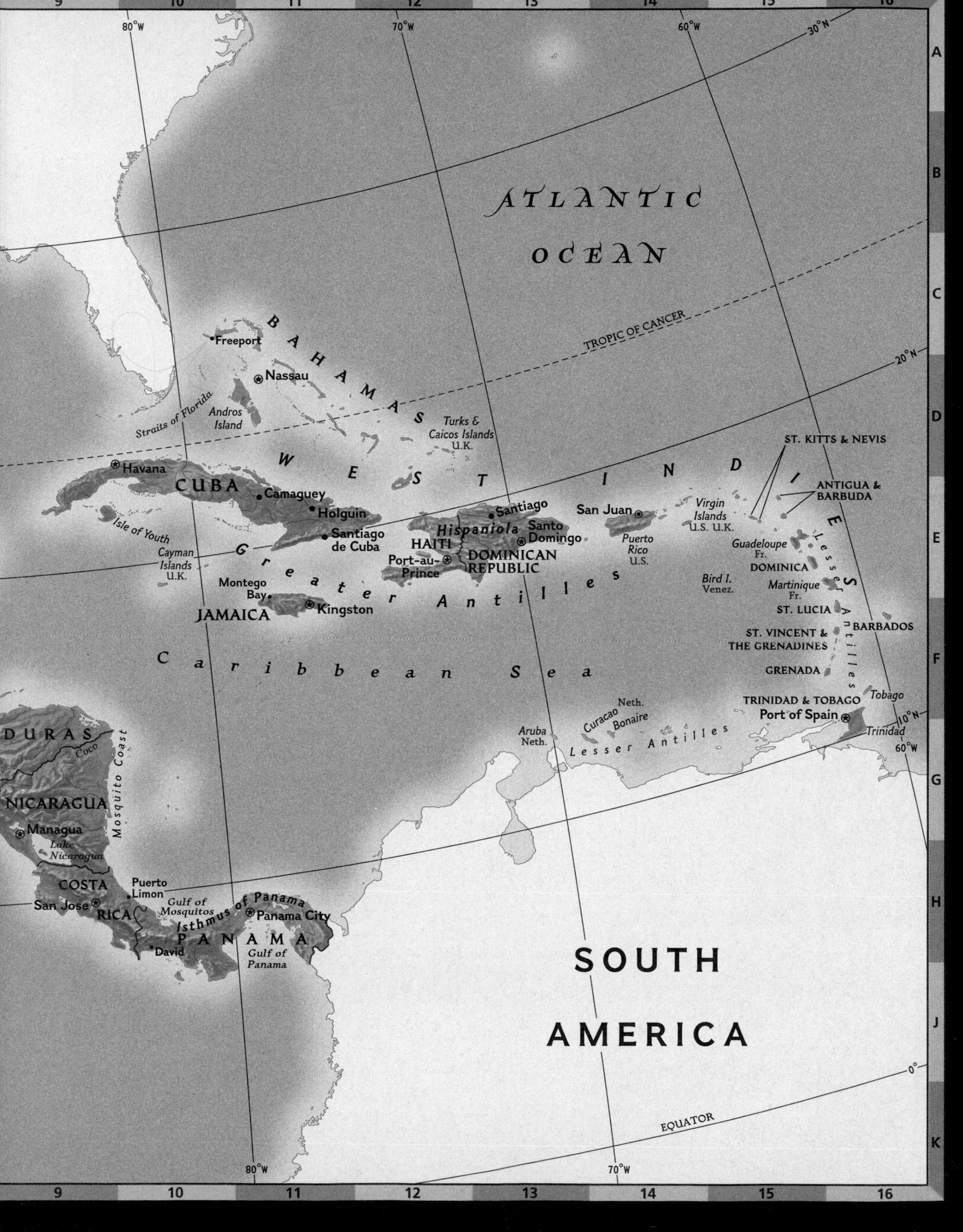

ATLANTIC OCEAN
TROPIC OF CANCER
BAHAMAS
Freeport
Nassau
Andros Island
Straits of Florida
Turks & Caicos Islands U.K.
WEST INDIES
Havana
CUBA
Camaguey
Holguin
Santiago de Cuba
Isle of Youth
Cayman Islands U.K.
Santiago
Hispaniola
HAITI
Port-au-Prince
Santo Domingo
DOMINICAN REPUBLIC
San Juan
Puerto Rico U.S.
Virgin Islands U.S. U.K.
ST. KITTS & NEVIS
ANTIGUA & BARBUDA
Guadeloupe Fr.
DOMINICA
Martinique Fr.
ST. LUCIA
BARBADOS
ST. VINCENT & THE GRENADINES
GRENADA
TRINIDAD & TOBAGO
Tobago
Port of Spain
Trinidad
Bird I. Venez.
Lesser Antilles
Montego Bay
Kingston
JAMAICA
Greater Antilles
Caribbean Sea
Aruba Neth.
Curacao
Bonaire
Neth.
Lesser Antilles
DURAS
Coco
Mosquito Coast
NICARAGUA
Managua
Lake Nicaragua
COSTA RICA
San Jose
Puerto Limon
Gulf of Mosquitos
Isthmus of Panama
Panama City
PANAMA
David
Gulf of Panama
SOUTH AMERICA
EQUATOR
80°W
70°W
60°W
30°N
20°N
10°N
0°

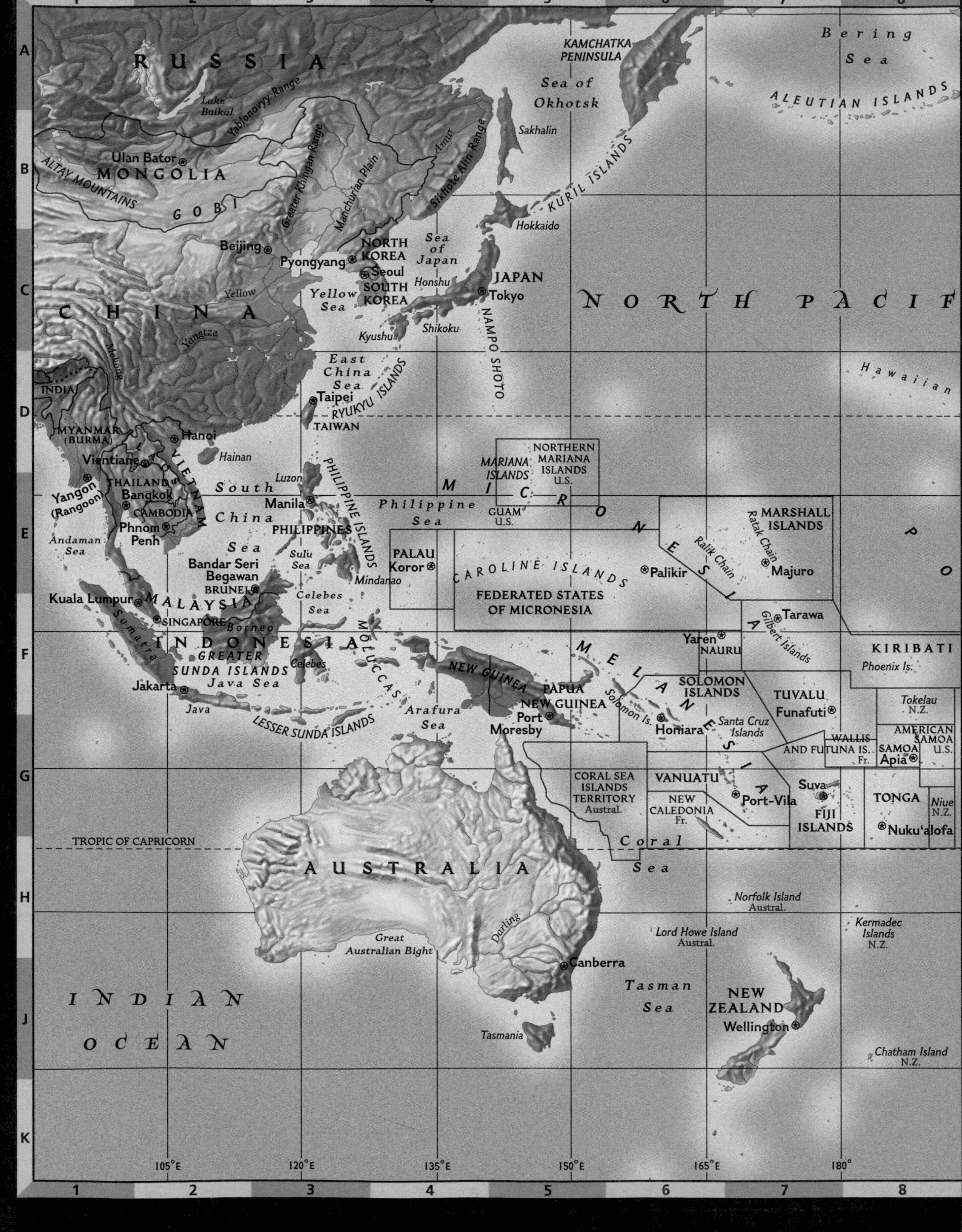
RUSSIA
KAMCHATKA PENINSULA
Bering Sea
Sea of Okhotsk
ALEUTIAN ISLANDS
Lake Baikal
Yablonovyy Range
Sakhalin
Ulan Bator
MONGOLIA
ALTAY MOUNTAINS
GOBI
Greater Khingan Range
Manchurian Plain
Amur
Sikhote Alin Range
KURIL ISLANDS
Hokkaido
Beijing
Pyongyang
NORTH KOREA
Seoul
SOUTH KOREA
Sea of Japan
Honshu
JAPAN
Tokyo
Yellow
Yellow Sea
CHINA
Yangtze
NORTH PACIF
Kyushu
Shikoku
NAMPO SHOTO
East China Sea
RYUKYU ISLANDS
Mekong
INDIA
Taipei
TAIWAN
Hawaiian
MYANMAR (BURMA)
Hanoi
LAOS
VIETNAM
Hainan
NORTHERN MARIANA ISLANDS U.S.
MARIANA ISLANDS
Vientiane
Yangon (Rangoon)
THAILAND
Bangkok
CAMBODIA
Phnom Penh
South China Sea
Luzon
Manila
PHILIPPINE ISLANDS
Philippine Sea
MICRONESIA
GUAM U.S.
MARSHALL ISLANDS
Ralik Chain
Ratak Chain
Majuro
Andaman Sea
PHILIPPINES
Sulu Sea
PALAU
Koror
CAROLINE ISLANDS
Palikir
Bandar Seri Begawan
BRUNEI
Mindanao
FEDERATED STATES OF MICRONESIA
Kuala Lumpur
MALAYSIA
Celebes Sea
SINGAPORE
Sumatra
Borneo
INDONESIA
MOLUCCAS
Celebes
Tarawa
Gilbert Islands
Yaren
NAURU
KIRIBATI
Phoenix Is.
GREATER SUNDA ISLANDS
Java Sea
Jakarta
Java
NEW GUINEA
PAPUA NEW GUINEA
Port Moresby
MELANESIA
Solomon Is.
SOLOMON ISLANDS
Honiara
Santa Cruz Islands
TUVALU
Funafuti
Tokelau N.Z.
LESSER SUNDA ISLANDS
Arafura Sea
WALLIS AND FUTUNA IS. Fr.
SAMOA
Apia
AMERICAN SAMOA U.S.
CORAL SEA ISLANDS TERRITORY Austral.
VANUATU
Port-Vila
NEW CALEDONIA Fr.
Suva
FIJI ISLANDS
TONGA
Nuku'alofa
Niue N.Z.
TROPIC OF CAPRICORN
Coral Sea
AUSTRALIA
Norfolk Island Austral.
Kermadec Islands N.Z.
Lord Howe Island Austral.
Great Australian Bight
Darling
Canberra
INDIAN OCEAN
Tasman Sea
NEW ZEALAND
Wellington
Tasmania
Chatham Island N.Z.
105°E
120°E
135°E
150°E
165°E
180°

PACIFIC RIM
PHYSICAL/POLITICAL
0 mi 1500
0 km 1500
MILLER CYLINDRICAL PROJECTION
NATIONAL GEOGRAPHIC SOCIETY
Gulf of Alaska
Kodiak I.
Alexander Archipelago
Queen Charlotte Islands
Vancouver Island
Coast Mountains
Cascade Range
ROCKY MOUNTAINS
GREAT PLAINS
CANADIAN SHIELD
Hudson Bay
CANADA
Missouri
Ottawa
Great Lakes
APPALACHIAN MTS.
CENTRAL LOWLAND
Washington
UNITED STATES
Mississippi
COASTAL PLAIN
ATLANTIC OCEAN
IC OCEAN
45°N
30°N
15°N
0°
15°S
30°S
45°S
Baja California
Gulf of California
Sierra Madre Occidental
Sierra Madre Oriental
MEXICO
Mexico City
Gulf of Mexico
TROPIC OF CANCER
Islands
HAWAII U.S.
Nassau
BAHAMAS
Havana
CUBA
JAMAICA
HAITI
DOMINICAN REPUBLIC
Santo Domingo
BELIZE
HONDURAS
Tegucigalpa
GUATEMALA
Guatemala City
San Salvador
EL SALVADOR
NICARAGUA
Managua
San Jose
COSTA RICA
Panama City
PANAMA
Caribbean Sea
Caracas
LLANOS
VENEZ.
Bogota
COLOMBIA
Kiritimati
Line Islands
EQUATOR
Galapagos Islands Ecua.
Quito
ECUADOR
AMAZON BASIN
BRAZIL
PERU
Lima
ANDES
BOLIVIA
La Paz
Marquesas Is.
Tuamotu Archipelago
COOK ISLANDS N.Z.
Society Is.
FRENCH POLYNESIA Fr.
Austral Is.
Pitcairn Island U.K.
POLYNESIA
SOUTH PACIFIC OCEAN
Santiago
ARGENTINA
CHILE
Chiloe Island
PATAGONIA
165°W
150°W
135°W
120°W
105°W
90°W
75°W
9 10 11 12 13 14 15 16
A B C D E F G H J K

TERRITORIAL EXPANSION OF THE UNITED STATES

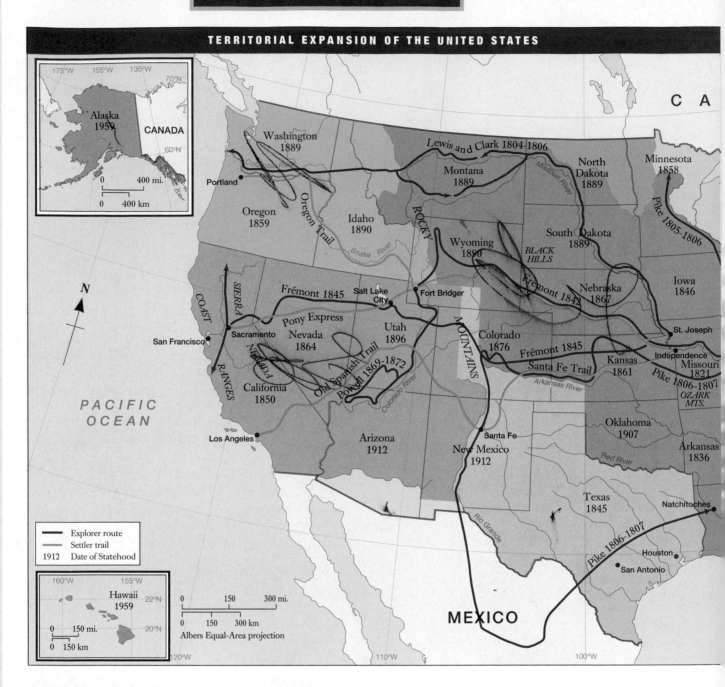

Explorer route
Settler trail
1912 Date of Statehood

Albers Equal-Area projection

Lewis and Clark 1804–1806
William Clark and Meriwether Lewis, guided by the Shoshone princess Sacajawea and the enslaved York, crossed the Rockies and reached the mouth of the Columbia River.

Zebulon Pike 1806–1807
Pike not only explored the Arkansas and Red Rivers of the Southwest but also entered Spanish territory. His reports on the rich overland trade with Mexico and on Spanish military weakness helped stimulate American expansion into Texas.

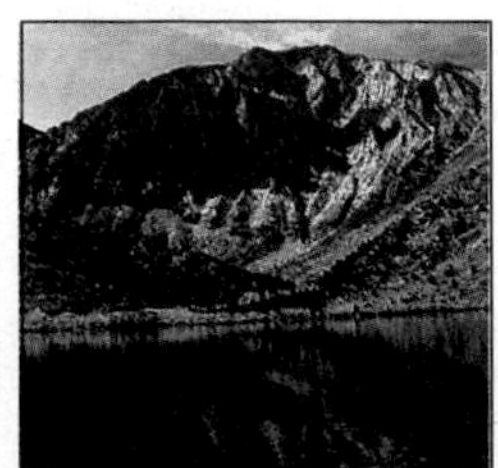

John Charles Frémont 1842–1844
Frémont's love of the wilderness inspired him to undertake expeditions to Wyoming, the Northwest, and California. His surveys charted America's westward expansion.

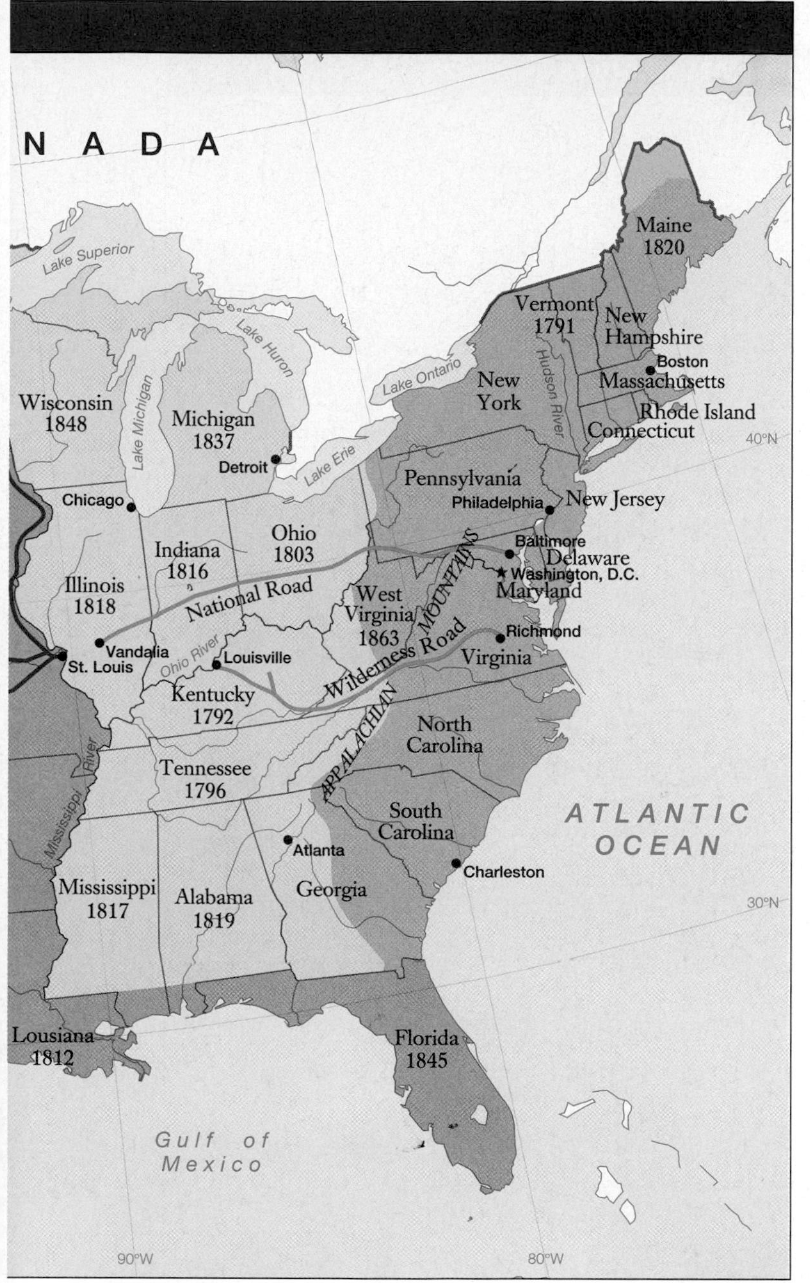

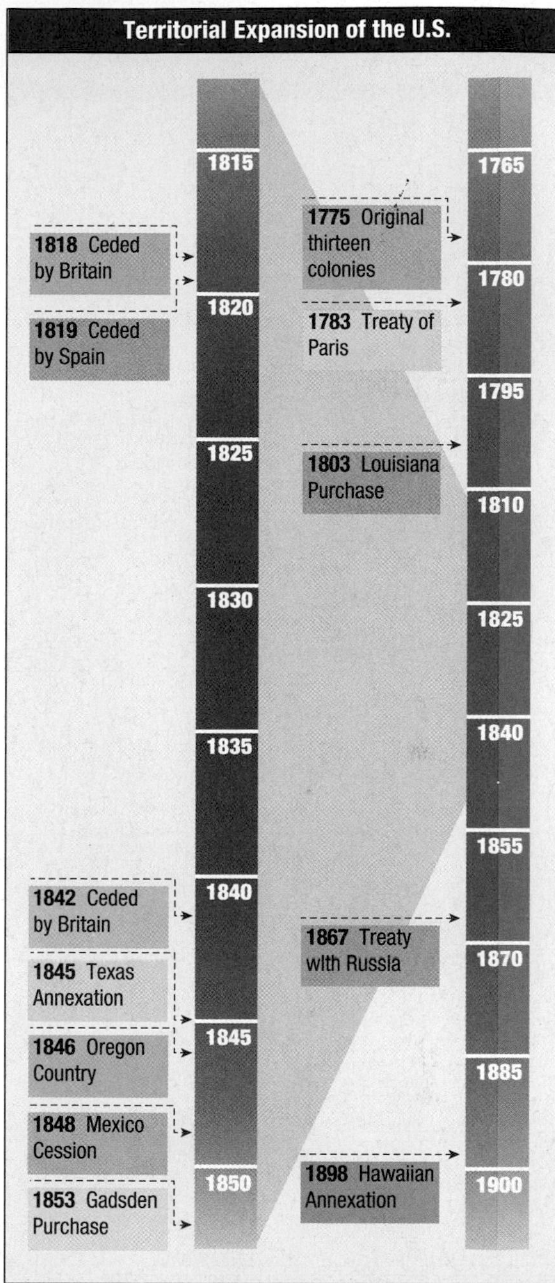

John Wesley Powell 1869
The Spanish explorer Coronado first discovered the Grand Canyon in 1540, but a party led by geologist and Native American scholar John Wesley Powell first saw the canyon from the Colorado River. The canyon extends for about 280 miles (451 km) and ranges in width from 4 to 18 miles (6.4 to 29 km).

Oregon Trail 1840s
Fur traders and missionaries opened this route stretching 2,000 miles (3,218 km) to Oregon. Pioneers undertook the difficult six months' journey in Conestoga wagons.

Promontory Point, Utah Territory, 1869
A golden spike marked the completion of the first transcontinental railroad linking the West Coast with the rest of the nation. The frontier steadily grew smaller as Americans settled in the vast empty spaces.

UNITED STATES CLIMATE REGIONS

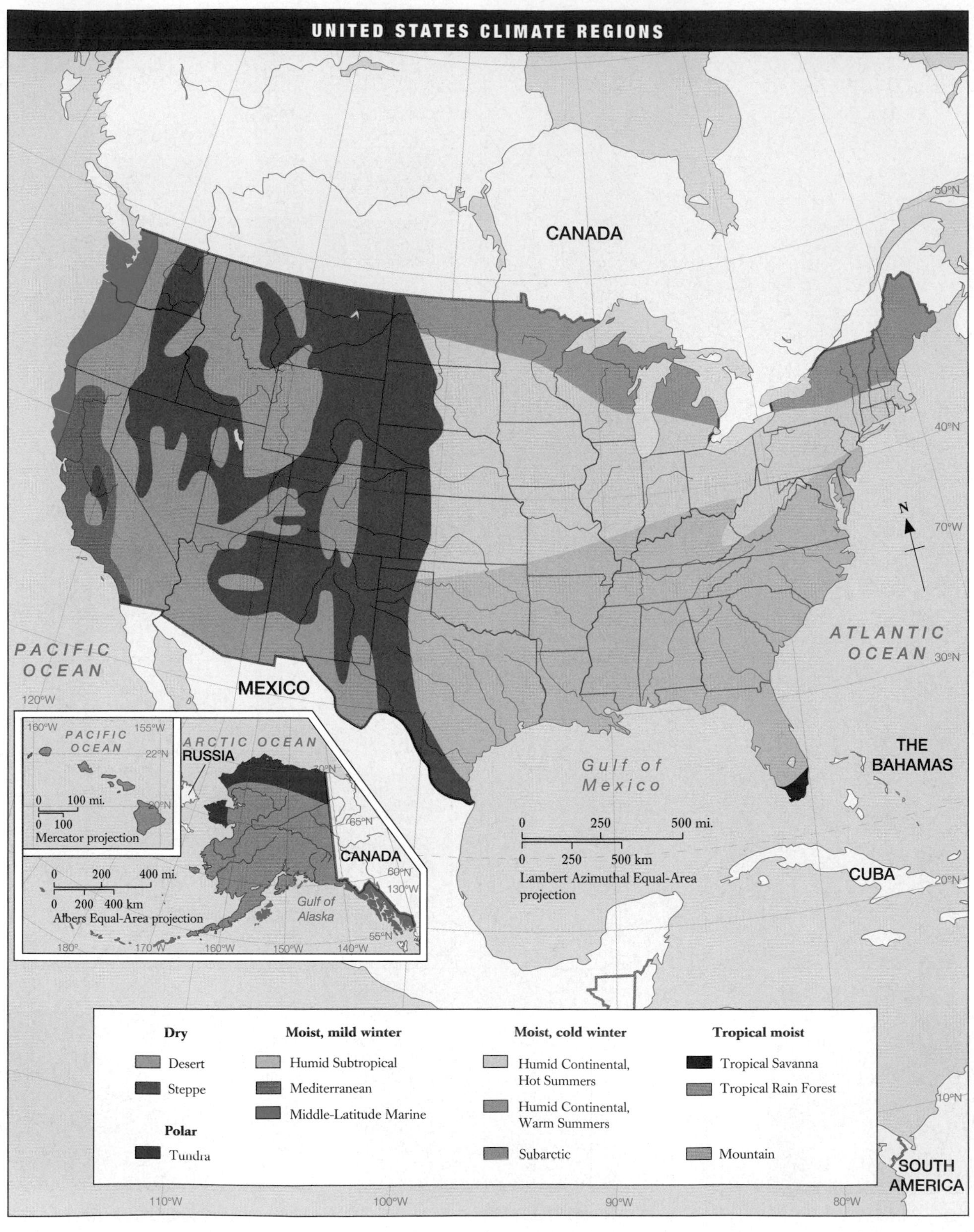
CANADA
PACIFIC OCEAN
MEXICO
ATLANTIC OCEAN
Gulf of Mexico
THE BAHAMAS
CUBA
SOUTH AMERICA
ARCTIC OCEAN
RUSSIA
Gulf of Alaska
0 250 500 mi.
0 250 500 km
Lambert Azimuthal Equal-Area projection
0 100 mi.
0 100
Mercator projection
0 200 400 mi.
0 200 400 km
Albers Equal-Area projection
Dry
Desert
Steppe
Polar
Tundra
Moist, mild winter
Humid Subtropical
Mediterranean
Middle-Latitude Marine
Moist, cold winter
Humid Continental, Hot Summers
Humid Continental, Warm Summers
Subarctic
Tropical moist
Tropical Savanna
Tropical Rain Forest
Mountain

Population of the United States

Year	Population		
1790	3,929,214	4.5	–
1800	5,308,483	6.1	35.1
1810	7,239,881	4.3	36.4
1820	9,638,453	5.5	33.1
1830	12,866,020	7.4	33.5
1840	17,069,453	9.8	32.7
1850	23,191,876	7.9	35.9
1860	31,443,321	10.6	35.6
1870	39,818,449	13.4	26.6
1880	50,155,783	16.9	26.0
1890	62,947,714	21.2	25.5
1900	75,994,575	25.6	20.7

Year	Population		
1910	91,972,266	31.0	21.0
1920	105,710,620	35.6	14.9
1930	122,775,046	41.2	16.1
1940	131,669,275	44.2	7.2
1950	151,325,798	50.7	14.5
1960	179,323,175	50.6	18.5
1970	203,302,031	57.4	13.4
1980	226,542,199	64.0	11.4
1990	248,718,301	70.3	9.8
2000*	274,634,000	77.7	10.5
2010**	297,716,000	84.2	8.3
2020**	322,742,000	91.3	8.4

Key:
Population per square mile of land
Percentage increase over preceding census

*estimated
**projected

Source: *Statistical Abstract of the United States,* 1999.

Population Distribution by Age

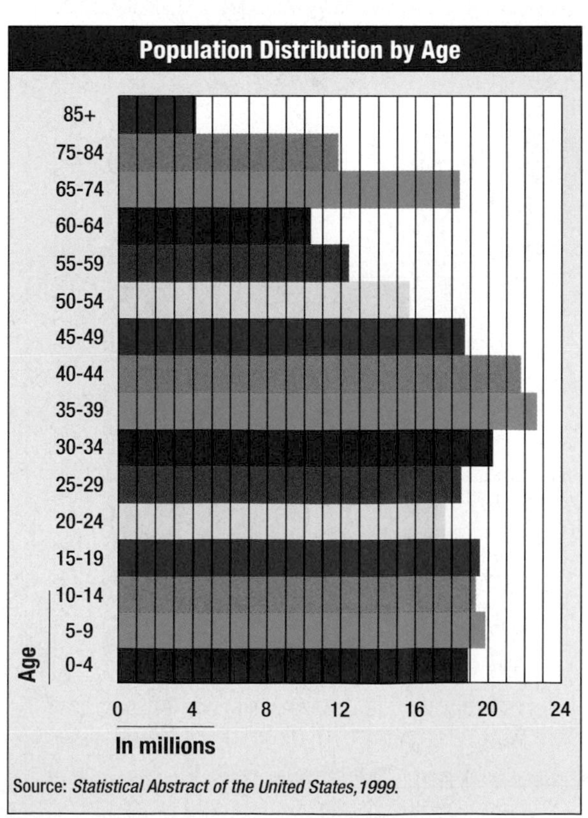

Source: *Statistical Abstract of the United States,1999.*

Major Religions in the United States

Roman Catholic Church 61,207,914
Southern Baptist Convention 15,891,514
United Methodist Church 8,496,047
National Baptist Convention, U.S.A. 8,200,000
Muslims 5,500,000
Church of God in Christ (Pentecostal) 5,499,875
Evangelical Lutheran Church in America 5,185,055
Church of Jesus Christ of Latter-Day Saints (Mormon) 4,923,100
Jews 4,075,000
Presbyterian Church (U.S.A.) 3,610,753
African Methodist Episcopal Church 3,500,000
Lutheran Church (Missouri Synod) 2,603,036
National Baptist Convention of America 2,500,000
Progressive National Baptist Convention 2,500,000
Assemblies of God 2,494,574
Episcopal Church 2,339,113
Orthodox Church in America 2,000,000
Greek Orthodox Diocese of America 1,954,500
Churches of Christ 1,800,000
American Baptist Churches in the U.S.A. 1,503,287
United Church of Christ 1,438,181
Hindu 1,285,000
African Methodist Episcopal Zion Church 1,252,369

Source: *The World Almanac 2000.*

Political Parties in Power in the Executive Branch

President	Party
George Washington, 1789–1797	Federalist
John Adams, 1797–1801	Federalist
Thomas Jefferson, 1801–1809	Democratic Republican
James Madison, 1809–1817	Democratic Republican
James Monroe, 1817–1825	Democratic Republican
John Quincy Adams, 1825–1829	Democratic Republican
Andrew Jackson, 1829–1837	Democratic
Martin Van Buren, 1837–1841	Democratic
William H. Harrison/John Tyler, 1841–1845	Whig
James K. Polk, 1845–1849	Democratic
Zachary Taylor/Millard Fillmore, 1849–1853	Whig
Franklin Pierce, 1853–1857	Democratic
James Buchanan, 1857–1861	Democratic
Abraham Lincoln, 1861–1865	Republican
Andrew Johnson, 1865–1869	Republican
Ulysses S. Grant, 1869–1877	Republican
Rutherford B. Hayes, 1877–1881	Republican
James A. Garfield/Chester A. Arthur, 1881–1885	Republican
Grover Cleveland, 1885–1889	Democratic
Benjamin Harrison, 1889–1893	Republican
Grover Cleveland, 1893–1897	Democratic
William McKinley, 1897–1901	Republican
Theodore Roosevelt, 1901–1909	Republican
William H. Taft, 1909–1913	Republican
Woodrow Wilson, 1913–1921	Democratic
Warren G. Harding, 1921–1923	Republican
Calvin Coolidge, 1923–1929	Republican
Herbert C. Hoover, 1929–1933	Republican
Franklin D. Roosevelt, 1933–1945	Democratic
Harry S. Truman, 1945–1953	Democratic
Dwight D. Eisenhower, 1953–1961	Republican
John F. Kennedy, 1961–1963	Democratic
Lyndon B. Johnson, 1963–1969	Democratic
Richard M. Nixon, 1969–1974	Republican
Gerald R. Ford, 1974–1977	Republican
James E. Carter, Jr., 1977–1981	Democratic
Ronald W. Reagan, 1981–1989	Republican
George H. W. Bush, 1989–1993	Republican
William J. Clinton, 1993–2001	Democratic
George W. Bush, 2001–	Republican

Federalist · Democratic Republican · Democratic · Whig · Republican

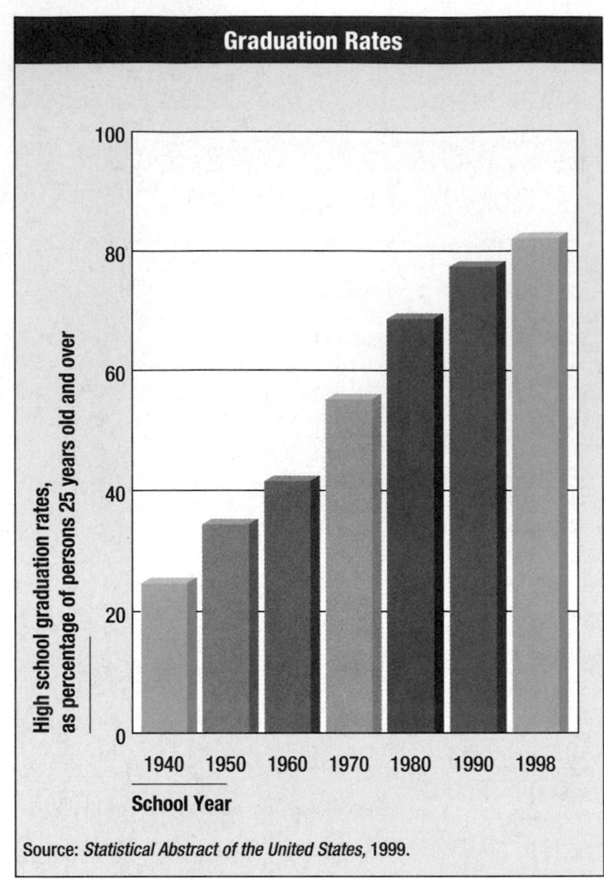

Source: *Statistical Abstract of the United States,* 1999.

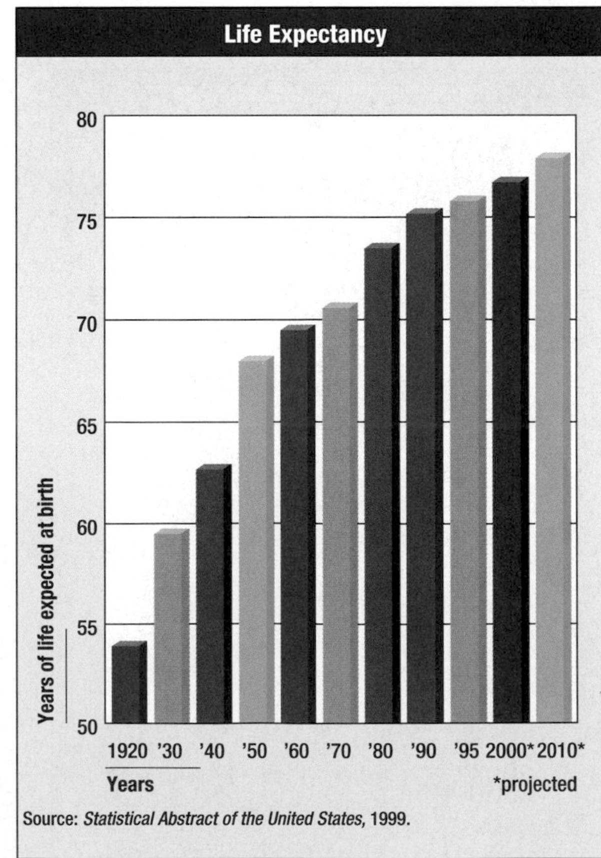

Source: *Statistical Abstract of the United States,* 1999.

The United States

STATE*	YEAR ADMITTED	POPULATION (1999)	LAND AREA (sq. mi.)	CAPITAL	LARGEST CITY	HOUSE REP. (1999)**
1. Delaware	1787	753,538	1,955	Dover	Wilmington	1
2. Pennsylvania	1787	11,994,016	44,820	Harrisburg	Philadelphia	21
3. New Jersey	1787	8,143,412	7,419	Trenton	Newark	13
4. Georgia	1788	7,788,240	57,919	Atlanta	Atlanta	11
5. Connecticut	1788	3,282,031	4,845	Hartford	Bridgeport	6
6. Massachusetts	1788	6,175,169	7,838	Boston	Boston	10
7. Maryland	1788	5,171,634	9,774	Annapolis	Baltimore	8
8. South Carolina	1788	3,885,736	30,111	Columbia	Columbia	6
9. New Hampshire	1788	1,201,134	8,969	Concord	Manchester	2
10. Virginia	1788	6,872,912	39,598	Richmond	Virginia Beach	11
11. New York	1788	18,196,601	47,224	Albany	New York	31
12. North Carolina	1789	7,650,789	48,718	Raleigh	Charlotte	12
13. Rhode Island	1790	990,819	1,045	Providence	Providence	2
14. Vermont	1791	593,740	9,249	Montpelier	Burlington	1
15. Kentucky	1792	3,960,825	39,732	Frankfort	Louisville	6
16. Tennessee	1796	5,483,535	41,219	Nashville	Memphis	9
17. Ohio	1803	11,256,654	40,953	Columbus	Columbus	19
18. Louisiana	1812	4,372,035	43,566	Baton Rouge	New Orleans	7
19. Indiana	1816	5,942,901	35,870	Indianapolis	Indianapolis	10
20. Mississippi	1817	2,768,619	46,914	Jackson	Jackson	5
21. Illinois	1818	12,128,370	55,593	Springfield	Chicago	20
22. Alabama	1819	4,369,862	50,750	Montgomery	Birmingham	7
23. Maine	1820	1,253,040	30,865	Augusta	Portland	2
24. Missouri	1821	5,468,338	68,898	Jefferson City	Kansas City	9
25. Arkansas	1836	2,551,373	52,075	Little Rock	Little Rock	4
26. Michigan	1837	9,863,775	56,809	Lansing	Detroit	16
27. Florida	1845	15,111,244	53,937	Tallahassee	Jacksonville	23
28. Texas	1845	20,044,141	261,194	Austin	Houston	30
29. Iowa	1846	2,869,413	55,874	Des Moines	Des Moines	5
30. Wisconsin	1848	5,250,446	54,314	Madison	Milwaukee	9
31. California	1850	33,145,121	155,973	Sacramento	Los Angeles	52
32. Minnesota	1858	4,775,508	79,617	St. Paul	Minneapolis	8
33. Oregon	1859	3,316,154	96,002	Salem	Portland	5
34. Kansas	1861	2,654,052	81,823	Topeka	Wichita	4
35. West Virginia	1863	1,806,928	24,087	Charleston	Charleston	3
36. Nevada	1864	1,809,253	109,806	Carson City	Las Vegas	2
37. Nebraska	1867	1,666,028	76,878	Lincoln	Omaha	3
38. Colorado	1876	4,056,133	103,729	Denver	Denver	6
39. North Dakota	1889	633,666	68,994	Bismarck	Fargo	1
40. South Dakota	1889	733,133	75,896	Pierre	Sioux Falls	1
41. Montana	1889	882,779	145,556	Helena	Billings	1
42. Washington	1889	5,756,361	66,581	Olympia	Seattle	9
43. Idaho	1890	1,251,700	82,751	Boise	Boise	2
44. Wyoming	1890	479,602	97,105	Cheyenne	Cheyenne	1
45. Utah	1896	2,129,836	82,168	Salt Lake City	Salt Lake City	3
46. Oklahoma	1907	3,316,154	68,679	Oklahoma City	Oklahoma City	6
47. New Mexico	1912	1,739,844	121,364	Sante Fe	Albuquerque	3
48. Arizona	1912	4,778,332	113,642	Phoenix	Phoenix	6
49. Alaska	1959	619,500	570,374	Juneau	Anchorage	1
50. Hawaii	1959	1,185,497	6,423	Honolulu	Honolulu	2
District of Columbia (Washington, D.C.)	–	519,000	61	–	–	–
United States of America	–	272,690,813	3,536,278	Washington, D.C.	New York	435

* Numbers denote the order in which states were admitted.
** Number of members in House of Representatives; based on 1990 census.

Presidents *of the* United States

★ ★

From George Washington to George W. Bush, this presidential gallery introduces the forty-three Presidents and highlights biographical information on each.

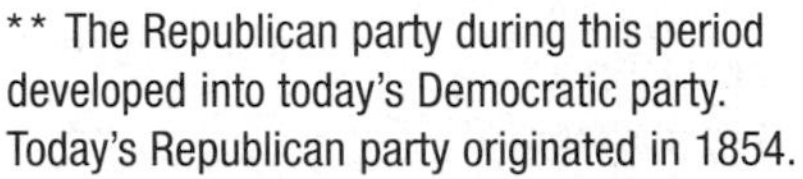

** The Republican party during this period developed into today's Democratic party. Today's Republican party originated in 1854.

George Washington

1789–1797

Born: 1732
Died: 1799
Born in: Virginia
Elected from: Virginia
Age when elected: 56
Occupations: Planter, Soldier
Party: None
Vice President: John Adams

John Adams

1797–1801

Born: 1735
Died: 1826
Born in: Massachusetts
Elected from: Massachusetts
Age when elected: 61
Occupations: Teacher, Lawyer
Party: Federalist
Vice President: Thomas Jefferson

Thomas Jefferson

1801–1809

Born: 1743
Died: 1826
Born in: Virginia
Elected from: Virginia
Age when elected: 57
Occupations: Planter, Lawyer
Party: Republican**
Vice Presidents: Aaron Burr, George Clinton

James Madison

1809–1817

Born: 1751
Died: 1836
Born in: Virginia
Elected from: Virginia
Age when elected: 57
Occupation: Planter
Party: Republican**
Vice Presidents: George Clinton, Elbridge Gerry

James Monroe

1817–1825

Born: 1758
Died: 1831
Born in: Virginia
Elected from: Virginia
Age when elected: 58
Occupation: Lawyer
Party: Republican**
Vice President: Daniel D. Tompkins

John Quincy Adams

1825–1829

Born: 1767
Died: 1848
Born in: Massachusetts
Elected from: Massachusetts
Age when elected: 57
Occupation: Lawyer
Party: Republican**
Vice President: John C. Calhoun

Andrew Jackson

1829–1837

Born: 1767
Died: 1845
Born in: South Carolina
Elected from: Tennessee
Age when elected: 61
Occupations: Lawyer, Soldier
Party: Democratic
Vice President: John C. Calhoun, Martin Van Buren

Martin Van Buren

1837–1841

Born: 1782
Died: 1862
Born in: New York
Elected from: New York
Age when elected: 54
Occupation: Lawyer
Party: Democratic
Vice President: Richard M. Johnson

William H. Harrison

1841

Born: 1773
Died: 1841
Born in: Virginia
Elected from: Ohio
Age when elected: 67
Occupations: Soldier, Planter
Party: Whig
Vice President: John Tyler

10

John Tyler

1841–1845

Born: 1790
Died: 1862
Born in: Virginia
Elected as V.P. from: Virginia
Succeeded: Harrison
Age when became President: 51
Occupation: Lawyer
Party: Whig
Vice President: None

11

James K. Polk

1845–1849

Born: 1795
Died: 1849
Born in: North Carolina
Elected from: Tennessee
Age when elected: 49
Occupation: Lawyer
Party: Democratic
Vice President: George M. Dallas

12

Zachary Taylor

1849–1850

Born: 1784
Died: 1850
Born in: Virginia
Elected from: Louisiana
Age when elected: 63
Occupation: Soldier
Party: Whig
Vice President: Millard Fillmore

13

Millard Fillmore

1850–1853

Born: 1800
Died: 1874
Born in: New York
Elected as V.P. from: New York
Succeeded: Taylor
Age when became President: 50
Occupation: Lawyer
Party: Whig
Vice President: None

14

Franklin Pierce

1853–1857

Born: 1804
Died: 1869
Born in: New Hampshire
Elected from: New Hampshire
Age when elected: 47
Occupation: Lawyer
Party: Democratic
Vice President: William R. King

15

James Buchanan

1857–1861

Born: 1791
Died: 1868
Born in: Pennsylvania
Elected from: Pennsylvania
Age when elected: 65
Occupation: Lawyer
Party: Democratic
Vice President: John C. Breckinridge

Abraham Lincoln

1861–1865

Born: 1809
Died: 1865
Born in: Kentucky
Elected from: Illinois
Age when elected: 51
Occupation: Lawyer
Party: Republican
Vice President: Hannibal Hamlin, Andrew Johnson

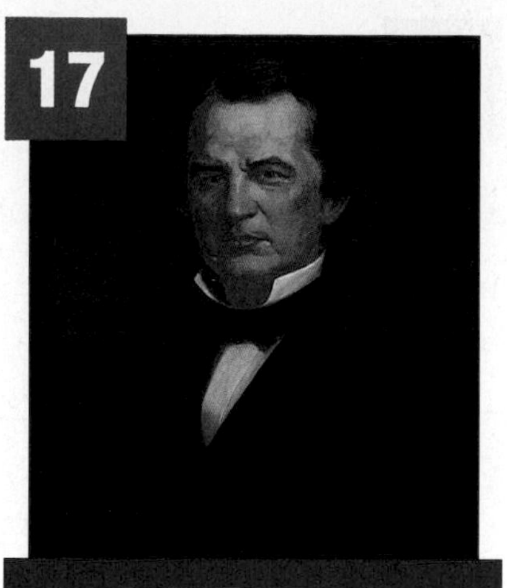

Andrew Johnson

1865–1869

Born: 1808
Died: 1875
Born in: North Carolina
Elected as V.P. from: Tennessee
Age when became President: 56
Succeeded: Lincoln
Occupation: Tailor
Party: Republican
Vice President: None

Ulysses S. Grant

1869–1877

Born: 1822
Died: 1885
Born in: Ohio
Elected from: Illinois
Age when elected: 46
Occupations: Farmer, Soldier
Party: Republican
Vice President: Schuyler Colfax, Henry Wilson

Rutherford B. Hayes

1877–1881

Born: 1822
Died: 1893
Born in: Ohio
Elected from: Ohio
Age when elected: 54
Occupation: Lawyer
Party: Republican
Vice President: William A. Wheeler

James A. Garfield

1881

Born: 1831
Died: 1881
Born in: Ohio
Elected from: Ohio
Age when elected: 49
Occupations: Lawyer, Politician
Party: Republican
Vice President: Chester A. Arthur

Chester A. Arthur

1881–1885

Born: 1830
Died: 1886
Born in: Vermont
Elected as V.P. from: New York
Succeeded: Garfield
Age when became President: 50
Occupations: Teacher, Lawyer
Party: Republican
Vice President: None

Grover Cleveland

1885–1889, 1893–1897

Born: 1837
Died: 1908
Born in: New Jersey
Elected from: New York
Age when elected: 47; 55
Occupation: Lawyer
Party: Democratic
Vice Presidents: Thomas A. Hendricks, Adlai E. Stevenson

Benjamin Harrison

1889–1893

Born: 1833
Died: 1901
Born in: Ohio
Elected from: Indiana
Age when elected: 55
Occupation: Lawyer
Party: Republican
Vice President: Levi P. Morton

William McKinley

1897–1901

Born: 1843
Died: 1901
Born in: Ohio
Elected from: Ohio
Age when elected: 53
Occupations: Teacher, Lawyer
Party: Republican
Vice Presidents: Garret Hobart, Theodore Roosevelt

Theodore Roosevelt

1901–1909

Born: 1858
Died: 1919
Born in: New York
Elected as V.P. from: New York
Succeeded: McKinley
Age when became President: 42
Occupations: Historian, Rancher
Party: Republican
Vice President: Charles W. Fairbanks

William H. Taft

1909–1913

Born: 1857
Died: 1930
Born in: Ohio
Elected from: Ohio
Age when elected: 51
Occupation: Lawyer
Party: Republican
Vice President: James S. Sherman

Woodrow Wilson

1913–1921

Born: 1856
Died: 1924
Born in: Virginia
Elected from: New Jersey
Age when elected: 55
Occupation: College Professor
Party: Democratic
Vice President: Thomas R. Marshall

Warren G. Harding

1921–1923

Born: 1865
Died: 1923
Born in: Ohio
Elected from: Ohio
Age when elected: 55
Occupations: Newspaper Editor, Publisher
Party: Republican
Vice President: Calvin Coolidge

Calvin Coolidge

1923–1929

Born: 1872
Died: 1933
Born in: Vermont
Elected as V.P. from: Massachusetts
Succeeded: Harding
Age when became President: 51
Occupation: Lawyer
Party: Republican
Vice President: Charles G. Dawes

Herbert C. Hoover

1929–1933

Born: 1874
Died: 1964
Born in: Iowa
Elected from: California
Age when elected: 54
Occupation: Engineer
Party: Republican
Vice President: Charles Curtis

Franklin D. Roosevelt

1933–1945

Born: 1882
Died: 1945
Born in: New York
Elected from: New York
Age when elected: 50
Occupations: Lawyer
Party: Democratic
Vice Presidents: John N. Garner, Henry A. Wallace, Harry S Truman

Harry S. Truman

1945–1953

Born: 1884
Died: 1972
Born in: Missouri
Elected as V.P. from: Missouri
Succeeded: Roosevelt
Age when became President: 60
Occupation: Clerk, Farmer
Party: Democratic
Vice President: Alben W. Barkley

Dwight D. Eisenhower

1953–1961

Born: 1890
Died: 1969
Born in: Texas
Elected from: New York
Age when elected: 62
Occupation: Soldier
Party: Republican
Vice President: Richard M. Nixon

35

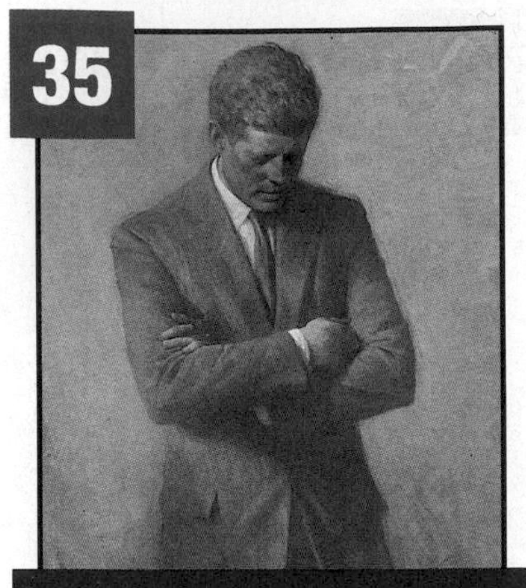

John F. Kennedy

1961–1963

Born: 1917
Died: 1963
Born in: Massachusetts
Elected from: Massachusetts
Age when elected: 43
Occupations: Author, Reporter
Party: Democratic
Vice President: Lyndon B. Johnson

36

Lyndon B. Johnson

1963–1969

Born: 1908
Died: 1973
Born in: Texas
Elected as V.P. from: Texas
Succeeded: Kennedy
Age when became President: 55
Occupation: Teacher
Party: Democratic
Vice President: Hubert H. Humphrey

37

Richard M. Nixon

1969–1974

Born: 1913
Died: 1994
Born in: California
Elected from: New York
Age when elected: 55
Occupation: Lawyer
Party: Republican
Vice Presidents: Spiro T. Agnew, Gerald R. Ford

38

Gerald R. Ford

1974–1977

Born: 1913
Born in: Nebraska
Appointed by Nixon as V.P. upon Agnew's resignation; assumed presidency upon Nixon's resignation
Age when became President: 61
Occupation: Lawyer
Party: Republican
Vice President: Nelson A. Rockefeller

39

James E. Carter, Jr.

1977–1981

Born: 1924
Born in: Georgia
Elected from: Georgia
Age when elected: 52
Occupations: Business, Farmer
Party: Democratic
Vice President: Walter F. Mondale

40

Ronald W. Reagan

1981–1989

Born: 1911
Born in: Illinois
Elected from: California
Age when elected: 69
Occupations: Actor, Lecturer
Party: Republican
Vice President: George H.W. Bush

George H.W. Bush

1989–1993

Born: 1924
Born in: Massachusetts
Elected from: Texas
Age when elected: 64
Occupation: Business
Party: Republican
Vice President: J. Danforth Quayle

William J. Clinton

1993–2001

Born: 1946
Born in: Arkansas
Elected from: Arkansas
Age when elected: 46
Occupation: Lawyer
Party: Democratic
Vice President: Albert Gore, Jr.

George W. Bush

2001–

Born: 1946
Born in: Connecticut
Elected from: Texas
Age when elected: 54
Occupation: Business
Party: Republican
Vice President: Richard B. Cheney

WORKING WITH PRIMARY SOURCES

Suppose that you have been asked to write a report on changes in your community over the past 25 years. Where would you get the information you need to begin writing? You would draw upon two types of information–primary sources and secondary sources.

Definitions

Primary sources are often first-person accounts by someone who actually saw or lived through what is being described. In other words, if you see a fire or live through a great storm and then write about your experiences, you are creating a primary source. Diaries, journals, photographs, and eyewitness reports are examples of primary sources. **Secondary sources** are secondhand accounts. For instance, if your friend experiences the fire or storm and tells you about it, or if you read about the fire or storm in the newspaper, and then you write about it, you are creating a secondary source. Textbooks, biographies, and histories are secondary sources.

Checking Your Sources

When you read primary or secondary sources, you should analyze them to figure out if they are dependable or reliable. Historians usually prefer primary sources to secondary sources, but both can be reliable or unreliable, depending on the following factors.

Time Span

With primary sources, it is important to consider how long after the event the primary source was written. Chances are the longer the time span between the event and the account, the less reliable the account is. As time passes, people often forget details and fill in gaps with events that never took place. Although we like to think we remember things exactly as they happened, the fact is we often remember them as we wanted them to occur.

Reliability

Another factor to consider when evaluating a primary source is the writer's background and reliability. First, try to determine how this person knows about what he or she is writing. How much does he or she know? Is the writer being truthful? Is the account convincing?

Opinions

When evaluating a primary source, you should also decide whether the account has been influenced by emotion, opinion, or exaggeration. Writers can have reasons to distort the truth to suit their personal

American History Primary Source Document Library

Find additional documents in the Glencoe Social Studies ***American History Primary Source Document Library***. This CD-ROM provides you with over 250 print documents and an audio document library.

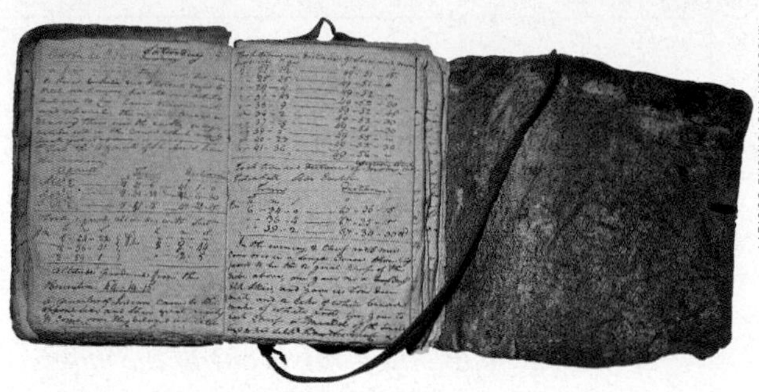
MISSOURI HISTORICAL SOCIETY

William Clark's log book

purposes. Ask yourself: Why did the person write the account? Do any key words or expressions reveal the author's emotions or opinions? You may wish to compare the account with one written by another witness to the event. If the two accounts differ, ask yourself why they differ and which is more accurate.

Interpreting Primary Sources

To help you analyze a primary source, use the following steps:

- **Examine the origins of the document.**
  You need to determine if it is a primary source.
- **Find the main ideas.**
  Read the document and summarize the main ideas in your own words. These ideas may be fairly easy to identify in newspapers and journals, for example, but are much more difficult to find in poetry.
- **Reread the document.**
  Difficult ideas are not always easily understood on the first reading.
- **Use a variety of resources.**
  Form the habit of using a dictionary, an encyclopedia, and maps. These resources are tools to help you discover new ideas and knowledge and check the validity of sources.

Classifying Primary Sources

Primary sources fall into different categories:

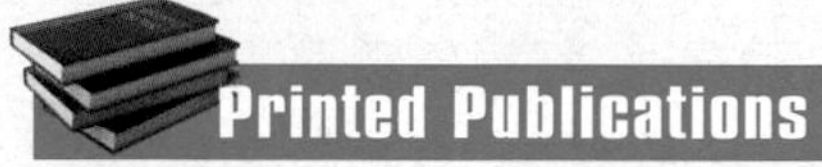

Printed Publications

Printed Publications include books such as autobiographies. Printed publications also include newspapers and magazines.

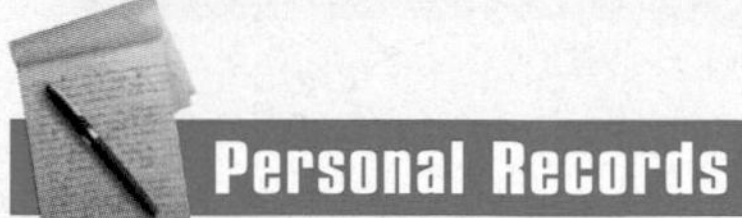

Personal Records

Personal Records are accounts of events kept by an individual who is a participant in or witness to these events. Personal records include diaries, journals, and letters.

Visual Materials

Visual Materials include a wide range of forms: original paintings, drawings, and sculpture; photographs; film; and maps.

Oral Histories

Oral Histories are chronicles, memoirs, myths, and legends that are passed along from one generation to another by word of mouth. Interviews are another form of oral history.

Songs and Poems

Songs and Poems include works that express the personal thoughts and feelings or political or religious beliefs of the writer, usually using rhyming and rhythmic language.

Artifacts

Artifacts are objects such as tools or ornaments. Artifacts present information about a particular culture or a stage of technological development.

For use with Units 1, "A Nation of Nations," and 2, "Rift and Reunion"

A New Nation

European settlers established colonies along the eastern coastline of North America, which was inhabited by many Native American peoples. A group of 13 English colonies won its independence in 1783 and formed the United States of America. Several decades later, the unity of the young nation was tested by a civil war.

Reader's Dictionary

discord: disagreement, conflict

late wars: the American Revolution

melancholy: sad

regiment: a military unit

For more primary sources to accompany Units 1 and 2, use the ***American History Primary Source Document Library*** CD-ROM.

Songs of Liberty

The following song is one of the many patriotic songs distributed in song books during the early 1800s.

The fruits of our country, our flocks and
 our fleeces,
What treasures immense, in our mountains
 that lie,
While discord is tearing Old Europe to pieces,
Shall amply the wants of the people supply;
New roads and canals, on the bosoms
 conveying,
Refinement and wealth through our forests
 shall roam,
And millions of freemen, with rapture
 surveying,
Shall shout out "O Liberty! this is thy home!"

The Oneida and the Use of Land

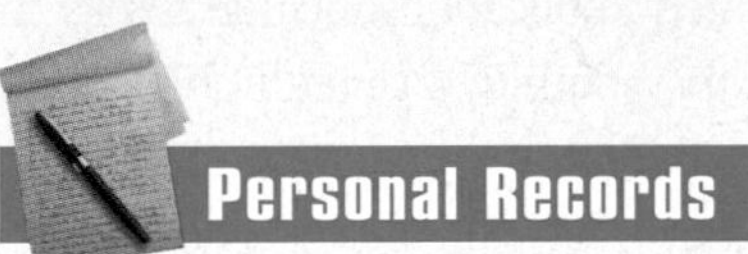

In March 1788 leaders of the Oneida people sent this message to the New York state legislature.

Brothers, we are your allies: we are a free people: our chiefs have directed us to speak to you, as such therefore, open your ears, and hear our words.

Brothers, in your late wars with the people on the other side of the great water, . . . We fought by your side. Our blood flowed together: and the bones of our warriors mingled with yours. . . . [W]e received an invitation to

SMITHSONIAN INSTITUTION

Flag flown at Fort McHenry during War of 1812

meet some of your chiefs, . . . Those chiefs, who then met us, will doubtless remember, how much we were disappointed, when they told us, they were only sent to buy our lands. . . .

Brothers, we are determined, then, never to sell any more. The experience of all the Indian nations to the east and south, has fully convinced us, that if we follow their example, we shall soon share their fate. We wish that our children and grandchildren may derive a comfortable living from the lands which the Great Spirit has given us and our forefathers. . . .

Brothers, we wish you to consider this matter well, and to do us justice. . . .

Retreat

After the Confederate victory at the Battle of Chickamauga in September 1863, a Union officer described his army's retreat:

The march was a melancholy one. All along the road for miles, wounded men were lying. They had crawled or hobbled slowly away from the fury of the battle, become exhausted, and lain down by the roadside to die. Some were calling the names and numbers of their regiments, but many had become too weak to do this . . . the army is simply a mob.

Looking for Relatives

Families that had been separated during slavery tried to reunite after the Civil War. Newspapers carried advertisements like the one shown here from African Americans seking information about missing relatives:

$200 reward. During the year 1849, Thomas Sample carried away from this city, as his slaves, our daughter Polly, and son, Geo. Washington, to the state of Mississippi, and [later] to Texas. . . . We will give $100 each for them, to any person who assists them, or either of them, to get to Nashville, or get word to us [about where to find them], if they are alive.

Interpreting Primary Sources

1. In the song, what does the phrase "treasures immense" mean?
2. Who are the "Brothers" that the Oneida leaders address? What are the Oneida asking?
3. How does the writer describe the Union forces after the Battle of Chickamauga?
4. What is the aim of the newspaper advertisement?

Activity

Making a Poster Make a poster advertising the new nation. Include reasons why people would want to settle in the United States.

For use with Units 3, "The Roots of a Modern Era," and 4, "The New Era of the Twenties"

A Modern Era Begins

After the Civil War, many Americans moved ahead optimistically. Thousands of settlers headed west to the new frontier. In the East, industries boomed and cities grew. Industrialization improved some citizens' standard of living but created new challenges for others. The growth of wealth was briefly interrupted by World War I. Afterward, Americans sought to forget the wartime memories during the roaring 1920s. The following excerpts examine this eventful time in the nation's history.

Reader's Dictionary

stampede: run away in panic

inclined: slanted or leaning

Harlem: New York neighborhood where many African Americans lived

treble: high-pitched musical notes

bass: low-pitched musical notes

For more primary sources to accompany Units 3 and 4, use the ***American History Primary Source Document Library*** CD-ROM.

On the Cattle Trail

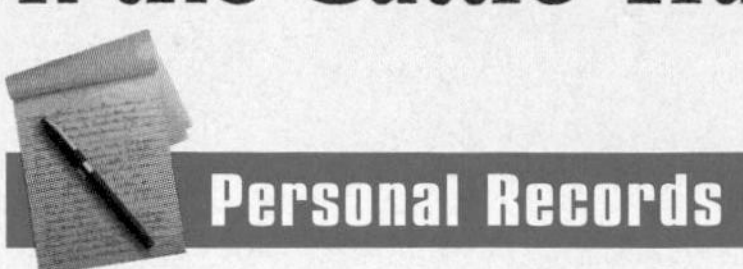

Cowhand George Duffield describes the troubles along a four-month trek from mid-Texas to Iowa in 1866.

April 29

. . . Started in evening from Salt Creek & traveled 5 miles to Alexanders Gap between Colorado & Brazos.

May 1

. . . Big Stampede lost 200 head of cattle.

May 4

Continued to hunt found 40 head day pleasant Sun shone once more. Heard that the other herd had stampeded & lost over 200.

May 13

Big Thunder Storm last night Stampede lost 100 Beeves [head of cattle] hunted all day found 50 all tired. Everything discouraging.

June 12

Hard Rain & Wind Big stampede & here we are among the Indians with 150 head of Cattle gone hunted all day & the Rain pouring down but with poor success Dark days are these to me Nothing but Bread & Coffee Hands all Growling & Swearing—everything wet and cold Beeves gone rode all day & gathered all but 35. . . .

Child Labor

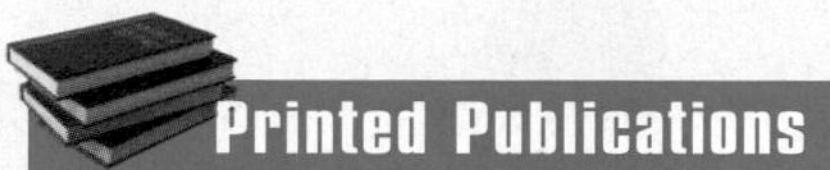

Printed Publications

Children as well as adults suffered in unhealthy working conditions, as the following description shows:

In a little room in this big, block shed—a room not twenty feet square—forty boys are picking their lives away. The floor of this room is an inclined plane, and a stream of coal pours constantly in. They work here, in this little black hole, all day and every day . . . picking away among the black coals, bending over till their little spines are curved. . . . Not three boys in this roomful could read or write. Shut in from everything that is pleasant, with no chance to learn, with no knowledge of what is going on about them. . . . They know nothing but the difference between slate and coal.

Young coal miners in Kingston, Pennsylvania

LIBRARY OF CONGRESS

Dream Boogie: Variation

Songs and Poems

Langston Hughes, a leading writer of the Harlem Renaissance, often drew inspiration for his poetry from jazz music and from his Harlem neighborhood.

Tinkling treble,
Rolling bass,
High noon teeth
In a midnight face,
Great long fingers
On great big hands,
Screaming pedals
Where his twelve-shoe lands,
Looks like his eyes
Are teasing pain,
A few minutes late
For the Freedom Train.

Interpreting Primary Sources

1. What crises did George Duffield face?
2. Why could so few child workers read or write?
3. What musical intrument is being played in Hughes' poem?

Activity

Writing a Poem Poetry often reflects the beat, or rhythm, of music and dance. Write a short poem that uses the rhythms of music you enjoy.

For use with Units 5, "Economic Crisis and the New Deal," and 6, "The United States Transformed"

THE GREAT DEPRESSION AND WORLD WAR II

The stock market crash of 1929 ushered in a decade-long depression. The carefree life of the 1920s was replaced by daily struggles for food, shelter, and jobs. When the United States joined the Allies in World War II, Americans were asked to continue saving and conserving resources to support the war effort. As you read, think about the hardships Americans faced during these times.

READER'S DICTIONARY

incinerator: a furnace that burns waste

paralysis: a state of being powerless to act

For more primary sources to accompany Units 5 and 6, use the ***American History Primary Source Document Library*** CD-ROM.

The Long Wait

Dorothea Lange was an American photographer who captured many powerful images of the Great Depression. The photograph below, "White Angel Bread Line," shows people waiting for food in San Francisco in 1933. Lange considered this her most famous photograph.

At the time, Lange made her living as a portrait photographer. She began to shoot street scenes such as this and hang them in her studio. As she told an interviewer: "The only comment I ever got was, 'What are you going to do with this kind of thing?' I didn't know. But I knew that picture was on my wall, and I knew that it was worth doing."

The Great Depression

In October 1929 the United States's stock market crashed—investors were ruined, businesses were destroyed, and millions of people lost their jobs. The 1930s brought a period of economic gloom, poverty, and despair. Joseph L. Heffernan, an Ohio mayor, describes life during the Great Depression in this excerpt.

As time went on, business conditions showed no improvement. Every night hundreds of homeless men crowded into the municipal incinerator, where they found warmth even though they had to sleep on heaps of garbage. In January 1931, I obtained the cooperation of the City Council to convert an abandoned police station into a "flophouse." The first night it was filled, and it has remained filled ever since. . . .

This descent from respectability, frequent enough in the best of times, has been hastened immeasurably by two years of business paralysis, and the people who have been affected in this manner must be numbered in millions. . . . I have seen thousands of these defeated, discouraged, hopeless men and women, cringing and fawning as they come to ask for public aid. It is a spectacle of national degeneration. . . .

On the Home Front

The US government appealed to civilians to support the World War II effort in many ways. This bulletin was posted in meat markets.

1] THE NEED IS URGENT–War in the Pacific has greatly reduced our supply of vegetable fats from the Far East. It is necessary to find substitutes for them. Fat makes glycerine. And glycerine makes explosives for us and our Allies—explosives to down Axis planes, stop their tanks, and sink their ships. We need millions of pounds of glycerine and you housewives can help supply it.

2] DON'T throw away a single drop of used cooking fat, bacon fat, meat drippings, fry fats—every kind you use. After you've got all the cooking good from them, pour them through a kitchen strainer into a clean, wide-mouthed can. Keep it in a cool dark place. . . .

3] TAKE THEM to your meat dealer when you've saved a pound or more. He is cooperating patriotically. He will pay you for your waste fats and get them started on their way to war industries.

INTERPRETING PRIMARY SOURCES

1. Why does Heffernan say people needed public aid in the 1930s?
2. How would you describe the mood of people in Lange's photograph?
3. For what purpose did the government ask people to save fats?

Researching Music Research to find songs of the 1930s that reflect the mood of the Depression. Present the lyrics and/or melodies to the class.

For use with Units 7, "The Postwar World," and 8, "Toward Equality and Social Reform"

POSTWAR CHANGES IN THE UNITED STATES

In the years following World War II, middle class Americans settled into life in the suburbs, enjoying the fruits of a booming economy. At the same time, they lived in fear of communism and nuclear threat during the Cold War. African Americans and women sought to expand the gains of equal rights they had enjoyed during the war. As you read these selections, think about the changes in United States society during these years.

READER'S DICTIONARY

fallout: particles of radioactive material that drift through the atmosphere after a nuclear explosion

Conelrad: (from "Control of Electromagnetic Radiation") an emergency radio broadcasting system that would replace normal broadcasts

Jim Crow laws: laws passed in the South in the late 1800s that enforced segregation and kept African Americans out of many public places

For more primary sources to accompany Units 7 and 8, use the ***American History Primary Source Document Library*** CD-ROM.

Fallout Fears

By 1961 fears of nuclear war were so great that the government urged people to be prepared for a nuclear attack. LIFE magazine reminded Americans what to do during such an attack.

The standard Civil Defense signal for an alert is a steady 3- to 5-minute blast of a siren or whistle. The warning to take cover is a 3-minute period of short blasts or a wailing siren. If an attack should come, however, the first warning you may get could be the flash itself. Your first move should be to close your eyes and bury your head in your arms or clothing to block out the light . The flash may last for several seconds, so keep covered until it begins to dim.

The shockwave will come next. Take cover so you will not be knocked down. If you are in a car, roll down windows to avoid flying glass and lie on the floor. Try to count the seconds between the flash and shockwave. This will help you estimate how far away the bomb has hit and how long you have to find better cover before the fallout can reach you. . . .

Wherever you are, try to reach a radio–preferably a battery radio since the electricity may be out–and tune it to 640 or 1240 on your dial, which are the Conelrad frequencies for emergency instructions. If you have a shelter, go to it immediately. . . .

A Tired Woman's Fight

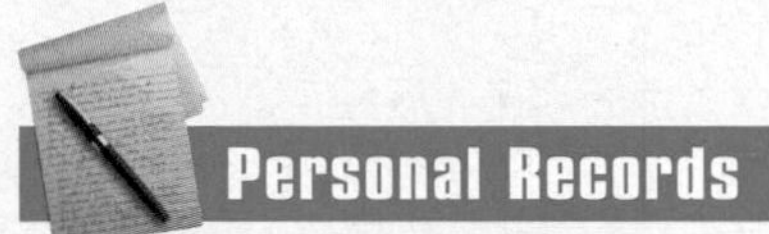

Rosa Parks's refusal to give up her seat on a bus helped spark the civil rights movement. In this selection, she answered a letter that asked, "How did you feel when you were on the bus?"

The custom of getting on the bus for black people in Montgomery in the 1950s was to pay at the front door, get off the bus, and then reenter through the back door to find a seat. Black people could not sit in the same rows with white people. This custom was humiliating.

When I sat down on the bus on the day I was arrested, I decided I must do what was right to do. People have said over the years that the reason I did not give up my seat was because I was tired. I did not think of being physically tired. My feet were not hurting. I was tired in a different way. I was tired of seeing so many men treated as boys and not called by their proper names or titles. I was tired of seeing children and women mistreated and disrespected because of the color of their skin. I was tired of Jim Crow laws, of legally enforced racial segregation.

I thought of the pain and the years of oppression and mistreatment that my people had suffered. I felt that way every day. December 1, 1955, was no different. Fear was the last thing I thought of that day. I put my trust in the Lord for guidance and help to endure whatever I had to face. I knew I was sitting in the right seat.

Working Women

During the 1960s and 1970s, women began demanding equal pay for equal work. Women such as Joanne Gus, a warehouse worker, filed lawsuits to get back pay from their employers. In this excerpt, Gus describes the difficulties she and her coworkers faced after receiving a disappointing $500 offer to settle their lawsuit.

. . . I was ready to cry. You can't realize all the aggravation and amount of work that had been done so far. The really sad part about it was that most of the women were willing to settle. They were afraid to take it any further. Well, I can be very stubborn, especially if I know I'm right about an issue. So I refused the offer for them all. Well, the next few days were really [awful] at work. Still, I knew I was worth more.

The case made it to federal court. A settlement gave 246 women $548,000 in back pay.

Interpreting Primary Sources

1. According to the LIFE magazine article, in what order would someone experience the effects of a nuclear attack?
2. How was Rosa Parks "tired" when she boarded the Montgomery bus?
3. How did Joanne Gus's attitude differ from those of her coworkers?

Analyzing Create a fictional account of a day in the life of a teenager in 1960. Your account may take the form of a diary, story, or play.

For use with Units 9, "The Troubled Years," and 10, "New Challenges"

CHALLENGES AND OPPORTUNITIES

The events during the Vietnam War era forever changed the way Americans viewed their country and the world. Within the next decades, the cold war ended and new advances in technology helped the world move forward. At the same time, problems such as war, poverty, and political oppression still plagued other parts of the world. To escape these problems, millions of immigrants came to the United States. As you examine these selections, think of the challenges and opportunities facing the United States today.

READER'S DICTIONARY

Viet Cong: communist guerilla forces in South Vietnam

cadremen: trained Viet Cong members

kangaroo court: a court set up outside the legal system that follows irregular or unfair procedures

Republicans: in Vietnam, forces of the U.S.-backed government of South Vietnam

interrogation: a formal and systematic questioning

Khmer Rouge: communist faction in Cambodia responsible for the deaths of millions of civilians

For more primary sources to accompany Units 9 and 10, use the ***American History Primary Source Document Library*** CD-ROM.

A Vietnamese Village

Many Vietnamese people felt trapped between the forces fighting over their country. Writer Le Ly Hayslip, who grew up in South Vietnam, describes what happened in her village, Ky La, during the war.

. . . The Republicans and Americans poured troops and firepower into the jungle around Ky La. . . . The Viet Cong had planned a three-day battle, but they had underestimated the colossal numbers of men and arms the enemy was willing to commit to prevent Ky La from falling into their hands. Inside the village, soldiers went from house to house, tearing everything apart to find the Viet Cong hideouts. Where anything suspicious was found, the house was burned and its occupants tied up and taken away for interrogation. Two thirds of my village disappeared this way. . . . So little was left that even the Viet Cong soon lost interest in Ky La as a prize of war. Instead, they turned their attention to the one thing they knew they could gain no matter what: a grip of terror on the survivors.

Despite–or perhaps because of–the terrible battle, the Viet Cong cadremen took even harsher steps to control us. They began by killing those they suspected of spying for the enemy, usually by taking the accused from their houses in the middle of the night and shooting them in the street–leaving the bodies for relatives to discover. Later, when government forces weren't around, the Viet Cong called villagers to special justice meetings . . .

during which they held kangaroo courts for the accused and shot them afterward. . . .

Naturally, these trials made us stay on our toes. . . . After a while, our fear of the Viet Cong–of false accusation by jealous neighbors or headstrong kids–was almost as strong as our fear of the Republicans.

Coming to America

In these selections, two teenagers explain why their families immigrated to the United States.

Ban is Cambodian, but she was born in a refugee camp in Thailand:

My parents decided it would be better to leave Cambodia because there was no food and no one could do anything unless the government said so. My father used to be an engineer. My mother was a teacher. They lived in an apartment in the city.

It was dangerous for them because the Khmer Rouge, who won the war, took over everything and killed lots of people who had worked in the city, who were educated. My parents were lucky they didn't get killed. But they were forced to leave the city and go work on farms planting rice. They weren't even able to stay together on the same farm. Then they decided to leave Cambodia.

Fernando came from Nicaragua at age six:

Life here is so easy compared to Nicaragua. . . . The reason my mom brought me out of Nicaragua was because of the war. There, when you are twelve or thirteen, they just give you a gun. You have to fight, and if you don't they come get you. I know, because I had a cousin who was seventeen. He didn't want to fight, and every day the soldiers came to the door and beat him up until he agreed to go. I remember that so well.

Presidential Elections in 2000

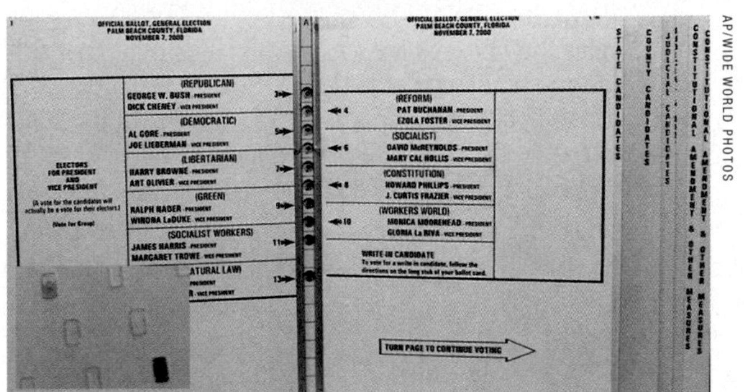

AP/WIDE WORLD PHOTOS

The presidential election of 2000 was the closest in United States history—and one of the most contested. Arguments arose on election day over the butterfly ballots, such as the one shown in the photograph, which some voters found confusing. Over the next few weeks, volunteers visually inspected and counted hundreds of thousands of individual ballots. Incompletely punched cards, such as the "dimpled" ballot shown in the inset, made the count difficult.

Interpreting Primary Sources

1. Do you think the people in Hayslip's village feared the government troops of the Viet Cong more? Explain.
2. What reasons for coming to America do Ban and Fernando share?
3. Why might it be difficult to tell how a vote was cast on a punch-out ballot?

Activity

Planning a Time Capsule Imagine that you are in charge of making a time capsule to be opened 100 years from now. List 10-12 items you would include and explain your choices.

Glossary

A

abolition The formal outlawing of slavery (p. 73)

abolitionism In the 1800s the movement to put an end to slavery in the United States (p. 155)

accommodation The policy under which certain African Americans accepted the results of white racism in order to achieve economic success (p. 283)

affirmative action government policies that award jobs, government contracts, promotions, admission to schools, and other benefits to minorities and women in order to make up for past discriminations (p. 915)

alliance A pact or association of nations joined in a common cause (p. 306)

amendment A written change or addition (p. 90)

amnesty An act by which the government grants pardon for crimes to a large group of individuals, usually in response to the group's acts of consolation (p. 185)

anarchism Opposition to any form of government; the theory that all governments should be abolished (p. 339)

annex To add or attach a new territory to an existing country (p. 294)

apartheid An official policy of racial segregation formerly mandated in South Africa (p. 880)

appeasement The policy of compromising or giving in to the demands of a hostile nation in the hope of maintaining peace (p. 496)

arbitration A method of settling a dispute by agreeing in advance to accept the decision of an impartial outsider (p. 271)

armistice An agreement to end hostilities (p. 222)

arms race Competition between the United States and the Soviet Union for greater military strength (p. 573)

assimilation The absorption of minority group members into the main culture of United States society (p. 737)

B

baby boom The unusually rapid population growth of the post-World War II period in the United States, lasting through the mid-1960s (p. 609)

backlash A strong, sudden reaction against an idea or policy (p. 809)

balance of power A condition in which the major powers are equal enough in strength to prevent the aggression of any and maintain the safety of all (p. 817)

bilingualism The use of two languages; the ability to use two languages with equal fluency (p. 737)

bipartisan coalition A group of Republicans and Democrats working together on issues (p. 906)

black codes Laws adopted in the South that severely restricted the rights of newly freed slaves (p. 185)

black power A movement to improve African American economic, political, and social conditions using African American leadership and organization, without the help of whites (p. 693)

black pride Pride in being African American; pride in one's African ancestry as well as one's American nationality (p. 691)

black separatism Concept, espoused by some African Americans in the United States, calling for the separation of the races (p.691)

blacklisting Efforts to brand people as Communists and prevent them from holding certain jobs (p. 647)

blitzkrieg An intensive attack, often combining air and land forces, from the German blitzkrieg, or "lightning war"; in World War II, the German bombing raids on England (p. 496)

bolshevism A radical socialist ideology; from Bolshevik, the name of V.I. Lenin's left-wing majority party during the Russian Revolution (p. 322)

bond Certificate that earns interest and is redeemed for cash on a specific date (p. 529)

bootlegger A person who made, sold, or transported illegal liquor (p. 398)

boycott An organized agreement not to buy or use a certain product or deal with a certain company or nation, in order to exert pressure for change (pp. 675)

brinksmanship Practice of attempting to keep the peace among nations by letting it be known that one will never back down and is prepared to cross the brink of war (p. 579)

C

cabinet A body of people appointed by the President to lead the various departments of government and to serve as the President's official advisers (p. 113)

capital Accumulated money or other material wealth that is devoted to the production of more wealth; material wealth acquired in business by an individual or company (p. 356)

capitalism An economic system based on open competition in a free market, in which individuals and companies own the means of production and operate for profit (p. 276)

carpetbagger A Northern opportunist who moved to the South and took advantage of unsettled post-Civil War conditions; scornfully dubbed carpetbagger, after a kind of homemade luggage that many of them carried (p. 190)

checks and balances The system by which each of the three branches of government prevents the others from gaining excessive power (p. 84)

civil disobedience A strategy for causing social change by means of nonviolent resistance to unfair laws (p. 679)

civil liberties Freedom to enjoy the rights guaranteed by the constitution of the state or nation (p. 546)

civil rights The political, economic, and social rights of a citizen; particularly, those guaranteed under the United States Constitution, such as the right to vote and the right to equal treatment under the law (p. 669)

climate The specific set of meteorological conditions that characterize an area (p. 14)

closed shop A system in which all workers in an industry are required to be union members. (p. 633)

coalition A temporary alliance (of nations, parties, for example) formed for a specific action or purpose (p. 701)

cold war The United States-Soviet conflict that followed World War II in which the two powers avoided military confrontation but opposed each other's political and economic goals (p. 567)

commune A group of people who live communally, with collective ownership and use of property, often having shared goals, philosophies, and ways of life (p. 751)

community policing A method of police patrolling that involves sending foot patrols into neighborhoods and establishing better relations between the police and the public (p. 922)

compensation Money or something in return for a loss (p. 742)

conglomerate A firm that has holdings in a variety of unrelated industries (p. 601)

conquistadors Spanish explorers who conquered the new lands they discovered (p. 32)

conscientious objector A person who refuses military service because of moral or religious principles (p. 789)

conscription Compulsory enrollment in military service; the draft (p. 315)

consensus decision-making A management style, such as that of President Dwight Eisenhower, based on general agreement (p. 654)

conservative era A period in presidential politics in which the role of government is limited and individuals depend less on the government for assistance (p. 781)

constitution A written document of a plan of government (p. 73)

consumer price index A measure of the change in the cost of goods and services as compared with their cost in a fixed time period; also called the cost-of-living index (p. 528)

containment After World War II, the United States policy of securing the peace by trying to contain communism, or keep it from expanding beyond its current borders (pp. 566, 769)

corollary A proposition added to another as a natural consequence or effect, such as Teddy Roosevelt's corollary to the Monroe Doctrine (p. 297)

corporation A group of individuals authorized by law to act as a single entity; a business owned by many investors (p. 356)

counterculture A culture of young people with values that run counter to those of the established culture (p. 749)

coup The act of seizing power and overthrowing the government (p. 305)

covert operation. A secret or undercover government mission (p. 588)

coverture A British law under which a woman's inherited property belonged to her husband (p. 74)

credit A delayed payment plan in which a purchaser puts money down and pays the balance in installments; time allowed for payment of something sold on trust (p. 381)

crime bill A bill that has provisions for more police on the streets, building prisons, adding new applications to the death penalty, and banning assault weapons (p. 899)

cultural diffusion The spread of customs, ways of life, and other products of human thought and work from one cultural group to another (p. 752)

culture of poverty After World War II, the hungry, homeless and largely invisible members of a generally affluent American society (p. 619)

D

deferment The postponement of a person's induction into military service for reasons such as health or occupation (p. 789)

deficit spending A government policy of borrowing money in order to spend more than is received in taxes (p. 539)

demagogue A leader who gains power by appealing to people's emotions and prejudices (p. 467)

demobilization The postwar process of dismissing the troops from military service and shifting citizens and businesses back to peacetime pursuits (p. 599)

depression A period of extended and severe decline in a nation's economy, marked by low production and high unemployment (p. 421)

deregulate To remove restrictions and regulations (p. 859)

détente During the cold war, an attempt to lessen the tension between the United States and the Communist powers (p. 817)

diplomacy The art or practice of conducting international relations (p. 298)

direct primary An election open to all voters in a party; in a direct primary, candidates are chosen by the voters rather than by the party leaders (p. 252)

disarmament The act or policy of reducing or destroying military weapons (p. 351)

discretionary income Money to buy what is wanted in addition to what is needed (pp. 599–600)

discrimination The denial of rights because of someone's race, religion, age, sex, or other quality (p. 478)

dissident One who disagrees with established beliefs and policies; before Gorbachev's presidency, a citizen of the USSR who spoke out against Soviet policies (p. 840)

dogfight Name given to clashes between enemy aircraft (p. 308)

dole Money or goods given as charity; during the Great Depression, government relief payments; to be "on the dole" was to receive such payments regularly (p. 455)

domino theory A theory that if one country fell to communism, other countries in turn would fall, just like dominoes (p. 770)

doughboys Nickname for the United States infantrymen in World War I (p. 315)

dove A person who supports the withdrawal of United States troops from war and favors a negotiated end to war (p. 791)

draft The selection of persons for a particular compulsory assignment; a system of selecting persons to serve in the military (p. 789)

due process The legal procedures that safeguard an individual's rights (p. 716)

E

e-commerce Companies that operate their business on the World Wide Web (p. 908)

egalitarian A culture with no recognized authority figures; where all are considered equal (p. 23)

electronic media Forms of communication transmitted electronically and reaching the general public; primarily, radio and television (p. 656)

emancipation Freedom from bondage; particularly, freedom of African Americans from slavery (p. 176)

embargo A restriction or stoppage of trade (pp. 117, 837)

emerging nation A developing country in Asia, Latin America, or Africa (p. 588)

emigrate To leave one country to settle in another (p. 309)

enfranchisement Attainment of the rights of citizenship, especially the right to vote (p. 682)

entrepreneur A small business owner (p. 752)

eugenics In the early 1900s, a movement advocating improving the human race by controlling hereditary factors in mating (p. 284)

evangelist A fundamentalist preacher (p. 397)

expansionism The policy or process of increasing a nation's land area by acquiring new territory (p. 219)

extended family A family unit that includes not only parents and children but also other relatives such as grandparents, aunts, uncles, and cousins (p. 734)

external tax A tax levied on goods coming into an area, such as the tax the British Parliament imposed on sugar entering the American colonies (p. 58)

F

family leave Unpaid leave of absence for the birth or adoption of a child or for the illness of a family member (p. 899)

fascism A strongly nationalistic ideology, named for the Fascist party of Italy; a government characterized by racism and militarism; a repressive one-party dictatorship (p. 494)

fascist A follower of a political philosophy that preached nationalism and racism (p. 494)

federal regulation Control by the federal government rather than by private interests (p. 481)

feminist Activist who works to attain political, economic, and social rights for women equal to those of men (p. 726)

filibuster The tactic of making extended speeches to delay or prevent a vote on a piece of legislation (p. 687)

flapper The 1920s girl—at least the one promoted in advertising and movies; named for the open galoshes she flapped around in (pp. 382–383)

flatboat A flat-bottomed, square-ended craft that was typically used to transport goods along inland waterways in the early 1800s (p. 132)

foreclosure The legal procedure for reclaiming a piece of property when the buyer is unable to keep up the mortgage payments (p. 431)

frontier The area where colonist-settled lands bordered on lands of Native Americans (p. 130)

fugitive A person who has escaped from slavery and is running from the law (p. 169)

fundamentalism In the United States, a Protestant movement characterized by the belief that the words of the Bible were inspired by God and should be interpreted literally and followed closely (p. 397)

G

generation gap The differences in values, tastes, and attitudes between members of different age groups, especially adolescents and their parents (p. 749)

geography The study of people, places, and environments (p. 6)

gerrymandering Dividing voting districts in a way that increases or decreases representation by a certain group or party (p. 190)

glasnost A Russian word for a policy of openness, begun by Soviet President Gorbachev, encouraging free expression and an end to party censorship (p. 868)

global economy System of worldwide trade (p. 883)

gospel tradition A type of music that combines the words of traditional Protestant hymns with various African musical styles (p. 167)

government boarding school A school at which Native American children were taught white cultural traditions (p. 201)

gross national product (GNP) The total value of all goods and services produced in a nation in a given year (p. 527)

guerrilla warfare Fighting by small, independent bands, using tactics such as sabotage and sudden ambushes (p. 774)

H

hard money Currency consisting of gold or silver coins as opposed to paper (p. 82)

hawk A person who supports the war effort (p. 791)

hippie A member of the counterculture (p. 749)

history The study of events and people over time (p. 13)

holding company A company that owns controlling shares of stock in other companies (p. 270)

homestead Land awarded by the United States government to settlers who would live on it and farm it for five years, under the Homestead Act of 1862 (p. 196)

horizontal integration The merger of competing companies in an industry, such as oil refining, in order to dominate that industry (p. 209)

human/environment interaction The interdependence of people and their surroundings (p. 9)

human rights Basic rights and freedoms assumed to belong to all people everywhere (p. 839)

I

immigrant Person who enters a country to live there (p. 236)

impeachment Charges of misconduct brought against a public official (p. 830)

imperialism The policy of establishing economic, political, and military dominance over weaker nations on humanitarian and moral grounds (p. 295)

impressed Forced into public service, as American sailors forced to serve on British vessels in the late 1700s (p. 115)

indentured servant A person who agreed to work for a set number of years in return for passage to the Colonies (p. 40)

indigenous The people who originally inhabit an area; natives (p. 32)

industrial productivity The amount of goods produced by one hour of labor (p. 355)

industrialism The movement from agriculture to manufacturing as the main source of economic growth (p. 205)

industrialist A person who deals with the commercial production and sale of goods and services (p. 362)

inflation A sharp, continuing rise in prices caused by too much money and credit relative to the available goods (pp. 527, 837)

initiative A reform that allowed citizens to introduce a bill to a legislature or to bypass the legislature and propose a new law by petition (p. 253)

injunction A court order requiring an individual or company to do something, such as end a strike (p. 217)

internationalism A policy of cooperation and involvement among nations (p. 347)

internal tax A tax levied on goods produced and consumed within an area, such as the stamp tax imposed by the British Parliament on the American colonies (p. 58)

interventionism The policy of intervening, or interfering, in the affairs of another nation; in World War II the position of those who opposed isolationism and believed the United States should give all possible support, short of war, to the Allied forces (pp. 347, 500)

irreconcilables During World War I, a group of senators who opposed a League of Nations and could not be reconciled to voting for it (p. 325)

isolationism Avoidance of conflicts and alliances with other nations; indifference to affairs outside the United States; at the beginning of World War II, a policy of forming no alliances and taking no sides (p. 502)

K

kachina A sacred doll of the Pueblo peoples (p. 47)

L

land reform Redistribution of property to land-poor peasants (p. 572)

legislature A committee empowered to make laws (p. 48)

liberal era A period when government promoted social progress (p. 783)

liberate To free from outside control (p. 744)

liberation theology The philosophy of a movement of Christian activists working for social justice, especially in Latin America (p. 820)

limited war Beginning in the Truman era, a policy of avoiding global war by confining the fighting to one area and using conventional weapons, not nuclear power (p. 574)

location The position on the earth's surface (p. 7)

lynching A mob action in which a person is executed without a trial, often by hanging (p. 178)

M

majority More than 50 percent of a group (p. 89)

mandate A clear expression of the wishes of voters, expressed by election results (pp. 701, 857)

margin To "buy on margin" means that the brokerage house lends money to someone to buy securities. If the stock goes up, all the profits (minus the interest charged on the loan) are the purchaser's (p. 420)

martyr A person who voluntarily suffers death rather than renounce religious principles; a person who dies or endures great suffering for a cause (p. 691)

mass media The methods by which information and entertainment are transmitted to large numbers of people; includes newspapers, television, and radio (pp. 381, 441)

massive retaliation The cold war policy of the United States under which aggression against any ally would be met with an immediate all-out nuclear strike (p. 579)

materialism Placing more importance on money and material goods than on intellectual, spiritual, and artistic concerns (p. 390)

melting pot A society in which a number of racial, ethnic, and cultural groups are absorbed and blended together; from a vessel used for melting metals (p. 283)

merger Combining competing firms in an industry into a single larger company; combining several companies or corporations into one larger firm (p. 208)

migration The movement of people from one country or region to another (p. 535)

militant A person who is aggressive in promoting a cause (p. 682)

military-industrial complex The vast, interwoven military establishment and arms industry (p. 583)

mission A Spanish settlement built to convert Native Americans to Christianity (p. 37)

missionary One who travels to many lands to convert people to Christianity (p. 220)

mobilization Preparation for war, including both military and civilian efforts (p. 315)

moratorium An official authorization to suspend payments, as of a debt; an officially authorized period of waiting (p. 454)

movement A theme referring to the flow of people, goods, ideas, and information from one place to another (p. 8)

muckraker A writer whose investigative articles or books attacked abuses such as child labor or corruption (p. 244)

mutual deterrence A theory that as long as accurate missiles capable of complete destruction target each other's countries, neither country will risk starting a nuclear war (p. 866)

N

national debt In the late 1700s, the amount of money owed to Americans and to other countries after the American Revolution; the total amount of money owed by the federal government (p. 113)

national liberation Freeing a nation from control by another nation (p. 769)

national market The nationwide economic system made possible by the transportation network in the United States (p. 206)

nationalist movement The activities of a group focused on freeing a nation from foreign influence and control (p. 801)

nationalization The process of changing a property or industry from private to government ownership; after World War II Iran's declaration that its oil fields, with their British-owned factories, were the property of the Iranian government (p. 590)

nativism A preference for native-born Americans over immigrants (p. 284)

negotiate To reach an agreement (p. 800)

neoconservatism The conservative philosophy of the Reagan presidency that opposed excessive bureaucracy, federal spending, and government intervention in people's private lives (p. 857)

neutral Not choosing a side in a conflict (p. 115)

neutrality The policy of remaining impartial in a dispute, including not taking sides in a war; the policy of remaining unallied (p. 306)

nomadic Wandering from place to place (p. 23)

nonviolent resistance The act of peacefully demonstrating for a change in policy without fighting authorities (p. 676)

nullification Before the Civil War, the right claimed by some states to reject, or render null and void, any federal law they believed violated the Constitution (p. 153)

O

oligopoly The control of an entire industry, such as meat packing, by a few major producers (p. 356)

P

pacification program A policy in which entire villages are uprooted and the people forced to move to cities or refugee camps (p. 775)

pacifism Opposition to the use of force (p. 40)

pardon To forgive; to pass over without punishment (p. 831)

penny auction Staged sale of property for pennies to friends, who simply returned the property later (p. 431)

perestroika A Russian word for restructuring; Soviet President Gorbachev's name for his economic policy, which favors less government intervention and more private initiative (p. 868)

perjury Lying under oath in a court of law (p. 910)

place A specific location (p. 8)

political machine A well-organized political organization that controls election results by awarding jobs and other favors in exchange for votes (p. 238)

pork barrel legislation Laws favoring projects of questionable necessity, bringing jobs and money into a legislator's district (p. 908)

pragmatist A person who is concerned with practical solutions to problems rather than with ideas and theories (p. 703)

presidio A Spanish settlement that served both as a trading center and as a garrison to defend Spanish territories (p. 37)

progressive A person who advocates reforms to confront the problems caused by industrialization and urbanization. (p. 243)

prohibition A ban on alcohol (p. 343)

propaganda A form of public information used to mold public opinion by employing techniques such as the use of emotionally charged language, name-calling, appeals to peer pressure, and the bandwagon approach (p. 317)

Q

quota A law limiting the number of immigrants (p. 401)

R

racism The idea that one race is superior to others, and that race determines a person's character or ability; prejudice and discrimination toward members of one racial group, usually a minority (p. 543)

radical Advocating political and social revolution (p. 338)

ratify To officially approve and accept (p. 81)

real income The amount of income earned, taking into account an increase in prices (p. 599)

realpolitik Practical politics; the view that a nation should pursue policies and make alliances based on its national interests (p. 817)

reapportionment A change in the number of legislative seats assigned to each state (p. 715)

recall A procedure that allows citizens to remove an elected official from office before the person's term officially ends (p. 253)

recession A period of declining productivity and reduced economic activity (p. 839)

referendum A process by which citizens vote directly for or against a political proposal or bill (p. 253)

region An area defined by one or more specific characteristics (p. 9)

regulatory commission A group whose responsibility it is to see that a company (or companies) is in compliance with existing laws (p. 275)

repatriation Return to a person's country of birth or citizenship (p. 433)

representation The right to be represented by delegates chosen in a free election; the election of officials who represent the views of a particular group (pp. 84, 735)

reservationists A group in the United States Congress who approved the idea of the League of Nations with reservations; they would support it if certain modifications were made to the proposal (p. 326)

resource management The scientific management of natural resources (p. 269)

revenue sharing A program through which the federal government returns some of its tax money to local governments (p. 810)

revivalism A religious movement that focused on individual religious experience rather than on church doctrine (p. 49)

revolution A violent effort to overthrow the government (p. 67)

right-to-work law Legislation outlawing union shops that require new workers to join (p. 633)

S

scientific management A management theory using efficiency experts to examine each work operation and find ways to minimize the time needed to complete it (p. 365)

scorched earth policy Policy of breaking the enemy's will by destroying food, shelter, and supplies (p. 178)

secede To withdraw formally from the Union (p. 153)

secession The act of officially withdrawing from a group (p. 172)

sectionalism A devotion to local interests over those of the larger group (p. 166)

sedentary Settled in one place (p. 23)

segregation The enforced separation of racial groups in schooling, housing, and other public areas (p. 668)

selectmen Elected officials in Puritan communities who decided such issues as taxes and land dispensation (p. 39)

self-determination The right of all people to decide what form of government they will live under (p. 305)

settlement house A neighborhood center providing educational and social services to needy people, established between 1889 and 1910 (p. 247)

sharecropping A system in which landowners provide farmers with land, seed, and supplies in exchange for a share in the crop (p. 189)

silent majority The great majority of Americans, whose opinions are not often heard (p. 809)

slave labor force A group of people enslaved by a master and made to work without pay (p. 85)

social gospel movement A movement emphasizing the application of Christian principles to social problems (p. 245)

socialism An economic theory advocating collective or government ownership of factories and other businesses instead of private ownership (p. 276)

soft money Donations of money to political parties that are to be used only for party-building activities, not political candidates (p. 910)

sonar technology Technology that detects submerged objects by means of sound waves (p. 511)

Southern strategy A plan designed to appeal directly to Southern white conservatives (p. 812)

speakeasy A club where liquor was sold in violation of the law (p. 398)

speculation A risky business venture involving buying or selling property in the hope of making a large, quick profit; making investments in the stock market (p. 419)

speculator A person who buys property, such as land or bonds, in the hope that its value will go up (p. 113)

spoils system An arrangement by which victorious parties or candidates reward their supporters with jobs, contracts, etc. (p. 152)

stagflation An unusual economic condition that combines a stagnant economy with rising prices (p. 837)

standard of living The material well-being of the individuals or groups in a society (p. 377)

status quo The current situation or condition (p. 73)

status symbol A possession thought to reflect a person's wealth, prestige, or superior position in society (p. 441)

stock A share in business ownership (p. 418)

strike An organized work stoppage used to force an employer to meet certain demands, such as for better wages, hours, and conditions (p. 215)

subsidy A government grant of money to an individual or company for a purpose thought to benefit society (p. 457)

suburb A community at the edge of a large city (p. 235)

suburbia The suburbs of a city; the suburban culture (p. 607)

suffrage The right to vote (p. 70)

supply-side economics A theory based on the belief that the key to economic vitality is reducing taxes—especially those on wealthy individuals and large corporations—and that lowering taxes would encourage saving and investment, which would lead to business expansion and more jobs (p. 858)

syndicate A chain of newspapers under central ownership; an agency that provides articles or features to a number of newspapers or magazines (p. 390)

T

tabloid A newspaper with small pages and large type (p. 390)

tariff A tax or fee on imported goods (p. 146)

temperance Moderation in, or total abstinence from, the use of alcoholic beverages (p. 155)

tenement A city apartment building, often a crowded, rundown rental apartment building in the slums (p. 235)

termination policy A policy to end the reservation system and terminate all federal services to Native American groups (p. 624)

territorial integrity A nation's right to protect its land and control its trade (p. 299)

textile Fabric, especially woven or knitted; cloth (p. 141)

totalitarian A government controlled by a single person or party; suppressing freedom and controlling every aspect of life (p. 494)

trade deficit A gap in value between a country's imports and exports caused by a country's buying more than it sells, thus creating an unfavorable balance of trade (p. 881)

transcontinental railroad A railway completed in 1869, connecting the eastern and western ends of the United States (p. 197)

treason Betrayal of one's government (p. 59)

trust A legal combination of companies brought together to gain control of an industry and reduce competition (p. 239)

turnpike A road on which travelers must pay tolls (p. 143)

unconditional surrender A surrender without any concessions (p. 509)

undocumented immigrant A person who lacks the legal papers necessary for residence in the United States (p. 735)

unemployment The condition of being out of work; the number of unemployed persons relative to the potential labor force (p. 421)

unfunded mandate A law that businesses or states must comply with, but for which Congress supplies no money (p. 907)

union A group of workers who are organized for the purpose of gaining better wages, hours, and other benefits (Also labor union or trade union) (p. 215)

unionization The organization of the workers in a particular industry into unions (p. 467)

union shop A shop in which new workers are required to join the union (p. 633)

universal coverage Health insurance for all (p. 895)

urbanization The growth of cities; the assumption of an urban way of life (p. 235)

V

vegetation The collection of plants that grow in a specific area (p. 14)

vertical integration The effort of a firm to reduce costs by controlling all aspects of production in an industry and eliminating payment of independent suppliers (p. 209)

vigilante A person who, without authority, dispenses justice (p. 647)

W

wage Daily pay (p. 142)

welfare capitalism Programs adopted by employers in order to convince workers that they did not need unions; for example, providing employees with doctors and nurses and organizing employee athletic teams (p. 358)

western passage A direct western route from Europe to Asia (p. 31)

whistle-stop tour Brief appearances by a political candidate in many communities, usually made from the rear platform of a train (p. 636)

white-collar worker A professional or office worker (p. 366)

women's liberation A movement by women to gain economic, legal, political, and social rights equal to those of men (p. 725)

working poor Members of the United States workforce with earnings too low for them to rise above poverty (p. 885)

Glosario

A

abolition/abolición Prohibición formal de la esclavitud

abolitionism/abolicionismo Movimiento que en el siglo XIX puso fin a la esclavitud en los Estados Unidos

accomodation/acomodación Política bajo la cual determinados afro-americanos aceptaron los resultados del racismo blanco para tener éxito económico

affirmative action/acción afirmativa Política de gobierno que les asigna trabajos, contratos gubernamentales, promociones, admisiones a escuelas, y otro beneficios a minorías y mujeres con el fin de enmendar discriminaciones pasadens

alliance/alianza Pacto o asociación de naciones unidas en una causa común

amendment/enmienda Un cambio o adición por escrito

amnesty/amnistía Ley por la cual el gobierno indulta a un gran grupo de individuos por los crímenes cometidos, generalmente en respuesta a las acciones de consuelo del grupo

anarchism/anarquismo Oposición a cualquier forma de gobierno; teoría de que todos los gobiernos deberían ser abolidos

annex/anexionar Añadir o adjuntar un territorio nuevo a un país ya existente

apartheid/apartheid Política oficial de segregación racial antiguamente en Suráfrica

appeasement/apaciguamiento Política de compromiso o aceptación de las exigencias de una nación hostil con la esperanza de mantener la paz

arbitration/arbitraje Método de arreglar una disputa comprometiéndose de antemano a aceptar la decisión de una persona imparcial

armistice/armisticio Acuerdo de poner fin a las hostilidades

arms race/carrera armamentista Competición entre los Estados Unidos y la Unión Soviética para poseer mayor poder militar

assimilation/asimilación Absorción de miembros de grupos minoritarios en la cultura principal de la sociedad de los Estados Unidos

B

baby boom/baby boom El rápido crecimiento inusual de la población durante el período de posguerra de la Segunda Guerra Mundial en los Estados Unidos, que duró hasta la mitad de los años 60

backlash/reacción Reacción fuerte y súbita contra una idea o política

balance of power/equilibrio de poder Condición en la cual los poderes más importantes son suficientemente iguales en fuerza para evitar cualquier agresión y mantener la seguridad de todos

bilingualism/bilingüismo Uso de dos lenguas; la habilidad de hablar dos lenguas con la misma fluidez

bipartisan coalition/coalición bipartita Grupo de republicanos y demócratas que trabajaban juntos en algunos asuntos

black codes/códigos negros Leyes adoptadas en el sur que restringían severamente los derechos de los negros recién liberados

black power/poder negro Movimiento afro-americano de los 60 cuya meta era trabajar para lograr objetivos económicos, políticos y sociales para los afro-americanos utilizando sus líderes y su organización, sin la ayuda de los blancos

black pride/orgullo negro Orgullo de ser afro-americano; orgullo de ser de ascendencia africana y de tener la nacionalidad americana

black separatism/separatismo negro Concepto, defendido por algunos afro-americanos de los Estados Unidos, que exige la seperación de las razas

blacklisting/poner en la lista negra Esfuerzos para tachar a ciertas personas de comunistas e impedir que realizaran determinados trabajos

blitz(krieg) Ataque intensivo, a menudo combinando las fuerzas aéreas y terrestres; del alemán blitzkrieg, o "guerra relámpago", los bombardeos alemanes sobre Inglaterra durante la Segunda Guerra Mundial

bolshevism/bolchevismo Ideología socialista radical; de Bolchevique, nombre del partido mayoritario de izquierdas liderado por Lenin durante la revolución rusa

bond/obligación Título que gana interés y que puede cobrarse en metálico en una fecha concreta

bootlegger/contrabandista de licores Persona que hacía, vendía o transportaba licor ilegalmente

boycott/boicot Un acuerdo organizado de no comprar o utilizar un determinado producto o de no relacionarse con una determinada compañía o nación para ejercer presión y que así se realicen cambios

brinksmanship/política de la cuerda floja Práctica para intentar mantener la paz entre las naciones dando a conocer que una nación nunca cederá y que está lista para cruzar el umbral de la guerra

C

cabinet/gabinete Cuerpo de personas nombradas por el presidente para dirigir los diferentes departamentos del gobierno y servir de consejeros al presidente

capital/capital Dinero acumulado u otra riqueza material que está destinada a la creación de más riqueza; riqueza material adquirida en los negocios por un individuo o por una compañía

capitalism/capitalismo Sistema económoico basado en la competición abierta en un mercado libre, en el cual los individuos y las compañías poseen los medios de producción y trabajan para obtener beneficios

carpetbaggers/politicastros Oportunistas del norte que fueron al sur y se aprovecharon de las condiciones allí inestables; se les apodó con el nombre despreciativo de politicastros por una especie de equipaje casero que llevaban

checks and balances/cheques y balances Sistema por el cual cada una de las tres ramas del gobierno impide que las otras ganen excesivo poder

civil desobedience/desobediencia civil Estrategia para provocar un cambio social mediante resistencia no violenta contra las leyes injustas

civil liberties/libertades civiles Libertad para disfrutar de los derechos que garantiza la constitución del estado o la nación

civil rights/derechos civiles Derechos políticos, económicos y sociales de un ciudadano; particularmente los que garantiza la Constitución de los Estados Unidos, como el derecho al voto y el derecho a la igualdad de trato ante la ley

climate/clima Conjunto específico de condiciones meteorológicas que caracterizan una zona

closed shop/closed shop Sistema en el cual a todos los trabajadores de una empresa se les pide que sean miembros del sindicato

coalition/coalición Alianza temporal (de naciones, partidos, por ejemplo) formada para una acción o propósito específicos

cold war/guerra fría El conflicto estadounidense-soviético que siguió a la Segunda Guerra Mundial en el cual las dos potencias evitaron el enfrentamiento militar, pero se opusieron mutuamente a sus intereses políticos y económicos

commune/comuna Un grupo de personas que viven en comuna, con posesión y uso colectivo de la sociedad, a menudo con objetivos, filosofías y estilos de vida compartidos

community policing/policía de la comunidad Método de patrullar de la policía que consiste en enviar patrullas a pie a los vecindarios y establecer unas relaciones mejores entre la policía y el público

compensation/compensación Dinero u otro bien que se ofrece a cambio de una pérdida

conglomerate/conglomerado Una compañía que tiene holdings en una diversidad de industrias que no están relacionadas entre sí

conquistadors/conquistadores Exploradores españoles que conquistaron las nuevas tierras que descubrieron

conscientious objector/objetor de conciencia Persona que se niega a hacer el servicio militar debido a principios morales o religiosos

conscription/reclutamiento Alistamiento obligatorio al servicio militar

concensus decision-making/toma de decisiones por consenso Un estilo administrativo como el del presidente Dwight Eisenhower, basado en el acuerdo general

conservative era/era conservadora Período de la política presidencial en el cual el papel del gobierno está limitado y los individuos dependen menos de la ayuda del gobierno

consumer price index/índice de precios al consumo Medida de cambio en el costo de los bienes y servicios en comparación con su costo en un período de tiempo fijo; también llamado índice del costo de la vida

containment/contención Después de la Segunda Guerra Mundial, la política de los Estados Unidos de asegurar la paz tratando de contener el comunismo, o impidiendo que se extendiera más allá de sus fronteras reales

corollary/corolario Una proposición que se añade a otra como una consecuencia o efecto natural, como el corolario de Teddy Roosevelt a la Doctrina de Monroe

corporation/corporación Grupo de individuos al que la ley autoriza a actuar como a una sola entidad; negocio que pertenece a muchos inversores

counter culture/contracultura Cultura de la gente joven con valores que se oponen a los valores de la cultura convencional

coup/golpe de estado Acto de hacerse con el poder y derrocar al gobierno

covert operation/operación secreta Misión secreta o clandestina del gobierno

coverture/cobertura Ley británica por la cual la propiedad heredada de una mujer pertenecía a su marido

credit/crédito Plan de pago demorado en el cual el comprador pone parte del dinero y paga el balance a plazos; tiempo permitido para pagar algo que se ha vendido a crédito

crime bill/proyecto de ley criminal Proyecto de ley que tiene disposiciones para destinar más policías en las calles, construir cárceles, incluir nuevas solicitudes para la pena de muerte y prohibir armas de ataque

cultural diffusion/difusión cultural Expansión de las costumbres, estilos de vida y otros productos del trabajo y pensamiento humano de un grupo cultural a otro

culture of poverty/cultura de la pobreza Después de la Segunda Guerra Mundial, las personas que pasaban hambre, las personas sin hogar y el gran número de miembros invisibles de una sociedad americana en general acaudalada

D

deferment/prórroga Aplazamiento de la incorporación de una persona al servicio militar por razones de salud u ocupación

deficit spending/gasto de déficit Política del gobierno de tomar dinero prestado para poder gastar más dinero del obtenido por los impuestos

demagogue/demagogo Líder que gana poder apelando a las emociones y prejuicios de la gente

demobilization/desmobilización Proceso de la posguerra de licenciar a las tropas del servicio militar para que los ciudadanos y los negocios vuelvan a sus tareas y objetivos propios de un período de paz

depression/depresión Período de una larga y severa decadencia en la economía de una nación, marcado por una baja producción y un alto índice de desempleo

deregulation/desregulación Acción de suprimir restricciones y reglas

détente/détente Intento de disminuir la tensión entre los Estados Unidos y las potencias comunistas durante la guerra fría

diplomacy/diplomacia Arte en la práctica de dirigir relaciones internacionales

direct primary/elecciones primarias Elecciones abiertas a todos los votantes de un partido, en unas elecciones primarias, son los votantes los que eligen a los candidatos y no los líderes del partido

disarmament/desarmamento Ley o política de reducción o destrucción de las armas militares

discretionary income/renta discrecional Dinero para comprar lo que se quiere además de lo que se necesita

discrimination/discriminación Negación de los derechos de una persona debido a su raza, religión, edad, sexo u otra cualidad

dissident/disidente Persona que no está de acuerdo con la política o creencias establecidas; antes de la presidencia de Gorbachev, ciudadano de la Unión Soviética que se manifestaba en contra de la política soviética

dogfight/combate aéreo Nombre que recibían los enfrentamientos entre aviones enemigos

dole/subsidio de paro Dinero o bienes dados en calidad de caridad; durante la Gran Depresión, pagos de beneficencia del gobierno; estar "acogido a la beneficencia" consistía en recibir estos pagos regularmente

domino theory/teoría del dominó Teoría según la cual tras la caída de un país en el comunismo, otros países a su vez también caerían, igual que los dominós

doughboys/doughboys Apodo con el que se conocía a los soldados de infantería de los Estados Unidos durante la Primera Guerra Mundial

dove/paloma Persona que apoya la retirada de las tropas de los Estados Unidos de la guerra y está a favor de la negociación para poner fin a la guerra

draft/destacamento Selección de personas para una particular misión obligatoria; sistema de selección de personas para servir militarmente

due process/proceso de reconocimiento Procedimientos legales que salvaguardan los derechos de un individuo

E

e-commerce/comercio electronico Empresas que cuyo negocio se opera por media de la web

egalitarian/igualitaria Cultura sin autoridades reconocidas, donde todas las personas se consideran iguales

electronic campaigning/campaña electrónica Estratégia de campaña política en la que un candidato intenta influenciar a los votantes mediante anuncios televisivos

electronic media/medios de comunicación electrónicos Formas de comunicación transmitida electrónicamente que llega a todo el público; radio y televisión principalmente

emancipation/emancipación Liberación de la esclavitud; en particular, liberación de la esclavitud de los afro-americanos

embargo/embargo Restricción o detención del comercio

emerging nation/nación emergente Países en vías de desarrollo de Asia, América Latina y África

emigrate/emigrar Dejar un país para establecerse en otro

enfranchisement/concesión de derechos políticos Obtención de los derechos de ciudadanía, especialmente el derecho al voto

entrepreneur/empresario Propietario de un pequeño negocio

eugenics/eugenesia Movimiento de principios del siglo XX para la mejora de la raza humana a través del control de los factores hereditarios mediante el emparejamiento

evangelist/evangelista Predicador fundamentalista

expansionism/expansionismo Política o proceso para incrementar el espacio físico de una nación adquiriendo nuevos territorios

extended family/familia ampliada Unidad familiar que incluye no sólo a los padres y a los hijos sino también a otros familiares, como abuelos, tíos y primos

external tax/impuesto exterior Impuesto exigido por los bienes que llegan a una zona, como el impuesto que impuso el Parlamento británico por el azúcar que llegaba a las colonias americanas

F

family leave/permiso familiar Permiso no pagado para ausentarse por el nacimiento o adopción de un hijo o por enfermedad de un miembro de la familia

fascism/fascismo Ideología altamente nacionalista cuyo nombre surgió para denominar al Partido fascista de Italia; gobierno caracterizado por el racismo y el militarismo; dictadura represiva de un solo partido

fascist/fascista Seguidor de una filosofía política que predicaba el nacionalismo y el racismo

federal regulation/regulación federal Control por parte del gobierno federal en vez de por parte de intereses privados

feminist/feminista Activista que trabaja para lograr derechos políticos, económicos y sociales para las mujeres iguales a los de los hombres

filibuster/obstruccionismo Táctica que consiste en dar largos discursos para demorar o impedir un voto para la creación de una ley

flapper/flapper Mujer característica de los años 20, por lo menos la que se promocionaba en la publicidad y en las películas; cuyo nombre hace referencia a los flecos de sus vestidos que giraban cuando se movían

flatboat/chalana Embarcación con el piso plano y los extremos cuadrados que se utilizaba para transportar bienes a lo largo de canales interiores a principios del siglo XIX

foreclosure/ejecución de una hipoteca Procedimiento legal para reclamar una parte de una propiedad cuando el comprador no puede mantener los pagos de la hipoteca

frontier/frontera Zona donde las tierras de los colonos establecidos hacían frontera con las tierras de los nativos americanos

fugitive/fugitivo Persona que escapó de la esclavitud y huía de la ley

fundamentalism/fundamentalismo Movimiento protestante en los Estados Unidos caracterizado por la creencia de que las palabras de la biblia fueron inspiradas por Dios y que por lo tanto deberían interpretarse literalmente y seguirse fielmente

G

generation gap/choque generacional Los diferentes valores, gustos y actitudes entre los miembros de grupos de diferentes edades, especialmente entre los adolescentes y sus padres

geography/geografía El estudio de la gente, lugares y entornos físicos

gerrymandering/división de los distritos electorales División de los distritos electorales de manera que aumente o disminuya la representación de un determinado grupo o partido

glasnost/glasnost Palabra rusa para denominar una política de apertura, empezó con el presidente Gorbachev, animando la libre expresión y poner fin a la censura de partido

global economy/economía global Sistema de comercio mundial

gospel tradition/tradición del gospel Tipo de música que combina las palabras de los himnos protestantes tradicionales con varios estilos de música africana

government boarding school/internado del gobierno Escuela en la que a los niños nativos americanos se les enseñaban las tradiciones culturales de los blancos

gross national product (GNP)/producto nacional bruto (PNB) El valor total de todos los bienes y servicios que se han producido en una nación en un año determinado

guerrilla warfare/guerra de guerrillas Lucha de bandas pequeñas e independientes, que utilizan tácticas como el sabotage y la emboscada

H

hard money/dinero fuerte Divisa consistente en monedas de oro o plata en oposición al papel moneda

hawk/halcón Persona que respalda el esfuerzo de la guerra

hippy/hippy Miembro de la contracultura

history/historia El estudio de los acontecimientos y de las personas a través del tiempo

holding company/holding Compañía que posee acciones predominantes del capital social en otras compañías

homestead/heredad Tierra concedida por el gobierno de los Estados Unidos a los colonos que allí vivieran y cultivaran durante cinco años, según la Ley de la heredad de 1862

horizontal integration/integración horizontal Fusión de compañías competitivas en una industria, como las de refinerías de petroleo, con la finalidad de dominar esa industria

human/environmental interaction/interacción ser humano/medio ambiente La interdependencia de las personas y el medio ambiente

human rights/derechos humanos Derechos y libertades básicas las cuales se asume que pertenecen a las personas de todos los lugares

I

immigrant/inmigrante Persona que entra en un país para vivir en él

impeachment/enjuiciamiento Cargos de mala conducta contra un funcionario público

imperialism/imperialismo Política que consiste en implantar un dominio económico, político y militar sobre naciones más debiles con motivos humanitarios y morales

impressment/requisición Práctica que consiste en forzar a la gente al servicio público, como los marineros americanos fueron forzados a sevir en los barcos británicos a finales del siglo XVIII

indentured servant/sirviente contratado Persona que aceptó trabajar por un número de años establecido a cambio de un pasaje para las colonias

indigenous/indígenas La gente que originariamente habita una zona; nativos

industrial productivity/productividad industrial Cantidad de bienes producidos en una hora de trabajo

industrialism/industrialismo El movimiento de la agricultura hacia la industria como la mayor fuente de crecimiento económico

industrialist/industrial Persona que se dedica a la producción comercial y a la venta de bienes y servicios

inflation/inflación Aumento agudo y continuo de los precios provocado por demasiado dinero y crédito relativo a los bienes disponibles

initiative/iniciativa Reforma que permitía a los ciudadanos introducir un decreto en una legislatura o evitar la legislatura y proponer una nueva ley por petición

injunction/requerimiento Una orden de la corte requiriendo que un individuo o una compañía haga algo, como terminar una huelga

internal tax/impuesto interior Impuesto exigido por los bienes que se producen y consumen dentro de una zona, como el impuesto del timbre fiscal impuesto por el Parlamento británico en las colonias americanas

interventionism/intervencionismo Política que consiste en intervenir, o interferir, en los asuntos de otra nación; en la Segunda Guerra Mundial la posición de aquellos que se oponían al aislacionismo y que creían que los Estados Unidos deberían ofrecer todo el apoyo posible a las fuerzas aliadas

irreconcilables/irreconciliables Durante la Primera Guerra Mundial un grupo de senadores que se opusieron a una Liga de Naciones y no pudieron reconciliarse para votar a su favor

isolationism/aislacionismo Evitar conflictos y alianzas con otras naciones; indiferencia a los asuntos que pasaban fuera de los Estados Unidos; a principios de la Segunda Guerra Mundial, política que consistía en no formar alianzas ni en ponerse de parte de nadie

K

kachina/kachina Muñeca sagrada de las gentes de Pueblo

L

land reform/reforma territorial Redistribución de propiedades a campesinos pobres sin tierras

legislature/legislatura Comité con poder para crear leyes

liberal era/era liberal Período en el que el gobierno promovió el progreso social

liberation theology/teología de liberación Filosofía de un movimiento de activistas cristianos que trabajaban a favor de la justicia social, especialmente en Latino América

limited war/guerra limitada Política que empezó con la era Truman y que consistía en evitar una guerra global confinando la lucha a una zona y utilizando armas covencionales, no poder nuclear

location/situación La posición sobre la superficie terrestre

lynching/linchamiento Una acción de la multitud en la que se ejecuta a una persona sin ser juzgada, generalmente en la horca

M

majority/mayoría Más del 50% de un grupo

mandate/mandato Una clara expresión de los deseos de los votantes, expresados en los resultados de las elecciones

margin/margen "Comprar al margen" significa que la casa de corretaje le presta dinero a alguien para comprar valores, si la bolsa sube, todos los beneficios (menos el interés que se cobra por el préstamo) son del comprador

martyr/mártir Persona que muere voluntariamente antes que renunciar a sus pricipios religiosos; persona que muere o que soporta un gran sufrimiento en defensa de una causa

mass media/medios de comunicación de masas Métodos mediante los cuales la información y el entretenimiento son transmitidos a un gran número de personas; incluyen periódicos, radio y televisión

massive retaliation/venganza masiva Política de la guerra fría de los Estados Unidos por la cual la agresión contra cualquier aliado se encontraría con una huelga nuclear incondicional

materialism/materialismo Dar más importancia al dinero y a los bienes materiales que a las cuestiones intelectuales, espirituales y artísticas

melting pot/crisol Sociedad en la cual un número de grupos raciales, étnicos y culturales se absorben y mezclan; de un recipiente que se utiliza para fundir metales

merger/fusión Conversión de compañías competitivas de una industria en una única compañía mayor; conversión de varias compañías o corporaciones en una compañía mayor

migration/migración Movimiento de gente de un país o región a otro

militant/militante Persona que es agresiva al promover una causa

military-industrial complex/complejo industrial militar El vasto y entrelazado establecimiento militar y la industria de las armas

mission/misión Colonia española construida para convertir al cristianismo a los nativos americanos

missionary/misionero Persona que viaja por muchos sitios para convertir a la gente al cristianismo

mobilization/mobilización Preparación para la guerra, incluyendo tanto esfuerzos militares como civiles

moratorium/moratoria Autorización oficial para suspender los pagos, como los de una deuda; un período de espera autorizado oficialmente

movement/movimiento Término que hace referencia al fluir de personas, bienes, ideas e información de un lugar a otro

muckraker/revelador de escándalos Escritor cuyos artículos de investigación o libros denunciaban abusos como el trabajo infantil o la corrupción

mutual deterrence/disuasión mútua Teoría que consiste en que siempre y cuando haya misiles precisos capaces de una destrucción total apuntando al otro país, ningún país se arriesgará a empezar una guerra nuclear

N

national debt/deuda nacional A finales del siglo XVII, la cantidad de dinero que se les debía a los americanos y a otros países después de la revolución americana; la cantidad total de dinero que se le debía al gobierno nacional

national liberation/liberación nacional Liberar a una nación del control de otra nación

national market/mercado nacional Sistema económico de dimensión nacional que es posible gracias a la red de transportes de los Estados Unidos

nationalist movement/movimiento nacionalista Las actividades de un grupo centradas en liberar a una nación de la influencia y control extranjero

nationalization/nacionalización El proceso de cambiar una propiedad o industria de un propietario privado al gobierno; después de la Segunda Guerra Mundial la declaración de Irán de que sus campos de petróleo, con sus fabricas pertenecientes a los británicos, eran propiedad del gobierno iraní

nativism/nativismo Preferencia de los americanos nativos por nacimiento sobre los inmigrantes

negotiate/negociar Llegar a un acuerdo

neoconservative/neoconservadora La filosofía conservadora de la presidencia Reagan que se oponía a la excesiva burocracia, al gasto federal y a la intervención del gobierno en la vida privada de las personas

neutral/neutral No estar de parte de nadie en un conflicto

neutrality/neutralidad Política que consistía en permanecer imparcial en una disputa, incluyendo el no ponerse de parte de nadie en una guerra; política de permanecer no aliado

nomadic/nómada Que va de un lugar a otro

nonviolent resistance/resistencia no violenta El acto de manifestarse pacíficamente para lograr un cambio en la política sin combatir a las autoridades

nullification/anulación Antes de la Guerra Civil, el derecho exigido por algunos estados para rechazar, o declarar nula cualquier ley federal que creían que violaba la Constitución

O

oligopoly/oligopolio El control de toda una industria, como la de envasado de carnes, por unos pocos productores importantes

P

pacification program/programa de pacificación Política bajo la cual pueblos enteros son desarraigados y se obliga a las personas a desplazarse hacia las ciudades o a campos de refugiados

pacifism/pacifismo Oposición al uso de la fuerza

pardon/perdón Perdonar; librarse del castigo

penny auction/subasta de penique Venta de propiedades que se realiza en un escenario para los amigos por tan solo unos peniques y que luego lo devuelven

perestroika/perestroika Palabra rusa que significa reestructura, nombre que denomina la política económica del presidente soviético Gorbachev, política que favorece una menor intervención del gobierno y una mayor iniciativa privada

perjury/perjurio Mintiendo bajo juramento ante un tribunal o corte

place/lugar Una posición específica

political machine/máquina política Una organización política bien organizada que controla los resultados electorales ofreciendo trabajos y otros favores a cambio de votos

porkbarrel legislation/legislación de fondos públicos Leyes que favorecen proyectos de cuestionable necesidad, creando empleos y proporcionando dinero en un distrito de un legislador

pragmatist/pragmático Persona interesada en las soluciones prácticas a los problemas en vez de resolverlos con ideas y teorías

presidio/presidio Poblado español que servía tanto de centro de comercio como para defender territorios españoles

progressive/progresista Persona que defiende las reformas para hacer frente a los problemas causados por la industrialización y la urbanización

prohibition/prohibición Prohibir el alcohol

propaganda/propaganda Una forma de información pública que se utiliza para crear en el público una opinión mediante la utilización de técnicas como el uso de un lenguaje con carga emocional, llamar por el nombre de pila, apelación a la presión de los semejantes y un enfoque de triunfo

Q

quota/cupo Ley que limita el número de inmigrantes

R

racism/racismo La idea de que una raza es superior a las otras, y que la raza determina el carácter y la habilidad de una persona; prejuicio y discriminación hacia los miembros de un grupo racial, generalmente una minoría

radical/radical A favor de la revolución política y social

ratify/ratificar Aceptar y aprobar oficialmente

real income/renta neta La cantidad de los ingresos profesionales, teniendo en cuenta el aumento de los precios

realpolitik/realpolitik Política práctica; la visión de que una nación debería perseguir políticas y hacer alianzas basadas en sus intereses nacionales

reapportionment/nueva repartición Cambio en el número de escaños legislativos asignados a cada estado

recall/revocación Procedimiento que permite a los ciudadanos retirar de su cargo a un funcionario elegido antes de que termine su período de mandato

recession/recesión Período de productividad en declive y de una actividad económica reducida

referendum/referéndum Proceso por el cual los ciudadanos votan directamente a favor o en contra de una propuesta política o decreto de ley

region/región Una zona caracterizada por una o más cualidades específicas

regulatory commision/comisión reguladora Grupo cuya responsabilidad es la de ver que una compañía (o compañías) cumple las leyes existentes

repatriation/repatriación Retorno de una persona a su país natal o de ciudadanía

representation/representación El derecho a ser representado por delegados escogidos en elecciones libres; la elección de funcionarios que representen las ideas de un partido en concreto

reservationists/reservacionistas Un grupo del congreso que aprobó la idea de la Liga de Naciones con reservas; apoyarían la idea si se hacían ciertas modificaciones a dicha propuesta

resource management/administración de recursos La administración científica de los recursos naturales

revenue sharing/reparto de impuestos Programa a través del cual el gobierno federal devuelve parte del dinero de los impuestos a los gobiernos locales

revivalism/evangelismo Movimiento religioso que se centra más en la experiencia religiosa individual que en la doctrina de la iglesia

revolution/revolución Un esfuerzo violento para derrocar al gobierno

right-to-work law/ley de derecho al trabajo Legislación que prohibía las union shops que requerían la unión de más trabajadores

S

scientific management/gestión científica Una teoría de gestión que utiliza expertos eficientes para examinar cada operación de trabajo y encontrar formas de minimizar el tiempo que se necesita para completarlo

scorched earth policy/táctica de bloqueo del avance enemigo Táctica que consiste en romper la voluntad del enemigo destruyéndole la comida, el refugio y las municiones

secede/separarse Retirarse formalmente de la Unión

secession/secesión Acto de retirarse oficialmente de un grupo

sectionalism/seccionalismo Devoción de los intereses locales sobre los del grupo mayor

sedentary/sedentario Asentado en un lugar

segregation/segregación La separación forzosa de los grupos raciales en las escuelas, los alojamientos y otros lugares públicos

selectmen/concejales Funcionarios elegidos en las comunidades puritanas que decidían sobre las cuestiones de impuestos y de reparto de tierras

self-determination/autodeterminación El derecho que tienen todas las personas a decidir la forma de gobierno bajo el cual les gustaría vivir

settlement house/centro social Un centro en el vecindario que facilita servicios sociales y educativos a la gente necesitada, establecido entre 1889 y 1910

sharecropping/aparcería Sistema por el cual los propietarios de tierras proporcionan tierras, semillas y maquinaria a los granjeros a cambio de un porcentaje de la cosecha

silent majority/mayoría silenciosa La gran mayoría de los americanos, cuyas opiniones no son a menudo escuchadas

slave labor force/mano de obra esclava Grupo de personas que pertenecen a un amo quien les hace trabajar sin cobrar

social gospel movement/movimiento social de gospel Movimiento que enfatiza la aplicación de los principios cristianos a los problemas sociales

socialism/socialismo Teoría económica que defiende la propiedad colectiva o gubernamental de las fábricas y otros negocios en vez de la propiedad privada

soft money/dinero blando Donativos de dinero a los partidos políticos exclusivamente para actividades que fortalecen el partido y no para candidatos políticos

sonar technology/tecnología sonar Tecnología que detecta objetos sumergidos mediante ondas sonoras

Southern strategy/estrategia sureña Plan diseñado para apelar directamente a los conservadores blancos del sur

speakeasy/despacho clandestino de bebidas Club donde se vende licor aun quebrantando la ley

speculation/especulación Aventura de negocios arriesgada que incluye la compra o venta de una propiedad con la esperanza de conseguir un gran beneficio rápidamente; invertir en la bolsa

speculator/especulador Persona que compra propiedades, como tierras o bonos, con la esperanza de que se incrementará su valor

spoils system/sistema de acaparamiento Acuerdo por el cual los partidos o candidatos victoriosos recompensan a sus seguidores con empleos, contratos, etc.

stagflation/inflación Condición económica inusual que combina una economía estancada con el aumento de los precios

standard of living/estilo de vida El bienestar material de los individuos o grupos de una sociedad

status quo/statu quo Estado de cosas en un determinado período

status symbol/símbolo de estatus La creencia de que las posesiones reflejaban la riqueza, prestigio o posición social superior de una persona en la sociedad

stocks/acciones Acciones de la propiedad del negocio

strike/huelga Paro organizado del trabajo que se utiliza para forzar al empleador a acceder a determinadas demandas, como mejores salarios, horarios y condiciones

subsidy/subsidio Dinero que concede el gobierno a un individuo o a una compañía con el propósito de beneficiar a la sociedad

suburb/suburbio Comunidad en las afueras de una gran ciudad

suburbia/suburbios Las afueras de una ciudad; la cultura suburbana

suffrage/sufragio Derecho al voto

supply-side economics/economía de supply-side Teoría basada en la creencia de que la clave de la vitalidad económica está en reducir los impuestos—especialmente los de los individuos ricos y las grandes compañías—y esta reducción de los impuestos animaría el ahorro y la inversión, lo cual llevaría a la expansión de los negocios y a la creación de más puestos de trabajo

syndicate/agencia de prensa Cadena de periódicos bajo dirección central; agencia que proporciona artículos o características a una serie de periódicos o revistas

T

tabloid/periódico sensacionalista Periódico de pequeñas páginas y grandes titulares—lectura ideal para los abarrotados y movedizos vagones del metro

tariff/tarifa Impuesto o cuota sobre los bienes importados

temperance/moderación Moderación, o abstinencia total, en el uso de bebidas alcohólicas

tenement/viviendas Edificio de apartamentos en la ciudad, a menudo un edificio de apartamentos poblados y de bajo alquiler en los barrios bajos

termination policy/política de terminación Política para poner fin al sistema de reserva y terminar con todos los servicios federales a los grupos de nativos americanos

territorial integrity/integridad territorial Protección de una nación de la violación de sus tierras y de sus derechos de comercio por otra nación

textile/industria textil Fábrica especialmente de prendas de lana y punto; telas

totalitarian/totalitario (Un gobierno) controlado por una sola persona o partido; que suprime la libertad y controla cada aspecto de la vida de las personas

trade deficit/déficit de comercio Un desequilibrio de los valores entre los bienes importados y exportados de un país debido a que dicho país ha comprado más de lo que ha vendido, creando así un balance desfavorable del comercio

transcontinental railroad/ferrocarril transcontinental Ferrocarril que se finalizó en 1869 y que unía los extremos este y oeste de los Estados Unidos

treason/traición Engaño del gobierno

trust/monopolio Combinación de compañías para ganar el control de una industria y reducir la competencia

turnpike/autovía Carretera en la que los conductores deben pagar peaje

U

unconditional surrender/rendición incondicional Rendición sin concesiones

undocumented immigrant/inmigrante indocumentado Persona que carece de los papeles legales necesarios para residir en los Estados Unidos

unemployment/desempleo La condición de estar sin trabajo; el número de personas desempleadas relativo al conjunto de trabajadores potenciales

unfunded mandate/mandato no remunerado Ley que los estados y los negocios deben acatar pero el congreso no proporciona dinero por ello

union/unión Grupo de trabajadores que están organizados con el propósito de ganar mejores salarios, horarios y otros beneficios (También sindicato)

unionization/sindicalización La organización de los trabajadores de una determinada industria dentro de los sindicatos

union shop/union shop Establecimiento que requería a sus nuevos trabajadores que se afiliaran al sindicato

universal coverage/cobertura universal Seguro sanitario que lo incluye todo

urbanization/urbanización El crecimiento de las ciudades; la pretensión de un estilo de vida urbano

V

vegetation/vegetación La colección de plantas que crecen en una zona específica

vertical integration/integración vertical El esfuerzo de una compañía para reducir costos mediante el control de todos los aspectos de producción de una industria y la eliminación del pago de proveedores independientes

vigilante/vigilante Persona que, sin autorización, administra justicia

W

wage/jornal Paga diaria

welfare capitalism/capitalismo benefactor Programas adoptados por los empleadores para convencer a los trabajadores de que no necesitan sindicatos; por ejemplo, proporcionando doctores y enfermeras a los empleados y organizando equipos de atletismo con los empleados

western passage/pasaje al oeste Una ruta directa hacia el oeste desde Europa hasta Asia

whistle-stop tour/gira por los apeaderos Breves apariciones de un cadidato político en muchas comunidades, generalmente en la plataforma trasera de un tren

white-collar worker/trabajador de cuello blanco Profesional o persona que trabaja en una oficina

women's liberation/liberación de la mujer Movimiento feminista para obtener los mismos derechos económicos, legales, políticos y sociales que los hombres

working poor/trabajo de pobres Miembros del cuerpo de trabajadores de los Estados Unidos cuyos salarios son demasiado bajos para permitirles salir de la pobreza

Index

Italicized page numbers refer to illustrations. Preceding the page number, abbreviations refer to a map (m), chart (c), photograph or other picture (p), graph (g), time line (t), cartoon (crt), or painting (ptg). Quoted material is referenced with the abbreviation (q) before the appropriate page number.

A

AAA. *See* Agricultural Adjustment Administration.
AARP. *See* American Association of Retired People.
ABC powers, 306
A&P. *See* Atlantic and Pacific Tea Company (A&P).
Abernathy, Ralph, 676, *p684*
***Abington* v. *Schempp,* (1963),** *c715*
abolitionism, 155–56, *t157,* 166; Brown, John, and, 162, *ptg163,* 171; Lincoln, Abraham, and, *q177*
abolitionists, 155–56, *p156, t157*
abolition of slavery, (Thirteenth Amendment 1865), *q104*
abortion, 727; Nixon court on, 731; Reagan and, 861
Abraham Lincoln Brigade, 494–95
Abzug, Bella, *p728,* 826
accommodation (policy of), 283
ACLU. *See* American Civil Liberties Union.
acquired immune deficiency syndrome (AIDS), 886, 921
activists, *c787,* 787–89
ADA. *See* Americans With Disabilities Act (ADA).
Adams, Abigail, *q71, q74, p74, q259*
Adams, John, *q60,* 67, 68, *q72, q914;* death of, 78; as President, *p72,* 112, 116
Adams, John Q., 151
Adams, Samuel, 58, 59, *p83,* 90
Adarand Constructors, 922, 923
***Adarand* v. *Pena* (1995),** 922–25
Addams, Jane, *q210, p242,* 242–43, 276; NAACP helped by, 283; unions supported by, 285
adjournment of congress, 93
advertising; in 1920s, 367, 381; department store use, 207; historians' view of, in political campaigns, 803, 877; after World War II, 600, 611, *p626;* during World War II, 526, 529
A.E.F. *See* American Expeditionary Force (A.E.F.).
advise and consent, congressional, *q98*
AFDC. *See* Aid to Families With Dependent Children.
affirmative action, 916–18
Afghanistan, invasion of, 840, *p840,* 841, 866
AFL. *See* American Federation of Labor.
Africa; human origins in, 16; President Clinton in, 910
African Americans; in 1990s, 916–18; affirmative action and, 916–18; Africa and, 678, 692; anti-slavery leaders, 155–56, *p156;* "Back to Africa" policy of, 342–43; and "black cabinet," 478; blues and, 371, 388–89; Bush and, 885; in Cabinet, 709; caste system for, 41; changes in polite term for, 692; Christian, 49–50; cities and, 236, 238, 247, 282, 341–343, 607, 622; Civilian Conservation Corps (CCC) and, 455–56, 479; as Civil War Soldiers, *p173,* 173–74, 176, 178–79; in Congress, *p188,* 189, 894, 899; in Continental Army, 54, 69, 75; as cowhands, *p197,* 198; crime and, 922; Daughters of the American Revolution (DAR) and, 476–77; Democratic party and, 478; in Detroit, 537, 622; discrimination and, 434, 542–46, 682; draft riots of Civil War and, 178; employment in World War II, 540–41, *c544,* 544; Eisenhower and, 509, 671, 672, 681; as "exodusters" to Kansas, 184; Fair Employment Practices Committee and, 544–46; feminism and, 724–25, 726; Fifteenth Amendment suffrage, (1870), *q105;* forced importation of, 34–35; free, 41, 54, 75; FERA and, 479; Ford Motor Company and, 342; free, in pre-Civil War South, 168; and Harlem Renaissance, 391–92; higher education and, 282; and home front during World War II, 534–36, 537, 540–41, 542–46, *m553;* jazz and, 388–89; illiteracy rate of, 283; immigrants and, 282; Kennedy, John F., and, *q681, 681–82, 684–86;* Kennedy, Robert, and, 680, 681, 682–84, 780, 781; Ku Klux Klan and, 399–401, 621–22; March on Washington Movement and, 543–44; Medal of Honor won by, 174; in middle class, 917, *c917;* migration from South of, *c341,* 341–43, 534–37, 540, *m553,* 622, 693, *q696;* military services and, 509, 544, 634, 789; music of, 166–67, 371, 388–389, 752–53; New Deal and, 478–79, 783; newspapers of, 180, 183, 543; Nixon and, 812–13; political parties and, 478; poll tax and, 479; population growth, 35, 49, 75; poverty among, 621–22, 885; during Progressive era, 281–83; as progressives, 247–48; Public Works Administration (PWA) and, 478; race riots involving. *See* race riots. Radical Republicans and, 186–87; during Reconstruction, 185, 186, 187, *p188,* 188–89, 190, 191; Republican, switching to Democratic party, 478; rhythm and blues (R&B), 752–53; rock music and, 752–53; Roosevelt, Eleanor, and, 478; Roosevelt, Franklin, and, 478–79, 538, 544; *Roots, q126–27;* segregation of. *See* segregation. slavery and: *See* slavery; slaves. Southern Alliance and, Southern Tenant Farmers' Union (STFU) and, *p465,* 466; in sports, 387–88, 585; street violence and, 920; as strike-breakers, 247, 341; suburbs and, 607; tenant farmers in Depression, 432–33; Truman and, 634–35, 637; unions and, 217; as Union soldiers, *p173,* 173–74, 176; and Vietnam War, 789; voting by, 186, *p186,* 187, *p188,* 189, 190, 282, 682, 689, *g689;* Woodrow Wilson and, 281; women, 894; in World War I, 315, *p315;* in World War II, *p509,* 509, 534–37, 540–41, 542–46, *m553. See also* civil rights; discrimination; minority groups; National Association for the Advancement of Colored People; racism.
African National Congress (ANC), 880–81
Africans; arts of, *p34;* culture of, 34, 49, *q126–27;* forced migration of, 34–35, 41, 49, 126–27
Afro-American Society, 791
Agee, James, 584
Agent Orange, *p774*
Agnew, Spiro, 813
agribusiness, 921
Agricultural Adjustment Act (1933), 481
Agricultural Adjustment Administration (AAA), 457, 465–66, 469, 470
Agricultural Marketing Act, 423–24. *See also* Farm Board.
Agricultural Workers Organizing Committee, 739
agriculture, 133, *m181;* domestication of plants and animals, 9, *t16,* 16–17; indigenous and imported, 33–34; vs. Industry, 213; Native American, 23, 25–26, 33–34; plantations, 33–34, 40–41, *m181;* technology and, 921. *See also* farms and farmers.
agriculture and industry (1860), *m181*
Aguinaldo, Emilio, 223, 292, 300
Aid to Families with Dependent Children (AFDC), 902, 907
AIDS. *See* acquired immunodeficiency syndrome (AIDS).
AIM. *See* American Indian Movement (AIM).
air conditioning and growth of Sunbelt, 815
airline industry; in 1930s, 484–85; deregulation of, 860, *crt860;* regulation of, 350
AJAX plan, 590
Alabama; civil rights in, 671, 686, 689. *See also* Anniston; Birmingham, Montgomery; Selma; grows as part of Sunbelt, 814, *m814*
Alabama, University of, 671, 686
Alamogordo (N. Mex.), 514, 518
Alaska; *p13; m23;* federal lands in, 843; gold in, 214, 221; Native Americans in, 744; as "Seward's folly," 221
Alaska Native Land Claims Settlement Act (1971), 744
Albert, Carl, 834
Albright, Madeleine, *p898*
Albuquerque (N. Mex.), 603
Alcatraz Island (Calif.), 744
alcohol, 257. *See also* Eighteenth Amendment; liquor; prohibition, temperance movement.
alcoholic beverages, prohibition of. *See* Prohibition.
Aldrin, Edwin ("Buzz"), 802, *p802*
Aleut, 29, 744
Alexandria (Egypt), 7
Algeria, 510
Algonquians, 26, *m26*
Alien Act (1798), 116
All-American Girls Baseball League, 554–55
Allen, Frederick Lewis, *q431*
Allende, Salvador, 821, *p821*
Alliance for Progress, 703
Allies; (World War I), *m307;* German war debts to, 350–51; Italy joins, 306–07; Triple Entente, 306; United States joins, 311; war debts of, to U.S., 350–51
***All Quiet on the Western Front* (Remarque),** *q309*
aluminum, 355
Alzheimer's Disease, 921
Amendments, Constitutional. *See* Constitution, United States.
America First. *See* Committee to Defend America First.
***America in the Twenties* (Perrett),** *q364*
American Alliance for Labor and Democracy, 318
American Anti-Slavery Society, 156, *t157*
American Civilization in the First Machine Age: 1890–1940, *q355*
American Civil Liberties Union (ACLU), 396
American Expeditionary Force (A.E.F.), 316, *p316*
American Federation of Labor (AFL), 216, 217, 286, 318; Boston police strike and, 341; membership, 216, 318, *c467*
***American Gothic* (Wood),** *ptg445*
American Independent Party, 782–83, *m783*
American Indian Defense Association, 480
American Indian Movement (AIM), 743, 744, *p758*
American Indians. *See* Native Americans.
American Liberty League, 469
American Medical Association, 345, 895
American Plan, 357–58
American Railway Union, 216–17
American Revolution; African Americans in, 54, *p55,* 75; American advantages in, 67, 68–69, *g69;* battles of, 60, 64, *m67, t68,* 69, *m77;* British strategy, 60, 68; causes of, 56,

57, 58–60, *t59;* end of, 68; women in, 70, *ptg 70,* 71, 74, *ptg 76*
Americans; in 1800s, 150–56; of colonial America, 36–41, 86–87, *p110–11;* earliest, 22–23, 31
***American Spirit, The* (Beveridge)**, *q295, q317*
American System, Clay's, 146–47
Americans Remember the Home Front, *q600*
American Tapestry, *q346, q347, q358*
American Telephone and Telegraph (AT&T), 365
American Tobacco Company, 273
Anaheim (Calif.), 400
anarchism, 339
Anasazi, 23–24, *p24*
ANC. *See* African National Congress (ANC).
Anderson, Marian, *p476,* 476–77
Andersonville (Ga.), 179
Andrews, Maxine, *q524*
Andrus, Cecil, 843
Angelus Temple, 397
Anglo-Persian Oil Company, 590
animals; imported species, 33, *ptg33,* 36, 122
Annapolis (U.S. Naval Academy), 730
Anniston (Ala.), 682
Antarctica, 879
Anthony, Susan B., 261, 725
anthracite coal strike, 271–72, *q272*
antibiotics, 550, 611
anticommunism; in 1950s, 631, 640–47, *t643*
Antietam, Battle of, 175, *m175*
Anti-Federalists, 80; constitutional views of, 88–90, *c89*
Antisaloon League, 343
antitrust laws; Harding and Coolidge and, 358; New Deal and, 456; Sherman Act and Roosevelt, Theodore, 269–71; Taft and, 273; World War II and, 539
Anzio beach (Italy), 510
apartment buildings, 24
Apollo program, 703
Appalachia; poverty in, 621, *c621*
Appalachian Mountains, *m12,* 14, *m131,* 132, 138; transport over, *p122–23*
Appalachian whites, 619, 620
appeasement, 496
Appomattox Court House, 179, 182
Aquideck (R.I.), 44
Arabs; oil embargo by, 819; in Persian Gulf War, 878; Soviet Union and, 819
Arawaks, 30
arbitration, 271, 272
archaeology, *q24*
architecture; moundbuilder, 24–25, *p25*
Arctic; Native American cultural area, *m28,* 29
Ardennes Forest (Belgium), 511
Area Redevelopment Act, 703
Aristide, Jean-Bertrand, 873, 898
Arizona, 34; as part of Sunbelt, *m814,* 814–15
Arkansas, civil rights in, 666, *p667,* 671–72, *p672;* Clinton and, 892, growth as part of Sunbelt, *m814,* 814; school reform and, 921
Armey, Richard, 900
Armistead, James ("James Lafayette"), 54, *p55*
Armistead, William, 54
Armour, 209
arms control, 818, 840
arms race; Bush and, 867; Carter and, 840–41; Eisenhower and, 579–80, *g581, t581,* 582; Kennedy and, 593; Nixon and, 818; Reagan and, 866–67; Truman and, 573. *See also* disarmament; nuclear weapons.
arms, right to bear, *q102*
Armstrong, Louis, *p389*
Armstrong, Neil, 802
Army, the Continental. *See* Continental Army.
Army, United States, *q95;* in the Constitution, *q95, q98, q102;* quartering the, *q102;* the standing, *q95*
Arneson, R. Gordon, *q517*
Arthur, Chester A., 194
Arthurdale (W. Va.), 450
Articles of Confederation (1781); flaws in, 82–83, *c89;* ratification of, 81–82, *t90*
Articles of the Constitution (1788), *q91–101. See also* Constitution, United States.
artists, 469
***Artists on WPA* (Sayer)**, *ptg469*
arts; African, 34, *p34;* folkart, p110; pre-columbian, 25
arts, federal funding for, 902
Aryans, 494
Ashdown, William, 380
Asia; cold war in, 571–75; foreign expansion into, *m299;* immigrants from, 298, 918; Japan and, 496–497, *m505;* trade route to, 30–31, 221; trade with, 220
Asian Americans; in Congress, 872, 894; feminism and, 726. *See also* specific individuals and Chinese Americans; Japanese Americans; Korean Americans.
assasination. *See* succession, presidential.
assembly, freedom of (1791), *q101*
assembly line, 355, 362–65
assimilation, 737, 743
Astaire, Fred, *p443*
astrolabe, *p8*
astronomy, 31
AT&T. *See* American Telephone and Telegraph (AT&T).
Atlanta (Ga.), 622, 681, 876, 920
Atlantic and Pacific Tea Co. (A&P), 357, 381
Atlantic Charter, 504
Atlantic Ocean; Europeans crossing the, 30–35, *m31;* ships seized in, 117
Atlantic Seaboard, 37, 38–40, 47, *m48*
Atlantis, 916
atomic bomb, 514–15, 516–19. *See also* nuclear weapons.
Atomic Energy Act (1954), 654
Austin, Richard, 343
Austin (Tex.), 433
Austria-Hungary, 306, 309, 316, *c316,* 323, 325
Austria, *m494,* 496, 564
Autobiography of Malcolm X, *q691*
automobiles and auto industry; in 1920s, 355, 360–61, *t360–61,* 378–80, *g379,* 384–85; in 1930s, 441–42; in 1950s, 599, 602–03, 606, 607, 660–61; air pollution and, 910; Bush and, 883; Corvette, 660–61; factory closings in Northeast and Midwest, 815; foreign cars' market share, 838, 883; Model A, 380; Model T, 361, 378, 379; oil embargo and, 838; Packard Roadster, *p360;* public services and, 361; Reagan and, 859, 860; technical developments, *t360–61;* tourism and, 378–80, 385; Volkswagen Beetle, 361; women's movement and, 383; after World War II, 599
Awakeners, 49–50
AWARE, 647
Axis Powers, 495, 504, 515
Ayatollah Khomeini. *See* Khomeini, Ruholla.
Ayres, Agnes, *p387*
Aztec, 32, *p32*

B

***Babbitt* (Lewis)**, *q376,* 391
***Baby and Child Care* (Spock)**, *q612*
baby boomers, 609–12; as Vietnam War protesters, *c787,* 787–89
"Back to Africa" policy, 342–43
Bacon, Nathaniel, 47–48
Bacon's Rebellion (1676), 47–48
Baer, George, 271–72, *q272*
Baez, Joan, *p753,* 786
Baghdad (Iraq), 878
Bahamas, 30
Bail and Punishment (1791), *q103*
Baker, Howard, 829
Baker, James, 871, 878, 881
Baker, Kenneth and Laura, 598–99
Baker, Newton D., 315
***Baker* v. *Carr* (1962)**, 715, *c715, m721*
Baklanov, Grigori, *q515*
balanced budget amendment, 909
balance of trade, 883
Balboa, Vasquo Núñez de, *m31*
Baldwin, James, *q622, q678*
Balkans, 897, *m897*
Ball, Lucille, 617, *p617*
Baltimore (Md.), 144
Baltimore and Ohio Railroad (B & O), 145
Bangladesh, 572
banishment, 44–45
banking system; in 1920s, 356; automobiles and, 380; Coughlin, Father Charles E., and, 467; crisis of, in 1930s, 454–55; deregulation of, and crisis, 884, *p884;* failures 1880–1915, *c279;* Federal Reserve System and, 278–79; Latin American debts and, 819–20; moratorium on, 454–55; New Deal and, 458; during Reconstruction, 190; Wilson, Woodrow, and, 278–79
Bank of Manhattan, 356
Bank of the United States; First, 114; Second, 146, 152–53
bankruptcy, 208
Baptists, 675
Bard, Ralph A., *q517*
Barents, William, 8
Barge Canal System (N.Y.), 149
Barnum, Phineas T., 182, 203, *p203*
Barrios, 618–19
Bart, Phil, *q358*
Barton, Bruce, 353–54, 367
baseball, 387, 388, 506, 554–55
Batista, Fulgencio, 591
Baton Rogue (La.), 176
Battle of Fallen Timbers, 134
Bausch and Lomb, 358
Baxter Street Court (Riis), *p234*
Bay of Pigs (Cuba), 592
Beals, Jessie Tarbox, *p237*
Beard, Charles, 243
Beard, Mary Ritter, 243
Beatles, 753, 756, *p756*
***Beat the Whites with the Red Wedge* (Lissitsky)**, *ptg322*
Begin, Menachem, *p841,* 841–42
Behrent, John, 65
Beiderbecke, Bix, 389
Beijing (China), 573, 879
Belgian Relief Committee, 350
Belgium, 306, 501, 511
Belk, Bill, 856
Belknap, William W., 190
Bell, Alexander Graham, *t205,* 206, 462
Bell, Fred, *p433*
Benin kingdom, 34, *p34*
Benton, Thomas Hart, 445, *ptg461*
Berkeley (University of California at), 786–87
Berlin (Germany); airlift, 569–71, *p569, p570;* wall, 703, 868, 874, *p874;* after World War II, 566; in World War II, 513, 515
Bernheim, Emily S., *q405*
Bernstein, Carl, 826, *q827*
Bernstein, Dorothe, *q435*
Berry, Chuck, 752–53
Bessemer converter, 204
Bessie, Alvah, 648
Best Years of Our Lives, The, *q630–31*
Bethlehem Steel, 359
Bethune, Mary McLeod, *p478,* 479
Beveridge, Albert J., 294, *q294, q295, t299, q300*

Bezos, Jeff, *p908*
Biberman, Herbert, 648
Bible, colonial America and, 42–45, 46; evolution vs., 396–97; schools and, 716
Biddle, Tony, 490
big band era, 532–33
big business; in 1920s, 354–59, 362–68; Harding–Coolidge administrations and, 349–50; Hoover and, 350; during Progressive era, 243; Roosevelt, Theodore, and, 269–71, 277; Taft and, 273; in World War I, 317–18; after World War II, 601–02
Big Four, 324
Big Stick philosophy, 352
Big Three, 564
bilingualism, 737
Bill of Rights (1791), *q101–103;* debate over, c89, 90; need for, 90; ratification of, *t90*; Virginia State, 73. *See also* Constitution, United States.
Bingham, George Caleb, *ptg37*
Bird, Caroline, 434
Birmingham (Ala.), *p410, p684,* 684–85, 691
bison, *p22*
Black, Hugo, *p714,* 716
black Americans. *See* African Americans.
black cabinet, 478
Black Caucus, 896
black codes, 185
Blackfeet, 28
blacklisting, 357, 647, 651
"Black Man Talks of Reaping, A" (Bontemps), 392
Blackmun, Harry, 813
Black Muslims, 343, 692
Black Panther party, 694, *p694,* 811, *p811*
black power, 693
black pride, 691–92
black separatism, 691, 692
blacksmiths, *p73*
Black Star Line, 343
"Black Tuesday," *ptg420, p428*
Blake, James, 674
"Bleeding Kansas," 162, 171
blind, care for, 155
blitz, 501–02
blitzkrieg, 496, 510
blockade runners, 176
blood plasma, 550, 551
"Blowin' in the Wind" (Dylan), *q748*
blue-collar workers, 365–66
Blue Lake (N. Mex.), 742–43, 745
blues, the, 388–89
blue stars on flags, 528
Bly, Nellie, 288, *p288*
B&O. *See* Baltimore and Ohio Railroad (B&O).
Boardman, Barrington, *q514*
Bogart, Humphrey, 507, 651
Bolick, Clint, *q925*
Bolsheviks, and Red Scare in United States, 340, 406. *See also* Russian Revolution.
bombings; in Chicago, 216; in New York, 341; in Oklahoma City, 919
Bonaparte, Napoleon, 131–32
bonds, federal government, *q94,* 113–14
bonds, government. *See* government bonds.
Bonnin, Gertrude, 480
Bontemps, Arna, *q392*
bonus army, *p426,* 426–27, 456
"Boogie Woogie Bugle Boy of Company B" (Price and Raye), *q526*
***Book of Daniel, The* (Doctorow),** *q558–59*
Book-of-the-Month Club, 390
books; in 1880s, 241; in 1920s, 389, 395; in 1930s, 440–41, 444–45
boom towns, during World War II, 536, 540–41
Boone, Daniel, *p65,* 130–31
Booth, John Wilkes, 180
bootleggers, 398–99
Borah, William, 325
Border Patrol, 406, *p406*
Bork, Robert, 829
***Born on the Fourth of July* (Kovic),** *q764–65*
Bosnia-Herzegovina, 897–98, *m897*
Boston (Mass.), 49, *t68*; Boston Massacre, *p59, t59*; Boston Tea Party, 59, 60; harbor, *t59,* 60; Hutchinson trial in, 42–45; Sugar Act protests, 57; Red Scare in, 340, 341; subway in, 235
Boston Harbor, *t59,* 59, 60
Boston Massacre, *t59, p59,* 59, 60
Boston Police Strike, 341
Boston Tea Party, 59
Boston University, 676
Boudinot, Elias, 139
Bourke-White, Margaret, *p424*
Boutros-Ghali, Boutros, *q868*
Bow, Clara, *p395*
Boxer Rebellion, 298
boxing, 387, 388
boycotts; of British goods, 59; civil rights and, 674–76, 678; embargo, 117, 141; grape, 733, 737, 738–41; Montgomery bus, 674–76; Supreme Court and, *t358,* 358; of tea ("Boston Tea Party"), 59, 60; by unions, 216
Boyle, Ralph ("Buzz"), 554
***bracero* program,** 407, 623, 735
Brady, James, 896
Brady Act, 896
branches of government. *See* checks and balances; Constitution, United States.
Brandeis, Louis, *p255,* 255–56
Brant, Joseph, *p46*
Braun, Carol Mosely, 894
Brazil, 820
Brezhnev, Leonid, *p818,* 818, 840
Briand, Aristide, 351
Bridgeport (Conn.), 920
brinkmanship, 579
Britain, Battle of, 501–02
Brooke, R.N., *ptg191*
Brooklyn Bridge, 194, *p195*
Brooks, Jack, 833
Brooks, John, *q619*
Brooks, Preston, 171, *crt171*
"Brother, Can You Spare a Dime?" (Harburg), *q424–25*
Brotherhood of Sleeping Car Porters, 544
Brown, John, 162, *ptg163,* 171
Brown, Linda, 670
Brown, Pat, 826
Brown University, 244
***Brown* v. *Board of Education* (1954),** 670–71
Bryan, William Jennings, 214, 309–10, *p396,* 396, 397
Buckland, William, *p41*
Buck, Pearl, 497
Budapest, 582
budget, balanced, 906, 911
budget deficit, *g839, g859,* 860–61
Buena Vista, *p169*
buffalo; Native American uses of, 28, *p29*
Buffalo (N.Y.), 266, 433
Bulganin, Nikolai, 581
Bulgaria, 316, 564
Bulge, Battle of the, 511
Bullitt, Bill, 490
Bull Moose party, 276–78, *crt277, m277*
Bull Run, First Battle of, 174, *m175*
bulrush house, *m28*
Bunche, Ralph, *q691*
Bundy, McGeorge, 772
Bureau of Corporations, 349
Bureau of Indian Affairs, 743, 744, 746
Bureau of Investigation, 340. *See also* Federal Bureau of Investigation (FBI).
Bureau of Standards, 350
Burger, Warren, 813, *c827, p827*
Burgess-Norton Company, 317
burial sites; moundbuilder, 24–25, *p25*
Burlington Railroad, 270
Burma, 513
Burr, Aaron, 103, *p116*
Busch, Irma, *q407*
Bush, George, 877, *q877;* arms limitations and, 867–68; China and, 879–80; Clinton vs., 892–93, *m893;* Cuba and, 873; Dukakis vs., 877, *p877;* economy and, 882–85, *crt883;* education and, 923; environment and, 903; Persian Gulf War and, *p878,* 878–79; post-cold war problems and, 877–78; Reagan and, 876, 877; Soviet Union and, 867–68; taxes and, 883
Bush, George W., 890–91, 912
Bush, Jeb, 918
business; in late 1800s, 208–09, 214; in 1920s, 349, 354–59, 362–68; in 1990s, 882–83; automobiles and, 379; cycles of, 1920–45, *g549;* during Great Depression, 424, 434–35; Hoover, Herbert, and, 350; managerial revolutions in, 208, 357; mass production in, 362–65; during Progressive era, 243; Reagan and, 857; Second New Deal and, 469–70; Taft, William Howard, and, 273; TVA and, 457–58; Whigs and, 153; white-collar workers in, 365–66; Wilson, Woodrow, and, 278–79; World War I and, 309, 310–11, 317–18; after World War II, 599, 601–02. *See also* big business; industry.
business administration, schools of, *p357*
business associations, *p357*
busing, school, 812–13
Butler, "Duckboards," *p408*
Butler Act, 396, 397
Butterfield, Alexander, *c827, p827,* 828–29
Byrnes, James F., 518

C

Cabeza de Vaca, Alvar Núñez, *q2–3,* 6
cabinet, the President's, 113
cable cars, 235
cable television, 859–60
Cabot, John (Giovanni Cabato), *m31*
Cahokia, settlement, 25
Calhoun, John C., 153, 169
California, *m28*; affirmative action and, 918; agriculture in, 198; anti-Chinese agitation in, 217, 405; Com-promise of 1850 and, 169–70; and grape boycott, 722, *p723,* 733, 736–37, 738–41, *p740;* illegal aliens and, 916; Japanese immigration to, 301; Ku Klux Klan in, 400; Mexico and, 169, 219; migration to, *m431,* 431–32; primary in 1968, 780; southern, as part of Sunbelt, *m814,* 814–15; Spanish, 37; after World War II, 600, 603, 610; during World War II and, 535, 540–41. *See also* Japanese Americans.
California Civil Rights Initiative (CCRI), 918
Calley, William, 792–93
Cambodia, 769, *m769,* 770, 773, 774, 793, 798–99, 800, 825, 879
Camelot, 706
camera. *See* photography.
Campbell, Ben Nighthorse, 894
Camp David (Md), 98
Camp David Accord, *p841,* 841–42
Camp meeting, 150, 153
Canada, *m31,* 48, *m161*; NAFTA and, 896; Newfoundland, 31, 37–38; Seven Years' War (French and Indian War) and, *m48,* 48–49; trade with, 881–82
canals, 128, *p129, p144,* 144–45, 149, 206
Cane Ridge (Ky.), 150, 153
Cantigny, 316
Capa, Robert, 489

Capone, Al, 399, *p399*
caravel, Portuguese, 31, *p31*
Caputo, Philip, *q773, q774*
Caribbean Sea, *m297*; in 1980s, *m872;* Seward and, 220–21; U.S. intervention in, *t297. See also* Bahamas; Cuba; Grenada; Haiti; Jamaica; Purerto Rico; Virgin Islands.
Carliss, George, 158
Carmichael, Stokely, *p690*, 690–91, 692–93
Carnegie, Andrew, *p204*, 204–05, *q205*, 209
Carnegie Endowment for International Peace, 642
Carnegie Steel Company, 216
Carolinas, 40–41. *See also* North Carolina; South Carolina.
Carpetbaggers, 190
Carranza, Venustiano, 306
Carswell, G. Harrold, 813
Carter, Jimmy, 840, *q840*, 893, administration of, 839–43, *t841;* Camp David Accord and, 841–42; economy and, 839; human rights and, 839–42; Iranian hostage crisis and, 842; Latin America and, 841
Cartier, Jacques, *m31*, 37
Casablanca Conference, 509
Cassino Pass, 510
caste system, racial, 41
Castro, Fidel, 591–93, *p593, p594*, 873
Catholicism; conversion to, 32
Catholics; Hispanic Americans as, 734; immigration by, 236, 284, *c284;* Kennedy as, 655, 656, 702–03; nominated for President, 402, 655, 656; and Sheen, Fulton J., 609; voting by, 403. *See also* Roman Catholic Church.
Catt, Carrie Chapman, 344, *p345*
cattle ranching, *p197*, 197–98
Cayuga, 26
CCC. *See* Civilian Conservation Corps (CCC).
census, 49, 143, 920
Central America; in 1980s, *m872;* Bush and Panama, 881; Hispanic Americans and, 734, 735; Native Americans in, 23, 32, 37; Reagan and, 870–73, *m872;* Wilson, Woodrow, and, 305–06. *See also* Caribbean; Latin America and names of specific countries.
Central Intelligence Agency (CIA), 588–590, 591–92, *m589;* Central America and, 871–72; Chile and, 821; domestic spying by, 794, 826, 833
Central Pacific Railroad, 199, *p199*
Central Powers, 306, *m307;* colonies of, 324–25
Chaco Canyon (N. Mex), 23–24
Chafee, Zechariah, Jr., 319
Chain, Ernst, 551
chain stores, 207, *p207*, 356, 357, 381
Chamberlain, Neville, *p496*, 496
Chambers, Whittaker, 642–43
Chaplin, Charlie, *p370*
Chaplin, Ralph, *q287*
Charbonneau, Toussaint, 132
charity; of Carnegie, Andrew, 204–05; in late 1800s, 210
Charles II of England, 40
Charles River (Mass.), 141
Charleston, Oscar, 387, *p388*
Charleston (S.C.); attack on Fort Sumter, 173; slave revolt in, 168
Charleston (the dance), 389
Chase, Salmon P., 188
Château-Thierry, 316
Chávez, César, 722, *p723*, 733, 736–37, *q737*, 739, *p739, q739*, 740, *p740*, 741
Chavez Ravine Naval Base, 537
"Checkers" speech, 653, *p653, q653*
checks and balances, federal government, 84–*c85. See also* Constitution, United States.
Cheever, John, *q612*
Cherokee, 48; alphabet, 135; Constitution of 1827, *q119*, 135; "Trail of Tears" and, *m135*, 136–39; treaty of 1775, 65
Cherokee County Central Labor Body, 460
Cherokee Phoenix, The, 135, 139
Chesapeake, 117
Chesapeake Bay (Va.), 176; battle at, 54, 68
Chevron, 884
Cheyenne, *p29*
Chiang Kai-shek (Jiang Jieshi), 497, 572–573
Chicago (Ill.), 149; in 1889, 230–31; Addams, Jane, of, *q210, p242*, 242–43; African Americans in, 341, 342, 622; blues and, 389; and Capone, Al, 399; Democrat convention of 1968 in, 781, *p781;* in Depression, 433; Haymarket riot in, 216; livestock market and meat packing in, 206; race riots in, 780; radioactive rain in, 582; during Reconstruction, 190; skyscrapers in, 356; South Side of, 389; stockyards, 244–45, *p245;* strike violence in, 216, 217
Chicago and Alton Railroad, 359
Chicago Defender, 342
***Chicago Tribune*, "Dewey Defeats Truman" headline in**, 636, *p636*
child care, 242, 538, 540, 917
child labor, *p233;* and children's march, 232; immigrants and, 285; Kelley, Horace and, 246–47; migrant farmworkers and, 623; Roosevelt, Eleanor, and, 460; Wilson, Woodrow, and, 279; during World War II, 538
Child Labor Act (1916), 345
children; in 1950s, 609–12, 620; in Civil War, *p192;* day care for, 242, 540; during Great Depression, 434, 435, 436; Hoover, Herbert, and, 350; of migrant farmers, 623; poverty among, 620, 885; during Progressive era, 242–43, 256–57; welfare reform proposals and, 902; during World War II, 538–39. *See also* child labor; education.
Children's Bureau, 273
Chile, 23, 820, 821
China; Carter and, 841; Communist party, 572–73, *t573;* democracy movement in, *p879*, 879–80; Hay and Open Door policy in, 299; immigrants from, 199, 217, 284, 298; Japanese and, 572–73; Johnson, Lyndon, and "loss of," 772; Korea and, 574–75; Nationalist party, 572, *t573;* Nixon and, 816, 817–18; People's Republic of, 573, 817–18; Polo, Marco and, 4; Taiwan and, 573, 817; trade with, 220, 298–99, *t299;* Treaty of Versailles and, 325; Truman and, 573, 637; United Nations and, 818; Vietnam and, 770, 771, 772; World War II and, 497, 572–73
China Incident, 497
Chinese Americans; discrimination against, 198, 217, 298; immigration laws and, 217, 284, 405, 852–53; in World War II, 540
Chinese Exclusion Act (1882), 217, 284, 405
Choctaw, 25, 48
Christianity; in 1950s, 608–09; among African Americans, 49–50; born-again, 857; of Cherokee, 135; China and, 298, *p298*; civil rights movement and, 674, 675, 676–77, 678, 686; of colonists, 32–33, 36–37, 42–45; conversion to, 20, 32, 33, 38, 47, 49–50, 135; European explorers and, 49–50; evangelical, 857; expansionism and, 220; and King, Martin Luther, Jr., 695; liberation theology in, *p820*, 820–21; Moral Majority and, 857; of Native Americans, 135; Philippines and, 223; and Second Great Awakening, 153–54; social gospel movement in, 245. *See also* Bible; missionaries; religion.
***Christianity and the Social Crisis* (Rauschenbusch)**, 245
Christian Voice, 857
Chrysler, Walter, 354
Chrysler Building, 356
churches, in 1950s, 608–09; civil rights and, 674, 675, 676, 678, 684, 685, 686, 695; in colonial America, 42–45; membership, 608–09; mill workers required to attend, 142. *See also* Christianity; religion.
Churchill, Winston; on appeasement, *q496;* on D-Day, *q510;* on Dulles, *q578–79;* on Hitler, *q503;* on "iron curtain," *q566–67, p567*, 865; on law enforcement, *q717;* on Royal Air Force, *q501;* Potsdam meeting and, 566; Roosevelt, Franklin, and, 504, 509, 527; Soviet Union and, *q503;* at Yalta, *p564*
CIA. *See* Central Intelligence Agency.
CIO. *See* Congress of Industrial Organizations.
***Cimarron* (Ferber)**, *q196*
circuit riders, 153
cities; in 1920s, 355–56, 399, 402–03; in 1950s, 618–20, 622; African Americans in, 236, 238, 247, 282, 341–42, 537, 693; attractions of, 235–36; automobiles and, 380; colonial era, *m53*; crime in, 237; during Great Depression, 424–25, 433–35; forms of government, *c251*, 251–52; growth of, 1870–1920, *g235, m235*, 235–37; industrial, 149; Johnson, Lyndon, and, 708–09; loss of political power in, 619; migration to suburbs from, 380, 605, 607, *g696;* mound-builder, 24–25; New Deal and, 469–70; political bosses in, 238, 252; population of, 1930, *m373;* poverty in, 618–20, 622; prehistoric, 24; problems of around 1900, 234; Progressive era and, 234–38; public services in, 237; the rise of, 148–49, *m148*; skyscrapers in, 355–56; after World War II, *g696;* during World War II, 536–38. *See also* housing; tenements.
Citizens' Advisory Council on the Status of Women, 726
civil disobedience, 544–45, 679, 684–85, 687–89, 786. *See also* non-violent resistance.
***Civil disobedience* (Thoreau)**, *q679*
Civilian Conservation Corps (CCC); begins, 455, *c481;* ends, 539; national parks and, 455; quotas in, 456; segregation and discrimination in, 456, 479
civil liberties; Nixon and, 811, 833; World War I and, 318–19; World War II and, 546–48. *See also* civil rights.
Civil Liberties Union, 319
civil rights; in 1950s, 669–72, 674–79, *t678;* in 1960s, *t678*, 680–89, *t687*, 690–95; advances, *t545; t678, t687;* antiwar movement and, 787; backlash against, 809; civil disobedience and, 544–45, 679, 682–83, 684–85, 687–89; deaths in movement, 686, 691; "Father" of movement for, 543–44; Little Rock and, 666, *p667*, 671–72, *p672;* and March on Washington, 686; and Montgomery bus boycott, 674–76, *p675, p676;* movement appraised, 695; under Nixon, *crt809*, 809, 812–13; nonviolent resistance and, 544–45, 676–77, 679, 682–83, 684–85, 687–89; Roosevelt, Franklin, and, 544; summer riots in 1965–1967 and, *m697;* Truman and, 634–35, 637; women's movement and, 724–25; World War II and, 542–48
Civil Rights Act; of 1866, 186, *t186*, 187; of 1875, nullified, 191; of 1957, 682; of 1960, 682; of 1964, 687, 708, 913; Title II of 1964 Act, 687; Title VII of 1964 act, 726, 730
Civil War, 172–80, 182–83; African Americans and, 172, *p173*, 173–74, 176–77, 178–79; blockade runners in, 176; costs of, *q104*, 177, 179; major battles of, *p174*, 174–76, *m175, t175*, 178–79, *m193;* navy and, 176; nurses in, 176, 177; resources compared, 173, *g177;* surrender ends, 179, 182; women's roles in, 176, 177, *p177*, 178

Clark, Champ, 275
Clark, Donald, *q920*
Clark, Jim, 687, 688, 689
Clark, William, 130, 132
Clay, Henry, *q117,* 146, *p146, p147,* 151; American system of 146–47; Bank of United States and, 146, 152; Compromise of 1850 and, 169–70; tariff controversy and, 146; War of 1812 and, *q117*
Clayton Antitrust Act (1914), 279
Clean Air Act (1990), 903
"clear and present danger," 319
Clemenceau, Georges, *q321,* 323, *q324*
Cleveland (Ohio), 208, *q209,* 342, 356, 433, *g696*
Cleveland, Grover, 194, 214, 217
Cliff Dwellers; Southwest, 23–24
Clinton, Bill, 892, *q893, p893, crt 896, p907, p918,* 912; affirmative action and, *p923, q923, q925;* Africa and, 910; Balkans and, 897; Brady Act and, 896; budget and, 894–96, 906, *p906;* Bush vs., *p892,* 892–93; crime bill and, 896; Dole vs., 907; economy and, 892–94, 908–09; family leave and, 896; Haiti and, 898–99; health care reform and, 894, 902; impeachment, 910–11; Kosovo and, 898; NAFTA and, 896–97; welfare reform and, 902, 909–10
Clinton, Hilary Rodham, 892, 895, 912
Clinton, DeWitt, 128, *p129*
clothing; colonial era, *p110–11;* Native American *q24;* ready-made, 377
clothing fashions, 378
Cloud, Henry Roe. *See* Roe Cloud, Henry.
coal, 209, 220, 271–72
coal miners; in 1920s, 378; in Appalachia, 621; strikes, 271–72, 341
coach travel, *p143*
coastal lowlands, *m12,* 14
Coast Ranges, *m12,* 14
Cobb, Frank, 311
Coca-Cola, 330–31
Coddington, William, *q43,* 44
codes of law, 45
Coeur d'Alene (Idaho), 216
coffee, 34
COFO. *See* Council of Federated Organizations (COFO).
Cohan, George M., 293
Coiner, Charles, 457
Cold Harbor (Va.), 178
cold war; beginning of, 563–67, *t567;* causes leading to, 563; declared, 567–68; developing nations and, 588; Eisenhower and, 578–83, 770; Johnson and, 772; Kennedy and, 592–93, 703, 704, 771–72; politics in U.S. during, 631, 640–47, *crt846;* Reagan and, 866–67
Cole, Thomas, *ptg133*
collective bargaining, 470, 633
colleges, 243–44, 383, 787, *c787. See also* universities.
Collier, John, *p479,* 479–80
Collins, Judy, 788–89
Collins, Michael, 802
Collinsville (Ill.), 319
Colombia, 297, 303, 735, 820
Colombine bombing, 920
colonial America, 30–53; culture of, 36–41, 86–87, *p110–11;* early European settlements (1565–1682), *t38;* French and Indian War (Seven Years' War), 48, 56, 57; Indian encounters, *See* Native Americans; population growth in, 35, 38, 39, 49, *m53;* self-government in, 32–34, 40–41, 75, 82, 85; three regions of, 38–41
Colorado, 169, 894
Colorado La Raza Unida, 735
Colson, Chuck, 826
Columbia University, 791
Columbus, Christopher, 4, 30–31, *q30, p30, m31,* 32, 35
Columbus (N. Mex.), 306
comic strips, 336, 447
Commerce, Department of, 350
Commitment and Community **(Kanter),** *q751*
Committee for a Sane Nuclear Policy (SANE), 582
Committee for the Restriction of Outdoor Advertising, 361
Committee on Public Information (CPI), 317, 318, 340
committees of correspondence, 59–60, *t59*
Committee to Defend America by Aiding the Allies, 502
Committee to Defend America First, 502
Committee to Re-elect the President (CREEP), 822, 826
common law, 45, 99
common man, courting the, 151–52
Common Sense **(Paine),** 66, *g74*
communes, 751, 752
communication media; 300 years of, *t86–87;* colonial era, 86–87
communism; in China, 572–73; containment of: *see* containment; "domino theory" and, 770, 821; fascism vs., 503, 509–10, 512–13; in Latin America, 591–93, 820–21, 870–72, 873; McCarthy, Joseph, and: *see* McCarthy, Joseph; Nixon and, 817; Reagan and Bush and, 866, 867; Red Scare concerning: *see* Red Scare; Rockefeller Center mural and, 472–75; Vietnam and, 769, 770, 771, 772; after World War II, 563–64, 566–68, 569–71, 572–73. *See also* anticommunism; Soviet Union.
Communist party(ies) in U.S., 340, 641–42, 648–49
community policing, 920
Compromise of 1850, 169–70, *m170*
Compromise, the Great, 84
computers, *t87,* 862–63, 921
Comstock Act (1873), 257
Comstock Lode, 198
concentration camps, 221, 511–12, *p512*
Concord (Mass.), 60, *p60,* 66, *t68,* 87
Conestogas, Wagons, *p122–23,* 133
Coney Island (N.Y.), 288, *p288–89*
Confederacy. *See* Confederate States of America.
Confederate States of America, 172, *m173,* 173, *g177*
Confederation, Articles of (1781), 81–83, *t90*
Confederation Congress, 81–83
Conference of Puerto Rican Women, 728
Congress; African Americans in, 894; American Revolution and, balance of power with executive, 825, 831; civil rights and, 686–87; declaration of war and, 95, 825, 831; environmental pollution and, 843, 910–11; feminism and, 730–31; First Continental, 60; first woman in, 315; Iran-*contra* scandal and, 872–73; Johnson, Andrew, and, 184–88; Nicaragua and, 872; Nixon and, 811, 813, 825, 828–29, 830–31, 832–35; religion and, 609; in Spanish-American War, 222; treaties and, 825; Truman and, 632–33, 635–36, 637; World War I and, 311, 315. *See also* House of Representatives; Senate.
Congressional Accountability Act (1995), *t901*
Congressional Budget and Impoundment Control Act (1974), 831
Congress, Second Continental, 66–67, *t68,* 81–82
Congressional Union, 93, 344
Congress of Industrial Organizations (CIO), 466–67, *t466, g467,* 538
Congress of Racial Equality (CORE), 544–45, 682, 683, 684, 690
Connecticut; state constitution, 73
Connor, Eugene ("Bull"), 685
conquistadors, Spanish, 32, 33, *p33,* 34, 37
Conrad, Marion, *q442*
conscientious objectors; in Vietnam War, 789; in World War I, 319
conscription. *See* military draft.
conservation and Theodore Roosevelt, 902–03
conservatives; backlash of, in 1970s, 809, 857–58; Clinton and, 901–03; Coolidge's support of, 349; Democrats as, 811; Harding's support of, 349; McCarthy, Joseph, and, 646; Nixon and, 810–13; Reagan and, 857–58; Roosevelt, Franklin, and, 468–69
Constitution, United States, *q91–109;* amendments to: *see* specific amendments e.g. First Amendment; debate and ratification of, 85, 88–90, *c89, t90,* 101; implied powers in, 114; making of, 80–81, 83–85, *t90;* need for, 81–83; Preamble to, *q80, q90, q91;* state ratification, 85, 89–90; slavery and, 84–85. *See also* Bill of Rights.
Constitutional Convention, 83–85
Constitution of the Cherokee Nation, *q119,* 137, q137
constitutions, state, 72–74
Construction of the Dam **(Gropper),** *ptg456*
consumerism, 207; in 1920s, *g377,* 377–78, 381; Roosevelt, Theodore, and, 272–73
consumer price index (CPI), in World War II, 528
containment; China and, 573; under Eisenhower, 579; Kennan's theory of, 566; under Kennedy, 703, 771; under Truman, 567–68, 574; Vietnam and, 769, 770, 771. *See also* cold war; domino theory.
Continental Army, 67–69, *t68, g69;* formation of 66; supply problems, 69
Continental Congress, First, 60
Continental Congress, Second, 66–67, *t68,* 81–82
Contract With America, 900–01, 902, *q902*
contras, 871–73, *m872*
Cooke, Alistair, *q702*
Cooke, Jay, 190
Coolidge, Calvin, 349, *q349;* background of, 348–49; on business, 349, *q354;* description of, by Richard Strout, *q346;* as governor during police strike, 341; on immigration, *q404*
Coral Sea, Battle of the, 513
CORE. *See* Congress of Racial Equality (CORE).
Corliss, George, 158
Cornell University, 246
Coronado Coal Co.* v. *United Mine Workers **(1925),** 358, *t358*
Coronado, Francisco Vásquez de, *m31*
corporations; in 1920s, 356–57, 357–58; in 1950s, 601–02; in 1990s, 884; and labor, 357–58
Cortés, Hernando *m31,* 32, 34
Corvette. *See* automobiles.
Costa Rica, 820, 871
cost of living after World War I, 341. *See also* inflation; Market Basket.
cotton; British mills buying Southern, 168; growth of, and slave labor, 165; *c165;* increase in production with cotton gin, 165, *q165;* machinery for, 206
cotton gin, 165, *p165*
Cotton, John, 42, 43
Coughlin, Charles E., 467–68, *p468*
Council of Federated Organizations (COFO), 684
Countercoup: the Struggle for Control of Iran **(Roosevelt),** *q587–88*
courts; juvenile, 256; strikes ended by, 286. *See also* Supreme Court.
Coventry (England), 501

covert operations. *See* Central Intelligence Agency.
cowhands, *p197,* 197–98
Cox, Archibald, *p827,* 828, 829
Cox, James M., 327, 347
Coxey, Jacob, 214
CPI. *See* Committee on Public Information (CPI).
Crawford, William, 151
credit, 380, 381
Creek, 25, 48
Creel, George, 317, 318, 322, 340
crime, 237, 896
crime bill, 896
Critical Thinking Skills; identifying assumptions, 712; recognizing bias, 625; detemining cause and effect, 249; making comparisons, 280; distinguishing fact from opinion, 657; making generalizations, 51; recognizing ideologies, 499; analyizing information, 119; synthesizing information, 393; predicting consequences, 864. *See also* Social Studies Skills; Study and Writing Skills.
Croatia, 897–98, *m897*
Cronkite, Walter, 704; on Vietnam War, *q777, q792;* Sadat and, 841
crops, 41, 133, *m181;* in 1920s, 377–78, 421; in colonial America, 40–41; frontier, 133; during Great Depression, 432–33, *m449,* 457, 465–66; overproduction in late 1800s, 213, *g213;* plantation, 33–34, *m181. See also* farms and farmers.
crossword puzzles, 389
Crow, 28
Crowe, Eyre, *ptg166*
Crozer Theological Seminary, 676
Crusade for Justice (Wells), *q248*
Cuba, 30; attempts to overthrow Castro in, 591–92; before Castro, 591, 820; Bush and, 873; Castro in, 591–92, *p593,* 873; Columbus and, 30; immigration to U.S. from, 735; independence for, 221–22; intervention by in other countries, 870, 871; Platt Amendment and, *t297;* Reagan and, 870, Soviet collapse and, 873; in Spanish-American War, 218, 221–22; Teller Amendment and, 299; U.S. intervention in, *t297*
Cuban Americans, 734
Cuban missile crisis, 592–93
culture; in 1920s, 370–71, 382–83, 386–92; in 1980s, 886–87; automobiles and, 380; conflicts in, in 1920s, 396–403; counter-, 748–55; during Great Depression, 440–41, 443–45; movies' effect on, 386–87
Cumberland Gap, (Ky.), 131
Cumberland (Md.), 144
currency, *q94,* Continental, 82, *p113*
Current Tax Payment Act (1943), *t527*
Curry, John Steuart, *ptg163,* 445
Curtis, Thomas, *crt846*
Cuzco (Peru), 32
Czechoslovakia; Communist party takes over, 568; democratic government regained, 868; Hitler and, *m494,* 496; splits into Czech Republic and Slovakia, 868; Yalta agreements and, 564
Czolgosz, Leon, 266–67, *q267*

D

Dachau, 512
Dade County (Fla.), 715
Dakotas, 28
Daladier, Edouard, 496
Dale, Thomas, 20
Daley, Richard, 781
Dallas (Tex.), 603, 704, 822
Da Nang (Vietnam), *m769,* 773
dance, 371, 389, 443, 507, 533, 617, 753–54
dance marathons, 371, 390
DAR. *See* Daughters of the American Revolution (DAR).
Darrow, Charles, 446
Darrow, Clarence, 366, *p396,* 397
Darwin, Charles, 210
Daughters of the American Revolution (DAR), 476
Davis, Daniel S., 542
Davis, Jefferson, 172–73
Davis, Paulina Wright, 259
Dawes, Charles G., 350–51
Dawes Plan, 350–51
Dawes Severalty Act (1887), 200, 201
Daye, Stephen, *t86*
Dayton (Ohio), 898
Dayton (Tenn.), 396
Dayton Peace Accord, 898
D'Cruz, Ben, *q885*
DC-3, 484–85
D-Day, 510, *m521*
deaf, care for, 155
Dean, John, 827, *p827,* 828
death penalty, 813
Debs, Eugene, 216, 217, 276, 277; during World War I, *p319,* 319
Declaration of Sentiments (1848), *q258*
Declaration of Independence, (1776), *q61–63,* 67, *t68, q71, t90*
Declaratory Act, (1766), 58, *t59*
Defense, Department of, 908
defense budget, 582, 703, 882–83, 901
deficit, 539, *g859,* 861, 883–84, 894, 900–01
Dekanawidah, *q26–27*
De Klerk, Frederik, 880–81
De la Garza, E. "Kika," 735
Delano (Calif.), 736, 739
De Large, Robert C., *p188*
Delaware, 40, *m53*
Delaware River, 39,
De Leon, Ponce, *m31*
de Lesseps, Ferdinand, 302–03
demobilization, 599
democracy, concepts of, 115,151–53
Democracy of Numbers, 151
Democratic Republicans, 115–16; party, 112, 115–16, 151; split by factions, 151
Democrats; in 1970s, 822; African American, 478; Chicago convention of 1968 of, 781, *p781;* civil rights and, 691; Clinton and, 892–94; Jackson's supporters begin party, 151; during Reconstruction, 190–91; "solid South" and, 671, 783, *m783,* 812; urban voters and, 403; after World War II, 634–35, 637
"demon rum," 155
Dempsey, Jack, *p387,* 388
Denmark, 39, 501
Denver (Colo.), 217
departments, government. *See* listings under department names.
department stores, 207
depression; in 1870s, 190, 208; in 1890s, 214. *See also* Great Depression; recession.
deregulation, 859–60, *crt860*
desert culture, 23–24
"Desert Fox," 510
deSoto, Fernando, *m31*
détente policy, 817–18
Detroit (Mich.); African Americans in, 537, 622, 693, *g696;* decrease in crime in, 922, *p923;* Ku Klux Klan in, 400; population, *g696;* race riots in, 537, 693
Deutsch, Helene, 613
De Vaca, Cabeza, *m31*
de Veer, Gerrit, 8
Dewey, George, 222, 223
De Witt, John, *q547*
Dewey, John, 256–57, *q257*
Dewey, Thomas E., 539, 635
Díaz, Porfirio, 305
Dickinson, John, 58
Didion, Joan, *q750*
Diem, Ngo Dinh. *See* Ngo Dinh Diem.
Dien Bien Phu, *m769,* 770
Diggers, 751
Dillingham, William, 405
Dillingham Commission, 284, 405–06
diphtheria, 611
direct primary, 252
Dirksen, Everett McKinley, 687
disarmament; Eisenhower and, 580, 581; nuclear weapons and, 840, 866–68; Washington Conference and, 351. *See also* nuclear weapons.
discrimination; in 1950s, 621–23; in 1990s, 916–18; in cities, 622; courts allow after Reconstruction, 191; Fair Employment Practices Committee and, 544–46; on frontier, 198; during Great Depression, 433, 434; against handicapped people, 918; in housing, 541, 607, 681, 682; against immigrants, 237, 405; against Mexicans and Mexican Americans, 198, 433, 456, 537–38, 736; in New Deal, 456, 470, 479; during Progressive era, 281–83; Roosevelt, Franklin, and, 479, 544; by unions, 541; against women, 436, 456, 477–78, 615, 917; during World War II, 537–38, 541, 542–48. *See also* racism.
diseases; acquired immunodeficiency syndrome (AIDS), 886, 921; diphtheria, 611; dysentery, 40, 117, 177, 309; influenza, 314, 611; in 1950s, 611; in 1960s, 749; in Civil War, 177; malaria, 177, 222, 302; measles, 234; Native Americans and colonial, 32–33, *p33;* polio, 453–54, 611; smallpox, 33; typhoid fever, 177, 611; of World War I soldiers, 309; yellow fever, 215, 222, 302, 303
Disney, Walt, 616; Davy Crockett and, 611; Disneyland and, 616; Mickey Mouse Club and, 610, 616
"Dispatches from the Front" (Pyle), *q488–89*
District of Columbia; 114; Brittish attack on, *crt118;* end of slave trade in, 169; Twenty-third Amendment give vote to, *q107. See also* Washington, D.C.
Dixiecrats, 634–35, 637
Dmytryk, Edward, 648
Doar, John, 680, *p834*
Doctorow, E. L., *q558–59*
dogfights, 308
Dog Swap, *ptg191*
Dole, Robert, *p900,* 901, 907, *q908*
Dollar Diplomacy, 298
dolls, 47, *p110*
Dominican Republic, 219, 297, *t297,* 305, 897
"domino theory," *q770,* 821. *See also* containment.
Donnelly, Ignatius, 212, *p212*
Dos Passos, John, 390, *q391,* 444, *q536*
"Double V" campaign, 543
doughboys, 316
Douglas, Helen Gahagan, 655
Douglas, Stephen A., 170, 171
Douglas, William, 566, *p714*
Douglas Aircraft Company, 485; DC-3 plane of, 484–85
Douglass, Frederick, 156, *p156,* 166, *q174*
***Down & Out in the Great Depression* (McElvaine),** *q425*
draft. *See* military draft.
Drake, Francis, 33
Dreiser, Theodore, *q230–31*
droughts, 213
Droz, Judy, 796
drugs; illegal, 237
Du Bois, W. E. B., *q189,* 283, *p283, q283;* Garvey, Marcus, and, 343

due process, *c715,* 716–17, 913
Dukakis, Michael, 340, 877
Duke family (tobacco industry), 209
Dulany, Daniel, 58
Dulles, John Foster, 578–79, *p579,* 588, 591
Dunkirk, 501, *p501*
Dunmore, Lord, *q75*
Dunne, Finley Peter, *q270*
***Duplex Printing Press Co.* v. *Deering* (1921),** *t358*
DuPont; corporation, 365; family, 354
Dust Bowl, 430–31, *m431, m437,* 438–39, *m439*
Dutch, 39
Dutch East Indies, 513
Duvalier, François, 873
Duvalier, Jean-Claude, 873
Dylan, Bob, 748, *p748, q748,* 753, *q789*
***Dynamic Sociology* (Ward),** 244
dysentery, 177, 309

E

Earhart, Amelia, 388
Earth Day, 784
earthworks, moundbuilder, 24–25, *p25*
Eastern Europe, 564, 565, 566, *t567,* 568. *See also* Europe.
Eastern North America, *m53, m57. See also* Atlantic Seaboard.
Eastern Woodland Native Americans, 25–27
East Germany, 571. *See also* Germany; Democratic Republic of (East).
East India Company, 59, *t59*
Eastland, James O., 683
Eastman, George, *t205*
East St. Louis (Ill.); Mississippian moundbuilder culture, 25
EC. *See* European Community (EC)
Eckford, Elizabeth Ann, 666
Economic Opportunity Act, 708
e-commerce, 908
economy; in 1800s, 113–14, 140–49, *m181;* in 1920s, 354–55; automobiles and, 379; baby boom and, 610; under Bush, 882–85, under Carter, *g839,* 839; under Clinton, 908; in colonial era, 37, 39; credit and, 381; crises, *t423;* under Ford, 837–39, *g839;* global, 883; in Great Depression, 421–22; under Kennedy, 703; money and, 213; New Deal and, 456–58, 465; under Nixon, *g839;* under Reagan, 858–61; and recession beginning during Reconstruction, 190; Roosevelt, Theodore, and, 269–73; during World War II, 527–29; after World War II, 599–600, 632–33
Ederle, Gertrude, *p388*
Edison, Thomas Alva, *t205,* 205–06, 240, *p240,* 241
Edmund Pettus Bridge, *p688*
education; in 1920s, 383; in 1950s, 610, 613; in 1990s, 893, 923–24; African Americans and, 188–89, 190, 282; arms race and, 582; baby boom and, 610, 613; in business management, 357; civil rights in, 670–72; in colonial America, 39, *p39,* 46–47; evolution vs. Bible in, 396–97; free public, 39, 155; GI Bill and, 599, 600; higher levels of, 256–57, *c787;* length of school year, *g256;* literacy increases, 256–57; of Native Americans, 46–47; need to improve quality of, 921; property taxes as funding for, 921; public, 39; reform movement for public, 921; slaves and, 168; women and, *g726,* 727. *See also* schools.
Education Amendments Act (1972), 730
Edwards, Malenda, 140–41, *q140*
EEOC. *See* Equal Employment Opportunity Commission (EEOC).
egalitarianism, 43; Native American, 23, 138
Egypt, 590–91, 819, 841–42, 878
Ehrlichman, John, 825, *crt825,* 828, 829, *p829*
Eighteenth Amendment (1919), *q105,* 343–44, 402. *See also* Prohibition.
Eighth Amendment (1791), *q103*
"Eight-hour orphans," 538
Eightieth Congress, 631, 632–33, 635–36
Eisenhower, Dwight D., *p578, t581,* 578–83, *q579;* African Americans and, 509; arms race and, 579–81; on atomic bombing of Japan, *q517;* background of, 578, 579; Bulganin and Khrushchev and, 581, 584; business and, 654; "Chance for Peace" speech of, 580; CIA and, 588–590, 591–92; civil rights and, 671, 672; consensus decision making by, 653–54; on costs of armaments, *q580;* Cuba and, 654; election of, to presidency, 578, 653; emerging nations and, 588; as general in World War II, 510; during Great Depression, 426–27; interstate highway system and, *q603,* 654, *g654, m655;* Iran and, 587–88, 590; Korea and, 575, 578; Latin America and, 591–92; massive retaliation policy of, 579–80; McCarthy and, 646; on military-industrial complex, *q583;* Native Americans and, 624; New Look policy of, 579; Nixon and, 653, *p653;* "open skies" proposal, 581; reelected, 654; on religion, *q609;* social policies of, 654–55; Sputnik and, 582, 654; Suez crisis and, 590–91; Vietnam and, 770, 771
Eisenhower Doctrine, 591
El Alamein, 510
Elbe River, 562
elderly, poverty among, 620, *p620*
elections; in 1800s, 116, 146, 147, 151–52; Congressional, *q91–92, q105,* 894, 899–900, Presidential, *q96–97, q103, p146, p147,* 151–52, 153, 890–93, 912, *m912*
Election of Senators, Direct, *q105*
electoral college, *q97, q103*
electors; District of Columbia, *q107;* presidential, *q97, q103,* 151
electricity; in 1920s, 377; appliance revolution, 442–43; during New Deal, 457–58, *p459;* Edison and, 205–06; lightbulb and, 205–06; to rural areas, 459, 539; use in motors, 206, 355; after World War II, 599
electronic bulletin boards (BBs), 87
Ellington, Edward ("Duke"), 533
Elliot, R. Brown, *p188*
Ellis, Clyde T., *q443*
Ellis Island, 236
Ellison, Ralph, *q668*
Ellsberg, Daniel, 799, 826
El Paso (Tex.), 735
El Salvador, 735, 820, 870–71, *p871*
emancipation, 176–77, *m179*
Emancipation Proclamation (1862), 176–77
Embargo Act (1807), 117, 141
embargo; of arms, to Yugoslav successor states, 897; of grain, to Soviet Union, 840; of military material for Japan, 504; of oil, by Saudi Arabia, 837–38
"Emergence of a Republican Majority, The" (Phillips), 811–12
Emergency Banking Act (1933), *c481*
Emergency Farm Mortgage Act (1933), *c481*
Emergency Price Control Act (EPCA) (1942), *t527*
Emergency Relief Act (1932), 426
emerging nations, 588–93
Emerson, Ralph Waldo, *q171*
Emlen, Anne, *q70*
***Emperor Jones* (O'Neill),** *p391*
Empire State Building, 356, 447
employment; in manufacturing, 1899, *m263;* by profession, 1800–1960, *c211. See* working women; during World War II, 530–31. *See also* Equal Employment Opportunity Commission (EEOC); unemployment.
***encomienda* policy,** 32
***Ends of Power, The* (Haldeman),** *q798*
Energy, Department of, *t841*
energy crisis, 836–38, 839
Enforcement Act (1870), 186, *t186,* 191
***Engel* v. *Vitale* (1962),** *c715,* 716, *q716*
England; colonists and settlers from, 36–37, *t38,* 38–39, 41, 66–69, *p110–11. See also* African Americans; Slavery; Native Americans as, 32–34, 48; New Amsterdam and, 40. *See also* Great Britain *(for events after 1707).*
English Channel, swimming the, 388, *p388*
Enola Gay, 514
Enslaved Africans; African culture drawn on by, 166–67; family strength of, 166; life of, on plantations, 166–68; physical abuse of, 166; religion of, and, 166–67; resistance and revolt by, 167–68, *t168;* Underground Railroad and, 167
entitlement programs, 902
environment; air pollution and, 910; agricultural effects, 9, 16–17; businesses and, 910; Carter and, 843; Civilian Conservation Corps (CCC) and, 455–56; cutbacks in protections for, 903; government regulation of, 842–43; housing adaptations to, 28–29, *m28, p29;* nuclear power and, 843; pollution of, 842–43, Reagan and, 860; Roosevelt, Theodore, and, 903; during World War II, 536
Environmental Protection Agency (EPA), 810, 842–43, 860, 903
EPA. *See* Environmental Protection Agency (EPA).
EPCA. *See* Emergency Price Control Act (EPCA).
equality; concepts of, 23, 27, 43, 138
Equal Pay Act (1963), 726
Equal Rights Amendment (ERA), *t728,* 730–31, *m759*
Equiano, Olaudah, *q34–35*
ERA. *See* Equal Rights Amendment (ERA).
Erie Canal, 128, *p129, p144,* 144–45, 149
Eriksson, Leif, 31
Ervin, Sam J., 828, 829, *p829*
***Escobedo* v. *Illinois* (1964),** *c715,* 716
Espionage Act (1917), 318, 319
Estevanico, 34
Estonia, 869
Ethiopia, Italian invasion of, 494
ethnic cleansing, 897
eugenics movement, 284, 405–06
Europe; alliances with countries in, 48, 68, 115, 116; in 1955, *m571;* in 1995, *m870;* Marshall Plan and, 568; Monroe Doctrine and, 219–20; neutrality during wars in, 115; and United States, in early twentieth century, 301; World War I and, *m307, m326;* World War II and, *m494, m511, m565;* Yalta agreements and, 564
European Community (EC), 817. *See also* European Union (formerly European Community).
European land claims (1763), *m48*
Europeans; colonial settlements of, 36–41, *t38,* 49; diseases brought by, 32–33; explorations by (1492–1550), *m31;* imported culture of, 33–34, 36–41, *p110–11*
European Union (formerly European Community), 896
evangelists, 397–98, 857
Evans, Hiram Wesley, 400–01

Evans, Oliver, 158
Everett, Edward, *p137,* 137–38
Evers, Charles, *p803*
Evers, Medgar, 686
Everything We Had, *q775, q801*
excise tax scandal, 190
executive branch, 84, *c85*; Constitutional description of, *q96,* 96–99
Executive Order 8802 (1941), 544
Executive Order 9066 (1942), 546–47
Exeter (NH), 45
Exodusters, 184
expansionism, 219, 220–23, *t299;* justified, 295
exploration; European (1492–1550), 31–34, *m31*; westward, 130, 132. *See also* travel.
explorers, African, 34–35; routes of European (1492–1550), 30–31, *m31*; westward, 130, 132
exports, *g295*

F

factories, in 1920s, 354–55, 357–59, 362–66; in 1990s, 917; assembly line child labor in, 232, *p233,* 345, 538; in cities, 235; during Great Depression, 434; New Deal and, 456–57, 466–67; after World War II, 599; during World War II, 527, 530–31
factory system, 140–43, *q140, c142, m181*
fads; in 1920s, 371, 382, 389; during World War II, 532
Fair Deal, 637, *crt637*
Fair Employment Practices Committee (FEPC), 544–46
Fair Labor Standards Act, 471, 481
Fall, Albert, 348
Falwell, Jerry, 857, *p857*
families; during Great Depression, 435–36; during World War II, *p523,* 538–39
Family Assistance Plan (FAP), 810–11
Family Leave Act, 896
FAP. *See* Family Assistance Plan.
Farm Board, 424
Farmer, James, 682
Farmers' Alliances, 214–15
farmers' cooperative, 214
farms and farmers; in 1800, 141; in 1860, *m181*; in late 1800s 213–215; in 1920s, *g377,* 377–78, 385, 421, 438–39; in 1950s, 602, *g602, p602*; in 1990s, 917; African American, 188–89, 190; in colonial America, 39, 40–41; Dust Bowl and, 430–31, *m437,* 438–39, *m439*; frontier, 133; grape boycott and, 722, *p723,* 733, 736–37, 738–41, *p740*; during Great Depression, 430–31, 432–33; highways and, 384–85; liquor tax and, 114; machinery on, 377, 385, 432, 438; migrant, 433, 623, *p623, m627,* 738–39; migration from Great Plains to California by, 431–32; move from farm to factories, 140–43; NAFTA and, 896; Native American, 23, 25–26; New Deal and, 457; organic, 917; percentage of population employed by, 602, 917. *See also* plantations, Populists and, 212, 213–15; poverty among, 623, *p623*; productivity of increases, 236; protests and rebellions by, *p82,* 82–83, 114, *p114*; railroads and, 213–214; Reagan and, 859; Second New Deal and, 470; size and population of, 602; subsidies for, 457; tenant. *See* tenant farmers; TVA and, 458; World War I and, 438; World War II and, 535, 537. *See also* agriculture.
Farm Security Administration (FSA) (1937), *c481*
Farm Workers Association. *See* United Farmworkers.
Farnsworth, Philo, 710
Farragut, David, 176
fashion; in 1920s, 382–83; in 1960s, 752; in automobiles, 378–380; fads, 382
Faubus, Orval, 671–72
Faulk, John Henry, 647
Faulkner, William, 391
FBI. *See* Federal Bureau of Investigation (FBI).
FCDA. *See* Federal Civil Defense Administration (FCDA).
FDIC. *See* Federal Deposit Insurance Corporation (FDIC).
FDR. *See* Roosevelt, Franklin D.
Federal Aid Road Act (1916), 385
Federal Bureau of Investigation (FBI); Hiss case and, 642, *p642;* New Left and, 794; Nixon and, 811, 826, 830, 833
Federal Civil Defense Administration (FCDA), 577
Federal Communications Commission (FCC), 860
Federal Deposit Insurance Corporation (FDIC), 458
Federal Election Campaign Act (1972), 831
Federal Emergency Relief Administration (FERA) (1933), 455, 457, 479, 481
Federal Employee Loyalty Program, 643–44
Federal Housing Administration (FHA) (1934), 481
Federalist Party, 112, 115–17
Federalists, 88–90, *c89,* 112, 115–17, 153
federal regulation. *See* regulation (business).
Federal Reserve Bank, 278–79
Federal Reserve Board, 278–79, 422, 883
Federal Trade Commission (FTC) (1914), 279, 349, 356
Feis, Herbert, 350
Fellowship of Reconciliation, 676
Feminine Mystique, The **(Friedan),** *q613–14,* 725
Feminism, 613–14; opposition to, 729, 731; revival of, in 1960s, 724–31
FEPC. *See* Fair Employment Practices Committee.
FERA. *See* Federal Emergency Relief Administration (FERA).
Ferber, Edna, *q196*
Ferdinand Maximilian. *See* Maximilian (Emperor of Mexico).
Ferris, Charles, 203
Ferris Wheel, 203, *p203*
FHA. *See* Federal Housing Administration.
Field, James G., 213
Fifth Amendment (1791), *q102,* 650, 651; "due process" clause of, *t715,* 716–17
Fifteenth Amendment (1870), *q105,* 186, *t186,* 708–09
Filipino Americans, 738, 739
Fillmore, Millard, 169–70
Finance. *See* Bank of the United States.
Finland, 39
Finley, James, *q150*
Finney, Charles Grandison, 154
Finnish colonists, 39
fireside chats, 459, *p482*
First Amendment (1791), *q101,* freedom of press, 799; freedom of speech, 319, 650; religion clause, 716
The First Americans **(Hakim),** *q24*
Fish, Hamilton, *q833*
fishing, 37, 132; Native American, 29
Fitch, Thomas, 87
Fitzgerald, F. Scott, *q334–35,* 390
flagpole sitting, 371, 382
Flaming Youth, 387
flappers, 382–83
flatboats, 128, *ptg129,* 133
Fleming, Alexander, 551
Flint (Mich.), 466, 600, 883
Florey, Howard, 551
Florida; illegal aliens and 916; in Reconstruction, 187; in Civil War, 172; Spanish explorers and Native Americans in, *q2–3*; population gain in World War II, 535; Spanish settlement in, 33, 37, *t38*; in Sunbelt, *m814,* 814
Flynn, Elizabeth Gurley, *p290*
Foley, Thomas, 899
food and diet; native and imported, 33; recipes, *q111*
Food and Drug Administration (FDA) (1938), 273, 727
food stamps, 858
football, 387
FOR. *See* Fellowship of Reconciliation (FOR).
Force Bill, 153
Ford, Gerald, 838, *q838;* administration of, *t841;* economy and, 837–39; named as vice president, 829–30; pardons Nixon, 831, 837; succeeds Nixon, 831, 835
Ford, Henry; assembly line and, 362, 364–65; on cars for every man, *q355;* employment policies of, 363–64; Model A car of, 380; Model T car of, 361, 378, 379; tractor by, 377; wages and, 363
Ford Motor Company, 342, 355, 362–65, 536; during World War II, 536
Fordson tractor, 377
foreclosures, 431
foreign aid, 588. *See also* Berlin airlift.
foreign policy, in 1790s, 114–16; in 1800s, 117–18; in 1920s, 350–52; under Bush, 878–80, 881–82; under Carter, 839–42; CIA and, 587–90, 821, 871–72; under Clinton, 896–99; under Eisenhower, 578–82, 590–91, 770–71; Jefferson's, 117; under Johnson, 772, 778–79; under Kennedy, 592–93, 771–72; Monroe Doctrine as cornerstone of, 219–20, 297–98, 305–06; under Nixon, 797–98, 799–800, 816–19, 821; during Progressive era, 294–301; under Reagan, 866–68, 870–73; under Roosevelt, Franklin, 497, 498, 502–05, 509, 563–64; under Roosevelt, Theodore, 296–301; under Truman, 565–68, 570, 571, 573, 574–75, 769; War Hawks and, 117–18; under Washington, George, 115–16; under Wilson, Woodrow, 305–06, 309–11, 322–25
Foreman, Avon, 382
forests; in Colonial America, *m15,* 25–26, 29; Roosevelt, Theodore, and conservation of, 269. *See also* woodlands.
Forest Service. *See* U.S. Forest Service.
Fort Des Moines, 315
Fort Sumter, 173
Four Freedoms, 525
442nd Regiment, 509
Fourteen Points; Atlantic Charter and, 504
Fourteenth Amendment (1868), 104–05, 186, *t186*
Fourth Amendment (1791), 102
France; Adams, John and, 115, 116; alliances with, 68, 115, 116; colonists from, 37–38, *p37, t38*; exploration by, *m31*; Fourteen Points and, 321, 323; Great Britain and, 68, 115; Indochina and, 768, 769–70; Jefferson and, 115, 117; Louisiana purchased from, 131–32; Monroe Doctrine and, 220; Normandy invasion, 510–11, *m511, m521*; Panama Canal and, 302–03; in Revolutionary War, *t68;* Revolution of 1789, 115; Treaty of Versailles and, 323, 324–25; Vietnam and, 768, 769–70; wars with England, 48, 56, 57; World War I and, 306–08, *m307, t308,* 315–16, *c316*; World War II and, 500–01, 510–11

Franck, James, *q517*
Franco, Francisco, 495
Frankfurter, Felix, 339, 340, 427
Franklin, Benjamin, *p50,* 89; at Constitutional Convention, 83, *q85*; in foreign affairs, 68; influence of, 50, 66; on Native Americans, *q27,* 46, *q47*; *Poor Richard's Almanack,* 50; as postmaster general, *p65*
Franz Ferdinand, murder of, 306, *p306*
Freedman's Bureau, 188–89, *p189*
Freedom of Information Act, 831
Freedom Riders, *p680,* 680–81, 682–83, *m683*
free enterprise. *See also* names of individual businesses.
Free Speech Movement (FSM), 786–87
freight routes. *See* transportation.
French and Indian War (Seven Years' War), 48, 56, 57
French Canadians; as immigrants, 402; Ku Klux Klan and, 400. *See also* Quebec.
French Revolution, 115
Fresh Kills (N.Y.), 905, *p905*
Friedan, Betty, 613–14, *p614, q614,* 725, 727, 728, 732, *p732, q732*
Friends (Quakers), *t38,* 40
***From Harding to Hiroshima* (Boardman),** *q514*
frontier; cattle ranching on, 197–98; farms on, 133; the moving, 130–32, *m131;* religion of the, 153–54
FSA. *See* Farm Security Administration.
FSM. *See* Free Speech Movement.
Fuchs, Klaus, 644
Fugard, Athol, *q881*
Fugitive Slave Law, 169, 176
Fulbright, William, 791
***Fullilove* v. *Klutznick* (1980),** 914
Fulton, Robert, *t145, t158*
fundamentalism, 397, 609
fur trade, 37–38, *ptg37*

G

Gabriel's Revolt, 168
Gage, Thomas George, 50, 59, 60
Galbraith, John Kenneth, *q702*
Gallipoli, Battle of, *t308*
Galveston (Tex.), 251–52
Gandhi, Mohandas, 677, 736
***Ganonsyoni* alliance,** 26–27
Garcia, John, 508
Garland, ex parte, 185
Garland, Judy, 651
Garrison, William Lloyd, 155, *p156, t157, q166, 259*
Garvey, Marcus, 342–43
Gary, Elbert, 341, 358
Gary (Ind.), 354
gasoline shortage, 361, 836. *See also* oil embargo.
Gatow airport (Berlin), 570
Geelan, Agnes, 344
"Gender gap," 861
General Dynamics, 882
General Electric Company, 358, 365
General History of Virginia, New-England, and the Summer Isles (Smith), *q17*
General Intelligence Division, 340
General Motors; Corvette by, 660–61; layoffs by, 883; sit-down strike at, 466–67; after World War II, 601
generation gap, 749
Geneva (Ill.), 317
Geneva (Switzerland), Eisenhower, Bulganin, and Khrushchev at, 581; Reagan and Gorbachev at, 867; Vietnamese agreement at (1954), 770
"Gentleman's Agreement," 284, 301
geography, themes of, 6–9; history vs., 13
George III of England; Proclamation of 1763, 57; war on colonies, 66, 67–69
Georgia, 41, *m53*; Cherokee expulsion from, 136–39; civil rights and, 681, 684, 689; in Civil War, 172, *m173, m175,* 178, 179, *m179, m180;* during Reconstruction, 185; reapportionment in, *m721;* in Sunbelt, *m814,* 814
German Americans; in World War I, 319
Germany; Democratic Republic of (East), 571; divided, 564, 566, 569–71; East. *See* Germany: Democratic Republic of; Federal Republic of (West), 571, *m571,* 868; Hitler and, 492–96, 501–02. *See also* Hitler, Adolf; Holocaust in, 511–12; immigrants from, 39, 49, 143; *Lusitania* and, 304, 310; neo-Nazis in, 869; reunification of, 868–69; Soviet Union and, 496, 563, 564, 566, 569–71; submarines of, 304, 308, 309–10, *p310,* 311, 503, 511; Treaty of Versailles and, 324, *p325;* war debts of, *p324,* 350–51; West. *See* Germany: Federal Republic of; in World War I, 306–09, *m307, t308,* 309–10, 311, *c316,* 316–17; World War II and, 496, 501–02, 503, 509–10, 511–13; Yalta agreements and, 564
Gerrymandering; African Americans and, 190, 921; Hispanic Americans and, 921; in 1990s, 920–21. *See also* redistricting.
Getty, J. Paul, 435
Gettysburg, Battle of, *m175,* 175–76
Ghana, 34, 678
GI Bill of Rights (1944), 599, 600–01, 607
Gibson Girl, 382
***Gideon* v. *Wainwright* (1963),** 713–14, *c715,* 716
"Gilded Age," 209
Gingrich, Newt, 899–901, *p900,* 907
Ginsberg, Allen, 749
Ginsburg, Ruth Bader, *p923, q923,* 924
Giumarra Vineyard Corporation, 740
glaciers, 22
glasnost, 868
Glass-Steagall Banking Act (1933), 458, *c481*
Glenn, John H., Jr., *p702,* 703, *p720*
Gluck, Sherna B., *q531*
GNP. *See* gross national product (GNP)
Goddard, Mary Katherine, *t86*
Goddard, Paulette, *p530*
gold; extracted after Civil War, 198
Goldmark, Josephine, 255–56
Goldwater, Barry, 708, 772, 835
golf, 387
***Gomillion* v. *Lightfoot* (1960),** *c715*
Gompers, Samuel, 216, 217, 318; strikes and, 341
***Gone With the Wind* (Mitchell),** *q440,* 440–41
***Gone With the Wind* (movie),** 443
Gonzales, Frank, 912
Gonzales Construction, 922
González, Henry B., 735
González, Rodolfo ("Corky"), 735
***Good Earth, The* (Buck),** 497
Good Neighbor Policy, 493
***"Good War, The"* (Terkel),** *q508, q512, q524*
Goodwin, Doris Kearns, *q706, q779*
Gorbachev, Mikhail, *p865,* 865–66, *p867,* 867–68, 869, *t869,* 873
Gorbachev, Raisa, 867
Gore, Albert, Jr., 890, 892, *p906,* 912
Gore, Tipper, 892
Gorgas, William C., 303
Gould, Chester, 447
Gould, Jay, 215
government; in colonial America, 39, 45, 50; commissioner style, *c251,* 251–52; corruption in, 238, 250–52; deficit spending by, 539, *q539,* 861, 883–84, 898, 901–02; reform of, 251–54; Roosevelt, Franklin, and, 480–81; state. *See* state government; three branches of, 84–*c85, q91–100*; unions and, 286; women in, 477; in World War II, 525, 527–29
government bonds, 529
government departments. *See* listings under department names.
governors, colonial, 50, 58, 72
Graham, Billy, 609, *p609,* 857
grain embargo, 840
Grand Exposition, 190
Grange, Red, 387
Grangers, 213–14
Grant, Jehu, 69
Grant, Madison, 406
Grant, Ulysses S.; in Civil War, 176, 178, *p178,* 179, *q179,* 182, *p182;* as President, 189–90
grape boycott, 722, *p723,* 733, 736–37, 738–41, *p740*
***Grapes of Wrath, The* (Steinbeck),** *q414–15, q444–45*
Grasso, Ella, 728
graves, Native American, 24–25, *p25*
Gray, Harold, 336
Great Atlantic and Pacific Tea Company (A&P), 207, 357
Great Awakening, 49
Great Basin, *m28*
Great Bear Lake, 14
Great Black Migration, 341–43. *See also* African Americans.
Great Britain; colonists from, 66–69, *p110–111*; France, wars with, 48, 56, 57; Jefferson and, 117; Persian Gulf War and, 878; Revolutionary War against, *m67,* 67–69, *t68, m77*; South's trade with, 168; Suez Crisis and, 591; Treaty of Versailles and, 323, 324; War of 1812 with, *p117,* 117–18, *p118,* 141; World War I and, 306, *m307,* 307–08, *t308,* 309, 310, 311, 316, *c316*; World War II and, 496, 501–04, 510–11, 563. *See also* England *(events before 1707).*
Great Compromise, 84
Great Crash, 418–20, *c419,* 421, 428, *p428*
Great Depression; businesses during, 424; causes, *c421,* 421–22; families during, 435–36; farmers during, 423–24, 430–32; Hoover, Herbert, and, 422–27. *See* New Deal; recovery from, 465, 481; unemployment during, 416, *p417,* 424–25, 433–36; World War II and, 515
Greater East Asia Co-Prosperity Sphere, 504
***Great Gatsby, The* (Fitzgerald),** *q334–35,* 390
Great Lakes, 14, *m53,* 145, 149, 655
Great Migration, 341–43
Great Plains, *m12,* 14; cattle ranching on, *p197,* 197–98, 206; Dust Bowl and, 438–39; migration from, 431–32; Native American cultural area, 28, *p29*; settling of, 197
Great Serpent Mound, *p25*
Great Society, 708–09; New Deal compared with, 709; Nixon and, 809, 810–11
Great War. *See* World War I.
Great White Fleet, *t299, p300,* 301, *m301*
Great Ziegfeld, The, 446, *p446*
Greece, 567, 568
Greeley, Horace, 177, 260
Green, Anne Bosanko, *q515*
Green Party, 912
Greensboro (N. C.), *p711*
Greenspan, Alan, *q908*
Greenwich (England), 7
Greenwood (Miss.), 690
Greer, 503
Grenada; invasion of, 870
***griot,* Mandinka,** 126-27
Gropper, William, *ptg456*
gross national product (GNP); under Reagan, 859; after World War II, 599; during World War II, 527

Grumman Corporation, 883
Guadalcanal, 513
Guam, 222, *t299,* 513
Guangzhou (China), 573
Guatemala, 735, 820
***Guernica* (Picasso),** *ptg495*
Gulf of Tonkin, 772
Gulf Oil, 884
Gullah people, 167
Gutenberg, Johannes, 4
Gutiérrez, José Angel, 735
Gypsies, 512

H

Haig, Alexander, 816, 835
Haight-Ashbury, 751
Haiphong (Vietnam), 769, *m769,* 800
Hair, 752
Hair, Penda, *q914–15*
Haiti; Louisiana Purchase and, 132; refugees from, 873, 898–99, U.S. intervention in, *t297,* 305
Hakim, Joy, *q24*
Haldeman, H. R., *q798,* 825, *crt825,* 828, 829, *p829*
Haley, Alex, *q126–27, p126*
Hamer, Fannie Lou, 691, *p691,* 724
Hamilton, Alexander, *p88*; *The Federalist* and, 88; Jefferson vs., 114–15; as Secretary of Tresury, 113–14
Hammermill Paper Company, 358
Hampton Institute, 282
Hanna, Mark, *q268*
Hanoi (Vietnam), 800
Harburg, E.Y. (Yip), *q424–425*
Harcourt, Brace, 390
Hardin, Lil, *p389*
Harding, Warren Gamaliel, 327, 346, *q347, p347,* 347–48
***Hard Times* (Terkel),** *q425, q431, q435, q441, q443, q467*
Hare Krishnas, 750
Harlan, John Marshall (I), *q282*
Harlan, John M. (II-grandson of above), *p714*
Harlem (N.Y.); Baldwin, James, and, *q622;* Columbia University and, 791; race riot in, 537; writers in: *see* Harlem Renaissance.
"Harlem" (Hughes), *q693*
Harlem Renaissance, 391–92
Harmony Society, 751
Harpers Ferry (W. Va.), 171
Harrington, Michael, *p619, q619,* 619–20, 708
Harris, Katherine, 912
Harris, Mark Jonathan, 534
Harrison, William Henry, 153
Harvard University, 39, 507; business school of, 357; Du Bois and, 283; Leary, Timothy, and, 749
***Harvest* (Jones),** *ptg480*
***Harvest of Death* (O'Sullivan),** *p174*
Havana (Cuba), 593
Havel, Vaclav, 868
Hawaii (state of), *p13*
Hawaiian Islands, 221, *p221, t299*
Hay, John, 299
Hay-Herrán Treaty (1903), 297
Hayden, Casey, 724–25, *p724*
Hayden, Tom, 788
Hayes, Janet Gray, 728
Hayes, Rutherford B., 190–91
Haymarket Riot, 216
Haynsworth, Clement, 813
Haywood, William D. ("Big Bill"), 287
H-bomb testing, 577–78, 580, *p580, c580,* 581, *t581,* 583
health. *See* public health.
health care; early plans for, 540; costs of, 884, *g895;* reform of coverage, 894–96, 902, *m903,* 908, 910–11
Health, Education and Welfare (HEW), Department of, 812
Heart Mountain (Wyo.), 547
Held, John, Jr., *ptg334*
Hell's Kitchen, 245
Hemingway, Ernest, 390
Hendrix, Jimi, 753, 756–57, *p757*
Henry, Patrick, 80–81, *p80*
Hepburn, Katherine, *q649,* 651
Hersch, Seymour, 792
Hershey Chocolate, 419
HEW. *See* Health, Education and Welfare (HEW), Department of.
Hiawatha, 26–27
***Hidden Persuaders, The* (Packard),** *q600*
Highlander Folk School, 675
Highland Park (Mich.), 363
Highway Act (1956), 603
highways, 65, 384–85, *m385,* 603
Hindenburg, Paul von, 495
Hingham (Mass.), 38
hippies, 749–51
Hirabayashi* v. *United States (1943), 548
Hirohito, Emperor, *p497*
Hiroshima (Japan), 514, *m514, p518,* 518–19
Hispanic Americans; in 1990s, 917, 920–21; affirmative action and, 920; bilingualism and, 737; *bracero* program and, 735; Bush and, 885; cities and, 607, 622, 623; Civilian Conservation Corps (CCC) and, 456; in Congress, 735, 894; as cowhands, 197, 198; crime and, 922; cultures of, 734; distribution of in 1970, *m734;* Fair Employment Practices Committee and, 545; as farmworkers, *p736,* 735–37, 738–41; feminism and, 726; history, 734–35; Kennedy, Robert, and, 780; in politics, 735; poverty among, 622–23, 885, 909; suburbs and, 607; United Farm Workers and, 722, *p723,* 733, 736–37, 738–41, *p740;* women as, 917; World War I and, 318; in World War II, 509, 537; as zoot-suiters, 537–38. *See also* Cuban Americans; Mexican Americans; Puerto Rican Americans.
Hispaniola, 30, 33. *See also* Dominican Republic; Haiti.
Hiss, Alger, 641, *p641,* 642–43, *q643, t643*
***Hitchman Coal Co.* v. *Mitchell* (1915),** *t358*
Hitler, Adolf, *p492, t493,* 494–95, 496, *p499,* 898; Franco aided by, 495; on government, *q499;* Jews and, 511–12; on purge of Nazi party, *q492;* racism and, 494; suicide by, 513; World War II and, 496, 509–11
HIV. *See* human immunodeficiency virus.
Hoar, George F., 292
Hobart, Garret, 267
hoboes, 436
Ho Chi Minh, 768, *p768, q769,* 771, *t771, q773,* 779
Ho Chi Minh Trail, 772–73, *p773, m777*
Hoffa, James R., 585
holding companies, 270, 356
Holly, Buddy, 753
Hollywood Ten, 648–651
Holmes, Oliver Wendell, Jr., 319, 642
holocaust, the, 511–12
***Home Front, The* (Harris, Mitchell, and Schechter),** *q528, q534*
"Homeless Family" (Lange), *p414*
homelessness, 435, 876
home ownership, 601, 607
Home Owners' Loan Act (1933), 481
Homestead Act (1862), 197, 438
homesteading, 196, 197, 213
Homestead Strike, 216, *p216*
***Home to Harlem* (McKay),** 392
Honduras, 871, *m872*
Honecker, Erich, 868
Hoover, Herbert, 422, *p422, q423;* background of, 350, 402, 422; bonus army, and, 426–27; description of, by Richard Strout, 347; Great Depression and, 423–24, 425–27; Roosevelt, Franklin, v., *p448,* 454; as Secretary of Commerce, 348, 349, 350, 395, 423; Smith, Al, v., 402–03, *p403;* World War I and, 317, 422–23
Hoover, J. Edgar, 340, 826
Hoovervilles, *p434,* 435
Hopis, 24
Hopkins, Harry, 432, 455, 469, 565
Hopper, Edward, 445
Hopper, Hedda, 387
Horinouchi, Bunjiro, *q406*
horses; Native American usage of, 33; settler usage of, 33, *p33,* 122
hot line, *c704*
household appliances, 599
House Judiciary Committee, 830, 832–34
House of Representatives; Adams, John Q., elected by, 151; African Americans in, 894, 899; Johnson, Andrew, and, 187–88; Nixon impeachment and, 830; Republicans capture in 1994, 899–903, *p900 See also* Congress.
House Un-American Activities Committee (HUAC), 641, *p641,* 642–43, 646, 648–51
housing; in 1950s, 607, 610, 621, 655; in cities, 1880–1920, 237–38; under Eisenhower, 655; under Fair Deal of Truman, 635, 637; GI Bill and, 600–01, 607; under Johnson, Lyndon, 709, *p709;* of Native Americans, 26, *c27, m28,* 28–29, *p29, q30;* public projects, 621, 810; in suburbs, 604–05, *p605*
Housing Act of 1949, 637
Housing and Urban Development (HUD), Department of, 709
Houston (Tex.), 356, 603
Howard, O. O., *p189*
Howard University, Law School, 670
Howe, Julia Ward, 261
***How the Other Half Lives* (Riis),** *q234*
HUAC. *See* House Un-American Activities Committee (HUAC).
Hubble Space Telescope, 845
HUD. *See* Housing and Urban Development (HUD), Department of.
Hudson Bay, *m31*
Hudson River, 128, 149
Hudson River School, *ptg133*
Hue (Vietnam), *m769,* 771, 776, *m777*
Huerta, Dolores, 722, 738
Huerta, Victoriano, 305–06
Hughes, Charles E., 310, 348, 351
Hughes, Langston, 391–92, *p392, q693*
Hugo, Victor, *q687*
Hull, Cordell, *p504*
Hull House, 242, 246, 247
human immunodeficiency virus (HIV), 921. *See also* acquired immune deficiency syndrome (AIDS).
human rights, 138, 839–42. *See also* civil liberties; civil rights.
Humphrey, Hubert, 691, 780, 781, 809, 822
Humphrey, William E., 356
Hundred Days, 454–459
Hungary, 324, 564, 582
Hunt, E. Howard, 824, 826
Hunt, Jane, 258
hunter-gatherers, 9, *t16*
Hurons, 26
Hurston, Zora Neale, 392
Hussein (King of Jordan), *q881*
Hussein, Saddam (Iraqi), 878
Huston, Tom, 826

Hutchinson, Anne, 39; trial of, 42–45, *p43*
Hutchinson, William, 42
Hyde Park (N.Y.), 716
hydrogen bomb. *See* nuclear weapons.

I

IBM. *See* International Business Machines (IBM).
Ice Age, 14, 16, 22–23
Ickes, Harold, 478
"If We Must Die" (McKay), 392
Igloo Houses, *m28*, 29
Il Duce, 493
Illinois, 132, 144, 205, 894
Illinois, 311
Illiteracy, 256, 283
immigrants; from 1880–1920, *g236, p236,* 236–37; in 1990s, 915–16; African Americans and, 282; Americanization of, 283–84; in cities, 236–37; colonial, 36–37, 38–40, *p110–11*; as Democrats, 153; deportation of, 623; Ford, Henry, and, 364; Ku Klux Klan and, 400; and melting pot, 283–84; mutual assistance societies of, 285; Palmer raids and, 340–41; prejudice against, 237, 405; during Progressive era, 285; progressives and, 283–85; undocumented, 623, 735, 736, 915; after World War I, 404–07. *See also countries of origin, e.g., Chinese Americans, German Americans.*
immigration; changes in law, 915, *c915*; Chinese and, 217, 284, 405, 407, 852–53; colonial era, *p110–11*; effects of, 407; eugenics movement and, 284, 405–06; Haiti and, 899; illegal, 623, 736; Japanese and, 284, 301, 406, 407; Jews and, 406, 407; Johnson, Lyndon, and, 709; Ku Klux Klan and, 400; literacy requirement, 284–85; open policy in, 404, 405; political radicals excluded, 284; Populist Party and, 213; quota system and, 401, 404, 406, 407; restrictions on, 284–85, 401, 404–07; sources of, *q401, g918, m927;* Southeast Asia and, 918
Immigration Act; of 1921, 401, 406, 407; of 1924, 401, 406, 407; of 1965, 407, 709, 915
Immigration and Nationality Act (1990), 915
Immigration and Naturalization Service (INS), 623, 736
Immigration Reform and Control Act (1986), 915
impeachment, Clinton, William Jefferson and, 911–12; Johnson, Andrew, and, 187–88; Nixon, Richard, and, 830–31, 832–35
imperialism, 295–301; opponents of, 295, 300
implied powers, 114
imports, 33–34, 36; slavery, 34–35; tariffs on, 146, 147
impoundment, 811, 831
impressment, 115, 117
Inca, 32
Inchon (Korea), 574
income, average annual, in 1920s, *g377*
income tax, 528, 858; home mortgage interest deduction on, 607
indentured servants, 40, 41, *p41*
independence; and the Constitution, *t90, q101*; early nationhood after, 78–90, 110–23
Independence Day (1776), *67*
Independence, (Mo.), 636
India, 572
Indiana, 135; Ku Klux Klan in, 400, 401; primary in, 780
Indianapolis (Ind.), 400
Indian Bureau, 479, 480
Indian Claims Commission (ICC), 744
Indian Removal Act (1830), 137
Indian Reorganization Act (1934), 479–80, *c481*
Indian Reserve, *m53*
indigo, 227
Indochina, 504, 769, *m769*
Indonesia, 572
"industrial democracy," 358–59
industrial productivity, 355; under Nixon and Ford, 837; in World War II, 527
Industrial Workers of the World (IWW), 287, 318, 319
industry; in 1860, *m181;* in 1920s, 350, 354–55, 356–59, 362–68; automobiles and, 838–39; baby boom and, 610; deregulation of, 859–60; exports by, 1860–1920, *g295;* under Ford, 837–39; Great Depression and, 421–22, 434; horizontal and vertical integration of, *g209;* New Deal and, 456–57, 465; in World War II, 527, 530; after World War II, 599. *See also* business.
INF. *See* Intermediate-Range Nuclear Forces Treaty (INF).
inflation; under Carter, 839, *g839;* under Ford, 837, 839, *g839;* under Reagan, 859, 860; in World War II, 527, 528; after World War II, 632, *c632*
influenza, 314, 611
initiative, 252-53
In Our Times **(Sullivan),** *q266*
Inouye, Daniel K., 872, *q872*
INS. *See* Immigration and Naturalization Service (INS)
installment plan, 380, 381
Institute for Justice, 915
interest rates under Bush, 883; under Ford, 839; under Reagan, 859
Interim Committee, 516–18
Interior, Department of the, 455, 478
Intermediate-Range Nuclear Forces Treaty (INF), 867
Internal Revenue Service (IRS), Nixon and, 811, 826, 833
International Business Machines (IBM), 350, 601
Internet, the, *t87,* 921
Interstate Commerce Commission, in 1920s, 349; segregation and, 683
interstate highway system, 603, 654, *g654, m655*
interventionism, 502, 525
Inuit, 29, 744
invasion; of the Americas by Europeans, 30–34
inventions, 202–03
investors and English Colonies, 38
Invisible Man **(Ellison),** *q668*
Invisible Scar, The **(Bird),** *q434*
Iowa, 921
Iran; Eisenhower and, 587–88, 590; hostage crisis, 842, 856; sale of arms to, 872; after World War II, 566
Iran-*contra* **scandal,** 872–73
Iraq, 878–79, *m889*
Ireland; immigrants from, 39, 41, 49, 143, 199, 284
Ireland, Sam, *q266*
iron, 205, 209
iron curtain, 566–67
"iron horse," 159
Iroquois Alliance (Ganonsyani), *m26*, 26–27, *c27*
irreconcilables, 325–26
isolationism; World War II and, 502, 525
Israel, 591, 819, 841–42, 878, 879, 881, *m889*
Issei, 546
Italy; immigrants from, 236; Treaty of Versailles and, 324, 325; World War I and, 306–07, *m307*, 316; World War II and, 501, 509, 510. *See also* Mussolini, Benito.
Itliong, Larry, 739
Iwo Jima, 513–514
IWW. *See* Industrial Workers of the World (IWW).

J

Jackson, Andrew, 151, *p151*; Cherokee and, 136–139, *p137, q137*; election of, as President, 151–52, *p152*; Second Bank of the United States, and, 152-53; tariffs and, 153; veto by, 147
Jackson, Jesse, *p876, q876,* 876–77
Jackson, Mahalia, 686
Jackson, William, 85
Jackson (Miss.), 683, 686
Jackson State University, 794, *p794*
Jamestown (Va.), 37, *t38*, 40; Powhatans and, 20
Japan; atomic bombing of, 514–15, 516–19; automobiles from, 838; China and, 497; emperor's role, 497; expansionist policy in nineteenth century, 300–01, 497; expansionist policy in 1930s, 496, 497, *m505;* immigrants from, 301, 546; immigration restriction and, 284, 301, 406; isolationist period of, 220; Pearl Harbor attack by, 505, *p506,* 506, 508, 509; Russia and, 300–01, 497, 564; trade with, 220, *p220;* Treaty of Versailles and, 325, *p325;* Vietnam and, 768; Washington Conference and, 351; World War II and, 505, 508, 513–515, 516–19
Japanese Americans; internment of, 546–48, *p546, p547;* Ku Klux Klan and, 400; in World War II, 509, 546–48
Jaworski, Leon, 829, 830, 833
Jay, John, 68, 115, *p115*
Jay Treaty (1795), 115, *crt115*
jazz, 388–89, 533
Jazz Age, 389
Jazz Singer, The, 386, 387
Jefferson, Thomas, 67; Bill of Rights and, 90; death of, 78; Declaration of Independence by, 67, *q67*; Hamilton vs., 114–15; philosophy of, *q78, q115*; as President, 78, 112, *p112*, 116, 117, 131–32; presidential campaign of, 103, 116; as Secretary of State, 113, 115; Virginia consitution and, 73
Jeffrey, Sharon, *q788*
Jesuits, 38
jewelry; Native American, 24–25
Jews/Jewish Americans; anti-Semitism during 1930s and, 407, 467–68; concentration camps and, 511–12; Hitler and, 494, 511–12; Holocaust involving, 511–12; immigration of, 236, 407; Ku Klux Klan and, 400
JFK. *See* Kennedy, John F.
Jiang Jieshi (Chiang Kai-shek), 497, 572–73
"Jim Crow" laws, 282
jitterbuggers, 533, 617
Job, The **(Lewis),** *q368*
Job Corps, 810
John Paul II (Pope), 866, 868
Johnson, Albert, 404, 406
Johnson, Andrew, 184–85, 186, 187–88
Johnson, Edward, *q43*
Johnson, Hiram, 325, 404, 406
Johnson, Lyndon B., *p705,* 706, *q706*; affirmative action and, 916; civil rights and, 671, 682, 687, 694, 707–08; Goldwater v., 708, 772; Great Society of, *q708,* 708–09, *p717*; Kennedy's policies and, 706, 707–08; Medicare and, 708; personality and career of, 706–07; reelection and, 778–79; as Vice President, 681; Vietnam War and, 706, *q772,* 772, 773, 776, *q777,* 777–79, *p779, q779*
John Wanamaker (store), 207

Jones, Bobby, 387
Jones, Joe, *ptg480*
Jones, Mary Harris ("Mother"), 215, *p215,* 232
Joplin, Janis, 753, *p755*
Joplin, Scott, 288
Jordan, Barbara, *p833, q833*
Jordan, 881, *m889*
Jordan Marsh, 207
***Journey Through Chaos* (Meyer),** *q538*
***Journey to Pennsylvania* (Mittelberger),** *q40*
***Joy Luck Club, The* (Tan),** *q852,* 852–53
judges; Supreme Court, *q98,* 116
judicial branch, 84–85, *c85;* constitutional description of, *q99–100*
Judiciary Act (1801), 116, 117
Judiciary Committee of the House of Representatives. *See* House Judiciary Committee.
Juffure (West Africa), 126–27
***Jungle, The* (Sinclair),** 244
Justice, Department of, 684, 811
Jutland, Battle of, 308

K

kachina dolls, 47
Kaiser, Henry J., 527, 540
Kalakaua, King, 221
Kamenshek, Dorothy ("Kammie"), *p555*
Kansas; African Americans in, 184, 191; cattle ranching in, 197; farming in, 213; slavery and, 162, 170–71
Kansas-Nebraska Act (1854), 170, *m170*
Kanter, Rosabeth Moss, *q751*
Karadzic, Radovan, 898
Kearns, Doris. *See* Goodwin, Doris Kearns.
Kearny, 503
Kelley, Florence, *q246,* 246–47, *q247,* 255
Kellogg, Frank, 351
Kellogg-Briand Pact (1928), 351
Kelly, Gene, 651
Kennan, George, 566
Kennedy, Edward, 826
Kennedy, Jacqueline, *p700, p705,* 706
Kennedy, John F., 701, *q701, p705;* administration of, 702–03, *c704;* affirmative action and, 916; assassination and funeral of, 687, 704–06, *p711,* 718; Bay of Pigs and, 592; civil rights and, 655, *p681, q681,* 681–82, 684–86, *q686,* 702, 704; cold war and, 592–93, 703, 704; Congress and, 704; Cuban missile crisis and, 560, *p561,* 592–93; family of, 700, *p701,* 705; glamorization of, 702–03; immigration quotas and, 407; Inaugural Address, 698, *q698, p700, q700–01,* 700–01; Latin America and, 703; New Frontier of, *q702;* Nixon v., 655–56, 681; Peace Corps of, *q698,* 698, *p699,* 703; space and, *p702,* 703, *p720;* Vietnam and, 656, *q771,* 771–72; women and, 725
Kennedy, Joseph P., 700
Kennedy, Robert; assassination of, 780–81; civil rights and, 680, 681, *p681,* 682–84; minorities and, 780; as presidential candidate, 778, 780; Vietnam War and, 778
Kennelly, Martin, 488
Kent State University, *p793,* 793–94
Kentucky, 177
Kerensky, Aleksandr, 322–23
Kerner Report, 694
Kerouac, Jack, 749
Keynes, John Maynard, 858
Khomeini, Ruholla, 842
Khrushchev, Nikita; Cuban missile crisis and, 592–93, *p594;* on Dulles, *q579;* Eisenhower and, 581, 582
Kilroy, 533
King, Coretta Scott, 676, 681, *p695*
King, Martin Luther, Jr., 675–77; 1960 election and, 681; on America's flaws, *q779;* assassination of, 694–95, 779–80, 809; Chávez and, 736; education of, 676; Freedom Riders and, 681–83; "I have a dream" speech, *p663, q686;* "I've been to the mountaintop" speech, *q695;* as leader, 676; "Letter from Birmingham Jail," *q685;* Montgomery bus boycott and, *p675, q675,* 675–76; nonviolence and, 676–77, *q679, q685;* Selma campaign and, 687–89; split with SNCC and, 690–91; Vietnam War and, 695, 791
King, Martin Luther, Sr., 681
King, Mary, 724–25
King Kong, 447
King Philip's War, 47
"King Philip" (Metacomet), 47
Kinte, Kunta, 126–27
Kissinger, Henry, 797–98, 799, 800, 816–19, 821, 825, *crt825*
"Kiss Me Clubs," 359
kivas, Anasazi, 23
Kline, Franz, *ptg558*
Knights of St. Crispin, 215
Knights of Labor, 215
Knox, Henry, *q83*
Knoxville (Tenn.), 342
Kokomo (Ind.), 400
Kongo kingdom, 34
Korea, 220, 300, 497, 574. *See also* Korean War.
Korean Airlines jet, attack on, 866
Korean War, 573, 574–75, *m574,* 637
***Korematsu* v. *United States* (1944),** 548
Kosovo, 898
Kovic, Ron, *q764,* 764–65
Kramer, John, 344
Krause, Allison, 794
Kroc, Ray, 760
Kronenwetter, Ralph, 640, 641
Ku Klux Klan; in 1920s, 399–401, *m400;* and African Americans in 1950s, 621–22, 671; during reconstruction, 187, *p187*
Kunen, James, 791
Kuwait, 878–79, *m889*

L

Labor, 215; in 1920s, 357–58; child, 246–47, 285, 345, 460, 538; factory system, 140–43, *q140*; immigrant vs. enslaved, 165–66; indentured, 40, 41, *p41*; and limiting the workday, 213, 215; NAFTA and, 882; Populist party and, 212–13; progressives and, 285–87; in textile mills, *q140,* 140–43; Truman and, 632–33; unions: *see* unions; women's, 140–43, *q140;* workers, 1800–1960, *c211;* workers' compensation and, 254, 279, 623; after World War I, 341; World War I and, 318; World War II and, 530–31, 539, 544
Labor, Department of, 455, 729–30, 740
***Labor Leaders in America* (Chávez),** *q737*
La Brigada, 591, 592
Lafayette, Marie Joseph, 54
La Follette, Robert; as govenor of Wisconsin, *crt250,* 250–51, *p252,* 252–53, 319; as irreconcilable, 325; as Republican, 276
La Guardia, Fiorello, 399
Laird, Melvin, 798, *crt825*
Lake Erie, 128, 144–45
Lake Michigan, 149
Lamont, Thomas W., *q309*
Lancaster (PA), 40, 123
landfills, 904–05
land grants; English royal, 40
Landon, Alfred, 471
landowners; African Americans as, 188–89, 190, 283
Landrum, Roger, *q698*
Lange, Dorothea, *p414, p425,* 425
Langeron, Roger, 500
languages, Native American, 46, 135, 137
Laos, 769, *m769,* 770, 773, 774, 798, 799, 800
La Raza Unida, 735, 741
Lardner, Ring, Jr., 648, 651
Las Casas, Bartolomé de, *q32,* 32-33
"latchkey children," 538
Latimer, Lewis, 241, *p241*
Latin America; in 1920s, 352; in 1950s and 1960s, 819; Bush and, 881–82, Carter and, 841; cold war in, 591–93, 820–21, 870–72, 873; debt in, 819–20; governments in, 820–21; Kennedy and, 592–93, 703; liberation theology and reform movements in, *p820,* 820–21; Nixon and, 821; Reagan and, 870–73; Roosevelt, Franklin, and, 493; U.S. intervention in, *t297,* 820–21, 841, 870–73, 881, 897–98; *See also* Central America; names of individual countries.
latitude, 7
Latvia, 869
Laughlin, Harry H., *q405*
Law, Nathaniel, 65
Lawrence (Kans.), 162
Lawson, John Howard, 648, *q649*
Lawton, Elizabeth Boyd, 361
LBJ. *See* Johnson, Lyndon Baines.
League of Nations, 323, 325–27, *crt327;* aggression in 1930s and, 497; United States and, 347
League of Women Voters, 730
Leary, Bob, *q435*
Leary, Timothy, 749
Lease, Mary E., *q212*
Le Duc Tho, 798
Lee, Henry, 114
Lee, Robert E., 172, 173, 175, 178, 179, *q179,* 182, *p182*
legislative branch, 84–85, *c85, q91,* 91–96; constitutional description of, *q91,* 91–96
legislatures; in colonial America, 45, 48, 50, 72–74, 90
Lekachman, Robert, *q843*
LeMay, Curtis, 782
Lend-Lease Act (1941), 502–03
Lenin, V. I., 322–23; and Rockefeller Center mural, 472, 473–74
Leningrad, siege of, 510
Lenni Lenape, *ptg40*
"Letter from Birmingham Jail" (King), *q685*
Leutze, Emanuel, *ptg70*
Levis, 226–27
Lewis and Clark Expedition, 130, 132, *p132*
Levitt & Sons, 604
Levittown, *m604,* 604–05, *p605,* 607
Lewis, John (of SNCC), 687, 688
Lewis, John L. (of UMW and CIO), *t466,* 502, 530
Lewis, Meriwether, 130, 132
Lewis, Sinclair, *q368, q376,* 391
Lewis, Sybil, *q534*
Lexington (Mass.), 60, 64, *p64,* 66, *t68,* 87
liberals; Kennedy and, 702, 703; Nixon and, 813; Truman and, 634
liberation theology, *p820,* 820–21
Liberator, The, *q166, q167*
Liberia, 301
Liberty Bonds, 314–15, 317
Liberty ships, 540, *p541*
Lichtenstein, Roy, 754
Liddy, G. Gordon, 826
Lieberman, Joseph, 912
"Like a Rolling Stone" (Dylan), *q748*
Lilienthal, David, *q539*
Liliuokalani, Queen, 221, *p221*

Limbaugh, Rush, 900
limited war, policy of, 574
Lincoln, Abraham, *p180;* and African Americans, 173–74, 176–77; assasination and funeral of, 180, *p180;* as Commander-in-Chief, 173, 174, 176, 178, 179–80; election as President, 172; and Emancipation Proclamation, 176–77; Reconstruction plans of, 179–80, 184, at Richmond, 172; Second Inaugural Address of, *q180;* Senate race by, 171
Lincoln Memorial Concert, 476–77
Lindbergh, Charles, 388, 394, *p394,* 484, 502, 503
Lindeux, Robert, *ptg138*
Lippmann, Walter, *q453*
liquor, taxes, 114
Lissitsky, El, *ptg322*
literacy; in colonial America, 39, *p39*
literacy tests, 284–85, 689
Literary Guild, 390
Lithuania, 869
"Little Boxes" (Reynolds), *q608*
"Little Orphan Annie," 336, 526
Little Richard, 616, *p616,* 752–53
Little Rock (Ark.), 666, *p667,* 671–72, *p672*
Livermore, Mary Rice, *p177*
livestock; imported, 33, *p33,* 36, 122
Lloyd, Henry Demarest, *q220*
Lloyd George, David, 323
lobbying; by railroads, 250; Wilson, Woodrow, and, 278
Locke, Alain, 391
Lodge, Henry Cabot, 326, 327,404, *q405,* 406
lodges, Iroquois, 26, *p26*
log cabins, *ptg133*
logging industry, 910
Logue, Sarah, 167
Loguen, Jerry, 167, *q167*
London, World War II and, 501–02, *p501,* 515
Lone Ranger, The, *p610*
Long, Jefferson H., *p188*
longhouses, 26, *p27, m28*
Long, Huey P., 468
Long Island (N.Y.), 44
longitude, 7
Longworth, Alice Roosevelt, 348
looms, textile, *c142*
Lopez, Pedro and Maria, 618–19, 622
Los Angeles (Calif.) (city); African Americans in, 622; growth of after World War II, 607, *m607;* Hispanic Americans and, 735; riots in, 693, *p693*
Los Angeles (Calif.) (county), 715
"Lost Generation," 390
Lott, Trent, *q906*
Louisiana; Civil War and, 172; and Long, Huey P., 468; in Reconstruction, 187; in Sunbelt, *m814,* 814; voting rights and, 253, 689
Louisiana Purchase, *m121,* 131–32, *m131, m161;* Missouri Compromise and, 168
Love Canal (N.Y.), 842
Lowell, Abbott Lawrence, 339
Lowell, Francis Cabot, 141–42
Lowell (Mass.), 142–43, 924
Low Income Home Energy Assistance Program, 909
Lowndes County Freedom Organization, 692–93
loyalty board, 644
Loyalty Leagues, 318
loyalty oaths, 647
LSD. *See* lysergic acid diethylamide.
Lucky Dragon, 581
Lucy, Autherine, 671
Ludlow Massacre, *m286*
lumber industry, 421
Lumpkin, Wilson, 137, *p137,* 138
Lusitania, 304, *p304,* 310
Luxembourg, World War II and, 501, 511
lynching, 247, *g247;* of German American, 319; Hoover, Herbert, and, 479; by Ku Klux Klan, 400, 622; Roosevelt, Franklin, and, 479; Truman and, 634
Lynd, Robert and Helen Merrell, 362, *q364,* 386
***Lyndon Johnson and the American Dream* (Goodwin),** *q706, q779*
lysergic acid diethylamide (LSD), 749

M

MacArthur, Douglas; bonus army and, 426–27; Korean War and, 574–75, *crt575;* in World War II, 514
machine politics, 238, 285; La Follette and, 251, 252–53; Wilson, Woodrow, and, 275
machines; in 1920s, 377; for farming, 377, 385, 415, 432
machine tools industry, 355
MacIntosh, Ebenezer, 56
Macy's, 207
Maddox, *t771*
Madero, Francisco, 305
Madison, James, 83, *p83,* 84, 89, 90; as President, 117–18, *crt118,* 147; as secretary of state, 116; veto by, 147
Maginot line, 501
Mailer, Norman, *q781*
mail-order business, *p208*
Maine, 168
Maine, 222
***Main Street* (Lewis),** 391
***Making Do: How Women Survived the '30s* (Westin),** *q436*
malaria, 177, 222 302, 303
Malcolm X, *q691, p692,* 692
Mali, 34
Maltz, Albert, 648
management, of large enterprises; in late 1800s, 208; in 1920s, 357
***Man at the Crossroads Looking with Hope and High Vision to the Choosing of a New and Better Future* (Rivera),** 472
Manchu Dynasty, 299
Manchukuo, 497
Manchuria, 300, 497
Mandan, 132
Mandela, Nelson, 880–81
Mandinka, 126–27
Manhattan Island (NY), 39, *p143*
Manifest Destiny, 219
Manila (Philippines), 515
Manila Bay, 222
***Man Nobody Knows, The* (Barton),** 353–54
Mansfield, Mike, *c827, p827*
manufacturing; in 1899, *m263;* beginning of, 140–43; computers in, 921; employee income in 1920s, *g377;* mass production of heavy industry goods, 205; military cutbacks and, 882–83; overtakes agriculture, 205
Mao Zedong (Mao Tse-tung), *p572,* 572–73; Nixon and, 818
Marbury* v. *Madison, 116–17
Marbury, William, 116–17
March on the Pentagon, 790–91
March on Washington, 686, *p686*
March on Washington Movement (MOWM), 544, 545
"March to the Sea," 178
Mariel Boatlift, 735
marijuana, 749–50
Market Basket, 64, 182, 240, 394, 428, 506, 584, 719, 802, 874
markets; in 1920s, 350, 352; Asian, 220, 298–99, 770; after Cold War, 881–82; expansionism and, 220, 294–95, 298–99
Marne, Second Battle of the, 316
"Marriage of the Waters," 128, *p129*
Married Woman's Property Act (1848), 259–60
Mars, 921
Marshall, George C., 510, 568, 573
Marshall, John; as Chief Justice, 101, 116–17, 136–39
Marshall, Thurgood, 670, *p670, q924*
Marshall Field (store), 207
Marshall Plan, 568
Martí, José, 221
Martine, Thomas E., 275
Marx, Karl, 323
Marx Brothers, *p429*
Maryland, 144, 145, 254, 535; Articles of Confederation ratification by, 81–82; colonial, *t38,* 40
masks, *p34,* 47
Mason, George, 73
Massachusetts, American Revolution and, 56, 58–60, 64, *t68;* Constitution (federal) and, 90; colonial, 36–37, *t38,* 38–39, 42–45, 47; Constitution (federal) and, 90; constitution (state) of, 74; loyalty oath for teachers, *q647;* Missouri Compromise and, 168; Sacco and Vanzetti trial and, 338–40; Shays, Daniel, and, *p82,* 82–83, *t90. See also* Concord (Mass.).
Massachusetts Bay Colony, 36, 39, 42–45
Massachusetts Spy, *p87*
massive retaliation policy, 579–80
mass media. *See* media.
materialism; in 1920s, 390
Mather, Cotton, *q49*
matriarchy, 26, *c27*
Mauldin, Bill, 510
Maximilian, (Emperor of Mexico), 220
Maynadier, Henry, *q200*
Mazo, Earl, 656
McAdoo, William Gibbs, 315, 317
McCain, Franklin, 678
McCarran Act (1950), 644
McCarthy, Eugene, 778, 779, 780
McCarthy, Joseph, 628, *p629, p645,* 645–46, *p646, p657*
McCarthyism, 645
McClintock, Mary Ann, 258
McCord, James W., 828
McCormick Harvesting Machine Company, 207, 216
McCoy, Joseph G., *q197*
McCullough* v. *Maryland, 101
McDonald's, *p760,* 760–61
McDonnell-Douglas, 882
McElvaine, Robert S., 425
McGinnis, Joe, 803
McGovern, George, 822, *q822,* 826
McKay, Claude, 391–92
McKinley, William; assassination of, *p266,* 266–67; Cuba and, 221–22; election of, 214; expansionism and, 221–22; Philippines and, 222–23, 292, 299–300; Roosevelt, Theodore, and, 267–68; Spanish-American War and, 221–23
McKissick, Floyd, 690
McNamara, Robert, 772, 790
McNamee, Graham, 374
McNeil, Joseph, 677
McPherson, Aimee Semple, 397, *p397*
McVeigh, Timothy, 920
Meade County (Kans.), 430
Meadlo, Paul, *q792*
Meany, George, 822
measles, 234
Meat Inspection Act (1906), 272
meatpacking, 206, 244–45, 272; mergers and, 209, 356
media; in 1920s, 375, 381; in 1930s, 444; Kennedy vs. Nixon and, 656, *p656,* 657; Nixon and, 813; Vietnam War and, 777, 791–93; in World War II, 525–26

Medical Care Act (1965), *c707*
medical discoveries, 550–51, *t550–51*
medical insurance, 894–95
Medicare and Medicaid, 708; Clinton and, 895, 902; Reagan and, 858. *See also* health care costs.
Mellon, Andrew, 348, 349, 354, 421
melting pot, 283–84
Memphis (Tenn.), *m175,* 176, 187, 248, 695, 715, 753
Mencken, H. L., 391
Menlo Park (N.J.), 205, 240
mental health care, 155
Meredith, James, 684, 690
Mergenthaler, Ottmar, *t205*
mergers; in late 1800s, 208–09; in 1890s, 239; 1895–1920, *g269;* in 1920s, 356; in 1950s, 601, in 1990s, 884
Merrimack, 176
Merrimack River (Mass.), 142-43
Mesa Verde (Col.), 24, *p24*
Metacom, (Philip), 47, *p47*
Metropolis, p364
Mexican Americans, 734–35; in 1950s, 622–23; in Depression, 433; as feminists, 728; and home front during World War II, 537–38; as immigrants, 402, 735; Ku Klux Klan and, 400; as migrant farmworkers, 623; as tenant farmers, 433. *See also* Hispanic Americans.
Mexican American War, 169, *p169,* 173, 219
Mexico, 23, 37; in 1960s and 1970s, 820, 821; *bracero* program and, 407, 623, 735; California and influence of, 198; cattle ranchers influenced by, 197; conquest of, 32, 34; French intervention in, 220; immigrants from, 623, 735, 736, NAFTA and, 896–97, Spanish and, 32, 34, 37; revolution in, 305–06
Meyer, Agnes E., 538
Miami (Fla.), 735, 781
Miami (Native American people), 134
Michigan, 454, *c466,* 537
Michigan, University of, 789
middle class, in 1890s, 239; in 1920s, 376–83; African Americans in, *t916,* 916–17; under Bush, 884; under Clinton, 907; suburbanization of, 603–07
Middle colonies, 37, 38–40
Middle Passage, *p35*
Middle East; Camp David Accord, 841–42; and energy crisis, *m837,* 837–38; Nixon and, 818–19; peace effort, 910–11, *p910;* Persian Gulf War in, *p878,* 878–79, *m889*
***Middletown* (Lynd),** *q364,* 386
Midvale Steel Works, 365
Midway, Battle of, 513
Midway Islands, 221
migrant farmworkers, 287, 623, *p623, m627,* 738–39
migration; African America forced, 34–35; Early European, 30–34; prehistoric, 16, 22–23, *m23;* during World War II, 534–36, *m535, m553*
militants; anti-war, 809; Native American, 743–44
military-industrial complex, 583
military; African Americans in, *p54,* 54, *p173,* 173–74, 315, *p315,* 509, 544; cuts in, 877–78, 882–83; minorities in, 509; Native Americans and U.S., 509; government by during Reconstruction, 185, *p185,* 188–89, 190–91; women in, 730. *See also* War, Department of; Navy, United States; West Point.
military draft; in Civil War, 178; lottery for, 315; peacetime, 502; in Vietnam War, *c789,* 789; in World War I, 315; in World War II, 502, 509
Milligan, ex parte, 185
mills. *See* steelmaking; textile mills.
Mills, C. Wright, *q365–66, q601*
Milosevic, Slobodan, 898
mineral resources, 25, 198, 205
Minh. *See* Ho Chi Minh.
minimum wage, under Eisenhower, 655; under Fair Deal of Truman, 635, 637; under Johnson, Lyndon, *c707;* under Kennedy, 703; for women, 345, 349
mining; *m181,* 198, 215, 271; in 1920s, *g377,* 421; child labor and, 232; Roosevelt, Franklin, and, 530; strikes in 216, 271–72, 530
Minneapolis (Minnesota), 892
minority groups; in 1950s, 601; Civilian Conservation Corps (CCC) and, 456, 479; in Congress, 894, 919; feminism and, 726; Ford, Henry, and, 364; Roosevelt, Franklin, and, 478–79, 538, 544, 547; Social Security Act and, 470; unions and, 217; in World War II, 509, 537–38, 542–48; *See also* African Americans; Asian Americans; Cuban Americans; Hispanic Americans; Japanese Americans; Jews/Jewish Americans; Korean Americans; Mexican Americans; Native Americans; Puerto Rican Americans; discrimination.
Minuteman, the, 60, *p64*
***Miranda* v. *Arizona* (1966),** *c715,* 716–717, *q717*
missionaries, 220; to China, 298, *p298. See also* Christianity.
missions, Spanish, 37, *p52*
Mississippi; civil rights and, 689, 691; Civil War and, 172; in Sunbelt, *m814,* 814; Reconstruction in, 185, 187. *See also* Jackson (Miss.).
Mississippi Freedom Democratic Party (MFDP), 691, *p691*
Mississippi Freedom Summer Project, 787
Mississippi River, 14, 145, 148, *p159;* in Civil War, *m175,* 176; flood of, 348–49, *p395*
Mississippi, University of, 684
Missouri, 602; in Civil War, 176–77; disagreements of admission of, 168
Missouri Compromise, 164, 168–69, *m170,* 170
Missouri River, 132, 148
Mitchell, Franklin D., 534
Mitchell, John, 811, *crt825,* 826, 829, *p829*
Mitchell, Margaret, *q440,* 440–41
Mitchell, Maria, 183
Mittelberger, Gottfried, *q40*
Moat, Hope, 436
Mobile (Ala.), 536, 814
mobilization, 315, 317–19
Model A car, 380
Model Cities Act, 709
***Model of Christian Charity, A,* (Winthrop),** *q36*
Model T car, 361, 378, 379, 380
Mohawk, 26, *m26, p46*
molasses, 57
Molotov, V. M., 565–66
money; Continental, 82, *p113;* credit and, 380, 381; Great Depression and, 422; hard, 82; "In God We Trust" added to, 609; silver and gold as, 82, 213, 214
"moneyed aristocracy" phrase, 151
Monitor, 176
monopolies, 269, *c270,* 270–71
Monopoly, 446
Monroe, James, 147, 151, 219; Louisiana Purchase and, 131–32; veto by, 147
Monroe Doctrine, 219, 220; Roosevelt, Theodore, and corollary to, *crt294,* 297–98, 305; Taft's Dollar Diplomacy and, 298, 305
Montana, 197
Montgomery (Ala.), 674–76, 680
Montgomery Improvement Association, 675
Montgomery Ward, *p208,* 361
Moody, Anne, *q684*
Moody, Paul, 141
Moon, Sun Myung, and "Moonies," 750
moon, NASA landing on, 802, *p802*
Moore, Michael, 883
moral majority, 857
Morehouse College, 676
Morgan, J. P., *q208,* 209, 264, *crt265,* 354; Roosevelt, Theodore, and, 270, 271, 272
Mormons, *p154,* 154
"morning in America," 856
Morocco, 301, 510, 879
Moscow, 510
Mosinee (Wis.), *p640,* 640–41
Morrow, 390
Mossadeg, Mohammed, 590
motion pictures and movies; in 1920s, 355, 370, 386–87, 395, 410–11, 429; in 1930s, 443–44, 446; in 1950s, 603, 609; in 1960s, 756, 803; in 1980s, 875; McCarthyism and, 648–51; musicals, 443; talkies, 387, 443; and World War II, 507, 525–26, *p552*
Motown, 585, 616
Mott, Lucretia C.; *p156,* 258, 259, 260
Mound Builders, 24–25, *p25*
MOWM. *See* March on Washington Movement.
Mowry, George, 387, *q388*
***Mr. Black Labor* (Davis),** 542
"Mr. Roosevelt Regrets" (Murray), 538
***Mrs. Schuyler Burning her Wheat Fields* (Leutze),** *ptg70*
***Ms.* magazine,** 728–29, *p729*
muckrakers, 244–45; workers' safety and, 254
Muir, John, *p268,* 269
Muller, Curt, 255
***Muller* v. *Oregon* (1903),** *p255,* 255–56
Muncie (Ind.), 357, 386
Munich Pact (1938), 496
Murao, Helen, 546
Murmansk (Russia), 323
Murphy, Frank, *c466*
Murphy, Harold, 513
Murray, Pauli, 538
Murray, Philip, 538
Muscle Shoals (Ala.), 343
Museum of Modern Art, 473
music; in 1860s, 183; in 1880s, 241; in 1920s, 388–89, 395, 429; in 1930s, 424–25; in 1950s, 585; in 1960s, 719, 848–49; in 1980s, 887; blues, 388–89; colonial era, 65, 110, 111; jazz, 388–89; ragtime, 288; rhythm and blues (R&B), 752–53; rock, 616–17, 749, 752–54, 756–57; in World War I, 293; in World War II, 507, 526, 533
musicals, 446, 585, 752
Muskie, Edmund, 822, 826
Muslims; in Bosnia, 897
Mussolini, Benito, 325, *p493,* 493–94, 495; France's surrender and, 501; Franco aided by, 495; rise of, 493–94
My Diplomatic Education, *q321*
My Lai massacre, 792–93

N

NAACP. *See* National Association for the Advancement of Colored People (NAACP)
Nader, Ralph, 912
NAFTA. *See* North American Free Trade Agreement (NAFTA)
Nagasaki, 515
Nanjing, 497, *p498*
Napoleon Bonaparte. *See* Bonaparte, Napoleon.
Napoleon III, 220
NASA. *See* National Aeronautics and Space Administration (NASA)

Nashville, 297
Nashville (Tenn.); civil rights and, 678
Nasser, Gamal Abdel, 591
Natchez (Miss.), 176
Natchez people, 25
Nation, *q295*
Nation at Risk, A, 923
National Advisory Commission on Civil Disorders, 694
National Aeronautics and Space Administration (NASA), 582, 654. 703, 844, 845, *t844–45*
National American Woman Suffrage Association (NAWSA), 253, 261, 344–45
National Association for the Advancement of Colored People (NAACP), 248, 283; affirmative action and, 924–25; vs. Randolph, A. Philip, 544; segregation and, 670–71, 684, 686, *q812;* in World War I, 315; in World War II, 544, 545
national bank. *See* Bank of the United States.
National Black Feminist Organization, 728
National Consumers League (NCL), 247, 255
national debt, federal bonds, 113–14; post-Revolutionary War, 82, 101, 113–14
National Dollar Stores, *p356*
National Empowerment Television, 900
National Endowment for the Arts (NEA), 902–03
National Endowment for the Humanities (NEH), 902–03
National Highway Traffic Safety Administration, 860
National Housing Act (1937), 481
National Housing Agency, 536
National Industrial Recovery Act (NIRA) (1933); industrial production and, 456–57, *c481;* labor and, 466, 467; Supreme Court and, 469, 470; Wagner Act and, 470
Nationalists (in China). *See* China.
nationalization of oil, 590
National Labor Relations Act (1935), 633, 739, 740
National Labor Relations Board (NLRB), 470, *c481*
National Liberation Front (NLF), 771, 773. *See also* Vietnam War.
National Negro Business League, *p357*
National Organization for Women (NOW), 727–28, 729, 731
National Origins Act (1924), 401, 404–07, 546
national parks and monuments, *t269,* 269, *m291,* 455, 903
National party, Cherokee, 139
National Recovery Administration (NRA), 456–57, 459, 478
National Republican party, 151, 153
National Rifle Association (NRA), 896
National Road, 144, 145
National Security Act (1947), 589
National Security Agency, 826
National Security Council (NSC), 573, 589; Reagan and, 873
National Socialist German Workers' party, 494
National Urban League, 248
National War Labor Board (NWLB), 527–28, 530, 531
National Woman's party (NWPC), 344, 345, 730
National Woman Suffrage Association, 261
National Women's Political Caucus, (NWPC), 728
National Women's Trade Union League, *p247*
National Youth Administration, 478, 539
Nationhood; early, 78–90, 110–23; territorial expansion and 128–39
Nation of Islam, 692
Native Americans, 27; in 1960s and 1970s, 742–45; African Americans compared with, 479; agriculture, 23, 25–26, 33–34; Aleut, 29, 744; Algonquian, 26; American Indian Movement (AIM), 743, 744, *p758;* Anasazi, 23–24, *p24;* Apache, *p200;* Arapaho, 201; Arawak, 30; Arctic cultural area, *m28,* 29; Aztec, 32, *ptg32;* Blackfeet, 28, 624; Cahokia people, 25; in Canada, Cayuga, Cherokee. *See* Cherokee; Cheyenne, 28, *p29;* 201, *t201;* Choctaw, 25, 48, 624; as Christians, 20, 32; Civilian Conservation Corps (CCC) and, 456; Cliff Dweller, 23–24; clothing, *q24;* colonial era settlers and, 20; as cowhands, 198; Creek, 25, 48; Crow, 28, 201; cultural areas (1500s to 1800s), *m28,* 28–29; Dakota, 28; Dawes Act and, *t480;* distribution of, *m26, m28,* 29, *m53, m121, m746, m747;* Eastern Native Groups (1500s), *m26;* Eastern Woodland, 25–27; education of, 46–47, 135, 743; egalitarianism among, 23, 27; Eisenhower and, 624, 743; enslavement of 32–33; environments of, 28–29; Europeans' diseases devastate, 32–33; feminism and, 726, 728; Great Plains cultural area, 28, *m28,* 29, *p29;* Hopi, 24, 624, 745; housing types for, 24, 25, 26, *c27,* 28–29, *m28, p29;* Huron, 26; Inca, 32; Indian Reorganization Act and, 479–80, 624; Inuit, 29, 744; Iroquois, 26–*c27,* 48; Iroquois Alliance, 26–27; lands reserved for, 47–48, *m53,* 57, 133–39; Lenni Lenape, *ptg40;* Mandan, 132; Marine Signal Corps and, 509; Mohawk, 26, *p46;* Mound Builders' culture of, 24–25, *p25;* Natchez, 25; Navajo, *t201, p479,* 509, 745; New Deal and, 479–80, 743; Nez Percé, *t201;* Nixon and, 742–43; Northwest Coast cultural area, 28–29; *m28;* Oglala Sioux, 201, *p201,* 743–44; Oneida, 26; Onondaga, 26; Ottawa, 57; Passamaquoddy, *c744, m744;* Penobscot, *c744, m744;* poverty among, 479, 624, 743, 747; Powhatans, 20; Proclamation of 1763 for, 57; Puyallup, 744; reservations for, 624, 746–47; second great removal of, 200–01, *m225;* in Revolutionary War, 69; Seminole, 624; in Senate, 894; Seneca, 26, 182; Shawnee, 134–35; Shoshone, 132; Sioux, 201, *t201,* 744. *See also* Oglala Sioux and Spanish explorers, *q2–3;* spiritual beliefs of, 742–43. *See also* religion, of Native Americans. Taos Pueblo, *q24,* 47, 742–43, 745; termination policy and, 624, 746; treaties with, 200, *t480;* Voluntary Relocation Program, 624, *p624,* 746; Wampanoag, 47; wars with, 47–48; wigwams, 26; Winnebago, *t201;* women as, 20–21, *p21,* 132; women leadership among, 20, 24, 26, *c27;* in World War II, 509, 540; Zuni, 24. *See also* Attucks, Crispus; Tecumseh; Tenskwatawa.
nativists, 284–85
naturalization, *q94*
NATO. *See* North Atlantic Treaty Organization (NATO).
Navajo, *t201, t479,* 509, 745
navigators, European, 30–31; in World War I, 316
Navy, United States; in Civil War, 176; in the Constitution, *q95, q98;* sea battles, *ptg117;* in War of 1812, *ptg117;* in World War II, 503
NAWSA. *See* National American Woman Suffrage Association (NAWSA).
Nazi party, 494. *See also* Hitler, Adolf.
NEA. *See* National Endowment for the Arts (NEA).
Nebraska; cattle ranching and, 197, Kansas-Nebraska Act and, 170, *m170;* primary, 780
"Necessary and proper" clause, 95
Negro Affairs Division of the National Youth Administration, 478
"Negro Artist and the Racial Mountain, The" (Hughes), 392
NEH. *See* National Endowment for the Humanities (NEH).
neoconservatism, 857
Netherlands, 501, 513; settlers from, 39. *See also* Dutch.
networks, communication, *t86–87*
Neustadt, Richard, *q705–06*
neutrality; international, 115; in World War I, 309–10; in World War II, 498
Neutrality Acts (1935, 1936), 498
Nevada, 169, 198
New Amsterdam, 39, 40
Newark (N.J.), 694
New Brunswick (N.J.), 400
New Deal; backlash against, 631–33; coalition ends, 783, 905; criticism of, 465–66, 467–69, 471, 641; end of, 539; Fair Deal vs. 637; farmers and, 439, 457, 465–66, 469, 470; First, 455–60; government's role changed by, 480–81; Great Society vs., 709; legislation of, *c481;* Second, 469–71; successes and failures of, 465; Supreme Court and, 469, 471; women and, 477–78
New England colonies, 36–37, 38–39
New Federalism, 810
Newfoundland, 504
New France, 37–38, *t38*
New Freedom (of Woodrow Wilson), 278–79
New Hampshire; constitutional ratification by, 90; primaries in, 778
New Jersey, *m53;* colonial woman suffrage in, 74; illegal aliens and, 919; vote for women in, 259
Newlands Reclamation Act (1902), 269
New Look, 579
New Mexico, 34, 169; Native Americans in, 742–43; Spanish, 37, 47; in Sunbelt, *m814,* 814
New Negro, The **(Locke),** 391
New Orleans (La.), 48, 131–32; Battle of, 118; in Civil War, 176; jazz in, 389
New Orleans Tribune, *q180, q183*
Newport (R.I), 210, *p210*
newspapers, *t86,* 87; in 1920s, 390; Red Scare and, 340, 341; Spanish-American War and, 222; strikes and, syndicates, 390; tabloids, 390; Vietnam War and, 777, 792–93, 799; women reporters on, 477, *p477*
New York (City), *p13,* 68, 144–45, *p145,* in 1950s, 618–19; Bronx in, *p18;* Brooklyn Bridge in, 194, *p195;* Coney Island in, 289, *p289;* Cubans in, 735; decrease in crime in, 920; Delancey Street in 1905, *p262;* in Depression, 425; in Civil War, 178; East Harlem in, 618–19; East Village in, 751; garbage and, 904–05; Erie Canal and, 128, 144–45; founding of, 39; Harlem in, 391–92, 537, 622; Hell's Kitchen in, 245; poverty in, 618; Prohibition in, 399; Puerto Ricans in, 622, 735; skyscrapers in, 356; Tammany Hall and, 238, *crt238;* Times Square in, *p337;* panic of 1873, 190
New York (State), 68, 144–45, *p145,* 147; illegal aliens and, 916; ratification of Constitution and, *p89,* 90; western land ceded by, 81
New Yorker, 389
New York Times, 416; Pentagon Papers and, 799
New York University, 357
Nez Percé, *t201*
Ngo Dinh Diem, *p770,* 770–72, 792
Nguyen Van Thieu, 773, 797, 800
Nicaragua, 735; canal proposals for *m302,* 302–03; *contras* and, 871–72; U.S. interventions in, *t297,* 352
Nichols, Terry, 920
Nineteenth Amendment (1920), *q106, p260,* 261, 343, *t344,* 344–45, 725
Niño, Pedro Alonso, 34

Nintendo, 928–29
Ninth Amendment (1791), *q106*
NIRA. *See* National Industrial Recovery Act (NIRA).
Nisei, 546
Nixon, Richard, 631, 810, *q810,* 825; affirmative action and, 917; background of, 809–10; California governor's election and, *q781;* character of, 825, 830; "Checkers" speech and, 653, *p653;* China and, 816, *p817,* 817–18; civil rights and, 655, 681, 809, *crt809,* 810, *q812,* 812–13; divisive tactics of, 809–10; Eisenhower and, 653; elected to Congress, 631, *p631;* "enemies list" of, 826; environmental protection and, 903; Ford pardon of, 831, 837; foreign policy of, *q810,* 816–19, 821; Great Society programs and, 810–11; Hiss and, 642–43; House Un-American Activities Committee and, 641, *p641,* 642; impeachment proceedings against, 830–31, 832–35; imperial presidency and, *crt825,* 825–26; Kennedy v., 655–56, 681; labor and, 740; Latin America and, 821; Middle East and, 818–19; *Miranda* and, 717; Native Americans and, 742–43; New Federalism of, 810–11; as presidential candidate, 656, 781–82, *p782, q782,* 782–83, *m783,* 808, 809; reelection campaign, 821–22, *q822;* resignation of, 806, *p807,* 830–31; "southern strategy" of, *crt809,* 811–12, 813; Vietnam War and, 782, 793, 797–801; Watergate and, *crt823,* 824–31, *t830, crt831;* welfare reform and, 810
Nixon Doctrine, 797
NLF. *See* National Liberation Front.
NLRB. *See* National Labor Relations Board (NLRB).
Nobel Peace Prize, 300
nomadic cultures, 23, 28, *p29*
non-violent resistance, 676–77, 679, 684–85, 687–89. *See also* civil disobedience.
Norden Systems, 885
Norfolk (Va.), 814
Norfolk navy yard, 176
Noriega, Manuel, 881
Normandy, 510
Norris, George, 343, 497
North; African American migration to, 191; during Reconstruction, 190; draft riots and, 178; Missouri Compromise and, 168–69; slavery and, 165–66; vs. South in Civil War, 172–80, *m173, g177*
North, Oliver, 873
North Africa; World War II and, 510, *m511*
North America; European exploration routes (1492–1550), 30–32, *m31*
North American Aviation, 542
North American Free Trade Agreement (NAFTA), 881–82, 896–97
North American Indian Women's Association, 728
North Atlantic Treaty Organization (NATO), 571, *m595,* 898
North Carolina, *m53;* Civil War and, 173, *m175;* 689; land ceded to Tennessee, *p81;* in Sunbelt, *m814,* 814; tobacco grown in, 165
North Dakota, 132, 197
Northeast, *m28,* 143
Northern Pacific Railroad, 270
Northern Securities Company, 270
North Korea, *m574,* 574
Northwest Coast villages; Native American, 28–29, *m28*
Northwestern University, 357
Northwest Ordinance (1787), 82, 132, 133–34, *q134,* 155
Norway, 501
Notes of a Native Son **(Baldwin),** *q622*
Nova Gallia (New France), 37–38, *t38*
November Revolution. *See* Russian Revolution.
NOW. *See* National Organization for Women (NOW).
NRA. *See* National Recovery Administration (NRA) *or* National Rifle Association (NRA).
nuclear freeze march, 867
nuclear power plants, 843, *p843*
nuclear weapons; arms control and, 818, 840–41; Bush and, 867–68; fallout from, *c580, p580,* 581, 582–83; Reagan and, 866–67; SALT and, 818, 840; Soviet Union and, 576–77, 580; test-ban treaties, 583, 867–68; United States and, 514–15, 566, 576–78, 580–81, 583. *See also* arms race; atomic bomb; disarmament.
nullification, theory of, 153
NWLB. *See* National War Labor Board (NWLB).
NWPC. *See* National Women's Political Caucus (NWPC).
nylon, 533, *t638,* 803

O

Oakland (Calif.), 694
O'Brien, John, *q883*
Ocala (Fla.), 214
Occupational Safety and Health Administration (OSHA), 810
OCD. *See* Office of Civilian Defense. (OCD).
O'Connor, Sandra Day, 861, *p861, q912, q914*
Odets, Clifford, 445
O'Donley, Carolyn, 865
OES. *See* Office of Economic Stabilization (OES).
Office of Civilian Defense (OCD), 525
Office of Economic Opportunity (OEO), 811
Office of Economic Stabilization (OES), *t527*
Office of Price Administration (OPA), *t527,* 528
Office of Production Management (OPM), *t527*
Office of War Information, 525
Ohio, 132, 134–35, 145, 147; Kent State University in, *p793,* 793–94; moundbuilder cultures in, 24–25, *p25;* oil refineries in, 208–09, *c209;* school reform and, 923; steelmaking in, 205
"Ohio Gang," 348
Ohio River valley, moundbuilder cultures in, 24–25
oil; industry and gasoline, *t361,* 361; Iranian, 590; OPEC embargo of, 361, 819
O'Keeffe, Georgia, *ptg355*
Okies, 431–32. *See also Grapes of Wrath* (Steinbeck).
Oklahoma; Cherokee and, 139; Cherokee Outlet land rush in, *p196,* 196–97; Plains Native Americans in, 200, 201
Oklahoma City (Okla.), 356, 919
Oldenburg, Claes, 754
oligopoly, 356
Olivas, Richard, *q665*
Oliver, Andrew, *crt56*
Oliver, Joseph ("King"), *p389,* 389
Olympic Games, 840, 880, 920
Omaha (Nebr.), 199, 212, 342
Omnibus Housing Act, *g707*
Oneidas, 26
O'Neill, Eugene, *p391*
O'Neill, Thomas ("Tip"), 834
One Woman's War **(Green),** *q515*
Onondagas, 26
On the Beach **(Shute),** 582–83, *p583*
OPA. *See* Office of Price Administration (OPA).
OPEC. *See* Organization of Petroleum Exporting Countries (OPEC).
Open Door policy, 299, 497, 505
open-hearth steelmaking, 204
open-shop associations, 357, 358
"open skies" idea, 581
Operation Mongoose, 592
Operation Overlord, 510
Operation Rolling Thunder, 772, 773
OPM. *See* Office of Production Management (OPM).
Oppenheimer, J. Robert, 514, 580
Oregon, *p13,* 219, 535; conservation and, 909; disputed ownership with Britain, 219; primary in, 780; workday limitations in, 255
Oregon, 296
Oregon Country, *m121*
Organization of Petroleum Exporting Countries (OPEC), 837–38, 839
Ornitz, Samuel, 648
OSHA. *See* Occupational Safety and Health Administration (OSHA)
O'Sullivan, Timothy, *p174*
Oswald, Lee Harvey, 705, 719
Ota, Peter, 548
Other America, The **(Harrington),** *q619,* 708
Otis, Elisha, *t205*
Otis, James, 58
Ottawa (Native Americans), 57
Ottoman Empire, 306, *t308,* 316. *See also* Turkey.
Our Country **(Strong),** *q237*
"Over There" (Cohan), 293
Ovington, Mary White, *q343*
Oyster Bay (N. Y.), 232

P

Pacific Ocean/islands; expansionism into, *t299,* 299–300; World War II and, *m505,* 513–14, *m514*
Pacific Railroad Act (1862), 199
pacifists, 40
packaging, 377
Packard, Vance, *q600*
Packard 1929 Roadster, *p360,* 360
Pahlavi, Mohammed Reza (Shah), 588, 590, 842
Paine, Thomas, 65, *p66, q70; Common Sense,* 66, *q74*
Pakistan, 572
Pale Horse, Pale Rider **(Porter),** 314–15, *q315*
Palestinian Liberation Organization (PLO), 819
Palmer, A. Mitchell, 340–41
Palmer Raids, 340–41
Pan-American Exhibition, 266
Panama, 297, 302–03, 841, 881
Panama Canal, *m296, p296,* 296–97, *m302,* 302–03, *p303;* Carter and, 841
Panic of 1873, 190
Panunzio, Constantine, *q405*
paper money; Continental, 82
Parchester Village, *p607*
Paris; in World War II, *p500*
Parker, Ely S., 182
Parkman, Francis, *q259*
Parks, Rosa, *p674,* 674–75
parks, *m291. See also* national parks.
Parsons, Louella, 387
parties, political; eighteenth century, 112, 114–16. *See also* political parties; specific party names.
Pascagoula (Miss.), 536
Passing of the Great Race, The **(Grant),** 405–06
patent medicines, 273
Patent Office, U.S., 203, 206
patents, *q95, t205*

Pathfinder, 916
Patterson, John, 681
Patton, George, *q551*
patronage, political, 152
Patrons of Husbandry, (Grange), 213–14
Paul, Alice, 344, *t344*
Peace Corps, 698, *p699*, 703, *p703*, 787
peace demonstrations, 777, 787–89
Peale, Charles Willson, *ptg68*
Peale, Norman Vincent, 609
Pearl Harbor (Hawaii), 221; attack on, 505, *m505, p506*, 506, 508, 524
Pech, Randy, 922, *p923, q923*
Pena, Federico, 912
penicillin, 551
Penn, William, *t38*, 40
Penney, J. C., 381
Penniman, Richard ("Little Richard"), 616, *p616*, 752–53
Pennsylvania, *m53*, 123, 147; colonial, *t38*, 40, 41, 50; state constitution of, 73–74; State House, *p83;* steelmaking in, 205; *See also* Philadelphia; Pittsburgh.
Pennsylvania Railroad, 204, 208
Pennsylvania, University of, 50
Penn, William, *t38*, 40
penny auctions, 431
Pentagon, March on, 790–91
Pentagon Papers, *t798*, 799, 826
People's (Populist) party, *p212*, 212–15, *m214*
"People's Lawyer," 255
People's party. *See* Populist party.
perestroika, 868
Pérez de Cuéllar, Javier, 871
Perkins, Frances, 477
Perot, H. Ross, 893, 900, 907
Perrett, Geoffrey, 364
Perry, Matthew, 220
Pershing, John J., 315–16
Persian Gulf War, *p878*, 878–79, *m889*
Peru, 32, 37, 820
Peterson, Esther, 725
Petroleum Building, 356
petroleum industry; and automobile, 355, 361
Philadelphia (Pa.), 40, 46, 50, *t68*, 158; Constitutionial Convention in, 83–84
Philadelphia Plan, 917, 923
Philippines; independence movement in, 222–23, 292, 299–300; Spanish-American War and, 222–23, *m223;* U.S. rule of, 222–23, 292, *t299, m299*, 299–300; in World War II, 504, 513, 514
Phillips, Kevin, 811–12
Phillips, Sam, 753
Phoenix (Ariz.), 603, *m847*
phonographs, 389, 848–49
photography; development of cameras, 202, *t205*, 206
Picasso, Pablo, *ptg390, ptg495*
picketers, 358
Pickett, George, 175–76
Pickford, Mary, 387
picture palaces, 410–11
Pierce, Charlotte Woodward, 261
Piggly Wiggly, 381
Pilgrim's Progress **(Bunyan)**, 244
Pinchot, Gifford, 269
Pine Ridge (S.Dak.) Reservation, 744
Pinkerton Detective Agency, 216
Pinochet, Augusto, 821
pioneers, western, *p122–23*, 133
piracy, 33, *q95*, 117
pit houses, *m28*, 29
Pittsburgh (Pa.), 204, 400
Pizarro, Francisco, 32
Plains. *See* Great Plains.
plantation economy, *m181;* enslaved labor for, 33–34, 40–41. *See* sugar plantations.
plastics, 638–39, *t638–39*, 661
Platt Amendment (1901), *t297*
Pledge of Allegiance, 609
Pleiku (Vietnam), 772
***Plessy* v. *Ferguson* (1896)**, 282, 669–70
PLO. *See* Palestinian Liberation Organization (PLO).
Plunkitt, George Washington, 238
Plymouth (Mass.), *t38*
Pocahontas, 20, *p21*
Poindexter, John, 873
"Poker Cabinet," 348
Poland, immigrants from, 236–37; Soviet Union and, 564, 565–66, *m565*, 866, 868; and Walesa, Lech, 868, *p868;* in World War II, *m494*, 496, 513; Yalta agreements and, 564
Police Strike (Boston), 341
polio, 453–54, 611
political parties; African Americans and, 478; beginnings of, 115–16; among Cherokee, 139; Communist, 340; during Progressive era, 238, 267–68, 275–278; Washington's warning about, 115–16. *See also* specific parties.
politics; in 1700s, 112–16; in 1800s, 112, 115–17, 146–47, 151–53; in 1990s, 842–94, *m893*, 898–99, 902–11, 912–15; corruption in, 238; machine. *See* machine politics. national v. regional, 146–47; religion and, 609; Sunbelt's importance in, 815; women in, *q726*, 727–29, *t728, crt729*
Polk, James K., 219, *p219*
polls; on H-bomb testing, 583; on Nixon's popularity, *g830;* on Lend-Lease Act, 502–03; on Truman-Dewey election, 636; on Vietnam War, *c795;* of voters in 1994 election, *c904*
poll tax, *q108*, 479
Polo, Marco, 4, *q4, p5*
pollution, 904; air, 903; Clean Air Act and, 903; Love Canal and, 842. *See also* environment.
Pollution Act of 1924, 350
Ponce de León, Luis, *m31*
Pontiac, chief, 57
Poor Richard's Almanack **(Franklin)**, 50
pop art, 754, *p754*
population growth; in 1800s, 143, 149; African American, 35, 49, 75; in colonial America, 35, 38, 39, 49–50, *m53*
Populist party, *p212*, 212–15, *m214*
pork barrel legislation, 902
Porter, Katherine Anne, 314–15, *q315*
Port Huron Statement, *q788*
Portraits in Color **(Ovington)**, *q343*
Portsmouth (R.I.), 44
Portugal, 31–32, *m31*
Portugal, explorers from, 11
potatoes, 33
Pottawatomi, 162
Potsdam Conference, 566
poverty; in 1920s, 377–78; in 1950s, 618–24, *p618;* in 1990s, 884–85, *p885*, 908–10, 915; among African Americans, 621–22, 885; in Appalachia, *c621;* during Great Depression, 424–25, 434–35, 471, 481, *c481;* Johnson, Lyndon, and war on, 704, 708–09; among Native Americans, 479, 624; New Deal and, 465–66, 468–71, 481; Reagan and, 858–59; of tenant farmers, 432–33, 465–66
Powell, Colin, *q882*
Powell, Lewis F., Jr., 813
Power of the Positive Woman, The **(Schlafly)**, 729
Powhatan, King, 20
Powhatans, 20
Poynter, Nelson, *q600*
Prague (Czechoslovakia), 512
Presidential Commission on the Status of Women, 725, 726, 730
Presidential Succession Act (1947), 97
President, United States; constitutional definition of, *q96–99;* duties and powers of the 84–85, *q85, q94, q98–99;* the first, *t90;* succession of, *q97, q106, q108;* veto power of, *q94*
presidios, Spanish, 37
Presley, Elvis, 617, *p617*, 753
press, freedom of the (1791), *q101*
Preston, Thomas, 59
Price, Hugh, 526, *q917*
price controls, 528, 633
prices; in 1800s, 123. See also Market Basket.
Prime Meridian, 7
primers, teaching, 39, *p39*
Princeton (N.J.), *p68*
Princeton University, 274, 275, 507
Principles of Scientific Management, The **(Taylor)**, 365
printing press; importance of, *t86, p87*
prison reform, 155
Privacy Act (1974), 831
Proclamation of 1763, 57
Proclamation Line (1763), *m57*
Progressive party, 634
progressives, 243; big business and, 243; child labor and, 246–47, *p246*, 344; church involvement in reform, 245; consumerism and, 272–73; economic reform by, 254–56; experts and, 243; expansionism,and, 294–95, *crt294;* government and social problems, 243, 244; high tariffs attached by, 278; League of Nations and, 325–26; muckrakers and 244–45; political reform by, *t246*, 246–48; 251–54, *crt254;* public education and, 256–57; racism and, 247–48, 325; social and moral reform by, 256–57; socialists, 285, 286; social scientists as, 243–44; suffrage and, 247, 344–45; Supreme Court opposes, 345; unions and, 285–87; and woman's issues, 253, 257; working conditions and, *p255*, 254–56, 341–42, 344; World War I and, 315, 317–18
Prohibition, 343–44, 398–99, 402, *p408, m409;* Eighteenth Amendment (1919), *q105;* repeal of (1933), *q107*. *See also* Twenty-first Amendment.
Project Gemini, 703
Project Head Start, 708, *p708*
Project Mercury, 703
Promentory (Utah), 199
propaganda; Fourteen Points and, 322; against Roosevelt, Franklin, 469; Soviet, 563, 588; in World war I, 317, *p317*
Prophet's Town, 135
Pulaski (Tenn.), *p187*
Protestants, 236, 284; Catholics and, 38, 48; settler groups, 40
Ptolemy, 31
Public Utility Holding Company Act (1935), 470–71, *c481*, 481
Public Works Administration (PWA), 456, 478, *c481*, 481
Pueblo Bonito (N. Mex.), 24
Pueblo people, 24, *m28*
Puerto Rican Americans, 734, 735
Puerto Ricans, as feminists, 728; as immigrants, 402, 622
Puerto Rico, 222, *m297, t297*
Pullman, George, 216
Pullman strike, 216–17, *m286*
Pumpkin Papers, 642–43
Pure Food and Drug Act (1906), 273
Purinton, Edward Earl, 354, *q354*, 359
Puritan colonies, 36–37, *p36*, 38–39, *t38;* dissension among, 42–45
Pusan (Korea), *m574*
PWA. *See* Public Works Administration (PWA).
Pyle, Ernie, 488, *p488, q488–89*

Q

quadrant, 31
Quakers (Friends), *t38,* 40; Hoover, Herbert, as, 422
Quayle, Dan, 892
Quebec, *t38, m53*
Queens (N.Y.), 619
Quota Board, 407
quota system, 401, 404, 406, 407, 918

R

RA. *See* Resettlement Administration (RA).
Rabin, Yitzhak, 881, *p881*
race riots in 1960s, 693–94, *m697;* in 1990s, 919; during Civil War, 178; after King, Martin Luther, Jr., assassination, 694–95, 779–80, 809; during Reconstruction, 187; in Watts, California, 693, *p693;* after World War I, 342; during World War II, 537
racism, 138; in 1950s, 607, 620, 621–24, 669, 671–72, 674–76, 677–78; accommodating, imperialism and, 295; European slave trade and, 34–35; progressives and, 247–248, 295; women and, during World War II, 542–48 *See also* discrimination.
Radcliffe College, 507
***Radiator Building, The* (O'Keeffe),** *ptg355*
radical feminism, 729
Radical Republicans, 186–189, 190
radicals, 338; Native Americans as, 743–44; Red Scare and, 340–41; Vanzetti and Sacco as, 338, *p338*
radio, *t87, t312–313.* 312–313; in 1920s, 389; in 1930s, 444, *p444,* 447; in 1960s, 749; fireside chats on, 459; fundamentalism and, 397; industry, 355; regulation, 350
radioactive fallout, *m580, p580,* 581, 582–83
radioactive rain, 582. *See also* radioactive fallout.
ragtime, 288
railroads, 145–46, *t145,* 148, 149, 158; in 1920s, 421; big business and, 209; discrimination and, 546; expansionism and, 295; highways and, *g654;* La Follette and, 250–51; managing, 208; mergers among, 269; national market and, *g206,* 206–209; political power of, 250–51; refrigerated cars for, *t205,* 206–207; regulation of, by state commissions, 254; settlement of west and, 197, *p198,* 198–199, 200, *p200;* steelmaking for, 204; strikes against, 215, 216–17, 530; worker safety on, 254
Rainbow Coalition, 919
Rainey, Gertrude ("Ma"), 389
Rainy, Joseph H., *p188*
ranches. *See* cattle ranching.
Randolph, A. Philip, *p543,* 543–44
Randolph, Edmund, *q80,* 84
Rankin, Jeanette, 315, *t344*
Raskob, John J., *q419*
ratification; of Articles of Confederation (1781), 81–82; of Bill of Rights (1791), *t90;* of the Constitution (1788), 85, *t90, q101;* of treaties, 98
rationing, 528, *c529*
Rauschenberg, Robert, 754
Rauschenbusch, Walter, 245, *q245,* 246, 247
Ravenel, Henry William, *q187*
Raye, Don, 526
REA. *See* Rural Electrification Act (REA).
Reader's Digest, 389
Reagan, Nancy, *p855*
Reagan, Ronald, 858, *q858, p866;* appeal of, 854, *p855,* 860; communism and, *q866,* 866–67, 870–73; conservative coalition for, 857–58; economic policies of, 857, 858–61; election of, 858; gender gap and, 861; as governor of California, 740; Hollywood Ten and, *q649;* inauguration of, 856, *q858;* Iran-*contra* scandal and, 872–73; Latin America and, 870–73; religious right and, 857; role of government and, 857, 858; South Africa and, 880; Soviet Union and, *q866,* 866–67; Supreme Court and, 861
Reaganomics, 858–61
realpolitik, 817–19, 821
reapers, 206, 207
reapportionment, 715, *c715, m721,* 920–21
rebellions; Bacon's (1676), 47–48; Popé's (1680), 47; Shays's (1787), *p82,* 82–83; Whiskey (1791), 114, *p114*
"rebel yell," 174
recall, 253
recession; under Bush, 882–85, 892–94; under Ford, 839; Reaganomics and, 859
Reclamation Act (1902), 269
Reconstruction, 184–91, *t186;* by Congress, 185–89; by Johnson, Andrew, 184–85
Reconstruction Finance Corporation (RFC), 426
recycling; in World War II, 525
Red Cloud, 201, *p201, q201*
red-hunting. *See* McCarthy, Joseph
redistricting, 715, *m721*
Red Scare, 327, 340–41; labor and, 341, 357; Seattle General Strike and, 341
***Red, White, and Black: The Peoples of Early America* (Nash),** *q26–27*
Reed, Esther De Berdt, *q75*
Reed, John, 323
referendum, 253
reference sources, 320
reform movements in 1830s and 1840s, 154–56
refrigerator, 377, 442, 599
Regan, Donald, 867
regionalism, 146–47
regulation (business); under Eisenhower, 654; under Harding and Coolidge, 349, 350; under Hoover, 350; during Progressive era, 254; under Roosevelt, Franklin, 456–57, 458, 468–69, 470–71, 527–28, 539, 545–46; under Roosevelt, Theodore, 269–71, 277
Rehnquist, William, 813
relief; First New Deal and, 455; Hoover and, 454; Second New Deal expands, 469–70. *See also* welfare.
religion; in 1800s, 150, 154–55; in 1920s, 397; in 1950s, 608–09; in 1960s, 750; Catholics in colonial America, 40, 42–45, 49–50; Eastern Orthodox, 236, 284; freedom of, 40, 45, *q101;* fundamentalism in, 397; of immigrants, 236, 284; Jewish. *See* Jews/Jewish Americans; of Native Americans, 742–43; Protestants, 236, 284, *g284;* Puritans and, 42–45; revivalism and, 49–50, 153–54; schools and, *c715,* 716; and Second Great Awakening, 153–54. *See also* Christianity and specific religions.
religious right, 857
Remarque, Erich Maria, *q309*
"remember the ladies" (Adams), *q71*
Remington, E. and Sons, 367
***repartimiento* policy,** 32
repatriation (Mexican), 433
Repeal of Prohibition, *q107*
representation; in colonial America, 50, *q71;* slavery and, 84–85; of women, *q71,* 155, 156
reproductive rights, 727
Republicans; African Americans and, 478; business support for, 214, 349; Clinton budget and, 899; loss of urban vote and, 403; New Deal and, 471; Nixon and, 631, 781–82, 830–31; Progressive, 325; Radical, 186–89, 190; Reagan and, 858; during Reconstruction, 186–89, 190; Roosevelt, Theodore, and 1912 split, 276–78; Roosevelt, Franklin, and, 471; Truman and, 635; victory in 1994, 903–05, *c904, crt905;* as Whigs, 153; Wilson, Woodrow, and, 324; after World War II, 631–33, 635–36, 637. *See also* Democratic Republicans; National Republicans.
reservationists, 326
reservations, 200, 201
Reserve Officers' Training Corps (ROTC), 789, 793
Resettlement Administration (RA) (1935), 450, 481
Reston, James, *q792*
Reuben James, 503
Revels, H. H., *p188*
Revere, Paul, *p47*
revivalism, 49–50
Revolutionary War. *See* American Revolution.
Reykjavik (Iceland), 867
Reyna, John C., *q742*
Reynolds, Malvina, *q608*
***Reynolds* v. *Sims* (1964),** *c715, q716*
RFD. *See* rural free delivery (RFD).
Rhineland, *m494,* 495
Rhode Island, 39, *m53;* state constitution, 73
Rhodes, James, 793
Richardson, Elliot, 828, 829
Richmond (Calif.), 527, *m540,* 540–41, *p607*
Richmond (Va.), Civil War and, 172, *p172, m175,* 178, 179; slave revolt in, 168, *t168;* trolley cars pioneered in, 235
***Richmond* v. *Croson* (1989),** 914
Rickover, Hyman, 222
Riddle, Albert, *q174*
Ride, Sally, *t845*
Ridge, John, *q138,* 139
Ridge, Major, 139, *q139*
Riis, Jacob, 234, *p234, q234, q236*
Rivera, Diego, 472–75, *p473, ptg474*
riverboats, 128, *p129,* 144, *p144*
river transportation, 144–45
roads and highways, 143–44; in 1920s, 355, 379; in 1950s, 603, 654, *g654, m655;* Anasazi, 23; Trail of Tears, *m135,* 136–39, *ptg138,* 139; turnpikes, 143–44; westward, 131, 133; Wilderness Road, 65, 131
robber barons, 210
Roberts, Grace, *p298*
Robinson, Jo Ann, 675
robots, 917
Rockefeller, John D., Jr., 354, 473, 475
Rockefeller, John D., Sr., 208–09, *g209, q209,* and Tarbell, Ida, 244
Rockefeller, Nelson, 472–75, *p473*
Rockefeller Center, 472–75
Rockford Peaches, *p555*
Rock 'n Roll, 616–17, 749, 752–54
Rocky Mountains, *m12,* 14, 198, 199
Rodino, Peter W., Jr., 833, *p833, q833,* 834, *p834*
Roe Cloud, Henry, 480
***Roe* v. *Wade* (1973), 731, 923**
***Roger and Me* (Moore), 883**
Rogers, Ginger, 443, *p443*
Rogers, J. A., 389
Rogers, Will (humorist); on Coolidge, 349; on Hoover, 350; on Roosevelt, Franklin, 459
Rogers, William (Secretary of State), 798
Rolfe, John, 20
Roman Catholic Church, 820. *See also* Catholics
Romania, 564
Rome, 510
Rome-Berlin-Tokyo Axis, 504
Rommel, Erwin, 510
***Room in a Tenement Flat* (Beals),** *p237*

Rooney, Andy, 562
Roosevelt, Eleanor, 450, 453, *p453, p460,* 507, 540; African Americans and, 478; Anderson, Marian, and, 476–77; Kennedy and, 725; political objectives of, 460; press conferences of, 477, *p477*
Roosevelt, Franklin D., *p452, p453,* 454, *q454, p504, p508;* African Americans and, 478–79, 538, 544, 635; Churchill and, 504, 509, 527; criticism of, 468–69, 471; death of, 513, 564; early life of, 453–54; election of, to presidency, 427, *m483;* fireside chats, 459, *p482;* First Inaugural Address, *p448, p452,* 452–53, *q453;* Good Neighbor policy of, 493; as governor, 454; holocaust and, 512; Hundred Days: *See* New Deal; influence of Eleanor on, 453, 460; Japanese Americans and, 547; Lend-Lease and, 502–03; marriage, *p453;* Munich Pact and, 496; Neutrality Acts and, 498; New Deal of: *See* New Deal; on NRA, *q459;* Pearl Harbor attack and, 506; polio and, 453–54; press and, 459; on racial equality, *q479;* reelection of, to fourth term, 539; reelection of, to second term, 471, *m483;* reelection of, to third term, 502, *m483;* Selective Training and Service Act and, 502; striking miners and, 530; Supreme Court and, 471; treaties and, 825; Truman and, 637; views of Hitler and Mussolini, 498; women appointed by, 477–78; World War II and, 490, 502, 509, 527, 530; at Yalta, 564, *p564,* 642
Roosevelt, Kermit (Kim), *p587,* 587–88, 590
Roosevelt, Theodore, 266, 267, *q267,* attempt to assassinate, 278; big business and trusts, 269–71, 277; Big Stick philosophy of, 296; "bully pulpit" of, 268; child labor and, 232; consumer issues and, 272–73; corollary to Monroe doctrine, 297–98; early political career, 267–68; environmental conservation and, *p268,* 268–69, *t269,* 902–03; foreign policy under, mediates peace between Russia and Japan, *t299,* 300; melting pot and, 284; moderate progressivism of, 268; Navy Department and, 218, 222, 267; Open Door plan and, Panama Canal and, *m296,* 296–97, *m302,* 303; personality, 268; personal life, 267; racism of, 283; Roosevelt, Eleanor, and, 453; and "Rough Riders," 218, *p218,* 223, 267; strikes and, 271–72; succeeds McKinley, 267; and Taft, 273, 276–77; Wilson, Woodrow, and, 277–78
Root, Elihu, 272
***Roots* (Haley),** *q126-27*
Rose, Ernestine, 259
Rosenberg, Ethel and Julius, *p643,* 644, *p644, q644, p658*
Rosenblum, Walter, 512
***Rosie the Riveter Revisited* (Gluck),** *q531*
Ross, Charles, 576
Ross, David, 775
Ross, John, *p137,* 137, 139
Rotary Club, 359
ROTC. *See* Reserve Officers' Training Corps.
"Rough Riders," 218, *p218*
Route 66, *m384,* 384–85
Rozzoni, Louis, *q739*
rubber industry, 355
Ruby, Jack, 705
Ruckelshaus, William, 829
***Rumor of War, A* (Caputo),** *q773, q774*
"Runnin' Wild," 389
rural areas, communes in, 751; electricity to, 470, 481; immigrants and, 401; poverty in, 620–21, 623, 624
Rural Electrification Act (REA) (1935), *p459,* 470, 481
rural free delivery (RFD), 361
Rush, Dr. Benjamin, *q75, p75*
***Rush Hour, New York* (Weber),** *ptg230*
Rusk, Dean, 772
Russell, Charles Edward, *q253*
Russell, C.P., *q380*
Russia; Bolshevik Revolution in, 308, 316, 322, 323, 338, 340; cooperation in space with, *p916,* 916–917; Fourteen Points and, 323; Roosevelt, Theodore, and, 300–01; World War I and, 306, *m307,* 307, *t308,* 308, 316, *c316,* 322–23. *See also* Soviet Union.
Russian Federation, 869
Russian Revolution, 308, 316, 322–23, 338, 340
Russo-Japanese War, 300–01, 497
Ruth, Babe, 374, *p375,* 387

S

Sabin, Albert, 611
Sacagawea, 132
Sacco, Nicola, 338, 339–40
***Sacramento (Calif.)*,** 199
Sadat, Anwar al-, *p841,* 841–42
Safeway, 381
Saigon (Vietnam), 766, 770, 800–01
sailing; ships, 31, *m31, p31, p36,* 36
St. Augustine (Fla.), 37, *t38*
St. Clair, James, 835
St. Lawrence River, 37
St. Lawrence Seaway, 655
St. Louis (Mo.), 148–49, *m148,* 374, 882
St. Louis Post-Dispatch, *q799*
St. Mihiel, 316, *p316*
sales and salesmanship, 366–67, 380–81
Salk, Jonas, 611
Salk vaccine, 611
SALT. *See* Strategic Arms Limitation Talks (SALT).
salvage in World War II, 525
Samoa, 221, *t299*
sanctions; against Haiti, 899; against South Africa, 880; against Soviet Union, 840
San Antonio (Tex.), 469–70, 735
Sandburg, Carl, *q176*
San Diego (Calif.), 536, 814, 882
Sandinistas, 871–72
Sandino, César Augusto, 352, *p352*
SANE. *See* Committee for a Sane Nuclear Policy (SANE).
San Fernando Valley (Calif.), 607
San Francisco (Calif.), 301, 348, 565; anti-Chinese mobs in, 217; cable cars in, 235; Haight-Ashbury in, 751
Sanger, Margaret, 257, *p257*
San Joaquin Valley (Calif.), 736
San Juan Hill, 218, 222, 223
Santa Anna, *p169*
Santoli, Al, *q801*
Sarajevo (Bosnia), 896, *m897,* 897–898
Saratoga (NY), *m67,* 68
Satterfield, Archie, 528
Saturday Night Massacre, 829
Saudi Arabia, 837, *m837,* 878, 882, *m889*
Savannah (Ga.), *m175,* 178
savings and loan institutions crisis, 884
Savio, Mario, 786, *p786, q786*
Schechter, Seven J., 534
Schlafly, Phyllis, 729, *p730,* 731
Schlesinger, Arthur M., Jr., *q619,* 704
School Children's Storm, 213
schools; in 1920s, 383; African American, 188–89, *p189,* 282; baby boom and, 610, *g610;* Bible banned in, 716; boarding, for Native Americans, 201; busing and, 812; Cherokee, in colonial era, 39; enrollment (1910–1970), *g610;* high schools increase, 256, *p256, g256;* segregation in, 189, 282, 669, *m669,* 670–72; during World War II, 536. *See also* education.
Schurz, Carl, *q295*
Schuster, Lincoln, 390
Schuyler, Mrs., *ptg70*
Schwab, Charles M., 359
scientific management, 365–66
SCLC. *See* Southern Christian Leadership Conference (SCLC).
Scopes, John, 396–97
Scopes Trial, 396–97
Scotland; immigrants from, 39
Scott, Adrian, 648
Scott, Coretta, 676, *p695*
Scott, Dred, 164, *p164*
Scott, Harriet, 164, *p164*
Screen Actors Guild, 649, 866
SDI. *See* Strategic Defense Initiative (SDI).
Sears, Roebuck, 361, 381
Seattle (Wash.), 217
Seattle General Strike, 341
secession, 153, 172, 173
Second Amendment (1791), *q102*
Second Great Awakening, 153–54
Second Inaugural Address (Lincoln), 179–80, *q180*
Second New Deal, 469–71. *See also* New Deal.
Second Reconstruction, 695
"Second War for Independence," 118
Secrettown Trestle, *p199*
sedentary cultures; Native American, 23, 28–29
Sedition Act (1798), 116
Sedition Amendment, (1918), 318, 319
segregation; in 1950s, 622, 666–72; Civilian Conservation Corps and, 456; *de facto,* 668–69; Dixiecrats and, 634–35; Fair Employment Practices Committee and, 544–46; in graduate education, *g673;* Nixon and, *q812;* passage of "Jim Crow" laws, 282; Roosevelt, Franklin, and, 477, 479; in schools, 622, 669, *m669,* 670–72; and tenant farmers, 464–65; in World War II, 509, 542–46
Selective Training and Service Act (1940), 502, 509
selectmen, 39
Selling of the President, The (McGinniss), 803
Selma (Ala.), 687–89, *p688*
***Selma, Lord, Selma* (Webb and Nelson),** *q688*
Senate; African Americans in, 894; direct election of senators, 253, *crt253;* filibustering in, 687; League of Nations and, 325–27; slavery and, 171; Treaty of Versailles rejected by, 327; women in, 894. *See also* Congress.
Senate Select Committee on Presidential Campaign Practices (Watergate Committee), 828–29, 833
Seneca Chief **flatboat,** 128, *p129*
Senecas, 26
Seneca Falls (N.Y.), 253, 258–61
Seoul (Korea), 574
"Separate but equal," 282, 669–70
separation of church and state, 45
Sequoya, 135, 137
Serbia, 306, 897–98, *m897*
sermon, Puritan, *q36*
servants, 40, 41, 49
service industries, 601–02
Sesame Street, *p711*
settlement houses, 242, 247, 285
settlement of the United States (1783–1900), *m131*
settlers; Jamestown (Va.), 20, 37, *t38,* 40; Native Americans and, 20, 133–39; pioneer western, *p122–23,* 133; prehistoric era, 22–23; westward expansion of (1783–1900), 130–39, *m131. See also* colonial America; immigrants.
Seventeenth Amendment, (1913), *q105,* 253
Seventh Amendment (1791), *q102*

Seven Years' War (French and Indian War), *m48,* 48, 56, 57
Seward, William, 219–21
"Seward's folly," 221
Shah of Iran, 587–88, 590, 842
Shakers, 154, 751
Shanghai (China), 497, 573
sharecropping, 189, 190, 213, 282, during Progressive era, 282
Share Our Wealth, 468
Shattuck, Jacob, *p82*
Shawnee solution, 134–35
Shays, Daniel, *p82,* 82–83
Shays's Rebellion (1787), *p82,* 82–83, *t90*
Sheen, Fulton J., 609
Shenandoah Valley (Va.), 178
Shepard, Alan, Jr., *c704, t844*
Sheppard-Towner Maternity Act (1921), 345
Sheridan, Philip Henry, 178, 179
Sherman, Roger, *p84*
Sherman, William Tecumseh, 178, *q185*
Sherman Antitrust Act (1890), 269–71, 279, strikes and, 286
Sherwood, Issac, 315
Shiloh, Battle of, 175
shipping, 143
ships and boats, 206; European colonist, *p36;* explorer, 31, *p31;* flatboats, *ptg37,* 128, *p129,* 133, 144; sailing, 31, *p31, p36;* slave, *q34–35, p35;* steamboats, 144, *t145,* 147, 148
Sholes, Christopher, *t205*
Shoong, Joe, *p356*
Shoshone, 132
"shot heard around the world," 60, 64
Shute, Nevil, *q582–83*
Sicily, 510
Sidisin, Ruth, *q775*
Sierra Nevada, 199
Silent Majority, 793
silk; during World War II, 533
silver; extracted after Civil War, 198; as legal tender, 213, 214
Simon and Schuster, 390
Simon, Richard, 390
Simpson, "Sockless Jerry," 212
Sims, William S., 316
Sinatra, Frank, 532
***Since Yesterday* (Allen),** *q431*
Sinclair, Upton, 244–45, *q245,* 246, 272
Singer Sewing Machine Company, 207
Singletary, Amos, *q88*
Sioux; Bonnin, Gertrude, of, 480
Sirica, John J., 827, *p827,* 828
***Sister Carrie* (Dreiser),** *q230–31*
sit-down strikes, 466–67
sit-ins, *p677,* 677–78, *p711*
Sixteenth Amendment (1913), *q105*
Sixth Amendment (1791), *q102*
skyscrapers, *p355,* 355–56
***Slave Market in Richmond, Virginia* (Crowe),** *ptg166*
slavery; abolition of, 75, *q104,* 155–56, *t157;* auctions, *p166, ptg166;* in colonial era, 32–34, 40–41, 75, 82, 85; constitutional compromise on, 85, 91; cotton gin and, 165, *m165;* dates of abolition in states, *m179;* economic basis for, 165; end to. *See* emancipation. framing of Constitution and, 85, 95; European trade in, 31; laws and customs to maintain, 168; Northwest Ordinance compromise (1787), 82, 132, 133–34, *q134,* 155; opposition to. *See* abolitionism, politics and; prohibited by Thirteenth Amendment, *t186;* Radical Republicans' feelings about, 166; in Spanish colonies, 32–34; states' rights and, 166. *See also* Compromise of 1850; emancipation; enslaved persons; Kansas-Nebraska Act; Missouri Compromise.
slaves. *See* enslaved Africans, or slavery.
***Slouching Towards Bethlehem* (Didion),** *q750*
Slovakia, 868
Slovenia, 896, *m897*
smallpox, 32–33, *p33,* 49
Smith, Al, 401, *p402*
Smith, Bessie, *p371,* 389
Smith College, 613
Smith, C.R., 484
Smith, James, Jr., 274, 275
Smith, John, *q17,* 20
***Smith* v. *Allwright* (1944),** 545
SNCC. *See* Student Nonviolent Coordinating Committee.
Social Darwinism, 210
social gospel movement, 245
Socialists, 216, 217, 276, 277; World War I and, 318, *p319,* 319
social reform; in 1800s, 154–56; in 1920s, 343–45; in 1954-to-1969 period, 717; and liberation theology, 820–21; and Roman Catholic Church, 820–821
social sciences and progressives, 243–44
Social Security, 464–65, 470, 635, 637, 654–55, 810, 902, 911
Social Security Act (1935), 470, *c481,* 910; Townsend and, 464–65
Social Studies Skills reading economic graphs, 549; interpreting images, 461; conducting interviews, 732; combining information from maps, 181; drawing inferences from maps, 437; reading a map, 10; analyzing news media, 925; interpreting political cartoons, 823; using reference materials, 320; reading statistical tables, 211; making telescoping time lines, 157; understanding public opinion polls, 795. *See also* Critical Thinking Skills; Study and Writing Skills.
Soil Conservation Act (1936), 439, 470, *c481*
Sojourner, 916, *p916*
Solidarity, 868
"Solidarity Forever" (Chaplin), *q287*
Solomon Islands, 513
Somalia, 879
Somme, Battle of, 307–08
Somoza, Anastasio, 871
Sons of Liberty, 58, 59
Soong Meiling, 497
Souter, David A., 914
South; African Americans, during Progressive era in, 281–83; African Americans, exodus from, 184, 341–43, 534, 535–36; annexation of Texas and, 169; colonial population of the, 35; cotton trade with England, 168; Democrats and, 671, 783, *m783,* 812; Missouri Compromise and, 168–69; vs. North in Civil War, 172–180, *g177;* Populism fails in, 214–15; Reconstruction in, 184–91; resistance to integration in, 671–72, 674–79, 680–89, 690–91, 692–93, 694–95, 812–13
South Africa, 880–81
South America, 23, 32, 37; African slaves in, 33–34; Hispanic Americans and, 734, 735; Native Americans in, 32, 33
South Braintree (Mass.), 338
South Carolina, *m53,* 153; Civil War and, 172, 173; constitution, 72; Reconstruction in, 187; in Sunbelt, *m814,* 814; voting rights and, 689
South Dakota, 197, 200
Southeast, *m28*
Southwest, *m28;* desert culture of, 23–24
Southern Alliance, 214–15
Southern Christian Leadership Conference (SCLC), 676, 678, 684, 690
Southern Manifesto, 671
Southern Tenant Farmers' Union (STFU), *p465,* 466
South Korea, 574
"Soviet Ark," 340
Soviet Union; Afghanistan and, 840, *p840,* 841, 866; Berlin and, 566, 569–71; breakup of, 868–70, *t869, p888;* Bush and, 867–68; Carter and, 840–41; China and, 572, 817, 818; cold war with: *see* cold war; Cuba and, 591–93, 871; Eastern Europe dominated by, 564, 565–66, 568, 569–71, 582, 868–69; Germany and, 496, 563, 564, 566, 569–71, 868–69; Gorbachev and, 865–66, 867–69; guerrilla activity supported by, 871; Iran and, 566; Kennedy, John F., and, 592–93; Nixon and, 818, 819; non-aggression pact with Nazi Germany, 496, 563; nuclear weapons and, 576, 580, 582, 583, 593, 818, 840; Poland and, 564, 565–66, 866, 868; Reagan and, 866–67; Spanish Civil War and, 495; Treaty of Versailles and, 324; United Nations and, 565; Vietnam and, 770, 771; view of United States and Allied Powers, 563; Wilson and Allies intervene in, 323; World War II and, 509–10, 512–13, 515; World War II, cost of to, 563; Yeltsin and, 869. *See also* Russia (events before 1917, after 1991).
Soyer, Moses, *ptg469*
SPAB. *See* Supply Priorities and Allocations Board (SPAB).
space program, 802, *p802,* 844–45, *t844–45,* 921. *See also* National Aeronautics and Space Administration (NASA).
Spain; California and, *m121;* civil war in, 495–96; colonists and settlers from, 37, *p37, t38;* Columbus and, 30–31; explorers from, *m31,* 32; in Americas, *q2–3;* exploration and conquests, 30–31, *m31,* 32–34; Florida and, *q2–3;* livestock and horses introduced to Americas by, *p33,* 33; Louisiana owned by, 131; Mexico and, 32; Missouri owned by, 131; Monroe Doctrine and, 219; Philippines and, 222; slave ships from, 34; territories of (1812), *m121, m161*
Spanish-American War, 218, 221–23, *m223*
Spanish Civil War, 495–96
Spanish conquest, 30–31, *m31,* 32–34
speakeasies, 398
speculators, 113
Spencer, Herbert, 210
spice trade, 31–32
Spirit of St. Louis, 394
spirituals (music), 110
Spock, Benjamin, 612, *p612, q612*
spoils system, 152
sports; in 1920s, 387–88; African Americans in, 387, 388, 910, *p910;* women in, 388, 555
spotted owl, 909
Spotsylvania (Va.), 178
Sprague, Jesse Rainsford, 380–81
Spreading the American Dream, 295
Springfield (Ill.), 180
Sproul Hall, 786
Sputnik, 582, 584
stagflation, 837, *g839*
Stalin, Joseph; Allies and, 503, 509, 527, 564, 566; anticommunism in U.S. and, 642, 649; Berlin and, 566, 569–71; China and, 572; death of, 578; Potsdam meeting and, 566; Tehran meeting with, 527; World War II and, 496, 509–10; at Yalta, 564, *p564*
Stalingrad, Battle of, 510
Stamp Act (1765), 58, 59, *t59*
standard of living; in 1920s, 377; credit and, during World War II, 527–28. *See also* Market Basket.
Standard Oil Company, 208–09, *g209,* 239, *crt239;* Taft, William Howard, and, 273; and Tarbell, Ida, 244
***Stand Up for America* (Wallace),** *q688*
Stanford, Leland, 199
Stanley, Thomas, *q671*

Stanton, Edwin, 187
Stanton, Elizabeth Cady, 258, *q258,* 259, *p259, q259,* 260, 261, 725
Stanton, Henry, 258, 260
Starling, Edmund, 459
Stars & Stripes, 562
Starr, Kenneth, 911
Star Wars, 868
state government; federal spending cuts and, 911; Progressive reforms of, 252–53; during Reconstruction, 187, 189, 190; statehood, *m121*
***State of the Nation* (Dos Passos),** *q536*
states; in 1812, *m121;* admission of new, *m121;* Articles of Confederation governing, 81–83, *c89;* Iroquois Alliance model for, 26–27; legislatures, 72–74, 90, 155; limitations on powers of, 84, *q96,* 153; post-Revolutionary debts, 113–14; powers reserved to the, 138; relations among the, *q100;* Western lands ceded by, 81–82
states' rights, 153, 635
States' Rights Democratic party, 634
steamboats, 144, *t145,* 147, 148, *p149, p159*
steam engines, 158–59, *p158–59*
steelmaking and steel industry; assembly line stimulates, 355; automobile industry and, 379, 815, 838; Carnegie and, 204, 209; factory closings in Northeast and Midwest, 815; foreign competition threatens, 838–39; heavy industry and, 205; new process in, 204; oil embargo and, 838; strike in, 341, 530
Stein, Gertrude, *ptg390*
Steinbeck, John, 385, *q414–15, q444–45,* 444
Steinem, Gloria, *p728, t728*
Stephenson, David, 400, 401
stereoscope, 202
Stevens, John Paul, *q914*
Stevens, Thaddeus, 186, *p187*
Stevenson, Adlai, 460, 653, 654
STFU. *See* Southern Tenant Farmers' Union (STFU).
Stimson, Henry L., 516–17, 519, 527
Stinson, Bob, 467
stock market, crash of, 418–21 regulation of, 458
Stokes, Rose Pastor, 318–19
Stone, Harlan Fiske, 458
Stone, I. F., *q780*
Stone, Lucy, 261
stores. *See* chain stores.
***Stories of John Cheever, The* (Cheever),** *q612*
Strabo, 7
Strategic Air Command, 867
Strategic Arms Limitation Talks (SALT), 818
Strategic Arms Limitation Treaty (SALT II), 840, 841
Strategic Defense Initiative (SDI), 866, 867
Stratton, Samuel W., 339
strikes, in 1800s, 143; in late 1800s, 216–17, *t217*; in 1920s, 358; in 1930s, 466–67; coal, 271–72, 341; pledge against during World War II, 530; Red Scare and, 341; steel workers, 216, *p216,* 341; after World War II, 599, 632
Stripling, Robert, 648
Strong, Josiah, *q237*
Strout, Richard, 346–47
Student Nonviolent Coordinating Committee (SNCC), 678–79, 684, 690–93, 724–25, 787; feminists and, 724–25; Vietnam War protesters and, 787
Students for a Democratic Society (SDS), *p788,* 788–89, 794; FBI and, 811; violence by, 794, 809
Student Volunteer Movement for Foreign Missions, 298
Studer, Helen, 531
Study and Writing Skills; analyzing secondary sources, 586; interpreting a primary source, 71; presenting statistical data, 673; identifying text patterns, 369. *See also* Critical Thinking Skills; Social Studies Skills.
submarines, in World War II, 503, 511
suburbs; automobiles and, *p547,* 603, 605; criticisms of, 608; early, 235; growth of, 603, 607; housing in, 604–05, *p605;* lifestyles in, 596, *p597,* 606, 608–14; recession hits, 885; transportation and, 235
subway, 235
Sudbury (Mass.), 38
Sudetenland, *m494,* 496
Suez Canal Crisis, 590–91, *p591*
suffrage, 74, 253, *p254,* 257, 258–61, 344–45. *See also* women's rights; voting.
Sugar Act (1764), 57
sugarcane plantations, 33–34, 37
Sullivan, Mark, 266
Sullivan, "Tim" (Big), *q255*
Sumner, Charles, 171, *crt171*
Sumner, William G., *q210*
***Sun Also Rises, The* (Hemingway),** 390
Sunbelt, 811, *m814,* 814–15, *m847*
Sun City (Ariz.), 815, *p815*
Sunday, Billy, *q309*
Supply Priorities and Allocations Board (SPAB), 527
supply-side economics, 858
Supreme Court, abortion and, 731; affirmative action and, 917, 922–25; antitrust cases and, 270; bilingual education and, 737; Cherokee and, 136–39; civil rights and, 191, 545, 548, 669, 682, 812; Coolidge's appointments to, 349; Dred Scott case and, 164, 171; due process and, 164, *c715,* 716–17; freedom of the press and, 799; freedom of speech and, 319, 650; gun control and, 899; Harding's appointments to, 349; Jackson refuses to obey, 136; Japanese internment and, 548; labor and, *t217,* 358; Marshall strengthens, 116–17; New Deal and, 469, 471; Nixon and, 813, 830, 835; powers of, 714 progressive legislation and, 344, 349 Reagan's appointments to, 861; during Reconstruction, 185, 191; redistricting and, 715, *c715, m721,* 919; religion and, *c715,* 716 Roosevelt, Franklin, and, 471; segregation and, 282, 669–71, 812; slavery and, 164, 171; term limits and, 709; "Warren Court," 713–17, *p714, c715,* 809; working conditions and, 344
Swanson, Gloria, 387
Sweden, 39
Sweeney, Thomas J., *q920*
Swift, Gustavus, 206, 209
swimming, 385
Swope, Gerard, 358
synthetics industry, 355
Syria, 878, *m889*

T

Tacoma (Wash.), 217
Taft, Robert, *q632*
Taft, William Howard, 272, *q272, p272, p273,* conservation and, 273; Dollar Diplomacy of, 298; Roosevelt, Theodore, and, 273, 276–77; trusts and, 273; Wilson, Woodrow, and, 275–278
Taft-Hartley Bill, 633, 637
Taiwan, 497, 573, 817
talk radio and 1994 election, 904
Tallahassee (Fla.), 3
Tammany Hall, 238, *crt238*
Tampico (Mexico), 305–06
Tan, Amy, *q852–53*
Taney, Roger, 164
Tannenberg, 308
Taos Pueblo people *q24,* 47
Tarbell, Ida, 244
tariffs, 146, 147, 153; Great Depression and, 422; North vs. South on, 168; Wilson, Woodrow, and, 278
taxation; British, 57–58; states' objections to, 81
taxes; American Revolution and, 57, 59, *t59;* under Articles of Confederation, 81, 82; under Bush, 883, 884; under Clinton, 898, 908; under Coolidge, 349; on gasoline, on liquor, 114; under Reagan, 858; in World War II, 528
Taylor, Frederick, 365–66
Taylor, Zachary, *p169,* 169–170
Taylor Society, 365
Tea Act (1773), 59, *t59*
teach-ins, 789
Teamsters Union, 585, 736
Teapot Dome Affair, 348
technology, 921, 922
Tecumseh, *ptg134*
teenagers during World War II, 538; violence and, in 1990s, 920–21
Teheran (Iran), 527, 842, 856
telegraph, 206
telephones, *t87, t205,* 206, 368, 462–63, *t462–63,* 803
televangelists, 857
television, *t710–711;* in 1950s, *p557,* 585, 599, 600, *p600,* 606, 609, *p610,* 610–11, 613, 616, *p617, p625,* 646; in 1960s, *p623,* 656, 704, 710, 711, 719, 757, *p845;* in 1970s, *p785;* in 1980s, 875, 887; Christian, 857; education on, *p711;* growth of, *t710–11,* 710–11; Kennedy vs. Nixon on, 656, *p656,* 657; national events on, 704–05, *p711;*
Teller Amendment, 299
temperance movement, 155, *crt155,* 257; immigrants' opposition to, 285
Templehof Airport (Berlin), 570
tenant farmers, 432–33, 465–66
***Ten Days That Shook the World* (Reed),** 323
tenements, *p234,* 234, *p237,* 237-38
Tennessee, 132; Civil War and, *m173, t175, m175,* 176; North Carolina land ceded to, *p81;* reapportionment in, 715; Scopes trial in, 396–97; settled, *m131;* statehood, 132; in Sunbelt, *m814,* 814
Tennessee Valley Authority (TVA), *t457,* 457–58, *m458,* 479, *c481*; African Americans and, 479; Eisenhower and, 654
tennis, 387
Tenskwatawa, 134–35
Tenth Amendment (1791), *q103*
Tenure of Office Act, 187
tepees, 28, *m28, p29*
Terkel, Studs, 425, 467, 508, 512, 524, 548
Terminal Tower, 356
termination policy, 624, 746
Terrell, Harry, 431
territories; admission to statehood, *m121,* 132; European, 36–41, 48–49, *m48, m121;* expansion of, 130–39; United States (1783–1900), *m131*
terrorism, 919–20
Terry, Peggy, 435
Tet offensive, 776–77, 778–79
Texas, annexation of, 219; cattle ranching and, 197; Civil War and, 172; defense jobs lost in, 882; illegal aliens and, 916; independence of, 169; during Reconstruction, 185; Spanish, 37; in Sunbelt, *m814,* 814
textile industry; in 1920s, 378, 421; productivity in, 206; strikes, *467;* in World War II, 535. *See also* factories.
textile production, 140–43, *p141*
Thayer, Webster, 338, 339
***Their Eyes Were Watching God* (Hurston),** 392
Thieu, Nguyen Van. *See* Nguyen Van Thieu.

Third Amendment (1791), *q102*
Third Reich, 495
thirteen colonies; in 1763, *m48, m161*
Thirteenth Amendment (1865), *q104, t186*
Tho, Le Duc. *See* Le Duc Tho.
Thomas, Clarence, *p913, q913,* 914
Thomas, Elmer, 426
Thomas, Isaiah, 87
Thomas, J. Parnell, 648, 650
Thoreau, Henry David, *q679*
Three Mile Island, 843, *p843*
Thurmond, Strom, 634–35, *q635*
Tiede, Tom, *q346, q347*
Tienanmen Square, 879
Tiffany, Joel, *t205*
Tilden, Samuel, 190
timber, 198
Timbuktu (Mali), 34
Time, 389
"Times They Are A-Changin', The" (Dylan), *q789*
tobacco; child labor in, 246; in colonial America, 40–41, grain replaces; 165; industry, 356
tobacco plantations, 34, 40–41
"togetherness," 610
Tojo, Hideki, 504–05
Tokyo (Japan), 514, 515
Toledo (Ohio), 425, 433
tolerance; religious, 40, 43–45, *q101*
toll roads, 143–44
Tontons Macoutes, 873
tools; of settlers, *p123*
Topaz (Utah), 547
Topeka (Kans.), 670
totalitarianism, 494
"To the Person Sitting in Darkness" (Twain), *q300*
tourism, 378–80, 385, 442
town meetings, 39, *p51*
Townsend, Francis E., 464–65, 467
Townshend Acts (1767), 59
tractors, 377, 385, 432
Tracy, Dick, 447
trade; in 1920s, 350, 352; in 1990s, 881–82; with Africa, 301; with Canada, 881–82; with China, 298–99, 497, 881; in colonial America, 33–34; deficit, 883–84; Embargo Act and, 117; European Union and, 881; Great Depression and, 421, 422; with Japan in 1930s, 496, 504; with Japan in 1980s and 1990s, 881; with Latin America, 352; and North American Free Trade Agreement (NAFTA), 881–82. *See also* markets; tariffs.
trade associations, 350
trading networks, 148–49, *m148;* Native American, 24–25
Traffic and Motor Vehicle Safety Act, *g707*
trailers, 442, 536
"Trail of Tears," *m135, ptg138,* 139
***Trail of Tears* (Lindeux),** *ptg138*
trains, 145–46, *t145,* 148, 149, 158, 159
transcontinental railroad, 159, 197, 198–99, 200, *p200. See also* railroads.
transistors, 863
transportation; in 1800s, 143–46, *t145, p145, m148;* canal, 128, *p129,* 144–45; Clay, Henry, and, 146–47; Conestoga wagon, *p122–23;* mass, 235; rail, 145–46, *t145, m148,* 148, 149, 158–59; road, 65, 131, 133, *p143,* 143–44, *m148;* routes, *m148;* water, 29, *ptg37,* 128, *p129,* 133, 134, *p144,* 144–45, *t145, m148,* 149, *p149. See also* trade.
Transportation, Department of, 922
trapping, *ptg37,* 37–38
Treasury, Department of, 529
treaties; with Native Americans, 40, *ptg40,* 65, 136, 138, 139; with French, 57
Treaty of Brest-Litovsk (1918), 322
Treaty of Greenville, 134, *ptg134*
Treaty of Guadalupe Hidalgo (1848), 169
Treaty of Paris (1783), 68, *t68, t90, m161*
Treaty of Versailles (1919), 324–25, *m326,* Hitler and, 493
Treaty party; Cherokee, 139
Triangle Shirtwaist Factory, *p255*
Tribune Tower, 356
"trickle down" effect, 884
Triple Entente, 306. *See also* Allies (World War I).
trolley cars, 235
Trotter, William Monroe, 281, *p281*
Truman, Harry S, 566, *q566,* 634; administration of, *t636;* atomic bomb and, 514–15, 516–19, 566; background of, 464–65; becomes President, 513, 564–65; Berlin and, 566; China and, 572–73; CIA and, 588–89; civil defense and, 577; civil rights and, *p634,* 634–35, *q635, crt637, q644;* communism and, 565–66, 567–68, 572–73, 574–75, 643–44; Democrats and, 634; Fair Deal and, 637; hydrogen bomb and, 577; Indochina and, 769, 771; Korea and, 574–75; labor and, 632–33, *q633;* on McCarthyism, *q646;* Native Americans and, 744; NATO and, 571; Potsdam meeting and, 566; Progressive party and, 634; reelection campaign, 634–36, *p635, p636, m659;* Soviet Union and, 565–66, 567–68, 572–73; United Nations and, 565; Vietnam and, 769, 771
Truman Doctrine, 567–68
Trumbo, Dalton, 648, 651
trusts, 239, 269–70, New Nationalism and, 277; Roosevelt, Theodore, and, 270–71; Taft, William Howard, and, 273; Wilson, Woodrow, and, 277–78
Truth, Sojourner, 156, *p156,* 166, 261, 916
Truth in Packaging Act, *g707*
Truth-in-Securities Act (1933), 458, *t481*
Tubman, Harriet, 167, *p167*
Tulsa (Okla.), 319, 342, 356
Tunisia, 510
Tunney, Gene, 388
Turkey, 567, 568, *m889*
Turner, Benjamin, *p188*
Turner, Nat, 168, *t168*
turnpikes, 143–44
Tuskegee Institute, *p282,* 282–83
TVA. *See* Tennessee Valley Authority (TVA).
Twain, Mark, 209, *q300*
Twelfth Amendment (1804), *q103*
***Twenties: Fords, Flappers, & Fanatics, The* (Mowry),** *q388*
Twentieth Amendment (1933), *q106*
Twenty-fifth Amendment (1967), *q108*
Twenty-first Amendment (1933), *q107*
Twenty-fourth Amendment (1964), *q108*
Twenty-second Amendment (1951), *q107*
Twenty-sixth Amendment (1971), *q109*
Twenty-third Amendment (1961), *q107*
Tyler, John, 98
typewriters, *t205,* 206, 367, 863
typhoid fever, 177, 611

U

UAW. *See* United Auto Workers.
U-boats; in World War II, 503, 511
UFW. *See* United Farm Workers (UFW).
Ukraine, 869–70
Underground Railroad, 167, *p167*
Underwood Tariff (1913), 278
unemployment; in 1870s, 190, 215; in 1890s, 214; in 1920s, 377–78, 421–22; under Bush, 882; under Carter, *q839;* in depression of 1870s, 208; Embargo Act and, 117; under Ford, 839, *q839;* Great Depression and, 416, *p417,* 424–25, 433–36; hoboes and, 436; New Deal and, 455–56, 469–70; under Reagan, 859, 860, 876; during Reconstruction, 190; after World War II, 531; WPA and, 469–70;
unemployment compensation, 655
Unification Church, 750
Union; in Civil War, *m173, g177;* Webster on Preserving, *q169;* Lincoln on preserving, *q177,* 179–80
Union of Russian Workers, 340
Union Pacific Railroad, 199, 270
Union, preserving the; tariff controversy and, 153
unions; before 1880, 215–16, *t217;* in 1920s, 358–59; in 1930s, 466–67; 544; autoworkers and, *t466–67;* coal mining and, *t358,* 530; immigration and, 217, 284; membership in, 217, 286, 358, *t358, g467,* 632; minorities and, 541; NAFTA and, 882, 897; NIRA and, 456–57, 466–67; during World War II, 530; pension plan mismanagement in, 884–85; progressives and, 285–87; resistance to, 216–17, 358–59, 466–67; skilled workers and, 215, 216; socialists in, 285, 286–87; steel workers, 341, 358–59; tenant farmers, 466–67; unskilled workers and, 217, 287; Wagner Act and, 470, 544; after World War II, 632; during World War II, 541. *See also* American Federation of Labor (AFL); Congress of Industrial Organizations (CIO).
United Auto Workers (UAW), 466–67
United Farm Workers (UFW), 722, *p723,* 733, 736–37, 738–41, *p740*
United Mine Workers (UMW), 215, 271–72
United Nations (UN); People's Republic of China admitted to, 818; El Salvador and, 871; formation of, 564, 565; Haiti and, 899; Iran and, 566; Korea and, 574; Persian Gulf War and, 879; South Africa and, 880; Yugoslavian breakup and, 868, 897–98
United States; 1776–1803, *m161;* in 1812, *m121;* climate regions of, 14, *p15;* geographic features of, *m12,* 13–14; human/environment interaction in, 16–17; location of, 13; movement in, 16; population density in, *m17;* regions of, *m10,* 13–14; vegetation regions of, 14, *p15. See* U.S. and name of organization.
United We Stand America, 900
Universal Negro Improvement Association, 343
universities; in 1920s, 357; in 1950s compared with 1960s, 787; arms race and, 582; civil rights and, *g673;* GI Bill and, 598–99, 600; Vietnam War protested at, 787–88, 789, 791, 793–94; during World War II, 507
urbanization, 148–49, 235, 402
Uruguay, 820
***U.S.A.* (Dos Passos),** 390, *q391*
U.S. Court of Claims, 744
U.S. Food Administration, 350
U.S. Forest Service, 269, 439
U.S. Marine Corps, 221, 305–06, 352
U.S. Navy; under Roosevelt, Theodore, *t299, p300, m301,* 301; in World War II, 503
U.S. Patent Office, 206
USS Constitution ("Old Ironsides"), *ptg117*
U.S. Steel Corporation, 209, 264, 358; strike against, 341; worker benefits paid out by, 358
U.S.* v. *Cruikshank (1876), 191
U.S.* v. *Nixon, 830–31
USSR. *See* Soviet Union.
Utah, 154, 169, 253, 923
utopian communities, 154

V

Valentino, Rudolph, *p387*
Van Buren, Martin, 153
Vance, Cyrus, 841
Vandalia (Ill.), 144
Vanderbilt, William, 210
Vane, Henry, 43, *p45*
Vanzetti, Bartolomeo, 338, 339–40, *q339*
vaqueros, 197, 198
Vassar College, 183
Vaudeville, 289
V-E Day, 513
Venezuela, 820
Vera Cruz, Philip, 739
Veracruz (Mexico), 305–06
Verdun, Battle of, 307
Verrazano, Giovanni da, *m31,* 37
Vesey, Denmark, 168
veterans, 898; after World War II, 630–31
Veterans Bureau, 348
Veterans' Village, 598–99
veto, presidential, 147, 152
Vicksburg (Miss.), 176
victory gardens, 525
Victory in Europe Day, 513
video games, 928–29
Vienna (Austria), 512
Vietcong (National Liberation Front), 771, 773–75, 797. *See also* Vietnam War.
Vietminh, 768–71, *t771*
Vietnam, *m769, t771, m805;* communism in, 769, 771; culture of, 775, 776, 779, 801; division of, *m769,* 770; French and, 768, 769–70; Geneva Pact (1954) on, 770; nationalism in, 768, 770; religion in, 770, 771, *p771;* social problems in, 770; South, 770–72; U.S. and, 573, 768. *See also* Vietnam War.
Vietnamization, 793, 797, *p797,* 799
Vietnam Veterans Memorial, *p801*
Vietnam War; bombing in, 772, 773–74; Cambodia and, 770, 773, 774, 793; chemical defoliation in, *p774;* "Christmas" bombings of, 800; costs of, 791, 801; deaths in, 773, 775, 777, *p792,* 792, 796, 797, 800, 801, *p801;* détente and, *p818;* domestic politics and, 778–79, 780–81, 782–83; draft and military service, *c789, p790, c799;* end of, *t798,* 799–801; events leading to U.S. involvement in, 768–72, *t771;* guerrilla warfare in, 774–75; Hawks vs. Doves in, 791; Martin Luther King, Jr., and, 695, 791; My Lai massacre in, 792–93; news media and, 777, 791–93; nurses in, *q775;* opposition to, 788–94, 796, 799, *g799;* pacification programs in, 775; peace talks in Paris, 797–800; Tet offensive in, 766, *p767,* 776–77, *m777,* 778–79, 791; Gulf of Tonkin Resolution and, 772; "Vietnamization" and, 793, 797, *p797,* 799
Villa, Pancho, 306
Viking exploration, 31
Vinland, 31
Vinson, Fred M., 670–71
Virginia, 41, 46, 47–48, *m53,* 78, 147; American Revolution and, *m67,* 68; in Civil War, 173, 174, *m175,* 178, 179, *m193;* bill of rights in, 73; constitutional ratification by, *p89,* 89–90; segregation and, 671, 689; state constitution, 73; in Sunbelt, *m814,* 814; tobacco grown in, 165; Western land ceded by, 81; in World War II, 535; Yorktown, 68. *See also* Richmond, Virginia.
Virginia, 176
Virgin Islands, *t297*
VISTA. *See* Volunteers in Service to America (VISTA).
Vladivostok, 323
Volkswagen Beetle, *t361*
Volstead Act, 343, 398, *p408*
Voluntary Relocation Policy, 624, 746
Volunteers in Service to America (VISTA), 708, 787
Voter Education Project, 683–84
voting; and Franklin Roosevelt, 478; by African Americans in 1960s, 682, 683–84, 689; by African Americans during Reconstruction, 186, *t186,* 187, *p188,* 189, 190; rights of African Americans, 282; rights of African Americans, under Kennedy, 682, 683–84; rights of African Americans, under Lyndon Johnson, 689; rights of African Americans revoked, 253–54; rights of women, 257. *See also* electoral votes; suffrage; rural v. city, Senate and reforms concerning.
Voting Rights Act of 1965, 689, 708–09, 812–13

W

Wade-Davis Bill (1864), 186
Wagner Act (1935), 470, 544
wagons, pioneer, *p122–23,* 133
***Waiting for Lefty* (Odets),** 445
Wake Island, *t299,* 513
Wales, 39
Walesa, Lech, 868, *p868*
Walker, Alice, *q664*
Walker, David, 155
Wallace, George; and civil rights, 687, *q688, q782;* as presidential candidate, 782, *q782, m783,* 812, 822; paralysis of, 822
Wallace, Henry A., 457, 634
Walls, Josiah T., *p188*
Walsh, Thomas J., 348
Waltham (Mass.), 141–42
Wampanoag, 47
Wamsutta, 47
War of 1812, 117–18, *p117–18,* 141
***War and Peace in the Nuclear Age* (Newhouse),** *q586*
war bonds, 529
War, Department of, 455, 512 *See also* Defense, Department of (after 1948).
Ward, Lester, *p243,* 243–44, *q244*
ward boss, 238
"war hawks," 117–18
Warhol, Andy, 754, *ptg754*
War Powers Act (1973), 831
War Production Board (WPB), 527
Warren, Earl, *p714,* 714–15, *q716,* 813; *Brown* decision and, *q671,* 671, 714; Japanese internment and, 547; Kennedy assassination and, 705; Nixon and, 809, 812–13; "Warren Court" and, 714–17, *p714, c715,* 809
Warren Commission, 705
Warren, Mercy, 65
Warsaw Pact, 571
washing machine, 442, 599
Washington, Booker T., *p282,* 282–83; Garvey, Marcus, and, 343
Washington, George; foreign policy of, 115–116; framing of Constitution and, 83, 84, 89, 90; national bank, and, 114; Native Americans and, 134; as President, *t90,* 113–16, 134; in Revolutionary War, 67, 68, *ptg68,* 75; Whiskey Rebellion and, 114
Washington, D.C., 114; British attack, *crt118;* civil rights demonstration in, 686, *p686* population, *g696;* race riots in, 342, 780; segregation of federal workers in, 281
Washington (state), 219, 535
Washington Conference (1921), 351
Washington Post; Watergate and, 826–28
Watergate, *crt823,* 824–31, *t830*
Watergate Committee, 828–29, 833
Waters, Walter W., 426
Watson, Thomas E., 350
Watson, Thomas J., 212, 215
Watt, James (inventor), 158
Watt, James (secretary of the interior), 860
Watts (Calif.), 693, *p693*
Wayne, Anthony, 134
Wayne, John, 526
WCTU. *See* Women's Christian Temperance Union (WCTU).
wealth; in 1990s, 884; distribution of in 1896 and 1910, 238–39; distribution of in 1920s, 422; Great Depression and, 422, 435
Weathermen (Weather Underground), 794, 809
Weaver, James B., 213, 214
Weaver, Robert, 709
Webb, Sheyann, *q688*
Weber, Max, *ptg230*
Webster, Daniel, 146, 152, *q169*
Welch, Joseph, 628, *p629*
Welcome Wagon, 608
Weld, Thomas, *q44*
welfare, under Nixon, 810; under Reagan, 858; reform proposals in 1994, 902–03, 907, 909, 910
welfare capitalism, 357, 358–59
Welfare Reform Act, 903, 909–10
Wells, Ida B., 247–48, *p248, q248*
***Wesberry* v. *Sanders* (1969),** *c715*
"We Shall Overcome," 688, 690, 786
West; anti-Chinese movement in, 217, 405; railroads transporting fruit and vegetables from, 207; settling the, 196–98. *See also* frontier.
West Africa, 126–27
Western Electric Company, 359
Western Federation of Miners, 216
Western lands; ceded by Native Americans, *m135;* ceded by states (1781), 81–82; migration into, 132–35; settlement of, 130–35, *m131. See also* territories.
Western revival, 153
Western Sahara, 879
West Germany, 571. *See also* Germany; Federal Republic of (West).
Westin, Jeane, 436
Westminster College, 566, 865
West Point (U.S. Military Academy), 173, 730
Westmoreland, William, 773, 776, *p776,* 777, 779
wheat, production and price of, 1860–1900, *g213*
Wheeler, Burton K., 348
Wheelright, John, 43–45
Whigs, 153
"Whip Inflation Now" (WIN), 839
Whiskey Rebellion (1791), 114, *p114*
"whistle-stop" tour, 636, *m659*
White, William Allen, 251, 276, 340–41, 348, 502
White, Edward H., 845
"White Angel Bread Line" (Lange), 425
White Army (vs. Bolsheviks), 322, 323
White Citizens' Council, 671, 675
"White City, The" (McKay), 392
***White Collar* (Mills),** *q365–66*
white collar workers, 365–66, 601, 885
Whitefield, George, *p49,* 50
"white flight," 541, 607
White House, the, 98, 151–52, p152; Roosevelt, Franklin, and, 459
Whiteman, Paul, 389
white supremacy, 215
Whitewater, 911
Whitney, Eli, 165, *q165*
Whitney, Richard, 418
***Why We Can't Wait* (King),** *q685*

wigwams, 26
Wilderness Road, 65, 131
wildlife, *p22, p132*
Willard, Frances, 257
Williamsburg (Va.), 46
Williams, Harrison, *q738, q739*
Williams, Hosea, 687, 688
Williams, Roger, 39, 44
Williams, Ted, 506
Willow Run (Mich.), 536
Wills, Frank, 824
Wills, Helen, 387
Wilson, John, *q42,* 43
Wilson, Woodrow, 322, *q322;* African Americans and, 281, 342; big business and trusts, and, 277–78, 279; early life, 275; Federal Reserve System and, 278–79; foreign policy under, 305–06, 309–11; Fourteen Points of, 321, 322; as Govenor of New Jersey, 274–75; Hughes vs., 310, *p311*; intervention in Latin America, 305–06; League of Nations and, 323, 325–27; *Lusitania* and, 304, 310; machine politics and, 274–75; opposition to immigration by, 284; policies rejected, 347; on populists, 275; progressive policies and, 274–75; Republicans and, 324; Roosevelt and Taft vs., 276–78, *crt277, m277*; treaty of Versailles and, *p321,* 321, 324-25; woman suffrage and, 344; World War I and, 304, 309–11, *q311,* 315
WIN. *See* Whip Inflation Now (WIN).
Winthrop, John, 36, *q36, q38–39,* 43–45, *q43, p45*
Wisconsin; La Follette's reforms in, 251, 252–53; primaries in, 779; railroad tax hike and, 250–51, 254
Wisconsin Idea, 252–53
Wisconsin, University of, 254
Wobblies, 287. *See also* Industrial Workers of the World (IWW).
Women's Campaign Fund, 728
Women's Christian Temperance Union (WCTU), 257
Women's Council of Defense, 317
Women's Joint Congressional Committee, 343
women's rights, movement, 65, 155, 156, *t344,* 724–31, *t728;* reproductive, 727; struggle for in 1800s, 725; to vote, 253, *p254, m344, t344,* 725; *See also* feminism; suffrage.
Women's Trade Union League, 318, 460
women; in 1920s, 367–68, 383; in 1950s, 601, 612–15; in 1960s, 724–31; in 1990s, 917–18; as abolitionists, 155, 156, 259–60, 261, 725; African Americans and, 261, 283, 724–25; after American Revolution, 74, 75; in cabinet, 477; as conservatives, 729, 731; cattle ranching and, 198; against Child Labor, 232, *p246,* 246–47; Civilian Conservation Corps (CCC) and, 456; during Civil War, 176, 177, 261; college educations for, 612; in Congress, 894; discrimination against, 456, 478, 531, 724–25; economic rights of, 726–27; in education, *g726,* 729; employment of, 367–68, 614–15; factory workers, 140–43, *p140, q140, p141;* fashions for, 382–83; frontier, 133; glass ceiling and, 920; during Great Depression, 435–36, 477; as homemakers, 612; Kennedy-Johnson era and, 724–28; in labor force, 917, 918, *c918*; as lawyers, 241; matriarchy of, 26, *c27;* as mill workers, *q140, p141, p140,* 140–43; minimum wage for, 286; minority, 726; New Deal and, 477–78; in politics, *q726,* 727, 728; in Progressive movement, 246–47, 253; in Puritan Massachusetts, 42–45; Reagan and, 861; reproductive rights of, 727; during Revolutionary War, 70, *ptg70,* 74–75; roles change for, *t613,* 724, *p725,* 725, 729, 731; Roosevelt, Franklin, and, 477–78; in space, 916–17; in sports, 554–55; on Supreme Court, 861, *p861, q922, p923, q923,* 924, *q924*; television portrayals of, *p617, p625, p785*; unions and, 215, 217; voting by, 258–61, *m344, t344: See also* suffrage; as white collar workers, 367–68, 614; working. *See* working women; World War I and, 261; during World War II, 530–31, 540–41, 554–55
women's rights, 155, 156; first article on, 65; to vote, 74
Women Strike for Peace, 790
Wood, Grant, *ptg445*
Wood, Robert E., 502
Wood, Sam, *q649*
Woodin, William, 454–55
Woods, Anna, *q188*
Woods, Tiger, 921, *p921*
Woodstock (N.Y.), 753, *p753*
Woodward, Bob, 826, *q827*
Woolworth, F. W., 207, *p207,* 381
Worcester, Samuel A., 136–39
***Worcester* v. *Georgia*,** 136–39
workday limitations; by Ford, Henry, 363; Hoover, Herbert, and, 350; populists and, 213; progressives and, 254–56; unions and, 215, 216, 286, 318
workers' compensation, 254, 279, 623
working women, *g726, g917,* 917; *in 1900, 254;* in 1920s, 367–68; in 1930s, 436, 477–78; in 1950s, 614–15, *g615;* in 1960s, 726–27; in 1970s and after, *g726,* 726–27; managerial positions and, 917/918; payment relative to men, 215, *c918*; unions and, 215, 217; during World War II, 531
Workmen's Compensation Law (1916), 254
Works Progress Administration (WPA) (1935), 469–70, 479, 481
World Series, 374
World Trade buildings, bombing of, 919
World War I, *m307, t308;* aftermath of, 338–45; deaths in, 309, 314, *c316,* 321; fighting in, 306–09, 315–17; mobilization for, 315; new weapons in, 307, 308; opposition to, *p318,* 318–19; origins of, 306; pacifism in, *p309*; submarine warfare in, 304, 308, 309–10, *p310,* 311; trench warfare in, *p308,* 308–09; Woodrow Wilson and, *q311,* 321, 323; U.S. enters, *t310,* 310–11; Zimmermann telegram and, 311
World War II, *m494, m505, m511, m514;* African Americans in, *p509,* 534–36, 537; Allied strategy, 509; appeasement and, 496; atomic bomb, use of in, 514–15, 516–19; costs of, 528, 563; deaths in, *c515;* economic legislation in, *c527;* end of, 562–566; immigration quotas and refugees in, 407; impact of, 534–39; invasion of France in, 500–01, 510, *m521;* invasion of Poland in, 496; Italy in, 501, 510; North African campaign, 510; Pearl Harbor attack and, 505, *p506,* 506, 508, 524 ; Roosevelt, Franklin. and, 502, 509, 527, 530; social change during, 534–39, 540–41, *m553,* 554–55; Soviet Union and, 509–10, 512–13, 515, 563; submarine warfare in, 503; unconditional surrender policy in, 509; U.S. vs. Japan in the Pacific, 513–15; volunteer efforts during, 525; wartime production in U.S., 526, 527, 540–41; women workers during, 530–31, 540, 554–55
Wounded Knee (S. Dak.), 743–44, *p758*
WPA. *See* Works Progress Administration (WPA).
WPB. *See* War Production Board (WPB).
Wright, Frank Lloyd, 502
Wright, Martha, 258
Wright's Ferry, 64
Wrigley, Philip, 554
Wyoming, 169, 197, 253

Y

Yale University, 507
Yalta Conference, 564, *p564,* 642
Yalu River, 574
Yamamoto, Isoroku, 505
"yellow-dog" contracts, 358
yellow fever, 215, 222, 247, 302, 303
Yeltsin, Boris, 869, *p888*
Yom Kippur War, 819, 837
York, Duke of, 40
Yorktown (Va.), 54, *t68*
Youth in Crisis, 538
Ypres, Second Battle of, 308
Yugoslavia, 868, 879; conflict among successor states, 897-98, *m897, p899*

Z

Zall, P.M., 47
Zhou Enlai, 818
Ziegfeld, Florenz, 446
zoot suits, 537–38
Zuñi, 24

Credits

TEXT

17 From *The Mapping of America* by Seymour I. Schwartz and Ralph E. Ehrenberg. Harry N. Abrams, Inc., Publishers, New York. Copyright © 1980 **24** From *Castaways, The Narrative of Alvar Núñez Cabeza de Vaca,* edited by Enrique Pupo-Walker, translated by Frances M. López-Morillas. University of California Press. Copyright © 1993 by The Regents of the University of California. **126** Excerpt from *Roots* by Alex Haley. Copyright © 1976 by Alex Haley. Used by permission of Doubleday, a division of Bantam Doubleday Dell Publishing Group, Inc. **230** From *Sister Carrie* by Theodore Dreiser. Copyright © 1900 by Doubleday, Page, and Co. **334** Reprinted with permission of Charles Scribner's Sons, an imprint of Macmillan Publishing Company, from *The Great Gatsby* (Authorized Text) by F. Scott Fitzgerald. Copyright © 1991, 1992 by Eleanor Lanahan, Matthew J. Bruccoli and Samuel J. Lanahan as Trustees under Agreement dated July 3, 1975 Created by Frances Scott Fitzgerald Smith. Copyright 1925 by Charles Scribner's Sons, renewal copyright 1953 by Frances Scott Fitzgerald Lanahan. **346** From *American Tapestry* by Tom Tiede. Copyright © 1988 by Tom Tiede. Reprinted with permission of Pharos Books. **353** Reprinted with permission of Macmillan Publishing Company from *The Man Nobody Knows* by Bruce Barton. Copyright 1925 by the Bobbs-Merrill Company, Inc. Copyright renewed 1952 by Bruce Barton. **365** From *White Collar: The American Middle Class* by C. Wright Mills. Copyright © 1951 by Oxford University Press, Inc.; renewed by Yaraslava Mills. Reprinted by permission of Oxford University Press, Inc. **376** Excerpt from *Babbitt* by Sinclair Lewis, copyright 1922 by Harcourt Brace Jovanovich, Inc., and renewed 1950 by Sinclair Lewis, reprinted by permission of Oxford University Press, Inc. **392** Reprinted by permission of Harold Ober Associates Incorporated. Copyright 1963 by Arna Bontemps. **414** From *The Grapes of Wrath* by John Steinbeck. Copyright © 1939, 1967 by John Steinbeck. Reprinted by permission of Viking Penguin, a division of Penguin Books USA Inc. **425, 431, 435, 441, 443** From *Hard Times: An Oral History of the Great Depression* by Studs Terkel. Copyright © 1970 by Studs Terkel. Reprinted by permission of Pantheon Books, a division of Random House Inc. **424** Copyright © 1932 (renewed) Warner Bros. Inc. All rights reserved. Used by permission. **488** From *Ernie's War: The Best of Ernie Pyle's World War II Dispatches* by David Nichols. Copyright © 1986 by David Nichols. Reprinted by permission of Random House Inc. **508, 512, 524, 548** From *The Good War: An Oral History of World War II* by Studs Terkel. Copyright © 1984 by Studs Terkel. Reprinted by permission of Pantheon Books, a division of Random House Inc. **526** "Boogie Woogie Bugle Boy": Words and music by Don Raye and Hughie Prince. Copyright © 1940, 1941 by MCA Music Publishing, a division of MCA, Inc., New York, NY 10019. Copyright renewed. Used by permission. All Rights Reserved. **528, 534** From *The Home Front* by Archie Satterfield, published by Playboy Press. Copyright © 1981 by Archie Satterfield. Reprinted by permission of the author. **538** Reprinted with permission from The Crisis Magazine. **548** From *Wyoming's War Years, 1941–1945* by T.A. Larson, University of Wyoming Press. Copyright © 1954. Reprinted by permission of T.A. Larson. **549** From "American Business Activity from 1790 to Today," Fifty-Ninth Edition, January 1988. Reprinted with permission of Ameritrust Company N.A. **558** From *The Book of Daniel* by E.L. Doctorow. Copyright © 1971 by E.L. Doctorow. Reprinted by permission of Random House Inc. **608** From the song "Little Boxes." Words and music by Malvina Reynolds. Copyright © 1962 Schroder Music Company (ASCAP). Renewed 1990 by Nancy Schimmel. Used by permission. **612** From *The Stories of John Cheever,* copyright © 1978. Reprinted by permission of Alfred A. Knopf, Inc. **622** From James Baldwin's *Notes of a Native Son.* Copyright 1955. Reprinted by permission of Beacon Press. **635** Excerpt from *Off the Record: The Private Papers of Harry S Truman* edited by Robert H. Ferrell. Copyright © 1980 by Robert H. Ferrell. Reprinted by permission of HarperCollins Publishers. **664** From *Circles on the Water* by Marge Piercy. Reprinted by permission of Alfred A. Knopf, Inc., "Women": From *Revolutionary Petunias and Other Poems,* copyright © by Alice Walker, reprinted by permission of Harcourt Brace. **665** "The Immigrant Experience": From "The Historical and Intellectual Presence of Mexican Americans" by Octavio Romano, *El Grito,* Vol. II, No. 2 (Winter, 1969). Grito Del Sol Collection, Berkeley, Calif. **688** Excerpt from *Stand Up for America* by George C. Wallace. Copyright © 1976 by George C. Wallace. Used by permission of Doubleday, a division of Bantam Doubleday Dell Publishing Group, Inc. **688** From *Selma, Lord, Selma: Girlhood Memories of the Civil-Rights Days,* by Sheyann Webb and Rachel West Nelson, as told to Frank Sikora, © 1980 The University of Alabama Press. Used by permission. **693** From *The Panther and the Lash* by Langston Hughes. Copyright 1951 by Langston Hughes. Reprinted by permission of Alfred A. Knopf. **748** "Blowin' in the Wind" by Bob Dylan. Copyright © transferred 1990 to Special Rider Music. All rights reserved. International copyright secured. Reprinted by permission; "Like a Rolling Stone," by Bob Dylan. Copyright © 1965 Warner Bros. Inc. All rights reserved. Used by permission. **764** From *Born on the Fourth of July* by Ron Kovic. Copyright © 1976 by Ron Kovic. Reprinted by permission of McGraw Hill Publishing Company. **789** "The Times They Are A-Changin'," by Bob Dylan. Copyright © 1962, 1964 Warner Bros. Inc. All rights reserved. Used by permission. **852** Reprinted by permission of The Putnam Publishing Group from *The Joy Luck Club* by Amy Tan. Copyright © 1989 by Amy Tan. **963** "Dream Boogie Variation" from *Collected Poems* by Langston Hughes. Copyright © 1994 by the Estate of Langston Hughes. Reprinted by permission of Alfred A. Knopf Inc. **967** Excerpt from *Dear Mrs. Parks: A Dialogue with Today's Youth.* Text copyright © 1996 by Rosa L. Parks. Reprinted by arrangement with Lee & Low Books, 95 Madison Avenue, New York, NY 10016. **968** From *When Heaven and Earth Changed Places,* by Le Ly Hayslip with Jay Wurts. Copyright © 1989 by Le Ly Hayslip and Charles Jay Wurts. Reprinted by permission from Doubleday.

MAPS

All interior maps by Mapping Specialists, Ltd., Madison, WI.

PHOTOGRAPHS

All border and background photos by John Soares with the exception of the *One Day in History* background photo by Doug Mindell. **Cover** N. Wright/National Motor Museum (c); Wesley Hitt/Liaison International (background); **Title page** Jeff Greenberg/Rainbow; **iv** Brown Brothers; **v** White House Historical Association; **vi** © Faith Ringgold Inc. (l); Photoplay Archives/LGI (r); **944** ©FPG International Corp. (c, r); © Randy Wells/Allstock (l); **945** ©FPG International Corp(l); © Greg Ryan/Sally Beyer/Allstock (c); © Tom Bean/Allstock (r); **950** © Rick Iwaskai/Allstock; **950–957,** White House Historical Association; **957** Bush 2000 Campaign.

The following credits are additions to or corrections of those found on page:
1 Laurie Platt Winfrey, Inc.; **17** World Perspectives; **115** New York State Historical Association, Cooperstown; **155** From the Collection of the Louisiana State Museum; **182** © 1984, Time-Life Books, Inc., from The Civil War Series, *Tenting Tonight,* photograph by Larry Sherer (bl); **199** Southern Pacific Lines; **201** S.J. Morrow Collection/W.H. Over State Museum; **202** Schmitt Collection/File photo by Ralph J. Brunke (l); **322** Courtesy Stephen White/© 1996 Artists Rights Society (ARS), New York/VG Bild-Kunst, Bonn (tr); **406** Photography Collection Harry Ransom Humanities Research Center, The University of Texas at Austin; **414** © The Dorothea Lange Collection, The Oakland Museum of California, The City of Oakland. Gift of Paul S. Taylor.; **425** © The Dorothea Lange Collection, The Oakland Museum of California, the city of Oakland. (br); **445** Cedar Rapids Museum of Art Archives, Gift of John B. Turner in Memory of Happy Yound Turner (tr); **463** Brooklyn Museum (bl); **495** © Copyright ARS. Centro de Arte Reina Sofia, Madrid, Spain/Art Resource, NY; **523** Alfred Eisenstaedt/LIFE Magazine ©Time Inc.; **585** © TM 1995 Dr. Seuss Enterprises, L.P. All rights reserved. (tr); **586** From *War and Peace in the Nuclear Age* by J. Newhouse. Reprinted by permission of Random House/Photo by Ralph Brunke.; **600** (inset) Corry/Archive; **621** University of Kentucky Libraries; **649** UPI/Bettmann Newsphotos (t); **649** UPI/Bettmann (tr, tc, br); Motion Picture & Television Photo Archive (bc); **650** UPI/Bettmann; **651** UPI/Bettmann; **706** photo by Frank Wolfe, Courtesy Lyndon Baines Johnson Library (b); Courtesy Benny Andrews (t); **729** Courtesy of Ms. Magazine; **730** UPI/Bettmann (br); **733** © Paul Fusco/Magnum Photos; **753** © J. Marshall/Gamma Liaison (c); **754** Collection of John Jenkins III/© 1996 Andy Warhol Foundation for the Visual Arts/ARS, New York; **803** Primrose is a registered trademark of F.W. Woolworth Co. (l); **827** © Bill Swersey/Gamma Liaison (c); UPI/Bettmann (all others); **875** The Carson Collection (c); **880** © Savino/Sipa Press; **899** © Dirck Halstead/Gamma Liaison; **913** File photo by Ralph J. Brunke; **923** © Bill Pugliano/Gamma Liaison; **958** Tom & Deeann McCarthy/The Stock Market; **959** Betty Crews/The Image Works; **961** Charles Thatcher/Tony Stone Images; **962** Lester Sloan/Woodfin Camp & Associates; **963** Ken Kerbs/Monkmeyer Press; **964** David Austen/Tony Stone Images; **965** Leif Skoogfors/Woodfin Camp & Associates; **966** Bob Daemmrich Photo, Inc.; **967** Michael Okoniewski/The Image Works; **968** Bob Daemmrich Photo, Inc.; **969** Bob Thomas/Tony Stone Images.

Diagraphics and Charts
Karl Gude **85, 142, 270, 645, 707, 895.** Arne Hurty **69, 165, 209;** Dennis Lowe **27, 529, 592, 790, 859;** David Puckett **296, 363, 379, 421, 503, 683;** All other charts and diagraphics by Ligature.